Open Secrets

The Dollar Power
of PACs in Congress

Open Secrets

The Dollar Power
of PACs in Congress

Larry Makinson

Center for Responsive Politics

Congressional Quarterly Inc.
1414 22nd Street N.W.
Washington, D.C. 20037

Library of Congress Cataloging-in-Publication Data

Open Secrets: The Dollar Power of PACs in Congress/Larry Makinson
    p.   cm.
    Includes index.
    ISBN 0-87187-579-9
    1. Campaign funds—United States. 2. Political action committees—United States.
3. United States. Congress—Elections, 1988.
I. Title.
JK1991.M26   1990
324.7'8'0973--dc20   90-2318
                                  CIP

Editorial, Research & Production Staff

Author and Project Director: Larry Makinson

Assistant Editor: Sheila Krumholz

Production and Research Assistants: Michael Levick
Wendy Martinek
Steve Pirozzi

Acknowledgments

Countless hours, days, weeks and months of painstaking research and production went into the publication of this reference work and dozens of people and organizations were extremely helpful in the process. *Open Secrets* was a project of the Center for Responsive Politics and its director, Ellen Miller, nurtured it from an idea to a finished product and won the enthusiasm — and support — of the foundations whose grants made it possible. Also assisting from the Center were Laura Weiss, the Center's media director; general counsel Paul Hoff; and volunteer intern Rebecca Schotland. The staff of the Federal Election Commission's Public Records Office provided invaluable assistance, as usual — most particularly Mike Dickerson, Kevin Fitzgerald and especially the office's director, Kent Cooper, who offered advice, assistance and encouragement at every step of this project, from original conception to its completion. Bob Biersack, the FEC's Supervisory Statistician and chief computer guru, provided critical assistance in unlocking the secrets of the FEC's computer database. Ed Zuckerman, publisher of *PACs and Lobbies* and the *Almanac of Federal PACs*, provided generous helpings of his advice, experience and unique perspective — as well as five boxes of corporate annual reports. Many of the hundreds of PAC treasurers and directors with whom we spoke were also quite helpful in providing an accurate picture of their PACs' perspectives and political agendas.

The funding that made this project possible came from major grants by the Joyce Foundation, the Arca Foundation, the Mary Reynolds Babcock Foundation, the J. Roderick MacArthur Foundation, and the Deer Creek Foundation. Computer equipment essential to the compiling of the data and its presentation was provided through a grant from Apple Computer Inc. Community Affairs.

The views expressed in this book are solely those of the Center for Responsive Politics.

The Center for Responsive Politics

The Center for Responsive Politics is a non-profit bipartisan research group in Washington, D.C. that studies Congress and related issues. Founded in 1983 by Senators Frank Church (D-Idaho) and Hugh Scott (R-Pa), it was designed to study Congress and examine potential reforms that could improve both its internal operation and its responsiveness to the American public. Over the years, the Center has published more than a dozen reports, monographs and books on issues ranging from congressional ethics to the dynamics between Congress and the news media. Money and politics has been one of its chief areas of concentration, and the Center was one of the first organizations to investigate the use of soft money in presidential elections. The Center's funding comes from a variety of foundations and private contributors. It is not associated with any political party or other organization, and serves as a non-partisan resource for the public, the academic community and the news media.

Contents

"Open Secrets"

The publication of this book is the culmination of a research project first conceived more than five and a half years ago, on a frigid December morning in Anchorage, Alaska. The author, one of a number of reporters at the *Anchorage Daily News* covering the 1984 state elections, was frustrated that despite intensive news coverage of the elections — and a model state campaign finance law — the voting public had gone to the polls with only the barest clues as to who was paying the bills for the candidates' campaigns. The politicians all knew where the money came from. So did the PACs, the lobbyists, the big contributors and other political insiders whose job it was to make the system work for themselves and their clients. The only ones in the dark were the voters.

In January, 1985, armed with a second-hand Macintosh computer, a stack of floppy disks, and a promise from *Daily News* editor Howard Weaver that he would run whatever stories I could dig up, I left my job at the paper and embarked on an open-ended odyssey on the trail of the money; setting up shop in a spare office down the hall from the Alaska Public Offices Commission and entering by hand into a computer database the details of more than 7,000 contributions to Alaska politicians.

Nine months later, in a 10-part series of articles in the *Anchorage Daily News*, the voters of Alaska finally learned who had paid for the previous elections, who the state's top contributors were, and which members of the state legislature received the lion's share of their largesse. The following spring, the original *Open Secrets* appeared — a 146 page volume that profiled Alaska's top 50 political contributors and identified in detail the source of contributions for each member of the Alaska legislature, using hundreds of charts and graphs to give the numbers life.

This book applies the format and philosophy of that original project, expands it, and applies it to the U.S. Congress.

In uncovering the patterns behind money and politics in Alaska, the chief problem was that nothing was computerized and all the public records were gathering dust in filing cabinets. When looking at the U.S. Congress, the problem is the opposite — so *much* is on computers that would-be investigators quickly find themselves buried in an avalanche of data. Whatever can be easily reported is seized upon — the names of the biggest PACs, the identities of the members who took the most money or ran the most expensive campaigns. But the currents and trends that underlie those surface details have remained — until now — largely invisible. *Open Secrets* attempts to bring them to the surface for all to see, and the reader will find much in this book that will raise both eyebrows and questions. Dig deeply into the money in politics and you inevitably find yourself exploring the intimate connection between American politics and American business, organized labor, and a diversity of ideological and single-issue interest groups.

This book probes those connections, but it makes no claims to presenting them all. Contributions from political action committees, which this book investigates, form only one element — albeit an important one — in the overall funding of American elections. Much work remains to be done uncovering the patterns in the large individual contributions which have become the mainstay of many politicians' fund-raising efforts. Future editions of *Open Secrets* will attempt to explore this area more fully.

In the meantime, this book provides a beginning. Far from bringing this project to a conclusion, it swings open the door to what will hopefully be a new phase in public examination of our politicians' benefactors. In that spirit, consider it not a neatly-wrapped analysis of money in politics, but a starting point for future research and a citizen's guide to the financial realities of modern American elections.

Larry Makinson
Center for Responsive Politics
August 7, 1990

Methodology

The process of compiling the materials for this book required many months of research, poring through reference materials and city directories in the stacks and reading rooms of the Library of Congress, scouring hundreds of annual reports, and telephoning several hundred businesses, labor unions and PAC managers in every corner of the nation.

PAC Classification System

The first step in the project was creating a classification system for the industries and interest groups that sponsor PACs. Since a majority of PACs come from the business world, the starting point was the Standard Industrial Codes (SIC codes) developed by the U.S. Government's Office of Management and Budget, and used widely by reference organizations, such as Standard & Poors, that publish business directories. The codes were then streamlined to eliminate fine lines of distinction between industries and to make them more relevant to the political realities of congressional committee jurisdictions.

No similar codes cover non-business PACs, so the Center developed its own, both for labor unions and for ideological and single-issue PACs. During the course of the project, the classification system underwent a continual evolution, as the real world patterns of PAC giving gradually became apparent. A complete list of the categories is included in Appendix A.

Identifying the PACs and Classifying the Contributions

The contemporary American business world does not lend itself to simple classification. Modern corporations are often extremely diversified in their lines of business — and in their political interests — and in recent years many have been buying and selling subsidiaries almost routinely. To adjust for this, the Center developed a multi-level system for classifying PACs with diversified sponsors. A primary code was assigned, based on the PAC sponsor's primary business or profit center; secondary codes were then added to account for subsidiary interests contributing more than 10 percent of its revenues or profits.

These multiple codes were then matched against the committee assignments of the candidates who received contributions. If the committee's jurisdiction did not relate to the PAC's main category, but did relate to a secondary code, that secondary code was used to classify the contribution. For example, a contribution from the Boeing PAC to a member of the Armed Services Committee was classified as a defense contribution. A similar contribution to a non-incumbent, or to someone sitting on a non-defense committee, would be classified under Boeing's primary category as an aircraft manufacturer. This system was used to determine unique categories for each of the nearly 115,000 PAC contributions that were made to federal candidates during the 1987-88 election cycle.

Compilation and Publication

Once all the data was collected and categorized, the final step was to arrange it in some order that would make it comprehensible — both for our own analysis and for readers of this book. Viewing that much data from only one angle would be limiting at best, so the information is presented here from a number of perspectives — profiles cover not only the finances of individual members, but of PACs, congressional committees, and specific industries. The interplay between different sectors is also highlighted, as in the "Targeting the Committees" section that compares average contributions to different committees by a variety of industries and interests. Wherever possible, the data is presented graphically, so readers can view not just the detail in the numbers but also the patterns. In all, the book contains more than 2,100 charts and graphs.

How We Did It

This entire project, from the first drafts of foundation proposals to the compiling of the databases, the charting and final desktop publishing, were done using Apple Macintosh™ computers. Printing of the final page proofs was done on an Apple LaserWriter II NTX printer. A large ensemble of software was used to gather and report the data. The workhorses included: 4th Dimension™ and FoxBase+/Mac™ for database work; Microsoft Excel™ and Microsoft Word™ for spreadsheet and word processing; DeltaGraph™ for the charts and graphs, and Aldus PageMaker™ for final page layout. All these companies — particularly PageMaker™ and DeltaGraph™ — provided helpful technical support along the way, and Aldus Corporation supplied an early copy of PageMaker 4.0 at a critical time to the project's completion. One computer (a Macintosh IIx with a two-page Apple Monitor) and one printer, (the LaserWriter II NTX) were provided through a grant from Apple Computer. All the other equipment and software was purchased at regular cost.

Accuracy was a constant concern and every attempt was made to present this data clearly and correctly. Readers who may find, or suspect, errors, are encouraged to contact the Center for Responsive Politics in Washington, D.C. Future editions of this book are planned for future election cycles, so any suggestions, or corrections, would be appreciated.

How to get the most from this book . . .

Open Secrets is arranged into five main sections, each of which explores the subject of PACs and Congress from a different angle. Here's a quick guide for using the book to its fullest:

1. The Big Picture

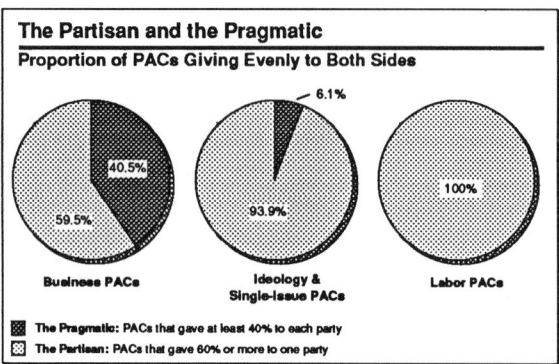

In this opening section, the overall patterns of PAC giving to candidates for Congress are highlighted. Among its features are a list of the 100 largest PAC sponsors contributing to federal campaigns in 1988, a review of the rising costs of winning election to Congress, and broad breakdowns showing differences in PAC giving between various industries, labor unions, and ideological/single-issue groups. One feature of particular note is the section, beginning on page 22, that examines the patterns by which different industries and interests appear to target their contributions at members of specific congressional committees.

2. Industry and Interest Group Profiles

One major finding of the study that led to this book is that PACs rarely give in isolation. Rather, PACs give in packs, and those packs often reflect the shared interests of particular industries. A member of the banking committee, for example, is likely to get money not from a single bank PAC, but from a dozen or more. This section examines the role of two dozen key industries and interest groups that play a major role in financing congressional campaigns.

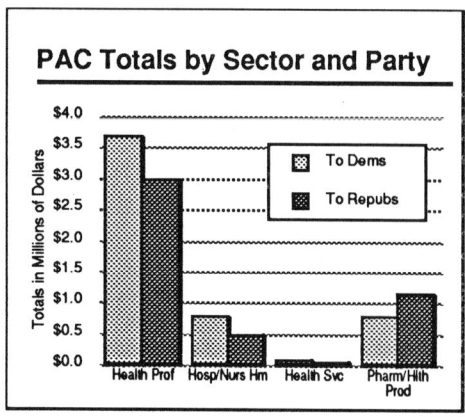

Included in each industry profile are lists of the top 20 PACs within that industry that contributed to 1988 federal campaigns, the top House and Senate recipients of their money, and charts showing the spending patterns of major subgroups within the industry. The industry profiles begin on page 41.

3. Committee Profiles

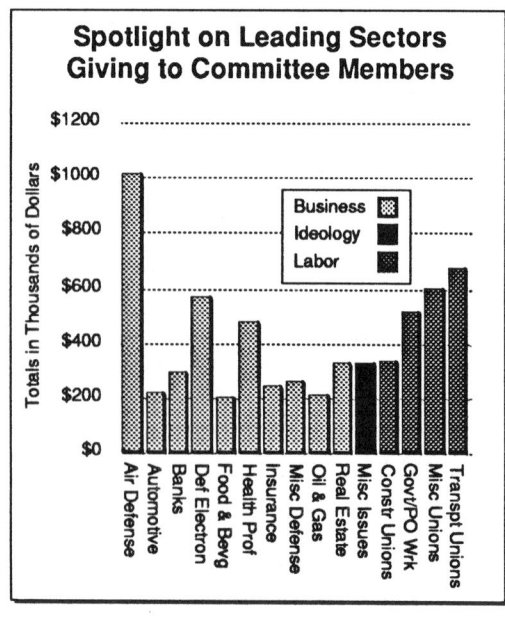

How much did defense contractors give to members of the House and Senate Armed Services committees? Which members of the tax-writing House Ways and Means Committee got the biggest totals from PACs in the last election? Which industries have interests that fall under the jurisdiction of the Interior committee? The answers to these questions can be found in section 3, which offers profiles of all 37 standing committees of the House and Senate. The profiles give the jurisdictions of each committee, a listing of their subcommittee chairmen and ranking Republicans, and a full list of the PAC dollars received by each member of the committee during the 1987-88 election cycle. An accompanying chart shows which industries gave the most to committee members, and a detailed list of the biggest PAC contributors is arranged both by dollars and by industry.

The Senate committee profiles begin on page 82, the House committees start on page 114. Within each house, the committees are arranged alphabetically.

4. Member Profiles

This is by far the largest section of the book, and includes two-page campaign finance profiles for every member of the U.S. House and Senate elected in 1988. The list includes all 435 members of the House and 33 senators. The senators' profiles are listed first, beginning on page 162. House profiles begin on page 230. A four-page introduction to the member profiles (on pages 158-161) explains the charts, graphs, PAC lists, interest group ratings and other elements and conventions used in describing the political finances of each member.

Included in the profiles are a variety of elements which will help identify the political leanings and financial backers of each member. Each member's 1988 committee assignments are listed, so the reader can easily follow the connection (or lack of it) between PAC contributions and the member's legislative assignments. A category chart shows how much of the member's PAC money came from each of 13 distinct industry and interest group sectors. Another chart gives a quick glance at the degree of spending and competition in the member's last three elections. An interest group ratings chart shows the member's voting record rating, as compiled by four key interest groups. And a customized listing of the member's biggest PAC contributors, arranged by specific industry or interest group, gives a comprehensive look at the sources of the member's 1988 campaign war chest.

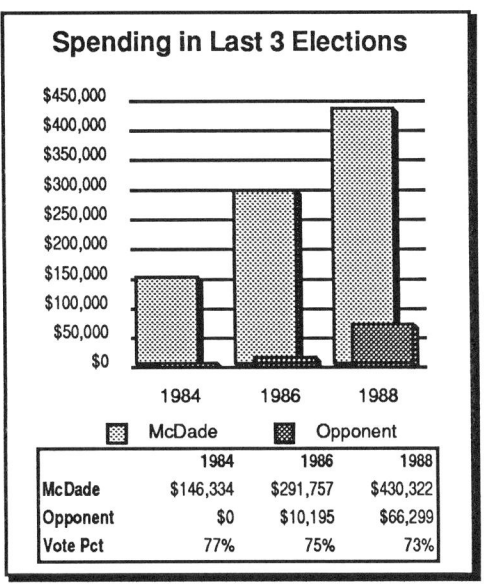

Spending in Last 3 Elections

	1984	1986	1988
McDade	$146,334	$291,757	$430,322
Opponent	$0	$10,195	$66,299
Vote Pct	77%	75%	73%

5. PAC Profiles

This 60-page section provides the names, locations, affiliations and primary industry or interest group classifications for all 1,113 PACs that gave $20,000 or more to federal candidates in the 1988 elections. Together, these PACs gave more than $147 million to candidates for federal office — 92.5 percent of all PAC giving. The profiles also give quick digests showing how the PAC distributed its funds. Included are the total number of candidates who received contributions, the average gift to House and Senate candidates, and the proportion of dollars that went to Democrats versus Republicans, incumbents versus non-incumbents, and House versus Senate or presidential candidates. The PACs are arranged alphabetically by sponsor (or by PAC name where there is no sponsor).

Federated Investors Inc		$41,300	32 Candidates		Dems:	54.5%
Financial Services Political Committee			Avg House:	$1,021	Senate:	60.5%
Pittsburgh, PA		Securities Investment	Avg Sen:	$1,562	Incumb:	91.5%

Appendices

At the end of the book are two appendices that clarify the PAC classification system used in this book, and offer an alternate index to find members of Congress from a particular state or district. Appendix A presents the detailed list of categories that was used to classify the nearly 3,300 PACs that contributed to federal candidates in the 1988 election. The appendix also includes the total dollars in PAC contributions given by PACs in each category during 1987-88. Appendix B lists the congressional delegations of each state, by district, and provides an index to the profile pages for each member.

	Short name	87-88 PAC Total
Banks & Lending Institutions		
Banks & lending institutions, general	Banks	$43,200
Commercial banks & bank holding companies	Comml Banks	$6,456,883
Savings banks and savings & loans	Sav Banks	$1,970,335
Credit unions	Credit Union	$516,238
Credit agencies & finance companies	Credit/Loans	$637,993

1.

The Big Picture

Open Secrets

The Price of Admission

Winning a seat in the U.S. Congress has become a very expensive proposition. In the 1988 elections, the average House winner spent about $390,000. Successful Senate races averaged just over $4 million. And those figures include *all* races — the great majority of which were waged by incumbents against unevenly matched opponents. For newcomers breaking in to Congress, the rates were even higher.

Newly elected House members spent anywhere from $183,000 to more than $1.4 million to win their seats; the average cost was $576,000. The price of admission for the 10 new Senators elected in 1988 ranged from $876,000 to nearly $7.5 million; the average for their campaigns was $3.27 million.

Incumbents — particularly in the House — had an easier time. Many incumbents faced only nominal opposition, against challengers with neither the name recognition nor the money to effectively compete.

Mismatched Races

Few House incumbents faced serious challenges in the 1988 elections. Of the 408 incumbents who sought new terms in the fall election, 402 were successfully reelected. Their *average* share of the vote was 72.4 percent — a margin of nearly three-to-one over their opponents. The gap in spending was even higher. As this chart illustrates, the great majority of challengers spent less than $100,000 in their campaigns. The largest group of incumbents spent between $250,000 and $500,000. Of those who spent more than a million, 14 were incumbents and two were challengers. Lopsided races were in fact the rule in 1988, not the exception. In more than half the races for the U.S. House, the winner outspent the loser by a factor of 10-to-one or greater. In all but six of those cases, the winner was an incumbent.

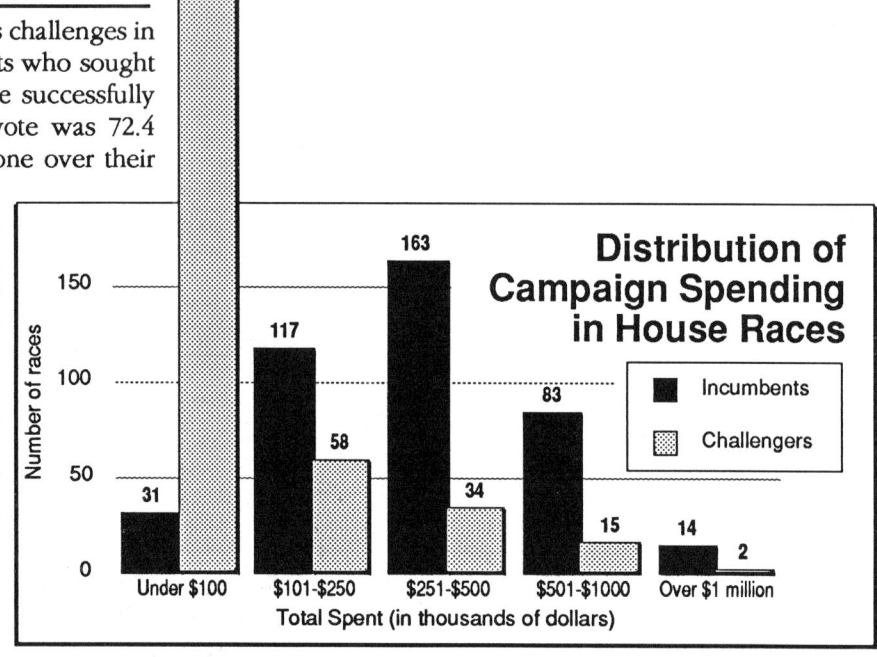

Average Spending 1974-88 House Incumbents vs. Challengers

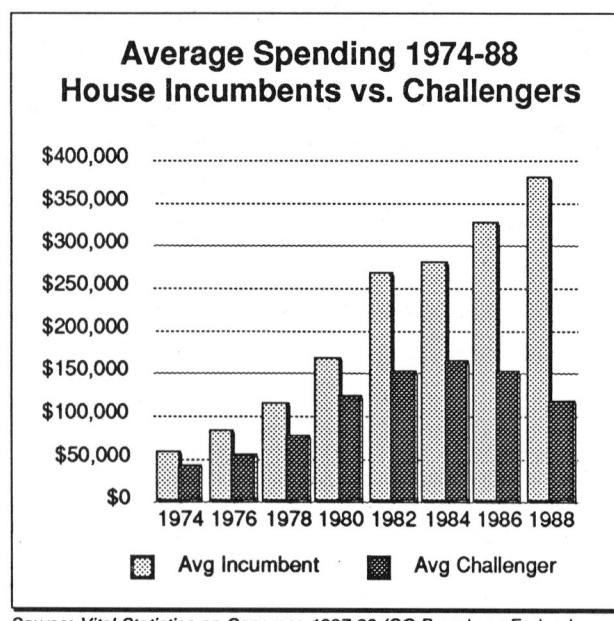

Source: *Vital Statistics on Congress 1987-88 (CQ Press)* and Federal Election Commission

Challengers Losing Ground in the Money Chase

In 1974, the first year that the Federal Election Commission compiled detailed records of spending in congressional races, the costs of campaigning for a seat in the U.S. House of Representatives were only a fraction of what they are today, and incumbents and challengers were fairly evenly matched. Campaign costs for both groups rose steadily throughout the late 1970s and early 80s, but since 1984 they have come to a parting of the ways. From 1986 onward, spending by challengers has actually *declined*, while House incumbents continue to spend ever-higher sums. In 1988, the average cost of a challenger's campaign was actually below the level of eight years earlier. At the same time, the gap in spending between incumbents and challengers has widened enormously — from about $16,000 in 1974 to more than $264,000 in 1988. The trend is continuing in the 1990 elections, as the mounting odds against beating incumbents have discouraged many serious challengers from entering the race at all.

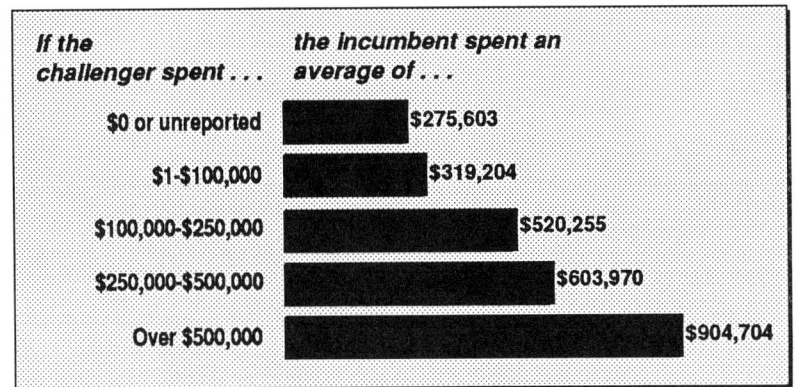

If the challenger spent...	the incumbent spent an average of...
$0 or unreported	$275,603
$1-$100,000	$319,204
$100,000-$250,000	$520,255
$250,000-$500,000	$603,970
Over $500,000	$904,704

Raising the Ante

Those House incumbents who did face relatively well-financed challengers in 1988 tended to respond by stepping up their own fundraising efforts and in most cases swamping the opposition. As seen in the chart at left, the level of spending by incumbents was directly proportional to the spending by their opponents.

What all these trends added up to in 1988 was an election that may have been the least competitive in American history. The House reelection rate of 98.5 percent was the highest since 1792 (though it was only slightly higher than the rate two years earlier). The disparity in spending between incumbents and challengers was unprecedented.

Who Pays the Bills

The dollars that drove winning campaigns 1988 came from different mixtures of sources, depending on the office and the status of the candidate. These pie charts highlight the differences.

Incumbent House members seeking reelection collected nearly half their campaign revenues from political action committees — about double the proportion collected by newcomers winning seats for the first time. Likewise, new candidates were much more likely to reach into their own pockets for the necessary campaign cash. Money from the candidates themselves accounted for nearly 12 percent of the revenues for new House members — over $80,000 on average, versus only 1.3 percent (about $5,000) among incumbents.

The proportion of personal dollars for newcomers to the Senate was even higher, but that average was heavily skewed by the campaign of Democrat Herb Kohl of Wisconsin, who took no money at all from PACs, and instead invested more than $7 million of his own money into his campaign.

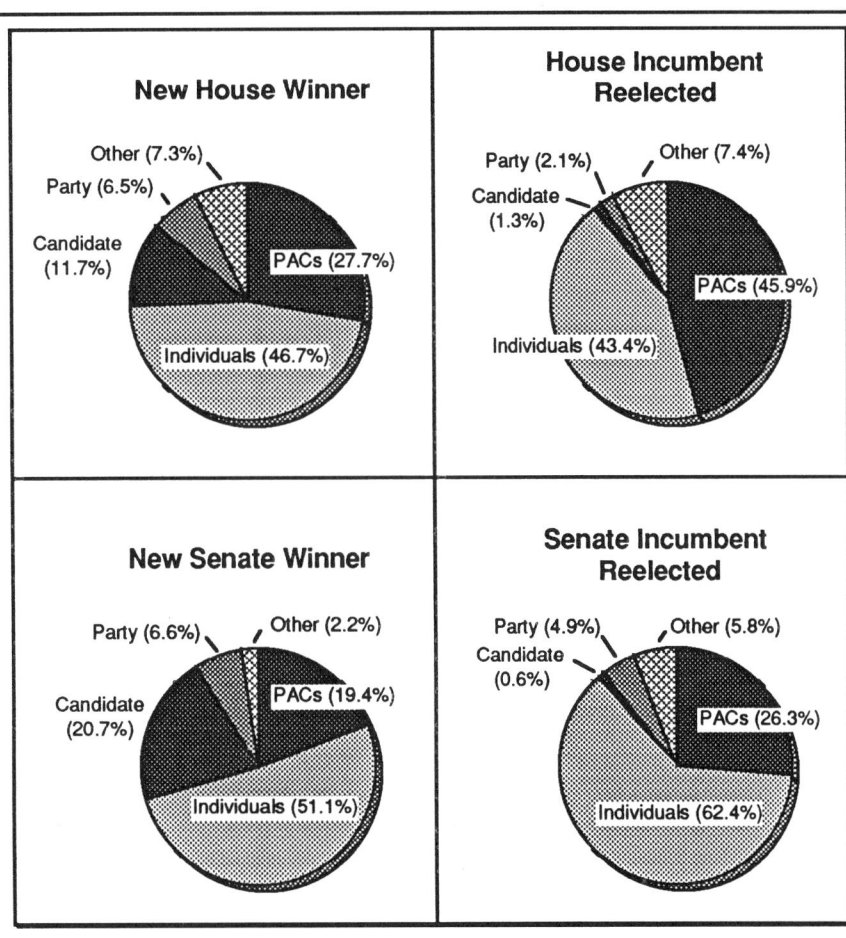

New House Winner
Other (7.3%)
Party (6.5%)
Candidate (11.7%)
PACs (27.7%)
Individuals (46.7%)

House Incumbent Reelected
Party (2.1%)
Other (7.4%)
Candidate (1.3%)
PACs (45.9%)
Individuals (43.4%)

New Senate Winner
Party (6.6%)
Other (2.2%)
Candidate (20.7%)
PACs (19.4%)
Individuals (51.1%)

Senate Incumbent Reelected
Party (4.9%)
Other (5.8%)
Candidate (0.6%)
PACs (26.3%)
Individuals (62.4%)

A Growing Dependency on PACs

With each new election cycle, more and more candidates for Congress — particularly for the U.S. House — are becoming dependent on ever larger sums of contributions from political action committees. The chart at left shows the slow but steady progression in the dependence of candidates on PAC dollars. In 1974 only 17 percent of the average House candidate's funds came from PACs. By 1988 the percentage had risen to 37 percent. Among winning candidates, the figures are even higher. Some 210 winning candidates got at least half their campaign funds from PACs; the overall average for House winners was 48.4 percent. Senate winners got considerably more dollars from PACs — just over $1 million on average — but that represented only one-fourth of the average Senator's total campaign revenues.

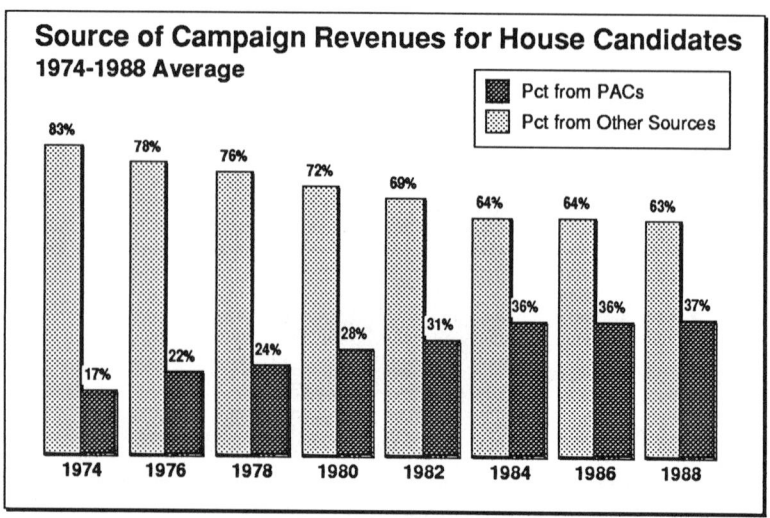

Source of Campaign Revenues for House Candidates
1974-1988 Average

- Pct from PACs
- Pct from Other Sources

Source: *Vital Statistics on Congress 1987-88 (CQ Press)* and Federal Election Commission

Where Newcomers Found the Money

Freshman Democrats and Republicans drew their PAC contributions from dramatically different sources, a fact that can be clearly seen in these two charts. Republican newcomers to Congress collected an average of just under $150,000 in PAC money — from a wide spectrum of business interests and single-issue/ideological groups. Financial interests were the biggest single business segment, contributing an average of $27,000, but ideological and single-issue PACs were the leading overall segment.

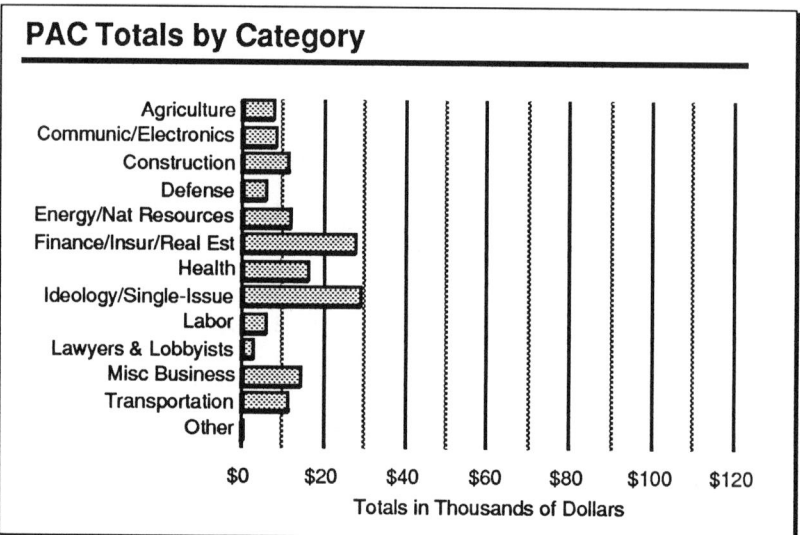

PAC Totals by Category

Totals in Thousands of Dollars

Average Freshman House Republican

Among Democrats, PAC dollars from labor unions far outweighed all other sources. First-term Democrats collected an average of nearly $110,000 from labor PACs in 1988, as opposed to just $66,000 from all segments of the business community combined. Ideological and single-issue issue PACs were also an important source of revenue — providing an average $38,500 for freshman Democrats. Much of that money came from "leadership" PACs sponsored by incumbent Democrats already serving in Congress.

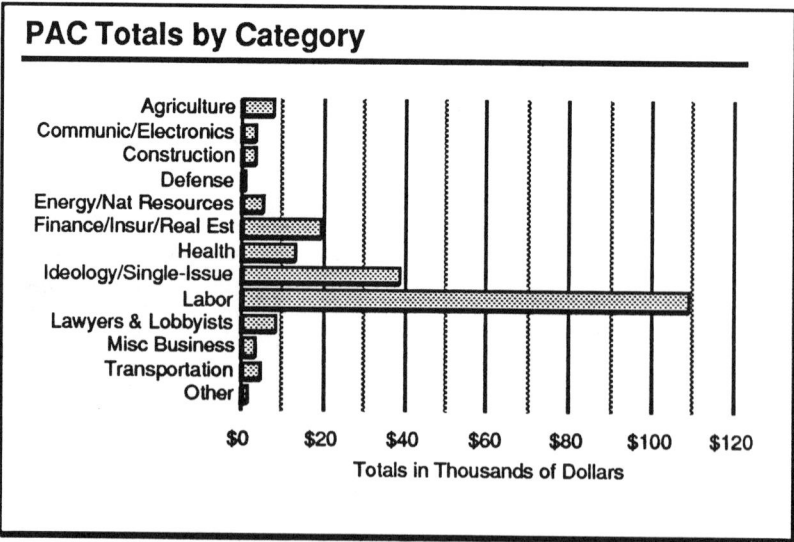

PAC Totals by Category

Totals in Thousands of Dollars

Average Freshman House Democrat

Incumbents Attract the PACs

The overall disparity in PAC contributions between incumbents and challengers is striking. Of the roughly $156 million in PAC dollars that went to congressional candidates in the 1988 elections, more than $118 million went to the campaigns of incumbents. Another $18.9 million went to candidates in races for open seats. The remaining $18.8 million was given to challengers.

Looked at another way, incumbent House members seeking reelection in 1988 received an average of $199,000 from PACs. The candidates who opposed them got an average of about $25,000. Open seat candidates averaged just under $156,000 in PAC contributions. In the Senate, the proportions were similar. Incumbents collected an average $1.22 million from PACs, versus $286,000 for challengers and $687,000 for open seat candidates.

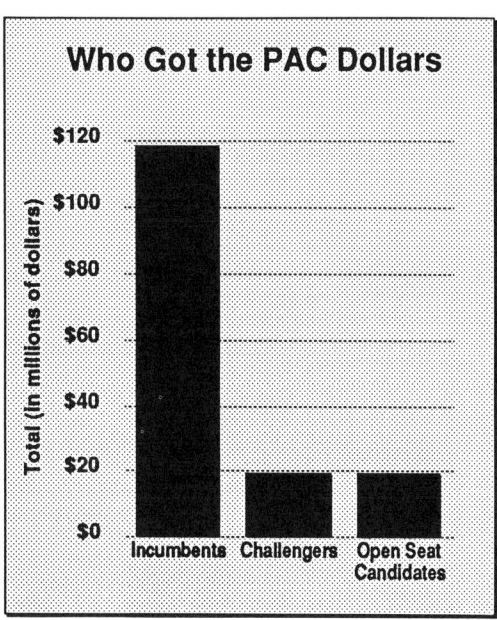

Who Got the PAC Dollars

PAC Totals by Category

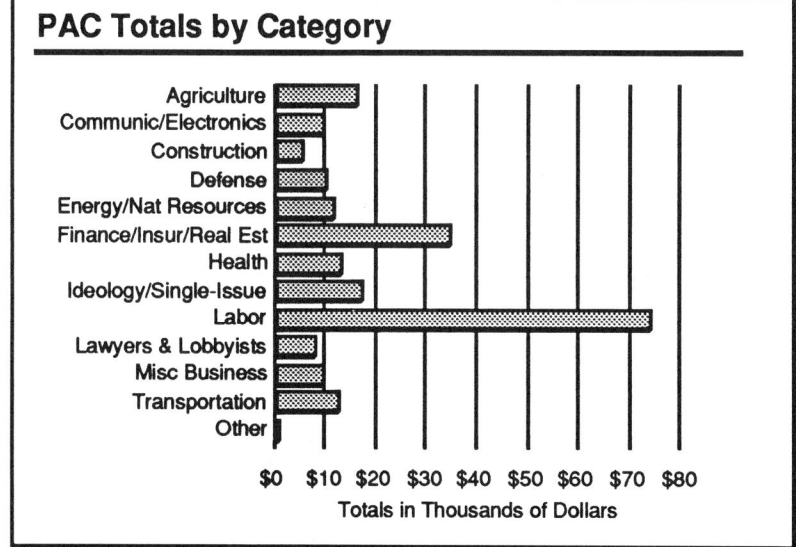

Totals in Thousands of Dollars

Average Incumbent House Republican

PAC Totals by Category

Totals in Thousands of Dollars

Average Incumbent House Democrat

Where Incumbents Found the Money

Once they're elected, Republicans still rely heavily on business PACs and Democrats still count on organized labor, but there is a leveling off in funds from the sources that got them there in the first place.

Most notable among Republican incumbents is the reduced reliance on ideological and single-issue PACs and the growing share of money from financial sector PACs.

Organized labor provides a slightly greater percentage of the funds for Republican incumbents than for GOP newcomers, but Republican members of Congress are still heavily tilted toward business PACs.

More apparent shifts are seen in the patterns of PAC giving to Democrats. While labor PACs are still the most important sector, their proportion of the total PAC dollars is considerably lessened with incumbency. Like the Republicans, the level of PAC contributions from financial, insurance and real estate PACs rises sharply in importance. So do several other business sectors.

The patterns for individual candidates tend to reflect their committee assignments. Many committees in Congress focus on specific industries, and the PACs that represent firms within those industries typically serve as important sources of campaign cash for the members of those committees — whether they are Democrats or Republicans.

Source of PAC Funds — House Freshmen vs. Incumbents

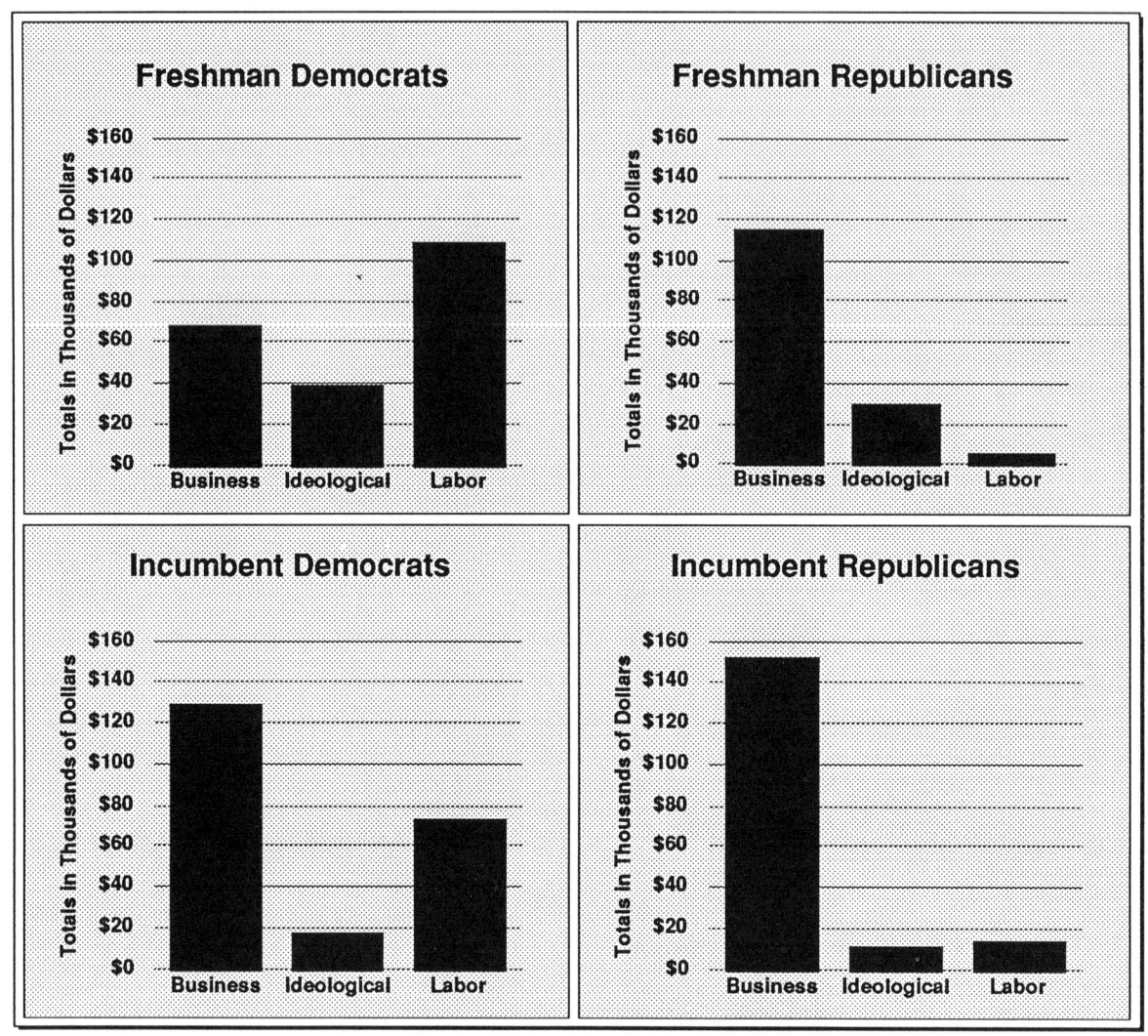

When viewed as three distinct groups of PACs — business, ideological and labor — significant contrasts in the source of PAC funds can be found between Democrats and Republicans, and between incumbents and newcomers to Congress. Freshmen Democrats win election to Congress largely on the strength of contributions from labor unions. In 1988, the average Democratic newcomer to the U.S. House collected nearly $110,000 in labor contributions, versus only $66,000 from all business PACs combined. Republicans averaged more than $115,000 from business PACs, and just $5,500 from labor.

Once a member has won election to Congress, however, the patterns shift — particularly among Democrats. Labor, while still more important than any other single business sector, is outweighed overall by business PACs. For Republicans, the emphasis on business PACs also grows, and the share of labor money — though still small — is higher than that of non-incumbents. For both parties, the share of ideological and single-issue PAC money declines with incumbency. Overall, business PACs gave about 83 percent of their money to incumbents, while ideological PACs gave only 55 percent. Unions gave two-thirds of their contributions to incumbents and one-third to challengers and candidates in open seat races.

Perhaps the most significant trend captured in these charts is the shifting emphasis amonfrom labor to business. Freshmen Democrats in 1988 entered Congress with 50.6 percent of their money coming from labor unions. For incumbents, the labor percentage declined to only one-third on average, and business giving — largely related to committee assignments — accounted for 58.5 percent of all PAC dollars.

Rules of the Game

The rules that govern the financing of federal elections can be complicated enough to keep a small army of Washington D.C. lawyers perpetually employed. But federal election laws are not so complicated that the average voter can't figure out the basics. Outlined below is an overview of the rules.

Who Can Contribute and Who Cannot

Any American citizen can contribute funds to candidates for federal office or to political parties. There is only one exception to this broad rule — individuals and owners of sole proprietorships that have contracts with the federal government. (That prohibition does not extend to employees, partners, officers, or shareholders of larger businesses with government contracts.)

Foreign nationals who do not have permanent residence in the United States are prohibited from contributing to *any* political candidates in the U.S. — at the federal, state, or local level.

Cash contributions exceeding an aggregate of $100 are also prohibited, no matter where they come from. And no candidate can accept an anonymous donation of more than $50.

Corporations, labor unions, national banks and federally chartered corporations are also prohibited from contributing to federal campaigns or parties. The prohibition against corporate giving has been a part of federal law since passage of the Tillman Act in 1907. In 1943, the ban was temporarily extended to labor unions as well. Four years later it was made permanent, with passage of the Taft-Hartley Act.

The Birth of PACs

Organized labor was quick to react to the new restrictions on its political giving. In 1943, the first modern "political action committee" was formed by the Congress of Industrial Organization (which later merged with the American Federation of Labor to form the AFL-CIO). The dollars the PAC distributed came not from the union treasury, but from voluntary contributions by its members. While such an arrangement was not specifically sanctioned by federal law, it was not prohibited either. Over the next 30 years the idea gradually caught on as other labor unions, corporations and business groups formed PACs of their own. But many groups held back. PACs were still a loophole in federal election laws; tolerated but not officially sanctioned.

In 1974, amid the post-Watergate climate of political reform, Congress gave PACs the green light. In its 1974 amendments to the Federal Election Campaign Act, Congress specifically sanctioned the formation of "political committees" to enable employees of corporations or labor unions, or members of political organizations, to pool their dollars and give to the candidates of their choice. At the same time, it gave PACs higher contribution limits than individual contributors, and set up the Federal Election Commission (FEC) to oversee elections and to collect and monitor campaign finance reports filed by PACs and candidates. It was an opening of the floodgates. By the end of 1974, 608 political action committees were officially recognized by the FEC. By 1990 that number had grown to more than 4,100. The dollars they pumped into federal elections mushroomed from $12.5 million in 1974 to over $159 million in 1988. The great majority of those dollars — then and now — went to finance the campaigns of incumbent members of Congress.

Contribution Limits

Candidates for Congress can spend as much money as they can raise — whether from their own pockets or from those of contributors — to wage their campaigns. No spending limits apply. *Contributors* to federal campaigns, on the other hand, *do* face limits on what they can give to a candidate or a national political party. The limits were set as part of the 1974 Federal Election Campaign Act, and they are summarized in the chart below:

Federal Campaign Spending Limits

	To any candidate or candidate committee	To any national party committee	To any PAC or other political committee	Total
Time period	per election*	per calendar year	per calendar year	per calendar year
Individual can give...	$1,000	$20,000	$5,000	$25,000
Multicandidate Committee† can give...	$5,000	$15,000	$5,000	No limit
Other Political Committee can give...	$1,000	$20,000	$5,000	No limit

SOURCE: Federal Election Commission

* Primary and general elections count as two separate elections; so this contribution can be effectively doubled during a normal election year in states with primaries.

† Multicandidate committees are those with more than 50 contributors, that have been registered for at least six months, and (with the exception of state party committees) have made contributions to five or more federal candidates.

Enforcement of the Campaign Laws

Enforcement of the federal campaign laws lies in the hands of the six-member Federal Election Commission in Washington, D.C. Appointed by the president to serve staggered six-year terms, the commission members are traditionally split 3-3 between Democrats and Republicans.

That 3-3 split is also common in many of the commission's votes, particularly when a ruling is likely to benefit one party over another. Many analysts and commentators have contended that the institutional paralysis which sometimes results was exactly what the drafters of the Federal Election Campaign Act had in mind — namely, to keep the commission from being too vigilant and too activist in its enforcement.

Over the years, the commission has come under considerable attack by critics on both sides of the political fence for its lack of direction in enforcing and interpreting the campaign finance law. While the commissioners have fairly regularly cited candidates and fined their campaigns for relatively minor offenses (and occasionally for serious ones), they have been unable to reach consensus on many larger issues affecting the conduct of federal elections.

One area for which the FEC has received substantial praise, however, is its role as a provider of campaign finance information to the public. The FEC has collected millions of pages of records since 1975 on the detailed financing of federal elections, and citizens curious about the identity of their representatives' financial backers can find a wealth of information in the FEC's files.

Public Disclosure

By law, every candidate for federal office must file periodic reports with the Federal Election Commission (FEC) in Washington, D.C., detailing both the income and expenditures of their campaign. Copies of these reports, which are timed to coincide with various high points in the two-year election cycle, must also be filed in the candidate's home state with the state election commission or equivalent agency.

Individual contributors who give an aggregate of $200 or more must be identified by name, address, occupation and employer. All PAC and party contributions, no matter how large or small, must also be itemized.

In addition, PACs themselves must file reports four times a year with the FEC in Washington, detailing both the contributions received by the PAC and the names of candidates and other groups that received the PAC's donations. While PACs are required to file at least quarterly, they may choose to file monthly if they wish — and many of the larger PACs do.

When it compiles the official records of PAC contributions, and records them on its computers, the FEC uses the reports filed by the PACs — *not* those reported by the candidates. Because of this, discrepancies are inevitable between the contributions reported by the candidates and those reported by the PACs.

Deciphering the candidates' FEC reports

Sifting through a candidate's FEC reports is not always an enlightening experience. Many candidates, instead of entering the full name of a PAC, or a hint of its sponsor, often enter the PAC's informal acronym. Even if you knew, for example, that the Association of Trial Lawyers of America was the nation's principal PAC representing lawyers, you might not be able to decode the PAC's shorthand name — ATLA — when it appears on a candidate's report.

Making matters worse, there are no conventions to PAC acronyms and no FEC guidelines to ensure that each PAC uses a unique name. In fact, there are many duplications of shortened PAC names. "APAC," for example, is the informal acronym for no fewer than three PACs: the Alltel Corporation PAC, the American Society of Association Executives PAC, and the Armco Employees PAC. Many other duplicates can also be found in the list of more than 4,000 currently-registered political action committees.

Aside from the acronyms, most PAC names are fairly self-explanatory — at least in naming the organization that sponsors them. There is nothing mysterious, for example, about the Boeing Company PAC or the Mid-America Dairymen. Identification becomes more difficult, however, when the PAC sponsor is less well known and the company's name offers no hint of its line of business. Without consulting a corporate directory on the shelves of the nearest business library, one might have difficulty knowing that Malone & Hyde is a major food wholesaler, that the Kaman Corporation is a defense contractor, or that the Summa Corporation runs a Las Vegas hotel and casino.

Many other PACs, particularly ideological or single-issue PACs, have names that can be maddeningly obscure. Few casual observers would guess, for instance, that the "Valley Education Fund" is actually the leadership PAC of former Democratic Congressman Tony Coelho of California, or that the "Committee for a Level Playing Field" represents banks that want Congress to allow them to begin offering stock brokerage services.

To assist those wanting to decipher the mysteries of PAC names that appear on candidates' FEC filings, the final section of this book, beginning on page 1103, identifies the primary interests of each PAC that gave $20,000 or more in the 1988 election cycle. But new PACs do spring up each election year, so the job of classifying the more obscure ones is a never-ending task.

Individual contributors present a different set of problems. Though candidates are required by law to list the name, address, occupation and employer of each contributor who gives $200 or more, this information is often incomplete. A July 1990 study by Citizen Action, a Washington public interest lobby group, found that 23 percent of FEC computerized records listed no occupation or employer at all.

Candidates who habitually omit this information from their filings rarely receive any penalties from the FEC. While full disclosure is a part of the law, it is routinely unenforced.

Where to find a candidate's reports

Any citizen can view current and past campaign spending reports filed by their own congressman or senator, or any other candidate for federal office. The central repository for these reports is the Public Records Office of the Federal Election Commission at 999 E Street NW, Washington, D.C. 20463. The FEC's toll-free phone number is 1-800-424-9530. In the Washington area, the number is 202-376-3140.

The FEC also maintains a number of remote computer terminals around the country, generally in the offices of the secretary of state or the state election commission. As of July 1990, some 23 states were equipped with FEC terminals. Computer printouts of candidate or PAC reports can be ordered either from the FEC in Washington or from these state offices with terminals. A nominal charge is made for the materials, generally calculated on the cost of reproducing each page. One caveat: itemized contribution reports for major campaigns, such as those for the U.S. Senate, can be quite lengthy, even when reduced to computer printouts. Browsing through them (and in some cases even picking them up and carrying them out the door) can be quite an effort.

Federal campaign records are also available on-line to anyone with a computer, a modem, and an interest in obtaining the information. The on-line fee is $25 an hour and new subscribers must first request the service in writing and include a deposit before receiving their password. The scope of services available on- line improved dramatically in early 1990. Among the data available are full contribution reports for any candidate or group of candidates (such as the congressional delegation from a particular state) and any PAC or groups of PACs. Recent FEC news releases — including those listing summary information such as Top 50 PAC contributor lists, and the latest national roundup of campaign spending by current candidates — are also available on-line.

Copies of the candidates' FEC filings are also available in the candidate's home state. The reports are filed with the secretary of state's office or the state election commission — or whichever other agency in the state monitors elections.

In addition to campaign reports, the FEC also publishes pre-election and post-election reports listing summary statistics on campaign spending and fund-raising by federal candidates, as well as a number of informative brochures outlining federal campaign finance laws and how it applies to candidates, PACs and contributors.

Filing deadlines

Members of Congress and candidates for Congress must file their FEC reports according to the schedules shown in the following charts. Each report must list all the candidate's contributions and expenditures during the reporting period. As the charts show, the schedules vary during election years and off years. In the course of a typical election year, a candidate for Congress may file as many as seven reports. In other years, only two reports are required.

Election Year Reporting Deadlines

Report	Deadline	Period covered
Pre-election reports	12 days before primary	Up to 20 days before the election
	12 days before general election	Up to 20 days before the election
Post-general report	30 days after general election	Up to 20 days after the election
Quarterly reports	Apr 15	Jan 1 - Mar 31
	Jul 15	Apr 1 - Jun 30
	Oct 15	July 1 - Sep 30
	Jan 31	Oct 1 - Dec 31 of previous year

NOTE: If two of the above deadlines closely coincide, a single report may be sufficient.

Non-election Year Reporting Deadlines

Report	Deadline	Period covered
Semi-annual reports	Jul 31	Jan 1 - Jun 30
	Jan 31	July 1 - Dec 31 of previous year

The Soft Money Loophole

In the eyes of many observers — and many political practitioners who make use of it — the principal loophole in the federal campaign spending law is something that has come to be called "soft money." In the broadest sense, soft money encompasses any contributions not regulated by federal election laws. The biggest single pockets of soft money are the contributions made to state and local party organizations, and those made to the national parties when earmarked for their local affiliates. Under the terms of the federal campaign laws, these contributions are exempted from the limitations and reporting requirements that apply to other contributions. Their use, however, is restricted.

Technically, soft money contributions may only be used to support state and local political activities, such as voter registration, get-out-the-vote drives, and the distribution of voter materials such as bumper stickers, campaign buttons and yard signs. The funds can also be used to finance political activities that jointly benefit state, local and federal candidates.

In practice, soft money funds have seeped into federal races in a big way, and have become an important means of supporting the parties' candidates for president and the U.S. Congress — particularly in key battleground states.

Unlike "hard money" contributions, which are subject to strict limits and full disclosure, "soft money" contributions have virtually no strings attached. This offers four main benefits to soft money contributors and recipients. Specifically:

- **Soft money is not subject to any contribution limits.** Contributions to candidates or federal party committees are subject to specific limits (outlined in the chart on page 8). Soft money contributions can be made for any amount at all. In 1988 the biggest single soft money contribution — to the Republican Party — exceeded $500,000. Two years earlier, a $1,000,000 soft money contribution was given to the Democratic Party by Joan Kroc, heiress to the McDonald's Hamburger fortune.

- **Soft money is not subject to federal disclosure requirements.** Unlike contributions to federal parties or to candidates, "soft money" contributions to state parties are subject to state disclosure laws, not federal laws. This means there is no record at the Federal Election Commission — or any other central location — of soft money contributions. There may or may not be records at the state level, depending on the campaign disclosure laws of the state where the contribution is made.

- **Soft money contributions can be made by anyone — including groups prohibited from making contributions to federal candidates or parties.** In federal campaigns, corporations and labor unions are explicitly prohibited from making direct contributions to federal candidates, federal parties, or federal PACs. Their soft money contributions are subject only to the restrictions passed by the legislatures in the individual states where the contributions are made. Many states currently allow corporate and labor union contributions.

- **Soft money offers an extra means of political giving for individuals who've already given the maximum to candidates and federal parties.** Under the federal election laws, individual contributors are limited to an annual maximum of $25,000 in contributions to all candidates, PACs and national parties. Once they've "maxed out" they can give no more — except in soft money. Using this device, wealthy contributors, often with the encouragement of the national parties, have been able to give substantially more than the nominal limit.

In the 1988 elections, both parties used soft money to bolster their parties' spending in presidential battleground states. A 1989 study by the Center for Responsive Politics found $28.5 million in soft money contributions to state parties in nine key states. Nineteen contributors — eight individuals and 11 corporations — gave $100,000 or more in those states. The contributions were found by painstakingly combing through thousands of microfiche and original records from the elections offices of the various states, as no records of the contributions are collected or recorded by the FEC or any other federal agency.

The national parties also raised money in other soft money accounts to enable wealthy contributors to exceed the nominal $25,000 limits. The Republican Party even organized "Team 100" — a select group of contributors (eventually numbering 249) who gave $100,000 or more to the party's soft money accounts. The Democrats were equally inventive in soliciting soft money donations from corporations, unions, and well-heeled individuals. In all, some 46 individuals gave the Democrats $100,000 or more. Between them, the parties are estimated to have raised between $40-$60 million in soft money in the 1988 elections, though the exact amount may never be known because no formal reporting of the money is required by federal law.

Independent Expenditures

Direct contributions to candidates are not the only outlet for political action committees wishing to influence elections. "Independent expenditures" — funds spent independently by PACs to either support or oppose a candidate — offer another, potentially powerful, option. Unlike regular PAC gifts to campaigns, which cannot exceed $10,000 for an election cycle, independent expenditures can total any amount at all. They may directly attack or support a candidate by name, but the expenditures (or the advertising they support) cannot be made in conjunction or coordination with the campaign or staff of any candidate. In all, 225 PACs spent a total of nearly $20.8 million in independent expenditures during the 1988 elections.

Nearly two thirds of that money — $13.6 million — was spent supporting or opposing candidates in the presidential race. Of that amount, more than $8.5 million came from a single group — the National Security PAC, which ran the controversial "Willie Horton" ads attacking Michael Dukakis's prisoner furlough program.

On the congressional level, independent expenditures played a relatively minor role in all but a handful of races. Eight Senate candidates and seven in the House were the beneficiaries of independent expenditure campaigns costing $100,000 or more. Two others — Sen. Howard Metzenbaum of Ohio and Massachusetts Congressman Joe Kennedy — were the targets of big-budget opposition campaigns. Sen. Robert Dole (R-Kan) also benefited from major independent expenditures, though most of that money was directed toward his presidential bid. The full list of candidates who were the subject of independent expenditure campaigns costing $100,000 or more can be seen in the chart on the facing page.

In all, 18 PACs spent $100,000 or more in independent expenditures in the 1988 elections. The following chart lists the PACs and the patterns by which they distributed it.

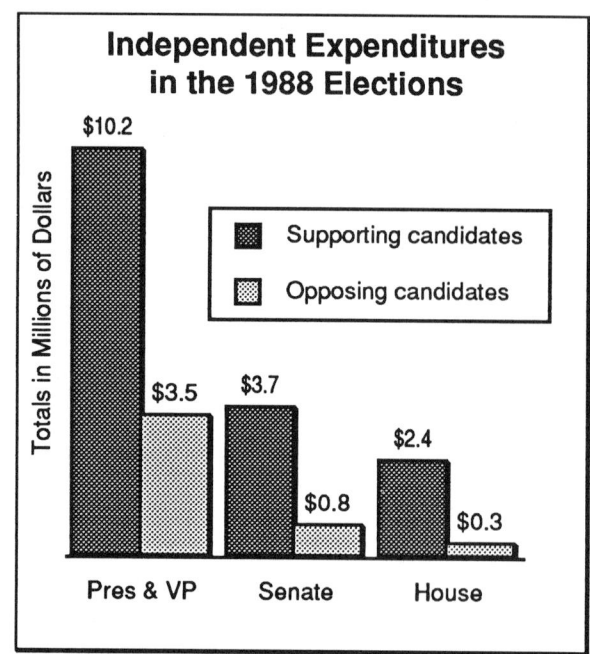

Independent Expenditures in the 1988 Elections

Top PACs Making Independent Expenditures in 1988

PAC	Total	Supporting	Opposing	No of cands	Pres/VP Avg	Senate Avg	House Avg
National Security PAC	$8,552,666	$8,552,666	$0	9	$8,177,502	$46,896	$0
National Rifle Assn	$1,527,832	$20,341	$1,507,491	6	$1,505,176	$2,269	$7,924
Auto Dealers & Drivers for Free Trade	$1,435,672	$1,412,222	$23,450	8	$0	$218,445	$62,500
National Assn of Realtors	$1,332,421	$1,332,421	$0	7	$0	$288,268	$151,177
National Right to Life PAC	$1,315,696	$1,102,842	$212,854	53	$83,836	$18,946	$1,784
Natl Cmte to Preserve Social Security	$1,133,952	$1,130,996	$2,956	285	$0	$19,783	$2,257
American Medical Assn	$838,202	$838,202	$0	15	$0	$60,473	$54,210
American Citizens for Political Action	$830,493	$426,941	$403,552	37	$47,138	$14,955	$18,946
Natl Congressional Club (Jesse Helms)	$645,141	$6,300	$638,841	2	$322,571	$0	$0
Americans United	$343,978	$0	$343,978	1	$0	$343,978	$0
Conservative Victory Committee	$320,094	$21,640	$298,454	12	$42,785	$4,119	$0
Council for National Defense	$263,362	$201,672	$61,690	239	$76,734	$1,701	$182
Committee for the Presidency	$191,918	$191,918	$0	1	$191,918	$0	$0
Mid-America Conservative PAC	$161,398	$0	$161,398	2	$143,909	$17,489	$0
National Council of Senior Citizens	$139,185	$97,359	$41,826	15	$80,457	$4,508	$128
National Conservative PAC	$119,240	$24,450	$94,790	14	$6,350	$8,878	$0
Conservative Campaign Fund	$107,407	$0	$107,407	2	$53,704	$0	$0
Public Affairs PAC	$105,040	$12,668	$92,372	3	$35,013	$0	$0

Most of those top-dollar campaigns were financed by PACs that were also major direct contributors to congressional candidates. Chief among them, as seen in the chart below, were the American Medical Association, the Realtors PAC, and the Auto Dealers and Drivers for Free Trade PAC, which represents dealers of Japanese autos.

In contrast to the presidential races, and a handful of Senate contests, most U.S. House candidates received only modest help, if any, from independent expenditures. Moderate-to-liberal candidates, mostly Democratic incumbents, were likely to benefit from spending by the National Committee to Preserve Social Security, which dispensed over $1.1 million in 1988 to support some 281 House and Senate candidates and oppose four others.

Top Beneficiaries and Targets of Independent Expenditures in 1988

Name	Office	Supporting	Opposing	Total	Principal PACs
Chic Hecht (R-Nev)	Sen	$731,110	$10,701	$741,811	Auto Dlrs/Driv for Free Trade ($521,539) American Medical Assn ($105,363) National Security PAC ($57,556)
Trent Lott (R-Miss)	Sen	$717,238	$0	$717,238	National Assn of Realtors ($348,498) Auto Dlrs/Driv for Free Trade ($319,126)
Howard Metzenbaum (D-Ohio)	Sen	$50,240	$428,733	$478,973	Americans United-OPPOSING ($343,978)
Connie Mack (R-Fla)	Sen	$422,831	$17,375	$440,206	Auto Dlrs/Driv for Free Trade ($326,050)
John Melcher (D-Mont)	Sen	$230,617	$6,896	$237,513	National Assn of Realtors ($228,038)
Joseph P. Kennedy II (D-Mass)	House	$1,506	$229,928	$231,434	Amer Citizens for Pol Action-OPPOSING ($229,928)
James V. Hansen (R-Utah)	House	$220,704	$688	$221,392	National Assn of Realtors ($155,287) American Medical Assn ($65,359)
Orrin Hatch (R-Utah)	Sen	$212,241	$0	$212,241	Amer Citizens for Pol Action ($152,500) National Security PAC ($57,741)
Robert Dole (R-Kan)	Pres/Sen	$197,649	$1,781	$199,430	Amer Citizens for Pol Action ($128,350)
Richard Stallings (D-Idaho)	House	$174,169	$6,044	$180,213	National Assn of Realtors ($126,450)
John Hiler (R-Ind)	House	$175,794	$477	$176,271	National Assn of Realtors ($166,236)
Bill Emerson (R-Mo)	House	$161,742	$0	$161,742	National Assn of Realtors ($152,600)
Ben Nighthorse Campbell (D-Colo)	House	$158,454	$0	$158,454	National Assn of Realtors ($155,312)
Malcolm Wallop (R-Wyo)	Senate	$150,759	$4,144	$154,903	Auto Dlrs/Driv for Free Trade ($88,862) National Security PAC ($58,082)
Leo McCarthy (D-Calif)	Sen cand	$146,554	$0	$146,554	Natl Cmte/Preserve Soc Secur ($133,129)
Dave Durenberger (R-Minn)	Sen	$143,104	$0	$143,104	American Medical Assn ($134,527)
Bill Sarpalius (D-Texas)	House	$131,560	$0	$131,560	American Medical Assn ($131,560)
Liz Patterson (D-SC)	House	$115,752	$0	$115,752	American Medical Assn ($112,994)

Profile of the Typical Congressional Winner

In 1988, the typical winning candidate for the U.S. House of Representatives . . . .

- **Was an incumbent.** In the 1988 November elections, 408 of the 435 seats were contested by incumbents seeking reelection. Of those 408 incumbents, 402 were successfully reelected, for a reelection rate of 98.5 percent — the highest percentage since the election of 1792.

- **Spent about $390,000.** The cost of winning election campaigns for the U.S. House in 1988 ranged from the $8,397 spent by veteran Democrat William Natcher of Kentucky to the more than $1.7 million spent by California Republican Bob Dornan. Of the 435 races, 110 winning campaigns cost $500,000 or more. Another 31 cost under $100,000; all were waged by incumbents seeking reelection.

- **Vastly outspent their opponent.** Many incumbents had only nominal opposition. And many of their challengers had an extremely difficult time collecting campaign funds. On average, losing candidates spent just under $116,000 — a figure that was lower than the average spent in 1980. It was the third election in a row where average spending by challengers actually declined. In more than half the races (230 out of 435) the winner spent at least *ten times* the amount spent by the loser. In nearly 85 percent of the races, the winner outspent the loser by a factor of two-to-one or more.

- **Collected about half their campaign funds from PACs.** The average winning candidate got almost $200,000 from political action committees in 1988. Eleven winning candidates (all incumbents) took no PAC money. They all won reelection easily.

- **Outpolled their opponent by nearly three-to-one.** The average winning House candidate in 1988 won election with 72.6 percent of the vote. Only 37 seats were won with 55 percent of the vote or less. In 61 races, the winners were unopposed or won with at least 95 percent of the vote.

- **Closed the election year with $128,000 in the bank.** While many losing candidates were struggling to repay debts, most House winners finished the 1988 election year with healthy balances in their campaign accounts that gave them a significant head start on challengers for the next election. Seventy-six House winners had leftover war chests of $250,000 or more. Another 75, however, closed the year with a net deficit in their campaign accounts. Among those elected for the first time in 1988, most closed the year with a deficit, the average end-of-year balance was a deficit of about $68,000.

In 1988, the typical winning candidate for the U.S. Senate . . . .

- **Was an incumbent.** Two-thirds of the winning candidates — 23 out of 33 — were incumbents who successfully won reelection. But the reelection rate for Senators, although high, was still lower than that of House members. In all, 23 incumbents won reelection and four lost — for an average reelection rate of 85 percent. But a considerably higher percentage of newcomers won election to the Senate than to the House. The 1988 elections brought 10 new faces to the Senate (for a turnover rate of 30 percent among the 33 running). In the House, 33 new candidates came to office for the first time — a turnover of less than 8 percent.

- **Spent just over $4 million.** The cost of Senate races has been escalating, like House races, at a rate roughly double the level of inflation. In 1988 that cost rose to an average of slightly more than $4 million. The range of spending in successful campaigns was wide; from Democrat Spark Matsunaga in Hawaii, who spent just $790,000 to win an easy reelection, to Republican Pete Wilson of California, whose race cost $14.6 million.

- **Faced fairly well financed opponents.** In contrast to U.S. House races, all Senate candidates in 1988 faced major party opponents — though some challengers waged only token campaigns. Ten of the 33 races were fairly competitive in spending, and in four races, the loser actually outspent the winner. But many races were runaways, both in votes and spending. Twenty-one winning Senate candidates outspent their opponents by at least two-to-one. Eight of them topped their challengers' spending by a margin of 10-to-1 or more.

- **Collected about $1 million — one quarter of their total revenues — from PACs.** While Senate campaigns rely much more heavily than house campaigns on contributions from individuals, the amount of PAC dollars poured into Senate campaigns was substantially higher than those given to House members. On average, Senate winners in 1988 drew just over $1 million in PAC funds, accounting for about one-fourth of their total campaign revenues. Two candidates — incumbents Pete Wilson of California and Lloyd Bentsen of Texas — drew more than $2 million each in PAC contributions. Wilson collected $2.4 million; Bentsen got more than $2.6 million. In 1988 Bentsen ran simultaneously for Vice President and for reelection to this Senate seat from Texas. Nearly all the PAC funds went to his Senate campaign committee.

- **Won election by a comfortable margin, but not a landslide.** Winning Senate candidates in 1988 captured an average 60.4 percent of the vote. One third of the 33 races were decided by less than 10 percentage points. Three Senators won with more than 70 percent of the overall vote. This is in striking contrast to U.S. House races, which were won by an *average* 72.6 percent at the polls, and reflects the fact that even in cases where incumbents are seeking reelection, opposition parties do try to recruit attractive candidates to contest the seat.

- **Spent most, but not all, of the money they raised.** Senate winners, unlike their counterparts in the House, tended to end the election year with relatively modest bank balances in their campaign accounts. Twelve winners ended with net deficits, and five closed out the election year with more than half a million dollars in the bank. One reason for the lower end-of-year balances by Senate winners is that they serve for six year terms. And although the pressures of money raising are never too far from an incumbent's mind, the breathing room between elections is considerably longer for Senators than for House members, who must run every two years and are therefore always raising funds for the next election.

The Rising Tide of PACs

Political action committees were born in the 1940s out of a perceived political necessity. When labor unions were prohibited from spending union treasury funds to contribute to federal candidates, they invented the idea of pooling donations from their members and presenting *that* money to the candidates instead. The idea appealed not only to labor unions, but to business and ideological groups as well, though the lack of a formal federal sanction for PACs kept many groups from setting up their own committees. When Congress passed the 1974 amendments to the Federal Election Campaign Act and officially sanctioned the concept of "political committees" the great PAC rush began. While the total number of political action committees has finally begun to taper off, the dollars they provide to federal candidates — and particularly to congressional incumbents — has continued to grow with each new election year.

A total of more than 4,800 political action committees were officially registered at the end of the 1988 election year. Of those, slightly less than 3,300 actually contributed funds to federal candidates. Many of those PACs were small-scale operations, sponsored by small

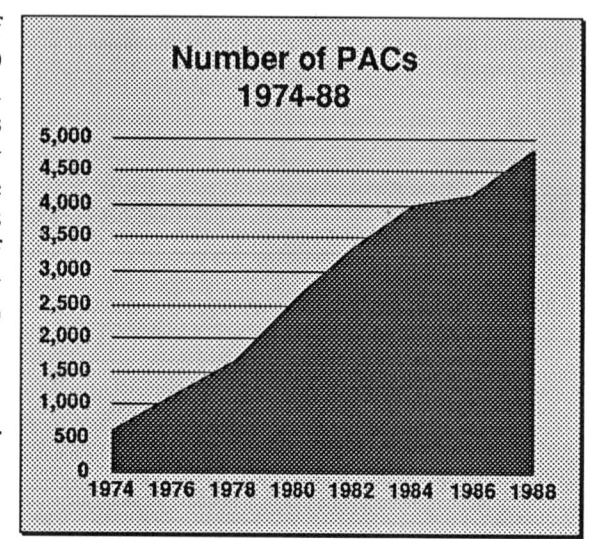

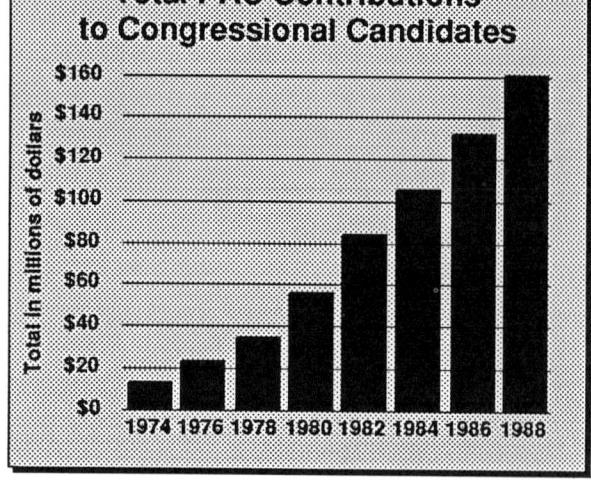

Source: Vital Statistics on Congress, 1987-1988 (CQ Press)

businesses, political clubs, or labor union locals, and contributed only to candidates in their own state or region. Less than one out of four of the registered PACs gave $20,000 or more to federal candidates; but those that did accounted for 93 percent of all PAC giving. The chart below shows the relative distribution of small, medium and large sized PACs, and their respective spending power in the 1988 elections.

This many PACs...	... gave this amount of money	... for this total impact
1,548	$0	
1,718	Less than $10,000	
458	$10,000-$20,000	
503	$20,001 - $50,000	
282	$50,001 - $100,000	
323	Over $100,000	

As is seen from this chart, the growth in the number of PACs may not be as significant as the growth in *large* PACs. One tenth of the total PAC community provided more than two-thirds of all the dollars in the 1987-88 election cycle. None of the charts on this page include the growing phenomenon of independent expenditures, made not directly to candidate's, but spent on their behalf — or against them. Such expenditures have shown their power in the past. In 1980, a well-financed campaign by the National Conservative PAC, or NCPAC, helped defeat enough liberal Democrats that the Republican party gained the balance of power in the U.S. Senate. And in 1988, the $8.5 million campaign of the National Security PAC introduced the name Willie Horton to millions of Americans and helped sabotage the campaign of Democratic presidential candidate Michael Dukakis.

With outstretched hands . . .

The rising financial clout of PACs is not something that has been forced upon members of Congress over their objections. Modern campaign techniques, centered around 30-second TV spots and highly targeted direct mail appeals, have prompted many incumbents to hire campaign consultants, pollsters, media advisers, fund-raisers and a retinue of specialists who are the behind-the-scenes operatives of today's high-tech campaigns. The pressures of raising the money it takes to pay for them all have forced nearly every incumbent to spend an increasing amount of time appealing to PACs and other contributors for funds.

While many incumbents faced only token opposition in the 1988 elections, many others had cause to use those funds to fend off aggressive challengers. The following charts show the members of Congress who relied the most heavily — and the least — on contributions from political action committees in the 1988 elections.

Top recipients of PAC contributions in 1987-88

House Members

Name	PAC Rcpts	Total Rcpts
Robert H. Michel (R-Ill)	$558,417	$877,026
Thomas S. Foley (D-Wash)	$554,640	$781,195
Jim Moody (D-Wis)	$519,503	$1,291,531
David E. Price (D-NC)	$489,658	$1,029,767
Mike Espy (D-Miss)	$480,490	$880,227
Robert T. Matsui (D-Calif)	$473,863	$917,025
Jim Jontz (D-Ind)	$471,225	$721,637
Thomas A. Luken (D-Ohio)	$468,185	$774,952
Byron L. Dorgan (D-ND)	$462,346	$687,234
John D. Dingell (D-Mich)	$459,242	$613,770

Senate Members

Name	PAC Rcpts	Total Rcpts
Lloyd Bentsen (D-Texas)	$2,499,811	$9,541,579
Pete Wilson (R-Calif)	$2,400,342	$14,515,245
Dave Durenberger (R-Minn)	$1,792,646	$6,761,554
Frank Lautenberg (D-NJ)	$1,631,341	$8,039,253
Jim Sasser (D-Tenn)	$1,620,300	$3,705,296
Donald W. Riegle Jr. (D-Mich)	$1,536,168	$4,186,389
John Heinz (R-Pa)	$1,481,333	$6,014,399
Jeff Bingaman (D-NM)	$1,403,255	$3,806,858
John Danforth (R-Mo)	$1,399,841	$4,753,327
Orrin Hatch (R-Utah)	$1,314,465	$4,268,515

House Members

Name	PAC Pct
Augustus F. Hawkins (D-Calif)	96.5%
Harley O. Staggers (D-WVa)	88.9%
Cardiss Collins (D-Ill)	88.4%
W. J. "Billy" Tauzin (D-La)	86.9%
William L. Clay (D-Mo)	82.1%
Jim Cooper (D-Tenn)	82.0%
Joe Kolter (D-Pa)	82.0%
Bernard J. Dwyer (D-NJ)	81.9%
Joseph M. Gaydos (D-Pa)	81.8%
Howard C. Nielson (R-Utah)	81.4%
William J. Coyne (D-Pa)	80.1%

Senate Members

Name	PAC Pct
James M. Jeffords (R-Vt)	65.5%
Robert C. Byrd (D-WVa)	65.1%
Malcolm Wallop (R-Wyo)	62.1%
Quentin N. Burdick (D-ND)	55.2%
Spark Matsunaga (D-Hawaii)	49.5%
Jim Sasser (D-Tenn)	44.1%
George Mitchell (D-Maine)	42.0%
William V. Roth Jr. (R-Del)	40.6%
Paul Sarbanes (D-Md)	38.5%
John Chafee (R-RI)	38.2%
Donald W. Riegle Jr. (D-Mich)	36.7%

Heaviest reliance on PAC dollars

Ten House members drew 80 percent or more of their 1988 campaign funds from PAC contributions. Several who did came from economically depressed districts. All won reelection.

Senate reliance on PAC contributions has historically been lower than in the House. On average, winning Senate candidates in 1988 drew about one-fourth of their campaign funds from PACs.

. . . And twelve members who said "No"

Of the 468 winning candidates elected to Congress in 1988, an even dozen won their seats without the help of PAC money. The liste included 11 House incumbents — all of whom won reelection by comfortable margins — and one Senate newcomer, Herb Kohl of Wisconsin. In place of the PACs, Kohl financed his campaign with $7 million of his own money. His turned his refusal to take PAC funds into a campaign asset, capitalizing on it with the slogan "He's nobody's man but yours."

Name	PAC Rcpts	Total Receipts
Bill Archer (R-Texas)	$0	$269,695
Anthony C. Beilenson (D-Calif)	$0	$150,275
Philip M. Crane (R-Ill)	$0	$466,894
Bill Goodling (R-Pa)	$0	$54,123
Bill Gradison (R-Ohio)	$0	$197,743
Andrew Jacobs Jr. (D-Ind)	$0	$35,731
Herb Kohl (D-Wis)	$0	$7,576,540
Jim Leach (R-Iowa)	$0	$206,618
Edward J. Markey (D-Mass)	$0	$484,173
William H. Natcher (D-Ky)	$0	$8,397
Ralph Regula (R-Ohio)	$0	$108,672
Mike Synar (D-Okla)	$0	$310,865

The Patterns in PAC Contributions

Pragmatism — not partisanship, and not political philosophy — appears to be the guiding principle behind many PAC contributions to congressional candidates, at least in the world of business PACs. Of the 1,113 PACs that gave $20,000 or more in the 1988 elections, 93 percent gave to members of both parties. One-third of those top-spending PACs — most of them within the business community — split their dollars fairly evenly between Democrats and Republicans, giving no more than 60 percent of their money to either side. Ideological and labor PACs were far more likely to concentrate their funds with candidates of a single political party, as seen in the chart below.

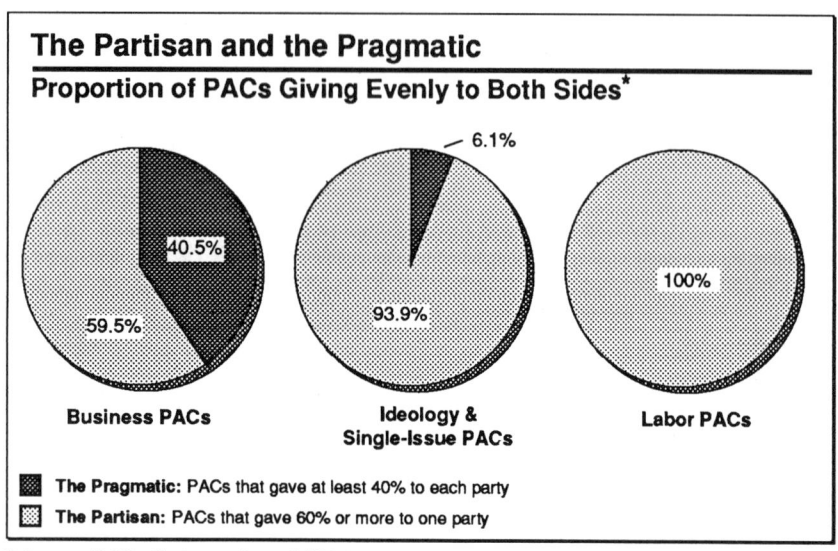

The Partisan and the Pragmatic

Proportion of PACs Giving Evenly to Both Sides*

— 6.1%

40.5%

59.5%

93.9%

100%

Business PACs

**Ideology &
Single-Issue PACs**

Labor PACs

■ **The Pragmatic:** PACs that gave at least 40% to each party

░ **The Partisan:** PACs that gave 60% or more to one party

* Among PACs that contributed $20,000 or more in 1987-88

Labor unions and ideological/single-issue PACs were the most likely to strongly favor one party over the other. That fact can also be seen in the chart below, which contrasts the proportion of dollars that each primary sector in the PAC community gave to members of each party.

The Three Primary PAC Sectors:
Business, Labor & Ideological/Single-Issue

While it is certainly possible to learn something about PAC behavior by looking at the overall patterns of PACs, it can be far more revealing to examine the many different segments of the PAC community one by one. It quickly becomes apparent that different groups of PACs behave differently. Labor and ideological PACs, for instance, distribute their money in a completely different pattern from business PACs — as the charts on this page show.

Business PACs gave almost exactly the same amount to Democrats as Republicans. Ideological PACs favored Democrats two-to-one. And labor PACs, long the stalwarts of the Democratic Party, favored the party's candidates by a ratio of more than nine-to-one when handing out their contributions.

This overwhelming proportion of labor contributions to Democratic candidates tips the scale in favor of that party in overall PAC contributions, even though business PACs as a group gave nearly three times as much money as labor PACs, and nearly twice as much as labor and ideological PACs combined. *(See the chart on the facing page).*

Within these three main categories of PACs many other patterns can be found. The rest of the book explores their differences and similarities in detail.

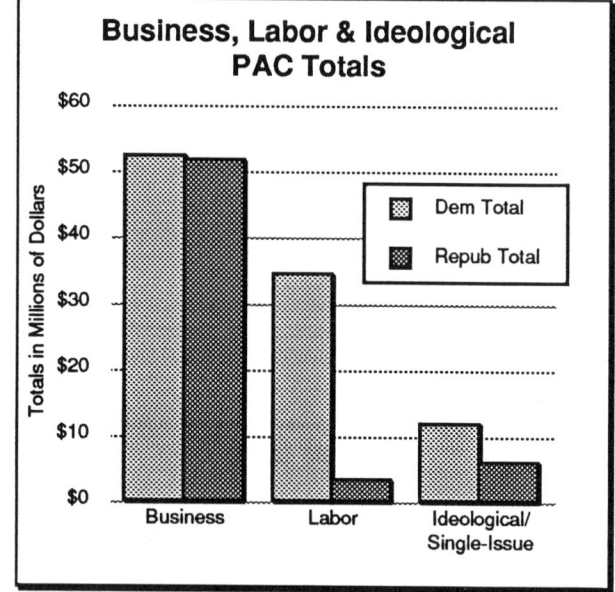

**Business, Labor & Ideological
PAC Totals**

Totals in Millions of Dollars

$60

$50

$40

$30

$20

$10

$0

□ Dem Total

▨ Repub Total

Business   Labor   Ideological/
Single-Issue

	Total	To Democrats	To Republicans	Dem Pct	Repub Pct
Business	$103,876,666	$52,234,895	$51,641,771	50.3%	49.7%
Ideology	$17,753,136	$11,790,709	$5,962,427	66.4%	33.6%
Labor	$37,573,622	$34,382,514	$3,191,108	91.5%	8.5%
Total	**$159,203,424**	**$98,408,118**	**$60,795,306**	**61.8%**	**38.2%**

The World of PACs from Three Different Angles

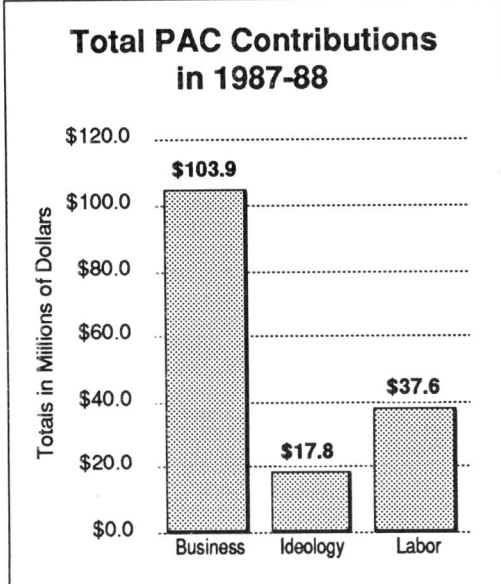

Total PAC Contributions in 1987-88

Totals in Millions of Dollars

- Business: $103.9
- Ideology: $17.8
- Labor: $37.6

The dollar power of business PACs can be clearly seen in the chart at left. With more than $100 million in contributions to federal candidates in the 1988 election cycle, PACs representing every industry from car dealers to morticians sought to help their political friends and win their favor. Compared to labor and ideological/single-issue PACs, their dollar power was overwhelming.

A different story emerges when you turn the chart on its ear and break apart the business PACs into their individual sectors. No business segment comes close to offering either party the dollars that labor PACs produce for Democrats. While business PACs were giving relatively equal amounts to members of both parties, labor put 91.5 percent of its PAC dollars into Democratic campaigns. Even ideological and single-issue PACs rank high compared with the many diverse components of the business and industrial PACs.

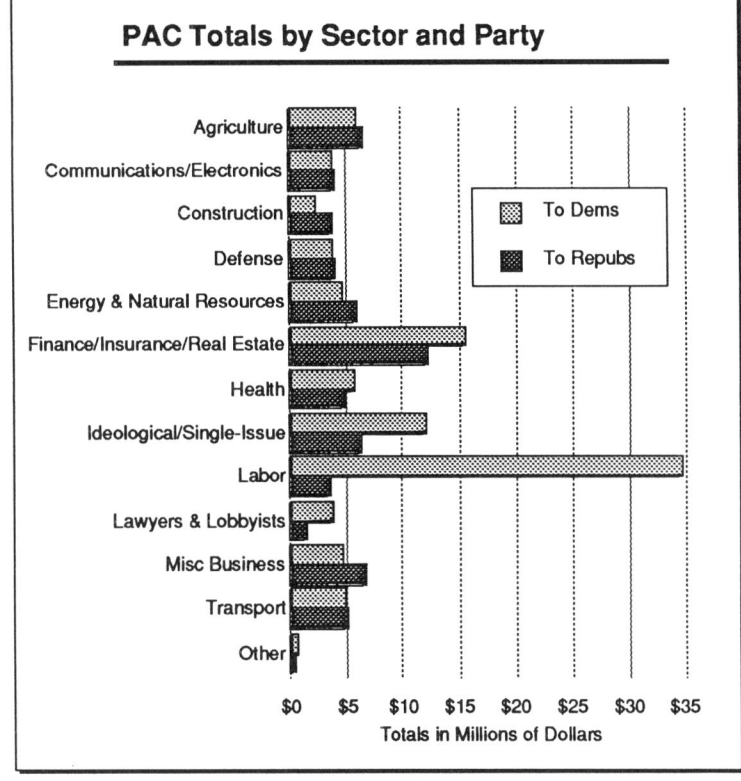

PAC Totals by Sector and Party

Legend:
- To Dems
- To Repubs

Sectors: Agriculture, Communications/Electronics, Construction, Defense, Energy & Natural Resources, Finance/Insurance/Real Estate, Health, Ideological/Single-Issue, Labor, Lawyers & Lobbyists, Misc Business, Transport, Other

Totals in Millions of Dollars

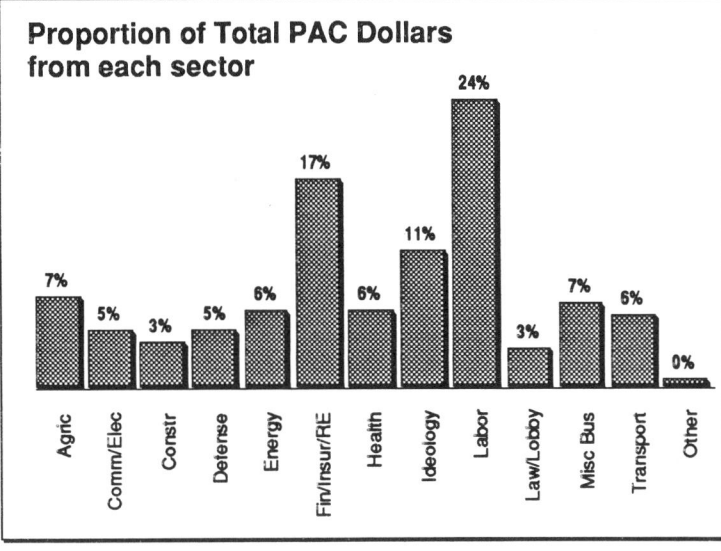

Proportion of Total PAC Dollars from each sector

- Agric: 7%
- Comm/Elec: 5%
- Constr: 3%
- Defense: 5%
- Energy: 6%
- Fin/Insur/RE: 17%
- Health: 6%
- Ideology: 11%
- Labor: 24%
- Law/Lobby: 3%
- Misc Bus: 7%
- Transport: 6%
- Other: 0%

After labor, the financial sector was the heaviest contributor to congressional campaigns, supplying 17 percent of all PAC dollars given in the 1988 elections. Banks, investment firms, insurance companies and Realtors combined to make it the biggest segment by far within the community of business PACs. What this chart doesn't show (but what can be seen in the pages that follow) is that many of those financial PACs gave with as much single-mindedness as labor — but in a different pattern. Instead of giving to members from one party, PACs representing such groups as accountants, commercial banks and insurance companies concentrated their funds on incumbent members of key congressional committees of strategic importance to the financial sector.

The Top 100 PAC Sponsors

Rank	PAC Sponsor	Total	Principal Category	Sector
1	National Assn of Realtors*	$3,047,269	Real Estate	Fin/Insur/Real Est
2	Teamsters Union*	$2,925,164	Transport Union	Labor
3	American Medical Assn*	$2,664,202	Doctors	Health
4	National Education Assn*	$2,151,029	Teachers Union	Labor
5	National Assn of Retired Federal Employees*	$1,986,400	Govt Union	Labor
6	Assn of Trial Lawyers of America*	$1,962,058	Lawyers	Law/Lobbyist
7	United Auto Workers*	$1,955,099	Manuf Union	Labor
8	National Assn of Letter Carriers*	$1,758,742	Postal Union	Labor
9	American Federation of State/County/Munic Employees	$1,658,386	Govt Union	Labor
10	Machinists/Aerospace Workers Union*	$1,524,780	Manuf Union	Labor
11	National Assn of Home Builders*	$1,462,756	Resid Constr	Construction
12	Marine Engineers Union*	$1,430,771	Seamen Union	Labor
13	Carpenters & Joiners Union*	$1,409,395	Constr Union	Labor
14	American Bankers Assn*	$1,345,083	Comml Banks	Fin/Insur/Real Est
15	National Assn of Life Underwriters	$1,329,150	Life Insurance	Fin/Insur/Real Est
16	AT&T	$1,305,112	Long Distance/Defense	Commun/Electric
17	Intl Brotherhood of Electrical Workers*	$1,237,170	Misc Union	Labor
18	Air Line Pilots Assn	$1,209,500	Transport Union	Labor
19	AFL-CIO*	$1,207,232	Labor Unions	Labor
20	National Auto Dealers Assn	$1,202,420	Auto Dealers	Transport
21	Food & Commercial Workers Union*	$1,175,210	Misc Union	Labor
22	Auto Dealers & Drivers for Free Trade	$1,158,700	Japanese Auto Dealers	Transport
23	National PAC	$1,134,500	Pro-Israel	Ideol/Single Issue
24	Seafarers International Union*	$1,108,945	Seamen Union	Labor
25	Operating Engineers Union*	$977,521	Constr Union	Labor
26	Laborers Union*	$920,645	Constr Union	Labor
27	American Institute of CPA's	$907,159	Accountants	Fin/Insur/Real Est
28	American Postal Workers Union*	$905,425	Postal Union	Labor
29	United Steelworkers	$902,150	Manuf Union	Labor
30	American Dental Assn*	$897,000	Dentists	Health
31	American Federation of Teachers*	$870,680	Teachers Union	Labor
32	Associated Milk Producers	$836,350	Dairy	Agriculture
33	United Transportation Union	$803,385	Railroad Union	Labor
34	Sheet Metal Workers Union*	$801,102	Constr Union	Labor
35	National Rifle Assn	$772,756	Pro-Guns	Ideol/Single Issue
36	United Parcel Service	$771,768	Delivery	Transport
37	Communications Workers of America*	$771,090	Misc Union	Labor
38	Associated General Contractors*	$748,975	Comml Constr	Construction
39	National Committee to Preserve Social Security	$744,650	Soc Security/Elderly	Ideol/Single Issue
40	US League of Savings Assn*	$704,601	Savings Banks	Fin/Insur/Real Est
41	National Committee for an Effective Congress	$684,616	Dem/Liberal	Ideol/Single Issue
42	American Academy of Ophthalmology	$644,000	Eye Doctors	Health
43	Philip Morris*	$623,380	Tobacco/Food Prod/Beer	Agriculture
44	Independent Insurance Agents of America	$612,167	Insurance	Fin/Insur/Real Est
45	Plumbers/Pipefitters Union*	$586,376	Constr Union	Labor
46	BellSouth*	$578,656	Phone Utility/Publishing	Commun/Electric
47	Federal Express Corp	$573,537	Air Freight	Transport
48	General Motors*	$555,469	Auto/Defense	Transport
49	Valley Education Fund (Rep. Tony Coelho)	$553,576	Dem Leaders	Ideol/Single Issue
50	Amalgamated Transit Union	$543,687	Transport Union	Labor

* Contributions came from more than one PAC affiliated with this sponsor

Top 100 Account for nearly half of all PAC dollars

These 100 corporations, labor unions, trade associations, professional societies and assorted interest groups were the heaviest hitters of the PAC community. Together, they **contributed a combined $77.2 million** to federal candidates in the 1988 elections — nearly half the total given by all PACs in the 1987-88 election cycle.

Labor unions were the dominant sector, accounting for 30 positions on the Top 100, and seven in the Top 10. In all, those 30 labor organizations accounted for a remarkable $33 million in direct contributions to candidates. The figure is even more remarkable when one considers that all labor PACs combined gave just $37.5 million. The figure is testimony to the fact that labor PAC dollars represent the most highly concentrated source of campaign cash in the entire PAC community. More than 91 percent of Labor's funds in the 1988 elections went to Democrats.

Rank	PAC Sponsor	Total	Principal Category	Sector
51	ACRE (Action Committee for Rural Electrification)*	$504,038	Rural Electric	Energy/Nat Resrce
52	Credit Union National Assn*	$471,630	Credit Union	Fin/Insur/Real Est
53	American Express*	$459,950	Securities/Credit	Fin/Insur/Real Est
54	Mid-America Dairymen	$458,650	Dairy	Agriculture
55	Chicago Mercantile Exchange	$449,400	Commodities	Agriculture
56	Majority Congress Committee (Rep. Jim Wright)	$447,220	Dem Leaders	Ideol/Single Issue
57	J P Morgan & Company	$445,900	Comml Banks	Fin/Insur/Real Est
58	Lockheed Corp	$441,834	Air Defense	Defense
59	National Beer Wholesalers Assn	$440,301	Liquor Whlsl	Misc Business
60	Ironworkers Union*	$433,375	Constr Union	Labor
61	Chicago Board of Trade	$424,350	Commodities	Agriculture
62	Waste Management Inc	$418,116	Waste Mgmt	Energy/Nat Resrce
63	Textron Inc	$411,431	Air Defense	Defense
64	American Hospital Assn	$409,127	Hospitals	Health
65	Citicorp	$401,223	Comml Banks	Fin/Insur/Real Est
66	National Rural Letter Carriers Assn	$398,280	Postal Union	Labor
67	Ladies Garment Workers Union	$393,929	Manuf Union	Labor
68	Northrop Corp	$383,517	Air Defense	Defense
69	FMC Corp	$382,345	Chemical/Defense	Defense
70	Rockwell International	$379,768	Air Defense	Defense
71	Barnett Banks of Florida	$375,700	Comml Banks	Fin/Insur/Real Est
72	Transportation Communication Union	$375,398	Transport Union	Labor
73	National Restaurant Assn*	$372,050	Restaurants	Misc Business
74	Dow Chemical*	$370,750	Chemicals/Oil/Pharm	Misc Business
75	General Electric*	$370,445	Electronics/Defense	Commun/Electric
76	Ford Motor Company*	$359,668	Auto/Defense	Transport
77	Food Marketing Institute	$358,574	Food Stores	Misc Business
78	Union Pacific Corp	$358,450	Railroads	Transport
79	Chrysler Corp	$355,008	Auto/Defense	Transport
80	United Technologies	$343,996	Air Defense	Defense
81	National Utility Contractors Assn	$337,500	Comml Constr	Construction
82	American Optometric Assn	$335,186	Eye Doctors	Health
83	American Family Corp	$334,900	Insurance	Fin/Insur/Real Est
84	American Crystal Sugar Corp	$334,575	Sugar	Agriculture
85	Texas Air*	$332,905	Airlines	Transport
86	Boeing Company	$325,485	Aircraft/Air Defense	Transport
87	McDonnell Douglas*	$320,800	Air Defense/Aircraft	Defense
88	Dairymen Inc*	$320,708	Dairy	Agriculture
89	Continental Telecom	$320,170	Phone Utility	Commun/Electric
90	Metropolitan Life*	$319,845	Life Insurance	Fin/Insur/Real Est
91	Service Employees International Union	$319,808	Misc Unions	Labor
92	Amoco Corp	$318,764	Oil & Gas	Energy/Nat Resrce
93	National Assn of Mutual Insurance Agents	$317,283	Insurance	Fin/Insur/Real Est
94	Campaign America (Sen. Bob Dole)	$313,861	Repub Leader	Ideol/Single Issue
95	National Federation of Independent Business	$310,349	Bus Assn	Misc Business
96	Mortgage Bankers Assn of America	$309,858	Mortgage Bank	Fin/Insur/Real Est
97	United Mine Workers	$309,068	Misc Union	Labor
98	Washington PAC	$308,650	Pro-Israel	Ideol/Single Issue
99	Morgan Stanley*	$306,700	Securities/Textiles	Fin/Insur/Real Est
100	Prudential Insurance*	$305,962	Insurance/Securities	Fin/Insur/Real Est

Financial interests were the second most pervasive on the Top 100 list. Seventeen PACs from the Finance, Insurance & Real Estate sector dispensed a total of just under $12 million. Leading the list — both of the finance sector and of all other PACs — was the Realtors PAC, which contributed more than $3 million to some 542 federal candidates.

Transportation PACs were next on the list. Ten transport PACs gave a combined $6 million. They were led by two groups of auto dealers — the National Auto Dealers Assn. and Auto Dealers & Drivers for Free Trade PAC, which represents dealers of Japanese cars. Health industry and ideological/single-issue PACs accounted for nearly $5 million each. The health PACs were led by the AMA PAC, which ranked third overall. The ideology sector included three "leadership PACs" sponsored by members of Congress.

Many of the PAC sponsors on the Top 100 list gave through multiple PACs. Labor unions gave both through their national union and through a number of locals. Corporations gave through the PACs of subsidiaries. Trade and professional associations chipped in from their regional affiliates.

Targeting the Committees

One of the first patterns that becomes apparent when reviewing the PAC contributions to incumbents in Congress is that the member's profile of contributors tends to parallel his or her committee assignments. Members of the Banking Committees in the House or Senate typically receive concentrations of money not only from bank PACs, but from related (and sometimes competing) financial concerns as well, like insurance companies and securities traders. Members sitting on industry-specific subcommittees (like the Aviation subcommittee of the House Public Works and Transportation Committee) often receive large concentrations of funds both from the corporate PACs involved in the industry and from labor PACs whose members provide the industry's workforce. The consistency of these patterns can be seen on the member profile pages (beginning on page 157), and in the committee profiles that begin on page 80.

It can also be seen in the following series of charts that show the average and total contributions given by specific industries to members of each congressional committee. To provide consistency, the averages include only those contributions given to members seeking reelection. House and Senate members who retired in 1988 (and thus were not raising money for their next election) are excluded, as are committee members who ran for higher office. Retiring members tend to collect much lower levels of PAC funds in their final term. Those seeking higher office — particularly House members running for the Senate — attract levels of PAC funds that are much higher than those of other House members. Both these extremes have been excluded, and the charts reflect the average contributions given to members running for reelection to their present office.

Average PAC Contributions to Each Committee*

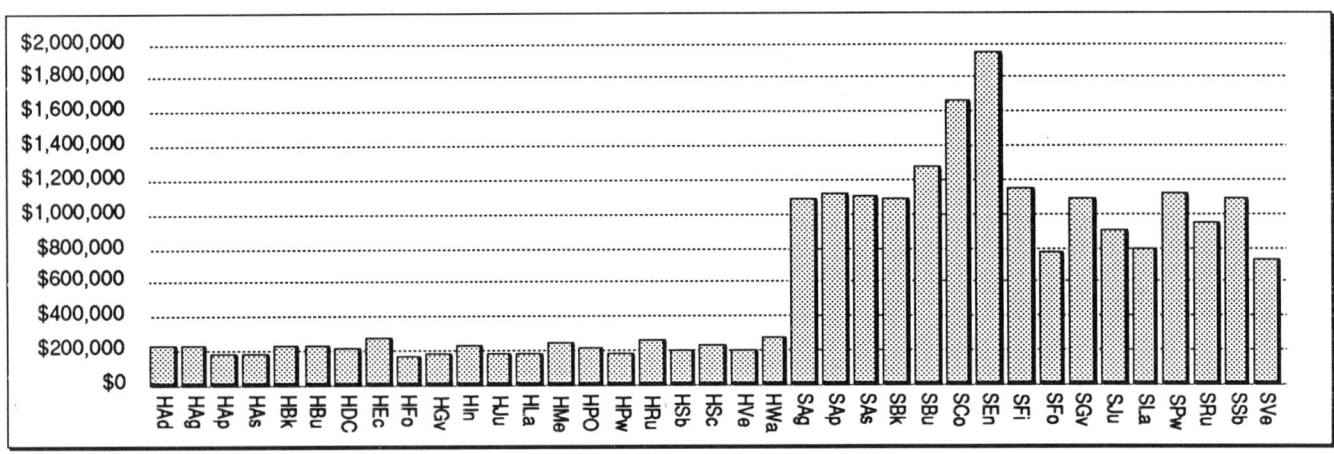

* Includes only those committee members running for reelection

House Committee Key	
HAd	House Administration
HAg	House Agriculture
HAp	House Appropriations
HAs	House Armed Services
HBk	House Banking, Finance & Urban Affairs
HBu	House Budget
HDC	House District of Columbia
HEc	House Energy & Commerce
HFo	House Foreign Affairs
HGv	House Government Operations
HIn	House Interior & Insular Affairs
HJu	House Judiciary
HLa	House Education & Labor
HMe	House Merchant Marine & Fisheries
HPO	House Post Office & Civil Service
HPw	House Public Works and Transportation
HRu	House Rules
HSb	House Small Business
HSc	House Science, Space & Technology
HVe	House Veterans' Affairs
HWa	House Ways & Means

Senate Committee Key	
SAg	Senate Agriculture, Nutrition & Forestry
SAp	Senate Appropriations
SAs	Senate Armed Services
SBk	Senate Banking, Housing & Urban Affairs
SBu	Senate Budget
SCo	Senate Commerce, Science & Transportation
SEn	Senate Energy & Natural Resources
SFi	Senate Finance
SFo	Senate Foreign Relations
SGv	Senate Governmental Affairs
SJu	Senate Judiciary
SLa	Senate Labor & Human Resources
SPw	Senate Environment & Public Works
SRu	Senate Rules & Administration
SSb	Senate Small Business
SVe	Senate Veterans' Affairs

Shotguns & Rifles: Different Approaches by Different Industries

Different industries have different philosophies about distributing their PAC dollars. The real estate industry, dominated in its political contributions by the Realtors PAC, spreads its money to nearly every member of Congress — largely without regard to the members' committee assignments. But most others — typified here by savings & loans — aim the largest share of their dollars squarely at the committees and subcommittees that oversee their industry.

Real Estate

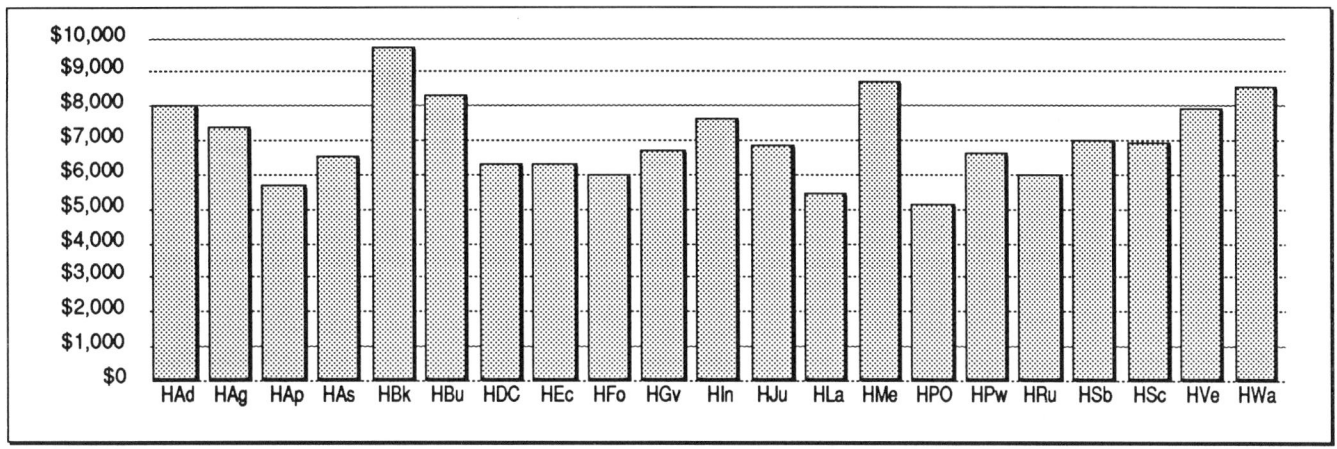

Savings Banks

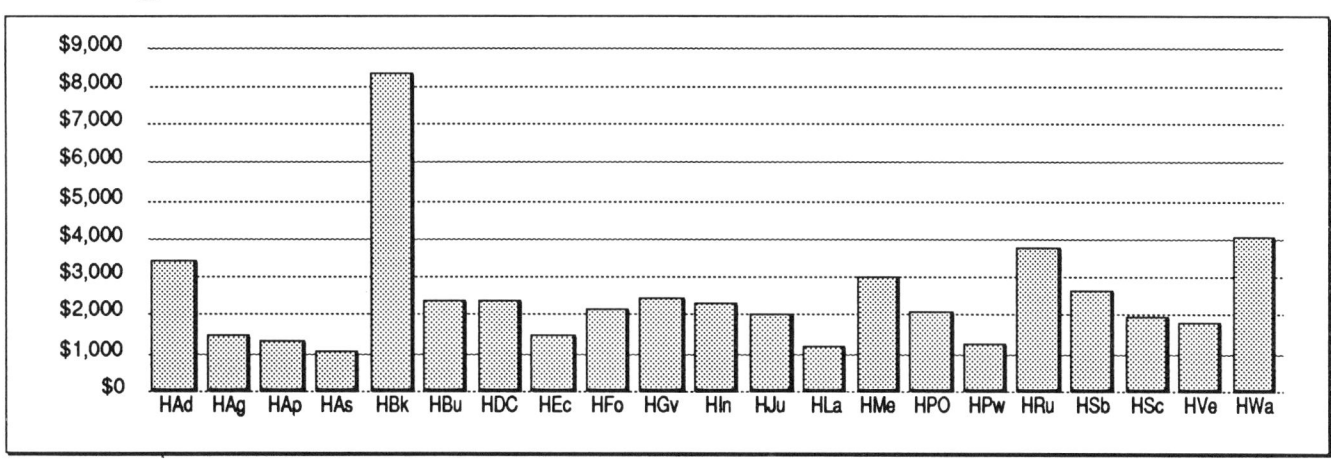

Apples and Oranges in the House & Senate

Average PAC contributions to Senate members are much higher than those to members of the House, but the connection between contributions and committee assignments are less apparent in the Senate. One reason is that House members sit on fewer committees than Senators, so their legislative agenda tends to be more concentrated in one field. Another is that only one third of the Senate seats come up for election in a given election year. Because of this, the level of PAC activity within a particular committee may have more to do with the number of committee members up for reelection than with any particular item on the committee's agenda.

The contrast between House and Senate can be seen clearly in the graphs below, spotlighting the telecommunications industry. Both charts illustrate the importance of the House Energy and Commerce Committee to the industry, but the priorities among Senate committees is less clear. Looking at the first chart, showing average contributions, no Senate committee dominates, though Commerce leads the rest.

In the bottom chart, which shows the *total* dollars going to members in each committee who are up for reelection, the importance of the House Energy and Commerce Committee is again plain to see. But in the Senate, the Finance Committee is now the most favored panel. Possibly this is a function of the committee's importance in writing tax laws, but another reason clearly affecting the figures was the fact that 11 members of the Finance Committee were seeking reelection in 1988 — far more than in any other Senate committee.

Telecommunications
Average contributions to Committee members seeking reelection

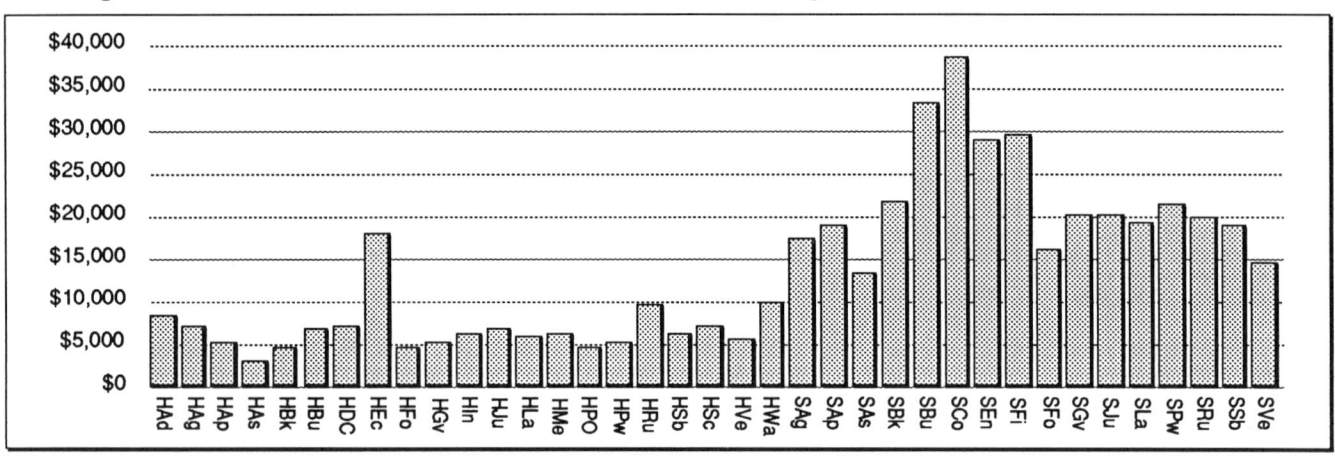

Telecommunications
Total contributions to Committee members seeking reelection

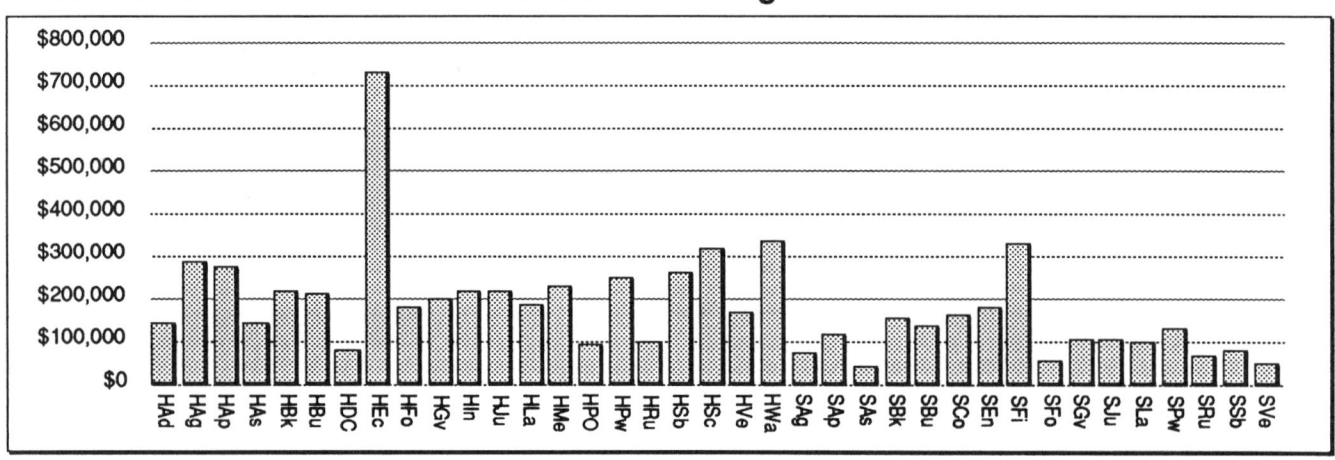

More Going on than Meets the Eye

A handful of industries — typified by the agriculture example below — show a pattern of funding to members of Senate committees that seems logical, considering the industry's interests. But the averages are quite often skewed by the mix of committee members who happen to be running that year. One reason the agriculture correlation was so strong in 1988 was that Pete Wilson of California was among the Agriculture Committee members running for reelection. Wilson drew more than $353,000 in agriculture-related contributions in his $14.6 million campaign — far more than any other member of Congress.

The chart at the bottom, tracing PAC contributions from government and postal worker unions, shows a case where the averages seem to have no relation at all to the interest group giving the money. The Governmental Affairs Committee oversees decisions affecting pay and working conditions of government and postal workers, but the biggest share of the unions' dollars went to the Energy & Natural Resources Committee. Again, the reason had more to do with who was running. Among the three Democrats on the Energy Committee running for reelection in 1988 was Howard Metzenbaum of Ohio. A liberal Democrat facing a strong challenge from a well-financed conservative opponent, Metzenbaum's race became a top priority in the labor community, and he eventually drew more contributions from labor PACs than anyone else in Congress. Metzenbaum's share skewed the average in the government and postal workers PAC distribution patterns, and shows once again the difficulties in drawing reliable parallels between committee assignments and PAC contributions in the U.S. Senate.

Patterns in the House— where members sit on fewer committees, and where each member runs for reelection every two years — are much more visible and much more consistent. For this reason, the charts on the following pages concentrate exclusively on House committees.

Agriculture

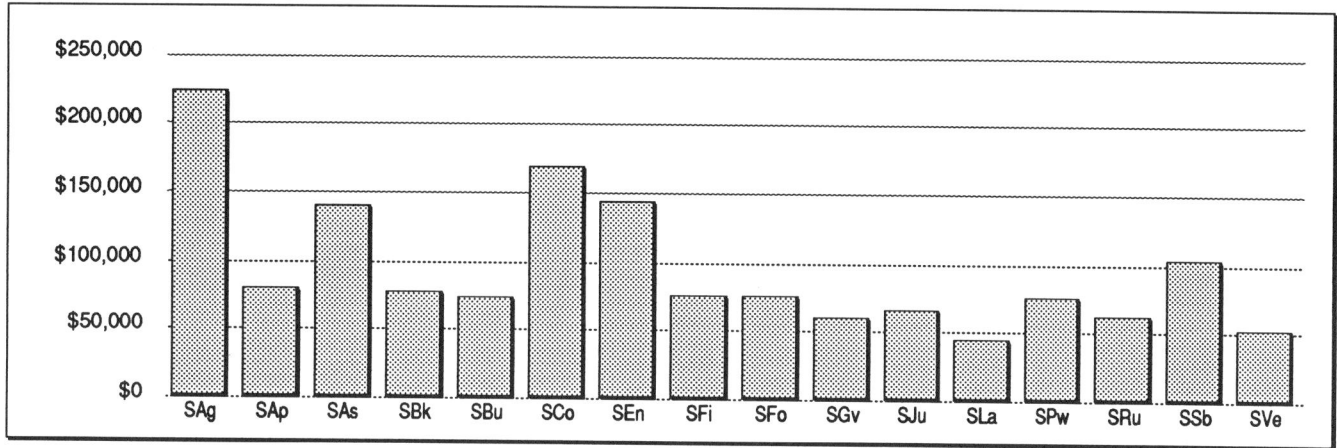

Government & Postal Worker Unions

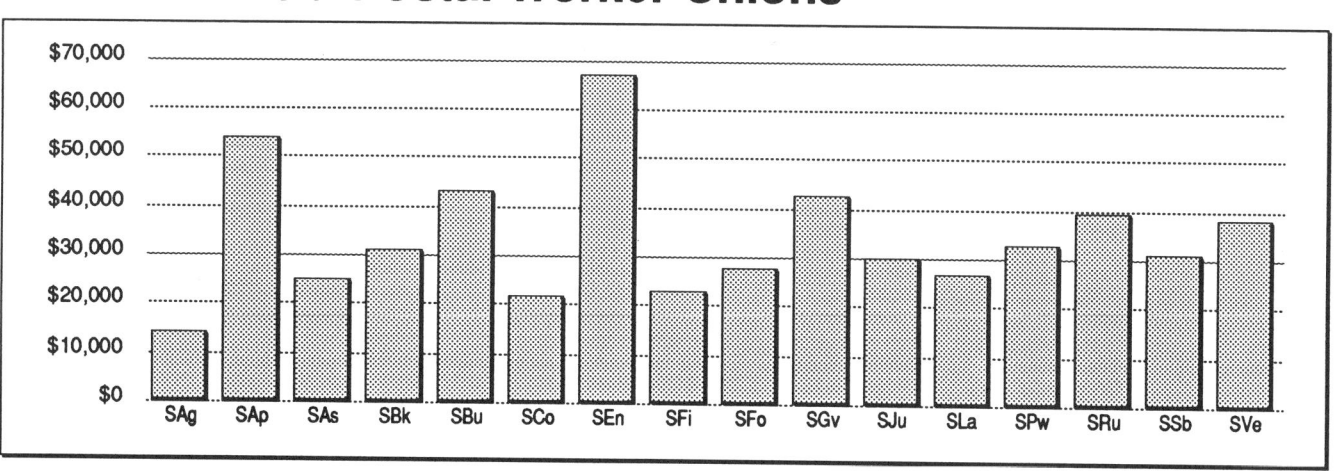

A complete key to the committee codes in these charts can be found on page 22.

25

A quick review of industry spending patterns on the following three pages provides an intuitive demonstration of committee jurisdictions in the U.S. House. The Agriculture and Defense charts offer no surprises, but several of the other charts make it clear even to a casual observer that the House Energy and Commerce Committee has a surprising breadth of responsibilities which affects many industries. The PACs have certainly taken notice, and so have the members. A seat on Energy and Commerce is considered a plum assignment, and competition for openings is often intense.

Agriculture

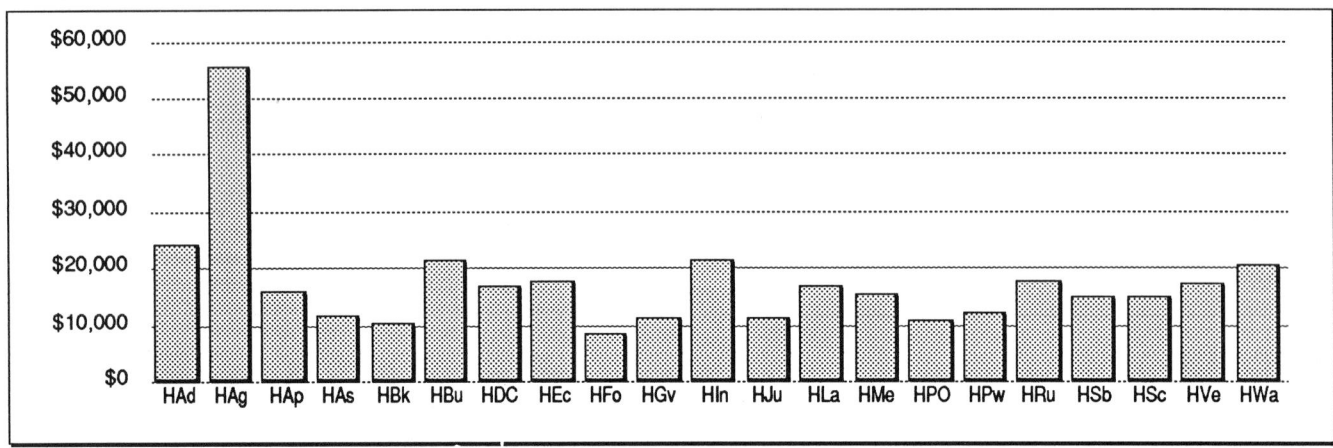

Communications & Electronics

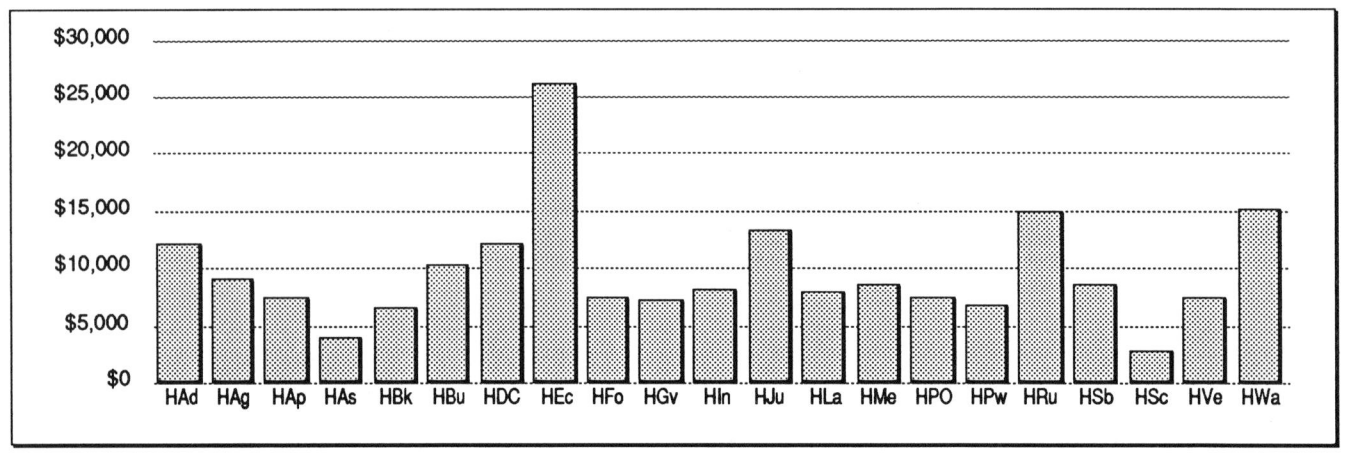

Defense

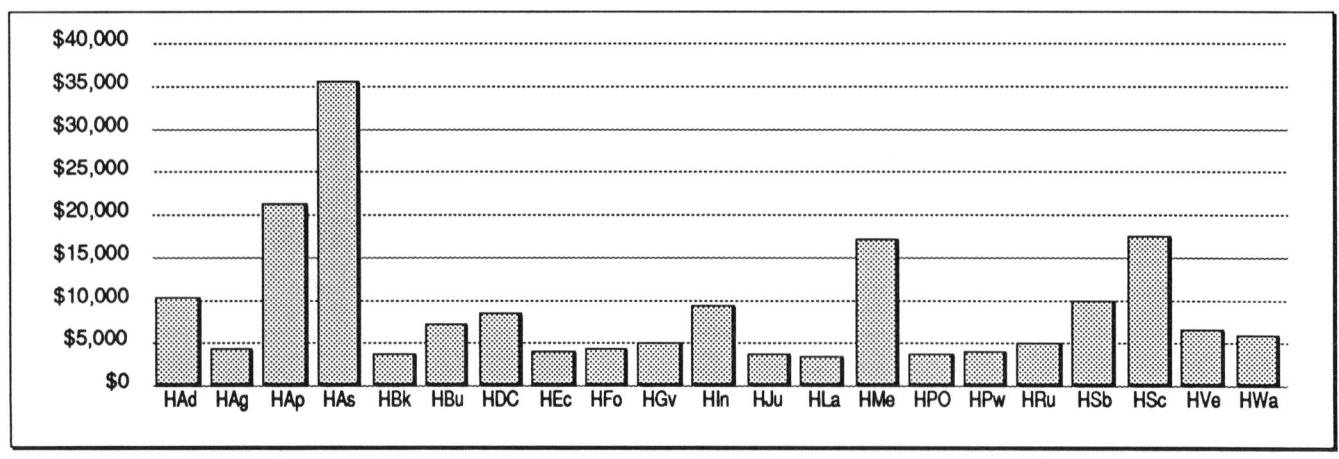

Energy & Natural Resources

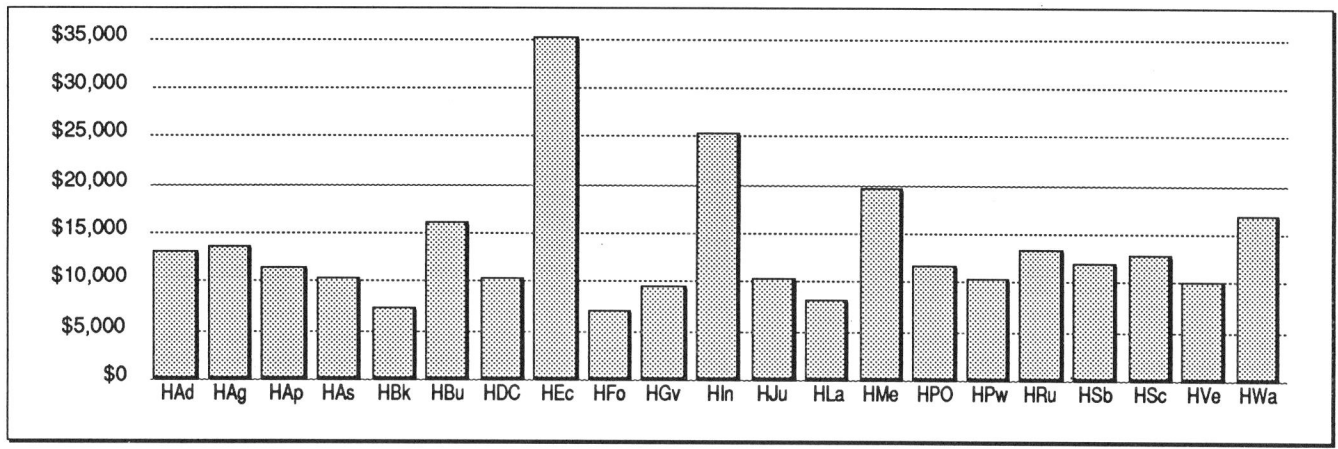

Finance, Insurance & Real Estate

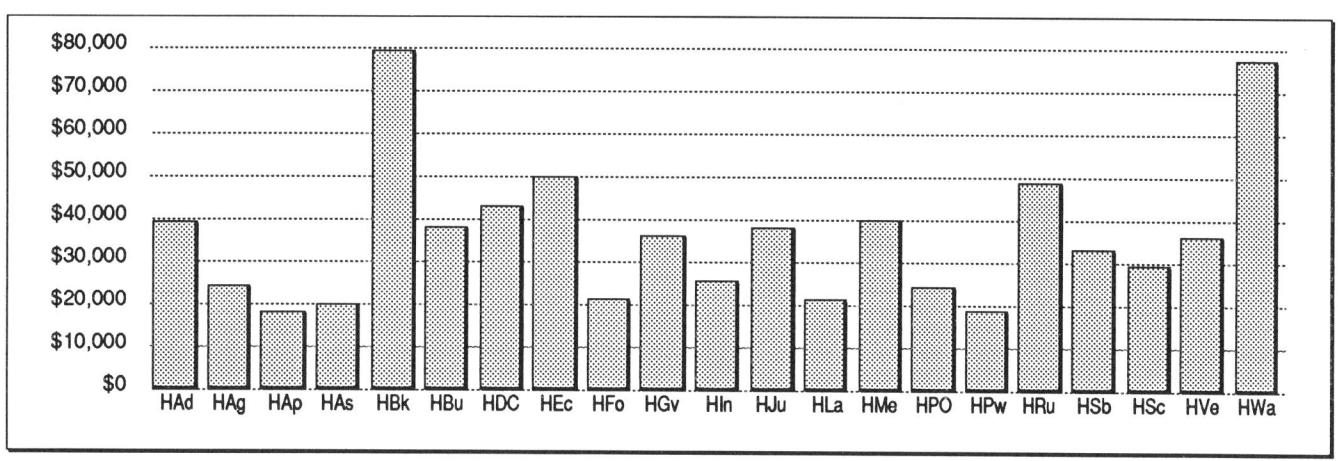

Health

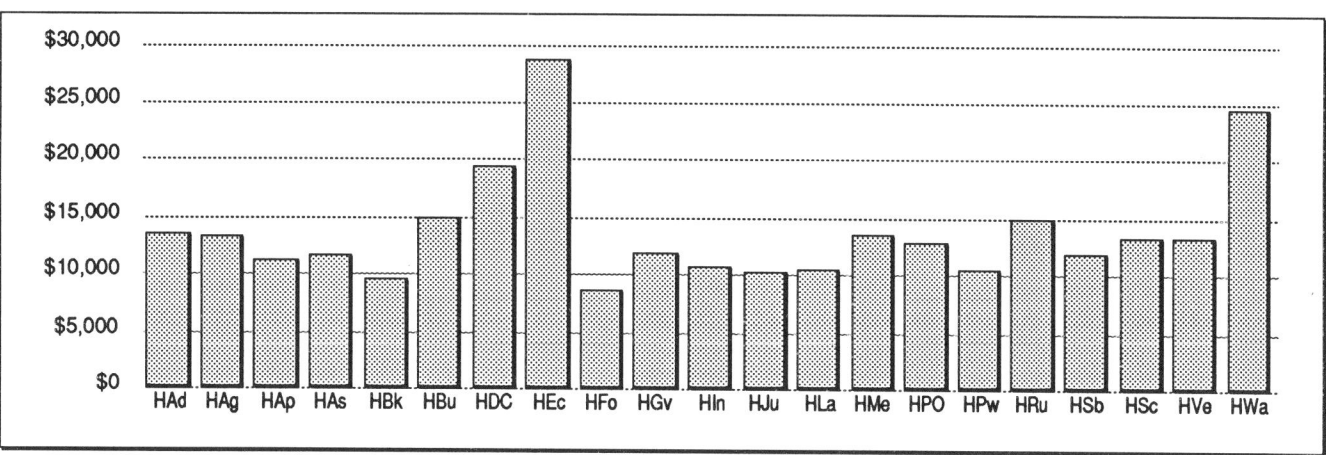

A complete key to the committee codes in these charts can be found on page 22.

Lawyers

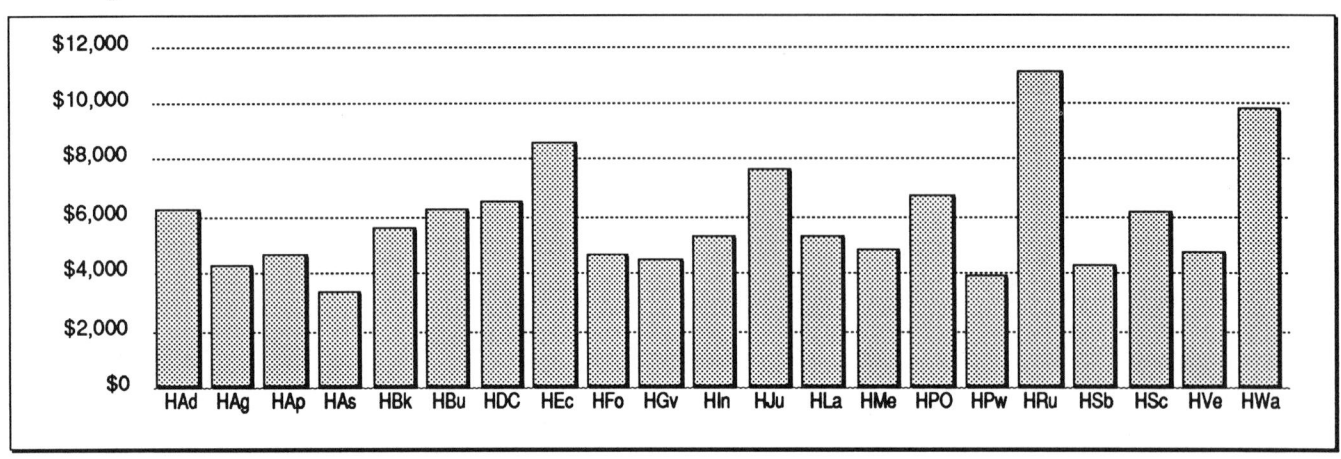

Transportation

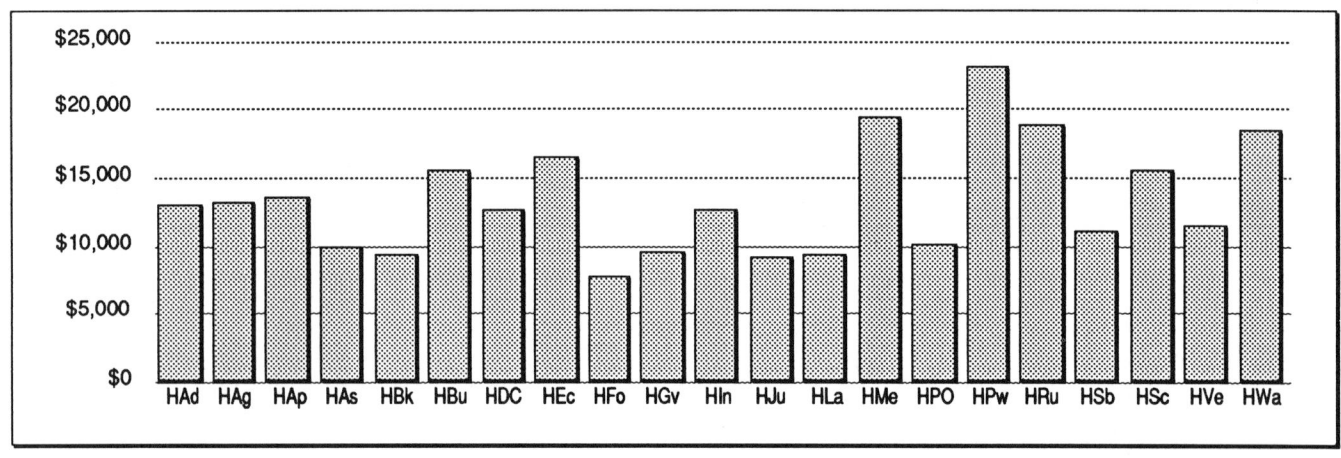

Pro-Israel

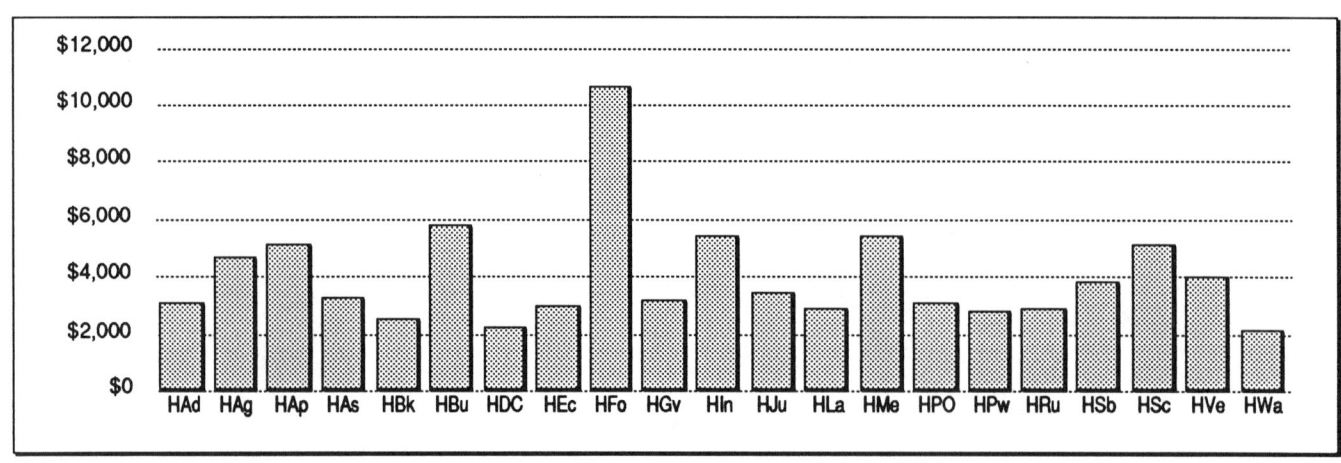

Tobacco: In a Class by Itself

As seen in the charts below, an interesting contrast can be found between the distribution of PAC funds from tobacco companies versus those of farmers producing other crops. There is also a difference between the types of companies that sponsor those PACs. Tobacco companies tend to be far more diversified, with many also branching into food processing and even liquor. The charts below clearly show the multiple interests of the big tobacco companies, versus the more mainline agricultural interests of cotton, sugar, fruit & vegetable, grain and other farmers.

Tobacco

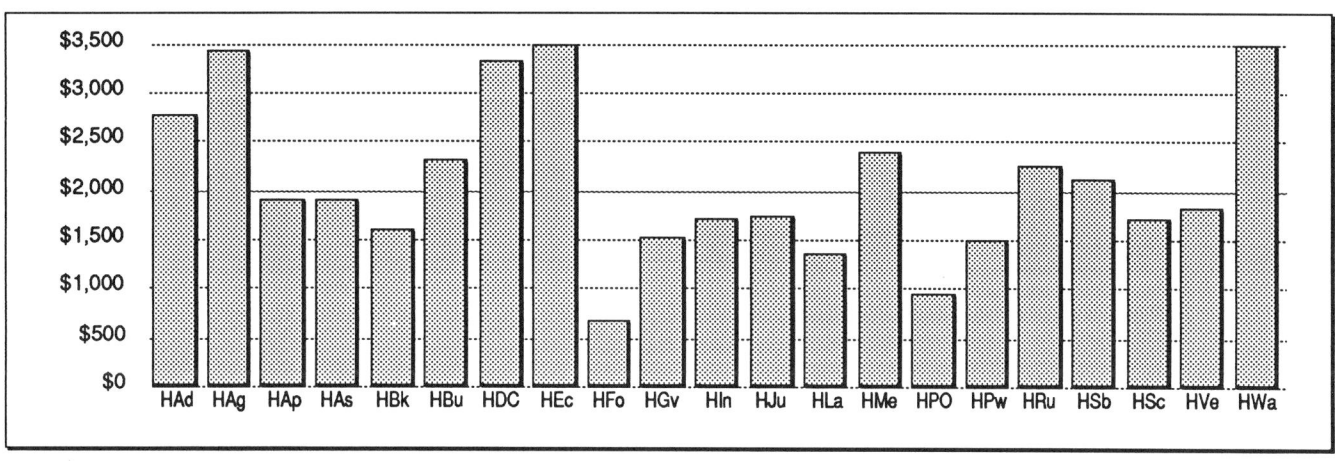

Non-Tobacco Crop Production

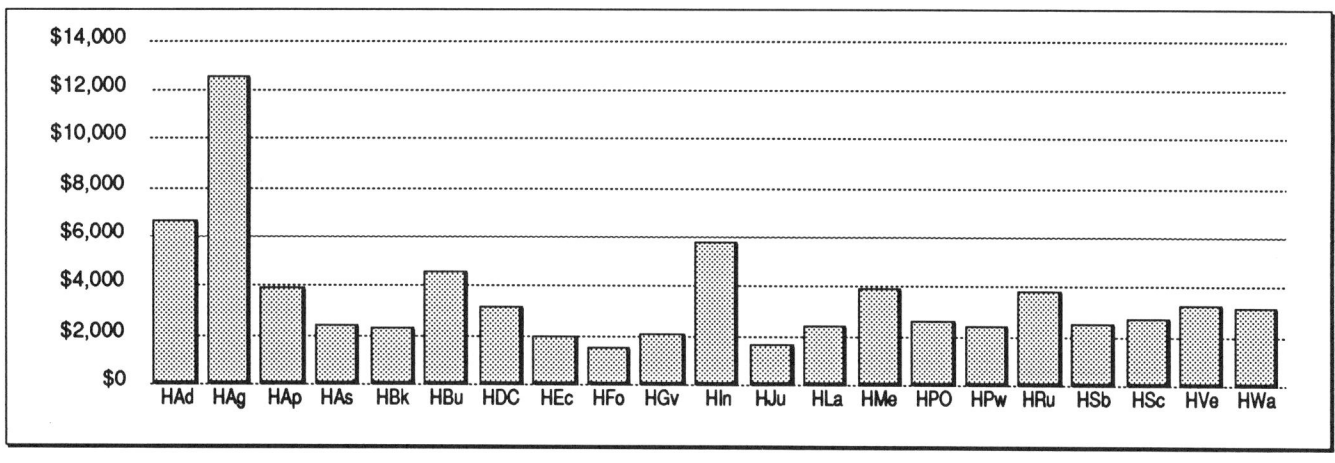

A complete key to the committee codes in these charts can be found on page 22.

Communications to Congress

Three different segments of the communications industry have three distinct sets of priorities on Capitol Hill. The telecommunications segment (made up of local and long distance telephone utilities, as well as companies providing telecom services and equipment) focuses most of its attention and money on the Energy and Commerce Committee, and particularly its subcommittee on Telecommunications and Finance. The broadcasting segment (made up principally of TV & radio stations and cable TV operators) also has its main focus on Energy and Commerce, but it shows a secondary interest in the Judiciary Committee. Those firms dealing directly in movie and recorded music production still have some interests with Energy and Commerce, but the number one priority for their PAC dollars is with members of the Judiciary Committee. One reason: copyright and patent laws concerning VCRs and other recording devices fall within Judiciary's jurisdiction.

Telecommunications

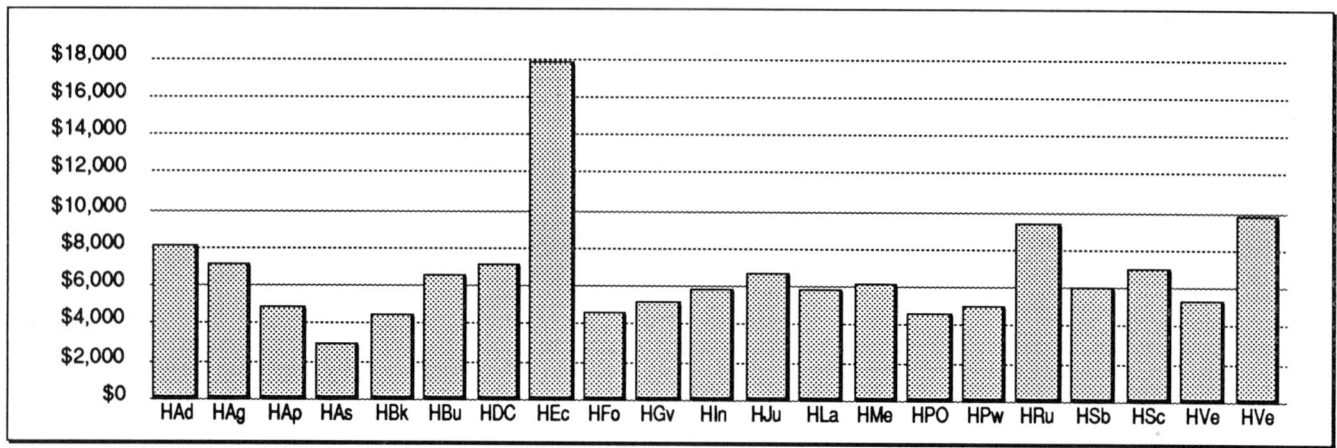

Broadcasting

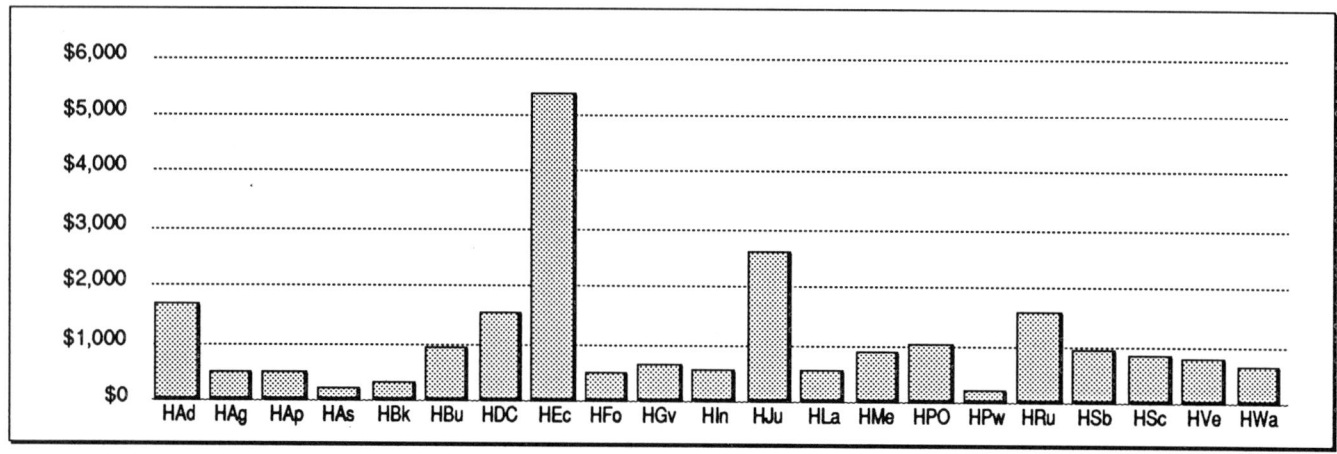

Movies & Music Production

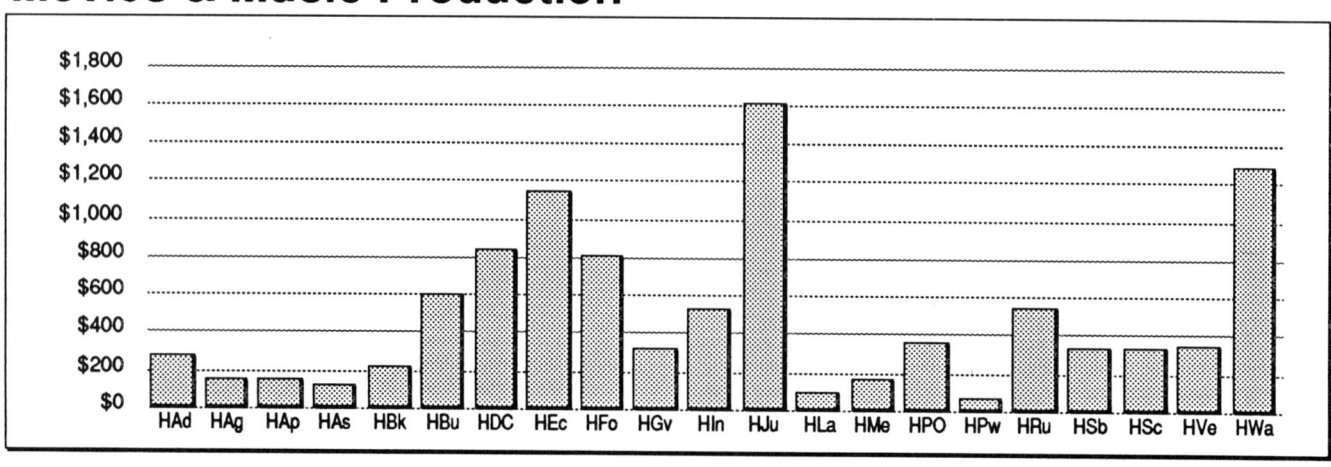

Construction

There are several different sectors of interests within the construction industry; the most clearly demarcated being that between contractors specializing in residential construction versus those dealing mainly in commercial and industrial projects, including public works. As the charts below illustrate, the PAC dollars from these two construction sectors take slightly different paths on Capitol Hill. Homebuilders made their biggest contributions to members of the Banking, Finance and Urban Affairs Committee, whose jurisdiction includes federal housing policy. Industrial contractors, on the other hand, gave most of their attention to the Public Works and Transportation Committee. Roadbuilders, dam builders and other large construction companies specializing in public works projects often earn large chunks of revenue from government contracts, and Public Works is the committee that sets those construction priorities.

Homebuilders

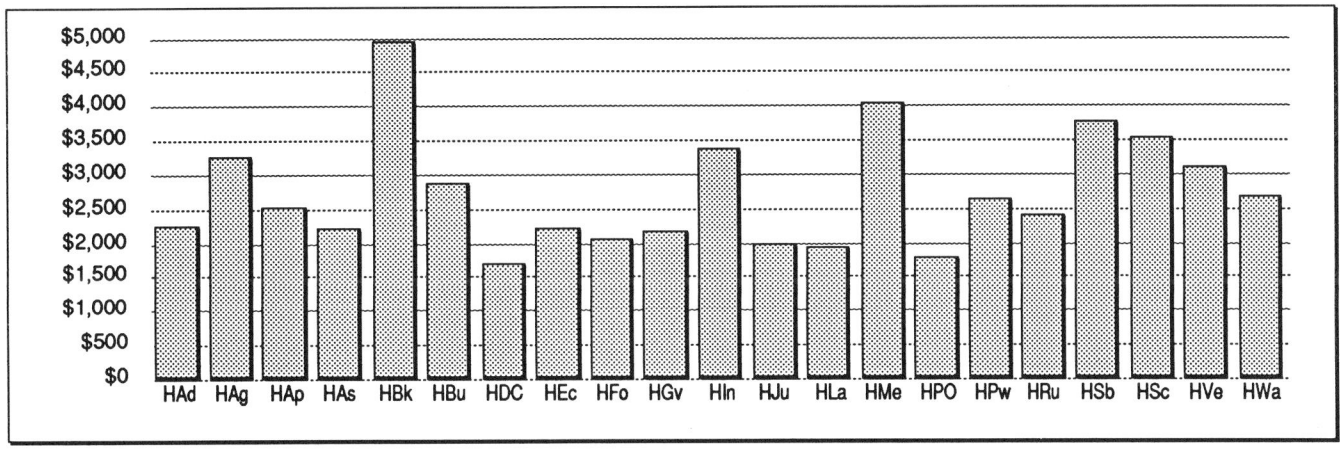

Commercial & Industrial Contractors

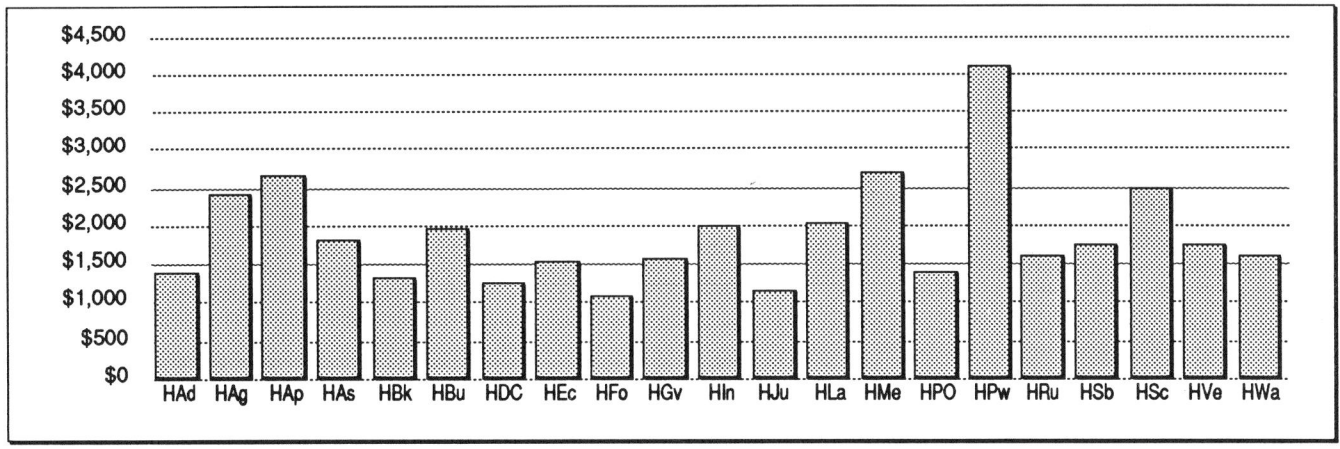

A complete key to the committee codes in these charts can be found on page 22.

Energy & Natural Resources

Energy and natural resource production also shows some variety in its contribution patterns. To the oil & gas industry, decisions made in any of three principal committees can have industry-wide repercussions. Most important of all, at least in the eyes of the PAC directors, is the Energy and Commerce Committee, which sets overall energy policy. The Interior Committee is also important, since it oversees not only the mining industry but also the vast tracts of public lands owned by the federal government in the energy-rich Western U.S. and Alaska. The Merchant Marine committee oversees the development of outer continental shelf — including offshore oil exploration and production. It is also the home for debate on oilspill liability laws. Electric utilities fall more specifically under the wing of Energy and Commerce, and particularly its subcommittee on Energy and Power. Mining companies also pay close attention to actions in Energy and Commerce, but direct their largest contributions to the Interior Committee, under whose jurisdiction mining falls.

Oil & Gas

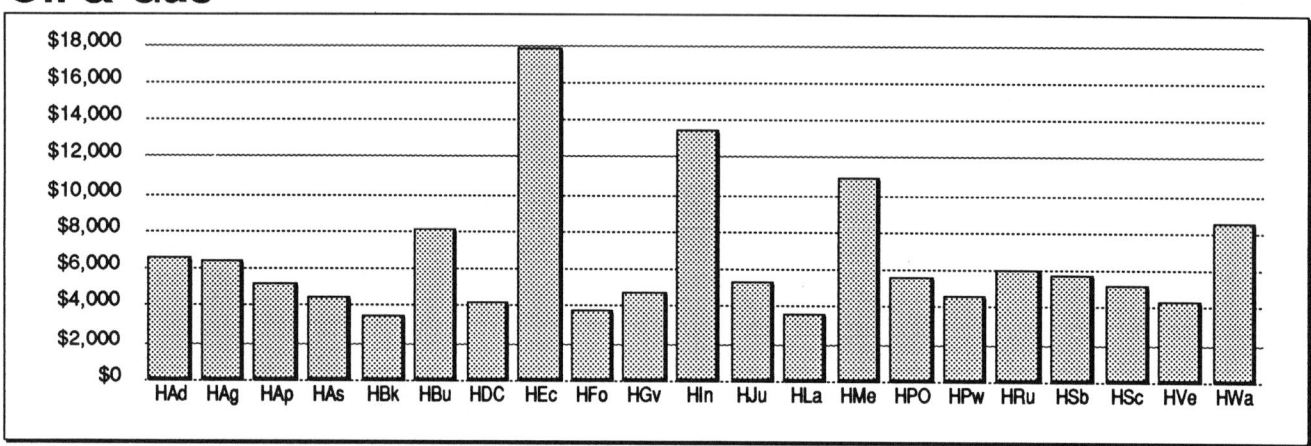

Electric Utilities

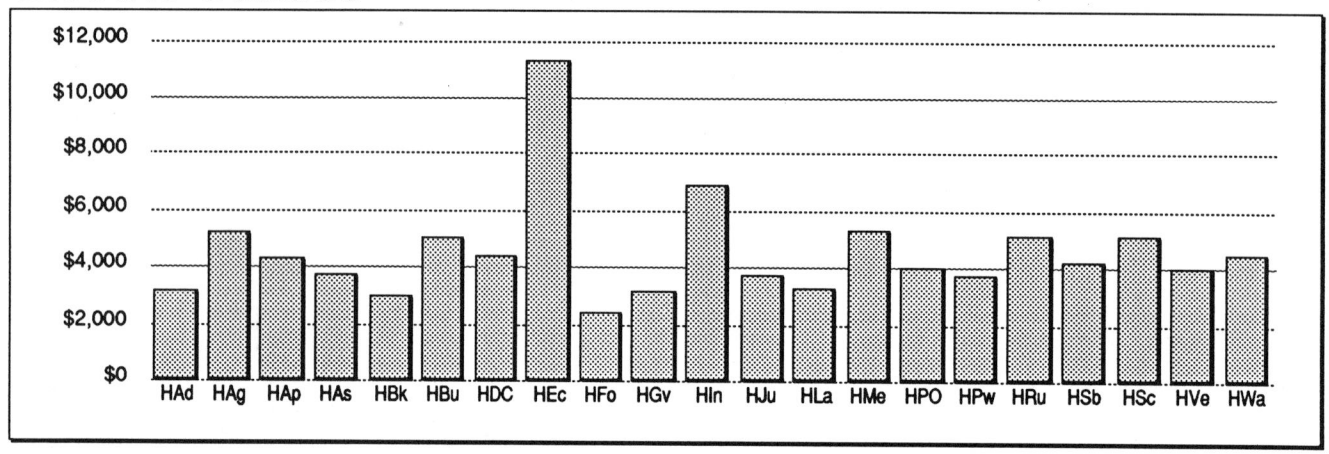

Mining

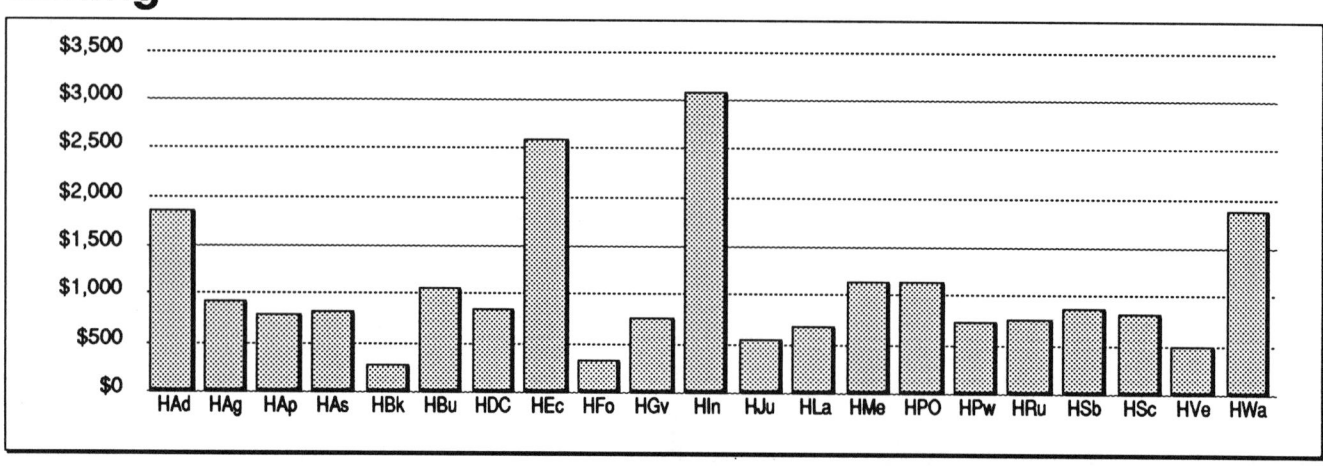

Financial Heavyweights

Three heavyweights of the financial community — commercial banks, securities companies, and insurance firms, show markedly different patterns in the distribution of their PAC funds to members of the House committees. Banks predominantly put their dollars with members of the Banking Committee. Securities companies give to a spectrum which includes Banking, Ways and Means, and Energy and Commerce (which oversees the securities industry in its Telecommunications and Finance subcommittee). To insurance companies, tax policy was a predominant issue in 1988, and members of the tax-writing Ways and Means committee were the chief beneficiaries of their PAC dollars.

Commercial Banks

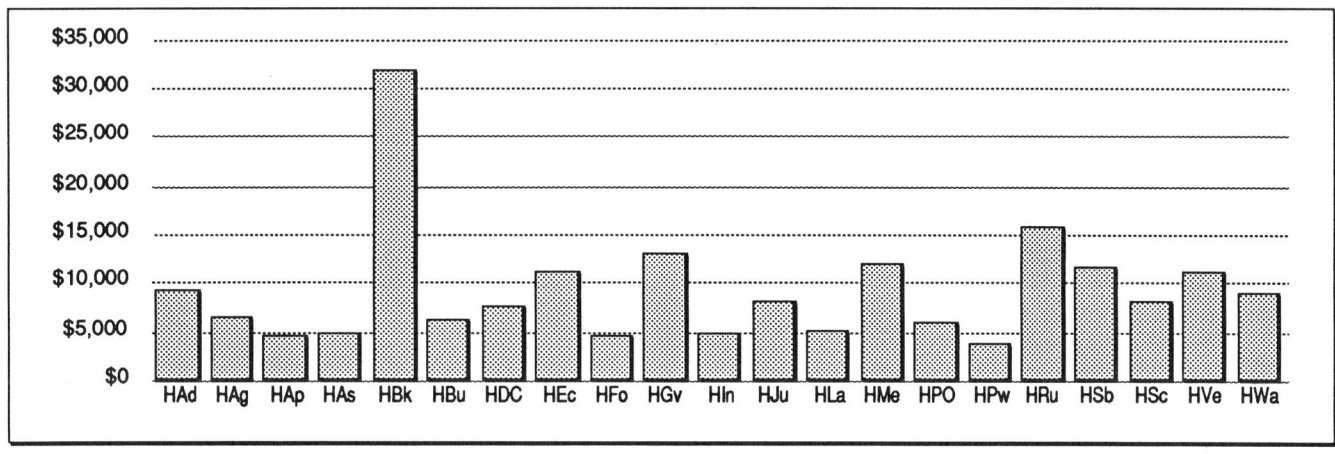

Securities

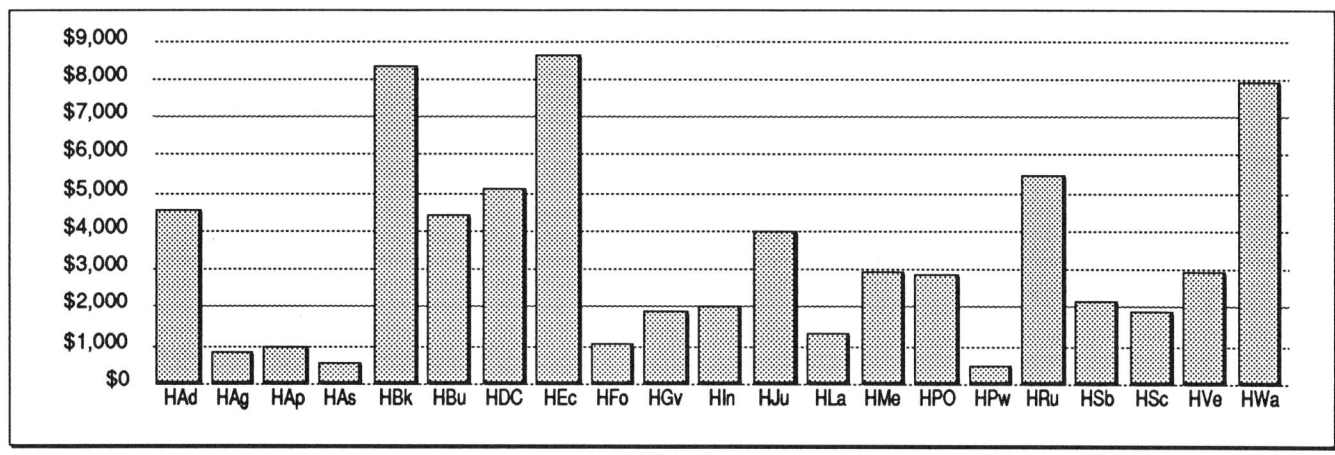

Insurance

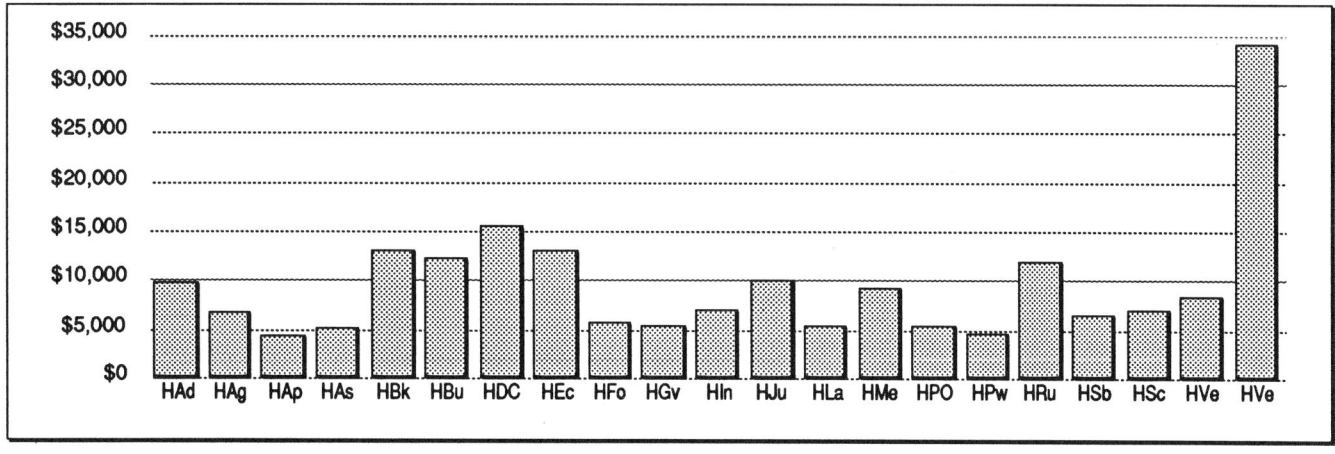

A complete key to the committee codes in these charts can be found on page 22.

Food & Beverage

The food & beverage industry was a major source of campaign funds to dozens of candidates in 1988, dispensing more than $5 million in PAC contributions. As the charts show, their interests were diverse. Food processors were most interested in agriculture committee matters. Beer, wine & liquor manufacturers and distributors were primarily concerned with tax policy, and so gave most of their biggest contributions to members of the Ways and Means Committee. To restaurants, however, minimum wage legislation is of vital importance — a matter that falls squarely under the jurisdiction of the Education and Labor Committee.

Food Processing

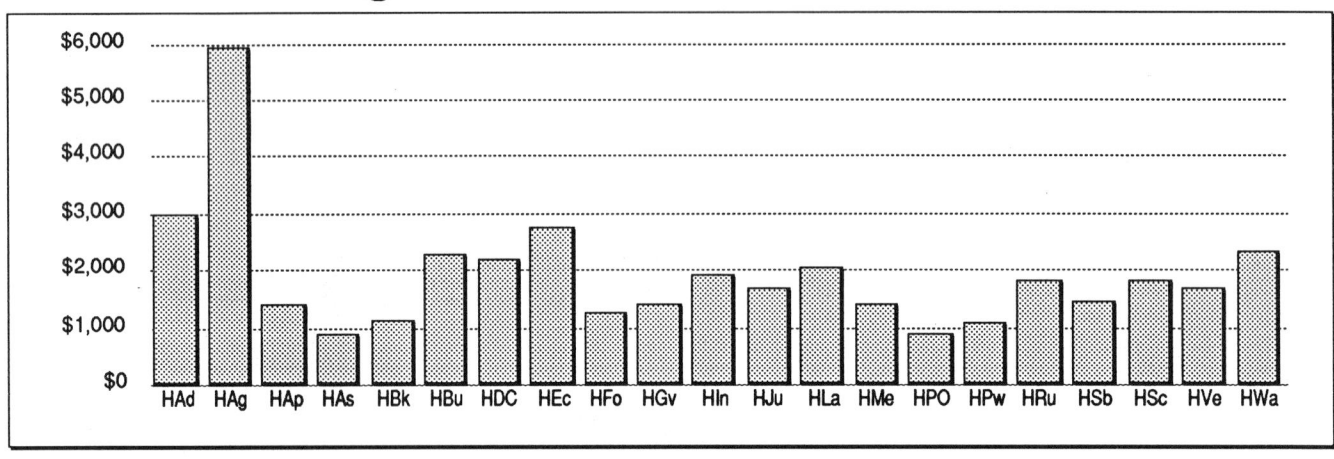

Beer, Wine & Liquor

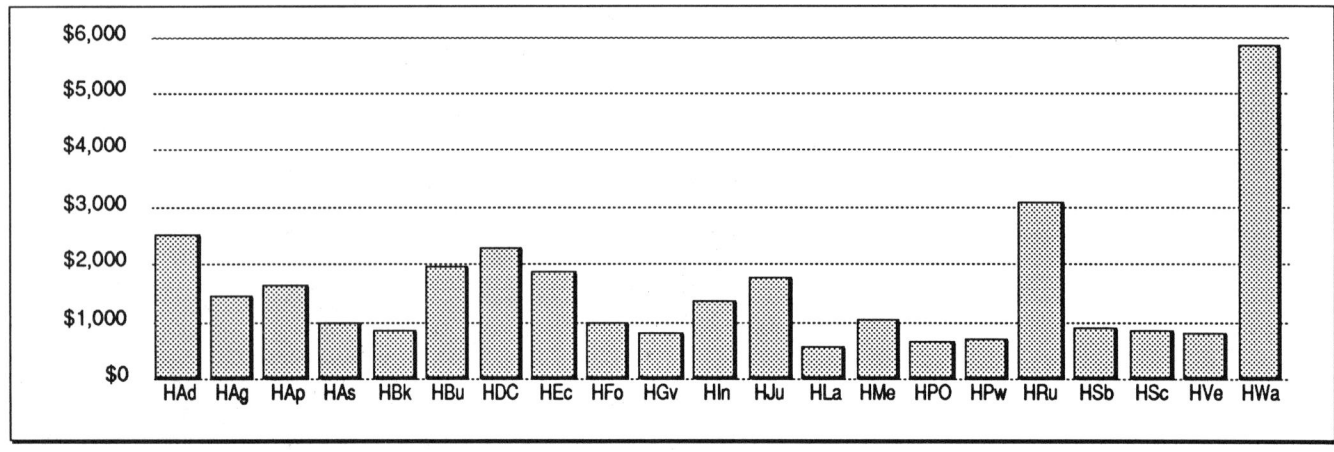

Restaurants

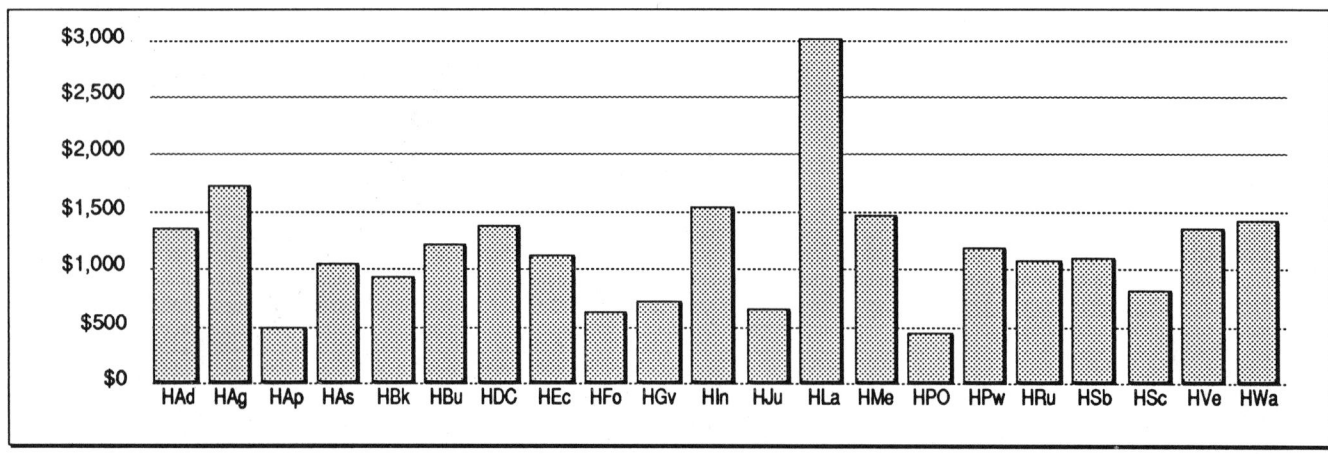

Stocks, Bonds & Pork Bellies

While there is considerable overlap in the interests of New York-based securities companies and Chicago-based commodities traders, the patterns in their PAC giving point out the differences as well. Commodities trading falls specifically under the jurisdiction of the agriculture committee, so members of that committee had the highest average contributions from the commodities sector. The Energy and Commerce Committee is the principal overseer of the securities industry, but the Banking Committee is the panel listening to most of the arguments of commercial banks that want Congress to allow them to expand into stock trading as a new service to their customers. Both sectors are also vitally interested in tax policies, as written by the Ways and Means Committee.

Another contrast between the two sectors does not show up on these charts, but is noteworthy. Most of the securities-related PACs are stock brokerage houses and investment banks that advise customers on the trading of stocks and bonds. The biggest commodities PACs are the exchanges themselves — the Chicago Board of Trade and the Chicago Mercantile Exchange. The New York, Philadelphia and Pacific Stock Exchanges also have PACs, but they are comparatively small.

Securities Trading

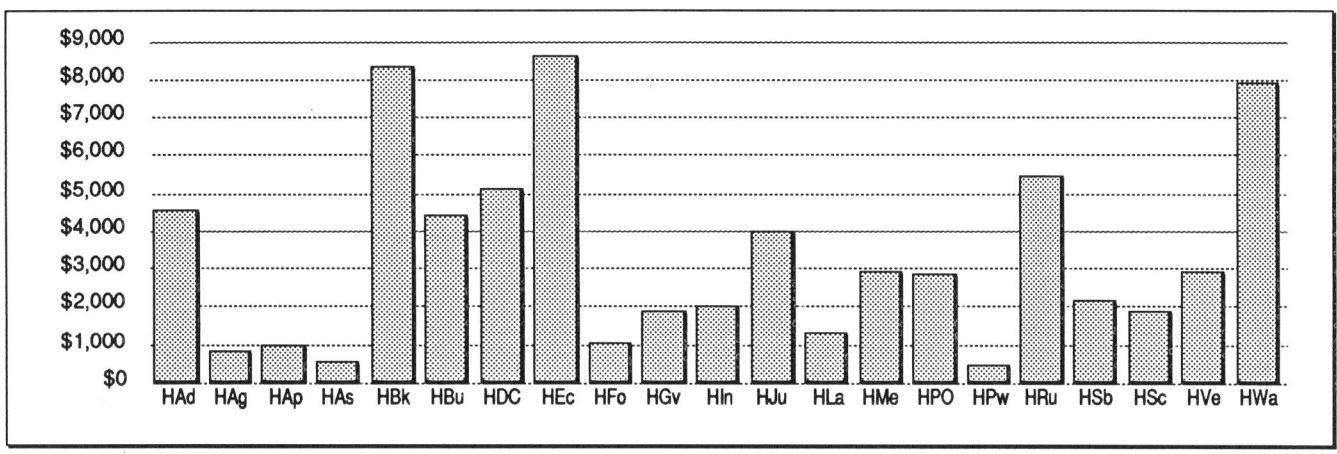

Commodities Trading

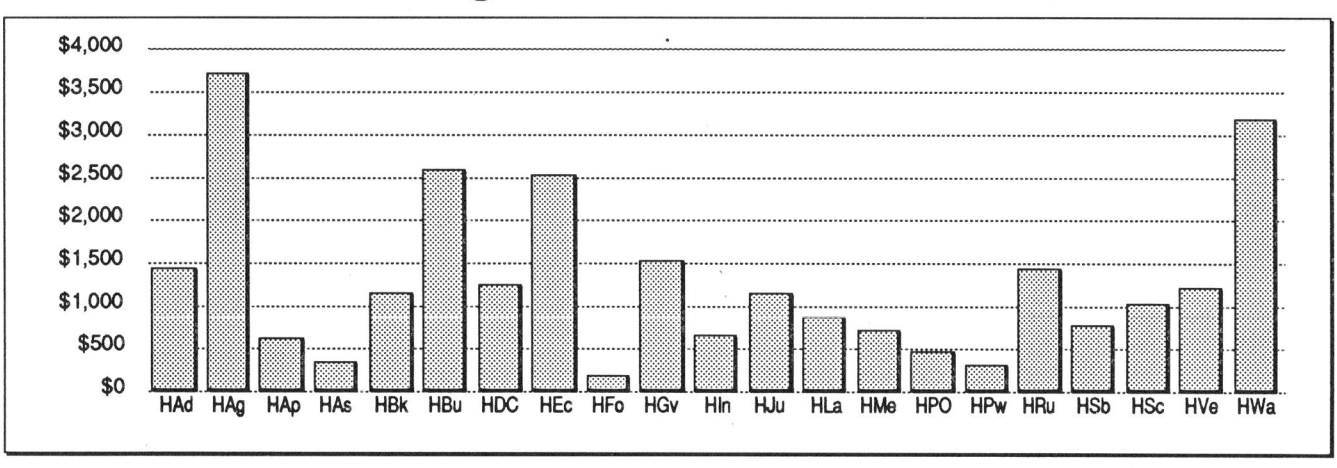

A complete key to the committee codes in these charts can be found on page 22.

Within the health care industry, the biggest concentration of PAC dollars is from the professional associations that represent the interests of health professionals. The American Medical Association's AMA PAC was the leader among them, and the nation's third largest PAC overall in 1987-88. Like other health professional groups, the AMA spread its donations to a wide spectrum of congressional incumbents. Hospitals and nursing homes, with fewer dollars to spend, were more selective. They targeted the biggest share of their contributions at the two committees — Energy & Commerce and Ways & Means — that have specific jurisdiction over health. Pharmaceutical manufacturers were equally selective, giving only token amounts to members on non health-related committees.

Health Professionals

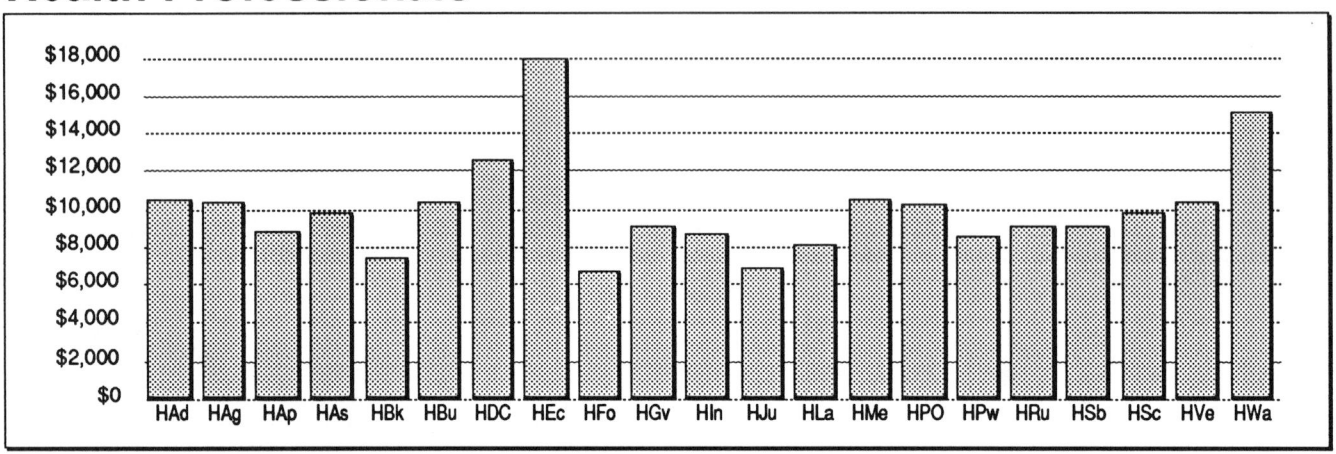

Hospitals & Nursing Homes

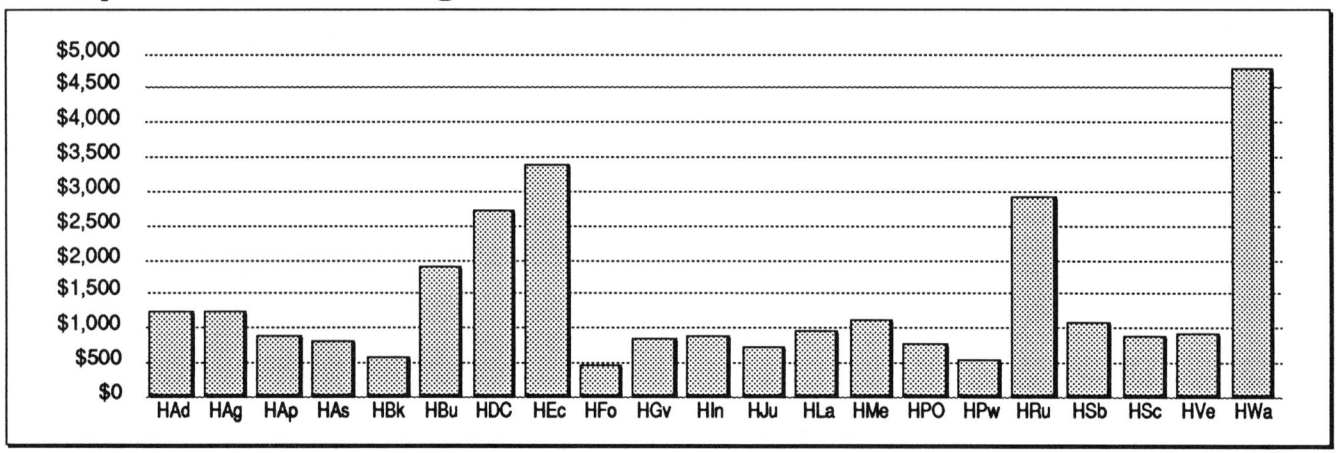

Pharmaceuticals/Health Products

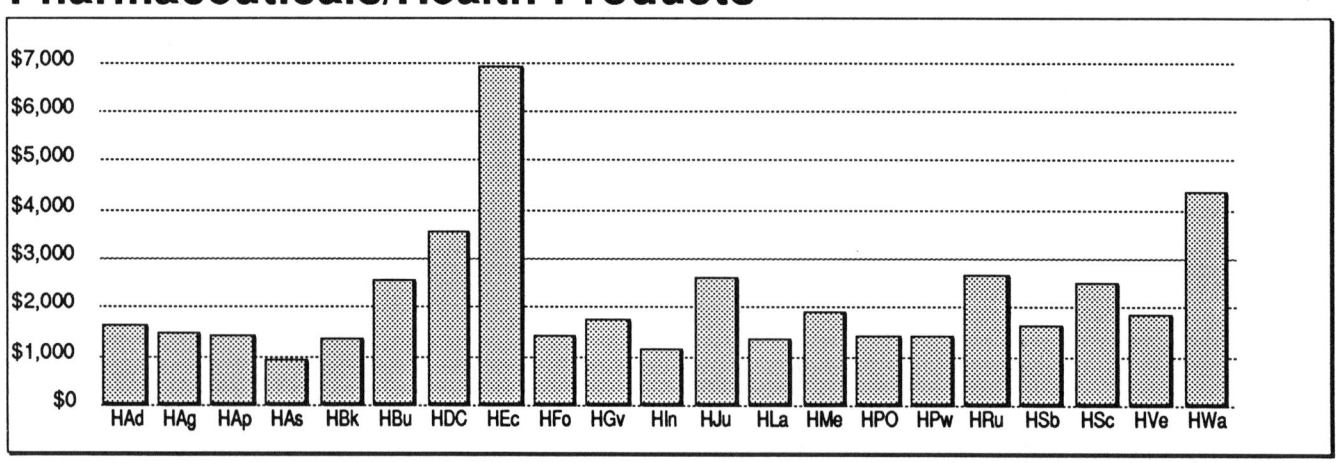

Diversity on the Labor Front

Taken as a whole, labor PACs steer their dollars more for reasons of party affiliation than committee assignment; the jumbled pattern of manufacturing unions, below, is typical. But there are exceptions. Public sector unions heavily target the Post Office and Civil Service Committee and several of the transportation unions aim their dollars carefully at members with transport-related assignments — particularly on the Public Works and Merchant Marine committees.

Government & Postal Worker Unions

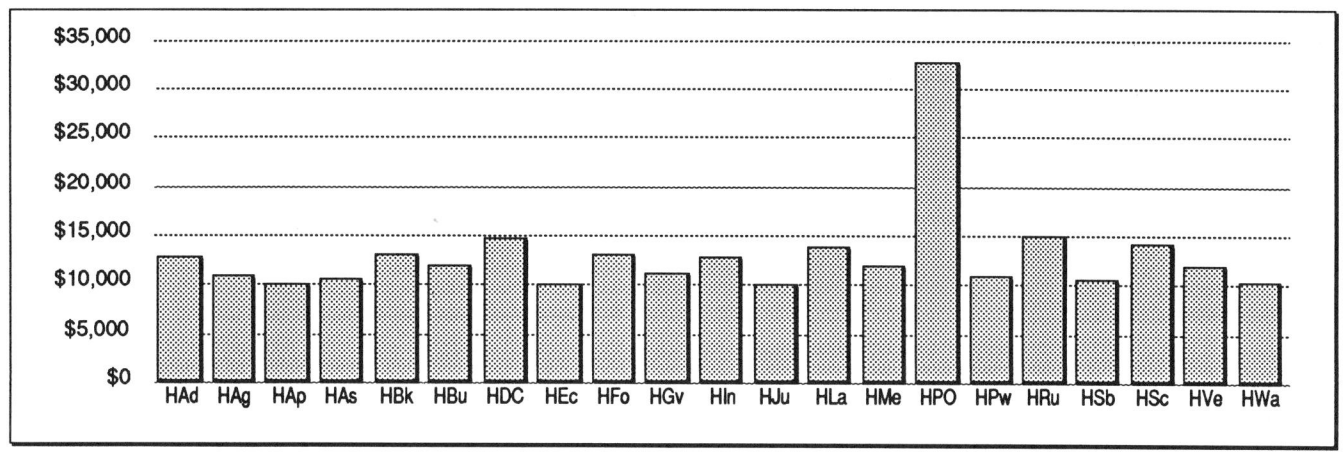

Transportation Unions

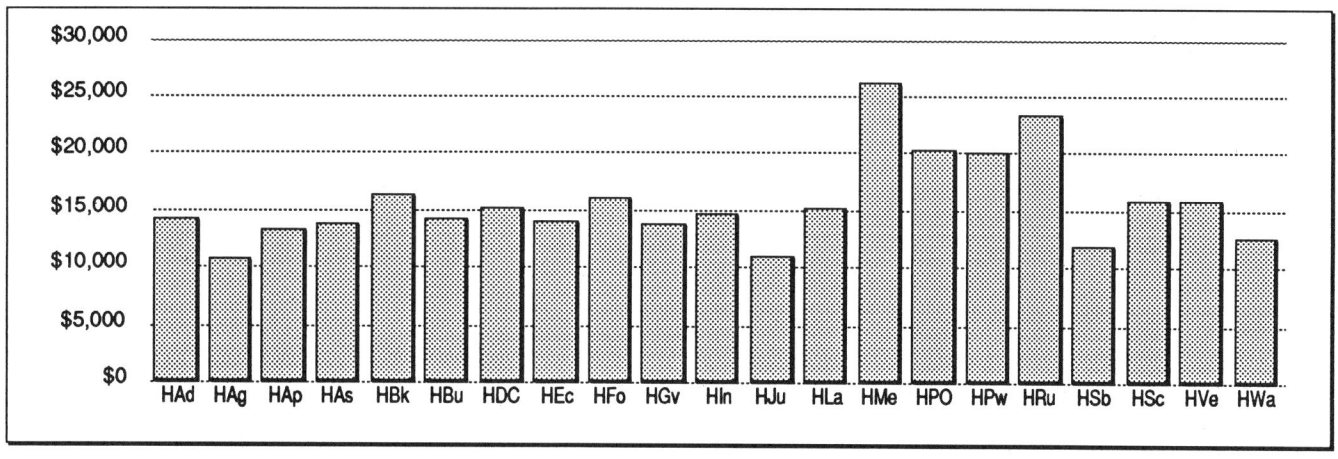

Manufacturing Unions

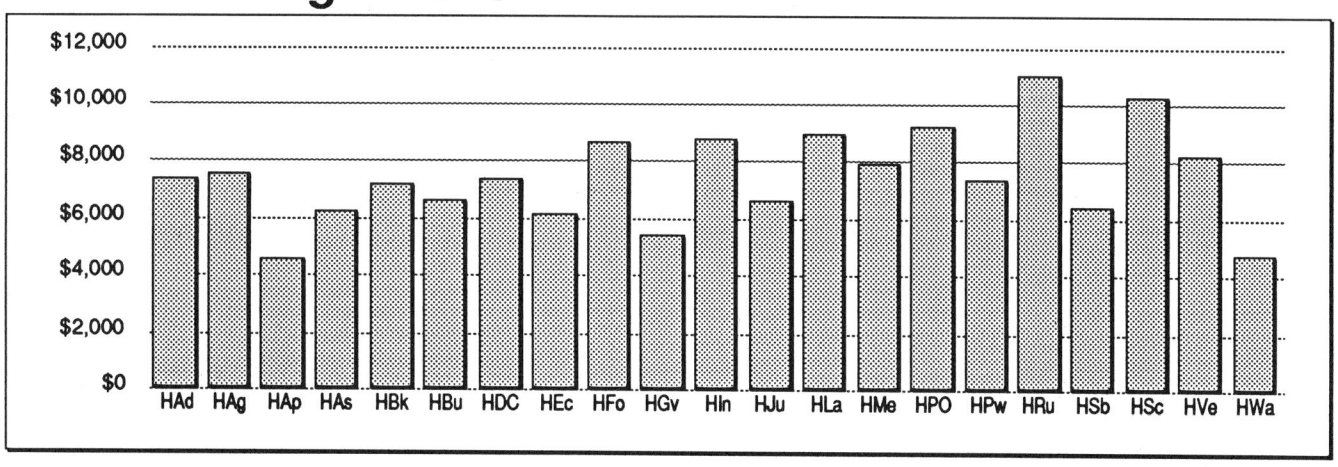

A complete key to the committee codes in these charts can be found on page 22.

Teamsters and the Merchant Marine Unions

Looking more closely at the different sectors within transportation unions, a striking contrast can be found between the Teamsters — one of the most diversified of all labor unions — and those unions dealing with sea transportation and America's struggling merchant marine. The Teamsters PAC was second only to the Realtors in dispensing contributions during the 1988 elections. The pattern by which it was distributed to members of different committees could hardly have been more diffuse.

The story was considerably different among the sea transport unions. The unions that supply marine engineers, longshoremen, and other workers for the nation's merchant shippers are much less diversified, and much more dependent on the health of their one particular industry. The pattern in their PAC contributions reflect that fact. Members of the House Merchant Marine and Fisheries Committee got an average of more than $15,000 each from sea transport unions, while members of most other committees got only a small fraction of that amount.

Teamsters

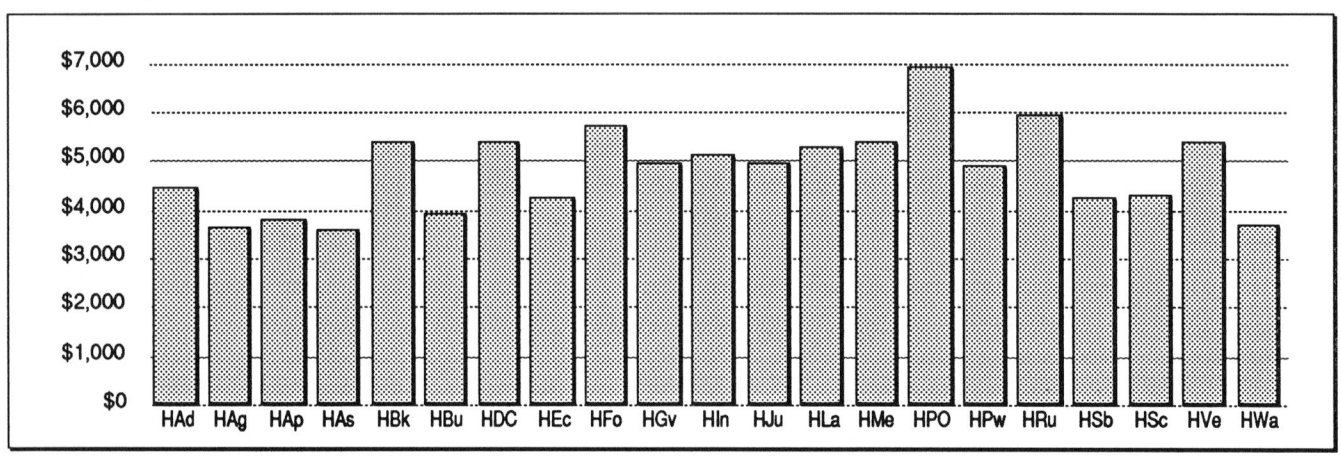

Sea Transport Unions

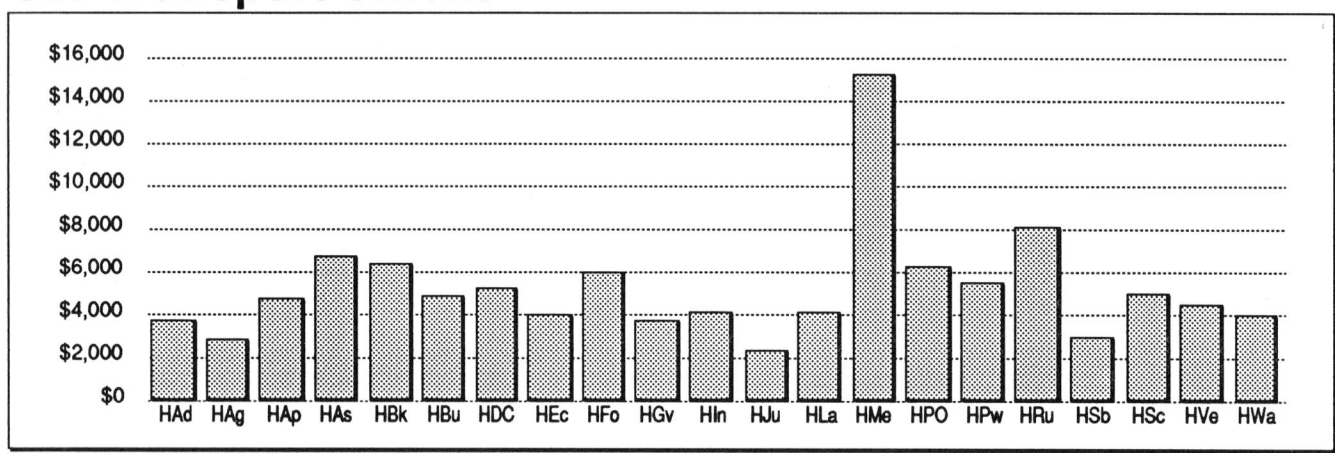

Union and Management: Giving Side by Side

One of the most revealing findings to emerge from an analysis of labor union PACs is that in some industries — particularly transportation — there may be more similarities than differences in the contribution patterns of corporate and labor PACs. Legislation that strengthens air carriers, railroads or the merchant marine results not only in higher corporate profits, but in secure jobs. An interesting footnote: while all labor PACs heavily preferred Democrats, transportation unions were the ones most likely to give a larger-than-normal share of their dollars to Republicans.

Air Transport & Unions

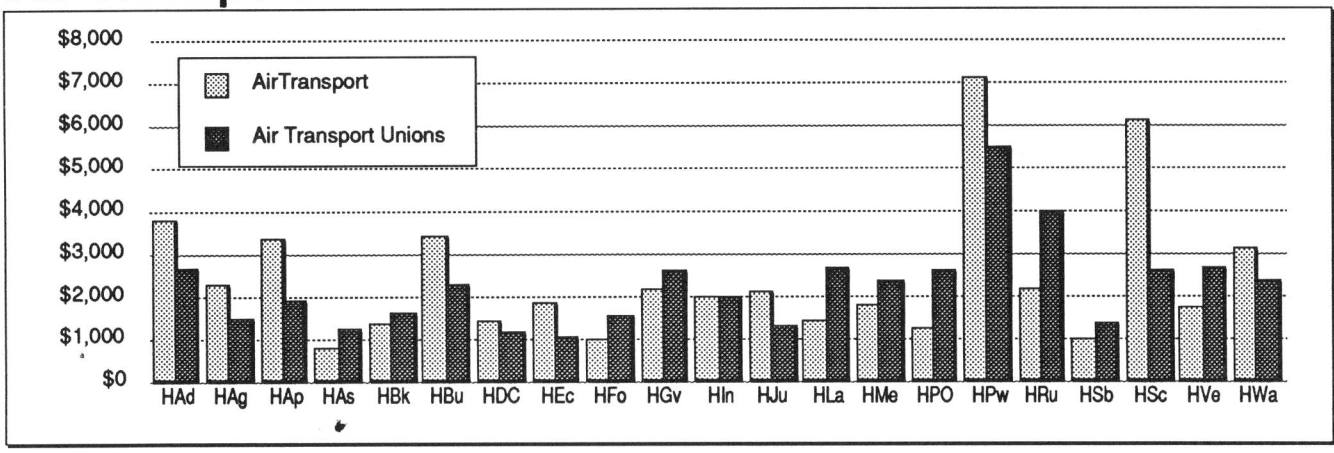

Railroads & Unions

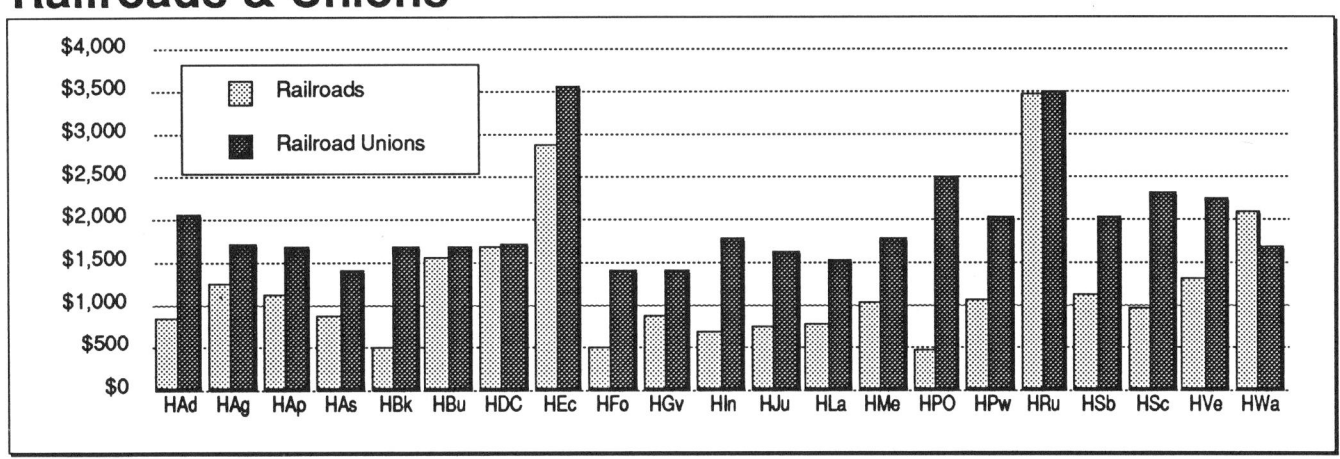

Sea Transport & Unions

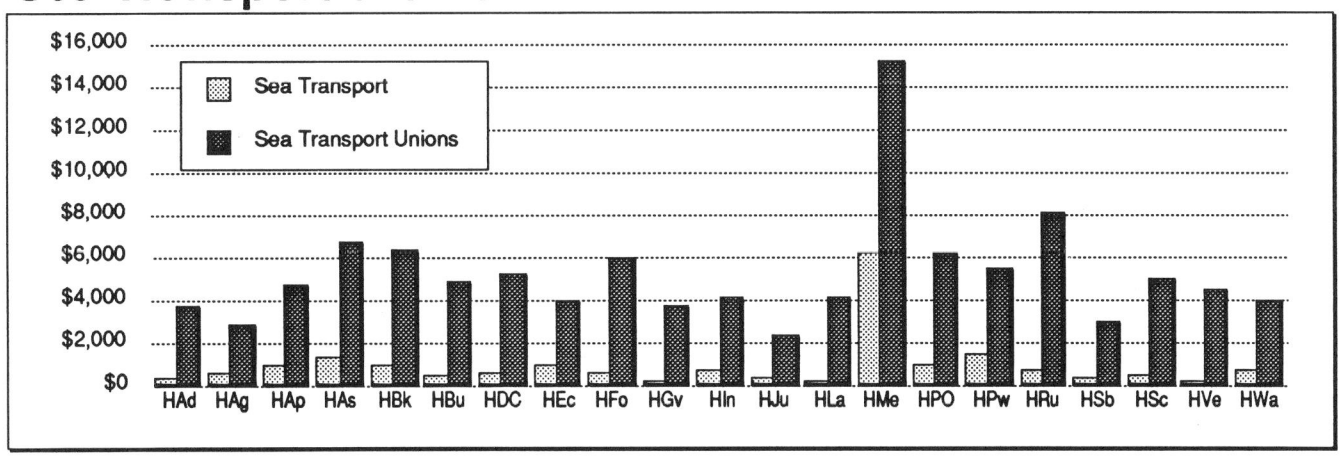

A complete key to the committee codes in these charts can be found on page 22.

2.

Industry Profiles

Open Secrets

Business PACs

Where the money came from . . .

The largest group of PACs by far is that connected with corporations, trade and professional associations that is loosely classified under the label of "business" PACs.

The PACs represented here come from every sector of American industry — sectors which are explored in greater detail on the following pages. Together, business PACs contributed more than $103 million to federal candidates in the 1988 elections —considerably more than all the labor and ideological/single-issue PACs combined.

The Finance/Insurance/Real Estate sector was the biggest (and richest) of the business PACs, contributing more than $27 million through more than 700 individual PACs. The sector was more than twice as large as the next highest groups, agriculture and "miscellaneous business," which includes a wide variety of manufacturing, service and sales related businesses.

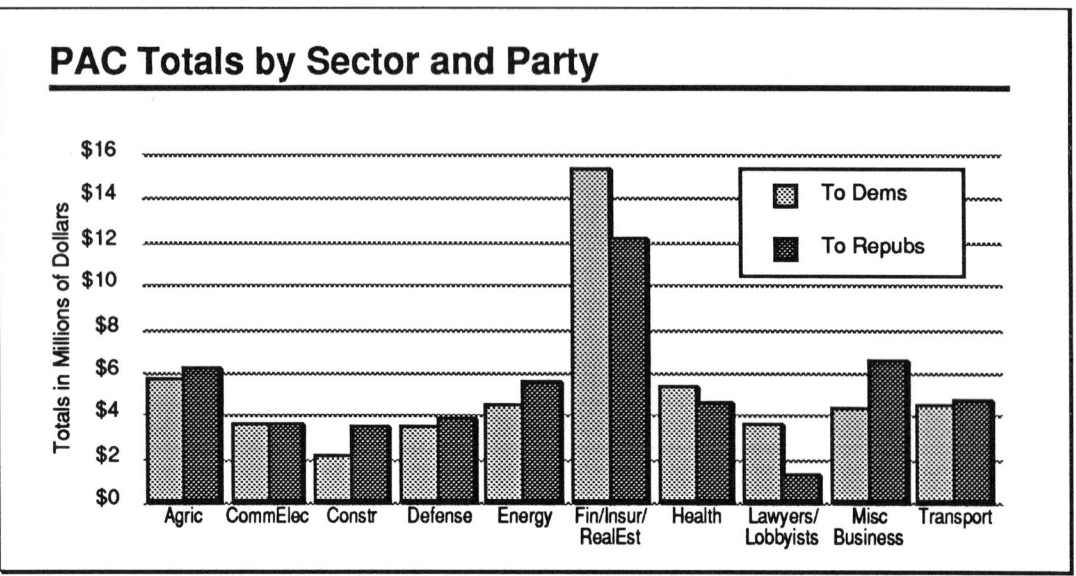

PAC Totals by Sector and Party

Category	Total	To Democrats	To Republicans	Dem Pct	Repub Pct
Agriculture	$11,686,211	$5,611,806	$6,074,405	48.0%	52.0%
Communications/Electronics	$7,170,043	$3,560,279	$3,609,764	49.7%	50.3%
Construction	$5,552,968	$2,087,035	$3,465,933	37.6%	62.4%
Defense	$7,181,439	$3,417,597	$3,763,842	47.6%	52.4%
Energy/Natural Resources	$9,845,920	$4,377,317	$5,468,603	44.5%	55.5%
Finance/Insurance/Real Estate	$27,333,774	$15,266,170	$12,067,604	55.9%	44.1%
Health	$9,865,952	$5,288,115	$4,577,837	53.6%	46.4%
Lawyers/Lobbyists	$4,796,745	$3,555,950	$1,240,795	74.1%	25.9%
Miscellaneous Business	$10,745,036	$4,297,377	$6,447,659	40.0%	60.0%
Transportation	$9,145,897	$4,448,396	$4,697,501	48.6%	51.4%
Business Total	**$103,323,985**	**$51,910,042**	**$51,413,943**	**50.2%**	**49.8%**

Where the money went . . .

During the 1970s and early 80s, business PACs tended to give the majority of their dollars to Republican candidates — the traditional allies of business interests. In the 1982 elections, for example, Republicans got 60 percent of the dollars from business

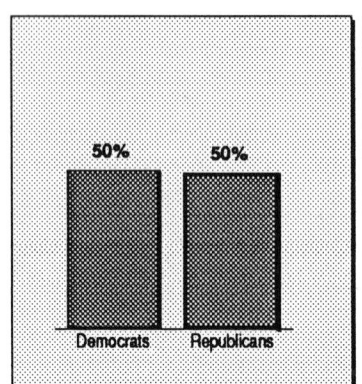

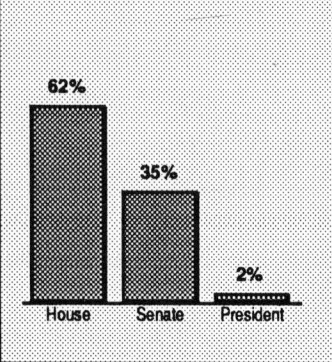

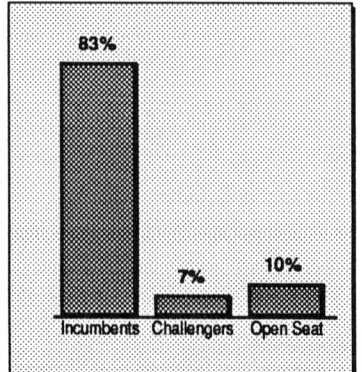

related PACs. Shortly after that election, the Democrats, led by Rep. Tony Coelho of California, began a concerted drive to attract more PAC dollars to Democrats. As the majority party in the U.S. House, Coelho argued, they controlled all the committee chairmanships, and thus were in a strong position to influence the shape of legislation. Many business PACs

Top 20 Business PACs

Rank	Total	PAC Sponsor or Affiliate	Type	To Dems	To Repubs	To Dems / To Repubs
1	$3,047,269	National Assn of Realtors	Real Estate	$1,630,452	$1,416,817	
2	$2,664,202	American Medical Assn*	Doctors	$1,276,445	$1,387,757	
3	$1,962,058	Assn of Trial Lawyers of America*	Lawyers	$1,688,708	$273,350	
4	$1,462,756	National Assn of Home Builders*	Resid Constr	$693,175	$769,581	
5	$1,345,083	American Bankers Assn*	Comml Banks	$742,525	$602,558	
6	$1,329,150	National Assn of Life Underwriters	Insurance	$726,350	$602,800	
7	$1,305,112	AT&T	Long Dist	$717,300	$587,812	
8	$1,202,420	National Auto Dealers Assn	Auto Dealers	$471,920	$730,500	
9	$1,158,700	Auto Dealers/Drivers for Free Trade	Auto Dealers	$303,400	$855,300	
10	$897,000	American Dental Assn*	Dentists	$452,200	$444,800	
11	$907,159	American Institute of CPA's	Accountants	$515,200	$391,959	
12	$836,350	Associated Milk Producers	Dairy	$569,750	$266,600	
13	$771,768	United Parcel Service	Delivery	$461,151	$310,617	
14	$748,975	Associated General Contractors*	Comml Constr	$206,600	$542,375	
15	$704,601	US League of Savings Assn*	Savings Banks	$445,001	$259,600	
16	$644,000	American Acad of Ophthalmology	Doctors	$300,500	$343,500	
17	$623,380	Philip Morris*	Tobacco	$358,793	$264,587	
18	$612,167	Indep Insurance Agents of America	Insurance	$372,133	$240,034	
19	$578,656	BellSouth Corp*	Phone Util	$320,030	$258,626	
20	$573,537	Federal Express Corp	Delivery	$378,950	$194,587	

* Contributions came from more than one PAC affiliated with this sponsor

Nine of the 25 PACs that gave $1 million or more to federal candidates in 1988 came from the business community. The National Association of Realtors was the biggest PAC in the nation, delivering more than $3 million to some 542 candidates. Unlike other groups that tended to concentrate their dollars on members of strategic committees, the Realtors gave considerable sums to just about everyone. Their average contribution was about $5,000.

Doctors, lawyers, homebuilders, bankers, insurance agents and auto dealers were also top-dollar players in the PAC arena in 1988, as they have been for many years. The largest corporate PAC was that of telecommunications giant AT&T, which directed its biggest block of contributions at members of the House Energy and Commerce Committee — the panel that oversees telecommunications policy in the House.

Of the top 20 business PACs, six came from the financial sector. Four others, led by the auto dealers, came from the transportation industry. Not a single company specializing in defense or energy production made the Top 20 list (though AT&T itself is a major defense contractor). During 1987-88, insurance PACs alone outspent the defense, communications and construction sectors. Close behind insurance were PACs representing commercial banks.

bought the argument, and the old patterns began to shift. In the 1988 elections, business PACs delivered more dollars to Democrats than to Republicans. The margin, however, was narrow, and for all practical purposes the business sectors split their dollars down the middle. But there were significant differences among the major industries, and particularly among narrower sectors within industries. Lawyers and lobbyists were the most reliably Democratic in 1988, delivering nearly three-quarters of their dollars to Democratic candidates. Financial and health PACs also gave more to the majority party, though by narrower margins. All the other industry groups gave more to Republicans, though in most cases the differences between the parties were slight. The most heavily Republican sector was the construction industry, which gave nearly $2 to Republicans for every $1 to Democrats. The miscellaneous business category was also solidly Republican. Within that category, manufacturing PACs tended to be the most conservative.

One clear pattern that sets apart business PACs from labor and ideological groups is their overwhelming preference for incumbents. Eighty-three percent of the dollars these PACs gave out in 1987-88 went to incumbents seeking reelection; only seven percent went to challengers. By way of comparison, labor PACs gave 21 percent to challengers; ideological and single-issue PACs gave 24 percent to challengers and another 21 percent to candidates for open seats. Business PACs were also by far the most pragmatic and the least partisan. Of the business PACs that gave $20,000 or more to federal candidates in 1988, 40.5 percent distributed their dollars fairly evenly between the parties, with neither party getting more than 60 percent of the total. Only six percent of ideological PACs were so even handed, and not a single large labor PACs split their dollars so evenly between Republicans and Democrats.

Agriculture

Where the money came from . . .

A powerful political force in Washington long before the age of political action committees, the agriculture industry has been quick to adapt to the PAC environment. In the 1988 election cycle some 277 agriculture-related PACs gave more than $12.7 million to federal candidates. Dairy producers, food processors, tobacco companies, commodities traders and forestry firms were all important sectors within the industry, but the single biggest source of PAC funds came from farmers and corporations engaged in crop production. Within the farming community, sugar growers led all others by a wide margin, but they were hardly alone in the field. The diversity of American agriculture can be seen in the remarkable variety of individual PACs, representing every segment of the industry. Georgia peanut farmers have their own PAC, so do Idaho potato processors, California pistachio growers, Tennessee Walking Horse breeders and dozens of others.

Companies providing agricultural services and equipment represent another important sector within the agriculture industry. Much of the PAC money in this group comes from chemical companies marketing everything from pesticides to growth hormones for livestock.

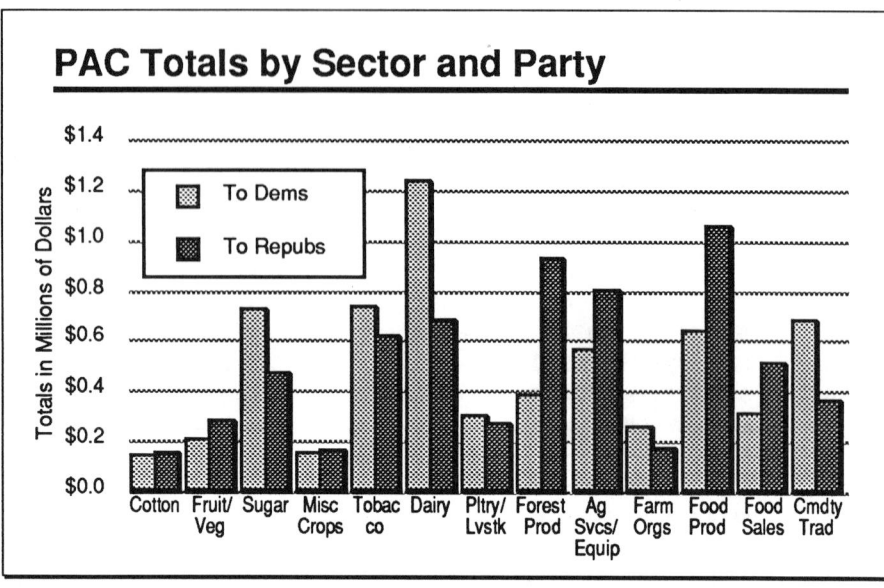

PAC Totals by Sector and Party

Category	Total	To Democrats	To Republicans	Dem Pct	Repub Pct
Cotton Growers	$283,403	$140,232	$143,171	49.5%	50.5%
Fruit/Veg Growers	$480,022	$202,270	$277,752	42.1%	57.9%
Sugar Growers	$1,186,301	$716,670	$469,631	60.4%	39.6%
Misc Crops	$310,045	$151,895	$158,150	49.0%	51.0%
Tobacco Products	$1,351,087	$734,344	$616,743	54.4%	45.6%
Dairy Production	$1,911,107	$1,227,897	$683,210	64.3%	35.7%
Poultry/Livestock	$557,626	$292,840	$264,786	52.5%	47.5%
Forest Products	$1,308,318	$383,479	$924,839	29.3%	70.7%
Agricultural Svcs & Equip	$1,359,081	$559,372	$799,709	41.2%	58.8%
Farm Organizations	$424,266	$252,780	$171,486	59.6%	40.4%
Food Processing	$1,689,528	$634,347	$1,055,181	37.5%	62.5%
Food Wholesale/Retail	$816,927	$312,680	$504,247	38.3%	61.7%
Commodities Trading	$1,044,050	$680,750	$363,300	65.2%	34.8%
Agriculture Total	**$12,721,761**	**$6,289,556**	**$6,432,205**	**49.4%**	**50.6%**

Where the money went . . .

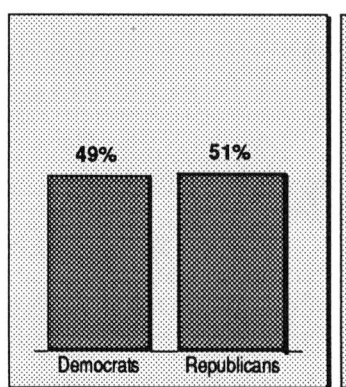

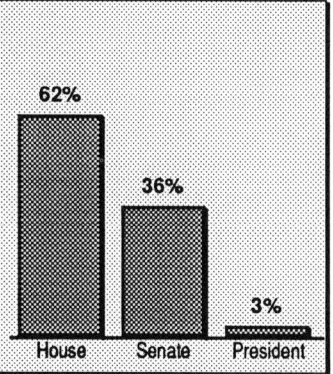

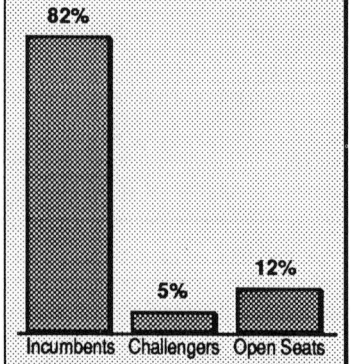

Overall, the industry split its contributions almost evenly between the parties, but there were wide variations between the different sectors. Dairy farmers and Chicago-based commodities traders were the most heavily Democratic, while forestry companies and food manufacturers strongly preferred Republicans.

Like all other business sectors, the industry gave an overwhelming proportion of its dollars to incumbents.

Top 20 Agriculture PACs

Rank	Total	PAC Sponsor or Affiliate	Type	To Dems	To Repubs	To Dems / To Repubs
1	$836,350	Associated Milk Producers	Dairy	$569,750	$266,600	
2	$605,080	Philip Morris*	Tobacco	$352,093	$252,987	
3	$458,650	Mid-America Dairymen	Dairy	$303,600	$155,050	
4	$449,400	Chicago Mercantile Exchange	Commodities	$282,900	$166,500	
5	$424,350	Chicago Board of Trade	Commodities	$284,650	$139,700	
6	$358,574	Food Marketing Institute	Food Stores	$155,255	$203,319	
7	$334,575	American Crystal Sugar Corp	Sugar	$195,425	$139,150	
8	$320,708	Dairymen Inc*	Dairy	$222,858	$97,850	
9	$260,675	RJR Nabisco†	Tobacco	$135,175	$125,500	
10	$242,811	National Cattlemen's Assn*	Livestock	$108,850	$133,961	
11	$220,700	Amer Sugarbeet Growers Assn	Sugar	$134,878	$85,822	
12	$208,500	Westvaco Corp	Forest Prod	$72,500	$136,000	
13	$194,557	Tobacco Institute	Tobacco	$103,876	$90,681	
14	$188,500	Amer Veterinary Medical Assn	Animal Hlth	$99,500	$89,000	
15	$186,577	ConAgra Inc*	Food Prod	$59,950	$126,627	
16	$160,550	Archer-Daniels-Midland Corp	Grain Trader	$90,950	$69,600	
17	$156,603	National Cotton Council	Cotton	$97,692	$58,911	
18	$148,500	American Sugar Cane League	Sugar	$97,100	$51,400	
19	$146,775	United States Tobacco Co	Tobacco	$57,650	$89,125	
20	$140,650	American Meat Institute	Meat Prod	$64,200	$76,450	

* Contributions came from more than one PAC affiliated with this sponsor.
† Does not include RJR Nabisco's Heublein subsidiary, which produces liquor products

The biggest recipients of the industry's PAC dollars were concentrated in the agriculture committees of the House and Senate. Leading the list by a country mile was Republican Pete Wilson of California, who collected more than $350,000 from agriculture-related interests — much of it from fruit and vegetable growers within his home state. Wilson waged a $14 million reelection campaign in 1988; some $2.4 million of that came from PACs. In second place was Richard Lugar of Indiana, the ranking Republican on the Senate Agriculture Committee. Besides Wilson and Lugar, three others on the top 10 Senate list were also Agriculture Committee members — David Karnes, Bob Dole and John Melcher.

Fully eight of the top 10 House recipients (everyone but Thomas Foley and Byron Dorgan) held seats on the House Agriculture Committee in 1988. Kika de la Garza was chairman of the committee and Edward Madigan was ranking Republican. Among the others on the list, Charlie Rose was a subcommittee chairman and Arlan Stangeland and Wally Herger were the senior minority members of two other subcommittees.

Top Senate Recipients

Rank	Name	Total	Status	W/L
1	Pete Wilson (R-Calif)	$353,029	Incumb	W
2	Richard Lugar (R-Ind)	$201,155	Incumb	W
3	Dave Durenberger (R-Minn)	$185,446	Incumb	W
4	Lloyd Bentsen (D-Texas)*	$170,900	Incumb*	W
5	David Karnes (R-Neb)	$168,400	Incumb	L
6	John Melcher (D-Mont)	$165,341	Incumb	L
7	Trent Lott (R-Miss)	$154,700	Open	W
8	Susan Engeleiter (R-Wis)	$130,036	Open	L
9	Bob Dole (R-Kan)	$127,032	Incumb†	†
10	George Voinovich (R-Ohio)	$123,689	Chall	L

* Bentsen ran simultaneously for Senate and Vice President in 1988.
† Dole ran for President in 1988. His Senate term expires in 1992

Top House Recipients

Rank	Name	Total	Status	W/L
1	Bill Emerson (R-Mo)	$129,400	Incumb	W
2	Thomas S. Foley (D-Wash)	$111,815	Incumb	W
3	Wally Herger (R-Calif)	$105,418	Incumb	W
4	Arlan Stangeland (R-Minn)	$104,500	Incumb	W
5	Bill Schuette (R-Mich)	$95,220	Incumb	W
6	Kika de la Garza (D-Texas)	$85,250	Incumb	W
7	Edward R. Madigan (R-Ill)	$84,473	Incumb	W
8	Fred Grandy (R-Iowa)	$84,400	Incumb	W
9	Charlie Rose (D-NC)	$74,250	Incumb	W
10	Byron L. Dorgan (D-ND)	$73,250	Incumb	W

Communications & Electronics

Where the money came from . . .

America's electronics and telecommunications industries — long the world leaders in high-technology research and development — are facing trying times these days, under pressure from competitors both at home and abroad. As if foreign competition from Japan were not enough, segments of the industry are competing against each other as they seek to carve out new territories in the high-tech future of electronic communications. The battleground for much of this competition is centered in Washington, as Congress debates alternative standards and regulations governing such emerging technologies as high-definition television, with its potential to provide new telecommunications services via home TV. The eventual guidelines Congress settles on could determine the pace of industry growth in the 1990s and beyond.

Major players in this debate are the cable TV industry and the seven regional Bell Telephone companies (the so-called "Baby Bells") that were created after the court-ordered breakup of AT&T in 1984. The telephone utilities — both local and long distance — are the prime source of PAC money in this sector. AT&T remains the undisputed giant within the industry. Its PAC dwarfed all others in 1988, giving more than $1.3 million to federal candi-

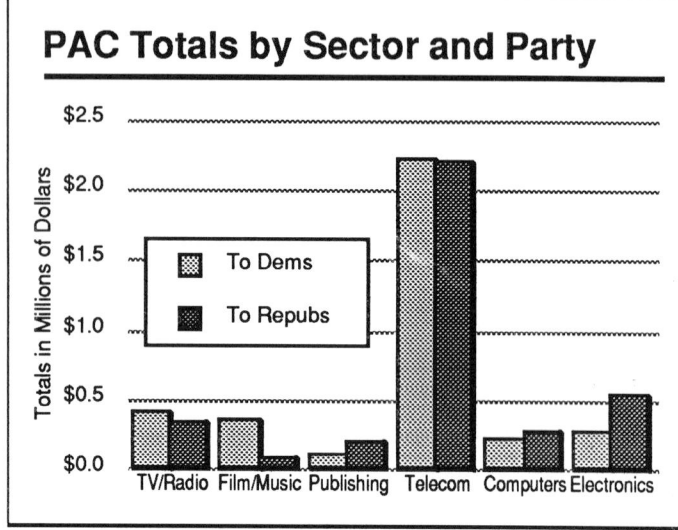

PAC Totals by Sector and Party

dates. But the Baby Bells are a powerful force in themselves. Together, these regional holding companies and their individual subsidiaries sponsored more than two dozen PACs, which gave a total of nearly $2 million in contributions during 1987-88. All seven regional Bell companies — BellSouth, US West, Bell Atlantic, Pacific Telesis, Ameritech, NYNEX, and Southwestern Bell — ranked among the top 11 telecommunications PACs. Most of the dollars they gave came from their subsidiary companies — utilities like New York Telephone, Illinois Bell, and Chesapeake & Potomac Telephone. In the chart on the following page the totals from each subsidiary are added together under their respective regional Bell parent.

Category	Total	To Democrats	To Republicans	Dem Pct	Repub Pct
TV/Radio Broadcasting	$740,373	$409,958	$330,415	55.4%	44.6%
Movies/Music Production	$429,448	$343,403	$86,045	80.0%	20.0%
Printing & Publishing	$292,906	$95,018	$197,888	32.4%	67.6%
Telecommunications	$4,402,406	$2,216,368	$2,186,038	50.3%	49.7%
Computer Products & Services	$488,114	$221,311	$266,803	45.3%	54.7%
Electronics Manufacturing	$816,797	$274,222	$542,575	33.6%	66.4%
Communications/Electronics Total	**$7,170,043**	**$3,560,279**	**$3,609,764**	**49.7%**	**50.3%**

Where the money went . . .

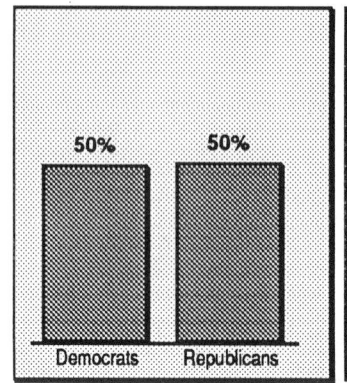

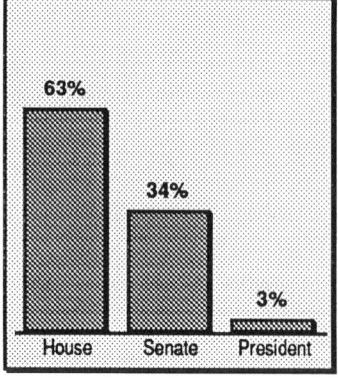

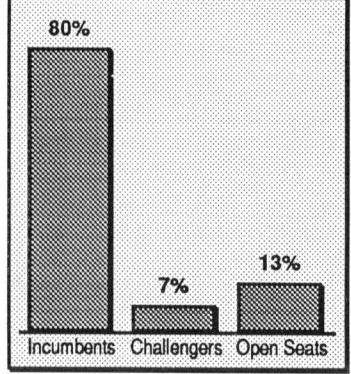

Democrats and Republicans benefited equally from the PAC dollars distributed by the electronics and telecommunications industries. The only segments to lean toward one party or the other were the film industry, which heavily favored Democrats, and electronics companies and printer-publishers, who gave about two-thirds of their money to Republicans.

Spotlight on Telecommunications

Top 20 Telecommunications PACs

Rank	Total	PAC Sponsor or Affiliate	Type	To Dems	To Repubs	To Dems / To Repubs
1	$1,305,112	AT&T	Long Dist	$717,300	$587,812	
2	$532,156	BellSouth Corp*	Phone Util	$319,280	$212,876	
3	$320,170	Continental Telecom	Phone Util	$103,550	$216,620	
4	$298,728	US West*	Phone Util	$172,445	$126,283	
5	$273,817	Bell Atlantic*	Phone Util	$142,218	$131,599	
6	$260,460	Pacific Telesis Group	Phone Util	$156,400	$104,060	
7	$260,174	Ameritech Corp*	Phone Util	$112,619	$147,555	
8	$248,995	GTE Corp*	Phone Util	$126,640	$122,255	
9	$228,484	United Telecommunications*	Phone Util	$47,684	$180,800	
10	$186,826	NYNEX Corp*	Phone Util	$78,161	$108,665	
11	$154,300	Southwestern Bell	Phone Util	$81,700	$72,600	
12	$131,578	Motorola Inc	Telecom Equip	$50,701	$80,877	
13	$122,354	US Telephone Assn	Phone Util	$78,464	$43,890	
14	$73,008	Comsat	Satellite Comm	$43,283	$29,725	
15	$56,433	MCI Telecommunications	Long Dist	$44,508	$11,925	
16	$44,384	Natl Telephone Co-Op Assn	Phone Util	$32,194	$12,190	
17	$41,975	Centel Corp	Phone Util	$20,300	$21,675	
18	$38,275	Alltel Corp	Phone Util	$21,725	$16,550	
19	$33,850	DSC Communications Corp	Telecom Equip	$22,100	$11,750	
20	$33,600	Penn Central Corp	Telecom Equip	$16,400	$17,200	

* Contributions came from more than one PAC affiliated with this sponsor

While more than 80 percent of the industry's PAC dollars went to incumbent members of Congress, there was still enough money left over for a handful of potential newcomers on the Senate side. Four of the top 10 Senate recipients of telecommunications PAC dollars were seeking open seats. A fifth, George Voinovich of Ohio, was challenging Democrat Howard Metzenbaum. John Danforth, the Missouri Republican who received the most from industry PACs, is the ranking minority member of the Senate Commerce Committee, the Senate group that deals most directly with telecommunications matters.

Center stage in the House of Representatives for the industry's struggles is the House Energy and Commerce Committee, and six of the top 10 recipients of telecom PAC dollars in the House were members of that committee in 1988. John Dingell, number one on the list, is chairman of the full committee. The other five all sit on the Telecommunications and Finance subcommittee, the specific panel that oversees industry affairs. Others on the Top 10 list are (or were) members of the House leadership.

Top Senate Recipients

Rank	Name	Total	Status	W/L
1	John Danforth (R-Mo)	$51,775	Incumb	W
2	George Voinovich (R-Ohio)	$46,900	Chall	L
3	Lloyd Bentsen (D-Texas)*	$44,720	Incumb*	W
4	Bob Dole (R-Kan)	$40,650	Incumb†	†
5	Susan Engeleiter (R-Wis)	$37,950	Open	L
6	Slade Gorton (R-Wash)	$36,600	Open	W
7	Al Gore (D-Tenn)	$34,750	Incumb†	†
8	John Heinz (R-Pa)	$33,868	Incumb	W
9	Connie Mack (R-Fla)	$33,650	Open	W
10	Chuck Robb (D-Va)	$32,500	Open	W

* Bentsen ran simultaneously for Senate and Vice President in 1988
† Dole and Gore both ran for President in 1988. Gore's Senate term expires in 1990. Dole's expires in 1992.

Top House Recipients

Rank	Name	Total	Status	W/L
1	John D. Dingell (D-Mich)	$41,030	Incumb	W
2	Al Swift (D-Wash)	$40,075	Incumb	W
3	Tom Tauke (R-Iowa)	$39,750	Incumb	W
4	Robert T. Matsui (D-Calif)	$38,300	Incumb	W
5	Don Ritter (R-Pa)	$31,425	Incumb	W
6	Richard A. Gephardt (D-Mo)	$30,250	Incumb*	W*
7	Jim Wright (D-Texas)	$30,000	Incumb	W
8	Robert H. Michel (R-Ill)	$29,850	Incumb	W
9	Dennis E. Eckart (D-Ohio)	$29,598	Incumb	W
10	Dan Coats (R-Ind)	$26,850	Incumb	W

* In 1988 Gephardt ran first for President, then for reelection to his U.S. House seat.

Construction

Where the money came from . . .

Homebuilders, public works contractors, project management firms, architects, engineers and a host of assorted subcontractors supplying everything from plumbing to air conditioning to cement make up this segment of American business — the nation's construction industry.

Many construction firms — particularly the biggest ones — are dependent for major portions of their work on decisions made in Washington. Government contracts to build new highways, bridges, dams and other public works projects can bring a substantial amount of business to a host of construction-related contractors and suppliers as well. Within the industry, the National Association of Homebuilders, which operates BUILD PAC, is by far the largest political action committee. BUILD gave more than $1.7 million to federal candidates in the 1988 elections, twice as much as the second-place Associated General Contractors, which primarily represents commercial and industrial contractors.

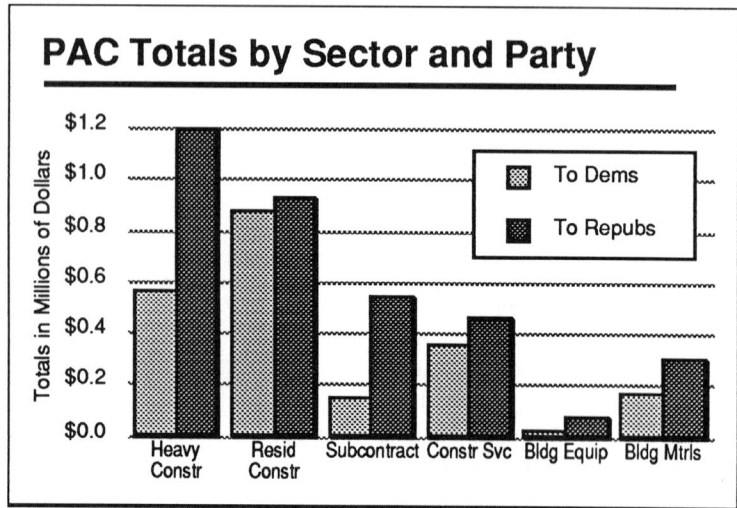

PAC Totals by Sector and Party

Category	Total	To Democrats	To Republicans	Dem Pct	Repub Pct
Industrial/Comm'l Contractors	$1,746,222	$553,834	$1,192,388	31.7%	68.3%
Home Builders	$1,790,256	$869,658	$920,598	48.6%	51.4%
Subcontractors	$669,216	$135,635	$533,581	20.3%	79.7%
Construction Services	$806,111	$349,850	$456,261	43.4%	56.6%
Bldg Equipment	$82,759	$12,950	$69,809	15.6%	84.4%
Bldg Materials	$458,404	$165,108	$293,296	36.0%	64.0%
Construction Total	**$5,552,968**	**$2,087,035**	**$3,465,933**	**37.6%**	**62.4%**

Where the money went . . .

The heavy construction segment of the industry, together with the many subcontractors' groups and companies, were strongly Republican in their distribution of PAC funds, despite the Democratic majorities in the U.S. House and Senate. Industrial contractors gave more than twice as much to G.O.P. members as to Democrats. Subcontractors and building equipment suppliers gave even higher proportions to the Republicans.

Though homebuilders, architects and engineering firms were somewhat more even-handed in their contributions, the industry overall was one of the most Republican-oriented of any within the PAC community, giving more than 62 percent of their total PAC dollars to Republicans and only 38 percent to Democrats.

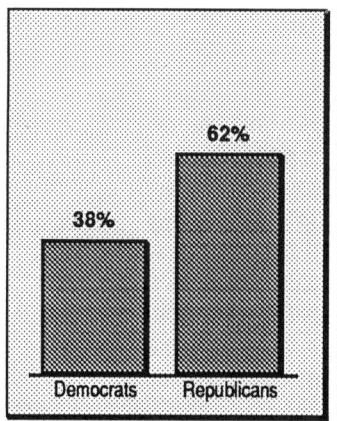

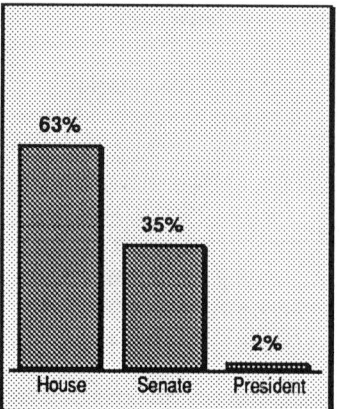

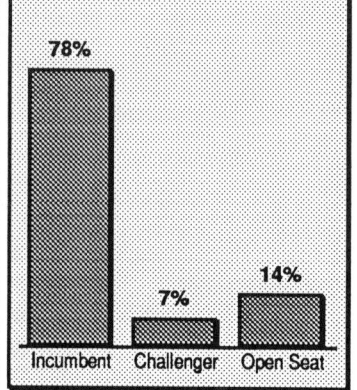

Top 20 Construction PACs

Rank	Total	PAC Sponsor or Affiliate	Type	To Dems	To Repubs	To Dems	To Repubs
1	$1,462,756	National Assn of Home Builders*	Resid Constr	$693,175	$769,581		
2	$748,975	Associated General Contractors*	Comml Constr	$206,600	$542,375		
3	$337,500	Natl Utility Contractors Assn	Comml Constr	$145,500	$192,000		
4	$217,500	Natl Electrical Contractors Assn	Electr Contr	$32,000	$185,500		
5	$205,535	Sheet Metal/Air Con Contractors	Plumb/AirCon	$57,635	$147,900		
6	$180,876	Associated Builders & Contractors	Builders	$17,150	$163,726		
7	$159,760	Manville Corp	Matls	$70,150	$89,610		
8	$122,450	Walter Industries*	Resid Constr	$86,950	$35,500		
9	$101,650	Natl Society of Prof Engineers	Engineers	$38,750	$62,900		
10	$98,650	Bechtel Corp	Comml Constr	$38,150	$60,500		
11	$94,648	Ch2M Hill	Engineers	$37,650	$56,998		
12	$93,439	Wall & Ceiling/Gypsum Contractors	Subcontr	$4,600	$88,839		
13	$88,275	American Consulting Engrs Council	Engineers	$30,250	$58,025		
14	$86,550	Fluor Corp	Comml Constr	$27,725	$58,825		
15	$80,338	Owens-Corning Fiberglas	Bldg Matls	$18,000	$62,338		
16	$77,808	American Supply Assn	Pipe Prod	$15,725	$62,083		
17	$74,700	Brown & Root	Comml Constr	$30,100	$44,600		
18	$61,600	Stone & Webster	Engineers	$33,100	$28,500		
19	$61,500	American Subcontractors Assn	Subcontr	$21,150	$40,350		
20	$59,855	Caterpillar Tractor	Bldg Equip	$7,550	$52,305		

* Contributions came from more than one PAC affiliated with this sponsor

The top recipient of construction industry contributions was California Republican Pete Wilson, whose 1988 Senate campaign was the most expensive in the country. In all, eight of the 10 leading Senate recipients of construction dollars were Republicans. The patterns of giving seemed more related to the general level of spending by the candidates than by any geographic considerations or committee assignments. Only half the top 10 recipients were incumbent senators.

Among House candidates there was a more even distribution between the parties, with six Republicans and four Democrats making the list. All were incumbents and five of the ten sat on the banking or public works committees. The banking committees in the House and Senate including housing under their jurisdiction. The public works committees guide the spending of federal dollars for road building, dams, and other public projects. Republican John Hiler of Indiana, the top House recipient of construction-related funds, was one of 20 House candidates to spend more than a million dollars in their 1988 campaigns. More than $344,000 of his campaign dollars came from PACs.

Top 10 Senate Recipients

Rank	Name	Total	Status	W/L
1	Pete Wilson (R-Calif)	$100,147	Incumb	W
2	Orrin Hatch (R-Utah)	$91,500	Incumb	W
3	Lloyd Bentsen (D-Texas)*	$88,925	Incumb*	W
4	George Voinovich (R-Ohio)	$81,762	Chall	L
5	Connie Mack (R-Fla)	$76,298	Open	W
6	Susan Engeleiter (R-Wis)	$73,070	Open	L
7	Dave Durenberger (R-Minn)	$72,075	Incumb	W
8	Jim Sasser (D-Tenn)	$68,450	Incumb	W
9	Trent Lott (R-Miss)	$65,726	Open	W
10	Slade Gorton (R-Wash)	$64,150	Open	W

* Bentsen ran simultaneously for Senate and Vice President in 1988

Top 10 House Recipients

Rank	Name	Total	Status	W/L
1	John Hiler (R-Ind)	$47,324	Incumb	W
2	Robert A. Roe (D-NJ)	$37,400	Incumb	W
3	Jack Brooks (D-Texas)	$36,600	Incumb	W
4	Arlan Stangeland (R-Minn)	$32,900	Incumb	W
5	Glenn M. Anderson (D-Calif)	$27,200	Incumb	W
6	Marge Roukema (R-NJ)	$27,000	Incumb	W
7	Robert J. Lagomarsino (R-Calif)	$26,800	Incumb	W
8	Jim Wright (D-Texas)	$26,500	Incumb	W
9	Dan L. Schaefer (R-Colo)	$25,550	Incumb	W
10	Steve Bartlett (R-Texas)	$25,460	Incumb	W

Defense

Where the money came from . . .

Defense contractors have always been major players in congressional politics; the dollars they dispense through their corporate PACs clearly shows it. Leading the industry in PAC spending were aerospace and electronics firms. Together they accounted for 87 percent of the $7.1 million given by all defense-related PACs.

Shipbuilding contractors — led by Tenneco and Litton Industries — added another $500,000. The remainder came from a variety of defense related services providing everything from research and development of weapons systems to overseas transportation of furniture for servicemen and their dependents.

The defense totals shown on these pages, and throughout this book, are conservative. Few U.S. corporations rely on defense work for the majority of their income, but many firms do some defense work or have defense-related subsidiaries. Under the system used to compile this book, PAC contributions from those firms were only counted as defense-related if they were given to a member sitting on the armed services or defense appropriations committees — panels that deal specifically with defense matters.

The wide diversification of many defense contractors can be seen in the list of Top 20 defense PACs on the facing page. The presence on the list of General Motors and Ford Motor Company, for example, is not due to the number of cars and trucks they sell to the armed forces, but to the fact that they own major defense-related subsidiaries. Nearly $300,000 of GM's PAC total came not from the parent company, but from the PAC of its subsidiary, Hughes Aircraft. Likewise, $137,00 of Ford's defense dollars came from BDM International, a major defense research and development firm. Since 1988, the slowdown in defense spending has moved many large corporations — the automakers included — to scale down their defense related enterprises, or even sell off their subsidiaries.

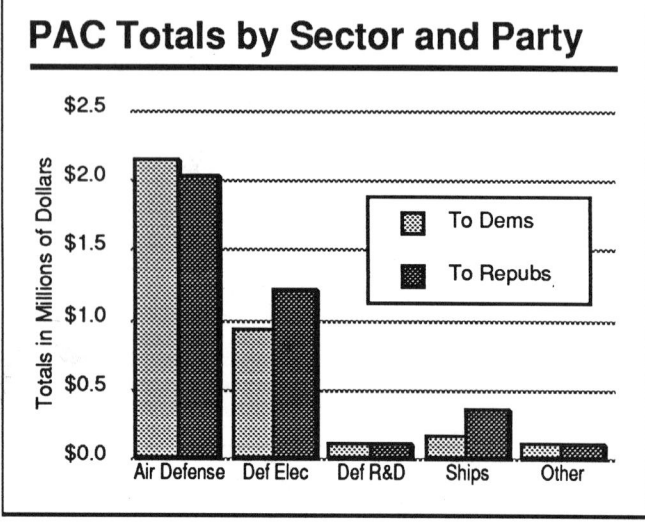

PAC Totals by Sector and Party

Category	Total	To Democrats	To Republicans	Dem Pct	Repub Pct
Defense Aerospace	$4,144,658	$2,131,522	$2,013,136	51.4%	48.6%
Defense Electronics	$2,114,116	$919,480	$1,194,636	43.5%	56.5%
Defense R&D	$207,700	$100,750	$106,950	48.5%	51.5%
Naval Shipbuilding	$501,325	$155,775	$345,550	31.1%	68.9%
Other Defense	$213,640	$110,070	$103,570	51.5%	48.5%
Defense Total	$7,181,439	$3,417,597	$3,763,842	47.6%	52.4%

Where the money went . . .

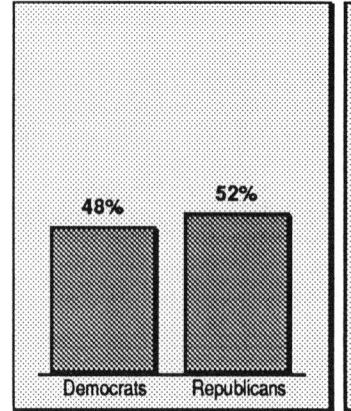

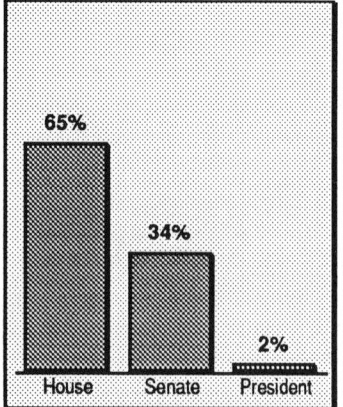

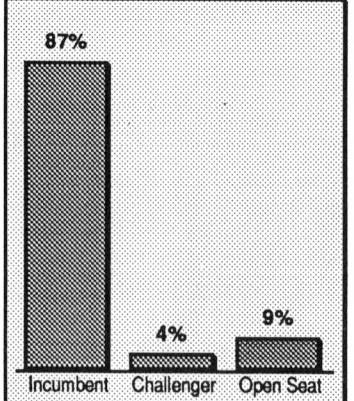

Except in a few unusual cases, where a candidate is particularly strong contender for an open congressional seat — or where they are opposing an avowed foe of the defense industry — non-incumbents need not apply for defense PAC money. Eighty-seven percent of the PACs' dollars went to incumbents — the highest rate of any sector within the PAC community.

Top 20 Defense PACs

Rank	Total	PAC Sponsor or Affiliate	Type	To Dems	To Repubs	To Dems	To Repubs
1	$441,834	Lockheed Corp	Air Defense	$210,400	$231,434		
2	$411,431	Textron Inc	Air Defense	$243,800	$167,631		
3	$383,517	Northrop Corp	Air Defense	$153,304	$230,213		
4	$379,768	Rockwell International	Air Defense	$151,183	$228,585		
5	$343,996	United Technologies	Air Defense	$143,357	$200,639		
6	$338,740	General Motors*	Electron/Air	$184,250	$154,490		
7	$320,800	McDonnell Douglas*	Air Defense	$180,050	$140,750		
8	$302,250	Harris Corp	Electron Def	$25,000	$277,250		
9	$296,125	Allied-Signal	Air Defense	$142,825	$153,300		
10	$285,049	General Dynamics	Air Defense	$173,149	$111,900		
11	$279,600	Tenneco Inc	Ships	$44,000	$235,600		
12	$253,404	Martin Marietta Corp	Air Defense	$125,338	$128,066		
13	$251,475	Grumman	Air Defense	$167,350	$84,125		
14	$217,975	Litton Industries	Ships	$75,675	$142,300		
15	$209,616	AT&T	Electron Def	$126,166	$83,450		
16	$208,648	TRW Inc	Electron Def	$94,550	$114,098		
17	$191,234	LTV Corp*	Air Defense	$126,750	$64,484		
18	$175,750	Ford Motor Company*	Elec/Air/R&D	$85,150	$90,600		
19	$167,500	Raytheon	Electron Def	$83,000	$84,500		
20	$117,850	Boeing Company	Air Defense	$69,550	$48,300		

NOTE: The totals in this chart do not include contributions from PAC sponsors' non-defense subsidiaries. Likewise, contributions from companies (such as Ford or AT&T) whose primary revenues come from non-defense sources, are counted here only when they gave to members of defense-related committees.

* Contributions came from more than one PAC affiliated with this sponsor

Nearly all the top House and Senate recipients of defense industry PAC dollars were members of the Armed Services committees or the Defense Appropriations subcommittees in their respective houses. Pete Wilson of California led the list in the Senate. Many of his defense dollars came from aerospace firms centered in southern California.

Among House members, Democrat Bill Chappell of Florida, who at the time was chairman of the House Defense Appropriations subcommittee, collected $182,000 from defense contractors — an amount second in the entire Congress only to Pete Wilson. Unlike the vast majority of House incumbents, Chappell was caught up in a very competitive (and expensive) reelection campaign. He was particularly vulnerable since he had come under investigation as part of the 1988 Pentagon procurement scandal — so vulnerable, in fact, that he became one of only six House incumbents to lose at the polls in the fall elections.

Many of the others on the House Top 10 list hold senior defense-related positions in Congress. Les Aspin is chairman of the Armed Services Committee. Bill Dickinson of Alabama is the committee's ranking Republican. Joseph McDade is the senior G.O.P. member of the Defense Appropriations subcommittee.

Top 10 Senate Recipients

Rank	Name	Total	Status	W/L
1	Pete Wilson (R-Calif)	$236,510	Incumb	W
2	Jeff Bingaman (D-NM)	$127,450	Incumb	W
3	Jim Sasser (D-Tenn)	$114,800	Incumb	W
4	Dennis DeConcini (D-Ariz)	$101,819	Incumb	W
5	Robert C. Byrd (D-WVa)	$91,166	Incumb	W
6	Trent Lott (R-Miss)	$85,500	Open	W
7	Lloyd Bentsen (D-Texas)*	$82,460	Incumb*	W
8	John Danforth (R-Mo)	$75,861	Incumb	W
9	Orrin Hatch (R-Utah)	$68,000	Incumb	W
10	Pete Dawkins (R-NJ)	$67,100	Chall	L

* Bentsen ran simultaneously for Senate and Vice President in 1988

Top 10 House Recipients

Rank	Name	Total	Status	W/L
1	Bill Chappell (D-Fla)	$182,000	Incumb	L
2	John P. Murtha (D-Pa)	$116,682	Incumb	W
3	Joseph M. McDade (R-Pa)	$101,800	Incumb	W
4	Les Aspin (D-Wis)	$101,200	Incumb	W
5	William L. Dickinson (R-Ala)	$92,550	Incumb	W
6	Roy Dyson (D-Md)	$89,300	Incumb	W
7	Charles Wilson (D-Texas)	$87,250	Incumb	W
8	Robert W. Davis (R-Mich)	$82,250	Incumb	W
9	Bill Hefner (D-NC)	$78,650	Incumb	W
10	James V. Hansen (R-Utah)	$61,400	Incumb	W

Energy & Natural Resources

Where the money came from . . .

In a nation that grew to world prominence by exploiting its abundant natural resources, then building new industries on the strength of its home-grown oil, gas, minerals and electricity, it is not surprising that energy producers still pack a powerful political punch on Capitol Hill.

Between them, the oil and gas industry and electrical power utilities dominated the PAC giving within the sector. In the 1988 elections, the oil industry gave just over $4 million in PAC dollars to candidates for federal office. Companies that transport natural gas through interstate pipelines added another $1.5 million, while power utilities gave $3 million. All three of those industries are subject to a raft of federal laws and regulations, as well as tax measures — like the oil depletion allowance — that are specific to their industries.

Mining interests played a comparatively smaller role within the PAC community, accounting for about $800,000 in contributions. That total, however, includes only those firms whose primary business is mining. Many oil and gas companies also operate coal and other mining subsidiaries.

The job of cleaning up the environment, and disposing of the prodigious amounts of trash and other wastes that are generated daily in America, is another segment within this industry group. In 1988, the waste management industry accounted for nearly $600,000 in PAC contributions.

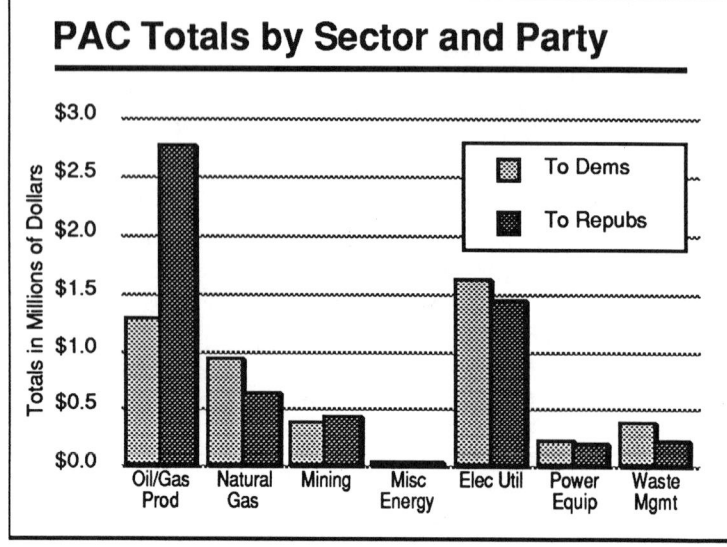

PAC Totals by Sector and Party

Category	Total	To Democrats	To Republicans	Dem Pct	Repub Pct
Oil & Gas Production/Marketing	$4,005,526	$1,256,210	$2,749,316	31.4%	68.6%
Natural Gas Distribution	$1,550,206	$915,949	$634,257	59.1%	40.9%
Mining	$802,205	$375,825	$426,380	46.8%	53.2%
Misc Energy	$55,750	$24,400	$31,350	43.8%	56.2%
Electric Utilities	$3,026,076	$1,599,926	$1,426,150	52.9%	47.1%
Power Plant Equipment	$406,157	$205,007	$201,150	50.5%	49.5%
Waste Mgmt	$593,401	$375,106	$218,295	63.2%	36.8%
Energy/Natural Resources Total	**$10,439,321**	**$4,752,423**	**$5,686,898**	**45.5%**	**54.5%**

The one energy sector whose PAC dollars take a more diffuse trail is the nuclear energy industry. No centralized PAC directs the industry's contributions, and though there are a small number of companies with PACs who do specialize in nuclear power plant construction and materials, the biggest players in the industry are the electric utilities who rely on nuclear powered generators, and the highly-diversified conglomerates, like Westinghouse, that build the plants.

Where the money went . . .

The oil and gas industry is among the most conservative in the entire business community, but the Republican slant of their PAC contributions is compensated somewhat by the Democratic leanings of interstate natural gas distributors. Electric utilities gave

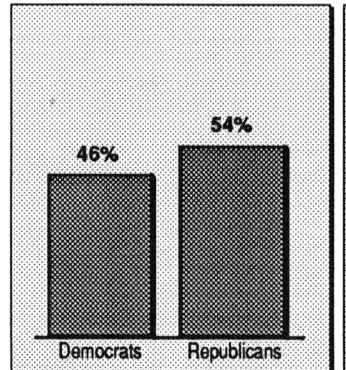

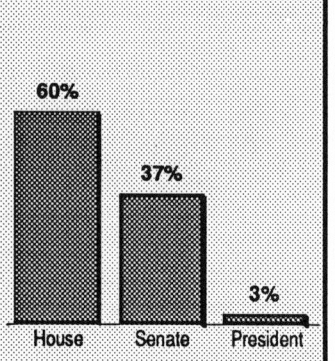

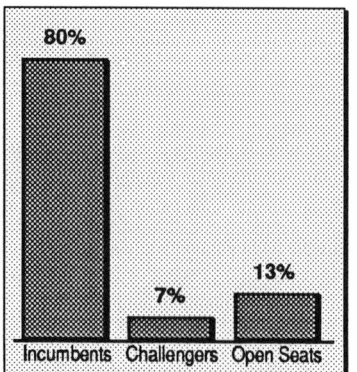

slightly more to Democrats than Republicans in the last election cycle, while mining interests narrowly preferred Republicans. Overall, the industry gave about 54 percent of its money to the G.O.P. and 46 percent to Democrats.

Top 20 Energy & Natural Resource PACs

Rank	Total	PAC Sponsor or Affiliate	Type	To Dems	To Repubs	To Dems / To Repubs
1	$504,038	ACRE (Act Cmte/Rural Electric)*	Rural Electric	$387,216	$116,822	
2	$418,116	Waste Management Inc	Waste Mgmt	$262,466	$155,650	
3	$318,764	Amoco Corp	Oil & Gas	$72,264	$246,500	
4	$296,748	Atlantic Richfield	Oil & Gas	$127,808	$168,940	
5	$277,815	Chevron Corp	Oil & Gas	$105,677	$172,138	
6	$267,035	Southern Company*	Elec Util	$136,385	$130,650	
7	$249,037	Phillips Petroleum	Oil & Gas	$52,950	$196,087	
8	$242,550	Mobil Oil	Oil & Gas	$47,550	$195,000	
9	$237,558	Coastal Corp	Natural Gas	$187,783	$49,775	
10	$188,126	Occidental Petroleum*	Oil & Gas	$102,201	$85,925	
11	$182,700	Petroleum Marketers Assn	Oil & Gas	$57,150	$125,550	
12	$167,850	Texas Utilities Electric Co*	Elec Util	$77,500	$90,350	
13	$164,105	Exxon Corp	Oil & Gas	$43,670	$120,435	
14	$161,270	Southern California Edison	Elec Util	$99,200	$62,070	
15	$155,075	Shell Oil	Oil & Gas	$47,150	$107,925	
16	$152,815	Texaco	Oil & Gas	$38,675	$114,140	
17	$152,000	Sun Company	Oil & Gas	$27,000	$125,000	
18	$143,625	Ashland Oil*	Oil & Gas	$69,325	$74,300	
19	$142,314	Pacific Enterprises	Natural Gas	$78,564	$63,750	
20	$136,277	Browning-Ferris Industries	Waste Mgmt	$85,827	$50,450	

* Contributions came from more than one PAC affiliated with this sponsor

A diverse mixture of companies populate the Top 20 list of energy-related PACs: four electric utilities, a dozen oil & gas producers, two natural gas distribution companies, and two firms specializing in waste management. Leading the list is ACRE, the Action Committee for Rural Electrification. This is the PAC that represents most of the nation's rural electric cooperatives.

On Capitol Hill, different facets of the nation's energy policy are overseen in a number of committees. In the Senate, the Energy and Natural Resources Committee plays the dominant role — though Environment and Public Works is also important to the industry, particularly in the battle over Clean Air legislation. In the House, the Energy and Commerce Committee is one of three centers of debate. Others are the Interior Committee (dealing with mining as well as resource extraction from federal lands), and the Merchant Marine and Fisheries panel, which oversees offshore oil exploration and oil spill liability. Rural electric utilities fall under the jurisdiction of the Agriculture Committees in the House and Senate.

Lloyd Bentsen, the Democratic Senator from oil-rich Texas, led all other recipients of energy-related PAC dollars in 1988. Fellow Westerners Malcolm Wallop of Wyoming and Chick Hecht of Nevada were also near the top of the list. Besides being from states where mining and energy are major industries, they also held seats on the Senate Energy Committee.

In the House, all the top money went to incumbents, and most of it went to members from energy-producing states who sit on energy-related committees. Five of the top 10 recipients held seats on the Energy and Power subcommittee of Energy and Commerce. Phil Sharp chaired the subcommittee and Norman Lent was ranking Republican. Two others were also members of Energy and Commerce — including John Dingell, the committee's chairman.

Top 10 Senate Recipients

Rank	Name	Total	Status	W/L
1	Lloyd Bentsen (D-Texas)*	$318,087	Incumb*	W
2	Malcolm Wallop (R-Wyo)	$216,877	Incumb	W
3	Chic Hecht (R-Nev)	$178,916	Incumb	L
4	George Voinovich (R-Ohio)	$173,823	Chall	L
5	John Heinz (R-Pa)	$128,197	Incumb	W
6	Quentin N. Burdick (D-ND)	$125,780	Incumb	W
7	Connie Mack (R-Fla)	$126,300	Open	W
8	Trent Lott (R-Miss)	$126,750	Open	W
9	Pete Wilson (R-Calif)	$116,697	Incumb	W
10	Slade Gorton (R-Wash)	$112,650	Open	W

* Bentsen ran simultaneously for Senate and Vice President in 1988

Top 10 House Recipients

Rank	Name	Total	Status	W/L
1	Joe L. Barton (R-Texas)	$88,407	Incumb	W
2	W.J. Tauzin (D-La)	$84,905	Incumb	W
3	Don Young (R-Alaska)	$81,975	Incumb	W
4	Philip R. Sharp (D-Ind)	$80,156	Incumb	W
5	Ralph M. Hall (D-Texas)	$79,988	Incumb	W
6	Robert J. Lagomarsino (R-Calif)	$66,228	Incumb	W
7	John D. Dingell (D-Mich)	$62,650	Incumb	W
8	Norman F. Lent (R-NY)	$59,600	Incumb	W
9	Dan L. Schaefer (R-Colo)	$58,969	Incumb	W
10	Michael A. Andrews (D-Texas)	$58,100	Incumb	W

Oil & Gas

Top 20 Oil & Gas PACs

Rank	Total	PAC Sponsor or Affiliate	Type	To Dems	To Repubs	To Dems / To Repubs
1	$318,764	Amoco Corp	Oil & Gas	$72,264	$246,500	
2	$296,748	Atlantic Richfield	Oil & Gas	$127,808	$168,940	
3	$277,815	Chevron Corp	Oil & Gas	$105,677	$172,138	
4	$249,037	Phillips Petroleum	Oil & Gas	$52,950	$196,087	
5	$242,550	Mobil Oil	Oil & Gas	$47,550	$195,000	
6	$237,558	Coastal Corp	Natural Gas	$187,783	$49,775	
7	$188,126	Occidental Petroleum*	Oil & Gas	$102,201	$85,925	
8	$182,700	Petroleum Marketers Assn	Oil & Gas	$57,150	$125,550	
9	$164,105	Exxon Corp	Oil & Gas	$43,670	$120,435	
10	$155,075	Shell Oil	Oil & Gas	$47,150	$107,925	
11	$152,815	Texaco	Oil & Gas	$38,675	$114,140	
12	$152,000	Sun Company	Oil & Gas	$27,000	$125,000	
13	$142,314	Pacific Enterprises	Natural Gas	$78,564	$63,750	
14	$134,525	Ashland Oil	Oil & Gas	$66,475	$68,050	
15	$118,951	Union Oil	Oil & Gas	$31,972	$86,979	
16	$117,383	Internorth Inc	Natural Gas	$58,033	$59,350	
17	$112,263	Enserch Corp	Natural Gas	$64,813	$47,450	
18	$108,000	Dallas Energy PAC	Oil & Gas	$5,000	$103,000	
19	$98,575	BP America	Oil & Gas	$33,375	$65,200	
20	$86,460	Mapco Inc	Oil & Gas	$10,000	$76,460	

* Contributions came from more than one PAC affiliated with this sponsor

Within the oil and gas industry there was some ideological distance between Republican-oriented oil producers and Democratic-leaning natural gas distribution companies. The differences were not all that deep, however, as both sides gave generously to members of both parties. More important than party affiliation, in the distribution of their funds, was geography and committee assignments within Congress.

The six Senate incumbents who ranked in the Top 10 list of oil & gas PAC recipients were all from Western states with major energy and resource extraction interests. Three of them — Malcolm Wallop, Jeff Bingaman and John Melcher — also held seats on the Energy and Natural Resources Committee. The logic explaining the heavy contributions to the third man on the list, however — Ohio Republican George Voinovich — is less apparent. The answer lies not so much with Voinovich, or with Ohio, but with the man he was challenging in 1988 — Democratic Senator Howard Metzenbaum. Metzenbaum, a liberal Democrat, has long been a thorn in the side of the oil and gas industry — fighting them on a variety of fronts, from their environmental record to their special tax benefits. Energy producers, as well as a lineup of companies from nearly every other business sector in the PAC community, gave Voinovich all the support they could muster. Metzenbaum won anyway, with 57 percent of the vote.

The list of Top House recipients reads like a roll call of Oil Patch representatives. Leading the list was Republican Don Young of Alaska, who sits on both the Interior and Merchant Marine Committees — both of strategic importance to oil producers. The only member on the top 10 from a non-oil producing state was Phil Sharp of Indiana. Sharp is chairman of the Energy and Power Subcommittee of the House Energy and Commerce Committee.

Top 10 Senate Recipients

Rank	Name	Total	Status	W/L
1	Lloyd Bentsen (D-Texas)*	$227,337	Incumb*	W
2	Malcolm Wallop (R-Wyo)	$141,617	Incumb	W
3	George Voinovich (R-Ohio)	$127,223	Chall	L
4	Chic Hecht (R-Nev)	$123,281	Incumb	L
5	Connie Mack (R-Fla)	$86,200	Open	W
6	Trent Lott (R-Miss)	$81,750	Open	W
7	Slade Gorton (R-Wash)	$74,250	Open†	W
8	Jeff Bingaman (D-NM)	$72,493	Incumb	W
9	Orrin Hatch (R-Utah)	$71,350	Incumb	W
10	John Melcher (D-Mont)	$69,569	Incumb	L

* Bentsen ran simultaneously for Senate and Vice President in 1988

Top 10 House Recipients

Rank	Name	Total	Status	W/L
1	Don Young (R-Alaska)	$57,325	Incumb	W
2	Joe L. Barton (R-Texas)	$49,957	Incumb	W
3	Robert J. Lagomarsino (R-Calif)	$48,803	Incumb	W
4	W.J. Tauzin (D-La)	$46,500	Incumb	W
5	Michael A. Andrews (D-Texas)	$42,400	Incumb	W
6	Jack Fields (R-Texas)	$41,700	Incumb	W
7	Ralph M. Hall (D-Texas)	$38,911	Incumb	W
8	Dan L. Schaefer (R-Colo)	$38,169	Incumb	W
9	Philip R. Sharp (D-Ind)	$37,756	Incumb	W
10	Jim Wright (D-Texas)	$37,400	Incumb	W

Electric Utilities

Rank	Total	PAC Sponsor or Affiliate	To Dems	To Repubs	To Dems / To Repubs
1	$504,038	ACRE (Action Cmte for Rural Electric)*	$387,216	$116,822	
2	$267,035	Southern Company*	$136,385	$130,650	
3	$167,850	Texas Utilities Electric Company*	$77,500	$90,350	
4	$161,270	Southern California Edison	$99,200	$62,070	
5	$126,550	Middle South Utilities*	$66,300	$60,250	
6	$89,363	Pacific Gas & Electric	$37,138	$52,225	
7	$86,039	Consumers Power Company	$44,529	$41,510	
8	$85,350	American Electric Power*	$46,500	$38,850	
9	$85,300	Edison Electric Institute	$38,800	$46,500	
10	$81,212	Houston Industries	$44,912	$36,300	
11	$78,423	Dominion Resources	$47,100	$31,323	
12	$70,400	Philadelphia Electric	$29,800	$40,600	
13	$63,545	Florida Power & Light	$27,750	$35,795	
14	$54,650	Baltimore Gas & Electric	$14,450	$40,200	
15	$54,100	Carolina Power & Light	$29,000	$25,100	
16	$53,500	Duke Power Company	$22,500	$31,000	
17	$49,948	Detroit Edison	$27,498	$22,450	
18	$43,900	New England Power Service Co	$17,600	$26,300	
19	$43,813	General Public Utilities	$20,383	$23,430	
20	$41,055	Public Service Electric & Gas	$22,233	$18,822	

* Contributions came from more than one PAC affiliated with this sponsor

A major revision of Clean Air legislation — which would mandate a major (and expensive) overhaul of many power utilities' pollution control equipment— has been a major concern of electric utilities in Congress for more than a decade. As the House and Senate have moved closer to final passage of a bill, the lobbying and the pace of PAC contributions have escalated.

The top-spending electricity PAC was ACRE, which represents rural electric cooperatives around the country. Ranking just below it was a collection of some of the largest power companies in the nation — both regional and local. Southern Company operates power utilities in four southern states — Georgia, Alabama, Mississippi and Florida. Middle South Utilities, based in New Orleans, supplies power to nearly 600,000 customers in Arkansas, Louisiana and Mississippi. Pacific Gas and Electric powers the homes and businesses of more than 11.2 million people in northern and Central California.

The names on the Top 10 recipients lists are slightly different than those receiving the biggest oil and gas contributions. Quentin Burdick, for example, chairs the Environment and Public Works Committee in the Senate — the panel in charge of clean air legislation. John Heinz of Pennsylvania counts the Pittsburgh steel mills among his constituents, while Robert Byrd of West Virginia represents the thousands of coal miners in that state who may lose jobs if demand for West Virginia's high-sulphur coal is cut back.

In the House, Ways and Means chairman Dan Rostenkowski came in third on the list. That committee has prime responsibility in the House for writing the nation's tax laws.

Top 10 Senate Recipients

Rank	Name	Total	Status	W/L
1	Lloyd Bentsen (D-Texas)*	$52,250	Incumb*	W
2	Quentin N. Burdick (D-ND)	$44,353	Incumb	W
3	John Heinz (R-Pa)	$39,367	Incumb	W
4	Chic Hecht (R-Nev)	$34,535	Incumb	L
5	Robert C. Byrd (D-WVa)	$34,300	Incumb	W
6	Connie Mack (R-Fla)	$31,600	Open	W
7	Malcolm Wallop (R-Wyo)	$27,760	Incumb	W
8	Wayne Dowdy (D-Miss)	$27,650	Open	L
9	Pete Wilson (R-Calif)	$25,125	Incumb	W
10	Chuck Robb (D-Va)	$24,550	Open	W

* Bentsen ran simultaneously for Senate and Vice President in 1988

Top 10 House Recipients

Rank	Name	Total	Status	W/L
1	Joe L. Barton (R-Texas)	$32,400	Incumb	W
2	Ralph M. Hall (D-Texas)	$30,877	Incumb	W
3	Dan Rostenkowski (D-Ill)	$29,100	Incumb	W
4	Philip R. Sharp (D-Ind)	$26,150	Incumb	W
5	W.J. Tauzin (D-La)	$22,598	Incumb	W
6	Larry S. Milner (R-Texas)	$19,850	Open	L
7	Robert T. Matsui (D-Calif)	$19,725	Incumb	W
8	John D. Dingell (D-Mich)	$19,450	Incumb	W
9	Norman F. Lent (R-NY)	$19,250	Incumb	W
10	Edward R. Madigan (R-Ill)	$17,770	Incumb	W

Finance, Insurance & Real Estate

Where the money came from . . .

Of all the sectors in American business — defense, energy, transportation, construction — none gave so much money to so many members of Congress as the financial community. Through a total of 733 individual PACs, a diversity of banks, insurance companies, real estate agencies, brokerage houses, accountants, commodity traders, loan companies and financial service firms of every description combined to give more than $27 million to federal candidates in the 1988 elections. Five dollars out of every six went to incumbents, and about 56 cents out of every dollar went to Democrats.

Insurance companies and commercial banks led the spending, accounting for over $14 million in contributions between them. The savings & loan industry, lately beset by scandal and insolvencies, was a comparatively small player, with less than $2 million in total contributions from PACs.

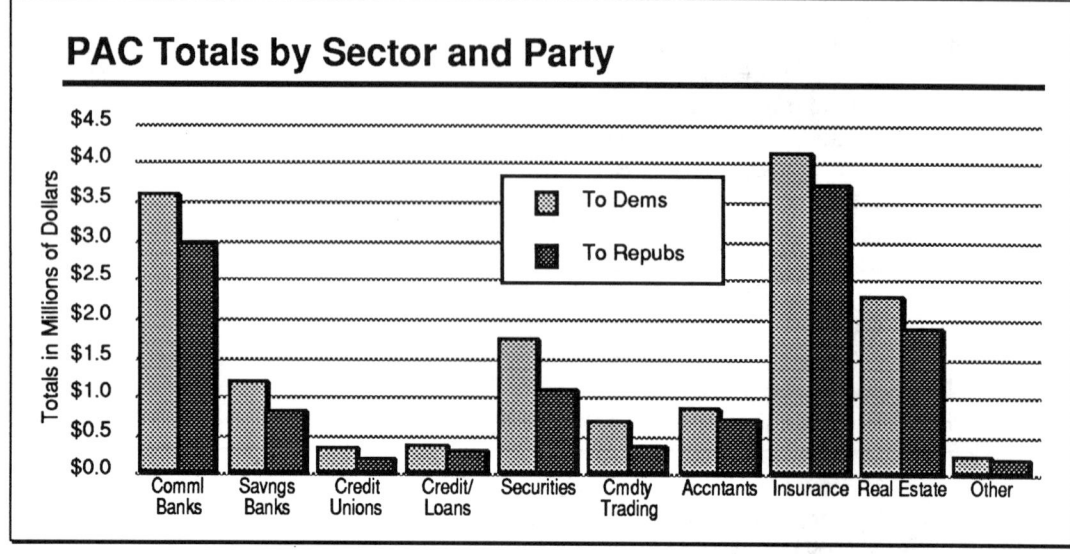

PAC Totals by Sector and Party

Category	Total	To Democrats	To Republicans	Dem Pct	Repub Pct
Commercial Banks	$6,500,083	$3,556,114	$2,943,969	54.7%	45.3%
Savings Banks	$1,970,085	$1,180,861	$789,224	59.9%	40.1%
Credit Unions	$516,238	$333,358	$182,880	64.6%	35.4%
Consumer Credit/Loans	$637,993	$346,636	$291,357	54.3%	45.7%
Securities Investment	$2,773,460	$1,714,539	$1,058,921	61.8%	38.2%
Commodities Trading*	$1,044,050	$680,750	$363,300	65.2%	34.8%
Accountants	$1,524,526	$831,771	$692,755	54.6%	45.4%
Insurance	$7,823,048	$4,110,040	$3,713,008	52.5%	47.5%
Real Estate	$4,137,626	$2,281,136	$1,856,490	55.1%	44.9%
Other Financial Services	$406,665	$230,965	$175,700	56.8%	43.2%
Finance/Insurance/Real Estate Total	**$27,333,774**	**$15,266,170**	**$12,067,604**	**55.9%**	**44.1%**

Though patterns of giving across the industry showed a consistent, if marginal, preference for Democrats, there were important differences in the way the money was distributed. The real estate industry — dominated by a single PAC, the National Association of Realtors — spread their dollars generously and widely. The Realtors PAC was the biggest in the nation, with gifts to a total of 542 candidates. Its average contribution was about $5,000.

Where the money went . . .

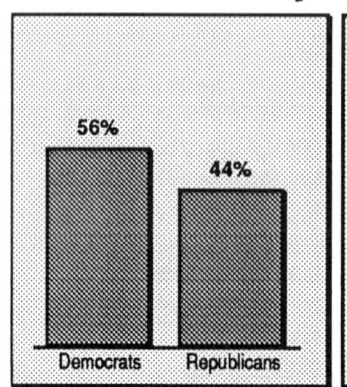

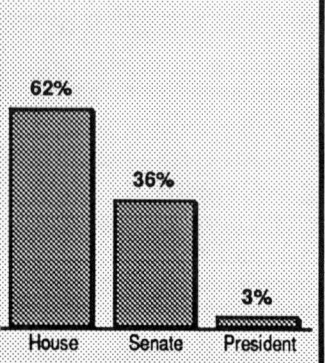

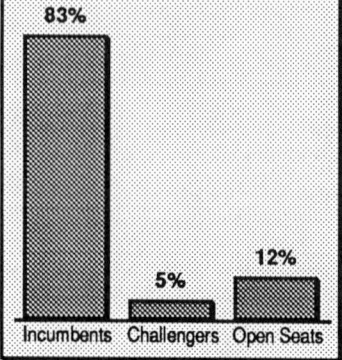

Other groups were more selective. The insurance industry, for example, targeted its largest gifts to members of the tax-writing House Ways and Means Committee and the Senate Finance Committee. Banking PACs also gave heavily to members of those committees, and to those sitting on the House and Senate banking committees.

Top 20 Finance, Insurance & Real Estate PACs

Rank	Total	PAC Sponsor or Affiliate	Type	To Dems	To Repubs	To Dems / To Repubs
1	$3,047,269	National Assn of Realtors*	Real Estate	$1,630,452	$1,416,817	
2	$1,345,083	American Bankers Assn*	Comml Banks	$742,525	$602,558	
3	$1,329,150	Natl Assn of Life Underwriters	Insurance	$726,350	$602,800	
4	$907,159	American Institute of CPA's	Accountants	$515,200	$391,959	
5	$704,601	US League of Savings Assn*	Savings Banks	$445,001	$259,600	
6	$612,167	Indep Insurance Agents of America	Insurance	$372,133	$240,034	
7	$471,630	Credit Union National Assn*	Credit Unions	$300,675	$170,955	
8	$459,950	American Express*	Securities/Cred	$283,171	$176,779	
9	$449,400	Chicago Mercantile Exchange	Commodities	$282,900	$166,500	
10	$445,900	J P Morgan & Co	Comml Banks	$230,150	$215,750	
11	$424,350	Chicago Board of Trade	Commodities	$284,650	$139,700	
12	$401,223	Citicorp	Comml Banks	$222,756	$178,467	
13	$375,700	Barnett Banks of Florida	Comml Banks	$191,700	$184,000	
14	$334,900	American Family Corp	Insurance	$194,450	$140,450	
15	$319,845	Metropolitan Life*	Insur/Securities	$210,593	$109,252	
16	$317,283	Natl Assn/Mutual Insurance Agents	Insurance	$156,108	$161,175	
17	$309,858	Mortgage Bankers Assn of America	Mrtg Banks	$182,308	$127,550	
18	$305,962	Prudential Insurance*	Insur/Securities	$189,012	$116,950	
19	$283,271	American Council of Life Insurance	Insurance	$152,776	$130,495	
20	$257,350	First Boston Corp	Invsmt Banks	$172,850	$84,500	

* Contributions came from more than one PAC affiliated with this sponsor

National trade associations led the list of top-spending PACs within the finance community, accounting for seven of the Top 20 spots. Two of the groups represent insurance companies and agents; the others represent Realtors, commercial bankers, savings banks, accountants, and credit unions. The biggest spending corporate PAC sponsor was American Express, which gave its money both through the PAC of its parent corporation, and through four other finance-related subsidiaries: Shearson Lehman Brothers, E. F. Hutton, Investors Diversified Services (IDS), and Fireman's Fund Insurance.

Texas Democrat Lloyd Bentsen, chairman of the tax-writing Senate Finance Committee, drew more than $636,000 from financial-related PACs — the biggest amount any member of Congress got from any sector of American business in the 1988 elections. Two others on the Senate Top 10 list (Dave Durenberger and Daniel Patrick Moynihan) also sat on the Finance Committee. Six others held seats on the Senate Banking Committee.

House Banking Committee chairman Fernand St Germain led all House recipients by a wide margin. Three other Banking Committee members also made the list, as did six members of the Ways and Means Committee – the panel that drafts tax laws in the House, and a panel of prime importance to the insurance industry in particular.

All 20 of the top recipients in the House and Senate were incumbents — a reflection of the finance industry's higher-than-average tendency to put their money into safe political bets. (In 1988, 85 percent of all Senate incumbents were successfully reelected; the reelection rate in the House was over 98 percent.)

Top 10 Senate Recipients

Rank	Name	Total	Status	W/L
1	Lloyd Bentsen (D-Texas)*	$636,672	Incumb*	W
2	Donald W. Riegle (D-Mich)	$450,220	Incumb	W
3	John Heinz (R-Pa)	$401,715	Incumb	W
4	Jim Sasser (D-Tenn)	$325,290	Incumb	W
5	John Chaffee (R-RI)	$319,775	Incumb	W
6	Dave Durenberger (R-Minn)	$305,545	Incumb	W
7	Pete Wilson (R-Calif)	$282,591	Incumb	W
8	Daniel Patrick Moynihan (D-NY)	$279,359	Incumb	W
9	David Karnes (R-Neb)	$271,778	Incumb	L
10	Terry Sanford (D-NC)	$271,349	Incumb	NR

* Bentsen ran simultaneously for Senate and Vice President in 1988

Top 10 House Recipients

Rank	Name	Total	Status	W/L
1	Fernand J. St Germain (D-RI)	$252,048	Incumb	L
2	Stephen L. Neal (D-NC)	$183,450	Incumb	W
3	Richard A. Gephardt (D-Mo)*	$181,826	Incumb*	W
4	Ronnie G. Flippo (D-Ala)	$174,563	Incumb	W
5	Byron L. Dorgan (D-ND)	$139,996	Incumb	W
6	Michael A. Andrews (D-Texas)	$131,384	Incumb	W
7	Robert T. Matsui (D-Calif)	$128,700	Incumb	W
8	Charles B. Rangel (D-NY)	$127,415	Incumb	W
9	John Hiler (R-Ind)	$127,275	Incumb	W
10	Carroll Hubbard (D-Ky)	$126,025	Incumb	W

* In 1988 Gephardt ran first for President, then for reelection to his U.S. House seat.

Banking

Top 20 Banking PACs

Rank	Total	PAC Sponsor or Affiliate	Type	To Dems	To Repubs	To Dems / To Repubs
1	$1,345,083	American Bankers Assn*	Comml Banks	$742,525	$602,558	
2	$704,601	US League of Savings Assn*	Savings Banks	$445,001	$259,600	
3	$471,630	Credit Union National Assn*	Credit Unions	$300,675	$170,955	
4	$445,900	J P Morgan & Co	Comml Banks	$230,150	$215,750	
5	$401,223	Citicorp	Comml Banks	$222,756	$178,467	
6	$375,700	Barnett Banks of Florida	Comml Banks	$191,700	$184,000	
7	$190,640	Chemical Bank*	Comml Banks	$113,141	$77,499	
8	$178,101	Citizens & Southern Natl Bank*	Comml Banks	$117,270	$60,831	
9	$177,290	Independent Bankers Assn	Comml Banks	$115,490	$61,800	
10	$170,450	Bankers Trust	Comml Banks	$102,500	$67,950	
11	$154,320	Chase Manhattan*	Comml Banks	$80,375	$73,945	
12	$131,560	NCNB Corp*	Comml Banks	$88,208	$43,352	
13	$130,857	Natl Council of Savings Insts	Savings Banks	$71,931	$58,926	
14	$124,940	Suntrust Banks*	Comml Banks	$92,190	$32,750	
15	$119,483	First Chicago Corp	Comml Banks	$74,458	$45,025	
16	$111,573	BankAmerica*	Comml Banks	$45,683	$65,890	
17	$104,425	Marine Midland Banks	Comml Banks	$43,175	$61,250	
18	$104,000	Security Pacific Corp	Comml Banks	$66,250	$37,750	
19	$95,875	Manufacturers Hanover	Comml Banks	$55,105	$40,770	
20	$90,775	Continental Illinois Corp	Comml Banks	$57,375	$33,400	

* Contributions came from more than one PAC affiliated with this sponsor

Top 10 Senate Recipients

Rank	Name	Total	Status	W/L
1	Donald W. Riegle (D-Mich)	$172,000	Incumb	W
2	Lloyd Bentsen (D-Texas)*	$163,697	Incumb*	W
3	David Karnes (R-Neb)	$141,150	Incumb	L
4	Pete Wilson (R-Calif)	$130,502	Incumb	W
5	Chic Hecht (R-Nev)	$125,749	Incumb	L
6	Terry Sanford (D-NC)	$123,000	Incumb	NR
7	Jim Sasser (D-Tenn)	$112,290	Incumb	W
8	John Chafee (R-RI)	$109,883	Incumb	W
9	John Heinz (R-Pa)	$108,901	Incumb	W
10	Bob Dole (R-Kan)	$92,890	Incumb†	†

* Bentsen ran simultaneously for Senate and Vice President. in 1988.
† Dole ran for President in 1988. His Senate term expires in 1992

Top 10 House Recipients

Rank	Name	Total	Status	W/L
1	Stephen L. Neal (D-NC)	$119,500	Incumb	W
2	Fernand J. St Germain (D-RI)	$115,900	Incumb	L
3	John Hiler (R-Ind)	$89,125	Incumb	W
4	Liz J. Patterson (D-SC)	$82,100	Incumb	W
5	Doug Barnard Jr. (D-Ga)	$81,150	Incumb	W
6	Carroll Hubbard (D-Ky)	$79,000	Incumb	W
7	David E. Price (D-NC)	$71,650	Incumb	W
8	Thomas R. Carper (D-Del)	$68,503	Incumb	W
9	Tom Ridge (R-Pa)	$66,400	Incumb	W
10	Norman D. Shumway (R-Calif)	$61,520	Incumb	W

The three components of the banking community spotlighted here — commercial banks, savings & loans, and credit unions — each support major national associations that provide the single biggest share of their political contributions. The American Bankers Association, the U.S. League of Savings Association, and the Credit Union National Association serve as the main conduit for the members of those three groups. But many of the nation's financial institutions also gave through PACs of their own. A total of 290 commercial banks delivered contributions through PACs or regional associations, as did 151 savings & loans. Most of these PACs were small, but their combined presence was powerful. Sen. Donald Riegle, for example, the leading congressional recipient, collected $172,000 from 77 different banking-related PACs.

Committee assignments in Congress were an obvious guidepost to PAC directors in the financial community. All 10 of the leading House recipients were members of the House Banking Committee. Fernand St Germain, the number two recipient, was the committee chairman until he lost his seat in 1988 following his indictment in an ethics scandal.

Seven of the top Senate recipients held seats on the Senate Banking Committee.

Securities & Commodities Investment

Top 20 Securities/Commodities PACs

Rank	Total	PAC Sponsor or Affiliate	Type	To Dems	To Repubs	To Dems / To Repubs
1	$449,400	Chicago Mercantile Exchange	Commodities	$282,900	$166,500	
2	$424,350	Chicago Board of Trade	Commodities	$284,650	$139,700	
3	$355,300	American Express*	Securities	$215,871	$139,429	
4	$257,350	First Boston Corp	Investmt Bank	$172,850	$84,500	
5	$230,300	Goldman Sachs	Investmt Bank	$150,300	$80,000	
6	$206,572	Investment Company Institute	Securities	$161,397	$45,175	
7	$206,000	Morgan Stanley & Co	Investmt Bank	$119,500	$86,500	
8	$147,366	Securities Industry Assn*	Securities	$98,616	$48,750	
9	$138,007	Merrill Lynch	Securities	$61,804	$76,203	
10	$122,833	Drexel Burnham Lambert	Securities	$53,833	$69,000	
11	$122,633	Prudential-Bache Securities	Securities	$74,233	$48,400	
12	$121,162	Salomon Brothers	Securities	$66,183	$54,979	
13	$96,200	Chicago Bd of Options Exchange	Commodities	$66,200	$30,000	
14	$86,900	PaineWebber*	Securities	$50,850	$36,050	
15	$74,150	Bear, Stearns & Co	Investmt Bank	$60,600	$13,550	
16	$73,707	Dean Witter Reynolds*	Securities	$44,307	$29,400	
17	$68,664	Public Securities Assn	Securities	$47,764	$20,900	
18	$55,450	Smith Barney	Securities	$24,850	$30,600	
19	$52,700	Kidder, Peabody	Securities	$33,700	$19,000	
20	$47,800	Commodity Exchange Inc	Commodities	$33,050	$14,750	

NOTE: The totals in this chart do not include contributions from PAC sponsors' subsidiaries that are engaged in other businesses.
* Contributions came from more than one PAC affiliated with this sponsor

Investment firms specializing in the trading of stocks, bonds and commodities on America's financial markets comprise a major portion of the finance industry and a substantial bloc of its PAC dollars. In all, securities and commodities traders gave more than $3.8 million to federal candidates in the 1988 elections. Leading the list were the Chicago-based commodities exchanges, which have a major impact not only in financial circles but also in the agriculture industry. Though they were far and away the largest financial exchanges to support PACs, they were not the only ones. The New York, American, Philadelphia and Pacific Stock Exchanges also operate PACs of their own.

American Express, which ranked third on the Top 20 securities list, operated three different investment-related PACs from its subsidiaries in 1988 — from Shearson Lehman Brothers, E. F. Hutton and Minneapolis-based IDS. Several other investment firms are owned by large conglomerates, and Prudential-Bache Securities is a subsidiary of Prudential Insurance. While insurance companies are free to own subsidiaries which trade stocks, commercial banks are not.[1] Anxious to branch into the lucrative business, and to begin offering stock investment services to their customers, the banks have been lobbying Congress heavily in recent years to loosen banking regulations.

[1] Investment banks, which specialize in securities trading, do not offer normal consumer banking services.

Top 10 Senate Recipients

Rank	Name	Total	Status	W/L
1	Lloyd Bentsen (D-Texas)*	$127,850	Incumb*	W
2	Daniel Patrick Moynihan (D-NY)	$93,678	Incumb	NR
3	John Heinz (R-Pa)	$87,707	Incumb	W
4	Donald W. Riegle (D-Mich)	$81,949	Incumb	W
5	Jim Sasser (D-Tenn)	$61,950	Incumb	W
6	Dave Durenberger (R-Minn)	$60,355	Incumb	W
7	Alfonse M. D'Amato (R-NY)	$59,000	Incumb	NR
8	John Chafee (R-RI)	$57,484	Incumb	W
9	David Karnes (R-Neb)	$52,850	Incumb	L
10	John Danforth (R-Mo)	$50,084	Incumb	W

* Bentsen ran simultaneously for Senate and Vice President in 1988

Top 10 House Recipients

Rank	Name	Total	Status	W/L
1	Fernand J. St Germain (D-RI)	$64,000	Incumb	L
2	Charles E. Schumer (D-NY)	$53,500	Incumb	W
3	Richard A. Gephardt (D-Mo)	$35,096	Incumb*	W*
4	Matthew J. Rinaldo (R-NJ)	$33,600	Incumb	W
5	Thomas S. Foley (D-Wash)	$33,500	Incumb	W
6	John D. Dingell (D-Mich)	$33,000	Incumb	W
7	Marty Russo (D-Ill)	$31,000	Incumb	W
8	Charles B. Rangel (D-NY)	$30,375	Incumb	W
9	Ronnie G. Flippo (D-Ala)	$28,500	Incumb	W
10	Norman F. Lent (R-NY)	$24,000	Incumb	W

* In 1988 Gephardt ran first for the Presidency, then for reelection to his U.S. House seat.

Insurance

Top 20 Insurance PACs

Rank	Total	PAC Sponsor or Affiliate	To Dems	To Repubs	To Dems / To Repubs
1	$1,329,150	National Assn of Life Underwriters	$726,350	$602,800	
2	$612,167	Indep Insurance Agents of America	$372,133	$240,034	
3	$334,900	American Family Corp	$194,450	$140,450	
4	$317,283	Natl Assn/Mutual Insurance Agents	$156,108	$161,175	
5	$283,271	American Council of Life Insurance	$152,776	$130,495	
6	$245,595	Metropolitan Life Insurance	$169,343	$76,252	
7	$244,608	Nat Assn of Independent Insurers	$51,794	$192,814	
8	$235,614	Casualty & Surety Agents Assn	$129,025	$106,589	
9	$198,084	Aetna Life & Casualty	$81,750	$116,334	
10	$195,750	Travelers Corp	$95,500	$100,250	
11	$194,725	Blue Cross & Blue Shield Assn*	$135,258	$59,467	
12	$188,798	Torchmark Corp	$80,550	$108,248	
13	$183,329	Prudential Insurance	$114,779	$68,550	
14	$178,487	Cigna Corp	$77,408	$101,079	
15	$175,879	Health Insurance Assn of America	$72,600	$103,279	
16	$171,800	Equitable Financial Services	$107,750	$64,050	
17	$163,265	Mass. Mutual Life Insurance	$120,221	$43,044	
18	$148,775	ITT Corp*	$61,800	$86,975	
19	$113,400	American International Group	$55,150	$58,250	
20	$112,000	TransAmerica Corp*	$58,250	$53,750	

* Contributions came from more than one PAC affiliated with this sponsor

Insurance companies have become a commanding presence in the world of political finance. In 1988 they surpassed even commercial banks in their total contributions. A total of 138 insurance related PACs delivered more than $7.8 million to federal candidates in the 1988 elections.

Much of that money was targeted to members of the congressional tax-writing committees — Ways and Means in the House and Finance in the Senate. Their principal concern was a provision within the 1988 revision of the tax laws that threatened to remove most tax advantages of "single-premium" life insurance policies.

The patterns in their top contributors list reflects that concern. Seven of the eight incumbent Senators on the list held seats on the Senate Finance Committee, and all 10 of the top House recipients were members of the Ways and Means Committee. In all, the insurance PACs distributed nearly $2.6 million dollars to the 56 Congressmen and Senators who sit on those two committees — an average of $46,000 per member.

Taxes were not the only item of interest to the insurance industry. Another perennial item on their legislative agenda is combating the efforts of commercial banks to begin offering stock-investment services to their customers. Currently, insurance companies may own securities-related subsidiaries; commercial banks may not. The insurance companies want to keep it that way.

Top 10 Senate Recipients

Rank	Name	Total	Status	W/L
1	Lloyd Bentsen (D-Texas)*	$212,750	Incumb*	W
2	Dave Durenberger (R-Minn)	$135,442	Incumb	W
3	John Danforth (R-Mo)	$131,125	Incumb	W
4	John Heinz (R-Pa)	$127,857	Incumb	W
5	George Voinovich (R-Ohio)	$125,575	Chall	L
6	John Chafee (R-RI)	$101,083	Incumb	W
7	Donald W. Riegle (D-Mich)	$100,950	Incumb	W
8	Susan Engeleiter (R-Wis)	$95,230	Open	L
9	Jim Sasser (D-Tenn)	$93,050	Incumb	W
10	George Mitchell (D-Maine)	$90,124	Incumb	W

* Bentsen ran simultaneously for Senate and Vice President in 1988

Top 10 House Recipients

Rank	Name	Total	Status	W/L
1	Byron L. Dorgan (D-ND)	$75,996	Incumb	W
2	Ronnie G. Flippo (D-Ala)	$64,555	Incumb	W
3	Pete Stark (D-Calif)	$56,000	Incumb	W
4	Michael A. Andrews (D-Texas)	$55,350	Incumb	W
5	Raymond J. McGrath (R-NY)	$53,961	Incumb	W
6	Charles B. Rangel (D-NY)	$52,690	Incumb	W
7	Thomas J. Downey (D-NY)	$52,450	Incumb	W
8	Beryl Anthony Jr. (D-Ark)	$50,500	Incumb	W
9	Bill Frenzel (R-Minn)	$50,197	Incumb	W
10	Ed Jenkins (D-Ga)	$47,097	Incumb	W

Real Estate

Top 20 Real Estate PACs

Rank	Total	PAC Sponsor or Affiliate	Type	To Dems	To Repubs	To Dems / To Repubs
1	$3,047,269	National Assn of Realtors*	RE Sales	$1,630,452	$1,416,817	
2	$309,858	Mortgage Bankers Assn of America	Mrtg Banking	$182,308	$127,550	
3	$74,250	Century 21 Real Estate	RE Sales	$41,250	$33,000	
4	$71,613	National Realty Committee	RE Devel	$49,113	$22,500	
5	$65,075	Amer Land Development Assn	RE Devel	$38,825	$26,250	
6	$62,300	First Union Corp	Mrgt Banking	$46,500	$15,800	
7	$54,650	American Land Title Assn	Title Insur	$30,700	$23,950	
8	$47,465	Irvine Company	RE Devel	$21,778	$25,187	
9	$43,400	General Development Corp	RE Devel	$29,400	$14,000	
10	$39,150	Federal National Mortgage Assn	Mrgt Banking	$23,100	$16,050	
11	$30,250	Commonwealth Financial Group	Mrgt Banking	$19,500	$10,750	
12	$30,125	Trammell Crow Co	RE Devel	$17,250	$12,875	
13	$27,034	National Apartment Assn	Bldg Mgmt	$9,400	$17,634	
14	$23,000	JMB Realty Corp	RE Devel	$21,500	$1,500	
15	$21,000	Real Estate Investment PAC	RE Devel	$12,350	$8,650	
16	$20,800	Soc of Real Estate Appraisers	RE Svcs	$9,900	$10,900	
17	$20,000	National Parking Assn	Bldg Mgmt	$15,000	$5,000	
18	$18,450	Newhall Land & Farming Co	RE Devel	$3,250	$15,200	
19	$16,750	Del Webb Corp	RE Devel	$9,750	$7,000	
20	$15,050	Lamar Corp	RE Sales	$12,200	$2,850	

* Contributions came from more than one PAC affiliated with this sponsor

Within the real estate industry, one single PAC — the Realtors PAC of the National Association of Realtors — was the predominant voice, accounting for three-quarters of the industry's total giving. It was, in fact, the biggest PAC in the nation in the 1988 elections, dispensing a total of more than $3 million to 542 federal candidates. An additional $1.3 million went out in independent expenditures on behalf of a handful of particularly favored candidates.

Within Congress, the chief jurisdiction over the housing industry is centered in the House and Senate Banking Committees. Tax policy is also important to the industry, so the House Ways and Means Committee and the Senate Finance Committee were other centers of attention for real estate PACs. Nine of the top 10 House recipients sat on either Ways and Means or the Banking Committee. Among Senate incumbents, Lloyd Bentsen chaired the Senate Finance Committee. Donald Riegle, John Heinz and Terry Sanford held seats on the Banking panel.

Direct PAC contributions were not the only vehicle through which the real estate industry delivered its funds. Seven candidates, listed below, benefited from independent expenditure campaigns of $100,000 or more waged on their behalf by the Realtors PAC.

Top Beneficiaries of Independent Expenditures by the Realtors PAC

Candidate	Office	Amount
Trent Lott (R-Miss)	Senate	$348,498
John Melcher (D-Mont)	Senate	$228,038
John Hiler (R-Ind)	House	$166,236
Ben Nighthorse Campbell (D-Colo)	House	$155,312
James V. Hansen (R-Utah)	House	$155,287
Bill Emerson (R-Mo)	House	$152,600
Richard Stallings (D-Idaho)	House	$126,450

Top 10 Senate Recipients

Rank	Name	Total	Status	W/L
1	Lloyd Bentsen (D-Texas)*	$60,500	Incumb*	W
2	Donald W. Riegle (D-Mich)	$36,450	Incumb	W
3	John Heinz (R-Pa)	$30,000	Incumb	W
4	Connie Mack (R-Fla)	$25,250	Open	W
5	Pete Wilson (R-Calif)	$25,004	Incumb	W
6	Terry Sanford (D-NC)	$25,000	Incumb	NR
7	Jim Sasser (D-Tenn)	$24,750	Incumb	W
8	Trent Lott (R-Miss)	$24,000	Open	W
9	Dennis DeConcini (D-Ariz)	$23,500	Incumb	W
10	Buddy MacKay (D-Fla)	$22,300	Open	L

* Bentsen ran simultaneously for Senate and Vice President in 1988
NR = Not Running in 1988

Top 10 House Recipients

Rank	Name	Total	Status	W/L
1	Robert T. Matsui (D-Calif)	$22,000	Incumb	W
2	Fernand J. St Germain (D-RI)	$20,000	Incumb	L
3	Ed Jenkins (D-Ga)	$19,700	Incumb	W
4	Michael A. Andrews (D-Texas)	$19,313	Incumb	W
5	Bill Thomas (R-Calif)	$18,250	Incumb	W
6	Steve Bartlett (R-Texas)	$17,700	Incumb	W
7	David E. Price (D-NC)	$17,650	Incumb	W
8	Stephen L. Neal (D-NC)	$17,300	Incumb	W
9	J. Alex McMillan (R-NC)	$17,000	Incumb	W
10	Howard Coble (R-NC)	$16,600	Incumb	W

Health

Where the money came from . . .

America's health care industry is a major player in Washington political circles. Its lobbyists are familiar figures in the halls of the Capitol and its PAC dollars help enrich the campaigns of nearly every member of Congress. Carefully monitoring the schedule of Medicare and Medicaid payments to doctors and other health care providers is of key legislative importance to the industry, as are a variety of other health related issues — including the occasional proposals calling for national health insurance.

Three main segments within the industry provide nearly all its PAC dollars. The biggest segment by far is made up of physicians and other health professionals. The American Medical Association is the largest doctors' organization in the country and its PAC is by far the leading health-related contributor to federal candidates. In the 1987-88 election cycle the AMA distributed more than $2.6 million to nearly 500 candidates for Congress. Of that, $2.3 million came from the national AMA PAC; the rest came from state affiliates around the country.

A variety of other national organizations representing specialists in various branches of medicine were also major contributors. Dentists, optometrists, orthopedists, podiatrists, and specialists in everything from eye surgery to root canal work support PACs of their own. So do a variety of non-physician specialists, including psychologists, pharmacists, chiropractors, physical therapists, dieticians and others. All are included in the health professionals category, as are PACs representing registered nurses.

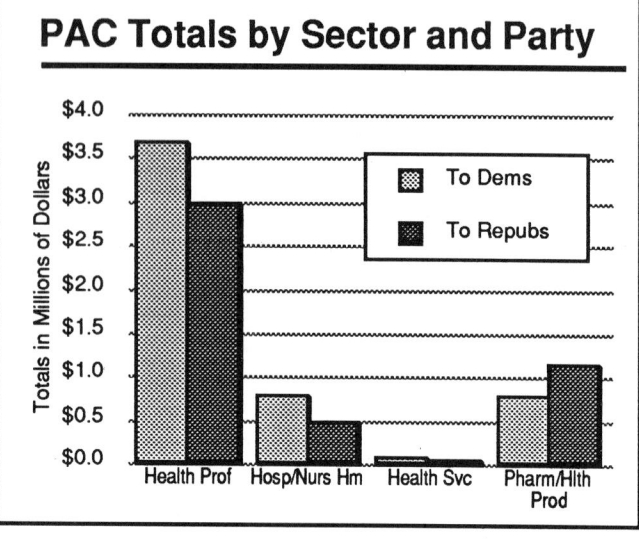

PAC Totals by Sector and Party

Category	Total	To Democrats	To Republicans	Dem Pct	Repub Pct
Health Professionals	$6,626,497	$3,665,883	$2,960,614	55.3%	44.7%
Hospitals/Nursing Homes	$1,213,847	$757,273	$456,574	62.4%	37.6%
Health Services	$111,483	$80,033	$31,450	71.8%	28.2%
Pharmaceuticals/Health Products	$1,914,125	$784,926	$1,129,199	41.0%	59.0%
Health Total	**$9,865,952**	**$5,288,115**	**$4,577,837**	**53.6%**	**46.4%**

Hospitals and nursing homes make up another important segment of the medical community — though a much smaller one than the health professionals. All told, they gave out $1.2 million in PAC contributions. The third leading sector within the industry consists of pharmaceutical manufacturers and companies that manufacture and distribute a variety of other health care products. The pharmaceutical makers comprised the biggest portion of PAC contributors within that group, giving out nearly $1.5 million of the $1.9 million sector total.

Where the money went . . .

As an industry, the health providers tended to favor Democrats slightly more than Republicans. This was true across the board, except for pharmaceutical companies, whose preference for Republicans was more reflective of the patterns seen within the chemical industry. Two thirds of the health industry's PAC dollars went to House candidates, and — as with every other sector of American business — the lion's share of contributions went to incumbents seeking reelection.

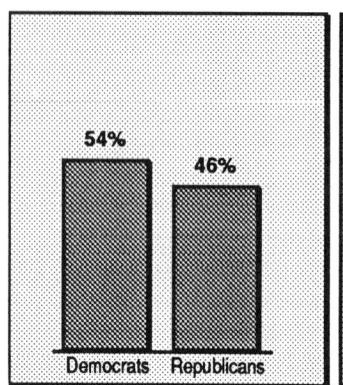

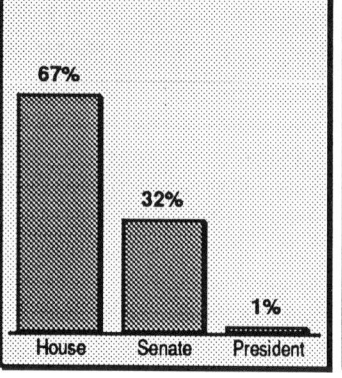

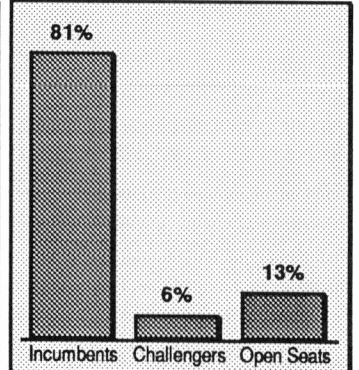

Top 20 Health PACs

Rank	Total	PAC Sponsor or Affiliate	Type	To Dems	To Repubs	To Dems	To Repubs
1	$2,664,202	American Medical Assn*	Doctors	$1,276,445	$1,387,757		
2	$897,000	American Dental Assn*	Dentists	$452,200	$444,800		
3	$644,000	Amer Acad of Ophthalmology	Doctors	$300,500	$343,500		
4	$409,127	American Hospital Assn	Hospitals	$277,918	$131,209		
5	$335,186	American Optometric Assn	Doctors	$203,066	$132,120		
6	$272,758	American Nurses Assn	Health Union	$244,133	$28,625		
7	$253,528	American Health Care Assn	Nursing Home	$155,564	$97,964		
8	$249,800	American Podiatry Assn	Doctors	$160,000	$89,800		
9	$193,545	Pfizer Inc	Pharmaceut	$93,850	$99,695		
10	$191,527	Abbott Laboratories	Pharmaceut	$56,175	$135,352		
11	$173,250	Cmte/Qual Orthopedic Hlth Care	Doctors	$81,450	$91,800		
12	$151,194	National Assn of Pharmacists	Pharmcists	$116,919	$34,275		
13	$143,500	Oral & Maxillofacial Surgeons	Dentists	$70,000	$73,500		
14	$143,115	American Chiropractic Assn*	Chiropractor	$103,065	$40,050		
15	$135,517	Fedn of American Hospitals	Hospitals	$81,283	$54,234		
16	$133,140	Eli Lilly & Co	Pharmaceut	$34,100	$99,040		
17	$117,600	Schering-Plough Corp	Pharmaceut	$42,050	$75,550		
18	$108,060	Warner-Lambert	Health Prod	$61,300	$46,760		
19	$105,825	Amer College/Emerg Physicians	Doctors	$64,950	$40,675		
20	$102,258	Amer Physical Therapy Assn	Health Pract	$62,950	$39,308		

* Contributions came from more than one PAC affiliated with this sponsor

No single committee within Congress has health care as its exclusive or primary jurisdiction. Rather, it falls within the aegis of specialized subcommittees on larger committees — specifically Finance in the Senate, Energy and Commerce, and Ways & Means in the House.

Dave Durenberger, who got more than anyone else from the health care industry, is the ranking Republican on the Health subcommittee in Senate Finance. George Mitchell, seventh on the list, was chairman of that subcommittee in 1988. Other members included Lloyd Bentsen, John Chafee and John Heinz.

In the House, leading recipient Henry Waxman is chairman of the Health and Environment subcommittee of the Energy and Commerce Committee. Edward Madigan is ranking Republican on that panel, and Doug Walgren is also a member. Pete Stark chairs the Health subcommittee on the Ways and Means Committee. Jim Moody and Beryl Anthony are subcommittee members.

In addition to direct contributions to their campaigns, several members of Congress benefited from substantial independent expenditures on their behalf by the AMA's PAC. Those members, and the amount spent on their behalf by the AMA, are listed below.

Top Beneficiaries of Independent Expenditures by the American Medical Association PAC

Candidate	Office	Amount
Dave Durenberger (R-Minn)	Senate	$134,527
Bill Sarpalius (D-Texas)	House	$131,560
Liz Patterson (D-SC)	House	$112,994
Chick Hecht (R-Nev)	Senate	$105,363
James V. Hansen (R-Utah)	House	$65,359

Top 10 Senate Recipients

Rank	Name	Total	Status	W/L
1	Dave Durenberger (R-Minn)	$186,711	Incumb	W
2	Lloyd Bentsen (D-Texas)*	$182,005	Incumb*	W
3	Orrin Hatch (R-Utah)	$147,100	Incumb	W
4	Pete Wilson (R-Calif)	$141,366	Incumb	W
5	John Chafee (R-RI)	$129,850	Incumb	W
6	John Heinz (R-Pa)	$115,385	Incumb	W
7	George Mitchell (D-Maine)	$104,259	Incumb	W
8	Daniel Patrick Moynihan (D-NY)	$103,180	Incumb	NR
9	John Danforth (R-Mo)	$87,450	Incumb	W
10	Jim Sasser (D-Tenn)	$83,215	Incumb	W

* Bentsen ran simultaneously for Senate and Vice President in 1988
NR = Not running in 1988

Top 10 House Recipients

Rank	Name	Total	Status	W/L
1	Henry A. Waxman (D-Calif)	$85,215	Incumb	W
2	Pete Stark (D-Calif)	$78,041	Incumb	W
3	Edward R. Madigan (R-Ill)	$67,515	Incumb	W
4	Robert H. Michel (R-Ill)	$66,800	Incumb	W
5	Jim Moody (D-Wis)	$61,500	Incumb	W
6	Ron Wyden (D-Ore)	$58,800	Incumb	W
7	Doug Walgren (D-Pa)	$55,550	Incumb	W
8	Beryl Anthony Jr. (D-Ark)	$53,350	Incumb	W
9	Robert T. Matsui (D-Calif)	$46,950	Incumb	W
10	Charles B. Rangel (D-NY)	$46,850	Incumb	W

Lawyers & Lobbyists

Where the money came from . . .

No other profession or industry is so naturally positioned to take an active role in the writing and rewriting the of the nation's laws as attorneys. Interpreting the nuances of law, after all, is the business of lawyers — one reason that more members of Congress come to public office from a career in the legal profession than from any other walk of life.

Political action committees representing lawyers and law firms contributed nearly $4.8 million to federal candidates in the 1988 elections. Almost $2 million of that total came from a single organization — the Association of Trial Lawyers of America (ATLA). The National ATLA PAC gave $1.92 million on its own; the rest came from affiliated state PACs around the country.

At first glance, the chart on the right might make it appear that lobbyists represent only a small portion of the legal community's PAC dollars, but in fact the line between lawyers and lobbyists is often a fuzzy one. While trial lawyers may have their own set of legislative priorities (for example, the issue of product liability), many attorneys centered in Washington specialize as agents for every variety of industry and interest group, advising them not only on litigation of existing laws, but on the creation of new laws or the revision of existing ones. Lobbying for these changes in legislation is one of the principal activities of law firms in Washington, so nearly every firm with a Washington office could conceivably be classified as a lobbyist. In addition to law firms, however, many other Washington businesses specialize in lobbying Congress and the administration. In the chart above, those companies alone are the ones grouped as "lobbyists." Often, their business extends to related fields as well, including public relations counseling and market research.

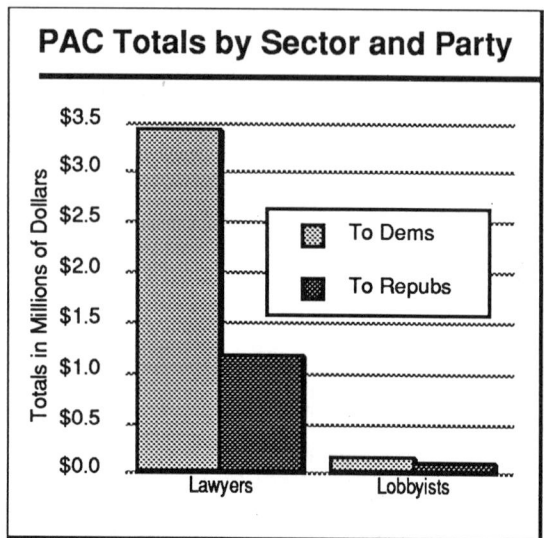

PAC Totals by Sector and Party

Category	Total	To Democrats	To Republicans	Dem Pct	Repub Pct
Lawyers	$4,557,750	$3,402,275	$1,155,475	74.6%	25.4%
Lobbyists	$238,995	$153,675	$85,320	64.3%	35.7%
Lawyers & Lobbyists Total	**$4,796,745**	**$3,555,950**	**$1,240,795**	**74.1%**	**25.9%**

Where the money went . . .

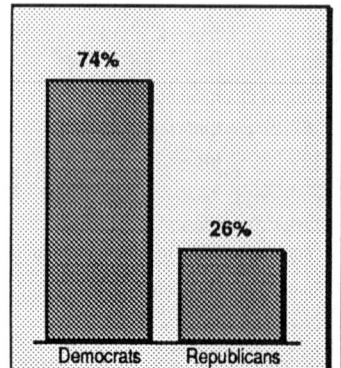

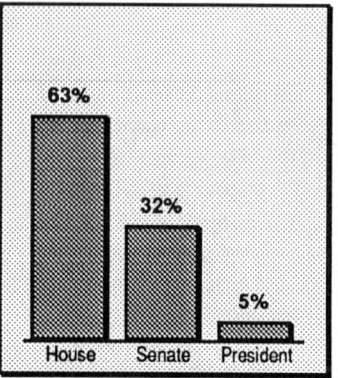

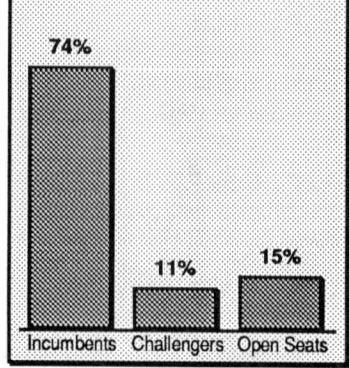

Overall, lawyers and lobbyists gave the biggest share of their PAC dollars — nearly three dollars out of every four — to Democrats. About the same proportion went to incumbents seeking reelection, and though that level is certainly high, the 26 percent that went to challengers and open seat candidates was the highest proportion given to non-incumbents of any sector in the business community.

Lawyers & Lobbyists Top 20 PACs

Rank	Total	PAC Sponsor or Affiliate	Type	To Dems	To Repubs	To Dems / To Repubs
1	$1,962,058	Assn of Trial Lawyers of America*	Lawyers	$1,688,708	$273,350	
2	$197,490	Akin, Gump, Hauer & Feld	Lawyers	$153,390	$44,100	
3	$116,640	Vinson, Elkins, Searls et al	Lawyers	$76,790	$39,850	
4	$99,840	Powell, Goldstein, Frazer & Murphy	Lawyers	$86,290	$13,550	
5	$97,294	Jones, Day, Reavis & Pogue	Lawyers	$43,598	$53,696	
6	$93,000	Kutak, Rock & Campbell	Lawyers	$62,300	$30,700	
7	$89,156	Williams & Jensen	Lawyers	$60,347	$28,809	
8	$86,028	Preston, Thorgrimson, Ellis & Holman	Lawyers	$62,342	$23,686	
9	$82,954	Verner, Liipfert, Bernhardt et al	Lawyers	$69,614	$13,340	
10	$71,150	Dickstein, Shapiro & Morin	Lawyers	$46,400	$24,750	
11	$70,680	Camp. Barsh, Bates & Tate	Lawyers	$57,830	$12,850	
12	$70,653	Wexler, Reynolds, Harrison & Schule	Lobbyist/PR	$49,442	$21,211	
13	$69,071	Kirkpatrick & Lockhart	Lawyers	$42,571	$26,500	
14	$66,725	Arnold & Porter*	Lawyer/Lobbyist	$49,250	$17,475	
15	$65,750	Fullbright & Jaworski	Lawyers	$41,000	$24,750	
16	$60,600	Manatt, Phelps, Rothenberg & Tunney	Lawyers	$37,000	$23,600	
17	$56,384	Kirkland & Ellis	Lawyers	$47,784	$8,600	
18	$56,312	Burson-Marsteller	Lobbyists/PR	$31,883	$24,429	
19	$55,450	Baker & Hostetler	Lawyers	$29,850	$25,600	
20	$54,455	Hill & Knowlton	Lobbyists/PR	$37,875	$16,580	

* Contributions came from more than one PAC affiliated with this sponsor

Lloyd Bentsen, the Democratic Senator who ran both for reelection and for Vice President on the Democratic ticket in 1988, towered over all other recipients of PAC dollars from lawyers and lobbying firms. Bentsen, who chairs the tax-writing Senate Finance Committee, got more than $132,000 from the groups — the vast majority of it (nearly $130,000) coming from lawyers. Bentsen's total was more than double the amount received by any other member of Congress. Though most of the money went to Bentsen's Senate reelection committee, the lawyers in particular showed a tendency to concentrate a higher-than-normal proportion of their PAC money on candidates in the presidential races. The second and third leading members of Congress receiving PAC contributions from law firm and lobbyist PACs were Republican Bob Dole of Kansas and Missouri Democrat Richard Gephardt — both of whom were actively running for President in early 1988. Not far behind was Democrat Al Gore of Tennessee, another Presidential candidate. George Bush also received nearly $60,000 from lawyers' PACs. All that money to presidential candidates was given fairly early in the election season; direct contributions to the candidates during the general election period are not allowed.

Overall, the top 20 House and Senate recipients of lawyer and lobbyist PAC dollars held a variety of committee assignments, with no one particular committee predominating. Seven of the top 10 Republicans, and all 10 of the House members were Democrats. Some 13 of the top 20 recipients were lawyers themselves.

Top 10 Senate Recipients

Rank	Name	Total	Status	W/L
1	Lloyd Bentsen (D-Texas)	$132,870	Incumb*	W
2	Bob Dole (R-Kan)	$54,450	Incumb†	†
3	John Heinz (R-Pa)	$48,865	Incumb	W
4	Quentin N. Burdick (D-ND)	$47,190	Incumb	W
5	Al Gore (D-Tenn)	$43,665	Incumb†	†
6	Huber H. Humphrey III	$43,445	Chall	L
7	Frank Lautenberg (D-NJ)	$42,900	Incumb	W
8	Pete Wilson (R-Calif)	$41,870	Incumb	W
9	Jim Sasser (D-Tenn)	$39,950	Incumb	W
10	Howard Metzenbaum (D-Ohio)	$38,250	Incumb	W

* Bentsen ran simultaneously for Senate and Vice President in 1988.
† Dole and Gore both ran for President in 1988. Gore's Senate term expires in 1990. Dole's expires in 1992.

Top 10 House Recipients

Rank	Name	Total	Status	W/L
1	Richard A. Gephardt (D-Mo)	$56,750	Incumb*	W*
2	Jim Wright (D-Texas)	$39,250	Incumb	W
3	Michael A. Andrews (D-Texas)	$31,750	Incumb	W
4	John Bryant (D-Texas)	$26,250	Incumb	W
5	Gerry Sikorski (D-Minn)	$26,036	Incumb	W
6	Mickey Leland (D-Texas)	$23,300	Incumb	W
7	Jim Moody (D-Wis)	$21,903	Incumb	W
8	Vic Fazio (D-Calif)	$21,825	Incumb	W
9	Jack Brooks (D-Texas)	$21,000	Incumb	W
10	Beryl Anthony Jr. (D-Ark)	$20,500	Incumb	W

* In 1988 Gephardt ran first for President, then for reelection to his U.S. House seat.

Miscellaneous Business

Where the money came from . . .

This catchall category encompasses a variety of disparate businesses from a wide range of industries — from steel manufacturers to travel agencies, beer distributors to funeral directors. Most of the industries here have an interest in a wide variety of legislative matters, but — aside from tax laws — few of those issues are concentrated under the jurisdiction of a particular committee or subcommittee in Congress. There are exceptions. Portions of the food and beverage industry — meat processors, for example — have specific interests dealt with by the agriculture committees. And a variety of heavy industrial companies have an interest in Clean Air legislation, which is handled by the Senate Environment and Public Works Committee and the Energy and Commerce Committee in the House.

The food and beverage industry was the biggest single source of PAC funds within the group, contributing more than $5 million during the 1987-88 election cycle. Manufacturing

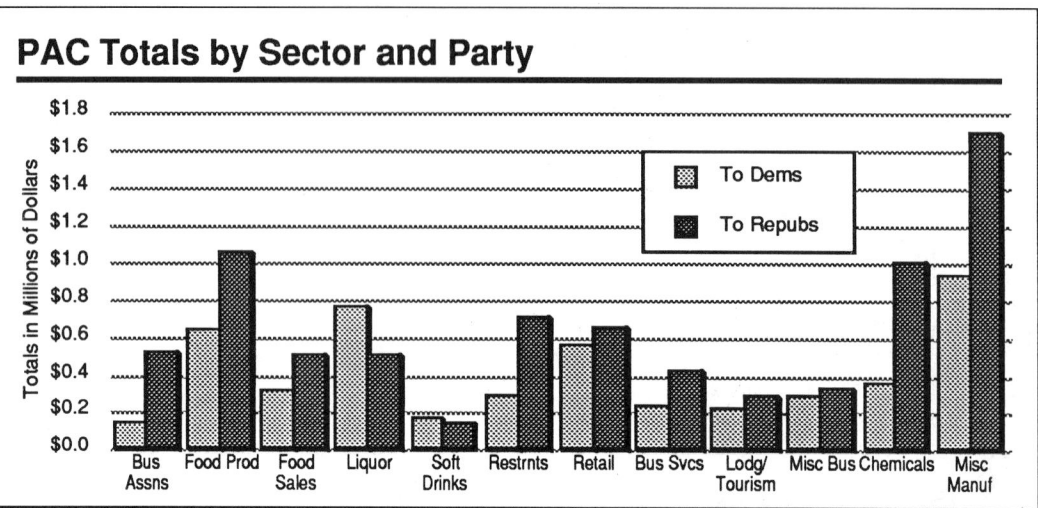

Category	Total	To Democrats	To Republicans	Dem Pct	Repub Pct
Business Assns	$660,074	$145,814	$514,260	22.1%	77.9%
Food Processing*	$1,689,528	$634,347	$1,055,181	37.5%	62.5%
Food Wholesale/Retail*	$816,927	$312,680	$504,247	38.3%	61.7%
Beer, Wine & Liquor	$1,266,723	$759,754	$506,969	60.0%	40.0%
Soft Drinks	$307,640	$168,990	$138,650	54.9%	45.1%
Restaurants	$985,236	$287,975	$697,261	29.2%	70.8%
Retail Sales	$1,211,109	$556,016	$655,093	45.9%	54.1%
Business Services	$647,839	$229,153	$418,686	35.4%	64.6%
Lodging/Tourism	$496,753	$215,925	$280,828	43.5%	56.5%
Other Businesses	$611,361	$280,354	$331,007	45.9%	54.1%
Chemicals	$1,353,896	$354,820	$999,076	26.2%	73.8%
Misc Manufacturing	$2,619,504	$926,470	$1,693,034	35.4%	64.6%
Misc Business Total	**$12,666,590**	**$4,872,298**	**$7,794,292**	**38.5%**	**61.5%**

firms, led by the chemical industry, gave just under $4 million. Department stores and others in the retail sales category gave a combined $1.2 million.

Where the money went . . .

Though there were some differences in PAC spending patterns within this miscellaneous group of businesses, there were many similarities as well. Manufacturing firms — whether they specialize in chemicals, home appliances, or microwave dinners — tended to show a strong preference for Republicans. So did most other businesses. Overall, the group gave about 62 percent of their dollars to G.O.P. candidates, leaving only 38 percent to the majority-party Democrats.

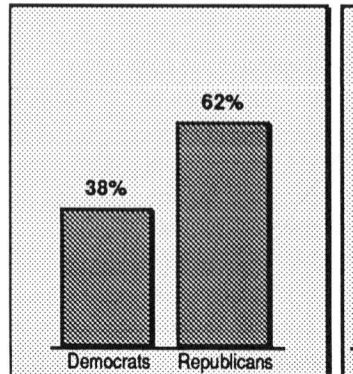

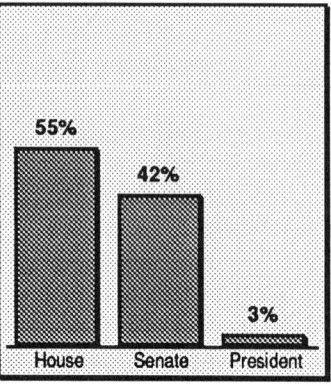

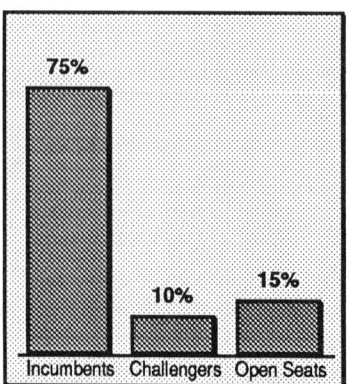

Top 20 Miscellaneous Business PACs

Rank	Total	PAC Sponsor or Affiliate	Type	To Dems	To Repubs	To Dems / To Repubs
1	$440,301	National Beer Wholsalers Assn	Beer	$276,752	$163,549	
2	$382,345	FMC Corp	Chemicals	$100,120	$282,225	
3	$372,050	National Restaurant Assn*	Restaurants	$113,750	$258,300	
4	$358,574	Food Marketing Institute	Food Stores	$155,255	$203,319	
5	$324,850	Dow Chemical*	Chemicals	$43,900	$280,950	
6	$310,349	Natl Fedn of Independent Business	Bus Assns	$35,861	$274,488	
7	$237,668	J C Penney Company	Retail Sales	$147,408	$90,760	
8	$230,100	McDonald's Corp	Restaurants	$74,750	$155,350	
9	$214,790	Coca-Cola Company	Soft Drinks	$128,190	$86,600	
10	$186,577	ConAgra Inc*	Food Prod	$59,950	$126,627	
11	$183,292	Pepsico Inc	Soft Drinks	$54,450	$128,842	
12	$173,150	Joseph E Seagram & Sons	Liquor	$130,100	$43,050	
13	$165,679	Wine & Spirits Whlslers of Amer	Liquor	$100,650	$65,029	
14	$159,800	General Mills*	Food Prod	$85,800	$74,000	
15	$159,079	Dun & Bradstreet	Mkt Research	$33,900	$125,179	
16	$140,650	American Meat Institute	Meat Prod	$64,200	$76,450	
17	$136,487	Business Industry PAC	Bus Assns	$7,885	$128,602	
18	$133,622	Natl Assn/Wholesale-Distributors	Wholesale	$33,522	$100,100	
19	$129,117	NL Industries*	Chemicals	$14,600	$114,517	
20	$128,300	American Textile Mfrs Institute	Textiles	$73,250	$55,050	

* Contributions came from more than one PAC affiliated with this sponsor

The contributors list for the miscellaneous business category shows some of the variety within the group. Food and beverage PACs — including three in the beer, wine & liquor industry — accounted for 11 of the Top 20 PACs. Three chemical companies also made the list. Besides its chemical interests, FMC Corporation is also a major defense contractor. Dow Chemical is notable in that its contributions came not from a single company PAC, but from nine separate PACs operating out of plants scattered around the country. The largest of them gave $62,000, but when combined the company's total PAC giving was more than $324,000.

The top recipients list shows this sector's heavy preference for Republicans. Nine of the top Senate recipients and seven of 10 in the House were members of the Republican minority. Leading the list was Ohio Republican George Voinovich, who mounted a well-financed challenge to Howard Metzenbaum—a liberal Democrat who has been a gadfly to a wide variety of business interests during his years in the Senate.

There was a decidedly pragmatic flavor to the Democrats who did make appearances on the top recipients list. Lloyd Bentsen and Dan Rostenkowski head the tax writing committees in their respective Houses. Thomas Foley during 1988 was House Majority Leader. (He became Speaker of the House when Jim Wright resigned in 1989). And John Dingell, the Michigan Democrat, is chairman of the House Energy and Commerce Committee — a panel with a wide jurisdiction encompassing virtually every sector of the business community.

Top 10 Senate Recipients

Rank	Name	Total	Status	W/L
1	George Voinovich (R-Ohio)	$291,159	Chall	L
2	Pete Wilson (R-Calif)	$273,128	Incumb	W
3	Trent Lott (R-Miss)	$237,717	Open	W
4	Orrin Hatch (R-Utah)	$222,247	Incumb	W
5	Lloyd Bentsen (D-Texas)*	$220,475	Incumb*	W
6	Dave Durenberger (R-Minn)	$216,689	Incumb	W
7	John Heinz (R-Pa)	$200,309	Incumb	W
8	Susan Engeleiter (R-Wis)	$193,523	Open	L
9	Connie Mack (R-Fla)	$184,080	Open	W
10	Pete Dawkins (R-NJ)	$184,055	Chall	L

* Bentsen ran simultaneously for Senate and Vice President in 1988

Top 10 House Recipients

Rank	Name	Total	Status	W/L
1	Robert H. Michel (R-Ill)	$85,989	Incumb	W
2	Bill Emerson (R-Mo)	$74,937	Incumb	W
3	Dan Rostenkowski (D-Ill)	$73,500	Incumb	W
4	Howard Coble (R-NC)	$64,105	Incumb	W
5	Bill Schuette (R-Mich)	$61,212	Incumb	W
6	Thomas S. Foley (D-Wash)	$58,743	Incumb	W
7	John Hiler (R-Ind)	$57,343	Incumb	W
8	Don Ritter (R-Pa)	$56,976	Incumb	W
9	John D. Dingell (D-Mich)	$51,800	Incumb	W
10	Barbara Vucanovich (R-Nev)	$50,776	Incumb	W

Transportation

Where the money came from . . .

In a nation that spans more than 2,000 miles from coast to coast, and another 1,000 from border to border, the transportation of goods, services and people from one location to another has always been a major industry. From the days when the railroads opened up the American West, transportation companies have relied on allies in Congress to keep their business rolling along. Likewise, competing segments within the industry — barge lines versus railroads, for example — have often sought to improve their market position at their competitors' expense.

Within the transportation sector, a variety of patterns in PAC spending can be found. In the automotive industry, for example, the big three auto manufacturers — though they are indisputably a powerful economic interest — played a relatively minor role in their political contributions, compared with the dealers who sell their products. Ford, General Motors and Chrysler (not counting their aerospace and defense-related subsidiaries) gave a combined $708,000 in PAC funds during 1987-88. But two auto dealer PACs — the National Auto Dealers Association and the Auto Dealers and Drivers for Free Trade PAC (which repre-

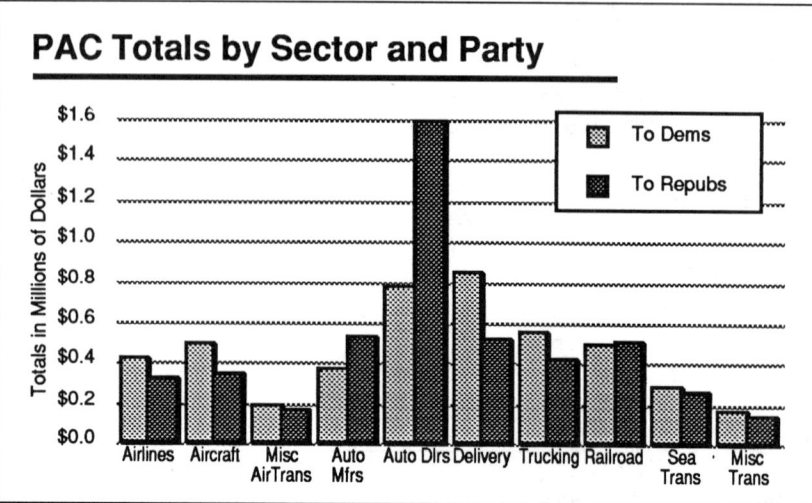

PAC Totals by Sector and Party

Category	Total	To Democrats	To Republicans	Dem Pct	Repub Pct
Airlines	$737,572	$412,950	$324,622	56.0%	44.0%
Aircraft & Aerospace Mfrs*	$844,866	$494,553	$350,313	58.5%	41.5%
Other Aviation	$352,339	$186,525	$165,814	52.9%	47.1%
Auto Manufacturing & Equipment	$899,014	$369,124	$529,890	41.1%	58.9%
Auto Dealers	$2,361,120	$775,320	$1,585,800	32.8%	67.2%
Package/Express Delivery	$1,359,655	$848,651	$511,004	62.4%	37.6%
Trucking	$975,789	$553,687	$422,102	56.7%	43.3%
Railroads	$998,656	$496,329	$502,327	49.7%	50.3%
Sea Transport	$546,631	$284,723	$261,908	52.1%	47.9%
Misc Transport	$307,251	$166,300	$140,951	54.1%	45.9%
Transportation Total	**$9,382,893**	**$4,588,162**	**$4,794,731**	**48.9%**	**51.1%**

* Does not include defense aerospace

sents dealers of Japanese cars) — handed out more than $2.2 million during the same period. The auto dealers gave two-thirds of their money to Republicans. Ford and GM slightly favored Republicans, while Chrysler gave 70 percent of its PAC dollars to Democrats.

The air transport industry — made up both of airlines and aircraft manufacturers, as well as a variety of related interests — gave just under $2 million. A surprisingly large PAC presence was also evident from the nation's two leading package delivery services, Federal Express and United Parcel Service. Their two PACs gave more than $1.3 million between them. Federal Express relies almost exclusively on air transport. UPS, which functions more as an alternative to the Postal Service, relies heavily on ground transport — though both services operate their own fleet of jets. Railroads, and the companies that service them, added about $1 million to the overall PAC total from the transport industry — about the same as trucking companies.

Where the money went . . .

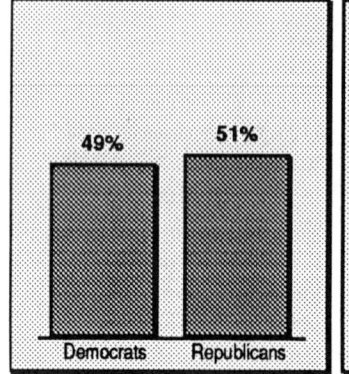

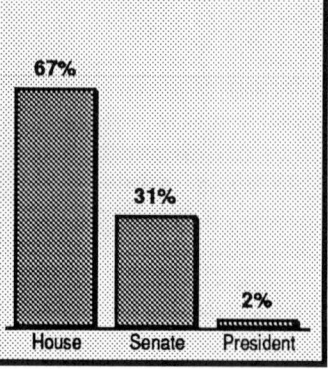

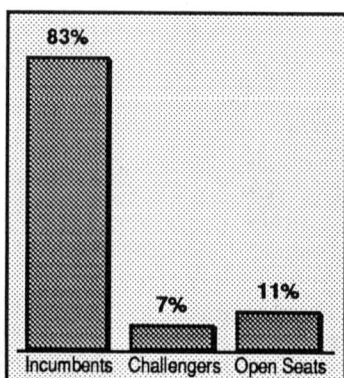

Top 20 Transportation PACs

Rank	Total	PAC Sponsor or Affiliate	Type	To Dems	To Repubs	To Dems / To Repubs
1	$1,202,420	National Auto Dealers Assn	Auto Dealers	$471,920	$730,500	
2	$1,158,700	Auto Dlrs/Drivers for Free Trade	Auto Dealers	$303,400	$855,300	
3	$771,768	United Parcel Service	Delivery	$461,151	$310,617	
4	$573,537	Federal Express Corp	Delivery	$378,950	$194,587	
5	$358,450	Union Pacific Corp	Railroad	$142,870	$215,580	
6	$332,905	Texas Air*	Airlines	$192,900	$140,005	
7	$329,733	Chrysler Corp*†	Auto/Aerospace	$214,633	$91,350	
8	$325,485	Boeing Co	Aircraft	$185,525	$139,960	
9	$290,089	Aircraft Owners & Pilots Assn	Genl Aviation	$155,775	$134,314	
10	$280,872	American Trucking Assns*	Trucking	$196,504	$84,368	
11	$203,458	Ford Motor Company	Auto/Aerospace	$106,208	$97,250	
12	$202,917	CSX Transportation Inc*	Rail/Sea Trans	$115,183	$87,734	
13	$198,688	General Motors	Auto/Aerospace	$79,858	$118,830	
14	$196,750	Norfolk Southern Corp*	Rail/Trucking	$121,400	$75,350	
15	$183,680	Yellow Freight System	Trucking	$118,050	$65,630	
16	$183,050	Eaton Corp	Auto Equip	$5,250	$177,800	
17	$124,649	American Airlines	Airlines	$74,750	$49,899	
18	$114,800	Consolidated Freightways	Trucking	$58,300	$56,500	
19	$113,070	Kansas City Southern	Railroad	$69,800	$43,270	
20	$95,600	Burlington Northern	Railroad	$56,025	$39,575	

* Contributions came from more than one PAC affiliated with this sponsor
† Does not include Chrysler's non-transport subsidiaries.

Since nearly all the common carriers — whether on land, sea or air — engage in interstate commerce, their operations come under varying degrees of federal jurisdiction. Within the House and Senate, that jurisdiction falls under the purview of several committees. The House Public Works and Transportation Committee oversees most of the industry, with two major exceptions: The House Merchant Marine & Fisheries Committee deals with ocean-going sea transport, and Energy and Commerce committee has jurisdiction over railroads. Within the Senate, the Commerce, Science and Transportation Committee is the center for transport policy.

Members of those committees were major recipients of transport industry PAC funds. Nine members of the House got $50,000 or more from transportation interests; three in the Senate got over $150,000.

At the top of the list were three Senate Commerce Committee members: Pete Wilson, Lloyd Bentsen and John Danforth. Danforth is the committee's ranking Republican. Dave Durenberger sits on the subcommittee on Environment and Public Works that oversees federal highway construction.

In the House, the top six recipients held seats on the Public Works and Transportation Committee. Glenn Anderson took over as committee chairman after the death of former chairman James J. Howard. Norman Mineta chaired the Aviation subcommittee; Newt Gingrich was that panel's ranking Republican and Robert Roe was a member of the Surface Transportation subcommittee. Republican Arlan Stangeland of Minnesota was the ranking Republican on the Water Resources subcommittee.

Top 10 Senate Recipients

Rank	Name	Total	Status	W/L
1	Pete Wilson (R-Calif)	$160,602	Incumb	W
2	Lloyd Bentsen (D-Texas)*	$159,040	Incumb*	W
3	John Danforth (R-Mo)	$152,026	Incumb	W
4	Dave Durenberger (R-Minn)	$99,986	Incumb	W
5	Frank Lautenberg (D-NJ)	$97,828	Incumb	W
6	Donald W. Riegle (D-Mich)	$97,551	Incumb	W
7	Slade Gorton (R-Wash)	$96,150	Open	W
8	Jim Sasser (D-Tenn)	$95,579	Incumb	W
9	Orrin Hatch (R-Utah)	$92,907	Incumb	W
10	Connie Mack (R-Fla)	$90,350	Open	W

* Bentsen ran simultaneously for Senate and Vice President in 1988

Top 10 House Recipients

Rank	Name	Total	Status	W/L
1	Glenn M. Anderson (D-Calif)	$78,900	Incumb	W
2	James J. Howard (D-NJ)*	$63,600	Incumb	†
3	Arlan Stangeland (R-Minn)	$57,620	Incumb	W
4	Newt Gingrich (R-Ga)	$57,150	Incumb	W
5	Norman Y. Mineta (D-Calif)	$55,618	Incumb	W
6	Robert A. Roe (D-NJ)	$52,875	Incumb	W
7	James H. Quillen (R-Tenn)	$51,350	Incumb	W
8	John R. Miller (R-Wash)	$51,060	Incumb	W
9	Thomas A. Luken (D-Ohio)	$50,890	Incumb	W
10	Bob Carr (D-Mich)	$48,526	Incumb	W

• Died Mar 25, 1988

Labor

Where the money came from . . .

The 17 million Americans who are members of organized labor unions represent a cross-section of the workforce that is as diverse as one can imagine. Union members drive trucks, deliver mail, build skyscrapers, teach children, print newspapers, and manufacture everything from bombers to safety pins. Even some individual unions are amazingly diverse. Teamsters, for example, can be found not only behind the wheels of tractor-trailers, but in canneries, dairies, building sites, and even in police departments.

Despite their diversity, however, the political action committees operated by labor unions are rock solid supporters of the Democratic Party. A look at their PAC contributions, in fact, shows that they may be the most solid rock that the Democrats stand on. Of the total $37 million that labor unions doled out in contributions in the 1987-88 election cycle, 91.5 percent — more than $34.3 million — went to Democrats. No other segment of the PAC community, with the exception of party-specific ideological PACs and those run by members of Congress, was as partisan in its distribution of funds. Nor did any segment have such a rich supply of available dollars. Unlike many business PACs, which

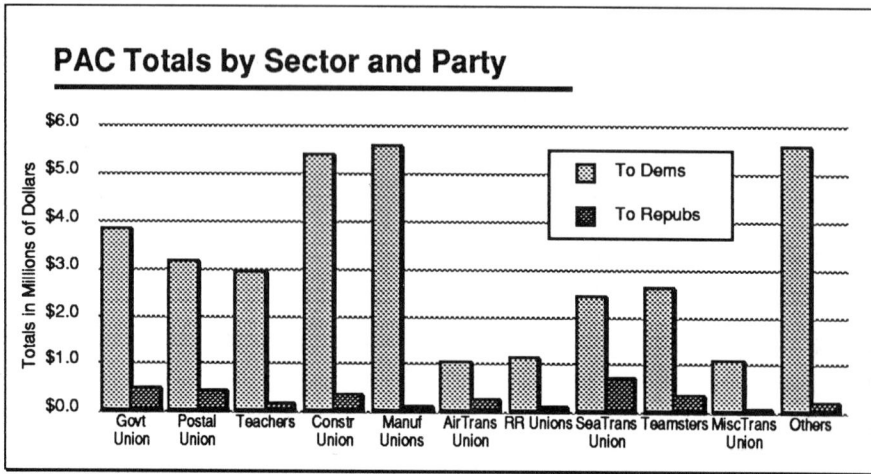

Category	Total	To Democrats	To Republicans	Dem Pct	Repub Pct
Govt Union	$4,265,298	$3,795,198	$470,100	89.0%	11.0%
Postal Unions	$3,558,977	$3,121,340	$437,637	87.7%	12.3%
Teachers	$3,021,709	$2,879,733	$141,976	95.3%	4.7%
Construction Unions	$5,706,655	$5,345,508	$361,147	93.7%	6.3%
Manufacturing Unions	$5,620,868	$5,512,768	$108,100	98.1%	1.9%
Air Transport Unions	$1,287,977	$1,021,477	$266,500	79.3%	20.7%
Railroad Unions	$1,226,339	$1,133,829	$92,510	92.5%	7.5%
Sea Transport Unions	$3,111,791	$2,393,716	$718,075	76.9%	23.1%
Teamsters	$2,925,164	$2,590,364	$334,800	88.6%	11.4%
Misc Transport Unions	$1,147,665	$1,075,094	$72,571	93.7%	6.3%
Other Unions	$5,701,179	$5,513,487	$187,692	96.7%	3.3%
Labor Total	**$37,573,622**	**$34,382,514**	**$3,191,108**	**91.5%**	**8.5%**

rely on fairly large contributions from corporate executives, labor unions traditionally rely on small amounts — often monthly deductions out of union dues — from their millions of members. The result is the biggest, most strategically directed bloc of campaign cash within the American political system.

Within the community of union PACs, there are some natural divisions of labor. Public sector unions — representing postal workers, teachers, and employees of state, federal and local governments — have become an increasingly important segment of the labor movement. Together they accounted for more than $10 million in PAC contributions in the '88 elections. Transportation unions added a total of $9.7 million in gifts to federal candidates. Construction unions, manufacturing unions, and service and miscellaneous unions together accounted for roughly equal thirds of the remaining $17 million from labor PACs.

Where the money went . . .

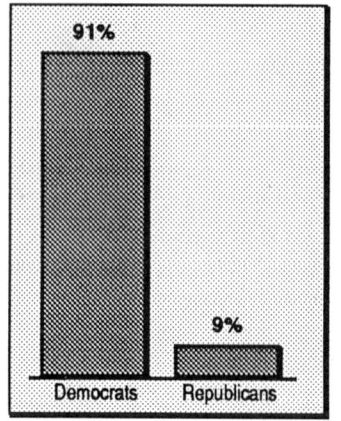

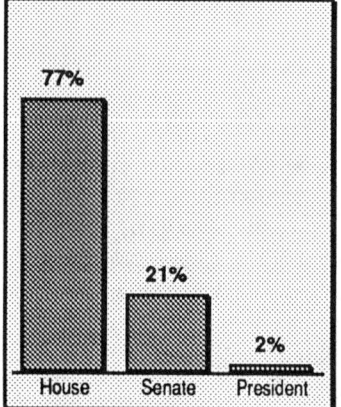

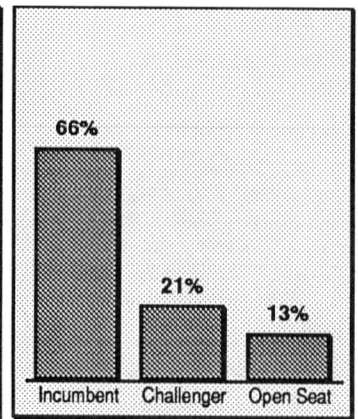

Top 20 Labor PACs

Rank	Total	PAC Sponsor or Affiliate	Type	To Dems	To Repubs	To Dems / To Repubs
1	$2,925,164	Teamsters Union*	Transpt Unions	$2,590,364	$334,800	
2	$2,151,029	National Education Assn*	Teachers	$2,030,003	$121,026	
3	$1,986,400	Natl Assn/Retired Federal Employ*	Govt Unions	$1,623,600	$362,800	
4	$1,955,099	United Auto Workers*	Manuf Unions	$1,932,449	$22,650	
5	$1,758,742	National Assn of Letter Carriers*	Postal Unions	$1,581,326	$177,416	
6	$1,658,386	Amer Fedn of St/Cnty/Munic Employ	Govt Unions	$1,597,086	$61,300	
7	$1,524,780	Machinists/Aerospace Wrkrs Union*	Manuf Unions	$1,508,780	$16,000	
8	$1,430,771	Marine Engineers Union*	Transpt Unions	$982,721	$448,050	
9	$1,409,395	Carpenters & Joiners Union*	Constr Unions	$1,316,088	$93,307	
10	$1,237,170	Intl Brthrhd of Electrical Workers*	Electrical	$1,189,820	$47,350	
11	$1,209,500	Air Line Pilots Assn	Transpt Unions	$951,500	$258,000	
12	$1,207,232	AFL-CIO*	Misc Unions	$1,175,332	$31,900	
13	$1,175,210	Food & Commercial Workers Union*	Misc Unions	$1,131,839	$41,371	
14	$1,108,945	Seafarers International Union*	Transpt Unions	$955,795	$153,150	
15	$977,521	Operating Engineers Union*	Constr Unions	$873,596	$103,925	
16	$920,645	Laborers Union*	Constr Unions	$859,845	$60,800	
17	$905,425	American Postal Workers Union*	Postal Unions	$842,850	$62,575	
18	$902,150	United Steelworkers	Constr Unions	$898,150	$4,000	
19	$870,680	American Federation of Teachers*	Teachers	$849,730	$20,950	
20	$803,385	United Transportation Union	Transpt Unions	$733,075	$70,310	

* Contributions came from more than one PAC affiliated with this sponsor

Fourteen labor union PACs gave $1 million or more to federal candidates in the 1988 elections. While most of the funds came from centralized PACs making donations nationwide, many individual PACs are run by union locals. The International Brotherhood of Electrical Workers, for example, gave just under $1.2 million through its national union and another $42,000 through 19 local IBEW chapters.

The combined might of union dollars was felt by dozens of candidates and incumbent members of Congress. A total of 116 federal candidates received $100,000 or more in labor contributions in 1987-88. All but two — Senators Lowell Weicker and John Heinz — were Democrats. Number one on the list of top recipients was Leo McCarthy, the California Lt. Governor who challenged, and eventually lost to, Republican incumbent Senator Pete Wilson. Two other Democratic challengers on the Top 10 Senate list used their funds to successfully defeat Republican incumbents. Richard Bryan in Nevada beat Republican Chic Hecht, and Bob Kerrey in Nebraska took over the seat held by David Karnes.

In the House, Labor's number one recipient was Thomas Ward, a Democratic lawyer from northcentral Indiana who two years earlier had come within 47 votes of beating Republican incumbent John Hiler. Hiler eventually prevailed in 1988, but only after spending more than a million dollars to defend his seat. Another top labor priority in 1988 was the New Jersey House seat won by Democrat Frank Pallone. Pallone collected $247,000 from 66 different labor PACs; enough to help finance a slim victory. Labor's pattern in its contributions has been to rally its forces in specially targeted races — either helping out a precariously-positioned Democratic incumbent, or financing the effort of a likely Democratic challenger. Overall, more than a third of labor PAC funds went to non-incumbents — a ratio considerably higher than that of business PACs.

Top 10 Senate Recipients

Rank	Name	Total	Status	W/L
1	Leo McCarthy (D-Calif)	$391,950	Chall	L
2	Frank Lautenberg (D-NJ)	$354,802	Incumb	W
3	Howard Metzenbaum (D-Ohio)	$346,750	Incumb	W
4	Wayne Dowdy (D-Miss)	$324,400	Open	L
5	Richard H. Bryan (D-Nev)	$314,800	Chall	W
6	Bob Kerrey (D-Neb)	$299,950	Chall	W
7	Hubert H. Humphrey III (D-Minn)	$297,375	Chall	L
8	Paul Sarbanes (D-Md)	$285,775	Incumb	W
9	Jim Sasser (D-Tenn)	$281,750	Incumb	W
10	Jeff Bingaman (D-NM)	$273,400	Incumb	W

Top 10 House Recipients

Rank	Name	Total	Status	W/L
1	Thomas W. Ward (D-Ind)	$255,800	Chall	L
2	Richard A. Gephardt (D-Mo)	$250,889	Incumb*	W*
3	Frank Pallone (D-NJ)	$247,100	Open	W
4	Nancy Pelosi (D-Calif)	$239,172	Incumb	W
5	Jim Jontz (D-Ind)	$236,450	Incumb	W
6	George J. Hochbrueckner (D-NY)	$225,074	Incumb	W
7	Peter H. Kostmayer (D-Pa)	$216,608	Incumb	W
8	Gary K. Hart (D-Calif)	$214,000	Chall	L
9	Jerry F. Costello (D-Ill)	$204,650	Incumb†	W
10	Louise M. Slaughter (D-NY)	$200,710	Incumb	W

* In 1988 Gephardt ran for President, then for reelection to his U.S. House seat.
† Costello ran twice in 1988; he won his seat in an August special election, then was elected to a full term in November

Government/Postal Worker Unions

Top 15 Government/Postal Worker Unions

Rank	Total	PAC Sponsor or Affiliate	Type	To Dems	To Repubs	To Dems	To Repubs
1	$1,986,400	Natl Assn of Retired Fed Employ*	Govt Unions	$1,623,600	$362,800		
2	$1,758,742	Natl Assn of Letter Carriers*	Postal Unions	$1,581,326	$177,416		
3	$1,658,386	Amer Fedn of St/Cnty/Munic Empl	Govt Unions	$1,597,086	$61,300		
4	$905,425	Amer Postal Workers Union*	Postal Unions	$842,850	$62,575		
5	$398,280	Natl Rural Letter Carriers Assn	Postal Unions	$323,224	$75,056		
6	$211,515	Amer Fedn of Govt Employees	Govt Unions	$195,715	$15,800		
7	$182,270	Natl League of Postmasters	Postal Unions	$122,920	$59,350		
8	$172,970	Natl Treasury Employees Union	Govt Unions	$162,970	$10,000		
9	$169,035	Natl Assn of Postmasters	Postal Unions	$123,245	$45,790		
10	$151,975	Intl Assn of Firefighters	Govt Unions	$145,675	$6,300		
11	$92,075	Natl Assn of Postal Supervisors	Postal Unions	$78,975	$13,100		
12	$31,100	Natl Fedn of Federal Employees	Govt Unions	$28,850	$2,250		
13	$30,830	Natl Alliance Postal/Federal Employ	Postal Unions	$30,580	$250		
14	$20,600	Federal Managers' Assn	Govt Unions	$16,200	$4,400		
15	$17,490	Natl Star Route Mail Contractors	Postal Unions	$13,440	$4,050		

* Contributions came from more than one PAC affiliated with this sponsor

One of the surprising features of government-sector unions — particularly those representing postal workers — is that there are so many of them. There is only one U.S. Postal Service, but its employees are represented by no fewer than 10 different PACs that contributed to federal candidates in the 1988 elections. Three PACs deal specifically with letter carriers — one concentrates on rural letter carriers, another with retirees. Postmasters and postal supervisors have three PACs of their own. Within the federal bureaucracy, Treasury Department workers have a PAC to themselves; so do federal managers. Biggest of all is the PAC representing retired federal employees, which gave out nearly $2 million in contributions.

In all, the government and postal worker PACs gave nearly $7.8 million to federal candidates during 1987-88. As with all other segments of the labor movement, the government employee PACs gave the vast majority of their PAC dollars to Democrats. But they also showed a tendency to pay extra attention to Congressmen and Senators who sit on committees important to public sector employees.

Jim Sasser, the Tennessee Democrat who topped all other candidates with more than $68,000 from government and postal worker PACs, served as chairman of the subcommittee on Senate Governmental Affairs that deals with Government Efficiency, Federalism, and the District of Columbia. Jeff Bingaman, also a member of that committee, held a seat on the subcommittee overseeing the Federal Civil Service and the U.S. Postal Service.

Two other Senate incumbents — Frank Lautenberg and Dennis DeConcini — were members of the Senate Appropriations Committee, the panel that actually doles out the money the federal government spends. DeConcini chaired the Treasury, Postal Service and General Government subcommittee.

Paul Sarbanes may have wound up on the Top 10 list for a different reason. He represents the state of Maryland — home to thousands of federal workers who work in and around Washington, D.C.

The top PAC recipient in the House of Representatives was Michigan Democrat William Ford, chairman of the House Post Office and Civil Service Committee. Four others on the Top 10 list also held seats on that committee. Steny Hoyer, who represents a portion of the Maryland suburbs outside the nation's capital, was a member of the Treasury, Postal Service and General Government Appropriations subcommittee.

Top 10 Senate Recipients

Rank	Name	Total	Status	W/L
1	Jim Sasser (D-Tenn)	$68,500	Incumb	W
2	Buddy MacKay (D-Fla)	$61,400	Open	L
3	Wayne Dowdy (D-Miss)	$59,950	Open	L
4	Richard H. Bryan (D-Nev)	$59,750	Chall	W
5	Frank Lautenberg (D-NJ)	$58,000	Incumb	W
6	Leo McCarthy (D-Calif)	$57,700	Chall	L
7	Mike Lowry (D-Wash)	$56,650	Open	L
8	Jeff Bingaman (D-NM)	$56,200	Incumb	W
9	Paul Sarbanes (D-Md)	$54,950	Incumb	W
10	Dennis DeConcini (D-Ariz)	$52,350	Incumb	W

Top 10 House Recipients

Rank	Name	Total	Status	W/L
1	William D. Ford (D-Mich)	$64,865	Incumb	W
2	Mary Rose Oakar (D-Ohio)	$58,900	Incumb	W
3	Frank McCloskey (D-Ind)	$57,350	Incumb	W
4	Mickey Leland (D-Texas)	$54,550	Incumb	W
5	Thomas W. Ward (D-Ind)	$49,300	Chall	L
6	George J. Hochbrueckner (D-NY)	$44,824	Incumb	W
7	Jim Jontz (D-Ind)	$44,600	Incumb	W
8	Frank Pallone (D-NJ)	$44,050	Open	W
9	Gary L. Ackerman (D-NY)	$43,900	Incumb	W
10	Steny H. Hoyer (D-Md)	$43,525	Incumb	W

Transportation Unions

Top 15 Transportation Union PACs

Rank	Total	PAC Sponsor or Affiliate	Type	To Dems	To Repubs	To Dems / To Repubs
1	$2,925,164	Teamsters Union*	Teamsters	$2,590,364	$334,800	
2	$1,430,771	Marine Engineers Union*	Sea Transpt	$982,721	$448,050	
3	$1,209,500	Air Line Pilots Assn	Air Transpt	$951,500	$258,000	
4	$1,108,945	Seafarers International Union*	Sea Transpt	$955,795	$153,150	
5	$803,385	United Transportation Union	RR Unions	$733,075	$70,310	
6	$543,687	Amalgamated Transit Union	Misc Transpt	$510,387	$33,300	
7	$375,398	Transportation Communication Union	Misc Transpt	$354,077	$21,321	
8	$221,780	Transport Workers Union	Misc Transpt	$205,180	$16,600	
9	$216,448	Masters, Mates and Pilots Union*	Sea Transpt	$159,448	$57,000	
10	$214,780	Intl Longshoremen Assn*	Sea Transpt	$167,655	$47,125	
11	$166,957	Brothrhood of Locomotive Engrs	RR Unions	$159,307	$7,650	
12	$138,127	Maintenance of Way Employees	RR Unions	$135,377	$2,750	
13	$89,472	Longshrmen/Warehousemen Union	Sea Transpt	$89,472	$0	
14	$77,270	Brotherhood of RR Signalmen	RR Unions	$71,020	$6,250	
15	$67,527	Assn of Flight Attendants	Air Transpt	$63,927	$3,600	

* Contributions came from more than one PAC affiliated with this sponsor

Within the labor community, and within the sector of transport unions in particular — lies an interesting example of unusual PAC behavior. While it has generally been assumed — correctly — that labor and business PACs tend to be natural adversaries in most bills that come before Congress, that is no longer entirely the case. For the sea transport unions in particular, which gave a higher proportion of their PAC dollars to Republicans than any other union group, the watchword was pragmatism. As the U.S. merchant marine industry has steadily lost ground to foreign competitors, sea transport unions have begun working to achieve consensus with their employers on bills in Congress affecting the industry's welfare. They have even played the lead role in financing congressional campaigns. In the 1988 elections, sea transport unions gave out $3.1 million in PAC contributions — nearly six times as much as the companies they work for. Much of that money was concentrated on the members — both Democrats and Republicans — who sit on the House Merchant Marine Committee.

Whether this is an aberration, or the first sign of a trend that may develop further as other industries face pressures from growing international competition, it is a point worth noting and a pattern worth watching in future election cycles.

Six of the top 10 recipients of transportation union PAC dollars in 1987-88 were members of the House Merchant Marine Committee, and contributions from sea transport unions formed a major share of that money. Typical was Maryland Republican Helen Delich Bentley — the only Republican to appear on any of the labor sector Top 10 lists. She collected nearly $39,000 from sea transport unions in the 1988 elections.

Many other transportation unions played major roles in supporting congressional candidates. Biggest of all was the Teamsters Union — the second-largest of all PAC contributors in 1988, with more than $2.9 million in total contributions. The Air Line Pilots Association, which gave 21 percent of its money to Republicans, led all air transport unions in spending.

Four railroad unions also appeared on the list of biggest transport unions. Like the merchant marine unions, railroad labor PACs also outspent the corporate side of their industry. Railroad companies gave just under $1 million in PAC contributions in 1987-88; railroad unions gave $1.2 million.

Top 10 Senate Recipients

Rank	Name	Total	Status	W/L
1	Leo McCarthy (D-Calif)	$96,800	Chall	L
2	Frank Lautenberg (D-NJ)	$93,302	Incumb	W
3	Howard Metzenbaum (D-Ohio)	$90,800	Incumb	W
4	Mike Lowry (D-Wash)	$89,100	Open	L
5	Bob Kerrey (D-Neb)	$74,250	Chall	W
6	Paul Sarbanes (D-Md)	$74,000	Incumb	W
7	Richard H. Bryan (D-Nev)	$73,250	Chall	W
8	Quentin N. Burdick (D-ND)	$68,250	Incumb	W
9	Jeff Bingaman (D-NM)	$62,250	Incumb	W
10	Jim Sasser (D-Tenn)	$61,000	Incumb	W

Top 10 House Recipients

Rank	Name	Total	Status	W/L
1	Nancy Pelosi (D-Calif)	$66,572	Incumb	W
2	Richard A. Gephardt (D-Mo)	$57,750	Incumb*	W*
3	Helen Delich Bentley (R-Md)	$55,900	Incumb	W
4	Thomas J. Manton (D-NY)	$54,281	Incumb	W
5	Roy Dyson (D-Md)	$51,400	Incumb	W
6	David E. Bonior (D-Mich)	$50,190	Incumb	W
7	Thomas W. Ward (D-Ind)	$49,050	Chall	L
8	George J. Hochbrueckner (D-NY)	$47,650	Incumb	W
9	Bill Alexander (D-Ark)	$46,475	Incumb	W
10	Glenn M. Anderson (D-Calif)	$46,000	Incumb	W

* In 1988 Gephardt ran first for President, then for reelection to his U.S. House seat.

Ideological/Single-Issue

Where the money came from ...

A world apart from the pragmatic and largely bipartisan business PACs, and the Democratically-aligned PACs that represent organized labor, are the third family of political action committees — those organized not around a business or a union, but around an idea, cause, or political party. Ideological and single-issue PACs have become significant players on the political landscape. They gave more than $17 million in direct contributions to federal candidates in the 1988 elections — and they spent a similar amount in independent expenditures, mainly targeted at influencing the race for President.

Though it may be conveniently conceived of as a distinct family within the PAC community, however, the PACs within this group are hardly a compatible collection. They represent every shade of political viewpoint, and many of them spend much of their money and time seeking to counteract the efforts of their adversaries. For issues which stir deep divisions within the American public — such as abortion, gun control, or defense spending — PACs have coalesced around both sides.

Not all the issues addressed by these PACs are so universal or broad as the issue of war and peace; many are quite specific.

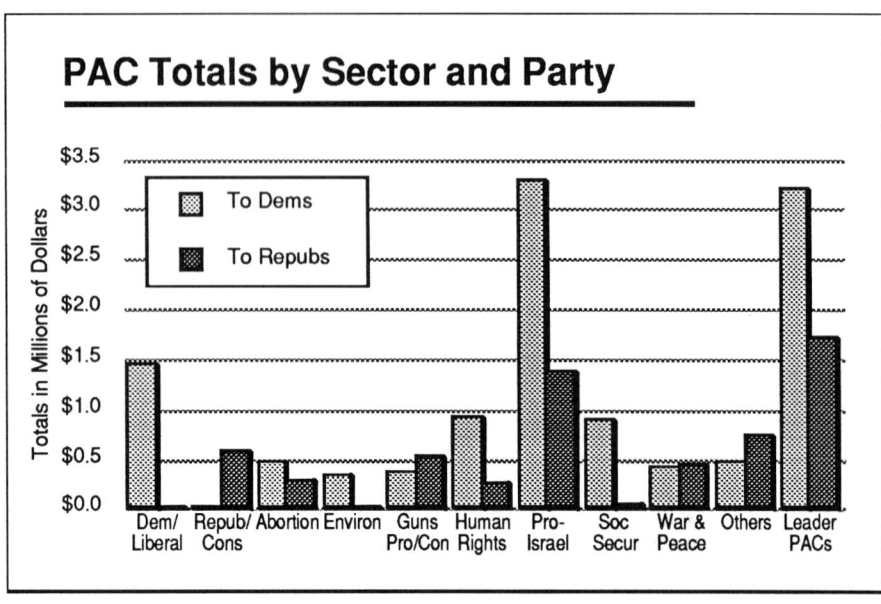

PAC Totals by Sector and Party

Category	Total	To Democrats	To Republicans	Dem Pct	Repub Pct
Democratic/Liberal	$1,442,212	$1,435,212	$7,000	99.5%	0.5%
Republican/Conservative	$589,991	$13,637	$576,354	2.3%	97.7%
Abortion Pro/Con	$759,085	$473,882	$285,203	62.4%	37.6%
Environmental Issues	$354,815	$343,024	$11,391	96.7%	3.2%
Guns Pro/Con	$890,806	$366,269	$524,537	41.1%	58.9%
Human Rights	$1,185,085	$925,618	$259,467	78.1%	21.9%
Pro-Israel	$4,642,372	$3,271,309	$1,371,063	70.5%	29.5%
Social Security/Senior Citizens	$935,350	$897,550	$37,800	96.0%	4.0%
Peace/Defense	$853,267	$406,207	$447,060	47.6%	52.4%
Other Issues	$1,178,931	$453,108	$726,223	38.4%	61.6%
Leadership PACs	$4,921,222	$3,204,893	$1,716,329	65.1%	34.9%
Ideological/Single-Issue Total	**$17,753,136**	**$11,790,709**	**$5,962,427**	**66.4%**	**33.6%**

There are PACs, for example, supporting animal rights; PACs opposing organized labor; PACs defending the rights of gays and lesbians; and PACs involved in every issue from historical preservation to toxic wastes. There are also a variety of ethnic and minority PACs whose interests revolve around a specific segment of the American population — as well as the interests of the citizens in their homelands. Armenian-Americans, for example, support no fewer than five individual PACs. Others promote the interests of Albanian-, Greek-, Latvian-, Korean-, Lithuanian-, Turkish-, Italian- and African-Americans; and there are PACs representing both American Indians and Indians from India.

Where the money went ...

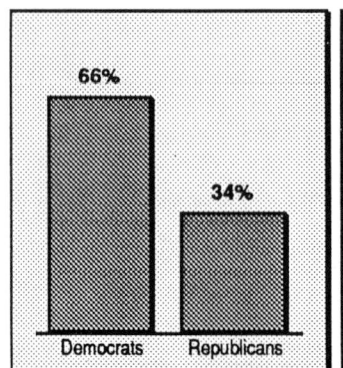

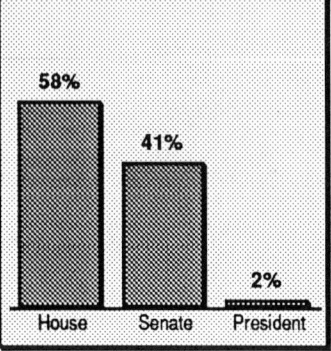

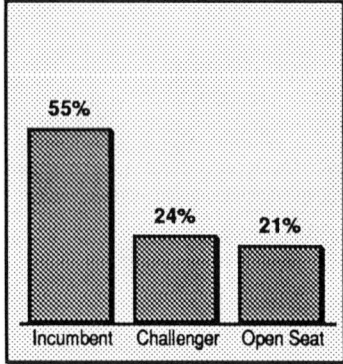

Top 20 Ideological/Single-Issue PACs

Rank	Total	PAC Name or Sponsor	Type	To Dems	To Repubs	To Dems / To Repubs
1	$1,134,500	National PAC	Pro-Israel	$720,000	$414,500	
2	$772,756	National Rifle Assn	Pro-Guns	$284,269	$488,487	
3	$744,650	Natl Cmte/Preserve Soc Security	Soc Security	$709,850	$34,800	
4	$684,616	National Cmte/Effective Congress	Dem/Liberal	$684,616	$0	
5	$553,576	Valley Education Fund	Dem Leaders	$553,576	$0	
6	$447,220	Majority Congress Committee	Dem Leaders	$447,220	$0	
7	$313,861	Campaign America	Repub Leader	$0	$313,861	
8	$308,650	Washington PAC	Pro-Israel	$237,900	$70,750	
9	$299,787	Public Service Research Council	Anti-Union	$6,750	$293,037	
10	$289,615	Hudson Valley PAC	Pro-Israel	$167,584	$122,031	
11	$287,400	KidsPAC	HealthWelfar	$260,400	$27,000	
12	$286,904	Sierra Club	Environment	$253,934	$32,970	
13	$285,823	Human Rights Campaign Fund	Gay Rights	$221,781	$59,042	
14	$271,660	Fund for America's Future	Repub Cands	$0	$271,660	
15	$264,924	Natl Abortion Rights Action Lge	Pro-Choice	$228,724	$36,200	
16	$261,800	Cmte for a Democratic Consensus	Dem Leaders	$261,800	$0	
17	$258,100	Senate Majority Fund	Dem Leaders	$258,100	$0	
18	$254,132	National Right to Life PAC	Pro-Life	$51,942	$202,190	
19	$243,830	Democrats for the 80's	Dem/Liberal	$243,830	$0	
20	$236,450	Joint Action Cmte for Political Affairs	Pro-Israel	$196,450	$40,000	

Foreign policy PACs are also active; whether seeking an end to apartheid in South Africa or the ouster of Fidel Castro from Cuba. Among this group, none is so large — or influential — as the 61 pro-Israel PACs, which gave a combined $4.6 million to federal candidates in the 1987-88 election cycle. Finally, there are the out-and-out ideological PACs. Here too every stripe of political perspective can be found, from mainstream to radical, left-wing to right-wing, and even a few in the middle. One PAC, for example, only gives to conservative Democrats, while another gives only to "progressive Republicans."

A subset of the ideological and party PACs are the so-called "leadership PACs" sponsored by individual members of Congress and other high-profile political figures. Often used as a tool for winning influence from their colleagues within the House and Senate, leadership PACs have become a favored tool for rewarding friends and punishing enemies on Capitol Hill. They have also become a financial force to be reckoned with, dispensing nearly $5 million in contributions in the 1988 elections.

Though they may represent every issue under the sun (and a few, like the SpacePAC, *beyond* the sun) one thing most single-issue and ideological PACs do have in common, is a tendency to back candidates from one political party or the other. They also have a higher-than-normal tendency to give money to non-incumbents. Only 55 percent of the PAC dollars from this group went to incumbents — as compared with 65 percent from labor unions and nearly 81 percent from business PACs.

Moved as they are by the passion of issues, the PACs that dispense ideological funds tend to be attracted to highly-competitive contests, often spotlighting an ideological gulf between the two opposing candidates. Such contests tend to be lightning rods for the ideological PAC community, attracting contributions at a furious pace from people on both sides of the issue.

Top 10 Senate Recipients

Rank	Name	Total	Status	W/L
1	Frank Lautenberg (D-NJ)	$410,417	Incumb	W
2	Howard Metzenbaum (D-Ohio)	$404,929	Incumb	W
3	Richard A. Licht (D-RI)	$305,647	Chall	L
4	Leo McCarthy (D-Calif)	$241,894	Chall	L
5	Jeff Bingaman (D-NM)	$240,444	Incumb	W
6	Mike Lowry (D-Wash)	$239,137	Open	L
7	Wayne Dowdy (D-Miss)	$234,398	Open	L
8	Dave Durenberger (R-Minn)	$226,735	Incumb	W
9	Bob Kerrey (D-Neb)	$208,972	Chall	W
10	Lowell P. Weicker Jr. (R-Conn)	$200,165	Incumb	L

Top 10 House Recipients

Rank	Name	Total	Status	W/L
1	Gary K. Hart (D-Calif)	$190,321	Chall	L
2	Anna Eshoo (D-Calif)	$174,821	Chall	L
3	Mike Espy (D-Miss)	$119,913	Incumb	W
4	Peter H. Kostmayer (D-Pa)	$111,584	Incumb	W
5	David Skaggs (D-Colo)	$109,987	Incumb	W
6	Jolene Unsoeld (D-Wash)	$106,014	Open	W
7	Rosemary S. Pooler (D-NY)	$101,099	Open	L
8	Wayne Owens (D-Utah)	$99,116	Incumb	W
9	John R. Miller (R-Wash)	$98,778	Incumb	W
10	Louise M. Slaughter (D-NY)	$97,140	Incumb	W

Pro-Israel

Top 20 Pro-Israel PACs

Rank	Total	PAC Name	To Dems	To Repubs	To Dems / To Repubs
1	$1,134,500	National PAC	$720,000	$414,500	
2	$308,650	Washington PAC	$237,900	$70,750	
3	$289,615	Hudson Valley PAC	$167,584	$122,031	
4	$236,450	Joint Action Cmte for Political Affairs	$196,450	$40,000	
5	$214,450	Desert Caucus	$138,450	$76,000	
6	$197,000	Citizens Organized PAC	$157,000	$40,000	
7	$178,100	Delaware Valley PAC	$125,350	$52,750	
8	$134,250	Women's Pro-Israel Natl PAC	$67,500	$66,750	
9	$133,250	Florida Congressional Cmte	$90,750	$42,500	
10	$127,000	St Louisians for Better Govt	$84,500	$42,500	
11	$120,000	Roundtable PAC	$83,500	$36,500	
12	$111,000	Pacific PAC	$111,000	$0	
13	$107,000	Multi-Issue PAC	$104,750	$2,250	
14	$104,000	San Franciscans for Good Govt	$82,000	$22,000	
15	$104,000	National Action Committee	$82,000	$22,000	
16	$96,000	MOPAC	$91,000	$5,000	
17	$90,400	Garden State PAC	$57,450	$32,950	
18	$80,450	Mid Manhattan PAC	$63,750	$16,700	
19	$79,200	Americans for Good Govt Inc	$44,200	$35,000	
20	$61,250	Heartland PAC	$44,250	$17,000	

Though the names of their PACs offer no clues as to the nature of their interest, the pro-Israel PACs are a well-known and potent political force on Capitol Hill — and they offer a potentially rich source of campaign funds for candidates in key congressional races. The primary concern of these PACs is continued U.S. support — both political and military — for the nation of Israel. Overwhelmingly, but not exclusively, they prefer Democrats; in all, 70 percent of their funds in 1988 went to candidates of that party. The PACs' tendency is to band together in a relatively small number of targeted races, compounding their funds to the candidate of their choice. Using this technique, the PACs delivered $245,000 in contributions to Democrat Howard Metzenbaum in Ohio, who was facing a serious and costly challenge in 1988 from Cleveland Mayor George Voinovich. Similar sums were received by New Jersey Democrat Frank Lautenberg, and Rhode Island Lt. Governor Richard Licht, who was seeking to upset incumbent Republican Senator John Chafee.

National PAC, or NATPAC, is the leading pro-Israel political action committee, dispensing over $1.1 million in the 1988 elections. Most of the other PACs are regionally based, and many draw their names — either explicitly or referentially — from the region in which their contributors live. The Desert Caucus, for example, is based in Tucson, Ariz.; MOPAC is based in Troy, Michigan — a suburb of Detroit, the Motor City.

Six of the top House recipients of pro-Israel PAC contributions held seats on the Foreign Affairs Committee, though none of the top Senate recipients sat on Foreign Relations.

Top 10 Senate Recipients

Rank	Name	Total	Status	W/L
1	Howard Metzenbaum (D-Ohio)	$245,085	Incumb	W
2	Frank Lautenberg (D-NJ)	$232,000	Incumb	W
3	Richard A. Licht (D-RI)	$228,600	Chall	L
4	Dave Durenberger (R-Minn)	$166,000	Incumb	W
5	Jeff Bingaman (D-NM)	$137,100	Incumb	W
6	Wayne Dowdy (D-Miss)	$128,600	Open	L
7	Lowell P. Weicker Jr. (R-Conn)	$123,500	Incumb	L
8	Bob Kerrey (D-Neb)	$85,000	Chall	W
9	Jim Sasser (D-Tenn)	$83,000	Incumb	W
10	Richard H. Bryan (D-Nev)	$80,250	Chall	W

Top 10 House Recipients

Rank	Name	Total	Status	W/L
1	John R. Miller (R-Wash)	$63,628	Incumb	W
2	Mike Espy (D-Miss)	$45,500	Incumb	W
3	Richard "Buck" O'Brien (D-Mont)	$38,250	Chall	L
4	Vin Weber (R-Minn)	$38,200	Incumb	W
5	Wayne Owens (D-Utah)	$35,800	Incumb	W
6	Sam Gejdenson (D-Conn)	$34,400	Incumb	W
7	Peter H. Kostmayer (D-Pa)	$34,250	Incumb	W
8	Gunn McKay (D-Utah)	$33,450	Chall	L
9	Lawrence J. Smith (D-Fla)	$33,100	Incumb	W
10	Howard Wolpe (D-Mich)	$32,500	Incumb	W

Leadership PACs

Top 20 Leadership PACs

Rank	Total	PAC Name and Sponsor	To Dems	To Repubs	To Dems / To Repubs
1	$553,576	Valley Education Fund (Tony Coelho)	$553,576	$0	
2	$447,220	Majority Congress Committee (Jim Wright)	$447,220	$0	
3	$313,861	Campaign America (Bob Dole)	$0	$313,861	
4	$271,660	Fund for America's Future (George Bush)	$0	$271,660	
5	$261,800	Cmte for a Democratic Consensus (Alan Cranston)*	$261,800	$0	
6	$258,100	Senate Majority Fund (Daniel Inouye)	$258,100	$0	
7	$213,115	Independent Action (Morris Udall)	$213,115	$0	
8	$205,000	24th Cong District of Calif PAC (Henry Waxman)	$205,000	$0	
9	$201,647	Pelican PAC (Bennett Johnston)	$201,647	$0	
10	$189,626	America's Leaders' Fund (Dan Rostenkowski)	$189,626	$0	
11	$186,769	Citizens for the Republic (Ronald Reagan)	$0	$186,769	
12	$170,000	Republican Majority Fund (Richard Lugar)	$0	$170,000	
13	$162,563	Catch the Spirit PAC (Bob Kasten)	$0	$162,563	
14	$139,800	Cmte for Democratic Opportunity (Bill Gray)	$139,800	$0	
15	$134,594	House Leadership Fund (Tom Foley)	$134,594	$0	
16	$123,916	Fund for a Democratic Majority (Edward Kennedy)	$123,916	$0	
17	$73,179	Conservative Victory Fund (Steve Symms)	$0	$73,179	
18	$67,423	Cmte for a Democratic Consensus (Marvin Leath)*	$67,423	$0	
19	$60,881	Fund for a Republican Majority (Ted Stevens)	$0	$60,881	
20	$56,600	Pax Americas (David Bonior)	$55,100	$1,500	

* Both California Sen. Alan Cranston and Texas Congressman Marvin Leath inadvertently settled on the same name for their leadership PACs. Leath's PAC has since been dissolved.

In a class by themselves — a category that might be termed "pragmatic ideological" — lie the so-called Leadership PACs. These are PACs sponsored by members of Congress, or other well known political leaders. Their dual purpose is to assist fellow party members in seeking election or reelection, and to win some measure of allegiance in return should the campaign be successful. The term "Leadership PAC" refers to the fact that these PACs have been widely used to bolster members' chances of being elected to leadership positions within the House and Senate — positions that are voted on by the members themselves in party caucuses.

During the 1988 election cycle, no fewer than 55 members of Congress — 30 Democrats and 25 Republicans — had formed or sponsored their own PACs. Together, they gave out more than $4.3 million of the total $4.9 million given by leadership PACs. Much of the rest came from PACs run by George Bush and Ronald Reagan. Nearly two-thirds of the leadership PACs' dollars went to Democrats.

In the past few years, leadership PACs have become a favorite instrument for incumbents who are not facing serious challenges to share the wealth with up-and-coming newcomers. Some 56 percent of the total dollars went to non-incumbents, with candidates in closely-fought elections collecting the most. Six of the top 10 Senate candidates were actually locked in battle against each other — Connie Mack vs. Buddy MacKay in Florida; Mike Lowry vs. Slade Gorton in Washington; and Howard Metzenbaum against George Voinovich in Ohio.

In the House, California Democrat Gary Hart (no relation to the former Colorado Senator) used his funds as part of a $1.6 million effort to unseat incumbent Republican Robert Lagomarsino. Hart eventually lost by just 0.4 percent of the vote.

Recent attempts at campaign reform legislation have targeted these PACs for elimination, but as long as they continue to be legal, they will likely remain popular tools by which incumbents hope to win friends and influence colleagues.

Top 10 Senate Recipients

Rank	Name	Total	Status	W/L
1	Buddy MacKay (D-Fla)	$98,000	Open	L
2	Mike Lowry (D-Wash)	$74,500	Open	L
3	Leo McCarthy (D-Calif)	$68,500	Chall	L
4	Frank Lautenberg (D-NJ)	$62,813	Incumb	W
5	Howard Metzenbaum (D-Ohio)	$57,500	Incumb	W
6	Connie Mack (R-Fla)	$56,757	Open	W
7	Conrad Burns (R-Mont)	$56,000	Chall	W
8	Chic Hecht (R-Nev)	$55,681	Incumb	L
9	George Voinovich (R-Ohio)	$55,452	Chall	L
10	Slade Gorton (R-Wash)	$53,502	Open	W

Top 10 House Recipients

Rank	Name	Total	Status	W/L
1	Gary K. Hart (D-Calif)	$55,500	Chall	L
2	Anna Eshoo (D-Calif)	$49,707	Chall	L
3	Louise M. Slaughter (D-NY)	$35,660	Incumb	W
4	David Skaggs (D-Colo)	$33,500	Incumb	W
5	George E. Brown Jr. (D-Calif)	$33,300	Incumb	W
6	Liz J. Patterson (D-SC)	$33,250	Incumb	W
7	Reese Lindquist (D-Wash)	$32,624	Chall	L
8	Jim Bates (D-Calif)	$32,000	Incumb	W
9	David J. Swarts (D-NY)	$30,000	Open	L
10	Bill Sarpalius (D-Texas)	$29,750	Open	W

A Potpourri of Issue PACs

Like metal filings drawn to a magnet, political action committees have coalesced around virtually every issue of interest — or dispute — among Americans. The amounts spent by one group versus another, and the proportions within each camp that go to Democrats versus Republicans, offer a fascinating glimpse at the political strategies of these specialized interest groups. The following mini-profiles present the highlights.

Abortion

A total of 18 anti-abortion or "Pro-Life" PACs and four pro-abortion or "Pro-Choice" PACs made direct contributions to federal candidates in the 1988 elections. Both sides also made independent expenditures in a number of races. Most of the Pro-Life PACs were organized under the national Right to Life organization, and that group's national PAC gave by far the biggest share of the group's money.

As can be seen in the chart at right, the Pro-Choice forces were decidedly Democratic in their contributions. Pro-Life groups mainly supported Republicans.

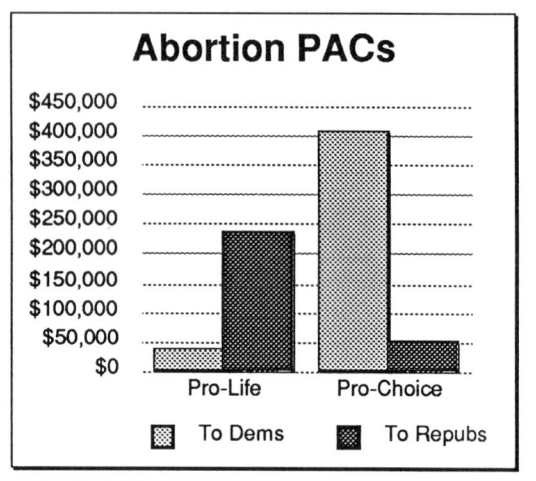

Leading Abortion Issue PACs	1987-88 Total
Pro-Life	**$301,711**
Natl Right to Life PAC	$254,132
Pro-Choice	**$457,374**
National Abortion Rghts Action League	$264,924
Voters for Choice/Friends of Family Planning	$174,450

Gun Control vs. Gun Ownership

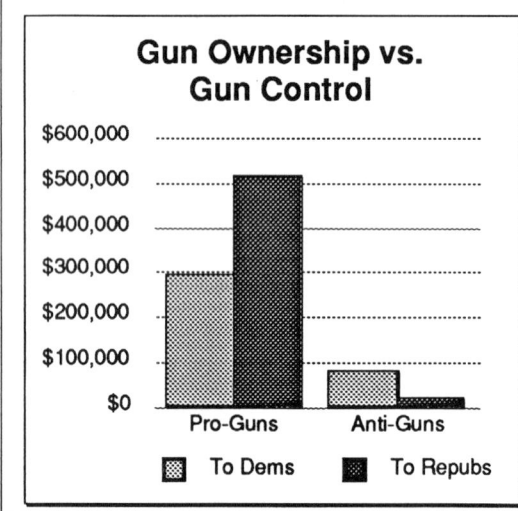

The National Rifle Association had the strongest presence by far among PACs dealing with the issue of gun control vs. gun owners' rights. Long an influential lobby on Capitol Hill, the NRA Political Victory Fund distributed more than three-quarters of a million dollars to 237 candidates in 1987-88. Many of its most favored recipients also got funds from Safari Club International, a hunters' rights group that shares the NRA's philosophy on gun ownership. On the opposite side of the issue, the Handgun Control Inc PAC gave funds to 123 candidates — predominantly Democrats. But the gun control group could muster only about 10 percent of the total spent by the pro-gun lobby.

Leading Pro-Gun and Anti-Gun PACs	1987-88 Total
Pro-Guns	**$802,906**
National Rifle Assn	$772,756
Safari Club International	$29,150
Anti-Guns	**$87,900**
Handgun Control Inc	$85,100

The Left and the Right

A total of 116 ideological PACs, on both the left and right of the political spectrum, contributed to federal candidates in the 1988 elections. Most were quite small, but the biggest liberal and conservative PACs were a major force — both through direct contributions and independent expenditures.

Leading Liberal & Conservative PACs	1987-88 Total
Democratic/Liberal PACs	**$1,442,212**
National Committee for an Effective Congress	$684,616
Democrats for the 80's	$243,830
Hollywood Women's Political Committee	$117,590
Republican/Conservative PACs	**$590,241**
Conservative Victory Committee	$84,352
National Conservative PAC	$83,481
American Citizens for Political Action	$67,400

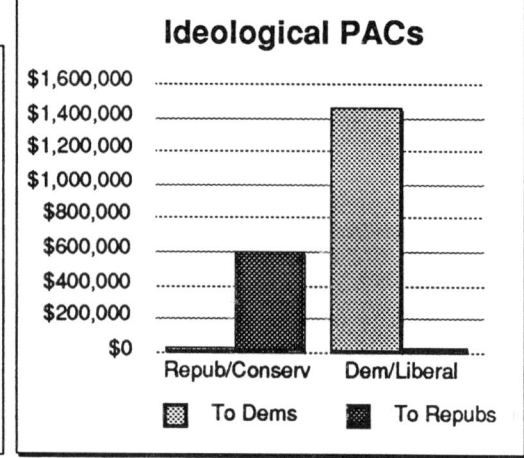

Human Rights

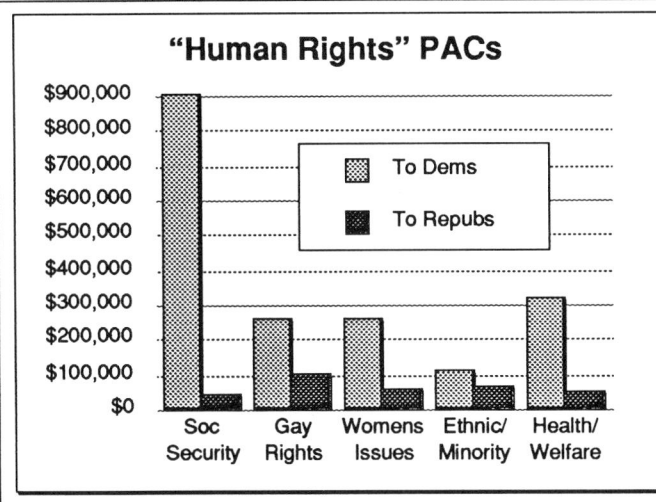

"Human Rights" PACs

Legend: To Dems / To Repubs

Categories: Soc Security, Gay Rights, Womens Issues, Ethnic/Minority, Health/Welfare

Groups seeking to improve the lot of the elderly, women, children, gays and ethnic minorities were all active in the PAC community in the 1988 elections. All together, they gave more than $2.1 million to federal candidates. By a wide margin, Democrats received the biggest share.

Human Rights PACs	1987-88 Total
Elderly/Social Security	**$935,350**
National Cmte to Preserve Social Security	$744,650
National Council of Senior Citizens	$190,700
Gay/Lesbian Rights	**$354,582**
Human Rights Campaign Fund	$285,823
Women's Issues	**$311,194**
Women's Campaign Fund	$121,012
Ethnic/Minority	**$165,747**
Health/Welfare	**$360,740**
KidsPAC	$287,400

War and Peace

While the threat of nuclear conflict with the Soviet Union may have faded in recent years, the level of debate between pro-military PACs and pro-peace PACs has simply shifted focus. Levels of defense spending in the post Cold War era are a concern of both groups, though their perspectives — and the distribution of their PAC dollars — are at opposite poles.

Leading Pro-Military and Pro-Peace PACs	1987-88 Total
Pro-Military	**$498,852**
Council for National Defense	$234,332
National Security PAC	$116,774
American Security Council	$65,446
Veterans of Foreign Wars	$52,500
Pro-Peace	**$354,815**
Council for a Lievable World/Peace PAC*	$189,407
SANE/Freeze Inc	$58,237

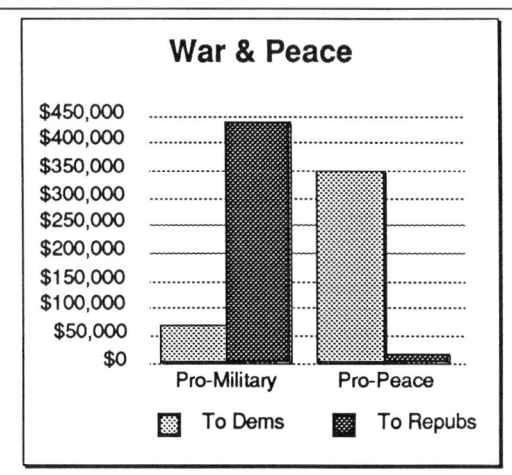

War & Peace

Categories: Pro-Military, Pro-Peace

Legend: To Dems / To Repubs

Other Single-Issue PACs

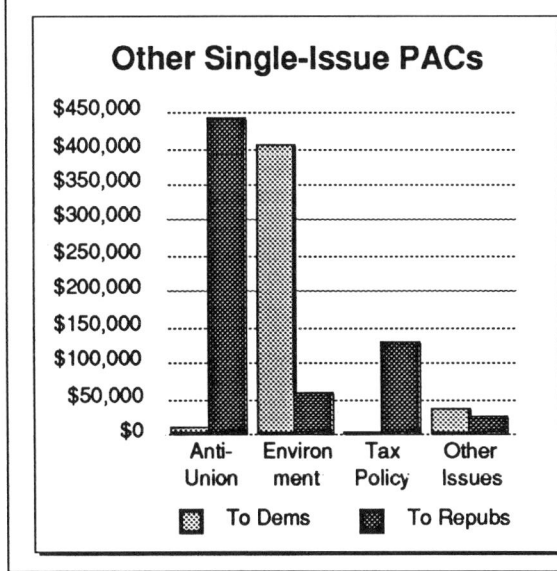

Other Single-Issue PACs

Categories: Anti-Union, Environment, Tax Policy, Other Issues

Legend: To Dems / To Repubs

Of the remaining single-issue PACs, the two largest groups are environmental PACs and organizations seeking to reduce the influence of labor unions in the American workplace. Largest by far on the environmental front is the Sierra Club. Among the anti-union PACs, the Public Service Research Council specifically opposes unionism among public employees. Promoting conservative fiscal policies is the chief concern of Ruff PAC, operated by financial newsletter publisher Howard Ruff.

Other Single-Issue PACs	1987-88 Total
Anti-Union	**$447,878**
Public Service Research Council	$299,787
Right to Work PAC	$148,091
Environmental Issues	**$459,951**
Sierra Club	$286,904
League of Conservation Voters*	$102,201
Tax Policy	**$126,679**
Ruff PAC	$125,079
Other Issues	**$57,565**

3.

Committee Profiles

Open Secrets

Introduction to the Committee Profiles

The committee profiles on the following pages present a unique picture of the relationship between PAC contributions and congressional committees. Most of the work that Congress does in shaping legislation takes place not on the floor of the House and Senate, but in meetings of committees and subcommittees. It is at this level that the language of bills is crafted, revised and debated, that congressional hearings are held and investigations are directed. For all these reasons, much of the attention of industry and interest group lobbyists — and PACs — is focused on deliberations within the specific committees that oversee their particular industry or interest. The section which follows examines the patterns in PAC contributions made in 1987-88 to members of each of the 37 standing committees of the House and Senate.

What the profiles contain

• Names of the chairman and ranking minority member of each committee and the ratio of seats between Democrats and Republicans.

• A full description of the committee's jurisdiction.

• A listing of each subcommittee, with its chairman and ranking minority member.

• A roster listing each committee member, and showing the amount of PAC contributions they received in 1987-88. The membership list includes those who served on the committee at any time during the 100th Congress — whether or not they ran for election in 1988. The members are arranged in descending order by the amount of PAC dollars they received.

• Top 20 PACs contributing to members of that committee.

• Total PAC contributions to all members of that committee from 13 broad categories of industries and interests. ➡

• A spotlight on the leading industry and interest group sectors that contributed to committee members during 1987-88. This is a more detailed breakdown of the general categories. For example, the general chart groups all finance, insurance and real estate PACs into one broad category. The spotlight chart breaks them down further, into Commercial Banks, Insurance Companies, Real Estate, etc.

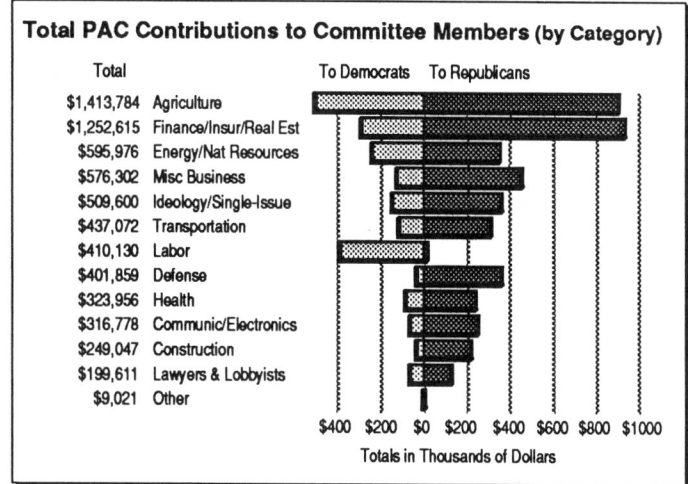

Total PAC Contributions to Committee Members (by Category)

Total		To Democrats	To Republicans
$1,413,784	Agriculture		
$1,252,615	Finance/Insur/Real Est		
$595,976	Energy/Nat Resources		
$576,302	Misc Business		
$509,600	Ideology/Single-Issue		
$437,072	Transportation		
$410,130	Labor		
$401,859	Defense		
$323,956	Health		
$316,778	Communic/Electronics		
$249,047	Construction		
$199,611	Lawyers & Lobbyists		
$9,021	Other		

$400 $200 $0 $200 $400 $600 $800 $1000
Totals in Thousands of Dollars

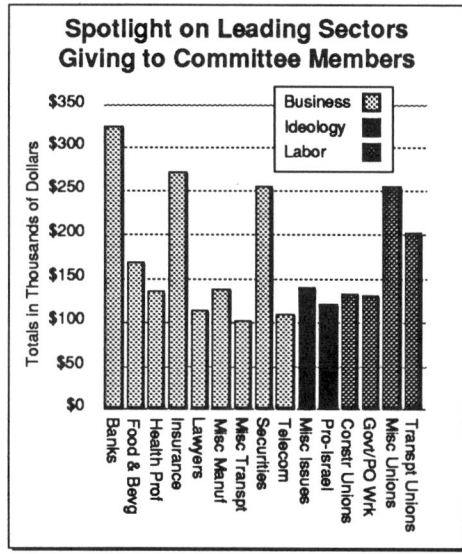

Spotlight on Leading Sectors Giving to Committee Members

Totals in Thousands of Dollars: $350, $300, $250, $200, $150, $100, $50, $0

Legend: Business, Ideology, Labor

Sectors: Banks, Food & Bevg, Health Prof, Insurance, Lawyers, Misc Manuf, Misc Transpt, Securities, Telecom, Misc Issues, Pro-Israel, Constr Unions, Govt/PO Wrk, Misc Unions, Transpt Unions

"Generic" Committees and "Specific" Committees

The format and information shown on the committee pages varies with the jurisdictional scope of the committee. Some "generic" committees (for example, the tax-writing committees or those dealing with foreign relations, veterans' affairs, or government operations) affect a broad range of industries and interest groups more or less equally. Other committees — such as Agriculture, Armed Services, or Energy and Commerce — have jurisdictions which focus on specific industries.

In generic committees, the PAC totals shown for committee members refer to the total dollars received by that member from *all* PACs. In the specific committees, the figure refers to the total received only from those PACs whose interests coincide with the committee's jurisdiction.

"Specific" committees also include one additional chart, highlighting those sectors most directly affected by the committee's actions.

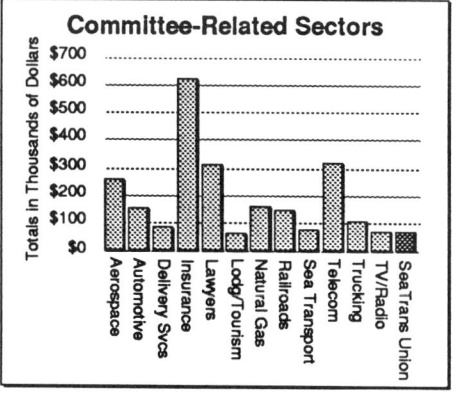

Committee-Related Sectors

Totals in Thousands of Dollars: $700, $600, $500, $400, $300, $200, $100, $0

Sectors: Aerospace, Automotive, Delivery Svcs, Insurance, Lawyers, Lodg/Tourism, Natural Gas, Railroads, Sea Transport, Telecom, Trucking, TV/Radio, SeaTrans Union

Senate Agriculture, Nutrition, and Forestry Committee

Patrick J. Leahy (D-Vt), Chairman
Richard G. Lugar (R-Ind), Ranking Republican

Party Ratio: 10 Democrats
9 Republicans

Jurisdiction: (1) Agricultural economics and research; (2) Agricultural extension services and experiment stations; (3) Agricultural production, marketing and stabilization of prices; (4) Agriculture and agricultural commodities; (5) Animal industry and diseases; (6) Crop insurance and soil conservation; (7) Farm credit and farm security; (8) Food from fresh waters; (9) Food stamp programs; (10) Forestry and forest reserves and wilderness areas other than those created from the public domain; (11) Home economics; (12) Home nutrition; (13) Inspection of livestock, meat, and agricultural products; (14) Pests and pesticides; (15) Plant industry, soils, and agricultural engineering; (16) Rural development, rural electrification, and watershed; (17) School nutrition programs. In addition, the committee is mandated to study and review matters relating to food, nutrition and hunger — both in the U.S. and in foreign countries — and rural areas, and to report on these matters periodically.

Subcommittees

Agricultural Credit
David L. Boren (D-Okla), Chairman
Rudy Boschwitz (R-Minn), Ranking Republican

Agricultural Production and Stabilization of Prices
John Melcher (D-Mont), Chairman
Jesse Helms (R-NC), Ranking Republican

Agricultural Research and General Legislation
Kent Conrad (D-ND), Chairman
Pete Wilson (R-Calif), Ranking Republican

Conservation and Forestry
Wyche Fowler Jr. (D-Ga), Chairman
Christopher (Kit) Bond (R-Mo), Ranking Republican

Domestic and Foreign Marketing and Product Promotion
David Pryor (D-Ark), Chairman
Thad Cochran (R-Miss), Ranking Republican

Nutrition and Investigations
Tom Harkin (D-Iowa), Chairman
Bob Dole (R-Neb), Ranking Republican

Rural Development and Rural Electrification
Howell T. Heflin (D-Ala), Chairman
Mitch McConnell (R-Ky), Minority Member

1987-88 Contributions to Committee Members from Committee-Related PACs

	Total from Cmte-Related PACs	Pct of Member's Total PACs
Pete Wilson (R-Calif)	$361,604	20%
Richard G. Lugar (R-Ind)	$200,530	26%
John Melcher (D-Mont)	$175,841	22%
David Karnes (R-Neb)	$172,400	19%
Bob Dole (R-Kan)[1]	$142,782	17%
Wyche Fowler Jr. (D-Ga)	$73,408	31%
John B. Breaux (D-La)	$59,808	22%
Howell Heflin (D-Ala)	$59,600	32%
Tom Harkin (D-Iowa)	$46,050	23%
Tom Daschle (D-SD)	$40,250	26%
Christopher S. Bond (R-Mo)	$39,100	29%
Kent Conrad (D-ND)	$33,755	23%
David Pryor (D-Ark)	$30,334	30%
Thad Cochran (R-Miss)	$8,700	44%
Edward Zorinsky (D-Neb)[2]	$7,647	59%
Mitch McConnell (R-Ky)	$6,750	16%
Patrick J. Leahy (D-Vt)	$4,750	63%
Rudy Boschwitz (R-Minn)	$3,550	19%
Jesse Helms (R-NC)	$2,825	32%
David L. Boren (D-Okla	$0	0%

Top 20 Committee-Related PAC Contributors to Committee Members in 1987-88

1	Chicago Board of Trade	$48,500
2	ConAgra Inc*	$46,650
3	Chicago Mercantile Exchange	$40,500
4	American Crystal Sugar Corp	$36,500
5	Archer-Daniels-Midland Corp	$35,000
6	Mid-American Dairymen	$33,200
7	ACRE (Action Cmte for Rural Electrification)*	$30,325
8	Dairymen Inc*	$29,500
9	Food Marketing Institute	$28,170
10	American Meat Institute	$27,500
11	Philip Morris	$23,980
12	National Cotton Council	$21,580
13	Dow Chemical*	$21,500
14	National Cattlemen's Assn*	$21,050
15	Associated Milk Producers	$20,500
16	FMC Corp	$19,975
17	Milk Industry Foundation	$19,500
18	American Veterinary Medical Assn	$19,000
19	American Sugar Cane League	$18,000
20	Westvaco Corp	$17,500

* Contributions came from more than one PAC affiliated with this sponsor.

Members in **boldface** ran for reelection in 1988

[1] Ran for President in 1988
[2] Died March 6, 1987

Summary

Dairy, sugar, tobacco and a variety of other agricultural subsidies and programs come under the jurisdiction of the Senate Agriculture Committee, making this panel crucially important to the nation's agriculture and food processing industries. The predominantly Republican slant of its PAC contributions in 1987-88 probably had more to do with the fact that four of the five committee members actively campaigning during that period were Republicans than with anything intrinsic to agricultural interests. Leading the list was California Republican Pete Wilson, who led all members of Congress (by a wide margin) in agriculture-related contributions.

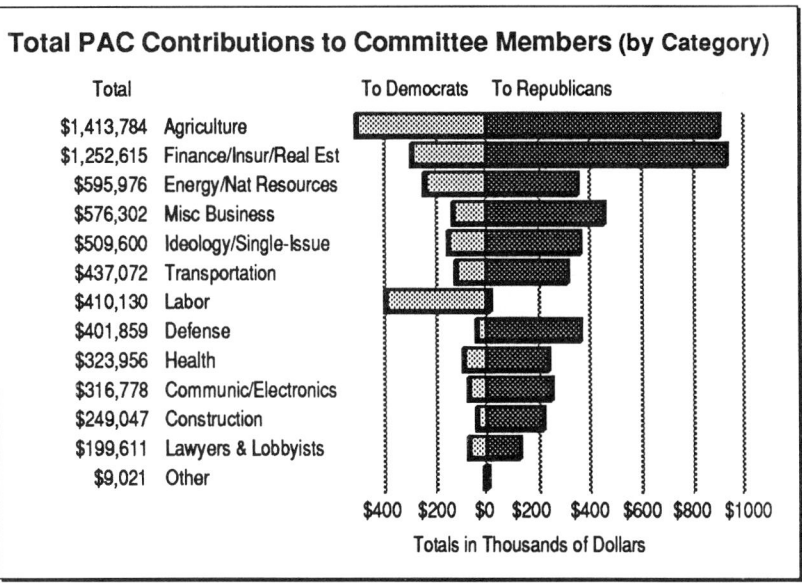

Total PAC Contributions to Committee Members (by Category)

Total	
$1,413,784	Agriculture
$1,252,615	Finance/Insur/Real Est
$595,976	Energy/Nat Resources
$576,302	Misc Business
$509,600	Ideology/Single-Issue
$437,072	Transportation
$410,130	Labor
$401,859	Defense
$323,956	Health
$316,778	Communic/Electronics
$249,047	Construction
$199,611	Lawyers & Lobbyists
$9,021	Other

Totals in Thousands of Dollars

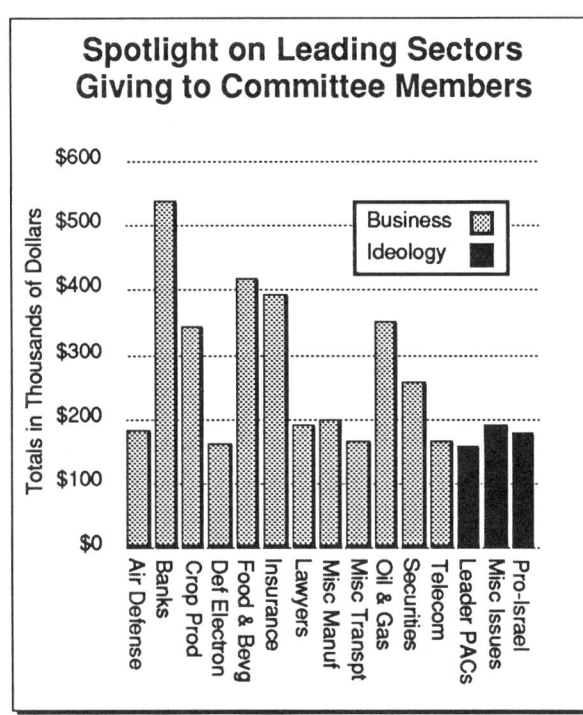

Spotlight on Leading Sectors Giving to Committee Members

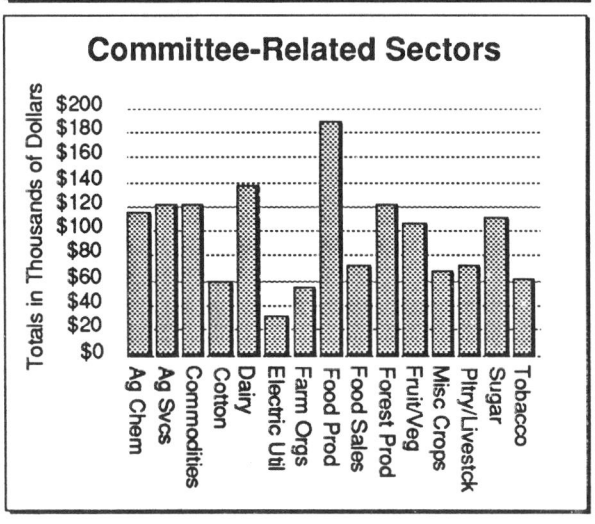

Committee-Related Sectors

Leading Committee-Related Sectors Giving to Committee Members

Agricultural Services & Supplies
- Agricultural Services $118,780
- Agricultural Chemicals $112,980

Commodities
- Commodity Trading $119,000

Crop Production
- Sugar Growers $108,584
- Fruit & Vegetable Growers $105,545
- Misc Crops $66,608
- Cotton Growers $56,680

Dairy
- Dairy Producers $133,700

Food Processing & Sales
- Food Processing $186,224
- Food Wholesale/Retail $69,470

Forestry
- Forest Products $120,518

Misc Agriculture
- Poultry & Livestock $69,300
- Farm Organizations $53,499

Tobacco Production & Marketing
- Tobacco $58,696

Other Committee-Related
- Rural Electric Utilities $29,325

Senate Appropriations Committee

John C. Stennis (D-Miss), Chairman
Mark O. Hatfield (R-Ore), Ranking Republican

Party Ratio: 16 Democrats
13 Republicans

Jurisdiction: (1) Appropriation of the revenue for the support of the Government; (2) Rescission of appropriations contained in appropriation acts; (3) The amount of new spending authority . . . which is to be effective for a fiscal year. Other committees of Congress may *authorize* the government to spend money on various projects and programs, but only the Appropriations committees of the House and Senate *appropriate* the funds.

Subcommittees

Agriculture, Rural Development, and Related Agencies
Quentin N. Burdick (D-ND), Chairman
Thad Cochran (R-Miss), Ranking Republican

Commerce, Justice, and State, The Judiciary, and Related Agencies
Ernest F. Hollings (D-SC), Chairman
Warren B. Rudman (R-NH), Ranking Republican

Defense
John C. Stennis (D-Miss), Chairman
Ted Stevens (R-Alaska), Ranking Republican

District of Columbia
Tom Harkin (D-Iowa), Chairman
Don Nickles (R-Okla), Ranking Republican

Energy and Water Development
J. Bennett Johnston (D-La), Chairman
Mark O. Hatfield (R-Ore), Ranking Republican

Foreign Operations
Daniel K. Inouye (D-Hawaii), Chairman
Robert W. Kasten, Jr. (R-Wis), Ranking Republican

HUD-Independent Agencies
William Proxmire (D-Wis), Chairman
Jake Garn (R-Utah), Ranking Republican

Interior and Related Agencies
Robert C. Byrd (D-WVa), Chairman
James A. McClure (R-Idaho), Ranking Republican

Labor, Health and Human Services, Education, and Related Agencies
Lawton Chiles (D-Fla), Chairman
Lowell P. Weicker Jr. (R-Conn), Ranking Republican

Legislative Branch
Dale Bumpers (D-Ark), Chairman
Charles E. Grassley (R-Iowa), Ranking Republican

Military Construction
Jim Sasser (D-Tenn), Chairman
Arlen Specter (R-Pa), Ranking Republican

Transportation and Related Agencies
Frank R. Lautenberg (D-NJ), Chairman
Alfonse M. D'Amato (R-NY), Ranking Republican

Treasury, Postal Service, and General Government
Dennis DeConcini (D-Ariz), Chairman
Pete V. Domenici (R-NM), Ranking Republican

1987-88 PAC Contributions to Committee Members

Frank R. Lautenberg (D-NJ) $1,403,242
Jim Sasser (D-Tenn) $1,381,554
Quentin N. Burdick (D-ND) $1,058,107
Dennis DeConcini (D-Ariz) $982,181
Lowell P. Weicker Jr. (R-Conn) $934,823
Robert C. Byrd (D-WVa) $918,764
Alfonse M. D'Amato (R-NY) $238,391
Tom Harkin (D-Iowa) $197,820
Ernest F. Hollings (D-SC) $178,750
Arlen Specter (R-Pa) $135,972
Ted Stevens (R-Alaska) $107,283
Harry Reid (D-Nev) $103,570
Mark O. Hatfield (R-Ore) $78,528
Daniel K. Inouye (D-Hawaii) $32,850
J. Bennett Johnston (D-La) $31,500

Bob Kasten (R-Wis) $24,165
Thad Cochran (R-Miss) $20,000
Charles E. Grassley (R-Iowa) $18,225
Barbara A. Mikulski (D-Md) $18,060
Don Nickles (R-Okla) $11,670
James A. McClure (R-Idaho) $7,650
Patrick J. Leahy (D-Vt) $7,538
Pete V. Domenici (R-NM) $7,300
Dale Bumpers (D-Ark) $4,950
Jake Garn (R-Utah) $2,850
John C. Stennis (D-Miss) $1,900
Warren B. Rudman (R-NH) $1,500
Lawton Chiles (D-Fla) $100
William Proxmire (D-Wis) $0

Members in **boldface** ran for reelection in 1988

Summary

The Appropriations Committee is the largest committee in the U.S. Senate; its 29 members have the job of doling out the dollars it takes to keep the government running. This makes its decisions especially important to those businesses that rely heavily on government contracts.

Pro-Israel PACs, with more than $566,000 in contributions, led all other sectors giving to the committee in 1987-88. More than half that total went to just two members — Democrats Frank Lautenberg of New Jersey and Jim Sasser of Tennessee. Lautenberg alone got $232,000 from pro-Israel PACs.

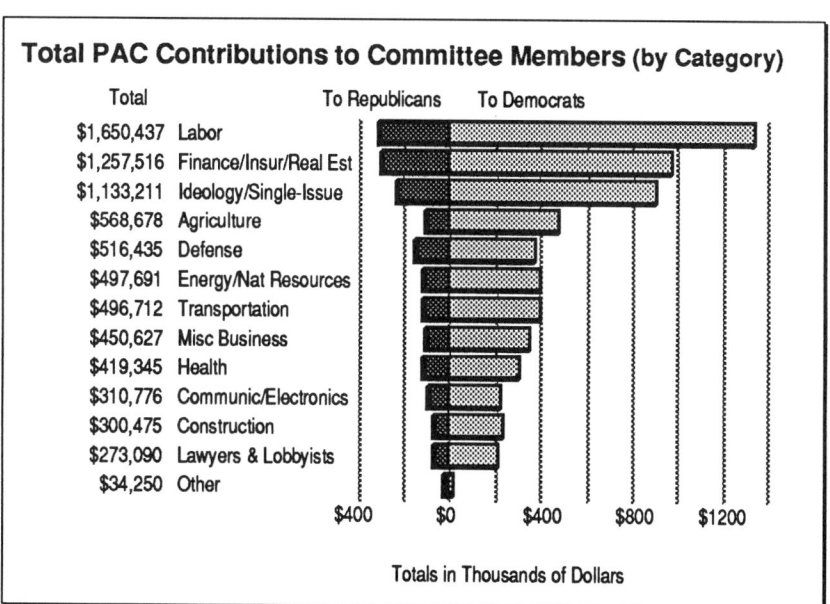

Total PAC Contributions to Committee Members (by Category)

Total	Category
$1,650,437	Labor
$1,257,516	Finance/Insur/Real Est
$1,133,211	Ideology/Single-Issue
$568,678	Agriculture
$516,435	Defense
$497,691	Energy/Nat Resources
$496,712	Transportation
$450,627	Misc Business
$419,345	Health
$310,776	Communic/Electronics
$300,475	Construction
$273,090	Lawyers & Lobbyists
$34,250	Other

Totals in Thousands of Dollars

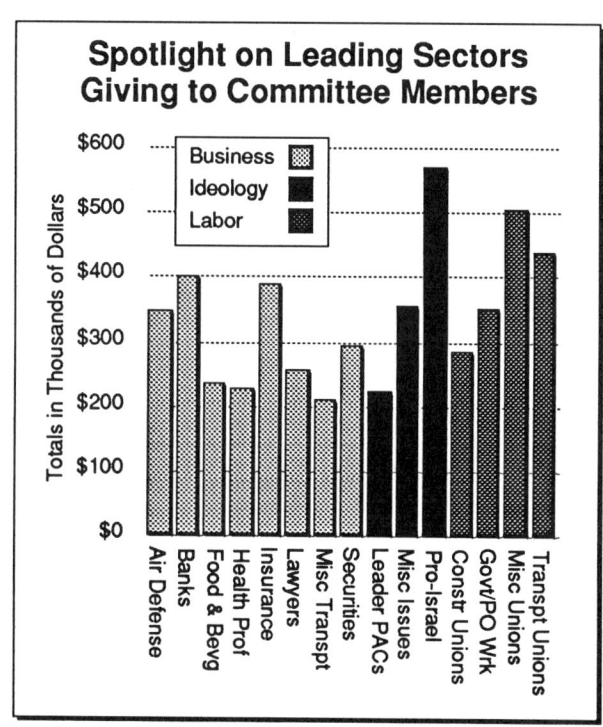

Spotlight on Leading Sectors Giving to Committee Members

Business, Ideology, Labor

Totals in Thousands of Dollars

Air Defense, Banks, Food & Bevg, Health Prof, Insurance, Lawyers, Misc Transpt, Securities, Leader PACs, Misc Issues, Pro-Israel, Constr Unions, Gov/PO Wrk, Misc Unions, Transpt Unions

Top 20 PAC Contributors to Committee Members in 1987-88

1	Assn of Trial Lawyers of America	$68,500
2	Federal Express Corp	$67,212
3	AT&T	$65,666
4	Teamsters Union*	$64,500
5	Air Line Pilots Assn	$62,500
6	National Assn of Letter Carriers	$62,000
7	American Bankers Assn*	$61,705
8	Chicago Mercantile Exchange	$61,000
9	Machinists/Aerospace Workers Union	$59,000
10	Laborers Union*	$58,500
11	AFL-CIO*	$56,050
12	National Assn of Retired Federal Employees	$55,700
13	Amer Fedn of State/County/Municipal Employees	$55,205
14	National Education Assn	$54,635
15	Marine Engineers Union*	$54,500
15	National Assn of Home Builders	$54,500
17	Carpenters Union	$52,500
18	Senate Majority Fund (Daniel Inouye)	$51,100
19	National Assn of Realtors	$49,600
20	Intl Brotherhood of Electrical Workers*	$49,000
20	United Parcel Service	$49,000

* Contributions came from more than one PAC affiliated with this sponsor.

Leading Sectors Giving to Committee Members

Business

Air Defense	$343,950
Banks	$395,327
Food & Beverage	$232,582
Health Professionals	$225,940
Insurance	$385,441
Lawyers	$254,090
Misc Transport	$208,948
Securities/Commodities Investment	$291,600

Ideological/Single-Issue

Leadership PACs	$220,408
Misc Issues	$349,653
Pro-Israel	$566,800

Labor

Construction Unions	$280,325
Govt & Postal Workers	$348,805
Misc Unions	$499,650
Transport Unions	$435,022

Senate Armed Services Committee

Sam Nunn (D-Ga), Chairman
John Warner (R-Va), Ranking Republican

Party Ratio: 11 Democrats
9 Republicans

Jurisdiction: (1) Aeronautical and space activities peculiar to or primarily associated with the development of weapons systems or military operations; (2) The common defense; (3) The Department of Defense, the Department of the Army, the Department of the Navy, and the Department of the Air Force, generally; (4) Maintenance and operation of the Panama Canal, including administration, sanitation, and government of the Canal Zone; (5) Military research and development; (6) National security aspects of nuclear energy; (7) Naval petroleum reserves, except those in Alaska; (8) Pay, promotion, retirement, and other benefits and privileges of members of the Armed Forces, including overseas education of civilian and military dependents; (9) Selective Service System; and (10) Strategic and critical materials necessary for the common defense. In addition, the committee is mandated to study and review, on a comprehensive basis, matters relating to the common defense policy of the United States and to report on them from time to time.

Subcommittees

Conventional Forces and Alliance Defense
Carl Levin (D-Mich), Chairman
Dan Quayle (R-Ind), Ranking Republican

Defense Industry and Technology
Jeff Bingaman (D-NM), Chairman
Phil Gramm (R-Texas), Ranking Republican

Manpower and Personnel
John Glenn (D-Ohio), Chairman
Pete Wilson (R-Calif), Ranking Republican

Projection Forces and Regional Defense
Edward M. Kennedy (D-Mass), Chairman
William S. Cohen (R-Maine), Ranking Republican

Readiness, Sustainability and Support
Alan J. Dixon (D-Ill), Chairman
Gordon J. Humphrey (R-NH), Ranking Republican

Strategic Forces and Nuclear Deterrence
J. James Exon (D-Neb), Chairman
Strom Thurmond (R-SC), Ranking Republican

1987-88 Contributions to Committee Members from Committee-Related PACs

	Total from Cmte-Related PACs	Pct of Member's Total PACs
Pete Wilson (R-Calif)	$244,319	13%
Jeff Bingaman (D-NM)	$127,450	12%
Phil Gramm (R-Texas)	$30,791	10%
Al Gore (D-Tenn)[1]	$29,766	5%
Alan J. Dixon (D-Ill)	$27,750	17%
Tim Wirth (D-Colo)	$27,650	19%
John Glenn (D-Ohio)[1]	$22,250	26%
Edward M. Kennedy (D-Mass)	$20,700	6%
Richard C. Shelby (D-Ala)	$17,250	8%
Strom Thurmond (R-SC)	$9,500	16%
John W. Warner (R-Va)	$7,360	42%
Steve Symms (R-Idaho)	$6,000	18%
Jim Exon (D-Neb)	$2,000	14%
Gordon J. Humphrey (R-NH)	$2,000	44%
John McCain (R-Ariz)	$1,540	6%
Dan Quayle (R-Ind)[2]	$1,000	4%
Sam Nunn (D-Ga)	$929	12%
Carl Levin (D-Mich)	$500	4%
William S. Cohen (R-Maine)	$0	0%
John C. Stennis (D-Miss)	$0	0%

Top 20 Committee-Related PAC Contributors to Committee Members in 1987-88

1	AT&T	$32,500
2	Textron Inc	$27,500
3	Ford Motor Company*	$21,200
4	LTV Aerospace & Defense	$20,500
5	Lockheed Corp	$18,500
6	General Motors*	$17,690
7	Continental Telecom	$17,000
8	McDonnell Douglas*	$16,250
9	Litton Industries	$15,500
10	General Dynamics	$15,099
11	Grumman	$14,550
12	Chrysler Corp*	$14,150
13	Allied-Signal	$13,500
14	FMC Corp	$12,575
15	Raytheon	$12,500
16	General Electric	$12,150
17	Martin Marietta Corp	$11,800
18	Northrop Corp	$11,344
19	United Technologies	$11,050
20	Computer Sciences Corp	$10,500

* Contributions came from more than one PAC affiliated with this sponsor.

Members in **boldface** ran for reelection in 1988

---

[1] Ran for President in 1988

[2] Ran for Vice President in 1988

Summary

Defense aerospace and electronics contractors were an important source of PAC dollars to the members of the Senate Armed Services Committee, but defense interests overall came in third place among the primary PAC categories giving to this committee — behind financial industry and labor PACs. This is partly due to the fact that Senators routinely sit on three or four major committees, and as many as a dozen subcommittees. This tends to spread out the spectrum of interests that contribute to their campaigns. Another reason is that only two committee members were up for reelection in 1988. Two others (John Glenn and Al Gore) were in the early race for President, but Democrats tend to draw considerably less from defense PACs than Republicans.

The presence of three major automakers on the committee's Top 20 defense-related PAC list relates less to the cars and trucks they sold to the military than to their defense-related subsidiaries. Hughes Aircraft, owned by GM, provided the bulk of that company's PAC funds, while Ford's BDM International, a defense research and development firm, gave four times as much as its parent company.

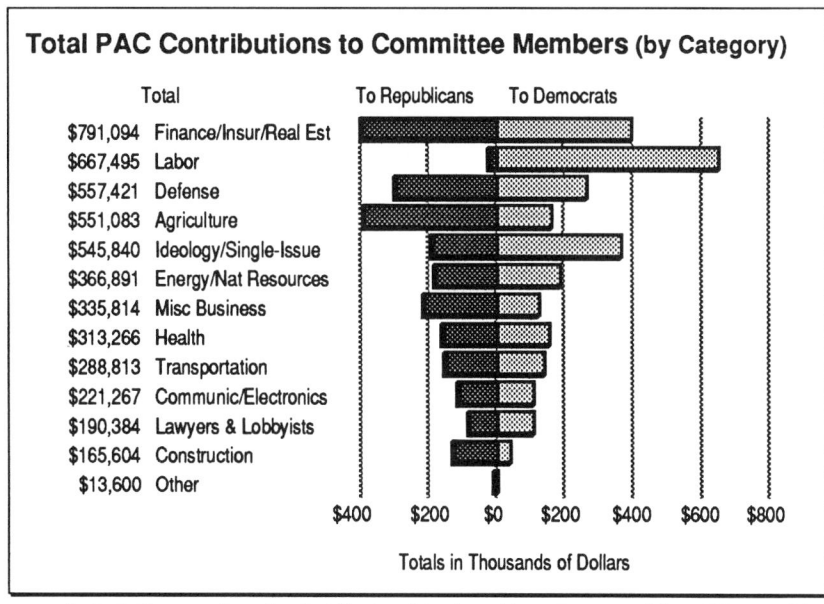

Total PAC Contributions to Committee Members (by Category)

Total		To Republicans	To Democrats
$791,094	Finance/Insur/Real Est		
$667,495	Labor		
$557,421	Defense		
$551,083	Agriculture		
$545,840	Ideology/Single-Issue		
$366,891	Energy/Nat Resources		
$335,814	Misc Business		
$313,266	Health		
$288,813	Transportation		
$221,267	Communic/Electronics		
$190,384	Lawyers & Lobbyists		
$165,604	Construction		
$13,600	Other		

Totals in Thousands of Dollars

Spotlight on Leading Sectors Giving to Committee Members

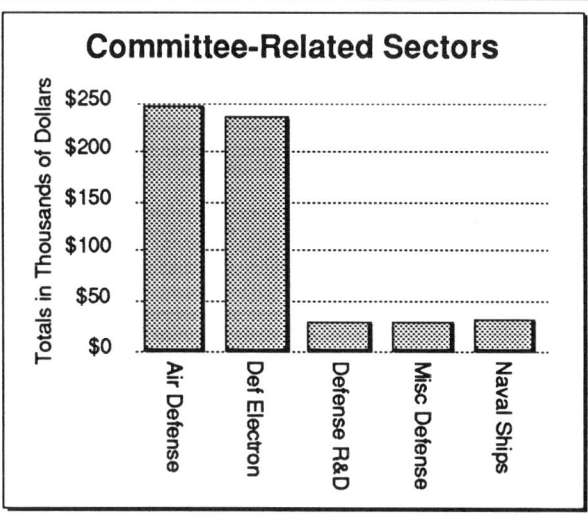

Committee-Related Sectors

Overall Leading Sectors Giving to Committee Members

Business

Air Defense	$244,012
Banks	$383,277
Crop Production	$160,089
Defense Electronics	$231,775
Food & Beverage	$195,989
Health Professionals	$137,129
Insurance	$197,588
Lawyers	$177,575
Oil & Gas	$221,416
Securities/Commodities Investment	$119,975

Ideological/Single-Issue

Misc Issues	$181,040
Pro-Israel	$253,900

Labor

Construction Unions	$123,800
Misc Unions	$229,620
Transport Unions	$161,075

Leading Committee-Related Sectors Giving to Committee Members

Air Defense	$244,012
Defense Electronics	$231,775
Defense R&D	$26,800
Misc Defense	$26,634
Naval Ships	$28,200

Senate Banking, Housing & Urban Affairs Committee

William Proxmire (D-Wis), Chairman
Jake Garn (R-Utah), Ranking Republican

Party Ratio: 11 Democrats
9 Republicans

Jurisdiction: (1) Banks, banking and financial institutions; (2) Financial aid to commerce and industry; (3) Deposit insurance; (4) Public and private housing (including veterans' housing); (5) Federal monetary policy (including Federal Reserve System); (6) Money and credit, including currency and coinage; (7) Issuance and redemption of notes; (8) Control of prices of commodities, rents, and services; (9) Urban development and urban mass transit; (10) Economic stabilization and defense production; (11) Export controls; (12) Export and foreign trade promotion; (13) Nursing home construction; (14) Renegotiation of Government contracts. In addition, the committee is mandated to study and review matters relating to international economic policy as it affects U.S. monetary affairs, credit, and financial institutions, economic growth, urban affairs, and credit, and to report on these matters periodically.

Subcommittees

Consumer Affairs
Christopher J. Dodd (D-Conn), Chairman
Phil Gramm (R-Texas), Ranking Republican

Housing and Urban Affairs
Alan Cranston (D-Calif), Chairman
Alfonse M. D'Amato (R-NY), Ranking Republican

International Finance and Monetary Policy
Paul S. Sarbanes (D-Md), Chairman
John Heinz (R- Pa), Ranking Republican

Securities
Donald W. Riegle Jr. (D-Mich), Chairman
William L. Armstrong (R-Colo), Ranking Republican

1987-88 Contributions to Committee Members from Committee-Related PACs

	Total from Cmte-Related PACs	Pct of Member's Total PACs
Donald W. Riegle Jr. (D-Mich)	$411,970	32%
John Heinz (R-Pa)	$378,115	28%
Jim Sasser (D-Tenn)	$304,790	22%
John H. Chafee (R-RI)	$290,775	28%
Terry Sanford (D-NC)	$260,349	44%
David Karnes (R-Neb)	$243,078	27%
Chick Hecht (R-Nev)	$231,090	23%
Alfonse M. D'Amato (R-NY)	$124,023	52%
Paul S. Sarbanes (D-Md)	$99,000	16%
Richard C. Shelby (D-Ala)	$91,763	43%
Phil Gramm (R-Texas)	$88,350	28%
Christopher S. Bond (R-Mo)	$53,894	40%
Alan J. Dixon (D-Ill)	$52,400	31%
Tim Wirth (D-Colo)	$45,710	31%
Alan Cranston (D-Calif)	$44,550	49%
Christopher J. Dodd (D-Conn)	$28,275	57%
Bob Graham (D-Fla)	$9,000	24%
Jake Garn (R-Utah)	$2,000	70%
William L. Armstrong (R-Colo)	$0	0%
William Proxmire (D-Wis)	$0	0%

Top 20 Committee-Related PAC Contributors to Committee Members in 1987-88

1	US League of Savings Assn*	$78,250
2	American Bankers Assn*	$68,700
3	J P Morgan & Co	$58,000
4	American Express*	$57,150
5	Citicorp	$56,249
6	Barnett Banks of Florida	$56,000
7	National Assn of Realtors	$53,674
8	National Assn of Mutual Insurance Agents	$52,500
9	Independent Insurance Agents of America	$52,148
10	American Family Corp	$51,000
11	First Boston Corp	$50,500
12	Investment Company Institute	$49,725
13	Bankers Trust	$46,500
14	National Assn of Home Builders	$43,500
15	Mortgage Bankers Assn of America	$41,500
16	Chemical Bank*	$40,600
17	Morgan Stanley & Co	$38,500
17	National Assn of Life Underwriters	$38,500
19	Credit Union National Assn*	$34,150
20	Prudential Insurance*	$33,300

* Contributions came from more than one PAC affiliated with this sponsor.

Members in **boldface** ran for reelection in 1988

Summary

The banking industry, a heavily regulated sector of American business, has become much more diversified in recent years, offering an ever-widening array of financial services. This diversification has come about as Congress (and the banking committees in particular) have gradually lifted the restrictions governing the industry. But banks are anxious for considerably more freedom — the ability to branch into stock brokerage services, for example — and the Senate Banking Committee has become one of the central battlegrounds for this ongoing debate.

The issue of bank deregulation, of course, concerns not only banks, but also their competitors — particularly major insurance companies, who have become increasingly active in the securities field. Accordingly, banking, insurance and securities companies were far and away the leading sources of PAC funds to members of the committee. Their dollars were split almost evenly between Republicans and Democrats.

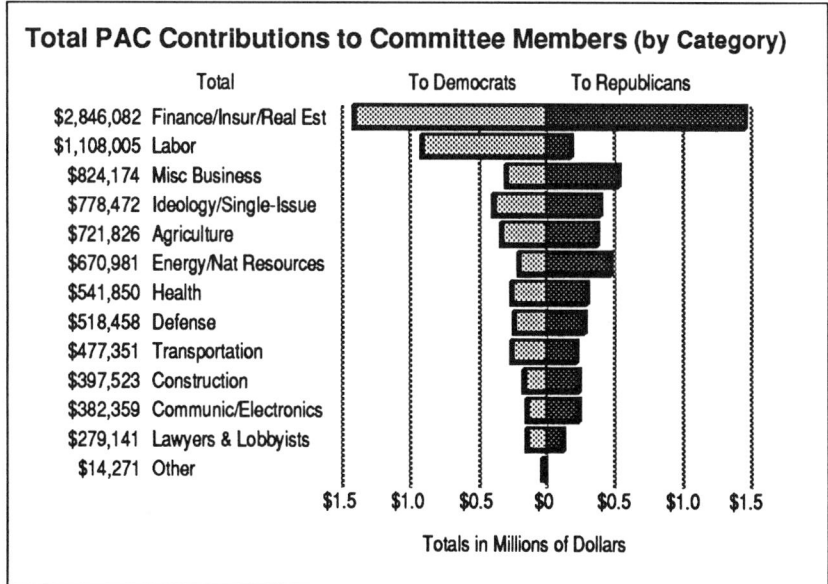

Total PAC Contributions to Committee Members (by Category)

Total	Category
$2,846,082	Finance/Insur/Real Est
$1,108,005	Labor
$824,174	Misc Business
$778,472	Ideology/Single-Issue
$721,826	Agriculture
$670,981	Energy/Nat Resources
$541,850	Health
$518,458	Defense
$477,351	Transportation
$397,523	Construction
$382,359	Communic/Electronics
$279,141	Lawyers & Lobbyists
$14,271	Other

Totals in Millions of Dollars

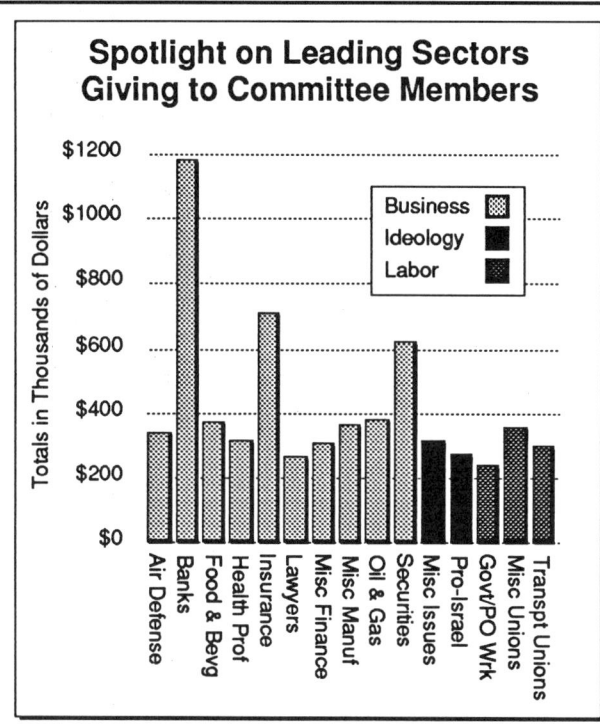

Spotlight on Leading Sectors Giving to Committee Members

Business, Ideology, Labor

Totals in Thousands of Dollars

Air Defense, Banks, Food & Bevg, Health Prof, Insurance, Lawyers, Misc Finance, Misc Manuf, Oil & Gas, Securities, Misc Issues, Pro-Israel, Govt/PO Wrk, Misc Unions, Transpt Unions

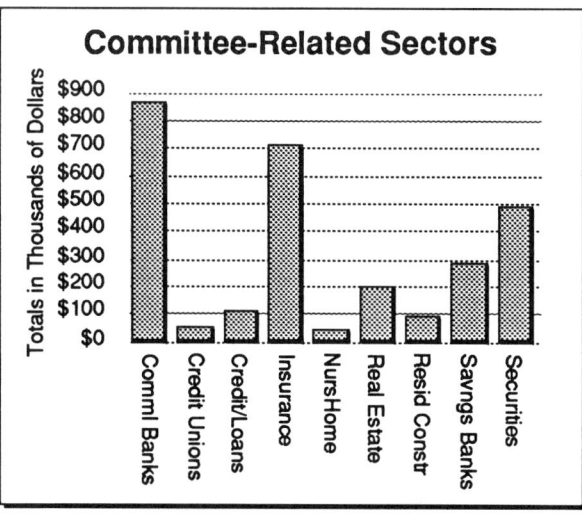

Committee-Related Sectors

Totals in Thousands of Dollars

Comml Banks, Credit Unions, Credit/Loans, Insurance, NursHome, Real Estate, Resid Constr, Savngs Banks, Securities

Overall Leading Sectors Giving to Committee Members

Business

Air Defense	$331,458
Banks	$1,168,842
Food & Beverage	$368,935
Health Professionals	$309,115
Insurance	$701,235
Lawyers	$261,891
Misc Finance	$298,271
Misc Manufacturing	$358,199
Oil & Gas	$372,227
Securities/Commodities Investment	$611,112

Ideological/Single-Issue

Misc Issues	$309,239
Pro-Israel	$265,800

Labor

Govt & Postal Workers	$232,630
Misc Unions	$347,125
Transport Unions	$290,225

Leading Committee-Related Sectors Giving to Committee Members

Banking

Commercial Banks	$855,106
Savings Banks	$272,311
Credit Unions	$41,425

Other Financial

Insurance	$701,235
Securities	$483,912
Consumer Credit/Loans	$98,821

Real Estate & Construction

Real Estate	$186,822
Residential Construction	$81,000

Other Committee-Related

Nursing Homes	$38,500

89

Senate Budget Committee

Lawton Chiles (D-Fla), Chairman
Pete V. Domenici (R-NM), Ranking Republican

Party Ratio: 13 Democrats
11 Republicans

Jurisdiction: (1) To report the matters needing to be reported by it under Titles III and IV of the Congressional Budget Act of 1974; (2) To make continuing studies of the effect on budget outlays of relevant existing and proposed legislation and to report the results of such studies to the Senate on a recurring basis; (3) To request and evaluate continuing studies of tax expenditures, to devise methods of coordinating tax expenditures, policies, and programs with direct budget outlays, and to report the results of such studies to the Senate on a recurring basis; (4) To review, on a continuing basis, the conduct by the Congressional Budget Office of its functions and duties; (5) To consider impoundment legislation required to be jointly referred to it, the Appropriations Committee, and other Senate Committees . . . and (6) To consider matters affecting the Congressional Budget process required to be referred to it and the Governmental Affairs Committee.

1987-88 PAC Contributions to Committee Members

Frank R. Lautenberg (D-NJ)	$1,403,242
Jim Sasser (D-Tenn)	$1,381,554
Donald W. Riegle Jr. (D-Mich)	$1,272,738
John C. Danforth (R-Mo)	$1,174,156
Terry Sanford (D-NC)	$588,339
Paul Simon (D-Ill)	$374,195
Wyche Fowler Jr. (D-Ga)	$233,489
Ernest F. Hollings (D-SC)	$178,750
Tim Wirth (D-Colo)	$148,811
Kent Conrad (D-ND)	$147,279
Christopher J. Dodd (D-Conn)	$50,009
Steve Symms (R-Idaho)	$33,605
J. Bennett Johnston (D-La)	$31,500
Dan Quayle (R-Ind)[1]	$25,658
Bob Kasten (R-Wis)	$24,165
Rudy Boschwitz (R-Minn)	$18,401
Charles E. Grassley (R-Iowa)	$18,225
Jim Exon (D-Neb)	$14,000
Don Nickles (R-Okla)	$11,670
Pete V. Domenici (R-NM)	$7,300
Nancy Landon Kassebaum (R-Kan)	$3,000
Warren B. Rudman (R-NH)	$1,500
William L. Armstrong (R-Colo)	$950
Lawton Chiles (D-Fla)	$100

Top 20 PAC Contributors to Committee Members in 1987-88

1	Independent Insurance Agents of America	$53,342
2	Teamsters Union	$52,900
3	Chicago Mercantile Exchange	$50,000
4	US League of Savings Assn*	$49,150
5	AFL-CIO*	$47,300
6	National Assn of Mutual Insurance Agents	$47,000
7	AT&T	$46,250
8	National Assn of Realtors	$45,025
9	Machinists/Aerospace Workers Union	$45,000
10	National Assn of Home Builders	$45,000
11	American Bankers Assn*	$44,600
12	Hudson Valley PAC	$42,500
12	United Transportation Union	$42,500
14	Air Line Pilots Assn	$39,500
15	Laborers Union*	$39,000
16	Operating Engineers Union*	$38,775
17	American Institute of CPA's	$38,500
18	Federal Express Corp	$38,400
19	American Medical Assn*	$37,759
20	Communications Workers of America	$36,000

* Contributions came from more than one PAC affiliated with this sponsor.

Members in **boldface** ran for reelection in 1988

1 Ran for Vice President in 1988

Summary

Perhaps no other document in the Western World is so important to as many people, yet understood by so few, as the federal government's annual budget. Weighty, befuddling, sometimes self-contradictory, and inevitably the subject of political wrangling and intense negotiation between the Congress and the administration, the budget is the blueprint for federal spending and federal programs for the coming fiscal year. This is the committee charged with shaping that budget into something both sides can live with.

In recent years, the budget deficit has been an ever-growing preoccupation of this committee. Finding ways to reduce it — at least on paper — has been a sometimes all-consuming task. Since federal spending — and the deficit in particular — affects the overall American economy, many industries have a more than casual interest in the committee's work. Financial interests led other PACs in 1987-88, with banks and insurance companies comprising the biggest individual sectors within the PAC community.

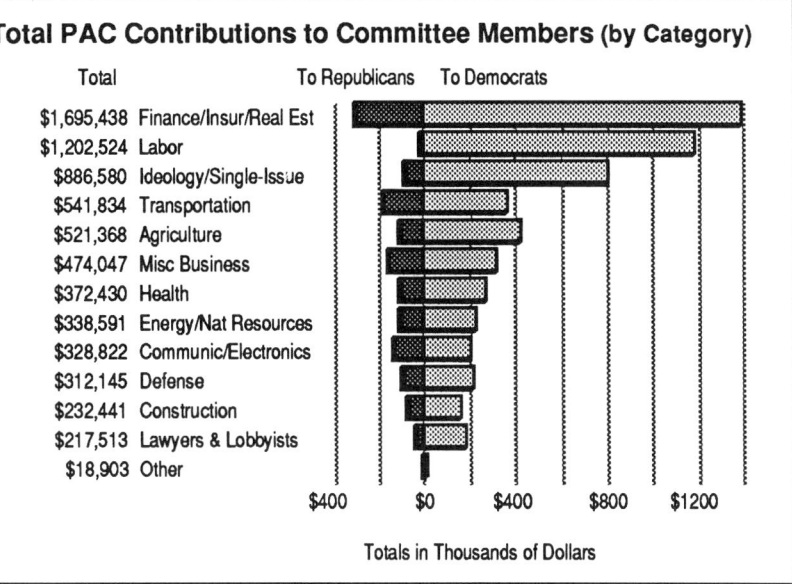

Total PAC Contributions to Committee Members (by Category)

Total	Category
$1,695,438	Finance/Insur/Real Est
$1,202,524	Labor
$886,580	Ideology/Single-Issue
$541,834	Transportation
$521,368	Agriculture
$474,047	Misc Business
$372,430	Health
$338,591	Energy/Nat Resources
$328,822	Communic/Electronics
$312,145	Defense
$232,441	Construction
$217,513	Lawyers & Lobbyists
$18,903	Other

Totals in Thousands of Dollars

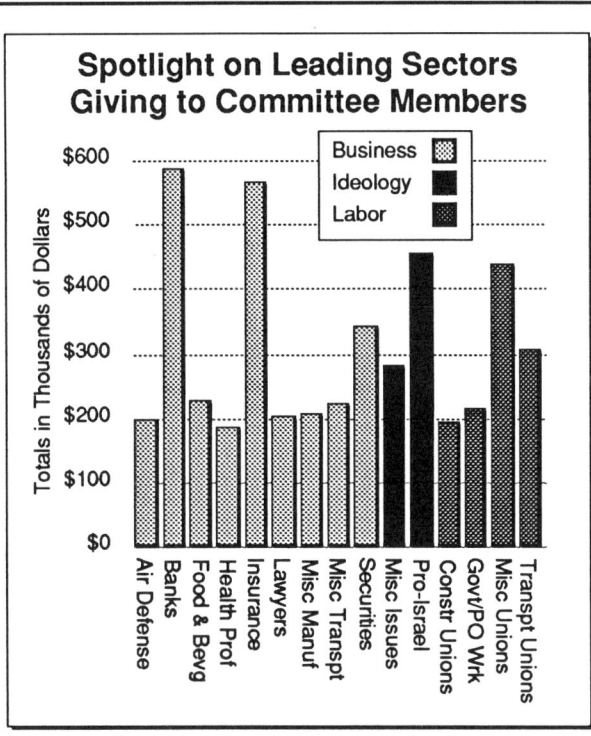

Spotlight on Leading Sectors Giving to Committee Members

Business
Ideology
Labor

Totals in Thousands of Dollars

Air Defense, Banks, Food & Bevg, Health Prof, Insurance, Lawyers, Misc Manuf, Misc Transpt, Securities, Misc Issues, Pro-Israel, Constr Unions, Govt/PO Wrk, Misc Unions, Transpt Unions

Leading Sectors
Giving to Committee Members

Business

Air Defense	$197,011
Banks	$581,060
Food & Beverage	$223,987
Health Professionals	$183,374
Insurance	$560,923
Lawyers	$199,138
Misc Manufacturing	$201,695
Misc Transport	$221,034
Securities/Commodities Investment	$339,309

Ideological/Single-Issue

Misc Issues	$277,186
Pro-Israel	$450,750

Labor

Construction Unions	$190,262
Govt & Postal Workers	$211,950
Misc Unions	$432,985
Transport Unions	$302,427

Senate Commerce, Science and Transportation Committee

Ernest F. Hollings (D-SC), Chairman
John C. Danforth (R-Mo), Ranking Republican

Party Ratio: 11 Democrats
9 Republicans

> **Jurisdiction:** (1) Interstate commerce; (2) Transportation; (3) Regulation of interstate common carriers, including railroads, buses, trucks, vessels, pipelines, and civil aviation; (4) Merchant marine and navigation; (5) Marine and ocean navigation, safety, and transportation, including navigational aspects of deepwater ports; (6) Coast Guard; (7) Inland waterways, except construction; (8) Communications; (9) Regulation of consumer products and services, including testing related to toxic substances, other than pesticides, and except for credit, financial services, and housing; (10) The Panama Canal and interoceanic canals generally, except as referred to the Committee on Armed Services; (11) Standards and measurement; (12) Highway safety; (13) Science, engineering, and technology research and development and policy; (14) Nonmilitary aeronautical and space sciences; (15) Transportation and commerce aspects of Outer Continental Shelf lands; (16) Marine fisheries; (17) Coastal Zone Management; (18) Oceans, weather, and atmospheric activities; (19) Sports. In addition, the committee is mandated to study and review all matters relating to science and technology, oceans policy, transportation, communications and consumer affairs, and to report on these matters periodically.

Subcommittees

Aviation
Wendell H. Ford (D-Ky), Chairman
Nancy Landon Kassebaum (R-Kan), Ranking Republican

Communications
Daniel K. Inouye (D-Hawaii), Chairman
Bob Packwood (R-Ore), Ranking Republican

Consumer
Albert Gore Jr. (D-Tenn), Chairman
John McCain (R-Idaho), Ranking Republican

Foreign Commerce and Tourism
John D. (Jay) Rockefeller IV (D-WVa), Chairman
Paul Trible (R-Va), Ranking Republican

Merchant Marine
John B. Breaux (D-La), Chairman
Ted Stevens (R-Alaska), Ranking Republican

Science, Technology, and Space
Donald W. Riegle Jr. (D-Mich), Chairman
Larry Pressler (R-SD), Ranking Republican

Surface Transportation
J. James Exon (D-Neb), Chairman
Robert W. Kasten Jr. (R-Wis), Ranking Republican

National Ocean Policy Study
Ernest F. Hollings (D-SC), Chairman
John C. Danforth (R-Mo), Ranking Republican

1987-88 Contributions to Committee Members from Committee-Related PACs

	Total from Cmte-Related PACs	Pct of Member's Total PACs
Lloyd Bentsen (D-Texas)[1]	$711,145	30%
John C. Danforth (R-Mo)	$407,828	35%
Pete Wilson (R-Calif)	$389,484	21%
Donald W. Riegle Jr. (D-Mich)	$336,496	26%
Al Gore (D-Tenn)[2]	$210,565	34%
Ernest F. Hollings (D-SC)	$114,750	64%
John B. Breaux (D-La)	$82,402	30%
Brock Adams (D-Wash)	$77,750	48%
Ted Stevens (R-Alaska)	$62,233	58%
Larry Pressler (R-SD)	$54,250	58%
John D. Rockefeller IV (D-WVa)	$34,666	36%
Paul S. Trible Jr. (R-Va)	$30,963	22%
Daniel K. Inouye (D-Hawaii)	$23,750	72%
John McCain (R-Ariz)	$13,040	47%
Jim Exon (D-Neb)	$11,500	82%
Bob Kasten (R-Wis)	$10,570	44%
Wendell H. Ford (D-Ky)	$3,850	36%
John Kerry (D-Mass)	$1,475	37%
Nancy Landon Kassebaum (R-Kan)	$0	0%
Bob Packwood (R-Ore)	-$1,646	35%

Members in **boldface** ran for reelection in 1988

[1] Ran simultaneously for Senate and Vice President in 1988
[2] Ran for President in 1988

Top 20 Committee-Related PAC Contributors to Committee Members in 1987-88

1	AT&T	$59,028
2	Federal Express Corp	$50,612
3	Auto Dealers & Drivers for Free Trade	$38,500
3	National Auto Dealers Assn	$38,500
5	Teamsters Union*	$37,500
5	Union Pacific Corp	$37,500
7	National Assn of Life Underwriters	$36,500
8	Marine Engineers Union*	$36,000
9	Texas Air*	$35,925
10	Air Line Pilots Assn	$33,000
11	Chrysler Corp	$32,600
12	American Family Corp	$32,000
12	National Assn of Mutual Insurance Agents	$32,000
14	American Trucking Assns	$30,220
15	United Parcel Service	$28,350
16	Pacific Telesis Group	$27,600
17	Independent Insurance Agents of America	$27,288
18	Northrop Corp	$25,440
19	Boeing Co	$25,000
20	Grumman	$24,125

* Contributions came from more than one PAC affiliated with this sponsor.

Summary

Under the wide umbrella of the Senate Commerce Committee's jurisdiction falls a variety of industries and interests ranging from cable TV operators to telephone utilities, oil companies to commercial fishermen, railroads to barge lines to interstate truckers. Disputes between competing segments within those industries ensure a perennially heavy schedule on the committee's agenda. One of the most contentious in recent years has been the battle over product liability laws, pitting lawyers on the one side against manufacturers on the other — with a host of other groups falling somewhere in between.

Banks and insurance companies were leading contributors to committee members in 1987-88. The top-spending PAC was AT&T, the nation's largest long distance telephone provider, and a key participant in telecommunications issues decided by the committee

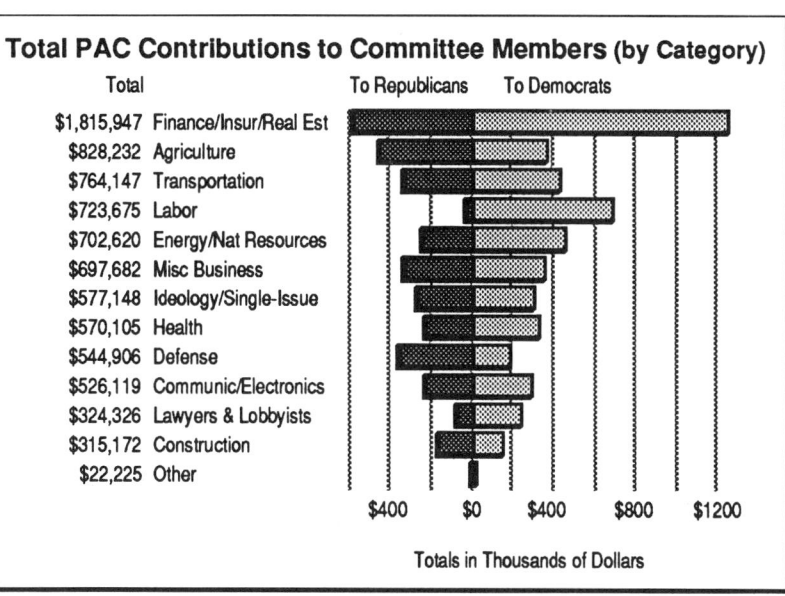

Total PAC Contributions to Committee Members (by Category)

Total		To Republicans	To Democrats
$1,815,947	Finance/Insur/Real Est		
$828,232	Agriculture		
$764,147	Transportation		
$723,675	Labor		
$702,620	Energy/Nat Resources		
$697,682	Misc Business		
$577,148	Ideology/Single-Issue		
$570,105	Health		
$544,906	Defense		
$526,119	Communic/Electronics		
$324,326	Lawyers & Lobbyists		
$315,172	Construction		
$22,225	Other		

$400 $0 $400 $800 $1200

Totals in Thousands of Dollars

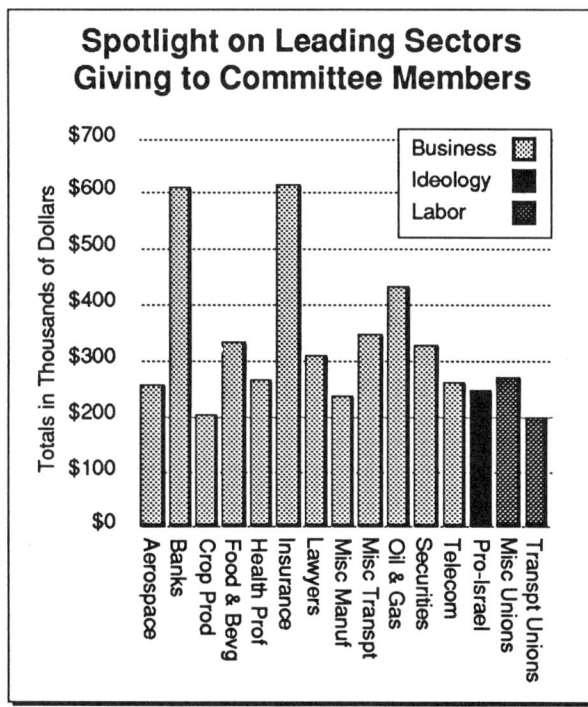

Spotlight on Leading Sectors Giving to Committee Members

Business / Ideology / Labor

Aerospace, Banks, Crop Prod, Food & Bevg, Health Prof, Insurance, Lawyers, Misc Manuf, Misc Transpt, Oil & Gas, Securities, Telecom, Pro-Israel, Misc Unions, Transpt Unions

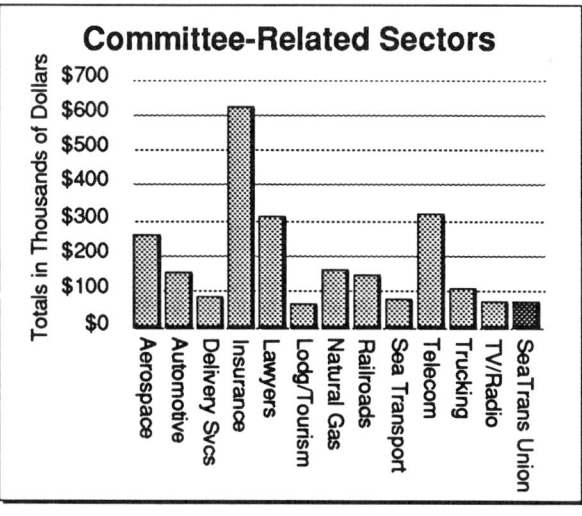

Committee-Related Sectors

Aerospace, Automotive, Delivery Svcs, Insurance, Lawyers, Lodg/Tourism, Natural Gas, Railroads, Sea Transport, Telecom, Trucking, TV/Radio, SeaTrans Union

Overall Leading Sectors Giving to Committee Members

Business

Air Defense	$252,012
Banks	$608,292
Crop Production	$198,632
Food & Beverage	$326,800
Health Professionals	$263,184
Insurance	$610,952
Lawyers	$302,267
Misc Manufacturing	$234,040
Misc Transport	$342,264
Oil & Gas	$430,346
Securities/Commodities Investment	$323,028
Telecommunications	$256,087

Ideological/Single-Issue

Pro-Israel	$242,600

Labor

Misc Unions	$266,080
Transport Unions	$196,150

Leading Committee-Related Sectors Giving to Committee Members

Transportation

Air Transport/Aerospace	$255,312
Automotive	$149,250
Railroads	$137,667
Trucking	$105,295
Delivery Services	$81,662
Sea Transport	$73,261
Sea Transport Unions	$66,150

Communications & Broadcasting

Telecommunications	$311,364
TV/Radio Broadcasting	$63,725

Other

Insurance	$610,952
Lawyers	$302,267
Natural Gas Distribution	$156,195
Lodging & Tourism	$56,100

Senate Energy and Natural Resources Committee

J. Bennett Johnston (D-La), Chairman
James A. McClure (R-Idaho), Ranking Republican

Party Ratio: 10 Democrats
9 Republicans

Jurisdiction: Oversight and legislative responsibilities, including (1) Strategic petroleum reserves; (2) Intergovernmental Relations; (3) Outer continental shelf leasing; (4) Investigation and oversight; (5) International energy affairs; (6) Natural gas pricing and regulation; (7) Utility policy; (8) Nuclear waste and insurance programs; (9) Territorial affairs, including commonwealths; (10) Free Associated States; and (11) Antarctica.

Subcommittees

Energy Regulation and Conservation
Howard M. Metzenbaum (D-Ohio), Chairman
Don Nickles (R-Okla), Ranking Republican

Energy Research and Development
Wendell H. Ford (D-Ky), Chairman
Pete V. Domenici (R-NM), Ranking Republican

Mineral Resources Development and Production
John Melcher (D-Mont), Chairman
Chic Hecht (R-Nev), Ranking Republican

Public Lands, National Parks and Forests
Dale Bumpers (D-Ark), Chairman
Malcolm Wallop (R-Wyo), Ranking Republican

Water and Power
Bill Bradley (D-NJ), Chairman
Daniel J. Evans (R- Wash), Ranking Republican

1987-88 Contributions to Committee Members from Committee-Related PACs

	Total from Cmte-Related PACs	Pct of Member's Total PACs
Malcolm Wallop (R-Wyo)	$206,877	22%
Chick Hecht (R-Nev)	$174,766	17%
Jeff Bingaman (D-NM)	$119,375	11%
John Melcher (D-Mont)	$102,219	13%
Lowell P. Weicker Jr. (R-Conn)	$49,500	5%
Wyche Fowler Jr. (D-Ga)	$28,700	12%
Tim Wirth (D-Colo)	$21,893	15%
Kent Conrad (D-ND)	$21,380	15%
Howard M. Metzenbaum (D-Ohio)	$26,041	3%
Bill Bradley (D-NJ)	$18,912	8%
J. Bennett Johnston (D-La)	$12,800	41%
Frank H. Murkowski (R-Alaska)	$10,500	19%
Mark O. Hatfield (R-Ore)	$9,500	12%
Wendell H. Ford (D-Ky)	$2,500	24%
James A. McClure (R-Idaho)	$1,500	20%
Don Nickles (R-Okla)	$1,000	8%
Dale Bumpers (D-Ark)	$0	0%
Pete V. Domenici (R-NM)	$0	0%
Daniel J. Evans (R-Wash)	$0	0%

Top 20 Committee-Related PAC Contributors to Committee Members in 1987-88

1	Amoco Corp	$35,200
2	Chevron Corp	$30,000
3	Atlantic Richfield	$27,486
4	Waste Management Inc	$26,200
5	ACRE (Action Cmte for Rural Electrification)*	$21,500
6	Southern Company*	$19,300
7	Shell Oil	$19,000
8	General Electric	$18,650
9	Coastal Corp	$17,500
10	Sierra Club	$17,343
11	Exxon Corp	$16,500
12	Mobil Oil	$16,000
13	Occidental Petroleum*	$15,250
14	Sun Company	$15,000
14	Tenneco Inc	$15,000
16	Cooper Industries	$13,750
17	Pacific Enterprises	$13,000
18	Phillips Petroleum	$12,998
19	Enserch Corp	$12,000
20	Peabody Coal	$11,250

* Contributions came from more than one PAC affiliated with this sponsor.

Members in **boldface** ran for reelection in 1988

Summary

Oil & gas policies, the interstate transportation of natural gas, the ever-deepening problem of nuclear waste disposal, and a host of other energy-related issues are the primary concern of the Senate Energy and Natural Resources Committee. Its domain, and the scope of its jurisdiction, range from oilfields on the North Slope of Alaska to the icefields of Antarctica and the oil and mineral-rich deposits beneath the seabed of the outer continental shelf.

As the world's largest consumer of energy, and one of its largest producers, the economic health of the United States has long been tied to the fortunes of the oil & gas industry — though the interests of the nation and the industry do not always coincide. Balancing those interests, and setting the nation's energy policy, is the charge of this committee.

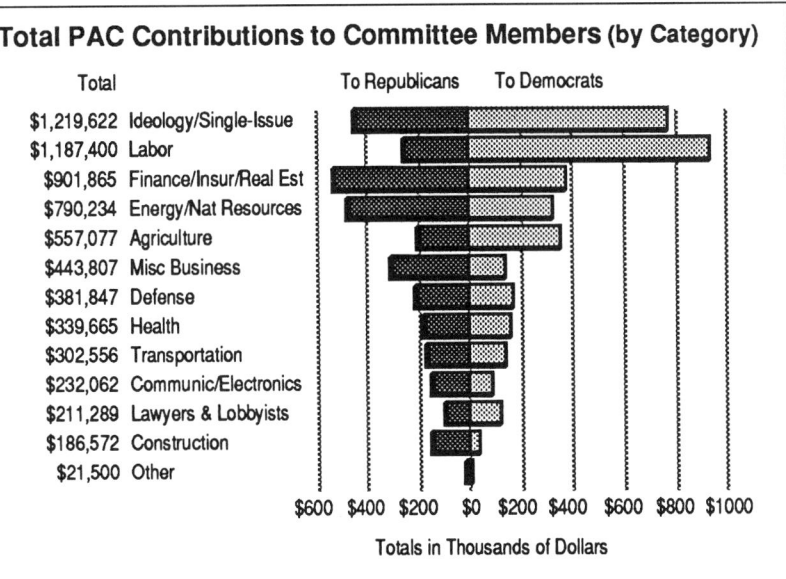

Total PAC Contributions to Committee Members (by Category)

Total		
$1,219,622	Ideology/Single-Issue	
$1,187,400	Labor	
$901,865	Finance/Insur/Real Est	
$790,234	Energy/Nat Resources	
$557,077	Agriculture	
$443,807	Misc Business	
$381,847	Defense	
$339,665	Health	
$302,556	Transportation	
$232,062	Communic/Electronics	
$211,289	Lawyers & Lobbyists	
$186,572	Construction	
$21,500	Other	

Totals in Thousands of Dollars

Oil & gas companies were by far the leading contributors to committee members in 1987-88 among businesses directly concerned with committee actions. Electric utilities, who are dependent on natural resources and whose industry is also regulated by the committee, were second on the PAC spending list, closely followed by natural gas distribution companies.

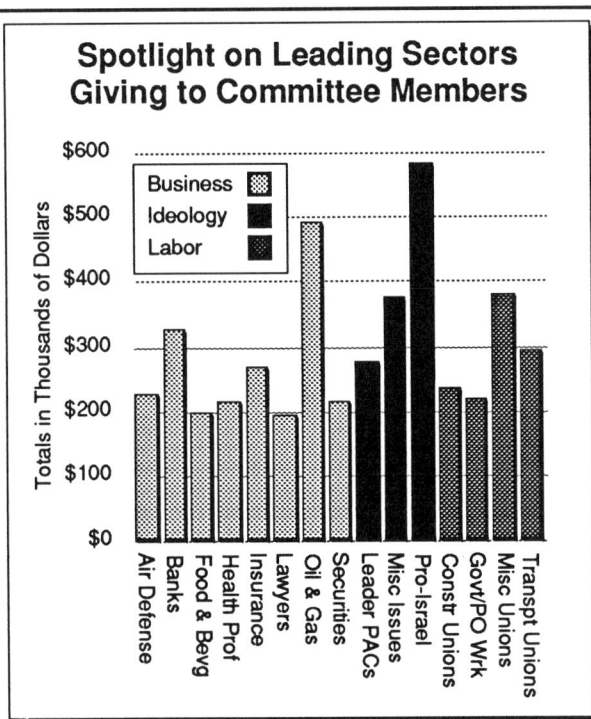

Spotlight on Leading Sectors Giving to Committee Members

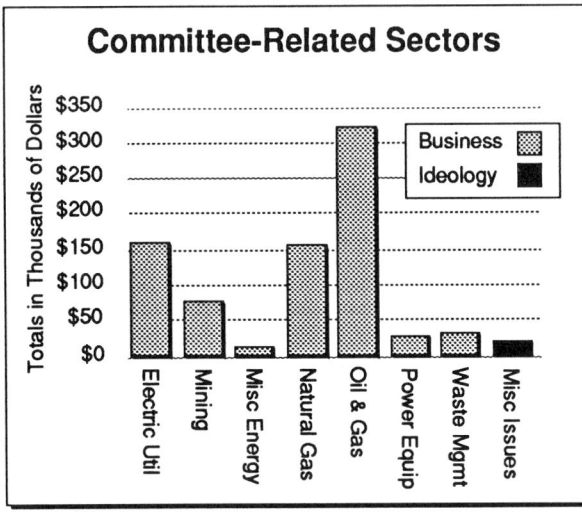

Committee-Related Sectors

Overall Leading Sectors Giving to Committee Members

Business

Air Defense	$224,746
Banks	$324,402
Food & Beverage	$195,351
Health Professionals	$213,659
Insurance	$266,863
Lawyers	$191,339
Oil & Gas	$488,408
Securities/Commodities Investment	$212,226

Ideological/Single-Issue

Leadership PACs	$271,815
Misc Issues	$373,689
Pro-Israel	$576,618

Labor

Construction Unions	$233,750
Govt & Postal Workers	$215,950
Misc Unions	$377,750
Transport Unions	$289,150

Leading Committee-Related Sectors Giving to Committee Members

Business

Electric Utilities	$154,732
Mining	$73,130
Misc Energy	$10,250
Natural Gas Distribution	$152,772
Oil & Gas	$318,136
Power Plant Equipment	$24,800
Waste Mgmt	$29,700

Ideological/Single-Issue

Environmental PACs	$17,343

Senate Environment and Public Works Committee

Quentin N. Burdick (D-ND), Chairman
Robert T. Stafford (R-Vt), Ranking Republican

Party Ratio: 9 Democrats
7 Republicans

Jurisdiction: (1) Environmental policy; (2) Environmental research and development; (3) Ocean dumping; (4) Fisheries and wildlife; (5) Environmental aspects of Outer Continental Shelf lands; (6) Solid waste disposal and recycling; (7) Environmental effects of toxic substances, other than pesticides; (8) Water resources; (9) Flood control and improvements of rivers and harbors, including environmental aspects of deepwater ports; (10) Public works, bridges, and dams; (11) Water pollution; (12) Air pollution; (13) Noise pollution; (14) Nonmilitary environmental regulation and control of nuclear energy; (15) Regional economic development; (16) Construction and maintenance of highways; (17) Public buildings and improved grounds of the United States generally, including Federal buildings in the District of Columbia. In addition, the committee is mandated to study and review matters relating to environmental protection, resource utilization and conservation, and to report on these matters periodically.

Subcommittees

Environmental Protection
George J. Mitchell (D-Maine), Chairman
John H. Chafee (R-RI), Ranking Republican

Hazardous Wastes and Toxic Substances
Max Baucus (D-Mont), Chairman
Dave Durenberger (R-Minn), Ranking Republican

Nuclear Regulation
John B. Breaux (D-La), Chairman
Alan K. Simpson (R-Wyo), Ranking Republican

Superfund and Environmental Oversight
Frank R. Lautenberg (D-NJ), Chairman
John Warner (R-Va), Ranking Republican

Water Resources, Transportation, and Infrastructure
Daniel P. Moynihan (D-NY), Chairman
Steve Symms (R-Idaho), Ranking Republican

1987-88 Contributions to Committee Members from Committee-Related PACs

	Total from Cmte-Related PACs	Pct of Member's Total PACs
Dave Durenberger (R-Minn)	$172,521	11%
Quentin N. Burdick (D-ND)	$158,550	15%
Frank Lautenberg (D-NJ)	$150,693	11%
John Chafee (R-RI)	$146,170	14%
Daniel Patrick Moynihan (D-NY)	$86,550	10%
John B. Breaux (D-La)	$48,280	18%
George Mitchell (D-Maine)	$41,500	6%
Max Baucus (D-Mont)	$22,300	8%
Larry Pressler (R-SD)	$21,500	23%
Alan K. Simpson (R-Wyo)	$16,000	16%
Harry Reid (D-Nev)	$13,770	13%
Barbara A. Mikulski (D-Md)	$5,750	32%
Steve Symms (R-Idaho)	$4,800	14%
Bob Graham (D-Fla)	$2,500	7%
John W. Warner (R-Va)	$2,000	11%
Robert T. Stafford (R-Vt)	$1,000	42%

Top 20 Committee-Related PAC Contributors to Committee Members in 1987-88

1	National Utility Contractors Assn	$45,500
2	Associated General Contractors	$44,000
3	Teamsters Union	$40,500
4	Waste Management Inc	$35,500
5	Marine Engineers Union*	$32,000
6	United Transportation Union	$27,500
7	Sierra Club	$25,619
8	American Trucking Assns	$24,698
9	Browning-Ferris Industries	$22,877
10	United Auto Workers	$22,500
11	Transport Workers Union*	$19,500
12	Seafarers International Union*	$19,400
13	Auto Dealers & Drivers for Free Trade	$18,000
14	Joseph E Seagram & Sons	$17,000
15	Chrysler Corp	$16,000
16	League of Conservation Voters	$15,319
17	Transportation Communication Union	$14,800
18	General Electric	$14,000
19	Maintenance of Way Employees	$14,000
20	ACRE (Action Cmte for Rural Electrification)*	$13,200

* Contributions came from more than one PAC affiliated with this sponsor.

Members in **boldface** ran for reelection in 1988

Summary

"Infrastructure" is not a glamorous word or a particularly inspiring political cause, but it is crucial to the health of the nation. The building and maintenance of the nation's highways, waterways and other public facilities is a central concern of this committee — and of many of the industries whose PACs supply campaign dollars to committee members.

But there is another side to development, one that often *does* inspire political action — the effect that our modern industrial infrastructure has on the environment of the planet. That too is a major preoccupation of this committee. Often, these dual responsibilities come together in a single issue, as in the continuing debate over nuclear power. Environmental groups, though not as numerous or as wealthy as industry PACs, do weigh in with PACs of their own. Both the Sierra Club and the League of Conservation Voters made the Top 20 list of committee-related PAC contributors.

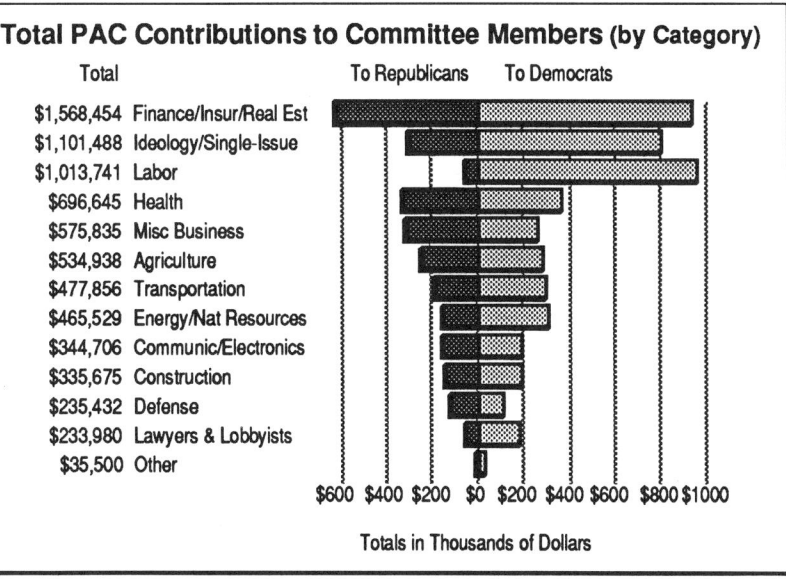

Total PAC Contributions to Committee Members (by Category)

Total	Category
$1,568,454	Finance/Insur/Real Est
$1,101,488	Ideology/Single-Issue
$1,013,741	Labor
$696,645	Health
$575,835	Misc Business
$534,938	Agriculture
$477,856	Transportation
$465,529	Energy/Nat Resources
$344,706	Communic/Electronics
$335,675	Construction
$235,432	Defense
$233,980	Lawyers & Lobbyists
$35,500	Other

Totals in Thousands of Dollars

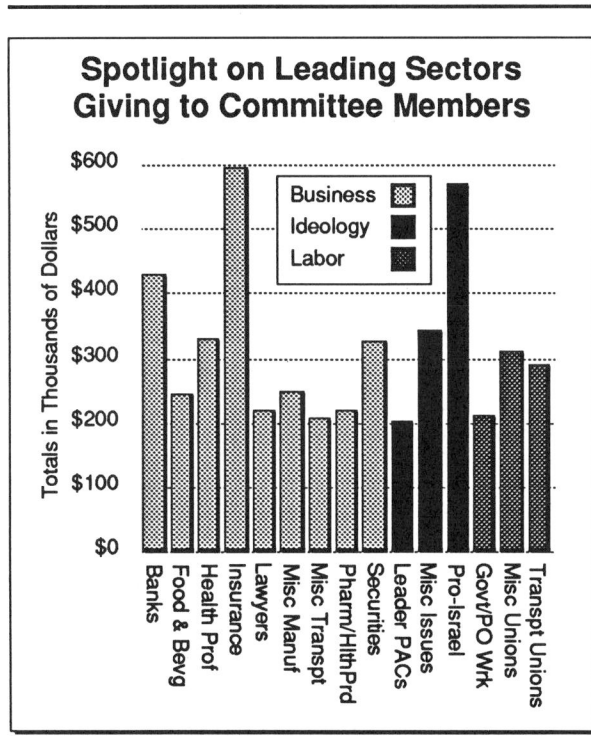

Spotlight on Leading Sectors Giving to Committee Members

Legend: Business, Ideology, Labor

Totals in Thousands of Dollars

Banks, Food & Bevg, Health Prof, Insurance, Lawyers, Misc Manuf, Misc Transpt, Pharm/HlthPrd, Securities, Leader PACs, Misc Issues, Pro-Israel, Govt/PO Wrk, Misc Unions, Transpt Unions

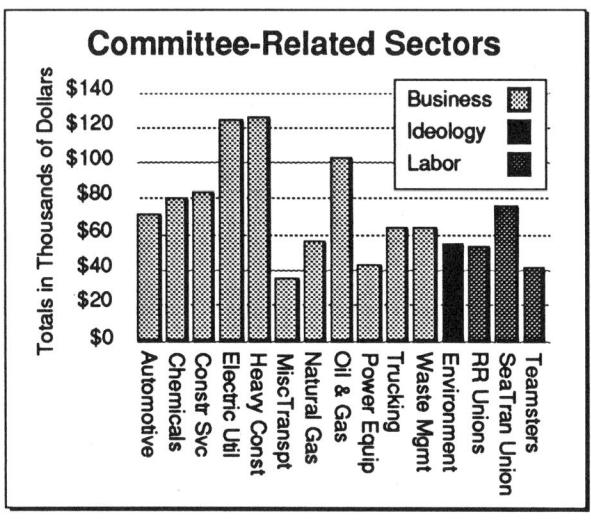

Committee-Related Sectors

Legend: Business, Ideology, Labor

Totals in Thousands of Dollars

Automotive, Chemicals, Constr Svc, Electric Util, Heavy Const, MiscTranspt, Natural Gas, Oil & Gas, Power Equip, Trucking, Waste Mgmt, Environment, RR Unions, SeaTran Union, Teamsters

Overall Leading Sectors Giving to Committee Members

Business

Banks	$424,517
Food & Beverage	$240,346
Health Professionals	$327,389
Insurance	$591,715
Lawyers	$217,280
Misc Manufacturing	$242,700
Misc Transport	$203,223
Pharmaceuticals/Health Products	$216,550
Securities/Commodities Investment	$322,767

Ideological/Single-Issue

Leadership PACs	$198,860
Misc Issues	$340,728
Pro-Israel	$565,550

Labor

Govt & Postal Workers	$206,985
Misc Unions	$305,500
Transport Unions	$285,802

Leading Committee-Related Sectors Giving to Committee Members

Business

Automotive	$69,600
Chemicals	$79,150
Construction Services	$82,400
Electric Utilities	$122,873
Heavy Construction	$124,250
Misc Transport	$34,300
Natural Gas Distribution	$55,670
Oil & Gas	$101,200
Power Plant Equipment	$41,300
Trucking	$62,673
Waste Mgmt	$63,177

Ideological/Single-Issue

Environmental PACs	$52,827

Labor

Railroad Unions	$52,250
Sea Transport Unions	$74,550
Teamsters	$40,500

Senate Finance Committee

Lloyd Bentsen (D-Tex), Chairman
Bob Packwood (R-Ore), Ranking Republican

Party Ratio: 11 Democrats
9 Republicans

Jurisdiction: (1) Except as provided in the Congressional Budget Act of 1974, revenue measures generally; (2) Except as provided in the Congressional Budget Act of 1974, the bonded debt of the United States; (3) The deposit of public moneys; (4) Customs, collection districts, and ports of entry and delivery; (5) Reciprocal trade agreements; (6) Transportation of dutiable goods; (7) Revenue measures relating to the insular possessions; (8) Tariffs and import quotas, and matters related thereto; (9) National social security; (10) General revenue sharing; (11) Health programs under the Social Security Act and health programs financed by a specific tax or trust fund.

Subcommittees

Energy and Agricultural Taxation
David L. Boren (D-Okla), Chairman
Malcolm Wallop (R-Wyo), Ranking Republican

Health
George J. Mitchell (D-Maine), Chairman
Dave Durenberger (R-Minn), Ranking Republican

International Debt
Bill Bradley (D-NJ), Chairman
William V. Roth Jr. (R-Del), Ranking Republican

International Trade
Spark M. Matsunaga (D-Hawaii), Chairman
John C. Danforth (R-Mo), Ranking Republican

Private Retirement Plans and Oversight of the Internal Revenue Service
David Pryor (D-Ark), Chairman
John Heinz (R-Pa), Minority Member

Social Security and Family Policy
Daniel P. Moynihan (D-NY), Chairman
Bob Dole (R-Kan), Ranking Republican

Taxation and Debt Management
Max Baucus (D-Mont), Chairman
John H. Chafee (R-RI), Ranking Republican

1987-88 PAC Contributions to Committee Members

Lloyd Bentsen (D-Texas)[1]	$2,342,276
Dave Durenberger (R-Minn)	$1,513,798
John Heinz (R-Pa)	$1,364,075
Donald W. Riegle Jr. (D-Mich)	$1,272,738
John C. Danforth (R-Mo)	$1,174,156
John H. Chafee (R-RI)	$1,042,170
Malcolm Wallop (R-Wyo)	$933,287
Daniel Patrick Moynihan (D-NY)	$906,891
Bob Dole (R-Kan)[2]	$838,482
William V. Roth Jr. (R-Del)	$772,046
George J. Mitchell (D-Maine)	$735,141
Spark M. Matsunaga (D-Hawaii)	$429,149
Max Baucus (D-Mont)	$277,660
Bill Bradley (D-NJ)	$231,472
Tom Daschle (D-SD)	$155,804
David Pryor (D-Ark)	$101,046
John D. Rockefeller IV (D-WVa)	$97,166
William L. Armstrong (R-Colo)	$950
David L. Boren (D-Okla)	$0
Bob Packwood (R-Ore)	-$4,646

Top 20 PAC Contributors to Committee Members in 1987-88

1	American Bankers Assn*	$107,900
2	American Express*	$105,309
3	American Institute of CPA's	$104,500
4	AT&T	$96,716
5	US League of Savings Assn*	$85,300
6	American Academy of Ophthalmology	$82,500
7	American Medical Assn*	$79,336
8	Associated General Contractors	$75,000
9	Prudential Insurance*	$72,367
10	American Dental Assn	$71,450
11	Union Pacific Corp	$69,500
12	National Assn of Realtors	$68,089
13	Independent Insurance Agents of America	$66,372
14	American Health Care Assn	$66,250
15	Metropolitan Life Insurance*	$66,199
16	Equitable Life*	$66,100
17	National Venture Capital Assn	$65,000
18	National Assn of Life Underwriters	$63,500
19	National Assn of Home Builders	$62,500
20	American Hospital Assn	$60,095

* Contributions came from more than one PAC affiliated with this group.

Members in **boldface** ran for reelection in 1988

---

[1] Ran simultaneously for Senate and Vice President in 1988
[2] Ran for President in 1988

Summary

With 11 committee members running for reelection in 1988 and a 12th — Robert Dole — running for President, it was hardly surprising that this committee drew substantially more PAC contributions in 1987-88 than any other in the Senate. But reelections were not the only reasons PACs had an interest here; Senate Finance is one of two congressional committees (House Ways and Means is the other) that debate and define the nation's tax laws.

Every industry in America — as well as every taxpayer — has a stake in decisions reached by this panel. Insurance companies and banks led the spending by PACs in 1988, a year the Congress considered, and eventually passed, a revision of the tax laws that had considerable bearing on a number of American industries.

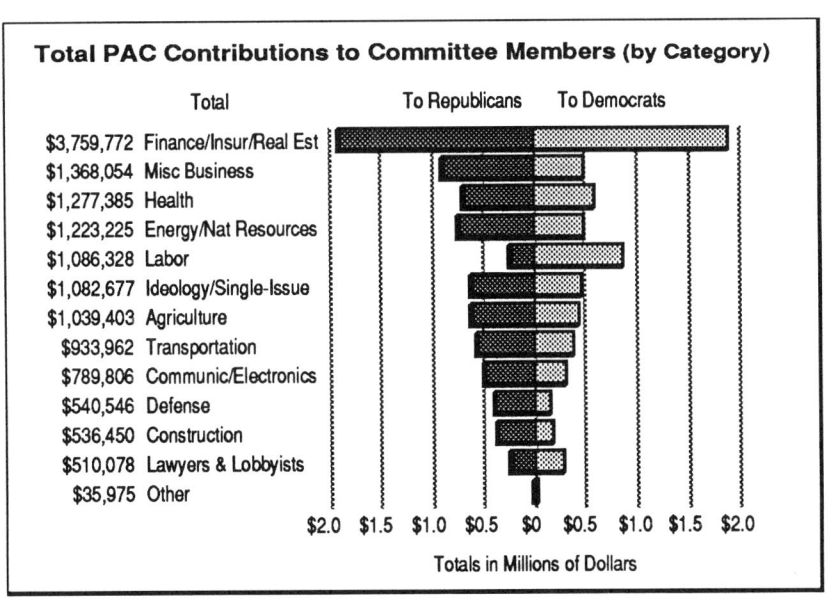

Total PAC Contributions to Committee Members (by Category)

	Total			To Republicans	To Democrats
$3,759,772	Finance/Insur/Real Est				
$1,368,054	Misc Business				
$1,277,385	Health				
$1,223,225	Energy/Nat Resources				
$1,086,328	Labor				
$1,082,677	Ideology/Single-Issue				
$1,039,403	Agriculture				
$933,962	Transportation				
$789,806	Communic/Electronics				
$540,546	Defense				
$536,450	Construction				
$510,078	Lawyers & Lobbyists				
$35,975	Other				

$2.0 $1.5 $1.0 $0.5 $0 $0.5 $1.0 $1.5 $2.0

Totals in Millions of Dollars

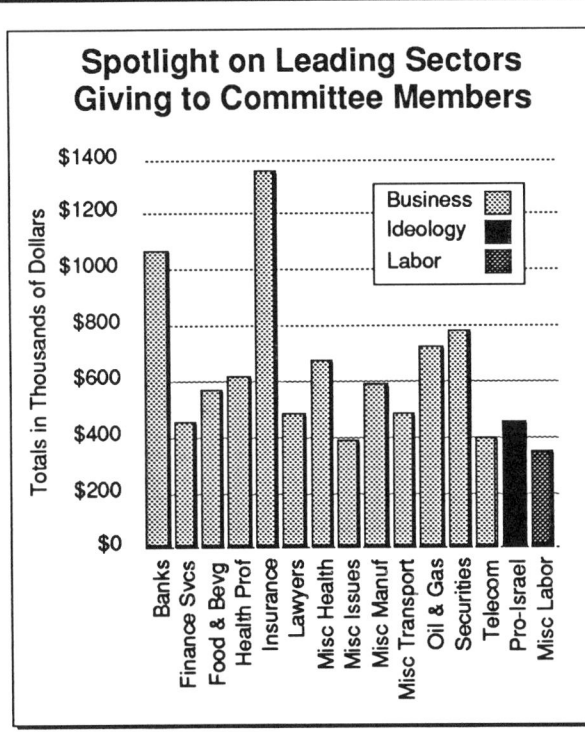

Spotlight on Leading Sectors Giving to Committee Members

Totals in Thousands of Dollars

Business, Ideology, Labor

Banks, Finance Svcs, Food & Bevg, Health Prof, Insurance, Lawyers, Misc Health, Misc Issues, Misc Manuf, Misc Transport, Oil & Gas, Securities, Telecom, Pro-Israel, Misc Labor

Leading Sectors
Giving to Committee Members

Business

Air Defense	$327,555
Banks	$1,057,039
Food & Beverage	$561,720
Health Professionals	$606,594
Insurance	$1,344,466
Lawyers	$478,678
Misc Finance	$445,836
Misc Manufacturing	$581,827
Misc Transport	$358,119
Oil & Gas	$715,739
Pharmaceuticals/Health Products	$384,285
Securities/Commodities Investment	$774,274
Telecommunications	$389,122

Ideological/Single-Issue

Misc Issues	$374,259
Pro-Israel	$446,883

Senate Foreign Relations Committee

Claiborne Pell (D-RI), Chairman
Jesse Helms (R-NC), Ranking Republican

Party Ratio: 10 Democrats
9 Republicans

Jurisdiction: (1) Relations of the United States with foreign nations generally; (2) Treaties and executive agreements, except reciprocal trade agreements; (3) Boundaries of the United States; (4) Protection of United States citizens abroad and expatriation; (5) Intervention abroad and declarations of war; (6) Foreign economic, military, technical, and humanitarian assistance;(7) United Nations and its affiliated organizations; (8) International conferences and congresses; (9) Diplomatic service; (10) International law as it relates to foreign policy; (11) Oceans and international environmental and scientific affairs as they relate to foreign policy; (12) International activities of the American National Red Cross and the International Committee of the Red Cross; (13) International aspects of nuclear energy, including nuclear transfer policy; (14) Foreign loans; (15) Measures to foster commercial intercourse with foreign nations and to safeguard American business interests abroad; (16) The World Bank group, the regional development banks, and other international organizations established primarily for development assistance purposes; (17) The International Monetary Fund and other international organizations established primarily for international monetary purposes (except that, at the request of the Committee on Banking, Housing, and Urban Affairs, any proposed legislation relating to such subjects reported by the Committee on Foreign Relations shall be referred to the Committee on Banking, Housing, and Urban Affairs); (18) Acquisition of land and buildings for embassies and legations in foreign countries; (19) National security and international aspects of trusteeships of the United States. In addition, the committee is mandated to study and review matters relating to the national security policy, foreign policy, and international economic policy as it relates to foreign policy of the U.S., and matters relating to food, hunger, and nutrition in foreign countries, and to report on these matters periodically.

Subcommittees

African Affairs
Paul Simon (D-Ill), Chairman
Nancy Landon Kassebaum (R-Kan), Minority Member

East Asian and Pacific Affairs
Alan Cranston (D-Calif), Chairman
Frank Murkowski (R-Alaska), Ranking Republican

European Affairs
Brock Adams (D-Wash), Chairman
Paul Trible (R-Va), Ranking Republican

International Economic Policy, Trade, Oceans and Environment
Terry Sanford (D-NC), Chairman
Jesse Helms (R-NC), Ranking Republican

Near Eastern and South Asian Affairs
Paul S. Sarbanes (D-Md), Chairman
Rudy Boschwitz (R-Minn), Ranking Republican

Terrorism, Narcotics and International Operations
John F. Kerry (D-Mass), Chairman
Mitch McConnell (R-Ky), Ranking Republican

Western Hemisphere and Peace Corps Affairs
Christopher J. Dodd (D-Conn), Chairman
Richard G. Lugar (R-Ind), Ranking Republican

War Powers (Special)
Joseph R. Biden Jr. (D-Del), Chairman
Larry Pressler (R-SD), Ranking Republican

1987-88 PAC Contributions to Committee Members

Daniel Patrick Moynihan (D-NY)	$906,891
Richard G. Lugar (R-Ind)	$784,528
Paul S. Sarbanes (D-Md)	$600,858
Terry Sanford (D-NC)	$588,339
Paul Simon (D-Ill)	$374,195
Brock Adams (D-Wash)	$161,631
Paul S. Trible Jr. (R-Va)	$142,983
Larry Pressler (R-SD)	$93,925
Alan Cranston (D-Calif)	$91,090
Frank H. Murkowski (R-Alaska)	$55,113
Christopher J. Dodd (D-Conn)	$50,009
Mitch McConnell (R-Ky)	$42,750
Joseph R. Biden Jr. (D-Del)[1]	$21,750
Rudy Boschwitz (R-Minn)	$18,401
Edward Zorinsky (D-Neb)[2]	$12,897
Jesse Helms (R-NC)	$8,735
John Kerry (D-Mass)	$4,012
Nancy Landon Kassebaum (R-Kan)	$3,000
Claiborne Pell (D-RI)	$1,800
Daniel J. Evans (R-Wash)	$1,725

Members in **boldface** ran for reelection in 1988

[1] Ran for President in 1988
[2] Died March 6, 1987

Top 20 PAC Contributors to Committee Members in 1987-88

1	National Assn of Realtors	$41,450
2	Teamsters Union	$37,900
3	National Assn of Home Builders	$34,500
4	National Assn of Letter Carriers	$33,500
5	AT&T	$31,862
6	American Institute of CPA's	$30,000
6	American Bankers Assn*	$30,000
8	AFL-CIO*	$29,954
9	US League of Savings Assn*	$29,650
10	American Medical Assn*	$29,000
11	Morgan Stanley & Co*	$28,600
12	United Transportation Union	$28,500
13	Intl Brotherhood of Electrical Workers*	$28,360
14	American Express*	$28,026
15	Machinists/Aerospace Workers Union	$28,000
16	National PAC	$27,500
17	National Assn of Mutual Insurance Agents	$27,000
18	Marine Engineers Union*	$26,000
19	United Steelworkers	$25,000
19	Washington PAC	$25,000

* Contributions came from more than one PAC affiliated with this sponsor.

Summary

Senate Foreign Relations is one committee in Congress that may be more important to the world community at large than to the PAC community at home. Since foreign nations and corporations based overseas are prohibited from making financial contributions to U.S. candidates, they must use other means than PACs to make their voices heard when the committee debates such issues as the level and focus of American foreign aid.

Of course, there are plenty of opinions within this country as to the direction of the nation's foreign policy. Correspondingly, there are many different PACs giving voice to those concerns through political contributions. Pro-Israel PACs are by far the biggest segment of this particular PAC community, but there are many others — from those seeking to oust Fidel Castro in Cuba to those seeking independence of the Baltic Republics or an end to persecution of Armenians. With the exception of the Pro-Israel PACs, and a handful of others, most are small both in size and dollars.

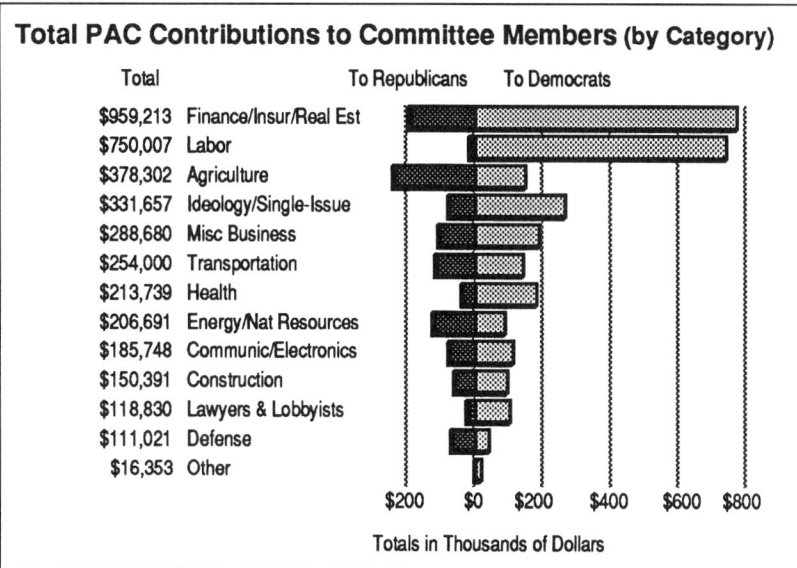

Total PAC Contributions to Committee Members (by Category)

Total	Category
$959,213	Finance/Insur/Real Est
$750,007	Labor
$378,302	Agriculture
$331,657	Ideology/Single-Issue
$288,680	Misc Business
$254,000	Transportation
$213,739	Health
$206,691	Energy/Nat Resources
$185,748	Communic/Electronics
$150,391	Construction
$118,830	Lawyers & Lobbyists
$111,021	Defense
$16,353	Other

Totals in Thousands of Dollars

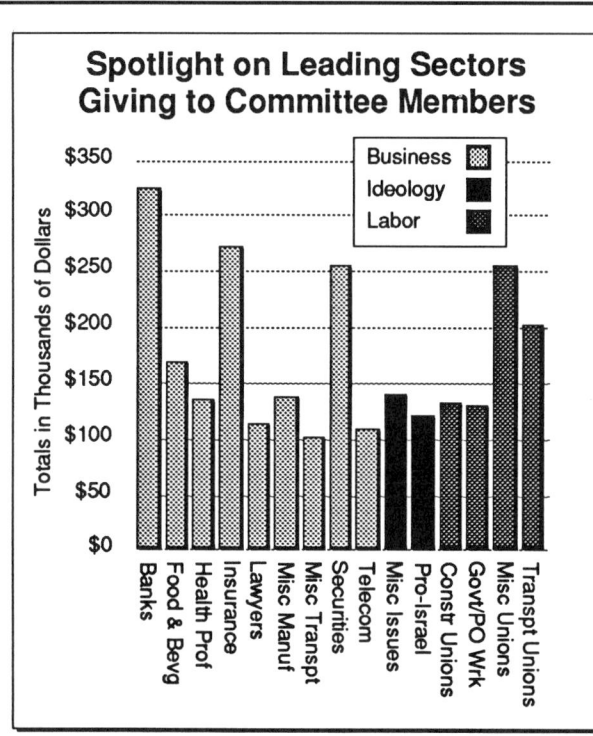

Spotlight on Leading Sectors Giving to Committee Members

Business / Ideology / Labor

Leading Sectors
Giving to Committee Members

Business

Banks	$321,800
Food & Beverage	$166,966
Health Professionals	$131,905
Insurance	$270,601
Lawyers	$110,955
Misc Manufacturing	$135,141
Misc Transport	$98,517
Securities/Commodities Investment	$254,287
Telecommunications	$106,112

Ideological/Single-Issue

Misc Issues	$137,786
Pro-Israel	$119,350

Labor

Construction Unions	$130,966
Govt & Postal Workers	$127,750
Misc Unions	$253,116
Transport Unions	$201,175

Senate Governmental Affairs Committee

John Glenn (D-Ohio), Chairman
William V. Roth Jr. (R-Del), Ranking Republican

Party Ratio: 8 Democrats
6 Republicans

Jurisdiction: (1) Except as provided in the Congressional Budget Act of 1974, budget and accounting measures, other than appropriations; (2) Organization and reorganization of the executive branch of the Government; (3) Intergovernmental relations; (4) Government information; (5) Municipal affairs of the District of Columbia, except appropriations therefor; (6) Federal Civil Service; (7) Status of officers and employees of the United States, including their classification, compensation, and benefits; (8) Postal Service; (9) Census and collection of statistics, including economic and social statistics; (10) Archives of the United States; (11) Organization and management of United States nuclear export policy; (12) Congressional organization, except for any part of the matter that amends the rules or orders of the Senate. In addition, the committee is mandated to (a) receive and examine reports of the U.S. Comptroller General and submit to the Senate recommendations relating thereto; (b) study the efficiency, economy, and effectiveness of the Government's agencies and departments; (c) evaluate the effects of laws enacted to reorganize the legislative and executive branches of the Government; (d) study the intergovernmental relationships between the U.S. and the states and municipalities, and between the U.S. and international organizations of which the U.S. is a member.

Subcommittees

Federal Services, Post Office, and Civil Service
David Pryor (D-Ark), Chairman
Ted Stevens (R-Alaska), Ranking Republican

Federal Spending, Budget, and Accounting
Lawton Chiles (D-Fla), Chairman
Warren B. Rudman (R-NH), Ranking Republican

Governmental Efficiency, Federalism, and the District of Columbia
Jim Sasser (D-Tenn), Chairman
John Heinz (R-Pa), Ranking Republican

Oversight of Government Management
Carl Levin (D-Mich), Chairman
William S. Cohen (R-Maine), Ranking Republican

Permanent Subcommittee on Investigations
Sam Nunn (D-Ga), Chairman
William V. Roth Jr. (R-Del), Ranking Republican

1987-88 PAC Contributions to Committee Members

Jim Sasser (D-Tenn)	$1,381,554
John Heinz (R-Pa)	$1,364,075
Jeff Bingaman (D-NM)	$1,086,814
William V. Roth Jr. (R-Del)	$772,046
George J. Mitchell (D-Maine)	$735,141
Paul S. Trible Jr. (R-Va)	$142,983
Ted Stevens (R-Alaska)	$107,283
David Pryor (D-Ark)	$101,046
John Glenn (D-Ohio)[1]	$85,881
Carl Levin (D-Mich)	$13,305
Sam Nunn (D-Ga)	$7,759
William S. Cohen (R-Maine)	$2,000
Warren B. Rudman (R-NH)	$1,500
Lawton Chiles (D-Fla)	$100

Top 20 PAC Contributors to Committee Members in 1987-88

1	American Institute of CPA's	$45,500
2	AT&T	$42,762
3	American Bankers Assn*	$41,500
4	Desert Caucus	$41,000
5	Assn of Trial Lawyers of America	$39,500
6	National Assn of Letter Carriers	$37,000
6	National Assn of Retired Federal Employees	$37,000
8	National Auto Dealers Assn	$36,500
9	National Assn of Life Underwriters	$35,500
10	American Medical Assn*	$35,350
11	National Assn of Home Builders	$35,000
12	American Dental Assn	$34,800
13	American Academy of Ophthalmology	$34,500
14	Federal Express Corp	$33,112
15	Independent Insurance Agents of America	$32,732
16	AFL-CIO*	$32,550
17	American Postal Workers Union	$32,000
17	National Assn of Mutual Insurance Agents	$32,000
19	American Express*	$31,500
20	Marine Engineers Union*	$31,500
20	National Assn of Realtors	$31,500

* Contributions came from more than one PAC affiliated with this sponsor.

Members in **boldface** ran for reelection in 1988

1 Ran for President in 1988

Summary

Other committees of Congress have more direct relevance to particular industries or interest groups than Senate Governmental Affairs, which focuses more on the government itself. The federal civil service and postal system fall within its purview, as does reorganization of executive branch agencies. Affairs relating to the District of Columbia are also debated here.

Postal and government employee union PACs gave a combined $242,000 to members of this committee during the 1987-88 election cycle.

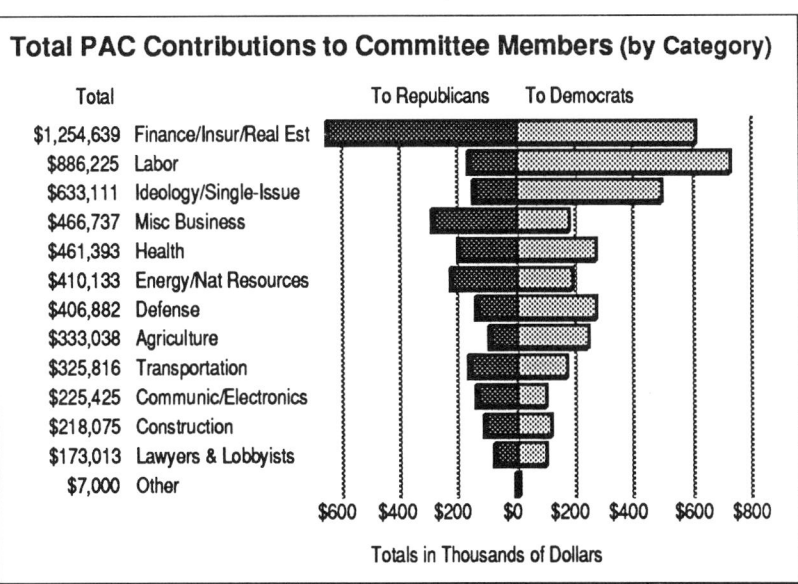

Total PAC Contributions to Committee Members (by Category)

Total		To Republicans To Democrats
$1,254,639	Finance/Insur/Real Est	
$886,225	Labor	
$633,111	Ideology/Single-Issue	
$466,737	Misc Business	
$461,393	Health	
$410,133	Energy/Nat Resources	
$406,882	Defense	
$333,038	Agriculture	
$325,816	Transportation	
$225,425	Communic/Electronics	
$218,075	Construction	
$173,013	Lawyers & Lobbyists	
$7,000	Other	

$600 $400 $200 $0 $200 $400 $600 $800

Totals in Thousands of Dollars

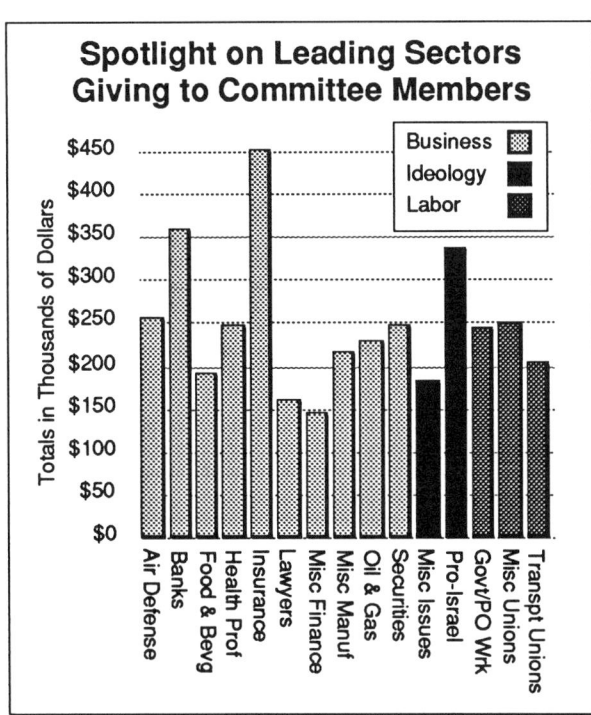

Spotlight on Leading Sectors Giving to Committee Members

Legend: Business, Ideology, Labor

Totals in Thousands of Dollars — $0 to $450

Categories: Air Defense, Banks, Food & Bevg, Health Prof, Insurance, Lawyers, Misc Finance, Misc Manuf, Oil & Gas, Securities, Misc Issues, Pro-Israel, Govt/PO Wrk, Misc Unions, Transpt Unions

Leading Sectors
Giving to Committee Members

Business

Air Defense	$255,406
Banks	$355,411
Food & Beverage	$188,877
Health Professionals	$243,924
Insurance	$447,673
Lawyers	$158,763
Misc Finance	$143,515
Misc Manufacturing	$215,424
Oil & Gas	$227,885
Securities/Commodities Investment	$244,540

Ideological/Single-Issue

Misc Issues	$180,167
Pro-Israel	$335,450

Labor

Govt & Postal Workers	$242,700
Misc Unions	$249,100
Transport Unions	$202,450

Senate Judiciary Committee

Joseph R. Biden, Jr. (D-Del), Chairman
Strom Thurmond (R-SC), Ranking Republican

Party Ratio: 8 Democrats
6 Republicans

> **Jurisdiction:** All areas not delegated to the subcommittees, including but not limited to: (1) Nominations; (2) Holidays, commemorations, Federal charters and celebrations; (3) Department of Justice oversight, authorization and budget; (4) Revision and codification of the statutes of the United States; (5) Criminal justice, including (a) criminal laws, (b) criminal judicial proceedings, (c) Rules of Criminal Procedure, (d) national penitentiaries, (e) Bureau of Prisons, (f) U.S. Parole Commission, (g) oversight of the Criminal Division of the U.S. Department of Justice, (h) juvenile justice, (i) Youthful Offenders Act, (j) oversight of the Office of Justice Programs. (Excluded from (5) above is criminal legislation delegated to the Subcommittee on the Constitution.)

Subcommittees

Antitrust, Monopolies and Business Rights
Howard M. Metzenbaum (D-Ohio), Chairman
Strom Thurmond (R-SC), Ranking Republican

Constitution
Paul Simon (D-Ill), Chairman
Arlen Specter (R-Pa), Ranking Republican

Courts and Administrative Practice
Howell T. Heflin (D-Ala), Chairman
Charles E. Grassley (R-Iowa), Ranking Republican

Immigration and Refugee Affairs
Edward M. Kennedy (D-Mass), Chairman
Alan K. Simpson (R-Wyo), Minority Member

Patents, Copyrights and Trademarks
Dennis DeConcini (D-Ariz), Chairman
Orrin G. Hatch (R-Utah), Ranking Republican

Technology and the Law
Patrick J. Leahy (D-Vt), Chairman
Gordon J. Humphrey (R-NH), Minority Member

1987-88 PAC Contributions to Committee Members

Orrin G. Hatch (R-Utah) $1,151,218
Howard M. Metzenbaum (D-Ohio) $1,025,894
Dennis DeConcini (D-Ariz) $982,181
Robert C. Byrd (D-WVa) $918,764
Paul Simon (D-Ill) $374,195
Edward M. Kennedy (D-Mass) $330,591
Howell Heflin (D-Ala) $185,200
Arlen Specter (R-Pa) $135,972
Alan K. Simpson (R-Wyo) $100,925
Strom Thurmond (R-SC) $59,000
Joseph R. Biden Jr. (D-Del)[1] $21,750
Charles E. Grassley (R-Iowa) $18,225
Patrick J. Leahy (D-Vt) $7,538
Gordon J. Humphrey (R-NH) $4,500

Top 20 PAC Contributors to Committee Members in 1987-88

1	AT&T	$52,816
2	Teamsters Union*	$47,600
3	United Transportation Union	$45,000
4	Federal Express Corp	$43,900
5	Laborers Union*	$41,000
6	Machinists/Aerospace Workers Union	$40,000
6	Senate Majority Fund (Daniel Inouye)	$40,000
8	Intl Brotherhood of Electrical Workers*	$36,860
9	National Beer Wholesalers Assn	$35,750
10	National Assn of Letter Carriers	$35,500
11	Carpenters Union*	$34,662
12	Operating Engineers Union*	$34,650
13	Chicago Mercantile Exchange	$34,000
14	AFL-CIO	$33,800
15	Ladies Garment Workers Union	$33,500
16	American Institute of CPA's	$33,000
17	Associated General Contractors	$32,250
18	Occidental Petroleum*	$32,100
19	American Postal Workers Union	$32,000
19	Chicago Board of Trade	$32,000

* Contributions came from more than one PAC affiliated with this sponsor.

Members in **boldface** ran for reelection in 1988

1 Ran for President in 1988

Summary

Besides overseeing the nation's criminal justice system, the Senate Judiciary Committee plays a crucial role in shaping the laws that regulate American business. From antitrust legislation to decisions over copyrights and patents, to new areas of the law arising from the birth of new high-tech industries, the committee plays a major role in defining the system of laws that governs the nation. Its jurisdiction over immigration matters also has important repercussions to those segments of the business community that rely on immigrant labor.

While all these issues make the Judiciary Committee important to American industry, it is perhaps better known by the public at large as the committee in Congress which holds hearings and makes recommendations on presidential nominations of cabinet officers, members of the Supreme Court, and other top government officials.

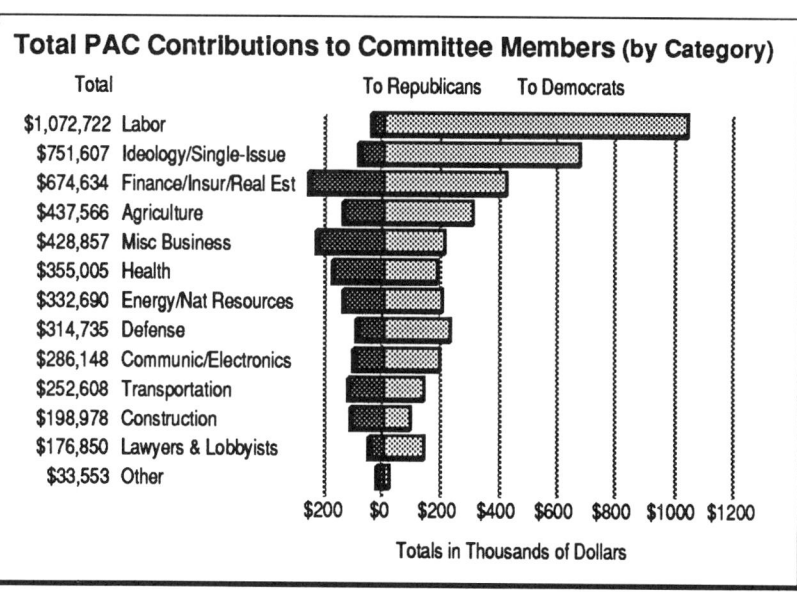

Total PAC Contributions to Committee Members (by Category)

Total	Category
$1,072,722	Labor
$751,607	Ideology/Single-Issue
$674,634	Finance/Insur/Real Est
$437,566	Agriculture
$428,857	Misc Business
$355,005	Health
$332,690	Energy/Nat Resources
$314,735	Defense
$286,148	Communic/Electronics
$252,608	Transportation
$198,978	Construction
$176,850	Lawyers & Lobbyists
$33,553	Other

Totals in Thousands of Dollars

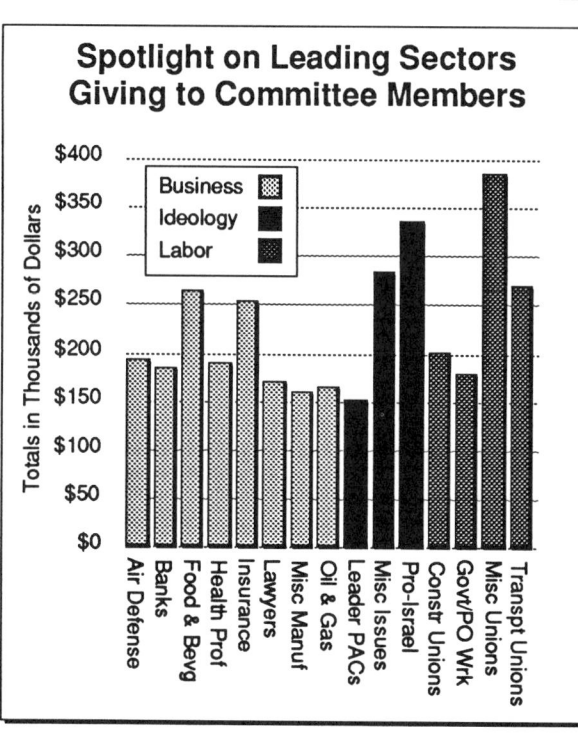

Spotlight on Leading Sectors Giving to Committee Members

Leading Sectors Giving to Committee Members

Business

Air Defense	$189,800
Banks	$182,462
Food & Beverage	$261,571
Health Professionals	$186,750
Insurance	$249,913
Lawyers	$167,975
Misc Manufacturing	$157,390
Oil & Gas	$163,955

Ideological/Single-Issue

Leadership PACs	$148,666
Misc Issues	$280,356
Pro-Israel	$331,835

Labor

Construction Unions	$199,362
Govt & Postal Workers	$176,050
Misc Unions	$383,185
Transport Unions	$266,625

Senate Labor and Human Resources Committee

Edward M. Kennedy (D-Mass), Chairman
Orrin G. Hatch (R-Utah), Ranking Republican

Party Ratio: 9 Democrats
7 Republicans

Jurisdiction: (1) Education, labor, health and public welfare; (2) Labor standards and labor statistics; (3) Wages and hours of labor; (4) Child labor; (5) Mediation and arbitration of labor disputes; (6) Convict labor and the entry of goods made by convicts into interstate commerce; (7) Regulation of foreign laborers; (8) Handicapped individuals; (9) Equal employment opportunity; (10) Occupational safety and health, including the welfare of miners; (11) Private pension plans; (12) Aging; (13) Railway labor and retirement; (14) Public health; (15) Arts and humanities; (16) Gallaudet College, Howard University, and Saint Elizabeths Hospital; (17) Biomedical research and development; (18) Student loans; (19) Agricultural colleges; (20) Domestic activities of the American Red Cross. The committee is also mandated to study and review matters relating to health, education and training, and public welfare, and to report thereon from time to time.

Subcommittees

Aging
Spark M. Matsunaga (D-Hawaii), Chairman
Thad Cochran (R-Miss), Ranking Republican

Children, Family, Drugs and Alcoholism
Christopher J. Dodd (D-Conn), Chairman
Strom Thurmond (R-SC), Ranking Republican

Education, Arts and Humanities
Claiborne Pell (D-RI), Chairman
Robert T. Stafford (R-Vt), Ranking Republican

Employment and Productivity
Paul Simon (D-Ill), Chairman
Gordon J. Humphrey (R-NH), Ranking Republican

Handicapped
Tom Harkin (D-Iowa), Chairman
Lowell P. Weicker Jr. (R-Conn), Ranking Republican

Labor
Howard M. Metzenbaum (D-Ohio), Chairman
Dan Quayle (R-Ind), Ranking Republican

1987-88 PAC Contributions to Committee Members

Orrin G. Hatch (R-Utah)	$1,151,218
Howard M. Metzenbaum (D-Ohio)	$1,025,894
Lowell P. Weicker Jr. (R-Conn)	$934,823
Spark M. Matsunaga (D-Hawaii)	$429,149
Paul Simon (D-Ill)	$374,195
Edward M. Kennedy (D-Mass)	$330,591
Tom Harkin (D-Iowa)	$197,820
Brock Adams (D-Wash)	$161,631
Strom Thurmond (R-SC)	$59,000
Christopher J. Dodd (D-Conn)	$50,009
Dan Quayle (R-Ind)[1]	$25,658
Thad Cochran (R-Miss)	$20,000
Barbara A. Mikulski (D-Md)	$18,060
Gordon J. Humphrey (R-NH)	$4,500
Robert T. Stafford (R-Vt)	$2,400
Claiborne Pell (D-RI)	$1,800

Top 20 PAC Contributors to Committee Members in 1987-88

1	Machinists/Aerospace Workers Union	$48,000
2	Teamsters Union*	$47,100
3	AT&T	$43,150
4	Air Line Pilots Assn	$38,000
5	Amer Fedn of State/County/Municipal Employees	$37,205
6	Carpenters Union*	$36,712
7	United Transportation Union	$36,600
8	Federal Express Corp	$35,800
9	National PAC	$35,000
9	Senate Majority Fund (Daniel Inouye)	$35,000
11	Laborers Union*	$34,500
12	American Dental Assn	$33,800
13	Auto Dealers & Drivers for Free Trade	$32,500
14	Operating Engineers Union*	$31,650
15	National Education Assn	$31,035
16	Seafarers International Union	$30,800
17	American Bankers Assn*	$30,505
18	American Postal Workers Union	$30,500
18	Washington PAC	$30,500
20	American Podiatry Assn	$30,000

* Contributions came from more than one PAC affiliated with this sponsor.

Members in **boldface** ran for reelection in 1988

---

1 Ran for Vice President in 1988

Summary

The Senate Labor Committee is the birthplace for many of the standards and rules that govern the American workplace. As such, it is of natural interest to the nation's labor unions, which provided more than $1 million in contributions to its members in 1987-88. But decisions about labor conditions affect not only workers, but also their employers, who must live by the rules. Consequently, many of the issues discussed and debated by the committee are closely followed by a wide cross-section of businesses and their PACs.

A glance at the chart below might make it appear that pro-Israel PACs are also keenly interested in decisions made by the Labor Committee. In fact, it was rather a particular member of the committee — Ohio Democrat Howard Metzenbaum — who drew most of their attention and money. Metzenbaum, long a supporter of Israel, found himself in a heated (and very expensive) battle for reelection against Cleveland Mayor George Voinovich. Pro-Israel PACs contributed more than $245,000 to Metzenbaum's successful campaign.

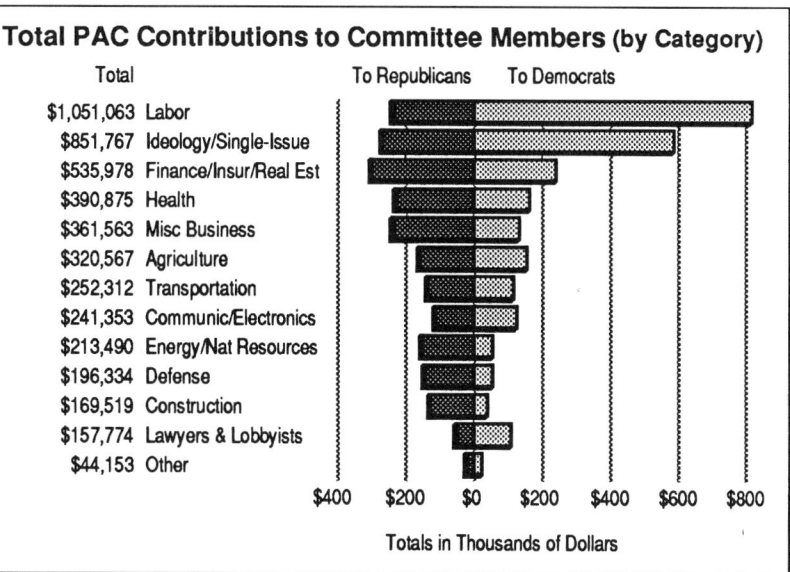

Total PAC Contributions to Committee Members (by Category)

Total	Category
$1,051,063	Labor
$851,767	Ideology/Single-Issue
$535,978	Finance/Insur/Real Est
$390,875	Health
$361,563	Misc Business
$320,567	Agriculture
$252,312	Transportation
$241,353	Communic/Electronics
$213,490	Energy/Nat Resources
$196,334	Defense
$169,519	Construction
$157,774	Lawyers & Lobbyists
$44,153	Other

Totals in Thousands of Dollars

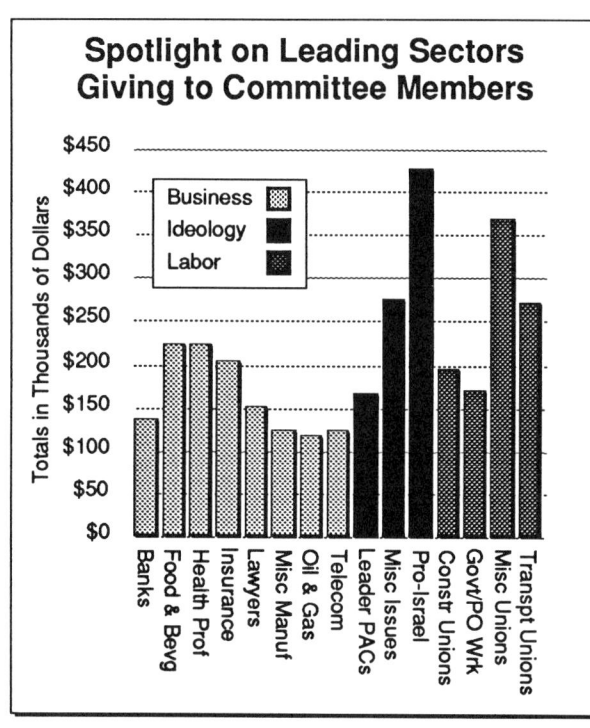

Spotlight on Leading Sectors Giving to Committee Members

Leading Sectors Giving to Committee Members

Business

Banks	$135,402
Food & Beverage	$221,377
Health Professionals	$220,825
Insurance	$202,267
Lawyers	$148,899
Misc Manufacturing	$122,390
Oil & Gas	$115,705
Telecommunications	$120,517

Ideological/Single-Issue

Leadership PACs	$164,571
Misc Issues	$273,011
Pro-Israel	$423,585

Labor

Construction Unions	$191,887
Govt & Postal Workers	$168,905
Misc Unions	$365,841
Transport Unions	$271,395

Senate Rules and Administration Committee

Wendell H. Ford (D-Ky), Chairman
Ted Stevens (R-Alaska), Ranking Republican

Party Ratio: 9 Democrats
7 Republicans

Jurisdiction: (1) Administration of the Senate Office Buildings and the Senate wing of the Capitol, including the assignment of office space. (2) Congressional organization relative to rules and procedures, and Senate rules and regulations, including floor and gallery rules. (3) Corrupt practices. (4) Credentials and qualifications of Members of the Senate, contested elections, and acceptance of incompatible offices. (5) Federal elections generally, including the election of the President, Vice President, and Members of the Congress. (6) Government Printing Office, and the printing and correction of the *Congressional Record*, as well as those matters provided for under rule XI. (7) Meetings of the Congress and attendance of Members. (8) Payment of money out of the contingent fund of the Senate or creating a charge upon the same (except that any resolution relating to substantive matter within the jurisdiction of any other standing committee of the Senate shall be first referred to such committee). (9) Presidential succession. (10) Purchase of books and manuscripts and erection of monuments to the memory of individuals. (11) Senate Library and statuary, art, and pictures in the Capitol and Senate Office Buildings. (12) Services to the Senate, including the Senate restaurant. (13) United States Capitol and congressional office buildings, the Library of Congress, the Smithsonian Institution (and the incorporation of similar institutions), and the Botanic Garden. The committee is also mandated to (A) make a continuing study of the organization and operation of the Congress of the United States and recommend improvements in such organization and operation with a view toward strengthening the Congress, simplifying its operations, improving its relationships with other branches of the U.S. Government, and enabling it better to meet it responsibilities under the Constitution of the United States; and (B) identify any court proceeding or action which, in its opinion, is of vital interest to the Congress as a constitutionally established institution of the Federal Government and call such proceeding or action to the attention of the Senate.

1987-88 PAC Contributions to Committee Members

Dennis DeConcini (D-Ariz)	$982,181
Robert C. Byrd (D-WVa)	$918,764
Daniel Patrick Moynihan (D-NY)	$906,891
Bob Dole (R-Kan)[1]	$838,482
Al Gore (D-Tenn)[1]	$624,450
Brock Adams (D-Wash)	$161,631
Ted Stevens (R-Alaska)	$107,283
Mark O. Hatfield (R-Ore)	$78,528
Christopher J. Dodd (D-Conn)	$50,009
Daniel K. Inouye (D-Hawaii)	$32,850
John W. Warner (R-Va)	$17,485
Wendell H. Ford (D-Ky)	$10,600
Jesse Helms (R-NC)	$8,735
James A. McClure (R-Idaho)	$7,650
Jake Garn (R-Utah)	$2,850
Claiborne Pell (D-RI)	$1,800

Top 20 PAC Contributors to Committee Members in 1987-88

1	Federal Express Corp	$48,712
2	AT&T	$45,166
3	National Assn of Home Builders	$40,500
4	National Assn of Letter Carriers	$35,000
5	Senate Majority Fund (Daniel Inouye)	$35,000
6	Teamsters Union*	$34,000
7	Associated General Contractors	$33,500
8	US League of Savings Assn*	$32,500
9	American Institute of CPA's	$32,000
10	Assn of Trial Lawyers of America	$30,000
11	Air Line Pilots Assn	$30,000
12	National PAC	$30,000
13	Marine Engineers Union*	$29,500
14	Auto Dealers & Drivers for Free Trade	$29,500
15	AFL-CIO*	$29,204
16	American Bankers Assn*	$28,000
17	Laborers Union*	$27,550
18	National Assn of Realtors	$27,249
19	Intl Brotherhood of Electrical Workers	$26,500
20	Carpenters Union*	$26,000

* Contributions came from more than one PAC affiliated with this sponsor.

Members in **boldface** ran for reelection in 1988

---

1 Ran for President in 1988

Summary

In any legislative body, the key to success often lies in a mastery of the body's rules and procedures. Those rules — from the assignment of office space to the conducting of business on the Senate floor and the rules governing federal elections — are debated within this committee.

As part of its role in setting election procedures, the committee is also at center stage in revising the laws governing campaign financing. The rules governing PACs, the spending limits and reporting requirements of contributors to federal campaigns, the oversight of the process by the Federal Election Commission — all these elements of American elections fall within the jurisdiction of the Senate Rules Committee.

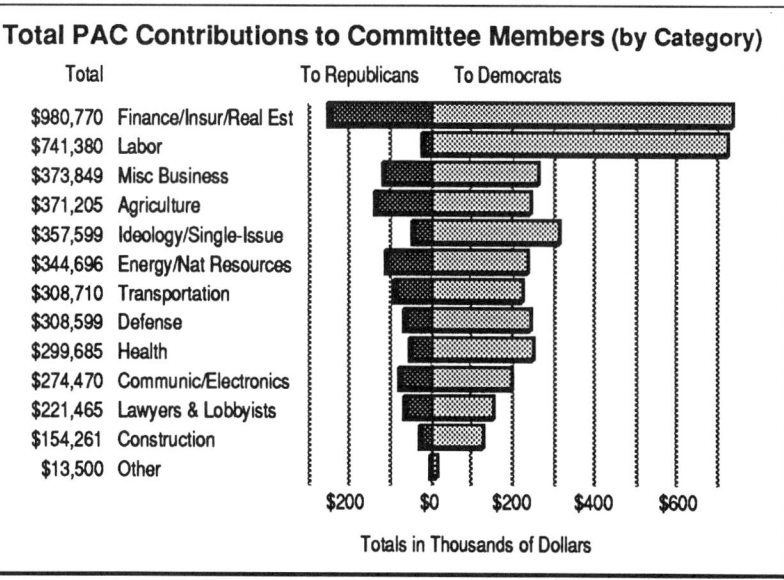

Total PAC Contributions to Committee Members (by Category)

Total	Category
$980,770	Finance/Insur/Real Est
$741,380	Labor
$373,849	Misc Business
$371,205	Agriculture
$357,599	Ideology/Single-Issue
$344,696	Energy/Nat Resources
$308,710	Transportation
$308,599	Defense
$299,685	Health
$274,470	Communic/Electronics
$221,465	Lawyers & Lobbyists
$154,261	Construction
$13,500	Other

Totals in Thousands of Dollars

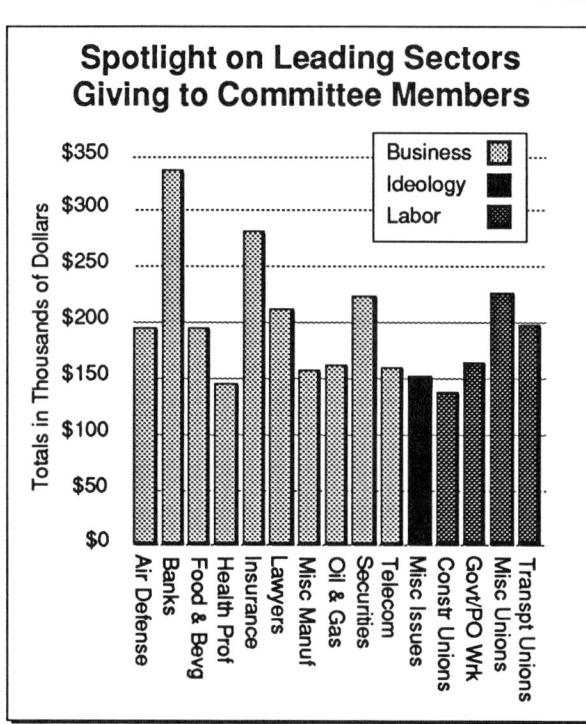

Spotlight on Leading Sectors Giving to Committee Members

Business, Ideology, Labor

Leading Sectors
Giving to Committee Members

Business

Air Defense	$194,250
Banks	$333,959
Food & Beverage	$193,149
Health Professionals	$143,480
Insurance	$278,391
Lawyers	$209,465
Misc Manufacturing	$154,000
Oil & Gas	$158,650
Securities/Commodities Investment	$222,028
Telecommunications	$156,708

Ideological/Single-Issue

Misc Issues	$148,923

Labor

Construction Unions	$135,854
Govt & Postal Workers	$163,000
Misc Unions	$225,026
Transport Unions	$194,900

Senate Small Business Committee

Dale Bumpers (D-Ark), Chairman
Lowell P. Weicker (R-Conn), Ranking Republican

Party Ratio: 10 Democrats
9 Republicans

Jurisdiction: (1) All legislation referred to the committee; (2) Jurisdiction over all matters related to the Small Business Administration; (3) Study and survey, through research and investigation, of all problems of American small business enterprises.

Subcommittees

Competition and Antitrust Enforcement
Tom Harkin (D-Iowa), Chairman
Malcolm Wallop (R-Wyo), Minority Member

Export Expansion
Jim Sasser (D-Tenn), Chairman
Rudy Boschwitz (R-Minn), Ranking Republican

Government Contracting and Paperwork Reduction
Alan J. Dixon (D-Ill), Chairman
Robert W. Kasten Jr. (R-Wis), Ranking Republican

Innovation, Technology and Productivity
Carl Levin (D-Mich), Chairman
Warren B. Rudman (R-NH), Ranking Republican

Rural Economy and Family Farming
Max Baucus (D-Mont), Chairman
Alfonse M. D'Amato (R-NY), Ranking Republican

Urban and Minority-Owned Business Development
John F. Kerry (D-Mass), Chairman
Christopher (Kit) Bond (R-Mo), Minority Member

1987-88 PAC Contributions to Committee Members

Jim Sasser (D-Tenn)	$1,381,554
Lowell P. Weicker Jr. (R-Conn)	$934,823
Malcolm Wallop (R-Wyo)	$933,287
David Karnes (R-Neb)	$895,504
Max Baucus (D-Mont)	$277,660
Alfonse M. D'Amato (R-NY)	$238,391
Tom Harkin (D-Iowa)	$197,820
Alan J. Dixon (D-Ill)	$167,450
Christopher S. Bond (R-Mo)	$133,459
Larry Pressler (R-SD)	$93,925
Bob Kasten (R-Wis)	$24,165
Rudy Boschwitz (R-Minn)	$18,401
Barbara A. Mikulski (D-Md)	$18,060
Carl Levin (D-Mich)	$13,305
Sam Nunn (D-Ga)	$7,759
Dale Bumpers (D-Ark)	$4,950
John Kerry (D-Mass)	$4,012
Warren B. Rudman (R-NH)	$1,500
David L. Boren (D-Okla)	$0

Top 20 PAC Contributors to Committee Members in 1987-88

1	American Bankers Assn*	$42,205
2	American Institute of CPA's	$41,500
3	Chicago Mercantile Exchange	$40,500
4	American Medical Assn*	$35,900
5	US League of Savings Assn*	$34,650
6	Assn of Trial Lawyers of America	$33,250
7	American Dental Assn	$33,000
8	United Parcel Service	$32,800
9	Auto Dealers & Drivers for Free Trade	$32,000
10	Teamsters Union	$31,000
11	Air Line Pilots Assn	$30,000
11	Machinists/Aerospace Workers Union	$30,000
11	National Venture Capital Assn	$30,000
14	Hudson Valley PAC	$29,733
15	American Express*	$29,526
16	AT&T	$29,500
17	Chicago Board of Trade	$29,000
17	J P Morgan & Co	$29,000
19	Campaign America (Bob Dole)	$28,557
20	National Assn of Life Underwriters	$28,000

* Contributions came from more than one PAC affiliated with this sponsor.

Members in **boldface** ran for reelection in 1988

Summary

Its statement of jurisdiction is the shortest of all Senate Committees, but the expanse of that jurisdiction reaches into every city and town across America. Overseeing the concerns of small business — from the corner grocery to the family farm — is the committee's charge, and considering the fact that both the corner grocery and the family farm are endangered species in America today, the concerns of small business are large indeed.

As with most committees in the Senate, the single biggest source of PAC funds to committee members came from financial sources, with banks and insurance companies leading the way. Among the handful of PACs concerned specifically with small business issues, the largest contributions came from the National Federation of Independent Business, which gave a total of $9,349 to committee members in 1987-88.

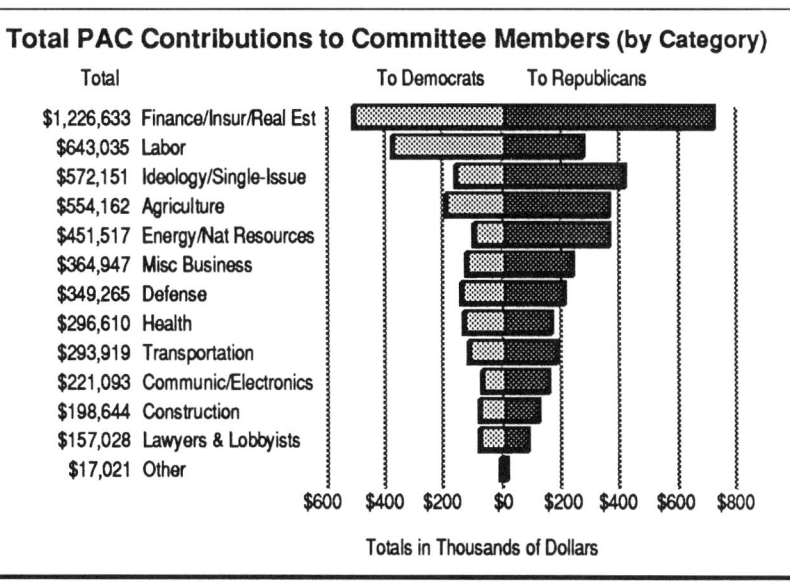

Total PAC Contributions to Committee Members (by Category)

Total		To Democrats	To Republicans
$1,226,633	Finance/Insur/Real Est		
$643,035	Labor		
$572,151	Ideology/Single-Issue		
$554,162	Agriculture		
$451,517	Energy/Nat Resources		
$364,947	Misc Business		
$349,265	Defense		
$296,610	Health		
$293,919	Transportation		
$221,093	Communic/Electronics		
$198,644	Construction		
$157,028	Lawyers & Lobbyists		
$17,021	Other		

Totals in Thousands of Dollars

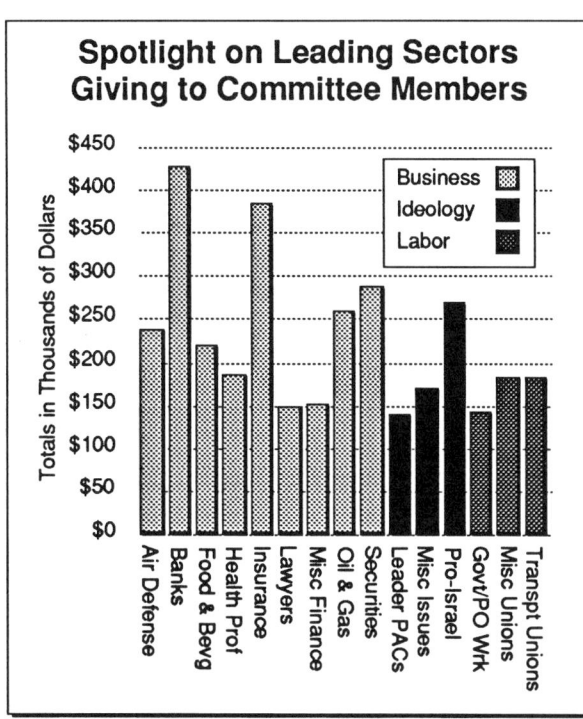

Spotlight on Leading Sectors Giving to Committee Members

Business
Ideology
Labor

Air Defense, Banks, Food & Bevg, Health Prof, Insurance, Lawyers, Misc Finance, Oil & Gas, Securities, Leader PACs, Misc Issues, Pro-Israel, Govt/PO Wrk, Misc Unions, Transpt Unions

Totals in Thousands of Dollars

Leading Sectors
Giving to Committee Members

Business

Air Defense	$234,390
Banks	$424,372
Food & Beverage	$217,452
Health Professionals	$182,115
Insurance	$381,320
Lawyers	$147,278
Misc Finance	$148,950
Oil & Gas	$257,467
Securities/Commodities Investment	$286,193

Ideological/Single-Issue

Leadership PACs	$137,804
Misc Issues	$167,714
Pro-Israel	$266,783

Labor

Govt & Postal Workers	$139,855
Misc Unions	$181,850
Transport Unions	$179,270

Senate Veterans' Affairs Committee

Alan Cranston (D-Calif), Chairman
Frank Murkowski (R-Alaska), Ranking Republican

Party Ratio: 6 Democrats
5 Republicans

> **Jurisdiction:** Veterans' measures generally; (2) Pensions of all wars of the U.S., general and special; (3) Life insurance issued by the Government on account of service in the Armed Forces; (4) Compensation of veterans; (5) Vocational rehabilitation and education of veterans; (5) Vocational rehabilitation and education of veterans; (6) Veterans' hospitals, medical care and treatment of veterans; (7) Soldiers' and sailors' civil relief; (8) Readjustment of servicemen to civil life; (9) National cemeteries.

No Subcommittees

1987-88 PAC Contributions to Committee Members

Dennis DeConcini (D-Ariz)	$982,181
George J. Mitchell (D-Maine)	$735,141
Spark M. Matsunaga (D-Hawaii)	$429,149
Arlen Specter (R-Pa)	$135,972
Alan K. Simpson (R-Wyo)	$100,925
John D. Rockefeller IV (D-WVa)	$97,166
Alan Cranston (D-Calif)	$91,090
Strom Thurmond (R-SC)	$59,000
Frank H. Murkowski (R-Alaska)	$55,113
Bob Graham (D-Fla)	$37,330
Robert T. Stafford (R-Vt)	$2,400

Top 20 PAC Contributors to Committee Members in 1987-88

1	American Bankers Assn	$38,000
2	Assn of Trial Lawyers of America	$34,000
3	AT&T	$32,666
4	Marine Engineers Union*	$29,000
5	American Institute of CPA's	$26,000
6	National Assn of Retired Federal Employees	$26,000
7	AFL-CIO*	$25,000
8	Laborers Union*	$25,000
9	Senate Majority Fund (Daniel Inouye)	$25,000
10	National Assn of Realtors	$21,700
11	Amer Fedn of State/County/Municipal Employees	$21,030
12	National Beer Wholesalers Assn	$20,500
13	Machinists/Aerospace Workers Union	$20,000
14	Pacific PAC	$19,000
15	Philip Morris*	$18,999
16	American Express*	$18,500
17	National Assn of Life Underwriters	$18,000
18	National Assn of Letter Carriers	$18,000
19	Air Line Pilots Assn	$17,500
20	Credit Union National Assn	$17,500

* Contributions came from more than one PAC affiliated with this sponsor.

Members in **boldface** ran for reelection in 1988

Summary

Insurance companies were the biggest overall contributors to members of the Senate Veterans Affairs Committee in 1987-88. While government life insurance to veterans does fall within its jurisdiction, most of the committee's work does not directly affect any particular segments of American business in a specific way. Perhaps because of this, the Veterans Committee has never been a central focus of PAC giving. Even the few PACs whose primary interest is Veterans Affairs gave a total of less than $4,000 to committee members during the 1988 election cycle.

Total PAC Contributions to Committee Members (by Category)

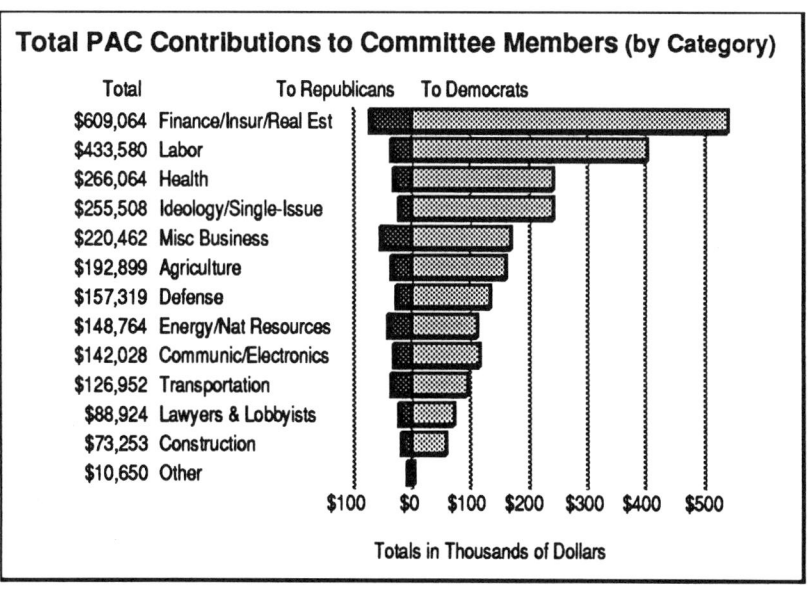

Total	Category
$609,064	Finance/Insur/Real Est
$433,580	Labor
$266,064	Health
$255,508	Ideology/Single-Issue
$220,462	Misc Business
$192,899	Agriculture
$157,319	Defense
$148,764	Energy/Nat Resources
$142,028	Communic/Electronics
$126,952	Transportation
$88,924	Lawyers & Lobbyists
$73,253	Construction
$10,650	Other

Totals in Thousands of Dollars

Spotlight on Leading Sectors Giving to Committee Members

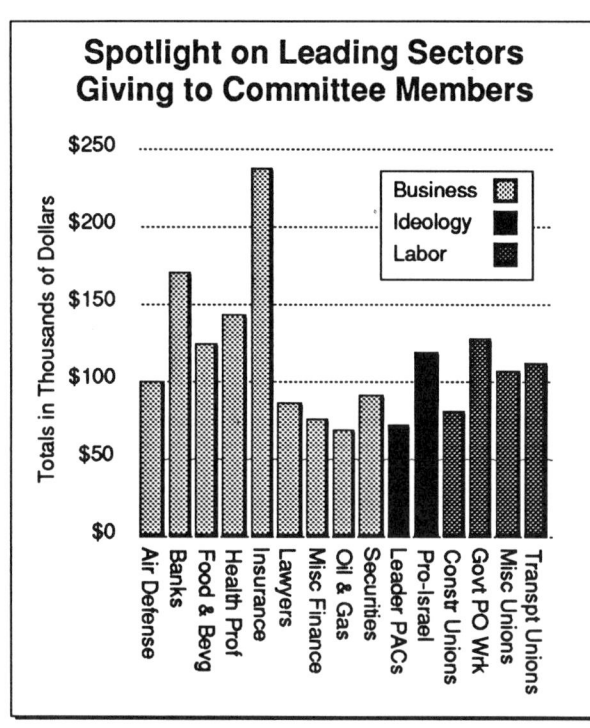

Leading Sectors Giving to Committee Members

Business

Air Defense	$98,550
Banks	$168,500
Food & Beverage	$122,562
Health Professionals	$140,609
Insurance	$235,474
Lawyers	$84,424
Misc Finance	$74,290
Oil & Gas	$67,800
Securities/Commodities Investment	$90,600

Ideological/Single-Issue

Leadership PACs	$71,000
Pro-Israel	$116,750

Labor

Construction Unions	$79,100
Govt & Postal Workers	$126,480
Misc Unions	$106,200
Transport Unions	$109,800

House Administration Committee

Frank Annunzio (D-Ill), Chairman
Bill Frenzel (R-Minn), Ranking Republican

Party Ratio: 12 Democrats
7 Republicans

Jurisdiction: (1) Appropriations from the contingent fund; (2) Auditing and settling of all accounts which may be charged to the contingent fund; (3) Employment of persons by the House, including clerks for Members and committees, and reporters of debates; (4) Matters relating to the Library of Congress and the House Library; statuary and pictures; acceptance or purchase of works of art for the Capitol; the Botanic Gardens; management of the Library of Congress, purchase of books and manuscripts; erection of monuments to the memory of individuals; (5) Matters relating to the Smithsonian Institution and the incorporation of similar institutions; (6) Expenditure of contingent fund of the House; (7) Matters relating to printing and correction of the Congressional Record; (8) Measures relating to accounts of the House generally; (9) Measures relating to assignment of office space for Members and committees; (10) measures relating to the disposition of useless executive papers; (11) Measures relating to the election of the President, Vice President, or Members of Congress; corrupt practices; contested elections; credentials and qualifications; and Federal elections generally; (12) Measures relating to services to the House, including the House Restaurant, parking facilities and administration of the House office Buildings and of the House wing of the Capitol; (13) Measures relating to the travel of Members of the House; (14) Measures relating to the raising, reporting and use of campaign contributions for candidates for office of Representative in the House of Representatives and of Resident Commissioner to the United States from Puerto Rico; (15) Measures relating to the compensation, retirement and other benefits of the Members, officers, and employees of the Congress.

Subcommittees

Accounts
Joseph M. Gaydos (D-Pa), Chairman
Robert E. Badham (R-Calif), Ranking Republican

Elections
Al Swift (D-Wash), Chairman
William M. Thomas (R-Calif), Ranking Republican

Libraries and Memorials
Mary Rose Oakar (D-Ohio), Chairwoman
Newt Gingrich (R-Ga), Ranking Republican

Office Systems
Charlie Rose (D-NC), Chairman
William M. Thomas (R-Calif), Ranking Republican

Personnel and Police
Leon E. Panetta (D-Calif), Chairman
Pat Roberts (R- Kan), Ranking Republican

Procurement and Printing
Ed Jones (D-Tenn), Chairman
Newt Gingrich (R-Ga), Ranking Republican

Total PAC Contributions to Committee Members

Tony Coelho (D-Calif)	$415,666
Mary Rose Oakar (D-Ohio)	$387,918
Bill Frenzel (R-Minn)	$301,078
Al Swift (D-Wash)	$286,312
Newt Gingrich (R-Ga)	$260,476
Jim Bates (D-Calif)	$244,955
Bill Thomas (R-Calif)	$215,150
Sam Gejdenson (D-Conn)	$208,800
Barbara F. Vucanovich (R-Nev)	$201,319
Charlie Rose (D-NC)	$177,500
William L. Dickinson (R-Ala)	$168,639
Leon E. Panetta (D-Calif)	$158,600
Frank Annunzio (D-Ill)	$156,200
Joe Kolter (D-Pa)	$146,606
Joseph M. Gaydos (D-Pa)	$142,850
William L. Clay (D-Mo)	$141,630
Pat Roberts (R-Kan)	$99,600
Robert E. Badham (R-Calif)[1]	$65,509
Ed Jones (D-Tenn)[1]	$3,000

Top 20 PAC Contributors to Committee Members in 1987-88

1	National Assn of Realtors	$114,475
2	Teamsters Union	$75,000
3	American Medical Assn	$71,275
4	National Assn of Retired Federal Employees	$59,600
5	National Education Assn	$59,200
6	United Auto Workers	$49,150
7	Assn of Trial Lawyers of America	$46,800
8	National Assn of Letter Carriers*	$46,625
9	AT&T	$45,700
10	Air Line Pilots Assn	$41,500
11	Machinists/Aerospace Workers Union*	$39,400
12	American Bankers Assn	$39,300
13	National Assn Life Underwriters	$37,500
14	National Assn of Home Builders	$35,800
15	Carpenters Union*	$34,800
16	Food & Commercial Workers Union*	$32,379
17	Operating Engineers Union*	$30,700
18	Associated Milk Producers	$30,500
19	American Institute of CPA's	$30,000
20	Auto Dealers & Drivers for Free Trade	$29,500

* Contributions came from more than one PAC affiliated with this sponsor.

[1] Did not run for reelection in 1988

Summary

Since the Committee on House Administration is more concerned with matters internal to the House than to the world of industry and commerce beyond it, the PAC contributions to its members show no exceptional patterns. Rather, they fairly typically mirror the overall patterns in industry giving to members of Congress, with labor providing the biggest share of the Democrats' money and financial interests giving the most to Republicans.

Fifteen of the top 20 PACs giving to members of the committee are also found on the Top 20 list of PACs giving to Congress as a whole.

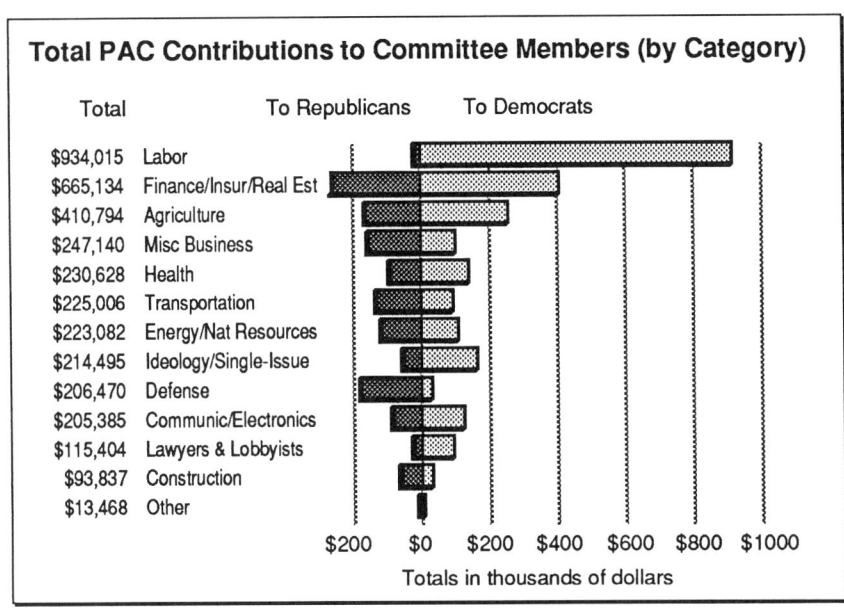

Total PAC Contributions to Committee Members (by Category)

Total		To Republicans	To Democrats
$934,015	Labor		
$665,134	Finance/Insur/Real Est		
$410,794	Agriculture		
$247,140	Misc Business		
$230,628	Health		
$225,006	Transportation		
$223,082	Energy/Nat Resources		
$214,495	Ideology/Single-Issue		
$206,470	Defense		
$205,385	Communic/Electronics		
$115,404	Lawyers & Lobbyists		
$93,837	Construction		
$13,468	Other		

Totals in thousands of dollars

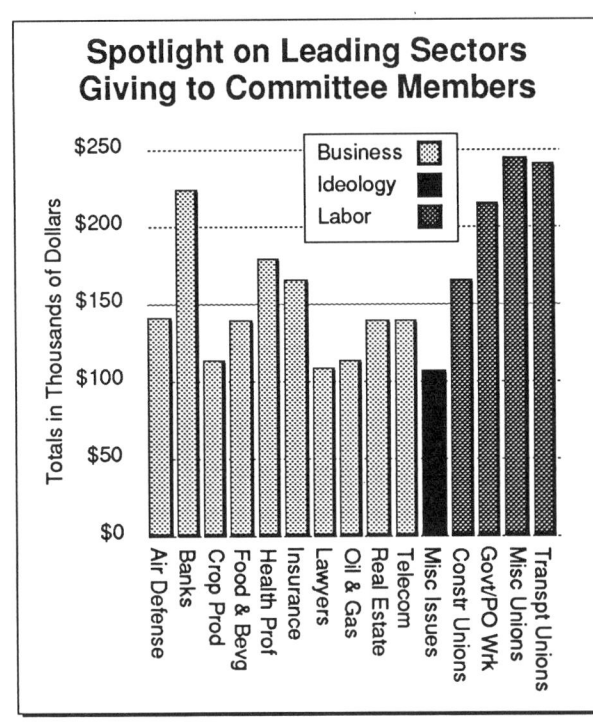

Spotlight on Leading Sectors Giving to Committee Members

- Business
- Ideology
- Labor

Leading Sectors Giving to Committee Members

Business

Air Defense	$140,270
Banks	$222,240
Crop Production	$112,010
Food & Beverage	$137,919
Health Professionals	$177,278
Insurance	$163,372
Lawyers	$106,850
Oil & Gas	$111,582
Real Estate	$137,625
Telecommunications	$137,935

Ideological/Single-Issue

Misc Issues	$105,395

Labor

Construction Unions	$162,950
Govt & Postal Workers	$212,575
Misc Unions	$243,085
Transportation Unions	$239,630

House Agriculture Committee

Kika de la Garza (D-Texas), Chairman
Edward R. Madigan (R-Ill) Ranking Republican

Party Radio: 26 Democrats
17 Republicans

Jurisdiction: (1) Adulteration of seeds, insect pests, and protection of birds and animals in forest reserves; (2) Agriculture generally; (3) Agricultural and industrial chemistry; (4) Agricultural colleges and experimental stations; (5) Agricultural economics and research; (6) Agricultural education extension services; (7) Agricultural production and marketing and stabilization of prices of agricultural products and commodities (not including distribution outside the United States); (8) Animal industry and diseases of animals; (9) Crop insurance and soil conservation; (10) Dairy industry; (11) Entomology and plant quarantine; (12) Extension of farm credit and farm security; (13) Forestry in general, and forest reserves other than those created from the public domain; (14) Human nutrition and home economics; (15) Inspection of livestock and meat products; (16) Plant industry, soils, and agricultural engineering; (17) Rural electrification; (18) Commodities exchanges; (19) Rural development.

Subcommittees

Cotton, Rice and Sugar
Jerry Huckaby (D-La), Chairman
Arlan Stangeland (R-Minn), Ranking Republican

Livestock, Dairy and Poultry
Charles W. Stenholm (D-Texas), Chairman
James M. Jeffords (R-Vt), Ranking Republican

Tobacco and Peanuts
Charlie Rose (D-NC), Chairman
Larry J. Hopkins (R-Ky), Ranking Republican

Wheat, Soybeans and Feed Grains
Dan Glickman (D-Kan), Chairman
Ron Marlenee (R-Mont), Ranking Republican

Conservation, Credit and Rural Development
Ed Jones (D-Tenn), Chairman
E. Thomas Coleman (R-Mo), Ranking Republican

Department Operations, Research, and Foreign Agriculture
George E. Brown Jr (D-Calif), Chairman
Pat Roberts (R-Kan), Ranking Republican

Total Agriculture-Related PAC Contributions to Committee Members

	Total from Cmte-Related PACs	Pct of Member's Total PACs
Bill Emerson (R-Mo)	$129,400	32%
James M. Jeffords (R-Vt)[1]	$116,950	17%
Wally Herger (R-Calif)	$105,418	41%
Arlan Stangeland (R-Minn)	$104,500	29%
Bill Schuette (R-Mich)	$95,220	33%
Kika de la Garza (D-Texas)	$85,250	66%
Edward R. Madigan (R-Ill)	$84,473	25%
Fred Grandy (R-Iowa)	$84,400	30%
Charlie Rose (D-NC)	$74,250	43%
Tony Coelho (D-Calif)	$72,569	17%
Glenn English (D-Okla)	$71,700	39%
Jerry Huckaby (D-La)	$61,586	47%
Mike Espy (D-Miss)	$60,300	13%
Clyde C. Holloway (R-La)	$59,350	21%
Steve Gunderson (R-Wis)	$56,400	40%
Dan Glickman (D-Kan)	$56,090	20%
Charles Hatcher (D-Ga)	$55,345	27%
Jim Jontz (D-Ind)	$54,650	11%
Robin Tallon (D-SC)	$54,650	23%
David R. Nagle (D-Iowa)	$51,050	12%
Tim Johnson (D-SD)	$51,050	16%
E. Thomas Coleman (R-Mo)	$50,816	29%
Ron Marlenee (R-Mont)	$47,400	26%
Richard H. Stallings (D-Idaho)	$47,100	18%
Charles W. Stenholm (D-Texas)	$46,650	42%
Pat Roberts (R-Kan)	$45,750	46%
Ben Nighthorse Campbell (D-Colo)	$45,405	15%
Bob Smith (R-Ore)	$43,250	31%
Harold L. Volkmer (D-Mo)	$42,025	19%
Leon E. Panetta (D-Calif)	$41,900	26%
Larry Combest (R-Texas)	$41,810	35%
Timothy J. Penny (D-Minn)	$41,300	33%

	Total from Cmte-Related PACs	Pct of Member's Total PACs
Jim Olin (D-Va)	$40,600	28%
Claude Harris (D-Ala)	$38,250	16%
Larry J. Hopkins (R-Ky)	$37,250	29%
H. Martin Lancaster (D-NC)	$29,350	22%
George E. Brown Jr. (D-Calif)	$27,900	10%
Sid Morrison (R-Wash)	$27,725	34%
Harley O. Staggers (D-WVa)	$18,450	14%
Tom Lewis (R-Fla)	$17,625	29%
Walter B. Jones (D-NC)	$12,000	13%
Ed Jones (D-Tenn)[2]	$1,500	50%

Top 20 Agriculture-Related PAC Contributors to Committee Members in 1987-88

1	Associated Milk Producers	$178,300
2	Mid-American Dairymen	$110,650
3	Dairymen Inc*	$75,850
4	American Crystal Sugar Corp	$67,900
5	Chicago Mercantile Exchange	$67,450
6	Chicago Board of Trade	$67,050
7	Philip Morris*	$66,050
8	National Cattlemen's Assn*	$60,086
9	ACRE (Action Cmte for Rural Electrification)*	$55,457
10	Food Marketing Institute	$52,100
11	American Meat Institute	$45,400
12	ConAgra Inc*	$43,600
13	American Sugarbeet Growers Assn	$43,575
14	RJR Nabisco*	$43,000
15	National Cotton Council	$38,336
16	Dow Chemical*	$38,150
17	American Veterinary Medical Assn	$32,000
18	Land O'Lakes Inc	$30,800
19	Southern Minnesota Beet Sugar Co-op	$28,550
20	American Sugar Cane League	$27,650

[1] Ran for U.S. Senate in 1988
[2] Did not run for reelection in 1988

* Contributions came from more than one PAC affiliated with this sponsor.

Summary

Agricultural interests — led by the dairy industry, sugar growers and food processors — were the single largest source of funding for members on the House Agriculture Committee, outweighing even the combined contributions from all labor unions. Together, the agriculture-related industries gave more than $2.1 million to committee members — an average of about $50,000 each.

Aside from traditional farming and food processing interests, Chicago-based commodity traders were another important source of contributions. So were firms producing agricultural chemicals, and rural electric cooperatives, whose industry is overseen by the Agriculture Committee. In all, four committee members received $100,000 or more from committee-related PACs and 18 others got $50,000 or more.

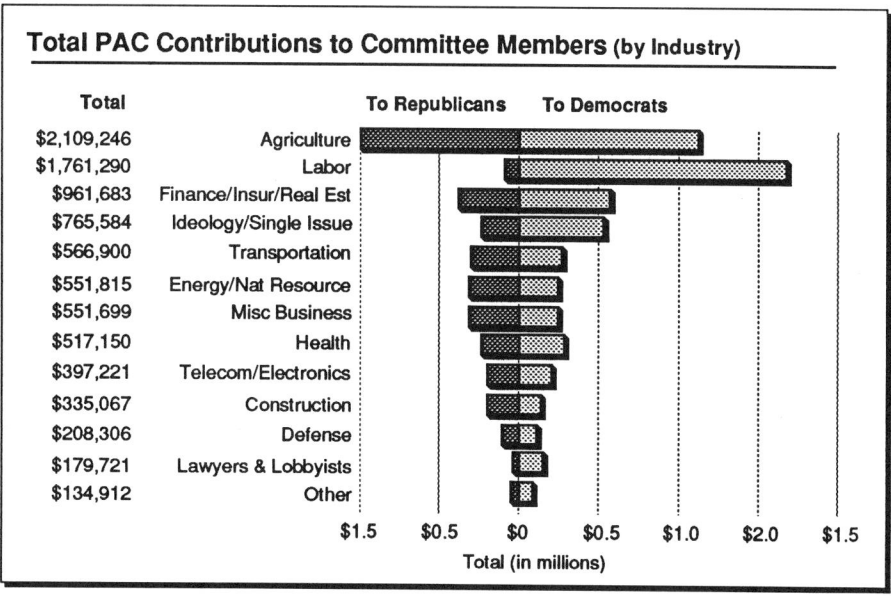

Total PAC Contributions to Committee Members (by Industry)

Total		To Republicans	To Democrats
$2,109,246	Agriculture		
$1,761,290	Labor		
$961,683	Finance/Insur/Real Est		
$765,584	Ideology/Single Issue		
$566,900	Transportation		
$551,815	Energy/Nat Resource		
$551,699	Misc Business		
$517,150	Health		
$397,221	Telecom/Electronics		
$335,067	Construction		
$208,306	Defense		
$179,721	Lawyers & Lobbyists		
$134,912	Other		

Total (in millions)

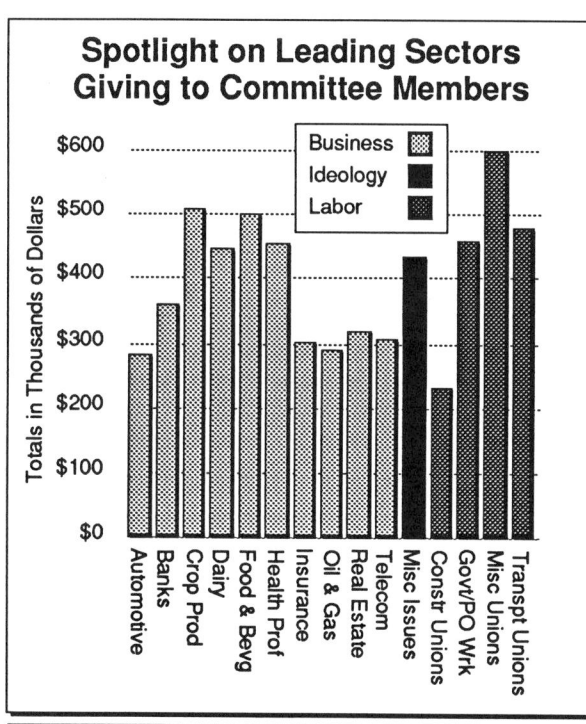

Spotlight on Leading Sectors Giving to Committee Members

Business
Ideology
Labor

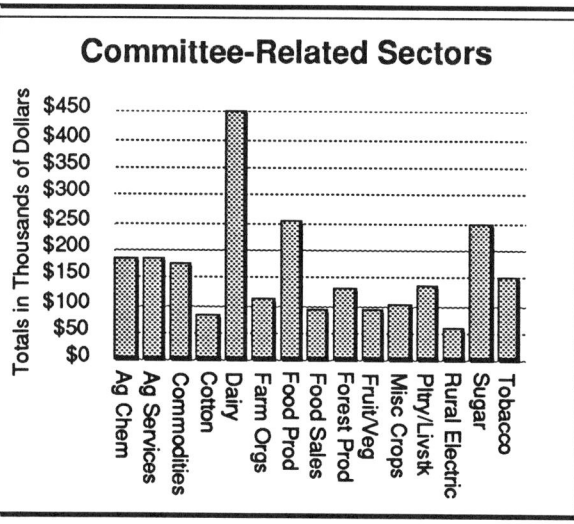

Committee-Related Sectors

Leading Agriculture-Related Sectors Giving to Committee Members

Business

Agricultural Services & Supplies
Agricultural Services $186,275
Agricultural Chemicals $180,975
Agricultural Equipment $18,575

Commodities
Commodities Trading $167,800

Crop Production
Sugar Growers $245,050
Misc Crops $99,175
Fruit/Vegetable Growers $91,810
Cotton Producers $77,796

Dairy
Dairy Producers $444,539

Food Processing & Sales
Food Processing $246,750
Food Retail/Wholesale $88,129

Forestry
Forest Products $127,188

Misc Agriculture
Poultry/Livestock $132,476
Farm Organizations $107,669

Tobacco Production & Marketing
Tobacco $145,950

Other Committee-Related
Rural Electric Utilities $56,307

117

House Appropriations Committee

Jamie L. Whitten (D-Miss), Chairman
Silvio O. Conte (R-Mass), Ranking Republican

Party Ratio: 35 Democrats
22 Republicans

Jurisdiction: (1) Appropriation of the revenue for the support of the Government; (2) Rescissions of appropriations contained in appropriation Acts; (3) Transfers of unexpended balances, and a variety of other duties involving the appropriation of government funds. Other committees of Congress may *authorize* the government to spend money on various projects and programs, but only the Appropriations committee *appropriates* the funds.

Subcommittees

Commerce, Justice, and State, The Judiciary and Related Agencies
Neal Smith (D-Iowa), Chairman
Harold Rogers (R-Ky), Ranking Republican

Defense
Bill Chappell (D-Fla), Chairman
Joseph M. McDade (R-Pa), Ranking Republican

District of Columbia
Julian C. Dixon (D-Calif), Chairman
Lawrence Coughlin (R-NJ), Ranking Republican

Energy and Water Development
Tom Bevill (D-Ala), Chairman
John T. Myers (R-Ind), Ranking Republican

Foreign Operations, Export Financing and Related Programs
David Obey (D-Wis), Chairman
Mickey Edwards (R-Okla), Ranking Republican

HUD-Independent Agencies
Edward P. Boland (D-Mass), Chairman
Bill Green (R-NY), Ranking Republican

Interior and Related Agencies
Sidney R. Yates (D-Ill), Chairman
Ralph Regula (R-Ohio), Ranking Republican

Labor, Health and Human Services, Education and Related Agencies
William H. Natcher (D-Ky), Chairman
Silvio O. Conte (R-Mass), Ranking Republican

Legislative Branch
Vic Fazio (D-Calif), Chairman
Jerry Lewis (R-Calif), Ranking Republican

Military Construction
W.G. (Bill) Hefner (D-NC), Chairman
Bill Lowery (R-Calif), Ranking Republican

Rural Development, Agriculture, and Related Agencies
Jamie L. Whitten (D-Miss), Chairman
Virginia Smith (R-Neb), Ranking Republican

Transportation and Related Agencies
William Lehman (D-Fla), Chairman
Lawrence Coughlin (R-Pa), Ranking Republican

Treasury, Postal Service, and General Government
Edward R. Roybal (D-Calif), Chairman
Joe Skeen (R-NM), Ranking Republican

Total PAC Contributions to Committee Members

Bill Chappell (D-Fla)	$422,427
Vic Fazio (D-Calif)	$378,783
William H. Gray III (D-Pa)	$377,752
Les AuCoin (D-Ore)	$340,400
Bill Alexander (D-Ark)	$320,524
John P. Murtha (D-Pa)	$310,815
David R. Obey (D-Wis)	$308,399
Bob Carr (D-Mich)	$277,673
Joseph M. McDade (R-Pa)	$271,620
Bill Hefner (D-NC)	$267,125
Carl D. Pursell (R-Mich)	$264,993
Charles Wilson (D-Texas)	$253,350
Steny H. Hoyer (D-Md)	$239,828
Martin Olav Sabo (D-Minn)	$237,550
Frank R. Wolf (R-Va)	$235,615
Vin Weber (R-Minn)	$232,704
Richard J. Durbin (D-Ill)	$220,305
Norman D. Dicks (D-Wash)	$213,189
Bill Lowery (R-Calif)	$182,415
Robert J. Mrazek (D-NY)	$176,931
Ronald D. Coleman (D-Texas)	$174,670
Tom DeLay (R-Texas)	$171,650
Neal Smith (D-Iowa)	$162,585
Jim Kolbe (R-Ariz)	$158,738
Jerry Lewis (R-Calif)	$156,400
Bill Green (R-NY)	$154,233
Lawrence Coughlin (R-Pa)	$150,851
Jack F. Kemp (R-NY)[2]	$150,339
Robert Lindsay Thomas (D-Ga)	$149,969
Bob Traxler (D-Mich)	$148,737
Louis Stokes (D-Ohio)	$147,800
Lindy Boggs (D-La)	$144,300
Virginia Smith (R-Neb)	$138,715
Jamie L. Whitten (D-Miss)	$135,400
William Lehman (D-Fla)	$131,750
Matthew F. McHugh (D-NY)	$129,633
Bob Livingston (R-La)	$127,834
Mickey Edwards (R-Okla)	$122,130
John Edward Porter (R-Ill)	$115,321
Bernard J. Dwyer (D-NJ)	$113,000
Alan B. Mollohan (D-WVa)	$112,890
C.W. Bill Young (R-Fla)	$109,600
Clarence E. Miller (R-Ohio)	$99,436
John T. Myers (R-Ind)	$96,500
Tom Bevill (D-Ala)	$94,350
Joseph D. Early (D-Mass)	$93,250
Joe Skeen (R-NM)	$87,050
Daniel K. Akaka (D-Hawaii)	$81,372
Wes Watkins (D-Okla)	$73,900
Silvio O. Conte (R-Mass)	$72,624
Julian C. Dixon (D-Calif)	$72,430
Harold Rogers (R-Ky)	$69,566
Edward R. Roybal (D-Calif)	$46,800
Edward P. Boland (D-Mass)[1]	$43,970
Sidney R. Yates (D-Ill)	$25,250
William H. Natcher (D-Ky)	$0
Ralph Regula (R-Ohio)	$0

[1] Did not run for reelection in 1988
[2] Ran for President in 1988

Summary

Businesses and industries that rely heavily on government contracts keep a sharp eye on the activities of the congressional appropriations committees — particularly defense contractors, whose fortunes may rise or fall depending on decisions reached by these panels. Three senior members of the Defense Appropriations subcommittee — Bill Chappell (D-Fla), John Murtha (D-Pa) and Joseph McDade (R-Pa) — each drew more than $100,000 from defense contractors in 1988. Chappell, who led all House members with $182,000 from the defense industry, nonetheless lost at the polls in November 1988, after being implicated in the Pentagon procurement scandal.

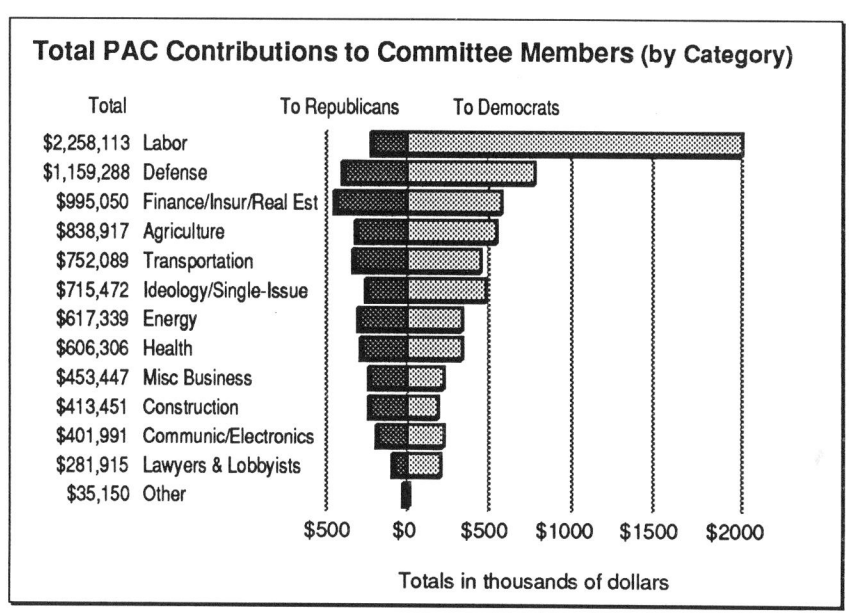

Total PAC Contributions to Committee Members (by Category)

Total		To Republicans	To Democrats
$2,258,113	Labor		
$1,159,288	Defense		
$995,050	Finance/Insur/Real Est		
$838,917	Agriculture		
$752,089	Transportation		
$715,472	Ideology/Single-Issue		
$617,339	Energy		
$606,306	Health		
$453,447	Misc Business		
$413,451	Construction		
$401,991	Communic/Electronics		
$281,915	Lawyers & Lobbyists		
$35,150	Other		

Totals in thousands of dollars

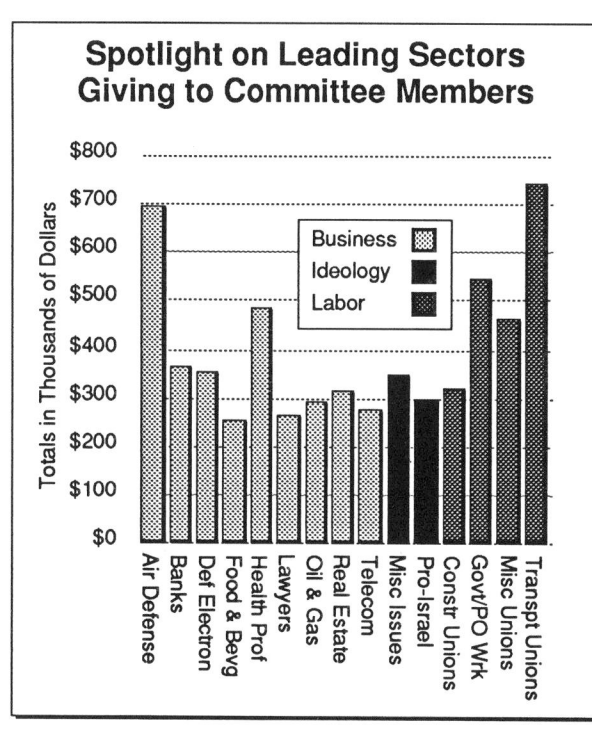

Spotlight on Leading Sectors Giving to Committee Members

Top 20 PAC Contributors to Committee Members in 1987-88

1	National Assn of Realtors	$251,407
2	American Medical Assn*	$234,816
3	Teamsters Union*	$213,100
4	National Assn/Retired Federal Employees	$179,150
5	National Education Assn	$159,150
6	National PAC	$135,000
7	Marine Engineers Union*	$131,750
8	National Assn of Home Builders	$123,589
9	AT&T	$122,367
10	National Assn of Letter Carriers	$111,700
11	United Auto Workers	$111,050
12	Assn of Trial Lawyers of America*	$107,200
13	Air Line Pilots Assn	$101,000
14	American Dental Assn	$100,850
15	Associated Milk Producers	$99,000
16	National Auto Dealers Assn	$89,550
17	General Motors*	$89,548
18	Seafarers International Union*	$89,100
19	Carpenters Union*	$88,150
20	Amer Fedn of State/County/Munic Employees	$84,583

* Contributions came from more than one PAC affiliated with this sponsor.

Leading Sectors Giving to Committee Members

Business

Air Defense	$690,267
Banks	$359,729
Defense Electronics	$346,546
Food & Beverage	$246,624
Health Professionals	$477,166
Lawyers	$260,924
Oil & Gas	$289,486
Real Estate	$311,885
Telecommunications	$272,793

Ideological/Single-Issue

Misc Issues	$342,688
Pro-Israel	$291,150

Labor

Construction Unions	$317,035
Govt & Postal Workers	$539,378
Misc Unions	$458,100
Transportation Unions	$737,855

House Armed Services Committee

Les Aspin (D-Wis), Chairman
William L. Dickinson (R-Ala), Ranking Republican

Party Ratio: 31 Democrats
20 Republicans

> **Jurisdiction:** (1) Common defense generally; (2) The Department of Defense generally, including the Department of the Army, Navy, and Air Force; (3) Ammunition depots; forts; arsenals; Army, Navy, and Air Force reservations and establishments; (4) Conservation, development, and use of naval petroleum and oil shale reserves; (5) Pay, promotion, retirement, and other benefits and privileges of members of the armed forces; (6) Scientific research and development in support of the armed services; (7) Selective service; (8) Size and composition of the Army, Navy and Air Force; (9) Soldiers' and sailors' homes; (10) Strategic and critical materials necessary for the common defense; (11) Military applications of nuclear energy. The committee also has oversight duties with respect to international arms control and disarmament, and military dependents' education.

Subcommittees

Investigations
Bill Nichols (D-Ala), Chairman
Larry J. Hopkins (R-Ky), Ranking Republican

Military Installations and Facilities
Ronald V. Dellums (D-Calif), Chairman
David O'B. Martin (R-NY), Ranking Republican

Military Personnel and Compensation
Beverly B. Byron (D-Md), Chairwoman
Herbert H. Bateman (R-Va), Ranking Republican

Procurement and Military Nuclear Systems
Samuel S. Stratton (D-NY), Chairman
Robert E. Badham (R-Calif), Ranking Republican

Readiness
Nicholas Mavroules (D-Mass), Chairman
John R. Kasich (R-Ohio), Ranking Republican

Research and Development
Les Aspin (D-Wis), Acting Chairman
William L. Dickinson (R-Ala), Ranking Republican

Seapower and Strategic and Critical Materials
Charles E. Bennett (D-Fla), Chairman
Floyd Spence (R-SC), Ranking Republican

Total Defense-Related PAC Contributions to Committee Members

	Total from Defense-Related PACs	Pct of Member's Total PACs		Total from Defense-Related PACs	Pct of Member's Total PACs
Les Aspin (D-Wis)	$101,700	38%	John M. Spratt (D-SC)	$29,050	21%
William L. Dickinson (R-Ala)	$94,164	59%	Norman Sisisky (D-Va)	$28,550	22%
Roy Dyson (D-Md)	$91,300	22%	Larry J. Hopkins (R-Ky)	$27,550	21%
Robert W. Davis (R-Mich)	$84,680	28%	Tommy F. Robinson (D-Ark)	$27,257	15%
James V. Hansen (R-Utah)	$63,250	26%	John G. Rowland (R-Conn)	$26,270	17%
Marilyn Lloyd (D-Tenn)	$58,200	18%	Albert G. Bustamante (D-Texas)	$25,650	17%
Herbert H. Bateman (R-Va)	$57,470	36%	Dennis M. Hertel (D-Mich)	$25,450	16%
Mac Sweeney (R-Texas)	$56,435	25%	John R. Kasich (R-Ohio)	$24,635	19%
Dave McCurdy (D-Okla)	$56,050	41%	David O'B. Martin (R-NY)	$24,600	35%
Beverly B. Byron (D-Md)	$55,384	38%	Joseph E. Brennan (D-Maine)	$23,300	8%
George "Buddy" Darden (D-Ga)	$53,700	22%	Sonny Montgomery (D-Miss)	$21,250	29%
Duncan L. Hunter (R-Calif)	$53,285	37%	Solomon P. Ortiz (D-Texas)	$21,150	21%
Richard Ray (D-Ga)	$50,417	38%	Owen B. Pickett (D-Va)	$20,100	10%
Jack Davis (R-Ill)	$45,123	18%	Arthur Ravenel (R-SC)	$18,850	15%
Jim Courter (R-NJ)	$44,977	28%	Frank McCloskey (D-Ind)	$18,750	6%
Ike Skelton (D-Mo)	$44,950	23%	Dan Daniel (D-Va)[2]	$17,300	63%
Floyd Spence (R-SC)	$44,812	23%	Charles E. Bennett (D-Fla)	$17,100	32%
Curt Weldon (R-Pa)	$41,277	19%	H. Martin Lancaster (D-NC)	$15,300	12%
Robert E. Badham (R-Calif)[1]	$38,181	58%	Thomas M. Foglietta (D-Pa)	$11,000	6%
Bob Stump (R-Ariz)	$37,900	29%	Nicholas Mavroules (D-Mass)	$10,200	10%
Earl Hutto (D-Fla)	$37,300	29%	Ben Blaz (R-Guam)[3]	$8,000	68%
Samuel S. Stratton (D-NY)[1]	$36,650	64%	Ronald V. Dellums (D-Calif)	$3,850	4%
Lynn Martin (R-Ill)	$35,050	20%	Patricia Schroeder (D-Colo)	$3,050	2%
Marvin Leath (D-Texas)	$33,400	38%	Barbara Boxer (D-Calif)	$2,250	1%
Jon Kyl (R-Ariz)	$33,089	19%	Lane Evans (D-Ill)	$1,700	1%
Bill Nichols (D-Ala)	$32,050	38%			
George J. Hochbrueckner (D-NY)	$29,550	7%			
Andy Ireland (R-Fla)	$29,050	18%			

[1] Did not run for reelection in 1988
[2] Died Jan 23, 1988
[3] Non-voting Delegate

Summary

The end of the Cold War and a general warming in international relations may be welcome news to most Americans, but it also signals hard times ahead for the defense industry. The House and Senate Armed Services Committees, along with the Defense Appropriations subcommittees, are at the center of the debate on how to cut back defense spending while not jeopardizing national security — or defense-related industries.

The patterns of PAC contributions within the committee reflect the industry's concern; defense contractors contributed more than $1.8 million to members of this committee in 1987-88, most of it from aerospace and electronics firms. Their contributions closely paralleled their position in the industry — 14 of the top 20 defense-related contributors to committee members were on the Pentagon's Top 20 contractors list, and all but Chrysler ranked among the top 30 in defense contracts.

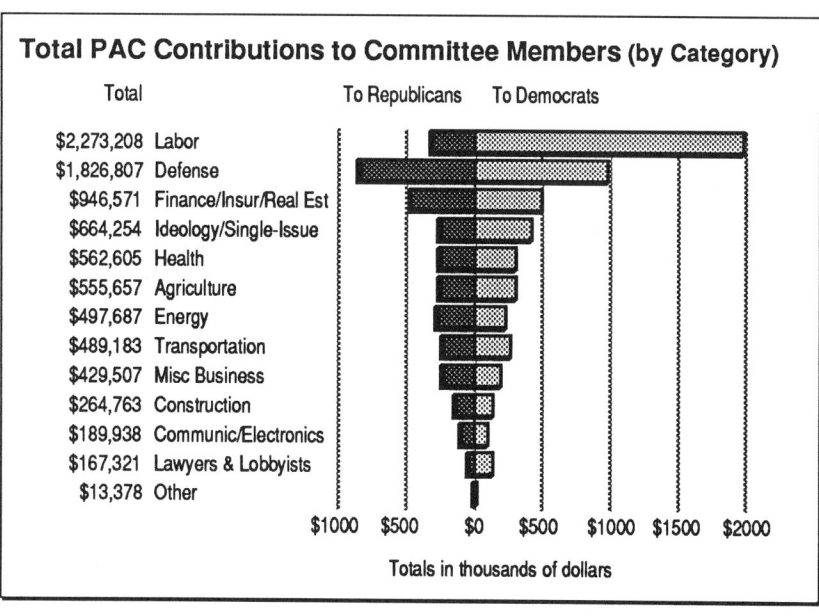

Total PAC Contributions to Committee Members (by Category)

Total		To Republicans · To Democrats
$2,273,208	Labor	
$1,826,807	Defense	
$946,571	Finance/Insur/Real Est	
$664,254	Ideology/Single-Issue	
$562,605	Health	
$555,657	Agriculture	
$497,687	Energy	
$489,183	Transportation	
$429,507	Misc Business	
$264,763	Construction	
$189,938	Communic/Electronics	
$167,321	Lawyers & Lobbyists	
$13,378	Other	

$1000 $500 $0 $500 $1000 $1500 $2000

Totals in thousands of dollars

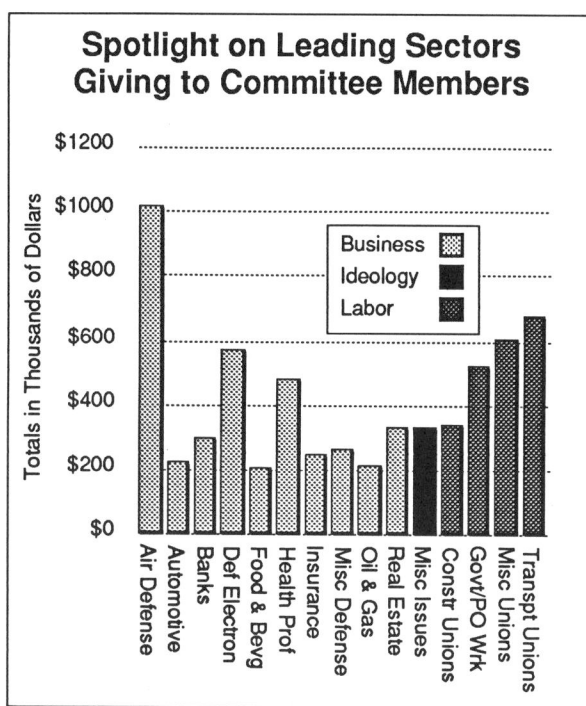

Spotlight on Leading Sectors Giving to Committee Members

Totals in Thousands of Dollars

Legend: Business, Ideology, Labor

Sectors: Air Defense, Automotive, Banks, Def Electron, Food & Bevg, Health Prof, Insurance, Misc Defense, Oil & Gas, Real Estate, Misc Issues, Constr Unions, Govt/PO Wrk, Misc Unions, Transpt Unions

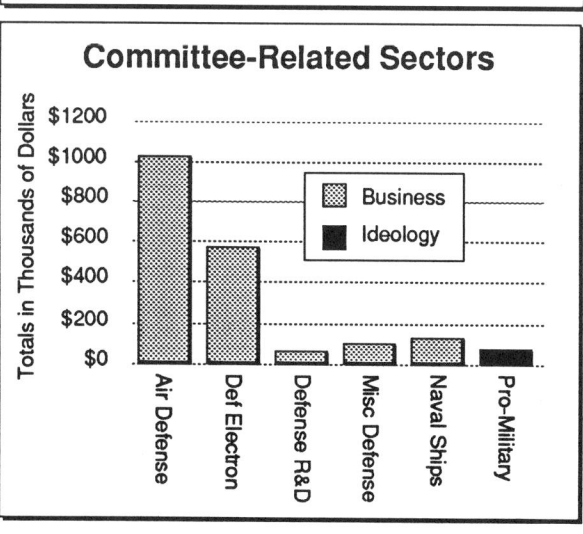

Committee-Related Sectors

Totals in Thousands of Dollars

Legend: Business, Ideology

Sectors: Air Defense, Def Electron, Defense R&D, Misc Defense, Naval Ships, Pro-Military

Top 20 Defense-Related PAC Contributors to Committee Members in 1987-88

1	AT&T	$105,700
2	Lockheed Corp	$91,850
3	McDonnell Douglas*	$89,150
4	Northrop Corp	$86,800
5	General Motors*	$82,900
6	Textron Inc	$75,100
7	General Dynamics	$72,250
8	United Technologies	$69,300
9	Boeing Co	$67,100
10	Grumman	$64,500
11	Rockwell International	$63,800
12	Raytheon*	$60,900
13	FMC Corp	$44,600
14	LTV Corp*	$43,600
15	Litton Industries	$42,350
16	Ford Motor Co*	$41,150
17	Chrysler Corp*	$41,025
18	Tenneco Inc	$38,000
19	Martin Marietta Corp	$37,400
20	General Electric	$34,000

* Contributions came from more than one PAC affiliated with this sponsor.

Leading Defense-Related Sectors Giving to Committee Members

Business

Air Defense	$1,006,604
Defense Electronics	$564,367
Defense R&D	$47,850
Misc Defense	$94,836
Naval Shipbuilding	$114,150

Ideological/Single-Issue

Pro-Military	$63,749

House Banking, Finance & Urban Affairs Committee

Fernand J. St Germain (D-RI), Chairman
Chalmers P. Wylie (R-Ohio), Ranking Republican

Party Ratio: 30 Democrats
20 Republicans

> **Jurisdiction:** (1) Banks and banking, including deposit insurance and Federal monetary policy; (2) money and credit, including currency and the issuance of notes and redemption thereof; gold and silver, including the coinage thereof; valuation and revaluation of the dollar; (3) Urban development; (4) Public and private housing; (5) Economic stabilization, defense production, renegotiation, and control of the price of commodities, rents, and services; (6) International finance; (7) Financial and Monetary organizations.

Subcommittees

Consumer Affairs and Coinage
Frank Annunzio (D-Ill), Chairman
John P. Hiler (R-Ind), Ranking Republican

Domestic Monetary Policy
Stephen L. Neal (D-NC), Chairman
Bill McCollum (R-Fla), Ranking Republican

Economic Stabilization
Mary Rose Oakar (D-Ohio), Chairwoman
Norman D. Shumway (R-Calif), Ranking Republican

Financial Institutions Supervision, Regulation and Insurance
Fernand J. St Germain (D-RI), Chairman
Chalmers P. Wylie (R-Ohio), Ranking Republican

General Oversight and Investigations
Carroll Hubbard (D-Ky), Chairman
Stan Parris (R-Va), Ranking Republican

Housing and Community Development
Henry B. Gonzalez (D-Texas), Chairman
Marge Roukema (R-NJ), Ranking Republican

International Development Institutions and Finance
Walter E. Fauntroy (D- DC), Chairman
Doug Bereuter (R-Neb), Ranking Republican

International Finance, Trade and Monetary Policy
Robert Garcia (D-NY), Chairman
Jim Leach (R-Iowa), Ranking Republican

Total Committee-Related PAC Contributions to Committee Members

	Total from Cmte-Related PACs	Pct of Member's Total PACs		Total from Cmte-Related PACs	Pct of Member's Total PACs
Fernand J. St Germain (D-RI)	$267,648	70%	Stan Parris (R-Va)	$76,500	42%
Stephen L. Neal (D-NC)	$188,500	45%	Bruce A. Morrison (D-Conn)	$75,250	34%
John Hiler (R-Ind)	$154,449	43%	John J. LaFalce (D-NY)	$72,550	52%
Carroll Hubbard (D-Ky)	$134,675	38%	Pat Swindall (R-Ga)	$70,950	37%
David E. Price (D-NC)	$127,000	27%	Barney Frank (D-Mass)	$69,975	43%
Joseph J. DioGuardi (R-NY)	$126,761	37%	Frank Annunzio (D-Ill)	$66,400	40%
Doug Barnard Jr. (D-Ga)	$126,200	72%	David Dreier (R-Calif)	$65,350	65%
Liz J. Patterson (D-SC)	$122,365	32%	Bill McCollum (R-Fla)	$64,200	55%
Chalmers P. Wylie (R-Ohio)	$105,669	65%	Bill Nelson (D-Fla)	$63,050	30%
Paul E. Kanjorski (D-Pa)	$105,500	36%	Joseph P. Kennedy II (D-Mass)	$55,620	22%
Thomas J. Manton (D-NY)	$104,750	34%	Marcy Kaptur (D-Ohio)	$54,400	27%
Mary Rose Oakar (D-Ohio)	$100,295	26%	Floyd H. Flake (D-NY)	$51,767	36%
Patricia Saiki (R-Hawaii)	$98,100	38%	Bruce F. Vento (D-Minn)	$51,250	27%
Tom Ridge (R-Pa)	$95,850	45%	Gerald D. Kleczka (D-Wis)	$47,650	35%
Tom McMillen (D-Md)	$95,533	25%	George C. Wortley (R-NY)[1]	$46,648	66%
Toby Roth (R-Wis)	$94,860	45%	Al McCandless (R-Calif)	$43,500	60%
J. Alex McMillan (R-NC)	$94,750	43%	Doug Bereuter (R-Neb)	$43,245	45%
Thomas R. Carper (D-Del)	$90,803	54%	Robert Garcia (D-NY)	$42,000	23%
Charles E. Schumer (D-NY)	$90,265	64%	Esteban Edward Torres (D-Calif)	$39,400	37%
H. James Saxton (R-NJ)	$89,564	45%	Gary L. Ackerman (D-NY)	$35,750	18%
Nancy Pelosi (D-Calif)	$87,955	17%	Henry B. Gonzalez (D-Texas)	$27,406	28%
Jim Bunning (R-Ky)	$87,898	37%	Kweisi Mfume (D-Md)	$20,310	26%
Steve Bartlett (R-Texas)	$85,900	37%	Walter Fauntroy (D-DC)[2]	$19,081	63%
Norman D. Shumway (R-Calif)	$84,820	56%	Jim Leach (R-Iowa)	$200	14%
Marge Roukema (R-NJ)	$82,846	45%	Stewart B. McKinney (R-Conn)[3]	-$500	100%
Ben Erdreich (D-Ala)	$81,700	48%	Buddy Roemer (D-La)[4]	-$1,000	133%
Richard H. Lehman (D-Calif)	$79,040	44%			

---

[1] Did not run for reelection in 1988
[2] Non-voting Delegate
[3] Died May 7, 1987
[4] Resigned Mar 14, 1988 to assume office as Governor of Louisiana

Summary

Many political observers point to the House Banking Committee, and its former chairman Fernand St Germain (D-RI), as a principal starting point of what later became the savings & loan crisis and government bailout. In the 1980s, St Germain led the committee through a substantial loosening in regulations and a dramatic increase in the ceiling on federal insurance for S&L deposits. Those moves helped transform many S&L's from staid institutions underwriting home loans into conduits for highly-speculative real estate ventures.

Though the S&L crisis has dominated public attention, however, PAC dollars from the S&L's were small potatoes compared with the funds that came to committee members (and to Congress as a whole) from commercial banks. They gave nearly $1.6 million to committee members in the last election cycle — an average of more than $30,000 per committee member. Realtors and home builders, whose industry also comes under the purview of the committee, were also major contributors.

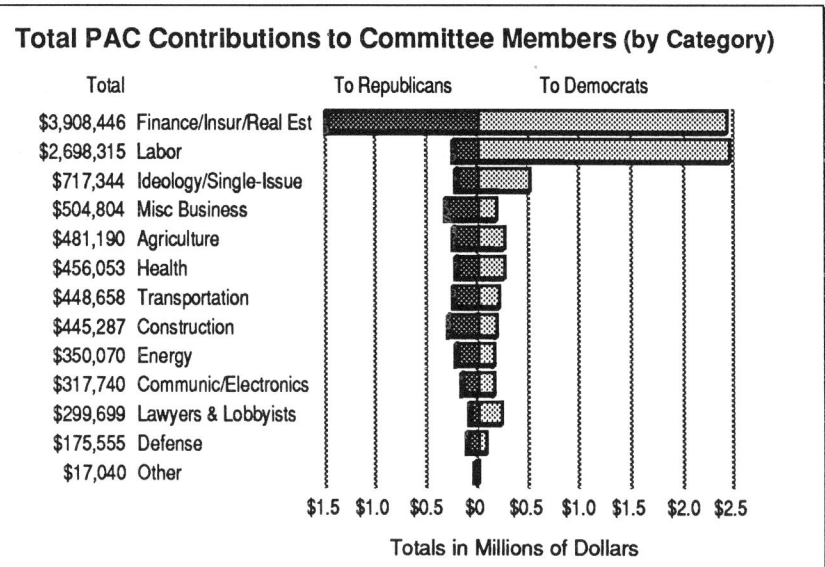

Total PAC Contributions to Committee Members (by Category)

Total		
$3,908,446	Finance/Insur/Real Est	
$2,698,315	Labor	
$717,344	Ideology/Single-Issue	
$504,804	Misc Business	
$481,190	Agriculture	
$456,053	Health	
$448,658	Transportation	
$445,287	Construction	
$350,070	Energy	
$317,740	Communic/Electronics	
$299,699	Lawyers & Lobbyists	
$175,555	Defense	
$17,040	Other	

To Republicans   To Democrats

$1.5 $1.0 $0.5 $0 $0.5 $1.0 $1.5 $2.0 $2.5

Totals in Millions of Dollars

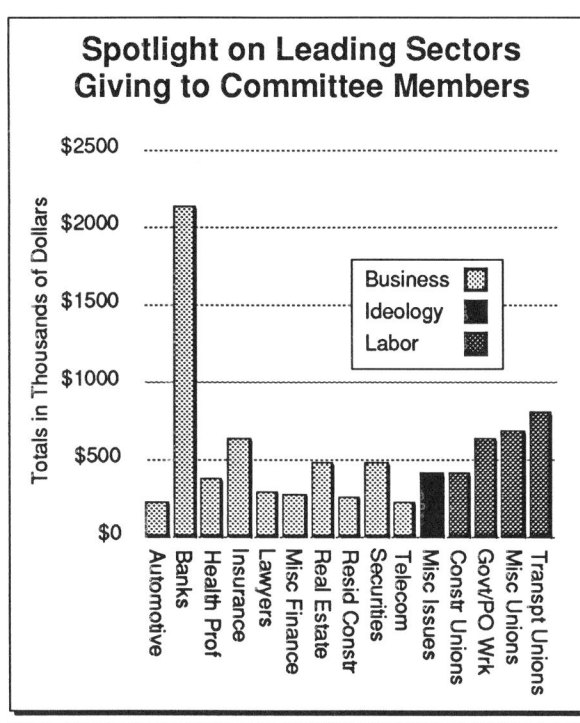

Spotlight on Leading Sectors Giving to Committee Members

Totals in Thousands of Dollars

Business
Ideology
Labor

Automotive, Banks, Health Prof, Insurance, Lawyers, Misc Finance, Real Estate, Resid Constr, Securities, Telecom, Misc Issues, Constr Unions, Govt/PO Wrk, Misc Unions, Transpt Unions

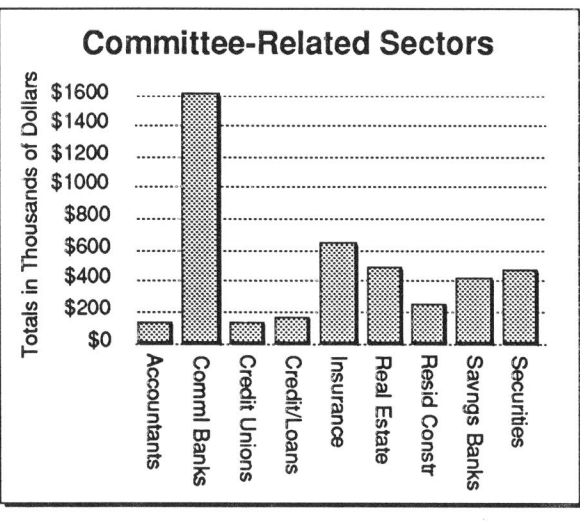

Committee-Related Sectors

Totals in Thousands of Dollars

Accountants, Comml Banks, Credit Unions, Credit/Loans, Insurance, Real Estate, Resid Constr, Savngs Banks, Securities

Top 20 Committee-Related PAC Contributors to Committee Members in 1987-88

1	National Assn of Realtors	$334,856
2	American Bankers Assn*	$293,675
3	National Assn of Home Builders*	$163,210
4	US League of Savings Assn*	$148,525
5	J P Morgan & Co	$131,150
6	Citicorp	$116,145
7	National Assn of Life Underwriters	$109,700
8	Independent Insurance Agents of America	$105,094
9	Barnett Banks of Florida	$104,600
10	Credit Union National Assn*	$96,300
11	Bankers Trust	$72,500
12	American Express*	$68,075
13	American Institute of CPA's	$66,400
14	Chemical Bank*	$56,923
15	First Boston Corp	$50,850
16	Mortgage Bankers Assn of America	$50,675
17	Chase Manhattan*	$50,425
18	Assn of Bank Holding Companies	$49,075
19	Goldman Sachs	$48,900
20	National Assn of Mutual Insurance Agents	$48,025

* Contributions came from more than one PAC affiliated with this sponsor.

Leading Committee-Related Sectors Giving to Committee Members

Banking
Commercial Banks ... $1,591,288
Savngs Banks ... $410,451
Credit Unions ... $121,550

Financial Services
Consumer Credit/Loans ... $147,800
Accountants ... $104,650

Other Financial
Insurance ... $631,990
Securities/Commodities Investment ... $462,125
Misc Finance ... $19,275

Real Estate & Construction
Real Estate ... $474,667
Residential Construction ... $240,852

House Budget Committee

William H. Gray III (D-Pa), Chairman
Delbert L. Latta (R-Ohio), Ranking Republican

Party Ratio: 21 Democrats
15 Republicans

Jurisdiction: (1) To report the matters required to be reported by it under titles III and IV of the Congressional Budget Act of 1974; (2) To make continuing studies of the effect on budget outlays of relevant existing and proposed legislation and to report the results of such studies to the House on a recurring basis; (3) To request and evaluate continuing studies of tax expenditures, to devise methods of coordinating tax expenditures, policies, and programs with direct budget outlays, and to report the results of such studies to the House on a recurring basis; and (4) To review, on a continuing basis, the conduct by the Congressional Budget Office of its functions and duties.

Task Forces

Budget Process
Butler Derrick (D-SC), Chairman

Community and Natural Resources
Howard Wolpe (D-Mich), Chairman

Defense and International Affairs
Vic Fazio (D-Calif), Chairman

Economic and Trade Policy
Mike Lowry (D-Wash), Chairman

Health
Martin Frost (D-Texas), Chairman

Human Resources
Pat Williams (D-Mont), Chairman

Income Security
Marty Russon (D-Ill), Chairman

State and Local Government
George Miller (D-Calif), Chairman

Total PAC Contributions to Committee Members

Connie Mack (R-Fla)[1]	$1,017,045
Buddy MacKay (D-Fla)[1]	$854,388
Mike Lowry (D-Wash)[1]	$684,405
Thomas S. Foley (D-Wash)	$554,640
Mike Espy (D-Miss)	$480,490
Vic Fazio (D-Calif)	$378,783
William H. Gray III (D-Pa)	$377,752
Butler Derrick (D-SC)	$370,841
Marty Russo (D-Ill)	$357,996
Jack Buechner (R-Mo)	$320,544
Ed Jenkins (D-Ga)	$310,397
Martin Frost (D-Texas)	$298,373
Jim Slattery (D-Kan)	$266,122
Howard Wolpe (D-Mich)	$262,274
Richard J. Durbin (D-Ill)	$220,305
Bill Thomas (R-Calif)	$215,150
Frank J. Guarini (D-NJ)	$213,835
Denny Smith (R-Ore)	$211,227
James L. Oberstar (D-Minn)	$206,320
Barbara Boxer (D-Calif)	$185,330
Don Sundquist (R-Tenn)	$182,103
Pat Williams (D-Mont)	$180,156
George Miller (D-Calif)	$179,984
Jim McCrery (D-La)	$158,446
Dick Armey (R-Texas)	$150,800
Charles E. Schumer (D-NY)	$137,325
Nancy L. Johnson (R-Conn)	$132,822
Mickey Edwards (R-Okla)	$122,130
Beau Boulter (R-Texas)	$117,993
Marvin Leath (D-Texas)	$94,900
Harold Rogers (R-Ky)	$69,566
Amo Houghton (R-NY)	$65,650
Delbert L. Latta (R-Ohio)[2]	$2,656
Chester G. Atkins (D-Mass)	$300
Bill Goodling (R-Pa)	$0
Bill Gradison (R-Ohio)	$0

Top 20 PAC Contributors to Committee Members in 1987-88

1	National Assn of Realtors*	$213,482
2	American Medical Assn*	$187,566
3	Teamsters Union*	$148,399
4	National Education Assn	$141,298
5	National Assn/Retired Federal Employees	$137,350
6	Assn of Trial Lawyers of America*	$122,750
7	National Assn of Letter Carriers	$100,200
8	United Auto Workers	$99,200
9	National Assn of Life Underwriters	$97,250
10	National Assn of Home Builders*	$95,498
11	Air Line Pilots Assn	$91,500
12	Marine Engineers Union*	$88,600
13	Amer Fedn of State/County/Munic Employees	$87,100
14	National PAC	$85,000
15	Carpenters Union*	$81,250
16	AT&T	$80,800
17	American Dental Assn*	$79,750
18	National Auto Dealers Assn	$75,750
19	Seafarers International Union*	$69,200
20	Auto Dealers & Drivers for Free Trade	$68,000

* Contributions came from more than one PAC affiliated with this sponsor.

1 Ran for U.S. Senate in 1988
2 Did not run for reelection in 1988

Summary

Members of the House Budget Committee received their PAC dollars from a cross-section of industries and interests that closely parallels that of Congress in general. Sixteen of the committee members' Top 20 PACs are also on the all-Congress Top 20 list.

As is typical of the PAC patterns in Congress, labor unions gave more than 90 percent of their dollars to Democrats, while business-related PACs spread their money fairly evenly between members of both parties. Ideological PACs also strongly favored Democrats on the committee — another trend that was common among congressional candidates in general.

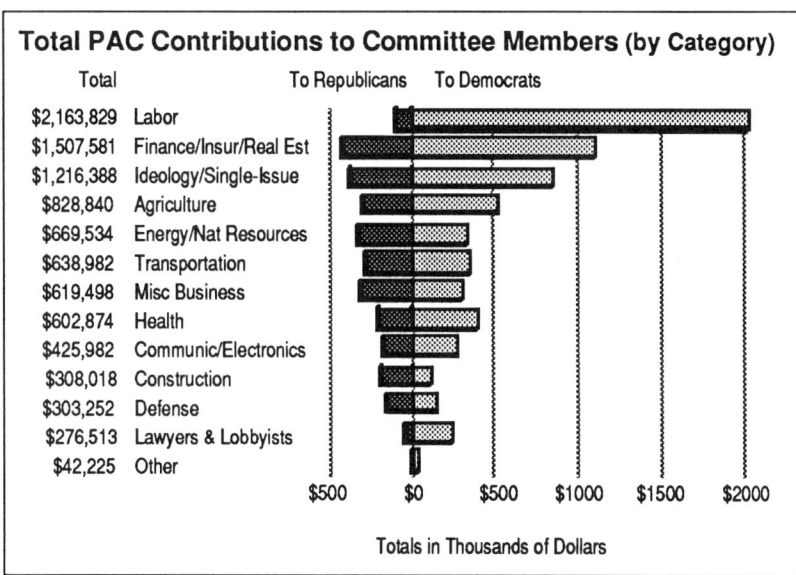

Total PAC Contributions to Committee Members (by Category)

Total	
$2,163,829	Labor
$1,507,581	Finance/Insur/Real Est
$1,216,388	Ideology/Single-Issue
$828,840	Agriculture
$669,534	Energy/Nat Resources
$638,982	Transportation
$619,498	Misc Business
$602,874	Health
$425,982	Communic/Electronics
$308,018	Construction
$303,252	Defense
$276,513	Lawyers & Lobbyists
$42,225	Other

Totals in Thousands of Dollars

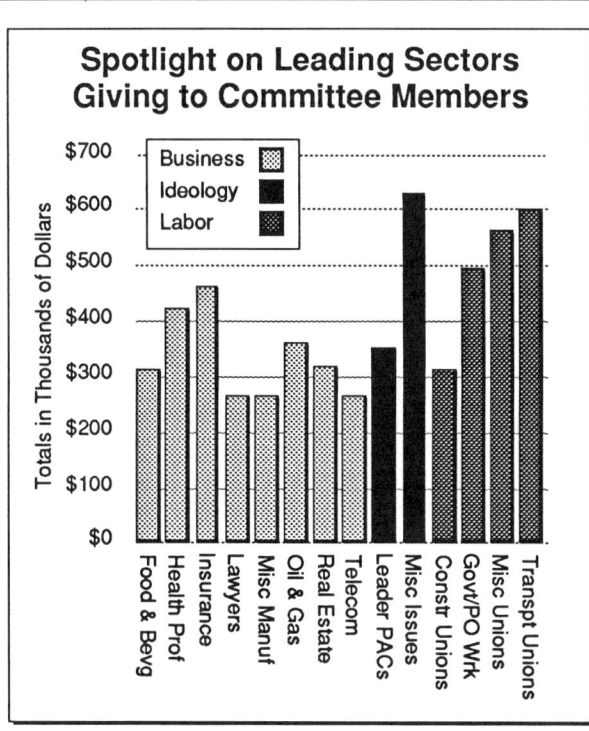

Spotlight on Leading Sectors Giving to Committee Members

Business / Ideology / Labor

Food & Bevg, Health Prof, Insurance, Lawyers, Misc Manuf, Oil & Gas, Real Estate, Telecom, Leader PACs, Misc Issues, Const Unions, Govt/PO Wrk, Misc Unions, Transpt Unions

Leading Sectors Giving to Committee Members

Business

Banks	$455,388
Food & Beverage	$308,836
Health Professionals	$418,666
Insurance	$457,658
Lawyers	$260,463
Misc Manufacturing	$262,899
Oil & Gas	$355,344
Real Estate	$313,885
Telecommunications	$263,125

Ideological/Single-Issue

Leadership PACs	$348,099
Misc Issues	$625,208

Labor

Construction Unions	$309,575
Govt & Postal Workers	$493,106
Misc Unions	$560,901
Transportation Unions	$599,349

House District of Columbia Committee

Ronald V. Dellums (D-Calif), Chairman
Stan Parris (R-Va), Ranking Republican

Party Ratio: 7 Democrats
4 Republicans

> **Jurisdiction:** (1) Local government, delegated authority, form, finances, operations and programs, of local government bodies, as authorized by . . . the U.S. Constitution—"Congress shall have the power to exercise exclusive legislation in all cases whatsoever over such District . . . "; (2) Political status, jurisdiction and boundaries of the District of Columbia; (3) The annual federal payment — pension fund financing for police, firefighters and teachers; (4) Delegate to the House of Representatives; courts: organization, operations; appointment and removal mechanisms and term of judges; (5) Organizations chartered by Congress: determination of tax-exempt status; (6) Planning and design of the national capital: (a) building height limitation, National Capital Planning Commission, protection of Old Georgetown, the Commission of Fine Arts; (7) Metropolitan regional affairs: (a) Washington Metropolitan Area Transit Authority, (b) emergency planning and procedures, Potomac River shoreline and water quality improvement; (8) The International Community.

Subcommittees

Fiscal Affairs and Health
Walter E. Fauntroy (D-DC), Chairman
Thomas J. Bliley Jr. (R-Va), Ranking Republican

Government Operations and Metropolitan Affairs
Alan Wheat (D-Mo), Chairman
Larry Combest (R-Texas), Ranking Republican

Judiciary and Education
Mervyn M. Dymally (D-Calif), Chairman
Lynn M. Martin (R-Ill), Ranking Republican

Total PAC Contributions to Committee Members

William H. Gray III (D-Pa)	$377,752
Pete Stark (D-Calif)	$325,428
Thomas J. Bliley (R-Va)	$270,350
Bruce A. Morrison (D-Conn)	$224,433
Alan Wheat (D-Mo)	$206,900
Romano L. Mazzoli (D-Ky)	$196,650
Lynn Martin (R-Ill)	$186,532
Stan Parris (R-Va)	$182,927
Mervyn M. Dymally (D-Calif)	$156,449
Larry Combest (R-Texas)	$119,800
Ronald V. Dellums (D-Calif)	$83,399
Walter Fauntroy (D-DC)[1]	$31,446
Stewart B. McKinney (R-Conn)[2]	-$500

Top 20 PAC Contributors to Committee Members in 1987-88

1	Teamsters Union	$58,500
2	Natl Assn of Realtors	$57,150
3	National Education Assn	$47,880
4	American Medical Assn	$45,955
5	Natl Assn/Retired Fed Employ	$40,500
6	United Auto Workers	$37,950
7	Natl Assn of Letter Carriers*	$33,430
8	Carpenters & Joiners Union*	$31,750
9	Marine Engineers Union*	$29,650
10	Assn of Trial Lawyers	$28,500
11	Natl Auto Dealers Assn	$27,350
12	Amer Fedn of St/Cnty/Munic Emp	$26,250
13	AT&T	$25,100
14	Natl Assn Life Underwriters	$24,800
15	American Bankers Assn*	$24,600
16	United Parcel Service	$23,825
17	Machinists/Aerospace Wrkrs Un*	$23,800
18	Amer Postal Workers Union	$22,350
19	Laborers Union*	$21,200
20	Natl Cmte/Preserve Soc Secur	$21,050

* Contributions came from more than one PAC affiliated with this sponsor.

[1] Non-voting Delegate
[2] Died May 7, 1987

Summary

Unlike every other city in America, the nation's capital is governed only partly by its own elected officials, and partly by the U.S. Congress, which has overseen the city's affairs since the District of Columbia was created in 1790. The degree of congressional control has lessened over the years, and the city now enjoys most benefits of home rule. But Congress still controls a major part of the district's purse strings, and decisions made in this committee affect the lives of every resident of Washington.

Since D.C. is not a state, its residents do not elect their own representative, but rather a "delegate" who may not vote for bills on the House floor. Delegates, however, *are* entitled to debate and vote on issues within the committees on which they serve.

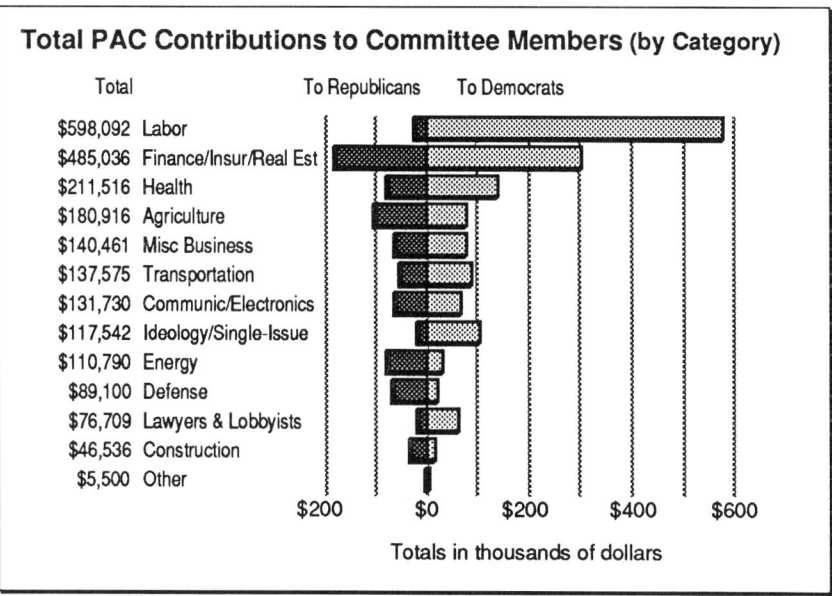

Total PAC Contributions to Committee Members (by Category)

Total	Category
$598,092	Labor
$485,036	Finance/Insur/Real Est
$211,516	Health
$180,916	Agriculture
$140,461	Misc Business
$137,575	Transportation
$131,730	Communic/Electronics
$117,542	Ideology/Single-Issue
$110,790	Energy
$89,100	Defense
$76,709	Lawyers & Lobbyists
$46,536	Construction
$5,500	Other

Totals in thousands of dollars

The only distinctive pattern in PAC contributions to members of the D.C. committee is a higher-than-normal proportion of dollars from government and postal workers, many of whom reside in the Washington, D.C. area.

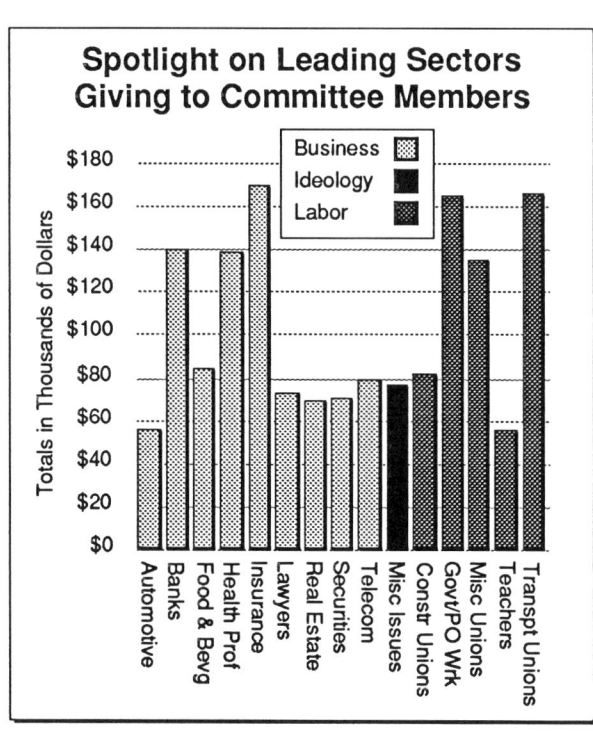

Spotlight on Leading Sectors Giving to Committee Members

Leading Sectors
Giving to Committee Members

Business

Automotive	$54,800
Banks	$138,461
Food & Beverage	$83,154
Health Professionals	$137,955
Insurance	$168,675
Lawyers	$72,365
Real Estate	$68,650
Securities/Commodities Investment	$69,700
Telecommunications	$77,795

Ideological/Single-Issue

Misc Issues	$75,292

Labor

Construction Unions	$81,150
Govt & Postal Workers	$162,960
Misc Unions	$133,992
Teachers Unions	$55,080
Transportation Unions	$164,910

127

House Education and Labor Committee

Augustus F. Hawkins (D-Calif), Chairman
James M. Jeffords (R-Vt), Ranking Republican

Party Ratio: 21 Democrats
13 Republicans

Jurisdiction: (1) Measures relating to education or labor generally; (2) Child labor; (3) Columbia Institution for the Deaf, Dumb, and Blind; Howard University; Freedman's Hospital; (4) Convict labor and the entry of goods made by convicts into interstate commerce; (5) Labor standards; (6) Labor statistics; (7) Mediation and arbitration of labor disputes; (8) Regulation or prevention of importation of foreign laborers under contract; (9) Food programs for children in schools; (10) United States Employees' Compensation Commission; (11) Vocational rehabilitation; (12) Wages and hours of labor; (13) Welfare of miners; (14) Work incentives programs. The committee also has a special oversight function with respect to domestic educational programs and institutions, and programs of student assistance, which are within the Jurisdiction of other committees.

Subcommittees

Elementary, Secondary, and Vocational Education
Augustus F. Hawkins (D-Calif), Chairman
William F. Goodling (R-Pa), Ranking Republican

Employment Opportunities
Matthew G. Martinez (D-Calif), Chairman
Steve Gunderson (R-Wis), Ranking Republican

Health and Safety
Joseph M. Gaydos (D-Pa), Chairman
Paul B. Henry (R-Mich), Ranking Republican

Human Resources
Dale E. Kildee (D-Mich), Chairman
Thomas J. Tauke (R-Iowa), Ranking Republican

Labor-Management Relations
William L. (Bill) Clay (D-Mo), Chairman
Marge Roukema (R-NJ), Ranking Republican

Labor Standards
Austin J. Murphy (D-Pa), Chairman
Thomas E. Petri (R-Wis), Ranking Republican

Postsecondary Education
Pat Williams (D-Mont), Chairman
E. Thomas Coleman (R-Mo), Ranking Republican

Total PAC Contributions to Committee Members

James M. Jeffords (R-Vt)[1]	$679,393
Jim Jontz (D-Ind)	$471,225
Thomas C. Sawyer (D-Ohio)	$312,904
Bill Richardson (D-NM)	$297,898
Fred Grandy (R-Iowa)	$294,944
Tom Tauke (R-Iowa)	$290,210
William D. Ford (D-Mich)	$267,901
Carl C. Perkins (D-Ky)	$264,300
Steve Bartlett (R-Texas)	$230,678
Matthew G. Martinez (D-Calif)	$218,900
Tommy F. Robinson (D-Ark)	$182,980
Marge Roukema (R-NJ)	$181,513
Pat Williams (D-Mont)	$180,156
E. Thomas Coleman (R-Mo)	$175,134
Peter J. Visclosky (D-Ind)	$157,250
Cass Ballenger (R-NC)	$153,375
Dick Armey (R-Texas)	$150,800
Joseph M. Gaydos (D-Pa)	$142,850
William L. Clay (D-Mo)	$141,630
Steve Gunderson (R-Wis)	$133,235
Austin J. Murphy (D-Pa)	$128,218
Timothy J. Penny (D-Minn)	$125,377
Major R. Owens (D-NY)	$125,085
Bob Wise (D-WVa)	$122,952
Thomas E. Petri (R-Wis)	$120,980
Charles A. Hayes (D-Ill)	$115,634
Augustus F. Hawkins (D-Calif)	$105,550
Dale E. Kildee (D-Mich)	$103,770
Harris W. Fawell (R-Ill)	$98,171
Paul B. Henry (R-Mich)	$97,425
Stephen J. Solarz (D-NY)	$59,605
Mario Biaggi (D-NY)[2]	$37,400
Chester G. Atkins (D-Mass)	$300
Bill Goodling (R-Pa)	$0

Top 20 PAC Contributors to Committee Members in 1987-88

1	Teamsters Union	$178,250
2	National Assn of Realtors*	$159,950
3	American Medical Assn*	$150,370
4	Assn of Trial Lawyers of America*	$122,800
5	National Education Assn	$119,222
6	Amer Fedn of State/County/Munic Employees	$118,635
7	United Auto Workers	$117,450
8	National Assn/Retired Federal Employees	$117,050
9	Letter Carriers Union*	$99,250
10	Air Line Pilots Assn	$89,500
11	American Federation of Teachers*	$82,225
12	Carpenters Union*	$79,000
13	Associated Milk Producers	$72,400
14	Machinists/Aerospace Wrkrs Union*	$69,400
15	Marine Engineers Union*	$68,020
16	Food & Commercial Workers Union*	$67,375
17	National Assn of Life Underwriters	$60,850
18	National Assn of Home Builders	$59,316
19	Seafarers International Union	$59,100
20	American Bankers Assn*	$58,275

* Contributions came from more than one PAC affiliated with this sponsor.

---

[1] Ran for U.S. Senate in 1988
[2] Resigned Aug 5, 1988

Summary

Not surprisingly, labor unions dominate the PAC contributions to members of the Education and Labor Committee. But decisions made by this panel affect virtually every American business, whether or not they employ union workers. Minimum wage laws, safety rules, and dozens of other labor-related standards and regulations fall within the purview of this committee.

Organized unions do have an enormous stake in the issues debated here, and they accounted for 13 of the Top 20 PAC contributors to committee members in 1987-88. By contrast, educational interests have never played a major role in the PAC world. With the exception of the two main teachers unions — the National Education Association and the American Federation of Teachers — education-related PACs gave only $162,000 to federal candidates during the 1988 elections. Nearly all represented schools dealing in vocational education.

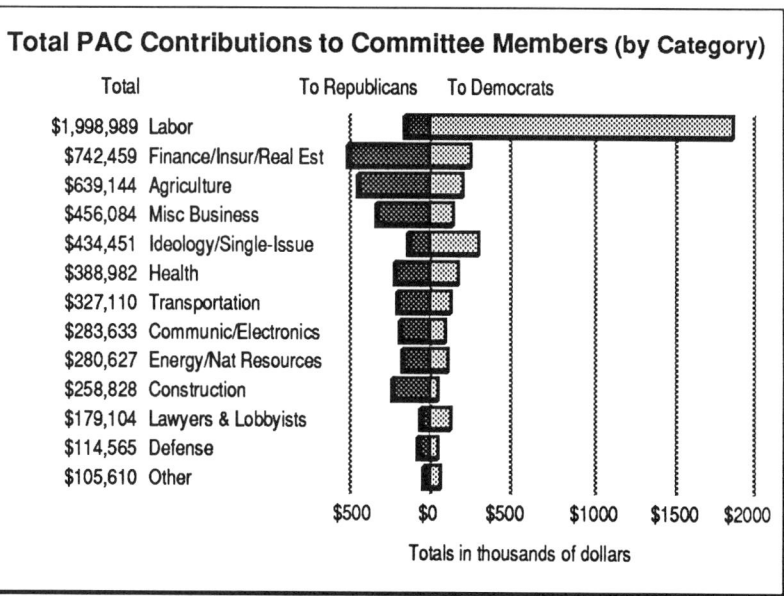

Total PAC Contributions to Committee Members (by Category)

Total	Category
$1,998,989	Labor
$742,459	Finance/Insur/Real Est
$639,144	Agriculture
$456,084	Misc Business
$434,451	Ideology/Single-Issue
$388,982	Health
$327,110	Transportation
$283,633	Communic/Electronics
$280,627	Energy/Nat Resources
$258,828	Construction
$179,104	Lawyers & Lobbyists
$114,565	Defense
$105,610	Other

Totals in thousands of dollars

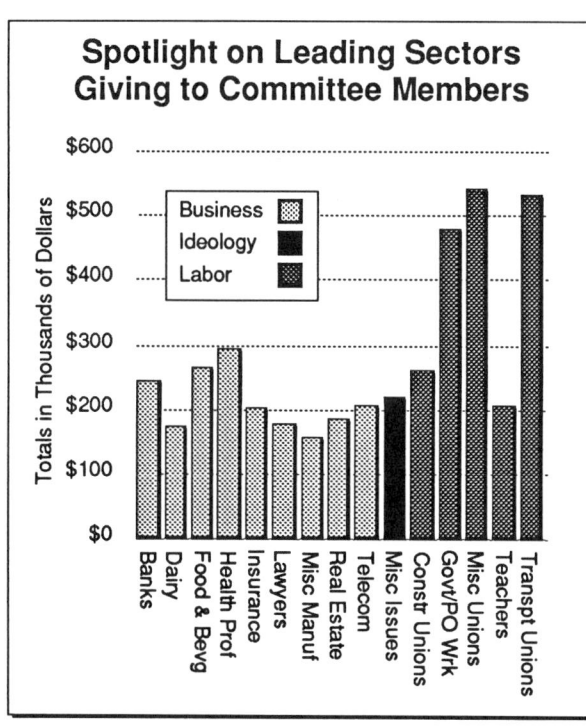

Spotlight on Leading Sectors Giving to Committee Members

Leading Sectors Giving to Committee Members

Business

Banks	$242,010
Dairy Producers	$168,725
Food & Beverage	$262,679
Health Professionals	$290,778
Insurance	$200,872
Lawyers	$173,925
Misc Manufacturing	$155,516
Real Estate	$184,486
Telecommunications	$202,391

Ideological/Single-Issue

Misc Issues	$216,850

Labor

Construction Unions	$256,595
Govt & Postal Workers	$473,790
Misc Unions	$536,166
Teachers Unions	$201,997
Transportation Unions	$530,441

House Energy and Commerce Committee

John D. Dingell (D-Mich), Chairman
Norman F. Lent (R-NY), Ranking Republican

Party Ratio: 25 Democrats
17 Republicans

Jurisdiction: (1) Interstate and foreign commerce generally; (2) National energy policy generally; (3) Measures relating to the exploration, production, storage, supply, marketing, pricing, and regulation of energy resources, including all fossil fuels, solar energy, and other unconventional or renewable energy resources; (4) Measures relating to the conservation of energy resources; (5) Measures relating to the commercial application of energy technology; (6) Measures relating to energy information generally; (7) Measures relating to (A) the generation and marketing of power (except by federally chartered or Federal regional power marketing authorities), (B) the reliability and interstate transmission of, and rate making for, all power, and (C) the siting of generation facilities; except the installation of interconnections between Government waterpower projects. (The committee's jurisdiction extends both to nuclear and nonnuclear facilities and energy). (8) Interstate energy compacts; (9) Measures relating to general management of the Department of Energy, and the management and all functions of the Federal Energy Regulatory Commission; (10) Inland waterways; (11) Railroads, including railroad labor, railroad retirement and unemployment, except revenue measures related thereto; (12) Regulation of interstate and foreign communication; (13) Securities and exchanges; (14) Consumer affairs and consumer protection; (15) Travel and tourism; (16) Public health and quarantine; (17) Health and health facilities, except health care supported by payroll deductions; (18) Biomedical research and development. The committee also has special oversight functions with respect to all laws, programs, and Government activities affecting nuclear and other energy.

Subcommittees

Commerce, Consumer Protection, and Competitiveness
James J. Florio (D-NJ), Chairman
William E. Dannemeyer (R-Calif), Ranking Republican

Energy and Power
Philip R. Sharp (D-Ind), Chairman
Carlos J. Moorhead (R-Calif), Ranking Republican

Health and the Environment
Henry A. Waxman (D-Calif), Chairman
Edward R. Madigan (R-Ill), Ranking Republican

Oversight and Investigations
John D. Dingell (D-Mich), Chairman
Thomas J. Bliley Jr. (R-Va), Ranking Republican

Telecommunications and Finance
Edward J. Markey (D-Mass), Chairman
Matthew J. Rinaldo (R-NJ), Ranking Republican

Transportation and Hazardous Materials
Thomas A. Luken (D-Ohio), Chairman
Bob Whittaker (R-Kan), Ranking Republican

Total Committee-Related PAC Contributions to Committee Members

	Total from Cmte-Related PACs	Pct of Member's Total PACs		Total from Cmte-Related PACs	Pct of Member's Total PACs
Wayne Dowdy (D-Miss)[1]	$284,849	31%	Matthew J. Rinaldo (R-NJ)	$159,657	57%
John D. Dingell (D-Mich)	$259,405	57%	Jim Cooper (D-Tenn)	$159,542	66%
Norman F. Lent (R-NY)	$254,739	72%	Jim Slattery (D-Kan)	$157,005	58%
Thomas A. Luken (D-Ohio)	$230,189	50%	Mickey Leland (D-Texas)	$154,450	43%
W.J. Tauzin (D-La)	$210,321	69%	Terry L. Bruce (D-Ill)	$151,005	54%
Edward R. Madigan (R-Ill)	$208,635	62%	Gerry Sikorski (D-Minn)	$149,540	41%
John Bryant (D-Texas)	$207,657	53%	Doug Walgren (D-Pa)	$145,931	52%
James J. Florio (D-NJ)	$196,261	55%	Bill Richardson (D-NM)	$144,976	49%
Joe L. Barton (R-Texas)	$193,717	68%	Carlos J. Moorhead (R-Calif)	$142,780	69%
Tom Tauke (R-Iowa)	$191,211	66%	Dan Coats (R-Ind)	$136,625	77%
Ralph M. Hall (D-Texas)	$185,738	77%	Sonny Callahan (R-Ala)	$131,850	52%
Dennis E. Eckart (D-Ohio)	$185,648	49%	Michael G. Oxley (R-Ohio)	$125,500	72%
Thomas J. Bliley (R-Va)	$183,475	68%	Cardiss Collins (D-Ill)	$120,355	58%
Rick Boucher (D-Va)	$181,850	48%	Bob Whittaker (R-Kan)	$117,900	77%
Dan L. Schaefer (R-Colo)	$177,123	52%	Michael Bilirakis (R-Fla)	$102,900	69%
Ron Wyden (D-Ore)	$172,623	54%	Howard C. Nielson (R-Utah)	$88,450	82%
Al Swift (D-Wash)	$170,707	59%	Jim Bates (D-Calif)	$82,700	36%
Jack Fields (R-Texas)	$168,964	65%	William E. Dannemeyer (R-Calif)	$80,500	66%
Don Ritter (R-Pa)	$166,978	58%	James H. Scheuer (D-NY)	$30,550	55%
Philip R. Sharp (D-Ind)	$160,681	54%	Mike Synar (D-Okla)	$200	64%
Henry A. Waxman (D-Calif)	$160,415	66%	Edward J. Markey (D-Mass)	-$725	257%

---

[1] Ran for U.S. Senate in 1988

Summary

During the 1987-88 election cycle, no other committee in Congress attracted as many dollars in PAC contributions as Energy and Commerce — a catch-all committee important to a wide spectrum of American businesses. The telecommunications, finance, health care and energy industries are the ones most directly affected by the decisions reached here, and they led the field in PAC giving, distributing a total of nearly $6 million to committee members. In all, the 42 members of Energy and Commerce collected $11.6 million from PACs in 1987-88, an average of more than $277,000 per member.

This abundance of PAC dollars is one reason that a seat on this powerful and wide-ranging committee is one of the most coveted assignments in the House of Representatives today.

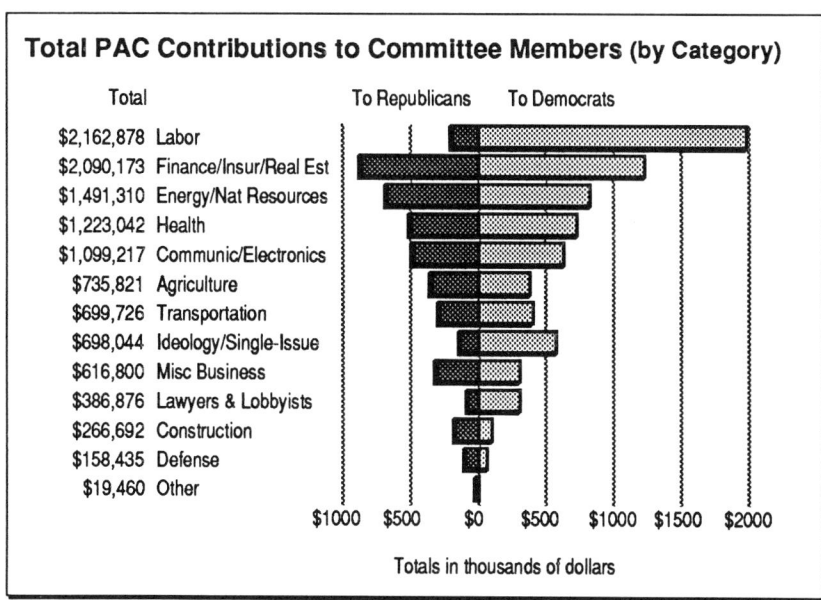

Total PAC Contributions to Committee Members (by Category)

Total	Category
$2,162,878	Labor
$2,090,173	Finance/Insur/Real Est
$1,491,310	Energy/Nat Resources
$1,223,042	Health
$1,099,217	Communic/Electronics
$735,821	Agriculture
$699,726	Transportation
$698,044	Ideology/Single-Issue
$616,800	Misc Business
$386,876	Lawyers & Lobbyists
$266,692	Construction
$158,435	Defense
$19,460	Other

Totals in thousands of dollars

Spotlight on Leading Sectors Giving to Committee Members

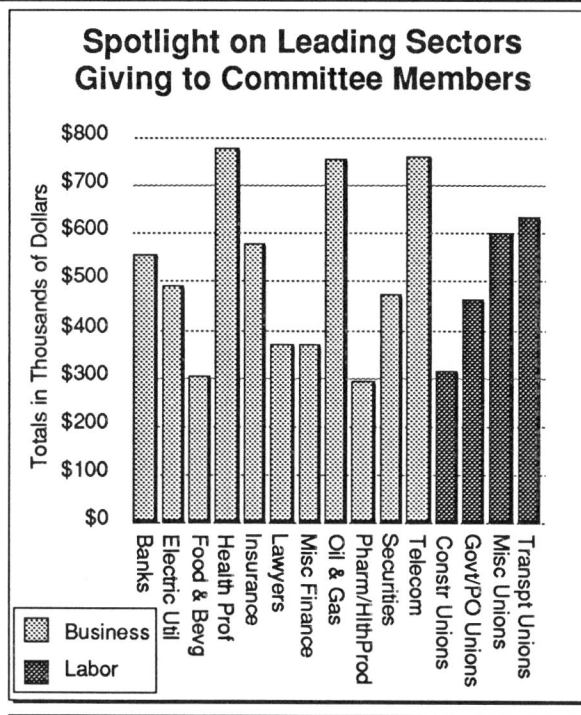

Committee-Related Sectors

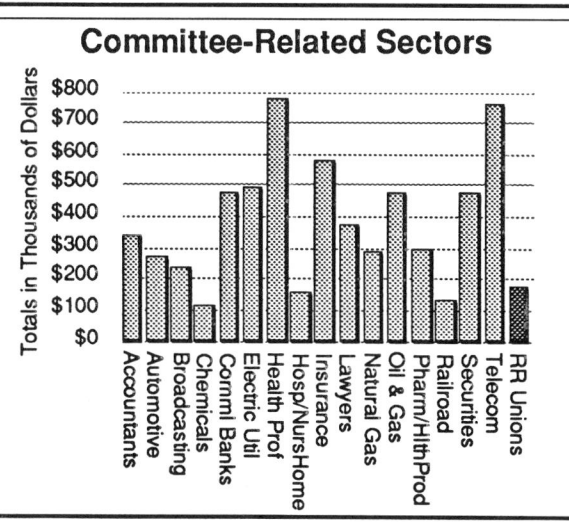

Top 20 Committee-Related PAC Contributors to Committee Members in 1987-88

1	American Medical Assn*	$246,560
2	American Institute of CPA's	$196,750
3	AT&T	$168,200
4	Assn of Trial Lawyers of America*	$147,783
5	American Bankers Assn*	$118,475
6	National Cable Television Assn	$116,790
7	American Dental Assn	$112,250
8	National Auto Dealers Assn	$106,690
9	United Transportation Union	$103,300
10	National Assn of Life Underwriters	$97,900
11	J P Morgan & Co	$81,750
12	BellSouth Corp*	$62,100
13	Auto Dealers & Drivers for Free Trade	$61,250
14	Pacific Telesis Group	$61,090
15	Southern Company*	$60,750
16	Bell Atlantic*	$53,195
17	National Assn of Broadcasters	$52,636
18	Chicago Board of Trade	$48,500
19	American Academy of Opthalmology	$48,500
20	American Optometric Assn	$48,181

* Contributions came from more than one PAC affiliated with this sponsor.

Leading Committee-Related Sectors Giving to Committee Members

Accountants	$332,939
Automotive	$263,439
Broadcasting	$225,259
Chemicals	$107,675
Commercial Banks	$473,333
Electric Utilities	$486,930
Health Professionals	$768,140
Hospitals & Nursing Homes	$148,513
Insurance	$571,494
Lawyers	$365,829
Natural Gas Distribution	$276,850
Oil & Gas Production	$470,582
Pharmaceuticals/Health Products	$286,656
Railroads	$125,354
Railroad Unions	$164,282
Securities/Commodities Investment	$468,313
Telecommunications	$753,600

House Foreign Affairs Committee

Dante B. Fascell (D-Fla), Chairman
William S. Broomfield (R-Mich), Ranking Republican

Party Ratio: 25 Democrats
17 Republicans

Jurisdiction: (1) Relations of the United States with foreign nations generally; (2) Acquisition of land and buildings for embassies and legations in foreign countries; (3) Establishment of boundary lines between the United States and foreign nations; (4) Foreign loans; (5) International conferences and congresses; (6) Intervention abroad and declarations of war; (7) Measures relating to the diplomatic service; (8) Measures to foster commercial intercourse with foreign nations and to safeguard American business interests abroad; (9) Neutrality; (10) Protection of American citizens abroad and expatriation; (11) The American National Red Cross; (12) United Nations Organizations; (13) Measures relating to international economic policy; (14) Export controls, including non-proliferation of nuclear technology and nuclear hardware; (15) International commodity agreements (other than those involving sugar), including all agreements for cooperation in the export of nuclear technology and nuclear hardware; (16) Trading with the enemy; (17) International education. The committee also has special oversight functions with respect to customs administration, intelligence activities relating to foreign policy, international financial and monetary organizations, and international fishing agreements.

Subcommittees

Africa
Howard Wolpe (D-Mich), Chairman
Dan Burton (R-Ind), Ranking Republican

Arms Control, International Security and Science
Dante B. Fascell (D-Fla), Chairman
William S. Broomfield (R-Mich), Ranking Republican

Asian and Pacific Affairs
Stephen J. Solarz (D-NY), Chairman
Jim Leach (R-Iowa), Ranking Republican

Europe and the Middle East
Lee H. Hamilton (D-Ind), Chairman
Benjamin A. Gilman (R-NY), Ranking Republican

Human Rights and International Organizations
Gus Yatron (D-Pa), Chairman
Gerald B. Solomon (R-NY), Ranking Republican

International Economic Policy and Trade
Don Bonker (D-Wash), Chairman
Toby Roth (R-Wis), Ranking Republican

International Operations
Daniel A. Mica (D-Fla), Chairman
Olympia J. Snowe (R-Maine), Ranking Republican

Western Hemisphere Affairs
George W. Crockett Jr. (D-Mich), Chairman
Robert J. Lagomarsino (R-Calif), Ranking Republican

Total PAC Contributions to Committee Members

Connie Mack (R-Fla)[1]	$1,017,045
Wayne Owens (D-Utah)	$455,310
Peter H. Kostmayer (D-Pa)	$416,321
Robert J. Lagomarsino (R-Calif)	$338,996
John R. Miller (R-Wash)	$333,560
James Bilbray (D-Nev)	$300,116
Lawrence J. Smith (D-Fla)	$289,543
James McClure Clarke (D-NC)	$278,867
Don Bonker (D-Wash)[1]	$267,642
Howard Wolpe (D-Mich)	$262,274
Sam Gejdenson (D-Conn)	$208,800
Howard L. Berman (D-Calif)	$207,317
Edward F. Feighan (D-Ohio)	$205,414
Gary L. Ackerman (D-NY)	$196,120
Toby Roth (R-Wis)	$180,814
Dante B. Fascell (D-Fla)	$176,934
Robert G. Torricelli (D-NJ)	$173,057
Daniel A. Mica (D-Fla)[1]	$171,280
Benjamin A. Gilman (R-NY)	$166,797
Mervyn M. Dymally (D-Calif)	$156,449
Mel Levine (D-Calif)	$153,500
Lee H. Hamilton (D-Ind)	$152,066
Dan Burton (R-Ind)	$141,170
Christopher H. Smith (R-NJ)	$124,881
Henry J. Hyde (R-Ill)	$121,407
Mike DeWine (R-Ohio)	$112,860
Tom Lantos (D-Calif)	$111,267
Jan Meyers (R-Kan)	$110,395
Gus Yatron (D-Pa)	$109,700
Doug Bereuter (R-Neb)	$99,120
Donald E. Lukens (R-Ohio)	$84,880
Morris K. Udall (D-Ariz)	$84,605
Gerry E. Studds (D-Mass)	$83,545
Robert K. Dornan (R-Calif)	$83,231
Gerald B.H. Solomon (R-NY)	$74,650
Olympia J. Snowe (R-Maine)	$72,300
Ted Weiss (D-NY)	$64,890
George W. Crockett (D-Mich)	$63,622
Stephen J. Solarz (D-NY)	$59,605
William S. Broomfield (R-Mich)	$57,700
Jaime B. Fuster (Pop Dem-Puerto Rico)[2]	$12,500
Ben Blaz (R-Guam)[2]	$11,800
Chester G. Atkins (D-Mass)	$300
Jim Leach (R-Iowa)	$0

[1] Ran for U.S. Senate in 1988
[2] Non-voting Delegate

Summary

Though its agenda of issues spans foreign policy issues around the world, the House Foreign Affairs Committee is not a center of great interest for the majority of the PAC community. There is one important exception, however — ideological and single-issue PACs whose main focus is foreign policy.

Among that group, none is more formidable on Capitol Hill than supporters of strong U.S. ties to Israel. Pro-Israel PACs are heavy contributors to Congress as a whole (giving more than $4.6 million in 1987-88), and to this committee in particular. Foreign Affairs members received a combined $459,000 from pro-Israel PACs in the last election cycle — an average of more than $11,000 per member.

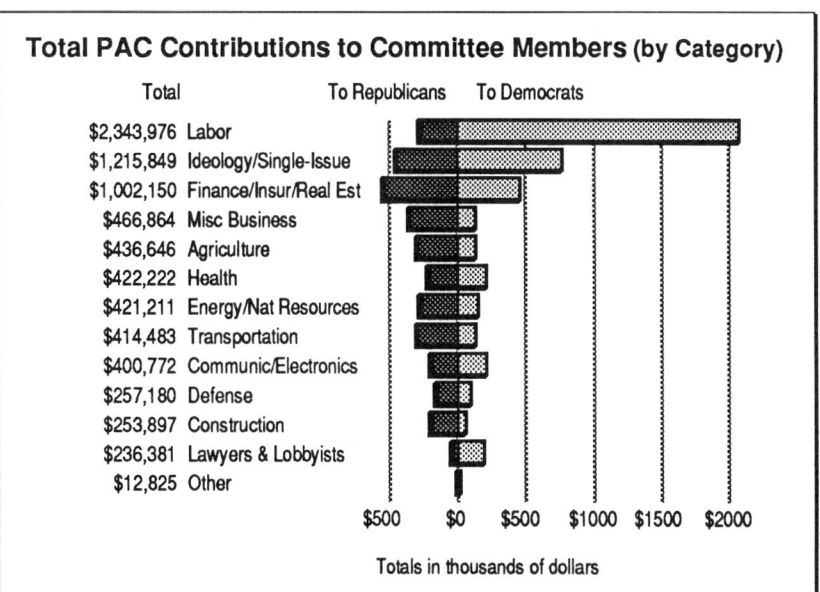

Total PAC Contributions to Committee Members (by Category)

Total		
$2,343,976	Labor	
$1,215,849	Ideology/Single-Issue	
$1,002,150	Finance/Insur/Real Est	
$466,864	Misc Business	
$436,646	Agriculture	
$422,222	Health	
$421,211	Energy/Nat Resources	
$414,483	Transportation	
$400,772	Communic/Electronics	
$257,180	Defense	
$253,897	Construction	
$236,381	Lawyers & Lobbyists	
$12,825	Other	

Totals in thousands of dollars

Spotlight on Leading Sectors Giving to Committee Members

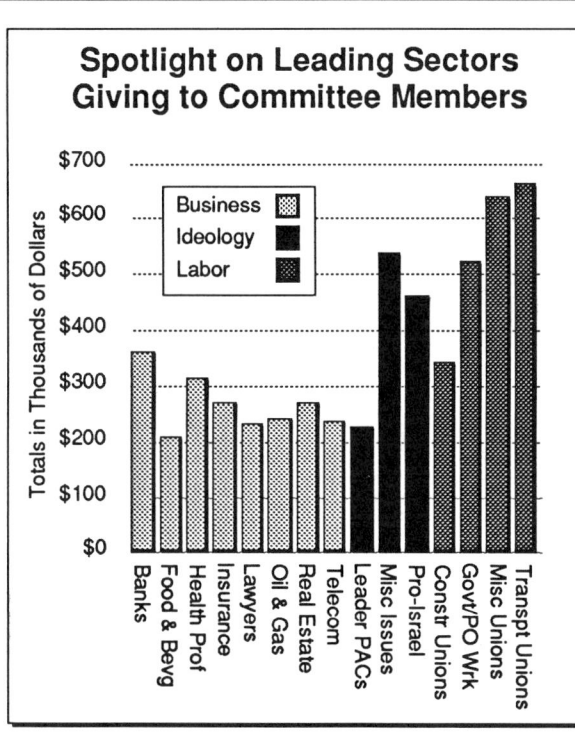

Business, Ideology, Labor

Top 20 PAC Contributors to Committee Members in 1987-88

1	National Assn of Realtors	$229,942
2	Teamsters Union*	$228,650
3	American Medical Assn*	$171,365
4	National Assn/Retired Federal Employees	$154,100
5	National Education Assn*	$144,705
6	Marine Engineers Union*	$136,001
7	United Auto Workers	$133,750
8	National Assn of Letter Carriers	$128,466
9	Assn of Trial Lawyers of America*	$116,400
10	National PAC	$115,000
11	Machinists/Aerospace Wrkrs Union	$105,250
12	Amer Fedn of State/County/Munic Employees	$93,046
13	Carpenters Union*	$85,590
14	National Assn of Home Builders	$81,850
15	Auto Dealers & Drivers for Free Trade	$81,000
16	Seafarers International Union*	$71,100
17	AT&T	$71,000
18	Intl Brotherhood of Electrical Workers*	$70,850
19	American Bankers Assn*	$70,575
20	National Assn of Life Underwriters	$67,800

* Contributions came from more than one PAC affiliated with this sponsor.

Leading Sectors Giving to Committee Members

Business

Banks	$355,359
Food & Beverage	$202,431
Health Professionals	$307,665
Insurance	$267,675
Lawyers	$225,781
Oil & Gas	$239,663
Real Estate	$267,392
Telecommunications	$232,670

Ideological/Single-Issue

Leadership PACs	$224,568
Misc Issues	$533,557
Pro-Israel	$459,624

Labor

Construction Unions	$337,912
Govt & Postal Workers	$519,692
Misc Unions	$637,015
Transportation Unions	$661,552

House Government Operations Committee

Jack Brooks (D-Texas), Chairman
Frank Horton (R-NY), Ranking Republican

Party Ratio: 24 Democrats
15 Republicans

Jurisdiction: (1) Budget and accounting measures, other than appropriations; (2) The overall economy and efficiency of Government operations and activities, including Federal procurement; (3) Reorganizations in the executive branch of the Government; (4) Intergovernmental relationships between the United States and the States and municipalities, and general revenue sharing; (5) National archives; (6) Measures providing for off-budget treatment of Federal agencies or programs.

Subcommittees

Commerce, Consumer and Monetary Affairs
Doug Barnard Jr. (D-Ga), Chairman
Larry E. Craig (R-Idaho), Ranking Republican

Employment and Housing
Tom Lantos (D-Calif), Chairman
Joseph J. DioGuardi (R-NY), Ranking Republican

Environment, Energy and Natural Resources
Mike Synar (D-Okla), Chairman
William F. Clinger Jr. (R-Pa), Ranking Republican

Government Activities and Transportation
Cardiss Collins (D-Ill), Chairwoman
Howard C. Nielson (R-Utah), Ranking Republican

Government Information, Justice, and Agriculture
Glenn English (D-Okla), Chairman
Al McCandless (R-Calif), Ranking Republican

Human Resources and Intergovernmental Relations
Ted Weiss (D-NY), Chairman
Jim Lightfoot (R-Iowa), Ranking Republican

Legislation and National Security
Jack Brooks (D-Texas), Chairman
Frank Horton (R-NY), Ranking Republican

Total PAC Contributions to Committee Members

Stephen L. Neal (D-NC) $411,180
Louise M. Slaughter (D-NY) $387,871
Joseph J. DioGuardi (R-NY) $338,765
Thomas C. Sawyer (D-Ohio) $312,904
Nancy Pelosi (D-Calif) $278,800
Jack Brooks (D-Texas) $276,562
James M. Inhofe (R-Okla) $262,222
Henry A. Waxman (D-Calif) $255,841
Matthew G. Martinez (D-Calif) $218,900
Cardiss Collins (D-Ill) $199,043
William F. Clinger Jr. (R-Pa) $189,036
Glenn English (D-Okla) $183,408
Jon Kyl (R-Ariz) $178,114
Doug Barnard Jr. (D-Ga) $176,171
Ben Erdreich (D-Ala) $173,850
Jim Lightfoot (R-Iowa) $166,077
Larry E. Craig (R-Idaho) $159,060
Albert G. Bustamante (D-Texas) $155,786
Dennis Hastert (R-Ill) $148,608
Joe Kolter (D-Pa) $146,606
Barney Frank (D-Mass) $141,635
John M. Spratt (D-SC) $140,970
Ed Towns (D-NY) $129,291
Gerald D. Kleczka (D-Wis) $129,283
Frank Horton (R-NY) $126,560
Major R. Owens (D-NY) $125,085
Bob Wise (D-WVa) $122,952
Beau Boulter (R-Texas) $117,993
Howard C. Nielson (R-Utah) $112,800
Tom Lantos (D-Calif) $111,267
Bill Grant (D-Fla) $102,100
Donald E. Lukens (R-Ohio) $84,880
John Conyers (D-Mich) $82,614

Christopher Shays (R-Conn) $79,702
Al McCandless (R-Calif) $75,500
Amo Houghton (R-NY) $65,650
Ted Weiss (D-NY) $64,890
Robert S. Walker (R-Pa) $43,875
Mike Synar (D-Okla) $0

Top 20 PAC Contributors to Committee Members in 1987-88

1	National Assn of Realtors	$215,900
2	American Medical Assn*	$202,435
3	Teamsters Union*	$190,500
4	American Institute of CPA's	$167,500
5	National Assn/Retired Federal Employees	$138,550
6	National Education Assn	$117,350
7	Assn of Trial Lawyers of America*	$112,100
8	American Bankers Assn*	$104,750
9	Air Line Pilots Assn	$96,500
10	Letter Carriers Union*	$89,600
11	Amer Fedn of State/County/Munic Employees	$87,045
12	AT&T	$74,667
13	United Auto Workers	$72,700
14	National PAC	$72,000
15	National Assn of Home Builders	$70,500
16	Marine Engineers Union*	$64,820
17	National Auto Dealers Assn	$63,950
18	Machinists/Aerospace Wrkrs Union*	$61,050
19	Carpenters Union*	$59,950
20	United Parcel Service	$54,280

* Contributions came from more than one PAC affiliated with this sponsor.

Summary

Despite a name which might make it seem preoccupied with affairs inside the federal bureaucracy, the Government Operations Committee has a wide-ranging jurisdiction that touches upon large segments of American business. Among other things, this committee has an important say in the reorganization of executive branch agencies — something that can have important repercussions on heavily-regulated industries.

Banking and other financial interests were an important element in the members' PAC contribution profile. The panel's Commerce, Consumer and Monetary Affairs subcommittee is of particular interest to that industry.

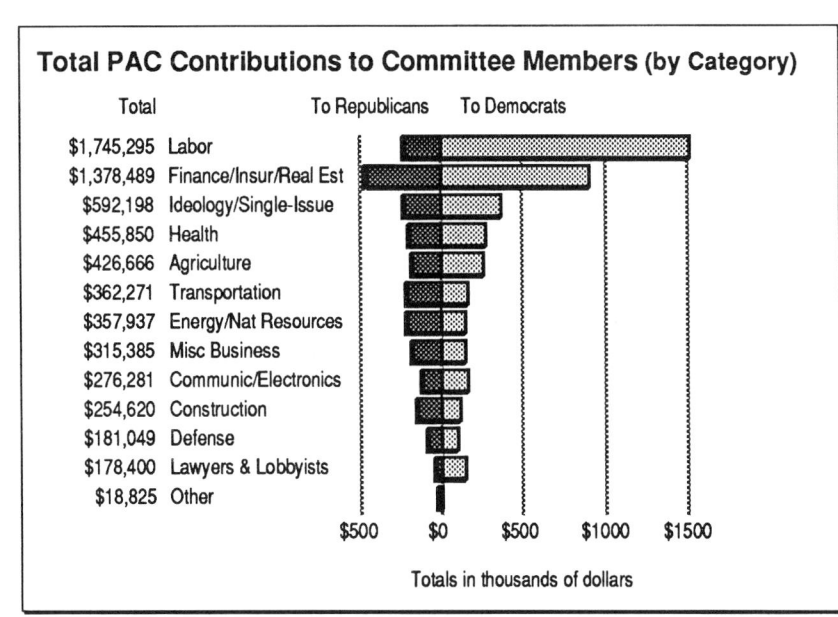

Total PAC Contributions to Committee Members (by Category)

Total	Category
$1,745,295	Labor
$1,378,489	Finance/Insur/Real Est
$592,198	Ideology/Single-Issue
$455,850	Health
$426,666	Agriculture
$362,271	Transportation
$357,937	Energy/Nat Resources
$315,385	Misc Business
$276,281	Communic/Electronics
$254,620	Construction
$181,049	Defense
$178,400	Lawyers & Lobbyists
$18,825	Other

Totals in thousands of dollars

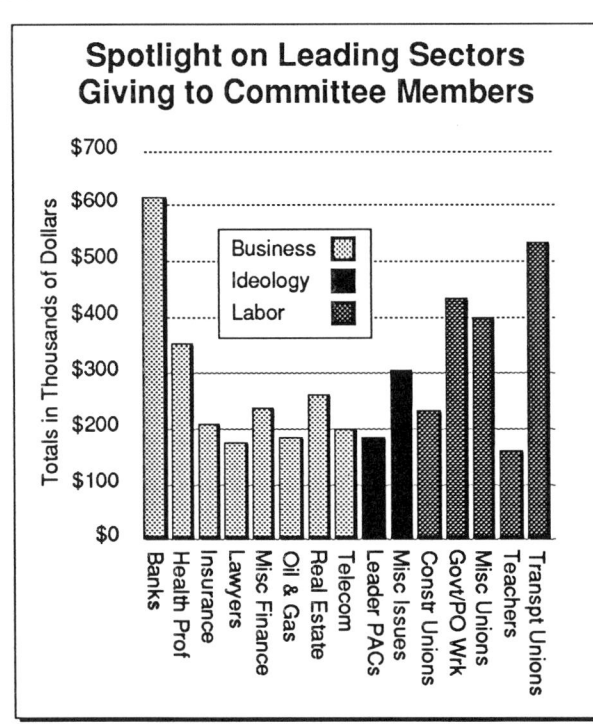

Spotlight on Leading Sectors Giving to Committee Members

Totals in Thousands of Dollars

Business
Ideology
Labor

Banks, Health Prof, Insurance, Lawyers, Misc Finance, Oil & Gas, Real Estate, Telecom, Leader PACs, Misc Issues, Constr Unions, Govt/PO Wrk, Misc Unions, Teachers, Transpt Unions

Leading Sectors Giving to Committee Members

Business

Banks	$613,385
Health Professionals	$349,985
Insurance	$205,874
Lawyers	$170,300
Misc Finance	$230,905
Oil & Gas	$181,740
Real Estate	$258,100
Telecommunications	$195,921

Ideological/Single-Issue

Leadership PACs	$179,604
Misc Issues	$300,644

Labor

Construction Unions	$227,925
Govt & Postal Workers	$430,245
Misc Unions	$396,395
Teachers Unions	$158,165
Transportation Unions	$532,565

House Interior and Insular Affairs Committee

Morris K. Udall (D-Ariz), Chairman
Don Young (R-Alaska), Ranking Republican

Party Ratio: 23 Democrats
14 Republicans

Jurisdiction: (1) Forest reserves and national parks created from the public domain; (2) Forfeiture of land grants and alien ownership, including alien ownership of mineral lands; (3) Geological survey; (4) Interstate compacts relating to apportionment of waters for irrigation purposes; (5) Irrigation and reclamation, including water supply for reclamation projects, and easements of public lands for irrigation projects, and acquisition of private lands when necessary to complete irrigation project; (6) Measures relating to the care and management of Indians, including the care and allotment of Indian lands and general and special measures relating to claims which are paid out of Indian funds; (7) Measures relating generally to the insular possessions of the United States, except those affecting the revenue and appropriations; (8) Military parks and battlefields; national cemeteries administered by the Secretary of the Interior, and parks within the District of Columbia; (9) Mineral land laws and claims and entries thereunder; (10) Mineral resources of the public lands; (11) Mining interest generally; (12) Mining schools and experimental stations; (13) Petroleum conservation on the public lands and conservation of the radium supply in the United States; (14) Preservation of prehistoric ruins and objects of interest on the public domain; (15) Public lands generally, including entry, easements, and grazing thereon; (16) Relations of the United States with the Indians and the Indian tribes; (17) Regulation of the domestic nuclear energy industry, including regulation of research and development reactors and nuclear regulatory research. The committee also has special oversight functions with respect to all programs affecting Indians and nonmilitary nuclear energy and research and development including the disposal of nuclear waste.

Subcommittees

Energy and the Environment
Morris K. Udall (D-Ariz), Chairman
Manuel Lujan Jr (R-NM), Ranking Republican

General Oversight and Investigations
Sam Gejdenson (D-Conn), Chairman
Denny Smith (R-Ore), Ranking Republican

Insular and International Affairs
Ron de Lugo (D-Virgin Islands), Chairman
Robert J. Lagomarsino (R-Calif), Ranking Republican

Mining and Natural Resources
Nick Joe Rahall II (D-WVa), Chairman
Larry E. Craig (R-Idaho), Ranking Republican

National Parks and Public Lands
Bruce F. Vento (D-Minn), Chairman
Ron Marlenee (R-Mont), Ranking Republican (Public Lands)
Robert J. Lagomarsino (R-Calif), Ranking Republican (Natl Parks)

Water and Power Resources
George Miller (D-Calif), Chairman
Charles Pashayan Jr. (R-Calif), Ranking Republican

Total Committee-Related PAC Contributions to Committee Members

	Total from Cmte-Related PACs	Pct of Member's Total PACs		Total from Cmte-Related PACs	Pct of Member's Total PACs
Philip R. Sharp (D-Ind)	$79,156	26%	Ben Nighthorse Campbell (D-Colo)	$18,190	6%
Don Young (R-Alaska)	$78,575	27%	Charles "Chip" Pashayan Jr. (R-Calif)	$17,950	17%
Robert J. Lagomarsino (R-Calif)	$66,228	20%	Morris K. Udall (D-Ariz)	$17,050	18%
Dick Cheney (R-Wyo)	$49,775	23%	Austin J. Murphy (D-Pa)	$16,071	13%
Barbara F. Vucanovich (R-Nev)	$48,357	24%	Beverly B. Byron (D-Md)	$15,900	11%
Bill Emerson (R-Mo)	$46,600	11%	Peter H. Kostmayer (D-Pa)	$13,361	3%
Ron Marlenee (R-Mont)	$36,950	20%	John Lewis (D-Ga)	$10,250	6%
Larry E. Craig (R-Idaho)	$36,425	23%	Peter A. DeFazio (D-Ore)	$8,327	4%
Elton Gallegly (R-Calif)	$31,561	20%	Richard H. Lehman (D-Calif)	$6,830	4%
Nick J. Rahall (D-WVa)	$30,800	18%	Peter J. Visclosky (D-Ind)	$6,750	4%
James V. Hansen (R-Utah)	$30,400	13%	Mel Levine (D-Calif)	$5,835	4%
Tony Coelho (D-Calif)	$30,100	7%	Bruce F. Vento (D-Minn)	$5,562	3%
George Miller (D-Calif)	$29,045	16%	Dale E. Kildee (D-Mich)	$3,850	4%
Denny Smith (R-Ore)	$28,761	13%	Sam Gejdenson (D-Conn)	$3,250	2%
Bill Richardson (D-NM)	$28,750	10%	Jaime B. Fuster (Pop Dem-Puerto Rico)[1]	$1,250	10%
Jerry Huckaby (D-La)	$27,850	21%	Ben Blaz (R-Guam)[1]	$950	8%
Richard H. Baker (R-La)	$23,600	19%	Edward J. Markey (D-Mass)	$695	409%
George "Buddy" Darden (D-Ga)	$22,625	9%	Ron de Lugo (R-Virgin Islands)[1]	$250	2%
John J. Rhodes (R-Ariz)	$20,950	17%	Manuel Lujan Jr. (R-NM)[2]	$50	1%
James McClure Clarke (D-NC)	$20,693	7%			
Wayne Owens (D-Utah)	$20,311	5%			

[1] Non-voting Delegate
[2] Did not run for reelection in 1988

Summary

Debates over the use and disposal of public lands are a central focus of the House Interior Committee — a focus that makes it vitally important to states in the Western U.S., where much of the land is still federally-owned. The committee is also vital to mining, oil & gas and other industries that extract natural resources from public lands through federal leases. In recent years, the committee has been a battleground for issues — like the Alaska Lands Bill — that have pitted the interests of industry against those of environmentalists trying to preserve the last vestiges of American wilderness.

The committee is also important to American territories and possessions, from Puerto Rico to Guam. Delegates from U.S. possessions may debate and vote on committee actions, but they may not vote for bills on the House floor.

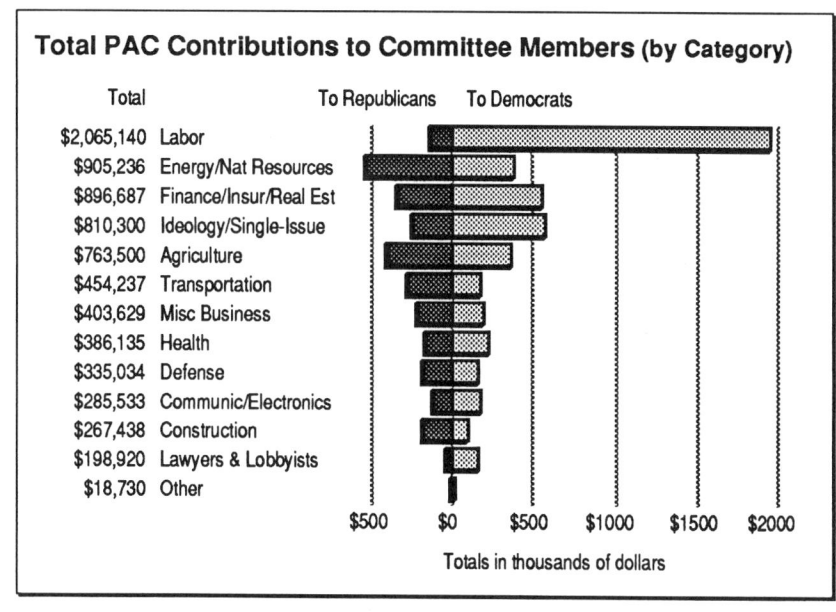

Total PAC Contributions to Committee Members (by Category)

Total		To Republicans	To Democrats
$2,065,140	Labor		
$905,236	Energy/Nat Resources		
$896,687	Finance/Insur/Real Est		
$810,300	Ideology/Single-Issue		
$763,500	Agriculture		
$454,237	Transportation		
$403,629	Misc Business		
$386,135	Health		
$335,034	Defense		
$285,533	Communic/Electronics		
$267,438	Construction		
$198,920	Lawyers & Lobbyists		
$18,730	Other		

Totals in thousands of dollars

Spotlight on Leading Sectors Giving to Committee Members

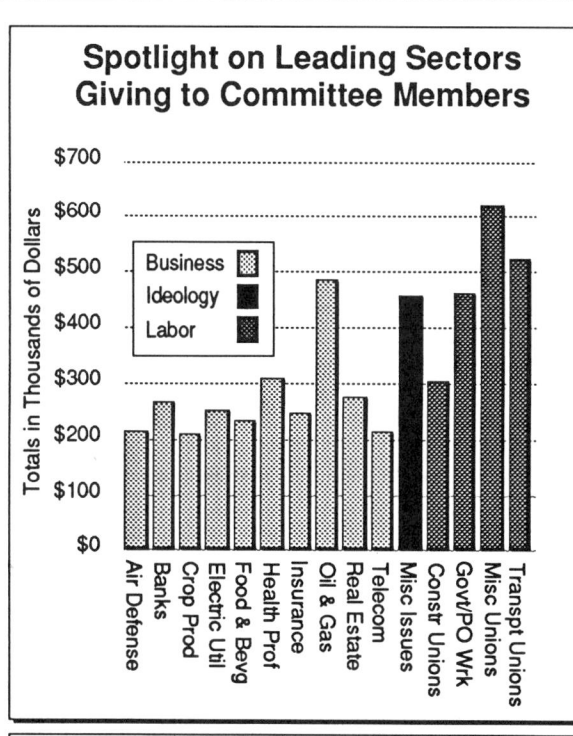

Committee-Related Sectors

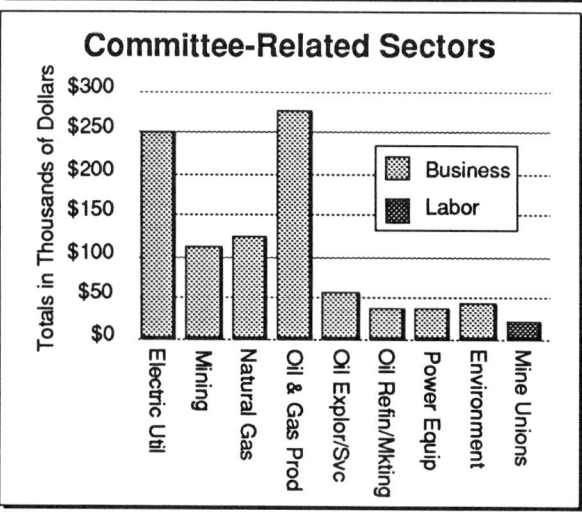

Top 20 Committee-Related PAC Contributors to Committee Members in 1987-88

1	Sierra Club	$36,638
2	ACRE (Action Cmte for Rural Electric)*	$32,650
3	Atlantic Richfield	$32,150
4	Litton Industries	$31,350
5	Chevron Corp	$31,250
6	Phillips Petroleum	$25,498
7	FMC Corp	$25,300
8	Southern California Edison	$25,000
9	Amoco Corp	$22,650
10	Southern Company	$21,525
11	Coastal Corp	$19,750
12	United Mine Workers	$19,200
13	BP America	$18,375
14	Pacific Gas & Electric	$18,055
15	Union Pacific Corp	$17,820
16	Exxon Corp	$16,900
17	Cooper Industries	$15,500
18	Pacific Enterprises	$15,065
19	Tenneco Inc	$15,000
20	Middle South Utilities*	$14,650

* Contributions came from more than one PAC affiliated with this sponsor.

Leading Committee-Related Sectors Giving to Committee Members

Business

Electric Utilities	$246,863
Mining	$109,650
Natural Gas Distribution	$122,796
Oil & Gas Production	$272,528
Oil Refining/Marketing	$32,729
Oilfield Exploration/Services	$52,370
Power Plant Equipment	$34,250

Ideological/Single-Issue

Environmental Issues	$40,847

Labor

Mine Worker Unions	$19,200

House Judiciary Committee

Peter W. Rodino Jr. (D-NJ), Chairman
Hamilton Fish Jr. (R-NY), Ranking Republican

Party Ratio: 21 Democrats
14 Republicans

Jurisdiction: (1) Judicial proceedings, civil and criminal generally; (2) Apportionment of Representatives; (3) Bankruptcy, mutiny, espionage, and counterfeiting; (4) Civil liberties; (5) Constitutional amendments; (6) Federal courts and judges; (7) Immigration and naturalization; (8) Interstate compacts generally; (9) Local courts in the Territories and possessions; (10) Measures relating to claims against the United States; (11) Meetings of Congress, attendance of Members and their acceptance of incompatible offices; ((12) National penitentiaries; (13) Patent Office; (14) Patents, copyrights, and trademarks; (15) Presidential succession; (16) Protection of trade and commerce against unlawful restraints and monopolies; (17) Revision and codification of the Statutes of the United States; (18) State and territorial boundary lines; (19) Communist and other subversive activities affecting the internal security of the United States.

Subcommittees

Administrative Law and Governmental Relations
Barney Frank (D-Mass), Chairman
Howard Coble (R-NC), Ranking Republican

Civil and Constitutional Rights
Don Edwards (D-Calif), Chairman
Jim Sensenbrenner Jr. (R-Wis), Ranking Republican

Courts, Civil Liberties, and the Administration of Justice
Robert W. Kastenmeier (D-Wis), Chairman
Carlos J. Moorhead (R-Calif), Ranking Republican

Crime
William J. Hughes (D-NJ), Chairman
Bill McCollum (R-Fla), Ranking Republican

Criminal Justice
John Conyers Jr. (D-Mich), Chairman
George W. Gekas (R-Pa), Ranking Republican

Immigration, Refugees, and International Law
Romano L. Mazzoli (D-Ky), Chairman
Patrick L. Swindall (R-Ga), Ranking Republican

Monopolies and Commercial Law
Peter W. Rodino Jr. (D-NJ), Chairman
Hamilton Fish Jr. (R-NY), Ranking Republican

Total PAC Contributions to Committee Members

John Bryant (D-Texas)	$390,757
Rick Boucher (D-Va)	$366,600
Lawrence J. Smith (D-Fla)	$289,543
Howard Coble (R-NC)	$282,524
Dan Glickman (D-Kan)	$277,290
Jack Brooks (D-Texas)	$276,562
Bruce A. Morrison (D-Conn)	$224,433
Carlos J. Moorehead (R-Calif)	$215,165
Benjamin L. Cardin (D-Md)	$208,148
Howard L. Berman (D-Calif)	$207,317
Edward F. Feighan (D-Ohio)	$205,414
Romano L. Mazzoli (D-Ky)	$196,650
Hamilton Fish (R-NY)	$196,388
Pat Swindall (R-Ga)	$191,356
Robert W. Kastenmeier (D-Wis)	$177,484
William E. Dannemeyer (R-Calif)	$143,472
Barney Frank (D-Mass)	$141,635
Charles E. Schumer (D-NY)	$137,325
Harley O. Staggers (D-WVa)	$131,953
Patricia Schroeder (D-Colo)	$129,785
Henry J. Hyde (R-Ill)	$121,407
Bill McCollum (R-Fla)	$117,835
Don Edwards (D-Calif)	$117,256
Mike DeWine (R-Ohio)	$112,860
William J. Hughes (D-NJ)	$112,150
F. James Sensenbrenner (R-Wis)	$109,839
Lamar Smith (R-Texas)	$95,732
D. French Slaughter Jr. (R-Va)	$94,496
Peter W. Rodino Jr. (D-NJ)[1]	$83,700

John Conyers (D-Mich)	$82,614
George W. Crockett (D-Mich)	$63,622
George W. Gekas (R-Pa)	$46,750
Dan Lungren (R-Calif)[1]	$13,100
Mike Synar (D-Okla)	$0

Top 20 PAC Contributors to Committee Members in 1987-88

1	National Assn of Realtors	$183,350
2	Teamsters Union	$156,225
3	Assn of Trial Lawyers of America*	$126,600
4	American Institute of CPA's	$126,000
5	American Medical Assn*	$115,516
6	National Assn/Retired Federal Employees	$108,850
7	National Education Assn	$101,450
8	United Auto Workers	$82,350
9	Letter Carriers Union*	$78,160
10	National Assn of Life Underwriters	$76,000
11	Machinists/Aerospace Workers Union	$66,900
12	Auto Dealers & Drivers for Free Trade	$63,800
13	AT&T	$63,417
14	Carpenters Union*	$61,000
15	American Bankers Assn*	$57,350
16	Amer Fedn of State/County/Munic Employees	$55,801
17	National Assn of Home Builders	$55,300
18	Operating Engineers Union*	$48,425
19	National Auto Dealers Assn	$47,400
20	National PAC	$45,000

* Contributions came from more than one PAC affiliated with this sponsor.

[1] Did not run for reelection in 1988

Summary

The shape of the American judicial and criminal justice system is the central focus of the House Judiciary Committee. It is a role that makes it important not only to lawyers, but to every sector of the American business community as well.

No particular industry, however, stands out in the pattern of PAC contributions to the committee's members. The distribution of dollars between various labor, business and ideological groups roughly parallels that of Congress as a whole.

Total PAC Contributions to Committee Members (by Category)

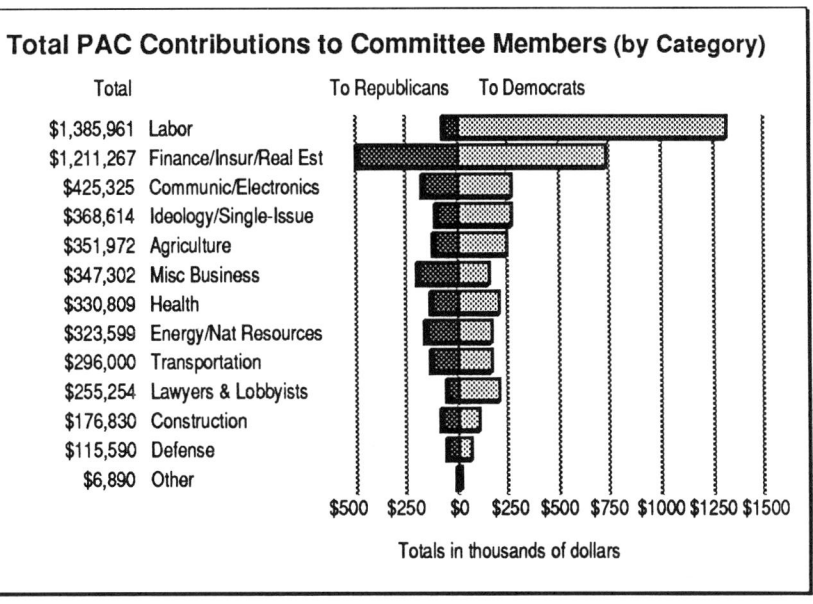

Total	Category
$1,385,961	Labor
$1,211,267	Finance/Insur/Real Est
$425,325	Communic/Electronics
$368,614	Ideology/Single-Issue
$351,972	Agriculture
$347,302	Misc Business
$330,809	Health
$323,599	Energy/Nat Resources
$296,000	Transportation
$255,254	Lawyers & Lobbyists
$176,830	Construction
$115,590	Defense
$6,890	Other

Totals in thousands of dollars

Spotlight on Leading Sectors Giving to Committee Members

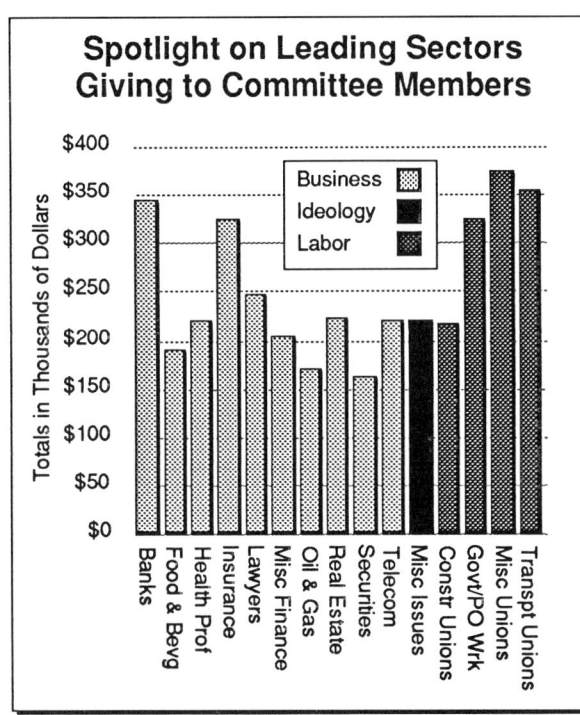

Leading Sectors Giving to Committee Members

Business

Banks	$342,143
Food & Beverage	$186,706
Health Professionals	$218,926
Insurance	$321,319
Lawyers	$246,735
Misc Finance	$200,155
Oil & Gas	$169,387
Real Estate	$221,950
Securities/Commodities Investment	$161,500
Telecommunications	$217,070

Ideological/Single-Issue

Misc Issues	$217,425

Labor

Construction Unions	$215,240
Govt & Postal Workers	$321,769
Misc Unions	$372,462
Transportation Unions	$352,485

House Merchant Marine and Fisheries Committee

Walter B. Jones (D-NC), Chairman
Robert W. Davis (R-Mich), Ranking Republican

Party Ratio: 25 Democrats
17 Republicans

Jurisdiction: (1) Merchant marine generally; (2) Oceanography and marine affairs, including coastal zone management; (3) Coast Guard, including lifesaving service, lighthouses, lightships and ocean derelicts; (4) Fisheries and wildlife, including research, restoration, refuges and conservation; (5) Measures relating to the regulation of common carriers by water (except matters subject to the jurisdiction of the Interstate Commerce Commission) and to the inspection of merchant marine vessels, lights and signals, lifesaving equipment and fire protection on such vessels; (6) Merchant marine officers and seamen; (7) Navigation and the laws relating thereto, including pilotage; (8) Panama Canal and the maintenance and operation of the Panama Canal, including the administration, sanitation and government of the Canal Zone; and interoceanic canals generally; (9) Registering and licensing of vessels and small boats; (10) Rules and international arrangements to prevent collisions at sea; (11) United States Coast Guard and Merchant Marine Academies, and State maritime academies; (12) International fishing agreements. The committee also oversees offshore oil and gas matters on the U.S. Outer Continental Shelf.

Subcommittees

Coast Guard and Navigation
Earl Hutto (D-Fla), Chairman
Robert W. Davis (R-Mich), Ranking Republican

Fisheries and Wildlife Conservation and the Environment
Gerry E. Studds (D-Mass), Chairman
Don Young (R-Alaska), Ranking Republican

Merchant Marine
Walter B. Jones (D-NC), Chairman
Norman F. Lent (R-NY), Ranking Republican

Oceanography
Mike Lowry (D-Wash), Chairman
Norman D. Shumway (R-Calif), Ranking Republican

Oversight and Investigations
Thomas M. Foglietta (D-Pa), Chairman
Claudine Schneider (R-RI), Ranking Republican

Panama Canal/Outer Continental Shelf
W. J. (Billy) Tauzin (D-La), Chairman
Jack Fields (R-Texas), Ranking Republican

Total Committee-Related PAC Contributions to Committee Members

	Total from Cmte-Related PACs	Pct of Member's Total PACs		Total from Cmte-Related PACs	Pct of Member's Total PACs
Don Young (R-Alaska)	$82,950	29%	Herbert H. Bateman (R-Va)	$25,000	16%
Helen Delich Bentley (R-Md)	$67,425	24%	Curt Weldon (R-Pa)	$23,500	11%
Robert W. Davis (R-Mich)	$52,850	17%	Owen B. Pickett (D-Va)	$22,250	11%
Jack Fields (R-Texas)	$52,325	20%	Joseph E. Brennan (D-Maine)	$22,000	8%
W.J. Tauzin (D-La)	$48,337	16%	Jim Bunning (R-Ky)	$21,900	9%
John R. Miller (R-Wash)	$45,200	13%	Gerry E. Studds (D-Mass)	$19,445	23%
Mike Lowry (D-Wash)[1]	$42,725	6%	Earl Hutto (D-Fla)	$19,350	15%
Glenn M. Anderson (D-Calif)	$40,400	15%	Thomas M. Foglietta (D-Pa)	$18,500	11%
Roy Dyson (D-Md)	$39,550	10%	Mario Biaggi (D-NY)[2]	$18,400	49%
Thomas J. Manton (D-NY)	$35,881	12%	Bob Clement (D-Tenn)	$18,000	5%
Walter B. Jones (D-NC)	$35,750	39%	Howard Coble (R-NC)	$17,650	6%
Patricia Saiki (R-Hawaii)	$35,350	14%	Norman D. Shumway (R-Calif)	$17,000	11%
Carroll Hubbard (D-Ky)	$34,875	10%	Claudine Schneider (R-RI)	$16,998	9%
Wally Herger (R-Calif)	$33,600	13%	Ernie Konnyu (R-Calif)	$16,450	12%
Norman F. Lent (R-NY)	$32,250	9%	Solomon P. Ortiz (D-Texas)	$13,250	13%
Mac Sweeney (R-Texas)	$29,600	13%	Douglas H. Bosco (D-Calif)	$12,600	11%
George J. Hochbrueckner (D-NY)	$28,250	7%	Robert A. Borski (D-Pa)	$12,500	6%
Don Bonker (D-Wash)[1]	$27,250	10%	Thomas R. Carper (D-Del)	$12,500	7%
H. James Saxton (R-NJ)	$27,107	14%	Dennis M. Hertel (D-Mich)	$11,500	7%
Robin Tallon (D-SC)	$26,871	11%	William O. Lipinski (D-Ill)	$10,950	11%

[1] Ran for U.S. Senate in 1988
[2] Resigned Aug 5, 1988

Summary

The House Merchant Marine and Fisheries Committee presents an interesting example of one of the often-overlooked realities of PAC giving — that the interests of labor unions and businesses are not always in conflict. Foreign competition and a dwindling American presence on the open seas have put labor and business together in trying to preserve what is left of the increasingly imperiled U.S. merchant marine. While the two sides do have their differences, they often work to achieve consensus on issues of basic interest to the survival of the industry, and the jobs it provides. The strong involvement of sea transport unions is especially apparent in the patterns of PAC giving, where the sea transport unions — dominated by the Marine Engineers union — actually outspent the business side of the industry by better than two-to-one in contributions to committee members.

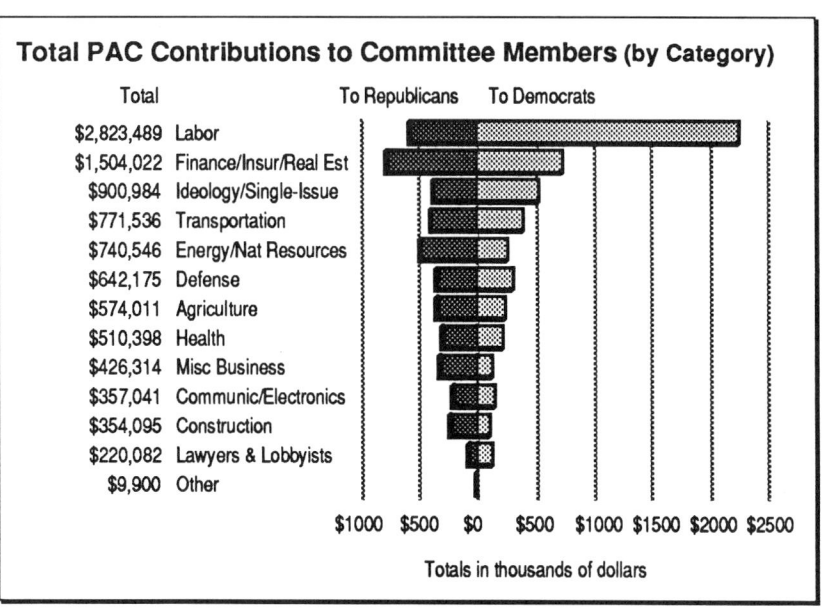

Total PAC Contributions to Committee Members (by Category)

Total	Category
$2,823,489	Labor
$1,504,022	Finance/Insur/Real Est
$900,984	Ideology/Single-Issue
$771,536	Transportation
$740,546	Energy/Nat Resources
$642,175	Defense
$574,011	Agriculture
$510,398	Health
$426,314	Misc Business
$357,041	Communic/Electronics
$354,095	Construction
$220,082	Lawyers & Lobbyists
$9,900	Other

Totals in thousands of dollars

Spotlight on Leading Sectors Giving to Committee Members

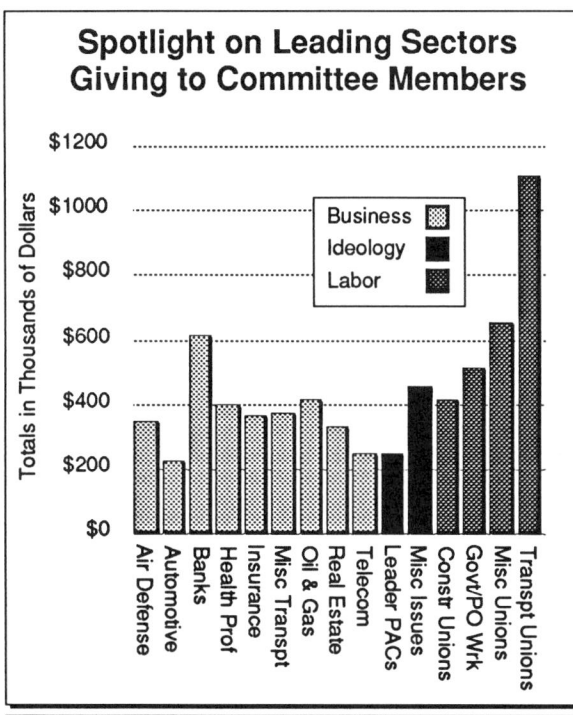

Legend: Business, Ideology, Labor

Sectors: Air Defense, Automotive, Banks, Health Prof, Insurance, Misc Transpt, Oil & Gas, Real Estate, Telecom, Leader PACs, Misc Issues, Const Unions, Govt/PO Wrk, Misc Unions, Transpt Unions

Committee-Related Sectors

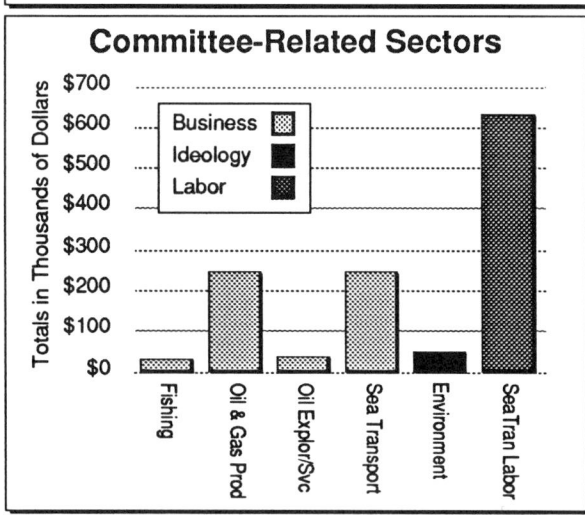

Legend: Business, Ideology, Labor

Sectors: Fishing, Oil & Gas Prod, Oil Explor/Svc, Sea Transport, Environment, SeaTran Labor

Top 20 Committee-Related PAC Contributors to Committee Members in 1987-88

1	Marine Engineers Union*	$321,350
2	Seafarers International Union*	$154,600
3	Masters, Mates & Pilots Union*	$77,750
4	American Pilots Assn	$54,600
5	International Longshoremen Assn	$38,631
6	CSX Corp*	$37,300
7	American President Lines	$35,150
8	Tenneco Inc	$33,300
9	Atlantic Richfield	$29,900
10	Matson Navigation	$29,450
11	National Fisheries Institute	$23,450
12	Boilermakers Union	$23,175
13	Chevron Corp	$22,325
14	BP America	$19,250
15	Amoco Corp	$19,050
16	Phillips Petroleum	$18,500
17	Exxon Corp	$18,050
18	Mobil Oil	$18,000
19	Crowley Maritime	$16,400
20	Texaco	$16,250

* Contributions came from more than one PAC affiliated with this sponsor.

Leading Sectors Giving to Committee Members

Business

Commercial Fishing	$25,750
Oil & Gas Production	$238,946
Oilfield Exploration/Services	$29,750
Sea Transport	$238,187

Ideological/Single-Issue

Environmental Issues	$40,728

Labor

Sea Transport Unions	$624,306

House Post Office and Civil Service Committee

William D. Ford (D-Mich), Chairman
Gene Taylor (R-Mo), Ranking Republican

Party Ratio: 13 Democrats
8 Republicans

> **Jurisdiction:** (1) Census and the collection of statistics generally; (2) All Federal Civil Service, including intergovernmental personnel; (3) Postal-savings banks; (4) Postal Service generally, including the railway mail service, and measures relating to ocean mail and pneumatic-tube service; but excluding post roads; (5) Status of officers and employees of the United States, including their compensation, classification, and retirement; (6) Hatch Act; (7) Holidays and celebrations; (8) Population and demography.

Subcommittees

Census and Population
Mervyn M. Dymally (D-Calif), Chairman
Constance A. Morella (R-Md), Ranking Republican

Civil Service
Patricia Schroeder (D-Colo), Chairwoman
Charles Pashayan Jr. (R-Calif), Ranking Republican

Compensation and Employee Benefits
Gary L. Ackerman (D-NY), Chairman
John T. Myers (R-Ind), Ranking Republican

Human Resources
Gerry Sikorski (D-Minn), Chairman
Dan Burton (R-Ind), Ranking Republican

Investigations
William D. Ford (D-Mich), Chairman
Gene Taylor (R-Mo), Ranking Republican

Postal Operations and Services
Mickey Leland (D-Texas), Chairman
Frank Horton (R-NY), Ranking Republican

Postal Personnel and Modernization
Frank McCloskey (D-Ind), Chairman
Don Young (R-Alaska), Ranking Republican

Total Committee-Related PAC Contributions to Committee Members

	Total from Cmte-Related PACs	Pct of Member's Total PACs
William D. Ford (D-Mich)	$54,865	21%
Mary Rose Oakar (D-Ohio)	$52,400	14%
Mickey Leland (D-Texas)	$47,300	13%
Frank McCloskey (D-Ind)	$46,600	14%
Gary L. Ackerman (D-NY)	$40,650	21%
Frank Horton (R-NY)	$37,700	29%
Constance A. Morella (R-Md)	$36,806	12%
Benjamin A. Gilman (R-NY)	$31,450	19%
Mervyn M. Dymally (D-Calif)	$30,100	19%
Gerry Sikorski (D-Minn)	$29,150	8%
Don Young (R-Alaska)	$26,700	9%
Robert Garcia (D-NY)	$24,800	14%
Patricia Schroeder (D-Colo)	$23,300	19%
William L. Clay (D-Mo)	$21,450	15%
Charles "Chip" Pashayan Jr. (R-Calif)	$14,650	14%
Gus Yatron (D-Pa)	$13,750	13%
Dan Burton (R-Ind)	$12,700	9%
Gene Taylor (R-Mo)[1]	$10,500	25%
John T. Myers (R-Ind)	$8,600	10%
Morris K. Udall (D-Ariz)	$6,850	7%
Stephen J. Solarz (D-NY)	$5,950	10%
Ron de Lugo (R-Virgin Islands)[2]	$3,250	20%

Top Committee-Related PAC Contributors to Committee Members in 1987-88

1	National Assn of Letter Carriers*	$149,850
2	National Assn/Retired Federal Employees	$132,450
3	American Postal Workers Union*	$102,450
4	National Assn of Postmasters	$33,350
5	National Rural Letter Carriers Assn	$31,806
6	National League of Postmasters	$24,390
7	National Assn of Postal Supervisors	$23,700
8	American Fedn of Govt Employees	$23,115
9	National Treasury Employees Union	$19,320
10	National Federation of Federal Employees	$11,650

* Contributions came from more than one PAC affiliated with this sponsor.

---

[1] Did not run for reelection in 1988
[2] Non-voting Delegate

Summary

Steelworkers, teamsters and assembly line operators may be popularly thought of as the mainstream of organized labor, but government employees and postal workers are an increasingly important segment of the labor community — and one which has begun to weigh in heavily with PAC contributions to members of Congress. The Post Office and Civil Service Committee is of particular interest to government and postal PACs, since it debates crucial issues ranging from salaries to government workers' participation in political activities.

Postal unions alone gave an average of more than $18,000 to each member of this committee; federal government employee unions added another $9,000 on average. Non-government unions were also generous, boosting labor PACs' total to more than $1.7 million to this 21-member committee. Overall, labor contributions accounted for 44 cents out of every dollar received in PAC contributions by members of this committee — the highest ratio of any committee in Congress.

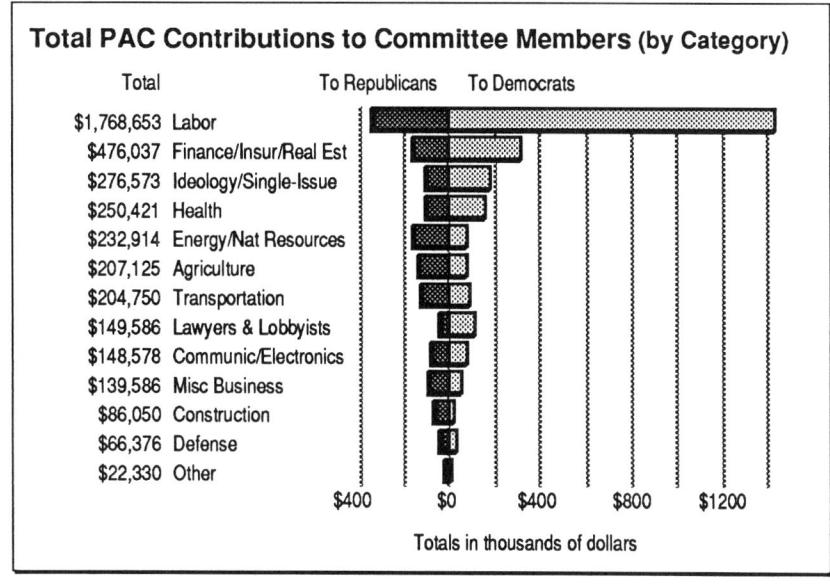

Total PAC Contributions to Committee Members (by Category)

Total	Category
$1,768,653	Labor
$476,037	Finance/Insur/Real Est
$276,573	Ideology/Single-Issue
$250,421	Health
$232,914	Energy/Nat Resources
$207,125	Agriculture
$204,750	Transportation
$149,586	Lawyers & Lobbyists
$148,578	Communic/Electronics
$139,586	Misc Business
$86,050	Construction
$66,376	Defense
$22,330	Other

Totals in thousands of dollars

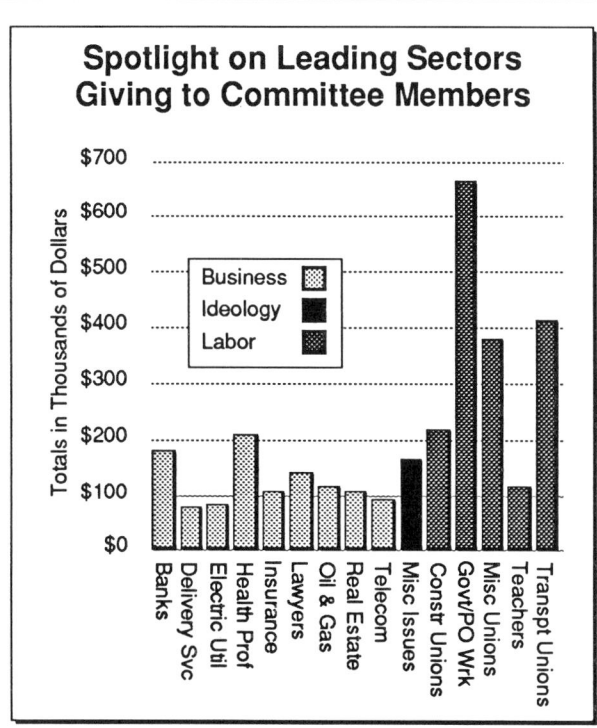

Spotlight on Leading Sectors Giving to Committee Members

Committee-Related Sectors

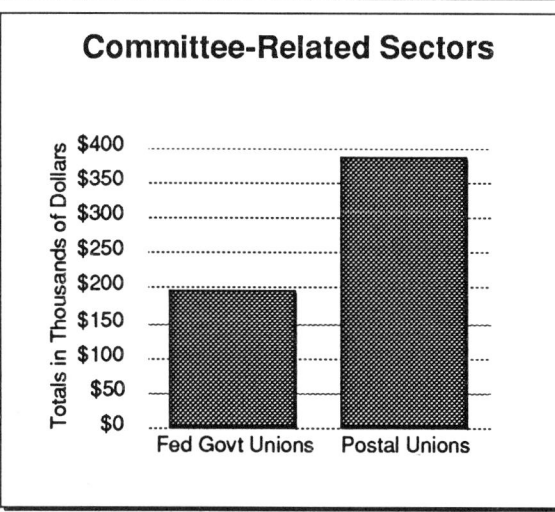

Leading Sectors Giving to Committee Members

Business
Banks	$173,813
Delivery Services	$72,100
Electric Utilities	$79,854
Health Professionals	$203,381
Insurance	$102,549
Lawyers	$138,315
Oil & Gas	$111,210
Real Estate	$101,350
Telecommunications	$90,103

Ideological
Misc Issues	$160,048

Labor

Government/Postal Workers
Federal Govt Unions	$194,985
Postal Worker Unions	$384,536
State & Local Govt Unions	$79,000

Other Unions
Constr Unions	$214,635
Misc Unions	$374,810
Teachers Unions	$112,275
Transportation Unions	$408,412

House Public Works and Transportation Committee

Glenn M. Anderson (D-Calif), Chairman
John Paul Hammerschmidt (R-Ark), Ranking Republican

Party Ratio: 30 Democrats
20 Republicans

Jurisdiction: (1) Flood control and improvement of rivers and harbors; (2) Measures relating to the Capitol Building and the Senate and the House Office Buildings; (3) Measures relating to the construction or maintenance of roads and post roads, other than appropriations therefor; but no bill providing general legislation in relation to roads may contain any provision for any specific road, nor may any bill in relation to a specific road embrace a provision in relation to any other specific road; (4) Measures relating to the construction or reconstruction, maintenance and care of the buildings and grounds of the Botanic Garden, the Library of Congress, and the Smithsonian Institution; (5) Measures relating to the purchase of sites and construction of post offices, customhouses, Federal courthouses, and Government buildings within the District of Columbia; (6) Oil and other pollution of navigable waters; (7) Public buildings and occupied or improved grounds of the United States generally; (8) Public works for the benefit of navigation, including bridges and dams (other than international bridges and dams); (9) Water power; (10) Transportation, including civil aviation except railroads, railroad labor, and pensions; (11) Roads and the safety thereof; (12) Water transportation subject to the jurisdiction of the Interstate Commerce Commission; (13) Related transportation regulatory agencies, except (A) the Interstate Commerce Commission as it relates to railroads, (B) Federal Railroad Administration, and (C) Amtrak.

Subcommittees

Aviation
Norman Y. Mineta (D-Calif), Chairman
Newt Gingrich (R-Ga), Ranking Republican

Economic Development
Gus Savage (D-Ill), Chairman
Bob McEwen (R-Ohio), Ranking Republican

Investigations and Oversight
James L. Oberstar (D-Minn), Chairman
William F. Clinger Jr. (R-Pa), Ranking Republican

Public Buildings and Grounds
Douglas H. Bosco (D-Calif), Chairman
Guy V. Molinari (R-NY), Ranking Republican

Surface Transportation
Glenn M. Anderson (D-Calif), Chairman
Bud Shuster (R-Pa), Ranking Republican

Water Resources
Henry J. Nowak (D-NY), Chairman
Arlan Stangeland (R-Minn), Ranking Republican

Total Committee-Related PAC Contributions to Committee Members

	Total from Cmte-Related PACs	Pct of Member's Total PACs		Total from Cmte-Related PACs	Pct of Member's Total PACs
Glenn M. Anderson (D-Calif)	$115,750	42%	Benjamin L. Cardin (D-Md)	$36,350	17%
Norman Y. Mineta (D-Calif)	$104,958	40%	Ed Towns (D-NY)	$35,950	25%
Robert A. Roe (D-NJ)	$93,100	35%	Sherwood Boehlert (R-NY)	$35,400	32%
James J. Howard (D-NJ)[1]	$91,500	46%	Henry J. Nowak (D-NY)	$33,920	36%
James L. Oberstar (D-Minn)	$81,100	39%	Jimmy Hayes (D-La)	$33,650	17%
Helen Delich Bentley (R-Md)	$76,650	27%	Ron Packard (R-Calif)	$32,540	29%
Newt Gingrich (R-Ga)	$73,200	28%	John Lewis (D-Ga)	$31,950	19%
Arlan Strangeland (R-Minn)	$68,820	19%	Bob McEwen (R-Ohio)	$31,900	22%
Bud Shuster (R-Pa)	$66,700	44%	Jim Lightfoot (R-Iowa)	$30,601	19%
David Skaggs (D-Colo)	$66,025	15%	Dean A. Gallo (R-NJ)	$29,170	20%
Carl C. Perkins (D-Ky)	$62,000	23%	William O. Lipinski (D-Ill)	$26,950	28%
John Paul Hammerschmidt (R-Ark)	$60,900	38%	Guy V. Molinari (R-NY)	$26,800	34%
Jim Chapman (D-Texas)	$57,370	21%	Thomas E. Petri (R-Wis)	$26,100	22%
Nick J. Rahall (D-WVa)	$53,850	31%	Nancy L. Johnson (R-Conn)	$25,920	17%
William F. Clinger Jr. (R-Pa)	$46,550	25%	Cass Ballenger (R-NC)	$25,180	17%
Louise M. Slaughter (D-NY)	$46,031	12%	Fred Upton (R-Mich)	$23,200	19%
James M. Inhofe (R-Okla)	$46,000	20%	Doug Applegate (D-Ohio)	$22,890	29%
Robert A. Borski (D-Pa)	$45,354	24%	J. Roy Rowland (D-Ga)	$22,650	19%
Bob Clement (D-Tenn)	$42,350	30%	Jerry F. Costello (D-Ill)	$20,250	16%
Don Sundquist (R-Tenn)	$42,150	24%	Lewis F. Payne Jr. (D-Va)	$19,950	14%
Joe Kolter (D-Pa)	$41,850	29%	James A. Traficant (D-Ohio)	$18,270	34%
Gus Savage (D-Ill)	$41,500	34%	Dennis Hastert (R-Ill)	$18,100	13%
Douglas H. Bosco (D-Calif)	$39,050	33%	Bill Grant (D-Fla)	$18,040	15%
Peter J. Visclosky (D-Ind)	$38,050	25%	Ron de Lugo (R-Virgin Islands)[2]	$8,750	54%
Bob Wise (D-WVa)	$37,443	32%	Tim Valentine (D-NC)	$8,000	14%
Peter A. DeFazio (D-Ore)	$37,158	16%	Kenneth J. Gray (D-Ill)[3]	$0	0%

[1] Died Mar 25, 1988
[2] Non-voting Delegate
[3] Did not run for reelection in 1988

Summary

The biggest PAC players on this committee are related to the American transportation industry — and those interests are represented not only by the airlines, trucking companies, railroads and freight services, but by the labor unions representing the people who drive the trucks, pilot the planes, and ride the rails across America. Together, transportation companies and transport unions gave more than $1.8 million to the committee's members.

The Committee also earmarks billions of dollars in federally-funded public works projects that are built each year in every congressional district in the nation — projects that employ thousands of construction workers and supply important revenues to the nation's building contractors, subcontractors, architects, engineers, and other construction-related businesses. Here too, the PAC dollars to committee members came both from the business and labor sectors of the industry, though most corporate PACs gave more to Republicans and all the labor PACs heavily favored Democrats.

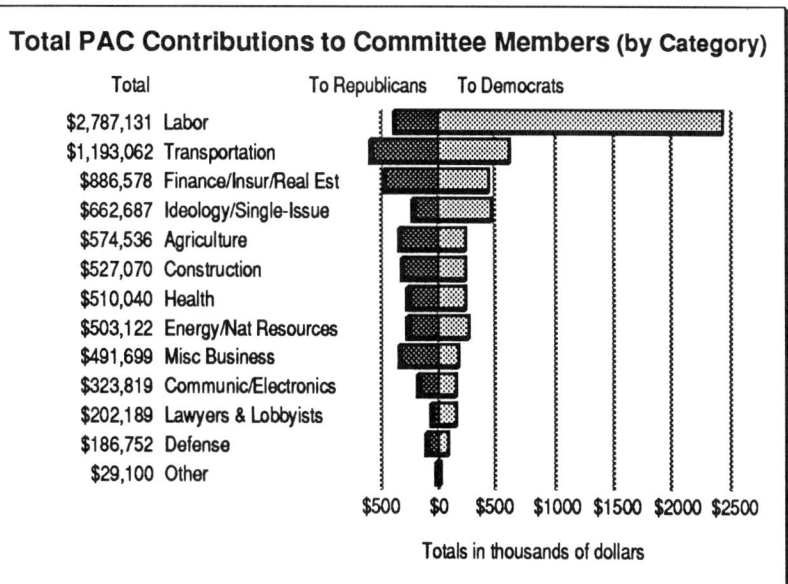

Total PAC Contributions to Committee Members (by Category)

Total	Category
$2,787,131	Labor
$1,193,062	Transportation
$886,578	Finance/Insur/Real Est
$662,687	Ideology/Single-Issue
$574,536	Agriculture
$527,070	Construction
$510,040	Health
$503,122	Energy/Nat Resources
$491,699	Misc Business
$323,819	Communic/Electronics
$202,189	Lawyers & Lobbyists
$186,752	Defense
$29,100	Other

Totals in thousands of dollars

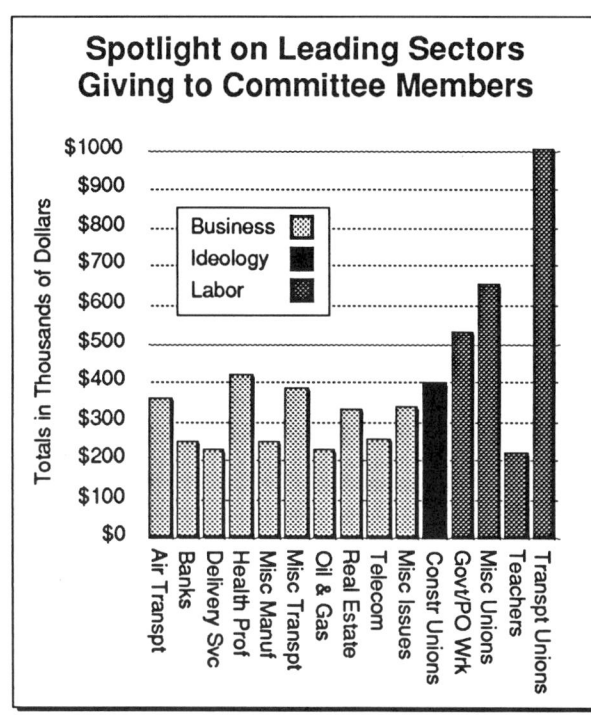

Spotlight on Leading Sectors Giving to Committee Members

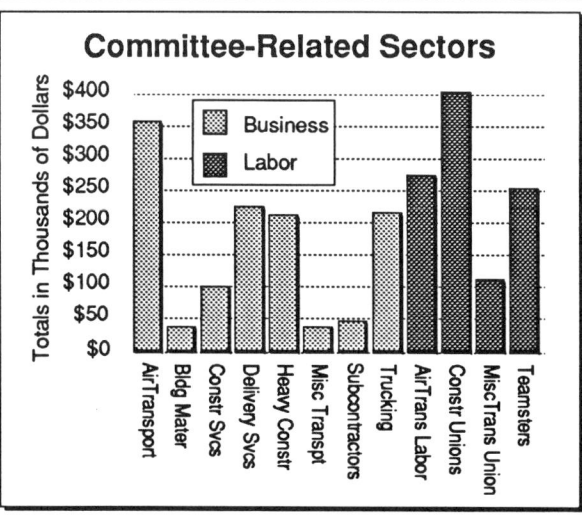

Committee-Related Sectors

Top 20 Committee-Related PAC Contributors to Committee Members in 1987-88

1	Air Line Pilots Assn	$256,500
2	Teamsters Union*	$247,900
3	United Parcel Service	$147,110
4	United Auto Workers	$145,100
5	Marine Engineers Union*	$128,300
6	National Utility Contractors Assn	$93,000
7	Seafarers International Union*	$90,100
8	Associated General Contractors	$76,650
9	Aircraft Owners & Pilots Assn	$74,506
10	Federal Express Corp	$71,050
11	Amalgamated Transit Union	$64,100
12	American Trucking Assns	$49,078
13	Norfolk Southern*	$44,250
14	Texas Air	$38,600
15	Yellow Freight System	$37,250
16	American Airlines	$32,350
17	Consolidated Freightways	$28,500
18	National Society of Professional Engineers	$26,550
19	Transportation Communication Union	$25,886
20	International Longshoremen Assn	$21,522

* Contributions came from more than one PAC affiliated with this sponsor.

Leading Committee-Related Sectors Giving to Committee Members

Business

Air Transport	$353,906
Bldg Materials	$33,750
Construction Services	$96,600
Delivery Services	$220,910
Heavy Construction	$210,450
Misc Transport	$34,600
Subcontractors	$45,060
Trucking	$213,746

Labor

Air Transport Unions	$272,450
Construction Unions	$397,215
Misc Transport Unions	$111,386
Teamsters	$247,900

145

House Rules Committee

Claude Pepper (D-Fla), Chairman
James H. Quillen (R-Tenn), Ranking Republican

Party Ratio: 9 Democrats
4 Republicans

Jurisdiction: (1) The rules and joint rules (other than rules or joint rules relating to the Code of Official Conduct), and order of business of the House; (2) Emergency waivers (under the Congressional Budget Act of 1974) of the required reporting date for bills and resolutions authorizing new budget authority; (3) Recesses and final adjournments of Congress.

Subcommittees

Legislative Process
Butler Derrick (D-SC), Chairman
Trent Lott (R-Miss), Ranking Republican

Rules of the House
Joe Moakley (D-Mass), Chairman
Gene Taylor (R-Mo), Ranking Republican

Total PAC Contributions to Committee Members

Trent Lott (R-Miss)[1]	$1,113,111
James H. Quillen (R-Tenn)	$413,800
Butler Derrick (D-SC)	$370,841
David E. Bonior (D-Mich)	$328,317
Martin Frost (D-Texas)	$298,373
Bart Gordon (D-Tenn)	$256,095
Claude Pepper (D-Fla)	$243,562
Alan Wheat (D-Mo)	$206,900
Joe Moakley (D-Mass)	$180,830
Tony P. Hall (D-Ohio)	$140,160
Gene Taylor (R-Mo)[2]	$41,550
Delbert L. Latta (R-Ohio)[2]	$2,656
Anthony C. Beilenson (D-Calif)	$0

Top 20 PAC Contributors to Committee Members in 1987-88

1	Assn of Trial Lawyers of America	$65,500
2	Teamsters Union*	$60,100
3	National Assn of Realtors	$51,400
4	Marine Engineers Union*	$50,500
5	American Bankers Assn*	$49,100
6	National Assn/Retired Federal Employees	$48,000
7	Air Line Pilots Assn	$45,000
8	United Auto Workers	$44,250
9	National Education Assn	$40,280
10	National Assn of Letter Carriers	$39,630
11	Federal Express Corp	$35,500
12	American Medical Assn*	$34,000
13	US League of Savings Assn*	$33,100
14	National Assn of Life Underwriters	$32,500
15	AT&T	$32,400
16	National Assn of Home Builders*	$32,200
17	National PAC	$30,000
18	Seafarers International Union	$29,940
19	BellSouth*	$28,200
20	United Transportation Union	$27,600

* Contributions came from more than one PAC affiliated with this sponsor.

[1] Ran for U.S. Senate in 1988
[2] Did not run for reelection in 1988

Summary

On the floor of the U.S. Senate, any Senator can offer an amendment to a bill under discussion, whether or not the amendment is germane to the bill itself. In the House, with its 435 members, such a policy could lead to a nightmare of legislative gridlock. To prevent that, the House is far more structured in its legislative procedures. Before any bill is brought to the House floor, specific rules are determined over whether amendments can be offered, and if so what type. Those rules — and a variety of other important legislative guidelines — are determined by the House Rules Committee.

While the shape of those rules can be important to a bill's passage, they do not specifically affect any particular industry or interest group more than any other. Correspondingly, PAC contributions to the committee came from a wide diversity of sources, and were reflective of the overall patterns of PAC giving to members of Congress in general.

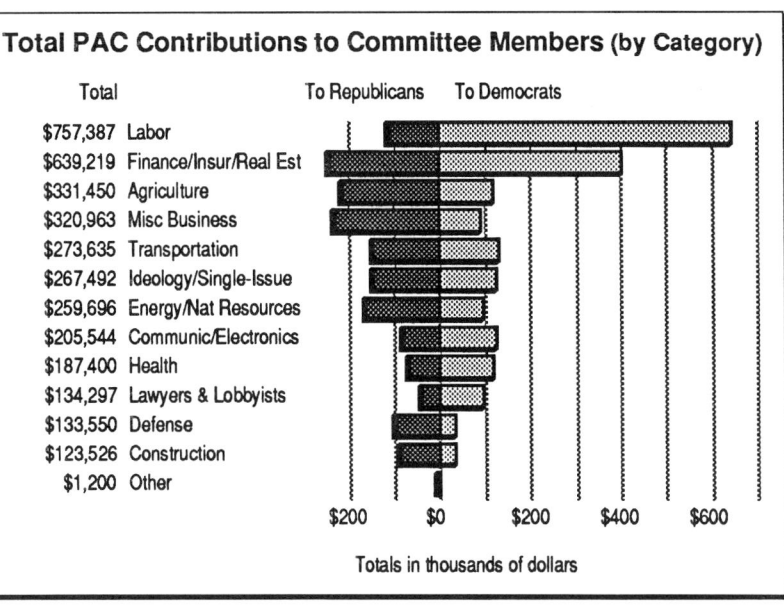

Total PAC Contributions to Committee Members (by Category)

Total		
$757,387	Labor	
$639,219	Finance/Insur/Real Est	
$331,450	Agriculture	
$320,963	Misc Business	
$273,635	Transportation	
$267,492	Ideology/Single-Issue	
$259,696	Energy/Nat Resources	
$205,544	Communic/Electronics	
$187,400	Health	
$134,297	Lawyers & Lobbyists	
$133,550	Defense	
$123,526	Construction	
$1,200	Other	

Totals in thousands of dollars

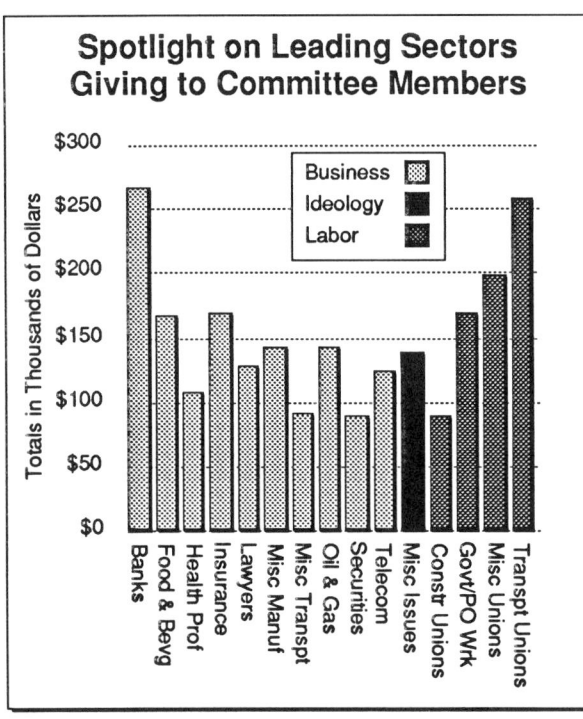

Spotlight on Leading Sectors Giving to Committee Members

Business, Ideology, Labor

Banks, Food & Bevg, Health Prof, Insurance, Lawyers, Misc Manuf, Misc Transpt, Oil & Gas, Securities, Telecom, Misc Issues, Const Unions, Govt/PO Wrk, Misc Unions, Transpt Unions

Leading Sectors
Giving to Committee Members

Business

Banks	$264,530
Food & Beverage	$165,400
Health Professionals	$106,050
Insurance	$167,539
Lawyers	$127,297
Misc Manufacturing	$140,800
Misc Transport	$89,785
Oil & Gas	$140,846
Securities/Commodities Investment	$86,550
Telecommunications	$122,534

Ideological/Single-Issue

Misc Issues	$136,015

Labor

Construction Unions	$87,550
Govt & Postal Workers	$168,430
Misc Unions	$196,277
Transportation Unions	$255,800

House Science, Space and Technology Committee

Robert A. Roe (D-NJ), Chairman
Manuel Lujan Jr. (R-NM), Ranking Republican

Party Ratio: 29 Democrats
19 Republicans

Jurisdiction: (1) Astronautical research and development, including resources, personnel, equipment and facilities; (2) Bureau of Standards, standardization of weights and measures and the metric system; (3) National Aeronautics and Space Administration; (4) National Aeronautics and Space Council; (5) National Science Foundation; (6) Outer space, including exploration and control thereof; (7) Science scholarships; (8) Scientific research, development, and demonstration, and projects therefor, and all federally owned or operated nonmilitary energy laboratories; (9) Civil aviation research and development; (10) Environmental research and development; (11) All energy research, development, and demonstration, and projects therefor, and all federally owned or operated nonmilitary energy laboratories; (12) National Weather Service. The committee also has oversight with respect to all nonmilitary research and development.

Subcommittees

Energy Research and Development
Marilyn Lloyd (D-Tenn), Chairwoman
Sid Morrison (R-Wash), Ranking Republican

International Scientific Cooperation
Ralph M. Hall (D-Texas), Chairman
Jim Sensenbrenner Jr. (R-Wis), Ranking Republican

Investigations and Oversight
Robert A. Roe (D-NJ), Chairman
Don Ritter (R-Pa), Ranking Republican

Natural Resources, Agricultural Research and Environment
James H. Scheuer (D-NY), Chairman
Claudine Schneider (R-RI), Ranking Republican

Science, Research and Technology
Doug Walgren (D-Pa), Chairman
Sherwood L. Boehlert R-NY), Ranking Republican

Space Science and Applications
Bill Nelson (D-Fla), Chairman
Robert S. Walker (R-Pa), Ranking Republican

Transportation, Aviation and Materials
Dave McCurdy (D-Okla) Chairman
Tom Lewis (R-Fla), Ranking Republican

Task Force on Technology Policy
Buddy MacKay (D-Fla) Chairman
Ron Packard (R-Calif), Ranking Republican

Total PAC Contributions to Committee Members

Buddy MacKay (D-Fla)[1]	$854,388
David E. Price (D-NC)	$489,658
David Skaggs (D-Colo)	$452,772
George J. Hochbrueckner (D-NY)	$416,961
David R. Nagle (D-Iowa)	$406,018
Tom McMillen (D-Md)	$392,492
Rick Boucher (D-Va)	$366,600
Jack Buechner (R-Mo)	$320,544
Marilyn Lloyd (D-Tenn)	$320,137
Constance A. Morella (R-Md)	$305,374
Don Ritter (R-Pa)	$293,454
Paul E. Kanjorski (D-Pa)	$286,370
Dan Glickman (D-Kan)	$277,290
George E. Brown (D-Calif)	$276,543
Norman Y. Mineta (D-Calif)	$275,360
Terry L. Bruce (D-Ill)	$274,737
Robert A. Roe (D-NJ)	$271,600
Jim Chapman (D-Texas)	$270,430
Richard H. Stallings (D-Idaho)	$265,739
Carl C. Perkins (D-Ky)	$264,300
Ralph M. Hall (D-Texas)	$242,743
Doug Walgren (D-Pa)	$232,214
Harold L. Volkmer (D-Mo)	$218,185
Bill Nelson (D-Fla)	$212,956
Jimmy Hayes (D-La)	$206,100
Claudine Schneider (R-RI)	$193,656
Robert G. Torricelli (D-NJ)	$173,057
Lee H. Hamilton (D-Ind)	$152,066
Ernie Konnyu (R-Calif)	$142,549
Dave McCurdy (D-Okla)	$142,272
Ron Packard (R-Calif)	$114,538
Joel Hefley (R-Colo)	$112,827
F. James Sensenbrenner (R-Wis)	$109,839
Robert C. Smith (R-NH)	$109,500
Harris W. Fawell (R-Ill)	$98,171
Paul B. Henry (R-Mich)	$97,425
Lamar Smith (R-Texas)	$95,732
D. French Slaughter Jr. (R-Va)	$94,496
Henry J. Nowak (D-NY)	$91,725
Sherwood Boehlert (R-NY)	$90,173
Sid Morrison (R-Wash)	$82,558
Christopher Shays (R-Conn)	$79,702
Tom Lewis (R-Fla)	$64,465
Tim Valentine (D-NC)	$58,650
James H. Scheuer (D-NY)	$55,600
James A. Traficant (D-Ohio)	$49,500
Robert S. Walker (R-Pa)	$43,875
Manuel Lujan Jr. (R-NM)[2]	$5,190

[1] Ran for U.S. Senate in 1988
[2] Did not run for reelection in 1988

Summary

As the mainstream of the American economy has shifted away from its old heavy industrial base into new high-tech and information industries, the attention of Congress has come to focus more and more on the legal and political ramifications of emerging technologies and the post-industrial economy. Much of the legislative debate on these new industries — and the unique new problems and legal challenges they present — has fallen into the jurisdiction of the Science, Space and Technology Committee. Formed in 1959, a year after the Russians launched Sputnik, the committee has also been deeply involved with the U.S. space program and NASA. The aviation and aerospace industry — both civilian and military — contributed a total of nearly $560,000 to committee members during the 1987-88 election cycle. Transport and aerospace-related unions also gave heavily, though mostly to Democrats.

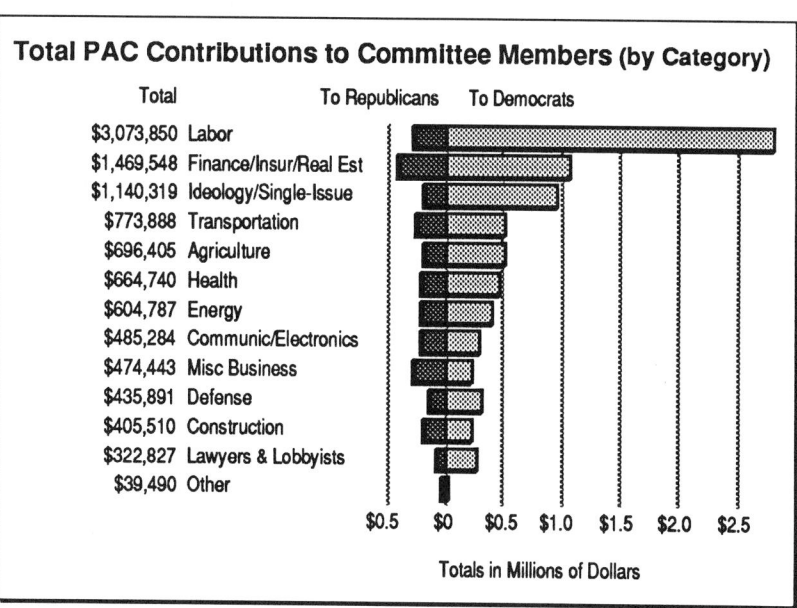

Total PAC Contributions to Committee Members (by Category)

Total	Category
$3,073,850	Labor
$1,469,548	Finance/Insur/Real Est
$1,140,319	Ideology/Single-Issue
$773,888	Transportation
$696,405	Agriculture
$664,740	Health
$604,787	Energy
$485,284	Communic/Electronics
$474,443	Misc Business
$435,891	Defense
$405,510	Construction
$322,827	Lawyers & Lobbyists
$39,490	Other

Totals in Millions of Dollars

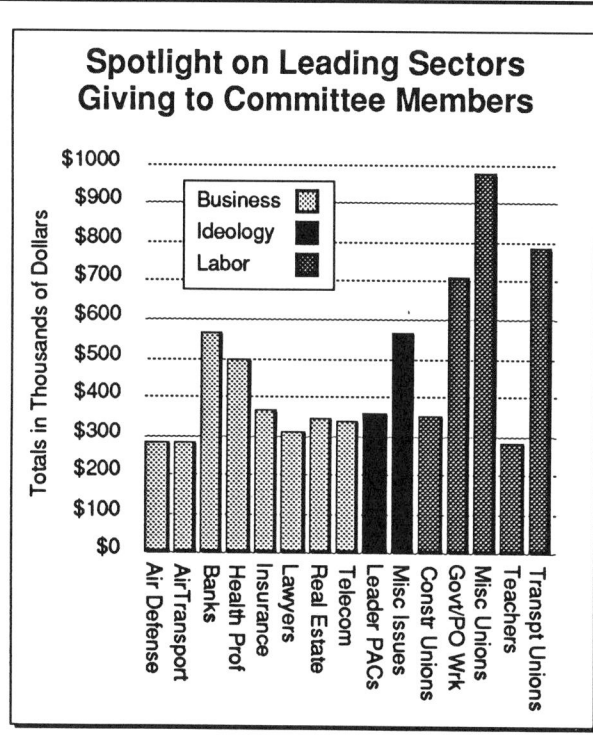

Spotlight on Leading Sectors Giving to Committee Members

Totals in Thousands of Dollars

Business / Ideology / Labor

Air Defense, Air Transport, Banks, Health Prof, Insurance, Lawyers, Real Estate, Telecom, Leader PACs, Misc Issues, Constr Unions, Gov/PO Wrk, Misc Unions, Teachers, Transpt Unions

Top 20 PAC Contributors to Committee Members in 1987-88

1	National Assn of Realtors	$289,283
2	American Medical Assn*	$264,490
3	National Assn/Retired Federal Employees	$217,000
4	Teamsters Union*	$211,750
5	Assn of Trial Lawyers of America*	$204,900
6	National Education Assn*	$202,205
7	National Assn of Letter Carriers*	$189,226
8	United Auto Workers	$188,050
9	National Assn of Home Builders	$153,750
10	Machinists/Aerospace Wrkrs Union*	$130,030
11	Amer Fedn of State/County/Munic Employees	$127,746
12	Air Line Pilots Assn	$120,500
13	National PAC	$117,000
14	Food & Commercial Wrks Union*	$112,800
15	Carpenters Union*	$110,406
16	United Steelworkers	$109,250
17	Marine Engineers Union*	$108,000
18	Intl Brotherhood of Electrical Workers*	$107,766
19	American Bankers Assn*	$107,600
20	AT&T	$103,850

* Contributions came from more than one PAC affiliated with this sponsor.

Leading Sectors Giving to Committee Members

Business

Air Defense	$278,161
Air Transport	$280,491
Banks	$557,171
Health Professionals	$491,865
Insurance	$356,575
Lawyers	$307,061
Real Estate	$336,258
Telecommunications	$335,357

Ideological/Single-Issue

Leadership PACs	$349,721
Misc Issues	$555,258

Labor

Construction Unions	$344,341
Govt & Postal Workers	$702,573
Misc Unions	$972,411
Teachers Unions	$277,013
Transportation Unions	$777,512

House Small Business Committee

John J. LaFalce (D-NY), Chairman
Joseph M. McDade (R-Pa), Ranking Republican

Party Ratio: 27 Democrats
17 Republicans

> **Jurisdiction:** (1) Assistance to and protection of small business, including financial aid; (2) Participation of small-business enterprises in Federal procurement and Government contracts. The committee also has oversight with respect to the problems of small business.

Subcommittees

Antitrust, Impact of Deregulation and Privatization
Dennis E. Eckart (D-Ohio), Chairman
John P. Hiler (R-Ind), Ranking Republican

Energy and Agriculture
Charles F. Hatcher (D-Ga), Chairman
David Dreier (R-Calif), Ranking Republican

Exports, Tourism and Special Problems
Norman Sisisky (D-Va), Chairman
Andy Ireland (R-Fla), Ranking Republican

Procurement, Innovation and Minority Enterprise Development
Ike Skelton (D-Mo), Chairman
Silvio O. Conte (R-Mass), Ranking Republican

Regulation and Business Opportunities
Ron Wyden (D-Ore), Chairman
William S. Broomfield (R-Mich), Ranking Republican

SBA and the General Economy
John J. LaFalce (D-NY), Chairman
Joseph M. McDade (R-Pa), Ranking Republican

Total PAC Contributions to Committee Members

David E. Price (D-NC)	$489,658
Thomas A. Luken (D-Ohio)	$468,185
Dennis E. Eckart (D-Ohio)	$382,028
John Hiler (R-Ind)	$344,741
Ron Wyden (D-Ore)	$316,772
Clyde C. Holloway (R-La)	$315,636
Ben Nighthorse Campbell (D-Colo)	$307,821
James Bilbray (D-Nev)	$300,116
Joseph M. McDade (R-Pa)	$271,620
Jim Cooper (D-Tenn)	$244,977
Peter A. DeFazio (D-Ore)	$235,589
Matthew G. Martinez (D-Calif)	$218,900
J. Alex McMillan (R-NC)	$214,455
Charles Hatcher (D-Ga)	$199,408
Romano L. Mazzoli (D-Ky)	$196,650
Ike Skelton (D-Mo)	$195,725
Elton Gallegly (R-Calif)	$163,825
Neal Smith (D-Iowa)	$162,585
Andy Ireland (R-Fla)	$162,389
Floyd H. Flake (D-NY)	$150,681
Dean A. Gallo (R-NJ)	$147,245
John J. LaFalce (D-NY)	$141,022
Jim Olin (D-Va)	$140,400
John J. Rhodes (R-Ariz)	$135,419
H. Martin Lancaster (D-NC)	$132,249
Richard Ray (D-Ga)	$131,117
Richard H. Baker (R-La)	$124,525
Larry Combest (R-Texas)	$119,800
Fred Upton (R-Mich)	$116,965
Gus Savage (D-Ill)	$116,218
Charles A. Hayes (D-Ill)	$115,634
Joel Hefley (R-Colo)	$112,827
Jan Meyers (R-Kan)	$110,395
Nicholas Mavroules (D-Mass)	$107,360
Esteban Edward Torres (D-Calif)	$106,780

Norman Sisisky (D-Va)	$101,886
David Dreier (R-Calif)	$101,850
Henry B. Gonzalez (D-Texas)	$100,387
D. French Slaughter Jr. (R-Va)	$94,496
John Conyers (D-Mich)	$82,614
Silvio O. Conte (R-Mass)	$72,624
Kweisi Mfume (D-Md)	$72,250
William S. Broomfield (R-Mich)	$57,700
Stewart B. McKinney (R-Conn)[1]	-$500

Top 20 PAC Contributors to Committee Members in 1987-88

1	National Assn of Realtors	$245,945
2	American Medical Assn*	$199,229
3	Teamsters Union	$181,650
4	National Assn/Retired Federal Employees	$151,650
5	National Education Assn	$133,783
6	National Assn of Home Builders	$125,750
7	National Assn of Letter Carriers	$117,750
8	Assn of Trial Lawyers of America*	$116,433
9	American Bankers Assn*	$102,250
10	National Auto Dealers Assn	$99,633
11	Machinists/Aerospace Wrkrs Union*	$99,350
12	United Auto Workers	$89,150
13	Auto Dealers & Drivers for Free Trade	$88,800
14	National PAC	$85,000
15	Amer Fedn of State/County/Munic Employees	$82,300
16	Food & Commercial Workers Union*	$74,174
17	Carpenters Union*	$73,970
18	AT&T	$71,700
19	Intl Brotherhood of Electrical Workers*	$64,150
20	National Assn of Life Underwriters	$63,350

* Contributions came from more than one PAC affiliated with this sponsor.

[1] Died May 7, 1987

150

Summary

Small businesses have always been an important constituency of Congress. Every congressional district in the land has its local chambers of commerce, with its bankers, lawyers, doctors, insurance agents, and real estate brokers — many of them taking a keen interest in those items of federal government policy that affect their businesses.

Judging from the patterns in PAC contributions over the 1987-88 election cycle, the banking industry has paid the closest attention of all. Financial institutions (predominately commercial banks) led all other business sectors with more than $626,000 in PAC donations. Health professionals (primarily physicians) were the second-leading source of revenue from business-related PACs.

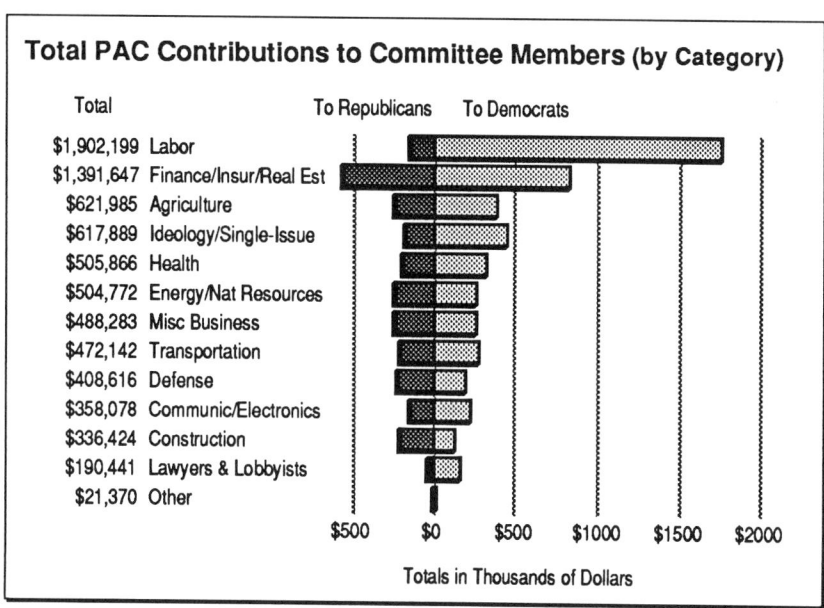

Total PAC Contributions to Committee Members (by Category)

Total	Category
$1,902,199	Labor
$1,391,647	Finance/Insur/Real Est
$621,985	Agriculture
$617,889	Ideology/Single-Issue
$505,866	Health
$504,772	Energy/Nat Resources
$488,283	Misc Business
$472,142	Transportation
$408,616	Defense
$358,078	Communic/Electronics
$336,424	Construction
$190,441	Lawyers & Lobbyists
$21,370	Other

Totals in Thousands of Dollars

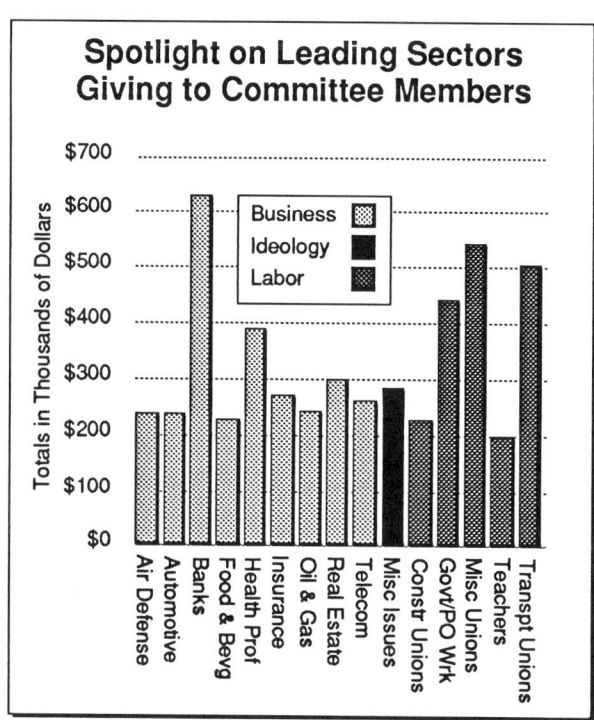

Spotlight on Leading Sectors Giving to Committee Members

Business / Ideology / Labor

Leading Sectors Giving to Committee Members

Business

Air Defense	$234,099
Automotive	$233,757
Banks	$626,578
Food & Beverage	$223,883
Health Professionals	$384,389
Insurance	$266,107
Oil & Gas	$237,957
Real Estate	$296,248
Telecommunications	$254,410

Ideological/Single-Issue

Misc Issues	$280,174

Labor

Construction Unions	$223,645
Govt & Postal Workers	$440,475
Misc Unions	$539,576
Teachers Unions	$195,293
Transportation Unions	$503,210

House Veterans' Affairs Committee

G.V. (Sonny) Montgomery (D-Miss), Chairman
Gerald B. Solomon (R-NY), Ranking Republican

Party Ratio: 21 Democrats
13 Republicans

Jurisdiction: (1) Veterans' measures generally; (2) Cemeteries of the United States in which veterans of any war or conflict are or may be buried, whether in the United States or abroad, except cemeteries administered by the Secretary of the Interior; (3) Compensation, vocational rehabilitation and education of veterans; (4) Life insurance issued by the Government on account of service in the Armed Forces; (5) Pensions of all the wars of the United States, general and special; (6) Compensation for service-related disability; (7) Readjustment of servicemen to civil life; (8) Soldiers' and sailors' civil relief; (9) Veterans' hospitals, medical care, and treatment of veterans.

Subcommittees

Compensation, Pension and Insurance
Douglas Applegate (D-Ohio), Chairman
Bob McEwen (R-Ohio), Ranking Republican

Education, Training and Employment
Wayne Dowdy (D-Miss), Chairman
Christopher H. Smith (R-NJ), Ranking Republican

Hospitals and Health Care
G.V. (Sonny) Montgomery (D-Miss), Chairman
John Paul Hammerschmidt (R-Ark), Ranking Republican

Housing and Memorial Affairs
Marcy Kaptur (D-Ohio), Chairwoman
Dan Burton (R-Ind), Ranking Republican

Oversight and Investigations
Lane Evans (D- Ill), Chairman
Bob Stump (R-Ariz), Ranking Republican

Total PAC Contributions to Committee Members

Wayne Dowdy (D-Miss)[1]	$904,557
Jim Jontz (D-Ind)	$471,225
Liz J. Patterson (D-SC)	$410,255
John Bryant (D-Texas)	$390,757
James J. Florio (D-NJ)	$359,310
Tim Johnson (D-SD)	$326,696
Paul E. Kanjorski (D-Pa)	$286,370
Joseph P. Kennedy II (D-Mass)	$272,840
Claude Harris (D-Ala)	$257,205
Jack Davis (R-Ill)	$251,809
Tom Ridge (R-Pa)	$211,711
Lane Evans (D-Ill)	$211,218
Marcy Kaptur (D-Ohio)	$201,740
Tommy F. Robinson (D-Ark)	$182,980
David A. Mica (D-Fla)[1]	$171,280
John Paul Hammerschmidt (R-Ark)	$166,700
Chalmers P. Wylie (R-Ohio)	$158,415
Michael Bilirakis (R-Fla)	$149,975
John G. Rowland (R-Conn)	$147,635
Bob McEwen (R-Ohio)	$144,266
Dan Burton (R-Ind)	$141,170
Harley O. Staggers (D-WVa)	$131,953
J. Roy Rowland (D-Ga)	$127,637
Timothy J. Penny (D-Minn)	$125,377
Christopher H. Smith (R-NJ)	$124,881
Don Edwards (D-Calif)	$117,256
Bob Stump (R-Ariz)	$114,546
Charles W. Stenholm (D-Texas)	$111,716
Robert C. Smith (R-NH)	$109,500
Robert K. Dornan (R-Calif)	$83,231
Gerald B.H. Solomon (R-NY)	$74,650
Sonny Montgomery (D-Miss)	$71,650
Doug Applegate (D-Ohio)	$66,751
Kenneth J. Gray (D-Ill)[2]	$7,750

Top 20 PAC Contributors to Committee Members in 1987-88

1	National Assn of Realtors	$214,350
2	American Medical Assn*	$180,494
3	Teamsters Union*	$177,800
4	National Assn/Retired Federal Employees	$122,000
5	National Assn of Letter Carriers*	$113,441
6	United Auto Workers	$110,350
7	Assn of Trial Lawyers of America*	$103,850
8	National Education Assn*	$98,300
9	American Bankers Assn*	$92,000
10	Carpenters Union*	$84,967
11	National Assn of Life Underwriters	$82,050
12	Air Line Pilots Assn	$81,500
13	National Assn of Home Builders	$79,919
14	National Auto Dealers Assn	$76,850
15	Machinists/Aerospace Wrkrs Union	$74,700
16	Operating Engineers Union*	$74,675
17	Associated Milk Producers	$73,950
18	National PAC	$70,000
19	Marine Engineers Union*	$66,450
20	Intl Brotherhood of Electrical Workers*	$66,000

* Contributions came from more than one PAC affiliated with this sponsor.

[1] Ran for U.S. Senate in 1988
[2] Did not run for reelection in 1988

Summary

The profile — and problems — of America's veterans have changed considerably over the past generation. The postwar boom of the late 1940s and early 50s, when veterans of World War II and Korea came home to raise new families, build new suburbs, and go on to college with the G.I. Bill has been replaced by the postwar trauma of Vietnam era vets, many of whom have still not been able to shake off the war's lingering effects.

The Veterans Affairs committee pays close attention to the needs of ex-servicemen and women, but the patterns of its PAC contributions reflect no special patterns apart from Congress as a whole.

Total PAC Contributions to Committee Members (by Category)

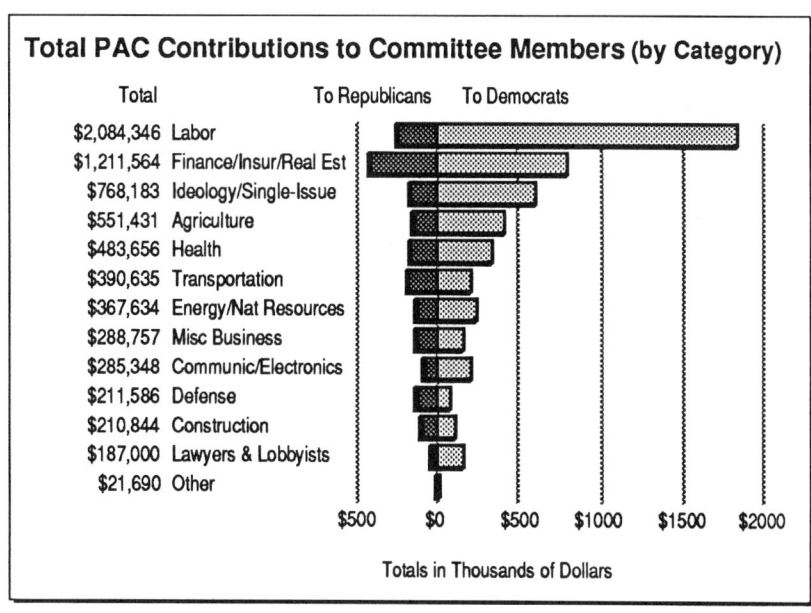

Total		
$2,084,346	Labor	
$1,211,564	Finance/Insur/Real Est	
$768,183	Ideology/Single-Issue	
$551,431	Agriculture	
$483,656	Health	
$390,635	Transportation	
$367,634	Energy/Nat Resources	
$288,757	Misc Business	
$285,348	Communic/Electronics	
$211,586	Defense	
$210,844	Construction	
$187,000	Lawyers & Lobbyists	
$21,690	Other	

To Republicans   To Democrats

Totals in Thousands of Dollars

Spotlight on Leading Sectors Giving to Committee Members

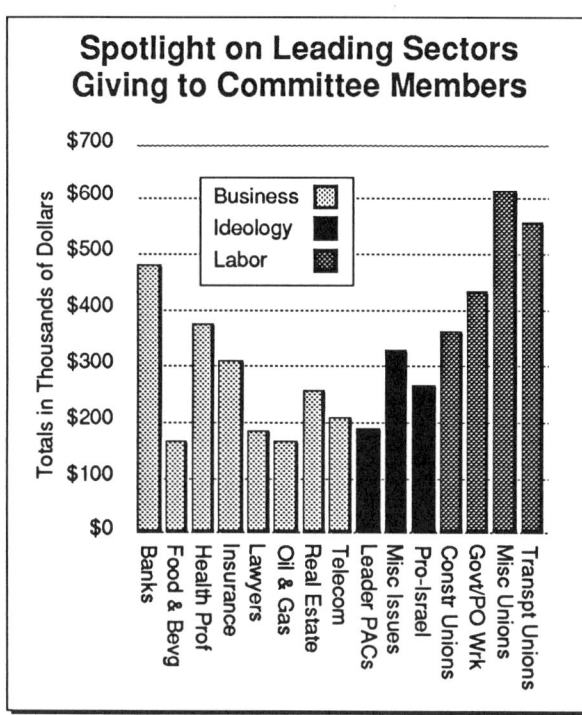

Leading Sectors Giving to Committee Members

Business

Banks	$475,216
Food & Beverage	$159,387
Health Professionals	$372,089
Insurance	$305,758
Lawyers	$179,040
Oil & Gas	$158,829
Real Estate	$250,740
Telecommunications	$201,542

Ideological/Single-Issue

Leadership PACs	$186,285
Misc Issues	$322,378
Pro-Israel	$263,650

Labor

Construction Unions	$359,164
Govt & Postal Workers	$428,936
Misc Unions	$613,835
Transportation Unions	$552,331

House Ways and Means Committee

Dan Rostenkowski (D-Ill), Chairman
Bill Archer (R-Texas), Ranking Republican

Party Ratio: 23 Democrats
13 Republicans

> **Jurisdiction:** (1) Customs, collection districts, and ports of entry and delivery; (2) Reciprocal trade agreements; (3) Revenue measures generally; (4) Revenue measures relating to the insular possessions; (5) The bonded debt of the United States; (6) The deposit of public moneys; (7) Transportation of dutiable goods; (8) Tax-exempt foundations and charitable trusts; (9) National social security, except (a) health care and facilities programs that are supported form general revenues as opposed to payroll deductions, and (b) work incentive programs.

Subcommittees

Trade
Sam M. Gibbons (D-Fla), Chairman
Philip M. Crane (R-Ill), Ranking Republican

Oversight
J.J. Pickle (D-Texas), Chairman
Richard T. Schulze (R-Pa), Ranking Republican

Select Revenue Measures
Charles B. Rangel (D-NY), Chairman
Guy Vander Jagt (R-Mich), Ranking Republican

Health
Fortney H. (Pete) Stark (D-Calif), Chairman
Willis D. Gradison Jr. (R-Ohio), Ranking Republican

Social Security
Andrew Jacobs Jr. (D-Ind), Chairman
Hal Daub (R-Neb), Ranking Republican

Human Resources
Thomas J. Downey (D-NY), Chairman
Hank Brown (R-Colo), Ranking Republican

Total PAC Contributions to Committee Members

Richard A. Gephardt (D-Mo)[1]	$882,414
Jim Moody (D-Wis)	$519,503
Robert T. Matsui (D-Calif)	$473,863
Byron L. Dorgan (D-ND)	$462,346
Ronnie G. Flippo (D-Ala)	$444,960
Dan Rostenkowski (D-Ill)	$433,198
Michael A. Andrews (D-Texas)	$399,785
Thomas J. Downey (D-NY)	$360,011
Charles B. Rangel (D-NY)	$358,625
Marty Russo (D-Ill)	$357,996
Beryl Anthony Jr. (D-Ark)	$352,042
Sam Gibbons (D-Fla)	$344,887
Pete Stark (D-Calif)	$325,428
Hal Daub (R-Neb)[2]	$310,675
Ed Jenkins (D-Ga)	$310,397
Bill Frenzel (R-Minn)	$301,078
Richard T. Schulze (R-Pa)	$264,420
Barbara B. Kennelly (D-Conn)	$264,103
Raymond J. McGrath (R-NY)	$251,324
Guy Vander Jagt (R-Mich)	$237,725
Bill Thomas (R-Calif)	$215,150
Frank J. Guarini (D-NJ)	$213,835
Harold E. Ford (D-Tenn)	$210,500
Sander M. Levin (D-Mich)	$193,430
Rod Chandler (R-Wash)	$191,478
Hank Brown (R-Colo)	$190,891
Don J. Pease (D-Ohio)	$189,677
William J. Coyne (D-Pa)	$156,075
E. Clay Shaw (R-Fla)	$153,750
Brian Donnelly (D-Mass)	$130,525
J. J. Pickle (D-Texas)	$46,463
Judd Gregg (R-NH)[3]	$38,010
Bill Archer (R-Texas)	$0
Philip M. Crane (R-Ill)	$0
Bill Gradison (R-Ohio)	$0
Andrew Jacobs (D-Ind)	$0

[1] Total includes PAC contributions received in both his Presidential and House reelection campaigns
[2] Ran for U.S. Senate in 1988
[3] Did not run for reelection in 1988

Top 20 PAC Contributors to Committee Members in 1987-88

1	National Assn of Realtors	$179,910
2	National Assn of Life Underwriters	$173,500
3	Assn of Trial Lawyers of America	$141,150
4	American Institute of CPA's	$139,400
5	American Medical Assn*	$138,151
6	Teamsters Union*	$129,600
7	National Education Assn	$107,575
8	Metropolitan Life*	$99,466
9	American Dental Assn	$98,250
10	American Bankers Assn*	$96,175
11	National Venture Capital Assn	$92,000
12	AT&T	$91,000
13	United Auto Workers	$89,050
14	Air Line Pilots Assn	$84,500
15	Amer Fedn of State/County/Munic Employees	$78,468
16	National Auto Dealers Assn	$76,950
17	Philip Morris*	$75,841
18	National Assn/Retired Federal Employees	$74,000
19	Letter Carriers Union*	$72,500
20	Seafarers International Union	$70,000

* Contributions came from more than one PAC affiliated with this sponsor.

Summary

No committee in the House of Representatives — and possibly in all of Congress — is more important to as wide a breadth of industries, interests and PACs as Ways and Means. Along with its counterpart, the Senate Finance Committee, this is where the first drafts of the nation's tax laws are written and where the final chapters (along with footnotes, abridgements, and special exceptions) are hammered into shape. Ways and Means operates in an arcane world of lawyers and tax accountants, but every comma, semicolon and parenthetical addendum is likely to mean millions or billions of dollars to individual companies and industries.

PAC gifts to its members reflect that political reality, and a glance at the patterns in industry giving provides a glimpse at those that feel themselves most in need of tax relief or tax benefits. During 1987-88, the insurance industry led the way, with more than $1.2 million in donations to committee members. At stake was a proposal within the 1988 tax bill to close a tax shelter that made "single premium" life insurance policies a profitable enterprise for insurance companies and clients alike. The loophole was eventually closed, at least partially.

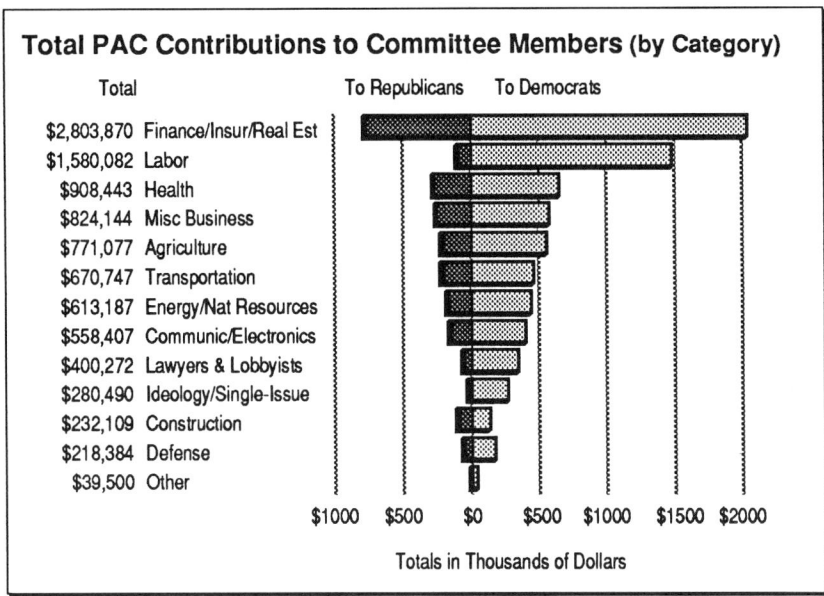

Total PAC Contributions to Committee Members (by Category)

Total	Category
$2,803,870	Finance/Insur/Real Est
$1,580,082	Labor
$908,443	Health
$824,144	Misc Business
$771,077	Agriculture
$670,747	Transportation
$613,187	Energy/Nat Resources
$558,407	Communic/Electronics
$400,272	Lawyers & Lobbyists
$280,490	Ideology/Single-Issue
$232,109	Construction
$218,384	Defense
$39,500	Other

Totals in Thousands of Dollars

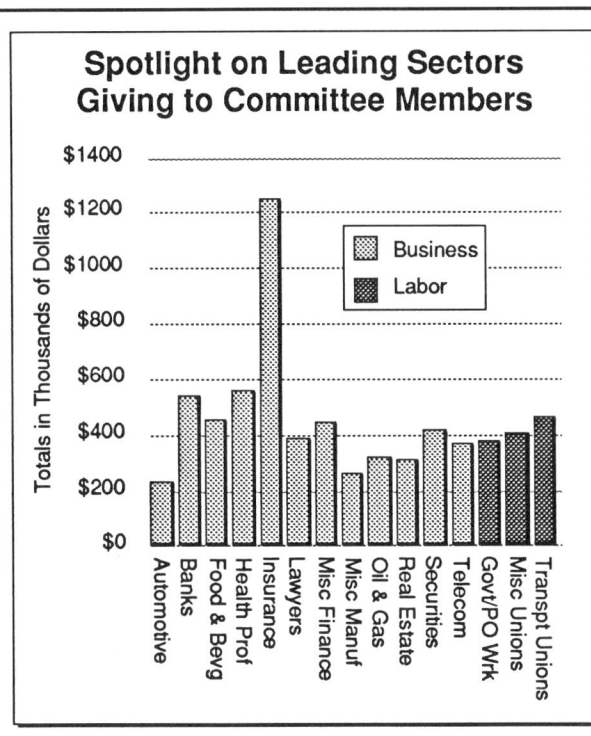

Spotlight on Leading Sectors Giving to Committee Members

Leading Sectors Giving to Committee Members

Business

Automotive	$222,515
Banks	$530,371
Food & Beverage	$448,212
Health Professionals	$554,926
Insurance	$1,241,186
Lawyers	$382,317
Misc Finance	$435,808
Misc Manufacturing	$254,013
Oil & Gas	$316,137
Real Estate	$306,198
Securities/Commodities Investment	$410,307
Telecommunications	$363,787

Labor

Govt & Postal Workers	$369,368
Misc Unions	$393,249
Transportation Unions	$452,425

4.

Member Profiles

Open Secrets

Introduction to the Member Profiles

Who's included in the Member Profiles

Every member of Congress *who was elected in 1988* has a two-page profile on the following pages. This includes members who have since died or resigned their seats. A full list, current as of Aug. 1, 1990, is presented in the following chart.

Members elected in 1988 who did not serve out their full terms*

Name	Date	Reason
Rep. Bill Nichols (D-Ala)	Dec 13, 88	Died
Rep. Dick Cheney (R-Wyo)	Mar 17, 89	Resigned to become Secretary of Defense
Rep. Claude Pepper (D-Fla)	May 30, 89	Died
Rep. Tony Coelho (D-Calif)	Jun 15, 89	Resigned
Rep. Jim Wright (D-Texas)	Jun 30, 89	Resigned
Rep. Mickey Leland (D-Texas)	Aug 7, 89	Died
Rep. Larkin Smith (R-Miss)	Aug 13, 89	Died
Rep. Guy Molinari (D-NY)	Jan 1, 90	Resigned to assume office as Borough President of Staten Island
Rep. Robert Garcia (D-NY)	Jan 7, 90	Resigned
Rep. James J. Florio (D-NJ)	Jan 16, 90	Resigned to assume office as Governor of New Jersey
Sen. Spark Matsunaga (D-Hawaii)	Apr 15, 90	Died

* As of Aug. 1, 1990

Two other House members gave up their seats after being appointed to fill vacancies in the U.S. Senate. On Jan. 3, 1989 Dan Coats (R-Ind) assumed the Indiana Senate seat vacated by Dan Quayle when Quayle became Vice President. And on May 16, 1990, Hawaii Democrat Daniel K. Akaka was appointed to the seat left vacant by the death of Spark Matsunaga. Both those Senate terms were due to expire in November 1990.

Who's __not__ included

• **Members of Congress who did not run in 1988.** Every two years one-third of the seats in the U.S. Senate are up for election. The 33 members who ran in 1988 are included in the following pages. The 67 members whose terms were not up are *not* included in the member profiles.

• **Members of Congress who lost in 1988.** Six House members and four U.S. Senators lost their reelection bids in the 1988 general elections. One additional House member — Republican Ernie Konnyu of California — lost in his Republican primary. A handful of others ran unsuccessfully for other offices. None of the losing incumbents are profiled.

• **Members of Congress elected *after* 1988.** Ten members of the House of Representatives were elected in special elections from early 1989 to mid-1990. Since this book examines only the 1988 elections, those members are not profiled here. They will be included in future editions of *Open Secrets*, just as members elected in special elections during 1987-88 are included in this volume.

Members Elected in 1989-90 Special Elections*

Name	Elected	Reason for Vacancy
Jill Long (D-Ind)	Mar 28, 89	Appointement of Dan Coats to U.S. Senate
Glen Browder (D-Ala)	Apr 4, 89	Death of Bill Nichols
Craig Thomas (R-Wyo)	Apr 26, 89	Resignation of Dick Cheney
Ileana Ros-Lehtinen (R-Fla)	Aug 29, 89	Death of Claude Pepper
Gary Condit (D-Calif)	Sep 12, 89	Resignation of Tony Coelho
Pete Geren (D-Texas)	Sep 12, 89	Resignation of Jim Wright
Gene Taylor (D-Miss)	Oct 17, 89	Death of Larkin Smith
Craig Washington (D-Texas)	Dec 9, 89	Death of Mickey Leland
Susan Molinari (R-NY)	Mar 20, 90	Resignation of Guy Molinari
Jose E. Serrano (D-NY)	Mar 20, 90	Resignation of Robert Garcia

* As of Aug. 1, 1990

What's included in the Member Profiles

Vital Statistics

Member's name, party affiliation, state and congressional district

Year first elected to this seat in Congress

Jim Cooper, D-Tenn (4)

1988 Committees & Subcommittees

Energy and Commerce
Oversight and investigations
Telecommunications and Finance
Transportation, Tourism and Hazardous Materials

Small Business
Regulation and Business Opportunities
SBA and the General Economy

> **First elected: 1982**
> Total receipts: $292,770
> Total from PACs: $244,977

Total PAC receipts in the 1988 campaign. This figure is also taken from the candidate's FEC filings.

Total receipts in 1988 campaign from all sources. This is the figure reported by the candidate in his or her FEC reports.

1988 committee and subcommittee assignments. These are the committee assignments that were held by the member *at the time of the 1988 election*. When the 101st Congress convened in January 1989, many members assumed new committee assignments, so these listings may no longer be current. They were current, however, when PACs were deciding where to place their contributions during the 1988 election season. Current committee assignments are listed for members who were elected to Congress for the first time in 1988.

Sources of Campaign Revenues

Each member's profile includes a pie chart that indicates the general sources of the candidate's 1988 campaign revenues. The percentages are derived from figures filed by the candidate with the Federal Election Commission. A maximum of five types of sources are detailed. Sources which accounted for less than one-half of one percent of the total revenues are not shown. The five sources are as follows:

PACs. The proportion of dollars that came from political action committees.

Individuals. The proportion of dollars that came in contributions from individuals.

Candidate. The proportion of dollars that were donated or loaned to the campaign by the candidate himself or herself.

Party. This figure includes two sources of funds provided by the candidate's political party — both the dollars directly contributed to the campaign by the party, and the dollars spent by the party on the candidate's behalf.

Other. This is a derived figure, calculated by subtracting the difference between total revenues reported by the candidate and the totals of the other categories. The most common sources of "other" revenues are loans made to the campaign and interest earned from the campaign's bank account.

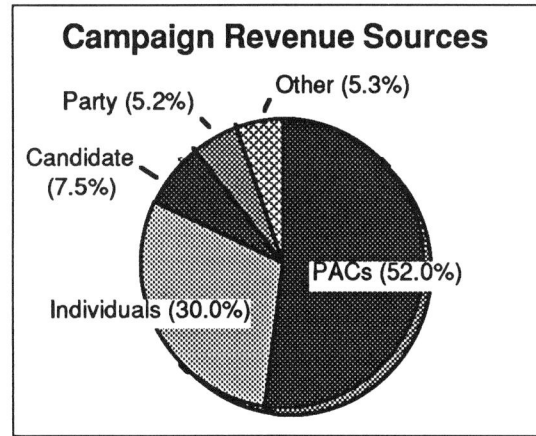

Campaign Revenue Sources

Party (5.2%)
Other (5.3%)
Candidate (7.5%)
Individuals (30.0%)
PACs (52.0%)

In order to allow for easy comparison of the sources of PAC funds among different candidates, each contribution was grouped into one of 13 broad categories. This chart shows how much money the member got from each. The categories are:

Agriculture. Also includes commodity traders, rural electric utilities & food processors.

Communications/Electronics. Includes telecommunications, broadcasting, printing and publishing, computer products and services, and electronics firms.

Construction and related services and equipment.

Defense. Defense contractors (like Boeing or General Motors) that earn most of their revenues from non-defense activities are *not* classified as defense, unless the member sits on a defense-related committee.

Energy & Natural Resources. Besides the oil & gas industry, this also includes electric utilities, mining companies and waste management, and related industries.

Finance, Insurance & Real Estate. Includes banks, stock brokerage and investment firms, insurance and real estate companies, accountants and all other financial services.

Health. Includes health professionals, hospitals, nursing homes pharmaceutical companies and others providing health services or products.

Ideology/Single-Issue. Also includes "leadership" PACs.

Labor. Includes all varieties of labor union PACs.

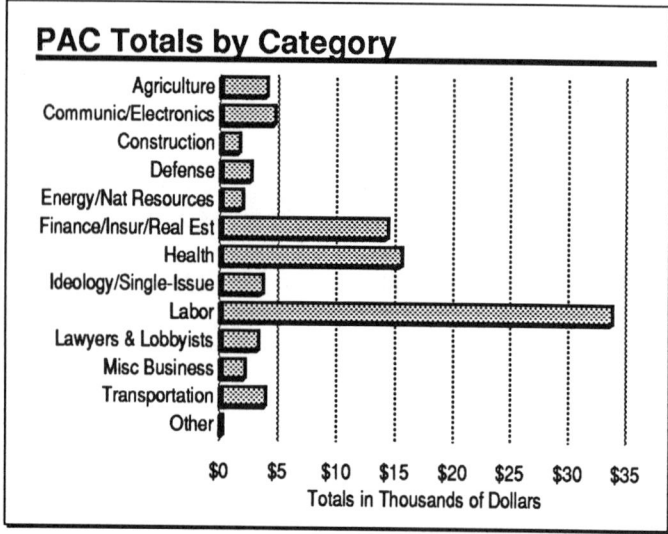

Lawyers & Lobbyists. Includes law firms and lawyer's professional associations, as well as other firms specializing in lobbying and public relations counseling.

Miscellaneous Businesses. This includes a wide variety of manufacturing, sales and service-related companies not classified elsewhere.

Transportation. Also includes non-defense aerospace manufacturers.

Other. Includes PACs that do not fit easily into the other categories, as well as those whose business or ideological interests could not be determined.

Spending in the Last Three Elections

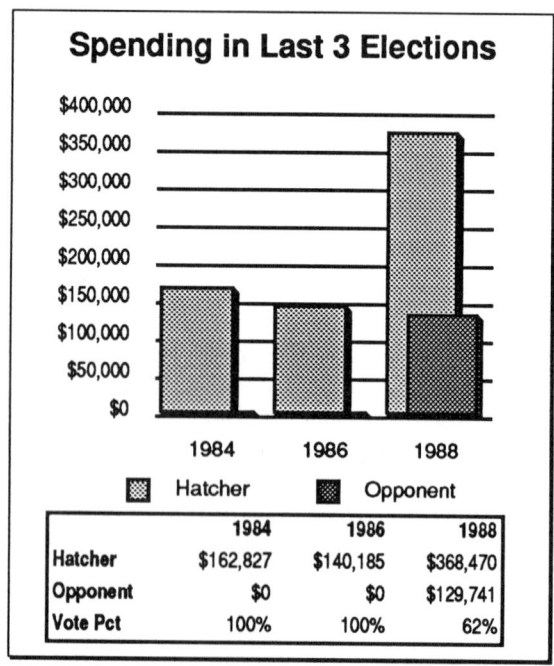

This chart shows at a glance the level of competition — both in votes and spending — that the member faced in his or her last three elections. It compares spending by the member and their chief opponents, and lists the percentage of the vote that the member received in each election.

One trend that these charts tend to show is that spending by incumbents in congressional elections is directly related to the spending of their opponents. Many incumbents, in 1988 as in previous years, spent relatively modest amounts in their reelection campaigns — unless they faced a challenger who was fairly well financed.

There were exceptions. Unusually large expenditures by an incumbent may also indicate a costly primary challenge — or it may be a sign that the member is building up his or her name recognition as a prelude to seeking higher office.

As a point of comparison, the average winning U.S. House campaign cost about $390,000 in 1988. Successful Senate races averaged just over $4 million.

PAC Contribution Profile

Health Professionals	**$35,733**
American Academy of Ophthalmology	$10,000
American Dental Assn	$3,500
American Medical Assn	$3,500
Corp for the Advancement of Psychiatry	$3,025
Oral & Maxillofacial Surgeons	$3,000
American Physical Therapy Assn	$2,779
American Podiatry Assn	$2,500
Others	$7,429
Insurance	**$38,158**
National Assn of Life Underwriters	$5,000
Casualty & Surety Agents Assn	$3,000
National Assn of Mutual Insurance Agents	$2,500
Others	$27,658
Oil & Gas	**$16,879**
Atlantic Richfield	$2,779
Chevron Corp	$2,500
Others	$11,600
Pharmaceuticals	**$15,954**
Abbott Laboratories	$3,500
Pfizer Inc	$2,500
Others	$9,954

This is a more detailed listing of the specific industries and interest groups that contributed to the member's 1988 campaign. The industry headings may be broad — or very specific — depending on the variety and number of PACs contributing to that member's campaign. Where possible, the listings go into greater detail when they relate to the member's committee assignment. For example, a member of the House Merchant Marine and Fisheries Committee may have a special listing for "Sea Transport Unions," while other members' profiles include those PACs under the more general category of "Transportation Unions."

Listed under the categories are the largest PACs in that group that contributed to the candidate. The PACs are arranged in descending order by the amount of their contribution. If contributions came from two or more PACs affiliated with the same sponsor, the total is shown and the sponsor's name is marked with an asterisk.

To make the source of each candidate's funds as clear as possible, the PACs are listed in most cases not by their official name, but by the name of their sponsoring or affiliated organization. This sponsorship may be formal or informal. Many PACs are officially connected with their parent organizations, while others may be legally "non-connected," even though its members all work for the same company or belong to the same union. The listing of corporate and union sponsors is *not* intended to imply that the organization contributed out of its corporate or union treasury. Such contributions are prohibited by federal law. Rather, PAC contributions come from *employees* of a company, or the members of a union — not from the organization itself.

Careful readers may notice that a particular company or PAC may sometimes appear under different categories in different candidates' profiles. This is because many companies have multiple interests. To accommodate that fact, the book uses a system which recognizes both primary and secondary classifications for diversified companies. *In cases where a member's committee assignments coincide with a secondary classification, the secondary code is the one used.* For example: the Boeing Company obtains most of its revenues from the manufacture and sale of commercial aircraft. It is also a major defense contractor. If one of its contributions goes to a member of the Armed Services Committee, or the Defense Appropriations Subcommittee, that contribution is considered to be defense-related. A Boeing contribution to a non-incumbent, or to a member who does not sit on a defense committee, is classified under the company's primary code as an aircraft manufacturer.

One important note: The PAC contributions listed on these pages were filed with the FEC not by the members who received them, but by the PACs that made the contribution. Occasional discrepancies between what the PACs report and what the candidates file are inevitable. The FEC's official computer records use the PAC reports as the final word; so does this book.

Interest Group Ratings

To provide an indication of the member's political perspective and voting record in Congress, a chart is included that shows the ratings given the member by four influential organizations that regularly monitor Congress and issue ratings based on each member's voting record on issues of interest to the groups. The higher the rating, the more favorably that member's voting record is viewed .

Two figures are included for most members: the groups' 1988 ratings, and the member's average rating over the previous five years. The four groups are:

ADA. Americans for Democratic Action. A liberal interest group which rates members on a wide variety of issues.

ACU. American Conservative Union. A conservative interest group which also rates members according to a wide spectrum of issues.

AFL-CIO. The nation's largest labor organization, comprising most of the nation's labor unions.

CCUS. Chamber of Commerce of the United States. A national business group representing local chambers of commerce, trade associations and a wide variety of businesses.

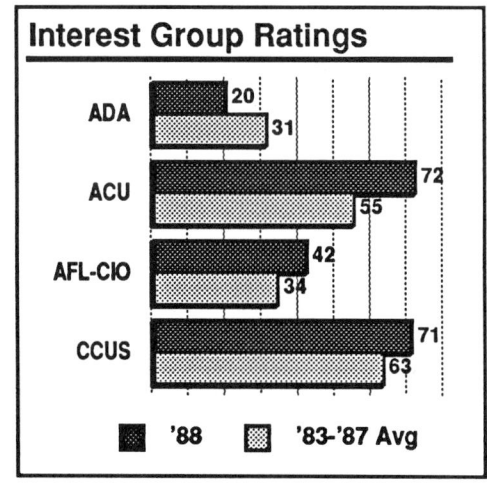

Interest Group Ratings

ADA	20 / 31
ACU	72 / 55
AFL-CIO	42 / 34
CCUS	71 / 63

■ '88   ▨ '83-'87 Avg

161

Lloyd Bentsen (D-Texas)

1988 Committees & Subcommittees

Finance (Chairman)
Health
International Trade
Private Retirement Plans and Oversight of the Internal Revenue Service

Commerce, Science and Transportation
Foreign Commerce and Tourism
Merchant Marine
Science, Technology and Space
National Ocean Policy Study

Select Intelligence

Joint Economic
Economic Growth, Trade and Taxes (Chairman)
Economic Goals and Intergovernmental Policy
Education and Health

Joint Taxation (Chairman)

PAC Contribution Profile

NOTE: The PAC contributions on these pages include funds that Bentsen received both in his U.S. Senate reelection race and his campaign seeking the nomination for vice president on the Democratic ticket. The total receipts listed in the box above, and the percentages in the pie chart at right, refer only to his Senate campaign.

Business

Automotive	....	$39,200
Auto Dealers & Drivers for Free Trade	....	$10,000
National Auto Dealers Assn	....	$10,000
Others	....	$19,200

Aviation & Aerospace	....	$56,000
American Airlines	....	$10,000
Federal Express Corp	....	$10,000
Texas Air	....	$10,000
Others	....	$26,000

Broadcasting/Entertainment	....	$42,715
MCA Inc	....	$10,000
Others	....	$32,715

Commercial Banks	....	$139,375
MBank	....	$12,500
NCNB Corp*	....	$12,100
Allied Bankshares	....	$11,000
Texas Commerce Bancshares*	....	$10,700
First City Bancorp	....	$10,500
American Bankers Assn	....	$10,000
Interfirst Corp	....	$10,000
Others	....	$62,575

Computers & Electronics	....	$45,800
None over $7,100		

Campaign Revenue Sources

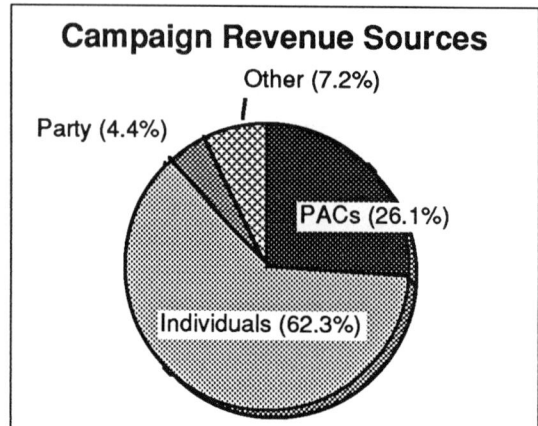

Other (7.2%)
Party (4.4%)
PACs (26.1%)
Individuals (62.3%)

PAC Totals by Category

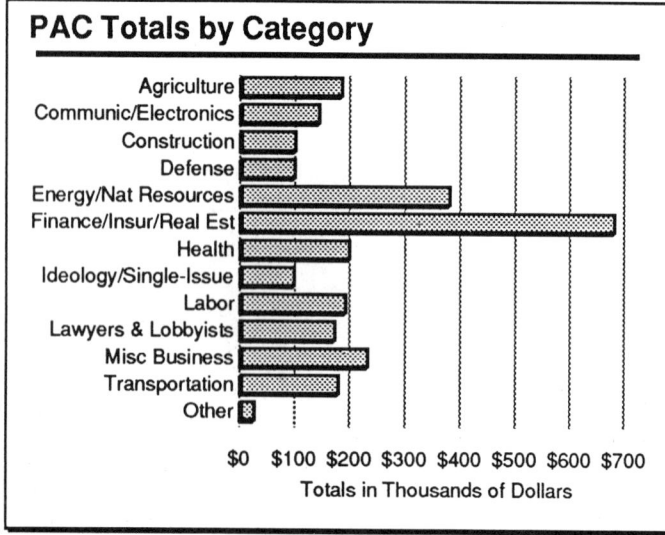

Agriculture
Communic/Electronics
Construction
Defense
Energy/Nat Resources
Finance/Insur/Real Est
Health
Ideology/Single-Issue
Labor
Lawyers & Lobbyists
Misc Business
Transportation
Other

$0 $100 $200 $300 $400 $500 $600 $700

Totals in Thousands of Dollars

Construction	....	$96,825
Associated General Contractors	....	$10,000
National Assn of Home Builders	....	$10,000
Others	....	$76,825

Consumer Credit & Loans	....	$37,500
Beneficial Management Corp	....	$10,000
Gulf + Western Industries	....	$10,000
Others	....	$17,500

Defense	....	$97,287
Litton Industries	....	$11,000
Textron Inc	....	$11,000
Others	....	$75,287

Electric Utilities	....	$62,900
Houston Industries	....	$11,000
Texas Utilities Electric Company*	....	$10,800
Others	....	$41,100

Food & Beverage	....	$84,950
National Beer Wholesalers Assn	....	$11,000
National Restaurant Assn	....	$10,000
Others	....	$63,950

Health Professionals	....	$84,355
American Academy of Ophthalmology	....	$10,000
American Dental Assn	....	$10,000
Others	....	$64,355

Hospitals & Nursing Homes	....	$59,000
American Hospital Assn	....	$11,000
Federation of American Hospitals	....	$11,000
American Health Care Assn	....	$10,000
Others	....	$27,000

Insurance	....	$233,650
National Assn of Life Underwriters	....	$12,000
United Services Auto Assn Group	....	$11,000
American Family Corp	....	$10,000

(continued on next page)

Insurance (cont'0

American International Group Inc	$10,000
Cigna Corp	$10,000
Equitable Financial Services	$10,000
Independent Insurance Agents of America	$10,000
Massachusetts Mutual Life Insurance	$10,000
Others	$150,650

Lawyers & Lobbyists $168,336

Lidell, Sapp	$15,000
Bracewell & Patterson	$11,000
Vinson, Elkins, Searls, Connally & Smith	$10,416
Assn of Trial Lawyers of America	$10,000
Baker & Botts	$10,000
Fullbright & Jaworski	$10,000
Johnson & Gibbs	$10,000
Jones, Day, Reavis & Pogue	$10,000
Others	$81,920

Oil & Gas $268,437

Internorth Inc	$15,000
Enserch Corp	$12,500
USX Corp*	$10,500
Amoco Corp	$10,000
Bass Brothers Enterprises	$10,000
Coastal Corp	$10,000
Valero Energy Corp	$10,000
Others	$190,437

Pharmaceuticals $44,250

None over $5,000

Real Estate $67,500

Trammell Crow Company	$10,000
Others	$57,500

Retail Sales $40,000

None over $8,500

Savings Banks & Credit Unions $59,872

Credit Union National Assn	$11,000
US League of Savings Assn	$10,000
Others	$38,872

Securities/Commodities Investment $133,850

Chicago Mercantile Exchange	$12,500
Chicago Board of Trade	$11,000
Investment Company Institute	$11,000
First Boston Corp	$10,000
Salomon Brothers	$10,000
Others	$79,350

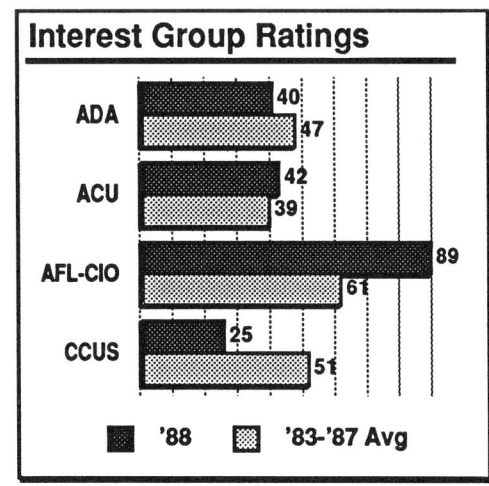

Interest Group Ratings

ADA 40 / 47
ACU 42 / 39
AFL-CIO 89 / 61
CCUS 25 / 51

■ '88   ▨ '83-'87 Avg

Telecommunications $48,820

GTE Corp*	$11,000
AT&T	$10,000
Others	$27,820

Trucking & Railroads $62,700

American Trucking Assns	$12,000
Union Pacific Corp	$11,000
Others	$39,700

Other Major Business PACs

Temple-Eastex Inc	$15,000	Packaging
Associated Milk Producers	$11,199	Dairy
National Venture Capital Assn	$11,000	Venture Cap
American Assn of Equipment Lessors	$10,000	Rentals
American Institute of CPA's	$10,000	Accountants
Browning-Ferris Industries	$10,000	Waste Mgmt
Waste Management Inc	$10,000	Waste Mgmt

Labor

Bldg Trades, Industrial & Other Unions $100,749

Food & Commercial Workers Union	$11,329
Others	$89,420

Government & Postal Workers $41,850

American Fedn of State/County/Munic Employees	$11,000
Others	$30,850

Transportation Unions $46,000

Marine Engineers Union*	$10,000
Teamsters Union*	$10,000
Others	$26,000

Ideological/Single-Issue

Pro-Israel $35,200

None over $5,000

Other Major Ideological/Single-Issue PACs

Cmte for a Demo Consensus (Alan Cranston)	$11,000	Dem Leaders
KidsPAC	$10,000	Health/Welfare

Independent expenditures supporting Bentsen

National Cmte to Preserve Social Security	$51,085

---

* Contributions came from more than one PAC affiliated
with this sponsor.

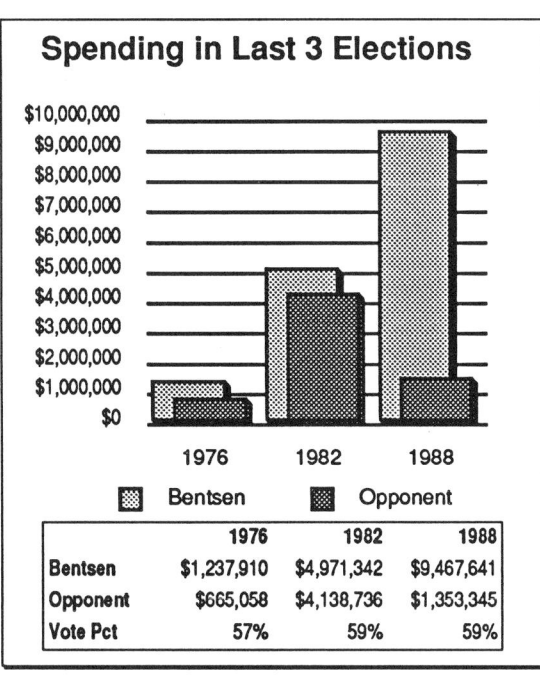

Spending in Last 3 Elections

▨ Bentsen   ▨ Opponent

	1976	1982	1988
Bentsen	$1,237,910	$4,971,342	$9,467,641
Opponent	$665,058	$4,138,736	$1,353,345
Vote Pct	57%	59%	59%

163

Jeff Bingaman (D-NM)

1988 Committees & Subcommittees

Total receipts: $3,806,858
Total from PACs: $1,403,255

Armed Services
Defense Industry and Technology (Chairman)
Readiness, Sustainability and Support
Strategic Forces and Nuclear Deterrence

Energy and Natural Resources
Public Lands, National Parks and Forests (Vice Chairman)
Energy Regulation and Conservation
Mineral Resources Development and Production

Governmental Affairs
Federal Services, Post Office and Civil Service
Federal Spending, Budget and Accounting
Oversight of Government Management

Joint Economic
Education and Health (Vice Chairman)
Economic Resources and Competitiveness
National Security Economics

PAC Contribution Profile

Business

Construction	**$22,050**
National Assn of Home Builders	$12,000
Others	$10,050
Dairy Producers	**$20,000**
Associated Milk Producers	$9,000
Dairymen Inc	$6,000
Others	$5,000
Defense	**$163,450**
BDM International	$12,250
Textron Inc	$11,000
McDonnell Douglas*	$9,000
Northrop Corp	$7,500
General Dynamics	$6,999
AT&T	$6,000
LTV Aerospace & Defense Company	$5,250
Allied-Signal	$5,000
Hughes Aircraft	$5,000
Lockheed Corp	$5,000
Others	$90,451
Electric Utilities	**$31,513**
Public Service Company of New Mexico	$5,963
ACRE (Action Committee for Rural Electrification)	$5,000
Others	$20,550
Financial Institutions	**$43,775**
American Bankers Assn	$13,150
US League of Savings Assn	$8,500
Credit Union National Assn	$8,000
Others	$14,125

Campaign Revenue Sources

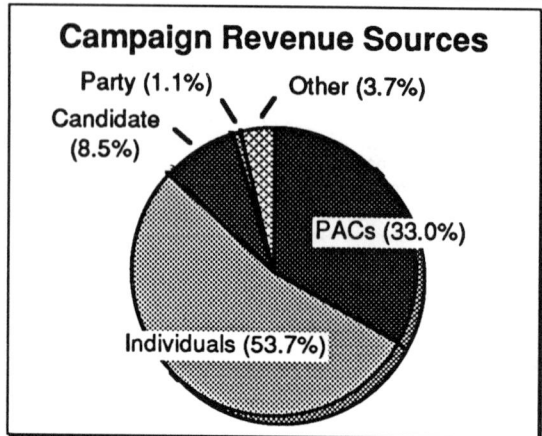

Party (1.1%)
Other (3.7%)
Candidate (8.5%)
PACs (33.0%)
Individuals (53.7%)

Food & Beverage	**$20,800**
None over $4,000	
Health Professionals	**$37,225**
American Academy of Ophthalmology	$5,000
American Podiatry Assn	$5,000
Others	$27,225
Hospitals & Nursing Homes	**$22,000**
American Hospital Assn	$10,000
American Health Care Assn	$5,000
Federation of American Hospitals	$5,000
Others	$2,000
Insurance	**$38,500**
National Assn of Life Underwriters	$9,500
Independent Insurance Agents of America	$6,500
Others	$22,500
Lawyers & Lobbyists	**$45,950**
Assn of Trial Lawyers of America	$15,000
Others	$30,950
Oil & Gas	**$96,892**
Chevron Corp	$8,750
Amoco Corp	$8,500
El Paso Company	$8,499
Valero Energy Corp	$7,000
Others	$64,143

PAC Totals by Category

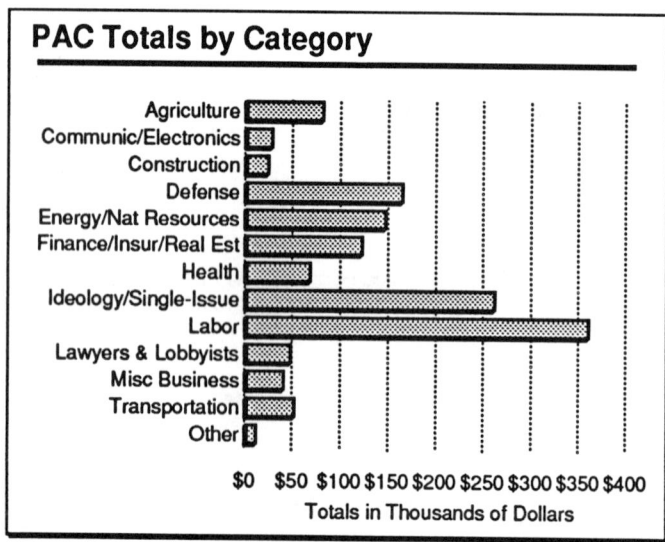

Agriculture
Communic/Electronics
Construction
Defense
Energy/Nat Resources
Finance/Insur/Real Est
Health
Ideology/Single-Issue
Labor
Lawyers & Lobbyists
Misc Business
Transportation
Other

$0 $50 $100 $150 $200 $250 $300 $350 $400
Totals in Thousands of Dollars

Other Major Business PACs

National Auto Dealers Assn	$12,000	Auto Sales
American Institute of CPA's	$10,000	Accountants
National Assn of Realtors	$7,900	RE Sales
Federal Express Corp	$7,500	Air Freight
American Crystal Sugar Corp	$6,000	Sugar
Chicago Board of Trade	$6,000	Commodities
United Parcel Service	$6,000	Delivery
Auto Dealers & Drivers for Free Trade	$5,500	JapanAutoSal
Chicago Mercantile Exchange	$5,000	Commodities

Labor

Bldg Trades, Industrial & Misc Unions...................$159,200
Carpenters & Joiners Union $14,000
United Steelworkers $13,000
Intl Brotherhood of Electrical Workers $12,000
Laborers' Political League $11,500
AFL-CIO* $11,000
United Auto Workers $10,500
Machinists/Aerospace Workers Union $10,000
Operating Engineers Union $10,000
Sheet Metal Workers Union $10,000
Bricklayers Union $9,000
Food & Commercial Workers Union $8,000
Plumbers/Pipefitters Union $8,000
Communications Workers of America $7,500
Boilermakers Union $5,000
Others $19,700

Government & Postal Workers.............................$78,400
National Assn of Letter Carriers $16,000
National Assn of Retired Federal Employees $13,000
American Postal Workers Union $12,000
American Fedn of State/County/Munic Employees $10,000
National Rural Letter Carriers Assn $9,500
National Treasury Employees Union $5,000
Others $12,900

Teachers Unions...$24,500
American Federation of Teachers $13,000
National Education Assn $11,500

Transportation Unions..$96,000
Teamsters Union $17,750
Seafarers International Union $15,000
Marine Engineers Union* $12,500
United Transportation Union $12,000
Air Line Pilots Assn $11,000
Transportation Communication Union.............................$7,750
Maintenance of Way Employees $5,500
Others $14,500

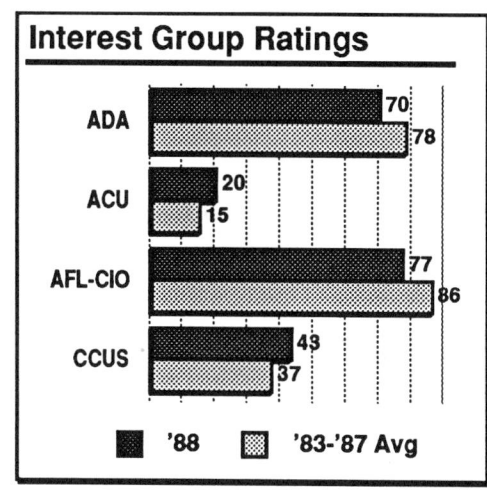

Interest Group Ratings

	'88	'83-'87 Avg
ADA	70	78
ACU	20	15
AFL-CIO	77	86
CCUS	43	37

Ideological/Single-Issue

Democratic/Liberal $21,493
Democrats for the 80's $10,000
National Cmte for an Effective Congress $9,993
Others $1,500

Democratic Leadership PACs.................................$34,494
Cmte for a Democratic Consensus (Alan Cranston) $10,000
Senate Majority Fund (Daniel Inouye)...........................$10,000
Pelican PAC (Bennett Johnston) $9,994
Others $4,500

Pro-Israel $148,600
Washington PAC $11,500
Delaware Valley PAC $11,000
Hudson Valley PAC $11,000
Citizens Organized PAC $10,000
Desert Caucus $10,000
National PAC $10,000
Pacific PAC $10,000
Roundtable PAC $5,500
Citizens Concerned for the National Interest $5,000
Joint Action Cmte for Political Affairs $5,000
Multi-Issue PAC $5,000
National Action Committee $5,000
San Franciscans for Good Government............................$5,000
St Louisians for Better Government $5,000
Others $39,600

Other Major Ideological/Single-Issue PACs

KidsPAC	$14,000	Health/Welfare
National Cmte to Preserve Social Security	$8,000	Elderly
Sierra Club	$6,907	Environment
National Abortion Rights Action League	$6,000	Pro-Choice
National Rifle Assn	$5,950	Pro-Guns
Free Cuba PAC	$5,000	ForeignPolcy
Voters for Choice/Friends of Fam Planning	$5,000	Pro-Choice

Independent expenditures opposing Bingaman
National Conservative PAC $79,099
Council for National Defense $6,044

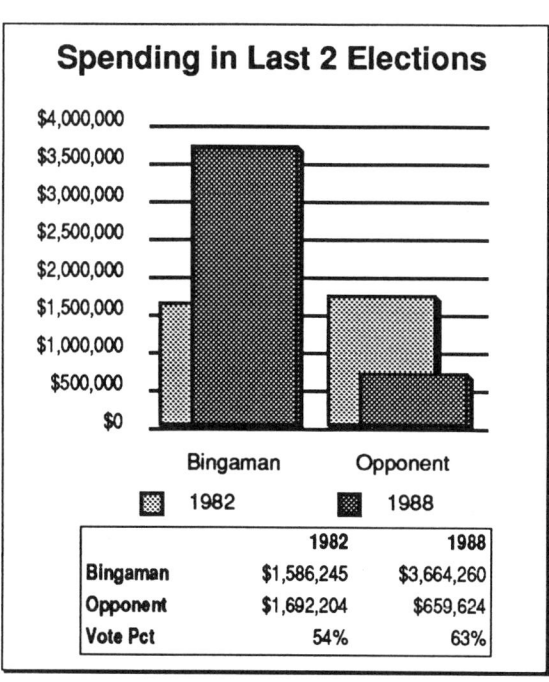

Spending in Last 2 Elections

	1982	1988
Bingaman	$1,586,245	$3,664,260
Opponent	$1,692,204	$659,624
Vote Pct	54%	63%

1982   1988

---

* Contributions came from more than one PAC affiliated
with this sponsor.

Richard H. Bryan (D-Nev)

1989-90 Committees & Subcommittees

First elected: 1988
Total receipts: $2,988,750
Total from PACs: $802,792

Banking, Housing and Urban Affairs
Consumer and Regulatory Affairs
Housing and Urban Affairs

Commerce, Science and Transportation
Consumer (Chairman)
Foreign Commerce and Tourism
Science, Technology and Space

Joint Economic Committee
Economic Resources and Competitiveness
Investment, Jobs and Prices
Technology and National Security

PAC Contribution Profile

Business

Air Transport/Air Freight	**$10,000**

Aircraft Owners & Pilots Assn	$4,000
Federal Express Corp	$4,000
Others	$2,000

Casinos & Gambling	**$50,516**

California Hotel & Casino PAC	$10,000
Bally Manufacturing	$9,500
Harrah's	$6,000
Circus Circus Enterprises	$5,766
Showboat Inc	$5,000
Summa Corp	$5,000
Union Plaza	$5,000
Others	$4,250

Commercial & Savings Banks	**$14,402**

American Bankers Assn	$2,500
Others	$11,902

Credit Unions	**$12,000**

Credit Union National Assn	$12,000

Food & Beverage	**$15,500**

Joseph E Seagram & Sons	$5,000
Southern Wine & Spirits	$4,000
Others	$6,500

Campaign Revenue Sources

Party (3.5%)   Other (3.8%)
Candidate (1.6%)
PACs (25.6%)
Individuals (65.5%)

Health Professionals	**$33,100**

American Academy of Ophthalmology	$10,000
American Nurses Assn	$7,000
American Dental Assn	$5,000
American Optometric Assn	$5,000
American Occupational Therapy Assn	$3,000
Others	$3,100

Insurance	**$48,999**

National Assn of Life Underwriters	$10,000
Independent Insurance Agents of America	$9,999
National Assn Mutual Insurance Agents	$7,000
Casualty & Surety Agents Assn	$4,500
American Council of Life Insurance	$3,500
Others	$14,000

Lawyers & Lobbyists	**$19,600**

Assn of Trial Lawyers of America	$10,000
Others	$9,600

Real Estate	**$18,250**

Del Webb Corp	$8,250
National Assn of Realtors	$6,000
Others	$4,000

Securities/Commodities Investment	**$14,000**

Chicago Mercantile Exchange	$5,000
Salomon Brothers	$3,000
Others	$6,000

Other Major Business PACs

Yellow Freight System	$7,500	Trucking
American Veterinary Medical Assn	$5,000	Veterinary
National Assn of Home Builders	$5,000	Resid Constr
American Hospital Assn	$3,000	Hospitals
Associated Milk Producers	$3,000	Dairy
MCA Inc	$2,500	Movies
National Assn of Social Workers	$2,500	Social Work
Union Pacific Corp	$2,500	Railroads

PAC Totals by Category

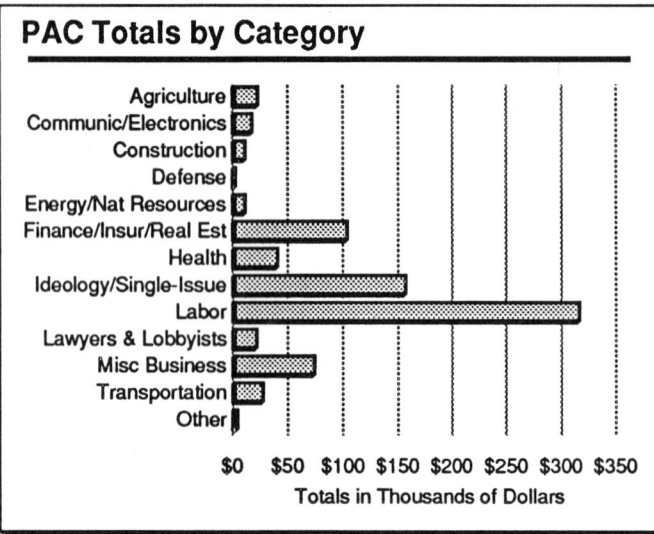

Agriculture
Communic/Electronics
Construction
Defense
Energy/Nat Resources
Finance/Insur/Real Est
Health
Ideology/Single-Issue
Labor
Lawyers & Lobbyists
Misc Business
Transportation
Other

$0 $50 $100 $150 $200 $250 $300 $350
Totals in Thousands of Dollars

Labor

Bldg Trades/Industrial/Misc Unions $161,800

AFL-CIO	$10,000
Carpenters & Joiners Union	$10,000
Communications Workers of America	$10,000
Food & Commercial Workers Union	$10,000
Intl Brotherhood of Electrical Workers	$10,000
Ironworkers Union	$10,000
Laborers' Western Political League	$10,000
Machinists/Aerospace Workers Union	$10,000
Operating Engineers Union	$10,000
Plumbers/Pipefitters Union	$10,000
United Auto Workers	$10,000
United Steelworkers	$7,500
Hotel/Restaurant Employees Union	$5,500
Service Employees International Union	$5,500
Amalgamated Clothing & Textile Workers	$5,000
Bricklayers Union	$5,000
Ladies Garment Workers Union	$5,000
Sheet Metal Workers Union	$5,000
Rubber Cork Linoleum Plastic Workers	$3,000
United Mine Workers	$2,500
Others	$7,800

Government & Postal Workers $59,750

American Fedn of State/County/Munic Employees	$10,000
National Assn of Letter Carriers	$10,000
National Assn of Retired Federal Employees	$10,000
National Rural Letter Carriers Assn	$10,000
National Treasury Employees Union	$8,000
American Postal Workers Union	$5,000
American Federation of Government Employees	$4,500
Others	$2,250

Teachers Unions $20,000

American Federation of Teachers	$10,000
National Education Assn	$10,000

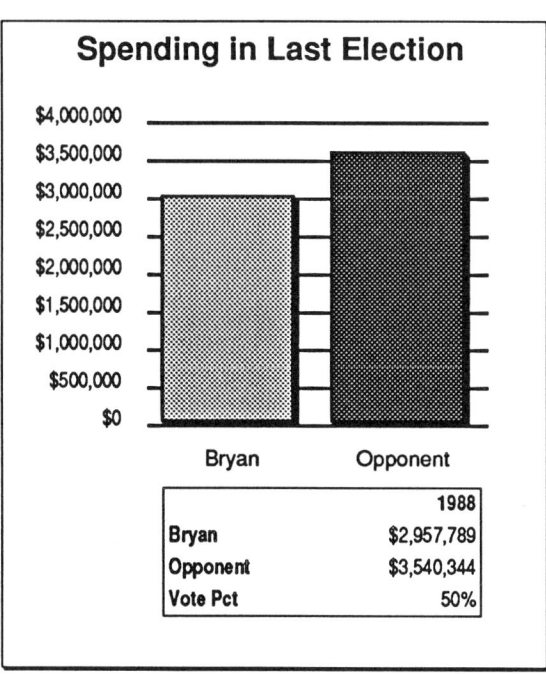

Spending in Last Election

	1988
Bryan	$2,957,789
Opponent	$3,540,344
Vote Pct	50%

Transportation Unions $73,250

Air Line Pilots Assn	$10,000
Marine Engineers Union	$10,000
Seafarers International Union	$10,000
Teamsters Union	$10,000
United Transportation Union	$10,000
Amalgamated Transit Union	$7,500
Transportation Communication Union	$6,500
Brotherhood of Locomotive Engineers	$2,500
International Longshoremen Assn	$2,500
Others	$4,250

Ideological/Single-Issue

Democratic/Liberal $19,300

Democrats for The 80's	$10,000
Religion and Tolerance PAC	$5,000
Others	$4,300

Democratic Leadership PACs $24,000

Committee for a Demo Consensus (Alan Cranston)	$10,000
Senate Majority Fund (Daniel Inouye)	$10,000
Others	$4,000

Health & Welfare Issues $12,500

KidsPAC	$10,000
National Community Action Foundation	$2,500

Pro-Israel $80,250

Hudson Valley PAC	$10,000
Joint Action Cmte for Political Affairs	$10,000
Washington PAC	$10,000
Citizens Organized PAC	$5,000
Desert Caucus	$5,000
MOPAC	$5,000
National PAC	$5,000
Pacific PAC	$5,000
San Franciscans for Good Govt	$5,000
Mid Manhattan PAC	$3,500
Multi-Issue PAC	$3,500
Others	$13,250

Senior Citizens/Social Security Issues $15,000

National Cmte to Preserve Social Security	$10,000
National Council of Sr Citizens	$5,000

Independent expenditures supporting Bryan

National Cmte to Preserve Social Security	$8,256

Independent expenditures opposing Bryan

Auto Dealers & Drivers for Free Trade	$23,450

Quentin N. Burdick (D-ND)

First elected: 1960
Total receipts: $2,061,729
Total from PACs: $1,186,056

1988 Committees & Subcommittees

Environment and Public Works (Chairman)
Water Resources, Transportation and Infrastructure

Appropriations
Agriculture, Rural Development and Related Agencies (Chairman)
Energy and Water Development
Interior and Related Agencies
Labor, Health and Human Services, Education and Related Agencies

Select Indian Affairs

Special Aging

PAC Contribution Profile

Business

Automotive **$20,250**

Auto Dealers & Drivers for Free Trade	$10,000
Others	$10,250

Construction **$60,000**

National Utility Contractors Assn	$11,000
Associated General Contractors	$10,000
National Assn of Home Builders	$8,500
Henley Group Inc	$5,000
Others	$25,500

Dairy Producers **$27,750**

Associated Milk Producers	$10,000
Mid-America Dairymen	$10,000
Others	$7,750

Defense **$21,900**

Textron Inc	$8,000
Allied-Signal	$5,000
Others	$8,900

Electric Utilities **$45,053**

ACRE (Action Committee for Rural Electrification)	$10,000
Others	$35,053

Financial Institutions **$26,450**

American Bankers Assn	$9,500
US League of Savings Assn	$6,500
Others	$10,450

Food & Beverage **$20,500**

National Beer Wholesalers Assn	$10,000
Others	$10,500

Health Professionals **$30,550**

American Podiatry Assn	$10,000
Others	$20,550

Insurance **$16,000**

National Assn of Life Underwriters	$8,000
Others	$8,000

Lawyers & Lobbyists **$49,940**

Assn of Trial Lawyers of America	$10,000
Fullbright & Jaworski	$6,000
Others	$33,940

Oil & Gas **$49,150**

None over $4,500

Real Estate **$15,650**

None over $4,000

Securities/Commodities Investment **$21,250**

Shearson Lehman Hutton	$8,000
Chicago Board of Trade	$5,000
Others	$8,250

Sugar Growers **$23,254**

American Crystal Sugar Corp	$10,000
Others	$13,254

Waste Management **$19,377**

Waste Management Inc	$10,000
Browning-Ferris Industries	$9,377

Campaign Revenue Sources

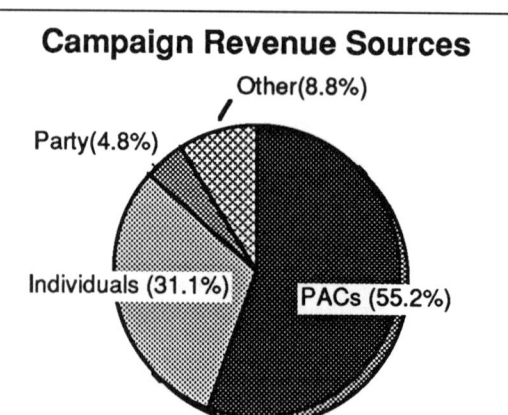

Other (8.8%)
Party (4.8%)
Individuals (31.1%)
PACs (55.2%)

Other Major Business PACs

Federal Express Corp	$7,000	Air Freight
American Hospital Assn	$6,250	Hospitals
American Institute of CPA's	$6,000	Accountants
Kansas City Southern	$6,000	Railroads
United Parcel Service	$6,000	Delivery
Lucas Aerospace	$5,822	AerospacePts
Northwestern Bell Telephone	$5,500	Phone Util
American Health Care Assn	$5,000	Nursing Home
Greyhound Corp	$5,000	Home Chem
RJR Nabisco	$5,000	Tobacco

PAC Totals by Category

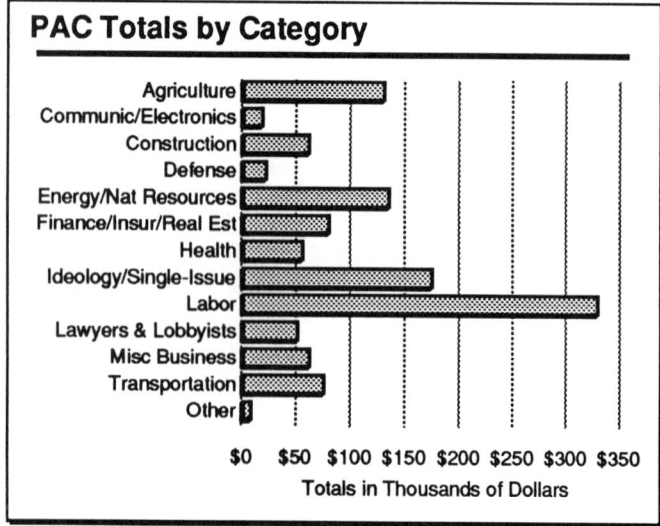

Agriculture
Communic/Electronics
Construction
Defense
Energy/Nat Resources
Finance/Insur/Real Est
Health
Ideology/Single-Issue
Labor
Lawyers & Lobbyists
Misc Business
Transportation
Other

$0 $50 $100 $150 $200 $250 $300 $350

Totals in Thousands of Dollars

Labor

Bldg Trades, Industrial & Misc Unions $148,800

AFL-CIO*	$11,000
Carpenters & Joiners Union	$10,000
Communications Workers of America	$10,000
Food & Commercial Workers Union	$10,000
Intl Brotherhood of Electrical Workers	$10,000
Laborers' Political League	$10,000
Machinists/Aerospace Workers Union	$10,000
United Auto Workers	$10,000
Operating Engineers Union*	$8,000
Ladies Garment Workers Union	$7,500
United Mine Workers	$7,000
Plumbers/Pipefitters Union	$6,500
Boilermakers Union	$6,000
Amalgamated Clothing & Textile Workers	$5,000
Others	$27,800

Government & Postal Workers $69,450

American Fedn of State/County/Munic Employees	$10,000
American Postal Workers Union	$10,000
National Assn of Letter Carriers	$10,000
National Assn of Retired Federal Employees	$10,000
National Assn of Postmasters	$5,150
American Fedn of Government Employees	$5,000
National Assn of Postal Supervisors	$5,000
National Rural Letter Carriers Assn	$5,000
Others	$9,300

Teachers Unions $20,000

American Federation of Teachers	$10,000
National Education Assn	$10,000

Interest Group Ratings

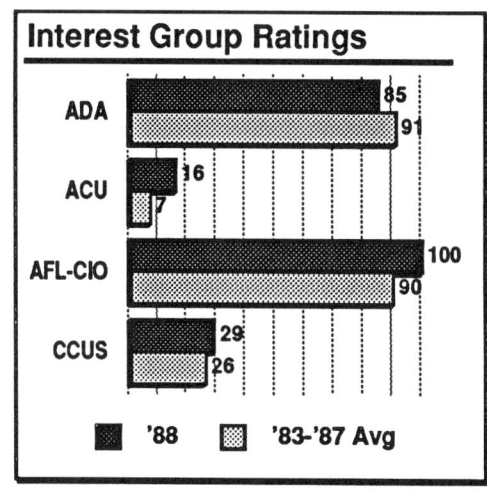

	’88	’83-’87 Avg

Transportation Unions $89,100

Air Line Pilots Assn	$10,000
Marine Engineers Union	$10,000
Masters, Mates & Pilots Union*	$10,000
Seafarers International Union*	$10,000
Teamsters Union	$10,000
United Transportation Union	$7,000
Amalgamated Transit Union	$6,000
International Longshoremen Assn	$5,000
Transportation Communication Union	$5,000
Others	$16,100

Ideological/Single-Issue

Democratic/Liberal $20,996

Democrats for The 80's	$10,000
National Cmte for an Effective Congress	$9,996
Others	$1,000

Democratic Leadership PACs $41,500

Committee for a Demo Consensus (Alan Cranston)	$10,000
Senate Majority Fund (Daniel Inouye)	$10,000
Fund for a Democratic Majority (Edward Kennedy)	$6,000
24th Cong District of California PAC (Henry Waxman)	$5,000
Pelican PAC (Bennett Johnston)	$5,000
Others	$5,500

Pro-Israel $69,050

Citizens Organized PAC	$10,000
Desert Caucus	$10,000
Washington PAC	$7,000
Delaware Valley PAC	$6,000
Hudson Valley PAC	$5,300
National PAC	$5,000
Others	$25,750

Other Major Ideological/Single-Issue PACs

KidsPAC	$10,000	Health/Welfare
National Rifle Assn	$9,900	Pro-Guns
National Cmte to Preserve Social Security	$5,000	Soc Secur

Independent expenditures opposing Burdick

Council for National Defense	$6,044

---

* Contributions came from more than one PAC affiliated with this sponsor.

Spending in Last 3 Elections

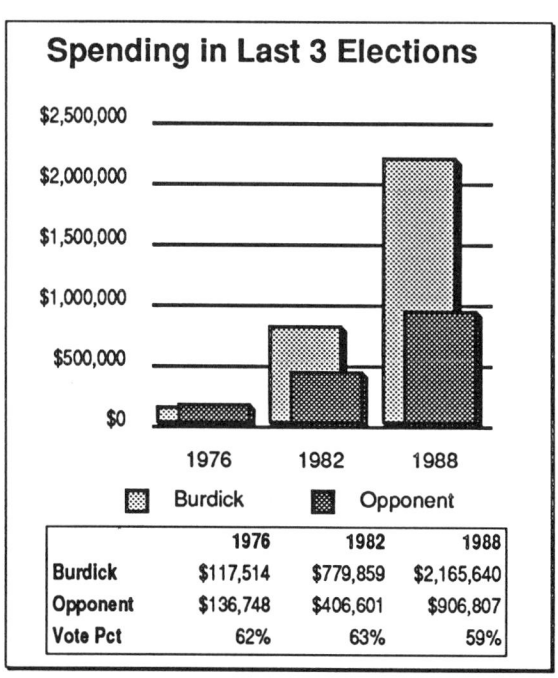

	1976	1982	1988
Burdick	$117,514	$779,859	$2,165,640
Opponent	$136,748	$406,601	$906,807
Vote Pct	62%	63%	59%

Conrad Burns (R-Mont)

First elected: 1988
Total receipts: $902,760
Total from PACs: $315,387

1989-90 Committees & Subcommittees

Commerce, Science and Transportation
Foreign Commerce and Tourism (Ranking Republican)
Communications
Surface Transportation

Energy and Natural Resources
Water and Power (Ranking Republican)
Energy Research and Development
Public Lands, National Parks and Forests

Small Business
Urban and Minority-Owned Business Development (Ranking Republican)
Rural Economy and Family Farming

PAC Contribution Profile

Business

Air Transport/Air Freight **$12,000**

    Federal Express Corp $10,000
    Eastern Airlines $2,000

Automotive **$21,000**

    Auto Dealers & Drivers for Free Trade $10,000
    National Auto Dealers Assn $5,000
    Eaton Corp $4,000
    General Motors $2,000

Chemicals **$7,000**

    NL Industries $5,000
    Dow Chemical* $2,000

Commercial Banks **$14,749**

    American Bankers Assn $10,000
    Norwest Corp $2,000
    Others $2,749

Construction **$25,500**

    Associated General Contractors $10,000
    Sheet Metal/Air Conditioning Contractors $5,000
    Manville Corp $3,000
    Wall & Ceiling/Gypsum Contractors $1,750
    Others $5,750

Campaign Revenue Sources

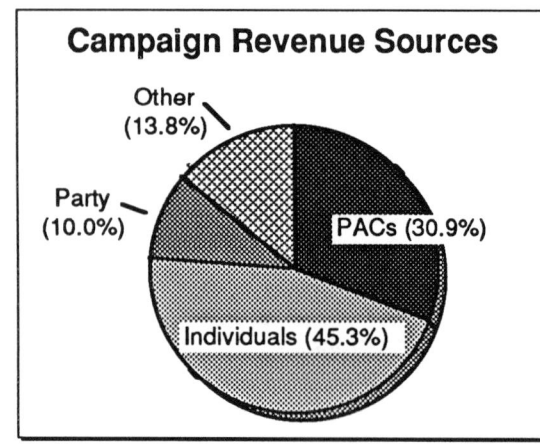

Other (13.8%)
Party (10.0%)
PACs (30.9%)
Individuals (45.3%)

Defense **$11,500**

    Harris Corp $3,000
    Northrop Corp $2,000
    Allied-Signal $1,500
    Martin Marietta Corp $1,500
    Tenneco Inc $1,500
    Others $2,000

Electric Utilities **$7,200**

    ACRE (Action Committee for Rural Electrification) $5,000
    Others $2,200

Electronics & Computers **$13,700**

    Cooper Industries $10,000
    General Electric $2,500
    Others $1,200

Food & Beverage **$17,650**

    Flowers Industries $5,000
    National Restaurant Assn $3,000
    American Bakers Assn $1,500
    Others $8,150

Forest Products **$7,000**

    International Paper Company $5,000
    Boise Cascade $2,000

Health Professionals **$6,000**

    American Medical Assn $5,000
    Others $1,000

Industrial Equipment & Materials **$5,750**

    Borg-Warner $2,500
    National Screw Machines Prod Assn $2,000
    Fuller Company $1,250

Insurance **$18,061**

    Torchmark Corp $5,000
    Independent Insurance Agents of America $2,561
    Aetna Life & Casualty $2,500
    National Assn of Independent Insurers $2,000
    Others $6,000

PAC Totals by Category

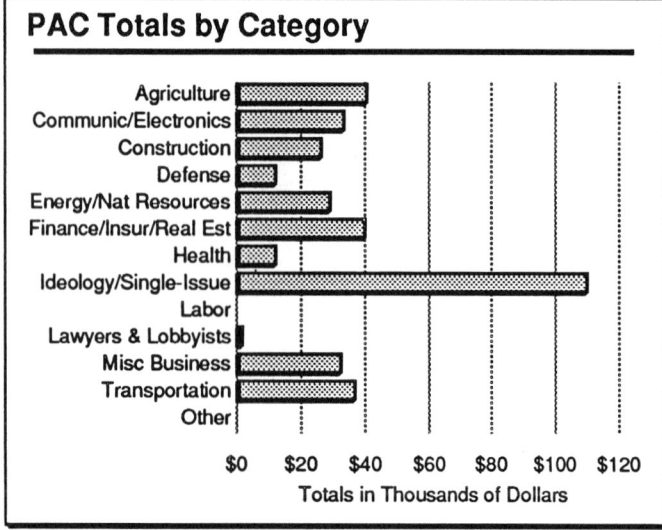

Agriculture
Communic/Electronics
Construction
Defense
Energy/Nat Resources
Finance/Insur/Real Est
Health
Ideology/Single-Issue
Labor
Lawyers & Lobbyists
Misc Business
Transportation
Other

$0 $20 $40 $60 $80 $100 $120

Totals in Thousands of Dollars

Oil & Gas **$17,200**

Dallas Energy PAC	$5,000
Chevron Corp	$2,000
Mapco Inc	$2,000
Forest Oil Corp	$1,500
HOUPAC	$1,500
Others	$5,200

Printing & Publishing **$5,996**

Printing Industries of America	$4,996
Others	$1,000

Sugar Growers **$7,000**

American Crystal Sugar Corp	$2,000
American Sugarbeet Growers Assn	$2,000
Others	$3,000

Telecommunications **$12,000**

Mountain Bell	$3,000
United Telecommunications	$3,000
AT&T	$2,000
Bell Atlantic	$1,500
Motorola Inc	$1,500
Others	$1,000

Tobacco **$13,500**

RJR Nabisco	$5,000
United States Tobacco Company	$5,000
Philip Morris	$2,000
Others	$1,500

Other Major Business PACs

National Fedn of Independent Business	$3,500	Sml Business
Dun & Bradstreet	$2,500	Mkt Research
Abbott Laboratories	$2,000	Pharmaceut
Drexel Burnham Lambert	$2,000	StocksInvest
National Coal Assn	$2,000	Coal
National Assn of Wholesale-Distributors	$2,000	Wholesale
Ecolab Inc	$1,500	BusinessSvcs
Pfizer Inc	$1,500	Pharmaceut
Williams & Jensen	$1,137	Lawyers
American Rental Assn	$1,001	Rentals

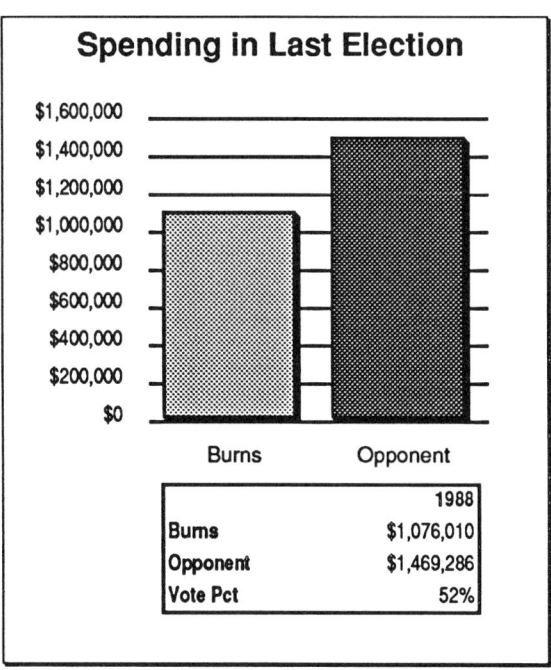

Spending in Last Election

	1988
Burns	$1,076,010
Opponent	$1,469,286
Vote Pct	52%

Ideological/Single-Issue

Pro-Defense PACs **$9,000**

Council for National Defense	$5,000
National Security PAC	$4,000

Pro-Israel **$28,800**

National PAC	$5,000
Women's Pro-Israel National PAC	$5,000
Hudson Valley PAC	$4,000
Desert Caucus	$2,000
Florida Congressional Cmte	$2,000
Roundtable PAC	$2,000
Garden State PAC	$1,800
Delaware Valley PAC	$1,500
Mid Manhattan PAC	$1,500
Others	$4,000

Republican Leadership PACs **$54,000**

Campaign America (Bob Dole)	$10,000
Catch the Spirit PAC (Bob Kasten)	$10,000
Citizens for the Republic (Ronald Reagan)	$5,000
Fund for America's Future (George Bush)	$5,000
Leadership - USA (James McClure)	$5,000
Republican Majority Fund (Richard Lugar)	$5,000
Heartland PAC of Missouri (Kit Bond)	$4,500
Plaid PAC (Rudy Boschwitz)	$4,000
Fund for a Republican Majority (Ted Stevens)	$3,000
Conservative Victory Fund (Steve Symms)	$1,500
Others	$1,000

Other Major Ideological/Single-Issue

Public Svc Research Council	$5,000	Anti-Union
Ruff PAC	$3,500	Tax Policy
Right to Work PAC	$3,000	Anti-Union
Conservatives Acting Together	$2,500	Repub/Conser
Repub Congressional Boosters Club	$2,000	Repub/Conser

Independent expenditures supporting Burns

Associated Builders & Contractors	$5,000

---

* Contributions came from more than one PAC affiliated
with this sponsor.

Robert C. Byrd (D-WVa)

1988 Committees & Subcommittees

First elected: 1958
Total receipts: $1,539,292
Total from PACs: $1,021,570

Majority Leader

Appropriations
Interior and Related Agencies (Chairman)
Defense
Energy and Water Development
Labor, Health and Human Services, Education and Related Agencies
Transportation and Related Agencies

Judiciary

Rules and Administration

Select Intelligence

PAC Contribution Profile

Business

Financial Institutions $45,000

    American Bankers Assn $10,000
    Credit Union National Assn $10,000
    US League of Savings Assn $10,000
    J P Morgan & Company $5,000
    Others $10,000

Construction $38,000

    Associated General Contractors $20,000
    National Assn of Home Builders $10,000
    Others $8,000

Defense..$95,166

    Northrop Corp $10,000
    Lockheed Corp $9,000
    AT&T $7,666
    Chrysler Corp $6,000
    Allied-Signal $5,000
    Grumman $5,000
    Hughes Aircraft $5,000
    McDonnell Douglas* $5,000
    Others $42,500

Electric Utilities $34,300

    American Electric Power $10,000
    Others $24,300

Food & Beverage $41,500

    National Beer Wholesalers Assn $10,000
    Occidental Petroleum $8,000
    Others $23,500

Campaign Revenue Sources

Other (11.6%)

Individuals (23.3%)

PACs (65.1%)

Health Professionals $22,750

    American Academy of Ophthalmology $5,000
    Others $17,750

Insurance...$32,021

    Metropolitan Life Insurance $5,000
    Others $27,021

Lawyers & Lobbyists $31,100

    Assn of Trial Lawyers of America $10,000
    Camp, Barsh, Bates & Tate $6,000
    Others $15,100

Mining $21,000

    Peabody Coal $8,500
    Others $12,500

Oil & Gas $47,350

    Tesoro Petroleum $7,000
    Ashland Oil $5,000
    Others $35,350

Railroads $18,100

    CSX Corp* $6,000
    Union Pacific Corp $5,000
    Others $7,100

Real Estate $15,850

    National Assn of Realtors $10,000
    Others $5,850

Securities/Commodities Investment $39,600

    Chicago Board of Trade $10,000
    Chicago Mercantile Exchange $10,000
    Morgan Stanley & Company $8,000
    Goldman Sachs $5,000
    Others $6,600

Telecommunications $29,928

    Pacific Telesis Group $6,000
    Bell Atlantic* $5,928
    Others $18,000

PAC Totals by Category

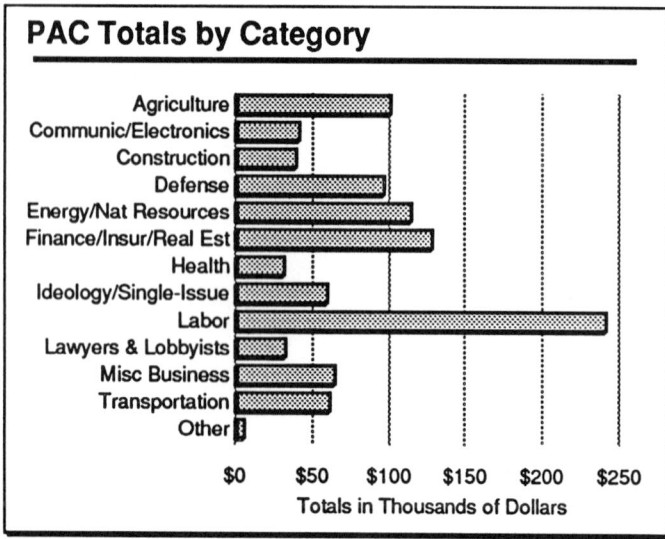

Agriculture
Communic/Electronics
Construction
Defense
Energy/Nat Resources
Finance/Insur/Real Est
Health
Ideology/Single-Issue
Labor
Lawyers & Lobbyists
Misc Business
Transportation
Other

$0 $50 $100 $150 $200 $250

Totals in Thousands of Dollars

Other Major Business PACs

Federal Express Corp	$10,000	Air Freight
J C Penney Company	$7,100	Dept Store
American Institute of CPA's	$7,000	Accountants
Philip Morris	$7,000	Tobacco
Westvaco Corp	$6,000	Paper Prod
Marriott Corp	$5,000	Hotel/Motel
National Cable Television Assn	$5,000	Cable TV
Waste Management Inc	$5,000	Waste Mgmt
Auto Dealers & Drivers for Free Trade	$4,000	JapanAutoSal
National Cotton Council	$4,000	Cotton

Labor

Bldg Trades, Industrial & Misc Unions $107,800

AFL-CIO*	$10,000
Laborers' Political League	$10,000
Operating Engineers Union	$10,000
Sheet Metal Workers Union	$10,000
United Mine Workers	$10,000
Carpenters & Joiners Union	$9,000
Ladies Garment Workers Union	$7,000
Amalgamated Clothing & Textile Workers	$6,000
Machinists/Aerospace Workers Union	$6,000
United Auto Workers	$6,000
Food & Commercial Workers Union	$5,000
Intl Brotherhood of Electrical Workers	$5,000
Others	$13,800

Government & Postal Workers $48,050

American Fedn of State/County/Munic Employees	$10,000
National Assn of Letter Carriers	$10,000
American Fedn of Government Employees	$7,000
National Assn of Retired Federal Employees	$6,000
American Postal Workers Union	$5,000
National Rural Letter Carriers Assn	$5,000
Others	$5,050

Teachers Unions $19,000

American Federation of Teachers	$10,000
National Education Assn	$9,000

Interest Group Ratings

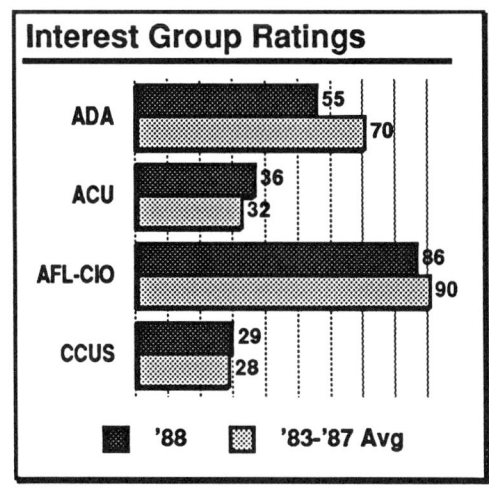

	'88	'83-'87 Avg
ADA	55	70
ACU	36	32
AFL-CIO	86	90
CCUS	29	28

Transportation Unions $65,200

United Transportation Union	$11,000
Air Line Pilots Assn	$10,000
Marine Engineers Union*	$10,000
Seafarers International Union	$10,000
Teamsters Union	$10,000
Amalgamated Transit Union	$7,500
Others	$6,700

Ideological/Single-Issue

Democratic Leadership PACs $12,500

Senate Majority Fund (Daniel Inouye)	$10,000
Fund for a Democratic Majority (Edward Kennedy)	$5,000
Pelican PAC (Bennett Johnston)	$5,000
Others	-$7,500

Other Major Ideological/Single-Issue PACs

National Cmte to Preserve Social Security	$7,000	Soc Secur
Democrats for The 80's	$6,000	Dem/Liberal
Free Cuba PAC	$5,000	ForeignPolcy
KidsPAC	$5,000	Health/Welfare
National PAC	$5,000	Pro-Israel

Independent expenditures supporting Byrd

National Cmte to Preserve Social Security	$8,146

Independent expenditures opposing Byrd

American Citizens for Political Action	$2,486

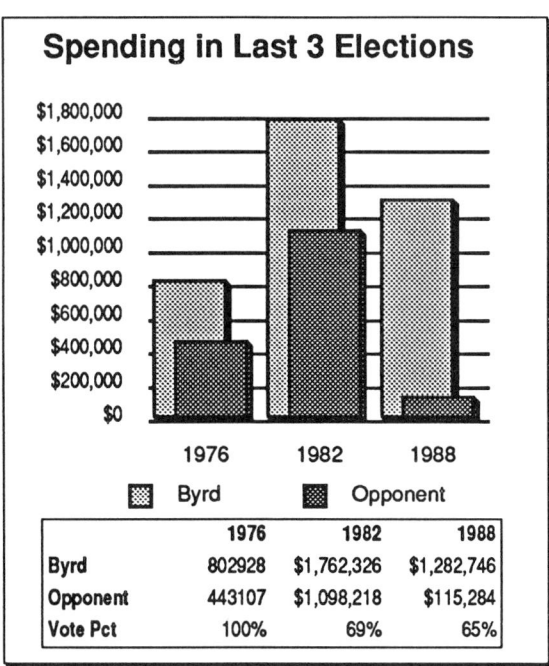

Spending in Last 3 Elections

	1976	1982	1988
Byrd	802928	$1,762,326	$1,282,746
Opponent	443107	$1,098,218	$115,284
Vote Pct	100%	69%	65%

Byrd ▨   Opponent ▨

---

* Contributions came from more than one PAC affiliated with this sponsor.

John H. Chafee (R-RI)

First elected: 1976
Total receipts: $3,005,907
Total from PACs: $1,180,695

1988 Committees & Subcommittees

Banking, Housing and Urban Affairs
Consumer Affairs
Housing and Urban Affairs

Environment and Public Works
Environmental Protection (Ranking Republican)
Hazardous Wastes and Toxic Substances
Water Resources, Transportation and Infrastructure

Finance
Taxation and Debt Management (Ranking Republican)
Health
International Trade

PAC Contribution Profile

Business

Accountants	**$20,500**
American Institute of CPA's	$10,000
Others	$10,500
Automotive	**$17,050**
Auto Dealers & Drivers for Free Trade	$9,000
Others	$8,050
Chemicals & Plastics	**$17,000**
None over $4,000	
Commercial Banks	**$94,233**
American Bankers Assn	$10,000
Barnett Banks of Florida	$10,000
Citicorp	$10,000
J P Morgan & Company	$8,000
Bankers Trust	$5,000
Others	$51,233
Construction	**$65,300**
Associated General Contractors	$10,000
National Utility Contractors Assn	$10,000
Others	$45,300
Defense	**$74,211**
General Dynamics	$10,000
Harris Corp	$10,000
Textron Inc	$10,000
United Technologies	$6,500
Allied-Signal	$5,500
Others	$32,211

Campaign Revenue Sources

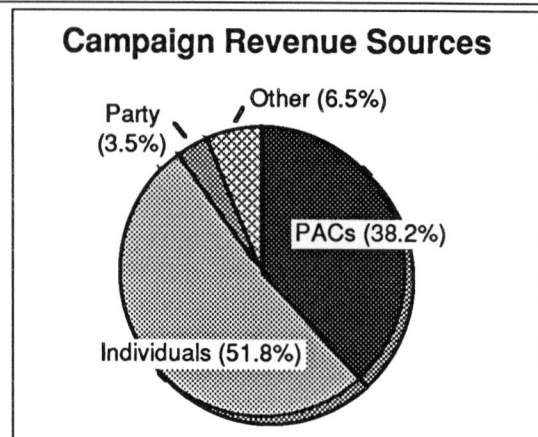

Party (3.5%)
Other (6.5%)
PACs (38.2%)
Individuals (51.8%)

Electronics & Computers	**$24,900**
Cooper Industries	$5,000
Honeywell Inc	$5,000
Others	$14,900
Food & Beverage	**$66,800**
Food Marketing Institute	$7,500
General Mills*	$6,000
ConAgra Inc	$5,000
McDonald's Corp	$5,000
National Restaurant Assn	$5,000
National Beer Wholesalers Assn	$5,000
Others	$33,300
Forest Products	**$19,250**
International Paper Company	$5,000
Others	$14,250
Health Professionals	**$73,600**
American Academy of Ophthalmology	$10,000
American Dental Assn	$10,000
American Medical Assn	$10,000
American Society of Cataract & Refractive Surgery	$5,000
American Nurses Assn	$5,000
American Optometric Assn	$5,000
American Podiatry Assn	$5,000
Others	$23,600
Hospitals & Nursing Homes	**$22,000**
American Hospital Assn	$10,000
American Health Care Assn	$5,000
Others	$7,000
Insurance	**$125,683**
Torchmark Corp	$9,666
American International Group inc	$9,500
Aetna Life & Casualty	$9,000
Equitable Financial Services	$9,000
American Family Corp	$7,000
Independent Insurance Agents of America	$7,000
National Assn of Independent Insurers	$5,000
Travelers Corp	$5,000
Others	$64,517

PAC Totals by Category

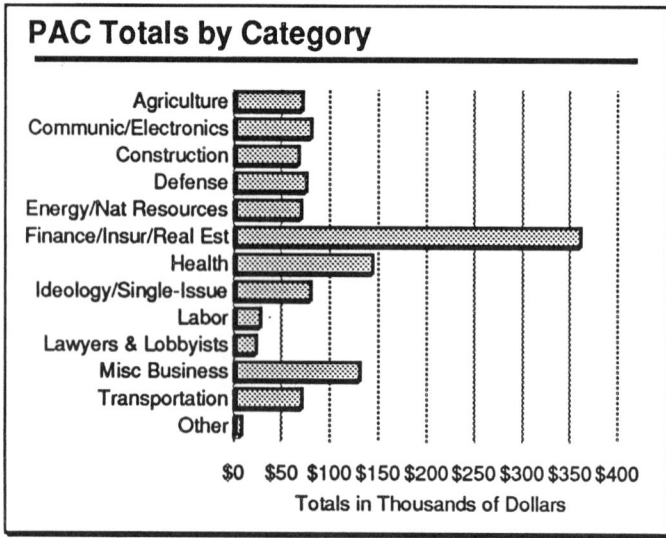

Agriculture
Communic/Electronics
Construction
Defense
Energy/Nat Resources
Finance/Insur/Real Est
Health
Ideology/Single-Issue
Labor
Lawyers & Lobbyists
Misc Business
Transportation
Other

$0 $50 $100 $150 $200 $250 $300 $350 $400
Totals in Thousands of Dollars

Lawyers & Lobbyists $21,325

    None over $2,000

Oil & Gas $17,035
    None over $2,500

Pharmaceuticals $41,400
    Ciba-Geigy Corp $7,150
    Abbott Laboratories $5,500
    Pfizer Inc $5,000
    Others $23,750

Real Estate $20,575
    Mortgage Bankers Assn of America $11,000
    Others $9,575

Savings Banks & Credit Unions $20,700
    US League of Savings Assn $8,000
    Credit Union National Assn $6,400
    Others $6,300

Securities/Commodities Investment $71,984
    Salomon Brothers $7,000
    Chicago Mercantile Exchange $6,000
    First Boston Corp $6,000
    Investment Company Institute $6,000
    Chicago Board of Trade $5,000
    FMR Corp $5,000
    Goldman Sachs $5,000
    Others $31,984

Telecommunications $30,185
    AT&T $9,900
    NYNEX Corp* $6,500
    Others $13,785

Trucking/Delivery $15,150
    United Parcel Service $6,500
    Others $8,650

Waste Management $15,500
    Waste Management Inc $8,000
    Others $7,500

Interest Group Ratings

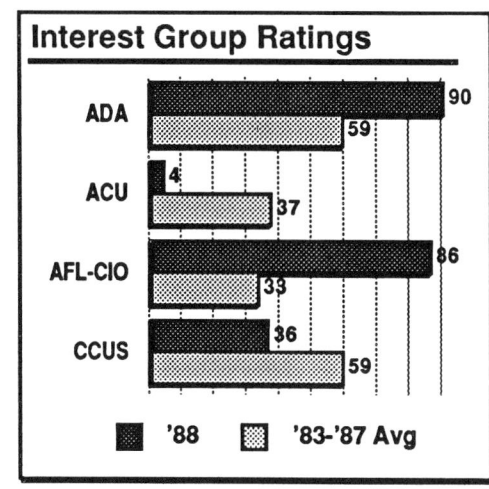

	'88	'83-'87 Avg
ADA	90	59
ACU	4	37
AFL-CIO	86	33
CCUS	36	59

■ '88   ▨ '83-'87 Avg

Other Major Business PACs

Union Pacific Corp ....$10,000 Railroads
Hallmark Cards ....$9,000 Publishing
Dun & Bradstreet ....$7,500 Mkt Research
Federal Express Corp ....$7,000 Air Freight
Stanley Works ....$5,400 Hardware
Hoechst Celanese Corp ....$5,000 Synth Fiber
National Cable Television Assn ....$5,000 CableTV

Labor

Labor Unions $25,450

    Laborers' Political League $6,000
    National Rural Letter Carriers Assn $5,000
    Others $14,450

Ideological/Single-Issue

Environmental Issues $17,937

    Sierra Club $9,250
    League of Conservation Voters $7,810
    Others $877

Republican Leadership PACs $29,500
    Republican Majority Fund (Richard Lugar) $10,000
    Campaign America (Bob Dole) $7,000
    Fund for America's Future (George Bush) $6,000
    Others $6,500

Other Major Ideological/Single-Issue PACs

Human Rights Campaign Fund ....$10,000 Gay Rights
National Abortion Rights Action League ......$5,000 Pro-Choice
National Cmte to Preserve Social Security ..$5,000 Elderly

Independent expenditures supporting Chafee

National Cmte to Preserve Social Security $3,287

---

* Contributions came from more than one PAC affiliated with this sponsor.

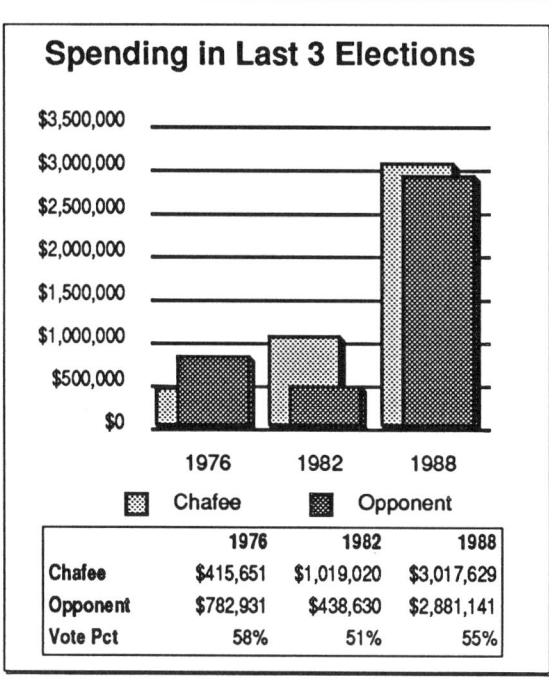

Spending in Last 3 Elections

	1976	1982	1988
Chafee	$415,651	$1,019,020	$3,017,629
Opponent	$782,931	$438,630	$2,881,141
Vote Pct	58%	51%	55%

▨ Chafee   ■ Opponent

John C. Danforth (R-Mo)

First elected: 1976
Total receipts: $4,753,327
Total from PACs: $1,399,841

1988 Committees & Subcommittees

Commerce, Science and Transportation (Ranking Republican)
National Ocean Policy Study (Ranking Republican)

Budget

Finance
International Trade (Ranking Republican)
International Debt
Taxation and Debt Management

PAC Contribution Profile

Business

Accountants	**$21,500**
American Institute of CPA's	$8,000
Touche Ross	$5,000
Others	$8,500
Air Transport/Air Freight	**$50,000**
Texas Air*	$12,000
McDonnell Douglas	$10,000
Federal Express Corp	$8,000
Boeing Company	$6,500
Others	$13,500
Automotive	**$36,650**
Chrysler Corp	$9,000
Auto Dealers & Drivers for Free Trade	$7,000
Ford Motor Company	$5,000
National Auto Dealers Assn	$5,000
Others	$10,650
Chemicals & Plastics	**$34,945**
Monsanto Company	$10,620
Others	$24,325
Commercial & Savings Banks	**$54,498**
American Bankers Assn	$10,000
US League of Savings Assn	$10,000
Boatmens Bankshares	$9,500
Others	$24,998

Campaign Revenue Sources

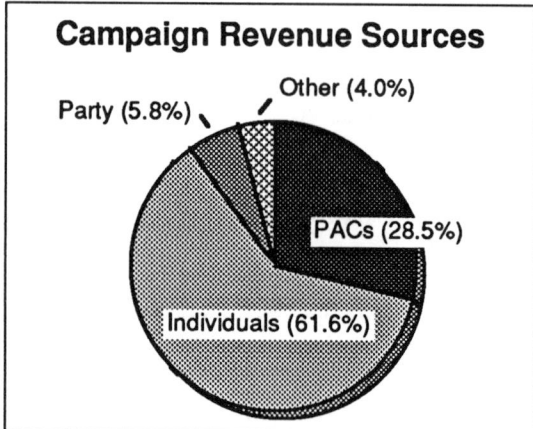

Party (5.8%)
Other (4.0%)
PACs (28.5%)
Individuals (61.6%)

Construction	**$60,750**
Associated General Contractors	$10,000
National Assn of Home Builders	$10,000
Heavy Constructors Assn	$6,000
Sheet Metal/Air Conditioning Contractors	$6,000
Sverdrup Corporation	$6,000
Others	$22,750
Defense	**$96,361**
Emerson Electric	$10,000
General Dynamics	$10,000
Northrop Corp	$9,000
Rockwell International	$9,000
Tenneco Inc	$7,000
Lockheed Corp	$6,000
Allied-Signal	$5,500
Harris Corp	$5,000
TRW Inc	$5,000
Others	$29,861
Electronics & Computers	**$28,250**
Cooper Industries	$5,000
Others	$23,250
Food & Beverage	**$55,169**
National Beer Wholesalers Assn	$7,149
Anheuser-Busch	$5,000
ConAgra Inc	$5,000
Others	$38,020
Health Professionals	**$35,000**
American Medical Assn	$8,500
American Academy of Ophthalmology	$7,000
American Dental Assn	$5,000
Oral & Maxillofacial Surgeons	$5,000
Others	$9,500
Insurance	**$142,125**
Business Mens Assurance Company	$10,000
National Assn of Life Underwriters	$10,000
National Assn of Independent Insurers	$8,200
National Assn of Mutual Insurance Agents	$8,000
Independent Insurance Agents of America	$7,999
General American Life Insurance	$7,500
Aetna Life & Casualty	$5,218
Torchmark Corp	$5,166
Cigna Corp	$5,000
Health Insurance Assn of America	$5,000
Travelers Corp	$5,000
Others	$65,042

PAC Totals by Category

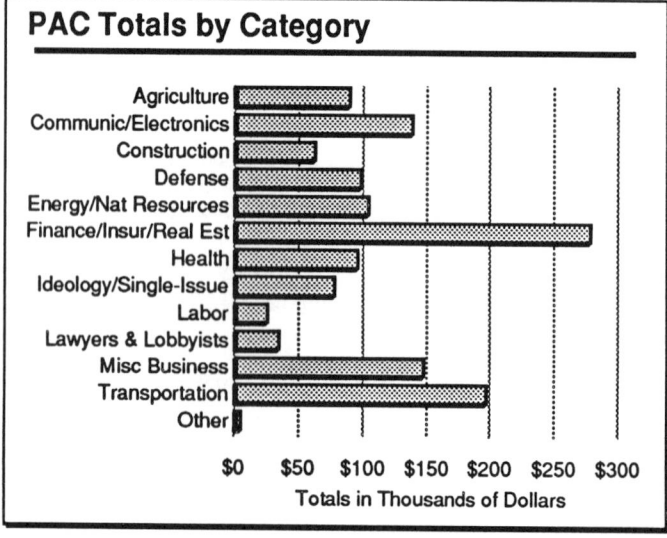

Agriculture
Communic/Electronics
Construction
Defense
Energy/Nat Resources
Finance/Insur/Real Est
Health
Ideology/Single-Issue
Labor
Lawyers & Lobbyists
Misc Business
Transportation
Other

$0 $50 $100 $150 $200 $250 $300

Totals in Thousands of Dollars

Lawyers & Lobbyists **$32,836**

> None over $3,500

Mining **$23,000**

    Peabody Coal $7,000
    Others $16,000

Oil & Gas **$50,655**

    Amoco Corp $5,000
    Mobil Oil $5,000
    Others $40,655

Pharmaceuticals **$41,500**

    Abbott Laboratories $6,000
    Johnson & Johnson $5,000
    Pfizer Inc $5,000
    Squibb Corp $5,000
    Others $20,500

Railroads **$40,600**

    Kansas City Southern $10,000
    Union Pacific Corp $10,000
    Others $20,600

Securities/Commodities Investment **$52,084**

    Goldman Sachs $10,000
    Chicago Board of Trade $5,000
    Chicago Mercantile Exchange $5,000
    Salomon Brothers $5,000
    Others $27,084

Telecommunications **$64,975**

    AT&T $9,000
    United Telecommunications $9,000
    Pacific Telesis Group $6,500
    Southwestern Bell $6,000
    Others $34,475

Television/Entertainment **$31,150**

    National Assn of Broadcasters $5,000
    National Cable Television Assn $5,000
    Others $21,150

Interest Group Ratings

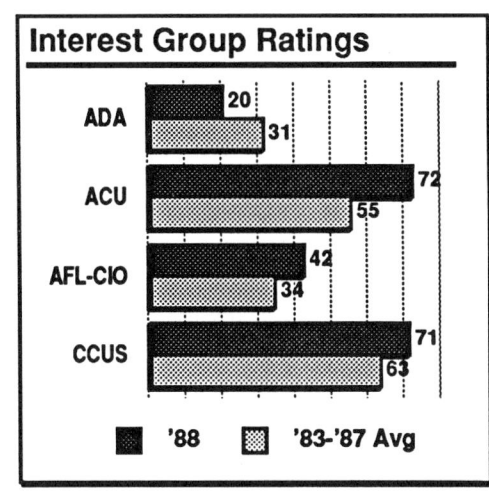

	'88	'83-'87 Avg
ADA	20	31
ACU	72	55
AFL-CIO	42	34
CCUS	71	63

Trucking/Delivery **$51,914**

    Yellow Freight System $10,000
    United Parcel Service $8,000
    American Trucking Assns $6,864
    Consolidated Freightways $6,000
    Others $21,050

Other Major Business PACs

Hallmark Cards	$10,000	Publishing
Mid-America Dairymen	$10,000	Dairy
May Department Stores	$7,750	Dept Store
American Health Care Assn	$6,000	Nursing Home
American Hospital Assn	$5,350	Hospitals
Missouri Farm Bureau*	$5,000	Farm Orgs
Triangle Industries	$5,000	Cans
Waste Management Inc	$5,000	Waste Mgmt

Labor

Labor Unions **$24,000**

    Marine Engineers Union* $9,000
    Teamsters Union $6,000
    Others $9,000

Ideological/Single-Issue

Pro-Israel **$38,000**

    St Louisians for Better Government $10,000
    Hudson Valley PAC $5,000
    National PAC $5,000
    Others $18,000

Republican Leadership PACs **$22,000**

    Fund for the Future Cmte (John Danforth) ...$5,000
    Republican Majority Fund (Richard Lugar) ...$5,000
    Others $12,000

---

* Contributions came from more than one PAC affiliated
with this sponsor.

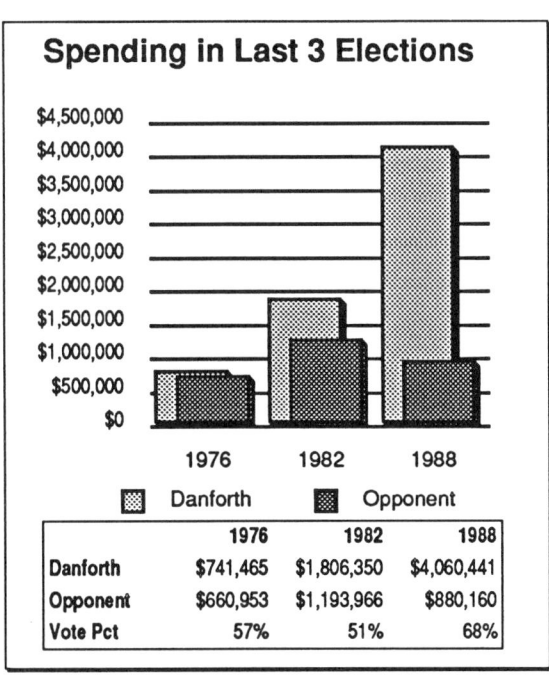

Spending in Last 3 Elections

	1976	1982	1988
Danforth	$741,465	$1,806,350	$4,060,441
Opponent	$660,953	$1,193,966	$880,160
Vote Pct	57%	51%	68%

Legend: Danforth, Opponent

Dennis DeConcini (D-Ariz)

First elected: 1976
Total receipts: $3,372,175
Total from PACs: $1,124,816

1988 Committees & Subcommittees

Appropriations
Treasury, Postal Service and General Government (Chairman)
Defense
Energy and Water Development
Foreign Operations
Interior and Related Agencies

Judiciary
Patents, Copyrights and Trademarks (Chairman)
Antitrust, Monopolies and Business Rights
Constitution
Courts and Administrative Practice
Technology and the Law

Rules and Administration

Veterans' Affairs

Select Indian Affairs
Special Investigations (Chairman)

Select Intelligence

Joint Library

Joint Printing

PAC Contribution Profile
Business

Accountants	**$20,800**
American Institute of CPA's	$10,000
Others	$10,800
Air Transport/Air Freight	**$19,750**
Texas Air	$7,500
Federal Express Corp	$6,500
Others	$5,750
Commercial Banks	**$42,950**
American Bankers Assn	$10,000
J P Morgan & Company	$10,000
Citicorp	$5,000
Others	$17,950
Construction	**$36,233**
National Assn of Home Builders	$10,000
Others	$26,233
Defense	**$118,519**
Allied-Signal	$10,000
AT&T	$10,000
Textron Inc	$10,000
Hughes Aircraft	$8,300
General Dynamics	$7,500
McDonnell Douglas*	$5,700
Motorola Inc	$5,219
Lockheed Corp	$5,000
Others	$56,800

Campaign Revenue Sources

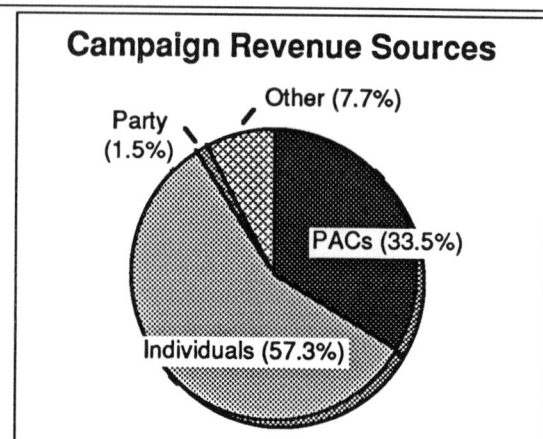

Other (7.7%)
Party (1.5%)
PACs (33.5%)
Individuals (57.3%)

Electric Utilities	**$16,000**
None over $3,000	
Food & Beverage	**$54,163**
National Beer Wholesalers Assn	$10,000
Wine & Spirits Wholesalers of America	$5,500
Joseph E Seagram & Sons	$5,000
Pepsico Inc	$5,000
Others	$28,663
Health Professionals	**$30,800**
American Medical Assn	$7,500
American Academy of Ophthalmology	$5,000
Others	$18,300
Insurance	**$70,150**
National Assn of Life Underwriters	$10,000
National Assn of Independent Insurers	$8,000
Metropolitan Life Insurance	$5,000
Aetna Life & Casualty	$4,500
Others	$42,650
Lawyers & Lobbyists	**$38,982**
Assn of Trial Lawyers of America	$10,000
Akin, Gump, Hauer & Feld	$5,000
Others	$23,982
Mining	**$15,400**
None over $4,400	
Oil & Gas	**$25,050**
None over $3,000	
Pharmaceuticals	**$35,955**
Warner-Lambert	$10,000
Abbott Laboratories	$6,355
Others	$19,600

PAC Totals by Category

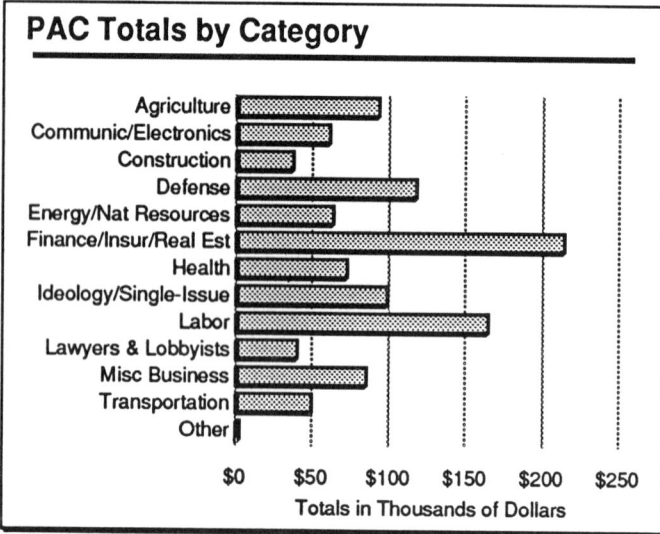

Agriculture
Communic/Electronics
Construction
Defense
Energy/Nat Resources
Finance/Insur/Real Est
Health
Ideology/Single-Issue
Labor
Lawyers & Lobbyists
Misc Business
Transportation
Other

$0 $50 $100 $150 $200 $250

Totals in Thousands of Dollars

Real Estate	....	$32,000
Estes Company	....	$10,000
National Assn of Realtors	....	$10,000
Others	....	$12,000

Savings Banks & Credit Unions	....	$20,400
US League of Savings Assn	....	$10,000
Credit Union National Assn	....	$5,000
Others	....	$5,400

Securities/Commodities Investment	....	$31,500
Chicago Mercantile Exchange	....	$10,000
Others	....	$21,500

Television/Entertainment	....	$38,662
Assn of Independent TV Stations	....	$6,000
Warner Communications	....	$6,000
MCA Inc	....	$5,000
National Cable Television Assn	....	$5,000
Turner Broadcasting System	....	$5,000
Others	....	$11,662

Other Major Business PACs

Sunkist Growers	....	$10,000	Fruit/Veg
Philip Morris	....	$7,999	Tobacco
Greyhound Corp	....	$7,700	Buses/Chem
United Parcel Service	....	$5,500	Delivery

Labor

Bldg Trades, Industrial & Other Unions	....	$72,540
Laborers' Western Political League	....	$10,000
Intl Brotherhood of Electrical Workers	....	$9,000
United Auto Workers	....	$6,000
Operating Engineers Union	....	$5,500
AFL-CIO	....	$5,000
Carpenters & Joiners Union	....	$5,000
Food & Commercial Workers Union	....	$5,000
Sheet Metal Workers Union	....	$5,000
Others	....	$22,040

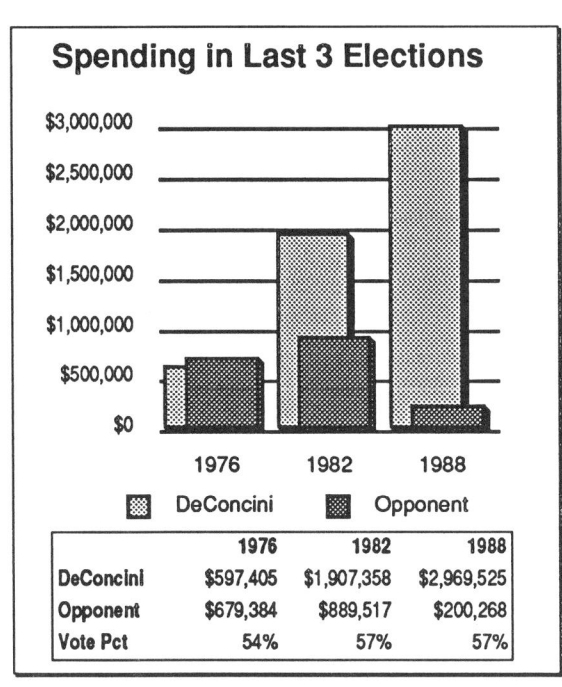

Spending in Last 3 Elections

Legend: ▨ DeConcini ▨ Opponent

	1976	1982	1988
DeConcini	$597,405	$1,907,358	$2,969,525
Opponent	$679,384	$889,517	$200,268
Vote Pct	54%	57%	57%

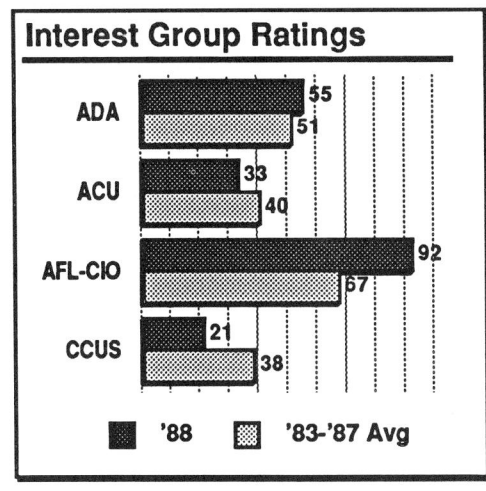

Interest Group Ratings

	'88	'83-'87 Avg
ADA	55	51
ACU	33	40
AFL-CIO	92	67
CCUS	21	38

Legend: ■ '88   ▨ '83-'87 Avg

Government & Postal Workers	....	$60,850
National Assn of Letter Carriers	....	$10,000
National Assn of Retired Federal Employees	....	$10,000
American Postal Workers Union	....	$8,000
National Rural Letter Carriers Assn	....	$7,350
National Treasury Employees Union	....	$6,050
American Fedn of State/County/Munic Employees	....	$5,000
Others	....	$14,450

Transportation Unions	....	$30,000
Air Line Pilots Assn	....	$10,000
Marine Engineers Union*	....	$7,000
Teamsters Union	....	$7,000
Others	....	$6,000

Ideological/Single-Issue

Democratic Leadership PACs	....	$28,500
Senate Majority Fund (Daniel Inouye)	....	$10,000
Campaign for American (Frank Lautenberg)	....	$5,000
Committee for a Demo Consensus (Alan Cranston)	....	$5,000
Pelican PAC (Bennett Johnston)	....	$5,000
Others	....	$3,500

Pro-Israel	....	$40,750
Washington PAC	....	$8,000
Desert Caucus	....	$5,000
National PAC	....	$5,000
Pacific PAC	....	$5,000
San Franciscans for Good Government	....	$5,000
Others	....	$12,750

Other Major Ideological/Single-Issue PACs

National Cmte to Preserve Social Security	$6,000	Elderly
Free Cuba PAC	$5,000	ForeignPolcy
KidsPAC	$5,000	Health/Welfare

Independent expenditures supporting DeConcini

National Cmte to Preserve Social Security	....	$20,780

* Contributions came from more than one PAC affiliated with this sponsor.

Dave Durenberger (R-Minn)

First elected: 1978
Total receipts: $6,761,554
Total from PACs: $1,792,646

1988 Committees & Subcommittees

Environment and Public Works
Environmental Protection
Superfund and Environmental Oversight
Water Resources, Transportation and Infrastructure

Finance
Health (Ranking Republican)
International Trade
Social Security and Family Policy

Special Aging

PAC Contribution Profile

Business

Air Transport/Air Freight	**$28,461**
Northwest Airlines	$6,211
Others	$22,250
Automotive	**$25,500**
Auto Dealers & Drivers for Free Trade	$10,000
Others	$15,500
Commercial & Savings Banks	**$65,508**
US League of Savings Assns*	$11,000
American Bankers Assn	$10,000
Others	$44,508
Construction	**$82,325**
National Electrical Contractors Assn	$11,000
Associated General Contractors	$9,500
National Assn of Home Builders	$9,000
National Utility Contractors Assn	$6,000
Others	$46,825
Dairy Producers	**$30,881**
Mid-America Dairymen	$10,000
Land O'Lakes Inc	$8,381
Associated Milk Producers	$7,000
Others	$5,500
Defense	**$55,161**
Textron Inc	$7,000
Others	$48,161
Electronics & Computers	**$30,900**
Honeywell Inc	$10,000
Others	$20,900

Campaign Revenue Sources

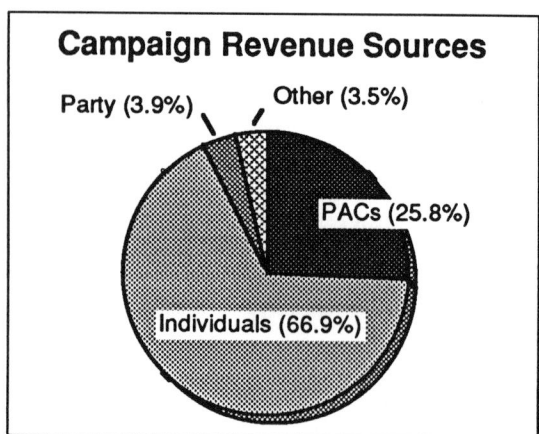

Party (3.9%)
Other (3.5%)
PACs (25.8%)
Individuals (66.9%)

Food & Beverage	**$112,746**
National Restaurant Assn	$10,000
General Mills	$9,500
McDonald's Corp	$8,250
Wine & Spirits Wholesalers of America	$7,000
ConAgra Inc	$6,500
Pillsbury Company	$6,250
Others	$65,246
Forest Products	**$33,294**
Potlatch Corp	$6,500
Others	$26,794
Grain Trading	**$25,000**
Archer-Daniels-Midland Corp	$10,000
Cargill Inc	$10,000
Others	$5,000
Health Professionals	**$96,050**
American Academy of Ophthalmology	$10,000
American Dental Assn	$10,000
American Medical Assn	$9,800
American Podiatry Assn	$7,000
American Assn of Nurse Anesthetists	$6,000
Others	$53,250
Hospitals & Nursing Homes	**$55,111**
American Health Care Assn	$10,000
American Hospital Assn	$9,800
Federation of American Hospitals	$9,500
Others	$25,811
Insurance	**$154,092**
Torchmark Corp	$10,000
Massachusetts Mutual Life Insurance	$9,942
St Paul Companies Inc	$9,750
Minnesota Mutual Life	$8,100
National Assn of Mutual Insurance Agents	$7,000
National Assn of Independent Insurers	$6,450
Health Insurance Assn of America	$6,000
Others	$96,850
Lawyers & Lobbyists	**$43,270**
None over $5,735	

PAC Totals by Category

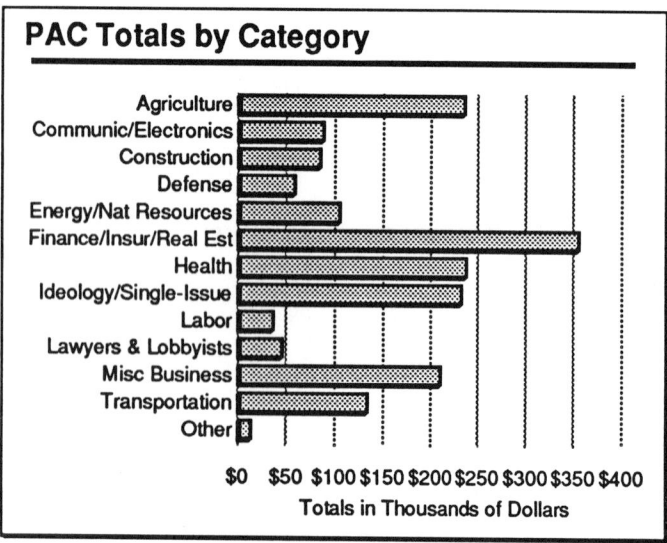

Agriculture
Communic/Electronics
Construction
Defense
Energy/Nat Resources
Finance/Insur/Real Est
Health
Ideology/Single-Issue
Labor
Lawyers & Lobbyists
Misc Business
Transportation
Other

$0 $50 $100 $150 $200 $250 $300 $350 $400

Totals in Thousands of Dollars

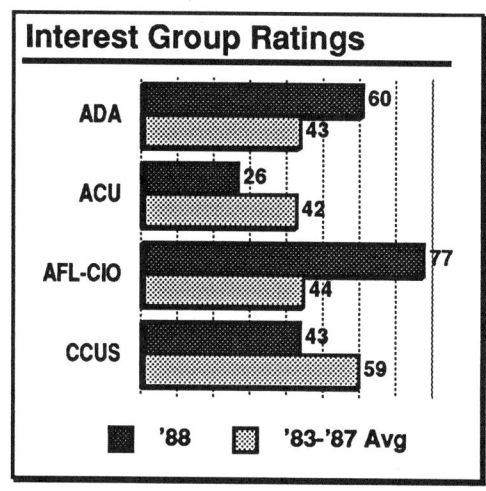
Oil & Gas *$55,285*

    Amoco Corp $6,000
    Petroleum Marketers Assn $6,000
    Others $43,285

Pharmaceuticals *$58,300*

    Eli Lilly & Company $10,000
    Others $48,300

Railroads *$29,150*

    Union Pacific Corp $9,000
    Others $20,150

Real Estate *$25,190*

    National Assn of Realtors $9,440
    Others $15,750

Securities/Commodities Investment *$87,419*

    Chicago Mercantile Exchange $12,000
    E F Hutton Group $7,500
    Chicago Board of Trade $6,000
    First Boston Corp $6,000
    Others $55,919

Sugar Growers *$29,601*

    American Crystal Sugar Corp $11,000
    Southern Minnesota Beet Sugar Co-op $7,000
    Others $11,601

Telecommunications *$41,285*

    AT&T $14,500
    Northwestern Bell Telephone $11,000
    Others $15,785

Trucking/Delivery *$35,825*

    United Parcel Service $7,100
    Others $28,725

Other Major Business PACs

American Institute of CPA's	$10,000	Accountants
Minnesota Mining & Manufacturing (3M)	$10,000	Indust Equip
Dun & Bradstreet	$8,750	Mkt Research
Baxter Healthcare Corp	$7,500	Med Supply
National Fedn of Independent Business	$7,084	Sml Business
National Venture Capital Assn	$7,000	Venture Cap
Bethlehem Steel	$6,500	Steel
Philip Morris	$6,000	Tobacco

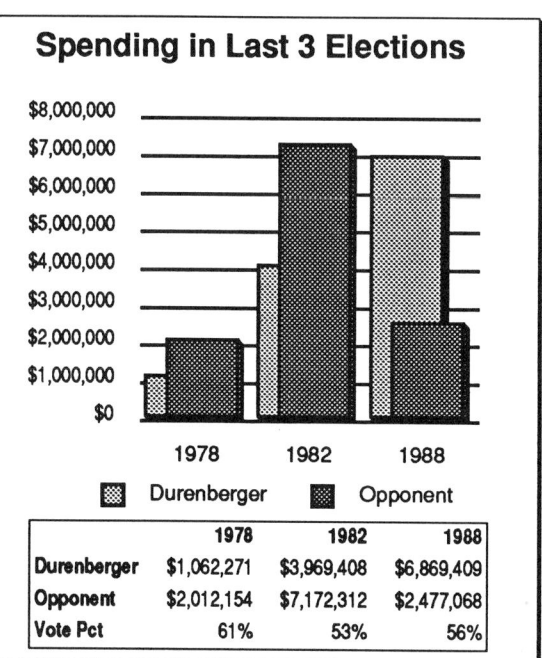

Spending in Last 3 Elections

▨ Durenberger   ■ Opponent

	1978	1982	1988
Durenberger	$1,062,271	$3,969,408	$6,869,409
Opponent	$2,012,154	$7,172,312	$2,477,068
Vote Pct	61%	53%	56%

Labor

Labor Unions *$34,000*

    National Assn of Retired Federal Employees $6,000
    Others $28,000

Ideological/Single-Issue

Pro-Israel *$169,500*

    Joint Action Cmte for Political Affairs $10,500
    Citizens Organized PAC $10,000
    Delaware Valley PAC $10,000
    Desert Caucus $10,000
    Florida Congressional Committee $10,000
    Maryland Assn for Concerned Citizens $10,000
    National PAC $10,000
    Washington PAC $10,000
    National Action Committee $7,500
    Garden State PAC $7,000
    Hudson Valley PAC $6,500
    Mid Manhattan PAC $6,000
    Others $62,000

Republican Leadership PACs *$30,797*

    Campaign America (Bob Dole) $10,000
    Republican Majority Fund (Richard Lugar) $10,000
    Others $10,797

Independent expenditures supporting Durenberger

American Medical Assn $134,527
Minnesota Citizens Concerned for Life $4,873
American Citizens for Political Action $3,704

* Contributions came from more than one PAC affiliated with this sponsor.

Slade Gorton (R-Wash)

First elected: 1980
Total receipts: $2,735,777
Total from PACs: $937,406

1989-90 Committees & Subcommittees

Agriculture, Nutrition and Forestry
Agricultural Credit
Conservation and Forestry
Domestic and Foreign Marketing and Product Promotion

Armed Services
Readiness, Sustainability and Support (Ranking Republican)
Projection Forces and Regional Defense
Strategic Forces and Nuclear Deterrence

Commerce, Science and Transportation
Consumer (Ranking Republican)
Communications
National Ocean Policy Study
Surface Transportation

PAC Contribution Profile

Business

Automotive	**$25,900**
Auto Dealers & Drivers for Free Trade	$10,000
Eaton Corp	$6,000
National Auto Dealers Assn	$5,000
Others	$4,900
Aviation & Air Freight	**$33,000**
Boeing Company	$10,000
Texas Air	$9,000
Federal Express Corp	$5,000
Others	$9,000
Business Associations	**$13,432**
National Fedn of Independent Business	$9,569
Others	$3,863
Chemicals	**$24,500**
Dow Chemical*	$6,000
NL Industries*	$6,000
FMC Corp	$5,000
Others	$7,500
Commercial & Savings Banks	**$68,005**
American Bankers Assn	$10,000
SeaFirst Bank	$10,000
US League of Savings Assn	$6,000
J P Morgan & Company	$5,000
Others	$37,005

Campaign Revenue Sources

- Party (11.1%)
- Other (1.5%)
- Candidate (3.0%)
- PACs (31.0%)
- Individuals (53.4%)

Construction	**$64,150**
Associated General Contractors	$10,000
Sheet Metal/Air Conditioning Contractors	$10,000
National Utility Contractors Assn	$8,000
National Assn of Home Builders	$5,000
National Electrical Contractors Assn	$5,000
National Society of Professional Engineers	$5,000
Others	$21,150
Defense	**$54,000**
Harris Corp	$10,000
Rockwell International	$7,000
BDM International	$5,000
Northrop Corp	$5,000
Others	$27,000
Electric Utilities	**$16,000**
None over $4,500	
Electronics & Computers	**$19,450**
Cooper Industries	$10,000
Others	$9,450
Fishing	**$10,500**
National Fisheries Institute	$10,000
Others	$500
Food & Beverage	**$72,499**
National Restaurant Assn	$6,000
Services Group of America	$6,000
Flowers Industries	$5,000
Food Marketing Institute	$5,000
McDonald's Corp	$5,000
Pepsico Inc	$5,000
Pillsbury Company	$5,000
Others	$35,499
Forest Products	**$48,864**
Simpson Investment Company	$10,000
Weyerhaeuser Company	$6,450
International Paper Company	$5,000
Willamette Industries	$5,000
Others	$22,414

PAC Totals by Category

- Agriculture
- Communic/Electronics
- Construction
- Defense
- Energy/Nat Resources
- Finance/Insur/Real Est
- Health
- Ideology/Single-Issue
- Labor
- Lawyers & Lobbyists
- Misc Business
- Transportation
- Other

$0 $20 $40 $60 $80 $100 $120 $140 $160

Totals in Thousands of Dollars

Health Professionals **$27,000**
    American Academy of Ophthalmology $10,000
    American Medical Assn $10,000
    American Dental Assn $5,000
    Others $2,000

Industrial Equipment & Materials **$11,000**
    None over $4,000

Insurance **$46,900**
    Safeco Corp...$5,100
    Aetna Life & Casualty $5,000
    Independent Insurance Agents of America.....................$5,000
    National Assn of Independent Insurers $5,000
    Others $26,800

Lawyers & Lobbyists **$11,000**
    None over $2,000

Oil & Gas **$74,250**
    Chevron Corp $10,000
    Dallas Energy PAC $10,000
    Amoco Corp $8,000
    Atlantic Richfield $5,000
    Exxon Corp $5,000
    Mobil Oil $5,000
    Others $31,250

Pharmaceuticals **$10,000**
    Eli Lilly & Company $5,000
    Others $5,000

Railroads & Railroad Services **$12,000**
    Union Pacific Corp..$7,000
    Others $5,000

Real Estate **$11,000**
    National Assn of Realtors $8,000
    Others $3,000

Sea Transport **$10,800**
    None over $3,000

Securities/Commodities Investment **$17,500**
    Chicago Mercantile Exchange $7,500
    Others $10,000

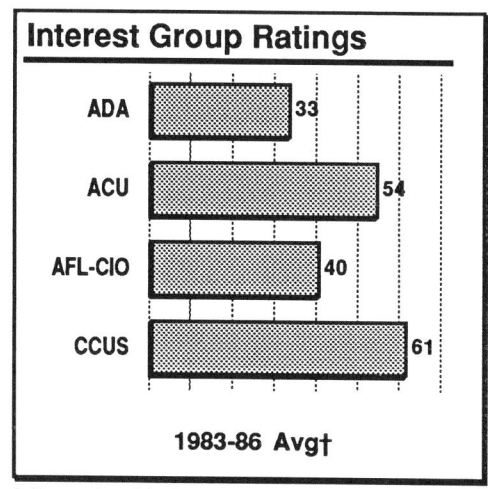

Interest Group Ratings

ADA — 33
ACU — 54
AFL-CIO — 40
CCUS — 61

1983-86 Avg†

† Gorton lost his Senate seat in the 1986 election

Telecommunications **$36,600**
    AT&T...$8,000
    Continental Telecom $6,000
    United Telecommunications $5,000
    Others $17,600

Television/Cable TV **$16,000**
    Assn of Independent TV Stations $9,000
    Others $7,000

Trucking **$10,450**
    None over $2,000

Other Major Business PACs

Dun & Bradstreet ....$6,000   Mkt Research
American Institute of CPA's ....$5,000   Accountants

Ideological/Single-Issue

Pro-Israel **$21,750**
    Citizens Organized PAC $5,000
    National PAC $5,000
    Others $11,750

Republican Leadership PACs **$48,502**
    Republican Majority Fund (Richard Lugar) $10,000
    Campaign America (Bob Dole)..$8,002
    Catch the Spirit PAC (Bob Kasten) $8,000
    Citizens for the Republic (Ronald Reagan) $5,000
    Fund for a Republican Majority (Ted Stevens)...............$5,000
    Fund for America's Future (George Bush) $5,000
    Others $7,500

Other Major Ideological/Single-Issue PACs

National Security PAC ....$6,000   Pro-Defense
Public Svc Research Council.......................$5,000   Anti-Union
Repub Congressional Boosters Club...........$5,000   Repub/Conser

Major Labor PACs

Marine Engineers Union ....$5,000   Seamen Union

Independent expenditures opposing Gorton

National Council of Senior Citizens $10,177

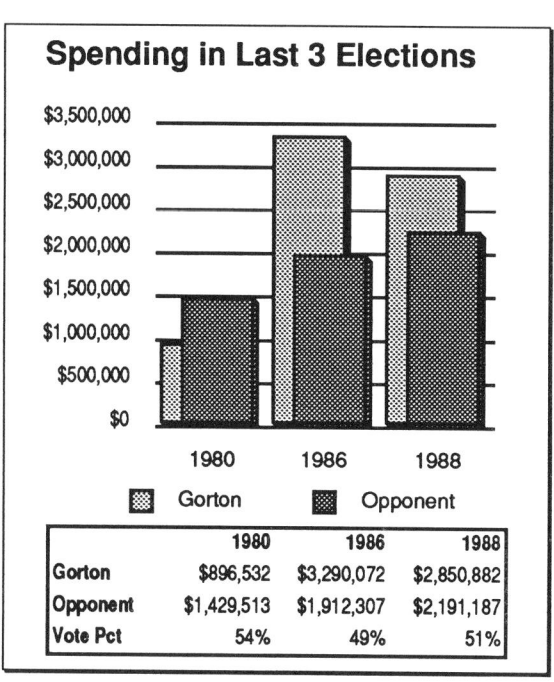

Spending in Last 3 Elections

Legend: Gorton / Opponent

	1980	1986	1988
Gorton	$896,532	$3,290,072	$2,850,882
Opponent	$1,429,513	$1,912,307	$2,191,187
Vote Pct	54%	49%	51%

---

* Contributions came from more than one PAC affiliated
with this sponsor.

Orrin G. Hatch (R-Utah)

1988 Committees & Subcommittees

Judiciary
Patents, Copyrights and Trademarks (Ranking Republican)
Antitrust, Monopolies and Business Rights
Constitution

Labor and Human Resources (Ranking Republican)
Children, Family, Drugs and Alcoholism
Education, Arts and Humanities
Employment and Productivity

Select Intelligence

PAC Contribution Profile

Business

Accountants	**$19,500**
American Institute of CPA's	$10,000
Others	$9,500
Air Transport/Air Freight	**$24,557**
Texas Air	$10,000
Federal Express Corp	$7,400
Others	$7,157
Automotive	**$26,000**
Auto Dealers & Drivers for Free Trade	$8,000
General Motors	$7,600
National Auto Dealers Assn	$6,000
Others	$4,400
Chemicals	**$24,900**
NL Industries*	$10,000
Others	$14,900
Commercial & Savings Banks	**$33,912**
American Bankers Assn	$10,000
Others	$23,912
Construction	**$99,900**
Wall & Ceiling/Gypsum Contractors	$10,950
Associated Builders & Contractors	$10,000
Associated General Contractors	$10,000
National Utility Contractors Assn	$10,000
Fluor Corp	$8,000
Sheet Metal/Air Conditioning Contractors	$6,000
National Electrical Contractors Assn	$5,000
Others	$39,950

Campaign Revenue Sources

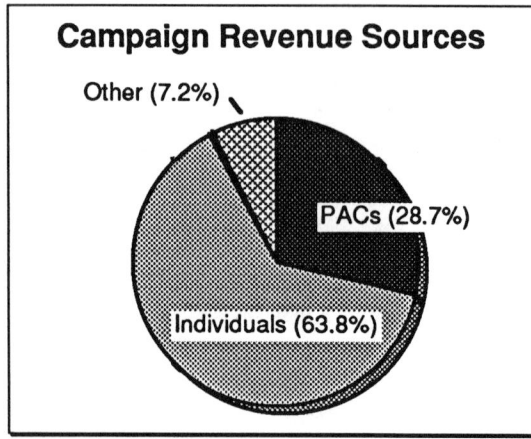

Other (7.2%)
PACs (28.7%)
Individuals (63.8%)

Defense	**$72,900**
Northrop Corp	$8,500
Harris Corp	$7,500
Litton Industries	$7,000
United Technologies	$6,000
Tenneco Inc	$5,500
Singer Company	$5,000
Others	$33,400
Food & Beverage	**$120,290**
National Restaurant Assn	$10,000
National Beer Wholesalers Assn	$10,000
S & A Restaurant Corp	$9,000
Food Marketing Institute	$8,500
Coca-Cola Company	$5,000
ConAgra Inc	$5,000
General Mills Restaurants	$5,000
IBP Inc	$5,000
McDonald's Corp	$5,000
Nutrasweet Company	$5,000
Pepsico Inc	$5,000
Winn-Dixie Stores	$5,000
Others	$42,790
Forest Products	**$25,325**
International Paper Company	$5,000
Others	$20,325
Health Professionals	**$64,550**
American Podiatry Assn	$10,500
American Medical Assn	$10,000
American Dental Assn	$9,050
American Academy of Ophthalmology	$9,000
Others	$26,000
Hospitals & Nursing Homes	**$31,126**
Care Enterprises	$7,000
American Health Care Assn	$5,000
American Hospital Assn	$5,000
Others	$14,126
Industrial Equipment & Materials	**$25,040**
National Tooling & Machining Assn	$10,500
Brush Wellman	$8,000
Others	$6,540
Insurance	**$89,842**
American Family Corp	$10,000
National Assn of Independent Insurers	$10,000
National Assn of Life Underwriters	$5,750
TransAmerica Insurance	$5,000
Others	$59,092
Lawyers & Lobbyists	**$36,000**
Baker & Botts	$7,000
Others	$29,000

PAC Totals by Category

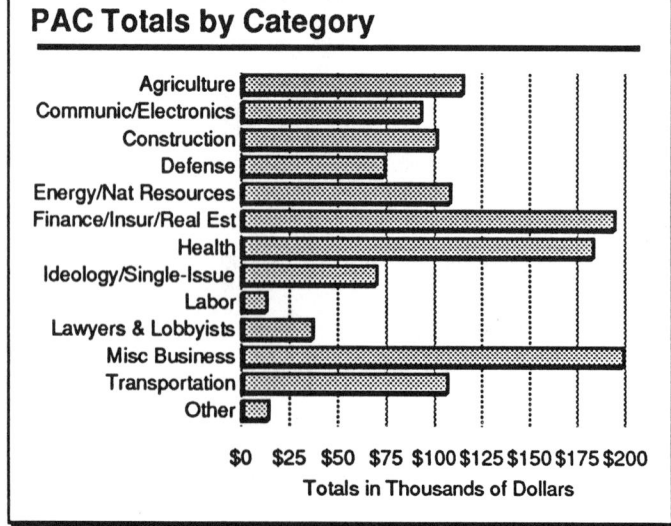

Agriculture
Communic/Electronics
Construction
Defense
Energy/Nat Resources
Finance/Insur/Real Est
Health
Ideology/Single-Issue
Labor
Lawyers & Lobbyists
Misc Business
Transportation
Other

$0 $25 $50 $75 $100 $125 $150 $175 $200
Totals in Thousands of Dollars

Oil & Gas	$73,350
BP America	$10,000
Amoco Corp	$5,000
Mobil Oil	$5,000
Others	$53,350

Pharmaceuticals	$70,010
Eli Lilly & Company	$7,000
Abbott Laboratories	$5,550
Ciba-Geigy Corp	$5,500
Pfizer Inc	$5,000
Warner-Lambert	$5,000
Others	$41,960

Real Estate	$22,184
National Assn of Realtors	$9,850
Century 21 Real Estate	$5,000
Others	$7,334

| Retail Sales | $19,014 |
| None over $3,250 | |

Securities/Commodities Investment	$19,900
Bear, Stearns & Company	$7,000
Others	$12,900

Telecommunications	$33,186
AT&T	$9,400
Others	$23,786

Television/Entertainment	$37,570
Assn of Independent TV Stations	$6,000
National Cable Television Assn	$5,000
Turner Broadcasting System	$5,000
Others	$21,570

Trucking/Delivery	$22,149
United Parcel Service	$5,500
American Trucking Assns	$5,249
Others	$11,400

Other Major Business PACs

Marriott Corp	$8,000	Hotel/Motel
Assn of Independent Colleges & Schools	$5,000	Education
Precision Metalforming Assn	$5,000	MetalProduct
Union Pacific Corp	$5,000	Railroads

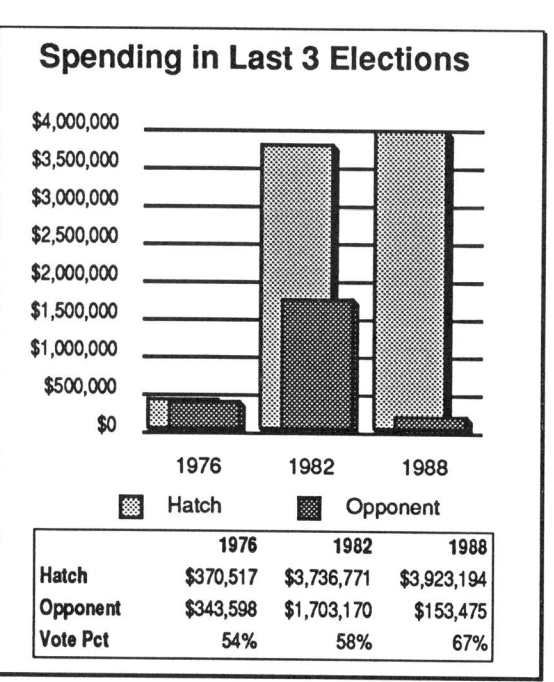

Spending in Last 3 Elections

	1976	1982	1988
Hatch	$370,517	$3,736,771	$3,923,194
Opponent	$343,598	$1,703,170	$153,475
Vote Pct	54%	58%	67%

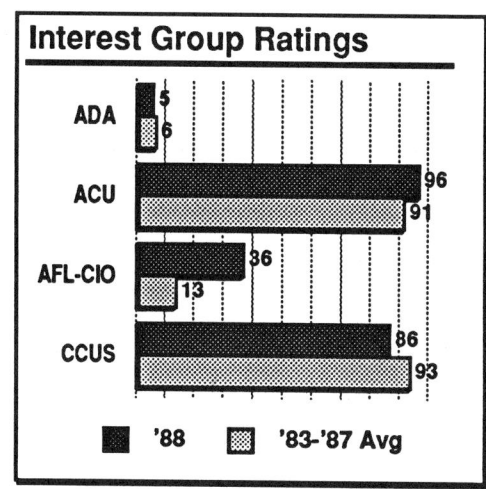

Interest Group Ratings

	'88	'83-'87 Avg
ADA	5	6
ACU	96	91
AFL-CIO	36	13
CCUS	86	93

Major Labor Union PACs

United Transportation Union	$6,000
Teamsters Local #745	$5,000

Ideological/Single-Issue

Republican Leadership PACs	$17,916
Catch the Spirit PAC (Bob Kasten)	$10,000
Republican Majority Fund (Richard Lugar)	$5,000
Others	$2,916

Other Major Ideological/Single-Issue PACs

National Rifle Assn	$8,450	Pro-Guns
Public Service Research Council	$6,250	Anti-Union
National Security PAC	$6,009	Pro-Defense
American Citizens for Political Action	$5,000	Repub/Conser
Congressional Majority Committee	$5,000	Repub/Conser
Free Cuba PAC	$5,000	Anti-Castro

Independent expenditures supporting Hatch

American Citizens for Political Action	$152,500
National Security PAC	$57,741

---

* Contributions came from more than one PAC affiliated with this sponsor.

John Heinz (R-Pa)

1988 Committees & Subcommittees

First elected: 1976
Total receipts: $6,014,399
Total from PACs: $1,481,333

Banking, Housing and Urban Affairs
International Finance and Monetary Policy (Ranking Republican)
Housing and Urban Affairs

Finance
Health
International Trade
Private Retirement Plans and Oversight of the Internal Revenue Service

Governmental Affairs
Government Efficiency, Federalism and the District of Columbia
(Ranking Republican)
Federal Spending, Budget and Accounting
Oversight of Government Management

Special Aging (Ranking Republican)

PAC Contribution Profile

Business

Chemicals	**$37,050**
Betz Laboratories	$5,000
FMC Corp	$5,000
NL Industries	$5,000
Pennwalt Corp	$5,000
Others	$17,050
Commercial Banks	**$72,901**
Mellon Bank	$9,151
Pittsburgh National Bank	$6,600
Meridian Bancorp/Reading, Pennsylvania	$6,117
Equimark Corp	$6,000
Independent Bankers Assn	$5,000
J P Morgan & Company	$5,000
Others	$35,033
Construction	**$63,700**
National Assn of Home Builders	$10,000
Associated General Contractors	$6,000
Dravo Corp	$5,000
Others	$42,700
Defense	**$59,236**
Rockwell International	$10,000
Allied-Signal	$7,000
Grumman	$5,775
Litton Industries	$5,000
Others	$31,461
Electric Utilities	**$39,367**
Philadelphia Electric	$9,400
ACRE (Action Committee for Rural Electrification)	$7,800
Duquesne Light Company	$6,182
Others	$15,985

Campaign Revenue Sources

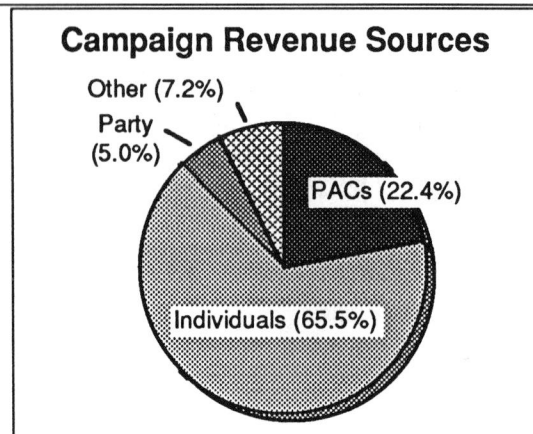

Other (7.2%)
Party (5.0%)
PACs (22.4%)
Individuals (65.5%)

Electronics & Computers	**$28,150**
Westinghouse Electric	$7,000
Others	$21,150
Food & Beverage	**$39,085**
ARA Services Inc	$7,500
McDonald's Corp	$5,000
Others	$26,585
Health Professionals	**$49,350**
American Academy of Ophthalmology	$10,000
American Dental Assn	$6,500
American Optometric Assn	$5,000
Others	$27,850
Insurance	**$138,457**
Cigna Corp	$10,000
National Assn of Life Underwriters	$10,000
National Assn of Mutual Insurance Agents	$10,000
Casualty & Surety Agents Assn	$8,000
Equitable Financial Services	$8,000
Independent Insurance Agents of America	$7,999
National Assn of Independent Insurers	$5,350
American Council of Life Insurance	$5,000
Associated Life Insurance	$5,000
Penn Mutual Life Insurance	$5,000
Others	$64,108
Lawyers & Lobbyists	**$50,865**
Kirkpatrick & Lockhart	$10,000
Wolf, Block, Schorr and Solis-Cohen	$10,000
Assn of Trial Lawyers of America	$5,500
Others	$25,365
Oil & Gas	**$52,785**
Atlantic Richfield	$8,000
USX Corp*	$6,750
Others	$38,035
Pharmaceuticals	**$47,385**
National Intergroup	$7,785
Smithkline Beckman	$7,000
Pfizer Inc	$5,000
Others	$27,600

PAC Totals by Category

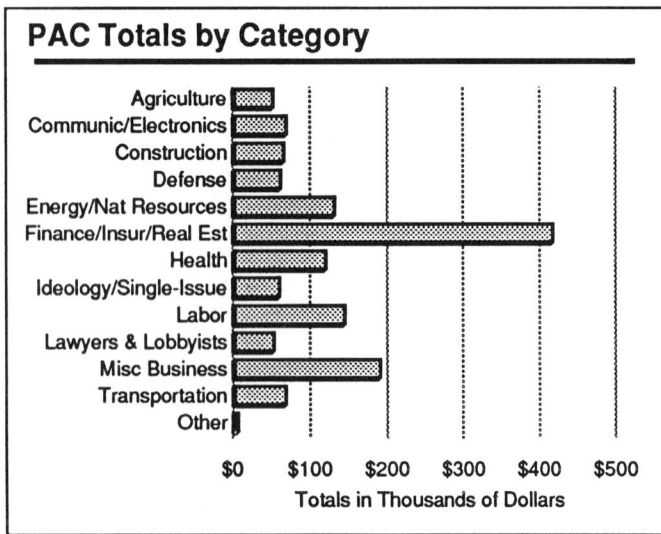

Agriculture
Communic/Electronics
Construction
Defense
Energy/Nat Resources
Finance/Insur/Real Est
Health
Ideology/Single-Issue
Labor
Lawyers & Lobbyists
Misc Business
Transportation
Other

$0 $100 $200 $300 $400 $500

Totals in Thousands of Dollars

Real Estate **$30,000**
    National Assn of Realtors $10,000
    Metropolitan Life Insurance $5,000
    Others $15,000

Savings Banks **$36,400**
    US League of Savings Assn* $9,000
    Home Savings of America $6,000
    Others $21,400

Securities/Commodities Investment **$89,707**
    Investment Company Institute $10,000
    Morgan Stanley & Company $7,000
    First Boston Corp $6,000
    Philadelphia Stock Exchange $5,500
    Chicago Board of Trade $5,000
    Goldman Sachs $5,000
    Others $51,207

Steel Producers **$32,570**
    Allegheny Ludlum Steel Corp $10,000
    Bethlehem Steel $8,800
    Others $13,770

Telecommunications **$33,868**
    AT&T $10,000
    Bell Atlantic* $9,497
    Others $14,371

Other Major Business PACs

American Institute of CPA's	$10,000	Accountants
Triangle Industries	$10,000	Cans
Union Pacific Corp	$10,000	Railroads
United Parcel Service	$8,000	Delivery
Boeing Company	$6,000	Aircraft
Fuller Company	$6,000	Indust Equip
National Venture Capital Assn	$6,000	Venture Cap
American Hospital Assn	$5,900	Hospitals
Alcoa	$5,000	Mining/Metals
Allegheny Intl Inc	$5,000	Appliances
American Health Care Assn	$5,000	Nursing Home
Associated Milk Producers	$5,000	Dairy
Gulf + Western Industries	$5,000	Credit/Loans

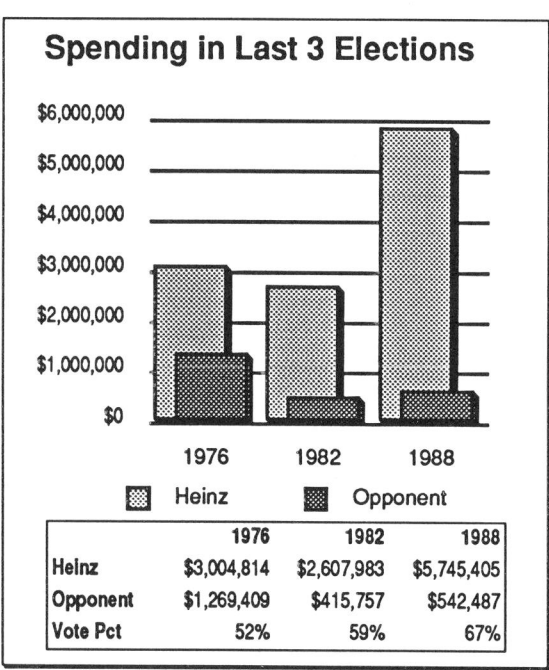

Spending in Last 3 Elections

	1976	1982	1988
Heinz	$3,004,814	$2,607,983	$5,745,405
Opponent	$1,269,409	$415,757	$542,487
Vote Pct	52%	59%	67%

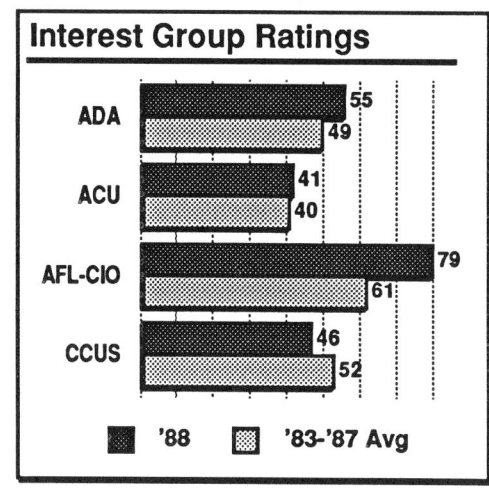

Interest Group Ratings

	'88	'83-'87 Avg
ADA	55	49
ACU	41	40
AFL-CIO	79	61
CCUS	46	52

Labor

Bldg Trades, Industrial & Other Unions **$61,475**
    Intl Brotherhood of Electrical Workers* $7,500
    National Education Assn $7,000
    Carpenters & Joiners Union $6,500
    Amalgamated Clothing & Textile Workers* $5,000
    American Federation of Teachers $5,000
    Others $30,475

Government & Postal Workers **$31,225**
    National Assn of Letter Carriers $6,000
    National Assn of Retired Federal Employees $6,000
    American Fedn of State/County/Munic Employees $5,000
    Others $14,225

Transportation Unions **$49,000**
    Marine Engineers Union* $10,000
    Teamsters Union $9,000
    United Transportation Union $6,000
    Air Line Pilots Assn $5,000
    Amalgamated Transit Union $5,000
    Others $14,000

Ideological/Single-Issue

Pro-Israel **$30,000**
    Desert Caucus $10,000
    Washington PAC $6,000
    National PAC $5,000
    Others $9,000

Other Major Ideological/Single-Issue PACs

Campaign America (Bob Dole)	$7,000	Repub Leader
Free Cuba PAC	$5,000	Anti-Castro
National Rifle Assn	$5,000	Pro-Guns
Republican Majority Fund (Richard Lugar)	$5,000	Repub Leader

---

* Contributions came from more than one PAC affiliated
with this sponsor.

James M. Jeffords (R-Vt)

First elected: 1988
Total receipts: $953,201
Total from PACs: $679,393

1988 House Committees & Subcommittees

Education and Labor (Ranking Republican)

Agriculture
Livestock, Dairy and Poultry (Ranking Republican)
Conservation, Credit and Rural Development

Select Aging
Retirement Income and Employment

PAC Contribution Profile

Business

Automotive **$13,000**

Auto Dealers & Drivers for Free Trade	$6,000
Chrysler Corp	$2,500
Others	$4,500

Chemicals **$11,850**

NL Industries*	$5,500
Others	$6,350

Construction **$56,616**

Associated General Contractors	$10,000
National Assn of Home Builders	$8,279
National Utility Contractors Assn	$7,000
Manville Corp	$5,000
National Electrical Contractors Assn	$5,000
Sheet Metal/Air Conditioning Contractors	$5,000
Associated Builders & Contractors	$3,500
Others	$12,837

Dairy Producers **$39,800**

Mid-America Dairymen	$10,000
Associated Milk Producers	$9,100
Dairymen Inc	$6,000
Agri-Mark Inc	$5,000
Land O'Lakes Inc	$4,500
Others	$5,200

Defense **$13,279**

Allied-Signal	$3,000
Others	$10,279

Campaign Revenue Sources

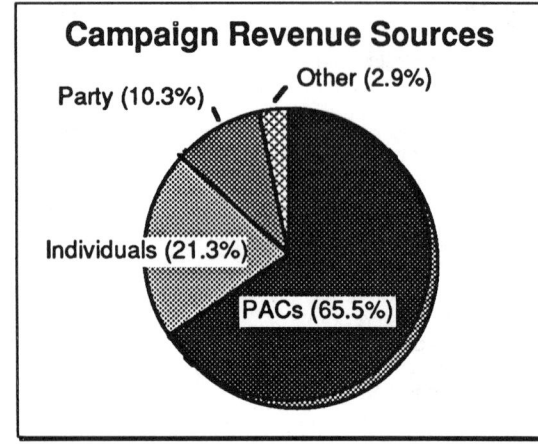

Party (10.3%)
Other (2.9%)
Individuals (21.3%)
PACs (65.5%)

Financial Institutions **$30,800**

American Bankers Assn	$10,000
Credit Union National Assn	$6,000
J P Morgan & Company	$5,000
Barnett Banks of Florida	$3,000
Independent Bankers Assn	$3,000
Others	$3,800

Food & Beverage **$34,629**

McDonald's Corp	$5,000
General Mills*	$3,500
Joseph E Seagram & Sons	$3,000
S & A Restaurant Corp	$3,000
National Restaurant Assn	$2,500
Others	$17,629

Health Professionals **$35,733**

American Academy of Ophthalmology	$10,000
American Dental Assn	$3,500
American Medical Assn	$3,500
Corp for the Advancement of Psychiatry	$3,025
Oral & Maxillofacial Surgeons	$3,000
American Physical Therapy Assn	$2,779
American Podiatry Assn	$2,500
Others	$7,429

Insurance **$38,158**

National Assn of Life Underwriters	$5,000
Casualty & Surety Agents Assn	$3,000
National Assn of Mutual Insurance Agents	$2,500
Others	$27,658

Oil & Gas **$16,879**

Atlantic Richfield	$2,779
Chevron Corp	$2,500
Others	$11,600

Pharmaceuticals **$15,954**

Abbott Laboratories	$3,500
Pfizer Inc	$2,500
Others	$9,954

Real Estate **$11,500**

National Assn of Realtors	$10,000
Others	$1,500

Retail Sales **$10,100**

None over $2,000

PAC Totals by Category

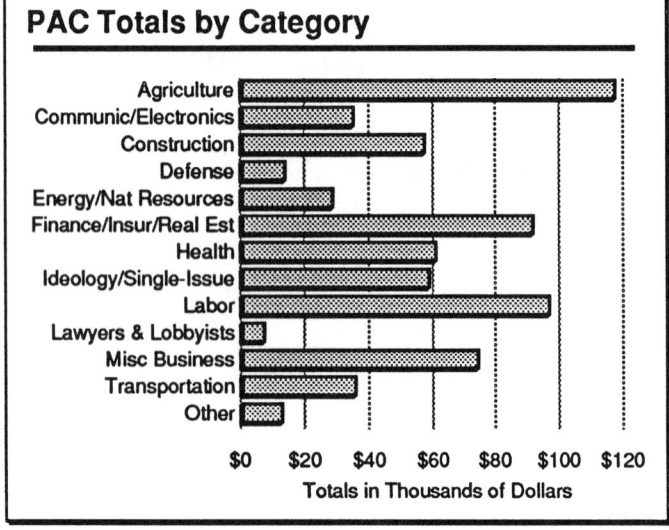

Category	
Agriculture	
Communic/Electronics	
Construction	
Defense	
Energy/Nat Resources	
Finance/Insur/Real Est	
Health	
Ideology/Single-Issue	
Labor	
Lawyers & Lobbyists	
Misc Business	
Transportation	
Other	

$0 $20 $40 $60 $80 $100 $120
Totals in Thousands of Dollars

Securities/Commodities Investment **$25,500**

Chicago Mercantile Exchange $10,000
Chicago Board of Trade $8,000
Salomon Brothers $2,500
Others $5,000

Telecommunications **$19,909**

AT&T $4,500
Others $15,409

Trucking/Delivery **$10,800**

American Trucking Assns $3,500
Others $7,300

Vocational Tech Schools **$11,200**

Assn of Independent Colleges and Schools $6,000
National Assn of Trade/Tech Schools $5,000
Others $200

Other Major Business PACs

Cooper Industries	$5,000	Electronics
American Institute of CPA's	$4,959	Accountants
Dun & Bradstreet	$3,500	Mkt Research
American Furniture Manufacturers Assn	$3,000	Furniture
American Veterinary Medical Assn	$3,000	Veterinary
American Hospital Assn	$3,000	Hospitals
RJR Nabisco	$3,000	Tobacco
American Meat Institute	$2,500	Feedlots
Continental Telecom	$2,500	Phone Util
National Assn of Wholesale-Distributors	$2,500	Wholesale
National Fedn of Independent Business	$2,500	Sml Business
Printing Industries of America	$2,500	Printing

Labor

Bldg Trades, Industrial & Misc Unions **$9,242**

Food & Commercial Workers Union $2,871
Others $6,371

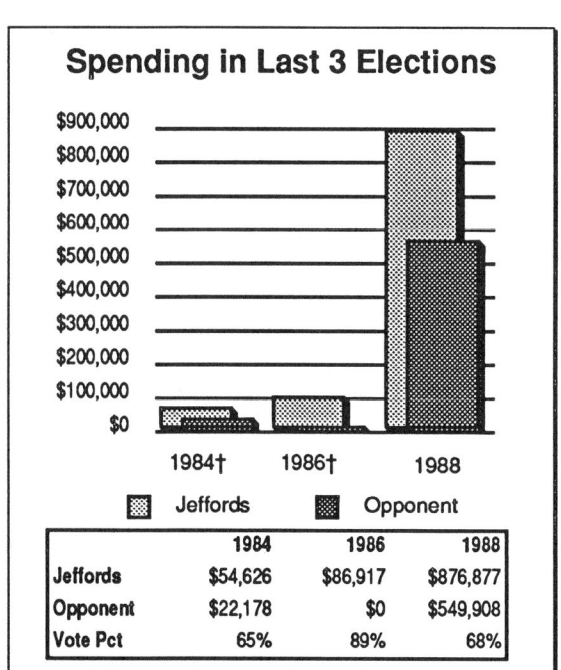

Spending in Last 3 Elections

Jeffords — Opponent

	1984	1986	1988
Jeffords	$54,626	$86,917	$876,877
Opponent	$22,178	$0	$549,908
Vote Pct	65%	89%	68%

† U.S. House races

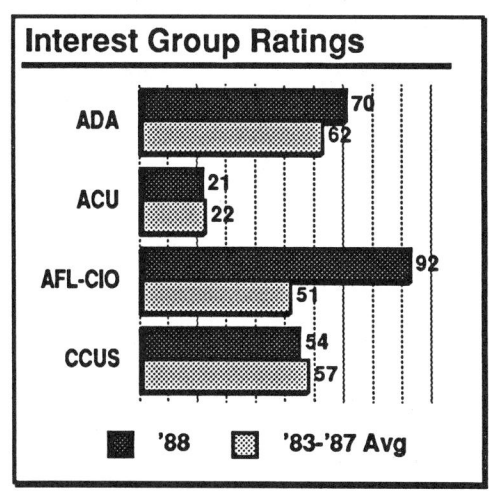

Interest Group Ratings

ADA 70 / 62
ACU 21 / 22
AFL-CIO 92 / 51
CCUS 54 / 57

■ '88   ▢ '83-'87 Avg

Government & Postal Workers **$37,500**

American Fedn of State/County/Munic Employees $10,000
National Assn of Letter Carriers $10,000
National Assn of Retired Federal Employees $6,000
American Postal Workers Union $5,000
National Rural Letter Carriers Assn $3,000
Others $3,500

Teachers Unions **$15,000**

National Education Assn $10,000
American Federation of Teachers $5,000

Transportation Unions **$34,350**

Air Line Pilots Assn $10,000
Teamsters Union $10,000
United Transportation Union $6,600
Amalgamated Transit Union $3,500
Others $4,250

Ideological/Single-Issue

Pro-Israel **$17,750**

Desert Caucus $5,000
Hudson Valley PAC $3,500
Florida Congressional Committee $2,500
San Franciscans for Good Government $2,500
Others $4,250

Republican Leadership PACs **$17,122**

Campaign America (Bob Dole) $5,000
Republican Majority Fund (Richard Lugar) $5,000
Catch the Spirit PAC (Bob Kasten) $4,500
Others $2,622

Other Major Ideological/Single-Issue PACs

Council for a Livable World	$5,569	Pro-Peace
Human Rights Campaign Fund	$5,000	Gay Rights
Republican Congressional Boosters Club	$3,000	Repub/Conser
National Community Action Found	$2,500	Health/Welfare

* Contributions came from more than one PAC affiliated
with this sponsor.

Edward M. Kennedy (D-Mass)

First elected: 1962
Total receipts: $3,589,933
Total from PACs: $356,747

1988 Committees & Subcommittees

Armed Services
Projection Forces and Regional Defense (Chairman)
Manpower and Personnel
Strategic Forces and Nuclear Deterrence

Judiclary
Immigration and Refugee Affairs (Chairman)
Antitrust, Monopolies and Business Rights
Constitution
Patents, Copyrights and Trademarks

Labor and Human Resources (Chairman)

Joint Economic
Fiscal and Monetary Policy (Chairman)
Investment, Jobs and Prices (Vice Chairman)
International Economic Policy

PAC Contribution Profile

Business

Defense	**$27,700**
AT&T	$5,500
Raytheon	$5,000
General Dynamics	$3,000
Grumman	$2,200
Chrysler Corp	$2,000
General Electric	$2,000
GTE Corp	$2,000
Lockheed Corp	$2,000
McDonnell Douglas	$2,000
Northrop Corp	$2,000
Delivery & Air Freight	**$7,500**
Federal Express Corp	$5,000
United Parcel Service	$2,500
Entertainment Industry	**$10,861**
MCA Inc	$4,861
Others	$6,000
Food & Beverage	**$15,000**
Occidental Petroleum	$5,000
Coca-Cola Company	$4,000
Others	$6,000

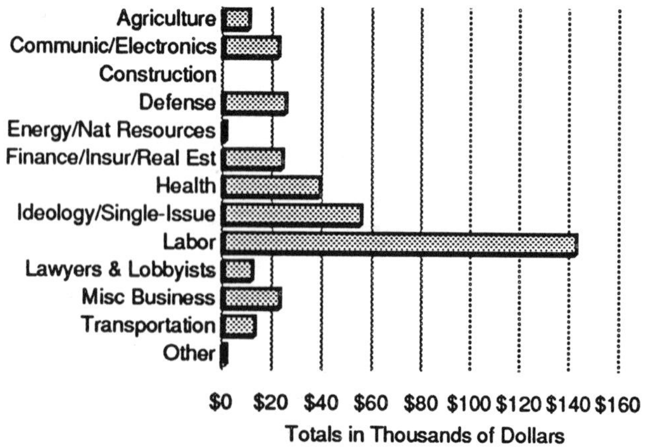

Campaign Revenue Sources

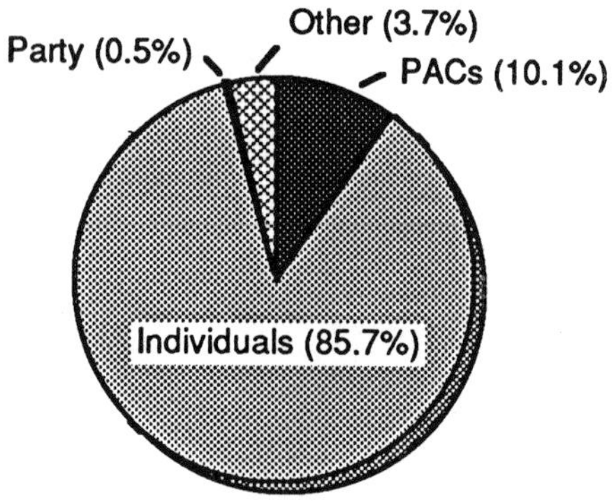

Party (0.5%)
Other (3.7%)
PACs (10.1%)
Individuals (85.7%)

Health Professionals	**$19,500**
American Dental Assn	$4,000
National Assn of Pharmacists	$4,000
American Society of Cataract & Refractive Surgery	$2,000
American Podiatry Assn	$2,000
Others	$7,500
Hospitals & Nursing Homes	**$6,500**
American Hospital Assn	$3,000
Others	$3,500
Insurance	**$11,000**
Health Insurance Assn of America	$2,000
Independent Insurance Agents of America	$2,000
Massachusetts Mutual Life Insurance	$2,000
Metropolitan Life Insurance	$2,000
Others	$3,000
Lawyers	**$11,250**
Meyer, Suoi, English & Klien	$2,000
RRD & B Good Government Cmte	$2,000
Swidler & Berlin	$2,000
Others	$5,250
Pharmaceuticals	**$8,750**
Johnson & Johnson	$2,000
Warner-Lambert	$2,000
Others	$4,750
Telecommunications	**$8,000**
New England Tel & Tel	$4,000
Pacific Telesis Group	$2,000
Others	$2,000

PAC Totals by Category

Agriculture
Communic/Electronics
Construction
Defense
Energy/Nat Resources
Finance/Insur/Real Est
Health
Ideology/Single-Issue
Labor
Lawyers & Lobbyists
Misc Business
Transportation
Other

$0 $20 $40 $60 $80 $100 $120 $140 $160
Totals in Thousands of Dollars

Other Major Business PACs

J C Penney Company	$4,000	Dept Store
Ocean Spray Cranberries Inc	$3,000	Fruit/Veg
Auto Dealers & Drivers for Free Trade	$2,500	JapanAutoSal
Society for Advncmt of Ambulatory Care	$2,500	OutpatntCare
Advest Group Inc	$2,000	StocksInvest
American Textile Manufacturers Institute	$2,000	Textiles
American Trucking Assns	$2,000	Trucking
National Apartment Assn	$2,000	Bldg Mgmt

Labor

Bldg Trades, Industrial & Misc Unions $86,500

Operating Engineers Union	$10,000
Carpenters & Joiners Union	$7,000
Communications Workers of America	$6,000
United Auto Workers	$5,500
AFL-CIO	$5,000
Amalgamated Clothing & Textile Workers	$5,000
Bricklayers Union	$5,000
Food & Commercial Workers Union	$5,000
Intl Brotherhood of Electrical Workers	$5,000
Ladies Garment Workers Union	$5,000
Service Employees International Union	$5,000
Sheet Metal Workers Union	$5,000
United Mine Workers	$5,000
United Steelworkers	$5,000
Laborers' Political League	$2,000
Plumbers/Pipefitters Union*	$2,000
Others	$4,000

Government & Postal Workers $28,500

American Postal Workers Union	$9,500
National Assn of Letter Carriers	$7,000
American Fedn of State/County/Munic Employees	$5,000
American Fedn of Government Employees	$4,000
Others	$3,000

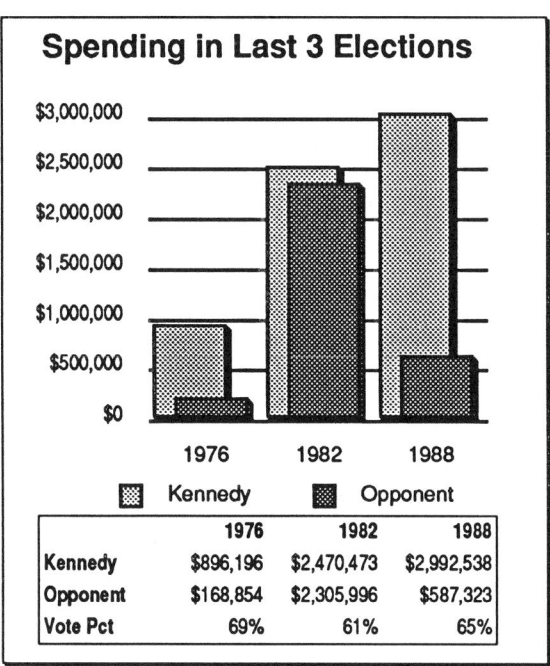

Spending in Last 3 Elections

	1976	1982	1988
Kennedy	$896,196	$2,470,473	$2,992,538
Opponent	$168,854	$2,305,996	$587,323
Vote Pct	69%	61%	65%

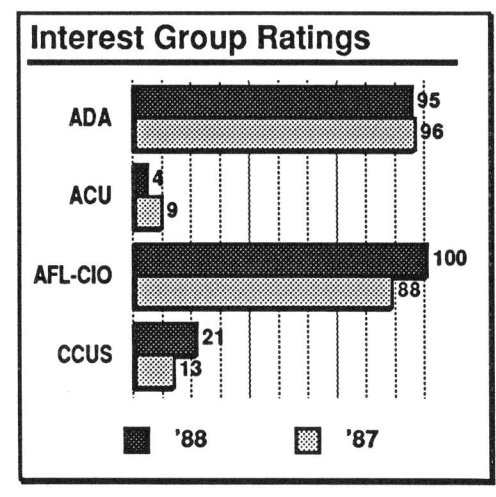

Interest Group Ratings

	'88	'87
ADA	95	96
ACU	4	9
AFL-CIO	100	88
CCUS	21	13

Teachers Unions $6,000

American Federation of Teachers	$5,000
Others	$1,000

Transportation Unions $20,900

Air Line Pilots Assn	$5,000
Amalgamated Transit Union	$5,000
United Transportation Union	$5,000
Teamsters Joint Council #10	$4,900
Seafarers International Union	$2,000
Others	-$1,000

Ideological/Single-Issue

Democratic/Liberal $7,494

Hollywood Women's Political Cmte	$5,000
Others	$2,494

Democratic Leadership PACs $6,250

Senate Majority Fund (Daniel Inouye)	$5,000
Others	$1,250

Health & Welfare Issues $6,500

KidsPAC	$5,000
Others	$1,500

Pro-Israel $25,000

Pacific PAC	$10,000
National PAC	$5,000
Washington PAC	$5,000
Others	$5,000

Other Major Ideological/Single-Issue PACs

Council for a Livable World	$2,607	Pro-Peace
National Cmte to Preserve Social Security	$2,000	Soc Secur

Independent expenditures supporting Kennedy

National Cmte to Preserve Social Security	$21,832

Independent expenditures opposing Kennedy

East Coast Conservative PAC	$16,312
Life Amendment PAC	$7,555
American Citizens for Political Action	$3,068

---

* Contributions came from more than one PAC affiliated with this sponsor.

Bob Kerrey (D-Neb)

1989-90 Committees & Subcommittees

First elected: 1988
Total receipts: $3,446,728
Total from PACs: $791,479

Agriculture, Nutrition and Forestry
Agricultural Production and Stabilization of Prices
Agricultural Research and General Legislation
Nutrition and Investigations

Appropriations
Agriculture, Rural Development and Related Agencies
District of Columbia
HUD — Independent Agencies
Treasury, Postal Service and General Government

PAC Contribution Profile

Business

Automotive **$10,200**

    Chrysler Corp $5,000
    National Auto Dealers Assn $5,000
    Others $200

Broadcasting/Entertainment **$10,750**
    None over $3,000

Construction **$13,500**

    Manville Corp $5,000
    Nebraska Associated General Contractors $5,000
    Others $3,500

Food & Beverage **$17,750**

    National Restaurant Assn $5,000
    Others $12,750

Health Professionals **$30,600**

    American Nurses Assn $7,000
    American Dental Assn $5,000
    American Optometric Assn $5,000
    Others $13,600

Insurance **$26,600**

    Mutual of Omaha $5,850
    National Assn of Life Underwriters $5,000
    Others $15,750

Lawyers & Lobbyists **$28,150**

    Assn of Trial Lawyers of America $10,000
    Kutak, Rock & Campbell $5,000
    Others $13,150

Campaign Revenue Sources

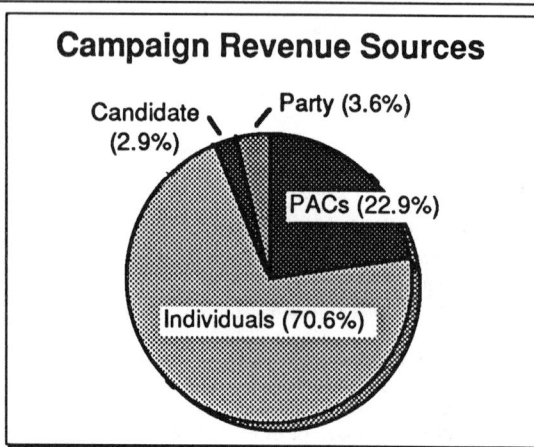

Candidate (2.9%)
Party (3.6%)
PACs (22.9%)
Individuals (70.6%)

Oil & Gas **$12,650**

    None over $2,650

Railroads & Railroad Services **$12,900**

    Union Pacific Corp $7,150
    Others $5,750

Securities/Commodities Investment **$16,250**

    Chicago Mercantile Exchange $5,000
    PaineWebber $5,000
    Others $6,250

Telecommunications **$22,000**

    AT&T $5,000
    Others $17,000

Other Major Business PACs

Federal Express Corp	$7,000	Air Freight
American Hospital Assn	$6,000	Hospitals
Mid-America Dairymen	$6,000	Dairy
American Orthotic/Prosthetic Assn	$5,000	Med Supply
American Express	$5,000	Credit/Loans
National Assn of Realtors	$5,000	RE Sales
Yellow Freight System	$5,000	Trucking

PAC Totals by Category

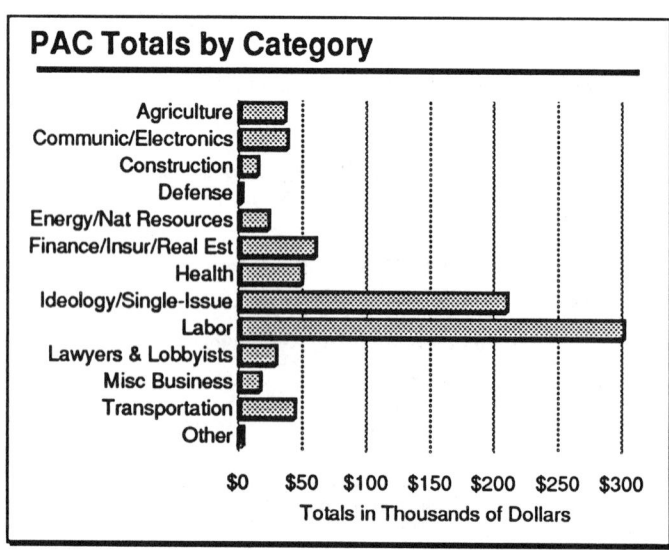

Agriculture
Communic/Electronics
Construction
Defense
Energy/Nat Resources
Finance/Insur/Real Est
Health
Ideology/Single-Issue
Labor
Lawyers & Lobbyists
Misc Business
Transportation
Other

$0 $50 $100 $150 $200 $250 $300

Totals in Thousands of Dollars

Labor

Bldg Trades/Industrial/Misc Unions $154,450

AFL-CIO*	$10,500
Carpenters & Joiners Union	$10,000
Communications Workers of America	$10,000
Food & Commercial Workers Union	$10,000
Intl Brotherhood of Electrical Workers	$10,000
Machinists/Aerospace Workers Union	$10,000
Operating Engineers Union*	$10,000
Sheet Metal Workers Union	$10,000
United Auto Workers	$10,000
United Steelworkers	$10,000
Laborers' Political League	$8,000
Plumbers/Pipefitters Union	$8,000
Rubber Cork Linoleum Plastic Workers	$5,900
Amalgamated Clothing & Textile Workers	$5,000
Boilermakers Union	$5,000
Others	$22,050

Government & Postal Workers $51,250

American Fedn of State/County/Munic Employees	$10,000
American Postal Workers Union	$10,000
National Assn of Letter Carriers	$8,000
National Treasury Employees Union	$8,000
National Assn of Retired Federal Employees	$5,000
National Rural Letter Carriers Assn	$5,000
Others	$5,250

Teachers Unions $20,000

American Federation of Teachers	$10,000
National Education Assn	$10,000

Transportation Unions $74,250

Air Line Pilots Assn	$10,000
Teamsters Union	$10,000
United Transportation Union	$10,000
Marine Engineers Union	$9,000
Transportation Communication Union	$8,500
Amalgamated Transit Union	$7,500
Seafarers International Union	$7,500
Transport Workers Union	$5,000
Others	$6,750

Ideological/Single-Issue

Democratic/Liberal $33,988

Democrats for The 80's	$10,000
National Cmte for an Effective Congress	$9,988
Hollywood Women's Political Cmte	$5,000
Religion and Tolerance PAC	$5,000
Others	$4,000

Democratic Leadership PACs.....................................$50,971

Senate Majority Fund (Daniel Inouye)	$15,000
Cmte for a Democratic Consensus (Alan Cranston)	$10,000
Independent Action (Morris Udall)	$8,000
Fund for a Democratic Majority (Ted Kennedy)	$7,500
Pelican PAC (Bennett Johnston)	$5,000
Others	$5,471

Pro-Israel $85,000

Washington PAC	$10,000
Multi-Issue PAC	$7,000
Citizens Organized PAC	$5,000
Desert Caucus	$5,000
Florida Congressional Cmte	$5,000
Joint Action Cmte for Political Affairs	$5,000
National PAC	$5,000
Pacific PAC	$5,000
Sacramento Area Good Govt Assn	$5,000
St Louisans for Better Govt	$5,000
Others	$28,000

Pro-Peace $15,025

Council for a Livable World	$8,638
Others	$6,387

Other Major Ideological/Single-Issue

KidsPAC	$7,500	Health/Welfare
National Cmte to Preserve Social Security	$5,000	Soc Secur

Independent expenditures supporting Kerrey

National Cmte to Preserve Social Security	$21,659

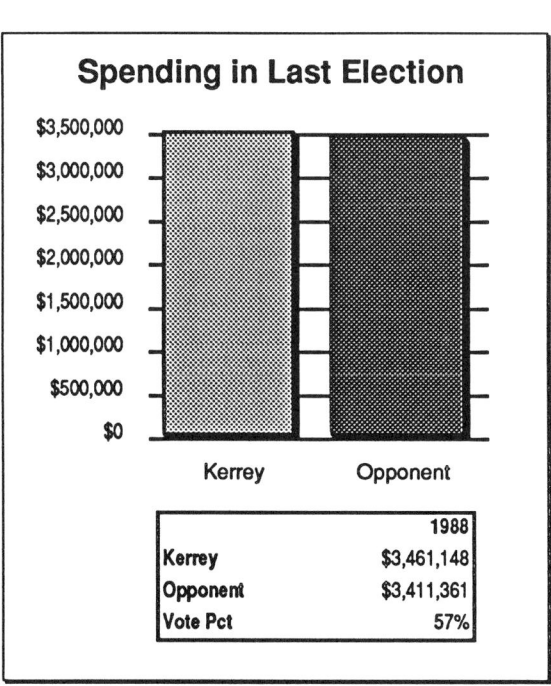

Spending in Last Election

	1988
Kerrey	$3,461,148
Opponent	$3,411,361
Vote Pct	57%

---

* Contributions came from more than one PAC affiliated
with this sponsor.

Herb Kohl (D-Wis)

First elected: 1988
Total receipts: $7,576,540
Total from PACs: $0

1989-90 Committees & Subcommittees

Governmental Affairs
Federal Services, Post Office and Civil Service
Government Information and Regulation
Oversight of Government Management
Permanent Subcommittee on Investigations

Judiciary
Antitrust, Monopolies and Business Rights
Courts and Administrative Practice
Technology and the Law

Special Aging

PAC Contribution Profile

Bakery, Confect & Tobacco Workers .... $1,500   FoodSvcUnion

NOTE: Kohl reported taking no PAC funds during his 1988 Senate campaign. The PAC listed above did report making a contribution, however, and that contribution is recorded in the official FEC records.

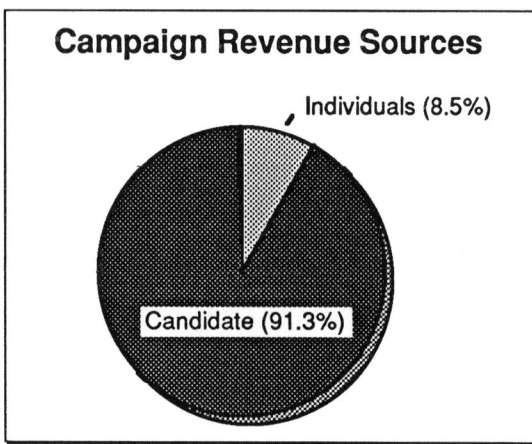

Campaign Revenue Sources

Individuals (8.5%)

Candidate (91.3%)

PAC Totals by Category

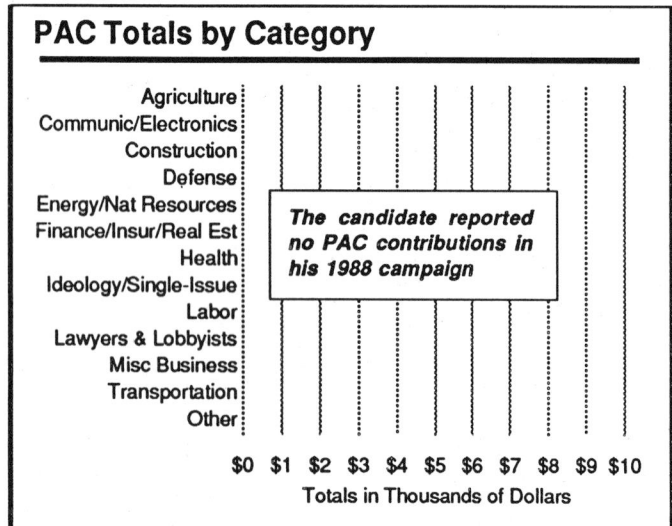

Agriculture
Communic/Electronics
Construction
Defense
Energy/Nat Resources
Finance/Insur/Real Est
Health
Ideology/Single-Issue
Labor
Lawyers & Lobbyists
Misc Business
Transportation
Other

The candidate reported no PAC contributions in his 1988 campaign

$0 $1 $2 $3 $4 $5 $6 $7 $8 $9 $10
Totals in Thousands of Dollars

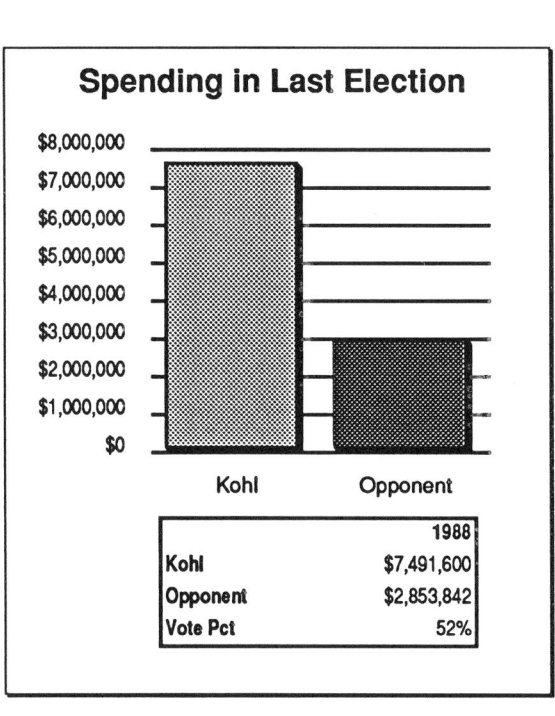

Spending in Last Election

	1988
Kohl	$7,491,600
Opponent	$2,853,842
Vote Pct	52%

195

Frank R. Lautenberg (D-NJ)

First elected: 1982
Total receipts: $8,039,253
Total from PACs: $1,631,341

1988 Committees & Subcommittees

Appropriations
Transportation and Related Agencies (Chairman)
Commerce, Justice, State, the Judiciary and Related Agencies
District of Columbia
Foreign Operations
HUD — Independent Agencies

Budget

Environment and Public Works
Superfund and Environmental Oversight (Chairman)
Environmental Protection
Hazardous Wastes and Toxic Substances

PAC Contribution Profile

Business

Air Transport/Air Freight	**$35,400**
Federal Express Corp	$11,000
Aircraft Owners & Pilots Assn	$10,000
Others	$14,400
Commercial Banks	**$47,922**
American Bankers Assn	$13,500
Others	$34,422
Construction	**$48,000**
National Assn of Home Builders	$11,000
National Utility Contractors Assn	$10,000
Others	$27,000
Consumer Credit & Loans	**$20,000**
Beneficial Management Corp	$13,500
Others	$6,500
Defense	**$28,300**
Allied-Signal	$10,500
Singer Company	$6,000
Others	$11,800
Entertainment Industry	**$38,499**
Gulf + Western Industries	$10,000
MCA Inc	$8,500
Others	$19,999
Insurance	**$92,250**
National Assn of Life Underwriters	$14,000
Prudential Insurance	$11,000
Independent Insurance Agents of America	$10,500
Mutual Benefit Life Insurance	$10,500
Home Group Inc	$10,000
Others	$36,250

Campaign Revenue Sources

Party (6.5%)
Other (4.1%)
Candidate (3.5%)
PACs (19.2%)
Individuals (66.8%)

Lawyers & Lobbyists	**$44,881**
Assn of Trial Lawyers of America	$10,000
Others	$34,881
Pharmaceuticals	**$59,650**
American Cyanimid*	$12,000
Hoffman-La Roche	$7,500
Warner-Lambert	$7,000
Others	$33,150
Real Estate	**$24,800**
National Assn of Realtors	$12,300
Others	$12,500
Savings Banks & Credit Unions	**$23,750**
None over $6,250	
Securities/Commodities Investment	**$59,500**
Chicago Mercantile Exchange	$9,000
E F Hutton Group	$7,500
Others	$43,000
Telecommunications	**$37,000**
AT&T	$10,000
New Jersey Bell Telephone	$10,000
Others	$17,000
Trucking/Delivery	**$29,948**
American Trucking Assns	$11,498
United Parcel Service	$10,000
Others	$8,450

Other Major Business PACs

Auto Dealers & Drivers for Free Trade .... $8,000   JapanAutoSal
Dun & Bradstreet .... $7,500   Mkt Research

PAC Totals by Category

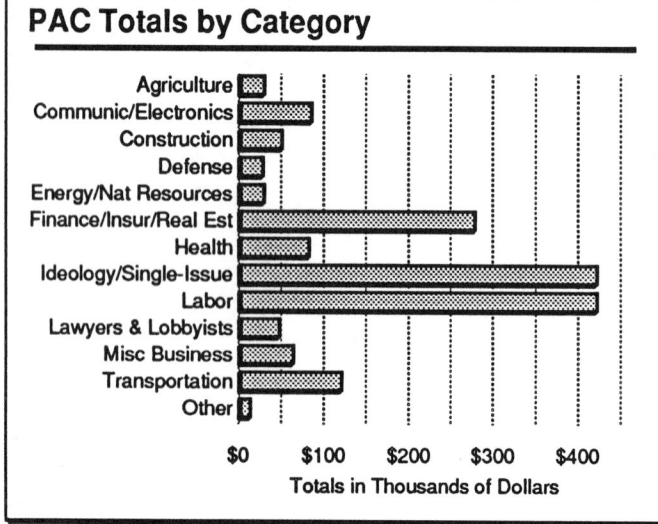

Agriculture
Communic/Electronics
Construction
Defense
Energy/Nat Resources
Finance/Insur/Real Est
Health
Ideology/Single-Issue
Labor
Lawyers & Lobbyists
Misc Business
Transportation
Other

$0 $100 $200 $300 $400
Totals in Thousands of Dollars

Labor

Bldg Trades, Industrial & Misc Unions	$210,000
Amalgamated Clothing & Textile Workers*	$12,500
United Auto Workers*	$12,000
Carpenters & Joiners Union*	$11,500
Intl Brotherhood of Electrical Workers*	$11,500
Laborers' Political League	$11,000
Service Employees International Union	$11,000
Machinists/Aerospace Workers Union	$10,500
AFL-CIO	$10,000
Bricklayers Union	$10,000
Communications Workers of America	$10,000
Food & Commercial Workers Union	$10,000
Operating Engineers Union*	$10,000
Plumbers/Pipefitters Union*	$10,000
United Steelworkers	$10,000
Electronic Machine Furniture Workers	$7,500
Sheet Metal Workers Union	$7,500
Others	$45,000

Government & Postal Workers	$66,681
American Fedn of State/County/Munic Employees	$13,181
National Assn of Letter Carriers	$11,000
American Postal Workers Union	$10,000
National Assn of Retired Federal Employees	$10,000
Others	$22,500

Teachers Unions	$21,000
National Education Assn	$11,000
American Federation of Teachers	$10,000

Transportation Unions	$121,552
Marine Engineers Union*	$15,000
United Transportation Union	$13,500
Air Line Pilots Assn	$12,500
Transportation Communication Union	$10,800
Amalgamated Transit Union	$10,452
Seafarers International Union*	$10,300
Teamsters Union	$10,000
Transport Workers Union	$9,500
Others	$29,500

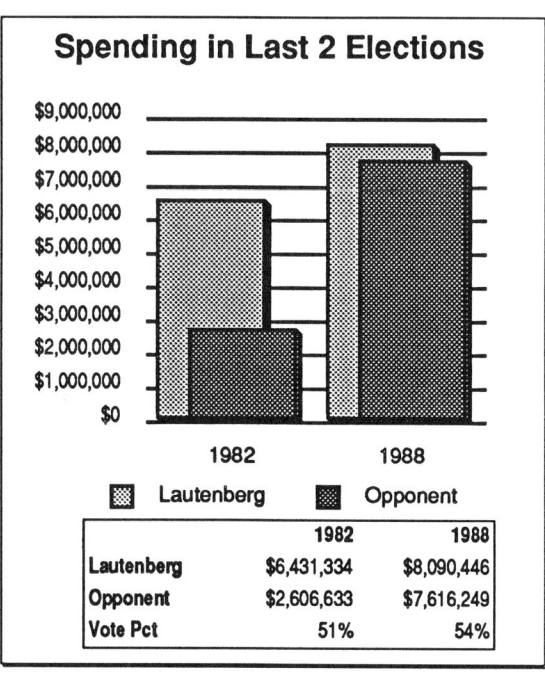

Spending in Last 2 Elections

	1982	1988
Lautenberg	$6,431,334	$8,090,446
Opponent	$2,606,633	$7,616,249
Vote Pct	51%	54%

Interest Group Ratings

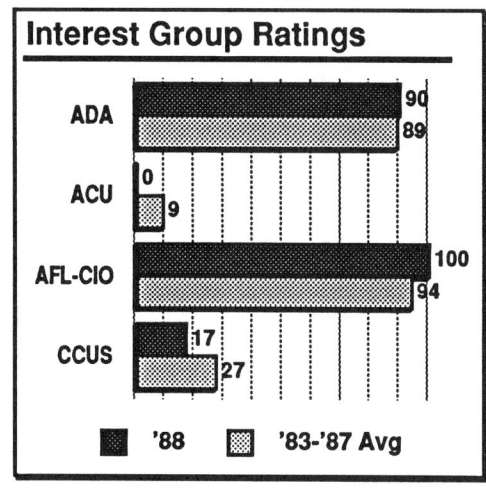

	'88	'83-'87 Avg
ADA	90	89
ACU	0	9
AFL-CIO	100	94
CCUS	17	27

Ideological/Single-Issue

Democratic/Liberal	$33,238
Democrats for The 80's	$10,000
National Cmte for an Effective Congress	$9,988
Others	$13,250

Democratic Leadership PACs	$62,813
Committee for a Demo Consensus (Alan Cranston)	$10,000
Fund for a Democratic Majority (Edward Kennedy)	$10,000
Senate Majority Fund (Daniel Inouye)	$10,000
Others	$32,813

Environmental Issues	$23,865
Sierra Club	$9,119
Others	$14,746

Pro-Israel	$240,750
Hudson Valley PAC	$12,500
Washington PAC	$11,500
Citizens Organized PAC	$10,000
Delaware Valley PAC	$10,000
Desert Caucus	$10,000
Joint Action Cmte for Political Affairs	$10,000
Mid Manhattan PAC	$10,000
MOPAC	$10,000
Multi-Issue PAC	$10,000
National Action Committee	$10,000
National PAC	$10,000
Pacific PAC	$10,000
San Franciscans for Good Government	$10,000
St Louisians for Better Government	$10,000
Maryland Assn for Concerned Citizens	$9,000
Citizens Concerned for the National Interest	$8,000
Florida Congressional Committee	$7,750
Heartland PAC	$7,000
Others	$65,000

Other Major Ideological/Single-Issue PACs

KidsPAC	$10,000	Health/Welfare
National Abortion Rights Action League	$10,000	Pro-Choice
Council for a Livable World	$8,676	Pro-Peace

* Contributions came from more than one PAC affiliated with this sponsor.

Joseph I. Lieberman (D-Conn)

First elected: 1988
Total receipts: $2,647,603
Total from PACs: $173,562

1989-90 Committees & Subcommittees

Environment and Public Works
Environmental Protection
Toxic Substances, Environmental Oversight, Research and Development
Water Resources, Transportation and Infrastructure

Governmental Affairs
General Services, Federalism and the District of Columbia
Oversight of Government Management
Permanent Subcommittee on Investigations

Small Business
Competition and Antitrust Enforcement
Export Expansion
Government Contracting and Paperwork Reduction

PAC Contribution Profile

Business

Airlines & Air Freight	**$2,000**
Federal Express Corp	$1,000
Texas Air	$1,000
Commercial & Savings Banks	**$8,210**
Fleet/Norstar Financial Group	$2,400
CBT Corp	$1,000
Citicorp	$1,000
Hartford National Corp	$1,000
World Savings & Loan	$1,000
Others	$1,810
Dairy	**$7,500**
Mid-America Dairymen	$5,000
Associated Milk Producers	$2,000
Others	$500
Department Stores	**$2,000**
Montgomery Ward	$2,000
Food & Beverage	**$2,000**
A E Staley Manufacturing Company	$1,000
Heublein	$1,000
Health Professionals	**$2,500**
American Chiropractic Assn	$1,500
Connecticut Medical Assn	$1,000

Campaign Revenue Sources

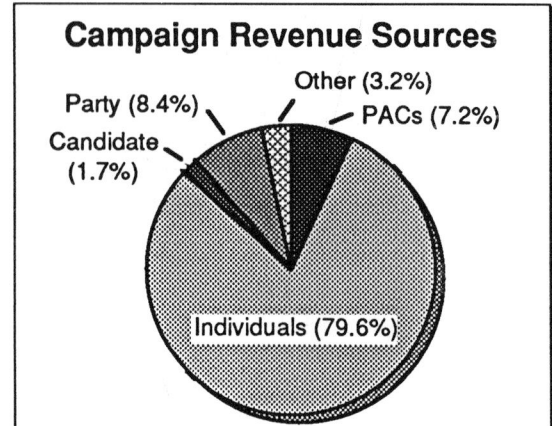

Other (3.2%)
Party (8.4%)
PACs (7.2%)
Candidate (1.7%)
Individuals (79.6%)

Insurance	**$8,400**
Insurance Assn of Connecticut	$5,000
Health Insurance Assn of America	$1,000
National Structured Settlements Assn	$1,000
Others	$1,400
Lawyers & Lobbyists	**$11,638**
Murtha, Cullina, Richter and Pinney	$2,000
Robinson & Cole	$2,000
Updike, Kelly & Spellacy	$1,100
Cummings & Lockwood	$1,000
Kirkpatrick & Lockhart	$1,000
Others	$4,538
Metal Cans	**$5,000**
Triangle Industries	$5,000
Securities Investment	**$14,500**
Donaldson, Lufkin & Jenrette	$7,500
Shearson Lehman Hutton	$5,000
Goldman Sachs	$1,000
PaineWebber	$1,000
Sugar Growers	**$2,000**
American Crystal Sugar Corp	$1,000
Others	$1,000
Tobacco	**$2,000**
Philip Morris	$2,000

Other Major Business PACs

Nevada Resort Assn	$1,500	Casinos/Gamb
ACRE (Action Cmte for Rural Electric)	$1,000	Rural Elect
Browning-Ferris Industries	$1,000	Waste Mgmt
General Development Corp	$1,000	RE Devel
General Instrument Corp	$1,000	Electronics
Kimberly-Clark	$1,000	Paper & Pulp
Lykes Bros Steamship Company	$1,000	SeaTransport

PAC Totals by Category

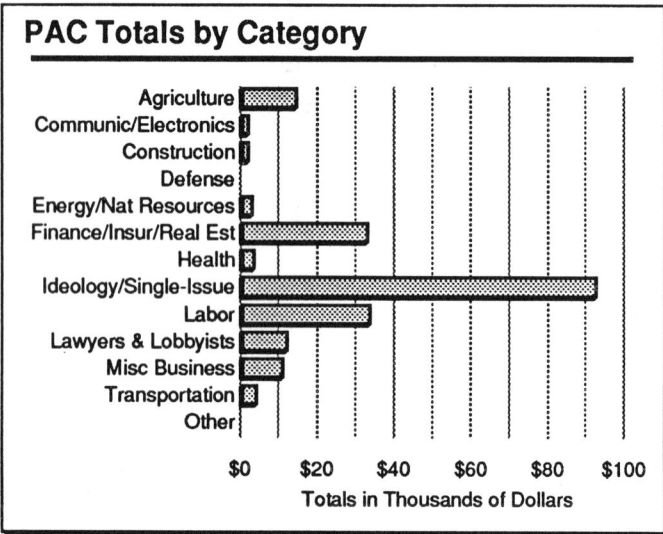

Agriculture
Communic/Electronics
Construction
Defense
Energy/Nat Resources
Finance/Insur/Real Est
Health
Ideology/Single-Issue
Labor
Lawyers & Lobbyists
Misc Business
Transportation
Other

$0 $20 $40 $60 $80 $100
Totals in Thousands of Dollars

Labor

Bldg Trades/Industrial/Service Unions **$13,700**

    Communications Workers of America $5,000
    Service Employees International Union $5,000
    Connecticut Union of Telephone Workers $2,000
    Office & Professional Employees Union $1,000
    Others $700

Government & Postal Workers **$4,500**

    National Treasury Employees Union $4,000
    Others $500

Teachers Unions **$5,000**

    American Federation of Teachers $5,000

Transportation Unions **$10,000**

    Teamsters Union $5,000
    United Auto Workers $5,000

Ideological/Single-Issue

Democratic/Liberal **$10,350**

    Democrats for The 80's $10,000
    Others $350

Democratic Leadership PACs **$37,067**

    Pelican PAC (Bennett Johnston) $10,000
    Cmte for a Democratic Consensus (Alan Cranston) $8,000
    Democratic Candidate Fund (Tip O'Neill) $5,500
    Campaign for America (Frank Lautenberg)....................$5,000
    Senate Majority Fund (Daniel Inouye) $5,000
    Valley Education Fund (Tony Coelho) $3,000
    Others $567

Other Candidate PACs **$3,500**

    HHH Fund (Hubert Humphrey III) $2,000
    Others $1,500

Environmental PACs **$9,759**

    League of Conservation Voters $4,945
    Sierra Club $4,625
    Others $189

Pro-Israel **$11,800**

    National PAC $5,000
    Hudson Valley PAC $2,500
    Americans for Good Govt Inc $2,000
    Garden State PAC $1,300
    Congressional Action Cmte of Texas $1,000

Other Major Ideological/Single-Issue PACs

Council for a Livable World ....$9,085   Pro-Peace
Free Cuba PAC ....$5,489   Anti-Castro
KidsPAC ....$5,000   Health/Welfare

Spending in Last Election

	1988
Lieberman	$2,570,779
Opponent	$2,731,294
Vote Pct	50%

Trent Lott (R-Miss)

First elected: 1988
Total receipts: $3,172,722
Total from PACs: $1,113,111

1988 House Committees & Subcommittees

Minority Whip

Rules
Legislative Process (Ranking Republican)
Rules of the House

PAC Contribution Profile

Business

Air Transport/Air Freight **$25,750**

Federal Express Corp	$10,000
Others	$15,750

Automotive **$20,000**

Auto Dealers & Drivers for Free Trade	$6,000
Eaton Corp	$5,000
Others	$9,000

Chemicals & Plastics **$31,600**

Dow Chemical*	$10,000
FMC Corp	$8,000
Others	$13,600

Construction **$65,726**

Associated General Contractors	$10,000
National Assn of Home Builders	$10,000
American Supply Assn	$5,000
Assoc Builders & Contractors	$5,000
National Electrical Contractors Assn	$5,000
Others	$30,726

Defense **$85,500**

Harris Corp	$10,000
Litton Industries	$10,000
Lockheed Corp	$10,000
Northrop Corp	$6,000
United Technologies	$6,000
Rockwell International	$5,500
Allied-Signal	$5,000
Mantech International	$5,000
(continued in next column)	

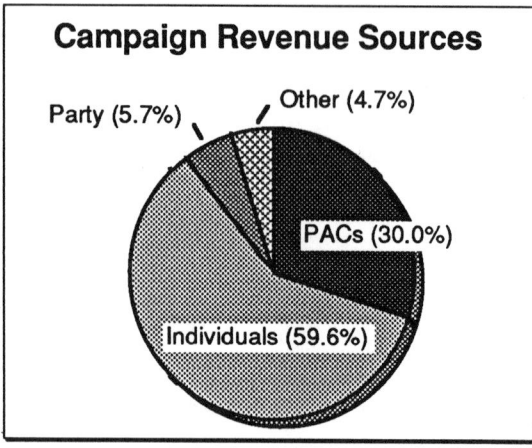

Campaign Revenue Sources

Party (5.7%)
Other (4.7%)
PACs (30.0%)
Individuals (59.6%)

Defense (cont'd)

Martin Marietta Corp	$5,000
Tenneco Inc	$5,000
Others	$18,000

Electric Utilities **$23,500**

Southern Company*	$10,000
Others	$13,500

Electronics & Computers **$20,550**

Cooper Industries	$5,000
Others	$15,550

Financial Institutions **$53,750**

US League of Savings Assn	$7,000
Bank of Mississippi	$6,000
American Bankers Assn	$5,000
Barnett Banks of Florida	$5,000
Credit Union National Assn	$5,000
J P Morgan & Company	$5,000
Others	$20,750

Food & Beverage **$94,600**

McDonald's Corp	$10,000
Food Marketing Institute	$8,000
American Meat Institute	$5,000
ConAgra Inc	$5,000
Jitney-Jungle Inc	$5,000
Malone & Hyde Inc	$5,000
National Restaurant Assn	$5,000
Others	$51,600

Forest Products **$41,000**

International Paper Company	$5,000
Union Camp Corp	$5,000
Westvaco Corp	$5,000
Others	$26,000

Insurance **$48,500**

National Assn of Life Underwriters	$10,000
Independent Insurance Agents of America	$6,000
Others	$32,500

Oil & Gas **$81,750**

Chevron Corp	$10,000
Amoco Corp	$8,000
Dallas Energy PAC	$5,000
Mobil Oil	$5,000
Petroleum Marketers Assn	$5,000
Others	$48,750

PAC Totals by Category

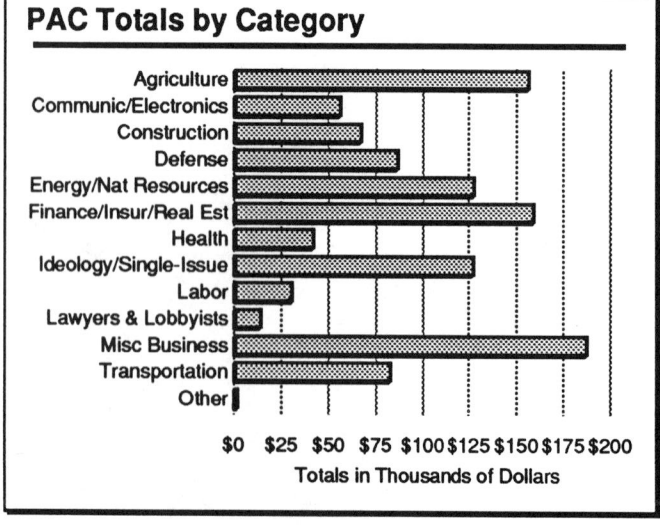

Agriculture
Communic/Electronics
Construction
Defense
Energy/Nat Resources
Finance/Insur/Real Est
Health
Ideology/Single-Issue
Labor
Lawyers & Lobbyists
Misc Business
Transportation
Other

$0 $25 $50 $75 $100 $125 $150 $175 $200

Totals in Thousands of Dollars

Pharmaceuticals **$19,800**

    Eli Lilly & Company $5,000
    Others $14,800

Real Estate **$24,000**

    National Assn of Realtors $10,000
    Century 21 Real Estate $5,000
    Others $9,000

Telecommunications **$27,750**

    AT&T $5,000
    Continental Telecom $5,000
    United Telecommunications $5,000
    Others $12,750

Tobacco **$19,000**

    RJR Nabisco...$6,000
    United States Tobacco Company $5,000
    Others $8,000

Trucking & Railroads **$22,750**

    Union Pacific Corp....................................$9,750
    United Parcel Service $8,000
    Others $5,000

Other Major Business PACs

American Furniture Manufacturers Assn	$9,000	Furniture
American Optometric Assn	$6,000	Eye Docs
National Fisheries Institute	$6,000	Fishing
American Institute of CPA's	$5,000	Accountants
American Dental Assn	$5,000	Dentists
Chicago Mercantile Exchange	$5,000	Commodities
Drexel Burnham Lambert	$5,000	StocksInvest
Dun & Bradstreet	$5,000	Mkt Research
National Assn of Wholesale-Distributors	$5,000	Wholesale
National Screw Machines Prod Assn	$5,000	Indust Equip
National Venture Capital Assn	$5,000	Venture Cap
National Fedn of Independent Business	$4,999	Sml Business

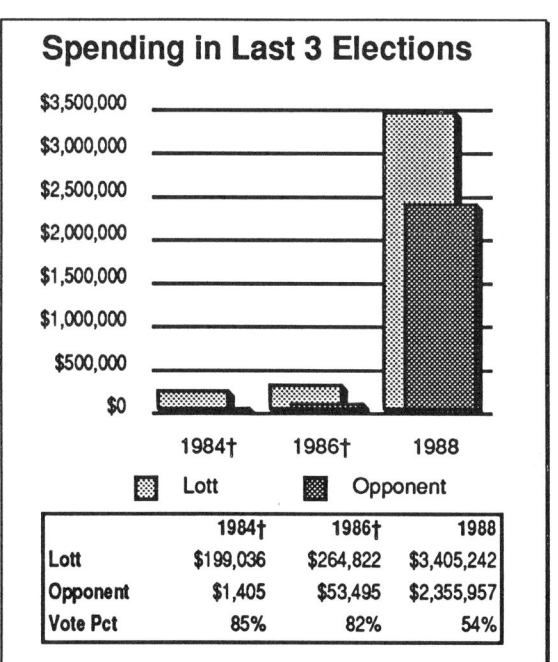

Spending in Last 3 Elections

	1984†	1986†	1988
Lott	$199,036	$264,822	$3,405,242
Opponent	$1,405	$53,495	$2,355,957
Vote Pct	85%	82%	54%

Legend: ▨ Lott   ▨ Opponent

† U.S. House races

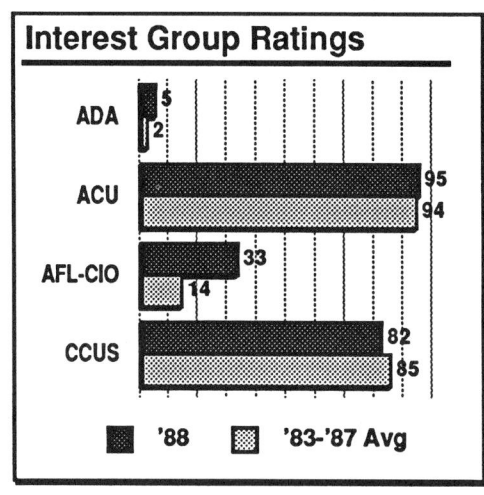

Interest Group Ratings

	'88	'83-'87 Avg
ADA	5	2
ACU	95	94
AFL-CIO	33	14
CCUS	82	85

Legend: ■ '88   ▨ '83-'87 Avg

Labor

Labor Unions..**$29,550**

    Marine Engineers Union* $11,000
    Air Line Pilots Assn $5,000
    National Assn of Retired Federal Employees $5,000
    Others $8,550

Ideological/Single-Issue

Republican/Conservative **$19,653**

    Black PAC $5,000
    Conservative Victory Cmte $5,000
    Others $9,653

Republican Leadership PACs **$49,627**

    Republican Majority Fund (Richard Lugar) $10,000
    Campaign America (Bob Dole)......................$6,000
    New Republican Victory Fund $6,000
    Catch the Spirit PAC (Bob Kasten) $5,000
    Citizens for the Republic (Ronald Reagan) $5,000
    Fund for America's Future (George Bush) $5,000
    Others $12,627

Other Major Ideological/Single-Issue PACs

National PAC	$10,000	Pro-Israel
Public Svc Research Council	$10,000	Anti-Union
National Security PAC	$8,000	Pro-Defense
National Rifle Assn	$5,000	Pro-Guns
Right to Work PAC	$5,000	Anti-Union

Independent expenditures supporting Lott

National Assn of Realtors	$348,498
Auto Dealers & Drivers for Free Trade	$319,126
National Security PAC	$49,556

* Contributions came from more than one PAC affiliated
with this sponsor.

Richard G. Lugar (R-Ind)

First elected: 1976
Total receipts: $3,608,098
Total from PACs: $836,846

1988 Committees & Subcommittees

Agriculture, Nutrition and Forestry (Ranking Republican)

Foreign Relations
Western Hemisphere and Peace Corps Affairs (Ranking Republican)
East Asian and Pacific Affairs
International Economic Policy, Trade, Oceans and Environment

PAC Contribution Profile

Business

Agricultural Chemicals	**$33,150**
Eli Lilly & Company	$9,000
FMC Corp	$5,000
Pfizer Inc	$5,000
Dow Chemical*	$3,000
Others	$11,150
Air Transport/Air Freight	**$14,875**
Federal Express Corp	$4,875
Eastern Airlines	$4,000
Others	$6,000
Automotive	**$29,625**
Auto Dealers & Drivers for Free Trade	$10,000
National Auto Dealers Assn	$8,000
General Motors	$4,125
Ford Motor Company	$4,000
Others	$3,500
Commercial & Savings Banks	**$50,411**
US League of Savings Assn*	$10,000
American Bankers Assn	$8,500
Banc One Corp*	$5,256
Citicorp	$4,500
Merchants National Corp	$3,180
Others	$18,975
Construction	**$50,150**
Associated General Contractors	$10,000
National Assn of Home Builders	$9,500
Associated Builders & Contractors	$5,000
Manufactured Housing Institute	$3,750
Others	$21,900

Campaign Revenue Sources

Party (4.9%)
Other (4.7%)
PACs (22.4%)
Individuals (68.0%)

Defense	**$51,420**
Northrop Corp	$7,000
Harris Corp	$5,000
United Technologies	$4,500
Colt Industries	$3,000
General Dynamics	$3,000
Lockheed Corp	$3,000
Textron Inc	$3,000
Others	$22,920
Electronics & Computers	**$10,500**
General Electric	$3,000
Others	$7,500
Food & Beverage	**$85,960**
ConAgra Inc	$10,000
Food Marketing Institute	$7,170
Kellogg Company	$4,168
Greyhound Corp	$4,000
Joseph E Seagram & Sons	$4,000
S & A Restaurant Corp	$4,000
Pillsbury Company	$3,397
A E Staley Manufacturing Company	$3,000
American Meat Institute	$3,000
Nabisco Brands Inc	$3,000
Pepsico Inc	$3,000
Others	$37,225
Forest Products	**$25,500**
Westvaco Corp	$10,000
Owens-Illinois	$3,000
Others	$12,500
Grain/Soybean Growers & Traders	**$12,600**
Archer-Daniels-Midland Corp	$5,500
Central Soya Company	$3,100
Others	$4,000
Health Professionals	**$16,325**
American Medical Assn	$6,000
American Academy of Ophthalmology	$5,000
Others	$5,325
Industrial Equipment & Materials	**$10,016**
None over $2,500	
Insurance	**$52,665**
Lincoln National Corp*	$8,750
National Assn of Life Underwriters	$6,750
National Assn of Mutual Insurance Agents	$5,000
National Assn of Independent Insurers	$3,550
Allstate Insurance	$3,000
Independent Insurance Agents of America	$3,000
Others	$22,615

PAC Totals by Category

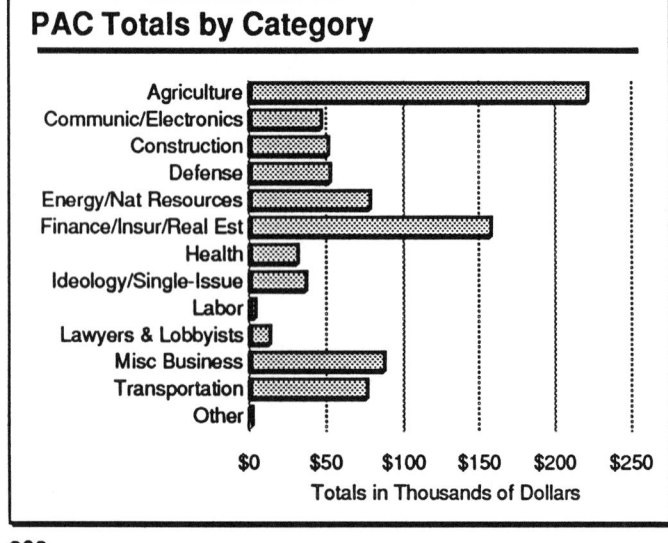

Agriculture
Communic/Electronics
Construction
Defense
Energy/Nat Resources
Finance/Insur/Real Est
Health
Ideology/Single-Issue
Labor
Lawyers & Lobbyists
Misc Business
Transportation
Other

$0 $50 $100 $150 $200 $250
Totals in Thousands of Dollars

Lawyers & Lobbyists	$12,250

None over $2,000

Mining & Metal Processing	$13,780
Alcoa	$5,000
Others	$8,780

Oil & Gas	$46,975
Amoco Corp	$5,000
Mobil Oil	$5,000
USX Corp	$3,100
Mapco Inc	$3,000
Tesoro Petroleum	$3,000
Others	$27,875

Real Estate	$14,500
National Assn of Realtors	$10,000
National Parking Assn	$3,000
Others	$1,500

Retail Sales	$13,000
Federated Dept Stores	$4,000
May Department Stores	$3,000
Others	$6,000

Securities/Commodities Investment	$56,350
Chicago Board of Trade	$10,000
Chicago Mercantile Exchange	$10,000
Morgan Stanley & Company	$5,000
Donaldson, Lufkin & Jenrette	$4,000
Merrill Lynch	$3,000
Salomon Brothers	$3,000
Others	$21,350

Telecommunications	$27,436
AT&T	$9,750
Ameritech Corp*	$4,886
Continental Telecom	$3,500
Others	$9,300

Trucking/Delivery	$13,975
United Parcel Service	$6,475
North American Van Lines	$4,000
Others	$3,500

Interest Group Ratings

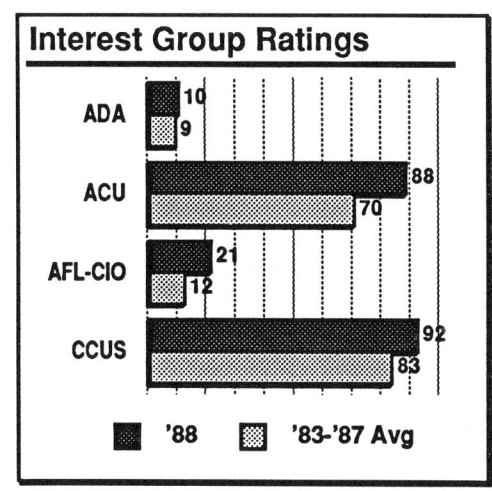

	'88	'83-'87 Avg
ADA	10	9
ACU	88	70
AFL-CIO	21	12
CCUS	92	83

Other Major Business PACs

Totem Ocean Trailer Express	$5,250	SeaTransport
Indiana Farm Bureau	$5,010	Farm Orgs
Navistar International	$5,000	Farm Equip
Peanut Butter & Nut Processors Assn	$5,000	Misc Crops
American Crystal Sugar Corp	$4,000	Sugar
Waste Management Inc	$4,500	Waste Mgmt
Abbott Laboratories	$3,500	Pharmaceut
ACRE (Action Cmte for Rural Electric)*	$3,375	Rural Elect
Credit Union National Assn	$3,000	Credit Union
National Venture Capital Assn	$3,000	Venture Cap
Union Pacific Corp	$3,000	Railroads

Ideological/Single-Issue

Republican Leadership PACs	$15,311
Campaign America (Bob Dole)	$6,000
Republican Majority Fund (Richard Lugar)	$5,000
Catch the Spirit PAC (Bob Kasten)	$3,000
Others	$1,311

Other Major Ideological/Single-Issue PACs

National PAC	$5,000	Pro-Israel
National Rifle Assn	$4,950	Pro-Guns

Spending in Last 3 Elections

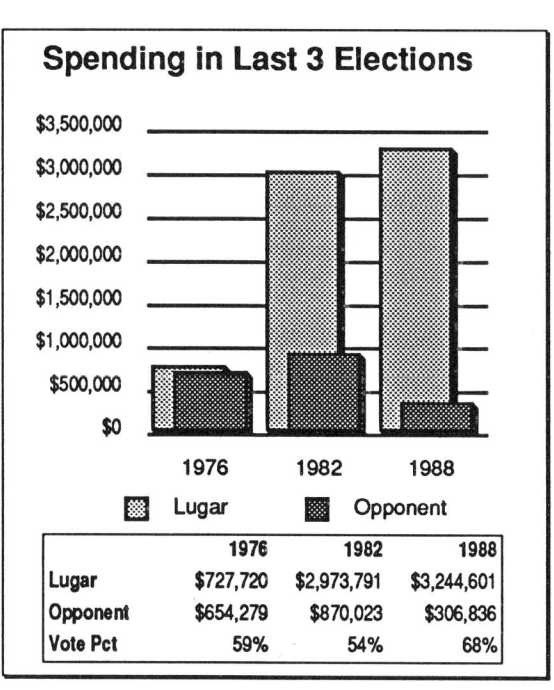

	1976	1982	1988
Lugar	$727,720	$2,973,791	$3,244,601
Opponent	$654,279	$870,023	$306,836
Vote Pct	59%	54%	68%

* Contributions came from more than one PAC affiliated with this sponsor.

Connie Mack (R-Fla)

First elected: 1988
Total receipts: $4,928,645
Total from PACs: $1,017,045

1988 House Committees & Subcommittees

Budget
Defense and International Affairs (Ranking Republican)
Income Security (Ranking Republican)
Health

Foreign Affairs
International Operations
Western Hemisphere Affairs

PAC Contribution Profile

Business

Air Transport/Air Freight	**$22,750**
Federal Express Corp	$10,000
Eastern Airlines	$9,250
Others	$3,500
Automotive	**$33,700**
Auto Dealers & Drivers for Free Trade	$11,500
Eaton Corp	$8,000
National Auto Dealers Assn	$7,300
Others	$6,900
Chemicals & Plastics	**$39,050**
Dow Chemical*	$10,000
FMC Corp	$9,600
NL Industries*	$5,500
Others	$13,950
Construction	**$76,298**
Associated General Contractors	$10,300
National Assn of Home Builders	$10,000
National Electrical Contractors Assn	$10,000
Assoc Builders & Contractors	$6,000
Manville Corp	$5,000
National Utility Contractors Assn	$5,000
Others	$29,998

Campaign Revenue Sources

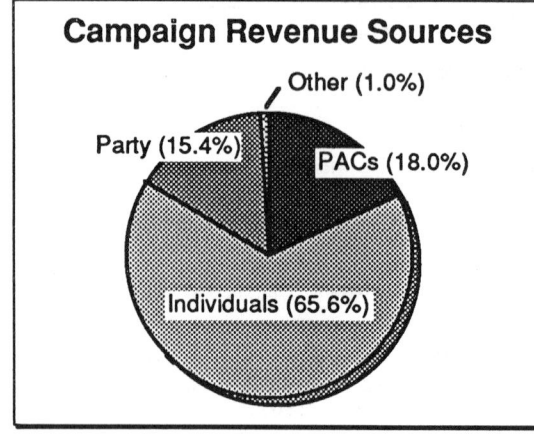

Other (1.0%)
Party (15.4%)
PACs (18.0%)
Individuals (65.6%)

Defense	**$63,100**
Harris Corp	$10,500
United Technologies	$7,000
Tenneco Inc	$5,500
Allied-Signal	$5,300
BDM International	$5,000
Northrop Corp*	$5,000
Others	$24,800
Electric Utilities	**$31,600**
Southern Company*	$9,100
Others	$22,500
Electronics & Computers	**$15,550**
Cooper Industries	$10,000
Others	$5,550
Financial Institutions	**$65,400**
American Bankers Assn	$10,000
Barnett Banks of Florida	$10,000
National Banks of Florida	$5,500
Florida League of Financial Institutions	$5,000
J P Morgan & Company	$5,000
Others	$29,900
Food & Beverage	**$55,400**
Coors Industries	$5,000
Flowers Industries	$5,000
Malone & Hyde Inc	$5,000
Pillsbury Company	$5,000
Others	$35,400
Forest Products	**$28,150**
International Paper Company	$5,000
Union Camp Corp	$5,000
Others	$18,150
Health Professionals	**$38,650**
American Dental Assn	$10,000
American Medical Assn	$7,800
American Optometric Assn	$5,600
American Academy of Ophthalmology	$5,000
Others	$10,250
Industrial Equipment & Materials	**$20,800**
National Screw Machines Producers Assn	$5,000
Others	$15,800

PAC Totals by Category

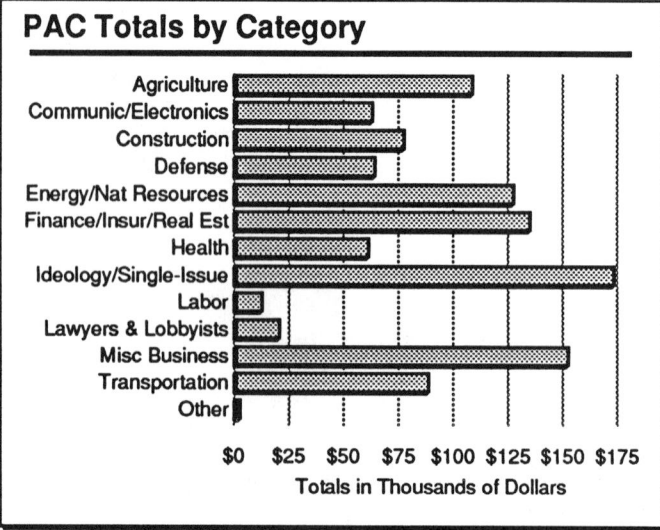

Agriculture
Communic/Electronics
Construction
Defense
Energy/Nat Resources
Finance/Insur/Real Est
Health
Ideology/Single-Issue
Labor
Lawyers & Lobbyists
Misc Business
Transportation
Other

$0 $25 $50 $75 $100 $125 $150 $175

Totals in Thousands of Dollars

Insurance *$35,400*

    None over $4,000

Lawyers & Lobbyists *$19,800*
    VSS&P FEDPAC $5,000
    Others $14,800

Oil & Gas *$86,200*
    Dallas Energy PAC $10,000
    Amoco Corp $8,300
    Chevron Corp $8,000
    Mobil Oil $7,500
    Petroleum Marketers Assn $5,000
    Union Oil $5,000
    Others $42,400

Real Estate *$25,250*
    National Assn of Realtors $10,000
    American Land Development Assn $5,000
    Others $10,250

Telecommunications *$34,150*
    Southern Bell $8,000
    AT&T $5,800
    United Telecommunications $5,600
    Others $14,750

Tobacco *$15,600*
    RJR Nabisco $5,000
    United States Tobacco Company $5,000
    Others $5,600

Trucking & Railroad Services *$23,200*
    Ryder System Inc $6,000
    Union Pacific Corp $6,000
    Others $11,200

Other Major Business PACs

National Fedn of Independent Business	$9,999	Sml Business
Chicago Mercantile Exchange	$5,000	Commodities
Eli Lilly & Company	$5,000	Pharmaceut
National Assn of Wholesale-Distributors	$5,000	Wholesale

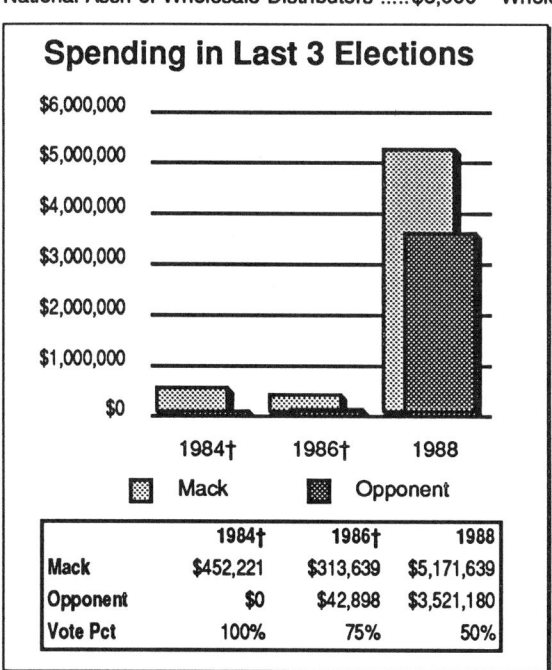

Spending in Last 3 Elections

Mack   Opponent

	1984†	1986†	1988
Mack	$452,221	$313,639	$5,171,639
Opponent	$0	$42,898	$3,521,180
Vote Pct	100%	75%	50%

† U.S. House races

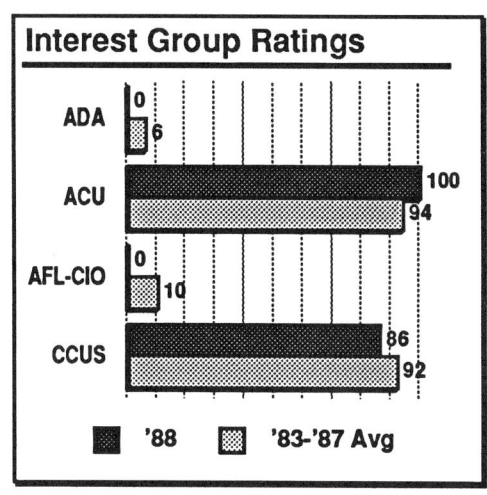

Interest Group Ratings

	'88	'83-'87 Avg
ADA	0	6
ACU	100	94
AFL-CIO	0	10
CCUS	86	92

■ '88   ▨ '83-'87 Avg

Ideological/Single-Issue

Pro-Israel *$33,622*

    National PAC $5,000
    Women's Pro-Israel National PAC $5,000
    Others $23,622

Republican/Conservative *$23,567*
    Conservative Victory Cmte $6,000
    Others $17,567

Republican Leadership PACs *$56,757*
    Catch the Spirit PAC (Bob Kasten) $11,077
    Citizens for the Republic (Ronald Reagan) ...$10,000
    Campaign America (Bob Dole) $9,880
    Fund for America's Future (George Bush) $6,000
    Republican Majority Fund (Richard Lugar) $5,000
    Others $14,800

Other Major Ideological/Single-Issue

Free Cuba PAC	$10,000	Anti-Castro
Public Service Research Council	$10,000	Anti-Union
National Security PAC	$7,969	Pro-Defense
Ruff PAC	$7,250	Tax Policy
Right to Work PAC	$6,343	Anti-Union
Council for National Defense	$5,000	Pro-Defense
National Right to Life PAC	$5,000	Pro-Life

Major Labor PACs

Marine Engineers Union*	$10,000	Seamen Union

Independent expenditures supporting Mack

Auto Dealers & Drivers for Free Trade	$326,050
National Security PAC	$42,175
National Right to Life PAC	$41,984
Council for National Defense	$7,542

Independent expenditures opposing Mack

National Council of Senior Citizens	$17,375

---

* Contributions came from more than one PAC affiliated
  with this sponsor.

Spark M. Matsunaga (D-Hawaii)

First elected: 1976
Total receipts: $1,092,028
Total from PACs: $525,233

1988 Committees & Subcommittees

Finance
International Trade (Chairman)
Energy and Agricultural Taxation
Taxation and Debt Management

Labor and Human Resources
Aging (Chairman)
Education, Arts and Humanities
Labor

Veterans' Affairs

Joint Taxation

PAC Contribution Profile
Business

Accountants **$10,750**

    American Institute of CPA's $5,000
    Others $5,750

Air Transport **$5,000**
    None over $2,000

Automotive **$9,550**

    Auto Dealers & Drivers for Free Trade $7,500
    National Auto Dealers Assn $2,050

Business Associations **$7,200**

    Small Business Council of America $6,200
    Others $1,000

Construction **$7,500**
    None over $2,000

Consumer Credit & Loans **$5,000**

    American Express $3,000
    Others $2,000

Defense **$6,500**
    None over $2,000

Campaign Revenue Sources

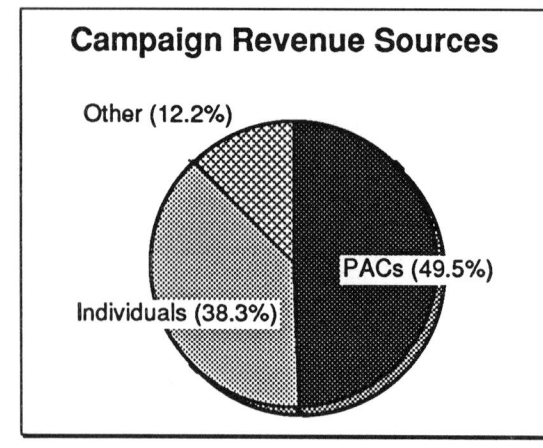

Other (12.2%)
PACs (49.5%)
Individuals (38.3%)

Financial Institutions **$24,000**

    American Bankers Assn $10,000
    US League of Savings Assn $3,000
    Credit Union National Assn $2,500
    Others $8,500

Food & Beverage **$25,000**

    Independent Bakers Assn $4,000
    Food Marketing Institute $3,000
    Nabisco Brands Inc $3,000
    National Restaurant Assn $3,000
    National Beer Wholesalers Assn $3,000
    Others $9,000

Health Professionals **$32,000**

    American Dental Assn $6,000
    American Assn of Nurse Anesthetists $4,500
    Co-op of American Physicians $3,000
    Oral & Maxillofacial Surgeons $3,000
    Others $15,500

Hospitals & Nursing Homes **$15,500**

    American Health Care Assn $5,000
    National Assn of Private Psychiatric Hospitals ... $3,000
    American Hospital Assn $2,500
    Others $5,000

Hotels/Motels **$5,500**

    American Hotel & Motel Assn $3,000
    Marriott Corp $2,500

Insurance **$39,700**

    Equitable Financial Services $6,000
    American Family Corp $5,000
    National Assn of Life Underwriters $4,000
    American International Group inc $2,500
    Others $22,200

Lawyers & Lobbyists **$18,499**

    Assn of Trial Lawyers of America $10,000
    Others $8,499

Oil & Gas **$17,750**

    Pacific Resources $4,000
    Pacific Enterprises $2,500
    Others $11,250

Pharmaceuticals **$5,500**
    None over $1,000

PAC Totals by Category

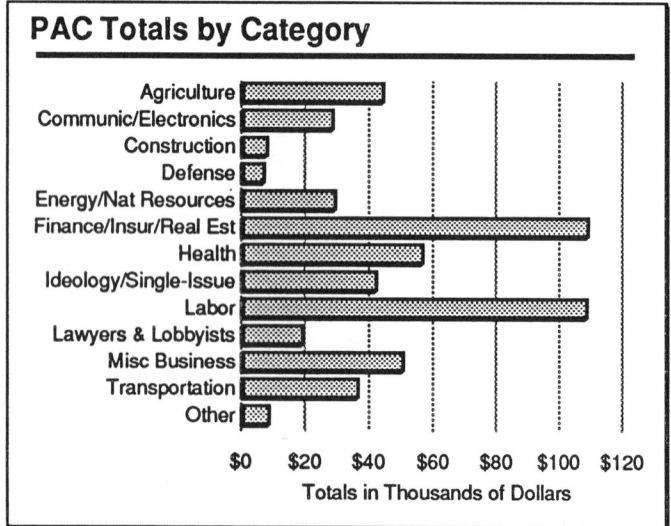

Agriculture
Communic/Electronics
Construction
Defense
Energy/Nat Resources
Finance/Insur/Real Est
Health
Ideology/Single-Issue
Labor
Lawyers & Lobbyists
Misc Business
Transportation
Other

$0 $20 $40 $60 $80 $100 $120

Totals in Thousands of Dollars

Real Estate **$16,500**

    National Assn of Realtors $10,000
    Others $6,500

Retail Sales **$14,500**

    J C Penney Company $5,000
    Others $9,500

Sea Transport **$8,500**

    Matson Navigation $5,000
    American President Lines $2,500
    Others $1,000

Securities/Commodities Investment **$16,500**

    Chicago Board of Trade $5,000
    E F Hutton Group $2,500
    Others $9,000

Sugar Growers **$7,000**

    American Crystal Sugar Corp $3,000
    Others $4,000

Telecommunications **$20,558**

    AT&T $10,000
    GTE Corp* $2,558
    Others $8,000

Television/Movies **$5,000**

    None over $2,000

Tobacco **$5,000**

    None over $2,000

Other Major Business PACs

National Assn of Trade/Tech Schools ....$3,000   Voc Tech
United Parcel Service ....$2,500   Delivery

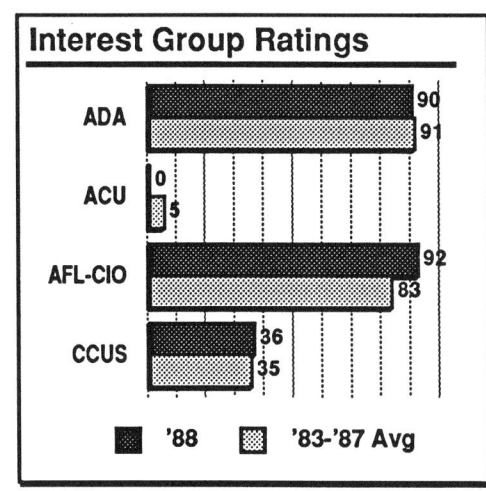

Interest Group Ratings

	'88	'83–'87 Avg
ADA	90	91
ACU	0	5
AFL-CIO	92	83
CCUS	36	35

Labor

Bldg Trades, Industrial & Other Unions **$45,550**

    Laborers' Western Political League $10,000
    Operating Engineers Union $7,000
    Carpenters & Joiners Union* $6,050
    AFL-CIO $5,000
    American Federation of Musicians $3,500
    National Education Assn $2,500
    Others $11,500

Government & Postal Workers **$34,800**

    American Fedn of State/County/Munic Employees $10,000
    National Assn of Letter Carriers $8,000
    American Postal Workers Union $5,000
    National Assn of Retired Federal Employees $5,000
    Others $6,800

Transportation Unions **$27,800**

    Marine Engineers Union $10,000
    Seafarers International Union $5,300
    Longshoremen/Warehousemen Union $4,500
    Air Line Pilots Assn $2,500
    Teamsters Union $2,500
    Others $3,000

Ideological/Single-Issue

Democratic Leadership PACs **$22,500**

    Senate Majority Fund (Daniel Inouye) $15,000
    Pelican PAC (Bennett Johnston) $5,000
    Others $2,500

Pro-Israel **$8,000**

    National PAC $5,000
    Others $3,000

Other Major Ideological/Single-Issue PACs

National Cmte to Preserve Social Security ..$5,000   Elderly
Council for a Livable World ....$2,600   Pro-Peace

Independent expenditures supporting Matsunaga

National Cmte to Preserve Social Security $2,447

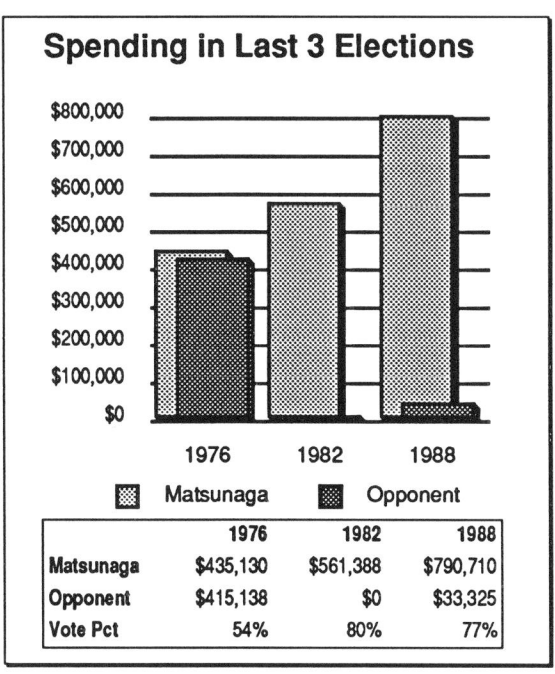

Spending in Last 3 Elections

	1976	1982	1988
Matsunaga	$435,130	$561,388	$790,710
Opponent	$415,138	$0	$33,325
Vote Pct	54%	80%	77%

Legend: ▨ Matsunaga   ▨ Opponent

---

* Contributions came from more than one PAC affiliated
  with this sponsor.

Howard M. Metzenbaum (D-Ohio)

First elected: 1976
Total receipts: $8,022,510
Total from PACs: $1,134,522

1988 Committees & Subcommittees

Energy and Natural Resources
Energy Regulation and Conservation (Chairman)
Energy Research and Development
Water and Power

Judiciary
Antitrust, Monopolies and Business Rights (Chairman)
Constitution
Courts and Administrative Practice

Labor and Human Resources
Labor (Chairman)
Aging
Handicapped

Aging
Health and Long-Term Care
Human Services

PAC Contribution Profile

Business

Air Transport/Air Freight **$15,000**

    Federal Express Corp $10,000
    Others $5,000

Entertainment Industry **$20,085**
    None over $4,000

Food & Beverage **$16,750**
    None over $5,500

Health Professionals **$43,000**
    American Podiatry Assn $10,000
    Others $33,000

Lawyers & Lobbyists **$60,250**
    Assn of Trial Lawyers of America $10,000
    Kirkland & Ellis $10,000
    Opperman & Paquin $10,000
    Akin, Gump, Hauer & Feld $6,000
    Fine, Kaplan & Black $6,000
    Others $18,250

Securities/Commodities Investment **$26,000**
    None over $5,500

Telecommunications **$22,500**
    AT&T $10,000
    Others $12,500

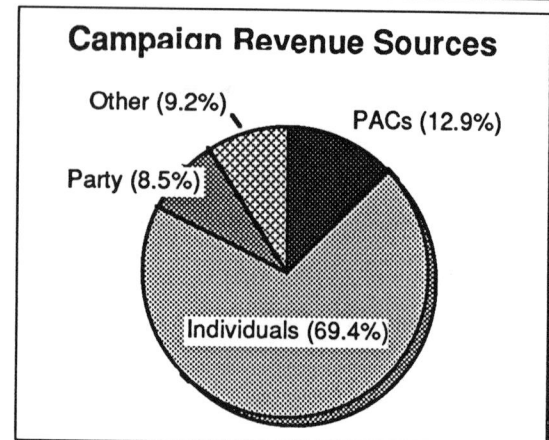

Campaign Revenue Sources

Other (9.2%)
PACs (12.9%)
Party (8.5%)
Individuals (69.4%)

Other Major Business PACs

Philips Industries .... $10,000   Const Prod

Labor

Bldg Trades, Industrial & Misc Unions **$240,949**

    United Auto Workers* $10,999
    AFL-CIO* $10,800
    Amalgamated Clothing & Textile Workers ... $10,000
    Boilermakers Union $10,000
    Bricklayers Union $10,000
    Carpenters & Joiners Union $10,000
    Communications Workers of America $10,000
    Electronic Machine Furniture Workers $10,000
    Food & Commercial Workers Union $10,000
    Intl Brotherhood of Electrical Workers $10,000
    Laborers' Political League $10,000
    Ladies Garment Workers Union $10,000
    Machinists/Aerospace Workers Union $10,000
    Operating Engineers Union $10,000
    Rubber Cork Linoleum Plastic Workers $10,000
    Service Employees International Union $10,000
    Sheet Metal Workers Union $10,000
    United Steelworkers $10,000
    United Mine Workers $9,900
    Ironworkers Union $7,000
    Others $42,250

Government & Postal Workers **$51,000**

    American Fedn of State/County/Munic Employees $10,000
    American Postal Workers Union $10,000
    National Assn of Letter Carriers $10,000
    National Assn of Retired Federal Employees $10,000
    Others $11,000

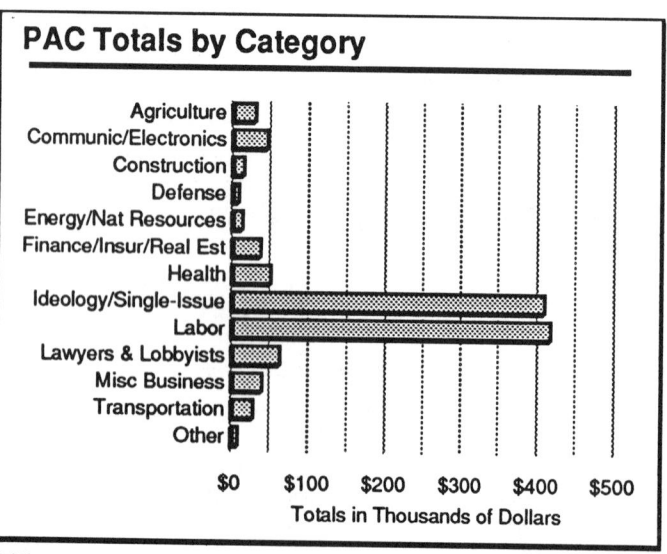

PAC Totals by Category

Agriculture
Communic/Electronics
Construction
Defense
Energy/Nat Resources
Finance/Insur/Real Est
Health
Ideology/Single-Issue
Labor
Lawyers & Lobbyists
Misc Business
Transportation
Other

$0 $100 $200 $300 $400 $500

Totals in Thousands of Dollars

Teachers Unions $20,000

American Federation of Teachers $10,000
National Education Assn $10,000

Transportation Unions $102,300

Air Line Pilots Assn $10,000
Amalgamated Transit Union $10,000
Marine Engineers Union $10,000
Seafarers International Union $10,000
United Transportation Union $10,000
Maintenance of Way Employees $8,500
Transport Workers Union $8,000
Transportation Communication Union $7,500
Assn of Flight Attendants $6,000
Others $22,300

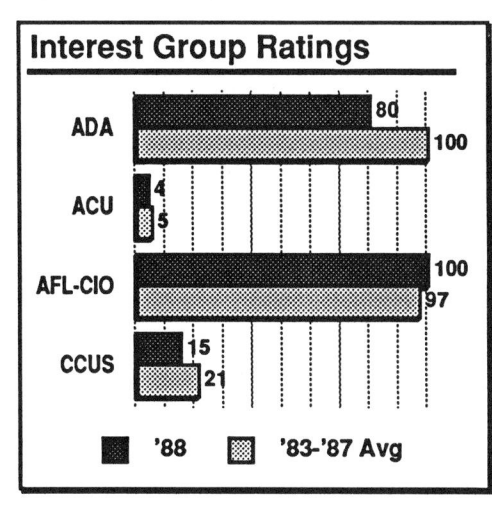

Ideological/Single-Issue

Democratic/Liberal $37,796

Democrats for The 80's $10,000
Religion and Tolerance PAC $10,000
National Cmte for an Effective Congress $9,996
Others $7,800

Democratic Leadership PACs $57,500

Campaign for American (Frank Lautenberg) $10,000
Committee for a Demo Consensus (Alan Cranston) $10,000
Senate Majority Fund (Daniel Inouye) $10,000
Independent Action (Morris Udall) $7,000
Others $20,500

Pro-Choice $15,000

National Abortion Rights Action League $10,000
Voters for Choice/Friends of Family Planning $5,000

Pro-Israel $246,085

Citizens Organized PAC $10,000
Delaware Valley PAC $10,000
Desert Caucus $10,000
Florida Congressional Committee $10,000
Garden State PAC $10,000
Hudson Valley PAC $10,000
Joint Action Cmte for Political Affairs $10,000
Maryland Assn for Concerned Citizens $10,000
MOPAC $10,000
Multi-Issue PAC $10,000
National PAC $10,000
Ocean State PAC $10,000
Pacific PAC $10,000
San Franciscans for Good Government $10,000
Washington PAC $10,000
Arizona Politically Interested Citizens $8,000
National Action Committee $8,000
Sacramento Area Good Government Assn $8,000
Heartland PAC $7,500
Mid Manhattan PAC $7,500
Others $57,085

Other Major Ideological/Single-Issue PACs

Natl Cmte to Preserve Social Security	$10,000	Soc Secur
Sierra Club	$9,936	Environment
Handgun Control Inc	$7,500	Anti-Guns
Council for a Livable World	$6,743	Pro-Peace

Independent expenditures supporting Metzenbaum

National Cmte to Preserve Social Security $45,060

Independent expenditures opposing Metzenbaum

Americans United $343,978
Life Amendment PAC $18,455
Mid-America Conservative PAC $17,489
Ruff PAC $17,466
Conservative Victory Committee $12,379

---

* Contributions came from more than one PAC affiliated
  with this sponsor.

George J. Mitchell (D-Maine)

First elected: 1980
Total receipts: $1,943,629
Total from PACs: $804,969

1988 Committees & Subcommittees

Environment and Public Works
Environmental Protection (Chairman)
Nuclear Regulation
Water Resources, Transportation and Infrastructure

Finance
Health (Chairman)
Social Security and Family Policy
International Trade

Governmental Affairs
Governmental Efficiency, Federalism and the District of Columbia
Oversight of Government Management
Permanent Subcommittee on Investigations

Veterans' Affairs

PAC Contribution Profile

Business

Air Transport/Air Freight	**$12,250**
Aircraft Owners & Pilots Assn	$4,500
Federal Express Corp	$4,250
Others	$3,500
Broadcasting/Entertainment	**$15,000**
Warner Communications	$4,000
Others	$11,000
Construction	**$23,000**
Associated General Contractors	$5,500
Walter Industries	$4,500
National Assn of Home Builders	$4,000
Others	$9,000
Defense	**$19,500**
Bath Iron Works	$5,000
Lockheed Corp	$5,000
Others	$9,500
Financial Institutions	**$35,550**
American Bankers Assn	$10,000
Credit Union National Assn	$10,000
Others	$15,550
Food & Beverage	**$30,000**
National Beer Wholesalers Assn	$6,000
Joseph E Seagram & Sons	$4,000
Wine & Spirits Wholesalers of America	$4,000
Others	$16,000

Campaign Revenue Sources

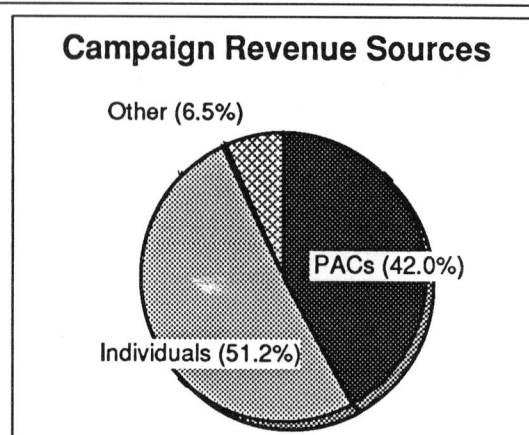

Other (6.5%)
PACs (42.0%)
Individuals (51.2%)

Health Professionals	**$56,509**
American Dental Assn	$6,500
American Podiatry Assn	$6,000
American Academy of Ophthalmology	$5,000
Anesthesia Service Medical Group	$5,000
National Assn of Pharmacists	$5,000
American Chiropractic Assn	$4,500
Co-op of American Physicians	$4,000
Others	$20,509
Hospitals & Nursing Homes	**$30,500**
American Health Care Assn	$9,500
American Hospital Assn	$5,000
Federation of American Hospitals	$5,000
Others	$11,000
Insurance	**$102,724**
National Assn of Mutual Insurance Agents	$8,500
Independent Insurance Agents of America	$7,724
Massachusetts Mutual Life Insurance	$7,500
Torchmark Corp	$7,000
National Assn of Life Underwriters	$6,500
Unum Life Insurance Company	$5,400
Equitable Financial Services	$5,000
Travelers Corp	$5,000
Blue Cross & Blue Shield Assn	$4,000
Metropolitan Life Insurance	$4,000
Prudential Insurance	$4,000
Others	$38,100
Lawyers & Lobbyists	**$21,700**
Assn of Trial Lawyers of America	$5,500
Verner, Liipfert, Bernhard & McPherson	$4,000
Others	$12,200
Pharmaceuticals	**$13,750**
Pfizer Inc	$4,000
Others	$9,750
Real Estate	**$19,500**
Mortgage Bankers Assn of America	$10,500
National Assn of Realtors	$5,000
Others	$4,000

PAC Totals by Category

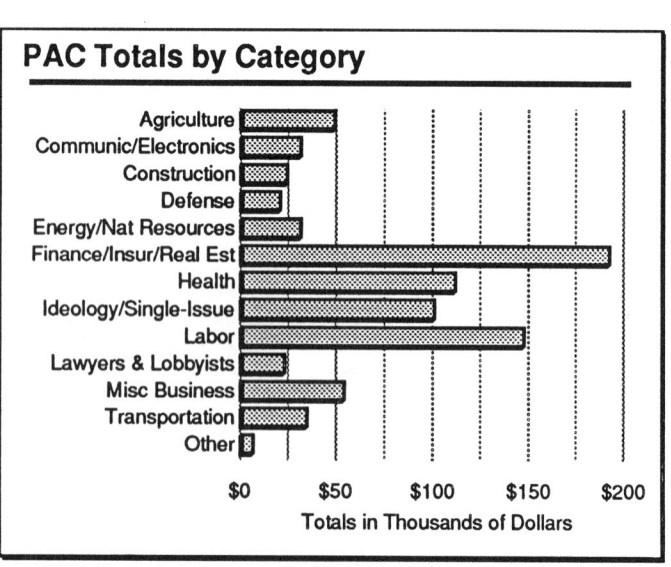

Agriculture
Communic/Electronics
Construction
Defense
Energy/Nat Resources
Finance/Insur/Real Est
Health
Ideology/Single-Issue
Labor
Lawyers & Lobbyists
Misc Business
Transportation
Other

$0 $50 $100 $150 $200

Totals in Thousands of Dollars

Securities/Commodities Investment **$26,500**
    E F Hutton Group $6,000
    First Boston Corp $5,000
    Others $15,500

Sugar Growers **$11,500**
    None over $3,250

Telecommunications **$12,250**
    AT&T $5,000
    Others $7,250

Tobacco **$11,000**
    Philip Morris $5,000
    Others $6,000

Other Major Business PACs

American Institute of CPA's	$6,000	Accountants
National Assn for Home Care	$5,000	Home Care
Auto Dealers & Drivers for Free Trade	$4,000	JapanAutoSal
Dun & Bradstreet	$4,000	Mkt Research
Henley Group Inc	$4,000	Altern Energy

Labor

Bldg Trades, Industrial & Other Unions **$71,500**
    AFL-CIO* $10,000
    Machinists/Aerospace Workers Union $10,000
    Communications Workers of America $5,000
    Ladies Garment Workers Union $5,000
    National Education Assn $5,000
    Operating Engineers Union $5,000
    Sheet Metal Workers Union $5,000
    United Auto Workers $5,000
    Others $21,500

Government & Postal Workers **$35,800**
    American Postal Workers Union $6,000
    American Fedn of State/County/Munic Employees $5,000
    National Assn of Letter Carriers $5,000
    National Assn of Retired Federal Employees $5,000
    National Treasury Employees Union $5,000
    Others $9,800

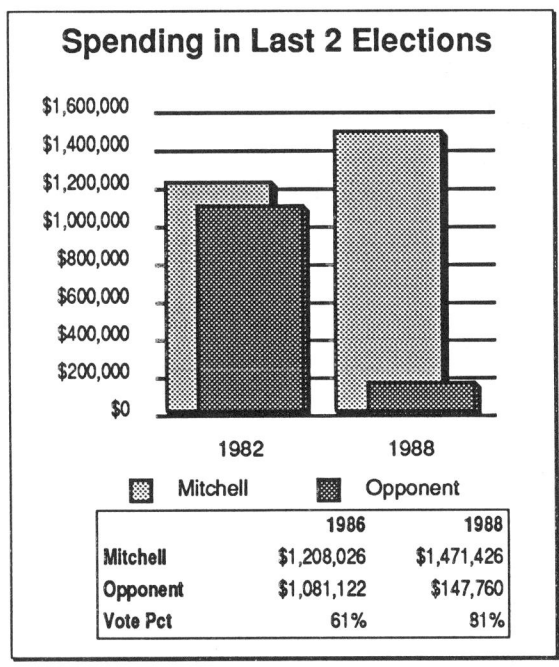

Spending in Last 2 Elections

Mitchell   Opponent

	1986	1988
Mitchell	$1,208,026	$1,471,426
Opponent	$1,081,122	$147,760
Vote Pct	61%	81%

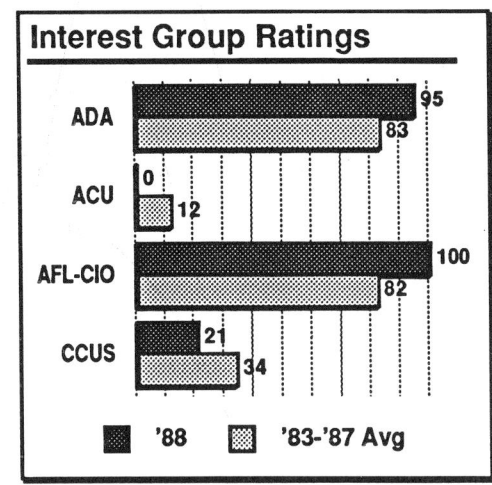

Interest Group Ratings

ADA — 95 ('88), 83 ('83–'87 Avg)
ACU — 0 ('88), 12 ('83–'87 Avg)
AFL-CIO — 100 ('88), 82 ('83–'87 Avg)
CCUS — 21 ('88), 34 ('83–'87 Avg)

■ '88   ▨ '83-'87 Avg

Transportation Unions **$39,000**
    Marine Engineers Union $10,000
    Air Line Pilots Assn $6,000
    Maintenance of Way Employees $5,000
    United Transportation Union $5,000
    Others $13,000

Ideological/Single-Issue

Democratic/Liberal **$10,034**
    Democrats for The 80's $5,000
    National Cmte for an Effective Congress $3,497
    Others $1,537

Democratic Leadership PACs **$10,020**
    Committee for a Demo Consensus (Alan Cranston) $5,000
    Fund for a Democratic Majority (Edward Kennedy) $5,000
    Others $20

Pro-Israel **$61,000**
    Citizens Organized PAC $10,000
    Desert Caucus $10,000
    Pacific PAC $10,000
    Hudson Valley PAC $6,500
    National PAC $5,000
    San Franciscans for Good Government $5,000
    Others $14,500

Other Major Ideological/Single-Issue PACs

Council for a Livable World	$6,300	Pro-Peace
Free Cuba PAC	$5,000	Anti-Castro
KidsPAC	$5,000	Health/Welfare

Independent expenditures supporting Mitchell

League of Conservation Voters	$8,731
National Cmte to Preserve Social Security	$3,390

---

* Contributions came from more than one PAC affiliated
  with this sponsor.

Daniel Patrick Moynihan (D-NY)

First elected: 1976
Total receipts: $5,811,946
Total from PACs: $1,225,712

1988 Committees & Subcommittees

Environment and Public Works
Water Resources, Transportation and Infrastructure (Chairman)
Environmental Protection
Nuclear Regulation

Finance
Social Security and Family Policy (Chairman)
International Trade
Taxation and Debt Management

Foreign Relations
Near Eastern and South Asian Affairs
Terrorism, Narcotics and International Operations

Rules and Administration

Joint Library

Joint Taxation

PAC Contribution Profile

Business

Broadcasting/Movies	**$25,700**
Gulf + Western Industries	$10,000
Others	$15,700
Commercial Banks	**$95,255**
American Bankers Assn*	$13,000
Manufacturers Hanover	$11,585
Chemical Bank	$10,370
J P Morgan & Company	$10,000
Citicorp	$9,000
Bankers Trust	$6,500
Marine Midland Banks	$6,000
Norstar Bancorp	$6,000
Chase Manhattan*	$5,900
Irving Bank	$5,000
Others	$11,900
Construction	**$38,500**
Associated General Contractors	$10,000
National Utility Contractors Assn	$9,000
National Assn of Home Builders	$5,000
Others	$14,500
Electric Utilities & Equipment	**$25,350**
None over $2,600	
Health Professionals	**$68,680**
New York Medical Assn	$10,000
American Academy of Ophthalmology	$9,000
Assn for Advancement of Psychology	$7,680
American Physical Therapy Assn	$5,000
American Society of Cataract & Refractive Surgery	$5,000
Others	$32,000

Campaign Revenue Sources

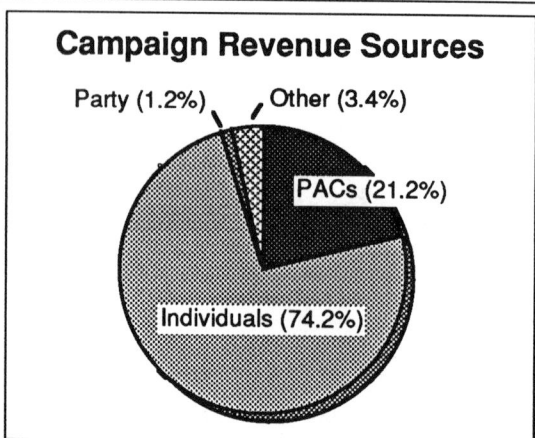

Party (1.2%) Other (3.4%)
PACs (21.2%)
Individuals (74.2%)

Insurance	**$84,987**
Metropolitan Life Insurance	$10,175
Continental Insurance	$9,812
Equitable Financial Services	$6,000
Travelers Corp	$5,500
American Council of Life Insurance	$5,000
Mutual Life Insurance of New York	$5,000
National Assn of Life Underwriters	$5,000
Others	$38,500
Lawyers & Lobbyists	**$47,050**
Assn of Trial Lawyers of America	$10,000
Verner, Liipfert, Bernhard & McPherson	$6,500
Others	$30,550
Pharmaceuticals	**$32,100**
Pfizer Inc	$5,100
Others	$27,000
Savings Banks	**$45,394**
US League of Savings Assn	$9,000
Dime Savings Bank of New York	$5,844
National Council of Savings Institutions	$5,000
Others	$25,550
Securities/Commodities Investment	**$121,178**
E F Hutton Group	$10,000
First Boston Corp	$10,000
Investment Company Institute	$9,822
PaineWebber	$7,750
Shearson Lehman Hutton	$7,500
Drexel Burnham Lambert	$7,000
Morgan Stanley & Company	$6,000
Salomon Brothers	$6,000
Bear, Stearns & Company	$5,000
Goldman Sachs	$5,000
Merrill Lynch	$5,000
Others	$42,106
Telecommunications	**$32,600**
NYNEX*	$10,600
AT&T	$8,000
Others	$14,000

PAC Totals by Category

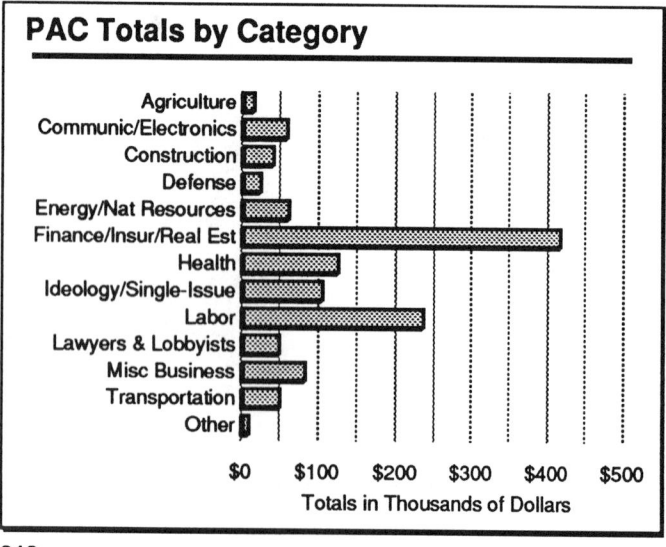

Agriculture
Communic/Electronics
Construction
Defense
Energy/Nat Resources
Finance/Insur/Real Est
Health
Ideology/Single-Issue
Labor
Lawyers & Lobbyists
Misc Business
Transportation
Other

$0 $100 $200 $300 $400 $500
Totals in Thousands of Dollars

Other Major Business PACs

American Institute of CPA's	$10,000	Accountants
Avon Products	$10,000	Cosmetics
Grumman	$10,000	Air Defense
National Venture Capital Assn	$10,000	Venture Cap
Triangle Industries	$10,000	Cans
Federal Express Corp	$9,000	Air Freight
American Hospital Assn*	$7,000	Hospitals
National Assn of Realtors	$7,000	RE Sales
American Health Care Assn	$6,000	Nursing Home
Arthur Young & Company	$5,000	Accountants
Mobil Oil	$5,000	Major Oil
Union Pacific Corp	$5,000	Railroads

Labor

Bldg Trades, Industrial & Other Unions	**$128,504**
Carpenters Union*	$10,000
Ladies Garment Workers Union	$10,000
Service Employees International Union	$10,000
AFL-CIO*	$9,954
Intl Brotherhood of Electrical Workers	$8,500
Communications Workers of America	$8,000
Operating Engineers Union*	$7,500
Sheet Metal Workers Union	$7,000
Laborers Union*	$6,250
United Steelworkers	$6,000
Amalgamated Clothing & Textile Workers*	$5,000
Bricklayers Union	$5,000
Food & Commercial Workers Union	$5,000
Ironworkers Union	$5,000
Machinists/Aerospace Workers Union	$5,000
National Education Assn	$5,000
Others	$15,300
Government & Postal Workers	**$34,500**
National Assn of Letter Carriers	$9,000
American Fedn of State/County/Munic Employees	$5,000
American Postal Workers Union	$5,000
National Assn of Retired Federal Employees	$5,000
Others	$10,500

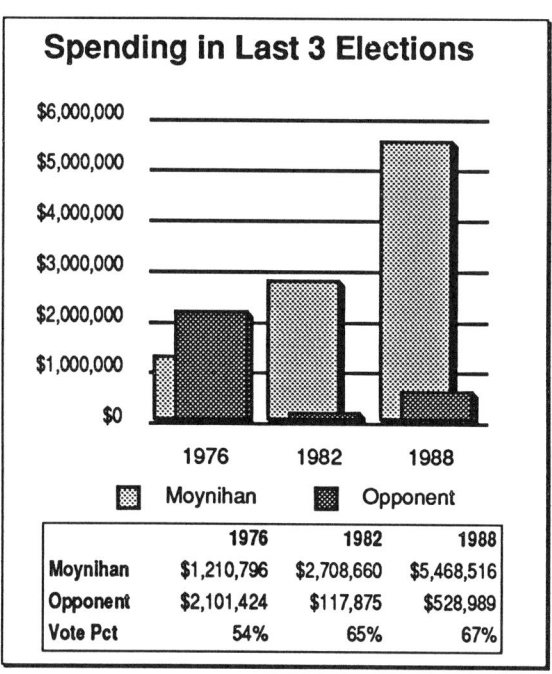

Spending in Last 3 Elections

	1976	1982	1988
Moynihan	$1,210,796	$2,708,660	$5,468,516
Opponent	$2,101,424	$117,875	$528,989
Vote Pct	54%	65%	67%

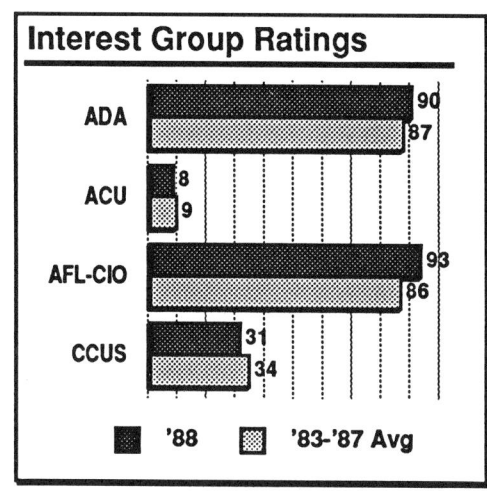

Interest Group Ratings

	'88	'83-'87 Avg
ADA	90	87
ACU	8	9
AFL-CIO	93	86
CCUS	31	34

Transportation Unions	**$65,550**
Air Line Pilots Assn	$10,000
Teamsters Union	$10,000
Transport Workers Union*	$10,000
United Transportation Union	$10,000
Marine Engineers Union*	$6,000
Amalgamated Transit Union	$5,000
Others	$14,550

Ideological/Single-Issue

Pro-Israel	**$33,000**
Washington PAC	$9,000
Chicagoans for Better Congress	$5,000
Citizens Concerned for the National Interest	$5,000
National PAC	$5,000
Others	$9,000

Other Major Ideological/Single-Issue PACs

National Cmte for an Effective Congress	$9,990	Dem/Liberal
National Cmte to Preserve Social Security	$7,000	Elderly
Religion and Tolerance PAC	$6,000	Dem/Liberal
Democrats for the 80's	$5,000	Dem/Liberal
Human Rights Campaign Fund	$5,000	Gay Rights
KidsPAC	$5,000	Health/Welfare

Independent expenditures supporting Moynihan

National Cmte to Preserve Social Security	$63,570

Independent expenditures opposing Moynihan

National Conservative PAC	$8,722
Council for National Defense	$6,044

* Contributions came from more than one PAC affiliated with this sponsor.

Donald W. Riegle Jr. (D-Mich)

First elected: 1976
Total receipts: $4,186,389
Total from PACs: $1,536,168

1988 Committees & Subcommittees

Banking, Housing and Urban Affairs
Securities (Chairman)
Housing and Urban Affairs

Budget

Commerce, Science and Transportation
Science, Technology and Space (Chairman)
Foreign Commerce and Tourism
Surface Transportation

Finance
Health
International Debt
International Trade

PAC Contribution Profile

Business

Accountants	**$25,000**
American Institute of CPA's	$10,000
Others	$15,000
Automotive	**$35,350**
Chrysler Corp	$8,100
National Auto Dealers Assn	$6,000
Others	$21,250
Aviation & Aerospace	**$41,100**
Boeing Company	$6,000
Others	$35,100
Commercial Banks	**$113,975**
American Bankers Assn*	$10,200
J P Morgan & Company	$10,000
Citicorp	$9,000
Bankers Trust	$7,000
Manufacturers Hanover	$6,250
Independent Bankers Assn	$6,000
Others	$65,525
Construction	**$26,000**
National Assn of Home Builders	$10,000
Others	$16,000
Food & Beverage	**$44,500**
National Beer Wholesalers Assn	$9,000
Joseph E Seagram & Sons	$6,000
Others	$29,500

Campaign Revenue Sources

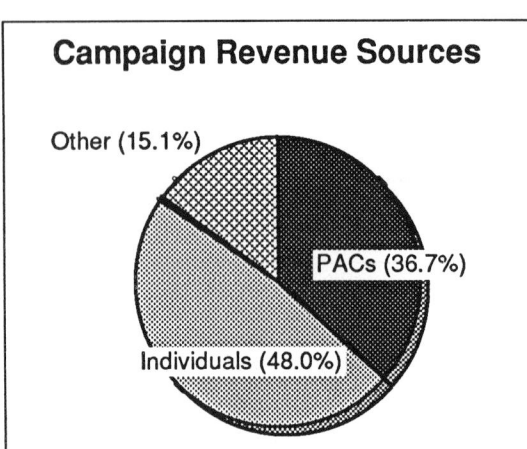

Other (15.1%)
PACs (36.7%)
Individuals (48.0%)

Health Professionals	**$52,150**
American Podiatry Assn	$7,500
American Academy of Ophthalmology	$6,000
American Society of Cataract & Refractive Surgery	$6,000
Assn for Advancement of Psychology	$6,000
Others	$26,650
Insurance	**$129,200**
Independent Insurance Agents of America	$10,000
National Assn of Life Underwriters	$10,000
National Assn of Mutual Insurance Agents	$10,000
TransAmerica Corp*	$10,000
Casualty & Surety Agents Assn	$9,000
Others	$80,200
Lawyers & Lobbyists	**$48,159**
Assn of Trial Lawyers of America	$10,000
Others	$38,159
Oil & Gas	**$21,275**
None over $5,750	
Real Estate	**$41,450**
Mortgage Bankers Assn of America	$10,000
National Assn of Realtors	$9,250
Others	$22,200
Savings Banks	**$66,325**
Columbia Savings & Loan (Beverly Hills)	$10,000
Home Savings of America	$10,000
Mercury Savings & Loan	$10,000
US League of Savings Assn*	$10,000
Others	$26,325
Securities/Commodities Investment	**$150,649**
Chicago Board of Trade	$10,000
Chicago Mercantile Exchange	$10,000
First Boston Corp	$10,000
Morgan Stanley & Company	$10,000
Drexel Burnham Lambert	$8,000
E F Hutton Group	$8,000
Shearson Lehman Hutton	$7,000
Oppenheimer Holdings Inc	$6,500
Others	$81,149

PAC Totals by Category

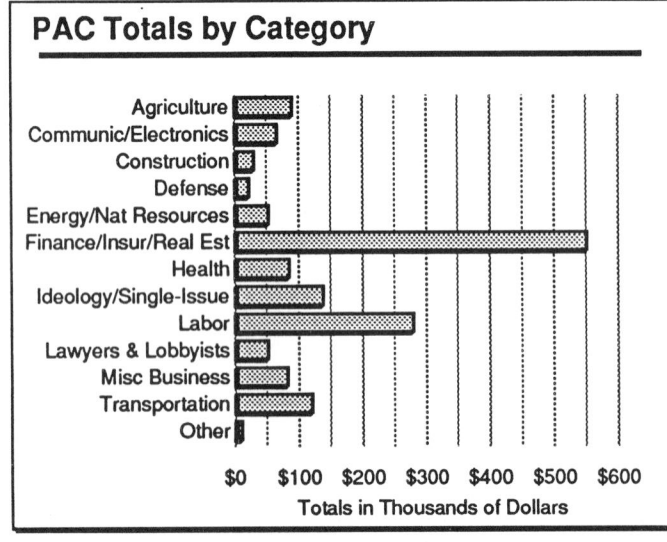

Agriculture
Communic/Electronics
Construction
Defense
Energy/Nat Resources
Finance/Insur/Real Est
Health
Ideology/Single-Issue
Labor
Lawyers & Lobbyists
Misc Business
Transportation
Other

$0 $100 $200 $300 $400 $500 $600
Totals in Thousands of Dollars

Telecommunications **$38,154**
     AT&T $10,000
     Michigan Bell Telephone $8,304
     Others $19,850

Trucking/Delivery **$26,801**
     American Trucking Assns $7,601
     Others $19,200

Other Major Business PACs

Credit Union National Assn*	$10,000	Credit Union
Triangle Industries	$10,000	Cans
Rockwell International	$8,600	Air Defense
Consumers Power Company	$8,200	Gas & Electr
Philip Morris	$7,500	Tobacco
Associated Milk Producers	$7,000	Dairy
American Hospital Assn	$6,500	Hospitals
Fidelity Management Research Company	$6,000	Finance Svcs
National Venture Capital Assn	$6,000	Venture Cap

Labor

Bldg Trades, Industrial & Other Unions **$163,950**
     AFL-CIO* $12,750
     National Education Assn $11,200
     Communications Workers of America $11,100
     Carpenters & Joiners Union $10,000
     Food & Commercial Workers Union $10,000
     Machinists/Aerospace Workers Union $10,000
     United Auto Workers $10,000
     Boilermakers Union* $9,100
     Intl Brotherhood of Electrical Workers $8,500
     Laborers' Political League $8,000
     Operating Engineers Union* $7,125
     Ironworkers Union $7,000
     Electronic Machine Furniture Workers $6,000
     Others $43,175

Government & Postal Workers **$46,200**
     American Fedn of State/County/Munic Employees $10,000
     National Assn of Retired Federal Employees $10,000
     American Postal Workers Union $7,000
     National Assn of Letter Carriers $6,000
     Others $13,200

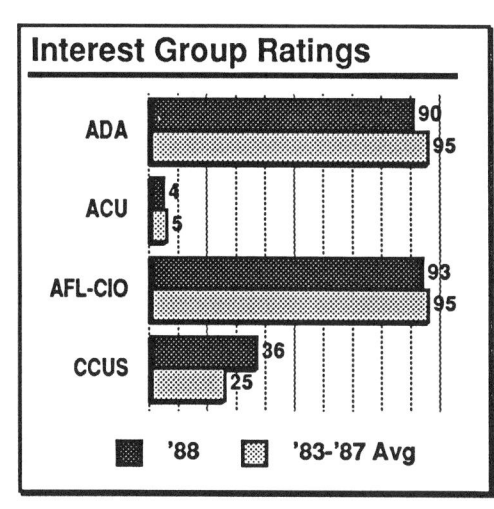

Interest Group Ratings

	'88	'83-'87 Avg
ADA	90	95
ACU	4	5
AFL-CIO	93	95
CCUS	36	25

■ '88   ▨ '83-'87 Avg

Transportation Unions **$65,500**
     Air Line Pilots Assn $10,000
     Marine Engineers Union* $10,000
     Seafarers International Union $10,000
     Teamsters Union $10,000
     Amalgamated Transit Union $6,000
     United Transportation Union $6,000
     Others $13,500

Ideological/Single-Issue

Democratic/Liberal **$21,090**
     Democrats for The 80's $10,000
     National Cmte for an Effective Congress $9,990
     Others $1,100

Democratic Leadership PACs **$24,000**
     Senate Majority Fund (Daniel Inouye).....................$10,000
     Fund for a Democratic Majority (Edward Kennedy) $6,000
     Others $8,000

Pro-Israel **$54,750**
     Citizens Organized PAC $10,000
     Others $44,750

Other Major Ideological/Single-Issue PACs

National Cmte to Preserve Social Security	$10,000	Elderly
KidsPAC	$6,000	Health/Welfare

Independent expenditures supporting Riegle

National Cmte to Preserve Social Security $37,790

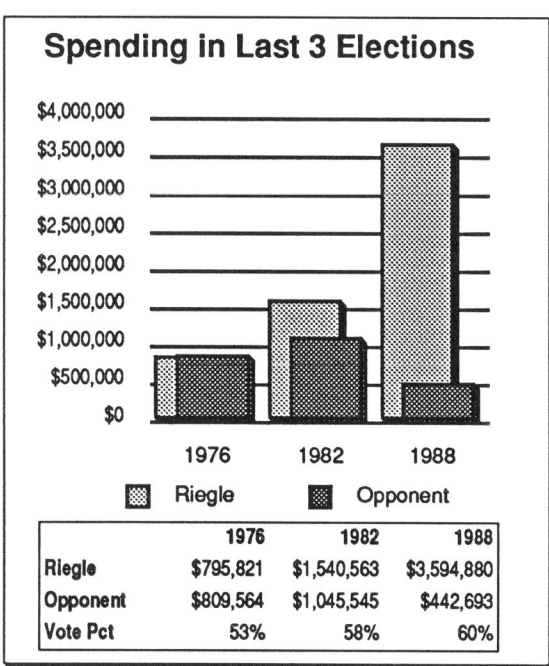

Spending in Last 3 Elections

	1976	1982	1988
Riegle	$795,821	$1,540,563	$3,594,880
Opponent	$809,564	$1,045,545	$442,693
Vote Pct	53%	58%	60%

▨ Riegle   ■ Opponent

---

* Contributions came from more than one PAC affiliated
with this sponsor.

215

Charles S. Robb (D-Va)

First elected: 1988
Total receipts: $3,198,630
Total from PACs: $911,763

1989-90 Committees & Subcommittees

Budget

Commerce, Science and Transportation
Consumer
National Ocean Policy Study
Science, Technology and Space
Surface Transportation

Foreign Relations
Near Eastern and South Asian Affairs
Terrorism, Narcotics and International Operations
Western Hemisphere and Peace Corps Affairs

PAC Contribution Profile

Business

Aviation & Air Freight	**$18,000**
Federal Express Corp	$9,000
Aircraft Owners & Pilots Assn	$4,000
Others	$5,000
Construction	**$36,350**
Associated General Contractors	$10,000
National Assn of Home Builders	$10,000
Others	$16,350
Defense	**$61,500**
Textron Inc	$10,000
BDM International	$5,000
TRW Inc	$5,000
Atlantic Research Corp	$4,000
Lockheed Corp	$4,000
Mantech International	$4,000
Others	$29,500
Electric Utilities	**$24,550**
Dominion Resources Inc	$10,000
Others	$14,550
Financial Institutions	**$48,200**
US League of Savings Assn	$6,000
American Bankers Assn	$5,000
Credit Union National Assn	$5,000
Virginia Bankers Assn	$5,000
Crestar Financial Corp	$4,000
Signet Bank	$4,000
Others	$19,200

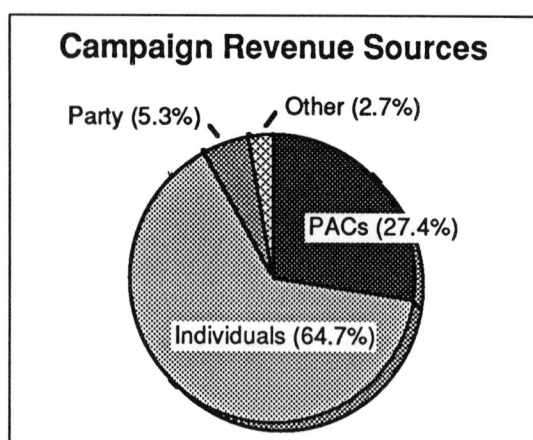

Campaign Revenue Sources

Party (5.3%)
Other (2.7%)
PACs (27.4%)
Individuals (64.7%)

Food & Beverage	**$38,050**
Food Marketing Institute	$5,000
General Mills*	$5,000
Others	$28,050
Forest Products	**$15,000**
Westvaco Corp	$5,000
Others	$10,000
Health Professionals	**$39,584**
American Medical Assn	$9,000
American Academy of Ophthalmology	$7,500
American Dental Assn	$5,000
American Optometric Assn	$5,000
Others	$13,084
Insurance	**$53,253**
National Assn of Life Underwriters	$10,000
Consolidated Healthcare Inc	$8,000
Independent Insurance Agents of America	$5,753
American Family Corp	$5,000
Others	$24,500
Lawyers & Lobbyists	**$31,700**
Assn of Trial Lawyers of America	$5,000
Kutak, Rock & Campbell	$4,000
Others	$22,700
Oil & Gas	**$52,847**
Amoco Corp	$5,000
Mobil Oil	$5,000
Others	$42,847
Real Estate	**$21,250**
National Assn of Realtors	$10,000
Century 21 Real Estate	$4,000
Others	$7,250
Securities/Commodities Investment	**$32,500**
Chicago Board of Trade	$5,000
Chicago Mercantile Exchange	$5,000
Merrill Lynch	$5,000
Shearson Lehman Hutton	$5,000
Others	$12,500

PAC Totals by Category

Agriculture
Communic/Electronics
Construction
Defense
Energy/Nat Resources
Finance/Insur/Real Est
Health
Ideology/Single-Issue
Labor
Lawyers & Lobbyists
Misc Business
Transportation
Other

$0 $25 $50 $75 $100 $125 $150 $175

Totals in Thousands of Dollars

Telecommunications	$32,500
AT&T	$10,000
Continental Telecom	$4,000
Others	$18,500

Television/Entertainment	$17,000
MCA Inc	$5,000
National Cable Television Assn	$5,000
Others	$7,000

Tobacco	$16,500
Philip Morris	$5,000
RJR Nabisco	$4,000
Others	$7,500

Trucking & Railroads	$15,000
Union Pacific Corp	$5,000
American Trucking Assns	$4,000
Others	$6,000

Other Major Business PACs

American Institute of CPA's	$5,000	Accountants
Associated Milk Producers	$5,000	Dairy
Chambers Development Company	$5,000	Waste Mgmt
National Auto Dealers Assn	$5,000	Auto Sales
Emhart Corp	$4,955	Indust Equip
Pittston Company	$4,250	Coal Mining
Abbott Laboratories	$4,000	Pharmaceut
Browning-Ferris Industries	$4,000	Waste Mgmt
Computer Sciences Corp	$4,000	Data Process
Orbital Sciences Corp	$4,000	Aerospace Equip

Labor

Bldg Trades, Industrial & Other Unions	$60,200
National Education Assn	$10,000
Carpenters & Joiners Union	$8,500
Intl Brotherhood of Electrical Workers	$7,500
Laborers' Political League	$7,000
AFL-CIO	$5,000
Food & Commercial Workers Union	$5,000
Others	$17,200

Government & Postal Workers	$24,250
National Assn of Retired Federal Employees	$7,000
American Fedn of State/County/Munic Employees	$5,000
National Assn of Letter Carriers	$5,000
Others	$7,250

Transportation Unions	$42,050
Marine Engineers Union*	$10,000
Seafarers International Union	$10,000
Teamsters Union*	$5,250
Air Line Pilots Assn	$5,000
United Transportation Union	$5,000
Others	$6,800

Ideological/Single-Issue

Democratic Leadership PACs	$22,500
Committee for a Demo Consensus (Alan Cranston)	$10,000
Pelican PAC (Bennett Johnston)	$5,000
Senate Majority Fund (Daniel Inouye)	$5,000
Others	$2,500

Pro-Israel	$33,000
National PAC	$10,000
Citizens Organized PAC	$5,000
Washington PAC	$5,000
Others	$13,000

Other Major Ideological/Single-Issue PACs $16,000

Democrats for The 80's	$6,000	Dem/Liberal
Free Cuba PAC	$5,000	ForeignPolcy
National Cmte to Preserve Social Security	$5,000	Elderly

Independent expenditures supporting Robb

National Cmte to Preserve Social Security	$20,154

Spending in Last Election

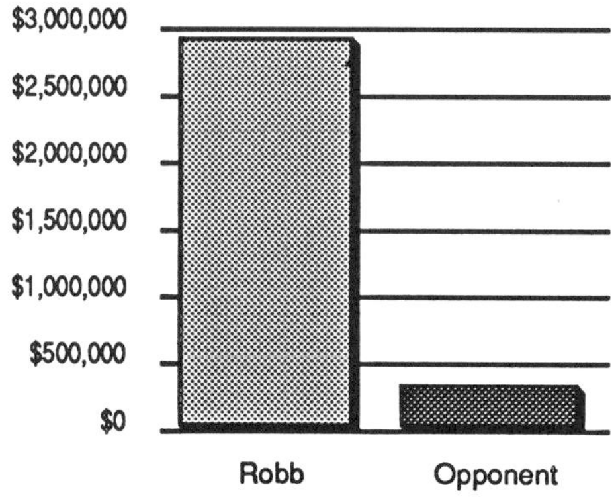

	1988
Robb	$2,881,666
Opponent	$292,229
Vote Pct	71%

---

* Contributions came from more than one PAC affiliated with this sponsor.

217

William V. Roth Jr. (R-Del)

Total receipts: $2,014,352

First elected: 1970
Total receipts: $2,014,352
Total from PACs: $875,041

1988 Committees & Subcommittees

Finance
International Debt (Ranking Republican)
International Trade
Taxation and Debt Management

Governmental Affairs
Permanent Subcommittee on Investigations (Ranking Republican)

Select Intelligence

Joint Economic
Economic Goals and Intergovernmental Policy
Economic Growth, Trade and Taxes
International Economic Policy

PAC Contribution Profile

Business

Accountants **$17,000**
American Institute of CPA's $10,000
Others $7,000

Air Transport/Air Freight **$11,400**
Federal Express Corp $4,400
Others $7,000

Automotive **$28,750**
National Auto Dealers Assn $10,000
Auto Dealers & Drivers for Free Trade $7,000
Chrysler Corp $4,000
Others $7,750

Chemicals **$13,500**
FMC Corp $4,000
Others $9,500

Commercial Banks **$55,950**
American Bankers Assn $10,000
J P Morgan & Company $9,000
Marine Midland Banks $6,000
Citicorp $5,000
Chemical Bank $4,500
Manufacturers Hanover $3,200
Others $18,250

Construction **$38,250**
Associated General Contractors $10,000
Associated Builders & Contractors $5,000
National Electrical Contractors Assn $5,000
National Utility Contractors Assn $4,500
Others $13,750

Campaign Revenue Sources

Party (5.0%)
Other (4.1%)
PACs (40.6%)
Individuals (50.3%)

Consumer Credit & Loans **$10,750**
Beneficial Management Corp $5,000
Household International $3,250
Others $2,500

Defense **$35,350**
Harris Corp $10,000
Tenneco Inc $5,000
Allied-Signal $4,500
Others $15,850

Food & Beverage **$40,500**
National Restaurant Assn $7,000
S & A Restaurant Corp $6,000
National Beer Wholesalers Assn $4,000
Others $23,500

Forest Products **$15,600**
Westvaco Corp $6,000
International Paper Company $5,000
Others $4,600

Health Professionals **$40,500**
American Academy of Ophthalmology $12,000
American Medical Assn $10,000
American Optometric Assn $4,000
American Dental Assn $3,800
Others $10,700

Insurance **$101,300**
American International Group Inc $10,000
National Assn of Independent Insurers $10,000
American Family Corp $8,000
National Assn of Life Underwriters $6,000
Torchmark Corp $6,000
Cigna Corp $5,000
Independent Insurance Agents of America $5,000
Health Insurance Assn of America $4,500
American Council of Life Insurance $4,000
Others $42,800

PAC Totals by Category

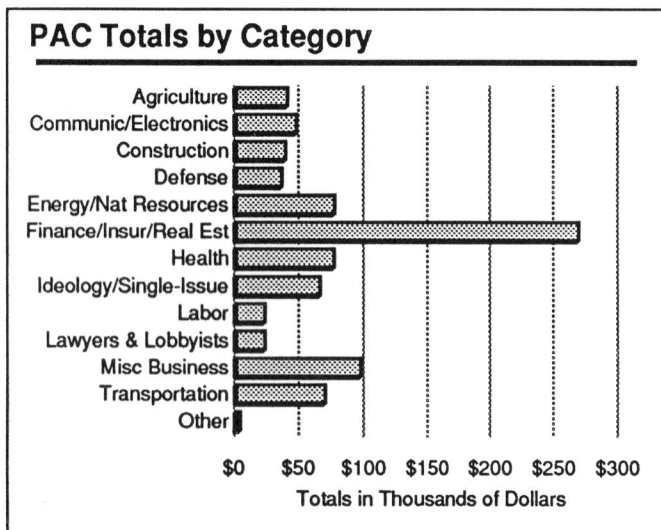

Agriculture
Communic/Electronics
Construction
Defense
Energy/Nat Resources
Finance/Insur/Real Est
Health
Ideology/Single-Issue
Labor
Lawyers & Lobbyists
Misc Business
Transportation
Other

$0 $50 $100 $150 $200 $250 $300
Totals in Thousands of Dollars

218

Lawyers & Lobbyists **$22,125**

    Assn of Trial Lawyers of America $10,000
    Others $12,125

Oil & Gas **$52,950**

    Amoco Corp $5,000
    Columbia Gas* $5,000
    Texaco $5,000
    Others $37,950

Pharmaceuticals **$24,500**

    Squibb Corp $4,000
    Others $20,500

Real Estate **$13,500**

    National Assn of Realtors $6,500
    Others $7,000

Retail Sales **$10,207**

    None over $3,000

Savings Banks & Credit Unions **$12,500**

    US League of Savings Assn $7,500
    Others $5,000

Securities/Commodities Investment **$49,250**

    Securities Industry Assn $5,250
    E F Hutton Group $5,000
    Merrill Lynch $5,000
    Salomon Brothers $5,000
    Others $29,000

Telecommunications **$30,650**

    Bell Atlantic* $8,000
    AT&T $7,400
    Others $15,250

Trucking/Delivery **$16,750**

    United Parcel Service $5,000
    Others $11,750

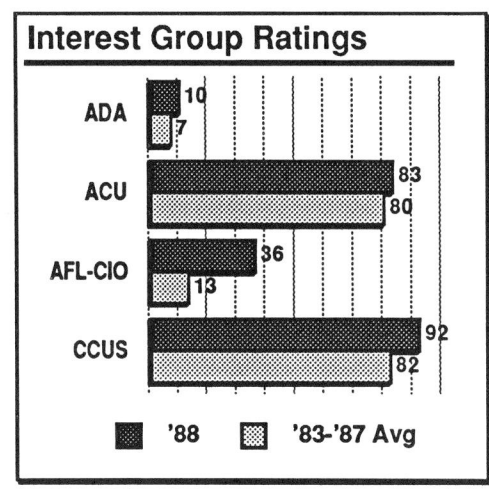

Other Major Business PACs

National Venture Capital Assn	$10,000	Venture Cap
American Assn of Equipment Lessors	$5,000	Rentals
Union Pacific Corp	$5,000	Railroads
American Health Care Assn	$4,750	Nursing Home
Avon Products	$4,000	Cosmetics
Cyprus Minerals Company	$4,000	Mining/Metals
General Electric	$4,000	Electronics

Labor

Government & Postal Workers **$21,000**

    National Assn of Retired Federal Employees $6,000
    National Assn of Letter Carriers $5,000
    Others $10,000

Ideological/Single-Issue

Pro-Israel **$13,500**

    Washington PAC $6,000
    Delaware Valley PAC $5,000
    Others $2,500

Republican Leadership PACs **$20,000**

    Republican Majority Fund (Richard Lugar) $10,000
    Catch the Spirit PAC (Bob Kasten) $5,000
    Campaign America (Bob Dole) $4,000
    Others $1,000

Other Major Ideological/Single-Issue PACs

Public Service Research Council	$10,000	Anti-Union
National Rifle Assn	$7,950	Pro-Guns
Council for National Defense	$5,605	Pro-Defense

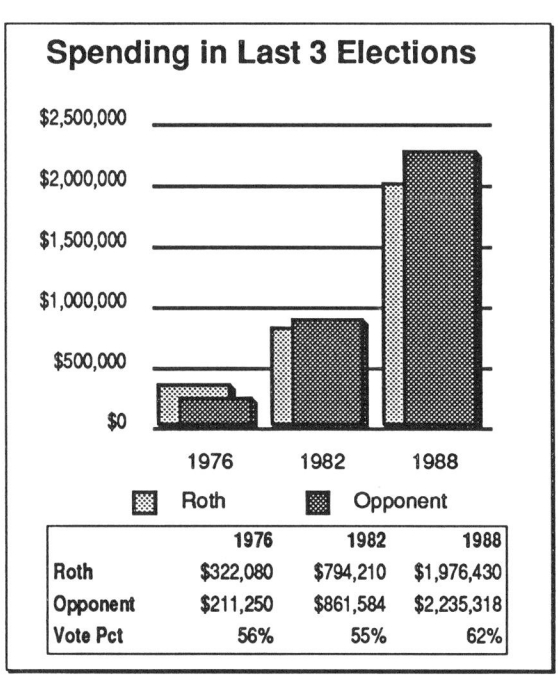

* Contributions came from more than one PAC affiliated
  with this sponsor.

Paul S. Sarbanes (D-Md)

First elected: 1976
Total receipts: $1,591,927
Total from PACs: $617,597

1988 Committees & Subcommittees

Banking, Housing and Urban Affairs
Housing and Urban Affairs
International Finance and Monetary Policy (Chairman)

Foreign Relations
Near Eastern and South Asian Affairs (Chairman)
European Affairs

Joint Economic (Chairman)
International Economic Policy (Chairman)
Investment, Jobs and Prices
National Security Economics

PAC Contribution Profile

Business

Accountants **$7,950**

    American Institute of CPA's $5,000
    Others $2,950

Automotive **$6,300**

    Chrysler Corp $4,000
    Others $2,300

Aviation & Aerospace **$8,000**

    Aircraft Owners & Pilots Assn $4,000
    Others $4,000

Construction **$19,750**

    National Assn of Home Builders $10,000
    Westvaco Corp $6,000
    Others $3,750

Consumer Credit & Loans **$6,000**

    None over $2,000

Dairy Producers **$7,000**

    Associated Milk Producers $3,000
    Dairymen Inc $3,000
    Others $1,000

Financial Institutions **$26,700**

    US League of Savings Assn $6,000
    American Bankers Assn $5,000
    Independent Bankers Assn $3,500
    Others $12,200

Campaign Revenue Sources

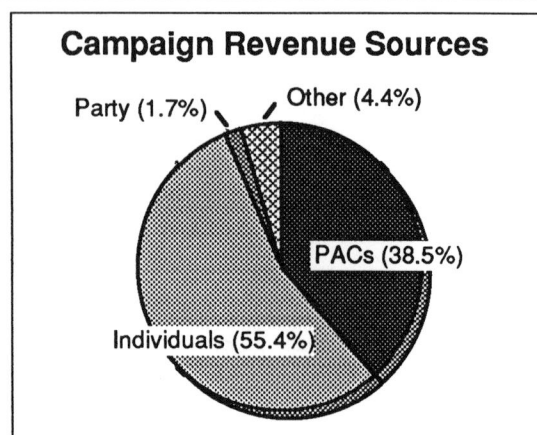

Party (1.7%)
Other (4.4%)
PACs (38.5%)
Individuals (55.4%)

Food & Beverage **$14,000**

    National Beer Wholesalers Assn $9,000
    Joseph E Seagram & Sons $4,000
    Others $1,000

Health Professionals **$7,000**

    None over $2,000

Insurance **$27,800**

    Independent Insurance Agents of America $8,000
    National Assn of Life Underwriters $7,500
    Casualty & Surety Agents Assn $4,000
    Travelers Corp $3,000
    Others $5,300

Lawyers **$17,000**

    Assn of Trial Lawyers of America $10,000
    Others $7,000

Securities/Commodities Investment **$29,750**

    Investment Company Institute $10,000
    First Boston Corp $5,000
    Alex Brown Inc $4,000
    Others $10,750

Telecommunications **$5,750**

    None over $1,750

Trucking/Delivery **$8,600**

    American Trucking Assns $3,500
    United Parcel Service $3,000
    Others $2,100

Other Major Business PACs

Triangle Industries .... $5,000   Cans
ACRE (Action Cmte for Rural Electric) .... $3,000   Rural Elect
Bethlehem Steel .... $3,000   Steel
General Electric .... $3,000   Electronics

PAC Totals by Category

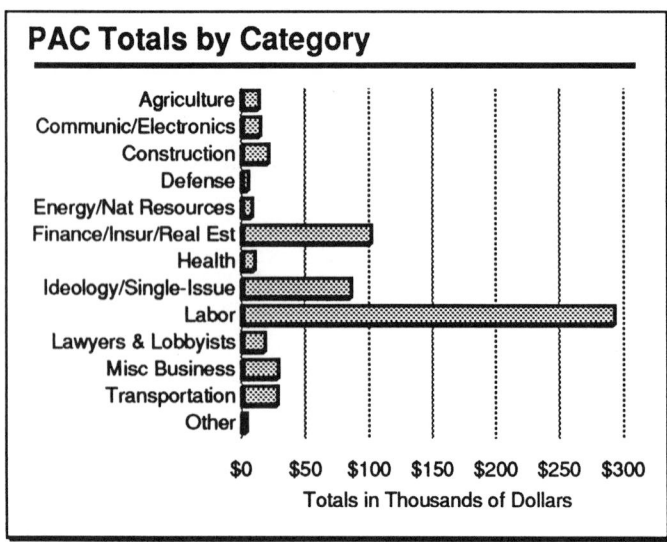

Agriculture
Communic/Electronics
Construction
Defense
Energy/Nat Resources
Finance/Insur/Real Est
Health
Ideology/Single-Issue
Labor
Lawyers & Lobbyists
Misc Business
Transportation
Other

$0 $50 $100 $150 $200 $250 $300

Totals in Thousands of Dollars

Labor

Bldg Trades, Industrial & Misc Unions.....................$136,825

Carpenters & Joiners Union $10,000
Intl Brotherhood of Electrical Workers.............$10,000
Sheet Metal Workers Union $10,000
United Auto Workers $10,000
United Steelworkers $10,000
Communications Workers of America............$7,500
Food & Commercial Workers Union................$7,100
AFL-CIO* $7,000
Boilermakers Union $7,000
Laborers' Political League $7,000
Ladies Garment Workers Union $7,000
Machinists/Aerospace Workers Union $7,000
Operating Engineers Union $7,000
Clothing/Textile Workers-Baltimore................$4,500
Plumbers/Pipefitters Union $4,000
Baltimore Bldg & Construction Trades Council $3,500
Bricklayers Union $3,000
Others $15,225

Government & Postal Workers $60,447

American Fedn of State/County/Munic Employees $14,497
National Assn of Letter Carriers $10,000
National Assn of Retired Federal Employees $10,000
American Postal Workers Union $8,000
National Rural Letter Carriers Assn $5,000
American Fedn of Government Employees $3,700
Others $9,250

Teachers Unions $20,000

American Federation of Teachers $10,000
National Education Assn $10,000

Spending in Last 3 Elections

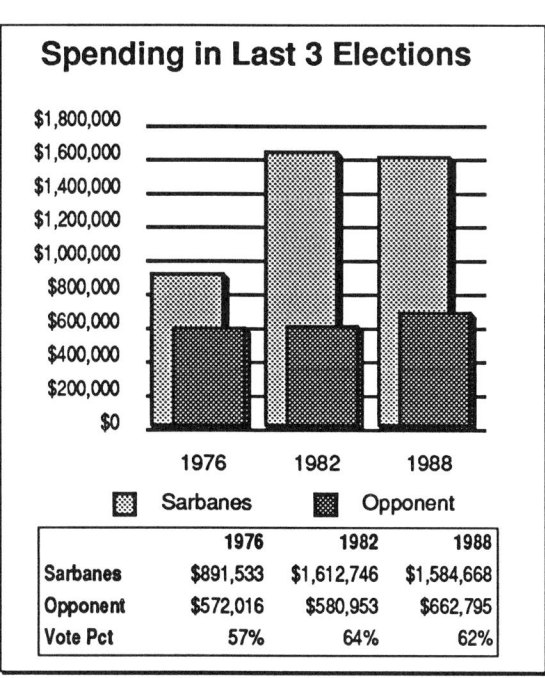

	1976	1982	1988
Sarbanes	$891,533	$1,612,746	$1,584,668
Opponent	$572,016	$580,953	$662,795
Vote Pct	57%	64%	62%

Interest Group Ratings

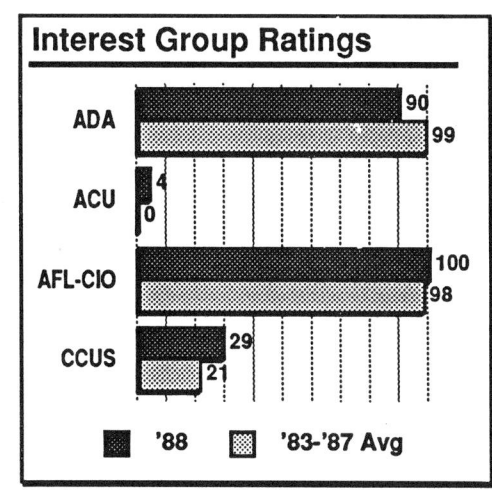

	'88	'83-'87 Avg
ADA	90	99
ACU	4	0
AFL-CIO	100	98
CCUS	29	21

Transportation Unions $74,000

Marine Engineers Union* $11,000
Masters, Mates & Pilots Union* $10,000
Seafarers International Union.........................$10,000
Teamsters Union $10,000
United Transportation Union $7,500
Air Line Pilots Assn.......................................$5,000
International Longshoremen Assn $5,000
Transportation Communication Union............$4,500
Amalgamated Transit Union $4,000
Others $7,000

Ideological/Single-Issue

Democratic/Liberal $11,533

Democrats for The 80's $5,000
National Cmte for an Effective Congress $4,996
Others $1,537

Democratic Leadership PACs.............................$15,000

Pelican PAC (Bennett Johnston) $5,000
Senate Majority Fund (Daniel Inouye) $5,000
Committee for a Demo Consensus (Alan Cranston)........$3,500
Others $1,500

Ethnic PACs $10,700

Dynamis $8,500
Others $2,200

Pro-Israel $38,000

Washington PAC $10,000
Hudson Valley PAC $6,000
National PAC $5,000
St Louisians for Better Government $5,000
Others $12,000

Other Major Ideological/Single-Issue PACs

KidsPAC ....$3,500   Health/Welfare

Independent expenditures supporting Sarbanes

National Cmte to Preserve Social Security $15,526

---

* Contributions came from more than one PAC affiliated
  with this sponsor.

Jim Sasser (D-Tenn)

1988 Committees & Subcommittees

First elected: 1976
Total receipts: $3,705,296
Total from PACs: $1,620,300

Appropriations
Military Construction (Chairman)
Agriculture, Rural Development and Related Agencies
Commerce, Justice, and State, the Judiciary and Related Agencies
Defense
Energy and Water Development

Banking, Housing and Urban Affairs
Housing and Urban Affairs
Securities

Budget

Governmental Affairs
Government Efficiency, Federalism and the District of Columbia
(Chairman)
Federal Services, Post Office and Civil Service
Permanent Subcommittee on Investigations

Small Business
Export Expansion (Chairman)
Government Contracting and Paperwork Reduction

PAC Contribution Profile

Business

Automotive	**$23,500**
Auto Dealers & Drivers for Free Trade	$11,000
National Auto Dealers Assn	$10,500
Others	$2,000
Commercial Banks	**$105,440**
American Bankers Assn*	$10,000
First American Corp	$10,000
First Tennessee National Corp	$10,000
J P Morgan & Company	$7,500
Citicorp	$7,000
Independent Bankers Assn	$6,750
Others	$54,190
Construction	**$73,200**
National Assn of Home Builders	$10,000
National Electrical Contractors Assn	$7,000
Sheet Metal/Air Conditioning Contractors	$6,500
Others	$49,700
Dairy Producers	**$22,000**
Dairymen Inc-Tennessee	$8,000
Associated Milk Producers	$6,500
Others	$7,500

Campaign Revenue Sources

Candidate (1.5%)
Other (3.5%)
PACs (44.1%)
Individuals (50.4%)

Defense	**$146,750**
Boeing Company	$12,000
Westinghouse Electric	$10,200
Textron Inc	$10,000
Martin Marietta Corp	$8,500
McDonnell Douglas*	$8,250
General Dynamics	$7,500
Long Island Aerospace PAC	$7,000
Lockheed Corp	$6,900
Others	$76,400
Food & Beverage	**$74,450**
National Beer Wholesalers Assn	$10,000
Others	$64,450
Health Professionals	**$59,615**
American Medical Assn	$15,000
American Dental Assn	$10,500
National Assn of Pharmacists	$7,490
Others	$26,625
Hospitals & Nursing Homes	**$29,250**
None over $5,500	
Insurance	**$112,600**
National Assn of Mutual Insurance Agents	$12,000
Independent Insurance Agents of America	$11,050
National Assn of Life Underwriters	$9,500
Casualty & Surety Agents Assn	$7,500
Others	$72,550
Lawyers & Lobbyists	**$45,550**
Assn of Trial Lawyers of America	$10,000
Others	$35,550
Oil & Gas	**$26,750**
None over $4,000	
Real Estate	**$32,000**
Mortgage Bankers Assn of America	$11,500
National Assn of Realtors	$10,000
Others	$10,500

PAC Totals by Category

Agriculture
Communic/Electronics
Construction
Defense
Energy/Nat Resources
Finance/Insur/Real Est
Health
Ideology/Single-Issue
Labor
Lawyers & Lobbyists
Misc Business
Transportation
Other

$0 $100 $200 $300 $400
Totals in Thousands of Dollars

Savings Banks & Credit Unions $32,600
- US League of Savings Assn $9,500
- Credit Union National Assn $6,750
- Others $16,350

Securities/Commodities Investment $88,850
- Investment Company Institute $10,500
- E F Hutton Group $10,000
- First Boston Corp $10,000
- Chicago Mercantile Exchange $9,500
- Others $48,850

Telecommunications $26,100
- South Central Bell Telephone $8,000
- AT&T $7,500
- Others $10,600

Tobacco $30,479
- United States Tobacco Company $7,000
- Philip Morris $6,979
- Others $16,500

Trucking/Delivery $27,729
- United Parcel Service $8,000
- Others $19,729

Other Major Business PACs

Federal Express Corp	$10,500	Air Freight
American Institute of CPA's	$10,000	Accountants

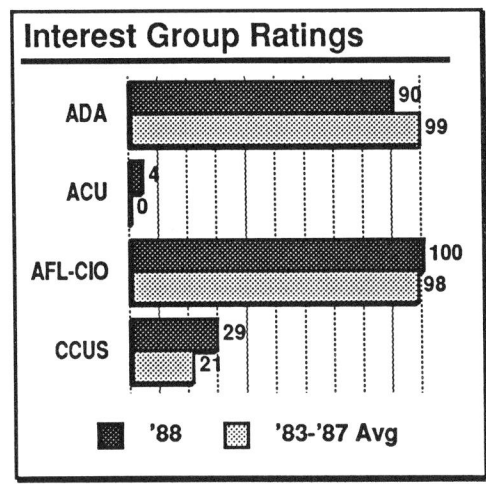

Interest Group Ratings

	'88	'83-'87 Avg
ADA	90	99
ACU	4	0
AFL-CIO	100	98
CCUS	29	21

■ '88   ▧ '83-'87 Avg

Labor

Bldg Trades, Industrial & Other Unions $156,850
- AFL-CIO* $10,300
- Communications Workers of America $10,000
- Machinists/Aerospace Workers Union $10,000
- Operating Engineers Union $10,000
- Sheet Metal Workers Union $10,000
- United Auto Workers $10,000
- United Steelworkers $10,000
- National Education Assn $9,500
- Carpenters & Joiners Union $8,500
- Laborers' Political League $8,500
- Amalgamated Clothing & Textile Workers $7,000
- American Federation of Teachers $7,000
- Electronic Machine Furniture Workers $6,500
- Others $39,550

Government & Postal Workers $74,500
- American Fedn of State/County/Munic Employees $11,000
- National Assn of Letter Carriers $11,000
- American Postal Workers Union $10,500
- National Assn of Retired Federal Employees $10,000
- National Assn of Postmasters $7,000
- National Rural Letter Carriers Assn $7,000
- Others $18,000

Transportation Unions $63,000
- Air Line Pilots Assn $10,000
- Teamsters Union $10,000
- Marine Engineers Union* $8,500
- United Transportation Union $8,000
- Amalgamated Transit Union $7,500
- Seafarers International Union $7,000
- Others $12,000

Ideological/Single-Issue

Democratic Leadership PACs $24,500
- Senate Majority Fund (Daniel Inouye) $10,000
- Others $14,500

Pro-Israel $84,000
- Citizens Organized PAC $10,000
- Desert Caucus $10,000
- Hudson Valley PAC $10,000
- Washington PAC $7,000
- Others $47,000

* Contributions came from more than one PAC affiliated
with this sponsor.

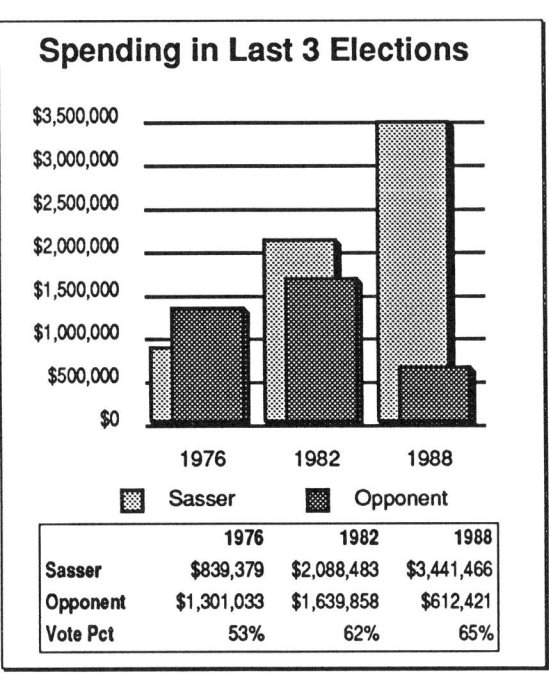

Spending in Last 3 Elections

▧ Sasser   ■ Opponent

	1976	1982	1988
Sasser	$839,379	$2,088,483	$3,441,466
Opponent	$1,301,033	$1,639,858	$612,421
Vote Pct	53%	62%	65%

Malcolm Wallop (R-Wyo)

First elected: 1976
Total receipts: $1,492,540
Total from PACs: $921,307

1988 Committees & Subcommittees

Finance
Energy and Agricultural Taxation (Ranking Republican)
International Trade
Taxation and Debt Management

Energy and Natural Resources
Public Lands, National Parks and Forests (Ranking Republican)
Mineral Resources Development and Production
Water and Power

Small Business
Competition and Antitrust Enforcement (Ranking Republican)
Export Expansion

PAC Contribution Profile

Business

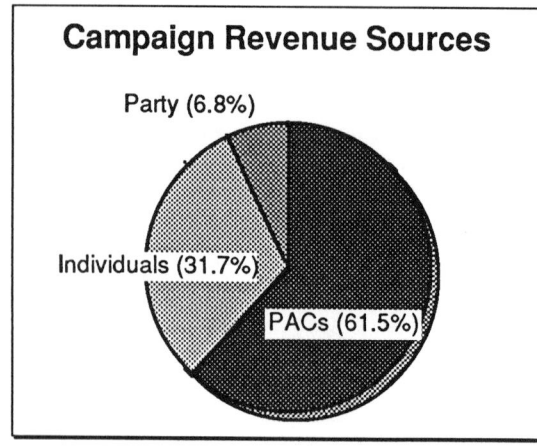

Campaign Revenue Sources

Party (6.8%)
Individuals (31.7%)
PACs (61.5%)

Accountants **$18,500**	
American Institute of CPA's $10,000	
Touche Ross $5,000	
Others $3,500	
Automotive **$20,200**	
National Auto Dealers Assn $10,000	
Auto Dealers & Drivers for Free Trade........$4,000	
Others $6,200	
Chemicals **$17,250**	
FMC Corp $10,000	
Others $7,250	
Commercial & Savings Banks **$29,033**	
American Bankers Assn $10,000	
J P Morgan & Company $8,000	
US League of Savings Assn $4,000	
Others $7,033	
Construction **$33,500**	
Associated General Contractors $10,000	
Others $23,500	

Defense **$66,861**

Harris Corp $10,000
Rockwell International $9,000
Northrop Corp $6,500
Textron Inc $6,500
TRW Inc $6,000
Martin Marietta Corp $4,286
Allied-Signal $4,000
Lockheed Corp $4,000
Others $16,575

Electric Utilities **$27,760**

Pacific Gas & Electric $5,000
Others $22,760

Food & Beverage **$43,633**

National Beer Wholesalers Assn $10,000
National Restaurant Assn $5,000
Wine & Spirits Wholesalers of America $4,000
Winn-Dixie Stores $4,000
Others $20,633

Health Professionals **$30,000**

American Medical Assn $10,000
American Academy of Ophthalmology $8,000
American Dental Assn $6,000
Others $6,000

Insurance **$80,193**

Torchmark Corp $9,834
National Assn of Independent Insurers $6,000
Aetna Life & Casualty $5,000
American Council of Life Insurance $4,000
American Family Corp $4,000
Prudential Insurance $4,000
US Fidelity & Guaranty $4,000
Others $43,359

Lawyers & Lobbyists **$30,750**

Assn of Trial Lawyers of America $4,750
Jones, Day, Reavis & Pogue $4,000
Others $22,000

Mining & Metal Processing **$29,500**

Cyprus Minerals Company $5,000
Mapco Inc $5,000
Peabody Coal $5,000
Others $14,500

PAC Totals by Category

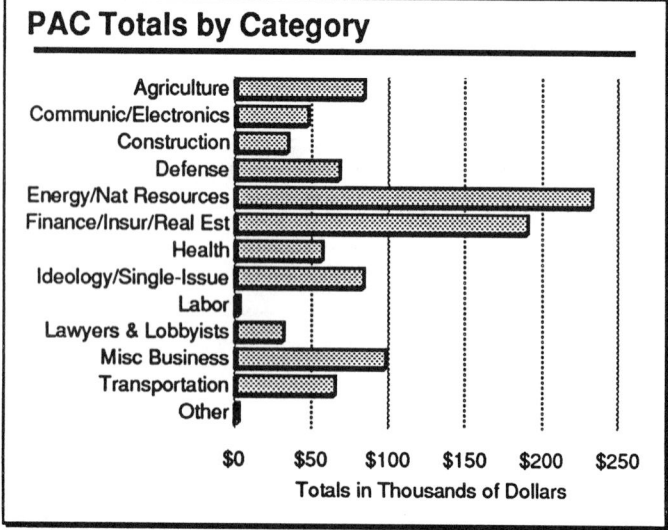

Agriculture
Communic/Electronics
Construction
Defense
Energy/Nat Resources
Finance/Insur/Real Est
Health
Ideology/Single-Issue
Labor
Lawyers & Lobbyists
Misc Business
Transportation
Other

$0 $50 $100 $150 $200 $250

Totals in Thousands of Dollars

Oil & Gas $156,967

Amoco Corp	$10,000
Atlantic Richfield	$10,000
Chevron Corp	$10,000
Union Pacific Corp	$10,000
Valero Energy Corp	$10,000
Enserch Corp	$7,500
Coastal Corp	$6,000
Exxon Corp	$5,000
Mobil Oil	$5,000
Shell Oil	$5,000
Tenneco Inc	$5,000
Texaco	$4,500
BP America	$4,000
Mesa PAC II	$4,000
Others	$60,967

Pharmaceuticals $21,500

Abbott Laboratories	$5,000
Pfizer Inc	$5,000
Eli Lilly & Company	$4,000
Others	$7,500

Securities/Commodities Investment $38,667

Merrill Lynch	$5,667
E F Hutton Group	$5,000
Chicago Board of Trade	$4,000
Drexel Burnham Lambert	$4,000
Morgan Stanley & Company	$4,000
Others	$16,000

Telecommunications $25,541

AT&T	$4,500
Others	$21,041

Tobacco $15,666

Philip Morris	$5,000
RJR Nabisco	$5,000
Others	$5,666

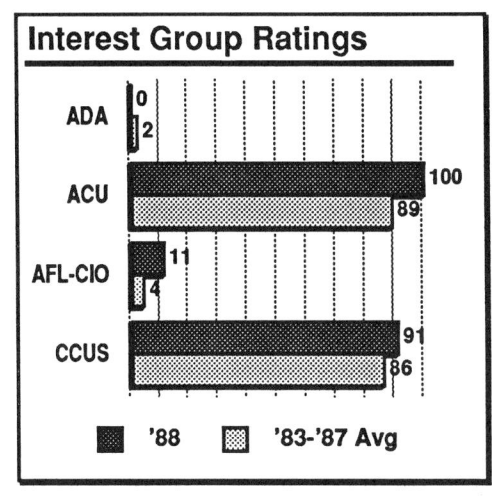

Interest Group Ratings

	'88	'83–'87 Avg
ADA	0	2
ACU	100	89
AFL-CIO	11	4
CCUS	91	86

Trucking/Delivery $20,727

United Parcel Service	$6,500
American Trucking Assns	$6,077
Others	$8,150

Other Major Business PACs

National Venture Capital Assn	$10,000	Venture Cap
National Cattlemen's Assn*	$6,000	Livestock
Waste Management Inc	$6,000	Waste Mgmt
American Horse Council	$4,500	Livestock
National Fedn of Independent Business	$4,500	Sml Business
American Assn of Equipment Lessors	$4,000	Rentals
American Crystal Sugar Corp	$4,000	Sugar
Dun & Bradstreet	$4,000	Mkt Research
Footwear Distributors PAC	$4,000	Shoes
General Electric	$4,000	NuclearEquip
Henley Group Inc	$4,000	Altern Energy
MCA Inc	$4,000	Movies
National Cable Television Assn	$4,000	CableTV

Ideological/Single-Issue

Republican Leadership PACs $34,297

Campaign America (Bob Dole)	$10,000
Republican Majority Fund (Richard Lugar)	$10,000
Fund for a Republican Majority (Ted Stevens)	$5,000
Catch the Spirit PAC (Bob Kasten)	$4,500
Others	$4,797

Other Major Ideological/Single-Issue PACs

National Rifle Assn	$8,764	Pro-Guns
Public Service Research Council	$7,000	Anti-Union
Right to Work PAC	$5,905	Anti-Union
Hudson Valley PAC	$5,233	Pro-Israel
National Security PAC	$5,009	Pro-Defense

Independent expenditures supporting Wallop

Auto Dealers & Drivers for Free Trade	$88,862
National Security PAC	$58,082

* Contributions came from more than one PAC affiliated with this sponsor.

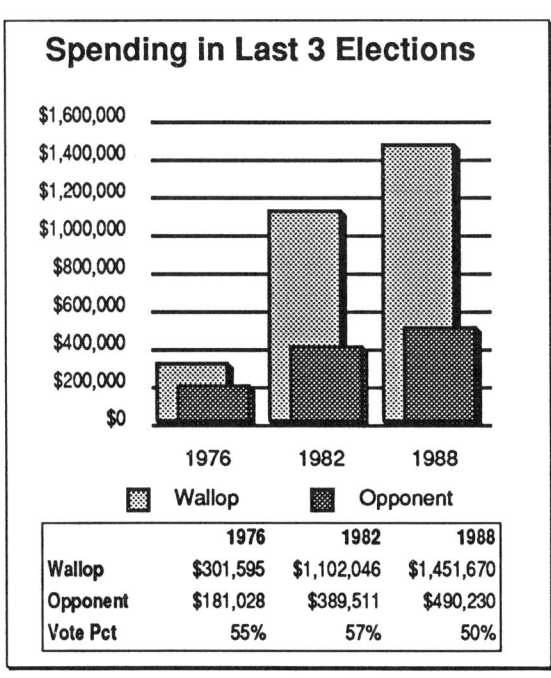

Spending in Last 3 Elections

	Wallop	Opponent

	1976	1982	1988
Wallop	$301,595	$1,102,046	$1,451,670
Opponent	$181,028	$389,511	$490,230
Vote Pct	55%	57%	50%

225

Pete Wilson (R-Calif)

1988 Committees & Subcommittees

First elected: 1982
Total receipts: $14,515,245
Total from PACs: $2,400,342

Agriculture, Nutrition and Forestry
Agricultural Research and General Legislation (Ranking Republican)
Agricultural Production and Stabilization of Prices
Domestic and Foreign Marketing and Product Promotion

Armed Services
Manpower and Personnel (Ranking Republican)
Conventional Forces and Alliance Defense
Strategic Forces and Nuclear Deterrence

Commerce, Science and Transportation
Communications
Foreign Commerce and Tourism
Science, Technology and Space
National Ocean Policy Study

Special Aging

Joint Economic
Economic Goals and Intergovernmental Policy
Education and Health
National Security Economics

PAC Contribution Profile

Business

Agricultural Chemicals	**$31,330**
Dow Chemical*	$10,000
Eli Lilly & Company	$10,000
Others	$11,330
Broadcasting/Entertainment	**$75,125**
MCA Inc	$11,000
Warner Communications	$11,000
Fox Inc	$10,000
Gulf + Western Industries	$10,000
Others	$33,125
Commercial Banks	**$72,744**
First Interstate Bank/California	$10,000
Others	$62,744
Construction	**$108,647**
Associated General Contractors	$10,000
Fluor Corp	$10,000
National Assn of Home Builders	$10,000
Sheet Metal/Air Conditioning Contractors	$10,000
Others	$68,647
Defense	**$322,309**
General Dynamics	$14,800
Northrop Corp	$13,240
McDonnell Douglas*	$11,500
Cubic Corp	$11,000
AT&T	$10,000
Continental Telecom	$10,000
(continued in next column)	

Campaign Revenue Sources

Other (3.8%)
Party (11.6%)
PACs (14.6%)
Individuals (70.1%)

Defense (cont'd)	
Harris Corp	$10,000
Litton Industries	$10,000
Lockheed Corp	$10,000
Morrison-Knudsen	$10,000
Textron Inc	$10,000
Others	$201,769
Electric Utilities	**$38,900**
Pacific Gas & Electric	$14,275
Southern California Edison	$10,000
Others	$14,625
Food & Beverage	**$102,690**
National Restaurant Assn	$10,000
Wine Institute	$9,999
Others	$82,691
Forest Products	**$57,548**
None over $7,299	
Fruit & Vegetable Growers	**$126,004**
California Almond Growers Exchange	$15,000
Sunkist Growers	$12,000
California Canning Peach Assn	$10,276
California Pistachio Assn	$10,000
Desert Grape Growers League/California	$10,000
Sun-Maid Growers of California	$9,999
Sunsweet Growers	$9,999
Others	$48,730
Health Professionals	**$62,529**
Co-op of American Physicians	$10,250
American Medical Assn	$10,000
Others	$42,279
Hospitals & Nursing Homes	**$50,158**
National Medical Enterprises Inc	$10,000
Others	$40,158

PAC Totals by Category

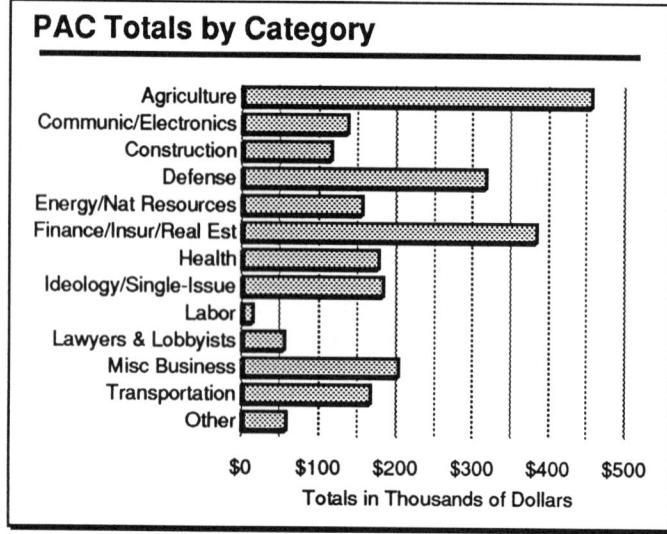

Agriculture
Communic/Electronics
Construction
Defense
Energy/Nat Resources
Finance/Insur/Real Est
Health
Ideology/Single-Issue
Labor
Lawyers & Lobbyists
Misc Business
Transportation
Other

$0 $100 $200 $300 $400 $500

Totals in Thousands of Dollars

| Insurance | .... | $84,923 |

Insurance **$84,923**
    National Assn of Independent Insurers $10,999
    TransAmerica Corp* $10,200
    Others $63,724

Lawyers & Lobbyists **$52,870**
    Irell & Manella $10,000
    Pillsbury, Madison & Sutro $10,000
    Others $32,870

Oil & Gas **$81,822**
    Atlantic Richfield $10,986
    Occidental Petroleum $10,000
    Pacific Enterprises $10,000
    Others $50,836

Pharmaceuticals **$35,779**
    Smithkline Beckman $10,000
    Others $25,779

Railroads & Railroad Services **$34,000**
    Union Pacific Corp $10,000
    Others $24,000

Real Estate **$47,254**
    Irvine Company $10,504
    National Assn of Realtors $10,500
    Kilroy Industries $10,000
    Others $16,250

Retail Sales **$39,923**
    Carter Hawley Hale Stores $15,000
    Others $24,923

Savings Banks **$107,641**
    Great Western Financial Corp $13,500
    US League of Savings Assn* $12,900
    Great American Federal Savings $10,500
    California Federal Savings & Loan $10,000
    Coast Federal Savings & Loan $10,000
    Home Federal Savings & Loan $10,000
    Others $40,741

Interest Group Ratings

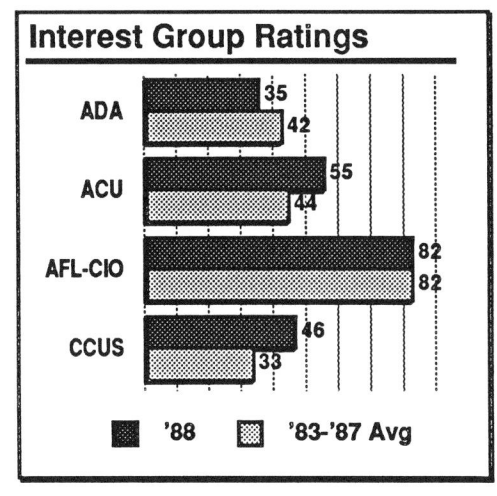

ADA — '88: 35, '83–'87 Avg: 42
ACU — '88: 55, '83–'87 Avg: 44
AFL-CIO — '88: 82, '83–'87 Avg: 82
CCUS — '88: 46, '83–'87 Avg: 33

■ '88   ▨ '83–'87 Avg

Sea Transport/Ship Repair **$37,900**
    Southwest Marine $14,500
    American President Lines $13,500
    Others $9,900

Securities/Commodities Investment **$37,012**
    Equitec Financial Group $10,000
    Others $27,012

Telecommunications **$33,286**
    Pacific Telesis Group $10,500
    Others $22,786

Other Major Business PACs

Calcot Ltd	$10,500	Cotton
Farmers' Rice Cooperative	$10,500	Crops
American Veterinary Medical Assn	$10,000	Veterinary
California Farm Bureau Federation	$10,000	Farm Orgs
Cooper Companies Inc	$10,000	Med Supply
National Auto Dealers Assn	$10,000	Auto Sales
Texas Air	$10,000	Airlines

Ideological/Single-Issue

Pro-Israel **$75,800**
    Desert Caucus $10,000
    Hudson Valley PAC $10,000
    National PAC $10,000
    St Louisians for Better Government $10,000
    Women's Pro-Israel National PAC $10,000
    Others $25,800

Republican Leadership PACs **$37,306**
    Catch the Spirit PAC (Bob Kasten) $10,000
    Others $27,306

Independent expenditures supporting Wilson

National Security PAC $58,336
Auto Dealers & Drivers for Free Trade $31,645

Spending in Last 2 Elections

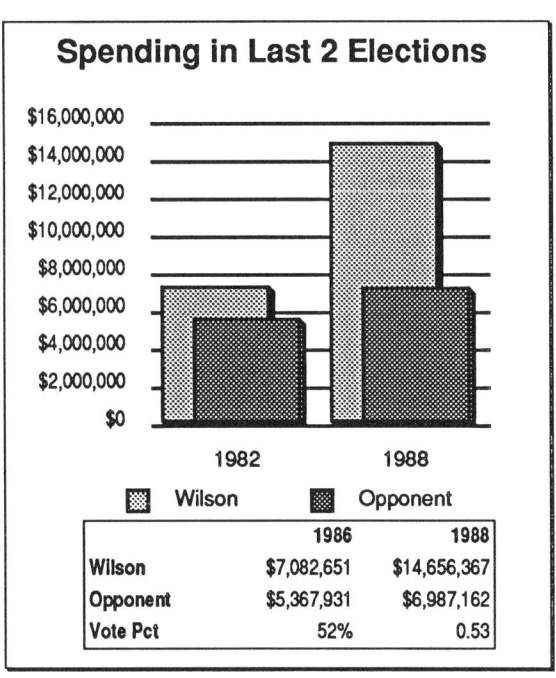

■ Wilson   ▨ Opponent

	1986	1988
Wilson	$7,082,651	$14,656,367
Opponent	$5,367,931	$6,987,162
Vote Pct	52%	0.53

* Contributions came from more than one PAC affiliated
with this sponsor.

227

Member Profiles

U.S. House of Representatives

Open Secrets

Gary L. Ackerman, D-NY (7)

First elected: 1983
Total receipts: $280,467
Total from PACs: $196,120

1988 Committees & Subcommittees

Banking, Finance and Urban Affairs
Housing and Community Development

Foreign Affairs
Asian and Pacific Affairs
Europe and the Middle East
Human Rights and International Organizations

Post Office and Civil Service
Compensation and Employee Benefits (Chairman)
Postal Personnel and Modernization

Select Hunger

PAC Contribution Profile

Business

Auto Dealers **$4,500**
    National Auto Dealers Assn $3,500
    Auto Dealers & Drivers for Free Trade $1,000

Commercial Banks **$6,150**
    American Bankers Assn $2,000
    Citicorp $1,750
    Bankers Trust $1,000
    Others $1,400

Health Professionals **$18,200**
    American Medical Assn $3,250
    American Podiatry Assn $2,500
    New York Medical Assn $2,500
    Corp for the Advancement of Psychiatry $1,750
    American Optometric Assn $1,500
    American Chiropractic Assn $1,000
    Assn for the Advancement of Psychology $1,000
    Washington Psychiatric Society $1,000
    Others $3,700

Insurance **$15,350**
    National Assn Life Underwriters $5,000
    Independent Insurance Agents of America $3,600
    CNA Financial Corp $1,500
    Blue Cross & Blue Shield Assn $1,250
    Others $4,000

Lawyers & Lobbyists **$3,500**
    Assn of Trial Lawyers of America $2,000
    Others $1,500

Campaign Revenue Sources

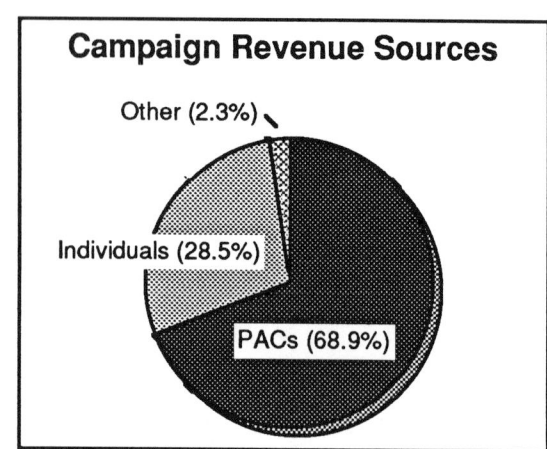

Other (2.3%)
Individuals (28.5%)
PACs (68.9%)

Package Delivery **$3,200**
    United Parcel Service $3,200

Real Estate **$4,000**
    National Assn of Realtors $3,500
    Others $500

Savings Banks **$3,500**
    Green Point Savings Bank $1,100
    US League of Savings Assn $1,000
    Others $1,400

Securities/Commodities Investment **$4,500**
    First Boston Corp $1,000
    Goldman Sachs $1,000
    Others $2,500

Other Major Business PACs

Healthcare Compare Corp .... $1,000   Financ Svcs

PAC Totals by Category

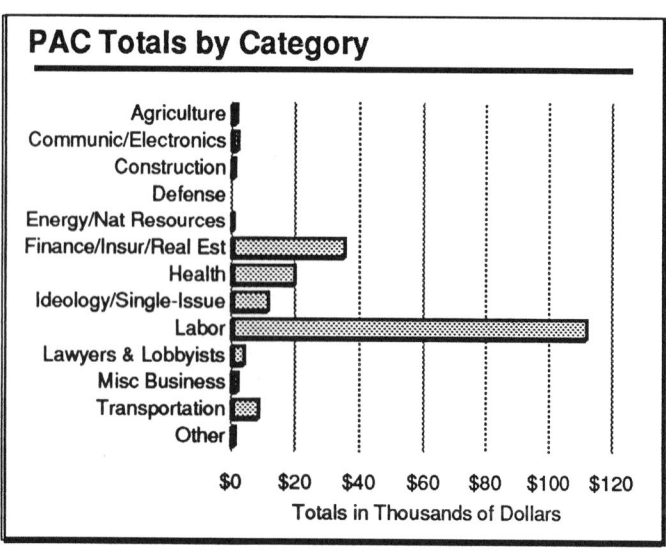

Agriculture
Communic/Electronics
Construction
Defense
Energy/Nat Resources
Finance/Insur/Real Est
Health
Ideology/Single-Issue
Labor
Lawyers & Lobbyists
Misc Business
Transportation
Other

$0 $20 $40 $60 $80 $100 $120

Totals in Thousands of Dollars

Labor

Bldg Trades/Industrial/Service Unions $27,900

Operating Engineers Local #15	$4,000
Carpenters & Joiners Union	$3,750
Intl Brotherhood of Electrical Workers	$3,200
Sheet Metal Workers Union	$2,500
AFL-CIO*	$2,250
Laborers' Political League	$2,250
Communications Workers of America	$1,500
Ladies Garment Workers Union	$1,250
United Mine Workers	$1,250
Food & Commercial Workers Union	$1,000
Machinists/Aerospace Workers Union	$1,000
Others	$3,950

Government & Postal Workers $43,900

National Assn of Letter Carriers	$10,000
National Assn of Retired Federal Employees	$10,000
American Postal Workers Union	$5,000
American Fedn of Government Employees	$4,000
National Treasury Employees Union	$3,000
American Fedn of State/County/Munic Employees	$2,000
National Federation of Federal Employees	$2,000
National Assn of Postmasters	$1,650
National Assn of Postal Supervisors	$1,500
International Assn of Firefighters	$1,250
National League of Postmasters	$1,000
National Rural Letter Carriers Assn	$1,000
Others	$1,500

Teachers Unions $8,800

National Education Assn	$4,500
American Federation of Teachers	$4,300

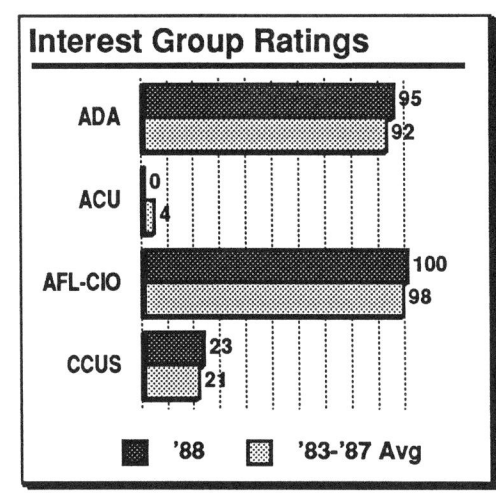

Interest Group Ratings

	'88	'83-'87 Avg
ADA	95	92
ACU	0	4
AFL-CIO	100	98
CCUS	23	21

Transportation Unions $30,650

Teamsters Union	$10,000
Marine Engineers Union*	$6,550
Air Line Pilots Assn	$2,000
Seafarers International Union	$2,000
United Transportation Union	$1,700
International Longshoremen Assn*	$1,650
Masters, Mates & Pilots Union	$1,500
Transport Workers Union	$1,500
Others	$3,750

Ideological/Single-Issue

Pro-Israel $5,750

National PAC	$5,000
Others	$750

Other Major Ideological/Single-Issue PACs

Valley Education Fund (Tony Coelho)	$2,000	Dem Leaders
National Cmte to Preserve Social Security	$1,000	Soc Secur

Independent expenditures supporting Ackerman

National Cmte to Preserve Social Security $1,604

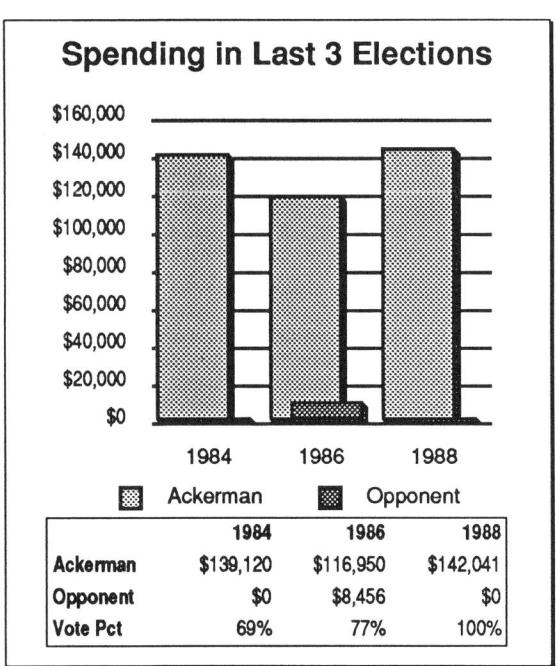

Spending in Last 3 Elections

	1984	1986	1988
Ackerman	$139,120	$116,950	$142,041
Opponent	$0	$8,456	$0
Vote Pct	69%	77%	100%

Legend: Ackerman, Opponent

* Contributions came from more than one PAC affiliated with this sponsor.

231

Daniel K. Akaka, D-Hawaii (2)

First elected: 1976
Total receipts: $255,470
Total from PACs: $81,372

1988 Committees & Subcommittees

Appropriations
Rural Development, Agriculture and Related Agencies
Treasury, Postal Service and General Government

Select Narcotics Abuse and Control

PAC Contribution Profile

Business

Construction **$1,400**
National Assn of Home Builders $1,100
Others $300

Dairy **$1,500**
Associated Milk Producers $1,000
Mid-American Dairymen $500

Electric Utilities **$2,250**
ACRE (Action Committee for Rural Electrification) $500
Public Service Company of New Mexico $500
San Diego Gas & Electric $500
Southern California Edison $500
Others $250

Financial Institutions **$9,030**
Bancorp Hawaii $2,000
First Hawaiian Inc $2,000
City Bank (Honolulu) $1,600
American Bankers Assn $1,000
Central Pacific Bank $900
Credit Union National Assn $800
US League of Savings Assn $500
Others $230

Food & Beverage **$2,200**
Wine & Spirits Wholesalers of America $1,000
A E Staley Manufacturing Company $500
Nabisco Brands Inc $500
Others $200

Fruit Growers **$2,000**
Castle & Cooke $1,000
Ocean Spray Cranberries Inc $1,000

Insurance **$1,500**
National Assn of Life Underwriters $1,000
Blue Cross & Blue Shield Assn $500

Lawyers **$3,000**
Assn of Trial Lawyers of America $2,000
Van Ness, Feldman, Sutcliffe & Curtis $500
Williams & Jensen $500

Real Estate **$7,000**
National Assn of Realtors $6,000
Bedford Properties $500
Mortgage Bankers Assn of America $500

Sea Transport **$4,500**
Matson Navigation $2,000
Alexander & Baldwin Inc $1,500
American President Lines $1,000

Sugar Growers **$1,500**
American Crystal Sugar Corp $500
American Sugarbeet Growers Assn $500
American Sugar Cane League $500

Telecommunications **$2,260**
GTE Corp* $1,260
AT&T $1,000

Campaign Revenue Sources

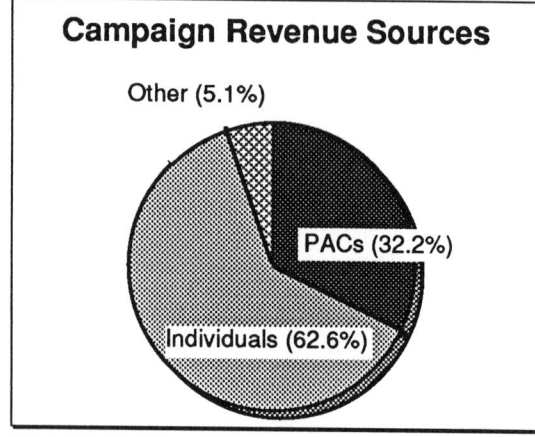

Other (5.1%)
PACs (32.2%)
Individuals (62.6%)

PAC Totals by Category

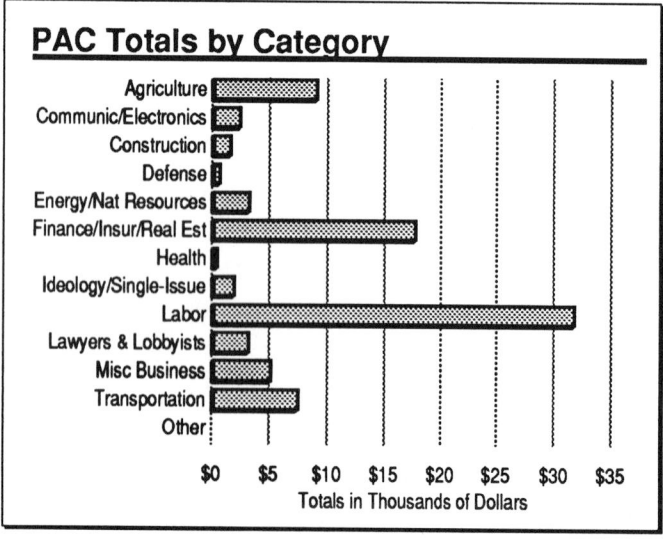

Agriculture
Communic/Electronics
Construction
Defense
Energy/Nat Resources
Finance/Insur/Real Est
Health
Ideology/Single-Issue
Labor
Lawyers & Lobbyists
Misc Business
Transportation
Other

$0 $5 $10 $15 $20 $25 $30 $35
Totals in Thousands of Dollars

Other Major Business PACs

Amfac Inc .... $1,000   Wholesale
J C Penney Company .... $1,000   Dept Store
Pirelli Cable .... $1,000   Indust Equip
American Assn of Crop Insurers .... $500   Ag Svcs
American Hotel & Motel Assn .... $500   Hotel/Motel
American Veterinary Medical Assn .... $500   Veterinary
American Trucking Assns .... $500   Trucking
Chicago Board of Trade .... $500   Commodities
Dyncorp .... $500   Air Defense
National Pest Control Assn .... $500   Pest Control
National Auto Dealers Assn .... $500   Auto Sales
Pacific Resources .... $500   Refine/Mktg
Texas Air .... $500   Airlines
Tobacco Institute .... $500   Tobacco
United Airlines .... $500   Airlines

Labor

Bldg Trades/Industrial/Misc Unions $14,350
Operating Engineers Union* $4,500
Laborers' Western Political League $4,000
Machinists/Aerospace Workers Union $1,500
United Auto Workers $1,500
Carpenters & Joiners Union $1,000
Food & Commercial Workers Union $1,000
Plumbers/Pipefitters Union $600
Others $250

Government & Postal Workers $8,950
National Assn of Retired Federal Employees $3,000
American Fedn of State/County/Munic Employees $2,000
National Assn of Letter Carriers $1,450
National Treasury Employees Union $1,000
American Federation of Government Employees $500
American Postal Workers Union $500
National Federation of Federal Employees $500

Teachers Unions $2,000
National Education Assn $2,000

Transportation Unions $6,300
Longshoremen/Warehousemen Union $2,500
Seafarers International Union $1,300
Air Line Pilots Assn $1,000
Assn of Flight Attendants $500
Transportation Communication Union $500
United Transportation Union $500

Ideological/Single-Issue

Ideological/Single-Issue PACs $1,750
Valley Education Fund (Tony Coelho) ....$1,000   Dem Leaders
National Cmte to Preserve Social Security .....$500   Soc Secur
Others $250

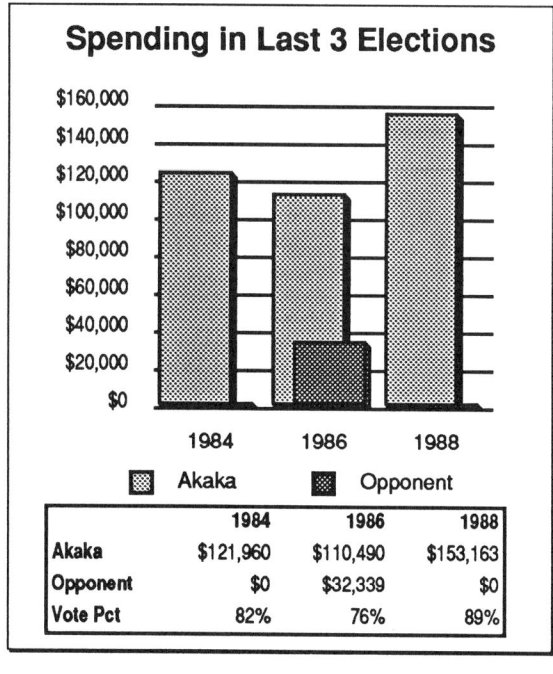

Spending in Last 3 Elections

	1984	1986	1988
Akaka	$121,960	$110,490	$153,163
Opponent	$0	$32,339	$0
Vote Pct	82%	76%	89%

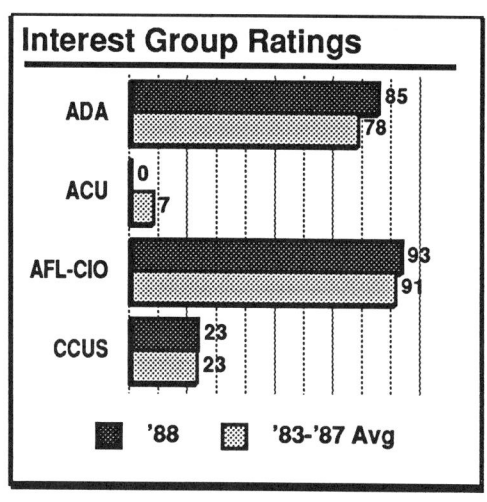

Interest Group Ratings

	'88	'83-'87 Avg
ADA	85	78
ACU	0	7
AFL-CIO	93	91
CCUS	23	23

* Contributions came from more than one PAC affiliated with this sponsor.

Bill Alexander, D-Ark (1)

First elected: 1968
Total receipts: $674,287
Total from PACs: $320,524

1988 Committees & Subcommittees

Appropriations
Commerce, Justice, State, the Judiciary and Related Agencies
Legislative Branch
Military Construction

PAC Contribution Profile

Business

Air Transport/Air Freight **$16,850**
    Federal Express Corp $10,000
    Boeing Company $3,100
    American Airlines $1,500
    Aircraft Owners & Pilots Assn $1,000
    Others $1,250

Automotive **$4,950**
    National Auto Dealers Assn $4,450
    Others $500

Commercial & Savings Banks **$5,250**
    American Bankers Assn $1,850
    US League of Savings Assn...$1,200
    Arkansas Savings & Loan League $1,000
    Independent Bankers Assn $1,000
    Others $200

Construction **$4,250**
    National Assn of Home Builders $1,500
    Associated General Contractors $1,000
    Others $1,750

Dairy **$11,200**
    Associated Milk Producers $6,500
    Mid-American Dairymen $2,500
    Dairymen Inc $1,700
    Others $500

Campaign Revenue Sources

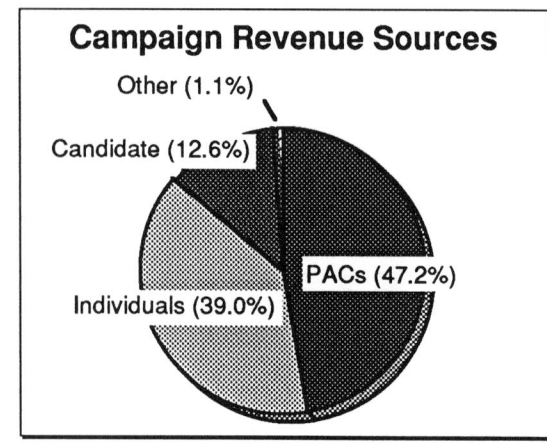

Other (1.1%)
Candidate (12.6%)
PACs (47.2%)
Individuals (39.0%)

Defense **$12,575**
    Rockwell International $2,700
    Lockheed Corp $1,850
    Textron Inc $1,500
    Hughes Aircraft $1,350
    LTV Aerospace & Defense Company $1,100
    Gencorp Inc $1,000
    Others $3,075

Electric Utilities **$5,000**
    Middle South Utilities* $4,000
    ACRE (Action Committee for Rural Electrification) $1,000

Grain Trading **$5,050**
    Archer-Daniels-Midland Corp $5,050

Health Professionals **$9,250**
    American Medical Assn $5,350
    National Assn of Pharmacists $2,400
    Others $1,500

Insurance **$10,400**
    National Assn of Life Underwriters $3,250
    American Family Corp $1,000
    Connecticut Mutual Life Insurance $1,000
    ITT Corp $1,000
    New England Mutual Life $1,000
    Others $3,150

Lawyers & Lobbyists **$10,800**
    Assn of Trial Lawyers of America $6,850
    Williams & Jensen $1,000
    Others $2,950

Sugar Growers **$5,800**
    American Sugar Cane League $2,000
    Minn-Dak Farmers Co-op $1,100
    Others $2,700

Telecommunications **$12,000**
    AT&T..$4,000
    Southwestern Bell $2,500
    GTE (Southwest) $1,750
    Continental Telecom $1,500
    US Telephone Assn..$1,000
    Others $1,250

PAC Totals by Category

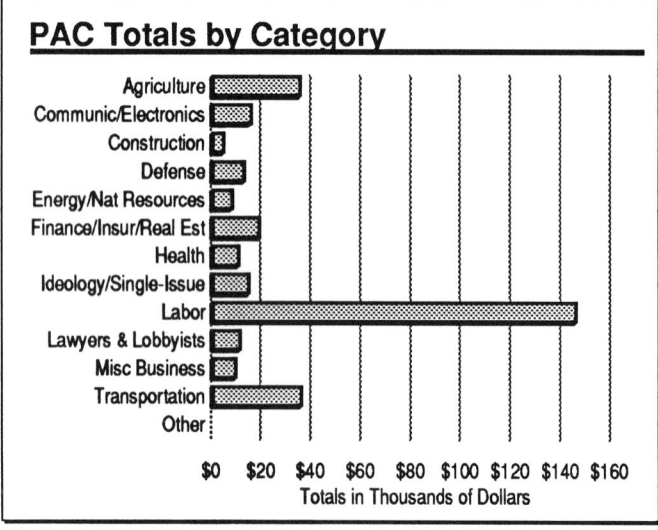

Agriculture
Communic/Electronics
Construction
Defense
Energy/Nat Resources
Finance/Insur/Real Est
Health
Ideology/Single-Issue
Labor
Lawyers & Lobbyists
Misc Business
Transportation
Other

$0 $20 $40 $60 $80 $100 $120 $140 $160
Totals in Thousands of Dollars

Tobacco **$3,350**
    RJR Nabisco $1,350
    Philip Morris $1,000
    Tobacco Institute $1,000

Trucking/Delivery **$9,450**
    United Parcel Service $3,950
    American Trucking Assns $1,500
    Consolidated Freightways $1,500
    Arkansas Best Corp $1,000
    North American Van Lines $1,000
    Others $500

Other Major Business PACs

CSX Corp*	$1,850	SeaTransport
National Assn of Realtors	$1,500	RE Sales
American Furniture Manufacturers Assn	$1,450	Furniture
National Cotton Council	$1,350	Cotton
National Beer Wholesalers Assn	$1,350	Liquor Whlsl
American Hotel & Motel Assn	$1,000	Hotel/Motel
Delaware North Companies	$1,000	Gambling
Greyhound Corp	$1,000	Home Chem
National Fisheries Institute	$1,000	Fishing
Riceland Foods	$1,000	Crops
Winn-Dixie Stores	$1,000	Food Stores

Labor

Bldg Trades/Industrial/Misc Unions **$61,500**
    Carpenters & Joiners Union $10,500
    United Auto Workers $10,000
    AFL-CIO* $6,200
    Machinists/Aerospace Workers Union $5,500
    Intl Brotherhood of Electrical Workers $3,500
    Operating Engineers Union $3,400
    Food & Commercial Workers Union $3,350
    United Steelworkers $3,000
    Laborers' Political League $2,850
    Sheet Metal Workers Union $2,500
    Communications Workers of America $2,000
    (continued in next column)

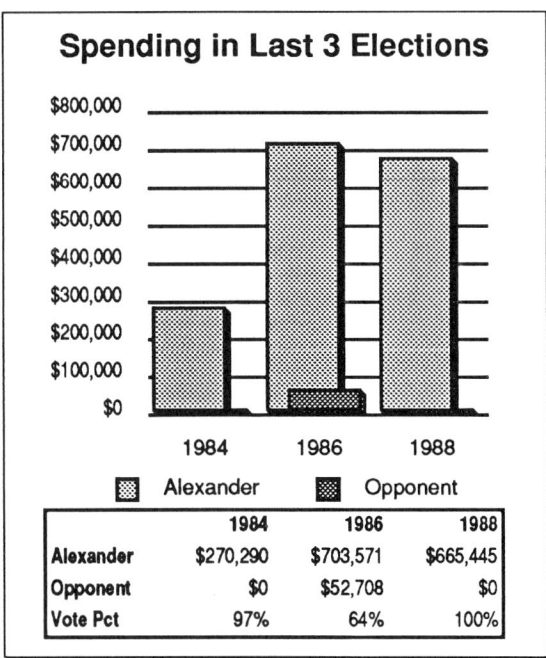

Spending in Last 3 Elections

	1984	1986	1988
Alexander	$270,290	$703,571	$665,445
Opponent	$0	$52,708	$0
Vote Pct	97%	64%	100%

■ Alexander ■ Opponent

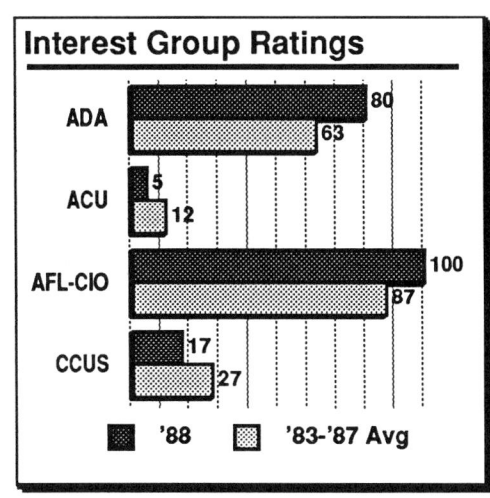

Interest Group Ratings

ADA — 80 ('88), 63 ('83–'87 Avg)
ACU — 5 ('88), 12 ('83–'87 Avg)
AFL-CIO — 100 ('88), 87 ('83–'87 Avg)
CCUS — 17 ('88), 27 ('83–'87 Avg)

■ '88   □ '83–'87 Avg

Labor (cont'd)
    Electronic Machinery Furniture Workers $1,500
    Plumbers/Pipefitters Union $1,350
    Amalgamated Clothing & Textile Workers $1,000
    Ladies Garment Workers Union $1,000
    Oil, Chemical & Atomic Workers Union $1,000
    Service Employees International Union $1,000
    Others $1,850

Government & Postal Workers **$31,050**
    National Assn of Retired Federal Employees .. $11,000
    American Fedn of State/County/Munic Employees ... $6,000
    National Assn of Letter Carriers $6,000
    American Postal Workers Union $3,200
    National Assn of Postmasters $1,300
    National Rural Letter Carriers Assn $1,000
    Others $2,550

Teachers Unions **$6,500**
    National Education Assn $6,500

Transportation Unions **$46,475**
    Teamsters Union $10,000
    International Longshoremen Assn* $7,950
    Seafarers International Union $7,500
    Marine Engineers Union* $6,500
    Air Line Pilots Assn $5,000
    United Transportation Union $3,000
    Amalgamated Transit Union $2,500
    Maintenance of Way Employees $1,225
    Brotherhood of Locomotive Engineers $1,150
    Transportation Communication Union $1,050
    Others $600

Ideological/Single-Issue

Pro-Gun Ownership **$9,900**
    National Rifle Assn $9,900

Other Major Ideological/Single-Issue PACs **$4,000**
National Cmte to Preserve Social Security .. $2,000 Soc Secur
Responsible Govt Fund (Ronnie Flippo) ..... $1,000 Dem Leaders
Valley Education Fund (Tony Coelho) .... $1,000 Dem Leaders

Independent expenditures supporting Alexander

National Cmte to Preserve Social Security $3,493

---

* Contributions came from more than one PAC affiliated
  with this sponsor.

Glenn M. Anderson, D-Calif (32)

First elected: 1968
Total receipts: $493,296
Total from PACs: $276,650

1988 Committees & Subcommittees

Merchant Marine and Fisheries
Fisheries and Wildlife Conservation and the Environment
Merchant Marine

Public Works and Transportation (Chairman)
Surface Transportation (Chairman)

PAC Contribution Profile

Business

Automotive	**$6,500**
Auto Dealers & Drivers for Free Trade	$5,250
Others	$1,250
Aviation & Air Freight	**$16,850**
Federal Express Corp	$7,000
Texas Air*	$2,000
McDonnell Douglas	$1,500
Trans World Airlines	$1,000
Others	$5,350
Bus Services	**$4,500**
National School Transport Assn	$2,250
American Bus Assn	$1,750
Others	$500
Construction	**$27,200**
Associated General Contractors	$6,000
National Assn of Home Builders	$3,500
National Utility Contractors Assn	$3,500
American Road & Trans Builders Assn	$2,000
Walter Industries	$2,000
National Society of Professional Engineers	$1,500
Parsons Corp	$1,500
American Consulting Engineers Council	$1,000
Bechtel Corp	$1,000
Others	$5,200
Defense	**$6,250**
Hughes Aircraft	$2,500
Northrop Corp	$1,500
Rockwell International	$1,000
Others	$1,250

Campaign Revenue Sources

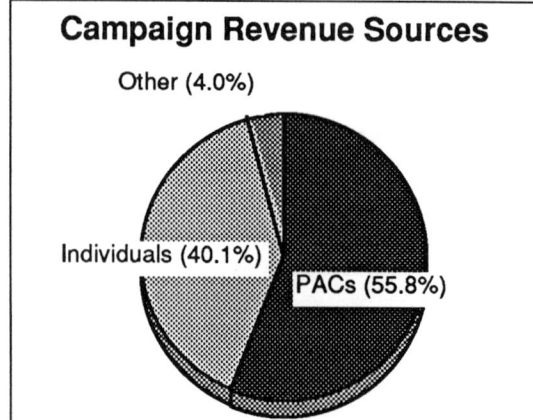

Other (4.0%)
Individuals (40.1%)
PACs (55.8%)

Electric Utilities	**$2,750**
Southern California Edison	$1,000
Others	$1,750
Food & Beverage	**$3,750**
National Beer Wholesalers Assn	$2,000
Food Marketing Institute	$1,500
Others	$250
Health Professionals	**$4,500**
American Medical Assn	$4,500
Lawyers & Lobbyists	**$4,500**
Preston, Thorgrimson, Ellis, & Holman	$1,000
Others	$3,500
Oil & Gas	**$19,050**
Atlantic Richfield	$5,500
Shell Oil	$1,500
Chevron Corp	$1,000
Edgington Oil Company	$1,000
Mobil Oil	$1,000
Pacific Enterprises	$1,000
Others	$8,050
Railroads & Railroad Services	**$4,000**
Union Pacific Corp	$1,500
Others	$2,500
Real Estate	**$12,750**
National Assn of Realtors	$6,000
Irvine Company	$5,750
Others	$1,000
Savings & Commercial Banks	**$9,100**
Mercury Savings & Loan	$4,000
US League of Savings Assn	$3,350
Others	$1,750
Sea Transport	**$13,350**
American President Lines	$3,750
American Pilots Assn	$2,000
CSX Corp*	$1,750
Crowley Maritime	$1,500
Matson Navigation	$1,250
Southwest Marine	$1,000
Others	$2,100
Telecommunications	**$3,250**
Pacific Telesis Group	$2,000
GTE Corp	$1,000
Others	$250

PAC Totals by Category

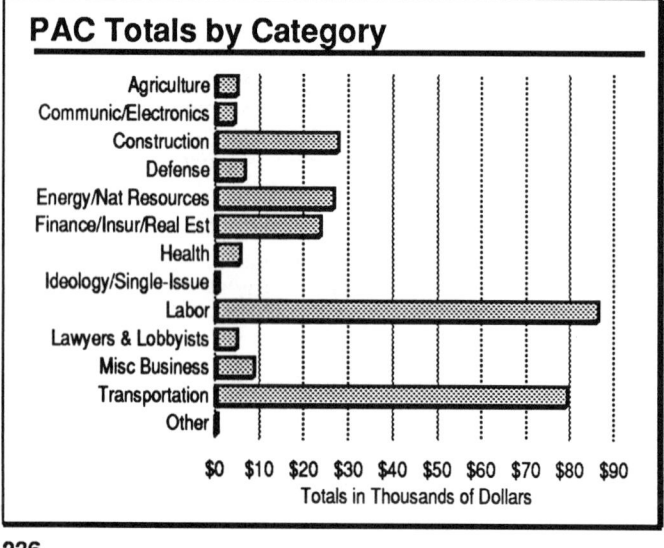

Agriculture
Communic/Electronics
Construction
Defense
Energy/Nat Resources
Finance/Insur/Real Est
Health
Ideology/Single-Issue
Labor
Lawyers & Lobbyists
Misc Business
Transportation
Other

$0 $10 $20 $30 $40 $50 $60 $70 $80 $90
Totals in Thousands of Dollars

Trucking/Delivery **$29,950**

United Parcel Service	$10,000
American Trucking Assns	$4,000
Consolidated Freightways	$4,000
Yellow Freight System	$2,500
North American Van Lines	$2,250
Roadway Services Inc	$1,500
Unigroup Inc	$1,050
Interstate Carriers Conference	$1,000
Paccar Inc	$1,000
Others	$2,650

Waste Management **$2,500**

Waste Management Inc	$2,500

Other Major Business PACs

American Society of Travel Agents	$1,500	Travel Agent
Energen Corp	$1,500	Indust Equip
American Hotel & Motel Assn	$1,250	Hotel/Motel
American Crystal Sugar Corp	$1,000	Sugar
National Coal Assn	$1,000	Coal

Labor

Bldg Trades/Industrial/Misc Unions **$23,000**

Carpenters & Joiners Union*	$6,000
Operating Engineers Union*	$6,000
Laborers' Western Political League	$2,000
Machinists/Aerospace Workers Union	$1,750
Plumbers/Pipefitters Union	$1,500
AFL-CIO*	$1,250
Food & Commercial Workers Union	$1,000
Oil, Chemical & Atomic Workers Union	$1,000
United Auto Workers	$1,000
Others	$1,500

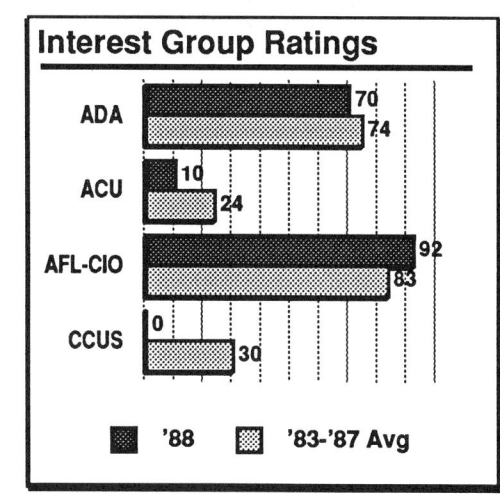

Interest Group Ratings

Group	'88	'83-'87 Avg
ADA	70	74
ACU	10	24
AFL-CIO	92	83
CCUS	0	30

■ '88   ▨ '83-'87 Avg

Government & Postal Workers **$12,000**

National Assn OF Retired Federal Employees	$5,000
American Fedn of State/County/Munic Employees	$3,000
National Assn of Letter Carriers	$2,000
American Postal Workers Union	$1,750
Others	$250

Sea Transport Unions **$14,000**

Marine Engineers Union*	$8,500
Seafarers International Union*	$3,000
Masters, Mates & Pilots Union	$1,250
Others	$1,250

Other Transport Unions **$32,000**

Air Line Pilots Assn	$10,000
Teamsters Union	$10,000
Amalgamated Transit Union	$5,500
United Transportation Union	$3,000
Transport Workers Union	$1,500
Transportation Communication Union	$1,000
Others	$1,000

Teachers Unions **$5,000**

National Education Assn	$4,500
United Teachers-Los Angeles	$500

Independent expenditures supporting Anderson

National Cmte to Preserve Social Security	$1,772

Spending in Last 3 Elections

	1984	1986	1988
Anderson	$410,127	$417,066	$457,410
Opponent	$63,989	$11,742	$20,608
Vote Pct	61%	69%	67%

▨ Anderson   ■ Opponent

* Contributions came from more than one PAC affiliated
with this sponsor.

237

Michael A. Andrews, D-Texas (25)

First elected: 1982
Total receipts: $638,035
Total from PACs: $399,785

1988 Committees & Subcommittees

Ways and Means
Public Assistance and Unemployment Compensation
Select Revenue Measures

PAC Contribution Profile

Business

Accountants	**$10,500**
American Institute of CPA's	$5,000
Touche Ross	$2,000
Others	$3,500
Air Transport	**$9,000**
Texas Air	$4,000
Eastern Airlines	$3,000
Others	$2,000
Automotive	**$8,500**
National Auto Dealers Assn	$6,500
Others	$2,000
Chemicals	**$8,800**
FMC Corp	$3,000
Others	$5,800
Commercial Banks	**$16,500**
American Bankers Assn	$5,000
First City Bancorp	$4,000
MBank	$2,000
Citicorp	$1,500
Others	$4,000
Construction	**$11,250**
National Assn of Home Builders	$3,000
Associated General Contractors	$2,500
Others	$5,750
Defense	**$10,850**
LTV Corp*	$3,500
Rockwell International	$1,500
Others	$5,850

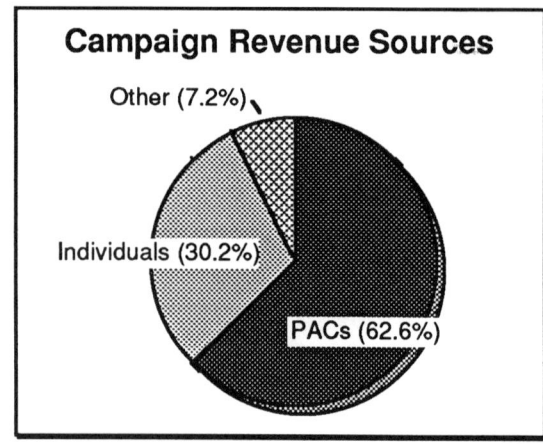

Campaign Revenue Sources

Other (7.2%)
Individuals (30.2%)
PACs (62.6%)

Electric Utilities	**$7,000**
Houston Industries	$3,500
Others	$3,500
Food & Beverage	**$13,750**
National Beer Wholesalers Assn	$2,500
National Restaurant Assn	$2,000
Wine & Spirits Wholesalers of America	$2,000
Joseph E Seagram & Sons	$1,500
Others	$5,750
Health Professionals	**$15,088**
American Medical Assn	$5,788
American Academy of Ophthalmology	$3,000
American Dental Assn	$2,000
Others	$4,300
Hospitals	**$4,263**
American Hospital Assn	$1,763
National Medical Enterprises Inc	$1,500
Others	$1,000
Insurance	**$55,850**
National Assn of Life Underwriters	$9,000
Torchmark Corp	$5,000
American Council of Life Insurance	$3,000
Equitable Financial Services	$3,000
Metropolitan Life Insurance	$3,000
Prudential Insurance	$2,500
Aetna Life & Casualty	$2,000
New York Life	$2,000
Northwestern Mutual Life	$2,000
American National Insurance Company	$1,500
Independent Insurance Agents of America	$1,500
TransAmerica Life Companies	$1,500
Others	$19,850
Lawyers	**$31,250**
Andrews, Kurth, Campbell & Jones	$5,000
Assn of Trial Lawyers of America	$5,000
Fullbright & Jaworski	$2,000
Vinson, Elkins, Searls, Connally & Smith	$2,000
Baker & Botts	$1,500
King & Spalding	$1,500
Kutak, Rock & Campbell	$1,500
Lidell, Sapp	$1,500
Baker & Hostetler	$1,250
Others	$10,000

PAC Totals by Category

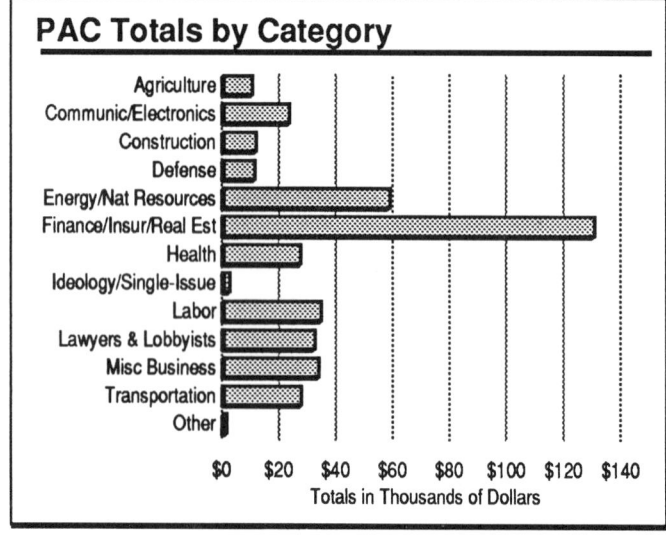

Agriculture
Communic/Electronics
Construction
Defense
Energy/Nat Resources
Finance/Insur/Real Est
Health
Ideology/Single-Issue
Labor
Lawyers & Lobbyists
Misc Business
Transportation
Other

$0 $20 $40 $60 $80 $100 $120 $140
Totals in Thousands of Dollars

Oil & Gas $42,400

Coastal Corp	$2,500
Atlantic Richfield	$2,000
Phillips Petroleum	$2,000
Shell Oil	$2,000
Texas Eastern Gas Transmission	$2,000
Transco Energy Company	$2,000
Valero Energy Corp	$2,000
International Assn of Drilling Contractors	$1,500
Occidental Petroleum*	$1,500
Petroleum Marketers Assn	$1,500
Texaco	$1,500
Others	$21,900

Pharmaceuticals $7,000

None over $1,000

Real Estate $19,313

National Assn of Realtors	$8,500
Century 21 Real Estate	$2,000
Trammell Crow Company	$2,000
Real Estate Investment PAC	$1,500
National Realty Committee	$1,313
Others	$4,000

Savings Banks & Credit Unions $5,300

US League of Savings Assn	$2,500
Others	$2,800

Securities/Commodities Investment $17,421

First Boston Corp	$2,000
Salomon Brothers	$2,000
Goldman Sachs	$1,500
Investment Company Institute	$1,500
Securities Industry Assn	$1,500
Shearson Lehman Hutton	$1,500
Others	$7,421

Telecommunications $17,550

GTE Corp*	$4,000
AT&T	$2,500
Southwestern Bell	$1,500
Others	$9,550

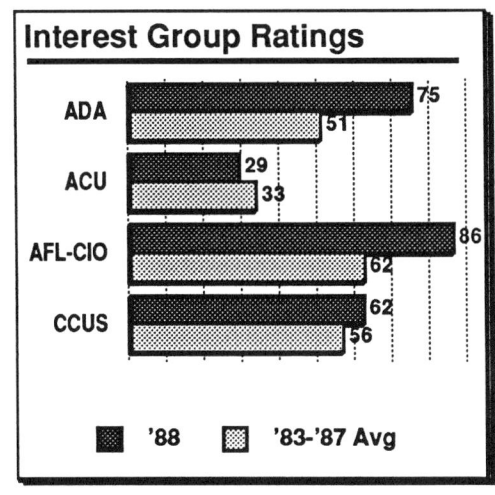

Interest Group Ratings

ADA: '88 = 75, '83-'87 Avg = 51
ACU: '88 = 29, '83-'87 Avg = 33
AFL-CIO: '88 = 86, '83-'87 Avg = 62
CCUS: '88 = 62, '83-'87 Avg = 56

■ '88 ▨ '83-'87 Avg

Other Major Business PACs

National Venture Capital Assn	$4,000	Venture Cap
Texas Farm Bureau	$2,500	Farm Orgs
American Assn of Equipment Lessors	$2,000	Rentals
Independent Coal Operators Assn	$2,000	Coal
Waste Management Inc	$2,000	Waste Mgmt
Browning-Ferris Industries	$1,500	Waste Mgmt
Freeport-McMoran Inc	$1,500	Other Mining
Household International	$1,500	Credit/Loans

Labor

Bldg Trades/Industrial/Other Unions $16,500

United Auto Workers	$3,500
Food & Commercial Workers Union	$2,500
Sheet Metal Workers Union	$2,500
United Steelworkers	$2,000
Carpenters & Joiners Union	$1,500
Others	$4,500

Government & Postal Workers $9,100

National Rural Letter Carriers Assn	$2,500
American Fedn of State/County/Munic Employees	$2,000
National Assn of Letter Carriers	$2,000
Others	$2,600

Teachers Unions $8,500

American Federation of Teachers	$5,500
National Education Assn	$3,000

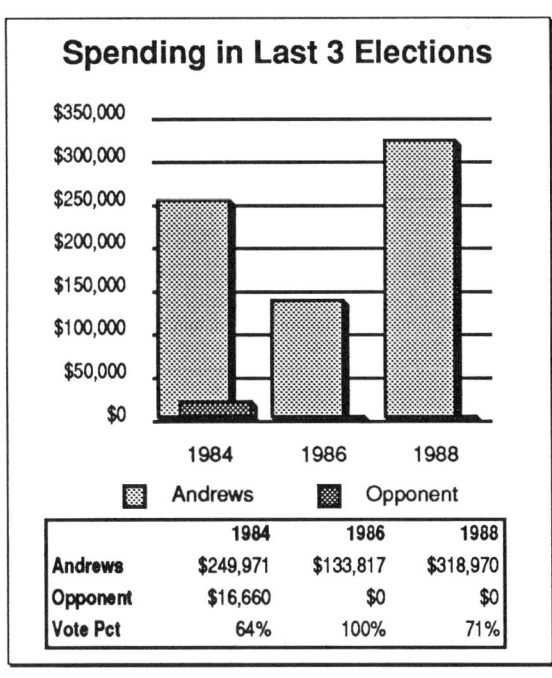

Spending in Last 3 Elections

▨ Andrews ■ Opponent

	1984	1986	1988
Andrews	$249,971	$133,817	$318,970
Opponent	$16,660	$0	$0
Vote Pct	64%	100%	71%

* Contributions came from more than one PAC affiliated with this sponsor.

Frank Annunzio, D-Ill (11)

1988 Committees & Subcommittees

First elected: 1964
Total receipts: $260,514
Total from PACs: $156,200

Banking, Finance and Urban Affairs
Consumer Affairs and Coinage (Chairman)
Economic Stabilization
Financial Institutions Supervision, Regulation and Insurance (Chairman)
General Oversight and Investigations

House Administration (Chairman)

Joint Library (Vice Chairman)

Joint Printing (Chairman)

PAC Contribution Profile

Business

Automotive	**$5,000**
National Auto Dealers Assn	$3,000
Auto Dealers & Drivers for Free Trade	$1,000
Chrysler Corp	$1,000
Commercial Banks	**$11,000**
Illinois Bankers Assn	$3,500
Independent Bankers Assn	$2,000
American Bankers Assn	$1,000
Continental Illinois Corp	$1,000
Others	$3,500
Construction	**$1,750**
National Assn of Home Builders	$1,000
Others	$750
Consumer Credit & Loans	**$7,450**
American Financial Services Assn	$2,000
Beneficial Management Corp	$2,000
Associated Credit Bureaus	$1,500
Others	$1,950
Insurance	**$12,000**
National Assn of Life Underwriters	$3,000
American Council of Life Insurance	$2,000
Casualty & Surety Agents Assn	$1,500
National Assn Mutual Insurance Agents	$1,500
Independent Insurance Agents of America	$1,000
Travelers Corp	$1,000
Others	$2,000

Campaign Revenue Sources

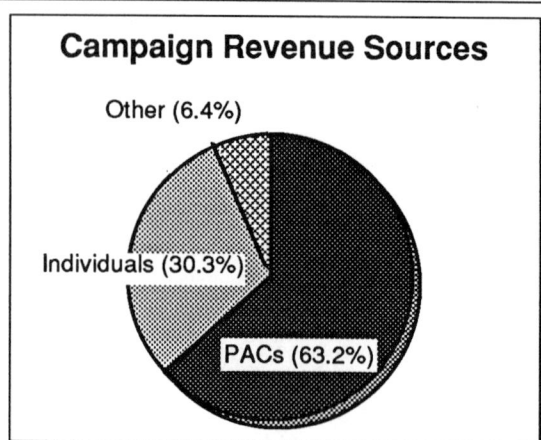

Other (6.4%)
Individuals (30.3%)
PACs (63.2%)

Lawyers & Lobbyists	**$12,250**
Assn of Trial Lawyers of America	$5,000
Camp, Barsh, Bates & Tate	$1,750
Kirkpatrick & Lockhart	$1,500
National Action Committee (Dave Evans)	$1,500
Akin, Gump, Hauer & Feld	$1,000
Others	$1,500
Office Machines	**$2,000**
Xerox Corp	$2,000
Real Estate	**$9,000**
National Assn of Realtors	$7,000
Mortgage Bankers Assn of America	$1,500
Others	$500
Savings Banks & Credit Unions	**$14,200**
US League of Savings Assn	$8,000
Credit Union National Assn	$1,500
American Savings Banks	$1,000
Home Savings of America	$1,000
Mid America Federal Savings & Loan	$1,000
Others	$1,700
Securities/Commodities Investment	**$11,500**
Chicago Board of Trade	$2,500
E F Hutton Group	$2,000
Municipal Securities Industry PAC	$2,000
First Boston Corp	$1,000
Investment Company Institute	$1,000
Morgan Stanley & Company	$1,000
Others	$2,000
Telecommunications	**$3,500**
AT&T	$2,000
Others	$1,500

Other Major Business PACs

Anheuser-Busch	$1,000	Beer
United Airlines	$1,000	Airlines

PAC Totals by Category

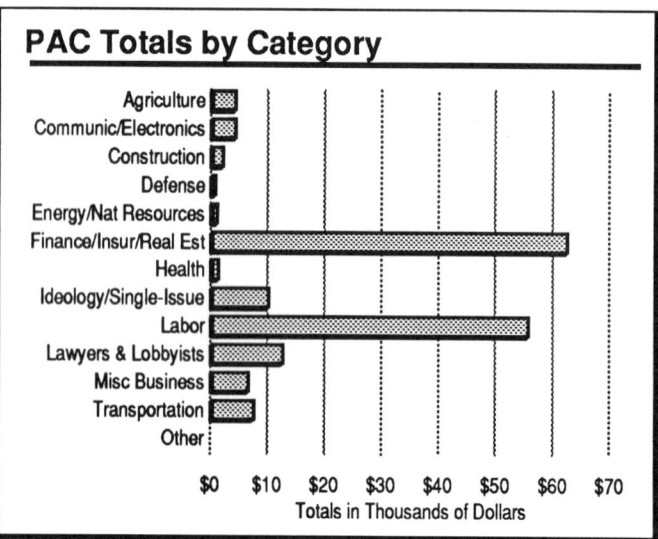

Category	
Agriculture	
Communic/Electronics	
Construction	
Defense	
Energy/Nat Resources	
Finance/Insur/Real Est	
Health	
Ideology/Single-Issue	
Labor	
Lawyers & Lobbyists	
Misc Business	
Transportation	
Other	

$0 $10 $20 $30 $40 $50 $60 $70
Totals in Thousands of Dollars

Labor

Bldg Trades/Industrial/Misc Unions $23,000
    Machinists/Aerospace Workers Union $5,000
    Laborers' Political League $4,000
    Operating Engineers Union $2,000
    Sheet Metal Workers Union $2,000
    AFL-CIO* $1,500
    Carpenters & Joiners Union $1,500
    Hotel/Restaurant Employees Union $1,500
    Service Employees International Union $1,500
    Food & Commercial Workers Union $1,000
    Intl Brotherhood of Electrical Workers $1,000
    Others $2,000

Government & Postal Workers $9,000
    National Assn of Retired Federal Employees $5,000
    American Federation of Government Employees $1,000
    American Fedn of State/County/Munic Employees $1,000
    National Assn of Letter Carriers $1,000
    Others $1,000

Teachers Unions $5,500
    National Education Assn $4,500
    American Federation of Teachers $1,000

Transportation Unions $17,800
    Teamsters Union $12,500
    Air Line Pilots Assn $2,500
    Seafarers International Union $2,000
    Others $800

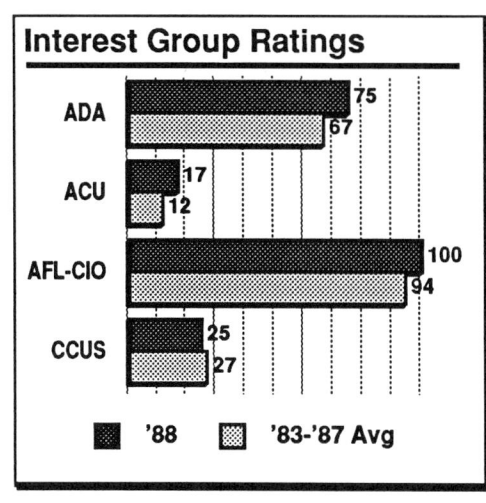

Interest Group Ratings

	'88	'83-'87 Avg
ADA	75	67
ACU	17	12
AFL-CIO	100	94
CCUS	25	27

Ideological/Single-Issue

Pro-Israel $5,000
    National PAC $5,000

Other Ideological/Single-Issue

Cmte of Concerned Italian-Americans $2,000	Ethnic Group
National Cmte to Preserve Social Security ..$1,000	Soc Secur
Valley Education Fund (Tony Coelho) $1,000	Dem Leaders

Independent expenditures supporting Annunzio

National Cmte to Preserve Social Security $2,751

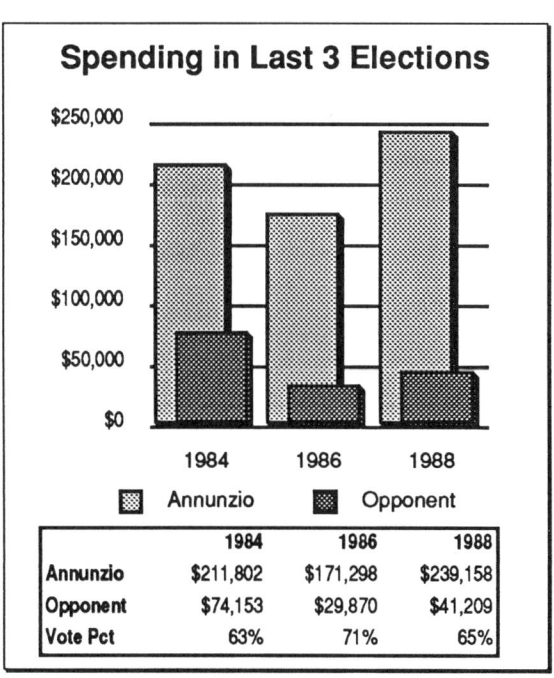

Spending in Last 3 Elections

	1984	1986	1988
Annunzio	$211,802	$171,298	$239,158
Opponent	$74,153	$29,870	$41,209
Vote Pct	63%	71%	65%

* Contributions came from more than one PAC affiliated
with this sponsor.

Beryl Anthony Jr., D-Ark (4)

1988 Committees & Subcommittees

Ways and Means
Health
Oversight

Select Children, Youth and Families

First elected: 1978
Total receipts: $547,244
Total from PACs: $352,042

PAC Contribution Profile

Business

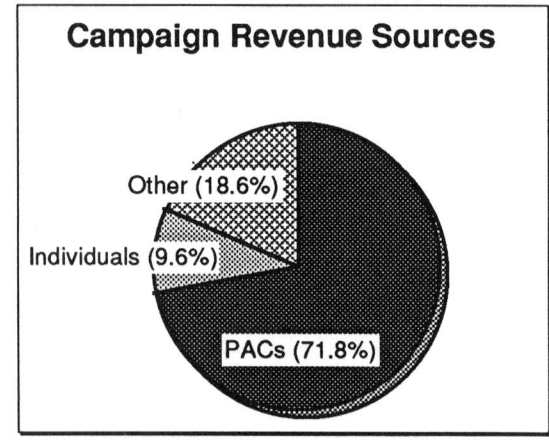

Campaign Revenue Sources

Other (18.6%)
Individuals (9.6%)
PACs (71.8%)

Accountants	**$9,000**
American Institute of CPA's	$5,000
Others	$4,000
Automotive	**$5,000**
National Auto Dealers Assn	$2,500
Others	$2,500
Aviation & Air Freight	**$8,500**
Federal Express Corp	$5,000
Others	$3,500
Construction	**$11,750**
Associated General Contractors	$2,000
National Assn of Home Builders	$2,000
National Utility Contractors Assn	$2,000
Others	$5,750
Dairy	**$5,000**
Associated Milk Producers	$3,000
Others	$2,000
Defense	**$14,050**
United Technologies	$2,000
General Dynamics	$1,750
Colt Industries	$1,500
TRW Inc	$1,500
Others	$7,300
Electronics	**$7,250**
Hewlett-Packard	$5,000
Others	$2,250

Financial Institutions	**$18,700**
Home Savings of America	$7,000
American Bankers Assn	$5,000
J P Morgan & Company	$2,000
US League of Savings Assn	$2,000
Others	$2,700
Food & Beverage	**$16,500**
National Beer Wholesalers Assn	$3,500
National Restaurant Assn	$2,500
Joseph E Seagram & Sons	$2,000
Others	$8,500
Forest Products	**$12,550**
Potlatch Corp	$5,000
International Paper Company	$2,000
Westvaco Corp	$2,000
Weyerhaeuser Company*	$1,500
Others	$2,050
Health Professionals	**$30,300**
American Medical Assn	$10,000
American Dental Assn	$5,000
American Academy of Ophthalmology	$3,000
American Nurses Assn	$3,000
Cmte for Quality Orthopedic Health Care	$2,000
Oral & Maxillofacial Surgeons	$2,000
American Optometric Assn	$1,500
Others	$3,800
Hospitals & Nursing Homes	**$9,500**
American Health Care Assn	$3,000
Federation of American Hospitals	$1,500
Others	$5,000
Insurance	**$51,000**
National Assn of Life Underwriters	$10,000
American Family Corp	$5,000
Torchmark Corp	$4,000
Metropolitan Life Insurance	$3,000
Travelers Corp	$2,500
Northwestern Mutual Life	$2,000
Prudential Insurance	$2,000
American Council of Life Insurance	$1,500
Health Insurance Assn of America	$1,500
Independent Insurance Agents of America	$1,500
Lincoln National Corp	$1,500
Others	$16,500

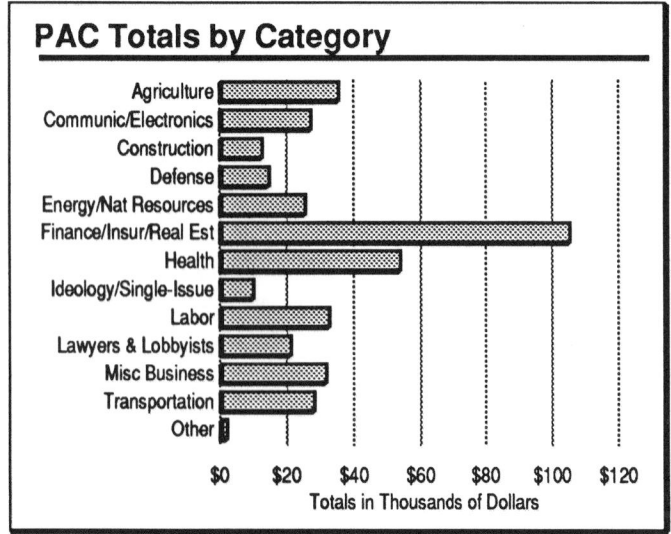

PAC Totals by Category

Agriculture
Communic/Electronics
Construction
Defense
Energy/Nat Resources
Finance/Insur/Real Est
Health
Ideology/Single-Issue
Labor
Lawyers & Lobbyists
Misc Business
Transportation
Other

$0 $20 $40 $60 $80 $100 $120
Totals in Thousands of Dollars

Lawyers **$20,500**
    Assn of Trial Lawyers of America $15,000
    Preston, Thorgrimson, Ellis & Holman $1,500
    Others $4,000

Oil & Gas **$18,850**
    Petroleum Marketers Assn $2,500
    Ashland Oil $1,500
    Others $14,850

Pharmaceuticals **$12,550**
    Pfizer Inc $2,000
    Schering-Plough Corp $2,000
    Eli Lilly & Company $1,500
    Others $7,050

Real Estate **$8,500**
    National Assn of Realtors $3,000
    American Resort & Residential Developers Assn $2,000
    Others $3,500

Securities/Commodities Investment **$13,975**
    Chicago Board of Trade $2,000
    Morgan Stanley & Company $2,000
    Assn of Private Pension Plans $1,975
    Others $8,000

Telecommunications **$17,550**
    AT&T $2,500
    Pacific Telesis Group $2,000
    Continental Telecom $1,500
    GTE (Southwest) $1,500
    Southwestern Bell $1,500
    Others $8,550

Trucking/Delivery **$8,770**
    Arkansas Best Corp $2,000
    Ryder System Inc $2,000
    United Parcel Service $1,250
    American Trucking Assns $1,020
    Others $2,500

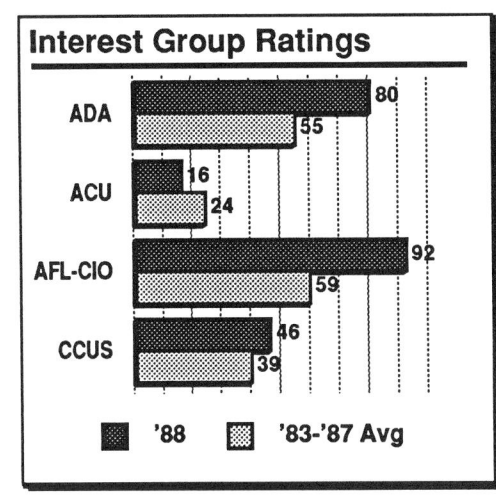

Interest Group Ratings

	'88	'83-'87 Avg
ADA	80	55
ACU	16	24
AFL-CIO	92	59
CCUS	46	39

Venture Capital **$6,000**
    National Venture Capital Assn $6,000

Other Major Business PACs
Union Pacific Corp .... $3,000   Railroads
Philip Morris .... $2,000   Tobacco
American Assn of Equipment Lessors .... $1,500   RentalsLabor

Labor

Bldg Trades/Industrial/Other Unions **$15,000**
    United Auto Workers $3,500
    Food & Commercial Workers Union $1,500
    Others $10,000

Teachers Unions **$6,000**
    National Education Assn $5,000
    Others $1,000

Transportation Unions **$11,000**
    Air Line Pilots Assn $5,000
    Marine Engineers Union* $2,000
    United Transportation Union $1,500
    Others $2,500

Ideological/Single-Issue

Ideological/Single-Issue **$9,500**
National PAC .... $5,000   Pro-Israel
National Cmte to Preserve Social Security .. $1,500   Soc Secur
Others $3,000

Independent expenditures supporting Anthony
National Cmte to Preserve Social Security $2,986

---

* Contributions came from more than one PAC affiliated
with this sponsor.

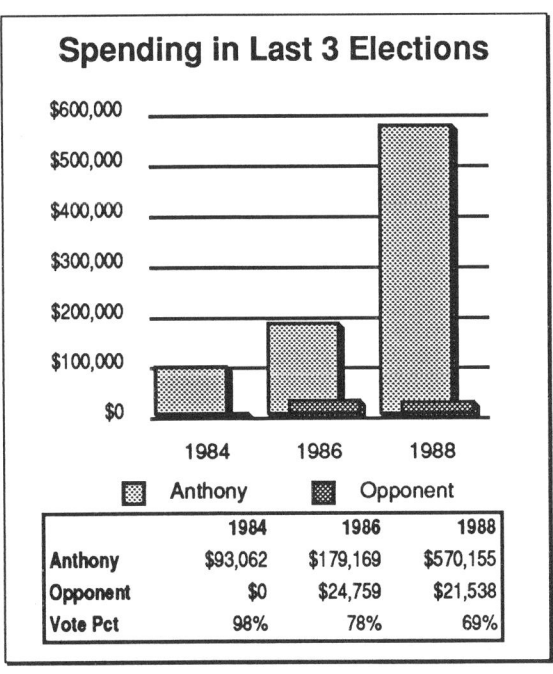

Spending in Last 3 Elections

	1984	1986	1988
Anthony	$93,062	$179,169	$570,155
Opponent	$0	$24,759	$21,538
Vote Pct	98%	78%	69%

Doug Applegate, D-Ohio (18)

1988 Committees & Subcommittees

First elected: 1976
Total receipts: $120,435
Total from PACs: $66,751

Public Works and Transportation
Economic Development
Surface Transportation
Water Resources

Veterans' Affairs
Compensation, Pension and Insurance (Chairman)
Oversight and Investigations

PAC Contribution Profile

Business

Chemicals	**$2,000**
Betz Laboratories	$2,000
Computers & Electronics	**$1,300**
NCR Corp	$1,000
Others	$300
Construction	**$3,000**
National Utility Contractors Assn	$2,000
Associated General Contractors	$500
National Assn of Home Builders	$500
Dairy	**$1,500**
Associated Milk Producers	$1,500
Electric Utilities	**$3,150**
American Electric Power*	$2,650
ACRE (Action Committee for Rural Electrification)	$500
Farm Organizations	**$2,250**
Ohio Farm Bureau Federation	$2,250
Health Professionals	**$1,750**
American Medical Assn	$1,000
American Chiropractic Assn	$500
Others	$250
Lawyers	**$2,000**
Assn of Trial Lawyers of America	$2,000

Oil & Gas	**$1,100**
East Ohio Gas	$500
USX Corp	$500
Others	$100
Real Estate	**$6,500**
National Assn of Realtors	$6,000
Mortgage Bankers Assn of America	$500
Savings & Commercial Banks	**$1,500**
Ohio Savings Assns League	$1,000
American Bankers Assn	$500
Steel Production	**$1,583**
Bethlehem Steel	$500
LTV Steel	$500
Others	$583
Telecommunications	**$3,000**
AT&T	$2,000
GTE Corp	$500
Ohio Bell Telephone	$500
Trucking/Delivery	**$4,940**
United Parcel Service	$2,250
Yellow Freight System	$600
Ryder System Inc	$550
American Trucking Assns	$540
National Assn of Truck Stop Operators	$500
North American Van Lines	$500

Other Major Business PACs

National Assn of Life Underwriters	$1,000	Life Insurance
Stone Container Corp	$1,000	Paper Packg
American Society of Travel Agents	$500	Travel Agent
American Sugar Cane League	$500	Sugar
Burlington Northern	$500	Railroads
Food Marketing Institute	$500	Food Stores
Ford Motor Company	$500	Auto Mfrs
Service Corporation International	$500	Funeral Svcs
Textile Rental Services Assn	$500	BusinessSvcs
Trans World Airlines	$500	Airlines
United Airlines	$500	Airlines

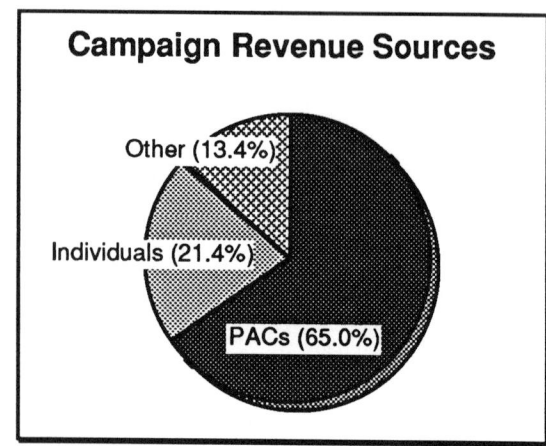

Campaign Revenue Sources

Other (13.4%)
Individuals (21.4%)
PACs (65.0%)

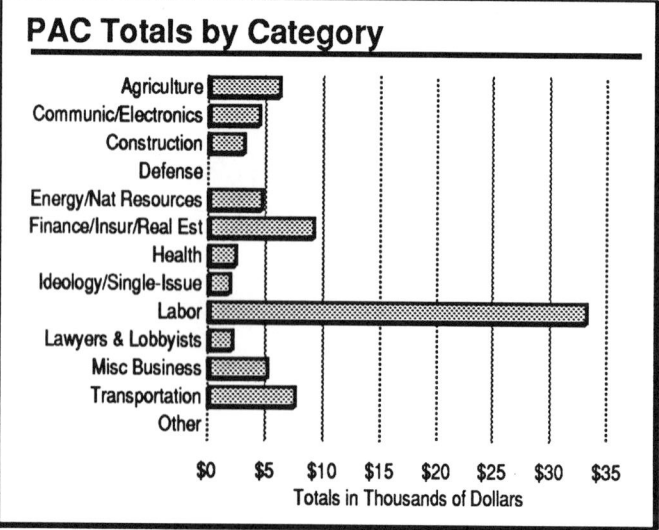

PAC Totals by Category

Agriculture
Communic/Electronics
Construction
Defense
Energy/Nat Resources
Finance/Insur/Real Est
Health
Ideology/Single-Issue
Labor
Lawyers & Lobbyists
Misc Business
Transportation
Other

$0 $5 $10 $15 $20 $25 $30 $35
Totals in Thousands of Dollars

Labor

Bldg Trades/Industrial/Misc Unions **$11,000**

Machinists/Aerospace Workers Union $2,000
Operating Engineers Union $2,000
Laborers' Political League $1,500
Carpenters & Joiners Union $1,000
Food & Commercial Workers Union............................$1,000
Intl Brotherhood of Electrical Workers.......................$1,000
Ladies Garment Workers Union $1,000
AFL-CIO $500
Plumbers/Pipefitters Union $500
United Auto Workers $500

Government & Postal Workers **$4,050**

National Assn/Retired Federal Employees $3,000
International Assn of Firefighters...................................$500
National League of Postmasters $500
National Assn of Postmasters $50

Transportation Unions **$18,000**

Teamsters Union $6,000
Air Line Pilots Assn $5,000
Marine Engineers District 2 Maritime Officers.................$2,000
United Transportation Union $1,500
Brotherhood of Locomotive Engineers $1,000
Brotherhood of Railway Carmen $1,000
Seafarers International Union $1,000
Assn of Flight Attendants $500

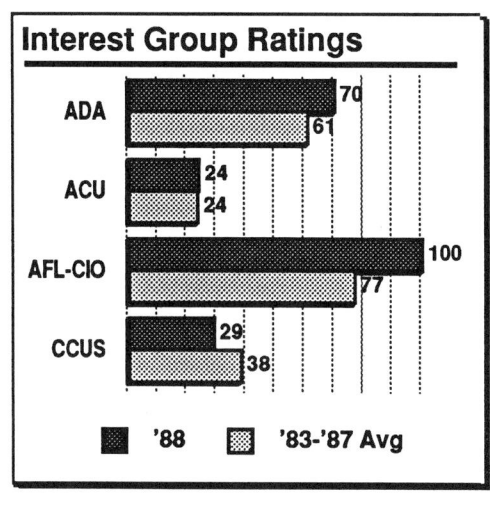

Ideological/Single-Issue

Ideological/Single-Issue PACs **$1,750**

Valley Education Fund (Tony Coelho) ....$1,000   Dem Leaders
National Assn for Uniformed Services ....$500   Pro-Military
Others $250

Independent expenditures supporting Applegate

National Cmte to Preserve Social Security $1,541

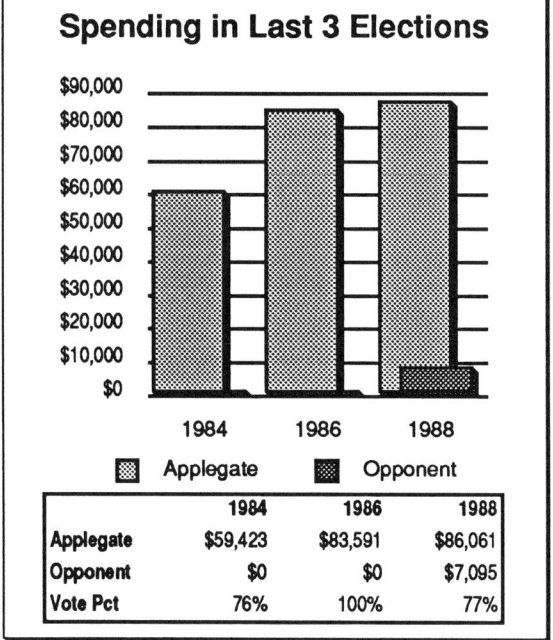

---

* Contributions came from more than one PAC affiliated
with this sponsor.

Bill Archer, R-Texas (7)

1988 Committees & Subcommittees

Ways and Means (Ranking Republican)

Joint Taxation

First elected: 1970
Total receipts: $269,695
Total from PACs: $0

Campaign Revenue Sources

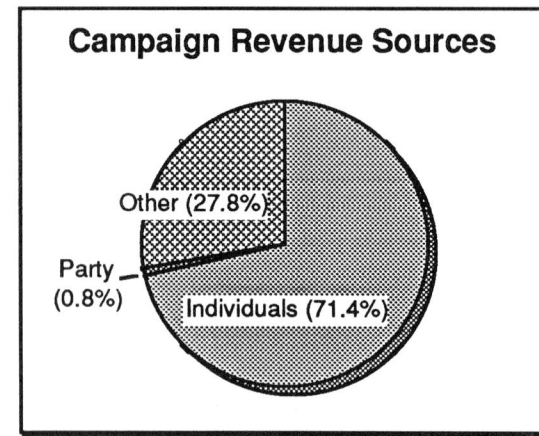

Other (27.8%)
Party (0.8%)
Individuals (71.4%)

PAC Contribution Profile

Lennox Industries	$1,000	Const Prod
McDonald's Corp	$1,000	Restaurants
Continental Telecom	$500	Phone Util
Mutual of Omaha	$500	Insurance
Alliance of Arts Advocates	$300	Other Ideolog

NOTE: Archer reported taking no PAC funds in his 1988 campaign. The PACs listed above did report making contributions to him during 1987-88, however, and those contributions are recorded in the official FEC records.

PAC Totals by Category

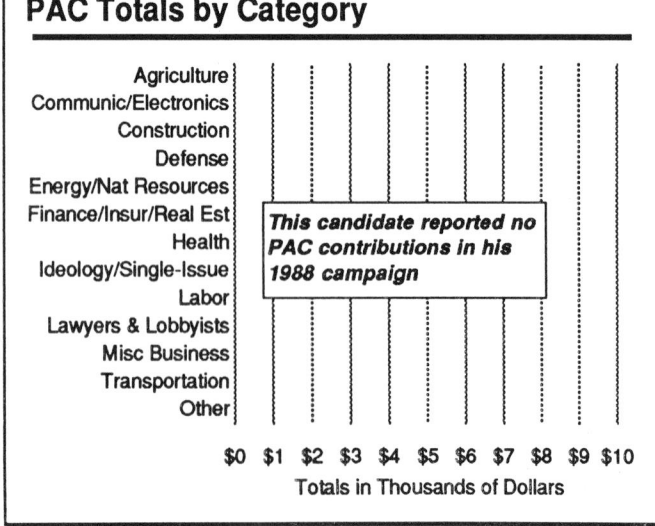

Agriculture
Communic/Electronics
Construction
Defense
Energy/Nat Resources
Finance/Insur/Real Est
Health
Ideology/Single-Issue
Labor
Lawyers & Lobbyists
Misc Business
Transportation
Other

This candidate reported no PAC contributions in his 1988 campaign

$0 $1 $2 $3 $4 $5 $6 $7 $8 $9 $10
Totals in Thousands of Dollars

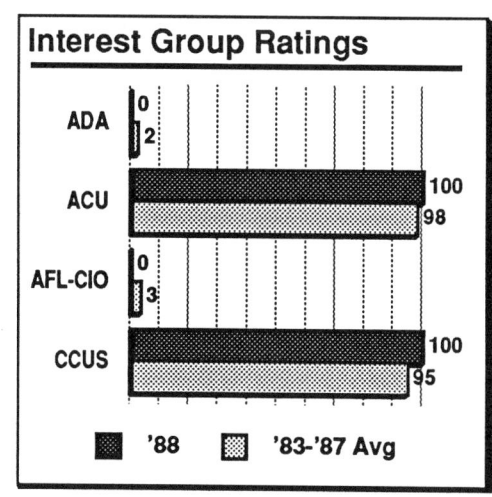

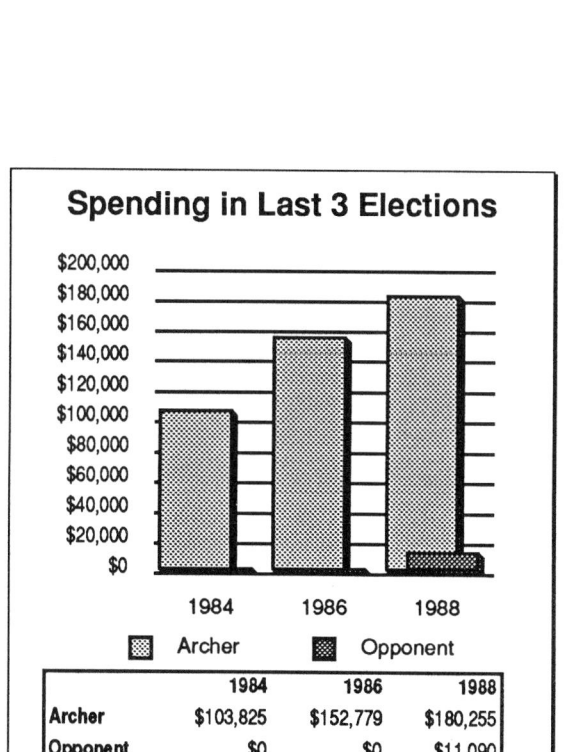

	1984	1986	1988
Archer	$103,825	$152,779	$180,255
Opponent	$0	$0	$11,090
Vote Pct	87%	87%	79%

Dick Armey, R-Texas (26)

1988 Committees & Subcommittees

Budget
Budget Process
Community and Natural Resources
Economic and Trade Policy

Education and Labor
Labor-Management Relations
Postsecondary Education

PAC Contribution Profile

Business

Automotive	$8,000
National Auto Dealers Assn	$4,750
Auto Dealers & Drivers for Free Trade	$2,000
Others	$1,250

Aviation	$2,200
American Airlines	$1,000
Others	$1,200

Chemicals	$3,250
Dow Chemical	$1,500
W R Grace & Company	$1,000
Others	$750

Construction	$10,350
National Utility Contractors Assn	$2,000
Associated General Contractors	$1,500
National Assn of Home Builders	$1,500
Others	$5,350

Defense	$14,201
LTV Aerospace & Defense Company	$2,750
E-Systems*	$2,351
Varo Inc	$2,000
Electrospace Systems Inc	$1,000
Harris Corp	$1,000
Rockwell International	$1,000
Others	$4,100

First elected: 1984
Total receipts: $419,632
Total from PACs: $150,800

Campaign Revenue Sources

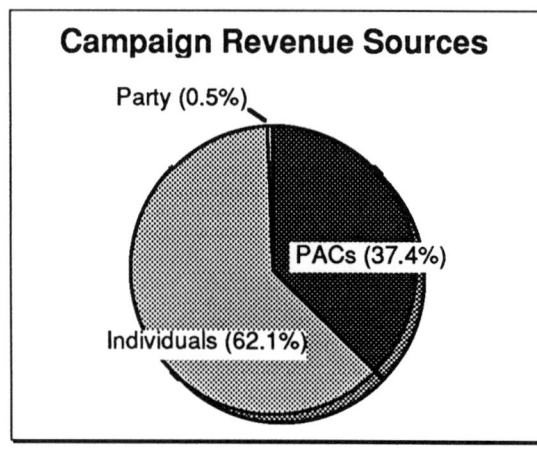

Party (0.5%)
PACs (37.4%)
Individuals (62.1%)

Electric Utilities	$9,300
Texas Utilities Electric Company*	$6,000
Texas-New Mexico Power Company	$1,500
Houston Industries	$1,000
Others	$800

Electronics & Computers	$6,600
Recognition Equipment Inc	$3,000
Texas Instruments	$1,250
Others	$2,350

Farm Organizations	$2,500
Texas Farm Bureau	$2,500

Financial Institutions	$5,700
Nowlin Savings Assn	$1,250
American Bankers Assn	$1,000
Credit Union National Assn	$1,000
NCNB Texas	$1,000
Others	$1,450

Food & Beverage	$8,350
National Restaurant Assn	$3,000
Food Marketing Institute	$1,500
Others	$3,850

Health Professionals	$7,850
American Medical Assn	$7,750
Others	$100

Insurance	$4,500
National Assn of Life Underwriters	$3,500
Others	$1,000

Lawyers	$3,000
Winstead, McGuire, Sechrest & Minick	$2,000
Johnson & Gibbs	$1,000

Oil & Gas	$18,450
Mesa PAC II	$5,000
Bass Brothers Enterprises	$1,250
Atlantic Richfield	$1,000
Hunt Oil Company	$1,000
Otis Company	$1,000
Phillips Petroleum	$1,000
Rosewood Corp	$1,000
Sun Company	$1,000
Others	$6,200

PAC Totals by Category

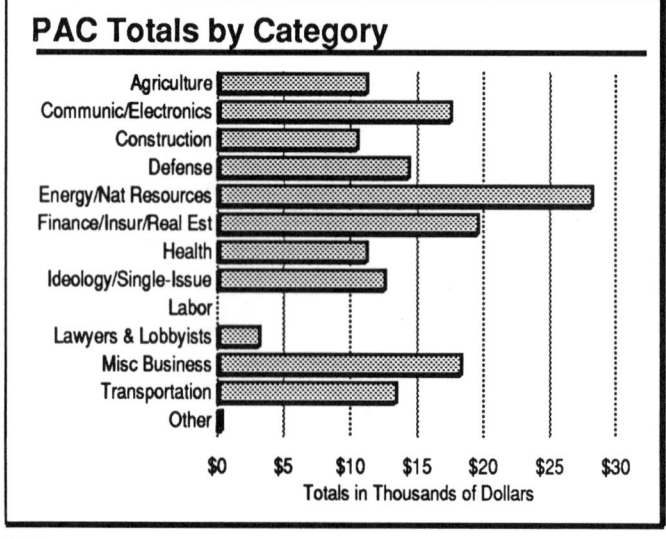

Agriculture
Communic/Electronics
Construction
Defense
Energy/Nat Resources
Finance/Insur/Real Est
Health
Ideology/Single-Issue
Labor
Lawyers & Lobbyists
Misc Business
Transportation
Other

$0 $5 $10 $15 $20 $25 $30
Totals in Thousands of Dollars

Paper Production $1,500
International Paper Company $1,000
Others $500

Pharmaceuticals $2,550
McKesson Corp $1,000
Others $1,550

Real Estate $9,000
National Assn of Realtors $5,500
Trammell Crow Company $2,000
Mortgage Bankers Assn of America $1,500

Retail Sales $2,800
J C Penney Company $1,000
National Assn of Chain Drug Stores $1,000
Others $800

Telecommunications $10,750
GTE (Southwest) $3,250
AT&T $3,000
Southwestern Bell $2,000
Penn Central Corp $1,000
United Telecommunications $1,000
Others $500

Other Major Business PACs

National Tooling & Machining Assn	$1,250	Indust Equip
Lone Star Steel*	$1,100	Steel
Bowling Proprietors Assn	$1,000	Amuse Ctr
Philip Morris	$1,000	Tobacco
Texas Cattle Feeders Assn	$1,000	Feedlots

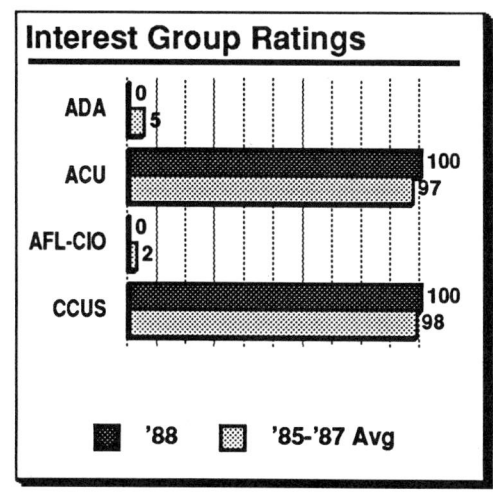

Interest Group Ratings

	'88	'85-'87 Avg
ADA	0	5
ACU	100	97
AFL-CIO	0	2
CCUS	100	98

■ '88   ☐ '85-'87 Avg

Ideological/Single-Issue

Anti-Union PACs $8,557
Right to Work PAC $7,807
Others $750

Other Major Ideological/Single-Issue PACs

Conservative Victory Cmte	$1,000	Repub/Conser
National Rifle Assn	$1,000	Pro-Guns

Spending in Last 3 Elections

	1984	1986	1988
Armey	$368,869	$558,559	$314,903
Opponent	$382,139	$133,785	$189,780
Vote Pct	51%	68%	69%

☐ Armey   ■ Opponent

---

* Contributions came from more than one PAC affiliated with this sponsor.

Les Aspin, D-Wis (1)

1988 Committees & Subcommittees

First elected: 1970
Total receipts: $618,045
Total from PACs: $265,249

Armed Services (Chairman)
Research and Development

PAC Contribution Profile

Business

Construction **$3,750**
    American Consulting Engineers Council $1,000
    Others $2,750

Dairy **$5,000**
    Associated Milk Producers $3,500
    Mid-American Dairymen $1,000
    Others $500

Defense **$101,200**
    Hughes Aircraft $6,000
    AT&T $5,000
    General Dynamics $5,000
    Grumman $5,000
    Kaman Corp $5,000
    United Technologies $5,000
    Boeing Company $4,000
    Lockheed Corp $4,000
    McDonnell Douglas* $4,000
    Rockwell International $3,600
    LTV Aerospace & Defense Company $3,500
    Textron Inc $3,250
    Colt Industries $3,000
    Loral Corp $3,000
    BDM International $2,500
    Litton Industries $2,500
    Tenneco Inc $2,500
    General Motors $2,050
    Gencorp Inc $2,000
    Northrop Corp $2,000
    (Continued in next column)

Campaign Revenue Sources

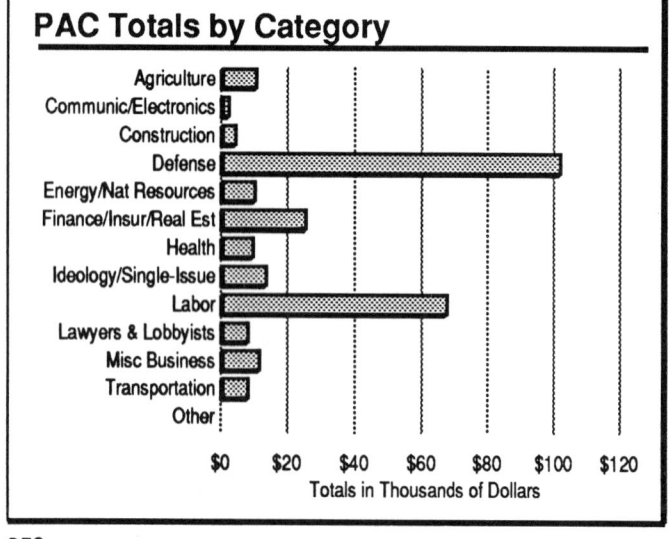

Other (12.5%)
PACs (43.0%)
Individuals (44.4%)

Defense (cont'd)
    Texas Instruments $2,000
    General Electric $1,900
    Bath Iron Works $1,500
    Beech Aircraft $1,500
    Emerson Electric* $1,500
    Martin Marietta Corp $1,500
    Allied-Signal $1,250
    Westinghouse Electric $1,150
    Raytheon $1,100
    AEL Industries Inc $1,000
    Cubic Corp $1,000
    Emhart Corp* $1,000
    FMC Corp $1,000
    Sequa Corp $1,000
    Singer Company $1,000
    TRW Inc $1,000
    Unisys Corp $1,000
    Others $6,900

Electric Utilities **$4,650**
    Wisconsin Electric Power Company $2,700
    ACRE (Action Committee for Rural Electrification) $1,000
    Others $950

Financial Institutions **$7,800**
    American Bankers Assn $2,000
    First Bank System Inc* $1,500
    Banc One Wisconsin $1,050
    Others $3,250

Food & Beverage **$3,750**
    National Beer Wholesalers Assn $2,000
    Others $1,750

Health Professionals **$7,850**
    American Podiatry Assn $2,000
    American Dental Assn $1,500
    American Optometric Assn $1,500
    American Medical Assn $1,350
    Others $1,500

Industrial Equipment & Materials **$6,050**
    Beloit Corp $2,000
    National Tooling & Machining Assn $1,600
    Aqua-Chem Inc $1,100
    Others $1,350

Insurance **$4,000**
    Northwestern Mutual Life $2,100
    Others $1,900

PAC Totals by Category

Agriculture
Communic/Electronics
Construction
Defense
Energy/Nat Resources
Finance/Insur/Real Est
Health
Ideology/Single-Issue
Labor
Lawyers & Lobbyists
Misc Business
Transportation
Other

$0 $20 $40 $60 $80 $100 $120

Totals in Thousands of Dollars

Lawyers **$7,600**
- Assn of Trial Lawyers of America $5,000
- Williams & Jensen $1,000
- Others $1,600

Real Estate **$9,999**
- National Assn of Realtors $7,749
- National Parking Assn $2,000
- Others $250

Tobacco **$3,200**
- Philip Morris $2,200
- Tobacco Institute $1,000

Other Major Business PACs

Waste Management Inc	$2,500	Waste Mgmt
Harley-Davidson Inc	$2,000	Motorcycles
Wisconsin Bell Telephone	$1,050	Phone Util
American Motors	$1,000	Auto Mfrs
Coastal Corp	$1,000	Natural Gas
Enserch Corp	$1,000	Natural Gas
GAF Corporation	$1,000	Chemicals
Paccar Inc	$1,000	Truck Mfrs
Stone Container Corp	$1,000	Paper Packg

Labor

Bldg Trades/Industrial/Misc Unions **$22,100**
- Carpenters & Joiners Union $3,250
- United Auto Workers $3,000
- Laborers' Political League $2,000
- AFL-CIO* $1,800
- Communications Workers of America $1,500
- Operating Engineers Union $1,500
- Ladies Garment Workers Union $1,250
- Food & Commercial Workers Union $1,100
- Ironworkers Union $1,000
- Machinists/Aerospace Workers Union $1,000
- Plumbers/Pipefitters Union $1,000
- Sheet Metal Workers Union $1,000
- United Steelworkers $1,000
- Others $1,700

Interest Group Ratings

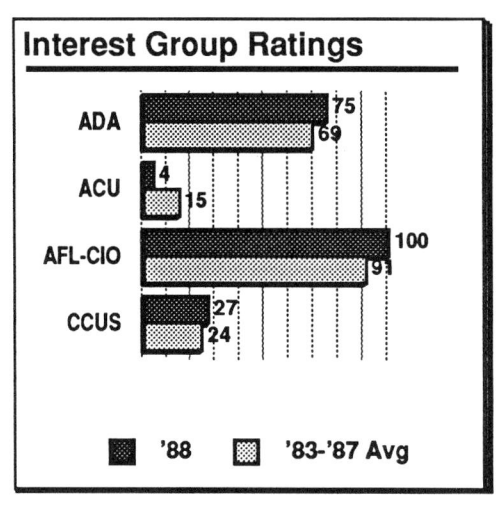

Government & Postal Workers **$14,500**
- National Assn of Retired Federal Employees $5,000
- National Assn of Letter Carriers $4,200
- American Fedn of State/County/Munic Employees ... $2,000
- American Postal Workers Union $1,000
- Others $2,300

Teachers Unions **$7,500**
- National Education Assn $5,000
- American Federation of Teachers $2,500

Transportation Unions **$22,800**
- Teamsters Union $10,000
- Marine Engineers Union* $6,000
- Air Line Pilots Assn $2,500
- International Longshoremen Assn $1,000
- Seafarers International Union $1,000
- Others $2,300

Ideological/Single-Issue

Pro-Israel **$11,500**
- National PAC $5,000
- Washington PAC $2,500
- Roundtable PAC $1,500
- Delaware Valley PAC $1,000
- Others $1,500

Independent expenditures supporting Aspin
National Cmte to Preserve Social Security $3,385

Spending in Last 3 Elections

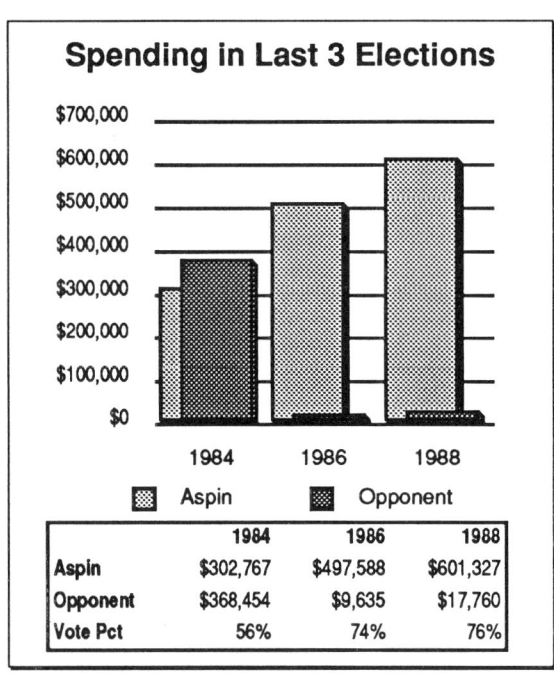

	1984	1986	1988
Aspin	$302,767	$497,588	$601,327
Opponent	$368,454	$9,635	$17,760
Vote Pct	56%	74%	76%

---

* Contributions came from more than one PAC affiliated
with this sponsor.

Chester G. Atkins, D-Mass (5)

First elected: 1984
Total receipts: $359,460
Total from PACs: $300

1988 Committees & Subcommittees

Budget
Budget Process
Community and Natural Resources
Defense and International Affairs

Education and Labor
Elementary, Secondary and Vocational Education
Employment Opportunities
Postsecondary Education

Foreign Affairs
Asian and Pacific Affairs
International Operations

Standards of Official Conduct

PAC Contribution Profile

League of Conservation Voters .... $749   Environment
Hudson Valley PAC .... $484   Pro-Israel
Farm Credit Council .... $250   Ag Services

NOTE: Atkins reported a total of $300 in PAC contributions in his 1988 campaign. The PACs listed above did report making contributions to him in 1987-88, however, and those contributions are recorded in the official FEC records.

Independent expenditures supporting Atkins

National Utility Contractors Assn $2,000
National Cmte to Preserve Social Security $1,538
League of Conservation Voters $587

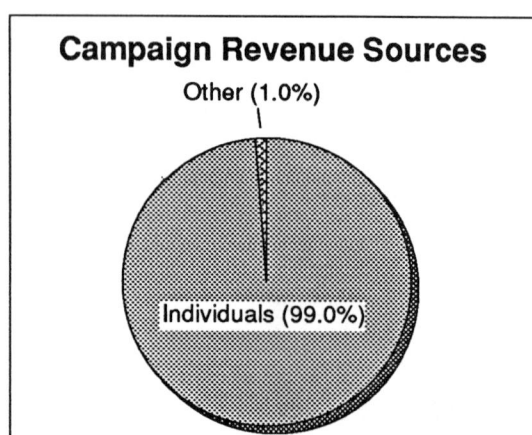

Campaign Revenue Sources

Other (1.0%)

Individuals (99.0%)

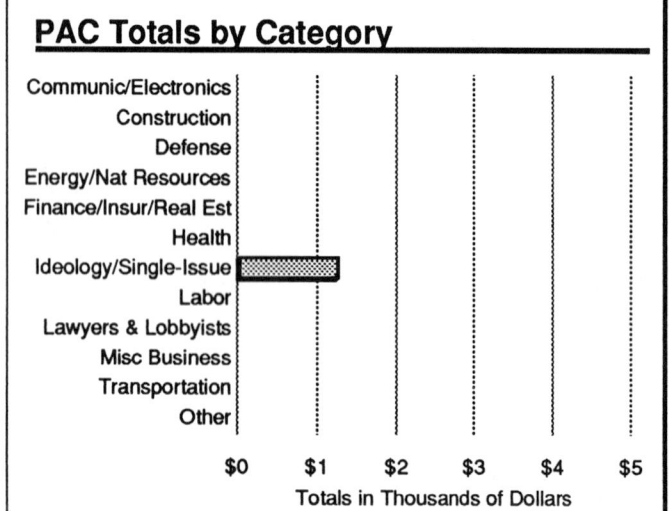

PAC Totals by Category

Category	
Communic/Electronics	
Construction	
Defense	
Energy/Nat Resources	
Finance/Insur/Real Est	
Health	
Ideology/Single-Issue	▨
Labor	
Lawyers & Lobbyists	
Misc Business	
Transportation	
Other	

$0 $1 $2 $3 $4 $5

Totals in Thousands of Dollars

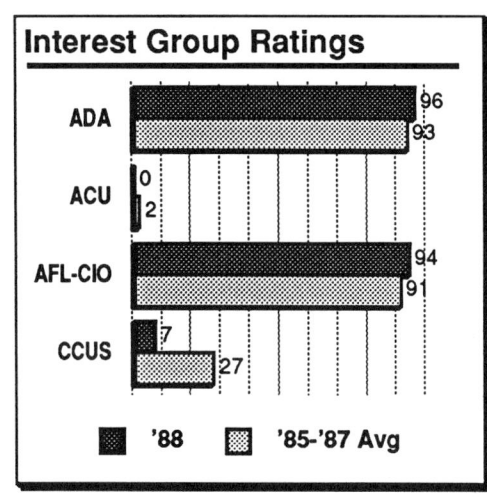

Interest Group Ratings

	'88	'85-'87 Avg
ADA	96	93
ACU	0	2
AFL-CIO	94	91
CCUS	7	27

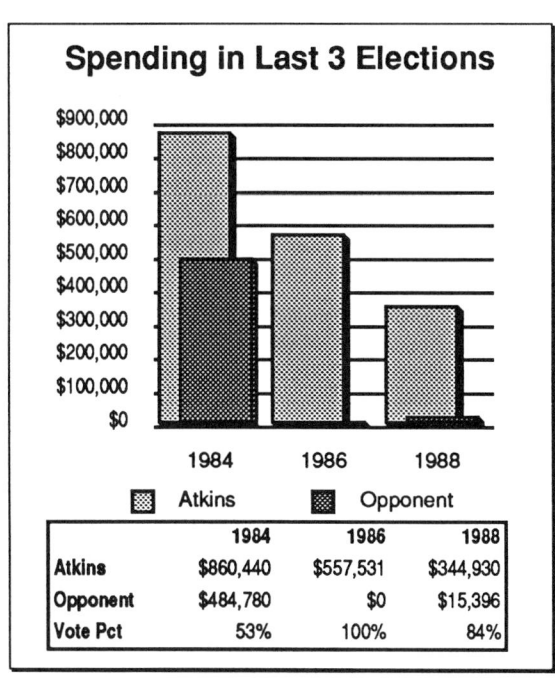

Spending in Last 3 Elections

	1984	1986	1988
Atkins	$860,440	$557,531	$344,930
Opponent	$484,780	$0	$15,396
Vote Pct	53%	100%	84%

Les AuCoin, D-Ore (1)

1988 Committees & Subcommittees

Appropriations
Defense
District of Columbia
Interior and Related Agencies

First elected: 1974
Total receipts: $724,149
Total from PACs: $340,400

Campaign Revenue Sources

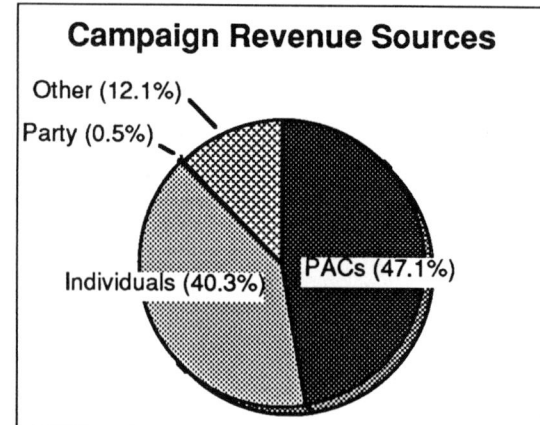

Other (12.1%)
Party (0.5%)
Individuals (40.3%)
PACs (47.1%)

PAC Contribution Profile

Business

Auto Dealers	**$6,000**
Auto Dealers & Drivers for Free Trade	$3,500
National Auto Dealers Assn	$2,500
Construction	**$10,539**
National Assn of Home Builders	$8,189
Blount Inc	$1,000
Others	$1,350
Defense	**$54,600**
General Dynamics	$5,350
Northrop Corp	$5,000
Textron Inc	$4,350
McDonnell Douglas*	$4,000
Hughes Aircraft	$3,500
Lockheed Corp	$3,500
AT&T	$3,000
Boeing Company	$3,000
LTV Aerospace & Defense Company	$2,900
General Electric	$2,200
Grumman	$2,000
TRW Inc	$1,850
E-Systems/Corporate Division	$1,500
Bath Iron Works	$1,050
Litton Industries	$1,050
Texas Instruments	$1,050
Motorola Inc	$1,000
Others	$8,300
Department/Variety Stores	**$6,400**
Fred Meyer Inc	$6,100
Others	$300

Electric Utilities	**$6,200**
Pacific Power & Light	$2,000
Portland General Electric Company	$1,850
Others	$2,350
Financial Institutions	**$19,050**
Credit Union National Assn	$8,000
American Bankers Assn	$3,500
US Bancorp*	$2,050
Rainier Bancorp	$1,500
National Council of Savings Institutions	$1,200
Others	$2,800
Forest Products	**$14,714**
National Forest Products Assn	$4,464
Mountain Fir Lumber Company	$2,200
Multnomah Plywood	$2,000
Weyerhaeuser Company*	$1,900
Georgia-Pacific Corp	$1,350
Boise Cascade	$1,150
Sun Studs Inc	$1,000
Others	$650
Health Professionals	**$10,100**
American Medical Assn	$7,500
National Assn of Pharmacists	$1,000
Others	$1,600
Lawyers & Lobbyists	**$17,330**
Assn of Trial Lawyers of America	$10,000
Stoel, Rives, Boley, Jones & Grey	$2,350
Garvey, Schubert & Barer	$1,800
Kirkland & Ellis	$1,000
Others	$2,180
Real Estate	**$11,850**
National Assn of Realtors	$8,800
Mortgage Bankers Assn of America	$2,200
Others	$850
Sea Transport	**$5,250**
United States Lines	$1,000
Others	$4,250
Telecommunications	**$5,250**
Pacific Northwest Bell	$3,350
Others	$1,900

PAC Totals by Category

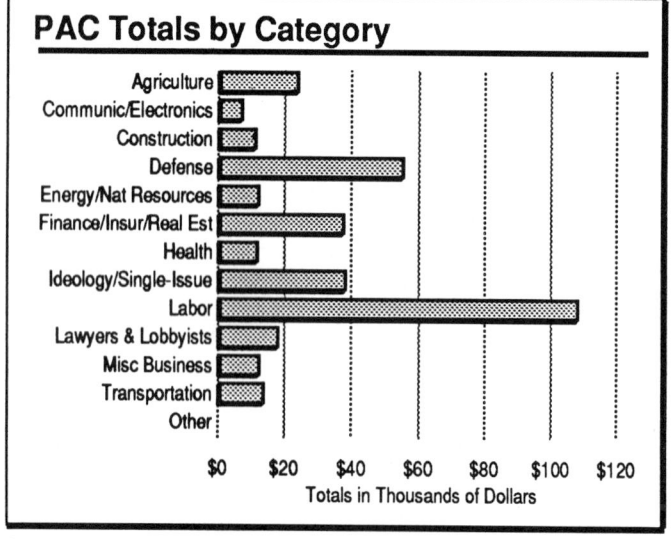

Agriculture
Communic/Electronics
Construction
Defense
Energy/Nat Resources
Finance/Insur/Real Est
Health
Ideology/Single-Issue
Labor
Lawyers & Lobbyists
Misc Business
Transportation
Other

$0 $20 $40 $60 $80 $100 $120
Totals in Thousands of Dollars

Other Major Business PACs

National Venture Capital Assn	$3,000	Venture Cap
Mid-American Dairymen	$2,700	Dairy
Waste Management Inc	$2,600	Waste Mgmt
Nike Inc	$2,350	Shoes
Chicago Mercantile Exchange	$1,350	Commodities
American Veterinary Medical Assn	$1,000	Veterinary
American Hospital Assn	$1,000	Hospitals
American Trucking Assns	$1,000	Trucking
Intel Corp	$1,000	Computer Part
Joseph E Seagram & Sons	$1,000	Wine&Liquor
National Assn of Life Underwriters	$1,000	Life Insurance
Northwest Natural Gas	$1,000	Natural Gas
Standard Insurance Company	$1,000	Insurance

Labor

Bldg Trades/Industrial/Misc Unions	**$35,200**
Carpenters & Joiners Union	$5,700
Food & Commercial Workers Union	$5,200
United Steelworkers	$4,000
Machinists/Aerospace Workers Union	$3,350
AFL-CIO*	$3,200
Intl Brotherhood of Electrical Workers	$2,500
Ironworkers Union	$2,500
Operating Engineers Union	$2,000
Laborers' Political League	$1,350
Bakery, Confectionery & Tobacco Workers	$1,000
Plumbers/Pipefitters Union	$1,000
Sheet Metal Workers Union	$1,000
United Auto Workers	$1,000
Others	$1,400

Government & Postal Workers	**$22,800**
National Assn of Letter Carriers	$7,950
National Assn of Retired Federal Employees	$7,000
American Fedn of State/County/Munic Employees	$4,000
American Postal Workers Union	$2,000
Others	$1,850

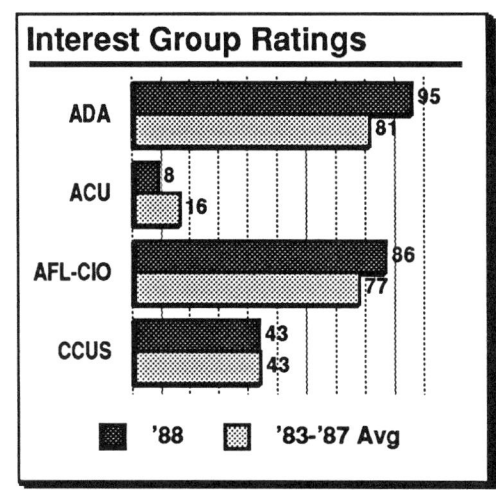

Interest Group Ratings

ADA — '88: 95, '83-'87 Avg: 81
ACU — '88: 8, '83-'87 Avg: 16
AFL-CIO — '88: 86, '83-'87 Avg: 77
CCUS — '88: 43, '83-'87 Avg: 43

■ '88   ▨ '83-'87 Avg

Teachers Unions	**$6,810**
National Education Assn	$3,700
Oregon Education Assn	$2,110
American Federation of Teachers	$1,000

Transportation Unions	**$42,700**
Marine Engineers Union	$10,000
Teamsters Union	$10,000
Seafarers International Union*	$9,600
United Transportation Union	$3,700
Masters, Mates & Pilots Union	$3,000
Longshoremen/Warehousemen Union	$2,000
Air Line Pilots Assn	$1,500
Amalgamated Transit Union	$1,000
Others	$1,900

Ideological/Single-Issue

Pro-Choice	**$15,500**
National Abortion Rights Action League	$10,000
Voters for Choice/Friends of Family Planning	$5,500

Pro-Israel	**$8,000**
National PAC	$5,000
Roundtable PAC	$1,000
Washington PAC	$1,000
Others	$1,000

Other Major Ideological/Single-Issue

Human Rights Campaign Fund	$5,000	Gay Rights
National Cmte to Preserve Social Security	$5,000	Soc Secur
Sierra Club	$1,106	Environment

Independent expenditures supporting AuCoin

National Cmte to Preserve Social Security	$3,769

Spending in Last 3 Elections

■ AuCoin   ■ Opponent

	1984	1986	1988
AuCoin	$841,614	$946,767	$542,224
Opponent	$655,136	$492,655	$11,741
Vote Pct	53%	62%	70%

---

* Contributions came from more than one PAC affiliated
with this sponsor.

Richard H. Baker, R-La (6)

1988 Committees & Subcommittees

First elected: 1986
Total receipts: $287,230
Total from PACs: $124,525

Interior and Insular Affairs
Energy and the Environment
Insular and International Affairs
Water and Power Resources

Small Business
Regulation and Business Opportunities
SBA and the General Economy

PAC Contribution Profile

Business

Auto Dealers	**$4,250**
National Auto Dealers Assn	$2,750
Auto Dealers & Drivers for Free Trade	$1,500
Chemicals	**$2,500**
Monsanto Company	$750
Others	$1,750
Commercial & Savings Banks	**$3,300**
First Commerce Corp	$1,500
Louisiana National Bank	$600
Others	$1,200
Construction	**$10,250**
National Assn of Home Builders	$6,000
Associated General Contractors	$1,500
Associated Builders & Contractors	$750
Others	$2,000
Dairy	**$4,500**
Associated Milk Producers	$2,000
Dairymen Inc-Louisiana	$2,000
Others	$500
Defense	**$2,950**
Harris Corp	$1,000
Others	$1,950
Electric Utilities	**$6,750**
Middle South Utilities*	$2,200
Gulf States Utilities	$750
Texas Utilities Electric Company*	$750
Others	$3,050

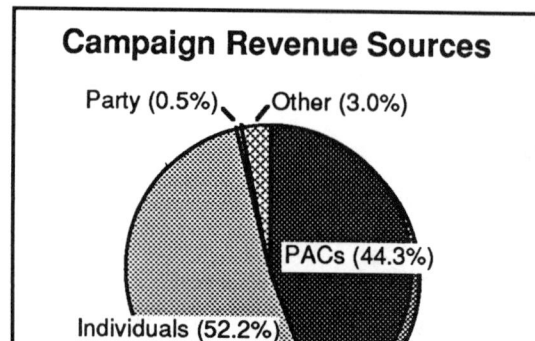

Campaign Revenue Sources

Party (0.5%)　Other (3.0%)
PACs (44.3%)
Individuals (52.2%)

Food & Beverage	**$6,250**
Malone & Hyde Inc	$2,000
Delchamps Inc	$1,000
Morrison Inc	$1,000
National Restaurant Assn	$1,000
Others	$1,250
Forest Products	**$2,550**
International Paper Company	$1,000
Georgia-Pacific Corp	$800
Others	$750
Health Professionals	**$7,249**
American Medical Assn	$4,999
American Academy of Ophthalmology	$1,500
Others	$750
Insurance	**$7,400**
National Assn of Life Underwriters	$2,500
Independent Insurance Agents of America	$1,800
American International Group Inc	$1,000
National Assn of Mutual Insurance Agents	$550
Others	$1,550
Lawyers	**$2,500**
Assn of Trial Lawyers of America	$2,000
Others	$500
Oil & Gas	**$15,350**
Shell Oil	$1,300
Exxon Corp	$1,000
Occidental Petroleum*	$1,000
Tenneco Inc	$1,000
Columbia Hydrocarbon Corp	$800
Mobil Oil	$750
Union Pacific Corp	$700
Atlantic Richfield	$550
BP America	$550
Chevron Corp	$550
Texaco	$550
Others	$6,600
Real Estate	**$5,500**
National Assn of Realtors	$5,000
Others	$500

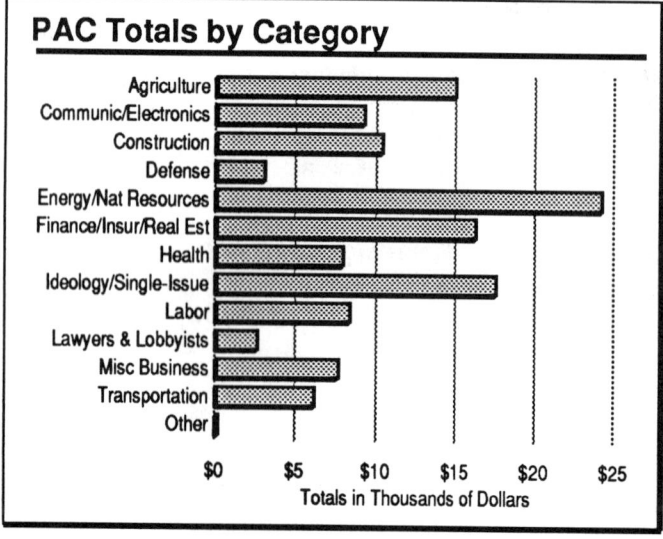

PAC Totals by Category

Agriculture
Communic/Electronics
Construction
Defense
Energy/Nat Resources
Finance/Insur/Real Est
Health
Ideology/Single-Issue
Labor
Lawyers & Lobbyists
Misc Business
Transportation
Other

$0　$5　$10　$15　$20　$25

Totals in Thousands of Dollars

Sugar Growers **$2,250**
    American Sugar Cane League $1,500
    Others $750

Telecommunications **$9,100**
    South Central Bell Telephone $6,000
    AT&T $3,100

Other Major Business PACs

Ciba-Geigy Corp	$550	Pharmaceut
Kansas City Southern	$550	Railroads

Labor

Labor Unions **$8,250**
    National Assn of Retired Federal Employees $7,000
    Seafarers International Union...............................$750
    Others $500

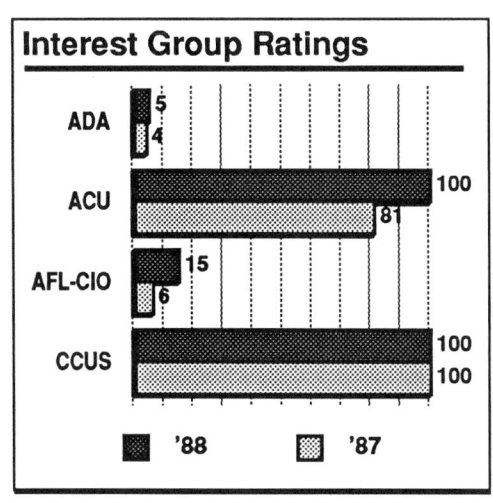

Interest Group Ratings

	'88	'87
ADA	5	4
ACU	100	81
AFL-CIO	15	6
CCUS	100	100

Ideological/Single-Issue

Pro-Israel **$8,100**
    National PAC $5,000
    Louisiana for American Security $2,750
    Others $350

Other Major Ideological/Single-Issue PACs

National Rifle Assn	$4,750	Pro-Guns
American Security Council	$1,643	Pro-Defense
New Republican Victory Fund (Trent Lott)	$1,000	Repub Leader

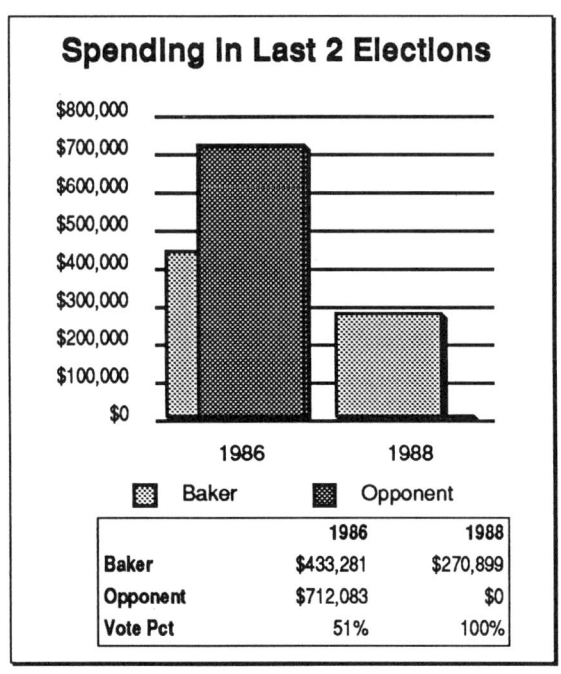

Spending In Last 2 Elections

	Baker	Opponent

	1986	1988
Baker	$433,281	$270,899
Opponent	$712,083	$0
Vote Pct	51%	100%

* Contributions came from more than one PAC affiliated with this sponsor.

Cass Ballenger, R-NC (10)

1988 Committees & Subcommittees

Education and Labor
Health and Safety
Labor-Management Relations

Public Works and Transportation
Aviation
Economic Development

First elected: 1986
Total receipts: $322,903
Total from PACs: $153,375

PAC Contribution Profile

Business

Campaign Revenue Sources

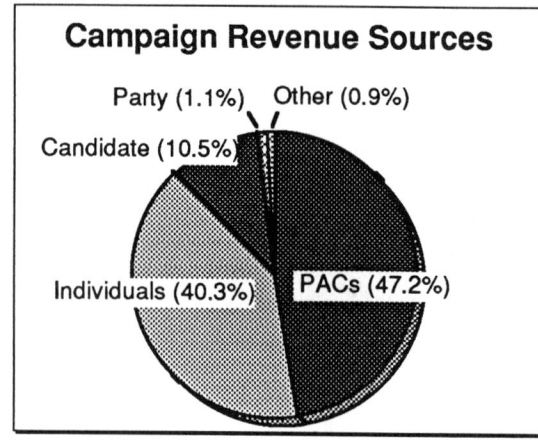

Party (1.1%)   Other (0.9%)
Candidate (10.5%)
Individuals (40.3%)   PACs (47.2%)

Air Transport & Equipment **$10,730**
Aircraft Owners & Pilots Assn $5,180
Eastern Airlines $3,000
Textron Inc $1,750
Others $800

Automotive **$8,000**
National Auto Dealers Assn $6,000
Auto Dealers & Drivers for Free Trade $1,500
Others $500

Building Contractors & Supplies **$11,850**
Associated General Contractors $2,500
National Utility Contractors Assn $2,000
Westvaco Corp $2,000
National Assn of Home Builders $1,500
American Subcontractors Assn $1,250
JA Jones Construction Company $1,000
Others $1,600

Chemicals **$5,100**
FMC Corp $3,000
Others $2,100

Commercial Banks **$3,750**
Branch Banking & Trust $1,000
First Union Corp $1,000
Others $1,750

Defense **$2,750**
United Technologies $1,250
Others $1,500

Electric Utilities **$5,500**
Duke Power Company $2,500
Carolina Power & Light $1,500
National Rural Electric Co-op Assn $1,000
Others $500

Food & Beverage **$10,350**
Food Marketing Institute $2,000
Hardee's Food Systems $2,000
National Restaurant Assn $2,000
Others $4,350

Health Professionals **$8,500**
American Medical Assn $2,750
American Academy of Ophthalmology $2,500
American Dental Assn $1,500
American Podiatry Assn $1,000
Others $750

Household & Office Products **$5,500**
American Furniture Manufacturers Assn $5,000
Others $500

Insurance **$5,500**
National Assn of Life Underwriters $3,000
Jefferson-Pilot Corp $1,500
Others $1,000

Oil Production & Marketing **$4,300**
Amoco Corp $1,500
Others $2,800

Real Estate **$8,000**
National Assn of Realtors $8,000

Telecommunications **$11,750**
Southern Bell $5,250
United Telecommunications $5,000
AT&T $1,000
Others $500

Textiles & Synthetic Fibers **$8,900**
Burlington Industries $2,050
Hoechst Celanese Corp $1,250
Cone Mills Corp $1,000
Dixie Yarns/TI-CARO $1,000
Springs Mills $1,000
Others $2,600

PAC Totals by Category

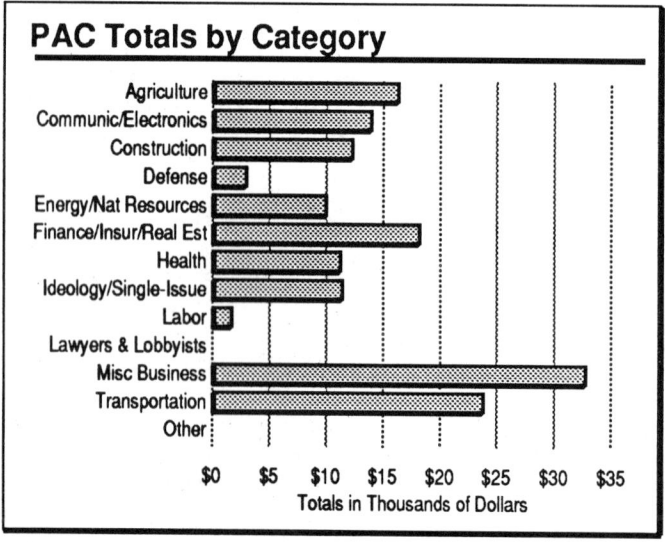

Agriculture
Communic/Electronics
Construction
Defense
Energy/Nat Resources
Finance/Insur/Real Est
Health
Ideology/Single-Issue
Labor
Lawyers & Lobbyists
Misc Business
Transportation
Other

$0 $5 $10 $15 $20 $25 $30 $35
Totals in Thousands of Dollars

Tobacco **$6,500**
      RJR Nabisco $3,500
      Philip Morris $2,000
      Others $1,000

Trucking/Delivery **$3,850**
      Carolina Freight Carriers $1,500
      United Parcel Service $1,250
      Others $1,100

Other Major Business PACs

PPG Industries	$3,000	Glass Prod
American Veterinary Medical Assn	$2,000	Veterinary
American Hospital Assn	$1,000	Hospitals
International Paper Company	$1,000	Paper Prod
International Mass Retail Assn	$1,000	Retail

Major Labor PACs

Seafarers International Union	$1,000	Seamen Union

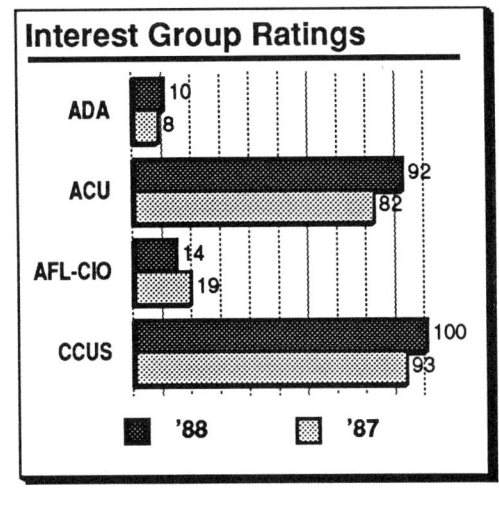

Ideological/Single-Issue

Pro-Israel **$9,250**
      National PAC $5,000
      Americans for Good Government Inc $1,000
      Hudson Valley PAC $1,000
      Roundtable PAC $1,000
      Others $1,250

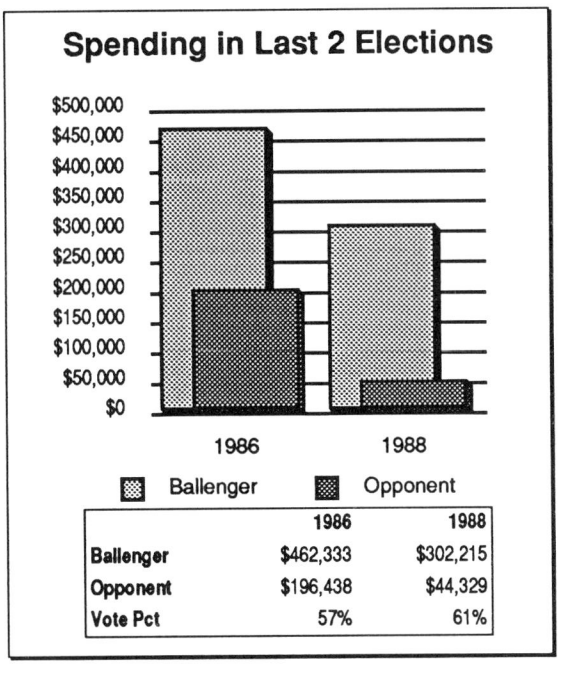

Doug Barnard Jr., D-Ga (10)

First elected: 1976
Total receipts: $285,060
Total from PACs: $176,171

1988 Committees & Subcommittees

Banking, Finance and Urban Affairs
Domestic Monetary Policy
Economic Stabilization
Financial Institutions Supervision, Regulation and Insurance
General Oversight and Investigations

Government Operations
Commerce, Consumer and Monetary Affairs (Chairman)

PAC Contribution Profile

Business

Campaign Revenue Sources

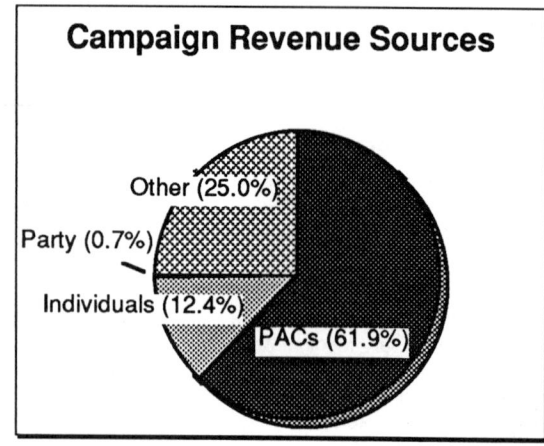

Other (25.0%)
Party (0.7%)
Individuals (12.4%)
PACs (61.9%)

Accountants	....	**$6,750**
American Institute of CPA's		$5,000
Arthur Young & Company		$750
Deloitte, Haskins & Sells		$500
Price Waterhouse		$500

Automotive & Trucking	....	**$7,250**
National Auto Dealers Assn		$3,000
Auto Dealers & Drivers for Free Trade		$2,500
American Trucking Assns		$1,000
Others		$750

Building Supplies & Contractors		**$6,600**
National Assn of Home Builders		$3,500
Associated General Contractors		$1,000
Manville Corp		$1,000
Others		$1,100

Commercial Banks		**$70,100**
American Bankers Assn		$10,000
J P Morgan & Company		$10,000
Citizens & Southern National Bank		$5,000
Citicorp		$4,500
Barnett Banks of Florida		$4,000
Security Pacific Corp		$3,500
Wells Fargo		$3,000
Chase Manhattan		$2,500
Consumer Bankers Assn		$2,500
First Atlanta Corp		$2,000
Suntrust Banks*		$2,000

(Continued in next column)

PAC Totals by Category

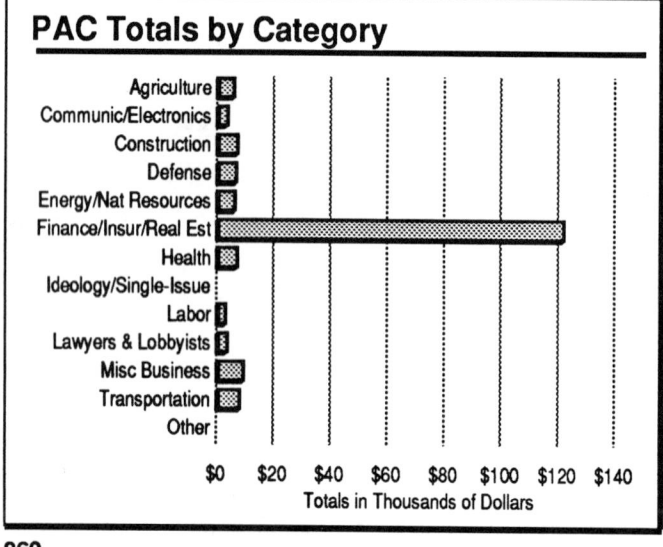

	Totals in Thousands of Dollars
Agriculture	
Communic/Electronics	
Construction	
Defense	
Energy/Nat Resources	
Finance/Insur/Real Est	
Health	
Ideology/Single-Issue	
Labor	
Lawyers & Lobbyists	
Misc Business	
Transportation	
Other	

$0 $20 $40 $60 $80 $100 $120 $140

Commercial Banks (cont'd)

BankAmerica		$1,500
Chemical Bank		$1,500
First Chicago Corp		$1,500
Manufacturers Hanover		$1,500
Continental Illinois Corp		$1,350
Ameritrust Company		$1,000
Assn of Bank Holding Companies		$1,000
Banc One Corp*		$1,000
Bank of Boston		$1,000
Bank South Corp		$1,000
Bankers Trust		$1,000
CB&T Bancshares		$1,000
First Railroad & Banking Company		$1,000
Irving Bank		$1,000
Marine Midland Banks		$1,000
Others		$3,750

Credit & Finance Companies		**$6,550**
Household International		$2,000
American Express		$1,500
American Financial Services Assn		$1,000
Others		$2,050

Defense	....	**$6,250**
Lockheed Corp		$2,500
Textron Inc		$1,000
Others		$2,750

Gas & Electric Utilities		**$5,750**
Atlanta Gas Light Company		$1,000
Southern Company*		$1,750
ACRE (Action Committee for Rural Electrification)		$3,000

Health Professionals		**$5,000**
American Medical Assn		$5,000

Insurance	....	**$8,000**
Travelers Corp		$1,500
Acacia Mutual Life Insurance		$1,000
American Family Corp		$1,000
Capital Holding Corp		$1,000
John Hancock Financial Service		$1,000
Sears		$1,000
Others		$1,500

Real Estate	....	**$12,000**
National Assn of Realtors		$8,000
First Union Corp		$2,000
National Assn of Independent Fee Appraisers		$2,000

Interest Group Ratings

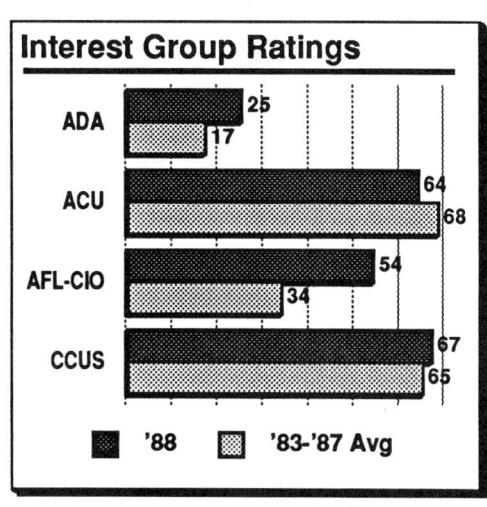

	'88	'83-'87 Avg
ADA	25	17
ACU	64	68
AFL-CIO	54	34
CCUS	67	65

Savings Banks & Credit Unions **$11,050**

Columbia Savings & Loan (Beverly Hills)	$2,000
US League of Savings Assn	$2,000
Credit Union National Assn	$1,500
Bankers 1st Federal Savings & Loan	$1,000
California Federal Savings & Loan	$1,000
Home Savings of America	$1,000
Others	$2,550

Securities & Commodities **$7,500**

Dean Witter Reynolds	$2,000
Chicago Board of Trade	$1,000
Merrill Lynch	$1,000
New York Stock Exchange	$1,000
Prudential-Bache Securities	$1,000
Others	$1,500

Other Major Business PACs

Southern Bell	$2,500	Phone Util
Winn-Dixie Stores	$1,000	Food Stores
Federated Department Stores	$1,000	Dept Store
Johnson & Johnson	$1,000	Health Prod
Powell, Goldstein, Frazer & Murphy	$1,000	Lawyers

Major Labor PACs

Teamsters Union	$1,000	Teamsters
Food & Commercial Workers Union	$1,000	Retail Union

Spending in Last 3 Elections

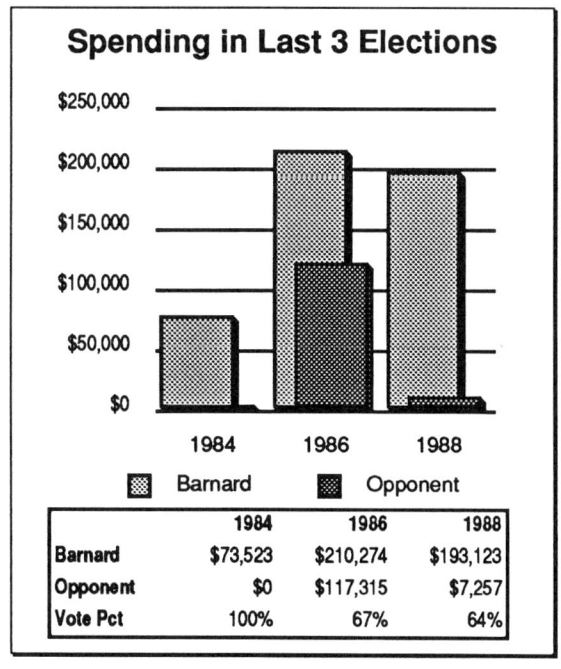

	1984	1986	1988
Barnard	$73,523	$210,274	$193,123
Opponent	$0	$117,315	$7,257
Vote Pct	100%	67%	64%

* Contributions came from more than one PAC affiliated with this sponsor.

Steve Bartlett, R-Texas (3)

First elected: 1982
Total receipts: $769,201
Total from PACs: $230,678

1988 Committees & Subcommittees

Banking, Finance and Urban Affairs
Financial Institutions Supervision, Regulation and Insurance
General Oversight and Investigations
Housing and Community Development

Education and Labor
Select Education (Ranking Republican)
Elementary, Secondary and Vocational Education
Labor Standards

PAC Contribution Profile

Business

Automotive & Trucking	**$7,750**
National Auto Dealers Assn	$4,000
Auto Dealers & Drivers for Free Trade	$1,500
Yellow Freight System	$1,000
Others	$1,250
Bldg Materials & Subcontractors	**$10,935**
National Electrical Contractors Assn	$2,000
Westvaco Corp	$2,000
Sheet Metal/Air Conditioning Contractors	$1,250
Albert H Halff Associates	$1,000
Lennox Industries	$1,000
National Concrete Masonry Assn	$1,000
Others	$2,685
Commercial & Industrial Construction	**$7,475**
Associated General Contractors	$2,500
Associated Builders & Contractors	$1,750
Fluor Corp	$1,750
Others	$1,475

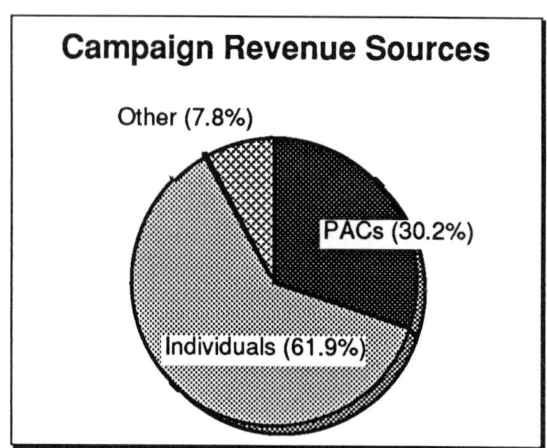

Campaign Revenue Sources

Other (7.8%)
PACs (30.2%)
Individuals (61.9%)

Commercial Banks	**$34,075**
American Bankers Assn	$5,000
J P Morgan & Company	$5,000
Texas Commerce Bancshares*	$3,500
NCNB Texas	$2,250
Barnett Banks of Florida	$2,000
MBank	$1,850
Bankers Trust	$1,500
Sun World Corp	$1,050
BankAmerica	$1,000
Chase Manhattan	$1,000
Chemical Bank	$1,000
Citicorp	$1,000
Citizens & Southern National Bank	$1,000
First City Bancorp	$1,000
Texas American Bancshares	$1,000
Others	$4,925
Computers & Electronics	**$7,150**
Electronic Data Systems	$1,950
Recognition Equipment Inc	$1,850
Texas Instruments	$1,500
Others	$1,850
Defense	**$7,635**
E-Systems*	$2,835
Harris Corp	$1,000
Rockwell International	$1,000
Others	$2,800
Food & Beverage	**$15,725**
Food Marketing Institute	$4,550
National Restaurant Assn	$4,000
McDonald's Corp	$1,000
Pepsico Inc	$1,000
Others	$5,175
Health Professionals	**$10,575**
American Medical Assn	$9,900
Others	$675

PAC Totals by Category

Category	
Agriculture	
Communic/Electronics	
Construction	
Defense	
Energy/Nat Resources	
Finance/Insur/Real Est	
Health	
Ideology/Single-Issue	
Labor	
Lawyers & Lobbyists	
Misc Business	
Transportation	
Other	

$0 $10 $20 $30 $40 $50 $60 $70 $80

Totals in Thousands of Dollars

Insurance **$8,450**

    TransAmerica Insurance $3,000
    Equitable Financial Services $1,100
    National Assn of Life Underwriters $1,050
    Travelers Corp $1,000
    Others $2,300

Lawyers & Lobbyists **$10,525**

    Winstead, McGuire, Sechrest & Minick $3,000
    Baker & Botts $1,750
    Johnson & Gibbs $1,750
    Jones, Day, Reavis & Pogue $1,050
    Hopkins & Sudder $1,000
    Others $1,975

Oil & Gas **$17,200**

    Halliburton Company* $2,000
    Enserch Corp $1,850
    Atlantic Richfield $1,525
    Dresser Industries $1,150
    Mesa PAC II $1,050
    Texaco $1,050
    Rosewood Corp $1,000
    Sun Company $1,000
    Others $6,575

Other Finance **$18,625**

    Arthur Young & Company $3,050
    Coopers & Lybrand* $1,850
    Dean Witter Reynolds $1,850
    Gulf + Western Industries $1,800
    American Financial Services Assn $1,550
    Nowlin Savings Assn $1,250
    Equifax Inc $1,000
    First Boston Corp $1,000
    Others $5,275

Interest Group Ratings

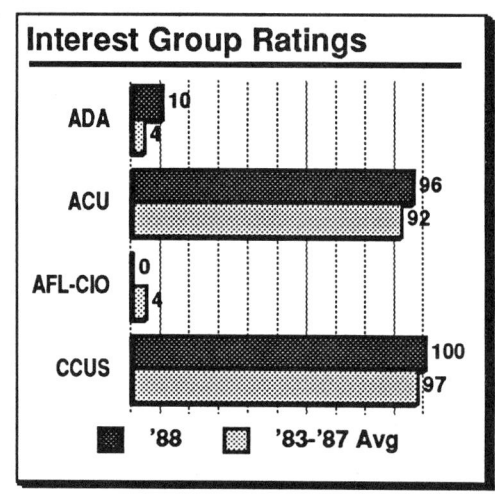

Real Estate **$16,650**

    National Assn of Realtors $10,000
    Commonwealth Financial Group $2,750
    Mortgage Bankers Assn of America $1,750
    Federal National Mortgage Assn $1,050
    Southland Financial Corp $1,000
    Others $100

Residential Construction **$7,050**

    Manufactured Housing Institute $1,850
    Centex Corp $1,750
    National Assn of Home Builders $1,750
    National Manufactured Housing Federation ...$1,150
    Others $550

Retail Sales **$10,978**

    International Mass Retail Assn $2,000
    J C Penney Company $1,850
    Southland Corp $1,828
    Federated Department Stores $1,000
    Others $4,300

Telecommunications **$6,000**

    AT&T $2,050
    GTE (Southwest) $1,950
    Southwestern Bell $1,500
    Others $500

Other Major Business PACs

Texas Utilities Electric Company*	$4,000	Electric Util
Texas Farm Bureau	$2,600	Farm Orgs
American Airlines	$1,950	Airlines
Lone Star Steel*	$1,550	Steel
Hoechst Celanese Corp	$1,200	SynthFiber
National Apartment Assn	$1,050	Bldg Mgmt
National Fedn of Independent Business	$1,050	Sml Business
Philip Morris	$1,037	Tobacco
Contran Corp	$1,000	Chemicals
Dow Chemical	$1,000	Chemicals
Holiday Inns	$1,000	Hotel/Motel
Texas Cattle Feeders Assn	$1,000	Feedlots
Texas/Southwestern Cattle Raisers	$1,000	Livestock
Xerox Corp	$1,000	Off Machines

Other Major Non-Business PACs

Teamsters Union	$1,750	Teamsters
Council for National Defense	$1,610	Pro-Defense

---

* Contributions came from more than one PAC affiliated
  with this sponsor.

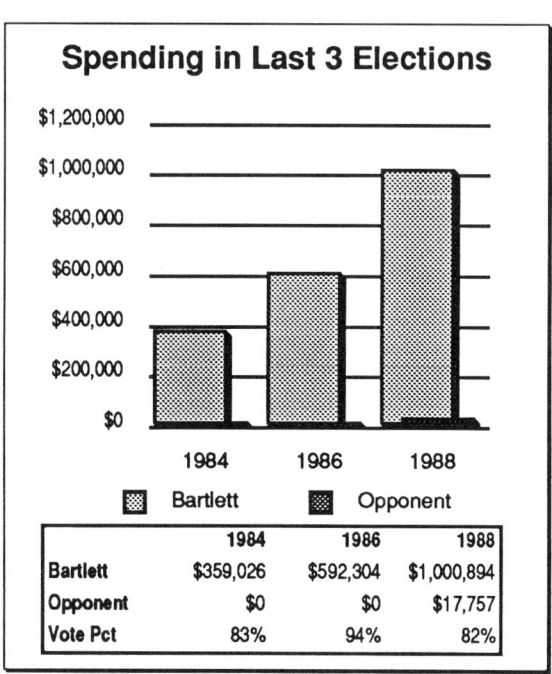

Spending in Last 3 Elections

	1984	1986	1988
Bartlett	$359,026	$592,304	$1,000,894
Opponent	$0	$0	$17,757
Vote Pct	83%	94%	82%

Joe L. Barton, R-Texas (6)

1988 Committees & Subcommittees

Energy and Commerce
Commerce, Consumer Protection and Competitiveness
Energy and Power

First elected: 1984
Total receipts: $750,559
Total from PACs: $288,083

PAC Contribution Profile

Business

Accountants **$5,600**
    American Institute of CPA's $5,000
    Others $600

Automotive **$12,150**
    National Auto Dealers Assn $6,550
    Auto Dealers & Drivers for Free Trade $3,500
    Others $2,100

Broadcasting/Cable TV **$3,300**
    National Cable Television Assn $2,000
    National Assn of Broadcasters $1,300

Chemicals **$5,150**
    NL Industries* $2,500
    Others $2,650

Commercial Banks **$13,160**
    First Bank & Trust $2,360
    American Bankers Assn $1,500
    NCNB Texas $1,500
    MBank $1,250
    Citizens & Southern National Bank $1,050
    Barnett Banks of Florida $1,000
    First City Bancorp $1,000
    Texas Commerce Bancshares $1,000
    Others $2,500

Campaign Revenue Sources

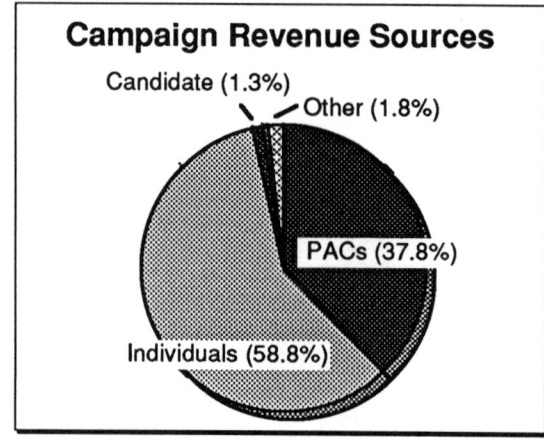

Candidate (1.3%)
Other (1.8%)
PACs (37.8%)
Individuals (58.8%)

Construction **$23,550**
    Owens-Corning Fiberglas $5,000
    National Assn of Home Builders $2,750
    Associated General Contractors $2,000
    Manville Corp $2,000
    Walter Industries $2,000
    Texas Industries $1,750
    Brown & Root $1,050
    Lennox Industries $1,000
    Others $6,000

Defense **$10,550**
    Textron Inc $1,600
    E-Systems* $1,550
    Electrospace Systems Inc $1,000
    Rockwell International $1,000
    Varo Inc $1,000
    Others $4,400

Electric Utilities **$32,400**
    Texas Utilities Electric Company* $10,000
    Houston Industries $5,000
    Southern Company* $3,000
    Public Service Company of New Hampshire* ... $1,100
    Central & South West Services $1,000
    Pacific Gas & Electric $1,000
    Others $11,300

Food & Beverage **$6,300**
    Morrison Inc $1,000
    Texas Restaurant Assn $1,000
    Others $4,300

Health Professionals **$17,050**
    American Medical Assn $11,750
    American Dental Assn $1,750
    American Academy of Ophthalmology $1,000
    Cmte for Quality Orthopedic Health Care $1,000
    Texas Medical Assn $1,000
    Others $550

Insurance **$10,750**
    Torchmark Corp $2,000
    American National Insurance Company $1,500
    American General Insurance Company $1,000
    National Assn of Life Underwriters $1,000
    Others $5,250

PAC Totals by Category

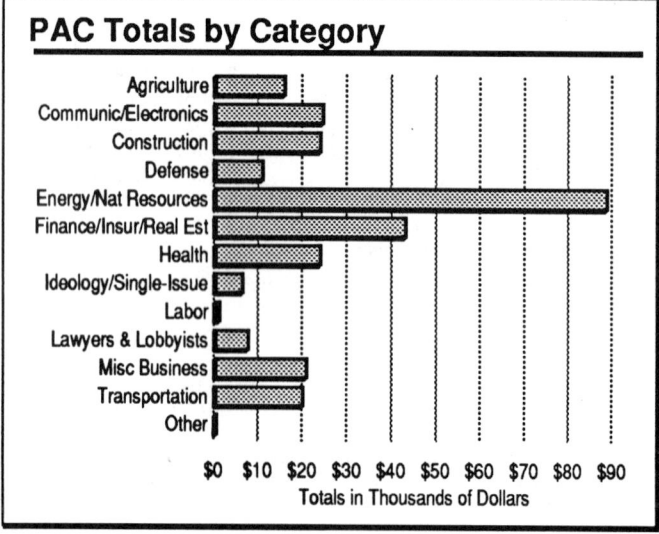

Agriculture
Communic/Electronics
Construction
Defense
Energy/Nat Resources
Finance/Insur/Real Est
Health
Ideology/Single-Issue
Labor
Lawyers & Lobbyists
Misc Business
Transportation
Other

$0 $10 $20 $30 $40 $50 $60 $70 $80 $90
Totals in Thousands of Dollars

Lawyers **$7,350**

Winstead, McGuire Sechrest & Minick	$2,000
Baker & Botts	$1,100
Johnson & Gibbs	$1,000
Others	$3,250

Oil & Gas **$50,207**

Atlantic Richfield	$5,750
Tenneco Inc	$2,500
Dow Chemical*	$2,250
Halliburton Company*	$2,000
Mesa PAC II	$2,000
Amoco Corp	$1,800
Internorth Inc	$1,800
American Petrofina	$1,500
Sun Company	$1,500
Enserch Corp	$1,250
Chevron Corp	$1,050
Columbia Hydrocarbon Corp	$1,050
Southland Corp	$1,007
HouPAC	$1,000
Hunt Committee for Sound Government	$1,000
Maxus Energy Corp	$1,000
Mitchell Energy & Development	$1,000
Phillips Petroleum	$1,000
Shell Oil	$1,000
Union Pacific Corp	$1,000
Valero Energy Corp	$1,000
Others	$16,750

Pharmaceuticals **$4,700**

Pfizer Inc	$1,000
Others	$3,700

Real Estate **$9,300**

National Assn of Realtors	$8,000
Others	$1,300

Retail Sales **$3,550**

Federated Department Stores	$1,000
J C Penney Company	$1,000
National Assn of Convenience Stores	$1,000
Others	$550

Interest Group Ratings

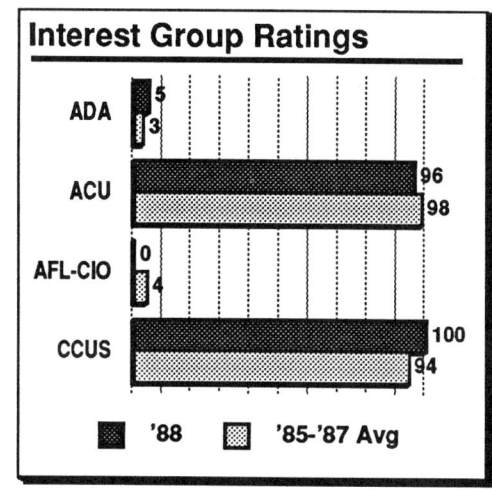

Securities/Commodities Trading **$3,550**

Morgan Stanley & Company	$1,000
Others	$2,550

Telecommunications **$19,300**

AT&T	$4,000
GTE (Southwest)	$2,500
Continental Telecom	$2,250
Southwestern Bell	$2,000
BellSouth Services	$1,550
United Telecommunications	$1,500
Bell Atlantic	$1,050
Pacific Telesis Group	$1,050
Others	$3,400

Tobacco **$4,250**

Philip Morris	$2,000
RJR Nabisco	$1,500
Others	$750

Other Major Business PACs

Texas Farm Bureau	$2,500	Farm Orgs
Texas Cattle Feeders Assn	$1,500	Feedlots
Lone Star Steel*	$1,300	Steel
Aircraft Owners & Pilots Assn	$1,250	Genl Aviation
Hoechst Celanese Corp	$1,250	Synth Fiber
United Parcel Service	$1,100	Delivery
Browning-Ferris Industries	$1,000	Waste Mgmt

Ideological/Single-Issue

Ideological & Leadership PACs **$5,590**

Conservative Victory Fund (Steve Symms)	$1,490	Repub Leader
Conservatives Acting Together	$1,000	Repub/Conser
Others	$3,100	

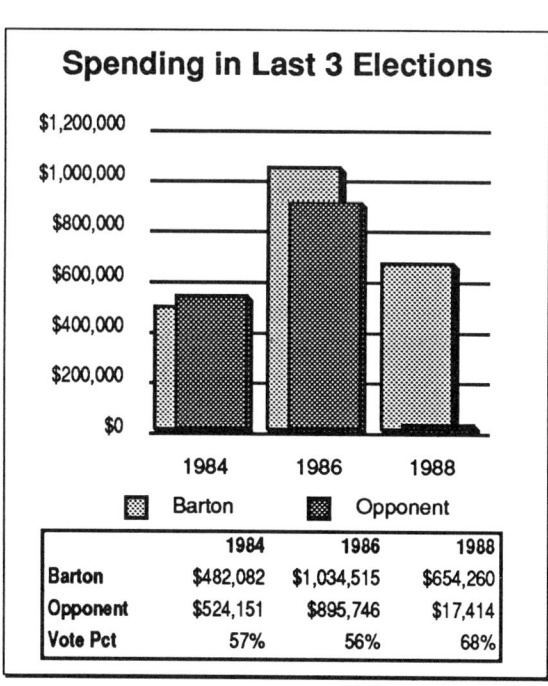

Spending in Last 3 Elections

	1984	1986	1988
Barton	$482,082	$1,034,515	$654,260
Opponent	$524,151	$895,746	$17,414
Vote Pct	57%	56%	68%

Barton   Opponent

---

* Contributions came from more than one PAC affiliated
with this sponsor.

Herbert H. Bateman, R-Va (1)

First elected: 1982
Total receipts: $293,109
Total from PACs: $159,640

1988 Committees & Subcommittees

Armed Services
Military Personnel and Compensation (Ranking Republican)
Seapower and Strategic and Critical Materials

Merchant Marine and Fisheries
Coast Guard and Navigation
Fisheries and Wildlife Conservation and the Environment
Merchant Marine

PAC Contribution Profile

Business

Automotive & Trucking **$6,500**
National Auto Dealers Assn $3,500
Auto Dealers & Drivers for Free Trade $2,000
Others $1,000

Building Contractors & Supplies..................................**$5,000**
Associated General Contractors $1,500
National Assn of Home Builders $1,250
National Utility Contractors Assn $1,000
Others $1,250

Commercial Banks **$9,250**
Virginia Bankers Assn $5,250
Dominion Bankshares Corp $2,000
Barnett Banks of Florida $1,000
Sovran Financial Corp $1,000

Defense..**$54,800**
Tenneco Inc $9,000
Continental Telecom $3,000
Lockheed Corp $2,750
McDonnell Douglas* $2,550
Textron Inc $2,500
Boeing Company $2,000
Rockwell International $2,000
Bath Iron Works $1,750
Hughes Aircraft $1,750
Raytheon $1,750
AT&T $1,500
General Electric $1,500
GTE Corp $1,500
Northrop Corp $1,500
(continued in next column)

Campaign Revenue Sources

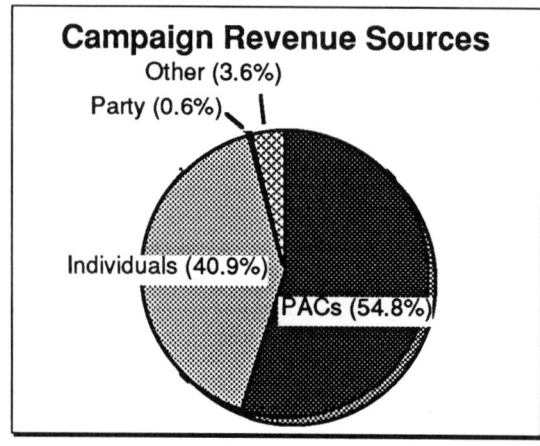

Other (3.6%)
Party (0.6%)
Individuals (40.9%)
PACs (54.8%)

Defense (cont'd)
United Technologies $1,500
BDM International $1,000
FMC Corp $1,000
Grumman $1,000
Harris Corp $1,000
Martin Marietta Corp $1,000
Singer Company $1,000
Others $12,250

Electric Utilities **$4,500**
Virginia ACRE $1,750
ACRE (Action Committee for Rural Electrification) $1,000
Dominion Resources Inc $1,000
Others $750

Food & Beverage **$2,540**
None over $1,000

Health Professionals **$13,500**
American Medical Assn $7,000
American Dental Assn $4,000
American Podiatry Assn $1,000
Others $1,500

Insurance **$4,500**
National Assn of Life Underwriters $3,000
Others $1,500

Oil & Gas **$3,500**
None over $750

Real Estate **$5,750**
National Assn of Realtors $5,250
Others $500

Sea Transport **$4,750**
American Pilots Assn $1,000
CSX Transportation Inc* $1,000
Matson Navigation $1,000
Others $1,750

Other Major Business PACs

National Fisheries Institute	$2,500	Fishing
Westvaco Corp	$2,000	Paper Prod
Philip Morris	$1,500	Tobacco
Waste Management Inc	$1,500	Waste Mgmt
American Textile Manufacturers Institute	$1,000	Textiles
Babcock & Wilcox	$1,000	PowerEquip
Pinkerton Tobacco	$1,000	Tobacco

PAC Totals by Category

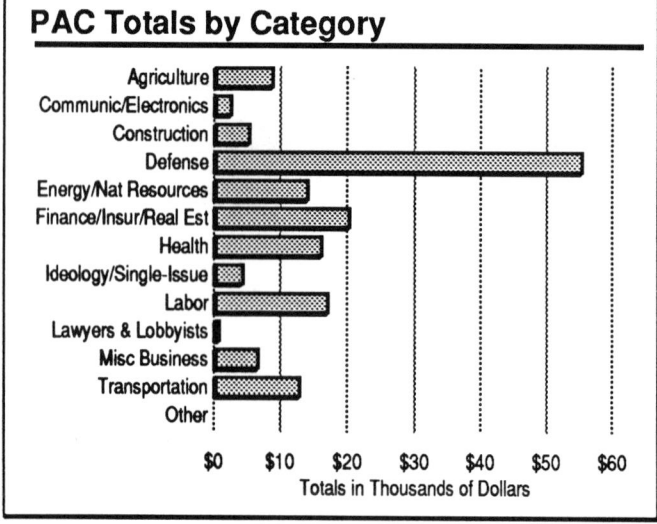

Category	
Agriculture	
Communic/Electronics	
Construction	
Defense	
Energy/Nat Resources	
Finance/Insur/Real Est	
Health	
Ideology/Single-Issue	
Labor	
Lawyers & Lobbyists	
Misc Business	
Transportation	
Other	

$0 $10 $20 $30 $40 $50 $60
Totals in Thousands of Dollars

Labor

Sea Transport Unions ***$14,500***
      Marine Engineers Union* $10,000
      Masters, Mates & Pilots Union $2,500
      Seafarers International Union $2,000

Other Major Labor PACs

National Assn of Retired Federal Employees .. $2,000   Fedl Workers

Ideological/Single-Issue

Pro-Defense PACs ***$2,420***
      None over $1,000

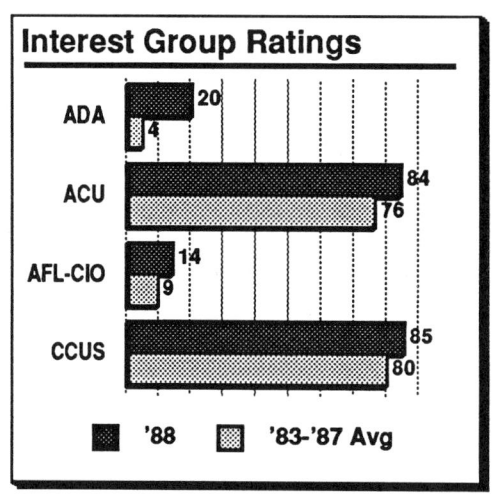

Interest Group Ratings

	'88	'83–'87 Avg
ADA	20	4
ACU	84	76
AFL-CIO	14	9
CCUS	85	80

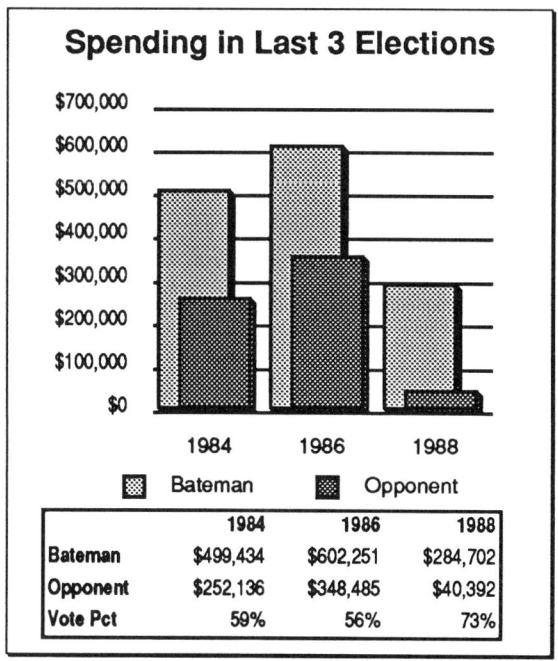

Spending in Last 3 Elections

	1984	1986	1988
Bateman	$499,434	$602,251	$284,702
Opponent	$252,136	$348,485	$40,392
Vote Pct	59%	56%	73%

---

* Contributions came from more than one PAC affiliated with this sponsor.

Jim Bates, D-Calif (44)

1988 Committees & Subcommittees

Energy and Commerce
Commerce, Consumer Protection and Competitiveness
Health and the Environment
Transportation, Tourism and Hazardous Materials

House Administration
Procurement and Printing (Chairman)
Elections

PAC Contribution Profile

Business

Accountants	*$6,450*
American Institute of CPA's	$5,000
Others	$1,450
Commercial & Savings Banks	*$4,925*
Great American Federal Savings	$1,125
American Bankers Assn	$1,000
California League of Savings Institutions	$1,000
Security Pacific Corp	$1,000
Others	$800
Health Professionals	*$21,800*
American Medical Assn	$4,300
American Dental Assn	$3,000
Anesthesia Service Medical Group	$3,000
American College of Emergency Physicians	$2,000
American Academy of Ophthalmology	$1,500
American Optometric Assn	$1,500
American Assn of Physicians from India	$1,000
American Podiatry Assn	$1,000
Cmte for Quality Orthopedic Health Care	$1,000
National Assn of Pharmacists	$1,000
Philippine Physicians in America	$1,000
Others	$1,500
Insurance	*$7,400*
American Family Corp	$5,000
Others	$2,400
Lawyers & Lobbyists	*$10,800*
Assn of Trial Lawyers of America	$10,000
Others	$800

First elected: 1982
Total receipts: $480,884
Total from PACs: $244,955

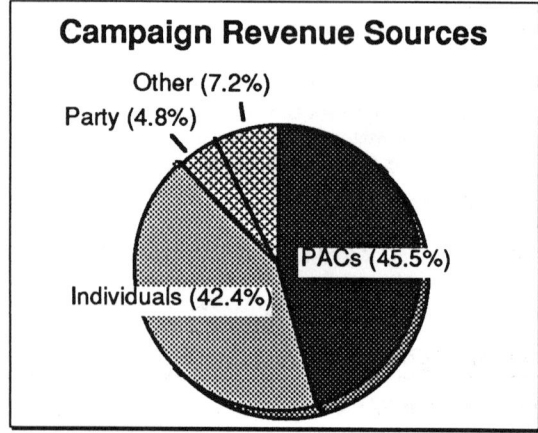

Campaign Revenue Sources

- Other (7.2%)
- Party (4.8%)
- PACs (45.5%)
- Individuals (42.4%)

Movies & Broadcasting	*$5,000*
National Cable Television Assn	$3,500
Others	$1,500
Real Estate	*$8,300*
National Assn of Realtors	$8,300
Securities & Commodities	*$3,450*
Chicago Mercantile Exchange	$1,250
Chicago Board of Trade	$1,000
Others	$1,200
Telecommunications	*$3,700*
Pacific Telesis Group	$2,150
US Telephone Assn	$1,000
Others	$550

Other Major Business PACs

Auto Dealers & Drivers for Free Trade	$2,500	JapanAutoSal
Waste Management Inc	$2,200	Waste Mgmt
Hotel del Coronado	$1,850	Hotel/Motel
Southern California Edison	$1,300	Electric Util
United Parcel Service	$1,150	Delivery
Cubic Corp	$1,050	Electron Def
Coastal Corp	$1,000	Natural Gas
Independent Coal Operators Assn	$1,000	Coal

PAC Totals by Category

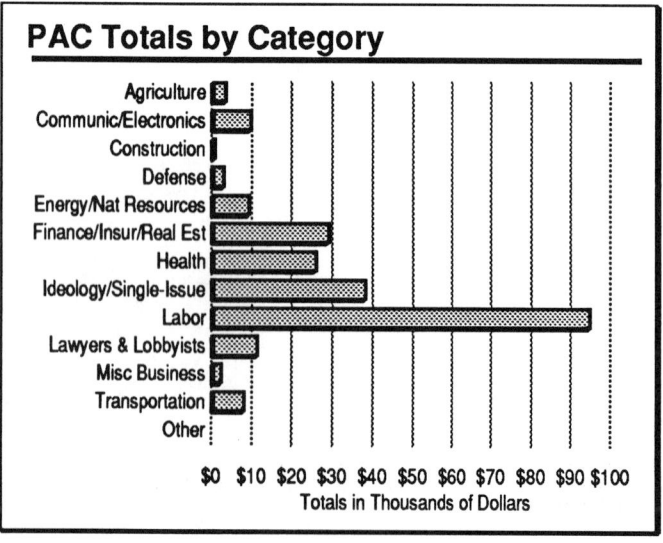

Agriculture
Communic/Electronics
Construction
Defense
Energy/Nat Resources
Finance/Insur/Real Est
Health
Ideology/Single-Issue
Labor
Lawyers & Lobbyists
Misc Business
Transportation
Other

$0 $10 $20 $30 $40 $50 $60 $70 $80 $90 $100

Totals in Thousands of Dollars

Labor

Bldg Trades/Industrial/Misc Unions $51,550

Food/Commercial Workers #1222	$9,600
Ironworkers Union	$7,800
AFL-CIO*	$6,300
Machinists/Aerospace Workers Union	$5,000
Carpenters & Joiners Union	$4,050
Laborers' Western Political League	$4,000
Intl Brotherhood of Electrical Workers...........................	$3,000
Sheet Metal Workers Union	$2,500
Operating Engineers Union	$2,000
Communications Workers of America	$1,500
Plumbers/Pipefitters Union	$1,500
United Auto Workers	$1,500
Others	$2,800

Government & Postal Workers $19,600

National Assn of Letter Carriers	$7,200
National Assn of Retired Federal Employees	$6,100
American Postal Workers Union	$3,200
American Fedn of State/County/Munic Employees	$2,000
Others	$1,100

Teachers Unions $5,975

National Education Assn	$5,675
Others	$300

Transportation Unions $17,200

Teamsters Union	$8,500
United Transportation Union	$2,200
Marine Engineers District 2 Maritime Officers	$1,500
Transportation Communication Union.............................	$1,200
Amalgamated Transit Union...	$1,000
Seafarers International Union	$1,000
Others	$1,800

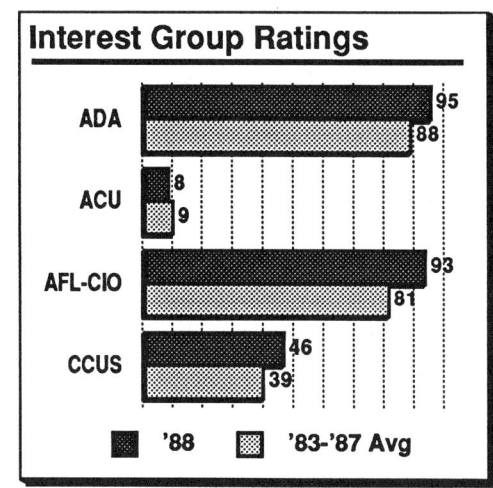

Interest Group Ratings

Ratings: ADA '88 95, '83-'87 Avg 88; ACU '88 8, '83-'87 Avg 9; AFL-CIO '88 93, '83-'87 Avg 81; CCUS '88 46, '83-'87 Avg 39.

■ '88   ▨ '83-'87 Avg

Ideological/Single-Issue

Democratic Leadership PACs $32,000

24th Cong Dist of California PAC (Henry Waxman)	$5,000
America's Leaders' Fund (Dan Rostenkowski)	$5,000
Cmte for a Democratic Consensus (Alan Cranston)	$5,000
Majority Congress Committee (Jim Wright)	$5,000
USA Committee (Jerry Brown)	$5,000
Valley Education Fund (Tony Coelho)	$5,000
Cmte for Democratic Opportunity (Bill Gray)	$1,000
House Leadership Fund (Tom Foley)	$1,000

Other Major Ideological & Single-Issue

Democratic Study Group Campaign Fund	$3,000
National Council of Senior Citizens	$1,000

Independent expenditures supporting Bates

Food/Commercial Workers Local #1222	$2,202

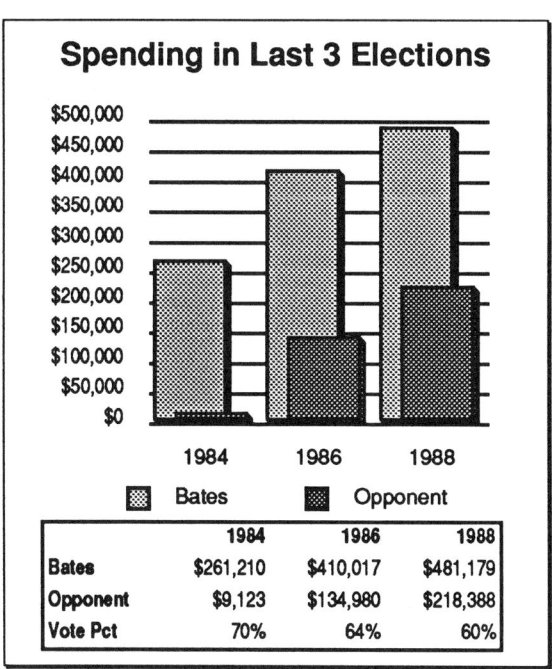

Spending in Last 3 Elections

	1984	1986	1988
Bates	$261,210	$410,017	$481,179
Opponent	$9,123	$134,980	$218,388
Vote Pct	70%	64%	60%

▨ Bates   ■ Opponent

---

* Contributions came from more than one PAC affiliated with this sponsor.

Anthony C. Beilenson, D-Calif (23)

First elected: 1976
Total receipts: $150,275
Total from PACs: $0

1988 Committees & Subcommittees

Rules
Rules of the House

Select Intelligence
Oversight and Evaluation (Chairman)

PAC Contribution Profile

American Health Care Assn .... $250   Nursing Homes

NOTE: Beilenson reported taking no PAC funds in his 1988 campaign. The PAC listed above did report making a contribution to him during 1987-88, however, and that contribution is recorded in the official FEC records.

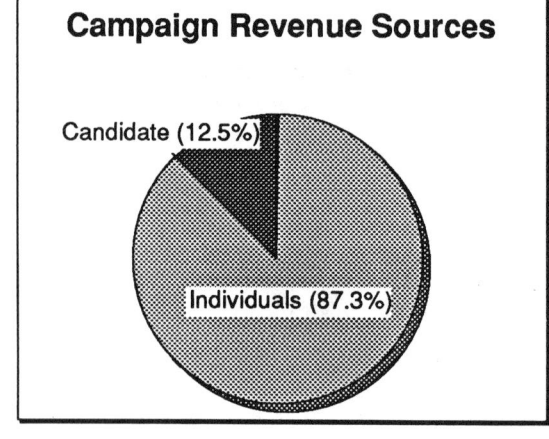

Campaign Revenue Sources

Candidate (12.5%)

Individuals (87.3%)

PAC Totals by Category

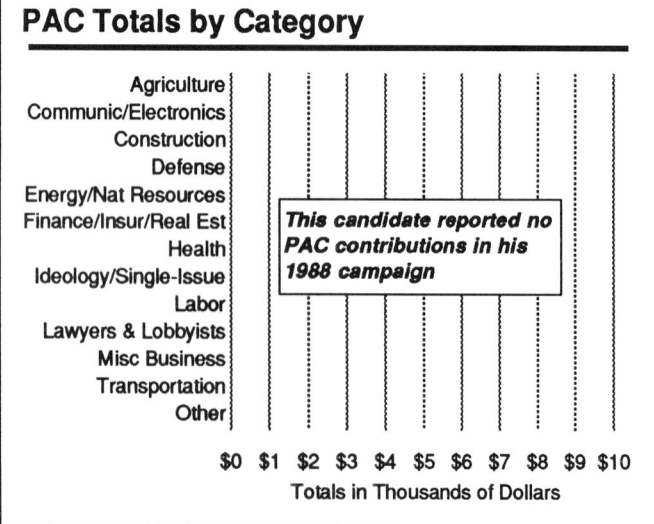

Agriculture
Communic/Electronics
Construction
Defense
Energy/Nat Resources
Finance/Insur/Real Est
Health
Ideology/Single-Issue
Labor
Lawyers & Lobbyists
Misc Business
Transportation
Other

This candidate reported no PAC contributions in his 1988 campaign

$0 $1 $2 $3 $4 $5 $6 $7 $8 $9 $10
Totals in Thousands of Dollars

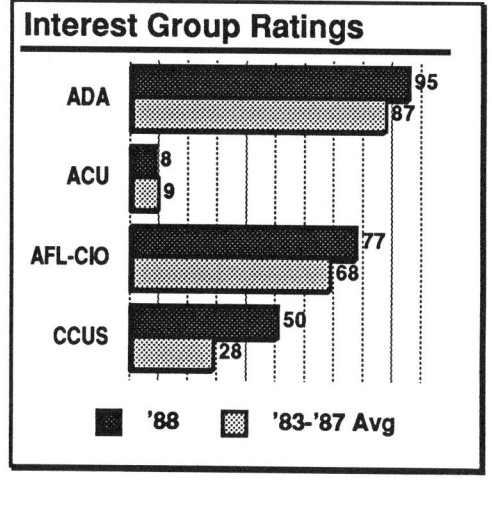

Interest Group Ratings

	'88	'83-'87 Avg
ADA	95	87
ACU	8	9
AFL-CIO	77	68
CCUS	50	28

'88   '83-'87 Avg

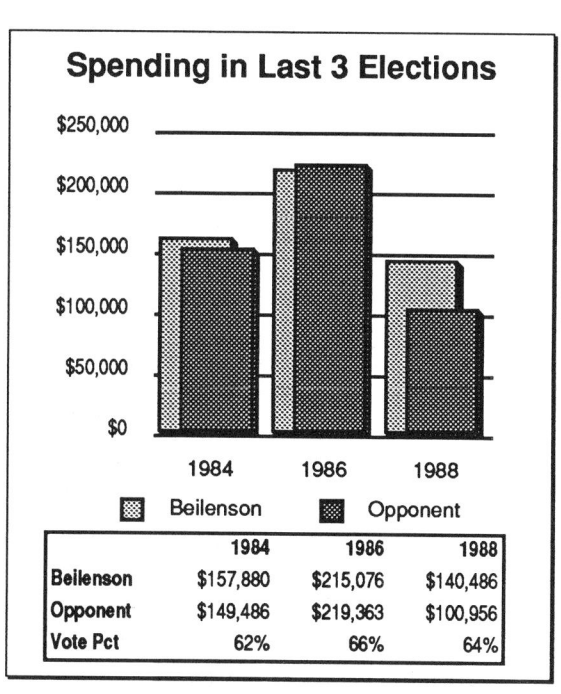

Spending in Last 3 Elections

	1984	1986	1988
Beilenson	$157,880	$215,076	$140,486
Opponent	$149,486	$219,363	$100,956
Vote Pct	62%	66%	64%

Charles E. Bennett, D-Fla (3)

First elected: 1948
Total receipts: $104,518
Total from PACs: $52,861

1988 Committees & Subcommittees

Armed Services
Seapower and Strategic and Critical Materials (Chairman)
Procurement and Military Nuclear Systems

Merchant Marine and Fisheries
Coast Guard and Navigation
Merchant Marine

PAC Contribution Profile

Business

Auto Dealers	*$6,000*
Auto Dealers & Drivers for Free Trade	$5,000
National Auto Dealers Assn	$1,000
Commercial & Savings Banks	*$3,350*
National Banks of Florida	$1,100
Barnett Banks of Florida	$1,000
Florida League of Financial Institutions	$1,000
Others	$250
Defense	*$16,600*
Grumman	$2,000
United Technologies	$1,500
McDonnell Douglas*	$1,250
Bath Iron Works	$1,000
Computer Sciences Corp	$1,000
General Dynamics	$1,000
Litton Industries	$1,000
GTE Corp	$550
AT&T	$500
EG&G Inc	$500
General Electric	$500
Gould Inc	$500
Hughes Aircraft	$500
Kaman Corp	$500
Lockheed Corp	$500
Loral Corp	$500
LTV Aerospace & Defense Company	$500

(Continued in next column)

Campaign Revenue Sources

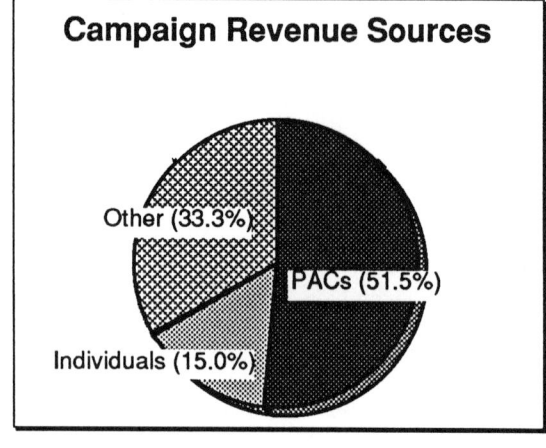

Other (33.3%)
PACs (51.5%)
Individuals (15.0%)

Defense (cont'd)

Martin Marietta Corp	$500
Raytheon	$500
Rockwell International	$500
Textron Inc	$500
Westinghouse Electric	$500
Others	$300
Lawyers	*$2,750*
Assn of Trial Lawyers of America	$2,500
Others	$250
Sea Transport	$3,000
CSX Transportation Inc	$600
American Pilots Assn	$500
American President Lines	$500
Crowley Maritime	$500
Lykes Bros Steamship Company	$500
Others	$400
Telecommunications	*$3,000*
Southern Bell	$3,000

Other Major Business PACs

Eastern Airlines	$2,000	Airlines
American Dental Assn	$1,000	Dentists
Associated General Contractors	$1,000	Comml Constr
Florida Citrus Mutual	$1,000	Fruit/Veg
Florida Medical Assn	$1,000	Doctors
Florida Rock Industries	$1,000	Stone/Concr
Stone Container Corp	$1,000	Paper Packg
Associated Milk Producers	$500	Dairy
Chevron Corp	$500	Major Oil
Florida Power & Light	$500	Electric Util
Internorth Inc	$500	Natural Gas
Prudential Insurance	$500	Insurance
Unigroup Inc	$500	Trucking

PAC Totals by Category

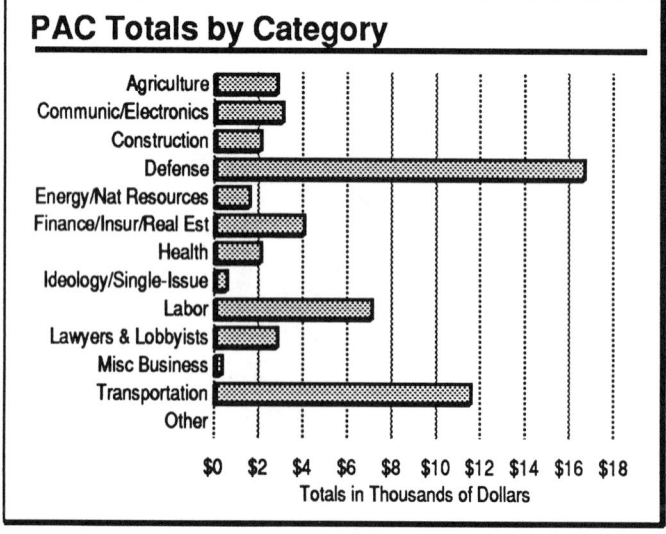

Totals in Thousands of Dollars

Labor

Labor Unions **$7,000**
    Laborers' Political League $1,500
    Food & Commercial Workers Union $1,000
    Marine Engineers District 2 Maritime Officers $1,000
    Seafarers International Union $1,000
    American Postal Workers Union $500
    Carpenters & Joiners Union $500
    Intl Brotherhood of Electrical Workers $500
    Operating Engineers Union $500
    United Transportation Union $500

Independent expenditures supporting Bennett

National Cmte to Preserve Social Security $3,118

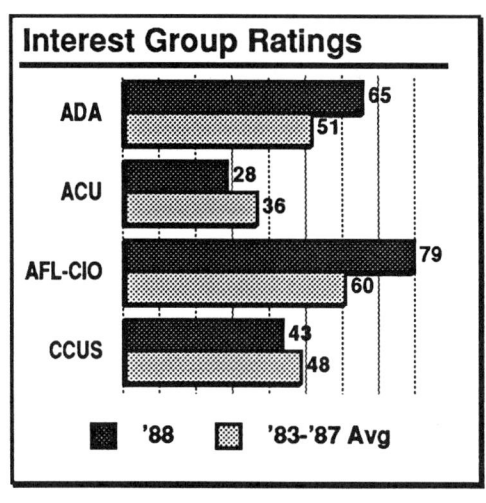

Interest Group Ratings

	'88	'83–'87 Avg
ADA	65	51
ACU	28	36
AFL-CIO	79	60
CCUS	43	48

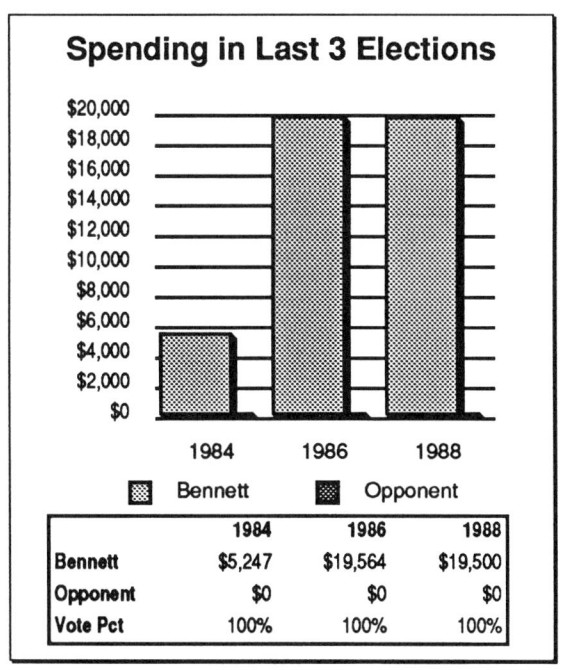

Spending in Last 3 Elections

	1984	1986	1988
Bennett	$5,247	$19,564	$19,500
Opponent	$0	$0	$0
Vote Pct	100%	100%	100%

☐ Bennett   ▨ Opponent

---

* Contributions came from more than one PAC affiliated
with this sponsor.

Helen Delich Bentley, R-Md (2)

First elected: 1984
Total receipts: $850,900
Total from PACs: $292,984

1988 Committees & Subcommittees

Merchant Marine and Fisheries
Merchant Marine
Oversight and Investigations
Panama Canal/Outer Continental Shelf

Public Works and Transportation
Economic Development
Investigations and Oversight
Water Resources

Select Aging
Health and Long-Term Care

PAC Contribution Profile

Business

Automotive	**$3,300**
National Auto Dealers Assn	$2,000
Others	$1,300
Commercial Banks	**$12,675**
MNC Financial Inc	$6,500
Mercantile Bankshares Corp	$1,000
Others	$5,175
Construction	**$18,050**
National Assn of Home Builders	$6,000
National Utility Contractors Assn	$3,500
National Electrical Contractors Assn	$2,000
Texas Industries	$1,300
Associated General Contractors	$1,250
Mechanical Contractors Assn of America	$1,000
Others	$3,000
Defense	**$14,550**
AAI Corp	$7,350
Martin Marietta Corp	$2,400
Lockheed Corp	$1,100
Others	$3,700
Electric Utilities	**$15,400**
Baltimore Gas & Electric	$10,000
Others	$5,400
Food & Beverage	**$6,500**
Jerrico Inc	$1,000
National Restaurant Assn	$1,000
Others	$4,500

Campaign Revenue Sources

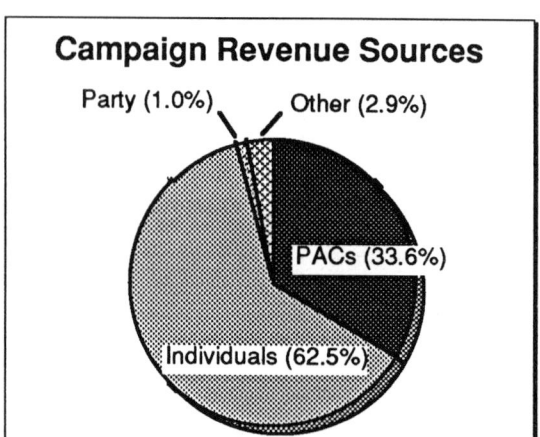

Party (1.0%)
Other (2.9%)
PACs (33.6%)
Individuals (62.5%)

Health Professionals	**$9,550**
American Medical Assn	$3,050
American Dental Assn	$2,500
American Academy of Ophthalmology	$2,000
Maryland Medical Assn	$2,000
Insurance	**$9,050**
US Fidelity & Guaranty	$2,500
National Assn of Life Underwriters	$2,000
Health Insurance Assn of America	$1,150
Others	$3,400
Oil & Gas Production/Marketing	**$12,300**
Mobil Oil	$3,000
Crown Central Petroleum	$1,150
Ashland Oil	$1,100
Sun Company	$1,000
Others	$6,050
Real Estate	**$10,300**
National Assn of Realtors	$10,000
Others	$300
Sea Transport	**$18,925**
CSX Transportation Inc*	$3,200
Matson Navigation	$3,000
American Pilots Assn	$2,500
American President Lines	$2,325
Lykes Bros Steamship Company	$2,050
Crowley Maritime	$1,350
Tenneco Inc	$1,000
United States Lines	$1,000
Others	$2,500
Steel	**$6,100**
Bethlehem Steel	$4,050
Others	$2,050

PAC Totals by Category

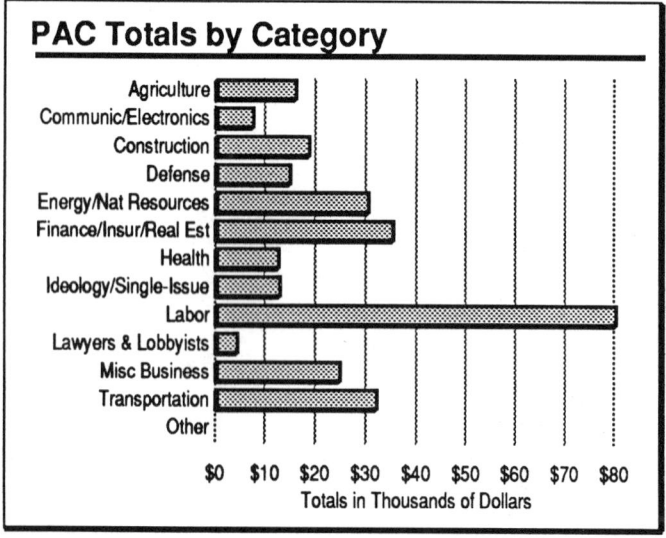

Totals in Thousands of Dollars

Categories (top to bottom): Agriculture, Communic/Electronics, Construction, Defense, Energy/Nat Resources, Finance/Insur/Real Est, Health, Ideology/Single-Issue, Labor, Lawyers & Lobbyists, Misc Business, Transportation, Other

Axis: $0 $10 $20 $30 $40 $50 $60 $70 $80

Trucking/Delivery $7,300
     United Parcel Service $3,450
     American Trucking Assns $1,050
     Others $2,800

Other Major Business PACs

Westvaco Corp	$4,000	Paper Prod
Associated Milk Producers	$2,000	Dairy
National Tooling & Machining Assn	$2,000	Indust Equip
AT&T	$1,650	LongDistance
J P Stevens & Company	$1,550	Textiles
Stone Container Corp	$1,500	Paper Packg
Chesapeake & Potomac Telephone	$1,400	Phone Util
Dairymen Inc	$1,300	Dairy
Philip Morris	$1,300	Tobacco
Business Industry PAC	$1,103	Bus Assns
Brown & Williamson Tobacco	$1,100	Tobacco
Waste Management Inc	$1,100	Waste Mgmt
Aircraft Owners & Pilots Assn	$1,050	GenlAviation
Corning Glass Works	$1,000	Glass Prod
Greater Washington Board of Trade	$1,000	Chamb/Cmrce
Second National Federal Savings Bank	$1,000	SavingsBanks

Interest Group Ratings

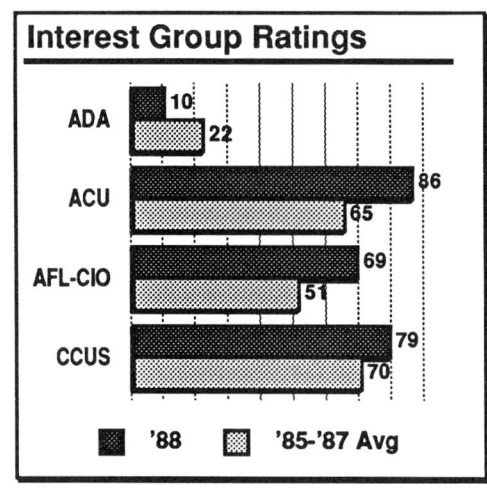

Labor

Bldg Trades/Industrial/Misc Unions $41,100
     Teamsters Union $10,000
     Air Line Pilots Assn $6,500
     Carpenters & Joiners Union* $6,250
     Operating Engineers Union $4,250
     Painters & Allied Trades Union $2,750
     Baltimore Bldg & Construction Trades Council $2,600
     National Assn of Letter Carriers $2,150
     Ironworkers Union $1,000
     National Assn of Retired Federal Employees $1,000
     Others $4,600

Sea Transport Unions...$38,850
     Marine Engineers Union* $10,000
     Seafarers International Union...............................$10,000
     International Longshoremen Assn $8,000
     Masters, Mates & Pilots Union Union* $7,000
     Boilermakers Union $2,350
     Maritime Union of America $1,500

Ideological/Single-Issue

Pro-Israel $9,750
     National PAC $5,000
     Hudson Valley PAC $2,500
     Others $2,250

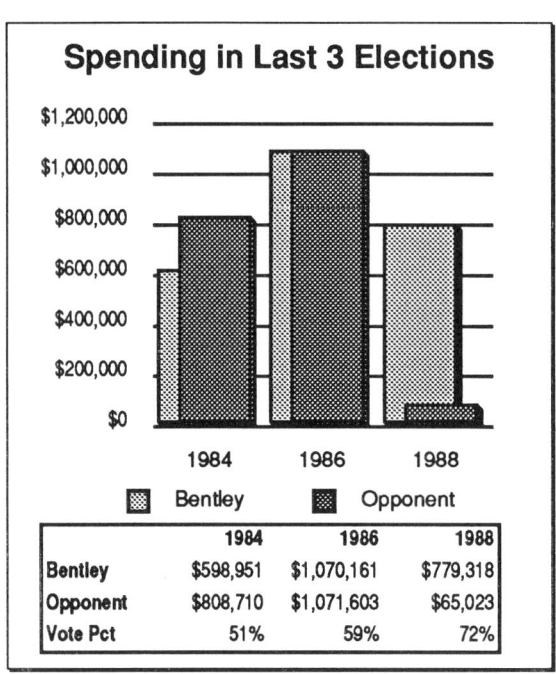

Spending in Last 3 Elections

	1984	1986	1988
Bentley	$598,951	$1,070,161	$779,318
Opponent	$808,710	$1,071,603	$65,023
Vote Pct	51%	59%	72%

* Contributions came from more than one PAC affiliated
with this sponsor.

Doug Bereuter, R-Neb (1)

First elected: 1978
Total receipts: $215,704
Total from PACs: $99,120

1988 Committees & Subcommittees

Banking, Finance and Urban Affairs
International Development Institutions and Finance (Ranking Republican)
Financial Institutions Supervision, Regulation and Insurance
Housing and Community Development

Foreign Affairs
Europe and the Middle East
International Economic Policy and Trade

Select Hunger

PAC Contribution Profile

Business

Auto Dealers **$4,000**
    National Auto Dealers Assn $2,000
    Auto Dealers & Drivers for Free Trade $2,000

Construction **$6,200**
    National Assn of Home Builders $2,000
    National Concrete Masonry Assn $1,000
    Nebraska Associated General Contractors $1,000
    Caterpillar Tractor $500
    Morton Building Inc $500
    Others $1,200

Electronics & Computers **$2,500**
    Valmont Industries $2,000
    Others $500

Financial Institutions **$21,345**
    American Bankers Assn $5,000
    Nebraska Bankers Assn $5,000
    Norwest Corp $2,000
    Barnett Banks of Florida $1,500
    Independent Bankers Assn $1,500
    Citicorp $1,000
    Credit Union National Assn $1,000
    BankAmerica $750
    Firstier Inc $545
    Chase Manhattan $500
    Commercial Federal Savings & Loan $500
    Sun Banks $500
    US League of Savings Assn $500
    Others $1,050

Campaign Revenue Sources

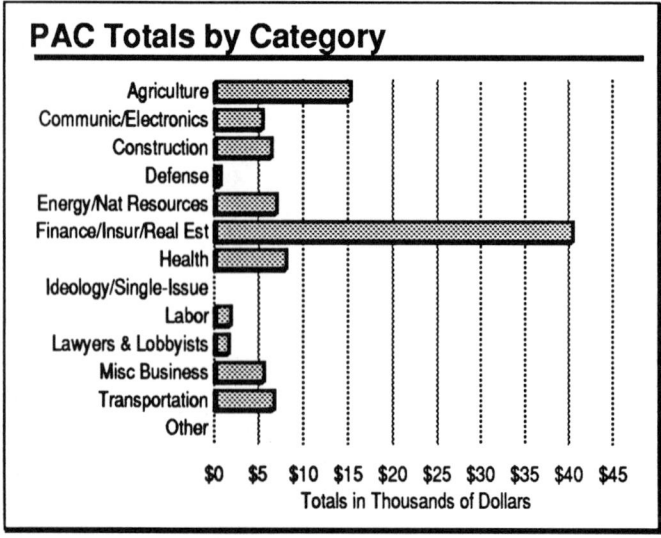

Party (4.0%)
Other (3.7%)
Individuals (47.6%)
PACs (44.7%)

Food & Beverage **$3,950**
    ConAgra Inc $1,750
    IBP Inc $1,000
    National Beer Wholesalers Assn $500
    Others $700

Grain Trading & Processing **$4,050**
    Cargill Inc $2,000
    Archer-Daniels-Midland Corp $1,250
    Continental Grain $500
    Others $300

Health Professionals **$6,250**
    American Medical Assn $4,000
    Nebraska Medical Assn $2,250

Industrial Equipment & Materials **$2,500**
    Square D Company $1,500
    Brunswick Corp $500
    Water Quality Assn $500

Insurance **$5,200**
    National Assn of Life Underwriters $2,500
    American Council of Life Insurance $1,000
    Independent Insurance Agents of America $700
    Mutual of Omaha $500
    Others $500

Oil & Gas **$4,850**
    Petroleum Marketers Assn $1,000
    Internorth Inc $750
    Amoco Corp $500
    Dresser Industries $500
    Mobil Oil $500
    Phillips Petroleum $500
    Tenneco Inc $500
    Others $600

PAC Totals by Category

Bar chart showing totals in thousands of dollars by category:
- Agriculture
- Communic/Electronics
- Construction
- Defense
- Energy/Nat Resources
- Finance/Insur/Real Est
- Health
- Ideology/Single-Issue
- Labor
- Lawyers & Lobbyists
- Misc Business
- Transportation
- Other

$0 $5 $10 $15 $20 $25 $30 $35 $40 $45
Totals in Thousands of Dollars

Real Estate $5,500

    National Assn of Realtors $5,000
    Mortgage Bankers Assn of America $500

Securities & Investment Banking $6,750

    Prudential-Bache Securities $2,000
    Goldman Sachs $1,500
    Municipal Securities Industry $1,000
    Chicago Mercantile Exchange $500
    E F Hutton Group $500
    Morgan Stanley & Company $500
    Others $750

Telecommunications $2,750

    AT&T $1,250
    Northwestern Bell Telephone $750
    Others $750

Other Major Business PACs

Farmland Industries	$1,000	Ag Svcs
Mid-American Dairymen	$1,000	Dairy
Smithkline Beckman	$1,000	Pharmaceut
Union Pacific Corp	$1,000	Railroads
American Express	$750	Credit/Loans
American Soybean Assn	$750	Soybeans
Sandoz Pharmaceuticals	$600	Pharmaceut
American Collectors Assn	$500	Credit/Loans
BHP-Utah International	$500	Metals/Mining
Boeing Company	$500	Aircraft
Kutak, Rock & Campbell	$500	Lawyers
Land O'Lakes Inc	$500	Dairy
Midwest Energy Company	$500	Gas & Electr
United Parcel Service	$500	Delivery
Xerox Corp	$500	Off Machines

Major Labor Union PACs

United Transportation Union	$1,500	RR Unions

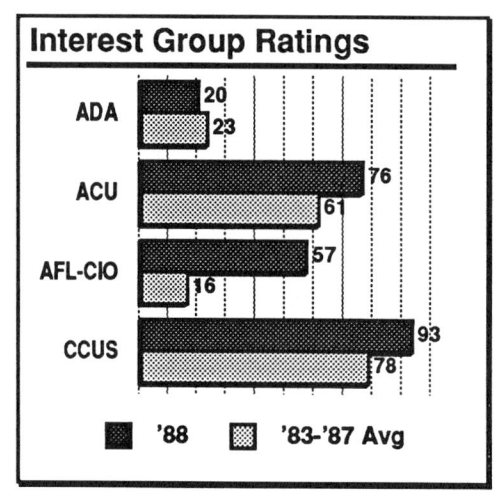

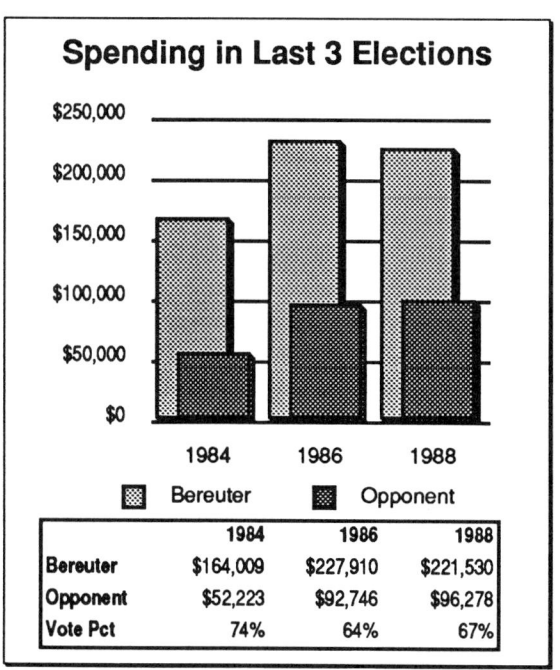

Howard L. Berman, D-Calif (26)

First elected: 1982
Total receipts: $528,296
Total from PACs: $207,317

1988 Committees & Subcommittees

Foreign Affairs
Arms Control, International Security and Science
International Economic Policy and Trade

Judiciary
Administrative Law and Governmental Relations
Courts, Civil Liberties and the Administration of Justice
Immigration, Refugees and International Law

PAC Contribution Profile

Business

Accountants	**$6,500**
American Institute of CPA's	$5,000
Others	$1,500
Commercial & Savings Banks	**$9,400**
American Bankers Assn	$1,500
Security Pacific Corp	$1,500
Mercury Savings & Loan	$1,200
American Savings & Loan Assn	$1,000
Columbia Savings & Loan (Beverly Hills)	$1,000
Others	$3,200
Defense	**$5,000**
Lockheed Corp	$3,500
Hughes Aircraft	$1,000
Others	$500
Entertainment Industry	**$16,500**
Fox Inc	$3,000
MCA Inc	$2,500
National Cable Television Assn	$2,500
Warner Communications	$2,000
Gulf + Western Industries	$1,500
ASCAP	$1,000
Lorimar-Telepictures Corp	$1,000
Motion Picture Assn of America	$1,000
Others	$2,000
Health Professionals	**$5,100**
American Medical Assn	$2,000
Co-op of American Physicians	$2,000
Corp for the Advancement of Psychiatry	$1,100

Campaign Revenue Sources

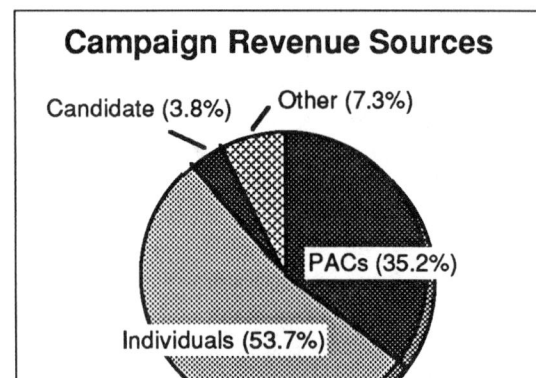

Candidate (3.8%)
Other (7.3%)
PACs (35.2%)
Individuals (53.7%)

Lawyers & Lobbyists	**$15,750**
Assn of Trial Lawyers of America	$5,000
California Trial Lawyers Assn	$5,000
Jones, Day, Reavis & Pogue	$1,400
Manatt, Phelps, Rothenberg & Tunney	$1,100
Akin, Gump, Hauer & Feld	$1,000
Others	$2,250
Real Estate	**$8,750**
National Assn of Realtors	$8,500
Others	$250
Telecommunications	**$7,000**
AT&T	$2,500
Pacific Telesis Group	$2,500
Comsat	$1,000
Others	$1,000

Other Major Business PACs

National Assn of Home Builders	$2,000	Resid Constr
TransAmerica Life Companies	$1,600	Life Insurance
Food Marketing Institute	$1,100	Food Stores
Southern California Edison	$1,100	Electric Util
Morgan Stanley & Company	$1,000	InvestmtBank
SGS North America	$1,000	BusinessSvcs
Sunkist Growers	$1,000	Fruit/Veg
West Publishing	$1,000	Books & Mags

PAC Totals by Category

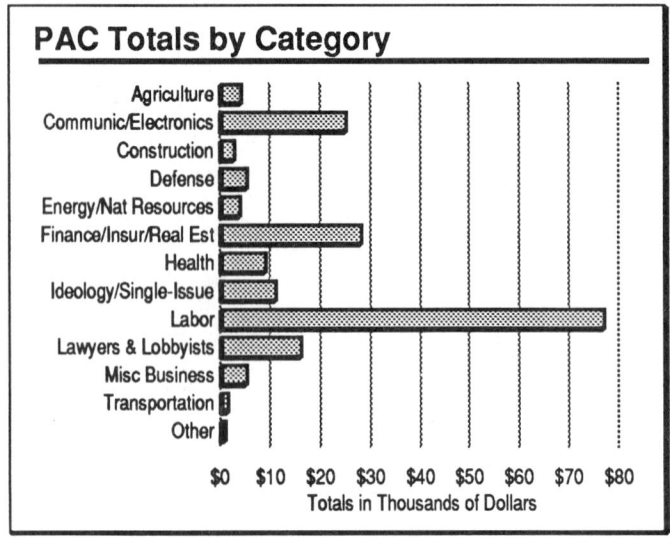

Agriculture
Communic/Electronics
Construction
Defense
Energy/Nat Resources
Finance/Insur/Real Est
Health
Ideology/Single-Issue
Labor
Lawyers & Lobbyists
Misc Business
Transportation
Other

$0 $10 $20 $30 $40 $50 $60 $70 $80
Totals in Thousands of Dollars

Labor

Bldg Trades/Industrial/Misc Unions **$44,700**

United Auto Workers $7,750
Operating Engineers Union* $6,500
Carpenters & Joiners Union* $5,800
Ironworkers Union $3,500
Plumbers/Pipefitters Union $3,500
AFL-CIO* $3,150
Laborers' Western Political League $3,000
Service Employees International Union $3,000
Machinists/Aerospace Workers Union $2,000
Bricklayers Union $1,800
Food & Commercial Workers Union $1,100
Others $3,600

Government & Postal Unions **$12,600**

American Fedn of State/County/Munic Employees $5,000
National Assn of Retired Federal Employees $3,000
American Postal Workers Union $1,100
National Assn of Letter Carriers $1,000
Others $2,500

Teachers Unions **$9,100**

National Education Assn $6,500
American Federation of Teachers $2,600

Transportation Unions **$10,750**

Teamsters Union $5,000
Seafarers International Union $1,600
United Transportation Union $1,400
Air Line Pilots Assn $1,000
Others $1,750

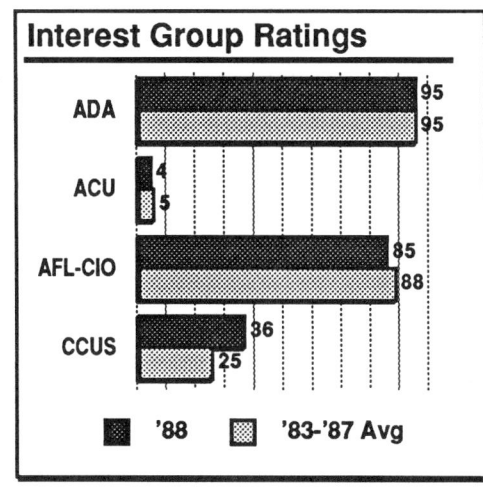

Ideological/Single-Issue

Ideological & Single-Issue **$10,720**

Hollywood Women's Political Cmte	$3,000	Dem/Lib
Pax Americas (David Bonior)	$1,000	Dem Leaders
Religion and Tolerance PAC	$1,000	Dem/Lib
Valley Education Fund (Tony Coelho)	$1,000	Dem Leaders
Washington PAC	$1,000	Pro-Israel
Others	$3,720	

Independent expenditures supporting Berman

National Cmte to Preserve Social Security $1,873

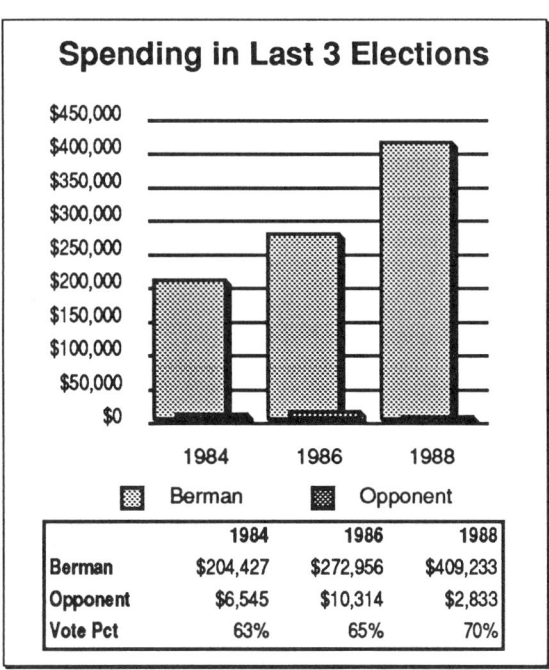

* Contributions came from more than one PAC affiliated with this sponsor.

Tom Bevill, D-Ala (4)

1988 Committees & Subcommittees

Appropriations
Energy and Water Development (Chairman)
Interior and Related Agencies
Military Construction

First elected: 1966
Total receipts: $206,806
Total from PACs: $94,350

PAC Contribution Profile

Business

Building Contractors	$8,400
National Utility Contractors Assn	$3,000
National Assn of Home Builders	$2,000
Walter Industries	$1,500
Associated General Contractors	$1,000
Others	$900

Commercial Banks	***$5,300***
Central Bancshares of the South	$1,200
Amsouth Bancorp	$1,100
American Bankers Assn	$1,000
First Alabama Bancshares	$750
Southtrust Corp	$750
Colonial Bancgroup	$500

Defense	***$2,450***
None over $500	

Electric Utilities	***$17,500***
Southern Company*	$6,500
ACRE (Action Committee for Rural Electrification)	$1,000
Public Service Company of NH/Yankee Division	$1,000
Southern California Edison	$1,000
Others	$8,000

Health Professionals	***$2,500***
American Dental Assn	$1,500
American Medical Assn	$1,000

Nuclear Power Equipment	***$3,000***
Westinghouse Electric	$1,500
General Atomics	$1,000
Others	$500

Campaign Revenue Sources

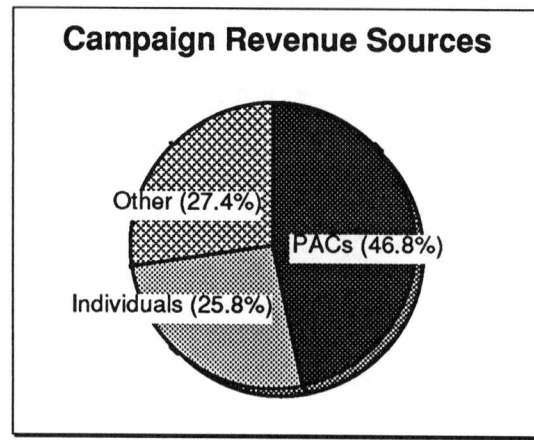

Other (27.4%)
PACs (46.8%)
Individuals (25.8%)

Oil & Gas	***$6,300***
Alagasco Inc	$1,250
Coastal Corp	$1,000
Southern Natural Resources	$1,000
Others	$3,050

Real Estate	***$6,600***
National Assn of Realtors	$6,000
Others	$600

Telecommunications	***$2,500***
South Central Bell Telephone	$1,500
AT&T	$1,000
Continental Telecom	$1,000

Other Major Business PACs

Intergraph Corp	$2,000	Comput Parts
Boeing Company	$1,600	Aircraft
Torchmark Corp	$1,500	Insurance
Alabama Farm Bureau Federation	$1,000	Farm Orgs
National Beer Wholesalers Assn	$1,000	Liquor Whlsl
National Coal Assn*	$1,000	Coal
Philip Morris	$1,000	Tobacco
United Parcel Service	$1,000	Delivery

PAC Totals by Category

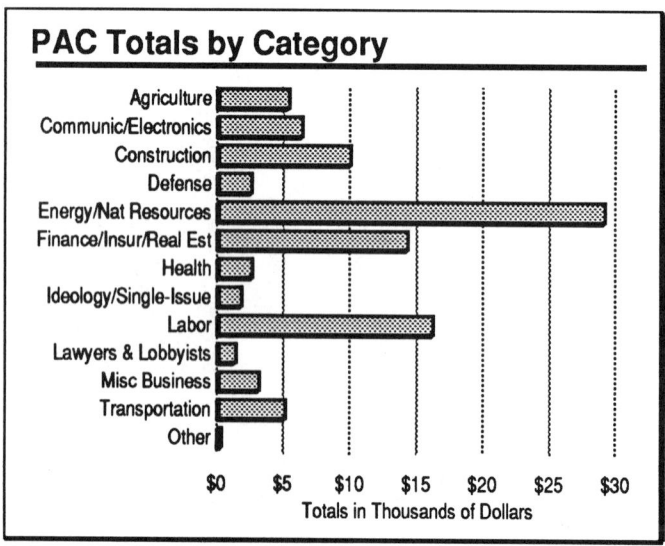

Agriculture
Communic/Electronics
Construction
Defense
Energy/Nat Resources
Finance/Insur/Real Est
Health
Ideology/Single-Issue
Labor
Lawyers & Lobbyists
Misc Business
Transportation
Other

$0 $5 $10 $15 $20 $25 $30
Totals in Thousands of Dollars

Labor

Postal Worker Unions ***$3,550***

    National Assn of Letter Carriers $2,000
    American Postal Workers Union $1,000
    Others $550

Other Labor Unions ***$12,500***

    Carpenters & Joiners Union $2,000
    Operating Engineers Union $2,000
    Laborers' Political League $1,500
    United Auto Workers $1,500
    Ladies Garment Workers Union $1,000
    Machinists/Aerospace Workers Union $1,000
    Seafarers International Union $1,000
    Others $2,500

Major Ideological/Single-Issue

National Cmte to Preserve Social Security ...... $1,000   Soc Secur

Independent expenditures supporting Bevill

National Cmte to Preserve Social Security $2,185

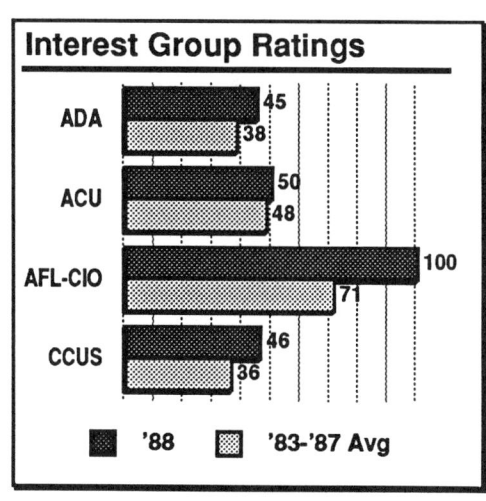

Interest Group Ratings

	'88	'83-'87 Avg
ADA	45	38
ACU	50	48
AFL-CIO	100	71
CCUS	46	36

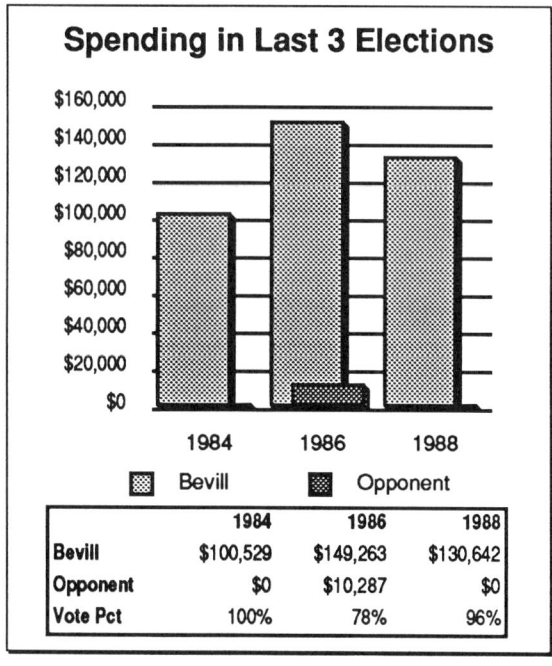

Spending in Last 3 Elections

	1984	1986	1988
Bevill	$100,529	$149,263	$130,642
Opponent	$0	$10,287	$0
Vote Pct	100%	78%	96%

* Contributions came from more than one PAC affiliated with this sponsor.

James Bilbray, D-Nev (1)

1988 Committees & Subcommittees

First elected: 1986
Total receipts: $669,014
Total from PACs: $300,116

Foreign Affairs
Africa
International Economic Policy and Trade

Small Business
Energy and Agriculture
Exports, Tourism and Special Problems

Select Aging
Housing and Consumer Interests

PAC Contribution Profile

Business

Casinos & Gambling	$18,141
California Hotel & Casino PAC	$3,500
Hilton Nevada Corp	$3,500
Circus Circus Enterprises	$3,391
Summa Corp	$2,500
Harrah's	$1,500
Caesars World	$1,000
Union Plaza	$1,000
Others	$1,750

Defense	$5,550
Gencorp Inc	$1,500
Others	$4,050

Health Professionals	$13,299
American Medical Assn	$7,499
American Academy of Ophthalmology	$3,500
American Dental Assn	$2,000
Others	$300

Insurance	$6,100
National Assn of Life Underwriters	$4,500
Independent Insurance Agents of America	$1,100
Others	$500

Lawyers & Lobbyists	$9,850
Assn of Trial Lawyers of America	$7,000
Akin, Gump, Hauer & Feld	$1,100
California Trial Lawyers Assn	$1,000
Others	$750

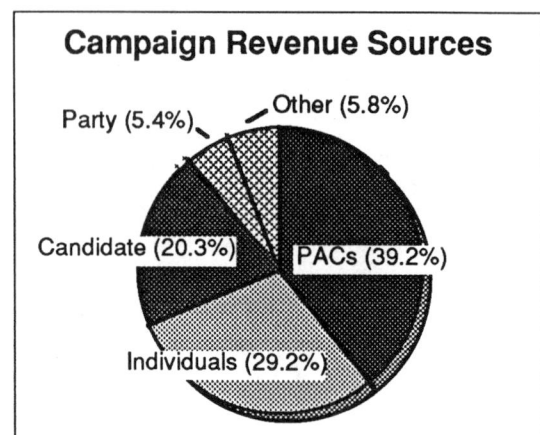

Campaign Revenue Sources

Party (5.4%)
Other (5.8%)
Candidate (20.3%)
PACs (39.2%)
Individuals (29.2%)

Oil & Gas	$6,450
Southwest Gas Corp	$3,800
Atlantic Richfield	$1,300
Others	$1,350

Real Estate	$12,200
National Assn of Realtors	$10,300
American Resort & Residential Developers Assn	$1,900

Residential Construction	$3,300
National Assn of Home Builders	$3,000
Others	$300

Telecommunications	$4,225
Pacific Telesis Group	$1,800
AT&T	$1,000
Centel Corp	$625
BellSouth Corp	$500
Others	$300

Other Major Business PACs

Associated Milk Producers	$2,000	Dairy
Freeport-McMoran Inc	$1,500	Other Mining
United Parcel Service	$1,500	Delivery
Philip Morris	$1,300	Tobacco
American Textile Manfacturers Institute	$1,100	Textiles
American Airlines	$1,100	Airlines
First Western Financial Corp	$1,000	SavingsBanks
Marriott Corp	$1,000	Hotel/Motel
Winn-Dixie Stores	$1,000	Food Stores

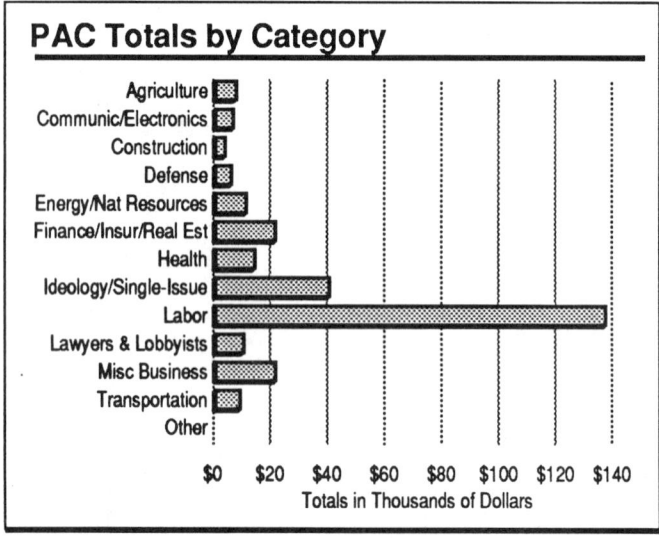

PAC Totals by Category

Agriculture
Communic/Electronics
Construction
Defense
Energy/Nat Resources
Finance/Insur/Real Est
Health
Ideology/Single-Issue
Labor
Lawyers & Lobbyists
Misc Business
Transportation
Other

$0 $20 $40 $60 $80 $100 $120 $140
Totals in Thousands of Dollars

Labor

Bldg Trades/Industrial/Misc Unions **$71,850**
    Machinists/Aerospace Workers Union $11,000
    Ironworkers Union $10,000
    Intl Brotherhood of Electrical Workers $8,000
    Food & Commercial Workers Union $7,300
    United Auto Workers* $6,100
    Carpenters & Joiners Union $6,000
    AFL-CIO* $5,000
    Laborers' Western Political League $5,000
    Sheet Metal Workers Union $2,500
    Operating Engineers Union $2,000
    United Steelworkers $2,000
    Plumbers/Pipefitters Union $1,750
    Boilermakers Union $1,400
    Hotel/Restaurant Employees Union $1,100
    Ladies Garment Workers Union $1,100
    Others $1,600

Government & Postal Workers **$30,700**
    National Assn of Letter Carriers $10,000
    National Assn of Retired Federal Employees $8,000
    American Fedn of State/County/Munic Employees $5,000
    International Assn of Firefighters $2,600
    American Postal Workers Union $2,000
    National Rural Letter Carriers Assn $2,000
    Others $1,100

Teachers Unions **$10,600**
    National Education Assn $10,000
    Others $600

Transportation Unions **$23,900**
    Teamsters Union $10,000
    Air Line Pilots Assn $3,000
    Seafarers International Union $3,000
    Marine Engineers Union* $2,900
    Transportation Communication Union $1,200
    Others $3,800

Interest Group Ratings

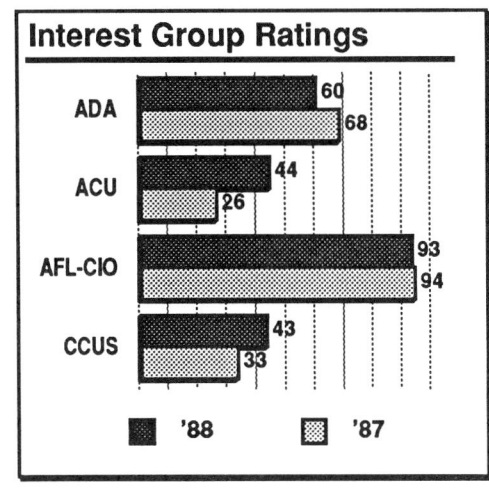

Ideological/Single-Issue

Democratic Leadership PACs **$12,000**
    24th Cong Dist of California PAC (Henry Waxman) $5,000
    Majority Congress Committee (Jim Wright) $3,000
    Valley Education Fund (Tony Coelho) $2,000
    Cmte for Democratic Opportunity (Bill Gray) $1,000
    Fund for a Democratic Majority (Ted Kennedy) $1,000

Pro-Israel **$16,750**
    National PAC $5,000
    Washington PAC $2,000
    Hudson Valley PAC $1,750
    Joint Action Cmte for Political Affairs $1,500
    Delaware Valley PAC $1,000
    Desert Caucus $1,000
    Florida Congressional Cmte $1,000
    Roundtable PAC $1,000
    Silver State PAC $1,000
    Others $1,500

Other Major Ideological/Single Issue
    National Rifle Assn $4,950
    Sierra Club $2,245
    National Cmte to Preserve Social Security $2,100
    National Council of Senior Citizens $1,000

Independent expenditures supporting Bilbray
National Cmte to Preserve Social Security $1,305

Independent expenditures opposing Bilbray
Council for National Defense $6,044

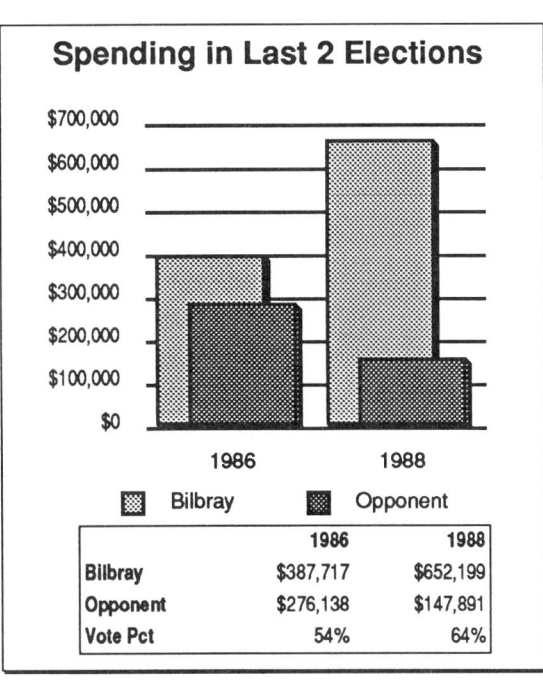

Spending in Last 2 Elections

	1986	1988
Bilbray	$387,717	$652,199
Opponent	$276,138	$147,891
Vote Pct	54%	64%

---

* Contributions came from more than one PAC affiliated
with this sponsor.

Michael Bilirakis, R-Fla (9)

First elected: 1982
Total receipts: $399,150
Total from PACs: $149,975

1988 Committees & Subcommittees

Energy and Commerce
Energy and Power
Oversight and Investigations
Transportation, Tourism and Hazardous Materials

Veterans' Affairs
Compensation, Pension and Insurance
Hospitals and Health Care

PAC Contribution Profile

Business

Campaign Revenue Sources

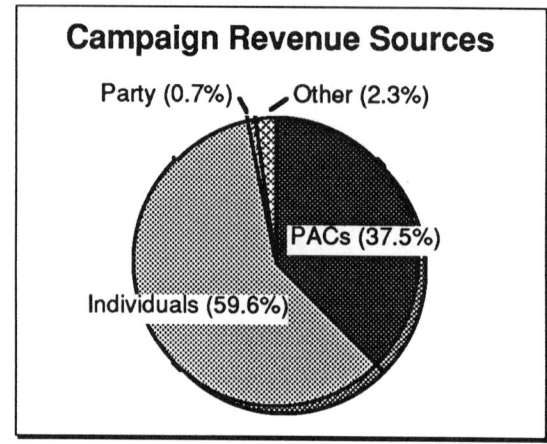

Party (0.7%)   Other (2.3%)
PACs (37.5%)
Individuals (59.6%)

Accountants	....	$8,300
American Institute of CPA's		$5,000
Touche Ross		$1,800
Coopers & Lybrand		$1,200
Others		$300

Automotive	....	$7,000
National Auto Dealers Assn		$4,600
Auto Dealers & Drivers for Free Trade		$1,500
Others		$900

Commercial Banks	....	$8,300
Barnett Banks of Florida		$3,000
NCNB Corp		$1,500
American Bankers Assn		$1,000
Citizens & Southern National Bank		$1,000
National Banks of Florida		$1,000
Others		$800

Defense	....	$3,200
Harris Corp		$1,000
United Technologies		$1,000
Others		$1,200

Drug Stores	....	$2,625
Jack Eckerd Corp		$1,350
Others		$1,275

Electric Utilities	....	$10,800
Southern Company*		$2,150
Florida Power & Light		$1,000
Others		$7,650

Food & Beverage	....	$3,000
None over $800		

Health Professionals	....	$14,600
American Dental Assn		$3,000
Florida Medical Assn		$3,000
American Medical Assn		$2,300
American Podiatry Assn		$1,500
American Academy of Ophthalmology		$1,000
American College of Emergency Physicians		$1,000
Others		$2,800

Insurance	....	$9,000
American Family Corp		$3,100
National Assn of Life Underwriters		$1,000
Others		$4,900

Oil & Gas	....	$11,350
Mobil Oil		$1,000
Others		$10,350

Pharmaceuticals	....	$4,000
Schering-Plough Corp		$1,000
Others		$3,000

Real Estate	....	$6,900
National Assn of Realtors		$6,300
Others		$600

Securities & Commodities	....	$5,450
Chicago Board of Trade		$1,000
Morgan Stanley & Company		$1,000
Others		$3,450

Telecommunications	....	$10,800
Southern Bell		$5,000
Pacific Telesis Group		$1,250
Corning Glass Works		$1,000
Others		$3,550

Tobacco	....	$5,500
Philip Morris		$2,400
RJR Nabisco		$1,000
Others		$2,100

TV & Radio	....	$2,900
National Cable Television Assn		$2,000
Others		$900

PAC Totals by Category

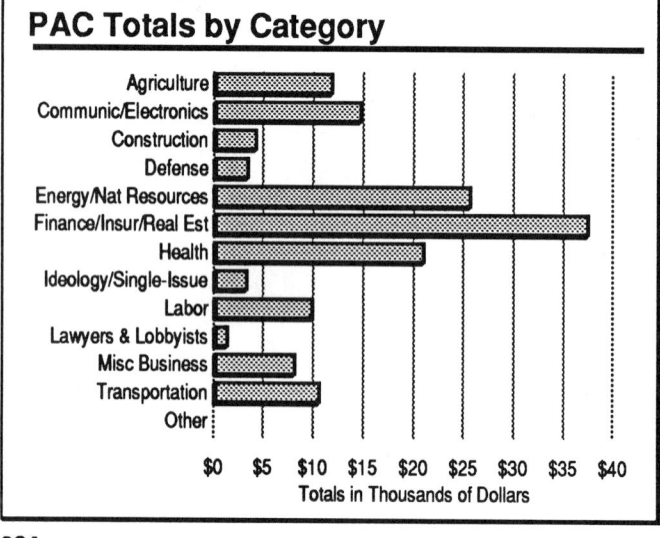

Agriculture
Communic/Electronics
Construction
Defense
Energy/Nat Resources
Finance/Insur/Real Est
Health
Ideology/Single-Issue
Labor
Lawyers & Lobbyists
Misc Business
Transportation
Other

$0 $5 $10 $15 $20 $25 $30 $35 $40
Totals in Thousands of Dollars

Other Major Business PACs

Walter Industries	$2,000	Resid Constr
Tampa Independent Dairy Farmers Assn	$1,000	Dairy

Labor

Labor Unions *$9,900*

National Assn of Retired Federal Employees	$5,000
Marine Engineers District 2 Maritime Officers	$2,500
Others	$2,400

Major Ideological/Single-Issue PACs

Dynamis	$1,000	Ethnic
National Cmte to Preserve Social Security	$1,000	Soc Secur

Independent expenditures supporting Bilirakis

National Cmte to Preserve Social Security	$2,637

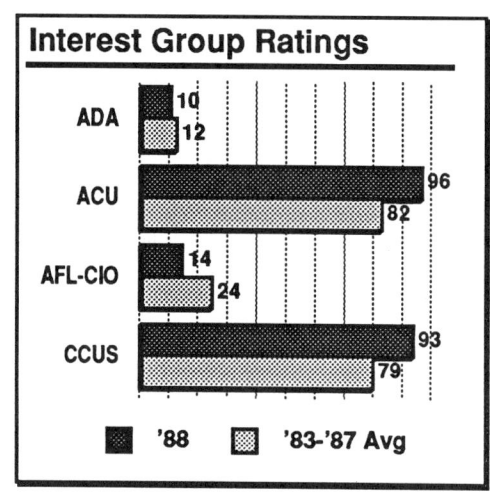

Interest Group Ratings

	'88	'83–'87 Avg
ADA	10	12
ACU	96	82
AFL-CIO	14	24
CCUS	93	79

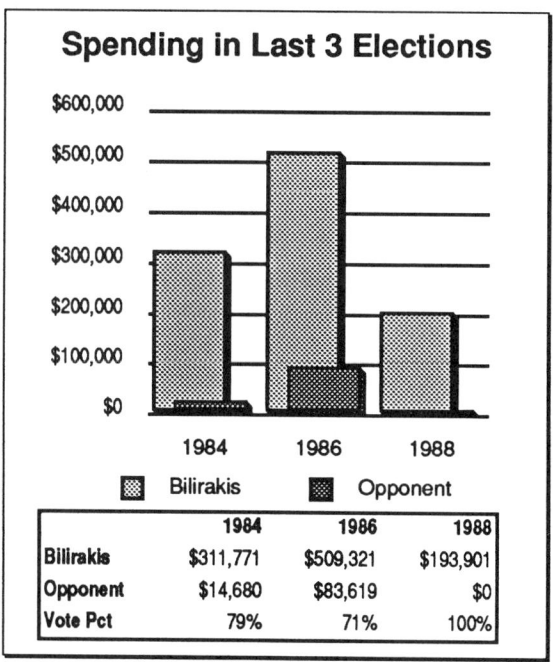

Spending in Last 3 Elections

	1984	1986	1988
Bilirakis	$311,771	$509,321	$193,901
Opponent	$14,680	$83,619	$0
Vote Pct	79%	71%	100%

Bilirakis · Opponent

---

* Contributions came from more than one PAC affiliated with this sponsor.

Thomas J. Bliley Jr., R-Va (3)

First elected: 1980
Total receipts: $467,449
Total from PACs: $270,350

1988 Committees & Subcommittees

District of Columbia
Fiscal Affairs and Health (Ranking Republican)
Judiciary and Education

Energy and Commerce
Oversight and Investigations (Ranking Republican)
Health and the Environment
Telecommunications and Finance

Select Children, Youth and Families

PAC Contribution Profile

Business

Accountants	**$13,400**
American Institute of CPA's	$6,800
Ernst & Whinney	$2,000
Coopers & Lybrand	$1,500
Arthur Young & Company	$1,200
Others	$1,900
Automotive	**$7,900**
National Auto Dealers Assn	$4,900
Auto Dealers & Drivers for Free Trade	$1,500
Others	$1,500
Broadcasting	**$8,400**
National Cable Television Assn	$5,000
National Assn of Broadcasters	$1,500
Others	$1,900
Builders & Bldg Supplies	**$7,150**
National Assn of Home Builders	$1,600
Associated General Contractors	$1,300
American Supply Assn	$1,000
Manville Corp	$1,000
Others	$2,250
Chemicals	**$3,250**
Ethyl Corp	$1,050
Others	$2,200

Campaign Revenue Sources

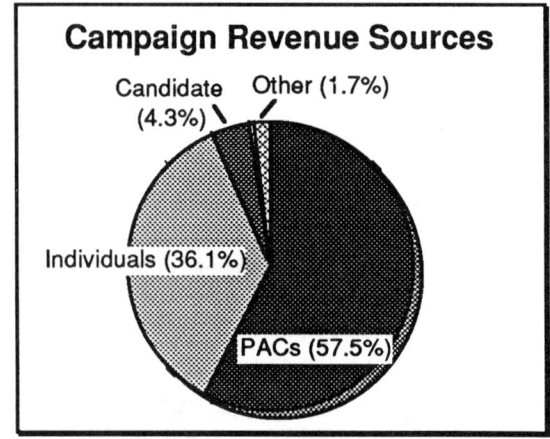

Candidate (4.3%)
Other (1.7%)
Individuals (36.1%)
PACs (57.5%)

Commercial Banks	**$15,530**
Virginia Bankers Assn	$5,250
J P Morgan & Company	$2,000
Signet Bank	$1,680
Sovran Financial Corp	$1,500
Crestar Financial Corp	$1,200
Barnett Banks of Florida	$1,000
Centerre Bank	$1,000
Citicorp	$1,000
Others	$900
Defense	**$5,900**
None over $900	
Electric Utilities	**$17,350**
Dominion Resources Inc	$3,650
Houston Industries	$1,500
Southern Company*	$1,150
New England Power Service Company	$1,100
Texas Utilities Electric Company*	$1,100
Others	$8,850
Food & Beverage	**$8,950**
National Beer Wholesalers Assn	$2,000
Pepsico Inc	$1,000
Others	$5,950
Forest Products	**$4,200**
Westvaco Corp	$3,000
Others	$1,200
Health Professionals	**$24,100**
American Medical Assn	$10,000
American Dental Assn	$3,500
American Podiatry Assn	$3,500
American Academy of Ophthalmology	$2,000
Cmte for Quality Orthopedic Health Care	$1,500
National Assn of Pharmacists	$1,200
Others	$2,400
Insurance	**$12,700**
American Council of Life Insurance	$1,500
National Assn of Life Underwriters	$1,500
Connecticut Mutual Life Insurance	$1,000
Consolidated Healthcare Inc	$1,000
Travelers Corp	$1,000
Others	$6,700

PAC Totals by Category

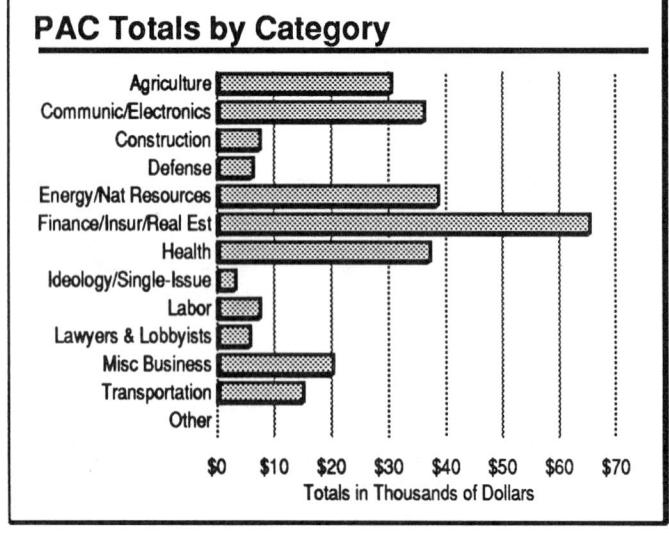

Totals in Thousands of Dollars

Categories shown: Agriculture, Communic/Electronics, Construction, Defense, Energy/Nat Resources, Finance/Insur/Real Est, Health, Ideology/Single-Issue, Labor, Lawyers & Lobbyists, Misc Business, Transportation, Other

Lawyers & Lobbyists $5,400
    Akin, Gump, Hauer & Feld $1,500
    Kleinfeld, Kaplan & Becker $1,500
    Others $2,400

Oil & Gas $14,650
    Tenneco Inc $3,000
    Mobil Oil $1,000
    Texas Eastern Gas Transmission $1,000
    Union Pacific Corp $1,000
    Others $8,650

Pharmaceuticals $10,350
    None over $800

Real Estate $6,000
    National Assn of Realtors $6,000

Securities/Commodities Investment $15,950
    E F Hutton Group $2,500
    First Boston Corp $2,000
    Morgan Stanley & Company $2,000
    Shearson Lehman Hutton $1,500
    Chicago Board of Trade $1,000
    Others $6,950

Sugar Growers $3,750
    None over $600

Telecommunications $27,370
    AT&T $10,000
    Chesapeake & Potomac Telephone $3,620
    Bell Atlantic $2,000
    BellSouth Corp* $1,300
    Comsat $1,100
    Pacific Telesis Group $1,050
    Continental Telecom $1,000
    Corning Glass Works $1,000
    DSC Communications Corp $1,000
    Others $5,300

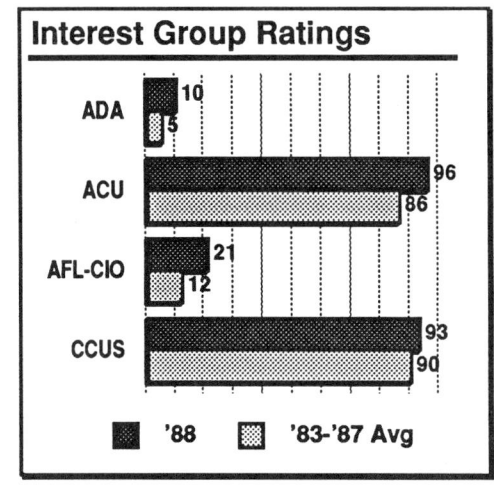

Interest Group Ratings

	'88	'83-'87 Avg
ADA	10	5
ACU	96	86
AFL-CIO	21	12
CCUS	93	90

Tobacco $14,600
    Philip Morris $5,500
    RJR Nabisco $2,700
    Tobacco Institute $1,400
    Pinkerton Tobacco $1,300
    United States Tobacco Company $1,200
    Universal Leaf Tobacco Company $1,000
    Others $1,500

Other Major Business PACs

Credit Union National Assn	$3,000	Credit Union
Reynolds Metals	$1,675	Metals/Mining
Stone Container Corp	$1,500	Paper Packg
Waste Management Inc	$1,200	Waste Mgmt
Greater Wash Board of Trade	$1,000	Chamb/Cmrce
Manor Healthcare Corp	$1,000	Nursing Home

Labor

Labor Unions $7,200
    Marine Engineers Union* $5,800
    Others $1,400

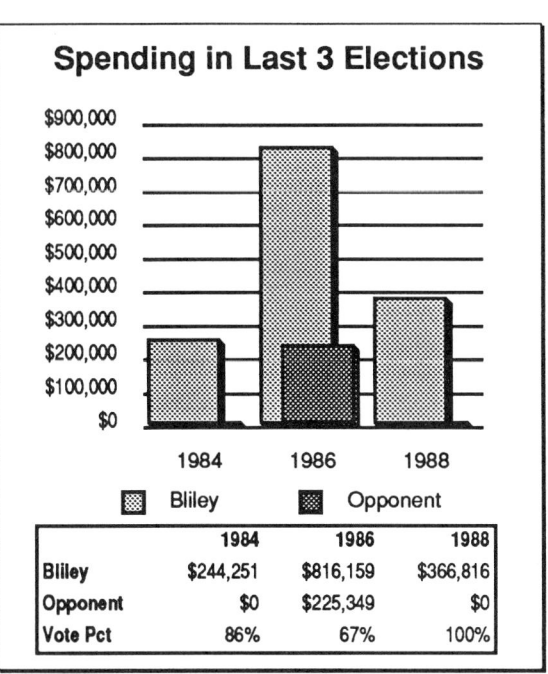

Spending in Last 3 Elections

	Bliley	Opponent

	1984	1986	1988
Bliley	$244,251	$816,159	$366,816
Opponent	$0	$225,349	$0
Vote Pct	86%	67%	100%

---

* Contributions came from more than one PAC affiliated
 with this sponsor.

Sherwood L. Boehlert, R-NY (25)

First elected: 1982
Total receipts: $235,512
Total from PACs: $90,173

1988 Committees & Subcommittees

Public Works and Transportation
Aviation
Economic Development
Surface Transportation

Science, Space and Technology
Science, Research and Technology (Ranking Republican)
International Scientific Cooperation

Select Aging
Health and Long-Term Care
Housing and Consumer Interests

PAC Contribution Profile

Business

Airlines & Aerospace	**$12,450**
Aircraft Owners & Pilots Assn	$2,000
Chrysler Corp	$1,300
Boeing Company	$1,000
Hercules Inc	$1,000
Lockheed Corp	$850
USAir Corp	$750
Allied-Signal	$550
General Dynamics	$550
Pan Am	$550
Textron Inc	$550
American Airlines	$500
General Electric	$500
Grumman	$500
Others	$1,850
Construction	**$6,500**
Associated General Contractors	$2,250
National Concrete Masonry Assn	$1,500
National Society of Professional Engineers	$1,500
National Assn of Home Builders	$1,000
Others	$250
Commercial & Savings Banks	**$2,750**
Chase Lincoln First Bank	$1,200
Citicorp	$1,000
Others	$550

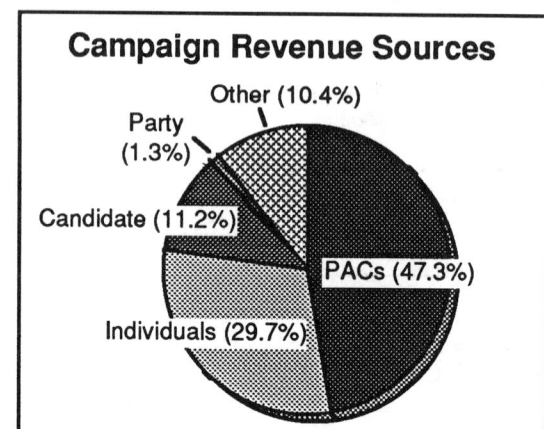

Campaign Revenue Sources

Other (10.4%)
Party (1.3%)
Candidate (11.2%)
PACs (47.3%)
Individuals (29.7%)

Dairy	**$6,400**
Associated Milk Producers	$5,000
Mid-American Dairymen	$1,000
Dairymen Inc	$500
Others	-$100
Food & Beverage	**$4,550**
Food Marketing Institute	$1,000
Wine & Spirits Wholesalers of America	$750
Independent Bakers Assn	$500
McDonald's Corp	$500
Nestle Enterprises Inc	$500
Pepsico Inc	$500
Others	$800
Health Professionals	**$8,230**
American Optometric Assn	$2,880
American Medical Assn	$2,250
American Dental Assn	$1,500
American Podiatry Assn	$1,000
Others	$600
Insurance	**$2,600**
Metropolitan Life Insurance	$750
National Assn Mutual Insurance Agents	$600
Kemper Insurance	$500
National Assn of Life Underwriters	$500
Others	$250
Real Estate	**$2,550**
National Assn of Realtors	$2,550
Telecommunications	**$4,750**
AT&T	$2,250
Continental Telecom	$2,000
New York Telephone	$500

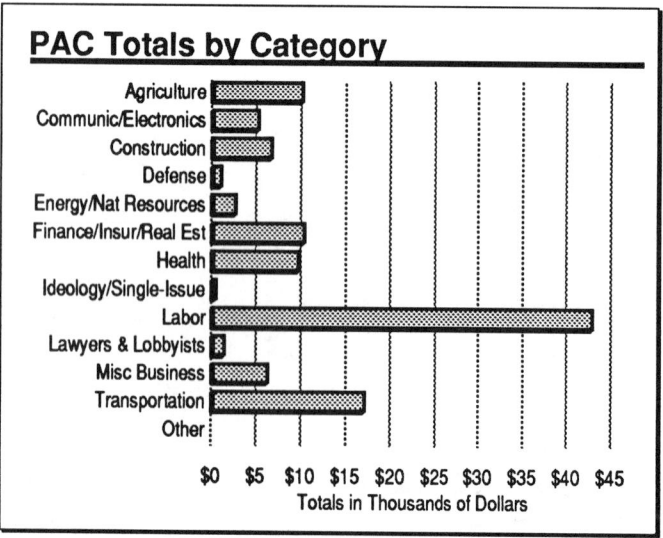

PAC Totals by Category

Agriculture
Communic/Electronics
Construction
Defense
Energy/Nat Resources
Finance/Insur/Real Est
Health
Ideology/Single-Issue
Labor
Lawyers & Lobbyists
Misc Business
Transportation
Other

$0 $5 $10 $15 $20 $25 $30 $35 $40 $45
Totals in Thousands of Dollars

Other Major Business PACs

United Parcel Service	$1,750	Delivery
Household International	$1,500	Credit/Loans
American Society of Travel Agents	$1,000	Travel Agent
Johnson & Johnson	$1,000	Health Prod
ACRE (Action Committee for Rural Electric)	$800	RuralElect
Borg-Warner	$750	Indust Equip
Chicago Mercantile Exchange	$750	Commodities
Goldman Sachs	$750	InvestmtBank
J P Stevens & Company	$750	Textiles
New York State Electric & Gas Corp	$750	Gas & Electr
Vorys, Sater, Seymour & Pease	$700	Lawyers
American Hotel & Motel Assn	$550	Hotel/Motel
CSX Transportation Inc	$550	Railroads
American Veterinary Medical Assn	$500	Veterinary
Amoco Corp	$500	Major Oil
Chicago & NorthWestern Transport	$500	Railroads
Corning Glass Works	$500	Glass Prod
Dow, Lohnes & Albertson	$500	Lawyers
National Assn of Convenience Stores	$500	Dept Store

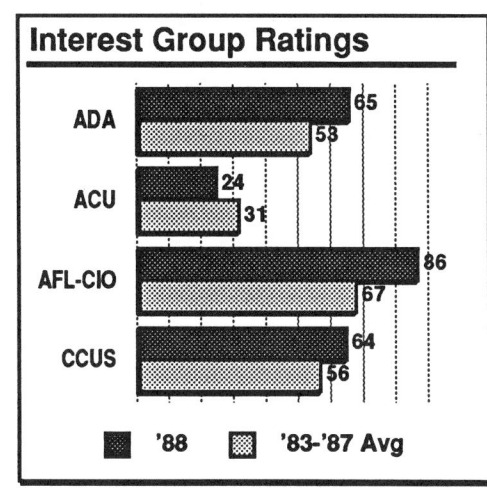

Interest Group Ratings

ADA — 65 ('88), 53 ('83–'87 Avg)
ACU — 24 ('88), 31 ('83–'87 Avg)
AFL-CIO — 86 ('88), 67 ('83–'87 Avg)
CCUS — 64 ('88), 56 ('83–'87 Avg)

■ '88　□ '83-'87 Avg

Labor

Bldg Trades/Industrial/Misc Unions $13,300

Food & Commercial Workers Union	$5,000
Operating Engineers Local #825	$5,000
Carpenters & Joiners Union	$1,500
Machinists/Aerospace Workers Union	$750
Ladies Garment Workers Union	$550
Others	$500
Teachers Unions	$4,500
National Education Assn	$4,500

Government & Postal Unions $7,150

American Fedn of State/County/Munic Employees	$2,000
National Assn of Letter Carriers	$2,000
National Assn of Retired Federal Employees	$2,000
National League of Postmasters	$550
National Rural Letter Carriers Assn	$550
Others	$50

Transportation Unions $17,750

Teamsters Union	$7,000
Air Line Pilots Assn	$5,000
Marine Engineers District 2 Maritime Officers	$3,000
Seafarers International Union	$1,500
Amalgamated Transit Union	$1,000
Others	$250

Major Ideological/Single-Issue PACs

National Rifle Assn	$1,250	Pro-Guns
Fund for America's Future (George Bush)	$500	Repub Cands
Sierra Club	$500	Environment

Independent expenditures supporting Boehlert

Teamsters Union	$2,000
New York Medical Assn	$1,000

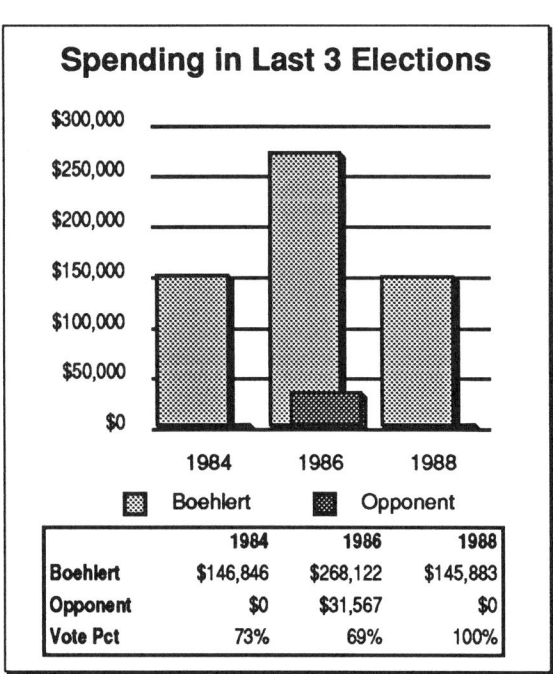

Spending in Last 3 Elections

■ Boehlert　■ Opponent

	1984	1986	1988
Boehlert	$146,846	$268,122	$145,883
Opponent	$0	$31,567	$0
Vote Pct	73%	69%	100%

Lindy Boggs, D-La (2)

1988 Committees & Subcommittees

Appropriations
Energy and Water Development
HUD-Independent Agencies
Legislative Branch

Select Children, Youth and Families

First elected: 1973
Total receipts: $266,033
Total from PACs: $144,300

PAC Contribution Profile

Business

Computers & Electronics	**$2,750**
Computer Sciences Corp	$1,500
Others	$1,250
Construction	**$5,500**
National Utility Contractors Assn	$2,000
National Assn of Home Builders	$1,000
Others	$2,500
Defense	**$7,300**
Avondale Industries	$1,500
Rockwell International	$1,000
Tenneco Inc	$1,000
Textron Inc	$1,000
Others	$2,800
Electric Utilities & Equipment	**$4,500**
McDermott Inc	$1,000
Middle South Utilities*	$1,000
Others	$2,500
Food & Beverage	**$3,500**
Winn-Dixie Stores	$1,000
Others	$2,500
Health Professionals	**$5,700**
American Medical Assn	$1,350
American Occupational Therapy Assn	$1,000
National Assn of Pharmacists	$1,000
Others	$2,350

Campaign Revenue Sources

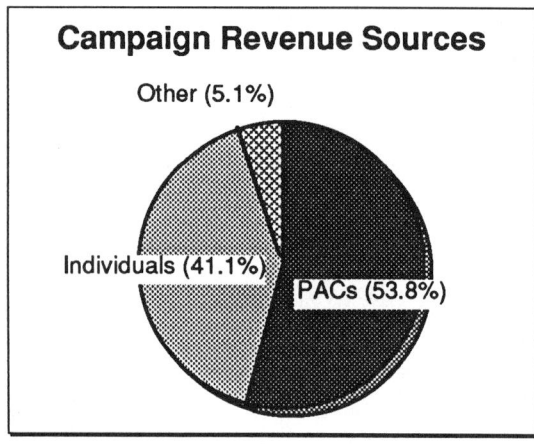

Other (5.1%)
Individuals (41.1%)
PACs (53.8%)

Hospitals & Health Services	**$3,750**
National Medical Enterprises Inc	$1,500
Others	$2,250
Insurance	**$4,000**
National Assn of Life Underwriters	$2,000
Others	$2,000
Lawyers & Lobbyists	**$8,000**
Assn of Trial Lawyers of America	$2,500
Jones, Walker, Waechter et al	$1,500
Others	$4,000
Oil & Gas	**$10,800**
Atlantic Richfield	$1,000
Shell Oil	$1,000
Others	$8,800
Other Crops & Dairy	**$5,250**
Associated Milk Producers	$1,000
Others	$4,250
Real Estate	**$7,500**
National Assn of Realtors	$5,000
Mortgage Bankers Assn of America	$2,000
Others	$500
Sea Transport	**$2,500**
Lykes Bros Steamship Company	$1,000
Others	$1,500
Securities Investment	**$6,000**
Thomson McKinnon Securities	$5,000
Investment Company Institute	$1,000
Sugar Growers	**$2,800**
American Sugar Cane League	$1,000
Others	$1,800
Surface Transport	**$4,750**
Auto Dealers & Drivers for Free Trade	$1,000
Kansas City Southern	$1,000
National Auto Dealers Assn	$1,000
Others	$1,750
Telecommunications	**$6,500**
South Central Bell Telephone	$5,000
AT&T	$1,000
Bell Atlantic	$500

PAC Totals by Category

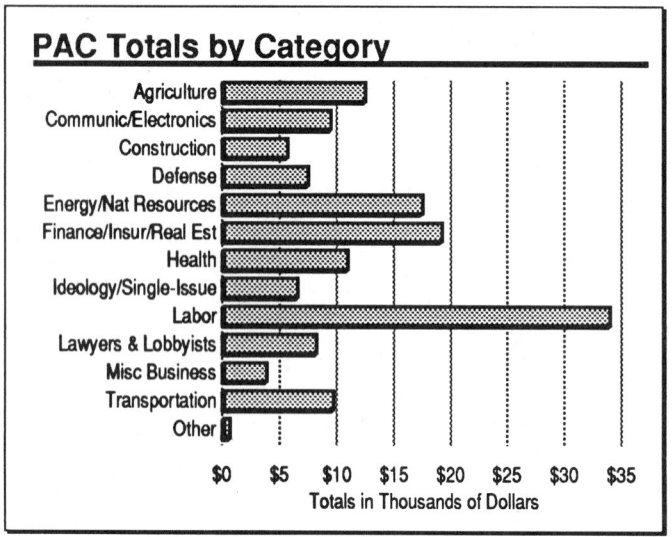

Agriculture
Communic/Electronics
Construction
Defense
Energy/Nat Resources
Finance/Insur/Real Est
Health
Ideology/Single-Issue
Labor
Lawyers & Lobbyists
Misc Business
Transportation
Other

$0 $5 $10 $15 $20 $25 $30 $35
Totals in Thousands of Dollars

Other Major Business PACs

Freeport-McMoran Inc	$1,000	Mining
J C Penney Company	$1,000	Dept Store

Labor

Bldg Trades/Industrial/Misc Unions	**$17,000**
United Auto Workers	$5,000
Machinists/Aerospace Workers Union	$2,500
Intl Brotherhood of Electrical Workers	$1,500
Operating Engineers Union	$1,500
AFL-CIO*	$1,000
American Nurses Assn	$1,000
Carpenters & Joiners Union	$1,000
Ladies Garment Workers Union	$1,000
Others	$2,500
Government & Postal Unions	**$7,300**
American Fedn of State/County/Munic Employees	$2,500
National Assn of Retired Federal Employees	$2,000
National Assn of Letter Carriers	$1,000
Others	$1,800
Teachers Unions	**$2,500**
National Education Assn	$2,500
Transportation Unions	**$8,000**
Marine Engineers Union*	$4,000
Seafarers International Union	$2,500
Others	$1,500

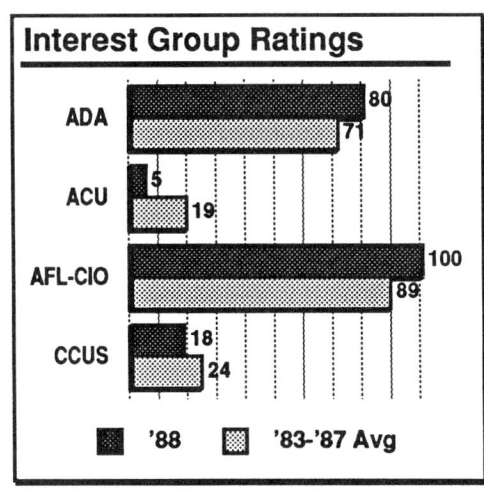

Interest Group Ratings

	'88	'83-'87 Avg
ADA	80	71
ACU	5	19
AFL-CIO	100	89
CCUS	18	24

Ideological/Single-Issue

Pro-Israel	**$2,500**
Louisiana for American Security	$2,000
Others	$500

Other Major Ideological & Single Issue

National Cmte to Preserve Social Security	$1,500	Soc Security
Human Rights Campaign Fund	$1,000	Gay Rights
KidsPAC	$1,000	Health/Welfare

Independent expenditures supporting Boggs

National Cmte to Preserve Social Security	$2,121

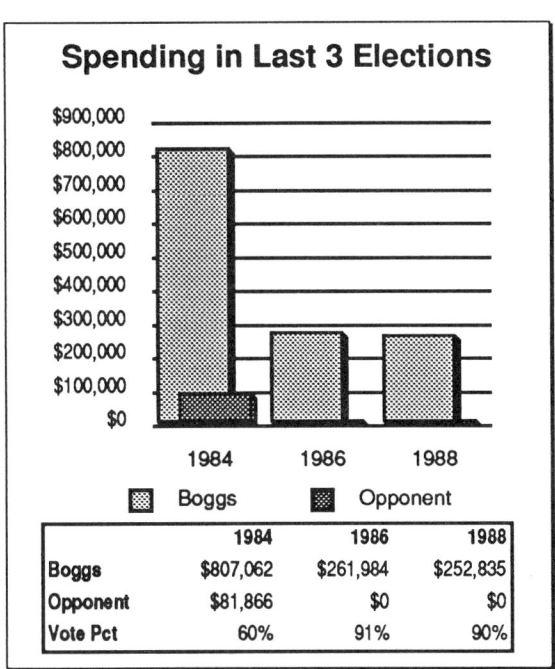

Spending in Last 3 Elections

	Boggs	Opponent

	1984	1986	1988
Boggs	$807,062	$261,984	$252,835
Opponent	$81,866	$0	$0
Vote Pct	60%	91%	90%

---

* Contributions came from more than one PAC affiliated with this sponsor.

David E. Bonior, D-Mich (12)

First elected: 1976
Total receipts: $475,462
Total from PACs: $328,317

1988 Committees & Subcommittees

Rules
Rules of the House

PAC Contribution Profile

Business

Campaign Revenue Sources

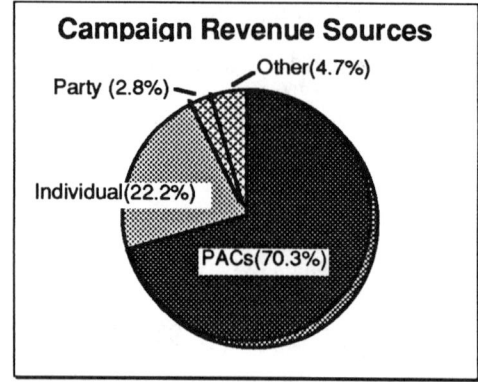

Other(4.7%)
Party (2.8%)
Individual(22.2%)
PACs(70.3%)

Automotive & Trucking $10,020

American Trucking Assns	$2,520
United Parcel Service	$2,250
Chrysler Corp	$2,000
Ford Motor Company	$1,500
Yellow Freight System	$1,000
Others	$750

Dairy $10,350

Associated Milk Producers	$4,000
Mid-American Dairymen	$3,500
Michigan Milk Producers Assn	$1,100
Dairymen Inc	$1,000
Others	$750

Electric Utilities $5,000

Consumers Power Company	$2,000
Detroit Edison	$2,000
ACRE (Action Committee for Rural Electrification)	$1,000

Financial Institutions $8,080

First National Bank/Mt Clemens	$1,080
American Bankers Assn	$1,000
Barnett Banks of Florida	$1,000
Michigan League of Savings Institutions	$1,000
Michigan Credit Union League	$1,000
Others	$3,000

Food & Beverage $11,100

Michigan Beer & Wine Wholesalers Assn	$2,100
Kellogg Company	$1,500
National Beer Wholesalers Assn	$1,500
A E Staley Manufacturing Company	$1,000
Anheuser-Busch	$1,000
Joseph E Seagram & Sons	$1,000
National Restaurant Assn	$1,000
Wine & Spirits Wholesalers of America	$1,000
Others	$1,000

PAC Totals by Category

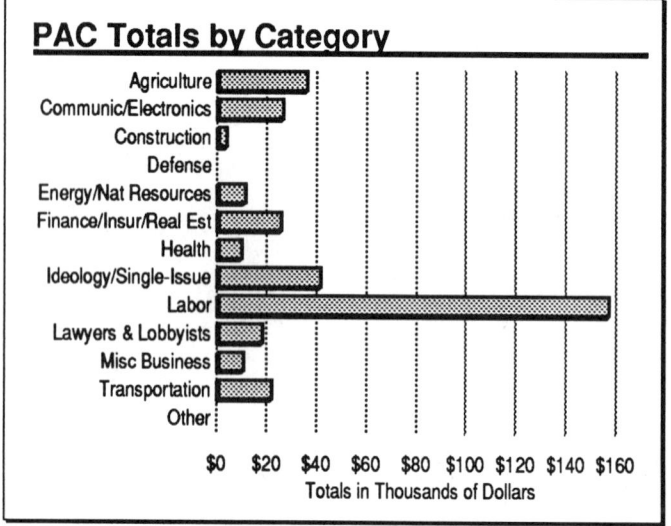

Category	
Agriculture	
Communic/Electronics	
Construction	
Defense	
Energy/Nat Resources	
Finance/Insur/Real Est	
Health	
Ideology/Single-Issue	
Labor	
Lawyers & Lobbyists	
Misc Business	
Transportation	
Other	

$0 $20 $40 $60 $80 $100 $120 $140 $160
Totals in Thousands of Dollars

Health Professionals $6,500

American Optometric Assn	$2,000
American Academy of Ophthalmology	$1,500
American Occupational Therapy Assn	$1,000
American Dental Assn	$1,000
Others	$1,000

Insurance $9,750

National Assn Mutual Insurance Agents	$1,500
Travelers Corp	$1,500
Blue Cross/Shield of Michigan	$1,250
American Council of Life Insurance	$1,000
Equitable Financial Services	$1,000
National Assn of Life Underwriters	$1,000
Prudential Insurance	$1,000
Others	$1,500

Lawyers & Lobbyists $17,340

Assn of Trial Lawyers of America	$10,000
Dickstein, Shapiro & Morin	$1,000
Holland & Hart	$1,000
Preston, Thorgrimson Ellis & Holman	$1,000
Verner, Liipfert Bernhard & McPherson	$1,000
Others	$3,340

Railroads $5,800

Kansas City Southern	$1,500
Norfolk Southern Corp	$1,500
CSX Transportation Inc	$1,300
Others	$1,500

Securities/Commodities Investment $9,500

Chicago Mercantile Exchange	$3,000
Chicago Board of Trade	$1,000
Commodity Exchange Inc	$1,000
First Boston Corp	$1,000
Investment Company Institute	$1,000
Morgan Stanley & Company	$1,000
Others	$1,500

Sugar Growers $9,700

American Crystal Sugar Corp	$2,000
American Sugarbeet Growers Assn	$2,000
Great Lakes Sugar Beet Growers	$1,700
Florida Sugar Cane League	$1,250
Southern Minnesota Beet Sugar Co-op	$1,000
Others	$1,750

Telecommunications $21,654

Michigan Bell Telephone	$4,154
AT&T	$4,000
Ameritech Corp	$3,000
BellSouth Corp*	$3,000

(continued on next page)

Telecommunications (cont'd)

US Telephone Assn	$2,500
Bell Atlantic	$1,500
Pacific Telesis Group	$1,000
U S West Inc	$1,000
Others	$1,500

Tobacco $6,500

Philip Morris	$3,500
Tobacco Institute	$1,500
Others	$1,500

Other Major Business PACs

National Cable Television Assn	$3,000	CableTV
Michigan Consolidated Gas	$2,200	Natural Gas
American Financial Services Assn	$1,500	Credit/Loans
Boat Owners Assn of the US	$1,500	Rec Boats
Northwest Airlines	$1,500	Airlines
Waste Management Inc	$1,500	Waste Mgmt
Boating PAC	$1,250	Rec Boats
International Council of Shopping Centers	$1,000	Retail
Manville Corp	$1,000	BldgMaterial
National Assn of Home Builders	$1,000	Resid Constr
National Assn of Realtors	$1,000	Real Estate

Labor

Bldg Trades/Industrial/Misc Unions $60,310

Food & Commercial Workers Union	$6,100
Carpenters & Joiners Union	$6,000
Boilermakers Union*	$5,500
Machinists/Aerospace Workers Union	$5,000
Operating Engineers Union*	$5,000
Plumbers/Pipefitters Union*	$3,950
AFL-CIO*	$3,910
Intl Brotherhood of Electrical Workers	$3,500
United Auto Workers	$3,500
Communications Workers of America	$2,500
United Mine Workers	$2,500
Laborers' Political League	$2,300
Ironworkers Union	$2,000
Ladies Garment Workers Union	$2,000
United Steelworkers	$1,200
Amalgamated Clothing & Textile Workers	$1,000
American Nurses Assn	$1,000
Electronic Machine Furniture Workers	$1,000
Hotel/Restaurant Employees Union	$1,000
Service Employees International Union	$1,000
Others	$350

Spending in Last 3 Elections

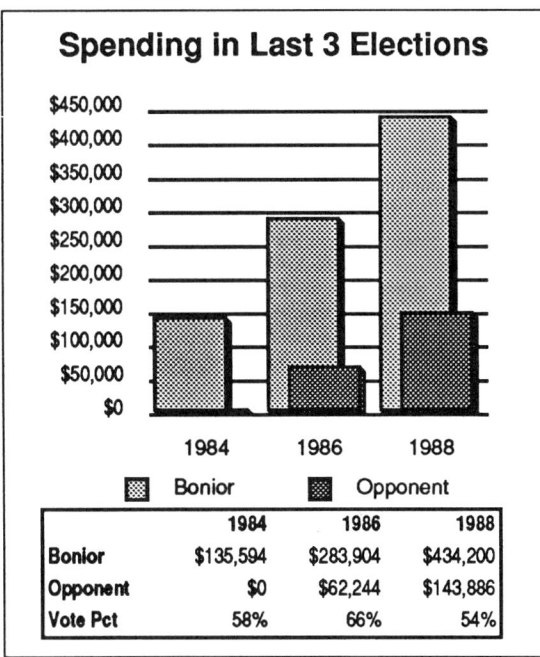

	1984	1986	1988
Bonior	$135,594	$283,904	$434,200
Opponent	$0	$62,244	$143,886
Vote Pct	58%	66%	54%

Interest Group Ratings

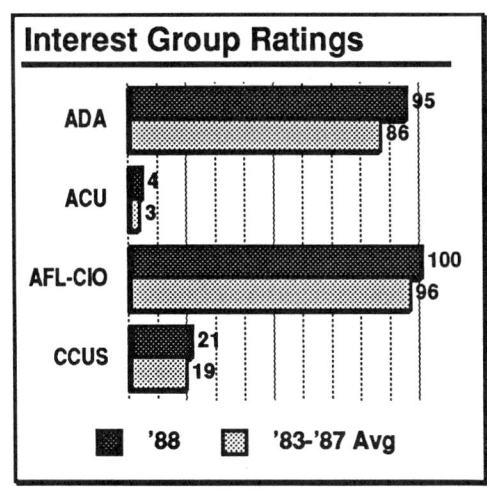

	'88	'83–'87 Avg
ADA	95	86
ACU	4	3
AFL-CIO	100	96
CCUS	21	19

Government & Postal Workers $18,500

National Assn of Letter Carriers	$9,700
American Fedn of State/County/Munic Employees	$7,000
National Assn of Retired Federal Employees	$7,000
American Postal Workers Union	$5,000
American Federation of Government Employees	$2,500
National Treasury Employees Union	$1,500
National Rural Letter Carriers Assn	$1,000
Others	$1,000

Sea Transport Unions $18,740

Marine Engineers Union*	$10,000
Seafarers International Union	$5,740
Masters, Mates & Pilots Union	$1,500
International Longshoremen Assn	$1,000
Others	$500

Other Transport Unions $31,450

Teamsters Union*	$10,100
Air Line Pilots Assn	$10,000
United Transportation Union	$5,100
Amalgamated Transit Union	$3,500
Brotherhood of Locomotive Engineers	$1,500
Transportation Communication Union	$1,250

Teachers Unions $12,050

National Education Assn	$10,000
American Federation of Teachers	$2,050

Ideological/Single-Issue

Democratic Leadership PACs $17,500

Majority Congress Committee (Jim Wright)	$5,000
Pax Americas (David Bonior)	$5,000
Valley Education Fund (Tony Coelho)	$3,500
Cmte for Democratic Opportunity (Bill Gray)	$2,500
America's Leaders' Fund (Dan Rostenkowski)	$1,000
Cmte for a Progressive Congress (David Obey)	$500

Other Major Ideological & Single Issue

12th Dist Demo Cmte	$9,800	Dem/Lib
KidsPAC	$4,000	Health/Welfare
National Right to Life PAC	$2,500	Pro-Life
National Cmte for Effective Congress	$2,497	Dem/Lib
Armenian Assembly of America	$1,000	Ethnic
Armenian-American PAC	$1,000	Ethnic

Independent expenditures supporting Bonior

National Cmte to Preserve Social Security	$2,175

* Contributions came from more than one PAC affiliated with this sponsor.

Robert A. Borski, D-Pa (3)

First elected: 1982
Total receipts: $337,723
Total from PACs: $189,654

1988 Committees & Subcommittees

Merchant Marine and Fisheries
Merchant Marine
Oceanography

Public Works and Transportation
Investigations and Oversight
Surface Transportation

Water Resources

Select Aging
Health and Long-Term Care

PAC Contribution Profile

Business

Commercial & Savings Banks **$3,050**
    None over $500

Construction **$3,250**
    National Assn of Home Builders $2,000
    Associated General Contractors $1,250

Electric Utilities **$3,200**
    Philadelphia Electric $1,700
    ACRE (Action Committee for Rural Electrification) $1,250
    Others $250

Health Professionals **$4,250**
    American Medical Assn $2,750
    Pennsylvania Medical Assn $1,250
    Others $250

Lawyers & Lobbyists **$4,750**
    Assn of Trial Lawyers of America $2,000
    Delaware Valley Leadership Fund $1,000
    Others $1,750

Real Estate **$4,750**
    National Assn of Realtors $4,750

Telecommunications **$6,000**
    AT&T $5,000
    Bell Telephone of Pennsylvania $1,000

Campaign Revenue Sources

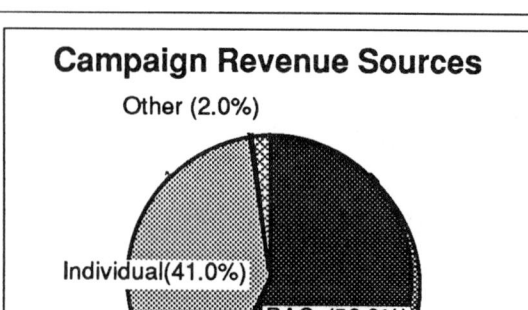

Other (2.0%)
Individual (41.0%)
PACs (56.9%)

Trucking/Delivery **$6,354**
    United Parcel Service $2,500
    Consolidated Freightways $2,000
    Others $1,854

Other Major Business PACs

National Assn of Life Underwriters	$1,500	Life Insurance
American Pilots Assn	$1,000	Sea Transport
Atlantic Richfield	$1,000	Major Oil
Budd Company	$1,000	Auto Equipmt
Pennwalt Corp	$1,000	Chemicals
Smithkline Beckman	$1,000	Pharmaceut
Waste Management Inc	$1,000	Waste Mgmt

PAC Totals by Category

Agriculture
Communic/Electronics
Construction
Defense
Energy/Nat Resources
Finance/Insur/Real Est
Health
Ideology/Single-Issue
Labor
Lawyers & Lobbyists
Misc Business
Transportation
Other

$0 $20 $40 $60 $80 $100 $120 $140
Totals in Thousands of Dollars

Labor

Bldg Trades/Industrial/Misc Unions $60,250

Ironworkers Union*	$10,000
United Auto Workers	$10,000
Sheet Metal Workers Union	$5,000
United Steelworkers	$5,000
Carpenters & Joiners Union	$4,000
Operating Engineers Union*	$4,000
Comm Workers Union Local #13000	$3,500
Machinists/Aerospace Workers Union	$3,000
AFL-CIO	$2,500
Plumbers/Pipefitters Union*	$2,000
Laborers' Political League	$1,500
Graphic Communications Union	$1,400
Ladies Garment Workers Union	$1,250
Amalgamated Clothing & Textile Workers*	$1,000
Boilermakers Union	$1,000
Food & Commercial Workers Union	$1,000
Intl Brotherhood of Electrical Workers	$1,000
Painters & Allied Trades Union	$1,000
Others	$2,100

Government & Postal Workers $32,345

American Fedn of State/County/Munic Employees	$12,095
National Assn of Retired Federal Employees	$10,000
National Assn of Letter Carriers	$6,500
American Postal Workers Union	$2,500
Others	$1,250

Teachers Unions $13,000

National Education Assn	$10,000
American Federation of Teachers	$3,000

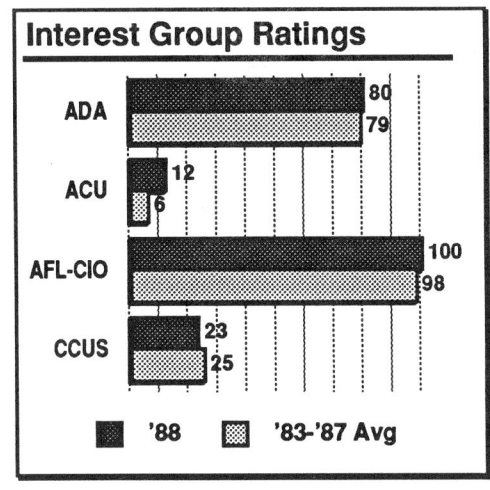

Interest Group Ratings

(Bar chart)
ADA: '88 = 80, '83–'87 Avg = 79
ACU: '88 = 12, '83–'87 Avg = 6
AFL-CIO: '88 = 100, '83–'87 Avg = 98
CCUS: '88 = 23, '83–'87 Avg = 25

■ '88   ▨ '83–'87 Avg

Transportation Unions $30,250

Teamsters Union*	$7,500
Marine Engineers District 2 Maritime Officers	$6,500
Air Line Pilots Assn	$5,000
Transport Workers Union	$3,000
Seafarers International Union	$2,000
Amalgamated Transit Union	$1,500
Transportation Communication Union	$1,250
United Transportation Union	$1,250
Masters, Mates & Pilots Union	$1,000
Others	$1,250

Ideological/Single-Issue

Pro-Israel $5,000

National PAC	$5,000

Other Major Ideological/Leadership PACs

Valley Education Fund (Tony Coelho) .... $1,000   Dem Leaders

Independent expenditures supporting Borski

National Cmte to Preserve Social Security $3,937

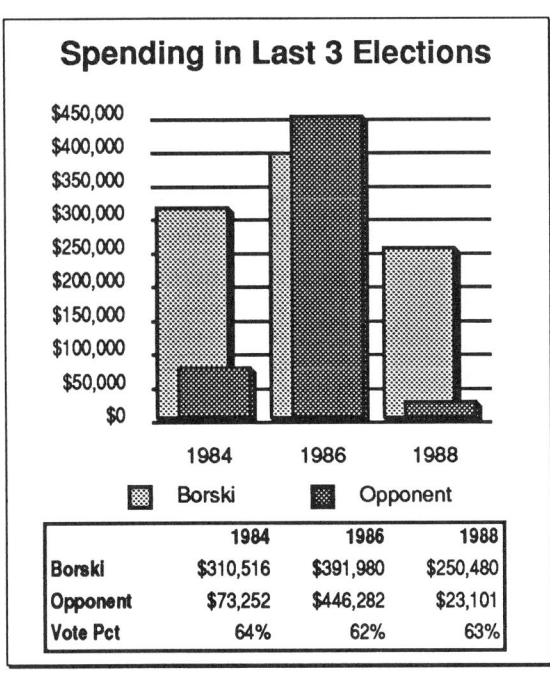

Spending in Last 3 Elections

(Bar chart with y-axis from $0 to $450,000)

▨ Borski   ■ Opponent

	1984	1986	1988
Borski	$310,516	$391,980	$250,480
Opponent	$73,252	$446,282	$23,101
Vote Pct	64%	62%	63%

* Contributions came from more than one PAC affiliated with this sponsor.

Douglas H. Bosco, D-Calif (1)

First elected: 1982
Total receipts: $252,328
Total from PACs: $119,638

1988 Committees & Subcommittees

Merchant Marine and Fisheries
Fisheries and Wildlife Conservation and the Environment
Panama Canal /Outer Continental Shelf

Public Works and Transportation
Public Buildings and Grounds (Chairman)
Aviation
Surface Transportation

PAC Contribution Profile

Business

Campaign Revenue Sources

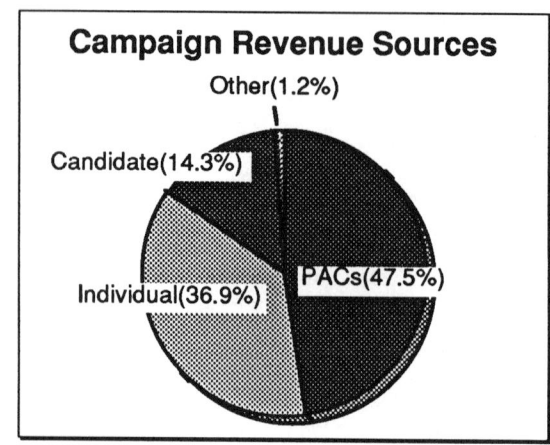

Other(1.2%)
Candidate(14.3%)
Individual(36.9%)
PACs(47.5%)

Air Transport **$4,000**
    Aircraft Owners & Pilots Assn $1,100
    Others $2,900

Automotive **$2,850**
    Auto Dealers & Drivers for Free Trade $2,500
    Others $350

Beer, Wine & Liquor **$2,700**
    Joseph E Seagram & Sons $1,000
    Others $1,700

Building Contractors & Engineers **$2,950**
    National Utility Contractors Assn $1,500
    Others $1,450

Forest Products **$3,600**
    Simpson Investment Company $2,100
    Louisiana-Pacific Corp $1,000
    Others $500

Health Professionals **$3,600**
    American Medical Assn $3,600

Lawyers & Lobbyists **$4,850**
    Assn of Trial Lawyers of America $2,500
    Others $2,350

Oil & Gas **$2,800**
    None over $600

Real Estate **$8,300**
    National Assn of Realtors $8,000
    Others $300

Trucking/Delivery **$5,650**
    United Parcel Service $3,350
    Enterprise Leasing Company $1,000
    Others $1,300

Other Major Business PACs

Pacific Telesis Group	$1,850	Phone Util
National Fisheries Institute	$1,500	Fishing
Arcata Corp	$1,000	Books & Mags
California Bankers Assn	$1,000	Comml Banks
Cargill Inc	$1,000	Grain Trader
Freeport-McMoran Inc	$1,000	Other Mining
National Assn of Life Underwriters	$1,000	Life Insurance
Stone Container Corp	$1,000	Paper Packg
Waste Management Inc	$1,000	Waste Mgmt

PAC Totals by Category

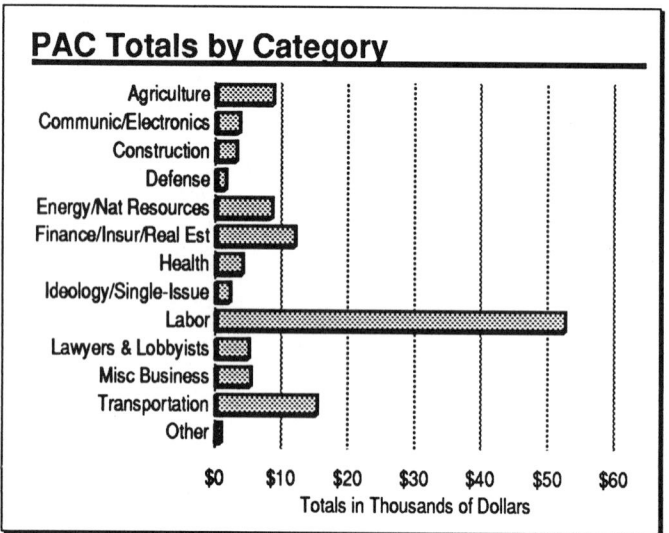

Agriculture
Communic/Electronics
Construction
Defense
Energy/Nat Resources
Finance/Insur/Real Est
Health
Ideology/Single-Issue
Labor
Lawyers & Lobbyists
Misc Business
Transportation
Other

$0 $10 $20 $30 $40 $50 $60

Totals in Thousands of Dollars

Labor

Bldg Trades/Industrial/Misc Unions *$13,900*

United Auto Workers	$3,300
Laborers' Western Political League	$3,000
Machinists/Aerospace Workers Union	$2,000
Carpenters & Joiners Union	$1,500
Operating Engineers Union*	$1,150
Food & Commercial Workers Union	$1,000
Intl Brotherhood of Electrical Workers	$1,000
Others	$950

Government & Postal Unions *$8,900*

National Assn of Retired Federal Employees	$6,000
International Assn of Firefighters	$1,200
American Postal Workers Union	$1,050
Others	$650

Sea Transport Unions *$7,700*

Marine Engineers Union	$3,500
Seafarers International Union	$2,000
Boilermakers Union	$1,000
Others	$1,200

Other Transport Unions *$17,000*

Air Line Pilots Assn	$7,500
Teamsters Union	$6,500
Amalgamated Transit Union	$1,000
Others	$2,000

Teachers Unions *$4,800*

National Education Assn	$4,800

Major Ideological/Single-Issue PACs

Valley Education Fund (Tony Coelho) .... $1,000   Dem Leaders

Independent expenditures supporting Bosco

National Cmte to Preserve Social Security	$2,677
Others	$303

Spending in Last 3 Elections

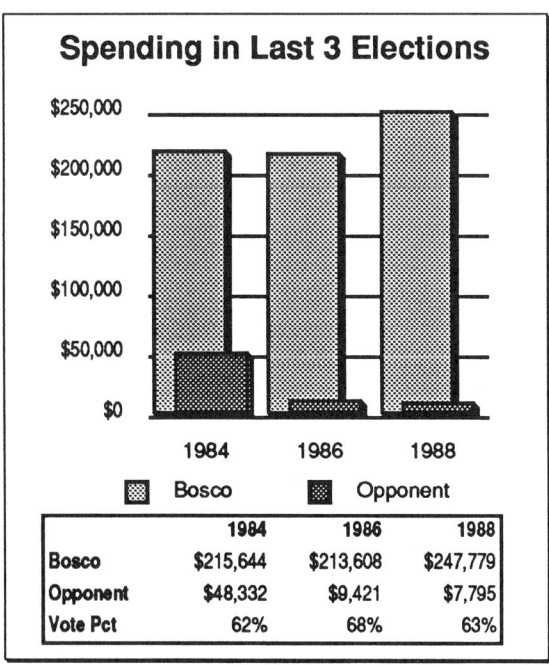

	1984	1986	1988
Bosco	$215,644	$213,608	$247,779
Opponent	$48,332	$9,421	$7,795
Vote Pct	62%	68%	63%

Interest Group Ratings

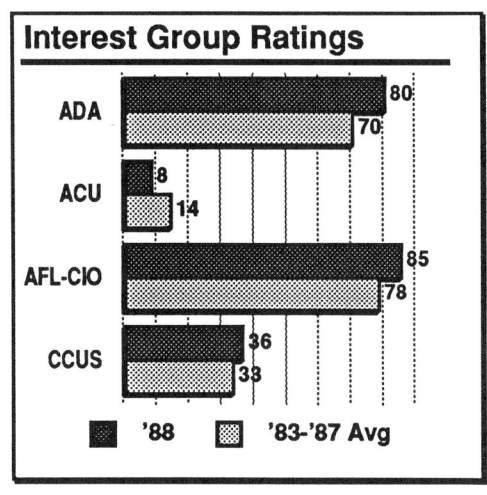

Group	'88	'83-'87 Avg
ADA	80	70
ACU	8	14
AFL-CIO	85	78
CCUS	36	33

* Contributions came from more than one PAC affiliated with this sponsor.

Rick Boucher, D-Va (9)

1988 Committees & Subcommittees

First elected: 1982
Total receipts: $616,821
Total from PACs: $366,600

Energy and Commerce
Oversight and Investigations
Telecommunications and Finance
Transportation, Tourism and Hazardous Materials

Judiciary
Courts, Civil Liberties and the Administration of Justice
Criminal Justice

Science, Space and Technology
Energy Research and Development

Select Aging
Housing and Consumer Interests
Retirement Income and Employment

PAC Contribution Profile

Business

Accountants	....	$24,000
American Institute of CPA's	....	$10,000
Touche Ross	....	$4,800
Coopers & Lybrand	....	$2,800
Ernst & Whinney	....	$2,000
Arthur Andersen & Company	....	$1,800
Others	....	$2,600

Aviation & Aerospace	....	$7,100
Pittston Company	....	$1,900
Aircraft Owners & Pilots Assn	....	$1,400
Federal Express Corp	....	$1,300
TRW Inc	....	$1,200
Others	....	$1,300

Broadcasting & Movies	....	$10,700
National Assn of Broadcasters	....	$4,600
Assn of Independent TV Stations	....	$2,300
Others	....	$3,800

Commercial Banks	....	$30,350
American Bankers Assn	....	$10,000
J P Morgan & Company	....	$5,000
Bankers Trust	....	$2,000
Chemical Bank	....	$2,000
Barnett Banks of Florida	....	$1,500
Chase Manhattan	....	$1,100
Others	....	$8,750

Defense	....	$7,050
Textron Inc	....	$2,100
Others	....	$4,950

Campaign Revenue Sources

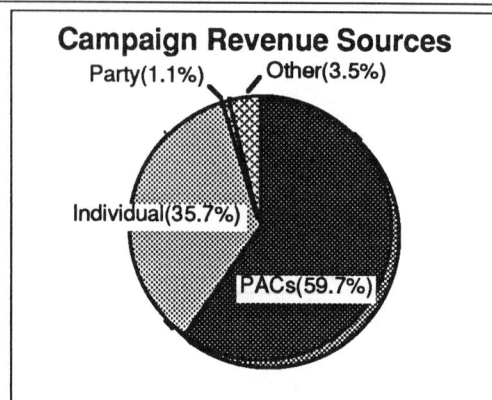

Party(1.1%) Other(3.5%)
Individual(35.7%)
PACs(59.7%)

Electric Utilities	....	$12,600
ACRE (Action Committee for Rural Electrification)*	....	$3,300
Dominion Resources Inc	....	$1,350
Southern Company*	....	$1,200
American Electric Power	....	$1,150
Others	....	$5,600

Food & Beverage	....	$6,250
None over $1,000		

Health Professionals	....	$12,350
American Medical Assn	....	$5,250
American Academy of Ophthalmology	....	$1,500
American Dental Assn	....	$1,500
National Assn of Pharmacists	....	$1,300
Others	....	$2,800

Insurance	....	$5,550
None over $800		

Lawyers & Lobbyists	....	$13,500
Assn of Trial Lawyers of America	....	$5,000
Akin, Gump, Hauer & Feld	....	$1,700
Rivkin, Radler, Dunne & Baye	....	$1,300
Others	....	$5,500

Mining	....	$6,000
Independent Coal Operators Assn	....	$2,000
Peabody Coal	....	$1,200
Others	....	$2,800

Oil & Gas	....	$15,500
Coastal Corp	....	$1,600
Columbia Natural Resources	....	$1,600
Sun Company	....	$1,500
Others	....	$10,800

Pharmaceuticals	....	$8,200
Warner-Lambert	....	$1,200
Ciba-Geigy Corp	....	$1,100
Others	....	$5,900

PAC Totals by Category

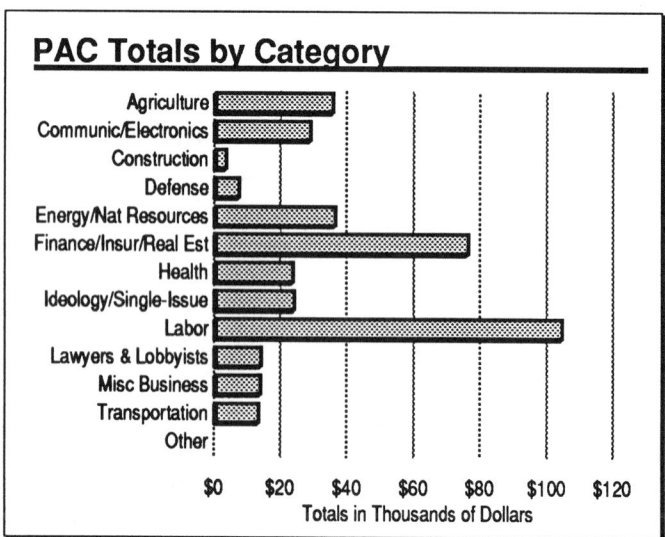

Agriculture
Communic/Electronics
Construction
Defense
Energy/Nat Resources
Finance/Insur/Real Est
Health
Ideology/Single-Issue
Labor
Lawyers & Lobbyists
Misc Business
Transportation
Other

$0 $20 $40 $60 $80 $100 $120
Totals in Thousands of Dollars

Securities/Commodities Investment $14,850

Securities Industry Assn	$1,700
Chicago Board of Trade	$1,500
Goldman Sachs	$1,500
Merrill Lynch	$1,100
Others	$9,050

Sugar Growers $5,900

American Crystal Sugar Corp	$1,400
American Sugarbeet Growers Assn	$1,100
Others	$3,400

Telecommunications $16,450

AT&T	$3,000
Corning Glass Works	$2,000
Chesapeake & Potomac Telephone	$1,500
Comsat	$1,200
Pacific Telesis Group	$1,050
Others	$7,700

Tobacco $13,650

Philip Morris	$5,000
RJR Nabisco	$4,300
Tobacco Institute	$1,500
Brown & Williamson Tobacco	$1,100
Others	$1,750

Other Major Business PACs

Dairymen Inc-Virginia	$3,500	Dairy
Hoechst Celanese Corp	$1,550	Synth Fiber
National Assn of Chain Drug Stores	$1,100	Drug Stores

Labor

Bldg Trades/Industrial/Misc Unions $55,400

United Auto Workers	$10,000
United Steelworkers	$10,000
Machinists/Aerospace Workers Union	$5,600
United Mine Workers	$5,600
Carpenters & Joiners Union	$4,000
Operating Engineers Union	$3,500

(Continued in next column)

Interest Group Ratings

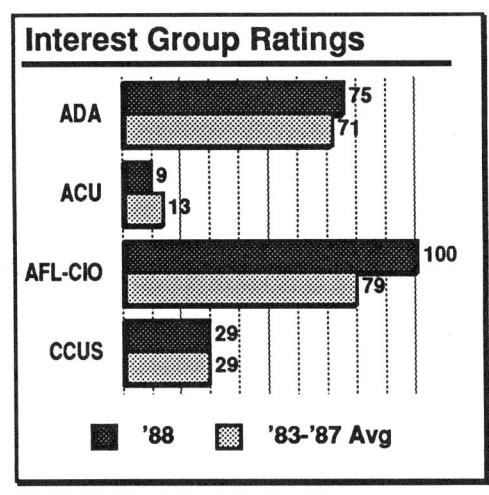

Labor (cont'd)

Intl Brotherhood of Electrical Workers	$3,000
Food & Commercial Workers Union	$2,800
Communications Workers of America	$2,300
Laborers' Political League	$2,300
Electronic Machine Furniture Workers	$1,300
Oil, Chemical & Atomic Workers Union	$1,100

Government & Postal Workers $25,050

National Assn of Letter Carriers	$9,300
National Assn of Retired Federal Employees	$5,000
American Postal Workers Union	$4,200
American Fedn of State/County/Munic Employees	$2,500
National Rural Letter Carriers Assn	$2,000
Others	$2,050

Teachers Unions $6,600

National Education Assn	$6,600

Transportation Unions $16,750

Teamsters Union	$6,000
United Transportation Union	$3,900
Marine Engineers Radio Officers #3	$2,000
Others	$4,850

Ideological/Single-Issue

Democratic/Liberal $5,300

National Cmte for an Effective Congress	$5,000
Others	$300

Pro-Gun Ownership $9,900

National Rifle Assn	$9,900

Pro-Israel $5,300

National PAC	$5,000
Others	$300

Independent expenditures supporting Boucher

National Cmte to Preserve Social Security	$1,257

---

* Contributions came from more than one PAC affiliated with this sponsor.

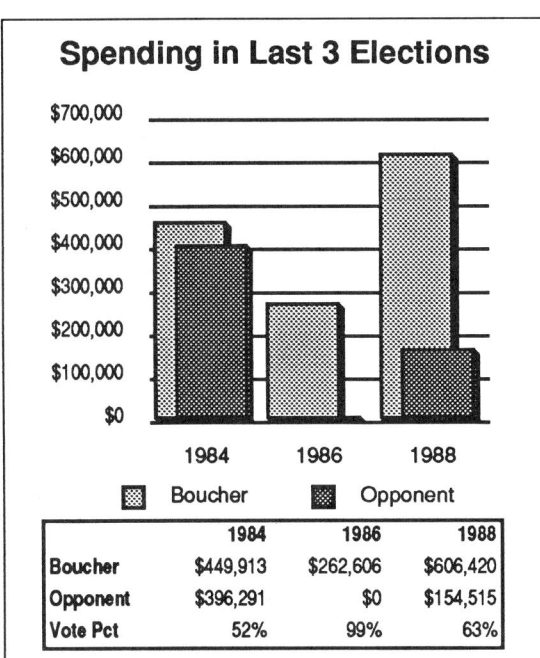

Spending in Last 3 Elections

	1984	1986	1988
Boucher	$449,913	$262,606	$606,420
Opponent	$396,291	$0	$154,515
Vote Pct	52%	99%	63%

Barbara Boxer, D-Calif (6)

First elected: 1982
Total receipts: $450,306
Total from PACs: $185,330

1988 Committees & Subcommittees

Armed Service
Investigations
Research and Development

Budget
Defense and International Affairs
Income Security
State and Local Government

Select Children, Youth and Families

Campaign Revenue Sources

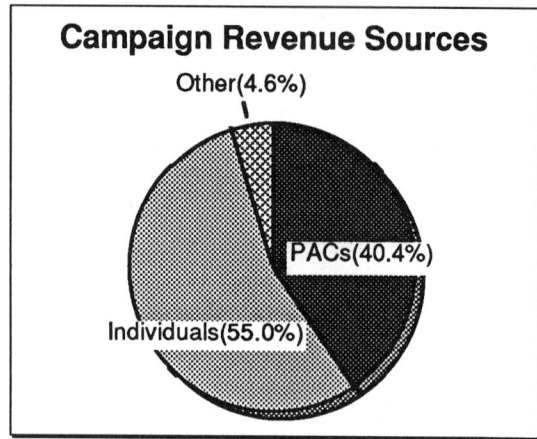

Other(4.6%)
PACs(40.4%)
Individuals(55.0%)

PAC Contribution Profile

Business

Construction	**$5,700**
Bechtel Corp	$2,000
National Assn of Home Builders	$2,800
Others	$900
Dairy	**$6,400**
Western United Dairymens Assn	$3,000
Associated Milk Producers	$1,500
Mid-American Dairymen	$1,300
Others	$600
Health Professionals	**$9,500**
American Medical Assn	$5,300
American Academy of Ophthalmology	$1,000
American Dental Assn	$1,000
Cmte for Quality Orthopedic Health Care	$1,000
Others	$1,200
Hospitals	**$2,500**
American Hospital Assn	$2,500
Insurance	**$3,600**
Massachusetts Mutual Life Insurance	$1,300
Farmers Group Inc	$1,000
National Assn of Life Underwriters	$1,000
Others	$300

Lawyers	**$4,250**
Assn of Trial Lawyers of America	$2,000
California Trial Lawyers Assn	$1,500
Others	$750
Real Estate	**$7,300**
National Assn of Realtors	$6,500
Others	$800
Sugar Growers	**$3,700**
California Beet Growers Assn	$2,000
Others	$1,700

Other Major Business PACs

United Parcel Service	$2,200	Delivery
National Venture Capital Assn	$2,000	Venture Cap
Pacific Gas & Electric	$1,900	Gas & Electr
Pacific Telesis Group	$1,450	Phone Util
Pacific Stock Exchange	$1,000	Securities

PAC Totals by Category

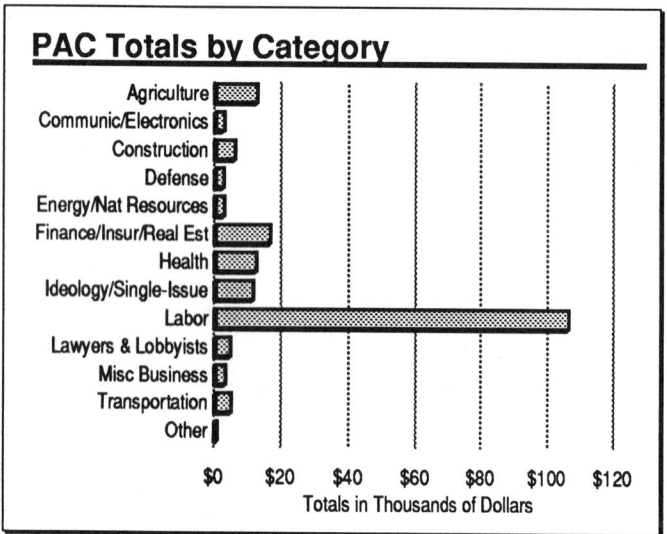

Agriculture
Communic/Electronics
Construction
Defense
Energy/Nat Resources
Finance/Insur/Real Est
Health
Ideology/Single-Issue
Labor
Lawyers & Lobbyists
Misc Business
Transportation
Other

$0 $20 $40 $60 $80 $100 $120

Totals in Thousands of Dollars

Labor

Bldg Trades/Industrial/Misc Unions $32,850

Machinists/Aerospace Workers Union	$5,550
United Auto Workers	$5,300
Carpenters & Joiners Union	$5,100
Laborers' Western Political League	$4,000
Food & Commercial Workers Union	$2,550
Sheet Metal Workers Union	$2,500
Service Employees International Union	$1,500
Hotel/Restaurant Employees Union	$1,250
AFL-CIO*	$1,000
Operating Engineers Union	$1,000
Others	$3,100

Government & Postal Workers $28,700

National Assn of Retired Federal Employees	$10,000
National Assn of Letter Carriers	$7,500
American Fedn of State/County/Munic Employees	$2,500
National Treasury Employees Union	$2,400
American Postal Workers Union	$2,100
American Federation of Government Employees	$1,500
Others	$2,700

Sea Transport Unions $17,800

Seafarers International Union*	$6,950
Marine Engineers Union*	$6,000
Longshoremen/Warehousemen Union	$3,250
Masters, Mates & Pilots Union	$1,100
Maritime Union of America	$500

Other Transport Unions $18,200

Teamsters Union	$10,000
Air Line Pilots Assn	$5,000
Others	$3,200

Teachers Unions $8,350

National Education Assn	$7,500
Others	$850

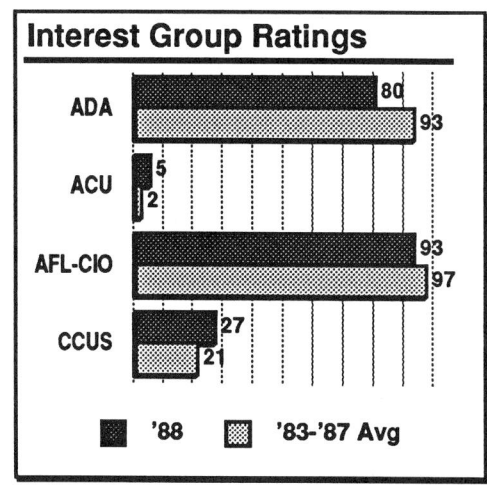

Interest Group Ratings

	'88	'83-'87 Avg
ADA	80	93
ACU	5	2
AFL-CIO	93	97
CCUS	27	21

Ideological/Single-Issue

Gay Rights $2,600

Human Rights Campaign Fund	$2,600

Other Major Ideological/Single Issue

Operation Grass Roots	$2,000	Dem/Lib
National Cmte to Preserve Social Security	$1,000	Soc Secur
Valley Education Fund (Tony Coelho)	$1,000	Dem Leaders

Independent expenditures supporting Boxer

Elections Cmte/Orange County	$2,000
National Cmte to Preserve Social Security	$2,264
Others	$1,192

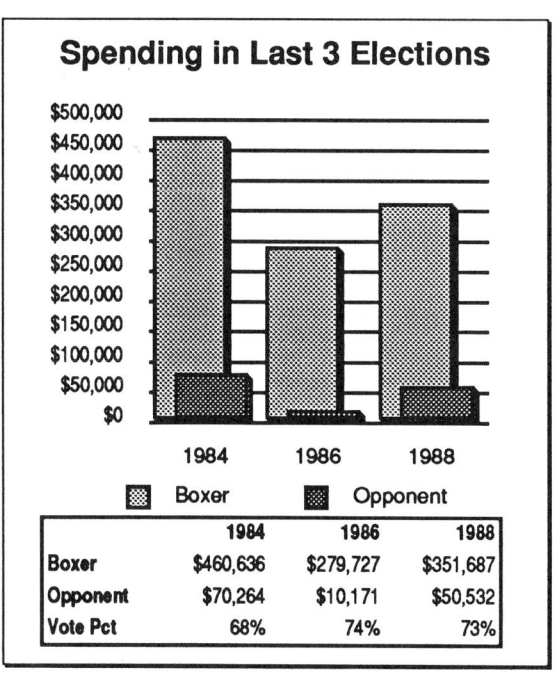

Spending in Last 3 Elections

	Boxer	Opponent

	1984	1986	1988
Boxer	$460,636	$279,727	$351,687
Opponent	$70,264	$10,171	$50,532
Vote Pct	68%	74%	73%

---

* Contributions came from more than one PAC affiliated with this sponsor.

Joseph E. Brennan, D-Maine (1)

First elected: 1986
Total receipts: $493,951
Total from PACs: $280,229

1988 Committees & Subcommittees

ArmedServices
Research and Development
Seapower and Strategic and Critical Materials

Merchant Marine and Fisheries
Coast Guard and Navigation
Merchant Marine
Panama Canal/Outer Continental Shelf

Select Hunger

PAC Contribution Profile

Business

Defense **$23,300**

Bath Iron Works	$7,000
AT&T	$3,500
United Technologies	$3,500
McDonnell Douglas*	$1,050
Chrysler Corp	$1,000
Grumman	$1,000
Raytheon	$1,000
Textron Inc	$1,000
Others	$4,250

Health Professionals **$5,750**

American Academy of Ophthalmology	$2,500
American Occupational Therapy Assn	$1,000
American Dental Assn	$1,000
National Assn of Pharmacists	$1,000
Others	$250

Insurance **$5,750**

Unum Life Insurance Company	$2,000
American Family Corp	$1,500
Independent Insurance Agents of America	$1,000
National Assn of Life Underwriters	$1,000
Others	$250

Lawyers **$8,000**

Assn of Trial Lawyers of America	$7,000
Verner, Liipfert Bernhard, & McPherson	$1,000

Campaign Revenue Sources

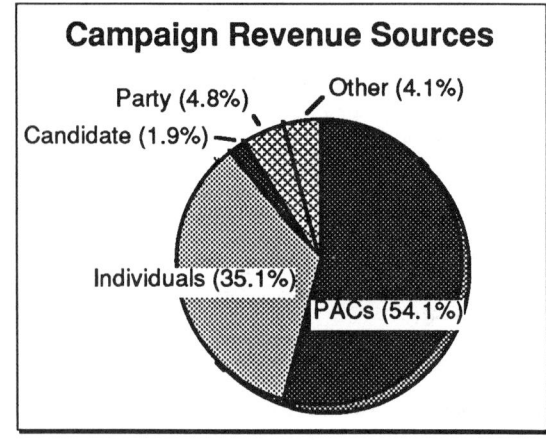

Party (4.8%)
Other (4.1%)
Candidate (1.9%)
Individuals (35.1%)
PACs (54.1%)

Real Estate **$8,500**

National Assn of Realtors	$8,000
Others	$500

Other Major Business PACs

National Assn of Home Builders	$2,000	Resid Constr
National Auto Dealers Assn	$2,000	Auto Sales
Fleet Bank of Maine	$1,900	Comml Banks
New England Tel & Tel	$1,875	Phone Util
Aircraft Owners & Pilots Assn	$1,500	GenlAviation
American Pilots Assn	$1,500	Sea Transport
American Bankers Assn	$1,000	Comml Banks
Associated Milk Producers	$1,000	Dairy
Duchossois Industries	$1,000	RR Equip
Freeport-McMoran Inc	$1,000	Other Mining
Joseph E Seagram & Sons	$1,000	Wine&Liquor
Maremont Corp	$1,000	Auto Equipmt
Matson Navigation	$1,000	Sea Transport
Mid-American Dairymen	$1,000	Dairy
Municipal Securities Industry	$1,000	Securities

PAC Totals by Category

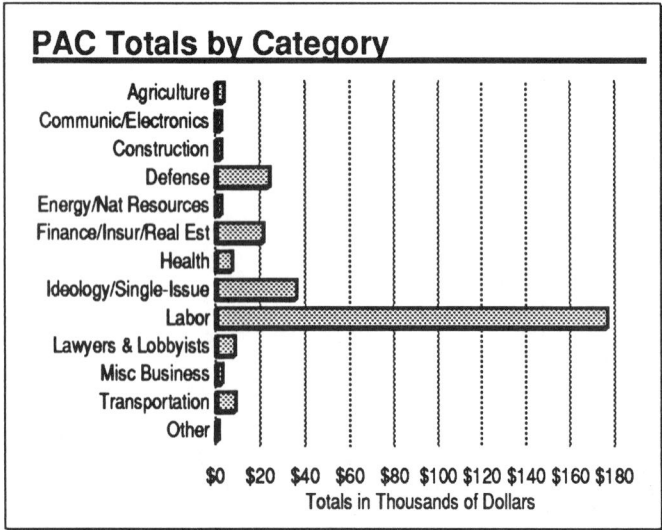

Totals in Thousands of Dollars

Labor

Bldg Trades/Industrial/Misc Unions **$93,137**

AFL-CIO*	$14,237
Food & Commercial Workers Union*	$11,500
Intl Brotherhood of Electrical Workers	$10,500
Machinists/Aerospace Workers Union	$10,000
United Auto Workers	$7,500
Carpenters & Joiners Union	$5,500
Ironworkers Union	$5,000
Operating Engineers Union	$4,000
United Paperworkers	$4,000
Boilermakers Union	$3,000
Rubber Cork Linoleum Plastic Workers	$3,000
Amalgamated Clothing & Textile Workers	$2,500
Laborers' Political League	$2,500
Sheet Metal Workers Union	$2,500
Bakery, Confectionery & Tobacco Workers	$2,325
Ladies Garment Workers Union	$1,500
American Nurses Assn	$1,125
Painters & Allied Trades Union	$1,000
Plumbers/Pipefitters Union	$1,000
Others	$450

Government & Postal Workers **$35,500**

American Fedn of State/County/Munic Employees	$10,000
National Assn of Letter Carriers	$10,000
National Assn of Retired Federal Employees	$10,000
American Postal Workers Union	$2,500
National Rural Letter Carriers Assn	$1,500
Others	$1,500

Sea Transport Unions **$19,000**

Marine Engineers Union*	$11,000
Seafarers International Union	$5,500
Masters, Mates & Pilots Union	$2,500

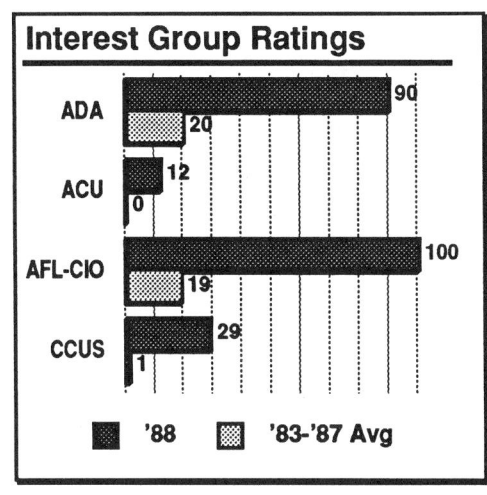

Interest Group Ratings

	'88	'83-'87 Avg
ADA	90	20
ACU	12	0
AFL-CIO	100	19
CCUS	29	1

Other Transport Unions **$20,827**

Teamsters Union	$7,500
Air Line Pilots Assn	$3,500
United Transportation Union	$3,000
Maintenance of Way Employees	$2,000
Amalgamated Transit Union	$1,500
Transportation Communication Union	$1,077
Brotherhood of Locomotive Engineers	$1,000
Others	$1,250

Teachers Unions **$8,500**

National Education Assn	$5,500
American Federation of Teachers	$3,000

Ideological/Single-Issue

Democratic/Liberal **$5,998**

National Cmte for an Effective Congress	$5,498
Others	$500

Democratic Leadership PACs **$17,500**

Valley Education Fund (Tony Coelho)	$6,500
Majority Congress Committee (Jim Wright)	$5,000
Cmte for the 100th Congress (Charles Rangel)	$3,000
Cmte for Democratic Opportunity (Bill Gray)	$2,000
House Leadership Fund (Tom Foley)	$1,000

Pro-Israel **$5,350**

National PAC	$5,000
Hudson Valley PAC	$350

Other Major Ideological/Single Issue

Council for a Livable World	$2,486	Pro-Peace
KidsPAC	$2,000	Health/Welfare
League of Conservation Voters	$1,000	Environment
National Council of Senior Citizens	$1,000	Elderly

Independent expenditures supporting Brennan

National Cmte to Preserve Social Security	$1,730

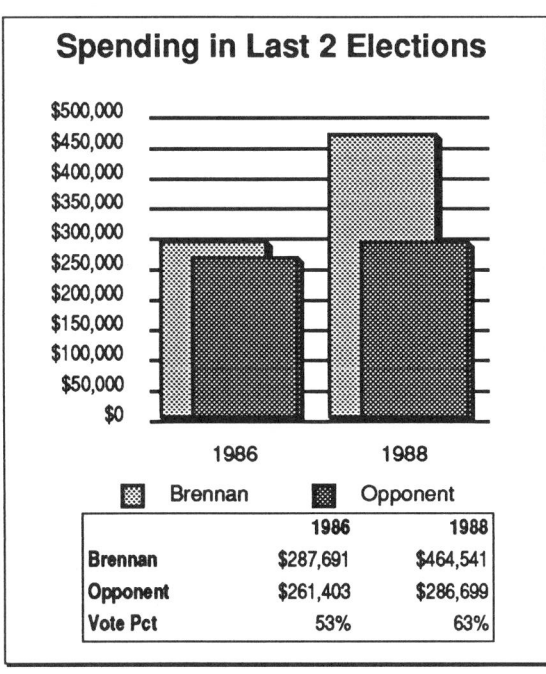

Spending in Last 2 Elections

	1986	1988
Brennan	$287,691	$464,541
Opponent	$261,403	$286,699
Vote Pct	53%	63%

Brennan / Opponent

* Contributions came from more than one PAC affiliated
with this sponsor.

Jack Brooks, D-Texas (9)

1988 Committees & Subcommittees

Government Operations (Chairman)
Legislation and National Security (Chairman)

Judiciary
Administrative Law and Governmental Relations
Monopolies and Commercial Law

First elected: 1952
Total receipts: $424,773
Total from PACs: $276,562

PAC Contribution Profile

Business

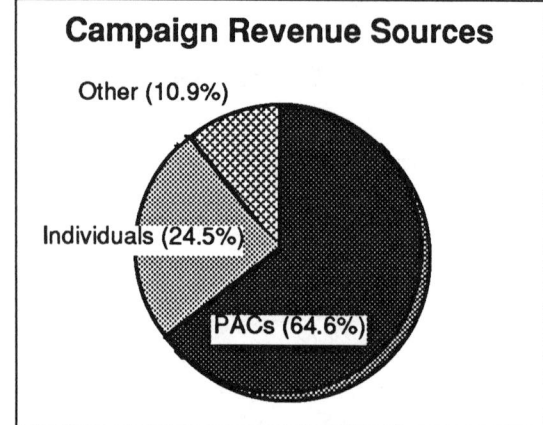

Campaign Revenue Sources

Other (10.9%)
Individuals (24.5%)
PACs (64.6%)

Accountants	**$9,500**
American Institute of CPA's	$5,000
Ernst & Whinney	$1,500
Others	$3,000
Air Transport/Air Freight	**$10,500**
Texas Air	$8,000
Others	$2,500
Automotive	**$7,000**
National Auto Dealers Assn	$5,000
Others	$2,000
Broadcasting & Movies	**$6,000**
National Cable Television Assn	$3,000
Others	$3,000
Commercial Banks	**$14,100**
J P Morgan & Company	$5,000
Independent Bankers Assn	$3,000
American Bankers Assn	$2,000
Others	$4,100
Computers & Electronics	**$5,500**
None over $1,000	

Construction	**$36,600**
Sheet Metal/AirCon Contractors	$10,000
National Electrical Contractors Assn	$7,000
National Assn of Home Builders	$3,500
Associated General Contractors	$3,000
Mechanical Contractors Assn of America	$3,000
National Society of Professional Engineers	$2,500
American Subcontractors Assn	$2,000
Others	$5,600
Defense	**$10,500**
Singer Company	$2,000
Rockwell International	$1,500
Others	$7,000
Food & Beverage	**$15,000**
National Beer Wholesalers Assn	$7,500
Pepsico Inc	$2,000
Occidental Petroleum	$5,500
Insurance	**$7,500**
National Assn of Life Underwriters	$3,000
Others	$4,500
Lawyers	**$21,000**
Assn of Trial Lawyers of America	$10,000
American Intellectual Prop Law Assn	$1,750
Others	$9,250
Oil & Gas	**$12,250**
Coastal Corp	$2,000
Texaco	$2,000
USX Corp*	$1,500
Others	$6,750
Real Estate	**$12,000**
National Assn of Realtors	$6,000
Commonwealth Financial Group	$4,000
Others	$2,000
Telecommunications	**$7,250**
AT&T	$2,000
Southwestern Bell	$1,500
GTE (Southwest)	$1,250
Others	$2,500
Tobacco	**$6,026**
Philip Morris	$2,500
Tobacco Institute	$1,026
Others	$2,500

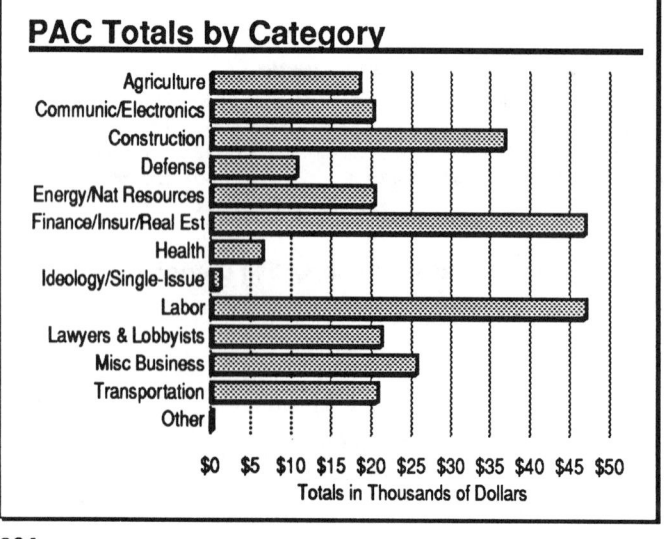

PAC Totals by Category

Agriculture
Communic/Electronics
Construction
Defense
Energy/Nat Resources
Finance/Insur/Real Est
Health
Ideology/Single-Issue
Labor
Lawyers & Lobbyists
Misc Business
Transportation
Other

$0 $5 $10 $15 $20 $25 $30 $35 $40 $45 $50
Totals in Thousands of Dollars

Other Major Business PACs

Houston Industries	$3,912	Electric Util
Westvaco Corp	$2,500	Paper Prod
Xerox Corp	$2,500	Off Machines
Mead Corp	$2,000	Paper Prod
Morgan Stanley & Company	$2,000	InvestmtBank
National Office Products Assn	$2,000	Off Machines
Waste Management Inc	$2,000	Waste Mgmt
J C Penney Company	$1,500	Dept Store

Labor

Bldg Trades/Industrial/Misc Unions $21,250

Sheet Metal Workers Union	$5,000
Operating Engineers Union	$3,000
Intl Brotherhood of Electrical Workers	$2,000
Laborers' Political League	$2,000
Others	$9,250

Government & Teachers Unions $9,000

National Education Assn	$4,000
American Fedn of State/County/Munic Employees	$2,000
National Assn of Retired Federal Employees	$2,000
Others	$1,000

Transportation Unions $16,000

Teamsters Union	$10,000
Marine Engineers District 2 Maritime Officers	$2,000
United Transportation Union	$2,000
Others	$2,000

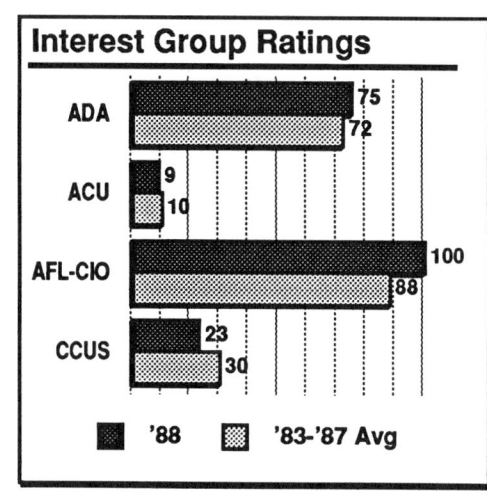

Interest Group Ratings

	'88	'83-'87 Avg
ADA	75	72
ACU	9	10
AFL-CIO	100	88
CCUS	23	30

■ '88   ▨ '83-'87 Avg

Major Ideological/Single-Issue PACs

KidsPAC	$2,000	HealthWelfare

Independent expenditures supporting Brooks

National Cmte to Preserve Social Security	$1,462

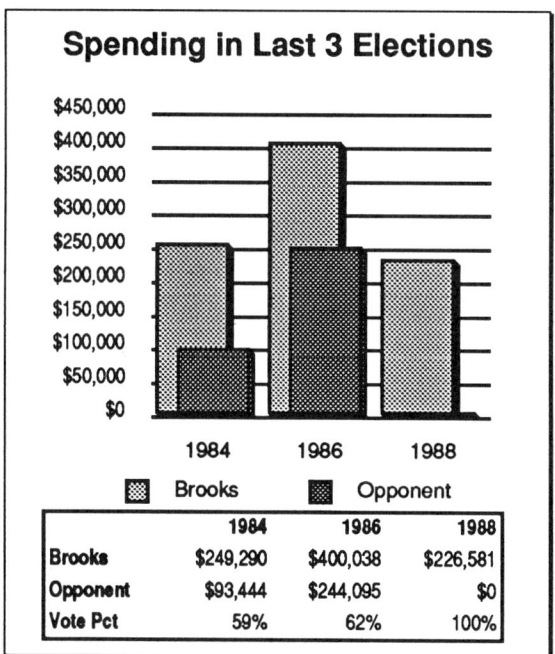

Spending in Last 3 Elections

▨ Brooks   ■ Opponent

	1984	1986	1988
Brooks	$249,290	$400,038	$226,581
Opponent	$93,444	$244,095	$0
Vote Pct	59%	62%	100%

---

* Contributions came from more than one PAC affiliated with this sponsor.

William S. Broomfield, R-Mich (18)

First elected: 1956
Total receipts: $235,699
Total from PACs: $57,700

1988 Committees & Subcommittees

Foreign Affairs (Ranking Republican)
Arms Control, International Security and Science (Ranking Republican)

Small Business
Regulation and Business Opportunities (Ranking Republican)

PAC Contribution Profile

Business

Automotive	*$5,300*
Auto Dealers & Drivers for Free Trade	$2,500
Budd Company	$1,500
Ford Motor Company	$1,000
Others	$300
Construction	*$7,500*
National Assn of Home Builders	$5,000
Associated General Contractors	$1,000
Mechanical Contractors Assn of America	$1,000
Ch2M Hill	$500
Defense	*$3,000*
General Dynamics	$1,000
Rockwell International	$1,000
Colt Industries	$500
McDonnell Douglas	$500
Financial Institutions	*$4,300*
American Bankers Assn	$1,000
Michigan League of Savings Institutions	$1,000
Michigan Credit Union League	$1,000
Comerica Inc	$500
National Bank of Detroit	$500
Others	$300

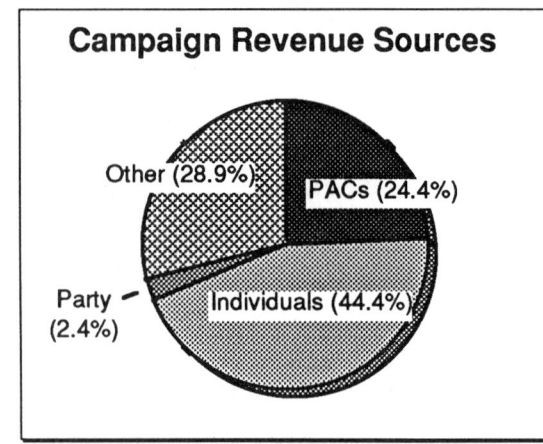

Campaign Revenue Sources

Other (28.9%)
PACs (24.4%)
Party (2.4%)
Individuals (44.4%)

Food & Beverage	*$5,400*
National Restaurant Assn	$2,000
Pepsico Inc	$1,000
Kellogg Company	$500
McDonald's Corp	$500
White Castle System	$500
Others	$900
Health Professionals	*$5,000*
American Medical Assn	$4,000
American Dental Assn	$1,000
Insurance	*$2,230*
National Assn of Life Underwriters	$1,000
Blue Cross/Shield of Michigan	$500
ITT Corp	$500
Others	$230
Real Estate	*$3,000*
National Assn of Realtors	$3,000
Telecommunications	*$5,620*
Michigan Bell Telephone	$3,620
AT&T	$2,000

Other Major Business PACs

Mobil Oil	$1,000	Major Oil
Schlussel, Lifton, Simon et al	$1,000	Lawyers
American Collectors Assn	$600	Credit/Loans
American Hospital Assn	$500	Hospitals
Consumers Power Company	$500	Gas & Electr
Deere & Company	$500	Farm Equip
Detroit Edison	$500	Electric Util
Dow Chemical/Midwest	$500	Chemicals
FMC Corp	$500	Chemicals
JSJ Corp	$500	Indust Equip
PPG Industries	$500	Glass Prod

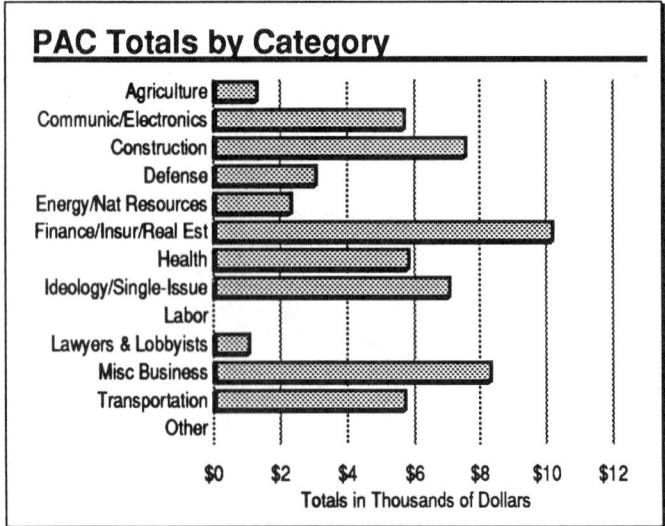

PAC Totals by Category

Agriculture
Communic/Electronics
Construction
Defense
Energy/Nat Resources
Finance/Insur/Real Est
Health
Ideology/Single-Issue
Labor
Lawyers & Lobbyists
Misc Business
Transportation
Other

$0 $2 $4 $6 $8 $10 $12

Totals in Thousands of Dollars

Ideological/Single-Issue

Pro-Israel **$5,500**

    National PAC $5,000
    Roundtable PAC $500

Other Major Ideological/Single-Issue PACs

National Albanian American PAC ....$1,000   Ethnic
Armenian Assembly of America ....$500   Ethnic

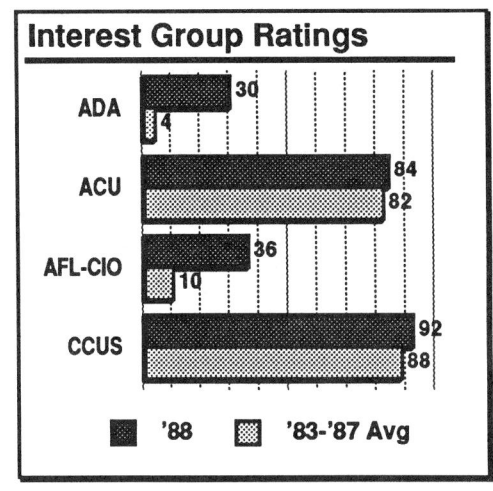

Interest Group Ratings

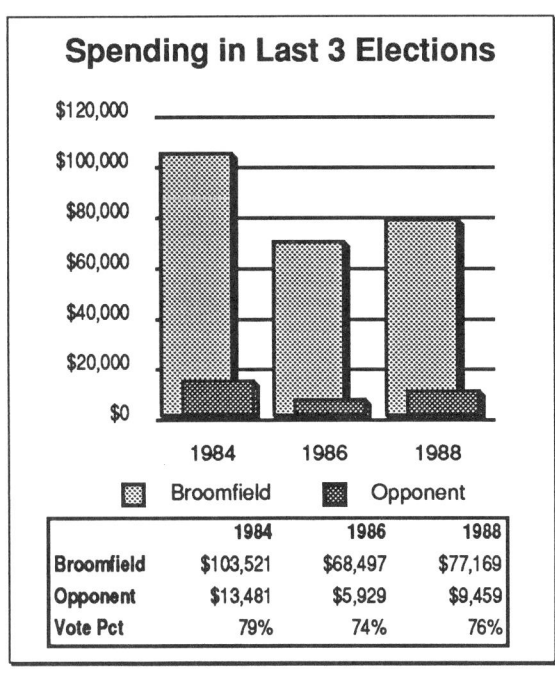

Spending in Last 3 Elections

	1984	1986	1988
Broomfield	$103,521	$68,497	$77,169
Opponent	$13,481	$5,929	$9,459
Vote Pct	79%	74%	76%

George E. Brown Jr., D-Calif (36)

First elected: 1962
Total receipts: $504,361
Total from PACs: $276,543

1988 Committees & Subcommittees

Agriculture
Department Operations, Research and Foreign Agriculture (Chairman)

Science, Space and Technology
Investigations and Oversight
Natural Resources, Agriculture Research and Environment
Science, Research and Technology
Space Science and Applications

PAC Contribution Profile

Business

Crop Production *$12,300*
    American Crystal Sugar Corp $1,500
    American Sugarbeet Growers Assn $1,500
    California Almond Growers Exchange $1,500
    Calcot Ltd $1,400
    Peanut Butter & Nut Processors Assn $1,000
    Sunkist Growers $1,000
    Others $4,400

Lawyers *$8,000*
    Assn of Trial Lawyers of America $5,000
    California Trial Lawyers Assn $3,000

Other Major Business PACs

American Veterinary Medical Assn	$3,500	Veterinary
National Assn of Realtors	$3,000	Real Estate
Auto Dealers & Drivers for Free Trade	$2,500	JapanAutoSal
United Parcel Service	$2,500	Delivery
Pacific Telesis Group	$2,100	Phone Util
Lockheed Corp	$2,000	Air Defense
ACRE (Action Committee for Rural Electric)	$1,500	RuralElect
American Bankers Assn	$1,000	Comml Banks
American Dental Assn	$1,000	Dentists
Chicago Mercantile Exchange	$1,000	Commodities
ConAgra Inc	$1,000	FoodProducts
Continental Telecom	$1,000	Phone Util
FMC Corp	$1,000	Chemicals
Food Marketing Institute	$1,000	Food Stores
National Society of Professional Engineers	$1,000	Engineers
Valmont Industries	$1,000	Electronics

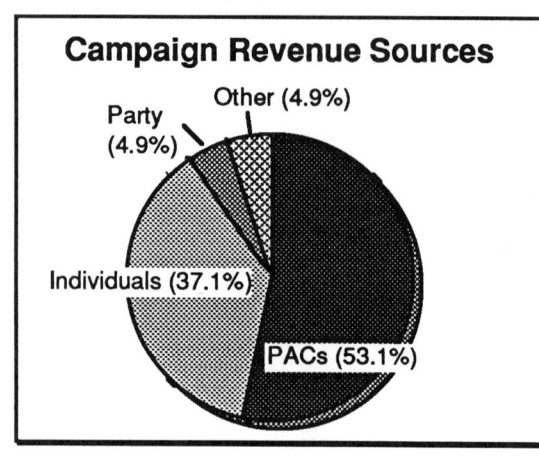

Campaign Revenue Sources

Other (4.9%)
Party (4.9%)
Individuals (37.1%)
PACs (53.1%)

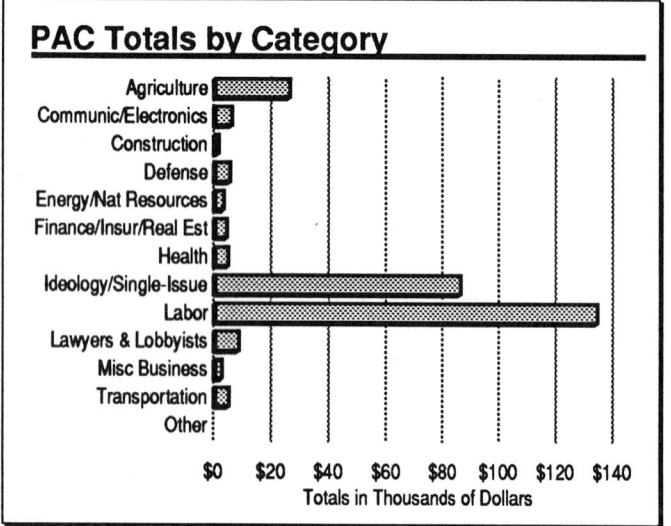

PAC Totals by Category

Agriculture
Communic/Electronics
Construction
Defense
Energy/Nat Resources
Finance/Insur/Real Est
Health
Ideology/Single-Issue
Labor
Lawyers & Lobbyists
Misc Business
Transportation
Other

$0 $20 $40 $60 $80 $100 $120 $140
Totals in Thousands of Dollars

Labor

Bldg Trades/Industrial/Misc Unions $74,136

Food & Commercial Workers Union	$8,000
United Steelworkers	$8,000
Carpenters & Joiners Union	$7,536
Intl Brotherhood of Electrical Workers	$7,500
United Auto Workers	$7,000
Machinists/Aerospace Workers Union	$5,500
AFL-CIO*	$5,000
Communications Workers of America	$5,000
Service Employees International Union	$5,000
Laborers' Western Political League	$3,000
Ironworkers Union	$2,000
Ladies Garment Workers Union	$2,000
Plumbers/Pipefitters Union	$2,000
Bakery, Confectionery & Tobacco Workers	$1,500
Operating Engineers Union	$1,500
Amalgamated Clothing & Textile Workers	$1,000
Others	$2,600

Government & Postal Workers $29,886

National Assn of Retired Federal Employees	$10,000
American Fedn of State/County/Munic Employees	$10,000
National Assn of Letter Carriers	$6,286
American Postal Workers Union	$3,600

Teachers Unions $11,000

National Education Assn	$8,000
American Federation of Teachers	$3,000

Transportation Unions $19,250

Teamsters Union	$10,000
Longshoremen/Warehousemen Union	$2,800
Seafarers International Union	$2,500
United Transportation Union	$1,500
Air Line Pilots Assn	$1,000
Others	$1,450

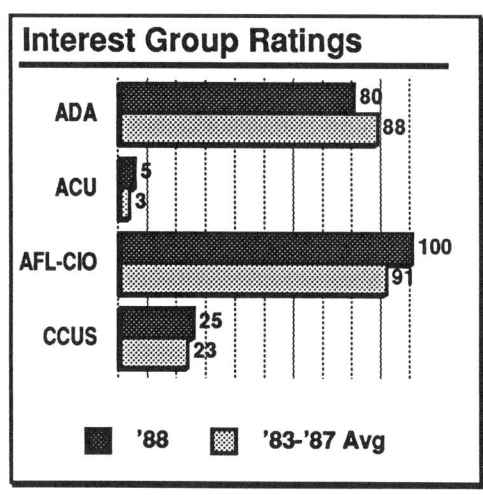

Interest Group Ratings

	'88	'83-'87 Avg
ADA	80	88
ACU	5	3
AFL-CIO	100	91
CCUS	25	23

Ideological/Single-Issue

Democratic/Liberal $17,500

Hollywood Women's Political Cmte	$9,000
National Cmte for an Effective Congress	$5,000
Democratic Study Group Campaign Fund	$3,000
Congressional Agenda 80's	$500

Democratic Leadership PACs $33,300

24th Cong Dist of California PAC (Henry Waxman)	$5,000
Cmte for a Democratic Consensus (Alan Cranston)	$5,000
House Leadership Fund (Tom Foley)	$5,000
Majority Congress Committee (Jim Wright)	$5,000
USA Committee (Jerry Brown)	$5,000
Valley Education Fund (Tony Coelho)	$5,000
America's Leaders' Fund (Dan Rostenkowski)	$2,500
Others	$800

Non-Congressional Candidate PACs $7,000

Friends of Roberti	$5,000
Friends of Edelman	$1,000
Rick Tuttle Campaign Cmte	$1,000

Pro-Israel $5,500

National PAC	$5,000
Others	$500

Senior Citizens Issues $6,000

National Cmte to Preserve Social Security	$3,000
National Council of Senior Citizens	$3,000

Other Major Ideological/Single Issue

National Abortion Rights Action League	$3,500	Pro-Choice
Sierra Club	$3,000	Environment
Southern California Freeze Voter	$3,000	Pro-Peace
Human Rights Campaign Fund	$2,250	Gay Rights
Handgun Control Inc	$1,000	Anti-Guns
Ohio Freeze Voter	$1,000	Pro-Peace
SpacePAC	$1,000	Other

Independent expenditures supporting Brown

National Cmte to Preserve Social Security	$1,490

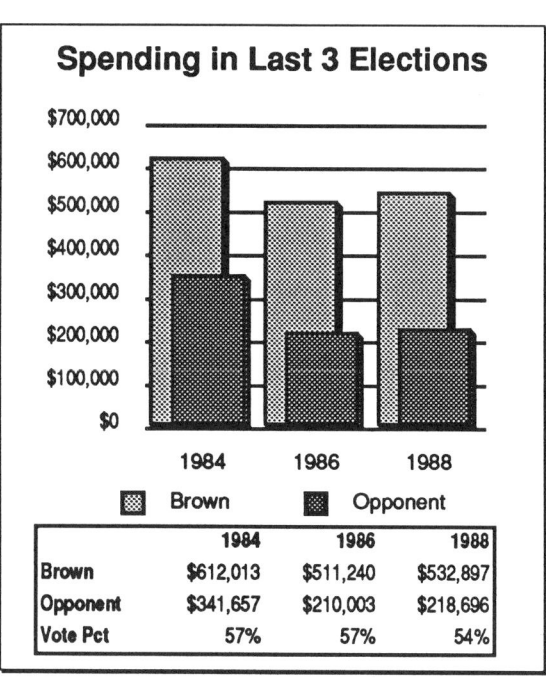

Spending in Last 3 Elections

	1984	1986	1988
Brown	$612,013	$511,240	$532,897
Opponent	$341,657	$210,003	$218,696
Vote Pct	57%	57%	54%

Legend: Brown / Opponent

---

* Contributions came from more than one PAC affiliated
  with this sponsor.

Hank Brown, R-Colo (4)

1988 Committees & Subcommittees

Standards of Official Conduct

Ways and Means
Public Assistance and Unemployment Compensation (Ranking Republican)
Select Revenue Measures

Select Hunger

First elected: 1980
Total receipts: $287,187
Total from PACs: $190,891

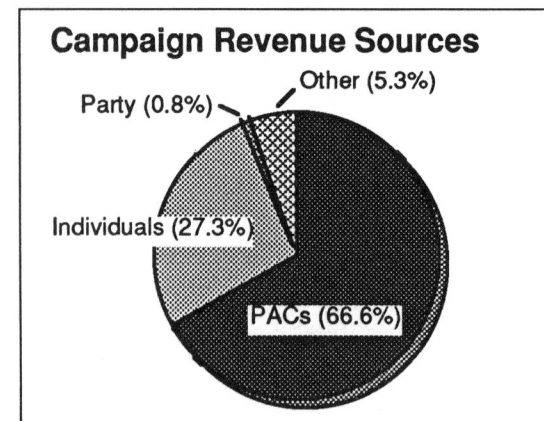

Campaign Revenue Sources

- Other (5.3%)
- Party (0.8%)
- Individuals (27.3%)
- PACs (66.6%)

PAC Contribution Profile

Business

Accountants	$16,500
American Institute of CPA's	$10,000
Deloitte, Haskins & Sells	$2,000
Ernst & Whinney	$2,000
Arthur Andersen & Company	$1,000
Arthur Young & Company	$500
National Society of Public Accountants	$500
Touche Ross	$500

Commercial Banks	$6,000
American Bankers Assn	$4,000
J P Morgan & Company	$1,000
Others	$1,000

Construction	$5,750
Associated General Contractors	$1,250
Manville Corp	$1,000
Others	$3,500

Defense	$5,100
Northrop Corp	$1,000
TRW Inc	$1,000
Others	$3,100

Food & Beverage	$10,250
National Restaurant Assn	$3,000
Food Marketing Institute	$1,750
National Beer Wholesalers Assn	$1,500
ConAgra Inc	$1,000
Others	$3,000

Health Professionals	$13,000
American Medical Assn	$7,750
American Dental Assn	$2,750
Cmte for Quality Orthopedic Health Care	$1,000
Others	$1,500

Insurance	$43,359
National Assn of Life Underwriters	$5,000
Midwestern United Life Insurance	$3,309
Great-West Life Assurance	$2,500
Northwestern Mutual Life	$2,500
American Council of Life Insurance	$2,000
Metropolitan Life Insurance	$2,000
New York Life	$2,000
Aetna Life & Casualty	$1,500
Mutual Life Insurance of New York	$1,500
Torchmark Corp	$1,500
Prudential Insurance	$1,350
Blue Cross & Blue Shield Assn	$1,250
Cigna Corp	$1,000
Connecticut Mutual Life Insurance	$1,000
Equitable Financial Services	$1,000
Georgia US Corp	$1,000
Guardian Life Insurance	$1,000
Massachusetts Mutual Life Insurance	$1,000
National Assn of Independent Insurers	$1,000
New England Mutual Life	$1,000
Principal Mutual Life Insurance	$1,000
Security Life of Denver	$1,000
Others	$6,950

Oil & Gas	$10,226
Atlantic Richfield	$1,500
Amoco Corp	$1,000
Mobil Oil	$1,000
Others	$6,726

Real Estate	$6,500
National Assn of Realtors	$3,750
American Resort & Residential Developers Assn	$1,000
Mortgage Bankers Assn of America	$1,000
Others	$750

Securities/Commodities Investment	$5,250
First Boston Corp	$2,000
Chicago Board of Trade	$1,000
Others	$2,250

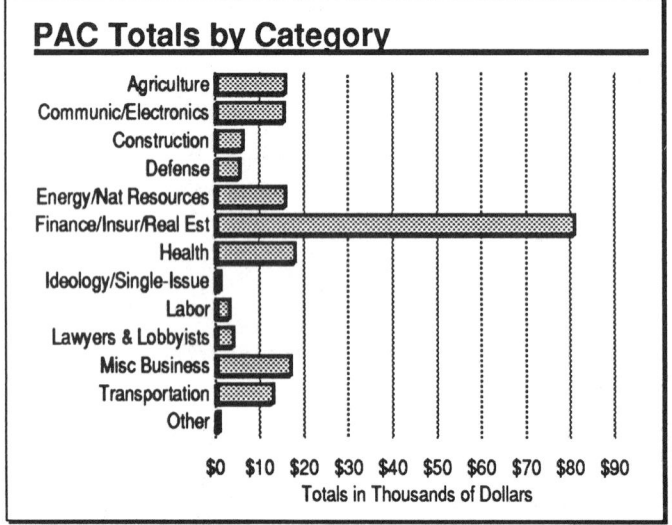

PAC Totals by Category

- Agriculture
- Communic/Electronics
- Construction
- Defense
- Energy/Nat Resources
- Finance/Insur/Real Est
- Health
- Ideology/Single-Issue
- Labor
- Lawyers & Lobbyists
- Misc Business
- Transportation
- Other

$0 $10 $20 $30 $40 $50 $60 $70 $80 $90
Totals in Thousands of Dollars

Telecommunications *$10,000*

Mountain Bell	$2,500
AT&T	$2,250
Others	$5,250

Other Major Business PACs

National Auto Dealers Assn	$2,750	Auto Sales
RJR Nabisco	$2,000	Tobacco
Texas Air	$2,000	Airlines
Philip Morris	$1,500	Tobacco
ACRE (Action Committee for Rural Electric)	$1,000	RuralElect
American Sugarbeet Growers Assn	$1,000	Sugar
American Hospital Assn	$1,000	Hospitals
Farmland Industries	$1,000	Ag Svcs
FMC Corp	$1,000	Chemicals
International Council of Shopping Centers	$1,000	Retail
J C Penney Company	$1,000	Dept Store
National Assn of Broadcasters	$1,000	TV/Radio
National Assn of Water Companies	$1,000	Water Util
Pfizer Inc	$1,000	Pharmaceut
Storage Technology Corp	$1,000	Comput Parts
Texas Cattle Feeders Assn	$1,000	Feedlots
US League of Savings Assn	$1,000	SavingsBanks
W R Grace & Company	$1,000	Chemicals
Williams & Jensen	$1,000	Lawyers
Worldcorp Inc	$1,000	AirTransport

Major Labor PACs

National Rural Letter Carriers Assn	$1,250	Postal Union
Marine Engrs District 2 Maritime Officers	$1,000	Seamen Union

Independent expenditures supporting Brown

Teamsters Union	$2,000
National School Transport Assn	$1,000

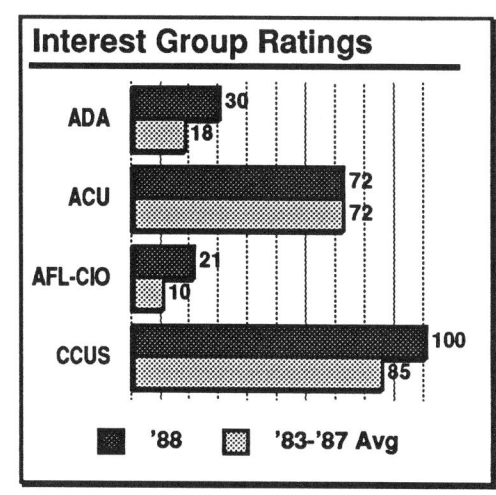

Interest Group Ratings

	'88	'83-'87 Avg
ADA	30	18
ACU	72	72
AFL-CIO	21	10
CCUS	100	85

■ '88   ▨ '83-'87 Avg

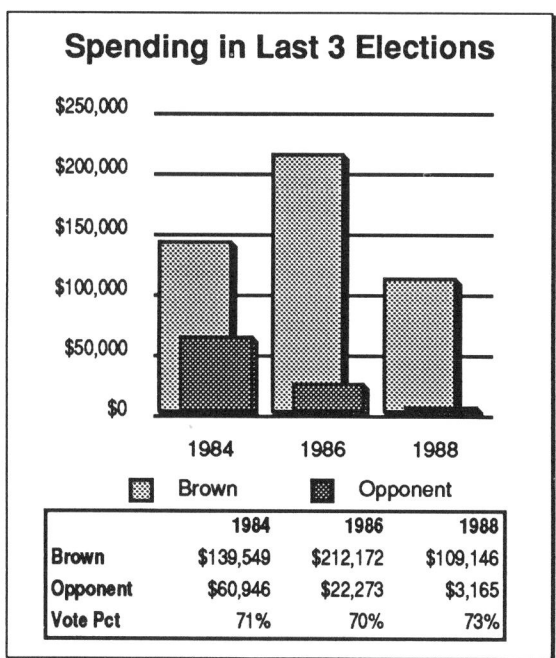

Spending in Last 3 Elections

▨ Brown   ■ Opponent

	1984	1986	1988
Brown	$139,549	$212,172	$109,146
Opponent	$60,946	$22,273	$3,165
Vote Pct	71%	70%	73%

Terry L. Bruce, D-III (19)

1988 Committees & Subcommittees

First elected: 1984
Total receipts: $457,955
Total from PACs: $274,737

Energy and Commerce
Energy and Power
Health and the Environment

Science, Space and Technology
Energy Research and Development
Science, Research and Technology

PAC Contribution Profile

Business

Accountants	**$5,850**
American Institute of CPA's	$5,000
Others	$850
Automotive	**$7,907**
National Auto Dealers Assn	$4,007
General Motors	$1,500
Ford Motor Company	$1,350
Chrysler Corp	$1,050
Commercial & Savings Banks	**$10,350**
Continental Illinois Corp	$2,350
J P Morgan & Company	$2,000
American Bankers Assn	$1,350
American Savings Banks	$1,000
Citicorp	$1,000
First Chicago Corp	$1,000
Others	$1,650
Dairy	**$5,300**
Associated Milk Producers	$2,500
Mid-American Dairymen	$2,500
Others	$300
Electric Utilities	**$10,775**
Illinois Power Company	$1,800
Southern Company*	$1,325
ACRE (Action Committee for Rural Electrification)	$1,050
Others	$6,600

Campaign Revenue Sources

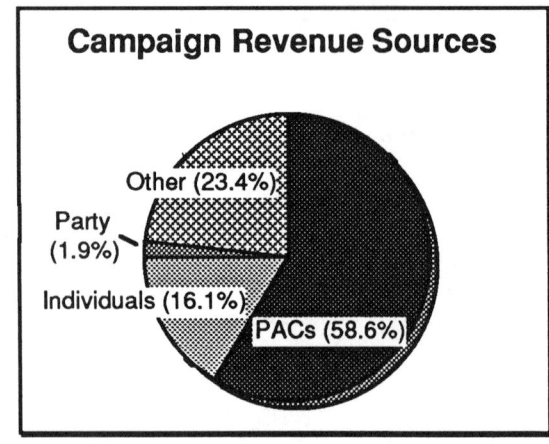

Other (23.4%)
Party (1.9%)
Individuals (16.1%)
PACs (58.6%)

Food & Beverage	**$9,750**
A E Staley Manufacturing Company	$2,000
Nutrasweet Company	$1,250
Joseph E Seagram & Sons	$1,000
Others	$5,500
Health Professionals	**$23,100**
American Medical Assn	$10,000
American Dental Assn	$4,000
American Academy of Ophthalmology	$2,000
American College of Emergency Physicians	$1,000
American Occupational Therapy Assn	$1,000
American Physical Therapy Assn	$1,000
American Podiatry Assn	$1,000
Cmte for Quality Orthopedic Health Care	$1,000
Others	$2,100
Insurance	**$6,800**
National Assn of Life Underwriters	$1,000
Others	$5,800
Lawyers	**$12,200**
Assn of Trial Lawyers of America	$10,000
Others	$2,200
Oil & Gas	**$18,079**
Amoco Corp	$1,300
Columbia Gas*	$1,050
Ashland Oil	$1,000
Others	$14,729
Pharmaceuticals	**$8,050**
Schering-Plough Corp	$1,200
Others	$6,850
Real Estate	**$7,800**
National Assn of Realtors	$7,500
Others	$300
Securities/Commodities Investment	**$13,400**
Chicago Board of Trade	$3,000
First Boston Corp	$2,000
Chicago Mercantile Exchange	$1,500
Chicago Board of Options Exchange	$1,000
Morgan Stanley & Company	$1,000
Prudential-Bache Securities	$1,000
Others	$3,900

PAC Totals by Category

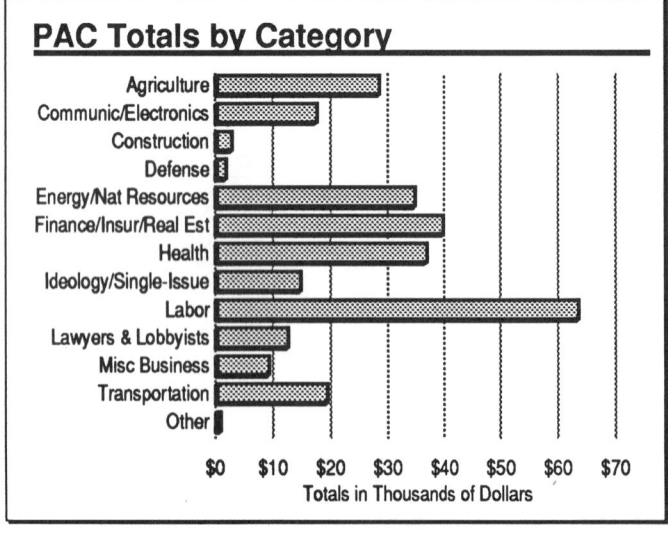

Agriculture
Communic/Electronics
Construction
Defense
Energy/Nat Resources
Finance/Insur/Real Est
Health
Ideology/Single-Issue
Labor
Lawyers & Lobbyists
Misc Business
Transportation
Other

$0 $10 $20 $30 $40 $50 $60 $70
Totals in Thousands of Dollars

Telecommunications	$13,383
Illinois Bell Telephone	$3,000
Continental Telecom	$1,750
Pacific Telesis Group	$1,250
US Telephone Assn	$1,233
Bell Atlantic	$1,000
Others	$5,150

Tobacco	$5,150
Philip Morris	$2,000
RJR Nabisco	$1,500
Others	$1,650

Trucking/Delivery	$4,100
United Parcel Service	$2,150
American Trucking Assns	$1,450
Others	$500

Other Major Business PACs

Aircraft Owners & Pilots Assn	$2,000	GenlAviation
National Cable Television Assn	$2,000	CableTV
National Assn of Home Builders	$1,500	Resid Constr
American Hospital Assn	$1,150	Hospitals
Allied-Signal	$1,000	Air Defense
American Supply Assn	$1,000	PipeProducts
National Coal Assn	$1,000	Coal
Valmont Industries	$1,000	Electronics
Waste Management Inc	$1,000	Waste Mgmt

Labor

Bldg Trades/Industrial/Misc Unions	$25,300
United Auto Workers	$7,300
Carpenters & Joiners Union	$4,500
Operating Engineers Union	$2,500
Intl Brotherhood of Electrical Workers	$2,000
Food & Commercial Workers Union	$1,750
Laborers' Political League*	$1,750
AFL-CIO*	$1,550
Plumbers/Pipefitters Union	$1,000
Others	$2,950

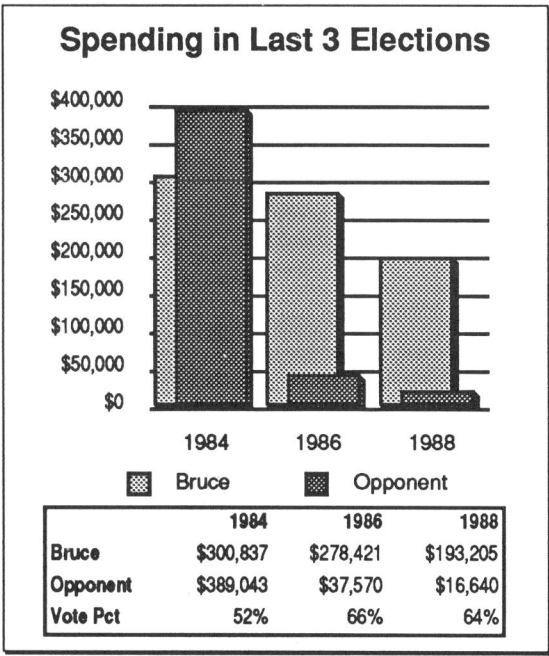

Spending in Last 3 Elections

	1984	1986	1988
Bruce	$300,837	$278,421	$193,205
Opponent	$389,043	$37,570	$16,640
Vote Pct	52%	66%	64%

Bruce ▨   Opponent ▩

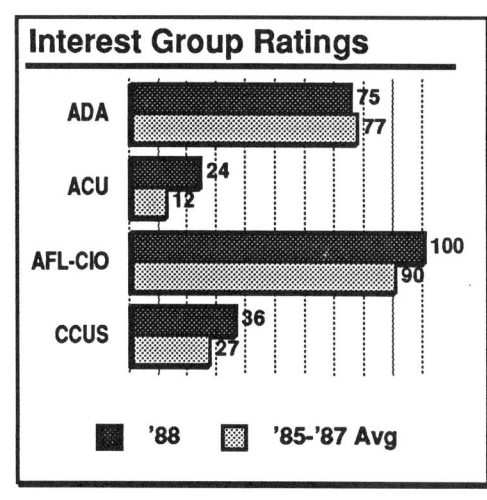

Interest Group Ratings

	'88	'85-'87 Avg
ADA	75	77
ACU	24	12
AFL-CIO	100	90
CCUS	36	27

■ '88   ▨ '85-'87 Avg

Government & Postal Workers	$11,100
American Fedn of State/County/Munic Employees	$5,000
National Assn of Retired Federal Employees	$3,500
American Postal Workers Union	$1,100
National Assn of Letter Carriers	$1,000
Others	$500

Teachers Unions	$10,000
National Education Assn	$10,000

Transportation Unions	$16,807
Teamsters Union	$5,000
Brotherhood of Locomotive Engineers	$3,257
Air Line Pilots Assn	$2,000
Marine Engineers District 2 Maritime Officers	$2,000
United Transportation Union	$2,000
Seafarers International Union	$1,000
Others	$1,550

Ideological/Single-Issue

Pro-Israel	$5,500
National PAC	$5,000
Others	$500

Other Major Ideological/Single-Issue PACs

National Rifle Assn	$2,500	Pro-Guns
National Right to Life PAC	$2,000	Pro-Life
National Cmte to Preserve Social Security	$1,000	Soc Secur
Valley Education Fund (Tony Coelho)	$1,000	Dem Leaders

Independent expenditures supporting Bruce

National Cmte to Preserve Social Security	$2,824

* Contributions came from more than one PAC affiliated with this sponsor.

John Bryant, D-Texas (5)

First elected: 1982
Total receipts: $889,511
Total from PACs: $390,757

1988 Committees & Subcommittees

Energy and Commerce
Energy and Power
Telecommunications and Finance

Judiciary
Courts, Civil Liberties and the Administration of Justice
Criminal Justice
Immigration, Refugees and International Law

Veterans' Affairs
Hospitals and Health Care

PAC Contribution Profile

Business

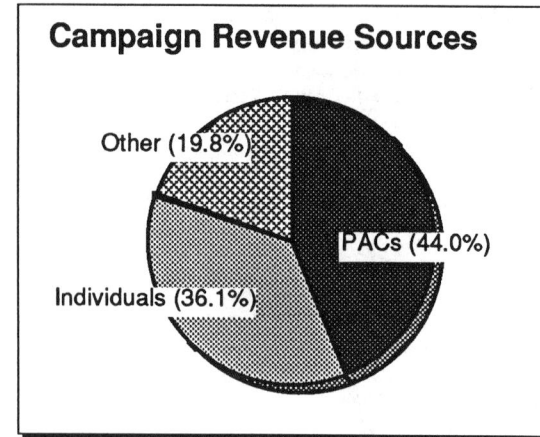

Campaign Revenue Sources

Other (19.8%)
PACs (44.0%)
Individuals (36.1%)

Accountants	**$9,000**
American Institute of CPA's	$5,000
Arthur Andersen & Company	$1,050
Others	$2,950
Air Transport	**$5,150**
Eastern Airlines	$2,300
American Airlines	$2,000
Others	$850
Automotive	**$6,450**
National Auto Dealers Assn	$5,300
Others	$1,150
Broadcasting & Movies	**$15,800**
Assn of Independent TV Stations	$6,000
Gulf + Western Industries	$2,000
National Cable Television Assn	$2,000
National Assn of Broadcasters	$1,200
Others	$4,600
Commercial Banks	**$14,350**
NCNB Texas	$6,750
J P Morgan & Company	$2,000
American Bankers Assn	$1,500
Others	$4,100

Construction	**$7,250**
National Assn of Home Builders	$3,000
Universal Services	$2,000
Manville Corp	$1,500
Others	$750
Electric Utilities	**$16,200**
Texas Utilities Electric Company*	$7,000
Houston Industries	$1,500
Central & South West Services	$1,250
Southern California Edison	$1,100
Others	$5,350
Food & Beverage	**$6,800**
None over $1,000	
Health Professionals	**$26,950**
American Medical Assn	$9,000
Texas Medical Assn	$3,250
American Academy of Ophthalmology	$2,500
American Dental Assn	$2,000
National Assn of Pharmacists	$2,000
American Optometric Assn	$1,100
American College of Emergency Physicians	$1,050
Others	$6,050
Insurance	**$9,350**
National Assn of Life Underwriters	$1,500
Independent Insurance Agents of America	$1,100
Others	$6,750
Lawyers & Lobbyists	**$26,250**
Assn of Trial Lawyers of America	$6,550
Johnson & Gibbs	$3,000
Vinson, Elkins, Searls, Conally & Smith	$3,000
Akin, Gump, Hauer & Feld	$2,000
Jones, Day, Reavis & Pogue	$2,000
Locke, Purnell, Rain, Harrell	$1,500
Arnold & Porter	$1,350
Others	$6,850
Oil & Gas	**$29,957**
Arkla Inc*	$2,550
Coastal Corp	$2,300
Michigan Consolidated Gas	$2,000
Phillips Petroleum	$2,000
Valero Energy Corp	$2,000
Shell Oil	$1,600
Atlantic Richfield	$1,300
Halliburton Company*	$1,250
Others	$14,957

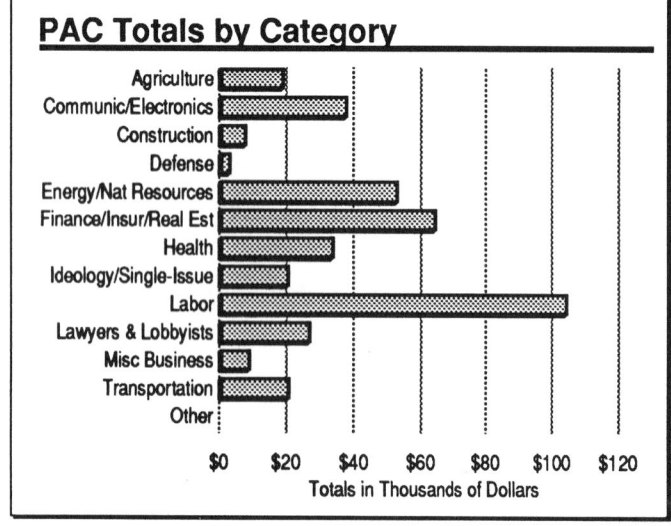

PAC Totals by Category

Agriculture
Communic/Electronics
Construction
Defense
Energy/Nat Resources
Finance/Insur/Real Est
Health
Ideology/Single-Issue
Labor
Lawyers & Lobbyists
Misc Business
Transportation
Other

$0 $20 $40 $60 $80 $100 $120
Totals in Thousands of Dollars

Real Estate	$10,600
National Assn of Realtors	$8,000
Trammell Crow Company	$2,000
Others	$600

Securities/Commodities Investment	$18,050
Investment Company Institute	$5,000
Travelers Corp	$1,250
Chicago Mercantile Exchange	$1,100
Others	$10,700

Telecommunications	$18,000
Corning Glass Works	$2,000
Southwestern Bell	$2,000
GTE (Southwest)	$1,750
Competitive Telecom Assn	$1,300
Pacific Telesis Group	$1,300
MCI Telecommunications	$1,050
Others	$8,600

Trucking/Delivery	$4,150
United Parcel Service	$1,800
Others	$2,350

Other Major Business PACs

Associated Milk Producers	$3,000	Dairy
Credit Union National Assn	$2,000	Credit Union
Recognition Equipment Inc	$2,000	Electronics
Philip Morris	$1,900	Tobacco
American Hospital Assn	$1,550	Hospitals
Electronic Data Systems	$1,500	Data Process
Waste Management Inc	$1,500	Waste Mgmt
Burlington Northern	$1,050	Railroads

Labor

Bldg Trades/Industrial/Misc Unions	$53,850
United Auto Workers	$10,000
Machinists/Aerospace Workers Union	$9,300
Communications Workers of America	$7,300
United Steelworkers	$6,000
Carpenters & Joiners Union	$3,200
Intl Brotherhood of Electrical Workers	$2,500
(continued in next column)	

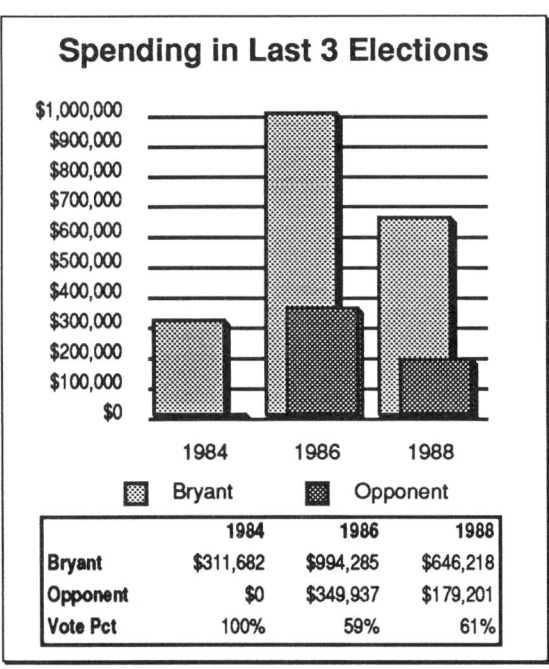

Spending in Last 3 Elections

	1984	1986	1988
Bryant	$311,682	$994,285	$646,218
Opponent	$0	$349,937	$179,201
Vote Pct	100%	59%	61%

Legend: ▨ Bryant   ▦ Opponent

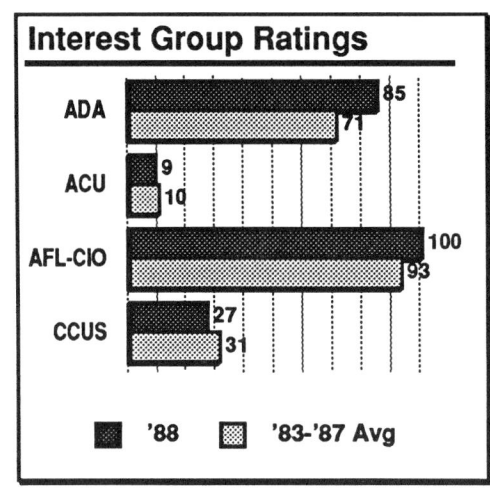

Interest Group Ratings

	'88	'83-'87 Avg
ADA	85	71
ACU	9	10
AFL-CIO	100	93
CCUS	27	31

Legend: ■ '88   ▨ '83-'87 Avg

Labor (cont'd)	
Electronic Machine Furniture Workers	$2,000
Office & Professional Employees Union	$2,000
Operating Engineers Union	$2,000
Laborers' Political League	$1,850
AFL-CIO*	$1,600
Food & Commercial Workers Union	$1,100
Ladies Garment Workers Union	$1,050
Others	$3,950

Government & Postal Workers	$18,000
National Assn of Letter Carriers	$6,600
National Assn of Retired Federal Employees	$5,000
American Postal Workers Union	$3,200
American Fedn of State/County/Munic Employees	$2,000
Others	$1,200

Teachers Unions	$9,700
National Education Assn	$9,700

Transportation Unions	$22,200
Teamsters Union	$10,000
Transport Workers Union	$3,000
United Transportation Union	$3,000
Air Line Pilots Assn	$1,500
Marine Engineers Radio Officers #3	$1,500
Brotherhood of Locomotive Engineers	$1,100
Others	$2,100

Ideological/Single-Issue

Democratic Leadership PACs	$5,000
Majority Congress Committee (Jim Wright)	$6,000
Others	-$1,000

Pro-Israel	$7,000
National PAC	$5,000
Others	$2,000

Other Major Ideological/Single Issue

National Cmte/Effective Congress	$3,497	Dem/Liberal
National Cmte to Preserve Social Security	$1,300	Soc Secur

Independent expenditures supporting Bryant

National Cmte to Preserve Social Security	$1,358
National Structured Settlements Assn	$1,217

* Contributions came from more than one PAC affiliated with this sponsor.

Jack Buechner, R-Mo (2)

First elected: 1986
Total receipts: $807,845
Total from PACs: $320,544

1988 Committees & Subcommittees

Budget
Defense and International Affairs
Economic and Trade Policy

Science, Space and Technology
Science, Research and Technology
Space Science and Applications

PAC Contribution Profile

Business

Campaign Revenue Sources

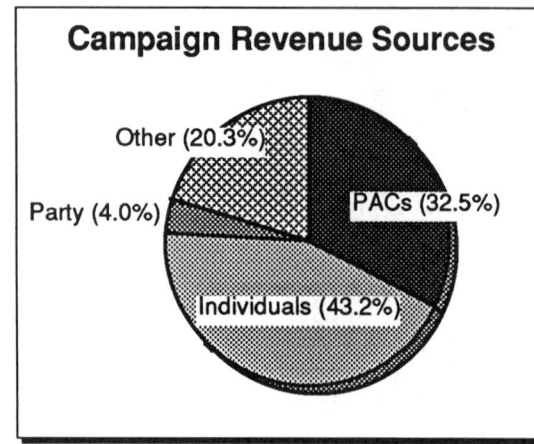

Other (20.3%)
Party (4.0%)
PACs (32.5%)
Individuals (43.2%)

Airlines & Aerospace	**$9,926**
Morton Thiokol	$2,000
Trans World Airlines	$1,900
United Technologies	$1,600
Sabreliner Corp	$1,276
Others	$3,150
Automotive & Trucking	**$19,800**
National Auto Dealers Assn	$5,850
Auto Dealers & Drivers for Free Trade	$5,000
Yellow Freight System	$2,000
Ford Motor Company	$1,100
Eaton Corp	$1,000
Enterprise Leasing Company	$1,000
Federal-Mogul Corp	$1,000
Others	$2,850
Chemicals	**$10,490**
Monsanto Company	$3,190
Chemtech Industries	$2,300
Mallinckrodt Inc	$2,200
Dow Chemical*	$1,550
Others	$1,250
Commercial Banks	**$5,150**
Boatmens Bankshares	$1,600
American Bankers Assn	$1,350
Centerre Bank	$1,000
Others	$1,200

Construction	**$15,900**
National Assn of Home Builders	$6,500
Sheet Metal/AirCon Contractors	$2,500
Associated General Contractors	$2,350
National Concrete Masonry Assn	$1,000
Sverdrup Corporation	$1,000
Others	$2,550
Defense	**$16,400**
McDonnell Douglas	$4,500
Tenneco Inc	$2,500
Harris Corp	$2,000
Lockheed Corp	$2,000
Emerson Electric	$1,000
Northrop Corp	$1,000
Others	$3,400
Food & Beverage	**$5,875**
Hardee's Food Systems	$1,000
National Restaurant Assn	$1,000
Others	$3,875
Health Professionals	**$10,250**
American Medical Assn	$4,000
American Academy of Ophthalmology	$2,500
American Dental Assn	$1,250
Cmte for Quality Orthopedic Health Care	$1,000
Missouri Medical Assn	$1,000
Others	$500
Industrial Equipment & Materials	**$5,000**
Hunter Engineering	$2,000
Hussmann Corp	$1,500
Minnesota Mining & Manufacturing (3M)	$1,000
National Tooling & Machining Assn	$500
Insurance	**$11,550**
National Assn of Life Underwriters	$2,750
General American Life Insurance	$1,500
Casualty & Surety Agents Assn	$1,350
Business Mens Assurance Company	$1,000
Shelter Mutual Insurance	$1,000
Others	$3,950
Lawyers & Lobbyists	**$10,050**
Assn of Trial Lawyers of America	$9,500
Fleishman-Hillard	$550

PAC Totals by Category

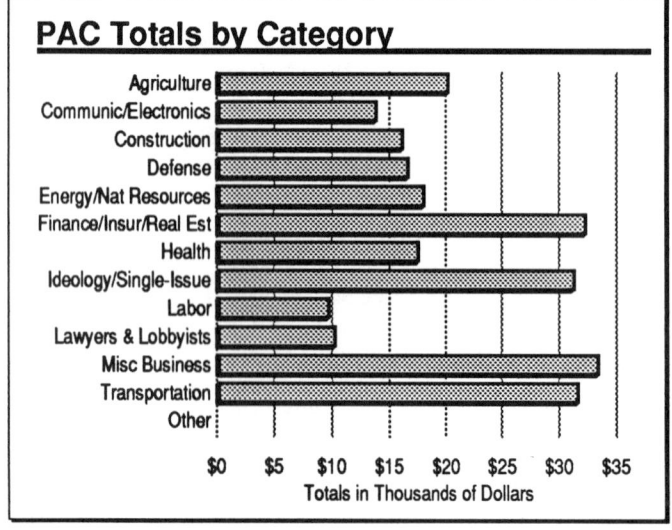

Category	
Agriculture	
Communic/Electronics	
Construction	
Defense	
Energy/Nat Resources	
Finance/Insur/Real Est	
Health	
Ideology/Single-Issue	
Labor	
Lawyers & Lobbyists	
Misc Business	
Transportation	
Other	

$0 $5 $10 $15 $20 $25 $30 $35
Totals in Thousands of Dollars

Oil & Gas	....	**$9,900**
Phillips Petroleum	....	$2,000
Mobil Oil	....	$1,000
Mustang Energy Corp	....	$1,000
Sun Company	....	$1,000
Others	....	$4,900

Pharmaceuticals	....	**$5,750**
None over $850		

Real Estate	....	**$12,075**
National Assn of Realtors	....	$9,750
Mortgage Bankers Assn of America	....	$2,200
Others	....	$125

Telecommunications	....	**$9,400**
Southwestern Bell	....	$2,850
AT&T	....	$2,300
Continental Telecom	....	$2,000
United Telecommunications	....	$1,000
Others	....	$1,250

Tobacco	....	**$5,050**
Philip Morris	....	$1,500
RJR Nabisco	....	$1,100
Tobacco Institute	....	$1,100
Others	....	$1,350

Other Major Business PACs

Business Industry PAC	.... $2,129	Bus Assns
Arch Mineral Corp	.... $2,000	Coal
Cooper Industries	.... $2,000	PowerEquip
Mid-American Dairymen	.... $2,000	Dairy
Missouri Farm Bureau/St Louis	.... $2,000	Farm Orgs
Kellwood Company	.... $1,500	Clothing
Deere & Company	.... $1,350	Farm Equip
Whirlpool Corp	.... $1,300	Appliances
Southland Corp	.... $1,257	Dept Store
Maytag Company	.... $1,250	Appliances
Waste Management Inc	.... $1,200	Waste Mgmt
Computer Dealers & Lessors Assn	.... $1,000	Computers
Precision Metalforming Assn	.... $1,000	MetalProduct
Printing Industries of America	.... $1,000	Printing
Stone Container Corp	.... $1,000	Paper Packg
Tandem Computers	.... $1,000	Comput Parts

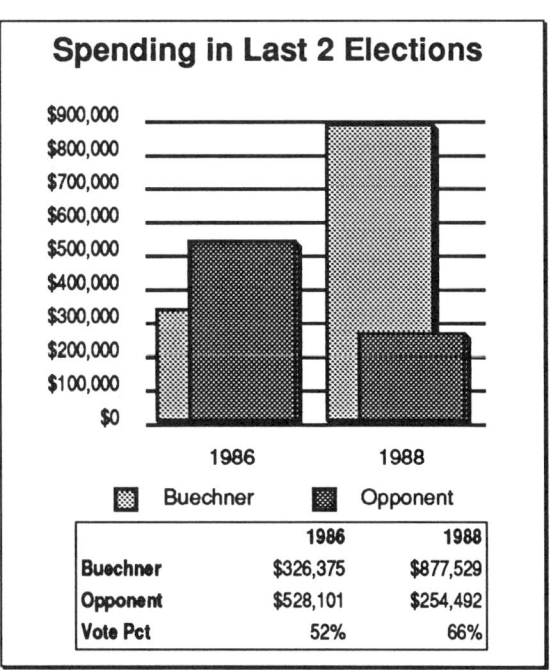

Spending in Last 2 Elections

	1986	1988
Buechner	$326,375	$877,529
Opponent	$528,101	$254,492
Vote Pct	52%	66%

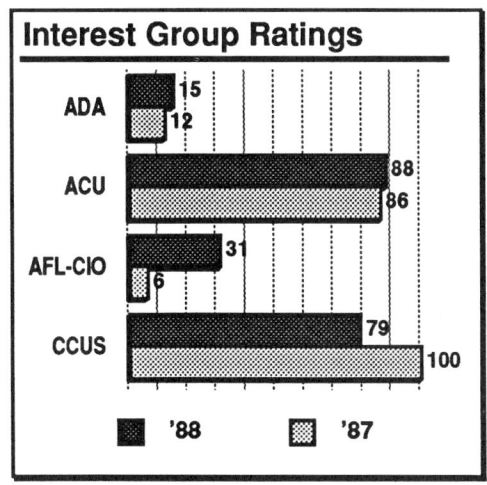

Interest Group Ratings

	'88	'87
ADA	15	12
ACU	88	86
AFL-CIO	31	6
CCUS	79	100

Labor

Labor Unions	....	**$9,500**
National Assn of Retired Federal Employees	....	$7,000
Air Line Pilots Assn	....	$2,000
Others	....	$500

Ideological/Single-Issue

Pro-Israel	....	**$19,750**
National PAC	....	$5,000
St Louisians for Better Government	....	$3,500
St Louis PAC	....	$2,000
Delaware Valley PAC	....	$1,000
Desert Caucus	....	$1,000
Florida Congressional Cmte	....	$1,000
Heartland PAC	....	$1,000
Roundtable PAC	....	$1,000
Women's Pro-Israel National PAC	....	$1,000
Others	....	$3,250

Other Major Ideological & Single-Issue

National Rifle Assn	.... $4,000	Pro-Guns
Council for National Defense	.... $2,760	Pro-Defense
Heartland PAC of Missouri (Kit Bond)	.... $1,000	Repub Leader

Independent expenditures supporting Buechner

Missouri Citizens for Life	....	$2,110

---

* Contributions came from more than one PAC affiliated
with this sponsor.

Jim Bunning, R-Ky (4)

First elected: 1986
Total receipts: $593,585
Total from PACs: $235,684

1988 Committees & Subcommittees

Banking, Finance and Urban Affairs
General Oversight and Investigations
Housing and Community Development
International Development Institutions and Finance
International Finance, Trade and Monetary Policy

Merchant Marine and Fisheries
Coast Guard and Navigation
Fisheries and Wildlife Conservation and the Environment

PAC Contribution Profile

Business

Automotive **$11,450**
    Auto Dealers & Drivers for Free Trade $6,500
    National Auto Dealers Assn $3,850
    Others $1,100

Building Contractors & Supplies **$12,668**
    National Assn of Home Builders $2,500
    Westvaco Corp $2,500
    Northern Kentucky Home Bldrs Assn $2,000
    National Electrical Contractors Assn $1,000
    Others $4,668

Commercial Banks **$32,600**
    American Bankers Assn $6,750
    Barnett Banks of Florida $2,500
    First Kentucky National Corp $2,500
    Bankers Trust $2,000
    J P Morgan & Company $2,000
    Chase Manhattan $1,950
    Citizens & Southern National Bank $1,500
    Kentucky Bankers Assn $1,250
    Continental Illinois Corp $1,150
    Others $11,000

Credit Unions **$5,400**
    Credit Union National Assn $2,500
    Kentucky Credit Union League $1,500
    National Assn of Fed Credit Unions $1,400

Electric & Power Utilities **$7,150**
    Cincinnati Gas & Electric $1,500
    Kentucky Utilities Company $1,000
    Others $4,650

Campaign Revenue Sources

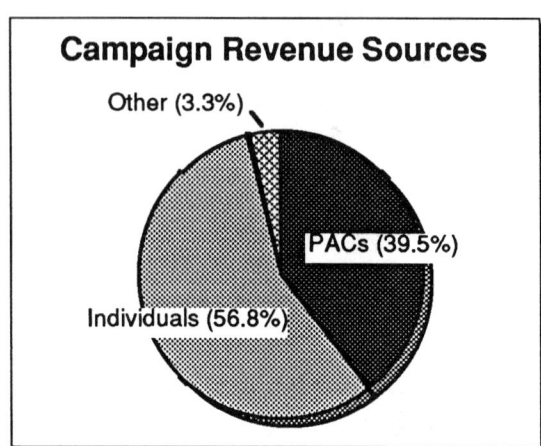

Other (3.3%)
PACs (39.5%)
Individuals (56.8%)

Food & Beverage **$13,000**
    Brown-Forman Distillers $2,300
    Jerrico Inc $1,300
    National Restaurant Assn $1,000
    Pepsico Inc $1,000
    Others $7,400

Health Professionals **$13,750**
    American Medical Assn $10,250
    American Academy of Ophthalmology $2,500
    Others $1,000

Insurance **$16,530**
    Independent Insurance Agents of America $3,205
    National Assn of Independent Insurers $2,500
    National Assn Mutual Insurance Agents $1,550
    Capital Holding Corp $1,100
    National Assn of Life Underwriters $1,100
    Others $7,075

Lawyers & Lobbyists **$6,550**
    Assn of Trial Lawyers of America $5,000
    Others $1,550

Oil & Gas **$9,100**
    Ashland Oil $1,300
    Atlantic Richfield $1,000
    Others $6,800

Real Estate **$8,800**
    National Assn of Realtors $5,700
    Federal National Mortgage Assn $1,350
    Century 21 Real Estate $1,000
    Others $750

Savings Banks **$7,200**
    Kentucky League of Savings Institutions $3,250
    US League of Savings Assn $1,450
    Great Financial Federal $1,000
    Others $1,500

PAC Totals by Category

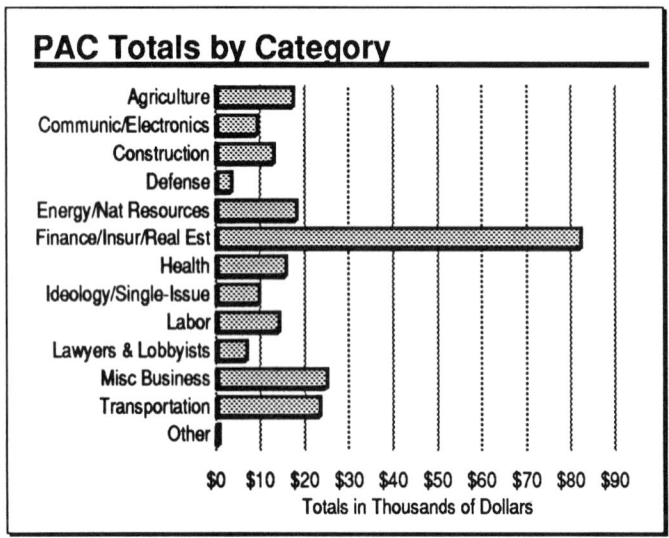

Agriculture
Communic/Electronics
Construction
Defense
Energy/Nat Resources
Finance/Insur/Real Est
Health
Ideology/Single-Issue
Labor
Lawyers & Lobbyists
Misc Business
Transportation
Other

$0 $10 $20 $30 $40 $50 $60 $70 $80 $90

Totals in Thousands of Dollars

Sea Transport	....	$5,050
CSX Transportation Inc*	....	$1,950
Others	....	$3,100

Telecommunications	....	$7,850
AT&T	....	$3,000
Cincinnati Bell	....	$2,200
Continental Telecom	....	$1,000
Others	....	$1,650

Tobacco	....	$6,650
Philip Morris	....	$1,850
RJR Nabisco	....	$1,400
Tobacco Institute	....	$1,100
Pinkerton Tobacco	....	$1,000
Others	....	$1,300

Other Major Business PACs

Touche Ross	$2,500	Accountants
Air Line Pilots Assn	$2,000	AirTrans Lab
United Parcel Service	$1,600	Delivery
Associated Milk Producers	$1,500	Dairy
Dow Corning Corp/Employees	$1,500	PlasticRubb
Square D Company	$1,500	Indust Equip
Norfolk Southern Corp	$1,400	Railroads
Goldman Sachs	$1,250	InvestmtBank
Litton Industries	$1,250	Ships
American Hotel & Motel Assn	$1,100	Hotel/Motel
Dairymen Inc-Kentucky	$1,100	Dairy
Dow Chemical*	$1,000	Chemicals
Federated Department Stores	$1,000	Dept Store
Stone Container Corp	$1,000	Paper Packg

Interest Group Ratings

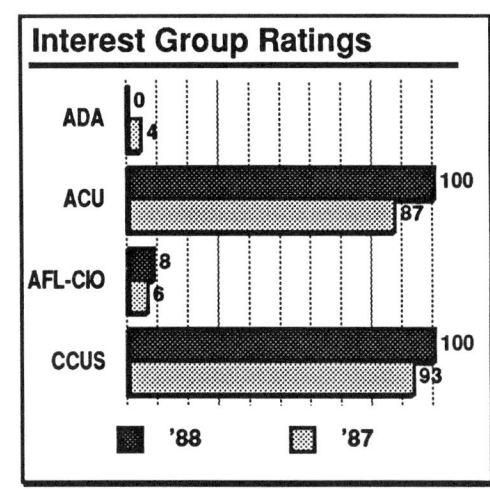

	'88	'87
ADA	0	4
ACU	100	87
AFL-CIO	8	6
CCUS	100	93

Labor

Sea Transport Unions	....	$10,500
Marine Engineers Union*	....	$9,500
Seafarers International Union	....	$1,000

Ideological/Single-Issue

Pro-Israel	....	$5,850
National PAC	....	$5,000
Others	....	$850

Other Major Ideological/Single-Issue PACs

National Rifle Assn	$1,300	Pro-Guns

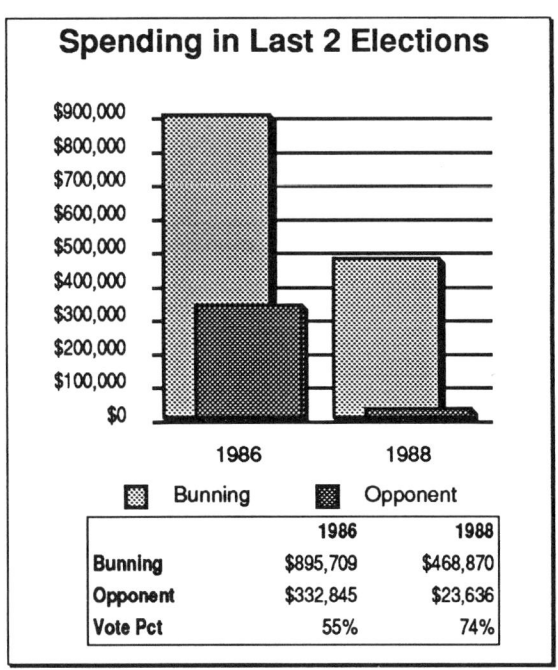

Spending in Last 2 Elections

Bunning • Opponent

	1986	1988
Bunning	$895,709	$468,870
Opponent	$332,845	$23,636
Vote Pct	55%	74%

---

* Contributions came from more than one PAC affiliated with this sponsor.

Dan Burton, R-Ind (6)

First elected: 1982
Total receipts: $383,915
Total from PACs: $141,170

1988 Committees & Subcommittees

Foreign Affairs
Africa (Ranking Republican)
Arms Control, International Security and Science

Post Office and Civil Service
Human Resources (Ranking Republican)
Census and Population

Veterans' Affairs
Housing and Memorial Affairs (Ranking Republican)
Oversight and Investigations

PAC Contribution Profile

Business

Automotive	***$8,700***
National Auto Dealers Assn	$4,700
Auto Dealers & Drivers for Free Trade	$2,000
Others	$2,000
Construction	***$5,650***
National Assn of Home Builders	$2,500
Associated General Contractors	$1,500
Others	$1,650
Dairy	***$9,500***
Associated Milk Producers	$7,500
Others	$2,000
Telecommunications	***$7,575***
Indiana Bell Telephone	$2,725
AT&T	$2,000
Continental Telecom	$1,500
Others	$1,350
Oil & Gas	***$3,800***
Mobil Oil	$1,000
Others	$2,800
Financial Institutions	***$5,550***
Credit Union National Assn	$2,100
Indiana League of Savings Institutions	$1,250
American Bankers Assn	$1,000
Others	$1,200
Food & Beverage	***$4,300***
None over $750	

Campaign Revenue Sources

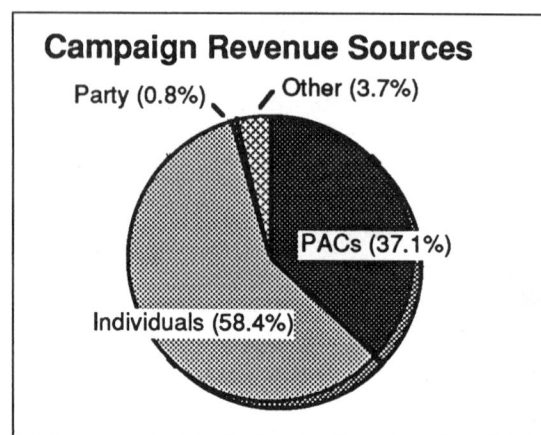

Party (0.8%) Other (3.7%)

PACs (37.1%)

Individuals (58.4%)

Health Professionals	***$9,600***
American Medical Assn	$4,750
American Dental Assn	$2,000
Indiana Medical Assn	$1,600
Others	$1,250
Insurance	***$12,570***
National Assn of Life Underwriters	$2,500
National Assn Mutual Insurance Agents	$2,250
American States Insurance Company	$1,750
Independent Insurance Agents of America	$1,700
Others	$4,370
Package Delivery	***$3,400***
United Parcel Service	$3,400
Real Estate	***$8,500***
National Assn of Realtors	$8,000
Others	$500

Other Major Business PACs

Indiana Farm Bureau	$2,500	Farm Orgs
Westvaco Corp	$1,500	Paper Prod
Maytag Company	$1,000	Appliances
Stone Container Corp	$1,000	Paper Packg

PAC Totals by Category

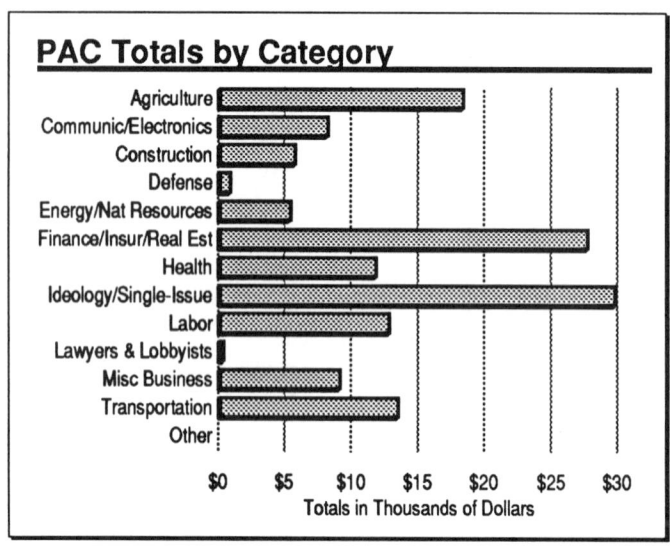

Agriculture
Communic/Electronics
Construction
Defense
Energy/Nat Resources
Finance/Insur/Real Est
Health
Ideology/Single-Issue
Labor
Lawyers & Lobbyists
Misc Business
Transportation
Other

$0 $5 $10 $15 $20 $25 $30
Totals in Thousands of Dollars

Labor

Government & Postal Workers $12,700

National Assn of Letter Carriers $5,500
National League of Postmasters $2,000
National Assn of Postmasters $1,500
National Assn of Retired Federal Employees $1,500
National Rural Letter Carriers Assn $1,000
Others $1,200

Ideological/Single-Issue

Pro-Israel $11,550

National PAC $5,000
Hudson Valley PAC $2,000
Washington PAC $1,500
Roundtable PAC $1,000
Others $2,050

Other Major Ideological/Single-Issue PACs

National Rifle Assn .... $7,450   Pro-Guns
Free Cuba PAC .... $5,000   Anti-Castro
Ruff PAC .... $3,000   Tax Policy

Independent expenditures supporting Burton

Hudson Valley PAC $1,000

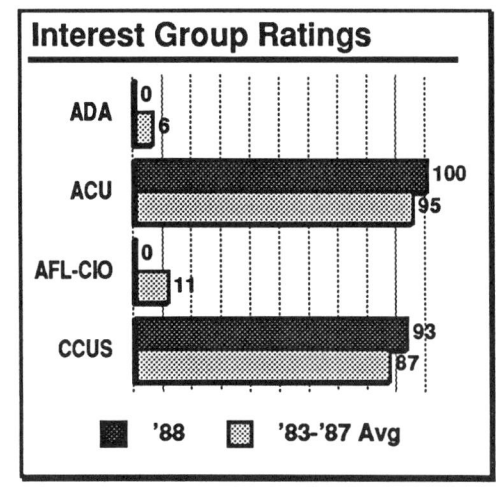

Interest Group Ratings

	'88	'83–'87 Avg
ADA	0	6
ACU	100	95
AFL-CIO	0	11
CCUS	93	87

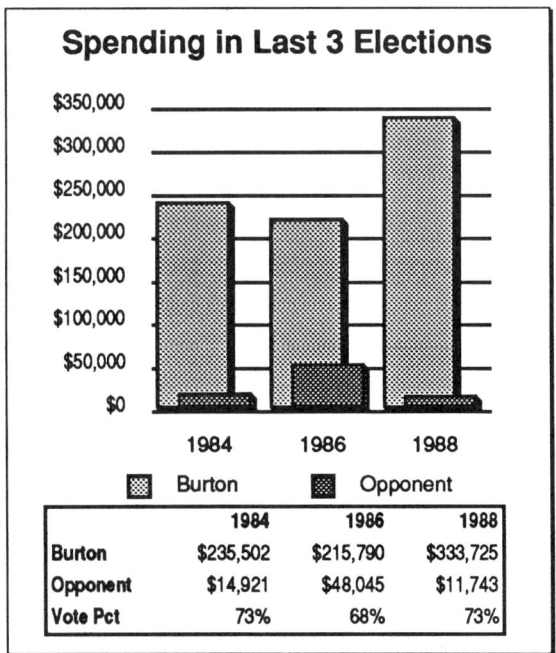

Spending in Last 3 Elections

	1984	1986	1988
Burton	$235,502	$215,790	$333,725
Opponent	$14,921	$48,045	$11,743
Vote Pct	73%	68%	73%

Albert G. Bustamante, D-Tex (23)

First elected: 1984
Total receipts: $280,485
Total from PACs: $155,786

1988 Committees & Subcommittees

Armed Services
Military Personnel and Compensation
Procurement and Military Nuclear Systems

Government Operations
Commerce, Consumer and Monetary Affairs
Environment, Energy and Natural Resources
Government Information, Justice and Agriculture

PAC Contribution Profile

Business

Accountants	**$5,000**
American Institute of CPA's	$5,000
Auto Dealers	**$4,000**
National Auto Dealers Assn	$4,000
Dairy	**$5,000**
Associated Milk Producers	$5,000
Defense	**$24,500**
Textron Inc	$2,300
GTE (Southwest)	$2,050
Rockwell International	$1,500
United Technologies	$1,300
Electronic Data Systems	$1,100
Singer Company	$1,100
General Dynamics	$1,000
Sequa Corp	$1,000
Others	$13,150
Electric Utilities	**$2,600**
Central Power & Light	$1,000
Houston Industries	$1,000
Others	$600

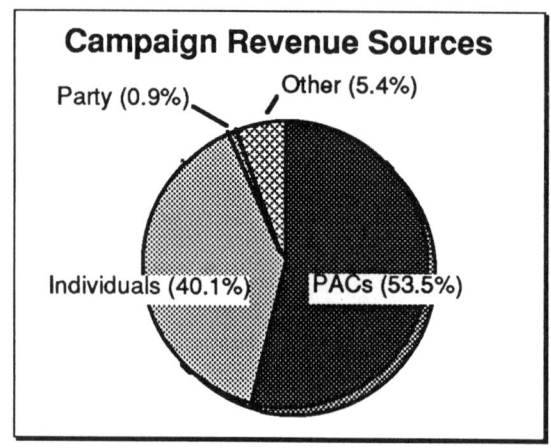

Campaign Revenue Sources

Party (0.9%)
Other (5.4%)
Individuals (40.1%)
PACs (53.5%)

Financial Institutions	**$2,850**
San Antonio Savings Assn	$1,000
Others	$1,850
Health Professionals	**$5,350**
American Podiatry Assn	$3,000
American Medical Assn	$1,600
Others	$750
Insurance	**$4,500**
United Services Auto Assn Group	$3,000
National Assn of Life Underwriters	$1,500
Oil & Gas	**$6,500**
Valero Energy Corp	$2,000
Tesoro Petroleum	$1,100
Coastal Corp	$1,000
Others	$2,400
Real Estate	**$5,350**
National Assn of Realtors	$5,350
Telecommunications	**$2,600**
Southwestern Bell	$2,000
Others	$600

Other Major Business PACs

Akin, Gump, Hauer & Feld	$1,150	Lawyers
United Parcel Service	$1,100	Delivery
Fullbright & Jaworski	$1,000	Lawyers
National Electrical Contractors Assn	$1,000	ElectricCont
Texas Cattle Feeders Assn	$1,000	Feedlots
Texas Restaurant Assn	$1,000	Restaurants
Waste Management Inc	$1,000	Waste Mgmt
Yellow Freight System	$1,000	Trucking

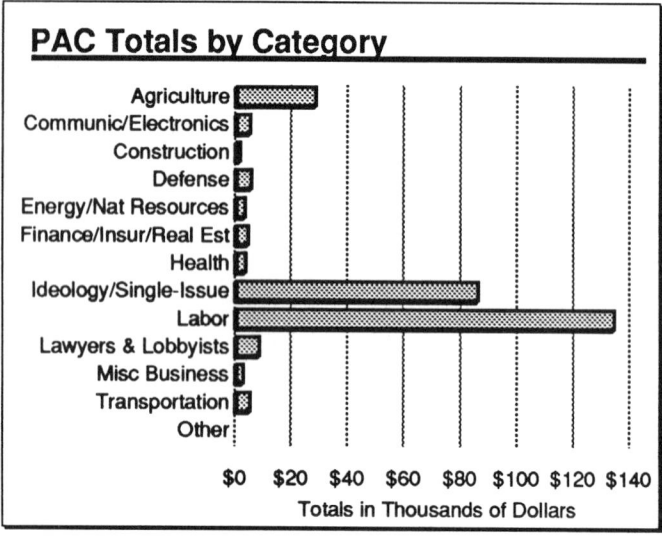

PAC Totals by Category

Agriculture
Communic/Electronics
Construction
Defense
Energy/Nat Resources
Finance/Insur/Real Est
Health
Ideology/Single-Issue
Labor
Lawyers & Lobbyists
Misc Business
Transportation
Other

$0 $20 $40 $60 $80 $100 $120 $140

Totals in Thousands of Dollars

Labor

Bldg Trades/Industrial/Misc Unions $18,000

Machinists/Aerospace Workers Union $2,500
Communications Workers of America $2,000
Intl Brotherhood of Electrical Workers.............................$2,000
United Steelworkers $2,000
Carpenters & Joiners Union $1,750
Laborers' Political League $1,500
Food & Commercial Workers Union.................................$1,350
Operating Engineers Union $1,000
Others $3,900

Government & Postal Workers $10,900

American Fedn of State/County/Munic Employees $3,000
National Assn of Retired Federal Employees $2,000
American Postal Workers Union $1,650
National Assn of Letter Carriers $1,600
Others $2,650

Teachers Unions $8,150

National Education Assn $7,500
Others $650

Transportation Unions $16,750

Teamsters Union $5,000
Transportation Communication Union.............................$2,350
Amalgamated Transit Union $2,000
Marine Engineers Union* $2,000
United Transportation Union $1,600
Air Line Pilots Assn $1,000
Seafarers International Union $1,000
Others $1,800

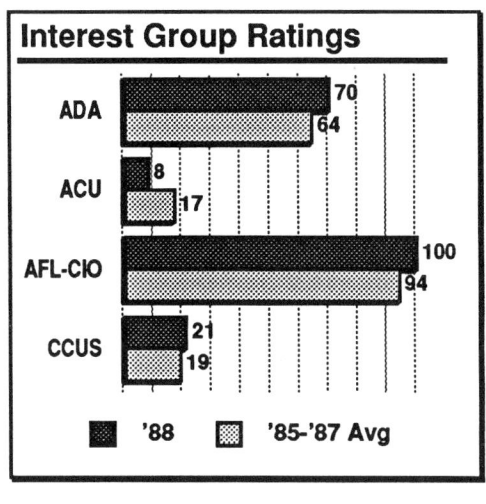

Interest Group Ratings

ADA — '88: 70, '85–'87 Avg: 64
ACU — '88: 8, '85–'87 Avg: 17
AFL-CIO — '88: 100, '85–'87 Avg: 94
CCUS — '88: 21, '85–'87 Avg: 19

■ '88   ▨ '85–'87 Avg

Ideological/Single-Issue

Pro-Israel $6,050

National PAC $5,000
Others $1,050

Other Major Ideological/Single-Issue PACs

Human Rights Campaign Fund ....$1,000   Gay Rights
Valley Education Fund (Tony Coelho) ....$1,000   Dem Leaders

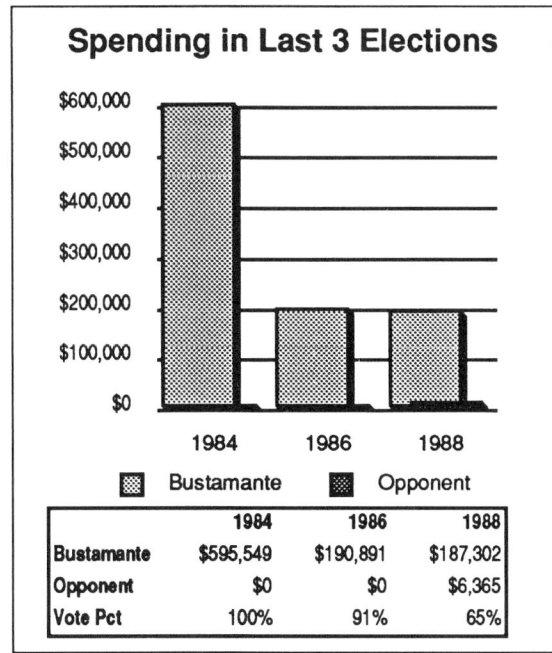

Spending in Last 3 Elections

▨ Bustamante   ■ Opponent

	1984	1986	1988
Bustamante	$595,549	$190,891	$187,302
Opponent	$0	$0	$6,365
Vote Pct	100%	91%	65%

---

* Contributions came from more than one PAC affiliated
with this sponsor.

Beverly B. Byron, D-Md (6)

First elected: 1978
Total receipts: $218,098
Total from PACs: $142,722

1988 Committees & Subcommittees

Armed Services
Military Personnel and Compensation (Chairwoman)
Investigations

Interior and Insular Affairs
National Parks and Public Lands
Water and Power Resources

Select Aging
Housing and Consumer Interests

PAC Contribution Profile

Business

Automotive	*$5,000*
National Auto Dealers Assn	$4,000
Goodyear	$1,000
Construction	*$4,800*
Associated General Contractors	$1,500
Associated Builders & Contractors	$1,000
National Utility Contractors Assn	$1,000
Others	$1,300
Dairy	*$3,500*
Associated Milk Producers	$2,500
Others	$1,000
Defense	*$54,134*
Grumman	$3,000
Kaman Corp	$3,000
Northrop Corp	$3,000
Lockheed Corp	$2,500
McDonnell Douglas	$2,500
AT&T	$2,000
General Dynamics	$2,000
Litton Industries	$2,000
Rockwell International	$2,000
Tenneco Inc	$2,000
Boeing Company	$1,500
General Electric	$1,500
Hughes Aircraft	$1,500
Textron Inc	$1,500

(Continued in next column)

Campaign Revenue Sources

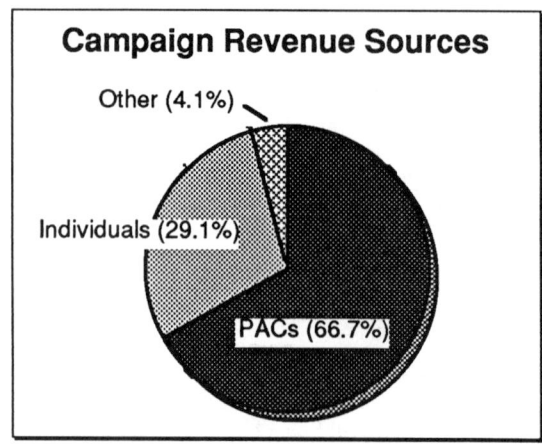

Other (4.1%)
Individuals (29.1%)
PACs (66.7%)

Defense (cont'd)	
United Technologies	$1,500
Fairchild Industries	$1,300
Allied-Signal	$1,000
Chrysler Corp	$1,000
FMC Corp	$1,000
LTV Aerospace & Defense Company	$1,000
Mantech International	$1,000
McDonnell Douglas Helicopter	$1,000
Raytheon	$1,000
TRW Inc	$1,000
Watkins-Johnson Company	$1,000
Westinghouse Electric	$1,000
Others	$11,334
Electric & Power Utilities	*$11,350*
Baltimore Gas & Electric	$3,500
Potomac Electric Power Company	$1,000
Others	$6,850
Food & Beverage	*$3,500*
Independent Bakers Assn	$1,000
National Restaurant Assn	$1,000
National Beer Wholesalers Assn	$1,000
Others	$500
Forest Products	*$4,750*
Westvaco Corp	$4,000
Others	$750
Health Professionals	*$14,250*
American Dental Assn	$4,000
American Medical Assn	$2,750
Maryland Medical Assn	$2,000
American Optometric Assn	$1,500
American Podiatry Assn	$1,500
American Academy of Ophthalmology	$1,000
American Assn for Marriage & Family Therapy	$1,000
Others	$500
Insurance	*$5,750*
National Assn of Life Underwriters	$2,000
Independent Insurance Agents of America	$1,000
National Assn/Independent Insurers	$1,000
Others	$1,750

PAC Totals by Category

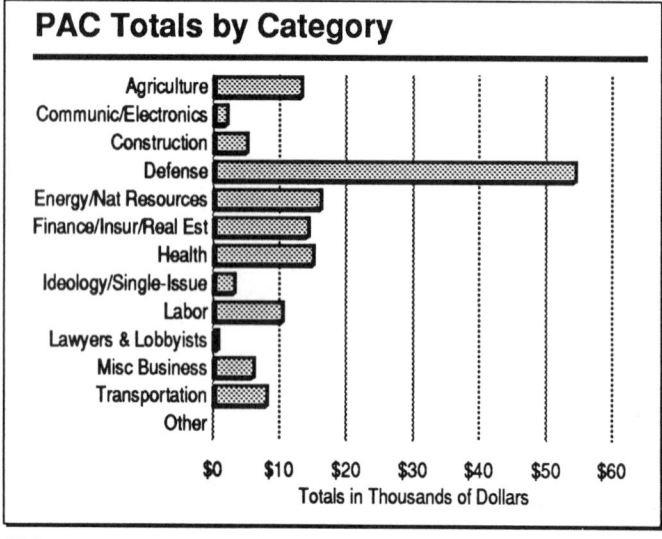

Agriculture
Communic/Electronics
Construction
Defense
Energy/Nat Resources
Finance/Insur/Real Est
Health
Ideology/Single-Issue
Labor
Lawyers & Lobbyists
Misc Business
Transportation
Other

$0 $10 $20 $30 $40 $50 $60
Totals in Thousands of Dollars

Oil & Gas *$3,300*
> None over $500

Real Estate *$5,000*
> National Assn of Realtors $5,000

Other Major Business PACs

Chesapeake & Potomac Telephone	$1,260	Phone Util
First Boston Corp	$1,000	InvestmtBank
Philip Morris	$1,000	Tobacco
Tobacco Institute	$1,000	Tobacco

Labor

Bldg Trades/Industrial/Misc Unions *$6,150*
> Seafarers International Union $1,500
> United Auto Workers $1,000
> United Transportation Union $1,000
> Others $2,650

Government & Postal Workers *$4,000*
> American Postal Workers Union $3,000
> National Assn of Retired Federal Employees $1,000

Major Ideological/Single-Issue

Valley Education Fund (Tony Coelho) .... $1,000   Dem Leaders

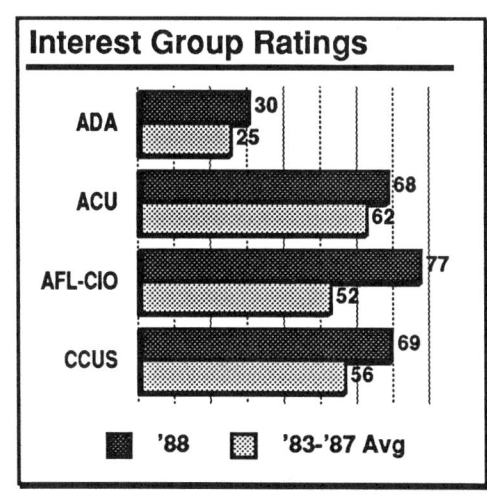

Interest Group Ratings

Spending in Last 3 Elections

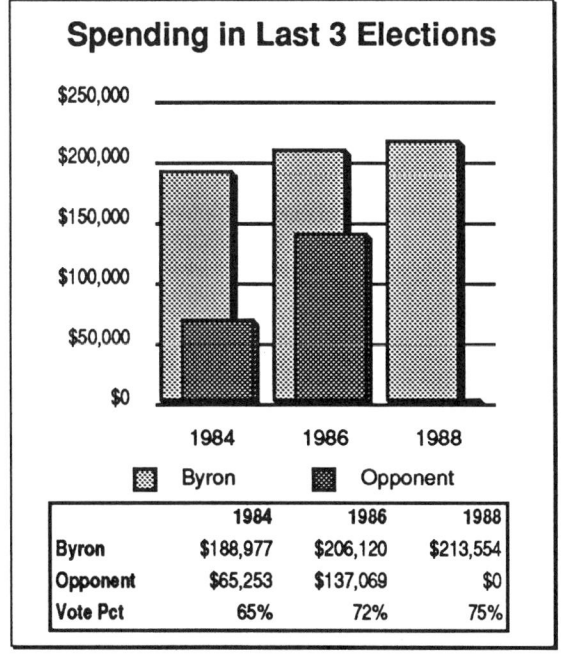

	1984	1986	1988
Byron	$188,977	$206,120	$213,554
Opponent	$65,253	$137,069	$0
Vote Pct	65%	72%	75%

---

* Contributions came from more than one PAC affiliated
  with this sponsor.

Sonny Callahan, R-Ala (1)

First elected: 1984
Total receipts: $596,631
Total from PACs: $252,301

1988 Committees & Subcommittees

Energy and Commerce
Energy and Power
Transportation, Tourism and Hazardous Materials

PAC Contribution Profile

Business

Accountants **$5,300**
    American Institute of CPA's $5,000
    Others $300

Automotive **$6,500**
    National Auto Dealers Assn $4,000
    Auto Dealers & Drivers for Free Trade $2,000
    Others $500

Broadcasting & Cable TV **$3,250**
    National Cable Television Assn $2,000
    National Assn of Broadcasters $1,000
    Others $250

Chemicals **$6,050**
    Dow Chemical* $2,300
    FMC Corp $1,000
    Others $2,750

Commercial Banks **$15,000**
    Amsouth Bancorp $5,000
    Central Bancshares of the South $5,000
    American Bankers Assn $2,500
    Barnett Banks of Florida $1,000
    Citicorp $1,000
    Others $500

Construction **$10,300**
    Walter Industries $3,300
    Associated General Contractors $2,500
    National Assn of Home Builders $1,500
    Others $3,000

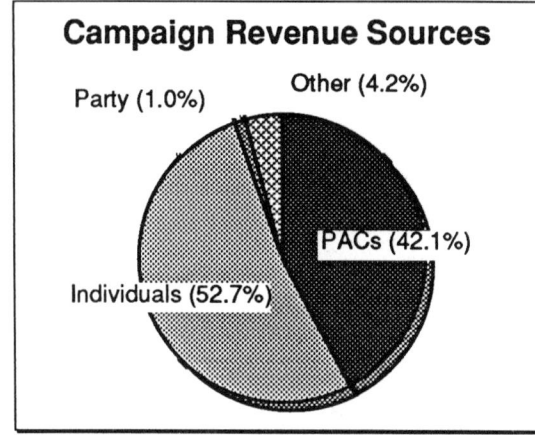

Campaign Revenue Sources

Party (1.0%)
Other (4.2%)
PACs (42.1%)
Individuals (52.7%)

Defense **$6,050**
    Hughes Aircraft $2,000
    Colt Industries $1,500
    Allied-Signal $1,000
    Others $1,550

Electric Utilities **$14,050**
    Southern Company* $6,700
    Texas Utilities Electric Company* $1,000
    Others $6,350

Food & Beverage **$11,150**
    Delchamps Inc $2,000
    Morrison Inc $1,900
    Hardee's Food Systems $1,000
    Jerrico Inc $1,000
    National Restaurant Assn $1,000
    Pepsico Inc $1,000
    Others $3,250

Forest Products **$11,500**
    Boise Cascade $2,000
    International Paper Company $2,000
    Scott Paper Company $2,000
    Westvaco Corp $1,500
    Champion International Corp $1,250
    Others $2,750

Health Professionals **$16,000**
    American Medical Assn $10,000
    American Dental Assn $2,500
    Cmte for Quality Orthopedic Health Care $1,500
    American College of Emergency Physicians $1,000
    Others $1,000

Insurance **$13,050**
    American Family Corp $2,500
    Torchmark Corp $2,000
    Independent Insurance Agents of America $1,250
    National Assn Mutual Insurance Agents $1,050
    National Assn of Life Underwriters $1,000
    Protective Life Corp $1,000
    Others $4,250

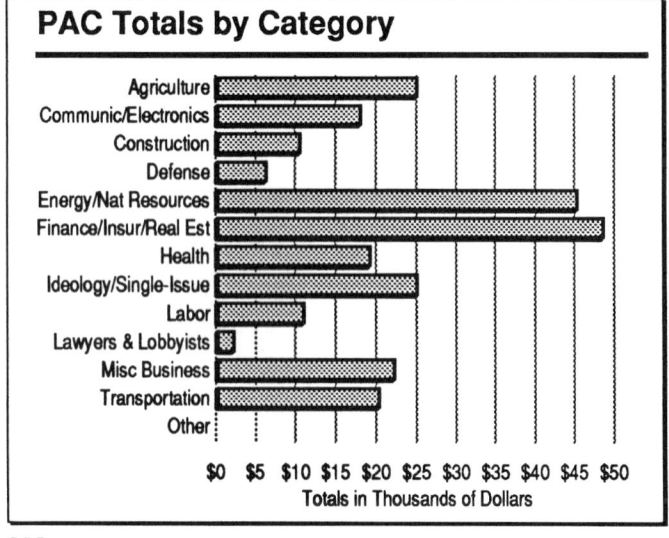

PAC Totals by Category

Category	Amount
Agriculture	
Communic/Electronics	
Construction	
Defense	
Energy/Nat Resources	
Finance/Insur/Real Est	
Health	
Ideology/Single-Issue	
Labor	
Lawyers & Lobbyists	
Misc Business	
Transportation	
Other	

Totals in Thousands of Dollars
$0 $5 $10 $15 $20 $25 $30 $35 $40 $45 $50

Oil & Gas **$25,250**
- Southern Natural Resources $3,250
- Alagasco Inc $1,500
- Tenneco Inc $1,250
- Chevron Corp $1,000
- Mobil Oil $1,000
- Phillips Petroleum $1,000
- Union Pacific Corp $1,000
- Others $15,250

Railroads **$2,800**
- Norfolk Southern Corp $1,000
- Others $1,800

Real Estate **$8,800**
- National Assn of Realtors $8,000
- Others $800

Savings Banks & Credit Unions **$4,700**
- 1st Southern Federal Savings & Loan $2,350
- Alabama Savings Assn $1,050
- Others $1,300

Telecommunications **$11,800**
- AT&T $7,000
- South Central Bell Telephone $2,250
- Continental Telecom $1,000
- Others $1,550

Textiles & Synthetic Fibers **$2,750**
- Westpoint Pepperell $1,250
- Others $1,500

Tobacco **$4,250**
- Philip Morris $1,500
- Batus Inc* $1,000
- RJR Nabisco $1,000
- Others $750

Trucking/Delivery **$5,300**
- United Parcel Service $1,500
- National Moving & Storage Assn $1,250
- Others $2,550

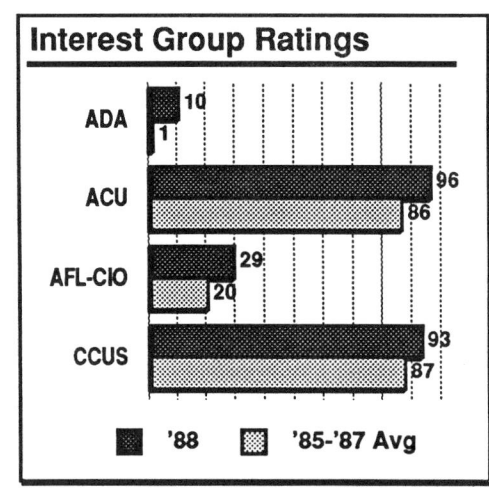

Interest Group Ratings

Legend: ■ '88   ▨ '85-'87 Avg

Other Major Business PACs

Intergraph Corp	$2,000	Comput Parts
Alabama Farm Bureau Federation	$1,550	Farm Orgs
Waste Management Inc	$1,500	Waste Mgmt
Ciba-Geigy Corp	$1,200	Pharmaceut
Business Industry PAC	$1,119	Bus Assns
Dravo Corp	$1,050	Other Mining
American Pilots Assn	$1,000	SeaTransport
Marriott Corp	$1,000	Hotel/Motel
Morgan Stanley & Company	$1,000	InvestmtBank
National Coal Assn	$1,000	Coal
Sirote, Permutt et al	$1,000	Lawyers
Stone Container Corp	$1,000	Paper Packg

Labor

Labor Unions **$10,750**
- Marine Engineers District 2 Maritime Officers $5,500
- National Assn of Retired Federal Employees $3,000
- Seafarers International Union $1,000
- Others $1,250

Ideological/Single-Issue

Pro-Israel **$19,750**
- Americans for Good Government Inc $5,000
- National PAC $5,000
- Desert Caucus $2,000
- Delaware Valley PAC $1,000
- Florida Congressional Cmte $1,000
- Garden State PAC $1,000
- Heartland PAC $1,000
- Hudson Valley PAC $1,000
- Roundtable PAC $1,000
- Others $1,750

Other Major Ideological/Single-Issue PACs

National Rifle Assn	$1,500	Pro-Guns
Council for National Defense	$1,082	Pro-Defense

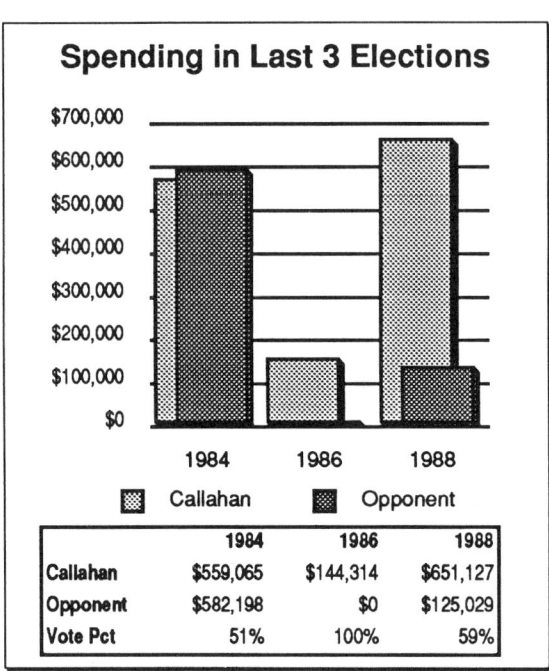

Spending in Last 3 Elections

Legend: ▨ Callahan   ■ Opponent

	1984	1986	1988
Callahan	$559,065	$144,314	$651,127
Opponent	$582,198	$0	$125,029
Vote Pct	51%	100%	59%

* Contributions came from more than one PAC affiliated
  with this sponsor.

Ben Nighthorse Campbell, D-Colo (3)

First elected: 1986
Total receipts: $503,919
Total from PACs: $307,821

1988 Committees & Subcommittees

Agriculture
Forests, Family Farms and Energy
Livestock, Dairy and Poultry

Interior and Insular Affairs
Mining and Natural Resources
Water and Power Resources

Small Business
Exports, Tourism and Special Problems

PAC Contribution Profile

Business

Aviation & Aerospace	**$4,450**
Aircraft Owners & Pilots Assn	$2,900
UNC Inc	$1,000
Others	$550
Commodities	**$2,500**
Chicago Mercantile Exchange	$1,500
Chicago Board of Trade	$1,000
Construction	**$6,500**
National Electrical Contractors Assn	$3,000
National Assn of Home Builders	$2,000
Others	$1,500
Dairy	**$23,980**
Associated Milk Producers	$7,000
Mid-American Dairymen	$6,500
Dairymens Mountain Assn	$5,730
Dairymen Inc	$2,000
Milk Marketing Inc	$1,500
Land O'Lakes Inc	$1,000
Others	$250
Electric Utilities	**$4,250**
ACRE (Action Committee for Rural Electrification)	$2,500
Others	$1,750
Food & Beverage	**$3,000**
National Restaurant Assn	$1,000
Winn-Dixie Stores	$1,000
Others	$1,000

Campaign Revenue Sources

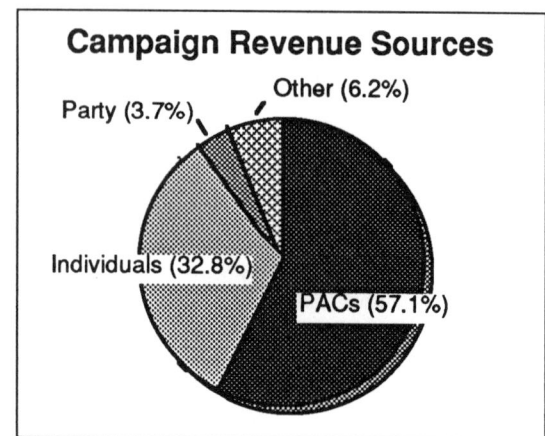

Other (6.2%)
Party (3.7%)
Individuals (32.8%)
PACs (57.1%)

Health Professionals	**$11,249**
American Medical Assn	$9,999
American Academy of Ophthalmology	$1,000
Others	$250
Insurance	**$6,000**
Independent Insurance Agents of America	$2,250
National Assn of Life Underwriters	$2,000
Security Life of Denver	$1,250
Others	$500
Lawyers	**$3,000**
Assn of Trial Lawyers of America	$2,500
Others	$500
Mining	**$3,150**
Cyprus Minerals Company	$1,500
Others	$1,650
Oil & Gas	**$9,670**
Amoco Corp	$1,500
Phillips Petroleum	$1,500
Atlantic Richfield	$1,250
W R Grace & Company	$1,000
Others	$4,420
Real Estate	**$7,000**
National Assn of Realtors	$7,000
Sugar Growers	**$4,900**
American Crystal Sugar Corp	$1,250
Others	$3,650
Telecommunications	**$6,000**
Mountain Bell	$3,500
AT&T	$2,000
Others	$500

PAC Totals by Category

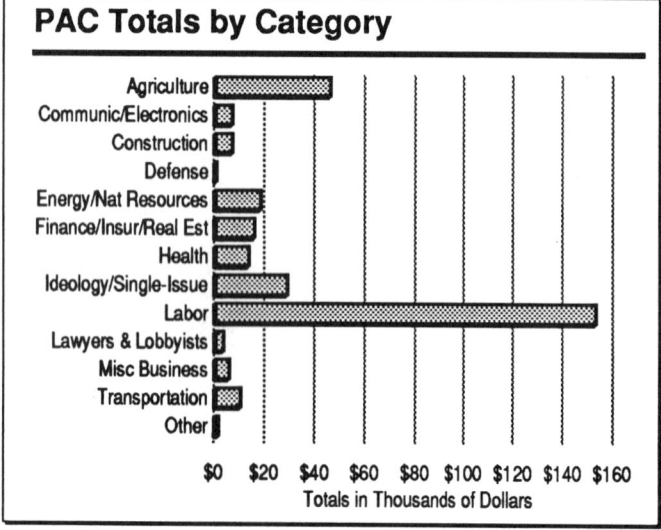

Totals in Thousands of Dollars

- Agriculture
- Communic/Electronics
- Construction
- Defense
- Energy/Nat Resources
- Finance/Insur/Real Est
- Health
- Ideology/Single-Issue
- Labor
- Lawyers & Lobbyists
- Misc Business
- Transportation
- Other

$0 $20 $40 $60 $80 $100 $120 $140 $160

Other Major Business PACs

National Auto Dealers Assn	$2,250	Auto Sales
Philip Morris	$1,750	Tobacco
American Veterinary Medical Assn	$1,000	Veterinary
Manville Corp	$1,000	Forestry
National Assn of Social Workers	$1,000	Social Work

Labor

Bldg Trades/Industrial/Misc Unions $77,950

Machinists/Aerospace Workers Union	$10,000
United Auto Workers	$10,000
Intl Brotherhood of Electrical Workers	$8,000
Food & Commercial Workers Union	$7,000
AFL-CIO*	$6,250
Carpenters & Joiners Union	$6,250
Communications Workers of America	$5,750
United Steelworkers	$5,500
Plumbers/Pipefitters Union	$2,500
Sheet Metal Workers Union	$2,500
Bakery, Confectionary & Tobacco Workers	$2,000
Laborers' Political League	$2,000
Operating Engineers Union	$2,000
Oil, Chemical & Atomic Workers Union	$1,750
Amalgamated Clothing & Textile Workers	$1,250
American Nurses Assn	$1,250
Ladies Garment Workers Union	$1,250
Ironworkers Union	$1,000
Others	$1,700

Government & Postal Workers $31,500

National Assn of Letter Carriers	$10,000
National Assn of Retired Federal Employees	$8,000
American Fedn of State/County/Munic Employees	$6,750
American Postal Workers Union	$3,000
National Rural Letter Carriers Assn	$2,000
International Assn of Firefighters	$1,000
Others	$750

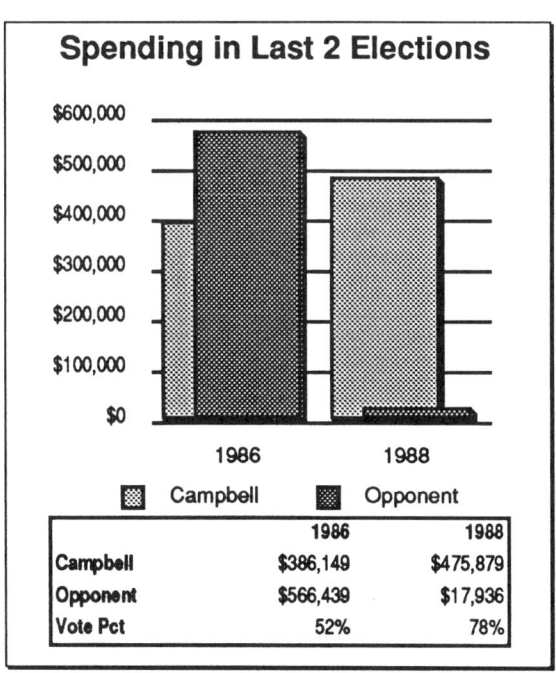

Spending in Last 2 Elections

	1986	1988
Campbell	$386,149	$475,879
Opponent	$566,439	$17,936
Vote Pct	52%	78%

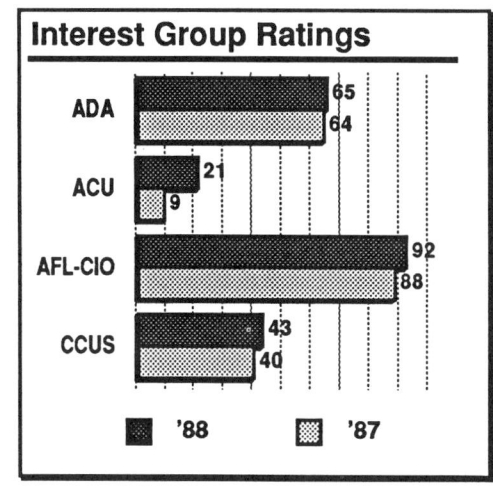

Interest Group Ratings

	'88	'87
ADA	65	64
ACU	21	9
AFL-CIO	92	88
CCUS	43	40

Teachers Unions $17,000

National Education Assn	$10,000
American Federation of Teachers	$7,000

Transportation Unions $27,300

Teamsters Union	$10,000
Air Line Pilots Assn	$4,500
Amalgamated Transit Union	$3,000
Marine Engineers Union	$2,500
Seafarers International Union	$2,500
United Transportation Union	$2,000
Transportation Communication Union	$1,300
Others	$1,500

Ideological/Single-Issue

Democratic Leadership PACs.....................................$10,000

Majority Congress Committee (Jim Wright)	$5,000
Cmte for the 100th Congress (Charles Rangel)	$3,000
Valley Education Fund (Tony Coelho)	$2,000

Pro-Israel $8,000

National PAC	$5,000
Delaware Valley PAC	$1,000
Roundtable PAC	$1,000
Others	$1,000

Other Major Ideological/Single-Issue PACs

National Cmte to Preserve Social Security	$2,000	Soc Secur
Council for a Livable World	$1,109	Pro-Peace
Human Rights Campaign Fund	$1,000	Gay Rights
National Council of Senior Citizens	$1,000	Soc Secur
Republican Congressional Boosters Club	$1,000	Repub/Conser
Women of Indian Nations PAC	$1,000	Ethnic

Independent expenditures supporting Campbell

National Assn of Realtors	$155,312
National Cmte to Preserve Social Security	$3,142

---

* Contributions came from more than one PAC affiliated
with this sponsor.

Tom Campbell, R-Calif (12)

1988-1989 Committees & Subcommittees

First elected: 1988
Total receipts: $1,445,770
Total from PACs: $235,383

Judiciary
Administrative Law and Governmental Relations
Economic and Commercial Law

Science, Space and Technology
Science, Research and Technology
Transportation, Aviation and Materials

Small Business
Antitrust, Impact of Deregulation and Privatization
SBA and the General Economy

PAC Contribution Profile

Business

Automotive **$8,250**
Auto Dealers & Drivers for Free Trade $5,000
Eaton Corp $2,000
New United Motor Manufacturing Inc $1,000
Others $250

Building Contractors & Supplies **$16,750**
National Assn of Home Builders $5,000
American Supply Assn $3,500
Associated General Contractors $2,500
Bechtel Corp $2,000
Sheet Metal/AirCon Contractors $2,000
National Electrical Contractors Assn $1,000
Others $750

Business Associations **$2,665**
Business Industry PAC $1,119
National Fedn of Independent Business $1,000
Others $546

Commercial Banks **$10,000**
American Bankers Assn $3,000
California Bankers Assn $2,000
Union Bank $1,500
First Interstate Bank/California $1,000
Wells Fargo $1,000
Others $1,500

Campaign Revenue Sources

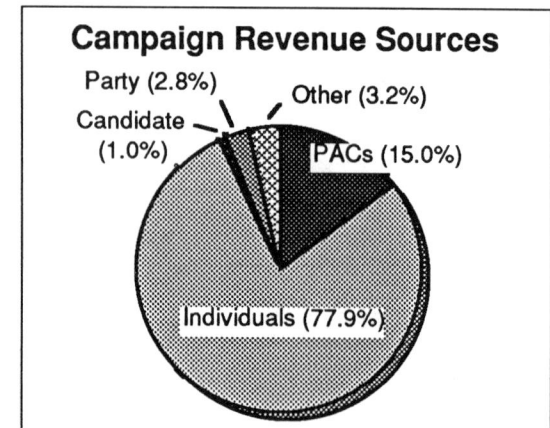

Party (2.8%)
Other (3.2%)
Candidate (1.0%)
PACs (15.0%)
Individuals (77.9%)

Computers & Electronics **$23,200**
National Semiconductor Corp $10,000
Recognition Equipment Inc $3,000
Intel Corp $2,500
Motorola Inc $1,500
Asian American Manufacturers Assn $1,000
Hewlett-Packard $1,000
Honeywell California $1,000
Tandem Computers $1,000
Others $2,200

Defense **$7,500**
Lockheed Corp $3,000
Harris Corp $2,000
United Technologies $1,000
Others $1,500

Electric & Power Utilities **$3,000**
Southern California Edison $1,500
Pacific Gas & Electric $1,000
Others $500

Food & Beverage **$6,500**
McLane Company $1,000
National Restaurant Assn $1,000
Pepsico Inc $1,000
Others $3,500

Health Professionals **$16,250**
American Medical Assn $10,000
American Academy of Ophthalmology $3,500
American Dental Assn $1,500
Co-op of American Physicians $1,000
Others $250

Insurance **$11,000**
National Assn of Life Underwriters $7,500
Others $3,500

Lawyers & Lobbyists **$5,300**
Pillsbury, Madison & Sutro $3,500
Others $1,800

PAC Totals by Category

Category	Totals in Thousands of Dollars
Agriculture	
Communic/Electronics	
Construction	
Defense	
Energy/Nat Resources	
Finance/Insur/Real Est	
Health	
Ideology/Single-Issue	
Labor	
Lawyers & Lobbyists	
Misc Business	
Transportation	
Other	

$0 $5 $10 $15 $20 $25 $30 $35 $40 $45

Market Research **$8,250**

    Dun & Bradstreet $8,250

Oil & Gas **$6,750**

    Chevron Corp $4,000
    Coastal Corp $1,000
    Others $1,750

Pharmaceuticals/Health Care Products **$11,100**

    Shaklee Corp $2,500
    Schering-Plough Corp $2,000
    Syntex (USA) Inc $2,000
    Abbott Laboratories $1,500
    Cooper Companies Inc..................................$1,000
    McKesson Corp $1,000
    Others $1,100

Real Estate **$6,300**

    National Assn of Realtors $5,000
    Newhall Land & Farming Company $1,000
    Others $300

Savings Banks **$2,250**

    None over $600

Telecommunications **$3,500**

    AT&T $1,000
    Continental Telecom $1,000
    GTE Corp $1,000
    Others $500

Venture Capital **$5,000**

    National Venture Capital Assn $5,000

Other Major Business PACs

Corning Glass Works	$2,000	Glass Prod
Duchossois Industries	$2,000	RR Equip
Viking Freight	$2,000	Trucking
Dean Witter Reynolds	$1,050	StocksInvest
American Hospital Assn	$1,000	Hospitals
Deere & Company	$1,000	Farm Equip
National Society of Professional Engineers	$1,000	Engineers
National Tooling & Machining Assn	$1,000	Indust Equip
Xerox Corp	$1,000	Off Machines

Spending in Last Election

	1988
Campbell	$1,440,639
Opponent	$1,089,570
Vote Pct	52%

Labor

Labor Unions..**$3,800**

    National Assn of Retired Federal Employees $3,000
    Others $800

Ideological/Single-Issue

Gay/Lesbian Rights **$12,499**

    Californians for Individual Rights/CiviLiberties $9,999
    Human Rights Campaign Fund $2,500

Pro-Israel **$5,000**

    Women's Pro-Israel National PAC $5,000

Republican/Conservative **$6,646**

    Lincoln Club of Northern California $5,000
    California Republican League $1,646

Republican Leadership PACs **$7,425**

    Fund for America's Future (George Bush) $5,000
    Campaign America (Bob Dole)......................$1,000
    Republican Leader's Fund (Bob Michel) $1,000
    Others $425

Other Major Ideological/Single-Issue PACs

Handgun Control Inc	$4,500	Anti-Guns
Public Service Research Council	$2,000	Anti-Union
Korean American National PAC	$1,000	Ethnic
Political Impact Coalition	$1,000	Pro-Peace

Benjamin L. Cardin, D-Md (3)

First elected: 1986
Total receipts: $405,789
Total from PACs: $208,148

1988 Committees & Subcommittees

Judiciary
Administrative Law and Governmental Relations
Courts, Civil Liberties and the Administration of Justice

Public Works and Transportation
Aviation
Public Buildings and Grounds
Water Resources

PAC Contribution Profile

Business

Accountants	**$5,705**
American Institute of CPA's	$5,000
Others	$705
Automotive	**$3,000**
National Auto Dealers Assn	$2,250
Others	$750
Aviation & Aerospace	**$4,100**
Aircraft Owners & Pilots Assn	$1,500
Others	$2,600
Broadcasting & Entertainment	**$4,550**
National Assn of Broadcasters	$1,000
ASCAP	$1,000
Others	$2,550
Chemicals	**$2,800**
FMC Corp	$1,500
W R Grace & Company	$1,300
Commercial Banks	**$10,006**
MNC Financial Inc	$2,000
First Maryland Bancorp	$1,250
Citicorp	$1,000
Mercantile Bankshares Corp	$1,000
Sovran Bank/Maryland	$1,000
Others	$3,756
Construction	**$4,250**
Associated General Contractors	$1,000
National Assn of Home Builders	$1,000
Others	$2,250

Campaign Revenue Sources

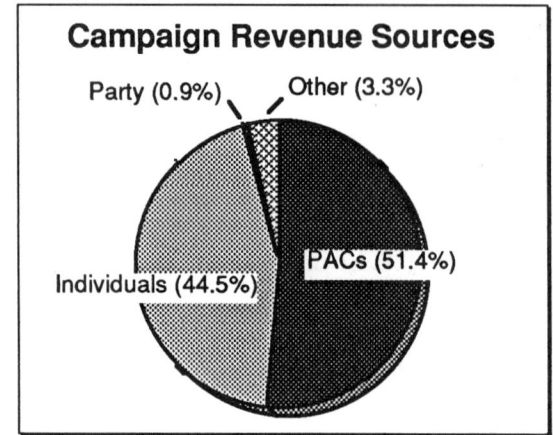

Party (0.9%)
Other (3.3%)
PACs (51.4%)
Individuals (44.5%)

Electric & Power Utilities	**$4,850**
Baltimore Gas & Electric	$2,100
Potomac Electric Power Company	$1,000
Others	$1,750
Food & Beverage	**$4,550**
Joseph E Seagram & Sons	$1,000
National Beer Wholesalers Assn	$1,000
Others	$2,550
Health Professionals	**$13,620**
American Medical Assn	$4,750
Maryland Medical Assn	$2,500
American Academy of Ophthalmology	$2,000
American Dental Assn	$1,500
Cmte for Quality Orthopedic Health Care	$1,000
Others	$1,870
Insurance	**$12,068**
National Assn of Independent Insurers	$2,286
National Assn of Life Underwriters	$1,500
Casualty & Surety Agents Assn	$1,000
Nationwide Corp	$1,000
New England Mutual Life	$1,000
Others	$5,282
Lawyers & Lobbyists	**$9,215**
Assn of Trial Lawyers of America	$5,000
Akin, Gump, Hauer & Feld	$1,500
Dow, Lohnes & Albertson	$1,000
Others	$1,715
Paper Production	**$3,000**
Westvaco Corp	$3,000
Pharmaceuticals	**$3,000**
None over $750	
Real Estate	**$3,250**
National Assn of Realtors	$3,250
Securities Investment	**$3,500**
Goldman Sachs	$1,500
Morgan Stanley & Company	$1,000
Others	$1,000
Telecommunications	**$4,750**
AT&T	$2,500
Chesapeake & Potomac Telephone	$1,750
Others	$500

PAC Totals by Category

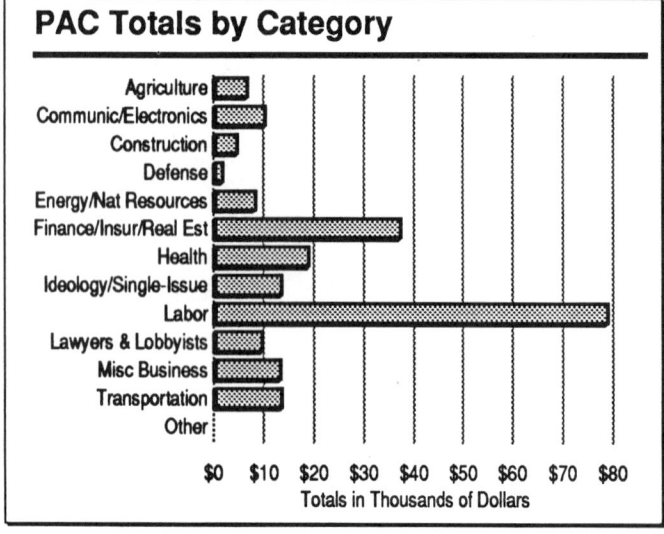

Agriculture
Communic/Electronics
Construction
Defense
Energy/Nat Resources
Finance/Insur/Real Est
Health
Ideology/Single-Issue
Labor
Lawyers & Lobbyists
Misc Business
Transportation
Other

$0 $10 $20 $30 $40 $50 $60 $70 $80
Totals in Thousands of Dollars

Trucking/Delivery		$4,400

United Parcel Service	$2,000
Others	$2,400

Other Major Business PACs

Credit Union National Assn	$1,300	Credit Union
American Hospital Assn	$1,000	Hospitals
Bethlehem Steel	$1,000	Steel
J C Penney Company	$1,000	Dept Store
Waste Management Inc	$1,000	Waste Mgmt
West Publishing	$1,000	Books & Mags

Labor

Bldg Trades/Industrial/Misc Unions	**$25,358**

Carpenters & Joiners Union	$4,000
Baltimore Bldg/Construction Trades Council	$3,140
Sheet Metal Workers Union	$2,500
Laborers' Political League	$2,250
Food & Commercial Workers Union	$2,000
Intl Brotherhood of Electrical Workers	$1,500
Operating Engineers Union	$1,500
United Auto Workers	$1,500
Ladies Garment Workers Union	$1,358
AFL-CIO*	$1,250
Machinists/Aerospace Workers Union	$1,000
Others	$3,360

Government & Postal Workers	**$20,578**

National Assn of Retired Federal Employees	$8,000
National Assn of Letter Carriers	$3,860
American Fedn of State/County/Munic Employees	$2,000
American Postal Workers Union	$1,750
National Rural Letter Carriers Assn	$1,718
National Treasury Employees Union	$1,000
Others	$2,250

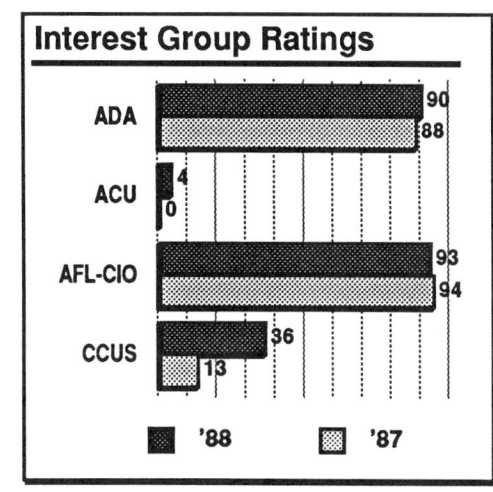

Interest Group Ratings

	'88	'87
ADA	90	88
ACU	4	0
AFL-CIO	93	94
CCUS	36	13

Teachers Unions	**$6,250**

National Education Assn	$3,750
American Federation of Teachers	$2,500

Transportation Unions	**$26,280**

Teamsters Union	$8,750
Air Line Pilots Assn	$5,000
Amalgamated Transit Union	$3,000
International Longshoremen Assn	$2,000
Marine Engineers Union*	$2,000
Seafarers International Union	$2,000
United Transportation Union	$1,500
Others	$2,030

Ideological/Single-Issue

Pro-Israel	**$7,500**

National PAC	$5,000
Mid Manhattan PAC	$1,500

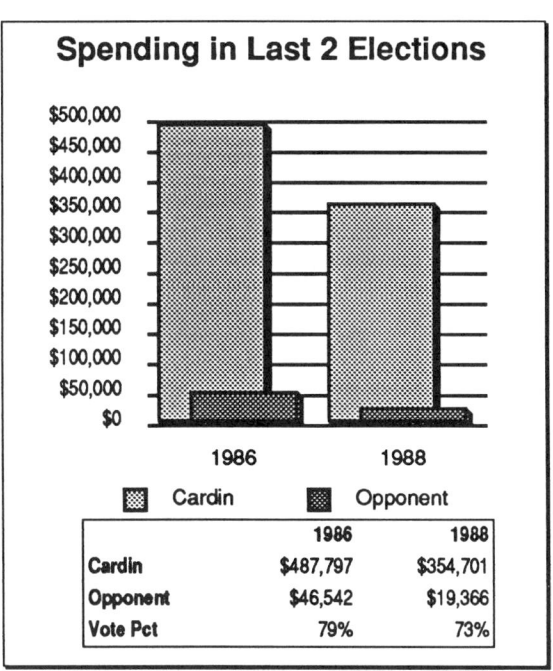

Spending in Last 2 Elections

	1986	1988
Cardin	$487,797	$354,701
Opponent	$46,542	$19,366
Vote Pct	79%	73%

Cardin — Opponent

---

* Contributions came from more than one PAC affiliated
with this sponsor.

333

Thomas R. Carper, D-Del (At Large)

First elected: 1982
Total receipts: $365,432
Total from PACs: $161,235

1988 Committees & Subcommittees

Banking, Finance and Urban Affairs
Financial Institutions Supervision, Regulation and Insurance
Housing and Community Development
International Finance, Trade and Monetary Policy

Merchant Marine and Fisheries
Coast Guard and Navigation
Fisheries and Wildlife Conservation and the Environment

PAC Contribution Profile

Business

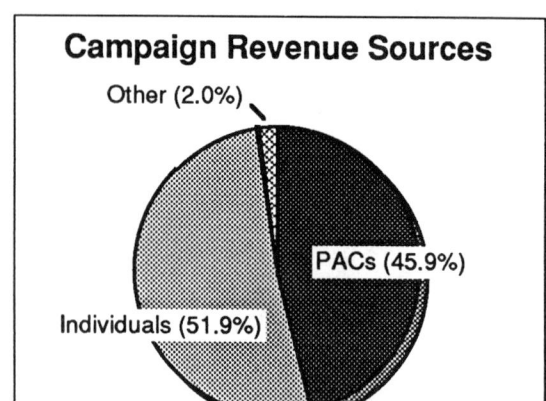

Campaign Revenue Sources

Other (2.0%)
PACs (45.9%)
Individuals (51.9%)

Commercial Banks.....................................	**$62,603**
American Bankers Assn	$10,000
J P Morgan & Company	$10,000
Citicorp	$4,250
Bankers Trust	$3,000
Marine Midland Banks	$3,000
Chemical Bank	$2,853
Barnett Banks of Florida	$2,500
First Chicago Corp	$2,500
Continental Illinois Corp	$2,250
Chase Manhattan	$2,000
Consumer Bankers Assn	$1,500
Security Pacific Corp	$1,500
Citizens & Southern National Bank	$1,300
Manufacturers Hanover	$1,125
Bank of New York	$1,000
Provident National Corp	$1,000
MNC Financial Inc	$825
Mellon Bank	$800
NCNB Corp	$800
Assn of Bank Holding Companies	$750
BankAmerica	$750
Meridian Bancorp	$750
Sun Banks	$750
Wells Fargo	$750
Wilmington Trust Company	$750
Others	$5,900
Consumer Credit & Loans.........................	**$3,650**
American Financial Services Assn	$1,250
Others	$2,400

Department Stores.....................................	**$2,000**
J C Penney Company	$2,000
Health Professionals	**$4,500**
American Medical Assn	$2,750
American Dental Assn	$1,000
Others	$750
Insurance..	**$3,250**
American International Group inc	$2,500
Others	$750
Lawyers & Lobbyists	**$2,000**
Akin, Gump, Hauer & Feld	$1,000
Others	$1,000
Real Estate	**$9,625**
National Assn of Realtors	$8,625
Others	$1,000
Savings Banks & Credit Unions	**$5,900**
US League of Savings Assn	$2,400
Credit Union National Assn	$1,000
National Council of Savings Institutions	$750
Others	$1,750
Sea Transport	**$4,750**
American Pilots Assn	$2,500
Tenneco Inc	$1,500
Others	$750
Securities Investment................................	**$3,250**
Dean Witter Reynolds	$1,000
New York Stock Exchange	$1,000
Shearson Lehman Hutton	$750
Others	$500
Telecommunications	**$3,375**
AT&T..	$1,500
Bell Atlantic	$1,000
Diamond State Telephone Company	$875

Other Major Business PACs

Chrysler Corp	$1,250	Auto Mfrs
Equifax Inc	$1,025	CreditReport
Hercules Inc	$1,000	Chemicals
ICI Americas Inc	$1,000	Pharmaceut
Kansas City Southern	$1,000	Railroads

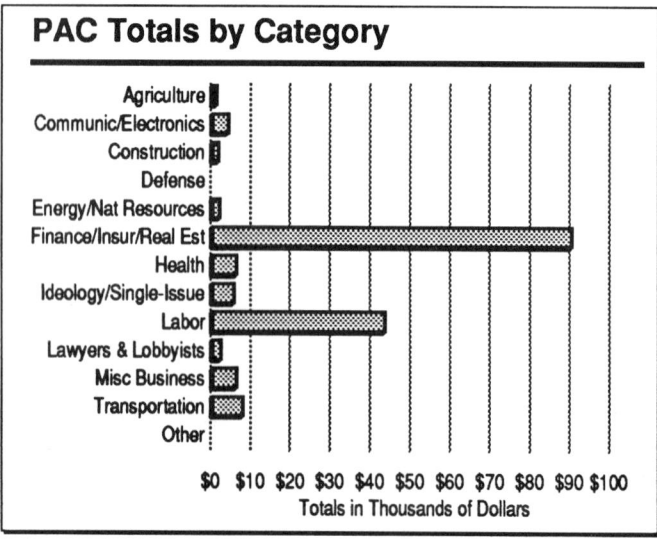

PAC Totals by Category

Agriculture
Communic/Electronics
Construction
Defense
Energy/Nat Resources
Finance/Insur/Real Est
Health
Ideology/Single-Issue
Labor
Lawyers & Lobbyists
Misc Business
Transportation
Other

$0 $10 $20 $30 $40 $50 $60 $70 $80 $90 $100
Totals in Thousands of Dollars

Labor

Bldg Trades/Industrial/Other Unions $23,470

    United Auto Workers $6,500
    Intl Brotherhood of Electrical Workers* $5,000
    Carpenters & Joiners Union $2,000
    Operating Engineers Union $2,000
    Food & Commercial Workers Union $1,250
    Laborers' Political League $1,250
    National Education Assn $1,250
    Machinists/Aerospace Workers Union $1,000
    Plumbers/Pipefitters Union* $1,000
    Others $2,220

Government & Postal Workers $6,500

    National Assn of Retired Federal Employees $4,000
    National Assn of Letter Carriers $1,000
    Others $1,500

Sea Transport Unions $7,250

    Marine Engineers District 2 Maritime Officers $3,500
    Seafarers International Union $3,000
    Boilermakers Union $750

Other Transportation Unions $5,850

    Air Line Pilots Assn $3,500
    United Transportation Union $600
    Others $1,750

Ideological/Single-Issue

Democratic/Liberal $2,500

    National Cmte for an Effective Congress $2,500

Pro-Israel $2,250

    Delaware Valley PAC $1,000
    Hudson Valley PAC $750
    Others $500

Interest Group Ratings

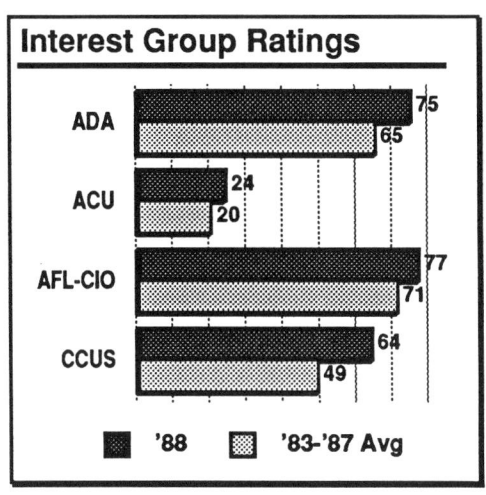

Spending in Last 3 Elections

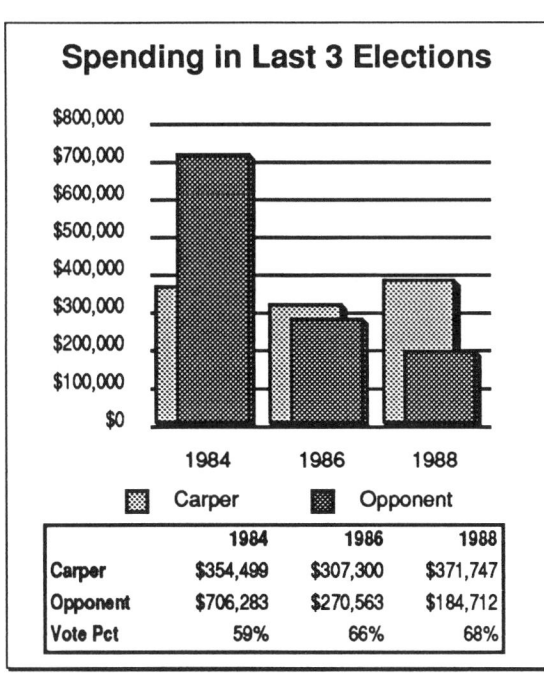

	1984	1986	1988
Carper	$354,499	$307,300	$371,747
Opponent	$706,283	$270,563	$184,712
Vote Pct	59%	66%	68%

* Contributions came from more than one PAC affiliated
  with this sponsor.

Bob Carr, D-Mich (6)

1988 Committees & Subcommittees

Appropriations
Commerce, Justice, State, the Judiciary and Related Agencies
Transportation and Related Agencies

Select Hunger

First elected: 1974
Total receipts: $534,741
Total from PACs: $277,673

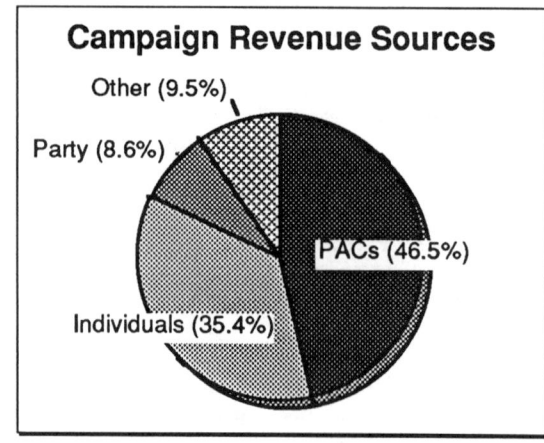

Campaign Revenue Sources

- Other (9.5%)
- Party (8.6%)
- PACs (46.5%)
- Individuals (35.4%)

PAC Contribution Profile

Business

Air Transport/Air Freight **$33,550**
Aircraft Owners & Pilots Assn $10,000
Texas Air $5,650
Boeing Company $2,000
Eastern Airlines $2,000
Federal Express Corp $1,500
Northwest Airlines $1,350
Genl Aviation Manufacturers Assn $1,250
American Assn of Airport Executives $1,200
American Airlines $1,200
Beech Aircraft $1,000
Trans World Airlines $1,000
Others $5,400

Automotive **$4,750**
General Motors $2,300
Ford Motor Company $1,000
Others $1,450

Broadcasting & Entertainment **$3,050**
None over $700

Construction **$8,025**
National Assn of Home Builders $2,500
Associated General Contractors $2,000
Sheet Metal/Air Conditioning Contractors $1,075
National Utility Contractors Assn $1,000
Others $1,450

Dairy **$8,700**
Associated Milk Producers $3,000
Mid-American Dairymen $3,000
Michigan Milk Producers Assn $1,150
Others $1,550

Defense **$8,050**
United Technologies $1,500
Emerson Electric* $1,450
Rockwell International $1,050
General Dynamics $1,000
Others $3,050

Electric Utilities **$10,349**
Consumers Power Company $4,274
Detroit Edison $1,300
ACRE (Action Committee for Rural Electrification) $1,200
Others $3,575

Financial Institutions **$3,900**
Michigan League of Savings Institutions $1,400
Michigan Credit Union League $1,100
Others $1,400

Food & Beverage **$3,275**
None over $675

Health Professionals **$13,050**
American Medical Assn $6,850
American Academy of Ophthalmology $3,000
American Dental Assn $1,500
Others $1,700

Insurance **$6,200**
National Assn of Life Underwriters $3,500
American Family Corp $1,000
National Assn Mutual Insurance Agents $1,000
Others $700

Lawyers **$4,100**
Akin, Gump, Hauer & Feld $1,400
Assn of Trial Lawyers of America $1,100
Others $1,600

Oil & Gas **$3,200**
None over $750

Real Estate **$8,650**
National Assn of Realtors $8,000
Mortgage Bankers Assn of America $650

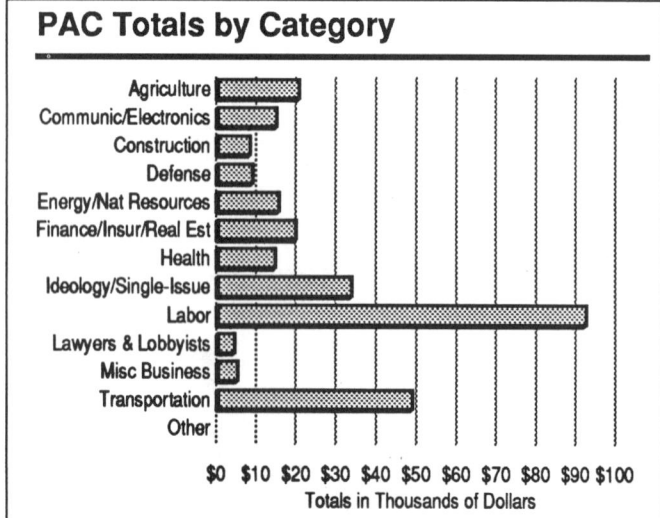

PAC Totals by Category

Agriculture
Communic/Electronics
Construction
Defense
Energy/Nat Resources
Finance/Insur/Real Est
Health
Ideology/Single-Issue
Labor
Lawyers & Lobbyists
Misc Business
Transportation
Other

$0 $10 $20 $30 $40 $50 $60 $70 $80 $90 $100
Totals in Thousands of Dollars

Telecommunications **$10,750**
    AT&T $4,250
    Michigan Bell Telephone $3,850
    Others $2,650

Tobacco **$4,050**
    Philip Morris $2,100
    Others $1,950

Trucking/Delivery **$6,826**
    American Trucking Assns $2,576
    United Parcel Service $2,550
    North American Van Lines $1,000
    Others $700

Other Major Business PACs

Michigan Farm Bureau	$1,500	Farm Orgs
American Sugarbeet Growers Assn	$1,100	Sugar
National Fisheries Institute	$1,000	Fishing

Labor

Bldg Trades/Industrial/Misc Unions **$39,850**
    United Auto Workers $10,000
    AFL-CIO $7,500
    Machinists/Aerospace Workers Union $4,000
    Boilermakers Local #169 ....$2,500
    Carpenters & Joiners Union $2,000
    Communications Workers of America $2,000
    Food & Commercial Workers Union $2,000
    Operating Engineers Union* $2,000
    Laborers' Political League $1,550
    Bricklayers Union $1,000
    Intl Brotherhood of Electrical Workers..................$1,000
    Ladies Garment Workers Union $1,000
    Plumbers/Pipefitters Union $1,000
    United Steelworkers $1,000
    Others $1,300

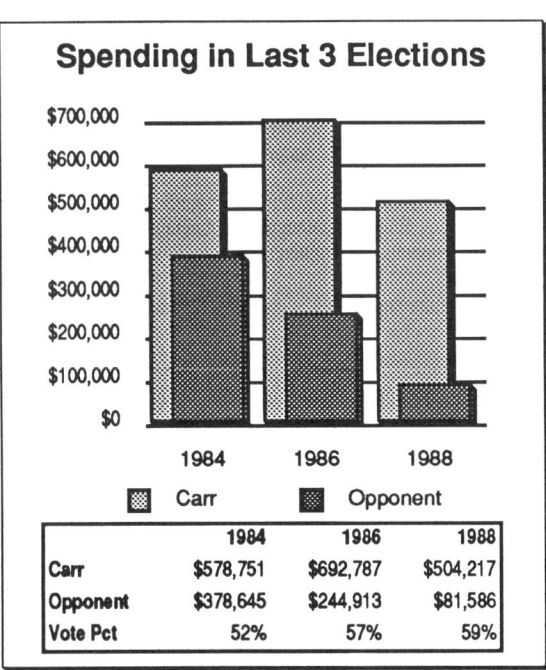

Spending in Last 3 Elections

Carr   Opponent

	1984	1986	1988
Carr	$578,751	$692,787	$504,217
Opponent	$378,645	$244,913	$81,586
Vote Pct	52%	57%	59%

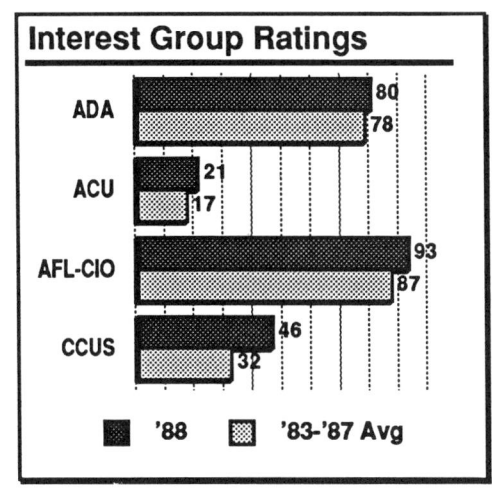

Interest Group Ratings

ADA 80 / 78
ACU 21 / 17
AFL-CIO 93 / 87
CCUS 46 / 32

■ '88   ▨ '83-'87 Avg

Government & Postal Workers **$8,125**
    National Assn of Retired Federal Employees $3,000
    American Fedn of State/County/Munic Employees $2,000
    National Assn of Letter Carriers $1,225
    Others $1,900

Teachers Unions **$8,050**
    National Education Assn $8,000
    Others $50

Transportation Unions **$36,100**
    Teamsters Union $10,000
    Marine Engineers District 2 Maritime Officers $7,000
    Seafarers International Union $5,500
    Amalgamated Transit Union $3,000
    Transport Workers Union $3,000
    United Transportation Union $2,650
    Air Line Pilots Assn $2,500
    Others $2,450

Ideological/Single-Issue

Democratic/Liberal **$10,600**
    Ingham County Democratic Party $9,500
    Congressional Agenda 80's $1,000
    Others $100

Pro-Israel **$13,350**
    National PAC $5,000
    MOPAC $2,500
    Delaware Valley PAC $2,000
    Joint Action Cmte for Political Affairs $1,500
    Hudson Valley PAC $1,000
    Others $1,350

Other Major Ideological/Single-Issue PACs

National Rifle Assn	$3,669	Pro-Guns
National Cmte to Preserve Social Security	$1,650	Soc Secur
Citizens for Public Education	$1,250	OtherIdeolog
KidsPAC	$1,000	HealthWelfar
Valley Education Fund (Tony Coelho)	$1,000	Dem Leaders

Independent expenditures supporting Carr

National Cmte to Preserve Social Security $1,001

---

* Contributions came from more than one PAC affiliated
  with this sponsor.

Rod Chandler, R-Wash (8)

First elected: 1982
Total receipts: $333,019
Total from PACs: $191,478

1988 Committees & Subcommittees

Ways and Means
Health
Oversight

PAC Contribution Profile

Business

Accountants **$6,500**
American Institute of CPA's $5,000
Ernst & Whinney $1,000
Others $500

Airlines & Aerospace **$8,350**
Boeing Company $2,750
Aircraft Owners & Pilots Assn $1,500
Texas Air $1,500
United Airlines $1,050
Eastern Airlines $1,000
Others $550

Automotive & Trucking **$7,600**
National Auto Dealers Assn $2,800
Auto Dealers & Drivers for Free Trade $1,500
Paccar Inc $1,000
Others $2,300

Commercial Banks **$10,100**
American Bankers Assn $2,500
J P Morgan & Company $2,000
U S Bancorp $2,000
Rainier Bancorp $1,500
Others $2,100

Campaign Revenue Sources

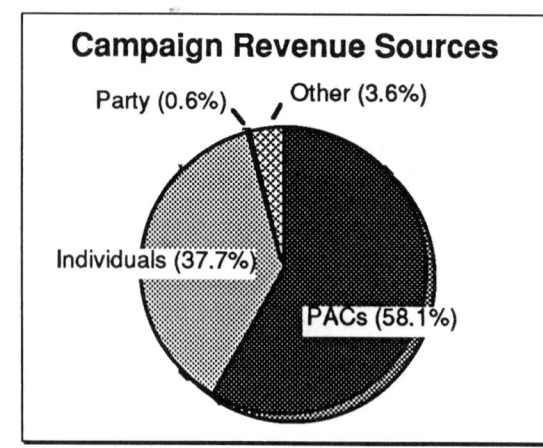

Party (0.6%)
Other (3.6%)
Individuals (37.7%)
PACs (58.1%)

Construction **$10,962**
National Assn of Home Builders $2,000
Associated General Contractors $1,500
Manville Corp $1,000
National Electrical Contractors Assn $1,000
National Society of Professional Engineers $1,000
National Utility Contractors Assn $1,000
Sheet Metal/Air Conditioning Contractors $1,000
Others $2,462

Defense **$3,400**
None over $800

Electric Utilities & Equipment **$3,300**
Puget Sound Power & Light $1,500
Combustion Engineering $1,000
Others $800

Electronics & Computers **$2,500**
General Electric $1,000
Others $1,500

Food & Beverage **$13,600**
Services Group of America $3,000
Miller Brewing Company $2,000
National Restaurant Assn $2,000
National Beer Wholesalers Assn $1,500
Food Marketing Institute $1,300
McDonald's Corp $1,000
McLane Company $1,000
Others $1,800

Forest Products **$3,800**
International Paper Company $1,000
Others $2,800

Health Professionals **$16,513**
American Dental Assn $3,000
American Medical Assn $2,300
American Academy of Ophthalmology $2,000
American Podiatry Assn $2,000
Cmte for Quality Orthopedic Health Care $2,000
Oral & Maxillofacial Surgeons $1,500
American College of Emergency Physicians $1,000
American Physical Therapy Assn $1,000
Others $1,713

PAC Totals by Category

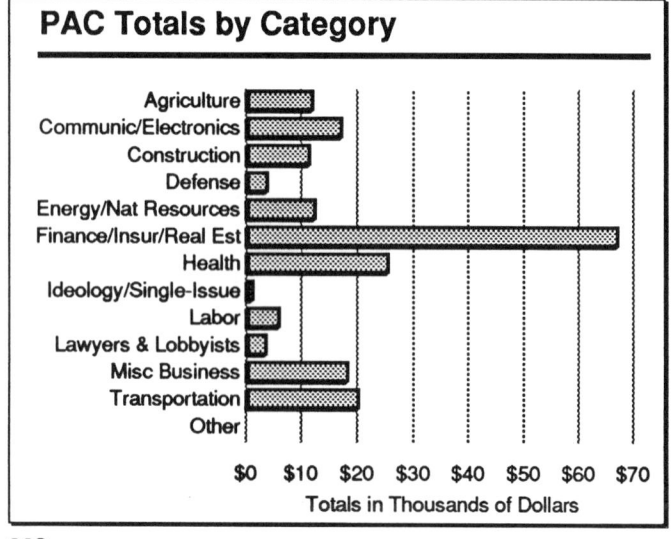

Agriculture
Communic/Electronics
Construction
Defense
Energy/Nat Resources
Finance/Insur/Real Est
Health
Ideology/Single-Issue
Labor
Lawyers & Lobbyists
Misc Business
Transportation
Other

$0 $10 $20 $30 $40 $50 $60 $70
Totals in Thousands of Dollars

Hospitals & Nursing Homes................................**$5,550**
   American Hospital Assn $1,500
   American Health Care Assn $1,000
   Federation of America Hospitals $1,000
   Others $2,050

Insurance..**$30,249**
   Mutual of Omaha* $2,050
   Equitable Financial Services $2,000
   Northwestern Mutual Life $2,000
   Aetna Life & Casualty $1,650
   Blue Cross & Blue Shield Assn $1,500
   Travelers Corp $1,500
   American Council of Life Insurance $1,299
   National Assn of Independent Insurers $1,100
   Massachusetts Mutual Life Insurance $1,000
   Metropolitan Life Insurance $1,000
   National Assn of Life Underwriters $1,000
   New York Life $1,000
   Prudential Insurance $1,000
   Standard Insurance Company $1,000
   Torchmark Corp..$1,000
   Others $10,150

Lawyers **$3,225**
   Williams & Jensen $1,000
   Others $2,225

Oil & Gas **$7,700**
   Atlantic Richfield $1,500
   Amoco Corp..$1,000
   Petroleum Marketers Assn $1,000
   Others $4,200

Pharmaceuticals **$3,000**
   None over $750

Real Estate **$7,500**
   National Assn of Realtors $6,000
   Mortgage Bankers Assn of America..................$1,000
   Others $500

Interest Group Ratings

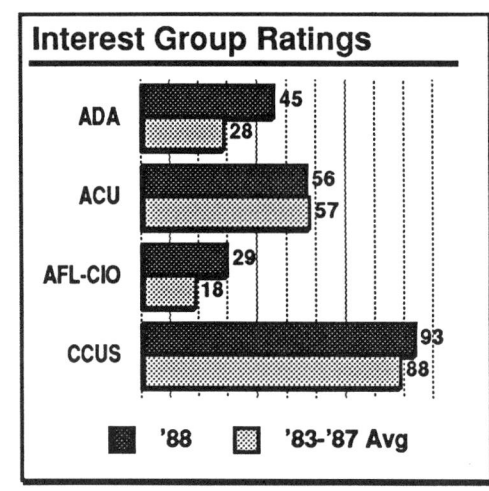

Savings Banks & Credit Unions **$3,600**
   Credit Union National Assn $1,850
   Washington Savings League $1,000
   Others $750

Securities Investment................................**$3,800**
   First Boston Corp $1,000
   Others $2,800

Small Business Organizations **$2,985**
   Small Business Council of America $2,000
   Others $985

Telecommunications **$12,450**
   Pacific Northwest Bell $3,150
   AT&T $2,000
   Continental Telecom $2,000
   Pacific Telesis Group $1,000
   United Telecommunications $1,000
   Others $3,300

Venture Capital **$4,000**
   National Venture Capital Assn $4,000

Other Major Business PACs

Printing Industries of America ....$1,257   Printing
Burlington Northern ....$1,000   Railroads
Corning Glass Works ....$1,000   Glass Prod
International Council of Shopping Centers ......$1,000   Retail

Labor

Labor Unions..**$5,500**
   Air Line Pilots Assn..$2,500
   American Fedn of State/County/Munic Employees $1,000
   National Rural Letter Carriers Assn $1,000
   Others $1,000

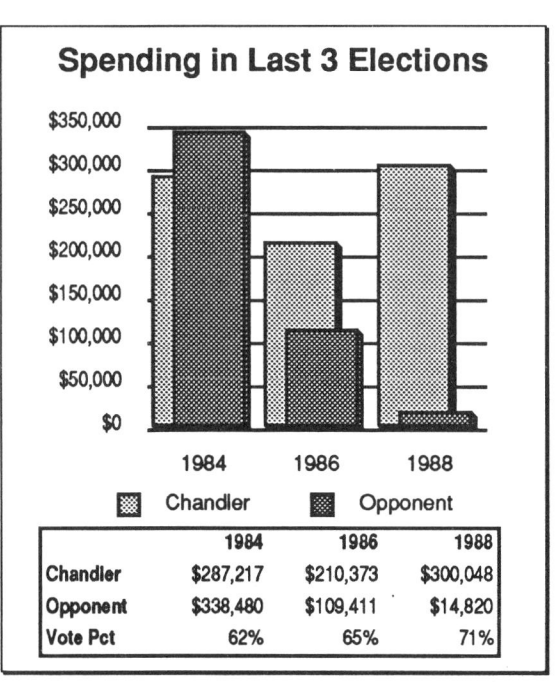

Spending in Last 3 Elections

	1984	1986	1988
Chandler	$287,217	$210,373	$300,048
Opponent	$338,480	$109,411	$14,820
Vote Pct	62%	65%	71%

---

* Contributions came from more than one PAC affiliated
  with this sponsor.

Jim Chapman, D-Texas (1)

First elected: 1986
Total receipts: $541,159
Total from PACs: $270,430

1988 Committees & Subcommittees

Public Works and Transportation
Aviation
Water Resources

Science, Space and Technology
Energy Research and Development
Science, Research and Technology
Space Science and Applications

PAC Contribution Profile

Business

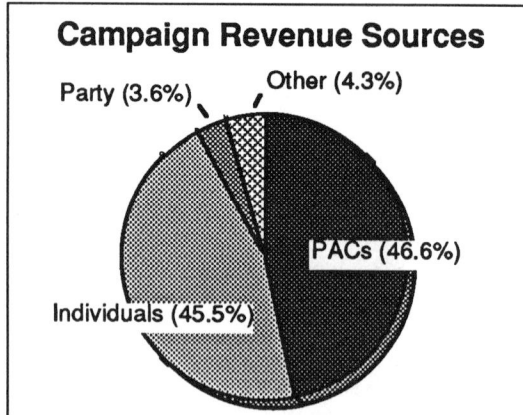

Campaign Revenue Sources

Party (3.6%)
Other (4.3%)
PACs (46.6%)
Individuals (45.5%)

Automotive	**$4,600**
National Auto Dealers Assn	$4,300
Others	$300
Aviation & Aerospace	**$24,300**
Texas Air	$7,000
American Airlines	$6,200
Aircraft Owners & Pilots Assn	$2,600
Textron Inc	$1,050
Morton Thiokol	$1,000
Others	$6,450
Construction	**$17,120**
National Assn of Home Builders	$10,000
Associated General Contractors	$3,000
Albert H Halff Associates	$1,000
Enserch Corp	$1,000
Others	$2,120
Dairy	**$14,300**
Associated Milk Producers	$9,500
Mid-American Dairymen	$4,500
Dairymen Inc	$300
Defense	**$3,150**
None over $900	
Electric Utilities	**$12,850**
Texas Utilities Electric Company*	$5,000
Houston Industries	$3,500
Central & South West Corp*	$2,250
Texas-New Mexico Power Company	$1,000
Others	$1,100

Food & Beverage	**$7,700**
National Restaurant Assn	$3,000
National Beer Wholesalers Assn	$1,000
Pepsico Inc	$1,000
Others	$2,700
Health Professionals	**$12,500**
American Medical Assn	$9,000
American Academy of Ophthalmology	$2,000
Texas Medical Assn	$1,000
Others	$500
Insurance	**$4,300**
National Assn of Life Underwriters	$3,000
Others	$1,300
Lawyers & Lobbyists	**$15,000**
Assn of Trial Lawyers of America	$10,000
Locke Purnell Rain Harrell	$2,500
Bracewell & Patterson	$1,100
Others	$1,400
Oil & Gas	**$10,857**
Occidental Oil & Gas	$2,507
Atlantic Richfield	$1,300
Bass Brothers Enterprises	$1,000
Mobil Oil	$1,000
Phillips Petroleum	$1,000
Texas Eastern Gas Transmission	$1,000
Others	$3,050
Real Estate	**$8,300**
National Assn of Realtors	$8,300
Sugar Growers	**$3,250**
None over $800	
Telecommunications	**$6,750**
GTE Corp*	$2,250
AT&T	$2,000
Southwestern Bell	$2,000
Others	$500
Tobacco	**$4,650**
Philip Morris	$2,100
RJR Nabisco	$1,000
Others	$1,550

PAC Totals by Category

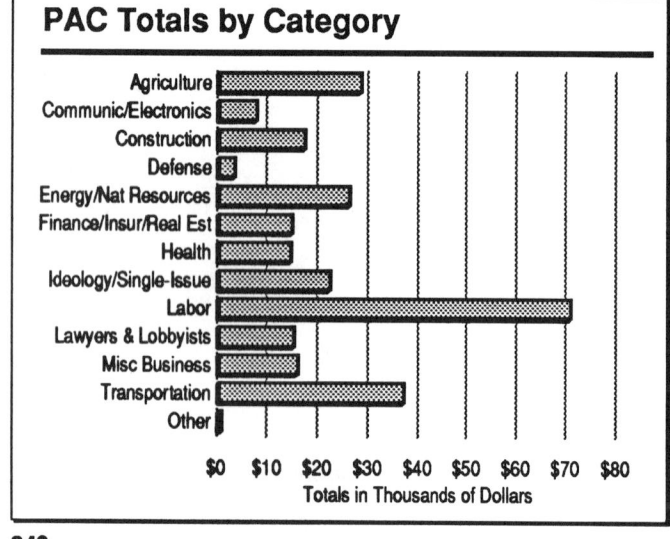

Agriculture
Communic/Electronics
Construction
Defense
Energy/Nat Resources
Finance/Insur/Real Est
Health
Ideology/Single-Issue
Labor
Lawyers & Lobbyists
Misc Business
Transportation
Other

$0 $10 $20 $30 $40 $50 $60 $70 $80
Totals in Thousands of Dollars

Trucking/Delivery...$5,850
    Yellow Freight System $2,300
    American Trucking Assns $1,100
    United Parcel Service $1,100
    Central Freight Inc $1,000
    Others $350

Other Major Business PACs

Lone Star Steel ....$2,050   Steel
J C Penney Company ....$1,100   Dept Store
American Hospital Assn ....$1,050   Hospitals
Freeport-McMoran Inc ....$1,000   Other Mining
International Paper Company ....$1,000   Paper Prod
Union Pacific Corp ....$1,000   Railroads

Labor

Bldg Trades/Industrial/Misc Unions $35,250
    United Auto Workers $15,000
    United Steelworkers $5,000
    Operating Engineers Union $4,000
    Carpenters & Joiners Union $3,600
    Intl Brotherhood of Electrical Workers $2,500
    Communications Workers of America $2,250
    Office & Prof Employees Union $1,000
    Others $1,900

Government & Postal Workers $15,350
    National Assn of Retired Federal Employees $8,000
    National Assn of Letter Carriers $2,600
    American Postal Workers Union $2,000
    Others $2,750

Teachers Unions $7,500
    National Education Assn $7,500

Transportation Unions $12,250
    Air Line Pilots Assn $5,000
    United Transportation Union $4,100
    Seafarers International Union $2,000
    Others $1,150

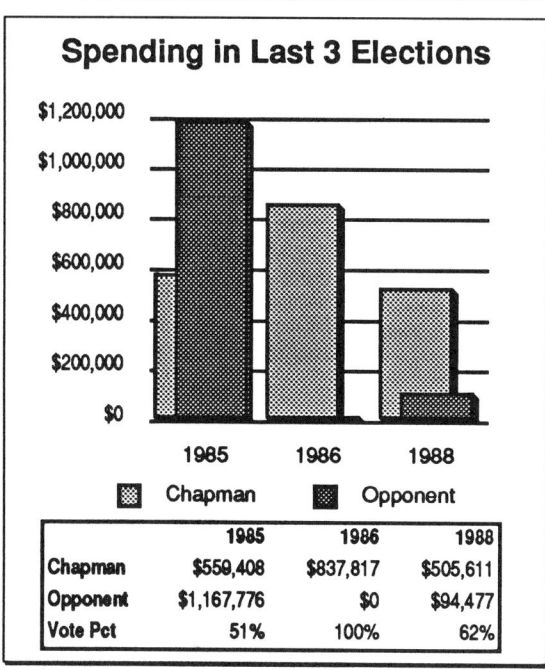

Spending in Last 3 Elections

	1985	1986	1988
Chapman	$559,408	$837,817	$505,611
Opponent	$1,167,776	$0	$94,477
Vote Pct	51%	100%	62%

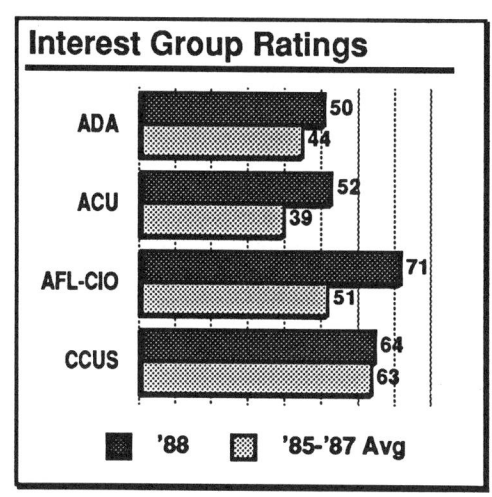

Interest Group Ratings

ADA   '88: 50   '85-'87 Avg: 44
ACU   '88: 52   '85-'87 Avg: 39
AFL-CIO   '88: 71   '85-'87 Avg: 51
CCUS   '88: 64   '85-'87 Avg: 63

■ '88   ▨ '85-'87 Avg

Ideological/Single-Issue

Democratic Leadership PACs.....................$14,500
    Majority Congress Committee (Jim Wright) $10,000
    Cmte for Democratic Opportunity (Bill Gray) $2,500
    Valley Education Fund (Tony Coelho) $2,000

Other Major Ideological/Single-Issue PACs
    National Rifle Assn $4,950
    National Cmte to Preserve Social Security $1,500
    TX PAC $1,000

Independent expenditures supporting Chapman

National Cmte to Preserve Social Security $1,337

---

* Contributions came from more than one PAC affiliated
  with this sponsor.

Dick Cheney, R-Wyo (At Large)

First elected: 1978
Total receipts: $295,437
Total from PACs: $216,983

1988 Committees & Subcommittees

Interior and Insular Affairs
National Parks and Public Lands
Water and Power Resources

Select Intelligence
Program and Budget Authorization (Ranking Republican)

PAC Contribution Profile

Business

Accountants	**$6,250**
American Institute of CPA's	$5,000
Others	$1,250
Air Transport	**$4,000**
Worldcorp Inc	$2,000
Eastern Airlines	$1,000
Texas Air	$1,000
Automotive & Trucking	**$12,000**
National Auto Dealers Assn	$4,000
Auto Dealers & Drivers for Free Trade	$3,500
Ford Motor Company	$1,000
IU International Corp	$1,000
Others	$2,500
Commercial & Savings Banks	**$9,500**
US League of Savings Assn	$3,000
American Bankers Assn	$2,500
Chase Manhattan	$1,000
Citicorp	$1,000
Wyoming Savings & Loan	$1,000
Others	$1,000
Construction	**$4,500**
Associated General Contractors	$1,500
National Assn of Home Builders	$1,000
Others	$2,000

Campaign Revenue Sources

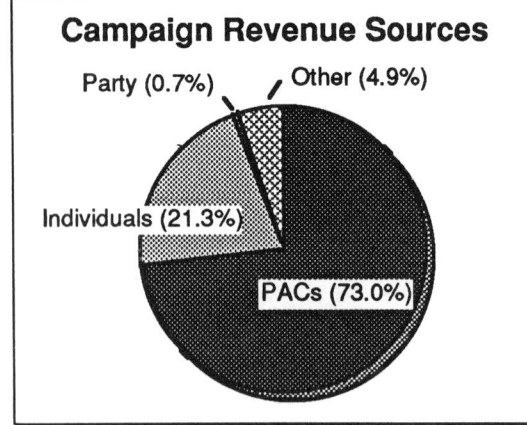

Party (0.7%)
Other (4.9%)
Individuals (21.3%)
PACs (73.0%)

Defense	**$10,000**
Lockheed Corp	$1,500
Martin Marietta Corp	$1,500
E-Systems/Corporate Division	$1,000
McDonnell Douglas	$1,000
TRW Inc	$1,000
United Technologies	$1,000
Others	$3,000
Electric Utilities & Equipment	**$11,525**
General Electric	$1,000
Middle South Utilities*	$1,000
Public Service Company of Colorado	$1,000
Others	$8,525
Food & Beverage	**$10,300**
National Restaurant Assn	$2,000
Pepsico Inc	$1,500
Food Marketing Institute	$1,000
Joseph E Seagram & Sons	$1,000
Nutrasweet Company	$1,000
Others	$3,800
Forest Products	**$3,250**
Boise Cascade	$1,000
Weyerhaeuser Company	$1,000
Others	$1,250
Health Professionals	**$16,000**
American Medical Assn	$10,000
American Dental Assn	$5,000
National Assn of Pharmacists	$1,000
Insurance	**$10,300**
Pacific Mutual Life	$1,500
Health Insurance Assn of America	$1,000
Independent Insurance Agents of America	$1,000
National Assn of Life Underwriters	$1,000
National Assn Mutual Insurance Agents	$1,000
Others	$4,800
Lawyers & Lobbyists	**$14,500**
Assn of Trial Lawyers of America	$10,000
Akin, Gump, Hauer & Feld	$1,000
Others	$3,500
Mining	**$10,750**
FMC Corp	$5,000
Dravo Corp	$1,000
Freeport-McMoran Inc	$1,000
National Coal Assn	$1,000
Others	$2,750

PAC Totals by Category

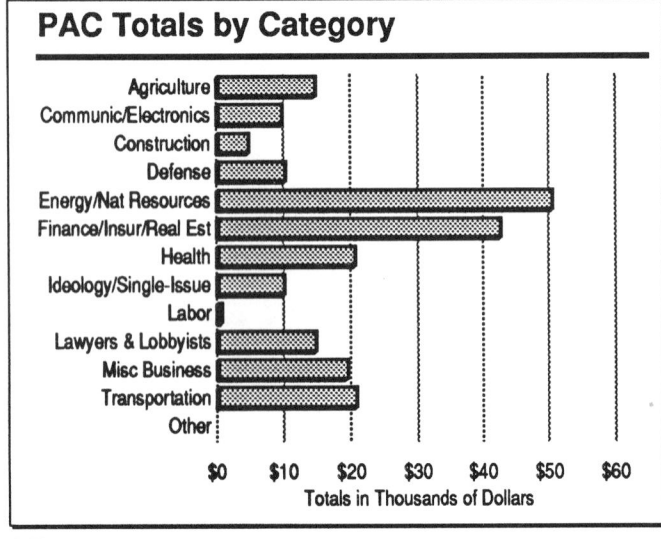

Agriculture
Communic/Electronics
Construction
Defense
Energy/Nat Resources
Finance/Insur/Real Est
Health
Ideology/Single-Issue
Labor
Lawyers & Lobbyists
Misc Business
Transportation
Other

$0 $10 $20 $30 $40 $50 $60

Totals in Thousands of Dollars

Oil & Gas $27,500

Tenneco Inc	$3,000
Atlantic Richfield	$2,000
Union Pacific Corp	$2,000
USX Corp*	$1,500
Chevron Corp	$1,000
Coastal Corp	$1,000
Columbia Hydrocarbon Corp	$1,000
Mobil Oil	$1,000
Petroleum Marketers Assn	$1,000
Sun Company	$1,000
Others	$13,000

Pharmaceuticals $3,800

Smithkline Beckman	$1,000
Others	$2,800

Real Estate $7,500

National Assn of Realtors	$5,500
Century 21 Real Estate	$1,000
Others	$1,000

Retail Sales $3,600

International Council of Shopping Centers	$1,000
Others	$2,600

Securities/Commodities Investment $9,552

Morgan Stanley & Company	$5,000
Chicago Mercantile Exchange	$2,000
First Boston Corp	$2,000
Others	$552

Telecommunications $5,750

AT&T	$2,500
Mountain Bell	$1,500
Others	$1,750

Tobacco $2,000

Philip Morris	$1,000
Others	$1,000

Interest Group Ratings

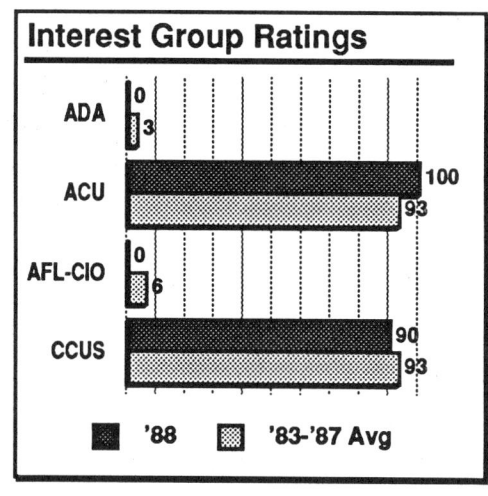

	'88	'83–'87 Avg
ADA	0	3
ACU	100	93
AFL-CIO	0	6
CCUS	90	93

Other Major Business PACs

American Sugarbeet Growers Assn	$1,000	Sugar
Hallmark Cards	$1,000	Publishing
Marriott Corp	$1,000	Hotel/Motel
Maytag Company	$1,000	Appliances
National Assn of Broadcasters	$1,000	TV/Radio
National Assn of Temporary Services	$1,000	EmployAgency
Santa Fe Southern Pacific	$1,000	Railroads
Texas Cattle Feeders Assn	$1,000	Feedlots

Ideological/Single-Issue

Ideological/Single-Issue $9,767

National PAC	$5,000	Pro-Israel
National Rifle Assn	$2,500	Pro-Guns
KidsPAC	$1,000	HealthWelfare
Others	$1,267	

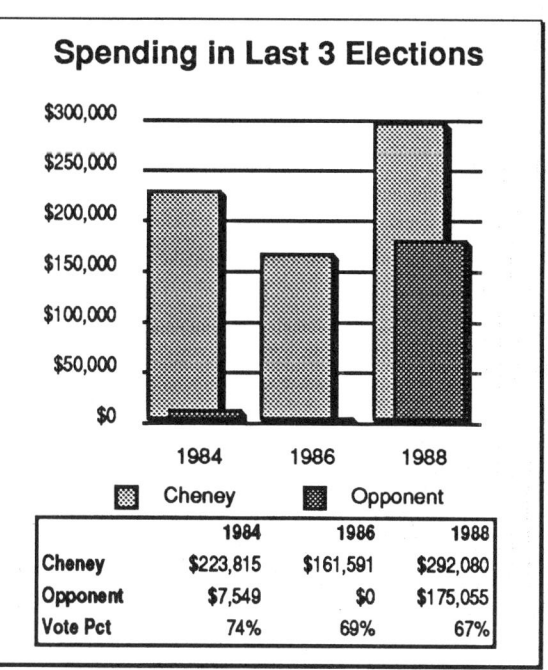

Spending in Last 3 Elections

	1984	1986	1988
Cheney	$223,815	$161,591	$292,080
Opponent	$7,549	$0	$175,055
Vote Pct	74%	69%	67%

* Contributions came from more than one PAC affiliated with this sponsor.

James McClure Clarke, D-NC (11)

First elected: 1986
Total receipts: $507,787
Total from PACs: $278,867

1988 Committees & Subcommittees

Foreign Affairs
Africa
Arms Control, International Security and Science

Interior and Insular Affairs
Energy and the Environment
Insular and International Affairs
National Parks and Public Lands

Select Aging
Human Services

PAC Contribution Profile

Business

Campaign Revenue Sources

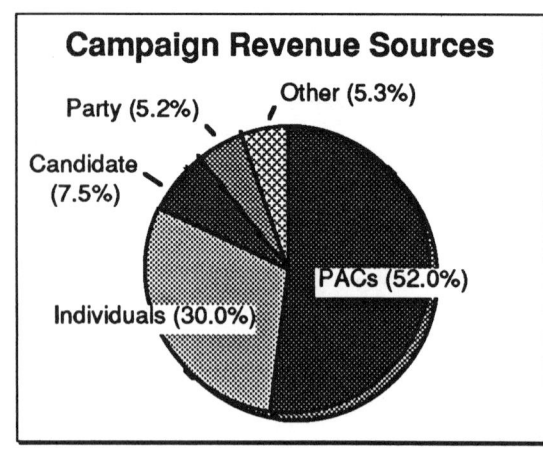

Party (5.2%)
Other (5.3%)
Candidate (7.5%)
Individuals (30.0%)
PACs (52.0%)

Electric Utilities	*$4,000*
ACRE (Action Committee for Rural Electrification)	$2,000
Carolina Power & Light	$2,000
Health Professionals	*$7,000*
American Medical Assn	$5,000
American Dental Assn	$1,500
Others	$500
Lawyers	*$7,750*
Assn of Trial Lawyers of America	$7,500
Others	$250
Real Estate	*$10,500*
National Assn of Realtors	$10,000
Others	$500
Telecommunications	*$3,750*
Southern Bell	$2,500
AT&T	$1,250
Textiles	*$3,800*
Burlington Industries	$1,300
Collins & Aikman Corp	$1,000
Others	$1,500
Tobacco	*$4,750*
Philip Morris	$2,000
RJR Nabisco	$2,000
Others	$750

Other Major Business PACs

Champion International Corp	$1,000	Paper Prod
Jefferson-Pilot Corp	$1,000	Insurance
National Assn of Social Workers	$1,000	Social Work
NCNB Corp	$1,000	Comml Banks
Winn-Dixie Stores	$1,000	Food Stores

PAC Totals by Category

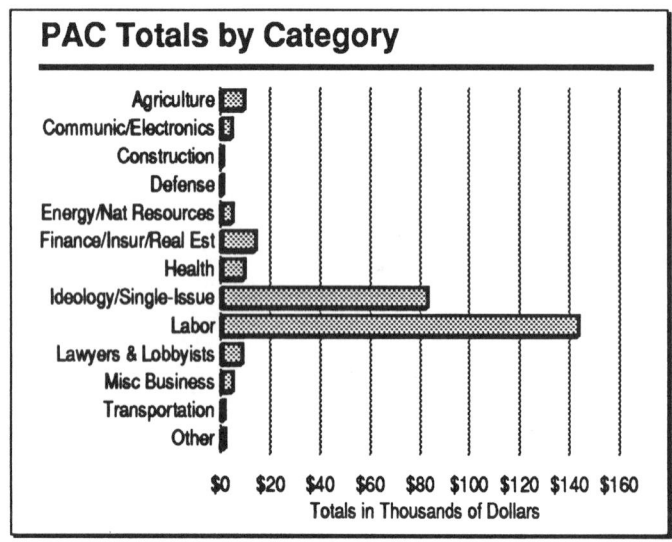

Agriculture
Communic/Electronics
Construction
Defense
Energy/Nat Resources
Finance/Insur/Real Est
Health
Ideology/Single-Issue
Labor
Lawyers & Lobbyists
Misc Business
Transportation
Other

$0 $20 $40 $60 $80 $100 $120 $140 $160
Totals in Thousands of Dollars

Labor

Bldg Trades/Industrial/Misc Unions $70,700

Machinists/Aerospace Workers Union	$10,000
Food & Commercial Workers Union*	$8,000
United Auto Workers	$7,750
AFL-CIO	$7,500
United Steelworkers	$6,000
Communications Workers of America	$5,500
Carpenters & Joiners Union	$4,000
Operating Engineers Union	$3,500
Intl Brotherhood of Electrical Workers	$3,000
Bakery, Confectionery & Tobacco Workers	$2,000
Rubber Cork Linoleum Plastic Workers	$2,000
Plumbers/Pipefitters Union	$1,750
Boilermakers Union	$1,500
Laborers' Political League	$1,250
Ladies Garment Workers Union	$1,250
Amalgamated Clothing & Textile Workers	$1,000
American Nurses Assn	$1,000
Electronic Machine Furniture Workers	$1,000
Sheet Metal Workers Union	$1,000
Others	$1,700

Government & Postal Workers $34,750

American Fedn of State/County/Munic Employees	$10,000
National Assn of Letter Carriers	$10,000
National Assn of Retired Federal Employees	$8,000
American Postal Workers Union	$4,000
Others	$2,750

Teachers Unions $10,000

National Education Assn	$10,000

Transportation Unions $25,750

Teamsters Union	$10,000
Amalgamated Transit Union	$4,500
Air Line Pilots Assn	$3,500
Seafarers International Union	$3,500
Marine Engineers District 2 Maritime Officers	$1,000
Others	$3,250

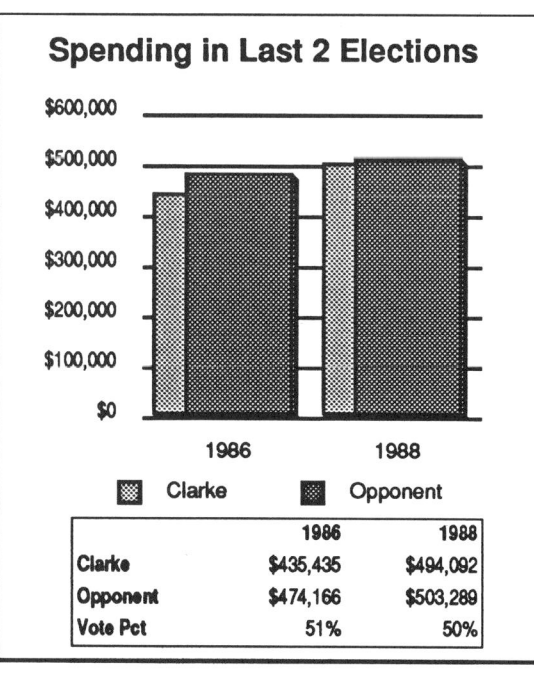

Spending in Last 2 Elections

	1986	1988
Clarke	$435,435	$494,092
Opponent	$474,166	$503,289
Vote Pct	51%	50%

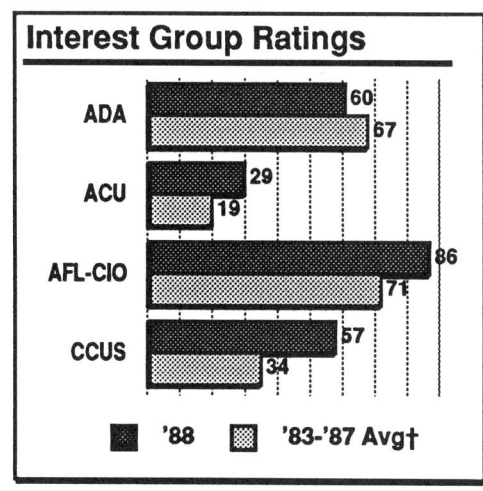

Interest Group Ratings

ADA 60 / 67
ACU 29 / 19
AFL-CIO 86 / 71
CCUS 57 / 34

■ '88   ▨ '83-'87 Avg†

Ideological/Single-Issue

Democratic/Liberal $16,495

National Cmte for an Effective Congress	$9,995
Class PAC	$5,000
Teamwork America	$1,000
Others	$500

Democratic Leadership PACs $22,000

Cmte for Democratic Opportunity (Bill Gray)	$6,000
Majority Congress Committee (Jim Wright)	$5,000
Cmte for the 100th Congress (Charles Rangel)	$3,000
America's Leaders' Fund (Dan Rostenkowski)	$2,000
House Leadership Fund (Tom Foley)	$2,000
Pax Americas (David Bonior)	$1,500
24th Cong Dist of California PAC (Henry Waxman)	$1,000
Valley Education Fund (Tony Coelho)	$1,000
Others	$500

Environmental $16,443

Sierra Club	$15,443
League of Conservation Voters	$1,000

Pro-Israel $20,800

National PAC	$10,000
Joint Action Cmte for Political Affairs	$2,000
Roundtable PAC	$1,500
Delaware Valley PAC	$1,000
Florida Congressional Cmte	$1,000
Washington PAC	$1,000
Others	$4,300

Other Major Ideological/Single-Issue PACs

National Cmte to Preserve Social Security	$2,000	Soc Secur
Council for a Livable World	$1,167	Pro-Peace
SANE/Freeze Inc	$1,100	Pro-Peace
National Council of Senior Citizens	$1,000	Soc Secur

Independent expenditures supporting Clarke

National Cmte to Preserve Social Security	$3,403

---

* Contributions came from more than one PAC affiliated
  with this sponsor.

William L. Clay, D-Mo (1)

First elected: 1968
Total receipts: $178,594
Total from PACs: $141,630

1988 Committees & Subcommittees

Education and Labor
Labor-Management Relations (Chairman)
Health and Safety

House Administration
Accounts
Elections
Libraries and Memorials

Post Office and Civil Service
Postal Operations and Services

PAC Contribution Profile

Business

Health Professionals **$6,000**
American Medical Assn $2,000
Oral & Maxillofacial Surgeons $1,500
American Dental Assn $1,000
Missouri Medical Assn $1,000
Others $500

Lawyers **$5,250**
Assn of Trial Lawyers of America $5,000
Others $250

Trucking/Delivery **$6,400**
United Parcel Service $4,650
Yellow Freight System $1,000
Others $750

Other Major Business PACs

Associated Milk Producers	$1,000	Dairy
National Assn of Home Builders	$1,000	Resid Constr
National Assn of Temporary Services	$1,000	EmployAgency
United Airlines	$1,000	Airlines

Campaign Revenue Sources

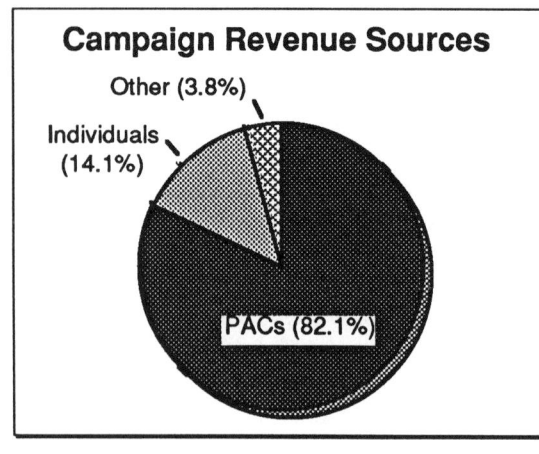

Other (3.8%)
Individuals (14.1%)
PACs (82.1%)

PAC Totals by Category

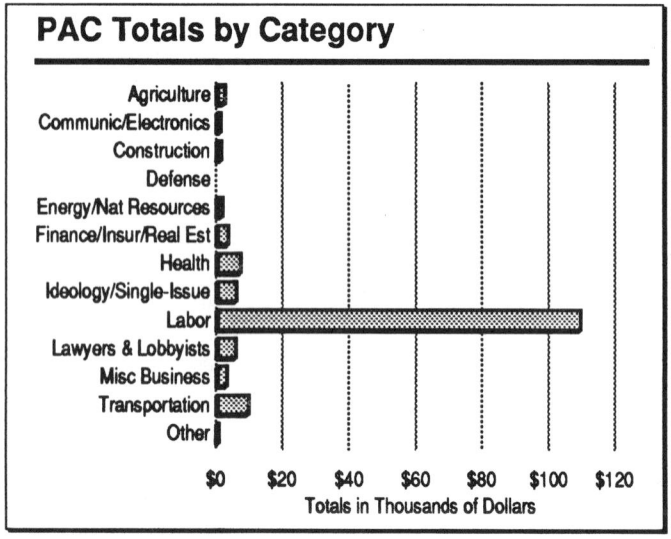

Agriculture
Communic/Electronics
Construction
Defense
Energy/Nat Resources
Finance/Insur/Real Est
Health
Ideology/Single-Issue
Labor
Lawyers & Lobbyists
Misc Business
Transportation
Other

$0 $20 $40 $60 $80 $100 $120
Totals in Thousands of Dollars

Labor

Bldg Trades/Industrial/Misc Unions $45,700

Operating Engineers Union	$7,500
United Auto Workers	$5,000
Food & Commercial Workers Union	$3,450
Intl Brotherhood of Electrical Workers*	$3,200
Machinists/Aerospace Workers*	$2,950
AFL-CIO*	$2,500
Carpenters & Joiners Union	$2,500
Ironworkers Union	$2,500
Laborers' Political League	$2,500
Sheet Metal Workers Union	$2,500
American Federation of Musicians	$2,000
Communications Workers of America	$1,250
United Steelworkers	$1,000
Bricklayers Union	$1,000
Others	$5,850

Government & Postal Workers $26,950

National Assn of Letter Carriers*	$5,950
American Fedn of State/County/Munic Employees	$5,000
American Postal Workers Union	$5,000
National Assn of Retired Federal Employees	$3,000
National Assn of Postmasters	$1,500
National League of Postmasters	$1,500
National Federation of Federal Employees	$1,250
National Alliance Postal/Federal Employees	$1,000
National Assn of Postal Supervisors	$1,000
Others	$1,750

Teachers Unions $8,975

National Education Assn	$7,750
American Federation of Teachers	$1,225

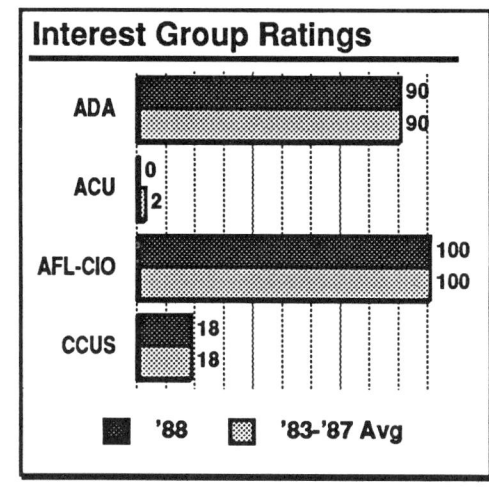

Interest Group Ratings

	'88	'83-'87 Avg
ADA	90	90
ACU	0	2
AFL-CIO	100	100
CCUS	18	18

■ '88   ▨ '83-'87 Avg

Transportation Unions $27,300

Teamsters Union	$10,000
Air Line Pilots Assn	$5,000
Seafarers International Union	$4,000
Marine Engineers District 2 Maritime Officers	$3,000
Amalgamated Transit Union	$1,800
Maritime Union of America	$1,250
Assn of Flight Attendants	$1,000
Others	$1,250

Ideological/Single-Issue

Ideological & Single-Issue $4,500

National Cmte to Preserve Social Security	$2,000	Soc Secur
St Louisians for Better Government	$1,000	Pro-Israel
Valley Education Fund (Tony Coelho)	$1,000	Dem Leaders
Others	$1,500	

Independent expenditures supporting Clay

Letter Carriers Branch #343	$2,000
Teamsters Union	$2,000
National Cmte to Preserve Social Security	$1,709

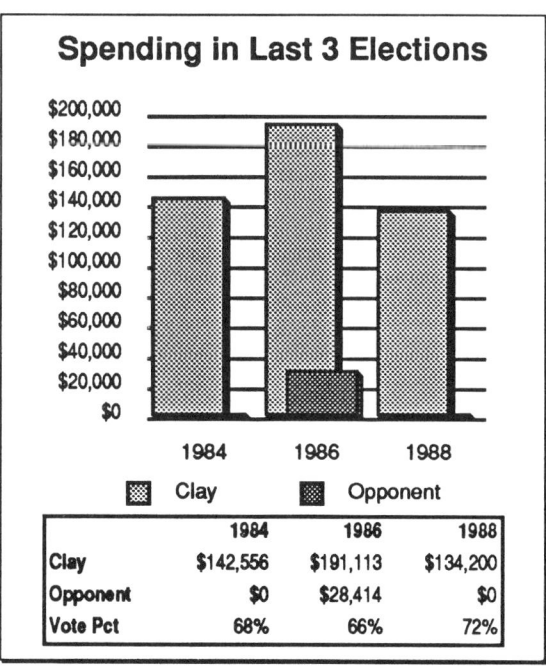

Spending in Last 3 Elections

	1984	1986	1988
Clay	$142,556	$191,113	$134,200
Opponent	$0	$28,414	$0
Vote Pct	68%	66%	72%

▨ Clay   ▨ Opponent

* Contributions came from more than one PAC affiliated with this sponsor.

Bob Clement, D-Tenn (5)

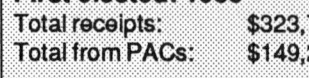

First elected: 1988
Total receipts: $323,734
Total from PACs: $149,200

1988 Committees & Subcommittees

Merchant Marine and Fisheries
Coast Guard and Navigation
Fisheries and Wildlife Conservation and the Environment

Public Works and Transportation
Investigations and Oversight
Public Buildings and Grounds
Surface Transportation

PAC Contribution Profile

NOTE: The PAC contributions listed on these pages include funds that Clement received in both of his 1988 races — the special election he won in January and the November general election in which he was elected to a full two-year term. The total receipts listed in the box above, and the percentages in the pie at right, refer only to the general election race.

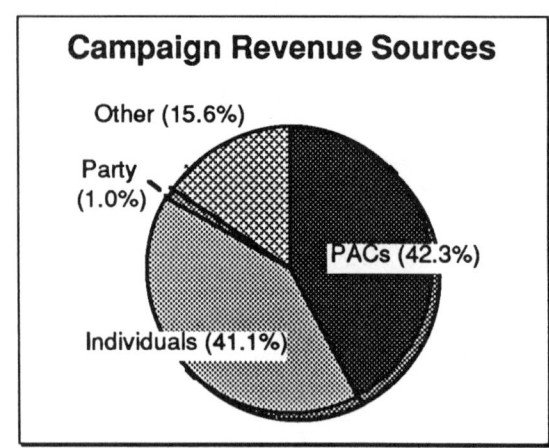

Campaign Revenue Sources

Other (15.6%)
Party (1.0%)
PACs (42.3%)
Individuals (41.1%)

Business

Air Freight	**$10,000**
Federal Express Corp	$10,000
Automotive & Trucking	**$10,100**
National Auto Dealers Assn	$4,250
Consolidated Freightways	$1,000
Paccar Inc	$1,000
United Parcel Service	$1,000
Others	$2,850
Commercial Banks	**$16,600**
Third National Corp	$5,500
Sovran Bank	$4,000
American Bankers Assn	$2,250
First American Corp	$2,000
First American Corp	$1,000
First Tennessee National Corp	$1,000
Others	$850
Construction	**$13,200**
National Assn of Home Builders	$10,000
Tennessee Road Builders Assn	$1,450
Associated Builders & Contractors	$1,000
Others	$750
Dairy	**$6,000**
Dairymen Inc-Tennessee	$3,000
Associated Milk Producers	$2,000
Mid-American Dairymen	$1,000

Food & Beverage	**$16,000**
Shoneys Inc	$12,000
Others	$4,000
Health Professionals	**$19,000**
American Medical Assn	$12,250
American Dental Assn	$3,500
American Academy of Ophthalmology	$2,000
Others	$1,250
Hospitals & Nursing Homes	**$9,450**
National Health Corp	$7,000
American Hospital Assn	$1,000
Others	$1,450
Insurance	**$14,450**
National Assn of Life Underwriters	$5,000
American General Insurance Company	$3,000
Independent Insurance Agents of America	$1,500
Mutual of Omaha	$1,500
Provident Life & Accident Insurance	$1,000
Others	$2,450
Lawyers	**$5,700**
Assn of Trial Lawyers of America	$5,000
Others	$700
Oil & Gas	**$6,300**
Atlantic Richfield	$1,000
Exxon Corp	$1,000
Others	$4,300
Real Estate	**$16,000**
National Assn of Realtors	$15,000
Others	$1,000
Telecommunications	**$6,000**
AT&T	$2,000
South Central Bell Telephone	$2,000
United Telecommunications	$1,000
Others	$1,000

PAC Totals by Category

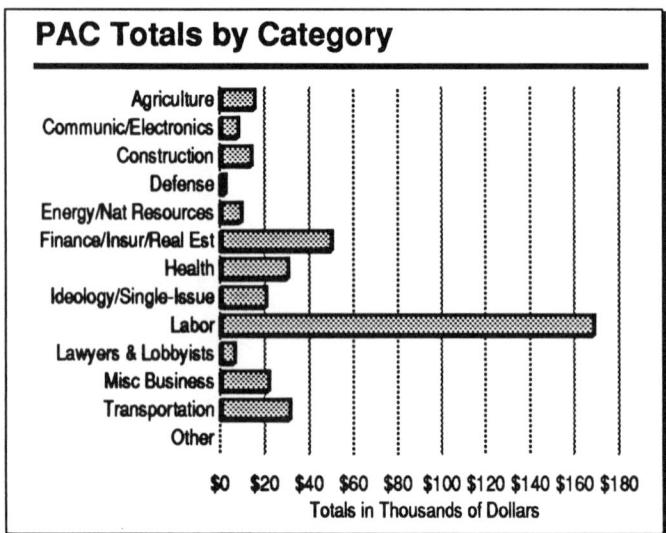

Agriculture
Communic/Electronics
Construction
Defense
Energy/Nat Resources
Finance/Insur/Real Est
Health
Ideology/Single-Issue
Labor
Lawyers & Lobbyists
Misc Business
Transportation
Other

$0 $20 $40 $60 $80 $100 $120 $140 $160 $180
Totals in Thousands of Dollars

Other Major Business PACs

Opryland USA	$2,850	Resorts
Aircraft Owners & Pilots Assn	$2,000	Genl Aviation
CSX Transportation Inc*	$1,750	Sea Transport
Philip Morris	$1,750	Tobacco
Tenneco Inc	$1,500	Sea Transport
Textron Inc	$1,500	Air Defense
ASCAP	$1,000	Live Music
Credit Union National Assn	$1,000	CreditUnion
Holiday Inns	$1,000	Hotel/Motel
RJR Nabisco	$1,000	Tobacco
Schering-Plough Corp	$1,000	Pharmaceut
Service Corporation International	$1,000	Funeral Svcs
Tennessee League of Savings Institutions	$1,000	SavingsBank
Tennessee Walking Horse Breeders	$1,000	Livestock

Labor

Bldg Trades/Industrial/Misc Unions	$82,450
United Auto Workers	$15,000
Machinists/Aerospace Workers Union	$13,000
AFL-CIO*	$8,250
Carpenters & Joiners Union	$8,000
United Steelworkers	$7,500
Intl Brotherhood of Electrical Workers	$5,000
Food & Commercial Workers Union	$4,500
Operating Engineers Union	$4,000
Laborers' Political League	$2,500
Sheet Metal Workers Union	$2,500
Communications Workers of America	$2,000
United Paperworkers	$2,000
Amalgamated Clothing & Textile Workers	$1,500
Plumbers/Pipefitters Union	$1,500
Ironworkers Union	$1,000
Rubber Cork Linoleum Plastic Workers	$1,000
Others	$3,200

Interest Group Ratings

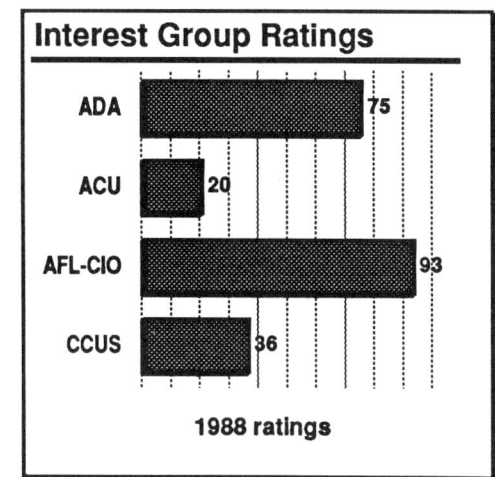

1988 ratings

ADA	75
ACU	20
AFL-CIO	93
CCUS	36

Government & Postal Workers	$27,500
National Assn of Retired Federal Employees	$9,000
American Fedn of State/County/Munic Employees	$7,500
National Assn of Letter Carriers	$7,000
American Postal Workers Union	$1,500
American Federation of Government Employees	$1,000
International Assn of Firefighters	$500
National League of Postmasters	$500
National Rural Letter Carriers Assn	$500

Teachers Unions	$12,250
National Education Assn	$7,750
American Federation of Teachers	$4,500

Transportation Unions	$45,750
Teamsters Union	$20,000
Amalgamated Transit Union	$7,500
Air Line Pilots Assn	$5,000
Seafarers International Union	$5,000
Marine Engineers District 2 Maritime Officers	$4,000
United Transportation Union	$2,000
Others	$2,250

Ideological/Single-Issue

Democratic Leadership PACs	$8,750
Majority Congress Committee (Jim Wright)	$5,000
Valley Education Fund (Tony Coelho)	$2,500
House Leadership Fund (Tom Foley)	$1,000
Others	$250

Pro-Israel	$5,250
National PAC	$5,000
Delaware Valley PAC	$250

Other Major Ideological/Single-Issue PACs

National Cmte for an Effective Congress	$2,497	Dem/Liberal
National Cmte to Preserve Social Security	$1,250	Soc Secur
Tennessee Freeze Voters	$1,000	Pro-Peace

Independent expenditures supporting Clement

National Cmte to Preserve Social Security	$2,134

---

* Contributions came from more than one PAC affiliated
with this sponsor.

Spending in Last 2 Elections

	1988 Special	1988
Clement	$938,492	$291,818
Opponent	$316,887	$0
Vote Pct	51%	100%

William F. Clinger Jr., R-Pa (23)

First elected: 1978
Total receipts: $405,262
Total from PACs: $189,036

1988 Committees & Subcommittees

Government Operations
Environment, Energy and Natural Resources (Ranking Republican)

Public Works and Transportation
Investigations and Oversight (Ranking Republican)
Economic Development
Surface Transportation

Select Aging
Housing and Consumer Interests
Human Services

PAC Contribution Profile

Business

Accountants	**$5,000**
American Institute of CPA's	$5,000
Automotive	**$7,050**
National Auto Dealers Assn	$3,900
Auto Dealers & Drivers for Free Trade	$2,000
Others	$1,150
Aviation	**$4,950**
Aircraft Owners & Pilots Assn	$2,000
Boeing Company	$1,000
Others	$1,950
Chemicals	**$3,950**
Betz Laboratories	$1,000
Others	$2,950
Commercial Banks	**$8,305**
American Bankers Assn	$4,000
PennBancorp	$1,625
Others	$2,680
Construction	**$19,900**
National Utility Contractors Assn	$5,500
Associated General Contractors	$2,800
National Assn of Home Builders	$2,200
American Consulting Engineers Council	$1,000
National Society of Professional Engineers	$1,000
Others	$7,400

Campaign Revenue Sources

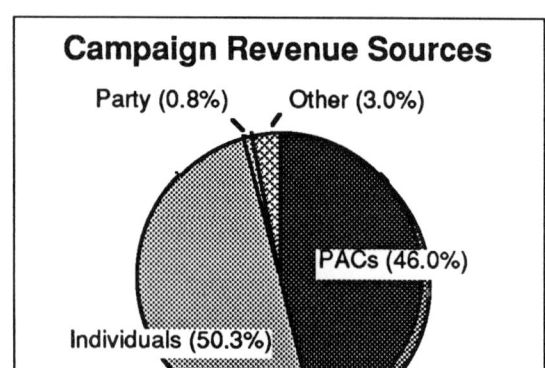

Party (0.8%)   Other (3.0%)
PACs (46.0%)
Individuals (50.3%)

Electric Utilities & Equipment	**$5,780**
ACRE (Action Committee for Rural Electrification)	$1,830
Gilbert Associates	$1,500
General Public Utilities	$1,200
Consumers Power Company	$1,000
Others	$250
Health Professionals	**$9,000**
American Medical Assn	$5,800
American Dental Assn	$2,000
Pennsylvania Medical Assn	$1,200
Insurance	**$5,300**
National Assn of Life Underwriters	$3,500
Others	$1,800
Lawyers	**$3,400**
Assn of Trial Lawyers of America	$2,300
Crowell & Moring	$600
Williams & Jensen	$500
Oil & Gas	**$21,690**
Columbia Gas Company*	$4,390
Tenneco Inc	$2,000
National Fuel Gas Corp	$1,700
Pennzoil Company	$1,250
Atlantic Richfield	$1,000
National Propane Gas Assn	$1,000
Sun Company	$1,000
Transco Energy Company	$1,000
Others	$8,350
Packaging & Glass Products	**$4,600**
Owens-Illinois	$1,600
Brockway Glass Company	$1,500
PPG Industries	$1,000
Others	$500
Real Estate	**$8,550**
National Assn of Realtors	$8,300
Others	$250
Sugar Growers	**$4,100**
American Sugarbeet Growers Assn	$1,400
Great Lakes Sugar Beet Growers	$1,000
Others	$1,700

PAC Totals by Category

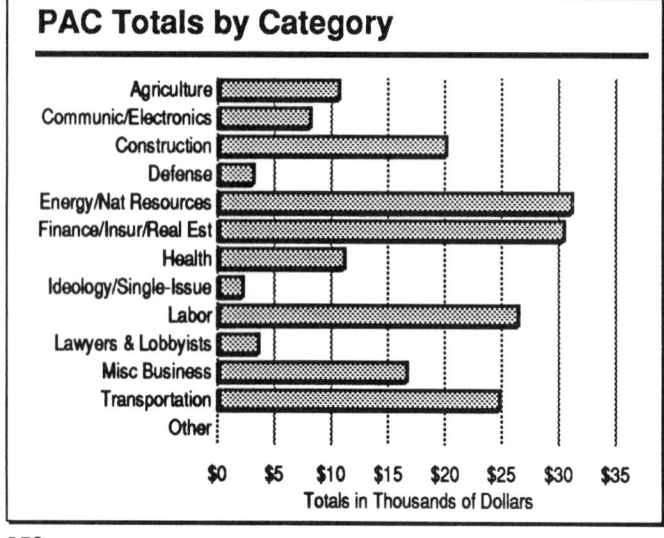

Agriculture
Communic/Electronics
Construction
Defense
Energy/Nat Resources
Finance/Insur/Real Est
Health
Ideology/Single-Issue
Labor
Lawyers & Lobbyists
Misc Business
Transportation
Other

$0 $5 $10 $15 $20 $25 $30 $35
Totals in Thousands of Dollars

Telecommunications *$7,400*

    AT&T $2,100
    Bell Telephone of Pennsylvania $1,650
    Continental Telecom $1,500
    Others $2,150

Trucking/Delivery *$8,500*

    United Parcel Service $3,700
    North American Van Lines $1,550
    American Trucking Assns $1,350
    Others $1,900

Other Major Business PACs

International Paper Company	$2,000	Paper Prod
Goldman Sachs	$1,750	Investmt Bank
Waste Management Inc	$1,600	Waste Mgmt
National Electric Sign Assn	$1,150	Outdoor Adv
Union Pacific Corp	$1,100	Railroads
American Textile Manufacturers Institute	$1,050	Textiles
Allied-Signal	$1,000	Air Defense
General Mills	$1,000	Food Prod
National Beer Wholesalers Assn	$1,000	Liquor Whlsl

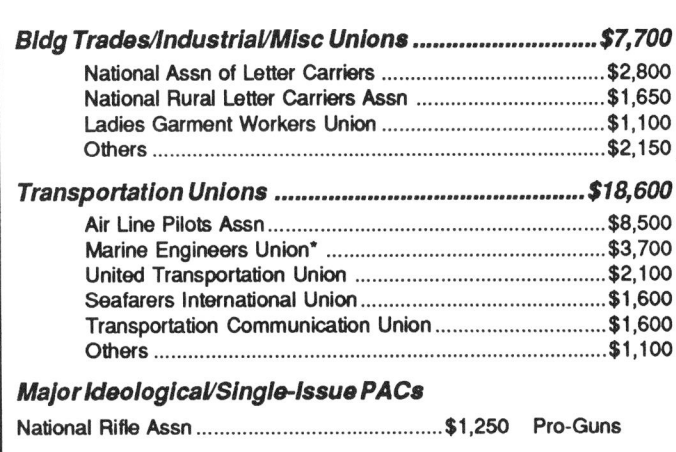

Interest Group Ratings

ADA 25 / 33
ACU 63 / 48
AFL-CIO 62 / 50
CCUS 86 / 67

■ '88   ▨ '83-'87 Avg

Labor

Bldg Trades/Industrial/Misc Unions *$7,700*

    National Assn of Letter Carriers $2,800
    National Rural Letter Carriers Assn $1,650
    Ladies Garment Workers Union $1,100
    Others $2,150

Transportation Unions *$18,600*

    Air Line Pilots Assn $8,500
    Marine Engineers Union* $3,700
    United Transportation Union $2,100
    Seafarers International Union $1,600
    Transportation Communication Union $1,600
    Others $1,100

Major Ideological/Single-Issue PACs

National Rifle Assn .... $1,250   Pro-Guns

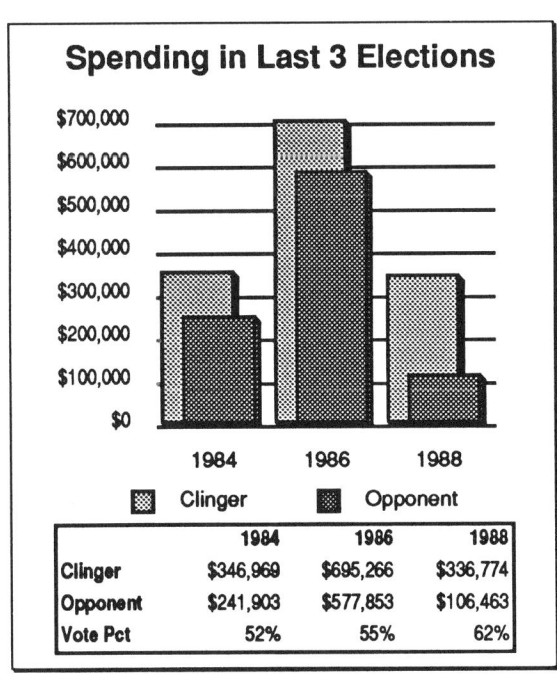

Spending in Last 3 Elections

▨ Clinger   ■ Opponent

	1984	1986	1988
Clinger	$346,969	$695,266	$336,774
Opponent	$241,903	$577,853	$106,463
Vote Pct	52%	55%	62%

---

* Contributions came from more than one PAC affiliated
  with this sponsor.

Dan Coats, R-Ind (4)

1988-1989 Committees & Subcommittees

Energy and Commerce
Health and the Environment
Oversight and Investigations
Telecommunications and Finance

Select Children, Youth and Families (Ranking Republican)

First elected: 1980
Total receipts: $351,827
Total from PACs: $190,152

PAC Contribution Profile

Business

Campaign Revenue Sources

Other (9.8%)
Party (0.8%)
PACs (50.3%)
Individuals (39.2%)

Agriculture	**$8,510**
Indiana Farm Bureau	$3,000
Navistar International	$1,510
Philip Morris	$1,500
Others	$2,500
Automotive & Trucking	**$11,000**
National Auto Dealers Assn	$4,250
North American Van Lines	$2,150
Auto Dealers & Drivers for Free Trade	$2,000
Others	$2,600
Commercial Banks	**$9,850**
Banc One Corp	$4,000
American Bankers Assn	$2,000
Lincoln Financial Corp	$1,300
Bankers Trust	$1,000
Others	$1,550
Defense	**$3,050**
United Technologies	$1,000
Others	$2,050
Electric Utilities	**$13,950**
Public Service Company of Indiana	$1,250
Southern Company*	$1,200
Middle South Utilities*	$1,000
Others	$10,500
Food & Beverage	**$7,850**
Central Soya Company	$1,700
Others	$6,150

Health Professionals	**$19,050**
American Medical Assn	$9,450
American Dental Assn	$3,500
Cmte for Quality Orthopedic Health Care	$1,500
Oral & Maxillofacial Surgeons	$1,500
American College of Emergency Physicians	$1,000
Others	$2,100
Insurance	**$15,575**
Lincoln National Corp	$2,875
National Assn of Life Underwriters	$2,500
National Assn of Independent Insurers	$1,250
American Council of Life Insurance	$1,000
Midwestern United Life Insurance	$1,000
Others	$6,950
Mining	**$3,550**
Phelps Dodge Corp	$1,050
Others	$2,500
Oil & Gas	**$9,300**
Atlantic Richfield	$1,000
Coastal Corp	$1,000
Union Pacific Corp	$1,000
Others	$6,300
Pharmaceuticals	**$10,550**
Eli Lilly & Company	$1,500
Pfizer Inc	$1,000
Others	$8,050
Real Estate	**$8,000**
National Assn of Realtors	$8,000
Securities/Commodities Investment	**$6,000**
Travelers Corp	$1,500
Chicago Board of Trade	$1,250
Morgan Stanley & Company	$1,000
Others	$2,250

PAC Totals by Category

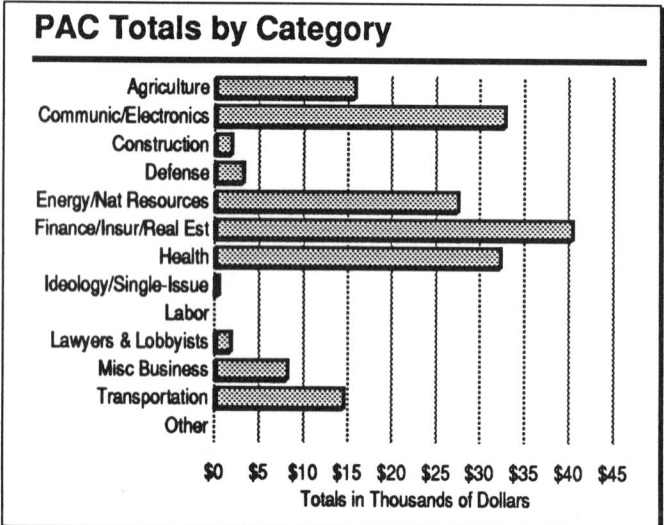

Agriculture
Communic/Electronics
Construction
Defense
Energy/Nat Resources
Finance/Insur/Real Est
Health
Ideology/Single-Issue
Labor
Lawyers & Lobbyists
Misc Business
Transportation
Other

$0 $5 $10 $15 $20 $25 $30 $35 $40 $45
Totals in Thousands of Dollars

Telecommunications **$27,350**

AT&T	$7,000
Indiana Bell Telephone	$2,300
United Telecommunications	$2,000
Continental Telecom	$1,500
GTE Corp	$1,300
Pacific Telesis Group	$1,250
BellSouth Services	$1,000
Corning Glass Works	$1,000
ITT Corp	$1,000
US Telephone Assn	$1,000
Others	$8,000

TV & Movies **$5,250**

National Cable Television Assn	$3,000
National Assn of Broadcasters	$1,000
Others	$1,250

Other Major Business PACs

Holiday Inns	$1,000	Hotel/Motel
National Assn of Home Builders	$1,000	Resid Constr
National Assn of Temporary Services	$1,000	EmployAgency

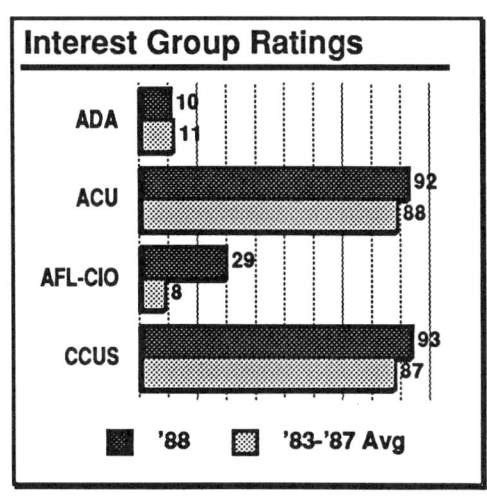

Interest Group Ratings

	'88	'83-'87 Avg
ADA	10	11
ACU	92	88
AFL-CIO	29	8
CCUS	93	87

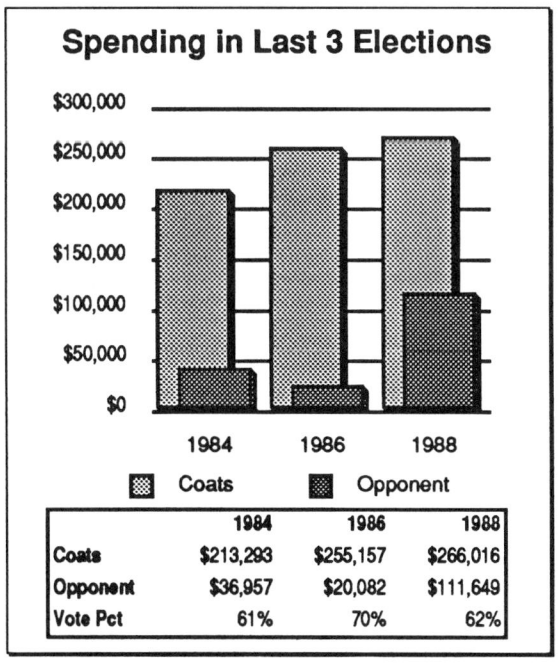

Spending in Last 3 Elections

	1984	1986	1988
Coats	$213,293	$255,157	$266,016
Opponent	$36,957	$20,082	$111,649
Vote Pct	61%	70%	62%

Coats / Opponent

---

* Contributions came from more than one PAC affiliated
  with this sponsor.

Howard Coble, R-NC (6)

First elected: 1984
Total receipts: $736,254
Total from PACs: $282,524

1988 Committees & Subcommittees

Judiciary
Administrative Law and Governmental Relations (Ranking Republican)
Courts, Civil Liberties and the Administration of Justice

Merchant Marine and Fisheries
Coast Guard and Navigation
Merchant Marine
Panama Canal/Outer Continental Shelf

PAC Contribution Profile

Business

Accountants	**$6,550**
American Institute of CPA's	$5,000
Others	$1,550
Automotive	**$19,200**
Auto Dealers & Drivers for Free Trade	$7,500
National Auto Dealers Assn	$6,850
Eaton Corp	$3,000
Dana Corp	$1,000
Others	$850
Broadcasting & Entertainment	**$11,300**
National Cable Television Assn	$4,000
National Assn of Broadcasters	$1,650
Motion Picture Assn of America	$1,250
ASCAP	$1,000
Others	$3,400
Business Associations	**$9,154**
National Fedn of Independent Business	$6,584
Business Industry PAC	$2,249
Others	$321
Chemicals	**$8,900**
Dow Chemical*	$4,500
Dow Corning Corp/Employees	$1,000
Sonoco Products	$1,000
Others	$2,400
Construction	**$14,650**
National Assn of Home Builders	$4,500
Associated General Contractors	$2,500
Wall & Ceiling/Gypsum Contractors	$1,100

(continued in next column)

Campaign Revenue Sources

Other (3.5%)
Party (7.8%)
PACs (37.6%)
Individuals (50.9%)

Construction (cont'd)	
American Subcontractors Assn	$1,000
Associated Builders & Contractors	$1,000
Caterpillar Tractor	$1,000
Others	$3,550
Defense	**$7,100**
Harris Corp	$1,500
Northrop Corp	$1,500
Textron Inc	$1,350
Martin Marietta Corp	$1,000
Others	$1,750
Electric Utilities	**$10,550**
Duke Power Company	$4,600
Carolina Power & Light	$2,000
National Rural Electric Co-op Assn	$1,000
Others	$2,950
Financial Institutions	**$11,050**
Credit Union National Assn	$3,200
US League of Savings Assn	$1,750
Barnett Banks of Florida	$1,500
Branch Banking & Trust	$1,000
Others	$3,600
Food & Beverage	**$8,000**
National Restaurant Assn	$2,000
Food Marketing Institute	$1,400
Morrison Inc	$1,000
Others	$3,600
Health Professionals	**$10,175**
American Medical Assn	$5,600
American Dental Assn	$2,000
American Optometric Assn	$1,575
Others	$1,000
Insurance	**$19,475**
National Assn of Life Underwriters	$7,000
Jefferson-Pilot Corp	$2,750
American Council of Life Insurance	$1,350
Independent Insurance Agents of America	$1,350
Casualty & Surety Agents Assn	$1,000
Integon Corp	$1,000
Loews Corp/Lorillard	$1,000
Others	$4,025
Lawyers	**$9,550**
Assn of Trial Lawyers of America	$6,750
Others	$2,800

PAC Totals by Category

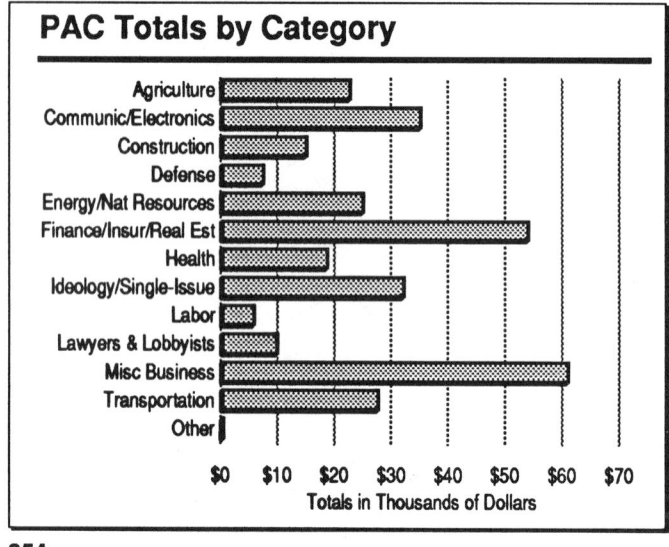

| Agriculture |
| Communic/Electronics |
| Construction |
| Defense |
| Energy/Nat Resources |
| Finance/Insur/Real Est |
| Health |
| Ideology/Single-Issue |
| Labor |
| Lawyers & Lobbyists |
| Misc Business |
| Transportation |
| Other |

$0 $10 $20 $30 $40 $50 $60 $70
Totals in Thousands of Dollars

Oil & Gas **$13,400**

Petroleum Marketers Assn	$2,000
Amoco Corp	$1,600
Phillips Petroleum	$1,500
Exxon Corp	$1,000
Mobil Oil	$1,000
Sun Company	$1,000
Others	$5,300

Packaging & Glass Products **$7,500**

PPG Industries	$4,000
Owens-Illinois	$1,500
Corning Glass Works	$1,000
Stone Container Corp	$1,000

Pharmaceuticals **$6,950**

Ciba-Geigy Corp	$1,700
Hoffman-La Roche	$1,600
Others	$3,650

Real Estate **$16,600**

National Assn of Realtors	$15,000
Mortgage Bankers Assn of America	$1,100
Others	$500

Telecommunications **$19,900**

Southern Bell	$8,250
United Telecommunications	$5,000
AT&T	$3,000
Continental Telecom	$1,000
Others	$2,650

Textiles **$17,050**

Cone Mills Corp	$6,000
Burlington Industries	$3,600
J P Stevens & Company	$1,750
American Textile Manfacturers Institute	$1,250
Collins & Aikman Corp	$1,100
Springs Mills	$1,000
Westpoint Pepperell	$1,000
Others	$1,350

Tobacco **$8,350**

RJR Nabisco	$3,500
Philip Morris	$3,000
Tobacco Institute	$1,500
Others	$350

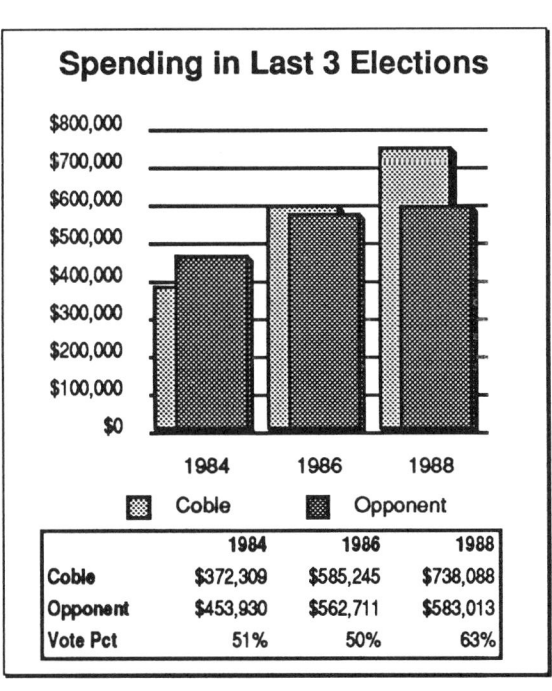

Spending in Last 3 Elections

	1984	1986	1988
Coble	$372,309	$585,245	$738,088
Opponent	$453,930	$562,711	$583,013
Vote Pct	51%	50%	63%

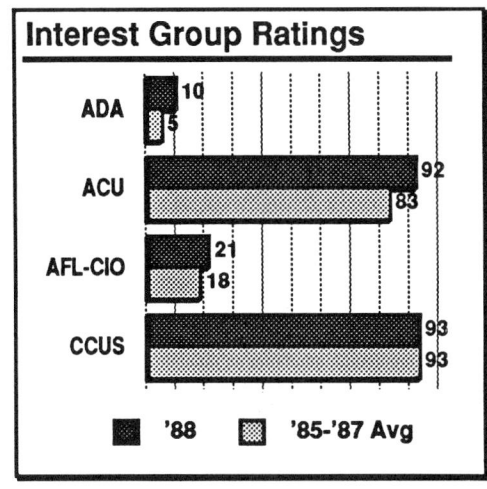

Interest Group Ratings

	'88	'85-'87 Avg
ADA	10	5
ACU	92	83
AFL-CIO	21	18
CCUS	93	93

Other Major Business PACs

American Furniture Manfacturers Assn	$2,850	Furniture
Blue Bell Inc	$2,000	Clothing
Cooper Industries	$2,000	Electronics
Weyerhaeuser Company	$1,750	Forestry
Dairymen Inc-North Carolina	$1,600	Dairy
Union Camp Corp	$1,350	Paper Prod
United Parcel Service	$1,350	Delivery
CSX Transportation Inc*	$1,300	SeaTransport
Precision Metalforming Assn	$1,000	MetalProduct
Square D Company	$1,000	Indust Equip
West Publishing	$1,000	Books & Mags

Labor

Labor Unions **$5,500**

Marine Engineers District 2 Maritime Officers	$5,500

Ideological/Single-Issue

Pro-Israel **$11,500**

National PAC	$5,000
Hudson Valley PAC	$1,250
Congressional Action Cmte of Texas	$1,000
Delaware Valley PAC	$1,000
Florida Congressional Cmte	$1,000
Roundtable PAC	$1,000
Others	$1,250

Other Major Ideological/Single-Issue PACs

Right to Work PAC	$5,000	Anti-Union
National Rifle Assn	$2,850	Pro-Guns
National Right to Life PAC	$2,709	Pro-Life
North Carolina Right to Life	$2,150	Pro-Life
Public Service Research Council	$1,600	Anti-Union
Council for National Defense	$1,457	Pro-Defense
Conservative Victory Cmte	$1,000	Repub/Conser
Policy Innovation PAC (Dick Armey)	$1,000	Repub Leader

Independent expenditures supporting Coble

National Right to Life PAC	$924
Others	$1,214

---

* Contributions came from more than one PAC affiliated
 with this sponsor.

Tony Coelho, D-Calif (15)

1988 Committees & Subcommittees

First elected: 1978
Total receipts: $837,955
Total from PACs: $415,666

House Majority Whip

Agriculture
Cotton, Rice and Sugar
Livestock, Diary and Poultry

House Administration
Accounts
Elections

Interior and Insular Affairs
National Parks and Public Lands
Water and Power Resources

PAC Contribution Profile

Business

Commercial Banks	$20,975
American Bankers Assn	$10,000
J P Morgan & Company	$3,500
First Interstate Bank/California	$2,600
Security Pacific Corp	$1,500
Others	$3,375

Dairy	$10,909
Associated Milk Producers	$4,500
Mid-American Dairymen	$3,000
Dairymen Inc	$2,500
Others	$909

Defense Aerospace	$12,750
Grumman	$2,500
Lockheed Corp	$2,500
McDonnell Douglas	$2,000
Others	$5,750

Food & Beverage	$34,250
National Beer Wholesalers Assn	$8,000
Wine Institute	$5,000
Food Marketing Institute	$2,000
Anheuser-Busch	$1,500
Nabisco Brands Inc	$1,500
Nutrasweet Company	$1,500
Wine & Spirits Wholesalers of America	$1,500
Joseph E Seagram & Sons	$1,250
Others	$12,000

Campaign Revenue Sources

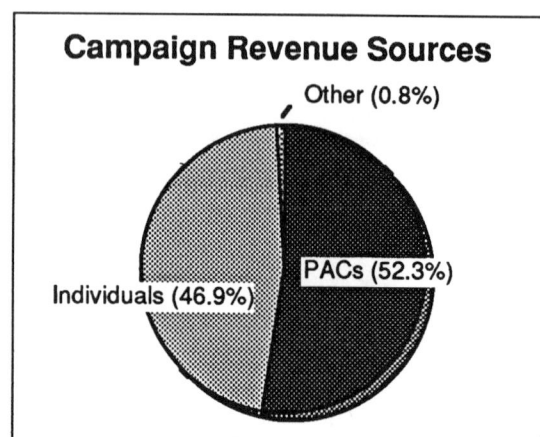

Other (0.8%)
PACs (52.3%)
Individuals (46.9%)

Fruits & Vegetables	$16,810
California Almond Growers Exchange	$5,250
Sun-Maid Growers of California	$2,500
Raisin Bargaining Assn	$1,750
Sunkist Growers	$1,500
Tri/Valley Growers	$1,460
Others	$4,350

Health Professionals	$20,250
American Medical Assn	$9,500
American Dental Assn	$5,000
American Optometric Assn	$1,500
American Nurses Assn	$1,250
Others	$3,000

Hospitals & Healthcare Services	$11,600
American Health Care Assn	$4,000
American Hospital Assn	$2,900
National Medical Enterprises Inc	$2,450
American Ambulance Assn	$1,500
Others	$750

Insurance	$25,500
National Assn of Life Underwriters	$9,000
American Council of Life Insurance	$2,500
Aetna Life & Casualty	$1,500
Independent Insurance Agents of America	$1,500
Metropolitan Life Insurance	$1,250
Others	$9,750

Lawyers & Lobbyists	$14,250
Assn of Trial Lawyers of America	$5,750
Dow, Lohnes & Albertson	$2,000
Others	$6,500

Oil & Gas	$21,000
Coastal Corp	$10,000
Union Pacific Corp	$2,000
Pacific Enterprises	$1,500
Others	$7,500

PAC Totals by Category

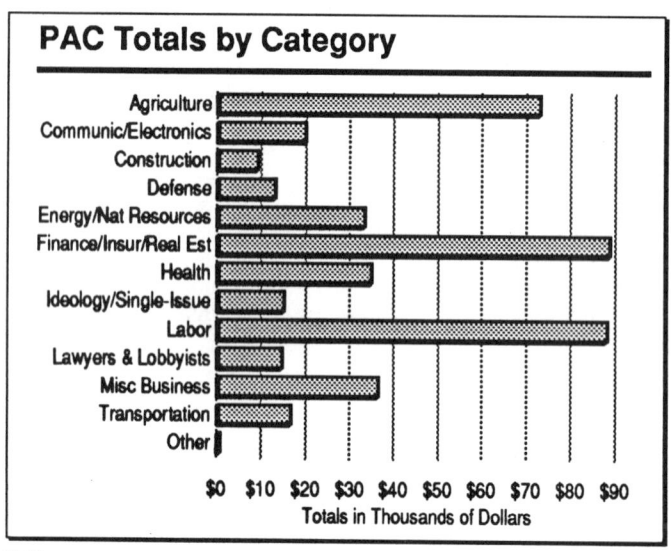

Agriculture
Communic/Electronics
Construction
Defense
Energy/Nat Resources
Finance/Insur/Real Est
Health
Ideology/Single-Issue
Labor
Lawyers & Lobbyists
Misc Business
Transportation
Other

$0 $10 $20 $30 $40 $50 $60 $70 $80 $90
Totals in Thousands of Dollars

Real Estate $11,750

National Assn of Realtors	$10,000
Newhall Land & Farming Company	$1,000
Others	$750

Savings Banks $10,395

Home Savings of America	$5,000
California League of Savings Institutions	$1,895
Others	$3,500

Securities/Commodities Investment $15,500

Goldman Sachs	$2,500
Commodity Exchange Inc	$1,500
Equitable Financial Services	$1,250
Prudential-Bache Securities	$1,250
Others	$9,000

Other Major Business PACs

American Institute of CPA's	$5,000	Accountants
AT&T	$5,000	LongDistance
Philip Morris	$3,500	Tobacco
Texas Air	$3,500	Airlines
Pacific Gas & Electric	$2,850	Gas & Electr
National Assn of Home Builders	$2,500	Resid Constr
Waste Management Inc	$2,500	Waste Mgmt
National Cable Television Assn	$2,250	CableTV
United Parcel Service	$2,250	Delivery
MCA Inc	$2,000	Movies
United States Tobacco Company	$2,000	Tobacco
Consolidated Freightways	$1,500	Trucking
J C Penney Company	$1,500	Dept Store
Montgomery Ward	$1,500	Dept Store
Westinghouse Electric	$1,500	NuclearEquip
Hallmark Cards	$1,250	Publishing

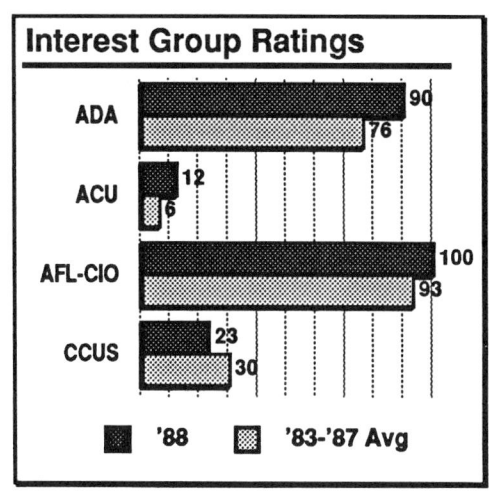

Interest Group Ratings

	'88	'83-'87 Avg
ADA	90	76
ACU	12	6
AFL-CIO	100	93
CCUS	23	30

Labor

Bldg Trades/Industrial/Misc Unions $51,475

Sheet Metal Workers Union	$7,500
United Auto Workers	$5,500
National Education Assn	$5,175
Carpenters & Joiners Union	$5,000
Operating Engineers Union*	$4,800
Laborers' Western Political League	$4,000
Machinists/Aerospace Workers Union	$3,000
Intl Brotherhood of Electrical Workers	$2,000
Ironworkers Union	$2,000
Plumbers/Pipefitters Union	$2,000
Bricklayers Union	$1,500
Communications Workers of America	$1,500
Painters & Allied Trades Union	$1,500
Food & Commercial Workers Union	$1,250
Others	$4,750

Government & Postal Workers $11,175

National Assn of Retired Federal Employees	$3,000
American Postal Workers Union	$1,500
International Assn of Firefighters	$1,500
National Rural Letter Carriers Assn	$1,500
National Assn of Letter Carriers	$1,375
Others	$2,300

Transportation Unions $24,800

Teamsters Union	$10,000
Air Line Pilots Assn	$5,000
Marine Engineers Union	$2,500
Amalgamated Transit Union	$2,000
Seafarers International Union	$2,000
Transportation Communication Union	$1,500
Others	$1,800

Ideological/Single-Issue

Ideological/Single-Issue $14,750

National Cmte to Preserve Social Security	$5,250	Soc Secur
Armenian-American PAC	$5,000	Ethnic
Human Rights Campaign Fund	$1,500	Gay Rights
Others	$3,000	

Independent expenditures supporting Coelho

National Cmte to Preserve Social Security	$1,798

Independent expenditures opposing Coelho

American Citizens for Political Action	$10,680

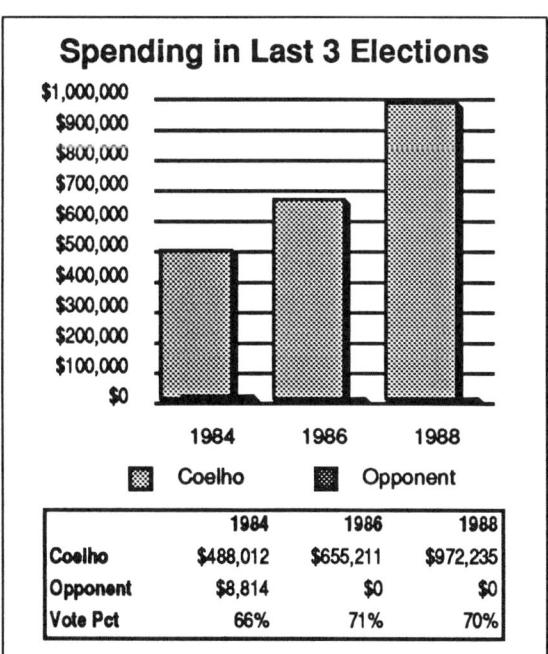

Spending in Last 3 Elections

	1984	1986	1988
Coelho	$488,012	$655,211	$972,235
Opponent	$8,814	$0	$0
Vote Pct	66%	71%	70%

Coelho — Opponent

---

* Contributions came from more than one PAC affiliated
  with this sponsor.

E. Thomas Coleman, R-Mo (6)

First elected: 1976	
Total receipts:	$305,961
Total from PACs:	$175,134

1988 Committees & Subcommittees

Agriculture
Conservation, Credit and Rural Development (Ranking Republican)
Department Operations, Research and Foreign Agriculture

Education and Labor
Postsecondary Education (Ranking Republican)
Human Resources

PAC Contribution Profile

Business

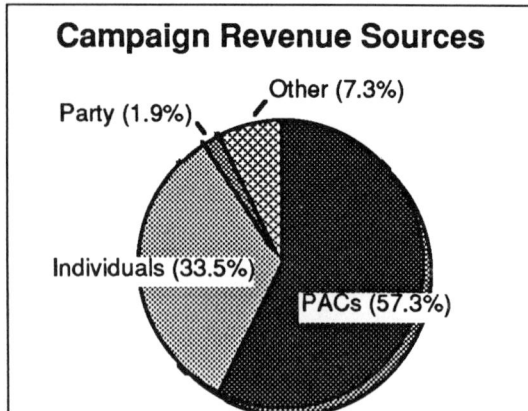

Campaign Revenue Sources

Other (7.3%)
Party (1.9%)
Individuals (33.5%)
PACs (57.3%)

Automotive	**$13,300**
Auto Dealers & Drivers for Free Trade	$6,000
National Auto Dealers Assn	$5,850
Ford Motor Company	$1,100
Others	$350
Commodities Trading	**$5,200**
Chicago Board of Trade	$3,000
Chicago Mercantile Exchange	$1,000
Others	$1,200
Construction	**$9,890**
Associated General Contractors	$2,700
National Utility Contractors Assn	$2,000
National Assn of Home Builders	$1,700
Sheet Metal/AirCon Contractors	$1,300
Others	$2,190
Dairy	**$6,700**
Mid-American Dairymen	$3,000
Associated Milk Producers	$2,500
Dairymen Inc	$700
Land O'Lakes Inc	$500
Defense	**$4,550**
Rockwell International	$1,000
Others	$3,550
Farm Organizations	**$3,650**
Missouri Farm Bureau Northwest District	$2,500
Others	$1,150

Financial Institutions	**$5,700**
American Bankers Assn	$1,000
Others	$4,700
Food & Beverage	**$16,450**
National Restaurant Assn	$2,000
Food Marketing Institute	$1,750
Pepsi-Cola Bottlers Assn	$1,750
ConAgra Inc	$1,500
A E Staley Manufacturing Company	$1,050
General Mills	$1,000
Pepsico Inc	$1,000
Pillsbury Company	$1,000
Others	$5,400
Forest Products	**$3,900**
Owens-Illinois	$2,000
Stone Container Corp	$1,000
Others	$900
Health Professionals	**$5,350**
American Medical Assn	$4,350
Missouri Medical Assn	$1,000
Insurance	**$9,044**
National Assn of Life Underwriters	$2,000
Business Mens Assurance Company	$1,500
General American Life Insurance	$1,000
Kansas City Life Insurance	$1,000
Shelter Mutual Insurance	$1,000
Others	$2,544
Lawyers	**$10,550**
Assn of Trial Lawyers of America	$10,000
Others	$550
Miscellaneous Agricultural	**$18,116**
Farmland Industries	$1,500
National Cattlemen's Assn	$1,166
American Veterinary Medical Assn	$1,000
Ecolab Inc	$1,000
Farm Credit Council	$1,000
Others	$12,450
Real Estate	**$8,660**
National Assn of Realtors	$8,000
Others	$660

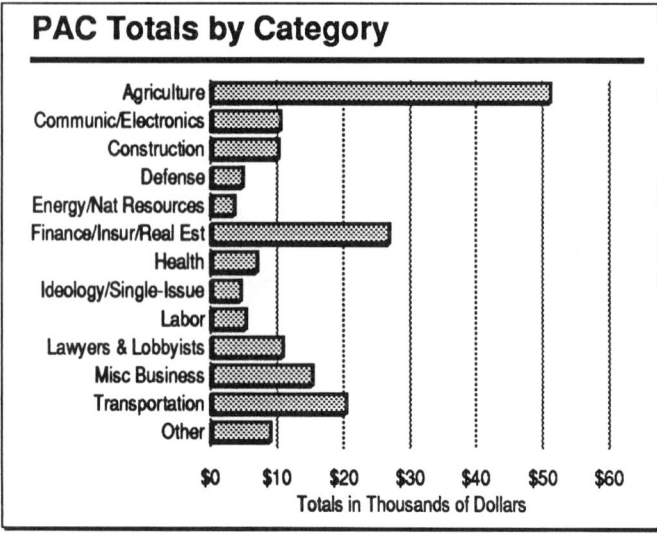

PAC Totals by Category

Agriculture
Communic/Electronics
Construction
Defense
Energy/Nat Resources
Finance/Insur/Real Est
Health
Ideology/Single-Issue
Labor
Lawyers & Lobbyists
Misc Business
Transportation
Other

$0 $10 $20 $30 $40 $50 $60
Totals in Thousands of Dollars

Interest Group Ratings

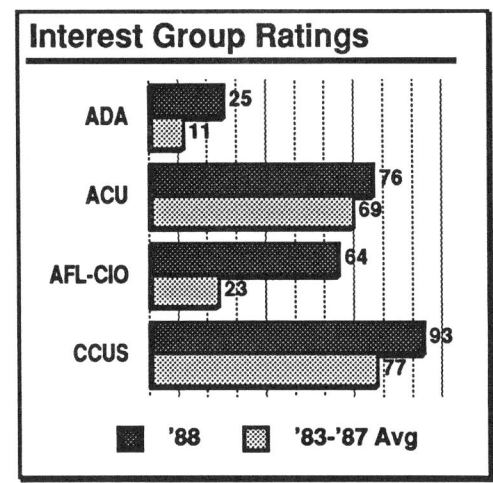

Group	'88	'83-'87 Avg
ADA	25	11
ACU	76	69
AFL-CIO	64	23
CCUS	93	77

■ '88   ▥ '83-'87 Avg

Sugar Growers **$2,950**

    American Sugarbeet Growers Assn $1,050
    Others $1,900

Telecommunications **$7,190**

    Southwestern Bell $2,500
    AT&T $1,600
    Continental Telecom $1,500
    Others $1,590

Trucking & Railroads **$4,650**

    Kansas City Southern $1,550
    Churchill Truck Lines $1,000
    Others $2,100

Vocational Tech Schools **$8,680**

    National Assn of Trade/Tech Schools $4,300
    Assn of Independent Colleges/Schools $2,580
    National Assn of Cosmetology Schools $1,400
    Others $400

Other Major Business PACs

Hallmark Cards	$2,440	Publishing
Higher Ed Mgmt/Resources Foundation	$1,732	Credit/Loans

Labor

Labor Unions **$5,000**

    Air Line Pilots Assn $1,500
    National Assn of Letter Carriers $1,500
    Others $2,000

Major Ideological/Single-Issue PACs

Council for National Defense .... $2,960   Pro-Defense

Independent expenditures supporting Coleman

Missouri Citizens for Life $2,110

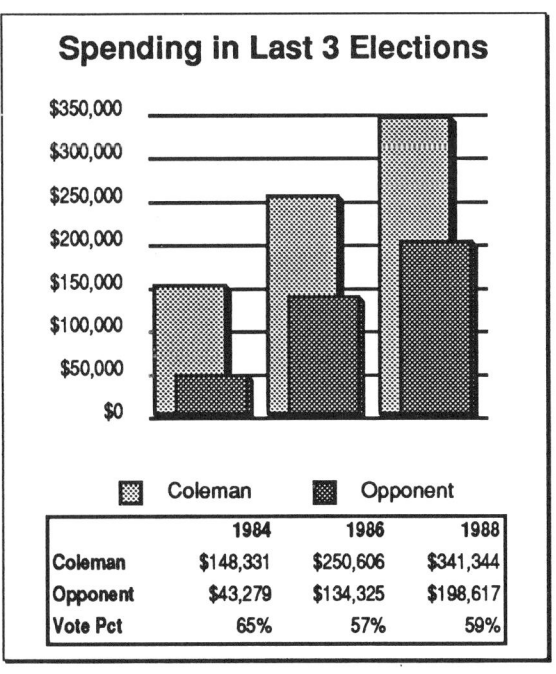

Spending in Last 3 Elections

	1984	1986	1988
Coleman	$148,331	$250,606	$341,344
Opponent	$43,279	$134,325	$198,617
Vote Pct	65%	57%	59%

▥ Coleman   ■ Opponent

Ronald D. Coleman, D-Texas (16)

First elected: 1982
Total receipts: $322,822
Total from PACs: $174,670

1988 Committees & Subcommittees

Appropriations
Military Construction
Treasury, Postal Service and General Government

PAC Contribution Profile

Business

Campaign Revenue Sources

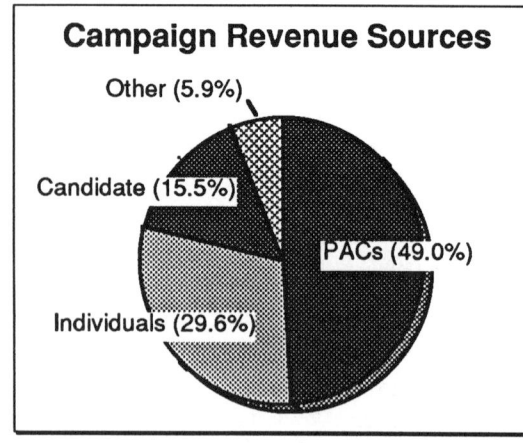

Other (5.9%)
Candidate (15.5%)
PACs (49.0%)
Individuals (29.6%)

Agriculture	**$5,750**
Philip Morris	$1,000
Others	$4,750

Airlines	**$3,350**
American Airlines	$1,800
Texas Air	$1,300
Others	$250

Commercial & Savings Banks	**$5,400**
MBank	$3,250
Texas Commerce Bancshares	$1,000
Others	$1,150

Construction	**$8,800**
Universal Services	$2,000
United Technologies	$1,600
Enserch Corp	$1,500
Associated General Contractors	$1,300
National Assn of Home Builders	$1,300
Others	$1,100

Defense	**$9,720**
LTV Aerospace & Defense Company	$1,500
BDM International	$1,100
Rockwell International	$1,100
TRW Inc	$1,000
Others	$5,020

Electric Utilities	**$4,700**
El Paso Electric	$3,750
Others	$950

Food & Beverage	**$3,400**
McDonald's Corp	$1,000
Others	$2,400

Health Professionals	**$4,300**
Texas Medical Assn	$2,000
American Medical Assn	$1,300
Others	$1,000

Lawyers	**$6,550**
Assn of Trial Lawyers of America	$5,000
Others	$1,550

Oil & Gas	**$8,200**
Atlantic Richfield	$1,700
El Paso Company	$1,500
Amoco Corp	$1,350
International Assn of Drilling Contractors	$1,100
Others	$2,550

Package Delivery	**$2,950**
United Parcel Service	$2,950

Real Estate	**$5,350**
National Assn of Realtors	$5,350

Telecommunications	**$3,500**
GTE (Southwest)	$1,500
Southwestern Bell	$1,500
Others	$500

Other Major Business PACs

National Assn of Life Underwriters	$1,500	Life Insurance
Independent Coal Operators Assn	$1,000	Coal
National Auto Dealers Assn	$1,000	Auto Sales

PAC Totals by Category

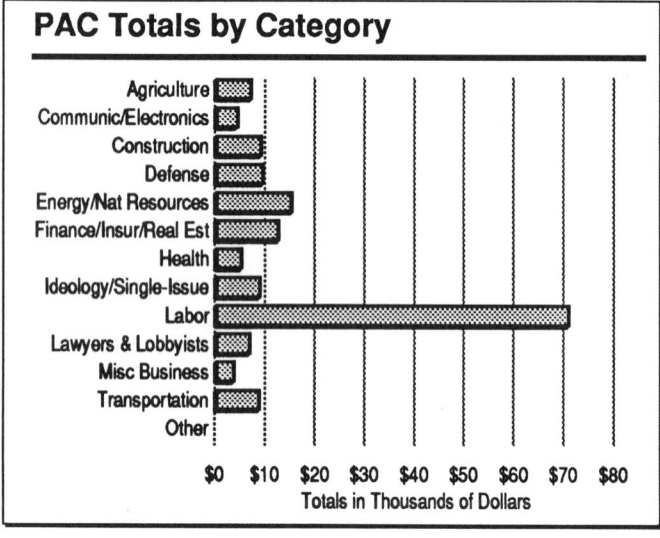

Agriculture
Communic/Electronics
Construction
Defense
Energy/Nat Resources
Finance/Insur/Real Est
Health
Ideology/Single-Issue
Labor
Lawyers & Lobbyists
Misc Business
Transportation
Other

$0 $10 $20 $30 $40 $50 $60 $70 $80
Totals in Thousands of Dollars

Labor

Bldg Trades/Industrial/Misc Unions $17,800
United Auto Workers $5,350
Carpenters & Joiners Union $2,500
Machinists/Aerospace Workers Union $1,650
Laborers' Political League $1,550
Intl Brotherhood of Electrical Workers $1,500
Operating Engineers Union $1,200
Amalgamated Clothing & Textile Workers $1,100
Others $2,950

Government & Postal Workers $25,400
National Assn of Retired Federal Employees $6,300
National Rural Letter Carriers Assn $4,850
American Postal Workers Unions $3,750
American Fedn of State/County/Munic Employees ... $3,000
National Assn of Letter Carriers $2,500
National Treasury Employees Union $2,350
Others $2,650

Teachers Unions $6,000
National Education Assn $6,000

Transportation Unions $21,350
Teamsters Union $7,000
Air Line Pilots Assn $4,000
Marine Engineers Union* $4,000
United Transportation Union $2,850
Seafarers International Union $2,000
Others $1,500

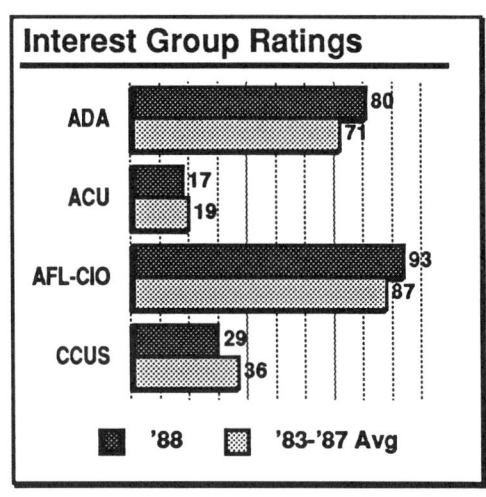

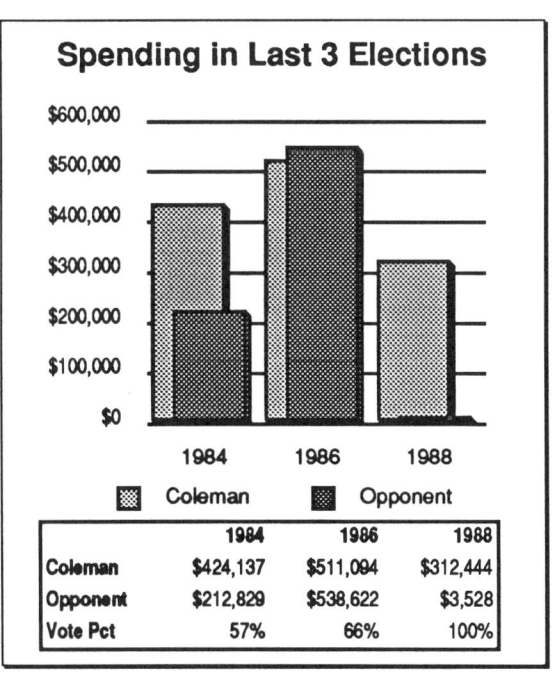

Ideological/Single-Issue

Democratic Leadership PACs $4,000
Valley Education Fund (Tony Coelho) $2,000
Cmte for a Democratic Consensus (Alan Cranston) $1,000
Majority Congress Committee (Jim Wright) $1,000

Other Major Ideological/Single-Issue PACs
National Cmte to Preserve Social Security ...... $1,650   Soc Secur
National Assn of Uniformed Services .... $1,250   Pro-Defense

Independent expenditures supporting Coleman
National Cmte to Preserve Social Security $1,087

---

* Contributions came from more than one PAC affiliated with this sponsor.

Cardiss Collins, D-III (7)

First elected: 1973
Total receipts: $235,058
Total from PACs: $199,043

1988 Committees & Subcommittees

Energy and Commerce
Commerce, Consumer Protection and Competitiveness
Health and the Environment
Telecommunications and Finance

Government Operations
Government Activities and Transportation (Chairwoman)

Select Narcotics Abuse and Control

PAC Contribution Profile

Business

Accountants	**$5,500**
American Institute of CPA's	$5,000
Others	$500
Agriculture	**$2,800**
American Crystal Sugar Corp	$1,000
Associated Milk Producers	$1,000
Others	$800
Airlines/Air Freight	**$3,500**
Federal Express Corp	$2,000
Texas Air	$1,000
Others	$500
Commercial Banks	**$10,600**
J P Morgan & Company	$5,000
American Bankers Assn	$1,500
Citicorp	$1,000
Continental Illinois Corp	$1,000
First Chicago Corp	$1,000
Others	$1,100
Electric Utilities	**$5,750**
Southern Company*	$1,000
Others	$4,750
Food & Beverage	**$2,500**
Whitman Corp	$1,000
Others	$1,500

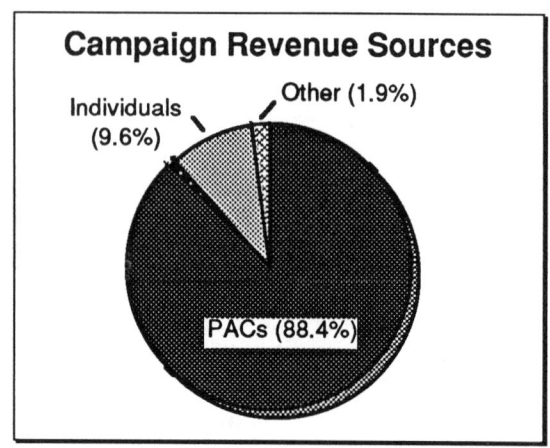

Campaign Revenue Sources

Individuals (9.6%)
Other (1.9%)
PACs (88.4%)

Health Professionals	**$9,050**
American Nurses Assn	$2,000
Oral & Maxillofacial Surgeons	$1,500
American College of Emergency Physicians	$1,000
Cmte for Quality Orthopedic Health Care	$1,000
National Assn of Pharmacists	$1,000
Others	$2,550
Insurance	**$21,811**
National Assn of Life Underwriters	$5,000
American Council of Life Insurance	$2,500
Independent Insurance Agents of America	$2,061
Metropolitan Life Insurance	$2,000
National Assn Mutual Insurance Agents	$1,500
American Family Corp	$1,000
Casualty & Surety Agents Assn	$1,000
Prudential Insurance	$1,000
Others	$5,750
Lawyers & Lobbyists	**$12,000**
Assn of Trial Lawyers of America	$10,000
Camp, Barsh, Bates & Tate	$1,000
Others	$1,000
Railroads	**$6,500**
Chicago & NorthWestern Transport	$2,000
Kansas City Southern	$1,000
Norfolk Southern Corp	$1,000
Others	$2,500
Real Estate	**$5,500**
National Assn of Realtors	$5,000
Others	$500
Securities & Commodities	**$15,750**
Chicago Board of Trade	$5,000
Chicago Mercantile Exchange	$5,000
Chicago Board of Options Exchange	$2,500
Investment Company Institute	$1,000
Travelers Corp	$1,000
Others	$1,250

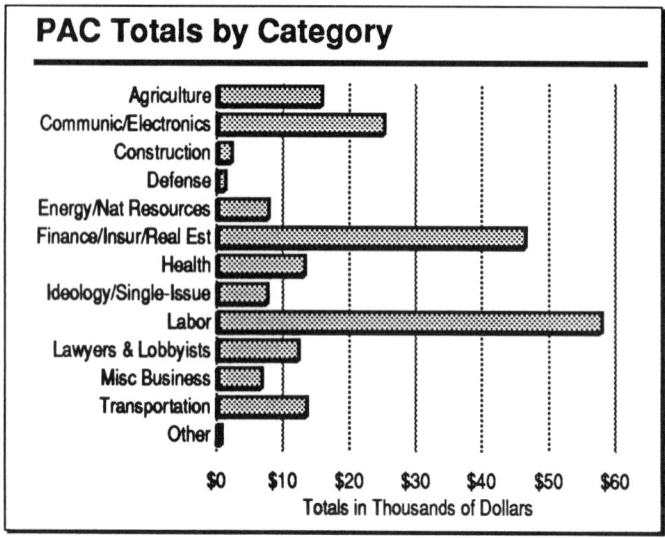

PAC Totals by Category

Agriculture
Communic/Electronics
Construction
Defense
Energy/Nat Resources
Finance/Insur/Real Est
Health
Ideology/Single-Issue
Labor
Lawyers & Lobbyists
Misc Business
Transportation
Other

$0 $10 $20 $30 $40 $50 $60
Totals in Thousands of Dollars

Telecommunications $14,194

AT&T	$5,000
BellSouth Corp*	$2,000
Illinois Bell Telephone	$2,000
Pacific Telesis Group	$1,250
Comsat	$1,000
Others	$2,944

Television/Cable TV $8,500

Tele-Communications Inc	$5,000
National Cable Television Assn	$2,000
National Assn of Broadcasters	$1,000
Others	$500

Trucking/Delivery $2,500

United Parcel Service	$2,000
Others	$500

Other Major Business PACs

National Assn of Home Builders	$1,500	Resid Constr
Schering-Plough Corp	$1,500	Pharmaceut
Computer Dealers & Lessors Assn	$1,000	Computers
Hallmark Cards	$1,000	Publishing
Health Industry Manufacturers Assn	$1,000	Med Supply

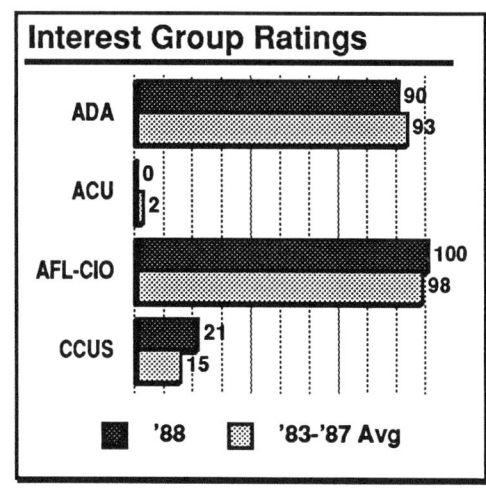

Interest Group Ratings

	'88	'83-'87 Avg
ADA	90	93
ACU	0	2
AFL-CIO	100	98
CCUS	21	15

■ '88   ▨ '83-'87 Avg

Labor

Bldg Trades/Industrial/Other Unions $16,750

National Education Assn	$5,500
AFL-CIO*	$1,500
Intl Brotherhood of Electrical Workers	$1,500
Machinists/Aerospace Workers Union	$1,500
Operating Engineers Union	$1,500
Carpenters & Joiners Union	$1,000
Food & Commercial Workers Union	$1,000
Laborers' Political League	$1,000
Ladies Garment Workers Union	$1,000
Others	$1,250

Government & Postal Workers $17,600

National Assn of Letter Carriers	$6,500
National Assn of Retired Federal Employees	$5,000
American Fedn of State/County/Munic Employees	$3,000
American Postal Workers Union	$1,500
Others	$1,600

Transportation Unions $23,250

Teamsters Union	$10,000
Air Line Pilots Assn	$5,000
Seafarers International Union	$3,000
United Transportation Union	$2,000
Marine Engineers Union*	$1,500
Others	$1,750

Ideological/Single-Issue

Pro-Israel $3,500

Hudson Valley PAC	$2,500
Others	$1,000

Other Major Ideological/Single-Issue PACs $3,823

National Cmte to Preserve Social Security	$1,500
Others	$2,323

Independent expenditures supporting Collins

National Cmte to Preserve Social Security	$2,042

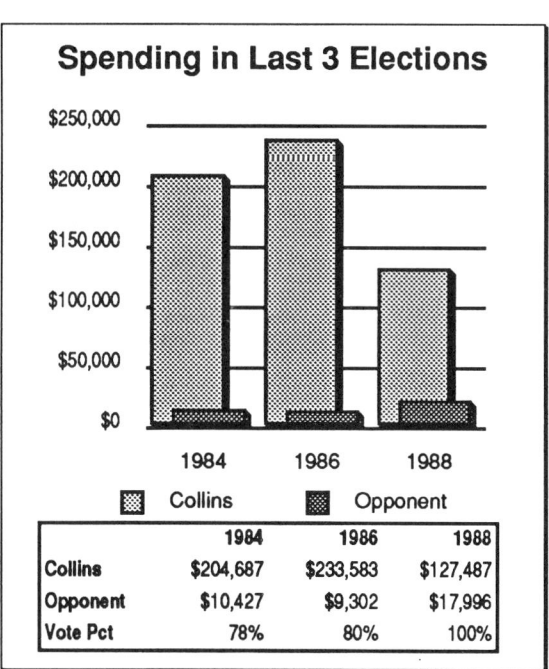

Spending in Last 3 Elections

	1984	1986	1988
Collins	$204,687	$233,583	$127,487
Opponent	$10,427	$9,302	$17,996
Vote Pct	78%	80%	100%

▨ Collins   ■ Opponent

---

* Contributions came from more than one PAC affiliated
with this sponsor.

Larry Combest, R-Texas (19)

First elected: 1984
Total receipts: $272,401
Total from PACs: $119,800

1988 Committees & Subcommittees

Agriculture
Conservation, Credit and Rural Development
Cotton, Rice and Sugar
Tobacco and Peanuts

District of Columbia
Government Operations and Metropolitan Affairs (Ranking Republican)
Fiscal Affairs and Health

Small Business
Energy and Agriculture
Regulation and Business Opportunities

Campaign Revenue Sources

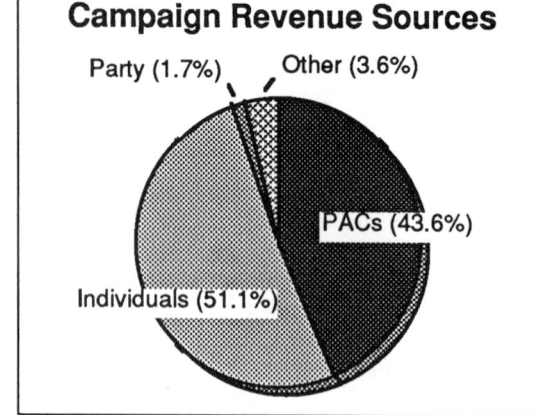

Party (1.7%) Other (3.6%)
PACs (43.6%)
Individuals (51.1%)

PAC Contribution Profile

Business

Agricultural Chemicals	**$4,500**
Dow Chemical*	$1,500
FMC Corp	$1,500
Others	$1,500
Automotive & Trucking	**$7,250**
National Auto Dealers Assn	$4,000
Auto Dealers & Drivers for Free Trade	$1,500
Yellow Freight System	$1,000
Others	$750
Building Contractors	**$4,500**
Associated General Contractors	$2,250
Others	$2,250
Commodity Trading	**$2,500**
Chicago Board of Trade	$1,000
Commodity Exchange Inc	$1,000
Others	$500
Cotton	**$4,060**
American Cotton Shippers Assn	$1,500
Plains Cotton Cooperative Assn	$1,060
Others	$1,500

Dairy	**$7,000**
Associated Milk Producers	$4,000
Dairymen Inc	$1,000
Mid-American Dairymen	$1,000
Milk Industry Foundation	$1,000
Electric Utilities	**$9,990**
Texas Utilities Electric Company*	$5,000
Southwestern Public Service Company	$2,740
Houston Industries	$1,500
Others	$750
Farm Organizations	**$3,750**
Texas Farm Bureau	$2,750
Others	$1,000
Food & Beverage	**$8,050**
National Restaurant Assn	$2,000
Food Marketing Institute	$1,000
Others	$5,050
Health Professionals	**$6,305**
American Medical Assn	$5,000
Texas Medical Assn	$1,055
Others	$250
Insurance	**$2,750**
American National Insurance Company	$1,500
National Assn of Life Underwriters	$1,000
Others	$250
Lawyers	**$3,000**
Assn of Trial Lawyers of America	$2,000
McCamish, Martin, Brown & Loeffler	$1,000
Livestock & Animal Health	**$7,100**
Texas Cattle Feeders Assn	$4,000
Texas/Southwestern Cattle Raisers	$1,000
Others	$2,100
Oil & Gas	**$10,250**
Enserch Corp	$1,000
Phillips Petroleum	$1,000
Others	$8,250
Real Estate	**$7,000**
National Assn of Realtors	$7,000

PAC Totals by Category

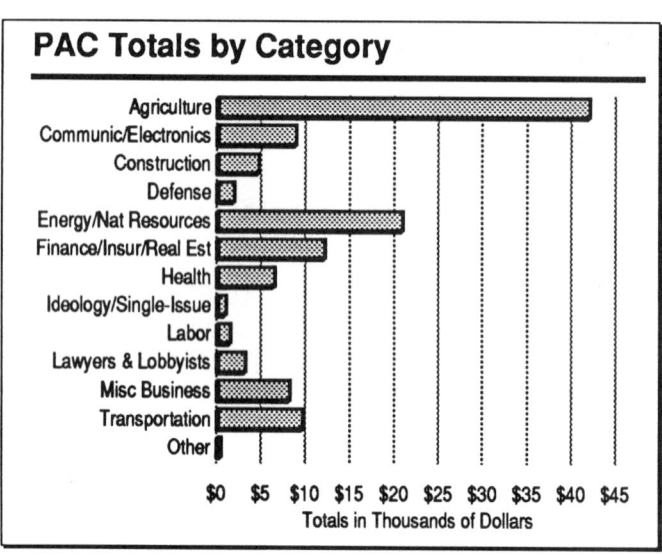

Agriculture
Communic/Electronics
Construction
Defense
Energy/Nat Resources
Finance/Insur/Real Est
Health
Ideology/Single-Issue
Labor
Lawyers & Lobbyists
Misc Business
Transportation
Other

$0 $5 $10 $15 $20 $25 $30 $35 $40 $45
Totals in Thousands of Dollars

Sugar Growers **$3,800**
    American Sugarbeet Growers Assn $1,000
    Others $2,800

Telecommunications **$7,000**
    GTE (Southwest) $2,500
    AT&T $2,000
    Southwestern Bell $1,500
    Others $1,000

Tobacco **$3,000**
    Philip Morris $2,000
    Others $1,000

Other Major Business PACs

American Textile Manfacturers Institute ....$1,000   Textiles

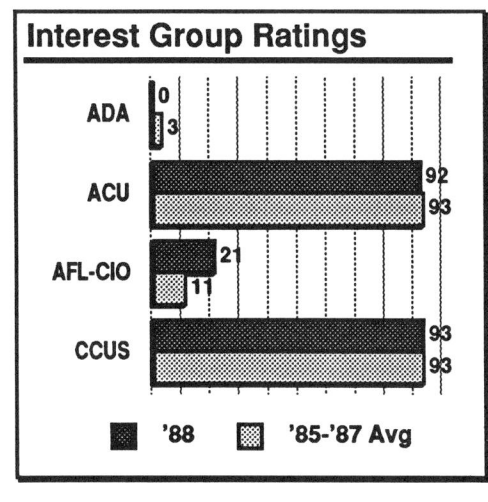

Interest Group Ratings

	'88	'85-'87 Avg
ADA	0	3
ACU	92	93
AFL-CIO	21	11
CCUS	93	93

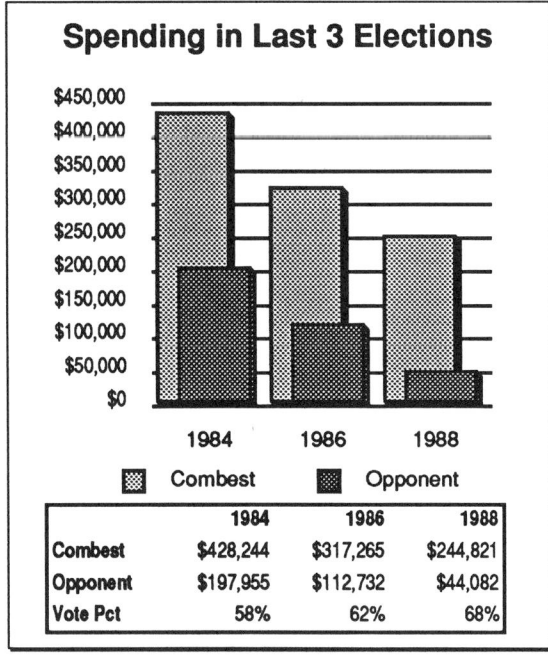

Spending in Last 3 Elections

Combest   Opponent

	1984	1986	1988
Combest	$428,244	$317,265	$244,821
Opponent	$197,955	$112,732	$44,082
Vote Pct	58%	62%	68%

* Contributions came from more than one PAC affiliated
   with this sponsor.

365

Silvio O. Conte, R-Mass (1)

First elected: 1958
Total receipts: $142,186
Total from PACs: $72,624

1988 Committees & Subcommittees

Appropriations (Ranking Republican)
Labor, Health and Human Services, Education and Related Agencies (Ranking Republican)
Legislative Branch
Transportation and Related Agencies

Small Business
Procurement, Innovation and Minority Enterprise Development (Ranking Republican)

PAC Contribution Profile

Business

Aviation	**$1,500**
Aircraft Owners & Pilots Assn	$1,000
Boeing Company	$500
Beer & Wine	**$3,000**
National Beer Wholesalers Assn	$1,500
Miller Brewing Company	$1,000
Wine Institute	$500
Broadcasting/Cable TV	**$2,500**
National Assn of Broadcasters	$1,000
National Cable Television Assn	$1,000
Viacom International	$500
Commercial/Industrial Construction	**$7,500**
National Utility Contractors Assn	$6,000
Associated General Contractors	$500
Bechtel Corp	$500
National Aggregates Assn	$500
Defense	**$1,700**
McDonnell Douglas	$700
American Systems Corp	$500
Colt Industries	$500
Health Professionals	**$8,500**
American Dental Assn	$4,000
Oral & Maxillofacial Surgeons	$1,500
American Medical Assn	$1,000
American Nurses Assn	$1,000
Assn for Advancement of Psychology	$500
Cmte for Quality Orthopedic Health Care	$500

Campaign Revenue Sources

Other (30.5%)
PACs (48.1%)
Party (1.4%)
Individuals (20.0%)

Industrial Equipment	**$1,500**
Pirelli Cable	$1,000
National Tooling & Machining Assn	$500
Insurance	**$1,500**
Travelers Corp	$1,000
National Assn of Life Underwriters	$500
Vocational Tech Schools	**$5,200**
National Assn of Trade/Tech Schools	$5,000
Others	$200

Other Major Business PACs

American Veterinary Medical Assn	$1,000	Veterinary
American Bankers Assn	$1,000	Comml Banks
AT&T	$1,000	LongDistance
Electrocom Automation Inc	$1,000	Comput Parts
Voluntary Hospitals of America	$1,000	Hospitals
Farm Credit Council	$500	Ag Svcs
FMC Corp	$500	Chemicals
Marriott Corp	$500	Hotel/Motel
National Assn of Social Workers	$500	Social Work
New England Power Service Company	$500	ElectricUtil
Petroleum Marketers Assn	$500	Gas Stations
Union Pacific Corp	$500	Railroads

PAC Totals by Category

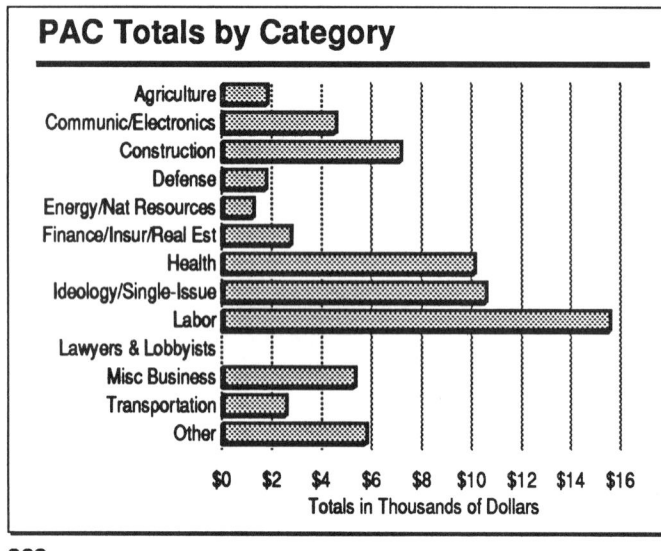

Totals in Thousands of Dollars

Labor

Labor Unions..$15,500

Teamsters Union	$5,000
National Assn of Letter Carriers	$3,000
Marine Engineers District 2 Maritime Officers	$2,000
Seafarers International Union	$1,500
American Fedn of State/County/Munic Employees	$1,000
Food & Commercial Workers Union	$1,000
Intl Brotherhood of Electrical Workers	$1,000
Transport Workers Union	$1,000

Ideological/Single-Issue

Pro-Israel...$5,000

National PAC	$5,000

Other Major Ideological/Single-Issue PACs

Human Rights Campaign Fund	$2,000	Gay Rights
KidsPAC	$1,500	HealthWelfare
National Council of Senior Citizens	$1,000	Soc Secur
Sierra Club	$500	Environment

Independent expenditures supporting Conte

National Cmte to Preserve Social Security $1,943

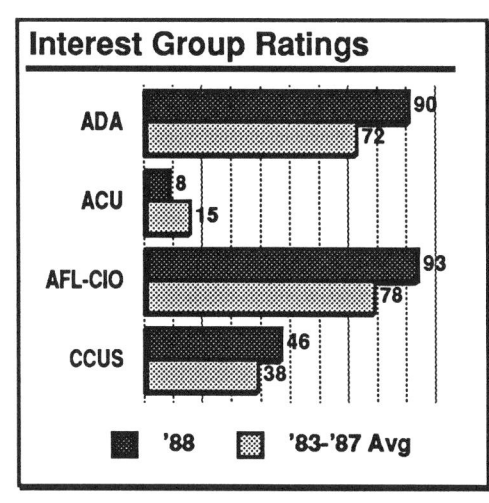

Interest Group Ratings

ADA 90 / 72
ACU 8 / 15
AFL-CIO 93 / 78
CCUS 46 / 38

■ '88   ▦ '83–'87 Avg

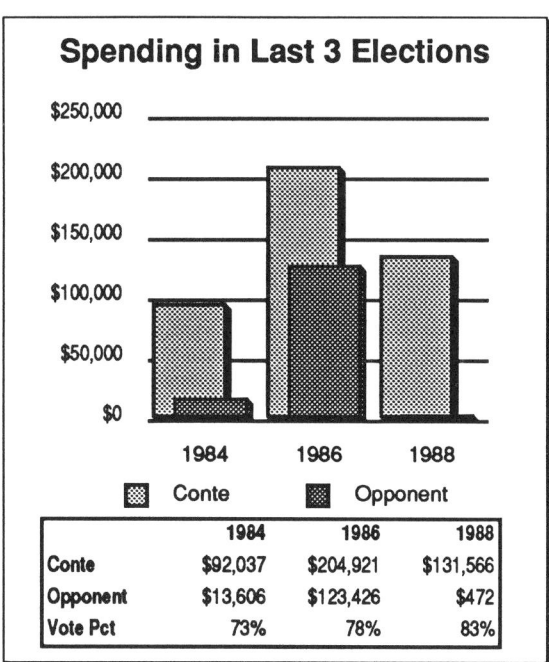

Spending in Last 3 Elections

▦ Conte   ■ Opponent

	1984	1986	1988
Conte	$92,037	$204,921	$131,566
Opponent	$13,606	$123,426	$472
Vote Pct	73%	78%	83%

John Conyers Jr., D-Mich (1)

First elected: 1964
Total receipts: $151,676
Total from PACs: $82,614

1988 Committees & Subcommittees

Government Operations
Human Resources and Intergovernmental Relations
Legislation and National Security

Judiciary
Criminal Justice (Chairman)
Civil and Constitutional Rights

Small Business
Procurement, Innovation and Minority Enterprise Development

PAC Contribution Profile

Business

Construction	**$8,200**
National Assn of Home Builders	$3,100
National Electrical Contractors Assn	$2,000
American Subcontractors Assn	$1,000
National Society of Professional Engineers	$1,000
Others	$1,100
Dairy	**$2,000**
Associated Milk Producers	$2,000
Electric Utilities	**$2,425**
Consumers Power Company	$1,450
Others	$975
Entertainment Industry	**$4,500**
MCA Inc	$1,300
ASCAP	$1,000
Others	$2,200
Financial Institutions	**$2,140**
Michigan Credit Union League	$1,000
Others	$1,140
Lawyers & Lobbyists	**$6,800**
Assn of Trial Lawyers of America	$5,000
Arnold & Porter	$1,000
Others	$800
Package Delivery	**$2,180**
United Parcel Service	$1,880
Others	$300

Campaign Revenue Sources

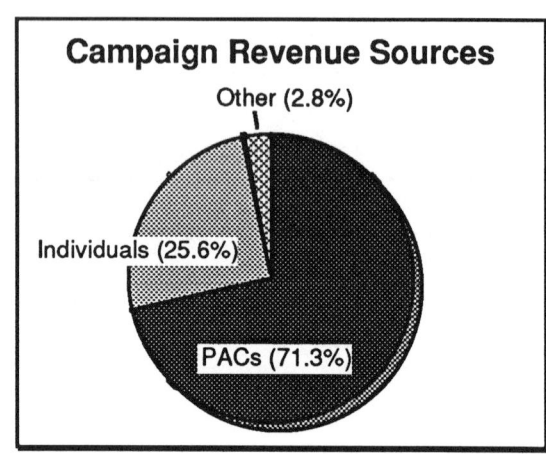

Other (2.8%)
Individuals (25.6%)
PACs (71.3%)

Other Major Business PACs

National Assn of Realtors	$1,150	Real Estate
Chrysler Corp	$1,000	Auto Mfrs
Xerox Corp	$1,000	Off Machines

PAC Totals by Category

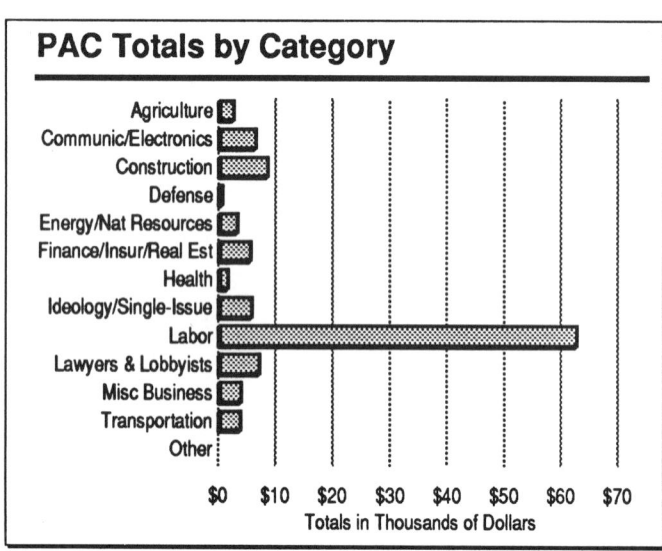

Agriculture
Communic/Electronics
Construction
Defense
Energy/Nat Resources
Finance/Insur/Real Est
Health
Ideology/Single-Issue
Labor
Lawyers & Lobbyists
Misc Business
Transportation
Other

$0 $10 $20 $30 $40 $50 $60 $70

Totals in Thousands of Dollars

Labor

Bldg Trades/Industrial/Misc Unions $22,165

Carpenters & Joiners Union	$3,500
Machinists/Aerospace Workers Union	$3,300
Food & Commercial Workers Union	$2,240
Operating Engineers Union*	$2,100
Intl Brotherhood of Electrical Workers	$1,500
United Auto Workers	$1,350
Laborers' Political League	$1,300
Others	$6,875

Government & Postal Workers $15,300

American Fedn of State/County/Munic Employees	$5,000
National Assn of Retired Federal Employees	$3,250
National Assn of Letter Carriers	$2,500
American Postal Workers Union	$1,550
Others	$3,000

Teachers Unions $6,175

National Education Assn	$4,150
American Federation of Teachers	$2,025

Transportation Unions $18,805

Teamsters Union	$7,500
Air Line Pilots Assn	$5,000
Maintenance of Way Employees	$1,565
Transportation Communication Union	$1,040
Seafarers International Union	$1,000
Others	$2,700

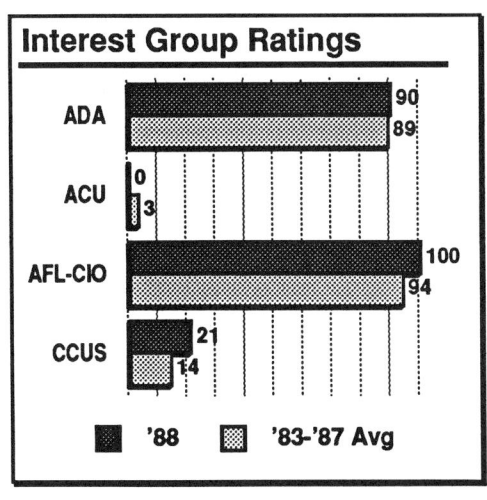

Interest Group Ratings

	'88	'83-'87 Avg
ADA	90	89
ACU	0	3
AFL-CIO	100	94
CCUS	21	14

Ideological/Single-Issue

Ideology/Single-Issue $5,021

National Assn of Arab-Americans	$2,000
Human Rights Campaign Fund	$1,225
Others	$1,796

Independent expenditures supporting Conyers

National Cmte to Preserve Social Security	$1,468

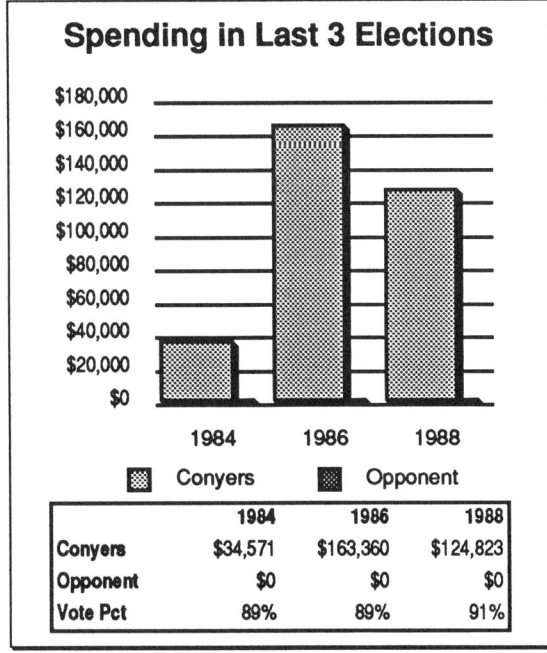

Spending in Last 3 Elections

	1984	1986	1988
Conyers	$34,571	$163,360	$124,823
Opponent	$0	$0	$0
Vote Pct	89%	89%	91%

* Contributions came from more than one PAC affiliated with this sponsor.

Jim Cooper, D-Tenn (4)

1988 Committees & Subcommittees

Energy and Commerce
Oversight and Investigations
Telecommunications and Finance
Transportation, Tourism and Hazardous Materials

Small Business
Regulation and Business Opportunities
SBA and the General Economy

First elected: 1982
Total receipts: $292,770
Total from PACs: $244,977

PAC Contribution Profile

Business

Accountants	**$16,283**
American Institute of CPA's	$10,000
Coopers & Lybrand	$2,733
Touche Ross	$2,000
Ernst & Whinney	$1,000
Others	$550
Air Transport/Air Freight	**$9,000**
Federal Express Corp	$7,000
Eastern Airlines	$1,000
Pittston Company	$1,000
Automotive	**$4,332**
National Auto Dealers Assn	$1,933
Others	$2,399
Commercial Banks	**$48,547**
American Bankers Assn	$10,000
J P Morgan & Company	$10,000
Bankers Trust	$4,500
First American Corp	$3,166
Citicorp	$3,000
Barnett Banks of Florida	$2,000
Security Pacific Corp	$2,000
Third National Corp	$2,000
First Chicago Corp	$1,333
Citizens & Southern National Bank	$1,000
Others	$9,548
Construction	**$2,750**
National Assn of Home Builders	$1,000
Others	$1,750

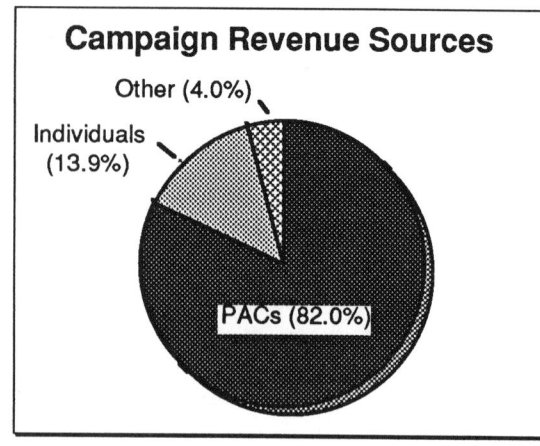

Campaign Revenue Sources

Other (4.0%)
Individuals (13.9%)
PACs (82.0%)

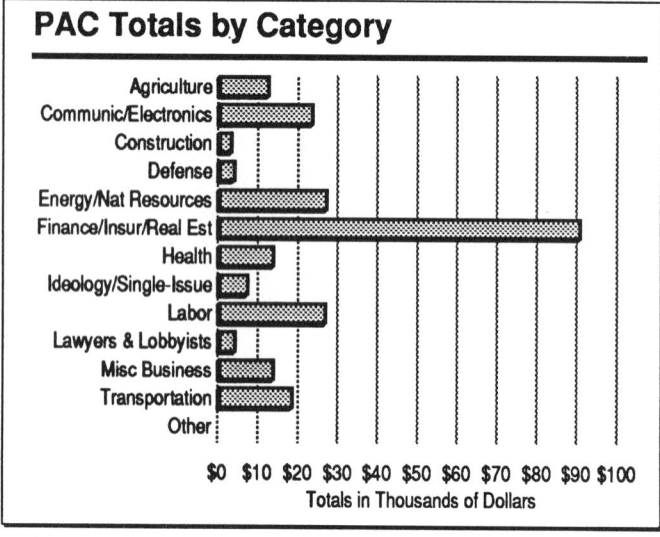

PAC Totals by Category

Agriculture
Communic/Electronics
Construction
Defense
Energy/Nat Resources
Finance/Insur/Real Est
Health
Ideology/Single-Issue
Labor
Lawyers & Lobbyists
Misc Business
Transportation
Other

$0 $10 $20 $30 $40 $50 $60 $70 $80 $90 $100
Totals in Thousands of Dollars

Dairy	**$3,033**
Associated Milk Producers	$1,500
Dairymen Inc-Tennessee	$1,233
Others	$300
Defense	**$3,499**
Textron Inc	$1,300
Others	$2,199
Electric Utilities	**$10,415**
Southern Company*	$2,050
ACRE (Action Committee for Rural Electrification)	$1,466
Others	$6,899
Food & Beverage	**$6,566**
Brown-Forman Distillers	$1,333
Joseph E Seagram & Sons	$1,000
Kellogg Company	$1,000
Pepsico Inc	$1,000
Others	$2,233
Health Professionals	**$6,865**
American Medical Assn	$2,800
National Assn of Pharmacists	$1,999
Others	$2,066
Insurance	**$9,981**
National Assn of Life Underwriters	$2,500
Independent Insurance Agents of America	$1,633
Others	$5,848
Lawyers & Lobbyists	**$3,748**
None over $883	
Mining	**$3,000**
Independent Coal Operators Assn	$1,000
Others	$2,000
Oil & Gas	**$11,129**
Mesa PAC II	$1,000
Others	$10,129
Pharmaceuticals	**$4,416**
Schering-Plough Corp	$1,500
Others	$2,916
Railroads & Railroad Services	**$2,000**
Norfolk Southern Corp	$1,100
Others	$900

Real Estate **$4,733**
National Assn of Realtors $3,300
Others $1,433

Securities/Commodities Investment **$11,631**
Chicago Board of Options Exchange $1,000
First Boston Corp $1,000
Morgan Stanley & Company $1,000
Travelers Corp $1,000
Others $7,631

Telecommunications **$16,932**
AT&T $2,100
South Central Bell Telephone $1,800
Pacific Telesis Group $1,750
National Telephone Co-op Assn $1,300
US Telephone Assn $1,200
Competitive Telecom Assn $1,000
NYNEX Corp $1,000
Others $6,782

Television/Broadcasting **$6,131**
National Cable Television Assn $2,000
National Assn of Broadcasters $1,266
Others $2,865

Tobacco **$3,899**
Philip Morris $2,499
Others $1,400

Other Major Business PACs

Waste Management Inc $1,266	Waste Mgmt
National Assn of Temporary Services $1,000	Employ Agency
Tenn League of Savings Institutions $1,000	Savings Banks

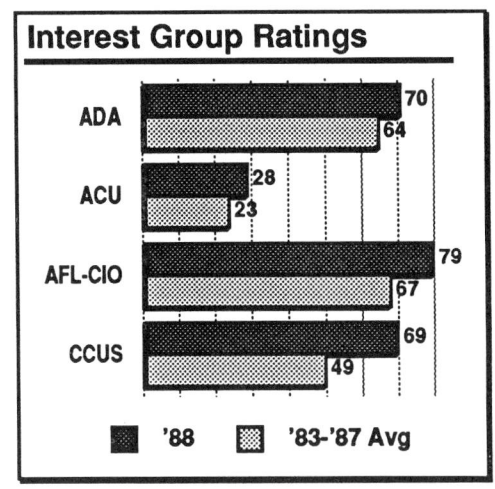

Interest Group Ratings

	'88	'83-'87 Avg
ADA	70	64
ACU	28	23
AFL-CIO	79	67
CCUS	69	49

■ '88   ▨ '83-'87 Avg

Labor

Bldg Trades/Industrial/Misc Unions **$8,600**
United Auto Workers $3,000
Food & Commercial Workers Union $1,500
Ladies Garment Workers Union $1,050
Intl Brotherhood of Electrical Workers $1,000
Others $2,050

Government & Postal Workers **$6,300**
National Assn of Retired Federal Employees $3,000
National Assn of Letter Carriers $2,000
Others $1,300

Teachers Unions **$2,833**
American Federation of Teachers $2,500
Others $333

Transportation Unions **$8,600**
Teamsters Union $5,000
United Transportation Union $1,500
Others $2,100

Ideological/Single-Issue

Pro-Israel **$5,000**
National PAC $5,000

Other Ideological/Single Issue

Valley Education Fund (Tony Coelho) ....$1,000   Dem Leaders

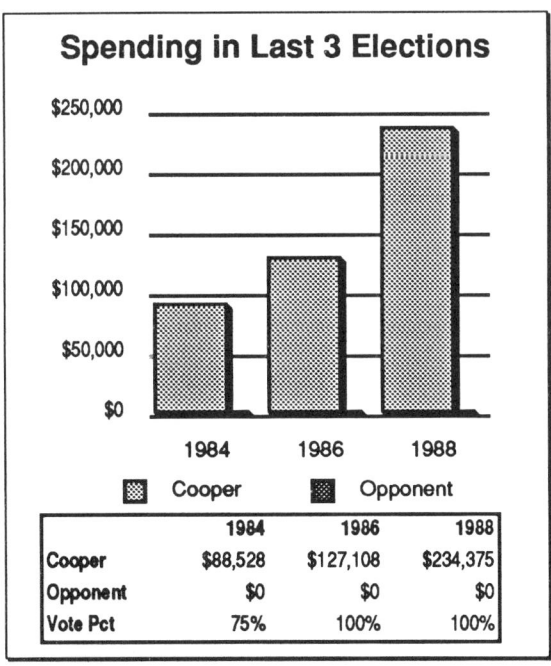

Spending in Last 3 Elections

▨ Cooper   ■ Opponent

	1984	1986	1988
Cooper	$88,528	$127,108	$234,375
Opponent	$0	$0	$0
Vote Pct	75%	100%	100%

---

* Contributions came from more than one PAC affiliated
with this sponsor.

Jerry F. Costello, D-III (21)

First elected: 1988
Total receipts: $285,503
Total from PACs: $123,381

1988 Committees & Subcommittees

Public Works and Transportation
Aviation
Surface Transportation
Water Resources

Science, Space and Technology
Energy Research and Development
Science, Research and Technology

Select Aging

PAC Contribution Profile

NOTE: The PAC contributions listed on these pages include funds that Costello received in both his 1988 races — the special election he won in August and the November general election in which he was elected to a full two-year term. The total receipts listed in the box above, and the percentages in the pie chart at right, refer only to the general election race.

Business

Coal Mining	**$2,250**
Peabody Coal	$2,250
Commercial Banks	**$11,450**
American Bankers Assn	$3,000
Boatmens Bankshares	$2,500
Illinois Bankers Assn	$1,500
Barnett Banks of Florida	$1,000
Centerre Bank	$1,000
Continental Illinois Corp	$1,000
Others	$1,450
Construction	**$3,250**
Sverdrup Corporation	$3,000
Others	$250
Credit Unions & Savings Banks	**$2,625**
Credit Union National Assn	$2,000
Others	$625
Dairy	**$4,000**
Mid-American Dairymen	$3,500
Associated Milk Producers	$500

Campaign Revenue Sources

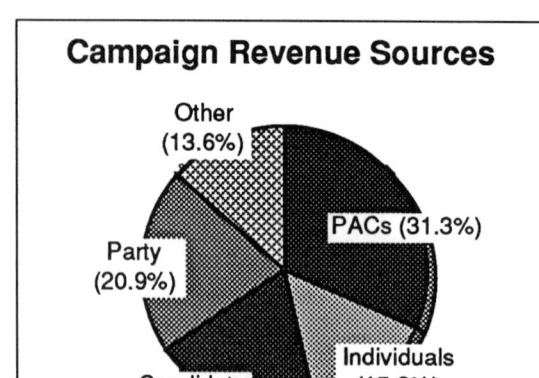

Other (13.6%)
PACs (31.3%)
Party (20.9%)
Individuals (15.2%)
Candidate (19.0%)

Farm Organizations	**$2,301**
Illinois Agricultural Assn	$2,301
Health Professionals	**$14,500**
American Academy of Ophthalmology	$5,000
American Medical Assn	$5,000
American Dental Assn	$1,500
American Chiropractic Assn	$1,000
Cmte for Quality Orthopedic Health Care	$1,000
Illinois Medical Assn	$1,000
Lawyers	**$9,250**
Assn of Trial Lawyers of America	$9,000
Others	$250
Oil & Gas	**$2,000**
None over $750	
Real Estate	**$15,000**
National Assn of Realtors	$15,000
Retail Sales	**$2,500**
None over $500	
Telecommunications	**$4,875**
Illinois Bell Telephone	$2,000
AT&T	$1,250
Continental Telecom	$1,000
Others	$625

Other Major Business PACs

Independent Insurance Agents of America	$1,000	Insurance
RJR Nabisco	$1,000	Tobacco

PAC Totals by Category

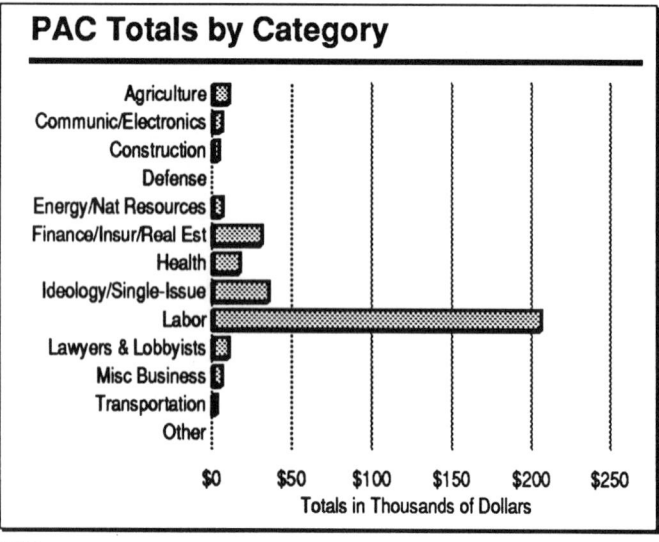

Agriculture
Communic/Electronics
Construction
Defense
Energy/Nat Resources
Finance/Insur/Real Est
Health
Ideology/Single-Issue
Labor
Lawyers & Lobbyists
Misc Business
Transportation
Other

$0 $50 $100 $150 $200 $250
Totals in Thousands of Dollars

Labor

Bldg Trades/Industrial/Misc Unions **$119,400**

Machinists/Aerospace Workers Union* $20,000
United Mine Workers $13,000
United Steelworkers $13,000
AFL-CIO* $10,500
Carpenters & Joiners Union $7,500
Intl Brotherhood of Electrical Workers $7,500
United Auto Workers $7,500
Food & Commercial Workers Union $7,000
Plumbers/Pipefitters Union $7,000
Communications Workers of America $5,000
Laborers' Political League* $3,500
Service Employees International Union $3,000
Bakery, Confectionery & Tobacco Workers $2,000
Boilermakers Union $2,000
Graphic Communications Union $1,500
Operating Engineers Union $1,500
Ladies Garment Workers Union $1,100
Bricklayers Union $1,000
Ironworkers Union $1,000
Painters & Allied Trades Union $1,000
Sheet Metal Workers Union $1,000
Others $2,800

Government & Postal Workers **$23,000**

National Assn of Letter Carriers $10,000
American Fedn of State/County/Munic Employees $5,500
National Assn of Retired Federal Employees $4,500
American Postal Workers Union $2,000
Others $1,000

Teachers Unions **$20,000**

National Education Assn $15,000
American Federation of Teachers $5,000

Interest Group Ratings

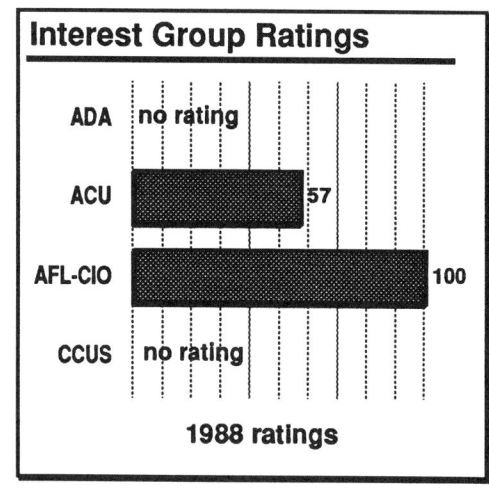

1988 ratings

Transportation Unions **$42,250**

Teamsters Union $20,000
Air Line Pilots Assn $5,000
Seafarers International Union $5,000
United Transportation Union $4,500
Amalgamated Transit Union $3,500
Marine Engineers District 2 Maritime Officers $2,500
Transportation Communication Union $1,250
Others $500

Ideological/Single-Issue

Democratic/Liberal **$5,000**

Class PAC $5,000

Democratic Leadership PACs **$20,500**

Majority Congress Committee (Jim Wright) $8,000
Valley Education Fund (Tony Coelho) $6,000
America's Leaders' Fund (Dan Rostenkowski) $3,000
Cmte for Democratic Opportunity (Bill Gray) $2,500
House Leadership Fund (Tom Foley) $1,000

Pro-Israel **$6,000**

National PAC $5,000
Others $1,000

Other Ideological/Single-Issue

National Rifle Assn .... $2,000   Pro-Guns
National Council of Senior Citizens .... $1,000   Soc Secur

Spending in Last 2 Elections

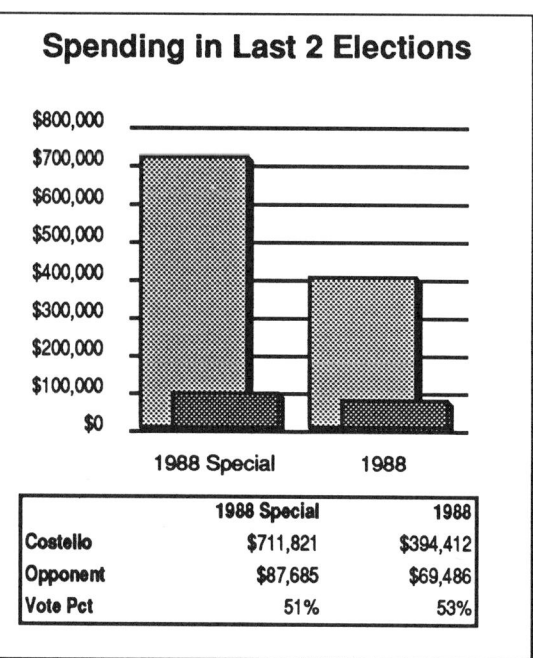

	1988 Special	1988
Costello	$711,821	$394,412
Opponent	$87,685	$69,486
Vote Pct	51%	53%

---

* Contributions came from more than one PAC affiliated
with this sponsor.

Lawrence Coughlin, R-Pa (13)

First elected: 1968
Total receipts: $396,262
Total from PACs: $150,851

1988 Committees & Subcommittees

Appropriations
District of Columbia (Ranking Republican)
HUD - Independent Agencies
Transportation and Related Agencies (Ranking Republican)

Select Narcotics Abuse and Control

PAC Contribution Profile

Business

Automotive	**$5,400**
Auto Dealers & Drivers for Free Trade	$2,000
Budd Company	$1,000
Others	$2,400
Aviation & Aerospace	**$14,800**
Eastern Airlines	$5,000
Aircraft Owners & Pilots Assn	$3,000
Boeing Company	$2,000
Others	$4,800
Chemicals	**$5,250**
FMC Corp	$2,250
Betz Laboratories	$1,000
Rohm and Haas Company	$1,000
Others	$1,000
Construction	**$16,800**
National Assn of Home Builders	$8,500
National Utility Contractors Assn	$2,500
Asplundh Tree Expert Company	$2,000
Associated General Contractors	$1,700
Toll Bros Inc	$1,000
Others	$1,100
Defense	**$11,700**
Hughes Aircraft	$1,550
Textron Inc	$1,500
United Technologies	$1,450
Lockheed Corp	$1,200
Rockwell International	$1,000
Others	$5,000

Campaign Revenue Sources

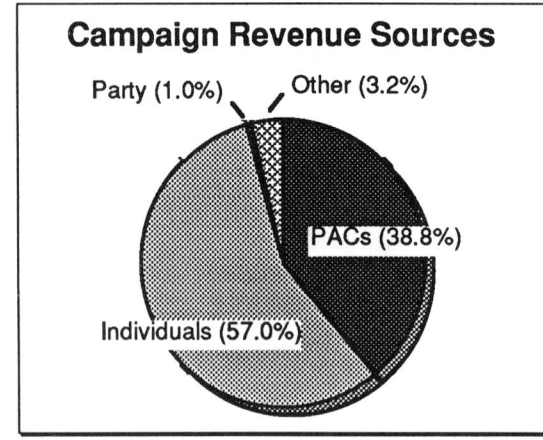

Party (1.0%) Other (3.2%)
PACs (38.8%)
Individuals (57.0%)

Electronics & Computers	**$3,750**
Electrocom Automation Inc	$1,000
Honeywell Pennsylvania	$1,000
Others	$1,750
Financial Institutions	**$4,650**
None over $750	
Food & Beverage	**$4,250**
Tasty Baking Company	$1,000
Winn-Dixie Stores	$1,000
Others	$2,250
Health Professionals	**$5,750**
American Medical Assn	$3,250
American Dental Assn	$2,000
Others	$500
Insurance	**$3,600**
National Assn of Life Underwriters	$1,000
Others	$2,600
Lawyers & Lobbyists	**$4,100**
Akin, Gump, Hauer & Feld	$1,000
Others	$3,100
Oil & Gas	**$3,000**
Atlantic Richfield	$1,250
Sun Company	$1,000
Others	$750
Pharmaceuticals	**$3,200**
Smithkline Beckman	$1,500
Johnson & Johnson	$1,000
Others	$700
Railroads & Railroad Services	**$6,700**
Union Pacific Corp	$4,000
Others	$2,700
Real Estate	**$6,950**
National Assn of Realtors	$6,000
Others	$950
Telecommunications	**$3,350**
AT&T	$2,000
Others	$1,350

PAC Totals by Category

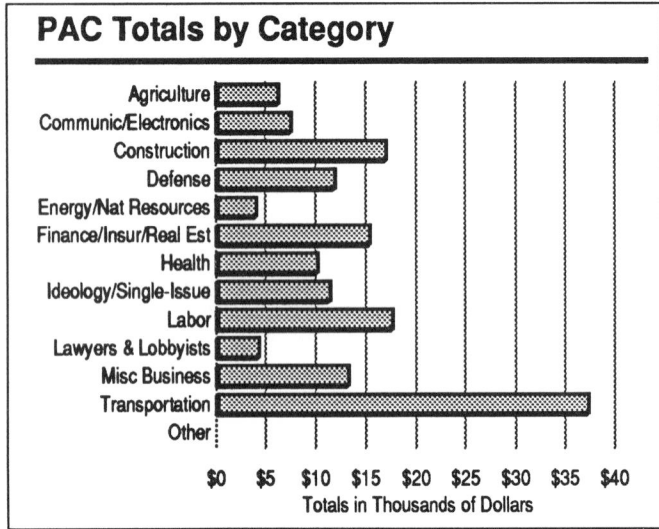

Agriculture
Communic/Electronics
Construction
Defense
Energy/Nat Resources
Finance/Insur/Real Est
Health
Ideology/Single-Issue
Labor
Lawyers & Lobbyists
Misc Business
Transportation
Other

$0 $5 $10 $15 $20 $25 $30 $35 $40
Totals in Thousands of Dollars

Tobacco **$2,400**
     Philip Morris $1,200
     Others $1,200

Trucking/Delivery.....................................**$7,509**
     United Parcel Service $4,050
     American Trucking Assns $2,359
     Others $1,100

Other Major Business PACs

Business Industry PAC ....$1,119 Bus Assns
Pennsylvania Shipbuilding Company ....$1,000 ShipBld/Repr

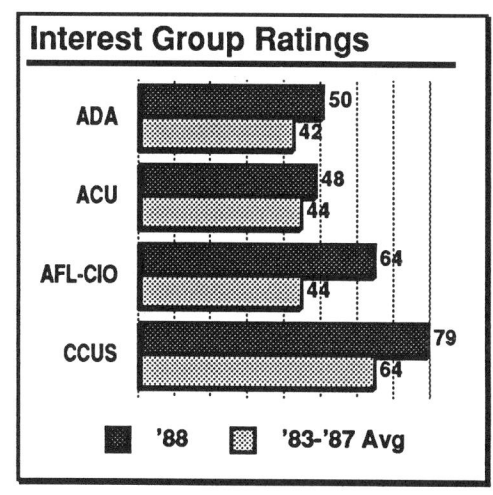

Interest Group Ratings

	'88	'83–'87 Avg
ADA	50	42
ACU	48	44
AFL-CIO	64	44
CCUS	79	64

Labor

Bldg Trades/Industrial/Other Unions **$4,600**
     National Education Assn $2,750
     National Assn of Letter Carriers $1,000
     Others $850

Transportation Unions **$12,850**
     Air Line Pilots Assn..............................$5,000
     Amalgamated Transit Union $3,000
     Marine Engineers District 2 Maritime Officers $1,000
     Seafarers International Union $1,000
     Transport Workers Union $1,000
     United Transportation Union $1,000
     Others $850

Ideological/Single-Issue

Pro-Israel **$7,850**
     National PAC $5,000
     Others $2,850

Other Major Ideological/Single-Issue PACs

KidsPAC ....$2,000 HealthWelfare

Independent expenditures supporting Coughlin

National Cmte to Preserve Social Security $4,095

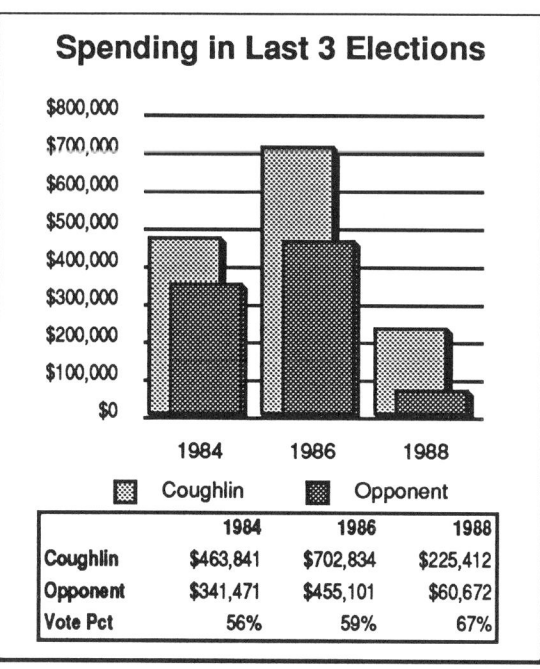

Spending in Last 3 Elections

	1984	1986	1988
Coughlin	$463,841	$702,834	$225,412
Opponent	$341,471	$455,101	$60,672
Vote Pct	56%	59%	67%

Jim Courter, R-NJ (12)

1988 Committees & Subcommittees

Armed Services
Procurement and Military Nuclear Systems
Research and Development

Select Aging
Health and Long-Term Care

First elected: 1978
Total receipts: $1,211,060
Total from PACs: $165,173

PAC Contribution Profile

Business

Auto Dealers	**$4,500**
Auto Dealers & Drivers for Free Trade	$2,500
National Auto Dealers Assn	$2,000
Commercial & Savings Banks	**$11,550**
American Bankers Assn	$3,000
Summit Bancorp	$2,100
SAPEC/NJ (New Jersey Savings Assn)	$2,000
First Fidelity Inc	$1,500
City Federal Savings & Loan	$1,000
Others	$1,950
Construction	**$8,750**
National Assn of Home Builders	$4,500
Associated General Contractors	$2,500
Blount Inc	$1,000
Others	$750
Consumer Credit & Loans	
Beneficial Management Corp	$7,000

Campaign Revenue Sources

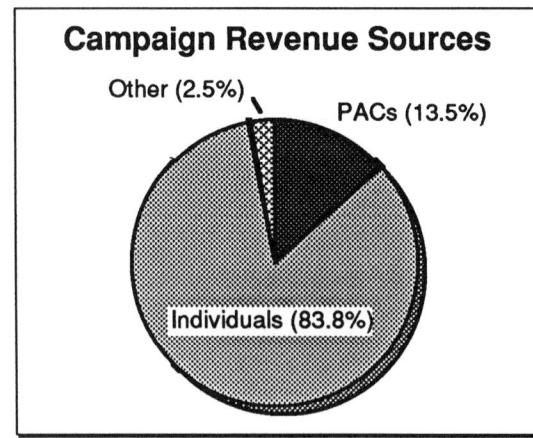

Other (2.5%)
PACs (13.5%)
Individuals (83.8%)

Defense	**$42,600**
AT&T	$3,600
Allied-Signal	$3,200
Lockheed Corp	$2,550
Harris Corp	$2,500
Singer Company	$2,350
Hughes Aircraft	$2,100
Tenneco Inc	$2,000
Northrop Corp	$1,700
Grumman	$1,350
Textron Inc	$1,350
United Technologies	$1,350
General Electric	$1,200
LTV Aerospace & Defense Company	$1,050
BDM International	$1,000
Boeing Company	$1,000
Electrospace Systems Inc	$1,000
General Dynamics	$1,000
ITT Corp	$1,000
Others	$11,300
Electric Utilities	**$6,472**
Public Service Electric & Gas	$3,000
Orange & Rockland Utilities	$2,500
Others	$972
Food & Beverage	**$4,900**
Brown-Forman Distillers	$1,500
Others	$3,400
Health Professionals	**$5,950**
American Medical Assn	$3,750
American Dental Assn	$2,000
Others	$200
Insurance	**$10,700**
Prudential Insurance	$4,350
Home Group Inc	$2,000
Chubb Corp	$1,000
National Assn of Life Underwriters	$1,000
Others	$2,350
Lawyers	**$3,000**
Assn of Trial Lawyers of America	$2,000
Wolf, Block, Schorr and Solis-Cohen	$1,000
Pharmaceuticals	**$8,600**
Sandoz Pharmaceuticals	$2,300
Johnson & Johnson	$2,000
Pfizer Inc	$1,000
Schering-Plough Corp	$1,000
Others	$2,300

PAC Totals by Category

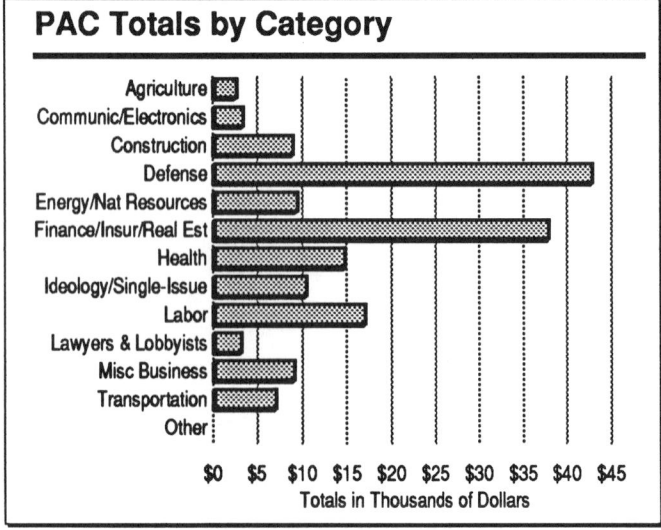

Agriculture
Communic/Electronics
Construction
Defense
Energy/Nat Resources
Finance/Insur/Real Est
Health
Ideology/Single-Issue
Labor
Lawyers & Lobbyists
Misc Business
Transportation
Other

$0 $5 $10 $15 $20 $25 $30 $35 $40 $45
Totals in Thousands of Dollars

Real Estate **$3,000**
    National Assn of Realtors $3,000

Securities Investment **$5,450**
    Prudential-Bache Securities $2,000
    Goldman Sachs $1,000
    Shearson Lehman Hutton $1,000
    Others $1,450

Telecommunications **$3,200**
    New Jersey Bell Telephone $2,200
    United Telecommunications $1,000

Other Major Business PACs

Deere & Company	$1,350	Farm Equip
United Parcel Service	$1,350	Delivery
Mobil Oil	$1,250	Major Oil
Hoechst Celanese Corp	$1,000	ManmadeFiber

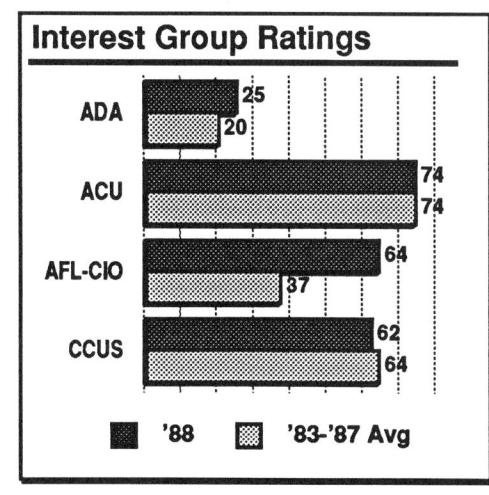

Interest Group Ratings

	'88	'83-'87 Avg
ADA	25	20
ACU	74	74
AFL-CIO	64	37
CCUS	62	64

Labor

Bldg Trades/Industrial/Other Unions **$11,800**
    Operating Engineers Local #825 .... $7,000
    Carpenters & Joiners Union $3,000
    National Assn of Retired Federal Employees $1,050
    Others $750

Transportation Unions **$5,000**
    Seafarers International Union $3,000
    Air Line Pilots Assn $1,000
    Marine Engineers District 2 Maritime Officers $1,000

Ideological/Single-Issue

Pro-Israel **$5,600**
    National PAC $5,000
    Others $600

Other Major Ideological/Single-Issue PACs

Amer Space Frontier Cmte (Bob Dornan) ..... $1,500   Repub Leader

Spending in Last 3 Elections

	1984	1986	1988
Courter	$409,609	$779,078	$1,333,882
Opponent	$90,759	$318,869	$17,334
Vote Pct	65%	63%	69%

C. Christopher Cox, R-Calif (40)

1988-1989 Committees & Subcommittees

First elected: 1988
Total receipts: $1,111,321
Total from PACs: $198,786

Government Operations
Commerce, Consumer and Monetary Affairs
Government Activities and Transportation

Public Works and Transportation
Economic Development
Public Buildings and Grounds
Surface Transportation
Water Resources

PAC Contribution Profile

Business

Automotive **$13,500**
National Auto Dealers Assn $7,000
Auto Dealers & Drivers for Free Trade $5,000
Mogul Corp $1,000
Others $500

Business Associations **$2,019**
Business Industry PAC $1,000
Others $1,019

Construction **$13,415**
National Assn of Home Builders $7,115
Fluor Corp $2,000
Associated General Contractors $1,250
Sheet Metal/Air Conditioning Contractors $1,000
Others $2,050

Defense **$14,000**
Textron Inc $3,000
Hughes Aircraft $1,500
Northrop Corp $1,500
General Dynamics $1,000
Litton Industries $1,000
Rockwell International $1,000
Others $5,000

Financial Institutions **$7,250**
American Bankers Assn $1,000
Credit Union National Assn $1,000
First Interstate Bank/California $1,000
Others $4,250

Campaign Revenue Sources

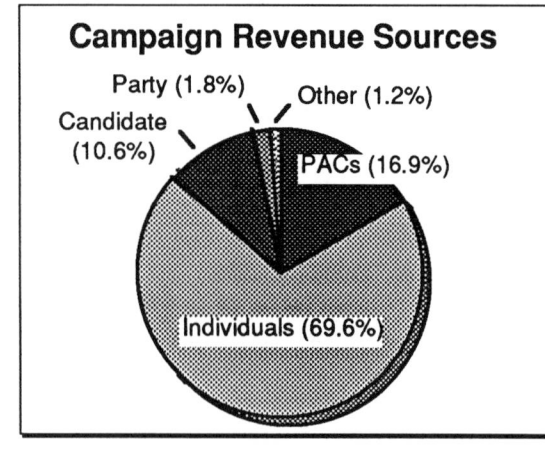

Party (1.8%)
Other (1.2%)
Candidate (10.6%)
PACs (16.9%)
Individuals (69.6%)

Food & Beverage **$4,550**
McLane Company $1,000
National Restaurant Assn $1,000
Pillsbury Company $1,000
Others $1,550

Health Professionals **$16,500**
American Medical Assn $10,000
American Academy of Ophthalmology $3,000
American Dental Assn $1,500
Assn of American Physicians/Surgeons $1,000
Others $1,000

Industrial Equipment & Materials **$2,750**
Parker-Hannifin $1,500
Others $1,250

Insurance **$11,250**
National Assn of Life Underwriters $5,000
National Assn Mutual Insurance Agents $2,000
Pacific Mutual Life $1,500
TransAmerica Life Companies $1,000
Others $1,750

Oil & Gas **$9,750**
Atlantic Richfield $3,500
Phillips Petroleum $1,000
Union Oil $1,000
Others $4,250

Pharmaceuticals **$3,000**
Smithkline Beckman $2,000
Pfizer Inc $1,000

Real Estate **$10,750**
National Assn of Realtors $10,000
Others $750

Retail Sales **$2,557**
Southland Corp $1,007
Carter Hawley Hale Stores $1,000
Others $550

Securities Investment **$2,300**
Drexel Burnham Lambert $1,000
Others $1,300

PAC Totals by Category

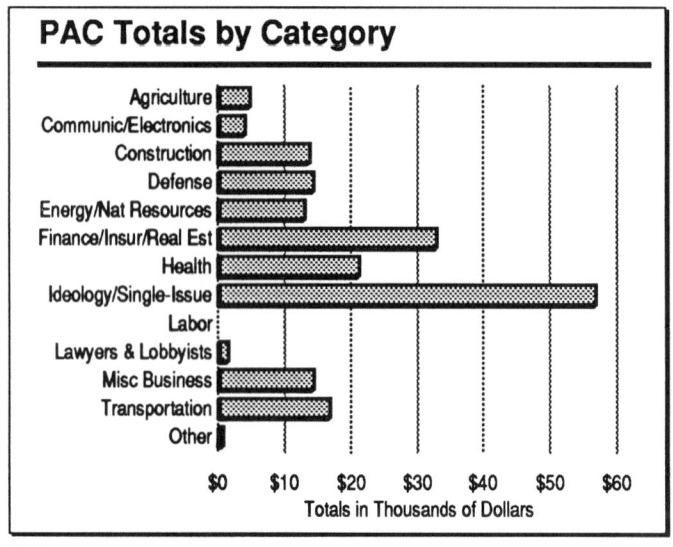

Agriculture
Communic/Electronics
Construction
Defense
Energy/Nat Resources
Finance/Insur/Real Est
Health
Ideology/Single-Issue
Labor
Lawyers & Lobbyists
Misc Business
Transportation
Other

$0 $10 $20 $30 $40 $50 $60
Totals in Thousands of Dollars

Telecommunications **$3,000**

    Continental Telecom $1,500
    AT&T $1,000
    Others $500

Other Major Business PACs

Baxter Healthcare Corp	$1,000	Med Supply
Dow Chemical*	$1,000	Chemicals
Federal Express Corp	$1,000	Delivery
Henley Group Inc	$1,000	Altern Enrgy
National Assn of Temporary Services	$1,000	Employ Agency
Southern California Edison	$1,000	ElectricUtil

Ideological/Single-Issue

Republican/Conservative $12,629

    American Citizens for Political Action $5,000
    America's PAC $2,000
    National Conservative PAC $1,279
    American Conservative Union $1,000
    Conservative Victory Committee $1,000
    Others $2,350

Republican Leadership PACs $16,628

    Conservative Victory Fund (Steve Symms) $5,028
    Citizens for the Republic (Ronald Reagan) $5,000
    National Congressional Club (Jesse Helms)...................$5,000
    Republican Leader's Fund (Bob Michel) $1,000
    Others $600

Other Major Ideological/Single-Issue

National Rifle Assn	$9,900	Pro-Guns
Council for National Defense	$5,000	Pro-Defense
National PAC	$5,000	Pro-Israel
Ruff PAC	$3,000	Tax Policy
Public Service Research Council	$1,750	Anti-Union
Right to Work PAC	$1,500	Anti-Union
National Security PAC	$1,000	Pro-Defense

Independent expenditures opposing Cox

American Council/Conservative Consensus $13,330

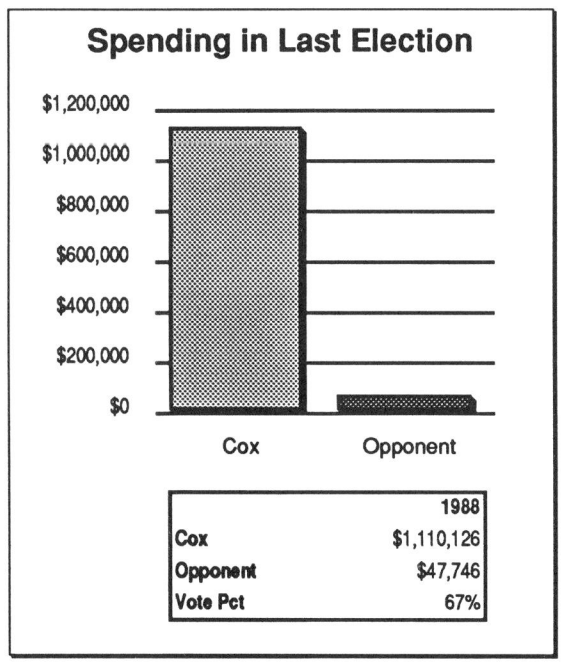

Spending in Last Election

	1988
Cox	$1,110,126
Opponent	$47,746
Vote Pct	67%

---

* Contributions came from more than one PAC affiliated
  with this sponsor.

William J. Coyne, D-Pa (14)

1988 Committees & Subcommittees

First elected: 1980
Total receipts: $168,698
Total from PACs: $156,075

Ways and Means
Health
Select Revenue Measures

PAC Contribution Profile

Business

Commercial Banks **$5,500**
American Bankers Assn $3,500
Pennsylvania Bankers Assn $1,500
Others $500

Electric Utilities **$1,750**
None over $750

Food & Beverage **$2,750**
National Beer Wholesalers Assn $1,000
Others $1,750

Health Professionals **$8,650**
Assn for Advancement of Psychology $2,000
Oral & Maxillofacial Surgeons $1,500
American Medical Assn $1,350
American Academy of Ophthalmology $1,000
Others $2,800

Hospitals & Nursing Homes **$2,750**
American Health Care Assn $1,500
Others $1,250

Campaign Revenue Sources

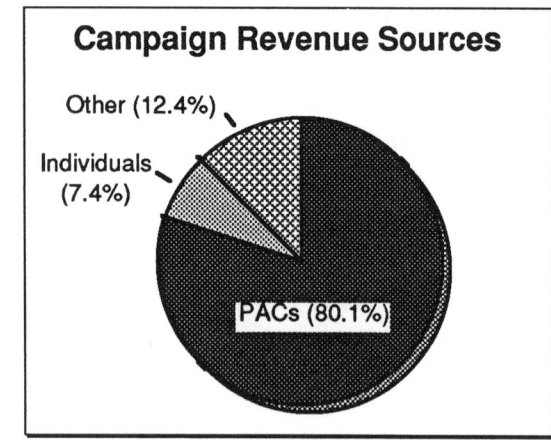

Other (12.4%)
Individuals (7.4%)
PACs (80.1%)

Insurance **$23,000**
Metropolitan Life Insurance $5,500
National Assn of Life Underwriters $5,000
American Council of Life Insurance $1,000
Cigna Corp $1,000
Connecticut Mutual Life Insurance $1,000
Massachusetts Mutual Life Insurance $1,000
New England Mutual Life $1,000
Northwestern Mutual Life $1,000
Prudential Insurance $1,000
Torchmark Corp $1,000
Travelers Corp $1,000
Others $3,500

Lawyers & Lobbyists **$10,000**
Assn of Trial Lawyers of America $5,500
Burson-Marsteller $1,500
Kirkpatrick & Lockhart $1,000
Others $2,000

Mining & Metal Processing **$3,000**
Dravo Corp $1,500
Alcoa $1,000
Others $500

Oil & Gas **$1,750**
USX Corp $1,000
Others $750

Real Estate **$3,000**
National Assn of Realtors $2,500
Others $500

Savings Banks & Credit Unions **$4,500**
US League of Savings Assn $2,000
Credit Union National Assn $1,000
Others $1,500

Securities/Commodities Investment **$3,500**
Chicago Board of Trade $1,000
Others $2,500

Telecommunications **$2,500**
AT&T $2,000
Others $500

Trucking **$2,000**
IU International Corp $1,000
Others $1,000

PAC Totals by Category

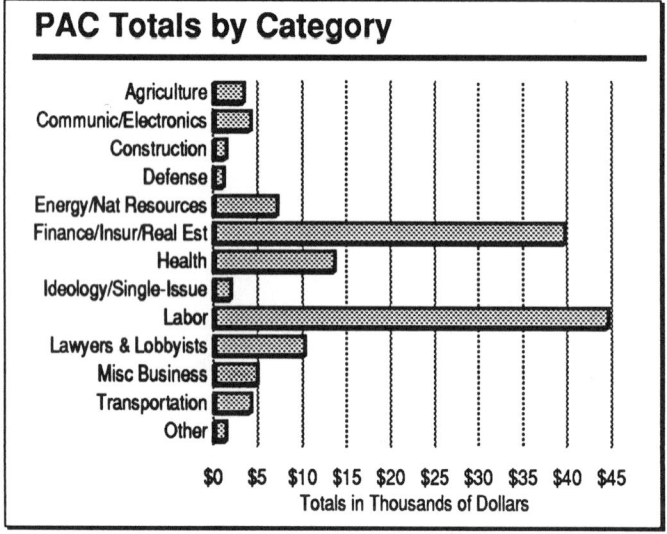

Agriculture
Communic/Electronics
Construction
Defense
Energy/Nat Resources
Finance/Insur/Real Est
Health
Ideology/Single-Issue
Labor
Lawyers & Lobbyists
Misc Business
Transportation
Other

$0 $5 $10 $15 $20 $25 $30 $35 $40 $45
Totals in Thousands of Dollars

Other Major Business PACs

Philip Morris	$1,500	Tobacco
National Assn of Home Builders	$1,000	Resid Constr

Labor

Bldg Trades/Industrial/Misc Unions $21,050

United Auto Workers	$5,000
Carpenters & Joiners Union	$3,500
Operating Engineers Union	$2,500
AFL-CIO*	$2,100
Laborers' Political League	$2,000
Bakery Confect & Tobacco Workers	$1,500
Machinists/Aerospace Workers Union	$1,500
Food & Commercial Workers Union	$1,000
Others	$1,950

Government & Postal Workers $5,300

American Fedn of State/County/Munic Employees	$2,000
National Assn of Letter Carriers	$1,000
National Rural Letter Carriers Assn	$1,000
Others	$1,300

Teachers Unions $5,500

National Education Assn	$4,500
American Federation of Teachers	$1,000

Transportation Unions $12,500

Teamsters Union	$5,000
Air Line Pilots Assn	$2,500
Marine Engineers District 2 Maritime Officers	$1,000
Seafarers International Union	$1,000
Transport Workers Union	$1,000
Others	$2,000

Major Ideological/Single-Issue PACs

Valley Education Fund (Tony Coelho)	$1,000	Dem Leaders

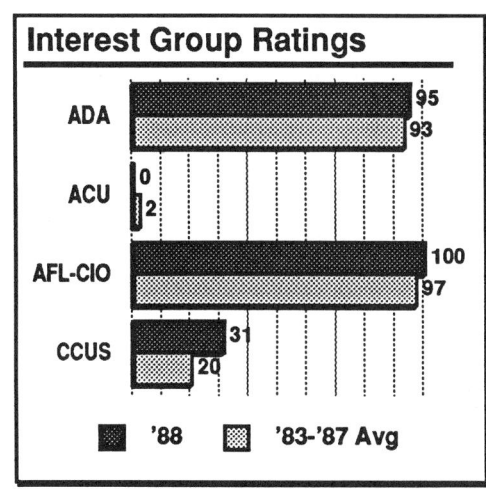

Interest Group Ratings

	'88	'83-'87 Avg
ADA	95	93
ACU	0	2
AFL-CIO	100	97
CCUS	31	20

■ '88   ▨ '83-'87 Avg

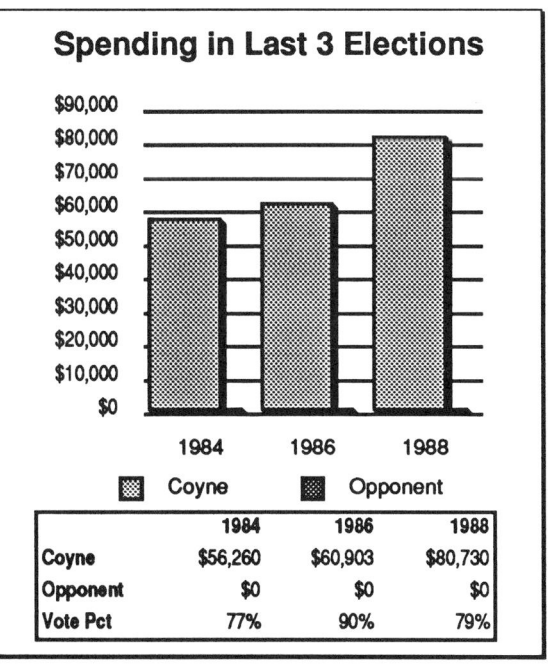

Spending in Last 3 Elections

▨ Coyne   ■ Opponent

	1984	1986	1988
Coyne	$56,260	$60,903	$80,730
Opponent	$0	$0	$0
Vote Pct	77%	90%	79%

---

* Contributions came from more than one PAC affiliated with this sponsor.

Larry E. Craig, R-Idaho (1)

1988 Committees & Subcommittees

Government Operations
Commerce, Consumer and Monetary Affairs (Ranking Republican)

Interior and Insular Affairs
Mining and Natural Resources (Ranking Republican)
Energy and the Environment
National Parks and Public Lands
Water and Power Resources

Standards of Official Conduct

First elected: 1980
Total receipts: $356,033
Total from PACs: $159,060

PAC Contribution Profile

Business

Accountants	**$5,500**
American Institute of CPA's	$5,000
Others	$500
Automotive	**$6,550**
National Auto Dealers Assn	$5,550
Others	$1,000
Commercial & Savings Banks	**$4,950**
American Bankers Assn	$2,500
Idaho Bank & Trust	$1,200
Others	$1,250
Construction	**$10,800**
Morrison-Knudsen	$4,050
National Assn of Home Builders	$2,600
Associated General Contractors	$1,550
Others	$2,600
Dairy	**$2,550**
Associated Milk Producers	$1,000
Dairymens Mountain Assn	$1,000
Others	$550
Electric Utilities	**$10,050**
Idaho Power Company	$3,550
ACRE (Action Committee for Rural Electrification)	$1,000
Washington Water Power Company	$1,000
Others	$4,500

Food & Beverage	**$7,050**
J R Simplot Company	$1,500
Food Marketing Institute	$1,050
Ampco Foods Inc	$1,000
Others	$3,500
Forest Products	**$12,900**
Boise Cascade	$5,000
Potlatch Corp	$5,000
Louisiana-Pacific Corp	$1,000
Others	$1,900
Health Professionals	**$11,999**
American Medical Assn	$9,999
American Optometric Assn	$1,000
Others	$1,000
Insurance	**$3,350**
National Assn of Life Underwriters	$2,500
Others	$850
Livestock	**$2,400**
National Cattlemen's Assn	$1,300
Others	$1,100
Mining	**$11,525**
FMC Corp	$2,000
Shell Oil	$1,100
Phelps Dodge Corp	$1,050
Freeport-McMoran Inc	$1,000
Others	$6,375
Oil & Gas	**$12,950**
Atlantic Richfield	$1,550
Phillips Petroleum	$1,500
Union Pacific Corp	$1,250
Chevron Corp	$1,100
Amoco Corp	$1,000
Mobil Oil	$1,000
Sun Company	$1,000
Others	$4,550

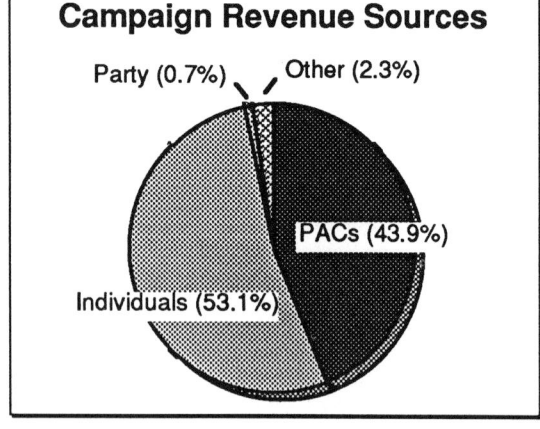

Campaign Revenue Sources

Party (0.7%)   Other (2.3%)
PACs (43.9%)
Individuals (53.1%)

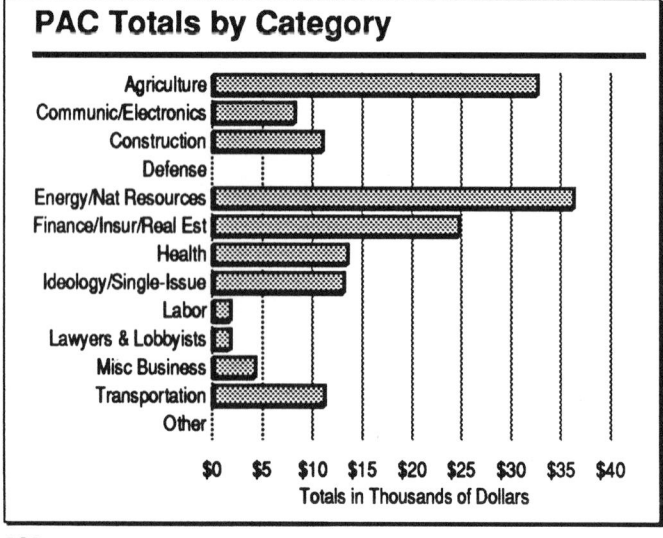

PAC Totals by Category

Agriculture
Communic/Electronics
Construction
Defense
Energy/Nat Resources
Finance/Insur/Real Est
Health
Ideology/Single-Issue
Labor
Lawyers & Lobbyists
Misc Business
Transportation
Other

$0 $5 $10 $15 $20 $25 $30 $35 $40
Totals in Thousands of Dollars

Railroads **$2,570**
> Kansas City Southern $1,820
> Others $750

Real Estate **$10,500**
> National Assn of Realtors $10,000
> Others $500

Sugar Growers **$4,300**
> American Sugarbeet Growers Assn $1,050
> Amalgamated Sugar Company $1,000
> Others $2,250

Telecommunications **$7,750**
> Mountain Bell $3,500
> AT&T $2,250
> Continental Telecom $1,500
> Others $500

Other Major Business PACs

Philip Morris ....$1,000   Tobacco

Major Labor Union PACs

National Assn of Retired Federal Employees .. $1,100   Fedl Workers

Ideological/Single-Issue

Pro-Gun Ownership **$10,900**
> National Rifle Assn $9,900
> Safari Club International $1,000

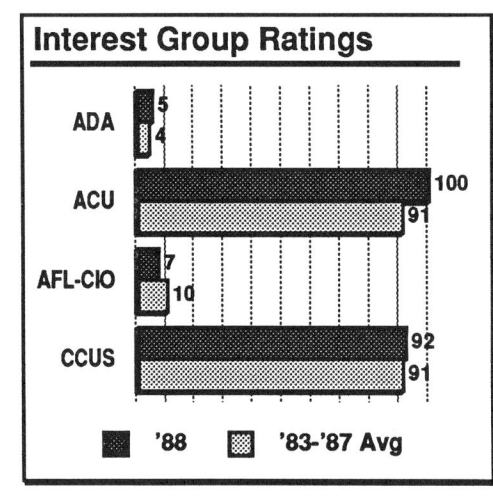

Interest Group Ratings

Group	'88	'83-'87 Avg
ADA	5	4
ACU	100	91
AFL-CIO	7	10
CCUS	92	91

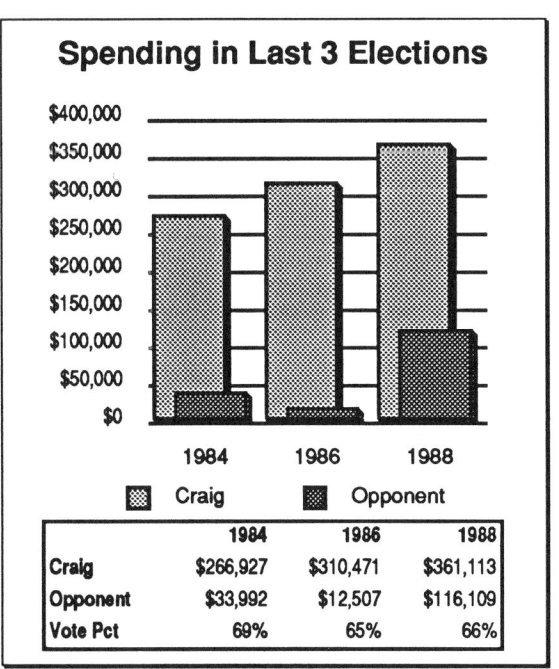

Spending in Last 3 Elections

	1984	1986	1988
Craig	$266,927	$310,471	$361,113
Opponent	$33,992	$12,507	$116,109
Vote Pct	69%	65%	66%

Philip M. Crane, R-Ill (12)

1988 Committees & Subcommittees

Ways and Means
Trade (Ranking Republican)
Social Security

First elected: 1969
Total receipts: $466,894
Total from PACs: $0

PAC Contribution Profile

AT&T	$1,000	LongDistance
Chicago Board of Trade	$1,000	Commodities
Interlake Inc	$500	Indust Equip
Mutual of Omaha	$500	Insurance
Nestle Enterprises Inc	$500	Food & Bevrg
Pacific Mutual Life	$500	Life Insurance
Torrington Company	$500	Auto Equipmt
Union Pacific Corp	$500	Railroads
Marion Laboratories	$300	Pharmaceut
Small Business Council of America	$271	Sml Business
Kemper Insurance	$250	Insurance
Talman Home Federal Savings & Loan	$250	SavingsBanks

NOTE: Crane reported taking no PAC funds in his 1988 campaign. The PACs listed above did report making contributions to him during 1987-88, however, and those contributions are recorded in the official FEC records.

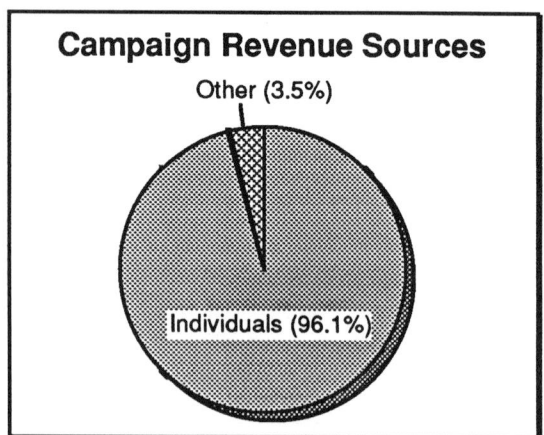

Campaign Revenue Sources

Other (3.5%)

Individuals (96.1%)

PAC Totals by Category

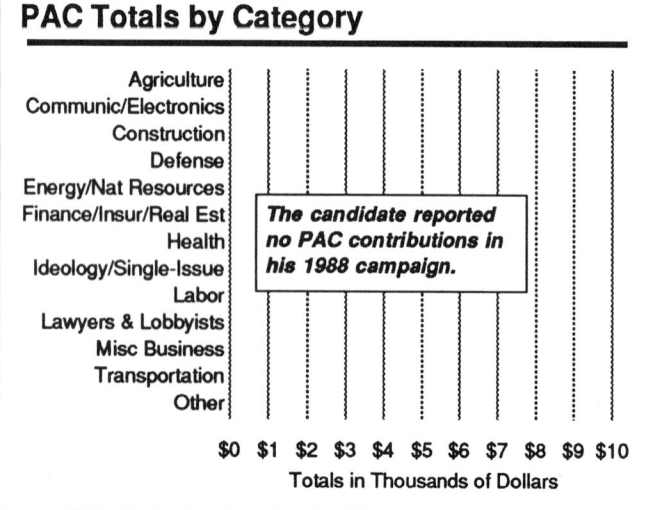

Agriculture
Communic/Electronics
Construction
Defense
Energy/Nat Resources
Finance/Insur/Real Est
Health
Ideology/Single-Issue
Labor
Lawyers & Lobbyists
Misc Business
Transportation
Other

The candidate reported no PAC contributions in his 1988 campaign.

$0 $1 $2 $3 $4 $5 $6 $7 $8 $9 $10
Totals in Thousands of Dollars

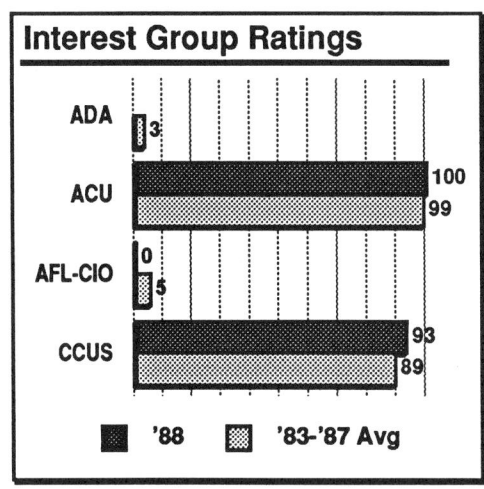

Interest Group Ratings

	'88	'83-'87 Avg
ADA		3
ACU	100	99
AFL-CIO	0	5
CCUS	93	89

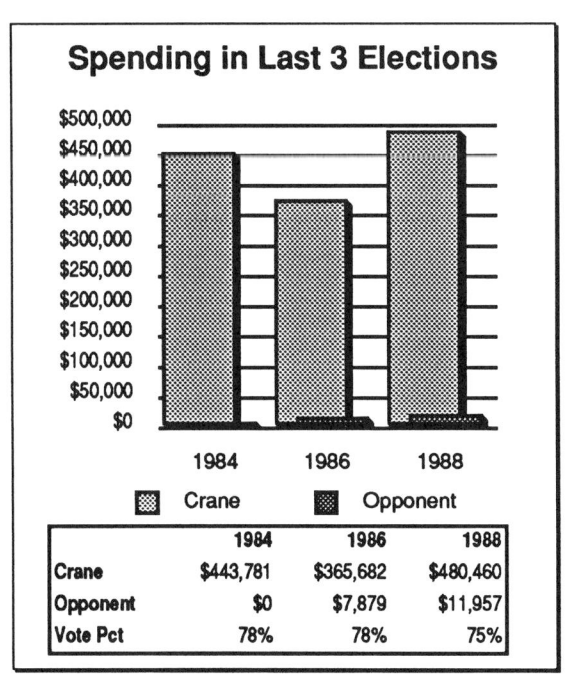

Spending in Last 3 Elections

	1984	1986	1988
Crane	$443,781	$365,682	$480,460
Opponent	$0	$7,879	$11,957
Vote Pct	78%	78%	75%

385

George W. Crockett Jr., D-Mich (13)

First elected: 1980
Total receipts: $97,827
Total from PACs: $63,622

1988 Committees & Subcommittees

Foreign Affairs
Western Hemisphere Affairs (Chairman)
Africa

Judiciary
Courts, Civil Liberties and the Administration of Justice
Crime

Select Aging
Retirement Income and Employment

PAC Contribution Profile

Business

Automotive	**$1,100**
Budd Company	$500
Others	$600
Dairy	**$1,000**
Associated Milk Producers	$1,000
Entertainment Industry	**$1,900**
Motion Picture Assn of America	$600
ASCAP	$500
National Cable Television Assn	$500
Others	$300
Financial Institutions	**$1,300**
Michigan Credit Union League	$1,000
Others	$300
Gas & Electric Utilities	**$2,200**
Detroit Edison	$1,000
Consumers Power Company	$600
Others	$600
Health Professionals	**$1,450**
American Medical Assn	$1,000
Others	$450
Lawyers	**$5,300**
Assn of Trial Lawyers of America	$5,000
Others	$300

Campaign Revenue Sources

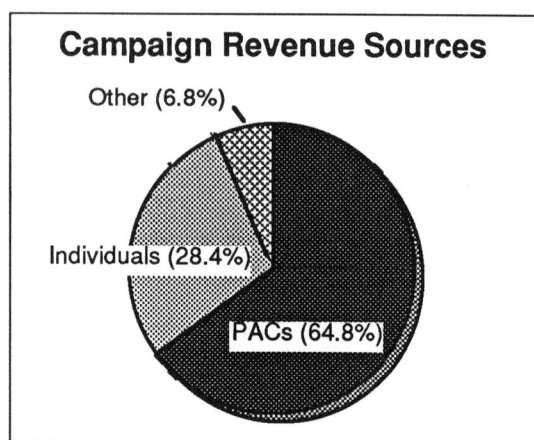

Other (6.8%)
Individuals (28.4%)
PACs (64.8%)

Sugar Growers	**$1,200**
None over $300	
Telecommunications	**$2,300**
AT&T	$1,500
Michigan Bell Telephone	$800

Other Major Business PACs

United Parcel Service	$1,150	Delivery
West Publishing	$1,000	Books & Mags
Ernst & Whinney	$800	Accountants
Blue Cross/Shield of Michigan	$500	Health Insur

PAC Totals by Category

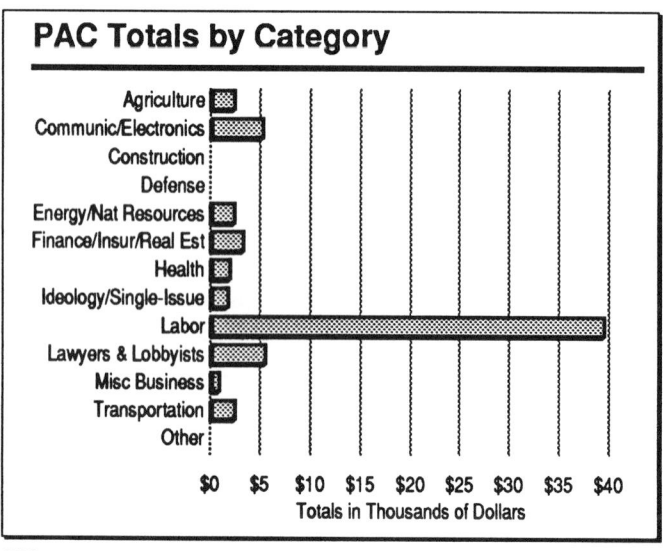

Agriculture
Communic/Electronics
Construction
Defense
Energy/Nat Resources
Finance/Insur/Real Est
Health
Ideology/Single-Issue
Labor
Lawyers & Lobbyists
Misc Business
Transportation
Other

$0 $5 $10 $15 $20 $25 $30 $35 $40
Totals in Thousands of Dollars

Labor

Bldg Trades/Industrial/Misc Unions $16,100

United Auto Workers	$5,000
Carpenters & Joiners Union	$2,500
Operating Engineers Union	$2,100
Laborers' Political League	$1,500
Machinists/Aerospace Workers Union	$1,500
AFL-CIO*	$1,200
Food & Commercial Workers Union	$1,000
Plumbers/Pipefitters Union	$500
Others	$800

Government & Postal Workers $7,400

National Assn of Retired Federal Employees	$3,000
American Fedn of State/County/Munic Employees	$2,500
American Postal Workers Union	$1,300
National Assn of Letter Carriers	$600

Teachers Unions $5,000

National Education Assn	$5,000

Transportation Unions $10,800

Teamsters Union	$7,500
Seafarers International Union	$1,500
Brotherhood of Locomotive Engineers	$600
Transportation Communication Union	$600
Others	$600

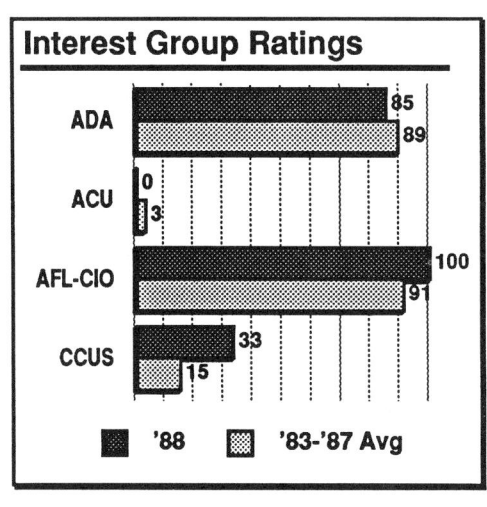

Interest Group Ratings

	'88	'83-'87 Avg
ADA	85	89
ACU	0	3
AFL-CIO	100	91
CCUS	33	15

■ '88   ▨ '83-'87 Avg

Ideological/Single-Issue

Ideological/Single-Issue $1,550

Handgun Control Inc	$600
National Assn of Arab-Americans	$600
Others	$350

Independent expenditures supporting Crockett

National Cmte to Preserve Social Security	$944

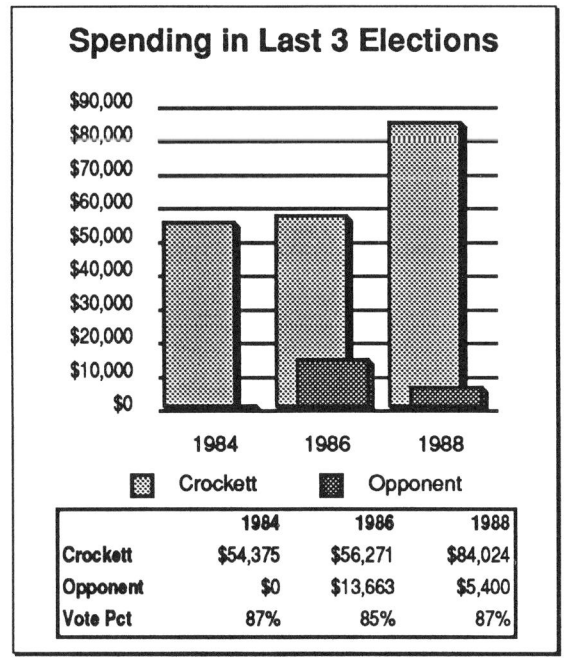

Spending in Last 3 Elections

	1984	1986	1988
Crockett	$54,375	$56,271	$84,024
Opponent	$0	$13,663	$5,400
Vote Pct	87%	85%	87%

▨ Crockett   ▨ Opponent

* Contributions came from more than one PAC affiliated with this sponsor.

William E. Dannemeyer, R-Calif (39)

First elected: 1978
Total receipts: $300,156
Total from PACs: $143,472

1988 Committees & Subcommittees

Energy and Commerce
Commerce, Consumer Protection and Competitiveness (Ranking Republican)
Energy and Power
Health and the Environment

Judiciary
Civil and Constitutional Rights
Monopolies and Commercial Law

PAC Contribution Profile

Business

Accountants	*$5,600*
American Institute of CPA's	$5,000
Others	$600
Automotive	*$5,850*
Auto Dealers & Drivers for Free Trade	$3,500
Others	$2,350
Cable TV & Movies	*$3,500*
Walt Disney Company	$2,500
National Cable Television Assn	$1,000
Construction	*$6,000*
Associated General Contractors	$1,300
National Assn of Home Builders	$1,000
Philips Industries	$1,000
Others	$2,700
Defense	*$6,975*
Hughes Aircraft	$1,950
Rockwell International	$1,425
Northrop Corp	$1,300
Others	$2,300
Electric Utilities	*$4,350*
None over $900	
Food & Beverage	*$3,900*
National Beer Wholesalers Assn	$1,000
Others	$2,900

Health Professionals	*$12,350*
American Medical Assn	$10,000
Cmte for Quality Orthopedic Health Care	$1,000
Others	$1,350
Insurance	*$13,050*
National Assn of Life Underwriters	$3,000
TransAmerica Insurance	$3,000
National Assn of Independent Insurers	$1,700
Travelers Corp	$1,000
Others	$4,350
Oil & Gas	*$17,650*
Atlantic Richfield	$2,000
Pacific Enterprises	$1,500
Shell Oil	$1,400
Chevron Corp	$1,250
Union Oil	$1,100
Petroleum Marketers Assn	$1,000
Others	$9,400

Campaign Revenue Sources

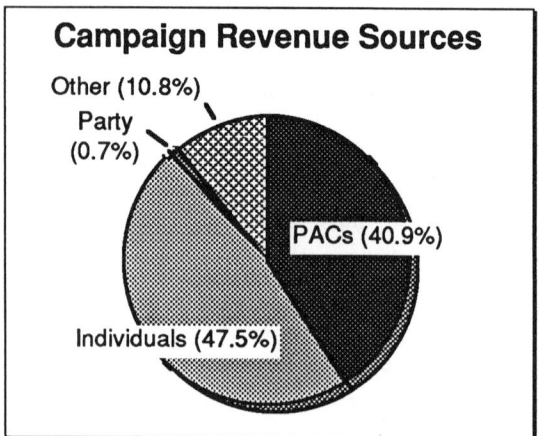

Other (10.8%)
Party (0.7%)
PACs (40.9%)
Individuals (47.5%)

PAC Totals by Category

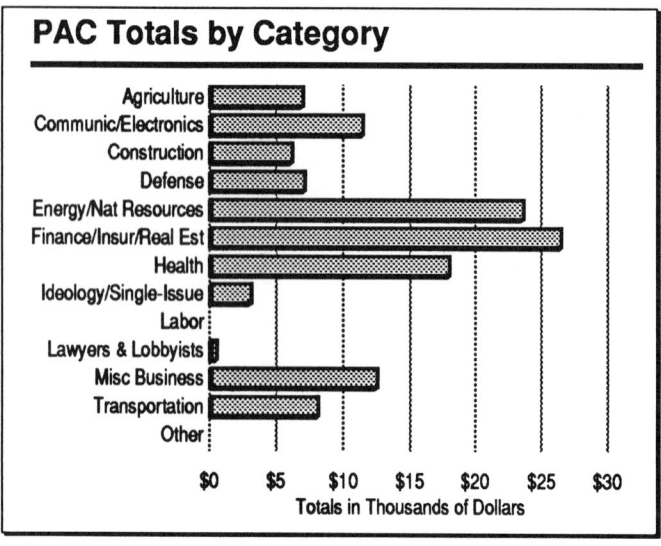

Totals in Thousands of Dollars

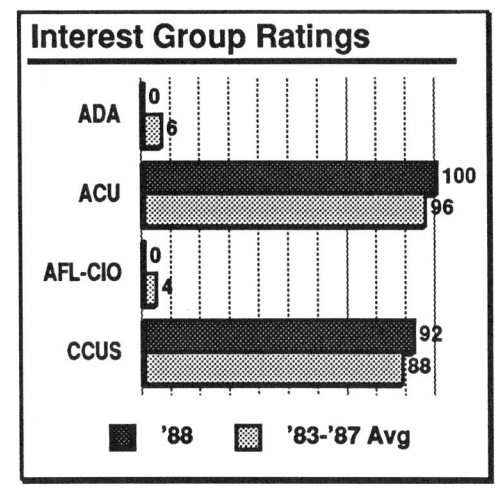

Interest Group Ratings

	'88	'83-'87 Avg
ADA	0	6
ACU	100	96
AFL-CIO	0	4
CCUS	92	88

Pharmaceuticals **$3,200**
    None over $600

Real Estate **$6,050**
    National Assn of Realtors $6,050

Retail Sales **$4,000**
    J C Penney Company $1,100
    Federated Department Stores $1,000
    Others $1,900

Telecommunications **$5,950**
    AT&T $2,000
    Pacific Telesis Group $1,900
    Others $2,050

Tobacco **$3,250**
    Philip Morris $1,500
    Others $1,750

Other Major Business PACs

American Health Care Assn	$2,000	Nursing Home
West Publishing	$1,000	Books & Mags

Major Ideological/Single-Issue PACs

Conservative Victory Fund (Steve Symms)	$1,303	Repub Leader

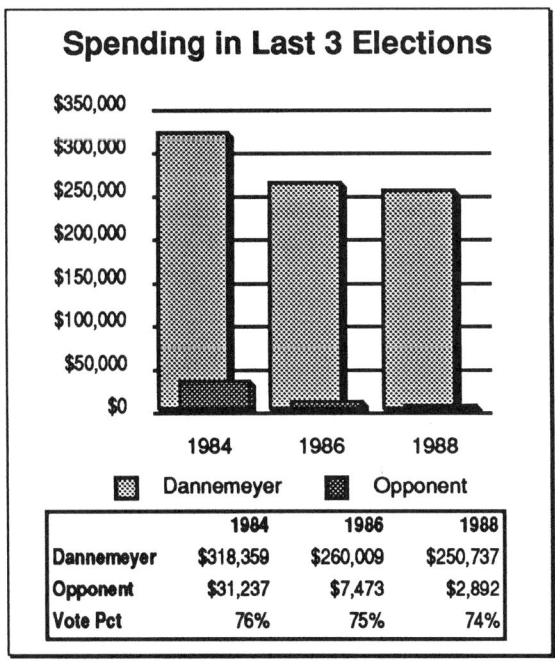

Spending in Last 3 Elections

	Dannemeyer	Opponent

	1984	1986	1988
Dannemeyer	$318,359	$260,009	$250,737
Opponent	$31,237	$7,473	$2,892
Vote Pct	76%	75%	74%

George "Buddy" Darden, D-Ga (7)

First elected: 1983
Total receipts: $448,399
Total from PACs: $241,375

1988 Committees & Subcommittees

Armed Services
Readiness
Research and Development

Interior and Insular Affairs
Energy and the Environment
Insular and International Affairs
National Parks and Public Lands

PAC Contribution Profile

Business

Auto Dealers	**$4,300**
National Auto Dealers Assn	$4,300
Building Contractors	**$6,800**
National Assn of Home Builders	$2,300
Associated General Contractors	$1,600
National Electrical Contractors Assn	$1,000
Sheet Metal/AirCon Contractors	$1,000
Others	$900
Commercial Banks	**$13,550**
Citizens & Southern National Bank	$5,000
Barnett Banks of Florida	$2,500
First Atlanta Corp	$2,000
Trust Company of Georgia	$1,550
Bank South Corp	$1,250
Others	$1,250
Dairy	**$3,000**
Dairymen Inc-Georgia	$2,700
Others	$300
Defense	**$50,050**
Lockheed Corp	$6,100
AT&T	$3,000
Northrop Corp	$3,000
Raytheon	$2,300
Rockwell International	$2,250
General Dynamics	$2,200
McDonnell Douglas*	$2,050
Boeing Company	$2,000
Textron Inc	$2,000

(Continued in next column)

Campaign Revenue Sources

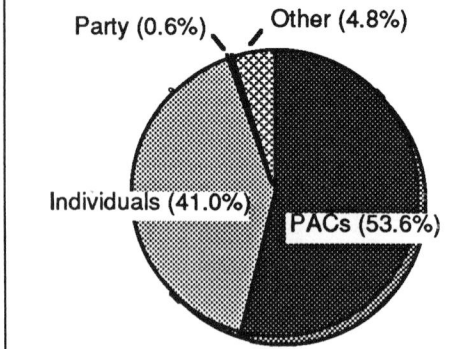

Party (0.6%)
Other (4.8%)
Individuals (41.0%)
PACs (53.6%)

PAC Totals by Category

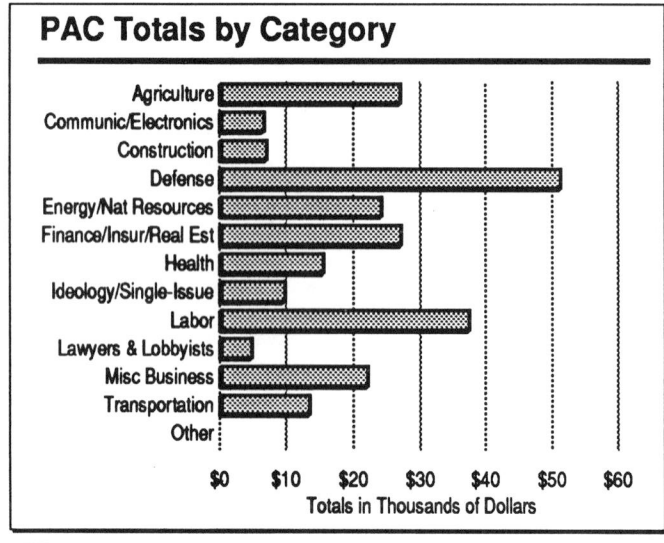

Agriculture
Communic/Electronics
Construction
Defense
Energy/Nat Resources
Finance/Insur/Real Est
Health
Ideology/Single-Issue
Labor
Lawyers & Lobbyists
Misc Business
Transportation
Other

$0 $10 $20 $30 $40 $50 $60
Totals in Thousands of Dollars

Defense (cont'd)	
TRW Inc	$1,600
Harris Corp	$1,500
Hughes Aircraft	$1,500
Tenneco Inc	$1,500
United Technologies	$1,450
Grumman	$1,400
LTV Aerospace & Defense Company	$1,100
Continental Telecom	$1,000
General Electric	$1,000
Martin Marietta Corp	$1,000
Others	$12,100
Electric Utilities	**$10,625**
Southern Company*	$3,350
ACRE (Action Committee for Rural Electrification)	$2,600
Others	$4,675
Food & Beverage	**$17,200**
Malone & Hyde Inc*	$3,000
National Restaurant Assn	$2,500
Coca-Cola Company	$2,300
Food Marketing Institute	$1,700
Kroger Company	$1,000
National Beer Wholesalers Assn	$1,000
Winn-Dixie Stores	$1,000
Others	$4,700
Forest Products	**$2,900**
None over $800	
Health Professionals	**$13,499**
American Medical Assn	$9,999
American Dental Assn	$1,500
Others	$2,000
Insurance	**$3,650**
National Assn of Life Underwriters	$1,500
Georgia US Corp	$1,000
Others	$1,150
Lawyers & Lobbyists	**$4,550**
Assn of Trial Lawyers of America	$2,000
King & Spalding	$1,000
Others	$1,550
Oil & Gas	**$8,800**
Atlanta Gas Light Company	$1,700
Chevron Corp	$1,400
Phillips Petroleum	$1,000
Others	$4,700

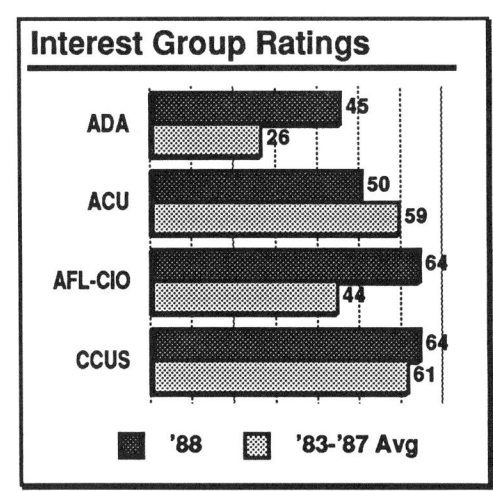

Interest Group Ratings

	'88	'83-'87 Avg
ADA	45	26
ACU	50	59
AFL-CIO	64	44
CCUS	64	61

Legend	
■ '88	▨ '83-'87 Avg

Real Estate *$8,600*

    National Assn of Realtors $7,000
    Others $1,600

Retail Sales *$3,250*

    National Assn of Convenience Stores $1,400
    Others $1,850

Telecommunications *$4,300*

    Southern Bell $4,050
    Others $250

Textiles *$3,900*

    American Textile Manufacturers Institute $1,000
    Others $2,900

Tobacco *$4,350*

    RJR Nabisco $2,000
    Others $2,350

Trucking/Delivery *$6,718*

    United Parcel Service $3,400
    Watkins Associated Industries $1,500
    Others $1,818

Other Major Business PACs

American Polygraph Assn	$2,103	Security Svc
Waste Management Inc	$1,600	Waste Mgmt
Columbia Pictures	$1,000	Movies
Gold Kist	$1,000	Poultry/Egg
Norfolk Southern Corp	$1,000	Railroads
Walter Industries	$1,000	Coal

Labor

Bldg Trades/Industrial/Misc Unions *$15,050*

    United Auto Workers $9,100
    Hotel/Restaurant Employees Union $3,850
    Others $2,100

Government & Postal Workers *$11,100*

    National Assn of Retired Federal Employees ...$5,000
    National Assn of Letter Carriers $3,700
    American Postal Workers Union $1,000
    Others $1,400

Transportation Unions *$11,000*

    Marine Engineers District 2 Maritime Officers ...$4,200
    Air Line Pilots Assn $2,500
    United Transportation Union $2,200
    Seafarers International Union $1,500
    Others $600

Ideological/Single-Issue

Democratic Leadership PACs *$4,000*

    Majority Congress Committee (Jim Wright) $3,000
    Valley Education Fund (Tony Coelho) $1,000

Other Major Ideological/Single-Issue PACs

American Security Council	$2,250	Pro-Defense
National Cmte to Preserve Social Security	$1,600	Soc Secur

Independent expenditures supporting Darden

National Cmte to Preserve Social Security $2,202

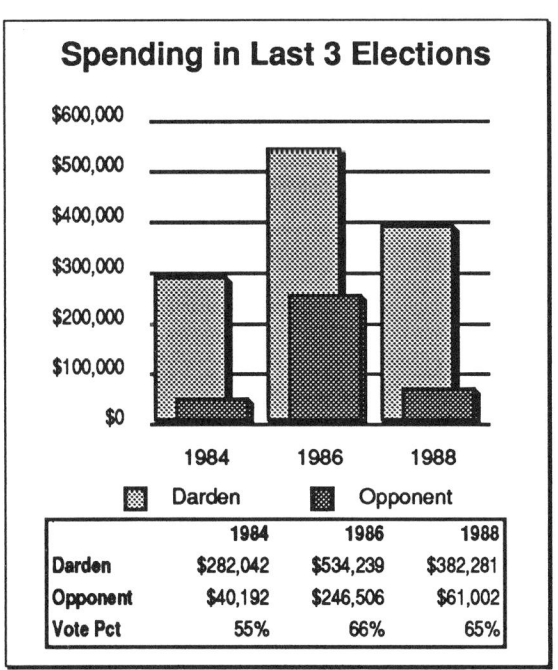

Spending in Last 3 Elections

	1984	1986	1988
Darden	$282,042	$534,239	$382,281
Opponent	$40,192	$246,506	$61,002
Vote Pct	55%	66%	65%

▨ Darden   ■ Opponent

* Contributions came from more than one PAC affiliated
  with this sponsor.

Robert W. Davis, R-Mich (11)

First elected: 1978
Total receipts: $582,616
Total from PACs: $310,059

1988 Committees & Subcommittees

Merchant Marine and Fisheries (Ranking Republican)
Coast Guard and Navigation (Ranking Republican)

Armed Services
Procurement and Military Nuclear Systems
Readiness
Research and Development

PAC Contribution Profile

Business

Building Contractors	**$5,400**
National Assn of Home Builders	$3,900
Associated General Contractors	$1,000
Others	$500
Defense	**$82,250**
Boeing Company	$8,000
United Technologies	$5,000
Lockheed Corp	$4,600
Northrop Corp	$4,300
AT&T	$4,000
Raytheon	$3,400
Tenneco Inc	$3,000
Rockwell International	$2,700
General Dynamics	$2,500
Textron Inc	$2,500
Harris Corp	$2,000
Harsco Corp	$2,000
General Motors	$1,950
LTV Aerospace & Defense Company	$1,850
Kaman Corp	$1,800
Sundstrand Corp*	$1,800
Hughes Aircraft	$1,550
Texas Instruments	$1,550
FMC Corp	$1,500
McDonnell Douglas	$1,500
Electronic Data Systems	$1,450
Martin Marietta Corp	$1,350
Bath Iron Works	$1,300
Chrysler Corp	$1,300
Ford Motor Company	$1,300
Gencorp Inc	$1,300

(Continued in next column)

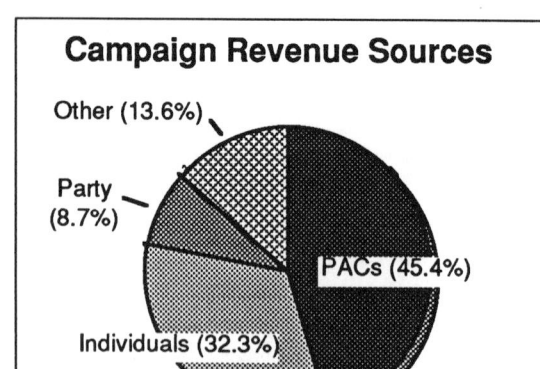

Campaign Revenue Sources

Other (13.6%)
Party (8.7%)
PACs (45.4%)
Individuals (32.3%)

Defense (cont'd)

General Electric	$1,300
Grumman	$1,300
Pneumo Abex Corp	$1,300
Allied-Signal	$1,250
GTE Corp	$1,150
Litton Industries	$1,100
Colt Industries	$1,000
TRW Inc	$1,000
Others	$7,350
Electric Utilities	**$10,025**
Consumers Power Company	$5,075
Detroit Edison	$2,100
Others	$2,850
Financial Institutions	**$5,525**
Michigan Credit Union League	$1,775
American Bankers Assn	$1,000
Michigan League of Savings Institutions	$1,000
Others	$1,750
Forest Products	**$5,100**
Champion International Corp	$1,400
Mead Corp	$1,300
Georgia-Pacific Corp	$1,100
Others	$1,300
Health Professionals	**$15,987**
American Medical Assn	$9,987
American Academy of Ophthalmology	$4,500
American Dental Assn	$1,500
Oil & Gas	**$16,945**
Michigan Consolidated Gas	$2,045
Phillips Petroleum	$2,000
Amoco Corp	$1,500
Michigan Petroleum PAC	$1,500
Exxon Corp	$1,000
Sun Company	$1,000
Zapata Corp	$1,000
Others	$6,900

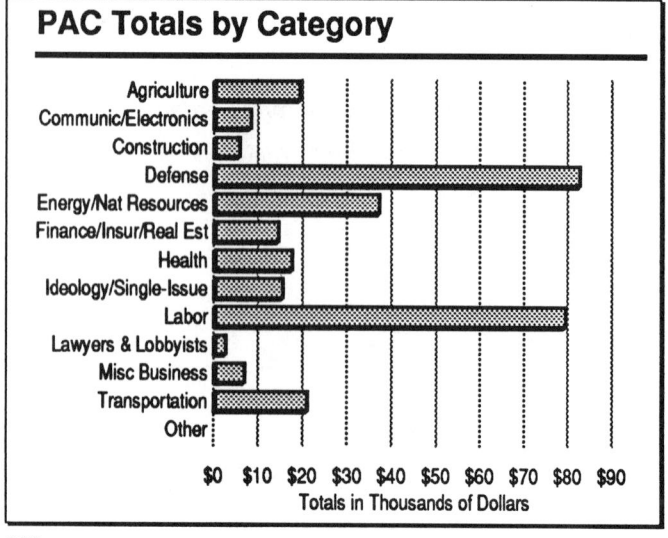

PAC Totals by Category

Agriculture
Communic/Electronics
Construction
Defense
Energy/Nat Resources
Finance/Insur/Real Est
Health
Ideology/Single-Issue
Labor
Lawyers & Lobbyists
Misc Business
Transportation
Other

$0 $10 $20 $30 $40 $50 $60 $70 $80 $90
Totals in Thousands of Dollars

Sea Transport...$16,600

American Pilots Assn	$3,300
CSX Transportation Inc*	$3,000
Boat Owners Assn of the US	$1,800
Matson Navigation	$1,800
American President Lines	$1,600
American Waterways Operators	$1,300
Crowley Maritime	$1,100
Lykes Bros Steamship Company	$1,100
Boating PAC	$1,000
Others	$600

Sugar Growers $5,750

Great Lakes Sugar Beet Growers	$1,800
American Crystal Sugar Corp	$1,600
American Sugarbeet Growers Assn	$1,500
Others	$850

Telecommunications $6,850

Michigan Bell Telephone	$6,350
Others	$500

Other Major Business PACs

Michigan Farm Bureau	$5,000	Farm Orgs
National Assn of Realtors	$5,000	Real Estate
KMS Fusion Inc	$4,500	Nuke Energy
Cleveland-Cliffs Iron Company	$3,300	Metals/Mining
National Assn of Life Underwriters	$2,000	Life Insurance
United Parcel Service	$1,650	Delivery
Stone Container Corp	$1,500	Paper Packg
American Hospital Assn	$1,300	Hospitals
Chicago & NorthWestern Transport	$1,300	Railroads
Dow Chemical/HQ Unit	$1,000	Chemicals
Garvey, Schubert & Barer	$1,000	Lawyers
Waste Management Inc	$1,000	Waste Mgmt

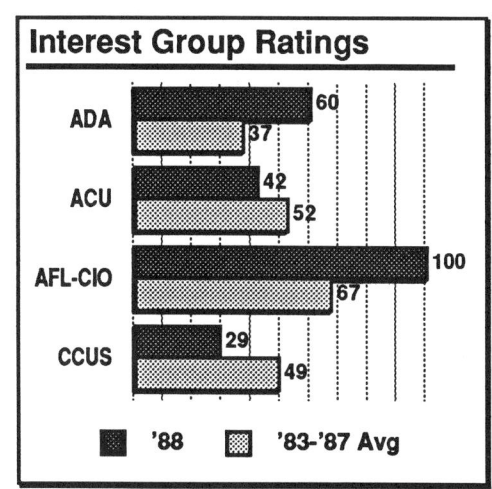

Interest Group Ratings

ADA — '88: 60, '83-'87 Avg: 37
ACU — '88: 42, '83-'87 Avg: 52
AFL-CIO — '88: 100, '83-'87 Avg: 67
CCUS — '88: 29, '83-'87 Avg: 49

■ '88   ▨ '83-'87 Avg

Labor

Bldg Trades/Industrial/Misc Unions $20,850

National Education Assn	$5,800
Carpenters & Joiners Union	$4,000
Communications Workers of America	$2,500
Food & Commercial Workers Union	$2,300
Intl Brotherhood of Electrical Workers	$2,300
Ladies Garment Workers Union	$1,100
Plumbers/Pipefitters Union	$1,000
Others	$1,850

Government & Postal Workers $21,600

National Assn of Letter Carriers	$10,000
National Assn of Retired Federal Employees	$8,000
National Rural Letter Carriers Assn	$1,500
National League of Postmasters	$1,000
Others	$1,100

Sea Transport Unions...............................$22,900

Seafarers International Union	$7,500
Marine Engineers Union*	$7,300
Masters, Mates & Pilots Union*	$7,100
International Longshoremen Assn	$1,000

Other Transportation Unions $13,600

Teamsters Union	$7,500
Air Line Pilots Assn	$4,000
Amalgamated Transit Union	$1,000
Others	$1,100

Ideological/Single-Issue

Pro-Gun Ownership....................................$9,900

National Rifle Assn	$9,900

Other Major Ideological/Single-Issue PACs

American Security Council	$1,250	Pro-Defense
National Cmte to Preserve Social Security	$1,000	Soc Secur
Republican Congressional Boosters Club	$1,000	Repub/Conser

Independent expenditures supporting Davis

National Cmte to Preserve Social Security	$1,869
National Rifle Assn	$1,448

---

* Contributions came from more than one PAC affiliated with this sponsor.

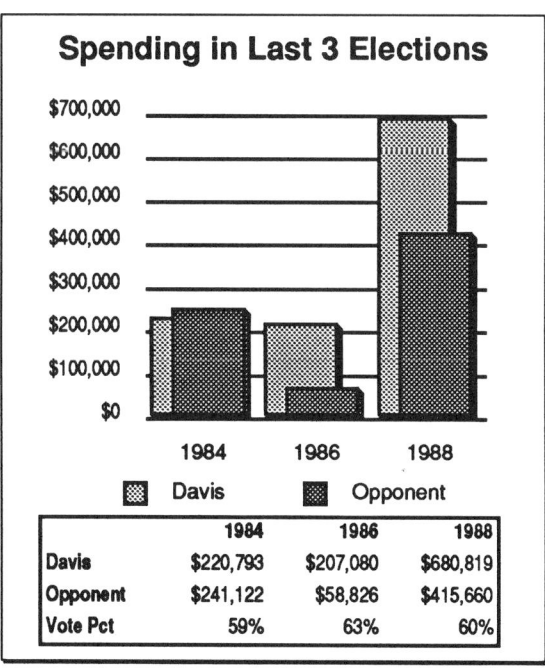

Spending in Last 3 Elections

■ Davis   ▨ Opponent

	1984	1986	1988
Davis	$220,793	$207,080	$680,819
Opponent	$241,122	$58,826	$415,660
Vote Pct	59%	63%	60%

E. "Kika" de la Garza, D-Texas (15)

First elected: 1964
Total receipts: $263,843
Total from PACs: $124,452

1988 Committees & Subcommittees

Agriculture (Chairman)

PAC Contribution Profile

Business

Campaign Revenue Sources

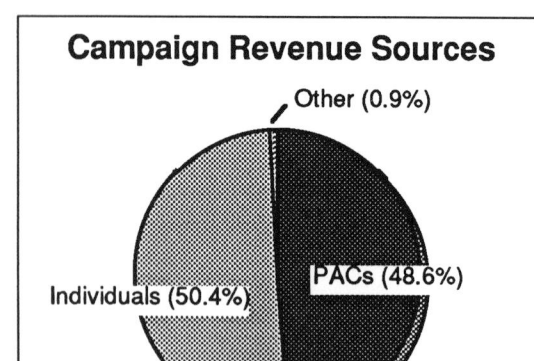

Other (0.9%)
Individuals (50.4%)
PACs (48.6%)

Agricultural Chemicals **$5,550**
    Eli Lilly & Company $1,000
    Monsanto Company $1,000
    Others $3,550

Agricultural Services **$4,200**
    American Veterinary Medical Assn $1,000
    Farm Credit Council $1,000
    Valmont Industries $1,000
    Others $1,200

Commercial Banks **$7,500**
    American Bankers Assn $5,500
    Independent Bankers Assn $2,000

Commodity Trading **$8,000**
    Chicago Mercantile Exchange $5,000
    Chicago Board of Trade $2,500
    Others $500

Construction **$2,850**
    National Utility Contractors Assn $2,000
    Others $850

Cotton **$4,500**
    American Cotton Shippers Assn $2,000
    National Cotton Council $1,500
    Others $1,000

Dairy **$11,500**
    Associated Milk Producers $4,500
    Dairymen Inc $2,500
    Mid-American Dairymen $1,500
    Borden Inc $1,000
    Milk Industry Foundation $1,000
    Others $1,000

Farm Organizations **$5,250**
    National Council of Farmer Co-ops $1,500
    Texas Farm Bureau $1,250
    Alabama Farm Bureau Federation $1,000
    National Farmers Organization $1,000
    Others $500

Food & Beverage **$9,000**
    Food Marketing Institute $1,500
    A E Staley Manufacturing Company $1,000
    ConAgra Inc $1,000
    General Mills $1,000
    IBP Inc $1,000
    Others $3,500

Fruits & Vegetables **$7,750**
    Desert Grape Growers League/California $2,000
    Sun-Maid Growers of California $2,000
    Florida Citrus Mutual $1,000
    Sunkist Growers $1,000
    Others $1,750

Lawyers **$5,300**
    Vinson, Elkins, Searls, Connally & Smith $2,500
    Assn of Trial Lawyers of America $2,000
    Others $800

Livestock & Poultry **$8,250**
    Texas/Southwestern Cattle Raisers $2,000
    King Ranch $1,000
    National Wool Growers Assn $1,000
    Texas Cattle Feeders Assn $1,000
    Others $3,250

Soybeans, Rice & Grain Growers **$4,000**
    American Rice Inc $1,000
    American Soybean Assn $1,000
    Others $2,000

PAC Totals by Category

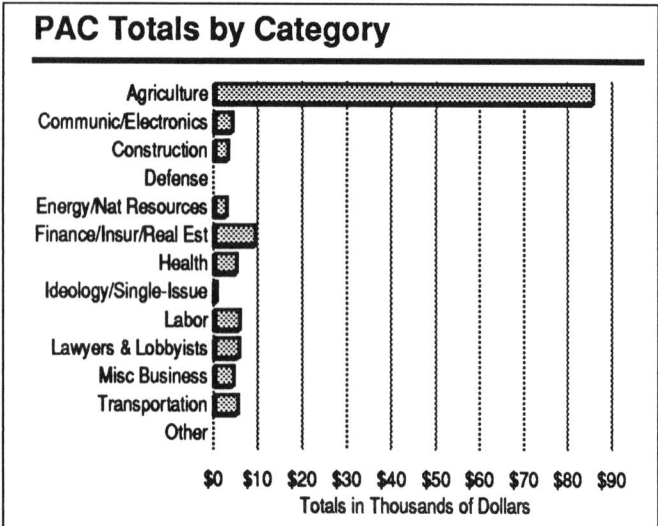

Agriculture
Communic/Electronics
Construction
Defense
Energy/Nat Resources
Finance/Insur/Real Est
Health
Ideology/Single-Issue
Labor
Lawyers & Lobbyists
Misc Business
Transportation
Other

$0 $10 $20 $30 $40 $50 $60 $70 $80 $90
Totals in Thousands of Dollars

Sugar Growers **$12,250**

    American Crystal Sugar Corp $5,000
    Florida Sugar Cane League $1,500
    American Sugar Cane League $1,000
    Minn-Dak Farmers Co-op $1,000
    Others $3,750

Telecommunications **$3,000**

    AT&T $1,000
    Southwestern Bell $1,000
    Others $1,000

Tobacco **$4,000**

    Philip Morris $2,500
    Others $1,500

Other Major Business PACs

National Auto Dealers Assn	$1,500	Auto Sales
ACRE (Action Committee for Rural Electric)	$1,000	RuralElect
American Medical Assn	$1,000	Doctors
Deere & Company	$1,000	Farm Equip
John Hancock Financial Service	$1,000	Insurance
National Pest Control Assn	$1,000	Pest Control
National Assn of Realtors	$1,000	Real Estate
Union Pacific Corp	$1,000	Railroads
United Parcel Service	$1,000	Delivery

Interest Group Ratings

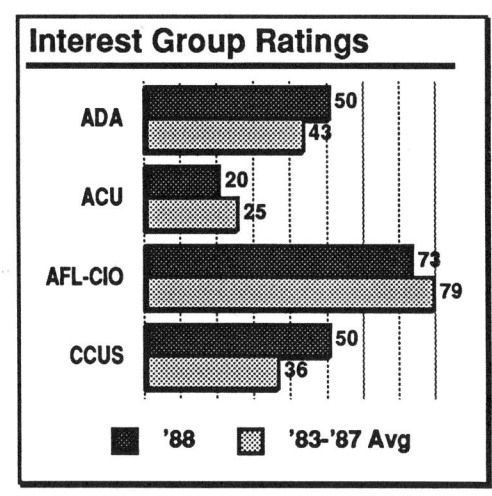

	'88	'83-'87 Avg
ADA	50	43
ACU	20	25
AFL-CIO	73	79
CCUS	50	36

Labor

Labor Unions **$5,500**

    American Fedn of State/County/Munic Employees $2,000
    Carpenters & Joiners Union $1,000
    Operating Engineers Union $1,000
    Others $1,500

Independent expenditures supporting de la Garza

American Sugarbeet Growers Assn $2,000
National Cmte to Preserve Social Security $1,091

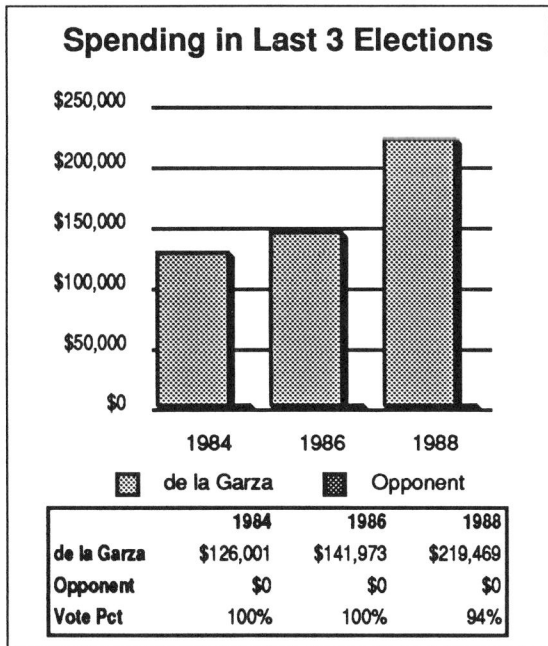

Spending in Last 3 Elections

	1984	1986	1988
de la Garza	$126,001	$141,973	$219,469
Opponent	$0	$0	$0
Vote Pct	100%	100%	94%

Peter A. DeFazio, D-Ore (4)

First elected: 1986
Total receipts: $327,640
Total from PACs: $235,589

1988 Committees & Subcommittees

Interior and Insular Affairs
General Oversight and Investigations
National Parks and Public Lands
Water and Power Resources

Public Works and Transportation
Aviation
Water Resources

Small Business
Regulation and Business Opportunities

PAC Contribution Profile

Business

Aviation/Air Freight **$3,600**
   None over $600

Commercial Banks **$3,000**
   US Bancorp $2,000
   American Bankers Assn $1,000

Dairy **$2,350**
   Associated Milk Producers $1,250
   Mid-American Dairymen $1,100

Electric Utilities **$4,100**
   Pacific Power & Light $1,500
   ACRE (Action Committee for Rural Electrification) $1,000
   Others $1,600

Forest Products **$2,600**
   Sun Studs Inc $1,250
   Others $1,350

Health Professionals **$10,487**
   American Medical Assn $7,487
   American Academy of Ophthalmology $2,500
   Others $500

Lawyers **$8,100**
   Assn of Trial Lawyers of America $5,000
   Stoel, Rives, Boley, Jones & Grey $1,500
   California Trial Lawyers Assn $1,000
   Others $600

Campaign Revenue Sources

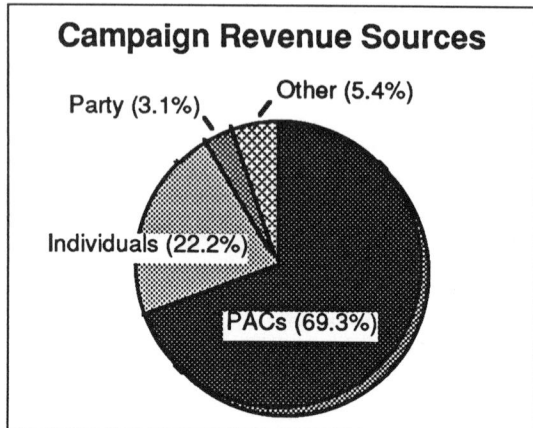

Party (3.1%)
Other (5.4%)
Individuals (22.2%)
PACs (69.3%)

Real Estate **$10,000**
   National Assn of Realtors $10,000

Residential Construction **$6,000**
   National Assn of Home Builders $6,000

Telecommunications **$4,800**
   Pacific Northwest Bell $3,000
   AT&T $1,300
   Others $500

Trucking/Delivery **$3,300**
   United Parcel Service $1,900
   Others $1,400

Other Major Business PACs

National Assn of Life Underwriters	$1,500	Life Insurance
Nike Inc	$1,500	Shoes
National Auto Dealers Assn	$1,000	Auto Sales

PAC Totals by Category

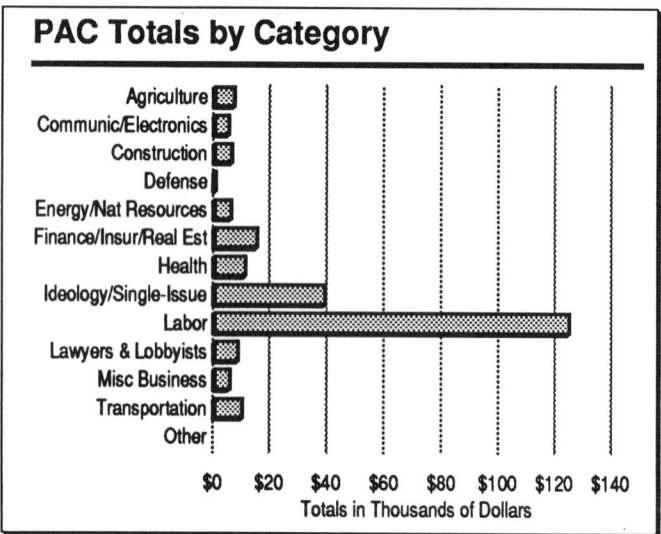

Agriculture
Communic/Electronics
Construction
Defense
Energy/Nat Resources
Finance/Insur/Real Est
Health
Ideology/Single-Issue
Labor
Lawyers & Lobbyists
Misc Business
Transportation
Other

$0 $20 $40 $60 $80 $100 $120 $140
Totals in Thousands of Dollars

Labor

Bldg Trades/Industrial/Misc Unions **$48,550**
- Machinists/Aerospace Workers Union $11,000
- Intl Brotherhood of Electrical Workers............................$6,300
- AFL-CIO* $5,600
- United Auto Workers $5,300
- Carpenters & Joiners Union $4,700
- Operating Engineers Union $4,000
- Food & Commercial Workers Union................................$3,300
- Service Employees International Union $2,000
- Ironworkers Union $1,000
- United Steelworkers $1,000
- Others $4,350

Government & Postal Workers **$33,650**
- American Fedn of State/County/Munic Employees $10,000
- National Assn of Letter Carriers $10,000
- National Assn of Retired Federal Employees $10,000
- American Federation of Government Employees $1,100
- Others $2,550

Teachers Unions **$12,500**
- National Education Assn $5,000
- Oregon Education Assn $5,000
- American Federation of Teachers $2,500

Transportation Unions **$29,758**
- Air Line Pilots Assn $8,500
- Marine Engineers Union* $5,000
- Teamsters Union $5,000
- Amalgamated Transit Union..$3,000
- United Transportation Union $2,700
- Transportation Communication Union.............................$1,936
- Seafarers International Union $1,000
- Others $2,622

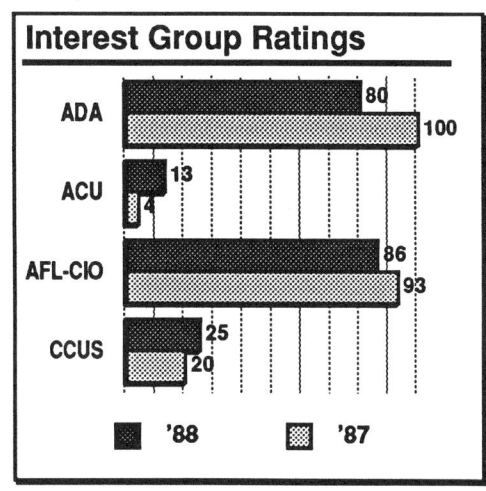

Interest Group Ratings

ADA: '88 80, '87 100
ACU: '88 13, '87 4
AFL-CIO: '88 86, '87 93
CCUS: '88 25, '87 20

■ '88   ▨ '87

Ideological/Single-Issue

Democratic/Liberal **$5,747**
- National Cmte for an Effective Congress $4,997
- Others $750

Democratic Leadership PACs **$3,000**
- Valley Education Fund (Tony Coelho) $3,000

Pro-Choice **$6,300**
- National Abortion Rights Action League $5,000
- Voters for Choice/Friends of Family Planning $1,300

Other Major Ideological/Single-Issue PACs

National Rifle Assn ....$9,900   Pro-Guns
National Cmte to Preserve Social Security ......$5,300   Soc Secur
Human Rights Campaign Fund ....$3,426   Gay Rights
Sierra Club ....$1,777   Environment
Council for a Livable World ....$1,167   Pro-Peace
Joint Action Cmte for Political Affairs ....$1,000   Pro-Israel

Independent expenditures supporting DeFazio

National Cmte to Preserve Social Security $4,886

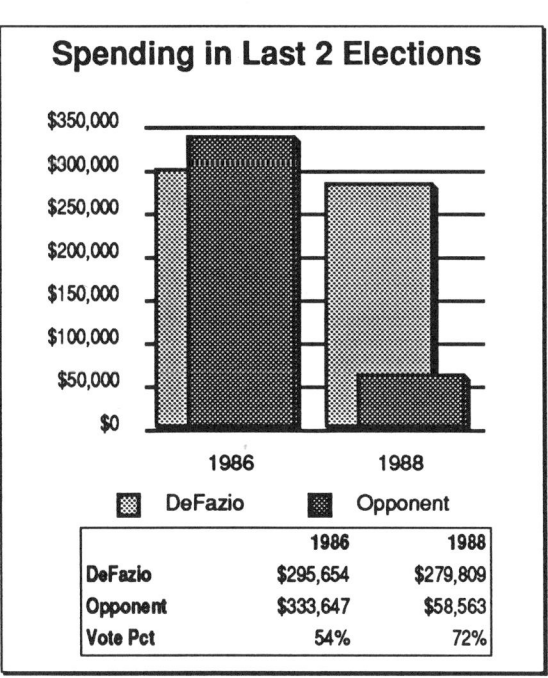

Spending in Last 2 Elections

	1986	1988
DeFazio	$295,654	$279,809
Opponent	$333,647	$58,563
Vote Pct	54%	72%

▨ DeFazio   ■ Opponent

---

* Contributions came from more than one PAC affiliated
with this sponsor.

Tom DeLay, R-Texas (22)

1988 Committees & Subcommittees

Appropriations
Military Construction
Transportation and Related Agencies

First elected: 1984
Total receipts: $364,837
Total from PACs: $171,650

Campaign Revenue Sources

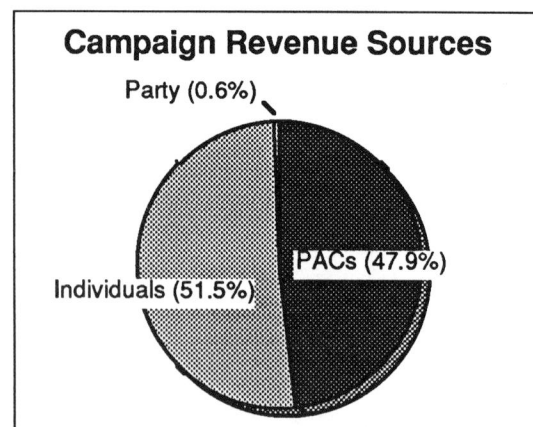

Party (0.6%)
PACs (47.9%)
Individuals (51.5%)

PAC Contribution Profile

Business

Air Transport/Air Freight	**$11,300**
Aircraft Owners & Pilots Assn	$4,400
Texas Air	$3,000
Federal Express Corp	$2,000
Others	$1,900
Automotive	**$6,550**
National Auto Dealers Assn	$4,800
Auto Dealers & Drivers for Free Trade	$1,500
Others	$250
Buses, Trucks & Taxi Service	**$8,700**
United Parcel Service	$2,300
International Taxicab Assn	$2,000
American Bus Assn	$1,300
Greyhound Lines	$1,000
Others	$2,100
Chemicals	**$9,600**
Dow Chemical	$6,000
FMC Corp	$1,000
Nalco Chemical Company	$1,000
Others	$1,600
Commercial Banks	**$10,000**
MBank	$5,000
Allied Bankshares	$2,000
NCNB Texas	$1,000
Texas American Bancshares	$1,000
Others	$1,000

Construction	**$16,100**
National Assn of Home Builders	$4,000
Associated General Contractors	$2,100
Texas Industries	$2,000
CRS Group Inc	$1,000
Fluor Corp	$1,000
Halliburton Company	$1,000
Tenneco Inc	$1,000
Others	$4,000
Defense	**$7,800**
Electrospace Systems Inc	$1,000
Others	$6,800
Electric Utilities	**$8,000**
Houston Industries	$3,000
Texas Utilities Electric Company*	$1,600
Others	$3,400
Farm Organizations	**$2,500**
Texas Farm Bureau	$2,500
Food & Beverage	**$8,550**
Food Marketing Institute	$1,850
National Beer Wholesalers Assn	$1,050
National Restaurant Assn	$1,000
Pepsico Inc	$1,000
Others	$3,650
Health Professionals	**$11,000**
American Medical Assn	$10,000
American Academy of Ophthalmology	$1,000
Insurance	**$4,800**
American National Insurance Company	$1,500
National Assn of Life Underwriters	$1,500
Others	$1,800
Lawyers & Lobbyists	**$6,978**
Assn of Trial Lawyers of America	$2,000
Akin, Gump, Hauer & Feld	$1,350
Locke Purnell Rain Harrell	$1,000
Mayor, Day & Caldwell	$1,000
Others	$1,628

PAC Totals by Category

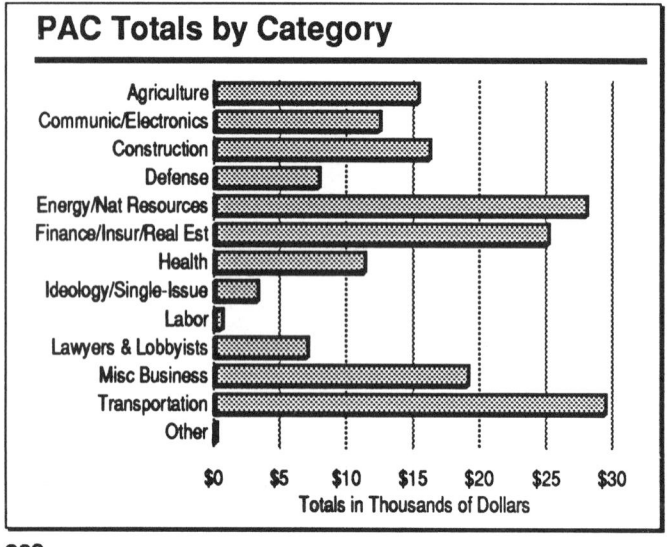

Agriculture
Communic/Electronics
Construction
Defense
Energy/Nat Resources
Finance/Insur/Real Est
Health
Ideology/Single-Issue
Labor
Lawyers & Lobbyists
Misc Business
Transportation
Other

$0 $5 $10 $15 $20 $25 $30
Totals in Thousands of Dollars

Oil & Gas **$18,100**

HOUPAC	$2,000
Columbia Hydrocarbon Corp	$1,550
Coastal Corp	$1,500
Mobil Oil	$1,250
Shell Oil	$1,100
Phillips Petroleum	$1,000
Texas Eastern Gas Transmission	$1,000
Others	$8,700

Real Estate **$9,500**

National Assn of Realtors	$8,000
Commonwealth Financial Group	$1,000
Others	$500

Telecommunications **$10,350**

GTE (Southwest)	$3,500
AT&T	$2,800
Southwestern Bell	$2,000
Penn Central Corp	$1,000
Others	$1,050

Tobacco **$5,050**

Philip Morris	$2,500
Tobacco Institute	$1,050
Others	$1,500

Other Major Business PACs

National Pest Control Assn	$1,800	Pest Control
J C Penney Company	$1,500	Dept Store
Cooper Industries	$1,000	Electronics
Texas Cattle Feeders Assn	$1,000	Feedlots

Ideological/Single-Issue

Ideological/Single-Issue **$2,700**

National Rifle Assn	$1,050
Others	$1,650

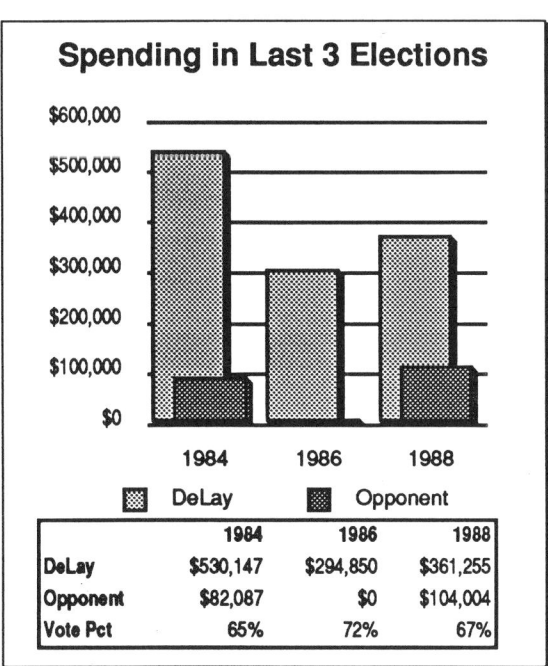

Spending in Last 3 Elections

	1984	1986	1988
DeLay	$530,147	$294,850	$361,255
Opponent	$82,087	$0	$104,004
Vote Pct	65%	72%	67%

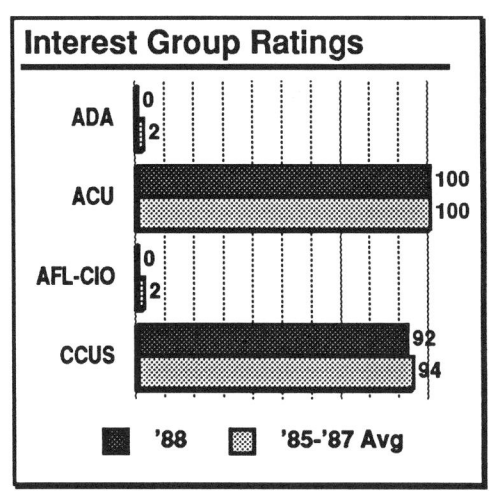

Interest Group Ratings

	'88	'85-'87 Avg
ADA	0	2
ACU	100	100
AFL-CIO	0	2
CCUS	92	94

■ '88   ▨ '85-'87 Avg

---

* Contributions came from more than one PAC affiliated with this sponsor.

Ronald V. Dellums, D-Calif (8)

First elected: 1970
Total receipts: $1,153,750
Total from PACs: $83,399

1988 Committees & Subcommittees

District of Columbia (Chairman)
Fiscal Affairs and Health
Judiciary and Education

Armed Services
Military Installations and Facilities (Chairman)
Investigations

PAC Contribution Profile

Business

Defense **$3,850**

McDonnell Douglas*	$1,050
General Dynamics	$1,000
Grumman	$600
Others	$1,200

Lawyers **$5,800**

Assn of Trial Lawyers of America	$5,000
O'Melveny & Myers	$800

Other Major Business PACs

American President Lines	$2,400	SeaTransport
United Parcel Service	$1,700	Delivery
World Savings & Loan	$1,000	SavingsBanks
ACRE (Action Committee for Rural Electric)	$800	RuralElect
Ch2M Hill	$500	Engineers
Greater Wash Board of Trade	$500	Chamb/Cmrce
Kansas City Southern	$500	Railroads
Maxima Corp	$500	Data Process
MCA Inc	$500	Movies
Motion Picture Assn of America	$500	Movies
National Assn of Social Workers	$500	Social Work
Wine Institute	$500	Wine&Liquor

Campaign Revenue Sources

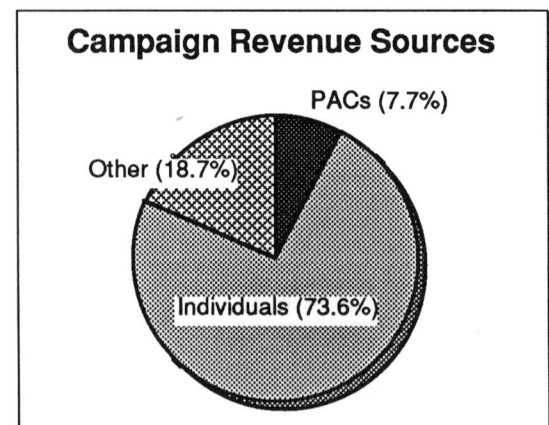

PACs (7.7%)
Other (18.7%)
Individuals (73.6%)

PAC Totals by Category

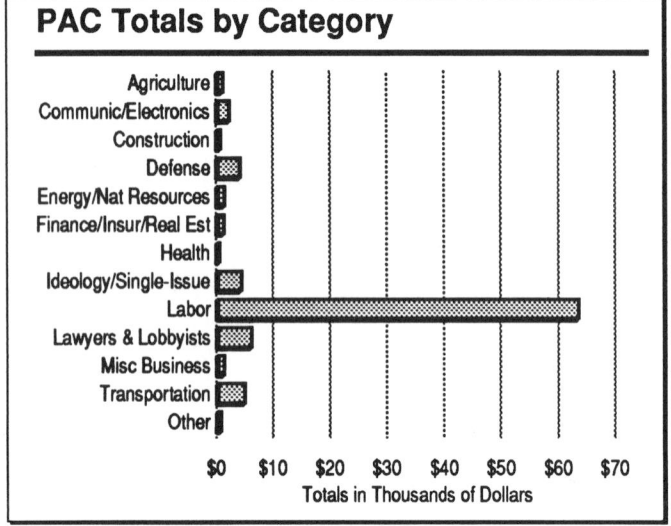

Agriculture
Communic/Electronics
Construction
Defense
Energy/Nat Resources
Finance/Insur/Real Est
Health
Ideology/Single-Issue
Labor
Lawyers & Lobbyists
Misc Business
Transportation
Other

$0 $10 $20 $30 $40 $50 $60 $70
Totals in Thousands of Dollars

Labor

Bldg Trades/Industrial/Misc Unions **$23,100**

Carpenters & Joiners Union	$4,750
Laborers' Western Political League	$3,000
Machinists/Aerospace Workers Union	$3,000
Food & Commercial Workers Union	$2,550
Operating Engineers Union	$2,500
United Auto Workers	$2,300
AFL-CIO*	$1,300
Ladies Garment Workers Union	$1,300
Hotel/Restaurant Employees Union	$850
United Mine Workers	$800
Plumbers/Pipefitters Union	$500
Others	$250

Government/Postal Workers **$17,600**

National Assn of Retired Federal Employees	$7,000
American Fedn of State/County/Munic Employees	$5,000
American Postal Workers Union	$2,600
National Assn of Letter Carriers*	$2,200
National Assn of Postmasters	$500
Others	$300

Teachers Unions **$4,500**

National Education Assn	$4,500

Transportation Unions **$18,000**

Teamsters Union	$6,000
Seafarers International Union	$3,500
Marine Engineers Union	$2,000
United Transportation Union	$1,500
Longshoremen/Warehousemen Union	$1,300
Masters, Mates & Pilots Union	$1,000
Maritime Union of America	$800
Transportation Communication Union	$600
Brotherhood of Locomotive Engineers	$500
Transport Workers Union	$500
Others	$300

Interest Group Ratings

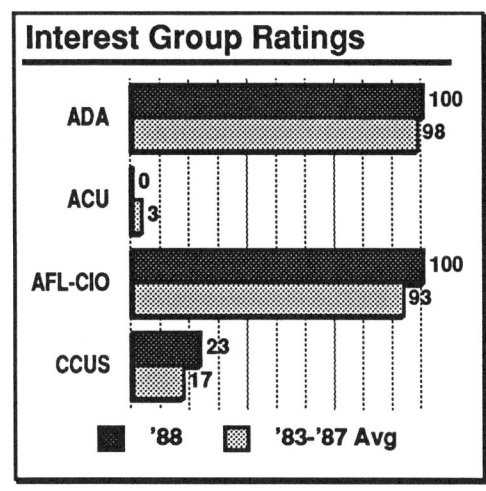

Ideological/Single-Issue

Ideological/Single-Issue **$3,720**

Valley Education Fund (Tony Coelho)	$1,000	Dem Leaders
Human Rights Campaign Fund	$500	Gay Rights
National Cmte to Preserve Social Security	$500	Soc Secur
Women's Pro-Israel National PAC	$500	Pro-Israel
Others	$1,220	

Independent expenditures supporting Dellums

National Cmte to Preserve Social Security $1,887

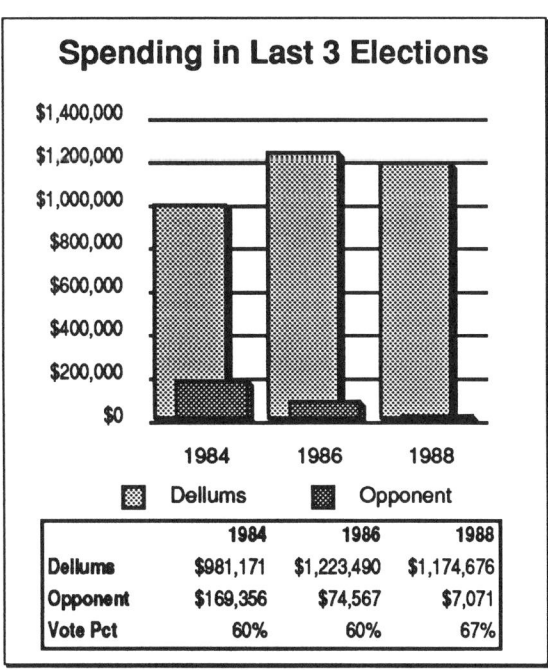

Spending in Last 3 Elections

	1984	1986	1988
Dellums	$981,171	$1,223,490	$1,174,676
Opponent	$169,356	$74,567	$7,071
Vote Pct	60%	60%	67%

* Contributions came from more than one PAC affiliated
  with this sponsor.

Butler Derrick, D-SC (3)

First elected: 1974	
Total receipts:	$579,468
Total from PACs:	$370,841

1988 Committees & Subcommittees

Budget
Budget Process (Chairman)
Economic and Trade Policy

Rules
Legislative Process (Chairman)

Select Aging
Health and Long-Term Care

Campaign Revenue Sources

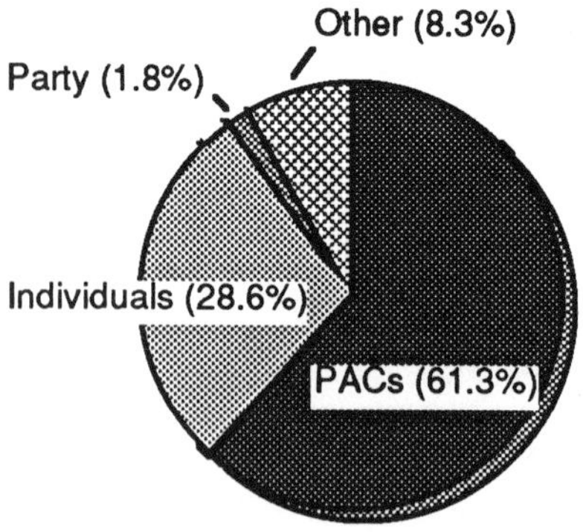

Other (8.3%)
Party (1.8%)
Individuals (28.6%)
PACs (61.3%)

PAC Contribution Profile

Business

Automotive ***$7,500***
- National Auto Dealers Assn $5,500
- Chrysler Corp $1,500
- Others $500

Aviation/Air Freight ***$6,800***
- Federal Express Corp $3,000
- Aircraft Owners & Pilots Assn $2,500
- Others $1,300

Commercial Banks ***$26,200***
- American Bankers Assn $10,000
- Citizens & Southern National Bank $4,000
- Bankers Trust $3,000
- South Carolina National Bank $2,000
- Others $7,200

Construction ***$7,250***
- Stone & Webster $2,000
- Owens-Corning Fiberglas $1,500
- Others $3,750

Consumer Credit & Loans ***$7,000***
- Beneficial Management Corp $2,500
- Others $4,500

Defense ***$8,900***
- Martin Marietta Corp $2,500
- EG&G Inc $1,500
- Others $4,900

PAC Totals by Category

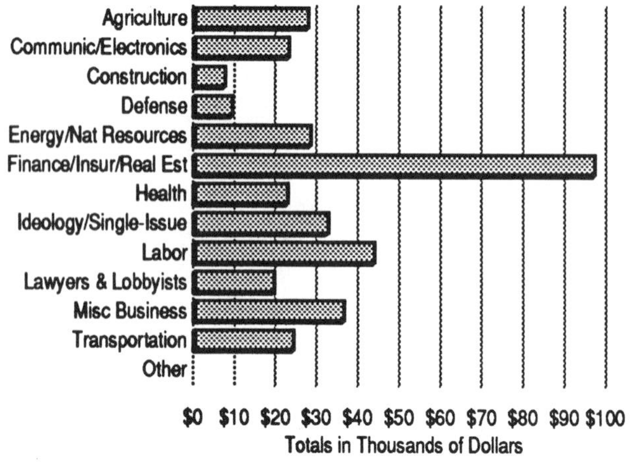

Agriculture
Communic/Electronics
Construction
Defense
Energy/Nat Resources
Finance/Insur/Real Est
Health
Ideology/Single-Issue
Labor
Lawyers & Lobbyists
Misc Business
Transportation
Other
$0 $10 $20 $30 $40 $50 $60 $70 $80 $90 $100
Totals in Thousands of Dollars

Electric Utilities & Equipment ***$8,800***
- ACRE (Action Committee for Rural Electrification) $4,500
- Duke Power Company $1,300
- Others $3,000

Food & Beverage ***$8,750***
- American Meat Institute $1,250
- Others $7,500

Health Professionals ***$11,750***
- American Medical Assn $7,500
- American Dental Assn $1,500
- Others $2,750

Insurance ***$22,500***
- National Assn of Life Underwriters $5,000
- Home Group Inc $2,000
- Independent Insurance Agents of America $2,000
- Acacia Mutual Life Insurance $1,750
- American Council of Life Insurance $1,500
- Travelers Corp $1,500
- Others $8,750

Lawyers & Lobbyists ***$19,157***
- Assn of Trial Lawyers of America $10,000
- Akin, Gump, Hauer & Feld $2,157
- Others $7,000

Oil & Gas ***$12,350***
- Coastal Corp $2,500
- Phillips Petroleum $2,000
- Others $7,850

Pharmaceuticals ***$7,000***
- Warner-Lambert $3,000
- Others $4,000

Real Estate ***$10,500***
- National Assn of Realtors $6,000
- Mortgage Bankers Assn of America $1,500
- National Realty Committee $1,500
- Others $1,500

Savings Banks & Credit Unions ***$16,250***
- Credit Union National Assn $7,000
- US League of Savings Assn $7,000
- Others $2,250

Securities/Commodities Investment $13,250

Drexel Burnham Lambert	$2,000
First Boston Corp	$2,000
Dean Witter Reynolds	$1,750
Chicago Mercantile Exchange	$1,500
Salomon Brothers	$1,500
Others	$4,500

Telecommunications $15,900

Southern Bell	$7,500
AT&T	$5,500
Others	$2,900

Textiles & Fibers $18,000

Springs Mills	$3,000
Burlington Industries	$2,500
Greenwood Mills	$2,000
American Textile Manufacturers Institute	$1,500
J P Stevens & Company	$1,500
Westpoint Pepperell	$1,500
Others	$6,000

Trucking & Railroads $9,550

American Trucking Assns	$1,500
Norfolk Southern Corp	$1,500
United Parcel Service	$1,500
Others	$5,050

Other Major Business PACs

Waste Management Inc	$5,000	Waste Mgmt
Associated Milk Producers	$3,000	Dairy
E I Du Pont De Nemours & Company	$2,500	Chemicals
Westinghouse Electric	$2,100	Electronics
American Hospital Assn	$2,000	Hospitals
FMC Corp	$2,000	Chemicals
National Cable Television Assn	$2,000	CableTV
Equifax Inc	$1,500	CreditReport
Mid-American Dairymen	$1,500	Dairy
National Cotton Council	$1,500	Cotton
Philip Morris	$1,500	Tobacco
Westvaco Corp	$1,500	Paper Prod
American Sugarbeet Growers Assn	$1,300	Sugar

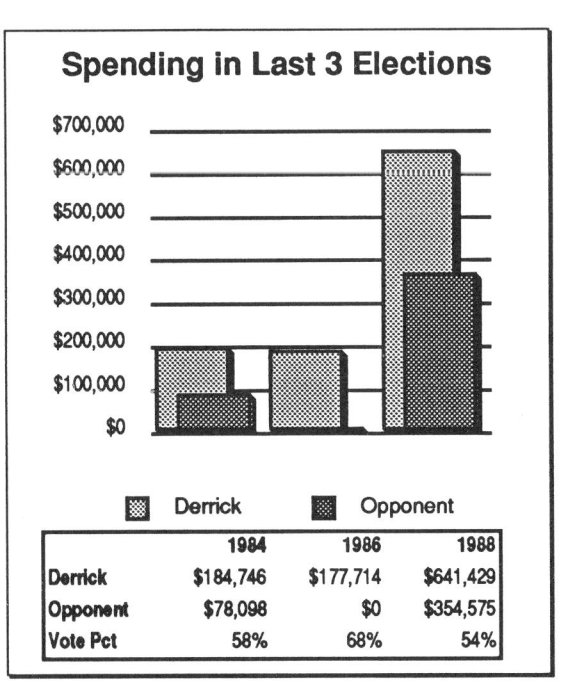

Spending in Last 3 Elections

	1984	1986	1988
Derrick	$184,746	$177,714	$641,429
Opponent	$78,098	$0	$354,575
Vote Pct	58%	68%	54%

Legend: ▒ Derrick ▓ Opponent

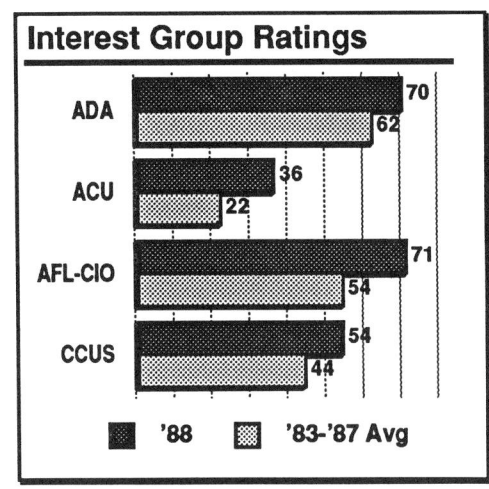

Interest Group Ratings

	'88	'83–'87 Avg
ADA	70	62
ACU	36	22
AFL-CIO	71	54
CCUS	54	44

■ '88   ▨ '83-'87 Avg

Labor

Bldg Trades/Industrial/Other Unions $12,850

National Education Assn	$3,250
United Auto Workers	$3,000
Communications Workers of America	$2,600
Others	$4,000

Government & Postal Workers $16,050

National Assn of Letter Carriers	$6,000
National Assn of Retired Federal Employees	$4,000
American Postal Workers Union	$2,500
National Rural Letter Carriers Assn	$1,500
Others	$2,050

Transportation Unions $14,500

Marine Engineers Union*	$8,500
Air Line Pilots Assn	$2,500
Seafarers International Union	$1,500
United Transportation Union	$1,500
Others	$500

Ideological/Single-Issue

Democratic Leadership PACs $14,000

24th Cong Dist of California PAC (Henry Waxman)	$5,000
Majority Congress Committee (Jim Wright)	$5,000
Valley Education Fund (Tony Coelho)	$2,000
Others	$2,000

Pro-Israel $7,000

National PAC	$5,000
Others	$2,000

Other Major Ideological/Single-Issue PACs

National Rifle Assn	$9,900

Independent expenditures supporting Derrick

National Cmte to Preserve Social Security	$2,710

---

* Contributions came from more than one PAC affiliated
  with this sponsor.

Mike DeWine, R-Ohio (7)

First elected: 1982
Total receipts: $312,200
Total from PACs: $112,860

1988 Committees & Subcommittees

Foreign Affairs
International Operations
Western Hemisphere Affairs

Judiciary
Civil and Constitutional Rights
Courts, Civil Liberties and the Administration of Justice

PAC Contribution Profile

Business

Accountants	**$5,850**
American Institute of CPA's	$5,000
Others	$850
Automotive	**$9,300**
Auto Dealers & Drivers for Free Trade	$6,500
National Auto Dealers Assn	$1,650
Others	$1,150
Broadcasting & Entertainment	**$5,550**
ASCAP	$1,000
National Cable Television Assn	$1,000
Others	$3,550
Chemicals	**$2,000**
FMC Corp	$1,000
Others	$1,000
Commercial & Savings Banks	**$3,675**
Ohio Bankers Assn	$1,000
Ohio Savings Assns League	$1,000
Others	$1,675
Construction	**$4,900**
National Assn of Home Builders	$1,500
Manville Corp	$1,000
National Utility Contractors Assn	$1,000
Others	$1,400
Electric Utilities	**$3,550**
Dayton Power & Light	$1,400
Ohio Edison	$1,400
Others	$750

Campaign Revenue Sources

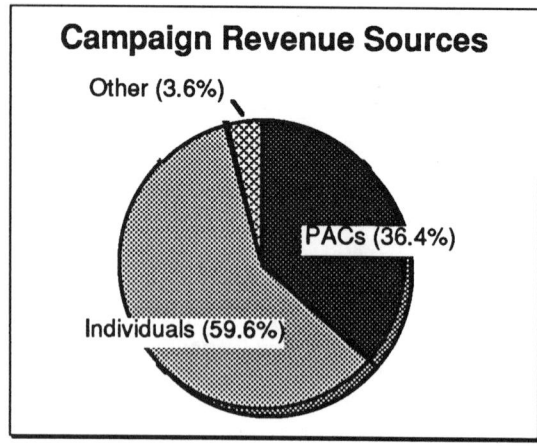

Other (3.6%)
PACs (36.4%)
Individuals (59.6%)

Food & Beverage	**$5,400**
Food Marketing Institute	$1,000
National Restaurant Assn	$1,000
Others	$3,400
Health Professionals	**$4,000**
American Medical Assn	$2,750
American Academy of Ophthalmology	$1,000
Others	$250
Insurance	**$7,850**
National Assn of Life Underwriters	$1,500
Nationwide Corp	$1,000
Travelers Corp	$1,000
Others	$4,350
Lawyers & Lobbyists	**$7,550**
Assn of Trial Lawyers of America	$5,250
Others	$2,300
Oil & Gas	**$3,770**
Columbia Gas Company*	$1,020
Others	$2,750
Pharmaceuticals	**$7,950**
Warner-Lambert	$1,600
Schering-Plough Corp	$1,500
Sandoz Pharmaceuticals	$1,000
Others	$3,850
Real Estate	**$6,250**
National Assn of Realtors	$6,000
Others	$250
Telephone Utility	**$7,550**
AT&T	$3,500
Ohio Bell Telephone	$1,400
Others	$2,650

Other Major Business PACs

Ohio Farm Bureau Federation	$1,250	Farm Orgs
Corning Glass Works	$1,000	Glass Prod
Navistar International	$1,000	Farm Equip
Owens-Illinois	$1,000	Paper Packg
Philip Morris	$1,000	Tobacco
PPG Industries	$1,000	Glass Prod
West Publishing	$1,000	Books & Mags

PAC Totals by Category

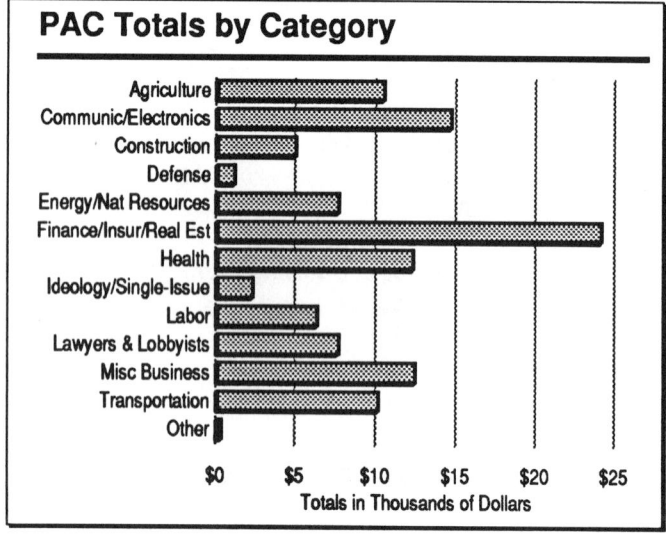

Agriculture
Communic/Electronics
Construction
Defense
Energy/Nat Resources
Finance/Insur/Real Est
Health
Ideology/Single-Issue
Labor
Lawyers & Lobbyists
Misc Business
Transportation
Other

$0 $5 $10 $15 $20 $25
Totals in Thousands of Dollars

Labor

Labor Unions ***$6,250***

    National Assn of Retired Federal Employees $4,000
    Teamsters Union $2,000
    Others $250

Independent expenditures supporting DeWine

Gulf + Western Industries $1,000

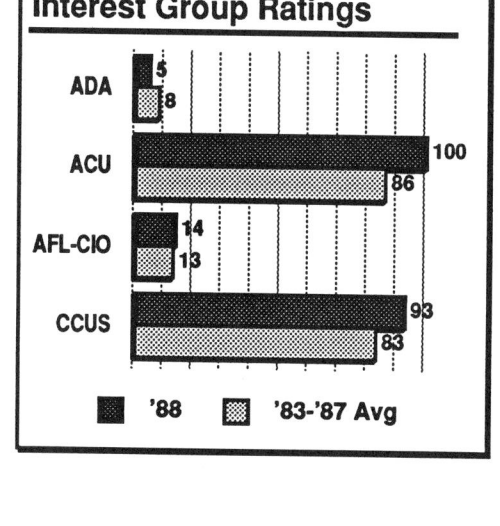

Interest Group Ratings

Group	'88	'83-'87 Avg
ADA	5	8
ACU	100	86
AFL-CIO	14	13
CCUS	93	83

■ '88 ▨ '83-'87 Avg

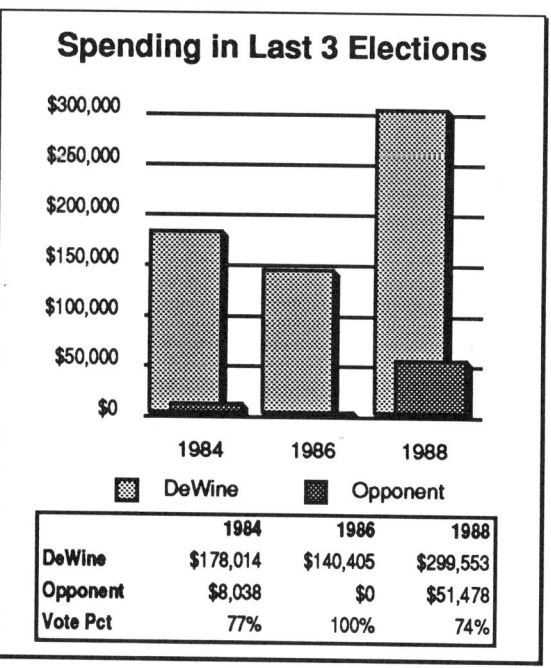

Spending in Last 3 Elections

	1984	1986	1988
DeWine	$178,014	$140,405	$299,553
Opponent	$8,038	$0	$51,478
Vote Pct	77%	100%	74%

▨ DeWine   ■ Opponent

---

* Contributions came from more than one PAC affiliated
  with this sponsor.

Bill Dickinson, R-Ala (2)

1988 Committees & Subcommittees

Armed Services (Ranking Republican)
Research and Development (Ranking Republican)
Military Installations and Facilities

House Administration
Office Systems
Personnel and Police

First elected: 1964
Total receipts: $304,708
Total from PACs: $168,639

PAC Contribution Profile

Business

Auto Dealers	**$2,500**
Auto Dealers & Drivers for Free Trade	$1,500
National Auto Dealers Assn	$1,000
Computers & Electronics	**$4,600**
Texas Instruments	$2,600
Intergraph Corp	$1,500
Others	$500
Defense	**$92,300**
Boeing Company	$8,000
McDonnell Douglas*	$6,250
Northrop Corp	$6,000
General Dynamics	$5,000
Grumman	$5,000
Hughes Aircraft	$5,000
Lockheed Corp	$4,750
Rockwell International	$4,000
Textron Inc	$4,000
LTV Aerospace & Defense Company	$3,750
FMC Corp	$2,500
Singer Company	$2,250
Colt Industries	$2,000
Martin Marietta Corp	$2,000
TRW Inc	$2,000
United Technologies	$2,000
Computer Sciences Corp	$1,500
General Electric	$1,500
Gould Inc	$1,500
Litton Industries	$1,500
Westinghouse Electric	$1,500
Allied-Signal	$1,250

(Continued in next column)

Campaign Revenue Sources

Party (1.0%)
Other (8.5%)
PACs (52.1%)
Individuals (38.4%)

Defense (cont'd)	
BDM International	$1,250
Chrysler Corp	$1,250
General Motors	$1,250
Morton Thiokol	$1,250
Bath Iron Works	$1,000
Emerson Electric*	$1,000
Gencorp Inc	$1,000
ITT Corp	$1,000
Raytheon	$1,000
Others	$9,050
Food & Beverage	**$5,550**
National Beer Wholesalers Assn	$2,000
National Restaurant Assn	$1,000
Others	$2,550
Health Professionals	**$4,500**
American Dental Assn	$1,500
American Medical Assn	$1,250
Cmte for Quality Orthopedic Health Care	$1,000
Others	$750
Oil & Gas	**$4,500**
Alagasco Inc	$1,000
Texaco	$1,000
Others	$2,500
Other Crops	**$3,500**
Alabama Peanut Producers Assn	$2,000
Others	$1,500
Real Estate	**$6,000**
National Assn of Realtors	$6,000
Telecommunications	**$6,500**
AT&T	$4,000
South Central Bell Telephone	$2,000
Others	$500
Tobacco	**$2,750**
Philip Morris	$1,000
Others	$1,750

PAC Totals by Category

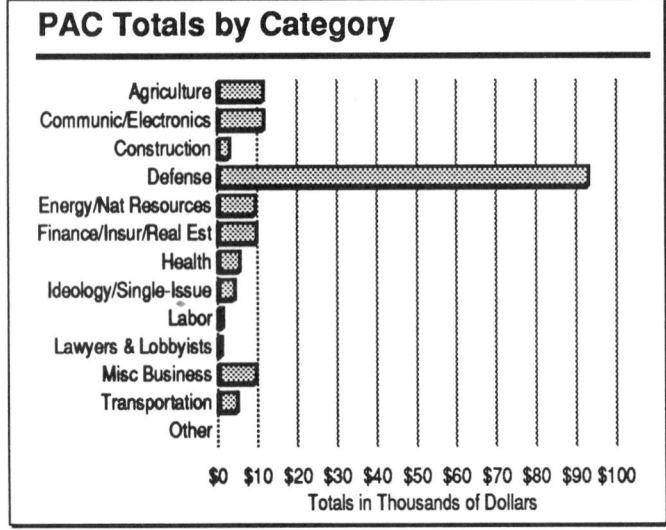

Agriculture
Communic/Electronics
Construction
Defense
Energy/Nat Resources
Finance/Insur/Real Est
Health
Ideology/Single-Issue
Labor
Lawyers & Lobbyists
Misc Business
Transportation
Other

$0 $10 $20 $30 $40 $50 $60 $70 $80 $90 $100
Totals in Thousands of Dollars

Other Major Business PACs

Southern Company*	$2,150	ElectricUtil
Alabama Farm Bureau Federation	$1,250	Farm Orgs
American Bankers Assn	$1,000	Comml Banks
Amsouth Bancorp	$1,000	Comml Banks
Dravo Corp	$1,000	Other Mining
National Assn of Life Underwriters	$1,000	Life Insurance
Stone Container Corp	$1,000	Paper Packg
Westpoint Pepperell	$1,000	Textiles

Ideological/Single-Issue

Ideological/Single-Issue		*$3,464*
American Security Council	$1,364	Pro-Defense
Public Service Research Council	$1,000	Anti-Union
Others	$1,100	

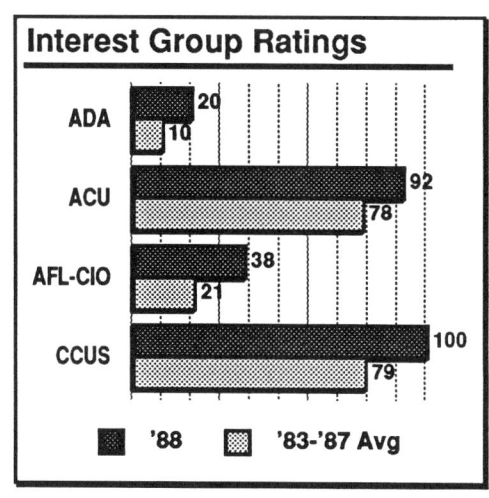

Interest Group Ratings

ADA 20 / 10
ACU 92 / 78
AFL-CIO 38 / 21
CCUS 100 / 79

■ '88   ▨ '83-'87 Avg

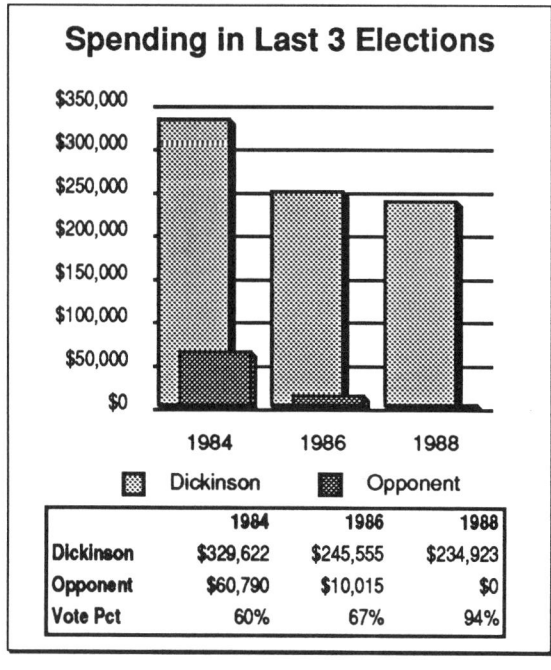

Spending in Last 3 Elections

	1984	1986	1988
Dickinson	$329,622	$245,555	$234,923
Opponent	$60,790	$10,015	$0
Vote Pct	60%	67%	94%

▨ Dickinson   ■ Opponent

---

* Contributions came from more than one PAC affiliated with this sponsor.

Norm Dicks, D-Wash (6)

First elected: 1976
Total receipts: $366,934
Total from PACs: $213,189

1988 Committees & Subcommittees

Appropriations
Defense
Interior and Related Agencies
Military Construction

PAC Contribution Profile

Business

Campaign Revenue Sources

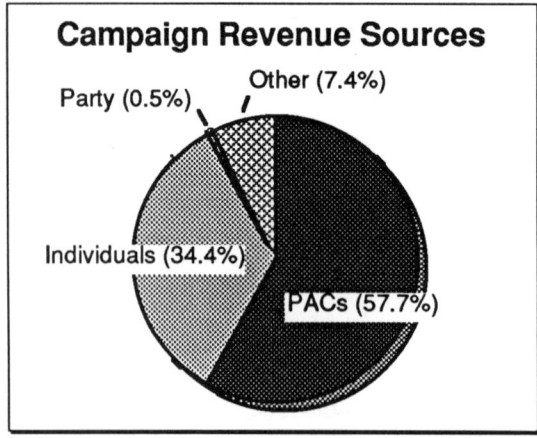

Other (7.4%)
Party (0.5%)
Individuals (34.4%)
PACs (57.7%)

Airlines & Aerospace **$2,800**
    None over $900

Automotive & Trucking **$5,050**
    Auto Dealers & Drivers for Free Trade $2,500
    Paccar Inc $2,000
    Others $550

Commercial & Savings Banks **$7,925**
    US Bancorp $2,050
    Washington Savings League $1,125
    Rainier Bancorp $1,000
    Others $3,750

Construction **$6,662**
    National Utility Contractors Assn $3,000
    Sheet Metal/AirCon Contractors $1,500
    Others $2,162

Defense **$53,450**
    Boeing Company $7,700
    Northrop Corp $3,500
    AT&T $3,000
    Grumman $3,000
    Hughes Aircraft $3,000
    McDonnell Douglas* $2,700
    Textron Inc $2,000
    United Technologies $1,750
    Lockheed Corp $1,700
    Raytheon $1,650
    BDM International $1,600
    Westinghouse Electric $1,550
    (Continued in next column)

PAC Totals by Category

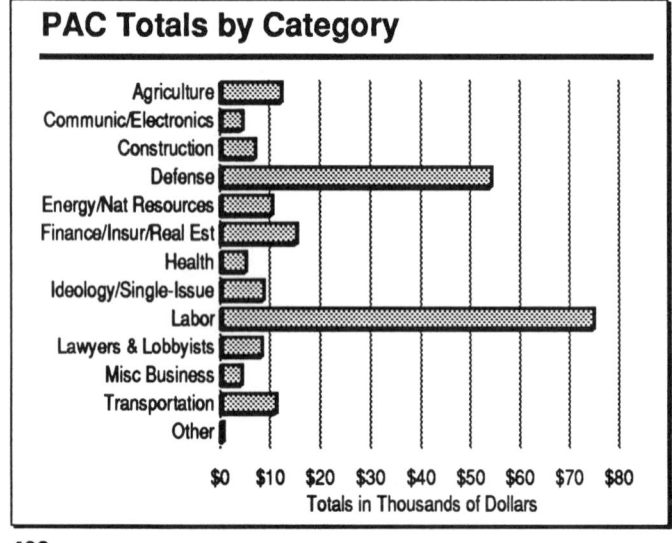

Totals in Thousands of Dollars

Defense (cont'd)
    General Dynamics $1,500
    General Electric $1,500
    Sundstrand Corp* $1,100
    Allied-Signal $1,000
    Tenneco Inc $1,000
    TRW Inc $1,000
    Others $13,200

Electric Utilities **$5,250**
    Puget Sound Power & Light $1,800
    Southern California Edison $1,500
    Others $1,950

Food & Beverage **$6,950**
    Services Group of America $2,000
    Food Marketing Institute $1,200
    National Restaurant Assn $1,000
    Others $2,750

Forest Products **$3,650**
    Weyerhaeuser Company $1,000
    Others $2,650

Health Professionals **$4,750**
    American Dental Assn $3,000
    American Medical Assn $1,250
    Others $500

Lawyers & Lobbyists **$7,900**
    Assn of Trial Lawyers of America $2,000
    Garvey, Schubert & Barer $1,100
    Preston, Thorgrimson, Ellis & Holman $1,100
    Others $3,700

Oil & Gas **$3,750**
    Burlington Northern $2,050
    Others $1,700

Real Estate **$4,650**
    National Assn of Realtors $4,050
    Others $600

Telecommunications **$3,050**
    Pacific Northwest Bell $2,750
    Others $300

Other Major Business PACs

Associated Milk Producers	$1,000	Dairy
Darigold/Northwest Dairymens Assn	$1,000	Dairy
National Assn of Life Underwriters	$1,000	Life Insurance

Labor

Bldg Trades/Industrial/Misc Unions $25,850

Machinists/Aerospace Workers Union	$5,300
Intl Brotherhood of Electrical Workers.............................	$3,000
United Steelworkers	$2,500
Food & Commercial Workers Union..................................	$2,000
Laborers' Political League	$2,000
Carpenters & Joiners Union	$1,850
United Auto Workers	$1,800
Operating Engineers Union*	$1,750
Oil, Chemical & Atomic Workers Union............................	$1,600
Ironworkers Union	$1,000
Office & Professional Employees Union	$1,000
Others	$2,050

Government & Postal Workers $14,450

National Assn of Retired Federal Employees	$5,000
National Assn of Letter Carriers	$3,100
American Fedn of State/County/Munic Employees	$2,000
American Federation of Government Employees	$1,150
Others	$3,200

Teachers Unions $4,600

National Education Assn	$4,000
Others	$600

Transportation Unions $29,650

Teamsters Union	$10,000
Marine Engineers Union*	$9,500
Air Line Pilots Assn	$2,500
Seafarers International Union	$2,000
United Transportation Union	$1,600
Longshoremen/Warehousemen Union	$1,500
Others	$2,550

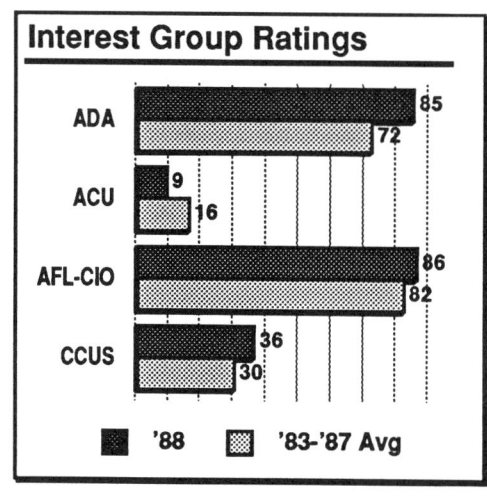

Ideological/Single-Issue

Pro-Israel $6,000

National PAC	$5,000
Washington PAC	$1,000

Other Ideological/Single-Issue

Valley Education Fund (Tony Coelho) ....$1,000   Dem Leaders

Independent expenditures supporting Dicks

National Cmte to Preserve Social Security $4,104

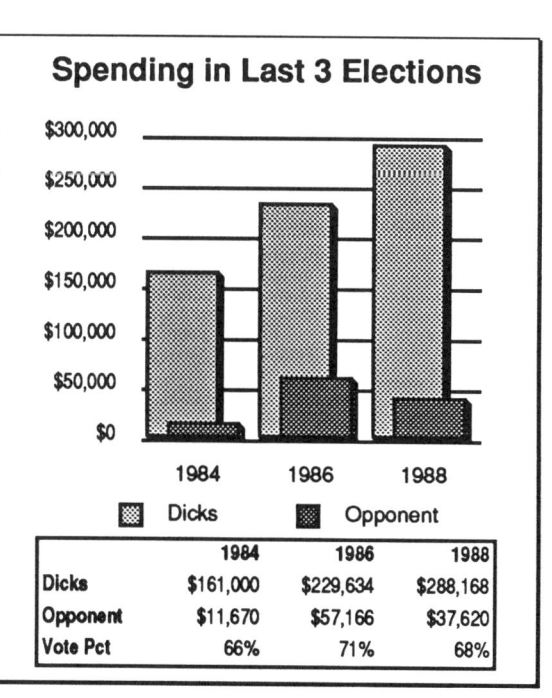

* Contributions came from more than one PAC affiliated
with this sponsor.

John D. Dingell, D-Mich (16)

First elected: 1955
Total receipts: $613,770
Total from PACs: $459,242

1988 Committees & Subcommittees

Energy and Commerce (Chairman)
Oversight and Investigations (Chairman)

PAC Contribution Profile

Business

Accountants	**$10,500**
American Institute of CPA's	$5,000
Others	$5,500
Automotive	**$14,000**
Ford Motor Company	$4,000
Chrysler Corp	$3,000
General Motors	$2,700
National Auto Dealers Assn	$1,500
Others	$2,800
Broadcasting & Entertainment	**$19,600**
National Cable Television Assn	$5,000
National Assn of Broadcasters	$4,000
MCA Inc	$3,000
Recording Industry Assn	$1,500
Others	$6,100
Electric Utilities	**$19,450**
Southern Company*	$4,250
Consumers Power Company	$3,500
Detroit Edison	$1,600
Idaho Power Company	$1,500
Others	$8,600
Financial Institutions	**$14,520**
US League of Savings Assn	$2,500
American Bankers Assn	$2,000
Independent Bankers Assn	$1,500
Michigan League of Savings Institutions	$1,500
Michigan Credit Union League	$1,320
National Bank of Detroit	$1,200
Others	$4,500

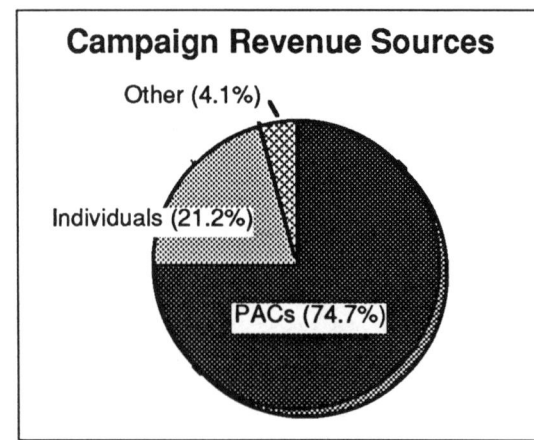

Campaign Revenue Sources

Other (4.1%)
Individuals (21.2%)
PACs (74.7%)

Food & Beverage	**$22,200**
Anheuser-Busch	$3,000
Joseph E Seagram & Sons	$2,000
Kellogg Company	$2,000
National Beer Wholesalers Assn	$2,000
Nutrasweet Company	$2,000
Coca-Cola Company	$1,500
Others	$9,700
Health Professionals	**$16,600**
American Dental Assn	$5,000
American Medical Assn	$2,500
American Academy of Ophthalmology	$2,000
American Chiropractic Assn	$1,100
Others	$6,000
Insurance	**$15,700**
National Assn of Life Underwriters	$2,500
American Family Corp	$2,000
American Council of Life Insurance	$1,500
Others	$9,700
Lawyers & Lobbyists	**$12,250**
Akin, Gump, Hauer & Feld	$2,000
Van Ness, Feldman, Sutcliffe & Curtis	$1,500
Others	$8,750
Oil & Gas	**$29,500**
Union Pacific Corp	$5,000
USX Corp	$3,000
Michigan Consolidated Gas	$2,700
Coastal Corp	$2,000
Ashland Oil	$1,500
Pacific Enterprises	$1,500
Others	$13,800
Pharmaceuticals	**$11,300**
Pfizer Inc	$2,000
Pharmaceutical Manufacturers Assn	$2,000
Others	$7,300
Securities/Commodities Investment	**$33,000**
First Boston Corp	$5,000
Investment Company Institute	$5,000
Goldman Sachs	$4,000
Morgan Stanley & Company	$4,000
Chicago Board of Options Exchange	$2,000
Philadelphia Stock Exchange	$2,000
E F Hutton Group	$1,500
Merrill Lynch	$1,500
Shearson Lehman Hutton	$1,500
Others	$6,500

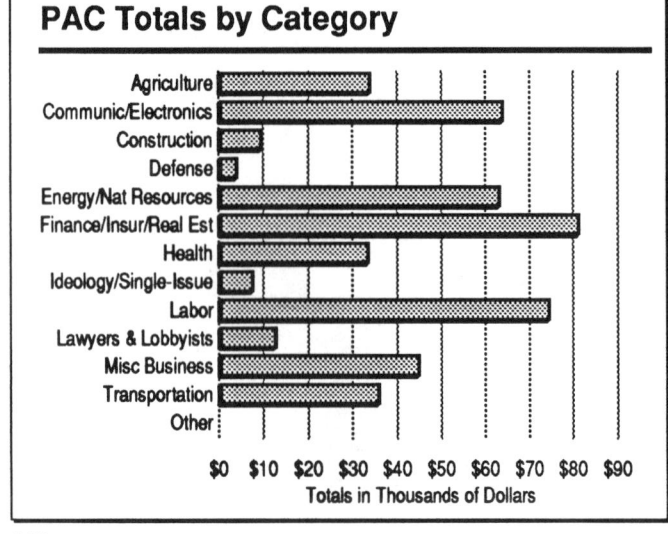

PAC Totals by Category

- Agriculture
- Communic/Electronics
- Construction
- Defense
- Energy/Nat Resources
- Finance/Insur/Real Est
- Health
- Ideology/Single-Issue
- Labor
- Lawyers & Lobbyists
- Misc Business
- Transportation
- Other

$0 $10 $20 $30 $40 $50 $60 $70 $80 $90

Totals in Thousands of Dollars

Telecommunications $41,030

AT&T	$8,500
Michigan Bell Telephone	$6,730
Pacific Telesis Group	$3,000
BellSouth Corp*	$2,500
Bell Atlantic	$2,000
Corning Glass Works	$2,100
US Sprint	$2,000
Southwestern Bell	$1,500
US West Inc	$1,500
Others	$11,200

Trucking & Railroads $14,300

American Trucking Assns	$3,000
United Parcel Service	$3,000
Consolidated Rail Corp	$1,500
Grand Trunk & Western Railroad	$1,300
Others	$5,500

Other Major Business PACs

National Assn of Realtors	$5,500	Real Estate
Philip Morris	$5,000	Tobacco
Associated Milk Producers	$4,000	Dairy
American Hospital Assn	$2,500	Hospitals
Waste Management Inc	$2,500	Waste Mgmt
Century 21 Real Estate	$2,000	Real Estate
Dow Chemical*	$2,000	Chemicals
Federal Express Corp	$2,000	Delivery
FMC Corp	$2,000	Chemicals
Mid-American Dairymen	$2,000	Dairy
Owens-Illinois	$2,000	Paper Packg
Walter Industries	$2,000	Resid Constr
Westvaco Corp	$2,000	Paper Prod
General Electric	$1,500	NuclearEquip
Hallmark Cards	$1,500	Publishing
Tobacco Institute	$1,500	Tobacco

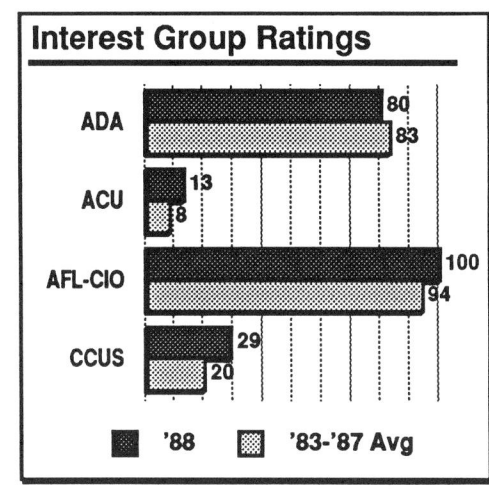

Interest Group Ratings

ADA 80 ('88), 83 ('83-'87 Avg)
ACU 13 ('88), 8 ('83-'87 Avg)
AFL-CIO 100 ('88), 94 ('83-'87 Avg)
CCUS 29 ('88), 20 ('83-'87 Avg)

■ '88   ▨ '83-'87 Avg

Labor

Bldg Trades/Industrial/Misc Unions $29,300

National Education Assn	$6,500
United Auto Workers	$2,500
Hotel/Restaurant Employees Union	$2,000
Laborers' Political League	$2,000
Machinists/Aerospace Workers Union	$2,000
Food & Commercial Workers Union	$1,800
AFL-CIO*	$1,600
Ladies Garment Workers Union	$1,500
Plumbers/Pipefitters Union*	$1,200
Others	$8,200

Government & Postal Workers $10,000

American Fedn of State/County/Munic Employees	$5,000
National Assn of Retired Federal Employees	$3,000
Others	$2,000

Transportation Unions $31,152

Teamsters Union*	$10,200
United Transportation Union	$5,000
Marine Engineers Unions	$3,100
Seafarers International Union	$2,900
Air Line Pilots Assn	$2,500
Transport Workers Union	$2,300
Transportation Communication Union	$1,300
Assn of Flight Attendants	$1,077
Others	$2,775

Major Ideological/Single-Issue

KidsPAC	$2,000	HealthWelfare
National Rifle Assn	$2,000	Pro-Guns

Independent expenditures supporting Dingell

National Cmte to Preserve Social Security	$2,003

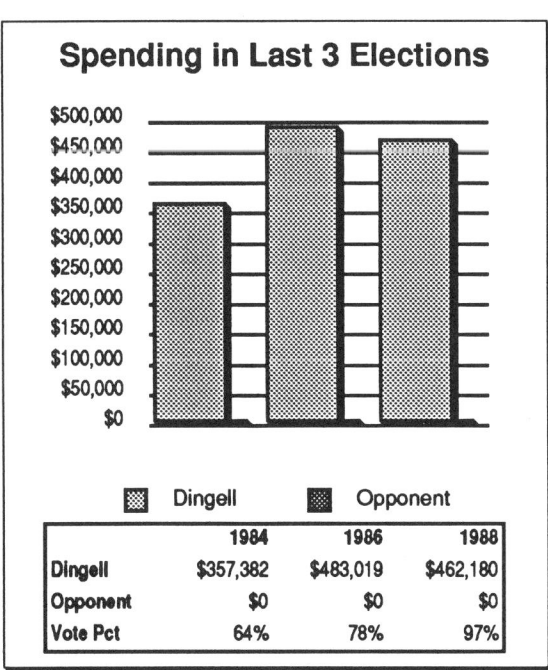

Spending in Last 3 Elections

▨ Dingell   ■ Opponent

	1984	1986	1988
Dingell	$357,382	$483,019	$462,180
Opponent	$0	$0	$0
Vote Pct	64%	78%	97%

---

* Contributions came from more than one PAC affiliated
  with this sponsor.

Julian C. Dixon, D-Calif (28)

First elected: 1978
Total receipts: $120,740
Total from PACs: $72,430

1988 Committees & Subcommittees

Appropriations
District of Columbia (Chairman)
Foreign Operations

Standards of Official Conduct (Chairman)

PAC Contribution Profile
Business

Agriculture **$3,300**
    Philip Morris $1,000
    Sunkist Growers $1,000
    Associated Milk Producers $500
    California Almond Growers Exchange $500
    Others $300

Casinos **$1,200**
    Summa Corp $1,200

Commercial & Savings Banks **$2,200**
    American Bankers Assn $1,000
    BankAmerica $600
    Great Western Financial Corp $600

Construction **$1,600**
    National Assn of Home Builders $1,000
    Parsons Corp $600

Defense **$2,100**
    Hughes Aircraft $600
    Lockheed Corp $600
    Others $900

Food & Beverage **$1,500**
    Coca-Cola Company $500
    National Beer Wholesalers Assn $500
    Wine Institute $500

Health Professionals **$3,600**
    American Medical Assn $3,000
    American Optometric Assn $600

Insurance **$2,250**
    Farmers Group Inc $1,000
    TransAmerica Life Companies $1,000
    Others $250

Natural Gas **$1,200**
    Pacific Enterprises $1,200

Real Estate **$6,000**
    National Assn of Realtors $6,000

Telecommunications **$1,650**
    AT&T $750
    Pacific Telesis Group $600
    Others $300

Other Major Business PACs

Kidder, Peabody $1,000	StocksInvest
United Parcel Service $750	Delivery
ASCAP $500	Live Music
Carter Hawley Hale Stores $500	Dept Store
Marriott Corp $500	Hotel/Motel
MCA Inc $500	Movies

Campaign Revenue Sources

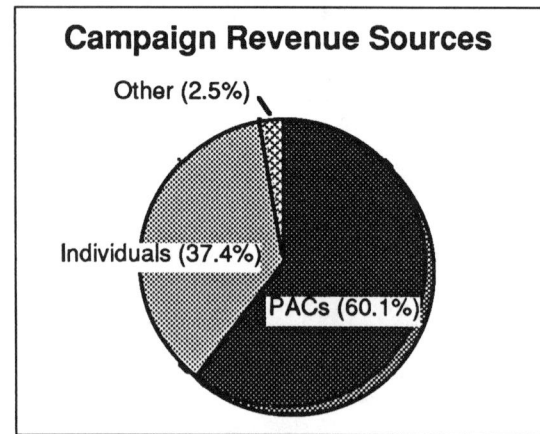

Other (2.5%)
Individuals (37.4%)
PACs (60.1%)

PAC Totals by Category

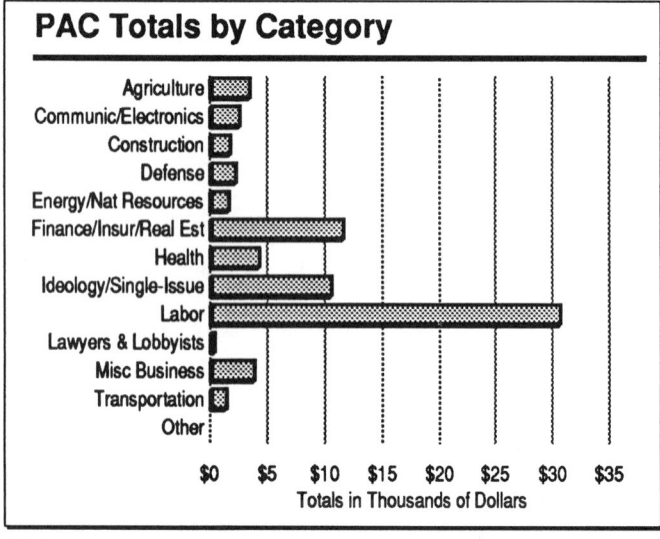

Agriculture
Communic/Electronics
Construction
Defense
Energy/Nat Resources
Finance/Insur/Real Est
Health
Ideology/Single-Issue
Labor
Lawyers & Lobbyists
Misc Business
Transportation
Other

$0 $5 $10 $15 $20 $25 $30 $35
Totals in Thousands of Dollars

Labor

Bldg Trades/Industrial/Misc Unions $12,600

    United Auto Workers $4,000
    Service Employees International Union $3,000
    Laborers' Western Political League $2,000
    Machinists/Aerospace Workers Union $1,500
    Food & Commercial Workers Union..............................$1,200
    Carpenters & Joiners Union $600
    Others $300

Government & Postal Workers $7,600

    National Assn of Retired Federal Employees $3,000
    American Fedn of State/County/Munic Employees $2,500
    American Postal Workers Union $900
    National Assn of Letter Carriers $900
    Others $300

Teachers Unions $7,900

    National Education Assn $5,500
    American Federation of Teachers $1,500
    United Teachers-Los Angeles $900

Transportation Unions $2,400

    Seafarers International Union $1,300
    Transportation Communication Union................................$600
    United Transportation Union $500

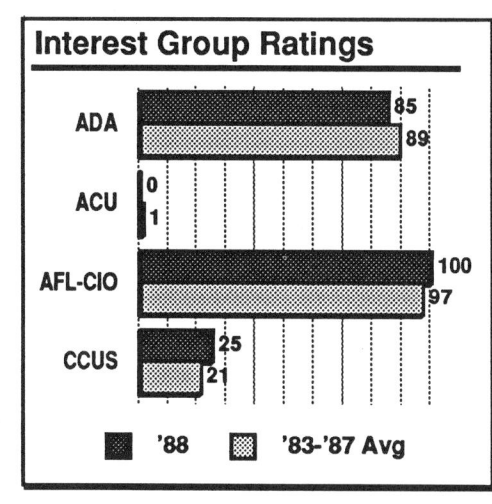

Interest Group Ratings

(ADA: '88 = 85, '83–'87 Avg = 89; ACU: '88 = 0, '83–'87 Avg = 1; AFL-CIO: '88 = 100, '83–'87 Avg = 97; CCUS: '88 = 25, '83–'87 Avg = 21)

■ '88   ▨ '83-'87 Avg

Ideological/Single-Issue

Pro-Israel $6,000

    National PAC $5,000
    Joint Action Cmte for Political Affairs $500
    Women's Pro-Israel National PAC $500

Other Major Ideological/Single-Issue PACs

Human Rights Campaign Fund ....$3,000   Gay Rights
National Cmte to Preserve Social Security ......$1,300   Soc Secur

Independent expenditures supporting Dixon

National Cmte to Preserve Social Security $1,411

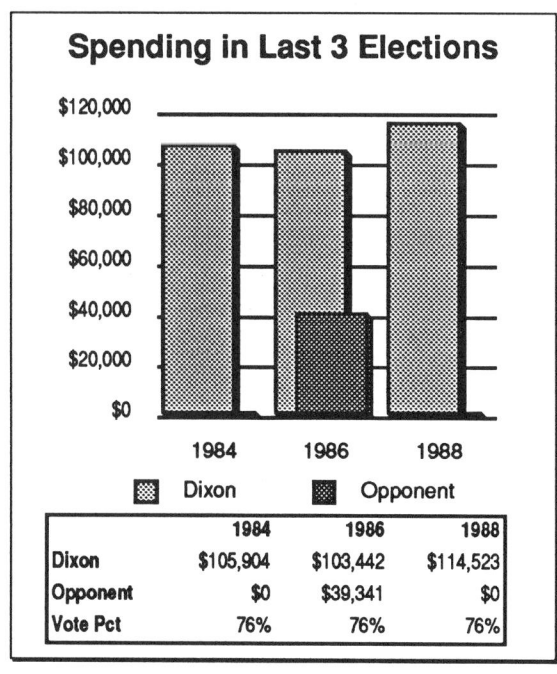

Spending in Last 3 Elections

	1984	1986	1988
Dixon	$105,904	$103,442	$114,523
Opponent	$0	$39,341	$0
Vote Pct	76%	76%	76%

▨ Dixon   ▨ Opponent

Brian Donnelly, D-Mass (11)

1988 Committees & Subcommittees

Ways and Means
Health
Public Assistance and Unemployment Compensation

First elected: 1978
Total receipts: $264,323
Total from PACs: $130,525

PAC Contribution Profile

Business

Accountants	**$6,000**
American Institute of CPA's	$5,000
Others	$1,000

Building Contractors	**$4,500**
National Assn of Home Builders	$3,000
American Road & Trans Builders Assn	$1,000
Others	$500

Commercial & Savings Banks	**$8,650**
American Bankers Assn	$2,000
US League of Savings Assn	$2,000
Bank of Boston	$1,500
J P Morgan & Company	$1,000
National Council of Savings Institutions	$1,000
Others	$1,150

Defense	**$4,200**
Bath Iron Works	$1,500
General Electric	$1,000
Raytheon	$1,000
Others	$700

Electric Utilities	**$4,500**
Boston Edison	$1,000
Com/Energy Services Company	$1,000
Edison Electric Institute	$1,000
New England Power Service Company	$1,000
Others	$500

Campaign Revenue Sources

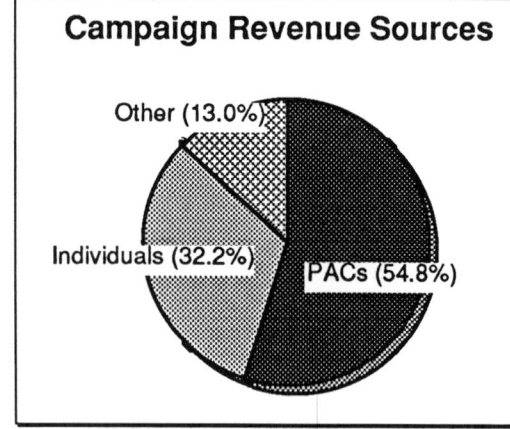

Other (13.0%)
Individuals (32.2%)
PACs (54.8%)

Food & Beverage	**$3,000**
Food Marketing Institute	$1,000
Joseph E Seagram & Sons	$1,000
Pepsi-Cola Bottlers Assn	$1,000

Health Professionals	**$10,200**
American Dental Assn	$4,000
Oral & Maxillofacial Surgeons	$1,500
American Physical Therapy Assn	$1,200
Cmte for Quality Orthopedic Health Care	$1,000
Co-op of American Physicians	$1,000
Others	$1,500

Hospitals & Nursing Homes	**$6,500**
American Hospital Assn	$3,000
American Health Care Assn	$1,000
Federation of American Hospitals	$1,000
Others	$1,500

Insurance	**$28,750**
Associated Life Insurance	$5,000
National Assn of Life Underwriters	$5,000
Massachusetts Mutual Life Insurance	$3,000
Metropolitan Life Insurance	$3,000
New England Mutual Life	$2,000
Liberty Mutual Insurance	$1,500
New York Life	$1,500
Prudential Insurance	$1,500
Blue Cross & Blue Shield Assn	$1,000
John Hancock Financial Service	$1,000
Northwestern Mutual Life	$1,000
Travelers Corp	$1,000
Others	$2,250

Lawyers	**$7,000**
Assn of Trial Lawyers of America	$5,000
Others	$2,000

Real Estate	**$4,000**
National Assn of Realtors	$3,000
Mortgage Bankers Assn of America	$1,000

Sea Transport	**$4,500**
Matson Navigation	$2,000
Crowley Maritime	$1,000
Sea-Land Corp	$1,000
Others	$500

PAC Totals by Category

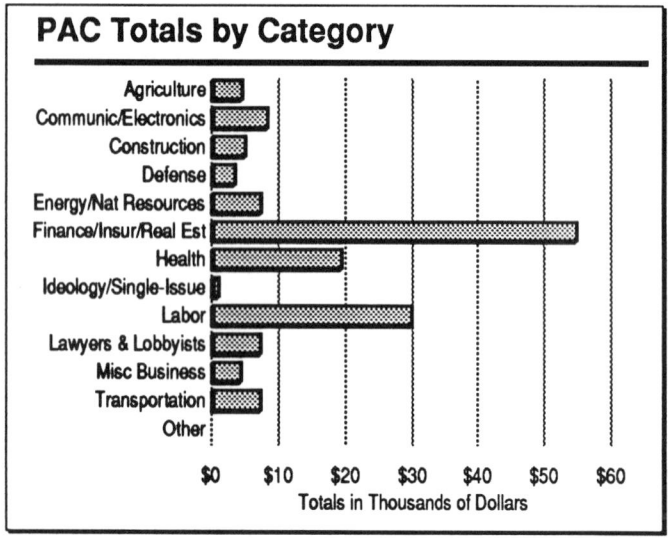

Agriculture
Communic/Electronics
Construction
Defense
Energy/Nat Resources
Finance/Insur/Real Est
Health
Ideology/Single-Issue
Labor
Lawyers & Lobbyists
Misc Business
Transportation
Other

$0 $10 $20 $30 $40 $50 $60

Totals in Thousands of Dollars

Securities & Commodities **$9,200**
 FMR Corp $5,200
 Chicago Board of Trade $2,000
 Public Securities Assn $1,000
 Others $1,000

Telecommunications **$6,500**
 AT&T $4,000
 New England Tel & Tel...$2,000
 Others $500

Other Major Business PACs

United Parcel Service	$1,500	Delivery
Bay State Gas Company	$1,100	Natural Gas
Chrysler Corp	$1,000	Auto Mfrs
Independent Coal Operators Assn	$1,000	Coal
International Council of Shopping Centers	$1,000	Retail
Ocean Spray Cranberries Inc	$1,000	Fruit/Veg

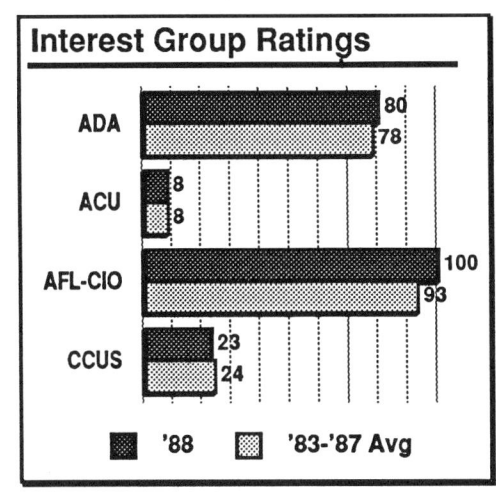

Interest Group Ratings

	'88	'83-'87 Avg
ADA	80	78
ACU	8	8
AFL-CIO	100	93
CCUS	23	24

Labor

Bldg Trades/Industrial/Misc Unions **$11,050**
 Ironworkers Union $2,500
 Machinists/Aerospace Workers Union $2,000
 Laborers' Political League $1,500
 Ladies Garment Workers Union $1,200
 Food & Commercial Workers Union $1,000
 Intl Brotherhood of Electrical Workers $1,000
 United Auto Workers $1,000
 Others $850

Government & Postal Workers **$5,000**
 American Fedn of State/County/Munic Employees $2,000
 National Rural Letter Carriers Assn $1,500
 National Assn of Retired Federal Employees $1,000
 Others $500

Teachers Unions **$2,500**
 American Federation of Teachers $2,000
 Others $500

Transportation Unions **$11,000**
 Teamsters Union $5,000
 Air Line Pilots Assn..$2,500
 Seafarers International Union..............................$2,000
 United Transportation Union $1,000
 Others $500

Independent expenditures supporting Donnelly

National Cmte to Preserve Social Security $1,657

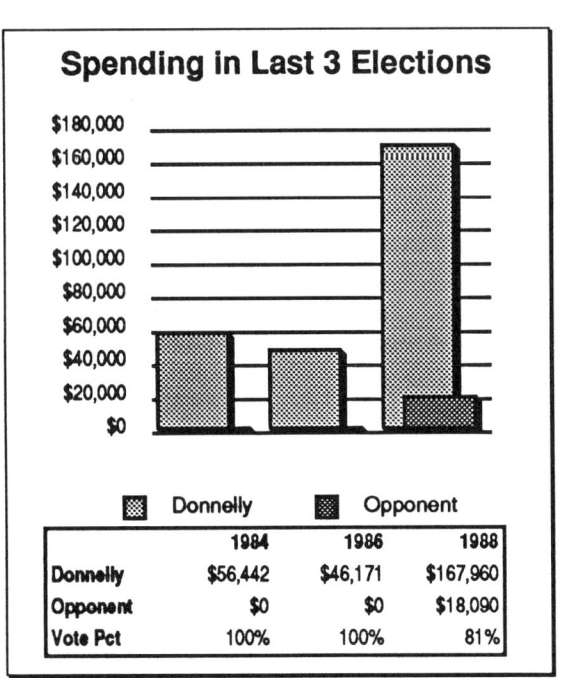

Spending in Last 3 Elections

	Donnelly	Opponent

	1984	1986	1988
Donnelly	$56,442	$46,171	$167,960
Opponent	$0	$0	$18,090
Vote Pct	100%	100%	81%

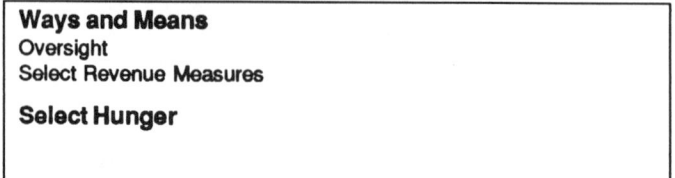

Byron L. Dorgan, D-ND (At Large)

First elected: 1980
Total receipts: $687,234
Total from PACs: $462,346

1988 Committees & Subcommittees

Ways and Means
Oversight
Select Revenue Measures

Select Hunger

PAC Contribution Profile

Business

Air Transport **$11,500**

Eastern Airlines	$5,000
Texas Air	$2,000
Northwest Airlines	$1,500
Others	$3,000

Beer, Wine & Liquor **$16,750**

Wine & Spirits Wholesalers of America	$5,000
National Beer Wholesalers Assn	$4,500
Joseph E Seagram & Sons	$3,500
Wine Institute	$1,500
Others	$2,250

Dairy **$16,000**

Associated Milk Producers	$7,500
Land O'Lakes Inc	$4,000
Mid-American Dairymen	$3,000
Dairymen Inc	$1,500

Financial Institutions **$20,500**

Credit Union National Assn	$10,000
US League of Savings Assn	$3,500
American Bankers Assn	$2,000
Norwest Corp	$2,000
Independent Bankers Assn	$1,500
National Assn of Federal Credit Unions	$1,500

Campaign Revenue Sources

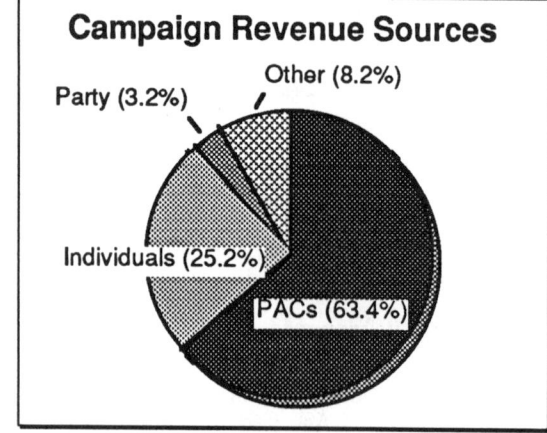

- Other (8.2%)
- Party (3.2%)
- Individuals (25.2%)
- PACs (63.4%)

Health Professionals **$18,250**

American Dental Assn	$4,000
American Optometric Assn	$3,000
National Assn of Pharmacists	$2,500
Corp for the Advancement of Psychiatry	$1,750
Assn for Advancement of Psychology	$1,500
Oral & Maxillofacial Surgeons	$1,500
Others	$4,000

Insurance **$75,996**

National Assn of Life Underwriters	$10,000
Massachusetts Mutual Life Insurance	$6,346
Metropolitan Life Insurance	$4,000
American Family Corp	$3,500
Prudential Insurance	$3,500
Torchmark Corp	$3,500
Equitable Financial Services	$3,000
New York Life	$3,000
Aetna Life & Casualty	$2,500
Health Insurance Assn of America	$2,000
Independent Insurance Agents of America	$2,000
Lincoln National Corp	$2,000
National Assn of Independent Insurers	$2,000
New England Mutual Life	$2,000
Northwestern Mutual Life	$2,000
Provident Life & Accident Insurance	$2,000
Travelers Corp	$2,000
American Council of Life Insurance	$1,500
American General Insurance Company	$1,500
Casualty & Surety Agents Assn	$1,500
John Hancock Financial Service	$1,500
Mutual Life Insurance of New York	$1,500
Pacific Mutual Life	$1,500
Others	$11,650

Lawyers & Lobbyists **$16,300**

Assn of Trial Lawyers of America	$5,000
Powell, Goldstein, Frazer & Murphy	$1,500
Rivkin, Radler, Dunne & Baye	$1,500
Others	$8,300

Livestock/Poultry & Animal Svcs **$10,600**

American Horse Council	$2,500
National Cattlemen's Assn	$2,500
Texas Cattle Feeders Assn	$2,000
Tyson Foods	$1,500
Others	$2,100

Real Estate **$9,000**

National Assn of Realtors	$5,000
Mortgage Bankers Assn of America	$1,500
Others	$2,500

PAC Totals by Category

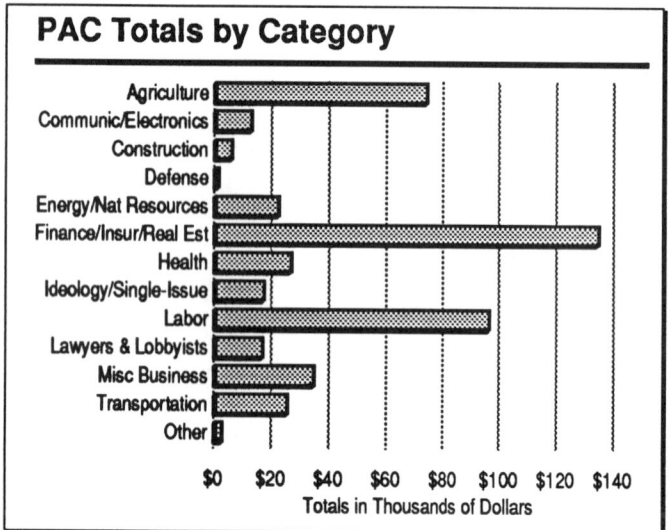

Category	
Agriculture	
Communic/Electronics	
Construction	
Defense	
Energy/Nat Resources	
Finance/Insur/Real Est	
Health	
Ideology/Single-Issue	
Labor	
Lawyers & Lobbyists	
Misc Business	
Transportation	
Other	

$0 $20 $40 $60 $80 $100 $120 $140
Totals in Thousands of Dollars

Interest Group Ratings

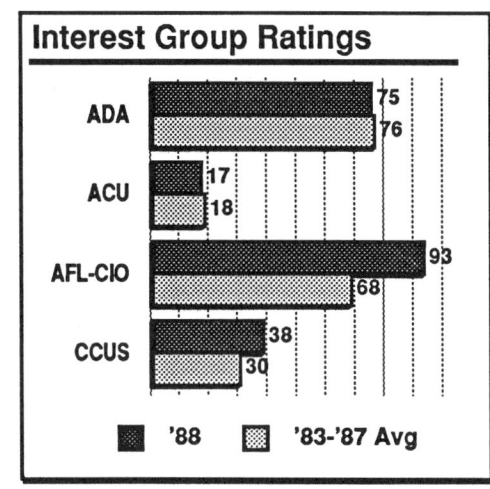

	'88	'83-'87 Avg
ADA	75	76
ACU	17	18
AFL-CIO	93	68
CCUS	38	30

Securities & Commodities Investment **$16,000**

    Chicago Board of Trade $3,000
    E F Hutton Group $2,000
    Commodity Exchange Inc $1,500

Securities Industry Assn **$1,500**

    Others $8,000

Other Major Business PACs

National Venture Capital Assn	$8,000	Venture Cap
Archer-Daniels-Midland Corp	$7,000	Grain Trader
American Institute of CPA's	$5,000	Accountants
AT&T	$4,000	LongDistance
ACRE (Action Committee for Rural Electric)	$3,500	RuralElect
American Crystal Sugar Corp	$3,500	Sugar
National Assn of Home Builders	$3,500	Resid Constr
American Hospital Assn	$3,000	Hospitals
Chrysler Corp	$2,500	Auto Mfrs
Food Marketing Institute	$2,500	Food Stores
National Auto Dealers Assn	$2,500	Auto Sales
Peabody Coal	$2,500	Coal
United Parcel Service	$2,500	Delivery
Coastal Corp	$2,000	Natural Gas
Federation of America Hospitals	$2,000	Hospitals
Freeport-McMoran Inc	$2,000	Mining
General Electric	$2,000	Electronics
National Assn of Wholesale-Distributors	$2,000	Wholesale
Philip Morris	$2,000	Tobacco
Winn-Dixie Stores	$2,000	Food Stores
National Farmers Organization	$1,750	Farm Orgs
American Assn of Equipment Lessors	$1,500	Rentals
American Sugarbeet Growers Assn	$1,500	Sugar
Employee Stock Ownership Assn	$1,500	Other
Farmland Industries	$1,500	Ag Svcs
J C Penney Company	$1,500	Dept Store
National Council of Farmer Co-ops	$1,500	Farm Orgs
Northwestern Bell Telephone	$1,500	Phone Util
US Beet Sugar Assn	$1,500	Sugar
National Telephone Co-op Assn	$1,250	Phone Util

Spending in Last 3 Elections

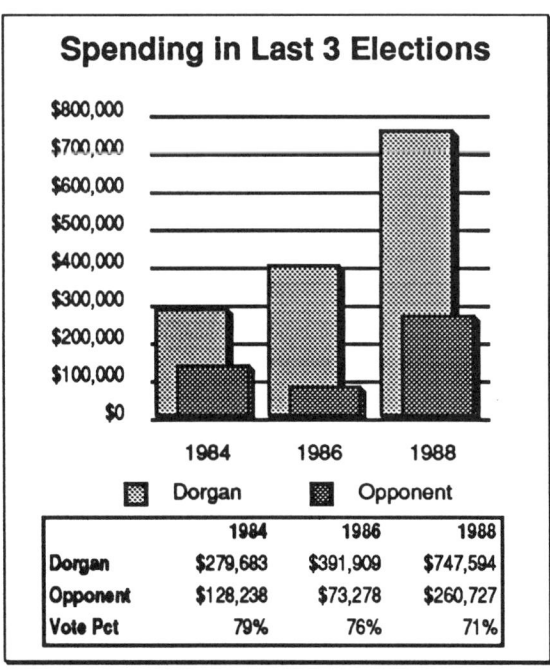

	1984	1986	1988
Dorgan	$279,683	$391,909	$747,594
Opponent	$128,238	$73,278	$260,727
Vote Pct	79%	76%	71%

Labor

Bldg Trades/Industrial/Misc Unions **$40,200**

    AFL-CIO* $5,200
    National Education Assn $5,500
    Carpenters & Joiners Union $4,000
    Machinists/Aerospace Workers Union $4,000
    Communications Workers of America $2,500
    American Federation of Teachers $2,000
    Intl Brotherhood of Electrical Workers $2,000
    Laborers' Political League $2,000
    United Auto Workers $2,000
    United Mine Workers $2,000
    Boilermakers Union $1,500
    Food & Commercial Workers Union $1,500
    Hotel/Restaurant Employees Union $1,500
    Plumbers/Pipefitters Union $1,500
    Sheet Metal Workers Union $1,500
    Others $1,500

Government & Postal Workers **$35,050**

    American Fedn of State/County/Munic Employees $10,000
    National Assn of Letter Carriers $8,000
    National Assn of Retired Federal Employees $5,000
    National Rural Letter Carriers Assn $5,000
    American Postal Workers Union $4,000
    Others $3,050

Transportation Unions **$20,450**

    Teamsters Union* $7,100
    Air Line Pilots Assn $6,000
    United Transportation Union $3,000
    Others $4,350

Major Ideological/Single-Issue

National PAC	$5,000	Pro-Israel
National Cmte to Preserve Social Security	$5,000	Soc Secur
Washington PAC	$1,500	Pro-Israel

Independent expenditures supporting Dorgan

National Cmte to Preserve Social Security $2,138

---

* Contributions came from more than one PAC affiliated
  with this sponsor.

417

Robert K. Dornan, R-Calif (38)

First elected: 1976
Total receipts: $1,731,883
Total from PACs: $83,231

1988 Committees & Subcommittees

Foreign Affairs
Africa
International Economic Policy and Trade
Western Hemisphere Affairs

Veterans' Affairs
Education, Training and Employment
Oversight and Investigations

Select Narcotics Abuse and Control

PAC Contribution Profile

Business

Automotive	*$5,250*
Auto Dealers & Drivers for Free Trade	$5,000
Others	$250
Construction	*$3,250*
Associated General Contractors	$1,000
National Assn of Home Builders	$1,000
Others	$1,250
Defense	*$11,300*
McDonnell Douglas	$3,000
Hughes Aircraft	$1,750
Rockwell International	$1,500
Northrop Corp	$1,200
Others	$3,850
Electronics & Computers	*$2,500*
Cooper Industries	$1,500
Others	$1,000
Food & Beverage	*$3,050*
Morrison Inc	$1,000
Papa Ginos	$1,000
Others	$1,050
Oil & Gas	*$3,850*
Amoco Corp	$1,000
Chevron Corp	$1,000
Mobil Oil	$1,000
Others	$850

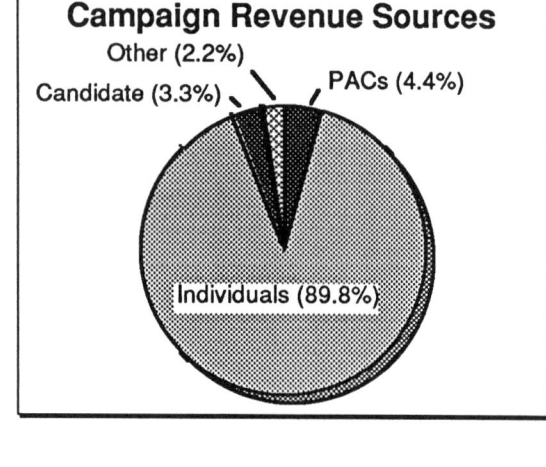

Campaign Revenue Sources

Other (2.2%)
Candidate (3.3%)
PACs (4.4%)
Individuals (89.8%)

Real Estate	*$7,250*
National Assn of Realtors	$6,000
Irvine Company	$1,000
Others	$250
Resorts/Movies	*$3,000*
Walt Disney Company	$3,000
Sugar Growers	*$3,050*
None over $750	

Other Major Business PACs

American Airlines	$1,000	Airlines
American Medical Assn	$1,000	Doctors
Philip Morris	$1,000	Tobacco

PAC Totals by Category

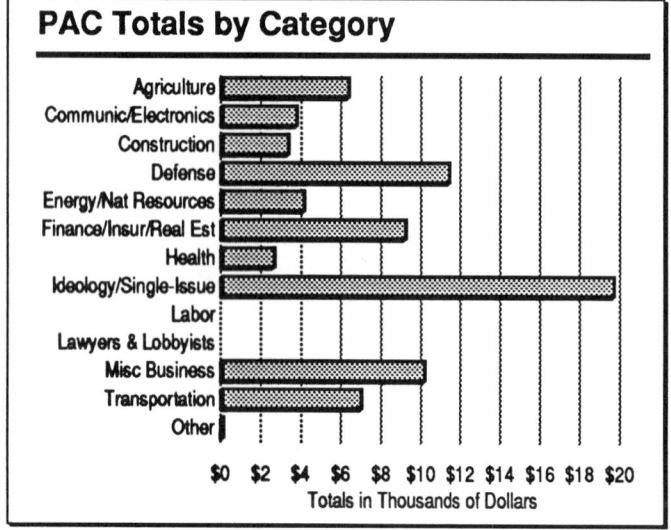

Totals in Thousands of Dollars

Agriculture
Communic/Electronics
Construction
Defense
Energy/Nat Resources
Finance/Insur/Real Est
Health
Ideology/Single-Issue
Labor
Lawyers & Lobbyists
Misc Business
Transportation
Other

$0 $2 $4 $6 $8 $10 $12 $14 $16 $18 $20

Ideological/Single-Issue

Pro-Defense **$5,837**
    Council for National Defense $5,087
    Others $750

Republican/Conservative **$6,242**
    Citizens for Moral Government.. $1,558
    American Citizens for Political Action $1,000
    Conservative Victory Cmte $1,000
    National Conservative PAC $1,000
    Others $1,684

Other Major Ideological/Single-Issue PACs

Conservative Victory Fund (Steve Symms) $1,250	Repub Leader
American Life Lobby $1,000	Pro-Life
Hudson Valley PAC $1,000	Pro-Israel
National Albanian American PAC $1,000	Ethnic
Ruff PAC $1,000	Tax Policy

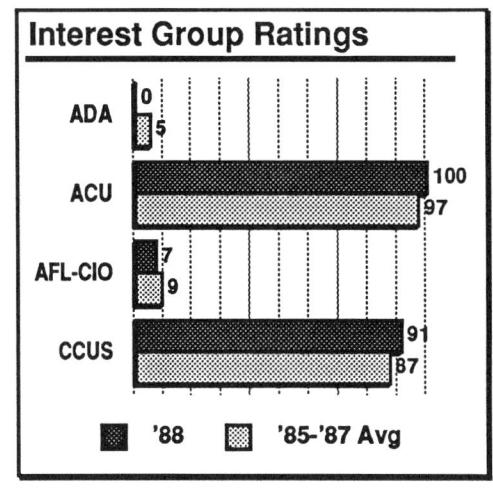

Interest Group Ratings

ADA 0 / 5
ACU 100 / 97
AFL-CIO 7 / 9
CCUS 91 / 87

■ '88   ▨ '85-'87 Avg

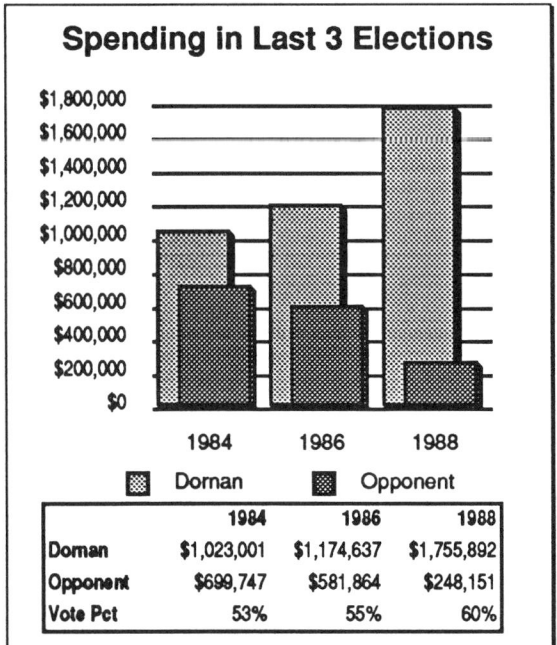

Spending in Last 3 Elections

▨ Dornan   ■ Opponent

	1984	1986	1988
Dornan	$1,023,001	$1,174,637	$1,755,892
Opponent	$699,747	$581,864	$248,151
Vote Pct	53%	55%	60%

Chuck Douglas, R-NH (2)

1988-1989 Committees & Subcommittees

First elected: 1988
Total receipts: $735,185
Total from PACs: $169,255

Government Operations
Commerce, Consumer and Monetary Affairs
Environment, Energy and Natural Resources

Judiciary
Administrative Law and Governmental Relations
Economic and Commercial Law

PAC Contribution Profile

Business

Air Transport	$2,000
Worldcorp Inc	$2,000

Automotive	$11,250
Auto Dealers & Drivers for Free Trade	$5,000
National Auto Dealers Assn	$5,000
Eaton Corp	$1,000
Others	$250

Building Contractors	$10,250
New Hampshire Home Builders	$5,000
Associated General Contractors	$2,500
National Assn of Home Builders	$2,500
Others	$250

Business Associations	$1,565
Business Industry PAC	$1,000
Others	$565

Dairy	$3,250
Associated Milk Producers	$3,000
Others	$250

Defense	$4,000
Lockheed Corp	$1,500
Harris Corp	$1,000
Others	$1,500

Electric Utilities	$5,500
None over $500	

Campaign Revenue Sources

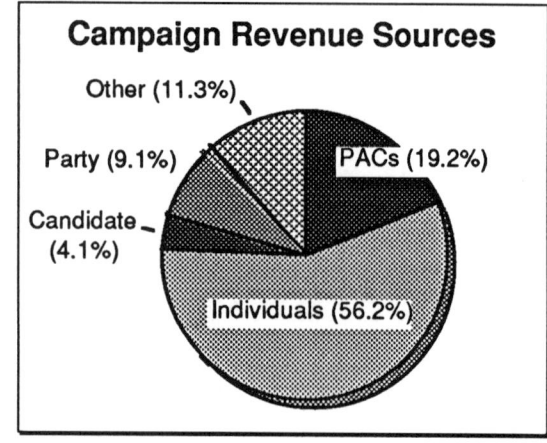

Other (11.3%)
Party (9.1%)
Candidate (4.1%)
PACs (19.2%)
Individuals (56.2%)

Financial Institutions	$7,750
New Hampshire Bankers Assn	$4,000
Bankeast Corp	$1,000
Citicorp	$1,000
Credit Union National Assn	$1,000
Others	$750

Food & Beverage	$3,750
Papa Ginos	$1,500
Coors Industries	$1,000
Others	$1,250

Health Professionals	$10,500
American Medical Assn	$5,000
American Academy of Ophthalmology	$3,000
American Dental Assn	$1,500
Others	$1,000

Insurance	$11,000
National Assn of Life Underwriters	$5,000
American International Group inc	$3,000
Chubb Corp	$1,000
Independent Insurance Agents of America	$1,000
National Assn Mutual Insurance Agents	$1,000

Labor Unions	$3,250
National Assn of Retired Federal Employees	$3,000
Others	$250

Lawyers	$11,300
Assn of Trial Lawyers of America	$10,000
Spear, Leeds & Kellogg	$1,000
Others	$300

Oil Companies	$2,500
None over $500	

Real Estate	$10,500
National Assn of Realtors	$10,000
Others	$500

Securities & Investing	$2,250
Cmte for Effective Government	$1,000
New York Stock Exchange	$1,000
Others	$250

PAC Totals by Category

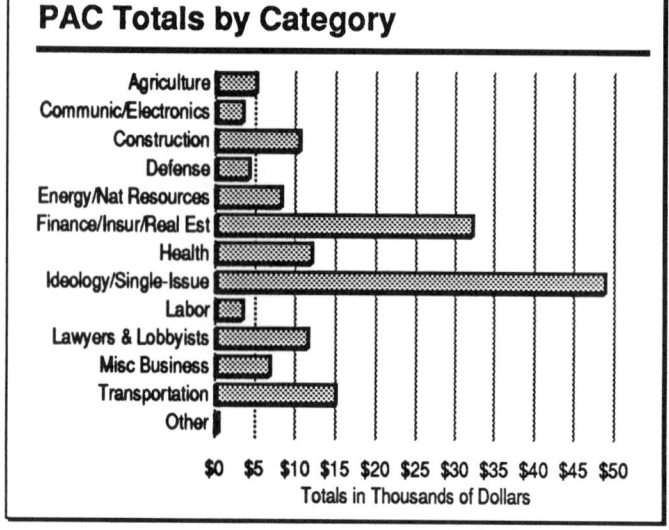

Agriculture
Communic/Electronics
Construction
Defense
Energy/Nat Resources
Finance/Insur/Real Est
Health
Ideology/Single-Issue
Labor
Lawyers & Lobbyists
Misc Business
Transportation
Other

$0 $5 $10 $15 $20 $25 $30 $35 $40 $45 $50
Totals in Thousands of Dollars

Telecommunications **$3,200**

    AT&T $2,000
    Continental Telecom $1,000
    Others $200

Other Major Business PACs

Philip Morris .... $1,000   Tobacco

Ideological/Single-Issue

Pro-Israel **$7,250**

    National PAC $5,000
    Hudson Valley PAC $1,000
    Others $1,250

Republican/Conservative **$10,057**

    Conservative Caucus PAC $4,500
    Fund for Conservative Majority $1,957
    Republican Congressional Boosters Club $1,000
    United Conservatives of America $1,000
    Others $1,600

Republican Leadership PACs **$16,866**

    Fund for America's Future (George Bush) $5,000
    Campaign for a New Majority (Jack Kemp) $4,000
    Campaign America (Bob Dole) $3,116
    Citizens for the Republic (Ronald Reagan) $2,500
    Republican Leader's Fund (Bob Michel) $1,000
    Others $1,250

Other Major Ideological/Single-Issue PACs

National Right to Life PAC .... $5,000   Pro-Life
Council for National Defense .... $2,755   Pro-Defense
Public Service Research Council .... $2,700   Anti-Union
Ruff PAC .... $1,500   Tax Policy
Bean-Jones Republican Congressional PAC .. $1,000   Repub Cands
Right to Work PAC .... $1,000   Anti-Union

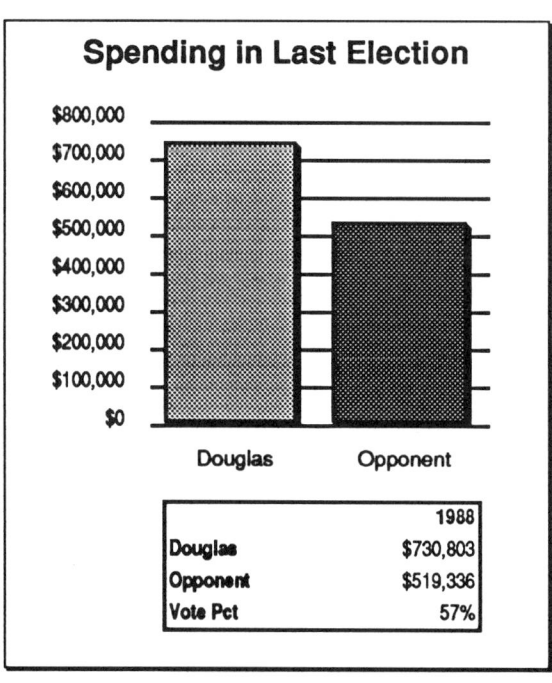

Spending in Last Election

	1988
Douglas	$730,803
Opponent	$519,336
Vote Pct	57%

Thomas J. Downey, D-NY (2)

First elected: 1974
Total receipts: $893,269
Total from PACs: $360,011

1988 Committees & Subcommittees

Ways and Means
Public Assistance and Unemployment Compensation (Acting Chairman)
Trade

Select Aging
Human Services (Acting Chairman)
Retirement Income and Employment

PAC Contribution Profile

Business

Accountants	**$11,500**
American Institute of CPA's	$5,000
Touche Ross	$5,000
Others	$1,500
Automotive	**$6,500**
Auto Dealers & Drivers for Free Trade	$5,000
Others	$1,500
Commercial Banks	**$16,520**
Chemical Bank	$2,520
American Bankers Assn	$2,000
Bankers Trust	$2,000
Chase Manhattan	$2,000
Citicorp	$2,000
J P Morgan & Company	$2,000
Irving Bank	$1,500
Others	$2,500
Defense	**$5,500**
Grumman	$4,000
Others	$1,500
Entertainment Industry	**$11,500**
Columbia Pictures	$2,500
MCA Inc	$2,500
Motion Picture Assn of America	$2,000
Recording Industry Assn	$1,500
Others	$3,000

Campaign Revenue Sources

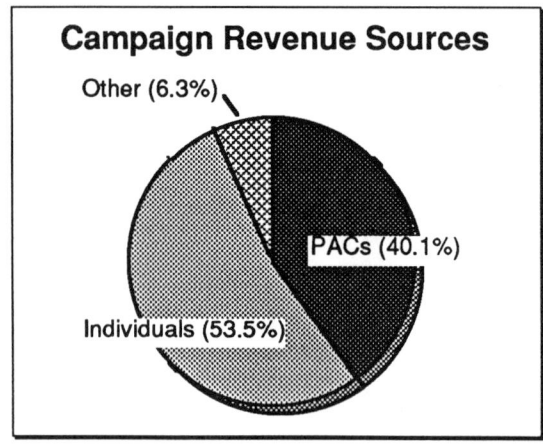

Other (6.3%)
PACs (40.1%)
Individuals (53.5%)

Food & Beverage	**$19,250**
Wine & Spirits Wholesalers of America	$4,000
National Beer Wholesalers Assn	$3,000
Joseph E Seagram & Sons	$2,000
General Mills*	$1,500
Others	$8,750
Health Professionals	**$15,100**
Assn for Advancement of Psychology	$5,000
New York Medical Assn	$1,600
American College of Emergency Physicians	$1,500
American Optometric Assn	$1,500
Corp for the Advancement of Psychiatry	$1,500
Others	$4,000
Hospitals & Nursing Homes	**$9,683**
American Hospital Assn	$3,783
American Health Care Assn	$2,900
National Assn of Private Psychiatric Hospitals	$1,500
Others	$1,500
Insurance	**$52,450**
Metropolitan Life Insurance	$9,000
National Assn of Life Underwriters	$5,000
New York Life	$5,000
Mutual Life Insurance of New York	$3,500
American International Group Inc	$3,000
Connecticut Mutual Life Insurance	$3,000
Massachusetts Mutual Life Insurance	$3,000
Northwestern Mutual Life	$3,000
Prudential Insurance	$3,000
American Council of Life Insurance	$2,000
Guardian Life Insurance	$2,000
Home Life Insurance	$1,500
John Hancock Financial Service	$1,500
Mutual Benefit Life Insurance	$1,250
Blue Cross & Blue Shield Assn	$1,200
Others	$5,500
Lawyers & Lobbyists	**$12,419**
Assn of Trial Lawyers of America	$5,000
Akin, Gump, Hauer & Feld	$2,000
Others	$5,419
Oil & Gas Marketing	**$4,500**
Northville Industries Corp	$1,000
Society of Independent Gasoline Marketers	$1,000
USX Corp	$1,000
Others	$1,500

PAC Totals by Category

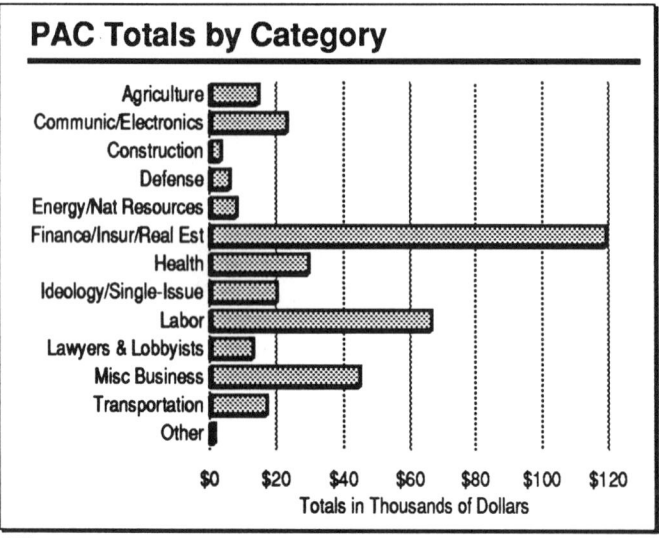

Agriculture
Communic/Electronics
Construction
Defense
Energy/Nat Resources
Finance/Insur/Real Est
Health
Ideology/Single-Issue
Labor
Lawyers & Lobbyists
Misc Business
Transportation
Other

$0 $20 $40 $60 $80 $100 $120
Totals in Thousands of Dollars

Real Estate $11,500
    National Assn of Realtors $8,000
    American Resort & Residential Development Assn $1,000
    Others $2,500

Retail Sales $7,000
    J C Penney Company $1,500
    Limited Inc $1,250
    Others $4,250

Savings Banks & Credit Unions $7,250
    US League of Savings Assn $2,500
    Others $4,750

Securities & Commodities Investment $17,000
    First Boston Corp $3,000
    Goldman Sachs $2,000
    Chicago Board of Trade $1,500
    Commodity Exchange Inc $1,500
    Others $9,000

Telecommunications $9,000
    New York Telephone $2,000
    AT&T $1,500
    Pacific Telesis Group $1,250
    US Telephone Assn $1,250
    Others $3,000

Other Major Business PACs

Triangle Industries	$10,000	Cans
National Venture Capital Assn	$3,000	Venture Cap
Milk Industry Foundation	$2,500	Dairy
Footwear Distributors PAC	$2,200	Shoes
American Express	$2,000	Credit/Loans
Philip Morris	$2,000	Tobacco
General Electric	$1,775	Electronics
CSX Transportation Inc	$1,500	Railroads
National Assn of Home Builders	$1,500	Resid Constr
National Custom Brokers Assn	$1,500	BusinessSvcs
United Parcel Service	$1,500	Delivery

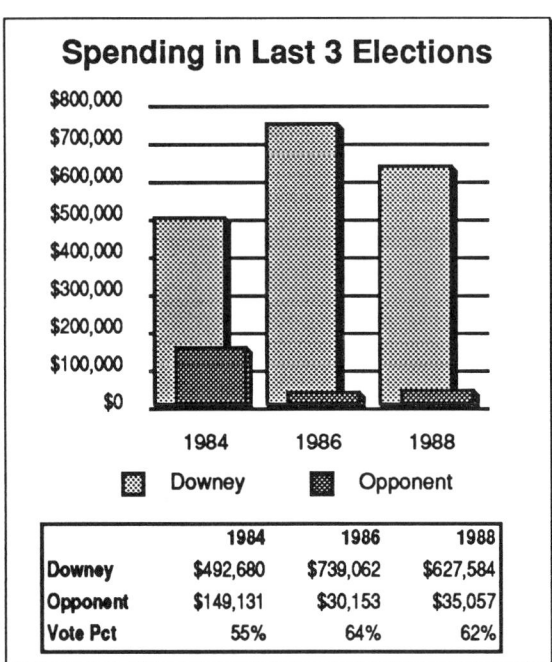

Spending in Last 3 Elections

	1984	1986	1988
Downey	$492,680	$739,062	$627,584
Opponent	$149,131	$30,153	$35,057
Vote Pct	55%	64%	62%

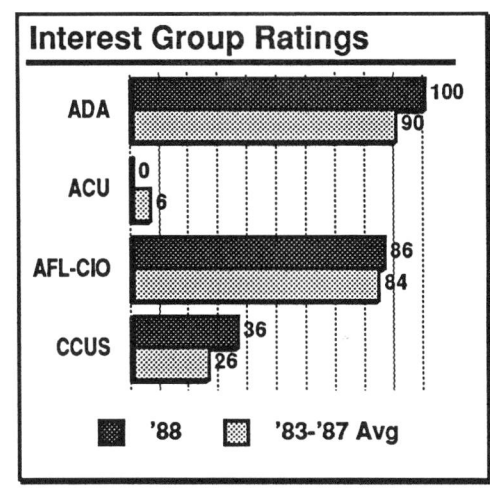

Interest Group Ratings

ADA 100 ('88), 90 ('83-'87 Avg)
ACU 0 ('88), 6 ('83-'87 Avg)
AFL-CIO 86 ('88), 84 ('83-'87 Avg)
CCUS 36 ('88), 26 ('83-'87 Avg)

■ '88   ▨ '83-'87 Avg

Labor

Bldg Trades/Industrial/Misc Unions $17,650
    Carpenters & Joiners Union* $6,000
    Food & Commercial Workers Union $2,150
    Laborers' Political League $2,000
    Hotel/Restaurant Employees Union $1,500
    Operating Engineers Union $1,500
    Others $4,500

Government & Postal Workers $20,122
    American Postal Workers Union $6,000
    National Assn of Retired Federal Employees $5,000
    National Assn of Letter Carriers $4,000
    American Fedn of State/County/Munic Employees $3,047
    Others $2,075

Teachers Unions $10,500
    National Education Assn $6,500
    American Federation of Teachers $4,000

Transportation Unions $17,300
    Teamsters Union $5,000
    United Transportation Union $2,500
    Seafarers International Union $2,000
    Transport Workers Union $2,000
    Others $5,800

Ideological/Single-Issue

Pro-Israel $8,000
    National PAC $5,000
    Others $3,000

Other Major Ideological/Single-Issue PACs

National Cmte for an Effective Congress	$4,070	Dem/Liberal
National Cmte to Preserve Social Security	$2,500	Society Secur

Independent expenditures supporting Downey

National Cmte to Preserve Social Security $1,560

---

* Contributions came from more than one PAC affiliated
  with this sponsor.

David Dreier, R-Calif (33)

First elected: 1980
Total receipts: $487,407
Total from PACs: $101,850

1988 Committees & Subcommittees

Banking, Finance and Urban Affairs
Financial Institutions Supervision, Regulation and Insurance
General Oversight and Investigations
Housing and Community Development

Small Business
Energy and Agriculture (Ranking Republican)

PAC Contribution Profile

Business

Agriculture	**$2,450**
Philip Morris	$1,000
Others	$1,450
Commercial Banks	**$31,200**
American Bankers Assn	$7,000
J P Morgan & Company	$5,000
Wells Fargo	$3,000
Bankers Trust	$2,000
First Interstate Bank/California	$2,000
Security Pacific Corp	$2,000
Assn of Bank Holding Companies	$1,600
Barnett Banks of Florida	$1,500
Union Bank	$1,500
BankAmerica	$1,250
Chase Manhattan	$1,000
Chemical Bank	$1,000
Citicorp	$1,000
Others	$1,350
Construction	**$4,750**
Simpson Investment Company	$1,250
Associated General Contractors	$1,000
National Assn of Home Builders	$1,000
Others	$1,500
Defense	**$3,750**
Lockheed Corp	$2,000
Others	$1,750

Campaign Revenue Sources

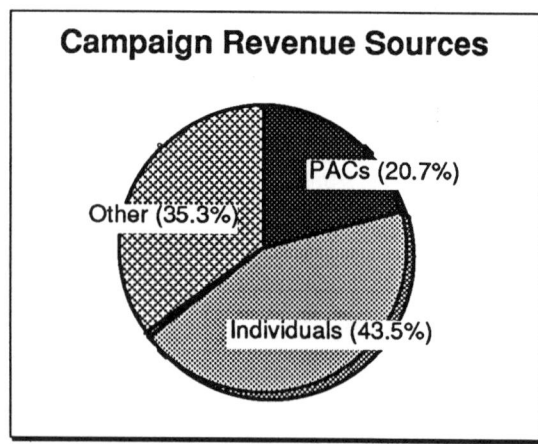

PACs (20.7%)
Other (35.3%)
Individuals (43.5%)

Health Professionals	**$2,750**
American Medical Assn	$2,500
Others	$250
Import Auto Dealers	**$3,500**
Auto Dealers & Drivers for Free Trade	$3,500
Insurance	**$8,250**
TransAmerica Insurance*	$3,500
Mortgage Insurance Companies of America	$1,500
Farmers Group Inc	$1,000
Travelers Corp	$1,000
Others	$1,250
Real Estate	**$3,500**
National Assn of Realtors	$3,500
Retail Sales	**$3,400**
Federated Department Stores	$1,000
Others	$2,400
Savings Banks	**$14,600**
California League of Savings Institute	$3,000
Home Savings of America	$2,500
California Federal Savings & Loan	$2,000
Coast Federal Savings & Loan	$1,750
Glendale Federal Savings & Loan	$1,000
Great Western Financial Corp	$1,000
Guarantee Savings	$1,000
Others	$2,350
Securities & Commodities Investment	**$2,500**
Drexel Burnham Lambert	$1,000
Others	$1,500

Other Major Business PACs

Credit Union National Assn	$1,500	Credit Union
United Parcel Service	$1,250	Delivery
Atlantic Richfield	$1,000	Major Oil
FMC Corp	$1,000	Chemicals
Honeywell California	$1,000	Electronics
Stone Container Corp	$1,000	Paper Packg

Other Major PACs

Free Enterprise USA PAC	$1,000	Unknown

PAC Totals by Category

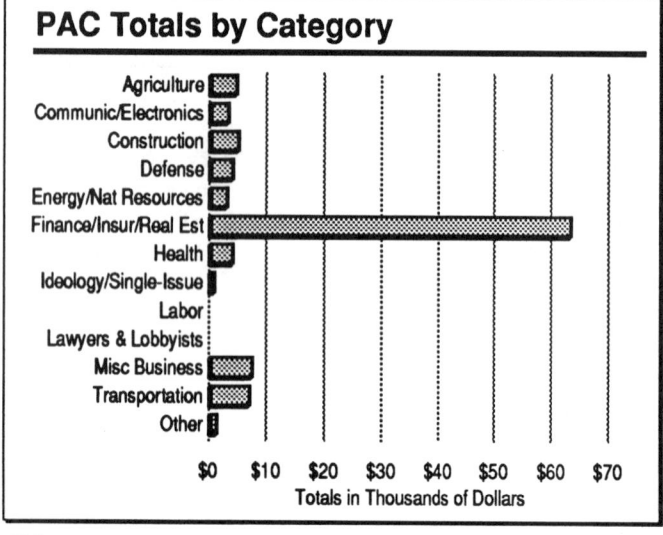

Totals in Thousands of Dollars

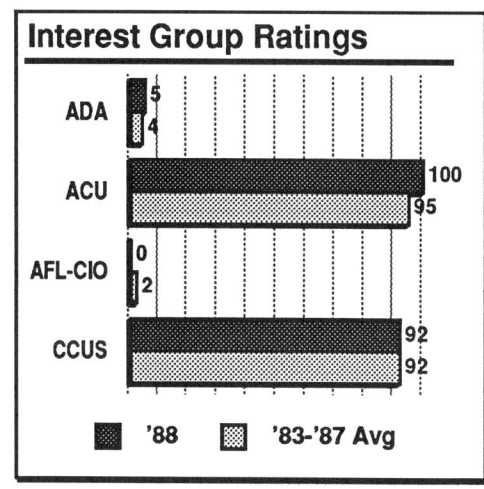

Interest Group Ratings

	'88	'83-'87 Avg
ADA	5	4
ACU	100	95
AFL-CIO	0	2
CCUS	92	92

■ '88   ▨ '83-'87 Avg

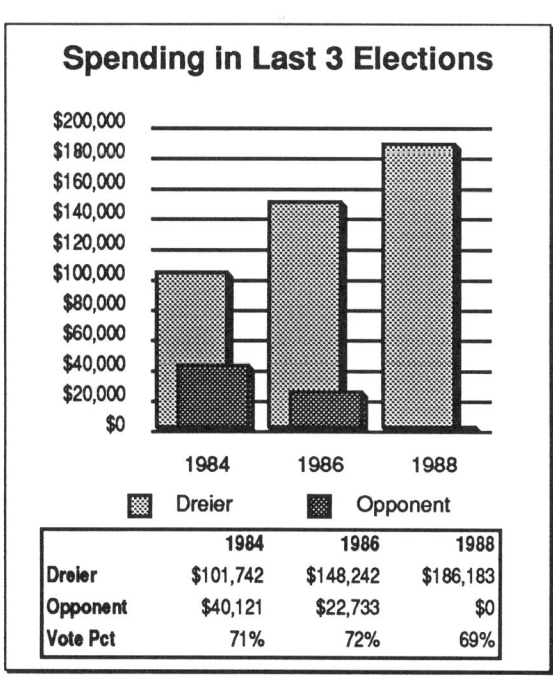

Spending in Last 3 Elections

▨ Dreier   ■ Opponent

	1984	1986	1988
Dreier	$101,742	$148,242	$186,183
Opponent	$40,121	$22,733	$0
Vote Pct	71%	72%	69%

---

* Contributions came from more than one PAC affiliated
with this sponsor.

John J. "Jimmy" Duncan Jr., R-Tenn (2)

First elected: 1988
Total receipts: $448,530
Total from PACs: $161,675

1988-1989 Committees & Subcommittees

Interior and Insular Affairs
General Oversight and Investigations
National Parks and Public Lands

Select Aging
Housing and Consumer Interests
Human Services

Public Works and Transportation
Aviation
Investigations and Oversight
Public Buildings and Grounds
Surface Transportation

PAC Contribution Profile

Business

Accountants	**$2,500**
American Institute of CPA's	$1,000
Others	$1,500
Air Transport/Air Freight	**$11,250**
Federal Express Corp	$7,000
Aircraft Owners & Pilots Assn	$1,000
Boeing Company	$1,000
Texas Air	$1,000
Others	$1,250
Automotive	**$3,500**
Auto Dealers & Drivers for Free Trade	$1,000
National Auto Dealers Assn	$1,000
Others	$1,500
Chemicals	**$3,300**
None over $500	
Construction	**$8,250**
National Assn of Home Builders	$2,500
Enserch Corp	$1,000
Sheet Metal/AirCon Contractors	$1,000
Tennessee Road Builders Assn	$1,000
Others	$2,750
Consumer Credit & Loans	**$2,500**
American Financial Services Assn	$1,000
Others	$1,500

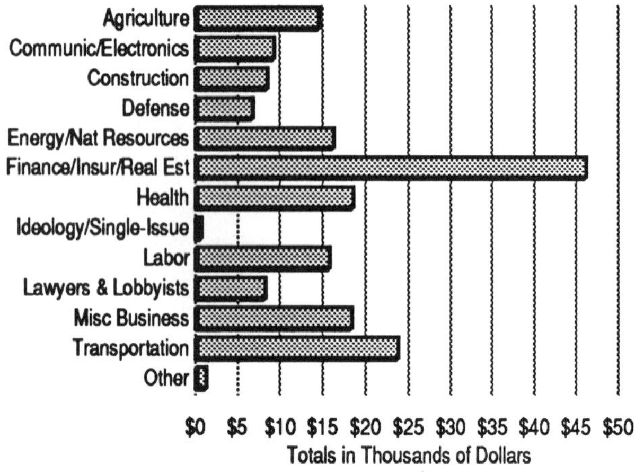

Campaign Revenue Sources

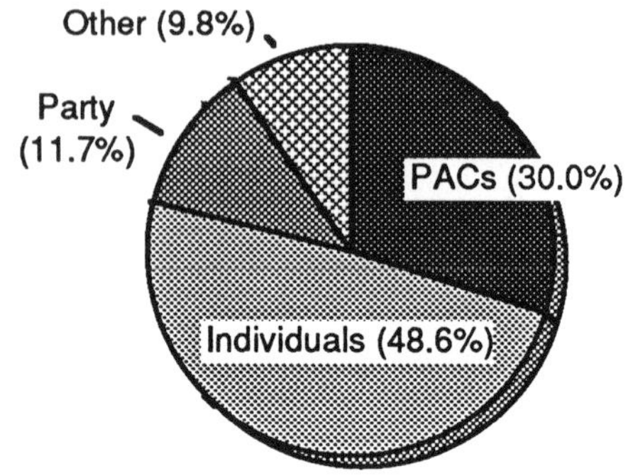

Other (9.8%)
Party (11.7%)
PACs (30.0%)
Individuals (48.6%)

Defense	**$6,500**
Colt Industries	$1,000
Northrop Corp	$1,000
Tenneco Inc	$1,000
Others	$3,500
Electronics & Computers	**$2,750**
General Electric	$1,000
Others	$1,750
Financial Institutions	**$7,000**
Citicorp	$1,000
Credit Union National Assn	$1,000
First American Corp	$1,000
US League of Savings Assn	$1,000
Others	$3,000
Food & Beverage	**$11,000**
National Beer Wholesalers Assn	$2,500
Malone & Hyde Inc	$2,000
Wine & Spirits Wholesalers of America	$1,500
Food Marketing Institute	$1,000
Joseph E Seagram & Sons	$1,000
Others	$3,000
Health Professionals	**$11,500**
American Podiatry Assn	$2,500
American Optometric Assn	$2,000
Cmte for Quality Orthopedic Health Care	$2,000
American Occupational Therapy Assn	$1,000
National Assn of Pharmacists	$1,000
Others	$3,000
Hospitals	**$4,500**
American Hospital Assn	$1,000
Federation of America Hospitals	$1,000
National Medical Enterprises Inc	$1,000
Others	$1,500

PAC Totals by Category

Agriculture
Communic/Electronics
Construction
Defense
Energy/Nat Resources
Finance/Insur/Real Est
Health
Ideology/Single-Issue
Labor
Lawyers & Lobbyists
Misc Business
Transportation
Other

$0 $5 $10 $15 $20 $25 $30 $35 $40 $45 $50
Totals in Thousands of Dollars

Hotels/Motels & Resorts..**$3,500**
    Holiday Inns $2,000
    American Hotel & Motel Assn.......................................$500
    Marriott Corp $500
    Walt Disney Company $500

Insurance...**$26,457**
    American Family Corp $3,000
    Equitable Financial Services $2,000
    Massachusetts Mutual Life Insurance $2,000
    Metropolitan Life Insurance $1,500
    Independent Insurance Agents of America $1,457
    Allstate Insurance $1,000
    American Council of Life Insurance $1,000
    Georgia US Corp $1,000
    Health Insurance Assn of America $1,000
    Mutual Life Insurance of New York $1,000
    National Assn of Life Underwriters $1,000
    New England Mutual Life $1,000
    New York Life $1,000
    Northwestern Mutual Life $1,000
    Others $7,500

Lawyers **$8,000**
    Assn of Trial Lawyers of America...........................$5,000
    Others $3,000

Mining & Metal Processing **$3,500**
    Alcoa $1,000
    Others $2,500

Oil & Gas **$11,000**
    Amoco Corp $1,000
    Shell Oil $1,000
    Sun Company $1,000
    Texaco $1,000
    Others $7,000

Real Estate **$3,000**
    None over $500

Securities & Commodities Investment.........................**$5,500**
    Chicago Board of Trade $1,000
    First Boston Corp $1,000
    Others $3,500

Telecommunications **$5,750**
    AT&T...$1,000
    NYNEX Corp $1,000
    South Central Bell Telephone $1,000
    Others $2,750

Tobacco **$2,500**
    Philip Morris $1,500
    Others $1,000

Trucking/Delivery..**$4,000**
    American Trucking Assns $1,000
    Consolidated Freightways $1,000
    Others $2,000

Other Major Business PACs
Employee Stock Ownership Assn ....$1,000   Other

Labor

Bldg Trades/Industrial/Misc Unions **$6,000**
    National Assn of Retired Federal Employees $2,000
    National Assn of Letter Carriers $1,000
    National Rural Letter Carriers Assn $1,000
    Others $2,000

Transportation Unions **$9,500**
    Air Line Pilots Assn...$5,000
    Marine Engineers Dist 2 Retirees $3,500
    Seafarers International Union..................................$1,000

Spending in Last Election

	1988
Duncan	$435,567
Opponent	$381,980
Vote Pct	56%

Richard J. Durbin, D-Ill (20)

First elected: 1982
Total receipts: $367,468
Total from PACs: $220,305

1988 Committees & Subcommittees

Appropriations
Rural Development, Agriculture and Related Agencies
Transportation and Related Agencies

Budget
Community and Natural Resources
Human Resources

Select Children, Youth and Families

PAC Contribution Profile

Business

Agricultural Services	**$2,200**
American Assn of Crop Insurers	$1,100
Others	$1,100
Air Transport	**$6,050**
Aircraft Owners & Pilots Assn	$2,800
Texas Air*	$1,100
Others	$2,150
Automotive	**$4,700**
National Auto Dealers Assn	$2,500
Chrysler Corp	$1,100
Others	$1,100
Commercial & Savings Banks	**$6,240**
First Chicago Corp	$1,350
American Savings Banks	$1,250
Continental Illinois Corp	$1,250
Others	$2,390
Construction	**$4,950**
National Assn of Home Builders	$2,200
National Electrical Contractors Assn	$1,000
Others	$1,750
Dairy	**$7,550**
Associated Milk Producers	$3,000
Mid-American Dairymen	$2,850
Land O'Lakes Inc	$1,000
Others	$700

Campaign Revenue Sources

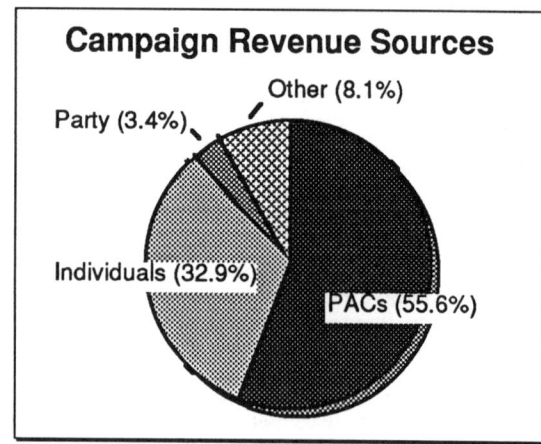

Other (8.1%)
Party (3.4%)
Individuals (32.9%)
PACs (55.6%)

Defense	**$2,550**
None over $750	
Food & Beverage	**$9,150**
A E Staley Manufacturing Company	$3,550
Food Marketing Institute	$1,000
McDonald's Corp	$1,000
Winn-Dixie Stores	$1,000
Others	$2,600
Grain Trading	**$3,000**
Archer-Daniels-Midland Corp	$3,000
Health Professionals	**$9,600**
American Medical Assn	$3,850
American Dental Assn	$2,500
American Dietetic Assn	$1,000
Cmte for Quality Orthopedic Health Care	$1,000
Others	$1,250
Insurance	**$8,750**
National Assn of Life Underwriters	$4,000
Independent Insurance Agents of America	$1,500
Franklin Life	$1,000
General American Life Insurance	$1,000
Others	$1,250
Lawyers	**$3,500**
Assn of Trial Lawyers of America	$1,350
Others	$2,150
Mining	**$3,000**
Peabody Coal	$1,500
Others	$1,500
Railroads	**$4,100**
CSX Transportation Inc	$1,000
Others	$3,100
Real Estate	**$6,750**
National Assn of Realtors	$6,000
Others	$750
Securities & Commodities Investment	**$9,500**
Chicago Board of Trade	$6,000
Chicago Mercantile Exchange	$2,500
Goldman Sachs	$1,000

PAC Totals by Category

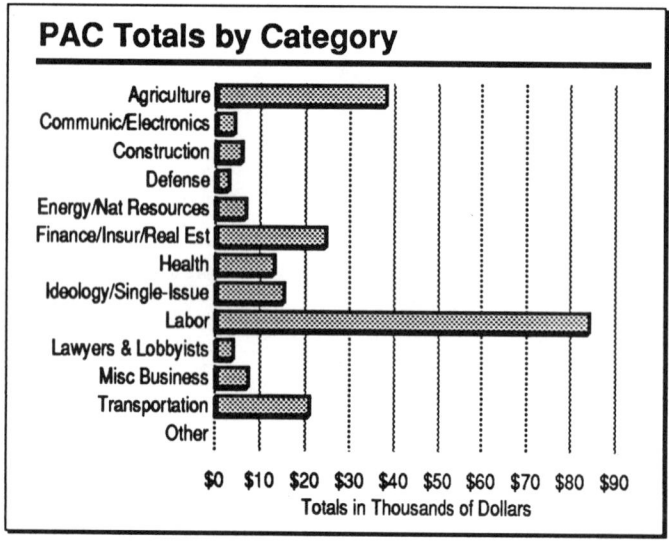

Totals in Thousands of Dollars

Agriculture
Communic/Electronics
Construction
Defense
Energy/Nat Resources
Finance/Insur/Real Est
Health
Ideology/Single-Issue
Labor
Lawyers & Lobbyists
Misc Business
Transportation
Other

$0 $10 $20 $30 $40 $50 $60 $70 $80 $90

Sugar Growers **$4,300**
    American Sugarbeet Growers Assn $1,500
    Others $2,800

Telecommunications **$3,750**
    AT&T $2,000
    Illinois Bell Telephone $1,000
    Others $750

Trucking/Delivery **$4,500**
    United Parcel Service $2,500
    American Trucking Assns $1,100
    Others $900

Other Major Business PACs

ACRE (Action Committee for Rural Electric) ...	$1,200	RuralElect
Waste Management Inc	$1,200	Waste Mgmt
Household International	$1,000	Credit/Loans
Montgomery Ward	$1,000	Dept Store

Labor

Bldg Trades/Industrial/Misc Unions **$28,900**
    United Auto Workers $5,700
    Machinists/Aerospace Workers* $4,000
    Carpenters & Joiners Union $3,700
    AFL-CIO* $2,600
    Sheet Metal Workers Union $2,500
    Laborers' Political League* $2,000
    Operating Engineers Union $2,000
    Plumbers/Pipefitters Union* $1,700
    Food & Commercial Workers Union $1,100
    Ladies Garment Workers Union $1,000
    Others $2,600

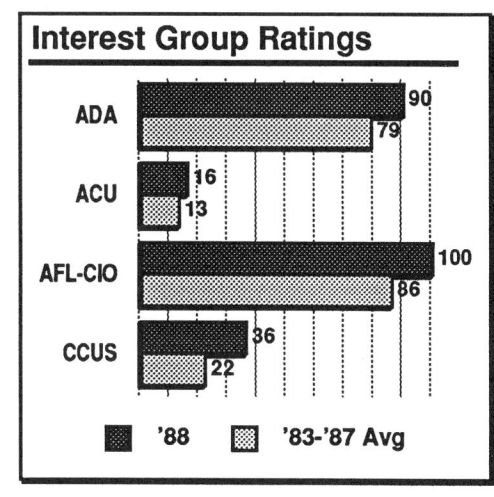

Interest Group Ratings

	'88	'83-'87 Avg
ADA	90	79
ACU	16	13
AFL-CIO	100	86
CCUS	36	22

Government & Postal Workers **$18,100**
    National Assn of Retired Federal Employees $8,500
    National Assn of Letter Carriers $4,200
    American Fedn of State/County/Munic Employees $2,000
    American Postal Workers Union $1,100
    Others $2,300

Teachers Unions **$13,600**
    National Education Assn $10,000
    American Federation of Teachers $3,600

Transportation Unions **$23,050**
    Air Line Pilots Assn...$7,500
    Teamsters Union $7,500
    United Transportation Union $3,000
    Amalgamated Transit Union $1,000
    Seafarers International Union $1,000
    Others $3,050

Ideological/Single-Issue

Pro-Israel **$11,450**
    National PAC $5,000
    St Louisians for Better Government $2,000
    Washington PAC $1,350
    Hudson Valley PAC $1,000
    Multi-Issue PAC $1,000
    Others $1,100

Other Major Ideological/Single-Issue PACs

Valley Education Fund (Tony Coelho)	$1,000	Dem Leaders
KidsPAC	$1,000	HealthWelfare

Independent expenditures supporting Durbin

National Cmte to Preserve Social Security	$3,471

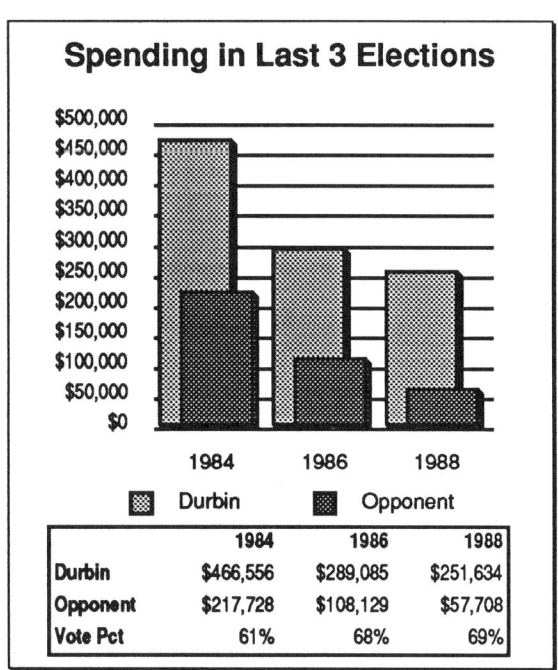

Spending in Last 3 Elections

Durbin / Opponent

	1984	1986	1988
Durbin	$466,556	$289,085	$251,634
Opponent	$217,728	$108,129	$57,708
Vote Pct	61%	68%	69%

* Contributions came from more than one PAC affiliated
with this sponsor.

Bernard J. Dwyer, D-NJ (6)

First elected: 1980
Total receipts: $136,330
Total from PACs: $113,000

1988 Committees & Subcommittees

Appropriations
Commerce, Justice, State, the Judiciary and Related Agencies
Labor, Health and Human Services, Education and Related Agencies

Select Intelligence
Oversight and Evaluation
Program and Budget Authorization

Standards of Official Conduct

PAC Contribution Profile

Business

Commercial & Savings Banks **$3,350**
SAPEC/NJ (New Jersey Savings Assn) $1,750
American Bankers Assn $1,000
Others $600

Construction **$6,100**
National Assn of Home Builders $4,600
Manville Corp $1,500

Defense **$4,400**
Hughes Aircraft $1,300
General Dynamics $1,000
Textron Inc $1,000
Others $1,100

Insurance **$9,700**
Independent Insurance Agents of America $2,400
National Assn of Mutual Insurance Agents $2,400
American International Group inc $1,100
Travelers Corp $1,000
Others $2,800

Medical Professionals **$7,700**
American Dental Assn $2,000
American Medical Assn $1,800
Cmte for Quality Orthopedic Health Care $1,300
Others $2,600

Pharmaceuticals **$5,400**
Johnson & Johnson $2,000
Merck & Company $1,000
Others $2,400

Campaign Revenue Sources

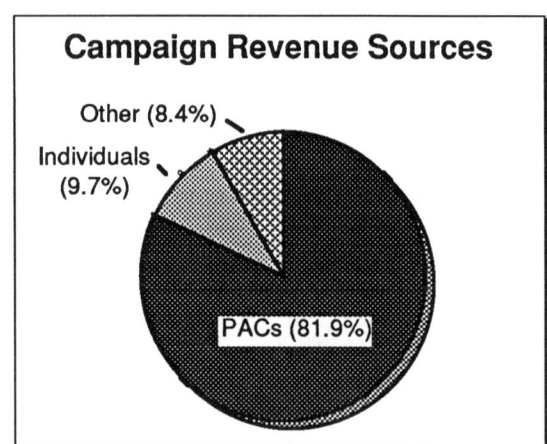

Other (8.4%)
Individuals (9.7%)
PACs (81.9%)

Real Estate **$2,600**
National Assn of Realtors $2,300
Others $300

Telecommunications **$3,650**
AT&T $1,750
New Jersey Bell Telephone $1,600
Others $300

Other Major Business PACs

GATX Corp .... $1,100   RR Svcs
National Assn of Trade/Tech Schools .... $1,000   Voc Tech

PAC Totals by Category

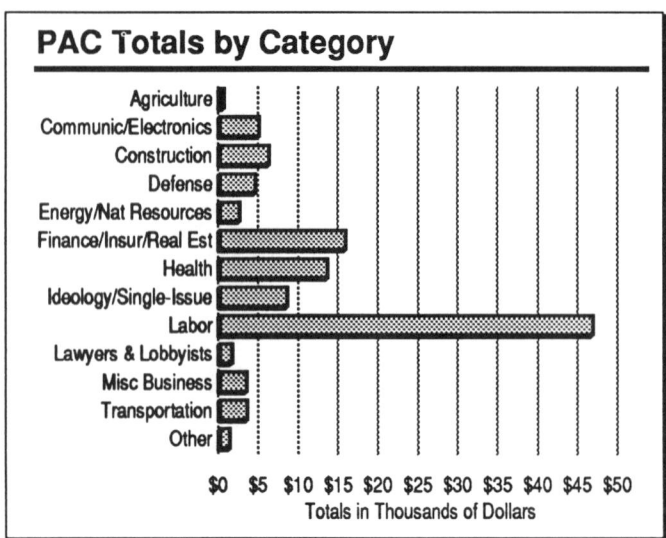

Agriculture
Communic/Electronics
Construction
Defense
Energy/Nat Resources
Finance/Insur/Real Est
Health
Ideology/Single-Issue
Labor
Lawyers & Lobbyists
Misc Business
Transportation
Other

$0 $5 $10 $15 $20 $25 $30 $35 $40 $45 $50
Totals in Thousands of Dollars

Labor

Bldg Trades/Industrial/Misc Unions $20,950
- Operating Engineers Union $6,800
- Plumbers/Pipefitters Local #9 ....$2,900
- Carpenters & Joiners Union $2,600
- United Auto Workers $2,600
- Food & Commercial Workers Union.................................$1,300
- Intl Brotherhood of Electrical Workers.............................$1,000
- Others $3,750

Government & Postal Workers $9,100
- National Assn of Retired Federal Employees $5,000
- American Fedn of State/County/Munic Employees $2,000
- National Assn of Letter Carriers $1,200
- Others $900

Teachers Unions $3,800
- National Education Assn $3,200
- Others $600

Transportation Unions $12,750
- Air Line Pilots Assn $3,500
- Marine Engineers District 2 Maritime Officers.................$2,000
- Seafarers International Union $2,000
- Teamsters Union $2,000
- AFL-CIO* $1,200
- Others $2,050

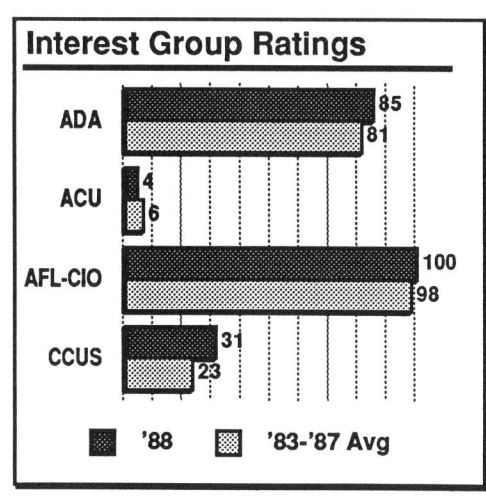

Interest Group Ratings

ADA 85 / 81
ACU 4 / 6
AFL-CIO 100 / 98
CCUS 31 / 23

■ '88   ▨ '83-'87 Avg

Ideological/Single-Issue

Democratic Leadership PACs.......................................$3,000
- America's Leaders' Fund (Dan Rostenkowski) $2,000
- Valley Education Fund (Tony Coelho) $1,000

Other Major Ideological/Single-Issue PACs

National Cmte to Preserve Social Security $2,600	Society Secur
Human Rights Campaign Fund $2,500	Gay Rights

Independent expenditures supporting Dwyer

National Cmte to Preserve Social Security $3,462

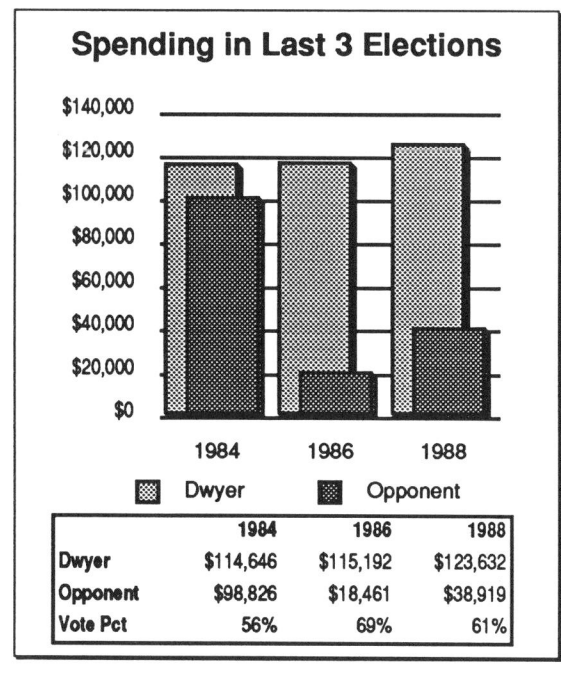

Spending in Last 3 Elections

	1984	1986	1988
Dwyer	$114,646	$115,192	$123,632
Opponent	$98,826	$18,461	$38,919
Vote Pct	56%	69%	61%

▨ Dwyer   ■ Opponent

Mervyn M. Dymally, D-Calif (31)

First elected: 1980
Total receipts: $488,149
Total from PACs: $156,449

1988 Committees & Subcommittees

District of Columbia
Judiciary and Education (Chairman)

Foreign Affairs
Asian and Pacific Affairs
International Operations

Post Office and Civil Service
Census and Population (Chairman)
Postal Personnel and Modernization

PAC Contribution Profile

Business

Defense..	**$5,500**
Hughes Aircraft	$1,250
Northrop Corp	$1,150
Lockheed Corp	$1,000
Others	$2,100
Electric Utilities	**$2,000**
Southern California Edison	$1,500
Others	$500
Package Delivery	**$5,100**
United Parcel Service	$5,100
Food & Beverage	**$3,362**
Occidental Petroleum	$2,100
Others	$1,262
Health Professionals	**$4,000**
American Medical Assn	$3,000
American Chiropractic Assn	$1,000
Oil & Gas	**$2,000**
None over $750	
Real Estate	**$2,000**
National Assn of Realtors	$2,000
Savings Banks	**$6,000**
Mercury Savings & Loan	$3,000
California League of Savings Institute	$2,000
US League of Savings Assn......................	$1,000

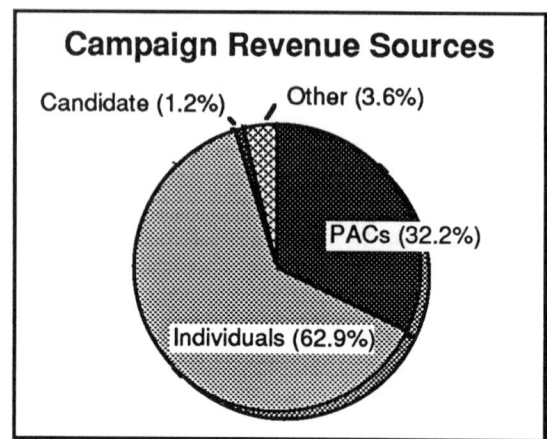

Campaign Revenue Sources

Candidate (1.2%)
Other (3.6%)
PACs (32.2%)
Individuals (62.9%)

Telecommunications	**$2,050**
Pacific Telesis Group	$1,050
AT&T	$1,000
Tobacco	**$2,250**
Philip Morris	$1,000
Others	$1,250

Other Major Business PACs

Farmers Group Inc	$1,100	Insurance
ASCAP	$1,000	Music Prod
Computer Sciences Corp	$1,000	Data Process
Morrison-Knudsen	$1,000	Comml Constr
Summa Corp	$1,000	Casinos/Gamb

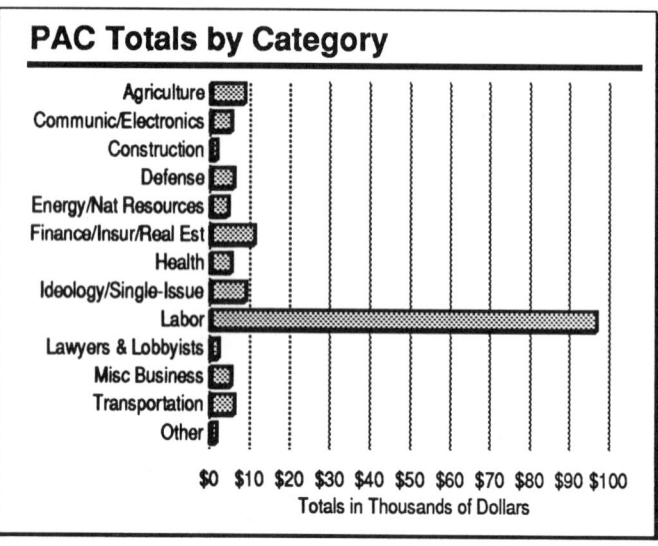

PAC Totals by Category

Agriculture
Communic/Electronics
Construction
Defense
Energy/Nat Resources
Finance/Insur/Real Est
Health
Ideology/Single-Issue
Labor
Lawyers & Lobbyists
Misc Business
Transportation
Other

$0 $10 $20 $30 $40 $50 $60 $70 $80 $90 $100
Totals in Thousands of Dollars

Labor

Bldg Trades/Industrial/Misc Unions $31,800

United Auto Workers $9,300
Carpenters & Joiners Union $4,800
Laborers' Western Political League $4,000
Machinists/Aerospace Workers Union $3,600
AFL-CIO* $2,000
Operating Engineers Union $2,000
Service Employees International Union $2,000
Food & Commercial Workers Union $1,450
Ladies Garment Workers Union $1,150
Others $1,500

Government & Postal Workers $32,350

National Assn of Letter Carriers $8,000
National Assn of Retired Federal Employees $7,000
American Postal Workers Union $3,600
National Alliance Postal/Federal Employees $3,300
American Fedn of State/County/Munic Employees $2,250
National Assn of Postmasters $2,100
National League of Postmasters $1,600
National Assn of Postal Supervisors $1,500
National Federation of Federal Employees $1,000
Others $2,000

Teachers Unions $9,800

National Education Assn $8,500
American Federation of Teachers $1,300

Transportation Unions $22,350

Teamsters Union* $10,000
Marine Engineers Union* $6,850
Seafarers International Union $2,000
United Transportation Union $1,200
Transport Workers Union $1,000
Others $1,300

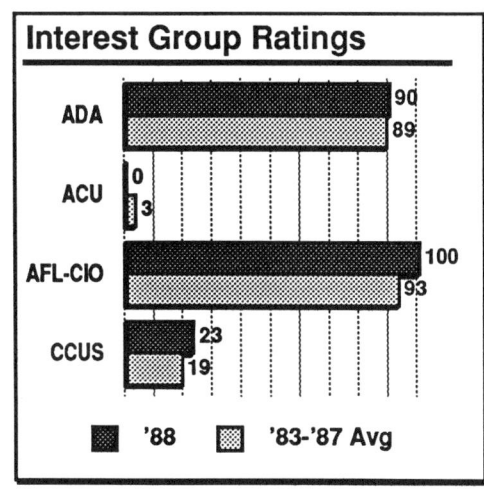

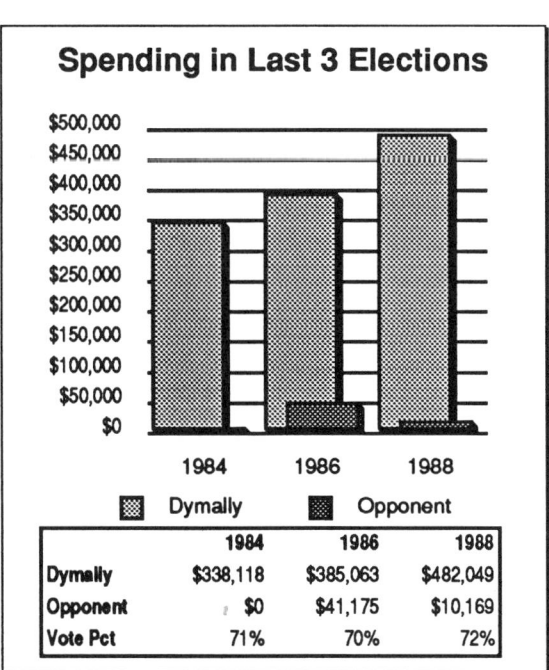

Ideological/Single-Issue

Ideological/Single-Issue $9,500

National Cmte to Preserve Social Security $5,250	Society Secur
Human Rights Campaign Fund $1,000	Gay Rights
Muslim PAC $1,000	UNKNOWN
National Assn of Arab-Americans $1,000	ForeignPolcy
Others $1,250	

Independent expenditures supporting Dymally

American Health & Beauty Aids Institute $2,000
National Cmte to Preserve Social Security $1,352

---

* Contributions came from more than one PAC affiliated with this sponsor.

Roy Dyson, D-Md (1)

1988 Committees & Subcommittees

Armed Services
Military Personnel and Compensation
Procurement and Military Nuclear Systems
Seapower and Strategic and Critical Materials

Merchant Marine and Fisheries
Fisheries and Wildlife Conservation and the Environment
Merchant Marine

First elected: 1980
Total receipts: $691,251
Total from PACs: $401,647

PAC Contribution Profile

Business

Defense...**$89,300**	
AAI Corp	$8,500
Mantech International	$7,000
BDM International	$5,000
Litton Industries	$5,000
Harsco Corp	$4,500
Northrop Corp	$4,500
Lockheed Corp	$3,500
Textron Inc	$3,500
McDonnell Douglas*	$3,250
Bath Iron Works	$2,500
General Dynamics	$2,500
Grumman	$2,500
Veda Inc	$2,500
Emhart Corp	$2,000
LTV Aerospace & Defense Company	$2,000
Morton Thiokol	$2,000
Raytheon	$2,000
Rockwell International	$2,000
Hughes Aircraft	$1,750
Kaman Corp	$1,500
Martin Marietta Corp	$1,500
United Technologies	$1,500
Westinghouse Electric	$1,500
Dyncorp	$1,200
FMC Corp	$1,050
Advanced Technology Inc	$1,000
Allied-Signal	$1,000
Chrysler Corp	$1,000
Gould Inc	$1,000
Long Island Aerospace PAC	$1,000
(Continued in next column)	

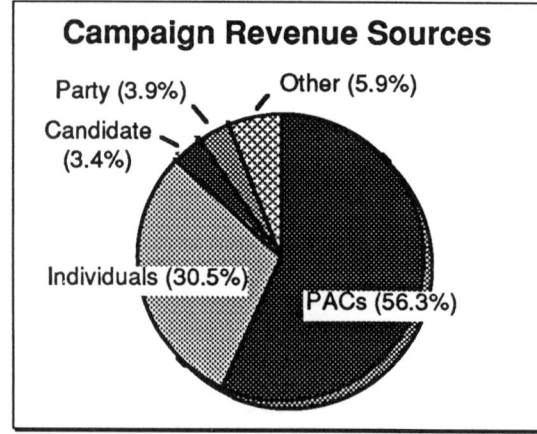

Campaign Revenue Sources

Party (3.9%)
Other (5.9%)
Candidate (3.4%)
Individuals (30.5%)
PACs (56.3%)

Defense (cont'd)	
Loral Corp	$1,000
Planning Research Corp	$1,000
Others	$7,550
Health Professionals **$16,850**	
American Medical Assn	$5,350
American Podiatry Assn	$4,000
Maryland Medical Assn	$3,500
American Dental Assn	$1,500
American Optometric Assn	$1,500
American Chiropractic Assn	$1,000
Real Estate **$11,500**	
National Assn of Realtors	$11,000
Others	$500

Other Major Business PACs

Assn of Trial Lawyers of America	$4,500	Lawyers
National Assn Life Underwriters	$3,500	Life Insur
Dairymen Inc	$3,000	Dairy
National Auto Dealers Assn	$3,000	Auto Sales
Philadelphia Electric	$3,000	Gas & Electr
Associated Milk Producers	$2,500	Dairy
MNC Financial Inc	$2,500	Comml Banks
American Sugarbeet Growers Assn	$2,300	Sugar
ACRE (Action Committee for Rural Electric) ...	$2,250	RuralElect
AT&T	$2,250	Long Distance
American Crystal Sugar Corp	$2,000	Sugar
Matson Navigation	$2,000	Sea Transport
American Trucking Assns	$1,500	Trucking
Boat Owners Assn of the US	$1,500	Rec Boats
Mid-American Dairymen	$1,500	Dairy
National Beer Wholesalers Assn	$1,500	Liquor Whlsl
Potomac Electric Power Company	$1,500	Electric Util
National Fisheries Institute	$1,300	Fishing
American President Lines	$1,250	SeaTransport
Mercantile Bankshares Corp	$1,250	Banks
Philip Morris	$1,200	Tobacco
First Maryland Bancorp	$1,100	Comml Banks
Bethlehem Steel	$1,088	Steel
Aircraft Owners & Pilots Assn	$1,000	GenlAviation
American Hospital Assn	$1,000	Hospitals
KMS Fusion Inc	$1,000	Nuke Energy
Michigan Bell Telephone	$1,000	Phone Util
National Assn of Home Builders	$1,000	Resid Constr
Preston, Thorgrimson, Ellis & Holman	$1,000	Lawyers
Tobacco Institute	$1,000	Tobacco
United Parcel Service	$1,000	Delivery
Waste Management Inc	$1,000	Waste Mgmt

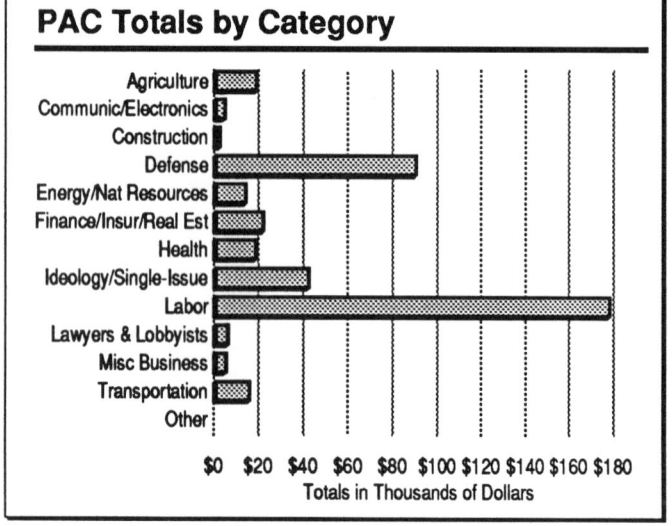

PAC Totals by Category

- Agriculture
- Communic/Electronics
- Construction
- Defense
- Energy/Nat Resources
- Finance/Insur/Real Est
- Health
- Ideology/Single-Issue
- Labor
- Lawyers & Lobbyists
- Misc Business
- Transportation
- Other

$0 $20 $40 $60 $80 $100 $120 $140 $160 $180
Totals in Thousands of Dollars

Labor

Bldg Trades, Industrial & Other Unions $80,888

Sheet Metal Workers Union	$8,500
Intl Brotherhood of Electrical Workers	$8,000
Food & Commercial Workers Union	$7,248
National Education Assn	$7,000
AFL-CIO*	$6,750
Machinists/Aerospace Workers Union	$6,500
Operating Engineers Union	$6,500
Carpenters & Joiners Union	$6,250
United Steelworkers	$5,000
Communications Workers of America	$4,800
Plumbers/Pipefitters Union*	$3,940
Laborers' Political League	$3,000
American Federation of Teachers	$2,000
Ironworkers Union	$2,000
Amalgamated Clothing & Textile Workers*	$1,500
Bakery, Confectionery & Tobacco Workers	$1,500
Rubber Cork Linoleum Plastic Workers	$1,500
United Mine Workers	$1,500
Baltimore Bldg & Construction Trades Council	$1,000
Graphic Communications Union	$1,000
Office & Professional Employees Union	$1,000
Painters & Allied Trades Union	$1,000
Others	$2,400

Government & Postal Workers $28,050

National Assn of Retired Federal Employees	$10,000
National Assn of Letter Carriers	$7,500
National Rural Letter Carriers Assn	$3,500
American Postal Workers Union	$3,000
American Federation of Government Employees	$1,250
National Treasury Employees Union	$1,000
Others	$1,800

Sea Transport Unions $30,500

Masters, Mates & Pilots Union*	$13,000
Marine Engineers Union*	$7,500
Seafarers International Union	$6,500
Boilermakers Union	$3,000
Others	$500

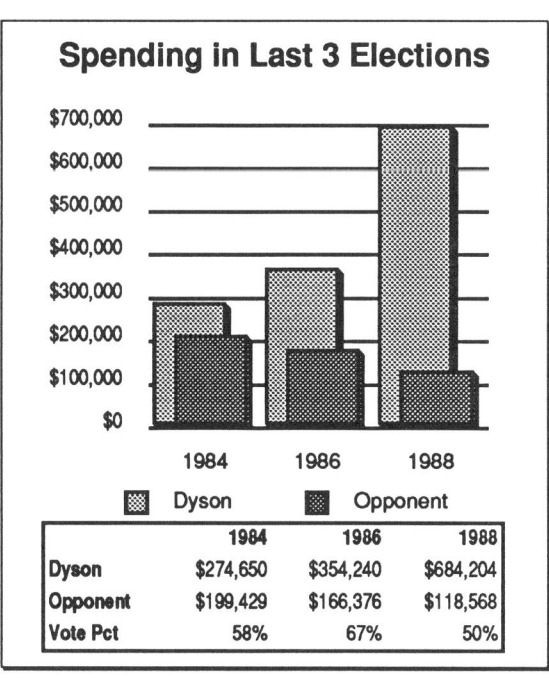

Spending in Last 3 Elections

	1984	1986	1988
Dyson	$274,650	$354,240	$684,204
Opponent	$199,429	$166,376	$118,568
Vote Pct	58%	67%	50%

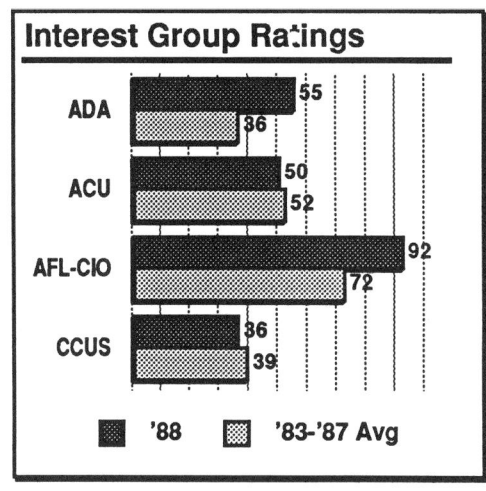

Interest Group Ratings

	'88	'83–'87 Avg
ADA	55	36
ACU	50	52
AFL-CIO	92	72
CCUS	36	39

Other Transportation Unions $28,900

United Auto Workers	$8,000
Teamsters Union	$6,000
United Transportation Union	$3,500
Brotherhood of Railroad Signalmen	$2,900
Air Line Pilots Assn	$2,000
Amalgamated Transit Union	$2,000
Brotherhood of Locomotive Engineers	$1,500
Transportation Communication Union	$1,500
Maintenance of Way Employees	$1,000
Others	$500

Ideological/Single-Issue

Democratic Leadership PACs $20,300

Valley Education Fund (Tony Coelho)	$7,000
Majority Congress Committee (Jim Wright)	$5,000
America's Leaders' Fund (Dan Rostenkowski)	$3,000
24th Congr Dist of California PAC (Henry Waxman)	$2,000
Cmte for Democratic Consensus (Marvin Leath)	$2,000
House Leadership Fund (Tom Foley)	$1,000
Others	$300

Other Major Ideological/Single-Issue PACs

National Rifle Assn	$5,950	Pro-Guns
National PAC	$5,000	Pro-Israel
Demo Study Group Campaign Fund	$3,000	Dem/Liberal
National Cmte to Preserve Social Security	$3,000	Soc Secur
American Security Council	$1,250	Pro-Defense
National Council of Senior Citizens	$1,000	Elderly

Independent Expenditures supporting Dyson

National Cmte to Preserve Social Security	$1,687

---

* Contributions came from more than one PAC affiliated with this sponsor.

Joseph D. Early, D-Mass (3)

First elected: 1974
Total receipts: $222,053
Total from PACs: $93,250

1988 Committees & Subcommittees

Appropriations
Commerce, Justice, State, the Judiciary and Related Agencies
Labor, Health and Human Services, Education and Related Agencies
Military Construction

PAC Contribution Profile
Business

Commercial & Savings Banks **$2,600**
American Bankers Assn $1,000
Others $1,600

Construction **$1,500**
National Assn of Home Builders $1,000
National Utility Contractors Assn $500

Defense **$2,500**
Textron Inc $1,500
Others $1,000

Health Professionals **$12,300**
American Dental Assn $4,000
American Medical Assn $1,250
American Academy of Ophthalmology $1,000
American Podiatry Assn $1,000
Corp for the Advancement of Psychiatry $1,000
Independent Allergists PAC $1,000
Others $3,050

Industrial Equipment & Materials **$2,000**
Pirelli Cable $1,000
Others $1,000

Insurance **$8,050**
Massachusetts Mutual Life Insurance $3,000
New England Mutual Life $1,000
State Mutual Life Assurance $1,000
Others $3,050

Campaign Revenue Sources

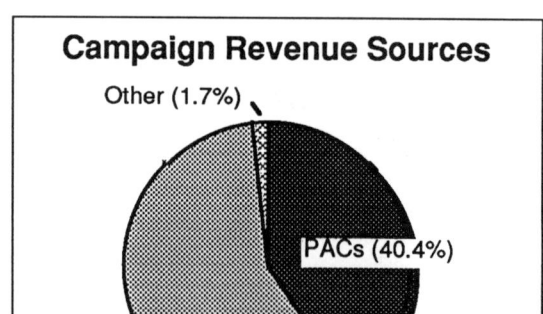

Other (1.7%)
PACs (40.4%)
Individuals (57.9%)

Lawyers & Lobbyists **$3,150**
Assn of Trial Lawyers of America $2,000
Others $1,150

Package Delivery **$3,000**
United Parcel Service $2,000
Federal Express Corp $1,000

Real Estate **$3,250**
National Assn of Realtors $3,250

Telecommunications **$3,750**
AT&T $2,000
New England Tel & Tel $1,000
Others $750

Other Major Business PACs

Ocean Spray Cranberries Inc .... $1,500 Fruit/Veg
Society for Advncmt of Ambulatory Care .... $1,500 OutpatntCare

PAC Totals by Category

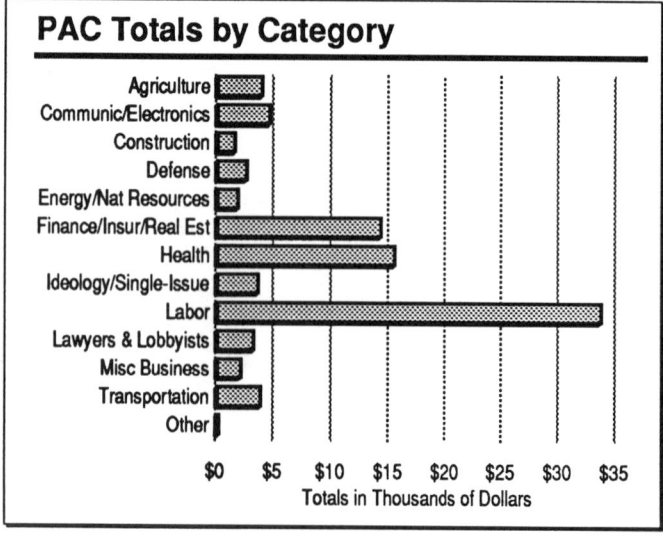

Agriculture
Communic/Electronics
Construction
Defense
Energy/Nat Resources
Finance/Insur/Real Est
Health
Ideology/Single-Issue
Labor
Lawyers & Lobbyists
Misc Business
Transportation
Other

$0 $5 $10 $15 $20 $25 $30 $35
Totals in Thousands of Dollars

Labor

Bldg Trades/Industrial/Misc Unions $14,800

Bricklayers Union	$2,000
Carpenters & Joiners Union	$2,000
Laborers' Political League	$1,500
Operating Engineers Union	$1,500
Machinists/Aerospace Workers Union	$1,250
United Auto Workers	$1,250
Food & Commercial Workers Union...................	$1,000
Ironworkers Union	$1,000
Others	$3,300

Government & Postal Workers $7,050

National Assn of Retired Federal Employees	$3,000
American Fedn of State/County/Munic Employees	$2,500
National Assn of Letter Carriers	$1,000
Others	$550

Transportation Unions $11,750

Teamsters Union	$10,000
Others	$1,750

Ideological/Single-Issue

Ideological/Single-Issue $3,500

Human Rights Campaign Fund	$1,000	Gay Rights
KidsPAC	$1,000	HealthWelfare
National Cmte to Preserve Social Security	$1,000	Society Secur
Others	$500	

Independent expenditures supporting Early

National Cmte to Preserve Social Security $1,858

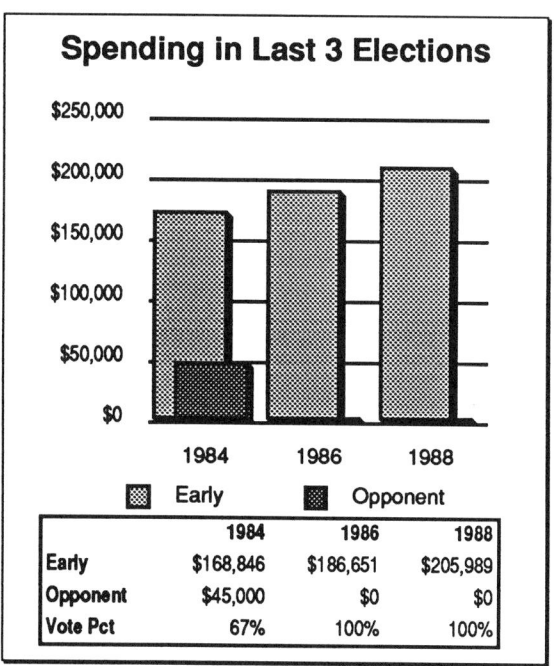

Spending in Last 3 Elections

	1984	1986	1988
Early	$168,846	$186,651	$205,989
Opponent	$45,000	$0	$0
Vote Pct	67%	100%	100%

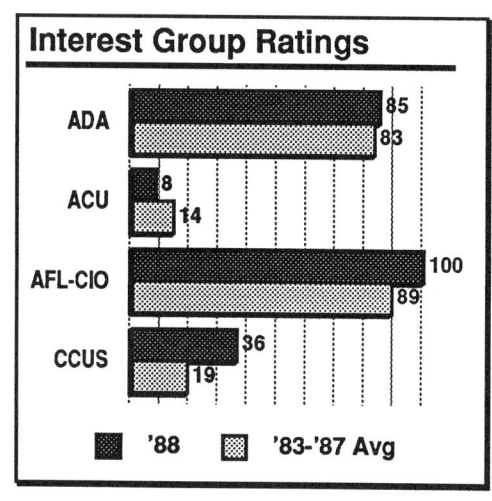

Interest Group Ratings

	'88	'83-'87 Avg
ADA	85	83
ACU	8	14
AFL-CIO	100	89
CCUS	36	19

Dennis E. Eckart, D-Ohio (11)

First elected: 1980
Total receipts: $569,638
Total from PACs: $382,028

1988 Committees & Subcommittees

Energy and Commerce
Commerce, Consumer Protection and Competitiveness
Oversight and Investigations
Telecommunications and Finance

Small Business
Antitrust, Impact of Deregulation and Privatization (Chairman)
Procurement, Innovation and Minority Enterprise Development

PAC Contribution Profile

Business

Accountants	**$15,450**
Touche Ross	$5,000
American Institute of CPA's	$4,000
Coopers & Lybrand	$1,850
Ernst & Whinney	$1,500
Arthur Young & Company	$1,100
Others	$2,000
Automotive & Trucking	**$12,200**
Ford Motor Company	$2,550
National Auto Dealers Assn	$2,500
General Motors	$1,700
American Trucking Assns	$1,550
Others	$3,900
Broadcasting/Entertainment	**$13,600**
National Cable Television Assn	$5,000
Assn of Independent TV Stations	$2,200
Tele-Communications Inc	$2,000
Others	$4,400
Commercial Banks	**$18,000**
American Bankers Assn	$2,500
Society Corp	$2,100
J P Morgan & Company	$2,000
Barnett Banks of Florida	$1,500
Banc One Corp	$1,200
Others	$8,700

Electric Utilities	**$8,950**
Centerior Energy Corp	$2,550
Southern Company*	$1,450
Southern California Edison	$1,200
Others	$3,750
Health Professionals	**$10,850**
American Medical Assn	$2,850
American Dental Assn	$1,850
American Optometric Assn	$1,700
National Assn of Pharmacists	$1,550
Others	$2,900
Lawyers & Lobbyists	**$17,250**
Assn of Trial Lawyers of America	$5,000
Akin, Gump, Hauer & Feld	$2,950
Burson-Marsteller	$1,200
Others	$8,100
Oil & Gas	**$16,250**
BP America	$1,700
CSX Transportation Inc	$1,550
Atlantic Richfield	$1,500
Chevron Corp	$1,350
USX Corp*	$1,200
Others	$8,950
Securities/Commodities Investment	**$18,750**
Investment Company Institute	$3,500
Morgan Stanley & Company	$3,000
Chicago Board of Trade	$2,000
First Boston Corp	$2,000
Shearson Lehman Hutton	$1,350
Drexel Burnham Lambert	$1,050
Securities Industry Assn	$1,050
Others	$4,800
Telecommunications	**$29,598**
AT&T	$5,000
Ohio Bell Telephone	$3,498
US Telephone Assn	$2,500
Corning Glass Works	$2,000
Pacific Telesis Group	$1,800
Bell Atlantic	$1,550
GTE Corp	$1,350
Others	$11,900

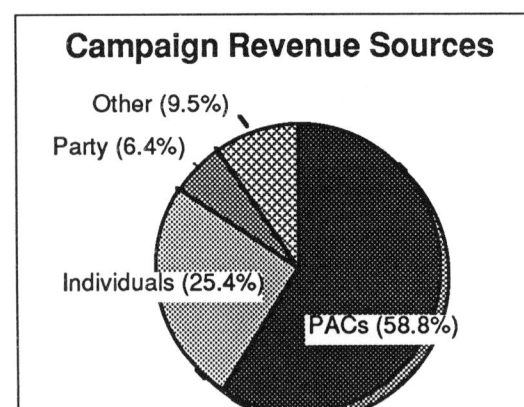

Campaign Revenue Sources

- Other (9.5%)
- Party (6.4%)
- Individuals (25.4%)
- PACs (58.8%)

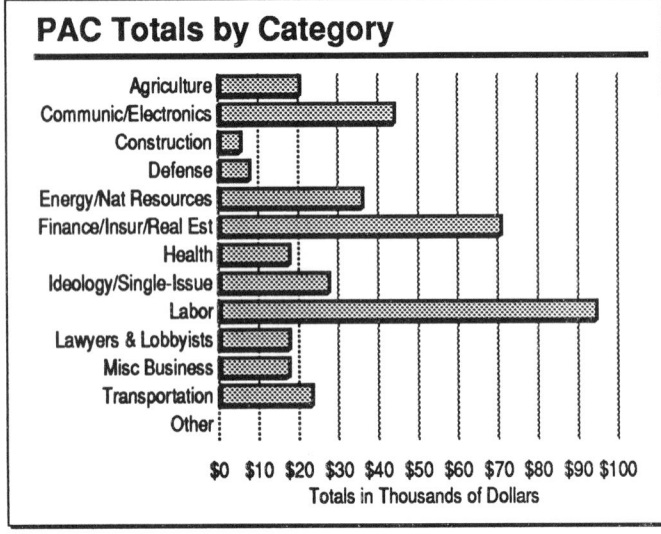

PAC Totals by Category

- Agriculture
- Communic/Electronics
- Construction
- Defense
- Energy/Nat Resources
- Finance/Insur/Real Est
- Health
- Ideology/Single-Issue
- Labor
- Lawyers & Lobbyists
- Misc Business
- Transportation
- Other

$0 $10 $20 $30 $40 $50 $60 $70 $80 $90 $100
Totals in Thousands of Dollars

Other Major Business PACs

National Assn of Realtors	$6,200	Real Estate
US League of Savings Assn	$5,050	Savings Banks
Federal Express Corp	$5,000	Air Freight
Triangle Industries	$4,000	Cans
Philip Morris	$2,800	Tobacco
TRW Inc	$2,750	Electron Def
Milk Marketing Inc	$1,650	Dairy
Associated Milk Producers	$1,500	Dairy
National Assn of Life Underwriters	$1,500	Life Insurance
RJR Nabisco	$1,500	Tobacco
Food Marketing Institute	$1,450	Food Stores
Mid-American Dairymen	$1,350	Dairy
National Assn of Chain Drug Stores	$1,350	Drug Stores
National Assn of Home Builders	$1,350	Resid Constr
Burroughs Wellcome	$1,200	Pharmaceut
Dow Chemical*	$1,200	Chemicals
Ohio Farm Bureau Federation	$1,100	Farm Orgs
American Council of Life Insurance	$1,050	Life Insurance
National Coal Assn	$1,050	Coal
Textron Inc	$1,050	Air Defense
Tobacco Institute	$1,050	Tobacco

Labor

Bldg Trades/Industrial/Misc Unions $51,050

Machinists/Aerospace Workers Union	$5,850
United Auto Workers	$5,850
Rubber Cork Linoleum Plastic Workers	$4,900
Food & Commercial Workers Union	$4,500
Intl Brotherhood of Electrical Workers	$4,500
Carpenters & Joiners Union	$4,000
Electronic Machine Furniture Workers	$3,500
United Steelworkers	$3,500
Communications Workers of America	$3,000
AFL-CIO	$2,350
Laborers' Political League	$1,550
Operating Engineers Union	$1,500
Amalgamated Clothing & Textile Workers	$1,350
Ladies Garment Workers Union	$1,200
Others	$3,500

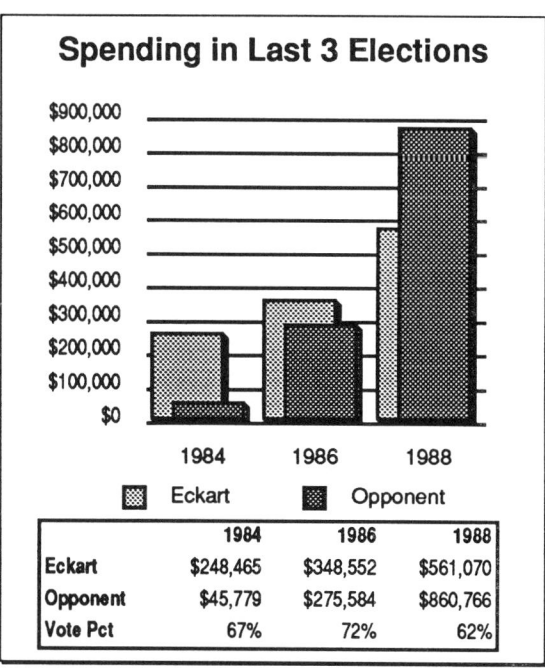

Spending in Last 3 Elections

	1984	1986	1988
Eckart	$248,465	$348,552	$561,070
Opponent	$45,779	$275,584	$860,766
Vote Pct	67%	72%	62%

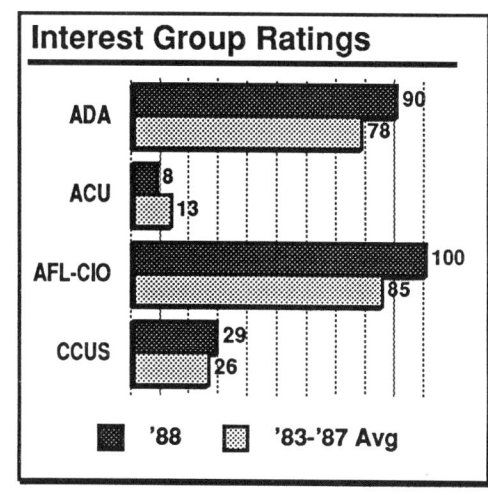

Interest Group Ratings

	'88	'83-'87 Avg
ADA	90	78
ACU	8	13
AFL-CIO	100	85
CCUS	29	26

Government, Postal & Teachers Unions $21,475

National Assn of Letter Carriers	$6,500
National Education Assn	$4,050
American Federation of Teachers	$3,000
National Assn of Retired Federal Employees	$3,000
International Assn of Firefighters	$2,525
Others	$2,400

Transportation Unions $21,500

Teamsters Union	$10,000
United Transportation Union	$3,100
Seafarers International Union	$3,000
Transport Workers Union	$2,000
Brotherhood of Locomotive Engineers	$1,200
Others	$2,200

Ideological/Single-Issue

Democratic Leadership PACs $13,000

Cmte for Democratic Opportunity (Bill Gray)	$4,000
Majority Congress Committee (Jim Wright)	$3,000
America's Leaders' Fund (Dan Rostenkowski)	$2,000
House Leadership Fund (Tom Foley)	$2,000
Valley Education Fund (Tony Coelho)	$2,000

Other Major Ideological/Single-Issue PACs

National PAC	$5,000	Pro-Israel
National Cmte for an Effective Congress	$2,500	Dem/Liberal
Delaware Valley PAC	$1,500	Pro-Israel
KidsPAC	$1,500	HealthWelfare

Independent expenditures supporting Eckart

National Cmte to Preserve Social Security	$1,157

---

* Contributions came from more than one PAC affiliated with this sponsor.

439

Don Edwards, D-Calif (10)

First elected: 1962
Total receipts: $166,689
Total from PACs: $117,256

1988 Committees & Subcommittees

Judiciary
Civil and Constitutional Rights (Chairman)
Criminal Justice
Monopolies and Commercial Law

Veterans' Affairs
Housing and Memorial Affairs
Oversight and Investigations

PAC Contribution Profile

Business

Broadcasting/Entertainment	*$4,300*
MCA Inc	$1,500
ASCAP	$1,000
Others	$1,800
Commercial & Savings Banks	*$2,400*
American Bankers Assn	$1,500
Others	$900
Construction	*$3,200*
National Assn of Home Builders	$1,500
National Utility Contractors Assn	$1,000
Others	$700
Food & Beverage	*$2,412*
National Beer Wholesalers Assn	$1,000
Others	$1,412
Health Professionals	*$2,500*
American Medical Assn	$1,500
Others	$1,000
Lawyers & Lobbyists	*$6,000*
Assn of Trial Lawyers of America	$4,000
California Trial Lawyers Assn	$1,000
Others	$1,000
Real Estate	*$6,800*
National Assn of Realtors	$5,700
Others	$1,100

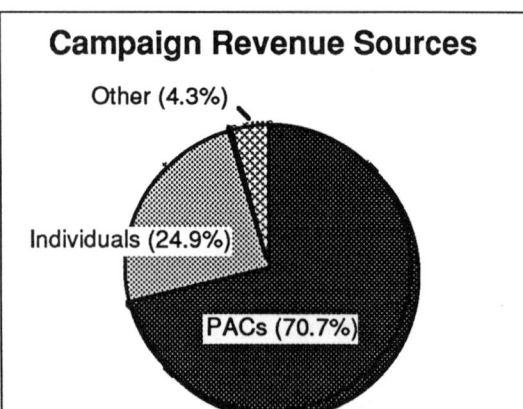

Campaign Revenue Sources

Other (4.3%)
Individuals (24.9%)
PACs (70.7%)

Sugar Growers	*$2,300*
None over $500	
Telecommunications	*$4,800*
Pacific Telesis Group	$2,300
AT&T	$2,000
Others	$500

Other Major Business PACs

FMC Corp	$1,500	Chemicals
United Parcel Service	$1,100	Delivery
Ernst & Whinney	$1,000	Accountants
Hewlett-Packard	$1,000	Electronics

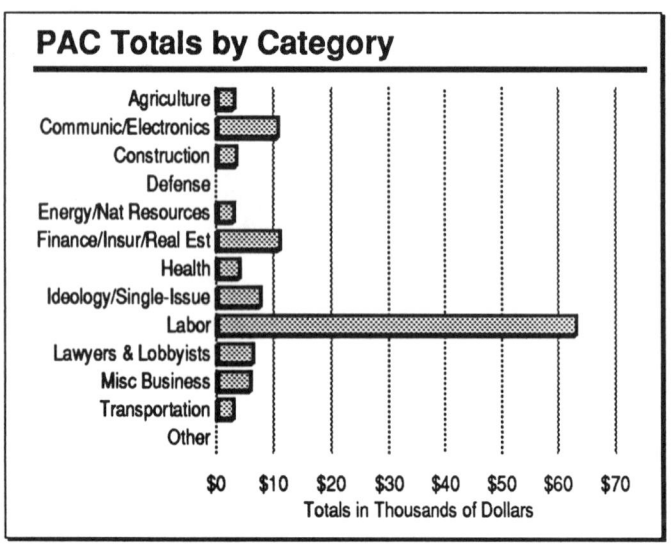

PAC Totals by Category

Agriculture
Communic/Electronics
Construction
Defense
Energy/Nat Resources
Finance/Insur/Real Est
Health
Ideology/Single-Issue
Labor
Lawyers & Lobbyists
Misc Business
Transportation
Other

$0 $10 $20 $30 $40 $50 $60 $70
Totals in Thousands of Dollars

Labor

Bldg Trades/Industrial/Misc Unions $22,100

Carpenters & Joiners Union	$2,500
United Auto Workers	$2,500
Intl Brotherhood of Electrical Workers	$2,000
Ironworkers Union	$2,000
Laborers' Western Political League	$2,000
Operating Engineers Union	$2,000
Communications Workers of America	$1,500
Food & Commercial Workers Union	$1,500
Machinists/Aerospace Workers Union	$1,100
Plumbers/Pipefitters Union	$1,000
Sheet Metal Workers Union	$1,000
Others	$3,000

Government & Postal Workers $15,600

National Assn of Retired Federal Employees	$5,000
Retired Letter Carriers PAC	$3,300
National Assn of Letter Carriers*	$2,900
American Fedn of State/County/Munic Employees	$2,500
Others	$1,900

Teachers Unions $8,130

National Education Assn	$8,000
Others	$130

Transportation Unions $16,900

Teamsters Union	$10,000
Air Line Pilots Assn	$2,500
Seafarers International Union	$2,000
Marine Engineers District 2 Maritime Officers	$1,000
Others	$1,400

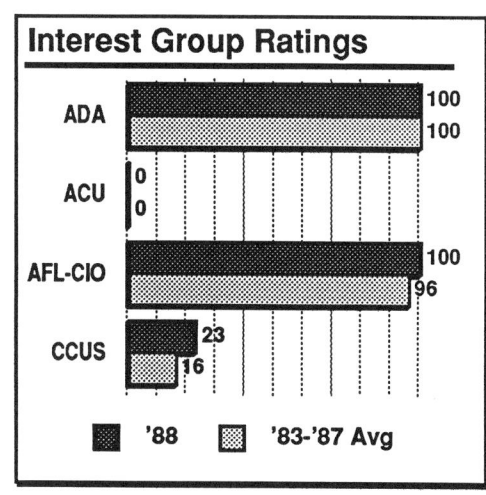

Interest Group Ratings

	'88	'83–'87 Avg
ADA	100	100
ACU	0	0
AFL-CIO	100	96
CCUS	23	16

Ideological/Single-Issue

Ideological/Single-Issue $7,330

Bay Area Munic Elections Cmte	$1,650	Gay Rights
National Abortion Rights Action League	$1,300	Pro-Choice
Human Rights Campaign Fund	$1,000	Gay Rights
Valley Education Fund (Tony Coelho)	$1,000	Dem Leaders
Others	$2,380	

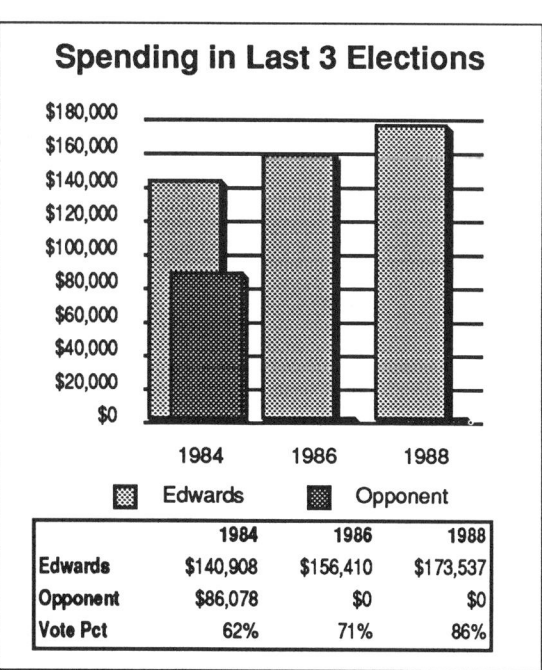

Spending in Last 3 Elections

	1984	1986	1988
Edwards	$140,908	$156,410	$173,537
Opponent	$86,078	$0	$0
Vote Pct	62%	71%	86%

---

* Contributions came from more than one PAC affiliated with this sponsor.

Mickey Edwards, R-Okla (5)

First elected: 1976
Total receipts: $340,042
Total from PACs: $122,130

1988 Committees & Subcommittees

Appropriations
Foreign Operations
Military Construction

Budget
Community and Natural Resources (Ranking Republican)
Budget Process
Economic and Trade Policy
Defense and International Affairs

PAC Contribution Profile

Business

Airlines & Aerospace **$5,450**
    Eastern Airlines $2,000
    American Airlines $1,350
    Texas Air $1,350
    Others $750

Automotive **$6,700**
    National Auto Dealers Assn $3,850
    Auto Dealers & Drivers for Free Trade $1,500
    Chrysler Corp $1,000
    Others $350

Chemicals **$2,700**
    FMC Corp $1,000
    Others $1,700

Commercial & Savings Banks **$4,775**
    Barnett Banks of Florida $1,000
    United Community Bankers $1,000
    Others $2,775

Construction **$6,500**
    National Assn of Home Builders $2,000
    Associated General Contractors $1,850
    National Utility Contractors Assn $1,000
    Others $1,650

Defense **$5,450**
    Rockwell International $1,700
    Sequa Corp $1,000
    Others $2,750

Campaign Revenue Sources

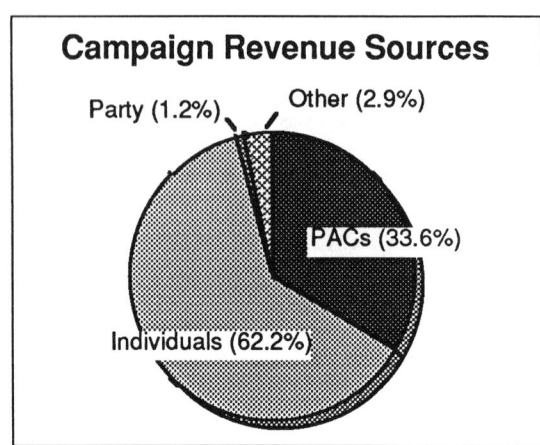

Party (1.2%)
Other (2.9%)
PACs (33.6%)
Individuals (62.2%)

Electric Utilities **$2,350**
    Oklahoma Gas & Electric $1,500
    Others $850

Health Professionals **$6,500**
    American Medical Assn $2,650
    Oklahoma Medical Assn $2,350
    American Dental Assn $1,000
    Others $500

Insurance **$4,000**
    Torchmark Corp $2,000
    National Assn of Life Underwriters $1,500
    Others $500

Lawyers & Lobbyists **$5,250**
    Akin, Gump, Hauer & Feld $2,350
    Hill & Knowlton $1,350
    Others $1,550

Oil & Gas **$18,398**
    Phillips Petroleum $4,998
    Others $13,400

Real Estate **$9,600**
    National Assn of Realtors $7,250
    Mortgage Bankers Assn of America $2,350

Telecommunications **$6,100**
    AT&T $3,000
    Southwestern Bell $2,100
    GTE (Southwest) $1,000

Trucking **$2,000**
    IU International Corp $1,500
    Others $500

Other Major Business PACs
Texas Cattle Feeders Assn .... $1,000   Feedlots

PAC Totals by Category

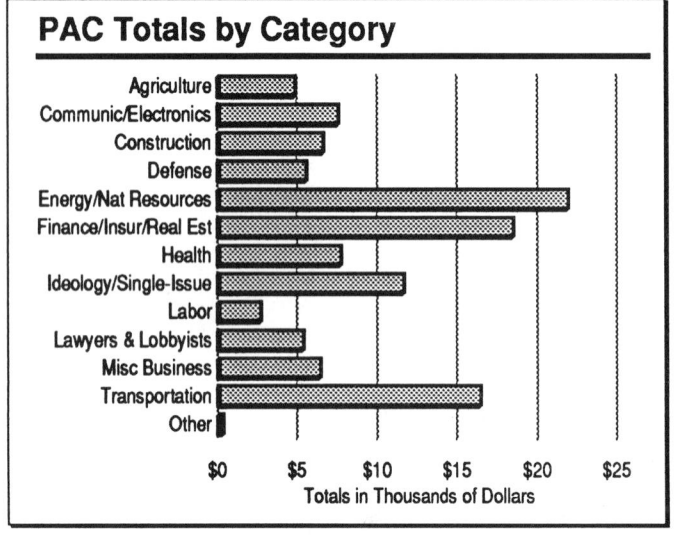

Agriculture
Communic/Electronics
Construction
Defense
Energy/Nat Resources
Finance/Insur/Real Est
Health
Ideology/Single-Issue
Labor
Lawyers & Lobbyists
Misc Business
Transportation
Other

$0 $5 $10 $15 $20 $25
Totals in Thousands of Dollars

Labor

Labor Unions ***$2,600***
    Laborers' Western Political League $1,000
    Others $1,600

Ideological/Single-Issue

Pro-Defense ***$3,712***
    Council for National Defense $2,112
    National Security PAC $1,000
    Others $600

Pro-Israel ***$6,750***
    National PAC $5,000
    Washington PAC $1,000
    Others $750

Independent expenditures supporting Edwards

American Medical Assn $2,000

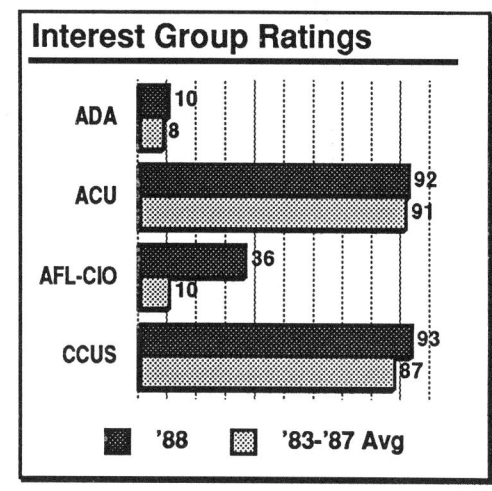

Interest Group Ratings

	'88	'83-'87 Avg
ADA	10	8
ACU	92	91
AFL-CIO	36	10
CCUS	93	87

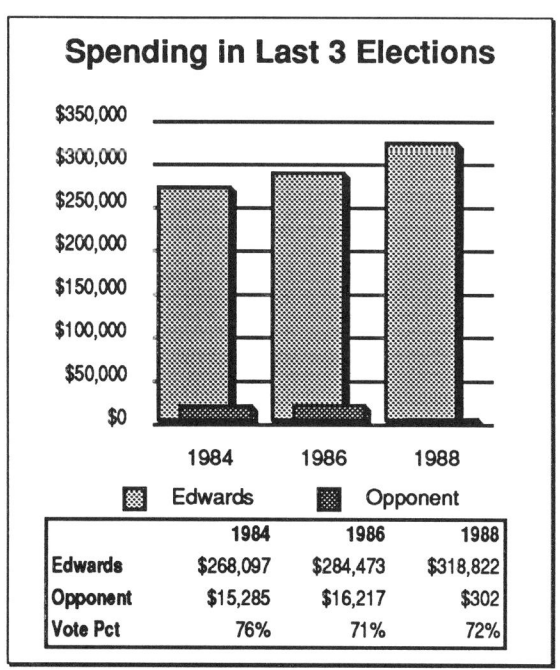

Spending in Last 3 Elections

	1984	1986	1988
Edwards	$268,097	$284,473	$318,822
Opponent	$15,285	$16,217	$302
Vote Pct	76%	71%	72%

Bill Emerson, R-Mo (8)

1988-1989 Committees & Subcommittees

First elected: 1980
Total receipts: $850,739
Total from PACs: $420,852

Foreign Affairs
Africa
Arms Control, International Security and Science
International Economic Policy and Trade

Small Business
Environment and Labor
Regulation, Business Opportunities and Energy

Select Hunger

PAC Contribution Profile
Business

Agricultural Services & Equipment	*$10,150*
Dow Chemical*	$3,100
American Assn of Crop Insurers	$1,550
Deere & Company	$1,500
Farmland Industries	$1,500
Others	$2,500
Automotive	*$27,750*
Auto Dealers & Drivers for Free Trade	$10,000
National Auto Dealers Assn	$10,000
Eaton Corp	$4,000
Ford Motor Company	$1,250
Others	$2,500
Construction	*$19,590*
National Assn of Home Builders	$8,000
Associated General Contractors	$5,000
Wall & Ceiling/Gypsum Contractors	$2,150
Associated Builders & Contractors	$1,500
Others	$2,940
Crop Production & Processing	*$31,250*
Fruits & Vegetables	$6,150
Cargill Inc	$5,000
National Cotton Council	$2,750
American Crystal Sugar Corp	$2,000
American Sugar Cane League	$1,750
American Sugarbeet Growers Assn	$1,500
RJR Nabisco	$1,250
Others	$10,850

Campaign Revenue Sources

Other (7.8%)
Party (6.9%)
PACs (43.2%)
Individuals (42.2%)

Dairy	*$16,750*
Mid-American Dairymen	$10,000
Associated Milk Producers	$5,000
Others	$1,750
Electric Utilities	*$10,600*
Union Electric	$2,500
Southern Company*	$1,750
Arkansas Power & Light	$1,500
Others	$4,850
Farm Organizations	*$11,000*
Missouri Farm Bureau*	$10,000
Others	$1,000
Food & Beverage	*$41,000*
Malone & Hyde Inc	$10,000
Food Marketing Institute	$4,000
National Restaurant Assn	$4,000
ConAgra Inc	$2,500
Pillsbury Company	$2,500
American Meat Institute	$2,000
General Mills*	$2,000
Others	$14,000
Forest Products	*$12,500*
Westvaco Corp	$6,000
Boise Cascade	$2,000
Potlatch Corp	$2,000
Others	$2,500
Health Professionals	*$12,875*
American Medical Assn	$8,875
American Academy of Ophthalmology	$1,500
American Dental Assn	$1,500
Others	$1,000
Insurance	*$15,500*
National Assn of Life Underwriters	$5,000
American Family Corp	$4,500
National Assn of Independent Insurers	$1,500
Others	$4,500

PAC Totals by Category

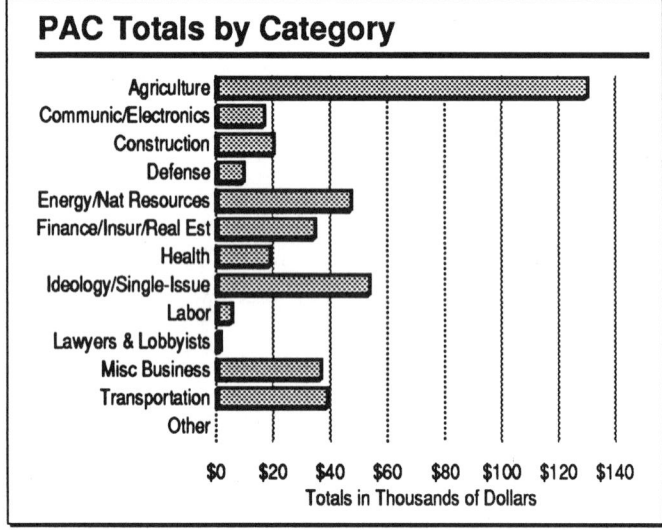

Agriculture
Communic/Electronics
Construction
Defense
Energy/Nat Resources
Finance/Insur/Real Est
Health
Ideology/Single-Issue
Labor
Lawyers & Lobbyists
Misc Business
Transportation
Other

$0 $20 $40 $60 $80 $100 $120 $140
Totals in Thousands of Dollars

Oil & Gas **$25,150**

Phillips Petroleum	$3,500
Cooper Industries	$3,000
Amoco Corp	$2,500
Atlantic Richfield	$1,250
Mobil Oil	$1,250
Others	$13,650

Real Estate **$10,100**

National Assn of Realtors	$10,000
Others	$100

Telecommunications **$13,800**

Continental Telecom	$4,000
AT&T	$3,500
Southwestern Bell	$3,000
United Telecommunications	$2,000
Others	$1,300

Other Major Business PACs

Chicago Mercantile Exchange	$3,000	Commodities
National Cattlemen's Assn	$3,000	Livestock
Business Industry PAC	$2,629	Bus Assns
FMC Corp	$2,500	Ag Chemicals
Monsanto Company	$2,500	Ag Chemicals
National Fedn of Independent Business	$2,500	Sml Business
Boatmens Bankshares	$2,000	Comml Banks
Corning Glass Works	$2,000	Glass Prod
Hunter Engineering	$2,000	Indust Equip
Martin Marietta Corp	$2,000	Air Defense
United Parcel Service	$2,000	Delivery
Peabody Coal	$1,750	Coal
American Bankers Assn	$1,500	Comml Banks
Chemtech Industries	$1,500	Chemicals
Chicago Board of Trade	$1,500	Commodities
Electronic Data Systems	$1,500	Data Process
Emerson Electric	$1,500	Electron Def
Mercantile Bancorp	$1,500	Comml Banks
Sabreliner Corp	$1,500	AerospacePts
Schering-Plough Corp	$1,500	Pharmaceut
Society of American Florists	$1,500	Florists
Yellow Freight System	$1,500	Trucking
American Health Care Assn	$1,350	Nursing Home
Gates Rubber Company	$1,300	PlasticRubb
McDonnell Douglas	$1,250	Air Defense

Major Labor PACs

National Assn of Retired Federal Employees	$2,000	Fedl Workers

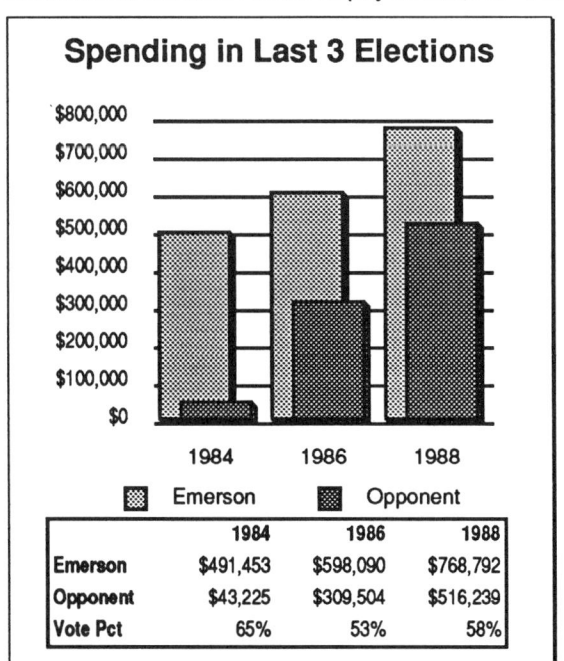

Spending in Last 3 Elections

	1984	1986	1988
Emerson	$491,453	$598,090	$768,792
Opponent	$43,225	$309,504	$516,239
Vote Pct	65%	53%	58%

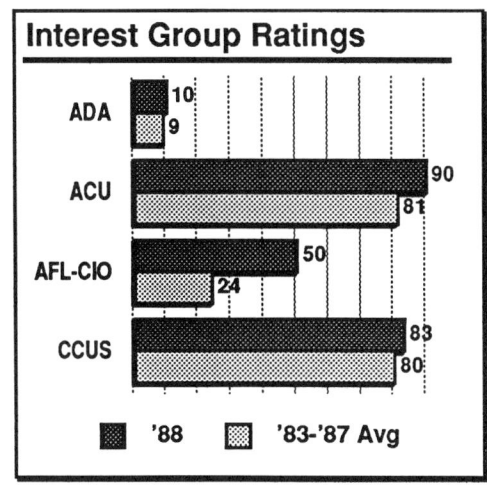

Interest Group Ratings

	'88	'83-'87 Avg
ADA	10	9
ACU	90	81
AFL-CIO	50	24
CCUS	83	80

Ideological/Single-Issue

Pro-Guns **$10,900**

National Rifle Assn	$9,900
Others	$1,000

Pro-Life **$11,000**

National Right to Life PAC	$10,000
Others	$1,000

Republican Leadership PACs **$19,289**

Fund for America's Future (George Bush)	$5,000
Fund for the Future Cmte (John Danforth)	$5,000
Campaign America (Bob Dole)	$4,522
Heartland PAC of Missouri (Kit Bond)	$2,000
Conservative Victory Fund (Steve Symms)	$1,267
Others	$1,500

Other Major Ideological/Single-Issue PACs

National Cmte to Preserve Social Security	$5,000	Society Secur
Public Service Research Council	$3,000	Anti-Union
Council for National Defense	$2,260	Pro-Defense

Independent expenditures supporting Emerson

National Assn of Realtors	$152,600
Missouri Farm Bureau/Southeast District	$4,837
Missouri Citizens for Life	$2,110
National Cmte to Preserve Social Security	$1,502

* Contributions came from more than one PAC affiliated
with this sponsor.

Eliot L. Engel, D-NY (19)

First elected: 1988
Total receipts: $172,088
Total from PACs: $99,600

1988-1989 Committees & Subcommittees

Foreign Affairs
Africa
Arms Control, International Security and Science
International Economic Policy and Trade

Small Business
Environment and Labor
Regulation, Business Opportunities and Energy

Select Hunger

PAC Contribution Profile

Business

Health Professionals	*$8,500*
American Medical Assn	$5,000
New York Medical Assn	$2,500
American Dental Assn	$1,000
Real Estate	*$3,000*
National Assn of Realtors	$3,000

Other Major Business PACs

AT&T	$1,000	LongDistance
ACRE (Action Committee for Rural Electricity)	$500	RuralElect
Associated Milk Producers	$500	Dairy
Independent Insurance Agents of America	$500	Insurance
International Paper Company	$500	Paper Prod
National Assn of Social Workers	$500	Social Work

Campaign Revenue Sources

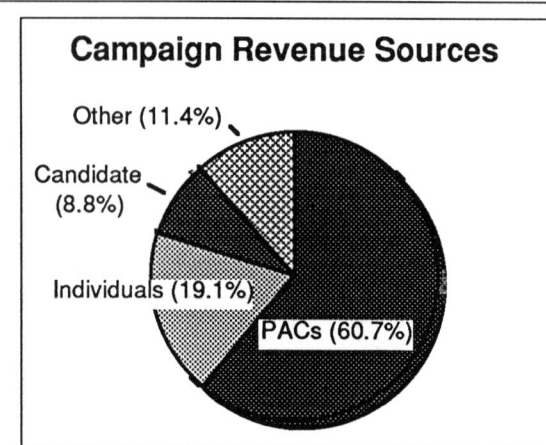

Other (11.4%)
Candidate (8.8%)
Individuals (19.1%)
PACs (60.7%)

PAC Totals by Category

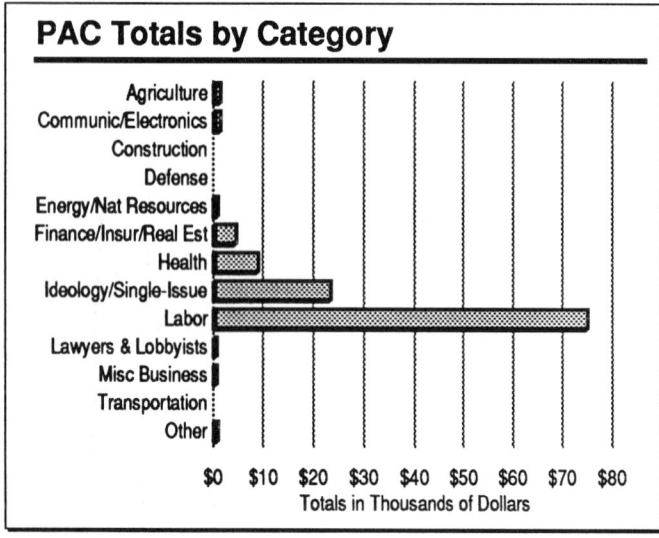

Totals in Thousands of Dollars

Labor

Government & Postal Workers **$25,000**

    American Fedn of State/County/Munic Employees $10,000
    National Assn of Letter Carriers $10,000
    American Postal Workers Union $5,000

Bldg Trades/Industrial/Misc Unions **$14,000**

    Machinists/Aerospace Workers Union $5,000
    AFL-CIO $3,500
    Intl Brotherhood of Electrical Workers.............................$2,000
    Hospital/Health Care Union Local #1199 ....$1,250
    Laborers' Political League $1,000
    Amalgamated Clothing & Textile Workers $750
    Ladies Garment Workers Union $500

Teachers Unions **$20,000**

    American Federation of Teachers $10,000
    National Education Assn $10,000

Transportation Unions **$17,100**

    Teamsters Union $10,000
    Seafarers International Union $2,500
    Marine Engineers Union..$2,000
    United Transportation Union $1,000
    Others $100

Ideological/Single-Issue

Democratic/Liberal **$1,500**

    National Cmte for an Effective Congress $1,000
    Americans for Democratic Action $500

Democratic Leadership PACs **$2,500**

    Cmte for Democratic Opportunity (Bill Gray).................$1,500
    Valley Education Fund (Tony Coelho) $1,500
    House Leadership Fund (Tom Foley) $1,000

Pro-Choice **$5,500**

    Prochoice Voter $2,500
    National Abortion Rights Action League $1,500
    Voters for Choice/Friends of Family Planning $1,000
    Citizens for Family Planning $500

Pro-Israel **$5,750**

    National PAC $5,000
    Washington PAC $500
    Others $250

Other Major Ideological/Single-Issue PACs

National Cmte to Preserve Social Security $3,000	Society Secur
Human Rights Campaign Fund $2,500	Gay Rights
Friends of Stanley Fink $500	NonCong Cand

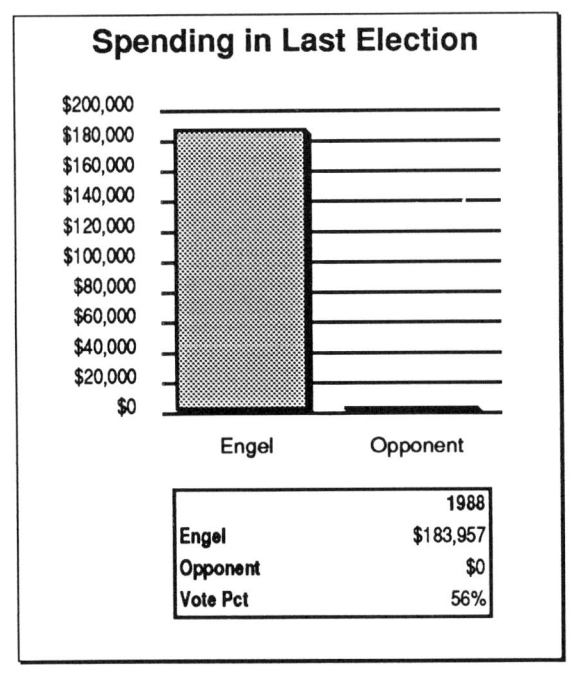

Spending in Last Election

	1988
Engel	$183,957
Opponent	$0
Vote Pct	56%

Glenn English, D-Okla (6)

First elected: 1974
Total receipts: $385,383
Total from PACs: $183,408

1988 Committees & Subcommittees

Agriculture
Conservation, Credit and Rural Development
Cotton, Rice and Sugar
Tobacco and Peanuts
Wheat, Soybeans and Feed Grains

Government Operations
Government Information, Justice and Agriculture (Chairman)

PAC Contribution Profile

Business

Agricultural Chemicals	**$3,650**
FMC Corp	$1,000
Others	$2,650
Agricultural Services	**$8,550**
American Assn of Crop Insurers	$3,250
Farm Credit Council	$1,450
Farmland Industries	$1,000
Others	$2,850
Automotive	**$4,500**
Auto Dealers & Drivers for Free Trade	$2,500
National Auto Dealers Assn	$1,750
Others	$250
Commercial & Savings Banks	**$10,900**
American Bankers Assn	$5,500
Independent Bankers Assn	$2,250
US League of Savings Assn	$1,000
United Community Bankers	$1,000
Others	$1,150
Commodities Trading	**$20,250**
Chicago Board of Trade	$8,500
Chicago Mercantile Exchange	$7,500
Commodity Exchange Inc	$2,500
Chicago Board of Options Exchange	$1,000
Others	$750
Construction	**$2,850**
National Assn of Home Builders	$1,000
Others	$1,850

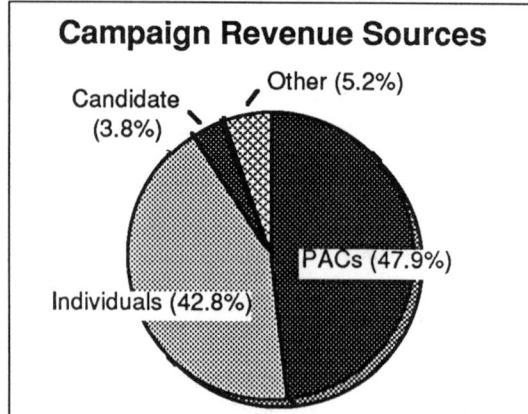

Campaign Revenue Sources

Other (5.2%)
Candidate (3.8%)
PACs (47.9%)
Individuals (42.8%)

Dairy	**$9,400**
Associated Milk Producers	$6,000
Mid-American Dairymen	$1,700
Dairymen Inc	$1,450
Others	$250
Defense	**$8,800**
Lockheed Corp	$2,800
United Technologies	$1,500
Textron Inc	$1,250
Others	$3,250
Electric Utilities	**$5,050**
Oklahoma Gas & Electric	$2,000
ACRE (Action Committee for Rural Electrification)	$1,300
Oklahoma ACRE	$1,000
Others	$750
Electronics & Computers	**$4,450**
Electronic Data Systems	$1,300
Others	$3,150
Farm Organizations	**$3,800**
National Farmers Organization	$1,350
Others	$2,450
Food & Beverage	**$9,900**
ConAgra Inc	$2,000
American Meat Institute	$1,250
Nabisco Brands Inc	$1,000
National Restaurant Assn	$1,000
National Beer Wholesalers Assn	$1,000
Others	$3,650
Insurance	**$3,600**
National Assn of Life Underwriters	$2,000
Others	$1,600
Lawyers & Lobbyists	**$5,200**
Assn of Trial Lawyers of America	$2,000
Williams & Jensen	$1,000
Others	$2,200
Livestock & Poultry	**$3,600**
National Cattlemen's Assn	$1,450
Texas Cattle Feeders Assn	$1,000
Others	$1,150
Oil & Gas	**$10,750**
Phillips Petroleum	$1,500
Texaco	$1,000
Others	$8,250

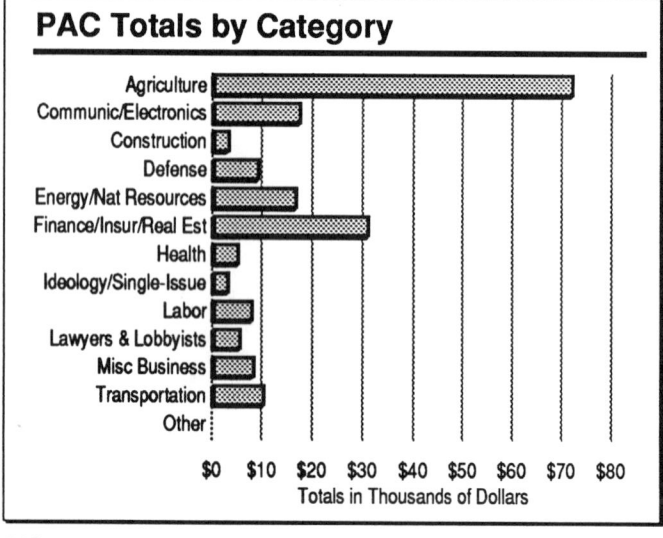

PAC Totals by Category

Agriculture
Communic/Electronics
Construction
Defense
Energy/Nat Resources
Finance/Insur/Real Est
Health
Ideology/Single-Issue
Labor
Lawyers & Lobbyists
Misc Business
Transportation
Other

$0 $10 $20 $30 $40 $50 $60 $70 $80
Totals in Thousands of Dollars

Other Crops **$5,800**
    National Cotton Council $1,250
    National Assn of Wheat Growers $1,250
    Riceland Foods $1,000
    Southwest Peanut Membership Organization $1,000
    Others $1,300

Package Delivery **$2,200**
    United Parcel Service $1,200
    Federal Express Corp $1,000

Real Estate **$10,500**
    National Assn of Realtors $10,000
    Others $500

Sugar Growers **$5,250**
    American Crystal Sugar Corp $2,000
    Others $3,250

Telecommunications **$11,800**
    AT&T $4,500
    Southwestern Bell $1,750
    GTE (Southwest) $1,500
    US Telephone Assn $1,250
    National Telephone Co-op Assn $1,200
    Others $1,600

Tobacco **$2,500**
    Philip Morris $1,000
    Others $1,500

Other Major Business PACs

Oklahoma Medical Assn	$1,500	Doctors
Care Enterprises	$1,000	Nursing Home
W R Grace & Company	$1,000	Chemicals

Interest Group Ratings

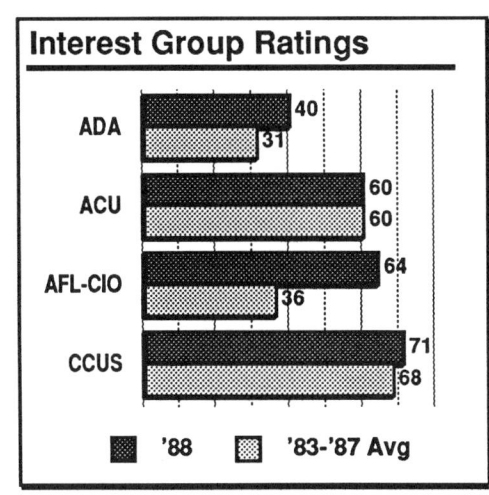

	'88	'83-'87 Avg
ADA	40	31
ACU	60	60
AFL-CIO	64	36
CCUS	71	68

Labor

Postal Worker Unions **$6,500**
    National Rural Letter Carriers Assn $3,000
    National Assn of Letter Carriers $2,000
    Others $1,500

Other Major Labor PACs

Food & Commercial Workers Union .... $1,000   Retail Union

Ideological/Single-Issue

Democratic Leadership PACs **$2,300**
    Valley Education Fund (Tony Coelho) $2,000
    Others $300

Spending in Last 3 Elections

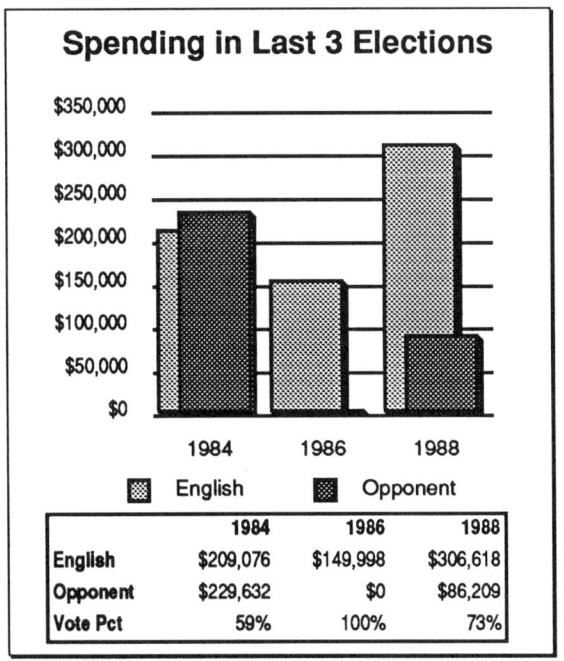

	1984	1986	1988
English	$209,076	$149,998	$306,618
Opponent	$229,632	$0	$86,209
Vote Pct	59%	100%	73%

449

Ben Erdreich, D-Ala (6)

First elected: 1982
Total receipts: $251,841
Total from PACs: $173,850

1988 Committees & Subcommittees

Banking, Finance and Urban Affairs
Financial Institutions Supervision, Regulation and Insurance
General Oversight and Investigations
Housing and Community Development

Government Operations
Commerce, Consumer and Monetary Affairs
Legislation and National Security

Select Aging
Health and Long-Term Care

PAC Contribution Profile

Business

Accountants	**$5,000**
American Institute of CPA's	$5,000
Commercial Banks	**$50,000**
American Bankers Assn	$10,000
Amsouth Bancorp	$5,000
Central Bancshares of the South	$5,000
First Alabama Bancshares	$3,250
Southtrust Corp	$2,500
Barnett Banks of Florida	$2,000
Citicorp	$2,000
J P Morgan & Company	$2,000
Bankers Trust	$1,500
Chemical Bank	$1,500
Citizens & Southern National Bank	$1,250
Continental Illinois Corp	$1,250
Assn of Bank Holding Companies	$1,200
Chase Manhattan	$1,050
First Chicago Corp	$1,050
Security Pacific Corp	$1,000
Others	$8,450
Construction	**$6,100**
Walter Industries	$2,500
National Electrical Contractors Assn	$1,000
Others	$2,600
Dairy	**$3,150**
Associated Milk Producers	$2,000
Others	$1,150

Campaign Revenue Sources

Other (13.5%)
Party (2.5%)
Individuals (19.8%)
PACs (64.1%)

Electric Utilities	**$4,650**
Alabama Power Company	$3,800
Others	$850
Health Professionals	**$3,050**
American Medical Assn	$1,550
American Dental Assn	$1,500
Insurance	**$6,650**
Torchmark Corp	$2,550
Independent Insurance Agents of America	$1,300
American Family Corp	$1,000
Others	$1,800
Lawyers & Lobbyists	**$3,400**
None over $900	
Oil & Gas	**$3,350**
Southern Natural Resources	$1,300
Alagasco Inc	$1,000
Others	$1,050
Real Estate	**$6,950**
National Assn of Realtors	$6,050
Others	$900
Savings Banks & Credit Unions	**$6,750**
US League of Savings Assn	$2,450
Others	$4,300
Sugar Growers	**$2,650**
None over $900	
Telecommunications	**$4,800**
AT&T	$2,300
South Central Bell Telephone	$1,500
Continental Telecom	$1,000

Other Major Business PACs

Alabama Farm Bureau Federation	$1,350	Farm Orgs
J C Penney Company	$1,300	Dept Store
National Auto Dealers Assn	$1,250	Auto Sales
Boeing Company	$1,000	Aircraft

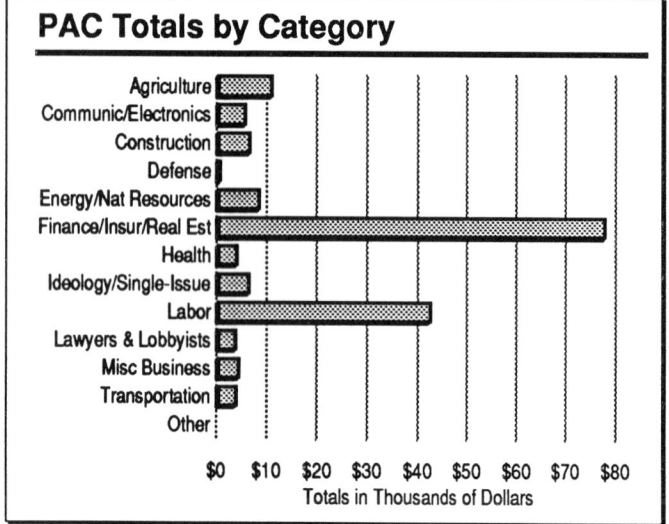

PAC Totals by Category

Agriculture
Communic/Electronics
Construction
Defense
Energy/Nat Resources
Finance/Insur/Real Est
Health
Ideology/Single-Issue
Labor
Lawyers & Lobbyists
Misc Business
Transportation
Other

$0 $10 $20 $30 $40 $50 $60 $70 $80
Totals in Thousands of Dollars

Labor

Bldg Trades/Industrial/Misc Unions $19,400

    United Steelworkers $4,000
    United Auto Workers $2,750
    Intl Brotherhood of Electrical Workers..............$2,500
    Carpenters & Joiners Union $2,000
    Food & Commercial Workers Union $1,550
    Laborers' Political League $1,250
    Bricklayers Union $1,050
    Plumbers/Pipefitters Union $1,000
    Others $3,300

Government & Postal Workers $8,650

    National Assn of Retired Federal Employees $5,000
    National Assn of Letter Carriers $1,600
    American Postal Workers Union $1,200
    Others $850

Teachers Unions $2,650

    American Federation of Teachers $2,000
    Others $650

Transportation Unions $11,250

    Teamsters Union $5,000
    Seafarers International Union $2,050
    Air Line Pilots Assn $1,000
    United Transportation Union $1,000
    Others $2,200

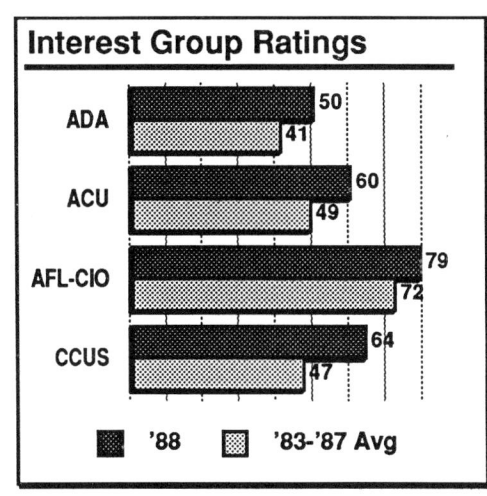

Ideological/Single-Issue

Pro-Israel $2,750

    Americans for Good Government Inc $1,000
    Roundtable PAC $1,000
    Others $750

Other Major Ideological/Single-Issue PACs

National Cmte to Preserve Social Security ......$1,000   Society Secur
Valley Education Fund (Tony Coelho) ....$1,000   Dem Leaders

Independent expenditures supporting Erdreich

National Cmte to Preserve Social Security $2,347

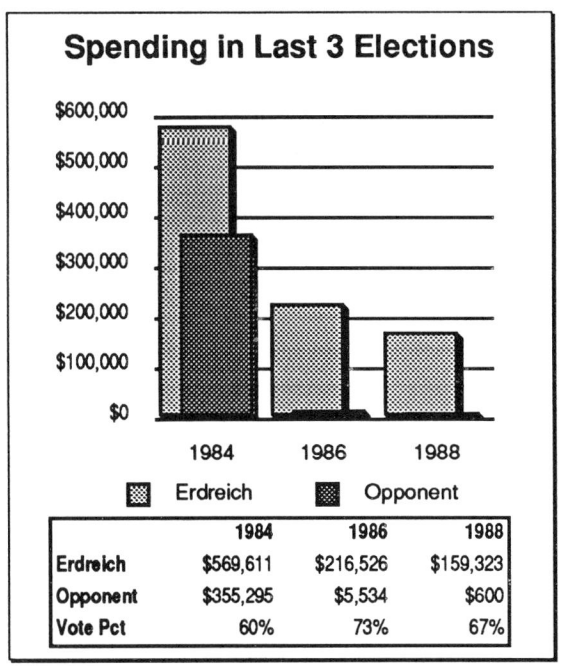

Spending in Last 3 Elections

	1984	1986	1988
Erdreich	$569,611	$216,526	$159,323
Opponent	$355,295	$5,534	$600
Vote Pct	60%	73%	67%

Mike Espy, D-Miss (2)

1988 Committees & Subcommittees

First elected: 1986
Total receipts: $880,227
Total from PACs: $480,490

Agriculture	Budget
Cotton, Rice and Sugar	Community and Natural Resources
Domestic Operations, Research and Foreign Agriculture	Economic and Trade Policy
Domestic Marketing, Consumer Relations and Nutrition	Human Resources
Wheat, Soybeans and Feed Grains	**Select Hunger**

PAC Contribution Profile

Business

Commercial & Savings Banks **$11,675**
- American Bankers Assn $2,500
- Grenada Bank $1,925
- Others $7,250

Construction **$12,500**
- National Assn of Home Builders $11,000
- Others $1,500

Dairy **$12,750**
- Associated Milk Producers $6,000
- Dairymen Inc-Mississippi $3,750
- Mid-American Dairymen $2,500
- Others $500

Food & Beverage **$10,700**
- Food Marketing Institute $1,700
- General Mills* $1,500
- McDonald's Corp $1,500
- A E Staley Manufacturing Company $1,050
- Others $4,950

Health Professionals **$19,317**
- American Medical Assn $8,767
- American Academy of Ophthalmology $3,500
- American Nurses Assn $2,750
- American Dental Assn $2,500
- Others $1,800

Insurance **$11,100**
- National Assn of Life Underwriters $4,000
- Independent Insurance Agents of America $2,250
- Others $4,850

Campaign Revenue Sources

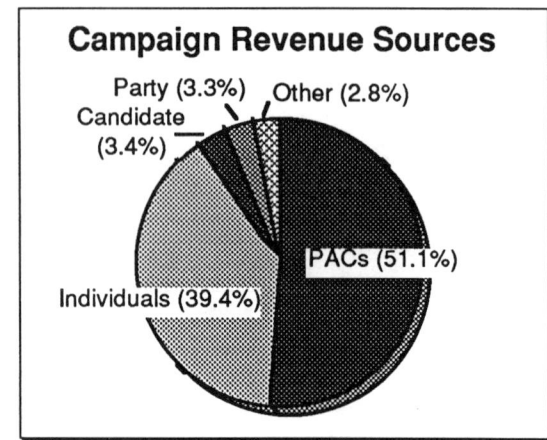

Party (3.3%)   Other (2.8%)
Candidate (3.4%)
PACs (51.1%)
Individuals (39.4%)

Lawyers & Lobbyists **$10,000**
- Assn of Trial Lawyers of America $9,000
- Others $1,000

Real Estate **$11,000**
- National Assn of Realtors $11,000

Other Major Business PACs

South Central Bell Telephone	$4,500	Phone Util
Federal Express Corp	$4,350	Delivery
National Assn of Social Workers	$3,000	Social Work
United Parcel Service	$2,800	Delivery
National Auto Dealers Assn	$2,500	Auto Sales
Sun-Maid Growers of California	$2,500	Fruit/Veg
AT&T	$2,000	LongDistance
Southern Company*	$1,750	ElectricUtil
American Crystal Sugar Corp	$1,500	Sugar
Chicago Mercantile Exchange	$1,500	Commodities
Middle South Utilities*	$1,500	ElectUtil
Mississippi ACRE(Action Cmte for Rural Elect)	$1,500	RuralElect
Philip Morris	$1,500	Tobacco
Sunsweet Growers	$1,500	Fruit/Veg
National Farmers Organization	$1,450	Farm Orgs
Alabama Farm Bureau Federation	$1,250	Farm Orgs

PAC Totals by Category

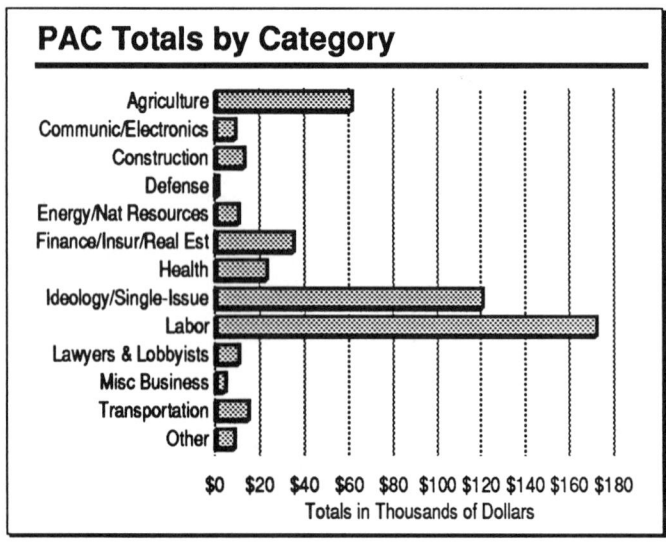

Totals in Thousands of Dollars

Labor

Bldg Trades/Industrial/Misc Unions $92,900

AFL-CIO*	$10,000
Food & Commercial Workers Union	$10,000
Intl Brotherhood of Electrical Workers	$10,000
Machinists/Aerospace Workers Union	$10,000
United Auto Workers	$10,000
Carpenters & Joiners Union	$8,000
United Steelworkers	$8,000
Plumbers/Pipefitters Union*	$5,500
Operating Engineers Union	$3,000
Sheet Metal Workers Union	$2,500
Laborers' Political League	$2,250
Bakery, Confectionery & Tobacco Workers	$2,000
Rubber Cork Linoleum Plastic Workers	$2,000
Ladies Garment Workers Union	$1,750
Electronic Machine Furniture Workers	$1,450
Communications Workers of America	$1,200
Others	$5,250

Government & Postal Workers $36,206

American Fedn of State/County/Munic Employees	$10,000
National Assn of Retired Federal Employees	$8,000
American Postal Workers Union	$6,000
National Assn of Letter Carriers	$5,000
National Rural Letter Carriers Assn	$2,456
American Federation of Government Employees	$1,750
Others	$3,000

Teachers Unions $15,250

National Education Assn	$10,000
American Federation of Teachers	$5,250

Transportation Unions $27,549

Teamsters Union	$9,999
Amalgamated Transit Union	$4,000
Air Line Pilots Assn	$3,500
United Transportation Union	$3,500
Seafarers International Union	$2,000
Transportation Communication Union	$1,500
Maintenance of Way Employees	$1,250
Others	$1,800

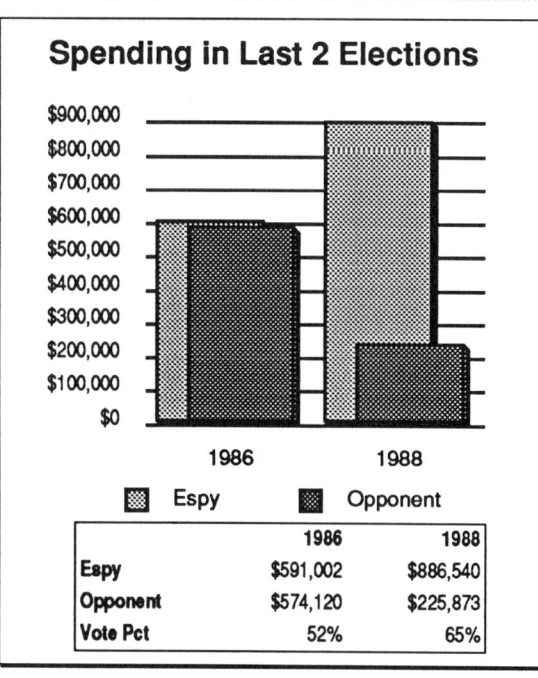

Spending in Last 2 Elections

	1986	1988
Espy	$591,002	$886,540
Opponent	$574,120	$225,873
Vote Pct	52%	65%

Interest Group Ratings

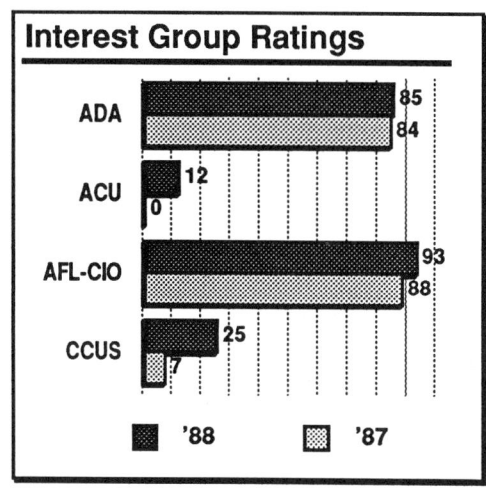

■ '88   ▨ '87

Ideological/Single-Issue

Democratic/Liberal $19,895

National Cmte for anEffective Congress	$7,495
Mississippians United for Progress	$5,100
Class PAC	$2,500
Others	$4,800

Democratic Leadership PACs...................................$18,100

Cmte for Democratic Opportunity (Bill Gray)	$5,000
Cmte for a Democratic Consensus (Alan Cranston)	$3,000
Cmte for the 100th Congress (Charles Rangel)	$3,000
Majority Congress Committee (Jim Wright)	$3,000
Valley Education Fund (Tony Coelho)	$2,000
Others	$2,100

Pro-Israel $45,500

Joint Action Cmte for Political Affairs	$5,500
Citizens Organized PAC	$5,000
National PAC	$5,000
Desert Caucus	$2,500
Florida Congressional Cmte	$2,500
Delaware Valley PAC	$2,250
Congressional Action Cmte of Texas	$2,000
Roundtable PAC	$2,000
Women's Pro-Israel National PAC	$2,000
City PAC	$1,500
Hudson Valley PAC	$1,500
Garden State PAC	$1,250
Multi-Issue PAC	$1,250
Others	$11,250

Other Major Ideological/Single-Issue PACs

National Rifle Assn	$12,400	Pro-Guns
21st Century PAC	$5,000	Unknown
National Abortion Rights Action League	$3,750	Pro-Choice
Americans Against Apartheid	$3,500	ForeignPolcy
KidsPAC	$3,500	HealthWelfare
National Cmte to Preserve Social Security	$3,250	Society Secur
Voters for Choice/Friends of Family Planning	$3,000	Pro-Choice
Bethune-Dubois PAC	$2,000	Ethnic
Council for a Livable World	$1,268	Pro-Peace

Independent expenditures supporting Espy

National Cmte to Preserve Social Security	$925

---

* Contributions came from more than one PAC affiliated
with this sponsor.

Lane Evans, D-Ill (17)

1988 Committees & Subcommittees

Armed Services
Research and Development

Veterans' Affairs
Oversight and Investigations (Chairman)
Compensation, Pension and Insurance
Education, Training and Employment

Select Children, Youth and Families

PAC Contribution Profile

Business

Commodities Trading	*$3,950*
Chicago Board of Trade	$2,000
Chicago Mercantile Exchange	$1,000
Others	$950
Dairy	*$8,200*
Associated Milk Producers	$3,500
Mid-American Dairymen	$2,500
Dairymen Inc	$1,700
Others	$500
Financial Institutions	*$3,250*
Credit Union National Assn	$2,500
Others	$750
Real Estate	*$4,250*
National Assn of Realtors	$4,250
Rural Electric Utilities	*$2,000*
ACRE (Action Committee for Rural Electrification)	$2,000
Sugar Growers	*$5,250*
American Crystal Sugar Corp	$1,450
American Sugarbeet Growers Assn	$1,100
Southern Minnesota Beet Sugar Co-op	$1,000
Others	$1,700

First elected: 1982
Total receipts: $461,211
Total from PACs: $211,218

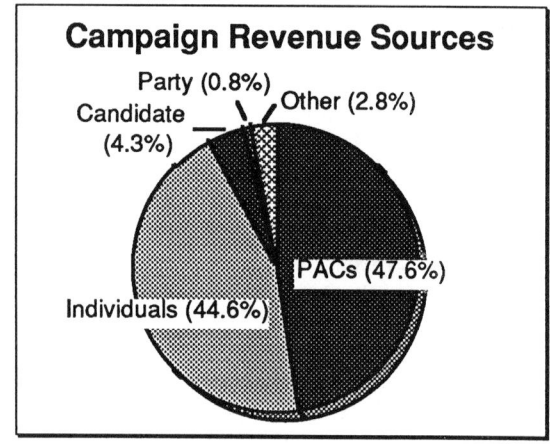

Campaign Revenue Sources

Party (0.8%)
Other (2.8%)
Candidate (4.3%)
PACs (47.6%)
Individuals (44.6%)

Other Major Business PACs

United Parcel Service	$1,100	Delivery
Crop Insurance Research Bureau	$1,022	Ag Svcs
National Assn of Home Builders	$1,000	Resid Constr
National Assn of Social Workers	$1,000	Social Work
Rural Caucus PAC	$1,000	Farm Orgs

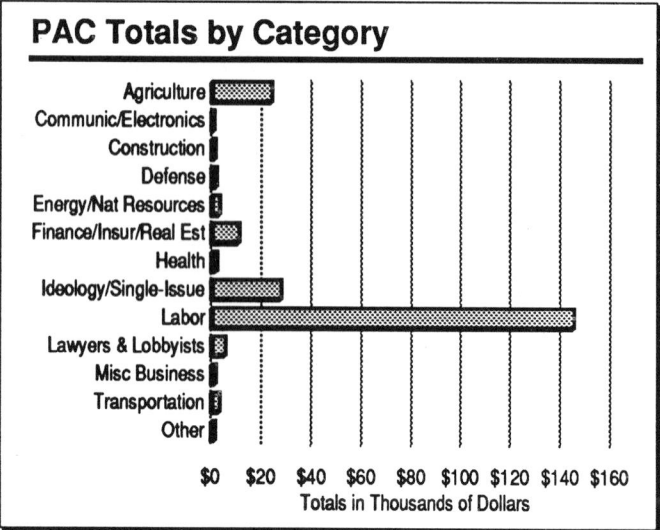

PAC Totals by Category

Agriculture
Communic/Electronics
Construction
Defense
Energy/Nat Resources
Finance/Insur/Real Est
Health
Ideology/Single-Issue
Labor
Lawyers & Lobbyists
Misc Business
Transportation
Other

$0 $20 $40 $60 $80 $100 $120 $140 $160
Totals in Thousands of Dollars

Labor

Bldg Trades/Industrial/Misc Unions $71,380

Machinists/Aerospace Workers Union	$10,000
United Auto Workers	$10,000
Carpenters & Joiners Union	$8,000
Operating Engineers Union*	$7,000
Food & Commercial Workers Union.............................	$5,000
Laborers' Political League*	$4,600
Ironworkers Union	$4,500
Intl Brotherhood of Electrical Workers.........................	$4,250
Alum Brick Glass Workers Local #105	$3,000
Sheet Metal Workers Union	$2,500
United Steelworkers	$2,000
Boilermakers Union	$1,750
Amalgamated Clothing & Textile Workers	$1,500
Ladies Garment Workers Union	$1,350
Bakery, Confectionery & Tobacco Workers	$1,250
United Mine Workers	$1,100
Rubber Cork Linoleum Plastic Workers	$1,000
Others	$2,580

Government/Postal Workers...................................... $35,270

American Fedn of State/County/Munic Employees	$10,000
National Assn of Letter Carriers	$10,000
National Assn of Retired Federal Employees	$8,000
American Postal Workers Union	$2,810
International Assn of Firefighters	$1,850
Others	$2,610

Teachers Unions $12,200

National Education Assn	$10,000
American Federation of Teachers	$2,200

Transportation Unions $25,950

Teamsters Union	$10,000
Seafarers International Union	$6,000
Air Line Pilots Assn	$3,000
Marine Engineers Union*	$2,500
United Transportation Union	$1,250
Others	$3,200

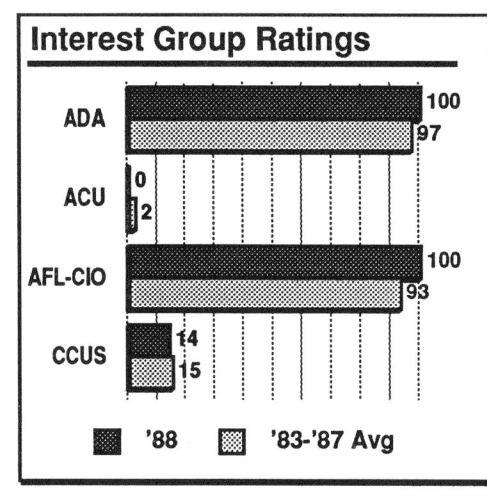

Interest Group Ratings

	'88	'83-'87 Avg
ADA	100	97
ACU	0	2
AFL-CIO	100	93
CCUS	14	15

Ideological/Single-Issue

Democratic Leadership PACs....................................... $9,300

Majority Congress Committee (Jim Wright)	$5,000
America's Leaders' Fund (Dan Rostenkowski)	$3,000
Valley Education Fund (Tony Coelho)	$1,000
Others	$300

Pro-Israel $3,750

Hudson Valley PAC	$1,000
Joint Action Cmte for Political Affairs	$1,000
Roundtable PAC	$1,000
Others	$750

Other Major Ideological/Single-Issue PACs

National Cmte for an Effective Congress.........	$7,495	Dem/Liberal
Assn of Trial Lawyers of America	$5,000	Lawyers
Human Rights Campaign Fund	$2,000	Gay Rights
National Abortion Rights Action League	$2,000	Pro-Choice

Independent expenditures supporting Evans

National Cmte to Preserve Social Security	$3,028

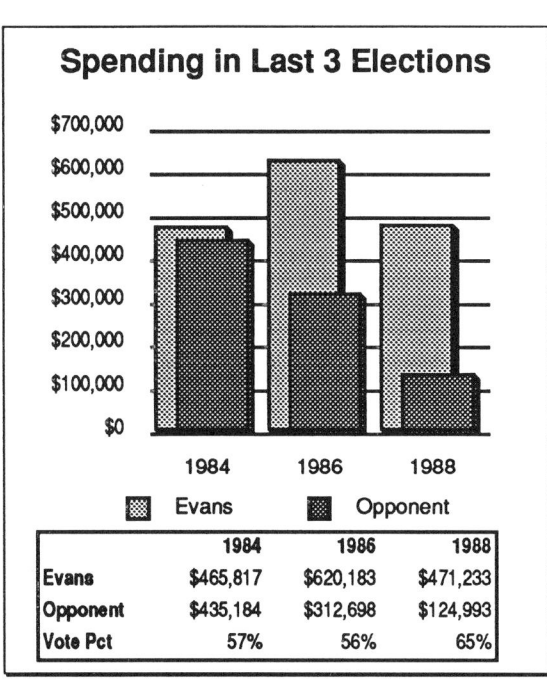

Spending in Last 3 Elections

	Evans	Opponent

	1984	1986	1988
Evans	$465,817	$620,183	$471,233
Opponent	$435,184	$312,698	$124,993
Vote Pct	57%	56%	65%

---

* Contributions came from more than one PAC affiliated with this sponsor.

Dante B. Fascell, D-Fla (19)

First elected: 1954
Total receipts: $490,976
Total from PACs: $176,934

1988 Committees & Subcommittees

Foreign Affairs (Chairman)
Arms Control, International Security and Science (Chairman)

Select Narcotics Abuse and Control

PAC Contribution Profile

Business

Air Transport **$3,500**
    Eastern Airlines $2,000
    Boeing Company $1,000
    Others $500

Construction **$3,000**
    Walter Industries $1,000
    Others $2,000

Defense **$9,500**
    General Dynamics $2,500
    Singer Company $1,000
    Textron Inc $1,000
    United Technologies $1,000
    Others $4,000

Electric Utilities **$2,500**
    ACRE (Action Committee for Rural Electrification) $1,000
    Florida Power & Light $1,000
    Others $500

Electronics & Computers **$3,000**
    Westinghouse Electric $1,000
    Others $2,000

Financial Institutions **$13,850**
    American Bankers Assn $3,000
    Barnett Banks of Florida $2,000
    Florida League of Financial Institutions $2,000
    National Banks of Florida $1,250
    Credit Union National Assn $1,000
    Guardian Savings & Loan $1,000
    US League of Savings Assn $1,000
    Others $2,600

Campaign Revenue Sources

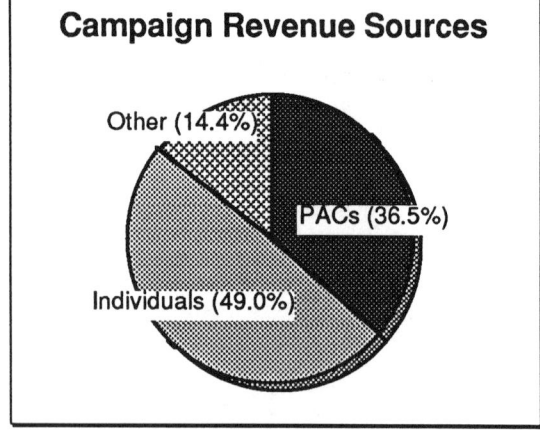

Other (14.4%)
PACs (36.5%)
Individuals (49.0%)

Food & Beverage **$4,000**
    Southern Wine & Spirits $2,000
    Pepsico Inc $1,000
    Others $1,000

Health Professionals **$8,000**
    American Medical Assn $5,000
    Florida Medical Assn $2,500
    Others $500

Lawyers & Lobbyists **$9,850**
    Assn of Trial Lawyers of America $5,000
    Akin, Gump, Hauer & Feld $1,000
    Kirkpatrick & Lockhart $1,000
    Others $2,850

Oil & Gas **$2,500**
    Internorth Inc $1,000
    Others $1,500

Real Estate **$7,500**
    National Assn of Realtors $6,000
    General Development Corp $1,000
    Others $500

Sugar Growers **$2,000**
    None over $500

Telecommunications **$7,000**
    AT&T $3,000
    Southern Bell $3,000
    Others $1,000

Other Major Business PACs

Ansell Inc	$1,000	Health Prod
FMC Corp	$1,000	Chemicals
Philip Morris	$1,000	Tobacco
Pirelli Cable	$1,000	Indust Equip
Riceland Foods	$1,000	Crops
United Parcel Service	$1,000	Delivery

PAC Totals by Category

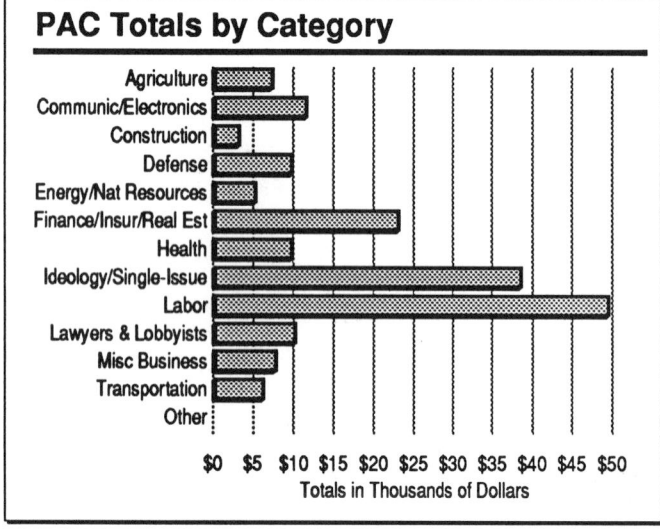

Agriculture
Communic/Electronics
Construction
Defense
Energy/Nat Resources
Finance/Insur/Real Est
Health
Ideology/Single-Issue
Labor
Lawyers & Lobbyists
Misc Business
Transportation
Other

$0 $5 $10 $15 $20 $25 $30 $35 $40 $45 $50
Totals in Thousands of Dollars

Labor

Bldg Trades/Industrial/Misc Unions $19,800

United Auto Workers	$3,500
Machinists/Aerospace Workers Union	$3,000
Ironworkers Union	$2,500
Communications Workers of America	$2,000
Laborers' Political League	$2,000
Carpenters & Joiners Union	$1,500
Food & Commercial Workers Union	$1,000
Intl Brotherhood of Electrical Workers	$1,000
Operating Engineers Union	$1,000
Others	$2,300

Government & Postal Workers $7,200

American Fedn of State/County/Munic Employees	$2,500
National Assn of Retired Federal Employees	$2,000
American Postal Workers Union	$1,000
National Assn of Letter Carriers	$1,000
Others	$700

Transportation Unions $22,250

Teamsters Union	$10,000
Air Line Pilots Assn	$5,000
Marine Engineers Union	$2,000
Seafarers International Union	$2,000
Transportation Communication Union	$1,000
Transport Workers Union	$1,000
Others	$1,250

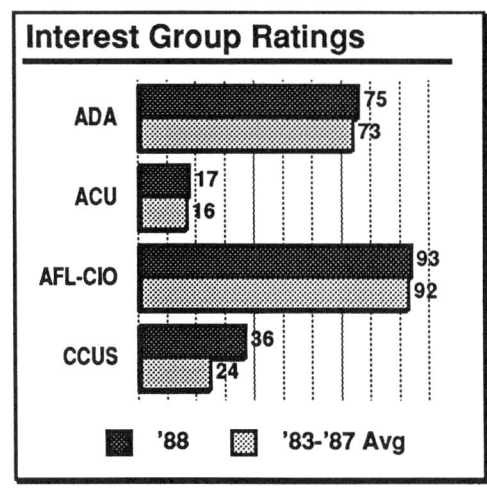

Interest Group Ratings

	'88	'83-'87 Avg
ADA	75	73
ACU	17	16
AFL-CIO	93	92
CCUS	36	24

Ideological/Single-Issue

Pro-Israel $24,250

National Action Committee (NACPAC)	$5,000
National PAC	$5,000
San Franciscans for Good Government	$5,000
Florida Congressional Cmte	$2,500
Washington PAC	$2,000
Roundtable PAC	$1,500
Hudson Valley PAC	$1,250
Joint Action Cmte for Political Affairs	$1,000
Others	$1,000

Other Major Ideological/Single-Issue PACs

Free Cuba PAC	$5,000	Anti-Castro
Armenian-American PAC	$2,000	Ethnic
National Albanian American PAC	$2,000	Ethnic
National Cmte to Preserve Social Security	$2,000	Society Secur

Independent expenditures supporting Fascell

National Cmte to Preserve Social Security	$2,513

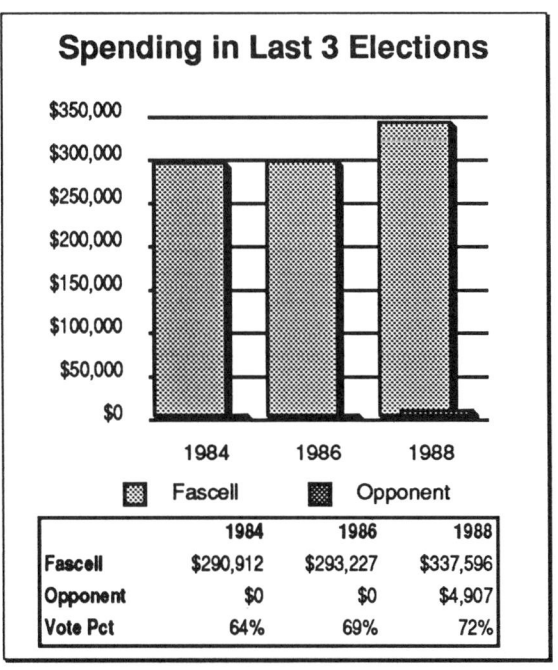

Spending in Last 3 Elections

	1984	1986	1988
Fascell	$290,912	$293,227	$337,596
Opponent	$0	$0	$4,907
Vote Pct	64%	69%	72%

Fascell · Opponent

Harris W. Fawell, R-Ill (13)

First elected: 1984
Total receipts: $292,896
Total from PACs: $98,171

1988 Committees & Subcommittees

Education and Labor
Elementary, Secondary and Vocational Education
Labor-Management Relations

Science, Space and Technology
Energy Research and Development
International Scientific Cooperation

Select Aging
Retirement Income and Employment

PAC Contribution Profile

Business

Aerospace	**$3,550**
Rockwell International	$1,400
Sundstrand Corp	$1,000
Others	$1,150
Automotive	**$6,250**
National Auto Dealers Assn	$3,750
Auto Dealers & Drivers for Free Trade	$1,500
Others	$1,000
Chemicals	**$2,500**
FMC Corp	$1,500
Nalco Chemical Company	$1,000
Commercial & Savings Banks	**$5,100**
First Chicago Corp	$1,250
American Bankers Assn	$1,000
Mid America Federal Savings & Loan	$1,000
Others	$1,850
Commodities Trading	**$2,750**
Chicago Board of Options Exchange	$1,000
Chicago Board of Trade	$1,000
Others	$750
Construction	**$6,100**
National Utility Contractors Assn	$2,000
Associated Builders & Contractors	$1,000
Others	$3,100

Campaign Revenue Sources

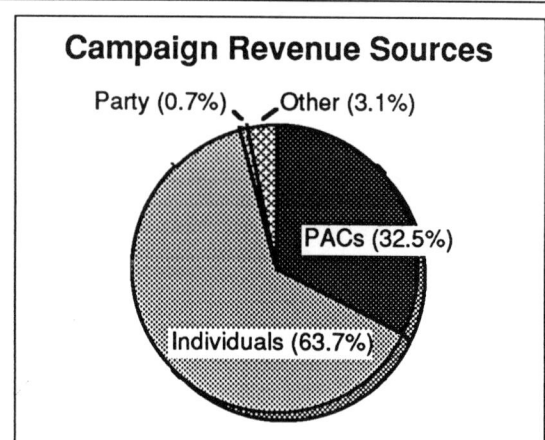

Party (0.7%) Other (3.1%)
PACs (32.5%)
Individuals (63.7%)

Electric Utilities & Equipment	**$2,000**
Commonwealth Edison	$1,250
Others	$750
Food & Beverage	**$10,350**
Food Marketing Institute	$2,000
National Restaurant Assn	$2,000
McDonald's Corp	$1,500
Others	$4,850
Health Professionals	**$6,500**
American Medical Assn	$5,000
American Dental Assn	$1,000
Others	$500
Industrial & Office Equipment	**$4,300**
Interlake Inc	$1,000
Others	$3,300
Insurance	**$4,800**
National Assn of Life Underwriters	$1,500
Others	$3,300
Lawyers	**$2,750**
Assn of Trial Lawyers of America	$2,000
Others	$750
Oil & Gas	**$2,900**
Nicor Inc	$1,400
Others	$1,500
Railroads & Equipment	**$2,900**
Duchossois Industries	$1,000
Others	$1,900
Real Estate	**$4,250**
National Assn of Realtors	$4,250

PAC Totals by Category

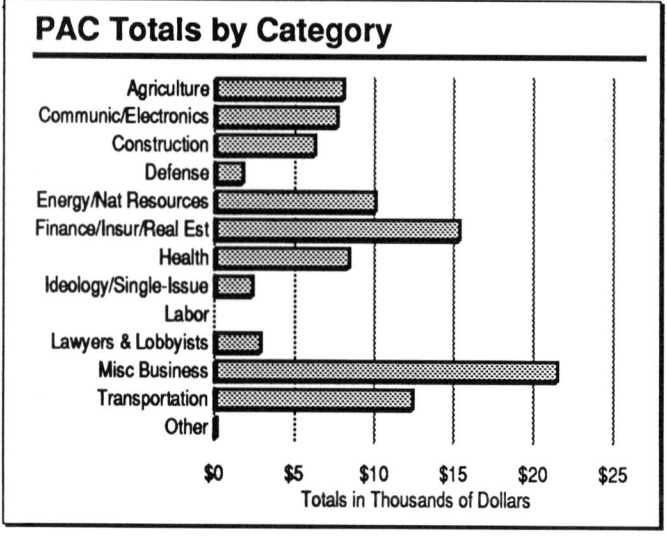

Agriculture
Communic/Electronics
Construction
Defense
Energy/Nat Resources
Finance/Insur/Real Est
Health
Ideology/Single-Issue
Labor
Lawyers & Lobbyists
Misc Business
Transportation
Other

$0 $5 $10 $15 $20 $25
Totals in Thousands of Dollars

Retail Sales & Mail Order **$5,550**

    Spiegel Inc $1,750

    Others $3,800

Telecommunications **$6,575**

    AT&T $2,500

    Illinois Bell Telephone $2,250

    Motorola Inc $1,000

    Others $825

Waste Management **$5,000**

    Waste Management Inc $5,000

Ideological/Single-Issue

Ideological/Single-Issue **$2,250**

Hudson Valley PAC ....$1,000   Pro-Israel

Others..$1,250

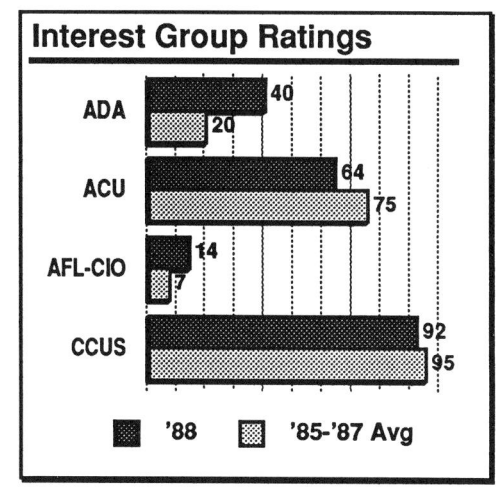

Interest Group Ratings

	'88	'85-'87 Avg
ADA	40	20
ACU	64	75
AFL-CIO	14	7
CCUS	92	95

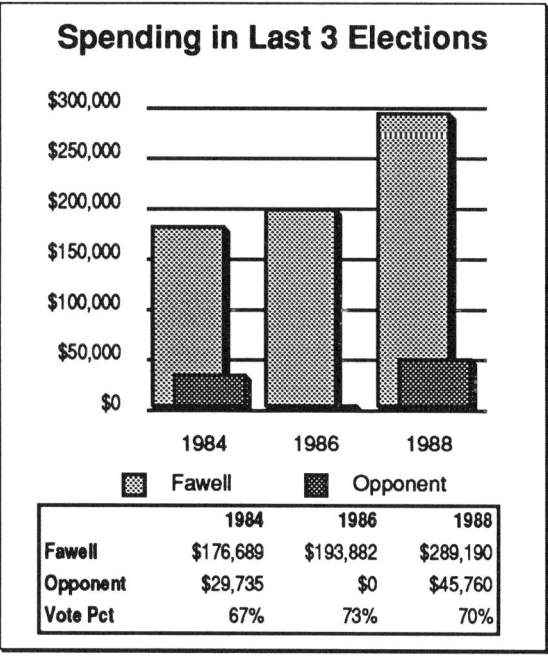

Spending in Last 3 Elections

	1984	1986	1988
Fawell	$176,689	$193,882	$289,190
Opponent	$29,735	$0	$45,760
Vote Pct	67%	73%	70%

Vic Fazio, D-Calif (4)

First elected: 1978
Total receipts: $622,357
Total from PACs: $378,783

1988 Committees & Subcommittees

Appropriations
Legislative Branch (Chairman)
Energy and Water Development
Military Construction

Budget
Defense and International Affairs (Chairman)

Budget Process
Community and Natural Resources
Income Security

Standards of Official Conduct

Select Hunger

PAC Contribution Profile

Business

Electric Utilities	**$14,100**
Southern California Edison	$5,500
Pacific Gas & Electric	$1,850
San Diego Gas & Electric	$1,200
Others	$5,550
Air Transport/Air Freight	**$8,150**
Boeing Company	$2,400
Texas Air	$2,350
Federal Express Corp	$2,200
Others	$1,200
Construction	**$13,200**
National Assn of Home Builders	$2,500
National Utility Contractors Assn	$2,500
Sheet Metal/AirCon Contractors	$1,750
Bechtel Corp	$1,500
Others	$4,950
Defense	**$17,950**
Northrop Corp	$3,050
McDonnell Douglas*	$2,150
United Technologies	$1,850
Lockheed Corp	$1,700
Martin Marietta Corp	$1,350
TRW Inc	$1,050
Others	$6,800
Financial Institutions	**$7,150**
BankAmerica	$1,500
Others	$5,650

Campaign Revenue Sources

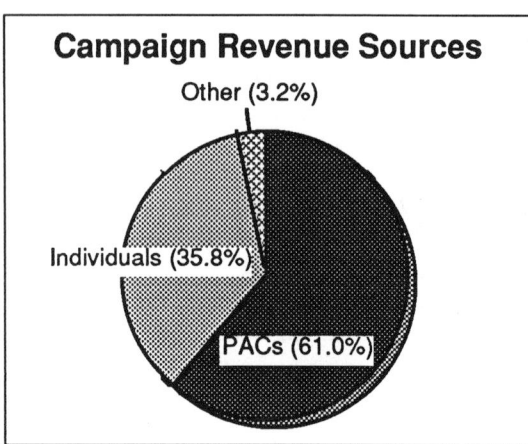

Other (3.2%)
Individuals (35.8%)
PACs (61.0%)

Food & Beverage	**$12,352**
Wine & Spirits Wholesalers of America	$2,900
National Beer Wholesalers Assn	$2,002
Others	$7,450
Fruit & Vegetable Growers	**$14,500**
California Almond Growers Exchange	$5,000
Desert Grape Growers League/California	$2,000
Sunkist Growers	$1,500
Tri/Valley Growers	$1,500
California Pistachio Assn	$1,250
Western Growers Assn	$1,250
Others	$2,000
Health Professionals	**$19,500**
American Medical Assn	$10,000
American Dental Assn	$3,000
American Optometric Assn	$2,150
Others	$4,350
Insurance	**$12,750**
National Assn of Life Underwriters	$3,000
TransAmerica Corp*	$2,250
Independent Insurance Agents of America	$1,350
Pacific Mutual Life	$1,250
Others	$4,900
Lawyers & Lobbyists	**$21,825**
Assn of Trial Lawyers of America	$6,100
California Trial Lawyers Assn	$3,000
Akin, Gump, Hauer & Feld	$1,700
Orrick, Herrington & Sutcliffe	$1,500
Williams & Jensen	$1,500
Others	$8,025
Oil & Gas	**$15,400**
Dow Chemical*	$2,750
Coastal Corp	$2,700
Atlantic Richfield	$1,500
Pacific Enterprises	$1,350
Others	$7,100

PAC Totals by Category

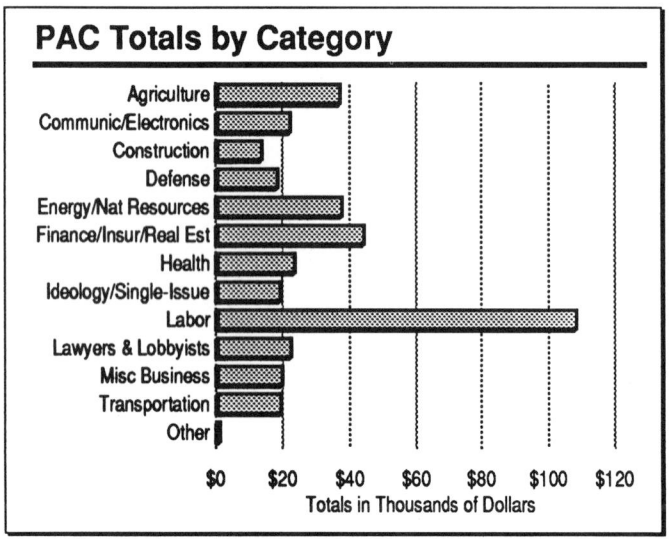

Agriculture
Communic/Electronics
Construction
Defense
Energy/Nat Resources
Finance/Insur/Real Est
Health
Ideology/Single-Issue
Labor
Lawyers & Lobbyists
Misc Business
Transportation
Other

$0 $20 $40 $60 $80 $100 $120
Totals in Thousands of Dollars

Real Estate **$16,228**

- National Assn of Realtors $9,900
- Irvine Company $4,628
- Others $1,700

Telecommunications **$8,550**

- Pacific Telesis Group $3,850
- AT&T $2,000
- Others $2,700

Television/Entertainment **$8,050**

- National Cable Television Assn $2,500
- MCA Inc $1,350
- Others $4,200

Other Major Business PACs

Associated Milk Producers	$3,500	Dairy
United Parcel Service	$2,850	Delivery
Carter Hawley Hale Stores	$2,000	Dept Store
KMS Fusion Inc	$2,000	Nuke Energy
General Electric	$1,700	Electronics
American Express	$1,500	Credit/Loans
American Trucking Assns	$1,500	Trucking
Pirelli Cable	$1,500	Indust Equip
Philip Morris	$1,400	Tobacco
Electronic Data Systems	$1,198	Data Process
National Council of Farmer Co-ops	$1,050	Farm Orgs

Labor

Bldg Trades/Industrial/Misc Unions **$39,800**

- Sheet Metal Workers Union $10,000
- Laborers' Western Political League $4,500
- Communications Workers of America $3,500
- Carpenters & Joiners Union $3,000
- Service Employees International Union $2,800
- Food & Commercial Workers Union $2,250
- Intl Brotherhood of Electrical Workers $2,000
- Ironworkers Union $2,000
- Machinists/Aerospace Workers Union $1,350
- United Mine Workers $1,350
- AFL-CIO* $1,200
- Painters & Allied Trades Union $1,125
- Others $4,725

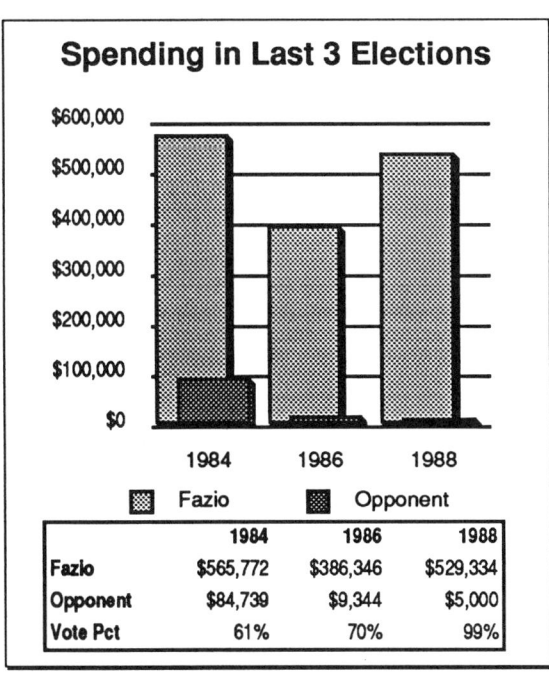

Spending in Last 3 Elections

	1984	1986	1988
Fazio	$565,772	$386,346	$529,334
Opponent	$84,739	$9,344	$5,000
Vote Pct	61%	70%	99%

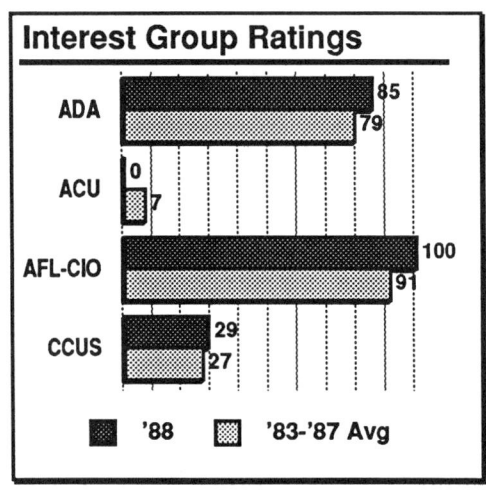

Interest Group Ratings

	'88	'83-'87 Avg
ADA	85	79
ACU	0	7
AFL-CIO	100	91
CCUS	29	27

Government & Postal Workers **$28,650**

- National Assn of Retired Federal Employees $10,000
- National Assn of Letter Carriers* $5,400
- American Postal Workers Union $3,000
- National Rural Letter Carriers Assn $3,000
- International Assn of Firefighters $1,850
- American Federation of Government Employees $1,350
- National Assn of Postal Supervisors $1,200
- Others $2,850

Teachers Unions **$8,700**

- National Education Assn $8,000
- Others $700

Transportation Unions **$30,625**

- Marine Engineers Union* $8,000
- Teamsters Union $7,500
- Air Line Pilots Assn $4,000
- United Transportation Union $3,200
- Amalgamated Transit Union $2,875
- Seafarers International Union $2,250
- Brotherhood of Locomotive Engineers $1,100
- Others $1,700

Ideological/Single-Issue

Ideological/Single-Issue **$16,100**

National PAC	$5,000	Pro-Israel
Human Rights Campaign Fund	$3,500	Gay Rights
National Cmte to Preserve Social Security	$2,350	Society Secur
Others	$5,250	

Independent expenditures supporting Fazio

- American Medical Assn $4,000
- National Cmte to Preserve Social Security $1,790

---

* Contributions came from more than one PAC affiliated with this sponsor.

Edward F. Feighan, D-Ohio (19)

First elected: 1982
Total receipts: $391,199
Total from PACs: $205,414

1988 Committees & Subcommittees

> **Foreign Affairs**
> Europe and the Middle East
> Human Rights and International Organizations
> International Economic Policy and Trade
>
> **Judiciary**
> Crime
> Monopolies and Commercial Law

PAC Contribution Profile

Business

Campaign Revenue Sources

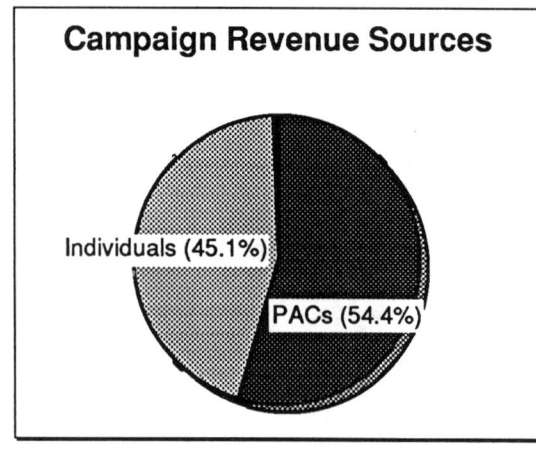

Individuals (45.1%) PACs (54.4%)

Accountants	**$7,250**
American Institute of CPA's	$5,000
Ernst & Whinney	$1,500
Others	$750
Automotive	**$3,000**
National Auto Dealers Assn	$2,500
Others	$500
Commercial & Savings Banks	**$9,000**
American Bankers Assn	$2,250
National City Corp	$1,100
Ohio Savings Assns League	$1,000
Society Corp	$1,000
Others	$3,650
Dairy	**$2,550**
Associated Milk Producers	$1,000
Others	$1,550
Defense	**$3,100**
TRW Inc	$2,250
Others	$850
Food & Beverage	**$3,000**
Food Marketing Institute	$2,000
Others	$1,000
Health Professionals	**$13,499**
American Medical Assn	$9,999
American Academy of Ophthalmology	$1,000
American Dental Assn	$1,000
Others	$1,500

Insurance	**$14,758**
National Assn of Life Underwriters	$4,000
Travelers Corp	$2,000
Independent Insurance Agents of America	$1,508
American Council of Life Insurance	$1,250
Nationwide Corp	$1,000
Others	$5,000
Lawyers & Lobbyists	**$11,625**
Assn of Trial Lawyers of America	$5,000
Baker & Hostetler	$3,000
Others	$3,625
Oil & Gas	**$2,300**
BP America	$1,500
Others	$800
Real Estate	**$10,750**
National Assn of Realtors	$10,000
Others	$750
Securities & Commodities Investment	**$2,350**
McDonald & Company Securities	$1,100
Others	$1,250
Telecommunications	**$4,250**
AT&T	$3,000
Others	$1,250
Television/Entertainment	**$3,000**
ASCAP	$1,000
Others	$2,000

Other Major Business PACs

National Assn of Social Workers .... $1,000   Social Work

PAC Totals by Category

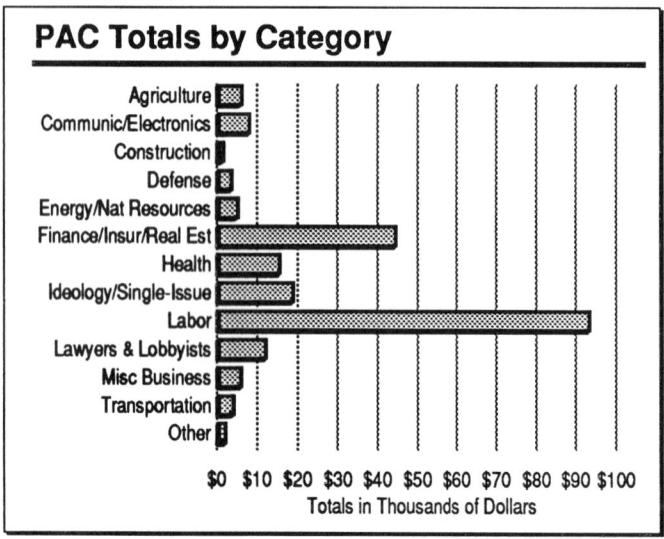

Category	
Agriculture	
Communic/Electronics	
Construction	
Defense	
Energy/Nat Resources	
Finance/Insur/Real Est	
Health	
Ideology/Single-Issue	
Labor	
Lawyers & Lobbyists	
Misc Business	
Transportation	
Other	

$0 $10 $20 $30 $40 $50 $60 $70 $80 $90 $100
Totals in Thousands of Dollars

Labor

Bldg Trades/Industrial/Misc Unions **$45,090**

Machinists/Aerospace Workers Union $10,000
United Auto Workers $5,000
United Steelworkers $5,000
Communications Workers of America $4,750
Intl Brotherhood of Electrical Workers* $3,250
Carpenters & Joiners Union $2,250
Plumbers/Pipefitters Union $2,250
Food & Commercial Workers Union $2,000
Ironworkers Union $2,000
Laborers' Political League $1,500
Operating Engineers Union $1,500
Electronic Machine Furniture Workers $1,250
Rubber Cork Linoleum Plastic Workers $1,000
Others $3,340

Government & Postal Workers **$10,780**

National Assn of Letter Carriers $3,000
American Fedn of State/County/Munic Employees $2,750
National Assn of Retired Federal Employees $2,500
American Postal Workers Union $1,000
Others $1,530

Teachers Unions **$11,250**

National Education Assn $10,000
American Federation of Teachers $1,250

Transportation Unions **$25,600**

Teamsters Union $10,000
Air Line Pilots Assn $4,000
United Transportation Union $3,000
Seafarers International Union $2,000
International Longshoremen Assn $1,500
Assn of Flight Attendants $1,250
Brotherhood of Locomotive Engineers $1,250
Marine Engineers District 2 Maritime Officers $1,000
Transport Workers Union $1,000
Others $600

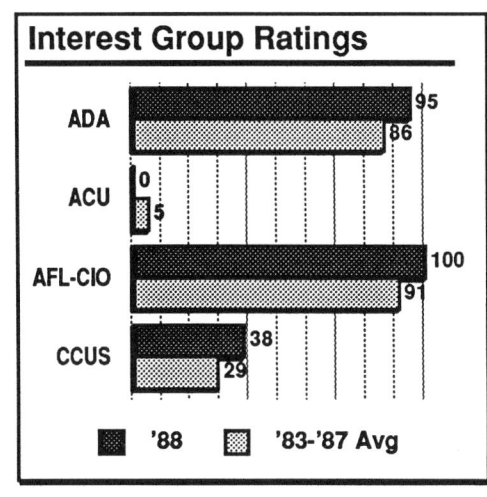

Interest Group Ratings

ADA 95 / 86
ACU 0 / 5
AFL-CIO 100 / 91
CCUS 38 / 29

■ '88   ▨ '83-'87 Avg

Ideological/Single-Issue

Democratic/Liberal **$5,248**

National Cmte for an Effective Congress $4,998
Others $250

Pro-Israel **$8,000**

National PAC $5,000
Hudson Valley PAC $1,000
Washington PAC $1,000
Others $1,000

Other Major Ideological/Single-Issue PACs

Handgun Control Inc .... $2,000   Anti-Guns
National Cmte to Preserve Social Security ...... $1,000   Society Secur

Independent expenditures supporting Feighan

National Cmte to Preserve Social Security $1,812

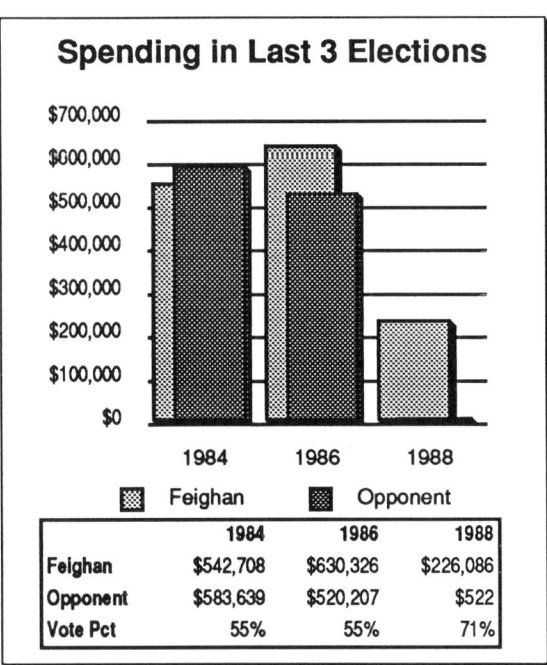

Spending in Last 3 Elections

	1984	1986	1988
Feighan	$542,708	$630,326	$226,086
Opponent	$583,639	$520,207	$522
Vote Pct	55%	55%	71%

▨ Feighan   ■ Opponent

---

* Contributions came from more than one PAC affiliated with this sponsor.

Jack Fields, R-Texas (8)

First elected: 1980
Total receipts: $510,950
Total from PACs: $270,975

1988 Committees & Subcommittees

Energy and Commerce
Energy and Power
Health and the Environment
Telecommunications and Finance

Merchant Marine and Fisheries
Panama Canal/Outer Continental Shelf (Ranking Republican)
Merchant Marine

PAC Contribution Profile

Business

Accountants	**$6,500**
American Institute of CPA's	$5,000
Others	$1,500
Automotive	**$6,700**
National Auto Dealers Assn	$4,350
Auto Dealers & Drivers for Free Trade	$2,000
Others	$350
Commercial Banks	**$9,850**
Allied Bankshares	$2,000
J P Morgan & Company	$2,000
American Bankers Assn	$1,500
Texas Commerce Bancshares	$1,500
Barnett Banks of Florida	$1,000
Others	$1,850
Construction	**$13,900**
National Assn of Home Builders	$3,500
Brown & Root	$2,000
Associated General Contractors	$1,350
3D/International Inc	$1,000
Fluor Corp	$1,000
Lennox Industries	$1,000
National Electrical Contractors Assn	$1,000
Others	$3,050
Electric Utilities	**$11,775**
Houston Industries	$3,000
Texas Utilities Electric Company*	$2,600
Others	$6,175

Campaign Revenue Sources

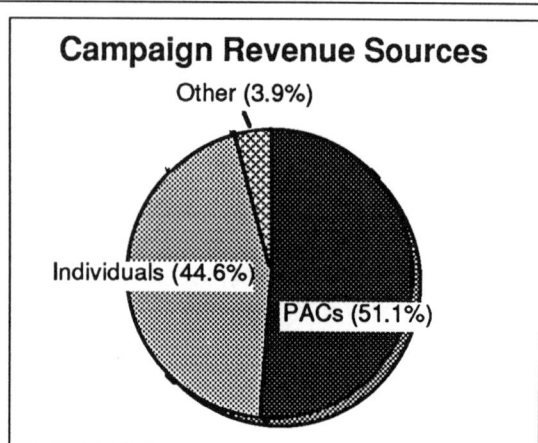

Other (3.9%)
Individuals (44.6%)
PACs (51.1%)

Food & Beverage	**$7,550**
Coca-Cola Company	$1,000
Jerrico Inc	$1,000
Malone & Hyde Inc	$1,000
National Beer Wholesalers Assn	$1,000
Pepsico Inc	$1,000
Others	$2,550
Health Professionals	**$21,200**
American Medical Assn	$10,700
American Dental Assn	$3,000
American Podiatry Assn	$1,500
Oral & Maxillofacial Surgeons	$1,500
American Academy of Ophthalmology	$1,000
American College of Emergency Physicians	$1,000
Cmte for Quality Orthopedic Health Care	$1,000
Others	$1,500
Insurance	**$9,850**
National Assn of Life Underwriters	$1,500
Independent Insurance Agents of America	$1,100
American General Insurance Company	$1,000
Torchmark Corp	$1,000
Others	$5,250
Lawyers	**$13,250**
Assn of Trial Lawyers of America	$5,000
Fullbright & Jaworski	$2,000
Akin, Gump, Hauer & Feld	$1,500
Baker & Botts	$1,500
Vinson, Elkins, Searls, Connally & Smith	$1,000
Others	$2,250

PAC Totals by Category

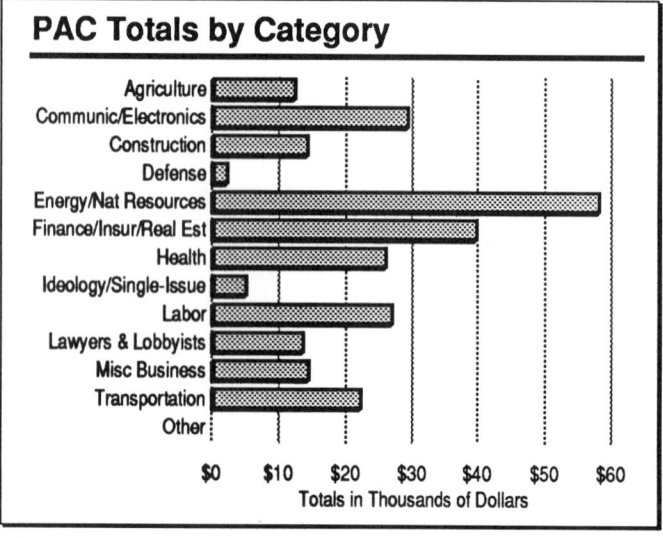

Totals in Thousands of Dollars

- Agriculture
- Communic/Electronics
- Construction
- Defense
- Energy/Nat Resources
- Finance/Insur/Real Est
- Health
- Ideology/Single-Issue
- Labor
- Lawyers & Lobbyists
- Misc Business
- Transportation
- Other

$0 $10 $20 $30 $40 $50 $60

Oil & Gas $41,700
Columbia Hydrocarbon Corp	$2,375
Texaco	$1,875
Mesa PAC II	$1,700
Atlantic Richfield	$1,500
Cooper Industries	$1,500
Tenneco Inc	$1,500
Coastal Corp	$1,375
Shell Oil	$1,375
Arkla Inc	$1,000
Baker Hughes Inc	$1,000
Dow Chemical	$1,000
Halliburton Company	$1,000
HOUPAC	$1,000
Internorth Inc	$1,000
Mitchell Energy & Development	$1,000
Mobil Oil	$1,000
Phillips Petroleum	$1,000
Texas Eastern Gas Transmission	$1,000
Union Pacific Corp	$1,000
Valero Energy Corp	$1,000
Others	$16,500

Real Estate $6,500
National Assn of Realtors	$6,000
Others	$500

Sea Transport $8,225
American Pilots Assn	$2,000
Lykes Bros Steamship Company	$1,200
American President Lines	$1,100
Others	$3,925

Securities & Commodities Investment $7,550
Chicago Board of Options Exchange	$1,000
Chicago Board of Trade	$1,000
First Boston Corp	$1,000
Goldman Sachs	$1,000
Morgan Stanley & Company	$1,000
Travelers Corp	$1,000
Others	$1,550

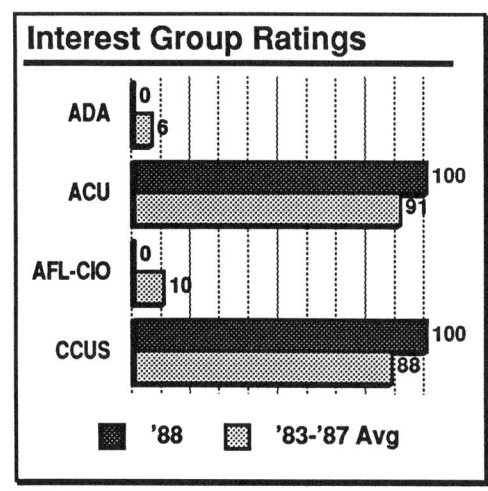

Interest Group Ratings

	'88	'83-'87 Avg
ADA	0	6
ACU	100	91
AFL-CIO	0	10
CCUS	100	88

■ '88   ▨ '83–'87 Avg

Telecommunications $18,950
AT&T	$5,000
GTE (Southwest)	$2,500
Southwestern Bell	$2,500
Pacific Telesis Group	$1,750
Bell Atlantic	$1,000
Comsat	$1,000
United Telecommunications*	$1,000
Others	$4,200

Television/Broadcasting $10,000
National Cable Television Assn	$8,000
Others	$2,000

Other Major Business PACs
Philip Morris	$1,200	Tobacco
American Airlines	$1,000	Airlines
Browning-Ferris Industries	$1,000	Waste Mgmt
Federal Express Corp	$1,000	Delivery
Federated Department Stores	$1,000	Dept Store
International Assn for Financial Planning	$1,000	FinancSvcs
Lone Star Steel	$1,000	Steel
NL Industries	$1,000	Chemicals
RJR Nabisco	$1,000	Tobacco
Texas Air	$1,000	Airlines
Texas Cattle Feeders Assn	$1,000	Feedlots
Texas/Southwestern Cattle Raisers	$1,000	Livestock

Labor

Bldg Trades/Industrial/Misc Unions $6,000
Teamsters Union	$5,000
United Transportation Union	$1,000

Sea Transport Unions $20,650
Marine Engineers Union*	$10,000
International Longshoremen Assn	$5,500
Masters, Mates & Pilots Union	$2,500
Seafarers International Union*	$2,150
Others	$500

Major Ideological/Single-Issue PACs
National Rifle Assn	$2,500	Pro-Guns
Black PAC	$1,000	Repub/Conser
Campaign America (Bob Dole)	$1,000	Repub Leader

---

* Contributions came from more than one PAC affiliated with this sponsor.

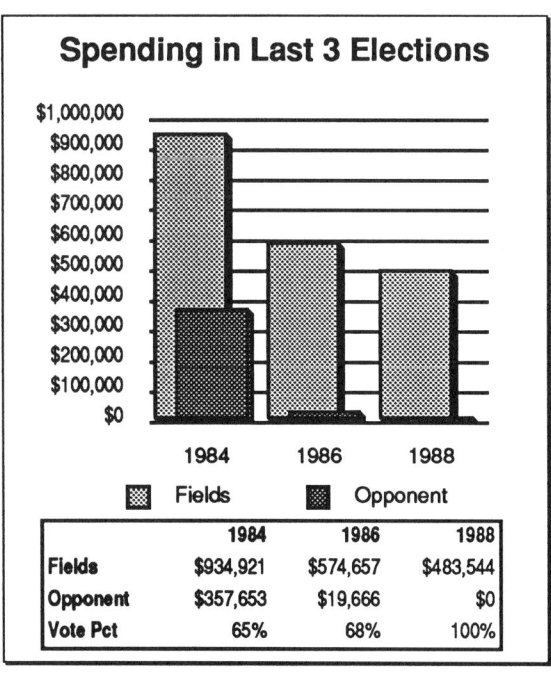

Spending in Last 3 Elections

▨ Fields   ■ Opponent

	1984	1986	1988
Fields	$934,921	$574,657	$483,544
Opponent	$357,653	$19,666	$0
Vote Pct	65%	68%	100%

Hamilton Fish Jr., R-NY (21)

First elected: 1968
Total receipts: $357,688
Total from PACs: $196,388

1988 Committees & Subcommittees

Judiciary (Ranking Republican)
Monopolies and Commercial Law (Ranking Republican)
Criminal Justice
Immigration, Refugees and International Law

PAC Contribution Profile

Business

Accountants	**$7,300**
American Institute of CPA's	$5,000
Ernst & Whinney	$1,300
Others	$1,000
Automotive	**$4,000**
Auto Dealers & Drivers for Free Trade	$2,500
Others	$1,500
Broadcasting & Entertainment	**$6,250**
National Assn of Broadcasters	$2,500
National Cable Television Assn	$1,000
Others	$2,750
Commercial Banks	**$9,450**
Citicorp	$4,000
J P Morgan & Company	$2,000
Chemical Bank	$1,000
Others	$2,450
Construction	**$3,000**
Ch2M Hill	$1,000
Manville Corp	$1,000
Others	$1,000
Dairy	**$2,500**
Associated Milk Producers	$2,000
Others	$500

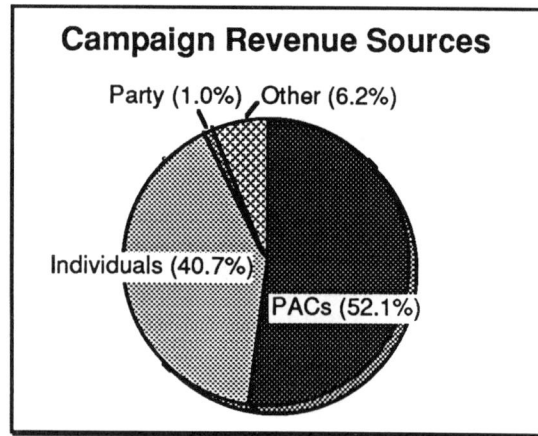

Campaign Revenue Sources

Party (1.0%) Other (6.2%)
Individuals (40.7%)
PACs (52.1%)

Food & Beverage	**$14,346**
Food Marketing Institute	$5,500
National Beer Wholesalers Assn	$4,000
Pepsico Inc	$2,046
Pepsi-Cola Bottlers Assn	$1,000
Others	$1,800
Health Professionals	**$8,850**
American Medical Assn	$4,350
New York Medical Assn	$2,500
American Dental Assn	$1,000
Others	$1,000
Insurance	**$25,213**
National Assn of Life Underwriters	$5,000
American Council of Life Insurance	$2,263
Travelers Corp	$2,000
Independent Insurance Agents of America	$1,500
National Assn of Independent Insurers	$1,150
National Assn of Mutual Insurance Agents	$1,100
Aetna Life & Casualty	$1,000
Allstate Insurance	$1,000
Casualty & Surety Agents Assn	$1,000
Crum & Forster Insurance	$1,000
Hartford Insurance	$1,000
Health Insurance Assn of America	$1,000
Prudential Insurance	$1,000
Others	$5,200
Lawyers & Lobbyists	**$3,400**
Akin, Gump, Hauer & Feld	$1,000
Preston, Thorgrimson, Ellis & Holman	$1,000
Others	$1,400
Oil & Gas	**$6,050**
Texaco	$2,000
Columbia Hydrocarbon Corp	$1,000
Others	$3,050
Pharmaceuticals	**$4,500**
Bristol-Myers	$1,000
Ciba-Geigy Corp	$1,000
Squibb Corp	$1,000
Others	$1,500
Railroads	**$3,000**
Consolidated Rail Corp	$1,000
Santa Fe Southern Pacific	$1,000
Others	$1,000

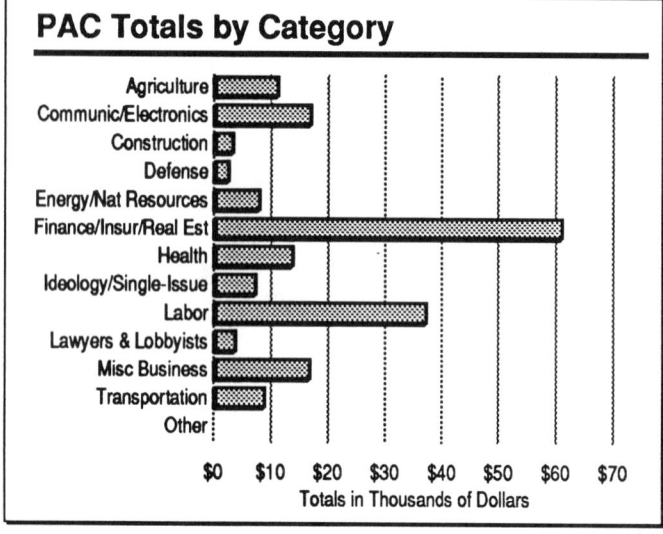

PAC Totals by Category

- Agriculture
- Communic/Electronics
- Construction
- Defense
- Energy/Nat Resources
- Finance/Insur/Real Est
- Health
- Ideology/Single-Issue
- Labor
- Lawyers & Lobbyists
- Misc Business
- Transportation
- Other

$0 $10 $20 $30 $40 $50 $60 $70
Totals in Thousands of Dollars

Real Estate $11,500
    National Assn of Realtors $10,000
    American Land Title Assn $1,000
    Others $500

Securities Investment $5,250
    Goldman Sachs $2,000
    Morgan Stanley & Company $2,000
    Others $1,250

Telecommunications $9,300
    AT&T $3,500
    New York Telephone $1,800
    Pacific Telesis Group $1,500
    Bell Atlantic $1,000
    BellSouth Corp* $1,000
    Others $500

Other Major Business PACs

Corning Glass Works	$2,000	Glass Prod
B F Goodrich	$1,000	Indust Equip
General Electric	$1,000	Electronics
International Council of Shopping Centers	$1,000	Retail
LTV Steel	$1,000	Steel
New York State Electric & Gas Corp	$1,000	Gas & Electr

Interest Group Ratings

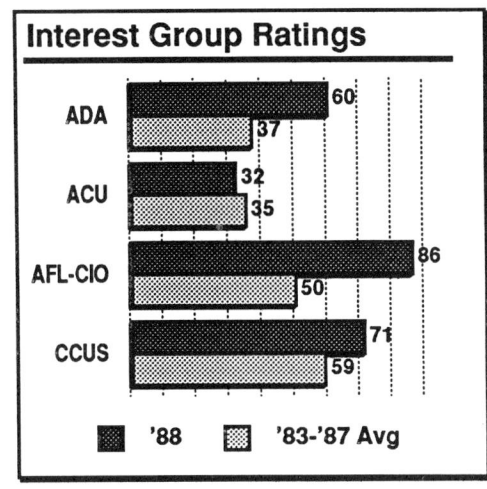

Labor

Bldg Trades/Industrial/Misc Unions $13,675
    Laborers' Political League $5,000
    Carpenters & Joiners Union $2,250
    Operating Engineers Union* $1,675
    Ladies Garment Workers Union $1,000
    Others $3,750

Government & Postal Workers $9,150
    National Assn of Retired Federal Employees $4,000
    National Assn of Letter Carriers $3,000
    American Fedn of State/County/Munic Employees $1,000
    Others $1,150

Transportation Unions $13,975
    Teamsters Union $8,975
    Air Line Pilots Assn $3,000
    Seafarers International Union $1,000
    United Transportation Union $1,000

Ideological/Single-Issue

Ideological/Single-Issue $6,950

National Rifle Assn	$4,950	Pro-Guns
KidsPAC	$1,000	HealthWelfare
Others	$1,000	

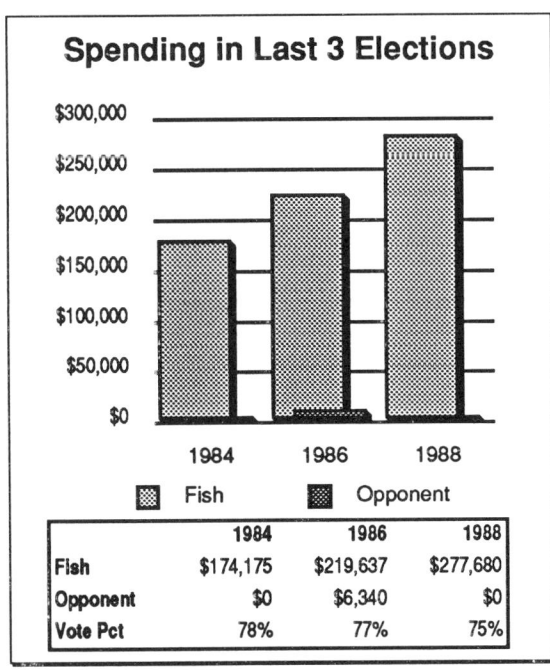

Spending in Last 3 Elections

	1984	1986	1988
Fish	$174,175	$219,637	$277,680
Opponent	$0	$6,340	$0
Vote Pct	78%	77%	75%

* Contributions came from more than one PAC affiliated
with this sponsor.

Floyd H. Flake, D-NY (6)

First elected: 1986
Total receipts: $344,391
Total from PACs: $150,681

1988 Committees & Subcommittees

Banking, Finance and Urban Affairs
Economic Stabilization
General Oversight and Investigations
Housing and Community Development

Small Business
Procurement, Innovation and Minority Enterprise Development
Regulation and Business Opportunities

Select Hunger

PAC Contribution Profile

Business

Commercial Banks **$22,247**
Citicorp $4,847
American Bankers Assn $4,000
Chemical Bank $2,150
Bankers Trust $1,500
Barnett Banks of Florida $1,000
Irving Bank $1,000
J P Morgan & Company $1,000
Marine Midland Banks $1,000
National Bankers Assn $1,000
New York State Bankers Assn $1,000
Others $3,750

Credit Unions **$3,750**
Credit Union National Assn $3,250
Others $500

Health Professionals **$2,750**
American Medical Assn $2,000
Others $750

Insurance **$3,500**
National Assn of Life Underwriters $1,000
Others $2,500

Lawyers & Lobbyists **$7,000**
Assn of Trial Lawyers of America $6,000
Others $1,000

Package Delivery **$3,000**
United Parcel Service $3,000

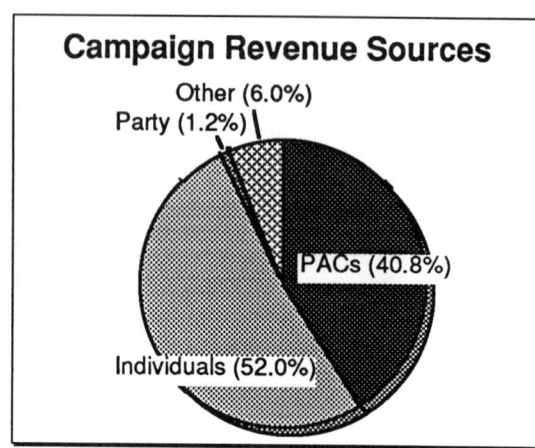

Campaign Revenue Sources

Other (6.0%)
Party (1.2%)
PACs (40.8%)
Individuals (52.0%)

Real Estate **$5,020**
National Assn of Realtors $4,250
Others $770

Savings Banks **$5,250**
US League of Savings Assn $3,500
Others $1,750

Securities & Commodities Investment **$8,750**
Goldman Sachs $2,000
Morgan Stanley & Company $1,500
Commodity Exchange Inc $1,250
First Boston Corp $1,000
Municipal Securities Industry $1,000
Others $2,000

Telecommunications **$2,700**
New York Telephone $1,800
AT&T $900

Tobacco **$2,000**
Philip Morris $1,500
Others $500

Other Major Business PACs

J C Penney Company .... $1,250   Dept Store
Equifax Inc .... $1,000   CreditReport
National Assn of Home Builders .... $1,000   Resid Constr

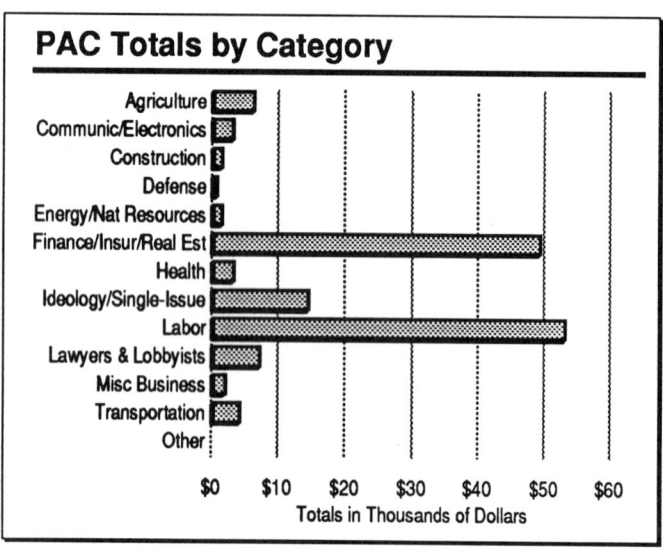

PAC Totals by Category

Agriculture
Communic/Electronics
Construction
Defense
Energy/Nat Resources
Finance/Insur/Real Est
Health
Ideology/Single-Issue
Labor
Lawyers & Lobbyists
Misc Business
Transportation
Other

$0 $10 $20 $30 $40 $50 $60
Totals in Thousands of Dollars

Labor

Bldg Trades/Industrial/Misc Unions $15,000

Carpenters & Joiners Union	$2,500
Machinists/Aerospace Workers Union	$1,750
Food & Commercial Workers Union	$1,500
Laborers' Political League	$1,500
Ladies Garment Workers Union	$1,400
AFL-CIO*	$1,250
Operating Engineers Union*	$1,200
Communications Workers of America	$1,000
Others	$2,900

Government & Postal Workers $19,450

National Assn of Letter Carriers	$5,750
American Fedn of State/County/Munic Employees	$5,000
National Assn of Retired Federal Employees	$5,000
American Postal Workers Union	$1,500
National Alliance Postal/Federal Employees	$1,000
Others	$1,200

Teachers Unions $5,750

National Education Assn	$5,750

Transportation Unions $12,700

Teamsters Union	$5,000
Transport Workers Union	$2,500
Marine Engineers District 2 Maritime Officers	$1,000
Seafarers International Union	$1,000
Others	$3,200

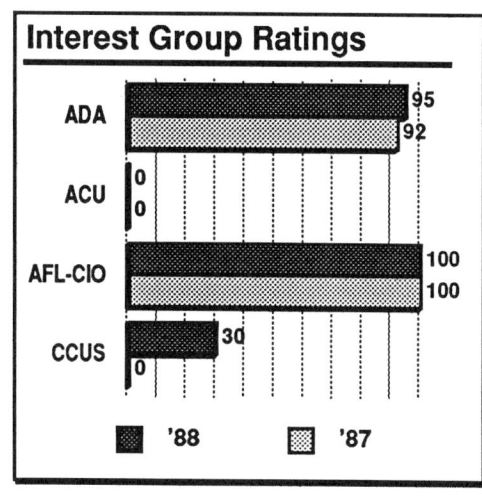

Interest Group Ratings

	'88	'87
ADA	95	92
ACU	0	0
AFL-CIO	100	100
CCUS	30	0

Ideological/Single-Issue

Pro-Israel $5,500

National PAC	$5,000
Others	$500

Pro-Life $7,000

National Right to Life PAC	$6,000
Black Americans for Life PAC	$1,000

Other Major Ideological/Single-Issue PACs

Valley Education Fund (Tony Coelho) ....$1,000   Dem Leaders

Independent expenditures supporting Flake

National Cmte to Preserve Social Security $1,363

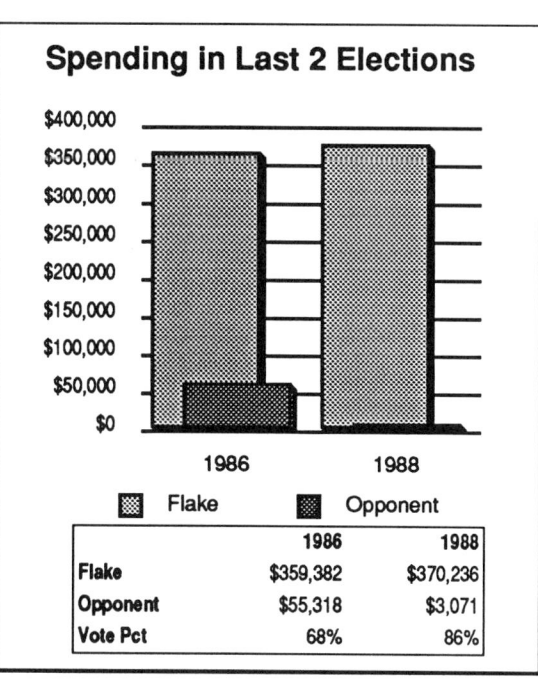

Spending in Last 2 Elections

	1986	1988
Flake	$359,382	$370,236
Opponent	$55,318	$3,071
Vote Pct	68%	86%

---

* Contributions came from more than one PAC affiliated with this sponsor.

Ronnie G. Flippo, D-Ala (5)

First elected: 1976
Total receipts: $711,580
Total from PACs: $444,960

1988 Committees & Subcommittees

Ways and Means
Human Resources
Select Revenue Measures

PAC Contribution Profile

Business

Accountants **$29,708**
American Institute of CPA's $10,000
Coopers & Lybrand $4,604
Touche Ross $4,604
Arthur Young & Company $3,000
Arthur Andersen & Company $2,000
Deloitte, Haskins & Sells $2,000
Ernst & Whinney $2,000
Others $1,500

Commercial Banks **$26,450**
American Bankers Assn $5,000
Central Bancshares of the South $5,000
J P Morgan & Company $5,000
Citicorp $3,000
Amsouth Bancorp $2,500
Others $5,950

Construction **$8,950**
Vulcan Materials Company $3,200
Walter Industries...$2,500
National Assn of Home Builders $1,250
Others $2,000

Defense **$21,750**
Singer Company $3,500
Lockheed Corp $3,000
Hughes Aircraft $2,000
United Technologies $2,000
BDM International $1,500
Rockwell International $1,200
Martin Marietta Corp $1,100
Others $7,450

Campaign Revenue Sources

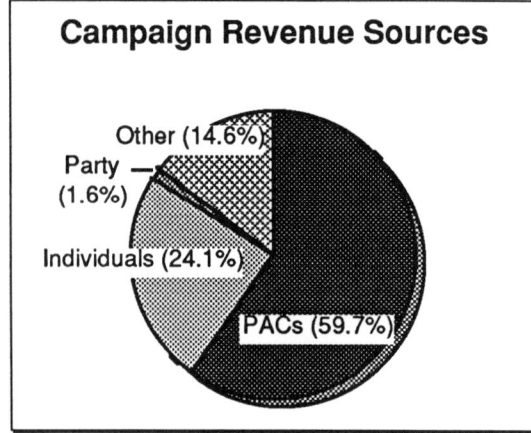

Other (14.6%)
Party (1.6%)
Individuals (24.1%)
PACs (59.7%)

PAC Totals by Category

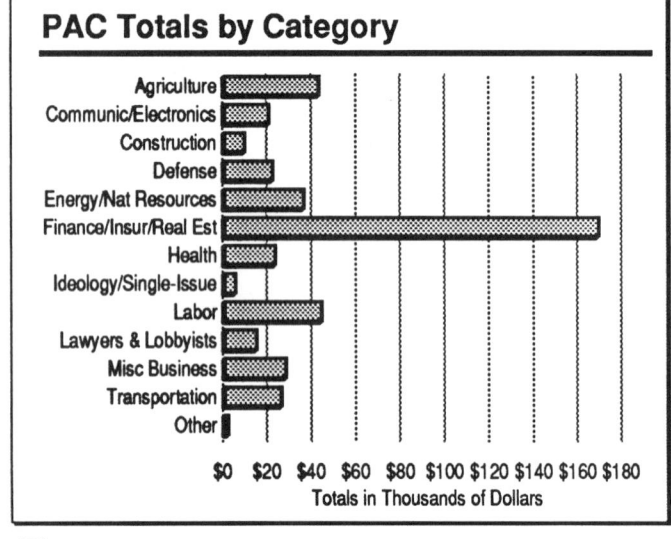

Agriculture
Communic/Electronics
Construction
Defense
Energy/Nat Resources
Finance/Insur/Real Est
Health
Ideology/Single-Issue
Labor
Lawyers & Lobbyists
Misc Business
Transportation
Other

$0 $20 $40 $60 $80 $100 $120 $140 $160 $180
Totals in Thousands of Dollars

Electric Utilities **$13,250**
Southern Company* $5,200
Middle South Utilities* $1,250
Others $6,800

Electronics & Computers **$6,250**
General Electric $2,000
Computer Sciences Corp $1,500
Intergraph Corp $1,500
Others $1,250

Food & Beverage **$16,750**
National Beer Wholesalers Assn $3,000
Food Marketing Institute $2,500
National Restaurant Assn $2,000
Wine & Spirits Wholesalers of America............$2,000
Winn-Dixie Stores $2,000
Others $5,250

Forest Products **$7,100**
Mead Corp $2,100
Union Camp Corp $1,500
Others $3,500

Health Professionals **$16,000**
American Medical Assn $5,000
American Dental Assn $4,000
American Academy of Ophthalmology $2,500
Cmte for Quality Orthopedic Health Care $2,000
National Assn of Pharmacists $1,500
American College of Emergency Physicians $1,000

Insurance **$65,055**
Torchmark Corp $10,000
National Assn of Life Underwriters $7,500
Equitable Financial Services $3,000
Massachusetts Mutual Life Insurance $2,605
American Council of Life Insurance $2,000
Casualty & Surety Agents Assn $2,000
Independent Insurance Agents of America $2,000
Metropolitan Life Insurance $2,000
Northwestern Mutual Life $2,000
American General Insurance Company $1,500
New England Mutual Life $1,500
New York Life $1,500
Others $27,450

Lawyers & Lobbyists **$14,500**
Assn of Trial Lawyers of America $5,000
Sirote, Permutt et al $1,500
Others $8,000

Oil & Gas **$15,300**
    Southern Natural Resources $2,200
    Chevron Corp $1,600
    Others $11,500

Real Estate **$8,500**
    National Assn of Realtors $6,000
    Others $2,500

Securities& Commodities Investment **$28,500**
    Investment Company Institute $7,000
    Chicago Board of Trade $4,000
    First Boston Corp $2,000
    Securities Industry Assn $2,000
    Prudential-Bache Securities $1,500
    Others $12,000

Telecommunications **$12,300**
    AT&T $4,500
    South Central Bell Telephone $3,000
    Continental Telecom $2,000
    Others $2,800

Tobacco **$7,250**
    Philip Morris $3,000
    RJR Nabisco $1,500
    Others $2,750

Other Major Business PACs

National Venture Capital Assn	$5,000	Venture Cap
Boeing Company	$3,500	Aircraft
Alabama Farm Bureau Federation	$3,000	Farm Orgs
National Auto Dealers Assn	$3,000	Auto Sales
Credit Union National Assn	$2,500	Credit Union
United Parcel Service	$2,500	Delivery
Small Business Council of America	$2,000	Sml Business
US League of Savings Assn	$2,000	Savings Banks
American Society of Assn Executives	$1,500	Other
American Bus Assn	$1,500	Bus Svcs
National Cotton Council	$1,500	Cotton
Norfolk Southern Corp	$1,500	Railroads
Tyson Foods	$1,500	Poultry/Egg
J C Penney Company	$1,200	Dept Store

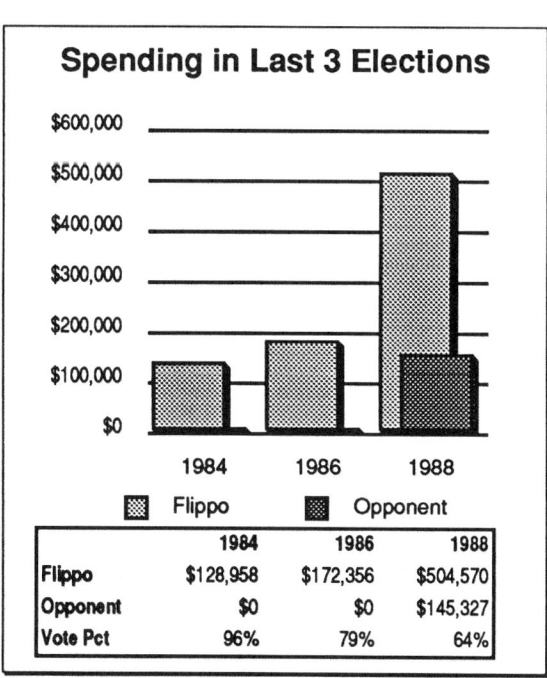

Spending in Last 3 Elections

Flippo ▨   Opponent ■

	1984	1986	1988
Flippo	$128,958	$172,356	$504,570
Opponent	$0	$0	$145,327
Vote Pct	96%	79%	64%

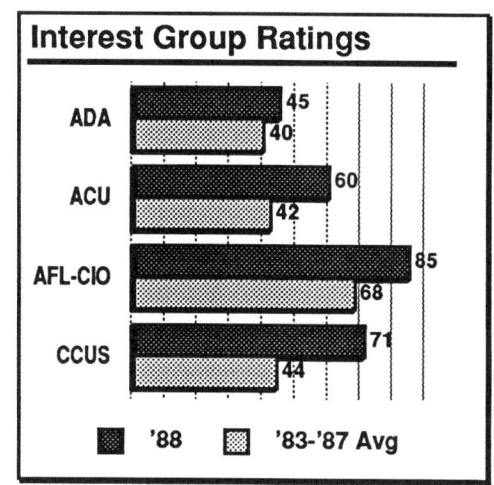

Interest Group Ratings

	'88	'83-'87 Avg
ADA	45	40
ACU	60	42
AFL-CIO	85	68
CCUS	71	44

■ '88   ▨ '83-'87 Avg

Labor

Bldg Trades/Industrial/Misc Unions **$13,500**
    United Auto Workers $4,000
    Carpenters & Joiners Union $2,500
    Laborers' Political League $1,500
    Others $5,500

Government & Postal Workers **$15,100**
    National Rural Letter Carriers Assn $7,000
    National Assn of Retired Federal Employees $3,000
    National Assn of Postmasters $1,600
    Others $3,500

Transportation Unions **$15,250**
    Teamsters Union $7,500
    Air Line Pilots Assn $5,000
    United Transportation Union $1,500
    Others $1,250

Major Ideological/Single-Issue PACs

National Cmte to Preserve Social Security	$2,000	Society Secur
Valley Education Fund (Tony Coelho)	$1,500	Dem Leaders
Americans for Good Government Inc	$1,200	Pro-Israel

Independent expenditures supporting Flippo

National Cmte to Preserve Social Security $2,358

---

* Contributions came from more than one PAC affiliated
with this sponsor.

James J. Florio, D-NJ (1)

First elected: 1974
Total receipts: $790,850
Total from PACs: $359,310

1988 Committees & Subcommittees

Energy and Commerce
Commerce, Consumer Protection and Competitiveness
Transportation and Hazardous Materials

Veterans' Affairs
Hospitals and Health Care
Housing and Memorial Affairs
Oversight and Investigations

Select Aging

PAC Contribution Profile

Business

Accountants $10,700
    American Institute of CPA's $5,000
    Coopers & Lybrand $3,100
    Others $2,600

Commercial Banks....................................$16,999
    Citicorp $4,999
    J P Morgan & Company $2,500
    American Bankers Assn $1,500
    Others $8,000

Health Professionals $18,300
    American Dental Assn $4,600
    American Medical Assn $2,500
    American Optometric Assn $2,100
    American Nurses Assn $2,000
    National Assn of Pharmacists $1,700
    American Physical Therapy Assn $1,100
    American Chiropractic Assn $1,100
    Co-op of American Physicians $1,100
    Others $2,100

Insurance $30,162
    Independent Insurance Agents of America $7,262
    Casualty & Surety Agents Assn $3,500
    National Assn of Life Underwriters $2,500
    Home Group Inc $2,000
    American Council of Life Insurance $1,100
    American International Group Inc $1,100
    (Continued in next column)

Campaign Revenue Sources

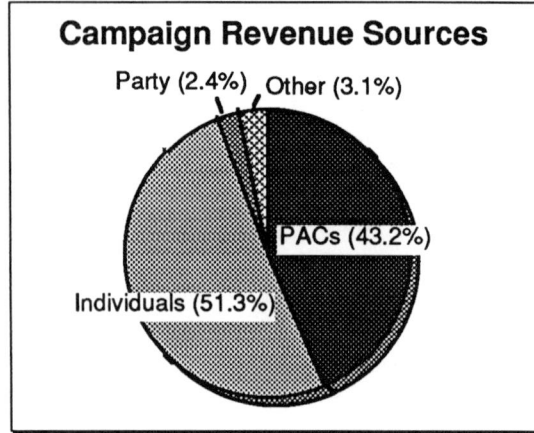

Party (2.4%)   Other (3.1%)
PACs (43.2%)
Individuals (51.3%)

Insurance (cont'd)
    Blue Cross & Blue Shield Assn $1,100
    Metropolitan Life Insurance $1,100
    National Assn Mutual Insurance Agents $1,100
    National Assn/Insurance Brokers $1,100
    Prudential Insurance $1,100
    Others $7,200

Lawyers & Lobbyists $13,000
    Assn of Trial Lawyers of America $5,000
    Camp, Barsh, Bates & Tate $1,050
    Others $6,950

Pharmaceuticals $17,550
    Johnson & Johnson $2,100
    American Home Products Corp $2,000
    Warner-Lambert $1,600
    Pharmaceutical Manufacturers Assn $1,500
    Squibb Corp $1,500
    Hoffman-La Roche $1,250
    Others $7,600

Railroads & Railroad Services $13,400
    ITEL Corp $4,000
    Consolidated Rail Corp $2,200
    Norfolk Southern Corp $1,200
    Kansas City Southern $1,100
    Others $4,900

Securities & Commodities Investment.....$20,000
    First Boston Corp $6,000
    Investment Company Institute $2,000
    Others $12,000

Telecommunications $14,400
    AT&T $4,000
    New Jersey Bell Telephone $2,500
    Pacific Telesis Group $2,000
    Corning Glass Works $1,500
    Ameritech Corp $1,100
    Bell Atlantic $1,100
    Others $2,200

PAC Totals by Category

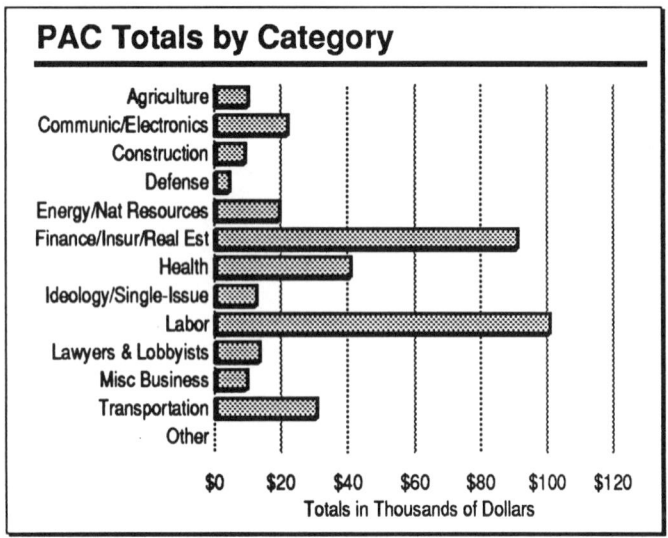

Totals in Thousands of Dollars

472

Other Major Business PACs

National Assn of Realtors	$4,100	Real Estate
National Assn of Home Builders	$3,000	Resid Constr
Walter Industries	$3,000	Resid Constr
Household International	$2,150	Credit/Loans
American Health Care Assn	$2,000	Nursing Home
National Auto Dealers Assn	$2,000	Auto Sales
National Cable Television Assn	$2,000	CableTV
Union Pacific Corp	$2,000	Independ Oil
American Express	$1,800	Credit/Loans
Mortgage Bankers Assn of America	$1,650	MortgageBank
American Society of Travel Agents	$1,600	Travel Agent
Chrysler Corp	$1,600	Auto Mfrs
General Electric	$1,600	NuclearEquip
United Parcel Service	$1,600	Delivery
Coastal Corp	$1,500	Natural Gas
Henley Group Inc	$1,500	Altern Energy
National Utility Contractors Assn	$1,500	Comml Constr
SAPEC/ NJ (New Jersey Savings Assn)	$1,500	SavingsBanks
US League of Savings Assn	$1,200	SavingsBanks
Aircraft Owners & Pilots Assn	$1,100	GenlAviation
American Financial Services Assn	$1,100	Credit/Loans
American Trucking Assns	$1,100	Trucking
CSX Transportation Inc	$1,100	Natural Gas
National Assn of Broadcasters	$1,100	TV/Radio
National Tour Brokers Assn	$1,100	Travel Agent
Owens-Illinois	$1,100	Paper Packg
Public Service Electric & Gas	$1,100	Gas & Electr
Ryder System Inc	$1,100	Car/Trk Rent
Society of Independent Gasoline Marketers	$1,100	Gas Stations
W R Grace & Company	$1,100	Independ Oil
Westinghouse Electric	$1,100	NuclearEquip
Tobacco Institute	$1,050	Tobacco

Labor

Bldg Trades/Industrial/Misc Unions $54,225

Operating Engineers Union*	$8,275
United Auto Workers	$8,100
Carpenters & Joiners Union	$5,500
Plumbers/Pipefitters Union*	$5,300
Laborers' Political League	$5,000
National Education Assn	$4,400
AFL-CIO*	$2,800
(Continued in next column)	

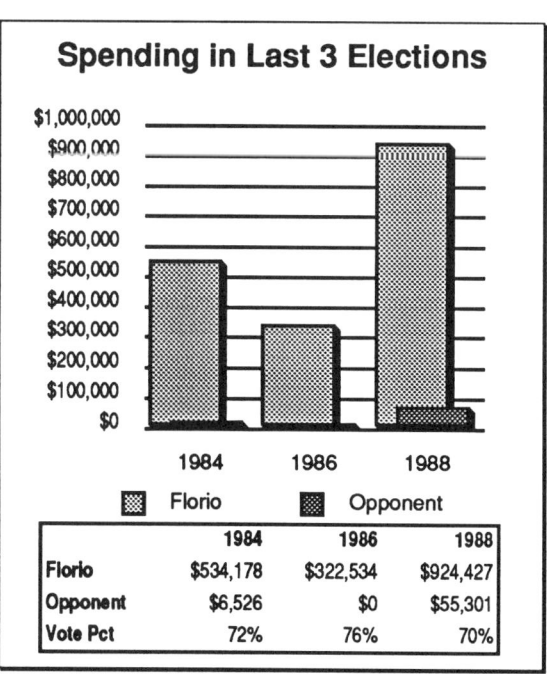

Spending in Last 3 Elections

	1984	1986	1988
Florio	$534,178	$322,534	$924,427
Opponent	$6,526	$0	$55,301
Vote Pct	72%	76%	70%

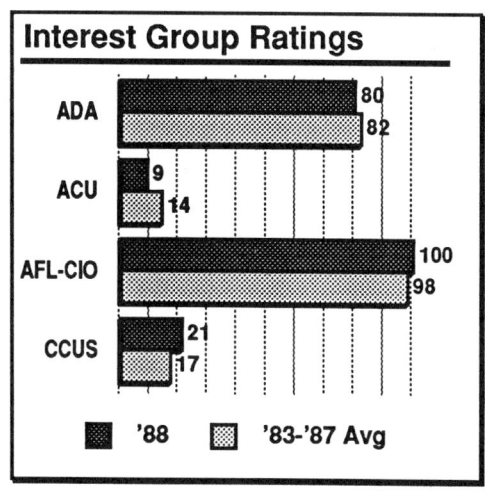

Interest Group Ratings

	'88	'83-'87 Avg
ADA	80	82
ACU	9	14
AFL-CIO	100	98
CCUS	21	17

■ '88   ▨ '83-'87 Avg

Labor (cont'd)

Hotel/Restaurant Employees Union	$2,250
American Federation of Teachers	$1,700
Graphic Communications Union	$1,500
Ladies Garment Workers Union	$1,400
Machinists/Aerospace Workers Union	$1,100
Oil, Chemical & Atomic Workers Union	$1,100
Service Employees International Union	$1,100
Others	$4,700

Government & Postal Workers $15,950

National Assn of Retired Federal Employees	$5,000
American Fedn of State/County/Munic Employees	$3,500
American Postal Workers Union	$2,500
National Assn of Letter Carriers	$1,700
National Rural Letter Carriers Assn	$1,650
National League of Postmasters	$1,100
Others	$500

Transportation Unions $30,000

United Transportation Union	$7,200
Teamsters Union*	$5,800
Air Line Pilots Assn	$5,000
Seafarers International Union	$2,500
Transport Workers Union	$2,400
Transportation Communication Union	$1,800
Amalgamated Transit Union	$1,500
Brotherhood of Locomotive Engineers	$1,100
Brotherhood of Railroad Signalmen	$1,100
Maintenance of Way Employees	$1,100
Others	$500

Ideological/Single-Issue

Democratic Leadership PACs.....................................$10,500

24th Congr Dist of California PAC (Henry Waxman)	$10,000
Others	$500

Independent expenditures supporting Florio

National Cmte to Preserve Social Security	$3,379

---

* Contributions came from more than one PAC affiliated with this sponsor.

Thomas M. Foglietta, D-Pa (1)

First elected: 1980
Total receipts: $335,167
Total from PACs: $172,700

1988 Committees & Subcommittees

Armed Services	**Merchant Marine and Fisheries**
Military Installations and Facilities	Oversight and Investigations (Chairman)
Seapower and Strategic and Critical Materials	Merchant Marine
	Oceanography

PAC Contribution Profile

Business

Commercial Banks	**$4,000**
Fidelity Bank	$1,000
Mellon Bank	$1,000
Others	$2,000
Defense	**$11,000**
Boeing Company	$2,000
McDonnell Douglas*	$1,250
Others	$7,750
Electric Utilities	**$2,500**
Philadelphia Electric	$1,500
Others	$1,000
Health Professionals	**$6,000**
American Academy of Ophthalmology	$2,000
American Medical Assn	$2,000
American Dental Assn	$1,500
Others	$500
Insurance	**$3,750**
Cigna Corp	$1,250
Penn Mutual Life Insurance	$1,000
Others	$1,500
Lawyers & Lobbyists	**$6,250**
Assn of Trial Lawyers of America	$4,500
Others	$1,750
Oil & Gas	**$2,250**
Atlantic Richfield	$1,000
Others	$1,250

Campaign Revenue Sources

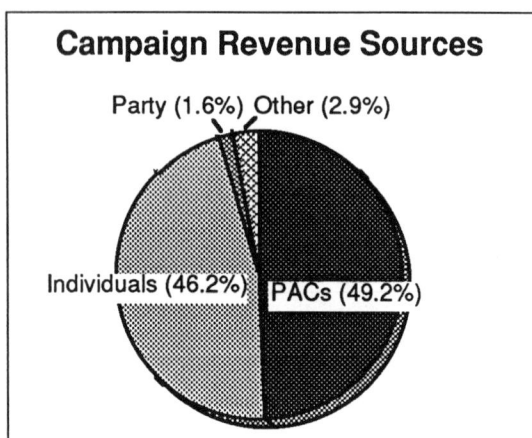

Party (1.6%) Other (2.9%)
Individuals (46.2%)
PACs (49.2%)

Real Estate	**$5,000**
National Assn of Realtors	$5,000
Sea Transport	**$3,750**
American Pilots Assn	$2,000
American President Lines	$1,000
Others	$750
Securities Investment	**$2,500**
Philadelphia Stock Exchange	$2,000
Others	$500

Other Major Business PACs

Waste Management Inc	$1,500	Waste Mgmt
Bethlehem Steel	$1,000	Steel
National Assn of Home Builders	$1,000	Resid Constr
Rohm and Haas Company	$1,000	Chemicals

PAC Totals by Category

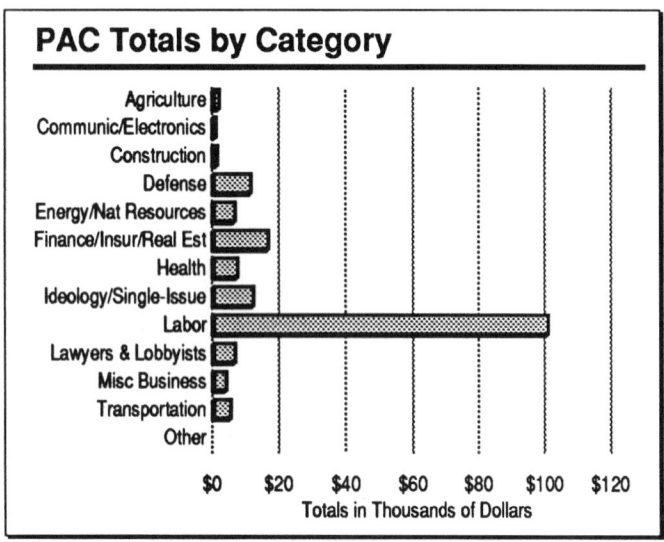

Totals in Thousands of Dollars

Labor

Bldg Trades/Industrial/Misc Unions $48,550

Carpenters & Joiners Union	$6,500
Sheet Metal Workers Union	$5,000
United Steelworkers	$5,000
Comm Workers Union Local #13000	$4,000
United Auto Workers	$4,000
Plumbers/Pipefitters Union*	$3,000
Intl Brotherhood of Electrical Workers*	$2,500
Machinists/Aerospace Workers Union	$2,500
Operating Engineers Union*	$2,500
AFL-CIO*	$2,000
Ladies Garment Workers Union	$2,000
Electronic Machine Furniture Workers	$1,750
Laborers' Political League	$1,750
Amalgamated Clothing & Textile Workers*	$1,500
Food & Commercial Workers Union	$1,500
Hotel/Restaurant Employees Union	$1,500
Others	$1,550

Government & Postal Workers $13,750

American Fedn of State/County/Munic Employees	$5,000
National Assn of Retired Federal Employees	$5,000
National Assn of Letter Carriers	$1,500
American Postal Workers Union	$1,000
Others	$1,250

Sea Transport Unions $13,500

Marine Engineers Union*	$7,500
Seafarers International Union	$3,000
International Longshoremen Assn	$1,500
Masters, Mates & Pilots Union	$1,000
Others	$500

Other Transportation Unions $17,000

Teamsters Union*	$10,000
Amalgamated Transit Union	$2,000
Air Line Pilots Assn	$1,500
United Transportation Union	$1,500
Transport Workers Union	$1,000
Others	$1,000

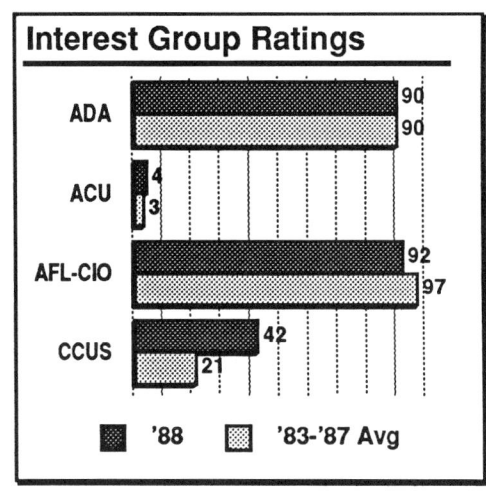

Interest Group Ratings

	'88	'83-'87 Avg
ADA	90	90
ACU	4	3
AFL-CIO	92	97
CCUS	42	21

Teachers Unions $7,500

National Education Assn	$5,000
American Federation of Teachers	$2,500

Ideological/Single-Issue

Democratic Leadership PACs $3,500

America's Leaders' Fund (Dan Rostenkowski)	$1,500
Democratic Candidate Fund (Tip O'Neill)	$1,000
Valley Education Fund (Tony Coelho)	$1,000

Pro-Israel $6,250

National PAC	$5,000
Others	$1,250

Other Major Ideological/Single Issue $2,000

National Cmte to Preserve Social Security	$1,000	Social Secur
Others	$1,000	

Independent expenditures supporting Foglietta

National Cmte to Preserve Social Security	$2,344

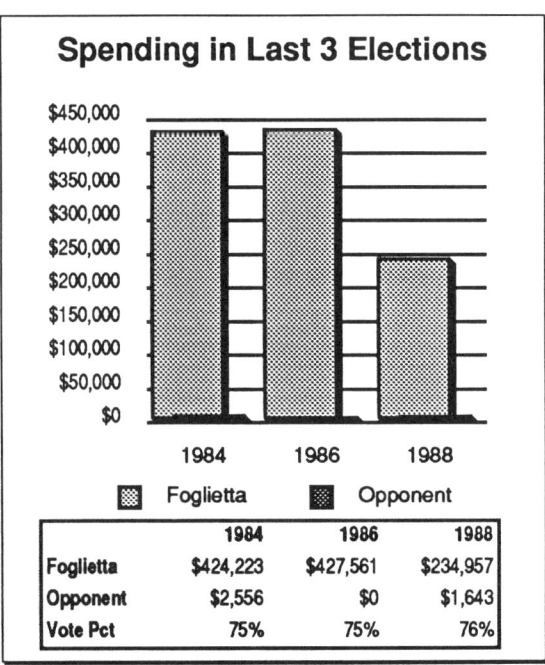

Spending in Last 3 Elections

Foglietta   Opponent

	1984	1986	1988
Foglietta	$424,223	$427,561	$234,957
Opponent	$2,556	$0	$1,643
Vote Pct	75%	75%	76%

---

* Contributions came from more than one PAC affiliated with this sponsor.

Thomas S. Foley, D-Wash (5)

First elected: 1964
Total receipts: $781,195
Total from PACs: $554,640

1988 Committees & Subcommittees

House Majority Leader

Budget

Select Intelligence

PAC Contribution Profile

Business

Automotive & Trucking	**$13,750**
Auto Dealers & Drivers for Free Trade	$3,500
National Auto Dealers Assn	$2,500
American Trucking Assns	$2,000
Others	$5,750
Aviation & Aerospace	**$12,500**
Boeing Company	$8,250
Others	$4,250
Commercial Banks	**$26,100**
American Bankers Assn	$3,500
J P Morgan & Company	$3,500
U S Bancorp	$3,000
Security Pacific Corp	$2,500
Chase Manhattan	$2,000
Others	$11,600
Crop Production & Processing	**$25,050**
Philip Morris	$4,000
National Cotton Council	$2,500
Archer-Daniels-Midland Corp	$2,000
Others	$16,550
Defense	**$18,500**
LTV Aerospace & Defense Company	$2,500
Allied-Signal	$2,000
Lockheed Corp	$2,000
Martin Marietta Corp	$2,000
Others	$10,000

Campaign Revenue Sources

Other (5.7%)

Individuals (22.6%)

PACs (71.7%)

Electric Utilities	**$16,500**
ACRE (Action Committee for Rural Electrification)	$2,500
Others	$14,000
Food & Beverage	**$37,050**
National Beer Wholesalers Assn	$3,000
Nabisco Brands Inc	$2,500
Wine & Spirits Wholesalers of America	$2,500
A E Staley Manufacturers Company	$2,000
American Meat Institute	$2,000
ConAgra Inc	$2,000
Food Marketing Institute	$2,000
Joseph E Seagram & Sons	$2,000
Pepsico Inc	$2,000
Others	$17,050
Forest Products	**$22,965**
Potlatch Corp	$4,999
Weyerhaeuser Company	$3,500
National Forest Products Assn	$3,116
Simpson Investment Company	$2,500
Westvaco Corp	$2,000
Others	$6,850
Health Professionals	**$18,249**
American Dental Assn	$5,000
American Medical Assn	$4,999
American Nurses Assn	$3,000
Others	$5,250
Insurance	**$21,500**
National Assn of Life Underwriters	$5,000
Metropolitan Life Insurance	$4,000
Independent Insurance Agents of America	$2,500
New York Life	$2,000
Others	$8,000
Lawyers & Lobbyists	**$18,541**
Baker & Botts	$2,541
Kirkpatrick & Lockhart	$2,000
Manatt, Phelps, Rothenberg & Tunney	$1,500
Others	$12,500
Oil & Gas	**$21,554**
Coastal Corp	$5,000
Chevron Corp	$2,500
Pennzoil Company	$2,500
Others	$11,554

PAC Totals by Category

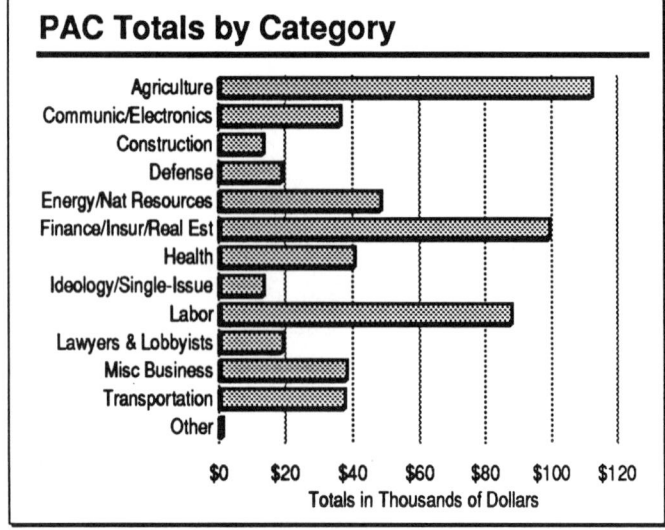

Totals in Thousands of Dollars

Agriculture, Communic/Electronics, Construction, Defense, Energy/Nat Resources, Finance/Insur/Real Est, Health, Ideology/Single-Issue, Labor, Lawyers & Lobbyists, Misc Business, Transportation, Other

$0 $20 $40 $60 $80 $100 $120

Real Estate **$16,000**

    National Assn of Realtors $10,000
    JMB Realty Corp $2,500
    Others $3,500

Savings Banks **$10,155**

    US League of Savings Assn $5,000
    Washington Mutual Savings Bank $2,000
    Others $3,155

Securities & Commodities Investment **$33,500**

    Chicago Mercantile Exchange $10,000
    Bear, Stearns & Company $5,000
    Chicago Board of Trade $5,000
    Morgan Stanley & Company $2,500
    Chicago Board of Options Exchange $2,000
    First Boston Corp $2,000
    Others $7,000

Telecommunications **$17,500**

    AT&T $8,000
    BellSouth Corp* $3,000
    Pacific Northwest Bell $2,000
    Others $4,500

Other Major Business PACs

National Assn of Home Builders	$9,000	Resid Constr
Waste Management Inc	$6,000	Waste Mgmt
American Health Care Assn	$5,000	Nursing Home
National Cable Television Assn	$5,000	Cable TV
National Cmte to Preserve Social Security	$5,000	Society Secur
National Assn of Broadcasters	$4,693	Radio/TV
American Institute of CPA's	$4,000	Accountants
General Electric	$3,000	Electronics
United Parcel Service	$3,000	Delivery
Eli Lilly & Company	$2,250	Pharmaceut
American Assn of Equipment Lessors	$2,000	Rentals
Associated Milk Producers	$2,000	Dairy
Mid-American Dairymen	$2,000	Dairy
Milk Industry Foundation	$2,000	Dairy
National Cattlemen's Assn	$2,000	Livestock
National Venture Capital Assn	$2,000	Venture Cap

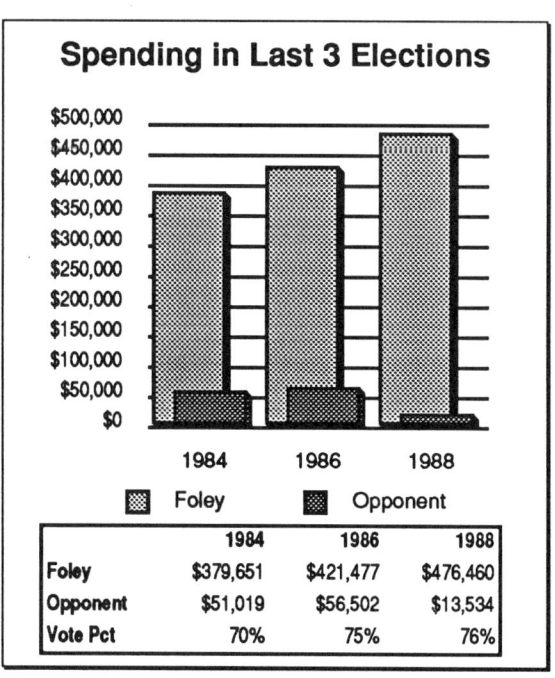

Spending in Last 3 Elections

	1984	1986	1988
Foley	$379,651	$421,477	$476,460
Opponent	$51,019	$56,502	$13,534
Vote Pct	70%	75%	76%

Foley   Opponent

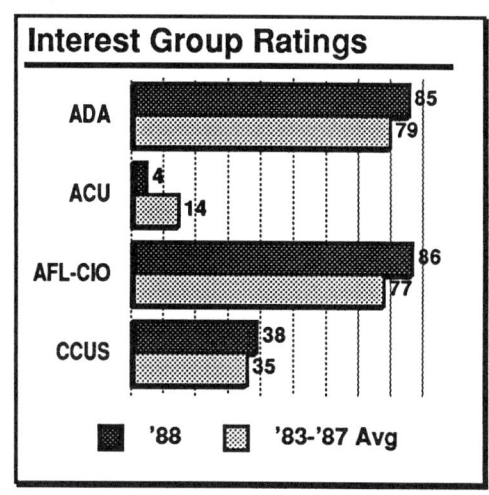

Interest Group Ratings

ADA — 85 ('88), 79 ('83-'87 Avg)
ACU — 4 ('88), 14 ('83-'87 Avg)
AFL-CIO — 86 ('88), 77 ('83-'87 Avg)
CCUS — 38 ('88), 35 ('83-'87 Avg)

■ '88   □ '83-'87 Avg

Labor

Bldg Trades/Industrial/Misc Unions **$45,550**

    National Education Assn $10,000
    Sheet Metal Workers Union $5,000
    United Steelworkers $5,000
    Carpenters & Joiners Union $4,000
    Laborers' Political League $4,000
    Operating Engineers Union* $3,250
    Food & Commercial Workers Union $2,500
    United Auto Workers $2,500
    Plumbers/Pipefitters Union $2,000
    Others $7,300

Government & Postal Workers **$15,000**

    American Fedn of State/County/Munic Employees $5,000
    National Assn of Retired Federal Employees $5,000
    National Rural Letter Carriers Assn $2,000
    Others $3,000

Transportation Unions **$26,750**

    Teamsters Union $7,000
    Air Line Pilots Assn $5,000
    United Transportation Union $3,000
    Marine Engineers Union $2,500
    International Longshoremen Asn $2,000
    Others $7,250

Major Ideological/Single-Issue PACs

National PAC .... $5,000   Pro-Israel

Independent expenditures supporting Foley

National Cmte to Preserve Social Security $4,180

---

* Contributions came from more than one PAC affiliated
with this sponsor.

Harold E. Ford, D-Tenn (9)

First elected: 1974
Total receipts: $298,096
Total from PACs: $210,500

1988 Committees & Subcommittees

Ways and Means
Oversight
Public Assistance and Unemployment Compensation

Select Aging
Health and Long-Term Care

PAC Contribution Profile

Business

Campaign Revenue Sources

Other (12.3%)
Party (1.3%)
Candidate (2.6%)
Individuals (18.8%)
PACs (65.1%)

Airlines & Air Freight	**$13,500**
Federal Express Corp	$10,000
Eastern Airlines	$3,000
Northwest Airlines	$1,000
Others	-$500
Automotive	**$2,000**
Chrysler Corp	$1,000
National Auto Dealers Assn	$1,000
Construction	**$2,086**
National Assn of Home Builders	$1,386
Others	$700
Electric Utilities	**$2,500**
Potomac Electric Power Company	$1,000
Others	$1,500
Financial Institutions	**$2,800**
Tennessee League of Savings Institutions	$1,000
Others	$1,800
Food & Beverage	**$4,500**
Food Marketing Institute	$1,000
Malone & Hyde Inc	$1,000
Stroh Brewery Company	$1,000
Wine & Spirits Wholesalers of America	$1,000
Others	$500

Health Professionals	**$5,250**
American Medical Assn	$1,500
American College of Emergency Physicians	$1,000
American Chiropractic Assn	$1,000
American Dental Assn	$1,000
Others	$750
Insurance	**$12,500**
National Assn of Life Underwriters	$6,000
Provident Life & Accident Insurance	$2,000
American Council of Life Insurance	$1,000
American General Insurance Company	$1,000
Cigna Corp	$1,000
Others	$1,500
Lawyers	**$9,250**
Assn of Trial Lawyers of America	$5,000
Citizens for Better Government	$2,000
Western Enterprise PAC	$1,000
Others	$1,250
Pharmaceuticals	**$4,200**
Schering-Plough Corp	$2,400
Sterling Drug	$1,500
Others	$300
Poultry	**$3,000**
Tyson Foods	$3,000
Railroads	**$3,000**
Norfolk Southern Corp	$1,500
CSX Transportation Inc	$1,000
Others	$500
Real Estate	**$4,500**
National Assn of Realtors	$3,500
Mortgage Bankers Assn of America	$1,000
Telecommunications	**$5,000**
South Central Bell Telephone	$4,500
Others	$500
Tobacco	**$4,000**
Philip Morris	$3,000
Others	$1,000
Trucking/Delivery	**$4,310**
United Parcel Service	$3,770
Others	$540

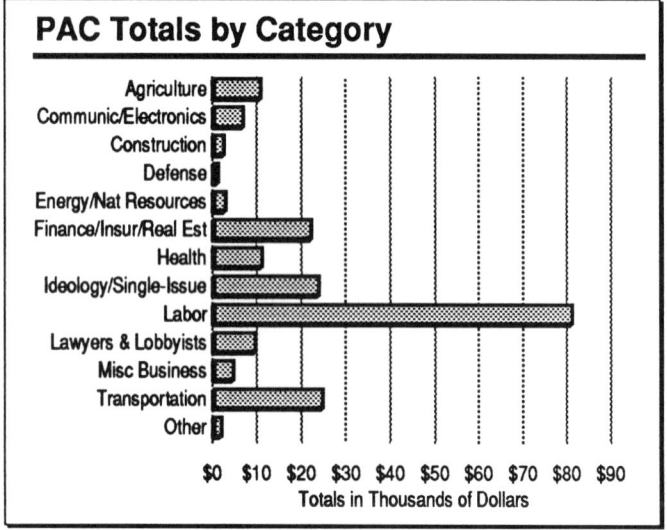

PAC Totals by Category

Agriculture
Communic/Electronics
Construction
Defense
Energy/Nat Resources
Finance/Insur/Real Est
Health
Ideology/Single-Issue
Labor
Lawyers & Lobbyists
Misc Business
Transportation
Other

$0 $10 $20 $30 $40 $50 $60 $70 $80 $90
Totals in Thousands of Dollars

Other Major Business PACs

Employee Stock Ownership Assn	$1,500	Other
Kelso & Company	$1,500	InvestmtBank
Chicago Board of Trade	$1,000	Commodities
J C Penney Company	$1,000	Dept Store
National Medical Enterprises Inc	$1,000	Hospitals
Westinghouse Electric	$1,000	Electronics

Labor

Bldg Trades/Industrial/Misc Unions $22,500

United Auto Workers	$4,000
AFL-CIO	$3,000
Carpenters & Joiners Union	$3,000
Laborers' Political League	$3,000
Machinists/Aerospace Workers Union	$2,000
Hotel/Restaurant Employees Union	$1,500
Amalgamated Clothing & Textile Workers	$1,000
Communications Workers of America	$1,000
Food & Commercial Workers Union	$1,000
Ladies Garment Workers Union	$1,000
Office & Professional Employees Union	$1,000
Plumbers/Pipefitters Union	$1,000

Government & Postal Workers $21,250

National Assn of Letter Carriers	$5,500
National Assn of Retired Federal Employees	$5,000
American Fedn of State/County/Munic Employees	$3,000
National Rural Letter Carriers Assn	$3,000
American Postal Workers Union	$1,500
National Assn of Postmasters	$1,000
National League of Postmasters	$1,000
Others	$1,250

Teachers Unions $9,000

National Education Assn	$5,000
American Federation of Teachers	$4,000

Interest Group Ratings

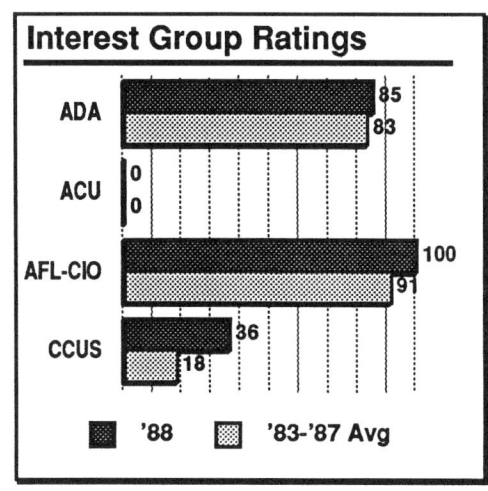

Transportation Unions $28,000

Teamsters Union	$12,000
Seafarers International Union	$5,000
United Transportation Union	$5,000
Marine Engineers District 2 Maritime Officers	$1,000
Maritime Union of America	$1,000
Transport Workers Union	$1,000
Others	$3,000

Ideological/Single-Issue

Democratic Leadership PACs $15,500

Congressional Black Caucus PAC	$8,000
Cmte for the 100th Congress (Charles Rangel)	$5,000
Valley Education Fund (Tony Coelho)	$2,000
Others	$500

Other Major Ideological/Single-Issue PACs

National Cmte to Preserve Social Security	$5,000	Society Secur
Tennesseans for Better Government	$1,500	Pro-Israel
Bethune-Dubois PAC	$1,000	Ethnic

Independent expenditures supporting Ford

National Cmte to Preserve Social Security	$2,022

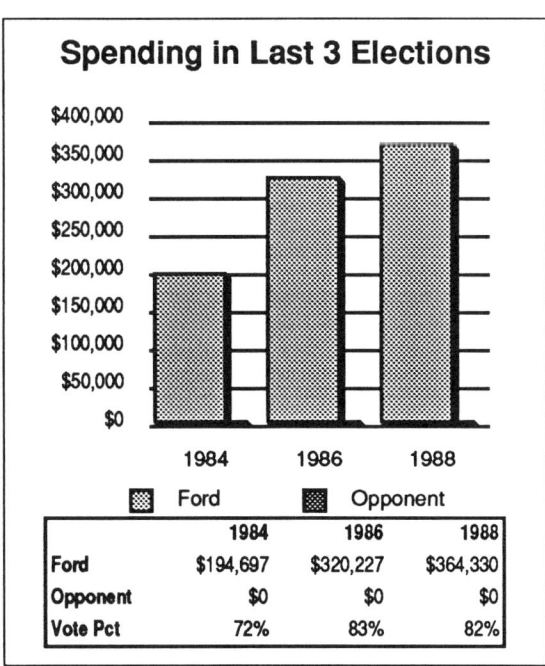

Spending in Last 3 Elections

	1984	1986	1988
Ford	$194,697	$320,227	$364,330
Opponent	$0	$0	$0
Vote Pct	72%	83%	82%

William D. Ford, D-Mich (15)

First elected: 1964
Total receipts: $335,331
Total from PACs: $267,901

1988 Committees & Subcommittees

Education and Labor
Elementary, Secondary and Vocational Education
Health and Safety
Labor-Management Relations
Postsecondary Education

Post Office and Civil Service (Chairman)
Investigations (Chairman)

PAC Contribution Profile

Business

Airlines/Air Freight	**$2,150**
None over $700	
Automotive	**$2,050**
None over $950	
Computers	**$2,450**
Electrocom Automation Inc	$2,000
Others	$450
Electric Utilities	**$2,390**
None over $940	
Employment Agencies	**$2,000**
Kelly Service Inc	$1,000
National Assn of Temporary Services	$1,000
Financial Institutions	**$5,760**
American Bankers Assn	$3,000
Michigan Credit Union League	$1,310
Michigan League of Savings Institutions	$1,000
Others	$450
Food & Beverage	**$3,400**
None over $850	
Health Professionals	**$5,900**
American Dental Assn	$3,000
Others	$2,900

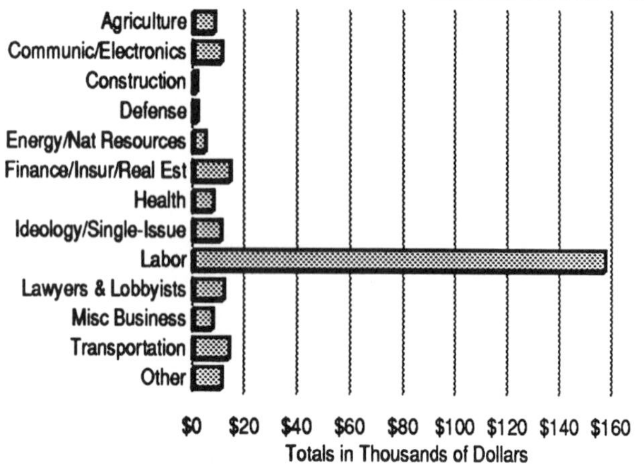

Campaign Revenue Sources

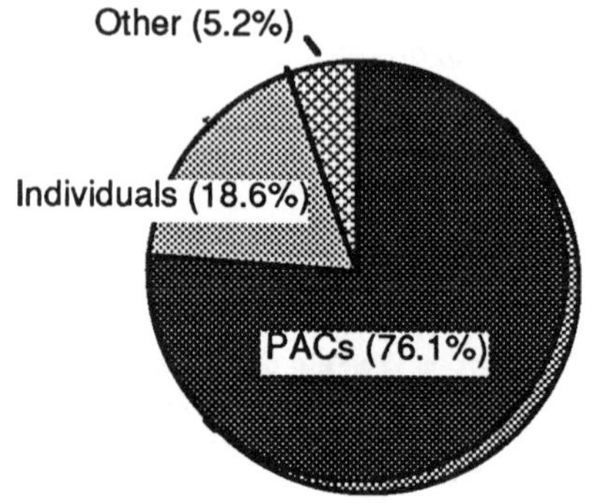

Other (5.2%)
Individuals (18.6%)
PACs (76.1%)

Insurance	**$5,700**
CNA Financial Corp	$2,400
National Assn of Life Underwriters	$2,000
Others	$1,300
Lawyers & Lobbyists	**$11,350**
Assn of Trial Lawyers of America	$10,000
Others	$1,350
Telecommunications	**$5,850**
Michigan Bell Telephone	$2,400
AT&T	$2,000
Others	$1,450
Tobacco	**$2,200**
Philip Morris	$1,000
Tobacco Institute	$850
Brown & Williamson Tobacco	$350
Trucking/Delivery	**$8,500**
United Parcel Service	$6,950
Others	$1,550
Vocational Tech Schools	**$10,490**
National Assn of Trade/Tech Schools	$4,700
Assn of Independent Colleges/Schools	$3,440
National Assn of Cosmetology Schools	$2,000
Others	$350

Other Major Business PACs

Higher Education Mgmt/Resources Found	$1,050	Credit/Loans
American Hospital Assn	$1,000	Hospitals
Associated Milk Producers	$1,000	Dairy

PAC Totals by Category

Agriculture
Communic/Electronics
Construction
Defense
Energy/Nat Resources
Finance/Insur/Real Est
Health
Ideology/Single-Issue
Labor
Lawyers & Lobbyists
Misc Business
Transportation
Other

$0 $20 $40 $60 $80 $100 $120 $140 $160
Totals in Thousands of Dollars

Labor

Bldg Trades, Industrial & Misc Unions $40,915

Machinists/Aerospace Workers Union $7,600
Operating Engineers Union* $6,590
Carpenters & Joiners Union $5,000
Int'l Brotherhood of Electrical Workers $4,000
Laborers' Political League $3,450
Food & Commercial Workers Union $3,220
Plumbers/Pipefitters Union* $1,680
Boilermakers Union* $1,375
AFL-CIO* $1,100
Communications Workers of America $1,100
Hotel/Restaurant Employees Union $1,000
Ironworkers Union $1,000
United Steelworkers $1,000
Others $2,800

Government & Postal Workers $64,865

American Fedn of State/County/Munic Employees $10,000
American Postal Workers Union $10,000
National Assn of Letter Carriers $10,000
National Assn of Retired Federal Employees $10,000
National Rural Letter Carriers Assn $6,000
National Assn of Postmasters $4,600
National Assn of Postal Supervisors $2,750
National League of Postmasters $2,590
American Federation of Government Employees $2,515
National Star Route Mail Contractors $1,940
National Treasury Employees Union $1,770
National Federation of Federal Employees $1,100
Others $1,600

Teachers Unions $13,800

National Education Assn $9,500
American Federation of Teachers $4,300

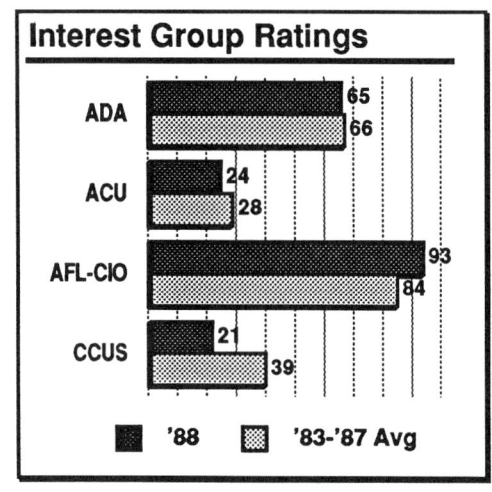

Interest Group Ratings

	'88	'83-'87 Avg
ADA	65	66
ACU	24	28
AFL-CIO	93	84
CCUS	21	39

Transportation Unions $37,200

United Auto Workers $10,000
Air Line Pilots Assn $5,000
Marine Engineers Union $5,000
Teamsters Union $5,000
Seafarers International Union $3,000
Amalgamated Transit Union $2,500
National Assn of Air Traffic Specialists $1,550
Brotherhood of Locomotive Engineers $1,200
Transport Workers Union $1,000
Others $2,950

Ideological/Single-Issue

Ideological/Single-Issue PACs $10,340

KidsPAC	$3,000	Health/Welfare
MOPAC	$2,500	Pro-Israel
Armenian Assembly of America	$1,000	Ethnic
Armenian-American PAC	$1,000	Ethnic
Valley Education Fund (Tony Coelho)	$1,000	Dem Leaders
Others	$1,840	

Independent Expenditures supporting Ford

Teamsters Union $2,000

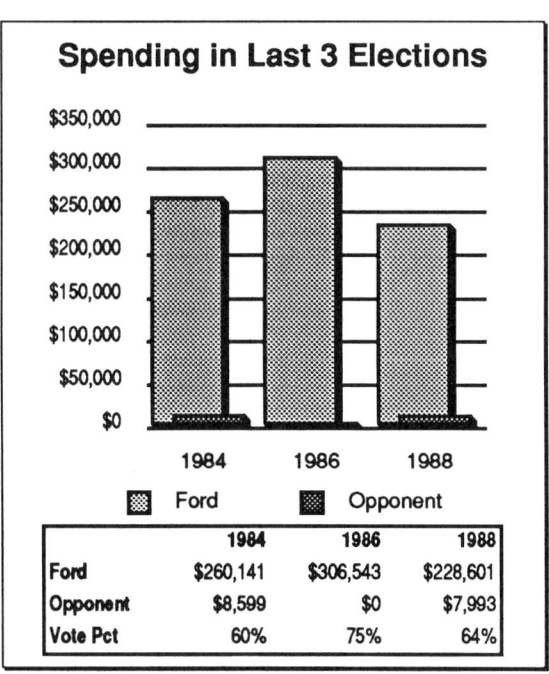

Spending in Last 3 Elections

	1984	1986	1988
Ford	$260,141	$306,543	$228,601
Opponent	$8,599	$0	$7,993
Vote Pct	60%	75%	64%

Ford   Opponent

---

* Contributions came from more than one PAC affiliated with this sponsor.

Barney Frank, D-Mass (4)

First elected: 1980
Total receipts: $431,299
Total from PACs: $141,635

1988 Committees & Subcommittees

Banking, Finance and Urban Affairs
Domestic Monetary Policy
Financial Institutions Supervision, Regulation and Insurance
Housing and Community Development

Government Operations
Employment and Housing
Legislation and National Security

Judiciary
Administrative Law and Governmental Relations (Chairman)
Immigration, Refugees and International Law

Select Aging
Health and Long-Term Care

PAC Contribution Profile

Business

Accountants	**$5,500**
American Institute of CPA's	$5,000
Others	$500
Broadcasting/Entertainment	**$4,500**
National Assn of Broadcasters	$1,500
Motion Picture Assn of America	$1,000
Others	$2,000
Commercial Banks	**$42,725**
J P Morgan & Company	$10,000
American Bankers Assn	$7,500
Citicorp	$3,000
Security Pacific Corp	$3,000
Chemical Bank	$2,500
Continental Illinois Corp	$2,500
Barnett Banks of Florida	$2,000
Chase Manhattan	$2,000
Bank of Boston	$1,750
Manufacturers Hanover	$1,575
Assn of Bank Holding Companies	$1,000
Bankers Trust	$1,000
First Chicago Corp	$1,000
Marine Midland Banks	$1,000
Others	$2,900
Construction	**$8,000**
National Assn of Home Builders	$4,500
Manville Corp	$1,000
Others	$2,500

Campaign Revenue Sources

PACs (36.4%)
Individuals (63.5%)

Health Professionals	**$3,350**
American Medical Assn	$1,350
Co-op of American Physicians	$1,000
Others	$1,000
Insurance	**$4,000**
New England Mutual Life	$1,500
John Hancock Financial Service	$1,000
Others	$1,500
Lawyers	**$8,500**
Assn of Trial Lawyers of America	$5,000
Lane & Edson	$1,000
Swidler & Berlin	$1,000
Others	$1,500
Real Estate/Mortgage Banking	**$3,500**
Mortgage Bankers Assn of America	$1,500
National Assn of Realtors	$1,500
Others	$500
Retail Sales	**$2,800**
Federated Department Stores	$1,000
International Council of Shopping Centers	$1,000
Others	$800
Savings Banks & Credit Unions	**$4,500**
National Council of Savings Institutions	$1,600
US League of Savings Assn	$1,500
Others	$1,400
Securities & Investment	**$3,100**
Shearson Lehman Hutton	$2,100
Dean Witter Reynolds*	$1,000
Telecommunications	**$4,000**
AT&T	$2,000
New England Tel & Tel	$2,000

PAC Totals by Category

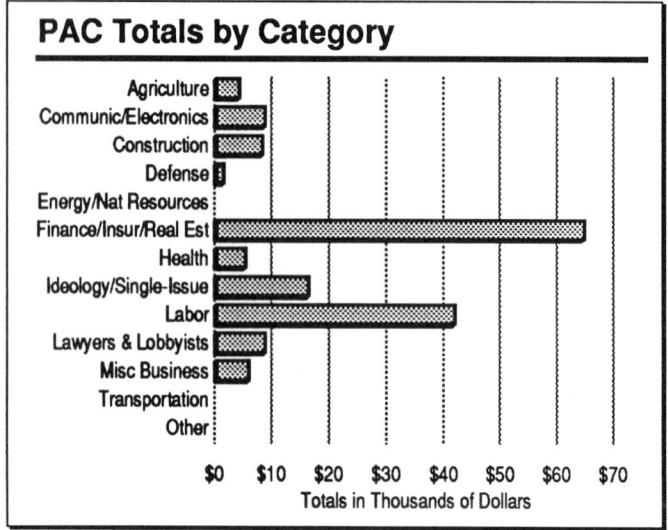

Agriculture
Communic/Electronics
Construction
Defense
Energy/Nat Resources
Finance/Insur/Real Est
Health
Ideology/Single-Issue
Labor
Lawyers & Lobbyists
Misc Business
Transportation
Other

$0 $10 $20 $30 $40 $50 $60 $70
Totals in Thousands of Dollars

Other Major Business PACs

Milk Industry Foundation	$2,000	Dairy
Food Marketing Institute	$1,500	Food Stores
American Textile Manufacturers Institute	$1,000	Textiles
American Health Care Assn	$1,000	Nursing Home

Labor

Bldg Trades/Industrial/Misc Unions	**$17,049**
United Auto Workers	$2,500
Carpenters & Joiners Union	$1,500
Intl Brotherhood of Electrical Workers	$1,500
Laborers' Political League	$1,500
Bricklayers Union	$1,250
Food & Commercial Workers Union	$1,249
AFL-CIO*	$1,000
Machinists/Aerospace Workers Union	$1,000
Operating Engineers Union	$1,000
Plumbers/Pipefitters Union	$1,000
Others	$3,550
Government & Postal Workers	**$9,250**
National Assn of Retired Federal Employees	$5,000
American Fedn of State/County/Munic Employees	$2,000
American Postal Workers Union	$1,000
Others	$1,250
Teachers Unions	**$2,000**
American Federation of Teachers	$1,000
National Education Assn	$1,000
Transportation Unions	**$13,250**
Teamsters Union	$10,000
Air Line Pilots Assn	$1,000
Seafarers International Union	$1,000
Others	$1,250

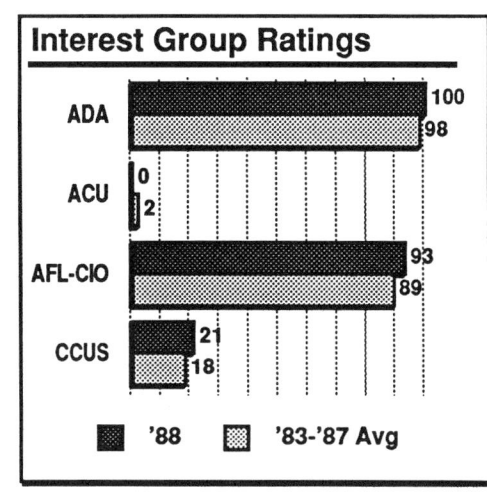

Interest Group Ratings

Group	'88	'83-'87 Avg
ADA	100	98
ACU	0	2
AFL-CIO	93	89
CCUS	21	18

Ideological/Single-Issue

Ideological/Single-Issue		**$16,000**
Emily's List	$5,000	WomensIssues
Human Rights Campaign Fund	$5,000	Gay Rights
KidsPAC	$3,000	HealthWelfare
Valley Education Fund (Tony Coelho)	$1,000	Dem Leaders
Others	$2,000	

Independent expenditures supporting Frank

National Cmte to Preserve Social Security	$1,762

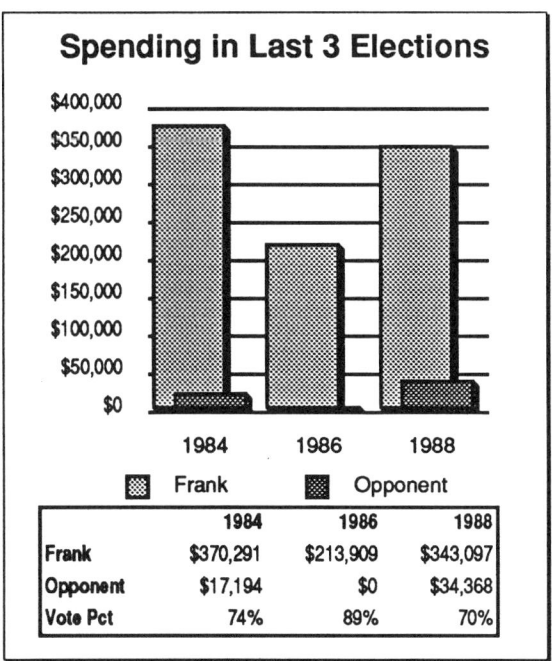

Spending in Last 3 Elections

	1984	1986	1988
Frank	$370,291	$213,909	$343,097
Opponent	$17,194	$0	$34,368
Vote Pct	74%	89%	70%

Frank ▨ Opponent ▩

---

* Contributions came from more than one PAC affiliated with this sponsor.

Bill Frenzel, R-Minn (3)

First elected: 1970
Total receipts: $497,281
Total from PACs: $301,078

1988 Committees & Subcommittees

House Administration (Ranking Republican)
Elections
Libraries and Memorials

Ways and Means
Public Assistance and Unemployment Compensation
Social Security
Trade

PAC Contribution Profile

Business

Campaign Revenue Sources

Other (9.3%)
Individuals (29.9%)
PACs (60.6%)

Accountants **$8,250**
American Institute of CPA's $5,000
Ernst & Whinney $1,500
Arthur Andersen & Company $1,000
Others $750

Automotive **$14,000**
Auto Dealers & Drivers for Free Trade $7,500
National Auto Dealers Assn $4,000
General Motors $1,000
Others $1,500

Commercial Banks **$18,500**
American Bankers Assn $5,000
J P Morgan & Company $5,000
Citicorp $3,000
Norwest Corp $1,500
Barnett Banks of Florida $1,000
Others $3,000

Construction **$9,350**
National Assn of Home Builders $2,000
American Supply Assn $1,000
Associated Builders & Contractors $1,000
Associated General Contractors $1,000
Others $4,350

Defense **$8,250**
Textron Inc $1,500
United Technologies $1,500
Northrop Corp $1,000
Others $4,250

Food & Beverage **$18,800**
National Restaurant Assn $2,000
Wine & Spirits Wholesalers of America $2,000
General Mills* $1,500
National Beer Wholesalers Assn $1,500
ConAgra Inc $1,150
Food Marketing Institute $1,000
Pepsico Inc $1,000
Pillsbury Company $1,000
Others $7,650

Health Professionals **$15,000**
American Medical Assn $7,000
American Dental Assn $3,000
Oral & Maxillofacial Surgeons $1,500
American Academy of Ophthalmology $1,000
American College of Emergency Physicians $1,000
Cmte for Quality Orthopedic Health Care $1,000
Others $500

Insurance **$50,197**
National Assn of Life Underwriters $10,000
Associated Life Insurance $4,000
Equitable Financial Services $3,000
Torchmark Corp $2,500
American Council of Life Insurance $2,247
Northwestern Mutual Life $2,000
Prudential Insurance $2,000
Independent Insurance Agents of America $1,500
Travelers Corp $1,500
Northwestern National Life $1,050
Aetna Life & Casualty $1,000
American International Group inc $1,000
Chubb Corp $1,000
Cigna Corp $1,000
Connecticut Mutual Life Insurance $1,000
Guardian Life Insurance $1,000
Health Insurance Assn of America $1,000
Lincoln National Corp $1,000
Mutual of Omaha* $1,000
National Assn Mutual Insurance Agents $1,000
National Assn of Independent Insurers $1,000
New England Mutual Life $1,000
Others $8,400

Oil & Gas **$8,250**
Atlantic Richfield $1,000
Exxon Corp $1,000
Mobil Oil $1,000
Others $5,250

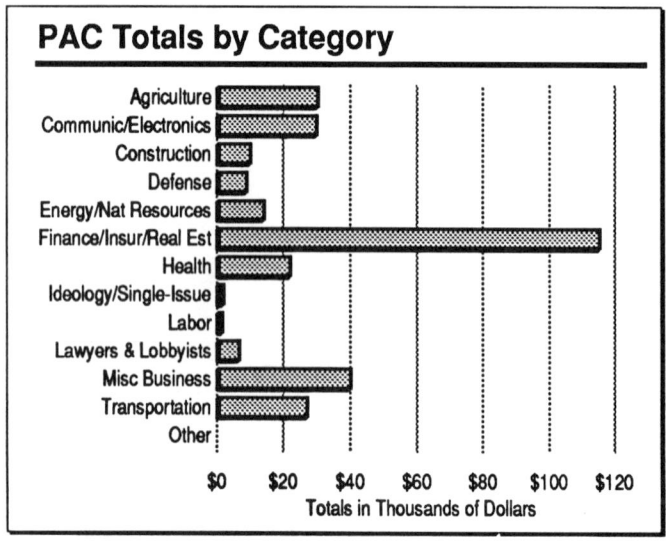

PAC Totals by Category

Agriculture
Communic/Electronics
Construction
Defense
Energy/Nat Resources
Finance/Insur/Real Est
Health
Ideology/Single-Issue
Labor
Lawyers & Lobbyists
Misc Business
Transportation
Other

$0 $20 $40 $60 $80 $100 $120
Totals in Thousands of Dollars

Interest Group Ratings

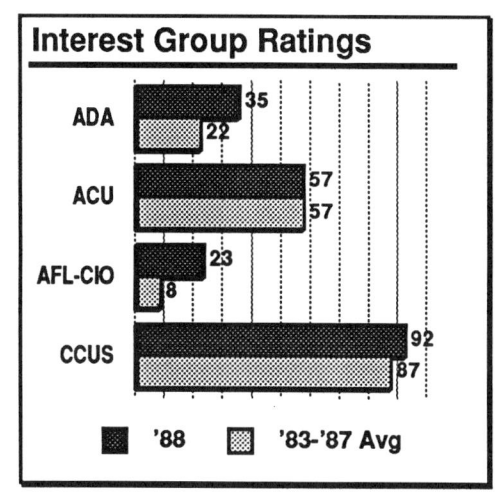

	'88	'83-'87 Avg
ADA	35	22
ACU	57	57
AFL-CIO	23	8
CCUS	92	87

Real Estate **$12,500**

National Assn of Realtors	$10,000
National Realty Committee	$1,000
Others	$1,500

Retail Sales **$8,900**

Dayton Hudson Corp	$1,000
International Council of Shopping Centers	$1,000
International Mass Retail Assn	$1,000
J C Penney Company	$1,000
Montgomery Ward	$1,000
Sears	$1,000
Others	$2,900

Securities & Commodities Investment **$15,040**

First Boston Corp	$2,000
Securities Industry Assn	$2,000
Dain Bosworth	$1,500
Chicago Board of Trade	$1,000
Goldman Sachs	$1,000
Merrill Lynch	$1,000
Morgan Stanley & Company	$1,000
Prudential-Bache Securities	$1,000
Public Securities Assn	$1,000
Salomon Brothers	$1,000
Others	$2,540

Telecommunications **$19,250**

AT&T	$5,500
Northwestern Bell Telephone	$5,000
Ameritech Corp	$1,500
BellSouth Corp	$1,250
Continental Telecom	$1,000
United Telecommunications	$1,000
Others	$4,000

Other Major Business PACs

National Venture Capital Assn	$4,000	Venture Cap
Philip Morris	$3,500	Tobacco
American Assn of Equipment Lessors	$2,500	Rentals
Southern Minnesota Beet Sugar Co-op	$2,500	Sugar
US League of Savings Assn	$2,500	SavingsBanks
Boeing Company	$2,000	Aircraft
Ecolab Inc	$2,000	BusinessSvcs
FMC Corp	$2,000	Chemicals
Honeywell Inc	$2,000	Electronics
Minnesota Truck Operators	$2,000	Trucking
Premark International	$2,000	PlasticRubb
Associated Milk Producers	$1,500	Dairy
Baker & Hostetler	$1,500	Lawyers
Cargill Inc	$1,500	Grain Trader
Deere & Company	$1,500	Farm Equip
National Custom Brokers Assn	$1,500	BusinessSvcs
General Electric	$1,150	Electronics
Abbott Laboratories	$1,000	Pharmaceut
American Crystal Sugar Corp	$1,000	Sugar
American Trucking Assns	$1,000	Trucking
Burlington Northern	$1,000	Railroads
Credit Union National Assn	$1,000	Credit Union
Dow Chemical*	$1,000	Chemicals
Hallmark Cards	$1,000	Publishing
International Paper Company	$1,000	Paper Prod
Marriott Corp	$1,000	Hotel/Motel
Mid-American Dairymen	$1,000	Dairy
National Council of Savings Institutions	$1,000	SavingsBanks
NCR Corp	$1,000	Computers
Pfizer Inc	$1,000	Pharmaceut
Potlatch Corp	$1,000	Forestry
Tobacco Institute	$1,000	Tobacco
Union Pacific Corp	$1,000	Railroads
Xerox Corp	$1,000	Off Machines

Major Labor PACs

Marine Engrs District 2 Maritime Officers	$1,000	Seamen Union

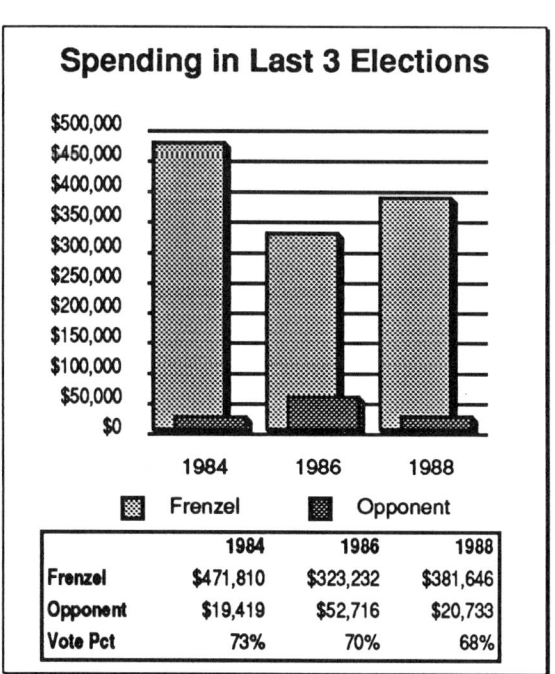

Spending in Last 3 Elections

	1984	1986	1988
Frenzel	$471,810	$323,232	$381,646
Opponent	$19,419	$52,716	$20,733
Vote Pct	73%	70%	68%

Frenzel · Opponent

---

* Contributions came from more than one PAC affiliated with this sponsor.

Martin Frost, D-Texas (24)

First elected: 1978
Total receipts: $590,973
Total from PACs: $298,373

1988 Committees & Subcommittees

Budget
Health (Chairman)
Budget Process
Defense and International Affairs

Rules
Legislative Process

PAC Contribution Profile

Business

Commercial Banks	**$27,650**
NCNB Corp*	$8,600
American Bankers Assn	$3,000
Chemical Bank	$2,000
MBank	$2,000
Bankers Trust	$1,500
Texas Commerce Bancshares*	$1,200
Chase Manhattan	$1,000
Citicorp	$1,000
Irving Bank	$1,000
Marine Midland Banks	$1,000
Security Pacific Corp	$1,000
Others	$4,350
Defense	**$12,000**
LTV Aerospace & Defense Company	$6,000
Textron Inc	$2,500
General Dynamics	$1,000
McDonnell Douglas	$1,000
Others	$1,500
Electric Utilities	**$10,050**
Texas Utilities Electric Company*	$4,000
Houston Industries	$1,000
Others	$5,050
Electronics & Computers	**$9,500**
Recognition Equipment Inc	$4,500
Electronic Data Systems	$3,500
Others	$1,500

Campaign Revenue Sources

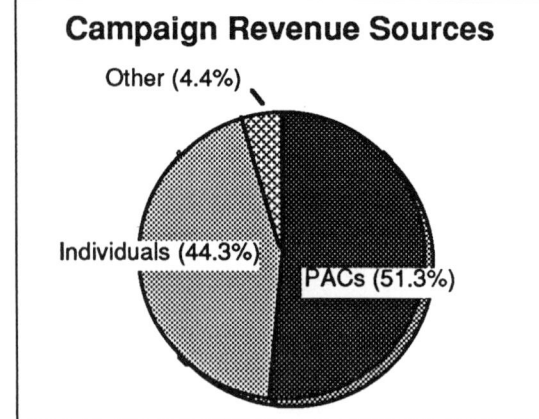

Other (4.4%)
Individuals (44.3%)
PACs (51.3%)

Health Professionals	**$20,250**
American Dental Assn	$3,000
Texas Medical Assn	$3,000
American Optometric Assn	$2,500
American Podiatry Assn	$2,500
American Academy of Ophthalmology	$1,500
American Society Cataract/Refractive Surgery	$1,500
American College of Emergency Physicians	$1,000
American Medical Assn	$1,000
American Nurses Assn	$1,000
Cmte for Quality Orthopedic Health Care	$1,000
Others	$2,250
Hospitals	**$11,750**
American Hospital Assn	$5,000
Voluntary Hospitals of America	$4,500
Others	$2,250
Insurance	**$11,973**
National Assn of Life Underwriters	$4,000
Independent Insurance Agents of America	$1,673
Travelers Corp	$1,500
Blue Cross & Blue Shield Assn	$1,000
Others	$3,800
Lawyers	**$20,150**
Assn of Trial Lawyers of America	$5,000
Johnson & Gibbs	$3,000
Akin, Gump, Hauer & Feld	$2,500
Vinson, Elkins, Searls, Connally & Smith	$2,000
Kutak, Rock & Campbell	$1,600
Lidell, Sapp	$1,100
Camp, Barsh, Bates & Tate	$1,000
Jones, Day, Reavis & Pogue	$1,000
Shank, Irwin, Conant, Lipshy, & Casterline	$1,000
Winstead, McGuire, Sechrest & Minick	$1,000
Others	$950
Oil & Gas	**$17,696**
Enserch Corp	$4,000
Valero Energy Corp	$2,846
Atlantic Richfield	$1,700
Halliburton Company*	$1,500
Internorth Inc	$1,100
Others	$6,550
Real Estate	**$11,500**
National Assn of Realtors	$8,000
Trammell Crow Company	$2,000
Mortgage Bankers Assn of America	$1,000
Others	$500

PAC Totals by Category

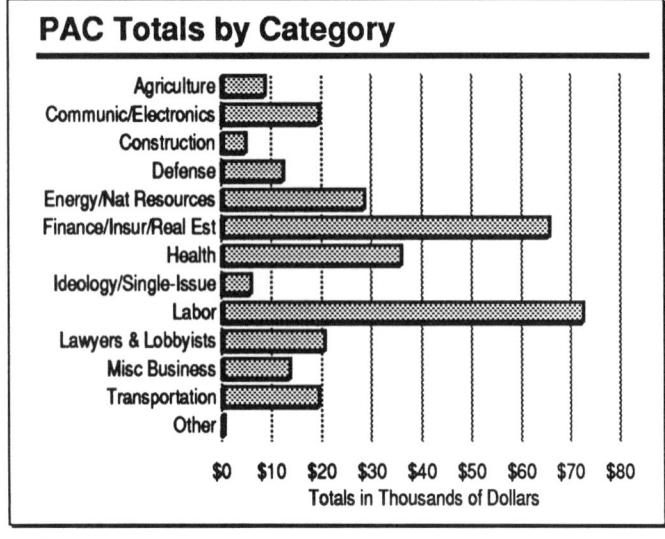

Agriculture
Communic/Electronics
Construction
Defense
Energy/Nat Resources
Finance/Insur/Real Est
Health
Ideology/Single-Issue
Labor
Lawyers & Lobbyists
Misc Business
Transportation
Other

$0 $10 $20 $30 $40 $50 $60 $70 $80
Totals in Thousands of Dollars

Retail Sales $9,000

J C Penney Company	$3,100
Zale Corp	$2,000
Federated Department Stores	$1,000
International Council of Shopping Centers	$1,000
Montgomery Ward	$1,000
Others	$900

Securities & Commodities Investment $8,000

Chicago Mercantile Exchange	$1,500
Securities Industry Assn*	$1,500
First Boston Corp	$1,000
Merrill Lynch	$1,000
Morgan Stanley & Company	$1,000
Others	$2,000

Telecommunications $8,500

AT&T	$3,000
GTE (Southwest)	$3,000
Southwestern Bell	$2,500

Other Major Business PACs

National Auto Dealers Assn	$5,000	Auto Sales
Associated Milk Producers	$3,500	Dairy
American Airlines	$2,500	Airlines
National Assn of Home Builders	$2,500	Resid Constr
Gulf + Western Industries	$2,000	Credit/Loans
Pepsico Inc	$1,500	Food & Bevrg
US League of Savings Assn	$1,500	Savings Banks
United Parcel Service	$1,250	Delivery
American Trucking Assns	$1,020	Trucking
American Financial Services Assn	$1,000	Credit/Loans
Associated General Contractors	$1,000	Comml Constr
Credit Union National Assn	$1,000	Credit Union
Eastern Airlines	$1,000	Airlines
Federal Express Corp	$1,000	Delivery
S & A Restaurant Corp	$1,000	Restaurants
Swift Independent Corp	$1,000	Meat Process
Union Pacific Corp	$1,000	Railroads
Waste Management Inc	$1,000	Waste Mgmt

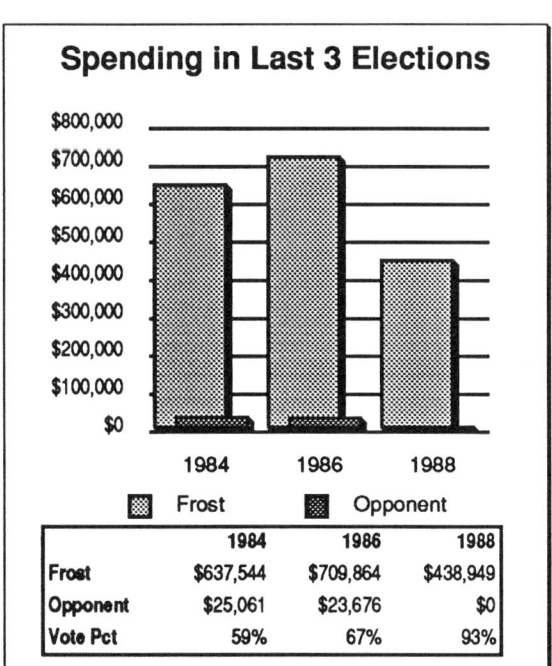

Spending in Last 3 Elections

	1984	1986	1988
Frost	$637,544	$709,864	$438,949
Opponent	$25,061	$23,676	$0
Vote Pct	59%	67%	93%

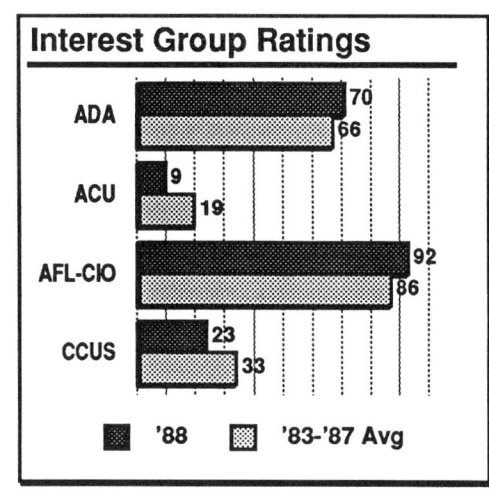

Interest Group Ratings

ADA 70 / 66
ACU 9 / 19
AFL-CIO 92 / 86
CCUS 23 / 33

■ '88   ▨ '83-'87 Avg

Labor

Bldg Trades/Industrial/Misc Unions $40,650

United Auto Workers	$10,000
Intl Brotherhood of Electrical Workers*	$6,100
Machinists/Aerospace Workers Union	$5,000
Food & Commercial Workers Union	$4,000
Carpenters & Joiners Union	$3,500
Operating Engineers Union	$3,500
Communications Workers of America	$3,350
Office & Professional Employees Union	$2,100
Laborers' Political League	$1,500
United Steelworkers	$1,000
Others	$600

Government, Postal & Teachers Unions $15,450

National Education Assn	$7,500
National Assn of Letter Carriers	$3,000
American Postal Workers Union	$2,000
American Fedn of State/County/Munic Employees	$1,000
National Assn of Retired Federal Employees	$1,000
Others	$950

Transportation Unions $16,000

Teamsters Union	$6,000
Seafarers International Union	$3,000
Transport Workers Union	$3,000
United Transportation Union	$3,000
Transportation Communication Union	$1,000

Major Ideological/Single-Issue PACs

National PAC	$5,000	Pro-Israel

---

* Contributions came from more than one PAC affiliated
with this sponsor.

Elton Gallegly, R-Calif (21)

First elected: 1986
Total receipts: $506,391
Total from PACs: $163,825

1988 Committees & Subcommittees

Interior and Insular Affairs
Insular and International Affairs
National Parks and Public Lands
Water and Power Resources

Small Business
Procurement, Innovation and Minority Enterprise Development
Regulation and Business Opportunities

PAC Contribution Profile

Business

Automotive	*$10,100*
Auto Dealers & Drivers for Free Trade	$9,000
Others	$1,100
Commercial & Savings Banks	*$7,000*
Valley Federal Savings & Loan	$2,200
Great Western Financial Corp	$1,200
Others	$3,600
Construction	*$13,350*
National Assn of Home Builders	$6,000
Sheet Metal/AirCon Contractors	$1,750
Pacifica PAC	$1,700
Associated General Contractors	$1,550
National Electrical Contractors Assn	$1,000
Others	$1,350
Dairy	*$2,500*
Associated Milk Producers	$2,500
Defense	*$20,850*
Lockheed Corp	$5,000
Hughes Aircraft	$3,700
Northrop Corp	$3,250
Emerson Electric	$2,250
Veda Inc	$1,350
Harris Corp	$1,200
Rockwell International	$1,000
Others	$3,100

Campaign Revenue Sources

Party (1.8%) Other (1.4%)
PACs (31.3%)
Individuals (65.5%)

Electric Utilities	*$3,850*
Southern California Edison	$1,000
Others	$2,850
Food & Beverage	*$3,350*
Nabisco Brands Inc	$1,250
National Restaurant Assn	$1,000
Others	$1,100
Fruits & Vegetables	*$2,200*
Sunkist Growers	$1,700
Others	$500
Health Professionals	*$12,450*
American Medical Assn	$6,200
American Academy of Ophthalmology	$2,500
Co-op of American Physicians	$2,100
Others	$1,650
Insurance	*$4,550*
National Assn of Life Underwriters	$1,500
Farmers Group Inc	$1,100
Others	$1,950
Oil & Gas	*$26,411*
Litton Industries	$11,000
Atlantic Richfield	$1,550
Chevron Corp	$1,550
Pacific Enterprises	$1,100
Halliburton Company	$1,000
Mobil Oil	$1,000
Shell Oil	$1,000
Union Oil	$1,000
Others	$7,211
Real Estate	*$12,250*
National Assn of Realtors	$8,450
Newhall Land & Farming Company	$2,700
Others	$1,100
Retail Sales	*$3,200*
J C Penney Company	$1,100
Others	$2,100

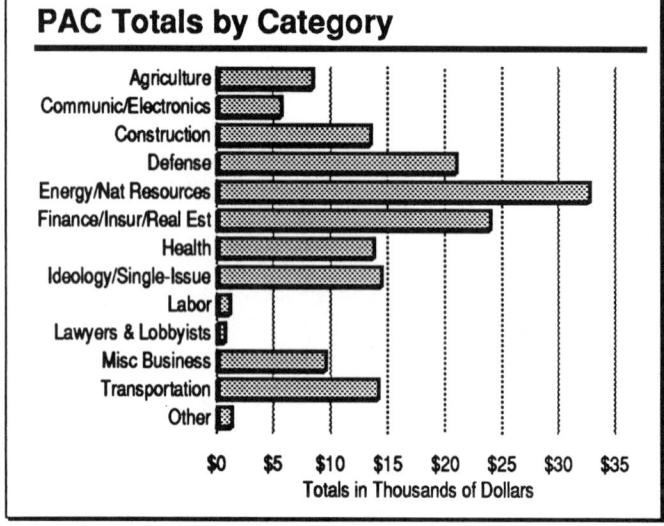

PAC Totals by Category

Agriculture
Communic/Electronics
Construction
Defense
Energy/Nat Resources
Finance/Insur/Real Est
Health
Ideology/Single-Issue
Labor
Lawyers & Lobbyists
Misc Business
Transportation
Other

$0 $5 $10 $15 $20 $25 $30 $35
Totals in Thousands of Dollars

Telecommunications **$4,300**
    GTE Corp $1,900
    Others $2,400

Other Major Business PACs

United Parcel Service	$2,250	Delivery
PGA Tour Inc	$1,050	Pro Sports
Republic Media Group	$1,050	Unknown
Philip Morris	$1,000	Tobacco
Walt Disney Company	$1,000	Resorts

Ideological/Single-Issue

Ideological/Single-Issue **$14,286**

National PAC	$5,000	Pro-Israel
National Rifle Assn	$4,950	Pro-Guns
Bernson PAC	$1,000	NonCong Cand
Women's Pro-Israel National PAC	$1,000	Pro-Israel
Others	$2,336	

Major Labor PACs

Marine Engrs District 2 Maritime Officers	$1,000	Seamens Union

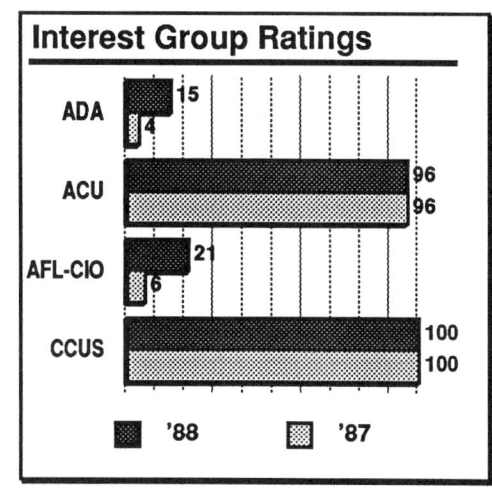

Interest Group Ratings

	'88	'87
ADA	15	4
ACU	96	96
AFL-CIO	21	6
CCUS	100	100

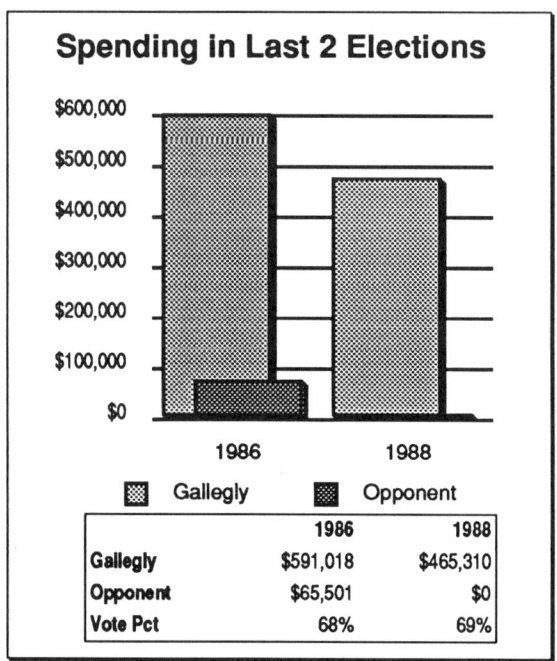

Spending in Last 2 Elections

	1986	1988
Gallegly	$591,018	$465,310
Opponent	$65,501	$0
Vote Pct	68%	69%

Dean A. Gallo, R-NJ (11)

First elected: 1984
Total receipts: $531,548
Total from PACs: $147,245

1988 Committees & Subcommittees

Public Works and Transportation
Public Buildings and Grounds
Surface Transportation
Water Resources

Small Business
Exports, Tourism and Special Problems
Procurement, Innovation and Minority Enterprise Development

PAC Contribution Profile

Business

Campaign Revenue Sources

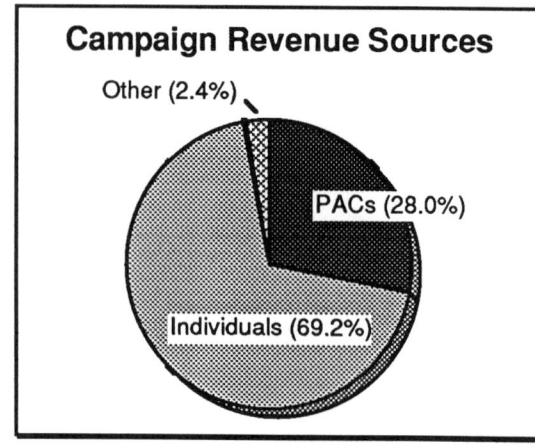

Other (2.4%)
PACs (28.0%)
Individuals (69.2%)

Automotive	**$7,000**
Auto Dealers & Drivers for Free Trade	$4,000
National Auto Dealers Assn	$2,500
Others	$500
Chemicals	**$3,000**
None over $750	
Commercial & Savings Banks	**$12,150**
SAPEC/NJ (New Jersey Savings Assn)	$3,000
American Bankers Assn	$2,000
City Federal Savings & Loan	$1,500
Midlantic National Bank	$1,250
Barnett Banks of Florida	$1,000
Others	$3,400
Construction	**$11,500**
National Assn of Home Builders	$5,500
National Utility Contractors Assn	$3,000
American Consulting Engineers Council	$1,000
Others	$2,000
Consumer Credit & Loans	**$2,000**
Beneficial Management Corp	$2,000
Defense	**$3,000**
Allied-Signal	$1,500
Others	$1,500
Electric & Power Utilities	**$2,945**
General Public Utilities	$1,695
Public Service Electric & Gas	$1,250

Food & Beverage	**$4,500**
Nabisco Brands Inc	$1,500
Food Marketing Institute	$1,000
National Restaurant Assn	$1,000
Others	$1,000
Health Professionals	**$6,750**
American Medical Assn	$4,000
American Dental Assn	$1,500
American Academy of Ophthalmology	$1,000
Others	$250
Insurance	**$8,000**
Chubb Corp	$1,000
Fireman's Fund Insurance	$1,000
National Assn of Life Underwriters	$1,000
Others	$5,000
Oil & Gas	**$3,500**
Columbia Natural Resources	$1,000
Others	$2,500
Pharmaceuticals	**$11,000**
Warner-Lambert	$2,850
Schering-Plough Corp	$2,250
Sandoz Pharmaceuticals	$1,750
Johnson & Johnson	$1,200
Hoffman-La Roche	$1,000
Others	$1,950
Real Estate	**$4,250**
National Assn of Realtors	$4,000
Others	$250
Securities Investment	**$2,000**
Dillon, Read & Company	$1,000
Others	$1,000
Telecommunications	**$5,060**
New Jersey Bell Telephone	$2,960
AT&T	$1,850
Others	$250

PAC Totals by Category

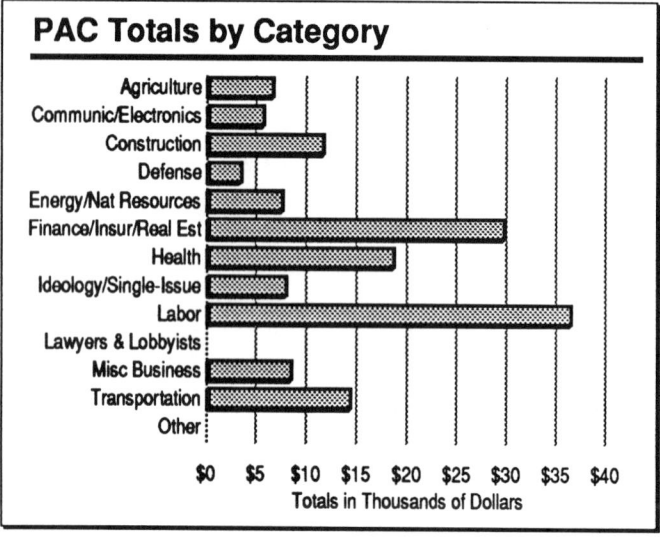

Agriculture
Communic/Electronics
Construction
Defense
Energy/Nat Resources
Finance/Insur/Real Est
Health
Ideology/Single-Issue
Labor
Lawyers & Lobbyists
Misc Business
Transportation
Other

$0 $5 $10 $15 $20 $25 $30 $35 $40
Totals in Thousands of Dollars

Trucking/Delivery *$5,420*

    United Parcel Service $2,550
    Maersk Inc $1,500
    Others $1,370

Other Major Business PACs

Texas Air .... $1,500   Airlines
Associated Milk Producers .... $1,000   Dairy
JSJ Corp .... $1,000   Indust Equip
National Society of Public Accountants .... $1,000   Accountants

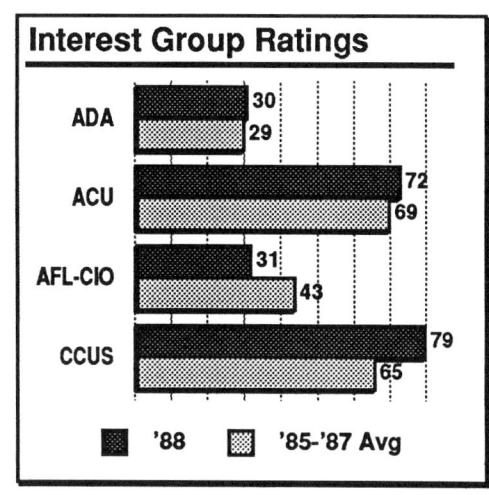

Interest Group Ratings

Group	'88	'85–'87 Avg
ADA	30	29
ACU	72	69
AFL-CIO	31	43
CCUS	79	65

■ '88   ▨ '85–'87 Avg

Labor

Bldg Trades/Industrial/Misc Unions *$15,750*

    Operating Engineers Local #825 .... $6,000
    Carpenters & Joiners Union $5,000
    Plumbers/Pipefitters Union* $2,500
    Laborers' Union* $2,000
    Others $250

Government & Postal Workers *$3,750*

    National Assn of Retired Federal Employees $2,500
    National Assn of Letter Carriers $1,000
    Others $250

Transportation Unions *$16,800*

    Marine Engineers Union* $5,500
    Air Line Pilots Assn $5,000
    Teamsters Union $3,500
    Seafarers International Union $2,000
    Others $800

Ideological/Single-Issue

Pro-Israel *$5,750*

    National PAC $5,000
    Others $750

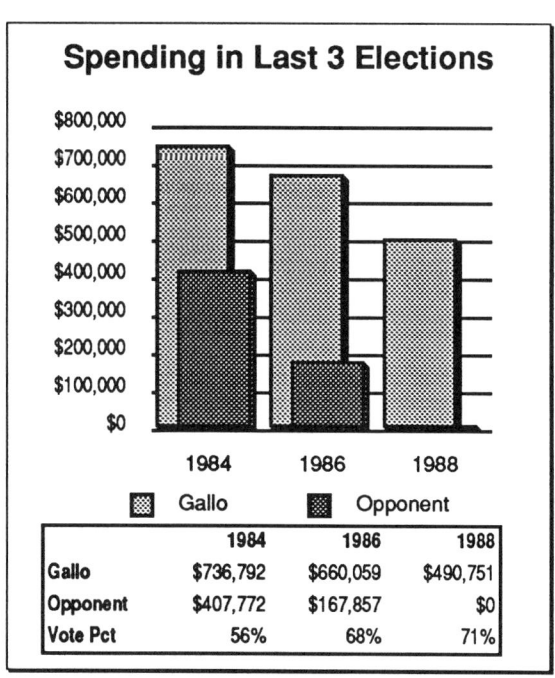

Spending in Last 3 Elections

	1984	1986	1988
Gallo	$736,792	$660,059	$490,751
Opponent	$407,772	$167,857	$0
Vote Pct	56%	68%	71%

▨ Gallo   ■ Opponent

---

* Contributions came from more than one PAC affiliated
with this sponsor.

Robert Garcia, D-NY (11)

First elected: 1978
Total receipts: $306,376
Total from PACs: $186,575

1988 Committees & Subcommittees

Banking, Finance and Urban Affairs
Economic Stabilization
Housing and Community Development
Policy Research and Insurance

Post Office and Civil Service
Census and Population
Postal Operations and Services

PAC Contribution Profile

Business

Commercial Banks	**$16,500**
Citicorp	$5,000
American Bankers Assn	$1,750
Assn of Bank Holding Companies	$1,500
Manufacturers Hanover	$1,300
Independent Bankers Assn	$1,000
Others	$5,950
Health Professionals	**$6,500**
New York Medical Assn	$5,000
Hospital/Health Care Union #1199	$1,000
Others	$500
Insurance	**$4,200**
Massachusetts Mutual Life Insurance	$2,100
Others	$2,100
Lawyers & Lobbyists	**$3,850**
National Action Committee	$1,500
Powell, Goldstein, Frazer & Murphy	$1,000
Others	$1,350
Real Estate	**$4,500**
National Assn of Realtors	$4,000
Others	$500
Savings Banks & Credit Unions	**$4,600**
New York Savings Assn League	$1,100
US League of Savings Assn	$1,000
Others	$2,500

Campaign Revenue Sources

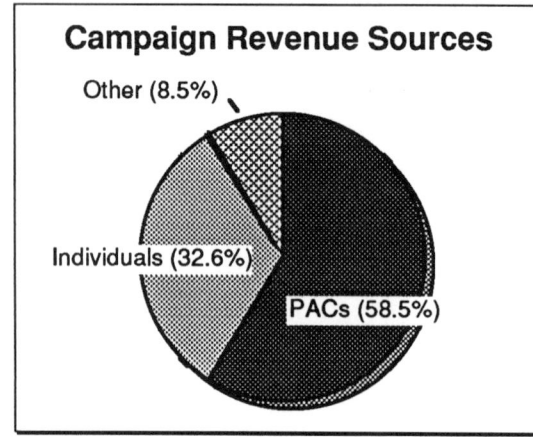

Other (8.5%)
Individuals (32.6%)
PACs (58.5%)

Securities Investment	**$8,750**
Goldman Sachs	$3,000
Investment Company Institute	$3,000
Prudential-Bache Securities	$1,000
Others	$1,750

Other Major Business PACs

United Parcel Service	$1,500	Delivery
AT&T	$1,000	Long Distance

PAC Totals by Category

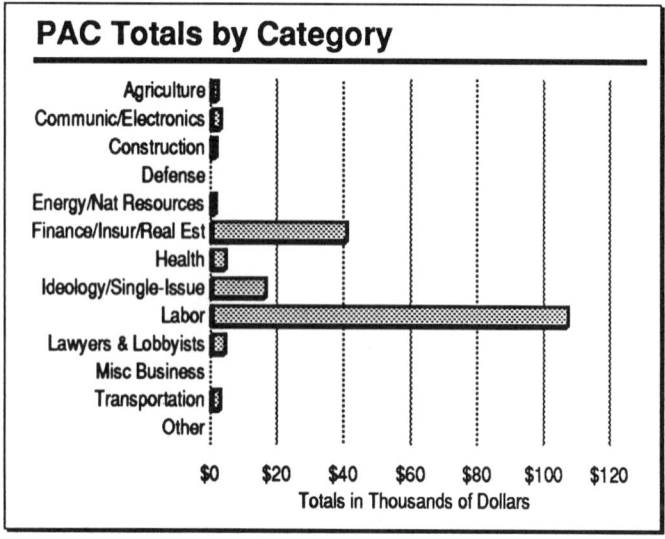

Totals in Thousands of Dollars

Labor

Bldg Trades/Industrial/Misc Unions $41,900

United Auto Workers	$7,000
Machinists/Aerospace Workers Union	$5,000
United Steelworkers	$5,000
AFL-CIO*	$4,500
Int'l Brotherhood of Electrical Workers....................	$3,500
Food & Commercial Workers Union..........................	$2,500
Plumbers/Pipefitters Union	$2,500
Ladies Garment Workers Union	$2,100
Carpenters & Joiners Union	$2,000
Laborers' Political League	$2,000
Amalgamated Clothing & Textile Workers	$1,000
Service Employees International Union	$1,000
Others	$3,800

Government & Postal Workers $30,550

National Assn of Letter Carriers	$10,000
American Postal Workers Union	$7,500
American Fedn of State/County/Munic Employees	$5,000
National Assn of Retired Federal Employees	$5,000
National Assn of Postal Supervisors	$1,000
Others	$2,050

Teachers Unions $4,700

National Education Assn	$4,500
Others	$200

Transportation Unions $28,606

Teamsters Union	$10,000
Transport Workers Union*	$6,000
International Longshoremen Assn*	$3,306
Seafarers International Union	$3,000
Transportation Communication Union......................	$2,300
Marine Engineers District 2 Maritime Officers................	$2,000
Amalgamated Transit Union.....................................	$1,000
Others	$1,000

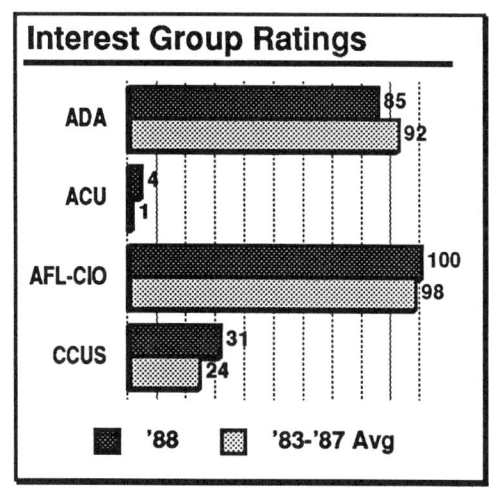

Interest Group Ratings

	'88	'83-'87 Avg
ADA	85	92
ACU	4	1
AFL-CIO	100	98
CCUS	31	24

Ideological/Single-Issue

Democratic Leadership PACs.....................................$14,000

24th Congr Dist of Calif PAC (Henry Waxman)	$5,000
Valley Education Fund (Tony Coelho)	$5,000
Majority Congress Committee (Jim Wright)	$3,000
Democratic Congressional Fund (Joe Moakley)	$1,000

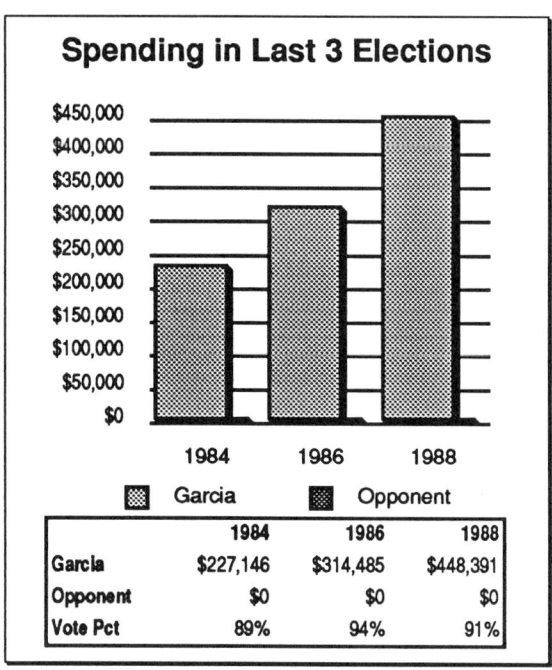

Spending in Last 3 Elections

| | Garcia | Opponent |

	1984	1986	1988
Garcia	$227,146	$314,485	$448,391
Opponent	$0	$0	$0
Vote Pct	89%	94%	91%

* Contributions came from more than one PAC affiliated
with this sponsor.

Joseph M. Gaydos, D-Pa (20)

First elected: 1968
Total receipts: $184,634
Total from PACs: $142,850

1988 Committees & Subcommittees

Education and Labor
Health and Safety (Chairman)
Postsecondary Education

House Administration
Accounts (Chairman)
Personnel and Police
Procurement and Printing

Standards of Official Conduct

Joint Printing

PAC Contribution Profile

Business

Commercial & Savings Banks	**$5,400**
American Bankers Assn	$1,000
Mellon Bank	$1,000
Others	$3,400
Dairy	**$2,500**
Associated Milk Producers	$1,000
Dairymen Inc-Pennsylvania	$1,000
Others	$500
Defense	**$3,000**
General Dynamics	$1,000
Hughes Aircraft	$1,000
Textron Inc	$1,000
Electric Utilities	**$4,000**
Philadelphia Electric	$1,500
ACRE (Action Committee for Rural Electrification)	$1,000
General Public Utilities	$1,000
Others	$500
Insurance	**$3,000**
Health Insurance Assn of America	$1,000
National Assn of Life Underwriters	$1,000
Others	$1,000
Lawyers & Lobbyists	**$7,500**
Assn of Trial Lawyers of America	$5,000
Burson-Marsteller	$1,000
Others	$1,500

Campaign Revenue Sources

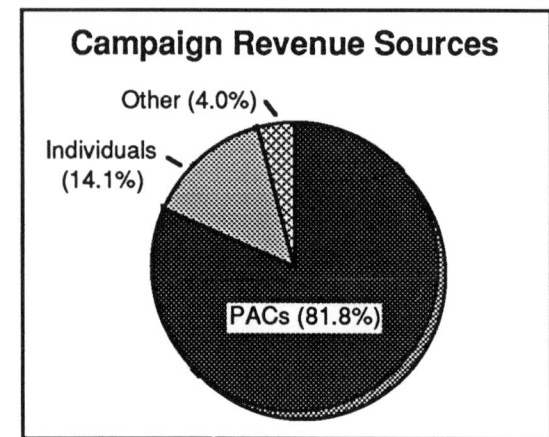

Other (4.0%)
Individuals (14.1%)
PACs (81.8%)

Oil & Gas	**$2,950**
USX Corp	$2,000
Peoples Natural Gas	$600
Others	$350
Real Estate	**$5,500**
National Assn of Realtors	$5,500
Residential Construction	**$2,000**
National Assn of Home Builders	$2,000
Steel Production	**$5,850**
Allegheny Ludlum Steel Corp	$1,500
Bethlehem Steel	$1,500
LTV Steel	$1,000
Wheeling-Pittsburgh Steel	$1,000
Others	$850
Sugar Growers	**$2,600**
American Crystal Sugar Corp	$1,000
American Sugarbeet Growers Assn	$1,000
Others	$600
Telecommunications	**$5,250**
AT&T	$1,750
Bell Telephone of Pennsylvania	$1,500
BellSouth Services	$1,000
Others	$1,000
Vocational Tech Schools	**$5,000**
National Assn of Trade/Tech Schools	$3,000
National Assn of Cosmetology Schools	$1,000
Superior Training Services	$1,000

Other Major Business PACs

American Hospital Assn	$1,300	Hospitals
Oral & Maxillofacial Surgeons	$1,000	Dentists
Russell, Rea & Zappala	$1,000	StocksInvest
Tobacco Institute	$1,000	Tobacco
Westinghouse Electric	$1,000	Electronics

PAC Totals by Category

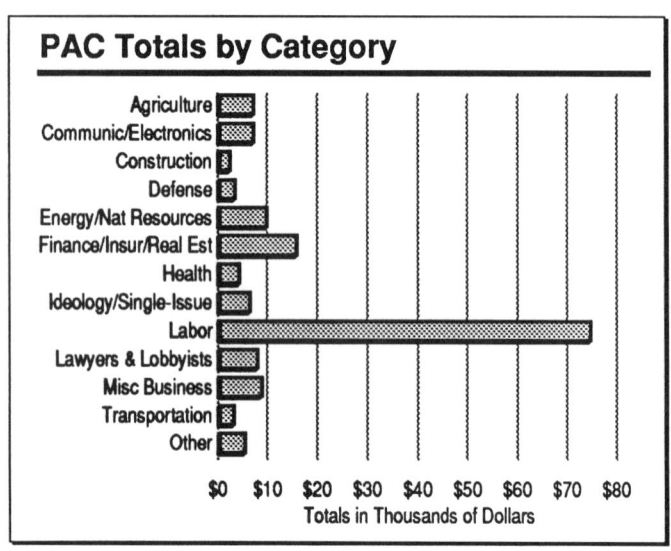

Agriculture
Communic/Electronics
Construction
Defense
Energy/Nat Resources
Finance/Insur/Real Est
Health
Ideology/Single-Issue
Labor
Lawyers & Lobbyists
Misc Business
Transportation
Other

$0 $10 $20 $30 $40 $50 $60 $70 $80
Totals in Thousands of Dollars

Labor

Bldg Trades/Industrial/Misc Unions $34,750

United Auto Workers	$7,000
AFL-CIO*	$3,500
Carpenters & Joiners Union	$3,500
Ironworkers Union	$3,000
Food & Commercial Workers Union	$2,000
Laborers' Political League	$2,000
Operating Engineers Union	$2,000
National Education Assn	$1,700
Intl Brotherhood of Electrical Workers	$1,500
United Mine Workers	$1,500
Machinists/Aerospace Workers Union	$1,000
Plumbers/Pipefitters Union	$1,000
Others	$5,050

Government & Postal Workers $14,500

National Assn of Retired Federal Employees	$6,000
National Assn of Letter Carriers	$2,500
American Fedn of State/County/Munic Employees	$2,000
American Postal Workers Union*	$2,000
American Federation of Government Employees	$1,000
Others	$1,000

Transportation Unions $25,000

Marine Engineers Union*	$8,000
Teamsters Union	$5,500
Air Line Pilots Assn	$3,000
Seafarers International Union	$3,000
United Transportation Union	$2,000
Transportation Communication Union	$1,000
Others	$2,500

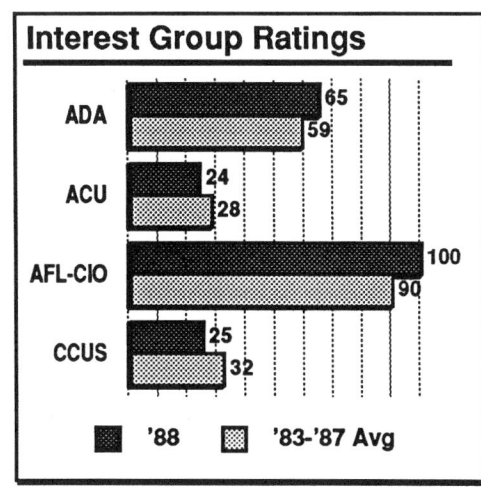

Interest Group Ratings

ADA: '88 = 65; '83-'87 Avg = 59
ACU: '88 = 24; '83-'87 Avg = 28
AFL-CIO: '88 = 100; '83-'87 Avg = 90
CCUS: '88 = 25; '83-'87 Avg = 32

■ '88   ▧ '83-'87 Avg

Ideological/Single-Issue

Democratic Leadership PACs $4,000

America's Leaders' Fund (Dan Rostenkowski)	$2,000
Valley Education Fund (Tony Coelho)	$2,000

Pro-Social Security $2,000

National Cmte to Preserve Social Security	$2,000

Independent expenditures to Gaydos

National Cmte to Preserve Social Security	$3,621

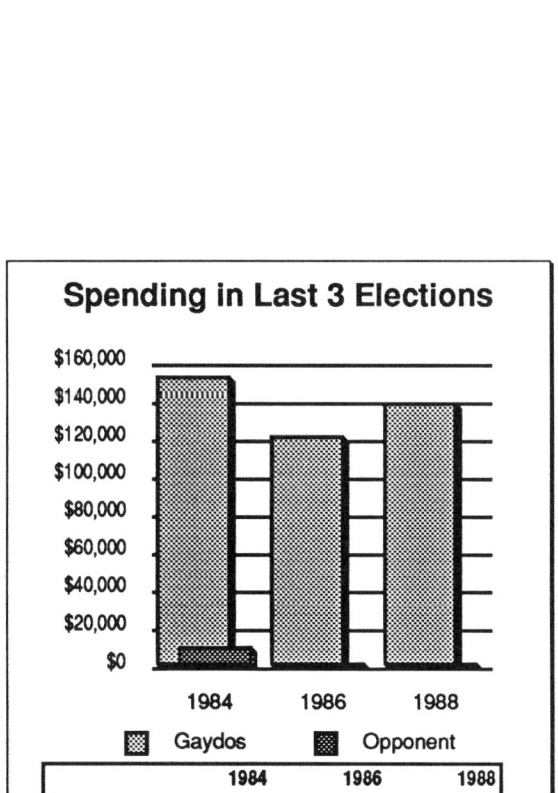

Spending in Last 3 Elections

■ Gaydos   ■ Opponent

	1984	1986	1988
Gaydos	$151,102	$119,321	$137,023
Opponent	$8,318	$0	$0
Vote Pct	76%	99%	99%

Sam Gejdenson, D-Conn (2)

First elected: 1980
Total receipts: $731,513
Total from PACs: $208,800

1988 Committees & Subcommittees

Foreign Affairs
International Economic Policy and Trade
Western Hemisphere Affairs

House Administration
Accounts
Office Systems

Interior and Insular Affairs
General Oversight and Investigations (Chairman)
Energy and the Environment

PAC Contribution Profile

Business

Consumer Credit & Loans..**$2,000**	
Household International $2,000	
Dairy **$8,000**	
Mid-American Dairymen $3,000	
Associated Milk Producers $2,000	
Dairymen Inc $2,000	
Agri-Mark Inc $1,000	
Defense..**$7,250**	
General Dynamics $3,000	
United Technologies $2,250	
Others $2,000	
Health Professionals **$4,150**	
American Dental Assn $1,000	
American Nurses Assn $1,000	
Corp for the Advancement of Psychiatry $1,000	
Others $1,150	
Insurance..**$2,800**	
None over $650	
Lawyers & Lobbyists **$4,900**	
Assn of Trial Lawyers of America $2,300	
Others $2,600	
Real Estate **$3,800**	
National Assn of Realtors $3,800	

Campaign Revenue Sources

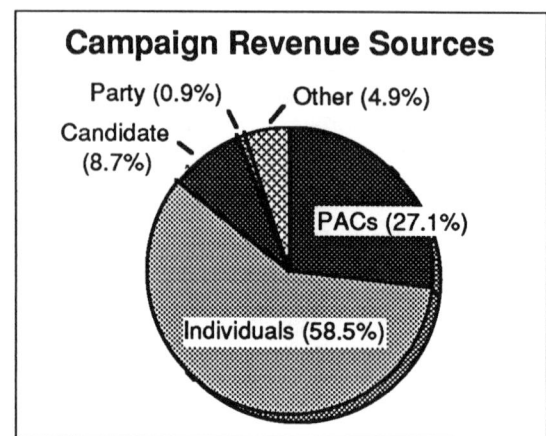

Party (0.9%) Other (4.9%)
Candidate (8.7%)
PACs (27.1%)
Individuals (58.5%)

Telecommunications **$2,600**
AT&T...$2,000
Others $600

Other Major Business PACs

Institute/Scrap Recycling Industries $1,800	Recycling
Stone Container Corp $1,250	Forestry
CBT Corp $1,000	Comml Banks
Joseph E Seagram & Sons $1,000	Wine&Liquor

PAC Totals by Category

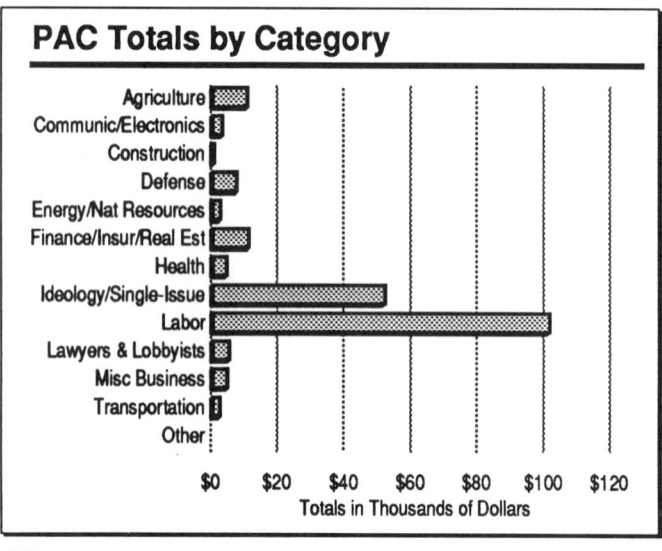

Agriculture
Communic/Electronics
Construction
Defense
Energy/Nat Resources
Finance/Insur/Real Est
Health
Ideology/Single-Issue
Labor
Lawyers & Lobbyists
Misc Business
Transportation
Other

$0 $20 $40 $60 $80 $100 $120
Totals in Thousands of Dollars

Labor

Bldg Trades/Industrial/Misc Unions $53,000

United Auto Workers	$10,000
Machinists/Aerospace Workers Union	$7,850
Connecticut Union of Telephone Workers	$5,000
Carpenters & Joiners Union*	$4,650
Intl Brotherhood of Electrical Workers	$4,500
AFL-CIO*	$3,550
Operating Engineers Union	$2,500
Sheet Metal Workers Union	$2,500
United Steelworkers	$2,000
Laborers' Political League	$1,750
Plumbers/Pipefitters Union	$1,500
Amalgamated Clothing & Textile Workers	$1,450
Boilermakers Union	$1,300
Ladies Garment Workers Union	$1,150
Food & Commercial Workers Union	$1,050
Ironworkers Union	$1,000
Service Employees International Union	$1,000
Others	$250

Government & Postal Workers $16,700

American Fedn of State/County/Munic Employees	$5,000
National Assn of Retired Federal Employees	$4,000
National Assn of Letter Carriers	$2,600
American Postal Workers Union	$1,300
National Treasury Employees Union	$1,300
Others	$2,500

Teachers Unions $12,900

National Education Assn	$7,400
American Federation of Teachers	$5,500

Transportation Unions $17,805

Teamsters Union	$5,000
Seafarers International Union	$3,000
International Longshoremen Assn	$2,600
Maintenance of Way Employees	$1,900
Transport Workers Union	$1,500
United Transportation Union	$1,500
Transportation Communication Union	$1,105
Others	$1,200

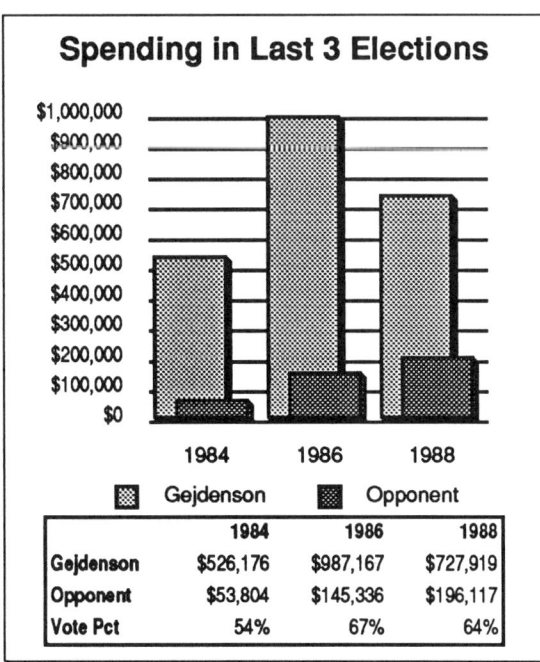

Spending in Last 3 Elections

	1984	1986	1988
Gejdenson	$526,176	$987,167	$727,919
Opponent	$53,804	$145,336	$196,117
Vote Pct	54%	67%	64%

Legend: Gejdenson, Opponent

Interest Group Ratings

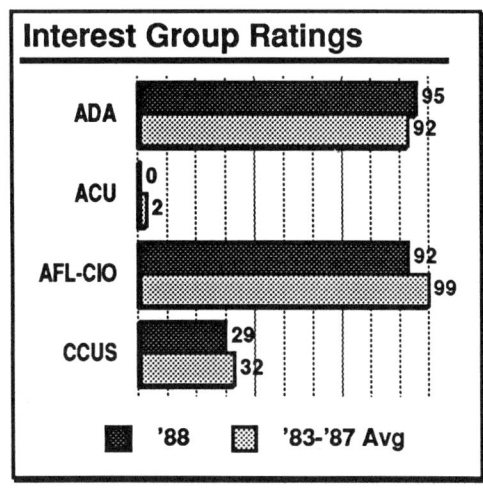

	'88	'83-'87 Avg
ADA	95	92
ACU	0	2
AFL-CIO	92	99
CCUS	29	32

Ideological/Single-Issue

Democratic Leadership PACs $11,700

24th Cong Dist of California PAC (Henry Waxman)	$5,000
Majority Congress Committee (Jim Wright)	$3,000
Valley Education Fund (Tony Coelho)	$2,000
House Leadership Fund (Tom Foley)	$1,000
America's Leaders' Fund (Dan Rostenkowski)	$700

Pro-Israel $34,400

Joint Action Cmte for Political Affairs	$6,000
Delaware Valley PAC	$4,000
Multi-Issue PAC	$4,000
Garden State PAC	$2,500
St Louisians for Better Government	$2,000
Washington PAC	$2,000
National Action Committee (NACPAC)	$1,500
Roundtable PAC	$1,500
Capital PAC	$1,000
Congressional Action Cmte of Texas	$1,000
Florida Congressional Cmte	$1,000
Hudson Valley PAC	$1,000
San Franciscans for Good Government	$1,000
Silver State PAC	$1,000
Women's Pro-Israel National PAC	$1,000
Others	$3,900

Other Major Ideological/Single-Issue PACs

Human Rights Campaign Fund	$2,000	Gay Rights
Sierra Club	$1,000	Environment

---

* Contributions came from more than one PAC affiliated
with this sponsor.

George W. Gekas, R-Pa (17)

First elected: 1982
Total receipts: $95,878
Total from PACs: $46,750

1988 Committees & Subcommittees

Judiciary
Criminal Justice (Ranking Republican)
Crime

PAC Contribution Profile

Business

Accountants	**$5,500**
American Institute of CPA's	$5,000
Ernst & Whinney	$500
Auto Dealers	**$4,750**
National Auto Dealers Assn	$3,250
Auto Dealers & Drivers for Free Trade	$1,500
Commercial & Savings Banks	**$1,750**
American Bankers Assn	$1,000
Pennsylvania Savings League	$500
Others	$250
Construction	**$3,000**
National Assn of Home Builders	$2,500
Others	$500
Food & Beverage	**$2,100**
Food Marketing Institute	$500
Pepsi-Cola Bottlers Assn	$500
Pepsico Inc	$500
Others	$600
Health Professionals	**$1,500**
American Medical Assn	$1,000
Cmte for Quality Orthopedic Health Care	$500
Insurance	**$3,050**
National Assn of Life Underwriters	$1,500
American Insurance Assn	$500
ITT Corp	$500
Others	$550

Campaign Revenue Sources

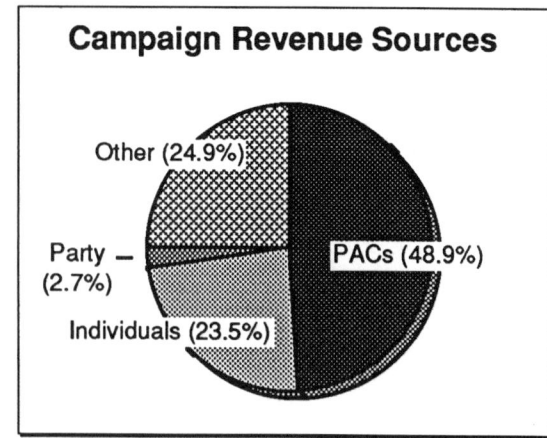

Other (24.9%)
Party (2.7%)
PACs (48.9%)
Individuals (23.5%)

Real Estate	**$6,000**
National Assn of Realtors	$6,000
Telecommunications	**$6,500**
AT&T	$4,000
Continental Telecom	$1,000
United Telecommunications	$1,000
Bell Telephone of Pennsylvania	$500

Other Major Business PACs

United Parcel Service	$1,350	Delivery
Harsco Corp	$1,100	Indust Equip
E F Hutton Group	$1,000	StocksInvest
Bethlehem Steel	$850	Steel
ACRE (Action Cmte for Rural Electricity)	$750	Rural Elect
Combustion Engineering	$750	PowerEquip
American Hospital Assn	$500	Hospitals
Associated Milk Producers	$500	Dairy
Colt Industries	$500	Air Defense
Mobil Oil	$500	Oil & Gas
Smithkline Beckman	$500	Pharmaceut
Sun Company	$500	Oil & Gas

Major Labor PACs

Seafarers International Union	$500	Seamen Union

Major Ideological/Single-Issue PACs

Dynamis	$1,000	Ethnic

PAC Totals by Category

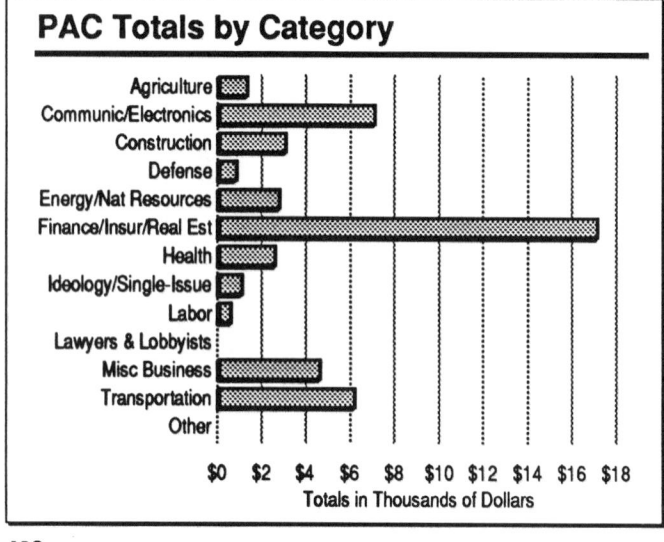

Agriculture
Communic/Electronics
Construction
Defense
Energy/Nat Resources
Finance/Insur/Real Est
Health
Ideology/Single-Issue
Labor
Lawyers & Lobbyists
Misc Business
Transportation
Other

$0 $2 $4 $6 $8 $10 $12 $14 $16 $18
Totals in Thousands of Dollars

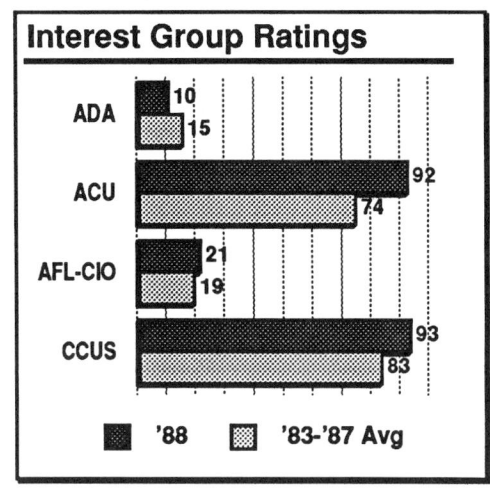

Interest Group Ratings

	'88	'83-'87 Avg
ADA	10	15
ACU	92	74
AFL-CIO	21	19
CCUS	93	83

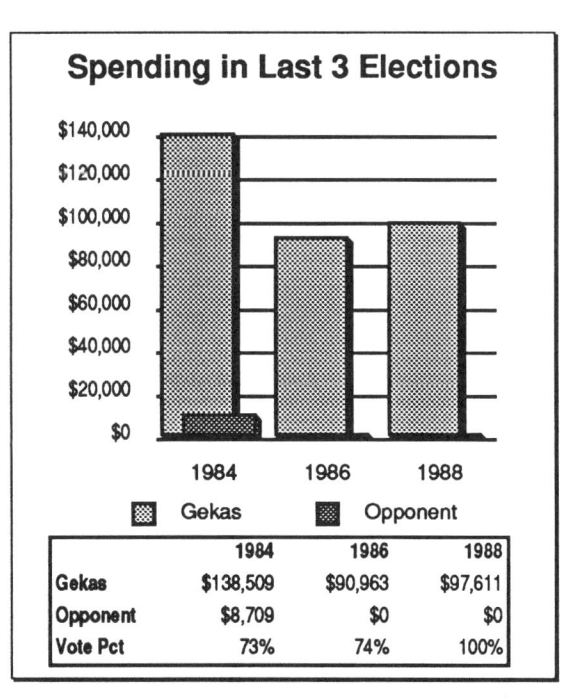

Spending in Last 3 Elections

	1984	1986	1988
Gekas	$138,509	$90,963	$97,611
Opponent	$8,709	$0	$0
Vote Pct	73%	74%	100%

Richard A. Gephardt, D-Mo (3)

First elected: 1976
Total receipts: $245,893
Total from PACs: $180,696

1988 Committees & Subcommittees

Ways and Means
Social Security
Trade

PAC Contribution Profile

NOTE: The PAC contributions listed on these pages include funds that Gephardt received in both his 1988 races — his bid for the Democratic nomination for president, and later his reelection campaign for his U.S. House seat. The total receipts listed in the box above, and the percentages in the pie chart at right, refer only to the U.S. House race.

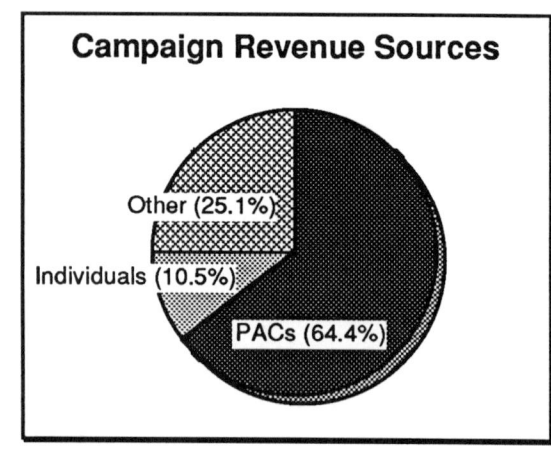

Campaign Revenue Sources

Other (25.1%)
Individuals (10.5%)
PACs (64.4%)

Business

Automotive & Trucking	**$27,850**
Yellow Freight System	$10,000
Chrysler Corp	$9,500
National Auto Dealers Assn	$5,000
Others	$3,350
Commercial Banks	**$39,725**
Centerre Bank	$5,500
American Bankers Assn	$5,000
Mercantile Bancorp	$5,000
Others	$24,225
Construction	**$20,250**
National Assn of Home Builders	$10,000
Others	$10,250
Dairy	**$12,000**
Associated Milk Producers	$8,000
Others	$4,000
Defense	**$24,500**
Emerson Electric	$5,000
General Dynamics	$5,000
Hughes Aircraft	$5,000
McDonnell Douglas	$5,000
Others	$4,500

Food & Beverage	**$30,125**
Occidental Petroleum	$10,000
McLane Company	$5,000
Wine Institute	$5,000
Others	$10,125
Health Professionals	**$18,200**
American Society Cataract/Refractive Surgery	$5,000
Others	$13,200
Hospitals & Nursing Homes	**$15,500**
American Hospital Assn	$7,000
Humana Inc	$5,000
Others	$3,500
Insurance	**$55,599**
General American Life Insurance	$10,000
Independent Insurance Agents of America	$9,999
American Family Corp	$5,000
Others	$30,600
Lawyers & Lobbyists	**$56,750**
Assn of Trial Lawyers of America	$10,000
Baker & Botts	$6,000
Vinson, Elkins, Searls, Connally & Smith	$6,000
Camp, Barsh, Bates & Tate	$5,000
Fullbright & Jaworski	$5,000
Pillsbury, Madison & Sutro	$5,000
Others	$19,750
Oil & Gas	**$20,746**
Valero Energy Corp	$6,396
Others	$14,350
Real Estate	**$18,775**
National Assn of Realtors	$5,750
National Realty Committee	$5,000
Trammell Crow Company	$5,000
Others	$3,025
Savings Banks	**$17,381**
US League of Savings Assn*	$6,600
Centrust Savings Bank	$5,000
Others	$5,781
Securities/Commodities Trading	**$35,096**
Chicago Mercantile Exchange	$10,000
Bear, Stearns & Company	$6,000
Chicago Board of Trade	$5,000
Others	$14,096

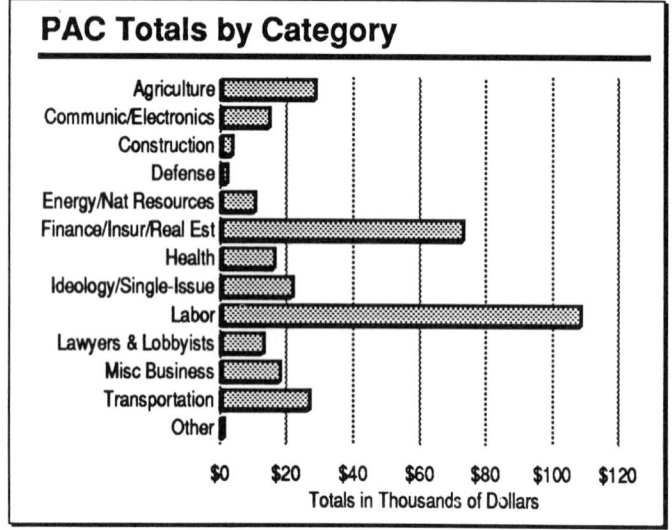

PAC Totals by Category

Agriculture
Communic/Electronics
Construction
Defense
Energy/Nat Resources
Finance/Insur/Real Est
Health
Ideology/Single-Issue
Labor
Lawyers & Lobbyists
Misc Business
Transportation
Other

$0 $20 $40 $60 $80 $100 $120
Totals in Thousands of Dollars

Telecommunications **$30,250**
- Southwestern Bell $6,500
- US Telephone Assn $5,000
- Others $18,750

Tobacco **$11,500**
- Philip Morris $7,500
- Others $4,000

Waste Management **$12,500**
- Waste Management Inc $6,000
- Chambers Development Company $5,000
- Others $1,500

Other Major Business PACs

Monsanto Company	$6,000	Chemicals
Federal Express Corp	$5,000	Delivery
Hallmark Cards	$5,000	Publishing
Henley Group Inc	$5,000	Altern Energy
Long Island Aerospace PAC	$5,000	AerospacePts
National Venture Capital Assn	$5,000	Venture Cap
Triangle Industries	$5,000	Cans
Tyson Foods	$5,000	Poultry/Egg

Labor

Bldg Trades/Industrial/Misc Unions **$140,889**
- United Auto Workers $15,000
- Intl Brotherhood of Electrical Workers* $14,444
- AFL-CIO $13,000
- Machinists/Aerospace Workers* $12,500
- Ironworkers Union $11,000
- Sheet Metal Workers Union $10,000
- Communications Workers of America $9,000
- Service Employees International Union $7,000
- United Mine Workers $5,100
- Amalgamated Clothing & Textile Workers $5,000
- Food & Commercial Workers Union $5,000
- Ladies Garment Workers Union $5,000
- United Paperworkers $5,000
- Others $23,845

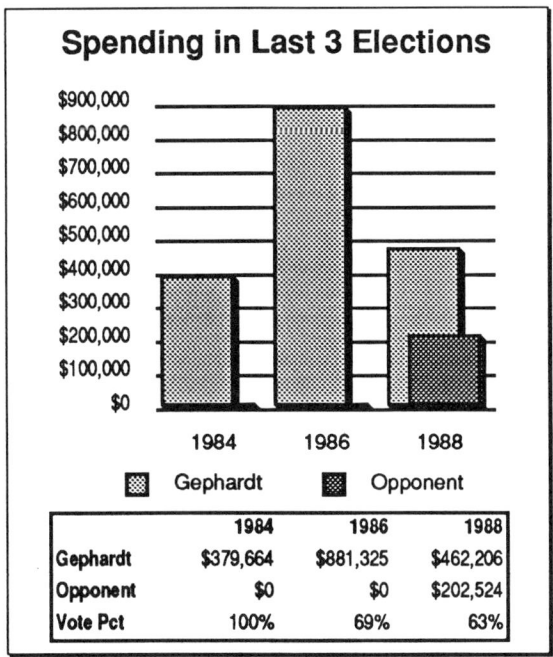

Spending in Last 3 Elections

	1984	1986	1988
Gephardt	$379,664	$881,325	$462,206
Opponent	$0	$0	$202,524
Vote Pct	100%	69%	63%

■ Gephardt   ■ Opponent

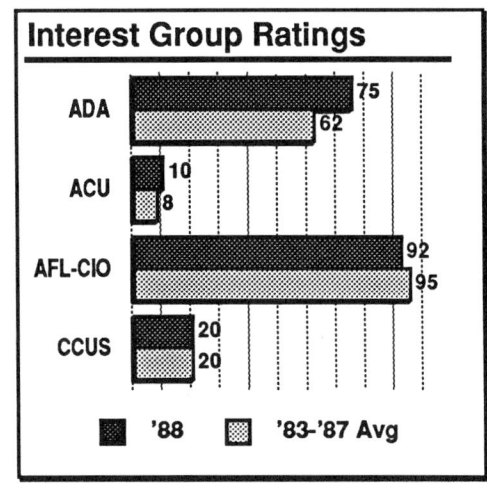

■ '88   ▨ '83-'87 Avg

Government & Postal Workers **$31,250**
- American Fedn of State/County/Munic Employees $10,000
- National Assn of Letter Carriers* $10,000
- American Postal Workers Union $8,000
- Others $3,250

Teachers Unions **$21,000**
- National Education Assn $15,000
- American Federation of Teachers $6,000

Transportation Unions **$57,750**
- Teamsters Union* $20,000
- Seafarers International Union $15,000
- Marine Engineers Union* $9,000
- Air Line Pilots Assn $5,000
- Transportation Communication Union $5,000
- Others $3,750

Ideological/Single-Issue

Democratic Leadership PACs **$21,334**
- America's Leaders' Fund (Dan Rostenkowski) $5,000
- Valley Education Fund (Tony Coelho) $5,000
- Others $11,334

Pro-Israel **$18,000**
- National PAC $10,000
- Others $8,000

Other Major Ideological/Single-Issue PACs

National Cmte to Preserve Social Security	$13,000	Social Secur
Democrats for The 80's	$5,000	Dem/Liberal
Free Cuba PAC	$5,000	Anti-Castro

Independent expenditures supporting Gephardt

Missouri Textile Committee $5,500

Independent expenditures opposing Gephardt

Missouri Citizens for Life $13,744
National Right to Life PAC $8,523

---

* Contributions came from more than one PAC affiliated with this sponsor.

Sam M. Gibbons, D-Fla (7)

1988 Committees & Subcommittees

First elected: 1962
Total receipts: $604,570
Total from PACs: $344,887

Ways and Means
Trade (Chairman)
Social Security

Joint Taxation

PAC Contribution Profile

Business

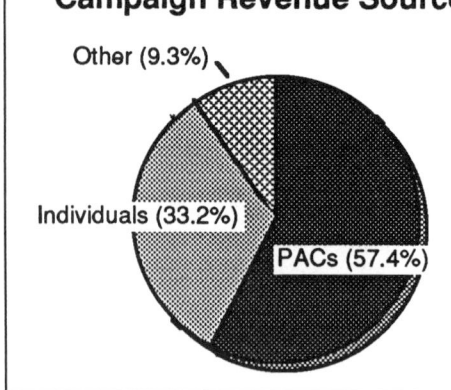

Campaign Revenue Sources

Other (9.3%)
Individuals (33.2%)
PACs (57.4%)

Accountants **$10,000**	
American Institute of CPA's $5,000	
Ernst & Whinney $1,500	
Others $3,500	

Automotive **$17,000**	
Auto Dealers & Drivers for Free Trade $10,000	
National Auto Dealers Assn $3,000	
General Motors $1,500	
Others $2,500	

Chemicals & Plastics **$9,500**	
FMC Corp $5,000	
Premark International $2,000	
W R Grace & Company $1,500	
Others $1,000	

Commercial & Savings Banks **$20,850**	
American Bankers Assn $3,000	
Citicorp $3,000	
US League of Savings Assn $3,000	
Barnett Banks of Florida $2,000	
J P Morgan & Company $2,000	
NCNB Corp $2,000	
Others $5,850	

Construction **$14,750**	
Walter Industries $4,000	
Lone Star Industries $3,000	
National Assn of Home Builders $2,500	
Associated General Contractors $1,500	
Others $3,750	

Defense **$15,684**
- United Technologies $2,684
- Singer Company $2,500
- Colt Industries $1,500
- Rockwell International $1,500
- Others $7,500

Electronics & Computers **$8,500**
- General Electric $2,000
- Others $6,500

Food & Beverage **$20,250**
- National Beer Wholesalers Assn $4,000
- Food Marketing Institute $2,000
- Joseph E Seagram & Sons $2,000
- National Restaurant Assn $2,000
- ConAgra Inc $1,200
- Others $9,050

Health Professionals **$13,000**
- American Dental Assn $2,500
- Florida Medical Assn $2,500
- American Medical Assn $2,000
- Oral & Maxillofacial Surgeons $1,500
- Others $4,500

Insurance **$42,150**
- Metropolitan Life Insurance $5,000
- National Assn of Life Underwriters $5,000
- Mutual Life Insurance of New York $4,000
- New York Life $3,000
- American Family Corp $2,500
- Massachusetts Mutual Life Insurance $2,000
- Prudential Insurance $2,000
- Mutual Benefit Life Insurance $1,500
- Northwestern Mutual Life $1,500
- TransAmerica Corp* $1,500
- Others $14,150

Lawyers & Lobbyists **$15,750**
- Assn of Trial Lawyers of America $5,000
- Holland & Knight $1,500
- Powell, Goldstein, Frazer & Murphy $1,250
- Others $8,000

Mining **$7,000**
- Freeport-McMoran Inc $2,000
- Peabody Coal $1,500
- Others $3,500

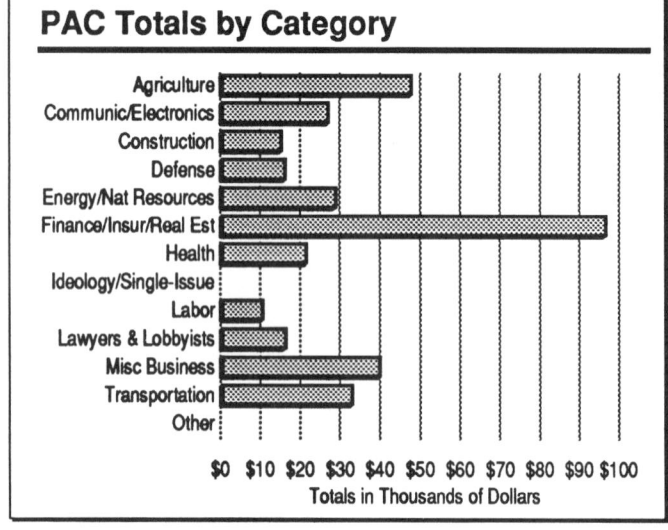

PAC Totals by Category

Agriculture
Communic/Electronics
Construction
Defense
Energy/Nat Resources
Finance/Insur/Real Est
Health
Ideology/Single-Issue
Labor
Lawyers & Lobbyists
Misc Business
Transportation
Other

$0 $10 $20 $30 $40 $50 $60 $70 $80 $90 $100
Totals in Thousands of Dollars

Oil & Gas **$15,288**
    Atlantic Richfield $2,000
    Petroleum Marketers Assn $1,500
    Others $11,788

Retail Sales **$9,500**
    Federated Department Stores $2,000
    Others $7,500

Securities & Commodities Investment **$9,000**
    First Boston Corp $2,000
    Securities Industry Assn $1,500
    Others $5,500

Telecommunications **$16,000**
    Southern Bell $4,000
    AT&T $2,000
    Pacific Telesis Group $1,750
    Bell Atlantic $1,500
    GTE Corp* $1,500
    US Telephone Assn $1,500
    Others $3,750

Tobacco **$10,000**
    United States Tobacco Company $5,000
    Philip Morris $3,000
    Cigar Assn of America $2,000

Other Major Business PACs

National Venture Capital Assn	$5,000	Venture Cap
Boeing Company	$4,000	Aircraft
Archer-Daniels-Midland Corp	$3,000	Grain Trader
Milk Industry Foundation	$3,000	Dairy
United Parcel Service	$3,000	Delivery
National Realty Committee	$2,500	Real Estate
American Express	$2,000	Credit/Loans
MCA Inc	$2,000	Movies
Westvaco Corp	$2,000	Paper Prod
American Crystal Sugar Corp	$1,500	Sugar
CF Industries	$1,500	Ag Chemicals
Corning Glass Works	$1,500	Glass Prod
International Hardwood Products Assn	$1,500	Forestry
Norfolk Southern Corp	$1,500	Railroads

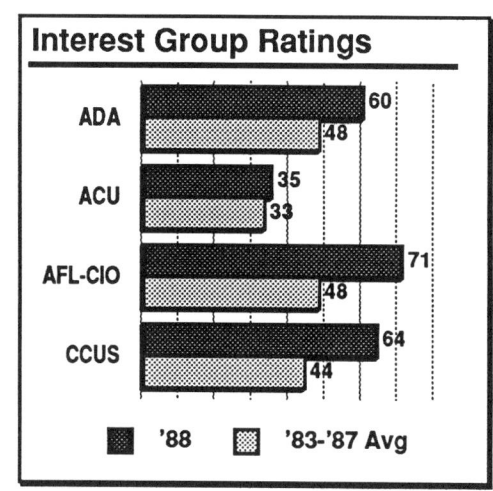

Interest Group Ratings

Legend: ■ '88   ▨ '83-'87 Avg

	'88	'83-'87 Avg
ADA	60	48
ACU	35	33
AFL-CIO	71	48
CCUS	64	44

Labor

Labor Unions **$10,000**
    American Fedn of State/County/Munic Employees $2,500
    National Education Assn $2,000
    Others $5,500

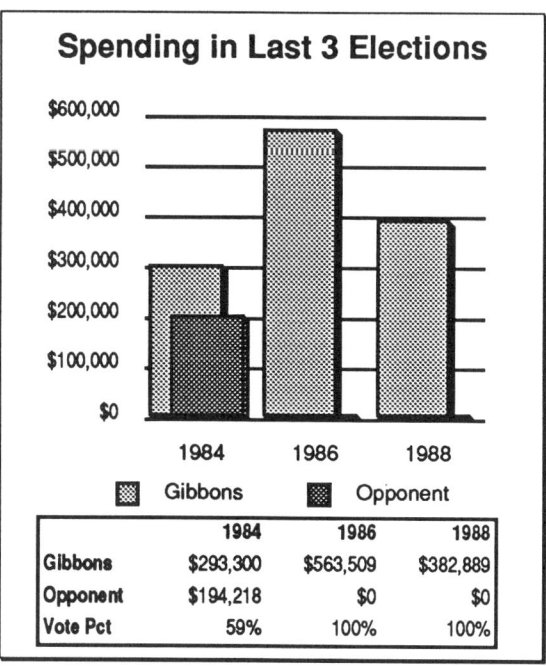

Spending in Last 3 Elections

Legend: ▨ Gibbons   ▦ Opponent

	1984	1986	1988
Gibbons	$293,300	$563,509	$382,889
Opponent	$194,218	$0	$0
Vote Pct	59%	100%	100%

---

* Contributions came from more than one PAC affiliated with this sponsor.

Paul E. Gillmor, R-Ohio (5)

1988-1989 Committees & Subcommittees

First elected: 1988
Total receipts: $742,123
Total from PACs: $317,870

Banking, Finance and Urban Affairs
Economic Stabilization
Financial Institutions Supervision, Regulation and Insurance
General Oversight and Investigations
Housing and Community Development

House Administration
Libraries and Memorials (Ranking Republican)
Accounts

Joint Library

PAC Contribution Profile

Business

Automotive	**$22,150**
National Auto Dealers Assn	$10,000
Eaton Corp	$7,000
Auto Dealers & Drivers for Free Trade	$2,500
Dana Corp	$1,000
Others	$1,650
Business Associations	**$5,128**
National Cooperative Business Assn	$2,500
Business Industry PAC	$2,121
Others	$507
Chemicals	**$5,150**
Dow Chemical*	$3,050
FMC Corp	$1,000
Others	$1,100
Commercial & Savings Banks	**$12,150**
National City Corp	$3,000
Ohio Bankers Assn	$2,000
Ohio Savings Assns League	$2,000
American Bankers Assn	$1,500
Ameritrust Company	$1,000
Others	$2,650
Construction	**$21,942**
National Assn of Home Builders	$10,000
Associated General Contractors	$3,500
Sheet Metal/AirCon Contractors	$2,000
Owens-Corning Fiberglas	$1,525
Manville Corp	$1,500
National Electrical Contractors Assn	$1,000
National Society of Professional Engineers	$1,000
Others	$1,417

Campaign Revenue Sources

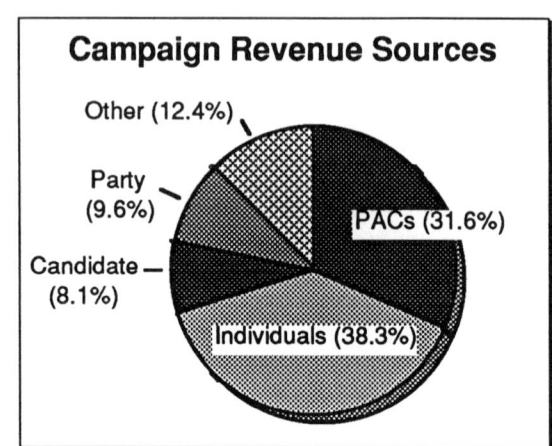

Other (12.4%)
Party (9.6%)
Candidate (8.1%)
Individuals (38.3%)
PACs (31.6%)

PAC Totals by Category

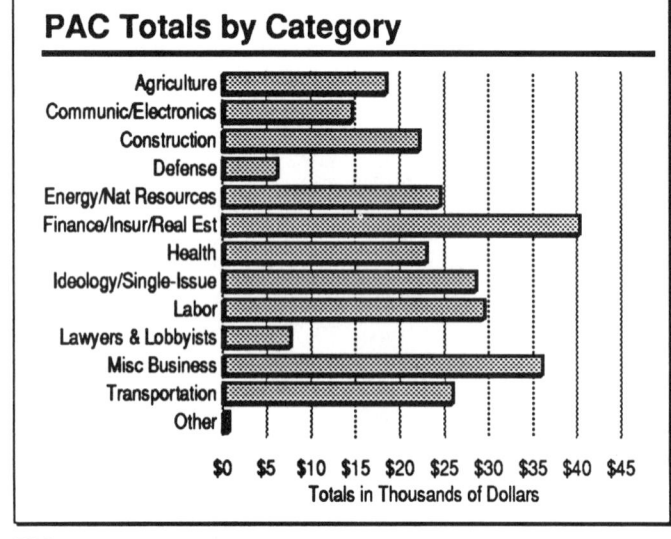

Agriculture
Communic/Electronics
Construction
Defense
Energy/Nat Resources
Finance/Insur/Real Est
Health
Ideology/Single-Issue
Labor
Lawyers & Lobbyists
Misc Business
Transportation
Other

$0 $5 $10 $15 $20 $25 $30 $35 $40 $45
Totals in Thousands of Dollars

Dairy	**$4,000**
Associated Milk Producers	$2,000
Mid-American Dairymen	$1,000
Others	$1,000
Defense	**$6,000**
United Technologies	$1,500
Harris Corp	$1,000
Others	$3,500
Electric Utilities	**$8,150**
Centerior Energy Corp	$3,500
American Electric Power*	$1,400
Cincinnati Gas & Electric	$1,000
Others	$2,250
Food & Beverage	**$8,500**
National Restaurant Assn	$2,000
McDonald's Corp	$1,500
Others	$5,000
Health Professionals	**$18,750**
American Medical Assn	$10,000
American Academy of Ophthalmology	$3,000
American Dental Assn	$2,500
American Nurses Assn	$2,000
Others	$1,250
Home Appliances	**$2,800**
Maytag Company	$1,500
Whirlpool Corp	$1,300
Industrial Equipment & Materials	**$7,100**
Brush Wellman	$6,000
Others	$1,100
Insurance	**$15,400**
National Assn of Life Underwriters	$5,000
National Assn Mutual Insurance Agents	$4,000
Nationwide Corp	$1,500
Independent Insurance Agents of America	$1,250
Others	$3,650

Lawyers **$7,500**
- Assn of Trial Lawyers of America $5,000
- Bricker & Eckler $1,000
- Others $1,500

Oil & Gas **$13,045**
- Ashland Oil $2,500
- Sun Company $1,500
- Columbia Gas Company* $1,345
- Amoco Corp $1,000
- Others $6,700

Real Estate **$10,500**
- National Assn of Realtors $10,000
- Others $500

Sugar Growers **$5,850**
- American Sugarbeet Growers Assn $1,750
- American Crystal Sugar Corp $1,500
- Others $2,600

Telecommunications **$11,600**
- AT&T $5,000
- Ohio Bell Telephone $2,450
- United Telecommunications* $1,350
- GTE Corp $1,000
- Others $1,800

Other Major Business PACs

Owens-Illinois	$2,500	Paper Packg
Mead Corp	$2,000	Paper Prod
Browning-Ferris Industries	$1,000	Waste Mgmt
Chambers Development Company	$1,000	Waste Mgmt
Cooper Industries	$1,000	Electronics
Corning Glass Works	$1,000	Glass Prod
L. M. Berry & Company	$1,000	Mail Advert
Libbey-Owens-Ford	$1,000	Glass Prod
Philip Morris	$1,000	Tobacco
Precision Metalforming Assn	$1,000	MetalProduct
RJR Nabisco	$1,000	Tobacco

Labor

Labor Unions **$29,250**
- National Education Assn $10,000
- Teamsters Union $8,000
- American Fedn of State/County/Munic Employees $2,500
- Intl Brotherhood of Electrical Workers $2,000
- Operating Engineers Union $2,000
- Seafarers International Union $1,500
- National Assn of Letter Carriers $1,000
- National Assn of Retired Federal Employees $1,000
- Others $1,250

Ideological/Single-Issue

Pro-Israel **$9,950**
- National PAC $5,000
- Heartland PAC $1,000
- Women's Pro-Israel National PAC $1,000
- Others $2,950

Republican Leadership PACs **$4,884**
- Campaign America (Bob Dole) $3,384
- Republican Leader's Fund (Bob Michel) $1,000
- Others $500

Other Major Ideological/Single-Issue PACs

National Rifle Assn	$4,950	Pro-Guns
Council for National Defense	$4,220	Pro-Defense
Public Service Research Council	$1,750	Anti-Union
Republican Congressional Boosters Club	$1,000	Repub/Conser

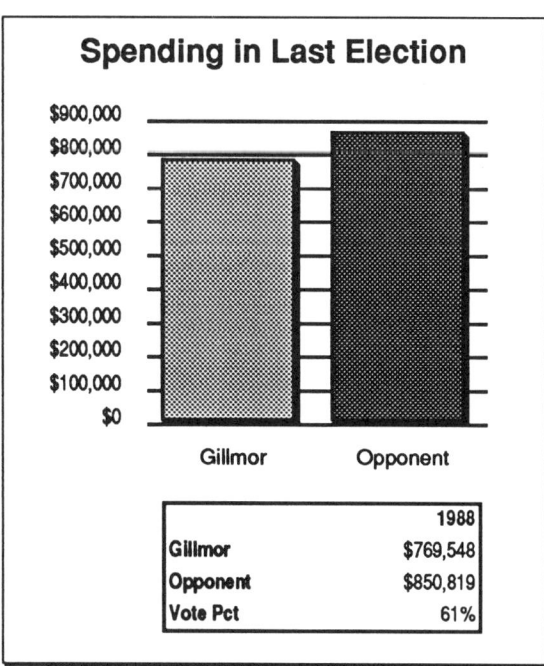

Spending in Last Election

	1988
Gillmor	$769,548
Opponent	$850,819
Vote Pct	61%

---

* Contributions came from more than one PAC affiliated with this sponsor.

Benjamin A. Gilman, R-NY (22)

First elected: 1972
Total receipts: $428,176
Total from PACs: $166,797

1988 Committees & Subcommittees

Foreign Affairs
Europe and the Middle East (Ranking Republican)
International Operations

Post Office and Civil Service
Human Resources
Investigations

Select Hunger

Select Narcotics Abuse and Control (Ranking Republican)

PAC Contribution Profile

Business

Commercial & Savings Banks	**$3,650**
Citicorp	$1,300
Others	$2,350
Dairy	**$6,150**
Associated Milk Producers	$5,000
Others	$1,150
Defense Aerospace	**$3,200**
Sequa Corp	$1,000
Others	$2,200
Electric & Power Utilities	**$4,915**
Orange & Rockland Utilities	$1,925
Consolidated Edison/New York	$1,100
New York State Electric & Gas Corp	$1,040
Others	$850
Package Delivery	**$4,300**
United Parcel Service	$4,300
Food & Beverage	**$2,600**
None over $800	
Forest Products	**$2,350**
International Paper Company	$1,450
Others	$900
Health Professionals	**$7,550**
New York Medical Assn	$3,900
American Medical Assn	$2,850
Others	$800

Insurance	**$2,200**
National Assn of Life Underwriters	$1,000
Others	$1,200
Lawyers & Lobbyists	**$2,250**
None over $600	
Pharmaceuticals	**$5,400**
Hoffman-La Roche	$1,650
Ciba-Geigy Corp	$1,300
Johnson & Johnson	$1,000
Others	$1,450
Real Estate	**$6,000**
National Assn of Realtors	$6,000
Sugar Growers	**$3,300**
None over $650	
Telecommunications	**$5,160**
Continental Telecom	$2,000
New York Telephone	$1,660
AT&T	$1,500

Other Major Business PACs

Shearson Lehman Hutton	$1,550	StocksInvest
Cooper Companies Inc	$1,050	Med Supply
Electrocom Automation Inc	$1,000	Comput Parts
National Assn of Home Builders	$1,000	Resid Constr

Campaign Revenue Sources

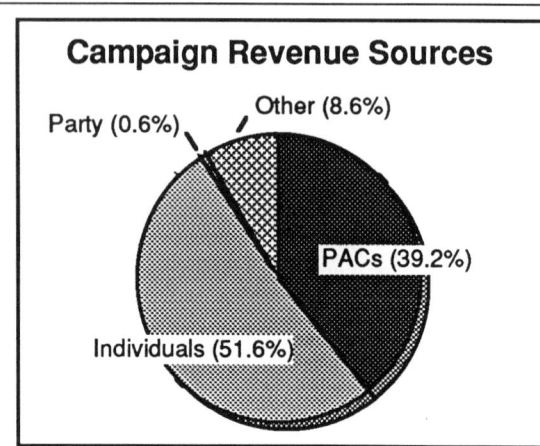

Party (0.6%)
Other (8.6%)
PACs (39.2%)
Individuals (51.6%)

PAC Totals by Category

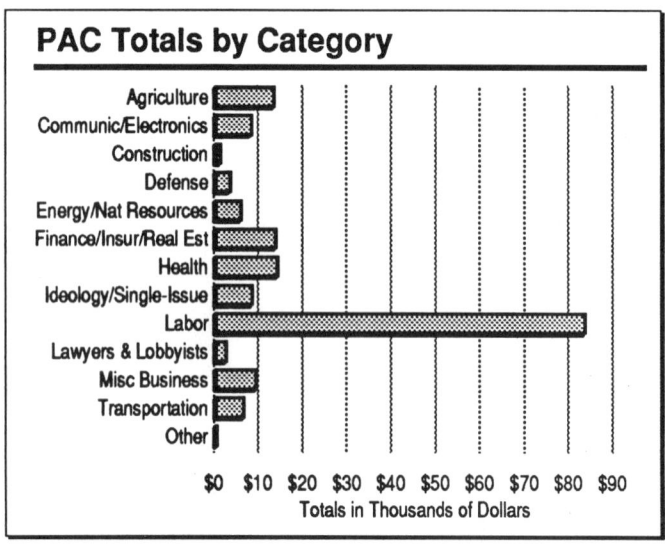

Agriculture
Communic/Electronics
Construction
Defense
Energy/Nat Resources
Finance/Insur/Real Est
Health
Ideology/Single-Issue
Labor
Lawyers & Lobbyists
Misc Business
Transportation
Other

$0 $10 $20 $30 $40 $50 $60 $70 $80 $90
Totals in Thousands of Dollars

Labor

Bldg Trades/Industrial/Misc Unions $28,140

Operating Engineers Union* $6,150
Laborers' Political League $5,000
Carpenters & Joiners Union* $3,740
United Auto Workers $3,500
Intl Brotherhood of Electrical Workers $1,800
Ladies Garment Workers Union $1,250
American Federation of Teachers $1,200
Utility Workers Union of America $1,200
Food & Commercial Workers Union $1,050
Others $3,250

Government & Postal Workers $32,950

National Assn of Letter Carriers $10,000
American Postal Workers Union $6,500
National Assn of Retired Federal Employees $6,000
National Rural Letter Carriers Assn $3,300
National Assn of Postal Supervisors $1,800
American Fedn of State/County/Munic Employees $1,500
National League of Postmasters $1,000
Others $2,850

Transportation Unions $22,200

Teamsters Union $6,650
Air Line Pilots Assn $5,000
Transport Workers Union* $2,150
Marine Engineers District 2 Maritime Officers $2,000
International Longshoremen Assn $1,500
Seafarers International Union $1,000
Others $3,900

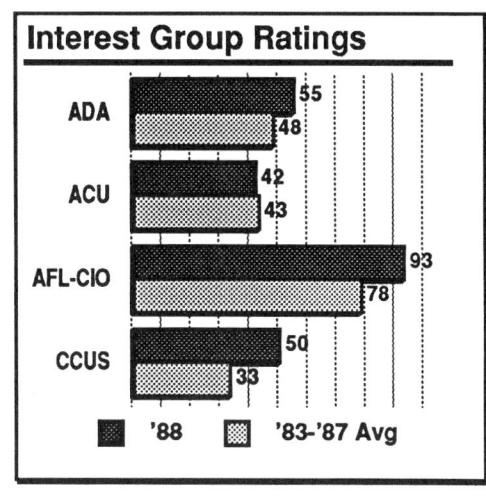

Interest Group Ratings

	'88	'83–'87 Avg
ADA	55	48
ACU	42	43
AFL-CIO	93	78
CCUS	50	33

Ideological/Single-Issue

Pro-Israel $7,000

National PAC $5,000
Washington PAC $2,000

Independent expenditures supporting Gilman

National Cmte to Preserve Social Security $1,667

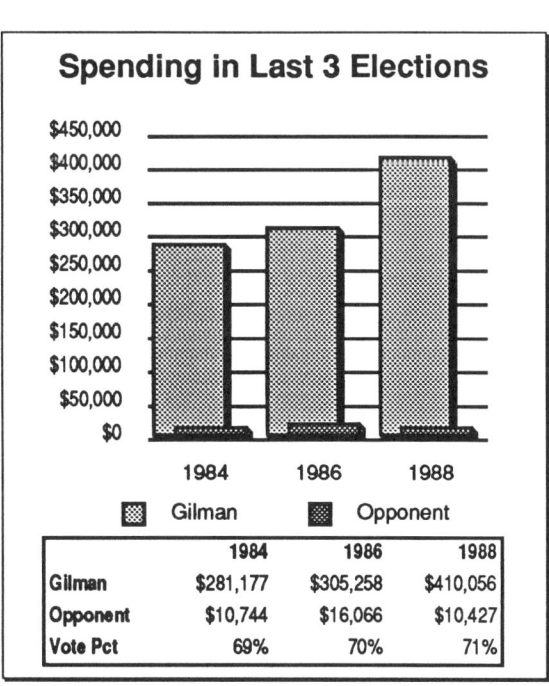

Spending in Last 3 Elections

	1984	1986	1988
Gilman	$281,177	$305,258	$410,056
Opponent	$10,744	$16,066	$10,427
Vote Pct	69%	70%	71%

*Contributions came from more than one PAC affiliated with this sponsor.

Newt Gingrich, R-Ga (6)

First elected: 1978
Total receipts: $851,786
Total from PACs: $260,476

1988 Committees & Subcommittees

House Administration
Libraries and Memorials (Ranking Republican)
Procurement and Printing (Ranking Republican)

Public Works and Transportation
Aviation (Ranking Republican)
Investigations and Oversight
Surface Transportation

Joint Library

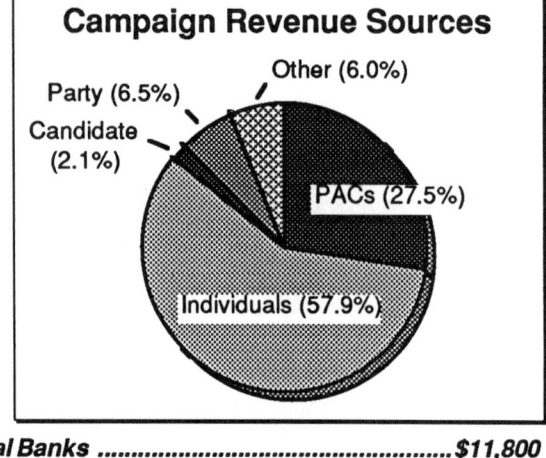

Campaign Revenue Sources

Other (6.0%)
Party (6.5%)
Candidate (2.1%)
PACs (27.5%)
Individuals (57.9%)

PAC Contribution Profile

Business

Automotive & Trucking **$16,050**
United Parcel Service $6,500
National Auto Dealers Assn $2,000
Auto Dealers & Drivers for Free Trade $1,500
General Motors $1,250
American Trucking Assns $1,000
Eaton Corp $1,000
Others $2,800

Aviation & Aerospace **$38,150**
Aircraft Owners & Pilots Assn $9,000
Delta Airlines $4,700
Northwest Airlines $2,600
Boeing Company $2,500
American Airlines $2,000
Federal Express Corp $2,250
Texas Air $2,000
Trans World Airlines $1,300
American Assn of Airport Executives $1,250
General Electric $1,000
General Aviation Manufacturers Assn $1,000
Loral Corp $1,000
United Airlines $1,000
United Technologies $1,000
USAir Corp $1,000
Others $4,550

Chemicals **$7,200**
Dow Chemical* $3,500
Nalco Chemical Company $1,000
Others $2,700

PAC Totals by Category

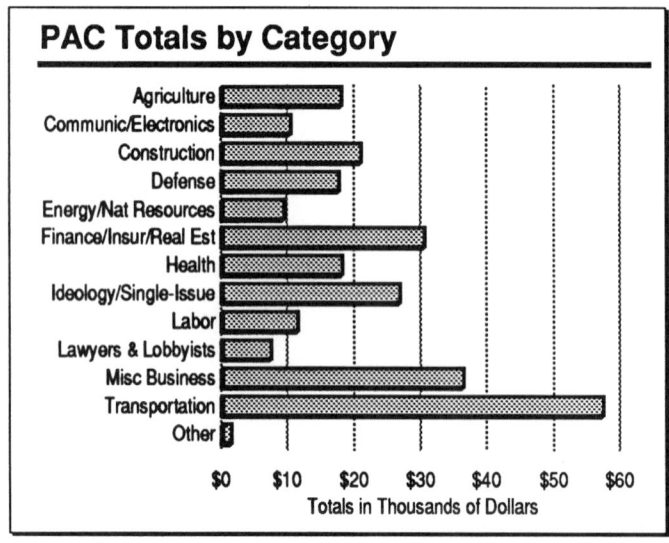

Totals in Thousands of Dollars

(categories: Agriculture, Communic/Electronics, Construction, Defense, Energy/Nat Resources, Finance/Insur/Real Est, Health, Ideology/Single-Issue, Labor, Lawyers & Lobbyists, Misc Business, Transportation, Other)

Commercial Banks **$11,800**
Citizens & Southern National Bank $3,100
First Atlanta Corp $2,700
Bank South Corp $2,000
Trust Company of Georgia $1,700
Barnett Banks of Florida $1,000
Others $1,300

Construction **$20,800**
National Assn of Home Builders $6,000
Associated General Contractors $5,000
Ch2M Hill $1,500
Owens-Corning Fiberglas $1,500
Wall & Ceiling/Gypsum Contractors $1,150
Manville Corp $1,000
Sheet Metal/AirCon Contractors $1,000
Others $3,650

Defense **$17,500**
Harris Corp $11,000
Lockheed Corp $1,750
Hughes Aircraft $1,250
Northrop Corp $1,250
Rockwell International $1,000
Others $1,250

Food & Beverage **$14,644**
Coca-Cola Company $3,500
Flowers Industries $2,000
S & A Restaurant Corp $2,000
National Restaurant Assn $1,000
National Beer Wholesalers Assn $1,000
Quaker Oats $1,000
Others $4,144

Forest Products **$5,000**
Westvaco Corp $1,500
International Paper Company $1,000
Others $2,500

Health Professionals **$16,450**
American Medical Assn $10,000
American Dental Assn $2,500
Georgia Medical Assn $1,200
American Optometric Assn $1,000
National Assn of Pharmacists $1,000
Others $750

Insurance **$6,150**
American Family Corp $2,750
National Assn of Life Underwriters $1,500
Others $1,900

Lawyers $7,254

Assn of Trial Lawyers of America	$2,000
King & Spalding	$2,000
Baker & Hostetler	$1,500
Others	$1,754

Real Estate $9,250

National Assn of Realtors	$8,250
First Union Corp	$1,000

Telecommunications $7,450

Southern Bell	$4,000
AT&T	$2,450
Continental Telecom	$1,000

Textiles $7,700

Burlington Industries	$1,300
Westpoint Pepperell	$1,300
J P Stevens & Company	$1,050
American Textile Manufacturers Institute	$1,000
Dixie Yarns/TI-CARO	$1,000
Milliken & Company	$1,000
Others	$1,050

Other Major Business PACs

National Fedn of Independent Business	$4,584	Sml Business
Dairymen Inc-Georgia	$3,250	Dairy
NCR Corp	$1,500	Computers
Owens-Illinois	$1,500	Paper Packg
ACRE (Action Committee for Rural Electric)	$1,250	RuralElect
Cooper Industries	$1,250	Electronics
Gold Kist	$1,250	Poultry/Egg
American Society of Travel Agents	$1,000	Travel Agent
Atlanta Gas Light Company	$1,000	Natural Gas
Browning-Ferris Industries	$1,000	Waste Mgmt
Common Sense PAC	$1,000	Unknown
Figgie International	$1,000	Security Svc
Fulton Federal Savings & Loan	$1,000	SavingsBanks
Georgia Power Company	$1,000	ElectricUtil
Mapco Inc	$1,000	Refine/Mktg
Maytag Company	$1,000	Appliances
Mobil Oil	$1,000	Major Oil

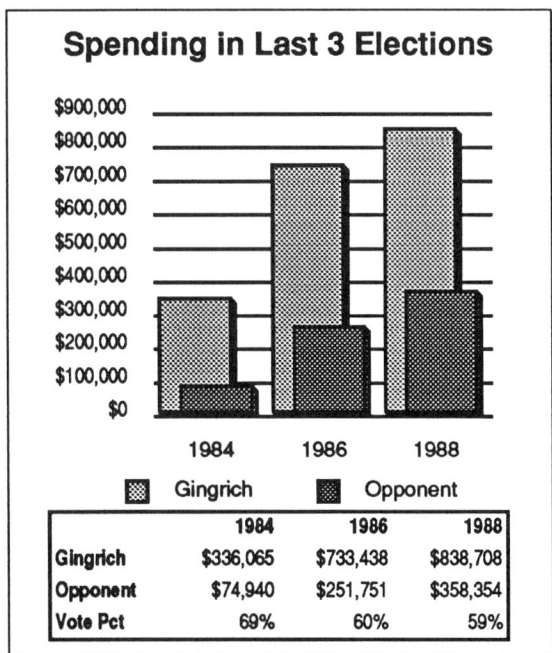

Spending in Last 3 Elections

	1984	1986	1988
Gingrich	$336,065	$733,438	$838,708
Opponent	$74,940	$251,751	$358,354
Vote Pct	69%	60%	59%

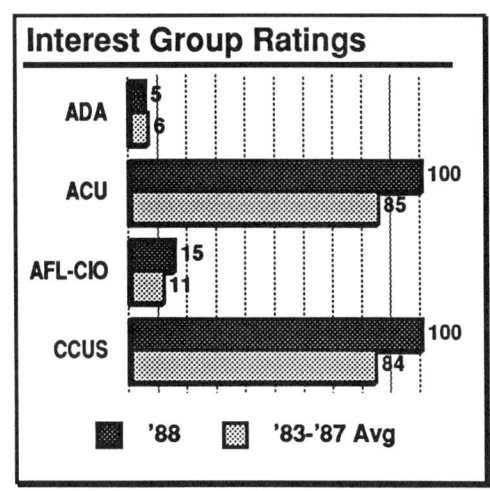

Interest Group Ratings

	'88	'83-'87 Avg
ADA	5	6
ACU	100	85
AFL-CIO	15	11
CCUS	100	84

Labor

Air Transport Unions $11,250

Air Line Pilots Assn	$10,000
Others	$1,250

Ideological/Single-Issue

Pro-Defense..$6,775

National Security PAC	$5,000
Council for National Defense	$1,525
Others	$250

Republican/Conservative $12,759

The Loose Group	$6,000
America's PAC	$3,000
Eagle Forum	$2,000
Conservative Victory Cmte	$1,000
Others	$759

Other Major Ideological/Single-Issue PACs

National Right to Life PAC	$1,560	Pro-Life
National Rifle Assn	$1,500	Pro-Guns
Ruff PAC	$1,250	Tax Policy

Independent expenditures supporting Gingrich

Life Amendment PAC	$2,348

---

* Contributions came from more than one PAC affiliated with this sponsor.

Dan Glickman, D-Kan (4)

First elected: 1976
Total receipts: $562,266
Total from PACs: $277,290

1988 Committees & Subcommittees

Agriculture
Department Operations, Research and Foreign Agriculture
Domestic Marketing, Consumer Relations and Nutrition
Wheat, Soybeans and Feed Grains (Chairman)

Judiciary
Administrative Law and Governmental Relations
Monopolies and Commercial Law

Science, Space and Technology
Transportation, Aviation and Materials

Select Intelligence
Legislation
Oversight and Evaluation

PAC Contribution Profile

Business

Aviation & Aerospace **$19,740**

Boeing Company	$3,525
Aircraft Owners & Pilots Assn	$2,750
United Technologies	$2,250
Texas Air*	$2,000
Beech Aircraft	$1,690
American Airlines	$1,450
Genl Aviation Manufacturers Assn	$1,450
Others	$4,625

Commercial & Savings Banks **$7,950**

American Bankers Assn	$2,500
US League of Savings Assn	$2,250
Kansas Bankers Assn	$1,000
Kansas League of Savings Institutions	$1,000
Others	$1,200

Crop Production & Trading **$11,800**

American Crystal Sugar Corp	$1,700
Archer-Daniels-Midland Corp	$1,700
American Sugarbeet Growers Assn	$1,400
National Assn of Wheat Growers	$1,400
Riceland Foods	$1,000
Others	$4,600

Defense **$8,850**

General Dynamics	$2,000
Textron Inc	$1,250
Allied-Signal	$1,000
Northrop Corp	$1,000
Rockwell International	$1,000
Others	$2,600

Campaign Revenue Sources

Party (1.0%)
Other (4.6%)
Individuals (46.2%)
PACs (48.2%)

Food & Beverage **$18,800**

ConAgra Inc	$2,000
Occidental Petroleum*	$2,000
American Meat Institute	$1,950
Food Marketing Institute	$1,650
General Mills	$1,500
A E Staley Manufacturing Company	$1,400
American Bakers Assn	$1,250
National Beer Wholesalers Assn	$1,200
Kellogg Company	$1,000
Pillsbury Company	$1,000
Others	$3,850

Insurance **$25,280**

National Assn of Life Underwriters	$5,000
National Assn Mutual Insurance Agents	$2,000
Aetna Life & Casualty	$1,950
American Council of Life Insurance	$1,500
Casualty & Surety Agents Assn	$1,500
Travelers Corp	$1,500
Independent Insurance Agents of America	$1,450
Allstate Insurance	$1,000
Cigna Corp	$1,000
Hartford Insurance	$1,000
Liberty Mutual Insurance	$1,000
National Assn of Independent Insurers	$1,000
US Fidelity & Guaranty	$1,000
Others	$4,380

Lawyers & Lobbyists **$10,305**

Akin, Gump, Hauer & Feld	$2,230
Kutak, Rock & Campbell	$1,250
Arnold & Porter	$1,200
Others	$5,625

Real Estate **$8,500**

National Assn of Realtors	$6,750
American Land Title Assn	$1,250
Others	$500

PAC Totals by Category

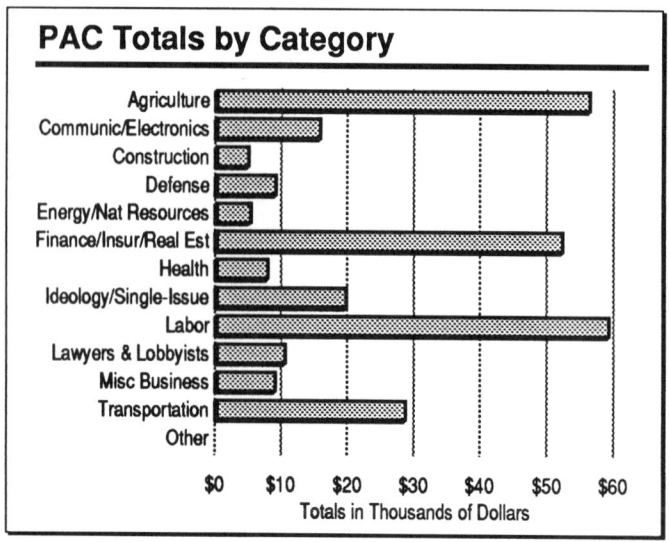

Agriculture
Communic/Electronics
Construction
Defense
Energy/Nat Resources
Finance/Insur/Real Est
Health
Ideology/Single-Issue
Labor
Lawyers & Lobbyists
Misc Business
Transportation
Other

$0 $10 $20 $30 $40 $50 $60
Totals in Thousands of Dollars

Securities & Commodities Investment $15,800

Chicago Board of Trade	$4,000
Chicago Mercantile Exchange	$3,200
Goldman Sachs	$2,500
Commodity Exchange Inc	$1,450
Futures Industry Assn	$1,450
Chicago Board of Options Exchange	$1,000
Morgan Stanley & Company	$1,000
Philadelphia Stock Exchange	$1,000
Others	$200

Other Major Business PACs

American Institute of CPA's	$5,000	Accountants
Auto Dealers & Drivers for Free Trade	$3,500	JapanAutoSal
National Assn of Home Builders	$2,500	Resid Constr
AT&T	$2,000	LongDistance
National Cable Television Assn	$2,000	CableTV
Southwestern Bell	$2,000	Phone Util
Texas Cattle Feeders Assn	$2,000	Feedlots
American Medical Assn	$1,750	Doctors
ACRE (Action Committee for Rural Electric)	$1,600	RuralElect
American Podiatry Assn	$1,500	Other MD
United Parcel Service	$1,300	Delivery
American Optometric Assn	$1,250	Eye Docs
National Farmers Organization	$1,200	Farm Orgs
Milk Industry Foundation	$1,150	Dairy
ASCAP	$1,000	Live Music
Continental Telecom	$1,000	Phone Util
Coopers & Lybrand	$1,000	Accountants
Deere & Company	$1,000	Farm Equip
Farm Credit Council	$1,000	Ag Svcs
Farmland Industries	$1,000	Ag Svcs
FMC Corp	$1,000	Ag Chemicals
Hallmark Cards	$1,000	Publishing
Kansas Chiropractic Assn	$1,000	Chiropractor
Riceland Foods	$1,000	Crops

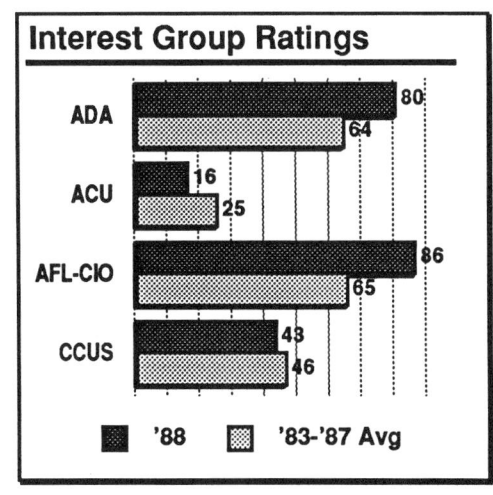

Interest Group Ratings

	'88	'83–'87 Avg
ADA	80	64
ACU	16	25
AFL-CIO	86	65
CCUS	43	46

Labor

Bldg Trades/Industrial/Misc Unions $37,025

Machinists/Aerospace Workers Union	$8,500
Communications Workers of America	$3,775
Food & Commercial Workers Union	$3,450
Sheet Metal Workers Union	$3,300
Rubber Cork Linoleum Plastic Workers	$3,000
National Education Assn*	$2,600
Operating Engineers Union	$2,500
United Auto Workers	$2,200
American Federation of Teachers	$2,000
Laborers' Political League	$1,700
Carpenters & Joiners Union	$1,000
Others	$3,000

Government & Postal Workers $13,500

National Assn of Letter Carriers	$7,000
National Assn of Retired Federal Employees	$5,000
American Postal Workers Union	$1,000
American Fedn of State/County/Munic Employees	$500

Transportation Unions $8,475

Air Line Pilots Assn	$2,500
Teamsters Union	$2,000
United Transportation Union	$1,575
Others	$2,400

Ideological/Single-Issue

Pro-Israel $17,200

National PAC	$5,000
Hudson Valley PAC	$2,500
St Louisians for Better Government	$2,500
Washington PAC	$1,750
Chai PAC	$1,250
Delaware Valley PAC	$1,000
National Action Committee (NACPAC)	$1,000
Roundtable PAC	$1,000
Others	$1,200

Other Major Ideological/Single-Issue PACs

Valley Education Fund (Tony Coelho)	$1,000	Dem Leaders

Independent expenditures supporting Glickman

National Cmte to Preserve Social Security	$3,155

---

* Contributions came from more than one PAC affiliated with this sponsor.

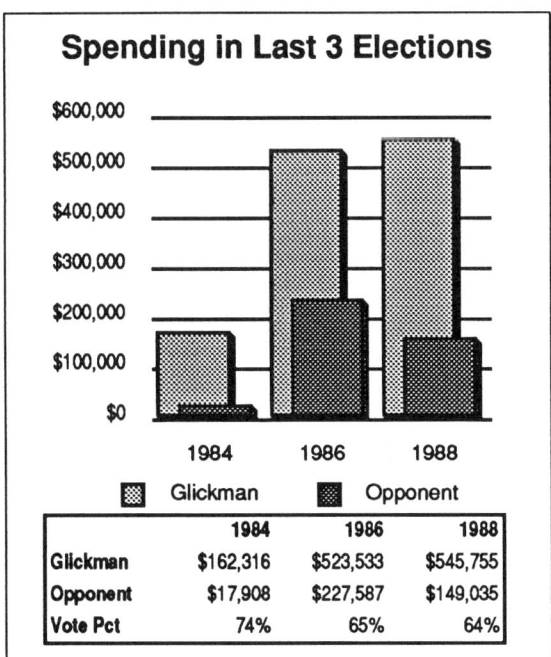

Spending in Last 3 Elections

	Glickman	Opponent

	1984	1986	1988
Glickman	$162,316	$523,533	$545,755
Opponent	$17,908	$227,587	$149,035
Vote Pct	74%	65%	64%

Henry B. Gonzalez, D-Texas (20)

First elected: 1961
Total receipts: $171,284
Total from PACs: $100,387

1988 Committees & Subcommittees

Banking, Finance and Urban Affairs
Housing and Community Development (Chairman)
Consumer Affairs and Coinage
Financial Institutions Supervision, Regulation and Insurance
General Oversight and Investigations

Small Business
Antitrust, Impact of Deregulation and Privatization

PAC Contribution Profile

Business

Campaign Revenue Sources

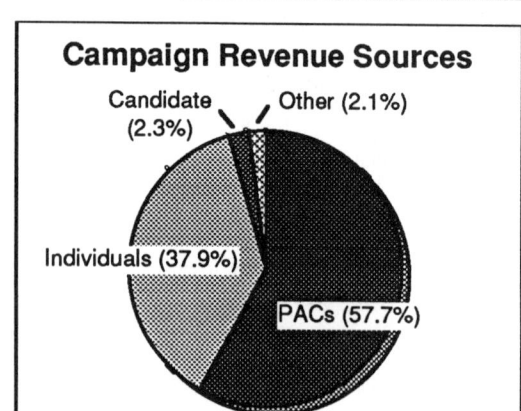

Candidate (2.3%)
Other (2.1%)
Individuals (37.9%)
PACs (57.7%)

Automotive	**$6,600**
National Auto Dealers Assn	$4,000
Auto Dealers & Drivers for Free Trade	$2,500
Others	$100

Construction	**$5,950**
National Assn of Home Builders	$2,500
Manville Corp	$1,000
National Concrete Masonry Assn	$1,000
Others	$1,450

Dairy	**$3,000**
Associated Milk Producers	$3,000

Financial Institutions	**$6,300**
American Bankers Assn	$1,000
Assn of Bank Holding Companies	$1,000
Credit Union National Assn	$1,000
Glendale Federal Savings & Loan	$1,000
Independent Bankers Assn	$1,000
Others	$1,300

Insurance	**$9,400**
Independent Insurance Agents of America	$5,000
National Assn of Life Underwriters	$3,000
American Council of Life Insurance	$1,200
Others	$200

Lawyers	**$6,550**
Assn of Trial Lawyers of America	$5,000
Fullbright & Jaworski	$1,000
Others	$550

Real Estate	**$7,556**
National Assn of Realtors	$4,356
Mortgage Bankers Assn of America	$2,000
Federal National Mortgage Assn	$1,000
Others	$200

Telecommunications	**$2,000**
GTE (Southwest)	$1,500
Others	$500

PAC Totals by Category

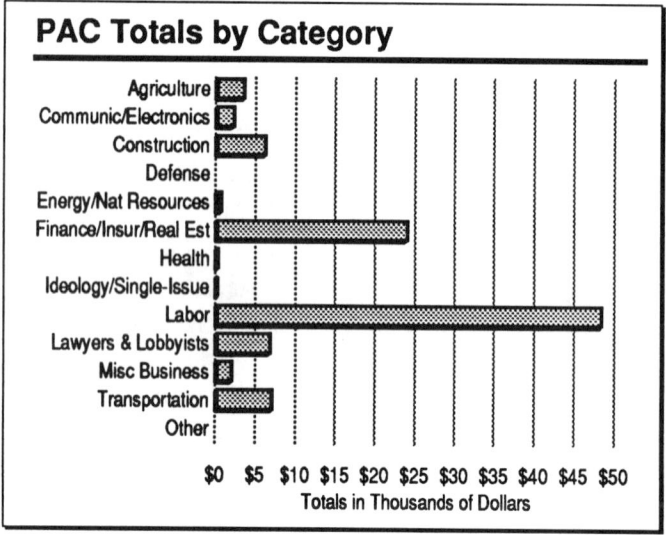

Agriculture
Communic/Electronics
Construction
Defense
Energy/Nat Resources
Finance/Insur/Real Est
Health
Ideology/Single-Issue
Labor
Lawyers & Lobbyists
Misc Business
Transportation
Other

$0 $5 $10 $15 $20 $25 $30 $35 $40 $45 $50
Totals in Thousands of Dollars

Labor

Bldg Trades/Industrial/Misc Unions **$18,120**

AFL-CIO $2,500
Carpenters & Joiners Union $2,500
Machinists/Aerospace Workers Union $2,500
Communications Workers of America $2,320
Laborers' Political League $1,500
Intl Brotherhood of Electrical Workers............$1,000
Ironworkers Union $1,000
Plumbers/Pipefitters Union $1,000
Sheet Metal Workers Union $1,000
United Steelworkers $1,000
Others $1,800

Government & Postal Workers **$9,750**

American Fedn of State/County/Munic Employees $3,000
National Assn of Retired Federal Employees $3,000
American Federation of Government Employees $1,500
National Assn of Letter Carriers $1,000
Others $1,250

Teachers Unions **$7,600**

National Education Assn $7,600

Transportation Unions **$12,650**

Teamsters Union $10,000
Seafarers International Union $1,000
United Transportation Union $1,000
Others $650

Independent expenditures supporting Gonzalez

National Cmte to Preserve Social Security $1,078

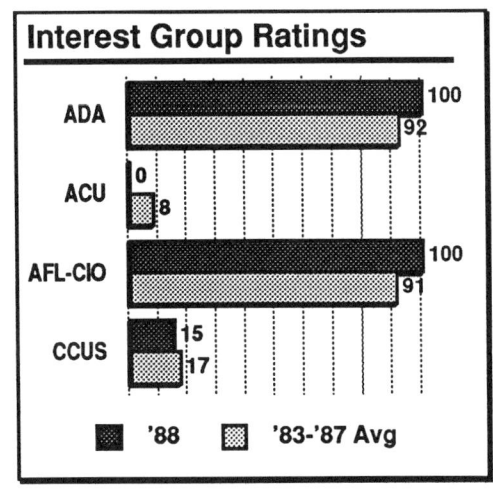

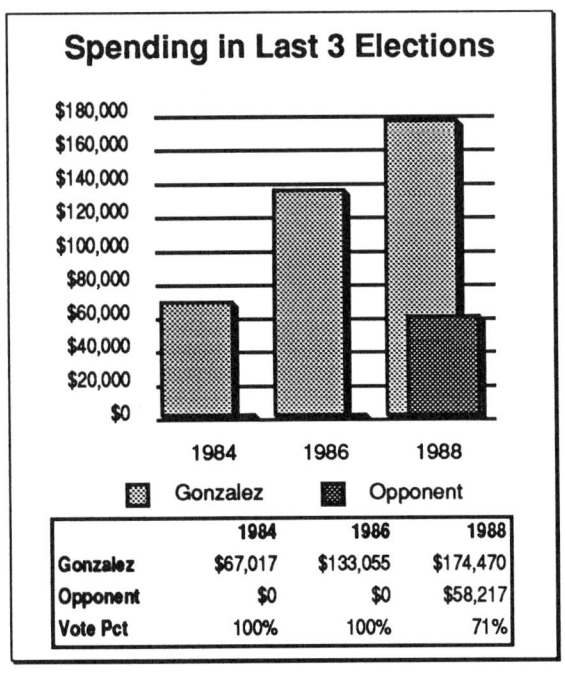

Bill Goodling, R-Pa (19)

1988 Committees & Subcommittees

Budget
Human Resources (Ranking Republican)
Health
Income Security

Education and Labor
Elementary, Secondary and Vocational Education (Ranking Republican)
Postsecondary Education

PAC Contribution Profile

Associated General Contractors	$1,000	Comml Constr
Mutual of Omaha	$500	Insurance
Bowling Proprietors Assn	$250	AmuseCtr

NOTE: Goodling reported taking no PAC funds in his 1988 campaign. The PACs listed above did report making contributions during 1987-88, however, and those contributions are recorded in the official FEC records.

First elected: 1974
Total receipts: $54,123
Total from PACs: $0

Campaign Revenue Sources

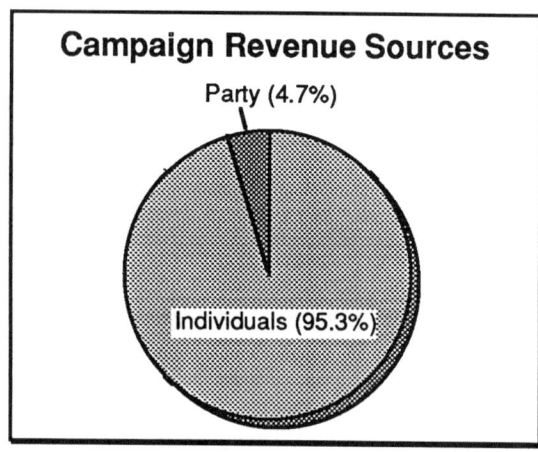

Party (4.7%)
Individuals (95.3%)

PAC Totals by Category

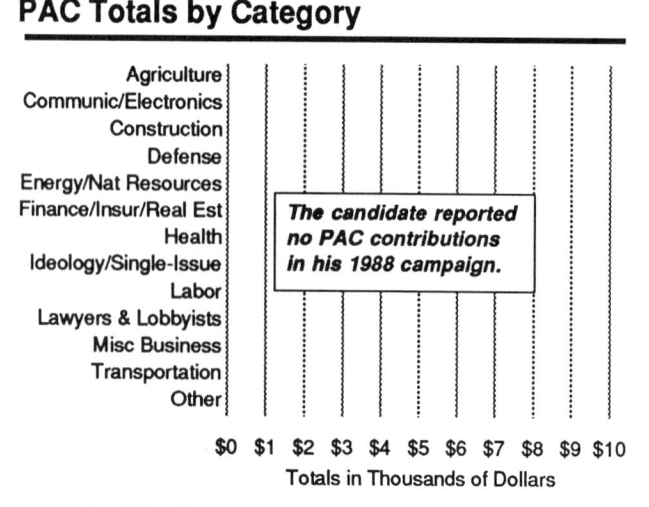

Agriculture
Communic/Electronics
Construction
Defense
Energy/Nat Resources
Finance/Insur/Real Est
Health
Ideology/Single-Issue
Labor
Lawyers & Lobbyists
Misc Business
Transportation
Other

The candidate reported no PAC contributions in his 1988 campaign.

$0 $1 $2 $3 $4 $5 $6 $7 $8 $9 $10
Totals in Thousands of Dollars

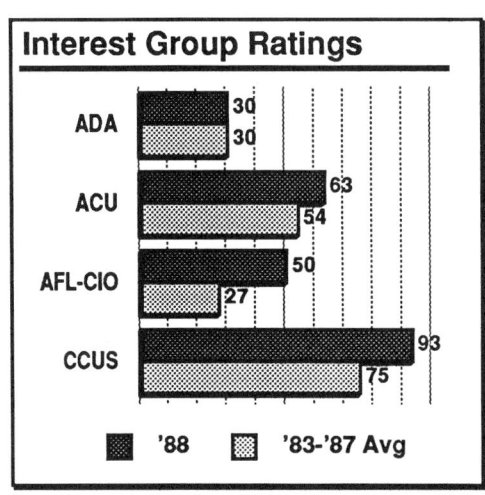

Interest Group Ratings

	'88	'83-'87 Avg
ADA	30	30
ACU	63	54
AFL-CIO	50	27
CCUS	93	75

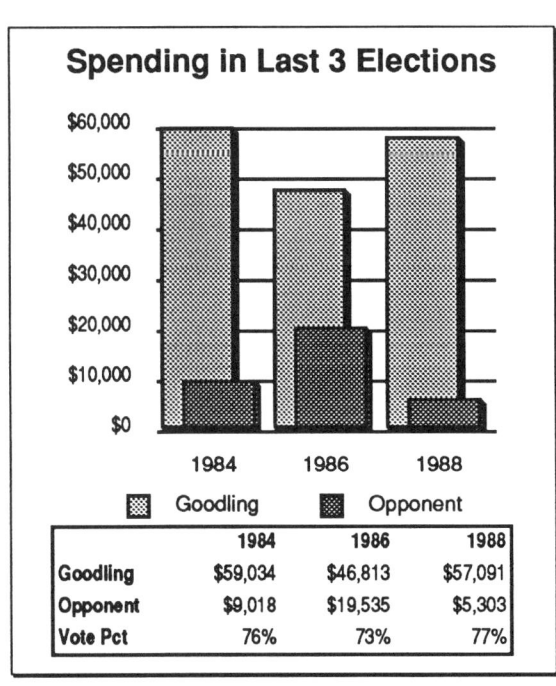

Spending in Last 3 Elections

	1984	1986	1988
Goodling	$59,034	$46,813	$57,091
Opponent	$9,018	$19,535	$5,303
Vote Pct	76%	73%	77%

515

Bart Gordon, D-Tenn (6)

First elected: 1984
Total receipts: $587,878
Total from PACs: $256,095

1988 Committees & Subcommittees

Rules
Legislative Process

Select Aging
Housing and Consumer Interests

PAC Contribution Profile

Business

Campaign Revenue Sources

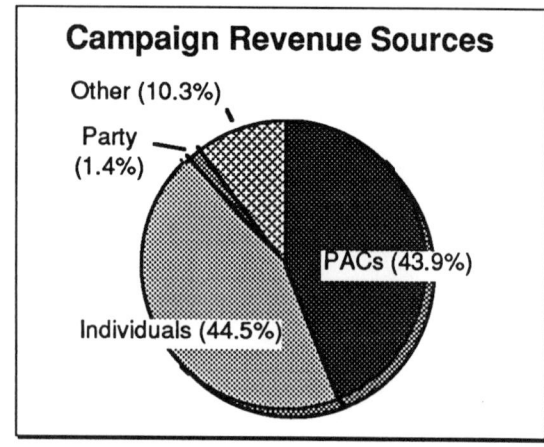

Other (10.3%)
Party (1.4%)
PACs (43.9%)
Individuals (44.5%)

Automotive	**$3,450**
National Auto Dealers Assn	$2,250
Others	$1,200
Aviation/Air Freight	**$12,350**
Federal Express Corp	$10,000
Aircraft Owners & Pilots Assn	$1,700
Others	$650
Commercial Banks	**$32,000**
American Bankers Assn	$10,000
First American Corp	$5,000
Bankers Trust	$2,500
Citicorp	$2,000
First Chicago Corp	$1,500
Citizens & Southern National Bank	$1,350
Marine Midland Banks	$1,350
Third National Corp	$1,100
Barnett Banks of Florida	$1,000
First Tennessee National Corp	$1,000
J P Morgan & Company	$1,000
Others	$4,200
Construction	**$8,000**
National Assn of Home Builders	$5,000
Tennessee Road Builders Assn	$1,000
Others	$2,000
Dairy	**$5,800**
Associated Milk Producers	$3,100
Dairymen Inc-Tennessee	$2,400
Others	$300

Defense	**$4,250**
Textron Inc	$1,400
Others	$2,850
Food & Beverage	**$8,100**
National Beer Wholesalers Assn	$1,150
Brown-Forman Distillers	$1,000
Hardee's Food Systems	$1,000
Shoneys Inc	$1,000
Others	$3,950
Health Professionals	**$7,900**
American Medical Assn	$2,300
American Optometric Assn	$1,300
National Assn of Pharmacists	$1,100
American Academy of Ophthalmology	$1,000
American Dental Assn	$1,000
Others	$1,200
Insurance	**$10,150**
Independent Insurance Agents of America	$2,950
National Assn of Life Underwriters	$2,000
National Assn Mutual Insurance Agents	$1,300
Others	$3,900
Lawyers & Lobbyists	**$6,950**
Assn of Trial Lawyers of America	$5,000
Others	$1,950
Oil & Gas	**$3,750**
Columbia Hydrocarbon Corp	$1,500
Others	$2,250
Real Estate	**$11,500**
National Assn of Realtors	$10,000
Mortgage Bankers Assn of America	$1,000
Others	$500
Savings Banks & Credit Unions	**$4,550**
US League of Savings Assn	$2,300
Tenn League of Savings Institutions	$1,000
Others	$1,250
Securities Investment	**$6,900**
Morgan Stanley & Company	$2,000
Dean Witter Reynolds	$1,350
Goldman Sachs	$1,000
Others	$2,550

PAC Totals by Category

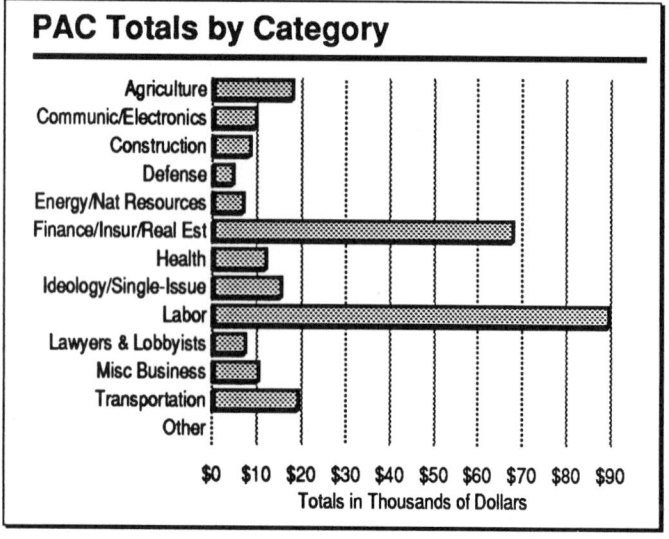

Agriculture
Communic/Electronics
Construction
Defense
Energy/Nat Resources
Finance/Insur/Real Est
Health
Ideology/Single-Issue
Labor
Lawyers & Lobbyists
Misc Business
Transportation
Other

$0 $10 $20 $30 $40 $50 $60 $70 $80 $90
Totals in Thousands of Dollars

Telecommunications	$6,250
South Central Bell Telephone	$3,100
AT&T	$1,900
Others	$1,250

Tobacco	$4,700
Philip Morris	$1,500
RJR Nabisco	$1,000
Others	$2,200

Other Major Business PACs

Schering-Plough Corp	$1,500	Pharmaceut
J C Penney Company	$1,350	Dept Store
ASCAP	$1,000	Live Music
Independent Coal Operators Assn	$1,000	Coal

Labor

Bldg Trades/Industrial/Misc Unions	$45,150
United Steelworkers	$10,000
United Auto Workers	$6,650
Carpenters & Joiners Union	$4,000
Intl Brotherhood of Electrical Workers	$4,000
Oil, Chemical & Atomic Workers Union	$3,600
AFL-CIO*	$2,400
Machinists/Aerospace Workers Union	$1,650
Laborers' Political League	$1,500
United Paperworkers	$1,500
Food & Commercial Workers Union	$1,350
Operating Engineers Union	$1,200
Plumbers/Pipefitters Union	$1,100
Rubber Cork Linoleum Plastic Workers	$1,000
Sheet Metal Workers Union	$1,000
Others	$4,200

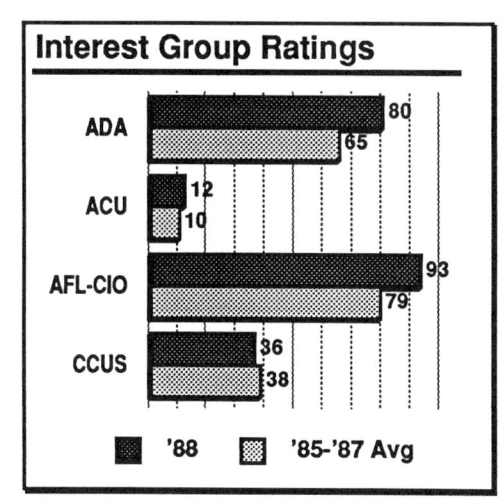
Government & Postal Workers	$14,850
National Assn of Retired Federal Employees	$6,000
National Assn of Letter Carriers	$2,000
National Assn of Postmasters	$1,200
American Fedn of State/County/Munic Employees	$1,000
American Postal Workers Union	$1,000
Others	$3,650

Teachers Unions	$4,350
National Education Assn	$2,450
American Federation of Teachers	$1,900

Transportation Unions	$24,650
Teamsters Union	$10,000
Air Line Pilots Assn	$5,000
Amalgamated Transit Union	$4,100
United Transportation Union	$2,300
Seafarers International Union	$1,700
Others	$1,550

Ideological/Single-Issue

Pro-Israel	$7,150
National PAC	$5,000
Others	$2,150

Other Major Ideological/Single-Issue PACs

National Cmte for an Effective Congress	$4,996	Dem/Liberal
National Cmte to Preserve Social Security	$1,300	Social Security
Valley Education Fund (Tony Coelho)	$1,000	Dem Leaders

Independent expenditures supporting Gordon

National Cmte to Preserve Social Security	$1,770

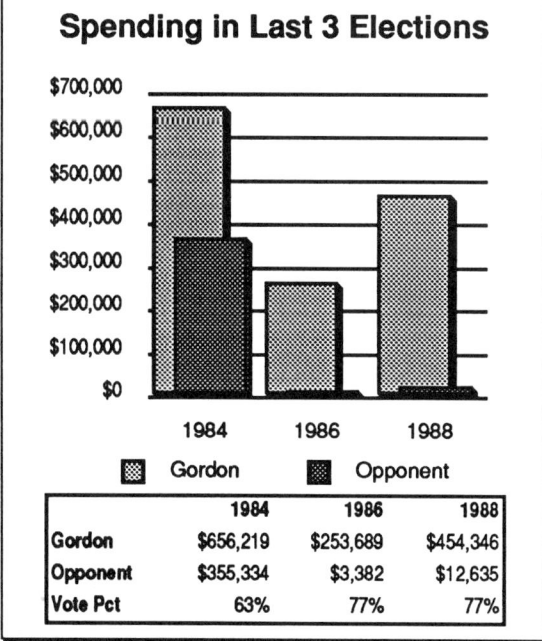

Spending in Last 3 Elections

■ Gordon   ■ Opponent

	1984	1986	1988
Gordon	$656,219	$253,689	$454,346
Opponent	$355,334	$3,382	$12,635
Vote Pct	63%	77%	77%

* Contributions came from more than one PAC affiliated with this sponsor.

Porter J. Goss, R-Fla (13)

First elected: 1988
Total receipts: $878,439
Total from PACs: $141,976

1988-1989 Committees & Subcommittees

Foreign Affairs
Arms Control, International Security and Science
Western Hemisphere Affairs

Merchant Marine and Fisheries
Coast Guard and Navigation
Oceanography

PAC Contribution Profile

Business

Automotive	**$3,250**
National Auto Dealers Assn	$3,000
Others	$250
Commercial Banks	**$14,650**
Barnett Banks of Florida	$5,000
American Bankers Assn	$2,000
Sun Banks	$1,750
Citizens & Southern National Bank	$1,500
First Florida Banks	$1,000
Others	$3,400
Construction	**$17,042**
National Assn of Home Builders	$11,992
Associated General Contractors	$1,000
National Society of Professional Engineers	$1,000
Others	$3,050
Electric Utilities	**$3,250**
ACRE (Action Committee for Rural Electrification)	$1,500
Florida Power & Light	$1,000
Others	$750
Food & Beverage	**$5,250**
Brown-Forman Distillers	$1,750
Malone & Hyde Inc	$1,000
Winn-Dixie Stores	$1,000
Others	$1,500

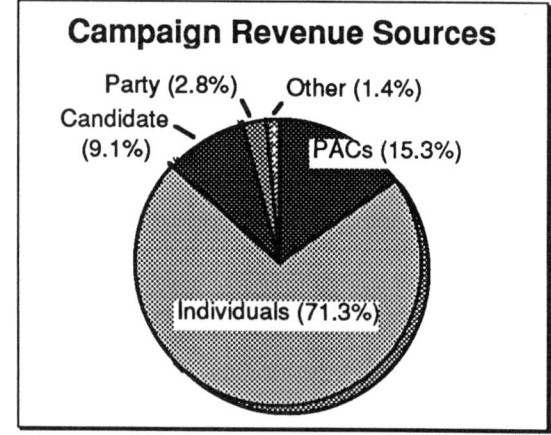

Campaign Revenue Sources

Party (2.8%)
Other (1.4%)
Candidate (9.1%)
PACs (15.3%)
Individuals (71.3%)

Health Professionals	**$22,750**
American Medical Assn	$10,000
American Academy of Ophthalmology	$6,500
Florida Medical Assn	$5,000
Others	$1,250
Insurance	**$2,050**
Independent Insurance Agents of America	$1,000
Others	$1,050
Oil & Gas	**$4,000**
None over $500	
Real Estate	**$13,300**
National Assn of Realtors	$10,000
American Land Development Assn	$1,500
General Development Corp	$1,000
Others	$800
Savings Banks & Credit Unions	**$3,800**
Florida League of Financial Institutions	$2,000
Credit Union National Assn	$1,000
Others	$800
Telecommunications	**$6,500**
United Telecommunications	$3,000
AT&T	$1,000
Continental Telecom	$1,000
General Telephone of Florida	$1,000
Others	$500
Waste Management	**$2,500**
Waste Management Inc	$2,000
Others	$500

Other Major Business PACs

Aircraft Owners & Pilots Assn	$1,150	Gen Aviation
Associated Milk Producers	$1,000	Dairy
Business Industry PAC	$1,000	Bus Assns
Coopers & Lybrand	$1,000	Accountants
Harris Corp	$1,000	Defense
National Assn of Temporary Services	$1,000	EmployAgency

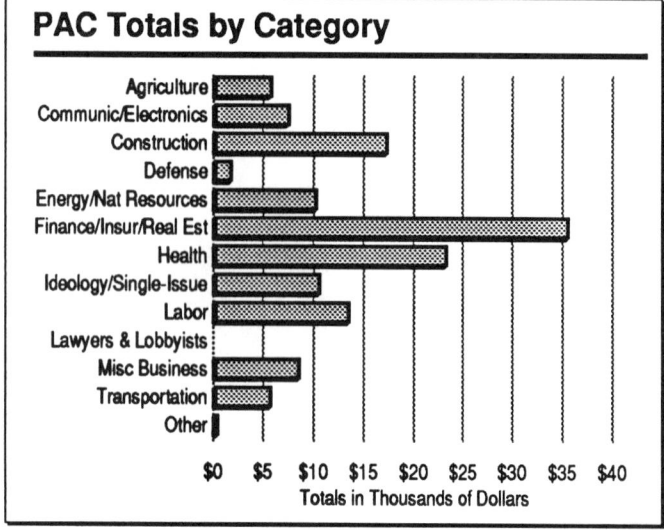

PAC Totals by Category

Agriculture
Communic/Electronics
Construction
Defense
Energy/Nat Resources
Finance/Insur/Real Est
Health
Ideology/Single-Issue
Labor
Lawyers & Lobbyists
Misc Business
Transportation
Other

$0 $5 $10 $15 $20 $25 $30 $35 $40
Totals in Thousands of Dollars

Labor

Labor Unions $13,250
National Education Assn $5,000
Air Line Pilots Assn $3,500
Marine Engineers Union* $2,500
National Assn of Letter Carriers $2,000
Others $250

Ideological/Single-Issue

Pro-Israel $6,750
National PAC $5,000
BayPAC $1,000
Others $750

Other Major Ideological/Single-Issue PACs

Council for National Defense ....$1,222   Pro-Defense

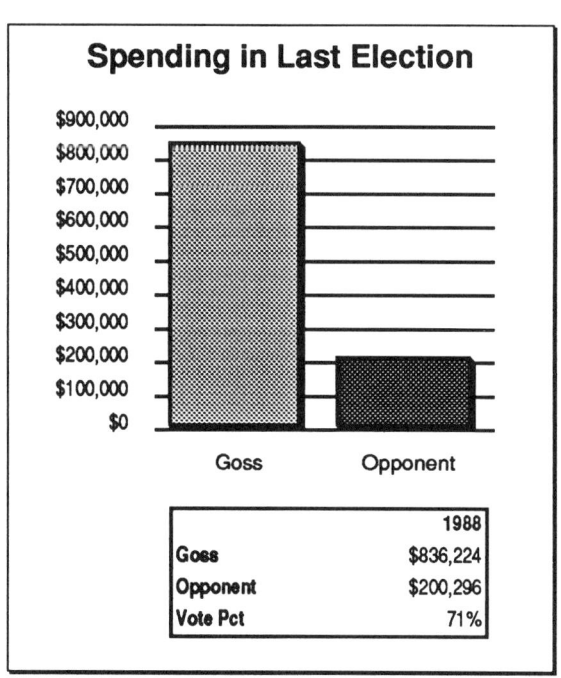

	1988
Goss	$836,224
Opponent	$200,296
Vote Pct	71%

* Contributions came from more than one PAC affiliated with this sponsor.

Bill Gradison, R-Ohio (2)

First elected: 1974
Total receipts: $197,743
Total from PACs: $0

1988 Committees & Subcommittees

Budget
Budget Process (Ranking Republican)
Economic and Trade Policy
Health
Income Security

Ways and Means
Health (Ranking Republican)
Public Assistance and Unemployment Compensation

PAC Contribution Profile

Pepsi-Cola Bottlers Assn ....$1,000 BevgBottling
Alltel Corp ....$300 Phone Util
American Health Care Assn............................$250 Nursing Home
Small Business Council of America ....$50 Sml Business

NOTE: Gradison reported taking no PAC funds in his 1988 campaign. The PACs listed above did report making contributions during 1987-88, however, and those contributions are recorded in the official FEC records.

Campaign Revenue Sources

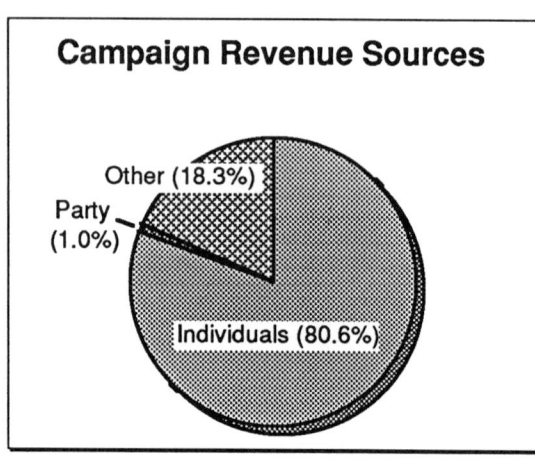

Other (18.3%)
Party (1.0%)
Individuals (80.6%)

PAC Totals by Category

Agriculture
Communic/Electronics
Construction
Defense
Energy/Nat Resources
Finance/Insur/Real Est
Health
Ideology/Single-Issue
Labor
Lawyers & Lobbyists
Misc Business
Transportation
Other

The candidate reported no PAC contributions in his 1988 campaign.

$0 $1 $2 $3 $4 $5 $6 $7 $8 $9 $10
Totals in Thousands of Dollars

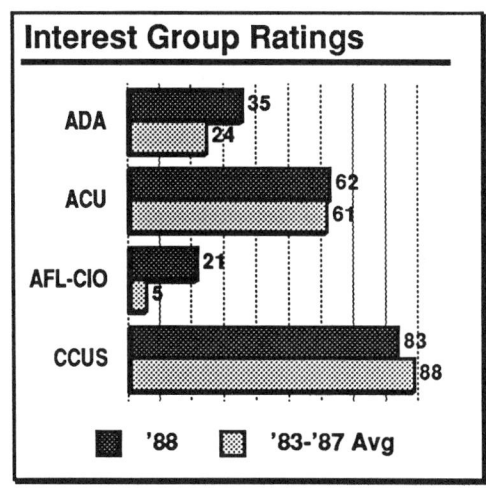

Interest Group Ratings

	'88	'83-'87 Avg
ADA	35	24
ACU	62	61
AFL-CIO	21	5
CCUS	83	88

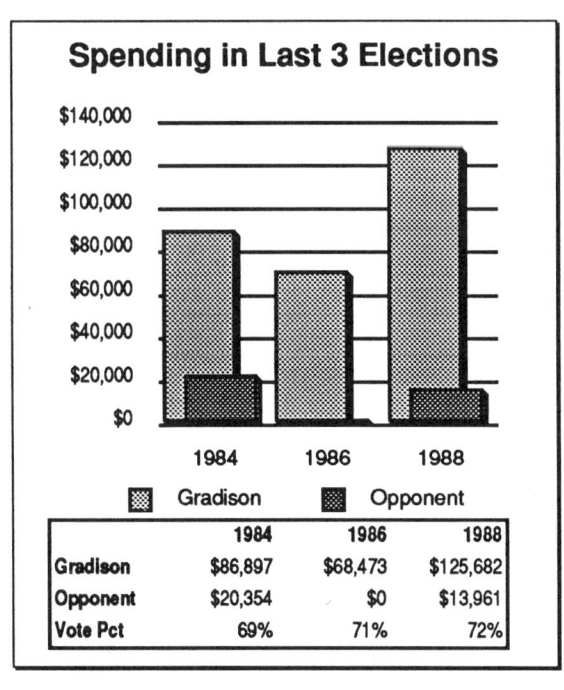

Spending in Last 3 Elections

Gradison   Opponent

	1984	1986	1988
Gradison	$86,897	$68,473	$125,682
Opponent	$20,354	$0	$13,961
Vote Pct	69%	71%	72%

521

Fred Grandy, R-Iowa (6)

First elected: 1986
Total receipts: $519,442
Total from PACs: $294,944

1988 Committees & Subcommittees

Agriculture
Conservation, Credit and Rural Development
Department Operations, Research and Foreign Agriculture
Wheat, Soybeans and Feed Grains

Education and Labor
Elementary, Secondary and Vocational Education
Employment Opportunities
Human Resources

Select Children, Youth and Families

PAC Contribution Profile

Business

Agricultural Chemicals	**$10,450**
Dow Chemical*	$2,300
FMC Corp	$2,250
Ecolab Inc	$1,000
Monsanto Company	$1,000
Others	$3,900
Automotive	**$15,250**
National Auto Dealers Assn	$8,500
Auto Dealers & Drivers for Free Trade	$5,000
Eaton Corp	$1,000
Others	$750
Commercial & Savings Banks	**$12,550**
US League of Savings Assns	$3,250
Hawkeye Bancorp	$3,000
American Bankers Assn	$2,500
Citicorp	$1,500
Norwest Corp	$1,000
Others	$1,300
Construction	**$19,487**
National Assn of Home Builders	$6,687
Associated General Contractors/Iowa	$1,800
Associated General Contractors	$1,750
Sheet Metal/AirCon Contractors	$1,750
Wall & Ceiling/Gypsum Contractors	$1,750
National Electrical Contractors Assn	$1,000
Others	$4,750

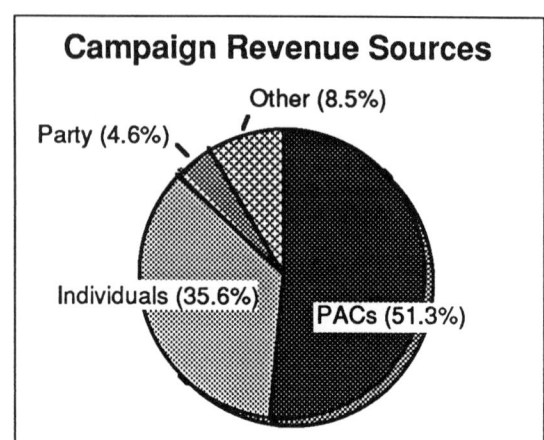

Campaign Revenue Sources

Other (8.5%)
Party (4.6%)
Individuals (35.6%)
PACs (51.3%)

Dairy	**$18,300**
Associated Milk Producers	$7,000
Mid-American Dairymen	$6,500
Land O'Lakes Inc	$2,000
Dairymen Inc	$1,750
Others	$1,050
Defense	**$7,000**
United Technologies	$1,250
Harris Corp	$1,000
Raytheon	$1,000
Rockwell International	$1,000
Others	$2,750
Electric Utilities	**$6,100**
Midwest Energy Company	$2,500
Interstate Power Company	$1,000
Others	$2,600
Food & Beverage	**$21,550**
General Mills*	$2,500
Hy-Vee Food Stores	$2,500
ConAgra Inc	$2,250
American Meat Institute	$2,000
National Restaurant Assn	$2,000
American Bakers Assn	$1,750
IBP Inc	$1,000
S & A Restaurant Corp	$1,000
Others	$6,550
Grain & Grain Trading	**$7,550**
Archer-Daniels-Midland Corp	$2,000
Cargill Inc	$2,000
AG Processing Inc	$1,000
American Soybean Assn	$1,000
Others	$1,550
Health Professionals	**$16,750**
American Medical Assn	$10,000
American Academy of Ophthalmology	$4,500
American Dental Assn	$1,500
Others	$750

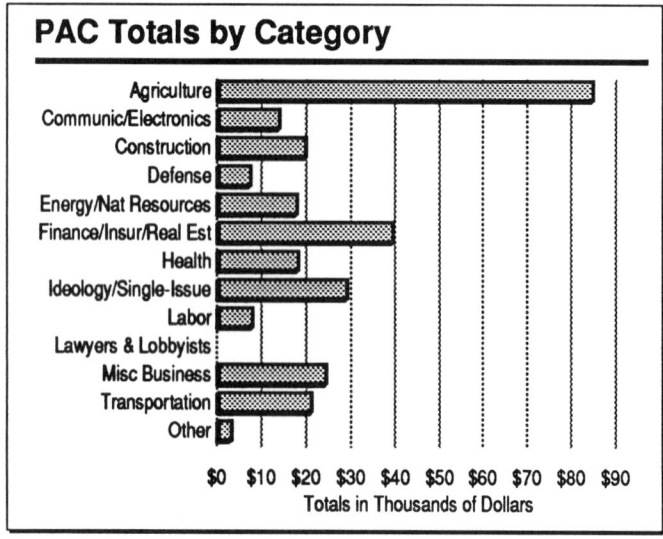

PAC Totals by Category

Agriculture
Communic/Electronics
Construction
Defense
Energy/Nat Resources
Finance/Insur/Real Est
Health
Ideology/Single-Issue
Labor
Lawyers & Lobbyists
Misc Business
Transportation
Other

$0 $10 $20 $30 $40 $50 $60 $70 $80 $90

Totals in Thousands of Dollars

Insurance $17,600

National Assn of Life Underwriters	$6,500
Independent Insurance Agents of America	$2,250
National Assn Mutual Insurance Agents	$1,250
Principal Mutual Life Insurance	$1,250
Casualty & Surety Agents Assn	$1,000
Prudential Insurance	$1,000
Others	$4,350

Oil & Gas $11,000

Phillips Petroleum	$2,000
Amoco Corp	$1,750
Atlantic Richfield	$1,000
Dallas Energy PAC	$1,000
Others	$5,250

Retail Sales $7,211

J C Penney Company	$1,250
Dayton Hudson Corp	$1,000
National Assn of Convenience Stores	$1,000
Walgreen Company	$1,000
Others	$2,961

Sugar Growers $5,400

American Crystal Sugar Corp	$1,250
American Sugarbeet Growers Assn	$1,250
Southern Minnesota Beet Sugar Co-op	$1,000
Others	$1,900

Telecommunications $9,900

Northwestern Bell Telephone	$2,750
AT&T	$1,500
NYNEX Corp	$1,250
Continental Telecom	$1,000
Motorola Inc	$1,000
United Telecommunications	$1,000
Others	$1,400

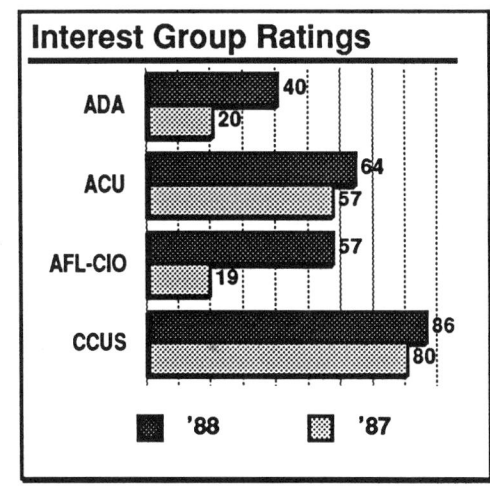

Interest Group Ratings

	'88	'87
ADA	40	20
ACU	64	57
AFL-CIO	57	19
CCUS	86	80

Other Major Business PACs

National Assn of Realtors	$5,875	Real Estate
Deere & Company	$3,000	Farm Equip
Philip Morris	$3,000	Tobacco
Iowa Farm Bureau Federation	$2,500	Farm Orgs
Maytag Company	$2,500	Appliances
Printing Industries of America	$2,151	Printing
Chicago Mercantile Exchange	$2,000	Commodities
Chicago & NorthWestern Transport	$1,500	Railroads
National Fedn of Independent Business	$1,500	Sml Business
American Feed Industry Assn	$1,400	Animal Feed
Chicago Board of Trade	$1,000	Commodities
Commodity Exchange Inc	$1,000	Commodities
Marriott Corp	$1,000	Hotel/Motel
Merck & Company	$1,000	Animal Health
Meredith Corp	$1,000	Books & Mags
National Cattlemen's Assn	$1,000	Livestock
Stone Container Corp	$1,000	Forestry

Labor

Labor Unions $7,500

National Assn of Retired Federal Employees	$4,000
National Assn of Letter Carriers	$2,000
Others	$1,500

Ideological/Single-Issue

Pro-Israel $11,750

National PAC	$5,000
Hudson Valley PAC	$3,000
Desert Caucus	$1,000
Roundtable PAC	$1,000
Others	$1,750

Other Major Ideological/Single-Issue PACs

Citizens for the Republic (Ronald Reagan)	$5,270	Repub Cands
National Right to Life PAC	$5,000	Pro-Life
National Rifle Assn	$2,250	Pro-Guns
Constitution Club	$2,000	Unknown
Minnesota Citizens Concerned for Life	$1,000	Pro-Life

Independent expenditures supporting Grandy

Iowa Bankers Assn	$1,000

* Contributions came from more than one PAC affiliated
  with this sponsor.

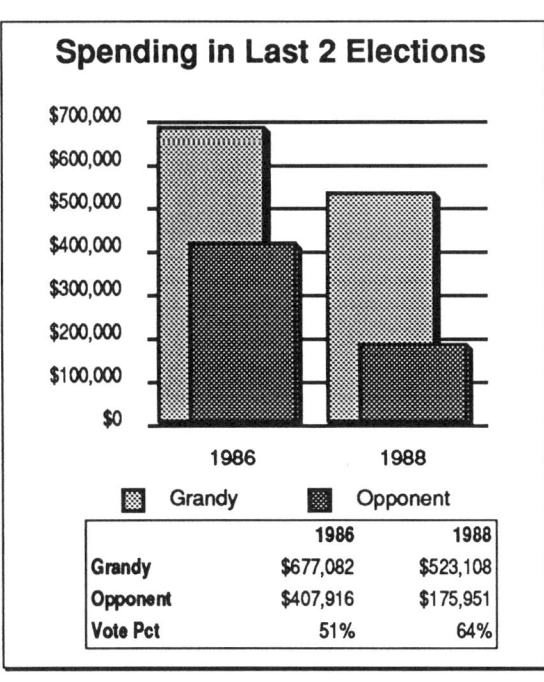

Spending in Last 2 Elections

	Grandy	Opponent

	1986	1988
Grandy	$677,082	$523,108
Opponent	$407,916	$175,951
Vote Pct	51%	64%

Bill Grant, R-Fla (2)

1988 Committees & Subcommittees

Government Operations
Employment and Housing
Government Information, Justice and Agriculture

Public Works and Transportation
Public Building and Grounds
Surface Transportation
Water Resources

PAC Contribution Profile

Business

Accountants	**$5,000**
American Institute of CPA's	$5,000
Air Transport/Air Freight	**$1,700**
None over $750	
Automotive	**$1,500**
National Auto Dealers Assn	$1,000
Others	$500
Commercial & Savings Banks	**$8,450**
Barnett Banks of Florida	$2,000
National Banks of Florida	$1,250
Southeast Banking Corp	$1,250
Florida League of Financial Institutions	$1,000
Others	$2,950
Construction	**$3,750**
National Society of Professional Engineers	$1,000
Others	$2,750
Defense	**$2,750**
None over $750	
Electric Utilities	**$15,700**
Southern Company*	$2,250
Middle South Utilities*	$1,550
Texas Utilities Electric Company*	$1,350
ACRE (Action Committee for Rural Electrification)	$1,250
Florida Power & Light	$1,000
Florida Power Corp	$1,000
Others	$7,300

Food & Beverage	**$2,500**
Winn-Dixie Stores	$1,000
Others	$1,500
Health Professionals	**$7,550**
Florida Medical Assn	$3,500
American Academy of Ophthalmology	$1,500
American Medical Assn	$1,250
American Optometric Assn	$1,000
Others	$300
Insurance	**$2,750**
National Assn of Life Underwriters	$1,500
Others	$1,250
Lawyers	**$3,250**
Assn of Trial Lawyers of America	$2,500
Others	$750
Oil & Gas	**$5,250**
Phillips Petroleum	$1,500
Others	$3,750
Real Estate	**$7,000**
National Assn of Realtors	$6,250
Others	$750
Sugar Growers	**$1,550**
None over $750	
Telecommunications	**$6,200**
Southern Bell	$3,000
AT&T	$1,200
Others	$2,000
Tobacco	**$1,750**
Philip Morris	$1,000
Others	$750
Trucking/Delivery	**$5,840**
American Trucking Assns	$1,540
United Parcel Service	$1,500
Consolidated Freightways	$1,000
Others	$1,800
Waste Management	**$2,000**
Waste Management Inc	$2,000

First elected: 1986
Total receipts: $264,955
Total from PACs: $102,100

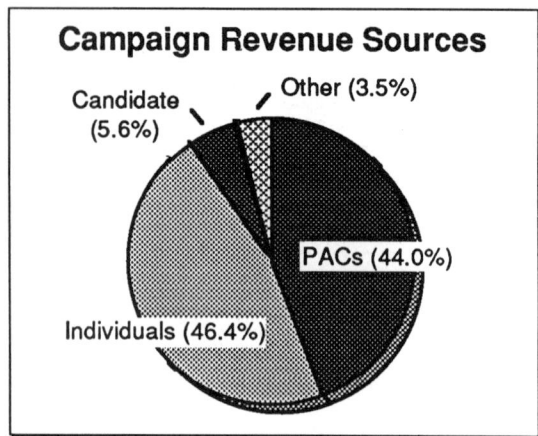

Campaign Revenue Sources

Candidate (5.6%)
Other (3.5%)
PACs (44.0%)
Individuals (46.4%)

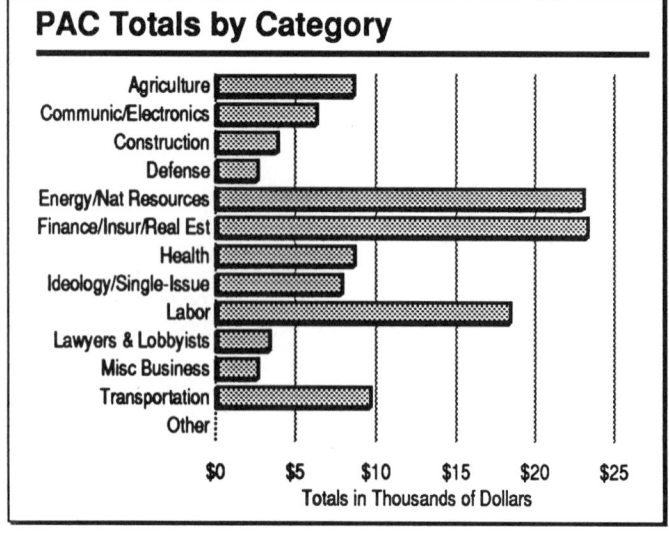

PAC Totals by Category

Agriculture
Communic/Electronics
Construction
Defense
Energy/Nat Resources
Finance/Insur/Real Est
Health
Ideology/Single-Issue
Labor
Lawyers & Lobbyists
Misc Business
Transportation
Other

$0 $5 $10 $15 $20 $25
Totals in Thousands of Dollars

Labor

Government & Postal Workers *$7,000*
   National Assn of Retired Federal Employees $3,000
   National Assn of Letter Carriers $2,500
   Others $1,500

Transportation Unions *$7,000*
   Air Line Pilots Assn $5,000
   United Transportation Union $1,000
   Others $1,000

Other Unions *$4,300*
   United Auto Workers $1,500
   National Education Assn $1,500
   Others $1,300

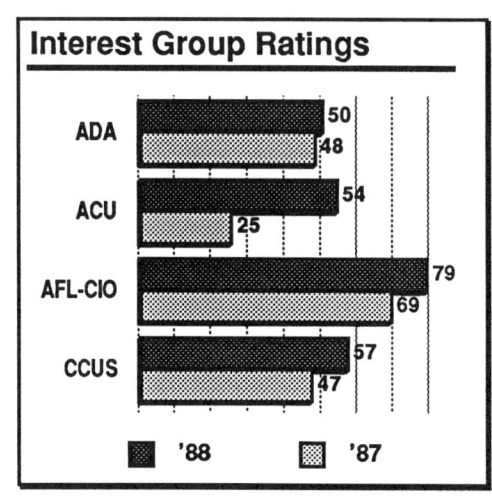

Interest Group Ratings

ADA 50 / 48
ACU 54 / 25
AFL-CIO 79 / 69
CCUS 57 / 47

■ '88   ▨ '87

Ideological/Single-Issue

Ideological/Single-Issue *$7,500*
   National PAC ....$5,000   Pro-Israel
   National Cmte to Preserve Social Security ......$1,000   Social Secur
   Valley Education Fund (Tony Coelho) ....$1,000   Dem Leaders
   Others $500

Independent expenditures supporting Grant

   National Cmte to Preserve Social Security $2,857

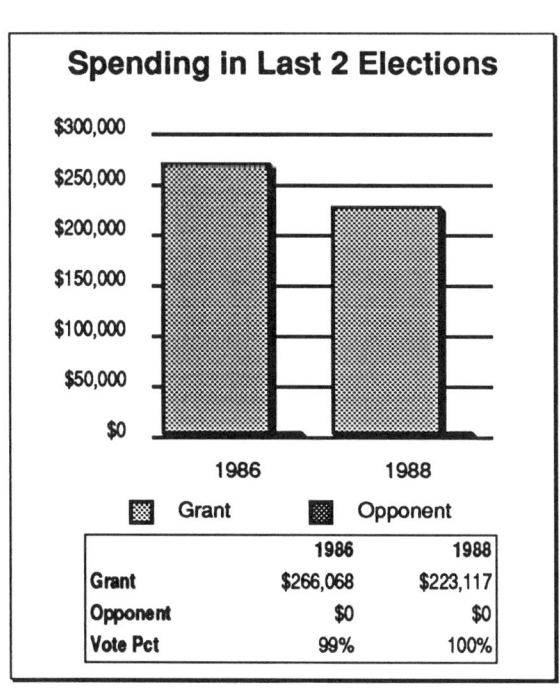

Spending in Last 2 Elections

	1986	1988
Grant	$266,068	$223,117
Opponent	$0	$0
Vote Pct	99%	100%

▨ Grant   ■ Opponent

---

* Contributions came from more than one PAC affiliated
with this sponsor.

William H. Gray III, D-Pa (2)

First elected: 1978
Total receipts: $656,859
Total from PACs: $377,752

1988 Committees & Subcommittees

Appropriations
Foreign Operations
Transportation and Related Agencies

Budget (Chairman)

District of Columbia
Fiscal Affairs and Health
Government Operations and Metropolitan Affairs

PAC Contribution Profile

Business

Air Transport/Air Cargo	**$6,750**
Boeing Company	$3,000
Federal Express Corp	$1,750
Texas Air	$1,000
Others	$1,000
Commercial Banks	**$13,350**
American Bankers Assn	$3,000
J P Morgan & Company	$2,500
Mellon Bank	$2,000
Others	$5,850
Construction	**$5,500**
National Assn of Home Builders	$3,500
Others	$2,000
Credit Unions & Savings Banks	**$10,200**
Credit Union National Assn	$5,000
US League of Savings Assn	$3,000
Atlantic Financial Federal	$1,200
Others	$1,000
Dairy	**$7,000**
Associated Milk Producers	$4,000
Dairymen Inc*	$2,000
Others	$1,000
Defense	**$5,250**
None over $1,000	

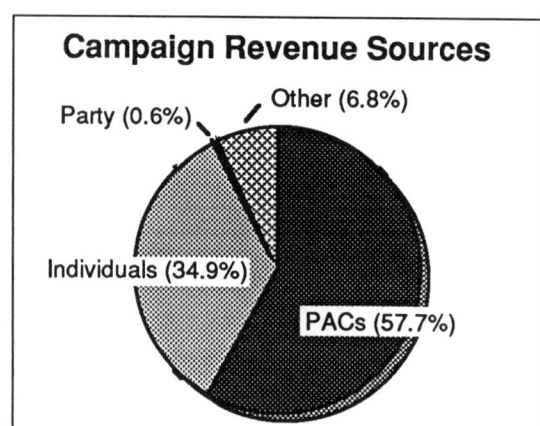

Campaign Revenue Sources

Party (0.6%)
Other (6.8%)
Individuals (34.9%)
PACs (57.7%)

Electric Utilities	**$5,850**
ACRE (Action Committee for Rural Electrification)	$3,500
Philadelphia Electric	$2,100
Others	$250
Food & Beverage	**$17,500**
Food Marketing Institute	$3,000
A E Staley Manufacturing Company	$2,000
American Meat Institute	$2,000
National Beer Wholesalers Assn	$2,000
Others	$8,500
Health Professionals	**$21,500**
American Dental Assn	$5,000
American Medical Assn	$4,500
American Academy of Ophthalmology	$2,000
American Physical Therapy Assn	$1,500
American Optometric Assn	$1,500
Corp for the Advancement of Psychiatry	$1,500
Others	$5,500
Hospitals & Nursing Homes	**$7,500**
American Hospital Assn	$3,500
Federation of America Hospitals	$1,500
Others	$2,500
Insurance	**$10,000**
Blue Cross & Blue Shield Assn	$1,500
Independent Insurance Agents of America	$1,500
Others	$7,000
Lawyers & Lobbyists	**$14,700**
Assn of Trial Lawyers of America	$5,000
Akin, Gump, Hauer & Feld	$2,000
Others	$7,700
Real Estate	**$9,000**
National Assn of Realtors	$5,500
Mortgage Bankers Assn of America	$2,500
Others	$1,000
Retail Sales	**$5,000**
Federated Department Stores	$2,500
J C Penney Company	$1,500
Others	$1,000
Securities/Commodities Investment	**$13,000**
Shearson Lehman Hutton	$7,500
Chicago Mercantile Exchange	$2,500
Goldman Sachs	$2,000
Others	$1,000

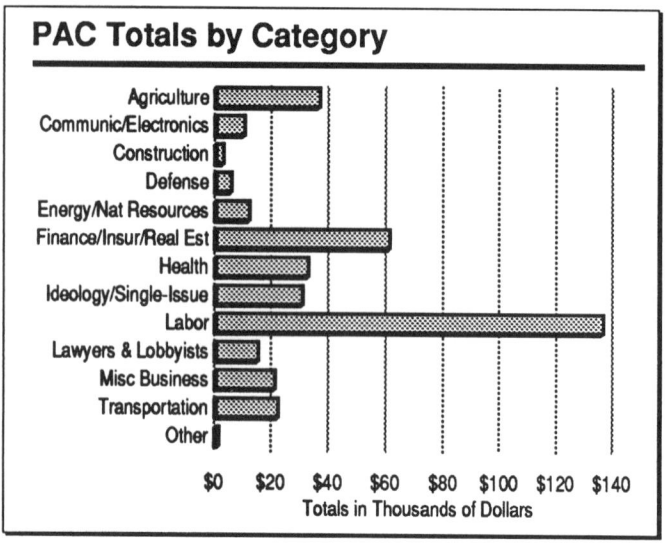

PAC Totals by Category

Agriculture
Communic/Electronics
Construction
Defense
Energy/Nat Resources
Finance/Insur/Real Est
Health
Ideology/Single-Issue
Labor
Lawyers & Lobbyists
Misc Business
Transportation
Other

$0 $20 $40 $60 $80 $100 $120 $140
Totals in Thousands of Dollars

Tobacco	$7,500
Philip Morris	$5,000
Others	$2,500

Trucking/Delivery	$5,650
United Parcel Service	$2,900
Others	$2,750

Venture Capital	$5,000
National Venture Capital Assn	$5,000

Other Major Business PACs

National Cotton Council	$3,000	Cotton
Atlantic Richfield	$1,500	Major Oil
Smithkline Beckman	$2,000	Pharmaceut
Pennwalt Corp	$2,000	Chemicals
Boating PAC	$2,000	Rec Boats
American Sugar Cane League	$2,500	Sugar
AT&T	$3,000	LongDistance

Labor

Bldg Trades/Industrial/Misc Unions	$47,200
Carpenters & Joiners Union	$8,500
Laborers' Union*	$7,250
United Steelworkers	$5,000
Operating Engineers Union*	$4,500
United Auto Workers	$4,500
Food & Commercial Workers Union	$3,500
Machinists/Aerospace Workers Union	$3,000
AFL-CIO*	$2,000
Intl Brotherhood of Electrical Workers	$2,000
Ladies Garment Workers Union	$1,400
Others	$5,550

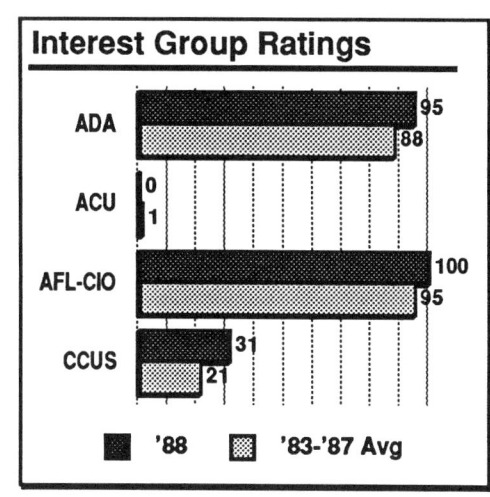

Interest Group Ratings

	'88	'83-'87 Avg
ADA	95	88
ACU	0	1
AFL-CIO	100	95
CCUS	31	21

Government & Postal Workers	$34,400
American Postal Workers Union	$7,500
American Fedn of State/County/Munic Employees	$6,000
National Assn of Letter Carriers	$5,000
National Assn of Retired Federal Employees	$5,000
National Assn of Postmasters	$3,400
National Alliance Postal/Federal Empoyees	$3,000
Others	$4,500

Teachers Unions	$11,400
National Education Assn	$10,000
American Federation of Teachers	$1,400

Transportation Unions	$42,000
Teamsters Union*	$11,000
Marine Engineers Union*	$7,000
Air Line Pilots Assn	$5,000
Amalgamated Transit Union	$5,000
Seafarers International Union	$3,500
Transport Workers Union	$3,000
Boilermakers Union	$2,000
Transportation Communication Union	$2,000
United Transportation Union	$1,500
International Longshoremen Assn	$1,200
Others	$800

Ideological/Single-Issue

Pro-Israel	$11,500
National PAC	$5,000
Washington PAC	$2,000
Others	$4,500

Other Major Ideological/Single-Issue PACs

National Cmte to Preserve Social Security	$8,000	Social Secur
Democraticcrats for The 80's	$5,000	Dem/Liberal
Human Rights Campaign Fund	$3,000	Gay Rights

Independent expenditures supporting Gray

National Cmte to Preserve Social Security	$2,659

Independent expenditures opposing Gray

American Citizens for Political Action	$1,063

---

* Contributions came from more than one PAC affiliated
 with this sponsor.

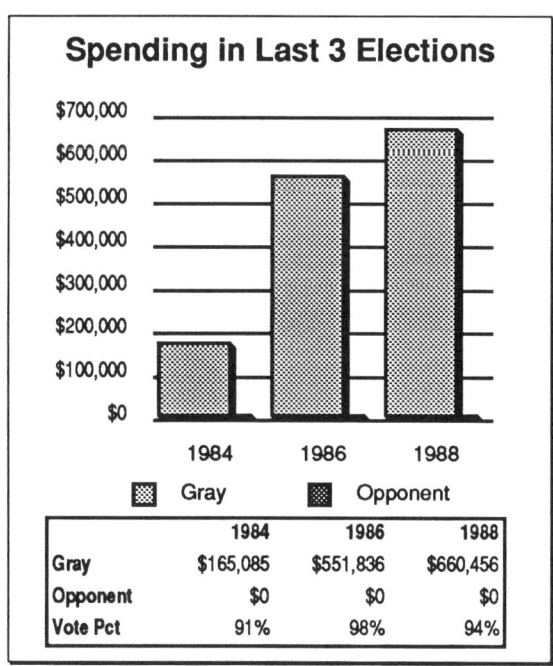

Spending in Last 3 Elections

Gray   Opponent

	1984	1986	1988
Gray	$165,085	$551,836	$660,456
Opponent	$0	$0	$0
Vote Pct	91%	98%	94%

Bill Green, R-NY (15)

1988 Committees & Subcommittees

Appropriations
HUD-Independent Agencies (Ranking Republican)
District of Columbia

First elected: 1978
Total receipts: $656,289
Total from PACs: $154,233

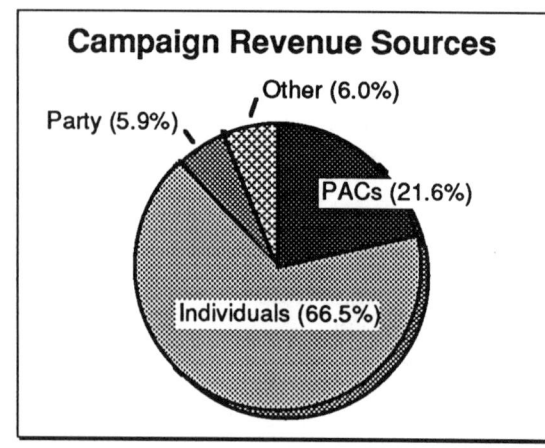

Campaign Revenue Sources

Other (6.0%)
Party (5.9%)
PACs (21.6%)
Individuals (66.5%)

PAC Contribution Profile

Business

Automotive	**$8,000**
Auto Dealers & Drivers for Free Trade	$7,500
Others	$500
Aviation & Aerospace	**$3,600**
TRW Inc	$1,800
Boeing Company	$1,500
Others	$300
Commercial Banks	**$14,785**
J P Morgan & Company	$5,000
Citicorp	$2,500
Marine Midland Banks	$2,500
Bankers Trust	$1,500
Chemical Bank	$1,235
American Bankers Assn	$1,000
Others	$1,050
Construction	**$13,250**
National Utility Contractors Assn	$6,000
National Assn of Home Builders	$5,000
National Society of Professional Engineers	$1,000
Others	$1,250
Defense	**$7,050**
Lockheed Corp	$1,300
Rockwell International	$1,300
United Technologies	$1,250
Others	$3,200
Electric Utilities	**$2,500**
None over $800	

Food & Beverage	**$2,600**
None over $500	
Insurance	**$6,060**
Metropolitan Life Insurance	$2,060
American International Group inc	$1,000
Equitable Financial Services	$1,000
Northwestern Mutual Life	$1,000
Others	$1,000
Lawyers	**$3,650**
Assn of Trial Lawyers of America	$2,000
Others	$1,650
Medical Professionals	**$5,300**
American Medical Assn	$2,300
American Dental Assn	$1,500
Others	$1,500
Pharmaceuticals	**$3,500**
Pfizer Inc	$1,000
Others	$2,500
Real Estate	**$5,900**
National Assn of Realtors	$4,800
Mortgage Bankers Assn of America	$1,100
Retail Sales	**$2,900**
Federated Department Stores	$1,000
Others	$1,900
Savings Banks	**$2,850**
Anchor Savings Bank	$1,000
Others	$1,850
Securities Investment	**$10,850**
Goldman Sachs	$2,500
Prudential-Bache Securities	$1,500
First Boston Corp	$1,000
Morgan Stanley & Company	$1,000
PaineWebber	$1,000
Others	$3,850
Telecommunications	**$4,500**
AT&T	$2,000
New York Telephone	$2,000
Others	$500

Other Major Business PACs

United Parcel Service	$1,400	Delivery
Pirelli Cable	$1,000	Indust Equip
Primerica Corp	$1,000	Credit/Loans

PAC Totals by Category

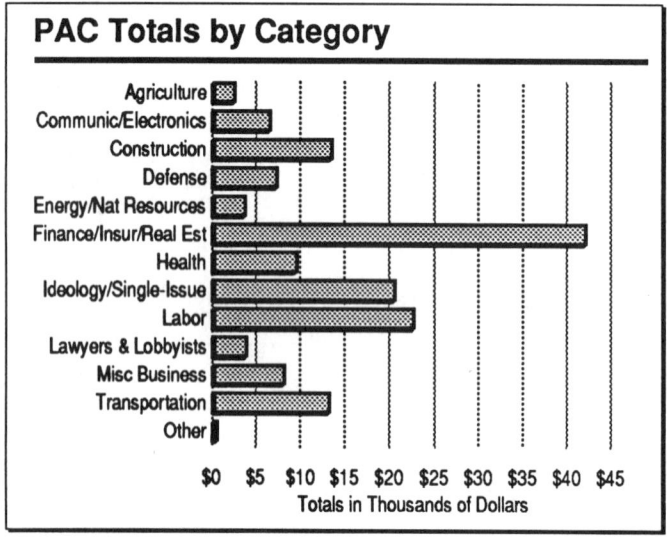

Agriculture
Communic/Electronics
Construction
Defense
Energy/Nat Resources
Finance/Insur/Real Est
Health
Ideology/Single-Issue
Labor
Lawyers & Lobbyists
Misc Business
Transportation
Other

$0 $5 $10 $15 $20 $25 $30 $35 $40 $45
Totals in Thousands of Dollars

Labor

Transportation Unions *$14,750*

    Teamsters Union $10,000
    Seafarers International Union $1,500
    Marine Engineers District 2 Maritime Officers $1,000
    Transportation Communication Union $1,000
    United Transportation Union $1,000
    Others $250

Other Unions *$7,700*

    National Education Assn $2,800
    Carpenters & Joiners Union $2,100
    Operating Engineers Local #15 .... $2,000
    Others $800

Ideological/Single-Issue

Pro-Israel *$6,500*

    National PAC $5,000
    Others $1,500

Other Major Ideological/Single-Issue PACs

National Abortion Rights Action League	$5,500	Pro-Choice
Sierra Club	$2,626	Environment
Human Rights Campaign Fund	$2,600	Gay Rights
KidsPAC	$1,000	HealthWelfare

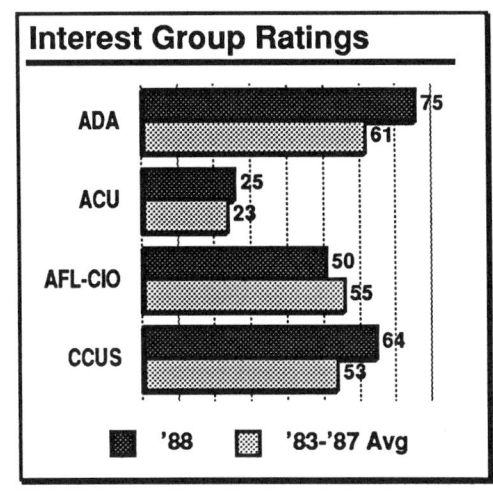

Interest Group Ratings

	'88	'83-'87 Avg
ADA	75	61
ACU	25	23
AFL-CIO	50	55
CCUS	64	53

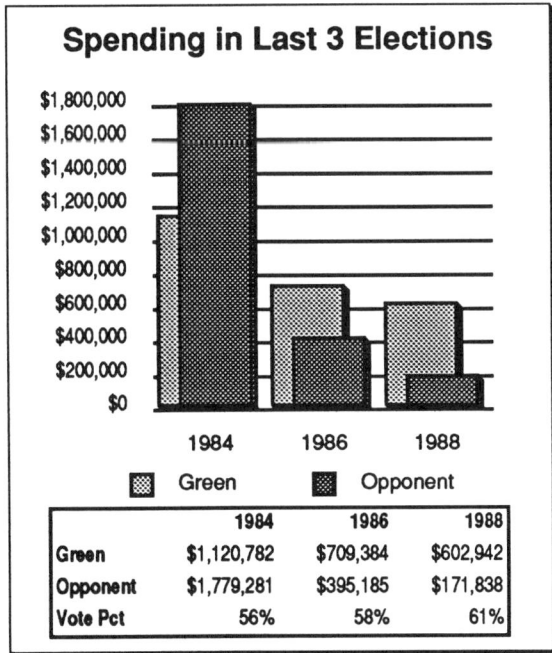

Spending in Last 3 Elections

	1984	1986	1988
Green	$1,120,782	$709,384	$602,942
Opponent	$1,779,281	$395,185	$171,838
Vote Pct	56%	58%	61%

Frank J. Guarini, D-NJ (14)

First elected: 1978
Total receipts: $465,653
Total from PACs: $213,835

1988 Committees & Subcommittees

Budget
Defense, and International Affairs
Economic and Trade Policy

Ways and Means
Trade

Select Narcotics Abuse and Control

PAC Contribution Profile

Business

Accountants **$6,000**
- American Institute of CPA's $5,000
- Ernst & Whinney $1,000

Financial Institutions **$13,150**
- US League of Savings Assn $3,000
- SAPEC/NJ (New Jersey Savings Assn) $2,250
- American Bankers Assn $2,000
- California Federal Savings & Loan $1,000
- Citicorp $1,000
- Credit Union National Assn $1,000
- National Westminster Bank/New Jersey $1,000
- Others $1,900

Food & Beverage **$5,800**
- National Beer Wholesalers Assn $2,000
- Joseph E Seagram & Sons $1,000
- Nabisco Brands Inc $1,000
- Others $1,800

Health Professionals **$7,000**
- American Medical Assn $3,500
- Oral & Maxillofacial Surgeons $1,500
- Others $2,000

Insurance **$43,250**
- National Assn of Life Underwriters $10,000
- Mutual Benefit Life Insurance $3,750
- Prudential Insurance $3,000
- Northwestern Mutual Life $2,500
- Metropolitan Life Insurance $2,000
- New York Life $2,000
- *(Continued in next column)*

Campaign Revenue Sources

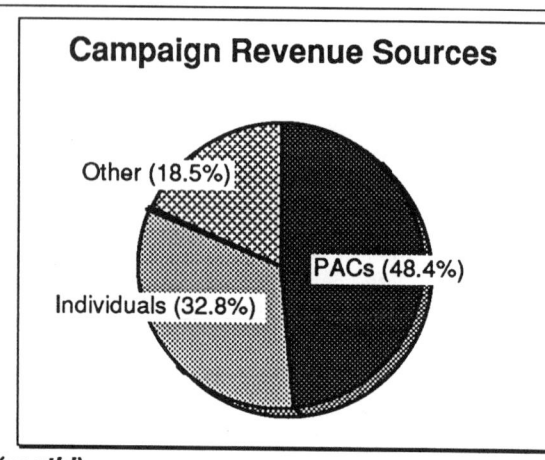

Other (18.5%)
PACs (48.4%)
Individuals (32.8%)

Insurance (cont'd)
- American Family Corp $1,500
- Health Insurance Assn of America $1,500
- Home Life Insurance $1,500
- Massachusetts Mutual Life Insurance $1,500
- New England Mutual Life $1,500
- Aetna Life & Casualty $1,000
- American Council of Life Insurance $1,000
- Chubb Corp $1,000
- Equitable Financial Services $1,000
- ITT Corp $1,000
- Mutual Life Insurance of New York $1,000
- National Assn Mutual Insurance Agents $1,000
- Pacific Mutual Life $1,000
- Principal Mutual Life Insurance $1,000
- Others $3,500

Lawyers & Lobbyists **$8,000**
- Assn of Trial Lawyers of America $5,000
- Hill & Knowlton $1,000
- Others $2,000

Pharmaceuticals **$6,300**
- Hoffman-La Roche $1,000
- ICI Americas Inc $1,000
- Johnson & Johnson $1,000
- Smithkline Beckman $1,000
- Warner-Lambert $1,000
- Others $1,300

Real Estate **$9,500**
- National Assn of Realtors $4,500
- National Realty Committee $3,000
- Mortgage Bankers Assn of America $1,500
- Others $500

Securities & Commodities Investment **$10,500**
- Prudential-Bache Securities $2,000
- Securities Industry Assn $2,000
- Chicago Board of Options Exchange $1,000
- Chicago Board of Trade $1,000
- First Boston Corp $1,000
- Shearson Lehman Hutton $1,000
- Others $2,500

PAC Totals by Category

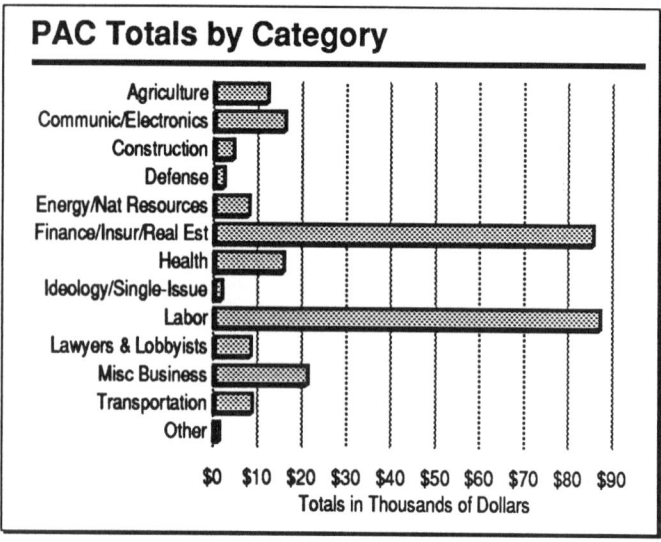

Category	
Agriculture	
Communic/Electronics	
Construction	
Defense	
Energy/Nat Resources	
Finance/Insur/Real Est	
Health	
Ideology/Single-Issue	
Labor	
Lawyers & Lobbyists	
Misc Business	
Transportation	
Other	

$0 $10 $20 $30 $40 $50 $60 $70 $80 $90
Totals in Thousands of Dollars

Telecommunications $12,800

Bell Atlantic	$2,500
New Jersey Bell Telephone	$2,500
AT&T	$2,250
Pacific Telesis Group	$1,500
Motorola Inc	$1,000
Others	$3,050

Tobacco $5,500

Philip Morris	$3,000
RJR Nabisco	$1,500
Tobacco Institute	$1,000

Other Major Business PACs

National Assn of Home Builders	$3,500	Resid Constr
National Venture Capital Assn	$3,000	Venture Cap
Corning Glass Works	$2,000	Glass Prod
J C Penney Company	$2,000	Dept Store
National Auto Dealers Assn	$2,000	Auto Sales
Cheese Importers Assn of America	$1,500	Dairy
American Hospital Assn	$1,250	Hospitals
Society of Independent Gasoline Marketers	$1,100	Gas Stations
Allegheny Ludlum Steel Corp	$1,000	Steel
Allied-Signal	$1,000	Air Defense
American Society of Assn Executives	$1,000	Other
American Textile Manufacturers Institute	$1,000	Textiles
American Trucking Assns	$1,000	Trucking
Bethlehem Steel	$1,000	Steel
Chrysler Corp	$1,000	Auto Mfrs
Gulf + Western Industries	$1,000	Credit/Loans
Henley Group Inc	$1,000	Altern Energy
International Council of Shopping Centers	$1,000	Retail
Motion Picture Assn of America	$1,000	Movies
National Bonded Warehouse Assn	$1,000	Warehouse
National Medical Enterprises Inc	$1,000	Hospitals
National Tooling & Machining Assn	$1,000	Indust Equip
SGS North America	$1,000	BusinessSvcs
W R Grace & Company	$1,000	Chemicals

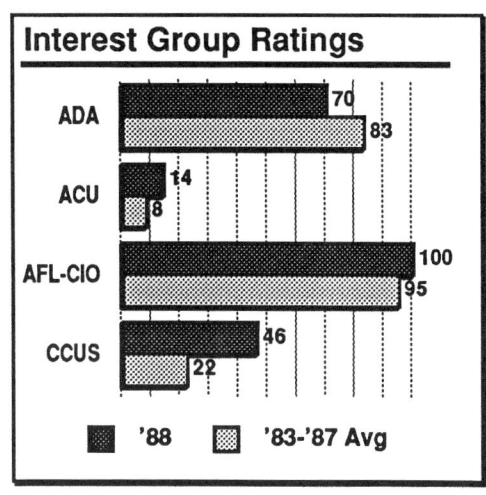

Interest Group Ratings

	'88	'83-'87 Avg
ADA	70	83
ACU	14	8
AFL-CIO	100	95
CCUS	46	22

Labor

Bldg Trades/Industrial/Misc Unions $36,655

Sheet Metal Workers Union	$7,500
Operating Engineers Union*	$5,000
Carpenters & Joiners Union	$4,500
United Auto Workers	$3,500
Intl Brotherhood of Electrical Workers	$2,500
Plumbers/Pipefitters Union*	$2,350
Laborers' Political League	$2,100
Hotel/Restaurant Employees Union	$2,000
AFL-CIO	$1,500
Machinists/Aerospace Workers Union	$1,500
Amalgamated Clothing & Textile Workers	$1,000
Electronic Machine Furniture Workers	$1,000
Food & Commercial Workers Union	$1,000
Others	$1,205

Government, Postal & Teachers Unions $18,800

American Fedn of State/County/Munic Employees	$5,000
National Assn of Letter Carriers	$3,200
National Education Assn	$3,100
National Assn of Retired Federal Employees	$3,000
American Postal Workers Union	$2,000
National Rural Letter Carriers Assn	$1,500
American Federation of Teachers	$1,000

Transportation Unions $31,325

Seafarers International Union	$7,500
International Longshoremen Assn	$6,000
Marine Engineers Union*	$5,000
Air Line Pilots Assn	$3,500
Teamsters Union	$3,000
Masters, Mates & Pilots Union	$2,775
United Transportation Union	$2,000
Others	$1,550

Other Major Ideological/Single-Issue PACs

Valley Education Fund (Tony Coelho)	$1,000	Dem Leaders

Independent expenditures supporting Guarini

National Cmte to Preserve Social Security	$2,671

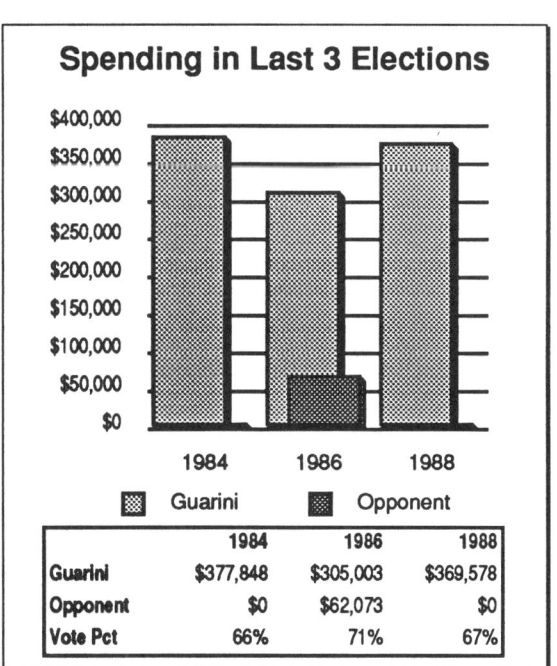

Spending in Last 3 Elections

	1984	1986	1988
Guarini	$377,848	$305,003	$369,578
Opponent	$0	$62,073	$0
Vote Pct	66%	71%	67%

(legend: ▨ Guarini   ▨ Opponent)

---

* Contributions came from more than one PAC affiliated with this sponsor.

531

Steve Gunderson, R-Wis (3)

First elected: 1980
Total receipts: $404,942
Total from PACs: $133,235

1988 Committees & Subcommittees

Agriculture
Conservation, Credit and Rural Development
Department Operations, Research and Foreign Agriculture
Livestock, Dairy and Poultry

Education and Labor
Employment Opportunities (Ranking Republican)
Elementary, Secondary and Vocational Education

PAC Contribution Profile

Business

Agricultural Chemicals **$4,650**
    Ecolab Inc $1,000
    Others $3,650

Agricultural Services **$2,550**
    None over $800

Automotive **$4,600**
    National Auto Dealers Assn $2,800
    Auto Dealers & Drivers for Free Trade $1,500
    Others $300

Commercial Banks **$9,500**
    American Bankers Assn $4,000
    Wisconsin Bankers Assn $1,200
    Banc One Wisconsin $1,000
    Norwest Corp $1,000
    Others $2,300

Commodities Trading **$4,050**
    Commodity Exchange Inc $2,000
    Chicago Board of Trade $1,500
    Others $550

Construction **$5,550**
    National Electrical Contractors Assn $2,000
    Associated General Contractors $1,100
    National Assn of Home Builders $1,100
    Others $1,350

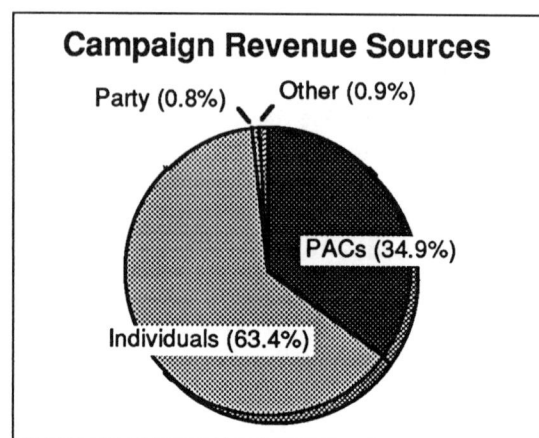

Campaign Revenue Sources

- Party (0.8%)
- Other (0.9%)
- PACs (34.9%)
- Individuals (63.4%)

Dairy **$17,600**
    Associated Milk Producers $6,000
    Land O'Lakes Inc $4,000
    Mid-American Dairymen $3,750
    Dairymen Inc $2,550
    Others $1,300

Electric Utilities **$5,157**
    ACRE (Action Committee for Rural Electrification) $2,807
    Others $2,350

Food & Beverage **$18,450**
    American Meat Institute $3,350
    Food Marketing Institute $3,100
    National Restaurant Assn $2,000
    ConAgra Inc $1,500
    G Heileman Brewing Company $1,400
    Pillsbury Company $1,000
    Others $6,100

Health Professionals **$4,900**
    American Medical Assn $2,550
    American Dental Assn $1,500
    Others $850

Insurance **$6,000**
    Northwestern Mutual Life $2,000
    National Assn of Life Underwriters $1,000
    Others $3,000

Poultry & Livestock **$3,250**
    None over $850

Real Estate **$6,550**
    National Assn of Realtors $6,550

PAC Totals by Category

Agriculture
Communic/Electronics
Construction
Defense
Energy/Nat Resources
Finance/Insur/Real Est
Health
Ideology/Single-Issue
Labor
Lawyers & Lobbyists
Misc Business
Transportation
Other

$0 $10 $20 $30 $40 $50 $60
Totals in Thousands of Dollars

Retail Sales	$4,600
National Assn of Chain Drug Stores	$1,150
National Assn of Convenience Stores	$1,000
Others	$2,450

Sugar Growers	$4,050
American Sugarbeet Growers Assn	$1,100
Others	$2,950

Telecommunications	$3,600
AT&T	$1,500
Wisconsin Bell Telephone	$1,000
Others	$1,100

Vocational Tech Schools	$6,450
National Assn of Trade/Tech Schools	$5,000
Others	$1,450

Other Major Business PACs

JSJ Corp	$1,500	Indust Equip
Deere & Company	$1,100	Farm Equip
Philip Morris	$1,050	Tobacco
Tenneco Inc	$1,000	Ships

Interest Group Ratings

	'88	'83-'87 Avg
ADA	45	27
ACU	54	52
AFL-CIO	79	28
CCUS	71	79

Labor

Labor Unions	$4,600
National Assn of Retired Federal Employees	$2,000
National Education Assn	$1,800
Others	$800

Ideological/Single-Issue

Republican Leadership PACs	$3,618
Campaign America (Bob Dole)	$3,118
Others	$500

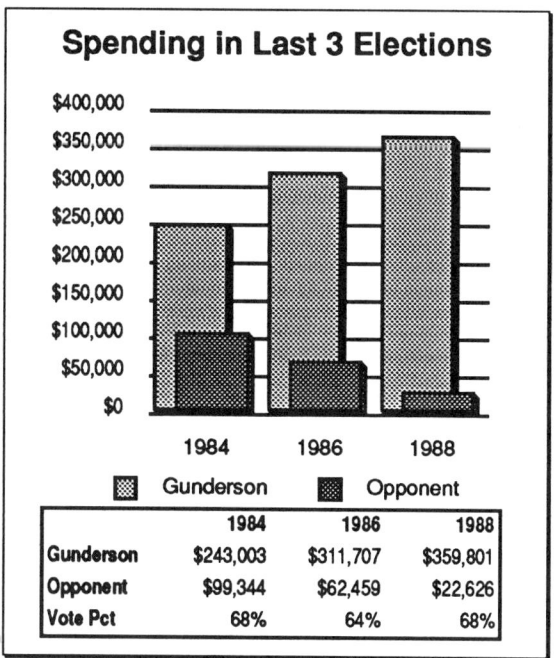

Spending in Last 3 Elections

	1984	1986	1988
Gunderson	$243,003	$311,707	$359,801
Opponent	$99,344	$62,459	$22,626
Vote Pct	68%	64%	68%

Ralph M. Hall, D-Texas (4)

First elected: 1980
Total receipts: $350,284
Total from PACs: $242,743

1988 Committees & Subcommittees

Energy and Commerce
Energy and Power
Health and the Environment
Telecommunications and Finance

Science, Space and Technology
International Scientific Cooperation (Chairman)
Space Science and Applications

PAC Contribution Profile

Business

Accountants	**$5,600**
American Institute of CPA's	$5,000
Others	$600
Automotive	**$10,700**
National Auto Dealers Assn	$6,900
Ford Motor Company	$1,400
General Motors	$1,100
Others	$1,300
Aviation & Aerospace	**$3,400**
None over $600	
Chemicals	**$7,700**
Eastman Kodak/Chemicals Division	$2,800
Hoechst Celanese Corp	$1,500
Union Carbide	$1,000
Others	$2,400
Commercial Banks	**$13,500**
J P Morgan & Company	$5,000
American Bankers Assn	$4,700
Barnett Banks of Florida	$1,000
First City Bancorp	$1,000
NCNB Texas	$1,000
Others	$800
Construction	**$7,450**
Associated General Contractors	$2,300
Stone & Webster	$1,100
Manville Corp	$1,000
Others	$3,050

Campaign Revenue Sources

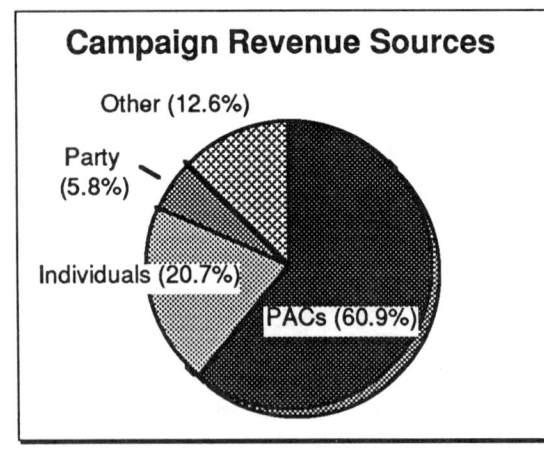

Other (12.6%)
Party (5.8%)
Individuals (20.7%)
PACs (60.9%)

Defense	**$6,255**
None over $855	
Electric Utilities & Equipment	**$34,477**
Texas Utilities Electric Company*	$9,750
Houston Industries	$4,000
Southern Company*	$2,450
General Atomics	$2,000
Texas-New Mexico Power Company	$1,577
Westinghouse Electric	$1,300
Pacific Gas & Electric	$1,100
Central & South West Corp*	$1,000
Others	$11,300
Farm Organizations	**$2,800**
Texas Farm Bureau	$2,500
Others	$300
Food & Beverage	**$7,950**
National Restaurant Assn	$2,000
National Beer Wholesalers Assn	$1,000
Winn-Dixie Stores	$1,000
Others	$3,950
Health Professionals	**$19,050**
American Medical Assn	$10,000
American Dental Assn	$3,500
American Academy of Ophthalmology	$1,500
American College of Emergency Physicians	$1,000
Others	$3,050
Insurance	**$7,000**
American Family Corp	$2,000
National Assn of Life Underwriters	$1,000
Others	$4,000
Lawyers & Lobbyists	**$9,100**
Assn of Trial Lawyers of America	$5,000
Others	$4,100
Mining & Metal Processing	**$3,900**
Independent Coal Operators Assn	$1,000
Others	$2,900

PAC Totals by Category

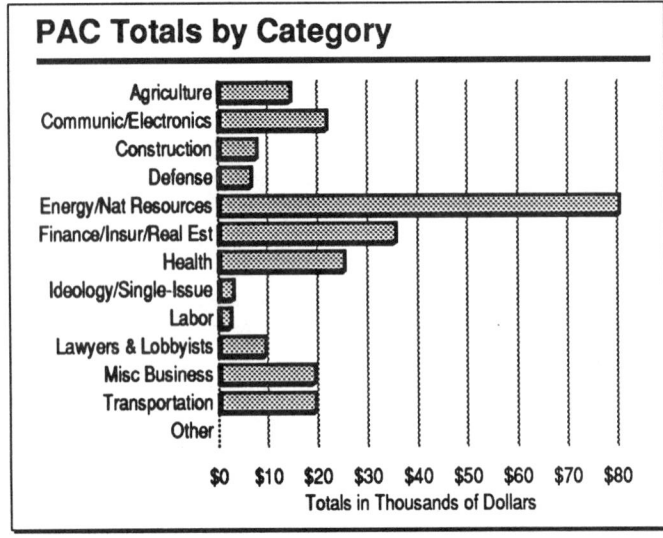

Agriculture
Communic/Electronics
Construction
Defense
Energy/Nat Resources
Finance/Insur/Real Est
Health
Ideology/Single-Issue
Labor
Lawyers & Lobbyists
Misc Business
Transportation
Other

$0 $10 $20 $30 $40 $50 $60 $70 $80
Totals in Thousands of Dollars

Oil & Gas $38,911

Enserch Corp	$2,600
Atlantic Richfield	$2,500
Columbia Natural Resources	$2,000
Phillips Petroleum	$2,000
Valero Energy Corp	$2,000
Amoco Corp	$1,850
Petroleum Marketers Assn	$1,750
Chevron Corp	$1,600
Union Pacific Corp	$1,600
USX Corp*	$1,300
Dow Chemical	$1,000
Maxus Energy Corp	$1,000
Mobil Oil	$1,000
Sun Company	$1,000
Tenneco Inc	$1,000
Others	$14,711

Pharmaceuticals $2,950

None over $800

Real Estate $6,600

National Assn of Realtors	$6,600

Securities & Commodities Investment $5,250

Chicago Board of Options Exchange	$1,000
Chicago Board of Trade	$1,000
Travelers Corp	$1,000
Others	$2,250

Telecommunications $16,450

AT&T	$5,000
Southwestern Bell	$2,000
Corning Glass Works	$1,500
Continental Telecom	$1,300
Comsat	$1,100
Pacific Telesis Group	$1,050
Bell Atlantic	$1,000
GTE (Southwest)	$1,000
Others	$2,500

Interest Group Ratings

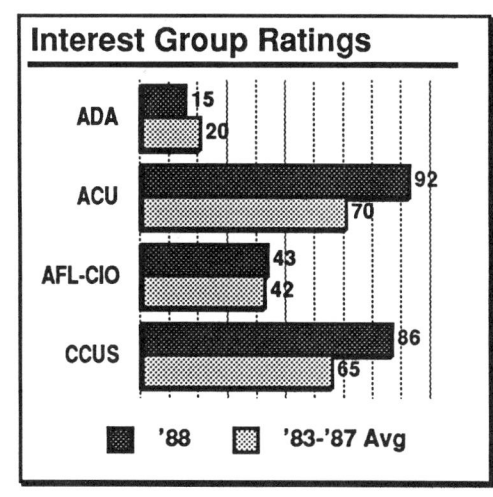

Television/Movies $3,200

National Cable Television Assn	$2,000
Others	$1,200

Other Major Business PACs

American Consulting Engineers Council	$1,800	Energy
Lone Star Steel*	$1,600	Steel
Associated Milk Producers	$1,500	Dairy
Universal Health Services	$1,250	Hospitals
Holiday Inns	$1,000	Hotel/Motel
Philip Morris	$1,000	Tobacco
Texas Cattle Feeders Assn	$1,000	Feedlots

Major Labor PACs

United Transportation Union	$1,600	RR Unions

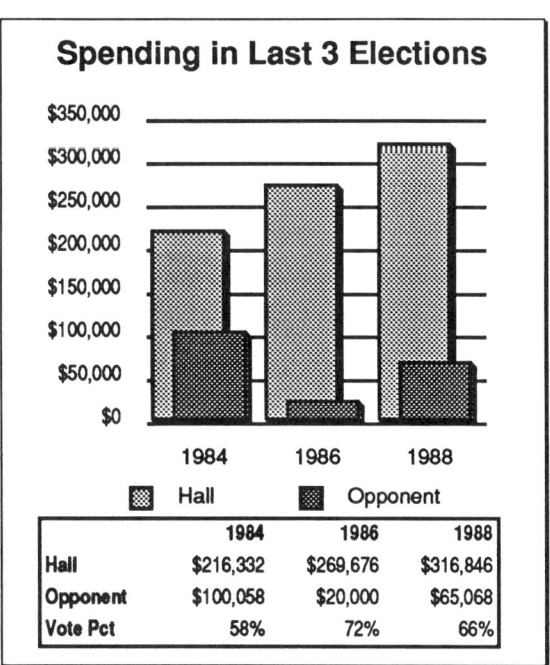

Spending in Last 3 Elections

	1984	1986	1988
Hall	$216,332	$269,676	$316,846
Opponent	$100,058	$20,000	$65,068
Vote Pct	58%	72%	66%

---

* Contributions came from more than one PAC affiliated with this sponsor.

Tony P. Hall, D-Ohio (3)

1988 Committees & Subcommittees

Rules
Rules of the House

Select Hunger

First elected: 1978
Total receipts: $216,111
Total from PACs: $140,160

PAC Contribution Profile

Business

Automotive	**$4,200**
National Auto Dealers Assn	$2,600
General Motors	$1,000
Others	$600
Construction	**$3,800**
National Assn of Home Builders	$1,600
Philips Industries	$1,600
Others	$600
Defense	**$2,600**
BDM International	$1,600
Others	$1,000
Electric Utilities	**$2,700**
None over $900	
Electronics & Computers	**$4,450**
NCR Corp	$1,700
Computer Sciences Corp	$1,000
Others	$1,750
Financial Institutions	**$9,200**
American Bankers Assn	$2,000
Ohio Savings Assns League	$1,500
Credit Union National Assn	$1,300
US League of Savings Assn	$1,200
National City Corp	$1,000
Society Corp	$1,000
Others	$1,200

Campaign Revenue Sources

Other (16.1%)
Individuals (21.4%)
PACs (62.5%)

Food & Beverage	**$4,250**
National Beer Wholesalers Assn	$2,000
Others	$2,250
Health Professionals	**$6,800**
American Medical Assn	$3,800
American Dental Assn	$1,000
American Podiatry Assn	$1,000
Others	$1,000
Insurance	**$6,900**
National Assn of Life Underwriters	$2,500
Travelers Corp	$1,000
Others	$3,400
Lawyers & Lobbyists	**$7,950**
Assn of Trial Lawyers of America	$5,000
Akin, Gump, Hauer & Feld	$1,200
Others	$1,750
Real Estate	**$4,550**
National Assn of Realtors	$4,000
Others	$550
Telecommunications	**$5,900**
AT&T	$2,500
Ohio Bell Telephone	$1,500
BellSouth Corp	$1,200
Others	$700

Other Major Business PACs

American Financial Services Assn	$1,600	Credit/Loans
United Parcel Service	$1,300	Delivery
Chicago Mercantile Exchange	$1,000	Commodities
Holiday Inns	$1,000	Hotel/Motel
Mead Corp	$1,000	Paper Prod
Ohio Farm Bureau Federation	$1,000	Farm Orgs

PAC Totals by Category

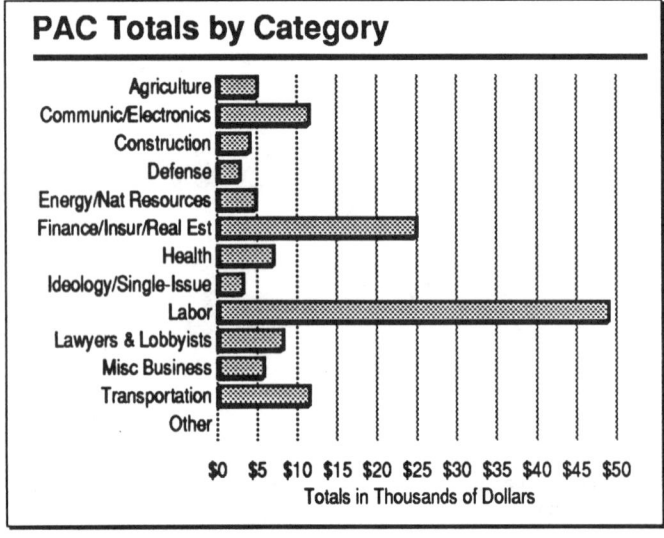

Totals in Thousands of Dollars

Labor

Bldg Trades/Industrial/Misc Unions $23,825

United Auto Workers	$7,100
Rubber Cork Linoleum Plastic Workers	$1,800
National Education Assn	$1,700
Carpenters & Joiners Union	$1,600
Communications Workers of America	$1,600
Electronic Machine Furniture Workers	$1,525
Operating Engineers Union	$1,500
Intl Brotherhood of Electrical Workers	$1,400
Laborers' Political League	$1,200
Ladies Garment Workers Union	$1,000
Plumbers/Pipefitters Union	$1,000
Others	$2,400

Government & Postal Workers $14,000

National Assn of Retired Federal Employees	$5,000
National Assn of Letter Carriers	$4,000
American Postal Workers Union	$1,600
American Fedn of State/County/Munic Employees	$1,000
Others	$2,400

Transportation Unions $10,900

Teamsters Union	$5,000
Air Line Pilots Assn	$1,500
Seafarers International Union	$1,400
United Transportation Union	$1,000
Others	$2,000

Major Ideological/Single-Issue PACs

Valley Education Fund (Tony Coelho) .... $1,000   Dem Leaders

Independent expenditures supporting Hall

National Cmte to Preserve Social Security $1,654

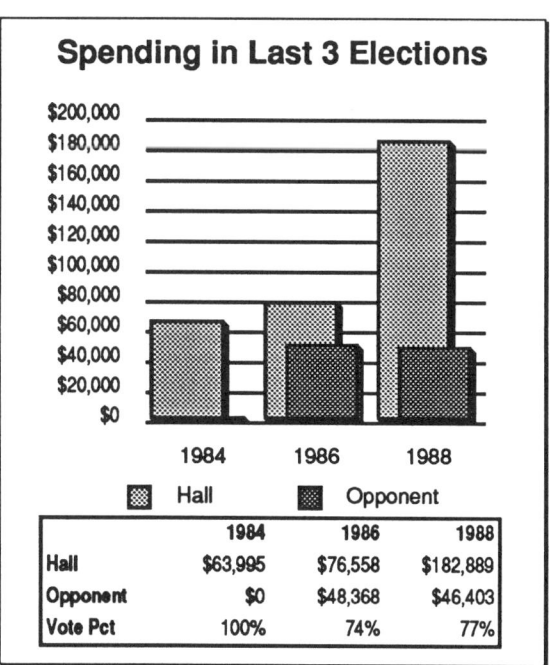

Spending in Last 3 Elections

	1984	1986	1988
Hall	$63,995	$76,558	$182,889
Opponent	$0	$48,368	$46,403
Vote Pct	100%	74%	77%

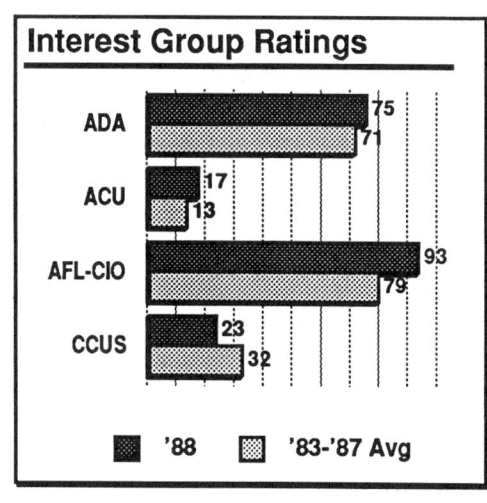

Interest Group Ratings

	'88	'83-'87 Avg
ADA	75	71
ACU	17	13
AFL-CIO	93	79
CCUS	23	32

■ '88   ▨ '83-'87 Avg

Lee H. Hamilton, D-Ind (9)

First elected: 1964
Total receipts: $369,547
Total from PACs: $152,066

1988 Committees & Subcommittees

Foreign Affairs
Europe and the Middle East (Chairman)
Arms Control, International Security and Science

Science, Space and Technology
Science, Research and Technology

Joint Economic (Vice Chairman)
Economic Goals and Intergovernmental Policy (Chairman)
Economic Growth, Trade and Taxes (Vice Chairman)
International Economic Policy (Vice Chairman)

PAC Contribution Profile

Business

Automotive	**$4,500**
Auto Dealers & Drivers for Free Trade	$2,500
Ford Motor Company	$1,500
Others	$500
Aviation & Aerospace	**$2,500**
Boeing Company	$1,000
TRW Inc	$1,000
Others	$500
Commercial & Savings Banks	**$6,500**
US League of Savings Assn	$2,000
American Bankers Assn	$1,000
Indiana League of Savings Institutions	$1,000
Others	$2,500
Construction	**$4,250**
National Assn of Home Builders	$3,000
Others	$1,250
Dairy	**$3,000**
Associated Milk Producers	$1,500
Dairymen Inc	$1,000
Others	$500
Defense	**$7,750**
General Dynamics	$1,500
Lockheed Corp	$1,250
Grumman	$1,000
Hughes Aircraft	$1,000
McDonnell Douglas	$1,000
Textron Inc	$1,000
Others	$1,000

Electric Utilities	**$4,300**
Indiana ACRE	$2,200
Public Service Company of Indiana	$1,100
ACRE (Action Committee for Rural Electrification)	$1,000
Farm Organizations	**$5,650**
Indiana Farm Bureau	$5,300
Others	$350
Food & Beverage	**$5,400**
Joseph E Seagram & Sons	$1,500
Occidental Petroleum	$1,000
Pillsbury Company	$1,000
Others	$1,900
Health Professionals	**$3,150**
American Medical Assn	$1,350
Eli Lilly & Company	$1,000
Others	$800
Insurance	**$2,550**
National Assn of Life Underwriters	$1,000
Others	$1,550
Oil & Gas	**$3,850**
Texas Gas Transmission Corp	$1,000
Others	$2,850
Real Estate	**$6,000**
National Assn of Realtors	$6,000
Telecommunications	**$6,400**
Continental Telecom	$2,000
Indiana Bell Telephone	$1,550
GTE Corp	$1,050
Others	$1,800

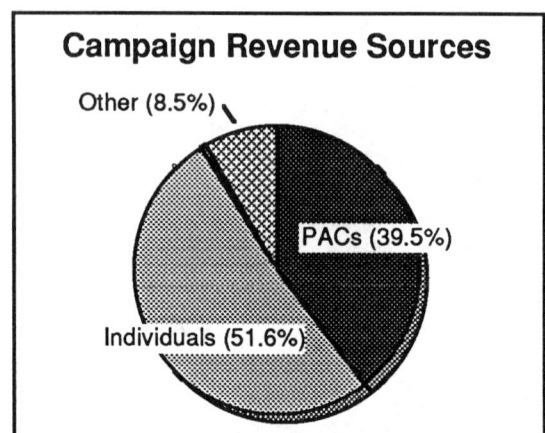

Campaign Revenue Sources

Other (8.5%)
PACs (39.5%)
Individuals (51.6%)

PAC Totals by Category

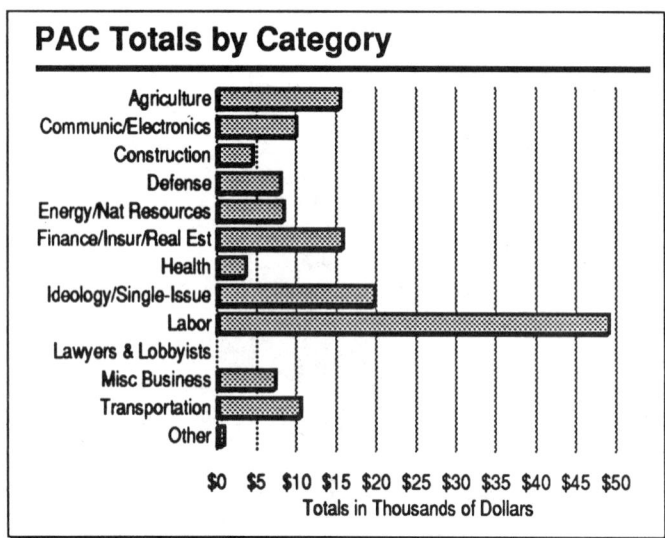

Agriculture
Communic/Electronics
Construction
Defense
Energy/Nat Resources
Finance/Insur/Real Est
Health
Ideology/Single-Issue
Labor
Lawyers & Lobbyists
Misc Business
Transportation
Other

$0 $5 $10 $15 $20 $25 $30 $35 $40 $45 $50
Totals in Thousands of Dollars

Other Major Business PACs

MCA Inc	$2,000	Movies
American Coml Barge Line Company	$1,500	SeaTransport
American Crystal Sugar Corp	$1,250	Sugar
United Parcel Service	$1,250	Delivery
Dun & Bradstreet	$1,000	Mkt Research
Tobacco Institute	$1,000	Tobacco

Labor

Bldg Trades/Industrial/Misc Unions $22,550
United Auto Workers	$10,000
United Steelworkers	$2,000
Machinists/Aerospace Workers Union	$1,750
Operating Engineers Union	$1,500
Food & Commercial Workers Union	$1,250
Ladies Garment Workers Union	$1,250
Oil, Chemical & Atomic Workers Union	$1,000
Others	$3,800

Government & Postal Workers $7,050
National Assn of Letter Carriers	$3,500
American Fedn of State/County/Munic Employees	$1,500
American Postal Workers Union	$1,000
Others	$1,050

Teachers Unions $2,750
National Education Assn	$2,750

Transportation Unions $16,500
Teamsters Union	$7,000
Masters Mates & Pilots Union	$5,000
United Transportation Union	$2,000
Brotherhood of Locomotive Engineers	$1,000
Others	$1,500

Interest Group Ratings

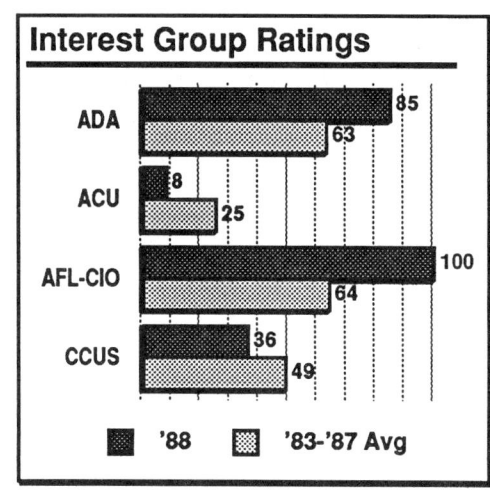

Ideological/Single-Issue

Pro-Israel $13,000
National PAC	$5,000
Washington PAC	$1,250
Gold Coast PAC	$1,000
Hudson Valley PAC	$1,000
Joint Action Cmte for Political Affairs	$1,000
National Action Committee (NACPAC)	$1,000
San Franciscans for Good Government	$1,000
South Florida Caucus	$1,000
Others	$750

Other Major Ideological/Single-Issue PACs
Free Cuba PAC	$2,000	Anti-Castro
National Assn of Arab-Americans	$1,750	ForeignPolicy
Hellenic American Council	$1,000	Ethnic
Valley Education Fund (Tony Coelho)	$1,000	Dem Leaders

Independent expenditures supporting Hamilton
National Cmte to Preserve Social Security	$1,017

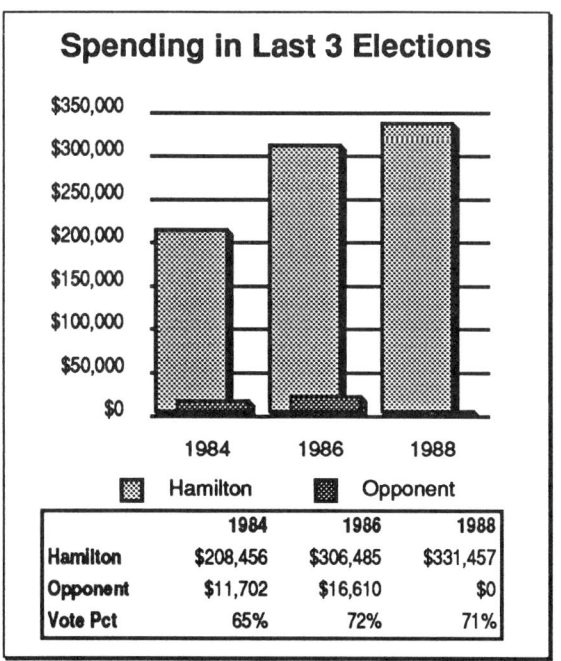

Spending in Last 3 Elections

	1984	1986	1988
Hamilton	$208,456	$306,485	$331,457
Opponent	$11,702	$16,610	$0
Vote Pct	65%	72%	71%

John Paul Hammerschmidt R-Ark (3)

First elected: 1966
Total receipts: $330,387
Total from PACs: $166,700

1988 Committees & Subcommittees

Public Works and Transportation (Ranking Republican)

Veterans' Affairs
Hospitals and Health Care (Ranking Republican)

Select Aging
Housing and Consumer Interests (Ranking Republican)

PAC Contribution Profile

Business

Air Transport	**$12,450**
Aircraft Owners & Pilots Assn	$3,600
Texas Air	$2,000
American Assn of Airport Executives	$1,100
Others	$5,750
Automotive	**$4,400**
National Auto Dealers Assn	$2,300
Auto Dealers & Drivers for Free Trade	$1,500
Others	$600
Commercial Banks	**$2,650**
American Bankers Assn	$1,000
Northwest National Bank	$1,000
Others	$650
Construction	**$16,500**
National Utility Contractors Assn	$4,000
Associated General Contractors	$3,600
National Assn of Home Builders	$3,100
Others	$5,800
Dairy	**$6,050**
Associated Milk Producers	$4,750
Mid-American Dairymen	$1,300
Electric Utilities	**$3,600**
ACRE (Action Committee for Rural Electrification)	$1,300
Arkansas Power & Light	$1,000
Others	$1,300
Electronics & Computers	**$2,300**
None over $600	

Campaign Revenue Sources

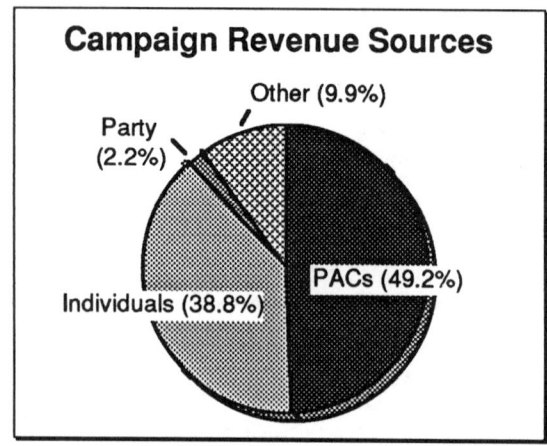

- Other (9.9%)
- Party (2.2%)
- Individuals (38.8%)
- PACs (49.2%)

Food & Beverage	**$5,400**
National Beer Wholesalers Assn	$2,000
Hiram Walker & Sons	$1,200
Others	$2,200
Health Professionals	**$15,900**
American Medical Assn	$6,000
Arkansas Medical Society	$4,000
American Podiatry Assn	$1,500
American Academy of Ophthalmology	$1,000
American Dental Assn	$1,000
Cmte for Quality Orthopedic Health Care	$1,000
Others	$1,400
Lawyers	**$7,350**
Assn of Trial Lawyers of America	$5,000
Others	$2,350
Oil & Gas	**$4,250**
None over $600	
Real Estate	**$4,200**
National Assn of Realtors	$3,600
Others	$600
Telecommunications	**$7,900**
Continental Telecom	$2,000
AT&T	$1,800
GTE (Southwest)	$1,600
Alltel Corp	$1,000
Southwestern Bell	$1,000
Others	$500
Trucking/Delivery	**$19,400**
United Parcel Service	$7,000
Consolidated Freightways	$3,000
Arkansas Best Corp	$2,500
North American Van Lines	$2,500
Yellow Freight System	$1,900
Others	$2,500

PAC Totals by Category

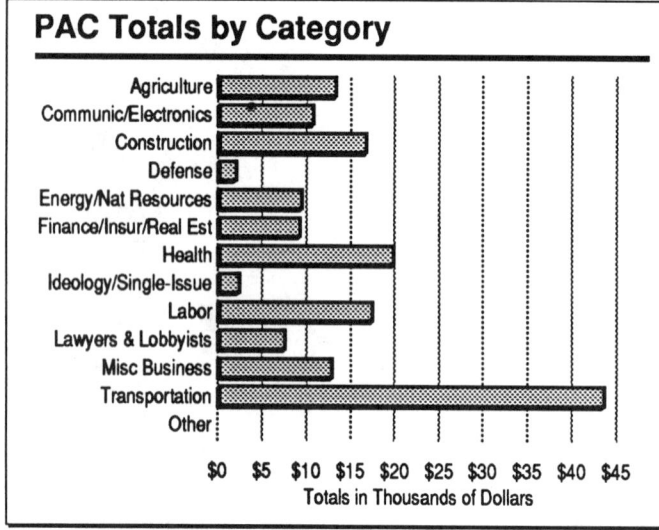

Totals in Thousands of Dollars

(Agriculture, Communic/Electronics, Construction, Defense, Energy/Nat Resources, Finance/Insur/Real Est, Health, Ideology/Single-Issue, Labor, Lawyers & Lobbyists, Misc Business, Transportation, Other)

$0 $5 $10 $15 $20 $25 $30 $35 $40 $45

Other Major Business PACs

Baxter Healthcare Corp	$1,100	Med Supply
American Assn of Equipment Lessors	$1,000	Rentals
Holiday Inns	$1,000	Hotel/Motel
J C Penney Company	$1,000	Dept Store
National Assn of Letter Carriers	$1,000	Postal Union
Riceland Foods	$1,000	Crops
Schering-Plough Corp	$1,000	Pharmaceut
Stephens Overseas Services	$1,000	FinancSvcs
Union Pacific Corp	$1,000	Railroads

Labor

Transportation Unions ***$16,200***
    Air Line Pilots Assn $10,000
    Marine Engineers District 2 Maritime Officers.................$2,500
    United Transportation Union $1,200
    Amalgamated Transit Union $1,000
    Others $1,500

Other Major Ideological/Single-Issue PACs

National Cmte to Preserve Social Security ......$1,000   Soc Secur

Independent expenditures supporting Hammerschmidt

National Cmte to Preserve Social Security $3,779

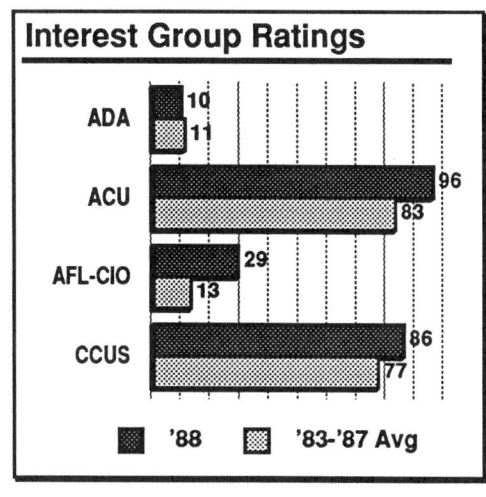

Interest Group Ratings

	'88	'83-'87 Avg
ADA	10	11
ACU	96	83
AFL-CIO	29	13
CCUS	86	77

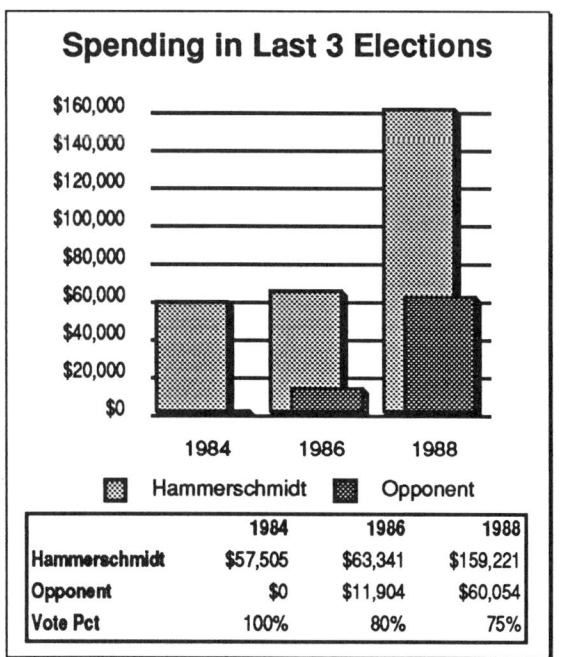

Spending in Last 3 Elections

Hammerschmidt   Opponent

	1984	1986	1988
Hammerschmidt	$57,505	$63,341	$159,221
Opponent	$0	$11,904	$60,054
Vote Pct	100%	80%	75%

Mel Hancock, R-Mo (7)

1988-1989 Committees & Subcommittees

First elected: 1988
Total receipts: $373,434
Total from PACs: $79,913

Public Works and Transportation
Aviation
Surface Transportation
Water Resources

Small Business
Regulation, Business Opportunities and Energy
SBA and the General Economy

Standards of Official Conduct

PAC Contribution Profile

Business

Automotive	**$10,250**
Auto Dealers & Drivers for Free Trade	$5,000
National Auto Dealers Assn	$5,000
General Motors	$250
Chemicals	**$2,250**
Dow Chemical*	$1,000
Others	$1,250
Commercial & Savings Banks	**$4,250**
United Missouri Bancshares	$1,200
Boatmens Bankshares	$1,000
Others	$2,050
Construction	**$6,250**
National Assn of Home Builders	$5,000
Associated General Contractors	$1,000
Others	$250
Defense	**$2,350**
Harris Corp	$1,000
Others	$1,350
Food & Beverage	**$3,550**
Malone & Hyde Inc	$1,000
National Restaurant Assn	$1,000
Others	$1,550
Health Professionals	**$7,500**
American Medical Assn	$5,000
American Academy of Ophthalmology	$2,000
Others	$500

Campaign Revenue Sources

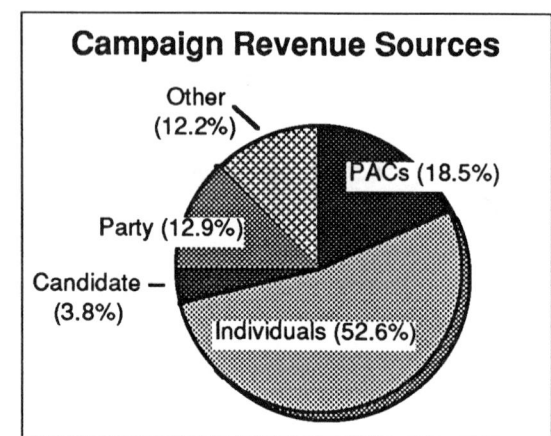

Other (12.2%)
PACs (18.5%)
Party (12.9%)
Candidate (3.8%)
Individuals (52.6%)

Insurance	**$8,300**
National Assn of Life Underwriters	$5,000
General American Life Insurance	$1,000
Independent Insurance Agents of America	$1,000
Others	$1,300
Oil & Gas	**$3,150**
Phillips Petroleum	$1,000
Others	$2,150
Real Estate	**$5,000**
National Assn of Realtors	$5,000
Telecommunications	**$3,000**
Continental Telecom	$2,000
United Telecommunications	$1,000

Other Major Business PACs

Associated Milk Producers	$1,000	Dairy
Cooper Industries	$1,000	Electronics
National Fedn of Independent Business	$1,000	Sml Business
RJR Nabisco	$1,000	Tobacco

PAC Totals by Category

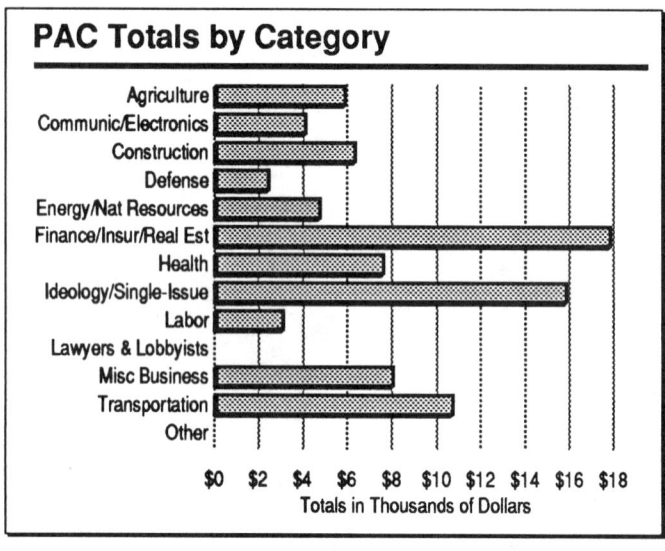

Totals in Thousands of Dollars

(Categories: Agriculture, Communic/Electronics, Construction, Defense, Energy/Nat Resources, Finance/Insur/Real Est, Health, Ideology/Single-Issue, Labor, Lawyers & Lobbyists, Misc Business, Transportation, Other)

Labor

Labor Unions ***$3,000***

    National Assn of Retired Federal Employees $2,500

    Others $500

Ideological/Single-Issue

Ideological/Single-Issue ***$11,902***

Public Service Research Council	$3,000	Anti-Union
Right to Work PAC	$2,500	Anti-Union
Council for National Defense	$2,252	Pro-Defense
Conservative Victory Cmte	$1,000	Repub/Conser
National Rifle Assn	$1,000	Pro-Guns
Republican Congressional Boosters Club	$1,000	Repub/Conser
Others	$1,150	

Republican Leadership PACs ***$3,850***

    Policy Innovation PAC (Dick Armey) $1,500

    Heartland PAC of Missouri (Kit Bond) $1,000

    Republican Leader's Fund (Bob Michel) $1,000

    Others $350

Independent expenditures supporting Hancock

Missouri Citizens for Life $1,317

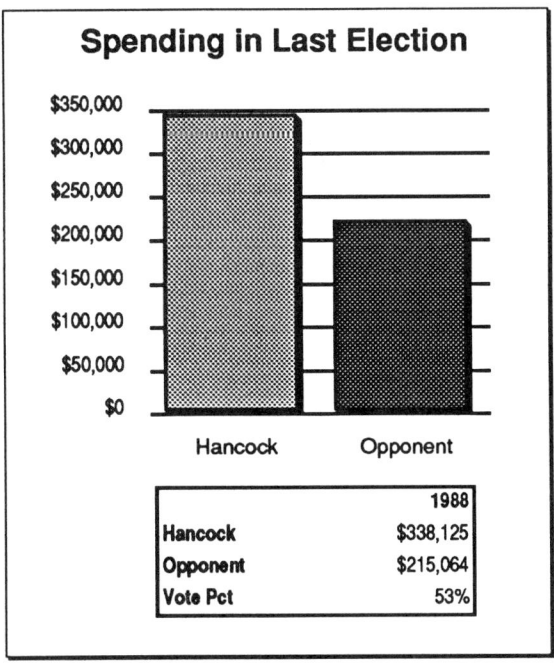

Spending in Last Election

	1988
Hancock	$338,125
Opponent	$215,064
Vote Pct	53%

* Contributions came from more than one PAC affiliated with this sponsor.

543

James V. Hansen, R-Utah (1)

First elected: 1980
Total receipts: $411,486
Total from PACs: $258,859

1988 Committees & Subcommittees

Armed Services
Procurement and Military Nuclear Systems
Readiness

Interior and Insular Affairs
General Oversight and Investigations
National Parks and Public Lands

Standards of Official Conduct

PAC Contribution Profile

Business

Auto Dealers	**$15,000**
Auto Dealers & Drivers for Free Trade	$10,000
National Auto Dealers Assn	$5,000
Aviation	**$3,750**
Aircraft Owners & Pilots Assn	$3,000
Others	$750
Business Organizations	**$8,756**
National Fedn of Independent Business	$7,130
Business Industry PAC	$1,119
Others	$507
Commercial Banks/Credit Unions	**$5,400**
Utah Ban Corp	$1,500
Barnett Banks of Florida	$1,000
Commercial Security Bancorp	$1,000
Credit Union National Assn	$1,000
Others	$900
Construction	**$17,050**
National Assn of Home Builders	$10,000
Associated General Contractors	$2,500
American Consulting Engineers Council	$1,300
Wall & Ceiling/Gypsum Contractors	$1,000
Others	$2,250

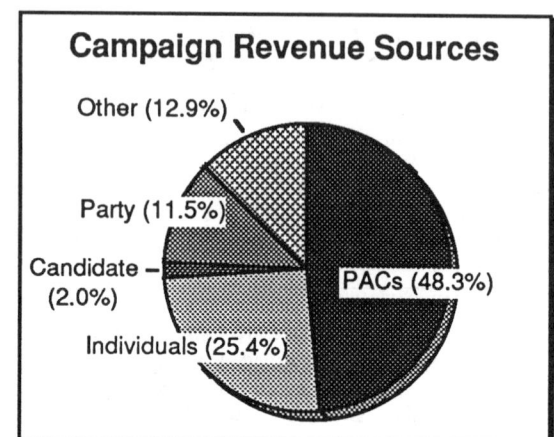

Campaign Revenue Sources

- Other (12.9%)
- Party (11.5%)
- Candidate (2.0%)
- Individuals (25.4%)
- PACs (48.3%)

Defense	**$61,150**
Litton Industries	$7,500
Morton Thiokol	$4,500
Lockheed Corp	$4,000
AT&T	$3,500
Northrop Corp	$3,500
Colt Industries	$2,100
Continental Telecom	$2,000
Eaton Corp	$2,000
Harris Corp	$2,000
McDonnell Douglas*	$2,000
FMC Corp	$1,950
Rockwell International	$1,750
United Technologies	$1,700
Boeing Company	$1,600
E-Systems/Corporate Division	$1,500
Textron Inc	$1,500
AAI Corp	$1,400
Hercules Inc	$1,300
Martin Marietta Corp	$1,250
TRW Inc	$1,050
Electrospace Systems Inc	$1,000
General Dynamics	$1,000
Grumman	$1,000
Hughes Aircraft	$1,000
Raytheon	$1,000
Tenneco Inc	$1,000
Unisys Corp	$1,000
Others	$6,050
Electric Utilities & Equipment	**$2,500**
General Atomics	$1,000
Others	$1,500
Food & Beverage	**$4,850**
JB's Big Boy Family Restaurant	$2,250
Pepsico Inc	$1,000
Others	$1,600

PAC Totals by Category

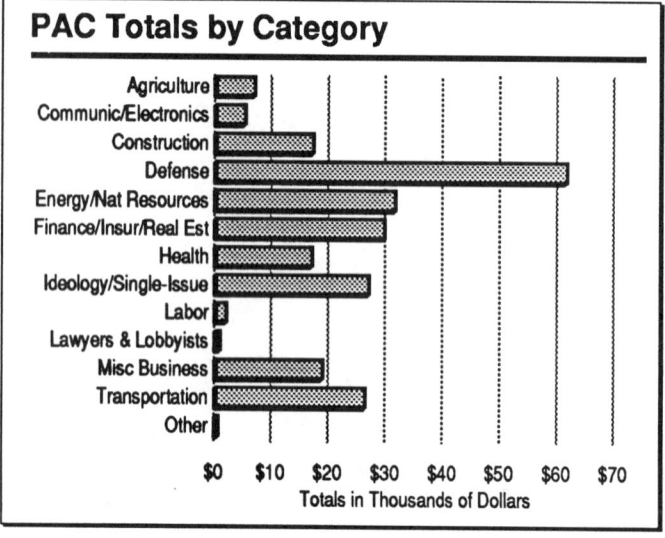

Agriculture
Communic/Electronics
Construction
Defense
Energy/Nat Resources
Finance/Insur/Real Est
Health
Ideology/Single-Issue
Labor
Lawyers & Lobbyists
Misc Business
Transportation
Other

$0 $10 $20 $30 $40 $50 $60 $70

Totals in Thousands of Dollars

Health Professionals **$16,250**
    American Medical Assn $10,000
    American Academy of Ophthalmology $4,500
    American Dental Assn $1,500
    Others $250

Industrial Equipment **$4,000**
    Brush Wellman $4,000

Insurance **$13,450**
    National Assn of Life Underwriters $7,500
    Casualty & Surety Agents Assn $1,500
    Independent Insurance Agents of America $1,500
    American Family Corp $1,000
    Others $1,950

Mining **$3,300**
    National Coal Assn $1,000
    Others $2,300

Oil & Gas **$24,600**
    Phillips Petroleum $3,000
    Cooper Industries $2,000
    Mountain Fuel Supply $1,550
    Amoco Corp $1,500
    Atlantic Richfield $1,500
    Chevron Corp $1,500
    BP America $1,250
    Texaco $1,100
    Exxon Corp $1,000
    Halliburton Company* $1,000
    Mobil Oil $1,000
    Sun Company $1,000
    Union Oil $1,000
    Union Pacific Corp $1,000
    Others $5,200

Real Estate **$10,500**
    National Assn of Realtors $10,000
    Others $500

Interest Group Ratings

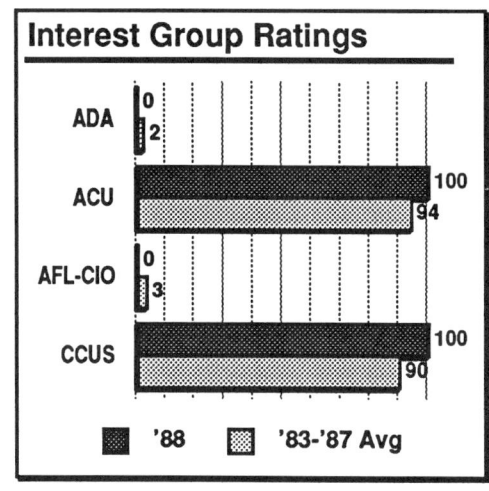

Legend: ■ '88 ▨ '83-'87 Avg

- ADA: '88 = 0; '83-'87 Avg = 2
- ACU: '88 = 100; '83-'87 Avg = 94
- AFL-CIO: '88 = 0; '83-'87 Avg = 3
- CCUS: '88 = 100; '83-'87 Avg = 90

Telecommunications **$5,000**
    Mountain Bell $5,000

Trucking/Delivery **$3,150**
    United Parcel Service $2,400
    Delivery
    Others $750

Other Major Business PACs

Marriott Corp	$2,500	Hotel/Motel
National Cattlemen's Assn	$1,250	Livestock
Deere & Company	$1,000	Farm Equip
Kimberly-Clark	$1,000	Paper Prod

Major Labor PACs

National League of Postmasters	$1,000	Postal Union

Ideological/Single-Issue

Pro-Guns **$10,900**
    National Rifle Assn $9,900
    Safari Club International $1,000

Republican Leadership PACs **$2,500**
    Policy Innovation PAC (Dick Armey) $1,000
    Others $1,500

Other Major Ideological/Single-Issue PACs

National Right to Life PAC	$3,500	Pro-Life
Public Service Research Council	$3,000	Anti-Union
Ruff PAC	$1,500	Tax Policy
Conservative Victory Cmte	$1,000	Repub/Conser
Republican Congressional Boosters Club	$1,000	Repub/Conser
Right to Work PAC	$1,000	Anti-Union

Independent expenditures supporting Hansen

National Assn of Realtors	$155,287
American Medical Assn	$65,359

Spending in Last 3 Elections

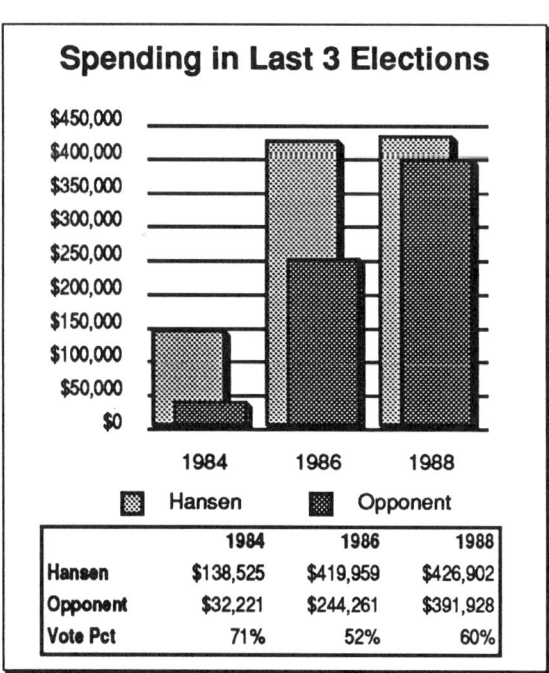

	1984	1986	1988
Hansen	$138,525	$419,959	$426,902
Opponent	$32,221	$244,261	$391,928
Vote Pct	71%	52%	60%

Legend: ▨ Hansen ■ Opponent

---

* Contributions came from more than one PAC affiliated with this sponsor.

Claude Harris, D-Ala (7)

1988 Committees & Subcommittees

Agriculture
Conservation, Credit and Rural Development
Cotton, Rice and Sugar
Forests, Family Farms and Energy
Livestock, Dairy and Poultry

Veterans' Affairs
Hospitals and Health Care

First elected: 1986
Total receipts: $405,426
Total from PACs: $257,205

PAC Contribution Profile

Business

Automotive	**$2,500**
National Auto Dealers Assn	$1,250
Auto Dealers & Drivers for Free Trade	$1,000
Others	$250
Commercial Banks	**$14,100**
Amsouth Bancorp	$3,750
Central Bancshares of the South	$3,750
First National Bank/Tuskaloosa	$3,000
Southtrust Corp	$1,350
American Bankers Assn	$1,250
Others	$1,000
Commodities Trading	**$3,350**
Chicago Mercantile Exchange	$1,850
Chicago Board of Trade	$1,500
Cotton	**$4,050**
National Cotton Council	$2,100
American Cotton Shippers Assn	$1,100
Others	$850
Dairy	**$4,750**
Dairymen Inc	$2,500
Associated Milk Producers	$1,500
Others	$750
Electric Utilities	**$4,610**
Southern Company*	$3,610
ACRE (Action Committee for Rural Electrification)	$1,000

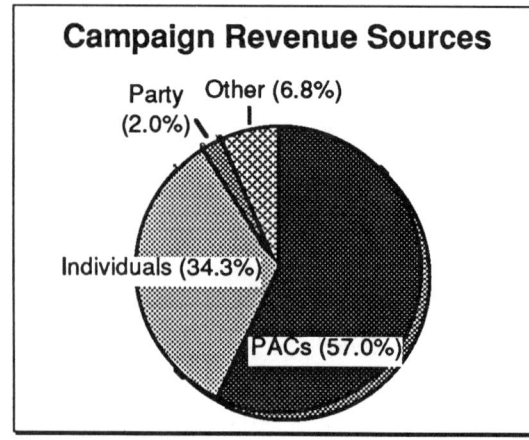

Campaign Revenue Sources

Party (2.0%)
Other (6.8%)
Individuals (34.3%)
PACs (57.0%)

Farm Organizations	**$5,750**
Alabama Farm Bureau Federation	$5,000
Others	$750
Food & Beverage	**$6,250**
Morrison Inc	$1,500
Malone & Hyde Inc	$1,000
National Restaurant Assn	$1,000
Others	$2,750
Health Professionals	**$12,750**
American Medical Assn	$8,000
American Dental Assn	$2,500
American Academy of Ophthalmology	$1,000
Others	$1,250
Insurance	**$8,850**
Torchmark Corp	$3,500
National Assn of Life Underwriters	$2,500
National Assn Mutual Insurance Agents	$1,550
Others	$1,300
Lawyers	**$2,750**
Assn of Trial Lawyers of America	$1,000
California Trial Lawyers Assn	$1,000
Others	$750
Oil & Gas	**$7,650**
Southern Natural Resources	$3,000
Alagasco Inc	$1,250
Others	$3,400
Peanut Growers	**$2,750**
Alabama Peanut Producers Assn	$2,250
Others	$500
Poultry & Livestock	**$3,100**
National Cattlemen's Assn	$1,000
Others	$2,100
Real Estate	**$10,350**
National Assn of Realtors	$9,600
Others	$750
Residential Construction	**$7,000**
National Assn of Home Builders	$5,000
Walter Industries	$2,000
Sugar Growers	**$4,350**
American Crystal Sugar Corp	$1,600
Others	$2,750

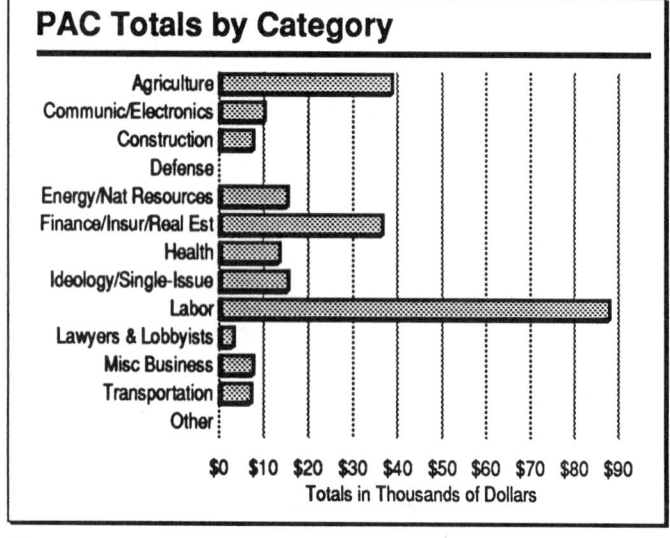

PAC Totals by Category

Agriculture
Communic/Electronics
Construction
Defense
Energy/Nat Resources
Finance/Insur/Real Est
Health
Ideology/Single-Issue
Labor
Lawyers & Lobbyists
Misc Business
Transportation
Other

$0 $10 $20 $30 $40 $50 $60 $70 $80 $90
Totals in Thousands of Dollars

Telecommunications **$8,750**

AT&T	$3,500
South Central Bell Telephone	$3,250
Continental Telecom	$2,000

Other Major Business PACs

American Institute of CPA's	$1,750	Accountants
American Veterinary Medical Assn	$1,000	Veterinary
CSX Transportation Inc	$1,000	Railroads
Philip Morris	$1,000	Tobacco
Westpoint Pepperell	$1,000	Textiles

Labor

Bldg Trades/Industrial/Misc Unions **$62,725**

United Auto Workers	$10,000
United Mine Workers	$10,000
Machinists/Aerospace Workers Union	$6,000
Heat/Frost/Asbestos Workers Union	$5,000
Intl Brotherhood of Electrical Workers	$5,000
United Steelworkers	$4,000
Operating Engineers Union	$3,500
AFL-CIO*	$3,125
Carpenters & Joiners Union	$3,000
Food & Commercial Workers Union	$2,500
Sheet Metal Workers Union	$2,500
Communications Workers of America	$2,000
Rubber Cork Linoleum Plastic Workers	$2,000
Laborers' Political League	$1,250
Others	$2,850

Government & Postal Workers **$11,350**

National Assn of Letter Carriers	$4,000
National Assn of Retired Federal Employees	$3,000
National Assn of Postmasters	$1,300
American Postal Workers Union	$1,200
American Fedn of State/County/Munic Employees	$1,000
Others	$850

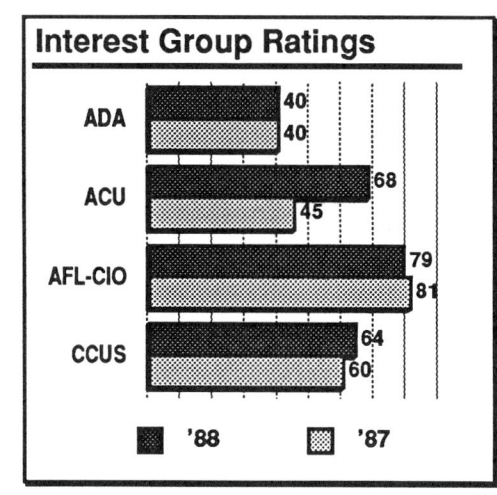

Interest Group Ratings

	'88	'87
ADA	40	40
ACU	68	45
AFL-CIO	79	81
CCUS	64	60

Transportation Unions **$13,450**

Teamsters Union	$10,000
United Transportation Union	$1,250
Seafarers International Union	$1,000
Others	$1,200

Ideological/Single-Issue

Democratic Leadership PACs **$4,250**

Valley Education Fund (Tony Coelho)	$2,000
Conservative Democratic PAC (Charles Stenholm)	$1,000
Responsible Government Fund (Ronnie Flippo)	$1,000
Others	$250

Pro-Israel **$9,500**

National PAC	$5,000
Americans for Good Government Inc	$2,500
Hudson Valley PAC	$1,000
Joint Action Cmte for Political Affairs	$1,000

Independent expenditures supporting Harris

National Cmte to Preserve Social Security	$2,055

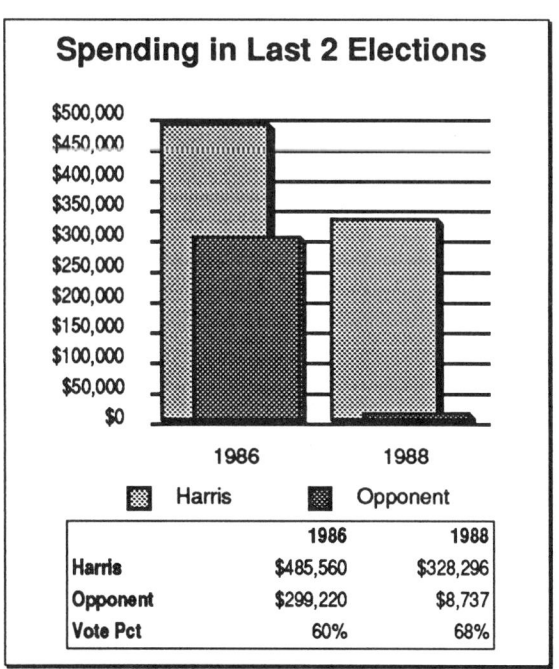

Spending in Last 2 Elections

	1986	1988
Harris	$485,560	$328,296
Opponent	$299,220	$8,737
Vote Pct	60%	68%

* Contributions came from more than one PAC affiliated with this sponsor.

Dennis Hastert, R-Ill (14)

1988 Committees & Subcommittees

First elected: 1986
Total receipts: $361,879
Total from PACs: $148,608

Government Operations
Government Activities and Transportation
Government Information, Justice and Agriculture

Public Works and Transportation
Surface Transportation
Water Resources

Select Children, Youth and Families

PAC Contribution Profile
Business

Accountants	**$5,000**
American Institute of CPA's	$5,000
Automotive	**$7,500**
National Auto Dealers Assn	$5,250
Auto Dealers & Drivers for Free Trade	$2,000
Others	$250
Chemicals	**$3,500**
Dow Chemical/Midwest	$1,000
FMC Corp	$1,000
Others	$1,500
Commodities Trading	**$2,500**
Chicago Board of Options Exchange	$1,000
Chicago Board of Trade	$1,000
Others	$500
Construction	**$8,860**
Associated General Contractors	$2,500
National Assn of Home Builders	$1,500
Caterpillar Tractor	$1,210
National Electrical Contractors Assn	$1,000
Sheet Metal/AirCon Contractors	$1,000
Others	$1,650
Dairy	**$2,250**
Associated Milk Producers	$2,000
Others	$250

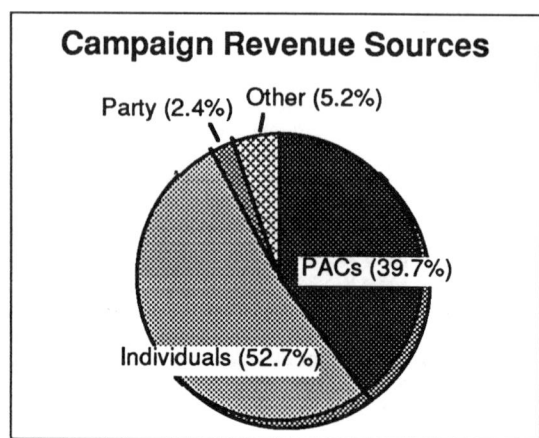

Campaign Revenue Sources

Party (2.4%)
Other (5.2%)
PACs (39.7%)
Individuals (52.7%)

Financial Institutions	**$4,761**
Mid America Federal Savings & Loan	$1,500
American Bankers Assn	$1,000
Credit Union National Assn	$1,000
Others	$1,261
Food & Beverage	**$5,800**
McDonald's Corp	$1,500
National Restaurant Assn	$1,000
Others	$3,300
General Aviation	**$2,000**
Aircraft Owners & Pilots Assn	$2,000
Health Professionals	**$14,350**
American Medical Assn	$10,000
American Academy of Ophthalmology	$4,000
Others	$350
Industrial Equipment & Materials	**$3,400**
Borg-Warner	$1,000
Others	$2,400
Insurance	**$5,182**
National Assn of Life Underwriters	$2,000
Kemper Insurance	$1,050
Others	$2,132
Oil & Gas	**$8,400**
Amoco Corp	$2,000
Nicor Inc	$1,350
Others	$5,050
Real Estate	**$11,500**
National Assn of Realtors	$10,000
Mortgage Bankers Assn of America	$1,250
Others	$250

PAC Totals by Category

Agriculture
Communic/Electronics
Construction
Defense
Energy/Nat Resources
Finance/Insur/Real Est
Health
Ideology/Single-Issue
Labor
Lawyers & Lobbyists
Misc Business
Transportation
Other

$0 $5 $10 $15 $20 $25 $30
Totals in Thousands of Dollars

Telecommunications **$13,470**

Illinois Bell Telephone	$4,600
Continental Telecom	$3,620
AT&T	$2,000
BellSouth Services	$1,000
Others	$2,250

Tobacco **$2,500**

Philip Morris	$2,000
Others	$500

Trucking/Delivery **$4,740**

United Parcel Service	$2,250
American Trucking Assns	$1,240
Others	$1,250

Other Major Business PACs

Chicago & NorthWestern Transport	$1,500	Railroad
Illinois Agricultural Assn	$1,315	Farm Orgs
Libbey-Owens-Ford	$1,050	Glass Prod
American Collectors Assn	$1,000	Credit/Loans
Masson, Grimm & Burgum	$1,000	Lawyers
Maytag Company	$1,000	Appliances
Owens-Illinois	$1,000	Paper Packg
Rockwell International	$1,000	AirDefense

Labor

Government & Postal Workers **$3,800**

National Assn of Retired Federal Employees	$2,000
National Assn of Letter Carriers	$1,000
Others	$800

Transportation Unions **$4,500**

Air Line Pilots Assn	$3,500
Others	$1,000

Interest Group Ratings

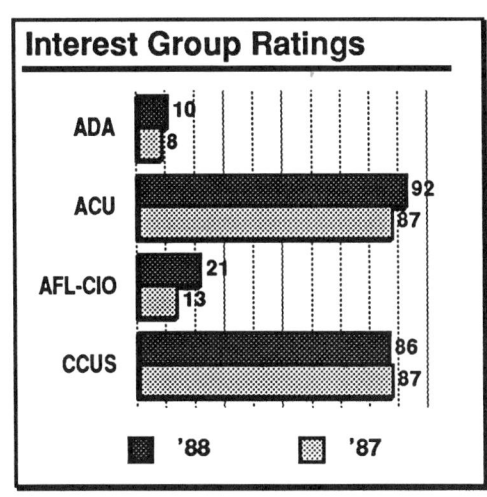

	'88	'87
ADA	10	8
ACU	92	87
AFL-CIO	21	13
CCUS	86	87

■ '88   ▨ '87

Ideological/Single-Issue

Pro-Israel **$5,850**

National PAC	$5,000
Others	$850

Other Major Ideological/Single-Issue PACs

National Rifle Assn	$2,250	Pro-Guns

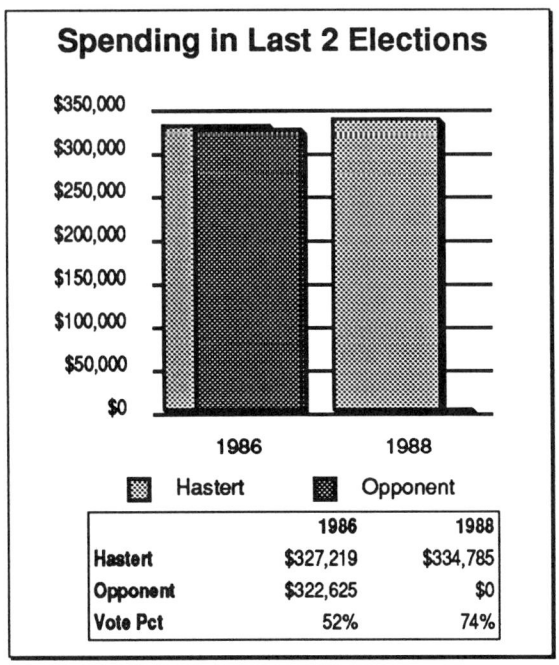

Spending in Last 2 Elections

▨ Hastert   ▨ Opponent

	1986	1988
Hastert	$327,219	$334,785
Opponent	$322,625	$0
Vote Pct	52%	74%

Charles Hatcher, D-Ga (2)

1988 Committees & Subcommittees

First elected: 1980
Total receipts: $348,158
Total from PACs: $199,408

Agriculture
Department Operations, Research and Foreign Agriculture
Forests, Family Farms and Energy
Tobacco and Peanuts

Small Business
Energy and Agriculture (Chairman)

PAC Contribution Profile

Business

Agricultural Chemicals	**$6,350**
Chemical Producers & Distributors Assn	$3,050
Freeport-McMoran Inc	$1,250
Chemical Specialties Manufacturers Assn	$1,050
Ecolab Inc	$1,000
Auto Dealers	**$7,250**
National Auto Dealers Assn	$4,750
Auto Dealers & Drivers for Free Trade	$2,500
Commercial Banks	**$9,250**
Citizens & Southern National Bank	$3,000
First Atlanta Corp	$2,300
Others	$3,950
Commodities Trading	**$2,550**
Chicago Board of Trade	$1,550
Chicago Mercantile Exchange	$1,000
Construction	**$4,800**
National Assn of Home Builders	$2,500
Associated General Contractors	$1,500
Others	$800
Dairy	**$13,900**
Dairymen Inc-Georgia	$6,900
Associated Milk Producers	$5,500
Mid-American Dairymen	$1,500
Defense	**$3,800**
Lockheed Corp	$2,500
Others	$1,300

Campaign Revenue Sources

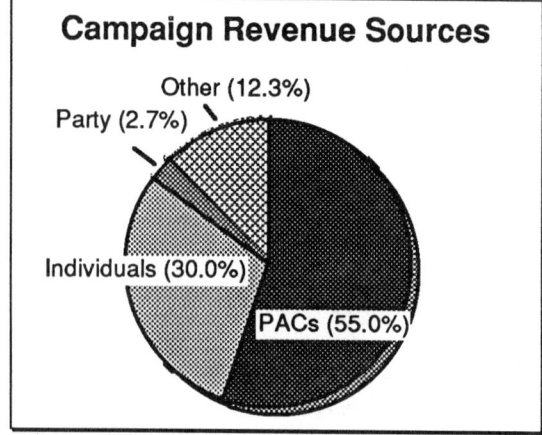

Other (12.3%)
Party (2.7%)
Individuals (30.0%)
PACs (55.0%)

Electrical Utilities	**$7,400**
ACRE (Action Committee for Rural Electrification)	$4,000
Southern Company*	$3,150
Others	$250
Farm Organizations	**$2,750**
Alabama Farm Bureau Federation	$1,850
Others	$900
Food & Beverage	**$8,500**
Coca-Cola Company	$3,500
Others	$5,000
Forest Products	**$4,520**
Union Camp Corp	$1,200
Georgia-Pacific Corp	$1,070
Others	$2,250
Health Professionals	**$12,999**
American Medical Assn	$9,999
American Academy of Ophthalmology	$2,000
American Podiatry Assn	$1,000
Household/Office Products	**$2,550**
International Sanitary Supply	$2,550
Insurance	**$5,450**
National Assn of Life Underwriters	$2,500
American Family Corp	$1,450
Others	$1,500
Lawyers	**$3,500**
Assn of Trial Lawyers of America	$2,000
King & Spalding	$1,000
Others	$500
Oil & Gas	**$4,750**
Petroleum Marketers Assn	$1,500
Amoco Corp	$1,250
Others	$2,000
Other Crop Production & Processing	**$3,725**
National Cotton Council	$1,500
Others	$2,225
Poultry & Eggs	**$2,750**
National Broiler Council	$1,300
Gold Kist	$1,200
Others	$250

PAC Totals by Category

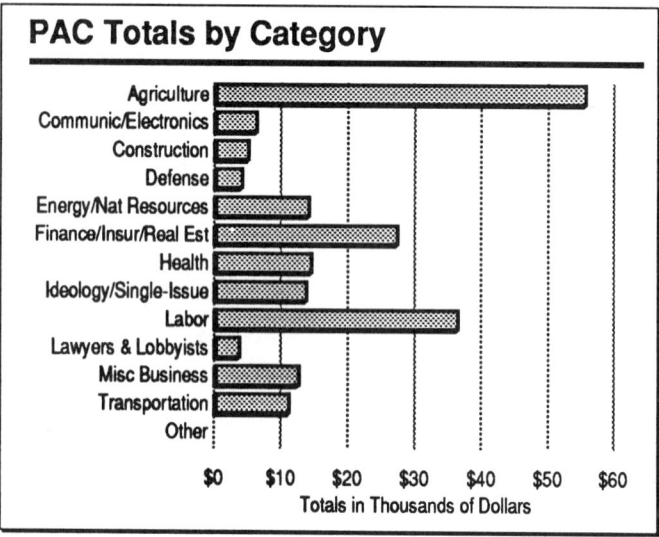

Agriculture
Communic/Electronics
Construction
Defense
Energy/Nat Resources
Finance/Insur/Real Est
Health
Ideology/Single-Issue
Labor
Lawyers & Lobbyists
Misc Business
Transportation
Other

$0 $10 $20 $30 $40 $50 $60
Totals in Thousands of Dollars

Real Estate **$10,500**
    National Assn of Realtors $10,000
    Others $500

Sugar Growers **$4,450**
    American Crystal Sugar Corp $1,600
    American Sugarbeet Growers Assn $1,350
    Others $1,500

Telecommunications **$6,000**
    Southern Bell $4,000
    AT&T $1,700
    Others $300

Textiles **$2,100**
    American Textile Manufacturers Institute $1,050
    Westpoint Pepperell $1,050

Tobacco **$6,600**
    Philip Morris $2,450
    RJR Nabisco $2,050
    Tobacco Institute $1,000
    Others $1,100

Other Major Business PACs

American Assn of Crop Insurers	$1,050	Ag Svcs
National Assn of Small Bus Invest Co's	$1,050	Sml Business
National Assn of Truck Stop Operators	$1,000	Trucking
Waste Management Inc	$1,000	Waste Mgmt

Interest Group Ratings

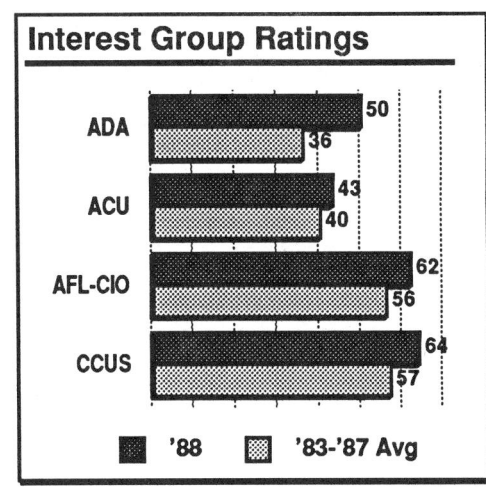

Labor

Bldg Trades/Industrial/Misc Unions **$5,750**
    Food & Commercial Workers Union $4,500
    Others $1,250

Government & Postal Workers **$7,500**
    National Assn of Retired Federal Employees $3,100
    National Assn of Letter Carriers $2,000
    American Postal Workers Union $1,300
    Others $1,100

Teachers Unions **$5,100**
    National Education Assn $5,100

Transportation Unions **$17,775**
    Teamsters Union $12,500
    United Transportation Union $3,650
    Transportation Communication Union $1,000
    Others $625

Ideological/Single-Issue

Democratic Leadership PACs **$9,750**
    Majority Congress Committee (Jim Wright) $5,000
    Valley Education Fund (Tony Coelho) $2,500
    House Leadership Fund (Tom Foley) $2,000
    Others $250

Pro-Guns **$3,000**
    National Rifle Assn $2,500
    Others $500

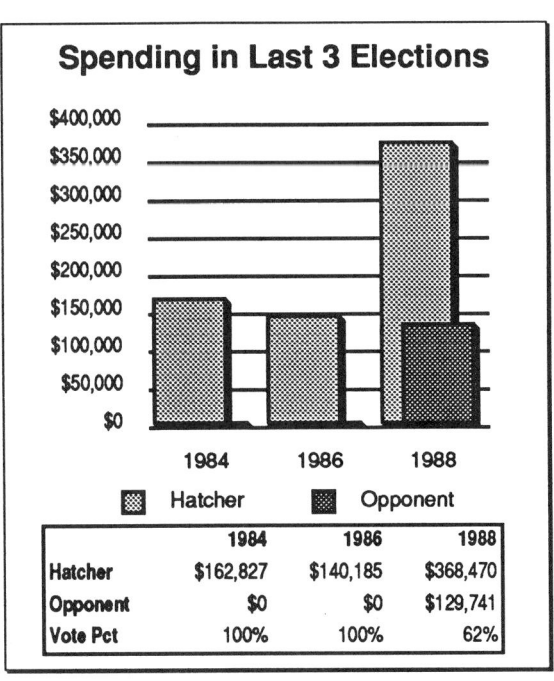

Spending in Last 3 Elections

	1984	1986	1988
Hatcher	$162,827	$140,185	$368,470
Opponent	$0	$0	$129,741
Vote Pct	100%	100%	62%

* Contributions came from more than one PAC affiliated
with this sponsor.

Augustus F. Hawkins, D-Calif (29)

First elected: 1962
Total receipts: $109,450
Total from PACs: $105,550

1988 Committees & Subcommittees

Education and Labor (Chairman)
Elementary, Secondary and Vocational Education (Chairman)

Joint Economic
Investment, Jobs and Prices (Chairman)
Economic Goals and Intergovernmental Policy
Education and Health

PAC Contribution Profile

Business

Health Professionals	**$9,250**
American Medical Assn	$5,350
American Dental Assn	$2,500
Others	$1,400
Real Estate	**$3,350**
National Assn of Realtors	$3,350
Telecommunications	**$4,000**
AT&T	$2,500
Pacific Telesis Group	$1,000
Others	$500
Vocational Tech Schools	**$7,650**
National Assn of Trade/Tech Schools	$4,000
Assn of Independent Colleges/Schools	$2,100
National Assn of Cosmetology Schools	$1,350
Others	$200

Other Major Business PACs

United Parcel Service	$1,200	Delivery
American Health Care Assn	$1,000	Nursing Home
National Assn of Temporary Services	$1,000	EmployAgency

Campaign Revenue Sources

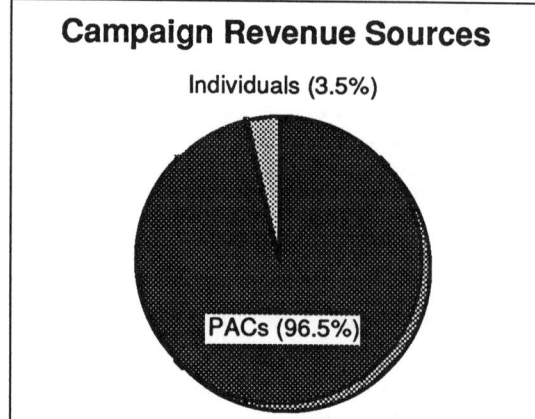

Individuals (3.5%)

PACs (96.5%)

PAC Totals by Category

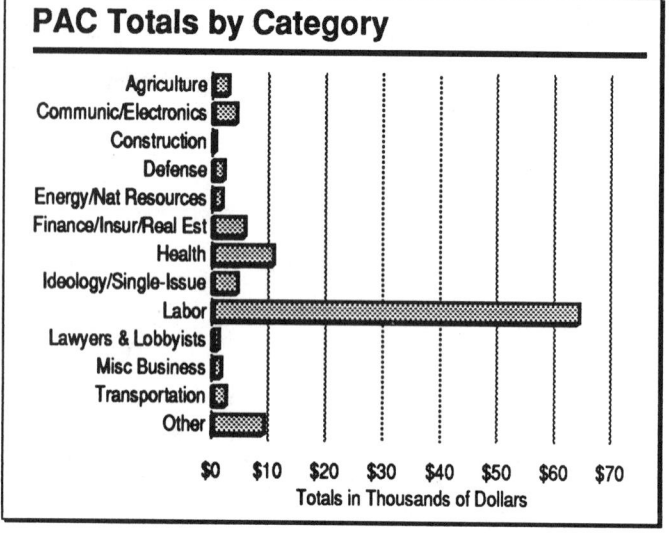

Totals in Thousands of Dollars

552

Labor

Bldg Trades/Industrial/Misc Unions $23,350

Operating Engineers Union	$3,500
Food & Commercial Workers Union	$3,000
Laborers' Western Political League	$3,000
United Auto Workers	$2,850
Plumbers/Pipefitters Union	$2,000
AFL-CIO*	$1,700
Carpenters & Joiners Union	$1,500
Machinists/Aerospace Workers Union	$1,500
Intl Brotherhood of Electrical Workers	$1,000
Others	$3,300

Government & Postal Workers $9,900

American Fedn of State/County/Munic Employees	$5,000
National Assn of Retired Federal Employees	$3,000
National Assn of Letter Carriers	$1,000
Others	$900

Teachers Unions $13,750

National Education Assn	$10,000
United Teachers-Los Angeles	$2,000
American Federation of Teachers	$1,750

Transportation Unions $17,050

Teamsters Union	$10,000
Air Line Pilots Assn	$2,500
Seafarers International Union	$2,000
Marine Engineers Union	$1,000
Others	$1,550

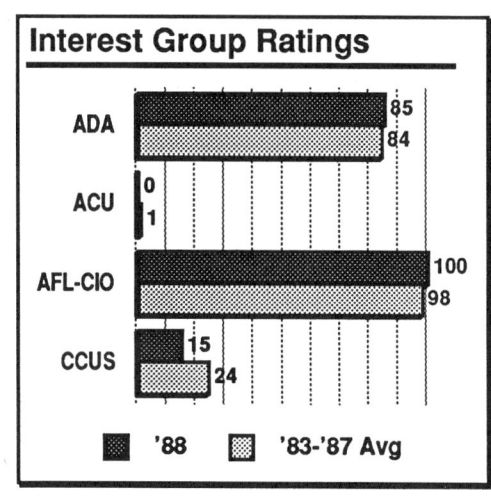

Interest Group Ratings

	'88	'83-'87 Avg
ADA	85	84
ACU	0	1
AFL-CIO	100	98
CCUS	15	24

Ideological/Single-Issue

Ideological/Single-Issue $4,200

National Cmte to Preserve Social Security	$1,350	Social Secur
KidsPAC	$1,000	HealthWelfare
Others	$1,850	

Independent expenditures supporting Hawkins

National Cmte to Preserve Social Security	$1,282

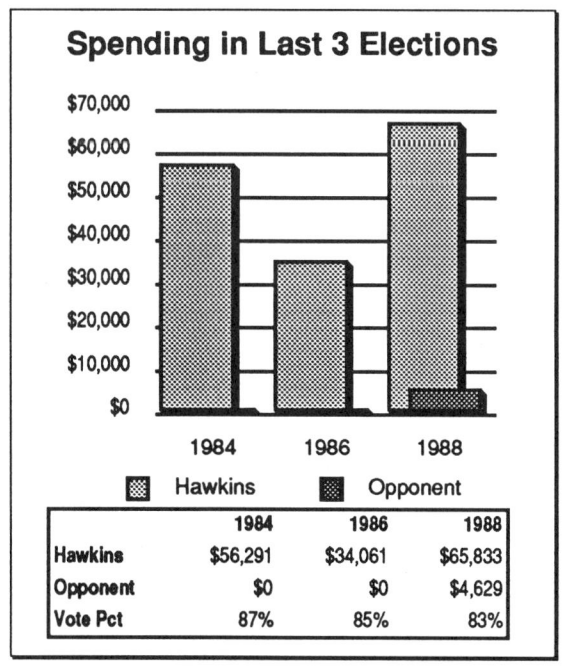

Spending in Last 3 Elections

	Hawkins	Opponent

	1984	1986	1988
Hawkins	$56,291	$34,061	$65,833
Opponent	$0	$0	$4,629
Vote Pct	87%	85%	83%

* Contributions came from more than one PAC affiliated with this sponsor.

Charles A. Hayes, D-III (1)

First elected: 1983
Total receipts: $150,960
Total from PACs: $115,634

1988 Committees & Subcommittees

Education and Labor
Elementary, Secondary and Vocational Education
Employment Opportunities
Labor-Management Relations
Postsecondary Education

Small Business
Procurement, Innovation and Minority Enterprise Development

PAC Contribution Profile

Business

Commodities Trading **$1,500**
    Chicago Board of Trade $1,000
    Chicago Mercantile Exchange $500

Dairy **$1,500**
    Associated Milk Producers $1,500

Lawyers **$5,000**
    Assn of Trial Lawyers of America $5,000

Package Delivery **$1,650**
    United Parcel Service $1,650

Real Estate **$8,000**
    National Assn of Realtors $8,000

Other Major Business PACs

Alabama Peanut Producers Assn	$500	Crops
Amoco Corp	$500	Major Oil
AT&T	$500	LongDistance
Illinois Bell Telephone	$500	Phone Util
National Assn of Life Underwriters	$500	Life Insurance
National Assn of Social Workers	$500	Social Work
National Assn of Trade/Tech Schools	$500	Voc Tech

Campaign Revenue Sources

Other (3.8%)
Individuals (21.0%)
PACs (75.0%)

PAC Totals by Category

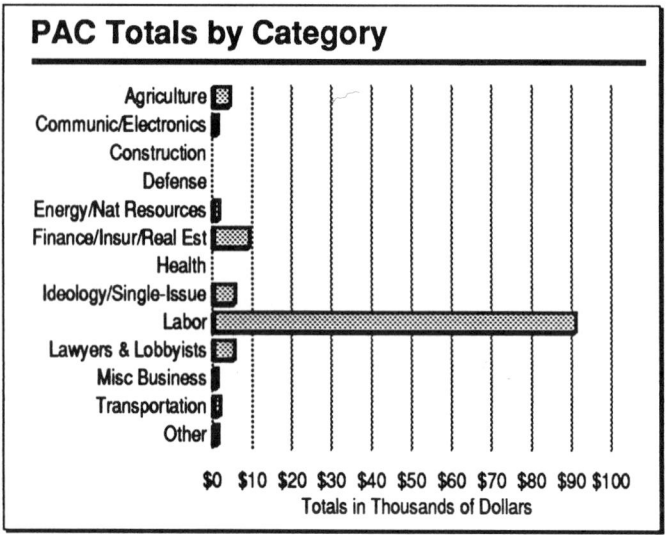

Totals in Thousands of Dollars

	$0	$10	$20	$30	$40	$50	$60	$70	$80	$90	$100

Agriculture
Communic/Electronics
Construction
Defense
Energy/Nat Resources
Finance/Insur/Real Est
Health
Ideology/Single-Issue
Labor
Lawyers & Lobbyists
Misc Business
Transportation
Other

Labor

Bldg Trades/Industrial/Misc Unions $41,434

United Auto Workers	$10,000
Food & Commercial Workers Union	$8,184
Machinists/Aerospace Workers Union	$4,300
Carpenters & Joiners Union	$3,000
United Steelworkers	$3,000
AFL-CIO	$2,250
Intl Brotherhood of Electrical Workers	$2,000
Laborers' Political League	$1,650
Operating Engineers Union	$1,500
Ladies Garment Workers Union	$1,450
Painters & Allied Trades Union	$1,000
Plumbers/Pipefitters Union	$1,000
Service Employees International Union	$800
Amalgamated Clothing & Textile Workers*	$550
Others	$750

Government & Postal Workers $17,700

American Fedn of State/County/Munic Employees	$10,000
National Assn of Retired Federal Employees	$3,000
National Assn of Letter Carriers	$2,200
American Postal Workers Union	$2,000
Others	$500

Teachers Unions $14,600

American Federation of Teachers	$9,600
National Education Assn	$5,000

Transportation Unions $16,800

Teamsters Union	$10,000
Air Line Pilots Assn	$2,500
Amalgamated Transit Union	$2,000
Seafarers International Union	$1,500
Transportation Communication Union	$800

Interest Group Ratings

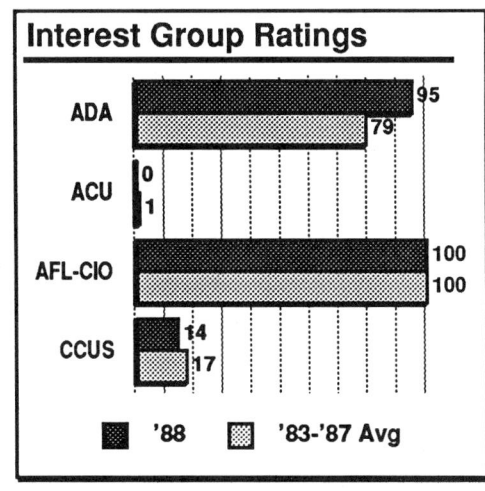

Ideological/Single-Issue

Democratic Leadership PACs $3,000

Valley Education Fund (Tony Coelho)	$3,000

Other Major Ideological/Single-Issue PACs

National Cmte to Preserve Social Security	$1,000	Social Secur
KidsPAC	$500	HealthWelfare

Independent expenditures supporting Hayes

National Cmte to Preserve Social Security	$2,136
National Assn of Letter Carriers	$1,000

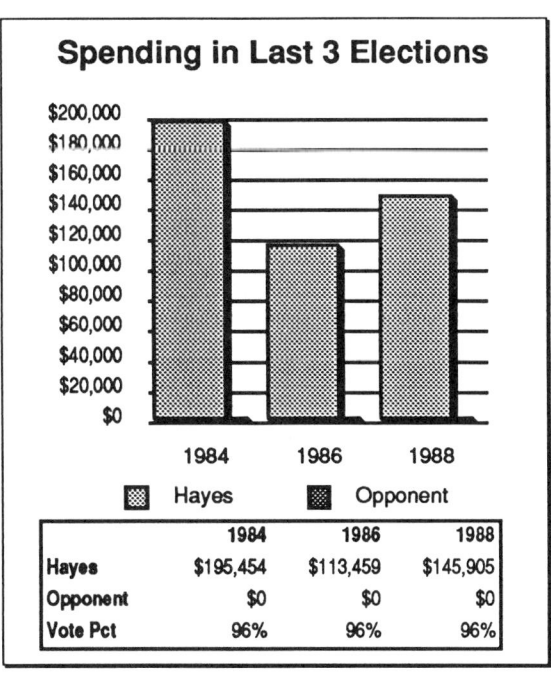

Spending in Last 3 Elections

	1984	1986	1988
Hayes	$195,454	$113,459	$145,905
Opponent	$0	$0	$0
Vote Pct	96%	96%	96%

---

* Contributions came from more than one PAC affiliated
with this sponsor.

Jimmy Hayes, D-La (7)

1988 Committees & Subcommittees

First elected: 1986
Total receipts: $304,917
Total from PACs: $206,100

Public Works and Transportation
Economic Development
Water Resources

Science, Space and Technology
Science, Research and Technology
Space Science and Applications
Transportation, Aviation and Materials

PAC Contribution Profile

Automotive **$3,050**
    National Auto Dealers Assn $2,100
    Others $950

Aviation & Aerospace **$8,600**
    Boeing Company $2,250
    Federal Express Corp $2,000
    Morton Thiokol $1,000
    Others $3,350

Commercial Banks **$2,200**
    None over $500

Construction **$10,750**
    National Assn of Home Builders $3,750
    Associated General Contractors $2,500
    National Society of Professional Engineers $1,000
    Others $3,500

Dairy **$3,750**
    Dairymen Inc-Louisiana $1,750
    Associated Milk Producers $1,500
    Others $500

Defense **$2,850**
    None over $850

Electric Utilities **$9,700**
    Middle South Utilities* $3,200
    Others $6,500

Food & Beverage **$3,000**
    Malone & Hyde Inc $1,000
    Others $2,000

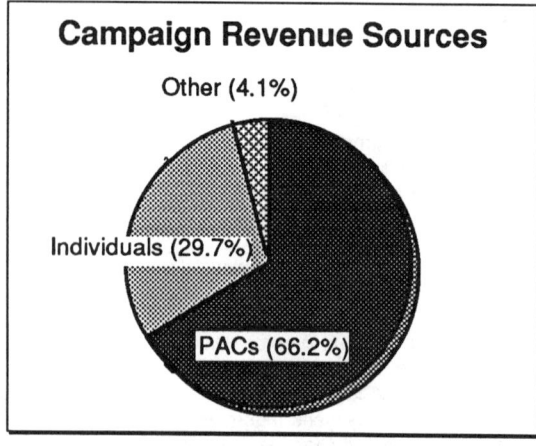

Campaign Revenue Sources

Other (4.1%)
Individuals (29.7%)
PACs (66.2%)

Health Professionals **$11,250**
    American Medical Assn $7,750
    Louisiana Medical Assn $2,500
    American Academy of Ophthalmology $1,000

Insurance **$5,500**
    National Assn of Life Underwriters $3,000
    Independent Insurance Agents of America $1,750
    Others $750

Lawyers & Lobbyists **$19,050**
    Assn of Trial Lawyers of America $14,500
    Jones, Walker, Waechter et al $2,000
    Others $2,550

Oil & Gas **$10,300**
    Atlantic Richfield $1,000
    Columbia Hydrocarbon Corp $1,000
    Others $8,300

Real Estate **$11,250**
    National Assn of Realtors $11,000
    Others $250

Telecommunications **$8,000**
    South Central Bell Telephone $5,000
    AT&T $3,000

Trucking/Delivery **$2,900**
    United Parcel Service $1,250
    Others $1,650

Other Major Business PACs

Greater Washington Board of Trade $1,750	Chamb/Cmrce
International Council of Shopping Centers $1,000	Retail
McDermott Inc $1,000	PowerEquip
PPG Industries $1,000	Glass Prod

PAC Totals by Category

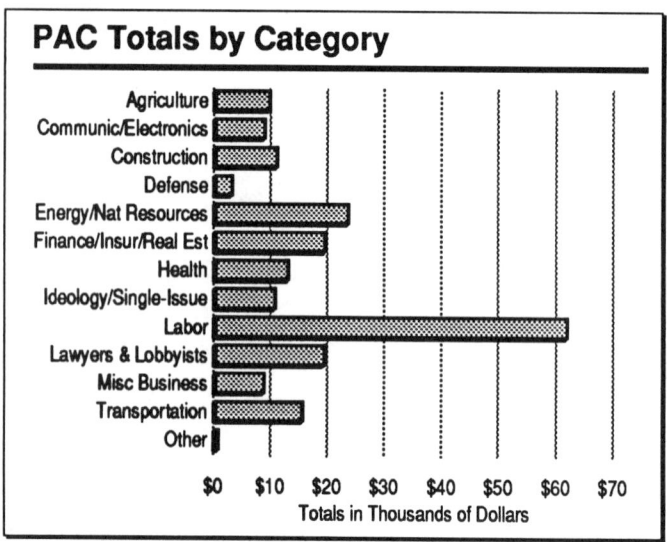

Agriculture
Communic/Electronics
Construction
Defense
Energy/Nat Resources
Finance/Insur/Real Est
Health
Ideology/Single-Issue
Labor
Lawyers & Lobbyists
Misc Business
Transportation
Other

$0 $10 $20 $30 $40 $50 $60 $70
Totals in Thousands of Dollars

Labor

Bldg Trades/Industrial/Misc Unions $29,650
United Auto Workers $10,000
Machinists/Aerospace Workers Union $6,000
AFL-CIO* $4,000
Intl Brotherhood of Electrical Workers $3,000
Food & Commercial Workers Union $2,500
Operating Engineers Union $1,000
Others $3,150

Government & Postal Workers $19,850
National Assn of Letter Carriers $11,100
American Fedn of State/County/Munic Employees $5,000
National Assn of Retired Federal Employees $3,000
Others $750

Teachers Unions $3,000
National Education Assn $3,000

Transportation Unions $9,100
Air Line Pilots Assn $2,500
Amalgamated Transit Union $2,000
United Transportation Union $1,600
Teamsters Union $1,000
Others $2,000

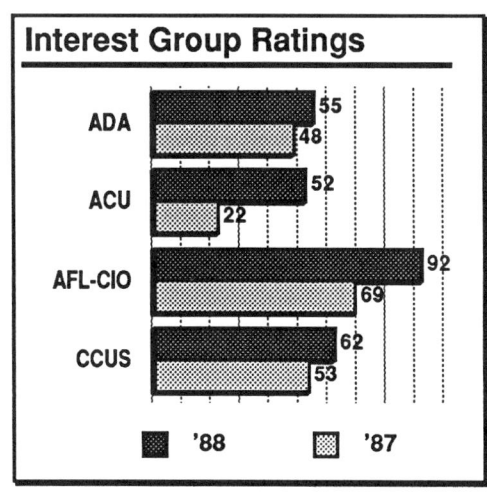

Ideological/Single-Issue

Democratic Leadership PACs $2,500
Valley Education Fund (Tony Coelho) $2,000
Others $500

Pro-Israel $5,500
National PAC $5,000
Others $500

Other Major Ideological/Single-Issue PACs
National Rifle Assn .... $1,100   Pro-Guns
National Cmte to Preserve Social Security ...... $1,050   Social Security

Independent expenditures supporting Hayes
National Cmte to Preserve Social Security $1,959
Louisiana Medical Assn $1,000

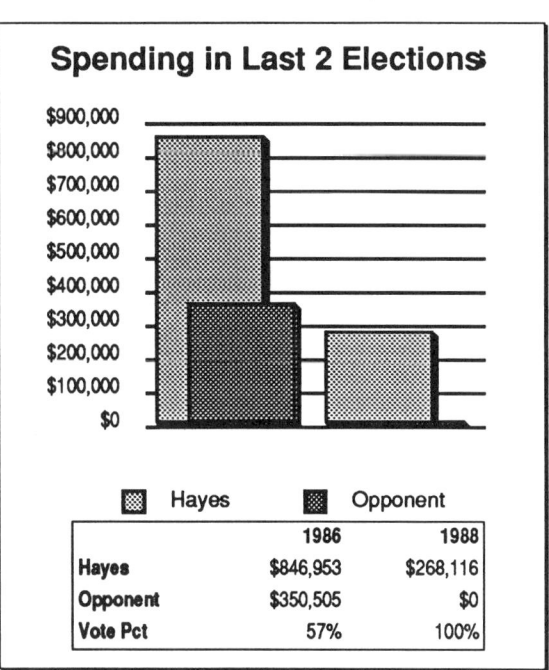

---

* Contributions came from more than one PAC affiliated
with this sponsor.

Joel Hefley, R-Colo (5)

1988 Committees & Subcommittees

Science, Space and Technology
Energy Research and Development
Natural Resources, Agriculture Research and Environment
Space Science and Applications

Small Business
SBA and the General Economy

First elected: 1986
Total receipts: $228,896
Total from PACs: $112,827

Campaign Revenue Sources

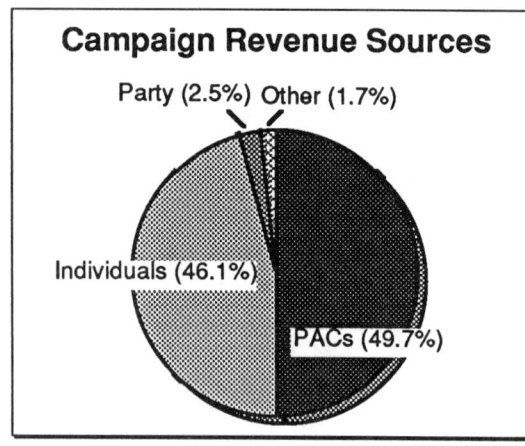

Party (2.5%) Other (1.7%)
Individuals (46.1%)
PACs (49.7%)

PAC Contribution Profile

Business

Air Transport/Air Freight **$2,750**
- Texas Air $1,400
- Federal Express Corp $1,000
- Others $350

Auto Dealers **$4,350**
- National Auto Dealers Assn $2,350
- Auto Dealers & Drivers for Free Trade $2,000

Business Organizations **$2,363**
- National Fedn of Independent Business $2,350
- Others $13

Construction **$10,200**
- National Assn of Home Builders $5,000
- Manville Corp $1,500
- National Electrical Contractors Assn $1,000
- Others $2,700

Defense **$13,700**
- AT&T $2,450
- Litton Industries $1,400
- TRW Inc $1,050
- Continental Telecom $1,000
- Others $7,800

Electric Utilities **$2,070**
- ACRE (Action Committee for Rural Electrification) $1,050
- Public Service Company of Colorado $1,020

Financial Institutions **$2,700**
- Credit Union National Assn $1,000
- Others $1,700

Food & Beverage **$4,050**
- McLane Company $1,000
- Others $3,050

Health Professionals **$10,998**
- American Medical Assn $8,648
- American Academy of Ophthalmology $2,000
- Others $350

Insurance **$4,920**
- National Assn of Life Underwriters $1,000
- Others $3,920

Oil & Gas **$7,150**
- Coastal Corp $1,350
- Chevron Corp $1,100
- Others $4,700

Printing & Publishing **$2,367**
- Printing Industries of America $1,367
- Looart Press $1,000

Real Estate **$7,050**
- National Assn of Realtors $6,000
- Mortgage Bankers Assn of America $1,050

Sugar Growers **$2,100**
- None over $700

Telecommunications **$2,500**
- Mountain Bell $2,500

Tobacco **$2,900**
- Philip Morris $2,900

TV/Cable TV **$2,785**
- Tele-Communications Inc $1,235
- Others $1,550

Other Major Business PACs

American Institute of CPA's	$1,050	Accountants
Associated Milk Producers	$1,000	Dairy
C A Norgren Company	$1,000	Indust Equip
Union Pacific Corp	$1,000	Railroads

PAC Totals by Category

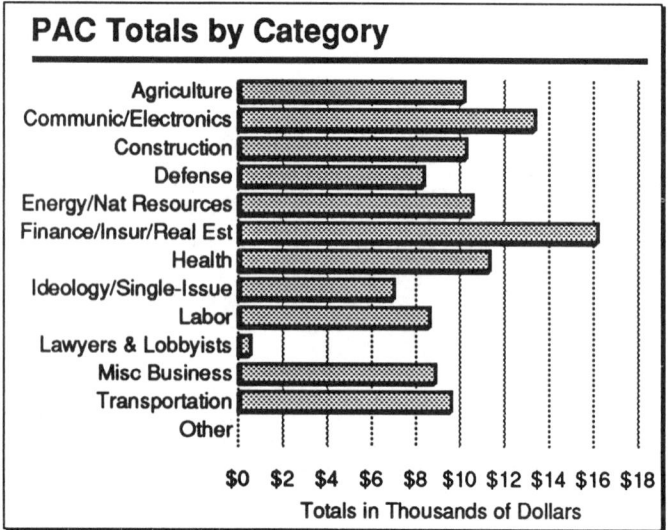

Agriculture
Communic/Electronics
Construction
Defense
Energy/Nat Resources
Finance/Insur/Real Est
Health
Ideology/Single-Issue
Labor
Lawyers & Lobbyists
Misc Business
Transportation
Other

$0 $2 $4 $6 $8 $10 $12 $14 $16 $18
Totals in Thousands of Dollars

Labor

Labor Unions **$8,500**
> National Assn of Retired Federal Employees $6,000
> Marine Engineers District 2 Maritime Officers $1,500
> Seafarers International Union $1,000

Ideological/Single-Issue

Pro-Israel **$5,000**
> National PAC $5,000

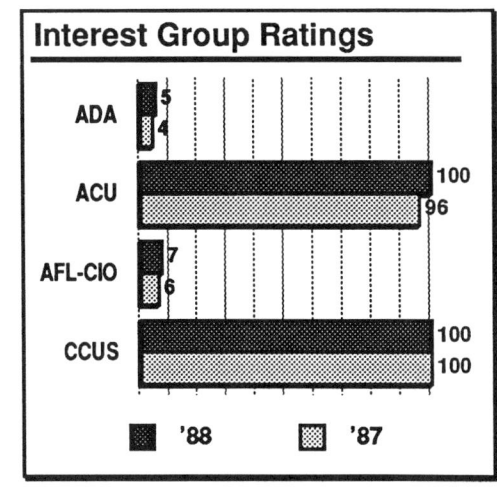

Interest Group Ratings

	'88	'87
ADA	5	4
ACU	100	96
AFL-CIO	7	6
CCUS	100	100

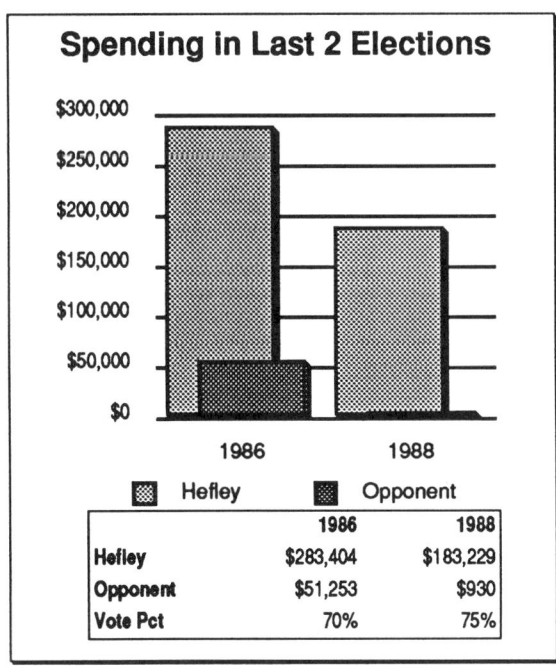

Spending in Last 2 Elections

| | Hefley | Opponent |
	1986	1988
Hefley	$283,404	$183,229
Opponent	$51,253	$930
Vote Pct	70%	75%

559

W. G. "Bill" Hefner, D-NC (8)

First elected: 1974
Total receipts: $432,432
Total from PACs: $267,125.

1988 Committees & Subcommittees

Appropriations
Military Construction (Chairman)
Defense

PAC Contribution Profile

Business

Campaign Revenue Sources

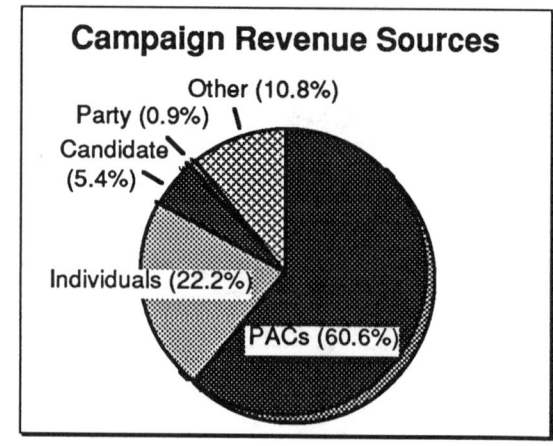

Other (10.8%)
Party (0.9%)
Candidate (5.4%)
Individuals (22.2%)
PACs (60.6%)

Construction	....	$10,750
National Concrete Masonry Assn		$2,000
Associated General Contractors		$1,500
JA Jones Construction Company		$1,500
National Assn of Home Builders		$1,500
Ch2M Hill		$1,000
Manville Corp		$1,000
Others		$2,250

Defense	....	$77,650
AT&T		$6,500
McDonnell Douglas*		$4,300
Singer Company		$4,000
Textron Inc		$4,000
Hughes Aircraft		$3,500
LTV Aerospace & Defense Company		$3,500
General Dynamics		$3,000
Grumman		$3,000
Rockwell International		$3,000
Raytheon		$2,500
United Technologies		$2,500
AEL Industries Inc		$2,000
General Electric		$2,000
Westinghouse Electric		$2,000
Penn Central Corp		$1,550
E-Systems/Corporate Division		$1,500
Ford Motor Company		$1,500
Litton Industries		$1,500
Lockheed Corp		$1,500
Gencorp Inc		$1,250
Talley Industries		$1,050
Allied-Signal		$1,000

(Continued in next column)

PAC Totals by Category

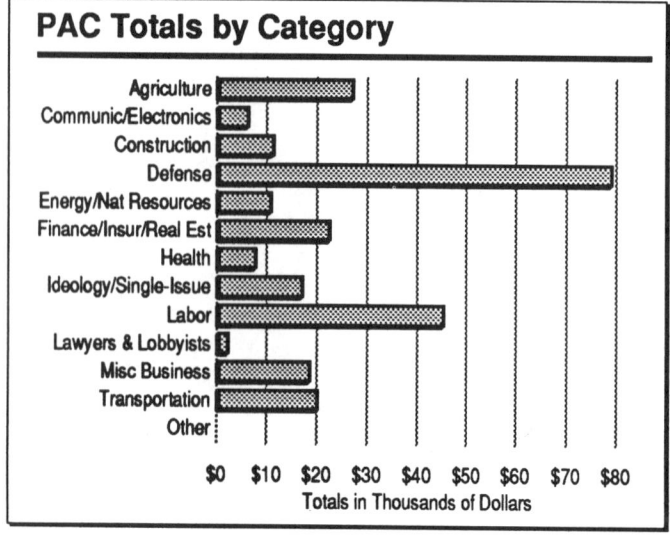

Totals in Thousands of Dollars

- Agriculture
- Communic/Electronics
- Construction
- Defense
- Energy/Nat Resources
- Finance/Insur/Real Est
- Health
- Ideology/Single-Issue
- Labor
- Lawyers & Lobbyists
- Misc Business
- Transportation
- Other

$0 $10 $20 $30 $40 $50 $60 $70 $80

Defense (cont'd)

Austin Powder Company		$1,000
Bath Iron Works		$1,000
Beech Aircraft		$1,000
Boeing Company		$1,000
FMC Corp		$1,000
Kaman Corp		$1,000
Martin Marietta Corp		$1,000
Northrop Corp		$1,000
Sundstrand Corp		$1,000
Tenneco Inc		$1,000
Texas Instruments		$1,000
TRW Inc		$1,000
Others		$9,000

Electric Utilities	....	$6,300
Duke Power Company		$1,800
Carolina Power & Light		$1,500
ACRE (Action Committee for Rural Electrification)		$1,000
Georgia Power Company		$1,000
Others		$1,000

Insurance	....	$9,750
National Assn Mutual Insurance Agents		$4,500
National Assn of Life Underwriters		$2,000
Independent Insurance Agents of America		$1,000
Jefferson-Pilot Corp		$1,000
Others		$1,250

Real Estate	....	$6,500
National Assn of Realtors		$3,500
First Union Corp		$2,000
Mortgage Bankers Assn of America		$1,000

Textiles	....	$10,750
Burlington Industries		$2,000
Collins & Aikman Corp		$1,500
Hoechst Celanese Corp		$1,500
J P Stevens & Company		$1,500
American Textile Manufacturers Institute		$1,000
Cone Mills Corp		$1,000
Springs Mills		$1,000
Others		$1,250

Tobacco	....	$13,250
Philip Morris		$4,000
RJR Nabisco		$4,000
Tobacco Institute		$2,250
Brown & Williamson Tobacco		$2,000
Others		$1,000

Trucking/Delivery $8,625

United Parcel Service	$1,625
National Tank Truck Carriers Inc	$1,250
Roadway Services Inc	$1,250
American Trucking Assns	$1,000
Consolidated Freightways	$1,000
Yellow Freight System	$1,000
Others	$1,500

Other Major Business PACs

Southern Bell	$5,500	Phone Util
National Auto Dealers Assn	$4,000	Auto Sales
American Medical Assn	$2,750	Doctors
Associated Milk Producers	$2,000	Dairy
Federal Express Corp	$2,000	Air Freight
US League of Savings Assn	$2,000	Savings Banks
NCNB Corp	$1,750	Comml Banks
American Furniture Manufacturers Assn	$1,500	Furniture
Norfolk Southern Corp	$1,500	Railroads
Quaker Oats	$1,500	Food Products
Dairymen Inc-North Carolina	$1,300	Dairy
Alcoa	$1,000	Metals/Mining
American Crystal Sugar Corp	$1,000	Sugar
American Bankers Assn	$1,000	Comml Banks
American Podiatry Assn	$1,000	Other MD
Coca-Cola Company	$1,000	Soft Drinks
Gulfstream Aerospace	$1,000	Aircraft
National Cotton Council	$1,000	Cotton
National Assn of Pharmacists	$1,000	Pharmacists
National Beer Wholesalers Assn	$1,000	Liquor Whlsl
National Broiler Council	$1,000	Poultry/Egg
Shoneys Inc	$1,000	Restaurants

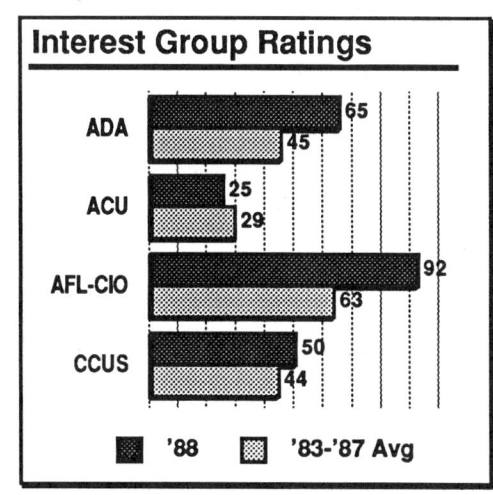

Interest Group Ratings

	'88	'83-'87 Avg
ADA	65	45
ACU	25	29
AFL-CIO	92	63
CCUS	50	44

Labor

Bldg Trades/Industrial/Misc Unions $15,000

National Education Assn	$10,000
United Auto Workers	$1,500
Ladies Garment Workers Union	$1,000
Machinists/Aerospace Workers Union	$1,000
Others	$1,500

Government & Postal Workers $10,500

National Assn of Retired Federal Employees	$7,000
National Assn of Letter Carriers	$2,000
American Fedn of State/County/Munic Employees	$1,000
Others	$500

Transportation Unions $19,250

United Transportation Union	$7,000
Marine Engineers Union*	$5,000
Air Line Pilots Assn	$3,500
Teamsters Union	$2,000
Others	$1,750

Ideological/Single-Issue

Democratic Leadership PACs $8,000

Majority Congress Committee (Jim Wright)	$5,000
House Leadership Fund (Tom Foley)	$3,000

Other Major Ideological/Single-Issue

National Rifle Assn	$4,950	Pro-Guns
National Cmte to Preserve Social Security	$2,000	Social Secur

Independent expenditures supporting Hefner

National Cmte to Preserve Social Security	$2,749

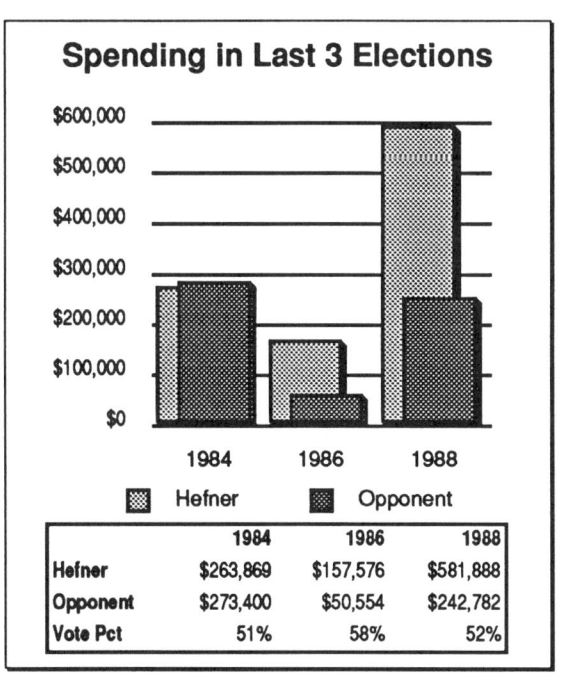

Spending in Last 3 Elections

	1984	1986	1988
Hefner	$263,869	$157,576	$581,888
Opponent	$273,400	$50,554	$242,782
Vote Pct	51%	58%	52%

Hefner / Opponent

---

* Contributions came from more than one PAC affiliated
with this sponsor.

Paul B. Henry, R-Mich (5)

1988 Committees & Subcommittees

First elected: 1984
Total receipts: $387,878
Total from PACs: $97,425

Education and Labor
Health and Safety (Ranking Republican)
Elementary, Secondary and Vocational Education
Employment Opportunities

Science, Space and Technology
Natural Resources, Agriculture Research and Environment
Science, Research and Technology

Select Aging
Retirement Income and Employment

PAC Contribution Profile

Business

Automotive	**$2,500**
None over $950	
Chemicals & Plastics	**$2,350**
None over $500	
Construction	**$16,450**
National Utility Contractors Assn	$4,500
Associated General Contractors	$1,600
National Assn of Home Builders	$1,500
Sheet Metal/AirCon Contractors	$1,500
Associated Builders & Contractors	$1,100
American Subcontractors Assn	$1,000
Wall & Ceiling/Gypsum Contractors	$1,000
Others	$4,250
Defense	**$2,800**
None over $600	
Electric & Power Utilities	**$3,000**
Consumers Power Company	$1,200
Others	$1,800
Financial Institutions	**$5,050**
Comerica Inc	$1,700
Michigan Credit Union League	$1,125
Michigan League of Savings Institute	$1,000
Others	$1,225

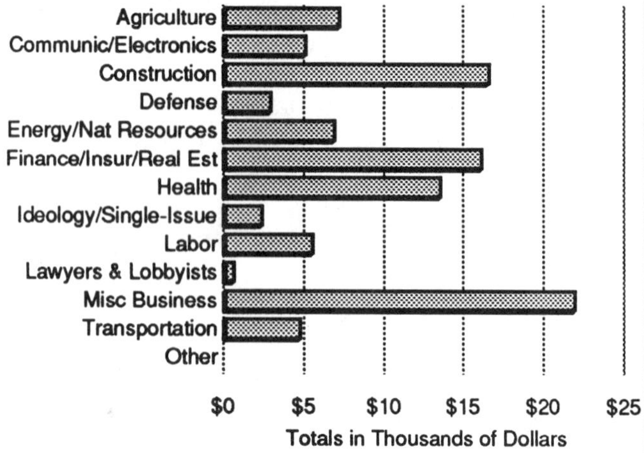

Campaign Revenue Sources

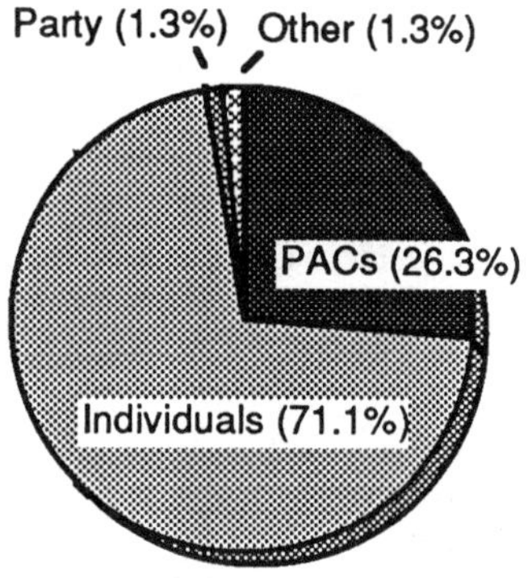

Party (1.3%) Other (1.3%)
PACs (26.3%)
Individuals (71.1%)

Food & Beverage	**$8,025**
National Restaurant Assn	$2,000
Food Marketing Institute	$1,100
Michigan Beer & Wine Wholesalers Assn	$1,075
McDonald's Corp	$1,000
Others	$2,850
Furniture	**$2,300**
American Furniture Manufacturers Assn	$1,950
Others	$350
Health Professionals	**$9,350**
American Medical Assn	$7,250
American Dental Assn	$1,500
Others	$600
Hospitals	**$2,125**
American Hospital Assn	$1,375
Others	$750
Industrial Equipment & Materials	**$2,500**
JSJ Corp	$2,000
Others	$500
Insurance	**$7,700**
National Assn of Life Underwriters	$1,500
American Insurance Assn	$1,000
Others	$5,200
Oil & Gas	**$3,500**
Michigan Consolidated Gas	$1,150
Others	$2,350
Real Estate	**$3,250**
National Assn of Realtors	$3,250
Retail Sales	**$4,700**
International Mass Retail Assn	$1,000
Others	$3,700

PAC Totals by Category

Agriculture
Communic/Electronics
Construction
Defense
Energy/Nat Resources
Finance/Insur/Real Est
Health
Ideology/Single-Issue
Labor
Lawyers & Lobbyists
Misc Business
Transportation
Other

$0 $5 $10 $15 $20 $25

Totals in Thousands of Dollars

Telecommunications *$4,200*
    Michigan Bell Telephone $1,900
    AT&T $1,500
    Others $800

Other Major Business PACs

National Assn of Wholesale-Distributors ....$1,200   Wholesale

Labor

Labor Unions *$5,400*
    National Assn of Retired Federal Employees $2,000
    Food & Commercial Workers Union................................$1,000
    Marine Engineers District 2 Maritime Officers.................$1,000
    Others $1,400

Major Ideological/Single-Issue PACs

Hudson Valley PAC ....$1,000   Pro-Israel

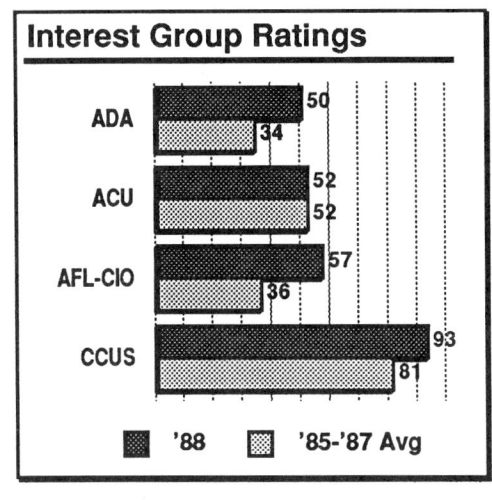

Interest Group Ratings

	'88	'85-'87 Avg
ADA	50	34
ACU	52	52
AFL-CIO	57	36
CCUS	93	81

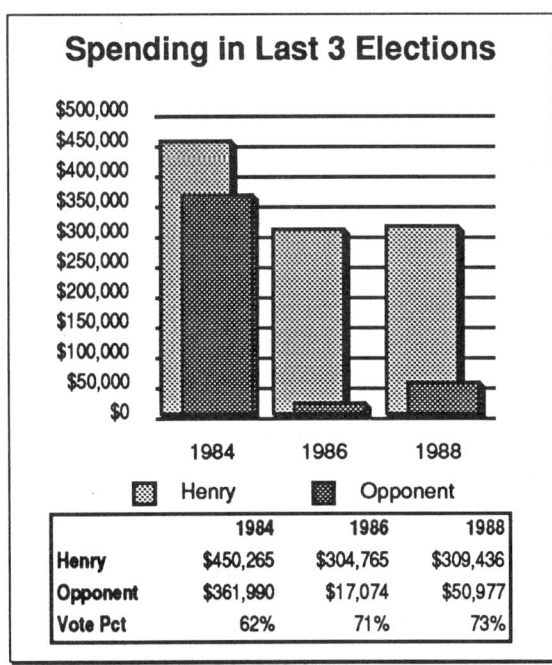

Spending in Last 3 Elections

	1984	1986	1988
Henry	$450,265	$304,765	$309,436
Opponent	$361,990	$17,074	$50,977
Vote Pct	62%	71%	73%

Wally Herger, R-Calif (2)

1988 Committees & Subcommittees

First elected: 1986
Total receipts: $691,969
Total from PACs: $258,675

Agriculture
Cotton, Rice and Sugar
Domestic Marketing, Consumer Relations and Nutrition
Forests, Family Farms and Energy

Merchant Marine and Fisheries
Fisheries and Wildlife Conservation and the Environment
Oceanography
Panama Canal/Outer Continental Shelf

Select Hunger

PAC Contribution Profile

Business

Agricultural Chemicals **$5,575**
Eli Lilly & Company	$1,050
FMC Corp	$1,000
Monsanto Company	$1,000
Others	$2,525

Automotive **$6,350**
Auto Dealers & Drivers for Free Trade	$5,000
National Auto Dealers Assn	$1,100
Others	$250

Construction **$19,100**
National Assn of Home Builders	$4,000
American Supply Assn	$3,250
Associated General Contractors	$2,500
Sheet Metal/AirCon Contractors	$2,300
National Electrical Contractors Assn	$2,000
Ch2M Hill	$1,300
Others	$3,750

Cotton Growers & Processors **$7,650**
Calcot Ltd	$3,000
National Cotton Council	$2,100
J G Boswell Company	$1,500
Others	$1,050

Dairy **$7,200**
Associated Milk Producers	$3,000
Milk Industry Foundation	$1,350
Dairymen Inc	$1,300
Western United Dairymens Assn	$1,000
Others	$550

Campaign Revenue Sources

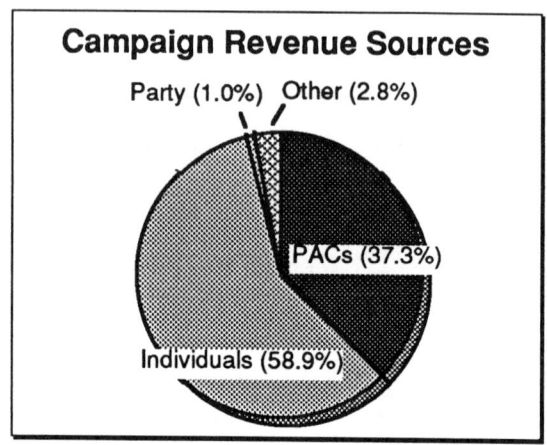

Party (1.0%) Other (2.8%)
PACs (37.3%)
Individuals (58.9%)

Defense **$5,450**
Textron Inc	$1,000
Others	$4,450

Financial Institutions **$8,100**
Barnett Banks of Florida	$1,000
California Bankers Assn	$1,000
Credit Union National Assn	$1,000
Others	$5,100

Food & Beverage **$18,592**
Nabisco Brands Inc	$2,600
American Meat Institute	$2,050
Wine Institute	$1,642
ConAgra Inc	$1,500
Food Marketing Institute	$1,300
National Beer Wholesalers Assn	$1,050
General Mills Restaurants	$1,000
National Restaurant Assn	$1,000
Pepsico Inc	$1,000
Safeway Stores	$1,000
Others	$4,450

Forest Products **$13,568**
Louisiana-Pacific Corp	$3,478
Manville Corp	$3,000
Simpson Investment Company	$1,550
National Forest Products Assn	$1,300
Weyerhaeuser Company*	$1,300
Stone Container Corp*	$1,250
Others	$1,690

Fruit & Vegetable Growers **$26,200**
California Almond Growers Exchange	$5,000
Desert Grape Growers League/California	$5,000
Sunsweet Growers	$4,700
California Canning Peach Assn	$2,100
Tri/Valley Growers	$1,750
California Pistachio Assn	$1,300
Diamond Walnut Growers	$1,200
Western Growers Assn	$1,000
Others	$4,150

PAC Totals by Category

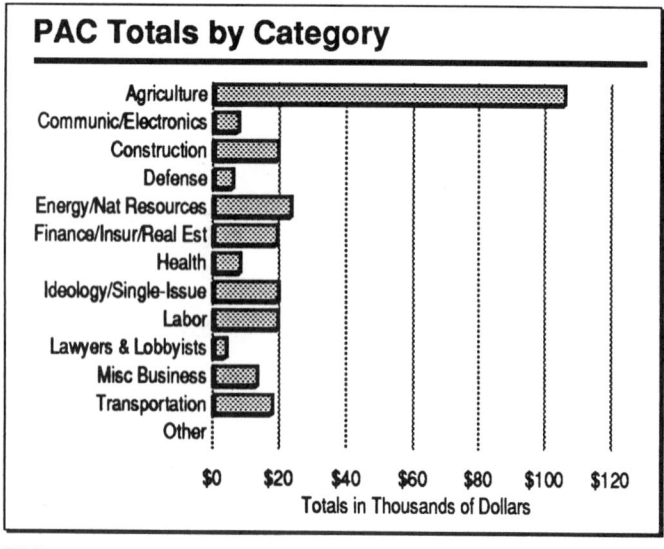

Agriculture
Communic/Electronics
Construction
Defense
Energy/Nat Resources
Finance/Insur/Real Est
Health
Ideology/Single-Issue
Labor
Lawyers & Lobbyists
Misc Business
Transportation
Other

$0 $20 $40 $60 $80 $100 $120
Totals in Thousands of Dollars

Health Professionals **$7,050**
  American Medical Assn $3,450
  American Academy of Ophthalmology $2,500
  Others $1,100

Livestock & Poultry **$5,350**
  National Cattlemen's Assn $1,400
  California Cattlemen's Assn $1,250
  Others $2,700

Oil & Gas **$16,300**
  Atlantic Richfield $1,550
  Halliburton Company $1,500
  National Propane Gas Assn $1,350
  Chevron Corp $1,100
  Phillips Petroleum $1,000
  Sun Company $1,000
  Others $8,800

Other Crops & Processing **$9,750**
  Farmers' Rice Cooperative $5,500
  Tobacco Institute $1,000
  Philip Morris $1,400
  Others $1,850

Real Estate **$7,100**
  National Assn of Realtors $6,850
  Others $250

Sea Transport **$5,400**
  Tenneco Inc $1,500
  Matson Navigation $1,250
  Others $2,650

Sugar Growers **$7,975**
  American Sugarbeet Growers Assn $1,475
  American Crystal Sugar Corp $1,350
  California Beet Growers Assn $1,200
  Others $3,950

Interest Group Ratings

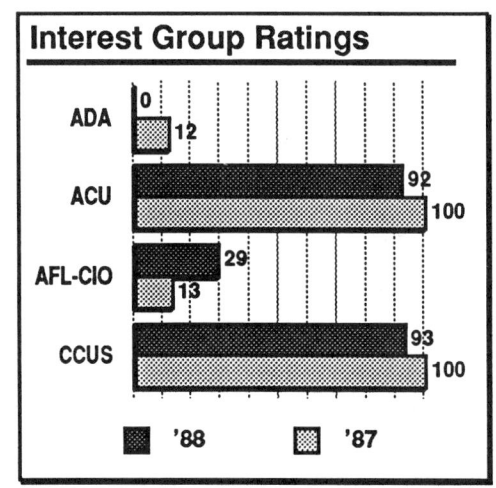

Telecommunications **$5,800**
  Continental Telecom $3,000
  Pacific Telesis Group $1,300
  AT&T $1,000
  Others $500

Other Major Business PACs

California Farm Bureau Federation	$4,150	Farm Orgs
Assn of Trial Lawyers of America	$2,750	Lawyers
National Assn of Life Underwriters	$2,500	Life Insurance
Marriott Corp	$2,000	Hotel/Motel
Pacific Gas & Electric	$1,400	Gas & Electr
National Fisheries Institute	$1,300	Fishing
Glenn Colusa PAC	$1,200	Ag Svcs
Southland Corp	$1,007	Dept Store
American Veterinary Medical Assn	$1,000	Veterinary
Chicago Mercantile Exchange	$1,000	Commodities

Labor

Sea Transport Unions **$15,050**
  Marine Engineers Union* $10,500
  Seafarers International Union $4,000
  Others $550

Other Major Labor PACs

National Assn of Retired Federal Employees	$4,000	Fed Workers

Ideological/Single-Issue

Ideological/Single-Issue **$19,112**

National Right to Life PAC	$5,250	Pro-Life
National Rifle Assn	$4,500	Pro-Guns
Conservative Victory Fund (Steve Symms)	$2,897	Repub Leader
Ruff PAC	$1,250	Tax Policy
Friends of Dronenburg	$1,000	NonCong Cand
Others	$4,215	

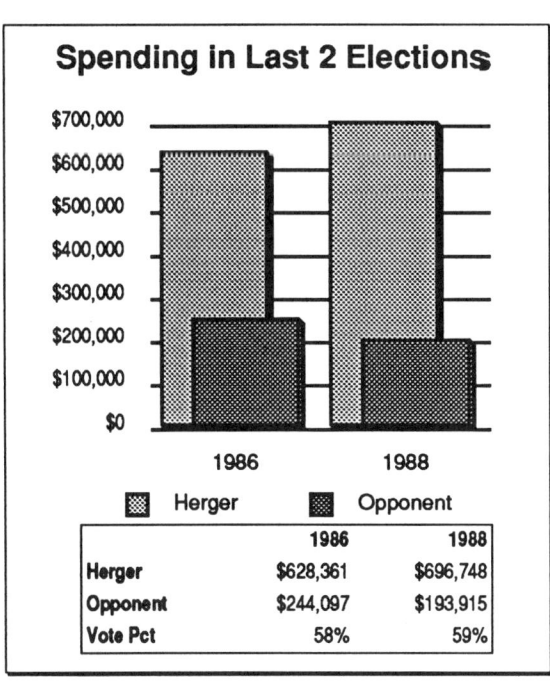

Spending in Last 2 Elections

	1986	1988
Herger	$628,361	$696,748
Opponent	$244,097	$193,915
Vote Pct	58%	59%

---

* Contributions came from more than one PAC affiliated with this sponsor.

Dennis M. Hertel, D-Mich (14)

First elected: 1980
Total receipts: $251,004
Total from PACs: $154,565

1988 Committees & Subcommittees

Armed Services
Military Personnel and Compensation
Research and Development

Merchant Marine and Fisheries
Coast Guard and Navigation
Fisheries and Wildlife Conservation and the Environment
Merchant Marine

Select Aging
Health and Long-Term Care

PAC Contribution Profile

Business

Commercial Banks/Credit Unions	**$3,370**
Comerica Inc	$1,250
Michigan Credit Union League	$1,170
Others	$950
Defense	**$25,450**
General Dynamics	$3,250
Lockheed Corp	$1,900
McDonnell Douglas*	$1,600
Textron Inc	$1,600
Chrysler Corp	$1,550
General Electric	$1,300
General Motors	$1,100
Mantech International	$1,000
Others	$12,150
Food & Beverage	**$2,160**
Michigan Beer & Wine Wholesalers Assn	$1,340
Others	$820
Health Professionals	**$6,500**
American Medical Assn	$4,000
American Dental Assn	$1,500
American Academy of Ophthalmology	$1,000
Lawyers	**$3,470**
Assn of Trial Lawyers of America	$2,500
Others	$970

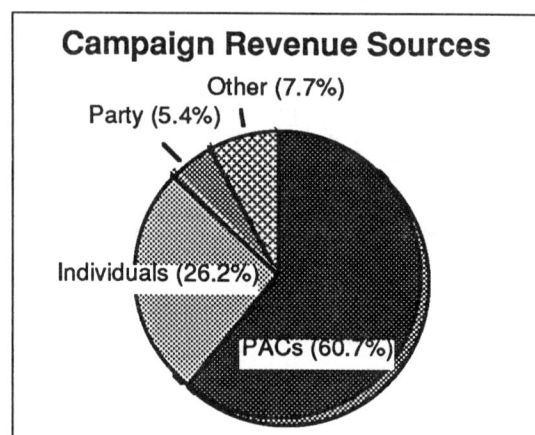

Campaign Revenue Sources

Other (7.7%)
Party (5.4%)
Individuals (26.2%)
PACs (60.7%)

Real Estate	**$3,500**
National Assn of Realtors	$3,500

Other Major Business PACs

KMS Fusion Inc	$1,600	Nuclear Energy
United Parcel Service	$1,500	Delivery
American Hospital Assn	$1,150	Hospitals
Great Lakes Sugar Beet Growers	$1,050	Sugar

PAC Totals by Category

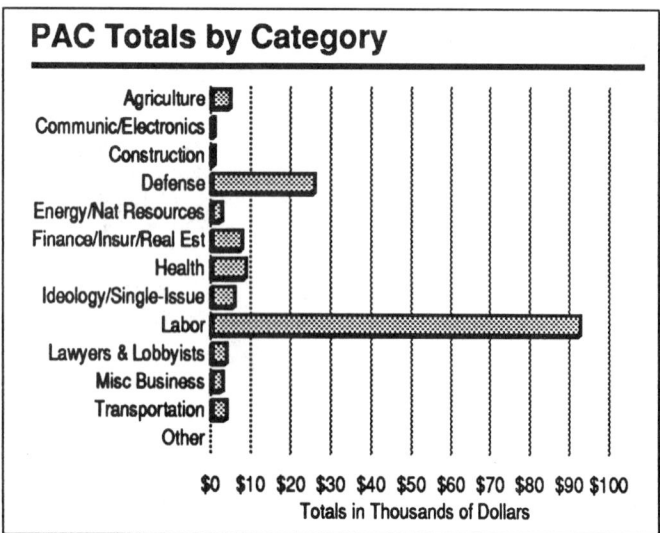

Totals in Thousands of Dollars

Labor

Bldg Trades/Industrial/Misc Unions $36,140

United Auto Workers	$10,000
Machinists/Aerospace Workers Union	$5,000
Carpenters & Joiners Union	$3,850
Food & Commercial Workers Union	$2,315
AFL-CIO	$2,000
Plumbers/Pipefitters Union*	$2,000
Communications Workers of America	$1,850
Laborers' Political League	$1,650
Intl Brotherhood of Electrical Workers	$1,500
Operating Engineers Union*	$1,350
Amalgamated Clothing & Textile Workers	$1,100
Others	$3,525

Government & Postal Workers $17,800

National Assn of Letter Carriers	$7,650
National Assn of Retired Federal Employees	$5,950
American Fedn of State/County/Munic Employees	$2,500
American Postal Workers Union	$1,300
Others	$400

Sea Transport Unions $9,600

Marine Engineers District 2 Maritime Officers	$4,750
Seafarers International Union	$3,350
International Longshoremen Assn	$1,000
Others	$500

Other Transport Unions $15,173

Teamsters Union	$10,000
Air Line Pilots Assn	$2,500
United Transportation Union	$1,200
Maintenance of Way Employees	$1,070
Others	$403

Teachers Unions $13,455

National Education Assn	$8,000
American Federation of Teachers	$5,455

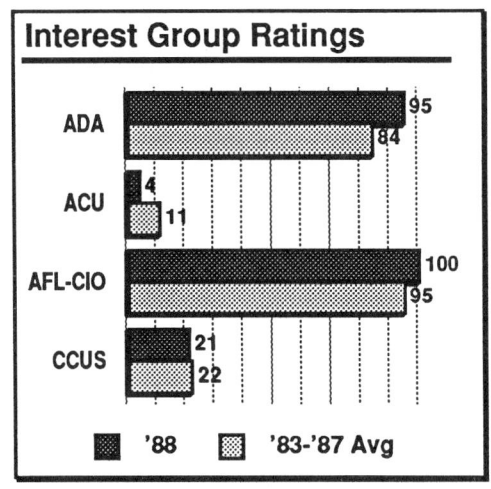

Interest Group Ratings

	'88	'83-'87 Avg
ADA	95	84
ACU	4	11
AFL-CIO	100	95
CCUS	21	22

■ '88   ☐ '83-'87 Avg

Ideological/Single-Issue

Ideological/Single-Issue $5,535

MOPAC	$2,500	Pro-Israel
American Latvian PAC	$1,200	Ethnic
Valley Education Fund (Tony Coelho)	$1,000	Dem Leaders
Others	$835	

Independent expenditures supporting Hertel

National Cmte to Preserve Social Security	$1,886

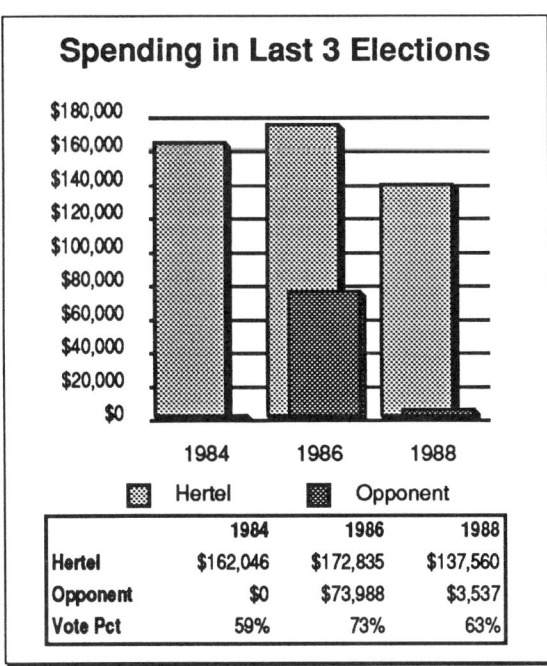

Spending in Last 3 Elections

	1984	1986	1988
Hertel	$162,046	$172,835	$137,560
Opponent	$0	$73,988	$3,537
Vote Pct	59%	73%	63%

☐ Hertel   ■ Opponent

---

* Contributions came from more than one PAC affiliated with this sponsor.

John P. Hiler, R-Ind (3)

1988 Committees & Subcommittees

Banking, Finance and Urban Affairs
Consumer Affairs and Coinage (Ranking Republican)
Financial Institutions Supervision, Regulation and Insurance
Housing and Community Development

Small Business
Antitrust, Impact of Deregulation and Privatization (Ranking Republican)

Campaign Revenue Sources

Other (14.0%)
Party (4.7%)
PACs (33.9%)
Individuals (47.4%)

PAC Contribution Profile

Business

Automotive	**$22,200**
Auto Dealers & Drivers for Free Trade	$7,500
Eaton Corp	$7,000
National Auto Dealers Assn	$4,350
Budd Company	$1,000
Dana Corp	$1,000
Federal-Mogul Corp	$1,000
Others	$350
Business Organizations	**$11,385**
National Fedn of Independent Business	$9,084
Business Industry PAC	$1,271
Others	$1,030
Commercial Banks	**$83,925**
American Bankers Assn	$10,000
Barnett Banks of Florida	$10,000
Banc One Corp*	$8,700
Citicorp	$6,000
J P Morgan & Company	$6,000
Bankers Trust	$5,000
Chase Manhattan	$4,000
Continental Illinois Corp	$3,000
Indiana National Corp	$2,500
National Bank of Detroit*	$2,350
BankAmerica	$2,200
Assn of Bank Holding Companies	$2,000
First Chicago Corp	$1,750
Merchants National Corp	$1,650
1st Source Corp	$1,600

(Continued in next column)

PAC Totals by Category

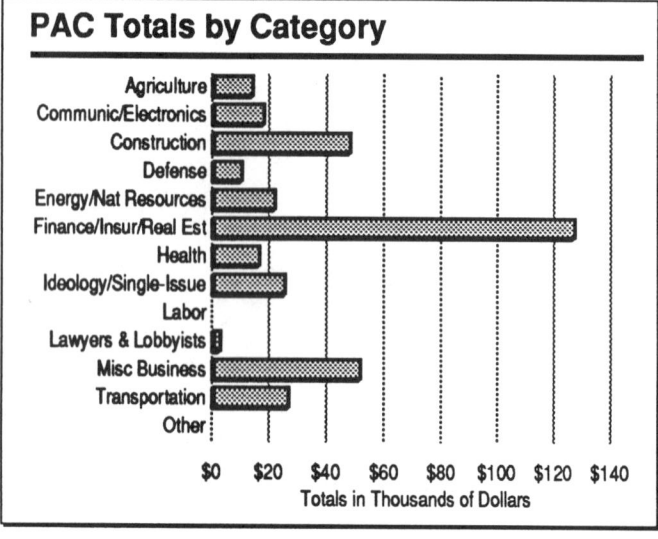

Totals in Thousands of Dollars

(Categories: Agriculture, Communic/Electronics, Construction, Defense, Energy/Nat Resources, Finance/Insur/Real Est, Health, Ideology/Single-Issue, Labor, Lawyers & Lobbyists, Misc Business, Transportation, Other)

Commercial Banks (cont'd)	
Consumer Bankers Assn	$1,450
Ameritrust Company	$1,200
Citizens & Southern National Bank	$1,200
First Bank System/Minnesota	$1,100
Chemical Bank	$1,000
US Bancorp	$1,000
Others	$10,225
Construction	**$47,324**
Manufactured Housing Institute	$10,174
National Assn of Home Builders	$10,000
Fleetwood Enterprises	$4,250
Associated General Contractors	$3,850
National Manufacturing Housing Federation	$2,750
National Electrical Contractors Assn	$2,000
Owens-Corning Fiberglas	$2,000
Caterpillar Tractor	$1,500
Deere & Company	$1,500
American Supply Assn	$1,000
Associated Builders & Contractors	$1,000
National Concrete Masonry Assn	$1,000
National Society of Professional Engineers	$1,000
Philips Industries	$1,000
Others	$4,300
Consumer Credit & Loans	**$12,750**
Credithrift Financial Mgmt Corp	$5,500
American Financial Services Assn	$2,000
Associated Credit Bureaus	$1,250
Beneficial Management Corp	$1,050
Gulf + Western Industries	$1,000
Others	$1,950
Defense	**$9,600**
Harris Corp	$2,000
Lockheed Corp	$1,250
Northrop Corp	$1,000
Tenneco Inc	$1,000
Others	$4,350
Food & Beverage	**$10,750**
National Restaurant Assn	$2,000
Central Soya Company	$1,000
Coors Industries	$1,000
Hardee's Food Systems	$1,000
McDonald's Corp	$1,000
Others	$4,750
Health Professionals	**$11,000**
American Medical Assn	$10,000
American Optometric Assn	$1,000

Insurance	$9,200
Connecticut Mutual Life Insurance	$1,000
Equitable Financial Services	$1,000
Liberty Mutual Insurance	$1,000
National Assn of Independent Insurers	$1,000
Sears	$1,000
Travelers Corp	$1,000
Others	$3,200

Oil & Gas	$14,564
Amoco Corp	$3,250
Phillips Petroleum	$3,000
Mobil Oil	$1,250
Sun Company	$1,000
Others	$6,064

Real Estate	$12,050
National Assn of Realtors	$10,000
Mortgage Bankers Assn of America	$1,200
Others	$850

Retail Sales	$8,407
J C Penney Company	$1,500
National Assn of Convenience Stores	$1,500
Southland Corp	$1,007
Federated Department Stores	$1,000
Others	$3,400

Telecommunications	$11,550
United Telecommunications	$5,500
Indiana Bell Telephone	$2,000
AT&T	$1,000
Continental Telecom	$1,000
Others	$2,050

Interest Group Ratings

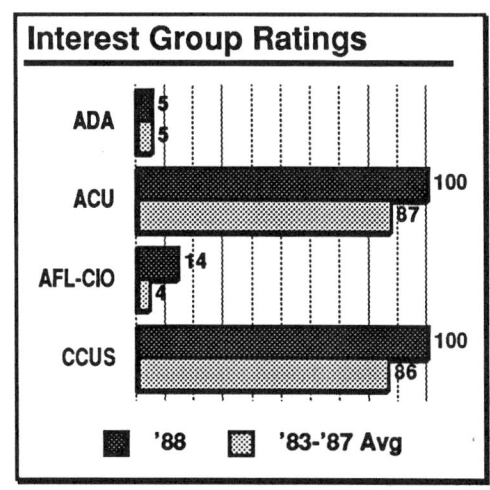

	'88	'83-'87 Avg

Other Major Business PACs

Indiana Farm Bureau	$5,000	Farm Orgs
Dow Chemical*	$3,500	Chemicals
Whirlpool Corp	$3,300	Appliances
Cooper Industries	$3,000	Electronics
Eli Lilly & Company	$2,750	Pharmaceut
Precision Metalforming Assn	$2,000	MetalProduct
Borg-Warner	$1,550	Indust Equip
Texas Utilities Electric Company*	$1,500	ElectricUtil
Southern Company*	$1,350	ElectricUtil
Santa Fe International Corp	$1,250	Trucking
FMC Corp	$1,200	Chemicals
American Business Products	$1,000	Printing
Bristol-Myers	$1,000	Pharmaceut
Credit Union National Assn	$1,000	Credit Union
Dean Witter Reynolds	$1,000	StocksInvest
Dow Corning Corp/Employees	$1,000	PlasticRubb
Hopkins & Sudder	$1,000	Lawyers
IMC Fertilizer Inc	$1,000	Ag Chemicals
Indiana League of Savings Institutions	$1,000	SavingsBanks
National Tooling & Machining Assn	$1,000	Indust Equip
R R Donnelley & Sons	$1,000	Publishing
Stone Container Corp	$1,000	Paper Packg
US League of Savings Assn	$1,000	SavingsBanks

Ideological/Single-Issue

Ideological/Single-Issue		$24,503
Public Service Research Council	$5,000	Anti-Union
National Rifle Assn	$4,950	Pro-Guns
National Right to Life PAC	$3,009	Pro-Life
Council for National Defense	$2,075	Pro-Defense
Policy Innovation PAC (Dick Armey)	$2,000	Repub Leader
15th District Committee (Edward Madigan)	$1,000	Repub Leader
Conservative Victory Cmte	$1,000	Repub/Conser
Conservative Victory Fund (Steve Symms)	$1,000	Repub Leader
Republican Congressional Boosters Club	$1,000	Repub/Conser
Right to Work PAC	$1,000	AntiUnion
Others	$2,469	

Independent expenditures supporting Hiler

National Assn of Realtors	$166,236
American Bankers Assn	$2,500
Banc One Indiana Corp	$2,000
Indiana Bankers Assn	$1,500
Ameritrust Company	$1,000

* Contributions came from more than one PAC affiliated
with this sponsor.

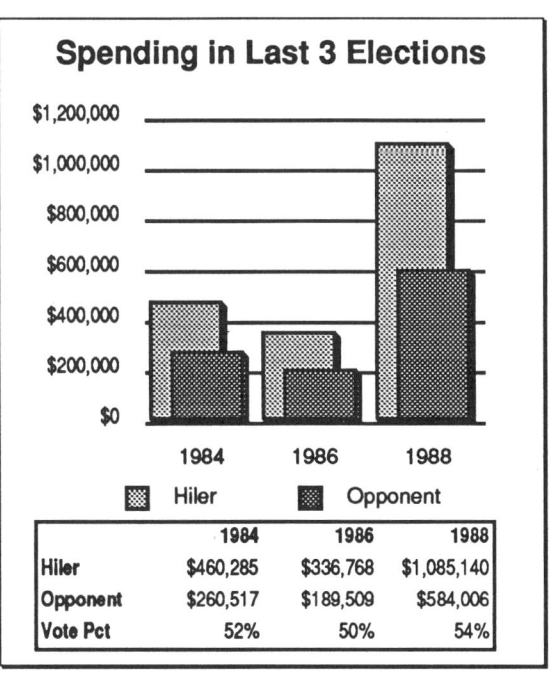

Spending in Last 3 Elections

	1984	1986	1988
Hiler	$460,285	$336,768	$1,085,140
Opponent	$260,517	$189,509	$584,006
Vote Pct	52%	50%	54%

Hiler   Opponent

Peter Hoagland, D-Neb (2)

1988-1989 Committees & Subcommittees

First elected: 1988
Total receipts: $860,865
Total from PACs: $323,400

Banking, Finance and Urban Affairs
Domestic Monetary Policy
Financial Institutions Supervision, Regulation and Insurance
General Oversight and Investigations
Housing and Community Development
International Development, Finance, Trade and Monetary Policy

Small Business
Exports, Tax Policy and Special Problems

PAC Contribution Profile

Business

Commercial & Savings Banks **$4,550**
  Commercial Federal Savings & Loan $3,000
  Others $1,550

Construction **$6,000**
  National Assn of Home Builders $5,000
  Centerra Corp $1,000

Dairy **$7,500**
  Mid-American Dairymen $5,000
  Associated Milk Producers $2,000
  Others $500

Electric Utilities **$3,000**
  ACRE (Action Committee for Rural Electrification) $2,500
  Others $500

Grain Production & Processing **$1,500**
  AG Processing Inc $1,000
  Others $500

Health Professionals **$6,000**
  American Chiropractic Assn $2,500
  American Optometric Assn $2,500
  Nebraska Chiropractors Assn $1,000

Insurance **$1,725**
  None over $975

Campaign Revenue Sources

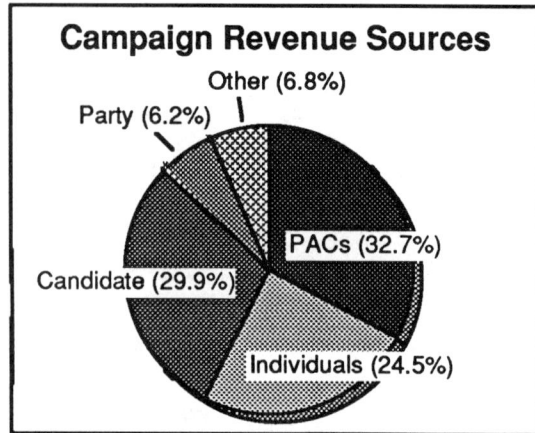

Other (6.8%)
Party (6.2%)
PACs (32.7%)
Candidate (29.9%)
Individuals (24.5%)

Lawyers **$11,650**
  Assn of Trial Lawyers of America $10,000
  Kutak, Rock & Campbell $1,000
  Others $650

Real Estate **$5,000**
  National Assn of Realtors $5,000

Telecommunications **$7,100**
  AT&T $4,000
  Northwestern Bell Telephone $3,100

Other Major Business PACs

Union Pacific Corp .... $1,500   Railroads
Yellow Freight System .... $1,500   Trucking

PAC Totals by Category

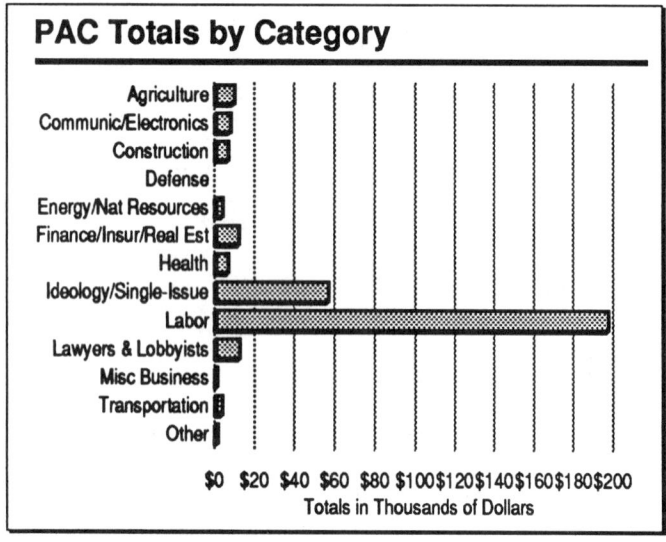

Agriculture
Communic/Electronics
Construction
Defense
Energy/Nat Resources
Finance/Insur/Real Est
Health
Ideology/Single-Issue
Labor
Lawyers & Lobbyists
Misc Business
Transportation
Other

$0 $20 $40 $60 $80 $100 $120 $140 $160 $180 $200
Totals in Thousands of Dollars

Labor

Bldg Trades/Industrial/Misc Unions $107,000

AFL-CIO*	$10,250
Carpenters & Joiners Union	$10,000
Food & Commercial Workers Union	$10,000
Intl Brotherhood of Electrical Workers	$10,000
Machinists/Aerospace Workers Union	$10,000
United Auto Workers	$10,000
Communications Workers of America	$9,800
United Steelworkers	$7,000
Service Employees International Union	$5,000
Plumbers/Pipefitters Union	$4,000
Rubber Cork Linoleum Plastic Workers	$4,000
Sheet Metal Workers Union	$3,500
Operating Engineers Union	$2,500
Bakery, Confectionery & Tobacco Workers	$2,000
Laborers' Political League	$2,000
Ironworkers Union	$1,500
Boilermakers Union	$1,000
Ladies Garment Workers Union	$1,000
Office & Professional Employees Union	$1,000
Others	$2,450

Government & Postal Workers $36,500

American Fedn of State/County/Munic Employees	$10,000
National Assn of Letter Carriers	$10,000
National Assn of Retired Federal Employees	$8,000
American Postal Workers Union	$5,000
International Assn of Firefighters	$1,500
American Federation of Government Employees	$1,250
Others	$750

Teachers Unions $15,000

National Education Assn	$10,000
American Federation of Teachers	$5,000

Transportation Unions $38,000

Teamsters Union	$10,000
Air Line Pilots Assn	$5,000
Amalgamated Transit Union	$5,000
Seafarers International Union	$5,000
United Transportation Union	$5,000
Transport Workers Union	$4,000
Transportation Communication Union	$2,000
Marine Engineers Union	$1,500
Others	$500

Ideological/Single-Issue

Democratic/Liberal $5,742

National Cmte for an Effective Congress	$4,998
Others	$744

Democratic Leadership PACs...................................$27,750

Independent Action (Morris Udall)	$6,000
Cmte for a Democratic Consensus (Marvin Leath)	$5,000
Majority Congress Committee (Jim Wright)	$5,000
Valley Education Fund (Tony Coelho)	$3,500
House Leadership Fund (Tom Foley)	$3,000
America's Leaders' Fund (Dan Rostenkowski)	$2,000
Cmte for Democratic Opportunity (Bill Gray)	$2,000
24th Cong Dist of California PAC (Henry Waxman)	$1,000
Others	$250

Pro-Israel $7,750

Joint Action Cmte for Political Affairs	$2,000
Roundtable PAC	$1,500
Multi-Issue PAC	$1,000
Others	$3,250

Senior Citizens/Social Security $8,000

National Cmte to Preserve Social Security	$5,000
National Council of Senior Citizens	$3,000

Other Major Ideological/Single-Issue PACs

Sierra Club	$4,500	Environment
Council for a Livable World	$2,311	Pro-Peace
Empire Leadership Fund (Mario Cuomo)	$1,000	Dem Cands
KidsPAC	$1,000	Health Welfare

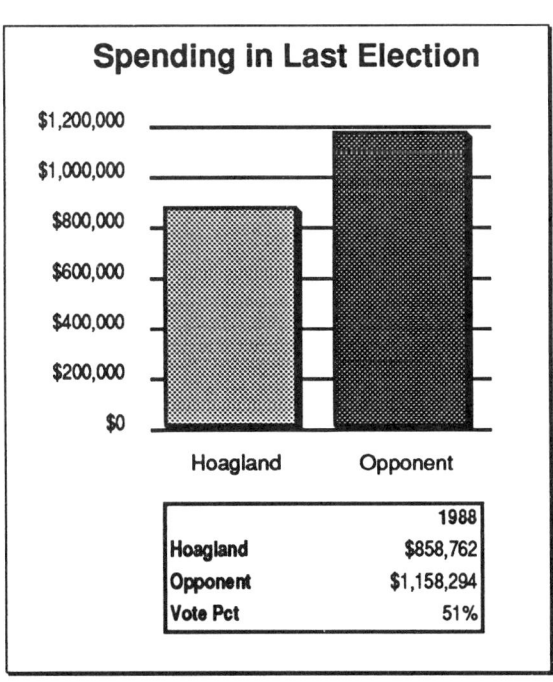

Spending in Last Election

	1988
Hoagland	$858,762
Opponent	$1,158,294
Vote Pct	51%

---

* Contributions came from more than one PAC affiliated with this sponsor.

George J. Hochbrueckner, D-NY (1)

First elected: 1986
Total receipts: $729,077
Total from PACs: $416,961

1988 Committees & Subcommittees

Armed Services
Readiness
Research and Development
Seapower and Strategic and Critical Materials

Merchant Marine and Fisheries
Coast Guard and Navigation
Merchant Marine

Science, Space and Technology
Energy Research and Development
Natural Resources, Agriculture Research and Environment
Science, Research and Technology

PAC Contribution Profile

Business

Auto Dealers	*$6,000*
National Auto Dealers Assn	$6,000
Construction	*$8,500*
National Assn of Home Builders	$7,500
Others	$1,000
Defense	*$29,050*
Grumman	$5,000
Raytheon	$3,650
Textron Inc	$2,000
Hughes Aircraft	$1,750
United Technologies	$1,450
Bath Iron Works	$1,250
Northrop Corp	$1,250
General Dynamics	$1,000
Harris Corp	$1,000
Lockheed Corp	$1,000
Rockwell International	$1,000
Others	$8,700
Health Professionals	*$21,750*
American Medical Assn	$11,500
American Academy of Ophthalmology	$3,000
American Optometric Assn	$2,000
American Dental Assn	$1,500
American Nurses Assn	$1,500
Corp for the Advancement of Psychiatry	$1,000
Others	$1,250

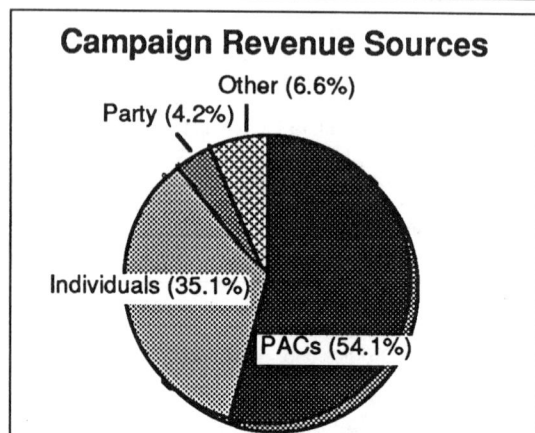

Campaign Revenue Sources

Other (6.6%)
Party (4.2%)
Individuals (35.1%)
PACs (54.1%)

Insurance	*$9,500*
National Assn of Life Underwriters	$4,500
Massachusetts Mutual Life Insurance	$1,000
Metropolitan Life Insurance	$1,000
Prudential Insurance	$1,000
Others	$2,000
Real Estate	*$13,000*
National Assn of Realtors	$13,000

Other Major Business PACs

Assn of Trial Lawyers of America	$4,000	Lawyers
Associated Milk Producers	$2,250	Dairy
AT&T	$1,500	LongDistance
Philip Morris	$1,500	Tobacco
American Hospital Assn	$1,250	Hospitals
Aircraft Owners & Pilots Assn	$1,000	GenlAviation
American Pilots Assn	$1,000	SeaTransport
National Assn of Social Workers	$1,000	Social Work
Union Savings Bank	$1,000	SavingsBanks

PAC Totals by Category

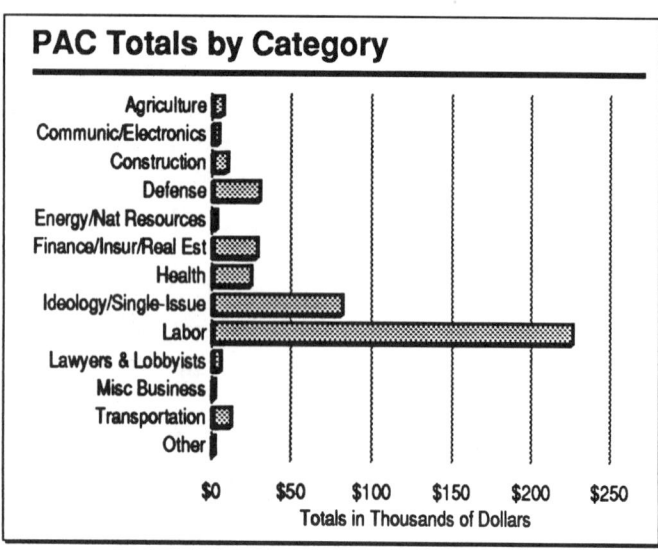

Totals in Thousands of Dollars

(Categories: Agriculture, Communic/Electronics, Construction, Defense, Energy/Nat Resources, Finance/Insur/Real Est, Health, Ideology/Single-Issue, Labor, Lawyers & Lobbyists, Misc Business, Transportation, Other)

Labor

Bldg Trades/Industrial/Misc Unions	*$112,600*
United Auto Workers	$11,000
Food & Commercial Workers Union	$10,000
Machinists/Aerospace Workers Union	$10,000
AFL-CIO*	$9,500
Carpenters & Joiners Union*	$9,500
Intl Brotherhood of Electrical Workers	$8,700
Sheet Metal Workers Union	$7,500
Communications Workers of America	$6,050
United Steelworkers	$6,000
Operating Engineers Union*	$5,250
Service Employees International Union	$5,000
Plumbers/Pipefitters Union	$3,100
Ironworkers Union	$3,000

(Continued in next column)

Labor (cont'd)

Laborers' Political League $2,500
Electrical Radio/Machine Workers $2,250
Bakery, Confectionary & Tobacco Workers $2,000
Rubber Cork Linoleum Plastic Workers $2,000
Boilermakers Union $1,500
Amalgamated Clothing & Textile Workers $1,250
Electronic Machine Furniture Workers $1,250
Graphic Communications Union $1,250
Ladies Garment Workers Union $1,250
United Mine Workers $1,000
Others $1,750

Government & Postal Workers $44,824

National Assn of Letter Carriers $12,000
National Assn of Retired Federal Employees $10,000
American Fedn of State/County/Munic Employees $7,749
American Postal Workers Union $6,500
Suffolk County Patrolmens Assn $2,375
American Federation of Government Employees $1,250
International Assn of Firefighters $1,000
National Rural Letter Carriers Assn $1,000
National Treasury Employees Union $1,000
Others $1,950

Sea Transport Unions $24,400

Marine Engineers Union* $11,500
Seafarers International Union $10,000
International Longshoremen Assn* $1,650
Masters, Mates & Pilots Union $1,250

Other Transport Unions $23,250

Teamsters Union $5,000
Amalgamated Transit Union $4,500
Air Line Pilots Assn $4,000
Transport Workers Union $3,500
United Transportation Union $2,250
Brotherhood of Locomotive Engineers $1,000
Maintenance of Way Employees $1,000
Others $2,000

Teachers Unions $20,000

American Federation of Teachers $10,000
National Education Assn $10,000

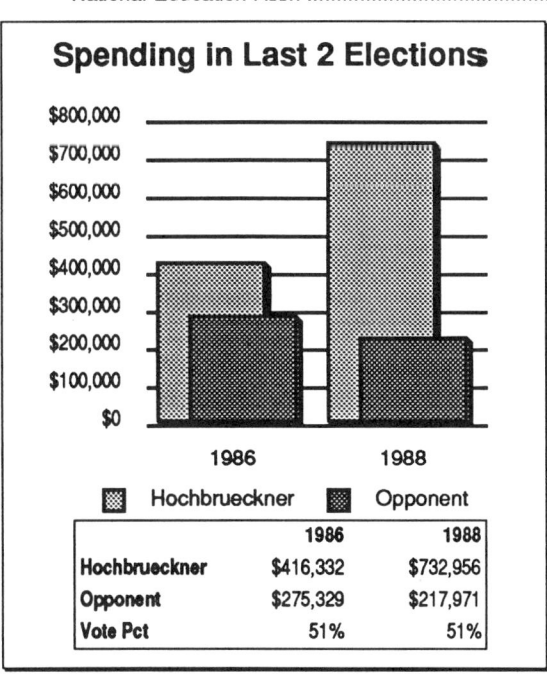

Spending in Last 2 Elections

	1986	1988
Hochbrueckner	$416,332	$732,956
Opponent	$275,329	$217,971
Vote Pct	51%	51%

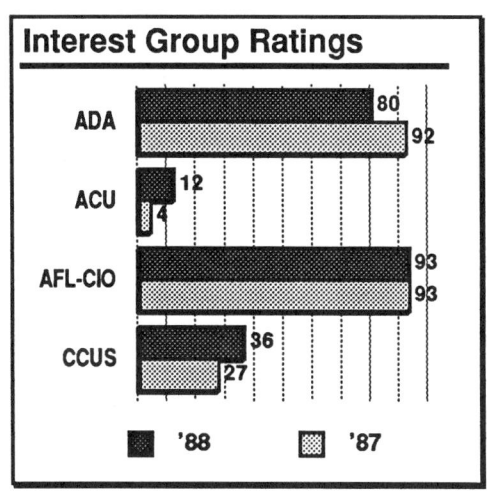

Interest Group Ratings

	'88	'87
ADA	80	92
ACU	12	4
AFL-CIO	93	93
CCUS	36	27

Ideological/Single-Issue

Democratic/Liberal $19,999

National Cmte for an Effective Congress $9,999
Class PAC $5,000
Democratic Study Group Campaign Fund $3,000
Americans for Democratic Action $1,000
Congressional Agenda 80's $1,000

Democratic Leadership PACs $25,201

24th Cong Dist of California PAC (Henry Waxman) $5,000
Majority Congress Committee (Jim Wright) $5,000
Valley Education Fund (Tony Coelho) $4,000
America's Leaders' Fund (Dan Rostenkowski) $3,201
Cmte for the 100th Congress (Charles Rangel) $3,000
Cmte for Democratic Opportunity (Bill Gray) $2,000
House Leadership Fund (Tom Foley) $2,000
Pax Americas (David Bonior) $1,000

Pro-Israel $18,800

Long Island PAC $7,500
National PAC $5,000
Joint Action Cmte for Political Affairs $3,000
Roundtable PAC $1,000
Washington PAC $1,000
Women's Pro-Israel National PAC $1,000
Others $300

Other Major Ideological/Single-Issue PACs

Sierra Club .... $5,939   Environment
National Cmte to Preserve Social Security ...... $4,250   Social Secur
Council for a Livable World .... $1,111   Pro-Peace
Handgun Control Inc .... $1,000   Anti-Guns
National Council of Senior Citizens .... $1,000   Social Secur
Ohio Freeze Voter .... $1,000   Pro-Peace

Independent expenditures supporting Hochbrueckner

National Cmte to Preserve Social Security $1,980

---

* Contributions came from more than one PAC affiliated
with this sponsor.

Clyde C. Holloway, R-La (8)

1988 Committees & Subcommittees

First elected: 1986
Total receipts: $690,080
Total from PACs: $315,636

Agriculture
Cotton, Rice and Sugar
Forests, Family Farms and Energy
Tobacco and Peanuts

Small Business
Energy and Agriculture
SBA and the General Economy

Select Children, Youth and Families

PAC Contribution Profile

Business

Agricultural Chemicals	**$11,500**
Dow Chemical*	$6,500
FMC Corp	$1,000
Freeport-McMoran Inc	$1,000
Others	$3,000
Automotive	**$22,000**
Auto Dealers & Drivers for Free Trade	$10,000
National Auto Dealers Assn	$9,500
Eaton Corp	$2,000
Others	$500
Business Organizations	**$6,590**
National Fedn of Independent Business	$5,180
Business Industry PAC	$1,119
Others	$291
Construction	**$19,000**
National Assn of Home Builders	$9,500
Associated General Contractors	$3,750
Texas Industries	$3,000
Associated Builders & Contractors	$1,250
Others	$1,500
Dairy	**$9,250**
Associated Milk Producers	$4,500
Dairymen Inc-Louisiana	$3,250
Mid-American Dairymen	$1,250
Others	$250

Campaign Revenue Sources

Other (8.1%)
Party (9.2%)
PACs (36.4%)
Individuals (46.3%)

Defense	**$7,750**
Allied-Signal	$1,000
Harris Corp	$1,000
Martin Marietta Corp	$1,000
Others	$4,750
Electric Utilities	**$13,000**
Central Louisiana Electric	$6,500
Middle South Utilities*	$4,000
Others	$2,500
Financial Institutions	**$4,060**
American Bankers Assn	$1,500
Credit Union National Assn	$1,000
Others	$1,560
Food & Beverage	**$14,200**
National Restaurant Assn	$3,000
Coors Industries	$2,000
American Meat Institute	$1,750
Food Marketing Institute	$1,750
ConAgra Inc	$1,300
Winn-Dixie Stores	$1,000
Others	$3,400
Forest Products	**$6,800**
Boise Cascade	$2,000
Willamette Industries	$2,000
International Paper Company	$1,000
Manville Corp	$1,000
Others	$800
Health Professionals	**$19,987**
American Medical Assn	$13,387
Louisiana Medical Assn	$2,100
American Academy of Ophthalmology	$2,000
Oral & Maxillofacial Surgeons	$1,500
American Dental Assn	$1,000
Insurance	**$6,000**
National Assn of Life Underwriters	$2,500
National Assn Mutual Insurance Agents	$1,000
Others	$2,500

PAC Totals by Category

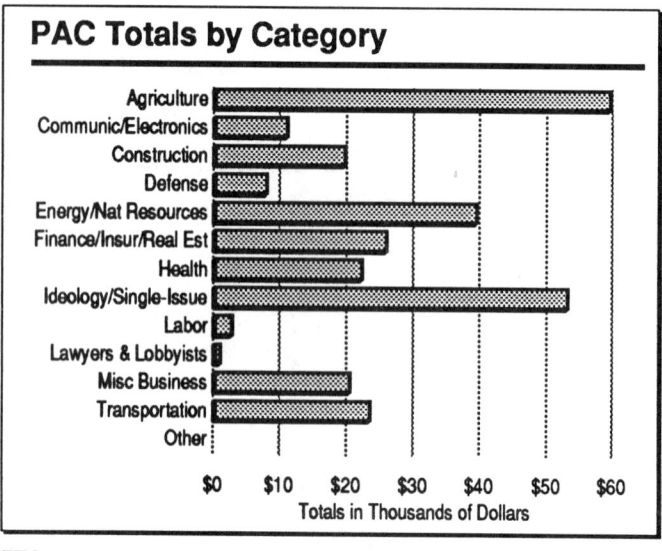

Totals in Thousands of Dollars

Agriculture
Communic/Electronics
Construction
Defense
Energy/Nat Resources
Finance/Insur/Real Est
Health
Ideology/Single-Issue
Labor
Lawyers & Lobbyists
Misc Business
Transportation
Other

$0 $10 $20 $30 $40 $50 $60

Oil & Gas **$24,750**

Murphy Oil	$2,000
Phillips Petroleum	$2,000
Amoco Corp	$1,500
Atlantic Richfield	$1,500
Columbia Hydrocarbon Corp	$1,500
Chevron Corp	$1,250
Marathon Oil	$1,250
Petroleum Marketers Assn	$1,250
Exxon Corp	$1,000
Halliburton Company*	$1,000
Mobil Oil	$1,000
Occidental Oil & Gas	$1,000
Shell Oil	$1,000
Sun Company	$1,000
Tenneco Inc	$1,000
Texaco	$1,000
Tidewater Inc	$1,000
Others	$3,500

Real Estate **$15,250**

National Assn of Realtors	$15,000
Others	$250

Sugar Growers **$7,850**

American Sugar Cane League	$2,000
American Crystal Sugar Corp	$1,500
Southern Minnesota Beet Sugar Co-op	$1,250
American Sugarbeet Growers Assn	$1,000
Others	$2,100

Telecommunications **$8,800**

South Central Bell Telephone	$4,500
AT&T	$3,000
United Telecommunications	$1,000
Others	$300

Tobacco **$6,300**

Philip Morris	$3,500
Tobacco Institute	$1,000
Others	$1,800

Spending in Last 2 Elections

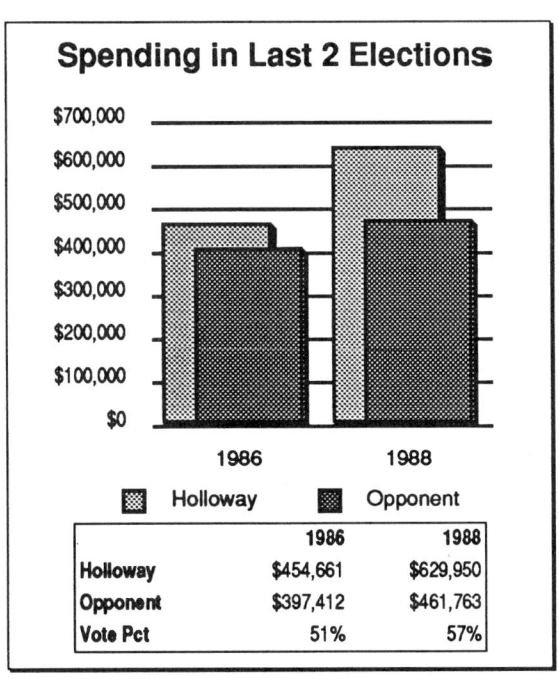

	1986	1988
Holloway	$454,661	$629,950
Opponent	$397,412	$461,763
Vote Pct	51%	57%

Interest Group Ratings

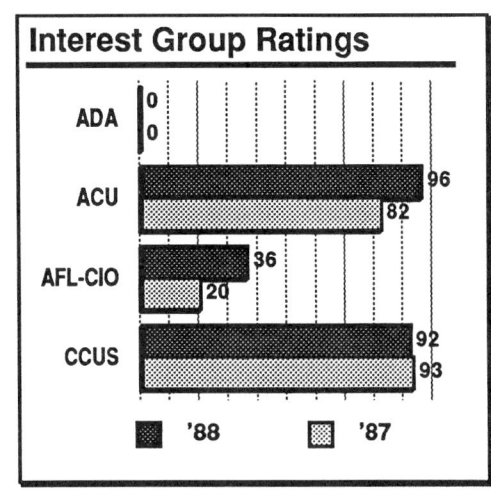

ADA '88 0, '87 0
ACU '88 96, '87 82
AFL-CIO '88 36, '87 20
CCUS '88 92, '87 93

■ '88   ▨ '87

Other Major Business PACs

Cooper Industries	$2,000	Electronics
National Assn of Retired Federal Employees	$2,000	Fedl Workers
National Cotton Council	$1,750	Cotton
Chicago Mercantile Exchange	$1,250	Commodities
American Cotton Shippers Assn	$1,000	Cotton
American Health Care Assn	$1,000	Nursing Home
Chicago Board of Trade	$1,000	Commodities
Nalco Chemical Company	$1,000	Chemicals
National Assn of Convenience Stores	$1,000	Dept Store
Society of American Florists	$1,000	Florists

Ideological/Single-Issue

Pro-Israel **$10,850**

Louisiana for American Security	$7,500
Citizens Organized PAC	$5,000
Roundtable PAC	$1,000
Washington PAC	$1,000
Others	-$3,650

Republican Leadership PACs **$13,026**

Fund for America's Future (George Bush)	$5,000
Conservative Victory Fund (Steve Symms)	$3,526
Campaign America (Bob Dole)	$2,500
15th District Committee (Edward Madigan)	$1,000
Policy Innovation PAC (Dick Armey)	$1,000

Other Major Ideological/Single-Issue PACs

National Rifle Assn	$10,900	Pro-Guns
Public Service Research Council	$5,500	Anti-Union
National Right to Life PAC	$3,835	Pro-Life
Ruff PAC	$3,000	Tax Policy
Council for National Defense	$1,040	Pro-Defense
Black PAC	$1,000	Repub/Conser
Conservative Victory Cmte	$1,000	Repub/Conser
Eagle Forum	$1,000	Repub/Conser
Republican Congressional Boosters Club	$1,000	Repub/Conser

* Contributions came from more than one PAC affiliated with this sponsor.

Larry J. Hopkins, R-Ky (6)

First elected: 1978
Total receipts: $356,281
Total from PACs: $134,335

1988 Committees & Subcommittees

Agriculture
Tobacco and Peanuts (Ranking Republican)
Livestock, Dairy and Poultry

Armed Services
Investigations (Ranking Republican)
Procurement and Military Nuclear Systems

PAC Contribution Profile

Business

Campaign Revenue Sources

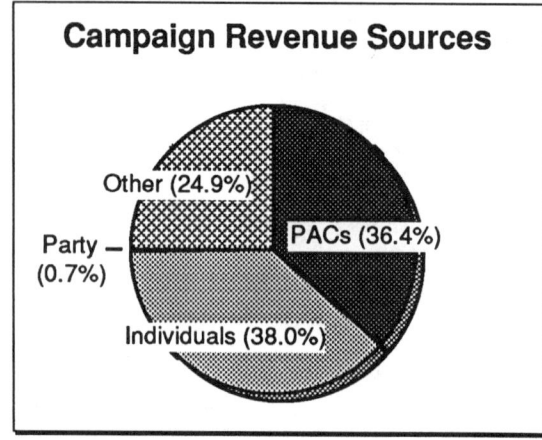

Other (24.9%)
PACs (36.4%)
Party — (0.7%)
Individuals (38.0%)

Auto Dealers	**$7,600**
Auto Dealers & Drivers for Free Trade	$5,000
National Auto Dealers Assn	$2,600
Commercial Banks/Credit Unions	**$2,700**
American Bankers Assn	$1,000
Others	$1,700
Construction	**$2,850**
Associated General Contractors	$1,000
Others	$1,850
Dairy	**$9,400**
Dairymen Inc-Kentucky	$5,000
Associated Milk Producers	$3,000
Others	$1,400
Defense	**$26,500**
McDonnell Douglas*	$2,600
Northrop Corp	$1,500
FMC Corp	$1,400
Textron Inc	$1,300
Hughes Aircraft	$1,200
E-Systems*	$1,150
AT&T	$1,100
Continental Telecom	$1,000
General Dynamics	$1,000
Others	$14,250
Electric Utilities	**$2,550**
Kentucky Utilities Company	$1,000
Others	$1,550

Food & Beverage	**$11,750**
Brown-Forman Distillers	$2,500
Food Marketing Institute	$1,200
Malone & Hyde Inc	$1,000
Winn-Dixie Stores	$1,000
Others	$6,050
Health Professionals	**$10,800**
American Medical Assn	$7,300
American Dental Assn	$2,000
American Academy of Ophthalmology	$1,000
Others	$500
Hospitals	**$3,500**
Humana Inc	$3,000
Others	$500
Lawyers	**$3,000**
Greenebaum, Doll & McDonald	$2,000
Stoll, Keenon & Park	$1,000
Oil & Gas	**$2,785**
Ashland Oil	$1,300
Others	$1,485
Paper Production	**$2,500**
Westvaco Corp	$2,500
Real Estate	**$6,000**
National Assn of Realtors	$6,000
Sugar Growers	**$2,950**
None over $900	
Tobacco	**$9,650**
Philip Morris	$3,500
RJR Nabisco	$2,000
Tobacco Institute	$1,200
Pinkerton Tobacco	$1,000
Others	$1,950

Other Major Business PACs

Chicago Board of Trade	$1,500	Commodities
Square D Company	$1,500	Indust Equip
South Central Bell Telephone	$1,300	Phone Util
National Assn of Life Underwriters	$1,000	Life Insurance
United Parcel Service	$1,000	Delivery

PAC Totals by Category

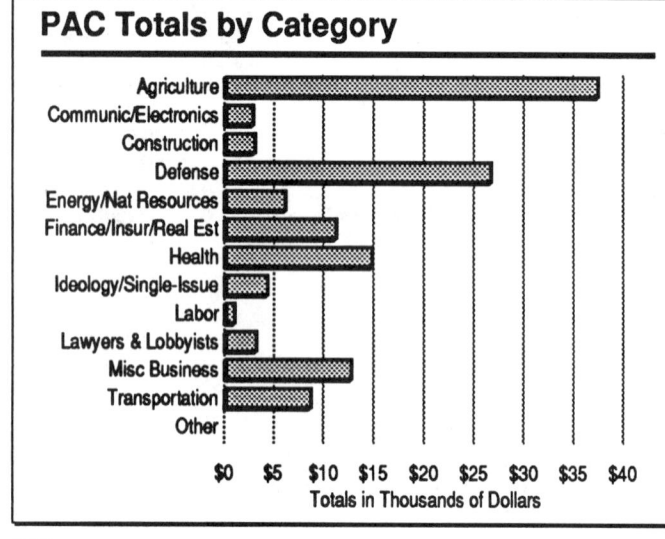

Totals in Thousands of Dollars

Ideological/Single-Issue

Ideological/Single-Issue **$4,150**		
National Rifle Assn $2,500	Pro-Guns	
Others...$1,650		

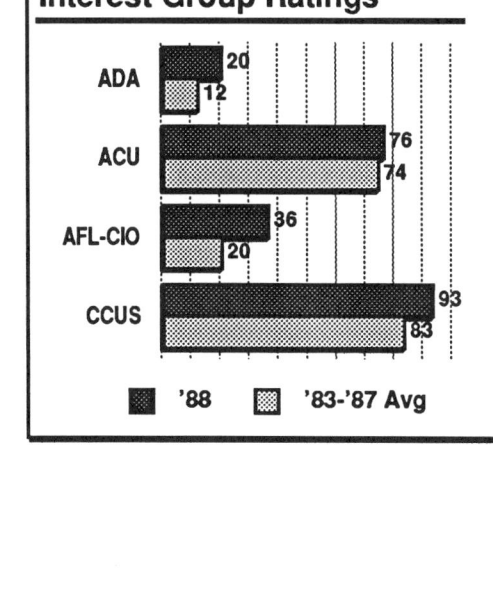

Interest Group Ratings

	'88	'83-'87 Avg
ADA	20	12
ACU	76	74
AFL-CIO	36	20
CCUS	93	83

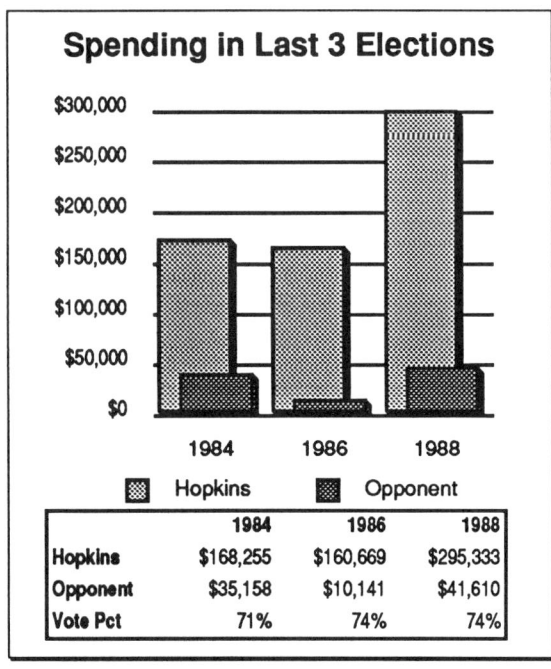

Spending in Last 3 Elections

	1984	1986	1988
Hopkins	$168,255	$160,669	$295,333
Opponent	$35,158	$10,141	$41,610
Vote Pct	71%	74%	74%

* Contributions came from more than one PAC affiliated with this sponsor.

Frank Horton, R-NY (29)

1988 Committees & Subcommittees

> **Government Operations** (Ranking Republican)
> Legislation and National Security (Ranking Republican)
>
> **Post Office and Civil Service**
> Postal Operations and Services (Ranking Republican)
> Civil Service

First elected: 1962
Total receipts: $163,751
Total from PACs: $126,560

PAC Contribution Profile

Business

Accountants **$7,700**
    American Institute of CPA's $5,000
    Arthur Andersen & Company $1,000
    Others $1,700

Commercial & Savings Banks **$2,025**
    None over $500

Construction **$3,950**
    Associated General Contractors $1,300
    National Society of Professional Engineers $1,000
    Others $1,650

Defense **$3,700**
    Aydin Corp $1,000
    Grumman $1,000
    Others $1,700

Food & Beverage **$2,400**
    National Restaurant Assn $1,000
    Others $1,400

Health Professionals **$6,100**
    American Medical Assn $3,800
    American Dental Assn $1,500
    Others $800

Office Machines **$3,500**
    Xerox Corp $2,500
    National Office Products Assn $1,000

Package Delivery **$2,600**
    United Parcel Service $2,600

Real Estate **$2,300**
    National Assn of Realtors $2,300

Telecommunications **$4,100**
    AT&T $3,500
    Others $600

Textiles **$7,500**
    Burlington Industries $2,000
    American Textile Manufacturers Institute $1,000
    J P Stevens & Company $1,000
    Others $3,500

Other Major Business PACs

Associated Milk Producers	$1,500	Dairy
Dow, Lohnes & Albertson	$1,000	Lawyers
Johnson & Johnson	$1,000	Health Prod
New York State Electric & Gas Corp	$1,000	Gas & Electr
Waste Management Inc	$1,000	Waste Mgmt

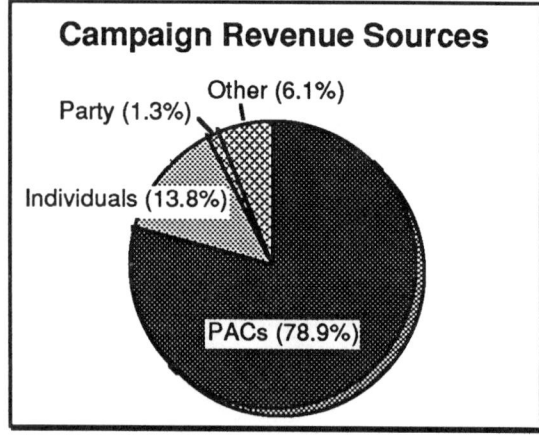

Campaign Revenue Sources

- Other (6.1%)
- Party (1.3%)
- Individuals (13.8%)
- PACs (78.9%)

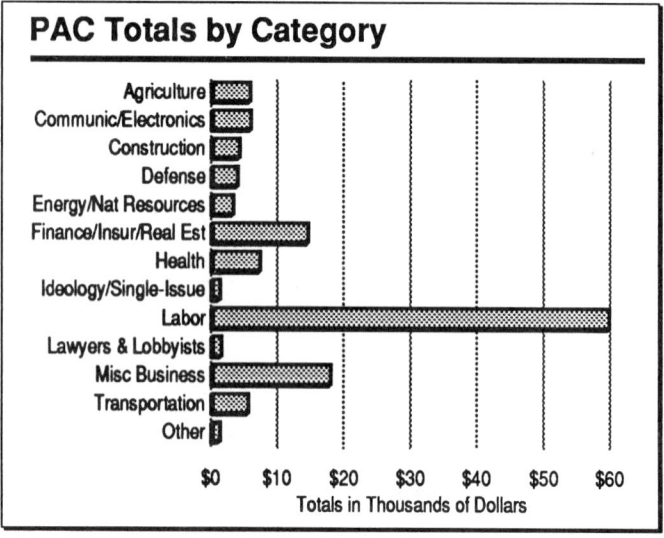

PAC Totals by Category

- Agriculture
- Communic/Electronics
- Construction
- Defense
- Energy/Nat Resources
- Finance/Insur/Real Est
- Health
- Ideology/Single-Issue
- Labor
- Lawyers & Lobbyists
- Misc Business
- Transportation
- Other

$0 $10 $20 $30 $40 $50 $60

Totals in Thousands of Dollars

Labor

Bldg Trades/Industrial/Misc Unions $9,500

Operating Engineers Union*	$3,000
Laborers' Political League	$2,000
Amalgamated Clothing & Textile Workers*	$1,400
Carpenters & Joiners Union	$1,000
Food & Commercial Workers Union	$1,000
Others	$1,100

Government & Postal Workers $39,200

American Postal Workers Union	$10,000
National Assn of Letter Carriers	$7,000
National Assn of Retired Federal Employees	$7,000
National Assn of Postmasters	$6,000
National Treasury Employees Union	$2,600
American Fedn of State/County/Munic Employees	$1,500
National Federation of Federal Employees	$1,200
National League of Postmasters	$1,000
National Rural Letter Carriers Assn	$1,000
Others	$1,900

Teachers Unions $2,800

National Education Assn	$2,800

Transportation Unions $8,050

Teamsters Union	$5,000
Air Line Pilots Assn	$2,500
Others	$550

Other Major Ideological/Single-Issue PACs

Common Sense PAC	$1,000	Unknown
National Cmte to Preserve Social Security	$1,000	Social Security

Independent expenditures supporting Horton

National Cmte to Preserve Social Security	$1,424

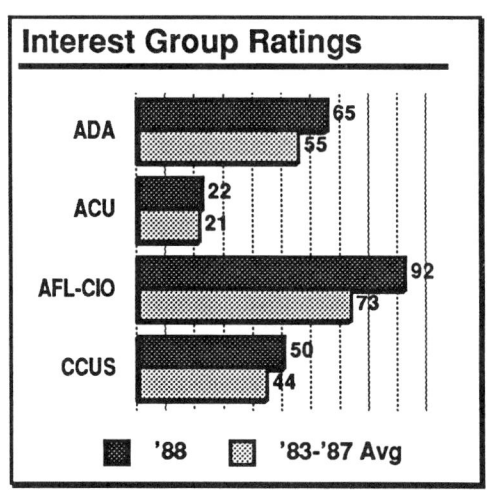

Interest Group Ratings

	'88	'83-'87 Avg
ADA	65	55
ACU	22	21
AFL-CIO	92	73
CCUS	50	44

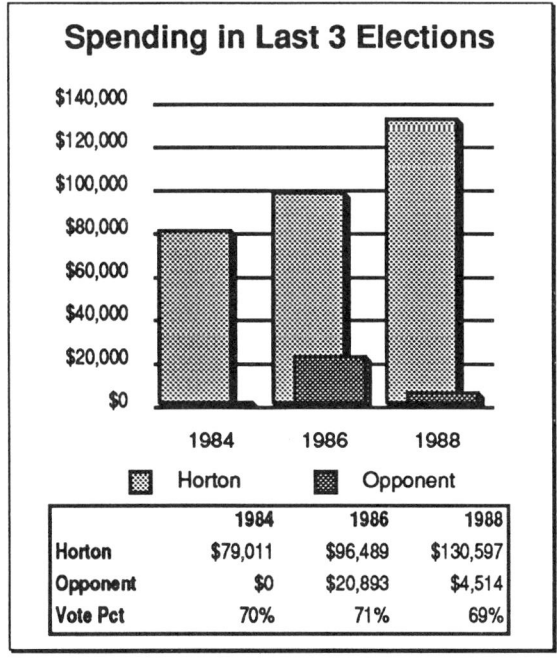

Spending in Last 3 Elections

	1984	1986	1988
Horton	$79,011	$96,489	$130,597
Opponent	$0	$20,893	$4,514
Vote Pct	70%	71%	69%

* Contributions came from more than one PAC affiliated with this sponsor.

Amo Houghton, R-NY (34)

First elected: 1986
Total receipts: $411,571
Total from PACs: $65,650

1988 Committees & Subcommittees

Budget
Economic Trade and Policy
Income Security

Government Operations
Commerce, Consumer and Monetary Affairs
Government Information, Justice and Agriculture

PAC Contribution Profile

Business

Accountants	**$5,000**
American Institute of CPA's	$5,000
Automotive	**$3,050**
Auto Dealers & Drivers for Free Trade	$2,500
Others	$550
Commercial Banks	**$8,000**
Citicorp	$5,000
American Bankers Assn	$1,000
Norstar Bancorp	$1,000
Others	$1,000
Defense	**$3,950**
None over $800	
Food & Beverage	**$2,400**
National Restaurant Assn	$1,000
Others	$1,400
Forest Products	**$4,000**
Westvaco Corp	$1,500
International Paper Company	$1,000
Weyerhaeuser Company*	$1,000
Others	$500
Health Professionals	**$11,500**
American Medical Assn	$5,000
New York Medical Assn	$2,500
American Academy of Ophthalmology	$2,000
American Dental Assn	$1,500
Others	$500

Insurance	**$3,150**
Metropolitan Life Insurance	$1,000
Others	$2,150
Oil & Gas	**$6,300**
Petroleum Marketers Assn	$1,300
Others	$5,000
Pharmaceuticals	**$3,000**
None over $800	
Real Estate	**$3,250**
National Assn of Realtors	$3,000
Others	$250
Telecommunications	**$3,400**
AT&T	$2,000
Others	$1,400

Other Major Business PACs

Corning Glass Works	$2,000	Glass Prod
Philip Morris	$1,100	Tobacco
Associated Milk Producers	$1,000	Dairy
Henley Group Inc	$1,000	Altern Energy
Owens-Illinois	$1,000	Paper Packg

Campaign Revenue Sources

Other (4.7%)
Party (0.7%)
PACs (20.6%)
Individuals (73.6%)

PAC Totals by Category

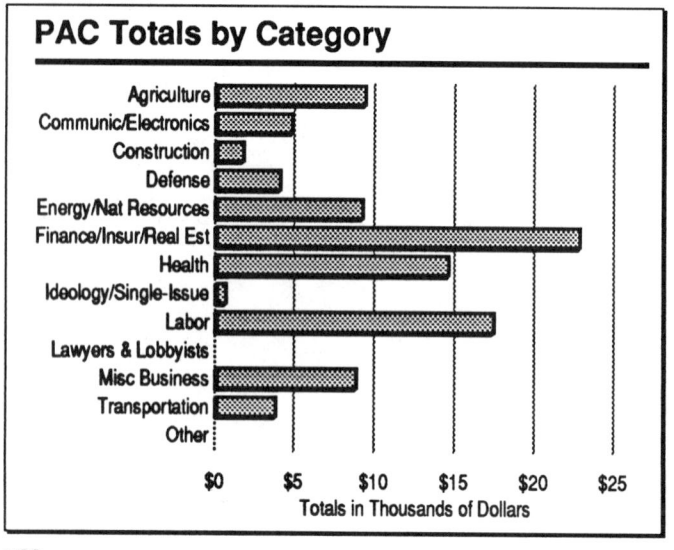

Agriculture
Communic/Electronics
Construction
Defense
Energy/Nat Resources
Finance/Insur/Real Est
Health
Ideology/Single-Issue
Labor
Lawyers & Lobbyists
Misc Business
Transportation
Other

$0 $5 $10 $15 $20 $25

Totals in Thousands of Dollars

Labor

Bldg Trades/Industrial/Misc Unions **$4,200**
    National Education Assn $2,500
    Others $1,700

Government & Postal Workers **$4,400**
    National Assn of Retired Federal Employees $4,000
    Others $400

Transportation Unions **$8,750**
    Teamsters Union $4,500
    Air Line Pilots Assn $1,500
    Seafarers International Union $1,500
    Marine Engineers District 2 Maritime Officers $1,000
    Others $250

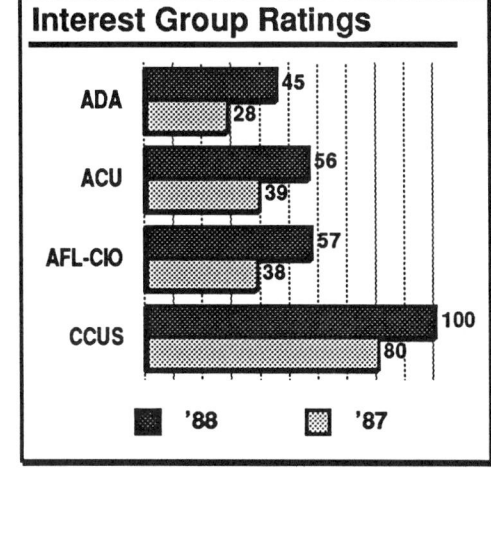

Interest Group Ratings

	'88	'87
ADA	45	28
ACU	56	39
AFL-CIO	57	38
CCUS	100	80

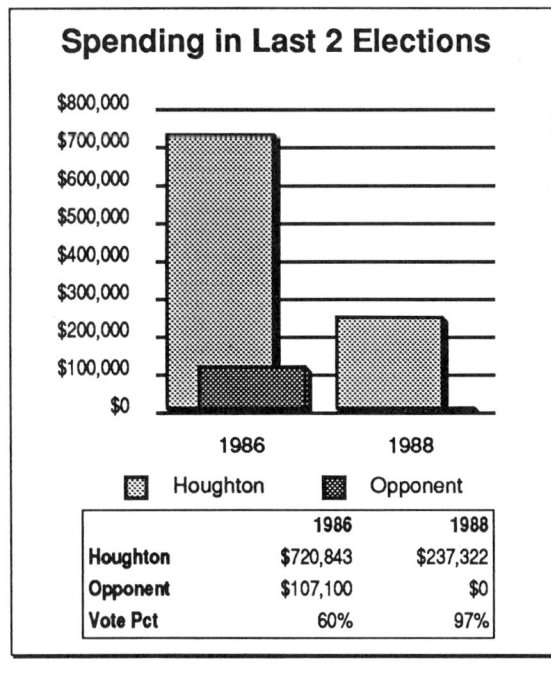

Spending in Last 2 Elections

Houghton   Opponent

	1986	1988
Houghton	$720,843	$237,322
Opponent	$107,100	$0
Vote Pct	60%	97%

---

* Contributions came from more than one PAC affiliated with this sponsor.

Steny H. Hoyer, D-Md (5)

1988 Committees & Subcommittees

Appropriations
District of Columbia
Labor, Health and Human Services, Education and Related Agencies
Treasury, Postal Service and General Government

First elected: 1981
Total receipts: $490,736
Total from PACs: $239,828

Campaign Revenue Sources

Other (9.7%)
Party (1.6%)
PACs (47.5%)
Individuals (41.2%)

PAC Contribution Profile

Business

Aviation & Aerospace	**$3,750**
Texas Air	$2,350
Aircraft Owners & Pilots Assn	$1,050
Others	$350
Construction	**$5,700**
National Assn of Home Builders	$4,500
Others	$1,200
Defense	**$6,975**
Litton Industries	$3,625
Others	$3,350
Financial Institutions	**$6,450**
American Bankers Assn	$1,500
Credit Union National Assn	$1,350
Sovran Bank/Maryland	$1,000
Others	$2,600
Food & Beverage	**$7,600**
Coca-Cola Company	$1,200
Others	$6,400
Health Professionals	**$13,200**
American Dental Assn	$4,000
American Podiatry Assn	$1,500
Oral & Maxillofacial Surgeons	$1,500
Corp for the Advancement of Psychiatry	$1,200
Cmte for Quality Orthopedic Health Care	$1,000
Others	$4,000

Hospitals & Health Care Facilities	**$3,200**
American Hospital Assn	$1,350
Others	$1,850
Insurance	**$7,800**
Blue Cross & Blue Shield Assn	$1,200
CNA Financial Corp	$1,050
Independent Insurance Agents of America	$1,050
Travelers Corp	$1,000
US Fidelity & Guaranty	$1,000
Others	$2,500
Lawyers & Lobbyists	**$13,650**
Assn of Trial Lawyers of America	$4,600
Akin, Gump, Hauer & Feld	$1,400
Laxalt, Washington, Perito & Dubuc	$1,000
Others	$6,650
Real Estate	**$4,800**
National Assn of Realtors	$3,100
Century 21 Real Estate	$1,000
Others	$700
Retail Sales	**$3,000**
J C Penney Company	$2,000
International Council of Shopping Centers	$1,000
Securities Investment	**$5,750**
Investment Company Institute	$4,000
Others	$1,750
Telecommunications	**$5,590**
AT&T	$1,500
Bell Atlantic	$1,400
Chesapeake & Potomac Telephone	$1,140
Others	$1,550
Trucking/Delivery	**$5,500**
United Parcel Service	$3,100
Others	$2,400

Other Major Business PACs

Greater Washington Board of Trade	$2,000	Chamb/Cmrce
CSX Transportation Inc	$1,050	Railroads
Associated Milk Producers	$1,000	Dairy
National Assn of Trade/Tech Schools	$1,000	Voc Tech

PAC Totals by Category

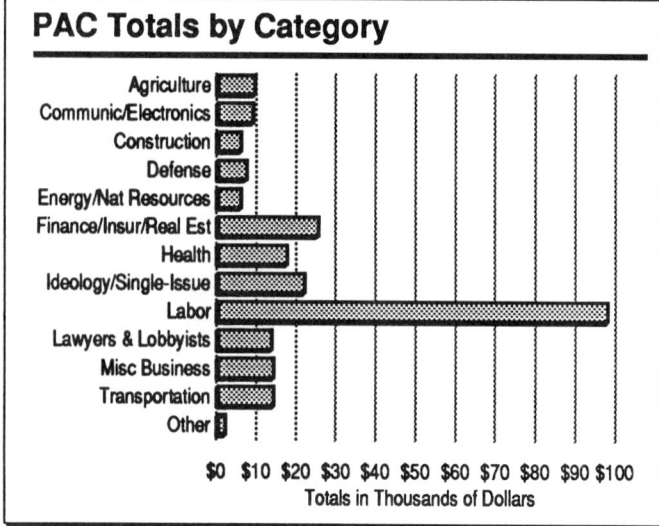

Agriculture
Communic/Electronics
Construction
Defense
Energy/Nat Resources
Finance/Insur/Real Est
Health
Ideology/Single-Issue
Labor
Lawyers & Lobbyists
Misc Business
Transportation
Other

$0 $10 $20 $30 $40 $50 $60 $70 $80 $90 $100
Totals in Thousands of Dollars

Labor

Bldg Trades/Industrial/Misc Unions $27,550

Food & Commercial Workers Union.................................$4,300
Intl Brotherhood of Electrical Workers.............................$2,500
Sheet Metal Workers Union $2,500
Plumbers/Pipefitters Union* $2,300
Carpenters & Joiners Union $2,200
Laborers' Political League $2,200
AFL-CIO* $1,850
United Auto Workers $1,700
Painters & Allied Trades Union $1,400
Ladies Garment Workers Union $1,350
Operating Engineers Union $1,000
Others $4,250

Government & Postal Workers $43,175

American Federation of Government Employees $7,550
National Treasury Employees Union $7,000
National Assn of Letter Carriers $6,225
National Assn of Retired Federal Employees $6,000
American Fedn of State/County/Munic Employees $4,650
National Rural Letter Carriers Assn $3,000
American Postal Workers Union $2,900
National League of Postmasters $1,350
National Assn of Postmasters $1,050
Others $3,450

Teachers Unions $7,400

National Education Assn $6,000
American Federation of Teachers $1,400

Transportation Unions $19,000

Teamsters Union $6,000
Air Line Pilots Assn $3,000
Seafarers International Union $2,900
United Transportation Union $1,700
Amalgamated Transit Union $1,000
Marine Engineers Union $1,000
Maritime Union of America $1,000
Others $2,400

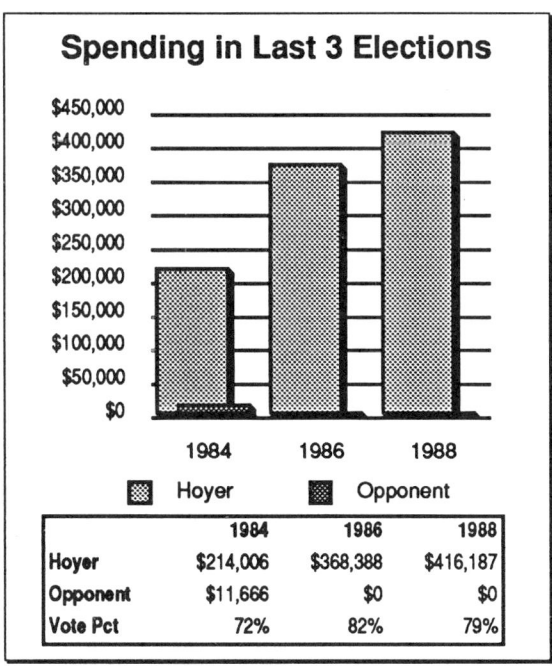

Spending in Last 3 Elections

Legend: ▨ Hoyer   ▧ Opponent

	1984	1986	1988
Hoyer	$214,006	$368,388	$416,187
Opponent	$11,666	$0	$0
Vote Pct	72%	82%	79%

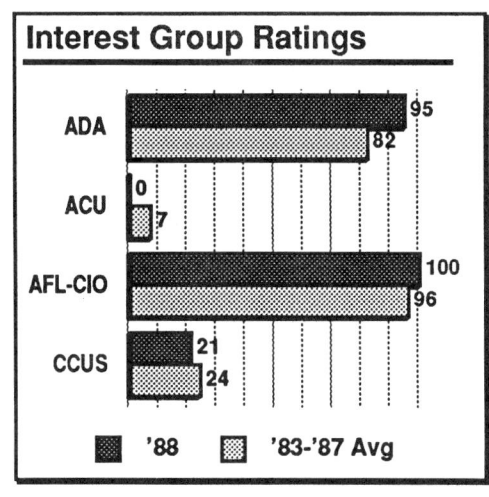

Interest Group Ratings

	'88	'83-'87 Avg
ADA	95	82
ACU	0	7
AFL-CIO	100	96
CCUS	21	24

Legend: ■ '88   ▧ '83-'87 Avg

Ideological/Single-Issue

Pro-Israel $4,000

Washington PAC $2,000
Others $2,000

Other Major Ideological/Single-Issue PACs

National Cmte to Preserve Social Security ......$5,350   Social Security
Human Rights Campaign Fund ....$5,332   Gay Rights
KidsPAC ....$3,000   HealthWelfare
Valley Education Fund (Tony Coelho) ....$1,000   Dem Leaders

Independent expenditures supporting Hoyer

National Cmte to Preserve Social Security $1,450

---

* Contributions came from more than one PAC affiliated
with this sponsor.

Carroll Hubbard Jr., D-Ky (1)

First elected: 1974
Total receipts: $518,338
Total from PACs: $356,663

1988 Committees & Subcommittees

Banking, Finance and Urban Affairs
General Oversight and Investigations (Chairman)
Domestic Monetary Policy
Financial Institutions Supervision, Regulation and Insurance
Housing and Community Development

Merchant Marine and Fisheries
Merchant Marine

PAC Contribution Profile

Business

Automotive	**$6,625**
National Auto Dealers Assn	$5,325
Others	$1,300
Commercial Banks	**$51,725**
Citicorp	$5,000
J P Morgan & Company	$5,000
Barnett Banks of Florida	$3,000
Citizens & Southern National Bank	$2,800
First Kentucky National Corp	$2,775
American Bankers Assn	$2,500
Bankers Trust	$2,500
Independent Bankers Assn	$2,350
Manufacturers Hanover	$2,075
Citizens Bank of Jackson	$2,000
Kentucky Bankers Assn	$1,875
Assn of Bank Holding Companies	$1,825
Chase Manhattan	$1,525
Chemical Bank	$1,500
Continental Illinois Corp	$1,375
Others	$13,625
Construction	**$20,750**
National Assn of Home Builders	$7,500
Westvaco Corp	$5,000
Manville Corp	$1,500
Owens-Corning Fiberglas	$1,500
Wall & Ceiling/Gypsum Contractors	$1,400
Others	$3,850

Campaign Revenue Sources

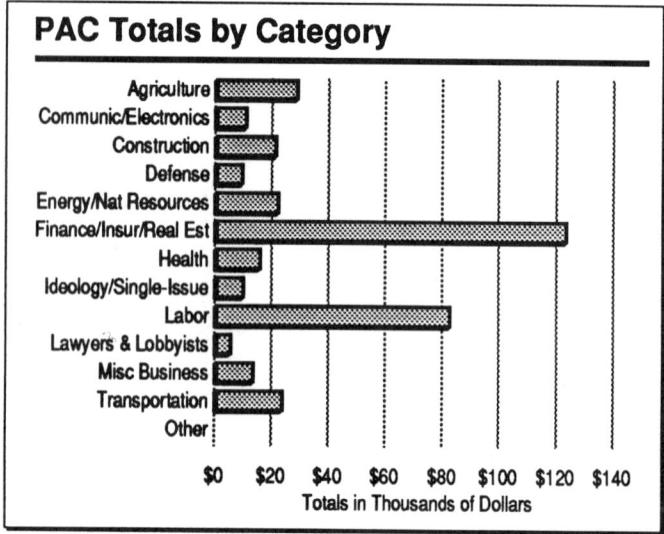

Other (7.1%)
Party (1.0%)
Individuals (22.7%)
PACs(69.2%)

Consumer Credit & Loans	**$6,775**
Creditthrift Financial Management Corp	$2,175
Household International	$1,550
Others	$3,050
Dairy	**$6,775**
Dairymen Inc-Kentucky	$4,075
Associated Milk Producers	$1,500
Others	$1,200
Defense	**$8,850**
Martin Marietta Corp	$1,275
Emerson Electric*	$1,150
Rockwell International	$1,025
Others	$5,400
Food & Beverage	**$6,390**
Jerrico Inc	$1,150
Occidental Petroleum	$1,125
Others	$4,115
Health Professionals	**$9,999**
American Medical Assn	$6,999
American Dental Assn	$1,400
Others	$1,600
Insurance	**$23,900**
National Assn of Life Underwriters	$5,750
Independent Insurance Agents of America	$5,375
Casualty & Surety Agents Assn	$1,775
National Assn Mutual Insurance Agents	$1,575
Capital Holding Corp	$1,425
Prudential Insurance	$1,275
Mortgage Insurance Companies of America	$1,175
Cigna Corp	$1,025
Others	$4,525
Oil & Gas	**$11,000**
Ashland Oil	$1,625
Shell Oil	$1,625
Others	$7,750
Real Estate	**$7,325**
National Assn of Realtors	$5,000
Mortgage Bankers Assn of America	$1,175
Others	$1,150

PAC Totals by Category

Agriculture
Communic/Electronics
Construction
Defense
Energy/Nat Resources
Finance/Insur/Real Est
Health
Ideology/Single-Issue
Labor
Lawyers & Lobbyists
Misc Business
Transportation
Other

$0 $20 $40 $60 $80 $100 $120 $140
Totals in Thousands of Dollars

Savings Banks $24,475

    US League of Savings Assn $7,450
    Kentucky League of Savings Institutions $5,750
    Great Western Financial Corp.......................................$5,000
    National Council of Savings Institutions $1,400
    Home Savings of America $1,375
    Others $3,500

Sea Transport $9,500

    American Pilots Assn $2,400
    CSX Transportation Inc* $1,575
    Tenneco Inc $1,500
    American President Lines $1,050
    Others $2,975

Securities & Commodities Investment $8,125

    Chicago Board of Trade $2,000
    Investment Company Institute $1,175
    E F Hutton Group $1,125
    Others $3,825

Telecommunications $6,875

    AT&T $2,475
    South Central Bell Telephone $1,775
    Others $2,625

Tobacco $8,725

    Philip Morris $2,700
    RJR Nabisco $1,575
    Batus Inc* $1,300
    Others $3,150

Other Major Business PACs

American Orthotic/Prosthetic Assn	$3,875	Med Supply
United Parcel Service	$2,200	Delivery
Credit Union National Assn	$1,925	Credit Union
General Electric	$1,575	Electronics
Boeing Company	$1,400	Aircraft
J C Penney Company	$1,375	Dept Store
National Fisheries Institute	$1,175	Fishing
Phelps Dodge Corp	$1,175	Metals/Mining
Peabody Coal	$1,125	Coal
Assn of Trial Lawyers of America	$1,025	Lawyers

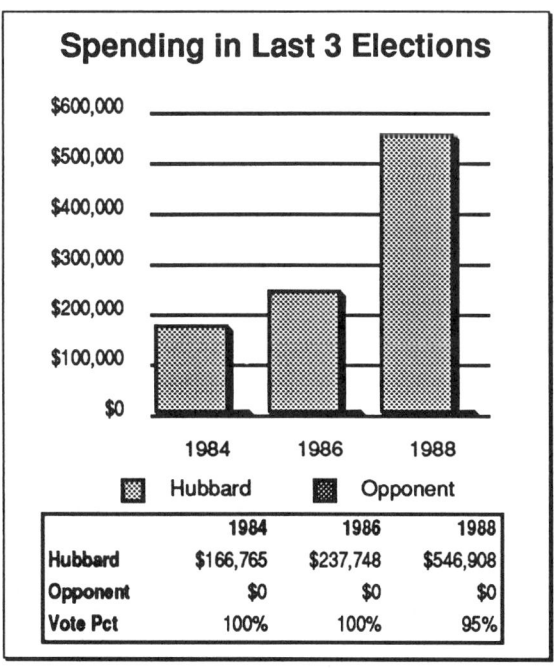

Spending in Last 3 Elections

	1984	1986	1988
Hubbard	$166,765	$237,748	$546,908
Opponent	$0	$0	$0
Vote Pct	100%	100%	95%

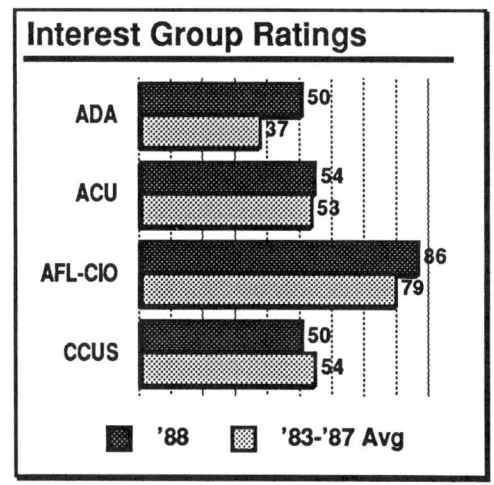

Interest Group Ratings

'88   '83–'87 Avg

	'88	'83–'87 Avg
ADA	50	37
ACU	54	53
AFL-CIO	86	79
CCUS	50	54

Labor

Bldg Trades/Industrial/Misc Unions $37,884

    United Auto Workers $15,000
    United Steelworkers $10,000
    United Mine Workers $3,534
    AFL-CIO $2,500
    Carpenters & Joiners Union $1,500
    Ladies Garment Workers Union $1,475
    Others $3,875

Government & Postal Workers $12,600

    National Assn of Retired Federal Employees $8,200
    National Assn of Letter Carriers $2,100
    American Postal Workers Union $1,200
    Others $1,100

Sea Transport Unions $15,975

    Marine Engineers Union* $8,700
    Masters, Mates & Pilots Union $2,850
    Seafarers International Union $1,800
    International Longshoremen Assn $1,200
    Boilermakers Union $1,025
    Others $400

Other Transportation Unions $15,500

    Teamsters Union $10,000
    Air Line Pilots Assn $2,500
    United Transportation Union $1,700
    Others $1,300

Ideological/Single-Issue

Ideological/Single-Issue	...**$7,299**	
National Rifle Assn	$3,100	Pro-Guns
National Right to Life PAC	$2,000	Pro-Life
Others	$2,199	

* Contributions came from more than one PAC affiliated with this sponsor.

Jerry Huckaby, D-La (5)

First elected: 1976
Total receipts: $266,854
Total from PACs: $131,650

1988 Committees & Subcommittees

Agriculture
Cotton, Rice and Sugar (Chairman)
Domestic Marketing, Consumer Relations and Nutrition
Wheat, Soybeans and Feed Grains

Interior and Insular Affairs
Energy and the Environment
National Parks and Public Lands

PAC Contribution Profile

Business

Automotive	*$2,400*
National Auto Dealers Assn	$2,100
Others	$300
Construction	*$2,500*
Texas Industries	$1,000
Others	$1,500
Cotton	*$9,886*
National Cotton Council	$4,486
American Cotton Shippers Assn	$2,000
J G Boswell Company	$1,300
Supima Assn of America	$1,300
Others	$800
Dairy	*$8,600*
Associated Milk Producers	$4,000
Dairymen Inc-Louisiana	$3,100
Mid-American Dairymen	$1,500
Electric Utilities	*$11,300*
Middle South Utilities*	$3,100
ACRE (Action Committee for Rural Electrification)	$1,100
Central Louisiana Electric	$1,000
Others	$6,100
Food & Beverage	*$7,700*
ConAgra Inc	$2,500
Malone & Hyde Inc	$2,000
A E Staley Manufacturing Company	$1,300
American Meat Institute	$1,300
Others	$600

Campaign Revenue Sources

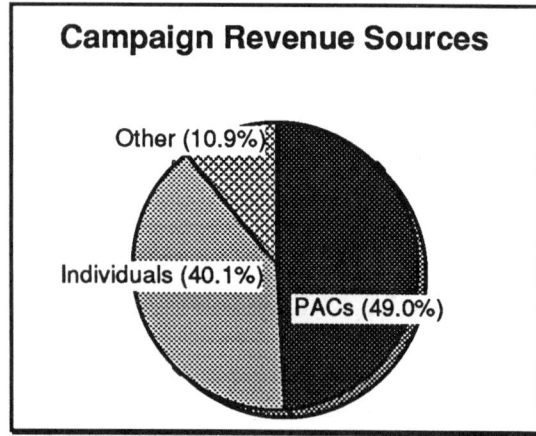

Other (10.9%)
Individuals (40.1%)
PACs (49.0%)

Forest Products	*$7,400*
Manville Corp	$2,000
Georgia-Pacific Corp	$1,000
International Paper Company	$1,000
Louisiana-Pacific Corp	$1,000
Stone Container Corp	$1,000
Others	$1,400
Lawyers	*$3,900*
Assn of Trial Lawyers of America	$2,000
McGlinchey, Stafford et al	$1,000
Others	$900
Mining	*$2,800*
Dravo Corp	$1,000
Others	$1,800
Oil & Gas	*$12,050*
Shell Oil	$1,400
Atlantic Richfield	$1,200
Sun Company	$1,000
Others	$8,450
Other Crops & Processing	*$8,400*
American Rice Inc	$3,000
Riceland Foods	$1,100
Archer-Daniels-Midland Corp	$1,000
Others	$3,300
Real Estate	*$5,000*
National Assn of Realtors	$5,000
Sugar Growers	*$10,350*
American Crystal Sugar Corp	$2,500
American Sugar Cane League	$2,000
Florida Sugar Cane League	$2,000
Others	$3,850
Telecommunications	*$8,000*
South Central Bell Telephone	$5,000
AT&T	$3,000

PAC Totals by Category

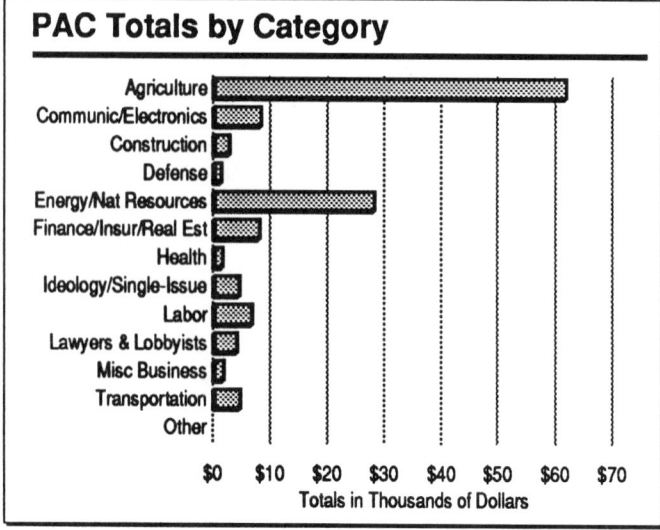

Agriculture
Communic/Electronics
Construction
Defense
Energy/Nat Resources
Finance/Insur/Real Est
Health
Ideology/Single-Issue
Labor
Lawyers & Lobbyists
Misc Business
Transportation
Other

$0 $10 $20 $30 $40 $50 $60 $70
Totals in Thousands of Dollars

Other Major Business PACs

Alabama Farm Bureau Federation	$1,300	Farm Orgs
American Medical Assn	$1,300	Doctors
American Textile Manufacturers Institute	$1,000	Textiles
Chicago Board of Trade	$1,000	Commodities
Louisiana Savings & Loan League	$1,000	SavingsBanks
National Assn of Life Underwriters	$1,000	Life Insurance
Texas Cattle Feeders Assn	$1,000	Feedlots

Labor

Labor Unions ***$6,500***
    National Assn of Retired Federal Employees $4,000
    Others $2,500

Ideological/Single-Issue

Ideological/Single-Issue ***$3,800***
Louisiana for American Security ....$2,000   Pro-Israel
Valley Education Fund (Tony Coelho) ....$1,000   Dem Leaders
Others $800

Independent expenditures supporting Huckaby

National Cmte to Preserve Social Security $2,033
American Sugarbeet Growers Assn $1,000

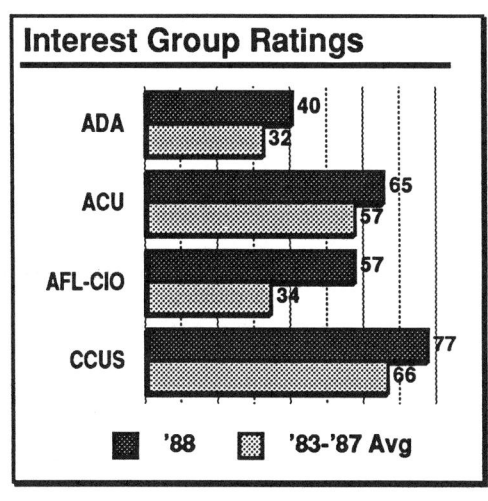

Interest Group Ratings

	ADA	ACU	AFL-CIO	CCUS
'88	40	65	57	77
'83-'87 Avg	32	57	34	66

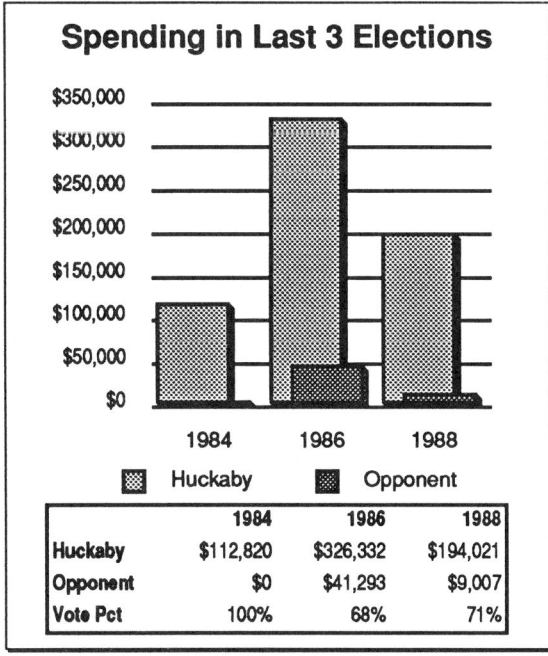

Spending in Last 3 Elections

■ Huckaby   ■ Opponent

	1984	1986	1988
Huckaby	$112,820	$326,332	$194,021
Opponent	$0	$41,293	$9,007
Vote Pct	100%	68%	71%

* Contributions came from more than one PAC affiliated with this sponsor.

William J. Hughes, D-NJ (2)

First elected: 1974
Total receipts: $283,532
Total from PACs: $112,150

1988 Committees & Subcommittees

Judiciary
Crime (Chairman)
Monopolies and Commercial Law

Merchant Marine and Fisheries
Coast Guard and Navigation
Fisheries and Wildlife Conservation and the Environment
Oceanography

Select Aging
Human Services

Select Narcotics Abuse and Control

PAC Contribution Profile

Business

Accountants	**$6,300**
American Institute of CPA's	$5,000
Others	$1,300
Financial Institutions	**$4,050**
American Bankers Assn	$2,000
SAPEC/NJ (New Jersey Savings Assn)	$1,000
Others	$1,050
Food & Beverage	**$4,000**
National Beer Wholesalers Assn	$1,300
Food Marketing Institute	$1,200
Others	$1,500
Health Professionals	**$2,500**
American Medical Assn	$2,500
Import Auto Dealers	**$2,500**
Auto Dealers & Drivers for Free Trade	$2,500
Insurance	**$3,550**
National Assn of Life Underwriters	$1,000
Others	$2,550
Lawyers	**$11,100**
Assn of Trial Lawyers of America	$10,000
Others	$1,100
Pharmaceuticals	**$2,000**
None over $500	

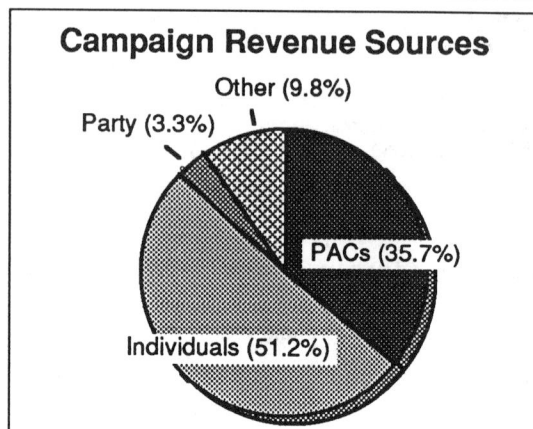

Campaign Revenue Sources

Other (9.8%)
Party (3.3%)
PACs (35.7%)
Individuals (51.2%)

Real Estate	**$6,950**
National Assn of Realtors	$6,450
Others	$500
Residential Construction	**$3,300**
National Assn of Home Builders	$3,300
Sea Transport	**$2,200**
American Pilots Assn	$1,000
Others	$1,200
Telecommunications	**$6,000**
New Jersey Bell Telephone	$3,000
AT&T	$2,000
Others	$1,000

Other Major Business PACs

Columbia Hydrocarbon Corp	$1,400	Natural Gas
Owens-Illinois	$1,100	Paper Packg
National Cable Television Assn	$1,000	CableTV
UNC Inc	$1,000	AerospacePts

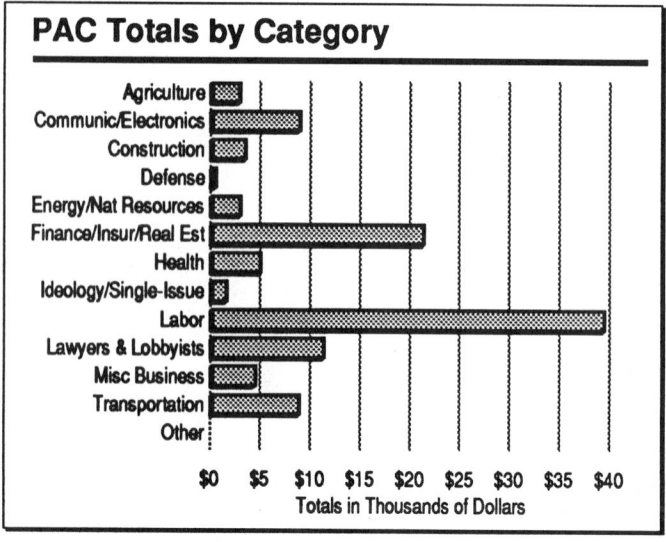

PAC Totals by Category

Agriculture
Communic/Electronics
Construction
Defense
Energy/Nat Resources
Finance/Insur/Real Est
Health
Ideology/Single-Issue
Labor
Lawyers & Lobbyists
Misc Business
Transportation
Other

$0 $5 $10 $15 $20 $25 $30 $35 $40
Totals in Thousands of Dollars

Labor

Bldg Trades/Industrial/Misc Unions **$19,100**

Operating Engineers Local #825	$5,600
Carpenters & Joiners Union	$4,400
Machinists/Aerospace Workers Union	$2,000
United Auto Workers	$2,000
Food & Commercial Workers Union	$1,300
Laborers' Political League	$1,300
Others	$2,500

Government & Postal Workers **$8,100**

National Assn of Retired Federal Employees	$5,000
National Assn of Letter Carriers	$1,200
American Fedn of State/County/Munic Employees	$1,000
Others	$900

Sea Transport Unions **$2,800**

Marine Engineers District 2 Maritime Officers	$1,000
Seafarers International Union	$1,000
Others	$800

Other Transportation Unions **$6,800**

Teamsters Union	$5,000
United Transportation Union	$1,200
Others	$600

Teachers Unions **$2,450**

National Education Assn	$2,450

Independent expenditures supporting Hughes

National Cmte to Preserve Social Security	$3,766

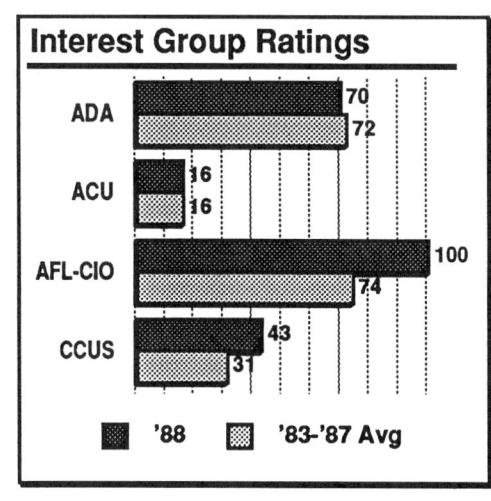

Interest Group Ratings

ADA — '88: 70, '83–'87 Avg: 72
ACU — '88: 16, '83–'87 Avg: 16
AFL-CIO — '88: 100, '83–'87 Avg: 74
CCUS — '88: 43, '83–'87 Avg: 31

■ '88   ▨ '83–'87 Avg

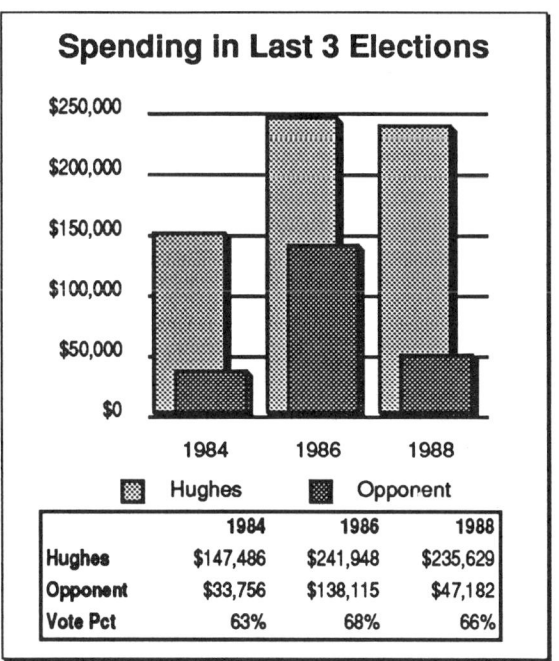

Spending in Last 3 Elections

▨ Hughes   ■ Opponent

	1984	1986	1988
Hughes	$147,486	$241,948	$235,629
Opponent	$33,756	$138,115	$47,182
Vote Pct	63%	68%	66%

Duncan Hunter, R-Calif (45)

First elected: 1980
Total receipts: $392,229
Total from PACs: $150,718

1988 Committees & Subcommittees

Armed Services
Research and Development
Seapower and Strategic and Critical Materials

Select Narcotics Abuse and Control

PAC Contribution Profile

Business

Campaign Revenue Sources

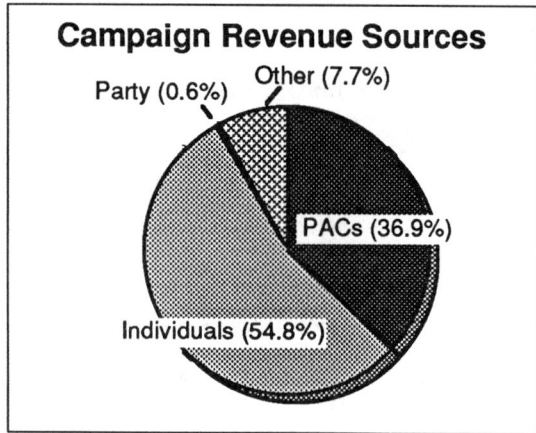

Party (0.6%)
Other (7.7%)
PACs (36.9%)
Individuals (54.8%)

Auto Dealers	$4,500
National Auto Dealers Assn	$3,000
Auto Dealers & Drivers for Free Trade	$1,500

Commercial & Savings Banks	$5,890
Great American Federal Savings	$1,680
Others	$4,210

Construction	$5,913
Associated General Contractors	$1,250
National Assn of Home Builders	$1,000
National Electrical Contractors Assn	$1,000
Others	$2,663

Defense	$49,970
Rohr Industries	$3,950
Cubic Corp	$3,050
Interlake Inc	$2,950
Morrison-Knudsen	$2,750
Lockheed Corp	$2,600
Rockwell International	$2,500
United Technologies	$2,250
General Dynamics	$2,100
General Atomics	$2,050
Continental Telecom	$2,000
Hughes Aircraft	$1,550
McDonnell Douglas*	$1,550
Textron Inc	$1,500
Computer Sciences Corp	$1,300
Boeing Company	$1,000
FMC Corp	$1,000

(continued in next column)

Defense (cont'd)

Grumman	$1,000
Northrop Corp	$1,000
Raytheon	$1,000
Tenneco Inc	$1,000
Others	$11,870

Electric & Power Utilities	$3,320
San Diego Gas & Electric	$1,750
Southern California Edison	$1,020
Others	$550

Health Professionals	$6,700
Anesthesia Service Medical Group	$2,700
American Medical Assn	$1,250
American Dental Assn	$1,000
Others	$1,750

Insurance	$3,050
National Assn of Life Underwriters	$1,850
Others	$1,200

Lawyers	$5,000
Assn of Trial Lawyers of America	$5,000

Real Estate	$6,250
National Assn of Realtors	$6,250

Sea Transport	$3,850
Southwest Marine	$2,750
Others	$1,100

Other Major Business PACs

United Parcel Service	$1,360	Delivery
Pacific Telesis Group	$1,020	Phone Util
McDonald's Corp	$1,000	Restaurants

PAC Totals by Category

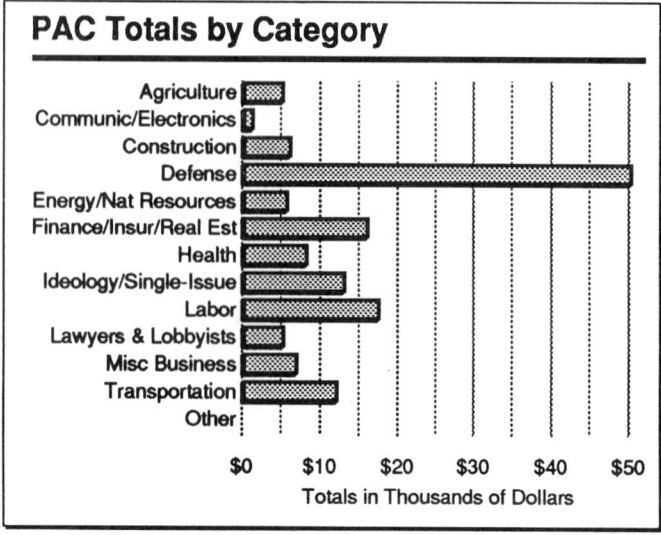

Agriculture
Communic/Electronics
Construction
Defense
Energy/Nat Resources
Finance/Insur/Real Est
Health
Ideology/Single-Issue
Labor
Lawyers & Lobbyists
Misc Business
Transportation
Other

$0 $10 $20 $30 $40 $50

Totals in Thousands of Dollars

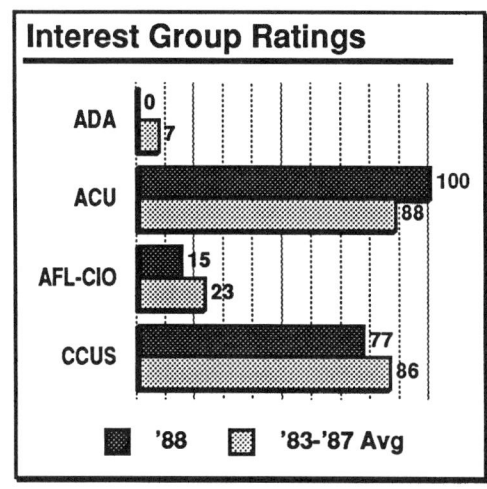

Interest Group Ratings

Labor

Labor Unions $17,250

Marine Engineers Union* $9,500
Teamsters Union $3,500
National Assn of Retired Federal Employees $2,000
Seafarers International Union $1,250
Masters, Mates & Pilots Union $1,000

Ideological/Single-Issue

Pro-Israel $5,500

National PAC $5,000
Others $500

Other Major Ideological/Single-Issue PACs

American Security Council .... $1,690 Pro-Defense
Conservative Order of Good Guys .... $1,200 Repub/Conser
American Citizens for Political Action .... $1,000 Repub/Conser
National Security PAC .... $1,000 Pro-Defense

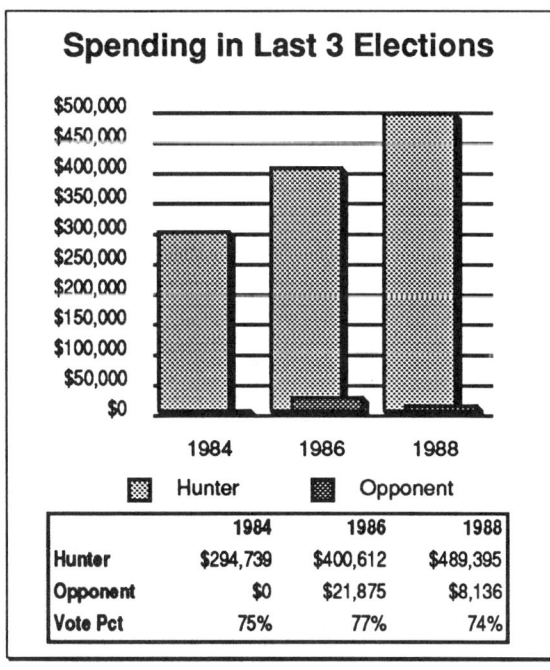

Spending in Last 3 Elections

	1984	1986	1988
Hunter	$294,739	$400,612	$489,395
Opponent	$0	$21,875	$8,136
Vote Pct	75%	77%	74%

* Contributions came from more than one PAC affiliated with this sponsor.

Earl Hutto, D-Fla (1)

1988 Committees & Subcommittees

Armed Services
Military Installations and Facilities
Readiness
Seapower and Strategic and Critical Materials

Merchant Marine and Fisheries
Coast Guard and Navigation
Fisheries and Wildlife Conservation and the Environment

PAC Contribution Profile

Business

Auto Dealers	**$9,000**
Auto Dealers & Drivers for Free Trade	$5,000
National Auto Dealers Assn	$4,000
Commercial & Savings Banks	**$7,950**
Barnett Banks of Florida	$2,000
Florida League of Financial Institutions	$2,000
Florida Bankers Assn	$1,250
Amsouth Bancorp	$1,000
Sun Banks	$1,000
Others	$700
Construction	**$3,750**
Associated General Contractors	$1,000
Others	$2,750
Defense	**$35,550**
Rockwell International	$2,750
AT&T	$2,000
Boeing Company	$2,000
BDM International	$1,500
Hughes Aircraft	$1,500
Lockheed Corp	$1,500
Tenneco Inc	$1,500
McDonnell Douglas*	$1,250
Bath Iron Works	$1,000
FMC Corp	$1,000
General Dynamics	$1,000
Grumman	$1,000
Harris Corp	$1,000
Northrop Corp	$1,000

(Continued in next column)

First elected: 1978
Total receipts: $212,973
Total from PACs: $109,186

Campaign Revenue Sources

Party (5.7%)
Candidate (6.2%)
Individuals (34.9%)
PACs (53.0%)

Defense (cont'd)

Penn Central Corp	$1,000
Textron Inc	$1,000
UNC Inc	$1,000
United Technologies	$1,000
Others	$11,550
Electric Utilities	**$4,800**
Southern Company*	$2,500
ACRE (Action Committee for Rural Electrification)	$1,000
Others	$1,300
Food & Beverage	**$4,000**
Delchamps Inc	$1,000
Food Marketing Institute	$1,000
General Mills Restaurants	$1,000
Winn-Dixie Stores	$1,000
Health Professionals	**$13,000**
American Medical Assn	$5,000
Florida Medical Assn	$5,000
American Optometric Assn	$1,500
American Dental Assn	$1,000
Others	$500
Insurance	**$2,250**
National Assn of Life Underwriters	$1,000
Others	$1,250
Oil & Gas	**$2,050**
Atlantic Richfield	$1,000
Others	$1,050
Real Estate	**$8,500**
National Assn of Realtors	$8,000
Others	$500
Sea Transport	**$7,000**
Boat Owners Assn of the US	$1,500
CSX Transportation Inc*	$1,500
American Pilots Assn	$1,000
Others	$3,000
Telecommunications	**$3,000**
Southern Bell	$3,000

Other Major Business PACs

Stone Container Corp	$1,500	Paper Packg
Florida Citrus Mutual	$1,400	Fruit/Veg
Champion International Corp	$1,000	Paper Prod

PAC Totals by Category

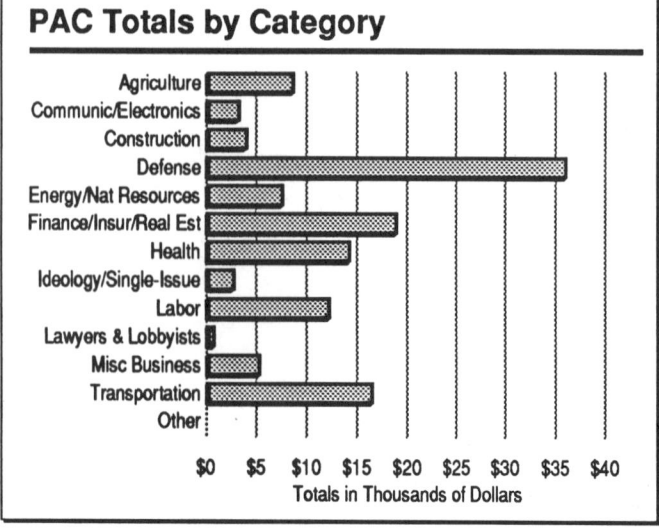

Agriculture	
Communic/Electronics	
Construction	
Defense	
Energy/Nat Resources	
Finance/Insur/Real Est	
Health	
Ideology/Single-Issue	
Labor	
Lawyers & Lobbyists	
Misc Business	
Transportation	
Other	

$0 $5 $10 $15 $20 $25 $30 $35 $40
Totals in Thousands of Dollars

Labor

Sea Transport Unions...**$11,000**

     Seafarers International Union $6,000
     Marine Engineers Union* $5,000

Other Major Labor PACs

Air Line Pilots Assn ....$1,000   AirTrans Lab

Major Ideological/Single-Issue PACs

National Security PAC ....$1,000   Pro-Defense
Valley Education Fund (Tony Coelho) ....$1,000   Dem Leaders

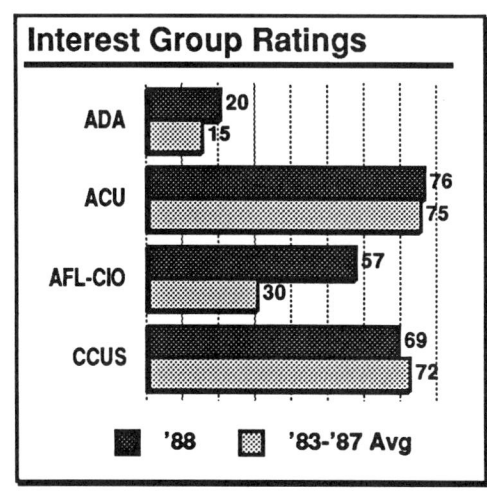

Interest Group Ratings

Group	'88	'83-'87 Avg
ADA	20	15
ACU	76	75
AFL-CIO	57	30
CCUS	69	72

■ '88   ▨ '83-'87 Avg

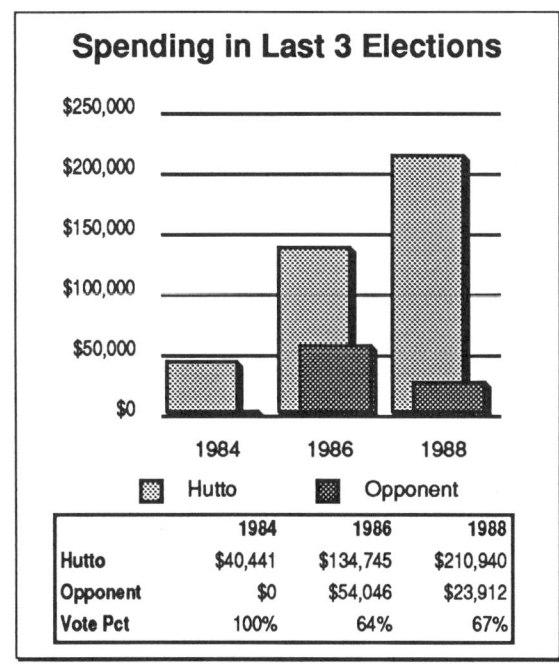

Spending in Last 3 Elections

▨ Hutto   ■ Opponent

	1984	1986	1988
Hutto	$40,441	$134,745	$210,940
Opponent	$0	$54,046	$23,912
Vote Pct	100%	64%	67%

---

* Contributions came from more than one PAC affiliated
with this sponsor.

Henry J. Hyde, R-III (6)

1988 Committees & Subcommittees

First elected: 1974
Total receipts: $304,349
Total from PACs: $121,407

Foreign Affairs
Arms Control, International Security and Science
Western Hemisphere Affairs

Judiciary
Courts, Civil Liberties and the Administration of Justice
Monopolies and Commercial Law

Select Intelligence (Ranking Republican)
Oversight and Evaluation
Program and Budget Authorization

PAC Contribution Profile

Business

Accountants **$6,000**
American Institute of CPA's $5,000
Others $1,000

Auto Dealers **$6,750**
National Auto Dealers Assn $5,250
Auto Dealers & Drivers for Free Trade $1,500

Broadcasting/Entertainment **$2,500**
None over $500

Chemicals **$2,750**
FMC Corp $2,500
Others $250

Commercial & Savings Banks **$11,550**
American Bankers Assn $3,000
Northern Trust Company $2,000
First Chicago Corp $1,500
Illinois Bankers Assn $1,400
US League of Savings Assn $1,250
Mid America Federal Savings & Loan $1,000
Others $1,400

Commodities & Securities Investment **$2,500**
Chicago Board of Trade $1,000
Morgan Stanley & Company $1,000
Others $500

Campaign Revenue Sources

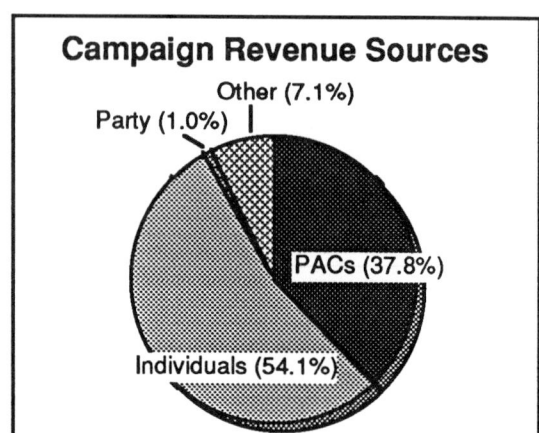

Other (7.1%)
Party (1.0%)
PACs (37.8%)
Individuals (54.1%)

Defense **$3,000**
None over $750

Food & Beverage **$8,750**
National Beer Wholesalers Assn $2,000
Quaker Oats $2,000
McDonald's Corp $1,000
Nutrasweet Company $1,000
Others $2,750

Health Professionals **$7,950**
American Medical Assn $6,500
Cmte for Quality Orthopedic Health Care $1,000
Others $450

Industrial Equipment & Materials **$3,650**
Illinois Tool Works $1,750
Others $1,900

Insurance **$11,100**
National Assn of Life Underwriters $2,000
Travelers Corp $1,500
American Family Corp $1,000
Others $6,600

Lawyers **$2,050**
None over $800

Oil & Gas **$3,550**
Mobil Oil $1,000
Others $2,550

Paper Production **$2,000**
International Paper Company $1,750
Others $250

Railroads & Railroad Equipment **$2,000**
Duchossois Industries $1,000
Others $1,000

PAC Totals by Category

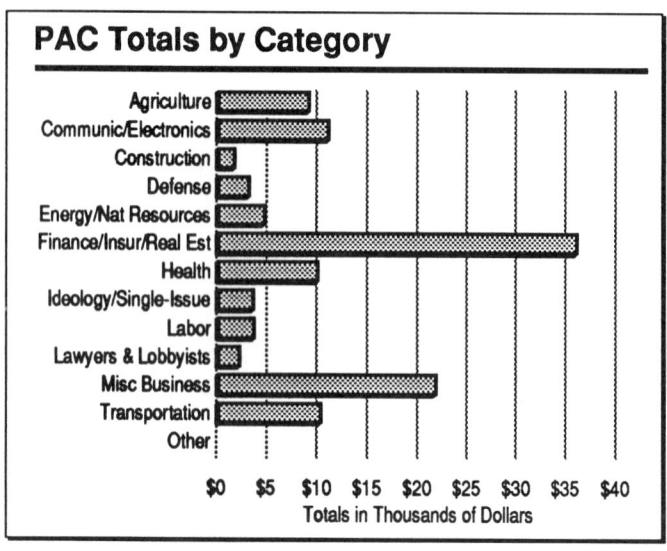

Agriculture
Communic/Electronics
Construction
Defense
Energy/Nat Resources
Finance/Insur/Real Est
Health
Ideology/Single-Issue
Labor
Lawyers & Lobbyists
Misc Business
Transportation
Other

$0 $5 $10 $15 $20 $25 $30 $35 $40
Totals in Thousands of Dollars

Interest Group Ratings

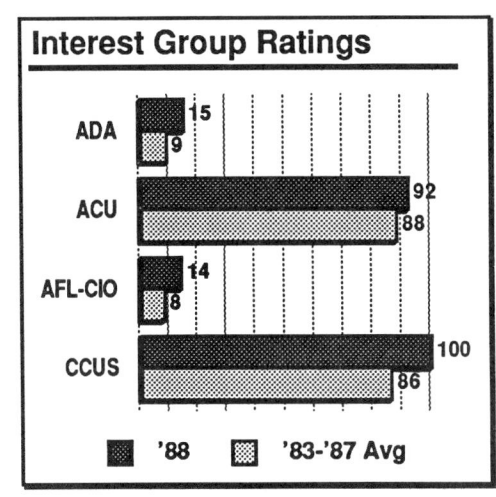

	'88	'83-'87 Avg
ADA	15	9
ACU	92	88
AFL-CIO	14	8
CCUS	100	86

Real Estate **$6,000**

National Assn of Realtors $6,000

Retail Sales **$5,300**

Walgreen Company $1,250
International Council of Shopping Centers $1,000
International Mass Retail Assn $1,000
Others $2,050

Telecommunications **$6,600**

Illinois Bell Telephone $3,000
AT&T $2,000
Others $1,600

Other Major Business PACs

American National Can Company	$1,300	Cans
Associated General Contractors	$1,000	Comml Constr
Commonwealth Edison	$1,000	ElectricUtil
Maytag Company	$1,000	Appliances
West Publishing	$1,000	Books & Mags

Labor

Labor Unions **$3,500**

National Assn of Retired Federal Employees $3,500

Major Ideological/Single-Issue PACs

American Citizens for Political Action	$1,000	Repub/Conser

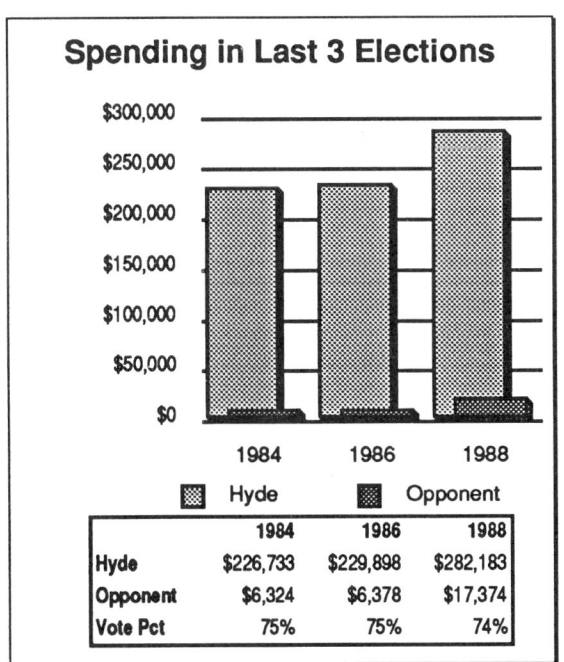

Spending in Last 3 Elections

	1984	1986	1988
Hyde	$226,733	$229,898	$282,183
Opponent	$6,324	$6,378	$17,374
Vote Pct	75%	75%	74%

James M. Inhofe, R-Okla (1)

1988 Committees & Subcommittees

First elected: 1986
Total receipts: $482,552
Total from PACs: $262,222

Government Operations
Commerce, Consumer and Monetary Affairs
Government Activities and Transportation

Public Works and Transportation
Aviation
Water Resources

Select Narcotics Abuse and Control

PAC Contribution Profile

Business

Accountants	**$5,000**
American Institute of CPA's	$5,000
Automotive	**$16,500**
National Auto Dealers Assn	$8,350
Auto Dealers & Drivers for Free Trade	$6,500
Ford Motor Company	$1,000
Others	$650
Aviation & Aerospace	**$21,450**
Aircraft Owners & Pilots Assn	$8,600
Texas Air	$3,000
American Airlines	$2,350
United Airlines	$1,150
Allied-Signal	$1,000
Others	$5,350
Business Organizations	**$2,100**
National Fedn of Independent Business	$2,100
Chemicals	**$2,650**
Greyhound Corp	$1,000
Others	$1,650
Construction	**$18,700**
National Electrical Contractors Assn	$7,000
Associated General Contractors	$3,650
National Assn of Home Builders	$2,500
Associated Builders & Contractors	$1,250
Halliburton Company	$1,000
National Society of Professional Engineers	$1,000
Sheet Metal/AirCon Contractors	$1,000
Others	$1,300

Campaign Revenue Sources

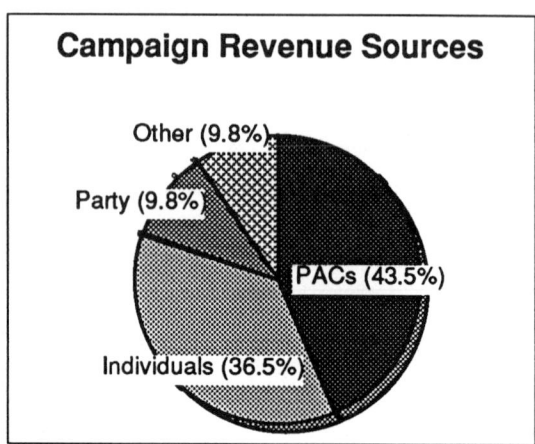

Other (9.8%)
Party (9.8%)
PACs (43.5%)
Individuals (36.5%)

Defense	**$7,400**
Rockwell International	$2,000
Harris Corp	$1,500
Electrospace Systems Inc	$1,250
Others	$2,650
Electric & Power Utilities	**$2,650**
Oklahoma Gas & Electric	$1,000
Others	$1,650
Financial Institutions	**$6,850**
US League of Savings Assn	$2,200
American Bankers Assn	$2,000
United Community Bankers	$1,000
Others	$1,650
Food & Beverage	**$5,600**
National Restaurant Assn	$2,000
National Beer Wholesalers Assn	$1,750
Others	$1,850
Health Professionals	**$15,675**
American Medical Assn	$7,675
American Dental Assn	$3,200
American Academy of Ophthalmology	$2,500
Oklahoma Medical Assn	$2,300
Insurance	**$11,200**
National Assn of Life Underwriters	$2,800
Independent Insurance Agents of America	$2,700
Casualty & Surety Agents Assn	$1,600
Metropolitan Life Insurance	$1,050
Connecticut Mutual Life Insurance	$1,000
Others	$2,050

PAC Totals by Category

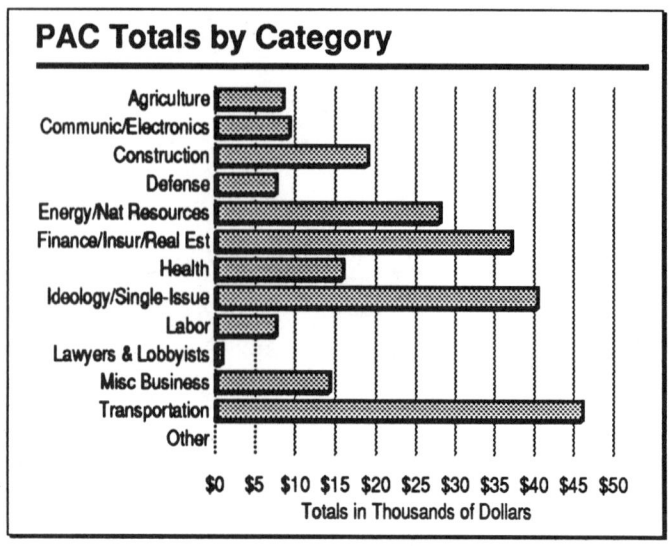

Agriculture
Communic/Electronics
Construction
Defense
Energy/Nat Resources
Finance/Insur/Real Est
Health
Ideology/Single-Issue
Labor
Lawyers & Lobbyists
Misc Business
Transportation
Other

$0 $5 $10 $15 $20 $25 $30 $35 $40 $45 $50
Totals in Thousands of Dollars

Oil & Gas	....	**$23,450**
Phillips Petroleum	....	$3,000
Sun Company	....	$3,000
Amoco Corp	....	$2,400
Mapco Inc	....	$2,300
Chevron Corp	....	$1,900
Occidental Oil & Gas	....	$1,600
Texaco	....	$1,200
Atlantic Richfield	....	$1,050
Mobil Oil	....	$1,000
Mustang Energy Corp	....	$1,000
Others	....	$5,000

Railroads	....	**$2,550**
Union Pacific Corp	....	$1,300
Others	....	$1,250

Real Estate	....	**$13,650**
National Assn of Realtors	....	$10,000
Mortgage Bankers Assn of America	....	$1,250
Society of Real Estate Appraisers	....	$1,050
Trammell Crow Company	....	$1,000
Others	....	$350

Sugar Growers	....	**$2,600**
None over $900		

Telecommunications	....	**$8,550**
AT&T	....	$3,500
Southwestern Bell	....	$2,050
GTE (Southwest)	....	$2,000
Others	....	$1,000

Trucking/Delivery	....	**$4,350**
United Parcel Service	....	$2,750
Others	....	$1,600

Other Major Business PACs

Philip Morris	....	$1,700	Tobacco
Brunswick Corp	....	$1,000	Indust Equip
Texas Cattle Feeders Assn	....	$1,000	Feedlots

Interest Group Ratings

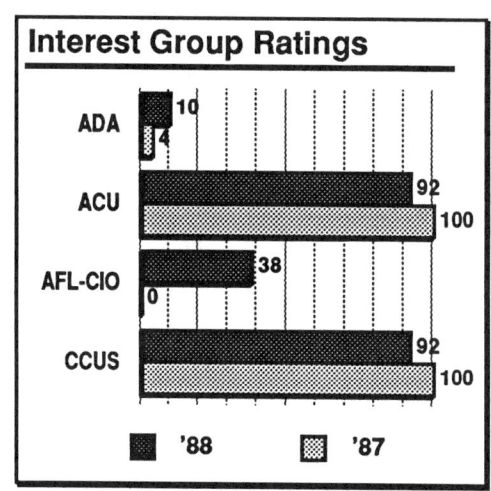

Labor

Labor Unions	....	**$7,400**
National Assn of Retired Federal Employees	....	$2,700
Seafarers International Union	....	$2,000
Air Line Pilots Assn	....	$1,000
Teamsters Local #523	....	$1,000
Others	....	$700

Ideological/Single-Issue

Anti-Union	....	**$4,650**
Public Service Research Council	....	$3,400
Right to Work PAC	....	$1,250

Pro-Guns	....	**$8,900**
National Rifle Assn	....	$8,900

Pro-Israel	....	**$5,500**
National PAC	....	$5,000
Others	....	$500

Republican Leadership/Conservative PACs	....	**$17,846**
Fund for America's Future (George Bush)	....	$5,500
Citizens for the Republic (Ronald Reagan)	....	$5,000
Conservative Victory Fund (Steve Symms)	....	$2,696
Campaign America (Bob Dole)	....	$2,650
Campaign for a New Majority (Jack Kemp)	....	$1,000
Policy Innovation PAC (Dick Armey)	....	$1,000
Republican Congressional Boosters Club	....	$1,000

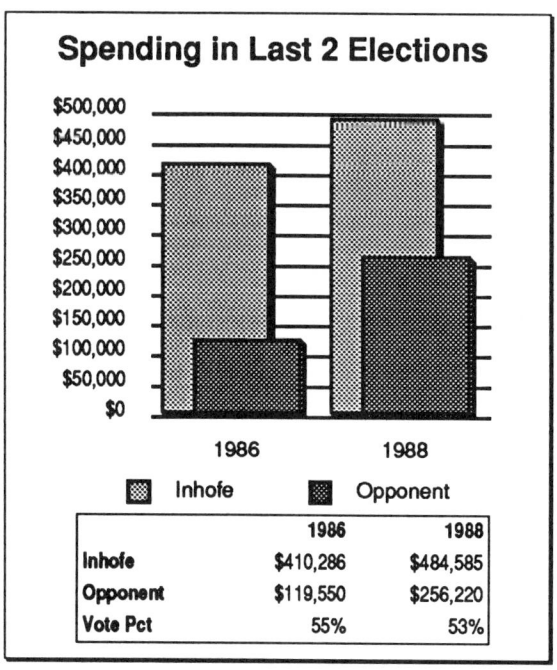

Spending in Last 2 Elections

	1986	1988
Inhofe	$410,286	$484,585
Opponent	$119,550	$256,220
Vote Pct	55%	53%

Andy Ireland, R-Fla (10)

1988 Committees & Subcommittees

Armed Services
Investigations
Procurement and Military Nuclear Systems

Small Business
Exports, Tourism and Special Problems (Ranking Republican)

First elected: 1976
Total receipts: $405,000
Total from PACs: $162,389

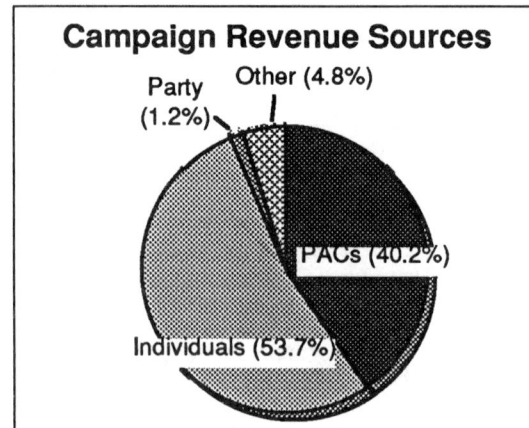

Campaign Revenue Sources

- Party (1.2%)
- Other (4.8%)
- PACs (40.2%)
- Individuals (53.7%)

PAC Contribution Profile

Business

Agricultural Chemicals	**$3,135**
IMC Fertilizer Inc	$2,100
Others	$1,035
Auto Dealers	**$7,000**
National Auto Dealers Assn	$5,000
Auto Dealers & Drivers for Free Trade	$2,000
Chemicals	**$3,250**
Greyhound Corp	$1,000
W R Grace & Company	$1,000
Others	$1,250
Commercial Banks	**$11,750**
Barnett Banks of Florida	$2,500
Citizens & Southern National Bank	$1,500
Florida Bankers Assn	$1,500
Sun Banks	$1,500
American Bankers Assn	$1,000
First Florida Banks	$1,000
National Banks of Florida	$1,000
Southeast Banking Corp	$1,000
Others	$750
Construction	**$11,300**
National Assn of Home Builders	$3,000
Wall & Ceiling/Gypsum Contractors	$2,300
Lone Star Industries	$1,500
American Subcontractors Assn	$1,000
Associated Builders & Contractors	$1,000
Associated General Contractors	$1,000
Others	$1,500

Defense	**$28,300**
FMC Corp	$3,000
AT&T	$2,000
Lockheed Corp	$2,000
McDonnell Douglas*	$2,000
United Technologies	$1,500
Allied-Signal	$1,000
BDM International	$1,000
Chrysler Corp	$1,000
Colt Industries	$1,000
General Dynamics	$1,000
Northrop Corp	$1,000
Rockwell International	$1,000
Textron Inc	$1,000
UNC Inc	$1,000
Others	$8,800
Electric Utilities	**$4,000**
ACRE (Action Committee for Rural Electrification)	$1,000
Florida Power & Light	$1,000
Others	$2,000
Food & Beverage	**$8,100**
Coca-Cola Company	$1,000
Food Marketing Institute	$1,000
National Beer Wholesalers Assn	$1,000
Winn-Dixie Stores	$1,000
Others	$4,100
Forest Products	**$2,500**
Westvaco Corp	$1,500
Others	$1,000
Health Professionals	**$13,478**
American Medical Assn	$5,478
Florida Medical Assn	$4,500
American Dental Assn	$2,000
Others	$1,500
Insurance	**$9,000**
National Assn of Life Underwriters	$2,500
Casualty & Surety Agents Assn	$1,500
Health Insurance Assn of America	$1,000
Independent Insurance Agents of America	$1,000
Travelers Corp	$1,000
US Fidelity & Guaranty	$1,000
Others	$1,000

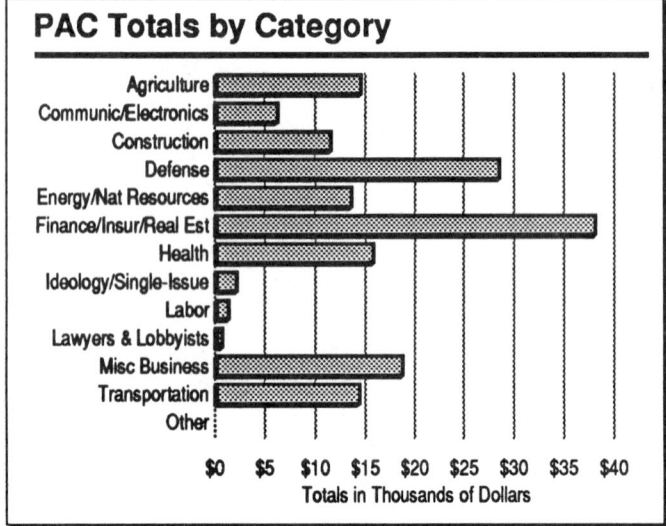

PAC Totals by Category

Categories (top to bottom): Agriculture, Communic/Electronics, Construction, Defense, Energy/Nat Resources, Finance/Insur/Real Est, Health, Ideology/Single-Issue, Labor, Lawyers & Lobbyists, Misc Business, Transportation, Other

Totals in Thousands of Dollars ($0, $5, $10, $15, $20, $25, $30, $35, $40)

Oil & Gas		$8,850
	Chevron Corp	$1,500
	Mobil Oil	$1,000
	Petroleum Marketers Assn	$1,000
	Others	$5,350

Pharmaceuticals		$2,100
	Abbott Laboratories	$1,000
	Others	$1,100

Real Estate		$9,750
	National Assn of Realtors	$6,750
	Mortgage Bankers Assn of America	$2,500
	Others	$500

Savings Banks		$3,450
	Florida League of Financial Institutions	$2,000
	Others	$1,450

Small Business Associations		$3,075
	National Assn of Sm Bus Invest Companies	$1,875
	National Fedn of Independent Business	$1,200

Telecommunications		$5,500
	Southern Bell	$3,000
	NYNEX Corp	$1,000
	Others	$1,500

Trucking/Delivery		$4,600
	United Parcel Service	$1,250
	Watkins Associated Industries	$1,250
	Others	$2,100

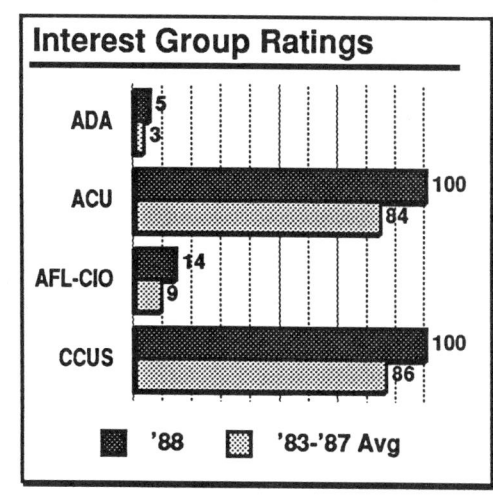

Interest Group Ratings

	'88	'83-'87 Avg
ADA	5	3
ACU	100	84
AFL-CIO	14	9
CCUS	100	86

Other Major Business PACs

National Venture Capital Assn	$2,000	Venture Cap
Owens-Illinois	$1,500	Paper Packg
National Tooling & Machining Assn	$1,250	Indust Equip
National Society of Public Accountants	$1,050	Accountants
American Furniture Manufacturers Assn	$1,000	Furniture
American Society of Travel Agents	$1,000	Travel Agent
National Assn of Wholesale-Distributors	$1,000	Wholesale

Major Labor PACs

Teamsters Union	$1,150	Teamsters

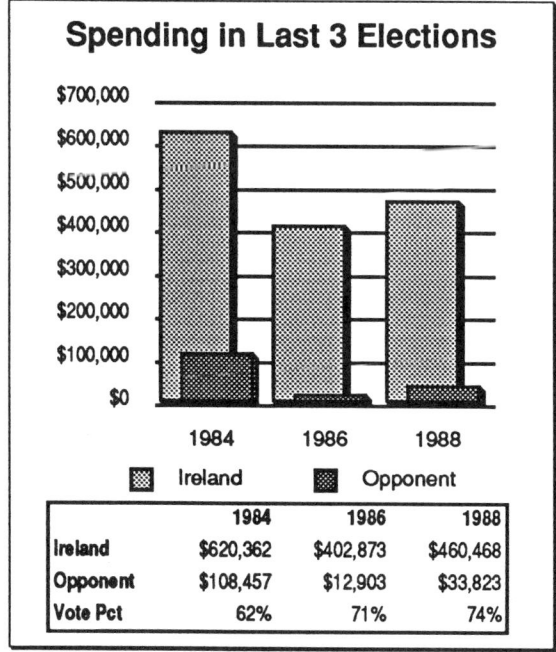

Spending in Last 3 Elections

	1984	1986	1988
Ireland	$620,362	$402,873	$460,468
Opponent	$108,457	$12,903	$33,823
Vote Pct	62%	71%	74%

Ireland ☐   Opponent ■

---

* Contributions came from more than one PAC affiliated with this sponsor.

Andrew Jacobs Jr., D-Ind (10)

First elected: 1964
Total receipts: $35,731
Total from PACs: $0

1988 Committees & Subcommittees

Ways and Means
Social Security (Chairman)
Oversight

PAC Contribution Profile

International Council of Shopping Centers .. $1,000   Retail
National Council of Senior Citizens .... $1,000   Social Security
Fleetwood Enterprises .... $500   Mobile Home

NOTE: Jacobs reported taking no PAC funds in his 1988 campaign. The PACs listed above did report making contributions during 1987-88, however, and those contributions are recorded in the official FEC records.

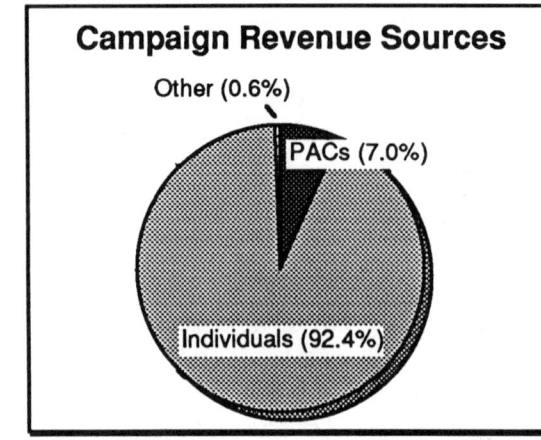

Campaign Revenue Sources

Other (0.6%)
PACs (7.0%)
Individuals (92.4%)

PAC Totals by Category

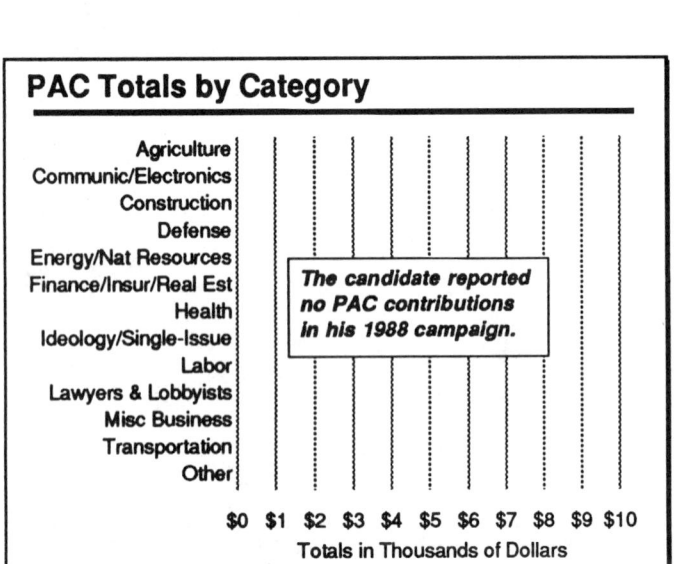

Agriculture
Communic/Electronics
Construction
Defense
Energy/Nat Resources
Finance/Insur/Real Est
Health
Ideology/Single-Issue
Labor
Lawyers & Lobbyists
Misc Business
Transportation
Other

The candidate reported no PAC contributions in his 1988 campaign.

$0 $1 $2 $3 $4 $5 $6 $7 $8 $9 $10
Totals in Thousands of Dollars

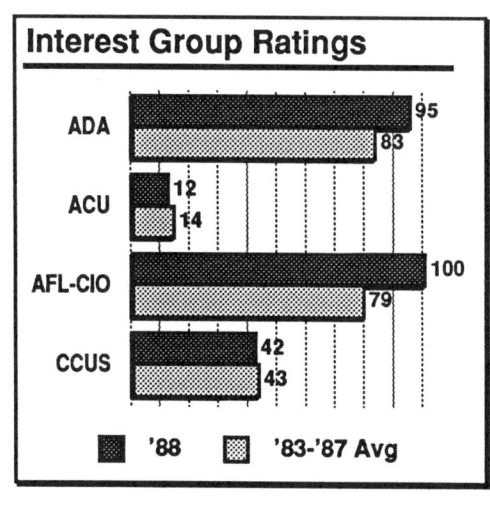

Interest Group Ratings

	'88	'83-'87 Avg
ADA	95	83
ACU	12	14
AFL-CIO	100	79
CCUS	42	43

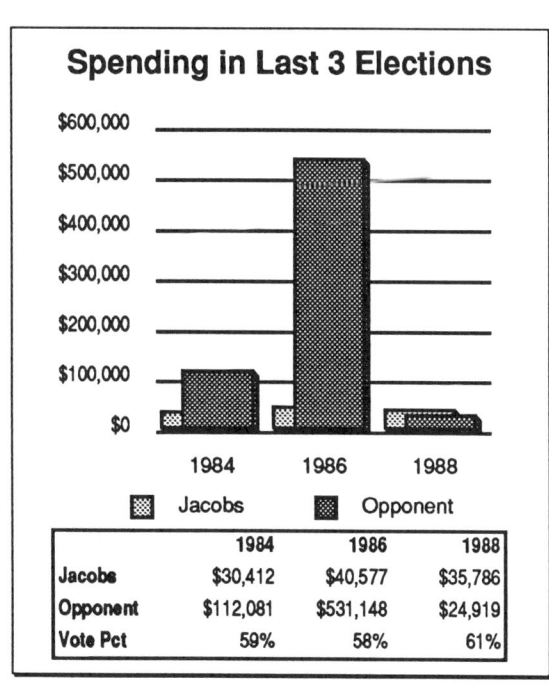

Spending in Last 3 Elections

	1984	1986	1988
Jacobs	$30,412	$40,577	$35,786
Opponent	$112,081	$531,148	$24,919
Vote Pct	59%	58%	61%

Craig T. James, R-Fla (4)

First elected: 1988
Total receipts: $316,314
Total from PACs: $7,295

1988-1989 Committees & Subcommittees

Judiciary
Administrative Law and Governmental Relations (Ranking Republican)
Civil and Constitutional Rights

Veterans' Affairs
Oversight and Investigations

Select Aging
Housing and Consumer Interests
Retirement Income and Employment

PAC Contribution Profile

Business

Real Estate

National Assn of Realtors $5,000

Other Business PACs

National Banks of Florida	$1,000	Comml Banks
Florida Power Corp	$500	ElectricUtil
Mapco Inc	$500	Refine/Mktg
Sears	$250	Retail

Ideological/Single-Issue PACs

Duval County Republican Party	$500	Repub/Conser
Public Service Research Council	$500	Anti-Union

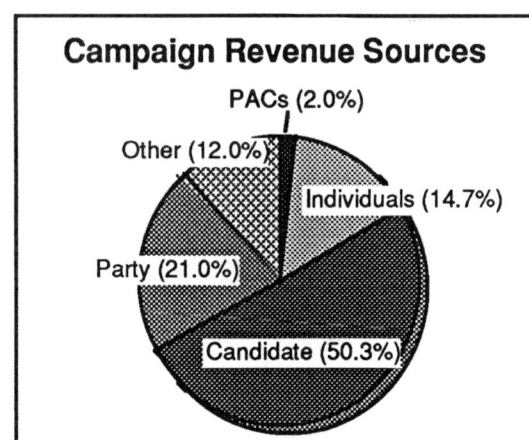

Campaign Revenue Sources

- PACs (2.0%)
- Other (12.0%)
- Individuals (14.7%)
- Party (21.0%)
- Candidate (50.3%)

PAC Totals by Category

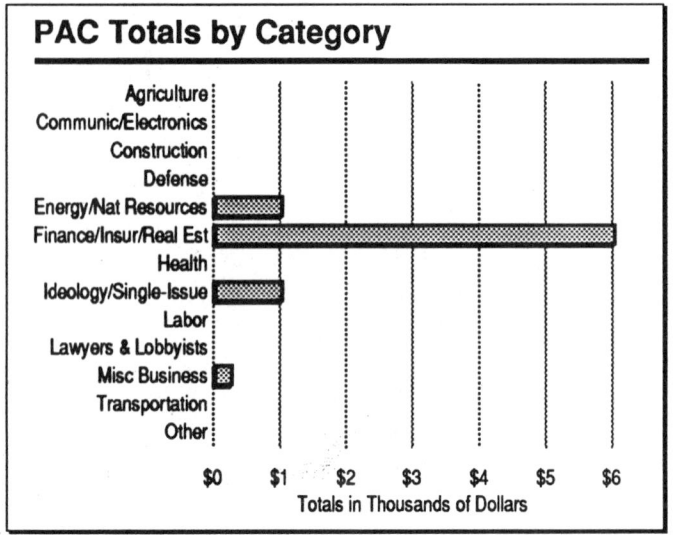

Agriculture
Communic/Electronics
Construction
Defense
Energy/Nat Resources
Finance/Insur/Real Est
Health
Ideology/Single-Issue
Labor
Lawyers & Lobbyists
Misc Business
Transportation
Other

$0 $1 $2 $3 $4 $5 $6

Totals in Thousands of Dollars

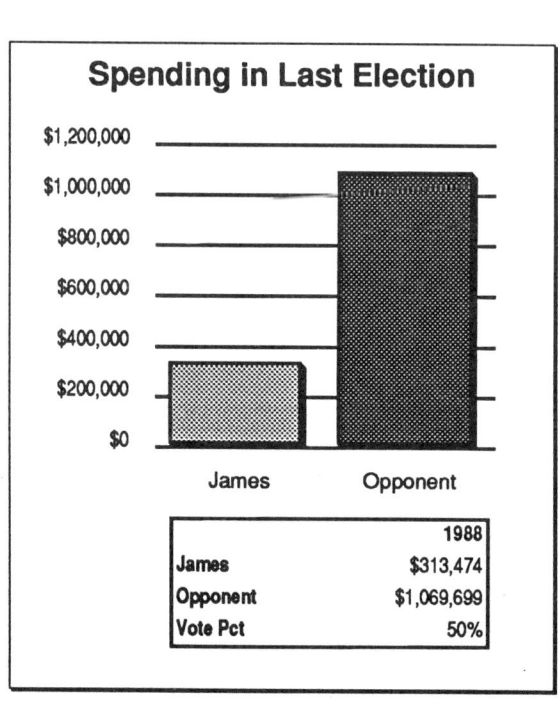

Spending in Last Election

	1988
James	$313,474
Opponent	$1,069,699
Vote Pct	50%

Ed Jenkins, D-Ga (9)

1988 Committees & Subcommittees

Budget
Community and Natural Resources
State and Local Government

Ways and Means
Trade

First elected: 1976
Total receipts: $453,174
Total from PACs: $310,397

PAC Contribution Profile

Business

Automotive	**$7,500**
National Auto Dealers Assn	$4,500
Ford Motor Company	$1,000
Others	$2,000
Commercial Banks	**$12,000**
American Bankers Assn	$5,000
Citizens & Southern National Bank	$2,000
Barnett Banks of Florida	$1,500
Citicorp	$1,500
J P Morgan & Company	$1,000
Others	$1,000
Construction	**$13,150**
National Assn of Home Builders	$3,500
Walter Industries	$3,500
National Utility Contractors Assn	$3,000
Associated General Contractors	$1,500
Manville Corp	$1,400
Others	$250
Defense	**$8,500**
Lockheed Corp	$3,500
Rockwell International	$1,000
Others	$4,000
Food & Beverage	**$13,350**
National Beer Wholesalers Assn	$3,000
National Restaurant Assn	$2,000
Winn-Dixie Stores	$2,000
Coca-Cola Company	$1,500
Food Marketing Institute	$1,000
Wine & Spirits Wholesalers of America	$1,000
Others	$2,850

Campaign Revenue Sources

Other (16.0%)

Individuals (18.0%)

PACs (65.9%)

PAC Totals by Category

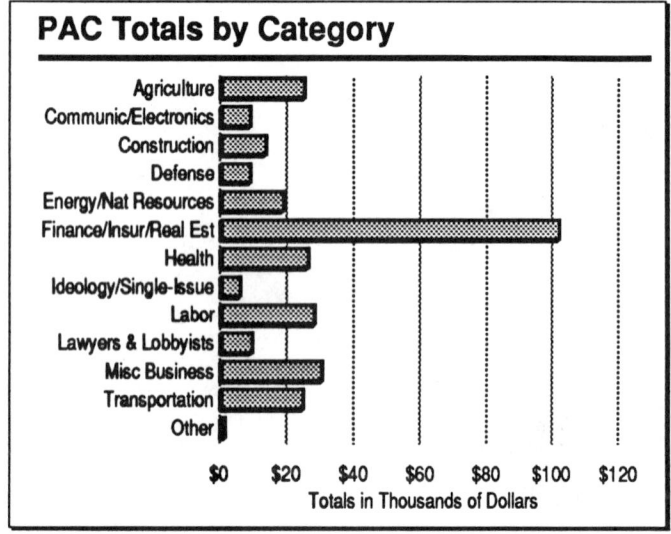

Agriculture
Communic/Electronics
Construction
Defense
Energy/Nat Resources
Finance/Insur/Real Est
Health
Ideology/Single-Issue
Labor
Lawyers & Lobbyists
Misc Business
Transportation
Other

$0 $20 $40 $60 $80 $100 $120
Totals in Thousands of Dollars

Health Professionals	**$19,000**
American Medical Assn	$10,000
American Dental Assn	$4,000
Oral & Maxillofacial Surgeons	$2,000
American College of Emergency Physicians	$1,000
Cmte for Quality Orthopedic Health Care	$1,000
Others	$1,000
Insurance	**$47,597**
National Assn of Life Underwriters	$10,000
Torchmark Corp	$5,000
Travelers Corp	$2,500
Massachusetts Mutual Life Insurance	$2,000
Metropolitan Life Insurance	$2,000
Northwestern Mutual Life	$1,500
American Council of Life Insurance	$1,000
American Family Corp	$1,000
American General Insurance Company	$1,000
Blue Cross & Blue Shield Assn	$1,000
Chubb Corp	$1,000
Connecticut Mutual Life Insurance	$1,000
Equitable Financial Services	$1,000
Georgia US Corp	$1,000
John Hancock Financial Service	$1,000
Liberty Mutual Insurance	$1,000
Mutual Life Insurance of New York	$1,000
New England Mutual Life	$1,000
New York Life	$1,000
Provident Life & Accident Insurance	$1,000
Prudential Insurance	$1,000
Others	$9,597
Lawyers & Lobbyists	**$9,000**
Assn of Trial Lawyers of America	$5,000
Dow, Lohnes & Albertson	$1,000
King & Spalding	$1,000
Others	$2,000
Real Estate	**$19,700**
National Assn of Realtors	$8,500
American Resort & Residential Development Assn	$5,000
Century 21 Real Estate	$4,000
National Realty Committee	$1,000
Others	$1,200
Securities & Commodities Investment	**$8,000**
Chicago Board of Trade	$2,000
First Boston Corp	$2,000
Chicago Board of Options Exchange	$1,000
Morgan Stanley & Company	$1,000
Others	$2,000

Interest Group Ratings

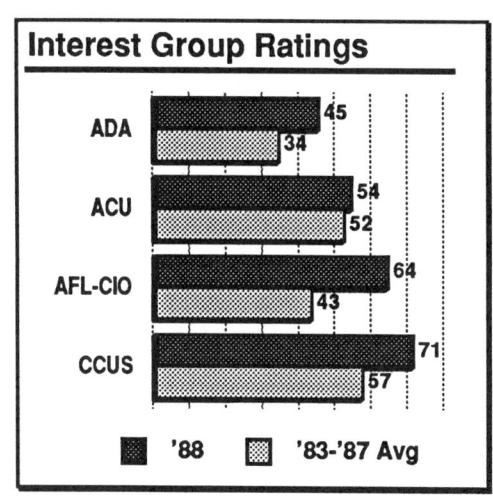

	'88	'83-'87 Avg
ADA	45	34
ACU	54	52
AFL-CIO	64	43
CCUS	71	57

Textiles **$8,750**

American Textile Manufacturers Institute	$1,000
American Yarn Spinners Assn	$1,000
Burlington Industries	$1,000
Cone Mills Corp	$1,000
Hoechst Celanese Corp	$1,000
Others	$3,750

Other Major Business PACs

American Institute of CPA's	$5,000	Accountants
National Venture Capital Assn	$5,000	Venture Cap
ACRE (Action Committee for Rural Electric)	$3,000	RuralElect
Southern Bell	$3,000	Phone Util
Philip Morris	$2,500	Tobacco
American Assn of Equipment Lessors	$2,000	Rentals
Eastern Airlines	$2,000	Airlines
National Cable Television Assn	$2,000	CableTV
RJR Nabisco	$2,000	Tobacco
United Parcel Service	$2,000	Delivery
Continental Telecom	$1,500	Phone Util
Delta Airlines	$1,500	Airlines
US League of Savings Assn	$1,500	SavingsBanks
Waste Management Inc	$1,500	Waste Mgmt
Westvaco Corp	$1,500	Paper Prod
American Society of Assn Executives	$1,000	Other
American Business Assn	$1,000	Bus Svcs
American Hospital Assn	$1,000	Hospitals
Atlanta Gas Light Company	$1,000	Natural Gas
Combustion Engineering	$1,000	PowerEquip
Consolidated Freightways	$1,000	Trucking
Federation of America Hospitals	$1,000	Hospitals
Georgia Power Company	$1,000	ElectricUtil
Holiday Inns	$1,000	Hotel/Motel
International Paper Company	$1,000	Paper Prod
International Council of Shopping Centers	$1,000	Retail
Johnson & Johnson	$1,000	Health Prod
National Coal Assn	$1,000	Coal
National Fedn of Independent Business	$1,000	Sml Business
Petroleum Marketers Assn	$1,000	Gas Stations
Pfizer Inc	$1,000	Pharmaceut
Schering-Plough Corp	$1,000	Pharmaceut
Union Pacific Corp	$1,000	Railroads

Labor

Bldg Trades/Industrial/Misc Unions **$14,500**

United Auto Workers	$8,500
National Education Assn	$2,500
Food & Commercial Workers Union	$1,500
Others	$2,000

Government & Postal Workers **$7,050**

National Rural Letter Carriers Assn	$4,000
American Fedn of State/County/Munic Employees	$1,000
National Assn of Letter Carriers	$1,000
Others	$1,050

Transportation Unions **$6,250**

Air Line Pilots Assn	$5,000
Seafarers International Union	$500
Others	$750

Major Ideological/Single-Issue PACs

National Cmte to Preserve Social Security	$5,000	Social Secur

Independent expenditures supporting Jenkins

National Cmte to Preserve Social Security	$2,226

Spending in Last 3 Elections

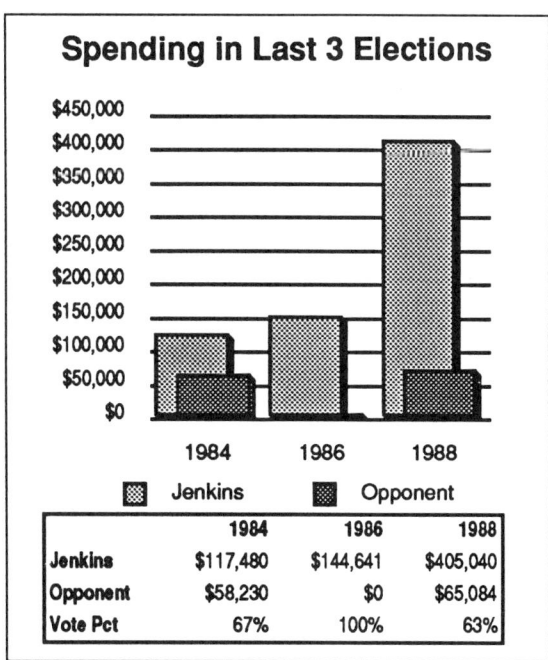

	1984	1986	1988
Jenkins	$117,480	$144,641	$405,040
Opponent	$58,230	$0	$65,084
Vote Pct	67%	100%	63%

Nancy L. Johnson, R-Conn (6)

First elected: 1982
Total receipts: $527,164
Total from PACs: $132,822

1988 Committees & Subcommittees

Budget
Health (Ranking Republican)
Economic and Trade Policy
Human Resources

Public Works and Transportation
Economic Development
Investigations and Oversight
Water Resources

Select Children, Youth and Families

PAC Contribution Profile

Business

Automotive	**$11,250**
Torrington Company	$5,000
National Auto Dealers Assn	$4,350
Auto Dealers & Drivers for Free Trade	$1,500
Others	$400
Aviation & Aerospace	**$3,350**
Texas Air*	$1,400
Others	$1,950
Commercial & Savings Banks	**$4,725**
Connecticut Bankers Assn	$1,250
CBT Corp	$1,000
Others	$2,475
Construction	**$11,350**
National Utility Contractors Assn	$2,000
Westvaco Corp	$2,000
Associated General Contractors	$1,650
National Assn of Home Builders	$1,500
Others	$4,200
Dairy	**$4,300**
Associated Milk Producers	$2,500
Agri-Mark Inc	$1,000
Others	$800
Defense	**$10,852**
United Technologies	$3,452
Kaman Corp	$2,500
Textron Inc	$2,000
General Dynamics	$1,000
Others	$1,900

Campaign Revenue Sources

Party (1.1%)
PACs (28.7%)
Individuals (70.3%)

Electronics & Computers	**$4,000**
Cooper Industries	$2,000
Others	$2,000
Food & Beverage	**$4,000**
Pepsi-Cola Bottlers Assn	$1,000
Others	$3,000
Hardware	**$3,000**
Stanley Works	$3,000
Health Professionals	**$9,500**
American Medical Assn	$5,000
American Dental Assn	$2,000
American Academy of Ophthalmology	$1,000
American Nurses Assn	$1,000
Others	$500
Industrial Equipment & Materials	**$5,700**
Emhart Corp	$3,400
Others	$2,300
Insurance	**$16,803**
Insurance Assn of Connecticut	$7,003
National Assn of Life Underwriters	$3,000
Independent Insurance Agents of America	$1,450
Others	$5,350
Oil & Gas	**$3,350**
Petroleum Marketers Assn	$1,000
Others	$2,350
Pharmaceuticals	**$3,100**
None over $500	
Power Utilities Equipment	**$2,700**
Combustion Engineering	$2,200
Others	$500
Real Estate	**$5,700**
National Assn of Realtors	$5,400
Others	$300

PAC Totals by Category

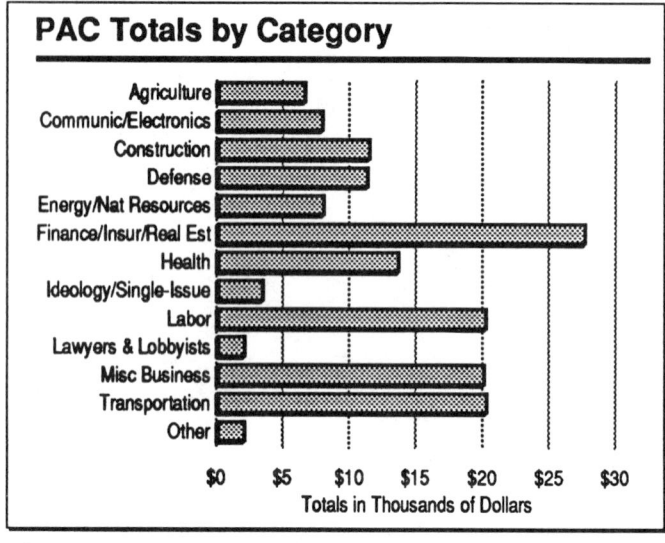

Totals in Thousands of Dollars

Agriculture
Communic/Electronics
Construction
Defense
Energy/Nat Resources
Finance/Insur/Real Est
Health
Ideology/Single-Issue
Labor
Lawyers & Lobbyists
Misc Business
Transportation
Other

$0 $5 $10 $15 $20 $25 $30

Telecommunications **$2,800**
    AT&T $2,000
    Others $800

Trucking/Delivery **$4,220**
    United Parcel Service $2,150
    Others $2,070

Other Major Business PACs

National Assn of Trade/Tech Schools	$2,000	Voc Tech
Corning Glass Works	$1,000	Glass Prod
Hallmark Cards	$1,000	Publishing
Holiday Corp	$1,000	Hotel/Motel
National Assn of Convenience Stores	$1,000	Dept Store

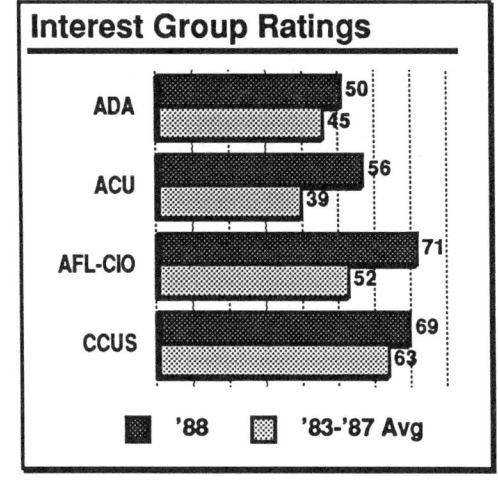

Interest Group Ratings

	'88	'83-'87 Avg
ADA	50	45
ACU	56	39
AFL-CIO	71	52
CCUS	69	63

Labor

Bldg Trades/Industrial/Misc Unions **$10,400**
    Teamsters Union $5,000
    Marine Engineers District 2 Maritime Officers $2,500
    Carpenters & Joiners Union $1,000
    Seafarers International Union $1,000
    Others $900

Government & Postal Workers **$4,400**
    National Assn of Retired Federal Employees $2,000
    National Assn of Letter Carriers $1,000
    Others $1,400

Teachers Unions **$5,300**
    National Education Assn $5,300

Major Ideological/Single-Issue PACs

Armenian-American PAC ....$1,000   Ethnic

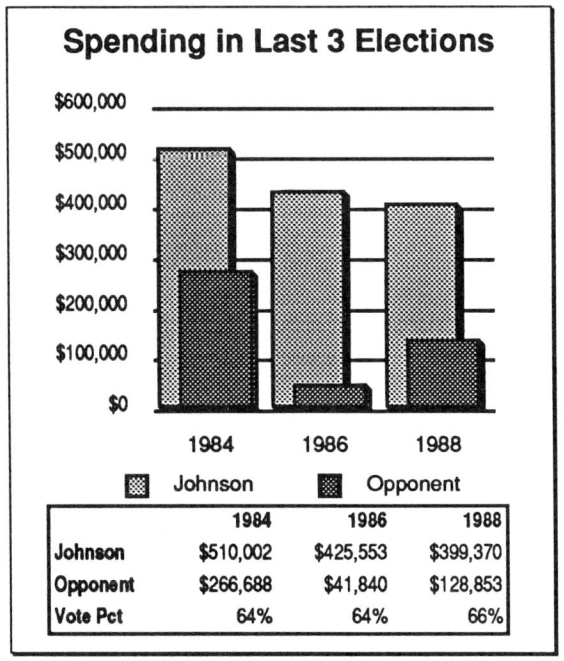

Spending in Last 3 Elections

	1984	1986	1988
Johnson	$510,002	$425,553	$399,370
Opponent	$266,688	$41,840	$128,853
Vote Pct	64%	64%	66%

---

* Contributions came from more than one PAC affiliated with this sponsor.

Tim Johnson, D-SD (At Large)

1988 Committees & Subcommittees

First elected: 1986
Total receipts: $676,225
Total from PACs: $326,696

Agriculture
Conservation, Credit and Rural Development
Forests, Family Farms and Energy
Livestock, Dairy and Poultry
Wheat, Soybeans and Feed Grains

Veterans' Affairs
Compensation, Pension and Insurance
Oversight and Investigations

PAC Contribution Profile

Business

Agricultural Services **$3,100**
American Veterinary Medical Assn $1,500
Others $1,600

Automotive **$2,750**
National Auto Dealers Assn $2,250
Others $500

Commercial Banks/Credit Unions **$8,500**
Citicorp $3,500
Norwest Corp $2,000
American Bankers Assn $1,250
Credit Union National Assn $1,250
Others $500

Dairy **$17,350**
Associated Milk Producers $8,000
Land O'Lakes Inc $4,000
Mid-American Dairymen $3,750
Dairymen Inc $1,350
Others $250

Electric Utilities **$2,500**
ACRE (Action Committee for Rural Electrification) $1,000
Others $1,500

Farm Organizations **$3,300**
Rural Caucus PAC $1,000
Others $2,300

Campaign Revenue Sources

Other (9.5%)
Party (4.4%)
PACs (45.2%)
Individuals (41.0%)

Food & Beverage **$7,350**
A E Staley Manufacturing Company $1,500
American Meat Institute $1,100
General Mills $1,000
Others $3,750

Health Professionals **$16,849**
American Medical Assn $9,999
American Academy of Ophthalmology $2,000
American Dental Assn $1,500
American Nurses Assn $1,000
American Optometric Assn $1,000
Others $1,350

Insurance **$3,800**
National Assn of Life Underwriters $2,500
Others $1,300

Lawyers **$6,000**
Assn of Trial Lawyers of America $5,000
Others $1,000

Poultry & Livestock **$3,600**
None over $800

Real Estate **$8,750**
National Assn of Realtors $8,000
Others $750

Residential Construction **$10,000**
National Assn of Home Builders $10,000

Securities & Commodities Investment **$5,600**
Chicago Mercantile Exchange $1,850
Chicago Board of Trade $1,500
Others $2,250

Sugar Growers **$7,850**
Southern Minnesota Beet Sugar Co-op $1,600
American Crystal Sugar Corp $1,100
American Sugarbeet Growers Assn $1,100
Great Lakes Sugar Beet Growers $1,000
Others $3,050

PAC Totals by Category

Agriculture
Communic/Electronics
Construction
Defense
Energy/Nat Resources
Finance/Insur/Real Est
Health
Ideology/Single-Issue
Labor
Lawyers & Lobbyists
Misc Business
Transportation
Other

$0 $20 $40 $60 $80 $100 $120 $140 $160 $180
Totals in Thousands of Dollars

Telecommunications *$2,500*

 Northwestern Bell Telephone $1,250
 Others $1,250

Other Major Business PACs

American Hospital Assn .... $2,242   Hospitals
National Assn of Social Workers .... $2,000   Social Work
Philip Morris .... $1,500   Tobacco

Labor

Bldg Trades/Industrial/Misc Unions *$81,410*

 Food & Commercial Workers Union $10,000
 Machinists/Aerospace Workers Union $10,000
 United Auto Workers $8,750
 AFL-CIO* $8,500
 Carpenters & Joiners Union $8,500
 Intl Brotherhood of Electrical Workers $7,500
 United Steelworkers $6,500
 Communications Workers of America $5,110
 Operating Engineers Union $3,500
 Sheet Metal Workers Union $3,500
 Laborers' Political League $1,750
 Bakery, Confectionery & Tobacco Workers $1,500
 Ladies Garment Workers Union $1,100
 Amalgamated Clothing & Textile Workers $1,000
 Ironworkers Union $1,000
 Plumbers/Pipefitters Union $1,000
 United Mine Workers $1,000
 Others $1,200

Government & Postal Workers *$41,350*

 American Fedn of State/County/Munic Employees $10,000
 National Assn of Letter Carriers $10,000
 American Postal Workers Union $9,000
 National Assn of Retired Federal Employees $8,000
 National Rural Letter Carriers Assn $2,250
 Others $2,100

Interest Group Ratings

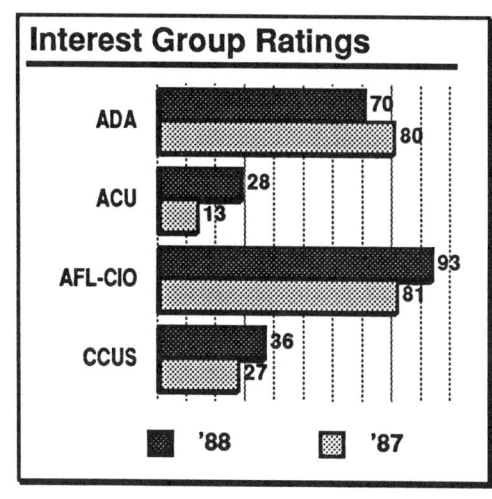

Teachers Unions *$13,000*

 National Education Assn $12,500
 Others $500

Transportation Unions *$28,050*

 Teamsters Union $10,000
 United Transportation Union $5,000
 Air Line Pilots Assn $3,500
 Marine Engineers Union $3,000
 Seafarers International Union $2,250
 Transportation Communication Union $1,350
 Others $2,950

Ideological/Single-Issue

Democratic/Liberal *$6,528*

 National Cmte for an Effective Congress $6,028
 Others $500

Democratic Leadership PACs *$10,000*

 Majority Congress Committee (Jim Wright) $6,000
 Valley Education Fund (Tony Coelho) $3,000
 Cmte for Democratic Opportunity (Bill Gray) $1,000

Pro-Israel *$11,000*

 National PAC $5,000
 Joint Action Cmte for Political Affairs $1,500
 Delaware Valley PAC $1,000
 Roundtable PAC $1,000
 Others $2,500

Other Major Ideological/Single-Issue PACs

National Rifle Assn .... $3,250   Pro-Guns
National Cmte to Preserve Social Security ...... $2,500   Social Secur
Sierra Club .... $1,500   Environment
Council for a Livable World .... $1,108   Pro-Peace
KidsPAC .... $1,000   HealthWelfare
National Council of Senior Citizens .... $1,000   Social Security

Independent expenditures supporting Johnson

National Cmte to Preserve Social Security $3,341

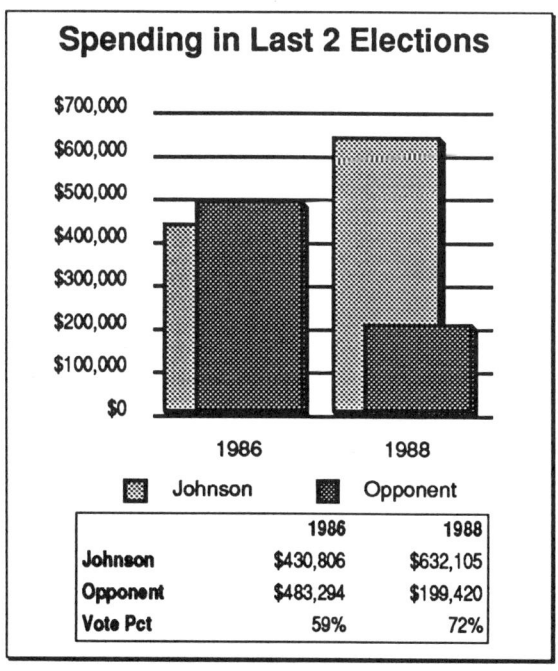

Spending in Last 2 Elections

	1986	1988
Johnson	$430,806	$632,105
Opponent	$483,294	$199,420
Vote Pct	59%	72%

---

* Contributions came from more than one PAC affiliated with this sponsor.

Harry A. Johnston, D-Fla (14)

First elected: 1988
Total receipts: $974,743
Total from PACs: $296,636

1988-1989 Committees & Subcommittees

Foreign Affairs
International Economic Policy and Trade
Western Hemisphere Affairs

Science, Space and Technology
Investigations and Oversight
Science, Research and Technology
Space Science and Applications

PAC Contribution Profile

Business

Automotive	**$6,000**
National Auto Dealers Assn	$5,000
Eaton Corp	$1,000
Commercial Banks	**$12,750**
Barnett Banks of Florida	$7,500
American Bankers Assn	$1,000
Chase Manhattan	$1,000
Sun Banks	$1,000
Others	$2,250
Defense	**$5,000**
United Technologies	$2,000
Martin Marietta Corp	$1,000
Others	$2,000
Food & Beverage	**$8,750**
National Restaurant Assn	$2,000
Pepsi-Cola Bottlers Assn	$2,000
General Mills*	$1,500
Coca-Cola Company	$1,000
Others	$2,250
Health Professionals	**$19,300**
American Academy of Ophthalmology	$4,000
American Medical Assn	$4,000
Florida Medical Assn	$3,500
American Chiropractic Assn	$2,300
American Dental Assn	$1,500
American Optometric Assn	$1,500
American Nurses Assn	$1,000
Others	$1,500

Insurance	**$10,700**
National Assn of Life Underwriters	$10,000
Others	$700
Lawyers & Lobbyists	**$12,750**
Assn of Trial Lawyers of America	$10,000
Holland & Knight	$1,000
Wolf, Block, Schorr, & Solis-Cohen	$1,000
Others	$750
Real Estate	**$10,250**
National Assn of Realtors	$8,000
General Development Corp	$1,000
Others	$1,250
Savings Banks	**$5,750**
Florida League of Financial Institutions	$3,000
US League of Savings Assn	$1,500
Others	$1,250
Securities Investment	**$3,050**
Kidder, Peabody	$2,000
Others	$1,050
Telecommunications	**$8,400**
Southern Bell	$5,000
GTE Corp*	$1,500
AT&T	$1,400
Others	$500

Campaign Revenue Sources

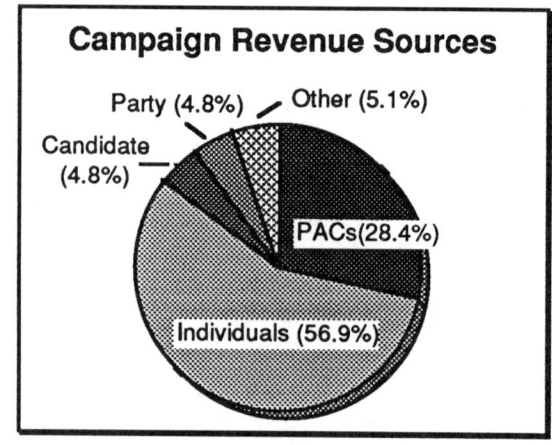

Party (4.8%)
Other (5.1%)
Candidate (4.8%)
PACs (28.4%)
Individuals (56.9%)

Other Major Business PACs

Florida Citrus Mutual	$1,850	Fruit/Veg
Waste Management Inc	$1,500	Waste Mgmt
American Business Products	$1,000	Printing
American Health Care Assn	$1,000	Nursing Home
Associated Builders & Contractors	$1,000	Builders
Associated General Contractors	$1,000	Comml Constr
Associated Milk Producers	$1,000	Dairy
Dairymen Inc	$1,000	Dairy
Florida Power & Light	$1,000	ElectricUtil
Mobil Oil	$1,000	Major Oil
National Assn of Social Workers	$1,000	Social Work
National Assn of Temporary Services	$1,000	EmployAgency
National Assn of Convenience Stores	$1,000	Dept Store

PAC Totals by Category

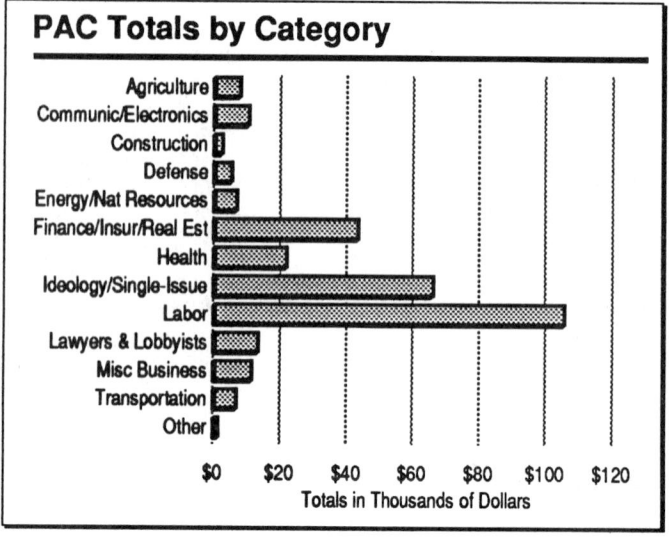

Agriculture
Communic/Electronics
Construction
Defense
Energy/Nat Resources
Finance/Insur/Real Est
Health
Ideology/Single-Issue
Labor
Lawyers & Lobbyists
Misc Business
Transportation
Other

$0 $20 $40 $60 $80 $100 $120

Totals in Thousands of Dollars

Labor

Bldg Trades/Industrial/Misc Unions $35,450

AFL-CIO $5,000
Communications Workers of America $5,000
Intl Brotherhood of Electrical Workers* $5,000
Machinists/Aerospace Workers Union $5,000
United Auto Workers $5,000
Laborers' Political League $2,500
Food/Commercial Workers Local #1222 .... $2,000
Plumbers/Pipefitters Union* $2,000
Carpenters & Joiners Union $1,750
Sheet Metal Workers Union $1,000
Others $1,200

Government & Postal Workers $23,500

National Assn of Letter Carriers $10,000
National Assn of Retired Federal Employees $6,000
American Fedn of State/County/Munic Employees $5,000
American Postal Workers Union $1,000
National Rural Letter Carriers Assn $1,000
Others $500

Teachers Unions $14,000

National Education Assn $10,000
American Federation of Teachers $4,000

Transportation Unions $32,000

Teamsters Union $10,000
Seafarers International Union $6,500
Marine Engineers Union* $6,000
Air Line Pilots Assn $5,000
Amalgamated Transit Union $1,000
Transport Workers Union $1,000
United Transportation Union $1,000
Others $1,500

Ideological/Single-Issue

Democratic/Liberal $7,248

National Cmte for Effective Congress $4,998
Teamwork America $1,000
Others $1,250

Democratic Leadership PACs $24,000

Valley Education Fund (Tony Coelho) $10,000
Majority Congress Committee (Jim Wright) $5,000
America's Leaders' Fund (Dan Rostenkowski) $3,000
Cmte for Democratic Opportunity (Bill Gray) $3,000
Democratic Congressional Fund (Joe Moakley) $1,000
House Leadership Fund (Tom Foley) $1,000
Independent Action (Morris Udall) $1,000

Pro-Choice $4,143

Voters for Choice/Friends of Family Planning $2,500
National Abortion Rights Action League $1,643

Pro-Israel $9,850

National Action Committee (NACPAC) $2,500
Women's Pro-Israel National PAC $2,500
Delaware Valley PAC $1,000
Joint Action Cmte for Political Afairs $1,000
Others $2,850

Senior Citizens/Social Security $6,000

National Cmte to Preserve Social Security $5,000
National Council of Senior Citizens $1,000

Other Major Ideological/Single-Issue PACs

Human Rights Campaign Fund .... $9,940   Gay Rights
Free Cuba PAC .... $1,000   Anti-Castro
Handgun Control Inc .... $1,000   Anti-Guns
Ohio Freeze Voter .... $1,000   Pro-Peace

Independent expenditures supporting Johnston

National Cmte to Preserve Social Security $7,986

Spending in Last Election

	1988
Johnston	$971,025
Opponent	$780,277
Vote Pct	55%

---

* Contributions came from more than one PAC affiliated
with this sponsor.

Ben Jones, D-Ga (4)

1988-1989 Committees & Subcommittees

Public Works and Transportation
Aviation
Surface Transportation
Water Resources

Veterans' Affairs
Compensation, Pension and Insurance
Housing and Memorial Affairs

PAC Contribution Profile

Business

Automotive	*$3,000*
National Auto Dealers Assn	$2,000
Others	$1,000
Commercial Banks	*$4,230*
Trust Company of Georgia	$1,100
First Atlanta Corp	$1,000
Others	$2,130
Commercial Fishing	*$4,000*
National Fisheries Institute	$4,000
Dairy	*$3,000*
Associated Milk Producers	$2,000
Dairymen Inc-Georgia	$1,000
Electric Utilities	*$3,900*
ACRE (Action Committee for Rural Electrification)	$3,000
Others	$900
Health Professionals	*$11,000*
American Nurses Assn	$4,000
American Medical Assn	$3,000
American Dental Assn	$1,500
American Academy of Ophthalmology	$1,000
Others	$1,500
Lawyers	*$7,950*
Assn of Trial Lawyers of America	$7,000
Others	$950

Real Estate	*$4,000*
National Assn of Realtors	$3,500
Others	$500

Other Major Business PACs

Coca-Cola Company	$1,500	Soft Drinks
Atlanta Gas Light Company	$1,000	Natural Gas

First elected: 1988
Total receipts: $522,594
Total from PACs: $265,606

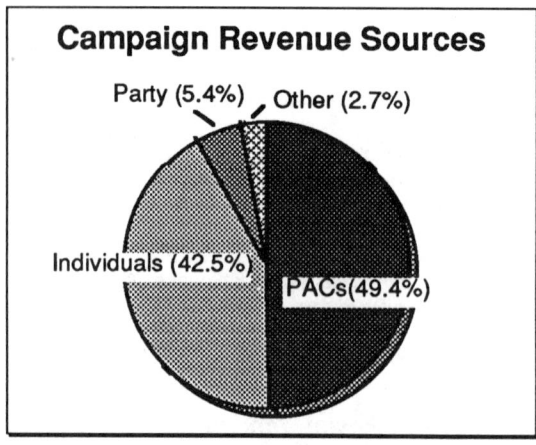

Campaign Revenue Sources

Party (5.4%) · Other (2.7%)
Individuals (42.5%)
PACs (49.4%)

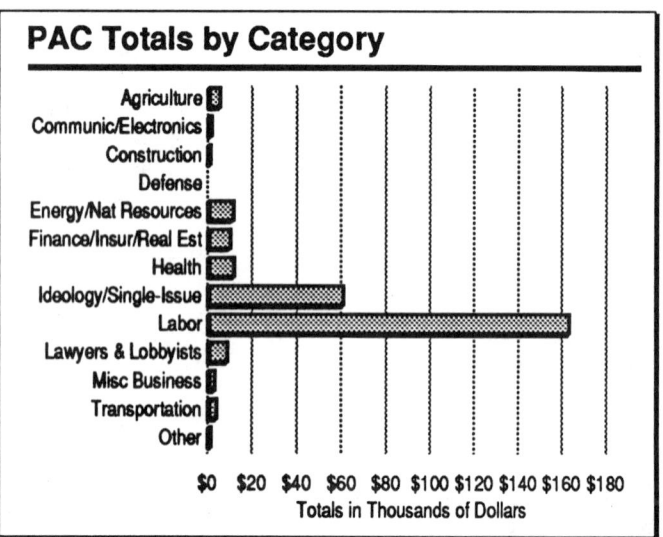

PAC Totals by Category

Agriculture
Communic/Electronics
Construction
Defense
Energy/Nat Resources
Finance/Insur/Real Est
Health
Ideology/Single-Issue
Labor
Lawyers & Lobbyists
Misc Business
Transportation
Other

$0 $20 $40 $60 $80 $100 $120 $140 $160 $180
Totals in Thousands of Dollars

Labor

Bldg Trades/Industrial/Misc Unions **$94,750**

Communications Workers of America	$10,000
Intl Brotherhood of Electrical Workers	$10,000
Machinists/Aerospace Workers Union	$10,000
United Auto Workers	$10,000
United Steelworkers	$10,000
AFL-CIO	$9,500
Food & Commercial Workers Union	$9,000
Sheet Metal Workers Union	$7,500
Carpenters & Joiners Union	$5,500
Plumbers/Pipefitters Union	$3,500
Laborers' Political League	$2,000
Rubber Cork Linoleum Plastic Workers	$2,000
Graphic Communications Union	$1,000
Ladies Garment Workers Union	$1,000
Operating Engineers Union	$1,000
Service Employees International Union	$1,000
Others	$1,750

Government & Postal Workers **$29,250**

American Fedn of State/County/Munic Employees	$10,000
National Assn of Letter Carriers	$10,000
National Assn of Retired Federal Employees	$6,000
American Postal Workers Union	$1,000
National Rural Letter Carriers Assn	$1,000
National Treasury Employees Union	$1,000
Others	$250

Teachers Unions **$15,000**

National Education Assn	$10,000
American Federation of Teachers	$5,000

Transportation Unions **$23,250**

Teamsters Union	$10,000
Amalgamated Transit Union	$3,000
Air Line Pilots Assn	$2,500
Seafarers International Union	$2,500
United Transportation Union	$1,500
Marine Engineers District 2 Maritime Officers	$1,000
Transport Workers Union	$1,000
Others	$1,750

Ideological/Single-Issue

Democratic/Liberal **$11,748**

National Cmte for an Effective Congress	$9,998
Democratic Study Group Campaign Fund	$1,000
Others	$750

Democratic Leadership PACs **$19,500**

Valley Education Fund (Tony Coelho)	$6,000
House Leadership Fund (Tom Foley)	$3,000
Majority Congress Committee (Jim Wright)	$3,000
America's Leaders' Fund (Dan Rostenkowski)	$2,000
Cmte for Democratic Opportunity (Bill Gray)	$2,000
Pax Americas (David Bonior)	$1,500
Empire Leadership Fund (Mario Cuomo)	$1,000
Independent Action (Morris Udall)	$1,000

Pro-Choice **$4,744**

National Abortion Rights Action League	$2,744
Voters for Choice/Friends of Family Planning	$2,000

Pro-Israel **$9,250**

National PAC	$5,000
Joint Action Cmte for Political Affairs	$1,000
Women's Pro-Israel National PAC	$1,000
Others	$2,250

Senior Citizens/Social Security **$7,000**

National Cmte to Preserve Social Security	$5,000
National Council of Senior Citizens	$2,000

Other Major Ideological/Single-Issue PACs

Sierra Club	$5,000	Environment
Handgun Control Inc	$1,000	Anti-Guns

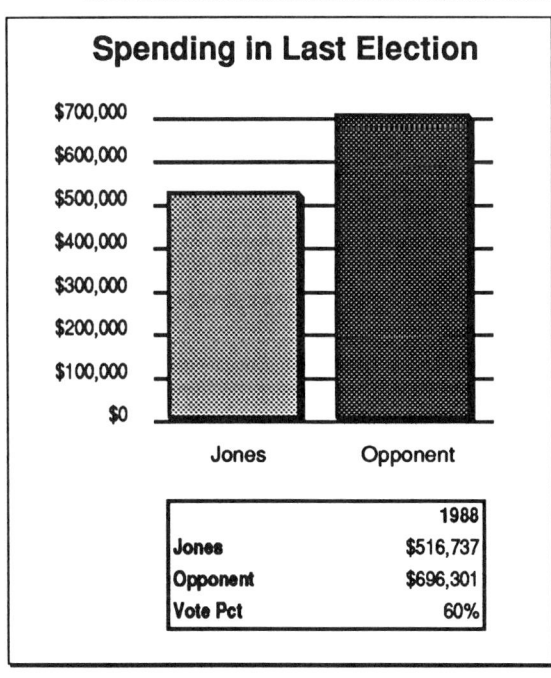

Spending in Last Election

	1988
Jones	$516,737
Opponent	$696,301
Vote Pct	60%

Walter B. Jones, D-NC (1)

First elected: 1966
Total receipts: $141,476
Total from PACs: $96,550

1988 Committees & Subcommittees

Agriculture
Tobacco and Peanuts
Wheat, Soybeans and Feed Grains

Merchant Marine and Fisheries (Chairman)
Merchant Marine (Chairman)

PAC Contribution Profile

Business

Auto Dealers **$3,000**
    National Auto Dealers Assn $3,000

Construction **$2,000**
    National Utility Contractors Assn $2,000

Dairy **$2,500**
    Associated Milk Producers $1,500
    Dairymen Inc-North Carolina $1,000

Defense **$2,500**
    Colt Industries $1,000
    Others $1,500

Electric Utilities **$2,250**
    None over $750

Food & Beverage **$1,500**
    Pepsico Inc $1,000
    Others $500

Health Professionals **$2,500**
    American Medical Assn $2,500

Insurance **$1,500**
    Jefferson-Pilot Corp $1,000
    Others $500

Lawyers **$6,750**
    Assn of Trial Lawyers of America $5,000
    Others $1,750

Oil & Gas **$8,750**
    Zapata Corp $1,500
    BP America $1,000
    Others $6,250

Real Estate **$4,000**
    National Assn of Realtors $3,000
    First Union Corp $1,000

Sea Transport **$14,000**
    American Pilots Assn $4,500
    Totem Ocean Trailer Express $1,500
    American President Lines $1,000
    Matson Navigation $1,000
    United States Lines $1,000
    Others $5,000

Sugar Growers **$1,500**
    American Crystal Sugar Corp $1,000
    American Sugar Cane League $500

Telecommunications **$4,500**
    Southern Bell $2,000
    United Telecommunications $2,000
    Others $500

Tobacco **$5,200**
    Philip Morris $2,000
    RJR Nabisco $2,000
    Others $1,200

Other Major Business PACs

Weyerhaeuser Company* .... $1,000   Forestry

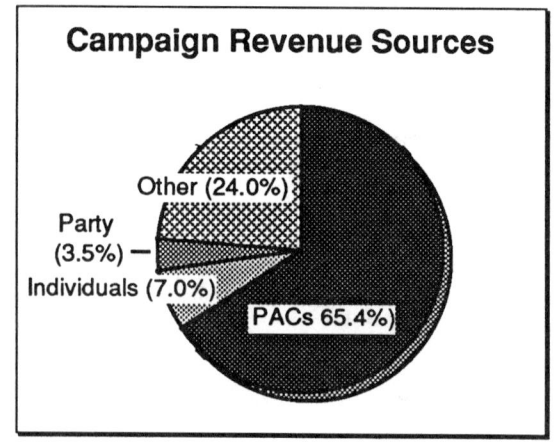

Campaign Revenue Sources

Other (24.0%)
Party (3.5%)
Individuals (7.0%)
PACs 65.4%

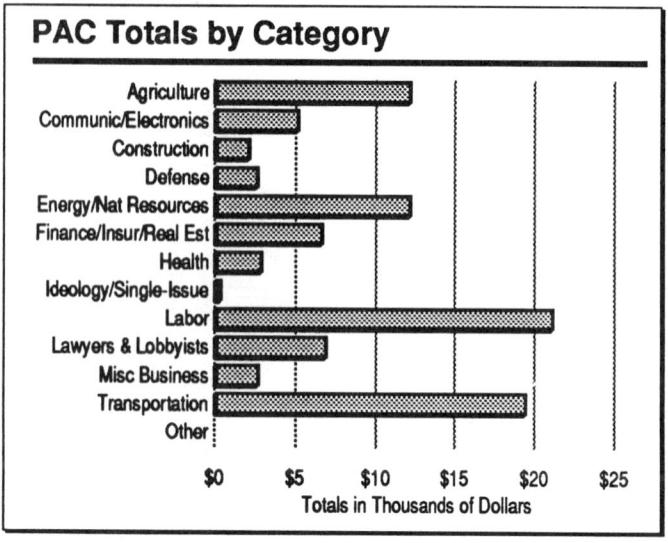

PAC Totals by Category

Agriculture
Communic/Electronics
Construction
Defense
Energy/Nat Resources
Finance/Insur/Real Est
Health
Ideology/Single-Issue
Labor
Lawyers & Lobbyists
Misc Business
Transportation
Other

$0 $5 $10 $15 $20 $25
Totals in Thousands of Dollars

Labor

Bldg Trades/Industrial/Misc Unions $7,000
        Carpenters & Joiners Union $2,000
        National Education Assn $2,000
        National Assn of Letter Carriers $1,000
        Others $2,000

Sea Transport Unions.....................................$14,000
        Marine Engineers Union* $9,000
        Seafarers International Union $2,500
        International Longshoremen Assn $1,000
        Masters, Mates & Pilots Union $1,000
        Others $500

Independent expenditures supporting Jones

National Cmte to Preserve Social Security $2,565

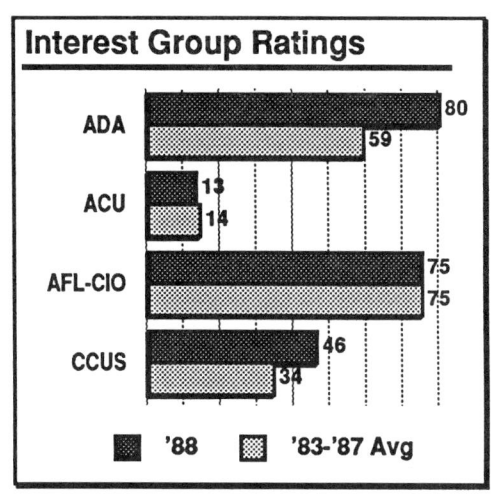

Interest Group Ratings

	'88	'83-'87 Avg
ADA	80	59
ACU	13	14
AFL-CIO	75	75
CCUS	46	34

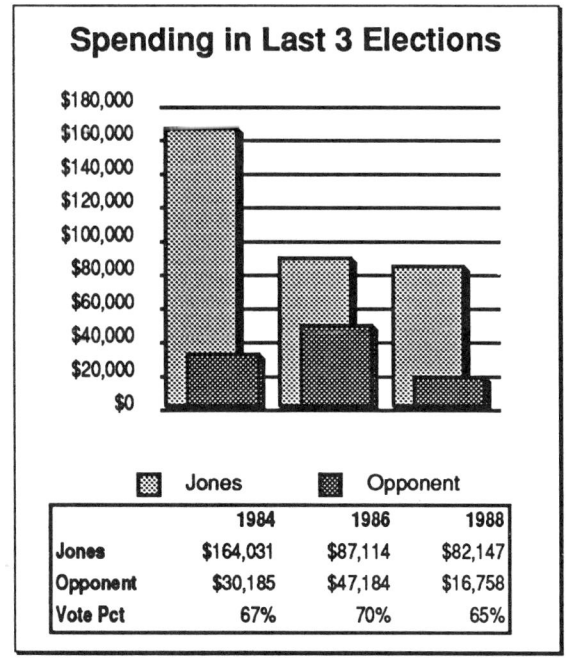

Spending in Last 3 Elections

	1984	1986	1988
Jones	$164,031	$87,114	$82,147
Opponent	$30,185	$47,184	$16,758
Vote Pct	67%	70%	65%

Jones   Opponent

* Contributions came from more than one PAC affiliated
with this sponsor.

Jim Jontz, D-Ind (5)

1988 Committees & Subcommittees

First elected: 1986
Total receipts: $721,637
Total from PACs: $471,225

Agriculture
Conservation, Credit and Rural Development
Forests, Family Farms and Energy
Wheat, Soybeans and Feed Grains

Education and Labor
Employment Opportunities
Labor-Management Relations

Veterans' Affairs
Education, Training and Employment

Select Aging
Retirement Income and Employment

PAC Contribution Profile

Business

Commercial Banks/Credit Unions **$8,555**
    American Bankers Assn $5,500
    Credit Union National Assn $1,150
    Others $1,905

Construction **$8,300**
    National Assn of Home Builders $7,500
    Others $800

Dairy & Eggs **$19,600**
    Associated Milk Producers $8,500
    Mid-American Dairymen $4,600
    Dairymen Inc $2,200
    Milk Marketing Inc $1,400
    United Egg Assn $1,150
    Others $1,750

Food & Beverage **$9,600**
    General Mills* $2,000
    Joseph E Seagram & Sons $1,500
    A E Staley Manufacturing Company $1,350
    American Meat Institute $1,250
    Others $3,500

Health Professionals **$16,950**
    American Medical Assn $3,250
    American Academy of Ophthalmology $2,500
    American Podiatry Assn $2,500
    National Assn of Pharmacists $2,000
    American Physical Therapy Assn $1,900
    American Nurses Assn $1,500
    Others $3,300

Campaign Revenue Sources

Party (5.6%)
Other (7.3%)
Individuals (27.5%)
PACs (59.6%)

Insurance **$9,600**
    National Assn of Life Underwriters $7,000
    Others $2,600

Lawyers **$16,250**
    Assn of Trial Lawyers of America $15,000
    Others $1,250

Real Estate **$11,000**
    National Assn of Realtors $11,000

Other Major Business PACs

National Assn of Trade/Tech Schools	$2,650	Voc Tech
ACRE (Action Committee for Rural Electric)	$2,500	RuralElect
National Assn of Social Workers	$2,500	Social Work
Superior Training Services	$2,200	Voc Tech
American Sugarbeet Growers Assn	$1,800	Sugar
American Crystal Sugar Corp	$1,650	Sugar
Philip Morris	$1,600	Tobacco
Chicago Board of Trade	$1,500	Commodities
Chicago Mercantile Exchange	$1,500	Commodities
Chrysler Corp	$1,450	Auto Manfr
Alabama Farm Bureau Federation	$1,350	Farm Orgs
American Hospital Assn	$1,350	Hospitals
Indiana ACRE	$1,350	RuralElect
Southern Minnesota Beet Sugar Co-op	$1,350	Sugar
National Council of Farmer Co-ops	$1,150	Farm Orgs
Rockwell International	$1,150	Air Defense

PAC Totals by Category

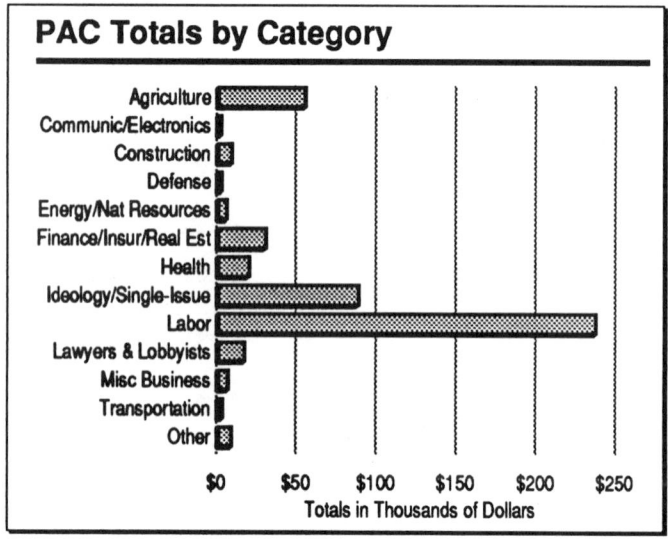

Agriculture
Communic/Electronics
Construction
Defense
Energy/Nat Resources
Finance/Insur/Real Est
Health
Ideology/Single-Issue
Labor
Lawyers & Lobbyists
Misc Business
Transportation
Other

$0 $50 $100 $150 $200 $250
Totals in Thousands of Dollars

Labor

Bldg Trades/Industrial/Misc Unions $126,750

AFL-CIO*	$10,500
Food & Commercial Workers Union	$10,000
Intl Brotherhood of Electrical Workers	$10,000
Machinists/Aerospace Workers Union	$10,000
Sheet Metal Workers Union	$10,000
United Auto Workers	$10,000
United Steelworkers	$10,000
Carpenters & Joiners Union	$8,100
Communications Workers of America	$7,800
Operating Engineers Union*	$6,250
United Mine Workers	$6,250
Service Employees International Union	$5,000
Laborers' Political League	$2,250
Plasterers/Cement Masons Union	$2,250
Bakery Confect & Tobacco Workers	$2,000
Rubber Cork Linoleum Plastic Workers	$2,000
Electronic Machine Furniture Workers	$1,750
Ladies Garment Workers Union	$1,550
Plumbers/Pipefitters Union	$1,500
United Paperworkers	$1,500
Oil, Chemical & Atomic Workers Union	$1,300
Boilermakers Union	$1,200
Painters & Allied Trades Union	$1,200
Others	$4,350

Government & Postal Workers $44,600

American Fedn of State/County/Munic Employees	$10,000
National Assn of Letter Carriers	$10,000
National Assn of Retired Federal Employees	$8,000
American Postal Workers Union	$6,500
National Rural Letter Carriers Assn	$4,050
American Federation of Government Employees	$1,950
International Assn of Firefighters	$1,500
Others	$2,600

Teachers Unions $20,000

American Federation of Teachers	$10,000
National Education Assn	$10,000

Transportation Unions $45,100

Teamsters Union	$10,000
Marine Engineers Union*	$9,100
Air Line Pilots Assn	$9,000
Amalgamated Transit Union	$4,500

(Continued in next column)

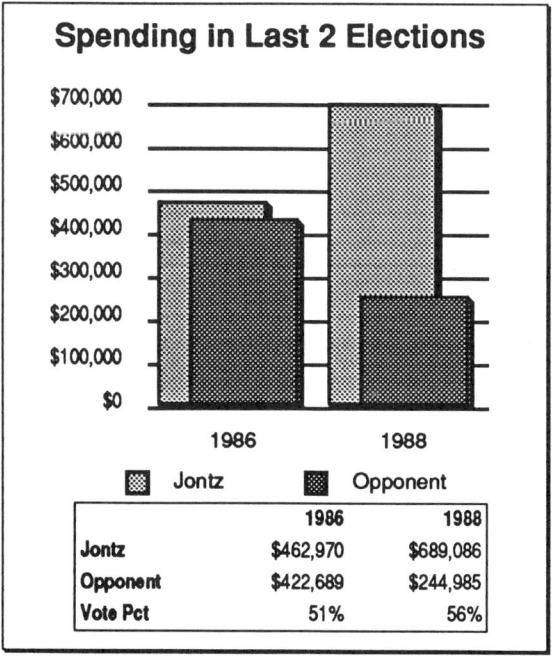

Spending in Last 2 Elections

	1986	1988
Jontz	$462,970	$689,086
Opponent	$422,689	$244,985
Vote Pct	51%	56%

Legend: ▨ Jontz   ▪ Opponent

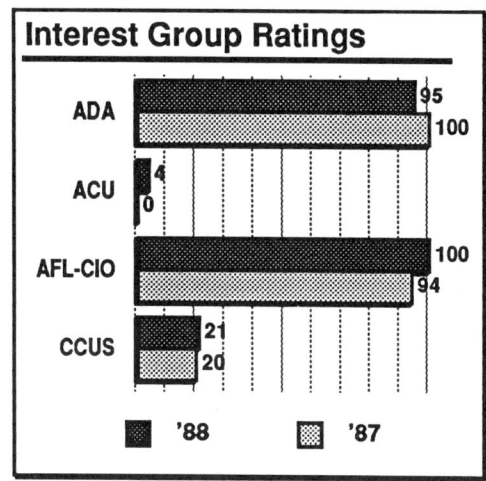

Interest Group Ratings

	'88	'87
ADA	95	100
ACU	4	0
AFL-CIO	100	94
CCUS	21	20

Legend: ■ '88   ▨ '87

Transportation Unions (cont'd)

Seafarers International Union	$3,600
Transportation Communication Union	$2,350
United Transportation Union	$2,150
International Longshoremen Assn	$1,300
Brotherhood of RR Signalmen	$1,050
Others	$2,050

Ideological/Single-Issue

Democratic/Liberal $20,896

National Cmte for an Effective Congress	$9,996
Class PAC	$5,000
Hollywood Womens Political Cmte	$3,500
Americans for Democratic Action	$1,500
Others	$900

Democratic Leadership PACs..................................$25,150

Valley Education Fund (Tony Coelho)	$8,000
24th Cong Dist of California PAC (Henry Waxman)	$5,000
Cmte for the 100th Congress (Charles Rangel)	$3,000
Majority Congress Committee (Jim Wright)	$3,000
Independent Action (Morris Udall)	$2,000
Cmte for Democratic Opportunity (Bill Gray)	$1,300
Others	$2,850

Pro-Israel $11,000

National PAC	$5,000
Joint Action Cmte for Political Affairs	$2,000
Roundtable PAC	$1,500
Others	$2,500

Other Major Ideological/Single-Issue PACs

Sierra Club	$9,871	Environment
National Rifle Assn	$5,450	Pro-Guns
National Cmte to Preserve Social Security	$3,950	Social Secur
KidsPAC	$2,000	HealthWelfare
Friends of the Earth	$1,809	Environment
National Council of Senior Citizens	$1,700	Social Secur
Voters for Choice/Friends of Family Planning	$1,500	Pro-Choice
Council for a Livable World	$1,261	Pro-Peace
Ohio Freeze Voter	$1,206	Pro-Peace
League of Conservation Voters	$1,100	Environment

Independent expenditures supporting Jontz

National Cmte to Preserve Social Security	$1,220

Independent expenditures opposing Jontz

Council for National Defense	$6,044

---

* Contributions came from more than one PAC affiliated with this sponsor.

Paul E. Kanjorski, D-Pa (11)

First elected: 1984
Total receipts: $431,513
Total from PACs: $286,370

1988 Committees & Subcommittees

Banking, Finance and Urban Affairs
Economic Stabilization
Financial Institutions Supervision, Regulation and Insurance
General Oversight and Investigations
Housing and Community Development

Science, Space and Technology
Energy Research and Development
Science, Research and Technology

Veterans' Affairs
Hospitals and Health Care

PAC Contribution Profile

Business

Aerospace	**$3,000**
Long Island Aerospace PAC	$2,000
TRW Inc	$1,000
Automotive	**$2,500**
National Auto Dealers Assn	$2,000
Chrysler Corp	$500
Commercial Banks	**$43,650**
American Bankers Assn	$5,000
Citicorp	$5,000
Marine Midland Banks	$2,250
Barnett Banks of Florida	$2,000
Pennsylvania Bankers Assn	$2,000
Chemical Bank	$1,750
First Chicago Corp	$1,750
Independent Bankers Assn	$1,750
United Penn Bank	$1,650
Bankers Trust	$1,500
Assn of Bank Holding Companies	$1,250
Citizens & Southern National Bank	$1,250
Meridian Bancorp	$1,250
Pittsburgh National Bank	$1,250
Philadelphia National Corp	$1,200
Mellon Bank	$1,150
First Bank System/Minnesota	$1,000
First Pennsylvania Corp	$1,000
Midlantic National Bank	$1,000
Others	$8,650
Construction	**$7,250**
National Assn of Home Builders	$3,500
Owens-Illinois	$2,000
National Concrete Masonry Assn	$1,000
Others	$750

Campaign Revenue Sources

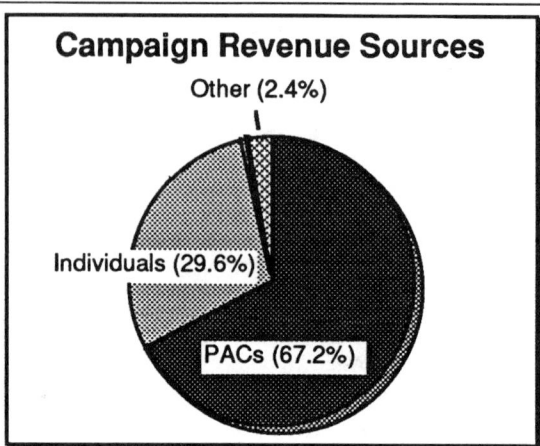

Other (2.4%)
Individuals (29.6%)
PACs (67.2%)

PAC Totals by Category

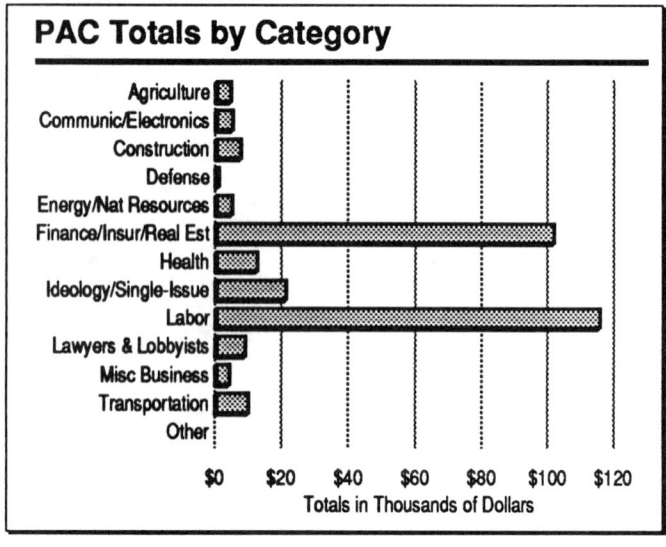

Agriculture
Communic/Electronics
Construction
Defense
Energy/Nat Resources
Finance/Insur/Real Est
Health
Ideology/Single-Issue
Labor
Lawyers & Lobbyists
Misc Business
Transportation
Other

$0 $20 $40 $60 $80 $100 $120
Totals in Thousands of Dollars

Dairy	**$3,000**
Associated Milk Producers	$1,500
Mid-American Dairymen	$1,000
Others	$500
Electric Utilities	**$3,150**
ACRE (Action Committee for Rural Electrification)	$1,750
Philadelphia Electric	$1,000
Others	$400
Health Professionals	**$9,495**
American Medical Assn	$8,000
Others	$1,495
Insurance	**$23,550**
National Assn of Life Underwriters	$8,250
National Assn Mutual Insurance Agents	$3,750
Casualty & Surety Agents Assn	$2,000
Capital Holding Corp	$1,250
Mortgage Insurance Companies of America	$1,250
Cigna Corp	$1,050
American Council of Life Insurance	$1,000
Independent Insurance Agents of America	$1,000
Prudential Insurance	$1,000
Others	$3,000
Lawyers & Lobbyists	**$8,450**
Assn of Trial Lawyers of America	$5,000
National Action Committee (Dave Evans)	$1,750
Others	$1,700
Real Estate	**$11,200**
National Assn of Realtors	$8,700
Mortgage Bankers Assn of America	$1,750
Others	$750
Savings Banks & Credit Unions	**$12,250**
Credit Union National Assn	$5,000
US League of Savings Assn	$2,000
Pennsylvania Savings League	$1,950
National Council of Savings Institutions	$1,500
National Assn of Federal Credit Unions	$1,000
Others	$800

Securities Investment **$9,500**

- First Boston Corp $2,000
- Goldman Sachs $2,000
- Prudential-Bache Securities $2,000
- Municipal Securitites Industry $1,500
- Morgan Stanley & Company $1,000
- Others $1,000

Telecommunications **$4,700**

- AT&T $1,500
- Bell Telephone of Pennsylvania $1,500
- Continental Telecom $750
- C-Tec Corp $700
- Others $250

Trucking/Delivery **$4,010**

- American Trucking Assns $2,810
- United Parcel Service $1,200

Other Major Business PACs

Merck & Company	$1,300	Pharmaceut
American Textile Manufacturers Institute	$1,000	Textiles

Labor

Bldg Trades/Industrial/Misc Unions **$50,450**

- United Auto Workers $8,000
- United Steelworkers $7,500
- Carpenters & Joiners Union $5,500
- Comm Workers Union Local #13000 .... $5,000
- Machinists/Aerospace Workers Union $4,500
- Intl Brotherhood of Electrical Workers $3,250
- Plumbers/Pipefitters Union* $2,700
- Food & Commercial Workers Union $2,500
- Sheet Metal Workers Union $2,500
- Laborers' Political League $2,000
- Operating Engineers Union $1,500
- Ladies Garment Workers Union $1,250
- AFL-CIO $1,000
- Boilermakers Union $1,000
- Others $2,250

Spending in Last 3 Elections

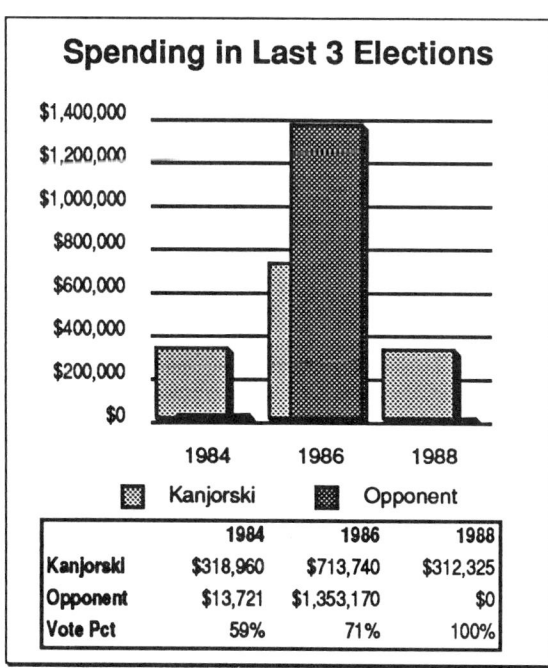

	1984	1986	1988
Kanjorski	$318,960	$713,740	$312,325
Opponent	$13,721	$1,353,170	$0
Vote Pct	59%	71%	100%

Interest Group Ratings

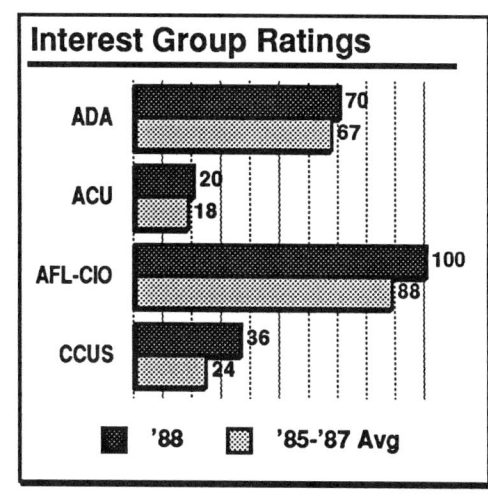

ADA 70 / 67
ACU 20 / 18
AFL-CIO 100 / 88
CCUS 36 / 24

■ '88   ▨ '85-'87 Avg

Government & Postal Workers **$28,800**

- National Assn of Retired Federal Employees $10,000
- National Assn of Letter Carriers $9,000
- American Fedn of State/County/Munic Employees .. $6,000
- American Postal Workers Union $2,500
- Others $1,300

Teachers Unions **$3,000**

- National Education Assn $3,000

Transportation Unions **$32,800**

- Teamsters Union* $11,000
- Seafarers International Union $6,000
- Marine Engineers Union* $5,000
- United Transportation Union $2,300
- Air Line Pilots Assn $2,000
- Brotherhood of Locomotive Engineers $1,250
- Transportation Communication Union $1,250
- Maintenance of Way Employees $1,000
- Transport Workers Union $1,000
- Others $2,000

Ideological/Single-Issue

Pro-Israel **$5,750**

- National PAC $5,000
- Others $750

Other Major Ideological/Single-Issue PACs

National Rifle Assn	$9,950	Pro-Guns
National Cmte to Preserve Social Security	$5,000	Social Secur

Independent expenditures supporting Kanjorski

National Cmte to Preserve Social Security $3,510

---

* Contributions came from more than one PAC affiliated with this sponsor.

Marcy Kaptur, D-Ohio (9)

First elected: 1982
Total receipts: $277,724
Total from PACs: $201,740

1988 Committees & Subcommittees

Banking, Finance and Urban Affairs
Economic Stabilization
Financial Institutions Supervision, Regulation and Insurance
Housing and Community Development

Veterans' Affairs
Housing and Memorial Affairs (Chairman)
Education, Training and Employment

PAC Contribution Profile

Business

Automotive	**$3,225**
Chrysler Corp	$1,800
Others	$1,425
Construction	**$9,425**
Owens-Illinois	$3,500
National Assn of Home Builders	$2,000
Owens-Corning Fiberglas	$1,525
Manville Corp	$1,500
Others	$900
Dairy	**$2,500**
Mid-American Dairymen	$1,100
Others	$1,400
Financial Institutions	**$16,750**
US League of Savings Assn	$3,500
Credit Union National Assn	$2,800
Ohio Savings Assns League	$2,250
Independent Bankers Assn	$2,100
Citicorp	$2,000
National Assn of Federal Credit Unions	$1,500
American Bankers Assn	$1,000
Others	$1,600
Insurance	**$17,850**
National Assn of Life Underwriters	$7,500
Independent Insurance Agents of America	$6,200
Massachusetts Mutual Life Insurance	$1,100
Others	$3,050

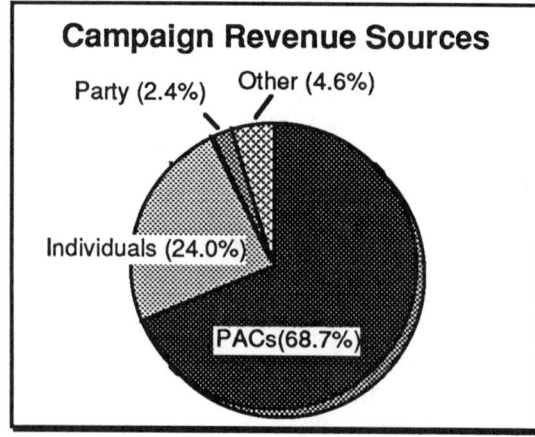

Campaign Revenue Sources

Party (2.4%)
Other (4.6%)
Individuals (24.0%)
PACs (68.7%)

Real Estate	**$10,700**
National Assn of Realtors	$8,000
Mortgage Bankers Assn of America	$2,100
Others	$600
Securities Investment	**$6,000**
Morgan Stanley & Company	$1,500
Prudential-Bache Securities	$1,000
Salomon Brothers	$1,000
Others	$2,500
Sugar Growers	**$3,050**
American Sugarbeet Growers Assn	$1,500
Others	$1,550

Other Major Business PACs

Precision Metalforming Assn	$2,000	MetalProduct
Ohio Farm Bureau Federation	$1,200	Farm Orgs
Libbey-Owens-Ford	$1,000	Glass Prod

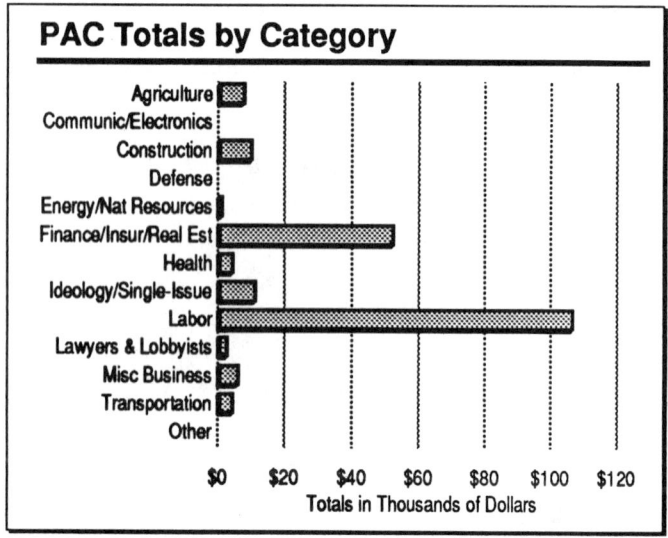

PAC Totals by Category

Agriculture
Communic/Electronics
Construction
Defense
Energy/Nat Resources
Finance/Insur/Real Est
Health
Ideology/Single-Issue
Labor
Lawyers & Lobbyists
Misc Business
Transportation
Other

$0 $20 $40 $60 $80 $100 $120
Totals in Thousands of Dollars

Labor

Bldg Trades/Industrial/Misc Unions $59,100

United Auto Workers	$10,000
Carpenters & Joiners Union	$6,200
Sheet Metal Workers Union	$6,000
Machinists/Aerospace Workers Union	$5,600
Heat/Frost/Asbestos Workers Union	$5,000
Operating Engineers Union	$3,100
Ironworkers Union	$3,000
Boilermakers Union*	$2,400
Food & Commercial Workers Union	$2,400
AFL-CIO*	$2,300
Communications Workers of America	$2,300
Laborers' Political League	$1,800
Intl Brotherhood of Electrical Workers	$1,500
Ladies Garment Workers Union	$1,500
Plumbers/Pipefitters Union*	$1,500
Rubber Cork Linoleum Plastic Workers	$1,000
United Steelworkers	$1,000
Others	$2,500

Government & Postal Workers $15,000

National Assn of Retired Federal Employees	$8,000
National Assn of Letter Carriers	$3,600
American Postal Workers Union	$2,100
American Fedn of State/County/Munic Employees	$1,000
Others	$300

Teachers Unions $5,300

National Education Assn	$5,300

Transportation Unions $26,500

Marine Engineers District 2 Maritime Officers	$7,000
International Longshoremen Assn	$5,800
Teamsters Union	$5,000
United Transportation Union	$2,650
Amalgamated Transit Union	$1,500
Seafarers International Union	$1,500
Brotherhood of Railroad Signalmen	$1,300
Others	$1,750

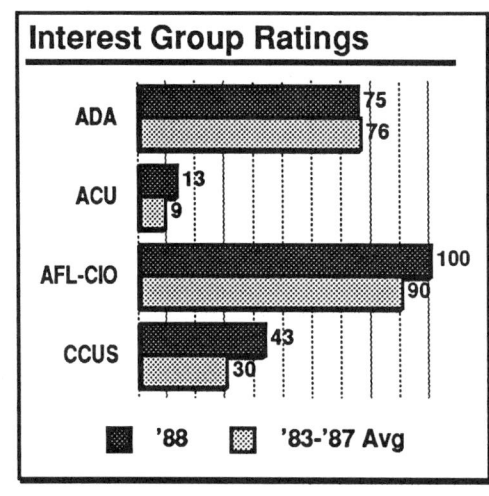

Interest Group Ratings

	'88	'83-'87 Avg
ADA	75	76
ACU	13	9
AFL-CIO	100	90
CCUS	43	30

■ '88   ▨ '83-'87 Avg

Ideological/Single-Issue

Democratic Leadership PACs $6,000

Majority Congress Committee (Jim Wright)	$5,000
Valley Education Fund (Tony Coelho)	$1,000

Other Major Ideological/Single-Issue $4,499

National Cmte for an Effective Congress	$2,499	Dem/Liberal
National Council of Senior Citizens	$1,000	Soc Secur
Others	$1,000	

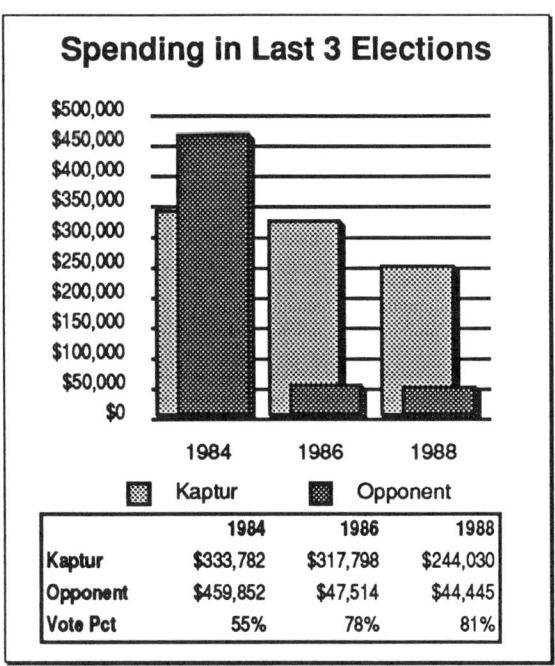

Spending in Last 3 Elections

▨ Kaptur   ■ Opponent

	1984	1986	1988
Kaptur	$333,782	$317,798	$244,030
Opponent	$459,852	$47,514	$44,445
Vote Pct	55%	78%	81%

* Contributions came from more than one PAC affiliated with this sponsor.

John R. Kasich, R-Ohio (12)

First elected: 1982
Total receipts: $370,579
Total from PACs: $130,486

1988 Committees & Subcommittees

Armed Services
Readiness (Ranking Republican)
Investigations

Campaign Revenue Sources

Other (6.9%)
Party (0.6%)
PACs(34.3%)
Individuals (58.3%)

PAC Contribution Profile

Business

Auto Dealers	**$8,750**
National Auto Dealers Assn	$4,750
Auto Dealers & Drivers for Free Trade	$4,000
Commercial & Savings Banks	**$5,250**
Banc One Corp	$1,000
Huntington Bancshares	$1,000
Ohio Bankers Assn	$1,000
Ohio Savings Assns League	$1,000
Others	$1,250
Construction	**$4,000**
National Electrical Contractors Assn	$1,000
Others	$3,000
Dairy	**$5,250**
Associated Milk Producers	$4,000
Others	$1,250
Defense	**$22,450**
AT&T	$4,000
Rockwell International	$2,000
Harsco Corp	$1,500
Lockheed Corp	$1,250
FMC Corp	$1,000
General Dynamics	$1,000
General Electric	$1,000
McDonnell Douglas*	$1,000
Textron Inc	$1,000
Others	$8,700

Electric Utilities	**$3,500**
American Electric Power*	$2,500
Others	$1,000
Food & Beverage	**$4,300**
Food Marketing Institute	$1,500
Others	$2,800
Health Professionals	**$6,750**
American Medical Assn	$3,000
American Dental Assn	$2,000
American Academy of Ophthalmology	$1,000
Others	$750
Insurance	**$7,050**
Nationwide Corp	$3,300
National Assn of Life Underwriters	$2,000
Independent Insurance Agents of America	$1,250
Others	$500
Lawyers	**$9,200**
Assn of Trial Lawyers of America	$5,000
Baker & Hostetler	$2,000
Bricker & Eckler	$1,250
Others	$950
Oil & Gas	**$3,550**
Ashland Oil	$1,500
Others	$2,050
Real Estate	**$7,950**
National Assn of Realtors	$7,450
Others	$500
Retail Sales	**$4,550**
Limited Inc	$2,000
Federated Department Stores	$1,000
International Mass Retail Assn	$1,000
Others	$550

Other Major Business PACs

United Parcel Service	$1,900	Delivery
Ohio Farm Bureau Federation	$1,650	Farm Orgs
505 King Ave Committee	$1,000	Unknown
Owens-Illinois	$1,000	Paper Packg

PAC Totals by Category

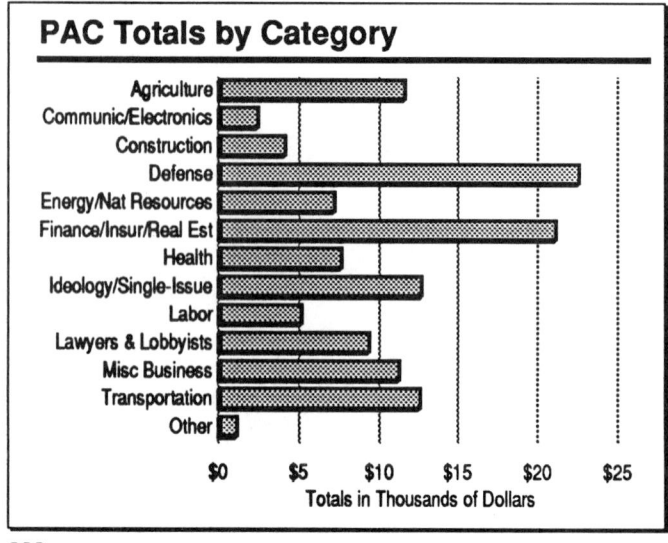

Agriculture
Communic/Electronics
Construction
Defense
Energy/Nat Resources
Finance/Insur/Real Est
Health
Ideology/Single-Issue
Labor
Lawyers & Lobbyists
Misc Business
Transportation
Other

$0 $5 $10 $15 $20 $25
Totals in Thousands of Dollars

Labor

Labor Unions ***$5,000***
    Teamsters Union $4,250
    Others $750

Ideological/Single-Issue

Ideological/Single-Issue ***$12,485***
National PAC ....$5,000   Pro-Israel
National Rifle Assn ....$3,750   Pro-Guns
American Security Council ....$1,135   Pro-Defense
Others..$2,600

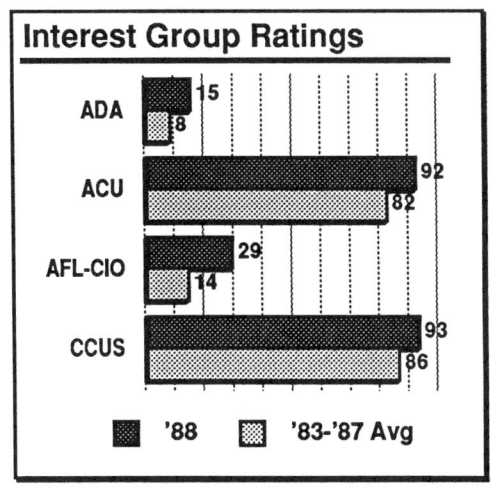

Interest Group Ratings

ADA — '88: 15, '83-'87 Avg: 8
ACU — '88: 92, '83-'87 Avg: 82
AFL-CIO — '88: 29, '83-'87 Avg: 14
CCUS — '88: 93, '83-'87 Avg: 86

■ '88　　▨ '83-'87 Avg

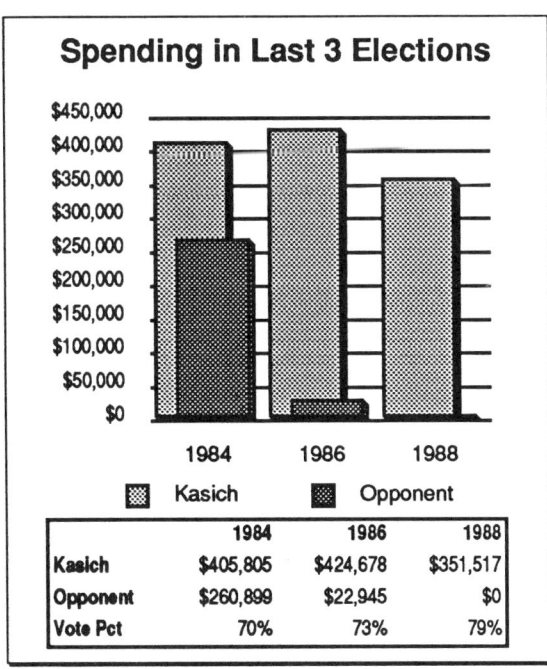

Spending in Last 3 Elections

	1984	1986	1988
Kasich	$405,805	$424,678	$351,517
Opponent	$260,899	$22,945	$0
Vote Pct	70%	73%	79%

▨ Kasich　　■ Opponent

---

* Contributions came from more than one PAC affiliated
with this sponsor.

Robert W. Kastenmeier, D-Wis (2)

First elected: 1958
Total receipts: $439,848
Total from PACs: $177,484

1988 Committees & Subcommittees

Judiciary
Courts, Civil Liberties and the Administration of Justice (Chairman)
Civil and Constitutional Rights

Select Intelligence
Legislation
Program and Budget Authorization

PAC Contribution Profile

Business

Credit Unions/Commercial Banks **$3,400**
    Credit Union National Assn $2,800
    Others $600

Dairy **$14,400**
    Associated Milk Producers $10,000
    Mid-American Dairymen $1,800
    Land O'Lakes Inc $1,600
    Dairymen Inc $1,000

Food & Beverage **$3,050**
    Food Marketing Institute $1,500
    Others $1,550

Insurance **$2,045**
    North Western Mutual Life $2,000
    Others $45

Lawyers & Lobbyists **$6,025**
    Opperman & Paquin $2,500
    Kirkpatrick & Lockhart $1,000
    Powell, Goldstein, Frazer & Murphy $1,000
    Others $1,525

Real Estate **$11,000**
    National Assn of Realtors $10,000
    Century 21 Real Estate $1,000

Rural Electric Utilities **$2,100**
    ACRE (Action Committee for Rural Electrification) $2,100

Campaign Revenue Sources

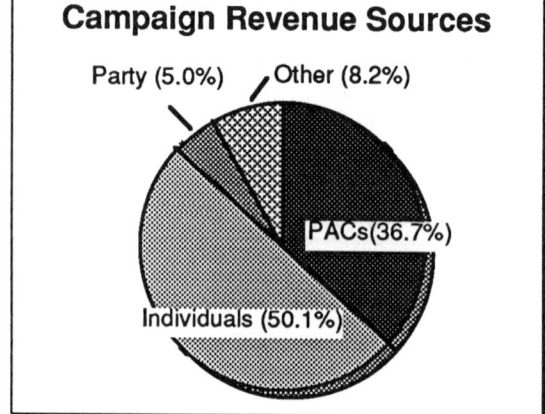

Party (5.0%)
Other (8.2%)
PACs (36.7%)
Individuals (50.1%)

Telecommunications **$5,400**
    AT&T $3,000
    US Telephone Assn $1,000
    Wisconsin Bell Telephone $1,000
    Others $400

Other Major Business PACs

American Veterinary Medical Assn	$1,500	Veterinary
West Publishing	$1,000	Books & Mags

PAC Totals by Category

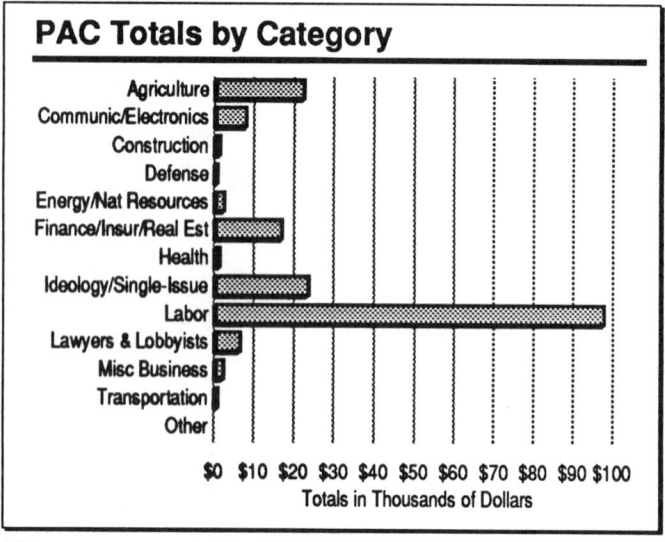

Agriculture
Communic/Electronics
Construction
Defense
Energy/Nat Resources
Finance/Insur/Real Est
Health
Ideology/Single-Issue
Labor
Lawyers & Lobbyists
Misc Business
Transportation
Other

$0 $10 $20 $30 $40 $50 $60 $70 $80 $90 $100
Totals in Thousands of Dollars

Labor

Bldg Trades/Industrial/Misc Unions **$43,490**

United Auto Workers $10,000
Machinists/Aerospace Workers Union $7,600
Food & Commercial Workers Union $7,440
Carpenters & Joiners Union $5,000
Operating Engineers Union $2,950
Laborers' Political League $2,000
Plumbers/Pipefitters Union $2,000
United Steelworkers $1,500
Boilermakers Union $1,000
Intl Brotherhood of Electrical Workers $1,000
Ladies Garment Workers Union $1,000
Others $2,000

Government & Postal Workers **$28,598**

National Assn of Letter Carriers $10,000
American Fedn of State/County/Munic Employees $8,988
National Assn of Retired Federal Employees $6,000
American Postal Workers Union $3,000
Others $610

Teachers Unions **$12,000**

National Education Assn $10,000
American Federation of Teachers $2,000

Transportation Unions **$13,100**

Teamsters Union $10,000
Air Line Pilots Assn $1,500
United Transportation Union $1,000
Others $600

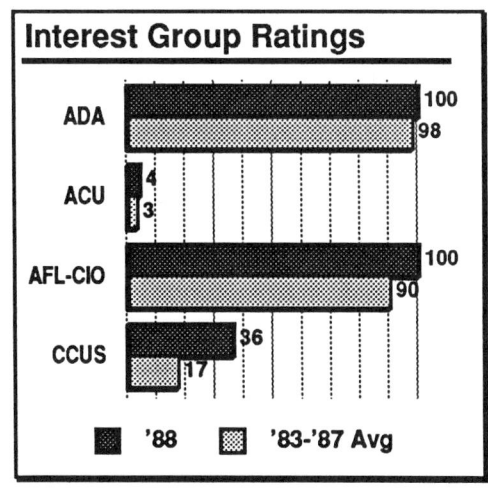

Interest Group Ratings

Ideological/Single-Issue

Democratic/Liberal **$7,240**

National Cmte for an Effective Congress $4,496
Congressional Agenda 80's $1,000
Teamwork America $1,000
Others $744

Democratic Leadership PACs **$7,500**

Majority Congress Committee (Jim Wright) $5,000
Cmte for Democratic Opportunity (Bill Gray) $2,000
Others $500

Other Major Ideological/Single-Issue PACs

Human Rights Campaign Fund $2,600	Gay Rights
National Cmte to Preserve Social Security $1,500	Social Secur
Council for a Livable World $1,000	Pro-Peace
KidsPAC $1,000	HealthWelfare
National Abortion Rights Action League $1,000	Pro-Choice

Independent expenditures supporting Kastenmeier

National Cmte to Preserve Social Security $3,008

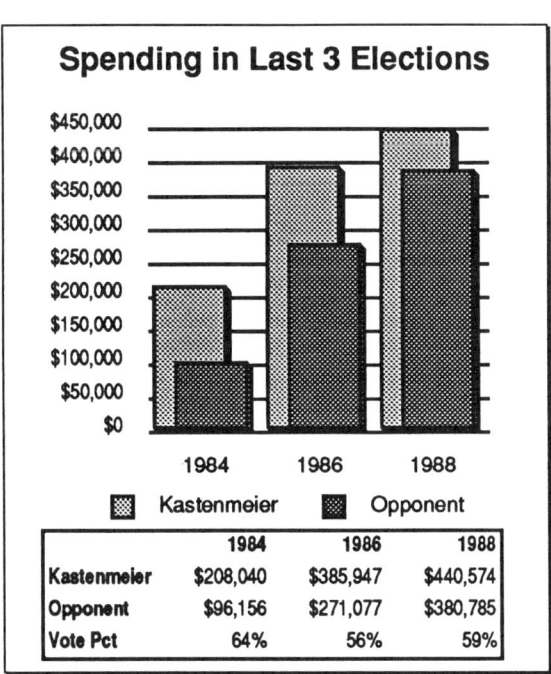

Spending in Last 3 Elections

	1984	1986	1988
Kastenmeier	$208,040	$385,947	$440,574
Opponent	$96,156	$271,077	$380,785
Vote Pct	64%	56%	59%

Joseph P. Kennedy II, D-Mass (8)

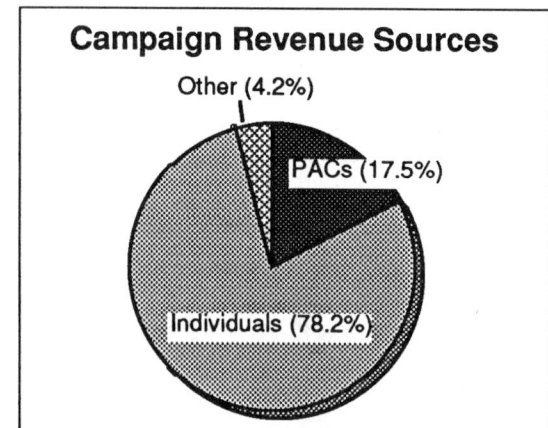

First elected: 1986
Total receipts: $1,399,337
Total from PACs: $272,840

1988 Committees & Subcommittees

Banking, Finance and Urban Affairs
Financial Institutions Supervision, Regulation and Insurance
Housing and Community Development
International Development Institutions and Finance

Veterans' Affairs
Education, Training and Employment
Hospitals and Health Care

Select Aging

PAC Contribution Profile

Business

Airlines & Aerospace	**$3,000**
Long Island Aerospace PAC	$2,000
Eastern Airlines	$1,000
Automotive	**$5,400**
Auto Dealers & Drivers for Free Trade	$5,100
Others	$300
Commercial Banks	**$20,950**
American Bankers Assn	$4,500
First Chicago Corp	$2,100
American Bankers Assn/Massachusetts	$1,700
Bankers Trust	$1,500
Citicorp	$1,500
Barnett Banks of Florida	$1,000
Others	$8,650
Consumer Credit & Loans	**$2,600**
American Financial Services Assn	$1,300
Others	$1,300
Defense	**$3,100**
Raytheon	$1,600
Bath Iron Works	$1,000
Others	$500
Fruit & Vegetable Growers	**$2,000**
Ocean Spray Cranberries Inc	$1,000
Raisin Bargaining Assn	$1,000

Campaign Revenue Sources

Other (4.2%)
PACs (17.5%)
Individuals (78.2%)

Health Professionals	**$3,300**
American Medical Assn	$1,300
American College of Emergency Physicians	$1,000
Others	$1,000
Insurance	**$8,950**
Independent Insurance Agents of America	$3,000
National Assn of Life Underwriters	$2,000
Massachusetts Mutual Life Insurance	$1,000
National Assn Mutual Insurance Agents	$1,000
Others	$1,950
Lawyers & Lobbyists	**$8,440**
Assn of Trial Lawyers of America	$4,500
California Trial Lawyers Assn	$1,000
Others	$2,940
Movies/Entertainment	**$2,800**
MCA Inc	$2,000
Others	$800
Natural Gas	**$2,050**
Bay State Gas Company	$1,000
Others	$1,050
Real Estate	**$6,240**
National Assn of Realtors	$4,350
Others	$1,890
Residential Construction	**$2,350**
National Assn of Home Builders	$1,750
Others	$600
Savings Banks & Credit Unions	**$5,980**
National Council of Savings Institutions	$3,300
US League of Savings Assn	$1,100
Others	$1,580
Securities & Commodities Investment	**$7,250**
Shearson Lehman Hutton	$2,550
Chicago Mercantile Exchange	$1,000
Others	$3,700
Soft Drinks & Liquor	**$3,850**
Coca-Cola Company	$2,300
Others	$1,550

PAC Totals by Category

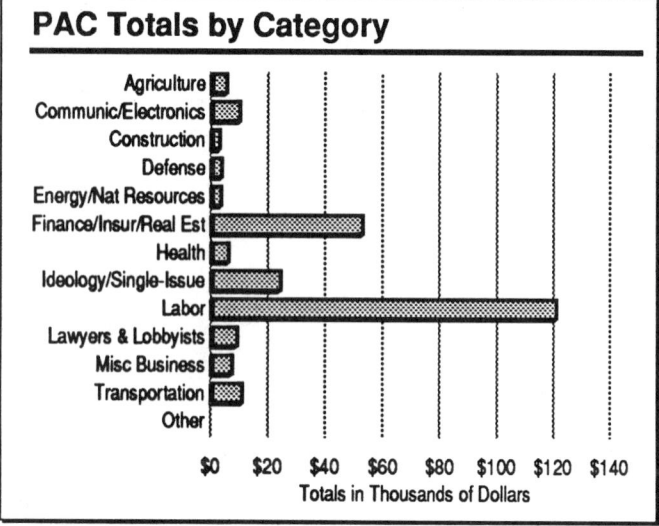

Agriculture
Communic/Electronics
Construction
Defense
Energy/Nat Resources
Finance/Insur/Real Est
Health
Ideology/Single-Issue
Labor
Lawyers & Lobbyists
Misc Business
Transportation
Other

$0 $20 $40 $60 $80 $100 $120 $140
Totals in Thousands of Dollars

Telecommunications **$6,700**

New England Tel & Tel	$3,400
AT&T	$2,500
Others	$800

Other Major Business PACs

J C Penney Company	$2,000	Dept Store
American Health Care Assn	$1,000	Nursing Home
Equifax Inc	$1,000	CreditReport
Mid-American Dairymen	$1,000	Dairy

Labor

Bldg Trades/Industrial/Misc Unions **$52,900**

Carpenters & Joiners Union	$7,200
Ironworkers Union	$6,250
Sheet Metal Workers Union	$6,000
Operating Engineers Union*	$5,750
Intl Brotherhood of Electrical Workers	$5,000
Laborers' Political League	$3,700
Plumbers/Pipefitters Union	$2,500
Food & Commercial Workers Union	$2,300
Service Employees International Union	$2,000
Electronic Machine Furniture Workers	$1,700
AFL-CIO*	$1,600
Communications Workers of America	$1,500
Ladies Garment Workers Union	$1,150
United Auto Workers	$1,000
United Steelworkers	$1,000
Others	$4,250

Government & Postal Workers **$29,825**

National Assn of Letter Carriers	$15,000
American Postal Workers Union	$6,000
National Assn of Retired Federal Employees	$3,000
American Fedn of State/County/Munic Employees	$2,500
National Treasury Employees Union	$1,500
Others	$1,825

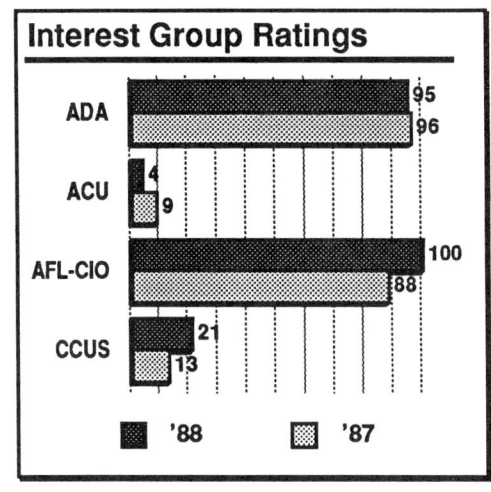

Interest Group Ratings

	'88	'87
ADA	95	96
ACU	4	9
AFL-CIO	100	88
CCUS	21	13

Teachers Unions **$11,100**

National Education Assn	$11,000
Others	$100

Transportation Unions **$26,350**

Seafarers International Union	$6,000
Marine Engineers District 2 Maritime Officers	$5,500
Teamsters Union	$5,000
Air Line Pilots Assn	$3,500
United Transportation Union	$2,500
Amalgamated Transit Union	$1,000
Others	$2,850

Ideological/Single-Issue

Democratic Leadership PACs **$6,100**

Valley Education Fund (Tony Coelho)	$5,000
Others	$1,100

Pro-Israel **$6,000**

National PAC	$5,000
Others	$1,000

Other Major Ideological/Single-Issue PACs

National Cmte to Preserve Social Security	$2,500	Social Secur
Business, Individuals & Government PAC	$2,000	Dem/Liberal
National Community Action Found	$2,000	HealthWelfar
Human Rights Campaign Fund	$1,500	Gay Rights
KidsPAC	$1,000	HealthWelfare

Independent expenditures supporting Kennedy

National Cmte to Preserve Social Security	$1,506

Independent expenditures opposing Kennedy

American Citizens for Political Action	$229,928

---

* Contributions came from more than one PAC affiliated with this sponsor.

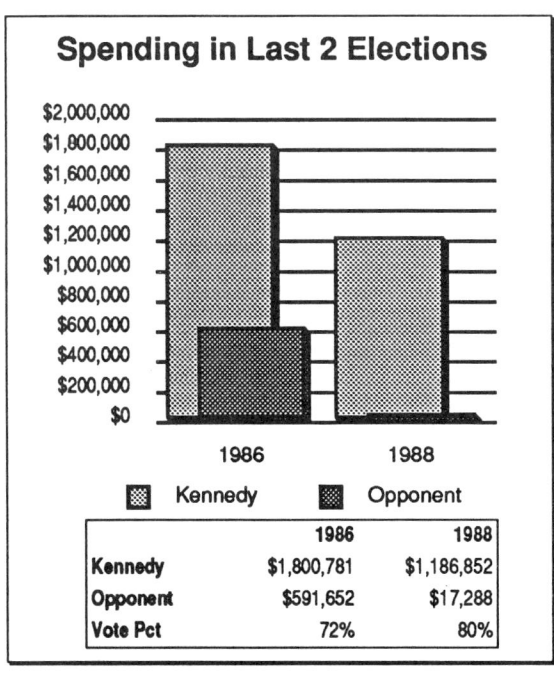

Spending in Last 2 Elections

	1986	1988
Kennedy	$1,800,781	$1,186,852
Opponent	$591,652	$17,288
Vote Pct	72%	80%

Legend: Kennedy, Opponent

Barbara B. Kennelly, D-Conn (1)

First elected: 1982
Total receipts: $448,010
Total from PACs: $264,103

1988 Committees & Subcommittees

Ways and Means
Public Assistance and Unemployment Compensation
Select Revenue Measures

Select Intelligence
Oversight and Evaluation
Program and Budget Authorization

PAC Contribution Profile

Business

Accountants	**$8,000**
American Inst of CPA's	$5,000
Coopers & Lybrand	$1,000
Ernst & Whinney	$1,000
Others	$1,000
Beer, Wine & Liquor	**$8,000**
Wine & Spirits Wholesalers of America	$2,000
National Beer Wholesalers Assn	$1,500
Anheuser-Busch	$1,000
Heublein	$1,000
Joseph E Seagram & Sons	$1,000
Smirnoff/Inglenook Distributors	$1,000
Others	$500
Defense	**$10,600**
United Technologies	$6,000
Textron Inc	$1,500
Allied-Signal	$1,000
Others	$2,100
Financial Institutions	**$12,975**
American Bankers Assn	$1,500
Citicorp	$1,500
US League of Savings Assn	$1,500
Connecticut Bankers Assn	$1,250
Credit Union National Assn	$1,000
Hartford National Corp	$1,000
National Assn of Federal Credit Unions	$1,000
National Council of Savings Institutions	$1,000
Others	$3,225

Campaign Revenue Sources

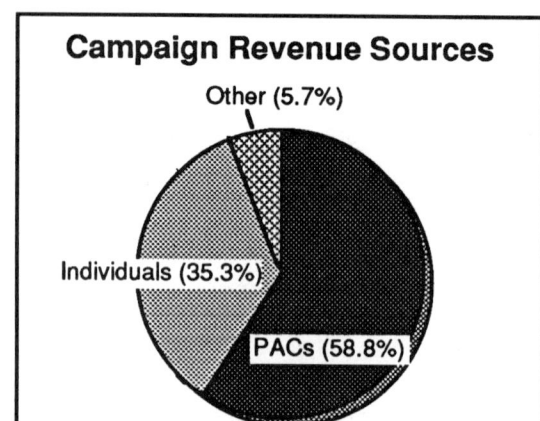

Other (5.7%)
Individuals (35.3%)
PACs (58.8%)

Health Professionals	**$15,150**
American Dental Assn	$4,000
American Medical Assn	$3,350
Oral & Maxillofacial Surgeons	$1,500
American College of Emergency Physicians	$1,000
American Nurses Assn	$1,000
American Optometric Assn	$1,000
Cmte for Quality Orthopedic Health Care	$1,000
Corp for the Advancement of Psychiatry	$1,000
Others	$1,300
Insurance	**$44,750**
National Assn of Life Underwriters	$10,000
Insurance Assn of Connecticut	$5,000
Independent Insurance Agents of America	$2,500
American Council of Life Insurance	$2,000
New England Mutual Life	$2,000
New York Life	$2,000
Health Insurance Assn of America	$1,500
North Western Mutual Life	$1,500
Mutual of Omaha	$1,250
American International Group inc	$1,000
Casualty & Surety Agents Assn	$1,000
Equitable Financial Services	$1,000
Lincoln National Corp	$1,000
Massachusetts Mutual Life Insurance	$1,000
Metropolitan Life Insurance	$1,000
National Assn of Independent Insurers	$1,000
Penn Mutual Life Insurance	$1,000
Prudential Insurance	$1,000
Torchmark Corp	$1,000
Others	$7,000
Lawyers & Lobbyists	**$10,990**
Assn of Trial Lawyers of America	$5,000
Murtha, Cullina, Richter, & Pinney	$2,000
Dickstein, Shapiro & Morin	$1,000
Wexler Reynolds Harrison & Schule	$1,000
Others	$1,990
Securities & Commodities Investment	**$11,500**
Investment Company Institute	$5,000
Chicago Board of Trade	$2,000
Assn of Private Pension Plans	$1,000
Public Securities Assn	$1,000
Others	$2,500

PAC Totals by Category

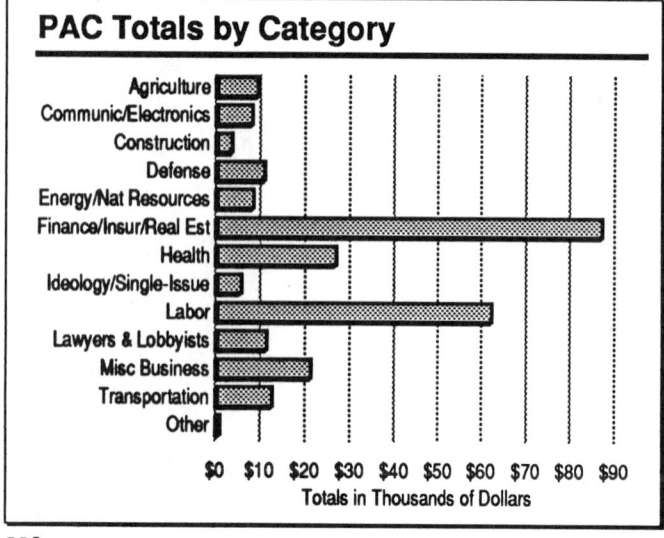

Agriculture
Communic/Electronics
Construction
Defense
Energy/Nat Resources
Finance/Insur/Real Est
Health
Ideology/Single-Issue
Labor
Lawyers & Lobbyists
Misc Business
Transportation
Other

$0 $10 $20 $30 $40 $50 $60 $70 $80 $90
Totals in Thousands of Dollars

Other Major Business PACs

Federal Express Corp	$5,000	Delivery
National Venture Capital Assn	$5,000	Venture Cap
National Assn of Realtors	$3,250	Real Estate
American Hospital Assn	$3,000	Hospitals
Corning Glass Works	$2,000	Glass Prod
Petroleum Marketers Assn	$2,000	Gas Stations
Philip Morris	$2,000	Tobacco
American Assn of Equipment Lessors	$1,500	Rentals
Combustion Engineering	$1,500	PowerEquip
Federation of America Hospitals	$1,500	Hospitals
Tyson Foods	$1,500	Poultry/Egg
Abbott Laboratories	$1,000	Pharmaceut
American Trucking Assns	$1,000	Trucking
Associated General Contractors	$1,000	Comml Constr
AT&T	$1,000	LongDistance
BellSouth Corp*	$1,000	Phone Util
Caterpillar Tractor	$1,000	BldgEqip
Greyhound Corp	$1,000	Home Chem
International Council of Shopping Centers	$1,000	Retail
J C Penney Company	$1,000	Dept Store
Johnson & Johnson	$1,000	Health Prod
Mortgage Bankers Assn of America	$1,000	MortgageBank
National Realty Committee	$1,000	Real Estate
NYNEX Corp	$1,000	Phone Util
Pacific Telesis Group	$1,000	Phone Util
Pfizer Inc	$1,000	Pharmaceut
Society of Independent Gasoline Marketers	$1,000	Gas Stations
Tobacco Institute	$1,000	Tobacco
United Parcel Service	$1,000	Delivery
Voluntary Hospitals of America	$1,000	Hospitals

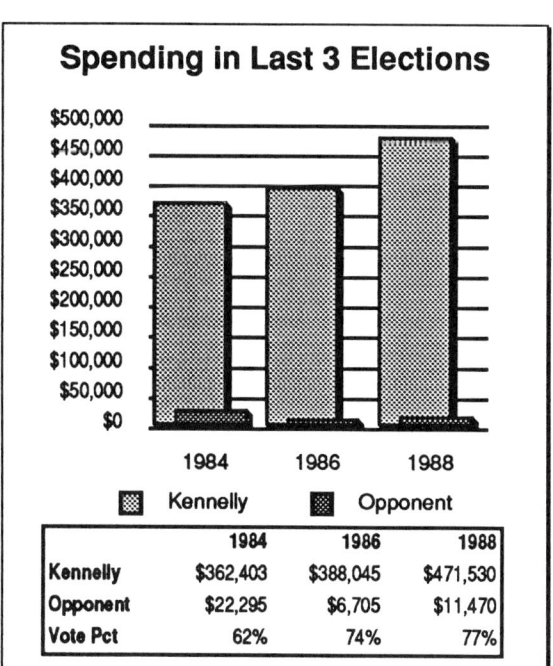

Spending in Last 3 Elections

	1984	1986	1988
Kennelly	$362,403	$388,045	$471,530
Opponent	$22,295	$6,705	$11,470
Vote Pct	62%	74%	77%

■ Kennelly   ■ Opponent

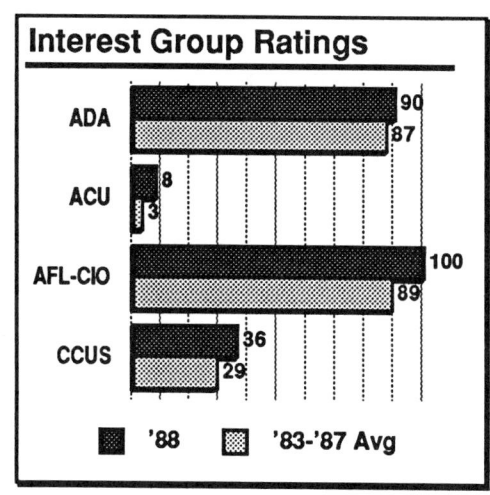

Interest Group Ratings

ADA 90 / 87
ACU 8 / 3
AFL-CIO 100 / 89
CCUS 36 / 29

■ '88   ▨ '83-'87 Avg

Labor

Bldg Trades/Industrial/Misc Unions $23,250

Conn Union of Telephone Workers	$5,000
Machinists/Aerospace Workers Union	$2,250
AFL-CIO*	$2,000
Carpenters & Joiners Union	$2,000
Laborers Political League	$2,000
United Steelworkers	$2,000
Operating Engineers Union	$1,500
Food & Commercial Workers Union	$1,000
Intl Brotherhood of Electrical Workers	$1,000
Ironworkers Union	$1,000
Service Employees International Union	$1,000
Sheet Metal Workers Union	$1,000
Others	$1,500

Government & Postal Workers $15,500

American Fedn of State/County/Munic Employees	$5,000
National Assn of Letter Carriers	$2,000
National Assn of Retired Federal Employees	$2,000
National Treasury Employees Union	$2,000
American Postal Workers Union	$1,000
International Assn of Firefighters	$1,000
National Rural Letter Carriers Assn	$1,000
Others	$1,500

Teachers Unions $8,000

National Education Assn	$5,000
American Federation of Teachers	$3,000

Transportation Unions $15,000

Teamsters Union	$7,500
Air Line Pilots Assn	$1,500
Seafarers International Union	$1,500
United Transportation Union	$1,500
Others	$3,000

Major Ideological/Single-Issue PACs

Valley Education Fund (Tony Coelho)	$2,000	Dem Leaders
KidsPAC	$1,000	HealthWelfare

Independent expenditures supporting Kennelly

National Cmte to Preserve Social Security	$3,829
National Structured Settlements Assn	$1,000

---

* Contributions came from more than one PAC affiliated with this sponsor.

Dale E. Kildee, D-Mich (7)

First elected: 1976
Total receipts: $152,246
Total from PACs: $103,770

1988 Committees & Subcommittees

Education and Labor
Human Resources (Chairman)
Elementary, Secondary and Vocational Education
Labor-Management Relations

Interior and Insular Affairs
National Parks and Public Lands
Water and Power Resources

PAC Contribution Profile

Business

Automotive	**$2,000**
Chrysler Corp	$900
Ford Motor Company	$600
General Motors	$500
Dairy	**$1,500**
Associated Milk Producers	$1,000
Mid-American Dairymen	$500
Electric & Power Utilities	**$1,500**
Consumers Power Company	$900
Detroit Edison	$600
Health Professionals	**$2,850**
American Medical Assn	$2,300
Others	$550
Lawyers	**$5,000**
Assn of Trial Lawyers of America	$5,000
Savings Banks/Credit Unions	**$1,500**
Michigan Credit Union League	$1,000
Michigan League of Savings Institutions	$500
Sugar Growers	**$1,400**
American Sugarbeet Growers Assn	$1,100
Others	$300
Telecommunications	**$1,450**
Michigan Bell Telephone	$1,200
Others	$250

Campaign Revenue Sources

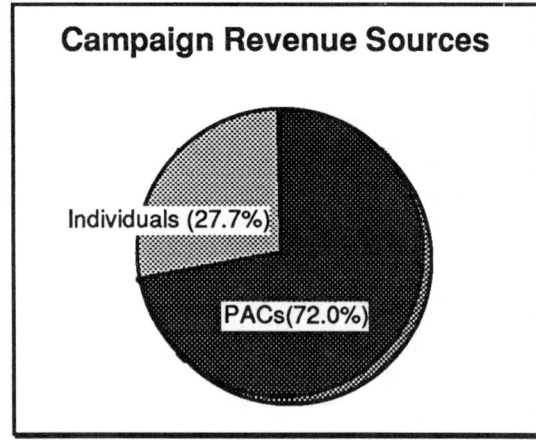

Individuals (27.7%)
PACs (72.0%)

Other Major Business PACs

Assn of Independent Colleges/Schools	$900	Voc Tech
United Parcel Service	$600	Delivery
American Hospital Assn	$500	Hospitals
Cmte for Farmworker Programs	$500	Social Work
ITT Corp	$500	Insurance
National Assn of Social Workers	$500	Social Work

PAC Totals by Category

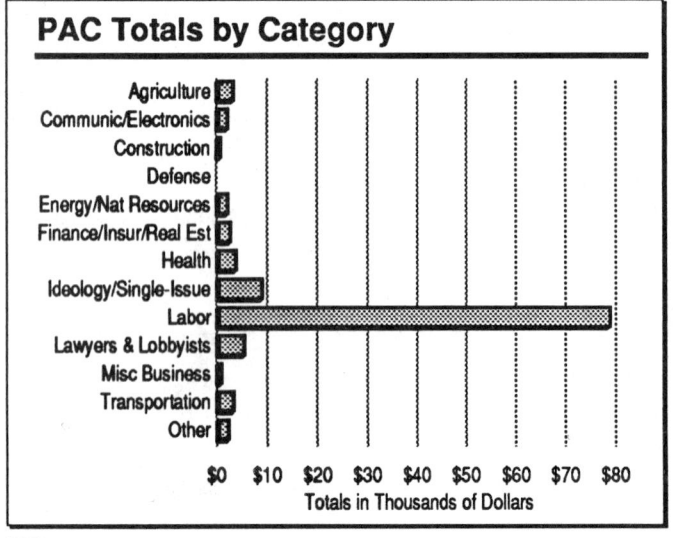

Agriculture
Communic/Electronics
Construction
Defense
Energy/Nat Resources
Finance/Insur/Real Est
Health
Ideology/Single-Issue
Labor
Lawyers & Lobbyists
Misc Business
Transportation
Other

$0 $10 $20 $30 $40 $50 $60 $70 $80
Totals in Thousands of Dollars

Labor

Bldg Trades/Industrial/Misc Unions $34,270

United Auto Workers	$10,000
Communications Workers of America	$5,000
Intl Brotherhood of Electrical Workers	$3,600
Carpenters & Joiners Union	$2,600
Machinists/Aerospace Workers Union	$2,000
Operating Engineers Union	$2,000
United Mine Workers	$1,550
AFL-CIO*	$1,500
Laborers' Political League	$1,500
Food & Commercial Workers Union	$1,300
Boilermakers Union	$800
Amalgamated Clothing & Textile Workers	$600
Hotel/Restaurant Employees Union	$600
Ladies Garment Workers Union	$600
Others	$620

Government & Postal Workers $16,050

National Assn of Letter Carriers	$4,500
American Fedn of State/County/Munic Employees	$3,500
National Assn of Retired Federal Employees	$3,000
American Postal Workers Union	$1,500
American Federation of Government Employees	$1,100
International Assn of Firefighters	$1,100
National League of Postmasters	$550
Others	$800

Teachers Unions $10,200

National Education Assn	$5,900
American Federation of Teachers	$4,300

Transportation Unions $17,800

Teamsters Union	$7,000
Air Line Pilots Assn	$5,000
United Transportation Union	$2,000
Seafarers International Union	$1,500
Transportation Communication Union	$1,100
Brotherhood of Locomotive Engineers	$600
Maintenance of Way Employees	$600

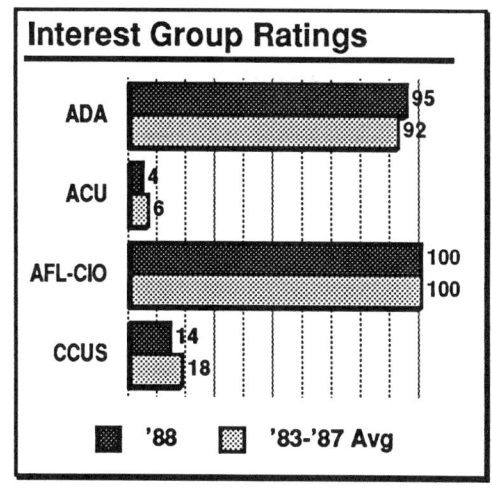

Interest Group Ratings

	'88	'83-'87 Avg
ADA	95	92
ACU	4	6
AFL-CIO	100	100
CCUS	14	18

Ideological/Single-Issue

Ideological/Single-Issue $8,500

National Community Action Found	$3,500	HealthWelfare
Valley Education Fund (Tony Coelho)	$2,000	Dem Leaders
KidsPAC	$1,000	HealthWelfare
National Council of Senior Citizens	$1,000	Social Security
Sierra Club	$500	Environment
Others	$500	

Independent expenditures supporting Kildee

National Cmte to Preserve Social Security	$1,530

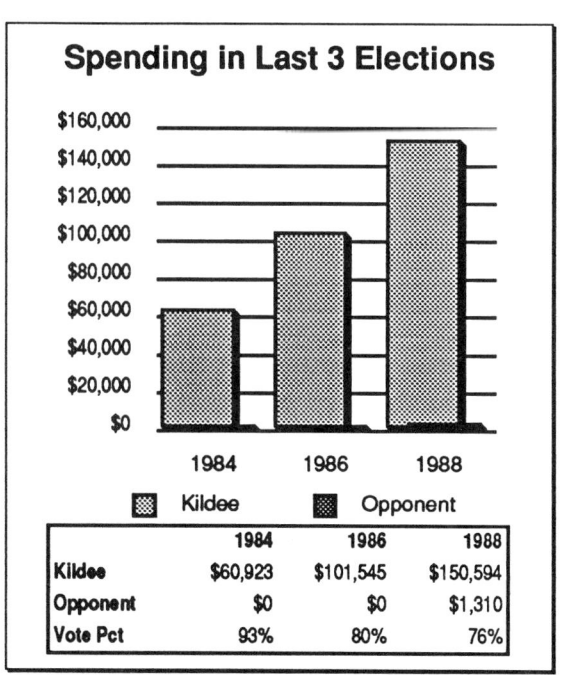

Spending in Last 3 Elections

	1984	1986	1988
Kildee	$60,923	$101,545	$150,594
Opponent	$0	$0	$1,310
Vote Pct	93%	80%	76%

Legend: Kildee, Opponent

---

* Contributions came from more than one PAC affiliated with this sponsor.

Gerald D. Kleczka, D-Wis (4)

First elected: 1984
Total receipts: $214,093
Total from PACs: $129,283

1988 Committees & Subcommittees

Banking, Finance and Urban Affairs
Financial Institutions Supervision, Regulation and Insurance
Housing and Community Development
International Development, Finance, Trade and Monetary Policy

Government Operations
Government Activities and Transportation
Legislation and National Security

PAC Contribution Profile

Business

Accountants	**$5,000**
American Institute of CPA's	$5,000
Automotive	**$2,700**
National Auto Dealers Assn	$2,000
Others	$700
Commercial Banks	**$18,300**
American Bankers Assn	$5,000
Banc One Corp*	$2,750
Norwest Corp	$2,000
Wisconsin Bankers Assn	$1,500
First Bank System*	$1,050
Citicorp	$1,000
Others	$5,000
Construction	**$2,500**
None over $850	
Dairy	**$2,700**
Associated Milk Producers	$1,500
Others	$1,200
Electric Utilities	**$2,400**
Wisconsin Electric Power Company	$1,700
Others	$700
Health Professionals	**$5,300**
American Medical Assn	$2,700
American Optometric Assn	$1,750
Others	$850

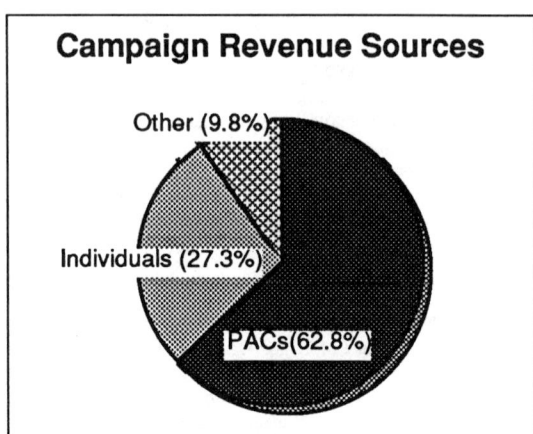

Campaign Revenue Sources

Other (9.8%)
Individuals (27.3%)
PACs (62.8%)

Insurance	**$5,300**
North Western Mutual Life	$2,050
Others	$3,250
Lawyers & Lobbyists	**$5,300**
Assn of Trial Lawyers of America	$4,600
Others	$700
Real Estate	**$8,950**
National Assn of Realtors	$8,600
Others	$350
Securities & Commodities Investment	**$7,700**
Municipal Securities Industry	$2,000
First Boston Corp	$1,000
Goldman Sachs	$1,000
Prudential-Bache Securities	$1,000
Others	$2,700

Other Major Business PACs

Waste Management Inc	$1,700	Waste Mgmt
Wisconsin Bell Telephone	$1,100	Phone Util

PAC Totals by Category

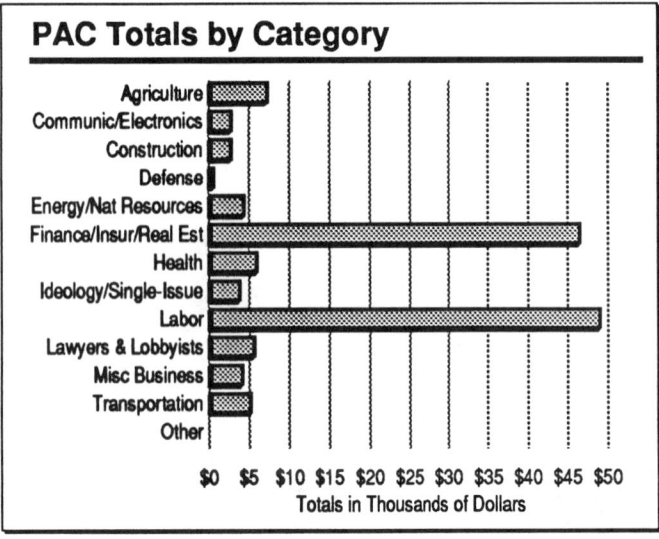

Totals in Thousands of Dollars

632

Labor

Bldg Trades/Industrial/Misc Unions $15,000
    United Auto Workers $3,200
    Carpenters & Joiners Union $1,700
    Laborers' Political League $1,550
    Operating Engineers Union $1,400
    AFL-CIO* $1,350
    Boilermakers Union $1,050
    Food & Commercial Workers Union $1,000
    Others $3,750

Government & Postal Workers $9,600
    National Assn of Retired Federal Employees $5,000
    National Assn of Letter Carriers $1,900
    American Fedn of State/County/Munic Employees $1,000
    Others $1,700

Teachers Unions $2,850
    National Education Assn $2,850

Transportation Unions $21,250
    Teamsters Union $10,000
    Air Line Pilots Assn $5,000
    Marine Engineers District 2 Maritime Officers $1,700
    Amalgamated Transit Union $1,000
    Seafarers International Union $1,000
    United Transportation Union $1,000
    Others $1,550

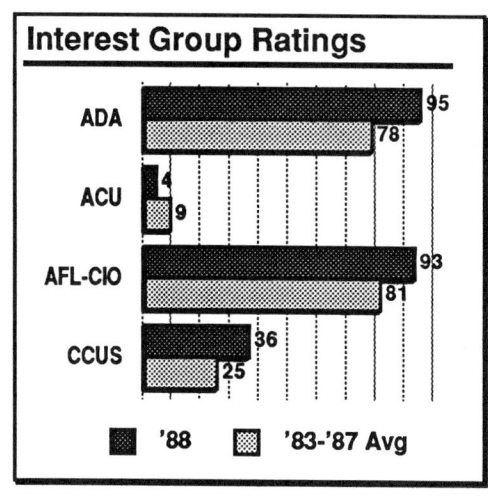

Interest Group Ratings

Ideological/Single-Issue

Democratic Leadership PACs $2,350
    Valley Education Fund (Tony Coelho) $2,000
    Others $350

Other Major Ideological/Single-Issue PACs
National Cmte to Preserve Social Security ...... $1,200   Social Secur

Independent expenditures supporting Kleczka
National Cmte to Preserve Social Security $3,759

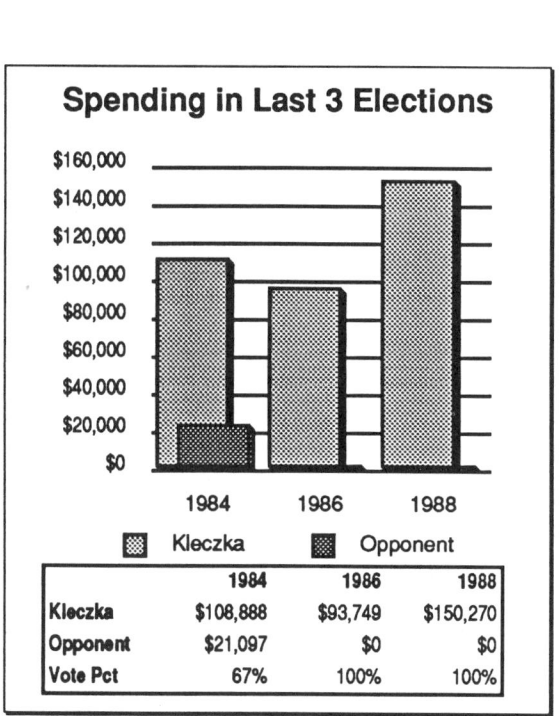

Spending in Last 3 Elections

	1984	1986	1988
Kleczka	$108,888	$93,749	$150,270
Opponent	$21,097	$0	$0
Vote Pct	67%	100%	100%

Kleczka   Opponent

---

* Contributions came from more than one PAC affiliated with this sponsor.

Jim Kolbe, R-Ariz (5)

1988 Committees & Subcommittees

Appropriations
Commerce, Justice, State, the Judiciary and Related Agencies
Military Construction

First elected: 1984
Total receipts: $419,090
Total from PACs: $158,738

PAC Contribution Profile

Business

Automotive	**$9,100**
National Auto Dealers Assn	$3,850
Auto Dealers & Drivers for Free Trade	$2,500
Federal-Mogul Corp	$2,000
Others	$750
Chemicals	**$3,500**
Greyhound Corp	$2,250
Others	$1,250
Commercial Banks	**$12,075**
Chase Bank of Arizona	$3,200
Arizona Bankers Assn	$1,500
First Interstate Bank of Arizona	$1,500
Valley National Bank of Arizona	$1,500
Arizona Bank	$1,450
Thunderbird Bank	$1,225
Others	$1,700
Construction	**$15,550**
Estes Company	$3,500
Associated General Contractors	$2,500
National Utility Contractors Assn	$2,500
National Assn of Home Builders	$1,000
National Society of Professional Engineers	$1,000
Others	$5,050
Cotton	**$5,000**
Calcot Ltd	$2,500
National Cotton Council	$1,250
Arizona Cotton Growers Assn	$1,000
Others	$250

Campaign Revenue Sources

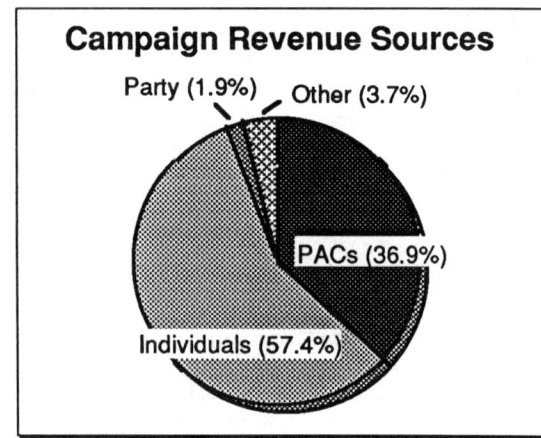

Party (1.9%)   Other (3.7%)
PACs (36.9%)
Individuals (57.4%)

Defense	**$12,100**
Hughes Aircraft	$4,500
Allied-Signal	$1,650
Textron Inc	$1,350
Emerson Electric	$1,000
Others	$3,600
Electric Utilities	**$2,500**
Arizona Public Service Company	$1,250
Others	$1,250
Electronics & Computers	**$2,600**
Honeywell Inc*	$1,000
Others	$1,600
Food & Beverage	**$3,800**
Pepsico Inc	$1,000
Others	$2,800
Health Professionals	**$9,350**
American Medical Assn	$6,250
American Dental Assn	$1,500
Others	$1,600
Insurance	**$5,200**
National Assn of Life Underwriters	$3,000
Others	$2,200
Irrigation Systems	**$2,500**
Salt River Valley Water Users	$2,500
Oil & Gas	**$8,050**
Southwest Gas Corp	$1,750
Circle K Corp	$1,000
Others	$5,300
Real Estate	**$8,300**
National Assn of Realtors	$5,000
Del Webb Corp	$2,000
Others	$1,300
Retail Sales	**$2,800**
National Assn of Convenience Stores	$1,000
Others	$1,800
Savings Banks/Credit Unions	**$4,900**
Merabank Federal Savings Bank	$1,100
Great American First Savings & Loan	$1,000
Others	$2,800

PAC Totals by Category

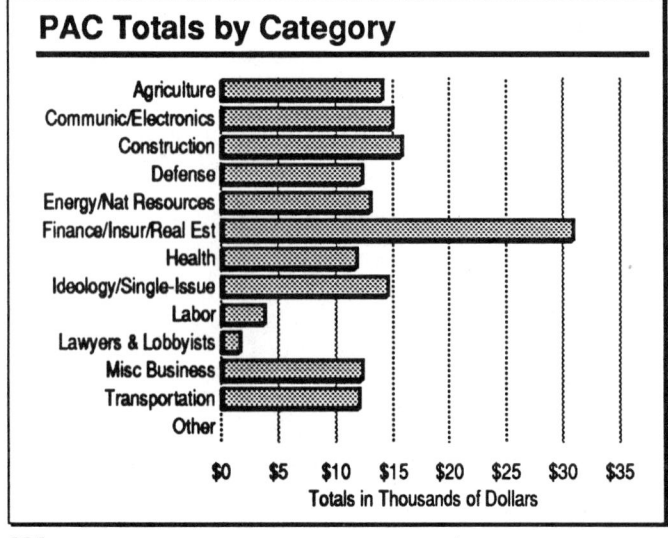

Agriculture
Communic/Electronics
Construction
Defense
Energy/Nat Resources
Finance/Insur/Real Est
Health
Ideology/Single-Issue
Labor
Lawyers & Lobbyists
Misc Business
Transportation
Other

$0 $5 $10 $15 $20 $25 $30 $35
Totals in Thousands of Dollars

Telecommunications *$9,050*

Mountain Bell	....$4,500
AT&T	....$3,000
Continental Telecom	....$1,000
Others	....$550

Television/Cable TV *$2,250*

National Cable Television Assn	....................................$1,250
Others	....$1,000

Other Major Business PACs

Stone Container Corp	....$1,500	Paper Packg
Abbott Laboratories	....$1,000	Pharmaceut
Fleishman-Hillard	....$1,000	Lobbyist/PR
National Assn of Temporary Services	.............$1,000	EmployAgency
Santa Fe Southern Pacific	...............................$1,000	Railroads

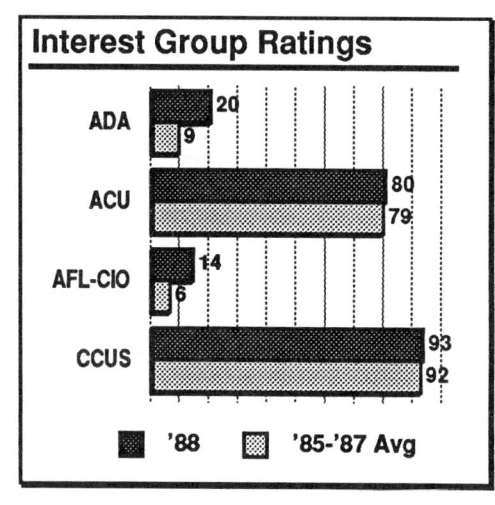

Labor

Labor Unions *$3,600*

National Assn of Retired Federal Employees	.................$2,000
Marine Engineers Union	....$1,000
Others	....$600

Ideological/Single-Issue

Pro-Gun Ownership *$4,950*

National Rifle Assn	....$4,950

Pro-Israel *$7,500*

National PAC	....$5,000
Roundtable PAC	....$1,500
Hudson Valley PAC	....$1,000

Other Major Ideological/Single-Issue PACs

Conservative Victory Fund (Steve Symms)	.....$1,102	Repub Leader

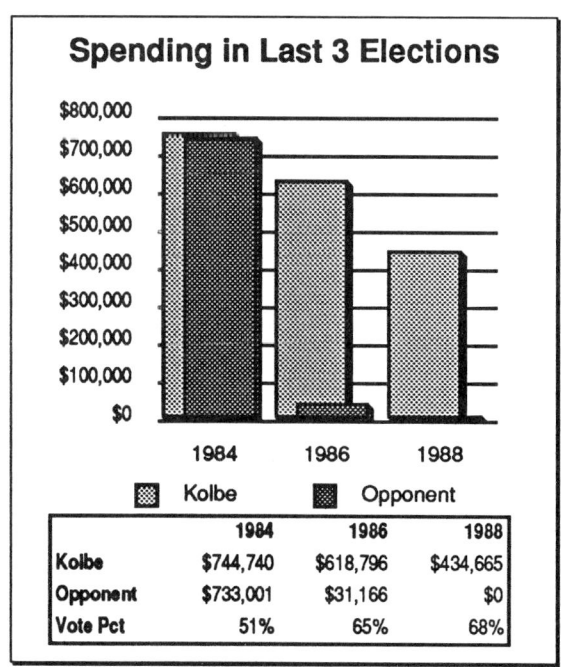

---

* Contributions came from more than one PAC affiliated with this sponsor.

Joe Kolter, D-Pa (4)

First elected: 1982
Total receipts: $175,980
Total from PACs: $146,606

1988 Committees & Subcommittees

Government Operations
Commerce, Consumer and Monetary Affairs
Government Activities and Transportation

House Administration
Accounts
Elections

Public Works and Transportation
Aviation
Investigations and Oversight
Surface Transportation

PAC Contribution Profile

Business

Accountants	**$5,000**
American Institute of CPA's	$5,000
Aviation & Aerospace	**$3,750**
Aircraft Owners & Pilots Assn	$1,000
Rockwell International	$1,000
Others	$1,750
Commercial & Savings Banks	**$3,250**
American Bankers Assn	$2,000
Others	$1,250
Construction	**$4,500**
National Assn of Home Builders	$2,000
National Utility Contractors Assn	$1,500
Others	$1,000
Dairy	**$3,500**
Associated Milk Producers	$1,500
Dairymen Inc-Pennsylvania	$1,000
Others	$1,000
Electric Utilities	**$2,600**
ACRE (Action Committee for Rural Electrification)	$1,000
Others	$1,600
Health Professionals	**$8,475**
American Medical Assn	$6,975
Pennsylvania Medical Assn	$1,500
Real Estate	**$5,000**
National Assn of Realtors	$4,750
Others	$250

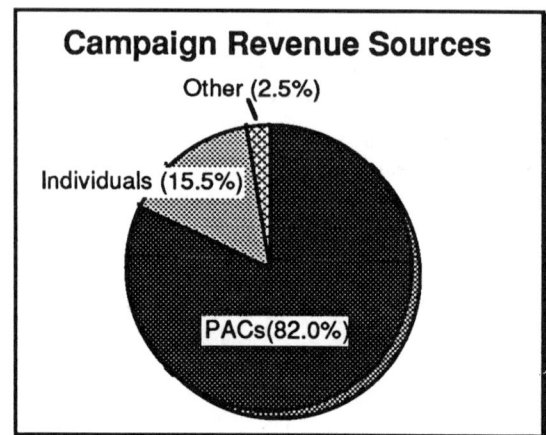

Campaign Revenue Sources

Other (2.5%)
Individuals (15.5%)
PACs (82.0%)

Steel Production	**$2,500**
None over $750	
Sugar Growers	**$3,500**
Great Lakes Sugar Beet Growers	$1,000
Others	$2,500
Telecommunications	**$4,500**
AT&T	$3,000
Bell Telephone of Pennsylvania	$1,500
Trucking/Delivery	**$5,850**
United Parcel Service	$2,500
American Trucking Assns	$1,250
Consolidated Freightways	$1,000
Others	$1,100

Other Major Business PACs

Food Marketing Institute	$1,000	Food Stores
Waste Management Inc	$1,000	Waste Mgmt

PAC Totals by Category

Bar chart showing PAC totals in thousands of dollars by category:

Category	
Agriculture	
Communic/Electronics	
Construction	
Defense	
Energy/Nat Resources	
Finance/Insur/Real Est	
Health	
Ideology/Single-Issue	
Labor	
Lawyers & Lobbyists	
Misc Business	
Transportation	
Other	

$0 $10 $20 $30 $40 $50 $60 $70 $80 $90

Totals in Thousands of Dollars

Labor

Bldg Trades/Industrial/Misc Unions $29,506

Machinists/Aerospace Workers Union $5,250	
United Auto Workers $5,000	
Carpenters & Joiners Union $2,500	
United Steelworkers $2,500	
Plumbers/Pipefitters Union* $2,250	
Intl Brotherhood of Electrical Workers.........................$1,700	
AFL-CIO* $1,500	
Laborers' Political League $1,500	
United Mine Workers $1,250	
Food & Commercial Workers Union..............................$1,000	
Ladies Garment Workers Union $1,000	
Operating Engineers Union $1,000	
Others $3,056	

Government & Postal Workers $14,700

National Assn of Retired Federal Employees $6,000
American Fedn of State/County/Munic Employees $2,500
National Assn of Letter Carriers $2,500
American Postal Workers Union $1,500
Others $2,200

Teachers Unions $6,000

National Education Assn $3,500
American Federation of Teachers $2,500

Transportation Unions $30,000

Air Line Pilots Assn $7,500
Teamsters Union $7,500
Marine Engineers Union* $4,000
Masters, Mates & Pilots Union $2,000
Transport Workers Union $1,750
United Transportation Union $1,750
Seafarers International Union $1,500
Amalgamated Transit Union.......................................$1,000
Others $3,000

Interest Group Ratings

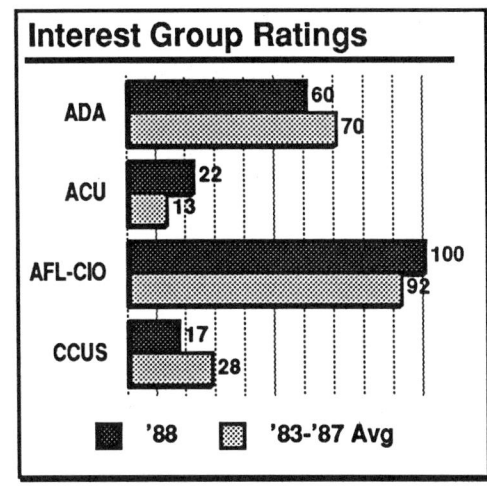

	'88	'83-'87 Avg
ADA	60	70
ACU	22	13
AFL-CIO	100	92
CCUS	17	28

Major Ideological/Single-Issue PACs

Valley Education Fund (Tony Coelho) ....$2,000   Dem Leaders
National Right to Life PAC ....$1,000   Pro-Life

Independent expenditures supporting Kolter

National Cmte to Preserve Social Security $3,612

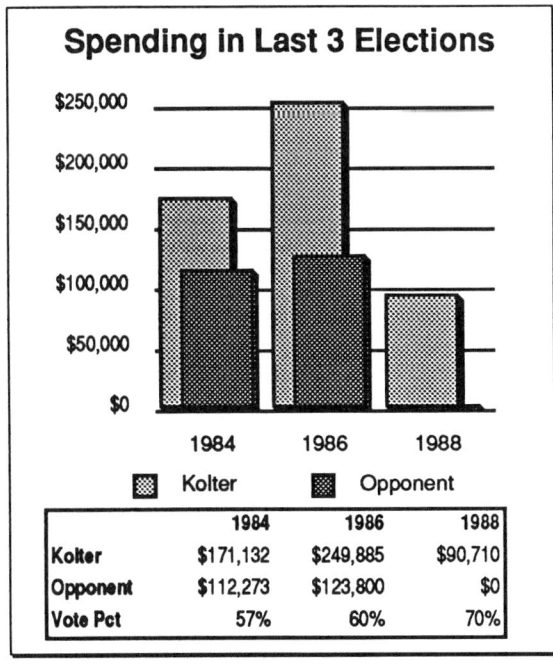

Spending in Last 3 Elections

	1984	1986	1988
Kolter	$171,132	$249,885	$90,710
Opponent	$112,273	$123,800	$0
Vote Pct	57%	60%	70%

---

* Contributions came from more than one PAC affiliated
with this sponsor.

Peter H. Kostmayer, D-Pa (8)

First elected: 1978
Total receipts: $1,148,687
Total from PACs: $416,321

1988 Committees & Subcommittees

Foreign Affairs
International Economic Policy and Trade
Western Hemisphere Affairs

Interior and Insular Affairs
Mining and Natural Resources
National Parks and Public Lands
Water and Power Resources

Select Hunger

PAC Contribution Profile
Business

Commercial Banks	**$6,400**
American Bankers Assn	$1,500
Others	$4,900
Defense	**$3,500**
AEL Industries Inc	$2,500
Others	$1,000
Health Professionals	**$7,000**
American Medical Assn	$2,000
American Nurses Assn	$2,000
American Optometric Assn	$2,000
Others	$1,000
Insurance	**$17,708**
American Family Corp	$10,000
National Assn of Life Underwriters	$5,000
Independent Insurance Agents of America	$1,658
Others	$1,050
Lawyers & Lobbyists	**$19,700**
Assn of Trial Lawyers of America	$10,000
Wolf, Block, Schorr, and Solis-Cohen	$5,000
Akin, Gump, Hauer & Feld	$1,500
Schnader Harrison Segal, & Lewis	$1,300
Others	$1,900
Oil & Gas	**$4,500**
Atlantic Richfield	$2,000
Others	$2,500

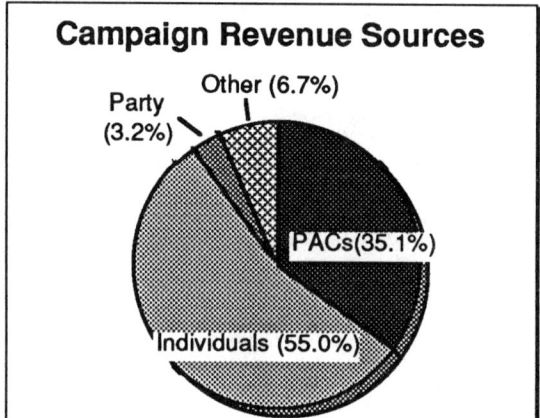

Campaign Revenue Sources

Party (3.2%)
Other (6.7%)
PACs (35.1%)
Individuals (55.0%)

Real Estate	**$10,000**
National Assn of Realtors	$10,000
Residential Construction	**$7,000**
National Assn of Home Builders	$5,000
Toll Bros Inc	$2,000
Securities & Commodities Investment	**$6,500**
None over $1,000	

Other Major Business PACs

AT&T	$2,500	LongDistance
National Assn of Social Workers	$2,000	Social Work
ACRE (Action Committee for Rural Electric)	$1,500	RuralElect
American Hospital Assn	$1,500	Hospitals
National Cable Television Assn	$1,500	CableTV

PAC Totals by Category

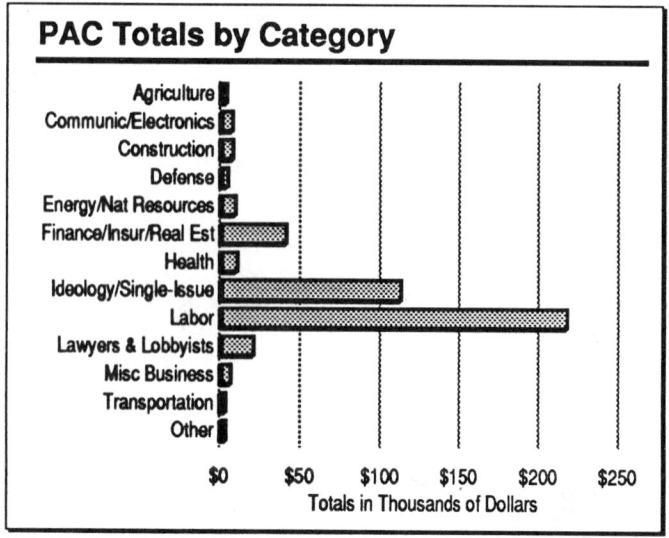

Totals in Thousands of Dollars

Agriculture
Communic/Electronics
Construction
Defense
Energy/Nat Resources
Finance/Insur/Real Est
Health
Ideology/Single-Issue
Labor
Lawyers & Lobbyists
Misc Business
Transportation
Other

$0 $50 $100 $150 $200 $250

Labor

Bldg Trades/Industrial/Misc Unions	**$117,425**
AFL-CIO*	$10,000
Comm Workers Union Local #13000	$10,000
Ironworkers Union	$10,000
Machinists/Aerospace Workers Union	$10,000
United Auto Workers	$10,000
United Steelworkers	$10,000
Food & Commercial Workers Union	$7,500
Intl Brotherhood of Electrical Workers*	$7,000
Carpenters & Joiners Union	$5,500
Plumbers/Pipefitters Union*	$4,500
Electronic Machine Furniture Workers	$4,000
Operating Engineers Union*	$3,500
Rubber Cork Linoleum Plastic Workers	$3,500
Laborers Political League	$2,500
Sheet Metal Workers Union	$2,500
Graphic Communications Union	$1,725
Glass/Molders/Pottery/Plastics Workers	$1,700
Bakery, Confectionary & Tobacco Workers	$1,500
Boilermakers Union	$1,500
Painters & Allied Trades Union	$1,500
Service Employees International Union	$1,500
Oil, Chemical & Atomic Workers Union	$1,250
Others	$6,250

Government & Postal Workers $40,933

American Fedn of State/County/Munic Employees	$11,983
National Assn of Letter Carriers	$10,000
National Assn of Retired Federal Employees	$6,500
American Postal Workers Union	$3,500
National Assn of Postmasters	$2,000
National Rural Letter Carriers Assn	$2,000
International Assn of Firefighters	$1,250
Others	$3,700

Teachers Unions $20,000

American Federation of Teachers	$10,000
National Education Assn	$10,000

Transportation Unions $38,250

Teamsters Union*	$10,000
Marine Engineers Union*	$5,000
Amalgamated Transit Union	$4,500
Air Line Pilots Assn	$3,500
Seafarers International Union	$3,000
Transport Workers Union	$3,000
Masters, Mates & Pilots Union	$2,500
United Transportation Union	$2,000
Transportation Communication Union	$1,600
Others	$3,150

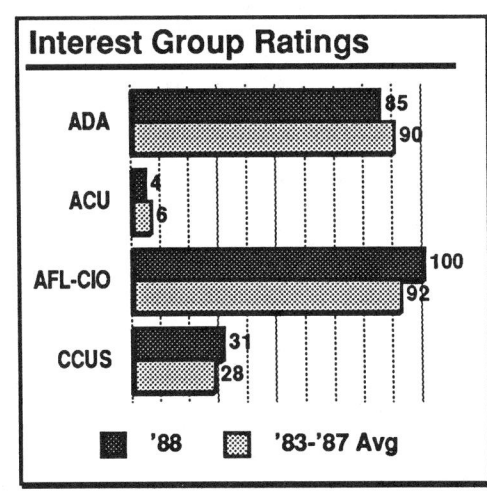

Interest Group Ratings

	'88	'83-'87 Avg
ADA	85	90
ACU	4	6
AFL-CIO	100	92
CCUS	31	28

Ideological/Single-Issue

Democratic/Liberal $14,246

National Cmte for an Effective Congress	$9,996
Hollywood Women's Political Cmte	$2,500
Others	$1,750

Democratic Leadership PACs $25,100

24th Cong Dist of California PAC (Henry Waxman)	$5,000
Cmte for Democratic Opportunity (Bill Gray)	$4,500
Valley Education Fund (Tony Coelho)	$4,000
Independent Action (Morris Udall)	$3,500
Majority Congress Committee (Jim Wright)	$3,000
Pax Americas (David Bonior)	$2,600
Others	$2,500

Pro-Choice $11,000

Voters for Choice/Friends of Family Planning	$6,000
National Abortion Rights Action League	$5,000

Pro-Israel $34,250

Joint Action Cmte for Political Affairs	$6,000
National PAC	$5,000
Hudson Valley PAC	$3,000
Desert Caucus	$2,500
Garden State PAC	$2,000
Women's Pro-Israel National PAC	$2,000
Roundtable PAC	$1,500
Washington PAC	$1,500
Others	$10,750

Other Major Ideological/Single-Issue PACs

National Cmte to Preserve Social Security	$5,500	Soc Secur
Human Rights Campaign Fund	$5,000	Gay Rights
Neighbor to Neighbor PAC	$4,089	ForeignPolicy
Sierra Club	$3,968	Environment
Council for a Livable World	$2,588	Pro-Peace
SANE/Freeze Inc	$2,000	Pro-Peace
League of Conservation Voters	$1,011	Environment

Independent expenditures supporting Kostmayer

National Cmte to Preserve Social Security	$3,517

Independent expenditures opposing Kostmayer

National Right to Life PAC	$1,313

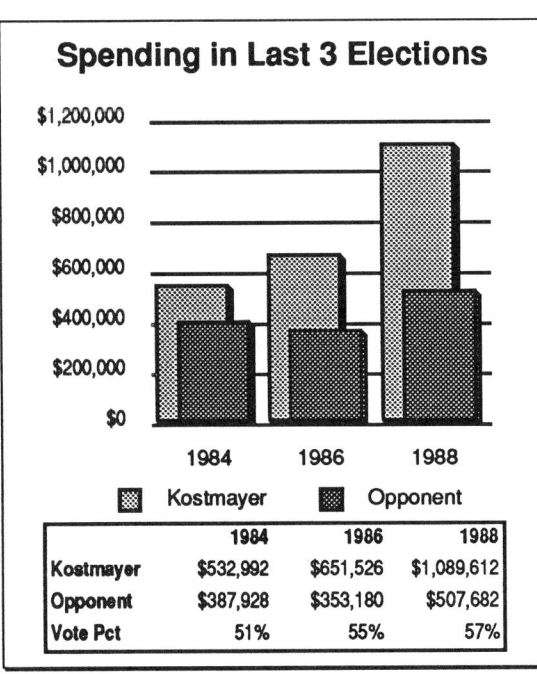

Spending in Last 3 Elections

	1984	1986	1988
Kostmayer	$532,992	$651,526	$1,089,612
Opponent	$387,928	$353,180	$507,682
Vote Pct	51%	55%	57%

Kostmayer   Opponent

---

* Contributions came from more than one PAC affiliated
with this sponsor.

639

Jon Kyl, R-Ariz (4)

1988 Committees & Subcommittees

Armed Services
Investigations
Military Personnel and Compensation

Government Operations
Employment and Housing
Environment, Energy and Natural Resources

PAC Contribution Profile

Business

Accountants	**$5,000**
American Institute of CPA's	$5,000
Automotive	**$4,250**
Auto Dealers & Drivers for Free Trade	$3,000
National Auto Dealers Assn	$1,000
Others	$250
Chemicals	**$8,650**
Greyhound Corp	$7,900
Others	$750
Commercial Banks	**$14,450**
Arizona Bankers Assn	$4,250
Valley National Bank of Arizona	$2,750
Chase Bank of Arizona	$2,250
Arizona Bank	$1,750
United Bank of Arizona	$1,100
Thunderbird Bank	$1,000
Others	$1,350
Construction	**$9,900**
National Utility Contractors Assn	$2,000
National Assn of Home Builders	$1,600
Associated General Contractors	$1,500
Philips Industries	$1,000
Others	$3,800

First elected: 1986
Total receipts: $497,313
Total from PACs: $178,114

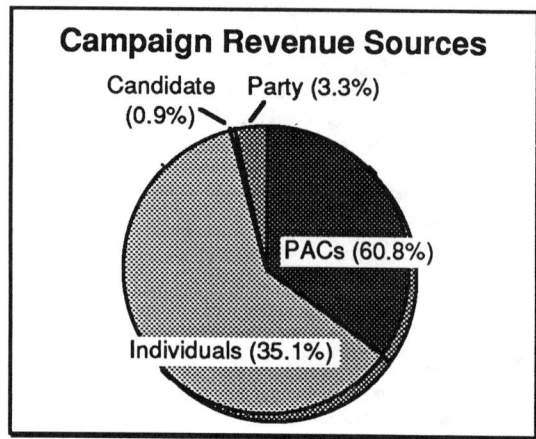

Campaign Revenue Sources

Candidate (0.9%)
Party (3.3%)
PACs (60.8%)
Individuals (35.1%)

Defense	**$31,300**
AT&T	$3,000
Talley Industries	$2,150
Textron Inc	$2,000
McDonnell Douglas*	$1,500
Rockwell International	$1,400
Allied-Signal	$1,250
Continental Telecom	$1,250
Motorola Inc	$1,250
Northrop Corp	$1,250
Colt Industries	$1,150
General Dynamics	$1,050
Boeing Company	$1,000
Honeywell Inc*	$1,000
Hughes Aircraft	$1,000
United Technologies	$1,000
Others	$10,050
Electric Utilities	**$2,250**
Arizona Public Service Company	$1,000
Others	$1,250
Food & Beverage	**$4,800**
Food Marketing Institute	$1,250
National Restaurant Assn	$1,000
Others	$2,550
Health Professionals	**$18,550**
American Medical Assn	$10,000
American Academy of Ophthalmology	$3,000
American Dental Assn	$3,000
Cmte for Quality Orthopedic Health Care	$1,000
Others	$1,550
Insurance	**$5,750**
National Assn of Life Underwriters	$3,000
Blue Cross & Blue Shield Assn*	$1,000
Others	$1,750
Irrigation Systems	**$2,500**
Salt River Valley Water Users	$2,500
Lawyers	**$5,100**
Assn of Trial Lawyers of America	$4,500
Others	$600
Mining & Metal Processing	**$3,250**
Phelps Dodge Corp	$2,250
Others	$1,000

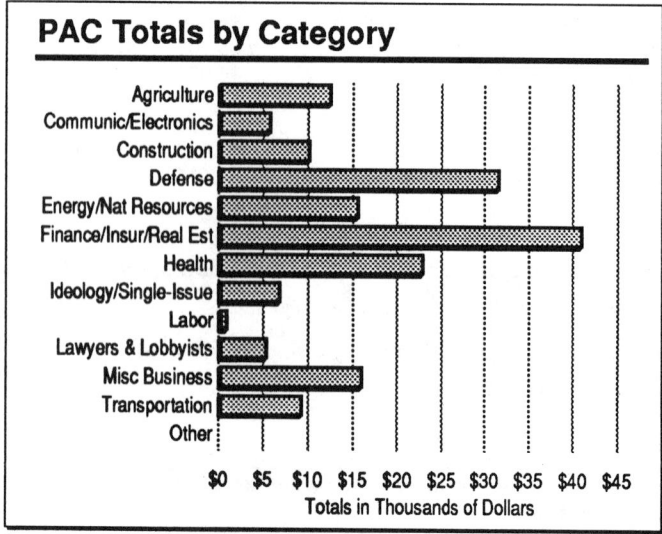

PAC Totals by Category

- Agriculture
- Communic/Electronics
- Construction
- Defense
- Energy/Nat Resources
- Finance/Insur/Real Est
- Health
- Ideology/Single-Issue
- Labor
- Lawyers & Lobbyists
- Misc Business
- Transportation
- Other

$0 $5 $10 $15 $20 $25 $30 $35 $40 $45
Totals in Thousands of Dollars

Oil & Gas	....	**$9,550**
	Southwest Gas Corp	$1,500
	El Paso Company	$1,300
	Amoco Corp	$1,250
	Atlantic Richfield	$1,000
	Others	$4,500

Pharmaceuticals	....	**$2,200**
	Abbott Laboratories	$1,250
	Others	$950

Real Estate	....	**$9,000**
	National Assn of Realtors	$6,250
	Del Webb Corp	$1,000
	Others	$1,750

Savings Banks	....	**$5,650**
	Sun State Savings & Loan	$2,000
	Merabank Federal Savings Bank	$1,500
	Great American First Savings & Loan	$1,250
	Others	$900

Telecommunications	....	**$5,000**
	Mountain Bell	$5,000

Other Major Business PACs

Maytag Company	....	$1,250	Appliances
Sunkist Growers	....	$1,250	Fruit/Veg
Santa Fe Southern Pacific	....	$1,150	Railroads
American Hospital Assn	....	$1,000	Hospitals
Stone Container Corp	....	$1,000	Paper Packg
United Parcel Service	....	$1,000	Delivery

Ideological/Single-Issue

Ideological/Single-Issue	....	**$6,539**
Execs for Free Enterprise Health Care	.... $1,250	HealthWelfare
Campaign America (Bob Dole)	.... $1,000	Repub Leader
Hudson Valley PAC	.... $1,000	Pro-Israel
Others	.... $3,289	

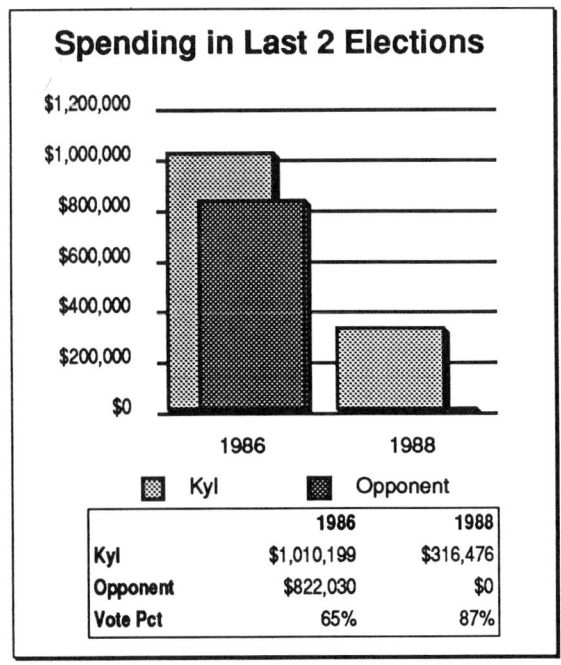

Spending in Last 2 Elections

	1986	1988
Kyl	$1,010,199	$316,476
Opponent	$822,030	$0
Vote Pct	65%	87%

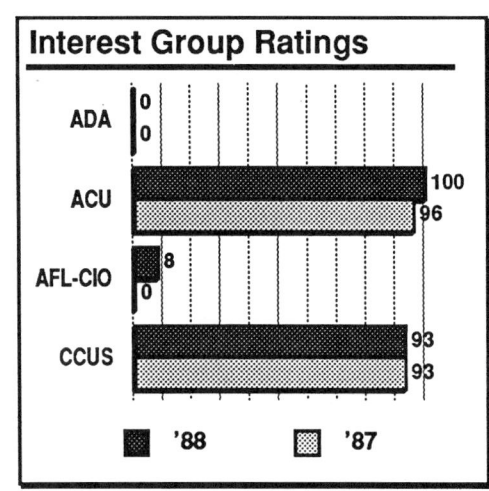

Interest Group Ratings

	'88	'87
ADA	0	0
ACU	100	96
AFL-CIO	8	0
CCUS	93	93

■ '88   ▨ '87

---

* Contributions came from more than one PAC affiliated
with this sponsor.

John J. LaFalce, D-NY (32)

First elected: 1974
Total receipts: $241,784
Total from PACs: $141,022

1988 Committees & Subcommittees

Banking, Finance and Urban Affairs
Economic Stabilization
Financial Institutions Supervision, Regulation and Insurance
International Development Institutions and Finance
International Finance, Trade and Monetary Policy

Small Business (Chairman)
SBA and the General Economy (Chairman)

PAC Contribution Profile

Business

Business Organizations	**$3,500**
American Assn of Mesbics	$1,000
National Assn of Sm Bus Invest Companies	$1,000
National Assn of Women Business Owners	$1,000
Others	$500
Commercial Banks	**$43,150**
J P Morgan & Company	$10,000
American Bankers Assn	$5,000
Security Pacific Corp	$3,000
Chase Lincoln First Bank	$2,500
Citicorp	$2,500
Norstar Bancorp	$2,500
Marine Midland Banks	$2,300
Bankers Trust	$2,000
Chemical Bank	$2,000
Barnett Banks of Florida	$1,500
Manufacturers Hanover	$1,500
Continental Illinois Corp	$1,250
BankAmerica	$1,000
Chase Manhattan	$1,000
Consumer Bankers Assn	$1,000
Others	$4,100
Consumer Credit & Loans	**$3,000**
Household International	$1,000
Others	$2,000
Health Professionals	**$4,500**
American Dental Assn	$2,000
New York Medical Assn	$1,500
National Assn of Pharmacists	$1,000

Campaign Revenue Sources

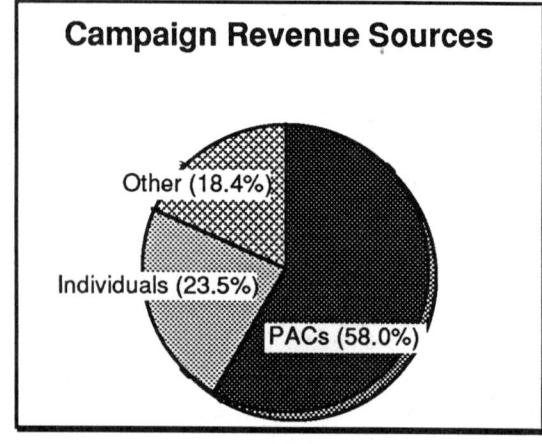

Other (18.4%)
Individuals (23.5%)
PACs (58.0%)

Lawyers	**$7,350**
Assn of Trial Lawyers of America	$5,000
Jones, Day, Reavis & Pogue	$1,000
Others	$1,350
Long Distance Telephone	**$2,000**
AT&T	$2,000
Real Estate	**$5,750**
National Assn of Realtors	$3,000
Federal National Mortgage Assn	$1,000
Mortgage Bankers Assn of America	$1,000
Others	$750
Savings Banks	**$11,150**
Goldome Bank for Savings	$3,100
Empire of America Federal Savings Bank	$1,500
US League of Savings Assn	$1,000
Others	$5,550
Securities & Commodities Investment	**$4,000**
Chicago-Mercantile Exchange	$1,000
Dean Witter Reynolds	$1,000
Others	$2,000
Waste Management	**$2,500**
Waste Management Inc	$2,000
Others	$500

Other Major Business PACs

National Venture Capital Assn	$2,000	Venture Cap
National Tooling & Machining Assn	$1,500	Indust Equip
American Veterinary Medical Assn	$1,000	Veterinary
Associated Milk Producers	$1,000	Dairy
J C Penney Company	$1,000	Dept Store
New York State Electric & Gas Corp	$1,000	Gas & Electr
United Parcel Service	$1,000	Delivery
Xerox Corp	$1,000	Off Machines

PAC Totals by Category

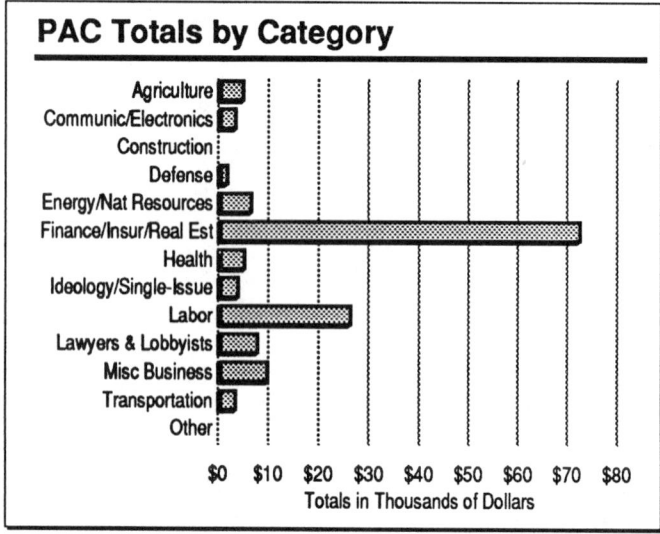

Agriculture
Communic/Electronics
Construction
Defense
Energy/Nat Resources
Finance/Insur/Real Est
Health
Ideology/Single-Issue
Labor
Lawyers & Lobbyists
Misc Business
Transportation
Other

$0 $10 $20 $30 $40 $50 $60 $70 $80
Totals in Thousands of Dollars

Labor

Bldg Trades/Industrial/Misc Unions $11,350
Operating Engineers Local #17 ....$2,000
Operating Engineers Local #832 ....$2,000
United Steelworkers $2,000
Intl Brotherhood of Electrical Workers $1,350
Food & Commercial Workers Union $1,000
Operating Engineers Local #463 ....$1,000
Others $2,000

Government & Postal Workers $2,350
National Assn of Retired Federal Employees $3,000
Others ....-$650

Teachers Unions $4,500
National Education Assn $4,500

Transportation Unions $7,650
Teamsters Union $5,000
Seafarers International Union $1,000
Others $1,650

Ideological/Single-Issue

Ideological/Single-Issue $2,998
National Cmte for an Effective Congress ....$2,498   Dem/Liberal
Others $500

Independent expenditures supporting LaFalce

National Cmte to Preserve Social Security $1,690
National Assn of Insurance Brokers $1,500

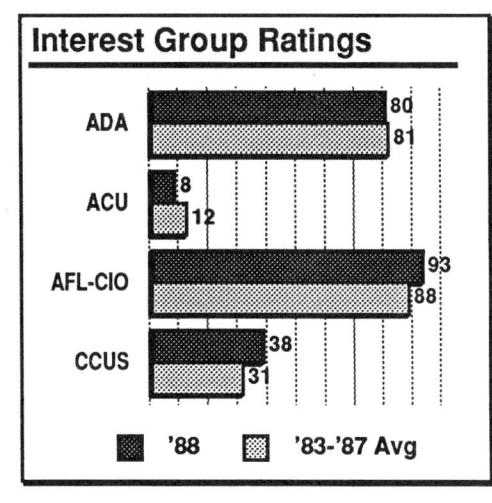

Interest Group Ratings

	'88	'83-'87 Avg
ADA	80	81
ACU	8	12
AFL-CIO	93	88
CCUS	38	31

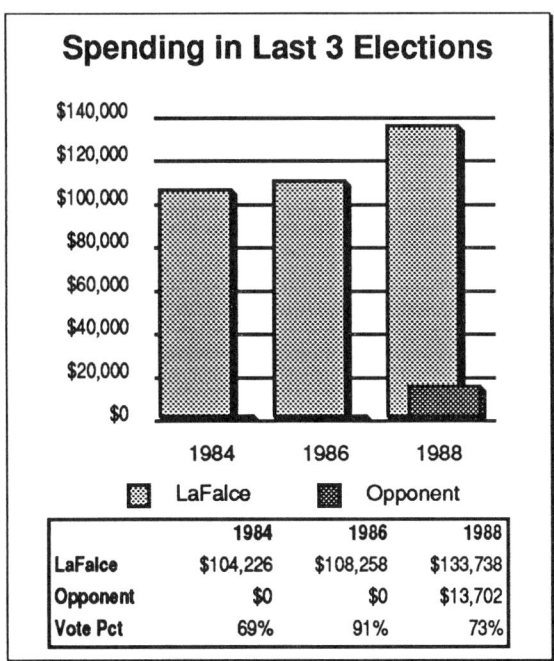

Spending in Last 3 Elections

	1984	1986	1988
LaFalce	$104,226	$108,258	$133,738
Opponent	$0	$0	$13,702
Vote Pct	69%	91%	73%

Robert J. Lagomarsino, R-Calif (19)

First elected: 1974
Total receipts: $1,226,229
Total from PACs: $338,996

1988 Committees & Subcommittees

Foreign Affairs
Western Hemisphere Affairs (Ranking Republican)
Asian and Pacific Affairs

Interior and Insular Affairs
Insular and International Affairs (Ranking Republican)
National Parks and Public Lands (Ranking Republican)

PAC Contribution Profile

Business

Automotive **$18,250**
- Auto Dealers & Drivers for Free Trade $8,500
- National Auto Dealers Assn $5,300
- Eaton Corp $3,000
- Others $1,450

Business Associations **$9,091**
- National Fedn of Independent Business $6,738
- Business Industry PAC $2,353

Construction **$26,800**
- National Assn of Home Builders $7,000
- Associated General Contractors $5,000
- Manville Corp $5,000
- Ameron Inc $2,000
- Associated Builders & Contractors $1,300
- National Electrical Contractors Assn $1,000
- Sheet Metal/AirCon Contractors $1,000
- Others $4,500

Defense **$32,050**
- Watkins-Johnson Company $5,000
- Rockwell International $4,850
- Raytheon $4,700
- Hughes Aircraft $4,500
- Northrop Corp $3,300
- Lockheed Corp $3,000
- Harris Corp $2,000
- General Dynamics $1,000
- Others $3,700

Campaign Revenue Sources

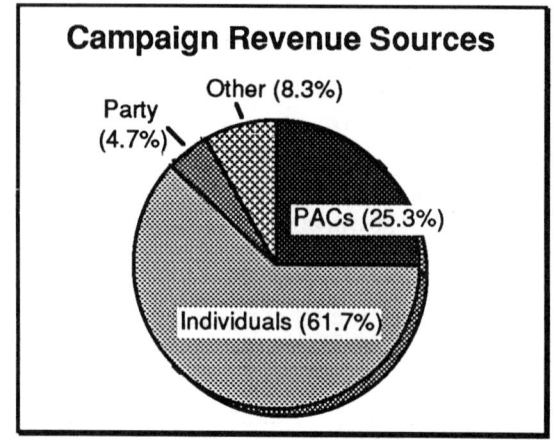

Other (8.3%)
Party (4.7%)
PACs (25.3%)
Individuals (61.7%)

Electric & Power Utilities **$12,225**
- Pacific Gas & Electric $3,500
- Southern California Edison $2,650
- Southern Company* $1,625
- Edison Electric Institute $1,050
- Texas Utilities Electric Company* $1,000
- Others $2,400

Financial Institutions **$14,260**
- American Bankers Assn $5,000
- BankAmerica $2,410
- First Interstate Bank/California $1,300
- Credit Union National Assn $1,000
- Glendale Federal Savings & Loan $1,000
- Others $3,550

Food & Beverage **$17,337**
- Wine Institute $5,254
- Wine & Spirits Wholesalers of America $2,400
- Coors Industries $2,033
- National Restaurant Assn $2,000
- Ampco Foods Inc $1,500
- Pepsico Inc $1,500
- Nabisco Brands Inc $1,000
- Others $1,650

Fruit & Vegetable Growers **$15,850**
- Sunkist Growers $5,000
- California Almond Growers Exchange $4,800
- Western Growers Assn $2,000
- California Canning Peach Assn $1,050
- Others $3,000

Health Professionals **$11,200**
- American Medical Assn $10,000
- Others $1,200

Oil & Gas **$48,803**
- Chevron Corp $5,050
- Halliburton Company $5,020
- Phillips Petroleum $4,998
- Litton Industries $3,500
- Amoco Corp $3,450
- Cooper Industries $3,000
- Tenneco Inc $3,000
- Atlantic Richfield $2,550
- Dow Chemical* $2,000
- Occidental Petroleum* $1,750
- Exxon Corp $1,500
- Sun Company $1,500
- Pacific Enterprises $1,400

(Continued in next column)

PAC Totals by Category

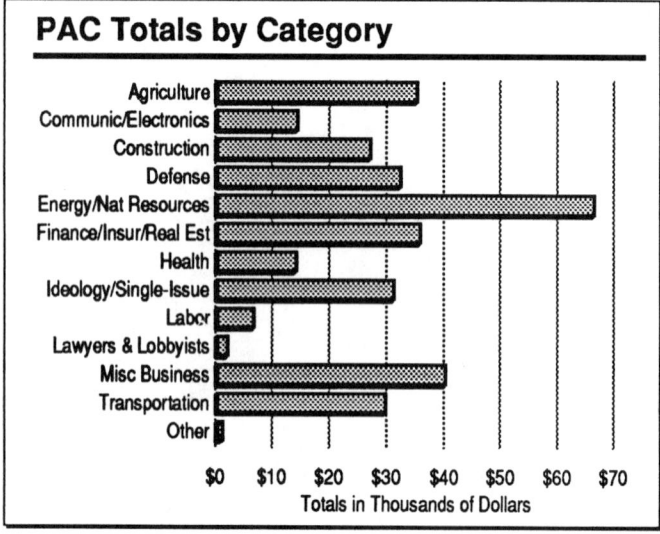

Agriculture
Communic/Electronics
Construction
Defense
Energy/Nat Resources
Finance/Insur/Real Est
Health
Ideology/Single-Issue
Labor
Lawyers & Lobbyists
Misc Business
Transportation
Other

$0 $10 $20 $30 $40 $50 $60 $70
Totals in Thousands of Dollars

Oil & Gas (cont'd)

Union Oil $1,385
Texaco $1,150
Independent Oil Producers' Agency $1,000
Mobil Oil $1,000
Shell Oil $1,000
Others $4,550

Real Estate **$11,600**

National Assn of Realtors $9,000
Newhall Land & Farming Company $1,250
Others $1,350

Telecommunications **$10,000**

Continental Telecom $3,000
Pacific Telesis Group $1,600
GTE Corp $1,550
AT&T $1,300
United Telecommunications $1,000
Others $1,550

Other Major Business PACs

California Farm Bureau Federation	$5,000	Farm Orgs
United Parcel Service	$2,860	Delivery
National Assn of Life Underwriters	$2,500	Life Insurance
American Financial Services Assn	$2,000	Credit/Loans
Minnesota Mining & Manufacturing (3M)	$2,000	Indust Equip
Pneumo Abex Corp	$1,621	AerospacePts
FMC Corp	$1,500	Metals/Mining
Western United Dairymens Assn	$1,320	Dairy
Nevada Resort Assn	$1,200	Casinos/Gamb
Borg-Warner	$1,150	Indust Equip
National Cattlemen's Assn	$1,050	Livestock
American Business Products	$1,000	Printing
American Consulting Engineers Council	$1,000	Engineers
American Sugarbeet Growers Assn	$1,000	Sugar
Carter Hawley Hale Stores	$1,000	Dept Store
Hercules Inc	$1,000	Chemicals
Holiday Inns	$1,000	Hotel/Motel
Institute/Scrap Recycling Industries	$1,000	Recycling
International Paper Company	$1,000	Paper Prod
International Sanitary Supply	$1,000	Hous/Off Prd
ITT Corp	$1,000	Insurance
Marriott Corp	$1,000	Hotel/Motel
Philip Morris	$1,000	Tobacco
Precision Metalforming Assn	$1,000	MetalProduct
TransAmerica Life Companies	$1,000	Life Insurance
Unisys Corp	$1,000	Comput Parts

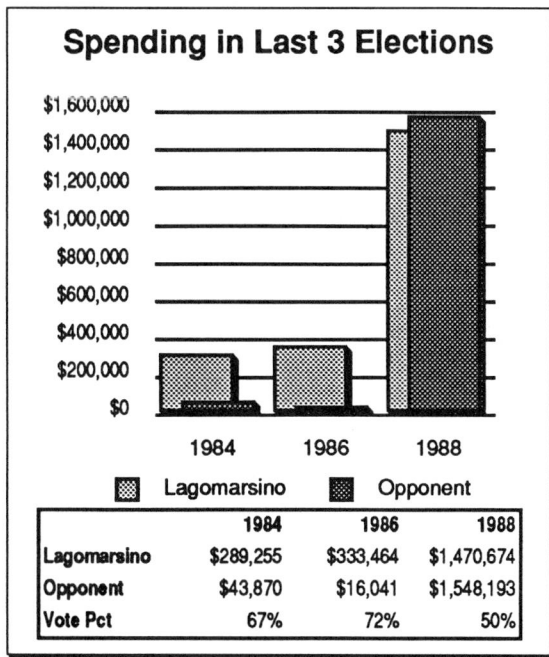

Spending in Last 3 Elections

■ Lagomarsino   ▨ Opponent

	1984	1986	1988
Lagomarsino	$289,255	$333,464	$1,470,674
Opponent	$43,870	$16,041	$1,548,193
Vote Pct	67%	72%	50%

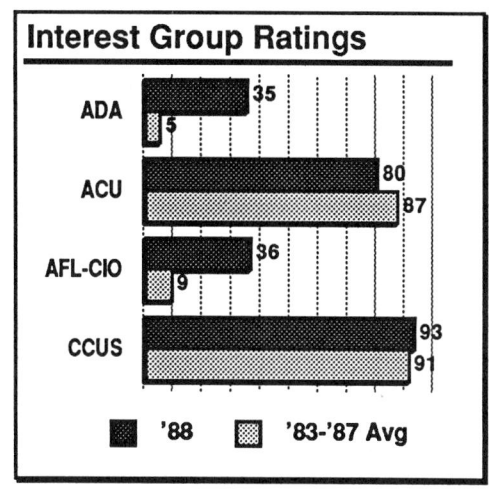

Interest Group Ratings

	'88	'83-'87 Avg
ADA	35	5
ACU	80	87
AFL-CIO	36	9
CCUS	93	91

■ '88   ▨ '83-'87 Avg

Labor

Labor Unions **$6,350**

National Assn of Retired Federal Employees $5,000
Masters Mates & Pilots Union $1,000
Others $350

Ideological/Single-Issue

Republican Leadership/Conservative PACs **$7,247**

Republican Congressional Boosters Club $2,000
Conservative Victory Fund (Steve Symms) $1,236
Conservative Victory Cmte $1,011
Campaign America (Bob Dole) $1,000
Policy Innovation PAC (Dick Armey) $1,000
Republican Majority Fund (Richard Lugar) $1,000

Other Major Ideological/Single-Issue PACs

Council for National Defense	$5,000	Pro-Defense
Women's Pro-Israel National PAC	$5,000	Pro-Israel
National Rifle Assn	$4,950	Pro-Guns
Public Service Research Council	$3,000	Anti-Union
National Right to Life PAC	$2,500	Pro-Life
Right to Work PAC	$1,000	Anti-Union

Independent expenditures supporting Lagomarsino

National Right to Life PAC $4,235

---

* Contributions came from more than one PAC affiliated
with this sponsor.

H. Martin Lancaster, D-NC (3)

First elected: 1986
Total receipts: $195,992
Total from PACs: $132,249

1988 Committees & Subcommittees

Agriculture
Tobacco and Peanuts

Armed Services
Investigations
Readiness

Small Business
Exports, Tourism and Special Problems
Procurement, Innovation and Minority Enterprise Development

PAC Contribution Profile

Business

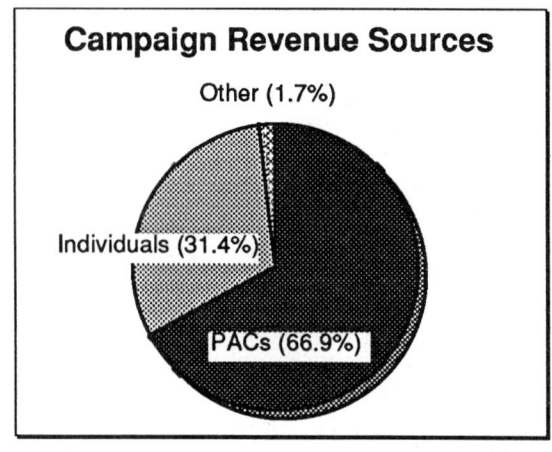

Campaign Revenue Sources

Other (1.7%)
Individuals (31.4%)
PACs (66.9%)

Aviation/Air Freight	**$2,800**
Federal Express Corp	$2,000
Others	$800
Commercial & Savings Banks	**$4,400**
US League of Savings Assn	$1,600
American Bankers Assn	$1,000
Barnett Banks of Florida	$1,000
Others	$800
Construction	**$6,100**
National Assn of Home Builders	$2,500
Associated General Contractors	$1,250
National Utility Contractors Assn	$1,000
Others	$1,350
Dairy	**$4,600**
Associated Milk Producers	$2,500
Dairymen Inc-North Carolina	$1,100
Mid-American Dairymen	$1,000
Defense	**$14,750**
AT&T	$1,750
Textron Inc	$1,250
Lockheed Corp	$1,000
Martin Marietta Corp	$1,000
McDonnell Douglas*	$1,000
Tenneco Inc	$1,000
Others	$7,750
Electric Utilities	**$3,200**
None over $550	$3,200

Food & Beverage	**$4,200**
National Restaurant Assn	$1,000
National Beer Wholesalers Assn	$1,000
Others	$2,200
Health Professionals	**$11,895**
American Medical Assn	$5,250
American Academy of Ophthalmology	$2,500
American Physical Therapy Assn	$1,350
Norht Carolina Society of Anesthesiologists	$1,195
National Assn of Pharmacists	$1,050
Others	$550
Insurance	**$7,386**
National Assn of Life Underwriters	$3,000
Independent Insurance Agents of America	$2,536
Others	$1,850
Lawyers & Lobbyists	**$2,250**
Assn of Trial Lawyers of America	$2,000
Others	$250
Real Estate	**$3,550**
National Assn of Realtors	$3,250
Others	$300
Sugar Growers	**$3,000**
None over $550	
Telecommunications	**$3,450**
Southern Bell	$2,000
Others	$1,450
Textiles	**$4,450**
Burlington Industries	$1,300
Others	$3,150
Tobacco	**$9,150**
Philip Morris	$3,300
RJR Nabisco	$2,000
Tobacco Institute	$1,400
Others	$2,450
Trucking/Delivery	**$3,750**
United Parcel Service	$1,600
Others	$2,150

PAC Totals by Category

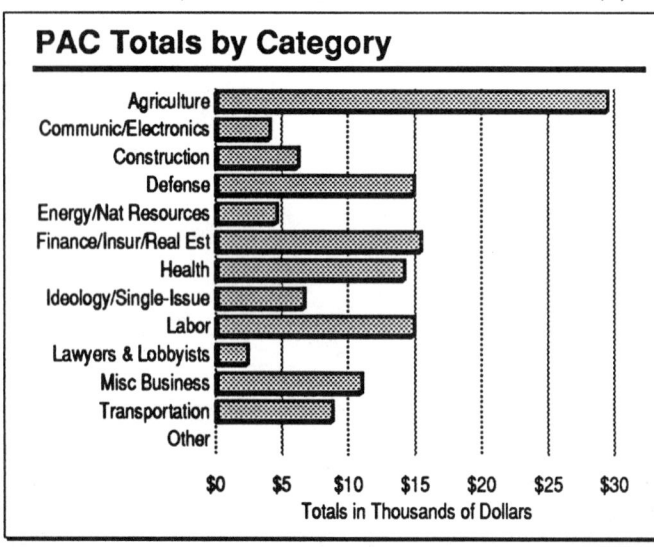

Totals in Thousands of Dollars

Categories (top to bottom): Agriculture, Communic/Electronics, Construction, Defense, Energy/Nat Resources, Finance/Insur/Real Est, Health, Ideology/Single-Issue, Labor, Lawyers & Lobbyists, Misc Business, Transportation, Other

X-axis: $0, $5, $10, $15, $20, $25, $30

Other Major Business PACs

National Cotton Council	$1,150	Cotton
American Furniture Manufacturers Assn	$1,050	Furniture
J C Penney Company	$1,000	Dept Store
National Auto Dealers Assn	$1,000	Auto Sales

Labor

Bldg Trades/Industrial/Misc Unions $6,350
> Air Line Pilots Assn $2,500
> National Education Assn $2,300
> Others $1,550

Government & Postal Workers $8,400
> National Assn of Retired Federal Employees $5,000
> National Assn of Letter Carriers $2,000
> Others $1,400

Ideological/Single-Issue

Democratic Leadership PACs $3,239
> Valley Education Fund (Tony Coelho) $3,239

Other Major Ideological/Single-Issue PACs
National Cmte to Preserve Social Security ...... $1,250   Soc Secur
National Rifle Assn .... $1,000   Pro-Guns

Independent expenditures supporting Lancaster
National Cmte to Preserve Social Security $1,840

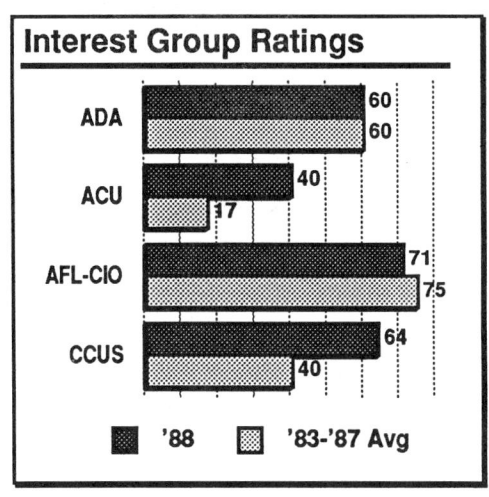

Interest Group Ratings

	'88	'83–'87 Avg
ADA	60	60
ACU	40	17
AFL-CIO	71	75
CCUS	64	40

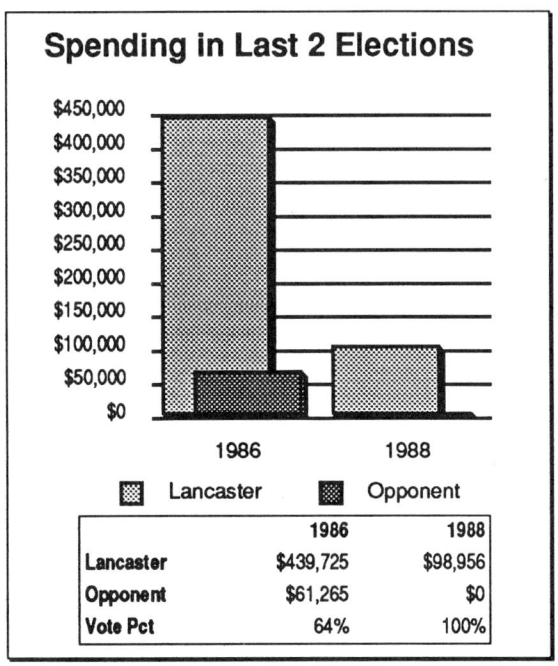

Spending in Last 2 Elections

	1986	1988
Lancaster	$439,725	$98,956
Opponent	$61,265	$0
Vote Pct	64%	100%

---

* Contributions came from more than one PAC affiliated with this sponsor.

Tom Lantos, D-Calif (11)

First elected: 1980
Total receipts: $386,453
Total from PACs: $111,267

1988 Committees & Subcommittees

Foreign Affairs
Arms Control, International Security and Science
Europe and the Middle East
Human Rights and International Organizations

Government Operations
Employment and Housing (Chairman)

Select Aging
Housing and Consumer Interests
Human Services

PAC Contribution Profile

Business

Accountants	***$5,000***
American Institute of CPA's	$5,000
Automotive	***$3,000***
National Auto Dealers Assn	$2,000
Chrysler Corp	$1,000
Defense	***$4,250***
Singer Company	$1,500
Lockheed Corp	$1,000
Others	$1,750
Health Professionals	***$2,250***
Corp for the Advancement of Psychiatry	$1,000
Others	$1,250
Lawyers & Lobbyists	***$3,500***
Assn of Trial Lawyers of America	$2,000
Others	$1,500
Real Estate	***$5,500***
National Assn of Realtors	$5,000
Others	$500
Waste Management	***$3,000***
Browning-Ferris Industries	$3,000

Other Major Business PACs

Boeing Company .... $1,000   Aircraft

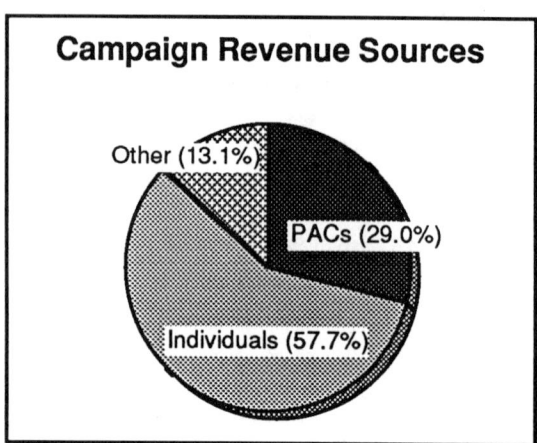

Campaign Revenue Sources

Other (13.1%)
PACs (29.0%)
Individuals (57.7%)

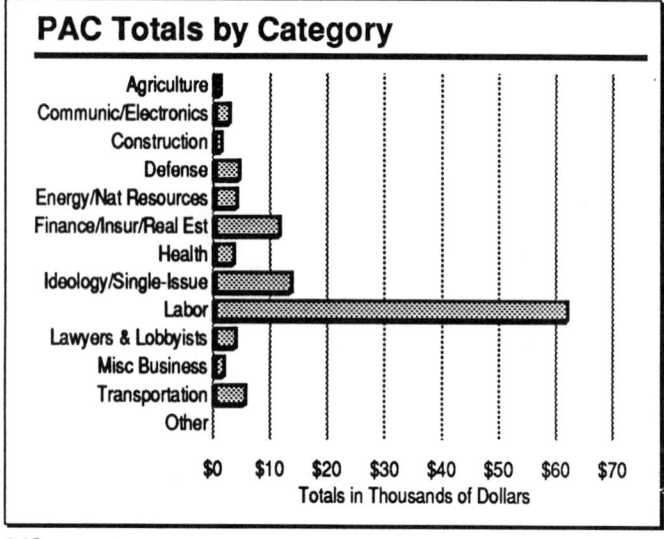

PAC Totals by Category

Agriculture
Communic/Electronics
Construction
Defense
Energy/Nat Resources
Finance/Insur/Real Est
Health
Ideology/Single-Issue
Labor
Lawyers & Lobbyists
Misc Business
Transportation
Other

$0 $10 $20 $30 $40 $50 $60 $70
Totals in Thousands of Dollars

Labor

Bldg Trades/Industrial/Misc Unions **$22,300**

Food & Commercial Workers Union $3,000
Machinists/Aerospace Workers Union $3,000
Plumbers/Pipefitters Union* $2,500
Carpenters & Joiners Union $2,000
Laborers' Western Political League $2,000
United Auto Workers $2,000
Operating Engineers Union $1,500
AFL-CIO* $1,000
Ladies Garment Workers Union $1,000
Oil, Chemical & Atomic Workers Union $1,000
United Steelworkers $1,000
Others $2,300

Government & Postal Workers **$11,200**

National Assn of Retired Federal Employees $6,000
American Postal Workers Union $1,500
American Fedn of State/County/Munic Employees $1,000
Others $2,700

Teachers Unions **$5,000**

National Education Assn $5,000

Transportation Unions **$23,100**

Teamsters Union $9,500
Marine Engineers Union* $4,500
Air Line Pilots Assn $3,500
Seafarers International Union $2,000
Masters, Mates & Pilots Union $1,000
United Transportation Union $1,000
Others $1,600

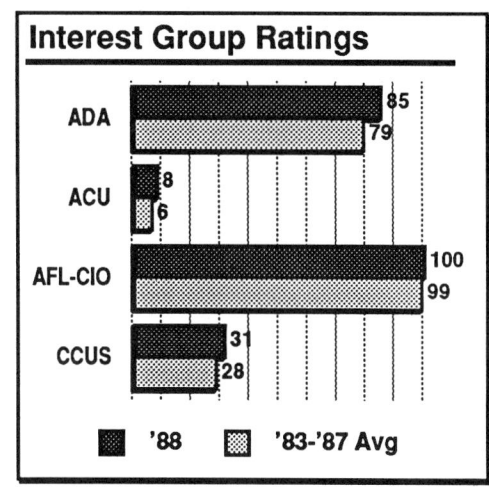

Interest Group Ratings

Legend: ■ '88   ▦ '83-'87 Avg

	'88	'83-'87 Avg
ADA	85	79
ACU	8	6
AFL-CIO	100	99
CCUS	31	28

Ideological/Single-Issue

Pro-Israel **$8,250**

National PAC $5,000
Washington PAC $1,500
Others $1,750

Other Major Ideological/Single-Issue PACs

National Albanian American PAC ....$2,000   Ethnic
National Cmte to Preserve Social Security ......$1,500   Soc Secur

Independent expenditures supporting Lantos

National Cmte to Preserve Social Security $2,458

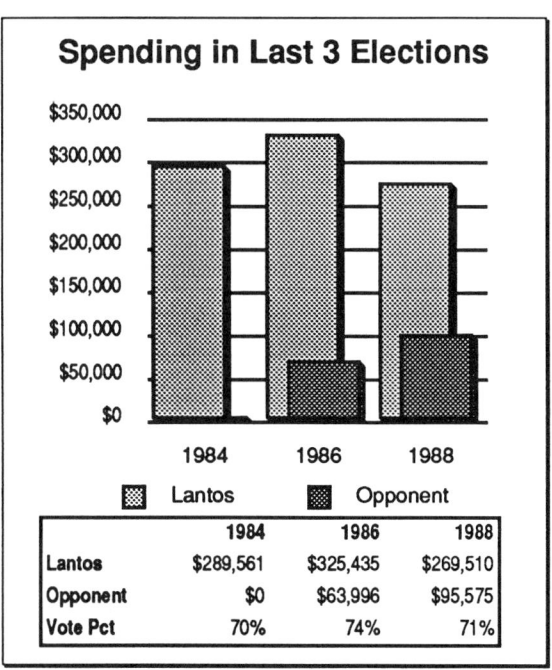

Spending in Last 3 Elections

Legend: ▦ Lantos   ■ Opponent

	1984	1986	1988
Lantos	$289,561	$325,435	$269,510
Opponent	$0	$63,996	$95,575
Vote Pct	70%	74%	71%

* Contributions came from more than one PAC affiliated with this sponsor.

Greg Laughlin, D-Texas (14)

First elected: 1988
Total receipts: $623,491
Total from PACs: $240,699

1988-1989 Committees & Subcommittees

Merchant Marine and Fisheries
Coast Guard and Navigation
Merchant Marine
Panama Canal/Outer Continental Shelf

Public Works and Transportation
Aviation
Surface Transportation
Water Resources

PAC Contribution Profile

Business

Auto Dealers	**$2,000**
National Auto Dealers Assn	$2,000
Construction	**$2,000**
Associated General Contractors	$2,000
Dairy	**$4,350**
Associated Milk Producers	$2,000
Mid-American Dairymen	$1,500
Others	$850
Defense	**$2,000**
Electrospace Systems Inc	$1,000
Others	$1,000
Electric Utilities	**$4,500**
ACRE (Action Committee for Rural Electrification)	$2,250
Central Power & Light	$1,000
Texas-New Mexico Power Company	$1,000
Others	$250
Health Professionals	**$7,000**
American Medical Assn	$5,000
American Nurses Assn	$1,500
Others	$500
Lawyers	**$14,000**
Assn of Trial Lawyers of America	$10,000
Vinson, Elkins, Searls, Connally & Smith	$2,000
Fullbright & Jaworski	$1,500
Others	$500

Life Insurance	**$1,500**
National Assn of Life Underwriters	$1,500
Oil & Gas	**$5,550**
Bass Brothers Enterprises	$1,000
Coastal Corp	$1,000
Phillips Petroleum	$1,000
Valero Energy Corp	$1,000
Others	$1,550
Real Estate	**$5,000**
National Assn of Realtors	$5,000
Trucking Companies	**$1,750**
Yellow Freight System	$1,500
American Trucking Assns	$250
Waste Management	**$3,000**
Browning-Ferris Industries	$3,000

Other Major Business PACs

Shearson Lehman Hutton	$1,000	StocksInvest
Winn-Dixie Stores	$1,000	Food Stores

Campaign Revenue Sources

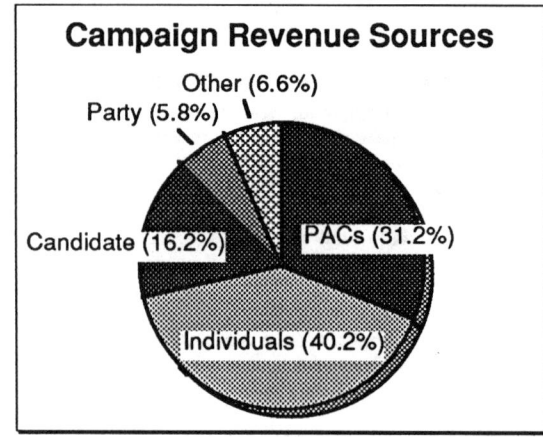

Other (6.6%)
Party (5.8%)
Candidate (16.2%)
PACs (31.2%)
Individuals (40.2%)

PAC Totals by Category

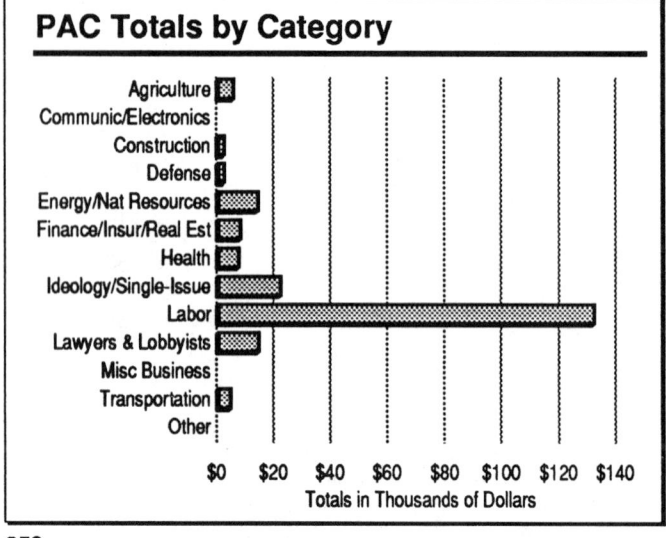

Totals in Thousands of Dollars

Agriculture
Communic/Electronics
Construction
Defense
Energy/Nat Resources
Finance/Insur/Real Est
Health
Ideology/Single-Issue
Labor
Lawyers & Lobbyists
Misc Business
Transportation
Other

$0 $20 $40 $60 $80 $100 $120 $140

Labor

Bldg Trades/Industrial/Misc Unions **$58,150**

Machinists/Aerospace Workers Union	$10,000
United Steelworkers	$10,000
United Auto Workers	$7,000
Communications Workers of America	$5,750
Food & Commercial Workers Union...............................	$5,000
Intl Brotherhood of Electrical Workers..........................	$4,500
Sheet Metal Workers Union	$3,500
AFL-CIO*	$2,800
Carpenters & Joiners Union	$2,750
Laborers' Political League	$2,450
Operating Engineers Union	$1,500
Ironworkers Union	$1,000
Office & Prof Employees Union	$1,000
Others	$900

Government & Postal Workers **$32,450**

National Assn of Letter Carriers	$10,000
National Assn of Retired Federal Employees	$9,000
American Fedn of State/County/Munic Employees	$7,500
American Postal Workers Union	$3,000
Others	$2,950

Teachers Unions **$12,500**

National Education Assn	$10,000
American Federation of Teachers	$2,500

Transportation Unions **$28,550**

Teamsters Union	$14,000
Seafarers International Union	$5,000
Air Line Pilots Assn	$4,000
Transport Workers Union	$2,000
United Transportation Union	$1,350
International Longshoremen Assn	$1,000
Others	$1,200

Ideological/Single-Issue

Democratic Leadership PACs **$13,500**

Valley Education Fund (Tony Coelho)	$7,000
Majority Congress Committee (Jim Wright)	$5,000
House Leadership Fund (Tom Foley)	$1,000
Others	$500

Other Major Ideological/Single-Issue PACs

National Cmte to Preserve Social Security	$5,000	Soc Secur
National Council of Senior Citizens	$1,000	Elderly

Independent expenditures supporting Laughlin

National Cmte to Preserve Social Security	$1,338

Spending in Last Election

	1988
Laughlin	$600,114
Opponent	$645,988
Vote Pct	53%

---

* Contributions came from more than one PAC affiliated with this sponsor.

Jim Leach, R-Iowa (1)

1988 Committees & Subcommittees

Banking, Finance and Urban Affairs
International Finance, Trade and Monetary Policy (Ranking Republican)
Domestic Monetary Policy
Financial Institutions Supervision, Regulation and Insurance

Foreign Affairs
Asian and Pacific Affairs (Ranking Republican)
Arms Control, International Security and Science

PAC Contribution Profile

Jones, Day, Reavis & Pogue	$500	Lawyers
Morton Building Inc	$500	Comml Constr
Occidental Petroleum	$250	Meat Process
Grinnell Mutual Reinsurance Company	$200	Insurance

NOTE: Leach reported taking no PAC funds in his 1988 campaign. The PACs listed above did report making contributions to him during 1987-88, however, and those contributions are recorded in the official FEC records.

First elected: 1976
Total receipts: $206,618
Total from PACs: $0

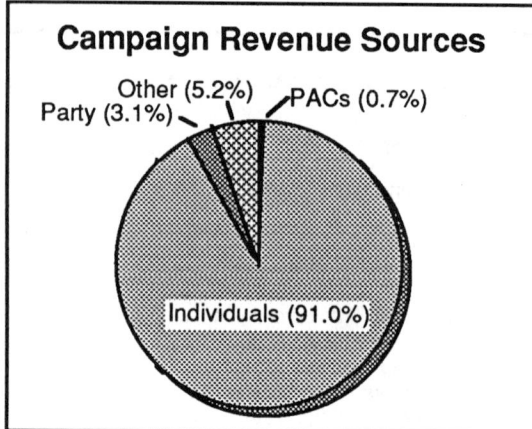

Campaign Revenue Sources

Other (5.2%)
Party (3.1%)
PACs (0.7%)
Individuals (91.0%)

PAC Totals by Category

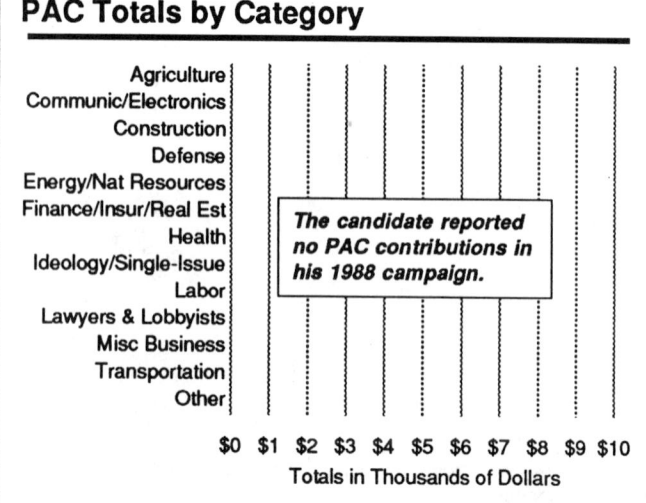

Agriculture
Communic/Electronics
Construction
Defense
Energy/Nat Resources
Finance/Insur/Real Est
Health
Ideology/Single-Issue
Labor
Lawyers & Lobbyists
Misc Business
Transportation
Other

The candidate reported no PAC contributions in his 1988 campaign.

$0 $1 $2 $3 $4 $5 $6 $7 $8 $9 $10
Totals in Thousands of Dollars

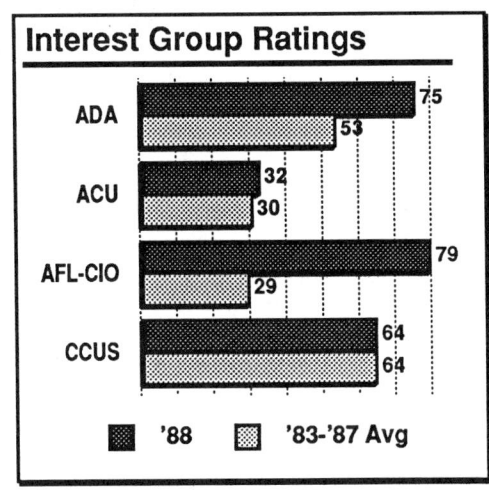

Interest Group Ratings

Group	'88	'83-'87 Avg
ADA	75	53
ACU	32	30
AFL-CIO	79	29
CCUS	64	64

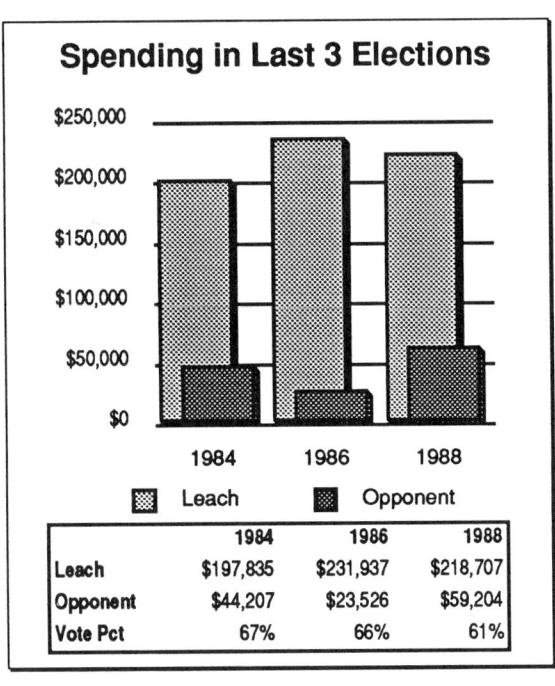

Spending in Last 3 Elections

	1984	1986	1988
Leach	$197,835	$231,937	$218,707
Opponent	$44,207	$23,526	$59,204
Vote Pct	67%	66%	61%

Marvin Leath, D-Texas (11)

First elected: 1978
Total receipts: $178,312
Total from PACs: $94,900

1988 Committees & Subcommittees

Armed Services
Military Installations and Facilities
Procurement and Military Nuclear Systems
Readiness

Budget
Defense and International Affairs

PAC Contribution Profile

Business

Airlines & Aerospace **$3,500**
    Eastern Airlines $2,000
    Gulfstream Aerospace $1,000
    Others $500

Construction **$2,250**
    None over $750

Defense **$30,150**
    AT&T $4,000
    General Dynamics $2,650
    Textron Inc $2,000
    McDonnell Douglas* $1,500
    Allied-Signal $1,000
    Boeing Company $1,000
    Electrospace Systems Inc $1,000
    FMC Corp $1,000
    Grumman $1,000
    Hughes Aircraft $1,000
    Singer Company $1,000
    Varo Inc $1,000
    Others $12,000

Electric Utilities & Equipment **$2,500**
    Houston Industries $1,000
    Others $1,500

Food & Beverage **$4,750**
    National Beer Wholesalers Assn $1,500
    Others $3,250

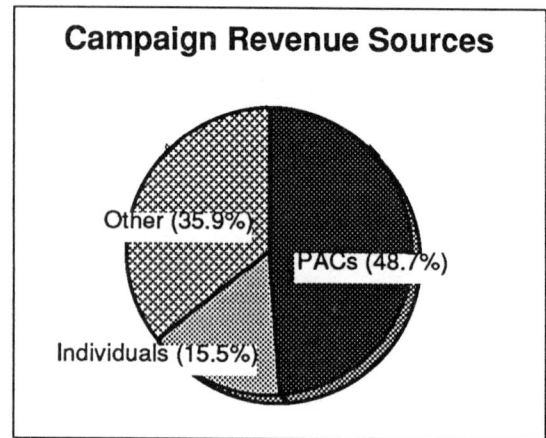

Campaign Revenue Sources

Other (35.9%)
PACs (48.7%)
Individuals (15.5%)

Health Professionals **$7,000**
    American Medical Assn $5,000
    American Dental Assn $2,000

Insurance **$3,000**
    National Assn of Life Underwriters $2,000
    United Services Auto Assn Group $1,000

Oil & Gas **$2,250**
    Valero Energy Corp $1,000
    Others $1,250

Real Estate **$5,500**
    National Assn of Realtors $5,000
    Others $500

Telecommunications **$2,000**
    Southwestern Bell $2,000

Tobacco **$2,250**
    RJR Nabisco $1,000
    Others $1,250

Other Major Business PACs

Alcoa	$1,000	Metals/Mining
American Hospital Assn	$1,000	Hospitals
Associated Milk Producers	$1,000	Dairy
Chicago Mercantile Exchange	$1,000	Commodities
National Auto Dealers Assn	$1,000	Auto Sales

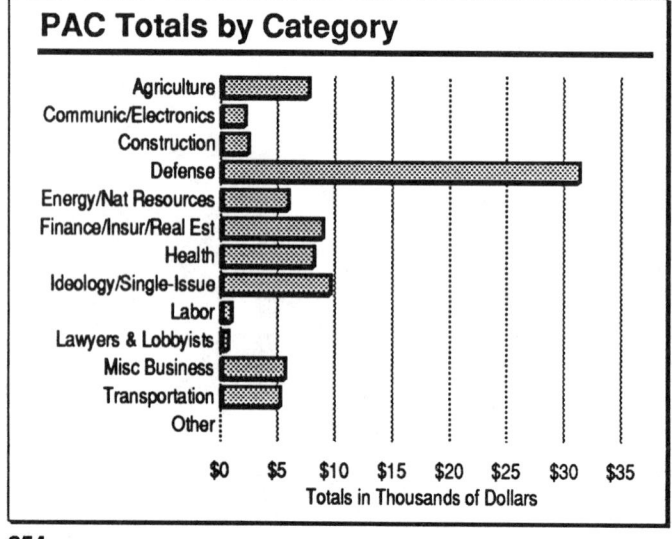

PAC Totals by Category

Agriculture
Communic/Electronics
Construction
Defense
Energy/Nat Resources
Finance/Insur/Real Est
Health
Ideology/Single-Issue
Labor
Lawyers & Lobbyists
Misc Business
Transportation
Other

$0 $5 $10 $15 $20 $25 $30 $35
Totals in Thousands of Dollars

Ideological/Single-Issue

Pro-Israel **$5,250**
    National PAC $5,000
    Others $250

Other Major Ideological/Single-Issue PACs

National Assn for Uniformed Services	$1,500	Pro-Defense
Valley Education Fund (Tony Coelho)	$1,000	Dem Leaders

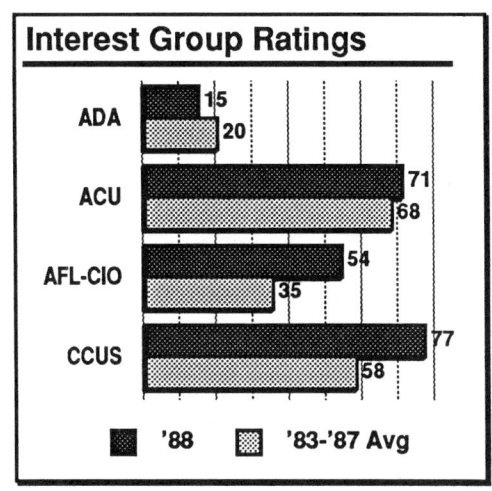

Interest Group Ratings

	'88	'83–'87 Avg
ADA	15	20
ACU	71	68
AFL-CIO	54	35
CCUS	77	58

■ '88   ▨ '83–'87 Avg

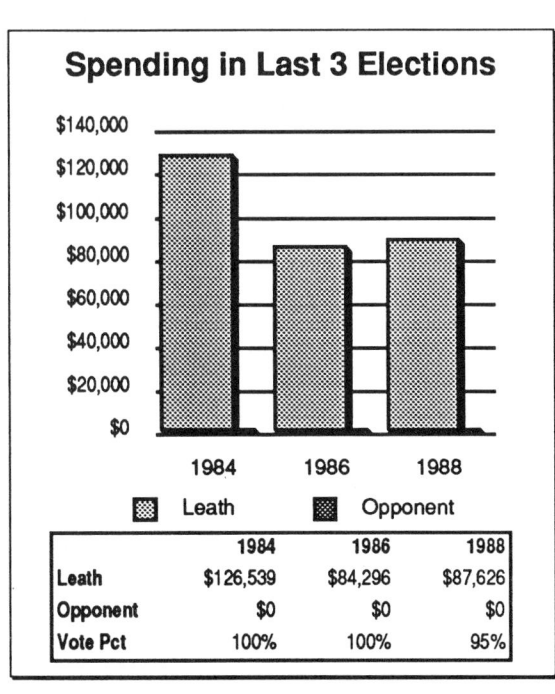

Spending in Last 3 Elections

▨ Leath   ■ Opponent

	1984	1986	1988
Leath	$126,539	$84,296	$87,626
Opponent	$0	$0	$0
Vote Pct	100%	100%	95%

---

* Contributions came from more than one PAC affiliated with this sponsor.

Richard H. Lehman, D-Calif (18)

First elected: 1982
Total receipts: $270,696
Total from PACs: $160,510

1988 Committees & Subcommittees

Banking, Finance and Urban Affairs
Financial Institutions Supervision, Regulation and Insurance
Housing and Community Development
International Finance, Trade and Monetary Policy

Interior and Insular Affairs
National Parks and Public Lands
Water and Power Resources

PAC Contribution Profile

Business

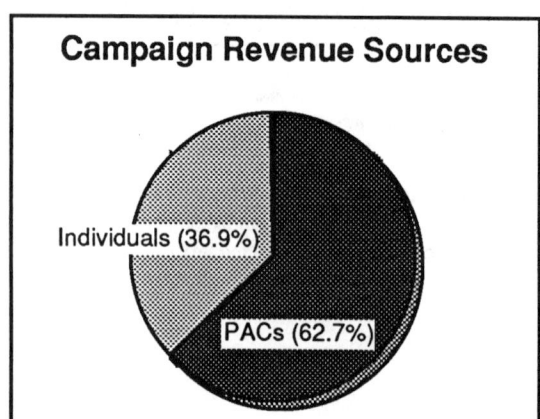

Campaign Revenue Sources

Individuals (36.9%)
PACs (62.7%)

Commercial Banks	**$10,250**
BankAmerica	$1,700
Security Pacific Corp	$1,500
American Bankers Assn	$1,350
Citicorp	$1,000
Others	$4,700

Electric Utilities	**$2,280**
Pacific Gas & Electric	$1,080
Others	$1,200

Fruit & Vegetable Growers	**$11,070**
California Almond Growers Exchange	$5,000
Tri/Valley Growers	$1,250
California Canning Peach Assn	$1,000
Sun-Maid Growers of California	$1,000
Sunsweet Growers	$1,000
Others	$1,820

Insurance	**$17,600**
National Assn of Life Underwriters	$7,150
Independent Insurance Agents of America	$3,200
National Assn Mutual Insurance Agents	$1,200
Pacific Mutual Life	$1,000
Prudential Insurance	$1,000
TransAmerica Life Companies	$1,000
Others	$3,050

Lawyers & Lobbyists	**$3,990**
Akin, Gump, Hauer & Feld	$1,050
Others	$2,940

Oil & Gas	**$2,850**
Pacific Enterprises	$2,000
Others	$850

Package Delivery	**$2,000**
Federal Express Corp	$1,000
United Parcel Service	$1,000

Real Estate	**$12,500**
National Assn of Realtors	$10,000
Century 21 Real Estate	$1,000
Others	$1,500

Residential Construction	**$7,000**
National Assn of Home Builders	$3,950
Manufactured Housing Institute	$1,400
Others	$1,650

Savings Banks	**$17,540**
Great Western Financial Corp	$5,350
US League of Savings Assn	$2,100
Coast Federal Savings & Loan	$1,390
Guarantee Savings	$1,200
Florida League of Financial Institutions	$1,000
Glendale Federal Savings & Loan	$1,000
World Savings & Loan	$1,000
Others	$4,500

Securities & Commodities Investment	**$11,700**
First Boston Corp	$3,000
Prudential-Bache Securities	$2,000
Goldman Sachs	$1,750
Morgan Stanley & Company	$1,500
Investment Company Institute	$1,400
Others	$2,050

Sugar Growers	**$2,100**
None over $700	

Other Major Business PACs

American Dental Assn	$1,500	Dentists
Pirelli Cable	$1,000	Indust Equip

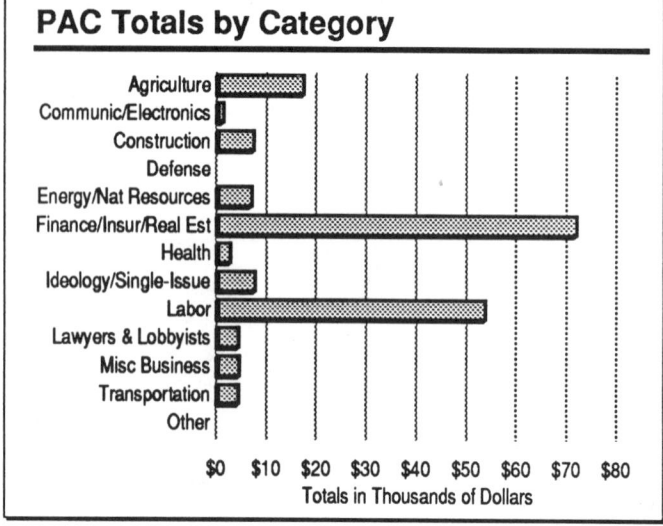

PAC Totals by Category

Agriculture
Communic/Electronics
Construction
Defense
Energy/Nat Resources
Finance/Insur/Real Est
Health
Ideology/Single-Issue
Labor
Lawyers & Lobbyists
Misc Business
Transportation
Other

$0 $10 $20 $30 $40 $50 $60 $70 $80
Totals in Thousands of Dollars

Labor

Bldg Trades/Industrial/Misc Unions $20,360
    Laborers' Western Political League $4,350
    United Auto Workers $3,200
    Operating Engineers Union* $2,110
    Machinists/Aerospace Workers Union $2,000
    Food & Commercial Workers Union $1,850
    Carpenters & Joiners Union $1,500
    Ironworkers Union $1,450
    Sheet Metal Workers Union $1,100
    AFL-CIO* $1,050
    Others $1,750

Government & Postal Workers $7,950
    National Assn of Retired Federal Employees $5,000
    National Assn of Letter Carriers $1,200
    Others $1,750

Teachers Unions $5,500
    National Education Assn $4,500
    American Federation of Teachers $1,000

Transportation Unions $19,600
    Teamsters Union $10,000
    Marine Engineers District 2 Maritime Officers $4,000
    Air Line Pilots Assn $2,000
    United Transportation Union $1,550
    Seafarers International Union $1,000
    Others $1,050

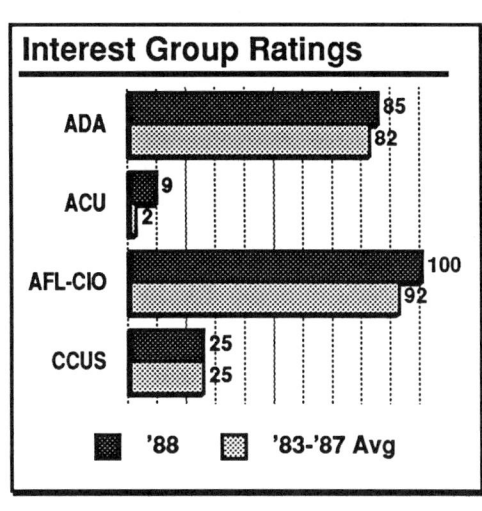

Interest Group Ratings

	'88	'83-'87 Avg
ADA	85	82
ACU	9	2
AFL-CIO	100	92
CCUS	25	25

Ideological/Single-Issue

Ethnic Groups $5,050
    Armenian National Committee $2,500
    Armenian Assembly of America $1,550
    Armenian-American PAC $1,000

Other Major Ideological/Single-Issue PACs
Valley Education Fund (Tony Coelho) .... $1,000   Dem Leaders

Independent expenditures supporting Lehman
National Cmte to Preserve Social Security $2,244

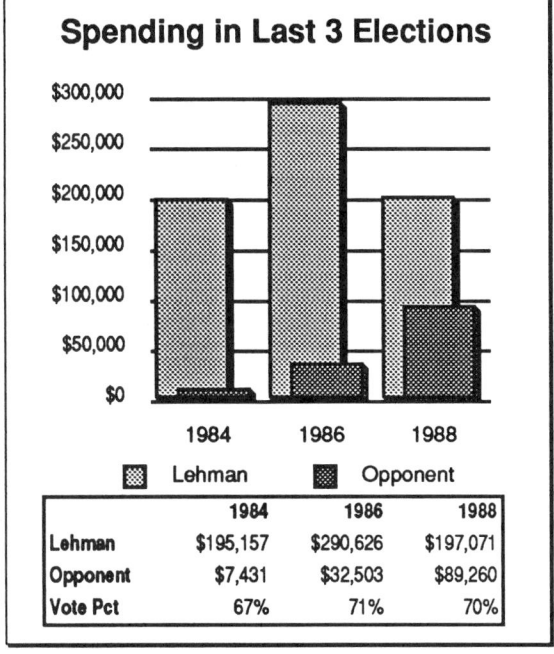

Spending in Last 3 Elections

	Lehman	Opponent

	1984	1986	1988
Lehman	$195,157	$290,626	$197,071
Opponent	$7,431	$32,503	$89,260
Vote Pct	67%	71%	70%

---

* Contributions came from more than one PAC affiliated with this sponsor.

William Lehman, D-Fla (17)

First elected: 1972
Total receipts: $324,062
Total from PACs: $131,750

1988 Committees & Subcommittees

Appropriations
Transportation and Related Agencies (Chairman)
Foreign Operations

Select Children, Youth and Families

PAC Contribution Profile

Business

Campaign Revenue Sources

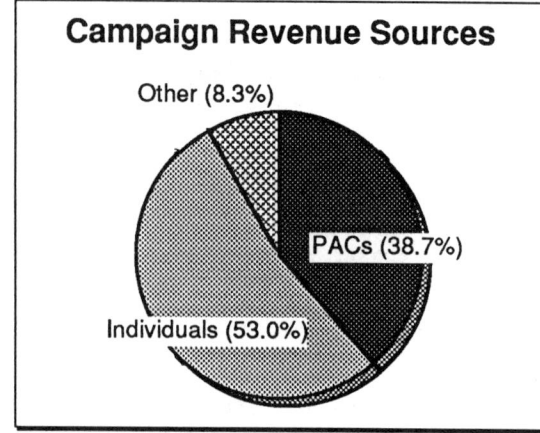

Other (8.3%)
PACs (38.7%)
Individuals (53.0%)

Automotive	**$3,300**
Auto Dealers & Drivers for Free Trade	$1,500
Others	$1,800
Aviation & Aerospace	**$13,550**
Federal Express Corp	$3,000
Eastern Airlines	$2,000
Aircraft Owners & Pilots Assn	$1,800
Boeing Company	$1,000
Genl Aviation Manufacturers Assn	$1,000
Texas Air	$1,000
Others	$3,750
Commercial & Savings Banks	**$6,700**
Barnett Banks of Florida	$1,500
Florida Bankers Assn	$1,000
Florida League of Financial Institutions	$1,000
National Banks of Florida	$1,000
Others	$2,200
Computer Equipment & Services	**$3,600**
Computer Sciences Corp	$2,000
Electrocom Automation Inc	$1,000
Others	$600
Construction	**$6,050**
National Utility Contractors Assn	$2,000
Associated General Contractors	$1,000
National Assn of Home Builders	$1,000
Others	$2,050

Defense	**$4,300**
Bath Iron Works	$1,000
Hughes Aircraft	$1,000
Others	$2,300
Fruit & Vegetable Growers	**$2,000**
Florida Citrus Mutual	$1,000
Ocean Spray Cranberries	$1,000
Health Professionals	**$2,250**
American Dental Assn	$1,000
Others	$1,250
Lawyers	**$7,550**
Assn of Trial Lawyers of America	$2,750
Powell, Goldstein, Frazer & Murphy	$1,000
Others	$3,800
Railroads & Railroad Equipment	**$3,900**
Union Pacific Corp	$1,000
Others	$2,900
Telecommunications	**$4,550**
Southern Bell	$3,000
AT&T	$1,000
Others	$550
Trucking/Delivery	**$9,000**
Consolidated Freightways	$2,500
Ryder System Inc	$2,500
United Parcel Service	$2,000
Others	$2,000

Other Major Business PACs

Boating PAC	$1,000	Rec Boats
Coopers & Lybrand	$1,000	Accountants
Florida Power & Light	$1,000	ElectricUtil
Internorth Inc	$1,000	Natural Gas
Securities Industry Assn	$1,000	Securities

PAC Totals by Category

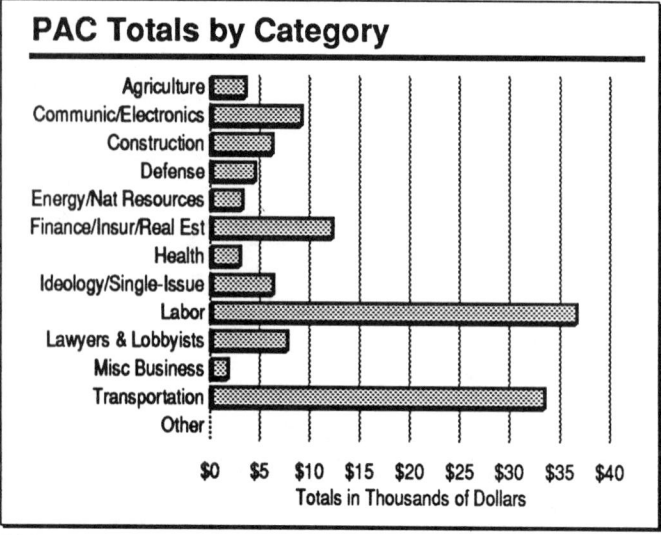

Agriculture
Communic/Electronics
Construction
Defense
Energy/Nat Resources
Finance/Insur/Real Est
Health
Ideology/Single-Issue
Labor
Lawyers & Lobbyists
Misc Business
Transportation
Other

$0 $5 $10 $15 $20 $25 $30 $35 $40
Totals in Thousands of Dollars

Labor

Bldg Trades/Industrial/Misc Unions $9,500
Carpenters & Joiners Union $2,500
AFL-CIO* $1,500
American Federation of Teachers $1,000
Intl Brotherhood of Electrical Workers $1,000
Ladies Garment Workers Union $1,000
Others $2,500

Government & Postal Workers $5,000
American Fedn of State/County/Munic Employees $2,500
National Assn of Letter Carriers $1,000
National Assn of Retired Federal Employees $1,000
Others $500

Transportation Unions $21,950
Amalgamated Transit Union $3,000
Transport Workers Union $3,000
Air Line Pilots Assn $2,500
Marine Engineers Union $2,500
Teamsters Union $2,500
United Transportation Union $2,500
Seafarers International Union $1,500
Transportation Communication Union $1,450
Maintenance of Way Employees $1,000
Others $2,000

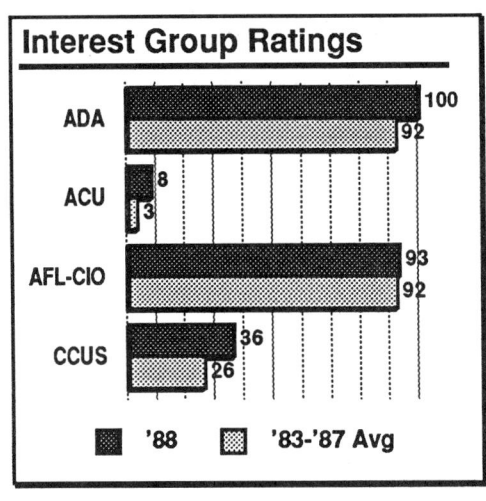

Interest Group Ratings

ADA — '88: 100, '83-'87 Avg: 92
ACU — '88: 8, '83-'87 Avg: 3
AFL-CIO — '88: 93, '83-'87 Avg: 92
CCUS — '88: 36, '83-'87 Avg: 26

■ '88   ▨ '83-'87 Avg

Ideological/Single-Issue

Ideological/Single-Issue $6,100
Assembly of Turkish-American Assns .... $1,000 Ethnic
Human Rights Campaign Fund .... $1,000 Gay Rights
National Cmte to Preserve Social Security ...... $1,000 Soc Secur
Washington PAC .... $1,000 Pro-Israel
Others $2,100

Independent expenditures supporting Lehman
National Cmte to Preserve Social Security $3,019

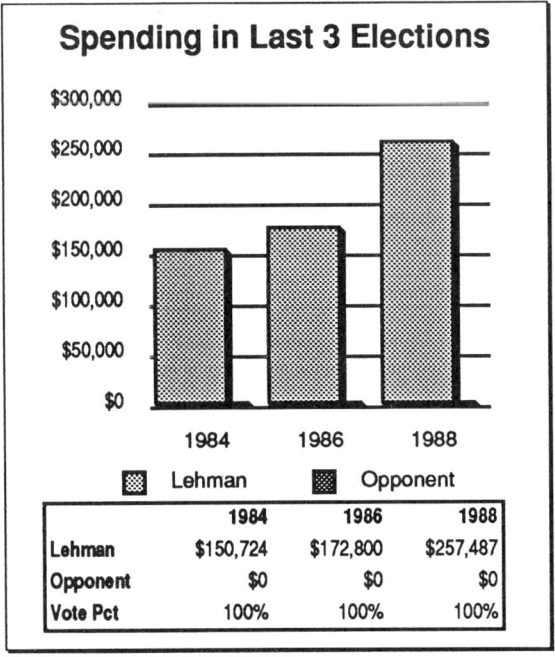

Spending in Last 3 Elections

■ Lehman   ■ Opponent

	1984	1986	1988
Lehman	$150,724	$172,800	$257,487
Opponent	$0	$0	$0
Vote Pct	100%	100%	100%

* Contributions came from more than one PAC affiliated
  with this sponsor.

Mickey Leland, D-Texas (18)

1988 Committees & Subcommittees

First elected: 1978
Total receipts: $532,832
Total from PACs: $346,525

Energy and Commerce
Energy and Power
Health and the Environment
Telecommunications and Finance

Post Office and Civil Service
Compensation and Employee Benefits
Postal Operations and Services (Chairman)
Compensation and Employee Benefits

Select Hunger (Chairman)

PAC Contribution Profile

Business

Accountants	**$5,500**
American Inst of CPA's	$4,900
Others	$600
Air Transport	**$4,700**
Texas Air	$3,500
Others	$1,200
Automotive	**$2,900**
National Auto Dealers Assn	$2,000
Others	$900
Commercial Banks	**$11,000**
First City Bancorp	$2,000
J P Morgan & Co	$2,000
American Bankers Assn	$1,600
Others	$5,400
Dairy	**$4,100**
Associated Milk Producers	$3,500
Others	$600
Electric Utilities	**$8,350**
Houston Industries	$5,000
Others	$3,350
Health Professionals	**$23,800**
American Medical Assn	$5,300
American Dental Assn	$4,300

Campaign Revenue Sources

Party (0.7%) Other (3.4%)
Individuals (29.8%)
PACs (66.1%)

American Pharmaceutical Assn	$3,100
American Academy of Ophthalmology	$1,500
American Podiatry Assn	$1,500
American Chiropractic Assn	$1,300
American Optometric Assn	$1,300
Others	$5,500
Lawyers & Lobbyists	**$23,300**
Assn of Trial Lawyers of America	$10,000
Vinson, Elkins, Searls et al	$4,000
Lidell, Sapp	$2,000
Fullbright & Jaworski	$1,500
Others	$5,800
Oil & Gas	**$19,400**
Arkla Inc*	$1,600
Enserch Corp	$1,500
Atlantic Richfield	$1,300
Chevron Corp	$1,300
Internorth Inc	$1,300
Cameron Iron Works	$1,100
Columbia Hydrocarbon Corp	$1,100
Others	$10,200
Package Delivery	**$7,100**
United Parcel Service	$6,600
Others	$500
Real Estate	**$6,850**
National Assn of Realtors	$4,550
Commonwealth Financial Group	$2,000
Others	$300
Securities & Commodities Investment	**$14,850**
Goldman Sachs	$4,000
Chicago Board of Trade	$2,000
E F Hutton Group	$1,100
Others	$7,750

PAC Totals by Category

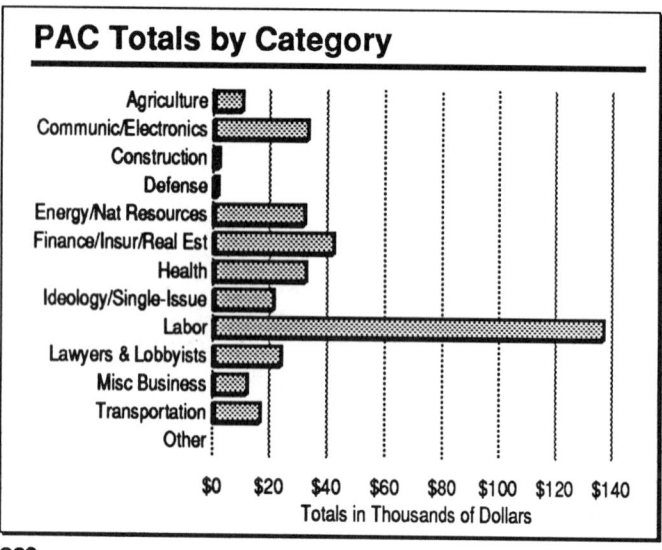

Agriculture
Communic/Electronics
Construction
Defense
Energy/Nat Resources
Finance/Insur/Real Est
Health
Ideology/Single-Issue
Labor
Lawyers & Lobbyists
Misc Business
Transportation
Other

$0 $20 $40 $60 $80 $100 $120 $140
Totals in Thousands of Dollars

Telecommunications	$18,050
GTE Corp*	$2,750
Pacific Telesis Group	$1,750
Southwestern Bell	$1,500
U S West Inc	$1,500
US Telephone Assn	$1,500
BellSouth Corp	$1,350
AT&T	$1,300
Others	$6,400

TV/Entertainment	$11,700
National Cable Television Assn	$5,000
Assn of Independent TV Stations	$1,700
National Assn of Broadcasters	$1,600
Others	$3,400

Other Major Business PACs

Independent Coal Operators Assn	$2,000	Coal
American Hospital Assn	$1,600	Hospitals
Hallmark Cards	$1,600	Publishing
Third Class Mail Assn	$1,400	Mail Order
Blue Cross & Blue Shield Assn	$1,300	Health Insur
Coca-Cola Co	$1,300	Soft Drinks
US League of Savings Assn	$1,100	SavingsBanks

Labor

Bldg Trades/Industrial/Misc Unions	$45,150
AFL-CIO*	$5,500
Communications Workers of America	$5,300
United Auto Workers	$5,300
Machinists/Aerospace Workers Union	$5,000
United Steelworkers	$5,000
Intl Brotherhood of Electrical Workers*	$4,000
Food & Commercial Workers Union	$3,550
Carpenters & Joiners Union	$3,000
Laborers' Political League	$1,900
Others	$6,600

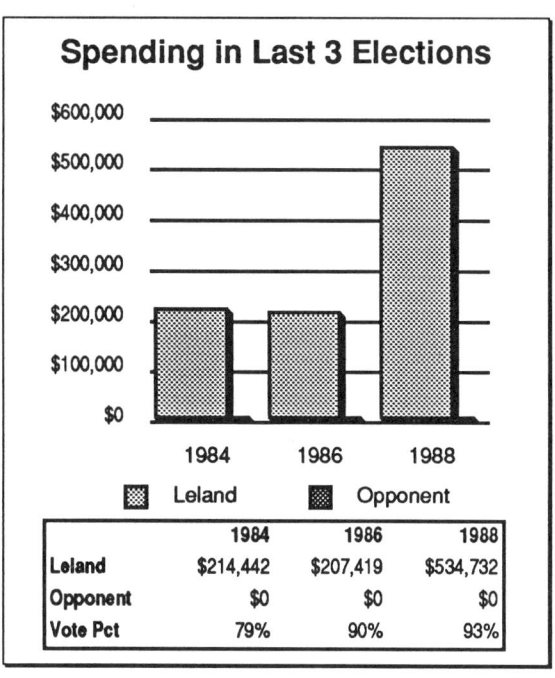

Spending in Last 3 Elections

Legend: Leland, Opponent

	1984	1986	1988
Leland	$214,442	$207,419	$534,732
Opponent	$0	$0	$0
Vote Pct	79%	90%	93%

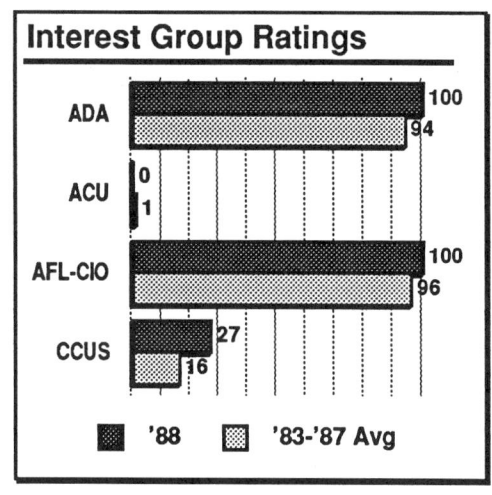

Interest Group Ratings

	'88	'83-'87 Avg
ADA	100	94
ACU	0	1
AFL-CIO	100	96
CCUS	27	16

Government & Postal Workers	$54,550
American Postal Workers Union*	$15,150
National Assn of Letter Carriers	$10,000
National Assn of Retired Federal Employees	$8,000
American Fedn of State/County/Munic Employees	$5,000
National Assn of Postmasters	$4,000
National Star Rte Mail Contractors	$2,800
International Assn of Firefighters*	$2,250
National Assn of Postal Supervisors	$2,100
National League of Postmasters	$1,600
National Rural Letter Carriers Assn	$1,600
Others	$2,050

Teachers Unions	$9,400
National Education Assn	$7,500
American Federation of Teachers	$1,900

Transportation Unions	$27,200
Teamsters Union	$10,000
United Transportation Union	$3,600
Seafarers International Union	$3,500
International Longshoremen Assn	$3,100
Amalgamated Transit Union	$2,000
Marine Engineers Union*	$2,000
Others	$3,000

Ideological/Single-Issue

Democratic Leadership PACs	$9,000
24th Cong Dist of Calif PAC (Henry Waxman)	$5,000
Majority Congress Committee (Jim Wright)	$2,000
Valley Education Fund (Tony Coelho)	$2,000

Pro-Israel	$7,000
National PAC	$5,000
Others	$2,000

Other Major Ideological/Single-Issue PACs

Human Rights Campaign Fund	$2,000	Gay Rights
National Cmte to Preserve Social Security	$1,300	Soc Secur

Independent expenditures supporting Leland

National Cmte to Preserve Social Security	$1,041

* Contributions came from more than one PAC affiliated
  with this sponsor.

Norman F. Lent, R-NY (4)

First elected: 1970
Total receipts: $589,323
Total from PACs: $357,749

1988 Committees & Subcommittees

Energy and Commerce (Ranking Republican)
Oversight and Investigations

Merchant Marine and Fisheries
Merchant Marine (Ranking Republican)

PAC Contribution Profile

Business

Accountants	**$23,300**
American Institute of CPA's	$10,000
Touche Ross	$5,000
Coopers & Lybrand	$2,800
Arthur Young & Company	$1,500
Ernst & Whinney	$1,500
Others	$2,500
Automotive	**$6,550**
Auto Dealers & Drivers for Free Trade	$2,250
Ford Motor Company	$1,250
Others	$3,050
Chemicals	**$6,250**
FMC Corp	$1,500
Others	$4,750
Commercial Banks	**$19,500**
J P Morgan & Company	$5,000
American Bankers Assn	$3,500
Citicorp	$2,500
Others	$8,500
Construction	**$10,850**
Walter Industries	$2,500
Sheet Metal/AirCon Contractors	$2,000
Others	$6,350
Defense	**$9,100**
Grumman	$1,500
United Technologies	$1,250
Others	$6,350

Campaign Revenue Sources

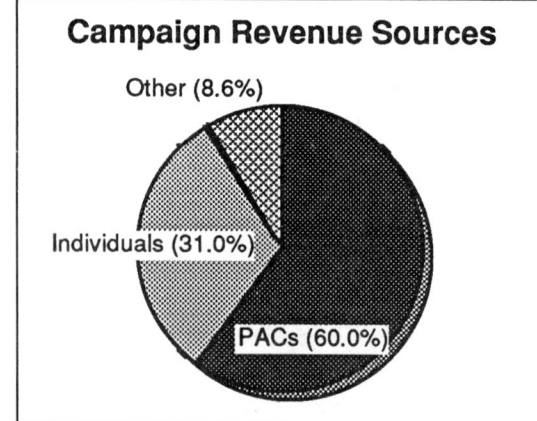

Other (8.6%)
Individuals (31.0%)
PACs (60.0%)

Electric Utilities	**$19,250**
Public Service Company of New Hampshire*	$2,400
Southern Company*	$1,800
Houston Industries	$1,500
New York State Electric & Gas Corp	$1,300
Southern California Edison	$1,300
Others	$10,950
Food & Beverage	**$9,300**
National Beer Wholesalers Assn	$2,000
Whitman Corp	$1,750
Others	$5,550
Health Professionals	**$21,350**
American Medical Assn	$5,250
American Dental Assn	$4,000
New York Medical Assn	$2,500
American College of Emergency Physicians	$2,000
American Podiatry Assn	$1,500
Cmte for Quality Orthopedic Health Care	$1,500
Others	$4,600
Hospitals & Nursing Homes	**$7,750**
American Health Care Assn	$5,000
Others	$2,750
Insurance	**$38,214**
American Council of Life Insurance	$3,383
Independent Insurance Agents of America	$3,381
National Assn of Life Underwriters	$2,500
Travelers Corp	$2,500
National Assn Mutual Insurance Agents	$2,250
Mutual of Omaha*	$1,750
Casualty & Surety Agents Assn	$1,500
Metropolitan Life Insurance	$1,500
National Assn of Independent Insurers	$1,500
Aetna Life & Casualty	$1,250
Cigna Corp	$1,250
Health Insurance Assn of America	$1,250
National Assn of Insurance Brokers	$1,250
Prudential Insurance	$1,250
Others	$11,700
Lawyers & Lobbyists	**$6,800**
None over $1,000	

PAC Totals by Category

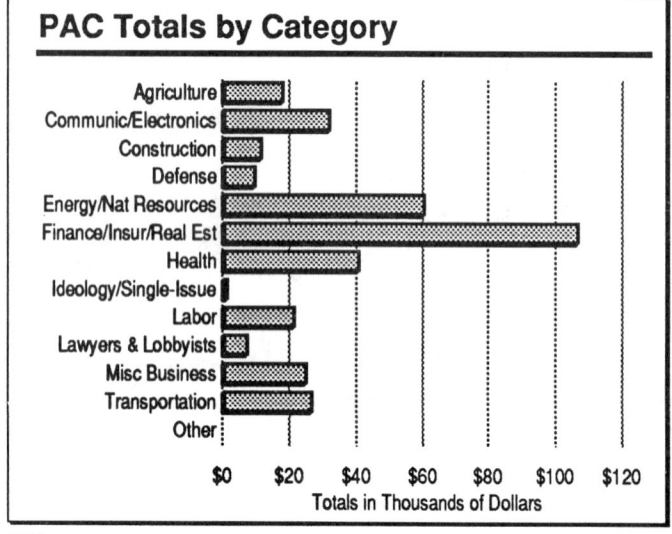

Agriculture
Communic/Electronics
Construction
Defense
Energy/Nat Resources
Finance/Insur/Real Est
Health
Ideology/Single-Issue
Labor
Lawyers & Lobbyists
Misc Business
Transportation
Other

$0 $20 $40 $60 $80 $100 $120
Totals in Thousands of Dollars

Oil & Gas $32,800
    Pacific Enterprises $2,050
    Columbia Natural Resources $2,000
    Enserch Corp $2,000
    Union Pacific Corp $2,000
    Atlantic Richfield $1,750
    Coastal Corp $1,500
    Others $21,500

Pharmaceuticals $9,950
    Schering-Plough Corp $1,500
    Others $8,450

Railroads $5,000
    None over $1,000

Real Estate $6,000
    National Assn of Realtors $5,750
    Others $250

Sea Transport $7,500
    CSX Transportation Inc* $2,500
    American Pilots Assn $2,000
    Others $3,000

Securities & Commodities Investment $24,000
    Morgan Stanley & Company $4,000
    First Boston Corp $3,000
    Goldman Sachs $2,500
    Chicago Board of Options Exchange $2,000
    Chicago Board of Trade $2,000
    New York Stock Exchange $1,500
    Others $9,000

Telecommunications $22,475
    AT&T $10,000
    BellSouth Corp $2,500
    Corning Glass Works $2,000
    New York Telephone $1,725
    Ameritech Corp $1,500
    Others $4,750

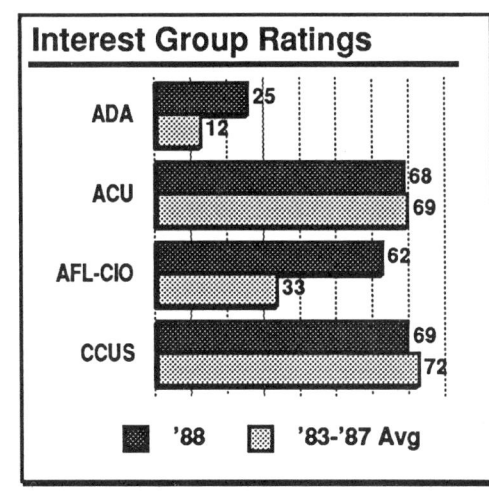

Tobacco $6,550
    Philip Morris $4,000
    Others $2,550

TV/Movies $7,750
    National Cable Television Assn $4,000
    National Assn of Broadcasters $1,750
    Others $2,000

Other Major Business PACs

United Parcel Service	$2,600	Delivery
Holiday Inns	$2,000	Hotel/Motel
Waste Management Inc	$2,000	Waste Mgmt
Browning-Ferris Industries	$1,500	Waste Mgmt
Owens-Illinois	$1,500	Paper Packg
Westvaco Corp	$1,500	Paper Prod

Labor

Bldg Trades/Industrial/Misc Unions $12,500
    National Assn of Retired Federal Employees ... $1,500
    Carpenters & Joiners Union* $4,000
    United Transportation Union $3,000
    Others $4,000

Sea Transport Unions $8,250
    Marine Engineers Union* $4,500
    Seafarers International Union $2,250
    Others $1,500

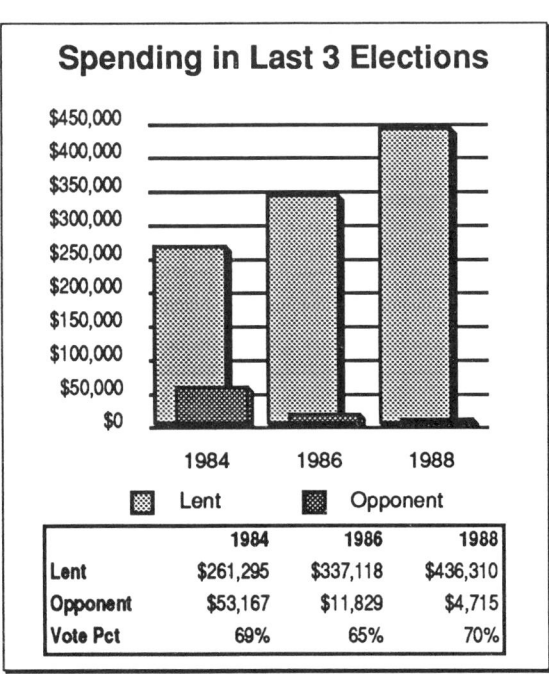

* Contributions came from more than one PAC affiliated with this sponsor.

Sander M. Levin, D-Mich (17)

First elected: 1982
Total receipts: $300,654
Total from PACs: $193,430

1988 Committees & Subcommittees

Ways and Means
Health
Social Security

Select Children, Youth and Families

PAC Contribution Profile

Business

Accountants **$6,250**
- American Institute of CPA's $5,000
- Others $1,250

Automotive **$3,375**
- None over $750

Electric Utilities **$3,125**
- Consumers Power Company $1,125
- Detroit Edison $1,000
- Others $1,000

Financial Institutions **$17,450**
- American Bankers Assn $5,000
- Comerica Inc $2,650
- Citicorp $1,500
- Michigan League of Savings Institutions $1,500
- US League of Savings Assn $1,500
- Credit Union National Assn $1,050
- Michigan Credit Union League $1,000
- National Bank of Detroit $1,000
- Others $2,250

Food & Beverage **$4,750**
- Joseph E Seagram & Sons $1,000
- Kellogg Company $1,000
- Others $2,750

Campaign Revenue Sources

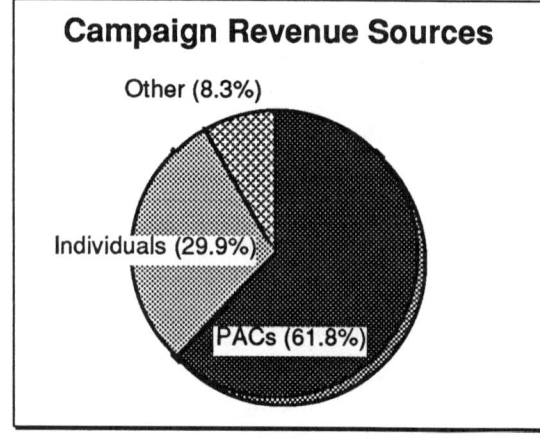

Other (8.3%)
Individuals (29.9%)
PACs (61.8%)

Health Professionals **$15,825**
- American Dental Assn $3,250
- American Medical Assn $2,000
- Oral & Maxillofacial Surgeons $1,500
- Assn for Advancement of Psychology $1,250
- American Podiatry Assn $1,000
- Others $6,825

Hospitals & Nursing Homes **$6,000**
- American Hospital Assn $2,750
- National Assn of Private Psychiatric Hospitals ... $1,500
- American Health Care Assn $1,250
- Others $500

Insurance **$14,775**
- Metropolitan Life Insurance $2,000
- Travelers Corp $1,500
- Chubb Corp $1,000
- National Assn of Life Underwriters $1,000
- North Western Mutual Life $1,000
- Others $8,275

Lawyers & Lobbyists **$10,500**
- Assn of Trial Lawyers of America $5,000
- Others $5,500

Oil & Gas **$2,750**
- Atlantic Richfield $1,000
- Others $1,750

Securities & Commodities Investment **$4,750**
- First Boston Corp $1,000
- Securities Industry Assn $1,000
- Others $2,750

Telecommunications **$5,430**
- AT&T $2,250
- Pacific Telesis Group $1,000
- Others $2,180

Other Major Business PACs

American Assn of Equipment Lessors	$1,500	Rentals
Boeing Company	$1,000	Aircraft
Federal Express Corp	$1,000	Delivery
General Electric	$1,000	Electronics
International Council of Shopping Centers	$1,000	Retail
Kelly Service Inc	$1,000	EmployAgency

PAC Totals by Category

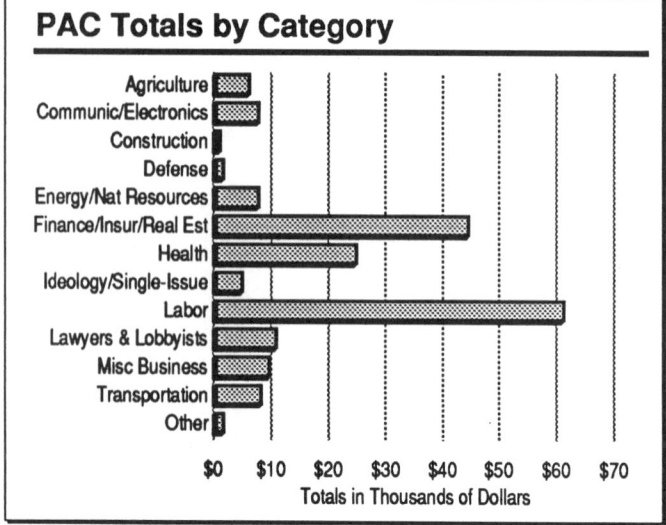

Agriculture
Communic/Electronics
Construction
Defense
Energy/Nat Resources
Finance/Insur/Real Est
Health
Ideology/Single-Issue
Labor
Lawyers & Lobbyists
Misc Business
Transportation
Other

$0 $10 $20 $30 $40 $50 $60 $70
Totals in Thousands of Dollars

Labor

Bldg Trades/Industrial/Misc Unions $28,425

United Auto Workers	$10,000
Carpenters & Joiners Union	$4,000
Operating Engineers Union*	$2,125
Machinists/Aerospace Workers Union	$2,000
Laborers' Political League	$1,750
Boilermakers Union*	$1,325
AFL-CIO*	$1,250
Others	$5,975

Government & Postal Workers $20,425

National Assn of Retired Federal Employees	$6,500
American Fedn of State/County/Munic Employees	$5,000
National Assn of Letter Carriers	$4,800
American Postal Workers Union	$1,750
National Rural Letter Carriers Assn	$1,250
Others	$1,125

Teachers Unions $4,800

National Education Assn	$4,250
Others	$550

Transportation Unions $7,125

Air Line Pilots Assn	$2,500
Seafarers International Union	$1,500
Others	$3,125

Major Ideological/Single-Issue PACs

National Council of Senior Citizens	$1,000	Soc Secur
Valley Education Fund (Tony Coelho)	$1,000	Dem Leaders

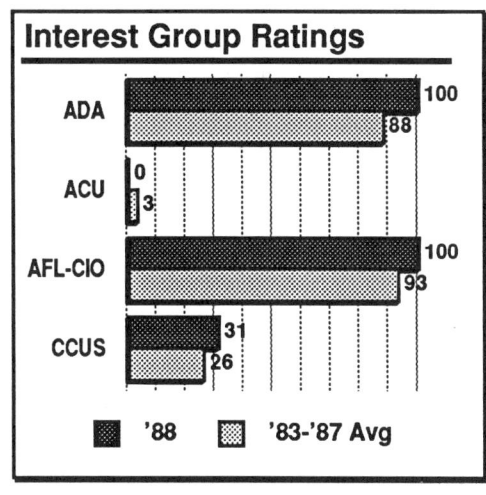

Interest Group Ratings

	'88	'83-'87 Avg
ADA	100	88
ACU	0	3
AFL-CIO	100	93
CCUS	31	26

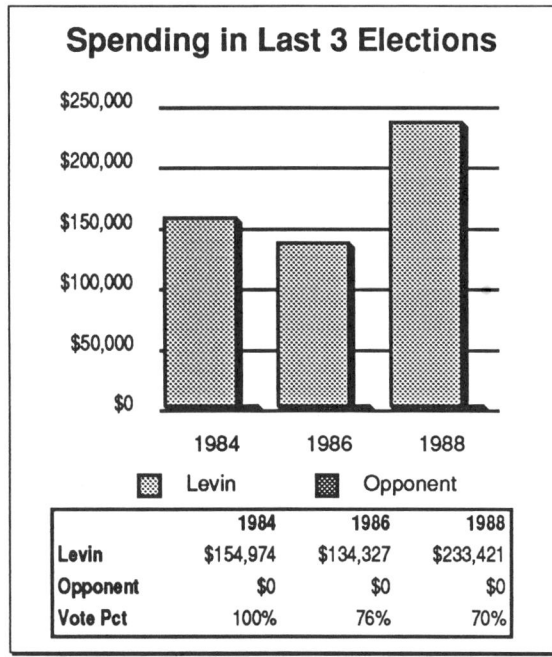

Spending in Last 3 Elections

Levin □   Opponent ■

	1984	1986	1988
Levin	$154,974	$134,327	$233,421
Opponent	$0	$0	$0
Vote Pct	100%	76%	70%

---

* Contributions came from more than one PAC affiliated with this sponsor.

665

Mel Levine, D-Calif (27)

First elected: 1982
Total receipts: $841,274
Total from PACs: $153,500

1988 Committees & Subcommittees

Foreign Affairs
Europe and the Middle East
International Economic Policy and Trade

Interior and Insular Affairs
Energy and the Environment
National Parks and Public Lands
Water and Power Resources

Select Narcotics Abuse and Control

PAC Contribution Profile

Business

Commercial Banks	**$3,450**
American Bankers Assn	$1,000
Others	$2,450
Defense	**$9,300**
Northrop Corp	$3,600
Lockheed Corp	$3,000
Hughes Aircraft	$1,200
Rockwell International	$1,200
Others	$300
Entertainment Industry	**$12,700**
Lorimar-Telepictures Corp	$4,000
MCA Inc	$2,600
Recording Industry Assn	$1,500
Fox Inc	$1,000
MGM/UA Communications	$1,000
Warner Communications	$1,000
Others	$1,600
Health Professionals	**$2,200**
American Medical Assn	$1,300
Others	$900
Hospitals & Nursing Homes	**$3,500**
Centinela Hospital	$2,000
Others	$1,500
Import Auto Dealers	**$5,000**
Auto Dealers & Drivers for Free Trade	$5,000

Campaign Revenue Sources

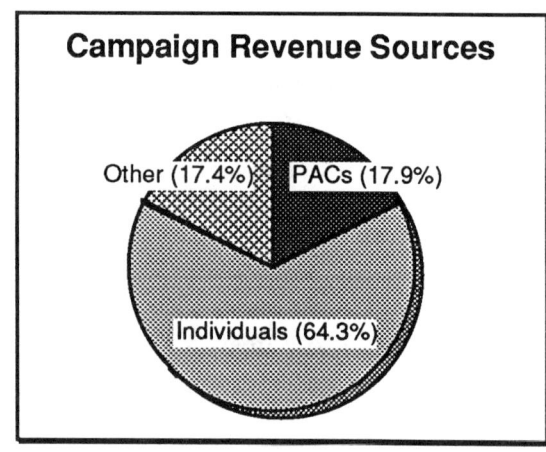

Other (17.4%) PACs (17.9%) Individuals (64.3%)

Insurance	**$2,200**
TransAmerica Life Companies	$1,000
Others	$1,200
Lawyers & Lobbyists	**$5,705**
Assn of Trial Lawyers of America	$2,000
Others	$3,705
Oil & Gas	**$3,515**
Pacific Enterprises	$3,015
Others	$500
Real Estate	**$9,050**
National Assn of Realtors	$8,450
Others	$600
Savings Banks	**$14,500**
Mercury Savings & Loan	$4,000
First Federal Savings Bank of California	$3,000
Great Western Financial Corp	$3,000
Home Savings of America	$3,000
Others	$1,500
Securities Investment	**$3,000**
Bear, Stearns & Company	$3,000
Telecommunications	**$4,400**
Pacific Telesis Group	$2,000
GTE Corp*	$1,200
AT&T	$1,000
Others	$200

Other Major Business PACs

National Assn of Home Builders	$1,000	Resid Constr
Walt Disney Company	$1,000	Resorts

PAC Totals by Category

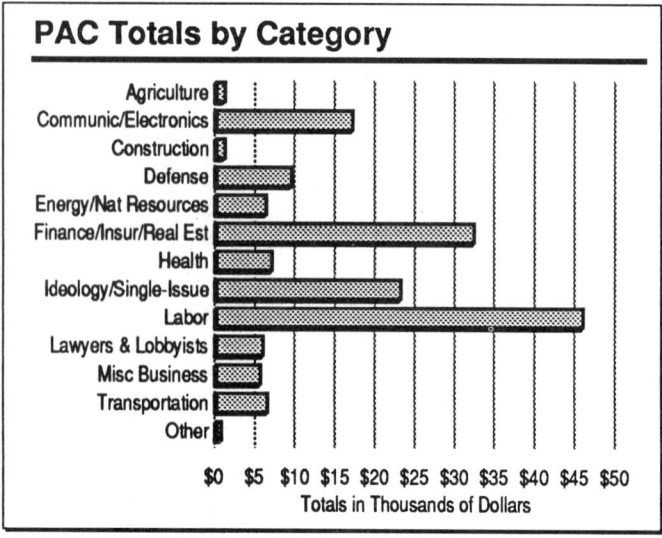

Totals in Thousands of Dollars

Labor

Bldg Trades/Industrial/Misc Unions $11,300

    Machinists/Aerospace Workers Union $2,300
    Carpenters & Joiners Union $2,100
    Laborers' Western Political League $2,000
    Food & Commercial Workers Union..............................$1,500
    United Auto Workers $1,300
    Plumbers/Pipefitters Union $1,000
    Others $1,100

Government & Postal Workers $10,500

    American Fedn of State/County/Munic Employees $5,000
    National Assn of Retired Federal Employees $3,000
    National Assn of Letter Carriers $1,000
    Others $1,500

Teachers Unions...$8,300

    National Education Assn $8,000
    American Federation of Teachers $300

Transportation Unions $15,700

    Teamsters Union $8,000
    Marine Engineers Union* $3,600
    Seafarers International Union $1,800
    Others $2,300

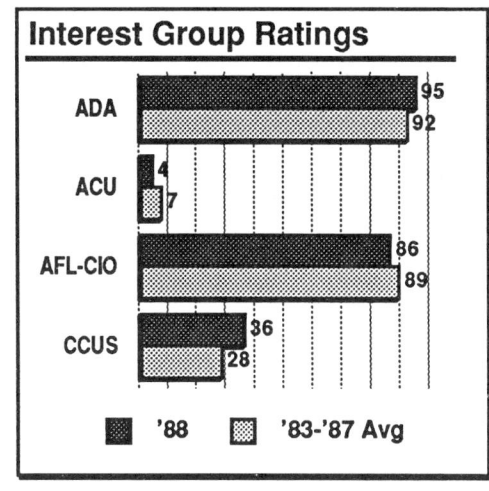

Interest Group Ratings

	'88	'83-'87 Avg
ADA	95	92
ACU	4	7
AFL-CIO	86	89
CCUS	36	28

Ideological/Single-Issue

Democratic/Liberal $14,900

    Religion and Tolerance PAC $6,000
    Hollywood Women's Political Cmte..................................$3,000
    Voter Guide '88 ....$3,000
    Business, Individuals & Government PAC $2,900

Pro-Israel $4,500

    Desert Caucus $2,500
    Others $2,000

Other Major Ideological/Single-Issue PACs

Pax Americas (David Bonior) ....$1,000   Dem Leaders

Independent expenditures supporting Levine

National Cmte to Preserve Social Security $2,340
Hudson Valley PAC $2,000
Five Towns PAC $1,500

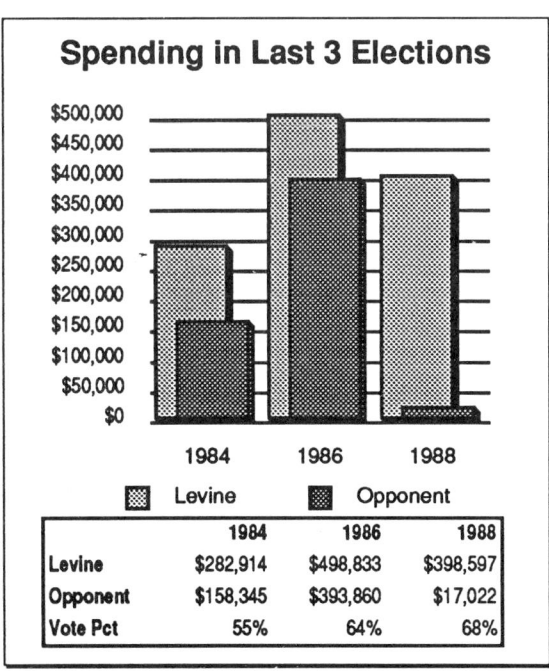

Spending in Last 3 Elections

	1984	1986	1988
Levine	$282,914	$498,833	$398,597
Opponent	$158,345	$393,860	$17,022
Vote Pct	55%	64%	68%

Levine   Opponent

* Contributions came from more than one PAC affiliated with this sponsor.

Jerry Lewis, R-Calif (35)

1988 Committees & Subcommittees

Appropriations
Legislative Branch (Ranking Republican)
Foreign Operations
HUD-Independent Agencies

First elected: 1978
Total receipts: $212,905
Total from PACs: $156,400

PAC Contribution Profile

Business

Automotive **$4,000**
Auto Dealers & Drivers for Free Trade $1,500
Chrysler Corp $1,000
National Auto Dealers Assn $1,000
Others $500

Aviation & Aerospace **$4,500**
American Airlines $1,500
Boeing Company $1,000
Federal Express Corp $1,000
TRW Inc $1,000

Commercial & Savings Banks **$6,000**
American Bankers Assn $1,500
California Bankers Assn $1,500
BankAmerica $1,000
US League of Savings Assn $1,000
Others $1,000

Construction **$18,250**
National Assn of Home Builders $10,000
Associated General Contractors $1,500
National Utility Contractors Assn $1,500
Sheet Metal/AirCon Contractors $1,000
Others $4,250

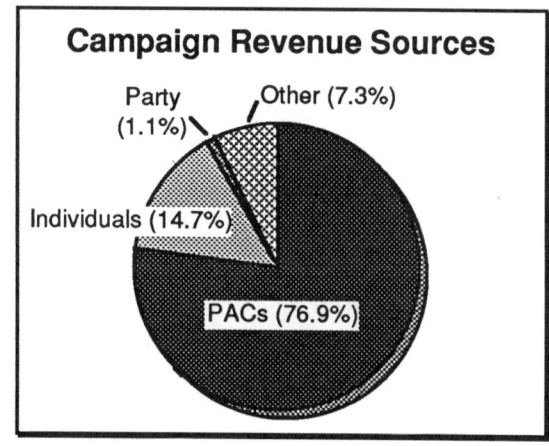

Campaign Revenue Sources

Party (1.1%)
Other (7.3%)
Individuals (14.7%)
PACs (76.9%)

Defense **$13,250**
General Dynamics $3,000
Lockheed Corp $2,000
United Technologies $1,500
McDonnell Douglas* $1,250
Dyncorp $1,000
Gencorp Inc $1,000
Northrop Corp $1,000
Rockwell International $1,000
Others $1,500

Electric Utilities **$4,900**
Southern California Edison $2,000
Pacific Gas & Electric $1,000
Others $1,900

Food & Beverage **$8,500**
Wine & Spirits Wholesalers of America $2,000
Pepsico Inc $1,000
Wine Institute $1,000
Winn-Dixie Stores $1,000
Others $3,500

Fruit & Vegetable Growers **$5,000**
California Pistachio Assn $1,000
Desert Grape Growers League/California $1,000
Sun-Maid Growers of California $1,000
Sunkist Growers $1,000
Others $1,000

Health Professionals **$12,000**
American Medical Assn $10,000
American Dental Assn $2,000

Insurance **$6,000**
Cigna Corp $1,000
National Assn of Life Underwriters $1,000
Pacific Mutual Life $1,000
TransAmerica Life Companies $1,000
Others $2,000

Lawyers & Lobbyists **$4,900**
Assn of Trial Lawyers of America $2,550
Others $2,350

Nursing Homes & Hospitals **$4,000**
American Health Care Assn $3,000
Others $1,000

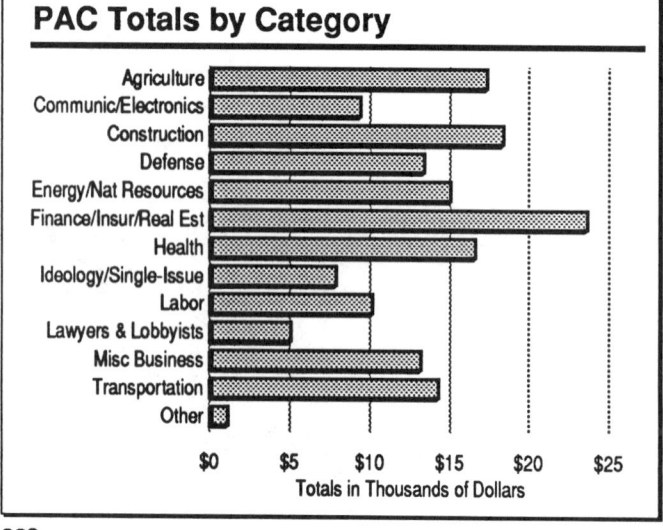

PAC Totals by Category

Category	
Agriculture	
Communic/Electronics	
Construction	
Defense	
Energy/Nat Resources	
Finance/Insur/Real Est	
Health	
Ideology/Single-Issue	
Labor	
Lawyers & Lobbyists	
Misc Business	
Transportation	
Other	

Totals in Thousands of Dollars
$0 $5 $10 $15 $20 $25

Oil & Gas $10,000
    Coastal Corp $2,000
    Pacific Enterprises $1,500
    Chevron Corp $1,000
    El Paso Company $1,000
    Others $4,500

Real Estate $11,000
    National Assn of Realtors $8,500
    Irvine Company $1,000
    Mortgage Bankers Assn of America $1,000
    Others $500

Sugar Growers $2,000
    American Sugarbeet Growers Assn $1,000
    Others $1,000

Telecommunications $7,250
    Continental Telecom $2,250
    Pacific Telesis Group $1,500
    AT&T $1,000
    BellSouth Services $1,000
    GTE Corp $1,000
    Others $500

Tobacco $3,500
    Philip Morris $2,000
    Tobacco Institute $1,000
    Others $500

Trucking/Delivery $2,300
    United Parcel Service $1,500
    Others $800

Other Major Business PACs

J C Penney Company .... $1,500   Dept Store
Chicago Mercantile Exchange .... $1,000   Commodities
Hercules Inc .... $1,000   Chemicals
J G Boswell Company .... $1,000   Cotton
Marriott Corp .... $1,000   Hotel/Motel
National Fedn of Independent Business ...... $1,000   Sml Business
Pirelli Cable .... $1,000   Indust Equip
Republic Communications .... $1,000   Unknown
Xerox Corp .... $1,000   Off Machines

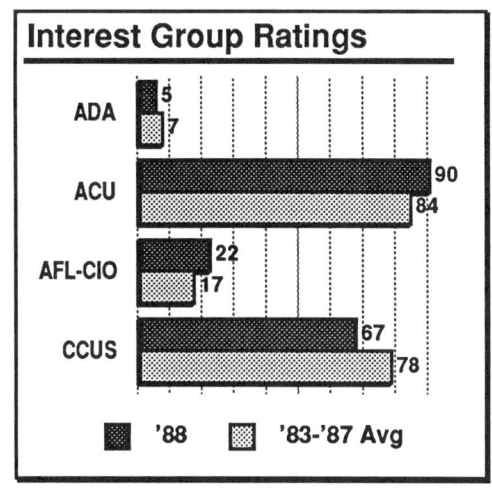

Labor

Transportation Unions $10,000
    Marine Engineers District 2 Maritime Officers $5,000
    Teamsters Union $2,500
    Air Line Pilots Assn $1,000
    Seafarers International Union $1,000
    Others $500

Ideological/Single-Issue

Pro-Israel $5,500
    National PAC $5,000
    Others $500

Major Ideological/Single-Issue PACs

Safari Club International .... $1,000   Hunting

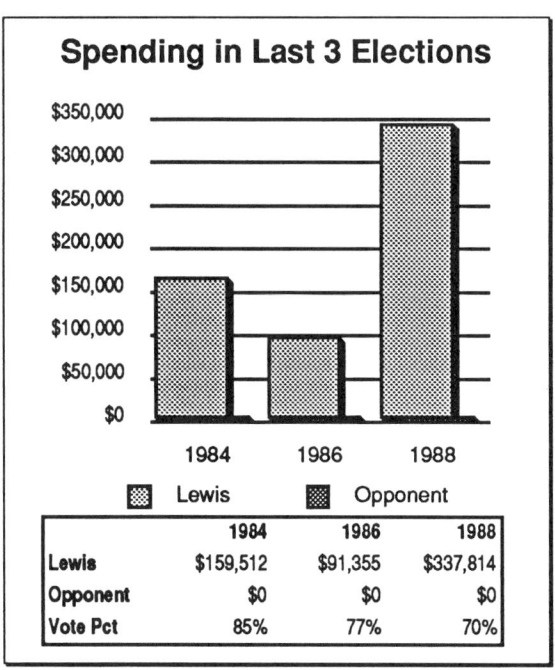

---

* Contributions came from more than one PAC affiliated
with this sponsor.

John Lewis, D-Ga (5)

1988 Committees & Subcommittees

Interior and Insular Affairs
Insular and International Affairs
National Parks and Public Lands

Public Works and Transportation
Economic Development
Public Buildings and Grounds
Water Resources

First elected: 1986
Total receipts: $193,584
Total from PACs: $142,915

PAC Contribution Profile

Business

Automotive **$4,600**
    National Auto Dealers Assn $4,000
    Others $600

Commercial Banks **$6,000**
    Citizens & Southern National Bank $2,000
    Trust Company of Georgia $1,300
    Barnett Banks of Florida $1,000
    Others $1,700

Construction **$2,650**
    National Assn of Home Builders $1,500
    Others $1,150

Electric Utilities **$3,900**
    Southern Company* $2,300
    ACRE (Action Committee for Rural Electrification) $1,300
    Others $300

Food & Beverage **$4,100**
    Coca-Cola Company $1,550
    Others $2,550

Health Professionals **$11,800**
    American Medical Assn $10,000
    American Academy of Ophthalmology $1,000
    Others $800

Lawyers **$3,450**
    Assn of Trial Lawyers of America $2,450
    Others $1,000

Campaign Revenue Sources

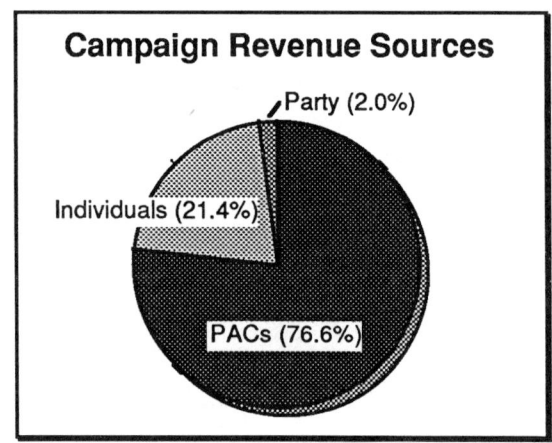

Party (2.0%)
Individuals (21.4%)
PACs (76.6%)

Oil & Gas **$4,650**
    None over $900

Package Delivery **$2,900**
    United Parcel Service $2,900

Real Estate **$6,900**
    National Assn of Realtors $6,600
    Others $300

Telecommunications **$6,800**
    Southern Bell $4,000
    AT&T $1,300
    Continental Telecom $1,000
    Others $500

Other Major Business PACs

Lockheed Corp	$1,500	Air Defense
Dairymen Inc-Georgia	$1,100	Dairy
Batus Inc*	$1,000	Tobacco
Federated Department Stores	$1,000	Dept Store
Waste Management Inc	$1,000	Waste Mgmt

PAC Totals by Category

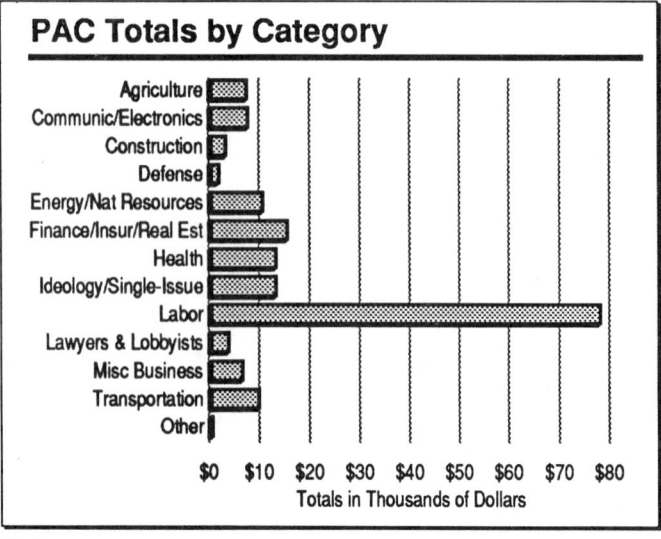

Agriculture
Communic/Electronics
Construction
Defense
Energy/Nat Resources
Finance/Insur/Real Est
Health
Ideology/Single-Issue
Labor
Lawyers & Lobbyists
Misc Business
Transportation
Other

$0 $10 $20 $30 $40 $50 $60 $70 $80
Totals in Thousands of Dollars

Labor

Bldg Trades/Industrial/Misc Unions $32,400

United Auto Workers	$6,800
Food & Commercial Workers Union	$4,000
Sheet Metal Workers Union	$4,000
Machinists/Aerospace Workers Union	$3,800
AFL-CIO*	$3,100
Carpenters & Joiners Union	$2,500
Intl Brotherhood of Electrical Workers	$2,000
Operating Engineers Union	$2,000
Laborers' Political League	$1,300
Others	$2,900

Government & Postal Workers $16,600

National Assn of Retired Federal Employees	$6,000
American Fedn of State/County/Munic Employees	$5,300
National Assn of Letter Carriers	$2,200
American Postal Workers Union	$1,400
Others	$1,700

Teachers Unions $8,100

American Federation of Teachers	$4,100
National Education Assn	$4,000

Transportation Unions $20,700

Teamsters Union	$10,000
Air Line Pilots Assn	$5,000
Amalgamated Transit Union	$2,500
Seafarers International Union	$1,500
Others	$1,700

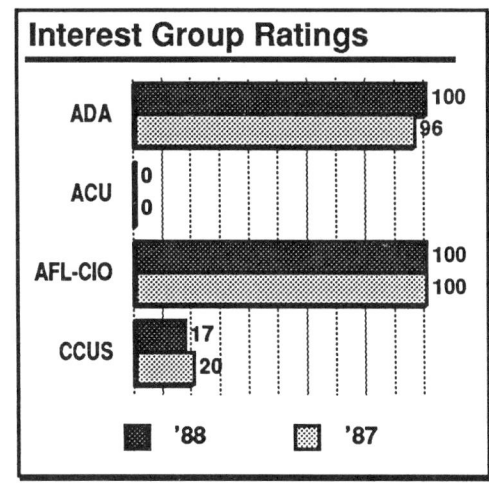

Interest Group Ratings

	'88	'87
ADA	100	96
ACU	0	0
AFL-CIO	100	100
CCUS	17	20

Ideological/Single-Issue

Pro-Israel $7,550

National PAC	$5,000
Hudson Valley PAC	$1,000
Joint Action Cmte for Political Affairs	$1,000
Others	$550

Other Major Ideological/Single-Issue PACs

Human Rights Campaign Fund	$1,600	Gay Rights
Valley Education Fund (Tony Coelho)	$1,000	Dem Leaders

Independent expenditures supporting Lewis

National Cmte to Preserve Social Security	$1,922

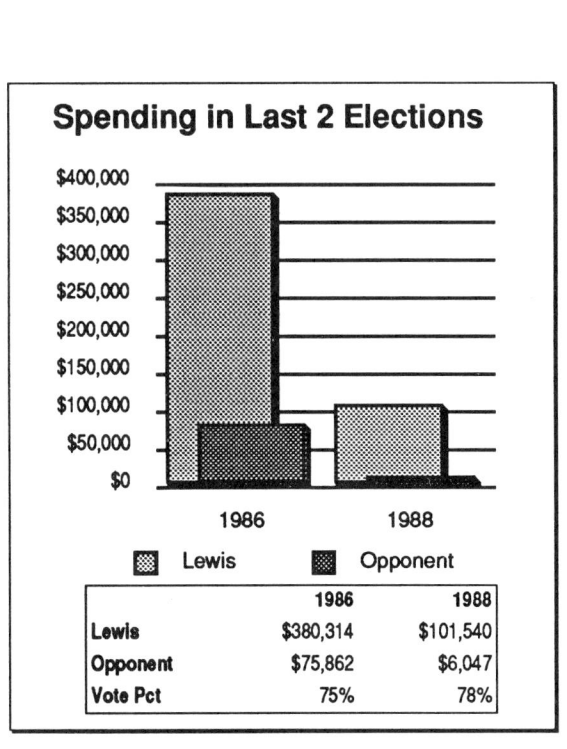

Spending in Last 2 Elections

Lewis   Opponent

	1986	1988
Lewis	$380,314	$101,540
Opponent	$75,862	$6,047
Vote Pct	75%	78%

---

* Contributions came from more than one PAC affiliated with this sponsor.

Tom Lewis, R-Fla (12)

First elected: 1982
Total receipts: $288,963
Total from PACs: $64,465

1988 Committees & Subcommittees

Agriculture
Cotton, Rice and Sugar
Domestic Marketing, Consumer Relations and Nutrition
Livestock, Dairy and Poultry

Science, Space and Technology
Transportation, Aviation and Materials (Ranking Republican)
Space Science and Applications

Select Narcotics Abuse and Control

PAC Contribution Profile

Business

Automotive	$3,250
Auto Dealers & Drivers for Free Trade	$2,000
National Auto Dealers Assn	$1,250
Aviation & Aerospace	**$3,750**
Aircraft Owners & Pilots Assn	$1,000
Boeing Company	$1,000
Others	$1,750
Commercial & Savings Banks	**$6,940**
Barnett Banks of Florida	$1,500
National Banks of Florida	$1,250
Florida League of Financial Institutions	$1,000
Others	$3,190
Construction	**$2,250**
Associated General Contractors	$1,250
Others	$1,000
Dairy	**$4,000**
Associated Milk Producers	$2,500
Others	$1,500
Defense	**$5,631**
Grumman	$1,250
Tenneco Inc	$1,000
Others	$3,381
Electric Utilities & Equipment	**$2,250**
None over $500	

Campaign Revenue Sources

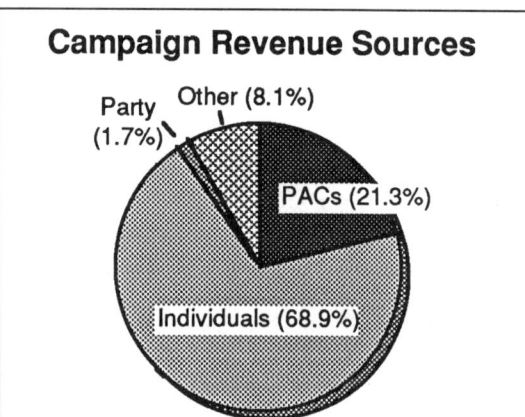

Party (1.7%)
Other (8.1%)
PACs (21.3%)
Individuals (68.9%)

Real Estate	$3,250
National Assn of Realtors	$3,000
Others	$250
Sugar Growers	**$4,250**
American Crystal Sugar Corp	$2,500
Others	$1,750
Telecommunications	**$6,000**
Southern Bell	$3,000
United Telecommunications	$1,000
Others	$2,000

Other Major Business PACs

Archer-Daniels-Midland Corp	$1,000	Grain Trader
Chicago Mercantile Exchange	$1,000	Commodities

PAC Totals by Category

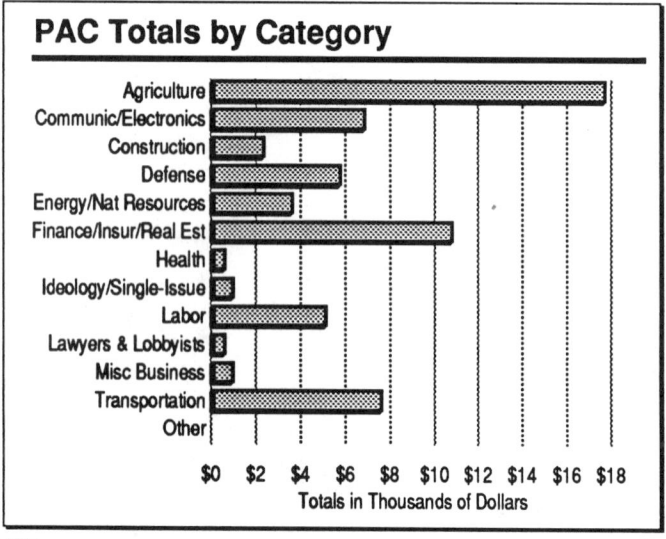

Agriculture
Communic/Electronics
Construction
Defense
Energy/Nat Resources
Finance/Insur/Real Est
Health
Ideology/Single-Issue
Labor
Lawyers & Lobbyists
Misc Business
Transportation
Other

$0 $2 $4 $6 $8 $10 $12 $14 $16 $18
Totals in Thousands of Dollars

Labor

Labor Unions **$5,000**

Marine Engineers District 2 Maritime Officers $2,500
Air Line Pilots Assn $1,500
Seafarers International Union $1,000

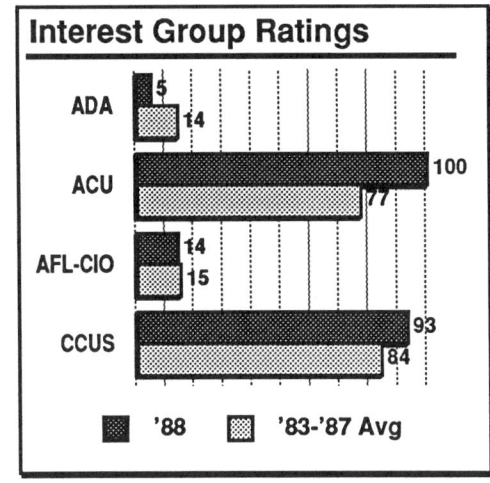

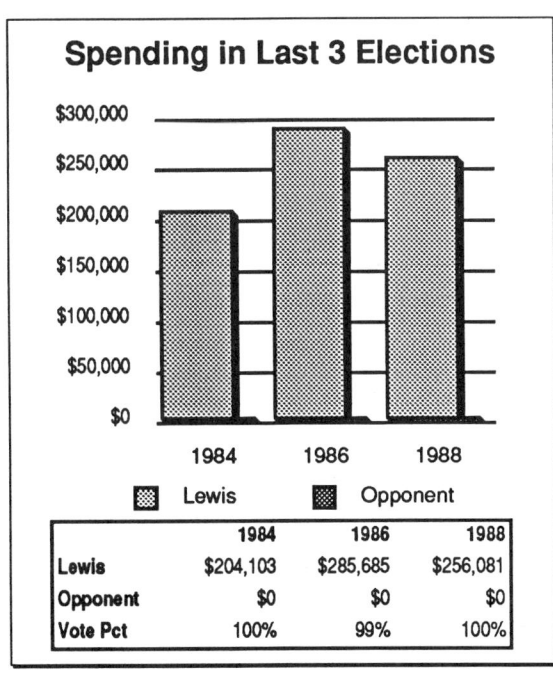

Jim Ross Lightfoot, R-Iowa (5)

First elected: 1984
Total receipts: $478,842
Total from PACs: $166,077

1988 Committees & Subcommittees

Government Operations
Human Resources and Intergovernmental Relations (Ranking Republican)

Public Works and Transportation
Aviation
Surface Transportation
Water Resources

Select Aging
Health and Long-Term Care

PAC Contribution Profile

Business

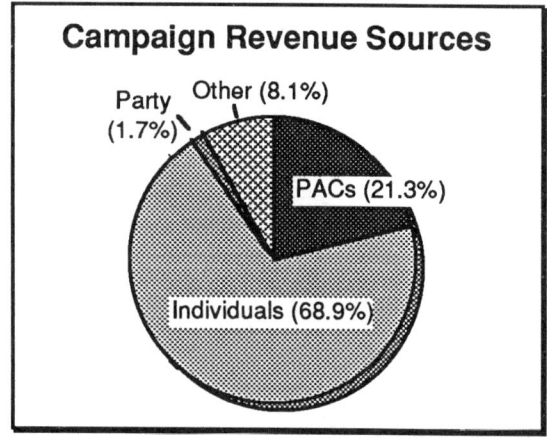

Campaign Revenue Sources

Party (1.7%)
Other (8.1%)
PACs (21.3%)
Individuals (68.9%)

Accountants	**$5,000**
American Institute of CPA's	$5,000
Automotive	**$7,750**
National Auto Dealers Assn	$5,500
Auto Dealers & Drivers for Free Trade	$2,000
Others	$250
Aviation & Aerospace	**$12,651**
Aircraft Owners & Pilots Assn	$8,651
Raytheon	$1,000
Others	$3,000
Commercial & Savings Banks	**$8,300**
Hawkeye Bancorp	$3,000
American Bankers Assn	$2,500
US League of Savings Assns	$1,200
Norwest Corp	$1,000
Others	$600
Construction	**$17,950**
National Assn of Home Builders	$5,000
Sheet Metal/AirCon Contractors	$2,400
Assoc Genl Contractors/Iowa	$2,000
Deere & Company	$2,000
Associated General Contractors	$1,250
Lennox Industries	$1,000
National Electrical Contractors Assn	$1,000
National Utility Contractors Assn	$1,000
Others	$2,300

Dairy	**$8,750**
Associated Milk Producers	$5,000
Mid-American Dairymen	$2,000
Land O'Lakes Inc	$1,500
Others	$250
Defense	**$2,500**
Rockwell International	$1,000
Others	$1,500
Electric Utilities	**$4,950**
Midwest Energy Company	$2,500
Others	$2,450
Farm Organizations	**$3,200**
Iowa Farm Bureau Federation	$2,700
Others	$500
Food & Beverage	**$7,450**
Hy-Vee Food Stores	$1,500
IBP Inc	$1,500
Food Marketing Institute	$1,000
Others	$3,450
Grain & Soybean Processing	**$2,300**
American Soybean Assn	$1,000
Cargill Inc	$1,000
Others	$300
Health Professionals	**$13,000**
American Medical Assn	$10,000
American Dental Assn	$2,000
American Optometric Assn	$1,000
Home Appliances	**$2,000**
Maytag Company	$2,000
Insurance	**$7,000**
National Assn of Life Underwriters	$3,000
Principal Mutual Life Insurance	$1,300
Others	$2,700
Oil & Gas	**$3,250**
None over $750	
Pharmaceuticals	**$3,150**
None over $500	

PAC Totals by Category

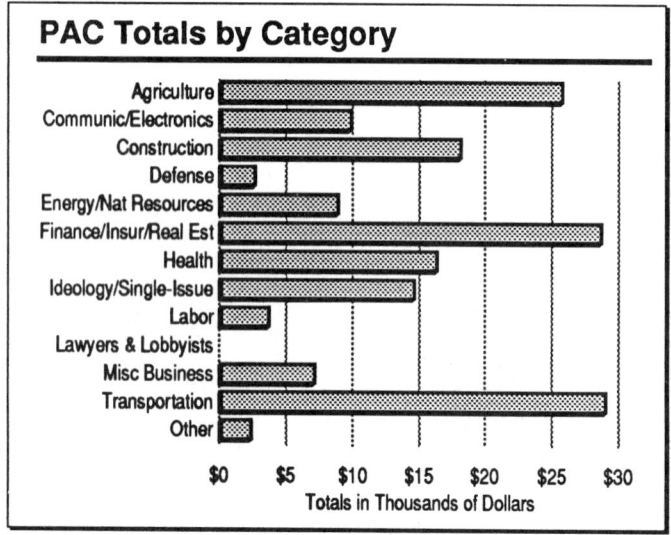

Totals in Thousands of Dollars

Agriculture
Communic/Electronics
Construction
Defense
Energy/Nat Resources
Finance/Insur/Real Est
Health
Ideology/Single-Issue
Labor
Lawyers & Lobbyists
Misc Business
Transportation
Other

$0 $5 $10 $15 $20 $25 $30

Real Estate **$8,250**
      National Assn of Realtors $7,750
      Others $500

Telecommunications **$7,800**
      North Western Bell Telephone $2,250
      AT&T $1,750
      Continental Telecom $1,500
      United Telecommunications $1,000
      Others $1,300

Trucking/Delivery **$4,750**
      United Parcel Service $2,500
      Others $2,250

Other Major Business PACs

American Commercial Barge Line Company ... $1,250   SeaTransport

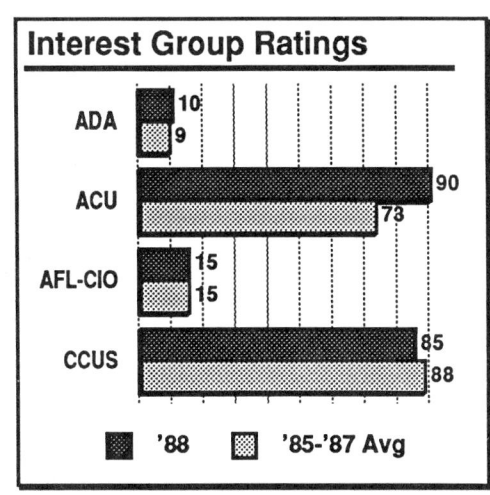

Labor

Labor Unions **$3,550**
      National Assn of Retired Federal Employees $3,000
      Others $550

Ideological/Single-Issue

Republican Leadership PACs **$10,250**
      Fund for America's Future (George Bush) $10,000
      Others $250

Other Major Ideological/Single-Issue PACs

Constitution Club ....$2,000   Unknown
National Rifle Assn ....$1,600   Pro-Guns

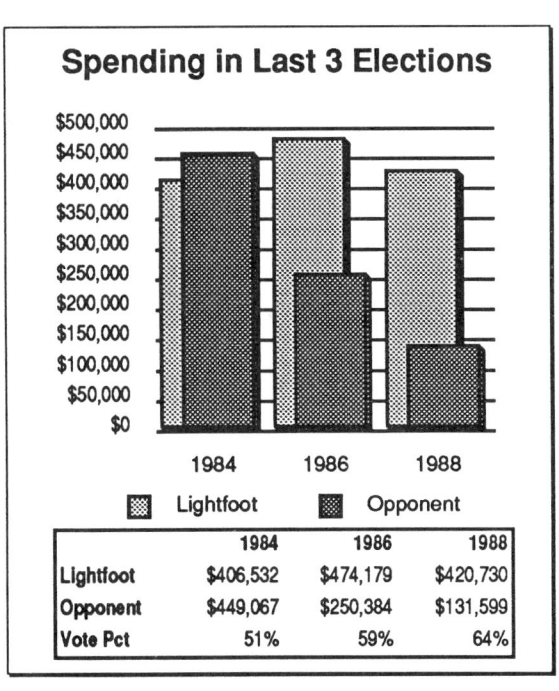

William O. Lipinski, D-Ill (5)

First elected: 1982
Total receipts: $154,568
Total from PACs: $96,464

1988 Committees & Subcommittees

Merchant Marine and Fisheries
Coast Guard and Navigation
Merchant Marine

Public Works and Transportation
Aviation
Economic Development
Surface Transportation

PAC Contribution Profile

Business

Aviation & Aerospace **$2,000**
    None over $500

Commodities Trading **$2,750**
    Chicago Mercantile Exchange $1,750
    Chicago Board of Trade $1,000

Construction **$1,250**
    National Utility Contractors Assn $1,000
    Others $250

Food & Beverage **$1,750**
    McDonald's Corp $1,250
    Others $500

Health Professionals **$2,350**
    American Medical Assn $2,250
    Others $100

Insurance **$1,500**
    National Assn of Life Underwriters $1,000
    Others $500

Lawyers **$4,250**
    Assn of Trial Lawyers of America $2,500
    Hopkins & Sudder $1,500
    Others $250

Real Estate **$4,900**
    National Assn of Realtors $4,900

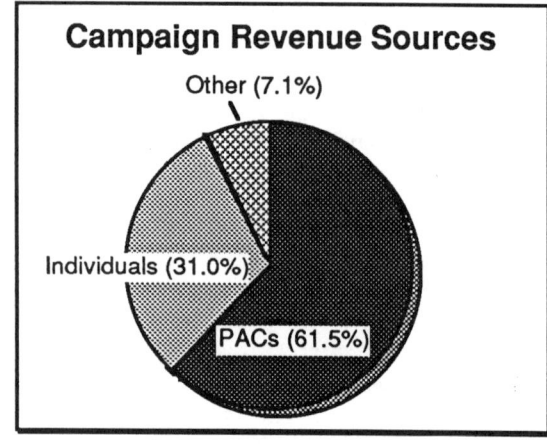

Campaign Revenue Sources

Other (7.1%)
Individuals (31.0%)
PACs (61.5%)

Sea Transport **$5,000**
    American President Lines $1,750
    Matson Navigation $1,500
    American Pilots Assn $1,000
    Others $750

Telecommunications **$2,350**
    Illinois Bell Telephone $2,100
    Others $250

Trucking/Delivery **$4,800**
    United Parcel Service $2,300
    Others $2,500

Other Major Business PACs

Waste Management Inc .... $1,000   Waste Mgmt

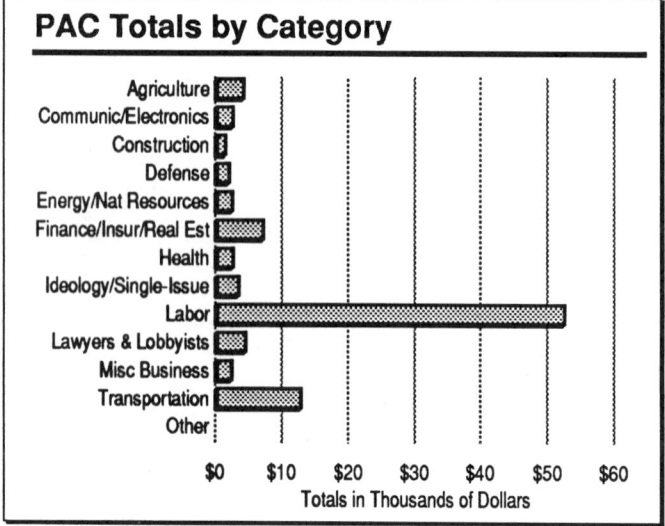

PAC Totals by Category

Category	
Agriculture	
Communic/Electronics	
Construction	
Defense	
Energy/Nat Resources	
Finance/Insur/Real Est	
Health	
Ideology/Single-Issue	
Labor	
Lawyers & Lobbyists	
Misc Business	
Transportation	
Other	

$0 $10 $20 $30 $40 $50 $60
Totals in Thousands of Dollars

Labor

Bldg Trades/Industrial/Misc Unions **$17,800**

    Carpenters & Joiners Union $3,000
    Intl Brotherhood of Electrical Workers $2,000
    Machinists/Aerospace Workers Union $1,750
    Laborers' Political League $1,500
    Operating Engineers Union $1,500
    Plumbers/Pipefitters Union $1,500
    Ladies Garment Workers Union $1,100
    Food & Commercial Workers Union $1,000
    Others $4,450

Government & Postal Workers **$7,300**

    National Assn of Retired Federal Employees $6,000
    Others $1,300

Sea Transport Unions **$5,700**

    Marine Engineers Union* $3,000
    Seafarers International Union $2,000
    Others $700

Other Transportation Unions **$14,950**

    Teamsters Union $6,000
    Air Line Pilots Assn $5,000
    Amalgamated Transit Union $1,000
    United Transportation Union $1,000
    Others $1,950

Teachers Unions **$6,500**

    National Education Assn $6,500

Interest Group Ratings

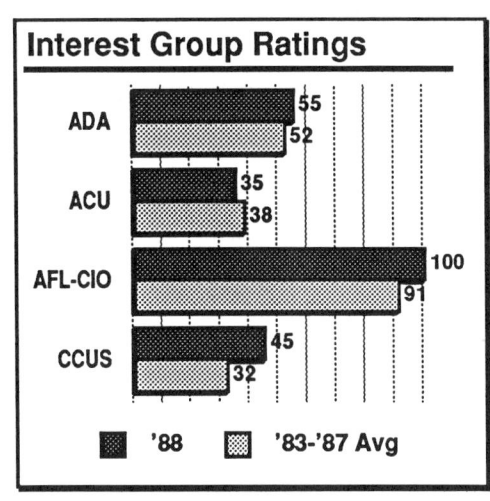

Ideological/Single-Issue

Democratic Leadership PACs **$1,500**

    Valley Education Fund (Tony Coelho) $1,000
    Others $500

Independent expenditures supporting Lipinski

National Cmte to Preserve Social Security $2,149

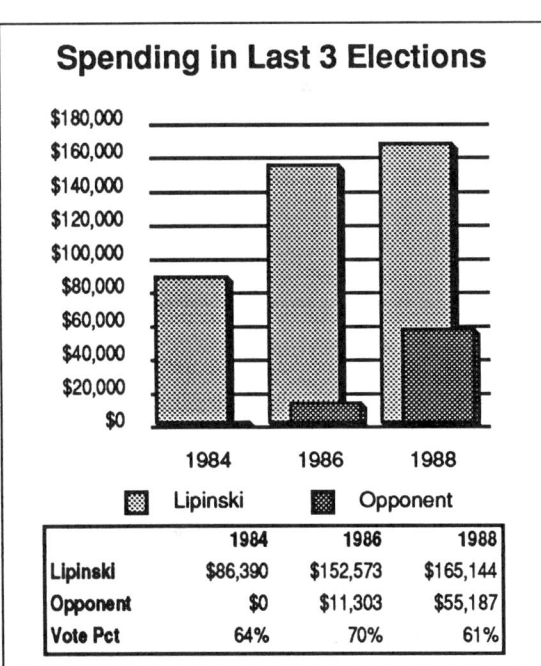

Spending in Last 3 Elections

	1984	1986	1988
Lipinski	$86,390	$152,573	$165,144
Opponent	$0	$11,303	$55,187
Vote Pct	64%	70%	61%

---

* Contributions came from more than one PAC affiliated
with this sponsor.

Bob Livingston, R-La (1)

1988 Committees & Subcommittees

Appropriations
Defense

Select Intelligence
Legislation (Ranking Republican)

First elected: 1977
Total receipts: $262,408
Total from PACs: $127,834

Campaign Revenue Sources

Party (0.6%)   Other (1.8%)

Individuals (45.7%)

PACs (52.0%)

PAC Contribution Profile

Business

Auto Dealers	**$5,100**
Auto Dealers & Drivers for Free Trade	$2,800
National Auto Dealers Assn	$2,300
Construction	**$2,800**
None over $850	
Defense	**$48,550**
Textron Inc	$7,000
Continental Telecom	$4,100
AT&T	$3,000
Northrop Corp	$2,700
Avondale Industries	$2,350
Lockheed Corp	$2,000
Martin Marietta Corp	$2,000
Tenneco Inc	$2,000
United Technologies	$1,850
General Dynamics	$1,800
General Electric	$1,800
McDonnell Douglas*	$1,800
FMC Corp	$1,500
Hughes Aircraft	$1,400
Boeing Company	$1,300
Rockwell International	$1,300
LTV Aerospace & Defense Company	$1,050
Gould Inc	$1,000
Others	$8,600
Electric Utilities & Equipment	**$6,000**
Middle South Utilities*	$4,600
McDermott Inc	$1,100
Others	$300

Food & Beverage	**$3,300**
Delchamps Inc	$1,000
Morrison Inc	$1,000
National Beer Wholesalers Assn	$1,000
Others	$300
Health Professionals	**$4,100**
American Dental Assn	$2,500
American Academy of Ophthalmology	$1,000
Others	$600
Hospitals	**$4,050**
National Medical Enterprises Inc	$2,500
Others	$1,550
Lawyers	**$4,850**
Assn of Trial Lawyers of America	$2,550
Adams & Reese	$1,000
Camp, Barsh, Bates & Tate	$1,000
Others	$300
Mining	**$2,050**
Dravo Corp	$1,000
Others	$1,050
Oil & Gas	**$15,800**
Louisiana Land & Exploration	$2,000
Shell Oil	$1,700
Atlantic Richfield	$1,500
Chevron Corp	$1,000
Exxon Corp	$1,000
Sun Company	$1,000
Texaco	$1,000
Others	$6,600

PAC Totals by Category

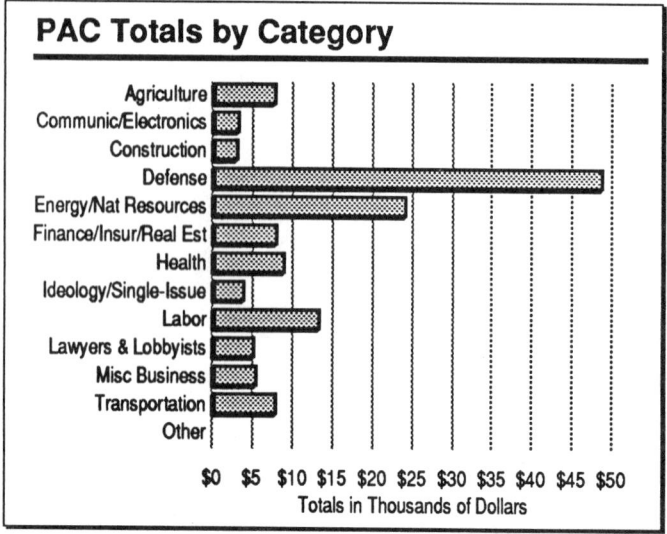

Totals in Thousands of Dollars

678

Real Estate **$5,000**
    National Assn of Realtors $5,000

Telecommunications **$3,000**
    South Central Bell Telephone $3,000

Tobacco **$2,400**
    Philip Morris $1,000
    Others $1,400

Other Major Business PACs

International Paper Company	$1,000	Paper Prod
National Assn of Life Underwriters	$1,000	Life Insurance
Ocean Spray Cranberries Inc	$1,000	Fruit/Veg
Stone Container Corp	$1,000	Paper Packg

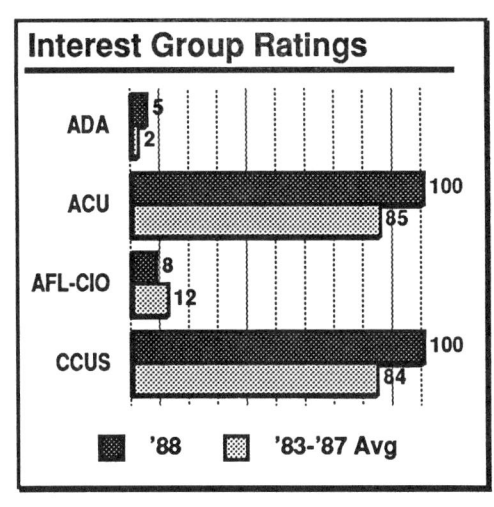

Interest Group Ratings

	'88	'83-'87 Avg
ADA	5	2
ACU	100	85
AFL-CIO	8	12
CCUS	100	84

■ '88   ▦ '83-'87 Avg

Labor

Labor Unions **$13,000**
    Marine Engineers Union* $5,500
    National Assn of Retired Federal Employees $3,000
    Air Line Pilots Assn...$2,500
    Seafarers International Union $1,500
    Others $500

Ideological/Single-Issue

Ideological/Single-Issue **$3,650**
Louisiana for American Security ....$2,000   Pro-Israel
Others $1,650

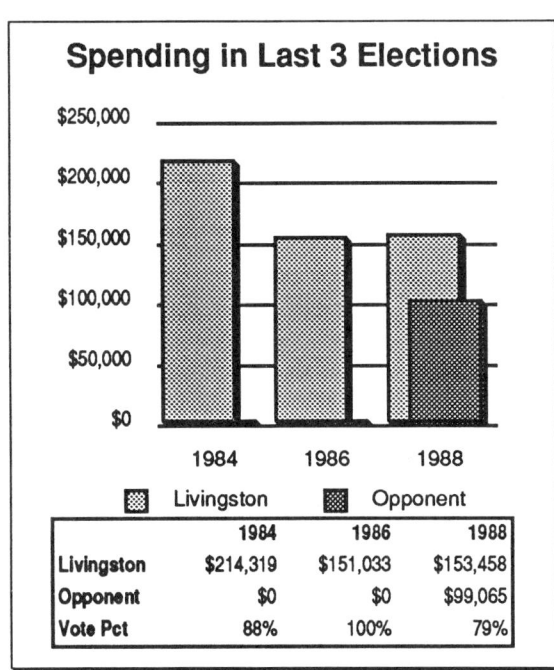

Spending in Last 3 Elections

■ Livingston   ▦ Opponent

	1984	1986	1988
Livingston	$214,319	$151,033	$153,458
Opponent	$0	$0	$99,065
Vote Pct	88%	100%	79%

---

* Contributions came from more than one PAC affiliated with this sponsor.

679

Marilyn Lloyd, D-Tenn (3)

First elected: 1974
Total receipts: $621,520
Total from PACs: $320,137

1988 Committees & Subcommittees

Armed Services
Procurement and Military Nuclear Systems

Science, Space and Technology
Energy Research and Development (Chairwoman)
International Scientific Cooperation

Select Aging
Housing and Consumer Interests
Retirement Income and Employment

PAC Contribution Profile

Business

Air Freight	**$10,000**
Federal Express Corp	$10,000
Auto Dealers	**$5,000**
National Auto Dealers Assn	$5,000
Construction	**$17,050**
National Assn of Home Builders	$5,000
Associated General Contractors	$2,500
Stone & Webster	$1,550
Bechtel Corp	$1,500
Ch2M Hill	$1,500
Fluor Corp	$1,000
Tennessee Road Builders Assn	$1,000
Others	$3,000
Defense	**$57,450**
Martin Marietta Corp	$6,000
Northrop Corp	$5,250
AT&T	$3,500
General Dynamics	$3,000
Lockheed Corp	$3,000
United Technologies	$3,000
McDonnell Douglas*	$2,750
Raytheon	$2,500
Boeing Company	$2,200
General Atomics	$2,000
Textron Inc	$1,750
Westinghouse Electric	$1,750

(Continued in next column)

Campaign Revenue Sources

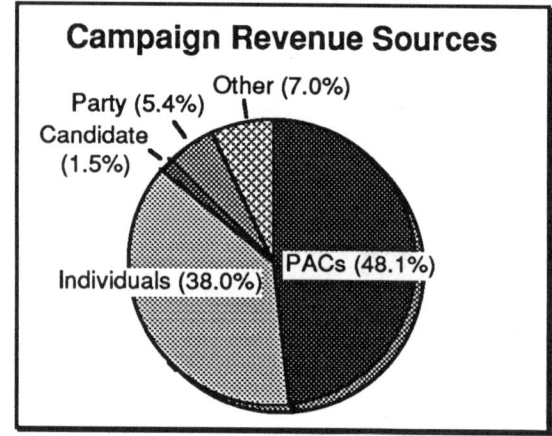

Party (5.4%)
Other (7.0%)
Candidate (1.5%)
Individuals (38.0%)
PACs (48.1%)

Defense (cont'd)

Chrysler Corp	$1,500
Hughes Aircraft	$1,500
Rockwell International	$1,500
General Electric	$1,250
Pneumo Abex Corp	$1,250
Continental Telecom	$1,000
E-Systems/Corporate Division	$1,000
EG&G Inc	$1,000
FMC Corp	$1,000
Kaman Corp	$1,000
LTV Aerospace & Defense Company	$1,000
Others	$7,750
Electric Utilities	**$9,200**
ACRE (Action Committee for Rural Electrification)	$1,750
Others	$7,450
Financial Institutions	**$8,550**
First American Corp	$2,000
Third National Corp	$2,000
American Bankers Assn	$1,000
Tenn League of Savings Institutions	$1,000
Others	$2,550
Health Professionals	**$14,687**
American Medical Assn	$9,937
American Dental Assn	$2,500
American Optometric Assn	$1,250
Others	$1,000
Insurance	**$8,350**
National Assn of Life Underwriters	$4,000
Provident Life & Accident Insurance	$3,850
Others	$500
Lawyers & Lobbyists	**$13,000**
Assn of Trial Lawyers of America	$12,000
Others	$1,000
Nuclear Power Plant Equipment	**$8,050**
Gilbert Associates	$3,500
Combustion Engineering	$2,300
KMS Fusion Inc	$1,250
Babcock & Wilcox	$1,000
Railroads & Railroad Equipment	**$6,000**
Duchossois Industries	$5,000
Norfolk Southern Corp	$1,000

PAC Totals by Category

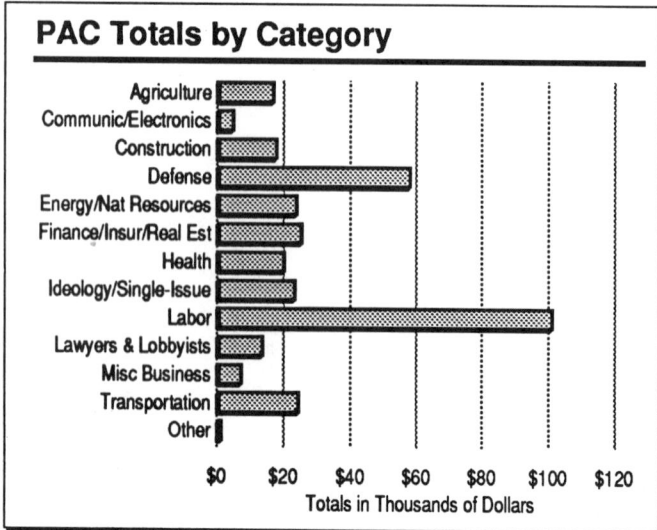

Agriculture
Communic/Electronics
Construction
Defense
Energy/Nat Resources
Finance/Insur/Real Est
Health
Ideology/Single-Issue
Labor
Lawyers & Lobbyists
Misc Business
Transportation
Other

$0 $20 $40 $60 $80 $100 $120
Totals in Thousands of Dollars

Real Estate **$5,750**
    National Assn of Realtors $5,750

Other Major Business PACs

Westvaco Corp	$2,000	Paper Prod
Schering-Plough Corp	$1,500	Pharmaceut
United Parcel Service	$1,250	Delivery
Service Corporation International	$1,000	Funeral Svcs
Dixie Yarns/TI-CARO	$1,000	Textiles
Burlington Industries	$1,000	Textiles
American Hospital Assn	$1,000	Hospitals
National Health Corp	$1,500	Nursing Home
Winn-Dixie Stores	$1,000	Food Stores
Arthur Young & Company	$2,000	Accountants
Petroleum Marketers Assn	$1,000	Gas Stations
South Central Bell Telephone	$3,250	Phone Util
Mid-American Dairymen................	$1,500	Dairy
Dairymen Inc-Tennessee	$1,750	Dairy
Philip Morris	$2,000	Tobacco

Labor

Bldg Trades/Industrial/Misc Unions **$52,750**
    Machinists/Aerospace Workers Union $10,000
    United Auto Workers $6,250
    Intl Brotherhood of Electrical Workers........................ $6,000
    AFL-CIO* $5,550
    Communications Workers of America $5,000
    United Steelworkers $5,000
    Food & Commercial Workers Union $4,500
    Carpenters & Joiners Union $3,000
    Office & Professional Employees Union $1,500
    Ladies Garment Workers Union $1,250
    Boilermakers Union $1,000
    Sheet Metal Workers Union $1,000
    Others $2,700

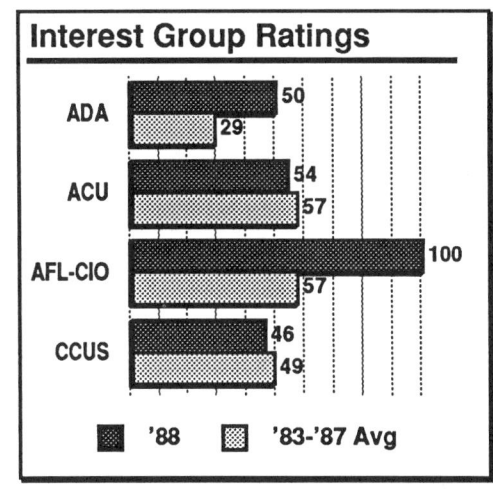

Interest Group Ratings

Legend: ■ '88　▨ '83-'87 Avg

- ADA: '88 = 50; '83-'87 Avg = 29
- ACU: '88 = 54; '83-'87 Avg = 57
- AFL-CIO: '88 = 100; '83-'87 Avg = 57
- CCUS: '88 = 46; '83-'87 Avg = 49

Government & Postal Workers **$18,100**
    National Assn of Letter Carriers $10,000
    National Assn of Retired Federal Employees $7,000
    Others $1,100

Teachers Unions **$10,000**
    National Education Assn $10,000

Transportation Unions **$19,550**
    Teamsters Union $10,000
    Marine Engineers District 2 Maritime Officers $2,500
    Amalgamated Transit Union $2,000
    Seafarers International Union $2,000
    Brotherhood of Locomotive Engineers $1,050
    United Transportation Union $1,000
    Others $1,000

Ideological/Single-Issue

Democratic Leadership PACs **$12,800**
    Majority Congress Committee (Jim Wright) $5,000
    Conservative Democratic PAC (Charles Stenholm) $2,000
    House Leadership Fund (Tom Foley) $2,000
    Valley Education Fund (Tony Coelho) $2,000
    Economic Security PAC (Mary Rose Oakar) $1,000
    Others $800

Other Major Ideological/Single-Issue PACs

National Rifle Assn	$4,500	Pro-Guns
National Cmte for an Effective Congress	$2,496	Dem/Liberal
National Right to Life PAC	$1,500	Pro-Life

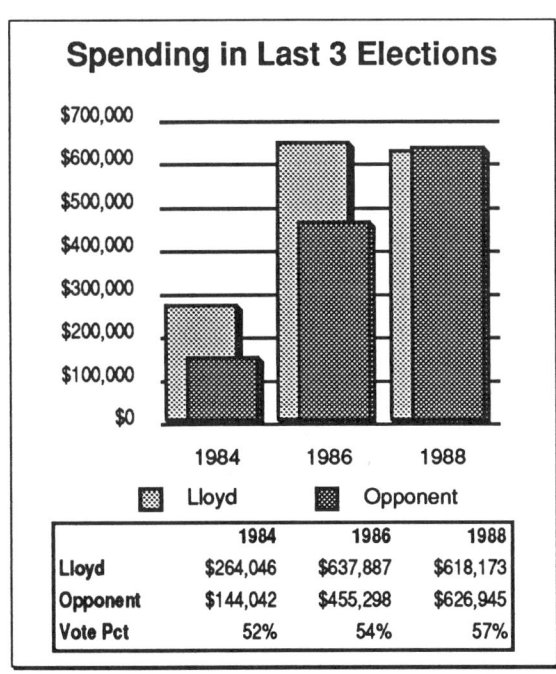

Spending in Last 3 Elections

Legend: ▨ Lloyd　■ Opponent

	1984	1986	1988
Lloyd	$264,046	$637,887	$618,173
Opponent	$144,042	$455,298	$626,945
Vote Pct	52%	54%	57%

---

* Contributions came from more than one PAC affiliated
with this sponsor.

Bill Lowery, R-Calif (41)

1988 Committees & Subcommittees

Appropriations
Military Construction (Ranking Republican)
Interior and Related Agencies
Treasury, Postal Service and General Government

First elected: 1980
Total receipts: $453,489
Total from PACs: $182,415

PAC Contribution Profile

Business

Automotive	**$4,000**
Auto Dealers & Drivers for Free Trade	$2,000
Others	$2,000
Aviation & Aerospace	**$7,100**
Rohr Industries	$3,650
Boeing Company	$1,000
Federal Express Corp	$1,000
Others	$1,450
Construction	**$13,525**
Morrison-Knudsen	$3,150
National Assn of Home Builders	$2,000
Associated General Contractors	$1,375
Bechtel Corp	$1,250
National Electrical Contractors Assn	$1,000
Others	$4,750
Defense	**$28,350**
Cubic Corp	$3,350
General Dynamics	$3,000
Gencorp Inc	$2,750
Lockheed Corp	$2,700
TRW Inc	$2,000
United Technologies	$1,850
Northrop Corp	$1,500
Textron Inc	$1,500
Hughes Aircraft	$1,300
Grumman	$1,100
Allied-Signal	$1,050
McDonnell Douglas	$1,000
Others	$5,250

Campaign Revenue Sources

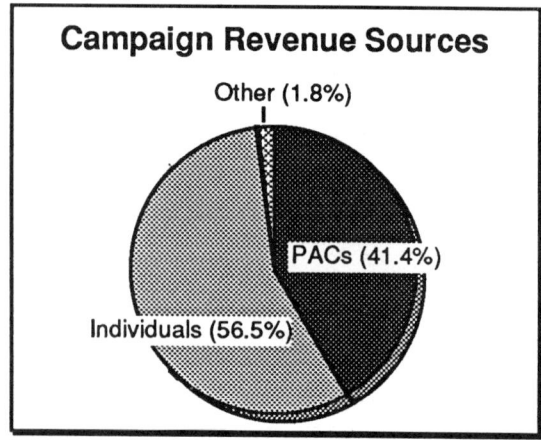

Other (1.8%)
PACs (41.4%)
Individuals (56.5%)

Department Stores	**$2,700**
Federated Department Stores	$1,000
Others	$1,700
Electric Utilities	**$12,600**
San Diego Gas & Electric	$2,400
Southern California Edison	$1,800
Texas Utilities Electric Company*	$1,000
Others	$7,400
Electronics & Computers	**$4,850**
Westinghouse Electric	$1,300
Computer Sciences Corp	$1,100
Others	$2,450
Financial Institutions	**$13,150**
Home Federal Savings & Loan	$2,250
US League of Savings Assn	$1,800
Great American Federal Savings	$1,500
Security Pacific Corp	$1,500
Credit Union National Assn	$1,150
Others	$4,950
Food & Beverage	**$4,220**
None over $800	
Forest Products	**$3,649**
National Forest Products Assn	$2,249
Others	$1,400
Fruit & Vegetable Growers	**$2,125**
None over $750	
Health Professionals	**$17,100**
American Medical Assn	$10,000
Anesthesia Service Medical Group	$4,450
American Dental Assn	$1,500
Others	$1,150
Hotels & Motels	**$2,800**
Hotel del Coronado	$2,000
Others	$800
Insurance	**$5,950**
Independent Insurance Agents of America	$1,600
National Assn of Life Underwriters	$1,500
Others	$2,850

PAC Totals by Category

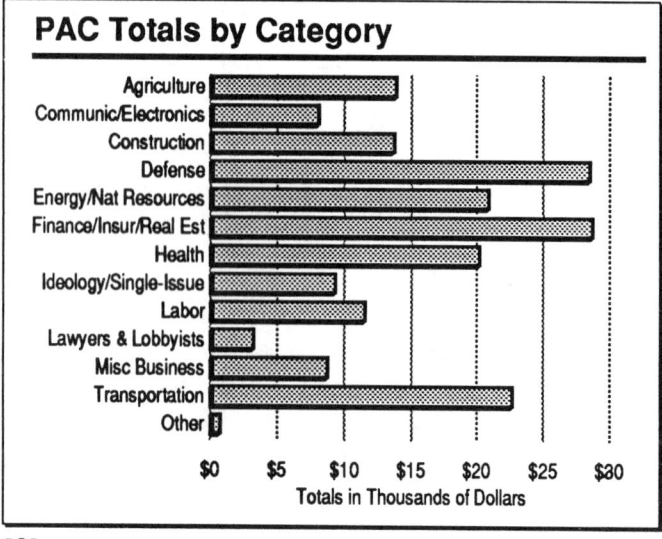

Agriculture
Communic/Electronics
Construction
Defense
Energy/Nat Resources
Finance/Insur/Real Est
Health
Ideology/Single-Issue
Labor
Lawyers & Lobbyists
Misc Business
Transportation
Other

$0 $5 $10 $15 $20 $25 $30
Totals in Thousands of Dollars

Lawyers $3,050
    Dow, Lohnes & Albertson $1,000
    Others $2,050

Oil & Gas $3,450
    None over $800

Real Estate $9,150
    National Assn of Realtors $7,550
    Mortgage Bankers Assn of America $1,600

Ship Building & Repair $7,371
    Southwest Marine $5,450
    California Small Bus Ship Repair Assn $1,071
    Others $850

Sugar Growers $2,900
    American Crystal Sugar Corp $2,350
    Others $550

Telecommunications $3,050
    Pacific Telesis Group $1,600
    Others $1,450

Other Major Business PACs

General Atomics	$1,850	NuclearEquip
American Tunaboat Assn	$1,300	Fishing
Hercules Inc	$1,000	Chemicals

Interest Group Ratings

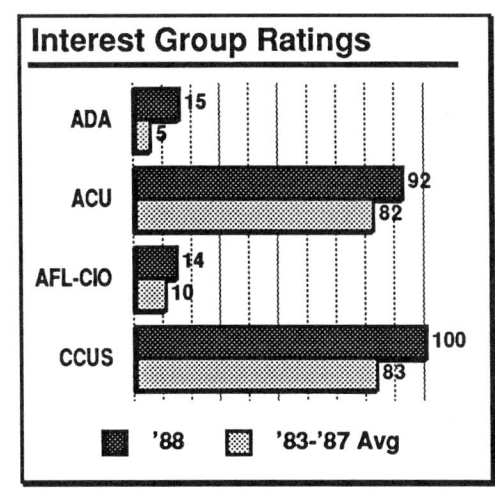

	'88	'83-'87 Avg
ADA	15	5
ACU	92	82
AFL-CIO	14	10
CCUS	100	83

Labor

Government & Postal Workers $4,500
    National Assn of Letter Carriers $1,500
    National Assn of Retired Federal Employees $1,000
    National Rural Letter Carriers Assn $1,000
    Others $1,000

Transportation Unions $6,250
    Marine Engineers District 2 Maritime Officers $3,500
    Seafarers International Union $1,000
    Others $1,750

Ideological/Single-Issue

Pro-Israel $5,500
    National PAC $5,000
    Others $500

Other Major Ideological/Single-Issue PACs

National Rifle Assn	$1,000	Pro-Guns

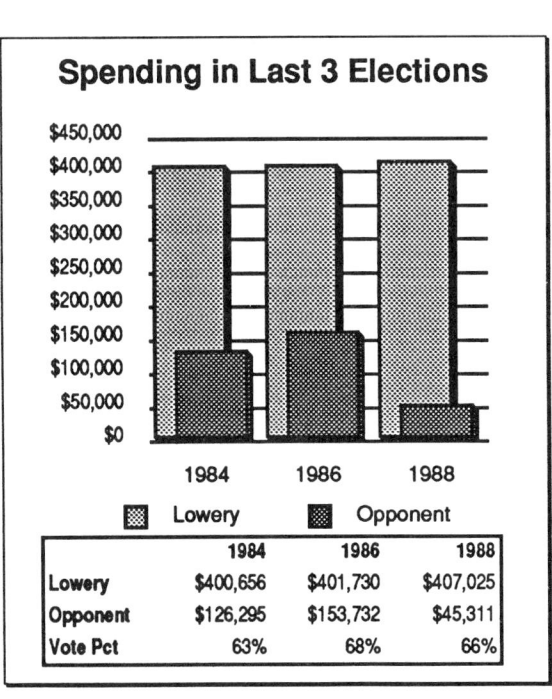

Spending in Last 3 Elections

	1984	1986	1988
Lowery	$400,656	$401,730	$407,025
Opponent	$126,295	$153,732	$45,311
Vote Pct	63%	68%	66%

    Lowery   Opponent

* Contributions came from more than one PAC affiliated
with this sponsor.

Nita M. Lowey, D-NY (20)

First elected: 1988
Total receipts: $1,338,147
Total from PACs: $164,175

1988-1989 Committees & Subcommittees

Education and Labor
Elementary, Secondary and Vocational Education
Human Resources
Postsecondary Education

Merchant Marine and Fisheries
Coast Guard and Navigation
Oceanography

Select Narcotics Abuse and Control

PAC Contribution Profile

Business

Health Professionals	***$7,750***
American Nurses Assn	$7,000
Others	$750
Insurance	***$2,000***
Independent Insurance Agents of America	$2,000
Lawyers	***$2,500***
Assn of Trial Lawyers of America	$2,500
Social Workers	***$2,000***
National Assn of Social Workers	$2,000

Other Major Business PACs

AT&T	$1,000	LongDistance
Philip Morris	$1,000	Tobacco

Campaign Revenue Sources

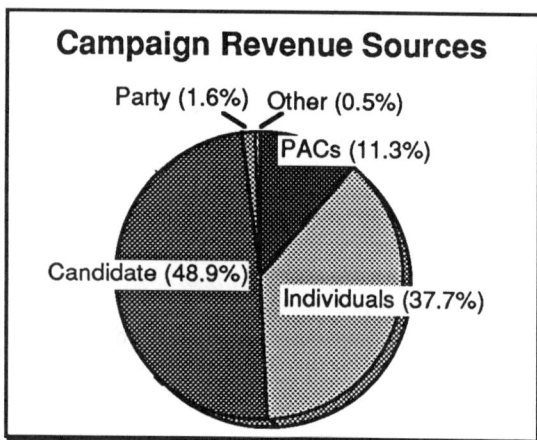

Party (1.6%) Other (0.5%)
PACs (11.3%)
Candidate (48.9%)
Individuals (37.7%)

PAC Totals by Category

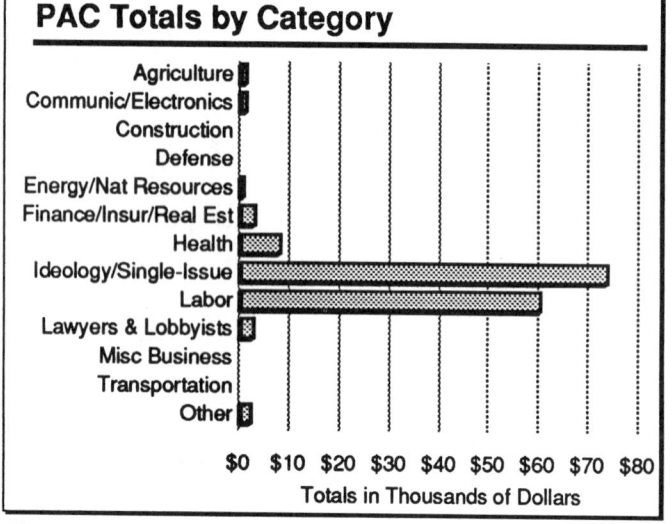

Agriculture
Communic/Electronics
Construction
Defense
Energy/Nat Resources
Finance/Insur/Real Est
Health
Ideology/Single-Issue
Labor
Lawyers & Lobbyists
Misc Business
Transportation
Other

$0 $10 $20 $30 $40 $50 $60 $70 $80
Totals in Thousands of Dollars

Labor

Bldg Trades/Industrial/Misc Unions $35,500

Machinists/Aerospace Workers Union	$5,000
Service Employees International Union	$5,000
Sheet Metal Workers Union	$5,000
United Auto Workers	$5,000
United Steelworkers	$5,000
AFL-CIO	$3,500
Intl Brotherhood of Electrical Workers...........................	$3,000
Communications Workers of America	$2,500
International Longshoremen Assn	$1,000
Others	$500

Government & Postal Workers $9,500

American Fedn of State/County/Munic Employees	$8,000
American Postal Workers Union	$1,500

Teachers Unions $15,000

National Education Assn	$10,000
American Federation of Teachers	$5,000

Ideological/Single-Issue

Democratic/Liberal $7,249

National Cmte for an Effective Congress	$4,999
Democratic Study Group Campaign Fund	$2,000
Others	$250

Democratic Leadership PACs....................................$17,000

Majority Congress Committee (Jim Wright)	$5,000
Empire Leadership Fund (Mario Cuomo)	$2,500
Independent Action (Morris Udall)	$2,500
Valley Education Fund (Tony Coelho)	$2,000
Cmte for Democratic Opportunity (Bill Gray)...................	$1,000
Cmte for a Progressive Congress (David Obey)..............	$1,000
Cmte for the 100th Congress (Charles Rangel)	$1,000
House Leadership Fund (Tom Foley)	$1,000
Others	$1,000

Pro-Choice $15,500

Prochoice Voter	$8,000
Citizens for Family Planning	$3,000
Voters for Choice/Friends of Family Planning	$3,000
National Abortion Rights Action League	$1,500

Pro-Israel $6,500

National PAC	$5,000
Joint Action Cmte for Political Affairs	$1,500

Womens Issues...$16,337

Women's Campaign Fund	$7,000
Emily's List..	$5,337
National Womens Political Caucus	$2,000
National Organization for Women	$1,000
National Womens Political Caucus	$1,000

Other Major Ideological/Single-Issue PACs

Human Rights Campaign Fund	$5,000	Gay Rights
National Council of Senior Citizens	$2,000	Soc Secur
KidsPAC	$1,500	HealthWelfare
Armenian-American PAC	$1,000	Ethnic

Spending in Last Election

	1988
Lowey	$1,309,873
Opponent	$1,567,129
Vote Pct	50%

Thomas A. Luken, D-Ohio (1)

First elected: 1976
Total receipts: $774,952
Total from PACs: $468,185

1988 Committees & Subcommittees

Energy and Commerce
Transportation, Tourism and Hazardous Materials (Chairman)
Oversight and Investigations

Small Business
Antitrust, Impact of Deregulation and Privatization
Regulation and Business Opportunities

Select Aging
Health and Long-Term Care

PAC Contribution Profile

Business

Campaign Revenue Sources

Party (2.1%) Other (6.0%)
Candidate 1.9%)
Individuals (32.4%)
PACs (57.6%)

Automotive	$19,100
Auto Dealers & Drivers for Free Trade	$7,000
National Auto Dealers Assn	$6,000
Ford Motor Company	$2,350
Chrysler Corp	$1,500
General Motors	$1,500
Others	$750

Construction	$14,750
Walter Industries	$4,000
National Assn of Home Builders	$2,750
Manville Corp	$1,750
Others	$6,250

Electric Utilities & Equipment	$20,529
Cincinnati Gas & Electric	$4,000
American Electric Power*	$1,750
Southern Company*	$1,700
General Electric	$1,500
Westinghouse Electric	$1,500
Henley Group Inc	$1,250
Others	$8,829

Food & Beverage	$15,600
Kroger Company	$2,050
Food Marketing Institute	$2,000
Others	$11,550

Health Professionals	$30,700
American Medical Assn	$7,500
American Optometric Assn	$5,000
American Dental Assn	$4,500
American Podiatry Assn	$3,750
National Assn of Pharmacists	$3,000
American College of Emergency Physicians	$1,500
Cmte for Quality Orthopedic Health Care	$1,500
Oral & Maxillofacial Surgeons	$1,500
Others	$2,450

Insurance	$24,000
National Assn of Life Underwriters	$5,000
Travelers Corp	$2,500
Union Central Life Insurance	$1,750
Independent Insurance Agents of America	$1,700
Casualty & Surety Agents Assn	$1,500
Others	$11,550

Oil & Gas	$15,860
Columbia Natural Resources	$2,310
CSX Transportation Inc	$1,550
Coastal Corp	$1,500
Union Pacific Corp	$1,500
Others	$9,000

Railroads & Railroad Services	$13,500
ITEL Corp	$5,000
Burlington Northern	$1,500
Kansas City Southern	$1,500
Santa Fe Southern Pacific	$1,500
Others	$4,000

Securities/Commodities Investment	$15,500
Investment Company Institute	$3,000
Chicago Board of Trade	$2,000
E F Hutton Group	$1,500
Securities Industry Assn	$1,500
Others	$7,500

Telecommunications	$15,475
AT&T	$7,000
Cincinnati Bell	$3,500
Ohio Bell Telephone	$1,675
Pacific Telesis Group	$1,250
Others	$2,050

Waste Management	$13,600
Browning-Ferris Industries	$5,000
Waste Management Inc	$5,000
National Solid Wastes Mgmt Assn	$3,000
Others	$600

PAC Totals by Category

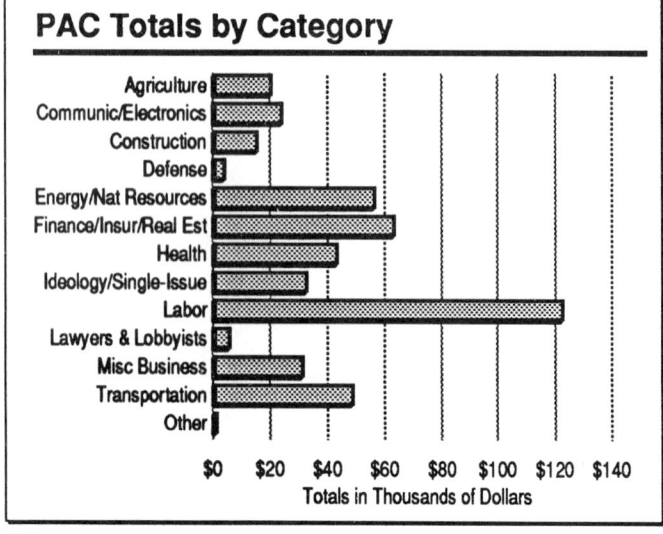

Agriculture
Communic/Electronics
Construction
Defense
Energy/Nat Resources
Finance/Insur/Real Est
Health
Ideology/Single-Issue
Labor
Lawyers & Lobbyists
Misc Business
Transportation
Other

$0 $20 $40 $60 $80 $100 $120 $140
Totals in Thousands of Dollars

Other Major Business PACs

National Assn of Realtors	$5,964	Real Estate
Avon Products	$5,007	Cosmetics
American Institute of CPA's	$5,000	Accountants
National Cable Television Assn	$3,500	CableTV
Federated Department Stores	$3,000	Dept Store
Banc One Corp	$2,500	Comml Banks
Owens-Illinois	$2,500	Paper Packg
Midland Enterprises	$2,324	SeaTransport
United Parcel Service	$2,166	Delivery
J P Morgan & Company	$2,000	Comml Banks
National Assn of Broadcasters	$2,000	TV/Radio
Philip Morris	$2,000	Tobacco
Touche Ross	$2,000	Accountants
Pearle Health Services	$1,850	Optical Svc
American Society of Travel Agents	$1,500	Travel Agent
Federation of America Hospitals	$1,500	Hospitals
Greyhound Corp	$1,500	Home Chem
Holiday Inns	$1,500	Hotel/Motel
Ohio Savings Assns League	$1,500	SavingsBanks

Labor

Bldg Trades/Industrial/Misc Unions $54,100

United Auto Workers	$8,500
Intl Brotherhood of Electrical Workers	$5,500
Food & Commercial Workers Union	$5,000
Machinists/Aerospace Workers Union	$5,000
Operating Engineers Union	$4,500
Laborers' Political League	$3,000
United Steelworkers	$3,000
AFL-CIO*	$2,750
Carpenters & Joiners Union	$2,500
Plumbers/Pipefitters Union	$2,500
Sheet Metal Workers Union	$2,500
Rubber Cork Linoleum Plastic Workers	$2,000
Ladies Garment Workers Union	$1,500
United Mine Workers	$1,500
Others	$4,350

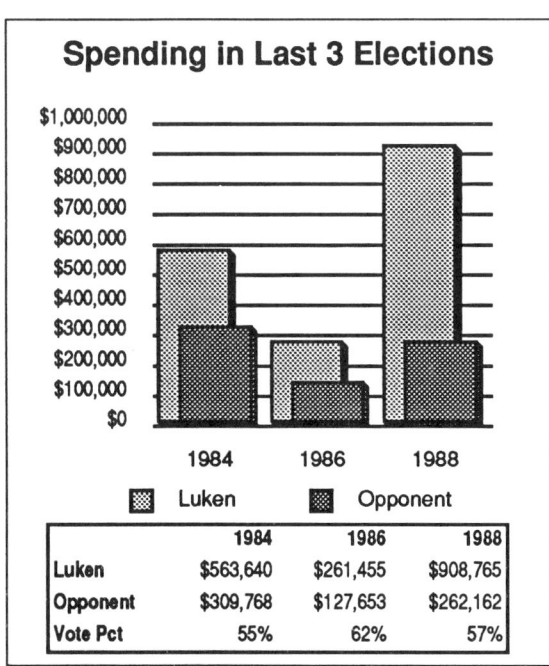

Spending in Last 3 Elections

Legend: Luken, Opponent

	1984	1986	1988
Luken	$563,640	$261,455	$908,765
Opponent	$309,768	$127,653	$262,162
Vote Pct	55%	62%	57%

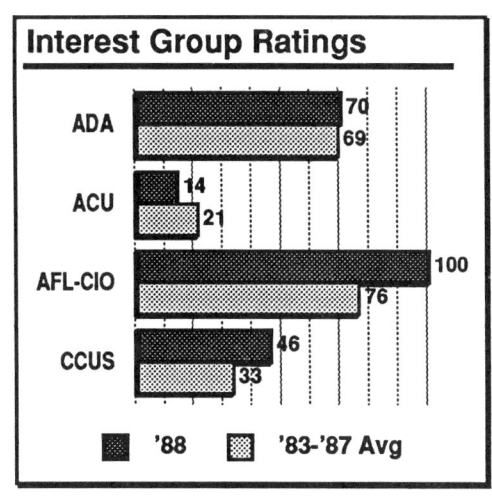

Interest Group Ratings

	'88	'83-'87 Avg
ADA	70	69
ACU	14	21
AFL-CIO	100	76
CCUS	46	33

Legend: ■ '88   ▦ '83-'87 Avg

Government & Postal Workers $20,300

National Assn of Retired Federal Employees	$7,000
National Assn of Letter Carriers	$6,200
American Postal Workers Union	$2,700
American Fedn of State/County/Munic Employees	$2,000
Others	$2,400

Teachers Unions $10,500

National Education Assn	$5,500
American Federation of Teachers	$5,000

Transportation Unions $36,850

United Transportation Union	$10,000
Seafarers International Union	$5,500
Teamsters Union	$5,000
Air Line Pilots Assn	$3,000
Marine Engineers Union*	$3,000
Amalgamated Transit Union	$2,000
International Longshoremen Assn	$2,000
Transportation Communication Union	$1,850
Brotherhood of Locomotive Engineers	$1,500
Brotherhood of Railroad Signalmen	$1,500
Others	$1,500

Ideological/Single-Issue

Democratic Leadership PACs $19,400

24th Cong Dist of California PAC (Henry Waxman)	$5,000
America's Leaders' Fund (Dan Rostenkowski)	$5,000
Majority Congress Committee (Jim Wright)	$5,000
House Leadership Fund (Tom Foley)	$3,000
Valley Education Fund (Tony Coelho)	$1,400

Other Major Ideological/Single-Issue PACs

National PAC	$5,000	Pro-Israel
Democratic Study Group Campaign Fund	$3,000	Dem/Liberal
KidsPAC	$1,500	HealthWelfare

* Contributions came from more than one PAC affiliated
  with this sponsor.

Donald E. "Buz" Lukens, R-Ohio (8)

First elected: 1986
Total receipts: $146,972
Total from PACs: $84,880

1988 Committees & Subcommittees

Foreign Affairs
Africa
Europe and the Middle East

Government Operations
Human Resources and Intergovernmental Relations
Legislation and National Security

PAC Contribution Profile

Business

Accountants **$5,880**
American Institute of CPA's $5,000
Others $880

Automotive **$6,150**
National Auto Dealers Assn $2,850
Auto Dealers & Drivers for Free Trade $1,500
Federal-Mogul Corp $1,000
Others $800

Commercial & Savings Banks **$4,550**
American Bankers Assn $2,500
Ohio Savings Assns League $1,000
Others $1,050

Construction **$5,200**
Associated General Contractors $1,300
National Assn of Home Builders $1,000
Others $2,900

Food & Beverage **$3,350**
American Meat Institute $1,750
Others $1,600

Health Professionals **$7,050**
American Academy of Ophthalmology $3,000
American Medical Assn $2,800
American Dental Assn $1,000
Others $250

Campaign Revenue Sources

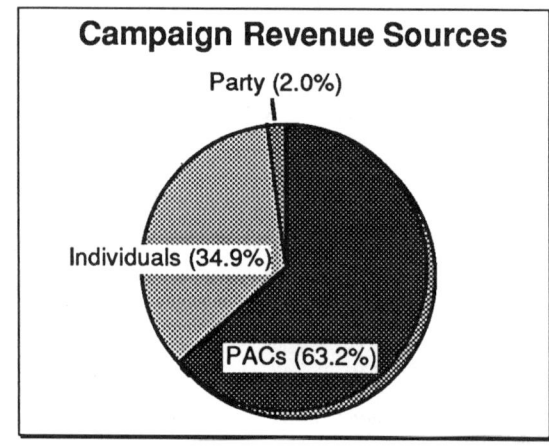

Party (2.0%)

Individuals (34.9%)

PACs (63.2%)

Insurance **$3,400**
National Assn of Life Underwriters $1,500
Others $1,900

Oil & Gas **$3,000**
None over $600

Paper Production **$2,300**
Westvaco Corp $2,000
Others $300

Real Estate **$6,600**
National Assn of Realtors $6,600

Telecommunications **$3,310**
AT&T $2,500
Others $810

Other Major Business PACs

Ohio Farm Bureau Federation .... $1,500 Farm Orgs
Associated Milk Producers .... $1,000 Dairy
Cincinnati Gas & Electric .... $1,000 Gas & Electr

PAC Totals by Category

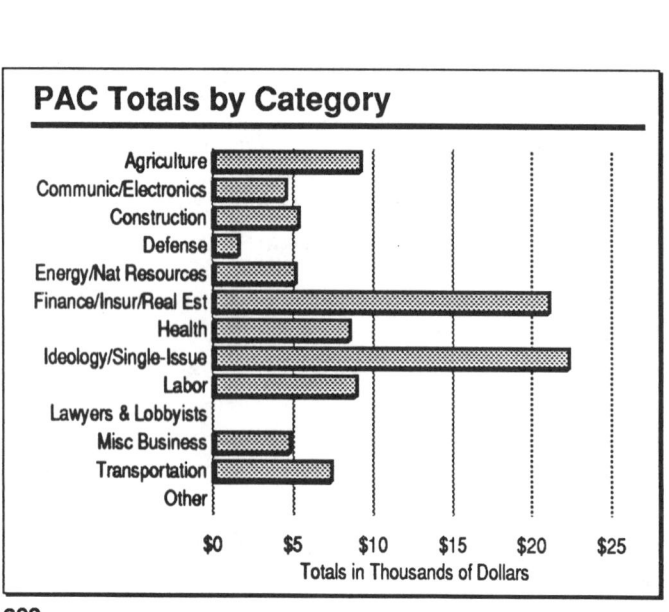

Totals in Thousands of Dollars

Labor

Labor Unions ***$8,800***

    Teamsters Union $5,000
    National Assn of Retired Federal Employees $2,000
    Air Line Pilots Assn $1,000
    Others $800

Ideological/Single-Issue

Pro-Defense ***$5,820***

    Council for National Defense $4,520
    Others $1,300

Pro-Israel ***$8,000***

    National PAC $5,000
    Hudson Valley PAC $2,500
    Others $500

Republican/Conservative ***$3,900***

    Southwest Ohio Concerned Citizens $1,000
    Others $2,900

Other Major Ideological/Single-Issue PACs

National Rifle Assn .... $1,500   Pro-Guns
Public Service Research Council .... $1,100   Anti-Union

Independent expenditures supporting Lukens

Teamsters Union $2,000

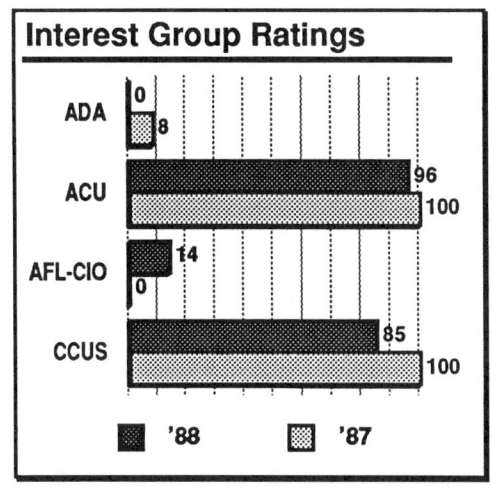

Interest Group Ratings

	'88	'87
ADA	0	8
ACU	96	100
AFL-CIO	14	0
CCUS	85	100

■ '88   ▨ '87

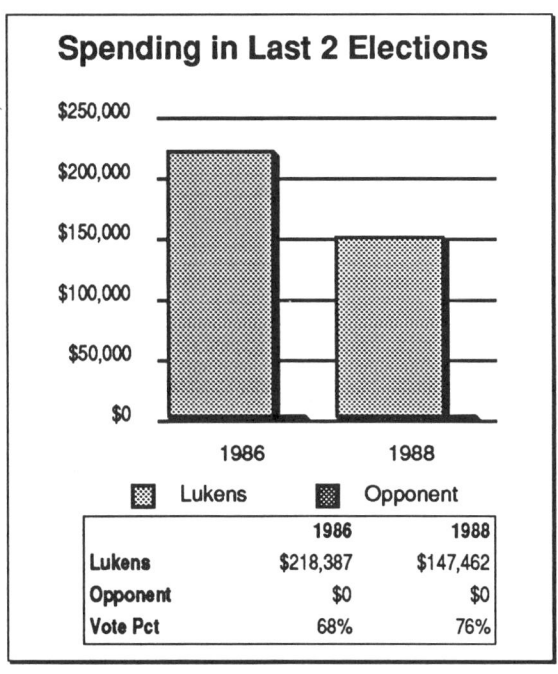

Spending in Last 2 Elections

	1986	1988
Lukens	$218,387	$147,462
Opponent	$0	$0
Vote Pct	68%	76%

▨ Lukens   ■ Opponent

Ronald K. Machtley, R-RI (1)

First elected: 1988
Total receipts: $417,449
Total from PACs: $81,524

1988-1989 Committees & Subcommittees

Armed Services
Military Personnel and Compensation
Readiness

Small Business
Procurement, Tourism and Rural Development

Select Children, Youth and Families

PAC Contribution Profile

Business

Auto Dealers	**$3,500**
National Auto Dealers Assn	$2,000
Auto Dealers & Drivers for Free Trade	$1,500
Business Organizations	**$4,869**
Business Industry PAC	$2,619
National Fedn of Independent Business	$1,500
Others	$750
Commercial Banks	**$3,075**
Fleet/Norstar Financial Group	$1,550
Others	$1,525
Construction	**$2,750**
Associated General Contractors	$2,000
Others	$750
Defense	**$6,000**
Litton Industries	$1,000
Lockheed Corp	$1,000
Raytheon	$1,000
Textron Inc	$1,000
Others	$2,000
Food & Beverage	**$1,250**
Pepsico Inc	$1,000
Others	$250
Health Professionals	**$8,000**
American Medical Assn	$5,000
American Academy of Ophthalmology	$2,000
American Dental Assn	$1,000

Insurance	**$4,000**
National Assn of Life Underwriters	$2,500
ITT Corp	$1,000
Others	$500
Oil & Gas	**$4,550**
Petroleum Marketers Assn	$1,500
Deblois Political Action Fund	$1,250
Amoco Corp	$1,000
Others	$800
Real Estate	**$10,000**
National Assn of Realtors	$10,000
Telecommunications	**$1,600**
Continental Telecom	$1,000
Others	$600

Other Major Business PACs

American Hospital Assn	$1,000	Hospitals
FMC Corp	$1,000	Chemicals
Precision Metalforming Assn	$1,000	MetalProduct
Stanley Works	$1,000	Hardware

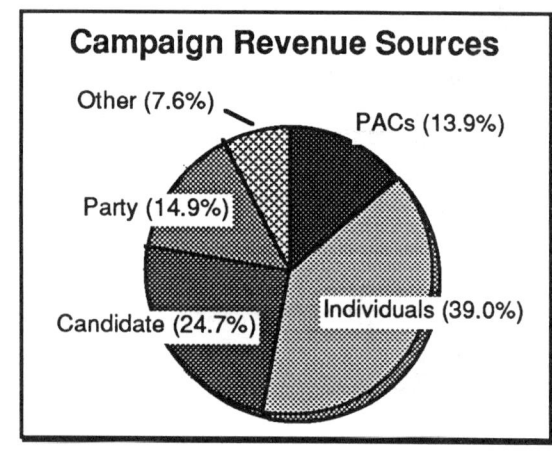

Campaign Revenue Sources

- Other (7.6%)
- PACs (13.9%)
- Party (14.9%)
- Candidate (24.7%)
- Individuals (39.0%)

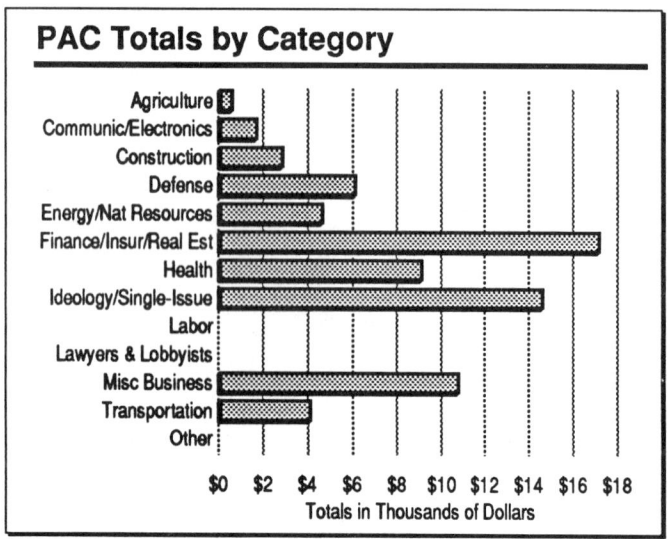

PAC Totals by Category

- Agriculture
- Communic/Electronics
- Construction
- Defense
- Energy/Nat Resources
- Finance/Insur/Real Est
- Health
- Ideology/Single-Issue
- Labor
- Lawyers & Lobbyists
- Misc Business
- Transportation
- Other

$0 $2 $4 $6 $8 $10 $12 $14 $16 $18
Totals in Thousands of Dollars

Ideological/Single-Issue

Republican Leadership/Conservative PACs $14,000

    Citizens for the Republic (Ronald Reagan) $5,000
    Fund for America's Future (George Bush) $5,000
    Republican Congressional Boosters Club $2,000
    Republican Leader's Fund (Bob Michel) $1,000
    Others $1,000

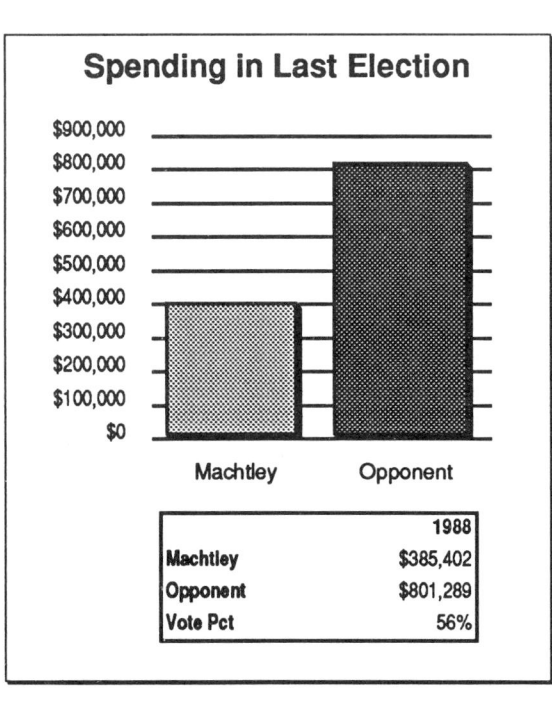

Spending in Last Election

	1988
Machtley	$385,402
Opponent	$801,289
Vote Pct	56%

691

Edward R. Madigan, R-Ill (15)

First elected: 1972
Total receipts: $500,508
Total from PACs: $333,315

1988 Committees & Subcommittees

Agriculture (Ranking Republican)

Energy and Commerce
Health and the Environment (Ranking Republican)

PAC Contribution Profile

Business

Agricultural Chemicals **$13,650**
- Ciba-Geigy Corp $2,000
- Dow Chemical* $2,000
- Eli Lilly & Company $2,000
- Freeport-McMoran Inc $1,500
- Pfizer Inc $1,250
- Others $4,900

Agricultural Services **$5,000**
- American Assn of Crop Insurers $1,500
- American Veterinary Medical Assn $1,500
- Farm Credit Council $1,500
- Others $500

Automotive **$9,000**
- National Auto Dealers Assn $3,000
- Auto Dealers & Drivers for Free Trade $2,000
- Ford Motor Company $1,750
- Others $2,250

Commercial & Savings Banks **$9,750**
- American Bankers Assn $2,500
- Continental Illinois Corp $1,250
- First Chicago Corp $1,250
- Others $4,750

Dairy **$4,800**
- Mid-American Dairymen $2,000
- Others $2,800

Campaign Revenue Sources

Other (10.3%)
Party (0.6%)
Individuals (22.3%)
PACs (66.8%)

Electric Utilities **$18,270**
- Illinois Power Company $3,070
- Texas Utilities Electric Company* $1,750
- Southern California Edison $1,250
- Others $12,200

Farm Organizations **$6,473**
- Illinois Agricultural Assn $3,973
- National Council of Farmer Co-ops $1,500
- Others $1,000

Food & Beverage **$20,000**
- National Beer Wholesalers Assn $2,000
- A E Staley Manufacturing Company $1,500
- Nutrasweet Company $1,500
- Others $15,000

Health Professionals **$33,850**
- American Medical Assn $4,500
- American Dental Assn $4,000
- American Academy of Ophthalmology $2,500
- Illinois Medical Assn $2,500
- Oral & Maxillofacial Surgeons $2,500
- American Assn of Nurse Anesthetist $2,000
- American College of Emergency Physicians $2,000
- American Physical Therapy Assn $2,000
- American Optometric Assn $2,000
- American Podiatry Assn $2,000
- American Nurses Assn $1,500
- Cmte for Quality Orthopedic Health Care $1,500
- Others $4,850

Hospitals & Nursing Homes **$12,165**
- American Health Care Assn $3,000
- American Hospital Assn $2,665
- National Assn of Private Psychiatric Hospitals $2,000
- Others $4,500

Lawyers & Lobbyists **$6,050**
- None over $1,000

Oil & Gas **$18,750**
- Union Pacific Corp $2,000
- CSX Transportation Inc $1,500
- Others $15,250

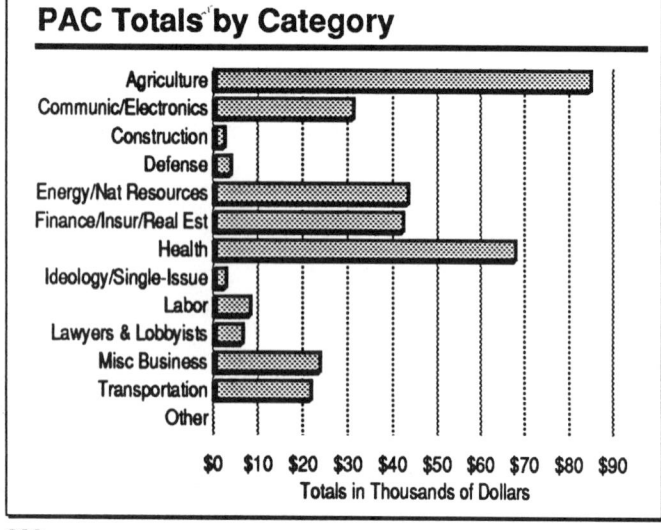

PAC Totals by Category

- Agriculture
- Communic/Electronics
- Construction
- Defense
- Energy/Nat Resources
- Finance/Insur/Real Est
- Health
- Ideology/Single-Issue
- Labor
- Lawyers & Lobbyists
- Misc Business
- Transportation
- Other

$0 $10 $20 $30 $40 $50 $60 $70 $80 $90
Totals in Thousands of Dollars

Pharmaceuticals $18,000
Abbott Laboratories $3,000
Upjohn Company $2,000
Schering-Plough Corp $1,500
Smithkline Beckman $1,500
Others $10,000

Railroads $7,050
Chicago & North Western Transport $3,000
Others $4,050

Securities & Commodities Investment $12,000
Chicago Mercantile Exchange $3,000
Chicago Board of Options Exchange $2,000
First Boston Corp $1,500
Merrill Lynch $1,500
Others $4,000

Sugar Growers $7,000
American Crystal Sugar Corp $2,500
American Sugar Cane League $1,500
Others $3,000

Telecommunications $26,300
Illinois Bell Telephone $5,000
AT&T $4,500
Corning Glass Works $2,500
BellSouth Corp* $2,000
US Telephone Assn $2,000
Pacific Telesis Group $1,750
Bell Atlantic $1,500
Others $7,050

Tobacco $6,000
Philip Morris $3,500
Others $2,500

Transportation $19,150
National Assn of Life Underwriters $2,500
Travelers Corp $2,500
Kemper Insurance $1,150
Others $13,000

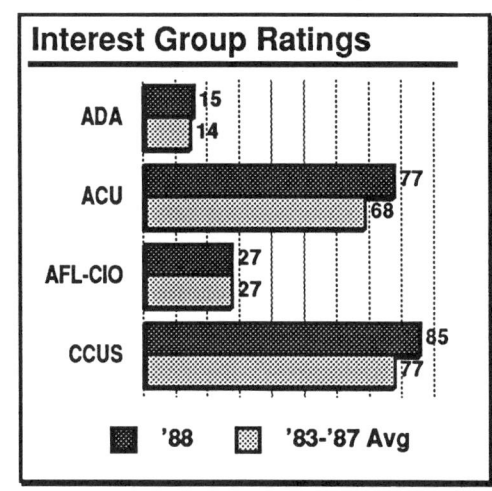

Interest Group Ratings

	'88	'83-'87 Avg
ADA	15	14
ACU	77	68
AFL-CIO	27	27
CCUS	85	77

Other Major Business PACs
National Assn of Realtors	$3,500	Real Estate
American Institute of CPA's	$2,500	Accountants
National Cable Television Assn	$2,500	CableTV
Archer-Daniels-Midland Corp	$2,000	Grain Trader
Cosmetic Toiletry & Fragrance Assn	$2,000	Cosmetics
Navistar International	$2,000	Farm Equip
Health Industry Manufacturers Assn	$1,500	Med Supply
National Assn of Broadcasters	$1,500	TV/Radio
United Parcel Service	$1,500	Delivery

Labor

Labor Unions...$7,850
National Education Assn $2,500
United Transportation Union $2,000
Others $3,350

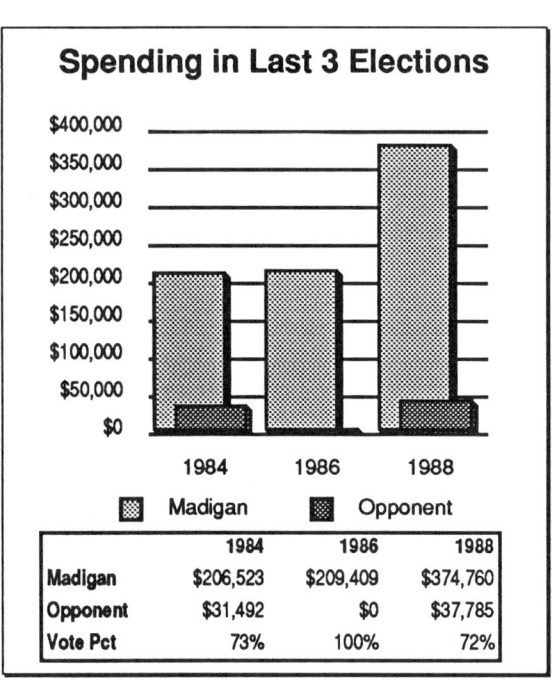

Spending in Last 3 Elections

	1984	1986	1988
Madigan	$206,523	$209,409	$374,760
Opponent	$31,492	$0	$37,785
Vote Pct	73%	100%	72%

Madigan / Opponent

* Contributions came from more than one PAC affiliated with this sponsor.

Thomas J. Manton, D-NY (9)

First elected: 1984
Total receipts: $424,381
Total from PACs: $262,545

1988 Committees & Subcommittees

Banking, Finance and Urban Affairs
Financial Institutions Supervision, Regulation and Insurance
Housing and Community Development
International Finance, Trade and Monetary Policy

Merchant Marine and Fisheries
Fisheries and Wildlife Conservation and the Environment
Panama Canal/Outer Continental Shelf

Select Aging
Retirement Income and Employment

PAC Contribution Profile

Business

Commercial Banks **$27,800**

American Bankers Assn	$5,000
Citicorp	$5,000
Bankers Trust	$2,000
Barnett Banks of Florida	$2,000
Chemical Bank	$1,500
Irving Bank	$1,500
Manufacturers Hanover	$1,450
Marine Midland Banks	$1,450
Chase Manhattan	$1,300
Security Pacific Corp	$1,300
Citizens & Southern National Bank	$1,000
Others	$4,300

Consumer Credit & Loans **$2,600**

None over $600

Dairy **$5,250**

Associated Milk Producers	$3,500
Mid-American Dairymen	$1,250
Others	$500

Health Professionals **$10,000**

American Medical Assn	$7,500
New York Medical Assn	$2,500

Campaign Revenue Sources

Other (3.8%)
Individuals (23.8%)
PACs (72.4%)

Insurance **$37,400**

Independent Insurance Agents of America	$10,000
National Assn of Life Underwriters	$10,000
National Assn Mutual Insurance Agents	$5,850
Casualty & Surety Agents Assn	$1,850
Equitable Financial Services	$1,750
American Council of Life Insurance	$1,300
Cigna Corp	$1,050
New York Life	$1,000
Travelers Corp	$1,000
Others	$3,600

Lawyers & Lobbyists **$8,450**

Assn of Trial Lawyers of America	$6,000
Others	$2,450

Oil & Gas **$6,800**

None over $850

Package Delivery **$2,950**

United Parcel Service	$2,950

Real Estate **$7,750**

National Assn of Realtors	$4,850
Metropolitan Life Insurance	$1,600
Others	$1,300

Residential Construction **$2,250**

National Assn of Home Builders	$2,000
Others	$250

Savings Banks & Credit Unions **$9,300**

US League of Savings Assn	$3,400
Credit Union National Assn	$1,600
National Council of Savings Institutions	$1,200
Others	$3,100

Securities & Commodities Investment **$18,150**

First Boston Corp	$4,000
Goldman Sachs	$2,500
Prudential-Bache Securities	$2,500
Securities Industry Assn*	$2,300
Investment Company Institute	$1,150
Morgan Stanley & Company	$1,000
PaineWebber	$1,000
Others	$3,700

Sugar Growers **$3,600**

American Sugarbeet Growers Assn	$1,400
Others	$2,200

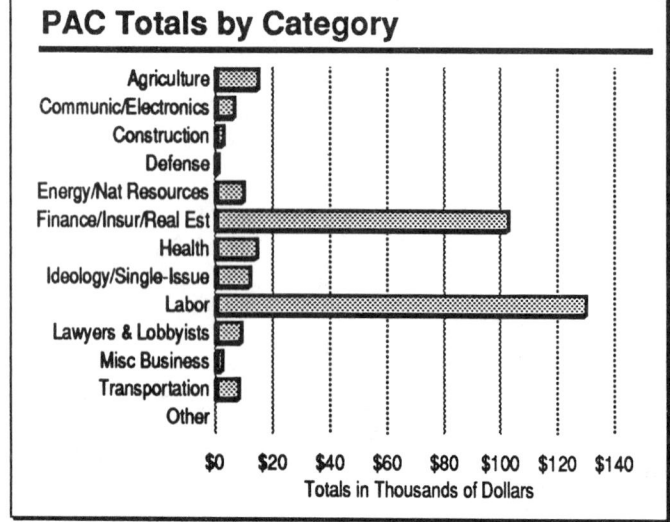

PAC Totals by Category

Agriculture
Communic/Electronics
Construction
Defense
Energy/Nat Resources
Finance/Insur/Real Est
Health
Ideology/Single-Issue
Labor
Lawyers & Lobbyists
Misc Business
Transportation
Other

$0 $20 $40 $60 $80 $100 $120 $140
Totals in Thousands of Dollars

Telecommunications **$5,000**

AT&T	$2,000
New York Telephone	$1,100
Others	$1,900

Other Major Business PACs

Southwest Peanut Membership Organ	$1,250	Crops
General Electric	$1,000	Electronics
Waste Management Inc	$1,000	Waste Mgmt
American Hospital Assn	$1,800	Hospitals
Boeing Company	$1,000	Aircraft

Labor

Bldg Trades/Industrial/Misc Unions **$39,500**

Ironworkers Union	$8,000
Sheet Metal Workers Union	$5,000
Bricklayers Union	$3,500
Carpenters & Joiners Union	$3,500
Operating Engineers Union*	$3,000
AFL-CIO*	$2,950
Communications Workers of America	$2,400
Laborers' Political League	$1,950
Food & Commercial Workers Union	$1,750
Intl Brotherhood of Electrical Workers	$1,500
Ladies Garment Workers Union	$1,250
Machinists/Aerospace Workers Union	$1,100
Others	$3,600

Government & Postal Workers **$27,650**

American Postal Workers Union	$9,250
National Assn of Retired Federal Employees	$8,000
American Fedn of State/County/Munic Employees	$5,000
National Assn of Letter Carriers	$4,000
Others	$1,400

Sea Transport Unions **$31,481**

International Longshoremen Assn*	$13,681
Marine Engineers Union*	$10,000
Seafarers International Union	$6,200
Masters, Mates & Pilots Union	$1,000
Others	$600

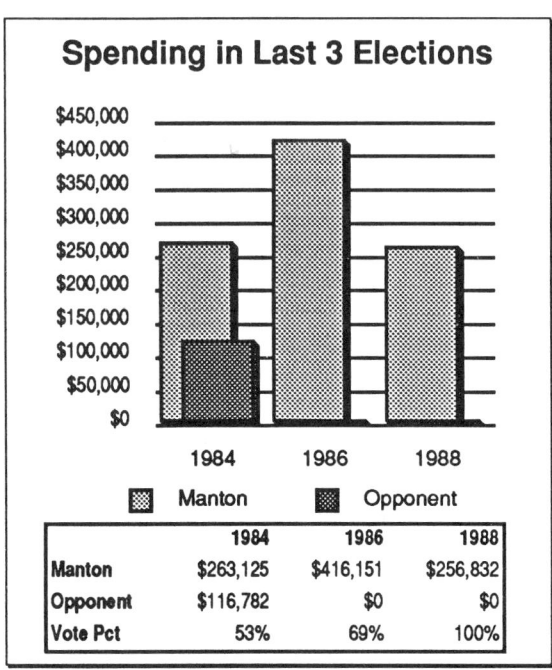

Spending in Last 3 Elections

	1984	1986	1988
Manton	$263,125	$416,151	$256,832
Opponent	$116,782	$0	$0
Vote Pct	53%	69%	100%

Interest Group Ratings

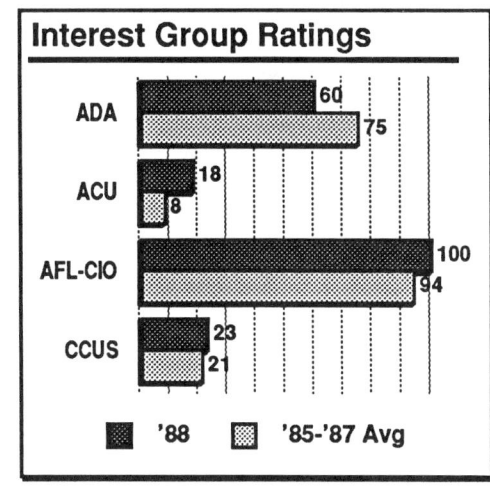

	'88	'85-'87 Avg
ADA	60	75
ACU	18	8
AFL-CIO	100	94
CCUS	23	21

Other Transportation Unions **$23,650**

Teamsters Union	$10,000
Air Line Pilots Assn	$4,500
United Transportation Union	$3,800
Transportation Communication Union	$1,150
Others	$4,200

Teachers Unions **$7,050**

National Education Assn	$6,850
United Federation of Teachers	$200

Ideological/Single-Issue

Democratic Leadership PACs **$2,500**

Valley Education Fund (Tony Coelho)	$2,500

Pro-Israel **$5,000**

National PAC	$5,000	Pro-Israel

Other Major Ideological/Single-Issue PACs

National Cmte to Preserve Social Security	$2,300	Soc Secur
National Cmte for an Effective Congress	$1,000	Dem/Liberal

Independent expenditures supporting Manton

National Cmte to Preserve Social Security	$1,282

* Contributions came from more than one PAC affiliated with this sponsor.

Edward J. Markey, D-Mass (7)

First elected: 1976
Total receipts: $484,173
Total from PACs: $0

1988 Committees & Subcommittees

Energy and Commerce
Telecommunications and Finance (Chairman)
Energy and Power

Interior and Insular Affairs
Energy and the Environment
Water and Power Resources

PAC Contribution Profile

Lane & Edson	$500	Lawyers
League of Conservation Voters	$493	Environment
Tanners' Council of America	$250	Livestock

NOTE: Markey reported taking no PAC funds in his 1988 campaign. The PACs listed above did report making contributions to him during 1987-88, however, and those contributions are recorded in the official FEC records.

Independent expenditures supporting Markey

National Cmte to Preserve Social Security	$1,947
League of Conservation Voters	$2,321

Campaign Revenue Sources

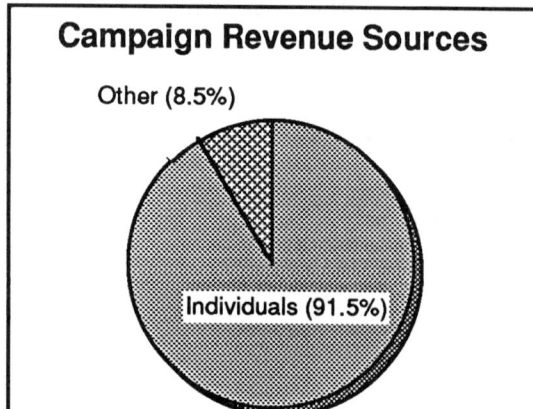

Other (8.5%)

Individuals (91.5%)

PAC Totals by Category

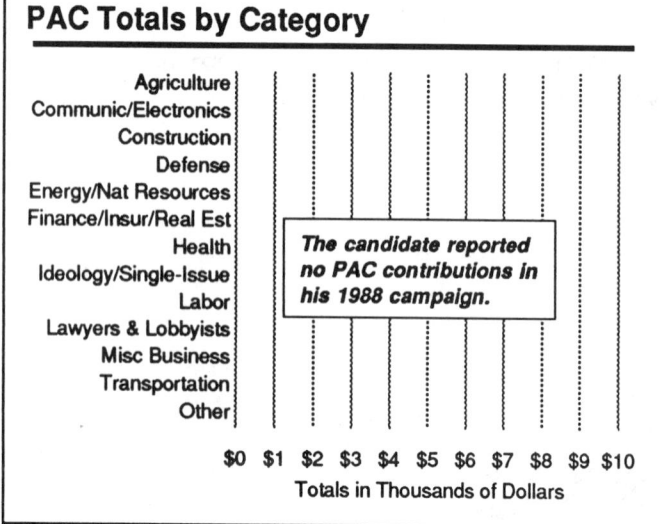

The candidate reported no PAC contributions in his 1988 campaign.

Agriculture
Communic/Electronics
Construction
Defense
Energy/Nat Resources
Finance/Insur/Real Est
Health
Ideology/Single-Issue
Labor
Lawyers & Lobbyists
Misc Business
Transportation
Other

$0 $1 $2 $3 $4 $5 $6 $7 $8 $9 $10
Totals in Thousands of Dollars

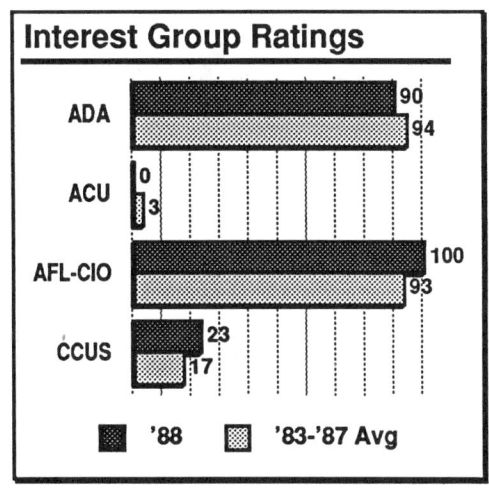

Interest Group Ratings

	'88	'83-'87 Avg
ADA	90	94
ACU	0	3
AFL-CIO	100	93
CCUS	23	17

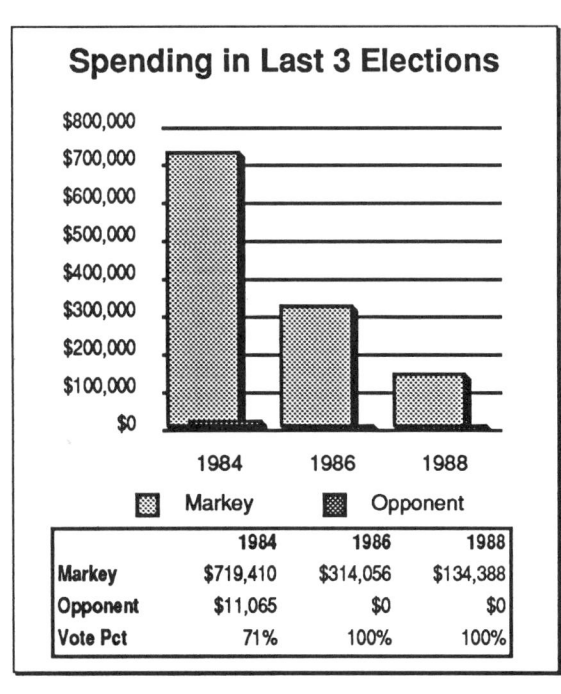

Spending in Last 3 Elections

	1984	1986	1988
Markey	$719,410	$314,056	$134,388
Opponent	$11,065	$0	$0
Vote Pct	71%	100%	100%

Ron Marlenee, R-Mont (2)

First elected: 1976
Total receipts: $416,031
Total from PACs: $171,992

1988 Committees & Subcommittees

Agriculture
Wheat, Soybeans and Feed Grains (Ranking Republican)
Forests, Family Farms and Energy

Interior and Insular Affairs
National Parks and Public Lands (Ranking Republican)
Energy and the Environment
Mining and Natural Resources

PAC Contribution Profile

Business

Agricultural Chemicals	**$2,900**
Ecolab Inc	$1,000
Others	$1,900
Automotive	**$13,500**
National Auto Dealers Assn	$7,000
Auto Dealers & Drivers for Free Trade	$6,000
Others	$500
Business Organizations	**$2,121**
Business Industry PAC	$1,119
National Fedn of Independent Business	$1,000
Others	$2
Mining	**$4,100**
FMC Corp	$1,000
Others	$3,100
Commercial Banks/Credit Unions	**$5,740**
American Bankers Assn	$3,000
Norwest Corp	$1,000
Others	$1,740
Construction	**$15,750**
National Assn of Home Builders	$7,500
Associated General Contractors	$5,000
Sheet Metal/AirCon Contractors	$1,000
Others	$2,250
Cotton	**$2,500**
Calcot Ltd	$1,500
Others	$1,000

Campaign Revenue Sources

Other (7.8%)
Party (8.7%)
PACs (38.4%)
Individuals (45.2%)

Dairy	**$5,800**
Associated Milk Producers	$3,000
Mid-American Dairymen	$1,500
Others	$1,300
Electric Utilities	**$10,950**
Montana ACRE(Action Committee for Rural Electric)	$1,500
Southern Company*	$1,500
Middle South Utilities*	$1,100
Texas Utilities Electric Company*	$1,000
Others	$5,850
Food & Beverage	**$3,850**
ConAgra Inc	$2,000
Others	$1,850
Forest Products	**$8,100**
Louisiana-Pacific Corp	$3,000
Westvaco Corp	$1,500
Boise Cascade	$1,000
Others	$2,600
General Aviation	**$3,000**
Aircraft Owners & Pilots Assn	$3,000
Grain & Soybean Production/Processing	**$4,350**
National Assn of Wheat Growers	$1,050
American Soybean Assn	$1,000
Cargill Inc	$1,000
Others	$1,300
Health Professionals	**$13,000**
American Medical Assn	$10,000
American Academy of Ophthalmology	$2,000
American Dental Assn	$1,000
Insurance	**$4,500**
National Assn of Life Underwriters	$1,500
National Assn Mutual Insurance Agents	$1,000
Others	$2,000

PAC Totals by Category

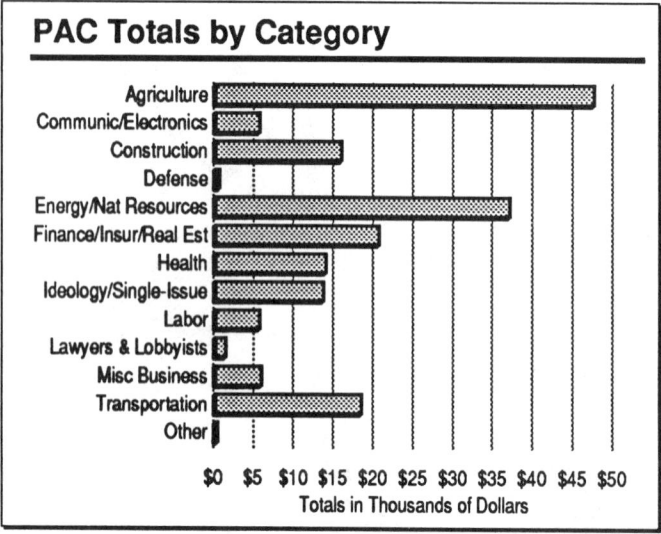

Category	
Agriculture	
Communic/Electronics	
Construction	
Defense	
Energy/Nat Resources	
Finance/Insur/Real Est	
Health	
Ideology/Single-Issue	
Labor	
Lawyers & Lobbyists	
Misc Business	
Transportation	
Other	

$0 $5 $10 $15 $20 $25 $30 $35 $40 $45 $50
Totals in Thousands of Dollars

Oil & Gas **$21,100**

Phillips Petroleum	$2,500
Cooper Industries	$2,000
Independent Energy Producers PAC	$2,000
Amoco Corp	$1,500
Chevron Corp	$1,500
Shell Oil	$1,250
Atlantic Richfield	$1,000
Exxon Corp	$1,000
Occidental Oil & Gas	$1,000
Sun Company	$1,000
Others	$6,350

Poultry & Livestock **$5,900**

National Cattlemen's Assn	$2,500
National Broiler Council	$1,000
Others	$2,400

Real Estate **$10,000**

National Assn of Realtors	$10,000

Sugar Growers **$8,800**

American Sugarbeet Growers Assn	$2,000
American Crystal Sugar Corp	$1,500
Southern Minnesota Beet Sugar Co-op	$1,000
US Beet Sugar Assn	$1,000
Others	$3,300

Telecommunications **$5,500**

Mountain Bell	$5,000
Others	$500

Other Major Business PACs

Philip Morris	$1,000	Tobacco

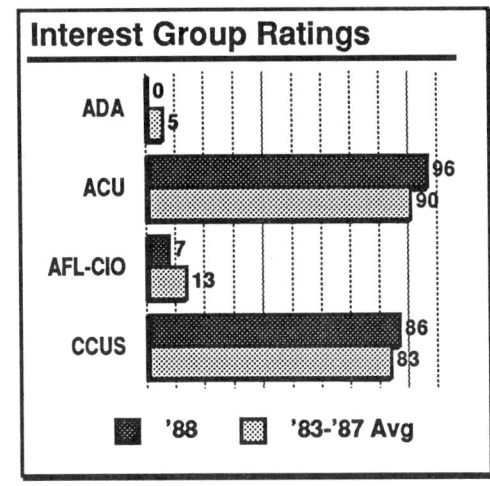

Interest Group Ratings

	'88	'83-'87 Avg
ADA	0	5
ACU	96	90
AFL-CIO	7	13
CCUS	86	83

Labor

Labor Unions **$5,500**

National Assn of Retired Federal Employees	$4,000
Seafarers International Union	$1,000
Others	$500

Ideological/Single-Issue

Pro-Gun Ownership **$9,950**

National Rifle Assn	$6,950
Safari Club International	$3,000

Republican Leadership PACs **$2,272**

Conservative Victory Fund (Steve Symms)	$1,272
Policy Innovation PAC (Dick Armey)	$1,000

Other Major Ideological/Single-Issue PACs

America's PAC	$1,000	Repub/Conser

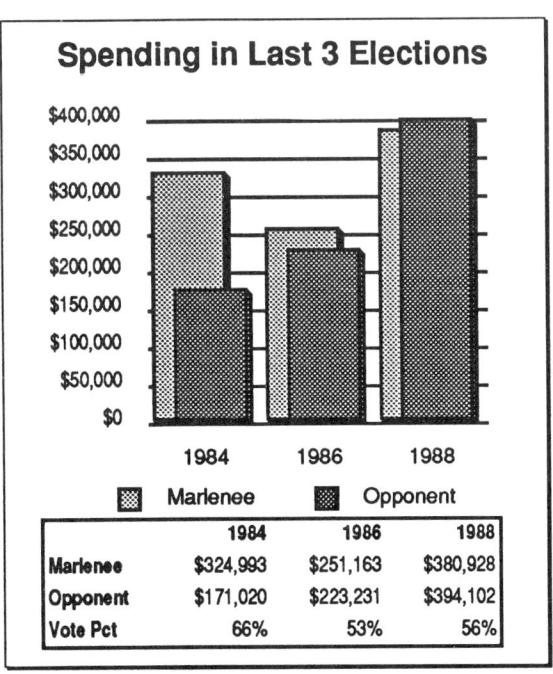

Spending in Last 3 Elections

	1984	1986	1988
Marlenee	$324,993	$251,163	$380,928
Opponent	$171,020	$223,231	$394,102
Vote Pct	66%	53%	56%

* Contributions came from more than one PAC affiliated with this sponsor.

David O'B. Martin, R-NY (26)

First elected: 1980
Total receipts: $133,256
Total from PACs: $84,316

1988 Committees & Subcommittees

Armed Services
Military Installations and Facilities (Ranking Republican)
Readiness

PAC Contribution Profile

Business

Auto Dealers	**$1,250**
Auto Dealers & Drivers for Free Trade	$1,000
Others	$250
Commercial & Savings Banks	**$1,600**
None over $750	
Construction	**$2,300**
Associated General Contractors	$1,000
National Assn of Home Builders	$1,000
Others	$300
Defense	**$24,100**
AT&T	$2,500
Boeing Company	$1,500
Continental Telecom	$1,500
McDonnell Douglas*	$1,500
Rockwell International	$1,250
FMC Corp	$1,000
General Electric	$1,000
Grumman	$1,000
Morrison-Knudsen	$1,000
Textron Inc	$1,000
United Technologies	$1,000
Others	$9,850
Electric Utilities	**$1,850**
New York State Electric & Gas Corp	$1,000
Others	$850

Campaign Revenue Sources

Other (16.0%)
Party (1.5%)
PACs (53.2%)
Individuals (29.3%)

Food & Beverage	**$3,250**
McDonald's Corp	$1,000
National Beer Wholesalers Assn	$1,000
Others	$1,250
Health Professionals	**$8,250**
New York Medical Assn	$4,000
American Medical Assn	$2,250
American Dental Assn	$1,500
Others	$500
Mining & Metals Processing	**$2,300**
Alcoa	$1,300
Reynolds Metals	$1,000
Paper Production	**$1,250**
International Paper Company	$1,000
Others	$250
Real Estate	**$4,000**
National Assn of Realtors	$4,000

Other Major Business PACs

Associated Milk Producers	$1,000	Dairy
Corning Glass Works	$1,000	Glass Prod

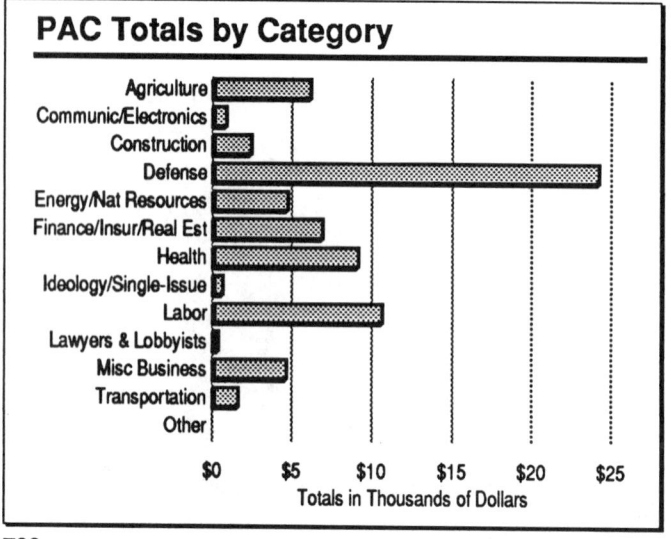

PAC Totals by Category

Agriculture
Communic/Electronics
Construction
Defense
Energy/Nat Resources
Finance/Insur/Real Est
Health
Ideology/Single-Issue
Labor
Lawyers & Lobbyists
Misc Business
Transportation
Other

$0 $5 $10 $15 $20 $25

Totals in Thousands of Dollars

Labor

Bldg Trades/Industrial/Misc Unions **$4,250**
    Carpenters & Joiners Union $1,500
    Others $2,750

Transportation Unions **$6,250**
    Marine Engineers Union* $3,250
    Seafarers International Union $2,000
    Others $1,000

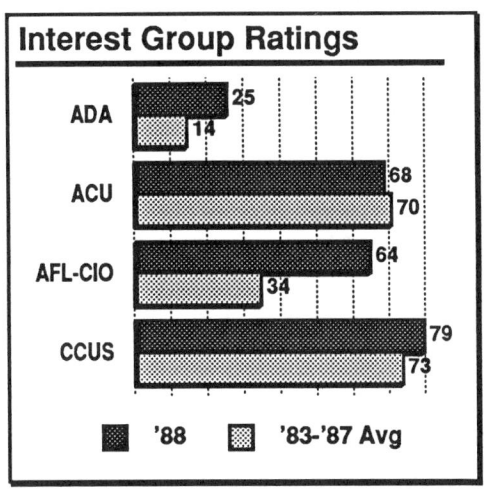

Interest Group Ratings

ADA — '88: 25, '83–'87 Avg: 14
ACU — '88: 68, '83–'87 Avg: 70
AFL-CIO — '88: 64, '83–'87 Avg: 34
CCUS — '88: 79, '83–'87 Avg: 73

■ '88　▨ '83–'87 Avg

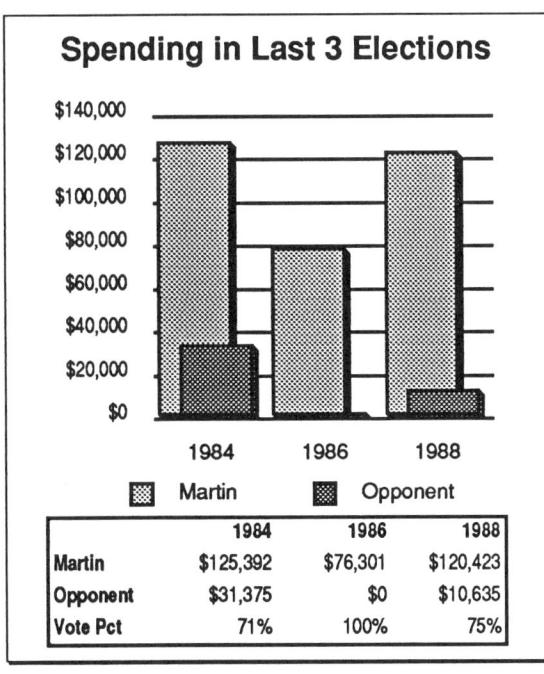

Spending in Last 3 Elections

	1984	1986	1988
Martin	$125,392	$76,301	$120,423
Opponent	$31,375	$0	$10,635
Vote Pct	71%	100%	75%

▨ Martin　▩ Opponent

---

* Contributions came from more than one PAC affiliated
with this sponsor.

Lynn Martin, R-Ill (16)

1988 Committees & Subcommittees

Armed Services
Military Installations and Facilities
Research and Development

District of Columbia
Judiciary and Education (Ranking Republican)
Government Operations and Metropolitan Affairs

First elected: 1980
Total receipts: $456,255
Total from PACs: $186,532

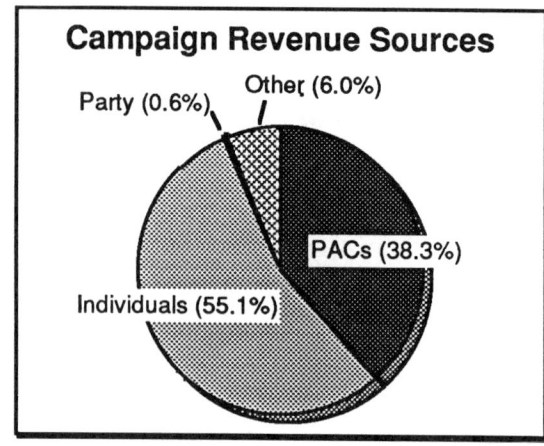

Campaign Revenue Sources

Party (0.6%)
Other (6.0%)
PACs (38.3%)
Individuals (55.1%)

PAC Contribution Profile

Business

Automotive	**$6,600**
National Auto Dealers Assn	$4,800
Auto Dealers & Drivers for Free Trade	$1,500
Others	$300
Commodities & Securities Investment	**$4,500**
Chicago Mercantile Exchange	$1,600
Chicago Board of Options Exchange	$1,000
Chicago Board of Trade	$1,000
Others	$900
Construction	**$6,450**
Associated General Contractors	$1,600
National Assn of Home Builders	$1,000
National Utility Contractors Assn	$1,000
Others	$2,850
Dairy	**$4,100**
Associated Milk Producers	$3,000
Others	$1,100
Defense	**$34,800**
AT&T	$4,000
Rockwell International	$2,500
Textron Inc	$2,000
Continental Telecom	$1,800
United Technologies	$1,500
General Electric	$1,400
Sundstrand Corp	$1,350
Northrop Corp	$1,300

(Continued in next column)

Defense (cont'd)	
Lockheed Corp	$1,200
McDonnell Douglas*	$1,100
FMC Corp	$1,000
Others	$15,650
Financial Institutions	**$12,250**
Credit Union National Assn	$2,800
American Bankers Assn	$2,500
First Chicago Corp	$2,500
Northern Trust Company	$1,700
Barnett Banks of Florida	$1,000
US League of Savings Assn	$1,000
Others	$750
Food & Beverage	**$8,750**
Food Marketing Institute	$2,100
McDonald's Corp	$1,000
Pillsbury Company	$1,000
Others	$4,650
Health Professionals	**$12,300**
American Medical Assn	$5,800
American Academy of Ophthalmology	$3,000
American Dental Assn	$2,500
Cmte for Quality Orthopedic Health Care	$1,000
Industrial Equipment & Materials	**$8,750**
Barber-Colman Company	$5,450
Others	$3,300
Insurance	**$8,275**
National Assn of Life Underwriters	$2,300
Kemper Insurance	$1,800
Others	$4,175
Lawyers	**$2,151**
None over $600	
Oil & Gas	**$5,900**
Nicor Inc	$1,300
American Gas Assn	$1,000
Mobil Oil	$1,000
Others	$2,600
Pharmaceuticals	**$3,700**
None over $900	

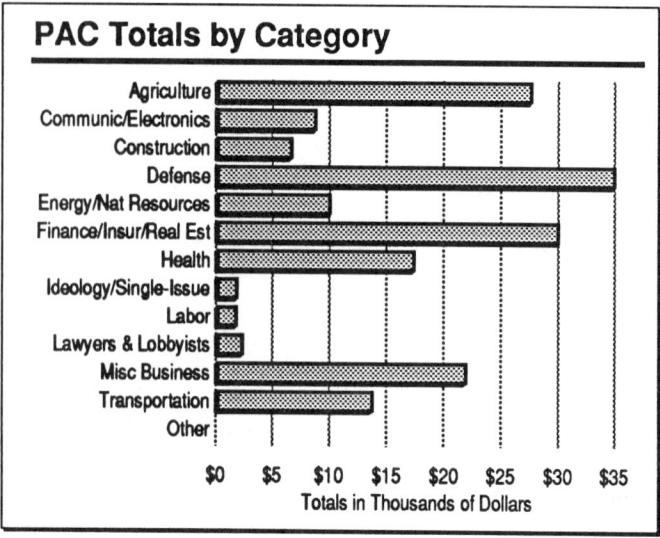

PAC Totals by Category

Agriculture
Communic/Electronics
Construction
Defense
Energy/Nat Resources
Finance/Insur/Real Est
Health
Ideology/Single-Issue
Labor
Lawyers & Lobbyists
Misc Business
Transportation
Other

$0 $5 $10 $15 $20 $25 $30 $35
Totals in Thousands of Dollars

Interest Group Ratings

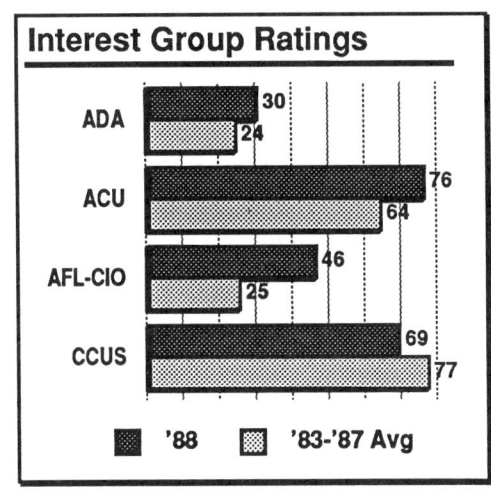

	'88	'83-'87 Avg
ADA	30	24
ACU	76	64
AFL-CIO	46	25
CCUS	69	77

Railroads **$3,100**
  Union Pacific Corp $1,000
  Others $2,100

Real Estate **$6,650**
  National Assn of Realtors $6,100
  Others $550

Retail Sales **$2,400**
  Montgomery Ward $1,000
  Others $1,400

Telecommunications **$5,450**
  Illinois Bell Telephone $3,750
  BellSouth Corp $1,400
  Others $300

Tobacco **$3,800**
  Philip Morris $2,000
  Others $1,800

Trucking/Delivery **$2,625**
  United Parcel Service $2,125
  Others $500

Other Major Business PACs

Household International	$1,400	Credit/Loans
Waste Management Inc	$1,400	Waste Mgmt
American Veterinary Medical Assn	$1,000	Veterinary
Calcot Ltd	$1,000	Cotton
Deere & Company	$1,000	Farm Equip
Ecolab Inc	$1,000	BusinessSvcs
Maytag Company	$1,000	Appliances
R R Donnelley & Sons	$1,000	Publishing
Stone Container Corp	$1,000	Paper Packg

Major Labor PACs

Teamsters Union	$1,000	Teamsters

Independent expenditures supporting Martin

American Medical Assn $1,000

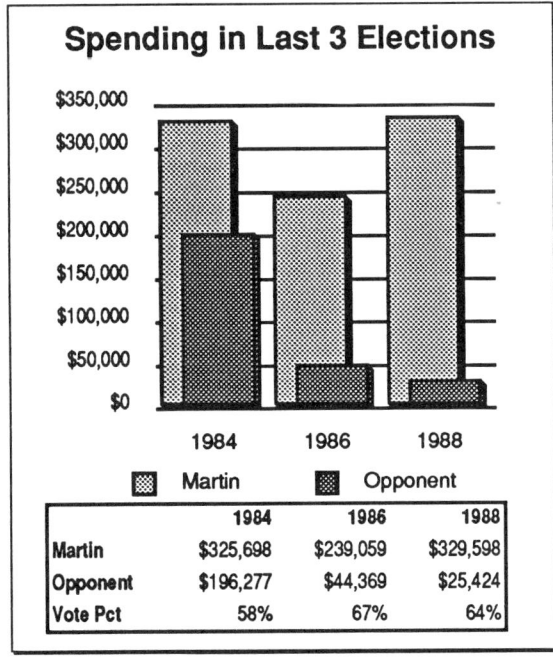

Spending in Last 3 Elections

	1984	1986	1988
Martin	$325,698	$239,059	$329,598
Opponent	$196,277	$44,369	$25,424
Vote Pct	58%	67%	64%

Martin ▨ Opponent ▨

* Contributions came from more than one PAC affiliated
  with this sponsor.

Matthew G. Martinez, D-Calif (30)

First elected: 1982
Total receipts: $437,775
Total from PACs: $218,900

1988 Committees & Subcommittees

Education and Labor
Employment Opportunities (Chairman)
Elementary, Secondary and Vocational Education
Select Education

Government Operations
Commerce, Consumer and Monetary Affairs
Environment, Energy and Natural Resources

Small Business
Antitrust, Impact of Deregulation and Privatization
Energy and Agriculture

Select Children, Youth and Families

PAC Contribution Profile

Business

Health Professionals	**$9,250**
Pathology Practice Assn	$5,000
American Medical Assn	$2,500
American Dental Assn	$1,000
Others	$750
Lawyers	**$10,250**
Assn of Trial Lawyers of America	$10,000
Others	$250
Real Estate	**$7,750**
National Assn of Realtors	$7,250
Others	$500
Residential Construction	**$2,000**
National Assn of Home Builders	$2,000
Telecommunications	**$2,050**
Pacific Telesis Group	$1,250
Others	$800

Other Major Business PACs

United Parcel Service	$1,150	Delivery
Southern California Edison	$1,100	ElectricUtil
National Assn of Trade/Tech Schools	$1,000	Voc Tech

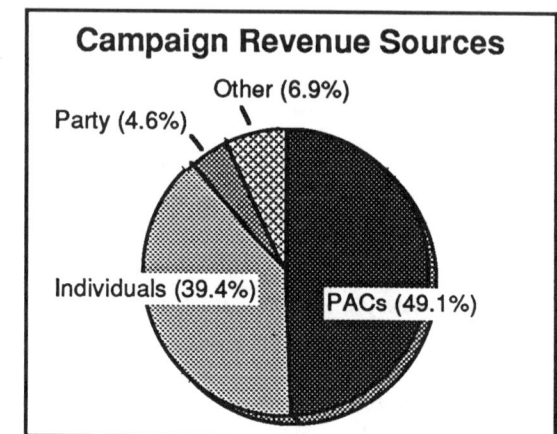

Campaign Revenue Sources

- Other (6.9%)
- Party (4.6%)
- Individuals (39.4%)
- PACs (49.1%)

PAC Totals by Category

- Agriculture
- Communic/Electronics
- Construction
- Defense
- Energy/Nat Resources
- Finance/Insur/Real Est
- Health
- Ideology/Single-Issue
- Labor
- Lawyers & Lobbyists
- Misc Business
- Transportation
- Other

$0 $20 $40 $60 $80 $100 $120 $140

Totals in Thousands of Dollars

Labor

Bldg Trades/Industrial/Misc Unions $59,950

Machinists/Aerospace Workers Union	$10,000
United Auto Workers	$10,000
Carpenters & Joiners Union*	$8,000
Laborers' Western Political League	$7,000
AFL-CIO*	$6,000
Food & Commercial Workers Union	$5,500
Intl Brotherhood of Electrical Workers	$3,500
United Steelworkers	$2,500
Operating Engineers Union*	$2,000
Service Employees International Union	$2,000
Communications Workers of America	$1,750
Others	$1,700

Government & Postal Workers $31,450

American Fedn of State/County/Munic Employees	$10,000
National Assn of Retired Federal Employees	$10,000
National Assn of Letter Carriers	$6,900
American Postal Workers Union	$2,500
International Assn of Firefighters	$1,300
Others	$750

Teachers Unions $15,000

American Federation of Teachers	$10,000
National Education Assn	$5,000

Transportation Unions $21,350

Teamsters Union	$10,000
Seafarers International Union	$3,500
Air Line Pilots Assn	$2,500
Marine Engineers District 2 Maritime Officers	$2,500
Transportation Communication Union	$1,950
Others	$900

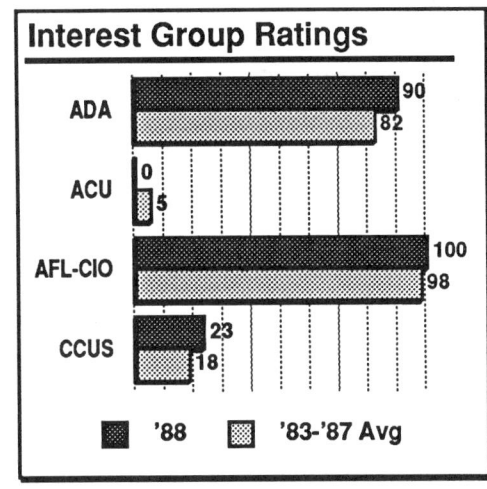

Interest Group Ratings

	'88	'83-'87 Avg
ADA	90	82
ACU	0	5
AFL-CIO	100	98
CCUS	23	18

Ideological/Single-Issue

Democratic Leadership PACs $19,000

24th Cong Dist of California PAC (Henry Waxman)	$5,000
Valley Education Fund (Tony Coelho)	$5,000
Majority Congress Committee (Jim Wright)	$4,000
House Leadership Fund (Tom Foley)	$2,000
America's Leaders' Fund (Dan Rostenkowski)	$1,000
Cmte for the 100th Congress (Charles Rangel)	$1,000
Economic Security PAC (Mary Rose Oakar)	$1,000

Gay/Lesbian Rights $3,500

Human Rights Campaign Fund	$2,500
Municipal Elections Cmte of Los Angeles	$1,000

Non-Congressional Candidate PACs $3,500

Rick Tuttle Campaign Cmte	$2,000
Citizens for Alatorre	$1,000
Others	$500

Pro-Israel $10,250

National PAC	$5,000
Women's Pro-Israel National PAC	$3,000
Joint Action Cmte for Political Affairs	$1,250
Others	$1,000

Other Major Ideological/Single-Issue PACs

National Cmte to Preserve Social Security	$2,750	Soc Secur
National Abortion Rights Action League	$1,500	Pro-Choice
Handgun Control Inc	$1,000	Anti-Guns
Hellenic American Council	$1,000	Ethnic

Independent expenditures supporting Martinez

National Cmte to Preserve Social Security	$1,575

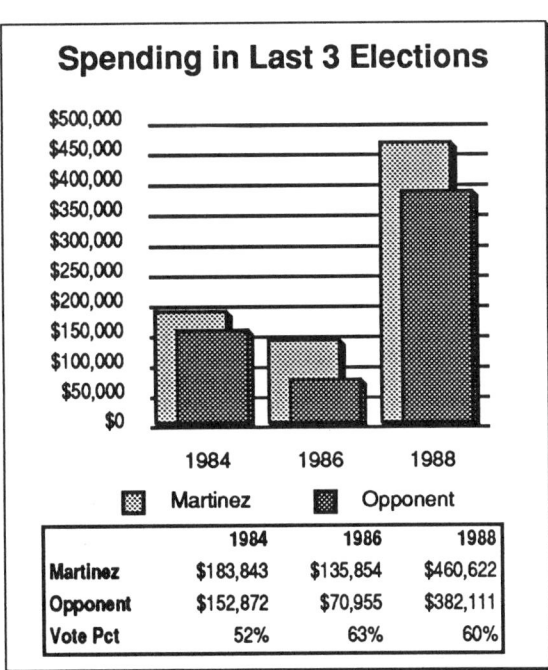

Spending in Last 3 Elections

	1984	1986	1988
Martinez	$183,843	$135,854	$460,622
Opponent	$152,872	$70,955	$382,111
Vote Pct	52%	63%	60%

Legend: Martinez / Opponent

---

* Contributions came from more than one PAC affiliated
with this sponsor.

Robert T. Matsui, D-Calif (3)

First elected: 1978
Total receipts: $917,025
Total from PACs: $473,863

1988 Committees & Subcommittees

Ways and Means
Public Assistance and Unemployment Compensation
Trade

PAC Contribution Profile

Business

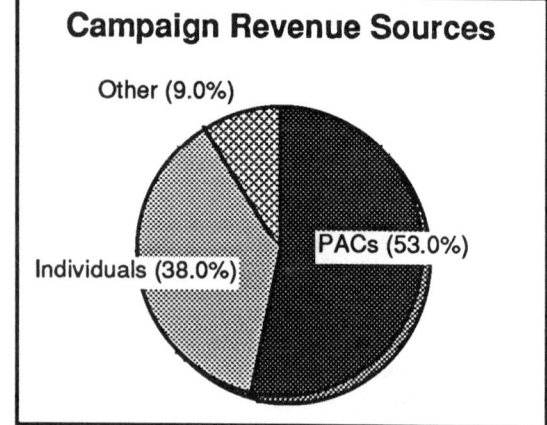

Campaign Revenue Sources

Other (9.0%)
PACs (53.0%)
Individuals (38.0%)

Commercial Banks **$22,500**
American Bankers Assn	$4,500
Wells Fargo	$4,500
Citicorp	$3,500
J P Morgan & Company	$3,000
Security Pacific Corp	$2,500
BankAmerica	$1,500
Others	$3,000

Electric Utilities **$19,725**
Southern California Edison	$3,500
Pacific Gas & Electric	$2,100
Southern Company*	$1,700
San Diego Gas & Electric	$1,125
Others	$11,300

Food & Beverage **$22,632**
National Beer Wholesalers Assn	$4,000
Wine & Spirits Wholesalers of America	$4,000
Food Marketing Institute	$2,250
National Restaurant Assn	$2,000
Joseph E Seagram & Sons	$1,500
Wine Institute	$1,132
Others	$7,750

Health Professionals **$30,100**
American Medical Assn	$11,500
American Dental Assn	$3,500
Co-op of American Physicians	$3,500
American Optometric Assn	$2,000
Cmte for Quality Orthopedic Health Care	$2,000
Others	$7,600

Hospitals & Nursing Homes **$11,750**
American Hospital Assn	$4,500
American Health Care Assn	$1,500
Others	$5,750

Insurance **$31,950**
Home Life Insurance	$3,500
Equitable Financial Services	$2,500
Metropolitan Life Insurance	$2,000
Prudential Insurance	$2,000
Connecticut Mutual Life Insurance	$1,750
Acacia Mutual Life Insurance	$1,500
Health Insurance Assn of America	$1,500
Massachusetts Mutual Life Insurance	$1,500
North Western Mutual Life	$1,500
Others	$14,200

Lawyers & Lobbyists **$18,371**
Assn of Trial Lawyers of America	$5,000
Dow, Lohnes & Albertson	$3,000
Others	$10,371

Oil & Gas **$22,384**
Pacific Enterprises	$3,500
Atlantic Richfield	$2,000
Society of Independent Gasoline Marketers	$2,000
Wickland Oil	$2,000
Petroleum Marketers Assn	$1,500
Columbia Gas Company*	$1,250
Union Oil	$1,084
Others	$9,050

Real Estate **$22,000**
National Assn of Realtors	$10,000
Century 21 Real Estate	$5,000
Real Estate Investment Trust	$2,000
Others	$5,000

Savings Banks **$13,250**
Home Savings of America	$4,500
US League of Savings Assn	$2,500
Great Western Financial Corp	$1,500
Others	$4,750

Securities & Commodities Investment **$19,500**
First Boston Corp	$2,000
Kidder, Peabody	$2,000
Securities Industry Assn	$2,000
Chicago Board of Trade	$1,500
Drexel Burnham Lambert	$1,500
E F Hutton Group	$1,500
Others	$9,000

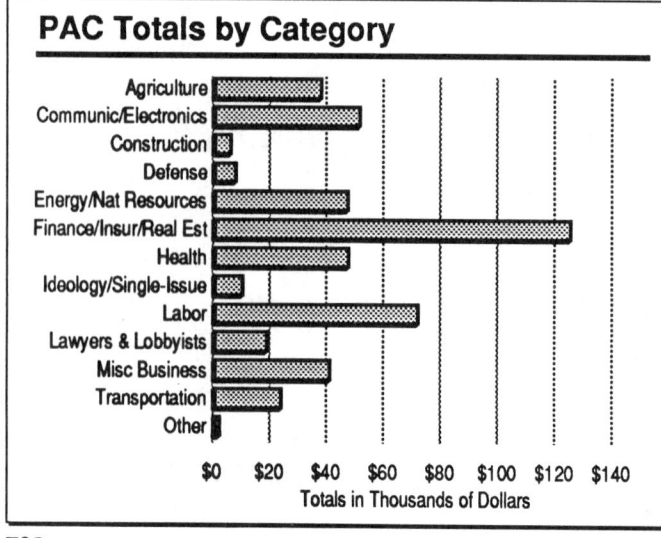

PAC Totals by Category

Category	
Agriculture	
Communic/Electronics	
Construction	
Defense	
Energy/Nat Resources	
Finance/Insur/Real Est	
Health	
Ideology/Single-Issue	
Labor	
Lawyers & Lobbyists	
Misc Business	
Transportation	
Other	

$0 $20 $40 $60 $80 $100 $120 $140
Totals in Thousands of Dollars

Telecommunications *$38,300*

Pacific Telesis Group	$6,500
Continental Telecom	$4,500
AT&T	$4,000
US Telephone Assn	$3,000
BellSouth Corp	$2,500
Bell Atlantic	$2,000
U S West Inc	$2,000
United Telecommunications	$2,000
GTE Corp	$1,500
Motorola Inc	$1,500
NYNEX Corp	$1,500
Southwestern Bell	$1,500
Others	$5,800

Other Major Business PACs

American Institute of CPA's	$5,000	Accountants
California Almond Growers Exchange	$5,000	Fruit/Veg
National Venture Capital Assn	$5,000	Venture Cap
Philip Morris	$4,041	Tobacco
Personal Injury Compensation PAC	$4,000	FinancSvcs
Triangle Industries	$4,000	Cans
J C Penney Company	$3,500	Dept Store
National Assn of Home Builders	$3,000	Resid Constr
Auto Dealers & Drivers for Free Trade	$2,500	JapanAutoSal
American Assn of Equipment Lessors	$2,000	Rentals
Boeing Company	$2,000	Aircraft
Aircraft Owners & Pilots Assn	$1,500	GenlAviation
American President Lines	$1,500	SeaTransport
Assn of Data Proc Service Organizations	$1,500	Data Process
Associated Milk Producers	$1,500	Dairy
Farmers' Rice Cooperative	$1,500	Crops
General Electric	$1,500	Electronics
MCA Inc	$1,500	Movies
National Assn of Wholesale Distributors	$1,500	Wholesale
United Parcel Service	$1,500	Delivery
Sheet Metal/AirCon Contractors	$1,250	Plumbing/AC

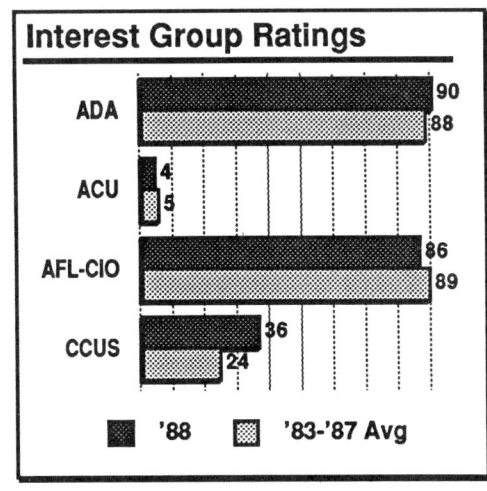

Interest Group Ratings

	'88	'83-'87 Avg
ADA	90	88
ACU	4	5
AFL-CIO	86	89
CCUS	36	24

Labor

Bldg Trades/Industrial/Misc Unions *$32,500*

United Auto Workers	$6,000
Laborers' Union*	$5,000
National Education Assn	$4,500
American Federation of Teachers	$2,500
Carpenters & Joiners Union	$2,500
Operating Engineers Union*	$2,250
Food & Commercial Workers Union	$2,000
Machinists/Aerospace Workers Union	$2,000
Plumbers/Pipefitters Union*	$1,500
Others	$4,250

Government & Postal Workers *$15,700*

National Assn of Retired Federal Employees	$6,000
American Fedn of State/County/Munic Employees	$2,700
International Assn of Firefighters	$2,000
National Assn of Letter Carriers	$2,000
Others	$3,000

Transportation Unions *$23,150*

Teamsters Union	$7,500
United Transportation Union	$4,000
Air Line Pilots Assn	$3,500
Marine Engineers District 2 Maritime Officers	$2,000
Seafarers International Union	$2,000
Brotherhood of Locomotive Engineers	$1,500
Transportation Communication Union	$1,150
Others	$1,500

Major Ideological/Single-Issue PACs

Valley Education Fund (Tony Coelho)	$2,000	Dem Leaders
National Cmte to Preserve Social Security	$2,000	Soc Secur

Independent expenditures supporting Matsui

National Cmte to Preserve Social Security	$2,184

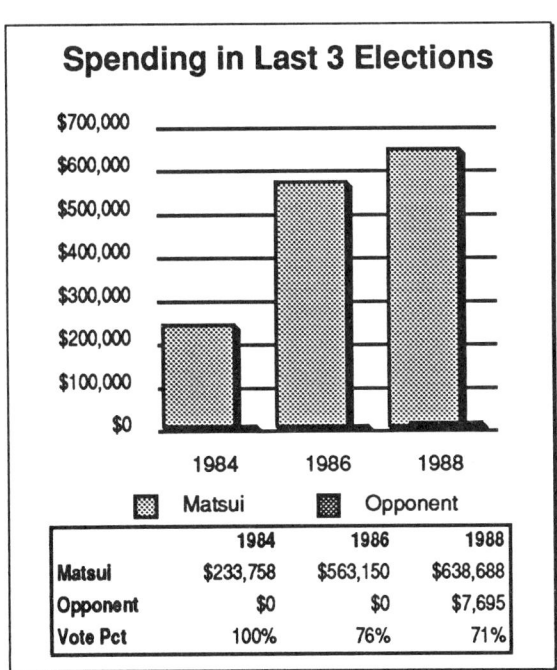

Spending in Last 3 Elections

	1984	1986	1988
Matsui	$233,758	$563,150	$638,688
Opponent	$0	$0	$7,695
Vote Pct	100%	76%	71%

Legend: Matsui, Opponent

---

* Contributions came from more than one PAC affiliated with this sponsor.

Nicholas Mavroules, D-Mass (6)

First elected: 1978
Total receipts: $349,184
Total from PACs: $107,360

1988 Committees & Subcommittees

Armed Services
Readiness (Chairman)
Procurement and Military Nuclear Systems

Small Business
Procurement, Innovation and Minority Enterprise Development

Select Intelligence
Legislation

PAC Contribution Profile

Business

Commercial Banks	**$4,450**
Bank of Boston	$2,200
American Bankers Assn	$1,000
Barnett Banks of Florida	$1,000
Others	$250
Construction	**$3,200**
American Consulting Engineers Council	$1,000
National Assn of Home Builders	$1,000
Stone & Webster	$1,000
Others	$200
Defense	**$10,200**
AT&T	$3,000
Mantech International	$1,500
Chrysler Corp	$1,000
Computer Sciences Corp	$1,000
FMC Corp	$1,000
Others	$2,700
Electric Utilities	**$2,550**
Boston Edison	$1,000
Others	$1,550
Food & Beverage	**$5,300**
Coca-Cola Company	$1,300
Food Marketing Institute	$1,000
McDonald's Corp	$1,000
Pepsi-Cola Bottlers Assn	$1,000
Others	$1,000

Campaign Revenue Sources

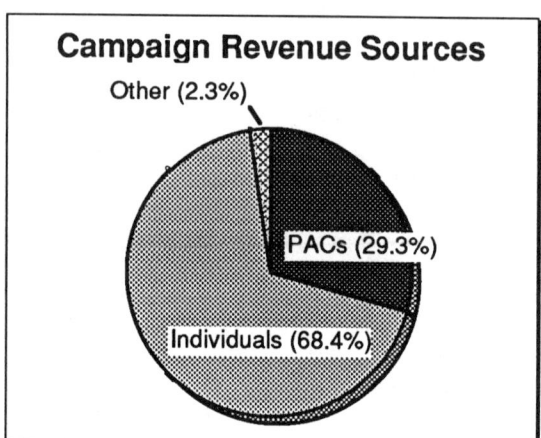

Other (2.3%)
PACs (29.3%)
Individuals (68.4%)

Health Professionals	**$3,350**
American Medical Assn	$2,350
American Dental Assn	$1,000
Insurance	**$2,000**
New England Mutual Life	$1,000
Others	$1,000
Oil & Gas	**$2,750**
Bay State Gas Company	$1,000
Chevron Corp	$1,000
Others	$750
Real Estate	**$3,000**
National Assn of Realtors	$3,000
Telecommunications	**$3,000**
New England Tel & Tel	$3,000

Other Major Business PACs

Coopers & Lybrand	$1,500	Accountants
National Assn of Sm Bus Invest Companies ...	$1,000	Sml Business
Ocean Spray Cranberries Inc	$1,000	Fruit/Veg
Tobacco Institute	$1,000	Tobacco
Xerox Corp	$1,000	Off Machines

PAC Totals by Category

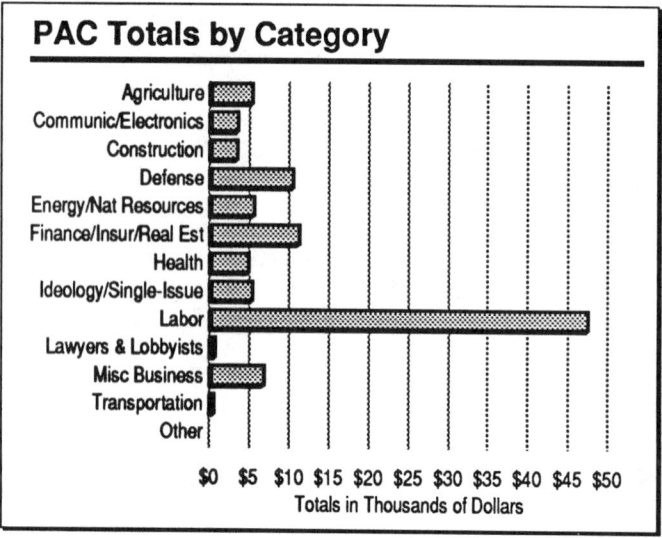

Totals in Thousands of Dollars

Labor

Bldg Trades/Industrial/Misc Unions $21,700

Carpenters & Joiners Union	$2,000
Electronic Machine Furniture Workers	$2,000
Laborers' Political League	$2,000
Operating Engineers Union	$2,000
AFL-CIO*	$1,500
Communications Workers of America	$1,500
Ironworkers Union	$1,500
Food & Commercial Workers Union	$1,000
Intl Brotherhood of Electrical Workers	$1,000
Ladies Garment Workers Union	$1,000
Machinists/Aerospace Workers Union	$1,000
National Education Assn	$1,000
United Auto Workers	$1,000
Others	$3,200

Government & Postal Workers $7,350

National Assn of Letter Carriers	$3,600
American Fedn of State/County/Munic Employees	$1,250
American Postal Workers Union	$1,000
Others	$1,500

Transportation Unions $18,223

Teamsters Union	$6,000
Marine Engineers Union	$3,000
Masters, Mates & Pilots Union	$2,173
Seafarers International Union	$2,000
Air Line Pilots Assn	$1,000
International Longshoremen Assn	$1,000
United Transportation Union	$1,000
Others	$2,050

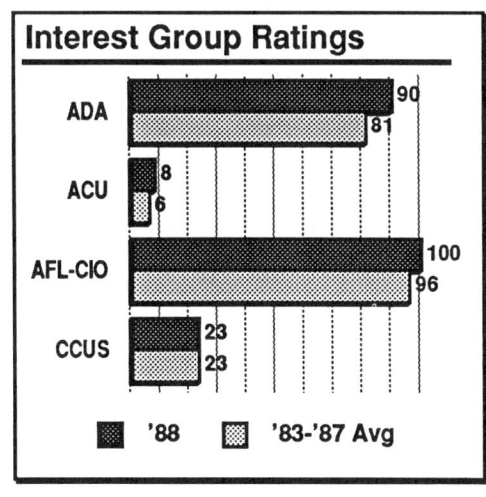

Interest Group Ratings

	'88	'83-'87 Avg
ADA	90	81
ACU	8	6
AFL-CIO	100	96
CCUS	23	23

Ideological/Single-Issue

Democratic Leadership PACs...$2,000

Valley Education Fund (Tony Coelho)	$2,000

Other Major Ideological/Single-Issue PACs

Dynamis ....$1,000   Ethnic

Independent expenditures supporting Mavroules

National Cmte to Preserve Social Security $1,932

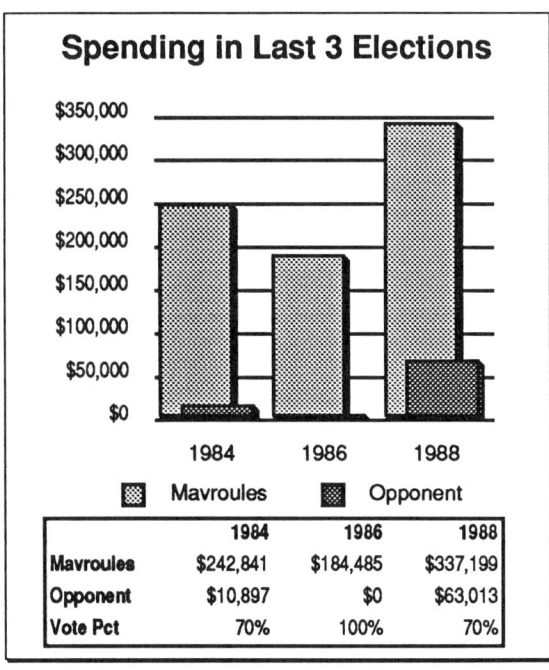

Spending in Last 3 Elections

	1984	1986	1988
Mavroules	$242,841	$184,485	$337,199
Opponent	$10,897	$0	$63,013
Vote Pct	70%	100%	70%

(legend: Mavroules, Opponent)

---

* Contributions came from more than one PAC affiliated
with this sponsor.

Romano L. Mazzoli, D-Ky (3)

First elected: 1970
Total receipts: $378,438
Total from PACs: $196,650

1988 Committees & Subcommittees

District of Columbia
Judiciary and Education

Judiciary
Immigration, Refugees and International Law (Chairman)
Crime
Monopolies and Commercial Law

Small Business
Regulation and Business Opportunities
SBA and the General Economy

PAC Contribution Profile

Business

Automotive **$9,800**
    Auto Dealers & Drivers for Free Trade $6,300
    National Auto Dealers Assn $2,600
    Others $900

Construction **$7,900**
    National Assn of Home Builders $5,000
    Others $2,900

Financial Institutions **$4,200**
    Liberty National Bancorp $1,100
    Citicorp $1,000
    Others $2,100

Food & Beverage **$17,890**
    National Restaurant Assn $2,000
    National Beer Wholesalers Assn $2,000
    Winn-Dixie Stores $2,000
    McDonald's Corp $1,500
    Pepsico Inc $1,500
    Brown-Forman Distillers $1,200
    Coca-Cola Company $1,100
    Hardee's Food Systems $1,000
    Jerrico Inc $1,000
    Others $4,590

Health Professionals **$3,800**
    American Medical Assn $2,300
    American Academy of Ophthalmology $1,000
    Others $500

Campaign Revenue Sources

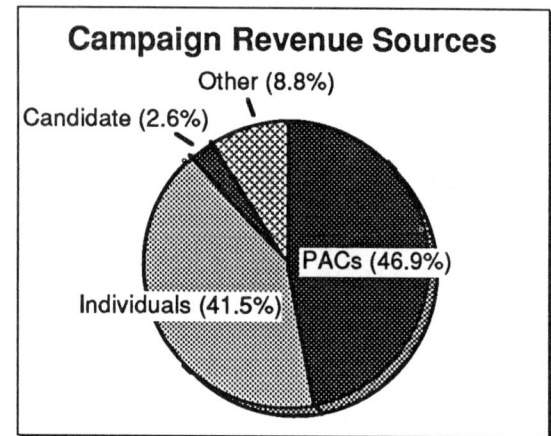

Other (8.8%)
Candidate (2.6%)
PACs (46.9%)
Individuals (41.5%)

Insurance **$14,650**
    National Assn of Life Underwriters $5,000
    National Assn of Independent Insurers $2,000
    Capital Holding Corp $1,300
    American Council of Life Insurance $1,200
    American Insurance Assn $1,000
    Others $4,150

Lawyers & Lobbyists **$4,650**
    Goldberg & Simpson $1,000
    Others $3,650

Medical Equipment **$3,000**
    American Orthotic/Prosthetic Assn $3,000

Package Delivery **$7,000**
    United Parcel Service $7,000

Paper Production **$2,000**
    Westvaco Corp $2,000

Real Estate **$8,850**
    National Assn of Realtors $8,000
    Others $850

Retail Sales **$2,050**
    International Council of Shopping Centers $1,000
    Others $1,050

Telecommunications **$7,900**
    South Central Bell Telephone $4,000
    AT&T $2,100
    Others $1,800

Tobacco **$2,600**
    Batus Inc* $1,800
    Others $800

PAC Totals by Category

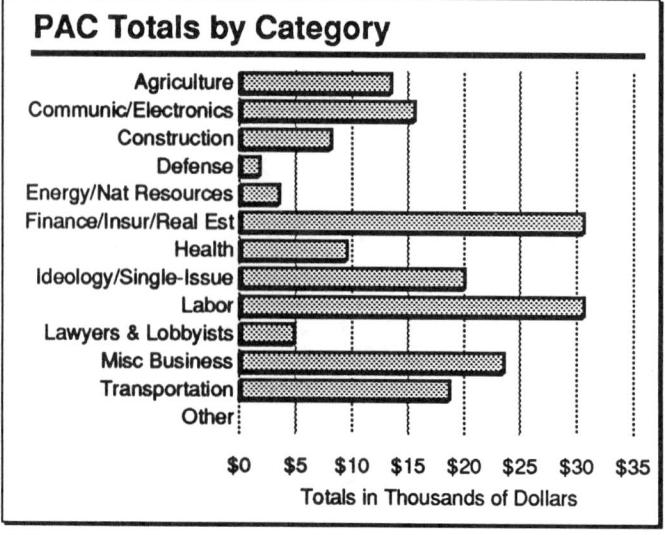

Category	
Agriculture	
Communic/Electronics	
Construction	
Defense	
Energy/Nat Resources	
Finance/Insur/Real Est	
Health	
Ideology/Single-Issue	
Labor	
Lawyers & Lobbyists	
Misc Business	
Transportation	
Other	

$0 $5 $10 $15 $20 $25 $30 $35

Totals in Thousands of Dollars

TV/Entertainment *$6,600*

    Assn of Independent TV Stations $1,100
    MCA Inc $1,000
    National Cable Television Assn $1,000
    Others $3,500

Other Major Business PACs

United Technologies	$1,300	Air Defense
General Electric	$1,215	Electronics
Handgun Control Inc	$1,100	Anti-Guns
American Institute of CPA's	$1,000	Accountants
Ashland Oil	$1,000	Refine/Mktg
Figgie International	$1,000	Security Svc
Kentucky Utilities Company	$1,000	ElectricUtil
National Fedn of Independent Business	$1,000	Sml Business
National Tooling & Machining Assn	$1,000	Indust Equip

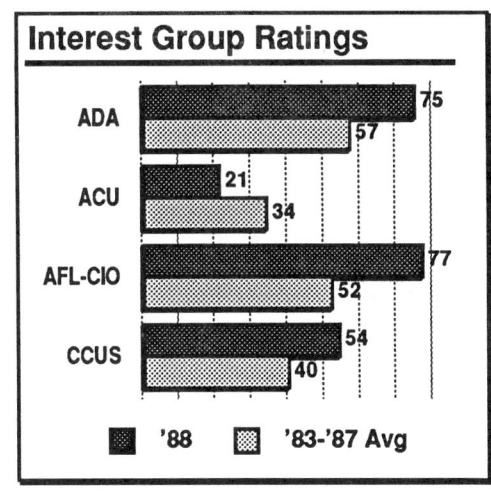

Interest Group Ratings

Legend: '88   '83-'87 Avg

	'88	'83-'87 Avg
ADA	75	57
ACU	21	34
AFL-CIO	77	52
CCUS	54	40

Labor

Bldg Trades/Industrial/Misc Unions *$2,100*

    Carpenters & Joiners Union $1,500
    Others $600

Government & Postal Workers *$8,850*

    National Assn of Letter Carriers $3,500
    National Assn of Retired Federal Employees $3,000
    American Postal Workers Union $1,000
    Others $1,350

Teachers Unions *$7,500*

    National Education Assn $7,500

Transportation Unions *$11,950*

    Teamsters Union $5,000
    United Transportation Union $2,300
    International Longshoremen Assn $1,500
    Marine Engineers District 2 Maritime Officers $1,000
    Others $2,150

Ideological/Single-Issue

Democratic Leadership PACs *$13,000*

    America's Leaders' Fund (Dan Rostenkowski) $10,000
    Conservative Democratic PAC (Charles Stenholm) $1,000
    Democratic Congressional Fund (Joe Moakley) $1,000
    Valley Education Fund (Tony Coelho) $1,000

Pro-Life *$5,150*

    National Right to Life PAC $5,000
    Others $150

Independent expenditures supporting Mazzoli

National Right to Life PAC $6,585
National Cmte to Preserve Social Security $2,473

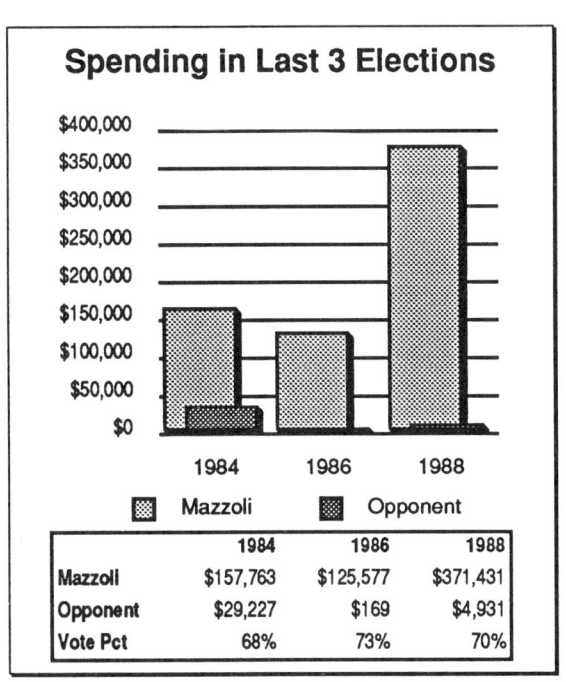

Spending in Last 3 Elections

Legend: Mazzoli   Opponent

	1984	1986	1988
Mazzoli	$157,763	$125,577	$371,431
Opponent	$29,227	$169	$4,931
Vote Pct	68%	73%	70%

---

* Contributions came from more than one PAC affiliated
  with this sponsor.

711

Al McCandless, R-Calif (37)

First elected: 1982
Total receipts: $129,505
Total from PACs: $75,500

1988 Committees & Subcommittees

Banking, Finance and Urban Affairs
Economic Stabilization
Financial Institutions Supervision, Regulation and Insurance
General Oversight and Investigations
International Development Institutions and Finance

Government Operations
Government Information, Justice and Agriculture (Ranking Republican)

PAC Contribution Profile

Business

Accountants	**$5,000**
American Institute of CPA's	$5,000
Automotive	**$2,400**
Auto Dealers & Drivers for Free Trade	$1,500
Others	$900
Commercial Banks	**$14,050**
American Bankers Assn	$3,750
Wells Fargo	$2,500
BankAmerica	$1,750
California Bankers Assn	$1,250
Chase Manhattan	$1,000
Others	$3,800
Construction	**$8,600**
National Assn of Home Builders	$2,500
Associated General Contractors	$1,600
Fleetwood Enterprises	$1,000
Manville Corp	$1,000
National Electrical Contractors Assn	$1,000
Others	$1,500
Health Professionals	**$2,300**
American Medical Assn	$2,300
Insurance	**$6,550**
TransAmerica*	$4,000
Others	$2,550
Real Estate	**$5,800**
National Assn of Realtors	$5,000
Others	$800

Campaign Revenue Sources

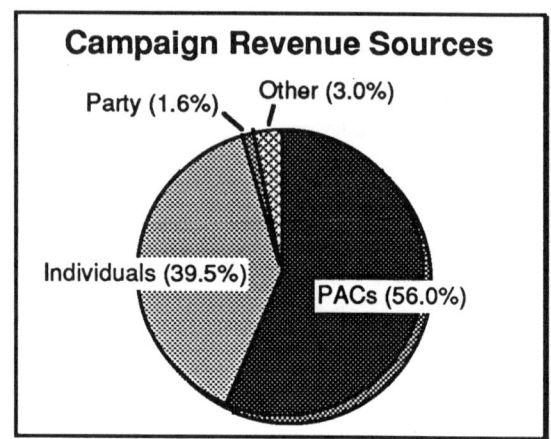

Party (1.6%)
Other (3.0%)
Individuals (39.5%)
PACs (56.0%)

Retail Sales	**$2,200**
None over $800	
Savings Banks & Credit Unions	**$5,300**
Coast Federal Savings & Loan	$1,250
California League of Savings Institutions	$1,000
Credit Union National Assn	$1,000
Glendale Federal Savings & Loan	$1,000
Others	$1,050
Telecommunications	**$2,900**
Continental Telecom	$1,500
Others	$1,400

Other Major Business PACs

American Veterinary Medical Assn	$1,000	Veterinary
Sunkist Growers	$1,000	Fruit/Veg

Major Ideological/Single-Issue PACs

National Rifle Assn	$1,300	Pro-Guns

PAC Totals by Category

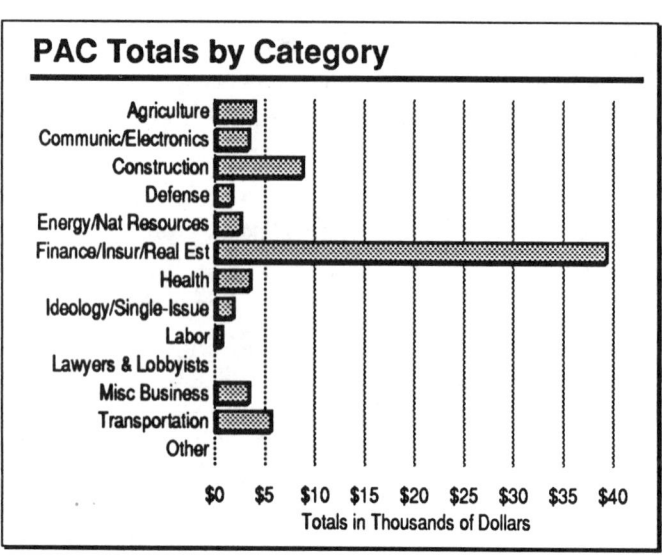

Agriculture
Communic/Electronics
Construction
Defense
Energy/Nat Resources
Finance/Insur/Real Est
Health
Ideology/Single-Issue
Labor
Lawyers & Lobbyists
Misc Business
Transportation
Other

$0 $5 $10 $15 $20 $25 $30 $35 $40
Totals in Thousands of Dollars

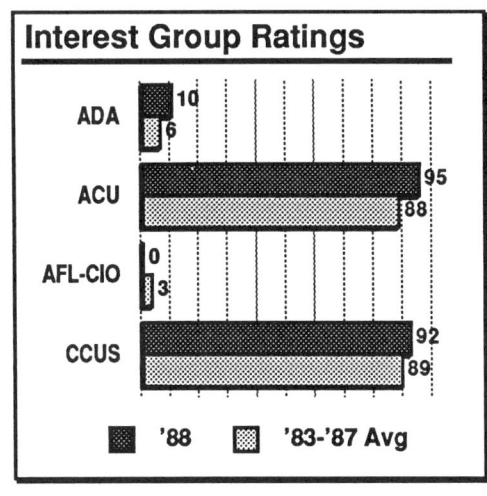

Interest Group Ratings

	'88	'83-'87 Avg
ADA	10	6
ACU	95	88
AFL-CIO	0	3
CCUS	92	89

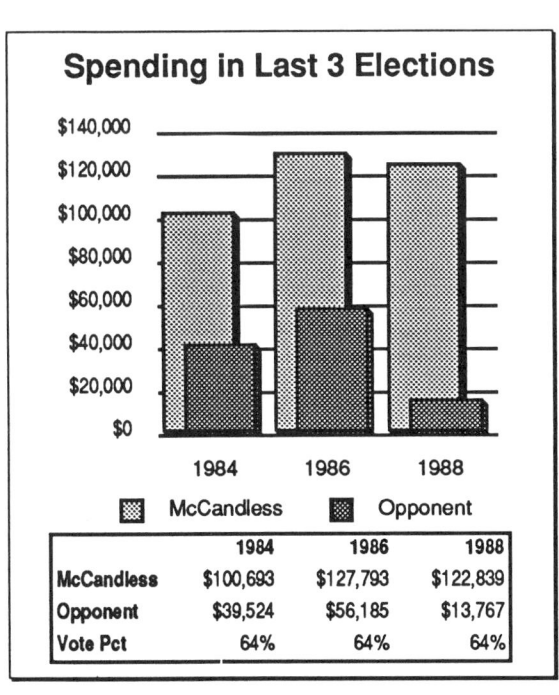

Spending in Last 3 Elections

	1984	1986	1988
McCandless	$100,693	$127,793	$122,839
Opponent	$39,524	$56,185	$13,767
Vote Pct	64%	64%	64%

Frank McCloskey, D-Ind (8)

1988 Committees & Subcommittees

Armed Services
Investigations
Research and Development

Post Office and Civil Service
Postal Personnel and Modernization (Chairman)
Human Resources

First elected: 1982
Total receipts: $549,096
Total from PACs: $342,058

PAC Contribution Profile

Business

Construction	**$8,300**
National Assn of Home Builders	$8,000
Others	$300
Defense	**$18,750**
AT&T	$3,000
United Technologies	$2,350
Continental Telecom	$2,000
Colt Industries	$1,100
General Motors	$1,100
McDonnell Douglas	$1,000
Others	$8,200
Electric Utilities	**$3,150**
ACRE (Action Committee for Rural Electrification)	$1,000
Others	$2,150
Farm Organizations	**$7,050**
Indiana Farm Bureau	$6,500
Others	$550
Financial Institutions	**$5,000**
Credit Union National Assn	$1,750
American Bankers Assn	$1,000
Others	$2,250
Food & Beverage	**$2,550**
None over $750	

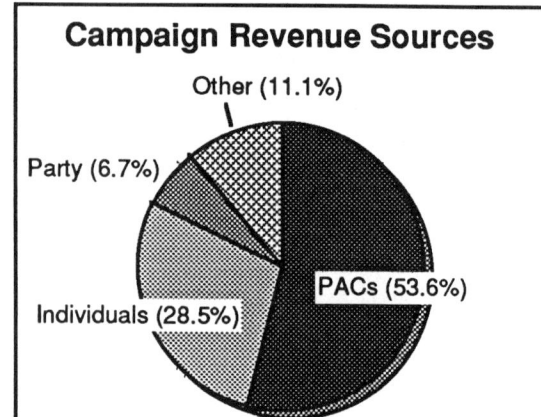

Campaign Revenue Sources

Other (11.1%)
Party (6.7%)
Individuals (28.5%)
PACs (53.6%)

Health Professionals	**$5,800**
American Medical Assn	$1,800
American Dental Assn	$1,500
American Nurses Assn	$1,000
Others	$1,500
Insurance	**$4,100**
National Assn of Life Underwriters	$3,000
Others	$1,100
Lawyers & Lobbyists	**$6,550**
Assn of Trial Lawyers of America	$6,000
Others	$550
Mining & Metal Processing	**$3,650**
Alcoa	$1,500
Peabody Coal	$1,400
Others	$750
Package Delivery	**$6,500**
United Parcel Service	$6,500
Real Estate	**$7,000**
National Assn of Realtors	$7,000
Sugar Growers	**$3,550**
American Crystal Sugar Corp	$1,600
Others	$1,950
Telecommunications	**$2,350**
Indiana Bell Telephone	$1,850
Others	$500

Other Major Business PACs

Dairymen Inc	$1,300	Dairy

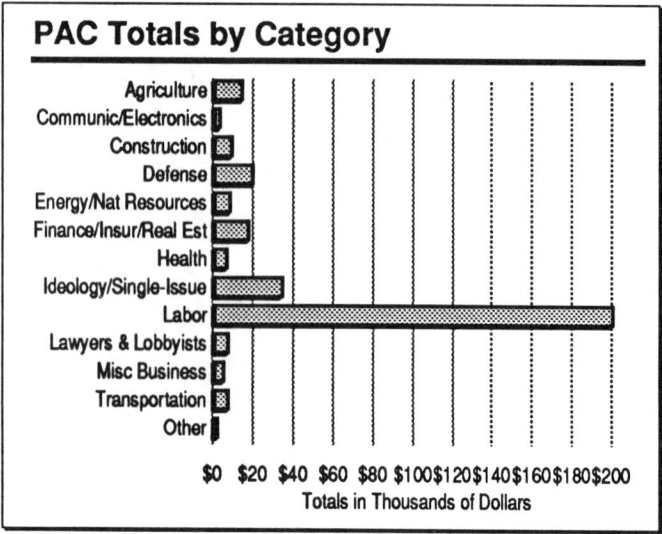

PAC Totals by Category

Category	
Agriculture	
Communic/Electronics	
Construction	
Defense	
Energy/Nat Resources	
Finance/Insur/Real Est	
Health	
Ideology/Single-Issue	
Labor	
Lawyers & Lobbyists	
Misc Business	
Transportation	
Other	

$0 $20 $40 $60 $80 $100 $120 $140 $160 $180 $200
Totals in Thousands of Dollars

Labor

Bldg Trades/Industrial/Misc Unions $100,149

Food & Commercial Workers Union	$10,000
Intl Brotherhood of Electrical Workers	$10,000
Machinists/Aerospace Workers Union	$10,000
Sheet Metal Workers Union	$10,000
United Auto Workers	$10,000
United Mine Workers	$10,000
AFL-CIO*	$9,999
Carpenters & Joiners Union	$6,800
United Steelworkers	$4,000
Laborers' Political League	$2,250
Bakery, Confectionary & Tobacco Workers	$2,000
Ironworkers Union	$2,000
Operating Engineers Union	$2,000
Rubber Cork Linoleum Plastic Workers	$2,000
Boilermakers Union	$1,500
Plumbers/Pipefitters Union	$1,500
Ladies Garment Workers Union	$1,400
Amalgamated Clothing & Textile Workers	$1,050
Glass/Molders/Pottery/Plastics Workers	$1,000
Oil, Chemical & Atomic Workers Union	$1,000
Others	$1,650

Government & Postal Workers $57,350

American Postal Workers Union	$10,000
National Assn of Letter Carriers	$10,000
National Assn of Retired Federal Employees	$10,000
American Fedn of State/County/Munic Employees	$9,900
National Rural Letter Carriers Assn	$5,500
National Star Route Mail Contractors	$2,600
National League of Postmasters	$2,300
National Assn of Postmasters	$1,650
American Federation of Government Employees	$1,600
National Assn of Postal Supervisors	$1,600
Others	$2,200

Teachers Unions $15,000

National Education Assn	$10,000
American Federation of Teachers	$5,000

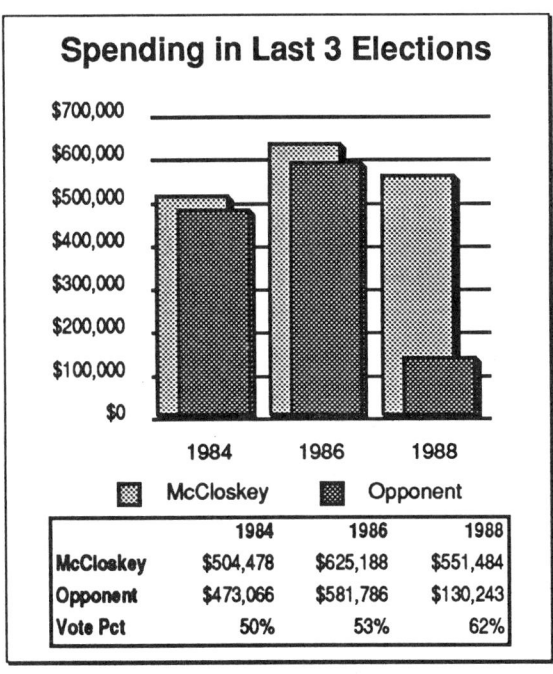

Spending in Last 3 Elections

	1984	1986	1988
McCloskey	$504,478	$625,188	$551,484
Opponent	$473,066	$581,786	$130,243
Vote Pct	50%	53%	62%

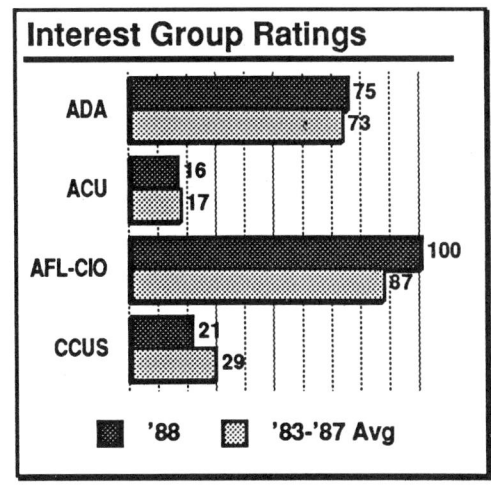

Interest Group Ratings

	'88	'83-'87 Avg
ADA	75	73
ACU	16	17
AFL-CIO	100	87
CCUS	21	29

Transportation Unions $26,850

Teamsters Union	$10,000
Marine Engineers Union	$3,500
Air Line Pilots Assn	$3,000
Amalgamated Transit Union	$2,000
United Transportation Union	$1,900
Masters, Mates & Pilots Union	$1,500
Seafarers International Union	$1,000
Others	$3,950

Ideological/Single-Issue

Democratic/Liberal $8,996

National Cmte for an Effective Congress	$8,496
Others	$500

Democratic Leadership PACs $10,500

Majority Congress Committee (Jim Wright)	$5,000
Valley Education Fund (Tony Coelho)	$4,000
24th Cong Dist of California PAC (Henry Waxman)	$1,000
Others	$500

Other Major Ideological/Single-Issue PACs

National Rifle Assn	$7,750	Pro-Guns
National Cmte to Preserve Social Security	$3,050	Soc Secur
National Council of Senior Citizens	$2,000	Soc Secur
Council for a Livable World	$1,110	Pro-Peace

Independent expenditures supporting McCloskey

National Cmte to Preserve Social Security	$1,367

---

* Contributions came from more than one PAC affiliated
with this sponsor.

Bill McCollum, R-Fla (5)

1988 Committees & Subcommittees

First elected: 1980
Total receipts: $303,806
Total from PACs: $117,835

Banking, Finance and Urban Affairs Domestic Monetary Policy (Ranking Republican) Financial Institutions Supervision, Regulation and Insurance Housing and Community Development	**Judiciary** Crime (Ranking Republican) Immigration, Refugees and International Law

PAC Contribution Profile

Business

Accountants	**$6,500**
American Institute of CPA's	$5,000
Ernst & Whinney	$1,000
Others	$500
Airlines	**$2,500**
Eastern Airlines	$2,000
Others	$500
Auto Dealers	**$2,500**
National Auto Dealers Assn	$1,000
Auto Dealers & Drivers for Free Trade	$1,500
Commercial Banks	**$23,850**
American Bankers Assn	$4,500
Barnett Banks of Florida	$4,000
J P Morgan & Company	$3,000
Citizens & Southern National Bank	$1,500
Independent Bankers Assn	$1,500
National Banks of Florida	$1,500
Chemical Bank	$1,100
Bankers Trust	$1,000
Southeast Banking Corp	$1,000
Others	$4,750
Construction	**$5,050**
Associated General Contractors	$1,000
National Assn of Home Builders	$1,000
National Concrete Masonry Assn	$1,000
Others	$2,050

Campaign Revenue Sources

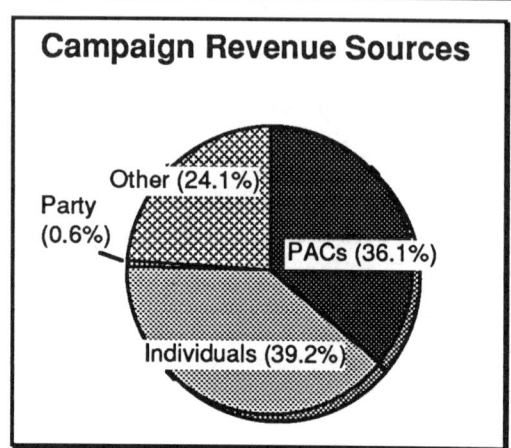

Other (24.1%)
Party (0.6%)
PACs (36.1%)
Individuals (39.2%)

Defense	**$2,500**
Harris Corp	$1,000
Others	$1,500
Food & Beverage	**$4,300**
McDonald's Corp	$1,000
National Beer Wholesalers Assn	$1,000
Others	$2,300
Insurance	**$13,500**
National Assn of Life Underwriters	$3,000
American Council of Life Insurance	$2,000
Independent Insurance Agents of America	$2,000
Others	$6,500
Lawyers & Lobbyists	**$7,000**
Akin, Gump, Hauer & Feld	$1,000
Baker & Hostetler	$1,000
Dickstein, Shapiro & Morin	$1,000
Gray, Harris & Robinson	$1,000
Others	$3,000
Pharmaceuticals	**$3,000**
Eli Lilly & Company	$1,000
Pfizer Inc	$1,000
Others	$1,000
Real Estate	**$4,000**
First Union Corp	$1,500
National Assn of Realtors	$1,000
Others	$1,500
Retail Sales	**$2,550**
Federated Department Stores	$1,000
Others	$1,550
Savings Banks	**$7,000**
US League of Savings Assn	$2,500
AmeriFirst Bank	$1,000
Glendale Federal Savings & Loan	$1,000
Others	$2,500

PAC Totals by Category

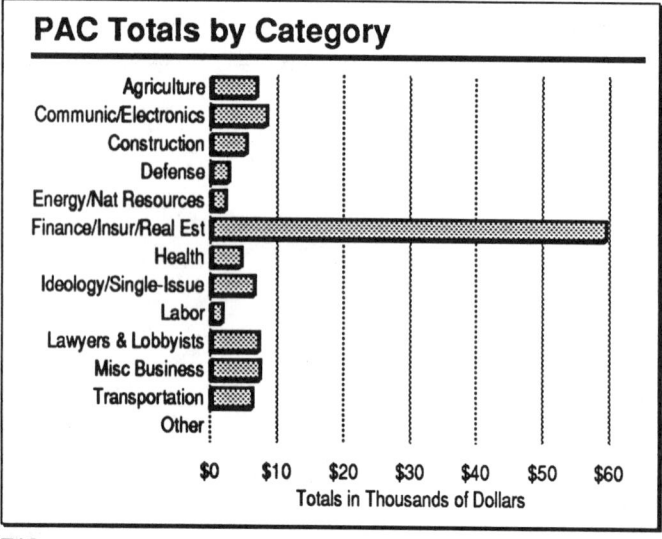

Agriculture
Communic/Electronics
Construction
Defense
Energy/Nat Resources
Finance/Insur/Real Est
Health
Ideology/Single-Issue
Labor
Lawyers & Lobbyists
Misc Business
Transportation
Other

$0 $10 $20 $30 $40 $50 $60

Totals in Thousands of Dollars

Securities & Commodities Investment **$6,500**
    Chicago Board of Options Exchange $1,000
    Chicago Board of Trade $1,000
    Chicago Mercantile Exchange $1,000
    First Boston Corp $1,000
    Others $2,500

Telecommunications **$6,550**
    Southern Bell $4,000
    AT&T $1,300
    Others $1,250

Other Major Business PACs

CSX Transportation Inc .... $1,000   Railroads
Internorth Inc .... $1,000   Natural Gas

Major Labor PACs

Seafarers International Union .... $1,000   Seamen Union

Ideological/Single-Issue

Pro-Israel **$5,000**
    National PAC $5,000

Independent expenditures supporting McCollum

National Cmte to Preserve Social Security $3,691

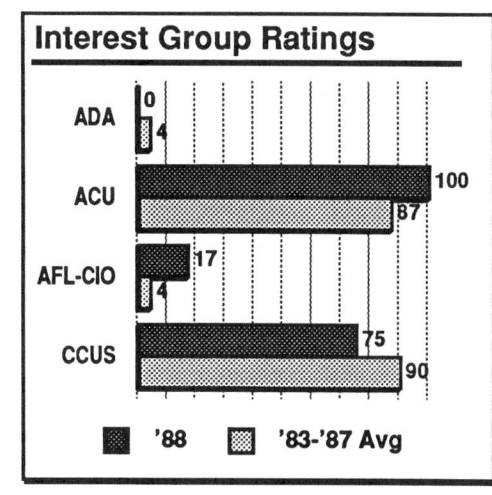

Interest Group Ratings

Group	'88	'83-'87 Avg
ADA	0	4
ACU	100	87
AFL-CIO	17	4
CCUS	75	90

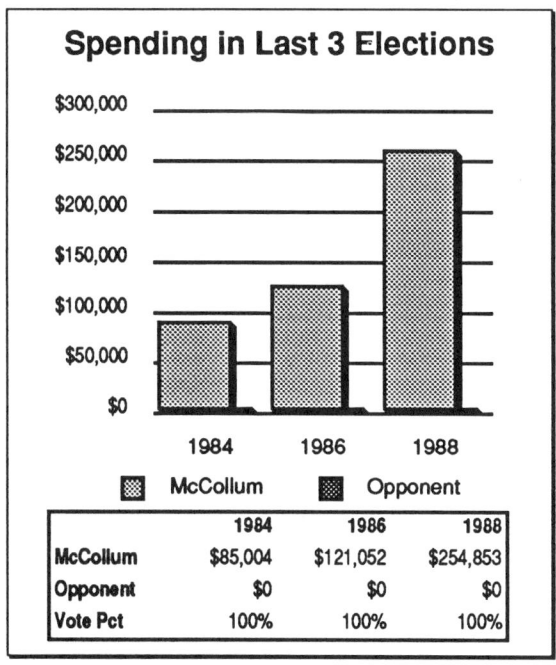

Spending in Last 3 Elections

	1984	1986	1988
McCollum	$85,004	$121,052	$254,853
Opponent	$0	$0	$0
Vote Pct	100%	100%	100%

Jim McCrery, R-La (4)

1988 Committees & Subcommittees

Budget
Defense and International Space
Economic and Trade Policy

First elected: 1988
Total receipts: $334,893
Total from PACs: $156,811

PAC Contribution Profile

NOTE: The PAC contributions listed on these pages include funds that McCrery received in both of his 1988 races — the special election he won in April and the November general election in which he was elected to a full two-year term. The total receipts listed in the box above, and the percentages in the pie chart at right, refer only to the general election race.

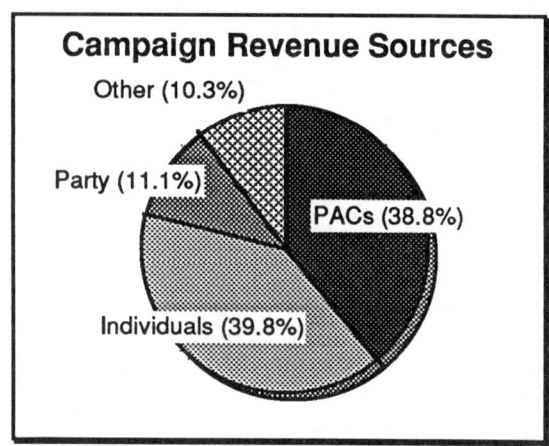

Campaign Revenue Sources

Other (10.3%)
Party (11.1%)
PACs (38.8%)
Individuals (39.8%)

Business

Automotive	....	$22,000
Auto Dealers & Drivers for Free Trade		$12,500
National Auto Dealers Assn		$5,750
Eaton Corp		$3,000
Others		$750

Business Associations		$3,323
National Fedn of Independent Business		$2,000
Business Industry PAC		$1,103
Others		$220

Chemicals		$6,350
Dow Chemical*		$4,500
Others		$1,850

Commercial Banks/Credit Unions		$2,750
Credit Union National Assn		$1,000
Louisiana Bankers Assn		$1,000
Others		$750

Construction		$22,100
National Assn of Home Builders		$10,000
Manville Corp		$3,000
Associated Builders & Contractors		$2,500
Associated General Contractors		$2,500
Brown & Root		$1,000
Lennox Industries		$1,000
Others		$2,100

Dairy	....	$2,750
Dairymen Inc-Louisiana		$1,250
Associated Milk Producers		$1,000
Others		$500

Defense	....	$8,500
Harris Corp		$3,000
Morton Thiokol		$1,500
Rockwell International		$1,000
Others		$3,000

Electric Utilities	....	$12,150
Middle South Utilities*		$2,100
Central Louisiana Electric		$2,000
ACRE (Action Committee for Rural Electrification)		$1,750
Louisiana ACRE		$1,200
Others		$5,100

Food & Beverage	....	$6,300
National Restaurant Assn		$2,000
Coors Industries		$1,000
Malone & Hyde Inc		$1,000
Pillsbury Company		$1,000
Others		$1,300

Forest Products	....	$24,285
International Paper Company		$8,000
Georgia-Pacific Corp*		$6,285
Boise Cascade		$3,500
Westvaco Corp		$2,500
Willamette Industries		$2,500
National Forest Products Assn		$1,250
Others		$250

Health Professionals	....	$14,250
American Medical Assn		$8,500
Louisiana Medical Assn		$2,500
American Optometric Assn		$1,750
American Dental Assn		$1,500

Insurance	....	$17,932
National Assn of Life Underwriters		$5,000
National Assn Mutual Insurance Agents		$4,500
American Council of Life Insurance		$2,282
Independent Insurance Agents of America		$1,100
US Fidelity & Guaranty		$1,100
Allstate Insurance		$1,000
Others		$2,950

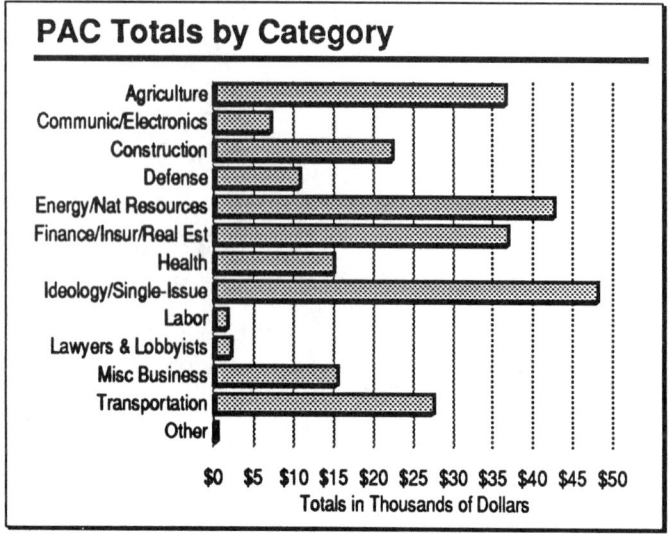

PAC Totals by Category

Agriculture
Communic/Electronics
Construction
Defense
Energy/Nat Resources
Finance/Insur/Real Est
Health
Ideology/Single-Issue
Labor
Lawyers & Lobbyists
Misc Business
Transportation
Other

$0 $5 $10 $15 $20 $25 $30 $35 $40 $45 $50
Totals in Thousands of Dollars

Lawyers	$2,000
Adams & Reese	$2,000

Oil & Gas	$30,735
Dallas Energy PAC	$7,000
Tenneco Inc	$3,000
Phillips Petroleum	$2,500
Union Oil	$2,035
Petroleum Marketers Assn	$2,000
Sun Company	$2,000
Arkla Inc	$1,250
Columbia Hydrocarbon Corp	$1,100
Amoco Corp	$1,000
Atlantic Richfield	$1,000
Mobil Oil	$1,000
Occidental Oil & Gas	$1,000
Texaco	$1,000
Others	$4,850

Real Estate	$16,000
National Assn of Realtors	$15,000
Mortgage Bankers Assn of America	$1,000

Telecommunications	$6,900
South Central Bell Telephone	$4,500
AT&T	$2,400

Tobacco	$3,000
Philip Morris	$1,500
RJR Nabisco	$1,000
Others	$500

Other Major Business PACs

Aircraft Owners & Pilots Assn	$1,500	GenlAviation
Cooper Industries	$1,000	PowerEquip
Kansas City Southern	$1,000	Railroads
National Assn of Retired Federal Employees	$1,000	Fedl Workers
United Parcel Service	$1,000	Delivery

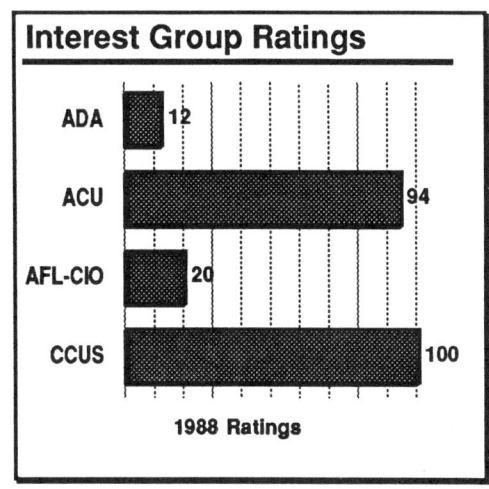

Interest Group Ratings

1988 Ratings

ADA	12
ACU	94
AFL-CIO	20
CCUS	100

Ideological/Single-Issue

Republican/Conservative	$5,223
National Conservative PAC	$1,867
Eagle Forum	$1,456
Republican Congressional Boosters Club	$1,000
Others	$900

Republican Leadership PACs	$19,250
Citizens for the Republic (Ronald Reagan)	$10,000
Fund for America's Future (George Bush)	$3,500
Republican Leader's Fund (Bob Michel)	$2,000
Campaign America (Bob Dole)	$1,000
Campaign for a New Majority (Jack Kemp)	$1,000
Policy Innovation PAC (Dick Armey)	$1,000
Others	$750

Other Major Ideological/Single-Issue PACs

Public Service Research Council	$9,500	Anti-Union
Louisiana for American Security	$5,000	Pro-Israel
National Rifle Assn	$4,950	Pro-Guns
National Right to Life PAC	$1,903	Pro-Life
Council for National Defense	$1,040	Pro-Defense

Independent expenditures supporting McCrery

National Cmte to Preserve Social Security	$1,267

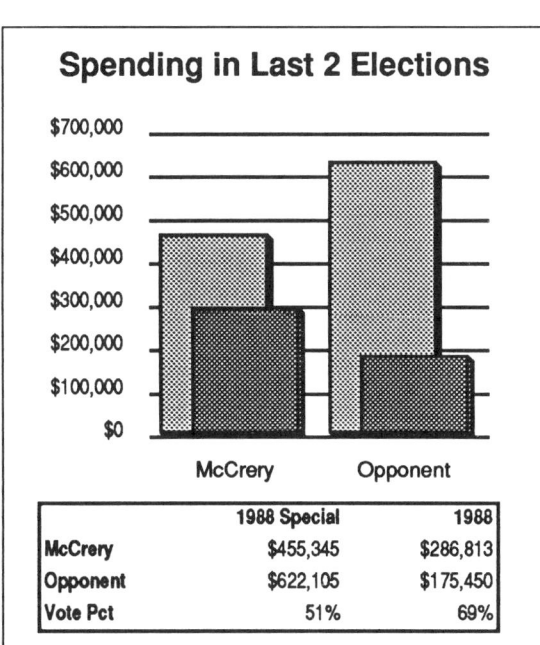

Spending in Last 2 Elections

	1988 Special	1988
McCrery	$455,345	$286,813
Opponent	$622,105	$175,450
Vote Pct	51%	69%

---

* Contributions came from more than one PAC affiliated with this sponsor.

Dave McCurdy, D-Okla (4)

1988 Committees & Subcommittees

Armed Services
Military Installations and Facilities
Research and Development

Science, Space and Technology
Transportation, Aviation and Materials (Chairman)
Natural Resources, Agriculture Research and Environment

First elected: 1980
Total receipts: $273,015
Total from PACs: $142,272

PAC Contribution Profile

Business

Automotive **$3,250**
    Auto Dealers & Drivers for Free Trade $3,000
    Others $250

Aviation & Aerospace **$4,300**
    Aircraft Owners & Pilots Assn $3,200
    Others $1,100

Commercial & Savings Banks **$2,750**
    American Bankers Assn $1,000
    United Community Bankers $1,000
    Others $750

Construction **$7,600**
    National Assn of Home Builders $3,750
    Associated General Contractors $1,250
    Albert H Halff Associates $1,000
    Others $1,600

Defense **$56,050**
    Textron Inc $5,000
    Boeing Company $4,000
    Rockwell International $3,500
    AT&T $3,000
    McDonnell Douglas* $3,000
    Northrop Corp $3,000
    LTV Aerospace & Defense Company $2,800
    General Dynamics $2,000
    Grumman $2,000
    GTE Corp* $1,750
    Lockheed Corp $1,700
    (continued in next column)

Campaign Revenue Sources

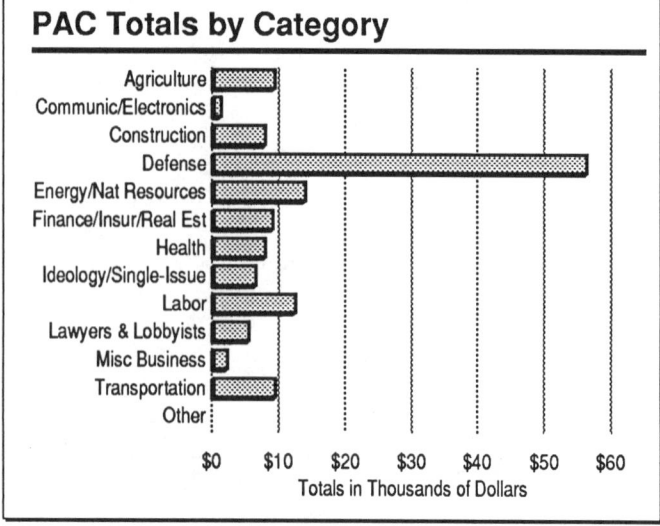

Other (9.8%)
PACs (50.7%)
Individuals (39.5%)

Defense (cont'd)
    Raytheon $1,550
    BDM International $1,500
    Singer Company $1,250
    Allied-Signal $1,200
    Hughes Aircraft $1,200
    United Technologies $1,200
    Gulfstream Aerospace $1,100
    Sequa Corp $1,000
    Others $14,300

Electric Utilities **$3,600**
    Oklahoma Gas & Electric $1,500
    Oklahoma ACRE $1,000
    Others $1,100

Health Professionals **$5,500**
    American Medical Assn $2,500
    Oklahoma Medical Assn $2,500
    Others $500

Insurance **$2,500**
    National Assn of Life Underwriters $1,500
    Torchmark Corp $1,000

Lawyers & Lobbyists **$5,150**
    Assn of Trial Lawyers of America $2,000
    Akin, Gump, Hauer & Feld $1,200
    Williams & Jensen $1,000
    Others $950

Oil & Gas **$9,750**
    Phillips Petroleum $1,200
    Halliburton Company $1,000
    Others $7,550

Real Estate **$3,000**
    National Assn of Realtors $3,000

Sugar Growers **$2,250**
    None over $600

Other Major Business PACs

Deere & Company	$1,350	Farm Equip
Philip Morris	$1,000	Tobacco
Southwestern Bell	$1,000	Phone Util

PAC Totals by Category

Agriculture
Communic/Electronics
Construction
Defense
Energy/Nat Resources
Finance/Insur/Real Est
Health
Ideology/Single-Issue
Labor
Lawyers & Lobbyists
Misc Business
Transportation
Other

$0 $10 $20 $30 $40 $50 $60

Totals in Thousands of Dollars

Labor

Bldg Trades/Industrial/Misc Unions **$5,300**
    Air Line Pilots Assn $2,500
    Food & Commercial Workers Union.............................$1,000
    Others $1,800

Government & Postal Workers **$6,800**
    National Assn of Retired Federal Employees $5,000
    Others $1,800

Ideological/Single-Issue

Pro-Israel **$5,250**
    National PAC $5,000
    Others $250

Other Major Ideological/Single-Issue PACs

Valley Education Fund (Tony Coelho) ....$1,000   Dem Leaders

Independent expenditures supporting McCurdy

National Cmte to Preserve Social Security $1,915

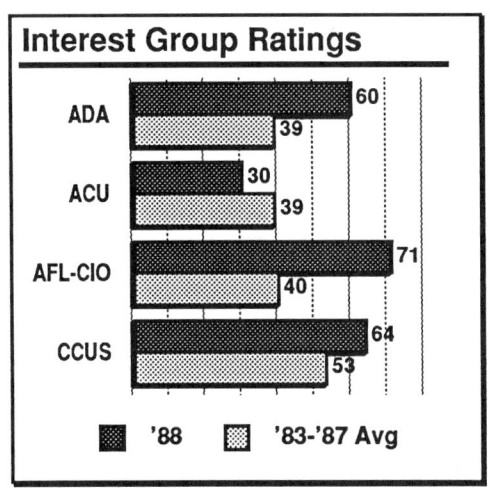

Interest Group Ratings

	'88	'83-'87 Avg
ADA	60	39
ACU	30	39
AFL-CIO	71	40
CCUS	64	53

■ '88   ▨ '83-'87 Avg

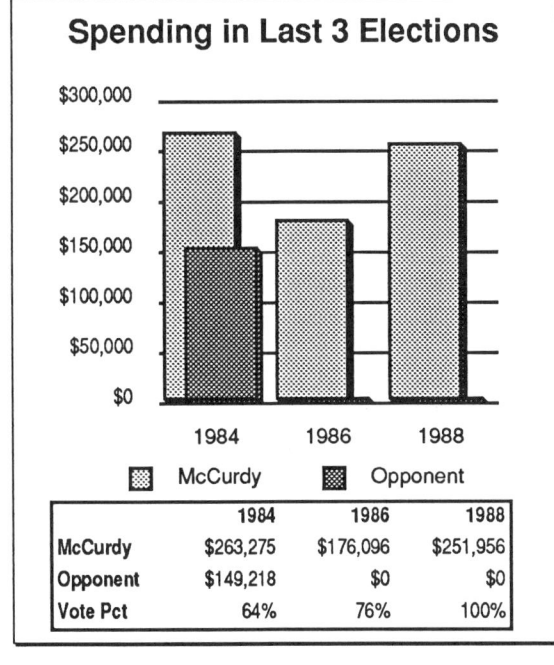

Spending in Last 3 Elections

▨ McCurdy   ▨ Opponent

	1984	1986	1988
McCurdy	$263,275	$176,096	$251,956
Opponent	$149,218	$0	$0
Vote Pct	64%	76%	100%

---

* Contributions came from more than one PAC affiliated
with this sponsor.

Joseph M. McDade, R-Pa (10)

1988 Committees & Subcommittees

First elected: 1962
Total receipts: $442,808
Total from PACs: $271,620

Appropriations
Defense (Ranking Republican)
Interior and Related Agencies

Small Business (Ranking Republican)
SBA and the General Economy (Ranking Republican)

PAC Contribution Profile

Business

Commercial & Savings Banks	**$5,000**
American Bankers Assn	$1,000
Independent Bankers Assn	$1,000
Others	$3,000
Construction	**$9,500**
National Assn of Home Builders	$2,500
National Utility Contractors Assn	$2,000
Associated General Contractors	$1,500
American Subcontractors Assn	$1,000
Stone & Webster	$1,000
Others	$1,500
Defense	**$101,800**
Northrop Corp	$8,000
Grumman	$5,000
Hughes Aircraft	$5,000
McDonnell Douglas*	$4,500
Tenneco Inc	$4,250
Boeing Company	$4,000
Lockheed Corp	$4,000
Raytheon	$3,500
Singer Company	$3,500
General Dynamics	$3,000
Textron Inc	$3,000
TRW Inc	$3,000
AT&T	$2,500
General Electric	$2,500
Rockwell International	$2,500
BDM International	$2,000
LTV Aerospace & Defense Company	$2,000
Martin Marietta Corp	$2,000
(continued in next column)	

Campaign Revenue Sources

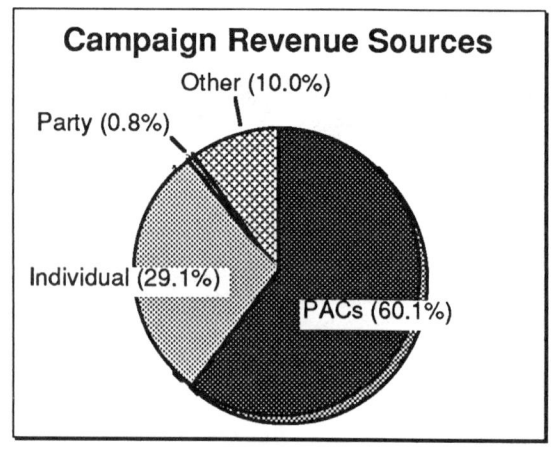

- Other (10.0%)
- Party (0.8%)
- Individual (29.1%)
- PACs (60.1%)

Defense (cont'd)

United Technologies	$2,000
Chrysler Corp	$1,500
Continental Telecom	$1,500
Emhart Corp*	$1,500
FMC Corp	$1,500
GTE Corp	$1,500
Harsco Corp	$1,500
Litton Industries	$1,500
Loral Corp	$1,500
Penn Central Corp	$1,500
Westinghouse Electric	$1,500
Computer Sciences Corp	$1,300
AEL Industries Inc	$1,000
Allied-Signal	$1,000
Beech Aircraft	$1,000
Dyncorp	$1,000
E-Systems/Corporate Division	$1,000
Electronic Data Systems	$1,000
Ford Motor Company	$1,000
Gencorp Inc	$1,000
Harris Corp	$1,000
Hazeltine Corp	$1,000
Pneumo Abex Corp	$1,000
Unisys Corp	$1,000
Others	$7,250
Health Professionals	**$6,000**
American Medical Assn	$3,000
American Dental Assn	$2,000
Others	$1,000
Insurance	**$5,770**
Metropolitan Life Insurance	$1,270
Cigna Corp	$1,000
John Hancock Financial Service	$1,000
National Assn of Life Underwriters	$1,000
Travelers Corp	$1,000
Others	$500
Lawyers	**$9,550**
Assn of Trial Lawyers of America	$5,000
Kleinfeld, Kaplan & Becker	$1,250
Kirkpatrick & Lockhart	$1,000
Others	$2,300
Oil & Gas	**$9,250**
Union Pacific Corp	$1,500
American Consulting Engineers Council	$1,000
Exxon Corp	$1,000
Others	$5,750

PAC Totals by Category

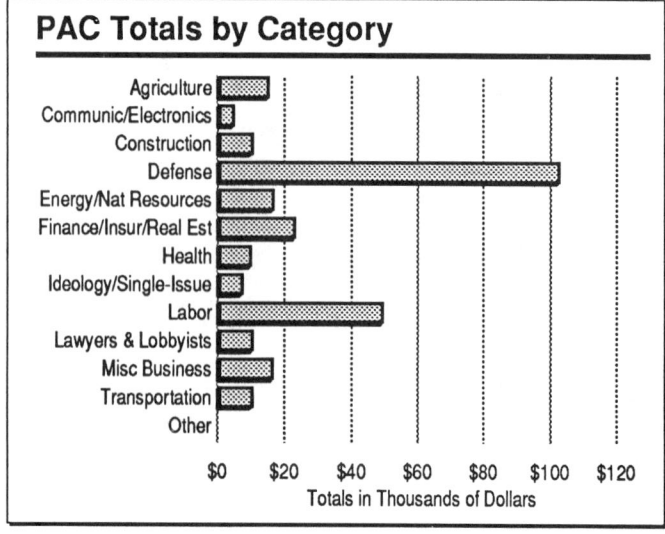

Category	
Agriculture	
Communic/Electronics	
Construction	
Defense	
Energy/Nat Resources	
Finance/Insur/Real Est	
Health	
Ideology/Single-Issue	
Labor	
Lawyers & Lobbyists	
Misc Business	
Transportation	
Other	

Totals in Thousands of Dollars
$0 $20 $40 $60 $80 $100 $120

| Railroad Equipment | .... | *$5,000* |
| Duchossois Industries | .... | $5,000 |

Real Estate	....	*$8,500*
National Assn of Realtors	....	$6,500
American Resort & Residential Developers Assn	....	$1,000
Others	....	$1,000

Other Major Business PACs

National Forest Products Assn	....	$3,300	Forestry
Philip Morris	....	$2,000	Tobacco
Pirelli Cable	....	$2,000	Indust Equip
Bell Telephone of Pennsylvania	....	$1,500	Phone Util
National Assn of Sm Bus Invest Companies	...	$1,500	Sml Business
Smithkline Beckman	....	$1,500	Pharmaceut
United Parcel Service	....	$1,500	Delivery
American Hospital Assn	....	$1,250	Hospitals
ACRE (Action Committee for Rural Electric)	...	$1,000	RuralElect
Air Products & Chemicals Inc	....	$1,000	Chemicals
American Veterinary Medical Assn	....	$1,000	Veterinary
Anheuser-Busch	....	$1,000	Beer
Associated Milk Producers	....	$1,000	Dairy
Babcock & Wilcox	....	$1,000	PowerEquip
Bethlehem Steel	....	$1,000	Steel
C-Tec Corp	....	$1,000	Commun Svc
Dravo Corp	....	$1,000	Other Mining
Greyhound Corp	....	$1,000	Home Chem
Hoechst Celanese Corp	....	$1,000	Synth Fiber
National Society of Public Accountants	....	$1,000	Accountants
National Tooling & Machining Assn	....	$1,000	Indust Equip
National Venture Capital Assn	....	$1,000	Venture Cap
Ocean Spray Cranberries Inc	....	$1,000	Fruit/Veg
RJR Nabisco	....	$1,000	Tobacco
Roadway Services Inc	....	$1,000	Trucking
Tobacco Institute	....	$1,000	Tobacco
Waste Management Inc	....	$1,000	Waste Mgmt
Wine & Spirits Wholesalers of America	....	$1,000	Liquor Whlsl

Interest Group Ratings

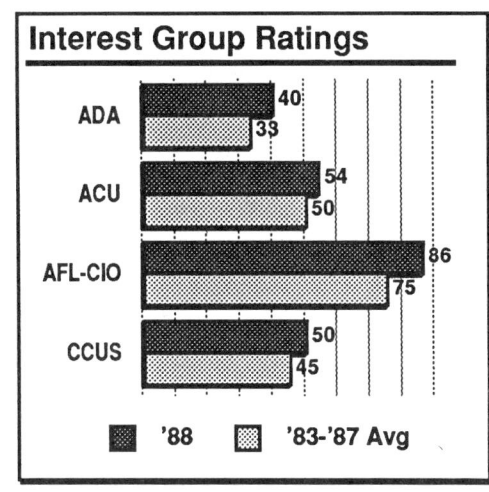

	'88	'83-'87 Avg
ADA	40	33
ACU	54	50
AFL-CIO	86	75
CCUS	50	45

Labor

Bldg Trades/Industrial/Misc Unions	....	*$16,800*
Carpenters & Joiners Union	....	$3,000
Laborers' Political League	....	$2,500
Operating Engineers Union	....	$2,000
Intl Brotherhood of Electrical Workers	....	$1,500
Boilermakers Union	....	$1,000
Food & Commercial Workers Union	....	$1,000
Ladies Garment Workers Union	....	$1,000
Machinists/Aerospace Workers Union	....	$1,000
Plumbers/Pipefitters Union	....	$1,000
United Mine Workers	....	$1,000
Others	....	$1,800

Government & Postal Workers	....	*$9,550*
National Assn of Retired Federal Employees	....	$6,000
National Assn of Letter Carriers	....	$2,000
Others	....	$1,550

Transportation Unions	....	*$22,250*
Teamsters Union	....	$7,500
Air Line Pilots Assn	....	$5,000
Marine Engineers Union*	....	$5,000
Seafarers International Union	....	$1,500
United Transportation Union	....	$1,500
Others	....	$1,750

Ideological/Single-Issue

| Pro-Israel | .... | *$5,000* |
| National PAC | .... | $5,000 |

Other Major Ideological/Single-Issue PACs

| KidsPAC | .... | $1,000 | HealthWelfare |

Independent expenditures supporting McDade

| National Cmte to Preserve Social Security | .... | $3,709 |

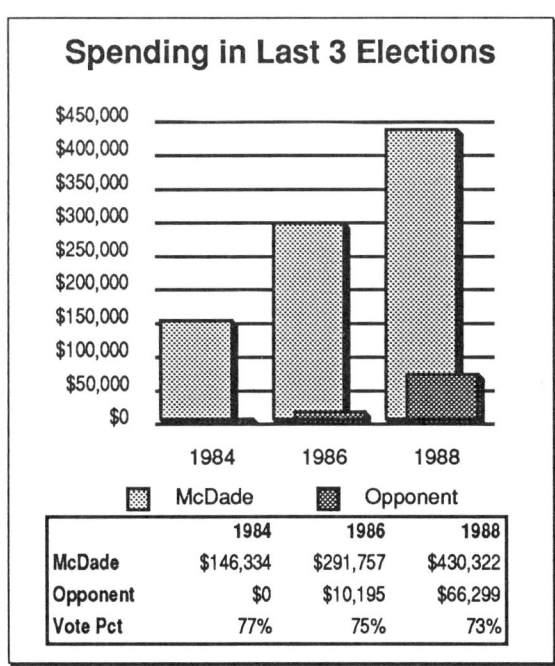

Spending in Last 3 Elections

	1984	1986	1988
McDade	$146,334	$291,757	$430,322
Opponent	$0	$10,195	$66,299
Vote Pct	77%	75%	73%

McDade   Opponent

---

* Contributions came from more than one PAC affiliated with this sponsor.

Jim McDermott, D-Wash (7)

First elected: 1988
Total receipts: $366,810
Total from PACs: $232,226

1988 Committees & Subcommittees

Banking, Finance and Urban Affairs
Financial Institutions Supervision, Regulation and Insurance
Housing and Community Development
International Development, Finance, Trade and Monetary Policy

District of Columbia
Fiscal Affairs and Health

Interior and Insular Affairs
National Parks and Public Lands
Water, Power and Off-shore Energy Resources

PAC Contribution Profile

Business

Construction	**$6,250**
Associated General Contractors	$2,500
National Assn of Home Builders	$2,500
Others	$1,250
Financial Institutions	**$10,150**
Credit Union National Assn	$2,000
Rainier Bancorp	$2,000
US Bancorp	$1,500
Washington Savings League	$1,500
American Bankers Assn	$1,000
Washington Mutual Savings Bank	$1,000
Others	$1,150
Health Professionals	**$32,250**
American Academy of Ophthalmology	$10,000
Corp for the Advancement of Psychiatry	$10,000
American Medical Assn	$5,000
American Dental Assn	$1,500
American Nurses Assn	$1,000
American Optometric Assn	$1,000
Assn for Advancement of Psychology	$1,000
Cmte for Quality Orthopedic Health Care	$1,000
Others	$1,750
Hospitals & Nursing Homes	**$3,450**
American Hospital Assn	$1,250
Others	$2,200
Import Auto Dealers	**$2,500**
Auto Dealers & Drivers for Free Trade	$2,500

Campaign Revenue Sources

Candidate (1.6%)
Other (2.6%)
Individuals (34.8%)
PACs (61.0%)

Lawyers	**$13,100**
Assn of Trial Lawyers of America	$10,000
Garvey, Schubert & Barer	$1,250
Others	$1,850
Oil & Gas	**$5,350**
Atlantic Richfield	$2,000
Phillips Petroleum	$2,000
Others	$1,350
Sea Transport	**$4,350**
Totem Ocean Trailer Express	$1,500
Others	$2,850
Securities Investment	**$2,750**
Smith Barney	$1,000
Others	$1,750
Telecommunications	**$3,500**
Pacific Northwest Bell	$2,000
AT&T	$1,000
Others	$500

Other Major Business PACs

Boeing Company	$1,000	Aircraft
National Assn of Social Workers	$1,000	Social Work
Services Group of America	$1,000	Food Whlsale
Waste Management Inc	$1,000	Waste Mgmt

PAC Totals by Category

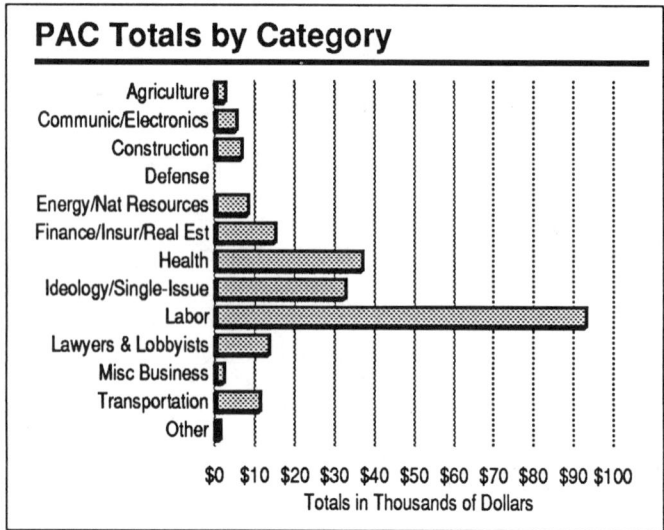

Agriculture
Communic/Electronics
Construction
Defense
Energy/Nat Resources
Finance/Insur/Real Est
Health
Ideology/Single-Issue
Labor
Lawyers & Lobbyists
Misc Business
Transportation
Other

$0 $10 $20 $30 $40 $50 $60 $70 $80 $90 $100
Totals in Thousands of Dollars

Labor

Bldg Trades/Industrial/Misc Unions $36,950
Machinists/Aerospace Workers Union $10,000
Food & Commercial Workers Union $5,000
United Steelworkers $5,000
AFL-CIO $2,500
Communications Workers of America $2,500
Laborers' Political League $2,500
Bakery, Confectionery & Tobacco Workers $2,000
Carpenters & Joiners Union $1,750
Operating Engineers Union $1,500
Ladies Garment Workers Union $1,000
Plumbers/Pipefitters Union $1,000
Service Employees International Union $1,000
Others $1,200

Government & Postal Workers $23,250
American Fedn of State/County/Munic Employees $10,000
National Assn of Letter Carriers $10,000
American Postal Workers Union $2,000
National Assn of Retired Federal Employees $1,000
Others $250

Teachers Unions $8,000
National Education Assn $5,000
American Federation of Teachers $3,000

Transportation Unions $24,500
Teamsters Union $10,000
Marine Engineers Union $5,000
Air Line Pilots Assn $2,500
Seafarers International Union $2,500
Amalgamated Transit Union $1,000
Longshoremen/Warehousemen Union $1,000
United Transportation Union $1,000
Others $1,500

Ideological/Single-Issue

Democratic Leadership PACs $14,000
Valley Education Fund (Tony Coelho) $5,000
Majority Congress Committee (Jim Wright) $3,000
24th Cong Dist of California PAC (Henry Waxman) $2,000
America's Leaders' Fund (Dan Rostenkowski) $1,000
Cmte for Democratic Opportunity (Bill Gray) $1,000
House Leadership Fund (Tom Foley) $1,000
Independent Action (Morris Udall) $1,000

Pro-Israel $6,000
National PAC $5,000
Others $1,000

Other Major Ideological/Single-Issue PACs

Human Rights Campaign Fund	$4,945	Gay Rights
National Cmte to Preserve Social Security	$3,000	Soc Secur
Sierra Club	$1,300	Environment
KidsPAC	$1,000	HealthWelfare
National Abortion Rights Action League	$1,000	Pro-Choice

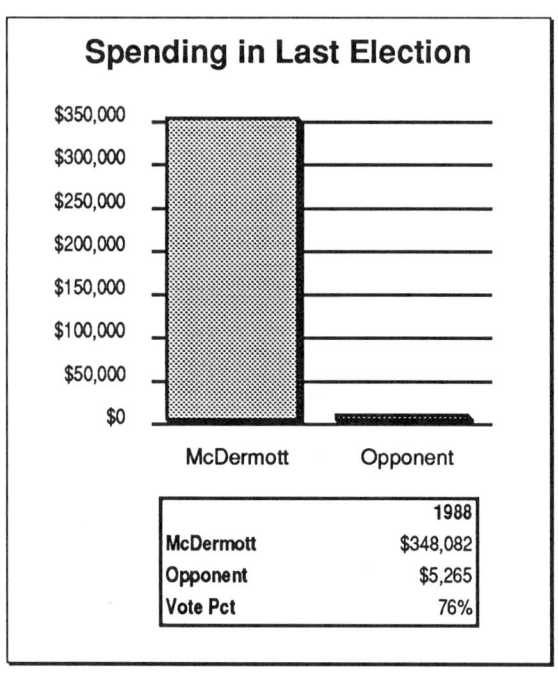

Spending in Last Election

	1988
McDermott	$348,082
Opponent	$5,265
Vote Pct	76%

Bob McEwen, R-Ohio (6)

1988 Committees & Subcommittees

First elected: 1980
Total receipts: $787,103
Total from PACs: $144,266

Public Works and Transportation
Economic Development (Ranking Republican)
Investigations and Oversight
Surface Transportation

Veterans' Affairs
Compensation, Pension and Insurance (Ranking Republican)
Hospitals and Health Care

PAC Contribution Profile

Business

Automotive **$5,100**
    National Auto Dealers Assn $2,300
    Auto Dealers & Drivers for Free Trade $2,000
    Others $800

Aviation & Aerospace **$2,500**
    None over $900

Bicycles & Motorcycles **$2,750**
    Huffy Corp $2,000
    Others $750

Chemicals **$3,350**
    Dow Chemical* $1,100
    Others $2,250

Commercial & Savings Banks **$6,850**
    National City Corp $2,000
    American Bankers Assn $1,500
    Ohio Bankers Assn $1,500
    Ohio Savings Assns League $1,000
    Others $850

Construction **$12,800**
    National Utility Contractors Assn $4,500
    Associated General Contractors $2,800
    National Assn of Home Builders $1,000
    Others $4,500

Dairy **$9,100**
    Associated Milk Producers $7,000
    Mid-American Dairymen $1,000
    Others $1,100

Campaign Revenue Sources

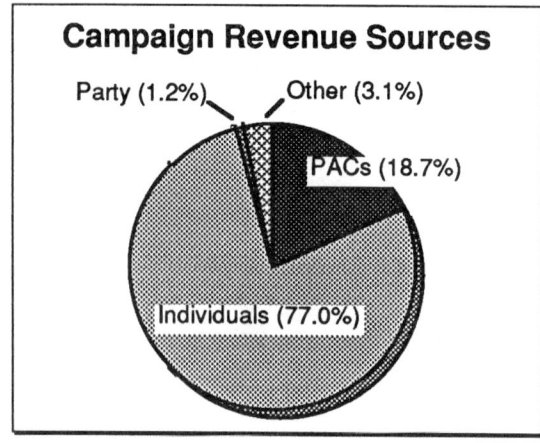

Party (1.2%)   Other (3.1%)
PACs (18.7%)
Individuals (77.0%)

PAC Totals by Category

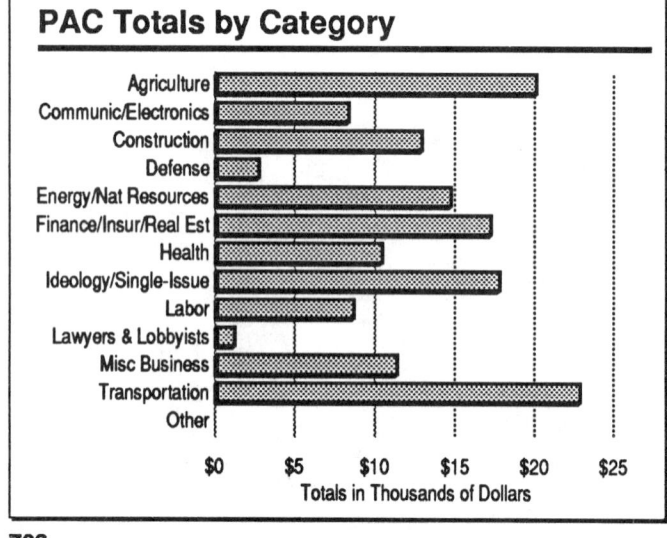

Agriculture
Communic/Electronics
Construction
Defense
Energy/Nat Resources
Finance/Insur/Real Est
Health
Ideology/Single-Issue
Labor
Lawyers & Lobbyists
Misc Business
Transportation
Other

$0 $5 $10 $15 $20 $25
Totals in Thousands of Dollars

Electric Utilities **$7,795**
    American Electric Power* $2,600
    Dayton Power & Light $2,400
    Cincinnati Gas & Electric $1,900
    Others $895

Food & Beverage **$3,050**
    Brown-Forman Distillers $1,000
    Others $2,050

Health Professionals **$8,550**
    American Medical Assn $5,000
    American Dental Assn $1,500
    American Academy of Ophthalmology $1,000
    Others $1,050

Insurance **$2,300**
    National Assn of Life Underwriters $1,000
    Others $1,300

Oil & Gas **$5,750**
    HOUPAC $1,000
    International Assn of Drilling Contractors $1,000
    Others $3,750

Paper Production **$3,600**
    Mead Corp $3,100
    Others $500

Real Estate **$8,000**
    National Assn of Realtors $8,000

Telecommunications **$6,550**
    AT&T $3,500
    Ohio Bell Telephone $1,000
    Others $2,050

Tobacco **$3,300**
    Philip Morris $1,500
    RJR Nabisco $1,000
    Others $800

Trucking/Delivery **$9,100**
    Paccar Inc $2,000
    American Trucking Assns $1,800
    Yellow Freight System $1,600
    United Parcel Service $1,550
    Others $2,150

Other Major Business PACs

L. M. Berry & Company	$2,500	Mail Advert
Ohio Farm Bureau Federation	$1,500	Farm Orgs
NCR Corp	$1,100	Computers
Illinois Central Railroad	$1,000	Railroads
PPG Industries	$1,000	Glass Prod

Labor

Labor Unions $8,550

Teamsters Union	$6,000
Air Line Pilots Assn	$2,500
Others	$50

Interest Group Ratings

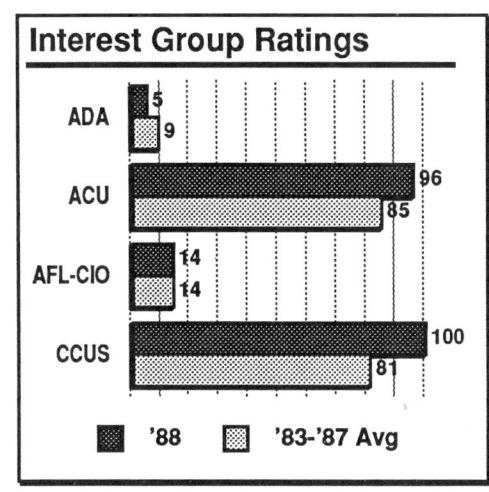

■ '88	▨ '83-'87 Avg

Ideological/Single-Issue

Republican/Conservative $2,250

American Citizens for Political Action	$1,000
Conservative Victory Committee	$1,000
Others	$250

Republican Leadership PACs $10,119

Campaign for a New Majority (Jack Kemp)	$5,000
Citizens for the Republic (Ronald Reagan)	$5,000
Others	$119

Other Major Ideological/Single-Issue PACs

National Rifle Assn	$2,500	Pro-Guns
National Security PAC	$1,000	Pro-Defense
Safari Club International	$1,000	Pro-Hunting

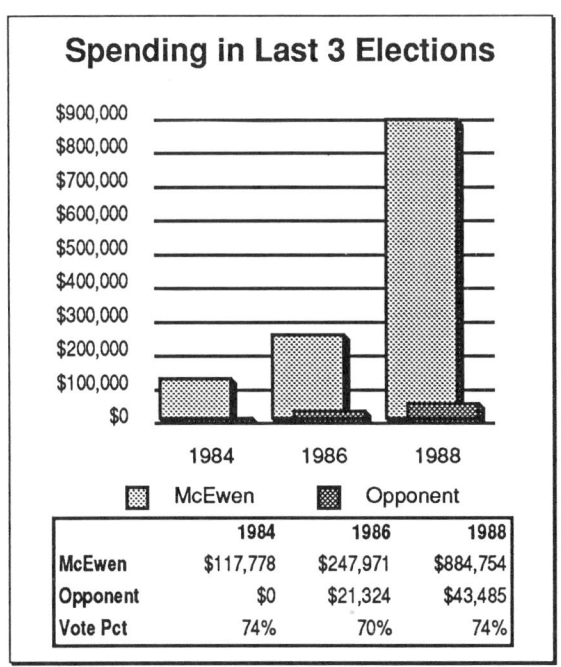

Spending in Last 3 Elections

	1984	1986	1988
McEwen	$117,778	$247,971	$884,754
Opponent	$0	$21,324	$43,485
Vote Pct	74%	70%	74%

* Contributions came from more than one PAC affiliated with this sponsor.

Raymond J. McGrath, R-NY (5)

First elected: 1980
Total receipts: $502,509
Total from PACs: $251,324

1988 Committees & Subcommittees

Ways and Means
Oversight
Select Revenue Measures

PAC Contribution Profile

Business

Commercial & Savings Banks **$16,360**
- J P Morgan & Company $5,000
- American Bankers Assn $3,000
- Citicorp $2,000
- Goldome Bank for Savings $1,500
- National Council of Savings Institutions $1,000
- Others $3,860

Defense **$12,000**
- Grumman $2,000
- Harris Corp $1,000
- Hughes Aircraft $1,000
- McDonnell Douglas $1,000
- Northrop Corp $1,000
- Textron Inc $1,000
- TRW Inc $1,000
- United Technologies $1,000
- Others $3,000

Food & Beverage **$13,250**
- Food Marketing Institute $2,000
- National Restaurant Assn $2,000
- Wine & Spirits Wholesalers of America $2,000
- National Beer Wholesalers Assn $1,500
- Joseph E Seagram & Sons $1,000
- Winn-Dixie Stores $1,000
- Others $3,750

Campaign Revenue Sources

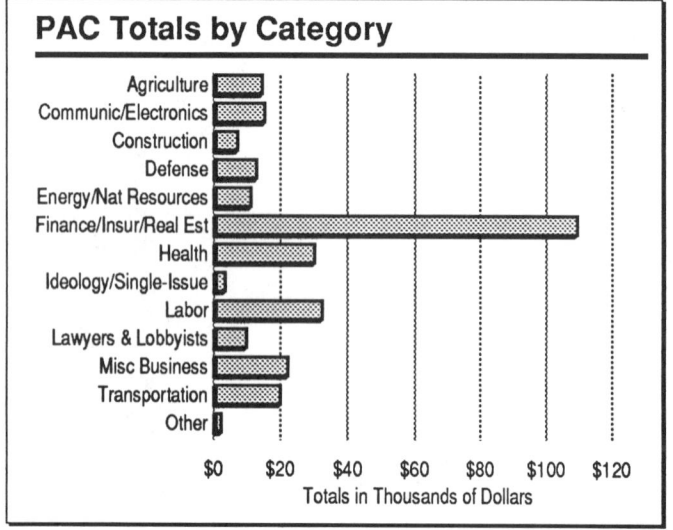

- Other (8.4%)
- Party (0.7%)
- PACs (55.8%)
- Individuals (35.0%)

Health Professionals **$16,500**
- New York Medical Assn $7,500
- American Dental Assn $3,000
- American Medical Assn $2,500
- Cmte for Quality Orthopedic Health Care $1,500
- American Optometric Assn $1,000
- Others $1,000

Insurance **$53,961**
- National Assn of Life Underwriters $10,000
- Torchmark Corp $6,000
- Metropolitan Life Insurance $5,480
- New York Life $4,074
- Massachusetts Mutual Life Insurance $3,500
- Mutual Life Insurance of New York $3,207
- Prudential Insurance $3,000
- American Council of Life Insurance $2,000
- Equitable Financial Services $2,000
- Guardian Life Insurance $2,000
- North Western Mutual Life $2,000
- Mutual of Omaha* $1,500
- Aetna Life & Casualty $1,000
- Health Insurance Assn of America $1,000
- Independent Insurance Agents of America $1,000
- John Hancock Financial Service $1,000
- New England Mutual Life $1,000
- Travelers Corp $1,000
- Others $3,200

Real Estate **$11,500**
- National Assn of Realtors $8,000
- Century 21 Real Estate $1,000
- Mortgage Bankers Assn of America $1,000
- Others $1,500

Securities & Commodities Investment **$14,900**
- First Boston Corp $3,000
- Salomon Brothers $2,900
- Chicago Board of Trade $2,000
- Goldman Sachs $2,000
- Chicago Board of Options Exchange $1,000
- Merrill Lynch $1,000
- Morgan Stanley & Company $1,000
- Public Securities Assn $1,000
- Others $1,000

PAC Totals by Category

Category	
Agriculture	
Communic/Electronics	
Construction	
Defense	
Energy/Nat Resources	
Finance/Insur/Real Est	
Health	
Ideology/Single-Issue	
Labor	
Lawyers & Lobbyists	
Misc Business	
Transportation	
Other	

$0 $20 $40 $60 $80 $100 $120
Totals in Thousands of Dollars

Telecommunications $12,500

AT&T	$2,500
New York Telephone	$2,000
Ameritech Corp	$1,000
Bell Atlantic	$1,000
BellSouth Corp*	$1,000
DSC Communications Corp	$1,000
International Telecharge Inc	$1,000
Others	$3,000

Other Major Business PACs

American Institute of CPA's	$5,000	Accountants
American Health Care Assn	$5,000	Nursing Home
Assn of Trial Lawyers of America	$5,000	Lawyers
Beneficial Management Corp	$3,000	Credit/Loans
Corning Glass Works	$3,000	Glass Prod
National Auto Dealers Assn	$3,000	Auto Sales
United Parcel Service	$2,750	Delivery
Philip Morris	$2,500	Tobacco
Associated General Contractors	$2,000	Comml Constr
Auto Dealers & Drivers for Free Trade	$2,000	JapanAutoSal
Independent Energy Producers PAC	$2,000	Energy
National Assn of Home Builders	$2,000	Resid Constr
American Assn of Equipment Lessors	$1,500	Rentals
American Society of Assn Executives	$1,500	Other
General Electric	$1,500	Electronics
Warner-Lambert	$1,500	Health Prod
Abbott Laboratories	$1,000	Pharmaceut
American Textile Manufacturers Institute	$1,000	Textiles
American Express	$1,000	Credit/Loans
American Supply Assn	$1,000	PipeProducts
Arnold & Porter	$1,000	Lawyers
Arthur Andersen & Company	$1,000	Accountants
Columbia Hydrocarbon Corp	$1,000	Natural Gas
Eastern Airlines	$1,000	Airlines
Federation of America Hospitals	$1,000	Hospitals
Ford Motor Company	$1,000	Auto Mfrs
Freeport-McMoran Inc	$1,000	Other Mining
General Motors	$1,000	Auto Mfrs
Gulf + Western Industries	$1,000	Credit/Loans
International Council of Shopping Centers	$1,000	Retail

(Continued in next column)

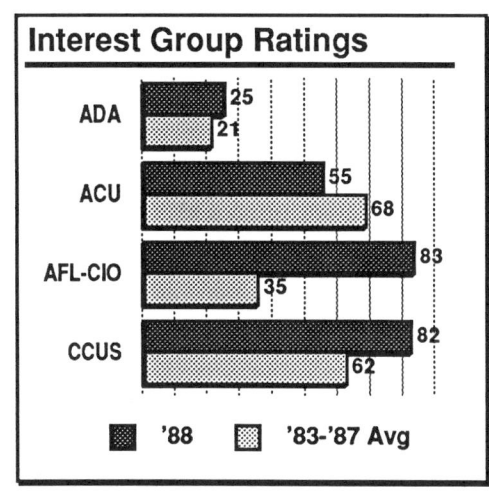

Interest Group Ratings

	'88	'83-'87 Avg
ADA	25	21
ACU	55	68
AFL-CIO	83	35
CCUS	82	62

Other Business PACs (cont'd)

Lucas Aerospace	$1,000	AerospacePts
National Assn of Wholesale-Distributors	$1,000	Wholesale
National Custom Brokers Assn	$1,000	BusinessSvcs
New England Power Service Company	$1,000	ElectricUtil
RJR Nabisco	$1,000	Tobacco
Ryder System Inc	$1,000	Car/Trk Rent
Sheet Metal/AirCon Contractors	$1,000	Plumbing/AC
Smithkline Beckman	$1,000	Pharmaceut
Tobacco Institute	$1,000	Tobacco

Labor

Bldg Trades/Industrial/Misc Unions $16,100

Carpenters & Joiners Union*	$4,500
National Assn of Retired Federal Employees	$3,000
American Fedn of State/County/Munic Employees	$2,500
National Rural Letter Carriers Assn	$1,500
Hotel/Restaurant Employees Union	$1,000
Ladies Garment Workers Union	$1,000
National Assn of Letter Carriers	$1,000
Others	$1,600

Transportation Unions $15,500

Air Line Pilots Assn	$5,000
Teamsters Union	$5,000
Marine Engineers District 2 Maritime Officers	$2,000
Seafarers International Union	$2,000
Others	$1,500

Major Ideological/Single-Issue PACs

National Cmte to Preserve Social Security	$2,000	Soc Secur

Independent expenditures supporting McGrath

National Cmte to Preserve Social Security	$2,009

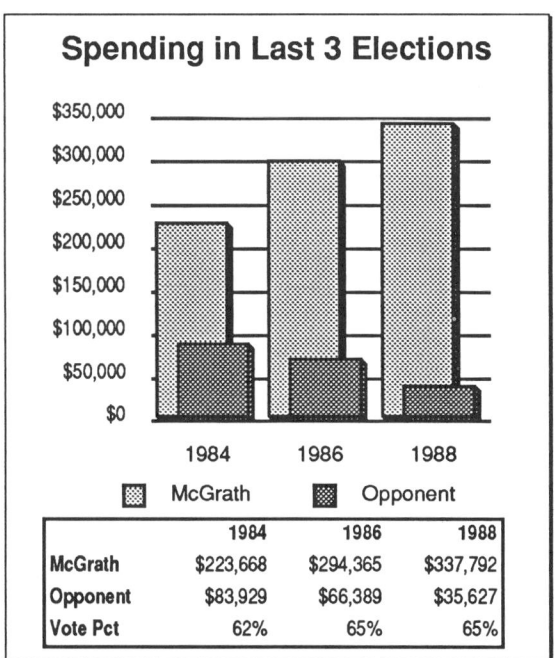

Spending in Last 3 Elections

	1984	1986	1988
McGrath	$223,668	$294,365	$337,792
Opponent	$83,929	$66,389	$35,627
Vote Pct	62%	65%	65%

Legend: McGrath, Opponent

---

* Contributions came from more than one PAC affiliated with this sponsor.

Matthew F. McHugh, D-NY (28)

First elected: 1974
Total receipts: $276,595
Total from PACs: $129,633

1988 Committees & Subcommittees

Appropriations
Foreign Operations
Rural Development, Agriculture and Related Agencies

Select Children, Youth and Families

Select Intelligence
Legislation (Chairman)
Oversight and Evaluation

PAC Contribution Profile

Business

Construction **$3,250**
 National Utility Contractors Assn $2,000
 Others $1,250

Dairy **$8,100**
 Associated Milk Producers $6,000
 Agri-Mark Inc $1,000
 Others $1,100

Defense **$6,600**
 Singer Company $2,800
 Grumman $2,300
 Others $1,500

Electric Utilities **$2,050**
 New York State Electric & Gas Corp $1,050
 Others $1,000

Financial Institutions **$6,150**
 Chase Lincoln First Bank $2,000
 Others $4,150

Health Professionals **$4,900**
 American Medical Assn $2,300
 American Dental Assn $1,500
 Others $1,100

Import Auto Dealers **$2,500**
 Auto Dealers & Drivers for Free Trade $2,500

Campaign Revenue Sources

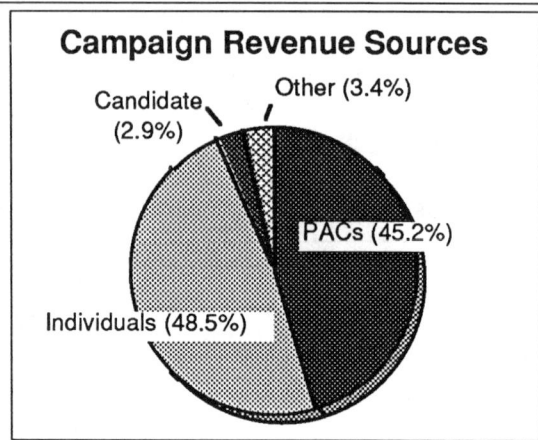

Candidate (2.9%)
Other (3.4%)
PACs (45.2%)
Individuals (48.5%)

Telecommunications **$3,700**
 AT&T $1,500
 Continental Telecom $1,000
 Others $1,200

Other Major Business PACs

American Veterinary Medical Assn	$1,500	Veterinary
American Assn of Crop Insurers	$1,000	Ag Svcs
Boeing Company	$1,000	Aircraft
General Electric	$1,000	Electronics
National Assn of Realtors	$1,000	Real Estate

PAC Totals by Category

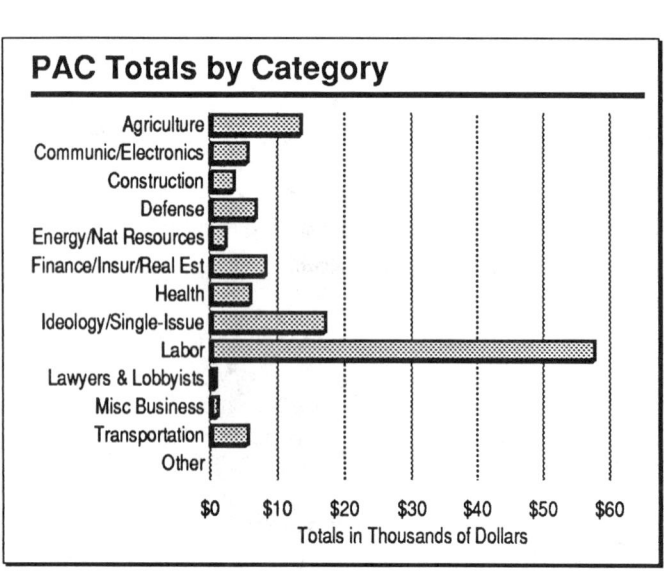

Agriculture
Communic/Electronics
Construction
Defense
Energy/Nat Resources
Finance/Insur/Real Est
Health
Ideology/Single-Issue
Labor
Lawyers & Lobbyists
Misc Business
Transportation
Other

$0 $10 $20 $30 $40 $50 $60
Totals in Thousands of Dollars

Labor

Bldg Trades/Industrial/Misc Unions $21,245
- Laborers' Political League $5,900
- Operating Engineers Union* $5,495
- AFL-CIO $2,500
- Communications Workers of America $2,000
- Machinists/Aerospace Workers Union $1,600
- Carpenters & Joiners Union $1,500
- Food & Commercial Workers Union $1,000
- Others $1,250

Government & Postal Workers $12,149
- National Assn of Retired Federal Employees $5,000
- National Assn of Letter Carriers $3,000
- American Fedn of State/County/Munic Employees $2,599
- Others $1,550

Teachers Unions $8,100
- National Education Assn $4,250
- American Federation of Teachers* $3,850

Transportation Unions $15,950
- Teamsters Union $10,000
- Seafarers International Union $1,500
- United Transportation Union $1,100
- Amalgamated Transit Union $1,000
- Others $2,350

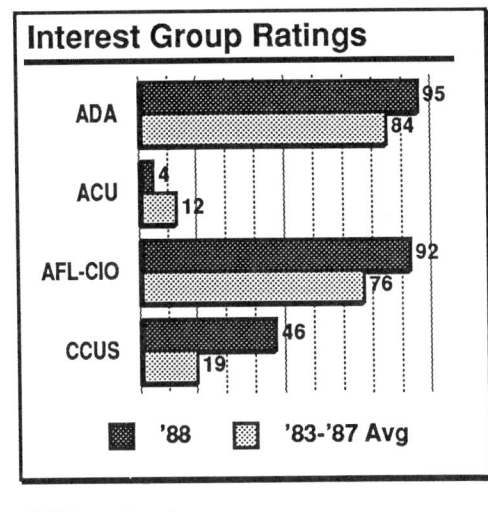

Ideological/Single-Issue

Democratic/Liberal $2,498
- National Cmte for an Effective Congress $2,498

Democratic Leadership PACs $2,000
- Valley Education Fund (Tony Coelho) $2,000

Pro-Israel $10,550
- National PAC $5,000
- Washington PAC $1,500
- Hudson Valley PAC $1,000
- Women's Pro-Israel National PAC $1,000
- Others $2,050

Independent expenditures supporting McHugh
National Cmte to Preserve Social Security $1,611

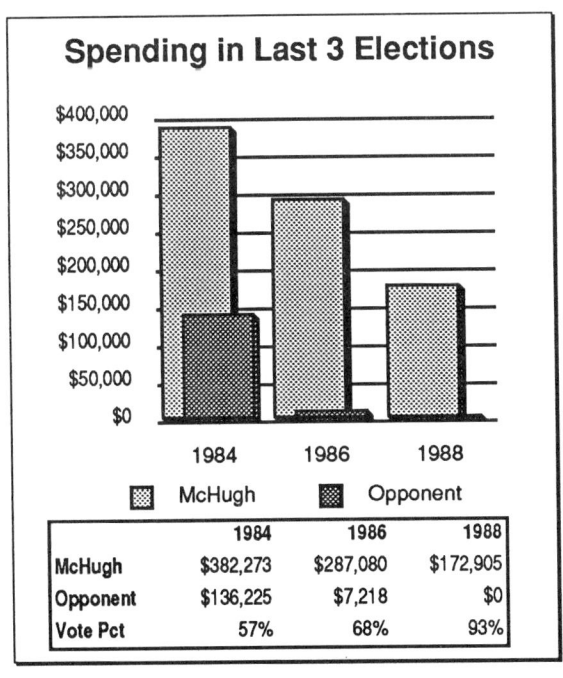

	1984	1986	1988
McHugh	$382,273	$287,080	$172,905
Opponent	$136,225	$7,218	$0
Vote Pct	57%	68%	93%

* Contributions came from more than one PAC affiliated with this sponsor.

731

Alex McMillan, R-NC (9)

First elected: 1984
Total receipts: $511,824
Total from PACs: $214,455

1988 Committees & Subcommittees

Banking, Finance and Urban Affairs
Economic Stabilization
Financial Institutions Supervision, Regulation and Insurance
General Oversight and Investigations
International Finance, Trade and Monetary Policy

Small Business
Regulation and Business Opportunities
SBA and the General Economy

Joint Economic
Economic Resources and Competitiveness

PAC Contribution Profile

Business

Automotive	**$10,150**
National Auto Dealers Assn	$5,750
Auto Dealers & Drivers for Free Trade	$3,500
Others	$900
Chemicals	**$7,950**
Dow Chemical*	$2,800
FMC Corp	$1,500
Others	$3,650
Commercial Banks	**$45,150**
American Bankers Assn	$10,000
J P Morgan & Company	$5,000
Bankers Trust	$3,000
Citicorp	$3,000
Barnett Banks of Florida	$2,500
First Chicago Corp	$2,500
Marine Midland Banks	$2,250
NCNB Corp	$2,000
Citizens & Southern National Bank	$1,800
Security Pacific Corp	$1,250
Central Carolina Bank & Trust	$1,200
Chase Manhattan	$1,150
Branch Banking & Trust	$1,000
Chemical Bank	$1,000
Others	$7,500
Construction	**$15,500**
National Assn of Home Builders	$5,500
Associated General Contractors	$2,500
JA Jones Construction Company	$1,200
Manville Corp	$1,000
Others	$5,300

Campaign Revenue Sources

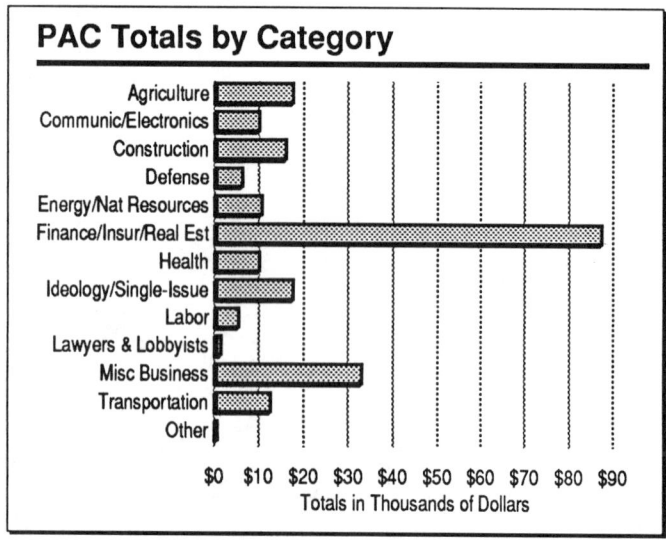

Party (0.5%)
PACs (43.4%)
Individuals (56.1%)

Consumer Credit & Loans	**$4,600**
American Financial Services Assn	$1,100
Barclays American Corp	$1,000
Others	$2,500
Defense	**$5,750**
Textron Inc	$1,700
Harris Corp	$1,000
Others	$3,050
Electric Utilities	**$5,650**
Duke Power Company	$3,550
Carolina Power & Light	$1,550
Others	$550
Food & Beverage	**$11,600**
Food Marketing Institute	$1,600
General Mills*	$1,000
Hardee's Food Systems	$1,000
Malone & Hyde Inc	$1,000
National Restaurant Assn	$1,000
Pepsico Inc	$1,000
Winn-Dixie Stores	$1,000
Others	$4,000
Health Professionals	**$5,800**
American Medical Assn	$2,800
American Dental Assn	$2,000
American Academy of Ophthalmology	$1,000
Industrial Equipment & Materials	**$2,250**
JSJ Corp	$1,000
Others	$1,250
Insurance	**$13,550**
Royal Indemnity	$1,350
Jefferson-Pilot Corp	$1,000
Travelers Corp	$1,000
Others	$10,200
Oil & Gas	**$4,450**
Mobil Oil	$1,000
Others	$3,450

PAC Totals by Category

Agriculture
Communic/Electronics
Construction
Defense
Energy/Nat Resources
Finance/Insur/Real Est
Health
Ideology/Single-Issue
Labor
Lawyers & Lobbyists
Misc Business
Transportation
Other

$0 $10 $20 $30 $40 $50 $60 $70 $80 $90
Totals in Thousands of Dollars

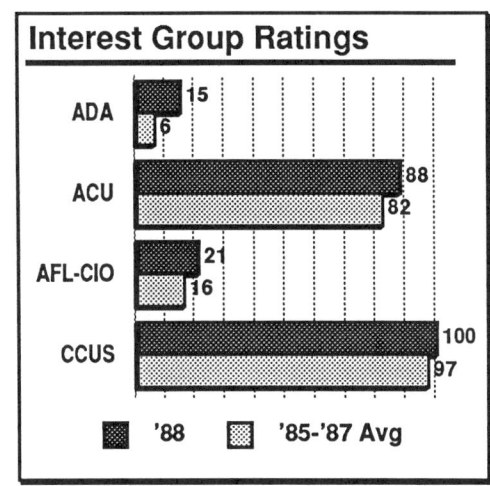

Interest Group Ratings

	'88	'85-'87 Avg
ADA	15	6
ACU	88	82
AFL-CIO	21	16
CCUS	100	97

Pharmaceuticals **$3,100**

    Sandoz Pharmaceuticals $1,200
    Others $1,900

Real Estate ***$17,000***

    National Assn of Realtors $8,300
    First Union Corp $6,000
    Mortgage Bankers Assn of America......................$2,200
    Others $500

Savings Banks & Credit Unions ***$3,950***

    National Council of Savings Institutions $1,350
    Credit Union National Assn $1,000
    Others $1,600

Sugar Growers ***$3,500***

    American Crystal Sugar Corp $1,100
    Southern Minnesota Beet Sugar Co-op $1,000
    Others $1,400

Telecommunications ***$8,950***

    Southern Bell $4,250
    United Telecommunications $3,000
    Others $1,700

Textiles ***$10,100***

    Cone Mills Corp $2,500
    Burlington Industries $1,200
    Collins & Aikman Corp $1,050
    American Textile Manufacturers Institute $1,000
    Hoechst Celanese Corp $1,000
    Others $3,350

Tobacco ***$5,850***

    RJR Nabisco $2,500
    Philip Morris $2,200
    Others $1,150

Other Major Business PACs

American Furniture Manufacturers Assn	$1,900	Furniture
American Institute of CPA's	$1,000	Accountants
Business Industry PAC	$1,000	Bus Assns
National Assn of Convenience Stores	$1,000	Dept Store

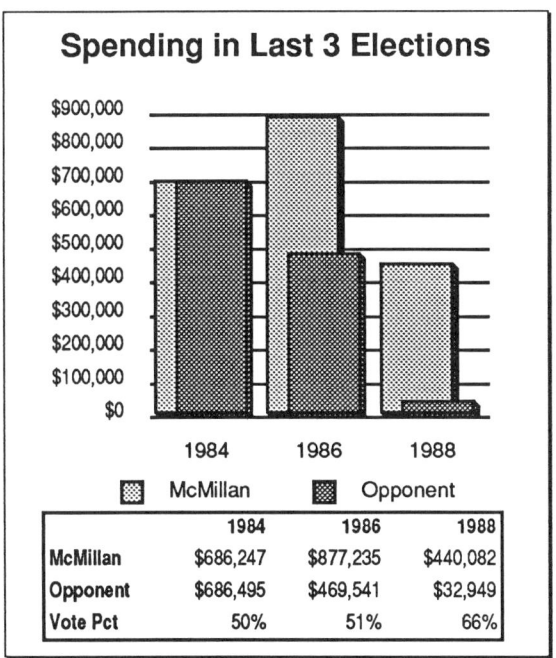

Spending in Last 3 Elections

	McMillan	Opponent

	1984	1986	1988
McMillan	$686,247	$877,235	$440,082
Opponent	$686,495	$469,541	$32,949
Vote Pct	50%	51%	66%

Labor

Labor Unions.. ***$4,950***

    Graphic Communications Union.......................$1,500
    National Assn of Retired Federal Employees $1,000
    Others $2,450

Ideological/Single-Issue

Pro-Israel ***$5,250***

    National PAC $5,000
    Others $250

Republican Leadership PACs ***$2,000***

    Catch the Spirit PAC (Bob Kasten) $2,000

Other Major Ideological/Single-Issue PACs

National Rifle Assn	$4,950	Pro-Guns
National Right to Life PAC	$2,600	Pro-Life

Independent expenditures supporting McMillan

National Right to Life PAC $3,740

---

* Contributions came from more than one PAC affiliated
with this sponsor.

Tom McMillen, D-Md (4)

First elected: 1986
Total receipts: $730,652
Total from PACs: $392,492

1988 Committees & Subcommittees

Banking, Finance and Urban Affairs
Economic Stabilization
Financial Institutions Supervision, Regulation and Insurance

Science, Space and Technology
Natural Resources, Agriculture Research and Environment
Space Science and Applications
Transportation, Aviation and Materials

PAC Contribution Profile

Business

Aviation & Aerospace **$10,350**
Federal Express Corp $2,350
UNC Inc $1,500
Boeing Company $1,100
Martin Marietta Corp $1,050
Others $4,350

Commercial Banks **$36,500**
American Bankers Assn $7,000
Citizens & Southern National Bank $3,000
Barnett Banks of Florida $2,500
Bankers Trust $2,000
First Maryland Bancorp $1,550
Assn of Bank Holding Companies $1,500
Banc One Corp* $1,500
Security Pacific Corp $1,500
Sovran Bank/Maryland $1,500
Citicorp $1,200
MNC Financial Inc $1,200
Independent Bankers Assn $1,050
Others $11,000

Construction **$10,400**
National Assn of Home Builders $7,100
Associated General Contractors $1,300
Others $2,000

Defense **$7,750**
General Dynamics $2,000
Lockheed Corp $1,150
BDM International $1,100
Rockwell International $1,100
Others $2,400

Campaign Revenue Sources

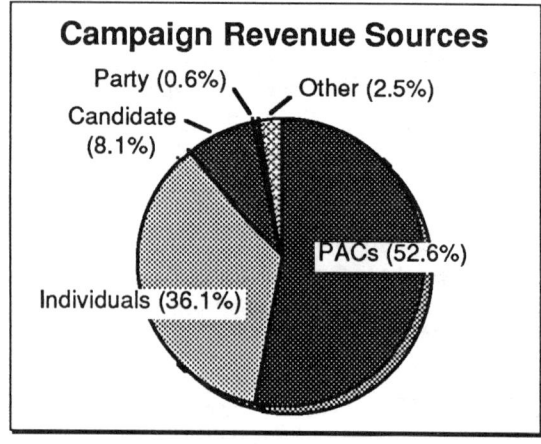

Party (0.6%)
Other (2.5%)
Candidate (8.1%)
PACs (52.6%)
Individuals (36.1%)

Electronics & Computers **$5,650**
Westinghouse Electric $1,450
General Electric $1,300
Others $2,900

Food & Beverage **$5,250**
A E Staley Manufacturers Company $1,100
Coca-Cola Company $1,050
Others $3,100

Health Professionals **$19,087**
American Medical Assn $8,587
American Dental Assn $4,000
Maryland Medical Assn $3,000
American Academy of Ophthalmology $2,000
Others $1,500

Insurance **$10,200**
Independent Insurance Agents of America $1,050
Others $9,150

Lawyers & Lobbyists **$17,650**
Assn of Trial Lawyers of America $5,000
Akin, Gump, Hauer & Feld $2,300
Verner, Liipfert, Bernhard & McPherson $2,300
Dow, Lohnes & Albertson $1,050
Others $7,000

Real Estate **$11,033**
National Assn of Realtors $7,933
Mortgage Bankers Assn of America $1,700
Others $1,400

Savings Banks & Credit Unions **$10,800**
US League of Savings Assn $4,200
Others $6,600

Securities Investment **$15,350**
Alex Brown Inc $2,000
Goldman Sachs $2,000
Prudential-Bache Securities $2,000
Investment Company Institute $1,300
Others $8,050

Telecommunications **$8,280**
AT&T $2,000
Chesapeake & Potomac Telephone $1,680
Southern Bell* $1,500
Comsat $1,300
Others $1,800

PAC Totals by Category

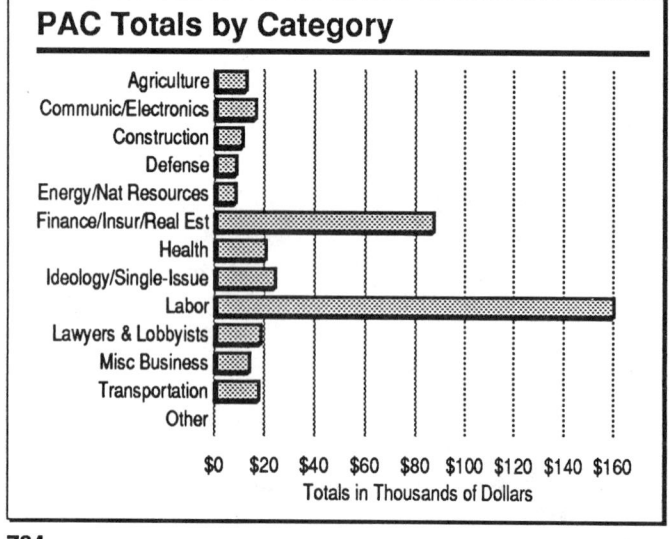

Agriculture
Communic/Electronics
Construction
Defense
Energy/Nat Resources
Finance/Insur/Real Est
Health
Ideology/Single-Issue
Labor
Lawyers & Lobbyists
Misc Business
Transportation
Other

$0 $20 $40 $60 $80 $100 $120 $140 $160
Totals in Thousands of Dollars

Other Major Business PACs

Dairymen Inc ....$2,600 Dairy
J C Penney Company ....$2,300 Dept Store
Greater Washington Board of Trade ....$2,000 Chamb/Cmrce
National Auto Dealers Assn ....$1,600 Auto Sales
Associated Milk Producers ....$1,500 Dairy
Dow Chemical* ....$1,500 Chemicals
United Parcel Service......................................$1,200 Delivery
ACRE (Action Committee for Rural Electric) ...$1,050 RuralElect
Columbia Hydrocarbon Corp ....$1,050 Natural Gas

Labor

Bldg Trades/Industrial/Misc Unions $71,050

Machinists/Aerospace Workers Union $10,000
Sheet Metal Workers Union $10,000
United Steelworkers $8,000
Carpenters & Joiners Union* $7,270
Food & Commercial Workers Union................................$6,000
Intl Brotherhood of Electrical Workers............................$6,000
AFL-CIO* $4,550
Operating Engineers Union $2,500
United Auto Workers $2,250
Bakery, Confectionery & Tobacco Workers $2,000
Baltimore Bldg/Construction Trades Council $2,000
Laborers' Political League $1,700
Amalgamated Clothing & Textile Workers* $1,300
Oil, Chemical & Atomic Workers Union..........................$1,300
Painters & Allied Trades Union $1,180
Others $5,000

Government & Postal Workers $37,330

American Fedn of State/County/Munic Employees $10,000
National Assn of Retired Federal Employees $8,500
National Assn of Letter Carriers $8,040
National Rural Letter Carriers Assn $2,800
American Postal Workers Union $1,940
American Federation of Government Employees $1,700
National League of Postmasters $1,550
Others $2,800

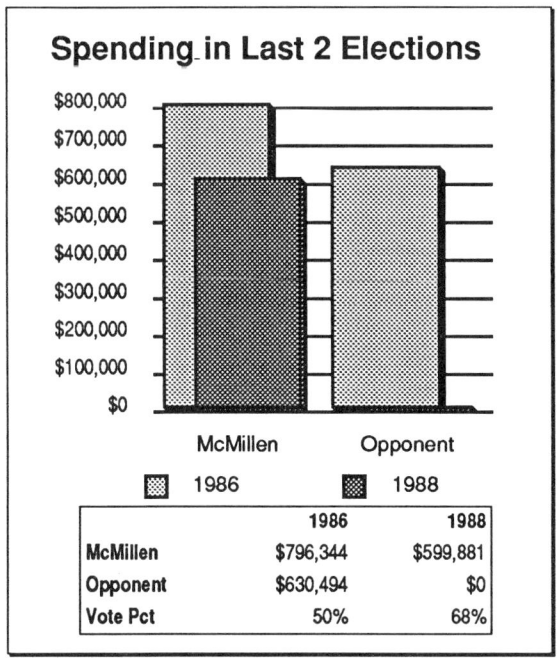

Spending in Last 2 Elections

	1986	1988
McMillen	$796,344	$599,881
Opponent	$630,494	$0
Vote Pct	50%	68%

McMillen — Opponent
☐ 1986 ■ 1988

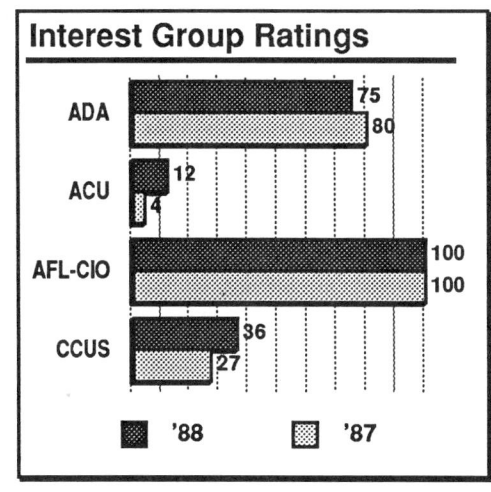

Interest Group Ratings

ADA — '88: 75, '87: 80
ACU — '88: 12, '87: 4
AFL-CIO — '88: 100, '87: 100
CCUS — '88: 36, '87: 27

■ '88   ☐ '87

Teachers Unions $10,108

National Education Assn $6,500
American Federation of Teachers $3,608

Transportation Unions $40,850

Teamsters Union $10,000
Marine Engineers Union* $7,100
Air Line Pilots Assn $7,000
Seafarers International Union..$5,000
Masters, Mates & Pilots Union $3,000
Amalgamated Transit Union $2,200
United Transportation Union $2,200
Transportation Communication Union $1,650
Others $2,700

Ideological/Single-Issue

Democratic Leadership PACs.....................................$8,250

Cmte for the 100th Congress (Charles Rangel)..............$3,000
Majority Congress Committee (Jim Wright) $3,000
Valley Education Fund (Tony Coelho) $2,000
Others $250

Pro-Israel $8,250

National PAC $5,000
Roundtable PAC $1,500
Others $1,750

Other Major Ideological/Single-Issue PACs

National Cmte to Preserve Social Security ......$3,350 Soc Secur
National Cmte for an Effective Congress.........$2,497 Dem/Liberal

Independent expenditures supporting McMillen

National Cmte to Preserve Social Security $1,359

Independent expenditures opposing McMillen

Council for National Defense $6,044

---

* Contributions came from more than one PAC affiliated
  with this sponsor.

Michael R. McNulty, D-NY (23)

First elected: 1988
Total receipts: $282,373
Total from PACs: $140,725

1988 Committees & Subcommittees

Armed Services
Readiness
Research and Development

Small Business
Exports, Tax Policy and Special Problems
Procurement, Tourism and Rural Development
Regulation Business Opportunities and Energy

Select Hunger

PAC Contribution Profile

Business

Commercial Banks	**$9,375**
Norstar Bancorp	$5,000
American Bankers Assn	$3,000
Chase Manhattan	$1,000
Others	$375
Health Professionals	**$17,500**
American Medical Assn	$5,000
New York Medical Assn	$5,000
American Dental Assn	$4,000
American Academy of Ophthalmology	$3,000
Others	$500
Insurance	**$6,500**
Independent Insurance Agents of America	$3,000
National Assn of Life Underwriters	$2,500
American International Group inc	$1,000
Lawyers	**$2,000**
Assn of Trial Lawyers of America	$2,000
Real Estate	**$5,000**
National Assn of Realtors	$5,000
Savings Banks	**$1,150**
None over $500	

Other Major Business PACs
AT&T ....$1,000   LongDistance

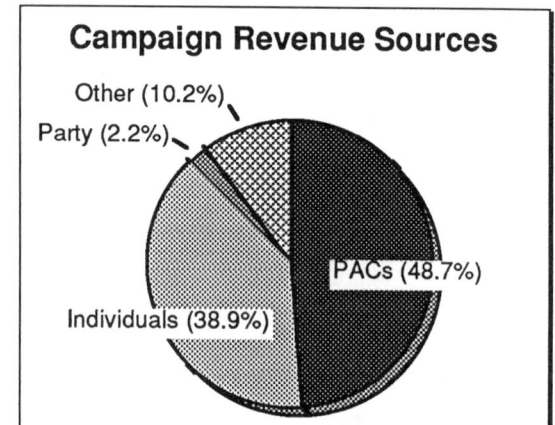

Campaign Revenue Sources

Other (10.2%)
Party (2.2%)
PACs (48.7%)
Individuals (38.9%)

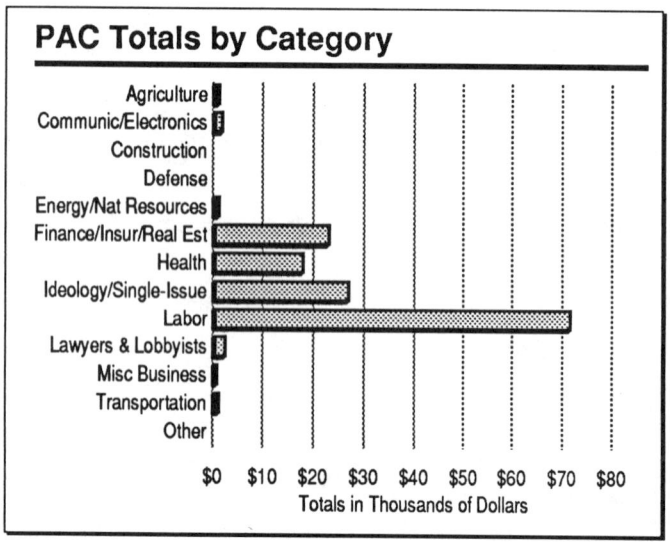

PAC Totals by Category

Agriculture
Communic/Electronics
Construction
Defense
Energy/Nat Resources
Finance/Insur/Real Est
Health
Ideology/Single-Issue
Labor
Lawyers & Lobbyists
Misc Business
Transportation
Other

$0 $10 $20 $30 $40 $50 $60 $70 $80

Totals in Thousands of Dollars

Labor

Bldg Trades/Industrial/Misc Unions $33,950

Food & Commercial Workers Union	$5,000
Intl Brotherhood of Electrical Workers	$5,000
United Auto Workers	$5,000
Laborers' Political League	$5,000
United Steelworkers	$3,000
Machinists/Aerospace Workers Union	$2,500
Ironworkers Union	$2,000
AFL-CIO	$1,000
Bricklayers Union	$1,000
Electrical Radio/Machine Workers	$1,000
Plumbers/Pipefitters Union	$1,000
Others	$2,450

Government & Postal Workers $17,500

American Fedn of State/County/Munic Employees	$5,000
American Postal Workers Union	$5,000
National Assn of Letter Carriers	$5,000
National Assn of Retired Federal Employees	$2,000
Others	$500

Teachers Unions $5,000

National Education Assn	$5,000

Transportation Unions $14,650

Teamsters Union	$5,000
Marine Engineers Union*	$3,000
Air Line Pilots Assn	$2,500
Seafarers International Union	$2,500
United Transportation Union	$1,000
Others	$650

Ideological/Single-Issue

Democratic Leadership PACs $15,500

Majority Congress Committee (Jim Wright)	$5,000
Valley Education Fund (Tony Coelho)	$5,000
Cmte for Democratic Opportunity (Bill Gray)	$2,500
America's Leaders' Fund (Dan Rostenkowski)	$1,000
Conservative Democratic PAC (Charles Stenholm)	$1,000
House Leadership Fund (Tom Foley)	$1,000

Pro-Israel $5,000

National PAC	$5,000

Social Security Issues $5,000

National Cmte to Preserve Social Security	$5,000

Other Major Ideological/Single-Issue PACs

National Cmte for an Effective Congress	$1,000	Dem/Liberal

Spending in Last Election

	1988
McNulty	$273,505
Opponent	$174,790
Vote Pct	62%

---

* Contributions came from more than one PAC affiliated with this sponsor.

Jan Meyers, R-Kan (3)

1988 Committees & Subcommittees

First elected: 1984
Total receipts: $201,229
Total from PACs: $110,395

Foreign Affairs
Europe and the Middle East
Human Rights and International Organizations

Small Business
Regulation and Business Opportunities
SBA and the General Economy

Select Aging
Health and Long-Term Care
Human Services

PAC Contribution Profile

Business

Automotive	**$3,750**
Auto Dealers & Drivers for Free Trade	$2,000
Others	$1,750
Aviation & Aerospace	**$4,750**
Beech Aircraft	$1,000
Boeing Company	$1,000
Federal Express Corp	$1,000
UNC Inc	$1,000
Others	$750
Business Associations	**$1,850**
National Fedn of Independent Business	$1,250
Others	$600
Chemicals	**$3,050**
Dow Chemical*	$1,100
Others	$1,950
Construction	**$10,850**
Associated General Contractors	$2,500
National Assn of Home Builders	$2,500
Sheet Metal/AirCon Contractors	$1,500
National Electrical Contractors Assn	$1,000
Others	$3,350
Financial Institutions	**$4,000**
Kansas Bankers Assn	$2,000
Others	$2,000
Food & Beverage	**$5,150**
Pepsico Inc	$1,250
National Restaurant Assn	$1,000
Others	$2,900

Campaign Revenue Sources

Party (1.0%)
Other (3.9%)
PACs (53.0%)
Individuals (42.1%)

Health Professionals	**$12,500**
American Medical Assn	$5,000
Kansas Medical Assn	$2,500
American Dental Assn	$1,500
American Academy of Ophthalmology	$1,000
Others	$2,500
Insurance	**$13,050**
National Assn of Life Underwriters	$3,500
Business Mens Assurance Company	$2,500
Mutual Benefit Life Insurance	$1,500
Kansas City Life Insurance	$1,250
Independent Insurance Agents of America	$1,000
Others	$3,300
Publishing	**$2,750**
Hallmark Cards	$2,250
Others	$500
Railroads	**$5,875**
Kansas City Southern	$3,000
Santa Fe Southern Pacific	$1,250
Burlington Northern	$1,125
Others	$500
Real Estate	**$3,600**
National Assn of Realtors	$2,500
Others	$1,100
Telecommunications	**$9,500**
AT&T	$3,000
Continental Telecom	$2,500
Southwestern Bell	$2,000
United Telecommunications	$2,000
Trucking/Delivery	**$3,530**
Yellow Freight System	$1,430
United Parcel Service	$1,250
Others	$850

PAC Totals by Category

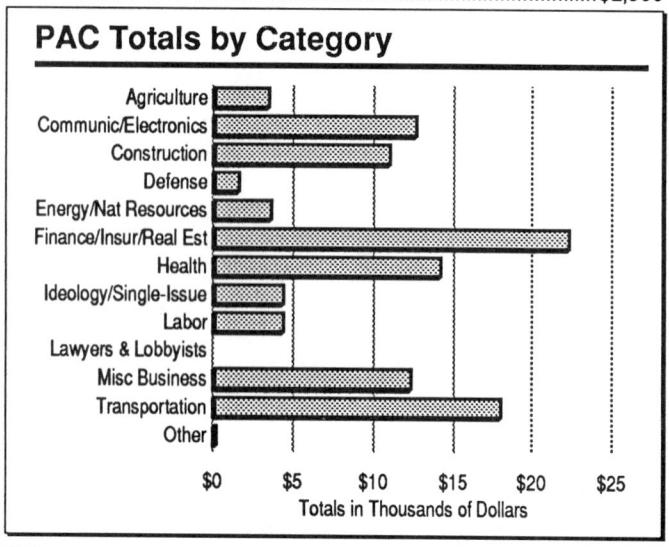

Totals in Thousands of Dollars

Agriculture
Communic/Electronics
Construction
Defense
Energy/Nat Resources
Finance/Insur/Real Est
Health
Ideology/Single-Issue
Labor
Lawyers & Lobbyists
Misc Business
Transportation
Other

$0 $5 $10 $15 $20 $25

Other Major Business PACs

American Hospital Assn	$1,000	Hospitals
H & R Block	$1,000	Tax Svcs

Labor

Labor Unions...**$4,250**

    National Education Assn* $2,250
    Marine Engineers Union $1,000
    National Assn of Retired Federal Employees $1,000

Ideological/Single-Issue

Pro-Israel **$3,000**

    Chai PAC $1,500
    Hudson Valley PAC $1,000
    Others $500

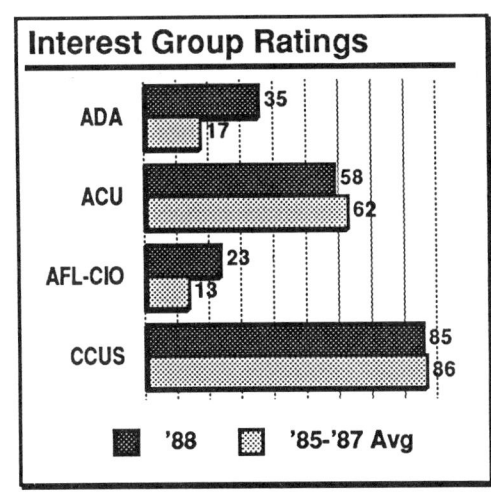

Interest Group Ratings

	'88	'85-'87 Avg
ADA	35	17
ACU	58	62
AFL-CIO	23	13
CCUS	85	86

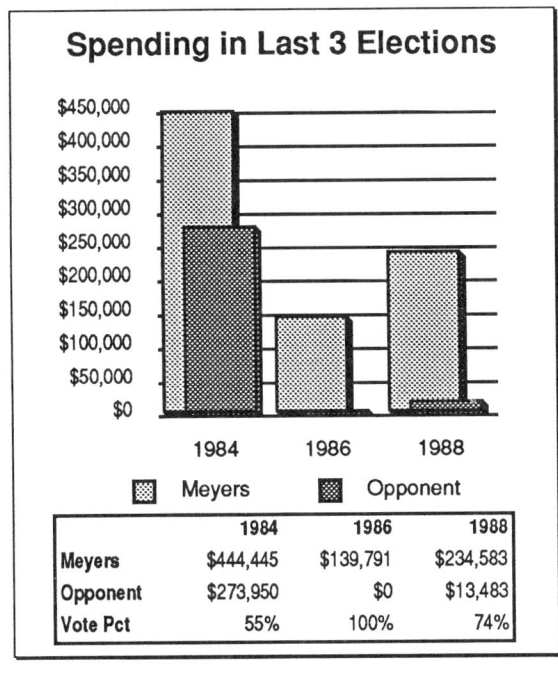

Spending in Last 3 Elections

Meyers / Opponent

	1984	1986	1988
Meyers	$444,445	$139,791	$234,583
Opponent	$273,950	$0	$13,483
Vote Pct	55%	100%	74%

---

* Contributions came from more than one PAC affiliated with this sponsor.

Kweisi Mfume, D-Md (7)

First elected: 1986
Total receipts: $130,466
Total from PACs: $72,250

1988 Committees & Subcommittees

Banking, Finance and Urban Affairs
Economic Stabilization
Housing and Community Development
International Development Institutions and Finance

Small Business
Export, Tourism and Special Problems
Procurement, Innovation and Minority Enterprise Development

Select Narcotics Abuse and Control

PAC Contribution Profile

Business

Commercial Banks	*$5,810*
American Bankers Assn	$2,000
Others	$3,810
Health Professionals	*$5,750*
American Medical Assn	$2,750
Maryland Medical Assn	$2,000
American Academy of Ophthalmology	$1,000
Lawyers	*$6,000*
Assn of Trial Lawyers of America	$6,000
Package Delivery	*$1,500*
United Parcel Service	$1,500
Real Estate	*$3,500*
National Assn of Realtors	$3,250
Others	$250
Savings Banks & Credit Unions	*$2,250*
US League of Savings Assn	$1,250
Others	$1,000
Securities Investment	*$6,250*
Alex Brown Inc	$2,000
Goldman Sachs	$1,500
Municipal Securities Industry	$1,000
Others	$1,750

Campaign Revenue Sources

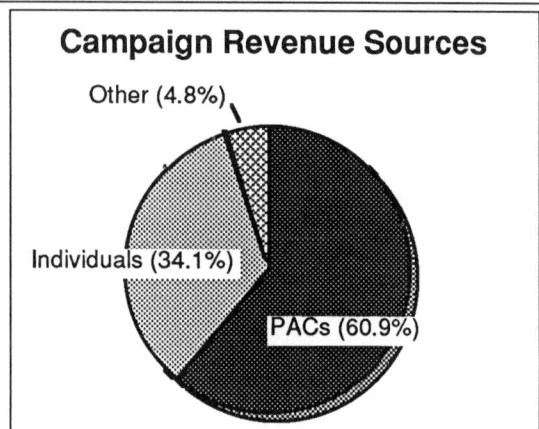

Other (4.8%)
Individuals (34.1%)
PACs (60.9%)

Other Major Business PACs

J C Penney Company	$1,000	Dept Store
Auto Dealers & Drivers for Free Trade	$1,000	JapanAutoSal

PAC Totals by Category

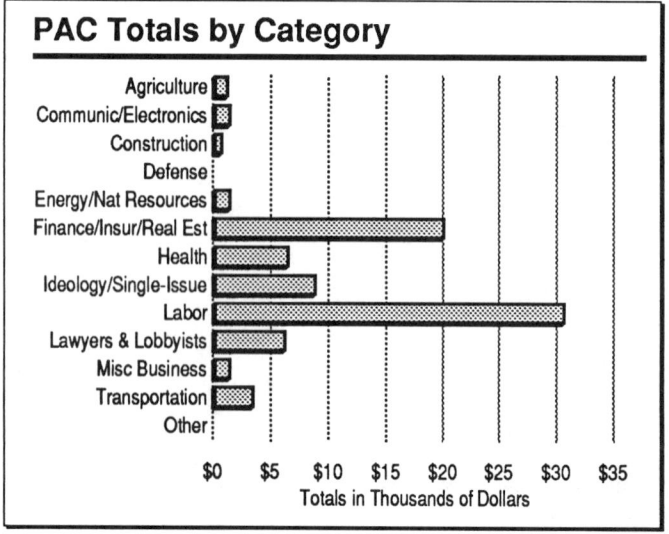

Agriculture
Communic/Electronics
Construction
Defense
Energy/Nat Resources
Finance/Insur/Real Est
Health
Ideology/Single-Issue
Labor
Lawyers & Lobbyists
Misc Business
Transportation
Other

$0 $5 $10 $15 $20 $25 $30 $35
Totals in Thousands of Dollars

Labor

Bldg Trades/Industrial/Misc Unions $13,650

AFL-CIO*	$1,750
Food & Commercial Workers Union	$1,750
Machinists/Aerospace Workers Union	$1,650
Carpenters & Joiners Union*	$1,620
United Auto Workers	$1,500
Operating Engineers Union	$1,000
Sheet Metal Workers Union	$1,000
Others	$3,380

Government & Postal Workers $7,950

American Fedn of State/County/Munic Employees	$2,500
National Assn of Letter Carriers	$2,300
American Postal Workers Union	$1,000
National Assn of Retired Federal Employees	$1,000
Others	$1,150

Teachers Unions $5,500

National Education Assn	$5,000
Others	$500

Transportation Unions $3,100

Seafarers International Union	$1,500
Others	$1,800

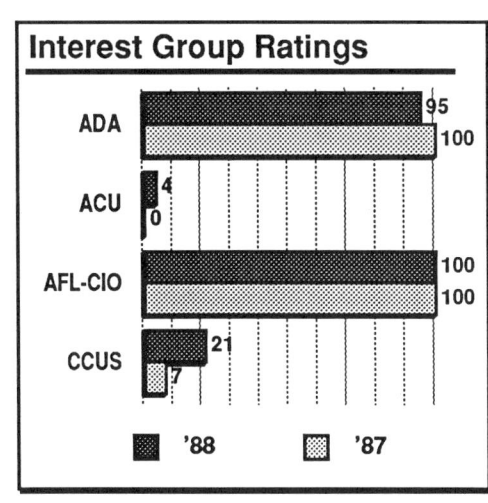

Interest Group Ratings

	'88	'87
ADA	95	100
ACU	4	0
AFL-CIO	100	100
CCUS	21	7

■ '88   ▨ '87

Ideological/Single-Issue

Pro-Israel $5,350

National PAC	$5,000
Others	$350

Other Major Ideological/Single-Issue PACs

National Cmte to Preserve Social Security	$1,500	Soc Secur
Valley Education Fund (Tony Coelho)	$1,000	Dem Leaders

Independent expenditures supporting Mfume

National Cmte to Preserve Social Security	$1,139

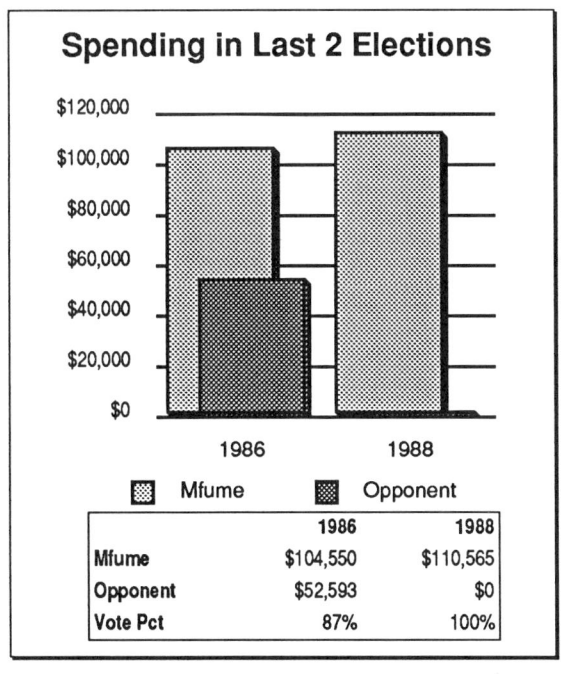

Spending in Last 2 Elections

	Mfume	Opponent

	1986	1988
Mfume	$104,550	$110,565
Opponent	$52,593	$0
Vote Pct	87%	100%

---

* Contributions came from more than one PAC affiliated with this sponsor.

741

Robert H. Michel, R-Ill (18)

1988 Committees & Subcommittees

Minority Leader

First elected: 1956
Total receipts: $877,026
Total from PACs: $558,417

PAC Contribution Profile

Business

Automotive	**$18,500**
Auto Dealers & Drivers for Free Trade	$6,000
National Auto Dealers Assn	$5,000
Ford Motor Company	$3,000
Chrysler Corp	$2,000
General Motors	$2,000
Others	$500

Commercial Banks	**$20,600**
American Bankers Assn	$10,000
J P Morgan & Company	$2,500
Barnett Banks of Florida	$2,000
First Chicago Corp	$2,000
Independent Bankers Assn	$2,000
Others	$2,100

Construction	**$22,395**
Caterpillar Tractor	$5,145
Associated General Contractors	$5,000
American Road & Transportation Builders Assn	$2,000
National Assn of Home Builders	$2,000
Sheet Metal/AirCon Contractors	$2,000
Others	$6,250

Defense	**$32,500**
McDonnell Douglas*	$5,500
Lockheed Corp	$3,000
Rockwell International	$3,000
General Dynamics	$2,500
Allied-Signal	$2,000
Grumman	$2,000
Hughes Aircraft	$2,000
Martin Marietta Corp	$2,000
Northrop Corp	$2,000
United Technologies	$2,000
Others	$6,500

Campaign Revenue Sources

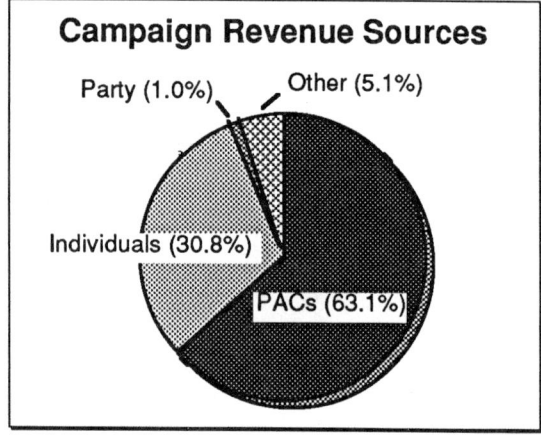

Party (1.0%) Other (5.1%)
Individuals (30.8%)
PACs (63.1%)

Electronics & Computers	**$13,600**
Westinghouse Electric	$3,500
General Electric	$2,000
Motorola Inc	$2,000
Others	$6,100

Food & Beverage	**$44,800**
National Beer Wholesalers Assn	$8,000
Food Marketing Institute	$5,000
A E Staley Manufacturing Company	$3,000
Anheuser-Busch	$2,000
Brown-Forman Distillers	$2,000
Hiram Walker & Sons	$2,000
Joseph E Seagram & Sons	$2,000
Pepsi-Cola Bottlers Assn	$2,000
Pepsico Inc	$2,000
Wine & Spirits Wholesalers of America	$2,000
Others	$14,800

Health Professionals	**$31,600**
American Dental Assn	$10,000
American Medical Assn	$8,000
American College of Emergency Physicians	$3,000
Illinois Medical Assn	$2,500
American Optometric Assn	$2,000
American Podiatry Assn	$2,000
Co-op of American Physicians	$2,000
Others	$2,100

Hospitals & Nursing Homes	**$15,000**
American Health Care Assn	$5,000
Beverly Enterprises	$3,000
Federation of America Hospitals	$2,000
National Medical Enterprises Inc	$2,000
Voluntary Hospitals of America	$2,000
Others	$1,000

Insurance	**$34,675**
National Assn of Life Underwriters	$5,000
Kemper Insurance	$2,175
American Council of Life Insurance	$2,000
CNA Financial Corp	$2,000
Equitable Financial Services	$2,000
Health Insurance Assn of America	$2,000
Independent Insurance Agents of America	$2,000
Metropolitan Life Insurance	$2,000
National Assn of Independent Insurers	$2,000
Travelers Corp	$2,000
Others	$11,500

PAC Totals by Category

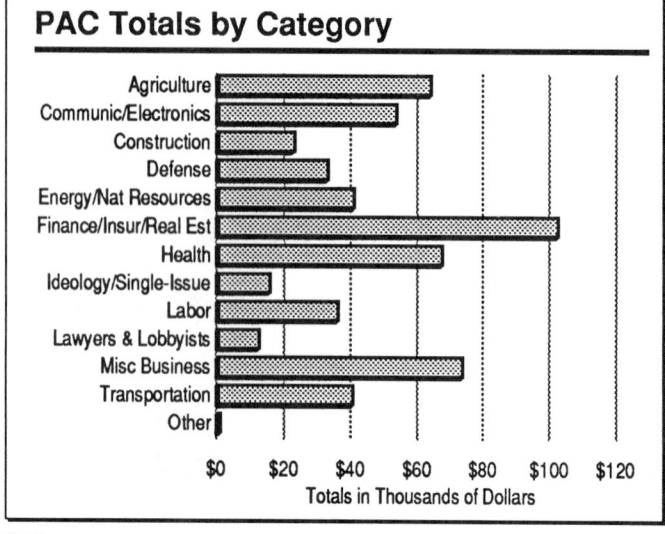

Agriculture
Communic/Electronics
Construction
Defense
Energy/Nat Resources
Finance/Insur/Real Est
Health
Ideology/Single-Issue
Labor
Lawyers & Lobbyists
Misc Business
Transportation
Other

$0 $20 $40 $60 $80 $100 $120
Totals in Thousands of Dollars

Lawyers & Lobbyists **$12,000**
    Assn of Trial Lawyers of America $5,000
    Others $7,000

Oil & Gas **$24,950**
    Amoco Corp $3,000
    Ashland Oil $2,000
    Atlantic Richfield $2,000
    Coastal Corp $2,000
    Phillips Petroleum $2,000
    Others $13,950

Pharmaceuticals **$20,200**
    Smithkline Beckman $6,000
    Abbott Laboratories $2,000
    American Home Products Corp $2,000
    Bristol-Myers $2,000
    Squibb Corp $2,000
    Sterling Drug $2,000
    Others $4,200

Real Estate **$14,500**
    National Assn of Realtors $10,000
    American Land Title Assn $2,000
    Mortgage Bankers Assn of America $2,000
    Others $500

Savings Banks & Credit Unions **$11,500**
    US League of Savings Assn $5,000
    Credit Union National Assn $3,000
    Others $3,500

Securities & Commodities **$20,500**
    Chicago Mercantile Exchange $7,500
    Chicago Board of Trade $5,000
    Morgan Stanley & Company $5,000
    E F Hutton Group $2,000
    Others $1,000

Telecommunications **$29,850**
    AT&T $7,000
    Illinois Bell Telephone $5,800
    BellSouth Corp* $5,000
    Bell Atlantic $4,000
    Pacific Telesis Group $2,000
    Others $6,050

Interest Group Ratings

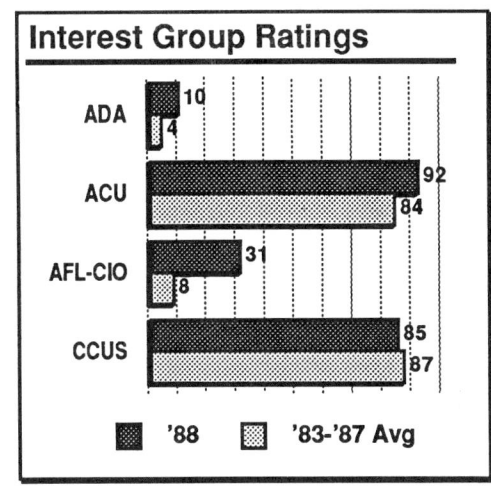

	'88	'83-'87 Avg
ADA	10	4
ACU	92	84
AFL-CIO	31	8
CCUS	85	87

Tobacco **$13,135**
    Philip Morris $4,000
    United States Tobacco Company $3,000
    Tobacco Institute $2,135
    RJR Nabisco $2,000
    Others $2,000

Other Major Business PACs

United Parcel Service	$5,915	Delivery
American Institute of CPA's	$5,000	Accountants
Archer-Daniels-Midland Corp	$5,000	Grain Trader
National Cable Television Assn	$5,000	CableTV
Federal Express Corp	$3,000	Delivery
Navistar International	$3,000	Farm Equip
Illinois Power Company	$2,860	Gas & Electr
ACRE (Action Committee for Rural Electric)	$2,000	RuralElect
American Assn of Equipment Lessors	$2,000	Rentals
American Hotel & Motel Assn	$2,000	Hotel/Motel
Bowling Proprietors Assn	$2,000	AmuseCtr
Deere & Company	$2,000	Farm Equip
FMC Corp	$2,000	Chemicals
Household International	$2,000	Credit/Loans
Interlake Inc	$2,000	Indust Equip
National Assn of Broadcasters	$2,000	TV/Radio
National Office Products Assn	$2,000	Off Machines
Society of American Florists	$2,000	Florists
Union Pacific Corp	$2,000	Railroads

Labor

Bldg Trades/Industrial/Misc Unions **$18,000**
    Laborers Union/Springfield, Ilinois $3,000
    National Rural Letter Carriers Assn $3,000
    Hotel/Restaurant Employees Union $2,000
    National Assn of Letter Carriers $2,000
    National Assn of Retired Federal Employees $2,000
    National League of Postmasters $2,000
    Others $4,000

Transportation Unions **$17,500**
    Air Line Pilots Assn $10,000
    Teamsters Union $5,000
    Marine Engineers Dist 2 Retirees $2,500

Major Ideological/Single-Issue PACs

National PAC .... $5,000   Pro-Israel

---

* Contributions came from more than one PAC affiliated
  with this sponsor.

Spending in Last 3 Elections

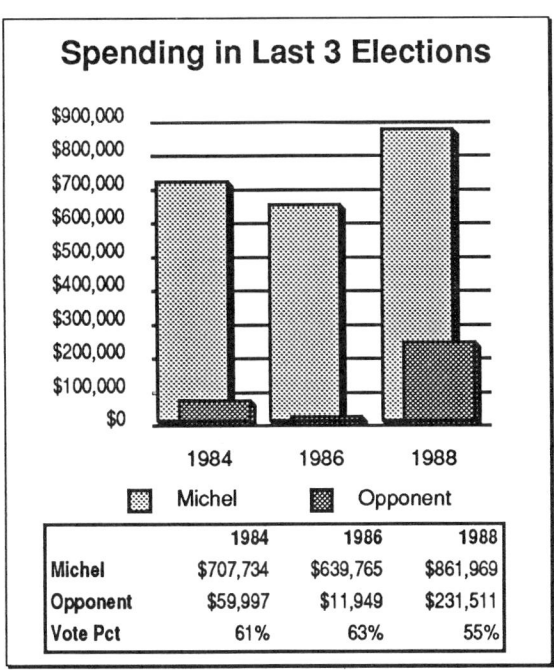

	Michel	Opponent

	1984	1986	1988
Michel	$707,734	$639,765	$861,969
Opponent	$59,997	$11,949	$231,511
Vote Pct	61%	63%	55%

Clarence E. Miller, R-Ohio (10)

First elected: 1966
Total receipts: $129,695
Total from PACs: $99,436

1988 Committees & Subcommittees

Appropriations
Defense

PAC Contribution Profile

Auto Dealers **$8,750**

    National Auto Dealers Assn $5,250
    Auto Dealers & Drivers for Free Trade $3,500

Construction **$8,000**

    Associated General Contractors $2,500
    Manville Corp $1,500
    National Assn of Home Builders $1,500
    Associated Builders & Contractors $1,000
    Others $1,500

Dairy **$4,600**

    Associated Milk Producers $3,500
    Others $1,100

Defense **$26,700**

    Hughes Aircraft $3,000
    AT&T $2,500
    Lockheed Corp $2,000
    Rockwell International $2,000
    United Technologies $1,500
    McDonnell Douglas* $1,050
    General Dynamics $1,000
    General Electric $1,000
    Northrop Corp $1,000
    Tenneco Inc $1,000
    Textron Inc $1,000
    Others $9,650

Electric Utilities **$1,750**

    American Electric Power* $1,250
    Others $500

Campaign Revenue Sources

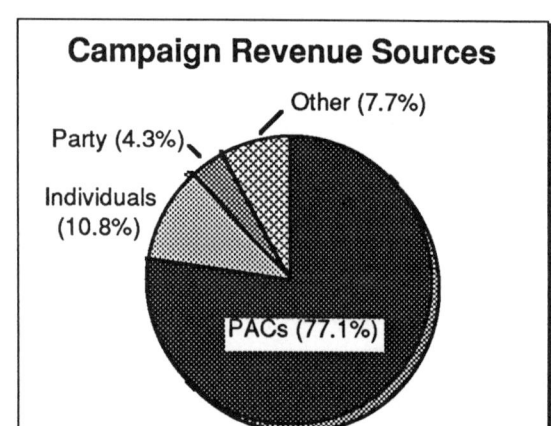

Other (7.7%)
Party (4.3%)
Individuals (10.8%)
PACs (77.1%)

Financial Institutions **$2,500**

    None over $500

Food & Beverage **$2,000**

    National Beer Wholesalers Assn $1,000
    Others $1,000

Health Professionals **$7,250**

    American Medical Assn $4,750
    American Dental Assn $2,000
    Others $500

Insurance **$2,750**

    National Assn of Life Underwriters $2,500
    Others $250

Oil & Gas **$4,050**

    Chevron Corp $1,250
    Ashland Oil $1,000
    Others $1,800

Real Estate **$8,000**

    National Assn of Realtors $8,000

Tobacco **$3,750**

    Philip Morris $2,000
    Tobacco Institute $1,000
    Others $750

Other Major Business PACs

Ohio Farm Bureau Federation .... $1,500   Farm Orgs

PAC Totals by Category

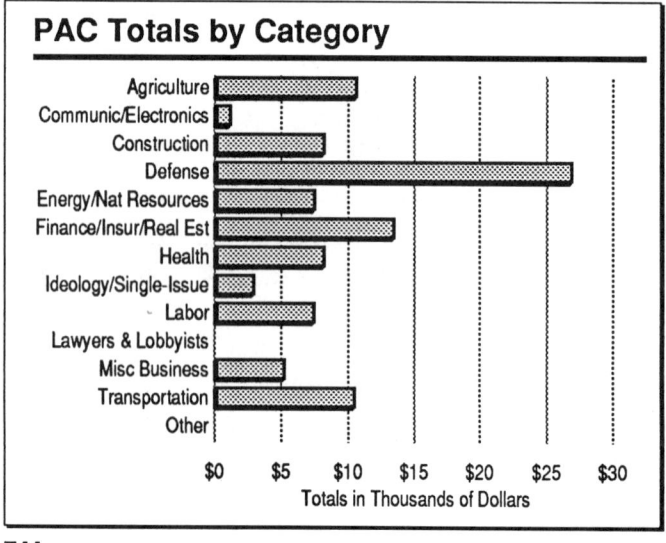

Agriculture
Communic/Electronics
Construction
Defense
Energy/Nat Resources
Finance/Insur/Real Est
Health
Ideology/Single-Issue
Labor
Lawyers & Lobbyists
Misc Business
Transportation
Other

$0 $5 $10 $15 $20 $25 $30
Totals in Thousands of Dollars

Labor

Labor Unions **$7,250**

    Marine Engineers District 2 Maritime Officers $3,500
    Teamsters Union $2,000
    United Auto Workers $1,000
    Others $750

Ideological/Single-Issue

Ideological/Single-Issue **$2,736**

Arizona Politically Interested Citizens .... $1,000   Pro-Israel
Others $1,736

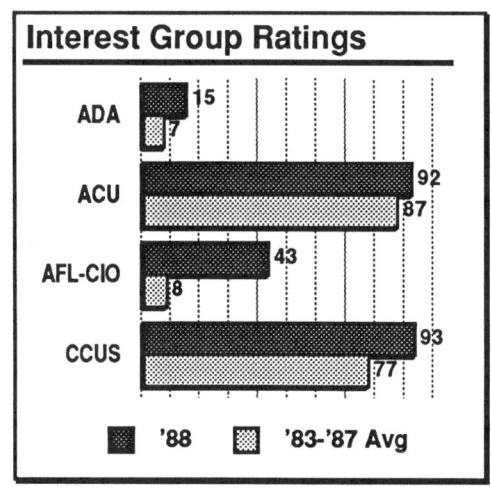

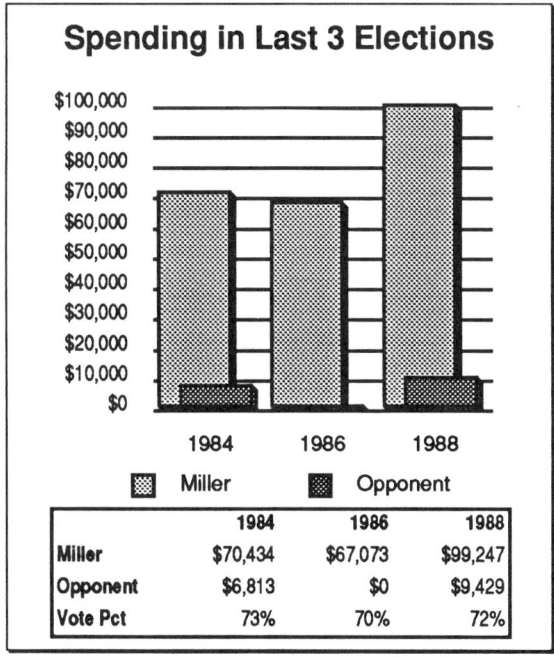

	1984	1986	1988
Miller	$70,434	$67,073	$99,247
Opponent	$6,813	$0	$9,429
Vote Pct	73%	70%	72%

---

* Contributions came from more than one PAC affiliated
  with this sponsor.

George Miller, D-Calif (7)

First elected: 1974
Total receipts: $429,305
Total from PACs: $179,984

1988 Committees & Subcommittees

Budget
State and Local Government (Chairman)
Budget Process
Defense and International Affairs
Income Security

Interior and Insular Affairs
Water and Power Resources (Chairman)
Energy and the Environment
General Oversight and Investigations
Mining and Natural Resources

Select Children, Youth and Families (Chairman)

PAC Contribution Profile

Business

Commodities/Securities Investment	**$2,150**
Chicago Board of Trade	$1,500
Others	$650
Construction	**$2,500**
National Assn of Home Builders	$1,600
Others	$900
Electric Utilities	**$14,125**
Southern California Edison	$7,000
Pacific Gas & Electric	$3,275
Pacific Power & Light	$1,000
Others	$2,850
Health Professionals	**$3,950**
American Medical Assn	$1,300
American Dental Assn	$1,000
Others	$1,650
Insurance	**$3,200**
Continental Insurance	$2,000
Others	$1,200
Lawyers	**$7,450**
Assn of Trial Lawyers of America	$2,550
California Trial Lawyers Assn	$2,000
Akin, Gump, Hauer & Feld	$1,200
Others	$1,700
Nuclear Power Equipment	**$3,500**
Bechtel Corp	$2,000
Others	$1,500

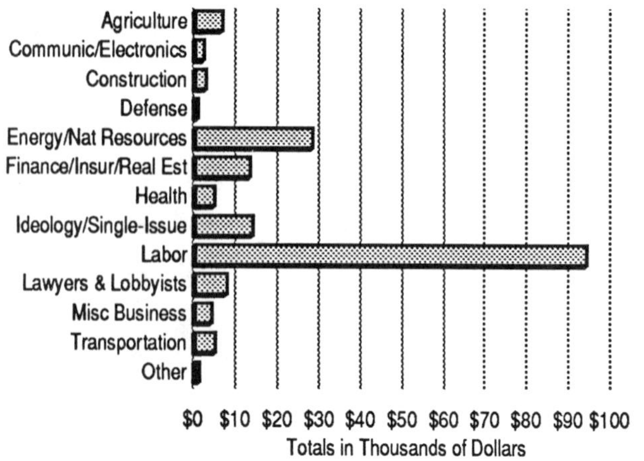

Campaign Revenue Sources

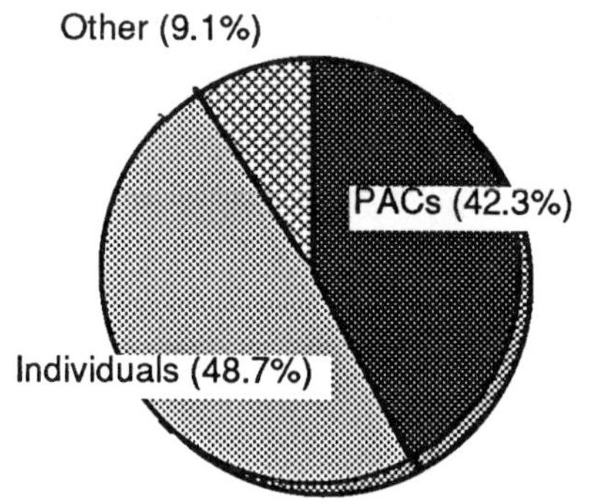

Other (9.1%)
PACs (42.3%)
Individuals (48.7%)

Oil & Gas	**$8,900**
Chevron Corp	$3,650
Atlantic Richfield	$1,600
Coastal Corp	$1,250
Others	$2,400
Real Estate	**$7,650**
National Assn of Realtors	$6,850
Others	$800
Sugar Growers	**$2,050**
None over $600	

Other Major Business PACs

Pacific Telesis Group	$1,300	Phone Util
Waste Management Inc	$1,100	Waste Mgmt
Auto Dealers & Drivers for Free Trade	$1,000	JapanAutoSal
Circus Circus Enterprises	$1,000	Casinos/Gamb
Kansas City Southern	$1,000	Railroads

PAC Totals by Category

Agriculture
Communic/Electronics
Construction
Defense
Energy/Nat Resources
Finance/Insur/Real Est
Health
Ideology/Single-Issue
Labor
Lawyers & Lobbyists
Misc Business
Transportation
Other

$0 $10 $20 $30 $40 $50 $60 $70 $80 $90 $100
Totals in Thousands of Dollars

Labor

Bldg Trades/Industrial/Misc Unions $35,950
Operating Engineers Union* $5,650
Laborers' Western Political League $4,000
Carpenters & Joiners Union $3,500
Intl Brotherhood of Electrical Workers $3,000
Plumbers/Pipefitters Union* $3,000
United Auto Workers $2,800
AFL-CIO* $2,100
Machinists/Aerospace Workers Union $2,000
Oil, Chemical & Atomic Workers Union $2,000
Food & Commercial Workers Union $1,800
Hotel/Restaurant Employees Union $1,500
Ironworkers Union $1,500
Sheet Metal Workers Union $1,450
Service Employees International Union $1,050
Others $600

Government & Postal Workers $21,350
American Fedn of State/County/Munic Employees $6,000
National Assn of Retired Federal Employees $5,000
National Assn of Letter Carriers* $4,000
International Assn of Firefighters $2,600
American Postal Workers Union $1,650
Others $2,100

Teachers Unions $9,025
National Education Assn $6,325
American Federation of Teachers $2,700

Transportation Unions $27,550
Teamsters Union $10,000
Seafarers International Union* $5,950
Longshoremen/Warehousemen Union $2,500
Amalgamated Transit Union $2,000
United Transportation Union $2,000
Air Line Pilots Assn $1,000
Marine Engineers District 2 Maritime Officers $1,000
Others $3,100

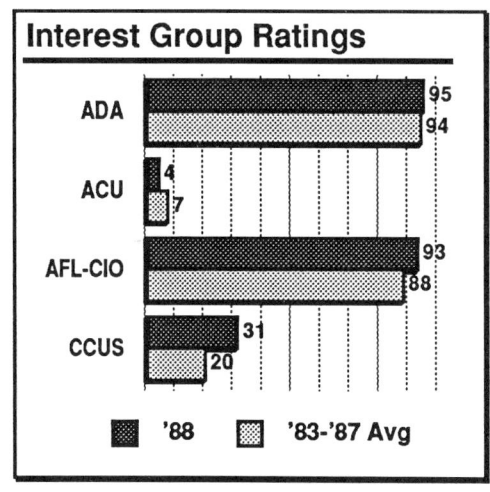

Interest Group Ratings

	'88	'83-'87 Avg
ADA	95	94
ACU	4	7
AFL-CIO	93	88
CCUS	31	20

Ideological/Single-Issue

Pro-Israel $6,250
Congressional Action Cmte of Texas $3,000
Delaware Valley PAC $2,500
Others $750

Other Major Ideological/Single-Issue PACs
Sierra Club	$2,200	Environment
National Cmte to Preserve Social Security	$1,800	Soc Secur
Valley Education Fund (Tony Coelho)	$1,000	Dem Leaders

Independent expenditures supporting Miller
American Ambulance Assn $2,000
National Cmte to Preserve Social Security $1,909

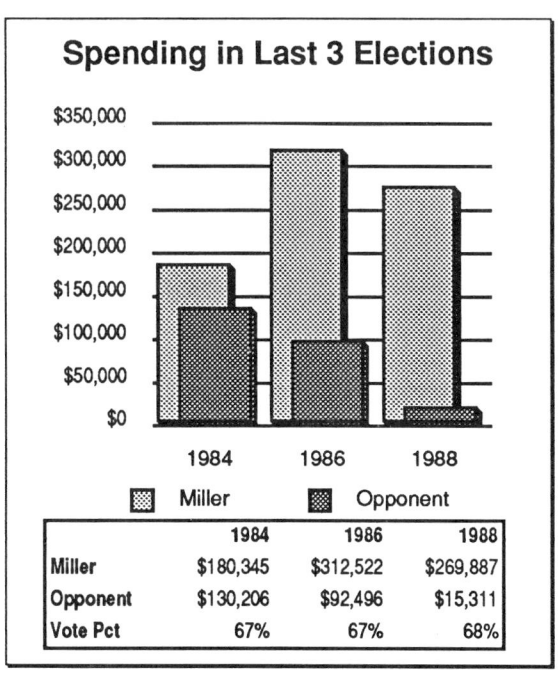

Spending in Last 3 Elections

Miller / Opponent

	1984	1986	1988
Miller	$180,345	$312,522	$269,887
Opponent	$130,206	$92,496	$15,311
Vote Pct	67%	67%	68%

* Contributions came from more than one PAC affiliated with this sponsor.

John Miller, R-Wash (1)

First elected: 1984
Total receipts: $1,328,979
Total from PACs: $333,560

1988 Committees & Subcommittees

Foreign Affairs
Human Rights and International Organizations
International Economic Policy and Trade

Merchant Marine and Fisheries
Fisheries and Wildlife Conservation and the Environment
Merchant Marine

PAC Contribution Profile

Business

Automotive	**$21,900**
Auto Dealers & Drivers for Free Trade	$15,000
National Auto Dealers Assn	$4,600
Eaton Corp	$1,500
Others	$800
Aviation & Aerospace	**$8,985**
Boeing Company	$7,210
Others	$1,775
Commercial & Savings Banks	**$8,410**
US Bancorp	$3,000
Rainier Bancorp	$1,410
Washington Savings League	$1,000
Others	$3,000
Construction	**$18,562**
National Assn of Home Builders	$7,500
Associated General Contractors	$6,000
National Utility Contractors Assn	$2,000
National Electrical Contractors Assn	$1,000
Others	$2,062
Defense	**$10,750**
Lockheed Corp	$2,100
Harris Corp	$2,000
E-Systems*	$1,750
General Dynamics	$1,250
Martin Marietta Corp	$1,000
Raytheon	$1,000
Others	$1,650

Campaign Revenue Sources

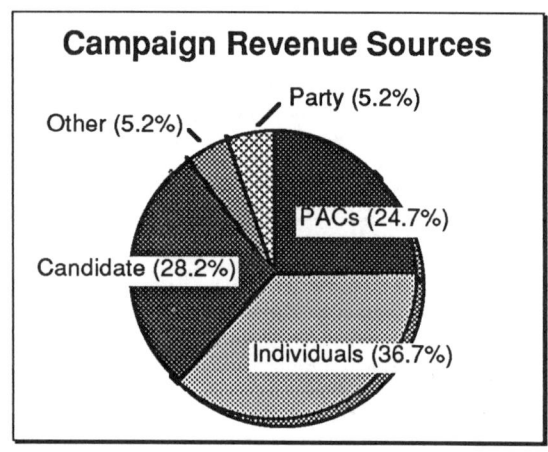

Other (5.2%)
Party (5.2%)
PACs (24.7%)
Candidate (28.2%)
Individuals (36.7%)

Electronics	**$9,550**
Cooper Industries	$3,000
Recognition Equipment Inc	$2,000
Honeywell Inc	$1,500
Esterline Corp	$1,000
Hewlett-Packard	$1,000
Others	$1,050
Food & Beverage	**$14,326**
Services Group of America	$5,375
National Restaurant Assn	$2,000
Peter Pan Seafoods	$1,250
Food Marketing Institute	$1,000
Pepsico Inc	$1,000
Pillsbury Company	$1,000
Others	$2,701
Forest Products	**$12,250**
Weyerhaeuser Company	$4,400
Simpson Investment Company	$3,250
Boise Cascade	$1,000
International Paper Company	$1,000
Others	$2,600
Health Professionals	**$19,749**
American Medical Assn	$9,899
American Optometric Assn	$6,500
American Nurses Assn	$1,500
American Dental Assn	$1,000
Others	$850
Insurance	**$9,800**
National Assn of Life Underwriters	$5,000
Safeco Corp	$2,000
Aetna Life & Casualty	$1,050
Others	$1,750
Oil & Gas	**$9,875**
Atlantic Richfield	$1,500
Chevron Corp	$1,300
Exxon Corp	$1,000
Mobil Oil	$1,000
Occidental Oil & Gas	$1,000
Phillips Petroleum	$1,000
Others	$3,075
Real Estate	**$10,550**
National Assn of Realtors	$10,000
Others	$550

PAC Totals by Category

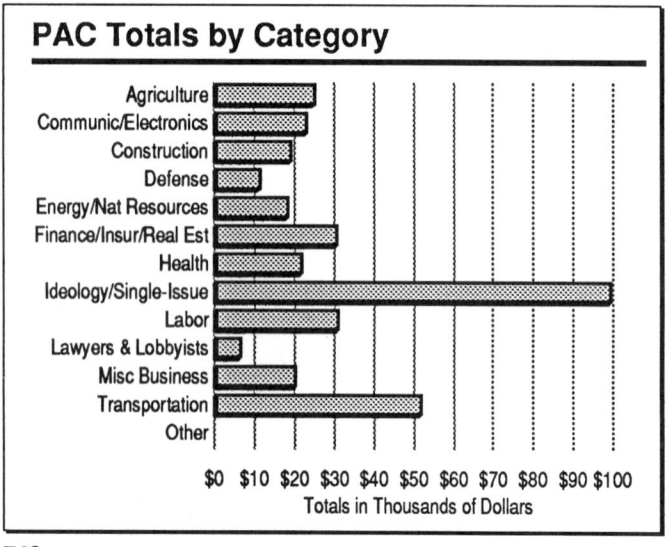

Agriculture
Communic/Electronics
Construction
Defense
Energy/Nat Resources
Finance/Insur/Real Est
Health
Ideology/Single-Issue
Labor
Lawyers & Lobbyists
Misc Business
Transportation
Other

$0 $10 $20 $30 $40 $50 $60 $70 $80 $90 $100
Totals in Thousands of Dollars

Sea Transport...$13,375

American Pilots Assn	$2,600
Matson Navigation	$2,500
American President Lines	$1,900
Crowley Maritime	$1,875
Totem Ocean Trailer Express	$1,875
Others	$2,625

Telecommunications $12,550

Pacific Northwest Bell	$5,600
United Telecommunications	$2,500
Continental Telecom	$2,000
GTE Corp	$1,450
AT&T	$1,000

Other Major Business PACs

Puget Sound Power & Light	$4,800	ElectricUtil
National Fedn of Independent Business	$2,584	Sml Business
Business Industry PAC	$2,128	Bus Assns
Garvey, Schubert & Barer	$2,000	Lawyers
Burlington Northern	$1,975	Railroads
United States Tobacco Company	$1,750	Tobacco
Perkins Coie	$1,500	Lawyers
United Parcel Service	$1,500	Delivery
National Fisheries Institute	$1,350	Fishing
Society of American Florists	$1,300	Florists
Southland Corp	$1,007	Dept Store
Foster, Pepper & Shefelman	$1,000	Lawyers
Fred Meyer Inc	$1,000	Dept Store
Santa Fe International Corp	$1,000	Trucking

Labor

Sea Transport Unions....................................$22,000

Marine Engineers Union*	$10,000
Seafarers International Union	$7,000
Masters, Mates & Pilots Union*	$4,500
Others	$500

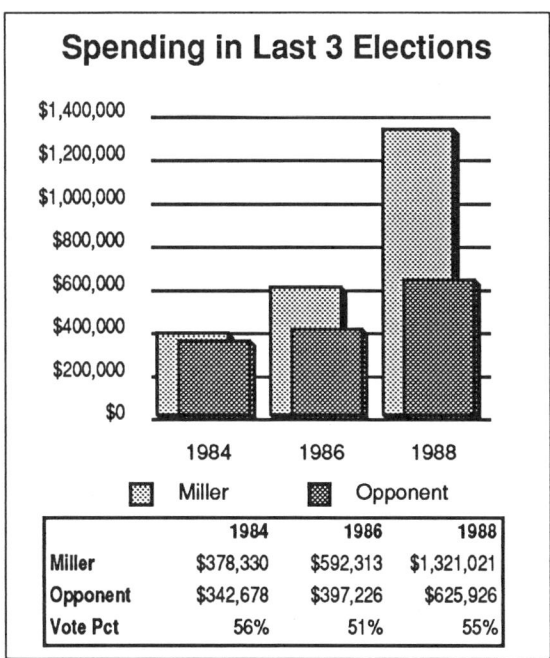

Spending in Last 3 Elections

	1984	1986	1988
Miller	$378,330	$592,313	$1,321,021
Opponent	$342,678	$397,226	$625,926
Vote Pct	56%	51%	55%

Miller   Opponent

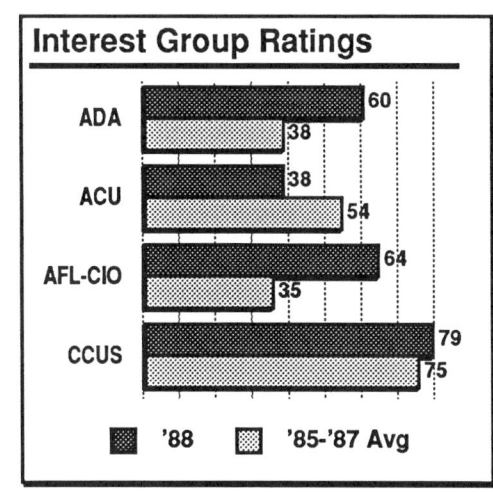

Interest Group Ratings

	'88	'85-'87 Avg
ADA	60	38
ACU	38	54
AFL-CIO	64	35
CCUS	79	75

Other Labor Unions $8,300

Air Line Pilots Assn	$2,500
Teamsters Union	$2,500
National Assn of Retired Federal Employees	$1,000
Others	$2,300

Ideological/Single-Issue

Gay/Lesbian Rights $17,000

Human Rights Campaign Fund	$10,000
Elections Cmte/Orange County	$7,000

Pro-Israel $63,628

Joint Action Cmte for Political Affairs	$10,000
National PAC	$10,000
Citizens Organized PAC	$5,000
Women's Pro-Israel National PAC	$5,000
Hudson Valley PAC	$4,698
Desert Caucus	$3,250
Roundtable PAC	$3,000
Americans for Good Government Inc	$2,500
Florida Congressional Cmte	$2,500
Garden State PAC	$2,000
Heartland PAC	$1,500
Maryland Assn for Concerned Citizens	$1,500
St Louisians for Better Government	$1,500
City PAC	$1,250
Capital PAC	$1,000
Committee for "18"	$1,000
East Midwood PAC	$1,000
Mid Manhattan PAC	$1,000
National Action Committee (NACPAC)	$1,000
Ocean State PAC	$1,000
Silver State PAC	$1,000
Others	$2,930

Republican Leadership PACs.........................$8,000

Fund for America's Future (George Bush)	$5,500
Fund for a Republican Majority (Ted Stevens)	$1,000
Policy Innovation PAC (Dick Armey)	$1,000
Others	$500

Other Major Ideological/Single-Issue PACs

Sierra Club	$5,000	Environment
League of Conservation Voters	$2,000	Environment
Public Service Research Council	$1,300	Anti-Union
Handgun Control Inc	$1,050	Anti-Guns

* Contributions came from more than one PAC affiliated with this sponsor.

Norman Y. Mineta, D-Calif (13)

First elected: 1974
Total receipts: $577,164
Total from PACs: $275,360

1988 Committees & Subcommittees

Public Works and Transportation
Aviation (Chairman)
Investigations and Oversight
Surface Transportation

Science, Space and Technology
Science, Research and Technology
Space Science and Applications

PAC Contribution Profile

Business

Aviation & Aerospace **$34,100**
Federal Express Corp $6,000
United Technologies $2,500
Boeing Company $2,000
LTV Aerospace & Defense Company $2,000
United Airlines $1,500
McDonnell Douglas $1,250
American Assn of Airport Executives $1,000
American Airlines $1,000
Chrysler Corp $1,000
Delta Airlines $1,000
General Dynamics $1,000
Genl Aviation Manufacturers Assn $1,000
Martin Marietta Corp $1,000
Northwest Airlines $1,000
Pan Am $1,000
Raytheon $1,000
Ryder System Inc $1,000
Trans World Airlines $1,000
USAir Corp $1,000
Worldcorp Inc $1,000
Others $4,850

Computers & Electronics **$9,000**
Computer Sciences Corp $1,500
National Semiconductor Corp $1,500
Asian American Manufacturers Assn $1,000
Tandem Computers $1,000
Westinghouse Electric $1,000
Others $3,000

Campaign Revenue Sources

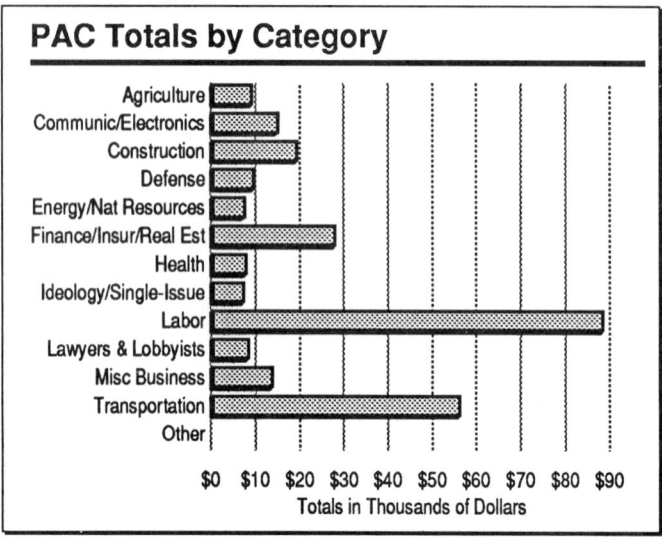

Other (9.7%)
PACs (45.8%)
Individuals (44.5%)

Construction **$18,840**
National Utility Contractors Assn $4,500
Sheet Metal/AirCon Contractors $2,590
Associated General Contractors $2,500
National Society of Professional Engineers $2,000
American Consulting Engineers Council $1,000
American Road & Transportation Bldrs Assn $1,000
Ch2M Hill $1,000
National Assn of Home Builders $1,000
Parsons Corp $1,000
Others $2,250

Defense **$9,000**
Lockheed Corp $2,250
Hughes Aircraft $1,500
E-Systems/Corporate Division $1,000
Hazeltine Corp $1,000
Litton Industries $1,000
Rockwell International $1,000
Others $1,250

Financial Institutions **$6,750**
American Bankers Assn $1,000
California Bankers Assn $1,000
Security Pacific Corp $1,000
Wells Fargo $1,000
Others $2,750

Health Professionals **$6,350**
American Medical Assn $3,850
Co-op of American Physicians $1,500
Others $1,000

Insurance **$9,650**
National Assn of Life Underwriters $3,000
Independent Insurance Agents of America $2,650
TransAmerica Life Companies $2,000
Travelers Corp $1,000
Others $1,000

Lawyers & Lobbyists **$7,850**
Crowell & Moring $1,000
Garvey, Schubert & Barer $1,000
Verner, Liipfert, Bernhard & McPherson $1,000
Others $4,850

PAC Totals by Category

Agriculture
Communic/Electronics
Construction
Defense
Energy/Nat Resources
Finance/Insur/Real Est
Health
Ideology/Single-Issue
Labor
Lawyers & Lobbyists
Misc Business
Transportation
Other

$0 $10 $20 $30 $40 $50 $60 $70 $80 $90
Totals in Thousands of Dollars

Real Estate **$7,500**
    National Assn of Realtors $7,000
    Others $500

Trucking/Delivery **$15,268**
    United Parcel Service $7,500
    Consolidated Freightways $2,500
    Yellow Freight System $1,500
    Viking Freight $1,018
    American Trucking Assns $1,000
    North American Van Lines $1,000
    Others $750

Other Major Business PACs

Waste Management Inc	$2,500	Waste Mgmt
American Assn of Equipment Lessors	$2,000	Rentals
Associated Milk Producers	$2,000	Dairy
FMC Corp	$2,000	Chemicals
National Venture Capital Assn	$2,000	Venture Cap
Pacific Telesis Group	$1,875	Phone Util
American Bus Assn	$1,000	Bus Svcs
American Express	$1,000	Credit/Loans
American Society of Travel Agents	$1,000	Travel Agent
AT&T	$1,000	LongDistance
Continental Telecom	$1,000	Phone Util
DGA International	$1,000	BusinessSvcs
Greater Washington Board of Trade	$1,000	Chamb/Cmrce
Mid-American Dairymen	$1,000	Dairy
Nabisco Brands Inc	$1,000	FoodProducts
National Beer Wholesalers Assn	$1,000	Liquor Whlsl
National Electric Sign Assn	$1,000	Advert/PR
Pacific Gas & Electric	$1,000	Gas & Electr
Santa Fe Southern Pacific	$1,000	Railroads
Southern California Edison	$1,000	ElectricUtil
Tobacco Institute	$1,000	Tobacco
Union Pacific Corp	$1,000	Railroads

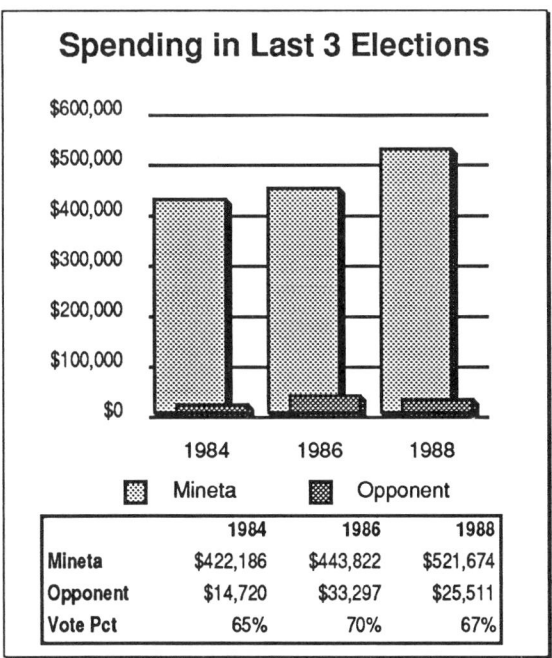

Spending in Last 3 Elections

	1984	1986	1988
Mineta	$422,186	$443,822	$521,674
Opponent	$14,720	$33,297	$25,511
Vote Pct	65%	70%	67%

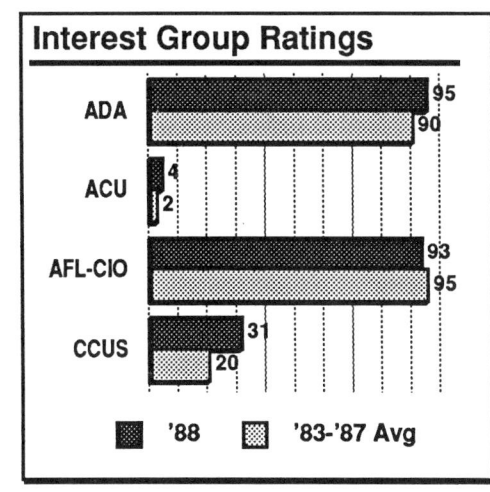

Interest Group Ratings

	'88	'83-'87 Avg
ADA	95	90
ACU	4	2
AFL-CIO	93	95
CCUS	31	20

Labor

Bldg Trades/Industrial/Misc Unions **$31,736**
    Carpenters & Joiners Union $4,500
    National Education Assn $4,500
    Machinists/Aerospace Workers Union $4,430
    Laborers' Western Political League $3,000
    Intl Brotherhood of Electrical Workers $2,916
    Food & Commercial Workers Union $2,600
    United Auto Workers $2,500
    Operating Engineers Union* $2,200
    AFL-CIO* $1,250
    Sheet Metal Workers Union $1,250
    Others $2,590

Government & Postal Workers **$15,630**
    National Assn of Retired Federal Employees $5,000
    National Assn of Letter Carriers $3,250
    American Postal Workers Union $2,350
    American Fedn of State/County/Munic Employees $1,500
    Retired Letter Carriers PAC $1,430
    National League of Postmasters $1,000
    Others $1,100

Transportation Unions **$40,500**
    Air Line Pilots Assn $10,000
    Teamsters Union $7,500
    Transport Workers Union $6,000
    Amalgamated Transit Union $4,000
    Assn of Flight Attendants $4,000
    Marine Engineers Union* $3,000
    Seafarers International Union $2,000
    United Transportation Union $1,500
    Transportation Communication Union $1,000
    Others $1,500

Ideological/Single-Issue

Ideological/Single-Issue **$6,195**
National Cmte to Preserve Social Security ......$2,000 Soc Secur
Valley Education Fund (Tony Coelho) ....$1,000 Dem Leaders
Washington PAC ....$1,000 Pro-Israel
Others $2,195

Independent expenditures supporting Mineta
National Cmte to Preserve Social Security $1,716

---

* Contributions came from more than one PAC affiliated
  with this sponsor.

Joe Moakley, D-Mass (9)

1988 Committees & Subcommittees

First elected: 1972
Total receipts: $385,654
Total from PACs: $180,830

Rules
Rules of the House (Chairman)

PAC Contribution Profile

Business

Accountants **$2,000**
    American Institute of CPA's $1,000
    Others $1,000

Aviation & Aerospace **$3,500**
    Federal Express Corp $1,000
    Others $2,500

Cable TV **$2,000**
    National Cable Television Assn $2,000

Commercial Banks **$11,600**
    American Bankers Assn $5,000
    Bank of Boston $1,200
    Barnett Banks of Florida $1,000
    Chase Manhattan $1,000
    Citicorp $1,000
    Others $2,400

Construction **$6,400**
    National Utility Contractors Assn $2,000
    Stone & Webster $1,400
    Manville Corp $1,000
    Others $2,000

Consumer Credit & Loans **$2,100**
    American Express $1,000
    Others $1,100

Defense **$5,800**
    Textron Inc $2,000
    Martin Marietta Corp $1,100
    Others $2,700

Campaign Revenue Sources

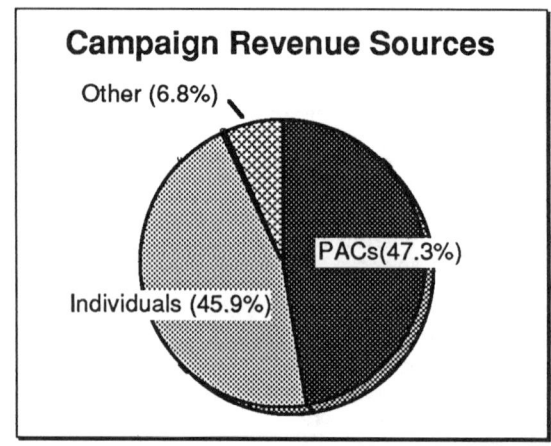

Other (6.8%)
PACs (47.3%)
Individuals (45.9%)

Electric Utilities **$3,000**
    Boston Edison $1,000
    Others $2,000

Food & Beverage **$6,950**
    General Mills* $1,500
    National Beer Wholesalers Assn $1,500
    Pillsbury Company $1,000
    Others $2,950

Health Professionals **$6,600**
    American Medical Assn $5,600
    American Podiatry Assn $1,000

Insurance **$22,166**
    Massachusetts Mutual Life Insurance $3,000
    National Assn of Life Underwriters $2,000
    New England Mutual Life $2,000
    American Council of Life Insurance $1,866
    John Hancock Financial Service $1,500
    National Assn Mutual Insurance Agents $1,500
    Travelers Corp $1,500
    Blue Cross & Blue Shield Assn $1,000
    Casualty & Surety Agents Assn $1,000
    Independent Insurance Agents of America $1,000
    Liberty Mutual Insurance $1,000
    Prudential Insurance $1,000
    Others $3,800

Lawyers & Lobbyists **$2,750**
    None over $500

Oil & Gas **$4,250**
    Coastal Corp $1,500
    Others $2,750

Railroads **$2,500**
    Norfolk Southern Corp $1,000
    Union Pacific Corp $1,000
    Others $500

Savings Banks & Credit Unions **$6,300**
    US League of Savings Assn $2,500
    National Council of Savings Institutions $2,000
    Credit Union National Assn $1,000
    Others $800

PAC Totals by Category

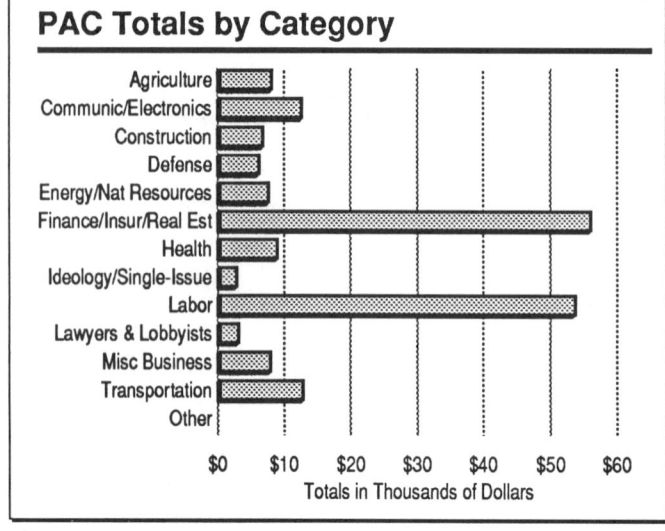

Categories (Totals in Thousands of Dollars): Agriculture, Communic/Electronics, Construction, Defense, Energy/Nat Resources, Finance/Insur/Real Est, Health, Ideology/Single-Issue, Labor, Lawyers & Lobbyists, Misc Business, Transportation, Other

Securities & Commodities **$12,500**

    Chicago Board of Trade $2,000
    Kidder, Peabody $2,000
    Shearson Lehman Hutton $2,000
    Dean Witter Reynolds* $1,900
    Investment Company Institute....................$1,500
    Investors Diversified Services $1,000
    Morgan Stanley & Company $1,000
    Others $1,100

Telecommunications **$8,980**

    AT&T $3,000
    New England Tel & Tel $2,380
    GTE Corp $2,200
    Others $1,400

Trucking/Delivery **$3,900**

    Ryder System Inc $2,000
    United Parcel Service $1,400
    Others $500

Other Major Business PACs

Ocean Spray Cranberries Inc	$1,500	Fruit/Veg
Greyhound Corp	$1,000	Hhold Chem

Labor

Bldg Trades/Industrial/Misc Unions **$20,500**

    Ironworkers Union $3,000
    Carpenters & Joiners Union $2,500
    Operating Engineers Union $2,500
    Laborers' Political League $1,500
    Machinists/Aerospace Workers Union $1,500
    National Education Assn $1,100
    AFL-CIO* $1,000
    Food & Commercial Workers Union............$1,000
    Ladies Garment Workers Union $1,000
    Plumbers/Pipefitters Union $1,000
    United Auto Workers $1,000
    Others $3,400

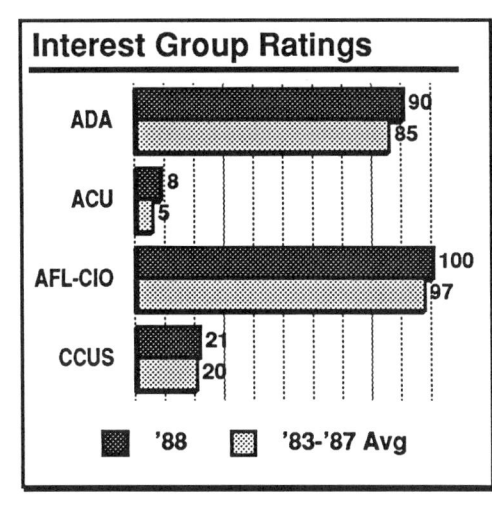

Interest Group Ratings

Group	'88	'83-'87 Avg
ADA	90	85
ACU	8	5
AFL-CIO	100	97
CCUS	21	20

Government & Postal Workers **$12,100**

    National Assn of Government Employees $3,000
    National Assn of Retired Federal Employees ...$3,000
    National Assn of Letter Carriers $1,500
    American Postal Workers Union $1,200
    American Fedn of State/County/Munic Employees $1,000
    National Treasury Employees Union $1,000
    Others $1,400

Transportation Unions **$20,700**

    Teamsters Union* $7,500
    Air Line Pilots Assn...................................$5,000
    Seafarers International Union $2,500
    United Transportation Union $2,300
    Marine Engineers Union $2,000
    Others $1,400

Major Ideological/Single-Issue PACs

Valley Education Fund (Tony Coelho) ....$1,000   Dem Leaders

Independent expenditures supporting Moakley

National Cmte to Preserve Social Security $1,620

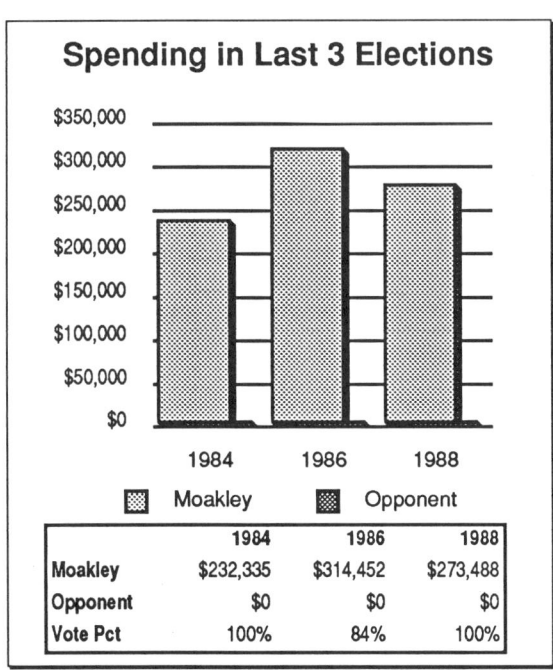

Spending in Last 3 Elections

	1984	1986	1988
Moakley	$232,335	$314,452	$273,488
Opponent	$0	$0	$0
Vote Pct	100%	84%	100%

Moakley   Opponent

---

* Contributions came from more than one PAC affiliated
with this sponsor.

Guy V. Molinari, R-NY (14)

First elected: 1980
Total receipts: $212,952
Total from PACs: $77,006

1988 Committees & Subcommittees

Public Works and Transportation
Public Buildings and Grounds (Ranking Republican)
Investigations and Oversight
Water Resources

PAC Contribution Profile

Campaign Revenue Sources

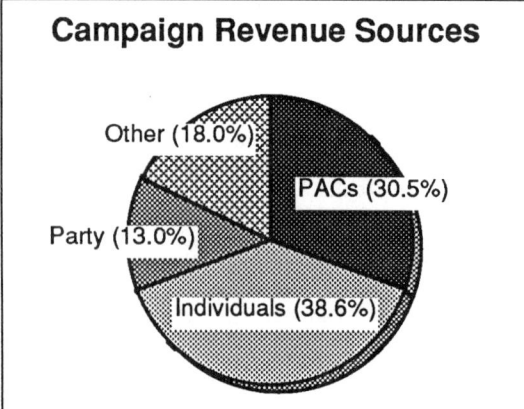

Other (18.0%)
PACs (30.5%)
Party (13.0%)
Individuals (38.6%)

Business

Auto Dealers	**$1,750**
Auto Dealers & Drivers for Free Trade	$1,500
Others	$250
Commercial & Savings Banks	**$2,775**
American Bankers Assn	$1,000
Anchor Savings Bank	$500
Others	$1,275
Construction	**$4,350**
National Utility Contractors Assn	$2,000
Associated General Contractors	$1,250
National Assn of Home Builders	$1,000
Others	$100
Food & Beverage	**$1,250**
Pepsico Inc	$1,000
Others	$250
Health Professionals	**$11,750**
American Medical Assn	$7,400
New York Medical Assn	$2,850
American Dental Assn	$1,000
American Podiatry Assn	$500
Insurance	**$2,900**
National Assn of Life Underwriters	$2,500
Others	$400
Oil & Gas	**$1,500**
Mobil Oil	$1,000
Brooklyn Union Gas Company	$500

Real Estate	**$5,000**
National Assn of Realtors	$5,000
Sea Transport	**$2,500**
United States Lines	$2,500
Securities Investment	**$2,000**
First Boston Corp	$1,000
Goldman Sachs	$500
PaineWebber	$500
Telecommunications	**$2,050**
AT&T	$1,500
New York Telephone	$550
Tobacco	**$1,750**
Philip Morris	$1,500
Others	$250
Trucking/Delivery	**$2,050**
United Parcel Service	$1,500
Others	$550

Other Major Business PACs

ASCAP	$500	Live Music
Delaware Otsego Corp	$500	Railroads

PAC Totals by Category

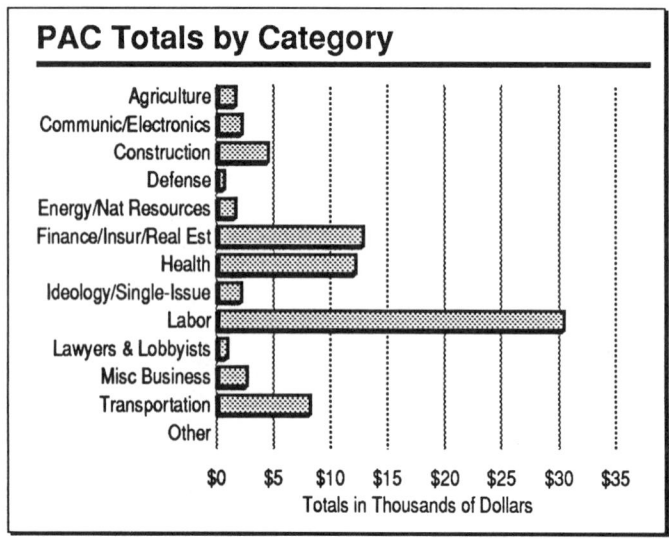

Categories (top to bottom): Agriculture, Communic/Electronics, Construction, Defense, Energy/Nat Resources, Finance/Insur/Real Est, Health, Ideology/Single-Issue, Labor, Lawyers & Lobbyists, Misc Business, Transportation, Other

Totals in Thousands of Dollars ($0, $5, $10, $15, $20, $25, $30, $35)

Labor

Construction Unions $3,000
    Carpenters & Joiners Union $2,000
    Operating Engineers Local #15 .... $1,000

Government & Postal Workers $6,250
    National Assn of Retired Federal Employees $5,000
    National Assn of Letter Carriers $500
    Police Assn of DC $500
    Others $250

Transportation Unions $21,000
    Air Line Pilots Assn $10,000
    Marine Engineers Union* $6,000
    Seafarers International Union $1,500
    Amalgamated Transit Union $1,000
    International Longshoremen Assn $1,000
    Transport Workers Union $1,000
    Transportation Communication Union $500

Ideological/Single-Issue

Ideological/Single-Issue $2,000
Fund for America's Future (George Bush) .... $500   Repub Cands
National Security PAC .... $500   Pro-Defense
Women's Pro-Israel National PAC .... $500   Pro-Israel
Others $500

Independent expenditures supporting Molinari
National Cmte to Preserve Social Security $1,501

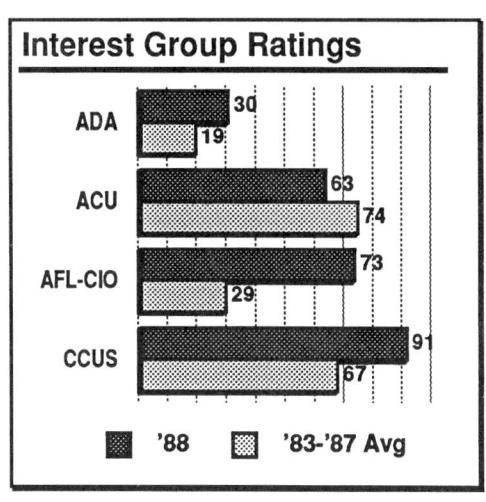

Interest Group Ratings

Group	'88	'83-'87 Avg
ADA	30	19
ACU	63	74
AFL-CIO	73	29
CCUS	91	67

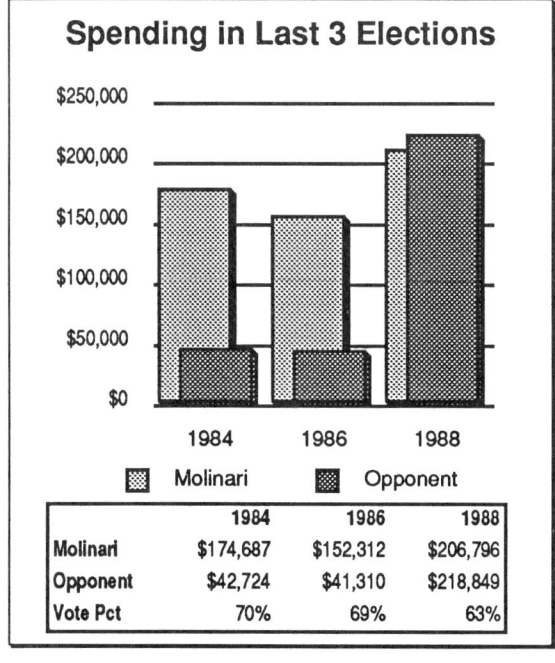

Spending in Last 3 Elections

	1984	1986	1988
Molinari	$174,687	$152,312	$206,796
Opponent	$42,724	$41,310	$218,849
Vote Pct	70%	69%	63%

Legend: Molinari, Opponent

---

* Contributions came from more than one PAC affiliated with this sponsor.

755

Alan B. Mollohan, D-WVa (1)

First elected: 1982
Total receipts: $168,119
Total from PACs: $112,890

1988 Committees & Subcommittees

Appropriations
Commerce, Justice, State, the Judiciary and Related Agencies
HUD-Independent Agencies

Standards of Official Conduct

PAC Contribution Profile

Business

Automotive **$2,150**
    National Auto Dealers Assn $1,000
    Others $1,150

Chemicals & Explosives............................**$3,100**
    Institute of Makers of Explosives $1,000
    Others $2,100

Construction **$10,800**
    Westvaco Corp $3,500
    United Technologies $3,200
    National Utility Contractors Assn $2,000
    Others $2,100

Dairy **$2,600**
    Associated Milk Producers $2,000
    Others $600

Defense...**$6,600**
    Hughes Aircraft $1,300
    Lockheed Corp $1,200
    General Dynamics $1,000
    Others $3,100

Health Professionals **$3,100**
    American Dental Assn $1,500
    American Medical Assn $1,300
    Others $300

Oil & Gas **$5,300**
    Mobil Oil $1,000
    Others $4,300

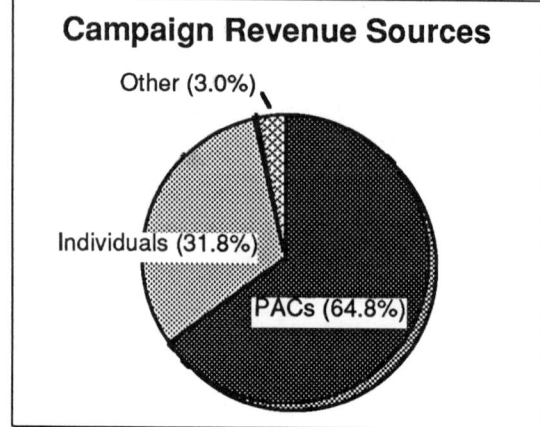

Campaign Revenue Sources

Other (3.0%)
Individuals (31.8%)
PACs (64.8%)

Real Estate **$2,100**
    National Assn of Realtors $1,800
    Others $300

Telecommunications **$2,767**
    Continental Telecom $1,000
    Others $1,767

Tobacco **$2,400**
    Philip Morris $1,500
    Others $900

Trucking/Delivery......................................**$2,100**
    United Parcel Service $1,500
    Others $600

Other Major Business PACs

American Cyanimid $1,000	Pharmaceut
American Hospital Assn $1,000	Hospitals
Borg-Warner $1,000	Indust Equip
National Assn of Life Underwriters $1,000	Life Insurance

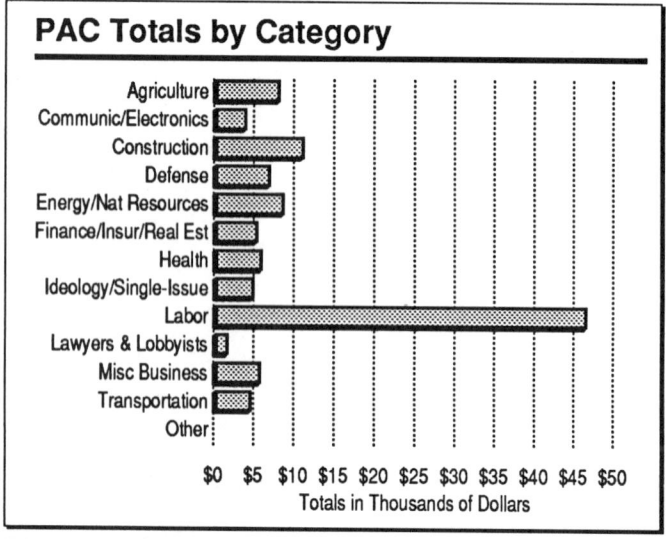

PAC Totals by Category

Agriculture
Communic/Electronics
Construction
Defense
Energy/Nat Resources
Finance/Insur/Real Est
Health
Ideology/Single-Issue
Labor
Lawyers & Lobbyists
Misc Business
Transportation
Other

$0 $5 $10 $15 $20 $25 $30 $35 $40 $45 $50
Totals in Thousands of Dollars

Labor

Bldg Trades/Industrial/Misc Unions $20,800
United Auto Workers $5,300
Intl Brotherhood of Electrical Workers $2,500
United Mine Workers $2,300
Operating Engineers Union $2,000
Food & Commercial Workers Union $1,500
Laborers' Political League $1,500
Carpenters & Joiners Union $1,000
United Steelworkers $1,000
Others $3,700

Government & Postal Workers $6,050
National Assn of Letter Carriers $1,600
American Postal Workers Union $1,300
National Assn of Retired Federal Employees $1,000
Others $2,150

Teachers Unions $2,600
National Education Assn $2,600

Transportation Unions $16,800
Teamsters Union $10,000
Marine Engineers Union* $2,000
Seafarers International Union $2,000
United Transportation Union $1,600
Others $1,200

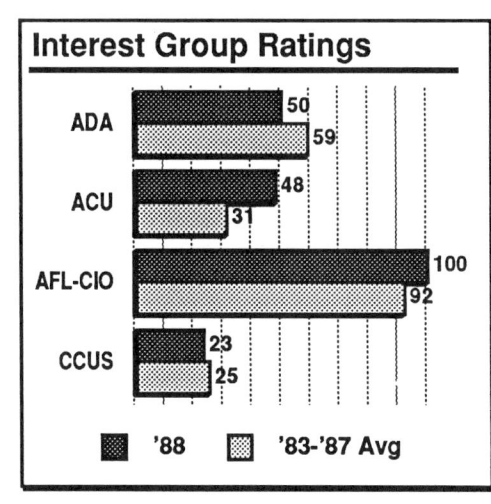

Interest Group Ratings

Key: ■ '88 ▨ '83–'87 Avg

	'88	'83–'87 Avg
ADA	50	59
ACU	48	31
AFL-CIO	100	92
CCUS	23	25

Ideological/Single-Issue

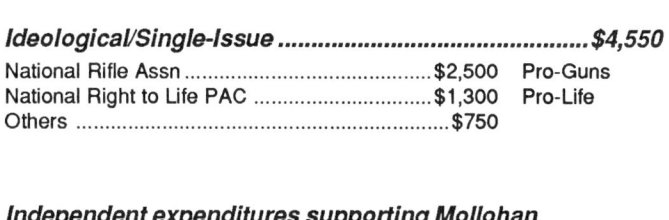

Ideological/Single-Issue $4,550
National Rifle Assn .... $2,500 Pro-Guns
National Right to Life PAC .... $1,300 Pro-Life
Others $750

Independent expenditures supporting Mollohan
National Cmte to Preserve Social Security $1,566

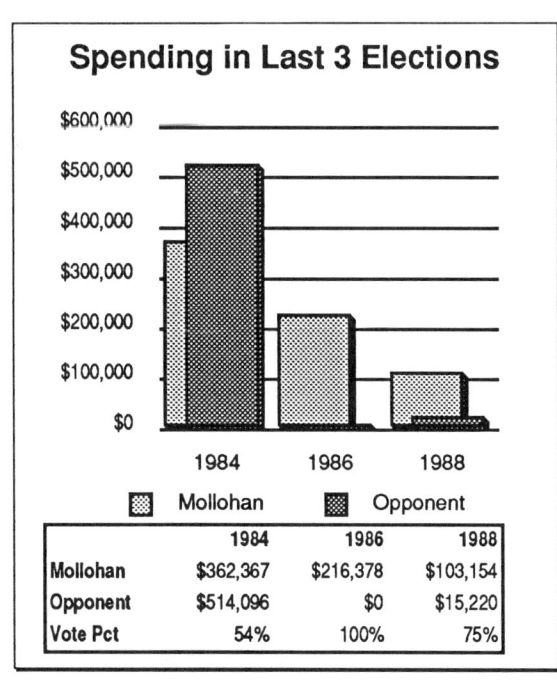

Spending in Last 3 Elections

Key: ▨ Mollohan ■ Opponent

	1984	1986	1988
Mollohan	$362,367	$216,378	$103,154
Opponent	$514,096	$0	$15,220
Vote Pct	54%	100%	75%

* Contributions came from more than one PAC affiliated with this sponsor.

G.V. "Sonny" Montgomery, D-Miss (3)

First elected: 1966
Total receipts: $148,077
Total from PACs: $71,650

1988 Committees & Subcommittees

Armed Services
Military Installations and Facilities
Military Personnel and Compensation

Veterans' Affairs (Chairman)
Hospitals and Health Care (Chairman)

PAC Contribution Profile

Business

Auto Dealers	**$4,500**
Auto Dealers & Drivers for Free Trade	$4,000
Others	$500
Commercial Banks	**$4,250**
Bank of Mississippi	$1,500
Grenada Bank	$1,000
Others	$1,750
Construction	**$4,000**
Associated General Contractors	$1,500
National Assn of Home Builders	$1,000
Others	$1,500
Defense	**$18,250**
Chrysler Corp	$1,500
AT&T	$1,000
General Dynamics	$1,000
Hughes Aircraft	$1,000
Litton Industries	$1,000
Lockheed Corp	$1,000
Northrop Corp	$1,000
Singer Company	$1,000
United Technologies	$1,000
Others	$8,750
Electric Utilities & Equipment	**$2,000**
Mississippi ACRE	$1,000
Others	$1,000

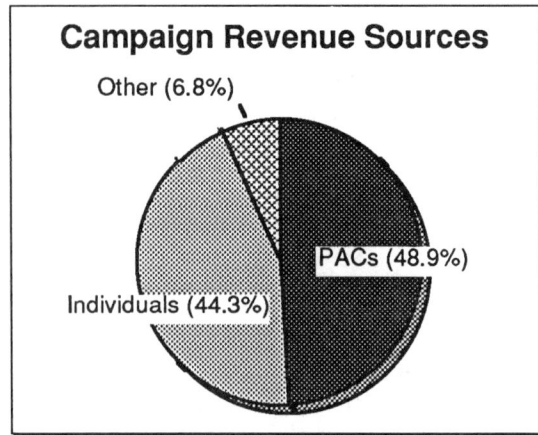

Campaign Revenue Sources

Other (6.8%)
PACs (48.9%)
Individuals (44.3%)

Food & Beverage	**$2,500**
Jitney-Jungle Inc	$1,000
National Beer Wholesalers Assn	$1,000
Others	$500
Health Professionals	**$6,000**
American Medical Assn	$1,500
American Dental Assn	$1,000
Cmte for Quality Orthopedic Health Care	$1,000
Others	$2,500
Insurance	**$5,000**
National Assn of Life Underwriters	$3,000
Others	$2,000
Lawyers	**$1,500**
Assn of Trial Lawyers of America	$1,000
Others	$500
Oil & Gas	**$2,700**
None over $500	
Sugar Growers	**$1,800**
None over $500	
Textiles	**$1,500**
Burlington Industries	$1,000
Others	$500
Tobacco	**$1,500**
None over $500	

Other Major Business PACs

South Central Bell Telephone .... $1,000 Phone Util

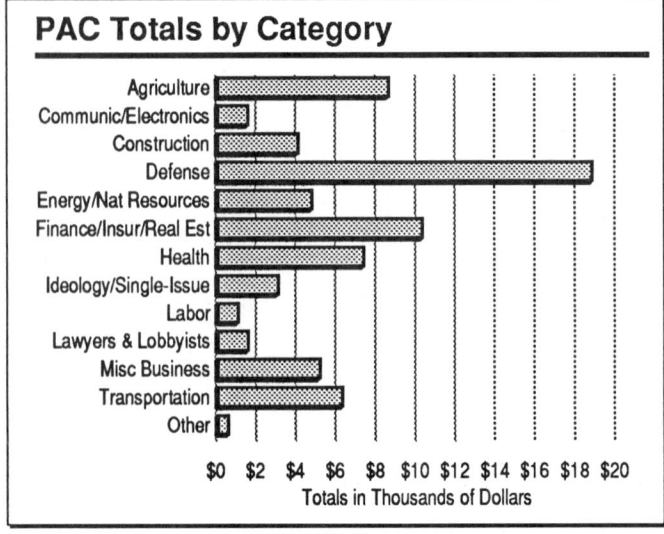

PAC Totals by Category

Agriculture
Communic/Electronics
Construction
Defense
Energy/Nat Resources
Finance/Insur/Real Est
Health
Ideology/Single-Issue
Labor
Lawyers & Lobbyists
Misc Business
Transportation
Other

$0 $2 $4 $6 $8 $10 $12 $14 $16 $18 $20
Totals in Thousands of Dollars

Ideological/Single-Issue

Pro-Defense PACs **$2,000**
    Veterans of Foreign Wars $1,000
    Others $1,000

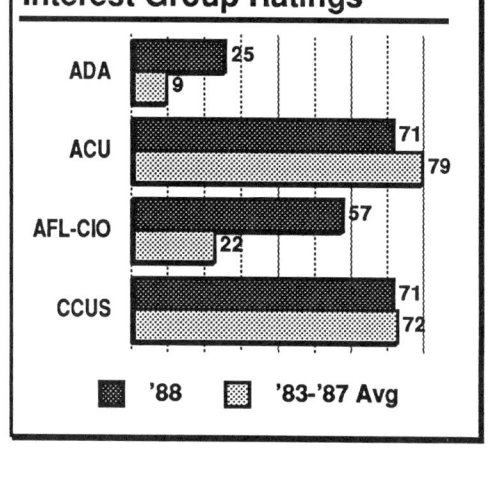

Interest Group Ratings

	'88	'83-'87 Avg
ADA	25	9
ACU	71	79
AFL-CIO	57	22
CCUS	71	72

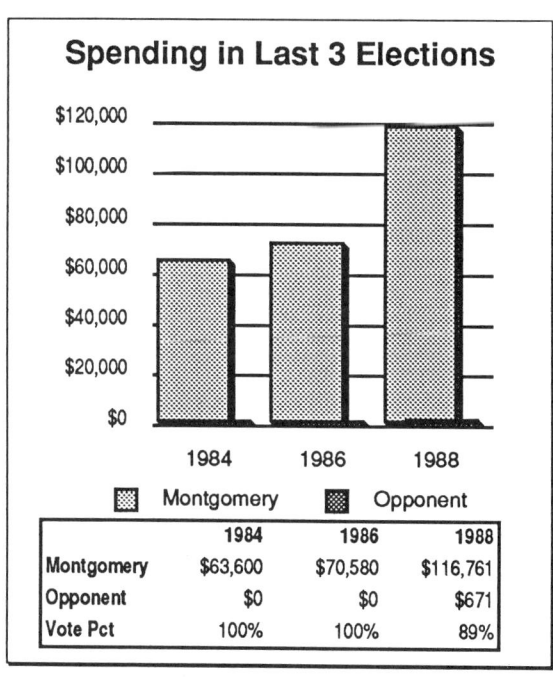

Spending in Last 3 Elections

	1984	1986	1988
Montgomery	$63,600	$70,580	$116,761
Opponent	$0	$0	$671
Vote Pct	100%	100%	89%

Jim Moody, D-Wis (5)

1988 Committees & Subcommittees

Ways and Means
Health
Social Security

First elected: 1982
Total receipts: $1,291,531
Total from PACs: $519,503

Campaign Revenue Sources

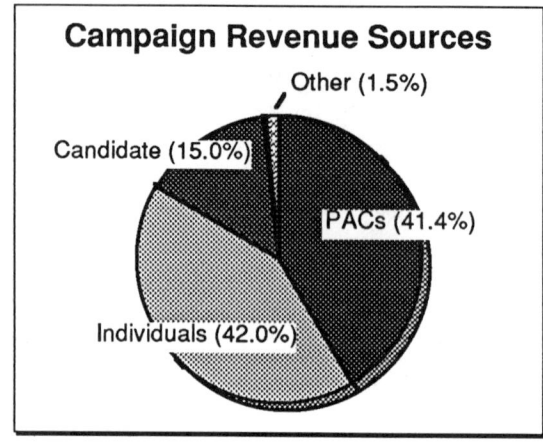

Other (1.5%)
Candidate (15.0%)
PACs (41.4%)
Individuals (42.0%)

PAC Contribution Profile

Business

Accountants **$15,050**
- Coopers & Lybrand $5,750
- American Institute of CPA's.....................$5,000
- Touche Ross $2,350
- Others $1,950

Financial Institutions **$21,150**
- US League of Savings Assn.....................$4,000
- Credit Union National Assn $3,500
- American Bankers Assn $3,000
- Wisconsin Bankers Assn $1,750
- First Chicago Corp $1,500
- Others $7,400

Food & Beverage **$19,605**
- Food Marketing Institute $3,605
- Wine & Spirits Wholesalers of America..........$2,200
- National Beer Wholesalers Assn $1,850
- Joseph E Seagram & Sons $1,500
- Others $10,450

Health Professionals **$36,500**
- American Physical Therapy Assn $4,850
- American Podiatry Assn $4,500
- American Medical Assn $4,250
- American Optometric Assn $3,850
- American Dental Assn $3,500
- American Occupational Therapy Assn $1,500
- American Nurses Assn $1,500
- Corp for the Advancement of Psychiatry $1,500
- Oral & Maxillofacial Surgeons $1,500
- Others $9,550

Hospitals & Nursing Homes **$15,850**
- American Hospital Assn $5,000
- American Health Care Assn $3,000
- Federation of America Hospitals $2,350
- National Assn of Private Psychiatric Hospitals.....$2,000
- Others $3,500

Insurance **$40,350**
- National Assn of Life Underwriters $5,000
- North Western Mutual Life $3,600
- Blue Cross & Blue Shield Assn* $2,250
- Mortgage Insurance Companies of America $2,100
- Equitable Financial Services $2,000
- Independent Insurance Agents of America $2,000
- Metropolitan Life Insurance $2,000
- New York Life $1,850
- Prudential Insurance $1,850
- Health Insurance Assn of America $1,500
- National Assn of Independent Insurers $1,500
- Others $14,700

Lawyers & Lobbyists **$21,903**
- Assn of Trial Lawyers of America $10,000
- Others $11,903

Real Estate **$13,000**
- National Assn of Realtors $8,500
- National Realty Committee $2,500
- Others $2,000

Securities/Commodities **$23,900**
- Chicago Board of Trade $5,000
- Chicago Mercantile Exchange $5,000
- Investment Company Institute $3,500
- First Boston Corp.................................$2,000
- Goldman Sachs $2,000
- Securities Industry Assn* $1,500
- Others $4,900

Venture Capital **$10,000**
- National Venture Capital Assn $10,000

PAC Totals by Category

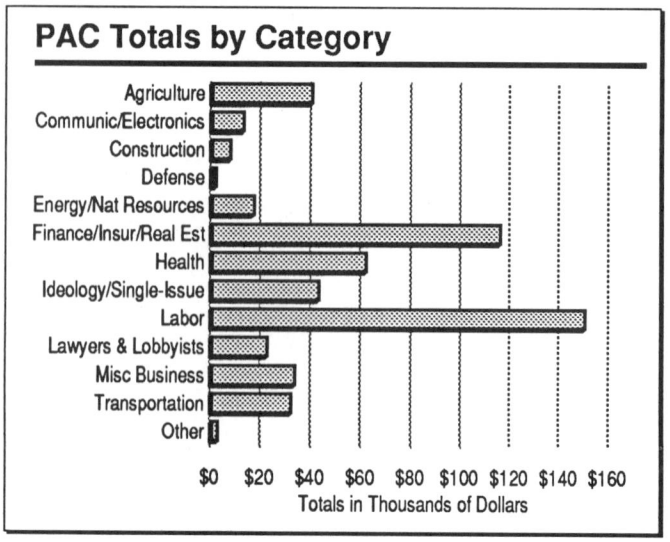

Agriculture
Communic/Electronics
Construction
Defense
Energy/Nat Resources
Finance/Insur/Real Est
Health
Ideology/Single-Issue
Labor
Lawyers & Lobbyists
Misc Business
Transportation
Other

$0 $20 $40 $60 $80 $100 $120 $140 $160
Totals in Thousands of Dollars

Other Major Business PACs

Tyson Foods	$6,000	Poultry/Egg
AT&T	$5,000	LongDistance
Waste Management Inc	$3,500	Waste Mgmt
Associated Milk Producers	$3,250	Dairy
United Parcel Service	$3,100	Delivery
National Auto Dealers Assn	$3,000	Auto Sales
Philip Morris	$3,000	Tobacco
International Taxicab Assn	$2,600	Taxis
Federal Express Corp	$2,500	Delivery
Wisconsin Electric Power Company	$2,050	ElectricUtil
Aircraft Owners & Pilots Assn	$2,000	GenlAviation
Archer-Daniels-Midland Corp	$2,000	Grain Trader
Auto Dealers & Drivers for Free Trade	$2,000	JapanAutoSal
National Assn of Home Builders	$2,000	Resid Constr
W R Grace & Company	$1,850	Chemicals
Motion Picture Assn of America	$1,668	Movies
American Textile Manufacturers Institute	$1,650	Textiles
American Assn of Equipment Lessors	$1,500	Rentals
Chicago & North Western Transport	$1,500	Railroads
Harley-Davidson Inc	$1,500	Motorcycles
Land O'Lakes Inc	$1,500	Dairy
MCA Inc	$1,500	Movies
Petroleum Marketers Assn	$1,500	Gas Stations

Labor

Bldg Trades/Industrial/Misc Unions $70,450

AFL-CIO*	$12,850
Food & Commercial Workers Union	$7,700
Carpenters & Joiners Union	$6,000
Sheet Metal Workers Union	$6,000
Communications Workers of America	$5,350
United Auto Workers	$4,850
Intl Brotherhood of Electrical Workers	$4,000
Operating Engineers Union	$3,700
Plumbers/Pipefitters Union	$3,000
Laborers' Political League	$2,600
Rubber Cork Linoleum Plastic Workers	$2,500
United Steelworkers	$2,000
Hotel/Restaurant Employees Union	$1,500
Others	$8,400

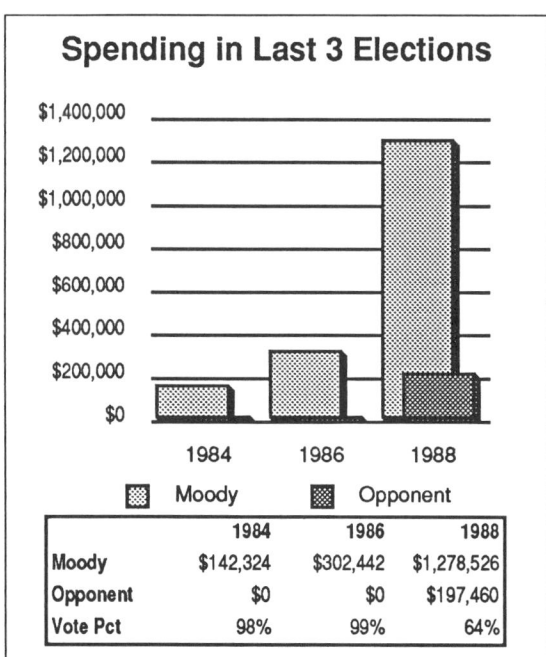

Spending in Last 3 Elections

	1984	1986	1988
Moody	$142,324	$302,442	$1,278,526
Opponent	$0	$0	$197,460
Vote Pct	98%	99%	64%

☐ Moody   ☐ Opponent

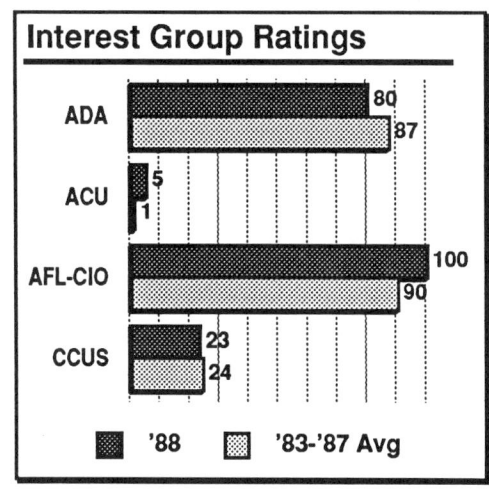

Interest Group Ratings

	'88	'83-'87 Avg
ADA	80	87
ACU	5	1
AFL-CIO	100	90
CCUS	23	24

■ '88   ☐ '83-'87 Avg

Government & Postal Workers $25,771

National Assn of Letter Carriers	$6,000
National Assn of Retired Federal Employees	$5,000
National Rural Letter Carriers Assn	$5,000
American Fedn of State/County/Munic Employees	$2,221
American Postal Workers Union	$2,000
International Assn of Firefighters	$1,500
Others	$4,050

Teachers Unions $14,050

National Education Assn	$9,500
American Federation of Teachers	$4,550

Transportation Unions $39,400

Teamsters Union	$10,000
Marine Engineers Union*	$7,500
Air Line Pilots Assn	$6,000
Seafarers International Union	$6,000
Amalgamated Transit Union	$3,500
United Transportation Union	$2,200
Maintenance of Way Employees	$1,500
Others	$2,700

Ideological/Single-Issue

Pro-Israel $27,600

Hudson Valley PAC	$5,000
Natlonal PAC	$5,000
San Franciscans for Good Government	$5,000
St Louisians for Better Government	$5,000
Washington PAC	$1,850
Others	$5,750

Other Major Ideological/Single-Issue PACs

America's Leaders' Fund (Dan Rostenkowski)	$5,000	Dem Leaders
Majority Congress Committee (Jim Wright)	$3,000	Dem Leaders

Independent expenditures supporting Moody

National Cmte to Preserve Social Security	$3,050

---

* Contributions came from more than one PAC affiliated with this sponsor.

Carlos J. Moorhead, R-Calif (22)

First elected: 1972
Total receipts: $397,417
Total from PACs: $215,165

1988 Committees & Subcommittees

Energy and Commerce
Energy and Power (Ranking Republican)
Telecommunications and Finance

Judiciary
Courts, Civil Liberties and the Administration of Justice (Ranking Republican)
Monopolies and Commercial Law

PAC Contribution Profile

Business

Campaign Revenue Sources

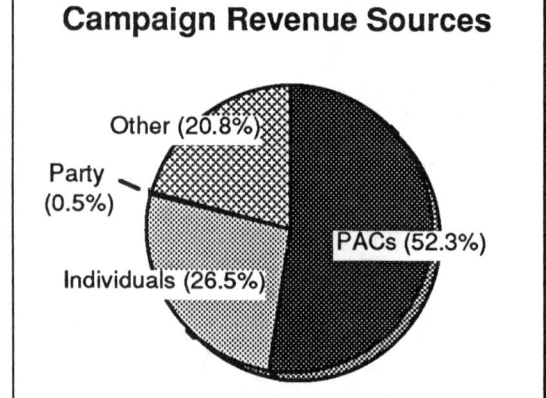

Other (20.8%)
Party (0.5%)
PACs (52.3%)
Individuals (26.5%)

Accountants	....	**$6,000**
American Institute of CPA's		$5,000
Others		$1,000

Automotive	....	**$7,200**
Auto Dealers & Drivers for Free Trade		$4,000
National Auto Dealers Assn		$1,100
Others		$2,100

Broadcasting/Entertainment	....	**$12,490**
National Cable Television Assn		$4,040
Walt Disney Company		$2,150
National Assn of Broadcasters		$1,100
ASCAP		$1,000
Motion Picture Assn of America		$1,000
Others		$3,200

Chemicals	....	**$2,600**
FMC Corp		$1,000
Others		$1,600

Commercial & Savings Banks	....	**$12,495**
J P Morgan & Company		$5,000
Glendale Federal Savings & Loan		$1,800
American Bankers Assn		$1,500
California League of Savings Institutions		$1,000
Others		$3,195

Construction	....	**$9,280**
National Assn of Home Builders		$2,000
Parsons Corp		$1,800
Associated General Contractors		$1,500
Jacobs Engineering Group		$1,180
Others		$2,800

Defense	....	**$9,000**
Lockheed Corp		$2,600
Mantech International		$1,000
Others		$5,400

Electric Utilities	....	**$16,850**
Southern Company*		$1,850
Southern California Edison		$1,600
Houston Industries		$1,500
San Diego Gas & Electric		$1,100
Pacific Gas & Electric		$1,050
Public Service Company of NH/Yankee Division		$1,000
Texas Utilities Electric Company*		$1,000
Others		$7,750

Food & Beverage	....	**$5,600**
National Beer Wholesalers Assn		$1,700
Others		$3,900

Health Professionals	....	**$12,065**
American Medical Assn		$7,950
American Dental Assn		$2,000
American Optometric Assn		$1,615
Others		$500

Insurance	....	**$17,090**
TransAmerica Insurance*		$5,000
National Assn of Life Underwriters		$2,000
National Assn Mutual Insurance Agents		$1,300
Aetna Life & Casualty		$1,100
Casualty & Surety Agents Assn		$1,100
Farmers Group Inc		$1,000
Pacific Mutual Life		$1,000
Others		$4,590

Lawyers & Lobbyists	....	**$3,890**
None over $800		

Oil & Gas	....	**$18,335**
Pacific Enterprises		$1,500
Columbia Hydrocarbon Corp		$1,100
Atlantic Richfield		$1,000
Petroleum Marketers Assn		$1,000
Sun Company		$1,000
Others		$12,735

PAC Totals by Category

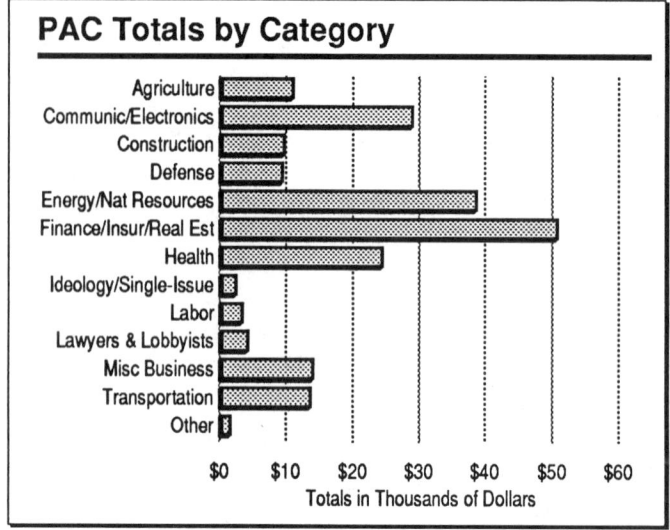

- Agriculture
- Communic/Electronics
- Construction
- Defense
- Energy/Nat Resources
- Finance/Insur/Real Est
- Health
- Ideology/Single-Issue
- Labor
- Lawyers & Lobbyists
- Misc Business
- Transportation
- Other

$0　$10　$20　$30　$40　$50　$60
Totals in Thousands of Dollars

Pharmaceuticals	....	**$9,950**
Schering-Plough Corp	....	$1,500
Merck & Company	....	$1,000
Others	....	$7,450

Real Estate	....	**$7,850**
National Assn of Realtors	....	$6,750
Others	....	$1,100

Securities/Commodities	....	**$8,300**
Morgan Stanley & Company	....	$1,500
Travelers Corp	....	$1,500
Investment Company Institute	....	$1,100
Chicago Board of Trade	....	$1,000
Others	....	$3,200

Telecommunications	....	**$15,570**
Pacific Telesis Group	....	$2,890
AT&T	....	$2,000
Continental Telecom	....	$2,000
GTE Corp	....	$1,130
Bell Atlantic	....	$1,100
Others	....	$6,450

Tobacco	....	**$3,600**
Philip Morris	....	$2,500
Others	....	$1,100

Other Major Business PACs

United Parcel Service	....	$1,785	Delivery
Maytag Company	....	$1,000	Appliances
Sunkist Growers	....	$1,000	Fruit/Veg
West Publishing	....	$1,000	Books & Mags

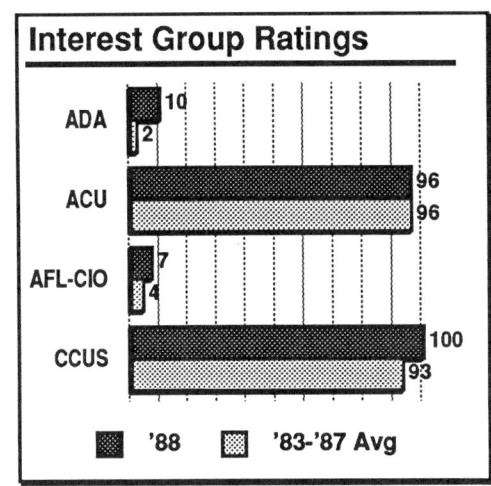

Labor

Labor Unions	....	**$3,000**
Teamsters Union	....	$2,500
Others	....	$500

Major Ideological/Single-Issue PACs

| Freedom PAC | .... | $1,210 | Unknown |
| Armenian-American PAC | .... | $1,000 | Ethnic |

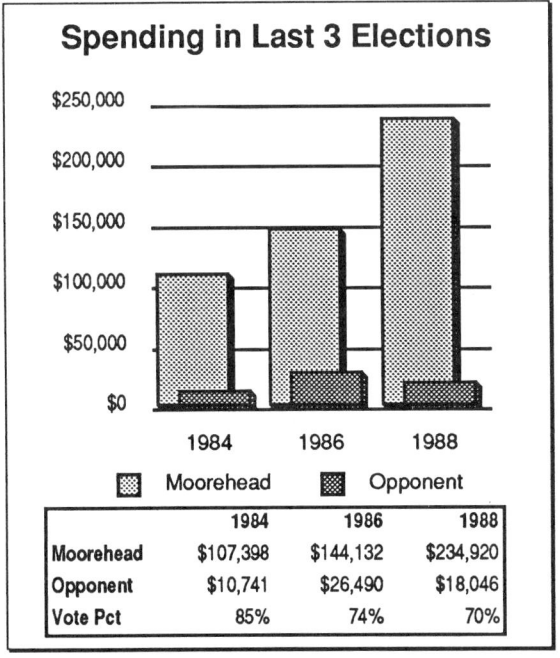

	1984	1986	1988
Moorehead	$107,398	$144,132	$234,920
Opponent	$10,741	$26,490	$18,046
Vote Pct	85%	74%	70%

---

* Contributions came from more than one PAC affiliated with this sponsor.

Constance A. Morella, R-Md (8)

First elected: 1986
Total receipts: $829,437
Total from PACs: $305,374

1988 Committees & Subcommittees

Post Office and Civil Service
Census and Population (Ranking Republican)
Compensation and Employee Benefits

Science, Space and Technology
Science, Research and Technology
Space Science and Applications

Select Aging
Human Services

Campaign Revenue Sources

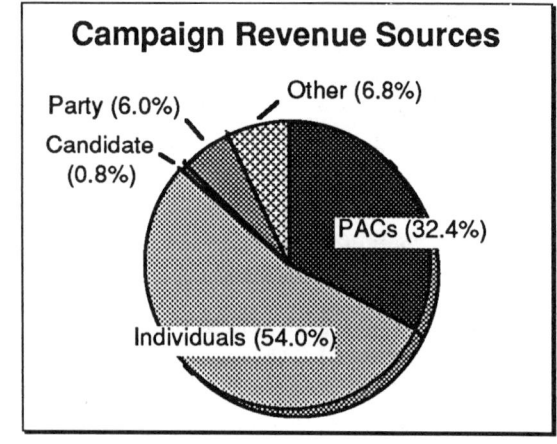

Party (6.0%)
Candidate (0.8%)
Other (6.8%)
PACs (32.4%)
Individuals (54.0%)

PAC Contribution Profile

Business

Automotive	**$11,750**
Auto Dealers & Drivers for Free Trade	$5,000
National Auto Dealers Assn	$4,000
Eaton Corp	$1,500
Others	$1,250
Business Associations	**$7,929**
Greater Washington Board of Trade	$6,000
Business Industry PAC	$1,129
Others	$800
Commercial Banks	**$10,350**
Crestar Financial Corp	$2,200
American Bankers Assn	$1,500
Citicorp	$1,000
Sovran Bank/Maryland	$1,000
Others	$4,650
Construction	**$20,500**
National Assn of Home Builders	$6,500
Associated Builders & Contractors	$2,750
Associated General Contractors	$2,750
National Society of Professional Engineers	$2,000
Bechtel Corp	$1,000
Manville Corp	$1,000
Others	$4,500

PAC Totals by Category

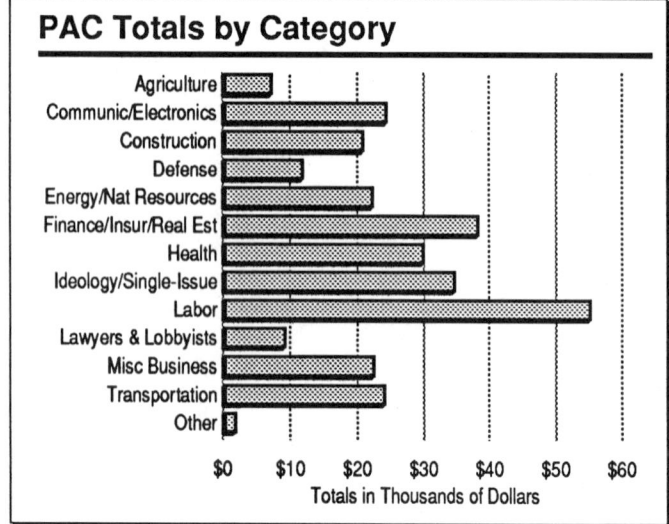

Agriculture
Communic/Electronics
Construction
Defense
Energy/Nat Resources
Finance/Insur/Real Est
Health
Ideology/Single-Issue
Labor
Lawyers & Lobbyists
Misc Business
Transportation
Other

$0 $10 $20 $30 $40 $50 $60
Totals in Thousands of Dollars

Defense	**$11,450**
Watkins-Johnson Company	$2,500
Lockheed Corp	$1,750
Rockwell International	$1,250
Allied-Signal	$1,000
BDM International	$1,000
Hughes Aircraft	$1,000
Others	$2,950
Electric & Power Utilities	**$14,200**
Baltimore Gas & Electric	$10,000
Potomac Electric Power Company	$1,350
Others	$2,850
Electronics & Computers	**$6,250**
Computer Sciences Corp	$2,750
Electronic Data Systems	$1,000
Others	$2,500
Food & Beverage	**$5,050**
National Restaurant Assn	$1,000
Safeway Stores	$1,000
Others	$3,050
Health Professionals	**$24,035**
American Medical Assn	$6,135
American Nurses Assn	$3,500
Maryland Medical Assn	$3,000
American Podiatry Assn	$2,500
American Dental Assn	$2,250
American Academy of Ophthalmology	$2,000
American Physical Therapy Assn	$1,850
Others	$2,800
Insurance	**$12,600**
National Assn of Life Underwriters	$3,000
GEICO Insurance	$2,250
CNA Financial Corp	$1,000
US Fidelity & Guaranty	$1,000
Others	$5,350
Lawyers & Lobbyists	**$8,850**
Assn of Trial Lawyers of America	$4,500
Fullbright & Jaworski	$1,500
Akin, Gump, Hauer & Feld	$1,250
Others	$1,600
Oil & Gas	**$5,700**
Mobil Oil	$1,000
Others	$4,700

Real Estate $11,500
    National Assn of Realtors $10,000
    Others $1,500

Telecommunications $16,000
    AT&T $5,500
    Chesapeake & Potomac Telephone $2,200
    Comsat $2,100
    Penn Central Corp..$2,000
    Continental Telecom $1,500
    Others $2,700

Other Major Business PACs

United Parcel Service	$2,500	Delivery
Martin Marietta Corp	$2,100	Space Equip
Marriott Corp	$2,000	Hotel/Motel
Goldman Sachs	$1,500	InvestmtBank
J C Penney Company	$1,500	Mail Order
National Assn of Temporary Services	$1,250	EmployAgency
Waste Management Inc	$1,250	Waste Mgmt
Cosmetic Toiletry & Fragrance Assn	$1,000	Cosmetics
Emhart Corp*	$1,000	Indust Equip
National Assn of Social Workers	$1,000	Social Work
Philip Morris	$1,000	Tobacco
Schering-Plough Corp	$1,000	Pharmaceut
TRW Inc	$1,000	Space Equip

Labor

Government & Postal Workers $42,056
    National Assn of Retired Federal Employees $10,000
    National Assn of Letter Carriers $7,000
    American Postal Workers Union $6,200
    American Fedn of State/County/Munic Employees $5,000
    National Rural Letter Carriers Assn $3,256
    American Federation of Government Employees $2,500
    National Treasury Employees Union $2,000
    National Assn of Postmasters $1,350
    National League of Postmasters $1,250
    National Assn of Postal Supervisors $1,000
    National Star Route Mail Contractors $1,000
    Others $1,500

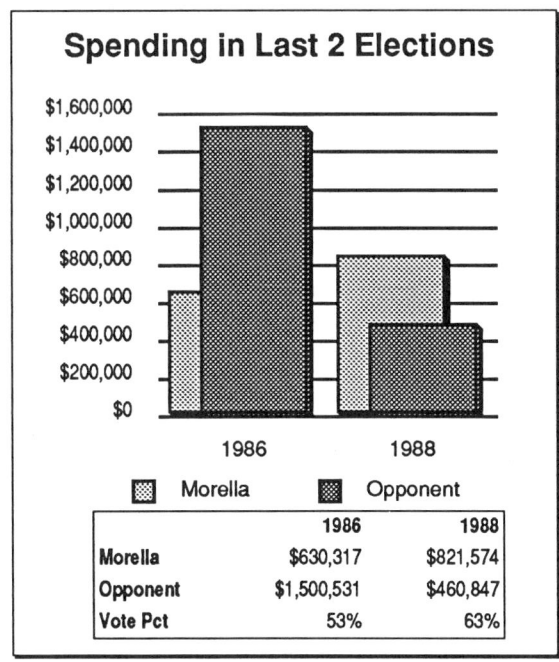

Spending in Last 2 Elections

	1986	1988
Morella	$630,317	$821,574
Opponent	$1,500,531	$460,847
Vote Pct	53%	63%

Interest Group Ratings

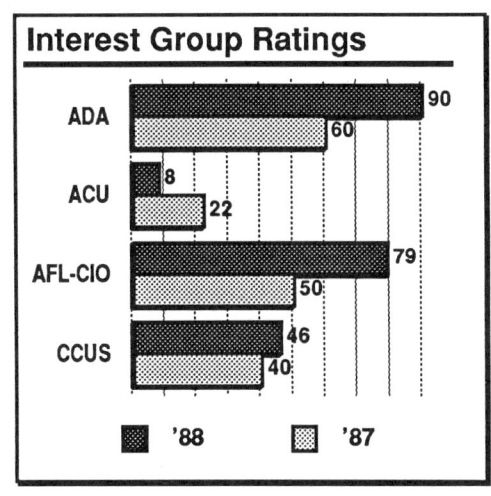

	'88	'87
ADA	90	60
ACU	8	22
AFL-CIO	79	50
CCUS	46	40

Other Unions $12,750
    Masters Mates & Pilots Union $3,000
    National Education Assn $3,000
    Air Line Pilots Assn.......................................$2,500
    Marine Engineers Union* $2,000
    American Federation of Teachers $1,000
    Others $1,250

Ideological/Single-Issue

Pro-Israel $8,450
    Joint Action Cmte for Political Affairs $1,500
    Congressional Action Cmte of Texas $1,000
    Florida Congressional Cmte $1,000
    Roundtable PAC $1,000
    Washington PAC $1,000
    Others $2,950

Womens Issues/Pro-Choice........................$10,650
    Women's Campaign Fund $8,000
    Voters for Choice/Friends of Family Planning $1,000
    Others $1,650

Other Major Ideological/Single-Issue PACs

Human Rights Campaign Fund	$5,706	Gay Rights
League of Conservation Voters	$2,000	Environment
Council for a Livable World	$1,172	Pro-Peace
Handgun Control Inc	$1,000	Anti-Guns
Pax Americas (David Bonior)	$1,000	Dem Leaders
Sierra Club	$1,000	Environment

Independent expenditures supporting Morella

National Cmte to Preserve Social Security $1,926

* Contributions came from more than one PAC affiliated
with this sponsor.

Bruce A. Morrison, D-Conn (3)

First elected: 1982
Total receipts: $490,274
Total from PACs: $224,433

1988 Committees & Subcommittees

Banking, Finance and Urban Affairs
Financial Institutions Supervision, Regulation and Insurance
Housing and Community Development
International Development Institutions and Finance

District of Columbia

Judiciary
Administrative Law and Governmental Relations
Courts, Civil Liberties and the Administration of Justice
Immigration, Refugees and International Law

Select Children, Youth and Families

PAC Contribution Profile

Business

Accountants	**$8,700**
American Institute of CPA's	$5,000
Touche Ross	$2,350
Deloitte, Haskins & Sells	$1,000
Others	$350
Broadcasting/Entertainment	**$7,950**
Warner Communications	$2,500
Recording Industry Assn	$1,050
ASCAP	$1,000
Others	$3,400
Defense	**$2,465**
United Technologies	$2,115
Others	$350
Financial Institutions	**$8,150**
CBT Corp	$1,800
Credit Union National Assn	$1,350
Others	$5,000
Insurance	**$39,000**
Independent Insurance Agents of America	$10,000
National Assn of Life Underwriters	$10,000
Insurance Assn of Connecticut	$5,000
National Assn Mutual Insurance Agents	$5,000
Casualty & Surety Agents Assn	$1,850
New England Mutual Life	$1,500
American Council of Life Insurance	$1,350
Others	$4,300

Campaign Revenue Sources

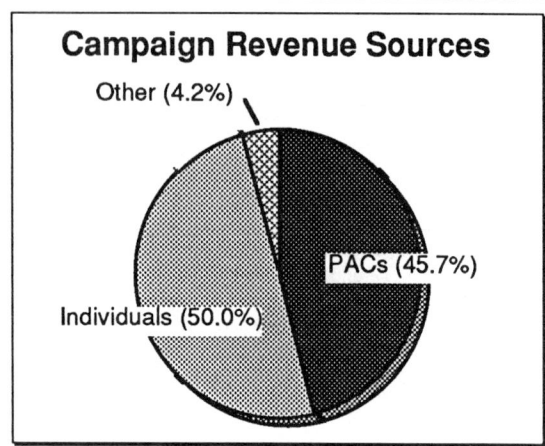

Other (4.2%)
PACs (45.7%)
Individuals (50.0%)

Lawyers & Lobbyists	**$10,444**
Assn of Trial Lawyers of America	$5,000
Akin, Gump, Hauer & Feld	$1,200
Updike, Kelly & Spellacy	$1,000
Others	$3,244
Liquor	**$2,450**
Heublein	$1,400
Others	$1,050
Real Estate	**$4,350**
National Assn of Realtors	$3,450
Others	$900
Securities Investment	**$12,700**
Goldman Sachs	$2,500
Investment Company Institute	$2,500
First Boston Corp	$2,000
Drexel Burnham Lambert	$1,350
Prudential-Bache Securities	$1,300
Dain Bosworth	$1,000
Others	$2,050
Telecommunications	**$5,350**
AT&T	$2,000
Pacific Northwest Bell	$1,000
Others	$2,350

Other Major Business PACs

American Dental Assn	$1,000	Dentists
Auto Dealers & Drivers for Free Trade	$1,000	JapanAutoSal
West Publishing	$1,000	Books & Mags

PAC Totals by Category

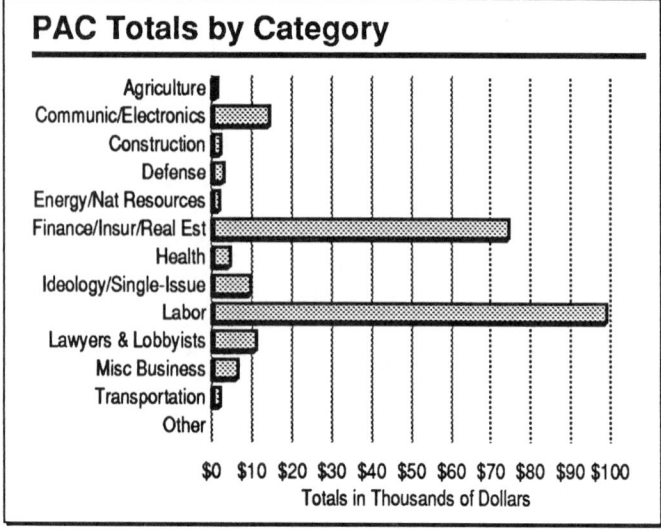

Agriculture
Communic/Electronics
Construction
Defense
Energy/Nat Resources
Finance/Insur/Real Est
Health
Ideology/Single-Issue
Labor
Lawyers & Lobbyists
Misc Business
Transportation
Other

$0 $10 $20 $30 $40 $50 $60 $70 $80 $90 $100
Totals in Thousands of Dollars

Labor

Bldg Trades/Industrial/Misc Unions $51,900

United Auto Workers	$10,850
Carpenters & Joiners Union*	$6,000
Laborers' Political League	$5,750
Machinists/Aerospace Workers Union	$5,700
Connecticut Union of Telephone Workers	$4,750
Food & Commercial Workers Union	$4,000
Sheet Metal Workers Union	$2,500
Intl Brotherhood of Electrical Workers	$2,000
Ironworkers Union	$2,000
United Steelworkers	$2,000
Ladies Garment Workers Union	$1,200
AFL-CIO	$1,000
Others	$4,150

Government & Postal Workers $20,550

American Postal Workers Union	$6,000
American Fedn of State/County/Munic Employees	$5,000
National Assn of Letter Carriers	$4,100
National Assn of Retired Federal Employees	$3,000
Others	$2,450

Teachers Unions $7,500

National Education Assn	$5,000
American Federation of Teachers	$2,500

Transportation Unions $18,550

Teamsters Union	$10,000
Seafarers International Union	$2,500
Amalgamated Transit Union	$1,500
United Transportation Union	$1,250
Marine Engineers District 2 Maritime Officers	$1,000
Others	$2,300

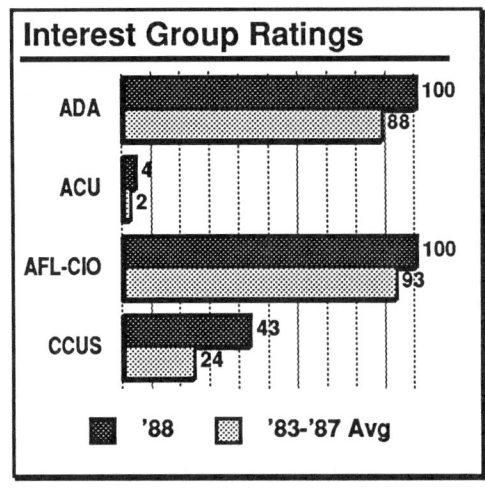

Interest Group Ratings

(ADA: '88 = 100, '83-'87 Avg = 88; ACU: '88 = 4, '83-'87 Avg = 2; AFL-CIO: '88 = 100, '83-'87 Avg = 93; CCUS: '88 = 43, '83-'87 Avg = 24)

■ '88 ▨ '83-'87 Avg

Ideological/Single-Issue

Democratic/Liberal $2,848

National Cmte for an Effective Congress	$2,498
Others	$350

Other Major Ideological/Single-Issue PACs

National Cmte to Preserve Social Security	$1,050	Soc Secur
Handgun Control Inc	$1,000	Anti-Guns
Sierra Club	$1,000	Environment
Valley Education Fund (Tony Coelho)	$1,000	Dem Leaders

Independent expenditures supporting Morrison

National Cmte to Preserve Social Security	$3,946

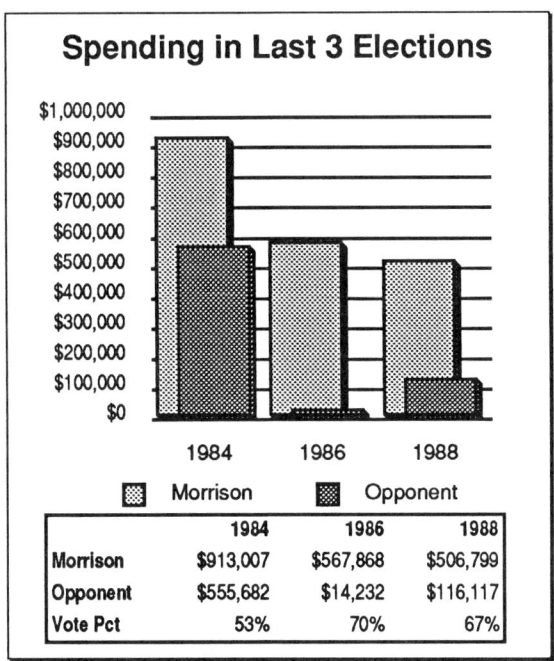

Spending in Last 3 Elections

▨ Morrison ▨ Opponent

	1984	1986	1988
Morrison	$913,007	$567,868	$506,799
Opponent	$555,682	$14,232	$116,117
Vote Pct	53%	70%	67%

* Contributions came from more than one PAC affiliated with this sponsor.

Sid Morrison, R-Wash (4)

First elected: 1980
Total receipts: $202,637
Total from PACs: $82,558

1988 Committees & Subcommittees

Agriculture
Forests, Family Farms and Energy (Ranking Republican)
Conservation, Credit and Rural Development
Department Operations, Research and Foreign Agriculture

Science, Space and Technology
Energy Research and Development (Ranking Republican)
Science, Research and Technology

Select Hunger

PAC Contribution Profile

Business

Agricultural Chemicals	**$2,800**
Ecolab Inc	$1,000
Others	$1,800
Auto Dealers	**$3,500**
National Auto Dealers Assn	$2,000
Auto Dealers & Drivers for Free Trade	$1,500
Aviation & Aerospace	**$3,050**
Boeing Company	$2,400
Others	$650
Commercial & Savings Banks	**$6,400**
American Bankers Assn	$2,500
US Bancorp	$1,200
Washington Savings League	$1,000
Others	$1,700
Commodities & Securities	**$4,000**
Chicago Board of Trade	$1,000
First Boston Corp	$1,000
Morgan Stanley & Company	$1,000
Others	$1,000
Construction	**$3,400**
Associated General Contractors	$1,300
Others	$2,100

Campaign Revenue Sources

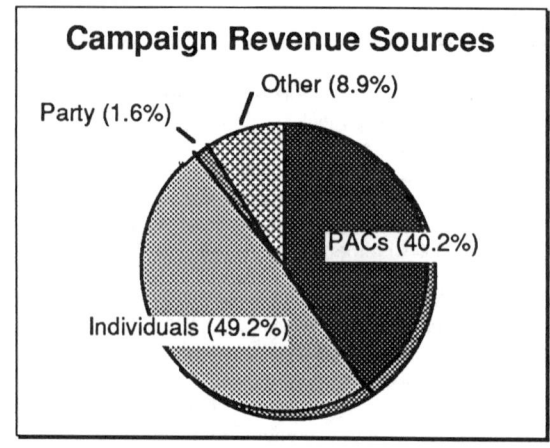

Other (8.9%)
Party (1.6%)
PACs (40.2%)
Individuals (49.2%)

Dairy	**$4,050**
Associated Milk Producers	$2,000
Darigold/Northwest Dairymens Assn	$1,600
Others	$450
Electric Utilities	**$2,300**
Pacific Power & Light	$1,000
Others	$1,300
Food & Beverage	**$6,000**
Ampco Foods Inc	$1,300
IBP Inc	$1,000
National Restaurant Assn	$1,000
Others	$2,700
Forest Products	**$5,850**
Boise Cascade	$1,000
Stone Container Corp	$1,000
Others	$3,850
Real Estate	**$6,000**
National Assn of Realtors	$6,000
Sugar Growers	**$2,050**
None over $600	
Telecommunications	**$8,500**
Pacific Northwest Bell	$3,000
AT&T	$2,500
Continental Telecom	$1,500
United Telecommunications	$1,000
Others	$500

Other Major Business PACs

505 King Ave Committee	$2,000	Unknown
American Medical Assn	$1,300	Doctors
National Assn of Life Underwriters	$1,000	Life Insurance
Peanut Butter & Nut Processors Assn	$1,000	Crops

PAC Totals by Category

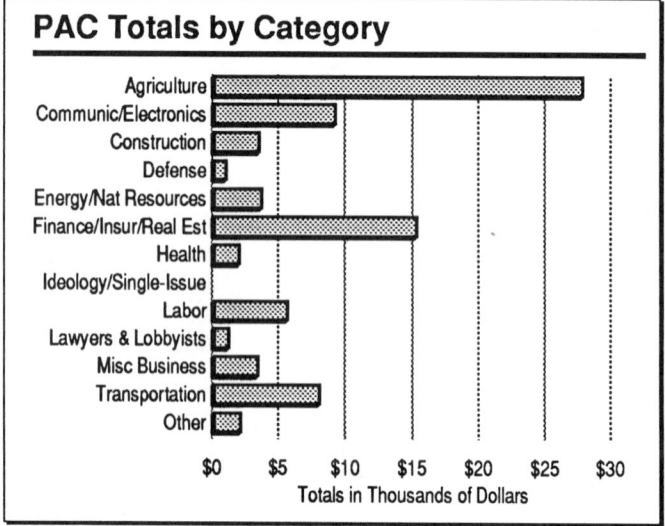

Agriculture
Communic/Electronics
Construction
Defense
Energy/Nat Resources
Finance/Insur/Real Est
Health
Ideology/Single-Issue
Labor
Lawyers & Lobbyists
Misc Business
Transportation
Other

$0 $5 $10 $15 $20 $25 $30
Totals in Thousands of Dollars

Labor

Labor Unions **$5,500**
    National Education Assn $4,000
    Teamsters Union $1,000
    Others $500

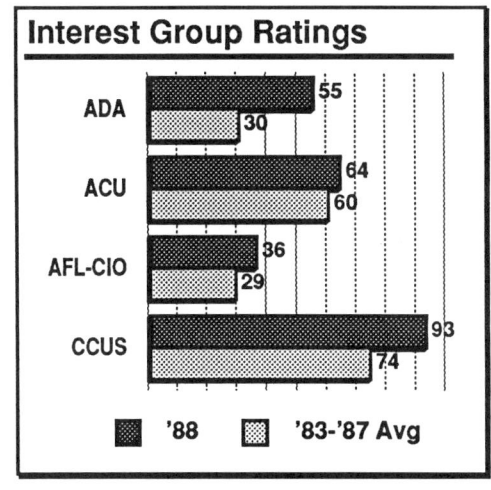

Interest Group Ratings

ADA 55 / 30
ACU 64 / 60
AFL-CIO 36 / 29
CCUS 93 / 74

'88   '83-'87 Avg

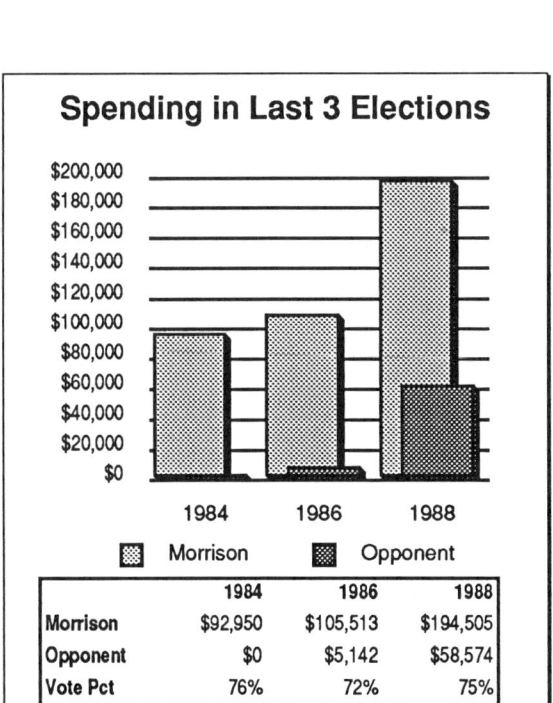

Spending in Last 3 Elections

	1984	1986	1988
Morrison	$92,950	$105,513	$194,505
Opponent	$0	$5,142	$58,574
Vote Pct	76%	72%	75%

Morrison   Opponent

Robert J. Mrazek, D-NY (3)

First elected: 1982
Total receipts: $447,902
Total from PACs: $176,931

1988 Committees & Subcommittees

Appropriations
Foreign Operations
Transportation and Related Agencies

PAC Contribution Profile

Business

Airlines & Aircraft	**$3,400**
Texas Air	$2,500
Others	$900
Automotive	**$2,400**
Auto Dealers & Drivers for Free Trade	$1,500
Others	$900
Computers & Electronics	**$2,250**
None over $800	
Construction	**$3,250**
CRS Group Inc	$1,450
National Assn of Home Builders	$1,300
Others	$500
Defense	**$9,100**
Grumman	$4,000
Textron Inc	$1,300
Hazeltine Corp	$1,150
Others	$2,650
Health Professionals	**$12,100**
American Medical Assn	$5,300
New York Medical Assn	$2,700
American Academy of Ophthalmology	$1,500
American Dental Assn	$1,500
Others	$1,100
Lawyers & Lobbyists	**$4,900**
None over $900	

Campaign Revenue Sources

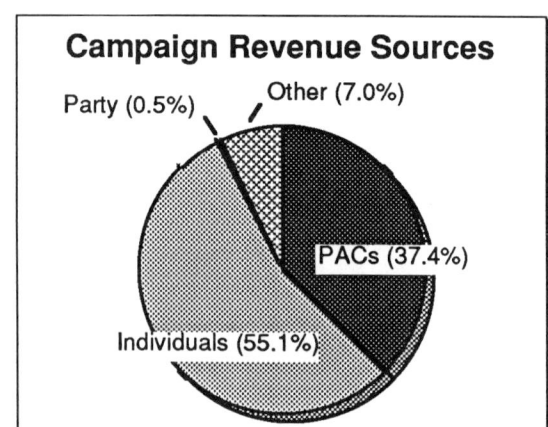

Party (0.5%)
Other (7.0%)
PACs (37.4%)
Individuals (55.1%)

Life Insurance	**$1,500**
National Assn of Life Underwriters	$1,500
Real Estate	**$6,200**
National Assn of Realtors	$5,600
Others	$600
Savings & Commercial Banks	**$1,905**
Union Savings Bank	$1,000
Others	$905
Telecommunications	**$2,204**
AT&T	$1,100
Others	$1,104
Trucking/Delivery	**$2,250**
United Parcel Service	$1,950
Others	$300
Wine & Liquor	**$4,100**
National Assn Beverage Importers	$1,300
Joseph E Seagram & Sons	$1,000
Others	$1,800

Other Major Business PACs

National Assn of Social Workers .... $1,000   Social Work

PAC Totals by Category

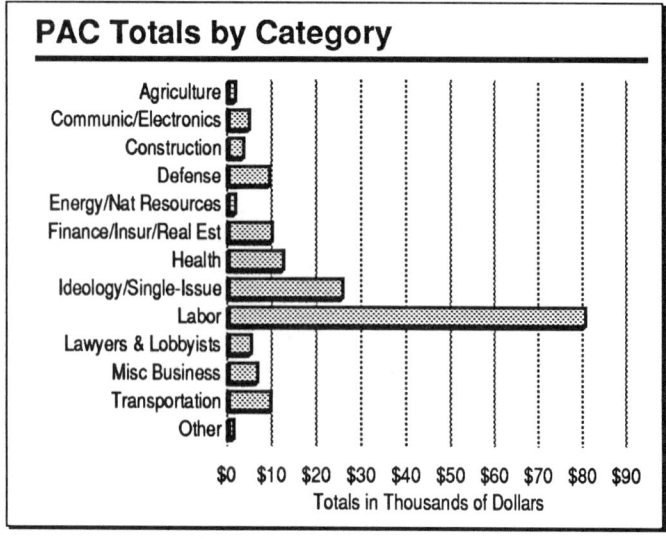

Agriculture
Communic/Electronics
Construction
Defense
Energy/Nat Resources
Finance/Insur/Real Est
Health
Ideology/Single-Issue
Labor
Lawyers & Lobbyists
Misc Business
Transportation
Other

$0 $10 $20 $30 $40 $50 $60 $70 $80 $90
Totals in Thousands of Dollars

Labor

Bldg Trades/Industrial/Misc Unions $24,700

Carpenters & Joiners Union* $6,300
Intl Brotherhood of Electrical Workers $3,500
Operating Engineers Union $2,500
Machinists/Aerospace Workers Union $2,300
Laborers' Political League $2,000
United Auto Workers $2,000
Food & Commercial Workers Union $1,300
Ironworkers Union $1,000
Others $3,800

Government & Postal Workers $17,284

American Fedn of State/County/Munic Employees $5,084
National Assn of Letter Carriers $5,000
National Assn of Retired Federal Employees $4,000
American Postal Workers Union $1,900
Others $1,300

Teachers Unions $8,600

National Education Assn $6,000
American Federation of Teachers $2,600

Transportation Unions $29,500

Air Line Pilots Assn $10,000
Teamsters Union $8,000
Marine Engineers District 2 Maritime Officers $2,500
Amalgamated Transit Union $2,000
Seafarers International Union $2,000
United Transportation Union $1,700
Transport Workers Union $1,500
Others $1,800

Interest Group Ratings

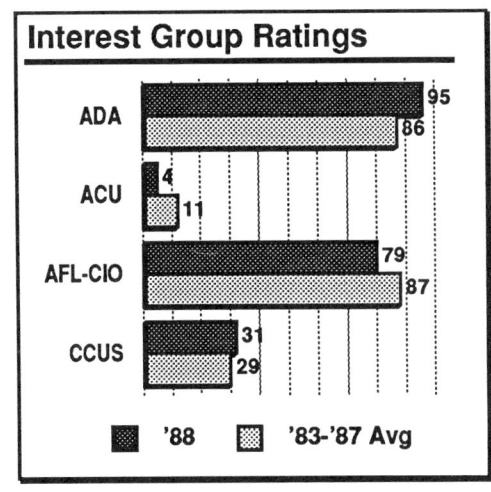

Legend: ■ '88   ▨ '83-'87 Avg

Group	'88	'83-'87 Avg
ADA	95	86
ACU	4	11
AFL-CIO	79	87
CCUS	31	29

Ideological/Single-Issue

Democratic/Liberal $5,278

National Cmte for an Effective Congress $5,028
Others $250

Pro-Israel $13,800

Long Island PAC $5,000
National PAC $5,000
Women's Pro-Israel National PAC $2,000
Joint Action Cmte for Political Affairs $1,000
Others $800

Other Major Ideological/Single-Issue PACs

National Cmte to Preserve Social Security ...... $2,100   Soc Secur
Handgun Control Inc .... $1,400   Anti-Guns
Human Rights Campaign Fund .... $1,000   Gay Rights
Valley Education Fund (Tony Coelho) .... $1,000   Dem Leaders

Independent expenditures supporting Mrazek

National Cmte to Preserve Social Security $2,275

Spending in Last 3 Elections

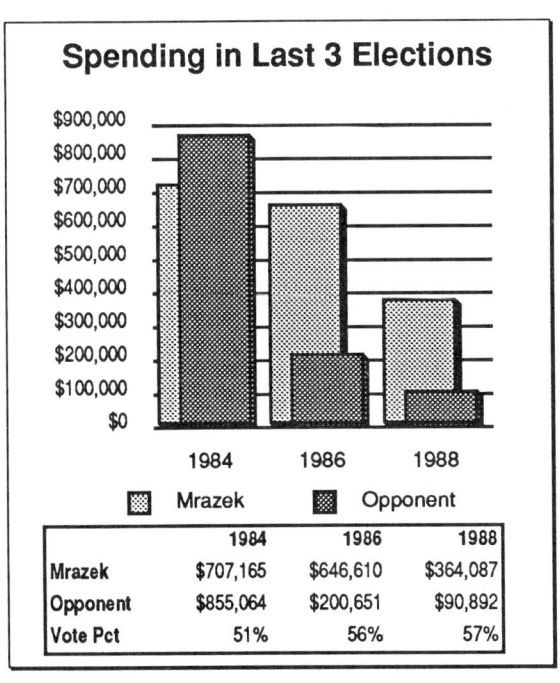

Legend: ▨ Mrazek   ■ Opponent

	1984	1986	1988
Mrazek	$707,165	$646,610	$364,087
Opponent	$855,064	$200,651	$90,892
Vote Pct	51%	56%	57%

---

* Contributions came from more than one PAC affiliated
with this sponsor.

Austin J. Murphy, D-Pa (22)

First elected: 1976
Total receipts: $173,164
Total from PACs: $128,218

1988 Committees & Subcommittees

Education and Labor
Labor Standards (Chairman)
Health and Safety
Labor-Management Relations

Interior and Insular Affairs
Energy and the Environment
Mining and Natural Resources

PAC Contribution Profile

Business

Commercial & Savings Banks **$2,700**
    Pennsylvania Savings League $1,000
    Others $1,700

Construction **$4,250**
    Manville Corp $2,000
    National Assn of Home Builders $1,000
    Others $1,250

Dairy **$1,750**
    Associated Milk Producers $1,000
    Others $750

Department & Drug Stores **$3,500**
    Walgreen Company $1,000
    Others $2,500

Electric Utilities **$7,121**
    Southern Company* $1,150
    ACRE (Action Committee for Rural Electrification) $1,100
    Others $4,871

Food & Beverage **$10,250**
    S & A Restaurant Corp $3,000
    National Restaurant Assn $2,000
    General Mills Restaurants $1,000
    Hardee's Food Systems $1,000
    Others $3,250

Forest Products **$3,250**
    Owens-Illinois $3,000
    Others $250

Campaign Revenue Sources

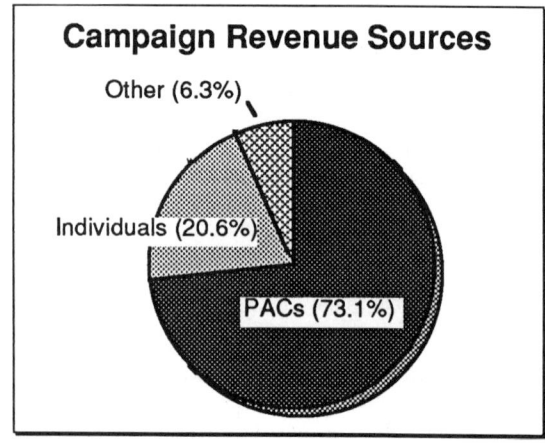

Other (6.3%)
Individuals (20.6%)
PACs (73.1%)

Lawyers & Lobbyists **$6,750**
    Assn of Trial Lawyers of America $5,000
    Others $1,750

Mining **$2,750**
    Cyrus Minerals Company $1,500
    Others $1,250

Oil & Gas **$3,900**
    Walter Industries $1,500
    Others $2,400

Power Plant Equipment **$2,050**
    Babcock & Wilcox $1,000
    Others $1,050

Real Estate **$5,000**
    National Assn of Realtors $5,000

Telecommunications **$3,300**
    Continental Telecom $1,500
    AT&T $1,000
    Others $800

Other Major Business PACs

American Medical Assn .... $1,250 Doctors
Allied-Signal .... $1,000 Air Defense
National Assn of Temporary Services .... $1,000 EmployAgency

PAC Totals by Category

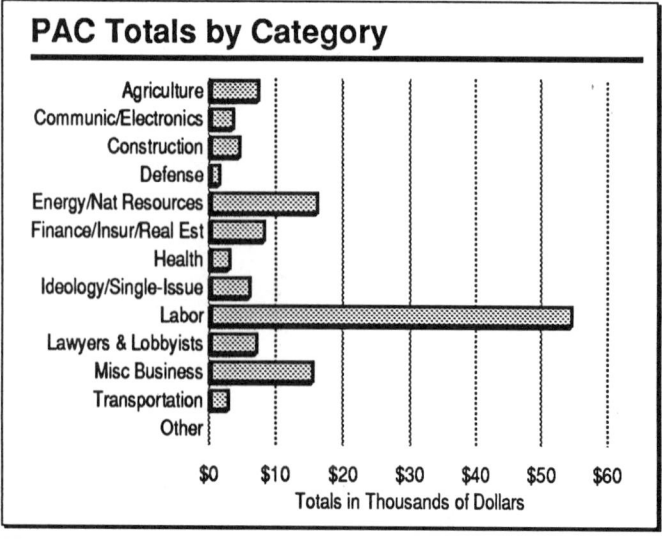

Agriculture
Communic/Electronics
Construction
Defense
Energy/Nat Resources
Finance/Insur/Real Est
Health
Ideology/Single-Issue
Labor
Lawyers & Lobbyists
Misc Business
Transportation
Other

$0 $10 $20 $30 $40 $50 $60
Totals in Thousands of Dollars

Labor

Bldg Trades/Industrial/Misc Unions $21,600

United Auto Workers $5,000
Carpenters & Joiners Union $3,000
Machinists/Aerospace Workers Union $1,600
Intl Brotherhood of Electrical Workers.............$1,500
Laborers' Political League $1,500
Food & Commercial Workers Union..................$1,250
AFL-CIO* $1,000
Ironworkers Union $1,000
Ladies Garment Workers Union $1,000
Operating Engineers Union $1,000
Plumbers/Pipefitters Union $1,000
Others $2,750

Government & Postal Workers $5,050

American Fedn of State/County/Munic Employees $2,000
National Assn of Letter Carriers $2,000
Others $1,050

Teachers Unions..$5,500

National Education Assn $5,500

Transportation Unions $22,000

Teamsters Union $7,500
Marine Engineers Union* $7,000
Seafarers International Union $2,500
United Transportation Union $1,500
Transport Workers Union $1,000
Others $2,500

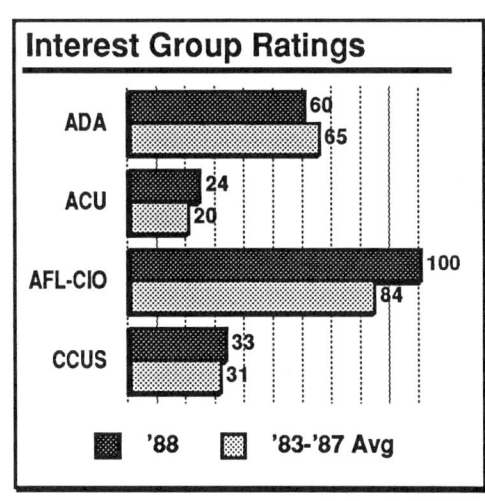

Ideological/Single-Issue

Pro-Gun Ownership $4,000

National Rifle Assn $3,000
Safari Club International $1,000

Other Major Ideological/Single-Issue PACs

Valley Education Fund (Tony Coelho) ....$1,000   Dem Leaders

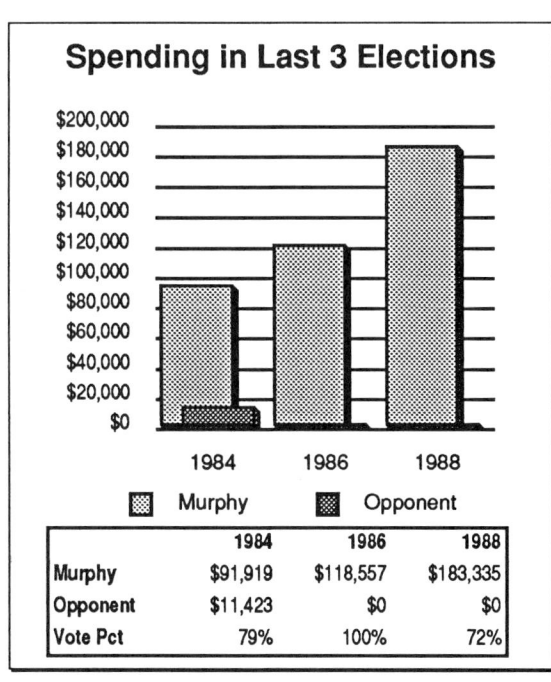

---

* Contributions came from more than one PAC affiliated
with this sponsor.

John P. Murtha, D-Pa (12)

First elected: 1974
Total receipts: $447,087
Total from PACs: $310,815

1988 Committees & Subcommittees

Appropriations
Defense
Interior and Related Agencies
Legislative Branch

PAC Contribution Profile

Business

Commercial & Savings Banks **$7,000**
- American Bankers Assn $3,000
- Mellon Bank $2,000
- Others $2,000

Dairy **$5,800**
- Associated Milk Producers $3,500
- Others $2,300

Defense **$116,682**
- AT&T $10,000
- Textron Inc $10,000
- McDonnell Douglas* $7,000
- Harsco Corp $6,000
- Northrop Corp $6,000
- Boeing Company $5,000
- Grumman $5,000
- Hughes Aircraft $5,000
- Lockheed Corp $5,000
- Raytheon $5,000
- General Dynamics $3,000
- LTV Aerospace & Defense Company $3,000
- Martin Marietta Corp $3,000
- United Technologies $3,000
- General Electric $2,500
- TRW Inc $2,500
- Long Island Aerospace PAC $2,432
- Allied-Signal $2,000
- Bath Iron Works $2,000
- Chrysler Corp $2,000
- Gencorp Inc $2,000
- General Motors $2,000
- *(Continued in next column)*

PAC Totals by Category

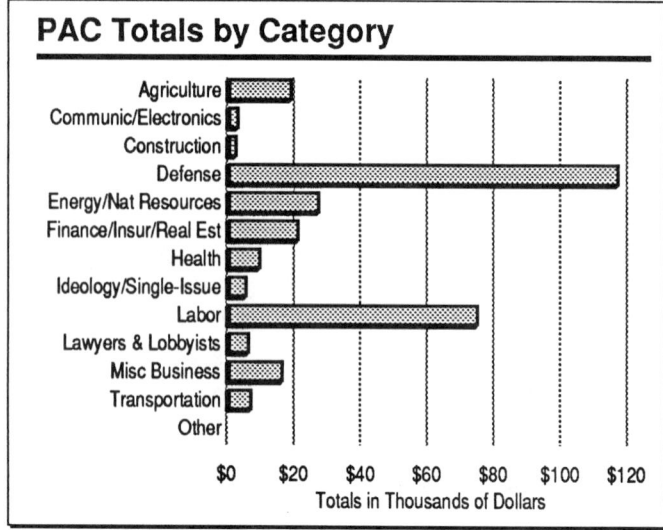

Totals in Thousands of Dollars

(Categories shown: Agriculture, Communic/Electronics, Construction, Defense, Energy/Nat Resources, Finance/Insur/Real Est, Health, Ideology/Single-Issue, Labor, Lawyers & Lobbyists, Misc Business, Transportation, Other)

Campaign Revenue Sources

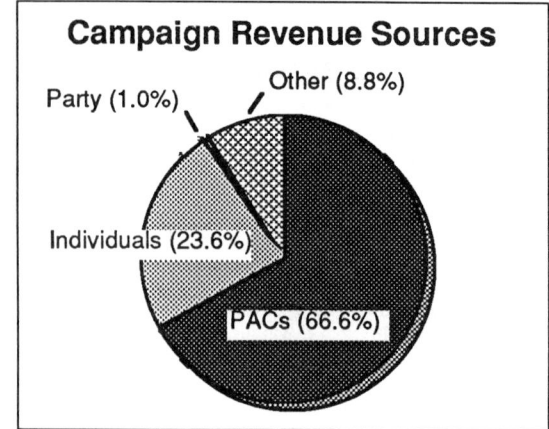

Party (1.0%)
Other (8.8%)
Individuals (23.6%)
PACs (66.6%)

Defense (cont'd)
- Hazeltine Corp $2,000
- Interlake Inc $2,000
- Pneumo Abex Corp $2,000
- Rockwell International $2,000
- Westinghouse Electric $2,000
- Litton Industries $1,500
- Others $11,750

Electric Utilities **$5,800**
- General Public Utilities $2,000
- ACRE (Action Committee for Rural Electrification) $1,500
- Others $2,300

Health Professionals **$4,500**
- American Medical Assn $2,000
- Others $2,500

Insurance **$5,500**
- American Council of Life Insurance $2,000
- Others $3,500

Lawyers & Lobbyists **$5,750**
- Akin, Gump, Hauer & Feld $2,000
- Assn of Trial Lawyers of America $2,000
- Burson-Marsteller $1,500
- Others $250

Oil & Gas **$15,100**
- USX Corp $5,000
- Chevron Corp $2,000
- Amoco Corp $1,500
- Others $6,600

Real Estate **$6,000**
- National Assn of Realtors $6,000

Steel Production **$8,650**
- Bethlehem Steel $3,000
- Armco Inc $2,000
- Inland Steel $1,250
- Others $2,400

Tobacco **$4,500**
- Philip Morris $1,500
- RJR Nabisco $1,500
- Tobacco Institute $1,500

Other Major Business PACs

American Hospital Assn	$2,500	Hospitals
Chicago Mercantile Exchange	$2,000	Commodities
Deere & Company*	$2,000	Farm Equip
Ocean Spray Cranberries Inc	$2,000	Fruit/Veg
Pirelli Cable	$2,000	Indust Equip
Shearson Lehman Hutton	$2,000	StocksInvest
Waste Management Inc	$2,000	Waste Mgmt
United Parcel Service	$1,500	Delivery

Labor

Bldg Trades/Industrial/Misc Unions $34,500

United Auto Workers	$6,000
Carpenters & Joiners Union	$3,500
Operating Engineers Union	$3,500
AFL-CIO*	$3,000
Intl Brotherhood of Electrical Workers	$2,500
Ironworkers Union	$2,500
Laborers' Political League	$2,000
Machinists/Aerospace Workers Union	$2,000
Plumbers/Pipefitters Union	$2,000
United Mine Workers	$2,000
Others	$5,500

Government & Postal Workers $10,850

National Assn of Retired Federal Employees	$5,000
American Fedn of State/County/Munic Employees	$2,000
National Assn of Letter Carriers	$2,000
American Postal Workers Union	$1,000
Others	$850

Teachers Unions $5,000

National Education Assn	$5,000

Transportation Unions $24,050

Teamsters Union	$10,000
Air Line Pilots Assn	$5,000
Seafarers International Union	$3,000
International Longshoremen Assn	$2,500
United Transportation Union	$2,000
Others	$1,550

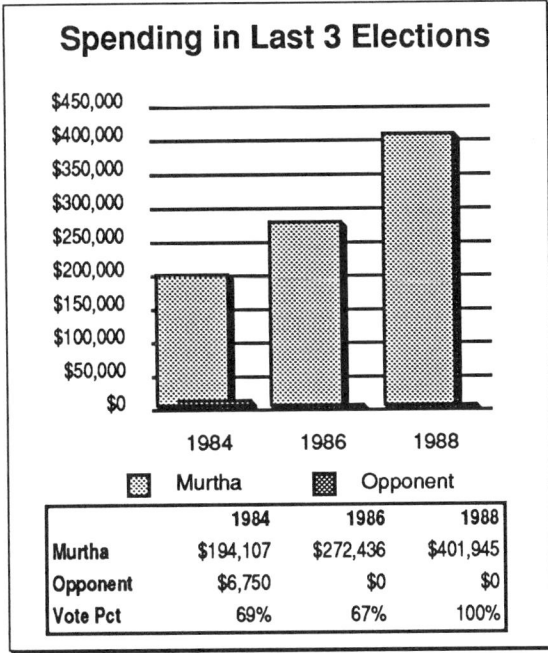

Spending in Last 3 Elections

Legend: Murtha, Opponent

	1984	1986	1988
Murtha	$194,107	$272,436	$401,945
Opponent	$6,750	$0	$0
Vote Pct	69%	67%	100%

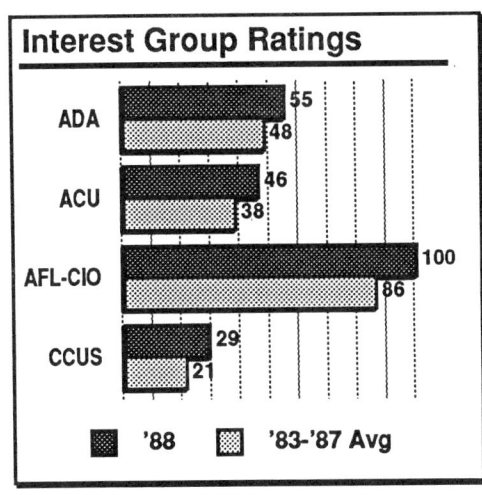

Interest Group Ratings

Group	'88	'83-'87 Avg
ADA	55	48
ACU	46	38
AFL-CIO	100	86
CCUS	29	21

Legend: '88, '83-'87 Avg

Ideological/Single-Issue

Ideological/Single-Issue $4,950

None over $1,000

Independent expenditures supporting Murtha

National Cmte to Preserve Social Security	$3,361

---

* Contributions came from more than one PAC affiliated with this sponsor.

John T. Myers, R-Ind (7)

First elected: 1966
Total receipts: $169,287
Total from PACs: $96,500

1988 Committees & Subcommittees

Appropriations
Energy and Water Development (Ranking Republican)
Legislative Branch
Rural Development, Agriculture and Related Agencies

Post Office and Civil Service
Compensation and Employee Benefits (Ranking Republican)
Postal Personnel and Modernization

Standards of Official Conduct (Ranking Republican)

PAC Contribution Profile

Business

Automotive	**$10,100**
National Auto Dealers Assn	$7,300
Auto Dealers & Drivers for Free Trade	$2,500
Others	$300
Construction	**$7,000**
National Assn of Home Builders	$2,000
Associated General Contractors	$1,300
Bechtel Corp	$1,000
National Utility Contractors Assn	$1,000
Others	$1,700
Dairy	**$3,800**
Associated Milk Producers	$3,000
Others	$800
Defense	**$2,650**
None over $900	
Electric Utilities & Equipment	**$5,649**
Indiana ACRE	$1,760
General Atomics	$1,000
Others	$2,889
Farm Organizations	**$3,300**
Indiana Farm Bureau	$3,000
Others	$300

Financial Institutions	**$4,653**
US League of Savings Assn	$1,900
American Bankers Assn	$1,000
Others	$1,753
Food & Beverage	**$2,300**
National Beer Wholesalers Assn	$1,000
Pillsbury Company	$1,000
Others	$300
Health Professionals	**$6,143**
American Medical Assn	$2,800
American Dental Assn	$2,000
Others	$1,343
Insurance	**$2,629**
None over $500	
Lawyers & Lobbyists	**$2,550**
Assn of Trial Lawyers of America	$2,250
Others	$300
Oil & Gas	**$2,000**
None over $300	
Real Estate	**$6,000**
National Assn of Realtors	$6,000
Telecommunications	**$5,400**
Continental Telecom	$2,500
Indiana Bell Telephone	$1,500
AT&T	$1,000
Others	$400

Other Major Business PACs

Dow Chemical*	$1,000	Ag Chemicals
Pirelli Cable	$1,000	Indust Equip
United Parcel Service	$1,000	Delivery

Campaign Revenue Sources

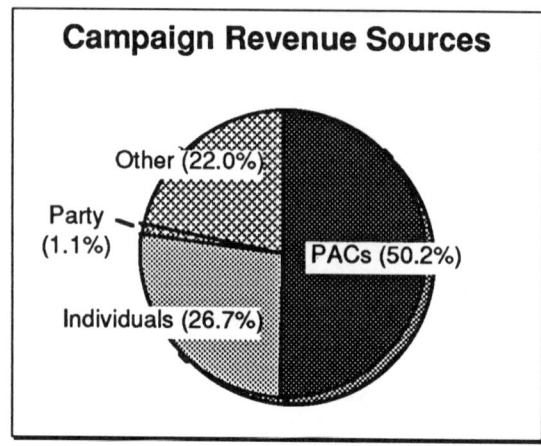

Other (22.0%)
Party (1.1%)
PACs (50.2%)
Individuals (26.7%)

PAC Totals by Category

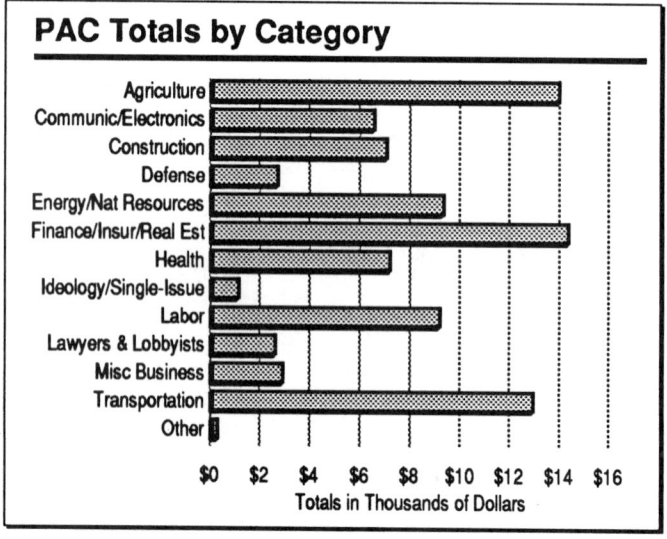

Agriculture
Communic/Electronics
Construction
Defense
Energy/Nat Resources
Finance/Insur/Real Est
Health
Ideology/Single-Issue
Labor
Lawyers & Lobbyists
Misc Business
Transportation
Other

$0 $2 $4 $6 $8 $10 $12 $14 $16
Totals in Thousands of Dollars

Labor

Labor Unions..**$9,100**

    National Assn of Retired Federal Employees $5,000
    National Assn of Postmasters $1,100
    National Assn of Letter Carriers $1,000
    Others $2,000

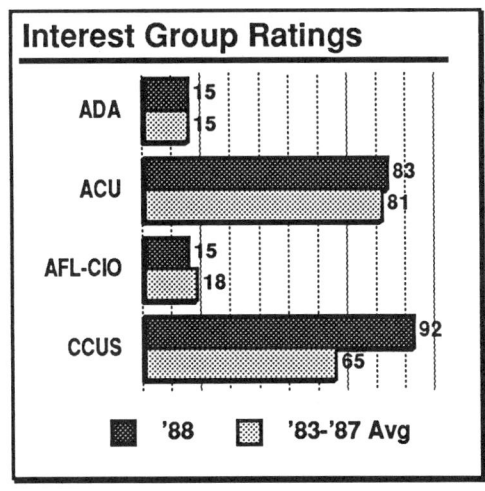

Interest Group Ratings

	'88	'83-'87 Avg
ADA	15	15
ACU	83	81
AFL-CIO	15	18
CCUS	92	65

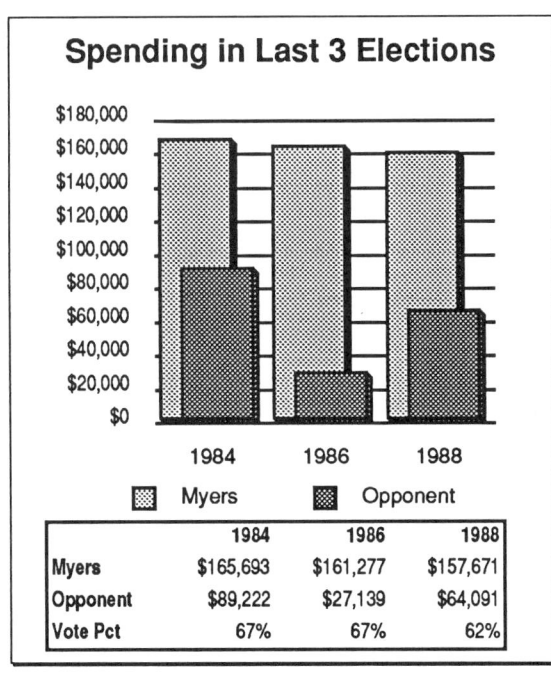

Spending in Last 3 Elections

	1984	1986	1988
Myers	$165,693	$161,277	$157,671
Opponent	$89,222	$27,139	$64,091
Vote Pct	67%	67%	62%

* Contributions came from more than one PAC affiliated with this sponsor.

Dave Nagle, D-Iowa (3)

1988 Committees & Subcommittees

First elected: 1986
Total receipts: $608,264
Total from PACs: $406,018

Agriculture
Conservation, Credit and Rural Development
Livestock, Dairy and Poultry
Wheat, Soybeans and Feed Grains

Science, Space and Technology
Science, Research and Technology
Space Science and Applications

PAC Contribution Profile

Business

Commercial Banks	**$18,750**
American Bankers Assn	$9,000
Hawkeye Bancorp	$3,000
Iowa Bankers Assn	$2,000
Independent Bankers Assn	$1,750
Barnett Banks of Florida	$1,500
Norwest Corp	$1,000
Others	$500
Construction	**$11,100**
National Assn of Home Builders	$10,000
Sheet Metal/AirCon Contractors	$1,000
Others	$100
Dairy	**$19,600**
Associated Milk Producers	$9,500
Mid-American Dairymen	$7,000
Dairymen Inc	$1,850
Land O'Lakes Inc	$1,000
Others	$250
Farm Organizations	**$5,700**
Iowa Farm Bureau Federation	$2,500
National Farmers Organization	$1,100
Rural Caucus PAC	$1,000
Others	$1,100
Health Professionals	**$22,988**
American Medical Assn	$19,238
American Academy of Ophthalmology	$2,000
American Optometric Assn	$1,000
Others	$750

Campaign Revenue Sources

Party (6.5%)
Candidate (3.0%)
Other (4.3%)
Individuals (22.2%)
PACs (64.0%)

Insurance	**$8,800**
National Assn of Life Underwriters	$3,000
Independent Insurance Agents of America	$2,100
Principal Mutual Life Insurance	$1,750
American Council of Life Insurance	$1,250
Others	$700
Lawyers & Lobbyists	**$13,750**
Assn of Trial Lawyers of America	$13,000
Others	$750
Real Estate	**$10,250**
National Assn of Realtors	$10,000
Others	$250
Savings Banks	**$5,650**
US League of Savings Assn*	$5,550
Others	$100
Telecommunications	**$6,800**
North Western Bell Telephone	$2,700
AT&T	$1,500
Others	$2,600

Other Major Business PACs

National Auto Dealers Assn	$3,000	Auto Sales
Philip Morris	$2,500	Tobacco
Chicago Board of Trade	$2,000	Commodities
Chicago Mercantile Exchange	$2,000	Commodities
Food Marketing Institute	$1,950	Food Stores
American Meat Institute	$1,750	Meat Process
ACRE (Action Committee for Rural Electric)	$1,500	RuralElect
Morton Thiokol	$1,250	Space Equip
American Crystal Sugar Corp	$1,100	Sugar
American Sugarbeet Growers Assn	$1,100	Sugar
American Retail Federation	$1,100	Retail
American Veterinary Medical Assn	$1,000	Veterinary

PAC Totals by Category

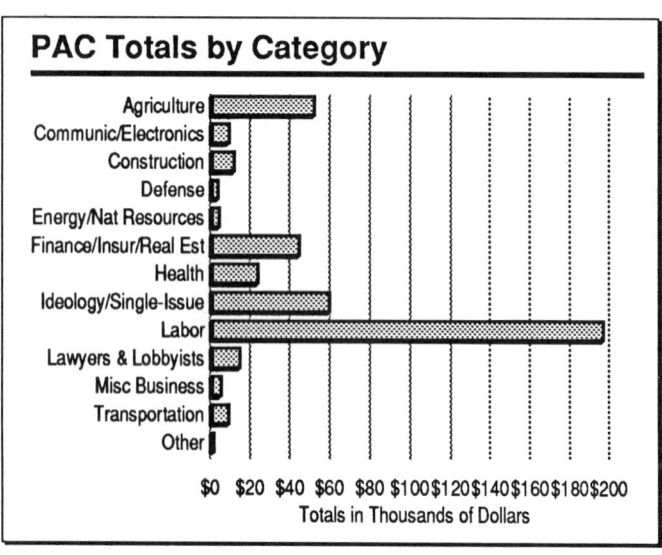

Agriculture
Communic/Electronics
Construction
Defense
Energy/Nat Resources
Finance/Insur/Real Est
Health
Ideology/Single-Issue
Labor
Lawyers & Lobbyists
Misc Business
Transportation
Other

$0 $20 $40 $60 $80 $100 $120 $140 $160 $180 $200
Totals in Thousands of Dollars

Labor

Bldg Trades/Industrial/Misc Unions $98,050

Intl Brotherhood of Electrical Workers	$14,000
United Auto Workers	$12,500
Machinists/Aerospace Workers Union	$11,000
AFL-CIO*	$10,000
Food & Commercial Workers Union	$9,250
Carpenters & Joiners Union	$8,000
United Steelworkers	$5,000
Sheet Metal Workers Union	$4,500
Communications Workers of America	$4,000
Operating Engineers Union	$4,000
Rubber Cork Linoleum Plastic Workers	$3,000
Laborers' Political League	$2,350
Ladies Garment Workers Union	$2,100
Plumbers/Pipefitters Union	$1,750
Amalgamated Clothing & Textile Workers	$1,100
Boilermakers Union	$1,100
Painters & Allied Trades Union	$1,000
Others	$3,400

Government & Postal Workers $41,000

National Assn of Retired Federal Employees	$11,000
American Fedn of State/County/Munic Employees	$10,000
National Assn of Letter Carriers	$10,000
American Postal Workers Union	$5,000
American Federation of Government Employees	$1,400
National Rural Letter Carriers Assn	$1,350
Others	$2,250

Teachers Unions $20,000

American Federation of Teachers	$10,000
National Education Assn	$10,000

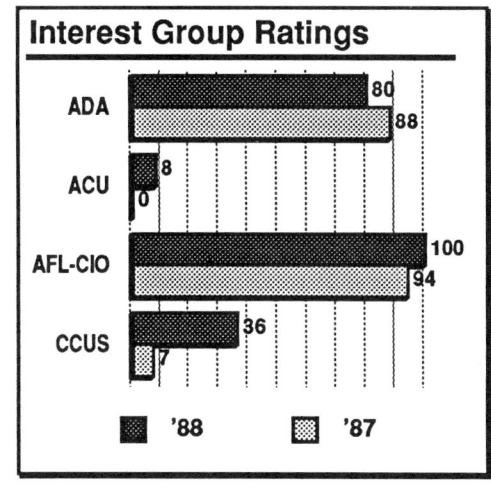

Interest Group Ratings

	'88	'87
ADA	80	88
ACU	8	0
AFL-CIO	100	94
CCUS	36	7

Transportation Unions $37,050

Teamsters Union*	$11,000
Seafarers International Union	$7,000
Air Line Pilots Assn	$5,000
Marine Engineers Union	$3,500
United Transportation Union	$3,100
Amalgamated Transit Union	$2,000
Transportation Communication Union	$1,850
Brotherhood of Locomotive Engineers	$1,250
Others	$2,350

Ideological/Single-Issue

Democratic/Liberal $13,497

National Cmte for an Effective Congress	$8,497
Class PAC	$2,500
Third District Central Cmte	$1,000
Others	$1,500

Democratic Leadership PACs $24,000

24th Cong Dist of California PAC (Henry Waxman)	$5,000
Majority Congress Committee (Jim Wright)	$5,000
Valley Education Fund (Tony Coelho)	$5,000
America's Leaders' Fund (Dan Rostenkowski)	$3,000
Independent Action (Morris Udall)	$2,000
Cmte for Democratic Opportunity (Bill Gray)	$1,500
Cmte for the 100th Congress (Charles Rangel)	$1,000
House Leadership Fund (Tom Foley)	$1,000
Others	$500

Pro-Israel $9,850

National PAC	$5,000
Joint Action Cmte for Political Affairs	$2,000
Multi-Issue PAC	$1,000
Washington PAC	$1,000
Others	$850

Other Major Ideological/Single-Issue PACs

National Cmte to Preserve Social Security	$5,500	Soc Secur
National Council of Senior Citizens	$2,000	Soc Secur
Sierra Club	$1,769	Environment
KidsPAC	$1,500	HealthWelfare
Council for a Livable World	$1,170	Pro-Peace

Independent expenditures supporting Nagle

National Cmte to Preserve Social Security	$2,861

---

* Contributions came from more than one PAC affiliated with this sponsor.

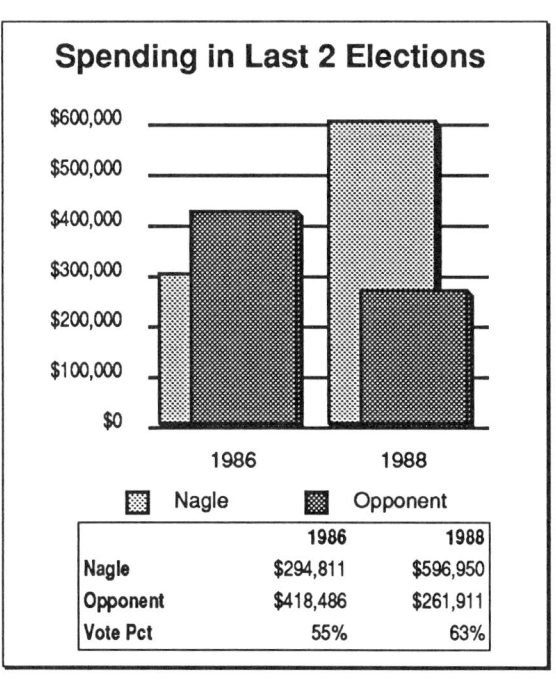

Spending in Last 2 Elections

	1986	1988
Nagle	$294,811	$596,950
Opponent	$418,486	$261,911
Vote Pct	55%	63%

Nagle / Opponent

William H. Natcher, D-Ky (2)

First elected: 1953
Total receipts: $8,397
Total from PACs: $0

1988 Committees & Subcommittees

Appropriations
Labor, Health and Human Services, Education and Related Agencies (Chairman)
District of Columbia
Rural Development, Agriculture and Related Agencies

PAC Contribution Profile

National Assn of Home Builders ....$1,000   Resid Constr

NOTE: Natcher reported taking no PAC funds in his 1988 campaign. The PAC listed above did report making a contribution to him during 1987-88, however, and that contribution is recorded in the official FEC records.

Independent expenditures supporting Natcher

National Cmte to Preserve Social Security $1,944

Campaign Revenue Sources

Individuals (2.3%)

Candidate (97.7%)

PAC Totals by Category

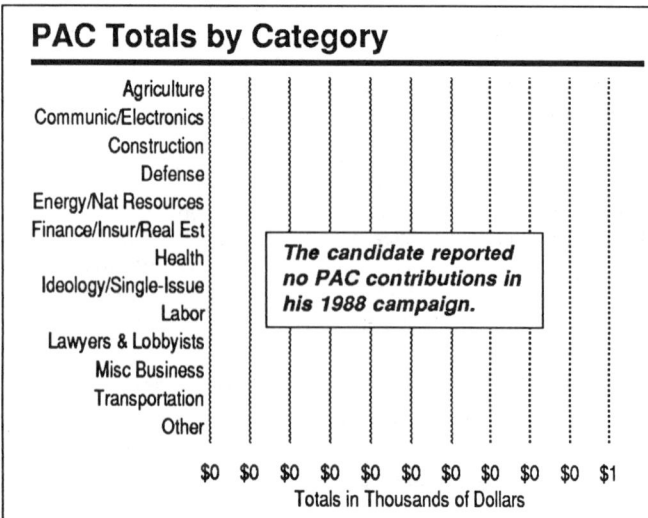

Agriculture
Communic/Electronics
Construction
Defense
Energy/Nat Resources
Finance/Insur/Real Est
Health
Ideology/Single-Issue
Labor
Lawyers & Lobbyists
Misc Business
Transportation
Other

The candidate reported no PAC contributions in his 1988 campaign.

$0 $0 $0 $0 $0 $0 $0 $0 $0 $0 $1
Totals in Thousands of Dollars

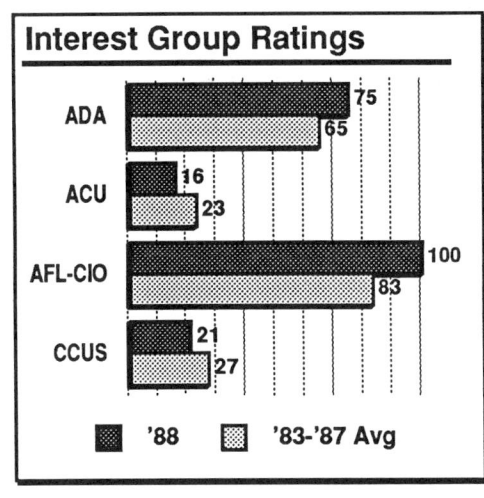

Interest Group Ratings

	'88	'83-'87 Avg
ADA	75	65
ACU	16	23
AFL-CIO	100	83
CCUS	21	27

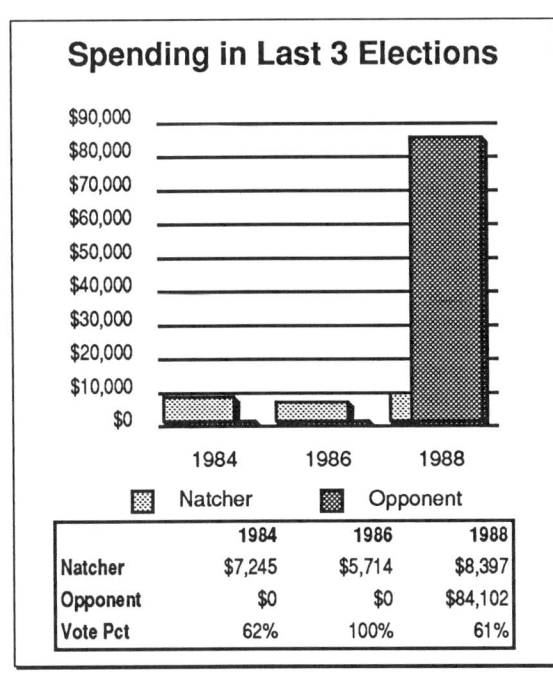

Spending in Last 3 Elections

	1984	1986	1988
Natcher	$7,245	$5,714	$8,397
Opponent	$0	$0	$84,102
Vote Pct	62%	100%	61%

Richard E. Neal, D-Mass (2)

First elected: 1988
Total receipts: $242,265
Total from PACs: $87,000

1989-90 Committees & Subcommittees

Banking, Finance and Urban Affairs
Economic Stabilization
General Oversight and Investigations
Housing and Community Development

Small Business
Procurement, Tourism and Rural Development

PAC Contribution Profile

Business

Construction	**$2,500**
National Assn of Home Builders	$2,500
Health Professionals	**$9,500**
American Medical Assn	$5,000
American Dental Assn	$2,500
American Academy of Ophthalmology	$2,000
Insurance...	**$7,820**
National Assn of Life Underwriters	$5,000
Massachusetts Mutual Life Insurance	$2,620
Others	$200
Lawyers	**$2,000**
Assn of Trial Lawyers of America	$2,000
Oil & Gas	**$2,500**
Coastal Corp...	$2,500
Paper Production...	**$2,000**
Westvaco Corp	$2,000
Real Estate	**$5,000**
National Assn of Realtors	$5,000
Telecommunications	**$5,000**
New England Tel & Tel......................................	$3,000
AT&T	$2,000

Campaign Revenue Sources

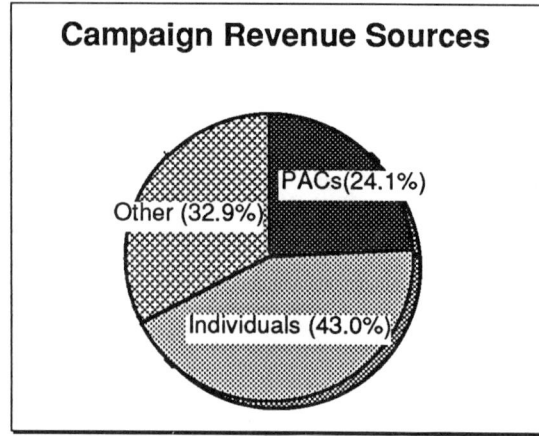

PACs(24.1%)
Other (32.9%)
Individuals (43.0%)

Other Major Business PACs

Auto Dealers & Drivers for Free Trade	$1,000	JapanAutoSal
Marriott Corp	$1,000	Hotel/Motel
American Bankers Assn	$500	Comml Banks
Bank of Boston	$500	Comml Banks
McDonald's Corp	$500	Restaurants
National Assn of Convenience Stores	$500	Dept Store
National Beer Wholesalers Assn	$500	Liquor Whlsl

PAC Totals by Category

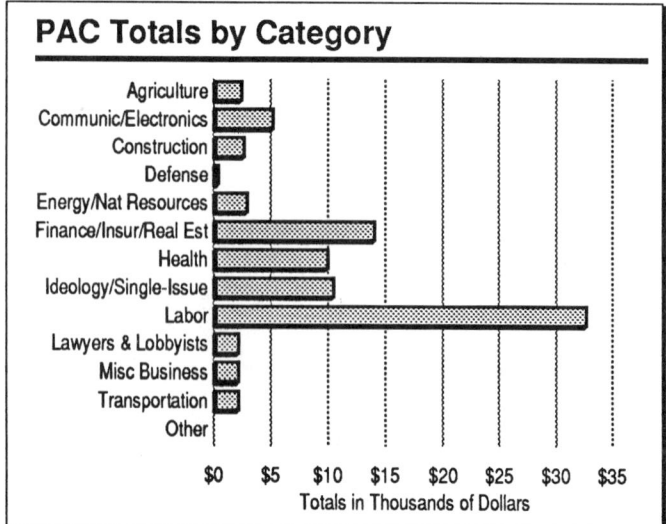

Category	
Agriculture	
Communic/Electronics	
Construction	
Defense	
Energy/Nat Resources	
Finance/Insur/Real Est	
Health	
Ideology/Single-Issue	
Labor	
Lawyers & Lobbyists	
Misc Business	
Transportation	
Other	

$0 $5 $10 $15 $20 $25 $30 $35
Totals in Thousands of Dollars

Labor

Bldg Trades/Industrial/Misc Unions $18,250
Food & Commercial Workers Union $5,000
Intl Brotherhood of Electrical Workers $2,750
AFL-CIO $2,500
Sheet Metal Workers Union $2,500
Carpenters & Joiners Union $1,500
Bricklayers Union $1,000
Communications Workers of America $1,000
Painters & Allied Trades Union $1,000
Boilermakers Union $500
Retail/Wholesale Dept Store Union $500

Government & Postal Workers $7,750
National Assn of Letter Carriers $5,000
American Fedn of State/County/Munic Employees $2,500
Others $250

Transportation Unions $6,500
Teamsters Union $5,000
United Transportation Union $1,000
Transportation Communication Union $500

Ideological/Single-Issue

Democratic Leadership PACs $2,000
America's Leaders' Fund (Dan Rostenkowski) $1,000
House Leadership Fund (Tom Foley) $1,000

Pro-Israel $5,250
National PAC $5,000
Others $250

Senior Citizens/Social Security $3,000
National Cmte to Preserve Social Security $3,000

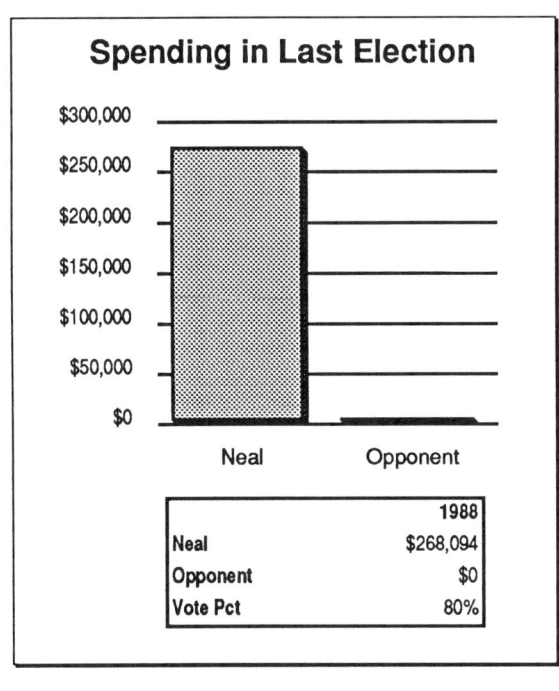

Spending in Last Election

	1988
Neal	$268,094
Opponent	$0
Vote Pct	80%

Stephen L. Neal, D-NC (5)

First elected: 1974
Total receipts: $715,578
Total from PACs: $411,180

1988 Committees & Subcommittees

Banking, Finance and Urban Affairs
Domestic Monetary Policy
Financial Institutions Supervision, Regulation and Insurance
Housing and Community Development
International Development, Finance, Trade and Monetary Policy

Government Operations
Legislation and National Security

PAC Contribution Profile

Business

Commercial Banks..$99,450

American Bankers Assn	$10,250
J P Morgan & Company	$10,000
Citicorp	$8,000
Chemical Bank	$6,000
Bankers Trust	$5,000
Assn of Bank Holding Companies	$4,000
Barnett Banks of Florida	$4,000
NCNB Corp	$4,000
Chase Manhattan	$3,500
First Chicago Corp	$3,500
Continental Illinois Corp	$3,250
Wells Fargo	$3,000
Marine Midland Banks	$2,750
Banc One Corp	$2,500
Citizens & Southern National Bank	$2,500
Manufacturers Hanover	$2,500
Consumer Bankers Assn	$2,000
Mellon Bank	$2,000
Security Pacific Corp	$2,000
BankAmerica	$1,500
Irving Bank	$1,500
First Bank System/Minnesota	$1,250
National City Corp	$1,250
Central Carolina Bank & Trust	$1,200
South Carolina National Bank	$1,100
Others	$10,900

Construction...$8,550

National Assn of Home Builders	$3,000
American Subcontractors Assn	$1,500
Others	$4,050

Campaign Revenue Sources

Party (4.0%)   Other (5.3%)
Candidate (3.2%)
Individuals (31.0%)
PACs (56.4%)

Dairy...$7,500

Associated Milk Producers	$3,000
Dairymen Inc-North Carolina	$2,500
Mid-American Dairymen	$1,500
Others	$500

Insurance...$13,450

Home Group Inc	$2,000
Mortgage Insurance Cos of America	$1,850
American International Group inc	$1,500
Integon Corp	$1,500
Others	$6,600

Lawyers & Lobbyists.......................................$10,500

Assn of Trial Lawyers of America	$5,000
Others	$5,500

Real Estate..$17,300

National Assn of Realtors	$10,000
First Union Corp	$3,250
Mortgage Bankers Assn of America	$1,500
Federal National Mortgage Assn	$1,300
Others	$1,250

Savings Banks & Credit Unions......................$20,050

US League of Savings Assn	$10,000
Credit Union National Assn	$4,500
National Council of Savings Institutions	$1,300
Others	$4,250

Securities/Commodities Investment...............$20,000

Chicago Board of Trade	$7,000
Chicago Mercantile Exchange	$5,000
First Boston Corp	$2,000
E F Hutton Group	$1,500
Others	$4,500

Telecommunications.......................................$12,500

AT&T	$7,000
Southern Bell	$3,500
Others	$2,000

Tobacco...$13,250

RJR Nabisco	$6,500
Philip Morris	$4,500
Tobacco Institute	$1,500
Others	$750

PAC Totals by Category

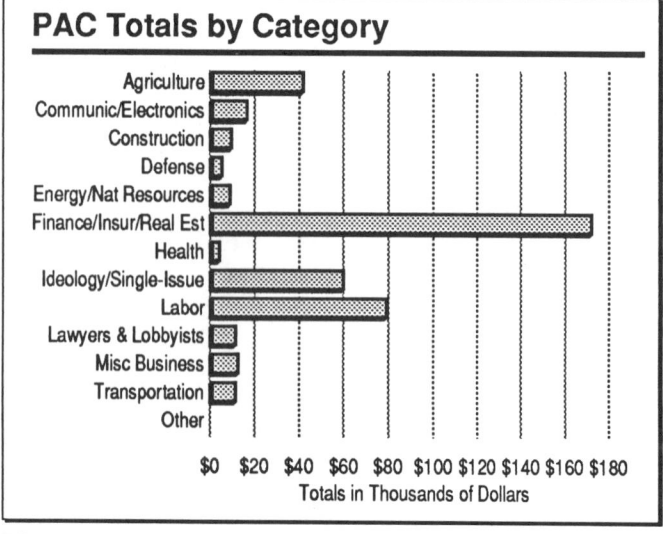

Category	
Agriculture	
Communic/Electronics	
Construction	
Defense	
Energy/Nat Resources	
Finance/Insur/Real Est	
Health	
Ideology/Single-Issue	
Labor	
Lawyers & Lobbyists	
Misc Business	
Transportation	
Other	

$0 $20 $40 $60 $80 $100 $120 $140 $160 $180
Totals in Thousands of Dollars

Other Major Business PACs

American Institute of CPA's	$5,000	Accountants
ACRE (Action Committee for Rural Electric)	$3,000	RuralElect
Boeing Company	$2,500	Aircraft
American Furniture Manufacturers Assn	$2,000	Furniture
J C Penney Company	$2,000	Dept Store
Textron Inc	$2,000	Air Defense
Piedmont Aviation	$1,750	Airlines
United Parcel Service	$1,750	Delivery
American Financial Services Assn	$1,500	Credit/Loans
Bay State Gas Company	$1,500	Natural Gas
Carolina Power & Light	$1,500	ElectricUtil
Computer Sciences Corp	$1,500	Data Process
Household International	$1,500	Credit/Loans
Burlington Industries	$1,400	Textiles
Southern Minnesota Beet Sugar Co-op	$1,250	Sugar
General Electric	$1,175	Electronics

Labor

Bldg Trades/Industrial/Misc Unions	**$25,550**
Communications Workers of America	$5,000
Food & Commercial Workers Union	$4,500
United Auto Workers	$4,500
AFL-CIO	$2,500
Food/Commercial Workers Local #1222	$2,000
Sheet Metal Workers Union	$2,000
Ladies Garment Workers Union	$1,500
Amalgamated Clothing & Textile Workers	$1,050
Others	$2,500

Government & Postal Workers	**$25,650**
National Assn of Letter Carriers	$10,000
National Assn of Retired Federal Employees	$7,000
American Fedn of State/County/Munic Employees	$3,000
American Postal Workers Union	$2,000
National Rural Letter Carriers Assn	$1,250
National Assn of Postmasters	$1,150
Others	$1,250

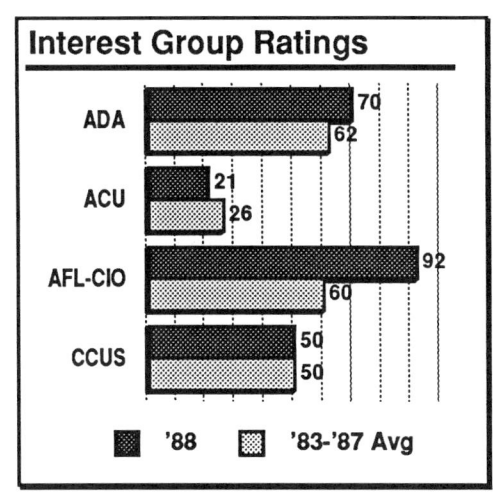

Interest Group Ratings

	'88	'83-'87 Avg
ADA	70	62
ACU	21	26
AFL-CIO	92	60
CCUS	50	50

Teachers Unions	**$10,000**
National Education Assn	$10,000

Transportation Unions	**$16,750**
Teamsters Union	$10,000
Seafarers International Union	$3,000
United Transportation Union	$2,500
Others	$1,250

Ideological/Single-Issue

Democratic/Liberal	**$12,671**
National Cmte for an Effective Congress	$9,171
Democratic Study Group Campaign Fund	$3,000
Others	$500

Democratic Leadership PACs	**$25,500**
24th Cong Dist of California PAC (Henry Waxman)	$5,000
Majority Congress Committee (Jim Wright)	$5,000
America's Leaders' Fund (Dan Rostenkowski)	$3,000
House Leadership Fund (Tom Foley)	$3,000
Valley Education Fund (Tony Coelho)	$3,000
Cmte for Democratic Opportunity (Bill Gray)	$2,000
Pax Americas (David Bonior)	$1,500
Others	$3,000

Other Major Ideological/Single-Issue PACs

National Abortion Rights Action League	$5,500	Pro-Choice
National Rifle Assn	$4,950	Pro-Guns
Voters for Choice/Friends of Family Planning	$3,000	Pro-Choice
Sierra Club	$2,614	Environment
National Cmte to Preserve Social Security	$2,000	Soc Secur

Independent expenditures supporting Neal

National Cmte to Preserve Social Security	$2,666

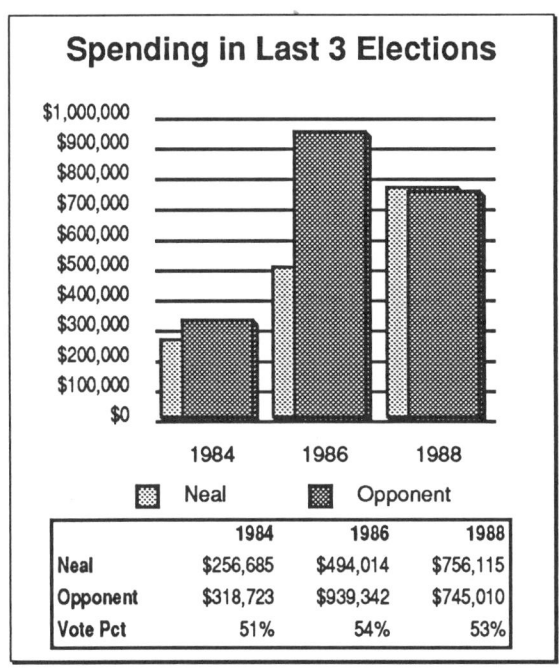

Spending in Last 3 Elections

	1984	1986	1988
Neal	$256,685	$494,014	$756,115
Opponent	$318,723	$939,342	$745,010
Vote Pct	51%	54%	53%

Neal · Opponent

Bill Nelson, D-Fla (11)

1988 Committees & Subcommittees

Banking, Finance and Urban Affairs
Financial Institutions Supervision, Regulation and Insurance

Science, Space and Technology
Space Science and Applications (Chairman)
Transportation, Aviation and Materials

First elected: 1978
Total receipts: $456,878
Total from PACs: $212,956

Campaign Revenue Sources

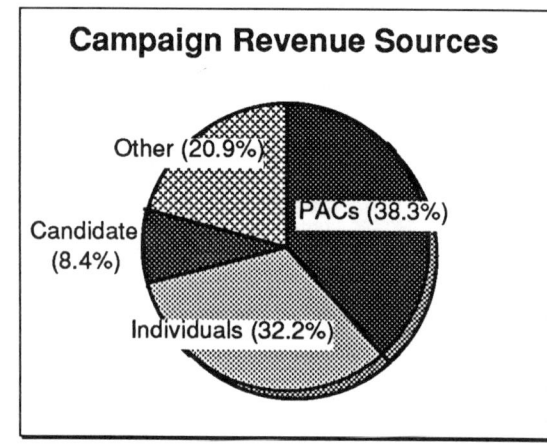

Other (20.9%)
Candidate (8.4%)
PACs (38.3%)
Individuals (32.2%)

PAC Contribution Profile

Business

Automotive **$7,150**

National Auto Dealers Assn	$5,050
Ford Motor Company	$1,050
Others	$1,050

Aviation & Aerospace **$18,700**

Boeing Company	$6,000
United Technologies	$2,400
Martin Marietta Corp	$2,350
Eastern Airlines	$1,550
Morton Thiokol	$1,200
TRW Inc	$1,150
Fairchild Industries	$1,050
Texas Air	$1,050
Others	$1,950

Computers & Electronics **$6,675**

Computer Sciences Corp	$3,000
General Electric	$2,325
Others	$1,350

Construction **$4,950**

None over $850

Defense **$29,450**

Harris Corp	$6,000
Lockheed Corp	$5,000
McDonnell Douglas	$3,000
Rockwell International	$3,000
Grumman	$2,350
General Dynamics	$2,000
Hughes Aircraft	$1,750
Textron Inc	$1,400
Litton Industries	$1,050
LTV Aerospace & Defense Company	$1,050
Others	$2,850

Electric Utilities **$3,350**

Teco Energy Inc	$1,000
Others	$2,350

Financial Institutions **$29,950**

Barnett Banks of Florida	$5,000
American Bankers Assn	$3,000
Florida League of Financial Institutions	$3,000
Citizens & Southern National Bank	$2,700
Glendale Federal Savings & Loan	$2,000
National Banks of Florida	$2,000
US League of Savings Assn	$1,400
Southeast Banking Corp	$1,100
Centrust Savings Bank	$1,000
Credit Union National Assn	$1,000
Sun Banks	$1,000
Others	$6,750

Food & Beverage **$4,350**

Food Marketing Institute	$1,000
General Mills Restaurants	$1,000
Winn-Dixie Stores	$1,000
Others	$1,350

Health Professionals **$11,800**

American Medical Assn	$5,150
Florida Medical Assn	$4,800
American Academy of Ophthalmology	$1,000
Others	$850

Hotels & Motels/Travel Agents **$6,100**

American Hotel & Motel Assn	$1,700
American Society of Travel Agents	$1,000
Holiday Corp	$1,000
Others	$2,400

PAC Totals by Category

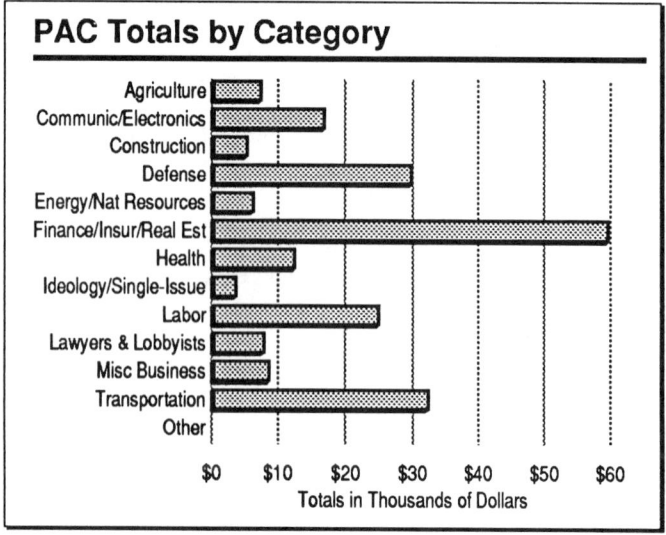

Totals in Thousands of Dollars

- Agriculture
- Communic/Electronics
- Construction
- Defense
- Energy/Nat Resources
- Finance/Insur/Real Est
- Health
- Ideology/Single-Issue
- Labor
- Lawyers & Lobbyists
- Misc Business
- Transportation
- Other

$0 $10 $20 $30 $40 $50 $60

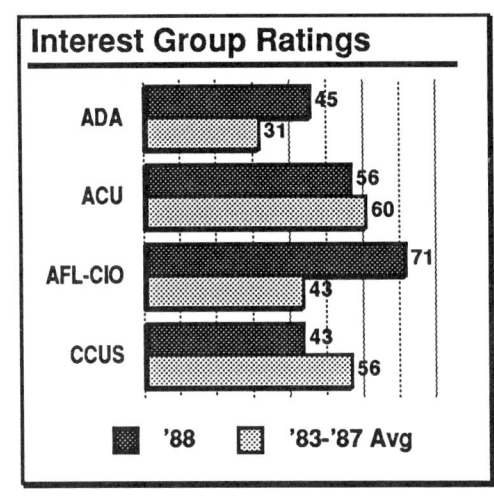

Insurance...$8,950
    ITT Corp $3,500
    Independent Insurance Agents of America $1,350
    Travelers Corp $1,000
    Others $3,100

Lawyers $7,500
    Assn of Trial Lawyers of America $2,850
    Baker & Hostetler $1,000
    Others $3,650

Oil & Gas $2,050
    None over $500

Real Estate $14,750
    National Assn of Realtors $10,000
    First Union Corp $1,500
    Others $3,250

Retail Sales $2,511
    Federated Department Stores $1,000
    Others $1,511

Securities/Commodities Investment $3,700
    Goldman Sachs $2,000
    Others $1,700

Telecommunications $9,300
    Southern Bell $4,000
    AT&T $2,050
    Continental Telecom $1,350
    Others $1,900

Other Major Business PACs

Greyhound Corp ....$1,700   Hhold Chem
A Duda & Sons ....$1,000   Fruit/Veg

Interest Group Ratings

	'88	'83-'87 Avg
ADA	45	31
ACU	56	60
AFL-CIO	71	43
CCUS	43	56

Labor

Bldg Trades/Industrial/Misc Unions $3,950
    United Auto Workers $1,350
    IBEW Local #606 ....$1,000
    Others $1,600

Government & Postal Workers $11,400
    National Assn of Retired Federal Employees $8,000
    National Assn of Letter Carriers $2,700
    Others $700

Teachers Unions $3,050
    National Education Assn $3,050

Transportation Unions $6,200
    Marine Engineers District 2 Maritime Officers $3,000
    Seafarers International Union $1,500
    Transport Workers Union $1,000
    Others $700

Ideological/Single-Issue

Ideological/Single-Issue $3,300
    Valley Education Fund (Tony Coelho) $1,000
    Others $2,300

Independent expenditures supporting Nelson

National Cmte to Preserve Social Security $4,769

Spending in Last 3 Elections

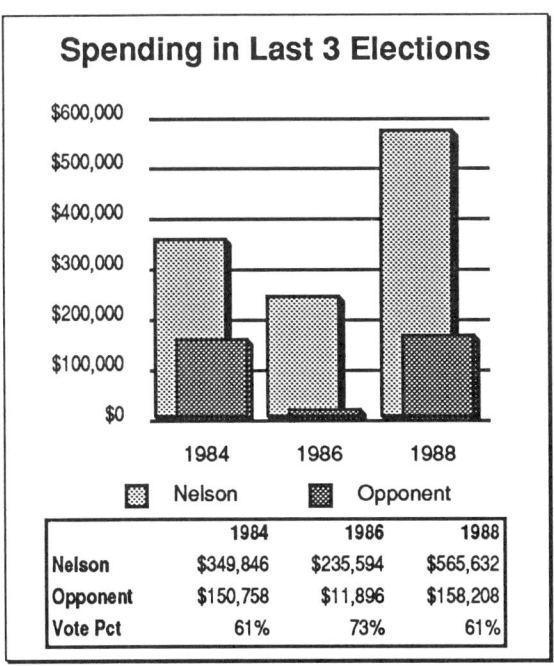

	1984	1986	1988
Nelson	$349,846	$235,594	$565,632
Opponent	$150,758	$11,896	$158,208
Vote Pct	61%	73%	61%

Bill Nichols, D-Ala (3)

1988 Committees & Subcommittees

Armed Services
Investigations (Chairman)
Military Personnel and Compensation
Readiness

First elected: 1966
Total receipts: $230,584
Total from PACs: $88,936

PAC Contribution Profile

Business

Automotive	**$1,500**
National Auto Dealers Assn	$1,000
Others	$500
Commercial Banks	**$2,700**
American Bankers Assn	$1,000
Amsouth Bancorp	$1,000
Others	$700
Computer Equipment	**$1,500**
Intergraph Corp	$1,500
Construction	**$3,050**
Associated General Contractors	$1,250
Others	$1,800
Defense	**$31,550**
FMC Corp	$2,500
General Atomics	$2,000
General Dynamics	$2,000
Hughes Aircraft	$2,000
Rockwell International	$2,000
Singer Company	$2,000
McDonnell Douglas*	$1,800
Boeing Company	$1,000
Continental Telecom	$1,000
Figgie International	$1,000
General Electric	$1,000
Grumman	$1,000
Northrop Corp	$1,000
Textron Inc	$1,000
United Technologies	$1,000
Others	$9,250

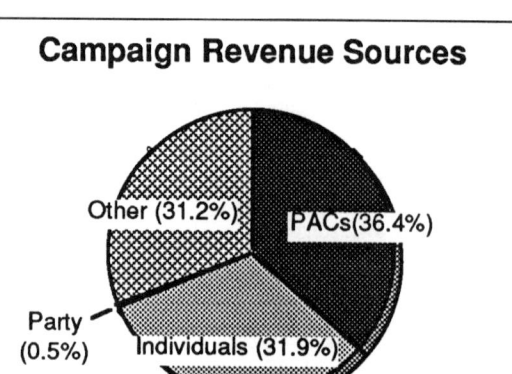

Campaign Revenue Sources

Other (31.2%)
PACs (36.4%)
Party (0.5%)
Individuals (31.9%)

Electric Utilities	**$1,900**
Southern Company*	$1,400
Others	$500
Food & Beverage	**$3,500**
National Beer Wholesalers Assn	$1,000
Others	$2,500
Health Professionals	**$6,750**
American Medical Assn	$4,250
American Dental Assn	$1,500
Others	$1,000
Mining & Metals Processing	**$1,750**
Dravo Corp	$1,000
Others	$750
Oil & Gas	**$2,250**
Alagasco Inc	$1,000
Others	$1,250
Paper Production	**$1,800**
Mead Corp	$1,000
Others	$800
Real Estate	**$5,750**
National Assn of Realtors	$5,750
Telecommunications	**$2,000**
South Central Bell Telephone	$2,000
Textiles & Clothing Manufacturers	**$2,800**
None over $550	

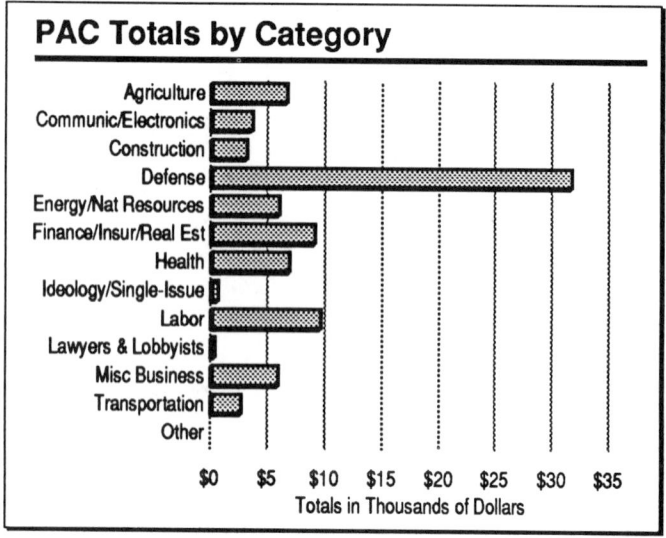

PAC Totals by Category

Agriculture
Communic/Electronics
Construction
Defense
Energy/Nat Resources
Finance/Insur/Real Est
Health
Ideology/Single-Issue
Labor
Lawyers & Lobbyists
Misc Business
Transportation
Other

$0 $5 $10 $15 $20 $25 $30 $35
Totals in Thousands of Dollars

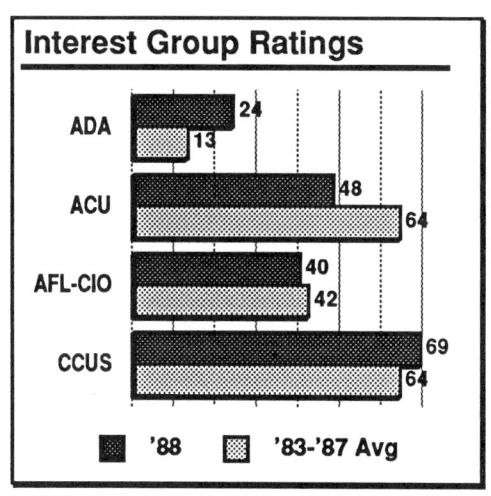

Interest Group Ratings

Labor

Government & Postal Workers $6,200
American Federation of Government Employees $5,000
Others $1,200

Other Unions $3,250
United Auto Workers $2,000
Seafarers International Union $1,000
Others $250

Independent expenditures supporting Nichols

National Cmte to Preserve Social Security $2,101

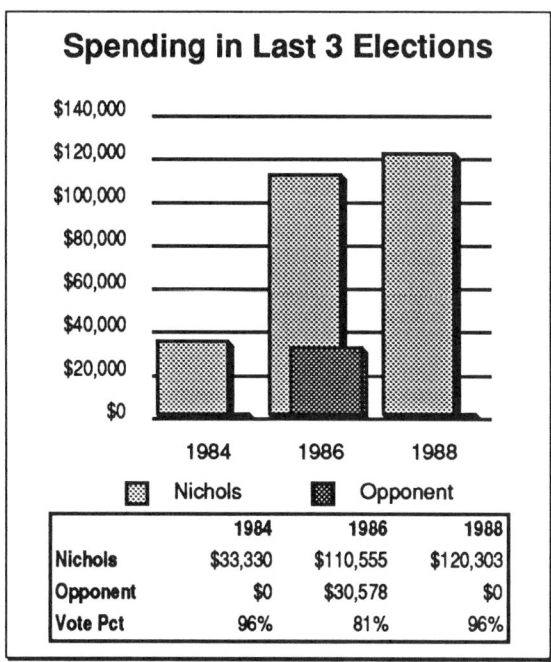

Spending in Last 3 Elections

	1984	1986	1988
Nichols	$33,330	$110,555	$120,303
Opponent	$0	$30,578	$0
Vote Pct	96%	81%	96%

Nichols   *Opponent*

* Contributions came from more than one PAC affiliated with this sponsor.

789

Howard C. Nielson, R-Utah (3)

First elected: 1982
Total receipts: $132,528
Total from PACs: $112,800

1988 Committees & Subcommittees

Energy and Commerce
Commerce, Consumer Protection and Competitiveness
Telecommunications and Finance

Government Operations
Government Activities and Transportation (Ranking Republican)

PAC Contribution Profile

Campaign Revenue Sources

Party (1.7%)
Other (3.4%)
Individuals (13.4%)
PACs (81.4%)

Business

Accountants	**$6,000**
American Institute of CPA's	$5,000
Others	$1,000
Air Transport	**$1,500**
Delta Airlines	$600
Texas Air	$600
Others	$300
Automotive	**$4,400**
National Auto Dealers Assn	$2,300
Auto Dealers & Drivers for Free Trade	$1,500
Others	$600
Chemicals	**$2,100**
Hercules Inc	$800
Others	$1,300
Commercial Banks	**$5,100**
J P Morgan & Company	$2,000
American Bankers Assn	$1,500
Commercial Security Bancorp	$1,000
Others	$600
Construction	**$4,050**
Associated General Contractors	$1,300
National Electrical Contractors Assn	$1,000
National Assn of Home Builders	$900
Others	$850

Defense	**$2,400**
Martin Marietta Corp	$600
Rockwell International	$600
Others	$1,200
Electric Utilities	**$4,450**
Southern Company*	$1,000
Southern California Edison	$800
ACRE (Action Committee for Rural Electrification)	$600
Edison Electric Institute	$600
Others	$1,450
Health Professionals	**$15,400**
American Medical Assn	$10,000
American Dental Assn	$3,500
Cmte for Quality Orthopedic Health Care	$1,000
Others	$900
Insurance	**$8,400**
National Assn of Life Underwriters	$4,500
National Assn of Independent Insurers	$1,100
National Assn Mutual Insurance Agents	$800
Casualty & Surety Agents Assn	$600
Others	$1,400
Mining & Metals Processing	**$3,300**
National Coal Assn	$600
Peabody Coal	$600
Others	$2,100
Oil & Gas	**$12,600**
Petroleum Marketers Assn	$1,000
Sun Company	$1,000
Union Pacific Corp	$900
Mountain Fuel Supply	$800
BP America	$700
Amoco Corp	$600
Columbia Hydrocarbon Corp	$600
CSX Transportation Inc	$600
Chevron Corp	$550
Others	$5,850
Pharmaceuticals	**$4,950**
Schering-Plough Corp	$1,500
Abbott Laboratories	$600
Ciba-Geigy Corp	$600
Hoffman-La Roche	$600
Others	$1,650

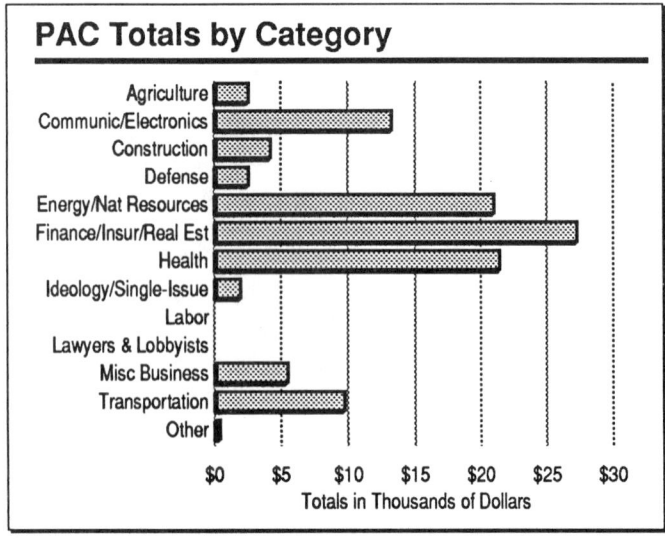

PAC Totals by Category

Agriculture
Communic/Electronics
Construction
Defense
Energy/Nat Resources
Finance/Insur/Real Est
Health
Ideology/Single-Issue
Labor
Lawyers & Lobbyists
Misc Business
Transportation
Other

$0 $5 $10 $15 $20 $25 $30
Totals in Thousands of Dollars

Real Estate **$3,500**
    National Assn of Realtors $3,200
    Others $300

Securities/Commodities Investment **$5,000**
    Chicago Board of Trade $1,000
    Travelers Corp $1,000
    Securities Industry Assn $600
    Others $2,400

Telecommunications **$11,800**
    AT&T $3,500
    Mountain Bell $3,000
    Continental Telecom $1,000
    BellSouth Corp* $900
    Bell Atlantic $600
    NYNEX Corp $600
    Others $2,200

Other Major Business PACs

Marriott Corp	$1,000	Hotel/Motel
National Assn of Broadcasters	$1,000	TV/Radio
United Parcel Service	$900	Delivery
Norfolk Southern Corp	$600	Railroads

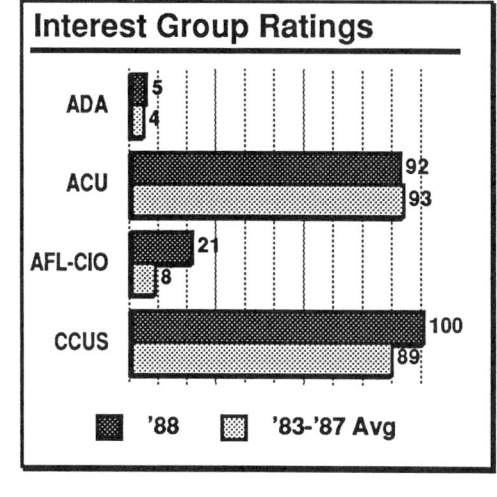

Interest Group Ratings

	'88	'83–'87 Avg
ADA	5	4
ACU	92	93
AFL-CIO	21	8
CCUS	100	89

■ '88   ▨ '83–'87 Avg

Major Ideological/Single-Issue PACs

Ruff PAC ....$600   Tax Policy

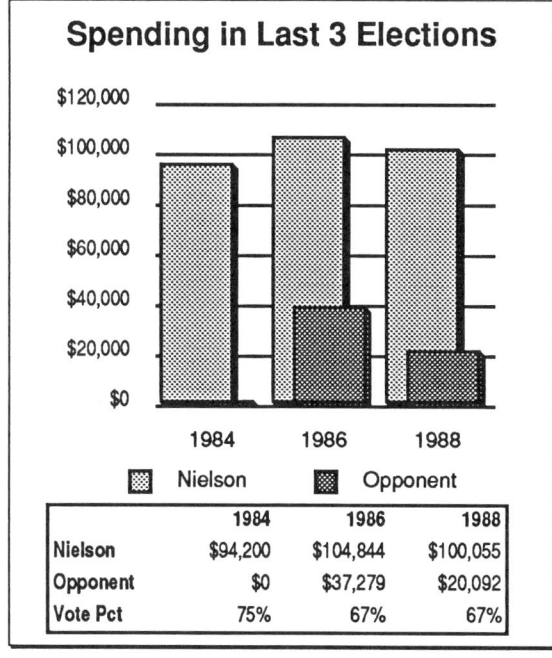

Spending in Last 3 Elections

▨ Nielson   ▨ Opponent

	1984	1986	1988
Nielson	$94,200	$104,844	$100,055
Opponent	$0	$37,279	$20,092
Vote Pct	75%	67%	67%

---

* Contributions came from more than one PAC affiliated
with this sponsor.

Henry J. Nowak, D-NY (33)

First elected: 1974
Total receipts: $122,806
Total from PACs: $91,725

1988 Committees & Subcommittees

Public Works and Transportation
Water Resources (Chairman)
Investigations and Oversight
Surface Transportation

Science, Space and Technology
Natural Resources, Agriculture Research and Environment
Science, Research and Technology

PAC Contribution Profile

Business

Air Transport **$1,200**
    None over $600

Bus Lines **$1,200**
    None over $900

Commercial & Savings Bank **$3,450**
    Chase Lincoln First Bank $1,450
    Goldome Bank for Savings $1,000
    Others $1,000

Construction **$11,100**
    National Utility Contractors Assn $5,000
    Associated General Contractors $1,300
    National Society of Professional Engineers $1,250
    Manville Corp $1,000
    National Assn of Home Builders $1,000
    Others $1,550

Defense **$2,400**
    LTV Aerospace & Defense Company $1,200
    Others $1,200

Food & Beverage **$1,500**
    National Beer Wholesalers Assn $1,000
    Others $500

Health Professionals **$1,300**
    New York Medical Assn $1,000
    Others $300

Lawyers **$2,500**
    Assn of Trial Lawyers of America $1,500
    California Trial Lawyers Assn $1,000

Real Estate **$4,100**
    National Assn of Realtors $2,800
    National Parking Assn $1,000
    Others $300

Telecommunications **$2,304**
    AT&T $1,500
    Others $804

Trucking/Delivery **$5,820**
    United Parcel Service $1,700
    Yellow Freight System $1,600
    North American Van Lines $1,300
    Others $1,220

Other Major Business PACs

Associated Milk Producers $1,000	Dairy
National Assn of Life Underwriters $1,000	Life Insurance
Delaware North Companies $1,000	Racetracks

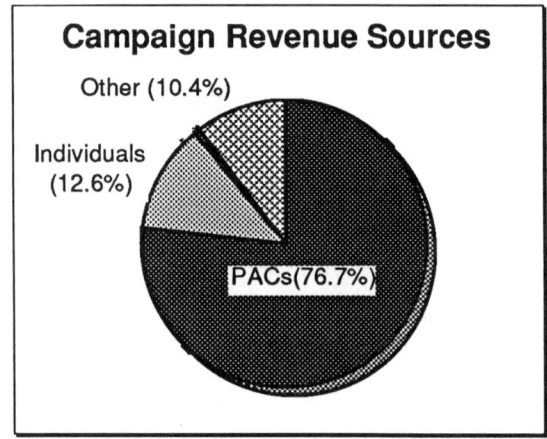

Campaign Revenue Sources

Other (10.4%)
Individuals (12.6%)
PACs (76.7%)

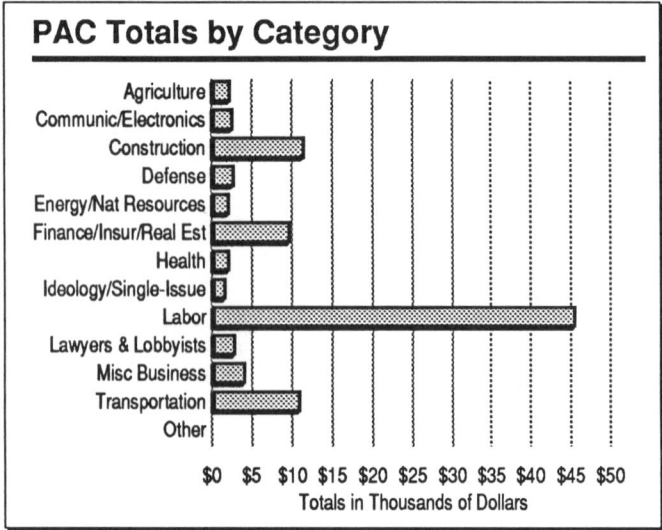

PAC Totals by Category

Agriculture
Communic/Electronics
Construction
Defense
Energy/Nat Resources
Finance/Insur/Real Est
Health
Ideology/Single-Issue
Labor
Lawyers & Lobbyists
Misc Business
Transportation
Other

$0 $5 $10 $15 $20 $25 $30 $35 $40 $45 $50
Totals in Thousands of Dollars

Labor

Bldg Trades/Industrial/Misc Unions $15,075

    Operating Engineers Local #17 ....$4,075
    Carpenters & Joiners Union $2,000
    United Steelworkers $2,000
    Laborers' Political League $1,500
    Food & Commercial Workers Union $1,000
    Sheet Metal Workers Union $1,000
    Others $3,500

Government & Postal Workers $8,800

    National Assn of Retired Federal Employees $5,000
    American Fedn of State/County/Munic Employees $2,000
    Others $1,800

Teachers Unions $4,500

    National Education Assn $4,500

Transportation Unions $16,800

    Air Line Pilots Assn $5,000
    Teamsters Union $5,000
    International Longshoremen Assn $1,800
    United Transportation Union $1,200
    Amalgamated Transit Union.............................$1,000
    Seafarers International Union $1,000
    Others $1,800

Independent expenditures supporting Nowak

National Cmte to Preserve Social Security $1,683

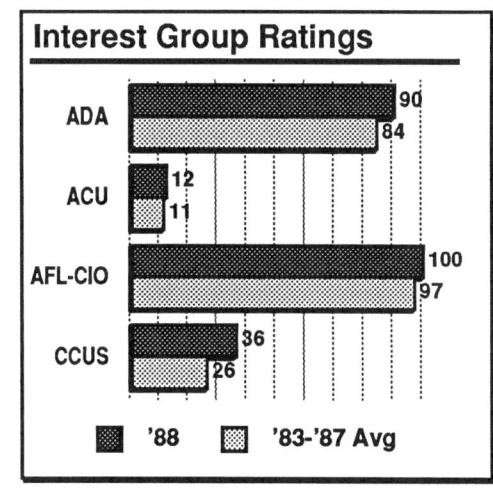

Interest Group Ratings

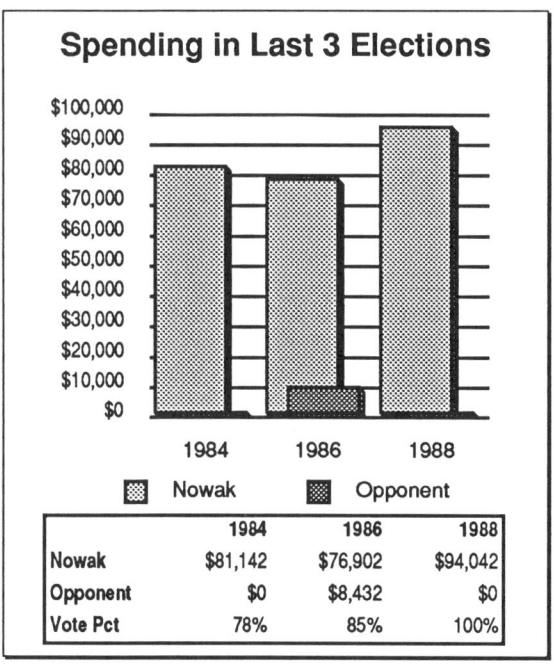

Spending in Last 3 Elections

	1984	1986	1988
Nowak	$81,142	$76,902	$94,042
Opponent	$0	$8,432	$0
Vote Pct	78%	85%	100%

Mary Rose Oakar, D-Ohio (20)

First elected: 1976
Total receipts: $691,256
Total from PACs: $387,918

1988 Committees & Subcommittees

Banking, Finance and Urban Affairs
Economic Stabilization (Chairwoman)
Financial Institutions Supervision, Regulation and Insurance
Housing and Community Development

House Administration
Libraries and Memorials (Chairwoman)
Accounts

Post Office and Civil Service
Compensation and Employee Benefits

Select Aging
Health and Long-Term Care
Retirement Income and Employment

Joint Library

PAC Contribution Profile

Business

Commercial Banks	**$37,320**
National City Corp	$5,450
Ameritrust Company	$5,050
Banc One Corp	$3,200
Society Corp	$3,100
Barnett Banks of Florida	$3,000
American Bankers Assn	$2,000
Chemical Bank	$2,000
Citicorp	$2,000
J P Morgan & Company	$2,000
Huntington Bank of Northeast Ohio	$1,970
Assn of Bank Holding Companies	$1,800
Others	$5,750
Construction	**$6,050**
National Assn of Home Builders	$2,250
Others	$3,800
Credit Unions	**$6,600**
Credit Union National Assn	$4,000
National Assn of Federal Credit Unions	$2,600
Dairy	**$6,000**
Associated Milk Producers	$4,000
Others	$2,000
Health Professionals	**$19,153**
American Nurses Assn	$5,053
American Chiropractic Assn	$2,500
American Podiatry Assn	$2,000
American Optometric Assn	$1,800
American Medical Assn	$1,500
Others	$6,300

Campaign Revenue Sources

Other (7.7%)
Party (0.6%)
PACs (55.2%)
Individuals (36.6%)

Insurance	**$11,350**
Independent Insurance Agents of America	$2,100
Blue Cross & Blue Shield Assn	$1,650
National Assn of Life Underwriters	$1,500
Casualty & Surety Agents Assn	$1,250
National Assn Mutual Insurance Agents	$1,250
Others	$3,600
Lawyers & Lobbyists	**$17,350**
Jones, Day, Reavis & Pogue	$5,000
Camp, Barsh, Bates & Tate	$3,000
Baker & Hostetler	$2,000
National Action Cmte (Dave Evans)	$1,500
Thompson, Hine and Flory	$1,500
Others	$4,350
Real Estate	**$10,000**
National Assn of Realtors	$7,300
Mortgage Bankers Assn of America	$1,250
Others	$1,450
Savings Banks	**$13,625**
US League of Savings Assn	$8,000
National Council of Savings Institutions	$1,500
Others	$4,125
Securities Investment	**$15,850**
Goldman Sachs	$2,500
Prudential-Bache Securities	$2,500
Municipal Securities Industry	$2,000
Investment Company Institute	$1,500
Others	$7,350

Other Major Business PACs

LTV Steel	$4,500	Steel
United Parcel Service	$4,300	Delivery
National Assn of Social Workers	$3,040	Social Work
AT&T	$2,500	LongDistance
BP America	$2,000	Major Oil
Rockwell International	$1,770	Air Defense
Chrysler Corp	$1,750	Auto Mfrs
National Assn for Home Care	$1,500	Home Care
Centerior Energy Corp	$1,200	ElectricUtil
American Financial Services Assn	$1,100	Credit/Loans

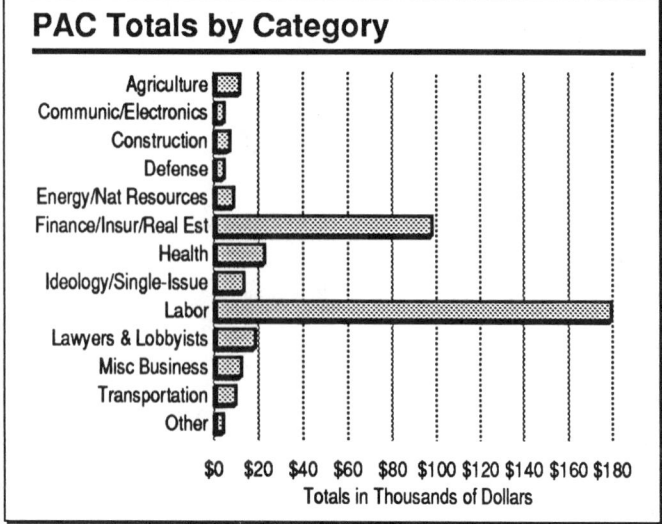

PAC Totals by Category

Agriculture
Communic/Electronics
Construction
Defense
Energy/Nat Resources
Finance/Insur/Real Est
Health
Ideology/Single-Issue
Labor
Lawyers & Lobbyists
Misc Business
Transportation
Other

$0 $20 $40 $60 $80 $100 $120 $140 $160 $180
Totals in Thousands of Dollars

Labor

Bldg Trades/Industrial/Misc Unions $76,879

United Auto Workers	$7,300
Sheet Metal Workers Union	$6,000
Machinists/Aerospace Workers Union	$5,500
Carpenters & Joiners Union	$5,000
Communications Workers of America	$5,000
Operating Engineers Union	$5,000
Plumbers/Pipefitters Union	$5,000
United Steelworkers	$5,000
Food & Commercial Workers Union	$4,679
AFL-CIO*	$3,450
Intl Brotherhood of Electrical Workers*	$3,400
Laborers' Political League	$3,000
United Mine Workers	$3,000
Service Employees International Union	$2,300
Boilermakers Union	$2,000
Rubber Cork Linoleum Plastic Workers	$2,000
Ladies Garment Workers Union	$1,550
Graphic Communications Union	$1,500
Ironworkers Union	$1,500
Hotel/Restaurant Employees Union	$1,250
Others	$3,450

Government & Postal Workers $58,900

National Assn of Letter Carriers	$15,000
National Assn of Retired Federal Employees	$10,000
American Postal Workers Union	$6,500
National Treasury Employees Union	$5,500
American Fedn of State/County/Munic Employees	$5,000
American Federation of Government Employees	$4,450
National Rural Letter Carriers Assn	$3,000
National Assn of Postal Supervisors	$2,000
International Assn of Firefighters	$1,500
Federal Managers' Assn	$1,100
National Federation of Federal Employees	$1,100
Others	$3,750

Teachers Unions $12,500

National Education Assn	$7,500
American Federation of Teachers	$5,000

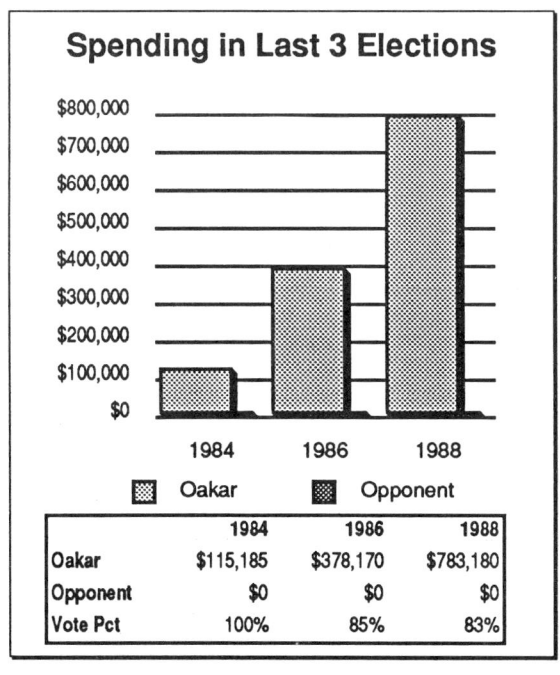

Spending in Last 3 Elections

	1984	1986	1988
Oakar	$115,185	$378,170	$783,180
Opponent	$0	$0	$0
Vote Pct	100%	85%	83%

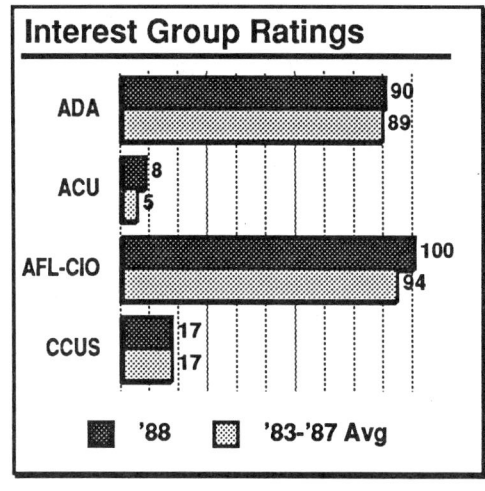

Interest Group Ratings

	'88	'83-'87 Avg
ADA	90	89
ACU	8	5
AFL-CIO	100	94
CCUS	17	17

Transportation Unions $30,000

Air Line Pilots Assn	$5,000
Teamsters Union	$5,000
International Longshoremen Assn	$4,000
United Transportation Union	$3,500
Seafarers International Union	$2,500
Maintenance of Way Employees	$2,000
Marine Engineers District 2 Maritime Officers	$2,000
Transportation Communication Union	$1,450
Brotherhood of Locomotive Engineers	$1,100
Others	$3,450

Ideological/Single-Issue

Ideological/Single-Issue $11,600

National Cmte to Preserve Social Security	$5,100	Soc Secur
National Assn of Arab-Americans	$3,750	ForeignPolcy
Others	$2,750	

Independent expenditures supporting Oakar

National Cmte to Preserve Social Security	$1,698

---

* Contributions came from more than one PAC affiliated with this sponsor.

James L. Oberstar, D-Minn (8)

First elected: 1974
Total receipts: $281,331
Total from PACs: $206,320

1988 Committees & Subcommittees

Budget
Budget Process
Community and Natural Resources
Defense, Foreign Policy and Space

Public Works and Transportation
Investigations and Oversight (Chairman)
Economic Development
Water Resources

PAC Contribution Profile

Business

Air Transport/Air Freight	**$22,400**
Federal Express Corp	$10,000
American Airlines	$3,300
Aircraft Owners & Pilots Assn	$2,900
Texas Air	$1,950
United Airlines	$1,400
Others	$2,850
Construction	**$9,100**
National Utility Contractors Assn	$4,500
Manville Corp	$1,000
National Assn of Home Builders	$1,000
Others	$2,600
Dairy	**$7,500**
Associated Milk Producers	$5,000
Land O'Lakes Inc	$1,500
Mid-American Dairymen	$1,000
Electric Utilities	**$2,440**
ACRE (Action Committee for Rural Electrification)	$1,000
Others	$1,440
Food & Beverage	**$3,100**
General Mills*	$1,500
Food Marketing Institute	$1,100
Others	$500
Forest Products	**$6,250**
Potlatch Corp	$5,000
Boise Cascade	$1,000
Others	$250

Campaign Revenue Sources

Other (8.9%)
Party (2.4%)
Individuals (17.7%)
PACs(70.9%)

Health Professionals	**$3,500**
American Medical Assn	$3,300
Others	$200
Lawyers	**$6,800**
Assn of Trial Lawyers of America	$5,000
Others	$1,800
Real Estate	**$3,800**
National Assn of Realtors	$3,000
Others	$800
Sugar Growers	**$4,350**
Southern Minnesota Beet Sugar Co-op	$2,500
American Crystal Sugar Corp	$1,300
Others	$550
Telecommunications	**$4,900**
North Western Bell Telephone	$2,700
National Telephone Co-op Assn	$1,200
AT&T	$1,000
Trucking Companies	**$12,600**
United Parcel Service	$3,500
Yellow Freight System	$2,250
Minnesota Truck Operators	$2,000
American Trucking Assns	$1,550
Consolidated Freightways	$1,500
North American Van Lines	$1,000
Others	$800
Waste Management	**$2,300**
Waste Management Inc	$2,000
Others	$300

Other Major Business PACs

Cleveland-Cliffs Iron Company	$1,800	Metals/Mining
National Auto Dealers Assn	$1,000	Auto Sales

PAC Totals by Category

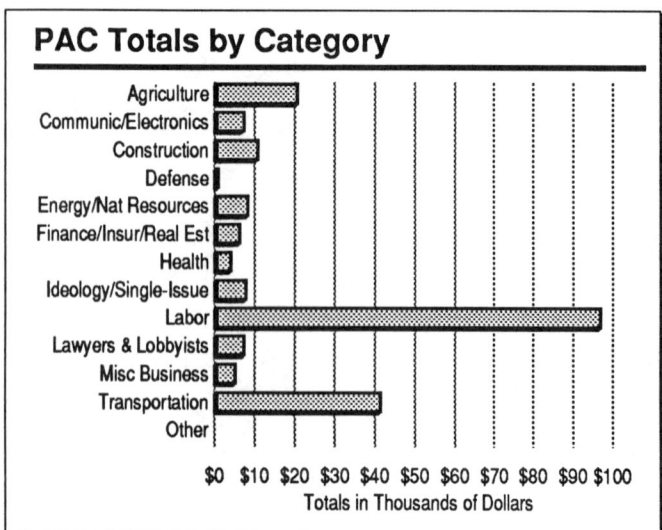

Agriculture
Communic/Electronics
Construction
Defense
Energy/Nat Resources
Finance/Insur/Real Est
Health
Ideology/Single-Issue
Labor
Lawyers & Lobbyists
Misc Business
Transportation
Other

$0 $10 $20 $30 $40 $50 $60 $70 $80 $90 $100
Totals in Thousands of Dollars

Labor

Bldg Trades/Industrial/Misc Unions $30,275

United Steelworkers	$5,000
Operating Engineers Union	$4,500
Carpenters & Joiners Union	$4,100
Intl Brotherhood of Electrical Workers	$4,000
Sheet Metal Workers Union	$2,500
United Auto Workers	$1,550
Laborers' Political League	$1,200
Food & Commercial Workers Union	$1,050
Ladies Garment Workers Union	$1,000
Others	$5,375

Government & Postal Workers $18,500

American Fedn of State/County/Munic Employees	$5,000
National Assn of Retired Federal Employees	$5,000
National Assn of Letter Carriers*	$3,700
American Postal Workers Union*	$2,250
Others	$2,550

Teachers Unions $7,550

American Federation of Teachers	$5,000
Minnesota Education Assn	$1,300
National Education Assn	$1,250

Transportation Unions $39,900

Teamsters Union*	$10,400
Air Line Pilots Assn	$10,000
Marine Engineers District 2 Maritime Officers	$5,000
Amalgamated Transit Union	$2,500
Seafarers International Union	$2,500
United Transportation Union	$2,100
Assn of Flight Attendants	$2,000
International Longshoremen Assn	$2,000
Transportation Communication Union	$1,150
Transport Workers Union	$1,000
Others	$1,250

Interest Group Ratings

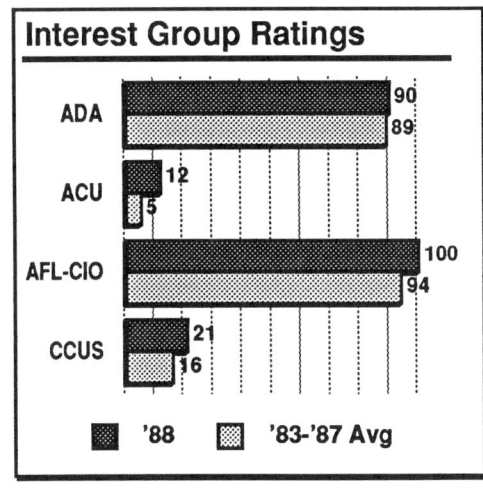

Ideological/Single-Issue

Ideological/Single-Issue $6,910

National Cmte to Preserve Social Security	$3,300	Soc Secur
National Right to Life PAC	$1,100	Pro-Life
Valley Education Fund (Tony Coelho)	$1,000	Dem Leaders
Others	$1,510	

Independent expenditures supporting Oberstar

National Cmte to Preserve Social Security	$2,095

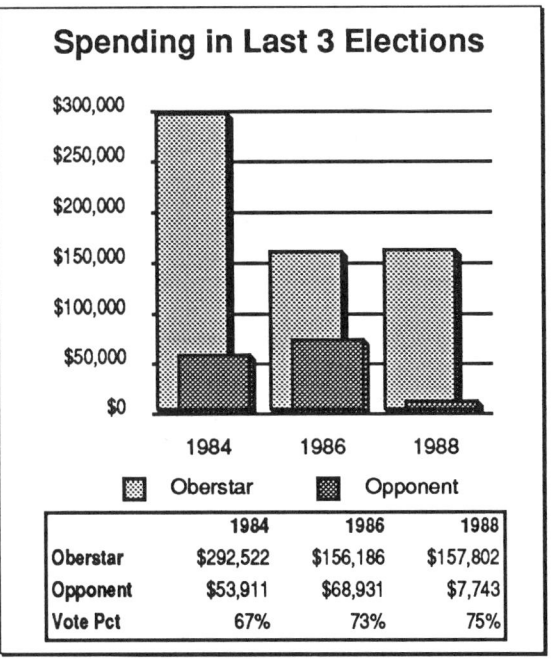

Spending in Last 3 Elections

	1984	1986	1988
Oberstar	$292,522	$156,186	$157,802
Opponent	$53,911	$68,931	$7,743
Vote Pct	67%	73%	75%

* Contributions came from more than one PAC affiliated with this sponsor.

David R. Obey, D-Wis (7)

First elected: 1969
Total receipts: $530,385
Total from PACs: $308,399

1988 Committees & Subcommittees

Appropriations
Foreign Operations (Chairman)
Labor, Health and Human Services, Education and Related Agencies
Legislative Branch

Joint Economic
Economic Resources and Competitiveness (Chairman)
National Security Economic (Vice Chairman)
Economic Growth, Trade and Taxes

PAC Contribution Profile

Business

Dairy	**$17,500**
Associated Milk Producers	$10,000
Land O'Lakes Inc	$3,500
Mid-American Dairymen	$3,000
Dairymen Inc	$1,000
Defense	**$4,000**
General Dynamics	$1,250
Others	$2,750
Electronics & Computers	**$4,250**
General Electric	$2,000
Westinghouse Electric	$1,250
Computer Sciences Corp	$1,000
Financial Institutions	**$5,550**
American Bankers Assn	$1,250
Banc One Wisconsin	$1,000
Citicorp	$1,000
Credit Union National Assn	$1,000
Others	$1,300
Food & Beverage	**$4,000**
National Beer Wholesalers Assn	$1,000
Others	$3,000
Health Professionals	**$9,600**
American Dental Assn	$4,000
American Medical Assn	$2,500
American Nurses Assn	$1,000
Others	$2,100

Campaign Revenue Sources

Other (7.8%)
Party (2.0%)
Individuals (34.9%)
PACs (55.3%)

Insurance	**$3,450**
Northwestern Mutual Life	$2,000
Blue Cross & Blue Shield Assn	$1,250
Wausau Insurance	$200
Lawyers & Lobbyists	**$14,000**
Assn of Trial Lawyers of America	$10,000
Williams & Jensen	$1,000
Others	$3,000
Sugar Growers	**$3,550**
American Crystal Sugar Corp	$1,500
Others	$2,050
Telecommunications	**$4,500**
AT&T	$2,000
US Telephone Assn	$1,000
Wisconsin Bell Telephone	$1,000
Others	$500

Other Major Business PACs

ACRE (Action Committee for Rural Electric)	$2,250	RuralElect
American Hospital Assn	$2,250	Hospitals
Chrysler Corp	$1,750	Auto Mfrs
United Parcel Service	$1,750	Delivery
Coastal Corp	$1,500	Natural Gas
Philip Morris	$1,500	Tobacco
Burlington Northern	$1,250	Railroads
National Farmers Organization	$1,250	Farm Orgs
Aircraft Owners & Pilots Assn	$1,000	GenlAviation
American Road & Transportation Bldrs Assn	$1,000	Comml Constr
Ansell Inc	$1,000	Health Prod
Assn of Independent Colleges/Schools	$1,000	Voc Tech
Boeing Company	$1,000	Aircraft
Chicago Mercantile Exchange	$1,000	Commodities
National Assn of Trade/Tech Schools	$1,000	Voc Tech
National Cable Television Assn	$1,000	CableTV
National Cooperative Business Assn	$1,000	BusinessAssn
Ocean Spray Cranberries Inc	$1,000	Fruit/Veg
Pirelli Cable	$1,000	Indust Equip
Society for Advncmt of Ambulatory Care	$1,000	OutpatntCare
Waste Management Inc	$1,000	Waste Mgmt

PAC Totals by Category

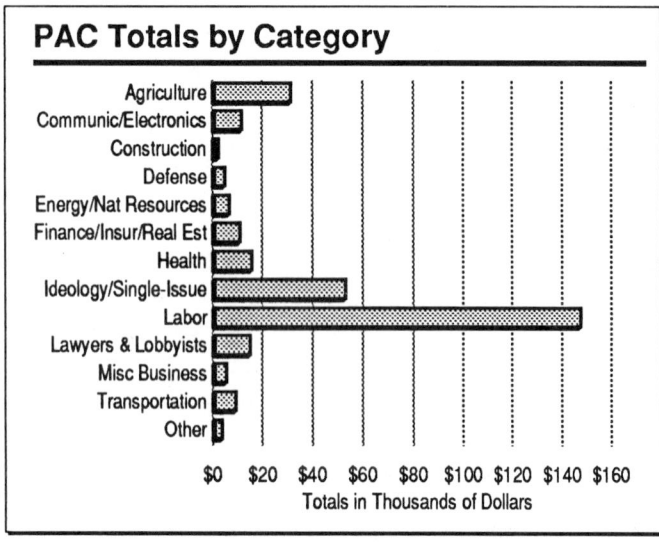

Agriculture
Communic/Electronics
Construction
Defense
Energy/Nat Resources
Finance/Insur/Real Est
Health
Ideology/Single-Issue
Labor
Lawyers & Lobbyists
Misc Business
Transportation
Other

$0 $20 $40 $60 $80 $100 $120 $140 $160
Totals in Thousands of Dollars

Labor

Bldg Trades/Industrial/Misc Unions **$73,350**
    United Auto Workers $10,000
    AFL-CIO* $6,250
    Plumbers/Pipefitters Union $6,250
    Communications Workers of America $6,000
    Carpenters & Joiners Union $5,000
    Intl Brotherhood of Electrical Workers $5,000
    Operating Engineers Union $5,000
    United Steelworkers $5,000
    Machinists/Aerospace Workers Union $4,250
    United Mine Workers $4,000
    Food & Commercial Workers Union $3,000
    Laborers' Political League $2,500
    Bricklayers Union $1,500
    United Paperworkers $1,500
    Ladies Garment Workers Union $1,350
    Amalgamated Clothing & Textile Workers $1,000
    Boilermakers Union $1,000
    Rubber Cork Linoleum Plastic Workers $1,000
    Service Employees International Union $1,000
    Sheet Metal Workers Union $1,000
    Others $1,750

Government & Postal Workers **$31,300**
    American Fedn of State/County/Munic Employees $10,000
    National Assn of Letter Carriers $9,500
    National Assn of Retired Federal Employees $5,000
    American Postal Workers Union $1,500
    International Assn of Firefighters $1,500
    American Federation of Government Employees $1,250
    National League of Postmasters $1,000
    National Rural Letter Carriers Assn $1,000
    Others $550

Teachers Unions **$16,550**
    American Federation of Teachers $10,000
    National Education Assn $6,550

Spending in Last 3 Elections

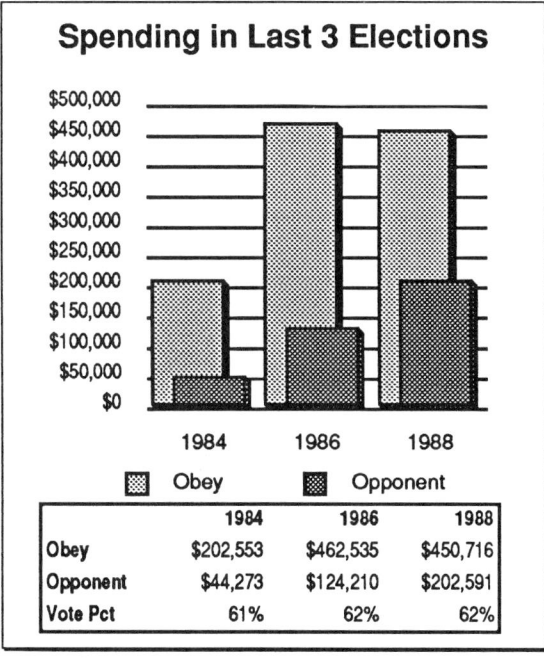

	1984	1986	1988
Obey	$202,553	$462,535	$450,716
Opponent	$44,273	$124,210	$202,591
Vote Pct	61%	62%	62%

Interest Group Ratings

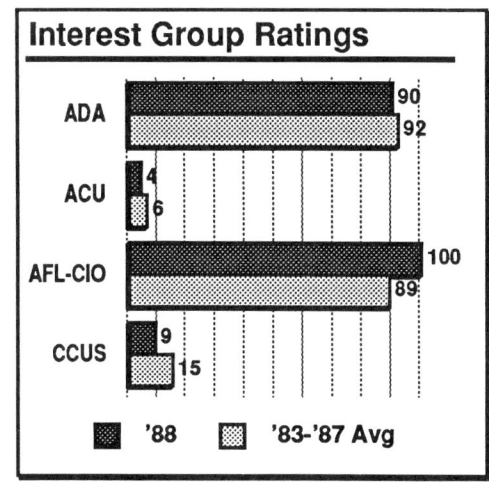

■ '88   □ '83-'87 Avg

Transportation Unions **$25,250**
    Teamsters Union $10,000
    Air Line Pilots Assn $5,000
    United Transportation Union $3,000
    Marine Engineers District 2 Maritime Officers $2,000
    Amalgamated Transit Union $1,500
    Transportation Communication Union $1,500
    Seafarers International Union $1,000
    Others $1,250

Ideological/Single-Issue

Democratic Leadership PACs **$6,000**
    Majority Congress Committee (Jim Wright) $5,000
    Valley Education Fund (Tony Coelho) $1,000

Pro-Israel **$29,750**
    Citizens Organized PAC $10,000
    National PAC $5,000
    Florida Congressional Committee $3,500
    Hudson Valley PAC $3,000
    National Action Committee (NACPAC) $3,000
    Joint Action Cmte for Political Affairs $1,000
    Roundtable PAC $1,000
    Others $3,250

Other Major Ideological/Single-Issue PACs

National Cmte to Preserve Social Security $3,250	Soc Secur
National Community Action Found $2,500	HealthWelfare
KidsPAC $2,000	HealthWelfare
Assembly of Turkish-American Assns $1,500	Ethnic
Free Cuba PAC $1,500	Anti-Castro
Hellenic American Council $1,000	Ethnic
National Rifle Assn $1,000	Pro-Guns
National Assn of Arab-Americans $1,000	ForeignPolcy
National Council of Senior Citizens $1,000	Soc Secur

Independent expenditures supporting Obey

National Cmte to Preserve Social Security $3,543

---

* Contributions came from more than one PAC affiliated
  with this sponsor.

Jim Olin, D-Va (6)

1988 Committees & Subcommittees

Agriculture
Domestic Marketing, Consumer Relations and Nutrition
Forests, Family Farms and Energy
Livestock, Dairy and Poultry

Small Business
Regulation and Business Opportunities
SBA and the General Economy

First elected: 1982
Total receipts: $321,705
Total from PACs: $140,400

PAC Contribution Profile

Business

Agricultural Chemicals	**$3,450**
None over $750	

Auto Dealers	**$6,500**
National Auto Dealers Assn	$4,000
Auto Dealers & Drivers for Free Trade	$2,500

Commercial & Savings Banks	**$8,850**
Virginia Bankers Assn	$2,500
US League of Savings Assn	$2,050
Crestar Financial Corp	$1,000
Dominion Bankshares Corp	$1,000
Sovran Financial Corp	$1,000
Others	$1,300

Commodities/Securities Investment	**$2,000**
Chicago Board of Trade	$1,150
Others	$850

Construction	**$4,250**
National Assn of Home Builders	$2,000
Others	$2,250

Dairy	**$3,850**
Milk Industry Foundation	$3,650
Others	$200

Electric Utilities	**$6,550**
ACRE (Action Committee for Rural Electrification)	$3,300
Dominion Resources Inc	$1,500
Others	$1,750

Campaign Revenue Sources

Party (2.0%)
Other (5.0%)
PACs (43.9%)
Individuals (49.1%)

Food & Beverage	**$12,100**
Food Marketing Institute	$2,500
American Meat Institute	$1,500
Pepsico Inc	$1,500
Kroger Company	$1,000
National Restaurant Assn	$1,000
Others	$4,600

Forest Products	**$3,150**
Westvaco Corp	$2,000
Others	$1,150

Health Professionals	**$2,700**
American Medical Assn	$1,350
American Academy of Ophthalmology	$1,000
Others	$350

Insurance	**$2,850**
National Assn of Life Underwriters	$1,000
Others	$1,850

Lawyers	**$2,000**
Assn of Trial Lawyers of America	$2,000

Poultry & Livestock	**$7,500**
National Cattlemen's Assn	$2,000
Texas Cattle Feeders Assn	$1,700
National Broiler Council	$1,200
National Turkey Federation	$1,000
Others	$1,600

Real Estate	**$3,850**
National Assn of Realtors	$3,850

Sugar Growers	**$5,050**
American Sugarbeet Growers Assn	$1,200
American Crystal Sugar Corp	$1,000
Others	$2,850

Tobacco	**$3,050**
Philip Morris	$1,200
Others	$1,850

Other Major Business PACs

American Assn of Crop Insurers	$1,200	Ag Svcs
United Parcel Service	$1,200	Delivery
AT&T	$1,000	LongDistance
Burlington Industries	$1,000	Textiles
Waste Management Inc	$1,000	Waste Mgmt

PAC Totals by Category

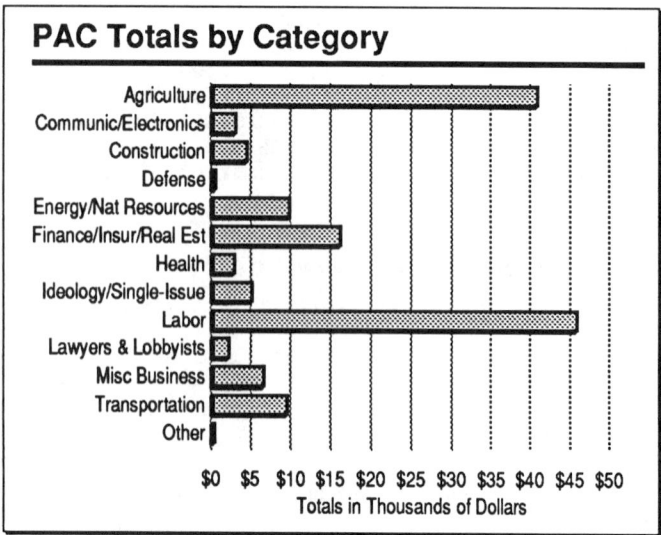

Agriculture
Communic/Electronics
Construction
Defense
Energy/Nat Resources
Finance/Insur/Real Est
Health
Ideology/Single-Issue
Labor
Lawyers & Lobbyists
Misc Business
Transportation
Other

$0 $5 $10 $15 $20 $25 $30 $35 $40 $45 $50
Totals in Thousands of Dollars

Labor

Bldg Trades/Industrial/Misc Unions **$12,850**
   Machinists/Aerospace Workers Union $3,100
   Food & Commercial Workers Union.................................$2,000
   National Education Assn $1,650
   Ladies Garment Workers Union $1,200
   Electronic Machine Furniture Workers $1,000
   Intl Brotherhood of Electrical Workers..........................$1,000
   Others $2,900

Government & Postal Workers **$15,150**
   National Assn of Retired Federal Employees $7,000
   National Assn of Letter Carriers $3,000
   American Fedn of State/County/Munic Employees $2,000
   American Federation of Government Employees $1,000
   Others $2,150

Transportation Unions **$17,500**
   Teamsters Union $10,000
   Seafarers International Union $2,650
   United Transportation Union $1,850
   Brotherhood of Railroad Signalmen $1,150
   Others $1,850

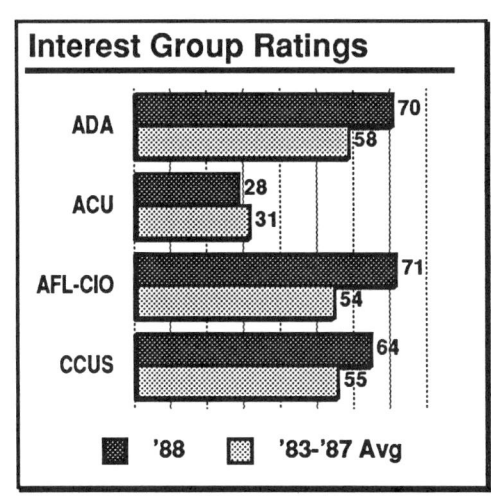

Interest Group Ratings

ADA — '88: 70 | '83-'87 Avg: 58
ACU — '88: 28 | '83-'87 Avg: 31
AFL-CIO — '88: 71 | '83-'87 Avg: 54
CCUS — '88: 64 | '83-'87 Avg: 55

■ '88   ▨ '83-'87 Avg

Ideological/Single-Issue

Democratic Leadership PACs.......................................**$4,500**
   Majority Congress Committee (Jim Wright) $3,000
   Valley Education Fund (Tony Coelho) $1,000
   Others $500

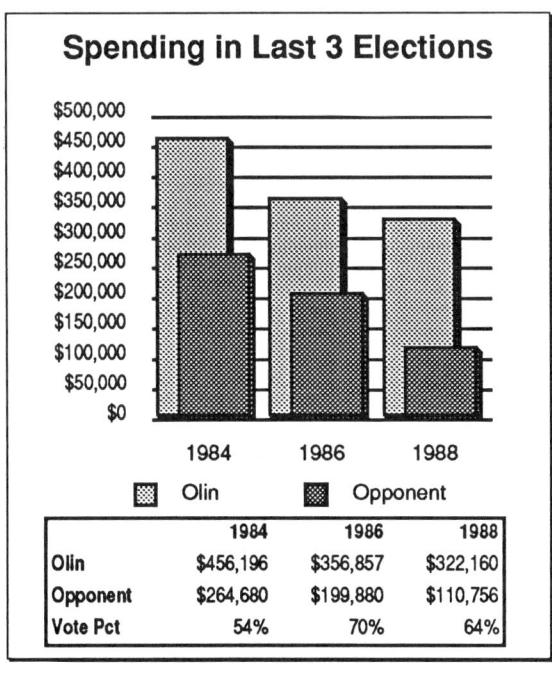

Spending in Last 3 Elections

▨ Olin   ▨ Opponent

	1984	1986	1988
Olin	$456,196	$356,857	$322,160
Opponent	$264,680	$199,880	$110,756
Vote Pct	54%	70%	64%

Solomon P. Ortiz, D-Texas (27)

First elected: 1982
Total receipts: $198,217
Total from PACs: $99,883

1988 Committees & Subcommittees

Armed Services
Investigations
Military Installations and Facilities
Seapower and Strategic and Critical Materials

Merchant Marine and Fisheries
Fisheries and Wildlife Conservation and the Environment
Panama Canal/Outer Continental Shelf

Select Narcotics Abuse and Control

PAC Contribution Profile

Business

Commercial Banks **$2,000**
    First City Bancorp $1,000
    MBank $1,000

Construction **$4,500**
    Associated General Contractors $1,000
    Brown & Root $1,000
    National Concrete Masonry Assn $1,000
    Others $1,500

Defense **$20,650**
    GTE (Southwest) $2,250
    Allied-Signal $1,000
    AT&T $1,000
    Bath Iron Works $1,000
    General Dynamics $1,000
    Lockheed Corp $1,000
    LTV Aerospace & Defense Company $1,000
    Northrop Corp $1,000
    Raytheon $1,000
    Rockwell International $1,000
    Singer Company $1,000
    Tenneco Inc $1,000
    Textron Inc $1,000
    Others $6,400

Insurance **$2,000**
    American General Insurance Company $1,000
    Others $1,000

Lawyers **$2,250**
    Assn of Trial Lawyers of America $2,000
    Others $250

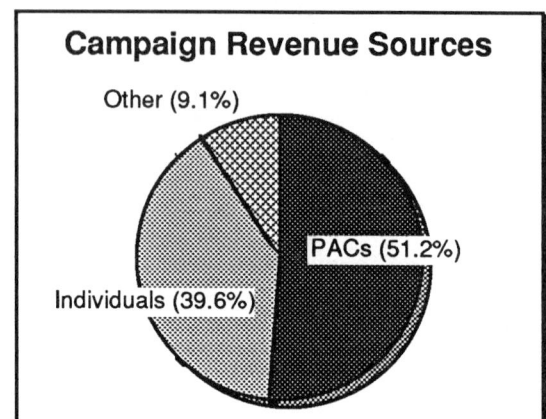

Campaign Revenue Sources

Other (9.1%)
PACs (51.2%)
Individuals (39.6%)

Oil & Gas **$8,650**
    Coastal Corp $3,000
    Valero Energy Corp $1,000
    Others $4,650

Real Estate **$8,000**
    National Assn of Realtors $8,000

Telecommunications **$2,600**
    Southwestern Bell $2,600

Other Major Business PACs

J C Penney Company	$1,500	Dept Store
Central Power & Light	$1,000	ElectricUtil
National Auto Dealers Assn	$1,000	Auto Sales
Union Pacific Corp	$1,000	Railroads

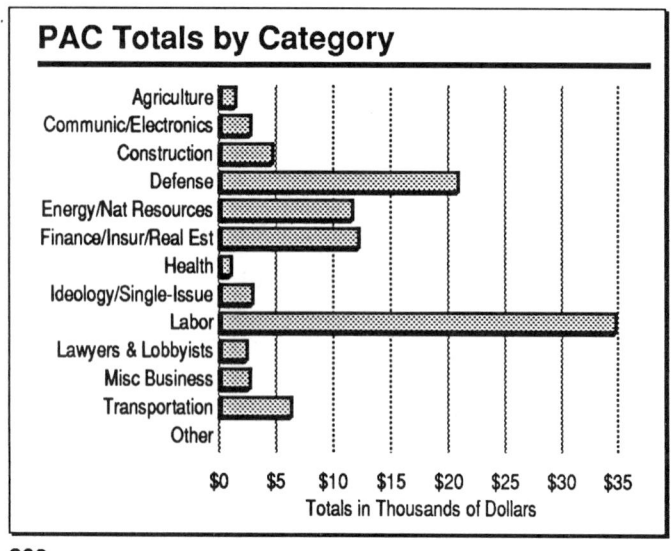

PAC Totals by Category

Agriculture
Communic/Electronics
Construction
Defense
Energy/Nat Resources
Finance/Insur/Real Est
Health
Ideology/Single-Issue
Labor
Lawyers & Lobbyists
Misc Business
Transportation
Other

$0 $5 $10 $15 $20 $25 $30 $35
Totals in Thousands of Dollars

Labor

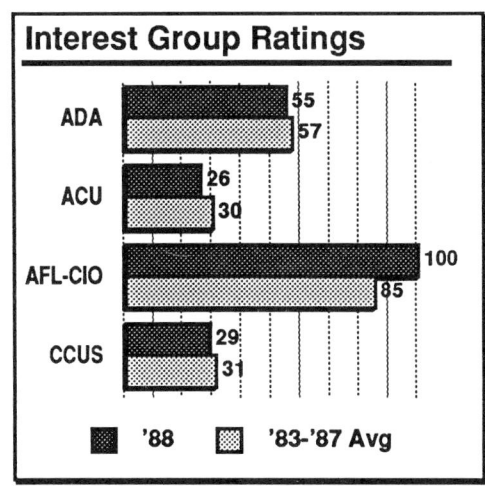

Bldg Trades/Industrial/Misc Unions $11,200
United Auto Workers	.........................$5,000
Intl Brotherhood of Electrical Workers	.............................$3,000
Carpenters & Joiners Union	....$1,000
Plumbers/Pipefitters Union	....$1,000
Others	....$1,200

Government & Postal Workers $9,200
National Assn of Retired Federal Employees	.................$4,000
National Assn of Letter Carriers	...................................$2,500
American Postal Workers Union	.....................................$1,200
American Fedn of State/County/Munic Employees	.........$1,000
Others	....$500

Teachers Unions $4,000
National Education Assn	....$3,500
Others	....$500

Transportation Unions $10,200
Marine Engineers District 2 Maritime Officers	.................$5,500
Seafarers International Union	....$1,500
Masters, Mates & Pilots Union	....$1,000
United Transportation Union	....$1,000
Others	....$1,200

Major Ideological/Single-Issue PACs
Valley Education Fund (Tony Coelho)	.............$1,500	Dem Leaders
National Cmte to Preserve Social Security	......$1,000	Soc Secur

Independent expenditures supporting Ortiz
National Cmte to Preserve Social Security	...................................$1,104

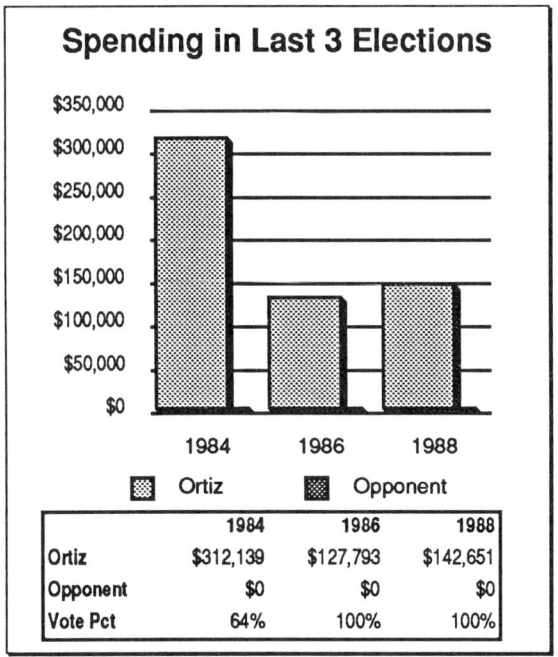

	1984	1986	1988
Ortiz	$312,139	$127,793	$142,651
Opponent	$0	$0	$0
Vote Pct	64%	100%	100%

Major R. Owens, D-NY (12)

First elected: 1982
Total receipts: $198,529
Total from PACs: $125,085

1988 Committees & Subcommittees

Education and Labor
Select Education (Chairman)
Elementary, Secondary and Vocational Education
Labor-Management Relations
Postsecondary Education

Government Operations
Government Activities and Transportation

PAC Contribution Profile

Business

Accountants	*$5,000*
American Institute of CPA's	$5,000
Health Professionals	*$8,200*
American Medical Assn	$6,350
American Optometric Assn	$600
American Academy of Ophthalmology	$500
Others	$750
Lawyers	*$5,000*
Assn of Trial Lawyers of America	$5,000
Life Insurance	*$2,050*
Metropolitan Life Insurance	$850
National Assn of Life Underwriters	$500
Others	$700
Package Delivery	*$2,300*
United Parcel Service	$2,300

Other Major Business PACs

Michigan Consolidated Gas	$600	Natural Gas
Coca-Cola Company	$500	Soft Drinks
National Assn of Home Builders	$500	Resid Constr
National Assn of Cosmetology Schools	$500	Voc Tech

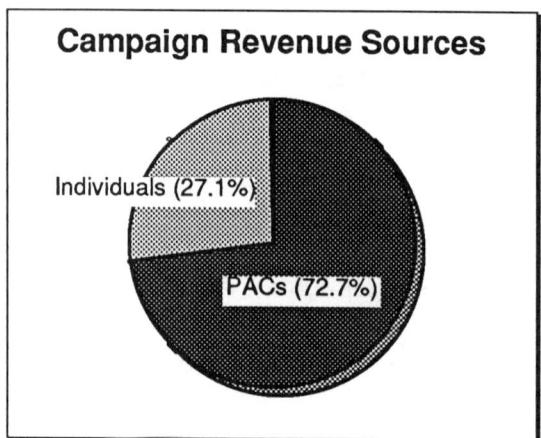

Campaign Revenue Sources

Individuals (27.1%)
PACs (72.7%)

PAC Totals by Category

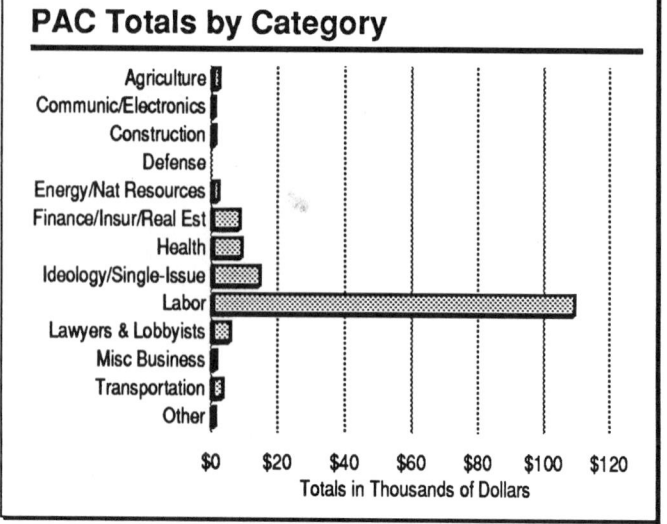

Agriculture
Communic/Electronics
Construction
Defense
Energy/Nat Resources
Finance/Insur/Real Est
Health
Ideology/Single-Issue
Labor
Lawyers & Lobbyists
Misc Business
Transportation
Other

$0 $20 $40 $60 $80 $100 $120
Totals in Thousands of Dollars

Labor

Bldg Trades/Industrial/Misc Unions **$26,200**

Food & Commercial Workers Union	$2,750
Machinists/Aerospace Workers Union	$2,600
Carpenters & Joiners Union	$2,500
Communications Workers of America	$2,500
AFL-CIO*	$2,100
Intl Brotherhood of Electrical Workers	$2,000
Laborers' Political League	$1,950
Electronic Machine Furniture Workers	$1,350
Ladies Garment Workers Union	$1,350
United Auto Workers	$1,350
Plumbers/Pipefitters Union	$1,000
Oil, Chemical & Atomic Workers Union	$850
Electrical Radio/Machine Workers	$750
Amalgamated Clothing & Textile Workers	$600
Hotel/Restaurant Employees Union	$600
Service Employees International Union	$600
Painters & Allied Trades Union	$500
Others	$850

Government & Postal Workers **$33,585**

American Fedn of State/County/Munic Employees	$14,685
National Assn of Retired Federal Employees	$10,000
National Assn of Letter Carriers	$3,550
National Alliance Postal/Federal Employees	$2,700
American Postal Workers Union	$1,700
American Federation of Government Employees	$600
Others	$350

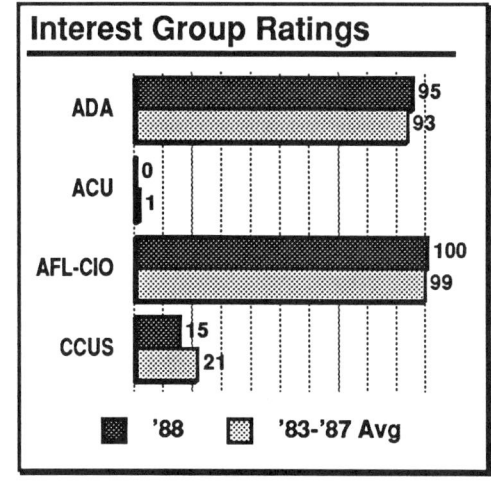

Interest Group Ratings

	'88	'83-'87 Avg
ADA	95	93
ACU	0	1
AFL-CIO	100	99
CCUS	15	21

Teachers Unions **$10,550**

National Education Assn	$7,000
American Federation of Teachers	$3,550

Transportation Unions **$38,210**

Teamsters Union	$15,000
Marine Engineers District 2 Maritime Officers	$6,120
Air Line Pilots Assn	$6,000
Transport Workers Union	$4,000
United Transportation Union	$2,100
Seafarers International Union	$1,500
Transportation Communication Union	$900
International Longshoremen Local #1814	$640
Brotherhood of Railroad Signalmen	$600
Amalgamated Transit Union	$500
Maritime Union of America	$500
Others	$350

Ideological/Single-Issue

Pro-Israel **$10,000**

National PAC	$10,000

Other Major Ideological/Single-Issue PACs

Valley Education Fund (Tony Coelho)	$1,000	Dem Leaders
National Cmte to Procorve Social Security	$850	Soc Secur
Human Rights Campaign Fund	$500	Gay Rights
National Abortion Rights Action League	$500	Pro-Choice

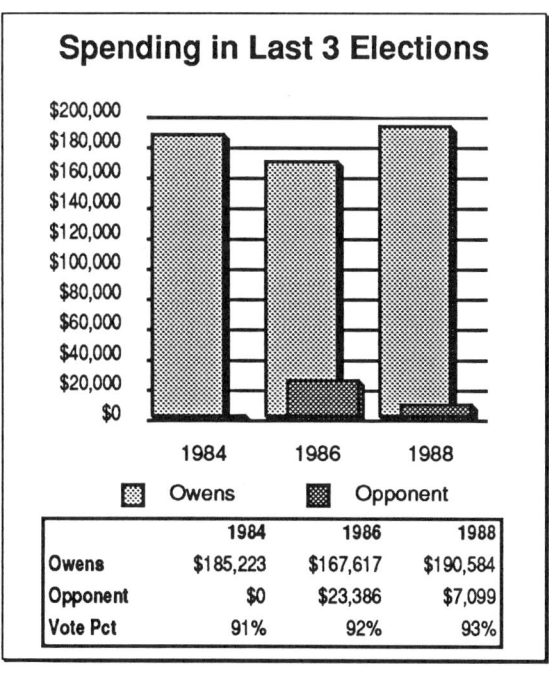

Spending in Last 3 Elections

	1984	1986	1988
Owens	$185,223	$167,617	$190,584
Opponent	$0	$23,386	$7,099
Vote Pct	91%	92%	93%

Owens   Opponent

---

* Contributions came from more than one PAC affiliated
  with this sponsor.

Wayne Owens, D-Utah (2)

First elected: 1986
Total receipts: $733,955
Total from PACs: $455,310

1988 Committees & Subcommittees

Foreign Affairs
Africa
Europe and the Middle East

Interior and Insular Affairs
Energy and the Environment
Mining and Natural Resources
National Parks and Public Lands
Water and Power Resources

PAC Contribution Profile

Business

Financial Institutions $10,220

US League of Savings Assn	$2,600
Commercial Security Bancorp	$2,300
Credit Union National Assn	$2,000
Citicorp	$1,250
Others	$2,070

Food & Beverage $6,050

National Restaurant Assn	$2,000
Coca-Cola Company	$1,750
McDonald's Corp	$1,000
Others	$1,300

Health Professionals $13,118

American Medical Assn	$7,368
American Dental Assn	$1,500
American Academy of Ophthalmology	$1,000
American Podiatry Assn	$1,000
National Assn of Pharmacists	$1,000
Others	$1,250

Insurance $21,886

National Assn of Life Underwriters	$7,500
Independent Insurance Agents of America	$5,136
National Assn Mutual Insurance Agents	$3,150
Metropolitan Life Insurance	$1,800
Casualty & Surety Agents Assn	$1,350
Travelers Corp	$1,000
Others	$1,950

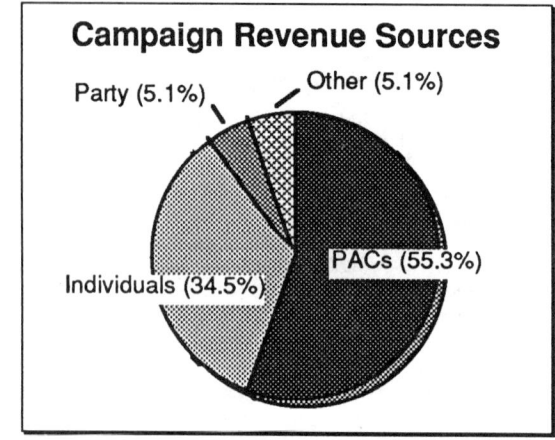

Campaign Revenue Sources

Party (5.1%)
Other (5.1%)
PACs (55.3%)
Individuals (34.5%)

Lawyers & Lobbyists $20,050

Assn of Trial Lawyers of America	$13,750
Akin, Gump, Hauer & Feld	$1,300
California Trial Lawyers Assn	$1,000
Dow, Lohnes & Albertson	$1,000
Others	$3,000

Oil & Gas $8,100

Litton Industries	$2,500
Williams Companies*	$1,500
Coastal Corp	$1,100
Others	$3,000

Real Estate $7,650

National Assn of Realtors	$6,150
National Realty Committee	$1,000
Others	$500

Telecommunications $12,050

Mountain Bell	$7,500
AT&T	$3,000
Continental Telecom	$1,000
Others	$550

Other Major Business PACs

National Assn of Home Builders	$5,500	Resid Constr
National Auto Dealers Assn	$4,800	Auto Sales
Associated Milk Producers	$3,000	Dairy
Marriott Corp	$3,000	Hotel/Motel
United Parcel Service	$2,450	Delivery
Mid-American Dairymen	$1,800	Dairy
American Hotel & Motel Assn	$1,500	Hotel/Motel
Archer-Daniels-Midland Corp	$1,000	Grain Trader

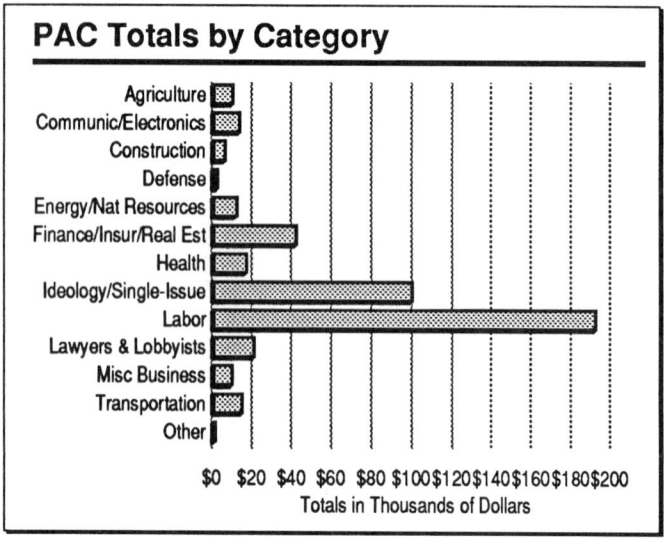

PAC Totals by Category

Agriculture
Communic/Electronics
Construction
Defense
Energy/Nat Resources
Finance/Insur/Real Est
Health
Ideology/Single-Issue
Labor
Lawyers & Lobbyists
Misc Business
Transportation
Other

$0 $20 $40 $60 $80 $100 $120 $140 $160 $180 $200
Totals in Thousands of Dollars

Labor

Bldg Trades/Industrial/Misc Unions $101,650

Intl Brotherhood of Electrical Workers* $11,000
Carpenters & Joiners Union $10,000
Food & Commercial Workers Union................................$10,000
Machinists/Aerospace Workers Union $10,000
United Auto Workers $10,000
AFL-CIO* $9,000
Sheet Metal Workers Union $7,500
United Steelworkers $7,500
Communications Workers of America...............................$6,300
Operating Engineers Union $5,000
Plumbers/Pipefitters Union $3,500
Service Employees International Union $3,000
Laborers' Political League $2,100
Bakery, Confectionery & Tobacco Workers $2,000
United Mine Workers $1,750
Hotel/Restaurant Employees Union $1,000
Others $2,000

Government & Postal Workers $33,600

American Fedn of State/County/Munic Employees $10,000
National Assn of Letter Carriers $10,000
National Assn of Retired Federal Employees $5,000
American Postal Workers Union $4,000
American Federation of Government Employees $1,800
Others $2,800

Teachers Unions $15,000

National Education Assn $10,000
American Federation of Teachers $5,000

Transportation Unions $41,451

Marine Engineers Union* $11,101
Teamsters Union $10,000
Air Line Pilots Assn $6,000
Seafarers International Union $6,000
Amalgamated Transit Union $2,500
United Transportation Union $2,300
Transportation Communication Union...............................$1,450
Brotherhood of Locomotive Engineers $1,000
Others $1,100

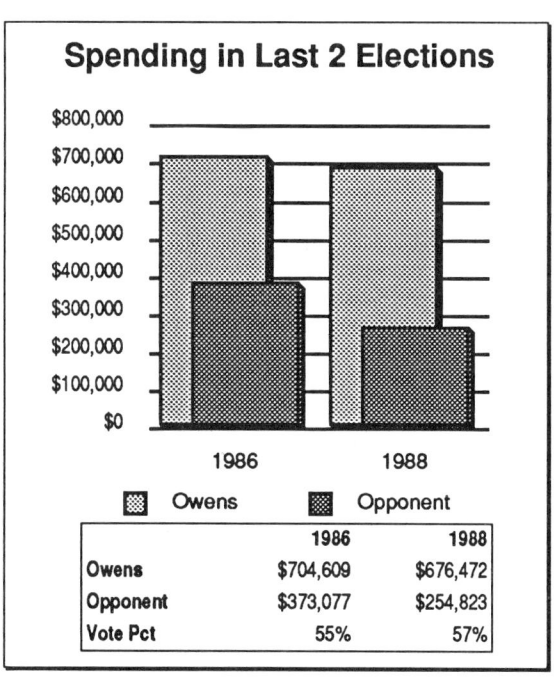

Spending in Last 2 Elections

	1986	1988
Owens	$704,609	$676,472
Opponent	$373,077	$254,823
Vote Pct	55%	57%

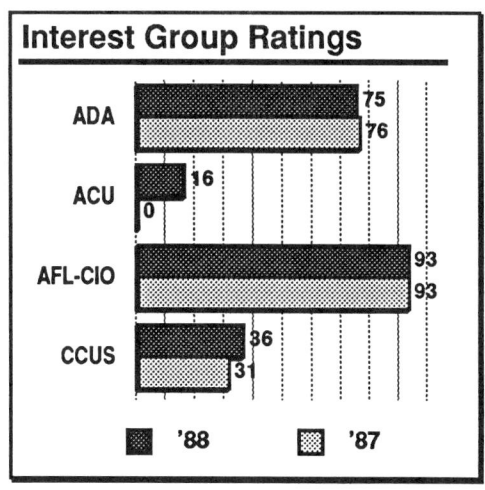

Interest Group Ratings

ADA 75 ('88), 76 ('87)
ACU 16 ('88), 0 ('87)
AFL-CIO 93 ('88), 93 ('87)
CCUS 36 ('88), 31 ('87)

■ '88   ▧ '87

Ideological/Single-Issue

Democratic/Liberal $12,744

National Cmte for an Effective Congress $7,494
Class PAC $3,500
Others $1,750

Democratic Leadership PACs...................................$21,500

24th Cong Dist of California PAC (Henry Waxman) $5,000
Majority Congress Committee (Jim Wright) $5,000
Valley Education Fund (Tony Coelho) $4,000
America's Leaders' Fund (Dan Rostenkowski) $3,000
Cmte for Democratic Opportunity (Bill Gray)...................$2,000
Empire Leadership Fund (Mario Cuomo) $1,000
House Leadership Fund (Tom Foley) $1,000
Others $500

Pro-Israel $35,800

Citizens Organized PAC...$5,000
National PAC $5,000
Delaware Valley PAC $2,500
Desert Caucus $2,500
Joint Action Cmte for Political Affairs $2,500
Roundtable PAC $2,500
Hudson Valley PAC $2,000
Washington PAC $2,000
National Action Committee (NACPAC) $1,750
Bi-County PAC $1,000
Florida Congressional Cmte $1,000
Heartland PAC $1,000
San Franciscans for Good Government............................$1,000
Women's Pro-Israel National PAC $1,000
Others $5,050

Other Major Ideological/Single-Issue PACs

National Rifle Assn ....$10,400 Pro-Guns
Sierra Club ....$6,500 Environment
National Cmte to Preserve Social Security ......$6,300 Soc Secur
National Council of Senior Citizens ....$2,000 Soc Secur
Council for a Livable World ....$1,261 Pro-Peace
League of Conservation Voters ....$1,011 Environment
KidsPAC ....$1,000 HealthWelfare

Independent expenditures supporting Owens

National Cmte to Preserve Social Security $12,035
Hudson Valley PAC $1,000

---

* Contributions came from more than one PAC affiliated
  with this sponsor.

Michael G. Oxley, R-Ohio (4)

First elected: 1981
Total receipts: $251,619
Total from PACs: $170,850

1988 Committees & Subcommittees

Energy and Commerce
Energy and Power
Oversight and Investigations
Telecommunications and Finance

Select Narcotics Abuse and Control

PAC Contribution Profile

Business

Accountants	**$6,600**
American Institute of CPA's	$5,000
Ernst & Whinney	$1,000
Others	$600
Automotive	**$5,300**
Auto Dealers & Drivers for Free Trade	$1,500
National Auto Dealers Assn	$1,300
Budd Company	$1,000
Others	$1,500
Commercial Banks	**$9,250**
J P Morgan & Company	$4,750
American Bankers Assn	$1,500
Barnett Banks of Florida	$1,000
Citicorp	$1,000
Ohio Bankers Assn	$1,000
Construction	**$4,600**
National Assn of Home Builders	$1,500
National Electrical Contractors Assn	$1,000
Others	$2,100
Dairy	**$2,800**
Associated Milk Producers	$2,500
Others	$300
Defense	**$4,750**
General Dynamics	$1,000
TRW Inc	$1,000
Others	$2,750

Campaign Revenue Sources

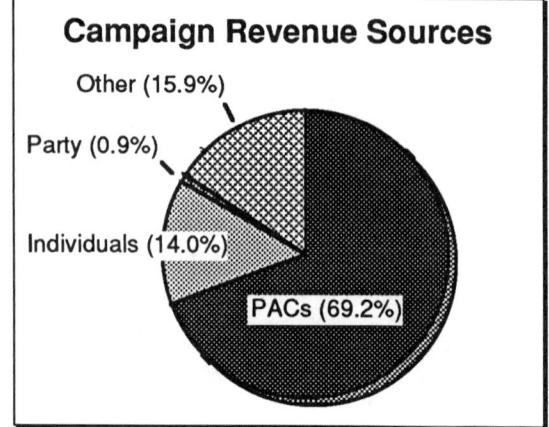

Other (15.9%)
Party (0.9%)
Individuals (14.0%)
PACs (69.2%)

Electric Utilities	**$17,150**
Public Service Company of Colorado	$1,900
Southern Company*	$1,500
Ohio Edison	$1,250
Texas Utilities Electric Company*	$1,000
Others	$11,500
Food & Beverage	**$8,100**
General Mills	$1,000
McDonald's Corp	$1,000
National Restaurant Assn	$1,000
National Beer Wholesalers Assn	$1,000
Others	$4,100
Health Professionals	**$10,050**
American Medical Assn	$5,300
American Dental Assn	$2,000
American Academy of Ophthalmology	$1,000
Cmte for Quality Orthopedic Health Care	$1,000
Others	$750
Insurance	**$8,800**
National Assn of Life Underwriters	$2,500
Independent Insurance Agents of America	$1,300
Others	$5,000
Lawyers & Lobbyists	**$6,850**
Assn of Trial Lawyers of America	$5,000
Others	$1,850
Oil & Gas	**$15,550**
Atlantic Richfield	$1,000
BP America	$1,000
Petroleum Marketers Assn	$1,000
Sun Company	$1,000
Union Pacific Corp	$1,000
Others	$10,550
Pharmaceuticals	**$7,450**
Schering-Plough Corp	$1,500
Others	$5,950
Real Estate	**$6,600**
National Assn of Realtors	$6,000
Others	$600
Securities/Commodities	**$7,450**
Chicago Board of Trade	$1,500
Travelers Corp	$1,000
Others	$4,950

PAC Totals by Category

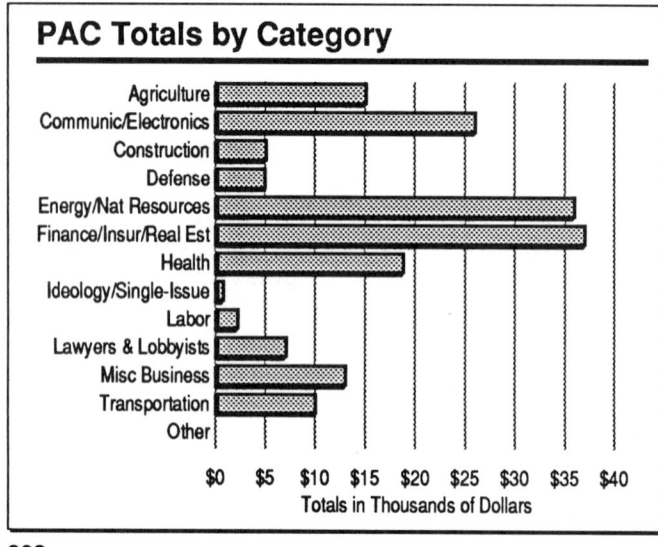

Agriculture
Communic/Electronics
Construction
Defense
Energy/Nat Resources
Finance/Insur/Real Est
Health
Ideology/Single-Issue
Labor
Lawyers & Lobbyists
Misc Business
Transportation
Other

$0 $5 $10 $15 $20 $25 $30 $35 $40
Totals in Thousands of Dollars

Telecommunications $19,000

AT&T	$7,500
Ohio Bell Telephone	$2,300
Michigan Bell Telephone	$1,300
Others	$7,900

Television/Cable TV $6,500

National Cable Television Assn	$5,000
Others	$1,500

Tobacco $3,850

Philip Morris	$1,600
United States Tobacco Company	$1,000
Others	$1,250

Other Major Business PACs

Owens-Illinois	$2,500	Paper Packg
Boeing Company	$1,000	Aircraft
National Assn of Truck Stop Operators	$1,000	Trucking

Labor

Labor Unions $2,000

Teamsters Union	$2,000

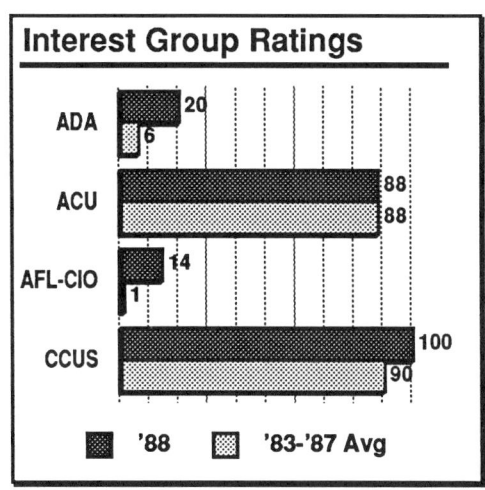

Interest Group Ratings

	'88	'83-'87 Avg
ADA	20	6
ACU	88	88
AFL-CIO	14	1
CCUS	100	90

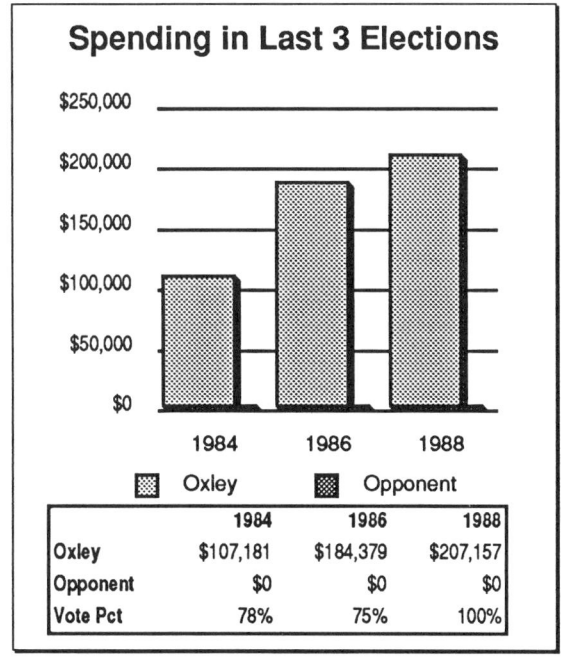

Spending in Last 3 Elections

	1984	1986	1988
Oxley	$107,181	$184,379	$207,157
Opponent	$0	$0	$0
Vote Pct	78%	75%	100%

---

* Contributions came from more than one PAC affiliated with this sponsor.

Ron Packard, R-Calif (43)

First elected: 1982
Total receipts: $215,956
Total from PACs: $114,538

1988 Committees & Subcommittees

Public Works and Transportation
Aviation
Surface Transportation
Water Resources

Science, Space and Technology
International Scientific Cooperation
Investigations and Oversight
Space Science and Applications

Select Children, Youth and Families

PAC Contribution Profile

Business

Automotive	**$3,750**
Auto Dealers & Drivers for Free Trade	$2,000
Others	$1,750
Aviation & Aerospace	**$15,850**
General Dynamics	$2,000
Aircraft Owners & Pilots Assn	$1,500
PSA Inc	$1,250
Allied-Signal	$1,000
Boeing Company	$1,000
Federal Express Corp	$1,000
Others	$8,100
Construction	**$11,250**
National Utility Contractors Assn	$2,500
Associated General Contractors	$1,500
National Assn of Home Builders	$1,500
National Electrical Contractors Assn	$1,000
Others	$4,750
Defense	**$5,000**
Rockwell International	$1,250
Others	$3,750
Electric Utilities	**$4,800**
Southern California Edison	$2,000
San Diego Gas & Electric	$1,000
Others	$1,800
Financial Institutions	**$2,600**
None over $750	

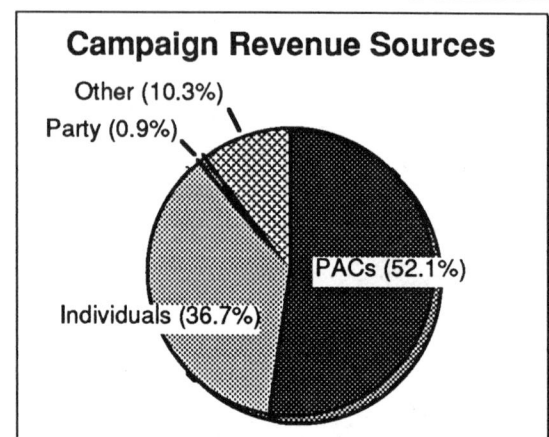

Campaign Revenue Sources

- Other (10.3%)
- Party (0.9%)
- PACs (52.1%)
- Individuals (36.7%)

Health Professionals	**$18,700**
American Medical Assn	$6,750
American Dental Assn	$5,200
Oral & Maxillofacial Surgeons	$3,000
American Academy of Ophthalmology	$2,000
Others	$1,750
Insurance	**$5,000**
National Assn of Life Underwriters	$1,750
Others	$3,250
Oil & Gas	**$2,500**
None over $750	
Real Estate	**$10,000**
National Assn of Realtors	$8,500
Irvine Company	$1,500
Telecommunications	**$2,250**
Pacific Telesis Group	$1,000
Others	$1,250
Trucking/Delivery	**$4,940**
United Parcel Service	$1,890
Consolidated Freightways	$1,500
Others	$1,550

Other Major Business PACs

Marriott Corp	$1,500	Hotel/Motel
American Veterinary Medical Assn	$1,000	Veterinary
Waste Management Inc	$1,000	Waste Mgmt

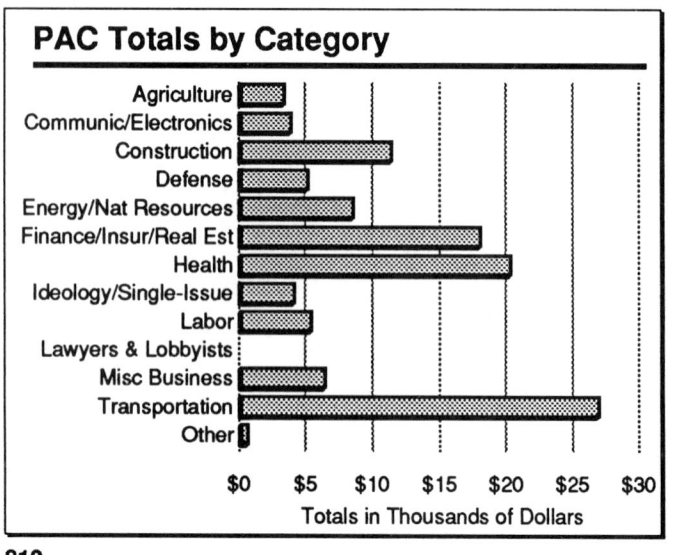

PAC Totals by Category

Categories: Agriculture, Communic/Electronics, Construction, Defense, Energy/Nat Resources, Finance/Insur/Real Est, Health, Ideology/Single-Issue, Labor, Lawyers & Lobbyists, Misc Business, Transportation, Other

Totals in Thousands of Dollars ($0 – $30)

Labor

Labor Unions $5,250
    Air Line Pilots Assn $3,500
    National Education Assn $1,000
    Others $750

Ideological/Single-Issue

Ideological/Single-Issue $4,000
National Rifle Assn ....$2,500   Pro-Guns
Others...$1,500

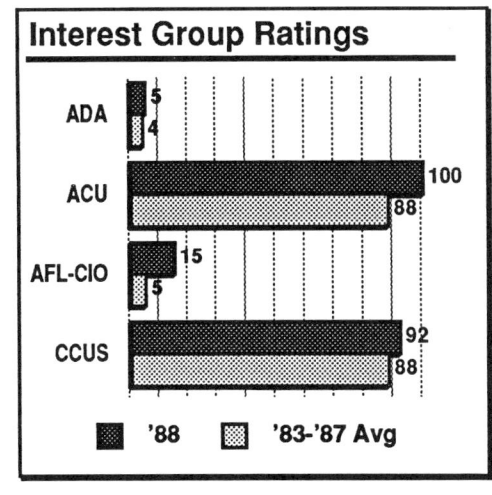

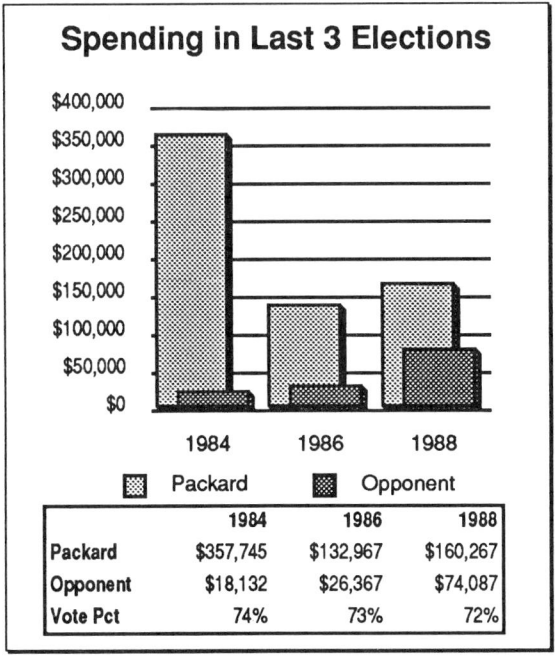

	1984	1986	1988
Packard	$357,745	$132,967	$160,267
Opponent	$18,132	$26,367	$74,087
Vote Pct	74%	73%	72%

Frank Pallone Jr., D-NJ (3)

First elected: 1988
Total receipts: $681,073
Total from PACs: $437,339

1989-90 Committees & Subcommittees

Merchant Marine and Fisheries
Fisheries and Wildlife Conservation and the Environment
Merchant Marine
Oversight and Investigations

Public Works and Transportation
Surface Transportation
Water Resources

Select Aging
Housing and Consumer Interests
Human Services

PAC Contribution Profile

Business

Auto Dealers **$2,000**
    National Auto Dealers Assn $2,000

Commercial & Savings Banks **$4,250**
    SAPEC/ NJ (New Jersey Savings Assn) $1,300
    Others $2,950

Construction **$6,825**
    National Assn of Home Builders $5,000
    Others $1,825

Electric Utilities **$2,000**
    Public Service Electric & Gas $1,500
    Others $500

Health Professionals **$18,900**
    American Medical Assn $10,000
    American Academy of Ophthalmology $3,000
    American Dental Assn $1,500
    American Optometric Assn $1,500
    American Podiatry Assn $1,000
    Others $1,900

Insurance **$14,650**
    National Assn of Life Underwriters $7,500
    Independent Insurance Agents of America $2,250
    Prudential Insurance $1,750
    Home Group Inc $1,000
    Others $2,150

Lawyers **$15,550**
    Assn of Trial Lawyers of America $15,000
    Others $550

Real Estate **$5,500**
    National Assn of Realtors $5,000
    Others $500

Trucking Companies **$3,150**
    North American Van Lines $1,850
    Yellow Freight System $1,000
    Others $300

Other Major Business PACs

Associated Milk Producers	$1,000	Dairy
AT&T	$1,000	LongDistance
Philip Morris	$1,000	Tobacco

Campaign Revenue Sources

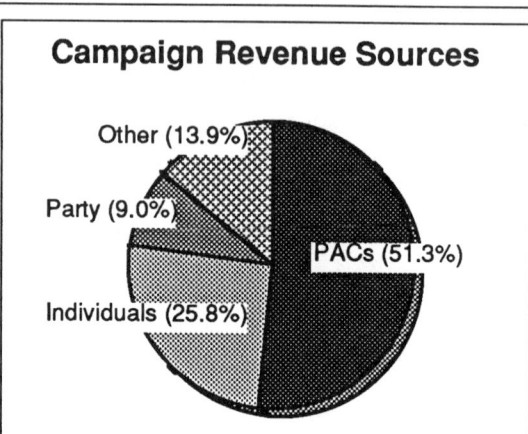

Other (13.9%)
Party (9.0%)
PACs (51.3%)
Individuals (25.8%)

PAC Totals by Category

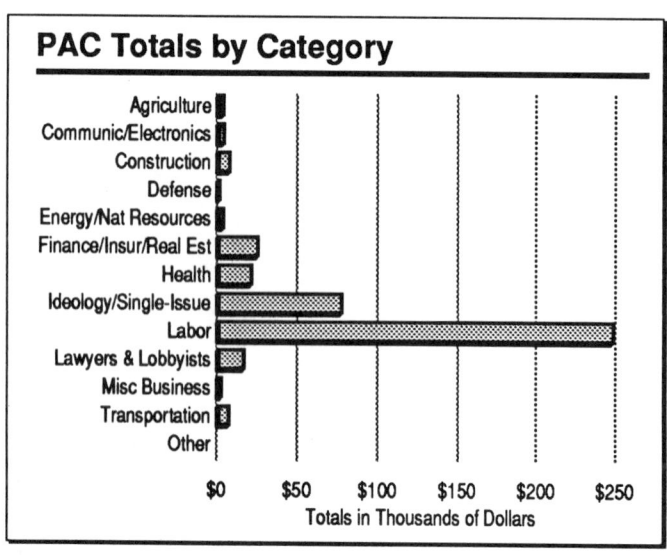

Agriculture
Communic/Electronics
Construction
Defense
Energy/Nat Resources
Finance/Insur/Real Est
Health
Ideology/Single-Issue
Labor
Lawyers & Lobbyists
Misc Business
Transportation
Other

$0 $50 $100 $150 $200 $250
Totals in Thousands of Dollars

Labor

Bldg Trades/Industrial/Misc Unions $144,050

AFL-CIO* $15,000
Machinists/Aerospace Workers Union $15,000
United Auto Workers $15,000
Food & Commercial Workers Union $12,500
Operating Engineers Local #68 .... $10,000
United Steelworkers $10,000
Plumbers/Pipefitters Union* $9,800
Carpenters & Joiners Union $8,500
Communications Workers of America $7,500
Operating Engineers Local #825 .... $6,200
Laborers' Political League $5,000
Intl Brotherhood of Electrical Workers $4,000
Rubber Cork Linoleum Plastic Workers $3,900
Ironworkers Union $2,500
Sheet Metal Workers Union $2,500
Bakery, Confectionery & Tobacco Workers $2,000
Bricklayers Union $2,000
New Jersey Industrial Union Council $2,000
Painters & Allied Trades Union $1,500
Ladies Garment Workers Union $1,250
Boilermakers Union $1,000
Electrical Radio/Machine Workers $1,000
Electronic Machine Furniture Workers $1,000
Heat & Frost Insulators/Asbestos Workers Union $1,000
Service Employees International Union $1,000
Others $2,900

Government & Postal Workers $44,050

American Fedn of State/County/Munic Employees $17,000
National Assn of Letter Carriers $10,000
National Assn of Retired Federal Employees $8,000
American Postal Workers Union $4,500
National Rural Letter Carriers Assn $1,250
National Assn of Postmasters $1,000
National Treasury Employees Union $1,000
Others $1,300

Teachers Unions $17,500

National Education Assn $10,000
American Federation of Teachers $7,500

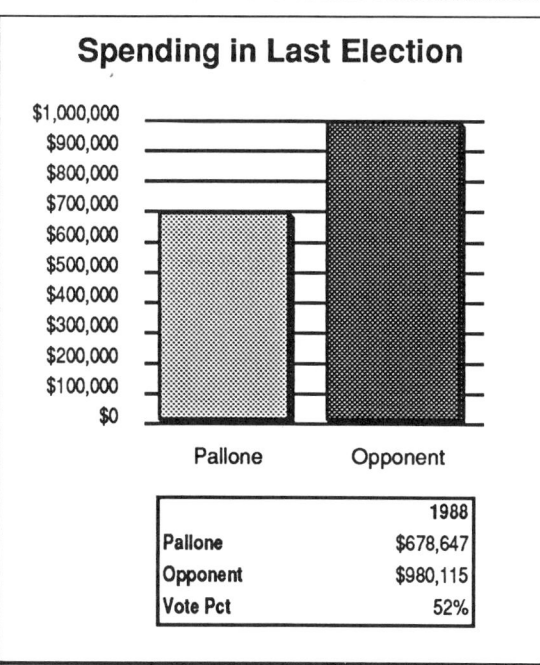

Spending in Last Election

	Pallone	Opponent

	1988
Pallone	$678,647
Opponent	$980,115
Vote Pct	52%

Transportation Unions $41,500

Seafarers International Union $10,000
Teamsters Union $10,000
Marine Engineers District 2 Maritime Officers $5,000
Amalgamated Transit Union $4,500
Air Line Pilots Assn $4,000
United Transportation Union $2,000
International Longshoremen Assn $1,500
Transport Workers Union $1,500
Transportation Communication Union $1,250
Others $1,750

Ideological/Single-Issue

Democratic/Liberal $12,361

National Cmte for an Effective Congress $12,061
Others $300

Democratic Leadership PACs $29,200

Majority Congress Committee (Jim Wright) $8,000
Valley Education Fund (Tony Coelho) $6,000
Cmte for a Democratic Consensus (Marvin Leath) $5,000
24th Cong Dist of California PAC (Henry Waxman) $3,000
Cmte for Democratic Opportunity (Bill Gray) $3,000
America's Leaders' Fund (Dan Rostenkowski) $2,000
House Leadership Fund (Tom Foley) $2,000
Others $200

Environmental PACs $17,143

Environmental Action $4,500
Sierra Club $3,988
Friends of the Earth $3,168
New Jersey Environmental Federation $2,966
League of Conservation Voters $1,521
New Jersey Environmental Voters Alliance $1,000

Pro-Israel $4,500

Desert Caucus $1,000
Joint Action Cmte for Political Affairs $1,000
Others $2,500

Senior Citizens Issues $7,000

National Cmte to Preserve Social Security $5,000
National Council of Senior Citizens $2,000

Other Major Ideological/Single-Issue PACs

Council for a Livable World .... $2,314 Pro-Peace
Armenian-American PAC .... $1,000 Ethnic
KidsPAC .... $1,000 HealthWelfare
New Jersey Legislative Action for Animals ...... $1,000 Animal Rights

Independent expenditures supporting Pallone

National Cmte to Preserve Social Security $4,070

---

* Contributions came from more than one PAC affiliated
with this sponsor.

Leon E. Panetta, D-Calif (16)

First elected: 1976
Total receipts: $318,076
Total from PACs: $158,600

1988 Committees & Subcommittees

Agriculture
Domestic Marketing, Consumer Relations and Nutrition (Chairman)
Department Operations, Research and Foreign Agriculture
Forests, Family Farms and Energy

House Administration
Personnel and Police (Chairman)
Elections

Select Hunger

Joint Printing

PAC Contribution Profile

Business

Commodity Trading	**$2,500**
Chicago Board of Trade	$2,000
Others	$500
Construction	**$3,750**
Sheet Metal/AirCon Contractors	$2,500
National Assn of Home Builders	$1,000
Others	$250
Dairy	**$7,000**
Associated Milk Producers	$4,000
Mid-American Dairymen	$1,500
Others	$1,500
Defense	**$2,500**
BDM International	$1,000
Others	$1,500
Electric Utilities	**$2,500**
ACRE (Action Committee for Rural Electrification)	$1,000
Others	$1,500
Financial Institutions	**$6,500**
American Bankers Assn	$2,500
Great Western Financial Corp	$1,000
Others	$3,000

Campaign Revenue Sources

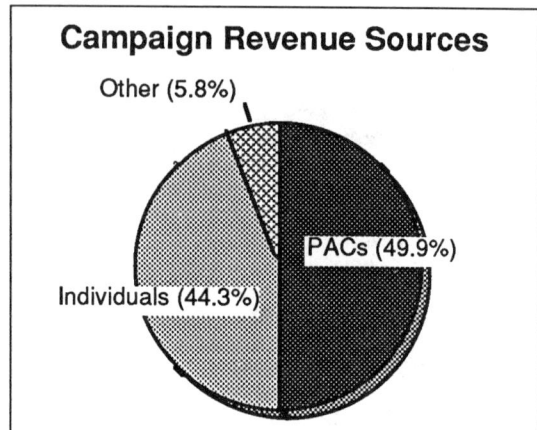

Other (5.8%)
PACs (49.9%)
Individuals (44.3%)

Food & Beverage	**$11,800**
Food Marketing Institute	$2,000
Wine Institute	$2,000
Wine & Spirits Wholesalers of America	$1,500
Ampco Foods Inc	$1,000
Pillsbury Company	$1,000
Winn-Dixie Stores	$1,000
Others	$3,300
Fruits & Vegetables	**$13,400**
Desert Grape Growers League/California	$5,000
Sun-Maid Growers of California	$2,500
California Almond Growers Exchange	$1,000
California Canning Peach Assn	$1,000
Sunkist Growers	$1,000
Tri/Valley Growers	$1,000
Western Growers Assn	$1,000
Others	$900
General Aviation	**$3,000**
Aircraft Owners & Pilots Assn	$3,000
Health Professionals	**$12,500**
American Medical Assn	$10,000
American Academy of Ophthalmology	$2,000
Others	$500
Insurance	**$2,250**
National Assn of Life Underwriters	$1,000
Others	$1,250
Lawyers & Lobbyists	**$5,750**
Assn of Trial Lawyers of America	$3,250
Dow, Lohnes & Albertson	$1,000
Others	$1,500
Oil & Gas	**$1,500**
None over $500	
Real Estate	**$10,000**
National Assn of Realtors	$9,500
Others	$500

PAC Totals by Category

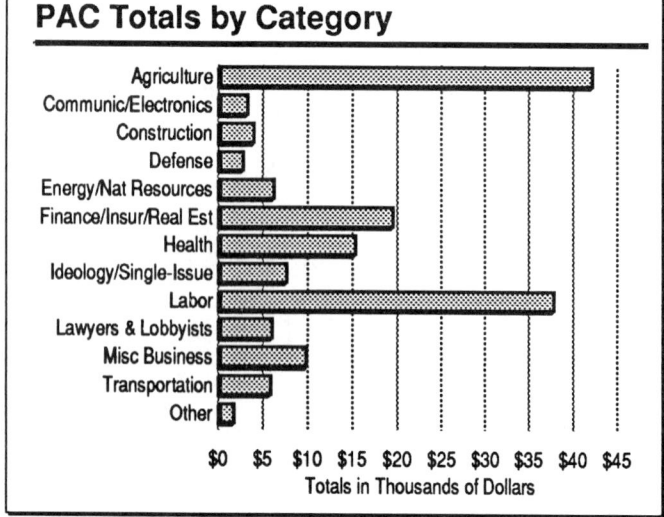

Agriculture
Communic/Electronics
Construction
Defense
Energy/Nat Resources
Finance/Insur/Real Est
Health
Ideology/Single-Issue
Labor
Lawyers & Lobbyists
Misc Business
Transportation
Other

$0 $5 $10 $15 $20 $25 $30 $35 $40 $45
Totals in Thousands of Dollars

Sugar Growers **$2,250**

    American Crystal Sugar Corp $1,000
    Others $1,250

Telecommunications **$2,250**

    Pacific Telesis Group $1,250
    Others $1,000

Waste Management **$2,000**

    Waste Management Inc $2,000

Other Major Business PACs

American Hospital Assn	$1,000	Hospitals
Chrysler Corp	$1,000	Auto Mfrs
International Council of Shopping Centers	$1,000	Retail
National Assn of Trade/Tech Schools	$1,000	Voc Tech
Philip Morris	$1,000	Tobacco
Stone Container Corp	$1,000	Forestry
Texas Cattle Feeders Assn	$1,000	Feedlots
Xerox Corp	$1,000	Off Machines

Labor

Bldg Trades/Industrial/Misc Unions **$13,950**

    Carpenters & Joiners Union $3,500
    Laborers' Western Political League $2,000
    United Auto Workers $2,000
    Machinists/Aerospace Workers Union $1,500
    Hotel/Restaurant Employees Union $1,250
    Food & Commercial Workers Union $1,200
    AFL-CIO* $1,000
    Operating Engineers Union $1,000
    Others $500

Government & Postal Workers **$10,750**

    National Assn of Retired Federal Employees $5,000
    National Rural Letter Carriers Assn $2,000
    American Fedn of State/County/Munic Employees $1,500
    National Assn of Letter Carriers* $1,500
    Others $750

Spending in Last 3 Elections

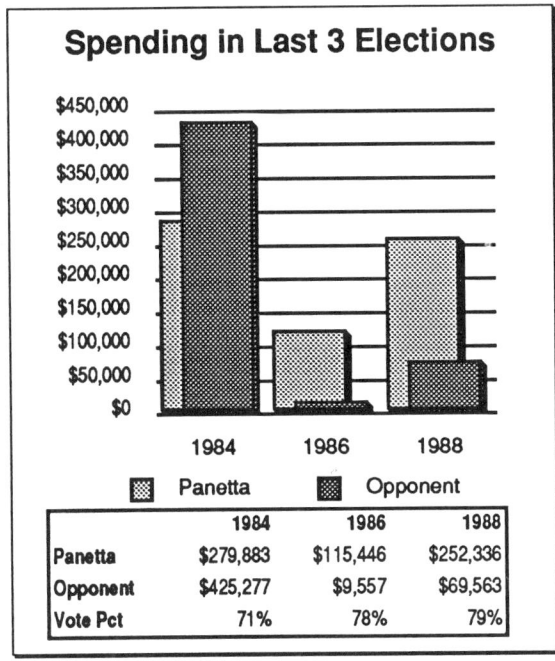

	1984	1986	1988
Panetta	$279,883	$115,446	$252,336
Opponent	$425,277	$9,557	$69,563
Vote Pct	71%	78%	79%

Interest Group Ratings

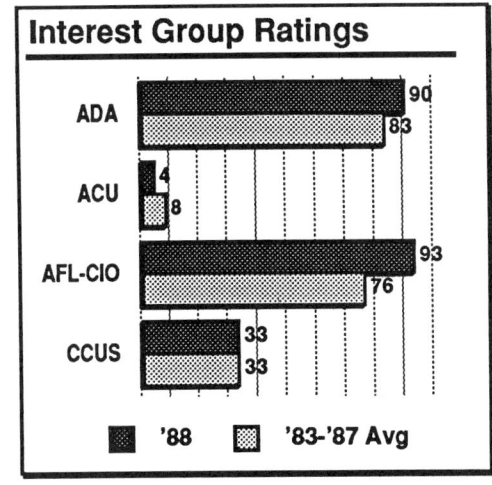

■ '88   ▨ '83-'87 Avg

Teachers Unions **$7,500**

    National Education Assn $7,000
    Others $500

Transportation Unions **$5,300**

    Air Line Pilots Assn...$1,500
    Marine Engineers District 2 Maritime Officers $1,000
    United Transportation Union $1,000
    Others $1,800

Ideological/Single-Issue

Pro-Israel **$2,000**

    Delaware Valley PAC $1,000
    Others $1,000

Social Security Issues **$5,000**

    National Cmte to Preserve Social Security $5,000

Independent expenditures supporting Panetta

National Cmte to Preserve Social Security $2,162

---

* Contributions came from more than one PAC affiliated
  with this sponsor.

Mike Parker, D-Miss (4)

1989-90 Committees & Subcommittees

Public Works and Transportation
Aviation
Surface Transportation
Water Resources

Veterans' Affairs
Compensation, Pension and Insurance
Housing and Memorial Affairs

First elected: 1988
Total receipts: $844,541
Total from PACs: $234,164

PAC Contribution Profile

Business

Automotive	....	**$3,500**
National Auto Dealers Assn	....	$2,000
Auto Dealers & Drivers for Free Trade	....	$1,000
Others	....	$500

Business Associations	....	**$2,103**
National Fedn of Independent Business	....	$1,500
Others	....	$603

Commercial & Savings Banks	....	**$3,710**
US League of Savings Assn	....	$1,000
Others	....	$2,710

Construction	....	**$3,000**
National Assn of Home Builders	....	$2,500
Others	....	$500

Dairy	....	**$6,500**
Associated Milk Producers	....	$4,500
Dairymen Inc-Mississippi	....	$1,500
Others	....	$500

Electric Utilities	....	**$4,450**
Southern Company*	....	$1,450
Mississippi ACRE (Action Cmte for Rural Electric)	....	$1,000
Others	....	$2,000

Food & Beverage	....	**$6,800**
McLane Company	....	$2,000
National Restaurant Assn	....	$1,000
Winn-Dixie Stores	....	$1,000
Others	....	$2,800

Campaign Revenue Sources

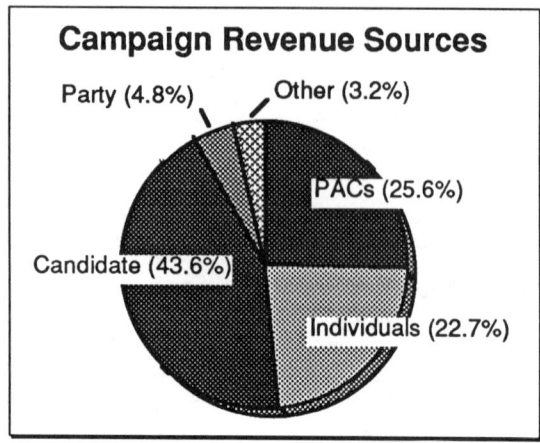

Party (4.8%)   Other (3.2%)
PACs (25.6%)
Candidate (43.6%)
Individuals (22.7%)

Forest Products	....	**$2,500**
International Paper Company	....	$2,000
Others	....	$500

Health Professionals	....	**$10,500**
American Medical Assn	....	$5,000
American Academy of Ophthalmology	....	$4,000
Others	....	$1,500

Insurance	....	**$10,750**
National Assn of Life Underwriters	....	$7,500
Casualty & Surety Agents Assn	....	$1,000
Independent Insurance Agents of America	....	$1,000
Others	....	$1,250

Lawyers	....	**$10,300**
Assn of Trial Lawyers of America	....	$10,000
Others	....	$300

Oil & Gas	....	**$5,000**
Amoco Corp	....	$1,500
Phillips Petroleum	....	$1,000
Others	....	$2,500

Real Estate	....	**$15,500**
National Assn of Realtors	....	$15,000
Others	....	$500

Telecommunications	....	**$7,300**
South Central Bell Telephone	....	$4,800
AT&T	....	$2,000
Others	....	$500

Tobacco	....	**$2,000**
Philip Morris	....	$2,000

Other Major Business PACs

National Assn of Temporary Services .... $1,000   EmployAgency

PAC Totals by Category

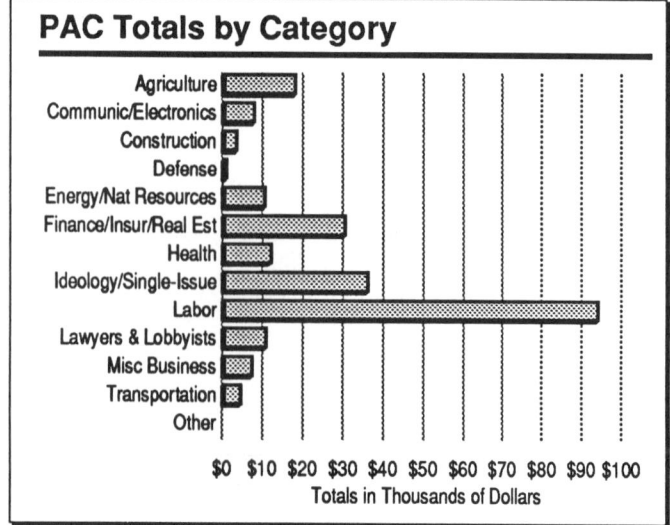

Category	
Agriculture	
Communic/Electronics	
Construction	
Defense	
Energy/Nat Resources	
Finance/Insur/Real Est	
Health	
Ideology/Single-Issue	
Labor	
Lawyers & Lobbyists	
Misc Business	
Transportation	
Other	

$0 $10 $20 $30 $40 $50 $60 $70 $80 $90 $100
Totals in Thousands of Dollars

Labor

Bldg Trades/Industrial/Misc Unions $48,200

Intl Brotherhood of Electrical Workers	$8,500
Food & Commercial Workers Union*	$6,000
Machinists/Aerospace Workers Union	$5,000
United Auto Workers	$5,000
Communications Workers of America	$4,000
Carpenters & Joiners Union	$3,750
AFL-CIO	$3,000
Electronic Machine Furniture Workers	$2,500
Sheet Metal Workers Union	$2,500
Laborers' Political League	$2,250
Bakery, Confectionery & Tobacco Workers	$2,000
Plumbers/Pipefitters Union	$2,000
Others	$1,700

Government & Postal Workers $19,250

National Assn of Letter Carriers	$10,000
American Fedn of State/County/Munic Employees	$5,000
American Postal Workers Union	$3,000
National Assn of Retired Federal Employees	$1,000
Others	$250

Teachers Unions $13,000

National Education Assn	$8,000
American Federation of Teachers	$5,000

Transportation Unions $13,100

Teamsters Union	$5,000
Air Line Pilots Assn	$2,500
Amalgamated Transit Union	$2,000
United Transportation Union	$2,000
Others	$1,600

Ideological/Single-Issue

Democratic Leadership PACs $20,750

Valley Education Fund (Tony Coelho)	$6,000
Majority Congress Committee (Jim Wright)	$5,000
Conservative Democratic PAC (Charles Stenholm)	$3,000
Cmte for Democratic Opportunity (Bill Gray)	$2,750
House Leadership Fund (Tom Foley)	$2,000
America's Leaders' Fund (Dan Rostenkowski)	$1,000
Empire Leadership Fund (Mario Cuomo)	$1,000

Pro-Israel $8,750

National PAC	$5,000
Joint Action Cmte for Political Affairs	$1,000
Others	$2,750

Other Major Ideological/Single-Issue PACs

National Cmte to Preserve Social Security	$4,000	Soc Secur
KidsPAC	$2,000	HealthWelfare

Independent expenditures supporting Parker

American Medical Assn	$94,101

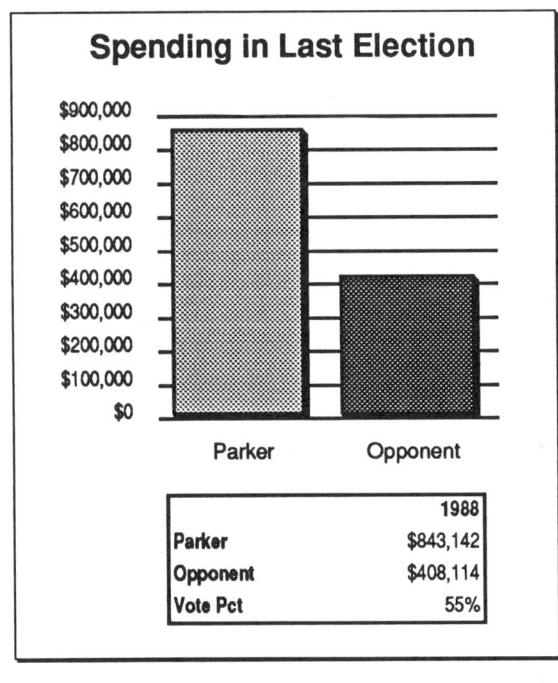

Spending in Last Election

	1988
Parker	$843,142
Opponent	$408,114
Vote Pct	55%

---

* Contributions came from more than one PAC affiliated with this sponsor.

Stan Parris, R-Va (8)

1988 Committees & Subcommittees

First elected: 1980
Total receipts: $632,755
Total from PACs: $182,927

Banking, Finance and Urban Affairs
General Oversight and Investigations (Ranking Republican)
Financial Institutions Supervision, Regulation and Insurance
Housing and Community Development
International Finance, Trade and Monetary Policy

District of Columbia (Ranking Republican)
Fiscal Affairs and Health
Government Operations and Metropolitan Affairs
Judiciary and Education

Select Narcotics Abuse and Control

PAC Contribution Profile

Business

Automotive	**$7,800**
National Auto Dealers Assn	$5,750
Auto Dealers & Drivers for Free Trade	$1,000
Others	$1,050
Business Associations	**$3,750**
Greater Washington Board of Trade	$3,750
Commercial Banks	**$27,550**
American Bankers Assn	$5,000
Virginia Bankers Assn	$5,000
Barnett Banks of Florida	$2,000
Crestar Financial Corp	$2,000
Assn of Bank Holding Companies	$1,750
American Security Bank	$1,500
Dominion Bankshares Corp	$1,500
Bankers Trust	$1,000
Chemical Bank	$1,000
Citicorp	$1,000
First Chicago Corp	$1,000
Independent Bankers Assn	$1,000
Sovran Financial Corp	$1,000
Others	$2,800
Construction	**$9,800**
Westvaco Corp	$2,000
Emhart Corp*	$1,850
National Assn of Home Builders	$1,600
Wall & Ceiling/Gypsum Contractors	$1,050
Associated General Contractors	$1,000
Others	$2,300

Campaign Revenue Sources

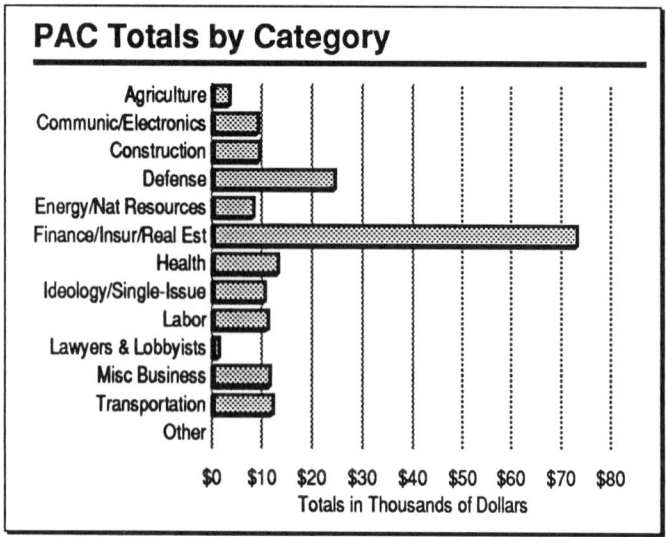

Party (2.2%)
Other (5.8%)
PACs (28.7%)
Individuals (63.3%)

Consumer Credit & Loans	**$2,500**
American Financial Services Assn	$1,250
Others	$1,250
Defense	**$24,085**
Tenneco Inc	$7,000
BDM International	$4,400
Mantech International	$1,300
Dyncorp	$1,250
Talley Industries	$1,100
Lockheed Corp	$1,035
Atlantic Research Corp	$1,000
Others	$7,000
Electric Utilities	**$5,100**
Dominion Resources Inc	$2,000
Virginia ACRE (Action Cmte for Rural Electric)	$1,250
Others	$1,850
Electronics & Computers	**$2,360**
Computer Sciences Corp	$1,610
Others	$750
Food & Beverage	**$3,552**
Coors Industries	$1,502
Others	$2,050
Health Professionals	**$11,500**
American Medical Assn	$10,000
American Dental Assn	$1,500
Insurance	**$18,800**
Independent Insurance Agents of America	$3,350
National Assn of Life Underwriters	$3,000
Casualty & Surety Agents Assn	$1,850
National Assn Mutual Insurance Agents	$1,800
Acacia Mutual Life Insurance	$1,500
American Council of Life Insurance	$1,300
Health Insurance Assn of America	$1,250
Travelers Corp	$1,000
Others	$3,750

PAC Totals by Category

Agriculture
Communic/Electronics
Construction
Defense
Energy/Nat Resources
Finance/Insur/Real Est
Health
Ideology/Single-Issue
Labor
Lawyers & Lobbyists
Misc Business
Transportation
Other

$0 $10 $20 $30 $40 $50 $60 $70 $80
Totals in Thousands of Dollars

Oil & Gas **$2,800**
    None over $750

Real Estate **$11,800**
    National Assn of Realtors $10,000
    Mortgage Bankers Assn of America.......................$1,000
    Others $800

Savings Banks & Credit Unions **$8,000**
    Credit Union National Assn $5,000
    National Council of Savings Institutions $1,550
    Atlantic Financial Federal $1,000
    Others $450

Securities/Commodities **$4,900**
    Investment Company Institute $1,100
    Federated Investors Inc..$1,000
    Others $2,800

Telecommunications **$5,700**
    Chesapeake & Potomac Telephone $2,000
    Continental Telecom $1,200
    AT&T $1,000
    United Telecommunications $1,000
    Others $500

Other Major Business PACs
Aircraft Owners & Pilots Assn ....$1,300   GenlAviation
Abbott Laboratories ....$1,000   Pharmaceut
Dickstein, Shapiro & Morin ....$1,000   Lawyers
Pinkerton Tobacco ....$1,000   Tobacco

Labor

Labor Unions **$10,750**
    National Assn of Retired Federal Employees $5,000
    Marine Engineers Union $4,000
    Police Assn of DC $1,000
    Others $750

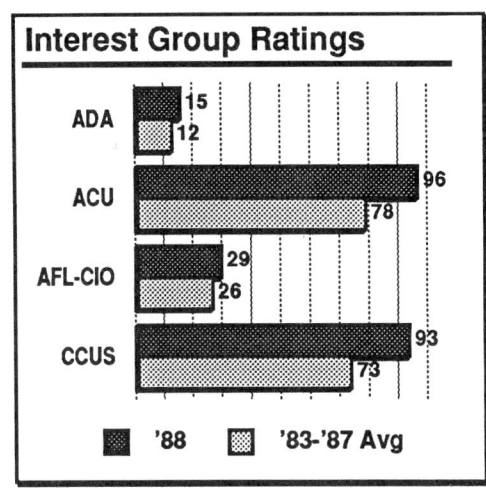

Interest Group Ratings

Group	'88	'83-'87 Avg
ADA	15	12
ACU	96	78
AFL-CIO	29	26
CCUS	93	73

Ideological/Single-Issue

Ideological/Single-Issue **$9,929**
National Rifle Assn ....$2,500   Pro-Guns
Council for National Defense ....$1,420   Pro-Defense
National Cmte to Preserve Social Security ......$1,250   Soc Secur
Ruff PAC ....$1,159   Tax Policy
National Assn for Uniformed Services ....$1,150   OtherIdeolog
Conservative Victory Cmte ....$1,000   Repub/Conser
Safari Club International ....$1,000   Pro-Hunting
Others $450

Independent expenditures supporting Parris
National Cmte to Preserve Social Security $1,013

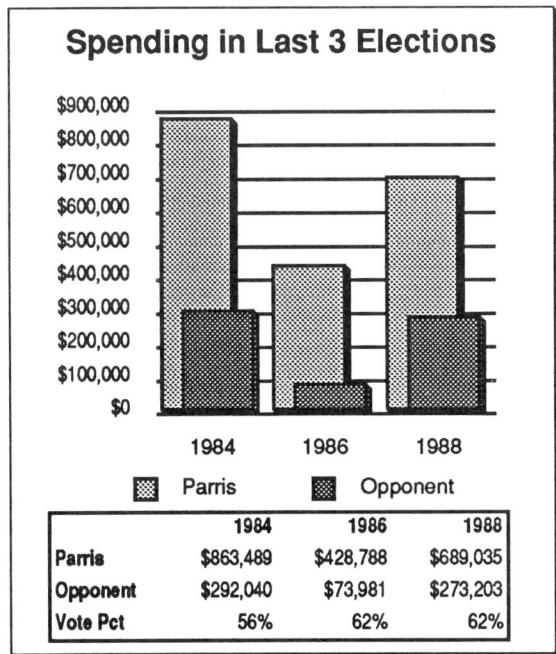

Spending in Last 3 Elections

	1984	1986	1988
Parris	$863,489	$428,788	$689,035
Opponent	$292,040	$73,981	$273,203
Vote Pct	56%	62%	62%

Parris   Opponent

Charles "Chip" Pashayan Jr., R-Calif (17)

First elected: 1978
Total receipts: $216,479
Total from PACs: $117,170

1988 Committees & Subcommittees

Interior and Insular Affairs
Water and Power Resources (Ranking Republican)
Energy and the Environment
National Parks and Public Lands

Post Office and Civil Service
Civil Service (Ranking Republican)
Postal Operations and Services

Standards of Official Conduct

PAC Contribution Profile

Business

Accountants	**$3,000**
American Institute of CPA's	$3,000
Automotive	**$2,300**
Auto Dealers & Drivers for Free Trade	$1,500
Others	$800
Commercial & Savings Banks	**$2,750**
American Bankers Assn	$1,000
Guarantee Savings	$1,000
Others	$750
Construction	**$4,350**
National Assn of Home Builders	$2,000
Associated General Contractors	$1,000
Others	$1,350
Cotton	**$2,950**
None over $850	
Electric Utilities	**$9,550**
Pacific Gas & Electric	$1,250
Public Service Company of NH/Yankee Division	$1,250
Others	$7,050
Fruits & Vegetables	**$14,975**
California Almond Growers Exchange	$5,000
Sun-Maid Growers of California	$3,000
Sunkist Growers	$1,675
Raisin Bargaining Assn	$1,650
California Pistachio Assn	$1,000
Others	$2,650

Campaign Revenue Sources

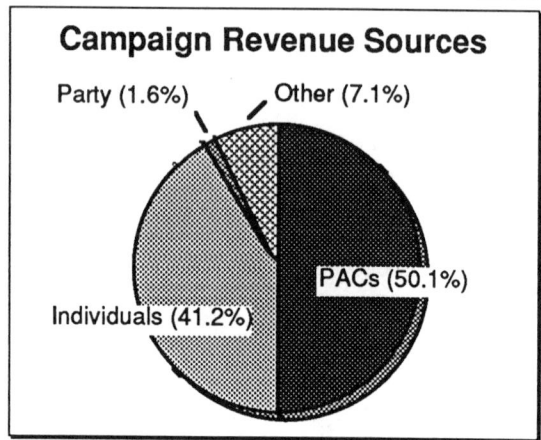

Party (1.6%)
Other (7.1%)
PACs (50.1%)
Individuals (41.2%)

Health Professionals	**$2,800**
American Medical Assn	$1,300
American Dental Assn	$1,000
Others	$500
Oil & Gas	**$6,300**
None over $750	
Package Delivery	**$2,900**
United Parcel Service	$2,900
Real Estate	**$6,250**
National Assn of Realtors	$6,000
Others	$250
Telecommunications	**$2,000**
Continental Telecom	$1,500
Others	$500
Tobacco	**$2,050**
None over $900	

Other Major Business PACs

National Assn of Life Underwriters	$1,500	Life Insurance
Associated Milk Producers	$1,250	Dairy
FMC Corp	$1,000	Metals/Mining

PAC Totals by Category

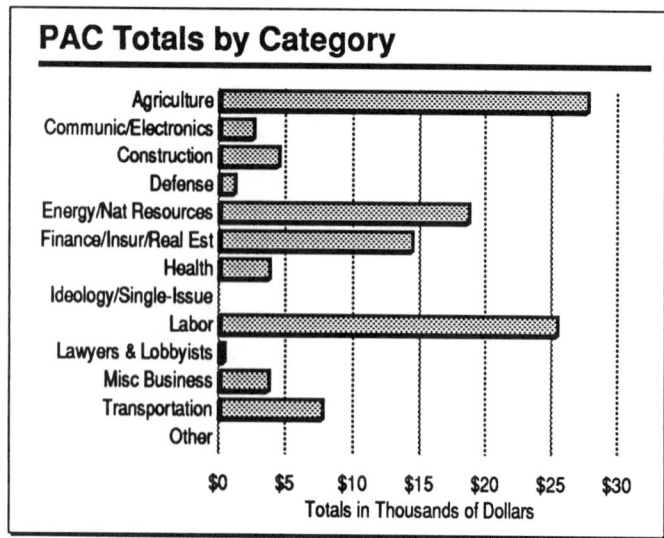

Totals in Thousands of Dollars

Agriculture
Communic/Electronics
Construction
Defense
Energy/Nat Resources
Finance/Insur/Real Est
Health
Ideology/Single-Issue
Labor
Lawyers & Lobbyists
Misc Business
Transportation
Other

Labor

Bldg Trades/Industrial/Misc Unions $10,350

Carpenters & Joiners Union $4,500	
Teamsters Union $2,500	
Air Line Pilots Assn $1,000	
Operating Engineers Union $1,000	
Others $1,350	

Government & Postal Workers $14,950

National Assn of Letter Carriers $7,000	
National Assn of Retired Federal Employees $2,500	
American Postal Workers Union $1,600	
National League of Postmasters $1,000	
Others $2,850	

Major Ideological/Single-Issue PACs

Armenian-American PAC $1,000	Ethnic	
Safari Club International $1,000	Pro-Hunting	

Independent expenditures supporting Pashayan

National Cmte to Preserve Social Security $1,573

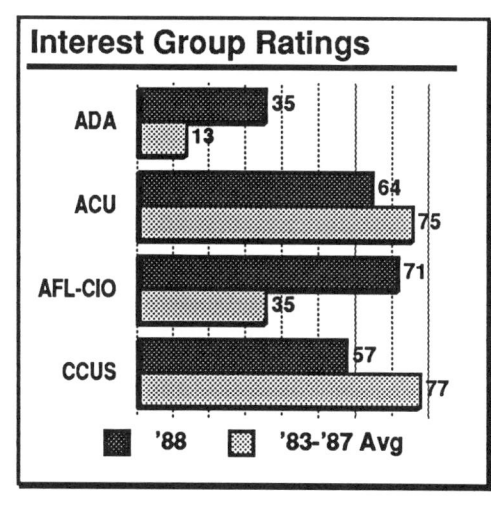

Interest Group Ratings

	'88	'83-'87 Avg
ADA	35	13
ACU	64	75
AFL-CIO	71	35
CCUS	57	77

■ '88 ▨ '83-'87 Avg

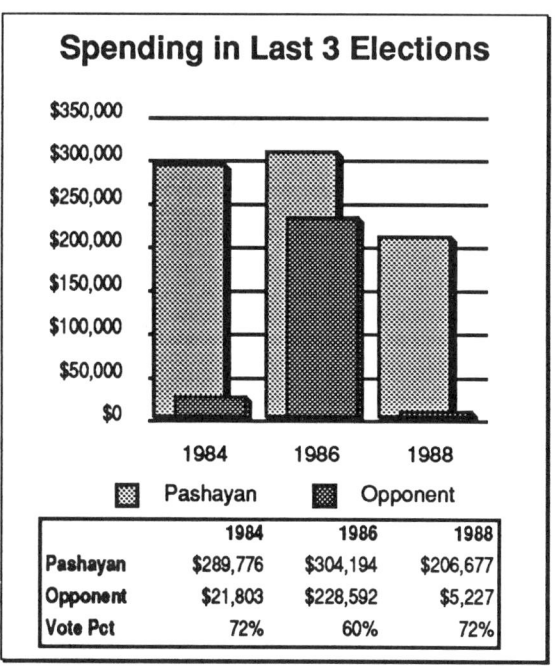

Spending in Last 3 Elections

▨ Pashayan   ■ Opponent

	1984	1986	1988
Pashayan	$289,776	$304,194	$206,677
Opponent	$21,803	$228,592	$5,227
Vote Pct	72%	60%	72%

* Contributions came from more than one PAC affiliated with this sponsor.

Liz J. Patterson, D-SC (4)

1988 Committees & Subcommittees

First elected: 1986
Total receipts: $974,666
Total from PACs: $410,255

Banking, Finance and Urban Affairs	Veterans' Affairs
Economic Stabilization	Education, Training and Employment
Financial Institutions Supervision, Regulation and Insurance	Housing and Memorial Affairs
General Oversight and Investigations	**Select Hunger**

PAC Contribution Profile

Business

Automotive	**$7,100**
National Auto Dealers Assn	$6,000
Others	$1,100
Business Associations	**$6,849**
National Fedn of Independent Business	$3,478
Business Industry PAC	$3,121
Others	$250
Commercial Banks	**$65,450**
American Bankers Assn	$18,500
Bankers Trust	$7,000
Citizens & Southern Corp*	$6,000
J P Morgan & Company	$3,100
Barnett Banks of Florida	$3,000
Continental Illinois Corp	$2,750
SC National Bank	$2,700
Chemical Bank	$2,550
Assn of Bank Holding Companies	$2,300
Consumer Bankers Assn	$1,600
Chase Manhattan	$1,550
First Chicago Corp	$1,500
NCNB Corp*	$1,500
Security Pacific Corp	$1,500
Independent Bankers Assn	$1,050
Others	$8,850
Construction	**$12,100**
National Assn of Home Builders	$4,500
American Subcontractors Assn	$1,750
Fluor Corp	$1,050
Others	$4,800

Campaign Revenue Sources

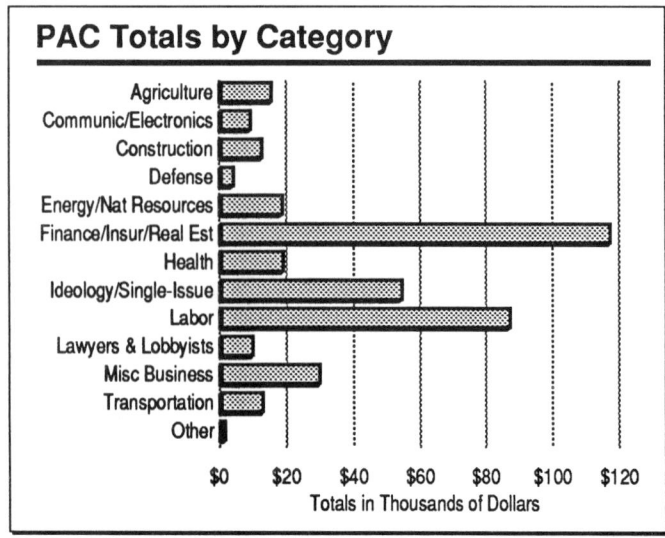

Party (3.6%)
Other (6.2%)
PACs (37.8%)
Candidate (30.5%)
Individuals (22.0%)

Electric Utilities	**$13,800**
Duke Power Company	$4,500
ACRE (Action Committee for Rural Electrification)	$3,850
Scana Corp	$3,200
Carolina Power & Light	$1,500
Others	$750
Food & Beverage	**$7,300**
National Restaurant Assn	$2,000
Winn-Dixie Stores	$2,000
Others	$3,300
Health Professionals	**$16,300**
American Medical Assn	$5,300
American Academy of Ophthalmology	$4,500
American Physical Therapy Assn	$2,000
American Nurses Assn	$1,850
American Optometric Assn	$1,500
Others	$1,150
Insurance	**$13,515**
Metropolitan Life Insurance	$3,115
Independent Insurance Agents of America	$2,050
Home Group Inc	$2,000
Liberty Corp	$1,500
Others	$4,850
Lawyers & Lobbyists	**$9,300**
Assn of Trial Lawyers of America	$6,500
Calif Trial Lawyers Assn	$1,000
Others	$1,800
Real Estate	**$13,350**
National Assn of Realtors	$10,000
First Union Corp	$2,100
Others	$1,250
Savings Banks & Credit Unions	**$16,650**
Credit Union National Assn	$7,000
US League of Savings Assn	$6,200
National Assn of Federal Credit Unions	$1,100
National Council of Savings Institutions	$1,050
Others	$1,300

PAC Totals by Category

Agriculture
Communic/Electronics
Construction
Defense
Energy/Nat Resources
Finance/Insur/Real Est
Health
Ideology/Single-Issue
Labor
Lawyers & Lobbyists
Misc Business
Transportation
Other

$0 $20 $40 $60 $80 $100 $120

Totals in Thousands of Dollars

Telecommunications *$7,650*
  Southern Bell $5,200
  AT&T $2,100
  Others $350

Textiles *$12,075*
  Springs Mills $3,000
  American Textile Manufacturers Institute $1,500
  Collins & Aikman Corp $1,250
  Others $6,325

Other Major Business PACs

J C Penney Company	$2,000	Dept Store
Lockheed Corp	$2,000	Air Defense
Philip Morris	$2,000	Tobacco
Phillips Petroleum	$2,000	Major Oil
American Hospital Assn	$1,500	Hospitals
Associated Milk Producers	$1,500	Dairy
Aircraft Owners & Pilots Assn	$1,300	GenlAviation
Securities Industry Assn	$1,300	Securities
American Financial Services Assn	$1,250	Credit/Loans
RJR Nabisco	$1,250	Tobacco

Labor

Bldg Trades/Industrial/Misc Unions *$33,450*
  Communications Workers of America $8,250
  United Auto Workers $5,800
  Food & Commercial Workers Union $5,000
  AFL-CIO* $4,200
  Intl Brotherhood of Electrical Workers $3,000
  Bakery, Confectionery & Tobacco Workers $2,000
  Ladies Garment Workers Union $1,750
  Others $3,450

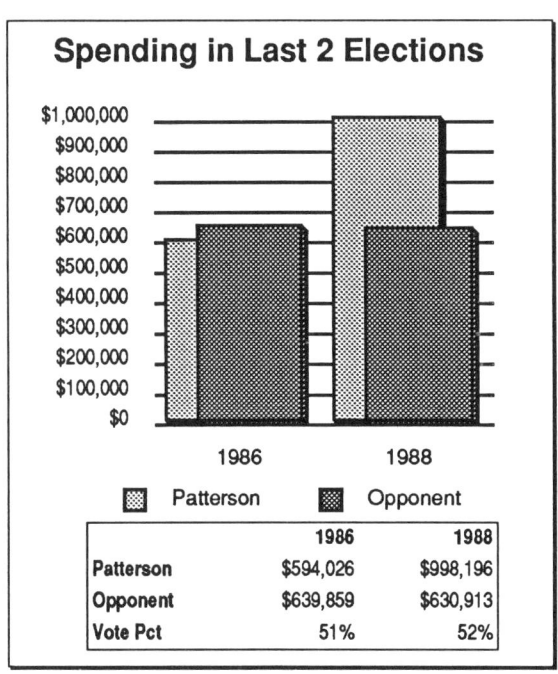

Spending in Last 2 Elections

	1986	1988
Patterson	$594,026	$998,196
Opponent	$639,859	$630,913
Vote Pct	51%	52%

Patterson   Opponent

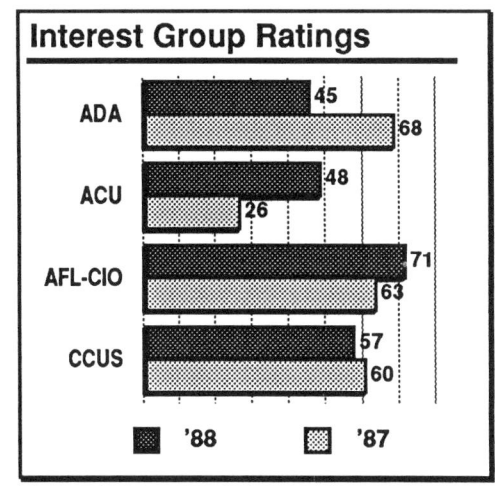

Interest Group Ratings

ADA — '88: 45, '87: 68
ACU — '88: 48, '87: 26
AFL-CIO — '88: 71, '87: 63
CCUS — '88: 57, '87: 60

■ '88   ▨ '87

Government & Postal Workers *$25,775*
  National Assn of Retired Federal Employees $11,000
  National Assn of Letter Carriers $8,725
  American Postal Workers Union $3,500
  National Treasury Employees Union $2,000
  National Rural Letter Carriers Assn $1,250
  Others ....-$700

Teachers Unions *$10,000*
  American Federation of Teachers $5,000
  National Education Assn $5,000

Transportation Unions *$17,250*
  Teamsters Union $8,000
  Air Line Pilots Assn $4,000
  Marine Engineers District 2 Maritime Officers $2,000
  Seafarers International Union $2,000
  Others $1,250

Ideological/Single-Issue

Democratic Leadership PACs *$33,250*
  Valley Education Fund (Tony Coelho) $6,000
  24th Cong Dist of California PAC (Henry Waxman) $5,000
  Majority Congress Committee (Jim Wright) $5,000
  America's Leaders' Fund (Dan Rostenkowski) $3,000
  Cmte for the 100th Congress (Charles Rangel) $3,000
  House Leadership Fund (Tom Foley) $3,000
  Cmte for Democratic Opportunity (Bill Gray) $2,000
  Conservative Democratic PAC (Charles Stenholm) $2,000
  Others $4,250

Other Major Ideological/Single-Issue PACs

Class PAC	$5,000	Dem/Liberal
National Cmte to Preserve Social Security	$2,550	Soc Secur
Joint Action Cmte for Political Affairs	$2,500	Pro-Israel
Women's Campaign Fund	$2,000	WomensIssues
KidsPAC	$1,500	HealthWelfare
National Womens Political Caucus	$1,500	WomensIssues
Council for a Livable World	$1,112	Pro-Peace

Independent expenditures supporting Patterson

American Medical Assn $112,994
National Cmte to Preserve Social Security $2,758

---

* Contributions came from more than one PAC affiliated
 with this sponsor.

Bill Paxon, R-NY (31)

1988 Committees & Subcommittees

First elected: 1988
Total receipts: $688,480
Total from PACs: $242,558

Banking, Finance and Urban Affairs
Economic Stabilization
Housing and Community Development
International Development, Finance, Trade and Monetary Policy
Policy Research and Insurance

Veterans' Affairs
Housing and Memorial Affairs

Select Narcotics Abuse and Control

PAC Contribution Profile

Business

Automotive $12,250
- Auto Dealers & Drivers for Free Trade $5,000
- National Auto Dealers Assn $3,750
- Eaton Corp $3,000
- Others $500

Business Associations...............................$3,017
- National Fedn of Independent Business $1,500
- Business Industry PAC $1,352
- Others $165

Chemicals & Plastics................................$4,250
- Dow Chemical* $1,500
- FMC Corp $1,000
- Others $1,750

Commercial Banks....................................$15,650
- Citicorp $3,500
- American Bankers Assn $3,000
- Marine Midland Banks $1,750
- Norstar Bancorp $1,550
- Chase Manhattan $1,500
- Chase Lincoln First Bank $1,100
- Bankers Trust $1,000
- Others $2,250

Construction $22,200
- National Assn of Home Builders $10,000
- Associated General Contractors $5,000
- Sheet Metal/AirCon Contractors $3,000
- American Supply Assn $1,100
- Others $3,100

Campaign Revenue Sources

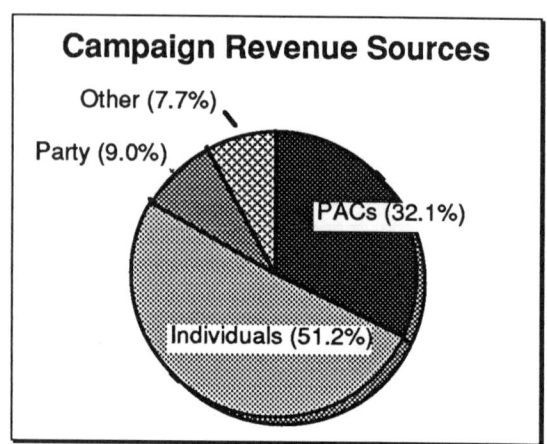

- Other (7.7%)
- Party (9.0%)
- PACs (32.1%)
- Individuals (51.2%)

Defense..$11,650
- Harris Corp $3,000
- Tenneco Inc $2,000
- Emerson Electric $1,000
- Lockheed Corp $1,000
- United Technologies $1,000
- Others $3,650

Electric Utilities $4,950
- New York State Electric & Gas Corp $4,000
- Others $950

Food & Beverage $11,216
- National Restaurant Assn $3,000
- Coors Industries $1,066
- Delaware North Companies $1,000
- Pepsi-Cola Bottlers Assn $1,000
- Pepsico Inc $1,000
- Others $4,150

Health Professionals $15,669
- American Medical Assn $8,960
- American Academy of Ophthalmology $3,000
- American Dental Assn $2,000
- National Assn of Pharmacists $1,000
- Others $709

Industrial Equipment/Materials..................$3,300
- Goulds Pumps Inc $1,200
- Minnesota Mining & Manufacturing (3M) $1,000
- Others $1,100

Insurance...$24,152
- National Assn of Life Underwriters $7,500
- Independent Insurance Agents of America $7,302
- American Family Corp $2,500
- American Council of Life Insurance $1,100
- Travelers Corp $1,000
- Others $4,750

PAC Totals by Category

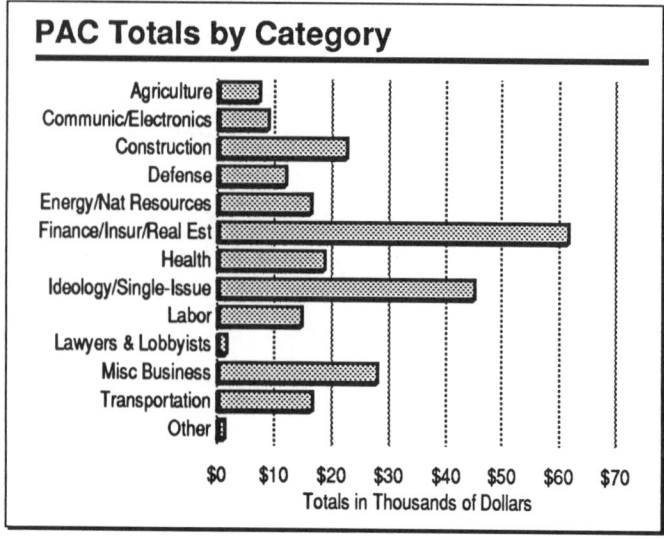

Totals in Thousands of Dollars

- Agriculture
- Communic/Electronics
- Construction
- Defense
- Energy/Nat Resources
- Finance/Insur/Real Est
- Health
- Ideology/Single-Issue
- Labor
- Lawyers & Lobbyists
- Misc Business
- Transportation
- Other

$0 $10 $20 $30 $40 $50 $60 $70

Oil & Gas $10,125
Phillips Petroleum $2,000
National Fuel Gas Corp $1,125
Amoco Corp $1,000
Sun Company $1,000
Others $5,000

Real Estate $11,500
National Assn of Realtors $10,000
Mortgage Bankers Assn of America $1,000
Others $500

Savings Banks & Credit Unions $6,425
Goldome Bank for Savings $2,500
Credit Union National Assn $1,600
National Council of Savings Institutions $1,250
Others $1,075

Securities Investment $3,000
New York Stock Exchange $1,000
Others $2,000

Telecommunications $6,300
AT&T $2,000
Motorola Inc $1,500
Continental Telecom $1,000
New York Telephone $1,000
Others $800

Other Major Business PACs
Cooper Industries	$2,000	Electronics
RJR Nabisco	$1,500	Tobacco
Delaware Otsego Corp	$1,200	Railroads
Southland Corp	$1,007	Dept Store
Corning Glass Works	$1,000	Glass Prod
Deere & Company	$1,000	Farm Equip
Holiday Inns	$1,000	Hotel/Motel
National Assn of Temporary Services	$1,000	EmployAgency
Philip Morris	$1,000	Tobacco

Labor

Labor Unions $14,350
National Assn of Letter Carriers $5,000
International Longshoremen Assn $3,000
Marine Engineers District 2 Maritime Officers $2,000
National Assn of Retired Federal Employees $2,000
American Fedn of State/County/Munic Employees .. $1,000
Others $1,350

Ideological/Single-Issue

Pro-Israel $6,250
National PAC $5,000
Others $1,250

Republican/Conservative $7,620
Conservative Victory Cmte $3,000
National Conservative PAC $1,918
Republican Congressional Boosters Club $1,000
Others $1,702

Republican Leadership PACs $15,250
Citizens for the Republic (Ronald Reagan) $5,000
Fund for America's Future (George Bush) $5,000
Policy Innovation PAC (Dick Armey) $2,000
Campaign for a New Majority (Jack Kemp) $1,000
Republican Leader's Fund (Bob Michel) $1,000
Others $1,250

Other Major Ideological/Single-Issue PACs
National Rifle Assn	$6,950	Pro-Guns
Public Service Research Council	$2,500	Anti-Union
Right to Work PAC	$2,500	Anti-Union
National Right to Life PAC	$1,361	Pro-Life
Ruff PAC	$1,150	Tax Policy
Common Sense PAC	$1,000	Unknown

Spending in Last Election

	1988
Paxon	$688,382
Opponent	$453,462
Vote Pct	53%

825

Donald M. Payne, D-NJ (10)

First elected: 1988
Total receipts: $545,049
Total from PACs: $201,177

1989-1990 Committees & Subcommittees

Education and Labor
Elementary, Secondary and Vocational Education
Labor Standards
Select Education

Foreign Affairs
Africa

Government Operations
Human Resources and Intergovernmental Relations

PAC Contribution Profile

Business

Auto Dealers	**$3,250**
National Auto Dealers Assn	$2,250
Auto Dealers & Drivers for Free Trade	$1,000
Electric Utilities	**$6,880**
Public Service Electric & Gas	$1,630
Dominion Resources Inc	$1,250
Others	$4,000
Financial Institutions	**$8,450**
American Bankers Assn	$2,500
National Westminster Bank/New Jersey	$1,250
Credit Union National Assn	$1,000
Midlantic National Bank	$1,000
Sovran Financial Corp	$1,000
Others	$1,700
Health Professionals	**$12,000**
American Medical Assn	$5,000
American Academy of Ophthalmology	$3,000
American Dental Assn	$1,500
Others	$2,500
Insurance	**$11,000**
National Assn of Life Underwriters	$5,000
Prudential Insurance	$1,250
Equitable Financial Services	$1,000
Home Group Inc	$1,000
Massachusetts Mutual Life Insurance	$1,000
Others	$1,750

Lawyers	**$5,000**
Assn of Trial Lawyers of America	$5,000
Pharmaceuticals	**$3,500**
Merck & Company	$1,000
Others	$2,500
Residential Construction	**$5,000**
National Assn of Home Builders	$5,000
Telecommunications	**$3,250**
New Jersey Bell Telephone	$2,000
AT&T	$1,000
Others	$250

Other Major Business PACs

American Hospital Assn	$1,050	Hospitals
Beneficial Management Corp	$1,000	Credit/Loans
Business Industry PAC	$1,000	Bus Assns
United Parcel Service	$1,000	Delivery

Campaign Revenue Sources

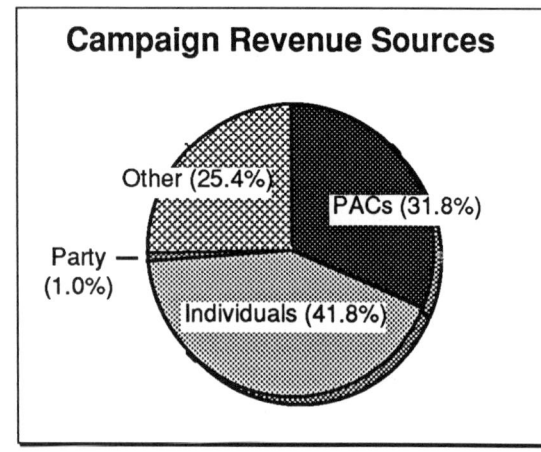

Other (25.4%)
PACs (31.8%)
Party — (1.0%)
Individuals (41.8%)

PAC Totals by Category

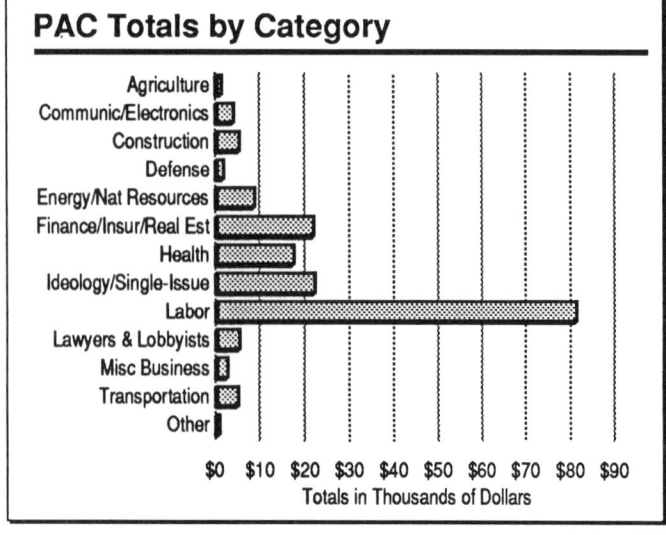

Totals in Thousands of Dollars

Labor

Bldg Trades/Industrial/Misc Unions $40,850

United Auto Workers	$10,000
Operating Engineers Local #68	$7,500
Food & Commercial Workers Union	$5,000
AFL-CIO	$3,000
Laborers' Political League	$3,000
Service Employees International Union	$3,000
Operating Engineers Local #825	$2,500
Machinists/Aerospace Workers Union	$2,000
New Jersey Industrial Union Council	$1,500
Carpenters & Joiners Union	$1,000
Others	$2,350

Government & Postal Workers $14,250

American Fedn of State/County/Munic Employees	$5,000
National Assn of Letter Carriers	$5,000
National Assn of Retired Federal Employees	$2,500
American Postal Workers Union	$1,000
Others	$750

Teachers Unions $3,000

American Federation of Teachers	$3,000

Transportation Unions $22,050

Air Line Pilots Assn	$5,000
Teamsters Union	$5,000
Seafarers International Union	$4,000
Marine Engineers Union*	$3,000
Amalgamated Transit Union	$1,500
Masters, Mates & Pilots Union	$1,000
United Transportation Union	$1,000
Others	$1,550

Ideological/Single-Issue

Democratic Leadership PACs $9,250

Valley Education Fund (Tony Coelho)	$5,000
Majority Congress Committee (Jim Wright)	$2,000
America's Leaders' Fund (Dan Rostenkowski)	$1,000
Cmte for Democratic Opportunity (Bill Gray) ...	$1,000
Others	$250

Pro-Israel $8,000

National PAC	$5,000
Others	$3,000

Other Major Ideological/Single-Issue PACs

National Cmte to Preserve Social Security	$2,500	Soc Secur
Teamwork America	$1,000	Dem/Liberal

Spending in Last Election

	1988
Payne	$413,338
Opponent	$0
Vote Pct	77%

---

* Contributions came from more than one PAC affiliated
with this sponsor.

827

Lewis F. Payne Jr., D-Va (5)

1989-1990 Committees & Subcommittees

Public Works and Transportation
Aviation
Economic Development
Public Buildings and Grounds

First elected: 1988
Total receipts: $280,435
Total from PACs: $127,850

PAC Contribution Profile

NOTE: The PAC contributions on these pages include funds that Payne received in both of his 1988 races — the special election he won in June and the November general election in which he was elected to a full two-year term. The total receipts listed in the box above, and the percentages in the pie chart at right, refer only to the general election race.

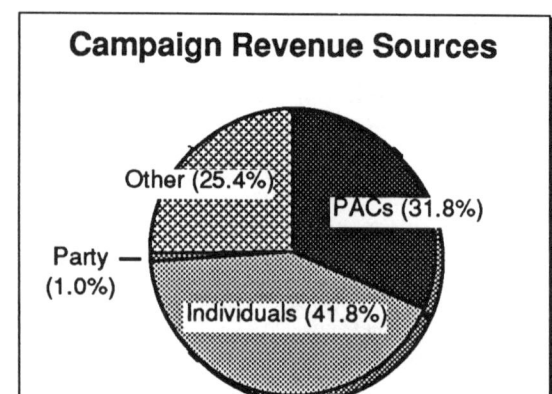

Campaign Revenue Sources

Other (25.4%)
PACs (31.8%)
Party — (1.0%)
Individuals (41.8%)

Business

Auto Dealers	**$3,250**
National Auto Dealers Assn	$3,250
Commercial & Savings Banks	**$14,450**
Virginia Bankers Assn	$8,000
Bankers Trust	$2,000
US League of Savings Assn	$2,000
Dominion Bankshares Corp	$1,000
Others	$1,450
Construction	**$11,500**
National Assn of Home Builders	$7,500
American Road & Transportation Bldrs Assn	$1,000
National Utility Contractors Assn	$1,000
Others	$2,000
Dairy	**$2,750**
Dairymen Inc-Virginia	$1,500
Mid-American Dairymen	$1,000
Others	$250
Electric Utilities & Equipment	**$7,750**
ACRE (Action Committee for Rural Electrification)	$2,500
Dominion Resources Inc	$2,250
Babcock & Wilcox	$1,500
Others	$1,500

Food & Beverage	**$2,500**
National Restaurant Assn	$1,000
Others	$1,500
Health Professionals	**$16,500**
American Medical Assn	$10,000
American Academy of Ophthalmology	$3,000
American Nurses Assn	$1,500
National Assn of Pharmacists	$1,000
Others	$1,000
Insurance	**$10,750**
National Assn of Life Underwriters	$5,000
Independent Insurance Agents of America	$3,500
Others	$2,250
Lawyers & Lobbyists	**$5,450**
Assn of Trial Lawyers of America	$3,000
McGuire, Woods, Battle & Booth	$1,000
Others	$1,450
Mining	**$3,500**
Independent Coal Operators Assn	$1,500
Pittston Company	$1,500
Others	$500
Oil & Gas	**$2,600**
Phillips Petroleum	$1,500
Others	$1,100
Real Estate	**$15,100**
American Land Development Assn	$7,600
National Assn of Realtors	$5,000
American Resort & Residential Developers Assn	$1,000
National Realty Committee	$1,000
Others	$500
Telecommunications	**$4,300**
Chesapeake & Potomac Telephone	$1,500
AT&T	$1,000
Continental Telecom	$1,000
Others	$800
Tobacco	**$4,750**
Philip Morris	$3,000
RJR Nabisco	$1,000
Others	$750

PAC Totals by Category

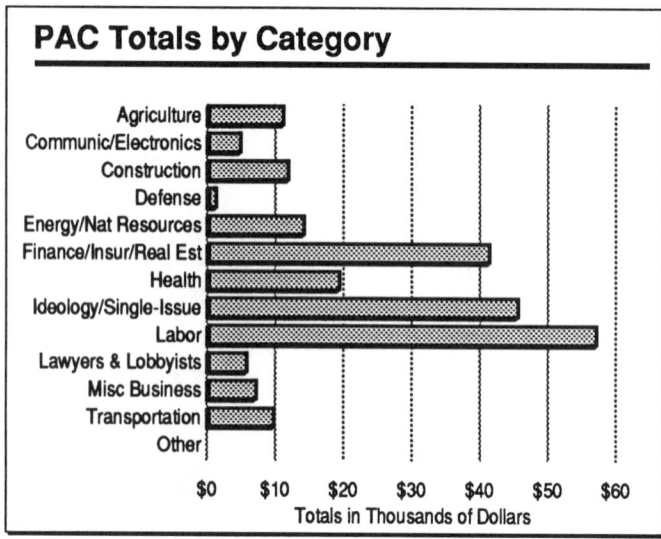

Agriculture
Communic/Electronics
Construction
Defense
Energy/Nat Resources
Finance/Insur/Real Est
Health
Ideology/Single-Issue
Labor
Lawyers & Lobbyists
Misc Business
Transportation
Other

$0 $10 $20 $30 $40 $50 $60
Totals in Thousands of Dollars

Interest Group Ratings

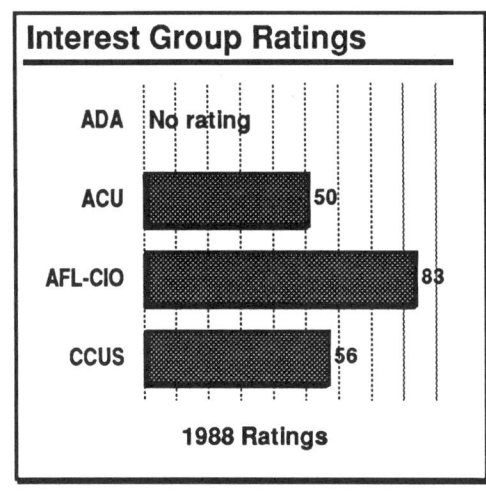

	1988 Ratings
ADA	No rating
ACU	50
AFL-CIO	83
CCUS	56

Trucking Companies **$3,000**

  American Trucking Assns $1,000
  North American Van Lines $1,000
  Yellow Freight System $1,000

Other Major Business PACs

Abbott Laboratories	$1,000	Pharmaceut
Allied-Signal	$1,000	Air Defense
American Hospital Assn	$1,000	Hospitals
Greater Washington Board of Trade	$1,000	Chamb/Cmrce
National Fedn of Independent Business	$1,000	Sml Business

Labor

Bldg Trades/Industrial/Misc Unions **$10,500**

  United Auto Workers $5,500
  Operating Engineers Union $1,500
  Carpenters & Joiners Union $1,000
  Others $2,500

Government & Postal Workers **$14,250**

  National Assn of Letter Carriers $9,000
  National Assn of Retired Federal Employees $3,000
  Others $2,250

Teachers Unions **$18,000**

  National Education Assn $18,000

Transportation Unions **$14,000**

  Teamsters Union $7,500
  Air Line Pilots Assn $2,500
  Seafarers International Union $2,500
  United Transportation Union $1,500

Ideological/Single-Issue

Democratic/Liberal **$6,999**

  National Cmte for an Effective Congress $4,999
  Class PAC $2,000

Democratic Leadership PACs....................................**$24,000**

  Majority Congress Committee (Jim Wright) $8,000
  Valley Education Fund (Tony Coelho) $5,000
  America's Leaders' Fund (Dan Rostenkowski) $4,000
  Conservative Democratic PAC (Charles Stenholm) $4,000
  House Leadership Fund (Tom Foley) $2,000
  Cmte for Democratic Opportunity (Bill Gray) $1,000

Pro-Israel **$5,500**

  National PAC $5,000
  Others $500

Other Major Ideological/Single-Issue PACs

National Cmte to Preserve Social Security	$4,500	Soc Secur
National Rifle Assn	$2,500	Pro-Guns
KidsPAC	$1,000	HealthWelfare

Independent expenditures supporting Payne

National Cmte to Preserve Social Security $1,093

Spending in Last 2 Elections

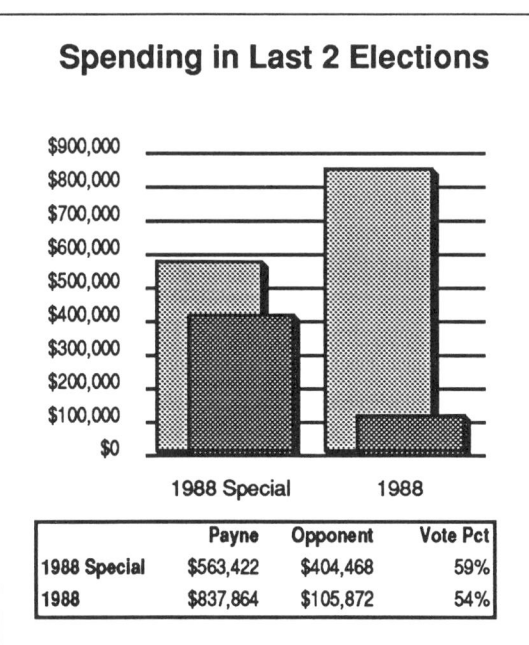

	Payne	Opponent	Vote Pct
1988 Special	$563,422	$404,468	59%
1988	$837,864	$105,872	54%

Don J. Pease, D-Ohio (13)

First elected: 1976
Total receipts: $292,904
Total from PACs: $189,677

1988 Committees & Subcommittees

Ways and Means
Public Assistance and Unemployment Compensation
Trade

Campaign Revenue Sources

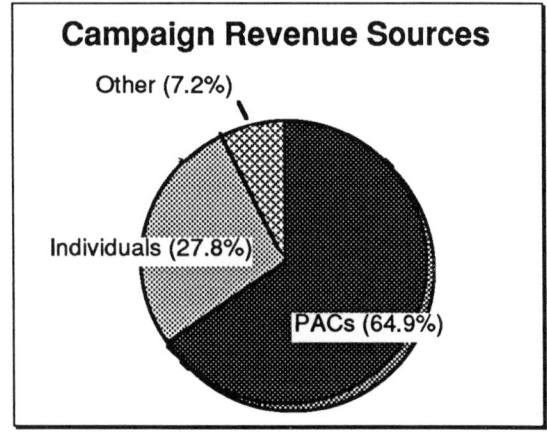

Other (7.2%)
Individuals (27.8%)
PACs (64.9%)

PAC Contribution Profile

Business

Accountants	**$6,500**
American Institute of CPA's	$5,000
Arthur Andersen & Company	$1,000
Others	$500
Automotive	**$3,500**
Chrysler Corp	$1,500
Others	$2,000
Commercial Banks	**$6,800**
American Bankers Assn	$2,000
Citicorp	$1,000
National City Corp	$1,000
Ohio Bankers Assn	$1,000
Society Corp	$1,000
Others	$800
Construction	**$2,800**
National Assn of Home Builders	$1,000
Others	$1,800
Dairy	**$6,000**
Associated Milk Producers	$1,500
Mid-American Dairymen	$1,500
Borden Inc	$1,000
Dairymen Inc	$1,000
Milk Marketing Inc	$1,000
Electronics & Computers	**$3,000**
General Electric	$1,000
NCR Corp	$1,000
Others	$1,000

Farm Organizations	**$2,000**
Ohio Farm Bureau Federation	$1,500
Others	$500
Food & Beverage	**$6,400**
National Beer Wholesalers Assn	$2,500
Pepsico Inc	$1,000
Wine & Spirits Wholesalers of America	$1,000
Winn-Dixie Stores	$1,000
Others	$900
Health Professionals	**$9,500**
American Dental Assn	$2,500
American Medical Assn	$2,250
American Academy of Ophthalmology	$1,000
American College of Emergency Physicians	$1,000
American Optometric Assn	$1,000
Cmte for Quality Orthopedic Health Care	$1,000
Others	$750
Insurance	**$11,500**
National Assn of Life Underwriters	$4,000
American Council of Life Insurance	$1,000
Chubb Corp	$1,000
Cigna Corp	$1,000
Health Insurance Assn of America	$1,000
ITT Corp	$1,000
Others	$2,500
Lawyers & Lobbyists	**$9,400**
Baker & Hostetler	$5,000
Jones, Day, Reavis & Pogue	$1,600
Kutak, Rock & Campbell	$1,000
Others	$1,800
Oil & Gas	**$7,250**
USX Corp	$2,000
BP America	$1,000
Petroleum Marketers Assn	$1,000
Society of Independent Gasoline Marketers	$1,000
Others	$2,250
Real Estate	**$7,500**
National Assn of Realtors	$6,500
Mortgage Bankers Assn of America	$1,000
Savings Banks & Credit Unions	**$5,425**
US League of Savings Assn	$2,500
Ohio Savings Assns League	$1,500
Credit Union National Assn	$1,000
Others	$425

PAC Totals by Category

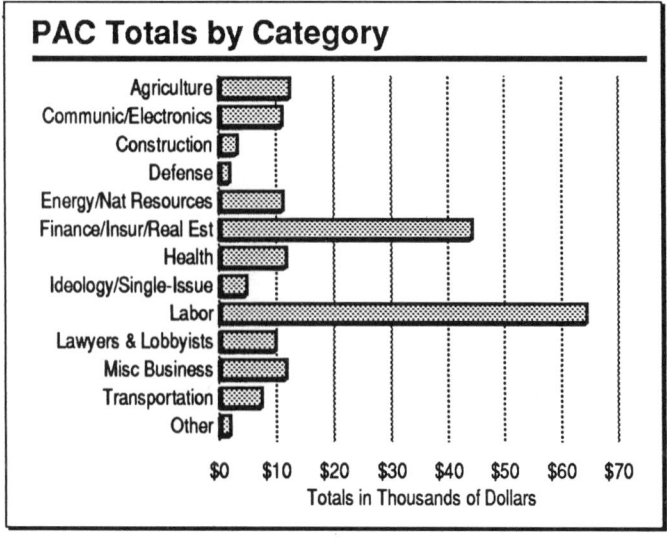

Categories: Agriculture, Communic/Electronics, Construction, Defense, Energy/Nat Resources, Finance/Insur/Real Est, Health, Ideology/Single-Issue, Labor, Lawyers & Lobbyists, Misc Business, Transportation, Other

Totals in Thousands of Dollars
($0 $10 $20 $30 $40 $50 $60 $70)

Securities/Commodities $4,000

Chicago Board of Trade	$1,000
Chicago Mercantile Exchange	$1,000
Kelso & Company	$1,000
Public Securities Assn	$1,000

Steel Production $2,613

Bethlehem Steel	$1,000
Others	$1,613

Telecommunications $7,182

AT&T	$2,500
United Telecommunications	$2,500
Others	$2,182

Venture Capital $4,000

National Venture Capital Assn	$4,000

Other Major Business PACs

Employee Stock Ownership Assn	$1,500	Other
Aircraft Owners & Pilots Assn	$1,000	GenlAviation
American Assn of Equipment Lessors	$1,000	Rentals
American Hospital Assn	$1,000	Hospitals
Babcock & Wilcox	$1,000	PowerEquip
Corning Glass Works	$1,000	Glass Prod
CSX Transportation Inc	$1,000	Railroads

Labor

Bldg Trades/Industrial/Misc Unions $30,620

United Auto Workers	$6,700
Carpenters & Joiners Union	$4,000
Machinists/Aerospace Workers Union	$3,000
Laborers' Political League	$2,500
Electronic Machine Furniture Workers	$2,000
Food & Commercial Workers Union	$2,000
Plumbers/Pipefitters Union	$2,000
Graphic Communications Union	$1,500
Intl Brotherhood of Electrical Workers	$1,500
(continued in next column)	

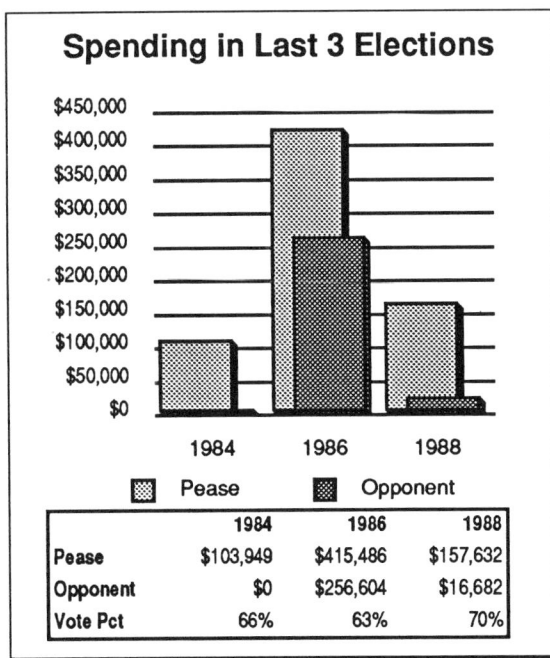

Spending in Last 3 Elections

Pease | Opponent

	1984	1986	1988
Pease	$103,949	$415,486	$157,632
Opponent	$0	$256,604	$16,682
Vote Pct	66%	63%	70%

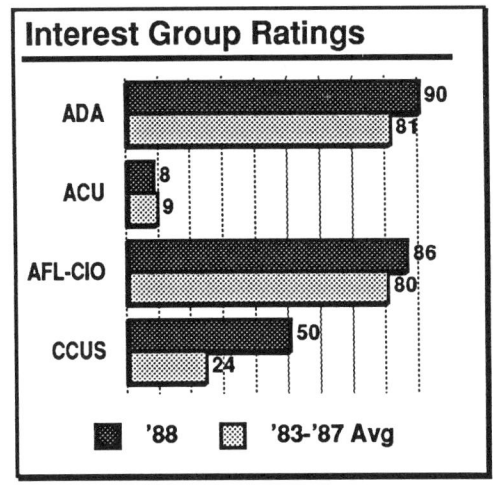

Interest Group Ratings

	'88	'83-'87 Avg
ADA	90	81
ACU	8	9
AFL-CIO	86	80
CCUS	50	24

Labor (cont'd)

Operating Engineers Union*	$1,020
AFL-CIO	$1,000
Sheet Metal Workers Union	$1,000
United Mine Workers	$1,000
Others	$1,400

Government & Postal Workers $14,350

National Assn of Retired Federal Employees	$4,500
National Rural Letter Carriers Assn	$2,700
American Postal Workers Union	$2,000
National Assn of Letter Carriers	$2,000
American Fedn of State/County/Munic Employees	$1,000
Others	$2,150

Teachers Unions $2,500

National Education Assn	$2,500

Transportation Unions $16,500

Teamsters Union	$5,000
Air Line Pilots Assn	$2,500
United Transportation Union	$2,000
Marine Engineers District 2 Maritime Officers	$1,500
Brotherhood of Locomotive Engineers	$1,000
Masters, Mates & Pilots Union	$1,000
Seafarers International Union	$1,000
Transportation Communication Union	$1,000
Others	$1,500

Ideological/Single-Issue

Ideological/Single-Issue $4,350

National Cmte to Preserve Social Security	$2,500	Soc Secur
National Council of Senior Citizens	$1,000	Soc Secur
Others	$850	

Independent expenditures supporting Pease

National Cmte to Preserve Social Security	$1,212

---

* Contributions came from more than one PAC affiliated
with this sponsor.

Nancy Pelosi, D-Calif (5)

First elected: 1987
Total receipts: $655,522
Total from PACs: $278,800

1988 Committees & Subcommittees

Banking, Finance and Urban Affairs
Consumer Affairs and Coinage
Housing and Community Development
International Development, Finance, Trade and Monetary Policy

Government Operations
Employment and Housing
Human Resources and Intergovernmental Relations

PAC Contribution Profile

NOTE: The PAC contributions on these pages include funds that Pelosi received both in 1988 and in the June 1987 special election in which she was first elected to Congress. The total receipts listed in the box above, and the percentages in the pie chart at right, refer only to her 1988 general election race.

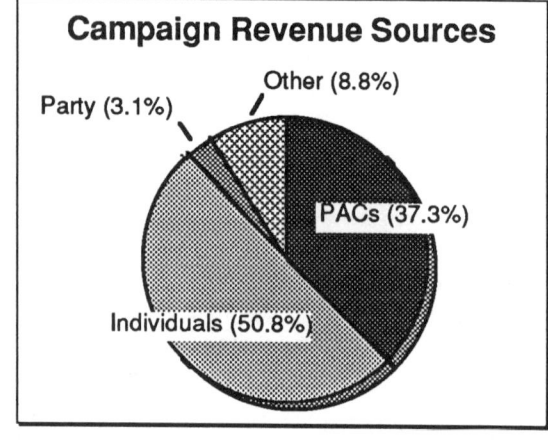

Campaign Revenue Sources

- Party (3.1%)
- Other (8.8%)
- PACs (37.3%)
- Individuals (50.8%)

Business

Accountants	**$5,000**
American Institute of CPA's	$5,000
Commercial Banks	**$31,500**
American Bankers Assn	$5,000
Wells Fargo	$3,500
BankAmerica	$3,400
California Bankers Assn	$3,000
Citicorp	$2,500
First Interstate Bank/California	$2,000
Security Pacific Corp	$2,000
Bankers Trust	$1,500
Chase Manhattan	$1,500
Union Bank	$1,500
Others	$5,600
Construction	**$16,600**
Sheet Metal/AirCon Contractors	$8,500
National Assn of Home Builders	$4,500
Bechtel Corp	$2,000
Others	$1,600
Electric Utilities	**$7,150**
Pacific Gas & Electric	$3,500
Southern California Edison	$1,500
Others	$2,150

Health Professionals	**$29,430**
American Medical Assn	$15,000
American Academy of Ophthalmology	$5,500
American Nurses Assn	$4,680
Co-op of American Physicians	$2,250
Others	$2,000
Insurance	**$10,105**
Independent Insurance Agents of America	$1,800
American Council of Life Insurance	$1,150
Others	$7,155
Lawyers & Lobbyists	**$11,950**
Assn of Trial Lawyers of America	$6,000
Pillsbury, Madison & Sutro	$3,000
California Trial Lawyers Assn	$1,500
Others	$1,450
Oil & Gas	**$10,600**
Occidental Petroleum	$6,000
Chevron Corp	$2,500
Others	$2,100
Real Estate	**$13,700**
National Assn of Realtors	$11,250
Mortgage Bankers Assn of America	$1,500
Others	$950
Savings Banks	**$12,950**
First Nationwide Bank	$2,500
US League of Savings Assn	$1,500
Coast Federal Savings & Loan	$1,250
Others	$7,700
Securities Investment	**$6,450**
None over $1,000	

Other Major Business PACs

Pacific Telesis Group	$3,050	Phone Util
American Hospital Assn	$2,500	Hospitals
McKesson Corp	$2,000	Pharmaceut
United Parcel Service	$1,800	Delivery
Dow Chemical/Midland	$1,500	Chemicals
Joseph E Seagram & Sons	$1,500	Wine&Liquor
Shaklee Corp	$1,500	Health Prod

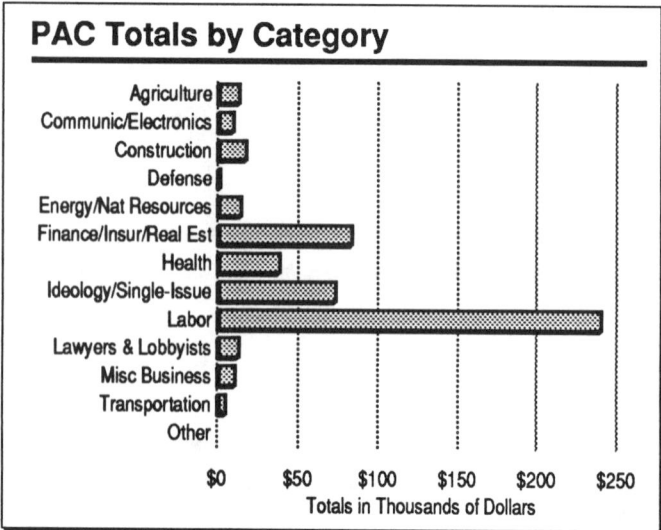

PAC Totals by Category

Categories (top to bottom): Agriculture, Communic/Electronics, Construction, Defense, Energy/Nat Resources, Finance/Insur/Real Est, Health, Ideology/Single-Issue, Labor, Lawyers & Lobbyists, Misc Business, Transportation, Other

Totals in Thousands of Dollars — axis: $0, $50, $100, $150, $200, $250

Labor

Bldg Trades/Industrial/Misc Unions $129,050

AFL-CIO*	$15,000
Machinists/Aerospace Workers Union	$15,000
Plumbers/Pipefitters Union	$15,000
United Auto Workers	$15,000
Operating Engineers Union*	$11,500
Sheet Metal Workers Union	$10,000
Laborers' Western Political League	$9,500
Communications Workers of America	$7,500
Carpenters & Joiners Union*	$6,500
Service Employees International Union	$5,500
Food & Commercial Workers Union	$4,000
Intl Brotherhood of Electrical Workers	$4,000
Ironworkers Union	$3,500
Ladies Garment Workers Union	$2,000
Hotel/Restaurant Employees Union	$1,500
Others	$3,550

Government & Postal Workers $22,800

American Fedn of State/County/Munic Employees	$8,500
National Assn of Letter Carriers	$7,500
National Assn of Retired Federal Employees	$3,000
American Postal Workers Union	$1,500
Others	$2,300

Teachers Unions $20,750

National Education Assn	$20,000
Others	$750

Transportation Unions $66,572

Teamsters Union	$20,000
Marine Engineers Union*	$11,000
Longshoremen/Warehousemen Union	$7,972
Seafarers International Union*	$7,950
Masters Mates & Pilots Union*	$6,500
Air Line Pilots Assn	$5,000
Transport Workers Union	$4,500
United Transportation Union	$1,600
Others	$2,050

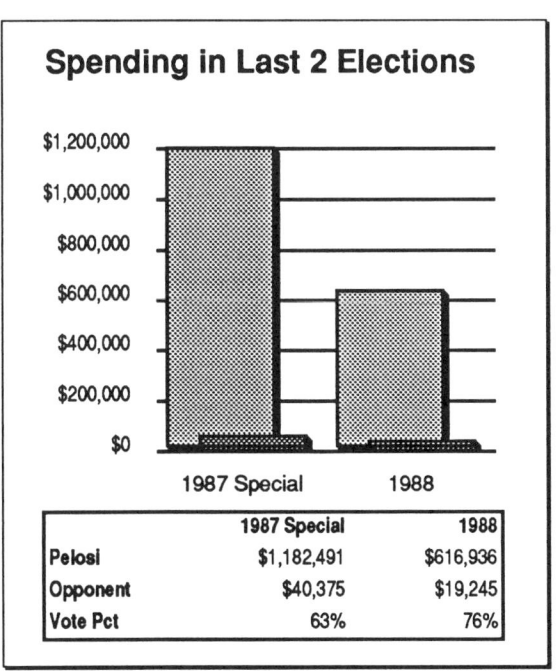

Spending in Last 2 Elections

	1987 Special	1988
Pelosi	$1,182,491	$616,936
Opponent	$40,375	$19,245
Vote Pct	63%	76%

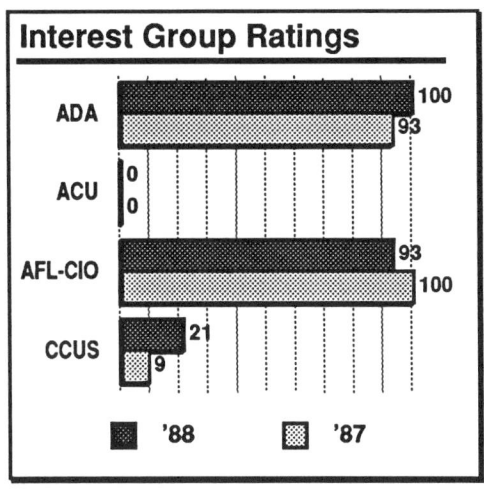

Interest Group Ratings

	'88	'87
ADA	100	93
ACU	0	0
AFL-CIO	93	100
CCUS	21	9

Ideological/Single-Issue

Democratic Leadership PACs..................................$26,300

Valley Education Fund (Tony Coelho)	$6,000
America's Leaders' Fund (Dan Rostenkowski)	$5,300
Cmte for a Democratic Consensus (Alan Cranston)	$5,000
Majority Congress Committee (Jim Wright)	$5,000
Others	$5,000

Pro-Israel $15,000

National PAC	$10,000
Washington PAC	$1,500
Others	$3,500

Womens Issues/Pro-Choice.....................................$17,200

Women's Political Committee	$6,000
Women's Political Fund	$3,200
Voters for Choice/Friends of Family Planning	$3,000
National Abortion Rights Action League	$2,250
Women's Campaign Fund	$1,500
Others	$1,250

Other Major Ideological/Single-Issue PACs

Human Rights Campaign Fund	$3,500	Gay/Lesbian
National Cmte to Preserve Social Security	$3,500	Soc Secur
Democrats for The 80's	$2,000	Dem/Liberal

Independent expenditures supporting Pelosi

National Cmte to Preserve Social Security	$2,197

---

* Contributions came from more than one PAC affiliated
with this sponsor.

Timothy J. Penny, D-Minn (1)

First elected: 1982
Total receipts: $284,554
Total from PACs: $125,377

1988 Committees & Subcommittees

Agriculture
Conservation, Credit and Rural Development
Wheat, Soybeans and Feed Grains

Education and Labor
Labor Standards

Veterans' Affairs
Compensation, Pension and Insurance
Hospitals and Health Care

Select Hunger

PAC Contribution Profile

Business

Automotive	**$6,800**
National Auto Dealers Assn	$4,050
Auto Dealers & Drivers for Free Trade	$2,500
Others	$250
Commodities/Securities	**$2,200**
Chicago Board of Trade	$1,500
Others	$700
Construction	**$3,250**
American Subcontractors Assn	$1,050
National Assn of Home Builders	$1,000
Others	$1,200
Dairy	**$13,800**
Associated Milk Producers	$6,700
Land O'Lakes Inc	$4,000
Mid-American Dairymen	$2,500
Others	$600
Financial Institutions	**$5,950**
American Bankers Assn	$2,000
Norwest Corp	$1,300
Others	$2,650
Food & Beverage	**$16,450**
National Restaurant Assn	$3,500
General Mills*	$3,300
S & A Restaurant Corp	$1,500
Food Marketing Institute	$1,300
American Meat Institute	$1,200
Hardee's Food Systems	$1,000
Pillsbury Company	$1,000
Others	$3,650

Campaign Revenue Sources

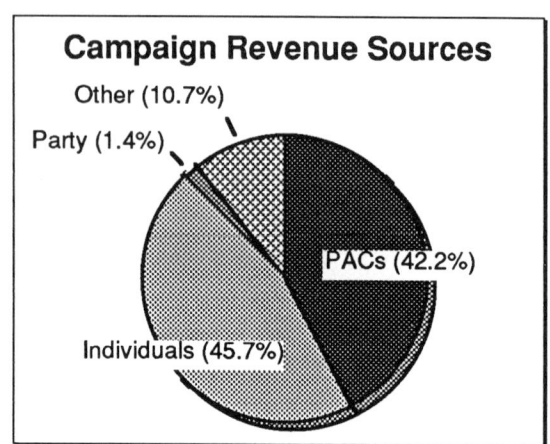

Other (10.7%)
Party (1.4%)
PACs (42.2%)
Individuals (45.7%)

Health Professionals	**$7,350**
American Medical Assn	$5,350
American Dental Assn	$1,500
Others	$500
Insurance	**$3,000**
National Assn of Life Underwriters	$1,000
Others	$2,000
Real Estate	**$7,600**
National Assn of Realtors	$6,000
Minnesota Assn of Realtors	$1,000
Others	$600
Retail Sales	**$5,657**
Southland Corp	$1,007
Dayton Hudson Corp	$1,000
Others	$3,650
Sugar Growers	**$6,250**
Southern Minnesota Beet Sugar Co-op	$2,500
American Crystal Sugar Corp	$2,200
Others	$1,550
Telecommunications	**$3,900**
North Western Bell Telephone	$2,500
Others	$1,400

Other Major Business PACs

Minnesota Truck Operators	$1,500	Trucking
Higher Ed Mgmt/Resources Found	$1,350	Credit/Loans
Ashland Oil	$1,000	Refine/Mktg
Honeywell Inc	$1,000	Electronics
Xerox Corp	$1,000	Off Machines

PAC Totals by Category

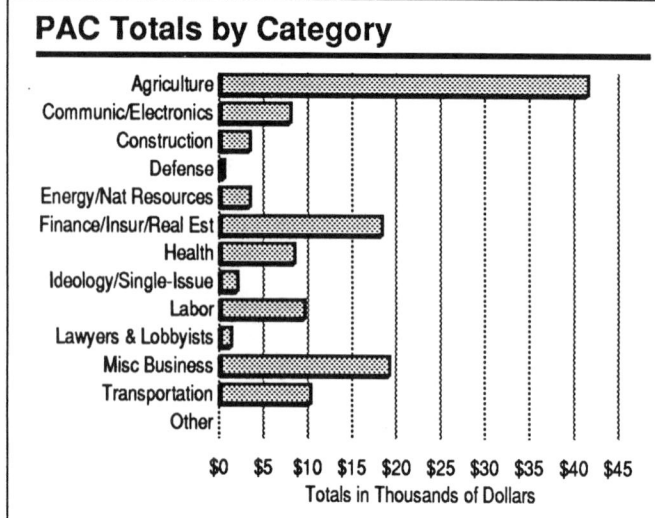

Agriculture
Communic/Electronics
Construction
Defense
Energy/Nat Resources
Finance/Insur/Real Est
Health
Ideology/Single-Issue
Labor
Lawyers & Lobbyists
Misc Business
Transportation
Other

$0 $5 $10 $15 $20 $25 $30 $35 $40 $45
Totals in Thousands of Dollars

Labor

Bldg Trades/Industrial/Misc Unions $3,050
    Carpenters & Joiners Union $1,000
    Others $2,050

Government & Postal Workers $3,050
    National Assn of Retired Federal Employees $1,500
    Others $1,550

Transportation Unions $3,300
    Air Line Pilots Assn $1,000
    Others $2,300

Major Ideological/Single-Issue PACs

Valley Education Fund (Tony Coelho) ....$1,000   Dem Leaders

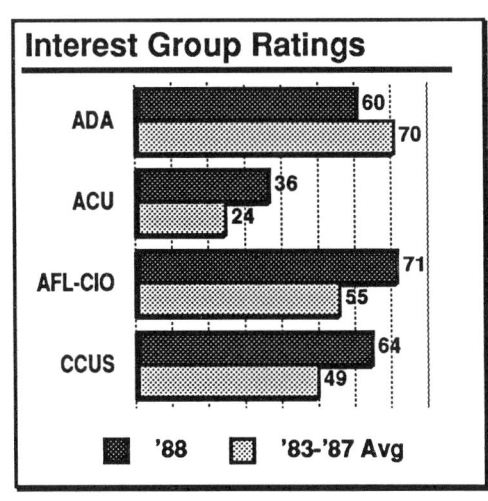

Interest Group Ratings

	'88	'83-'87 Avg
ADA	60	70
ACU	36	24
AFL-CIO	71	55
CCUS	64	49

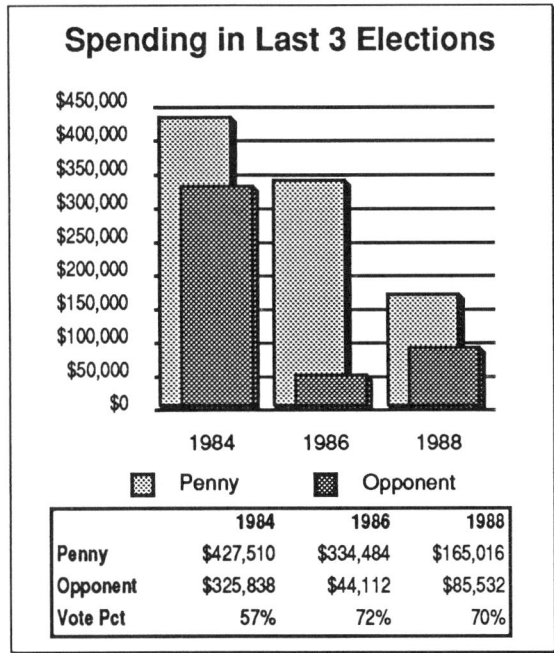

Spending in Last 3 Elections

	1984	1986	1988
Penny	$427,510	$334,484	$165,016
Opponent	$325,838	$44,112	$85,532
Vote Pct	57%	72%	70%

* Contributions came from more than one PAC affiliated
with this sponsor.

Claude Pepper, D-Fla (18)

First elected: 1962
Total receipts: $434,858
Total from PACs: $243,562

1988 Committees & Subcommittees

Rules (Chairman)
Legislative Process
Rules of the House

Select Aging
Health and Long-Term Care (Chairman)

Campaign Revenue Sources

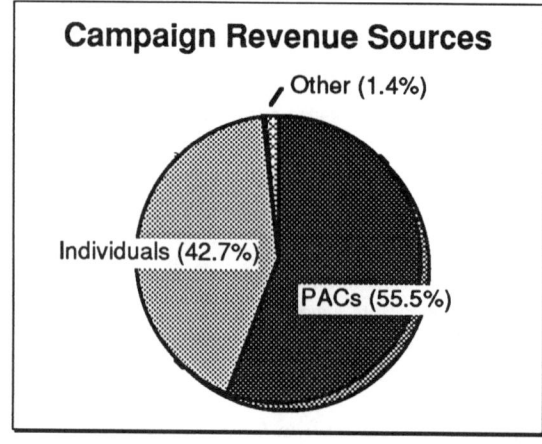

Other (1.4%)
Individuals (42.7%)
PACs (55.5%)

PAC Contribution Profile

Business

Commercial Banks..**$21,600**
American Bankers Assn $5,500
Barnett Banks of Florida $3,500
Citizens & Southern National Bank $2,000
National Banks of Florida $2,000
Southeast Banking Corp $2,000
Independent Bankers Assn $1,500
Sun Banks $1,500
Citicorp $1,000
Florida Bankers Assn $1,000
NCNB Corp $1,000
Others $600

Electric Utilities **$5,750**
ACRE (Action Committee for Rural Electrification) $1,000
American Electric Power $1,000
Edison Electric Institute $1,000
Others $2,750

Health Professionals **$11,050**
American Dental Assn $2,000
American Society Cataract/Refract Surgery $1,500
American Assn of Nurse Anesthetist.............................$1,000
American Physical Therapy Assn $1,000
American Optometric Assn...$1,000
American Podiatry Assn $1,000
Corp for the Advancement of Psychiatry $1,000
National Assn of Pharmacists $1,000
Others $1,550

Insurance..**$4,000**
Blue Cross & Blue Shield Assn* $2,500
Others $1,500

Lawyers & Lobbyists **$15,800**
Assn of Trial Lawyers of America.................................$10,000
Akin, Gump, Hauer & Feld $1,000
Camp, Barsh, Bates & Tate $1,000
Dickstein, Shapiro & Morin $1,000
Western Enterprise PAC $1,000
Others $1,800

Real Estate **$6,000**
General Development Corp $2,000
First Union Corp $1,500
National Assn of Realtors $1,500
Mortgage Bankers Assn of America...............................$1,000

Savings Banks & Credit Unions **$6,950**
US League of Savings Assn...$3,000
Centrust Savings Bank $1,000
Credit Union National Assn $1,000
Florida League of Financial Institutions $1,000
Others $950

Securities/Commodities **$4,500**
Chicago Mercantile Exchange $1,000
Federated Investors Inc...$1,000
Others $2,500

Telecommunications **$11,000**
Southern Bell $5,000
AT&T...$2,500
Pacific Telesis Group $2,000
Others $1,500

PAC Totals by Category

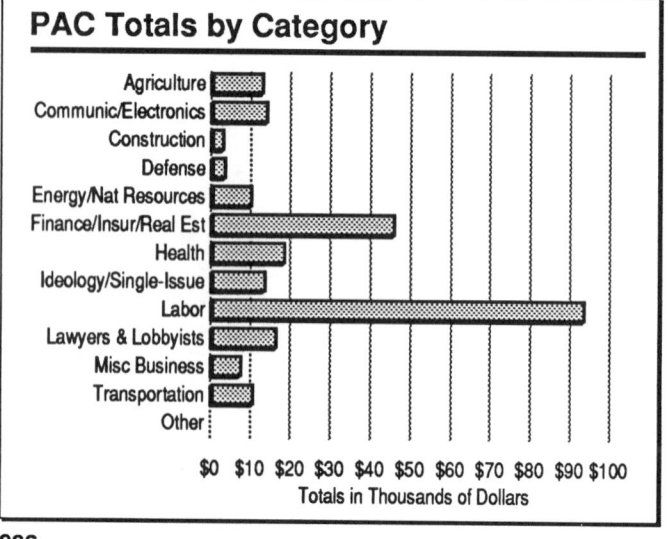

Agriculture
Communic/Electronics
Construction
Defense
Energy/Nat Resources
Finance/Insur/Real Est
Health
Ideology/Single-Issue
Labor
Lawyers & Lobbyists
Misc Business
Transportation
Other

$0 $10 $20 $30 $40 $50 $60 $70 $80 $90 $100
Totals in Thousands of Dollars

Other Major Business PACs

Associated Milk Producers	$2,500	Dairy
National Beer Wholesalers Assn	$2,000	Liquor Whlsl
American Financial Services Assn	$1,500	Credit/Loans
Allied-Signal	$1,000	Air Defense
American Sugarbeet Growers Assn	$1,000	Sugar
Boat Owners Assn of the US	$1,000	Rec Boats
Computer Sciences Corp	$1,000	Data Process
CSX Transportation Inc	$1,000	Railroads
Florida Sugar Cane League	$1,000	Sugar
Household International	$1,000	Credit/Loans
Internorth Inc	$1,000	Natural Gas
Manor Healthcare Corp	$1,000	Nursing Home
Medical Equipment Suppliers	$1,000	Med Supply
National Restaurant Assn	$1,000	Restaurants
National Assn for Home Care	$1,000	Home Care
National Assn of Home Builders	$1,000	Resid Constr
National Assn of Temporary Services	$1,000	EmployAgency
National Assn of Private Psychiatric Hospitals	$1,000	Hospitals
Norfolk Southern Corp	$1,000	Railroads
Ryder System Inc	$1,000	Car/Trk Rent
Sears	$1,000	Retail
Union Pacific Corp	$1,000	Railroads
United Parcel Service	$1,000	Delivery
Waste Management Inc	$1,000	Waste Mgmt

Labor

Bldg Trades/Industrial/Misc Unions $36,000

Machinists/Aerospace Workers Union	$5,000
Sheet Metal Workers Union	$5,000
Operating Engineers Union*	$3,500
Carpenters & Joiners Union	$3,000
United Auto Workers	$3,000
Intl Brotherhood of Electrical Workers*	$2,500
Plumbers/Pipefitters Union	$2,500
Ladies Garment Workers Union	$2,000
United Steelworkers	$2,000
Hotel/Restaurant Employees Union	$1,500
Laborers' Political League	$1,500
Communications Workers of America	$1,300

(Continued in next column)

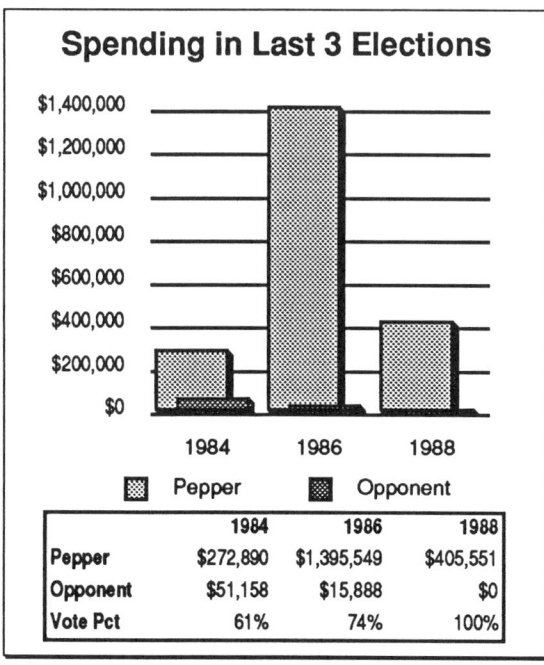

Spending in Last 3 Elections

	1984	1986	1988
Pepper	$272,890	$1,395,549	$405,551
Opponent	$51,158	$15,888	$0
Vote Pct	61%	74%	100%

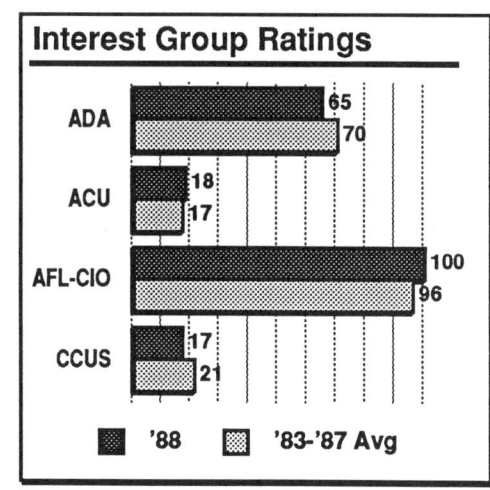

Interest Group Ratings

	'88	'83–'87 Avg
ADA	65	70
ACU	18	17
AFL-CIO	100	96
CCUS	17	21

■ '88   ▨ '83–'87 Avg

Labor (cont'd)

AFL-CIO	$1,000
Food & Commercial Workers Union	$1,000
Others	$1,200

Government & Postal Workers $15,500

National Assn of Retired Federal Employees	$5,000
National Assn of Letter Carriers	$3,000
American Fedn of State/County/Munic Employees	$2,500
American Postal Workers Union	$2,000
National League of Postmasters	$1,000
Others	$2,000

Teachers Unions $6,000

National Education Assn	$3,500
American Federation of Teachers	$2,500

Transportation Unions $35,500

International Longshoremen Assn	$7,500
United Transportation Union	$7,500
Air Line Pilots Assn	$5,000
Teamsters Union	$5,000
Marine Engineers Union*	$4,500
Seafarers International Union	$2,000
Transportation Communication Union	$1,500
Brotherhood of Locomotive Engineers	$1,000
Others	$1,500

Ideological/Single-Issue

Senior Citizens Issues $7,000

National Cmte to Preserve Social Security	$6,000
National Council of Senior Citizens	$1,000

Other Major Ideological/Single-Issue PACs

Free Cuba PAC	$5,000	Anti-Castro

Independent expenditures supporting Pepper

National Cmte to Preserve Social Security	$2,504

---

* Contributions came from more than one PAC affiliated
with this sponsor.

Carl C. Perkins, D-Ky (7)

First elected: 1984
Total receipts: $418,749
Total from PACs: $264,300

1988 Committees & Subcommittees

Education and Labor
Elementary, Secondary and Vocational Education
Postsecondary Education

Public Works and Transportation
Aviation

Science, Space and Technology
Science, Research and Technology
Space Science and Applications

PAC Contribution Profile

Business

Aviation & Aerospace **$9,800**
   Federal Express Corp $6,350
   Others $3,450

Dairy **$7,450**
   Associated Milk Producers $3,750
   Dairymen Inc-Kentucky $2,200
   Mid-American Dairymen $1,500

Defense **$2,250**
   Lockheed Corp $1,200
   Others $1,050

Electric Utilities **$3,100**
   Kentucky Utilities Company $1,000
   Others $2,100

Insurance **$2,550**
   National Assn of Life Underwriters $1,500
   Others $1,050

Lawyers **$11,250**
   Assn of Trial Lawyers of America $10,000
   Others $1,250

Mining **$3,700**
   Cyprus Minerals Company $1,850
   Independent Coal Operators Assn $1,000
   Others $850

Sugar Growers **$4,100**
   American Crystal Sugar Corp $1,200
   Others $2,900

Campaign Revenue Sources

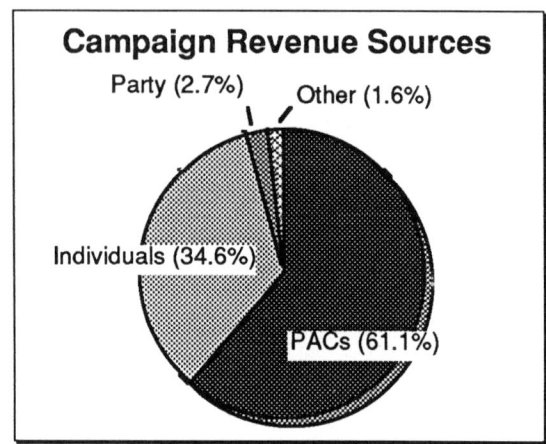

Party (2.7%)
Other (1.6%)
Individuals (34.6%)
PACs (61.1%)

Telecommunications **$4,150**
   South Central Bell Telephone $2,050
   AT&T $1,350
   Others $750

Tobacco **$5,050**
   Tobacco Institute $1,200
   Philip Morris $1,000
   Pinkerton Tobacco $1,000
   RJR Nabisco $1,000
   Others $850

Trucking/Delivery **$4,750**
   United Parcel Service $2,550
   American Trucking Assns $1,000
   Others $1,200

Vocational Tech Schools **$8,700**
   National Assn of Trade/Tech Schools $4,700
   Assn of Independent Colleges/Schools ... $3,000
   National Assn of Cosmetology Schools ... $1,000

Other Major Business PACs
Higher Ed Mgmt/Resources Found .... $1,350   Credit/Loans
Lamar Corp .... $1,000   Real Estate

PAC Totals by Category

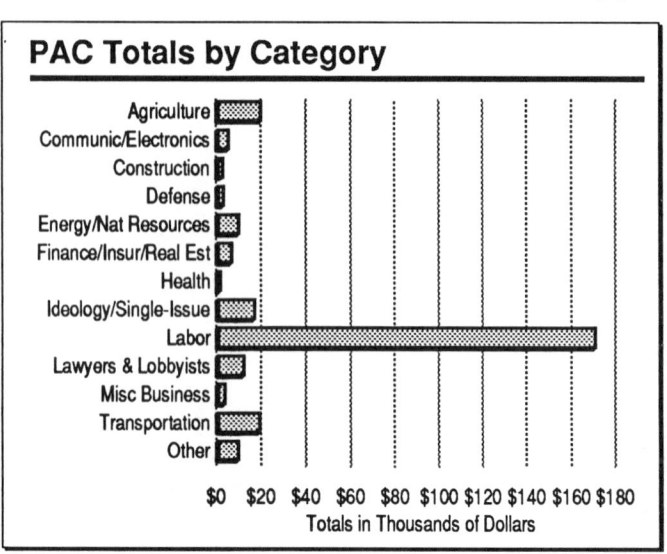

Agriculture
Communic/Electronics
Construction
Defense
Energy/Nat Resources
Finance/Insur/Real Est
Health
Ideology/Single-Issue
Labor
Lawyers & Lobbyists
Misc Business
Transportation
Other

$0 $20 $40 $60 $80 $100 $120 $140 $160 $180
Totals in Thousands of Dollars

Labor

Bldg Trades/Industrial/Misc Unions **$71,350**

United Auto Workers $10,000
United Steelworkers $10,000
Carpenters & Joiners Union $8,200
Machinists/Aerospace Workers Union $7,000
United Mine Workers $6,450
AFL-CIO* $5,400
Communications Workers of America $5,000
Food & Commercial Workers Union $4,000
Intl Brotherhood of Electrical Workers $3,500
Operating Engineers Union $3,500
Laborers' Political League $2,650
Electronic Machinery Furniture Workers $1,350
Ladies Garment Workers Union $1,350
Others $2,950

Government & Postal Workers **$34,700**

American Fedn of State/County/Munic Employees $10,000
National Assn of Letter Carriers $8,700
National Assn of Retired Federal Employees $8,000
National Rural Letter Carriers Assn $3,700
American Postal Workers Union $2,000
Others $2,300

Teachers Unions **$20,600**

National Education Assn $11,000
American Federation of Teachers $9,600

Transportation Unions **$43,100**

Teamsters Union $10,000
Seafarers International Union $8,500
Marine Engineers Union* $7,350
Air Line Pilots Assn $6,000
United Transportation Union $3,900
Transportation Communication Union $1,450
Amalgamated Transit Union $1,000
International Longshoremen Assn $1,000
Others $3,900

Interest Group Ratings

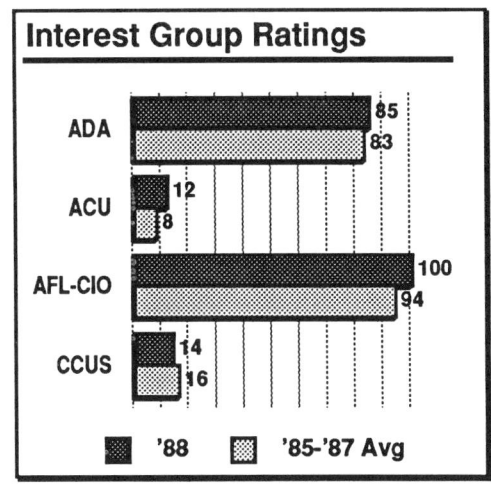

Ideological/Single-Issue

Democratic Leadership PACs **$4,000**

Valley Education Fund (Tony Coelho) $3,000
Cmte for Democratic Opportunity (Bill Gray) $1,000

Other Major Ideological/Single-Issue PACs

National Rifle Assn .... $9,900   Pro-Guns
National Cmte to Preserve Social Security ...... $1,700   Soc Secur

Independent expenditures supporting Perkins

National Cmte to Preserve Social Security $2,298

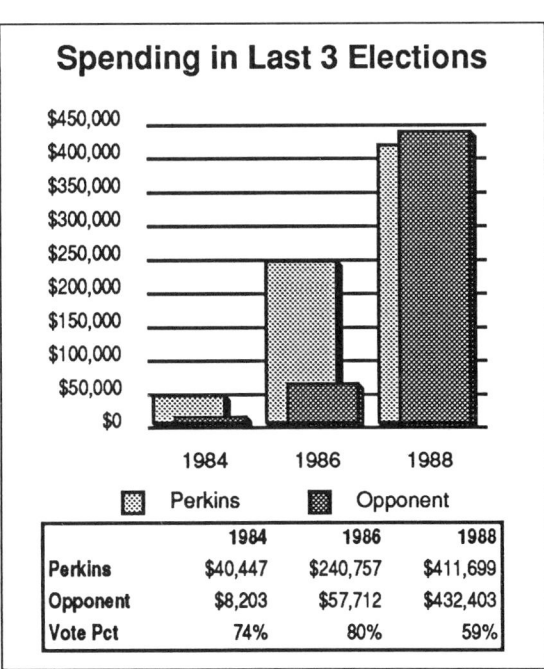

Spending in Last 3 Elections

	1984	1986	1988
Perkins	$40,447	$240,757	$411,699
Opponent	$8,203	$57,712	$432,403
Vote Pct	74%	80%	59%

* Contributions came from more than one PAC affiliated
with this sponsor.

Thomas E. Petri, R-Wis (6)

First elected: 1979
Total receipts: $258,876
Total from PACs: $120,980

1988 Committees & Subcommittees

Education and Labor Labor Standards (Ranking Republican) Elementary, Secondary and Vocational Education Labor-Management Relations	**Public Works and Transportation** Aviation Surface Transportation Water Resources **Standards of Official Conduct**

PAC Contribution Profile

Business

Automotive **$5,000**
    National Auto Dealers Assn $2,750
    Auto Dealers & Drivers for Free Trade $1,500
    Others $750

Aviation & Aerospace **$6,000**
    Texas Air $1,250
    Others $4,750

Commercial & Savings Banks **$4,450**
    US League of Savings Assn $1,250
    American Bankers Assn $1,000
    Others $2,200

Construction **$13,850**
    National Utility Contractors Assn $3,000
    American Supply Assn $1,500
    National Assn of Home Builders $1,000
    National Electrical Contractors Assn $1,000
    Others $7,350

Dairy **$9,250**
    Associated Milk Producers $6,000
    Mid-American Dairymen $1,250
    Land O'Lakes Inc $1,000
    Others $1,000

Electric Utilities **$2,420**
    Wisconsin Electric Power Company $1,000
    Others $1,420

Campaign Revenue Sources

Other (14.7%)
Party (1.1%)
PACs (46.6%)
Individuals (37.3%)

Food & Beverage **$12,300**
    Hardee's Food Systems $2,000
    National Restaurant Assn $2,000
    Food Marketing Institute $1,750
    Jerrico Inc $1,000
    Pepsico Inc $1,000
    Others $4,550

Forest Products **$3,900**
    International Paper Company $2,050
    Others $1,850

Health Professionals **$4,620**
    American Medical Assn $4,370
    Others $250

Hotels/Motels **$2,250**
    Holiday Inns $1,000
    Others $1,250

Insurance **$6,320**
    Northwestern Mutual Life $2,000
    Others $4,320

PAC Totals by Category

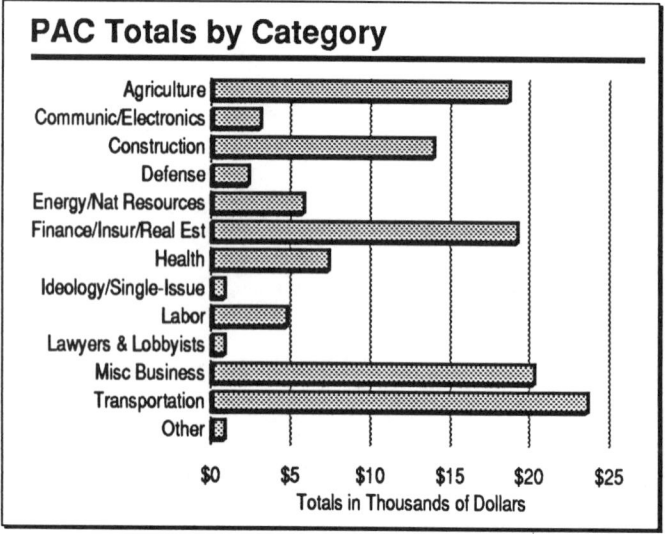

Agriculture
Communic/Electronics
Construction
Defense
Energy/Nat Resources
Finance/Insur/Real Est
Health
Ideology/Single-Issue
Labor
Lawyers & Lobbyists
Misc Business
Transportation
Other

$0 $5 $10 $15 $20 $25
Totals in Thousands of Dollars

Railroads $2,250

    None over $500

Real Estate $6,550

    National Assn of Realtors $6,550

Retail Sales $4,650

    J C Penney Company $1,000
    National Assn of Convenience Stores $1,000
    Others $2,650

Telecommunications $2,250

    Wisconsin Bell Telephone $1,000
    Others $1,250

Trucking/Delivery $6,000

    United Parcel Service $1,750
    Consolidated Freightways $1,000
    Others $3,250

Other Major Business PACs

American Institute of CPA's	$1,500	Accountants
Brunswick Corp	$1,000	Indust Equip
FMC Corp	$1,000	Chemicals
National Assn of Temporary Services	$1,000	EmployAgency
Tenneco Inc	$1,000	Ships
Waste Management Inc	$1,000	Waste Mgmt

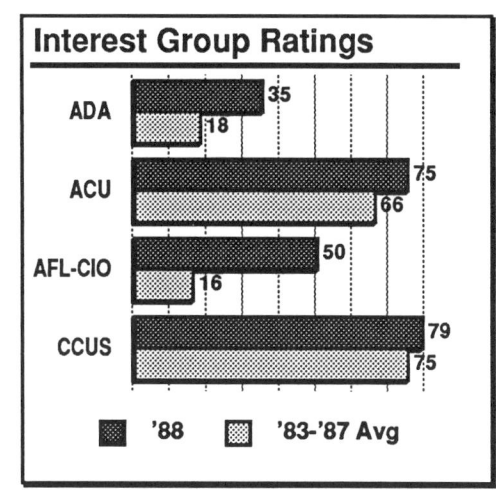

Interest Group Ratings

	'88	'83-'87 Avg
ADA	35	18
ACU	75	66
AFL-CIO	50	16
CCUS	79	75

Labor

Labor Unions...$4,640

    National Assn of Retired Federal Employees $2,000
    Others $2,640

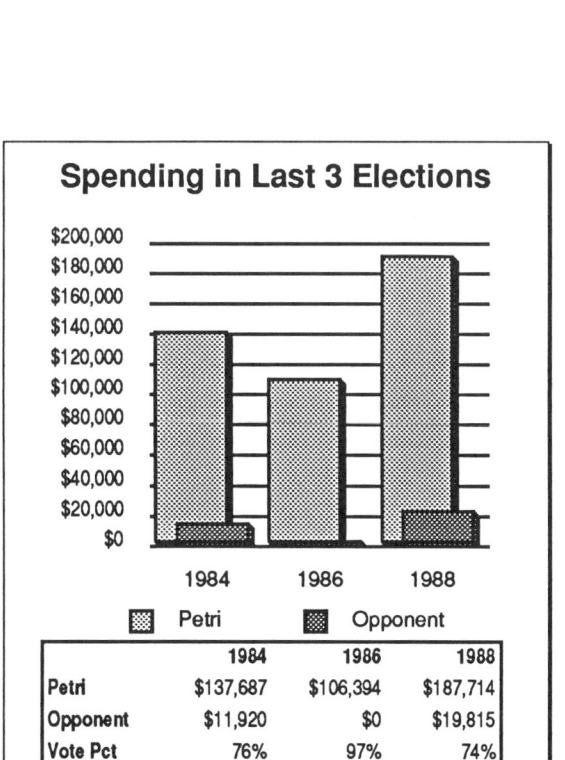

Spending in Last 3 Elections

	1984	1986	1988
Petri	$137,687	$106,394	$187,714
Opponent	$11,920	$0	$19,815
Vote Pct	76%	97%	74%

841

Owen B. Pickett, D-Va (2)

First elected: 1986
Total receipts: $437,439
Total from PACs: $215,810

1988 Committees & Subcommittees

Armed Services
Military Personnel and Compensation
Research and Development
Seapower and Strategic and Critical Materials

Merchant Marine and Fisheries
Coast Guard and Navigation
Merchant Marine

PAC Contribution Profile

Business

Accountants **$14,300**
American Institute of CPA's $10,000
Deloitte, Haskins & Sells $2,000
Ernst & Whinney $2,000
Others $300

Auto Dealers **$7,000**
Auto Dealers & Drivers for Free Trade............$4,000
National Auto Dealers Assn $3,000

Commercial Banks...**$10,000**
Virginia Bankers Assn $5,000
Crestar Financial Corp $2,000
Dominion Bankshares Corp $2,000
Sovran Financial Corp $1,000

Construction **$6,600**
National Assn of Home Builders $6,600

Defense...**$19,800**
Mantech International $2,000
BDM International $1,500
Lockheed Corp $1,200
Raytheon $1,200
Textron Inc $1,200
AT&T $1,000
Tenneco Inc $1,000
Others $10,700

Electric Utilities **$2,700**
Dominion Resources Inc $1,000
Others $1,700

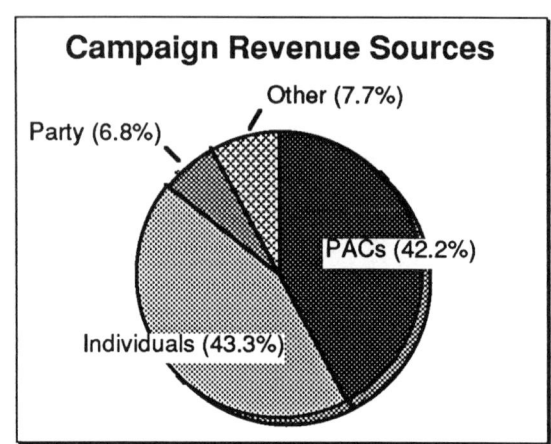

Campaign Revenue Sources

Other (7.7%)
Party (6.8%)
PACs (42.2%)
Individuals (43.3%)

Health Professionals **$15,400**
American Medical Assn $10,000
American Dental Assn $1,800
American Academy of Ophthalmology $1,500
Cmte for Quality Orthopedic Health Care $1,000
Others $1,100

Insurance..**$3,300**
National Assn of Life Underwriters $3,000
Others $300

Lawyers **$4,000**
Assn of Trial Lawyers of America $4,000

Nursing Homes **$2,000**
American Health Care Assn $1,500
Others $500

Oil & Gas **$2,150**
Mobil Oil $1,000
Others $1,150

Real Estate **$8,600**
National Assn of Realtors $8,600

Sea Transport **$2,400**
American Pilots Assn $1,500
Others $900

Other Major Business PACs
Burlington Industries ....$1,000   Textiles

PAC Totals by Category

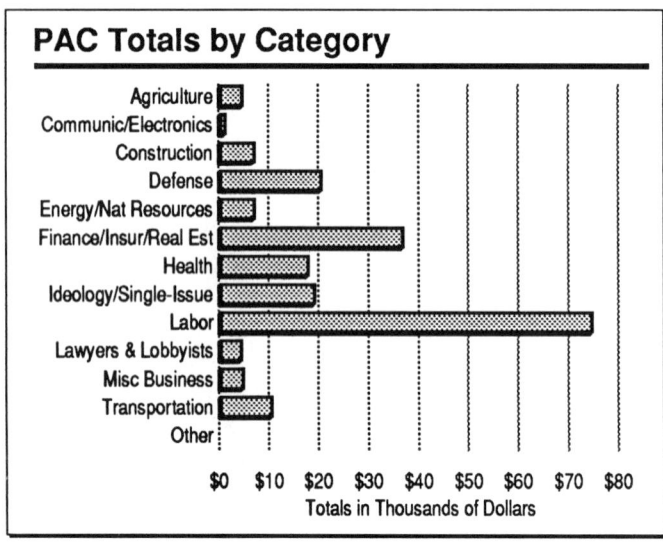

Agriculture
Communic/Electronics
Construction
Defense
Energy/Nat Resources
Finance/Insur/Real Est
Health
Ideology/Single-Issue
Labor
Lawyers & Lobbyists
Misc Business
Transportation
Other

$0 $10 $20 $30 $40 $50 $60 $70 $80
Totals in Thousands of Dollars

Labor

Bldg Trades/Industrial/Misc Unions $24,900

Carpenters & Joiners Union $5,500
Operating Engineers Union $4,000
Machinists/Aerospace Workers Union $3,000
United Auto Workers $3,000
Food & Commercial Workers Union..............................$2,500
Laborers' Political League $1,500
AFL-CIO $1,300
Intl Brotherhood of Electrical Workers..........................$1,000
Plumbers/Pipefitters Union $1,000
Others $2,100

Government & Postal Workers $16,500

National Assn of Retired Federal Employees $7,000
American Fedn of State/County/Munic Employees $2,500
National Assn of Letter Carriers $2,100
American Postal Workers Union $2,000
Others $2,900

Sea Transport Unions....................................$17,100

Marine Engineers Union* $11,100
Seafarers International Union $5,000
International Longshoremen Assn $1,000

Other Transportation Unions $4,800

Teamsters Union $2,500
Others $1,200
United Transportation Union $1,100

Teachers Unions $11,000

National Education Assn $10,000
American Federation of Teachers $1,000

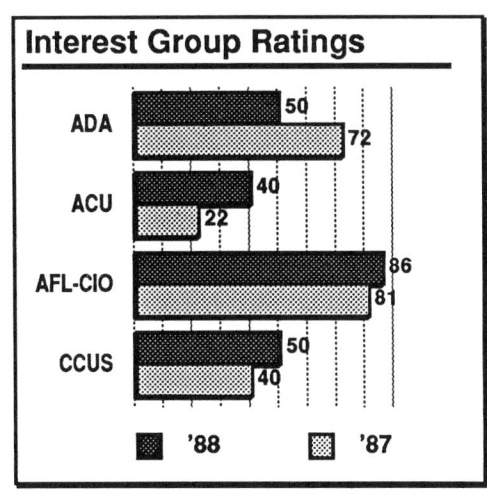
Ideological/Single-Issue

Democratic Leadership PACs......................................$10,000

Cmte for the 100th Congress (Charles Rangel)..............$3,000
Majority Congress Committee (Jim Wright) $3,000
America's Leaders' Fund (Dan Rostenkowski) $2,000
Valley Education Fund (Tony Coelho) $2,000

Pro-Choice $2,800

Voters for Choice/Friends of Family Planning $1,500
National Abortion Rights Action League $1,300

Pro-Israel $5,000

National PAC $5,000

Independent expenditures supporting Pickett

National Cmte to Preserve Social Security $1,291

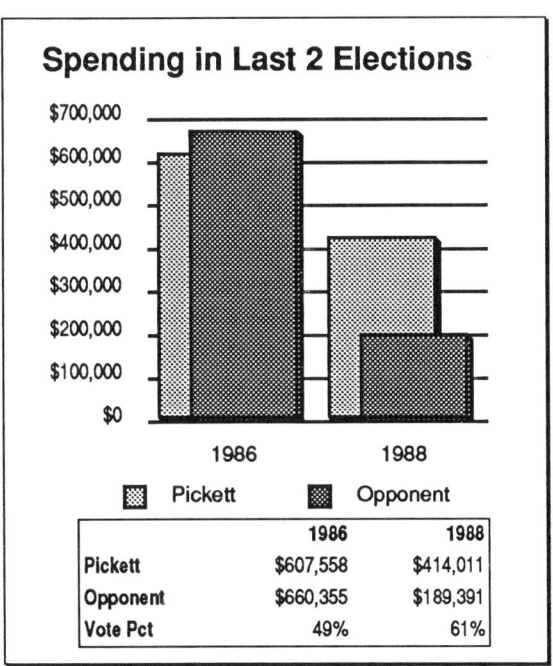

Spending in Last 2 Elections

	1986	1988
Pickett	$607,558	$414,011
Opponent	$660,355	$189,391
Vote Pct	49%	61%

---

* Contributions came from more than one PAC affiliated
with this sponsor.

J. J. "Jake" Pickle, D-Texas (10)

First elected: 1963
Total receipts: $172,746
Total from PACs: $46,463

1988 Committees & Subcommittees

Ways and Means
Oversight (Chairman)
Health

Joint Taxation

PAC Contribution Profile

Business

Auto Dealers	**$2,000**
Auto Dealers & Drivers for Free Trade	$1,000
National Auto Dealers Assn	$1,000
Commercial & Savings Banks	**$6,750**
American Bankers Assn	$1,000
Citicorp	$1,000
Independent Bankers Assn	$1,000
Investment Company Institute	$1,000
MBank	$1,000
US League of Savings Assn	$1,000
NCNB Texas	$500
Others	$250
Construction	**$2,500**
Associated General Contractors	$1,500
National Assn of Home Builders	$1,000
Department Stores	**$2,500**
J C Penney Company	$1,500
Federated Department Stores	$1,000
Electronics & Computers	**$2,200**
General Electric	$1,000
Motorola Inc	$1,000
Others	$200
Food & Beverage	**$2,750**
Joseph E Seagram & Sons	$1,000
National Beer Wholesalers Assn	$1,000
Swift Independent Corp	$1,000
Others	-$250

Campaign Revenue Sources

Other (15.9%)
Party (0.5%)
PACs (27.5%)
Individuals (56.0%)

Health Professionals	**$4,800**
Cmte for Quality Orthopedic Health Care	$2,500
American Academy of Ophthalmology	$1,000
American Medical Assn	$1,000
Others	$300
Insurance	**$8,000**
Torchmark Corp	$5,000
Equitable Financial Services	$1,000
National Assn of Life Underwriters	$1,000
TransAmerica Life Companies	$1,000
Others	$0
Lawyers	**$1,500**
Bracewell & Patterson	$1,000
Preston, Thorgrimson, Ellis & Holman	$1,000
Dickstein, Shapiro & Morin	$500
Others	-$1,000
Oil & Gas	**$7,263**
Amoco Corp	$1,000
Ashland Oil	$1,000
Dresser Industries	$1,000
Internorth Inc	$1,000
Petroleum Marketers Assn	$1,000
Shell Oil	$1,000
Enserch Corp	$763
Texas Eastern Gas Transmission	$500

Other Major Business PACs

Texas/Southwestern Cattle Raisers	$1,500	Livestock
American Hospital Assn	$1,000	Hospitals
Coalition of Publicly Traded Partnershps	$1,000	BusinessAssn
Employee Stock Ownership Assn	$1,000	Other
National Assn of Realtors	$1,000	Real Estate
Temple-Eastex Inc	$1,000	Packaging
Bristol-Myers	$500	Pharmaceut
Chicago Board of Trade	$500	Commodities
Freeport-McMoran Inc	$500	Other Mining
GTE (Southwest)	$500	Phone Util
Marriott Corp	$500	Hotel/Motel
Southwestern Bell	$500	Phone Util
United Parcel Service	$500	Delivery

PAC Totals by Category

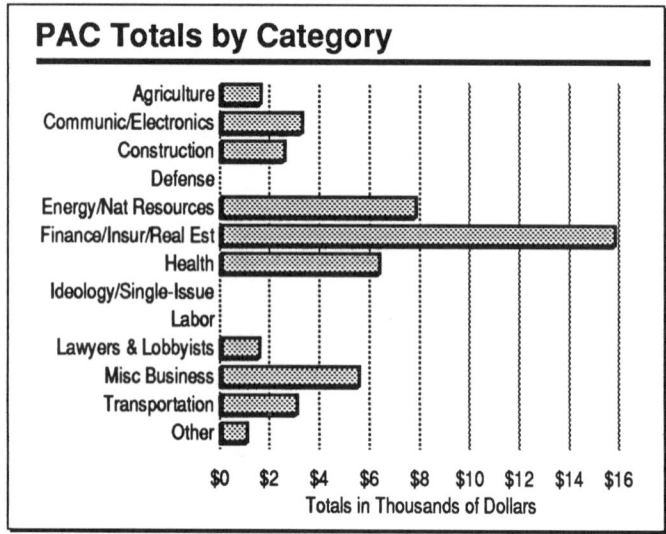

Agriculture
Communic/Electronics
Construction
Defense
Energy/Nat Resources
Finance/Insur/Real Est
Health
Ideology/Single-Issue
Labor
Lawyers & Lobbyists
Misc Business
Transportation
Other

$0 $2 $4 $6 $8 $10 $12 $14 $16
Totals in Thousands of Dollars

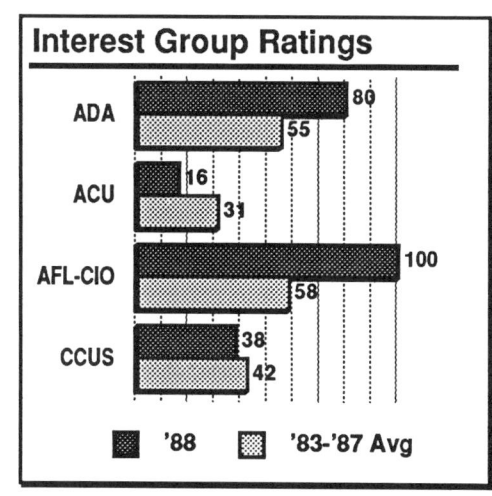

Interest Group Ratings

	'88	'83-'87 Avg
ADA	80	55
ACU	16	31
AFL-CIO	100	58
CCUS	38	42

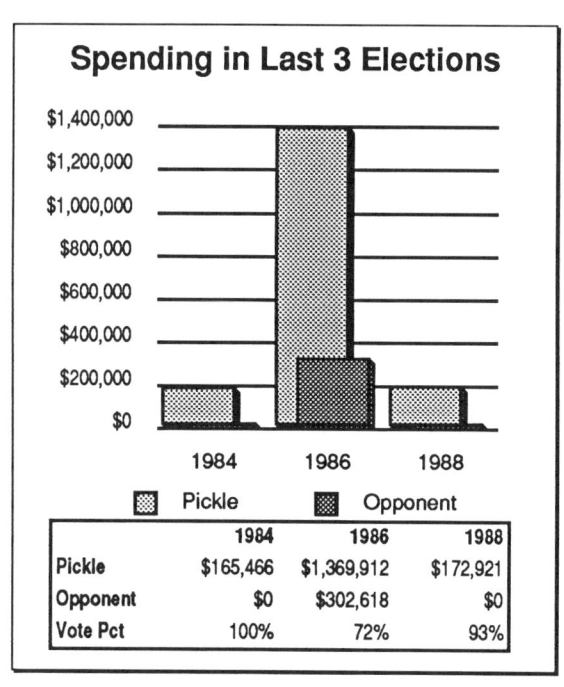

Spending in Last 3 Elections

	1984	1986	1988
Pickle	$165,466	$1,369,912	$172,921
Opponent	$0	$302,618	$0
Vote Pct	100%	72%	93%

845

John Porter, R-Ill (10)

1988 Committees & Subcommittees

Appropriations
Foreign Operations
Labor, Health and Human Services, Education and Related Agencies
Legislative Branch

First elected: 1980
Total receipts: $245,366
Total from PACs: $115,321

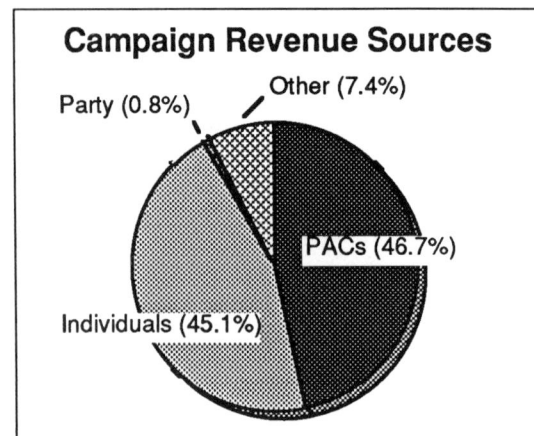

Campaign Revenue Sources

Party (0.8%)
Other (7.4%)
PACs (46.7%)
Individuals (45.1%)

PAC Contribution Profile

Business

Automotive	**$6,400**
National Auto Dealers Assn	$3,350
Auto Dealers & Drivers for Free Trade	$2,000
Others	$1,050
Commercial Banks	**$4,025**
First Chicago Corp	$1,325
American Bankers Assn	$1,000
Others	$1,700
Construction	**$3,500**
Manville Corp	$2,000
Others	$1,500
Food & Beverage	**$9,950**
Kraft Inc	$1,350
Pepsico Inc	$1,350
McDonald's Corp	$1,000
Nutrasweet Company	$1,000
Others	$5,250
Health Professionals	**$8,350**
American Medical Assn	$3,350
American Dental Assn	$2,000
Oral & Maxillofacial Surgeons	$1,500
Others	$1,500
Industrial Equipment & Materials	**$4,350**
Square D Company	$1,500
Others	$2,850
Insurance	**$7,000**
National Assn of Life Underwriters	$1,000
Others	$6,000

Oil & Gas	**$2,550**
None over $600	
Paper & Pulp Mills	**$2,250**
Westvaco Corp	$2,000
Others	$250
Pharmaceuticals	**$4,300**
Abbott Laboratories	$2,000
Others	$2,300
Plastics & Chemicals	**$2,150**
Premark International	$1,000
Others	$1,150
Real Estate	**$6,700**
National Assn of Realtors	$6,350
Others	$350
Retail Sales	**$3,200**
International Mass Retail Assn	$1,000
Walgreen Company	$1,000
Others	$1,200
Telecommunications	**$5,500**
Illinois Bell Telephone	$2,200
AT&T	$2,000
Others	$1,300
Vocational Tech Schools	**$5,550**
National Assn of Trade/Tech Schools	$5,000
Others	$550

Other Major Business PACs

Baxter Healthcare Corp	$1,750	Med Supply
IMC Fertilizer Inc	$1,050	Ag Chemicals
American National Can Company	$1,000	Cans
Chicago Board of Trade	$1,000	Commodities
R R Donnelley & Sons	$1,000	Publishing

PAC Totals by Category

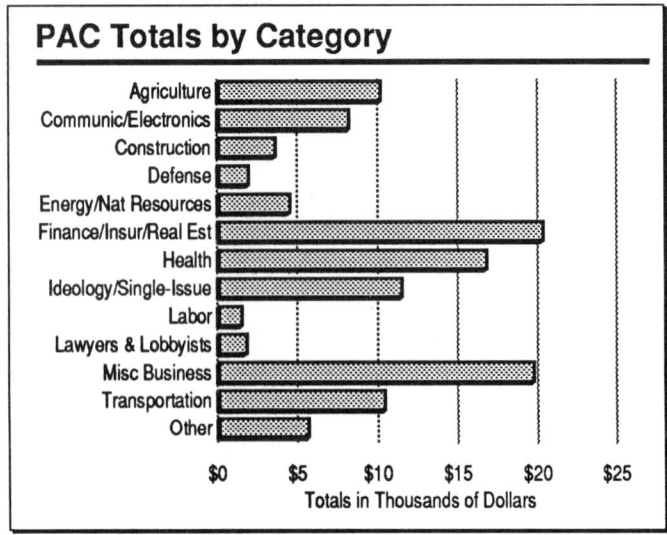

Agriculture
Communic/Electronics
Construction
Defense
Energy/Nat Resources
Finance/Insur/Real Est
Health
Ideology/Single-Issue
Labor
Lawyers & Lobbyists
Misc Business
Transportation
Other

$0 $5 $10 $15 $20 $25

Totals in Thousands of Dollars

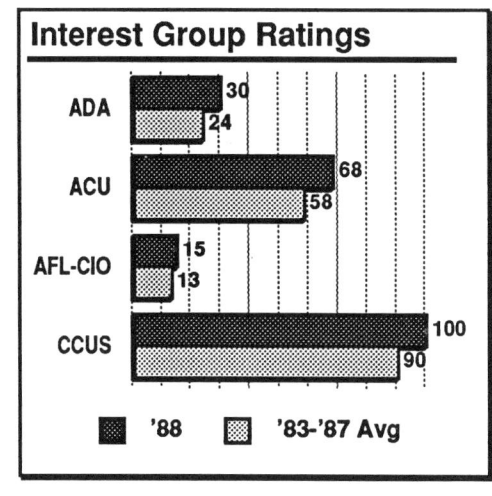

Major Labor PACs

National Assn of Retired Federal Employees ..$1,000   Fedl Workers

Ideological/Single-Issue

Pro-Israel ***$6,000***
        National PAC $5,000
        Others $1,000

Other Major Ideological/Single-Issue PACs

Fifth Horseman PAC ....$2,500   Dem/Lib
Handgun Control Inc ....$1,000   Anti-Guns
KidsPAC ....$1,000   HealthWelfare

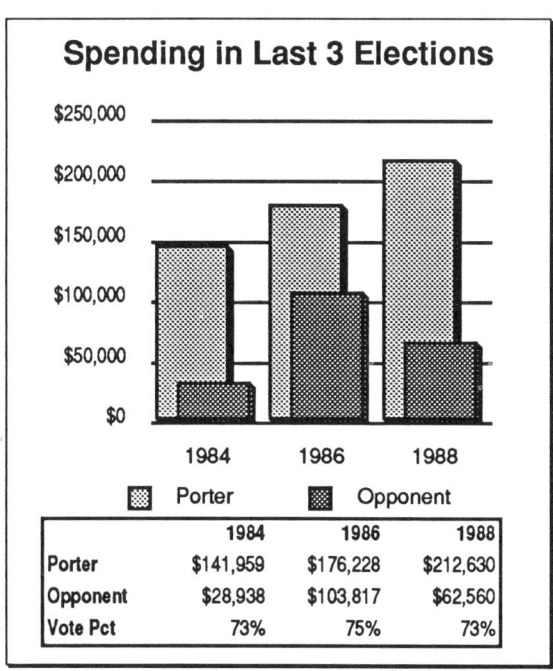

Spending in Last 3 Elections

	1984	1986	1988
Porter	$141,959	$176,228	$212,630
Opponent	$28,938	$103,817	$62,560
Vote Pct	73%	75%	73%

Glenn Poshard, D-Ill (22)

First elected: 1988
Total receipts: $430,248
Total from PACs: $248,970

1989-1990 Committees & Subcommittees

Education and Labor
Elementary, Secondary and Vocational Education
Human Resources
Postsecondary Education

Small Business
Environment and Labor
Procurement, Tourism and Rural Development

PAC Contribution Profile

Business

Campaign Revenue Sources

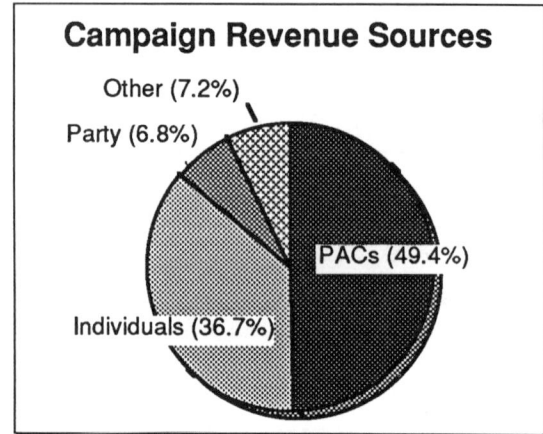

Other (7.2%)
Party (6.8%)
PACs (49.4%)
Individuals (36.7%)

Auto Dealers	**$3,000**
National Auto Dealers Assn	$3,000
Commodities/Securities	**$1,700**
Chicago Mercantile Exchange	$1,500
Others	$200
Dairy	**$4,500**
Mid-American Dairymen	$2,500
Associated Milk Producers	$2,000
Farm Organizations	**$4,087**
Illinois Agricultural Assn	$3,637
Others	$450
Financial Institutions	**$3,750**
Credit Union National Assn	$1,500
American Bankers Assn	$1,000
Others	$1,250
Health Professionals	**$8,500**
American Academy of Ophthalmology	$4,000
American Dental Assn	$1,500
American Medical Assn	$1,000
American Optometric Assn	$1,000
Others	$1,000
Insurance	**$5,100**
National Assn of Life Underwriters	$5,000
Others	$100
Lawyers	**$5,000**
Assn of Trial Lawyers of America	$5,000

Real Estate	**$10,000**
National Assn of Realtors	$10,000
Telecommunications	**$2,200**
Continental Telecom	$2,000
Others	$200

Other Major Business PACs

Allied-Signal	$1,000	Air Defense
American Hospital Assn	$1,000	Hospitals
National Assn of Social Workers	$1,000	Social Work

PAC Totals by Category

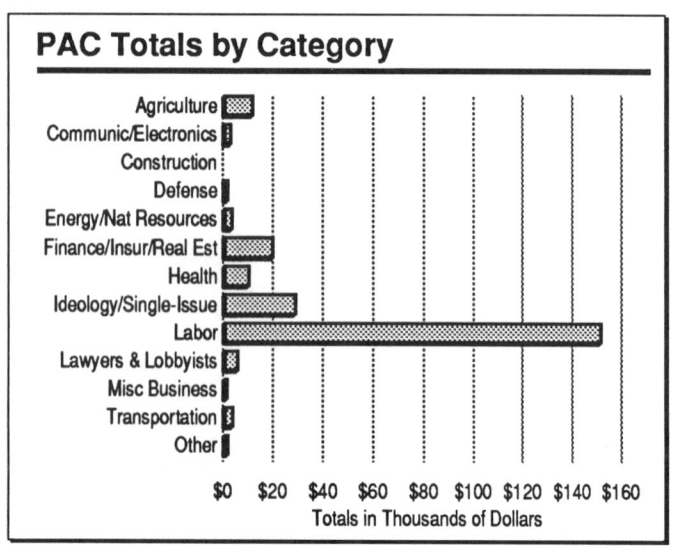

Agriculture
Communic/Electronics
Construction
Defense
Energy/Nat Resources
Finance/Insur/Real Est
Health
Ideology/Single-Issue
Labor
Lawyers & Lobbyists
Misc Business
Transportation
Other

$0 $20 $40 $60 $80 $100 $120 $140 $160
Totals in Thousands of Dollars

Labor

Bldg Trades/Industrial/Misc Unions $88,150
Intl Brotherhood of Electrical Workers $10,000
Machinists/Aerospace Workers Union $10,000
United Auto Workers $10,000
United Mine Workers $10,000
United Steelworkers $8,000
Laborers' Political League* $7,750
AFL-CIO $7,500
Carpenters & Joiners Union $6,500
Food & Commercial Workers Union $5,000
Sheet Metal Workers Union $3,500
Bakery, Confectionery & Tobacco Workers $2,000
Ladies Garment Workers Union $1,050
Graphic Communications Union $1,000
Operating Engineers Union $1,000
Plumbers/Pipefitters Union $1,000
Service Employees International Union $1,000
Others $2,850

Government & Postal Workers $31,150
American Fedn of State/County/Munic Employees $10,000
National Assn of Letter Carriers* $8,500
National Assn of Retired Federal Employees $5,000
American Postal Workers Union $4,000
International Assn of Firefighters $1,000
National Rural Letter Carriers Assn $1,000
Others $1,650

Teachers Unions $15,000
National Education Assn $10,000
American Federation of Teachers $5,000

Transportation Unions $16,350
Teamsters Union $10,000
Air Line Pilots Assn $2,500
Amalgamated Transit Union $1,000
Others $2,850

Ideological/Single-Issue

Democratic Leadership PACs $13,500
Majority Congress Committee (Jim Wright) $5,000
Valley Education Fund (Tony Coelho) $5,000
Cmte for Democratic Opportunity (Bill Gray) $1,500
America's Leaders' Fund (Dan Rostenkowski) $1,000
House Leadership Fund (Tom Foley) $1,000

Pro-Israel $7,250
National PAC $5,000
Chicagoans for Better Congress $1,000
Others $1,250

Other Major Ideological/Single-Issue PACs

National Cmte to Preserve Social Security	$5,000	Soc Secur
National Council of Senior Citizens	$1,000	Soc Secur
National Rifle Assn	$1,000	Pro-Guns

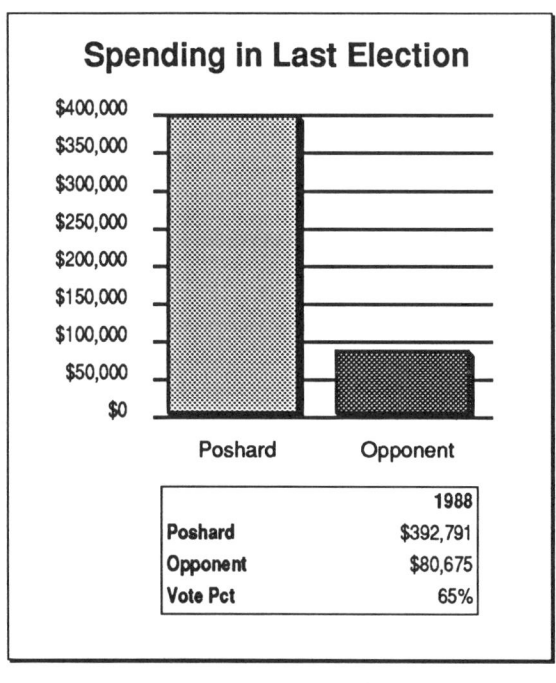

Spending in Last Election

	1988
Poshard	$392,791
Opponent	$80,675
Vote Pct	65%

---

* Contributions came from more than one PAC affiliated with this sponsor.

David E. Price, D-NC (4)

1988 Committees & Subcommittees

First elected: 1986
Total receipts: $1,029,767
Total from PACs: $489,658

Banking, Finance and Urban Affairs
Economic Stabilization
Financial Institutions Supervision, Regulation and Insurance

Science, Space and Technology
Investigations and Oversight
Science, Research and Technology

Small Business
Antitrust, Impact of Deregulation and Privatization
Regulation and Business Opportunities

PAC Contribution Profile

Business

Commercial Banks	**$56,750**
American Bankers Assn	$10,500
Bankers Trust	$7,000
J P Morgan & Company	$7,000
Barnett Banks of Florida	$3,000
Citizens & Southern National Bank	$2,800
Chase Manhattan	$2,050
Chemical Bank	$1,800
Central Carolina Bank & Trust	$1,750
Branch Banking & Trust	$1,700
NCNB Corp	$1,550
Continental Illinois Corp	$1,500
First Chicago Corp	$1,500
Marine Midland Banks	$1,300
Consumer Bankers Assn	$1,250
Independent Bankers Assn	$1,150
Banc One Corp*	$1,100
Others	$9,800
Construction	**$14,350**
National Assn of Home Builders	$9,750
Manufactured Housing Institute	$1,200
Others	$3,400
Electric Utilities	**$9,400**
Carolina Power & Light	$2,000
National Rural Electric Co-op Assn	$1,000
Others	$6,400

Campaign Revenue Sources

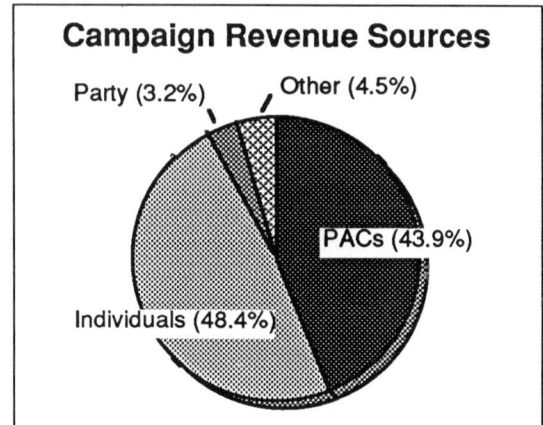

Party (3.2%)
Other (4.5%)
PACs (43.9%)
Individuals (48.4%)

Health Professionals	**$14,829**
American Medical Assn	$6,279
American Academy of Ophthalmology	$3,000
American Nurses Assn	$2,500
Others	$3,050
Insurance	**$14,700**
National Assn of Life Underwriters	$2,500
Home Group Inc	$2,000
Jefferson-Pilot Corp	$2,000
Independent Insurance Agents of America	$1,600
Others	$6,600
Lawyers & Lobbyists	**$12,800**
Assn of Trial Lawyers of America	$10,500
Others	$2,300
Real Estate	**$17,650**
National Assn of Realtors	$10,500
First Union Corp	$4,300
Mortgage Bankers Assn of America	$1,400
Others	$1,450
Savings Banks & Credit Unions	**$14,900**
US League of Savings Assn	$8,900
Credit Union National Assn	$2,400
National Council of Savings Institutions	$1,700
Others	$1,900

PAC Totals by Category

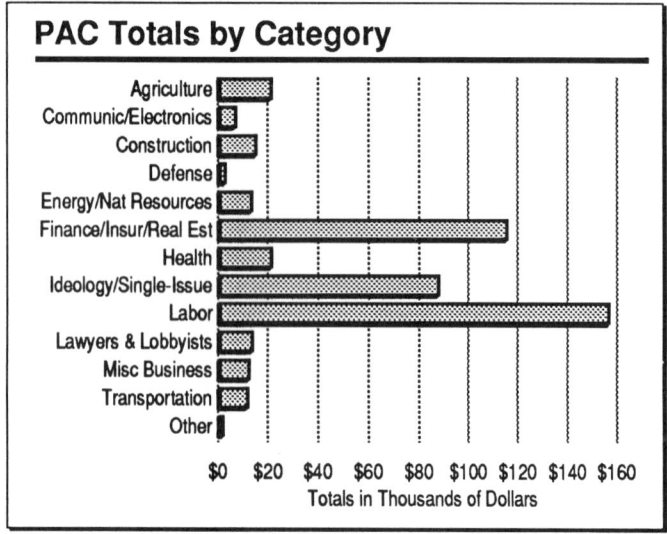

Agriculture
Communic/Electronics
Construction
Defense
Energy/Nat Resources
Finance/Insur/Real Est
Health
Ideology/Single-Issue
Labor
Lawyers & Lobbyists
Misc Business
Transportation
Other

$0 $20 $40 $60 $80 $100 $120 $140 $160
Totals in Thousands of Dollars

Other Major Business PACs

National Auto Dealers Assn	$4,500	Auto Sales
Associated Milk Producers	$3,500	Dairy
Southern Bell	$3,425	Phone Util
American Hospital Assn	$3,350	Hospitals
RJR Nabisco	$2,500	Tobacco
Philip Morris	$2,300	Tobacco
American Financial Services Assn	$2,250	Credit/Loans
American Airlines	$1,900	Airlines
Beneficial Management Corp	$1,650	Credit/Loans
Textron Inc	$1,600	Air Defense
Cone Mills Corp	$1,500	Textiles
Nabisco Brands Inc	$1,500	FoodProducts

(Continued on the next column)

Other Business PACs (cont'd)

Waste Management Inc	$1,500	Waste Mgmt
Burlington Industries	$1,400	Textiles
AT&T	$1,350	LongDistance
Household International	$1,300	Credit/Loans
Dairymen Inc-North Carolina	$1,100	Dairy
J C Penney Company	$1,100	Dept Store
Tobacco Institute	$1,100	Tobacco

Labor

Bldg Trades/Industrial/Misc Unions	**$65,800**
United Steelworkers	$10,000
Machinists/Aerospace Workers Union	$9,900
United Auto Workers	$8,100
Communications Workers of America	$8,000
AFL-CIO*	$7,500
Food & Commercial Workers Union*	$7,000
Intl Brotherhood of Electrical Workers	$5,500
Bakery, Confectionery & Tobacco Workers	$2,000
Ladies Garment Workers Union	$1,500
Electron Mach Furniture Workers	$1,300
Others	$5,000
Government & Postal Workers	**$38,700**
National Assn of Letter Carriers	$15,000
National Assn of Retired Federal Employees	$10,000
American Fedn of State/County/Munic Employees	$5,000
American Postal Workers Union	$2,000
International Assn of Firefighters	$2,000
National Rural Letter Carriers Assn	$2,000
Others	$2,700
Teachers Unions	**$12,300**
National Education Assn	$9,900
American Federation of Teachers	$2,400
Transportation Unions	**$38,900**
United Transportation Union	$10,100
Teamsters Union	$10,000
Marine Engineers Union*	$5,600
Seafarers International Union	$4,600
Amalgamated Transit Union	$4,000
Air Line Pilots Assn	$3,000
Transportation Communication Union	$1,400
Others	$200

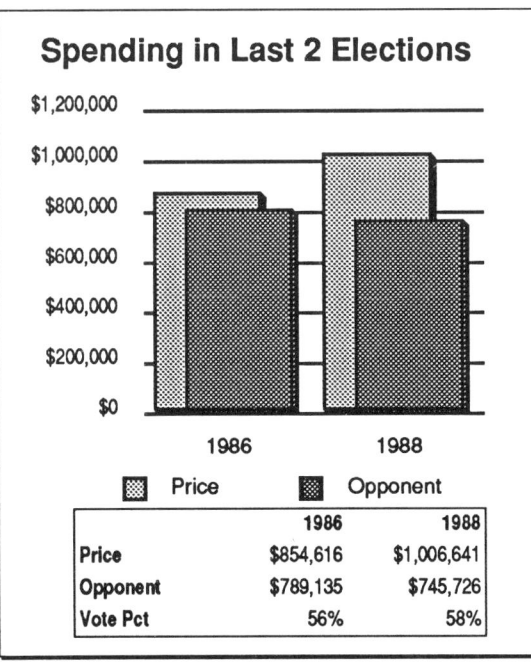

Spending in Last 2 Elections

	1986	1988
Price	$854,616	$1,006,641
Opponent	$789,135	$745,726
Vote Pct	56%	58%

■ Price   ▨ Opponent

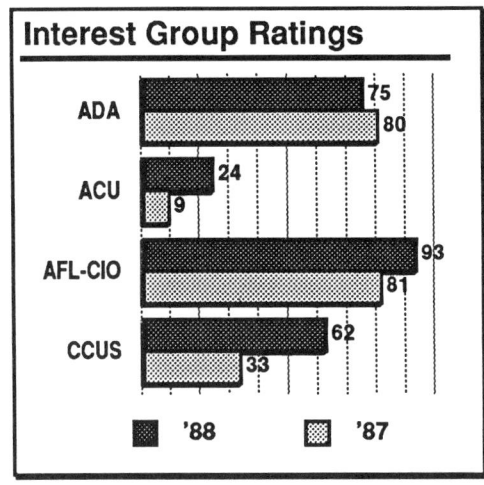

Interest Group Ratings

	'88	'87
ADA	75	80
ACU	24	9
AFL-CIO	93	81
CCUS	62	33

■ '88   ▨ '87

Ideological/Single-Issue

Democratic/Liberal	**$18,792**
National Cmte for an Effective Congress	$8,492
Class PAC	$5,000
Democratic Study Group Campaign Fund	$3,000
Others	$2,300
Democratic Leadership PACs	**$27,500**
24th Cong Dist of California PAC (Henry Waxman)	$7,000
Independent Action (Morris Udall)	$4,000
Valley Education Fund (Tony Coelho)	$4,000
America's Leaders' Fund (Dan Rostenkowski)	$3,000
Majority Congress Committee (Jim Wright)	$3,000
Cmte for Democratic Opportunity (Bill Gray)	$2,000
Others	$4,500
Pro-Choice	**$8,000**
National Abortion Rights Action League	$5,500
Voters for Choice/Friends of Family Planning	$2,500
Pro-Israel	**$15,000**
National PAC	$5,000
Joint Action Cmte for Political Affairs	$2,500
Maryland Assn for Concerned Citizens	$2,000
Hudson Valley PAC	$1,250
Others	$4,250

Other Major Ideological/Single-Issue PACs

National Cmte to Preserve Social Security	$5,300	Soc Secur
SANE/Freeze Inc	$4,131	Pro-Peace
Council for a Livable World	$2,109	Pro-Peace
National Council of Senior Citizens	$2,000	Soc Secur
Sierra Club	$2,000	Environment
KidsPAC	$1,500	HealthWelfare

Independent expenditures supporting Price

National Cmte to Preserve Social Security	$2,177

---

* Contributions came from more than one PAC affiliated
with this sponsor.

Carl D. Pursell, R-Mich (2)

First elected: 1976
Total receipts: $811,384
Total from PACs: $264,993

1988 Committees & Subcommittees

Appropriations
Energy and Water Development
Labor, Health and Human Services, Education and Related Agencies

Campaign Revenue Sources

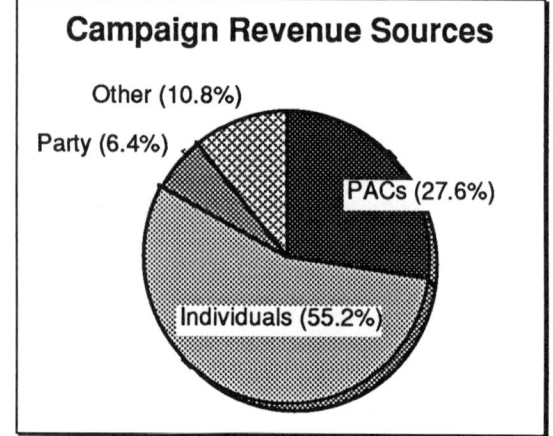

Other (10.8%)
Party (6.4%)
PACs (27.6%)
Individuals (55.2%)

PAC Contribution Profile

Business

Automotive	**$25,850**
Auto Dealers & Drivers for Free Trade	$10,000
Chrysler Corp	$2,600
Ford Motor Company	$2,600
General Motors	$2,400
Federal-Mogul Corp	$2,000
National Auto Dealers Assn	$1,900
Dana Corp	$1,500
Eaton Corp	$1,250
Budd Company	$1,000
Others	$600
Business Associations	**$4,090**
National Fedn of Independent Business	$2,581
Business Industry PAC	$1,161
Others	$348
Construction	**$22,300**
National Assn of Home Builders	$8,300
Sheet Metal/AirCon Contractors	$5,000
Associated General Contractors	$2,500
Bechtel Corp	$1,000
Mechanical Contractors Assn of America	$1,000
National Utility Contractors Assn	$1,000
Walbridge Aldinger	$1,000
Others	$2,500
Dairy	**$2,000**
Michigan Milk Producers Assn	$1,500
Others	$500
Defense	**$3,550**
None over $800	

PAC Totals by Category

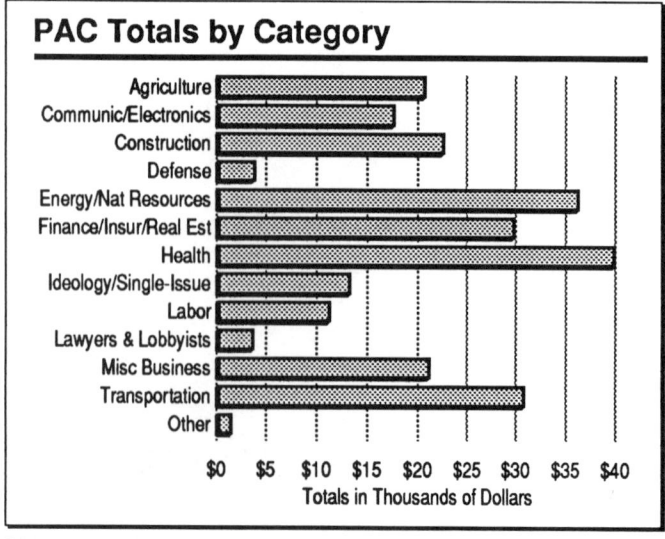

Category	
Agriculture	
Communic/Electronics	
Construction	
Defense	
Energy/Nat Resources	
Finance/Insur/Real Est	
Health	
Ideology/Single-Issue	
Labor	
Lawyers & Lobbyists	
Misc Business	
Transportation	
Other	

$0 $5 $10 $15 $20 $25 $30 $35 $40
Totals in Thousands of Dollars

Electric Utilities	**$17,325**
Consumers Power Company	$7,875
Detroit Edison	$3,400
Southern Company*	$1,000
Others	$5,050
Farm Organizations	**$7,500**
Michigan Farm Bureau	$7,500
Financial Institutions	**$11,450**
Comerica Inc	$4,250
American Bankers Assn	$2,000
Michigan League of Savings Institutions	$1,700
Manufacturers National Bank	$1,000
Michigan Credit Union League	$1,000
Security Bancorp	$1,000
Others	$500
Food & Beverage	**$9,689**
Kellogg Company	$2,589
Stroh Brewery Company	$2,300
Michigan Beer & Wine Wholesalers Assn	$1,450
National Restaurant Assn	$1,000
Others	$2,350
Health Professionals	**$30,535**
American Medical Assn	$9,735
American Academy of Ophthalmology	$4,500
American Dental Assn	$4,000
American Optometric Assn	$3,900
American Nurses Assn	$2,300
American Podiatry Assn	$1,000
Corp for the Advancement of Psychiatry	$1,000
Independent Allergists PAC	$1,000
Others	$3,100
Hospitals & Nursing Homes	**$2,750**
American Hospital Assn	$2,250
Others	$500
Industrial Equipment & Materials	**$2,500**
Pirelli Cable	$1,000
Others	$1,500
Insurance	**$7,050**
National Assn of Life Underwriters	$2,500
Blue Cross & Blue Shield*	$2,450
Health Insurance Assn of America	$1,300
Others	$800

Lawyers & Lobbyists *$3,400*
    None over $800

Oil & Gas *$15,750*
    Dow Chemical* $4,500
    Phillips Petroleum $2,000
    Michigan Consolidated Gas $1,800
    Michigan Petroleum PAC $1,700
    Amoco Corp $1,000
    Sun Company $1,000
    Others $3,750

Pharmaceuticals *$5,150*
    Warner-Lambert $1,600
    Pfizer Inc $1,000
    Upjohn Company $1,000
    Others $1,550

Power Plant Equipment *$4,800*
    Cooper Industries $3,000
    KMS Fusion Inc $1,000
    Others $800

Real Estate *$10,500*
    National Assn of Realtors $10,000
    Others $500

Retail Sales *$2,700*
    None over $500

Sugar Growers *$5,050*
    American Sugarbeet Growers Assn $1,800
    Great Lakes Sugar Beet Growers $1,650
    American Crystal Sugar Corp $1,000
    Others $600

Telecommunications *$13,068*
    Michigan Bell Telephone $6,968
    AT&T $2,350
    BellSouth Corp* $1,300
    Continental Telecom $1,000
    Others $1,450

Interest Group Ratings

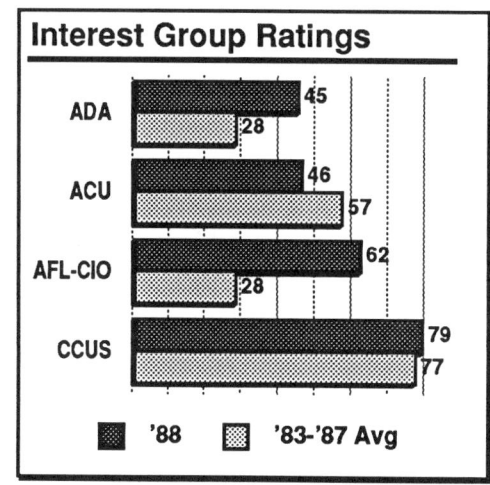

	'88	'83-'87 Avg
ADA	45	28
ACU	46	57
AFL-CIO	62	28
CCUS	79	77

Other Major Business PACs

Electronic Data Systems	$1,300	Data Process
Whirlpool Corp	$1,300	Appliances
United Parcel Service	$1,250	Delivery
National Assn of Trade/Tech Schools	$1,000	Voc Tech
Ocean Spray Cranberries Inc	$1,000	Fruit/Veg
Precision Metalforming Assn	$1,000	MetalProduct

Labor

Labor Unions *$10,950*
    Marine Engineers Union* $4,000
    National Assn of Retired Federal Employees $3,000
    Air Line Pilots Assn $2,000
    Masters Mates & Pilots Union $1,000
    Others $950

Ideological/Single-Issue

Pro-Israel *$8,000*
    National PAC $5,000
    Delaware Valley PAC $2,000
    Desert Caucus $1,000

Republican Leadership/Conservative PACs *$4,000*
    Republican Congressional Boosters Club $2,000
    Modern PAC (Bill Green) $1,000
    Others $1,000

Other Major Ideological/Single-Issue PACs
KidsPAC ....$1,000   HealthWelfare

Spending in Last 3 Elections

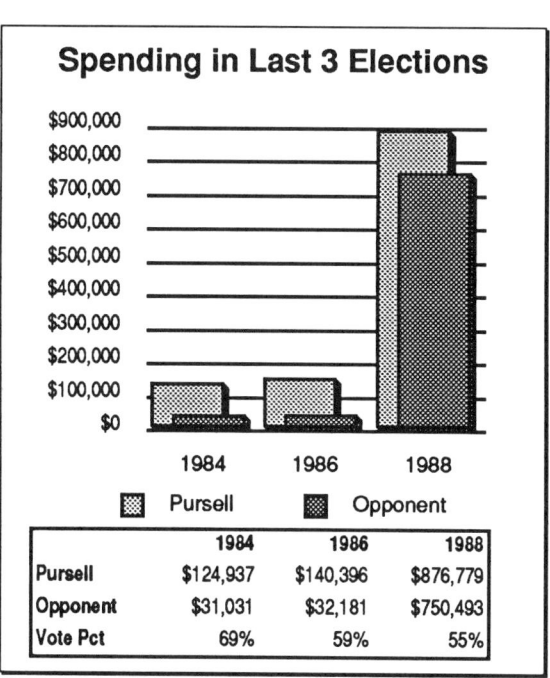

	Pursell	Opponent

	1984	1986	1988
Pursell	$124,937	$140,396	$876,779
Opponent	$31,031	$32,181	$750,493
Vote Pct	69%	59%	55%

* Contributions came from more than one PAC affiliated
  with this sponsor.

James H. Quillen, R-Tenn (1)

First elected: 1962
Total receipts: $617,030
Total from PACs: $413,800

1988 Committees & Subcommittees

Rules (Ranking Republican)

PAC Contribution Profile

Campaign Revenue Sources

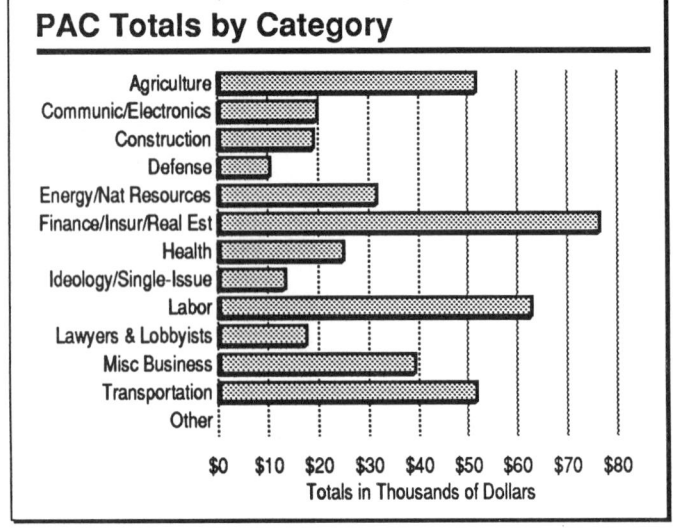

Other (13.0%)

Individuals (19.7%)

PACs (67.0%)

Business

Automotive	**$15,000**
Auto Dealers & Drivers for Free Trade	$6,000
National Auto Dealers Assn	$5,000
Others	$4,000
Aviation/Air Freight	**$11,750**
Federal Express Corp	$10,000
Others	$1,750
Broadcasting/Entertainment	**$6,750**
National Cable Television Assn	$3,500
Others	$3,250
Chemicals	**$6,250**
Eastman Kodak/Chemicals Division	$2,000
Others	$4,250
Commercial Banks	**$21,000**
American Bankers Assn	$3,500
Third National Corp	$2,500
Barnett Banks of Florida	$2,000
First Tennessee National Corp	$2,000
Assn of Bank Holding Companies	$1,500
BankAmerica	$1,500
First American Corp	$1,500
Others	$6,500
Construction	**$18,600**
National Assn of Home Builders	$10,000
Others	$8,600

Dairy	**$22,500**
Associated Milk Producers	$10,000
Dairymen Inc-Tennessee	$10,000
Mid-American Dairymen	$1,500
Others	$1,000
Defense	**$10,000**
Raytheon	$2,000
Gencorp Inc	$1,500
Others	$6,500
Electric Utilities	**$13,850**
Southern Company*	$1,550
Others	$12,300
Food & Beverage	**$20,250**
Malone & Hyde Inc	$2,000
National Beer Wholesalers Assn	$2,000
Wine & Spirits Wholesalers of America	$2,000
Others	$14,250
Health Professionals	**$13,000**
American Medical Assn	$5,750
American Dental Assn	$4,000
American Podiatry Assn	$2,000
Others	$1,250
Insurance	**$25,000**
National Assn of Life Underwriters	$5,000
National Assn Mutual Insurance Agents	$3,000
American Council of Life Insurance	$2,000
Provident Life & Accident Insurance	$1,700
American Family Corp	$1,500
American General Insurance Company	$1,500
Independent Insurance Agents of America	$1,500
Travelers Corp	$1,500
Others	$7,300
Lawyers & Lobbyists	**$17,100**
Assn of Trial Lawyers of America	$10,000
Kutak, Rock & Campbell	$1,500
Others	$5,600
Oil & Gas	**$11,750**
None over $1,000	
Pharmaceuticals	**$7,400**
Abbott Laboratories	$1,500
Schering-Plough Corp	$1,500
Others	$4,400

PAC Totals by Category

Agriculture
Communic/Electronics
Construction
Defense
Energy/Nat Resources
Finance/Insur/Real Est
Health
Ideology/Single-Issue
Labor
Lawyers & Lobbyists
Misc Business
Transportation
Other

$0 $10 $20 $30 $40 $50 $60 $70 $80

Totals in Thousands of Dollars

Real Estate **$10,500**
    National Assn of Realtors $8,000
    Mortgage Bankers Assn of America $2,000
    Others $500

Savings Banks & Credit Unions **$7,250**
    US League of Savings Assn $4,000
    Others $3,250

Securities/Commodities Investment **$7,750**
    Morgan Stanley & Company $2,000
    Securities Industry Assn* $1,500
    Others $4,250

Sugar Growers **$7,000**
    None over $1,000

Telecommunications **$8,300**
    South Central Bell Telephone $2,000
    AT&T $1,500
    Others $4,800

Textiles **$7,000**
    Cherokee Textile Mills $3,000
    Others $4,000

Trucking/Delivery **$8,800**
    United Parcel Service $3,000
    American Trucking Assns* $2,500
    Others $3,300

Other Major Business PACs

J C Penney Company	$3,000	Retail
Waste Management Inc	$3,000	Waste Mgmt
American Pilots Assn	$2,000	Sea Transport
Philip Morris	$2,000	Tobacco
American Financial Services Assn	$1,500	Credit/Loans
American Furniture Manufacturers Assn	$1,500	Furniture
American Institute of CPA's	$1,500	Accountants

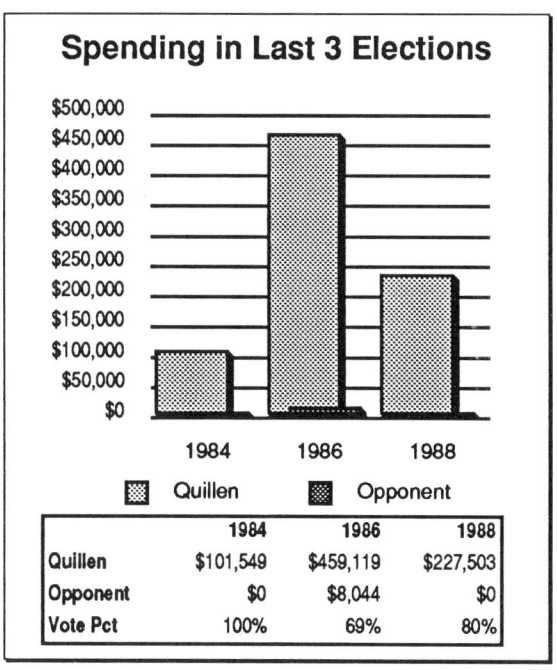

Spending in Last 3 Elections

	1984	1986	1988
Quillen	$101,549	$459,119	$227,503
Opponent	$0	$8,044	$0
Vote Pct	100%	69%	80%

Quillen   Opponent

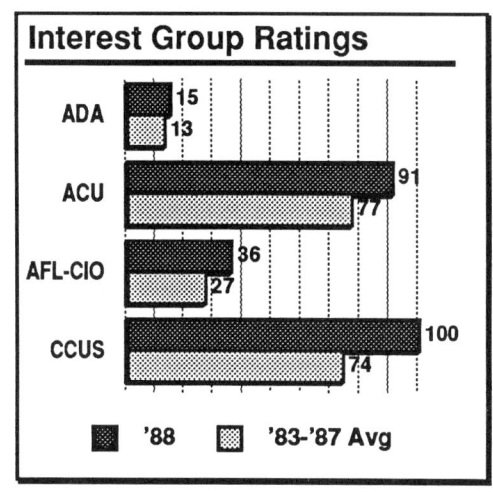

Interest Group Ratings

	'88	'83-'87 Avg
ADA	15	13
ACU	91	77
AFL-CIO	36	27
CCUS	100	74

■ '88   ▨ '83-'87 Avg

Labor

Bldg Trades/Industrial/Misc Unions **$7,500**
    National Education Assn $3,000
    Communications Workers of America $2,000
    Others $2,500

Government & Postal Workers **$14,000**
    National Assn of Retired Federal Employees $5,000
    National Assn of Postmasters $3,500
    National Assn of Letter Carriers $3,000
    Others $2,500

Transportation Unions **$40,900**
    Marine Engineers Union* $10,000
    Seafarers International Union $10,000
    Teamsters Union $10,000
    Air Line Pilots Assn $5,000
    United Transportation Union $2,500
    Others $3,400

Ideological/Single-Issue

Ideological/Single-Issue **$12,900**
National Rifle Assn .... $10,900   Pro-Guns
Others $2,000

Independent expenditures supporting Quillen

National Cmte to Preserve Social Security $2,532

---

* Contributions came from more than one PAC affiliated
  with this sponsor.

Nick J. Rahall II, D-WVa (4)

First elected: 1976
Total receipts: $333,159
Total from PACs: $175,442

1988 Committees & Subcommittees

Interior and Insular Affairs
Mining and Natural Resources (Chairman)
Energy and the Environment
National Parks and Public Lands

Public Works and Transportation
Economic Development
Surface Transportation

PAC Contribution Profile

Business

Air Transport **$3,500**
   None over $750

Commercial & Savings Banks **$2,000**
   US League of Savings Assn $1,000
   Others $1,000

Construction **$5,250**
   National Utility Contractors Assn $3,000
   Westvaco Corp $1,000
   Others $1,250

Dairy **$3,750**
   Associated Milk Producers $2,000
   Dairymen Inc $1,000
   Others $750

Defense **$2,000**
   None over $750

Electric Utilities **$3,500**
   None over $750

Lawyers **$3,250**
   Assn of Trial Lawyers of America $2,000
   Others $1,250

Mining **$6,350**
   National Coal Assn* $1,000
   Peabody Coal $1,000
   Pittston Company $1,000
   Others $3,350

Campaign Revenue Sources

Other (18.9%)

PACs (51.8%)

Individuals (29.1%)

Oil & Gas **$12,200**
   Walter Industries $1,500
   Ashland Oil $1,150
   Atlantic Richfield $1,000
   Coastal Corp $1,000
   Others $7,550

Railroads **$2,000**
   CSX Transportation Inc $1,000
   Others $1,000

Real Estate **$2,000**
   National Assn of Realtors $2,000

Sugar Growers **$2,050**
   None over $750

Telecommunications **$2,250**
   Chesapeake & Potomac Telephone $1,000
   Continental Telecom $1,000
   Others $250

Tobacco **$3,750**
   Philip Morris $1,750
   RJR Nabisco $1,000
   Others $1,000

Trucking/Delivery **$12,450**
   United Parcel Service $3,900
   Consolidated Freightways $2,000
   American Trucking Assns $1,250
   Eastern Central Motor Carriers $1,000
   North American Van Lines $1,000
   Others $3,300

Waste Management **$2,000**
   Waste Management Inc $2,000

Other Major Business PACs

American Medical Assn	$1,250	Doctors
National Auto Dealers Assn	$1,250	Auto Sales
American Coml Barge Line Company	$1,000	SeaTransport
National Beer Wholesalers Assn	$1,000	Liquor Whlsl

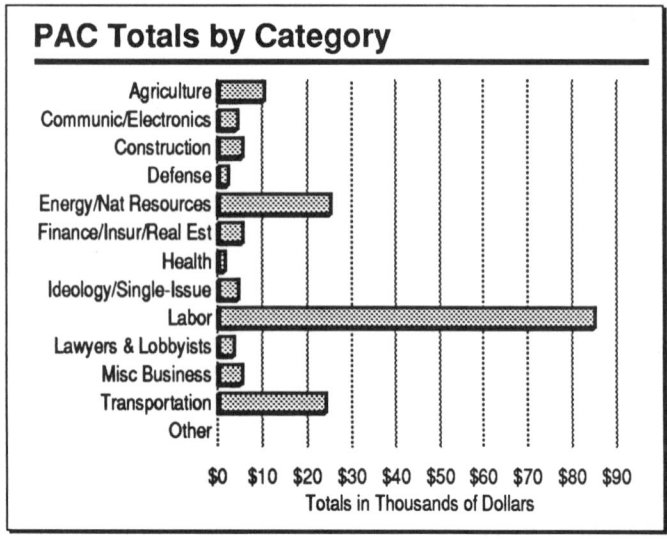

PAC Totals by Category

Agriculture
Communic/Electronics
Construction
Defense
Energy/Nat Resources
Finance/Insur/Real Est
Health
Ideology/Single-Issue
Labor
Lawyers & Lobbyists
Misc Business
Transportation
Other

$0 $10 $20 $30 $40 $50 $60 $70 $80 $90
Totals in Thousands of Dollars

Labor

Bldg Trades/Industrial/Misc Unions **$37,200**

United Mine Workers $7,500
United Auto Workers $5,750
AFL-CIO* $4,250
Operating Engineers Union $4,000
Carpenters & Joiners Union $2,500
Ironworkers Union $2,000
Intl Brotherhood of Electrical Workers.............$1,500
Laborers' Political League $1,500
Machinists/Aerospace Workers Union $1,500
Food & Commercial Workers Union..................$1,000
United Steelworkers $1,000
Others $4,700

Government & Postal Workers **$10,675**

National Assn of Letter Carriers $3,175
American Fedn of State/County/Munic Employees $2,000
National Assn of Retired Federal Employees $2,000
American Postal Workers Union $1,750
Others $1,750

Teachers Unions **$4,600**

National Education Assn $4,600

Transportation Unions **$32,150**

Teamsters Union $10,000
Air Line Pilots Assn $5,000
Marine Engineers Union* $4,500
United Transportation Union $4,000
Amalgamated Transit Union............................$3,750
Seafarers International Union $2,000
Others $2,900

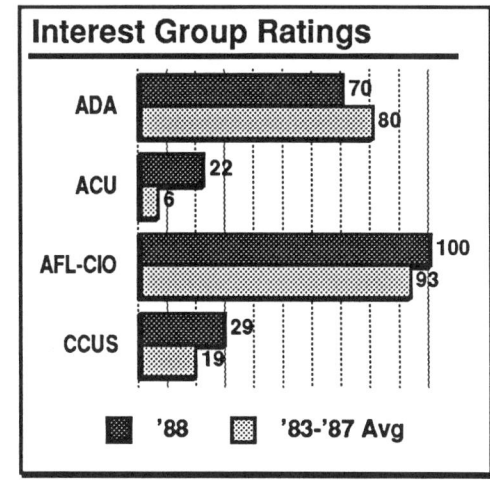

Interest Group Ratings

ADA — '88: 70, '83-'87 Avg: 80
ACU — '88: 22, '83-'87 Avg: 6
AFL-CIO — '88: 100, '83-'87 Avg: 93
CCUS — '88: 29, '83-'87 Avg: 19

■ '88   □ '83-'87 Avg

Ideological/Single-Issue

Democratic Leadership PACs **$2,000**

Pax Americas (David Bonior) $1,000
Valley Education Fund (Tony Coelho) $1,000

Other Major Ideological/Single-Issue PACs

National Cmte to Preserve Social Security ......$1,000   Soc Secur

Independent expenditures supporting Rahall

National Cmte to Preserve Social Security $1,759

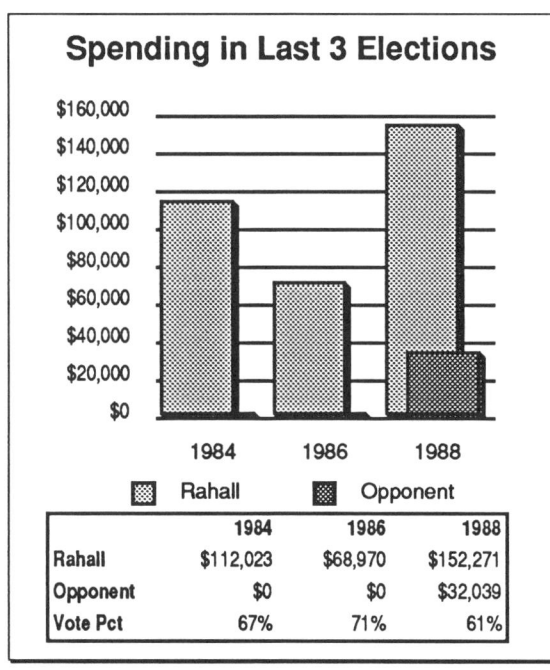

Spending in Last 3 Elections

■ Rahall   ■ Opponent

	1984	1986	1988
Rahall	$112,023	$68,970	$152,271
Opponent	$0	$0	$32,039
Vote Pct	67%	71%	61%

* Contributions came from more than one PAC affiliated
with this sponsor.

Charles B. Rangel, D-NY (16)

First elected: 1970
Total receipts: $583,012
Total from PACs: $358,625

1988 Committees & Subcommittees

Ways and Means
Select Revenue Measures (Chairman)
Oversight

Select Narcotics Abuse and Control (Chairman)

PAC Contribution Profile
Business

Accountants **$9,500**
- American Institute of CPA's $5,000
- Touche Ross $2,000
- Ernst & Whinney $1,500
- Others $1,000

Financial Institutions **$22,350**
- Citicorp $6,250
- American Bankers Assn $3,000
- Credit Union National Assn $2,500
- J P Morgan & Company $2,500
- US League of Savings Assn $1,500
- Chemical Bank $1,050
- Others $5,550

Food & Beverage **$17,350**
- Joseph E Seagram & Sons $2,000
- National Beer Wholesalers Assn $2,000
- Wine & Spirits Wholesalers of America $2,000
- Brown-Forman Distillers $1,500
- Coca-Cola Company $1,500
- McDonald's Corp $1,500
- Others $6,850

Health Professionals **$26,800**
- Assn for Advancement of Psychology $8,000
- American Medical Assn $5,550
- American Dental Assn $4,250
- New York Medical Assn $2,250
- American Optometric Assn $1,500
- American College of Emergency Physicians ... $1,250
- Others $4,000

Campaign Revenue Sources

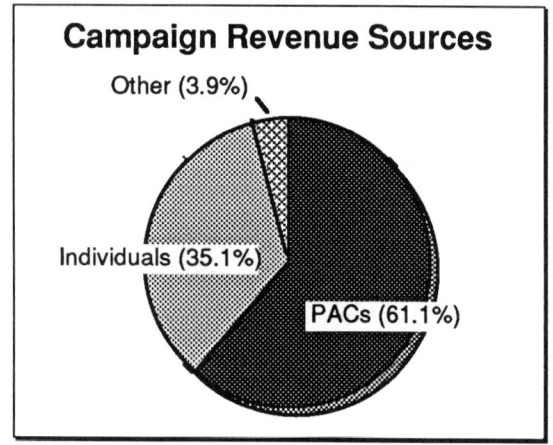

- Other (3.9%)
- Individuals (35.1%)
- PACs (61.1%)

Hospitals **$5,250**
- Federation of America Hospitals $2,000
- Others $3,250

Insurance **$53,190**
- Metropolitan Life Insurance $10,065
- American Family Corp $5,000
- Equitable Financial Services $5,000
- National Assn of Life Underwriters $4,000
- Massachusetts Mutual Life Insurance $3,000
- American Council of Life Insurance $2,000
- Mutual Life Insurance of New York $2,000
- New York Life $2,000
- North Western Mutual Life $2,000
- American International Group inc $1,500
- Connecticut Mutual Life Insurance $1,500
- Mutual Benefit Life Insurance $1,500
- Travelers Corp $1,500
- Blue Cross & Blue Shield Assn $1,125
- Others $11,000

Lawyers & Lobbyists **$14,450**
- Assn of Trial Lawyers of America $5,000
- Baker & Hostetler $1,500
- Others $7,950

Pharmaceuticals **$11,100**
- Smithkline Beckman $3,000
- Upjohn Company $1,100
- Others $7,000

Real Estate **$8,000**
- National Assn of Realtors $7,000
- Others $1,000

Securities/Commodities Investment **$30,375**
- Goldman Sachs $5,500
- First Boston Corp $4,000
- Investment Company Institute $3,000
- Bear, Stearns & Company $2,500
- Commodity Exchange Inc $2,000
- Drexel Burnham Lambert $2,000
- Morgan Stanley & Company $2,000
- Public Securities Assn $1,625
- Prudential-Bache Securities $1,250
- Others $6,500

PAC Totals by Category

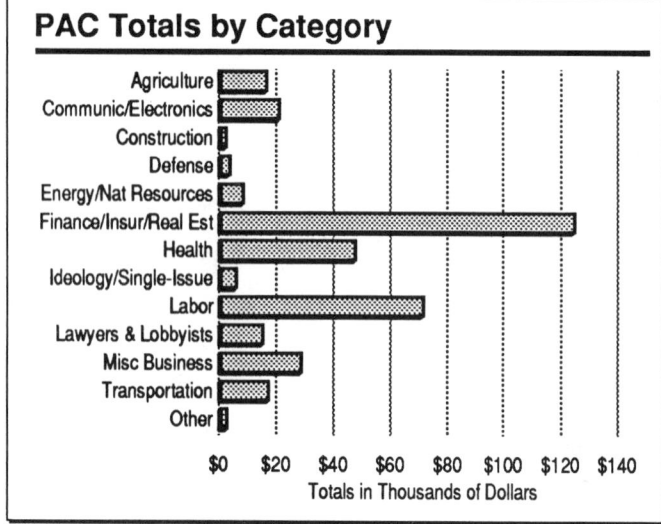

- Agriculture
- Communic/Electronics
- Construction
- Defense
- Energy/Nat Resources
- Finance/Insur/Real Est
- Health
- Ideology/Single-Issue
- Labor
- Lawyers & Lobbyists
- Misc Business
- Transportation
- Other

$0 $20 $40 $60 $80 $100 $120 $140
Totals in Thousands of Dollars

Telecommunications **$12,600**

AT&T	$5,000
Pacific Telesis Group	$2,000
Bell Atlantic	$1,500
New York Telephone	$1,475
Others	$2,625

Tobacco **$7,200**

Philip Morris	$4,000
RJR Nabisco	$2,700
Others	$500

Trucking/Delivery **$7,500**

United Parcel Service	$5,000
American Trucking Assns	$1,500
Others	$1,000

Other Major Business PACs

General Electric	$2,000	Electronics
Gulf + Western Industries	$2,000	Credit/Loans
American Assn of Equipment Lessors	$1,500	Rentals
Employee Stock Ownership Assn	$1,500	Other
Ford Motor Company	$1,500	Auto Mfrs
Grumman	$1,500	Air Defense
Union Pacific Corp	$1,500	Railroads
United Airlines	$1,500	Airlines
W R Grace & Company	$1,500	Chemicals
MCA Inc	$1,250	Movies
Avon Products	$1,150	Cosmetics
Warner-Lambert	$1,100	Health Prod

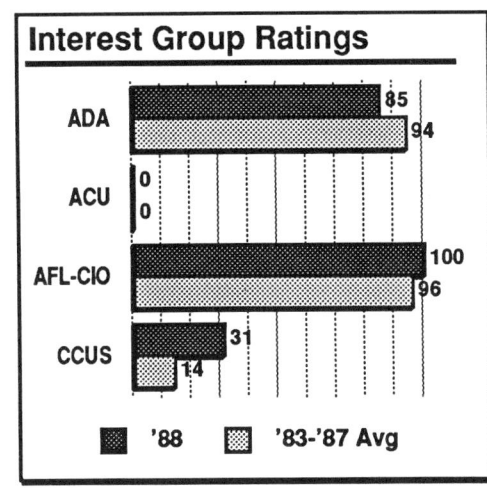

Interest Group Ratings

Ratings:
- ADA: '88 = 85, '83-'87 Avg = 94
- ACU: '88 = 0, '83-'87 Avg = 0
- AFL-CIO: '88 = 100, '83-'87 Avg = 96
- CCUS: '88 = 31, '83-'87 Avg = 14

Legend: ■ '88   ▨ '83-'87 Avg

Labor

Bldg Trades/Industrial/Misc Unions **$19,200**

United Auto Workers	$4,000
Laborers' Political League	$2,500
Operating Engineers Union	$2,500
AFL-CIO*	$2,300
Food & Commercial Workers Union	$2,000
Ladies Garment Workers Union	$1,800
Others	$4,100

Government & Postal Workers **$19,500**

American Postal Workers Union	$5,500
American Fedn of State/County/Munic Employees	$5,000
National Rural Letter Carriers Assn	$3,500
National Assn of Letter Carriers	$2,000
National Assn of Retired Federal Employees	$2,000
Others	$1,500

Teachers Unions **$7,250**

National Education Assn	$4,625
American Federation of Teachers	$2,625

Transportation Unions **$24,625**

Teamsters Union	$10,000
Air Line Pilots Assn	$5,000
Seafarers International Union	$3,000
Marine Engineers Union*	$2,000
United Transportation Union	$1,500
Transport Workers Union	$1,250
Others	$1,875

Major Ideological/Single-Issue PACs

KidsPAC	$1,500	HealthWelfare

Independent expenditures supporting Rangel

National Cmte to Preserve Social Security	$1,117

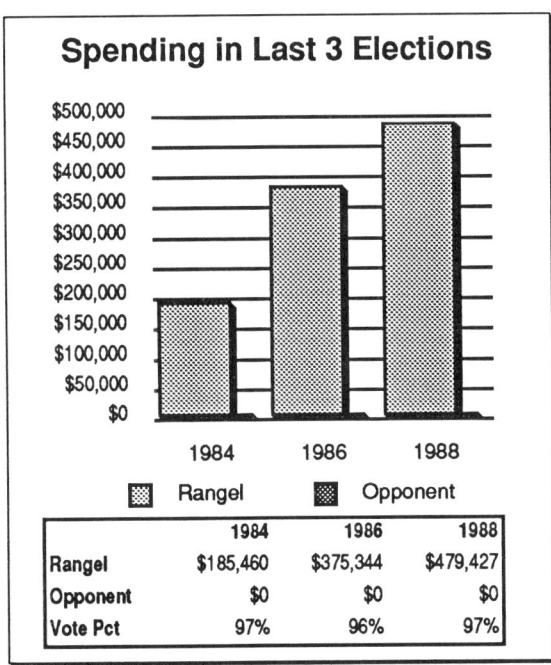

Spending in Last 3 Elections

Legend: ▨ Rangel   ■ Opponent

	1984	1986	1988
Rangel	$185,460	$375,344	$479,427
Opponent	$0	$0	$0
Vote Pct	97%	96%	97%

---

* Contributions came from more than one PAC affiliated with this sponsor.

Arthur Ravenel Jr., R-SC (1)

First elected: 1986
Total receipts: $273,828
Total from PACs: $141,080

1988 Committees & Subcommittees

Armed Services
Military Installations and Facilities
Military Personnel and Compensation

PAC Contribution Profile

Business

Auto Dealers	**$7,000**
National Auto Dealers Assn	$5,000
Auto Dealers & Drivers for Free Trade	$2,000
Chemicals	**$3,050**
Eastman Kodak/Chemicals Division	$1,300
Dow Chemical/Southeast Region	$1,000
Others	$750
Construction	**$10,550**
National Assn of Home Builders	$7,500
Associated General Contractors	$1,300
Others	$1,750
Defense	**$18,550**
Lockheed Corp	$2,600
CSX Transportation Inc*	$1,200
AT&T	$1,050
General Dynamics	$1,000
Northrop Corp	$1,000
Rockwell International	$1,000
Others	$10,700
Electric Utilities	**$3,350**
Duke Power Company	$1,300
ACRE (Action Committee for Rural Electrification)	$1,050
Carolina Power & Light	$1,000
Financial Institutions	**$6,725**
South Carolina National Bank	$2,000
Citizens & Southern National Bank	$1,000
Others	$3,725

Campaign Revenue Sources

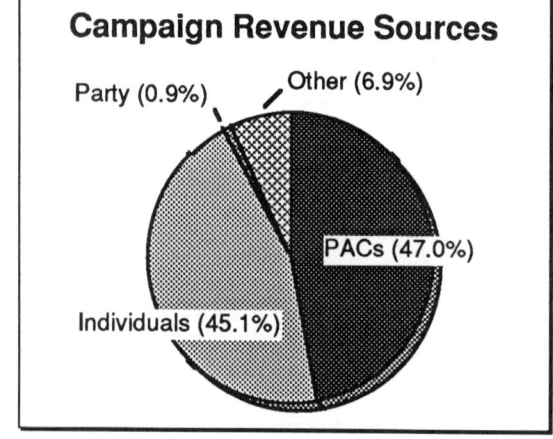

Party (0.9%)
Other (6.9%)
PACs (47.0%)
Individuals (45.1%)

Food & Beverage	**$4,100**
National Beer Wholesalers Assn	$1,300
Hardee's Food Systems	$1,000
Winn-Dixie Stores	$1,000
Others	$800
Health Professionals	**$14,400**
American Medical Assn	$5,250
American Academy of Ophthalmology	$4,500
American Podiatry Assn	$2,000
American Dental Assn	$1,500
Others	$1,150
Insurance	**$2,100**
National Assn of Life Underwriters	$1,000
Others	$1,100
Oil & Gas	**$3,600**
None over $550	
Paper Production	**$4,750**
Westvaco Corp	$3,000
International Paper Company	$1,000
Others	$750
Real Estate	**$10,500**
National Assn of Realtors	$10,000
Others	$500
Telecommunications	**$4,300**
Southern Bell	$3,800
Others	$500
Textiles	**$2,350**
Springs Mills	$1,000
Others	$1,350

Other Major Business PACs

Associated Milk Producers .... $1,000 Dairy

PAC Totals by Category

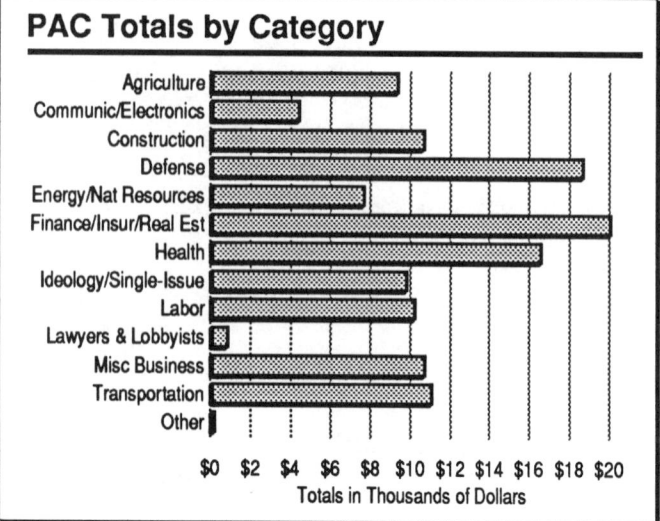

Agriculture
Communic/Electronics
Construction
Defense
Energy/Nat Resources
Finance/Insur/Real Est
Health
Ideology/Single-Issue
Labor
Lawyers & Lobbyists
Misc Business
Transportation
Other

$0 $2 $4 $6 $8 $10 $12 $14 $16 $18 $20
Totals in Thousands of Dollars

Labor

Government & Postal Workers **$7,650**	
National Assn of Retired Federal Employees	$5,000
National Assn of Letter Carriers	$1,500
Others	$1,150

Other Unions **$2,450**	
Marine Engineers Union*	$2,000
Others	$450

Ideological/Single-Issue

Ideological/Single-Issue **$9,700**		
National Rifle Assn	$4,950	Pro-Guns
Desert Caucus	$1,000	Pro-Israel
South Carolinians for Rep Govorment	$1,000	Pro-Israel
Others	$2,750	

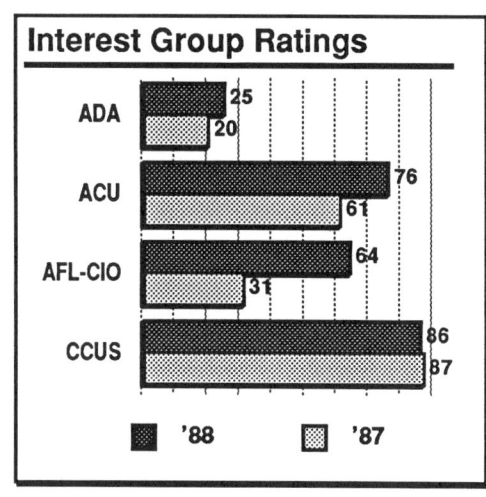

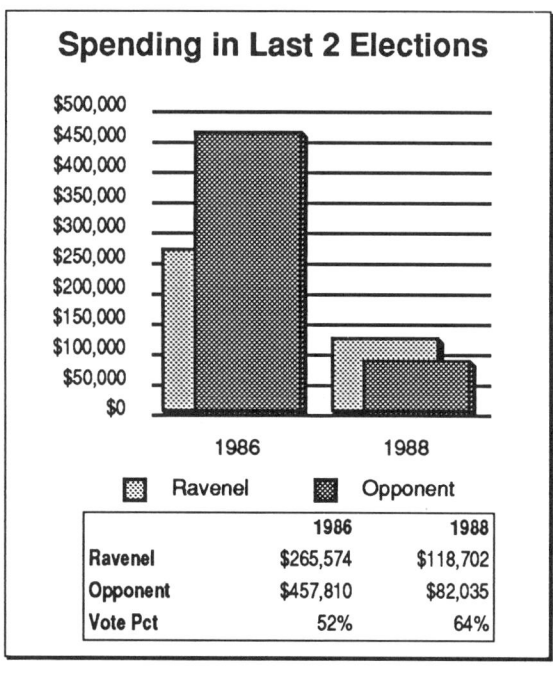

---

* Contributions came from more than one PAC affiliated
with this sponsor.

Richard Ray, D-Ga (3)

1988 Committees & Subcommittees

Armed Services
Military Personnel and Compensation
Procurement and Military Nuclear Systems
Readiness

Small Business
Energy and Agriculture

First elected: 1982
Total receipts: $281,295
Total from PACs: $131,117

PAC Contribution Profile
Business

Auto Dealers	**$2,850**
Auto Dealers & Drivers for Free Trade	$2,500
National Auto Dealers Assn	$350
Commercial Banks	**$8,600**
Trust Company of Georgia	$2,500
Citizens & Southern National Bank	$2,050
CB&T Bancshares	$2,000
First Atlanta Corp	$1,250
Others	$800
Construction	**$7,000**
Associated General Contractors	$2,500
National Assn of Home Builders	$1,750
Walter Industries	$1,000
Others	$1,750

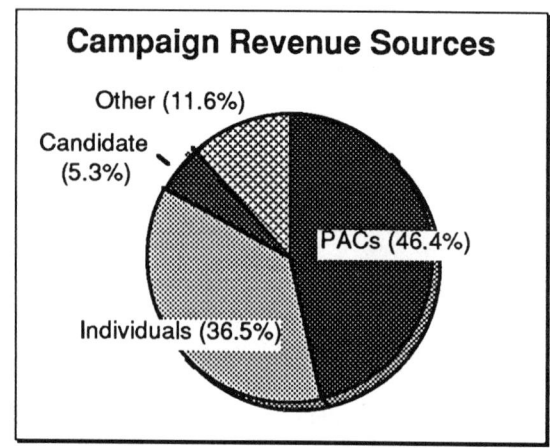

Campaign Revenue Sources

Other (11.6%)
Candidate (5.3%)
PACs (46.4%)
Individuals (36.5%)

Defense	**$50,167**
Northrop Corp	$4,250
McDonnell Douglas*	$3,550
Lockheed Corp	$3,500
Boeing Company	$3,000
Textron Inc	$2,500
Hughes Aircraft	$2,000
Grumman	$1,950
Litton Industries	$1,700
AT&T	$1,500
Continental Telecom	$1,500
Gulfstream Aerospace	$1,450
United Technologies	$1,350
E-Systems/Corporate Division	$1,017
General Dynamics	$1,000
Long Island Aerospace PAC	$1,000
Rockwell International	$1,000
TRW Inc	$1,000
Others	$16,900
Food & Beverage	**$4,500**
Coca-Cola Company	$1,000
National Beer Wholesalers Assn	$1,000
Others	$2,500
Forest Products	**$3,600**
Westvaco Corp	$1,500
Others	$2,100
Health Professionals	**$6,100**
American Medical Assn	$3,300
American Dental Assn	$1,500
American Optometric Assn	$1,300
Insurance	**$3,050**
American Family Corp	$1,100
Others	$1,950
Lawyers	**$3,150**
Assn of Trial Lawyers of America	$1,000
King & Spalding	$1,000
Others	$1,150
Oil & Gas	**$3,100**
Petroleum Marketers Assn	$1,500
Others	$1,600
Pest Control	**$2,450**
National Pest Control Assn	$1,500
Others	$950

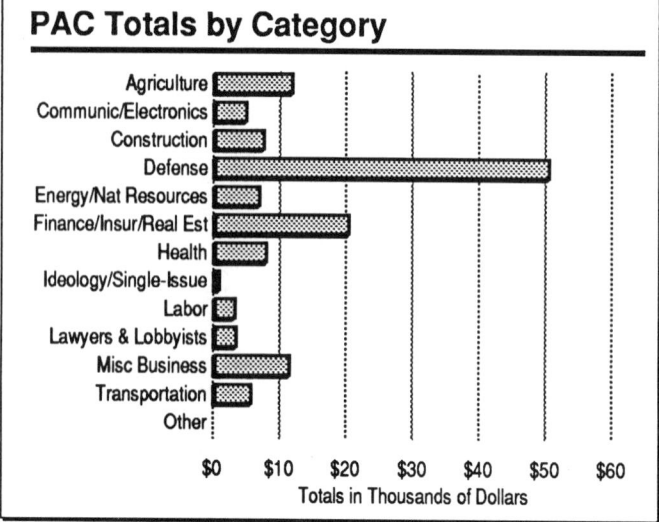

PAC Totals by Category

Agriculture
Communic/Electronics
Construction
Defense
Energy/Nat Resources
Finance/Insur/Real Est
Health
Ideology/Single-Issue
Labor
Lawyers & Lobbyists
Misc Business
Transportation
Other

$0 $10 $20 $30 $40 $50 $60
Totals in Thousands of Dollars

Real Estate $7,250
     National Assn of Realtors $6,500
     Others $750

Telecommunications $2,500
     Southern Bell $2,500

Textiles $2,100
    None over $800

Tobacco $2,150
     Philip Morris $1,200
     Others $950

Other Major Business PACs

Georgia Power Company .... $1,400   ElectricUtil
Gold Kist .... $1,000   Poultry/Egg
Maytag Company .... $1,000   Appliances

Labor

Labor Unions $2,900
     National Assn of Retired Federal Employees $1,300
     United Transportation Union $1,100
     Others $500

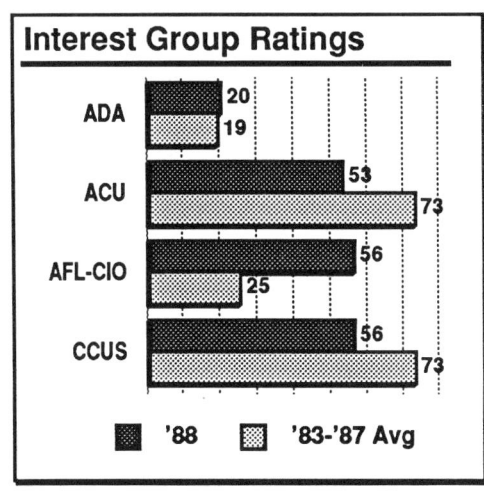

Interest Group Ratings

Group	'88	'83-'87 Avg
ADA	20	19
ACU	53	73
AFL-CIO	56	25
CCUS	56	73

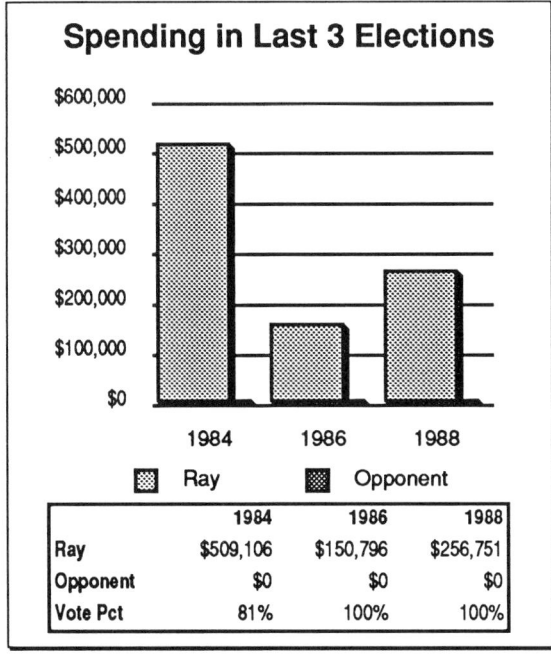

Spending in Last 3 Elections

	1984	1986	1988
Ray	$509,106	$150,796	$256,751
Opponent	$0	$0	$0
Vote Pct	81%	100%	100%

---

* Contributions came from more than one PAC affiliated
with this sponsor.

Ralph Regula, R-Ohio (16)

First elected: 1972
Total receipts: $108,672
Total from PACs: $0

1988 Committees & Subcommittees

Appropriations
Interior and Related Agencies (Ranking Republican)
Commerce, Justice, State, the Judiciary and Related Agencies
District of Columbia

Select Aging
Health and Long-Term Care (Ranking Republican)

PAC Contribution Profile

National Assn of Home Builders .... $1,000   Resid Constr
Morton Building Inc .... $500   Comml Constr
Long Island Aerospace PAC .... $432   AerospacePts
Conf of National Park Concessioners .... $250   Lodging/Tour

NOTE: Regula reported taking no PAC funds in his 1988 campaign. The PACs listed above did report making contributions to him during 1987-88, however, and those contributions are recorded in the official FEC records.

Campaign Revenue Sources

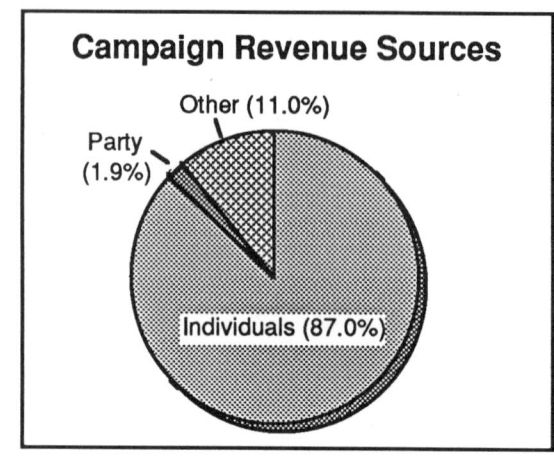

Other (11.0%)
Party (1.9%)
Individuals (87.0%)

PAC Totals by Category

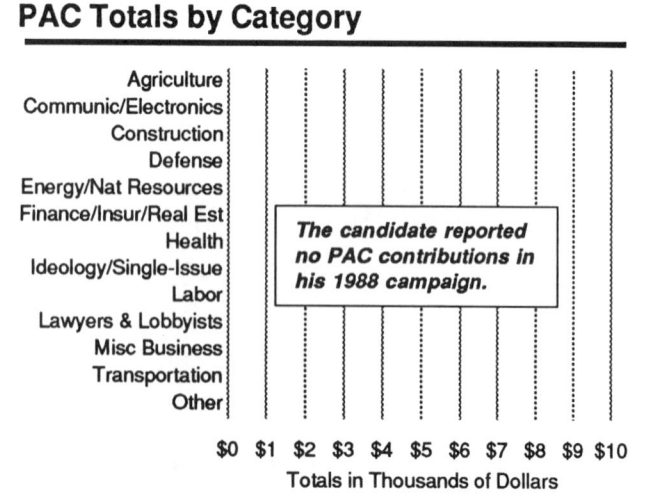

Agriculture
Communic/Electronics
Construction
Defense
Energy/Nat Resources
Finance/Insur/Real Est
Health
Ideology/Single-Issue
Labor
Lawyers & Lobbyists
Misc Business
Transportation
Other

The candidate reported no PAC contributions in his 1988 campaign.

$0 $1 $2 $3 $4 $5 $6 $7 $8 $9 $10
Totals in Thousands of Dollars

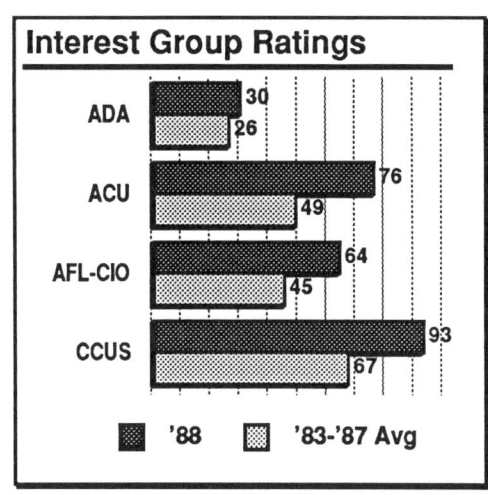

Interest Group Ratings

	'88	'83-'87 Avg
ADA	30	26
ACU	76	49
AFL-CIO	64	45
CCUS	93	67

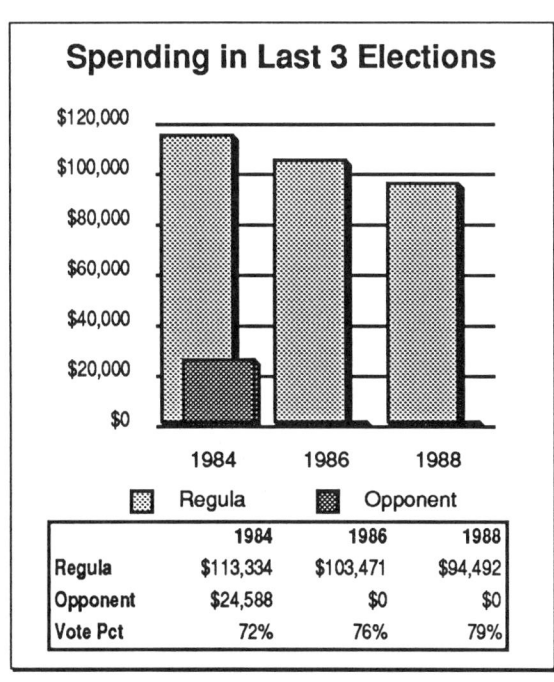

Spending in Last 3 Elections

	1984	1986	1988
Regula	$113,334	$103,471	$94,492
Opponent	$24,588	$0	$0
Vote Pct	72%	76%	79%

John J. Rhodes III, R-Ariz (1)

First elected: 1986
Total receipts: $293,044
Total from PACs: $135,419

1988 Committees & Subcommittees

Interior and Insular Affairs
Energy and the Environment
National Parks and Public Lands
Water and Power Resources

Small Business
Antitrust, Impact of Deregulation and Privatization
Procurement, Innovation and Minority Enterprise Development

PAC Contribution Profile

Business

Agricultural Services	**$1,625**
Salt River Valley Water Users	$1,625
Automotive	**$4,900**
National Auto Dealers Assn	$2,800
Auto Dealers & Drivers for Free Trade	$1,500
Others	$600
Aviation & Aerospace	**$1,550**
None over $550	
Chemicals	**$2,800**
Greyhound Corp	$2,800
Commercial Banks	**$9,500**
First Interstate Bank of Arizona	$2,500
Chase Bank of Arizona	$1,500
Arizona Bank	$1,250
Valley National Bank of Arizona	$1,100
Arizona Bankers Assn	$1,000
Others	$2,150
Construction	**$4,150**
American Homebuilders PAC	$1,000
Others	$3,150
Defense	**$10,200**
McDonnell Douglas*	$3,750
Talley Industries	$1,800
Others	$4,650

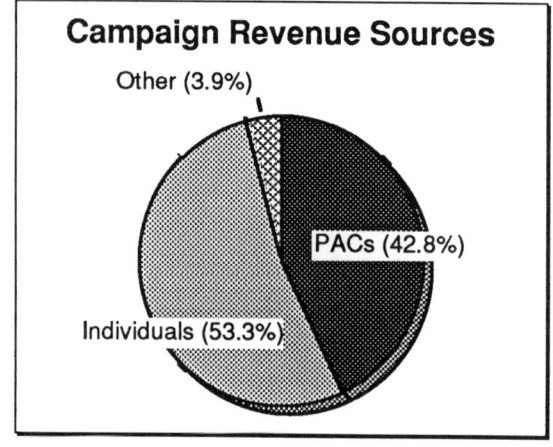

Campaign Revenue Sources

Other (3.9%)
PACs (42.8%)
Individuals (53.3%)

Electric Utilities	**$5,250**
Arizona Public Service Company	$1,000
Others	$4,250
Electronics & Computers	**$4,350**
Motorola Inc	$3,000
Others	$1,350
Food & Beverage	**$4,350**
Malone & Hyde Inc	$1,000
McLane Company	$1,000
Safeway Stores	$1,000
Others	$1,350
Health Professionals	**$7,050**
American Medical Assn	$3,550
American Academy of Ophthalmology	$3,000
Others	$500
Insurance	**$5,800**
National Assn of Life Underwriters	$2,500
Connecticut Mutual Life Insurance	$1,000
Others	$2,300
Lawyers	**$5,250**
Assn of Trial Lawyers of America	$5,250
Mining	**$3,050**
Phelps Dodge Corp	$1,000
Others	$2,050
Oil & Gas	**$11,650**
Litton Industries	$1,300
Circle K Corp	$1,250
Southwest Gas Corp	$1,250
Mobil Oil	$1,000
Others	$6,850
Real Estate	**$5,050**
National Assn of Realtors	$4,500
Others	$550
Savings Banks & Credit Unions	**$2,750**
Great American First Savings & Loan	$1,000
Others	$1,750
Securities Investment	**$2,500**
Kidder, Peabody	$2,500

PAC Totals by Category

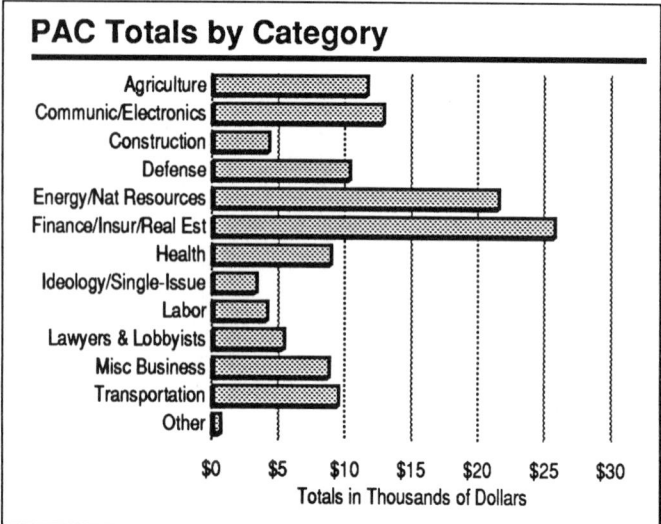

Agriculture
Communic/Electronics
Construction
Defense
Energy/Nat Resources
Finance/Insur/Real Est
Health
Ideology/Single-Issue
Labor
Lawyers & Lobbyists
Misc Business
Transportation
Other

$0 $5 $10 $15 $20 $25 $30
Totals in Thousands of Dollars

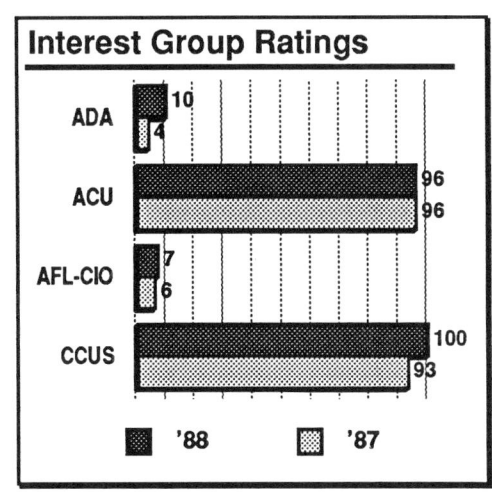

Interest Group Ratings

	'88	'87
ADA	10	4
ACU	96	96
AFL-CIO	7	6
CCUS	100	93

Telecommunications **$8,390**

Mountain Bell $5,000
AT&T $3,000
Others $390

Tobacco **$1,750**

Philip Morris $1,250
Others $500

Trucking/Delivery **$1,400**

United Parcel Service $1,150
Others $250

Labor

Labor Unions **$4,000**

National Assn of Retired Federal Employees $2,500
National League of Postmasters $1,000
Others $500

Ideological/Single-Issue

Ideological/Single-Issue **$3,185**

Council for National Defense ....$1,635   Pro-Defense
Others..$1,550

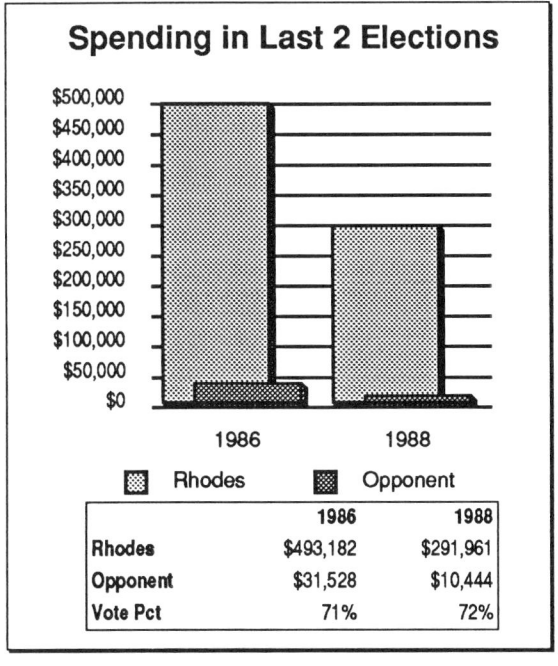

Spending in Last 2 Elections

	1986	1988
Rhodes	$493,182	$291,961
Opponent	$31,528	$10,444
Vote Pct	71%	72%

Rhodes   Opponent

* Contributions came from more than one PAC affiliated
with this sponsor.

Bill Richardson, D-NM (3)

First elected: 1982
Total receipts: $456,787
Total from PACs: $297,898

1988 Committees & Subcommittees

Education and Labor
Elementary, Secondary and Vocational Education

Energy and Commerce
Commerce, Consumer Protection and Competitiveness
Energy and Power
Telecommunications and Finance

Interior and Insular Affairs
National Parks and Public Lands
Water and Power Resources

Select Aging
Housing and Consumer Interests
Human Services

Select Intelligence
Legislation

PAC Contribution Profile

Business

Accountants	**$5,850**
American Institute of CPA's	$5,000
Others	$850
Aviation & Aerospace	**$5,000**
Texas Air	$2,500
Aircraft Owners & Pilots Assn	$1,000
UNC Inc	$1,000
Others	$500
Broadcasting/Entertainment	**$8,876**
National Cable Television Assn	$3,000
National Assn of Broadcasters	$1,650
Others	$4,226
Electric Utilities	**$6,600**
Public Service Company of New Mexico	$1,250
Others	$5,350
Food & Beverage	**$9,300**
General Mills*	$2,500
National Restaurant Assn	$2,000
McDonald's Corp	$1,000
National Beer Wholesalers Assn	$1,000
Others	$2,800
Health Professionals	**$19,100**
American Medical Assn	$6,050
American Dental Assn	$3,500
New Mexico Medical Assn	$2,050

(continued in next column)

Campaign Revenue Sources

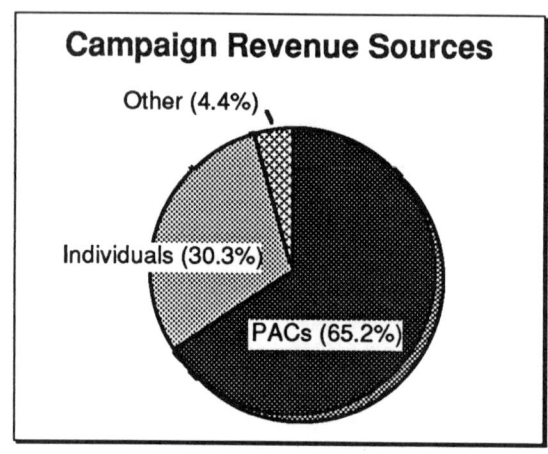

Other (4.4%)
Individuals (30.3%)
PACs (65.2%)

Health Professionals (cont'd)

American Academy of Ophthalmology	$2,000
American Optometric Assn	$1,600
National Assn of Pharmacists	$1,050
American College of Emergency Physicians	$1,000
Others	$1,850
Insurance	**$17,000**
National Assn of Life Underwriters	$5,000
National Assn Mutual Insurance Agents	$3,250
Torchmark Corp	$2,000
Independent Insurance Agents of America	$1,300
Others	$5,450
Lawyers & Lobbyists	**$9,150**
Akin, Gump, Hauer & Feld	$2,750
Dow, Lohnes & Albertson	$1,000
Others	$5,400
Oil & Gas	**$15,600**
Atlantic Richfield	$1,750
Chevron Corp	$1,700
El Paso Company	$1,450
Walter Industries	$1,000
Others	$9,700
Pharmaceuticals	**$8,850**
Schering-Plough Corp	$1,050
Others	$7,800
Securities/Commodities	**$10,100**
Investment Company Institute	$2,000
Drexel Burnham Lambert	$1,750
Securities Industry Assn	$1,300
Chicago Board of Options Exchange	$1,000
Chicago Board of Trade	$1,000
First Boston Corp	$1,000
Morgan Stanley & Company	$1,000
Others	$1,050

PAC Totals by Category

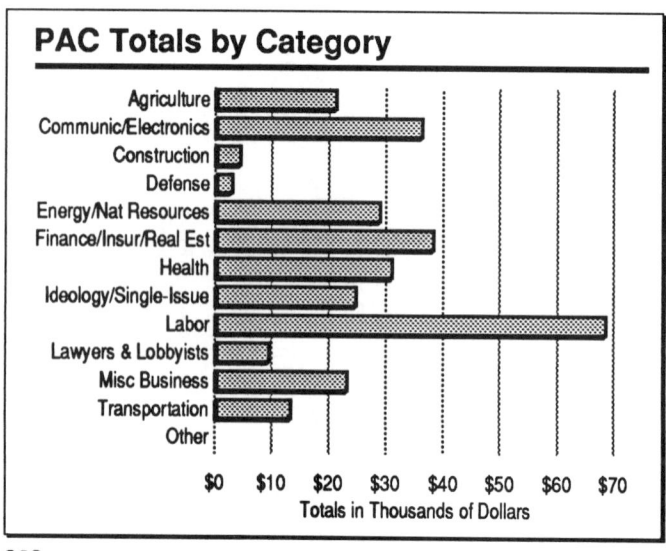

Categories (top to bottom): Agriculture, Communic/Electronics, Construction, Defense, Energy/Nat Resources, Finance/Insur/Real Est, Health, Ideology/Single-Issue, Labor, Lawyers & Lobbyists, Misc Business, Transportation, Other

Totals in Thousands of Dollars ($0, $10, $20, $30, $40, $50, $60, $70)

Telecommunications **$21,700**

AT&T	$2,750
Mountain Bell	$2,250
Pacific Telesis Group	$2,250
Continental Telecom	$2,000
Corning Glass Works	$2,000
Bell Atlantic	$1,950
GTE Corp*	$1,750
US Telephone Assn	$1,500
BellSouth Services	$1,200
Others	$4,050

Tobacco **$6,950**

Philip Morris	$4,100
RJR Nabisco	$1,500
Others	$1,350

Other Major Business PACs

Hallmark Cards	$4,250	Publishing
Associated Milk Producers	$4,000	Dairy
National Assn of Realtors	$3,050	Real Estate
Manville Corp	$2,000	BldgMaterial
National Assn of Chain Drug Stores	$2,000	Drug Stores
American Bankers Assn	$1,500	Comml Banks
Owens-Illinois	$1,350	Forestry
Borg-Warner	$1,300	Indust Equip
Chrysler Corp	$1,300	Auto Mfrs
National Assn of Wholesale-Distributors	$1,300	Wholesale
United Parcel Service	$1,300	Delivery
American Hospital Assn	$1,250	Hospitals
Fluor Corp	$1,250	Metals/Mining
Citicorp	$1,000	Comml Banks
FMC Corp	$1,000	Chemicals
Marriott Corp	$1,000	Hotel/Motel
Waste Management Inc	$1,000	Waste Mgmt

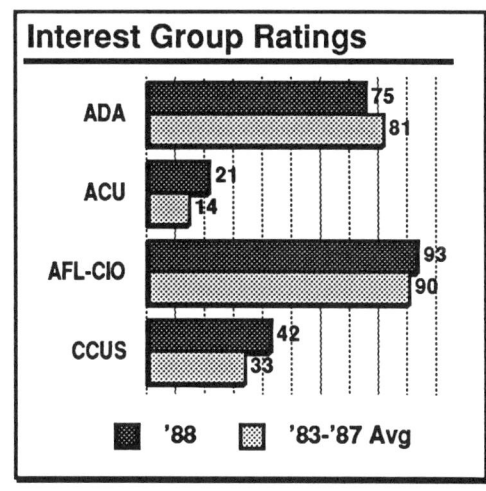

Interest Group Ratings

	'88	'83-'87 Avg
ADA	75	81
ACU	21	14
AFL-CIO	93	90
CCUS	42	33

Labor

Bldg Trades/Industrial/Misc Unions **$36,500**

United Auto Workers	$5,000
Carpenters & Joiners Union	$4,500
Food & Commercial Workers Union	$4,250
Intl Brotherhood of Electrical Workers	$4,000
United Steelworkers	$2,500
National Education Assn	$2,300
Operating Engineers Union	$2,000
Laborers' Political League	$1,500
Machinists/Aerospace Workers Union	$1,300
Plumbers/Pipefitters Union	$1,250
AFL-CIO*	$1,200
United Mine Workers	$1,100
Others	$5,600

Government & Postal Workers **$12,550**

American Fedn of State/County/Munic Employees	$5,000
National Assn of Retired Federal Employees	$3,000
National Assn of Letter Carriers	$2,900
American Postal Workers Union	$1,300
Others	$350

Transportation Unions **$19,200**

Teamsters Union	$10,000
Transportation Communication Union	$2,400
United Transportation Union	$2,350
Air Line Pilots Assn	$1,500
Seafarers International Union	$1,500
Others	$1,450

Ideological/Single-Issue

Pro-Israel **$7,000**

National PAC	$5,000
Hudson Valley PAC	$1,000
Others	$1,000

Other Major Ideological/Single-Issue PACs

Free Cuba PAC	$6,108	Anti-Castro
National Cmte for an Effective Congress	$2,497	Dem/Liberal
National Cmte to Preserve Social Security	$2,350	Soc Secur
America's Leaders' Fund (Dan Rostenkowski)	$1,577	Dem Leaders
KidsPAC	$1,000	HealthWelfare
National Rifle Assn	$1,000	Pro-Guns
Safari Club International	$1,000	Pro-Hunting
Valley Education Fund (Tony Coelho)	$1,000	Dem Leaders

---

* Contributions came from more than one PAC affiliated
 with this sponsor.

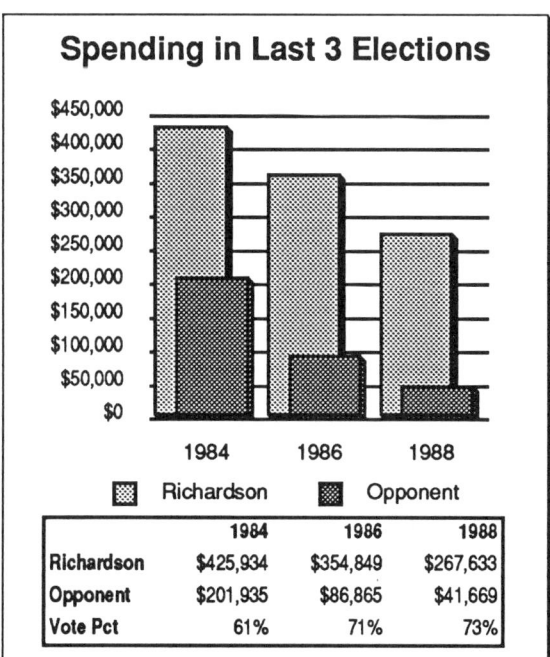

Spending in Last 3 Elections

Richardson   Opponent

	1984	1986	1988
Richardson	$425,934	$354,849	$267,633
Opponent	$201,935	$86,865	$41,669
Vote Pct	61%	71%	73%

Tom Ridge, R-Pa (21)

1988 Committees & Subcommittees

First elected: 1982
Total receipts: $419,770
Total from PACs: $211,711

Banking, Finance and Urban Affairs
Consumer Affairs and Coinage
Financial Institutions Supervision, Regulation and Insurance
Housing and Community Development

Veterans' Affairs
Education, Training and Employment
Hospitals and Health Care

Select Aging
Health and Long-Term Care
Housing and Consumer Interests

PAC Contribution Profile

Business

Automotive	***$3,750***
National Auto Dealers Assn	$3,000
Others	$750
Commercial Banks	***$59,400***
American Bankers Assn	$10,000
Citicorp	$5,000
J P Morgan & Company	$5,000
Barnett Banks of Florida	$4,000
Bankers Trust	$3,500
Marine Bank	$2,600
Chemical Bank	$2,050
Chase Manhattan	$2,000
Security Pacific Corp	$2,000
PennBancorp	$1,900
Independent Bankers Assn	$1,750
Mellon Bank	$1,650
Continental Illinois Corp	$1,500
Philadelphia National Corp	$1,500
Marine Midland Banks	$1,300
Citizens & Southern National Bank	$1,250
First Chicago Corp	$1,000
Hamilton Bank	$1,000
Meridian Bancorp	$1,000
Others	$9,400
Construction	***$6,500***
National Assn of Home Builders	$3,000
Associated General Contractors	$1,000
Others	$2,500
Consumer Credit & Loans	***$2,650***
None over $750	

Campaign Revenue Sources

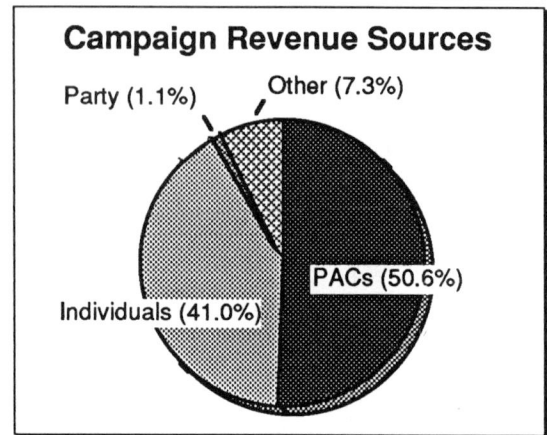

Party (1.1%) Other (7.3%)

PACs (50.6%)

Individuals (41.0%)

Dairy	***$6,750***
Associated Milk Producers	$5,500
Others	$1,250
Electric Utilities	***$5,850***
General Public Utilities	$2,250
Philadelphia Electric	$1,750
ACRE (Action Committee for Rural Electrification)	$1,350
Others	$500
Health Professionals	***$5,250***
American Medical Assn	$3,250
American Dental Assn	$2,000
Insurance	***$8,850***
Travelers Corp	$1,500
Mortgage Insurance Cos of America	$1,350
American Council of Life Insurance	$1,000
National Assn of Independent Insurers	$1,000
Others	$4,000
Lawyers & Lobbyists	***$4,500***
Assn of Trial Lawyers of America	$2,250
Kirkpatrick & Lockhart	$1,000
Others	$1,250
Oil & Gas	***$4,800***
National Fuel Gas Corp	$1,500
Others	$3,300
Real Estate	***$9,750***
National Assn of Realtors	$8,000
Others	$1,750
Savings Banks & Credit Unions	***$7,000***
Pennsylvania Savings League	$2,250
Credit Union National Assn	$2,000
US League of Savings Assn	$1,000
Others	$1,750

PAC Totals by Category

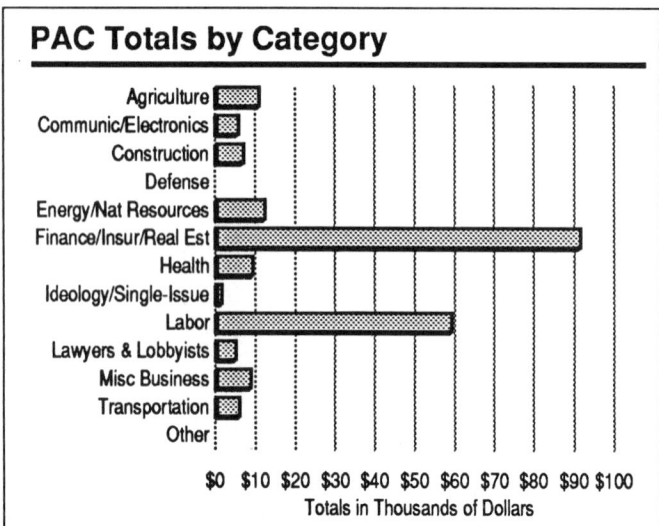

Agriculture
Communic/Electronics
Construction
Defense
Energy/Nat Resources
Finance/Insur/Real Est
Health
Ideology/Single-Issue
Labor
Lawyers & Lobbyists
Misc Business
Transportation
Other

$0 $10 $20 $30 $40 $50 $60 $70 $80 $90 $100
Totals in Thousands of Dollars

Telecommunications $4,500

Bell Telephone of Pennsylvania	$1,500
AT&T	$1,000
Bell Atlantic	$1,000
Others	$1,000

Other Major Business PACs

International Paper Company	$2,000	Paper Prod
National Tooling & Machining Assn	$2,000	Indust Equip
Business Industry PAC	$1,119	Bus Assns
Allegheny Ludlum Steel Corp	$1,000	Steel
American Health Care Assn	$1,000	Nursing Home
First Boston Corp	$1,000	InvestmtBank
National Grape Company-Operative Assn	$1,000	Fruit/Veg
Smithkline Beckman	$1,000	Pharmaceut

Interest Group Ratings

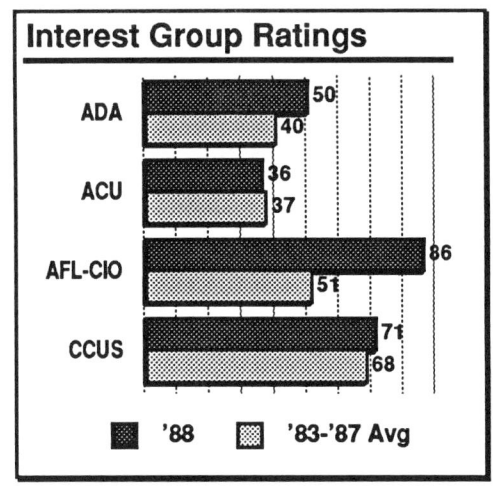

Labor

Bldg Trades/Industrial/Misc Unions $16,767

Intl Brotherhood of Electrical Workers	$3,000
Ironworkers Union	$2,500
Carpenters & Joiners Union	$2,267
Plumbers/Pipefitters Union*	$1,600
Operating Engineers Union	$1,500
Food & Commercial Workers Union	$1,000
Laborers' Political League	$1,000
Others	$3,900

Government & Postal Workers $12,050

National Assn of Letter Carriers	$7,500
American Postal Workers Union	$2,000
American Federation of Government Employees	$1,000
American Fedn of State/County/Munic Employees	$1,000
Others	$550

Transportation Unions $29,871

Teamsters Union*	$14,500
Air Line Pilots Assn	$5,000
Marine Engineers Union*	$5,000
Seafarers International Union	$2,000
Transportation Communication Union	$1,371
Masters, Mates & Pilots Union	$1,000
Others	$1,000

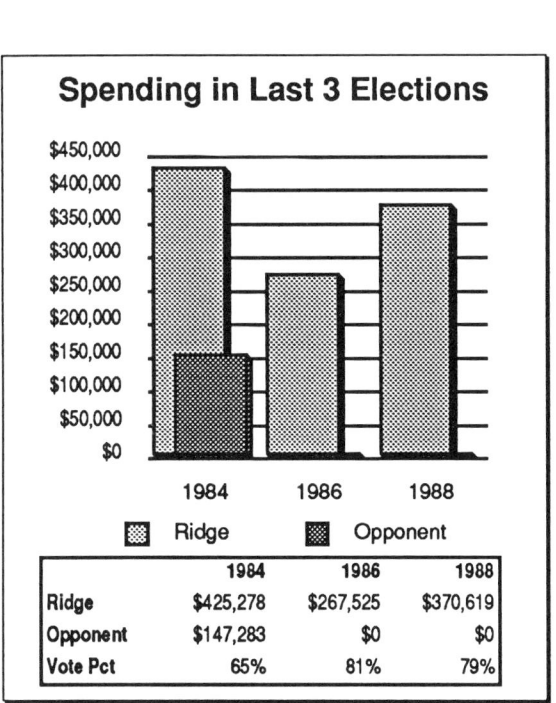

Spending in Last 3 Elections

	1984	1986	1988
Ridge	$425,278	$267,525	$370,619
Opponent	$147,283	$0	$0
Vote Pct	65%	81%	79%

---

* Contributions came from more than one PAC affiliated with this sponsor.

Matthew J. Rinaldo, R-NJ (7)

First elected: 1972
Total receipts: $607,728
Total from PACs: $271,527

1988 Committees & Subcommittees

Energy and Commerce
Telecommunications and Finance (Ranking Republican)
Commerce, Consumer Protection and Competitiveness

Select Aging (Ranking Republican)
Health and Long-Term Care

PAC Contribution Profile

Business

Accountants	**$14,156**
American Institute of CPA's	$5,000
Touche Ross	$2,300
Deloitte, Haskins & Sells	$1,556
Coopers & Lybrand	$1,300
Arthur Andersen & Company	$1,000
Arthur Young & Company	$1,000
Ernst & Whinney	$1,000
Price Waterhouse	$1,000
Automotive	**$2,600**
National Auto Dealers Assn	$2,000
Others	$600
Commercial Banks	**$21,350**
J P Morgan & Company	$5,000
American Bankers Assn	$2,500
Bankers Trust	$1,000
Barnett Banks of Florida	$1,000
Citicorp	$1,000
Midlantic National Bank	$1,000
Others	$9,850
Construction	**$7,350**
National Assn of Home Builders	$5,000
National Utility Contractors Assn	$1,500
Others	$850
Electric Utilities	**$5,850**
Public Service Electric & Gas	$1,550
Others	$4,300

Campaign Revenue Sources

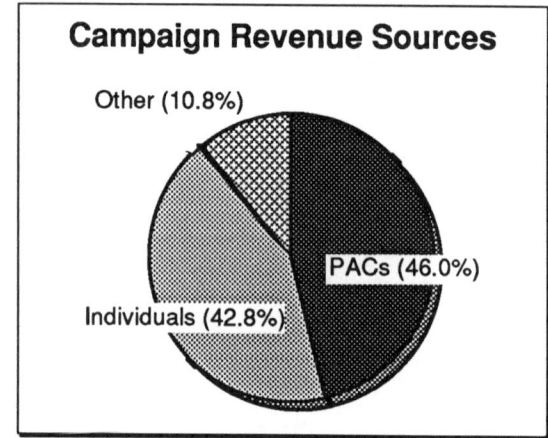

Other (10.8%)
PACs (46.0%)
Individuals (42.8%)

Health Professionals	**$12,600**
American Medical Assn	$4,100
American Dental Assn	$2,500
Cmte for Quality Orthopedic Health Care	$2,000
Others	$4,000
Insurance	**$14,350**
National Assn of Life Underwriters	$2,950
Chubb Corp	$1,000
Others	$10,400
Lawyers & Lobbyists	**$3,500**
None over $600	
Nursing Homes & Hospitals	**$5,550**
American Health Care Assn	$5,000
Others	$550
Oil & Gas	**$6,800**
Mesa PAC II	$1,000
Pacific Enterprises	$1,000
Petroleum Marketers Assn	$1,000
Others	$3,800
Pharmaceuticals	**$7,550**
Hoffman-La Roche	$1,700
Schering-Plough Corp	$1,500
Others	$4,350
Real Estate	**$3,850**
National Assn of Realtors	$3,550
Others	$300
Savings Banks	**$3,350**
SAPEC/ NJ (New Jersey Savings Assn)	$2,500
Others	$850
Securities/Commodities	**$33,600**
Goldman Sachs	$7,300
Chicago Board of Trade	$3,000
Chicago Mercantile Exchange	$3,000
First Boston Corp	$3,000
Investment Company Institute	$3,000
Morgan Stanley & Company	$2,500
Chicago Board of Options Exchange	$2,000
E F Hutton Group	$2,000
Travelers Corp	$1,500
Prudential-Bache Securities	$1,300
Dean Witter Reynolds	$1,000
Others	$4,000

PAC Totals by Category

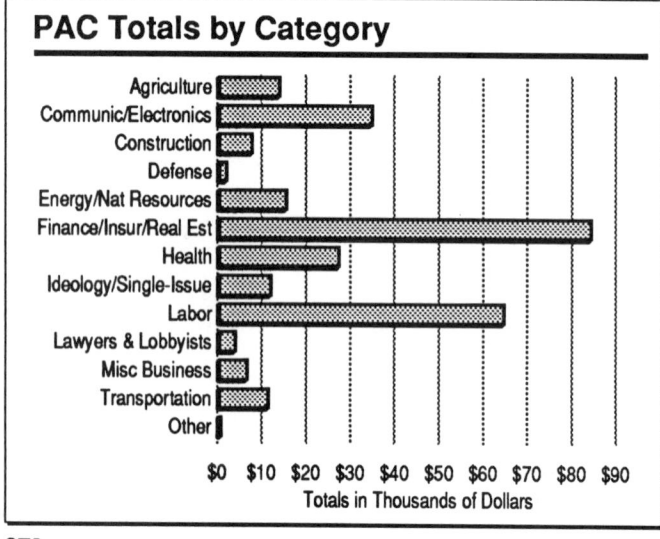

Agriculture
Communic/Electronics
Construction
Defense
Energy/Nat Resources
Finance/Insur/Real Est
Health
Ideology/Single-Issue
Labor
Lawyers & Lobbyists
Misc Business
Transportation
Other

$0 $10 $20 $30 $40 $50 $60 $70 $80 $90
Totals in Thousands of Dollars

Telecommunications **$23,951**

    AT&T $10,000
    New Jersey Bell Telephone $3,500
    Bell Atlantic $2,000
    Pacific Telesis Group $1,600
    Others $6,851

Television/Movies **$10,100**

    National Cable Television Assn $5,000
    Assn of Independent TV Stations $1,200
    MCA Inc $1,000
    National Assn of Broadcasters $1,000
    Others $1,900

Tobacco **$3,900**

    Philip Morris $2,500
    Others $1,400

Trucking/Delivery **$3,365**

    United Parcel Service $2,500
    Others $865

Other Major Business PACs

Texas Air	$1,500	Airlines
FMC Corp	$1,000	Chemicals
GATX Corp	$1,000	RR Svcs
Holiday Inns	$1,000	Hotel/Motel

Labor

Bldg Trades/Industrial/Misc Unions **$29,750**

    Operating Engineers Union* $6,200
    Laborers' Political League $5,200
    United Auto Workers $3,600
    Carpenters & Joiners Union $2,500
    National Education Assn $2,300
    Food & Commercial Workers Union $1,600
    Intl Brotherhood of Electrical Workers $1,500
    Machinists/Aerospace Workers Union $1,300
    AFL-CIO* $1,200
    Others $4,350

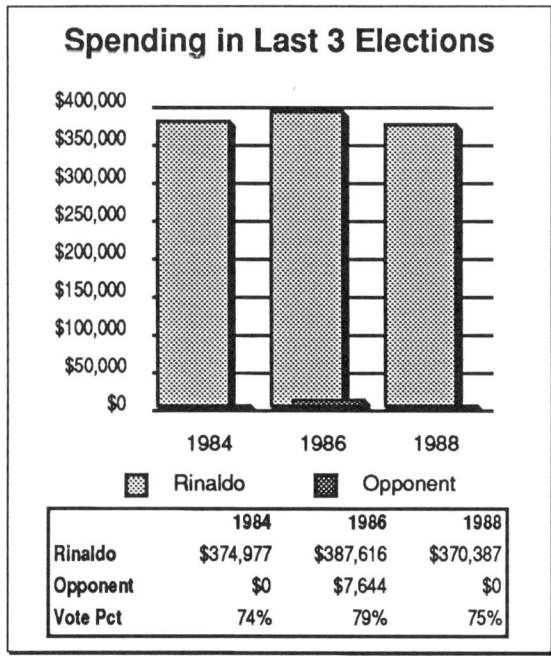

Spending in Last 3 Elections

Legend: Rinaldo, Opponent

	1984	1986	1988
Rinaldo	$374,977	$387,616	$370,387
Opponent	$0	$7,644	$0
Vote Pct	74%	79%	75%

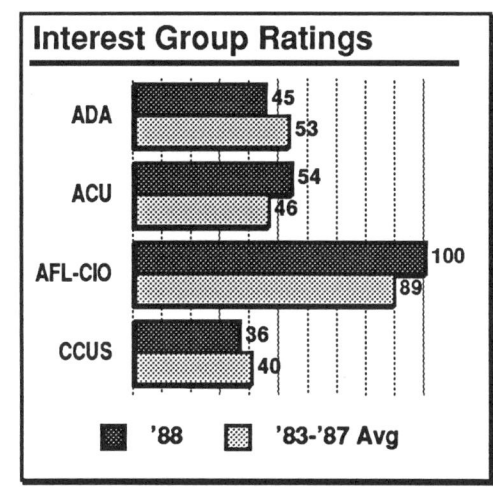

Interest Group Ratings

	'88	'83-'87 Avg
ADA	45	53
ACU	54	46
AFL-CIO	100	89
CCUS	36	40

Legend: ■ '88   ▨ '83-'87 Avg

Government & Postal Unions **$10,050**

    National Assn of Retired Federal Employees $4,000
    American Fedn of State/County/Munic Employees $2,000
    National Assn of Letter Carriers $2,000
    Others $2,050

Transportation Unions **$24,350**

    Teamsters Union $10,000
    Air Line Pilots Assn $5,000
    Marine Engineers District 2 Maritime Officers $3,500
    Seafarers International Union $2,000
    United Transportation Union $1,500
    Others $2,350

Ideological/Single-Issue

Ideological/Single-Issue **$11,550**

National PAC	$5,000	Pro-Israel
National Cmte to Preserve Social Security	$5,000	Soc Secur
Sierra Club	$1,000	Environment
Others	$550	

Independent expenditures supporting Rinaldo

    National Cmte to Preserve Social Security $3,558

---

* Contributions came from more than one PAC affiliated
with this sponsor.

Don Ritter, R-Pa (15)

1988 Committees & Subcommittees

Energy and Commerce
Commerce, Consumer Protection and Competitiveness
Telecommunications and Finance

Science, Space and Technology
Investigations and Oversight (Ranking Republican)
Science, Research and Technology

First elected: 1978
Total receipts: $759,713
Total from PACs: $293,454

PAC Contribution Profile

Business

Accountants	**$13,250**
American Institute of CPA's	$5,000
Coopers & Lybrand	$3,250
Touche Ross	$2,000
Arthur Young & Company	$1,000
Deloitte, Haskins & Sells	$1,000
Others	$1,000
Automotive	**$7,500**
National Auto Dealers Assn	$5,250
Others	$2,250
Chemicals & Plastics	**$11,875**
Air Products & Chemicals Inc	$4,375
Dow Corning Corp/Employees	$1,500
FMC Corp	$1,250
Betz Laboratories	$1,000
Rohm and Haas Company	$1,000
Others	$2,750
Commercial Banks	**$13,662**
J P Morgan & Company	$5,000
American Bankers Assn	$4,500
Citicorp	$1,000
Merchants Bancorp	$1,000
Others	$2,162
Construction	**$10,000**
National Assn of Home Builders	$5,000
Associated General Contractors	$1,750
Others	$3,250

Campaign Revenue Sources

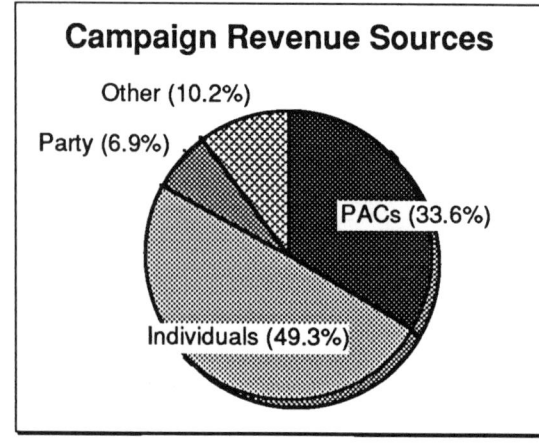

Other (10.2%)
Party (6.9%)
PACs (33.6%)
Individuals (49.3%)

Electric Utilities	**$16,916**
General Public Utilities	$3,016
Southern Company*	$2,400
Southern California Edison	$1,250
Philadelphia Electric	$1,000
Texas Utilities Electric Company*	$1,000
Others	$8,250
Food & Beverage	**$9,600**
National Beer Wholesalers Assn	$1,250
Miller Brewing Company	$1,000
National Restaurant Assn	$1,000
Pepsico Inc	$1,000
Stroh Brewery Company	$1,000
Others	$4,350
Health Professionals	**$8,000**
American Medical Assn	$5,250
American Dental Assn	$2,500
Others	$250
Industrial Equipment & Materials	**$8,800**
Fuller Company	$7,000
Others	$1,800
Insurance	**$15,675**
National Assn of Life Underwriters	$2,000
American Council of Life Insurance	$1,500
Independent Insurance Agents of America	$1,500
National Assn of Independent Insurers	$1,500
Casualty & Surety Agents Assn	$1,250
Cigna Corp	$1,250
Liberty Mutual Insurance	$1,000
Others	$5,675
Oil & Gas	**$19,125**
Union Pacific Corp	$2,250
Cooper Industries	$2,000
Amoco Corp	$1,750
Phillips Petroleum	$1,500
Dow Chemical*	$1,000
Mobil Oil	$1,000
Rosewood Corp	$1,000
Sun Company	$1,000
Others	$7,625

PAC Totals by Category

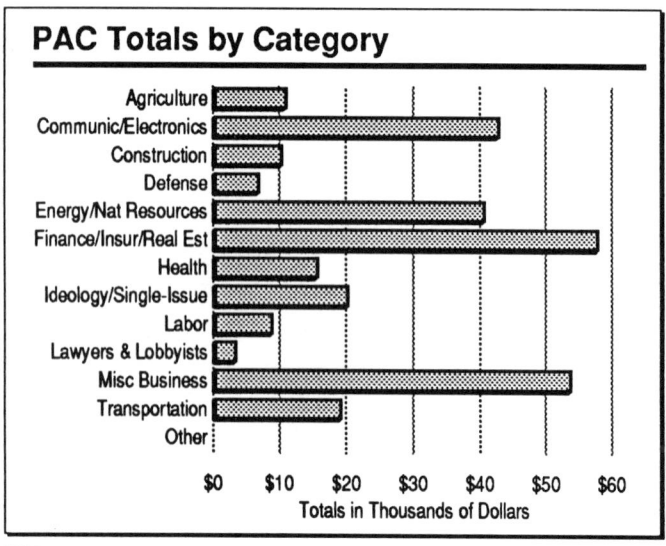

Agriculture
Communic/Electronics
Construction
Defense
Energy/Nat Resources
Finance/Insur/Real Est
Health
Ideology/Single-Issue
Labor
Lawyers & Lobbyists
Misc Business
Transportation
Other

$0 $10 $20 $30 $40 $50 $60
Totals in Thousands of Dollars

Real Estate **$9,225**
   National Assn of Realtors $8,975
   Others $250

Securities/Commodities Investment **$7,000**
   Chicago Board of Trade $2,000
   Morgan Stanley & Company $1,000
   Others $4,000

Steel Production **$6,650**
   Bethlehem Steel $4,400
   Others $2,250

Telecommunications **$31,425**
   AT&T $10,000
   BellSouth Corp* $2,750
   Ameritech Corp $2,000
   Pacific Telesis Group $1,750
   Bell Telephone of Pennsylvania $1,675
   Bell Atlantic $1,500
   Continental Telecom $1,500
   NYNEX Corp $1,250
   Corning Glass Works $1,000
   Harris Corp $1,000
   U S West Inc...$1,000
   United Telecommunications $1,000
   US Telephone Assn $1,000
   Others $4,000

Television/Movies **$6,750**
   National Assn of Broadcasters $1,000
   National Cable Television Assn $4,000
   Others $1,750

Interest Group Ratings

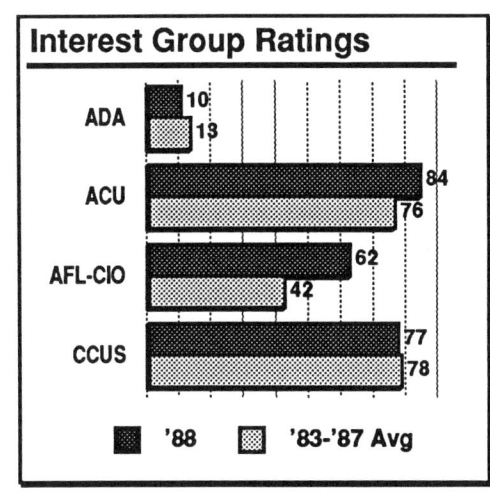

	'88	'83-'87 Avg
ADA	10	13
ACU	84	76
AFL-CIO	62	42
CCUS	77	78

Other Major Business PACs

American Veterinary Medical Assn	$5,000	Veterinary
US Fedn of Small Businesses	$2,500	Sml Business
Hallmark Cards	$2,300	Publishing
Rockwell International	$2,250	Air Defense
Mack Trucks	$1,800	Truck Mfrs
United Parcel Service	$1,550	Delivery
Owens-Illinois	$1,500	Paper Packg
United Technologies	$1,500	Space Equip
National Fedn of Independent Business	$1,350	Sml Business
Atlantic Apparel Contractors Assn	$1,250	Clothing
Northrop Corp	$1,250	Air Defense
Smithkline Beckman	$1,250	Pharmaceut
Business Industry PAC	$1,121	Bus Assns
American Textile Manufacturers Institute	$1,000	Textiles
Burlington Industries	$1,000	Textiles
National Society of Professional Engineers	$1,000	Energy
Precision Metalforming Assn	$1,000	MetalProduct
Stanley Works	$1,000	Hardware
Xerox Corp	$1,000	Off Machines

Labor

Labor Unions...**$8,500**
   Marine Engineers Union* $3,500
   Teamsters Union $2,500
   Masters Mates & Pilots Union $1,000
   Seafarers International Union $1,000
   Others $500

Ideological/Single-Issue

Ideological/Single-Issue **$17,885**
Hudson Valley PAC	$4,000	Pro-Israel
Conservatives Acting Together	$3,500	Repub/Conser
Ruff PAC	$3,000	Tax Policy
Public Service Research Council	$2,500	Anti-Union
Campaign for a New Majority (Jack Kemp)	$1,250	Repub Leader
American Latvian PAC	$1,200	Ethnic
National Right to Life PAC	$1,000	Pro-Life
Republican Congressional Boosters Club	$1,000	Repub/Conser
Others	$1,685	

---

* Contributions came from more than one PAC affiliated
   with this sponsor.

Spending in Last 3 Elections

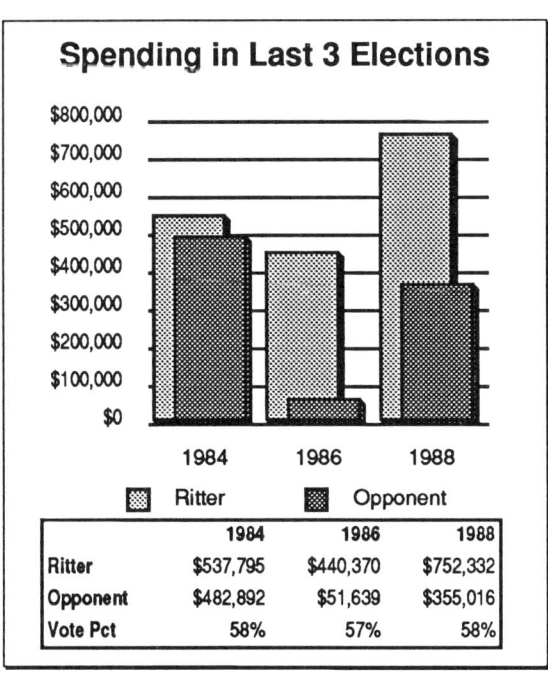

	Ritter	Opponent

	1984	1986	1988
Ritter	$537,795	$440,370	$752,332
Opponent	$482,892	$51,639	$355,016
Vote Pct	58%	57%	58%

Pat Roberts, R-Kan (1)

First elected: 1980
Total receipts: $191,584
Total from PACs: $99,600

1988 Committees & Subcommittees

Agriculture
Department Operations, Research and Foreign Agriculture (Ranking Republican)
Tobacco and Peanuts
Wheat, Soybeans and Feed Grains

House Administration
Personnel and Police (Ranking Republican)
Accounts
Elections

Joint Library

Joint Printing

PAC Contribution Profile

Business

Agricultural Chemicals **$12,100**
  FMC Corp $2,000
  ConAgra Inc $1,500
  Ecolab Inc $1,500
  Ciba-Geigy Corp $1,000
  Others $6,100

Agricultural Services **$5,000**
  American Assn of Crop Insurers $1,000
  American Veterinary Medical Assn $1,000
  Farmland Industries $1,000
  Others $2,000

Auto Dealers **$4,800**
  Auto Dealers & Drivers for Free Trade $2,500
  National Auto Dealers Assn $2,300

Commercial & Savings Banks **$6,250**
  American Bankers Assn $3,500
  Independent Bankers Assn $1,300
  US League of Savings Assn $1,000
  Others $450

Commodities Trading **$2,000**
  Chicago Board of Trade $1,000
  Chicago Mercantile Exchange $1,000

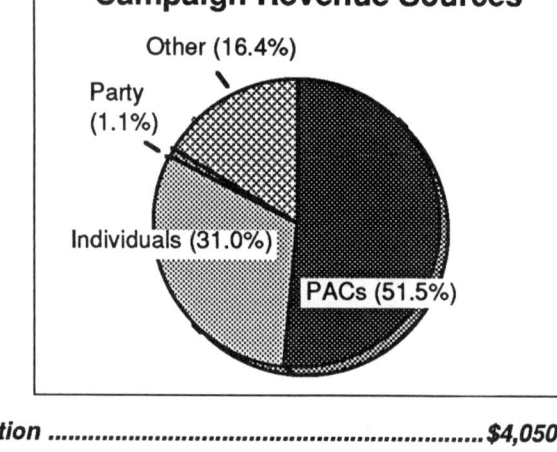

Campaign Revenue Sources

- Other (16.4%)
- Party (1.1%)
- Individuals (31.0%)
- PACs (51.5%)

Construction **$4,050**
  National Assn of Home Builders $2,000
  Associated General Contractors $1,300
  Others $750

Food & Beverage **$8,200**
  Food Marketing Institute $1,100
  IBP Inc $1,000
  Pillsbury Company $1,000
  Others $5,100

Grain & Soybean Production/Processing **$4,200**
  Archer-Daniels-Midland Corp $1,500
  Cargill Inc $1,000
  Others $1,700

Health Professionals **$7,600**
  Kansas Medical Assn $5,000
  American Dental Assn $1,300
  Kansas Chiropractic Assn $1,000
  Others $300

Insurance **$2,400**
  None over $500

Livestock **$3,250**
  Texas Cattle Feeders Assn $1,500
  National Cattlemen's Assn $1,100
  Others $650

Pharmaceuticals **$3,950**
  Sterling Drug $1,300
  Smithkline Beckman $1,000
  Others $1,650

Railroads **$2,100**
  Santa Fe Southern Pacific $1,000
  Others $1,100

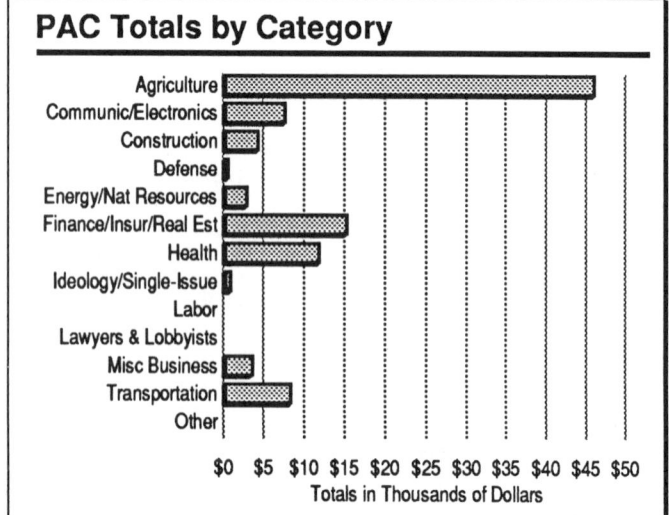

PAC Totals by Category

- Agriculture
- Communic/Electronics
- Construction
- Defense
- Energy/Nat Resources
- Finance/Insur/Real Est
- Health
- Ideology/Single-Issue
- Labor
- Lawyers & Lobbyists
- Misc Business
- Transportation
- Other

$0 $5 $10 $15 $20 $25 $30 $35 $40 $45 $50
Totals in Thousands of Dollars

Real Estate **$6,300**
    National Assn of Realtors $6,300

Sugar Growers **$3,200**
    American Crystal Sugar Corp $1,300
    Others $1,900

Telecommunications **$7,100**
    AT&T $3,000
    Continental Telecom $2,000
    Southwestern Bell $1,600
    Others $500

Tobacco **$2,350**
    Philip Morris $1,000
    Others $1,350

Other Major Business PACs
Avery Inc ....$1,000   Adhesives

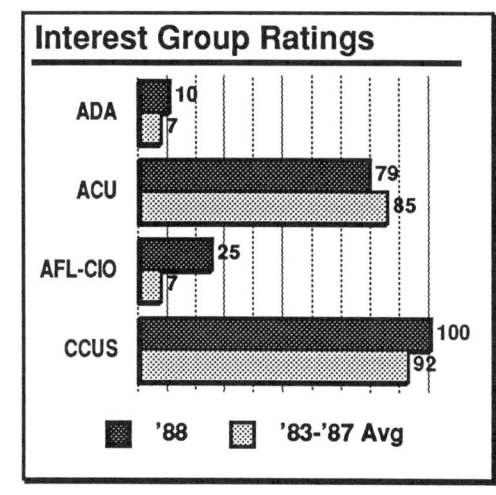

Interest Group Ratings

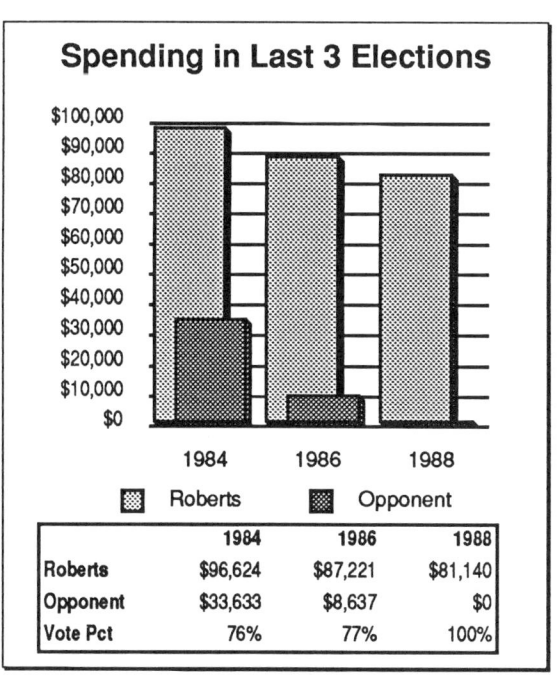

Spending in Last 3 Elections

	1984	1986	1988
Roberts	$96,624	$87,221	$81,140
Opponent	$33,633	$8,637	$0
Vote Pct	76%	77%	100%

Tommy F. Robinson, R-Ark (2)

First elected: 1984
Total receipts: $503,328
Total from PACs: $182,980

1988 Committees & Subcommittees

Armed Services
Military Installations and Facilities
Readiness

Education and Labor
Elementary, Secondary and Vocational Education
Labor Standards
Postsecondary Education

Veterans' Affairs
Hospitals and Health Care

Select Aging
Human Services

PAC Contribution Profile

Business

Auto Dealers	**$6,850**
National Auto Dealers Assn	$4,350
Auto Dealers & Drivers for Free Trade	$2,500
Construction	**$1,500**
Associated General Contractors	$1,000
Others	$500
Dairy	**$1,600**
Associated Milk Producers	$1,000
Others	$600
Defense	**$26,050**
Northrop Corp	$4,000
AT&T	$3,000
GTE (Southwest)	$2,500
Continental Telecom	$2,000
United Technologies	$1,600
FMC Corp	$1,350
Rockwell International	$1,200
Others	$10,400
Electric Utilities	**$3,850**
ACRE (Action Committee for Rural Electrification)	$2,500
Middle South Utilities*	$1,350
Financial Institutions	**$2,350**
First Commercial Bank/Little Rock	$1,000
Others	$1,350

Campaign Revenue Sources

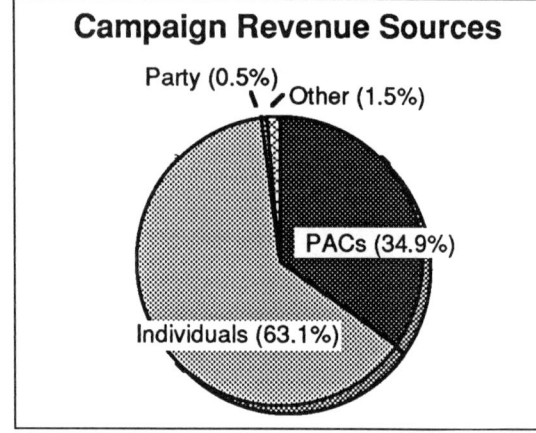

Party (0.5%)
Other (1.5%)
PACs (34.9%)
Individuals (63.1%)

Food & Beverage	**$11,500**
National Restaurant Assn	$5,000
General Mills Restaurants	$2,000
McDonald's Corp	$1,000
Safeway Stores	$1,000
Others	$2,500
Health Professionals	**$14,000**
American Medical Assn	$10,000
American Dental Assn	$2,000
Cmte for Quality Orthopedic Health Care	$1,000
Others	$1,000
Hospitals & Nursing Homes	**$2,750**
Beverly Enterprises	$2,000
Others	$750
Insurance	**$3,700**
Torchmark Corp	$2,000
National Assn of Life Underwriters	$1,000
Others	$700
Lawyers	**$4,000**
Wallace, Dover & Dixon	$3,000
California Trial Lawyers Assn	$1,000
Real Estate	**$10,350**
National Assn of Realtors	$10,000
Others	$350
Telecommunications	**$2,200**
Southwestern Bell	$1,000
Others	$1,200
Trucking/Freight	**$3,050**
Arkansas Best Corp	$1,500
Others	$1,550

PAC Totals by Category

Agriculture
Communic/Electronics
Construction
Defense
Energy/Nat Resources
Finance/Insur/Real Est
Health
Ideology/Single-Issue
Labor
Lawyers & Lobbyists
Misc Business
Transportation
Other

$0 $5 $10 $15 $20 $25 $30 $35 $40 $45 $50
Totals in Thousands of Dollars

Other Major Business PACs

Stephens Overseas Services	$3,000	FinancSvcs
American Hotel & Motel Assn	$1,000	Hotel/Motel
National Assn of Trade/Tech Schools	$1,000	Voc Tech
Riceland Foods	$1,000	Rice
Schering-Plough Corp	$1,000	Pharmaceut
Stone Container Corp	$1,000	Paper Packg

Labor

Bldg Trades/Industrial/Misc Unions $24,400

Carpenters & Joiners Union	$4,700
United Auto Workers	$3,000
Food & Commercial Workers Union	$2,350
Intl Brotherhood of Electrical Workers	$2,000
Machinists/Aerospace Workers Union	$2,000
Laborers' Political League	$1,850
Operating Engineers Union	$1,500
Communications Workers of America	$1,350
AFL-CIO*	$1,050
Plumbers/Pipefitters Union	$1,000
Others	$3,600

Government & Postal Workers $5,600

American Fedn of State/County/Munic Employees	$2,500
National Assn of Letter Carriers	$1,000
National Assn of Retired Federal Employees	$1,000
Others	$1,100

Transportation Unions $18,800

Teamsters Union	$10,000
Air Line Pilots Assn	$4,000
United Transportation Union	$1,500
Seafarers International Union	$1,000
Others	$2,300

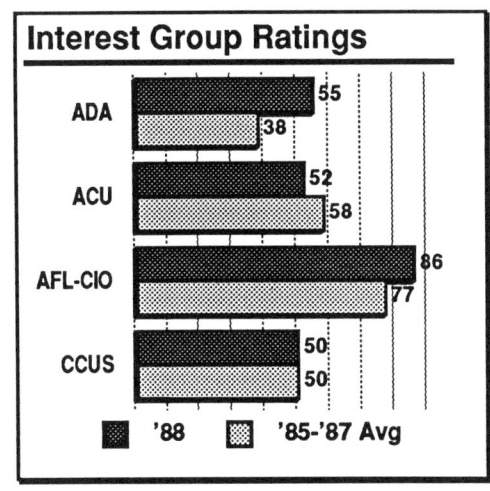

Interest Group Ratings

	'88	'85-'87 Avg
ADA	55	38
ACU	52	58
AFL-CIO	86	77
CCUS	50	50

Ideological/Single-Issue

Democratic Leadership PACs $6,500

Majority Congress Committee (Jim Wright)	$5,000
Valley Education Fund (Tony Coelho)	$1,000
Others	$500

Pro-Israel $8,500

National PAC	$5,000
Delaware Valley PAC	$1,000
Hudson Valley PAC	$1,000
Louisiana for American Security	$1,000
Others	$500

Other Major Ideological/Single-Issue PACs

National Rifle Assn	$1,000	Pro-Guns

Independent expenditures supporting Robinson

National Cmte to Preserve Social Security	$2,727

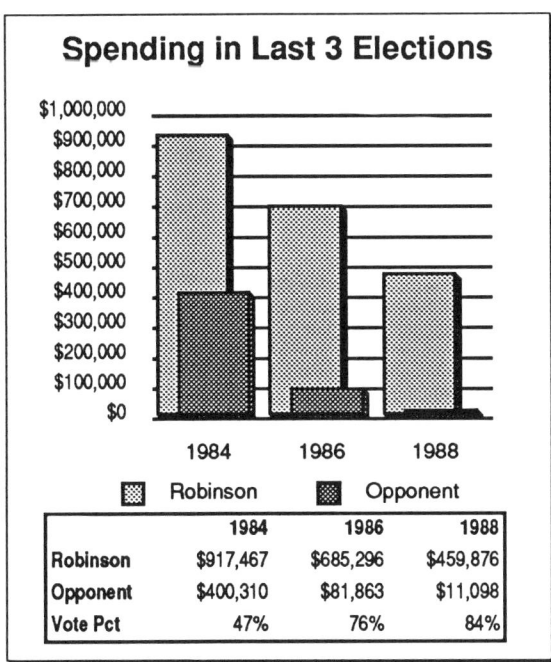

Spending in Last 3 Elections

	1984	1986	1988
Robinson	$917,467	$685,296	$459,876
Opponent	$400,310	$81,863	$11,098
Vote Pct	47%	76%	84%

Robinson ▨   Opponent ▨

* Contributions came from more than one PAC affiliated with this sponsor.

Robert A. Roe, D-NJ (8)

First elected: 1969
Total receipts: $490,884
Total from PACs: $271,600

1988 Committees & Subcommittees

Public Works and Transportation
Investigations and Oversight
Surface Transportation
Water Resources

Science, Space and Technology (Chairman)
Investigations and Oversight (Chairman)

Select Intelligence
Program and Budget Authorization

PAC Contribution Profile

Business

Aviation & Aerospace **$30,500**
    Boeing Company $5,000
    McDonnell Douglas $4,000
    Martin Marietta Corp $3,000
    Morton Thiokol $3,000
    TRW Inc $3,000
    United Technologies $3,000
    Long Island Aerospace PAC $2,500
    Fairchild Industries $1,500
    Seal-Tech Space $1,000
    Sundstrand Corp* $1,000
    Trans World Airlines $1,000
    USAir Corp $1,000
    Others $1,500

Construction **$37,400**
    National Assn of Home Builders $8,500
    National Utility Contractors Assn $8,500
    National Society of Professional Engineers $2,500
    American Road & Transportation Builders Assn $2,000
    Associated General Contractors $2,000
    Deere & Company* $2,000
    Engineers & Architects Assn $2,000
    Enserch Corp $1,500
    National Society of Professional Surveyors $1,300
    American Consulting Engineers Council $1,000
    Ch2M Hill $1,000
    Dravo Corp $1,000
    Parsons Corp $1,000
    Stone & Webster $1,000
    Others $2,100

Campaign Revenue Sources

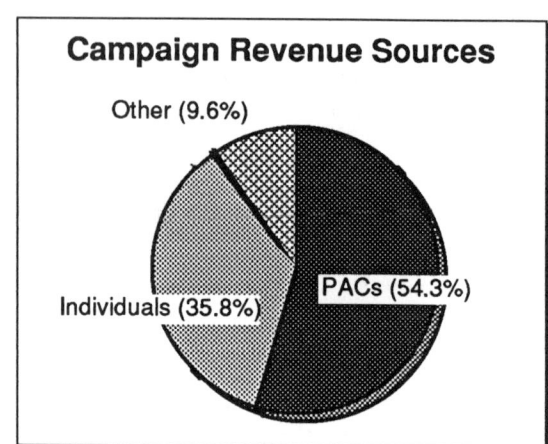

Other (9.6%)
Individuals (35.8%)
PACs (54.3%)

Defense Aerospace & Electronics **$36,500**
    Rockwell International $6,000
    Grumman $5,000
    Lockheed Corp $5,000
    Singer Company $5,000
    General Dynamics $3,000
    Hughes Aircraft $3,000
    Allied-Signal $2,000
    Hazeltine Corp $2,000
    LTV Aerospace & Defense Company $2,000
    Atlantic Research Corp $1,000
    Gencorp Inc $1,000
    Textron Inc $1,000
    Others $500

Electric Utilities & Equipment **$5,050**
    General Atomics $2,000
    Public Service Electric & Gas $1,150
    Combustion Engineering $1,000
    Others $900

Electronics & Computers **$7,125**
    General Electric $2,125
    Computer Sciences Corp $2,000
    Westinghouse Electric $2,000
    Others $1,000

Financial Institutions **$5,050**
    American Bankers Assn $3,000
    SAPEC/ NJ (New Jersey Savings Assn) $1,450
    Others $600

Insurance **$2,000**
    ITT Corp $1,000
    Mutual Benefit Life Insurance $1,000

Lawyers & Lobbyists **$3,500**
    Assn of Trial Lawyers of America $2,000
    Powell, Goldstein, Frazer & Murphy $1,000
    Others $500

PAC Totals by Category

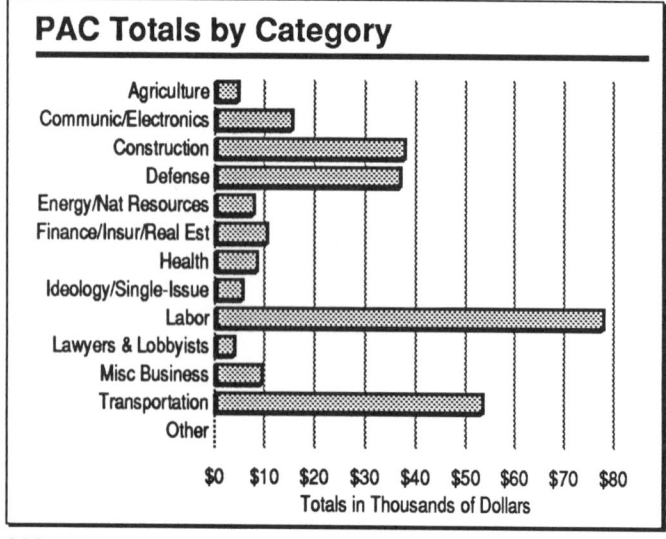

Agriculture
Communic/Electronics
Construction
Defense
Energy/Nat Resources
Finance/Insur/Real Est
Health
Ideology/Single-Issue
Labor
Lawyers & Lobbyists
Misc Business
Transportation
Other

$0 $10 $20 $30 $40 $50 $60 $70 $80
Totals in Thousands of Dollars

Pharmaceuticals **$6,500**
    American Cyanimid $3,000
    Hoffman-La Roche $2,000
    Johnson & Johnson $1,000
    Others $500

Real Estate **$3,000**
    National Assn of Realtors $3,000

Telecommunications **$7,950**
    AT&T $2,750
    New Jersey Bell Telephone..........................$2,450
    Pacific Telesis Group $1,250
    Comsat $1,000
    Others $500

Trucking/Freight **$16,950**
    United Parcel Service $3,950
    Yellow Freight System $3,000
    American Trucking Assns $2,000
    Eastern Central Motor Carriers $2,000
    North American Van Lines $2,000
    Roadway Services Inc $1,500
    Consolidated Freightways $1,000
    Ryder System Inc $1,000
    Others $500

Other Major Business PACs

Potters Industries	$3,000	Glass Prod
American Bus Assn	$2,000	Bus Svcs
Ocean Spray Cranberries Inc	$2,000	Fruit/Veg
Pirelli Cable	$2,000	Indust Equip
National Coal Assn	$1,500	Coal
American Coml Barge Line Company	$1,000	SeaTransport
American Veterinary Medical Assn	$1,000	Veterinary
American Medical Assn	$1,000	Doctors
Emhart Corp	$1,000	Indust Equip
Ford Motor Company	$1,000	Auto Mfrs
National Electric Sign Assn	$1,000	Advert/PR
Union Camp Corp	$1,000	Paper Prod

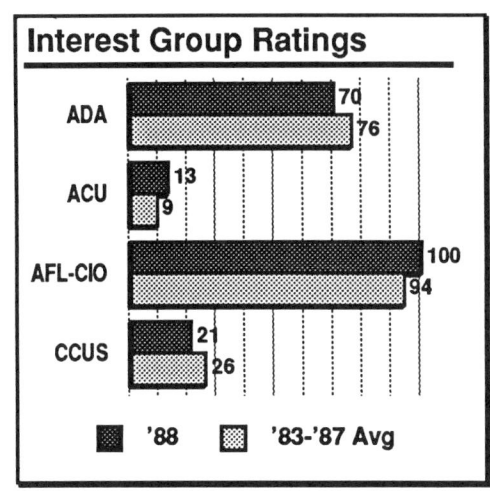

Interest Group Ratings

ADA: 70 ('88), 76 ('83-'87 Avg)
ACU: 13 ('88), 9 ('83-'87 Avg)
AFL-CIO: 100 ('88), 94 ('83-'87 Avg)
CCUS: 21 ('88), 26 ('83-'87 Avg)

■ '88 ▨ '83-'87 Avg

Labor

Bldg Trades/Industrial/Misc Unions **$41,600**
    Operating Engineers Union* $10,000
    Carpenters & Joiners Union $6,000
    Machinists/Aerospace Workers Union $5,000
    Laborers' Political League $4,500
    Plumbers/Pipefitters Union* $3,750
    United Auto Workers $3,000
    National Education Assn $2,800
    AFL-CIO* $2,000
    Food & Commercial Workers Union $1,600
    Intl Brotherhood of Electrical Workers $1,000
    Ladies Garment Workers Union $1,000
    Others $950

Government & Postal Workers **$5,800**
    National Assn of Letter Carriers $2,800
    American Fedn of State/County/Munic Employees $2,000
    American Postal Workers Union $1,000

Transportation Unions **$30,050**
    Air Line Pilots Assn $10,000
    Teamsters Union $10,000
    Seafarers International Union.........................$2,750
    Marine Engineers District 2 Maritime Officers $2,500
    Amalgamated Transit Union $2,000
    United Transportation Union $2,000
    Others $800

Ideological/Single-Issue

Ideological/Single-Issue **$5,200**

Free Cuba PAC	$1,000	Anti-Castro
Great Lakes Space Tech Assn	$1,000	OtherIdeolog
National Cmte to Preserve Social Security	$1,000	Soc Secur
SpacePAC	$1,000	OtherIdeolog
Others	$1,200	

Independent expenditures supporting Roe

National Cmte to Preserve Social Security $3,354

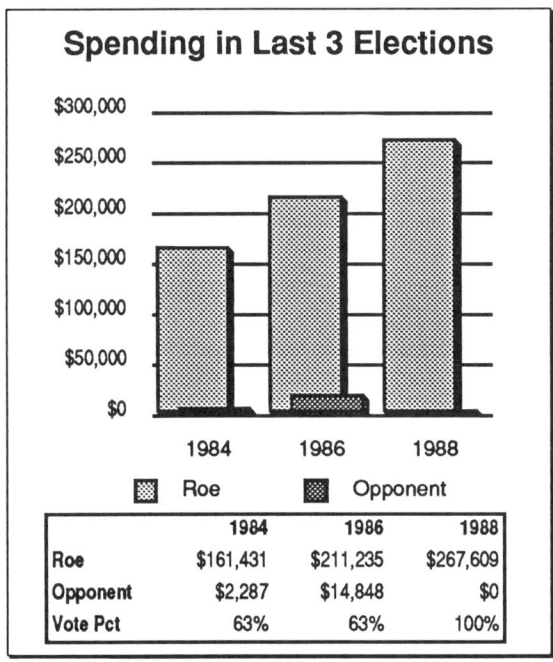

Spending in Last 3 Elections

▨ Roe ■ Opponent

	1984	1986	1988
Roe	$161,431	$211,235	$267,609
Opponent	$2,287	$14,848	$0
Vote Pct	63%	63%	100%

---

* Contributions came from more than one PAC affiliated
  with this sponsor.

Harold Rogers, R-Ky (5)

1988 Committees & Subcommittees

First elected: 1980
Total receipts: $177,242
Total from PACs: $69,566

Appropriations
Commerce, Justice, State, the Judiciary and Related Agencies (Ranking Republican)

Budget
Budget Process
Defense and International Affairs
Economic and Trade Policy

Campaign Revenue Sources

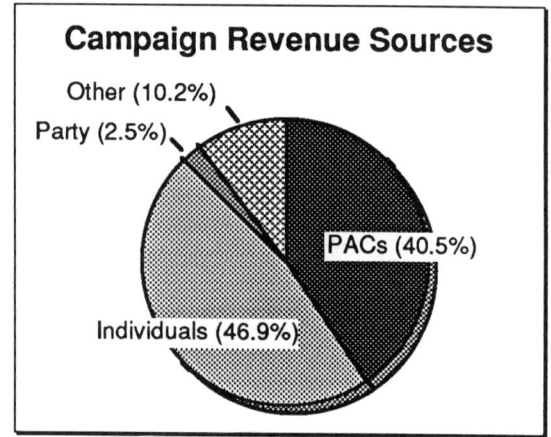

Other (10.2%)
Party (2.5%)
PACs (40.5%)
Individuals (46.9%)

PAC Contribution Profile

Business

Automotive	**$2,600**
Auto Dealers & Drivers for Free Trade	$1,500
National Auto Dealers Assn	$800
Others	$300
Construction	**$1,600**
National Assn of Home Builders	$1,000
Others	$600
Dairy	**$2,600**
Associated Milk Producers	$2,000
Others	$600
Electric Utilities	**$5,000**
Kentucky Utilities Company	$1,000
Texas Utilities Electric Company*	$600
American Electric Power	$550
Teco Energy Inc	$500
Others	$2,350
Food & Beverage	**$2,900**
Jerrico Inc	$800
ConAgra Inc	$600
Food Marketing Institute	$600
Others	$900
Health Professionals	**$10,500**
American Medical Assn	$10,000
Cmte for Quality Orthopedic Health Care	$500

Insurance	**$1,300**
National Assn of Life Underwriters	$1,000
Others	$300
Lawyers & Lobbyists	**$2,900**
Assn of Trial Lawyers of America	$2,000
Others	$900
Mining	**$1,400**
National Coal Assn	$600
Cyprus Minerals Company	$500
Others	$300
Oil & Gas	**$4,450**
Ashland Oil	$700
Atlantic Richfield	$600
Sun Company	$500
Others	$2,650
Railroads	**$1,200**
Union Pacific Corp	$600
Others	$600
Real Estate	**$3,782**
National Assn of Realtors	$3,482
Others	$300
Sugar Growers	**$1,500**
None over $300	
Telecommunications	**$8,850**
South Central Bell Telephone	$2,200
AT&T	$2,000
Continental Telecom	$1,500
GTE Corp	$550
NYNEX Corp	$500
Southwestern Bell	$500
US West Inc	$500
US Telephone Assn	$500
Others	$600

PAC Totals by Category

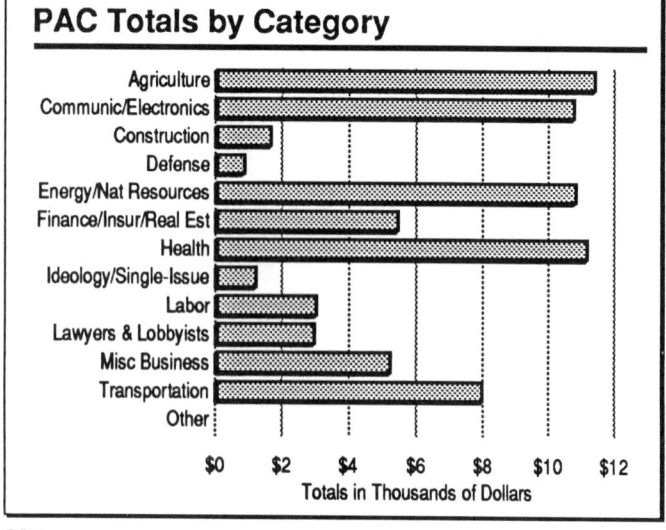

Agriculture
Communic/Electronics
Construction
Defense
Energy/Nat Resources
Finance/Insur/Real Est
Health
Ideology/Single-Issue
Labor
Lawyers & Lobbyists
Misc Business
Transportation
Other

$0 $2 $4 $6 $8 $10 $12
Totals in Thousands of Dollars

Textiles **$2,300**

    American Textile Manufacturers Institute $600
    American Yarn Spinners Assn $500
    Others $1,200

Tobacco **$3,700**

    Philip Morris $1,500
    Pinkerton Tobacco $1,000
    Tobacco Institute $600
    Others $600

Trucking/Delivery **$2,900**

    United Parcel Service $2,300
    Others $600

TV/Broadcasting **$1,100**

    National Assn of Broadcasters $1,100

Other Major Business PACs

Westvaco Corp ....$1,000   Paper Prod
American Veterinary Medical Assn ....$500   Veterinary
Colt Industries ....$500   Air Defense
Computer Sciences Corp ....$500   Data Process

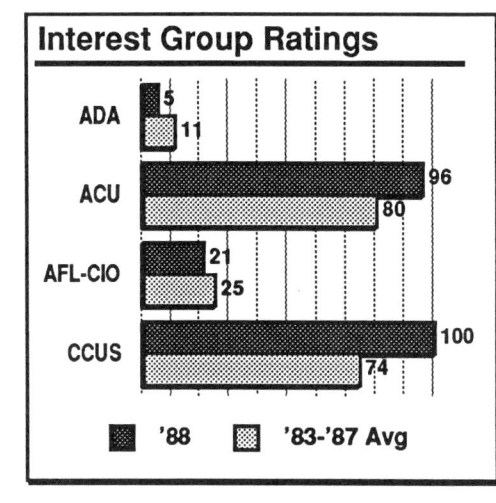

Interest Group Ratings

Group	'88	'83–'87 Avg
ADA	5	11
ACU	96	80
AFL-CIO	21	25
CCUS	100	74

■ '88   ▢ '83-'87 Avg

Labor

Labor Unions **$2,950**

    Marine Engineers District 2 Maritime Officers $1,250
    Air Line Pilots Assn $500
    Others $1,200

Major Ideological/Single-Issue PACs

National Security PAC ....$600   Pro-Defense

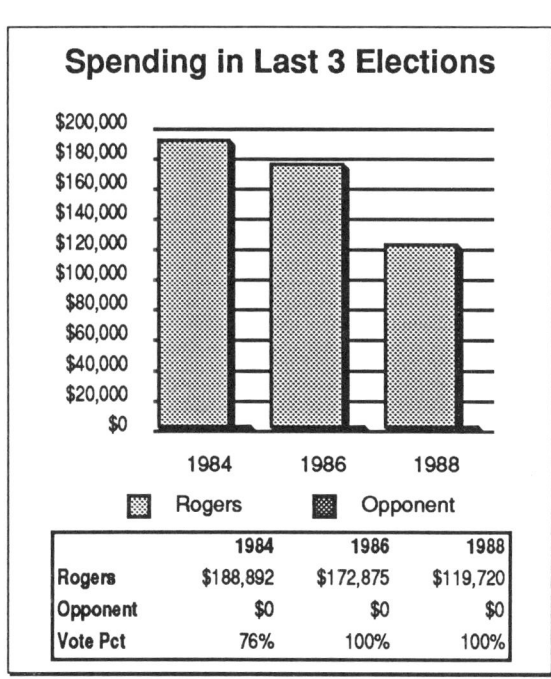

Spending in Last 3 Elections

■ Rogers   ■ Opponent

	1984	1986	1988
Rogers	$188,892	$172,875	$119,720
Opponent	$0	$0	$0
Vote Pct	76%	100%	100%

* Contributions came from more than one PAC affiliated
  with this sponsor.

Dana Rohrabacher, R-Calif (42)

1989-1990 Committees & Subcommittees

First elected: 1988
Total receipts: $521,565
Total from PACs: $186,427

District of Columbia
Judiciary and Education (Ranking Republican)
Government Operations and Metropolitan Affairs

Science, Space and Technology
Space Science and Applications
Transportation, Aviation and Materials

PAC Contribution Profile

Business

Automotive	**$10,250**
Auto Dealers & Drivers for Free Trade	$5,000
National Auto Dealers Assn	$5,000
Others	$250
Construction	**$7,250**
National Assn of Home Builders	$5,000
Associated General Contractors	$1,000
Sheet Metal/AirCon Contractors	$1,000
Others	$250
Defense	**$6,050**
Northrop Corp	$1,550
Hughes Aircraft	$1,500
Lockheed Corp	$1,000
TRW Inc	$1,000
Others	$1,000
Financial Institutions	**$6,600**
American Bankers Assn	$1,000
Credit Union National Assn	$1,000
US League of Savings Assn	$1,000
Others	$3,600
Food & Beverage	**$4,800**
J R Simplot Company	$1,000
McLane Company	$1,000
National Restaurant Assn	$1,000
Others	$1,800

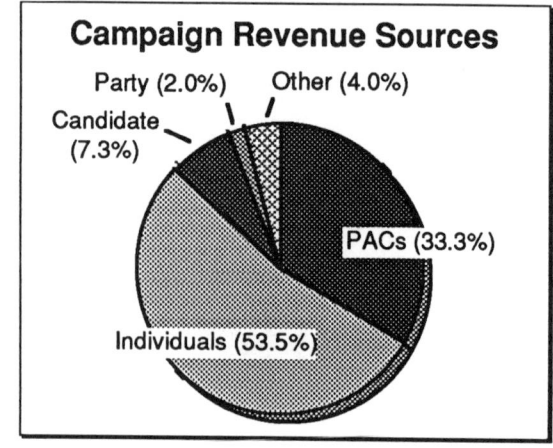

Campaign Revenue Sources

- Party (2.0%)
- Other (4.0%)
- Candidate (7.3%)
- PACs (33.3%)
- Individuals (53.5%)

Health Professionals	**$25,500**
American Medical Assn	$10,000
American Chiropractic Assn	$5,000
California Chiropractic Assn	$5,000
American Academy of Ophthalmology	$3,000
American Dental Assn	$1,500
Cmte for Quality Orthopedic Health Care	$1,000
Insurance	**$4,000**
National Assn of Life Underwriters	$2,500
Others	$1,500
Oil & Gas	**$9,650**
Atlantic Richfield	$2,500
Amoco Corp	$1,000
Mobil Oil	$1,000
Union Oil	$1,000
Others	$4,150
Real Estate	**$12,000**
National Assn of Realtors	$10,000
Irvine Company	$1,000
Others	$1,000
Retail Sales	**$2,957**
Southland Corp	$1,007
Carter Hawley Hale Stores	$1,000
Others	$950
Shipbuilding & Repair	**$2,650**
Southwest Marine	$2,500
Others	$150
Telecommunications	**$2,250**
Continental Telecom	$1,000
Others	$1,250
Tobacco	**$2,250**
Philip Morris	$1,000
RJR Nabisco	$1,000
Others	$250

Other Major Business PACs

National Assn of Wholesale-Distributors	$1,250	Wholesale
Business Industry PAC	$1,000	Bus Assns
Henley Group Inc	$1,000	Altern Energy
National Assn of Temporary Services	$1,000	EmployAgency
PPG Industries	$1,000	Glass Prod
Southern California Edison	$1,000	ElectricUtil
Union Pacific Corp	$1,000	Railroads

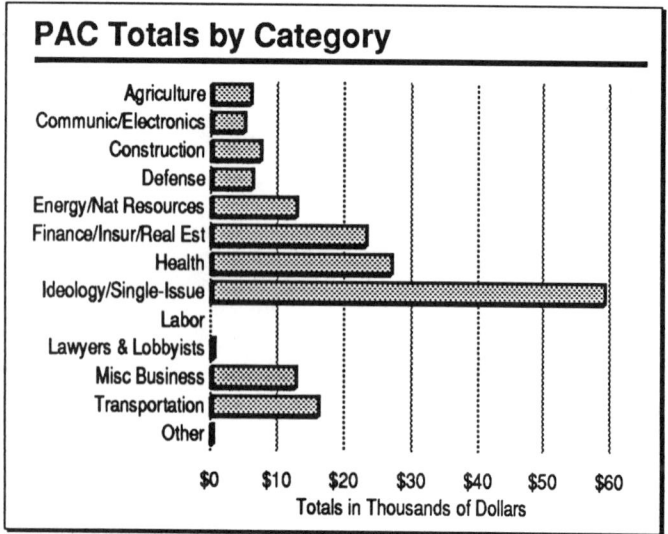

PAC Totals by Category

- Agriculture
- Communic/Electronics
- Construction
- Defense
- Energy/Nat Resources
- Finance/Insur/Real Est
- Health
- Ideology/Single-Issue
- Labor
- Lawyers & Lobbyists
- Misc Business
- Transportation
- Other

$0 $10 $20 $30 $40 $50 $60

Totals in Thousands of Dollars

Ideological/Single-Issue

Republican/Conservative $22,426

American Citizens for Political Action	$10,000
America's PAC	$6,000
Free Congress PAC	$2,000
National Conservative PAC	$1,426
Eagle Forum	$1,000
Others	$2,000

Republican Leadership PACs $14,656

Citizens for the Republic (Ronald Reagan)	$5,000
Campaign America (Bob Dole)	$4,906
Conservative Victory Fund (Steve Symms)	$1,150
American Enterprise PAC (Bill Lowery)	$1,000
National Congressional Club (Jesse Helms)	$1,000
Republican Leader's Fund (Bob Michel)	$1,000
Others	$600

Other Major Ideological/Single-Issue PACs

Council for National Defense	$5,000	Pro-Defense
National Rifle Assn	$4,950	Pro-Guns
Ruff PAC	$3,500	Tax Policy
National Right to Life PAC	$2,416	Pro-Life
Right to Work PAC	$1,500	Anti-Union
Gun Owners of America	$1,000	Pro-Guns
Korean American National PAC	$1,000	Ethnic
Public Service Research Council	$1,000	Anti-Union

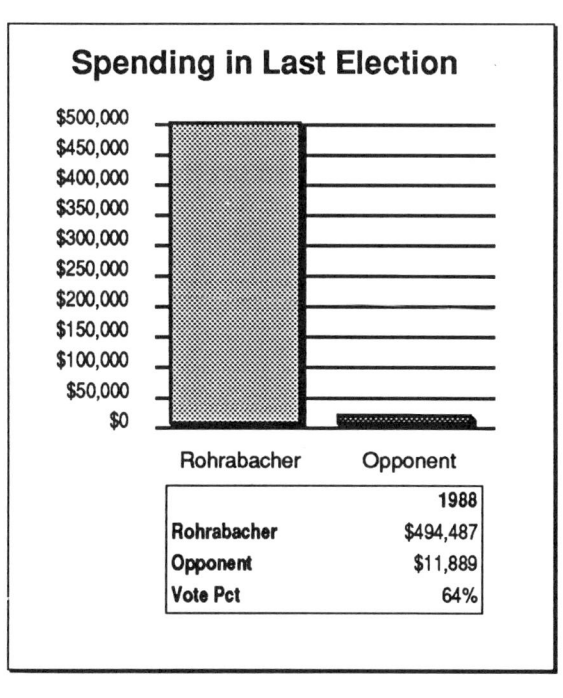

Spending in Last Election

	1988
Rohrabacher	$494,487
Opponent	$11,889
Vote Pct	64%

Charlie Rose, D-NC (7)

1988 Committees & Subcommittees

Agriculture
Tobacco and Peanuts (Chairman)
Department Operations, Research and Foreign Agriculture
Livestock, Dairy and Poultry

House Administration
Office Systems (Chairman)
Elections

PAC Contribution Profile

Business

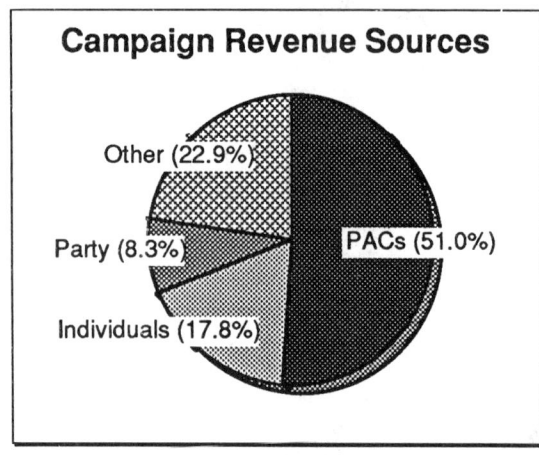

Campaign Revenue Sources

Other (22.9%)
Party (8.3%)
PACs (51.0%)
Individuals (17.8%)

Agricultural Chemicals	$9,250
FMC Corp	$2,000
Ciba-Geigy Corp	$1,000
Eli Lilly & Company	$1,000
Monsanto Company	$1,000
Others	$4,250

Automotive	$4,250
National Auto Dealers Assn	$3,750
Others	$500

Commercial & Savings Banks	$5,800
American Bankers Assn	$3,500
Others	$2,300

Commodities Trading	$5,250
Chicago Mercantile Exchange	$3,000
Chicago Board of Trade	$2,000
Others	$250

Dairy	$16,100
Associated Milk Producers	$7,000
Dairymen Inc-North Carolina	$3,200
Mid-American Dairymen	$3,000
Land O'Lakes Inc	$1,000
Others	$1,900

Electric Utilities	$2,750
ACRE (Action Committee for Rural Electrification)	$1,000
Carolina Power & Light	$1,000
Others	$750

Farm Organizations	$4,250
Alabama Farm Bureau Federation	$1,250
National Farmers Orgsnization	$1,000
Norht Carolina Farm Bureau Federation	$1,000
Others	$1,000

Food & Beverage	$12,000
A E Staley Manufacturing Company	$2,250
ConAgra Inc	$1,500
Food Marketing Institute	$1,000
General Mills*	$1,000
Hardee's Food Systems	$1,000
National Beer Wholesalers Assn	$1,000
Winn-Dixie Stores	$1,000
Others	$3,250

Health Professionals	$5,500
American Medical Assn	$5,000
Others	$500

Insurance	$3,000
Jefferson-Pilot Corp	$1,000
National Assn of Life Underwriters	$1,000
Others	$1,000

Lawyers & Lobbyists	$3,250
Assn of Trial Lawyers of America	$2,000
Others	$1,250

Peanut Growers	$3,250
Alabama Peanut Producers Assn	$1,000
Southwest Peanut Membership Organization	$1,000
Others	$1,250

Real Estate	$4,500
National Assn of Realtors	$3,500
Others	$1,000

Sugar Growers	$7,000
American Crystal Sugar Corp	$3,000
Florida Sugar Cane League	$1,000
Others	$3,000

Telecommunications	$7,250
AT&T	$5,000
Southern Bell	$1,000
Others	$1,250

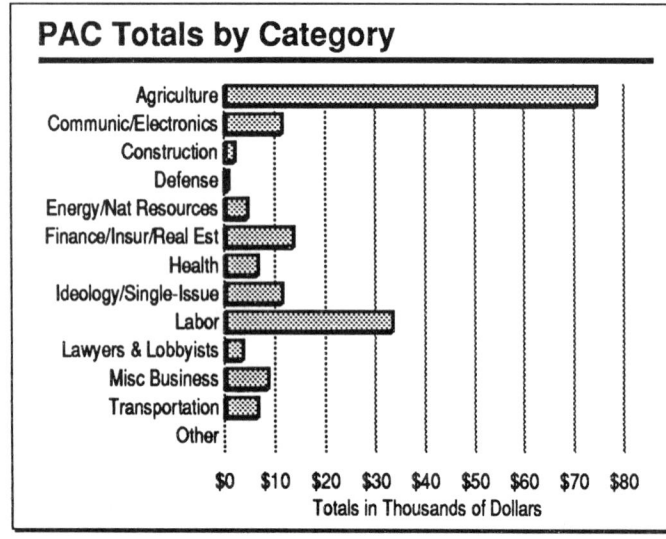

PAC Totals by Category

Agriculture
Communic/Electronics
Construction
Defense
Energy/Nat Resources
Finance/Insur/Real Est
Health
Ideology/Single-Issue
Labor
Lawyers & Lobbyists
Misc Business
Transportation
Other

$0 $10 $20 $30 $40 $50 $60 $70 $80
Totals in Thousands of Dollars

Tobacco $16,050

RJR Nabisco	$5,000
United States Tobacco Company	$3,500
Philip Morris	$2,300
Tobacco Institute	$2,000
National Assn Tobacco Distributors	$1,000
Others	$2,250

Other Major Business PACs

National Cable Television Assn	$2,000	CableTV
National Assn of Home Builders	$1,500	Resid Constr
American Assn of Crop Insurers	$1,000	Ag Svcs
Corning Glass Works	$1,000	Glass Prod
General Electric	$1,000	Electronics
Phillips Petroleum	$1,000	Major Oil

Labor

Bldg Trades/Industrial/Misc Unions $7,000

United Auto Workers	$3,250
Food & Commercial Workers Union	$1,250
Others	$2,500

Government & Postal Workers $13,750

National Assn of Letter Carriers	$5,000
National Assn of Retired Federal Employees	$5,000
American Fedn of State/County/Munic Employees	$2,000
American Postal Workers Union	$1,000
Others	$750

Teachers Unions $5,000

National Education Assn	$5,000

Transportation Unions $7,250

United Transportation Union	$3,000
Air Line Pilots Assn	$1,000
Marine Engineers District 2 Maritime Officers	$1,000
Teamsters Union	$1,000
Others	$1,250

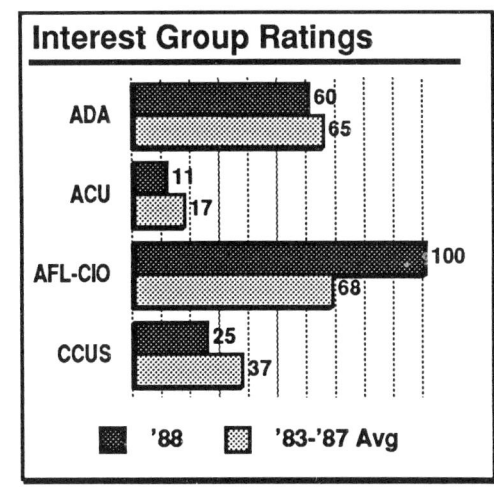

Interest Group Ratings

	'88	'83-'87 Avg
ADA	60	65
ACU	11	17
AFL-CIO	100*	68
CCUS	25	37

Ideological/Single-Issue

Pro-Israel $6,000

National PAC	$5,000
Hudson Valley PAC	$1,000

Other Major Ideological/Single-Issue PACs

National Cmte for an Effective Congress	$2,496	Dem/Liberal
Valley Education Fund (Tony Coelho)	$1,000	Dem Leaders

Independent expenditures supporting Rose

National Cmte to Preserve Social Security	$2,078

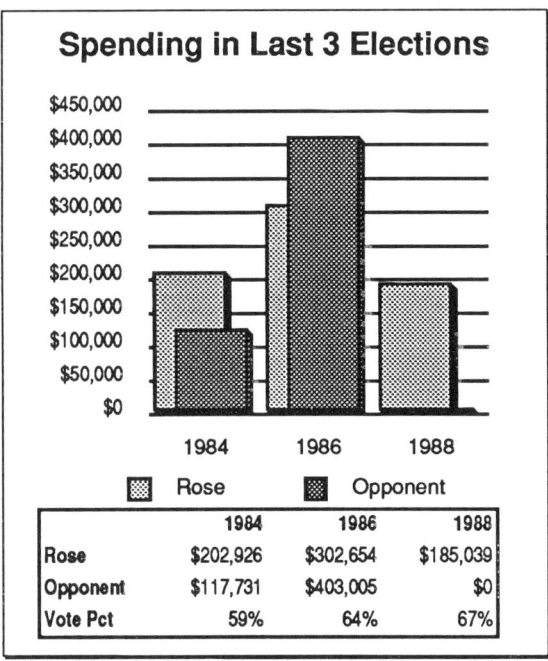

Spending in Last 3 Elections

	1984	1986	1988
Rose	$202,926	$302,654	$185,039
Opponent	$117,731	$403,005	$0
Vote Pct	59%	64%	67%

Rose   Opponent

---

* Contributions came from more than one PAC affiliated with this sponsor.

Dan Rostenkowski, D-Ill (8)

First elected: 1958
Total receipts: $866,341
Total from PACs: $433,198

1988 Committees & Subcommittees

Ways and Means (Chairman)
Trade

Joint Taxation (Vice Chairman)

PAC Contribution Profile

Business

Campaign Revenue Sources

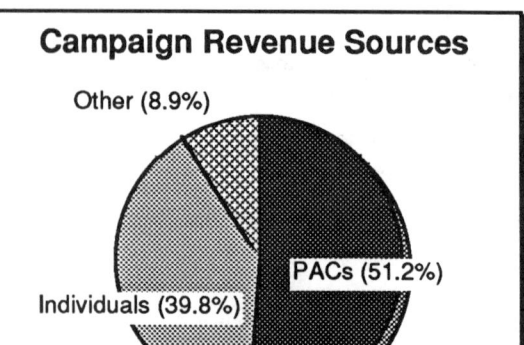

Other (8.9%)
PACs (51.2%)
Individuals (39.8%)

Automotive	**$20,500**
Auto Dealers & Drivers for Free Trade	$10,000
National Auto Dealers Assn	$5,000
Ford Motor Company	$4,000
Others	$1,500

Casinos/Gambling	**$10,000**
Circus Circus Enterprises	$5,000
Bally Manufacturing	$2,000
Others	$3,000

Commercial & Savings Banks	**$22,200**
First Chicago Corp	$5,000
Home Savings of America	$5,000
J P Morgan & Company	$5,000
American Bankers Assn	$3,000
Others	$4,200

Defense	**$16,000**
Emerson Electric	$5,000
Allied-Signal	$2,000
Rockwell International	$2,000
Others	$7,000

Electric Utilities	**$29,100**
Southern California Edison	$3,000
Middle South Utilities*	$2,500
Commonwealth Edison	$2,000
Texas Utilities Electric Company*	$2,000
Southern Company*	$1,750
Others	$17,850

Electronics & Computers	**$10,000**
General Electric	$3,000
Zenith Electronics Corp	$3,000
Others	$4,000

Food & Beverage	**$19,000**
National Beer Wholesalers Assn	$5,000
Kellogg Company	$2,000
Kraft Inc	$2,000
McDonald's Corp	$1,500
Others	$8,500

Health Professionals	**$10,500**
American Dental Assn	$5,000
Oral & Maxillofacial Surgeons	$3,000
Others	$2,500

Insurance	**$19,500**
American Family Corp	$5,000
National Assn of Life Underwriters	$3,000
TransAmerica Corp*	$2,500
Aetna Life & Casualty	$2,000
Allstate Insurance	$2,000
CNA Financial Corp	$2,000
Others	$3,000

Lawyers	**$18,100**
Assn of Trial Lawyers of America	$10,000
Kirkland & Ellis	$5,000
Others	$3,100

Oil & Gas	**$13,500**
Pacific Enterprises	$5,000
Amoco Corp	$2,000
Chevron Corp	$2,000
Others	$4,500

Railroads	**$10,000**
Union Pacific Corp	$5,000
Chicago & North Western Transport	$2,000
Illinois Central Railroad	$1,000
Kansas City Southern	$1,000
Santa Fe Southern Pacific	$1,000

Real Estate	**$12,000**
National Assn of Realtors	$10,000
Others	$2,000

PAC Totals by Category

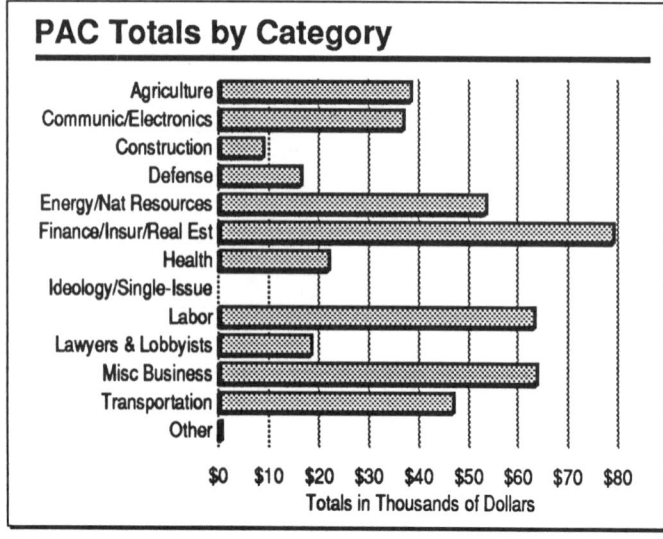

Agriculture
Communic/Electronics
Construction
Defense
Energy/Nat Resources
Finance/Insur/Real Est
Health
Ideology/Single-Issue
Labor
Lawyers & Lobbyists
Misc Business
Transportation
Other

$0 $10 $20 $30 $40 $50 $60 $70 $80
Totals in Thousands of Dollars

Retail Sales...**$12,250**

Federated Department Stores	$2,000
Sears	$2,000
Carson Pirie Scott & Company	$1,500
Others	$6,750

Securities & Commodities Investment...........**$22,500**

Chicago Mercantile Exchange	$5,000
Salomon Brothers	$5,000
Investment Company Institute	$2,500
Chicago Board of Options Exchange	$2,000
Chicago Board of Trade	$2,000
Others	$6,000

Telecommunications.................................**$14,000**

AT&T	$5,000
Illinois Bell Telephone	$4,000
Others	$5,000

Other Major Business PACs

American Health Care Assn	$5,000	Nursing Home
Federal Express Corp	$5,000	Delivery
Henley Group Inc	$5,000	Altern Energy
Household International	$5,000	Credit/Loans
MCA Inc	$5,000	Movies
National Assn of Home Builders	$5,000	Resid Constr
Navistar International	$5,000	Farm Equip
Waste Management Inc	$5,000	Waste Mgmt
Beneficial Management Corp	$3,000	Credit/Loans
United Airlines	$3,000	Airlines
Associated General Contractors	$2,500	Comml Constr
Premark International	$2,500	PlasticRubb
American Assn of Equipment Lessors	$2,000	Rentals
Archer-Daniels-Midland Corp	$2,000	Grain Trader
Associated Milk Producers	$2,000	Dairy
FMC Corp	$2,000	Chemicals
Minnesota Mining & Manufacturing (3M)	$2,000	Indust Equip
National Assn of Wholesale-Distributors	$2,000	Wholesale
Stone Container Corp	$2,000	Paper Packg
Sundstrand Corp	$2,000	AerospacePts
United States Tobacco Company	$2,000	Tobacco
Warner Communications	$2,000	Broadcast
Ernst & Whinney	$1,500	Accountants
Nalco Chemical Company	$1,500	Chemicals

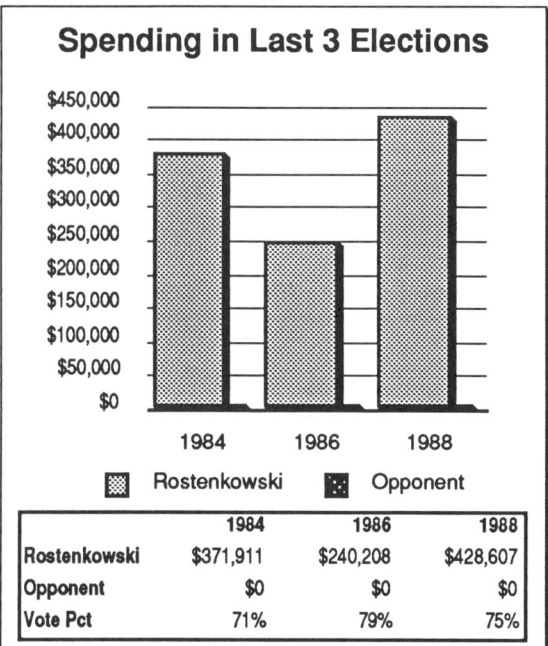

Spending in Last 3 Elections

Legend: ▨ Rostenkowski ▦ Opponent

	1984	1986	1988
Rostenkowski	$371,911	$240,208	$428,607
Opponent	$0	$0	$0
Vote Pct	71%	79%	75%

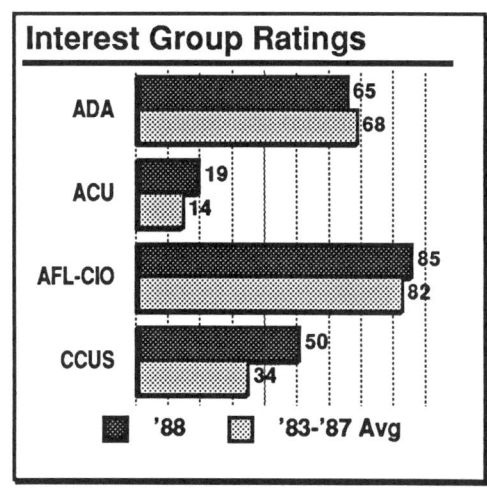

Interest Group Ratings

	'88	'83-'87 Avg
ADA	65	68
ACU	19	14
AFL-CIO	85	82
CCUS	50	34

Legend: ■ '88   ▨ '83-'87 Avg

Labor

Bldg Trades/Industrial/Misc Unions...........**$25,000**

AFL-CIO Bldg/Const Trades Dept	$6,000
Food & Commercial Workers Union	$6,000
Hotel/Restaurant Employees Union	$5,000
Carpenters & Joiners Union	$2,500
Sheet Metal Workers Union	$2,500
Others	$3,000

Government & Postal Workers...................**$10,000**

American Fedn of State/County/Munic Employees	$5,000
National Assn of Letter Carriers	$5,000

Teachers Unions..**$10,000**

National Education Assn	$10,000

Transportation Unions..............................**$18,000**

Marine Engineers District 2 Maritime Officers	$7,500
Seafarers International Union	$5,000
Teamsters Union	$5,000
Others	$500

---

* Contributions came from more than one PAC affiliated
with this sponsor.

Toby Roth, R-Wis (8)

1988 Committees & Subcommittees

First elected: 1978
Total receipts: $339,852
Total from PACs: $180,814

Banking, Finance and Urban Affairs
Economic Stabilization
Financial Institutions Supervision, Regulation and Insurance
Housing and Community Development

Foreign Affairs
International Economic Policy and Trade (Ranking Republican)
Asian and Pacific Affairs

PAC Contribution Profile

Business

Automotive	**$6,350**
Auto Dealers & Drivers for Free Trade	$3,000
National Auto Dealers Assn	$2,550
Others	$800
Chemicals	**$3,050**
FMC Corp	$2,000
Others	$1,050
Commercial Banks	**$40,900**
American Bankers Assn	$10,000
J P Morgan & Company	$5,000
Banc One Corp*	$2,750
Barnett Banks of Florida	$2,500
Citicorp	$2,500
Assn of Bank Holding Companies	$2,300
Norwest Corp	$2,000
Wisconsin Bankers Assn	$1,800
Independent Bankers Assn	$1,500
Bankers Trust	$1,000
First Chicago Corp	$1,000
Others	$8,550
Construction	**$13,000**
National Assn of Home Builders	$3,000
Associated General Contractors	$1,250
American Cement Trade Alliance	$1,000
National Concrete Masonry Assn	$1,000
Owens-Illinois	$1,000
Others	$5,750

Campaign Revenue Sources

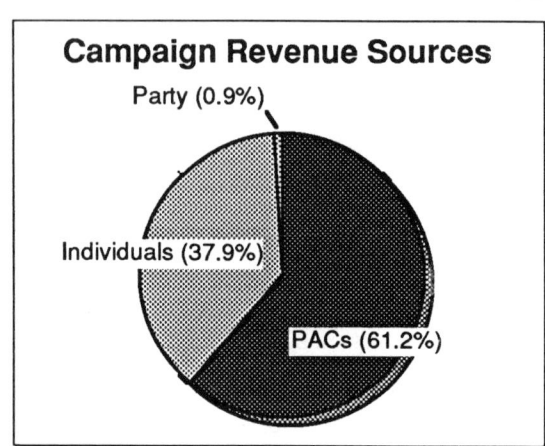

Party (0.9%)
Individuals (37.9%)
PACs (61.2%)

Consumer Credit & Loans	**$2,950**
None over $800	
Dairy	**$10,100**
Associated Milk Producers	$5,500
Land O'Lakes Inc	$2,600
Mid-American Dairymen	$1,500
Others	$500
Defense	**$7,050**
Textron Inc	$1,550
Rockwell International	$1,000
Tenneco Inc	$1,000
Others	$3,500
Electric Utilities & Equipment	**$4,725**
Combustion Engineering	$1,500
Wisconsin Electric Power Company	$1,000
Others	$2,225
Food & Beverage	**$6,900**
Nabisco Brands Inc	$3,500
Others	$3,400
Insurance	**$23,868**
Independent Insurance Agents of America	$2,406
American International Group inc	$2,400
National Assn Mutual Insurance Agents	$2,100
National Assn of Independent Insurers	$2,100
Northwestern Mutual Life	$2,050
Aid Assn for Lutherans	$1,600
Cigna Corp	$1,500
Casualty & Surety Agents Assn	$1,300
Mortgage Insurance Cos of America	$1,300
American Council of Life Insurance	$1,212
Guardian Life Insurance	$1,100
National Assn Life Companies	$1,000
Travelers Corp	$1,000
Others	$2,800

PAC Totals by Category

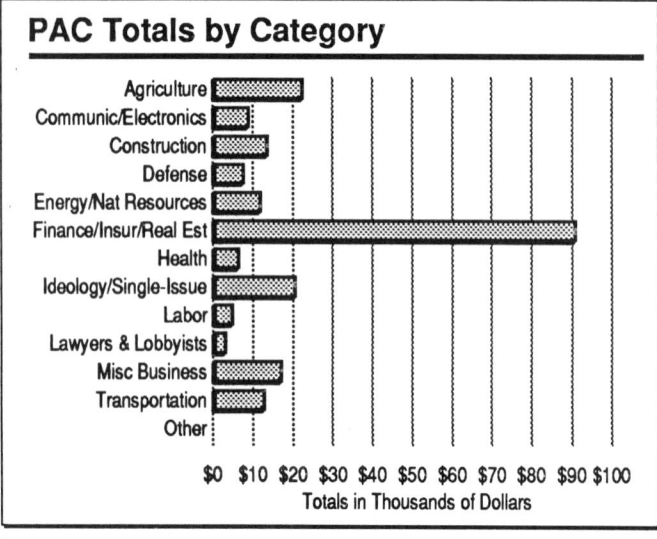

Agriculture
Communic/Electronics
Construction
Defense
Energy/Nat Resources
Finance/Insur/Real Est
Health
Ideology/Single-Issue
Labor
Lawyers & Lobbyists
Misc Business
Transportation
Other

$0 $10 $20 $30 $40 $50 $60 $70 $80 $90 $100
Totals in Thousands of Dollars

Interest Group Ratings

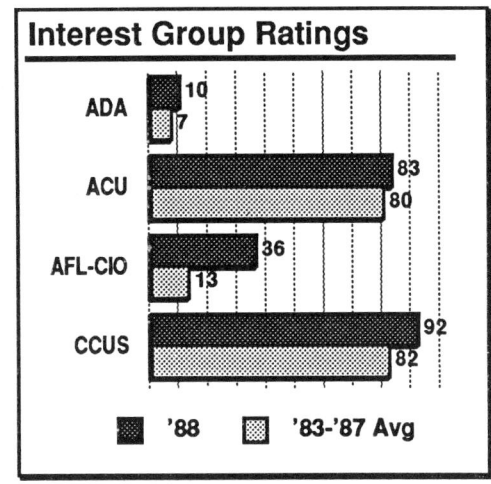

Group	'88	'83-'87 Avg
ADA	10	7
ACU	83	80
AFL-CIO	36	13
CCUS	92	82

■ '88   ▨ '83-'87 Avg

Lawyers & Lobbyists **$2,500**
    None over $600

Oil & Gas **$6,550**
    Mobil Oil $2,500
    National Propane Gas Assn $1,000
    Others $3,050

Paper Products **$4,250**
    Fort Howard Corp $1,600
    Green Bay Packaging $1,300
    International Paper Company $1,000
    Others $350

Pharmaceuticals **$3,000**
    Pfizer Inc $3,000

Real Estate **$12,692**
    National Assn of Realtors $8,292
    Mortgage Bankers Assn of America $1,800
    Metropolitan Life Insurance $1,250
    Others $1,350

Savings Banks & Credit Unions **$5,600**
    US League of Savings Assn $3,100
    Credit Union National Assn $1,300
    Others $1,200

Securities/Commodities Investment **$4,150**
    First Boston Corp $2,000
    Others $2,150

Telecommunications **$6,950**
    AT&T $1,500
    Wisconsin Bell Telephone $1,200
    Ameritech Corp $1,000
    Motorola Inc $1,000
    Telocator Network of America $1,000
    United Telecommunications $1,000
    Others $250

Other Major Business PACs

American Medical Assn	$1,800	Doctors
American Hotel & Motel Assn	$1,250	Hotel/Motel
Direct Selling Assn	$1,000	Direct Sales
Philip Morris	$1,000	Tobacco
Walt Disney Company	$1,000	Resorts

Labor

Labor Unions **$4,200**
    National Assn of Retired Federal Employees $2,000
    Teamsters Union $1,500
    Others $700

Ideological/Single-Issue

Pro-Gun Ownership **$8,000**
    National Rifle Assn $7,000
    Safari Club International $1,000

Republican/Conservative **$3,548**
    Conservative Caucus PAC $1,000
    Conservative Victory Committee $1,000
    Others $1,548

Republican Leadership PACs **$6,300**
    Catch the Spirit PAC (Bob Kasten) $5,000
    Others $1,300

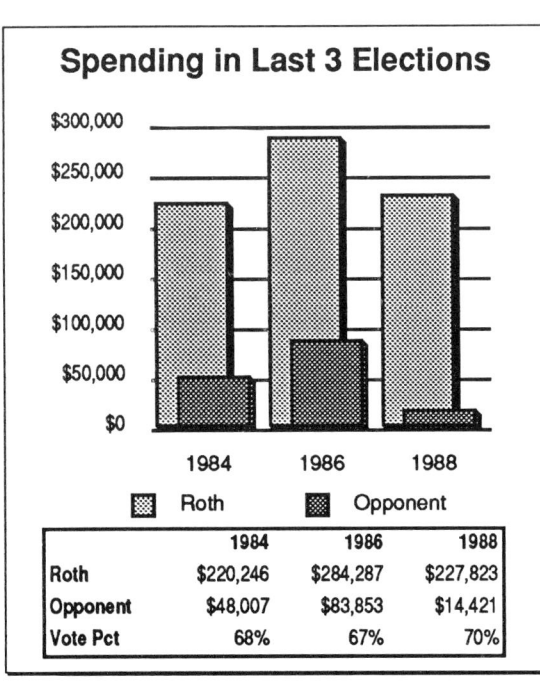

Spending in Last 3 Elections

	1984	1986	1988
Roth	$220,246	$284,287	$227,823
Opponent	$48,007	$83,853	$14,421
Vote Pct	68%	67%	70%

▨ Roth   ■ Opponent

* Contributions came from more than one PAC affiliated with this sponsor.

Marge Roukema, R-NJ (5)

1988 Committees & Subcommittees

First elected: 1980
Total receipts: $406,469
Total from PACs: $181,513

Banking, Finance and Urban Affairs
Housing and Community Development (Ranking Republican)
Financial Institutions Supervision, Regulation and Insurance
International Development Institutions and Finance

Education and Labor
Labor-Management Relations (Ranking Republican)
Elementary, Secondary and Vocational Education
Postsecondary Education

Select Hunger

PAC Contribution Profile

Business

Automotive	**$3,900**
Auto Dealers & Drivers for Free Trade	$1,500
Others	$2,400
Commercial Banks	**$23,420**
Citicorp	$4,000
American Bankers Assn	$2,500
New Jersey Bankers Assn	$2,000
Midlantic National Bank	$1,550
Barnett Banks of Florida	$1,500
Chemical Bank	$1,270
Bankers Trust	$1,000
Irving Bank	$1,000
Others	$8,600
Construction	**$27,000**
National Assn of Home Builders	$10,000
National Utility Contractors Assn	$4,000
National Electrical Contractors Assn	$2,000
Westvaco Corp	$1,500
Associated Builders & Contractors	$1,200
Manufactured Housing Institute	$1,150
National Concrete Masonry Assn	$1,000
Others	$6,150
Consumer Credit & Loans	**$2,700**
None over $900	
Electric Utilities	**$3,800**
Orange & Rockland Utilities	$1,800
Public Service Electric & Gas	$1,100
Others	$900

Campaign Revenue Sources

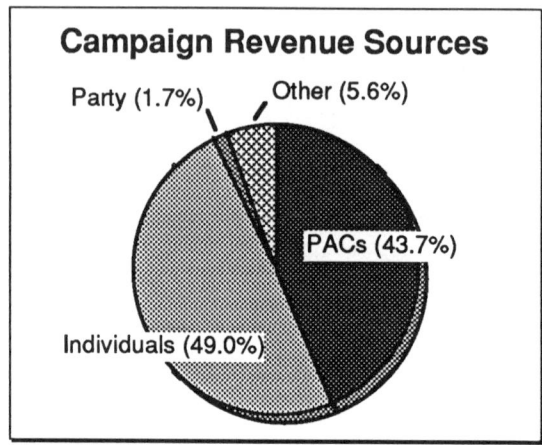

Party (1.7%)
Other (5.6%)
PACs (43.7%)
Individuals (49.0%)

Food & Beverage	**$6,650**
Food Marketing Institute	$1,100
S & A Restaurant Corp	$1,000
Others	$4,550
Health Professionals	**$6,440**
American Medical Assn	$2,800
Oral & Maxillofacial Surgeons	$1,500
Others	$2,140
Industrial Equipment & Materials	**$2,800**
Borg-Warner	$1,100
Others	$1,700
Insurance	**$10,550**
National Assn of Life Underwriters	$1,300
Travelers Corp	$1,000
Others	$8,250
Lawyers & Lobbyists	**$2,850**
None over $600	
Oil & Gas	**$2,200**
Amoco Corp	$1,100
Others	$1,100
Pharmaceuticals	**$8,850**
Sandoz Pharmaceuticals	$1,400
Hoffman-La Roche	$1,200
Sterling Drug	$1,200
Johnson & Johnson	$1,000
Schering-Plough Corp	$1,000
Others	$3,050
Real Estate	**$10,176**
National Assn of Realtors	$5,600
Mortgage Bankers Assn of America	$1,500
Federal National Mortgage Assn	$1,200
Others	$1,876

PAC Totals by Category

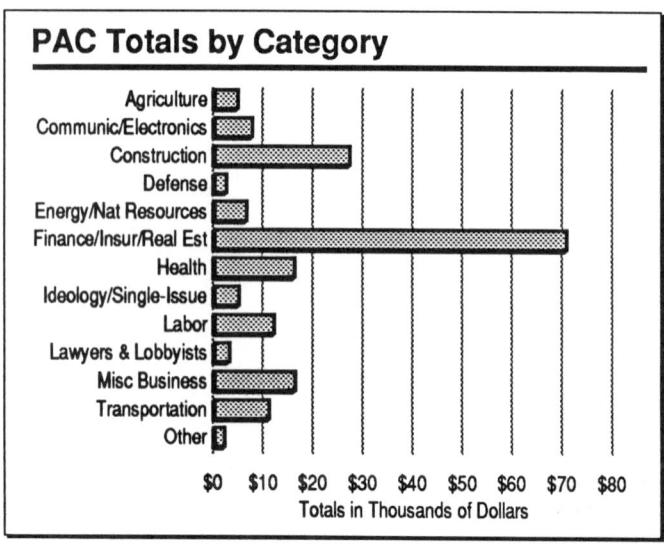

Agriculture
Communic/Electronics
Construction
Defense
Energy/Nat Resources
Finance/Insur/Real Est
Health
Ideology/Single-Issue
Labor
Lawyers & Lobbyists
Misc Business
Transportation
Other

$0 $10 $20 $30 $40 $50 $60 $70 $80
Totals in Thousands of Dollars

Savings Banks & Credit Unions $12,650

SAPEC/ NJ (New Jersey Savings Assn) $3,000
Credit Union National Assn $2,300
US League of Savings Assn $1,400
National Council of Savings Institutions $1,100
Howard Savings Bank $1,000
Others $3,850

Securities Investment $11,000

Goldman Sachs $2,500
Municipal Savings Industry $1,200
Donaldson, Lufkin & Jenrette $1,000
First Boston Corp $1,000
Morgan Stanley & Company $1,000
Others $4,300

Telecommunications $6,800

AT&T $2,000
New Jersey Bell Telephone $1,600
Penn Central Corp $1,200
Others $2,000

Textiles/Fibers $2,100

Hoechst Celanese Corp $1,000
Others $1,100

Trucking & Freight $3,000

United Parcel Service $1,200
Others $1,800

Other Major Business PACs

Texas Air	$1,600	Airlines
Bowling Proprietors Assn	$1,300	AmuseCtr
United Technologies	$1,200	Air Defense
International Paper Company	$1,000	Paper Prod
National Assn of Temporary Services ...	$1,000	EmployAgency
National Assn of Trade/Tech Schools ...	$1,000	Voc Tech

Interest Group Ratings

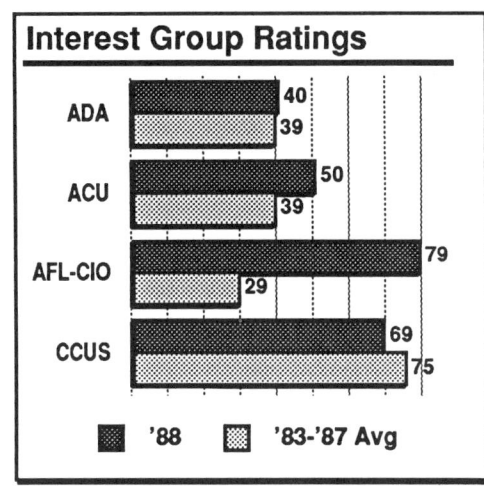

Labor

Government & Postal Workers $5,400

National Assn of Retired Federal Employees $3,000
American Fedn of State/County/Munic Employees $1,500
Others $900

Transportation Unions $6,000

Air Line Pilots Assn $3,500
Marine Engineers Union $1,000
Teamsters Union $1,000
Others $500

Ideological/Single-Issue

Ideological/Single-Issue $4,250

Armenian-American PAC	$1,000	Ethnic
KidsPAC	$1,000	HealthWelfare
Others	$2,250	

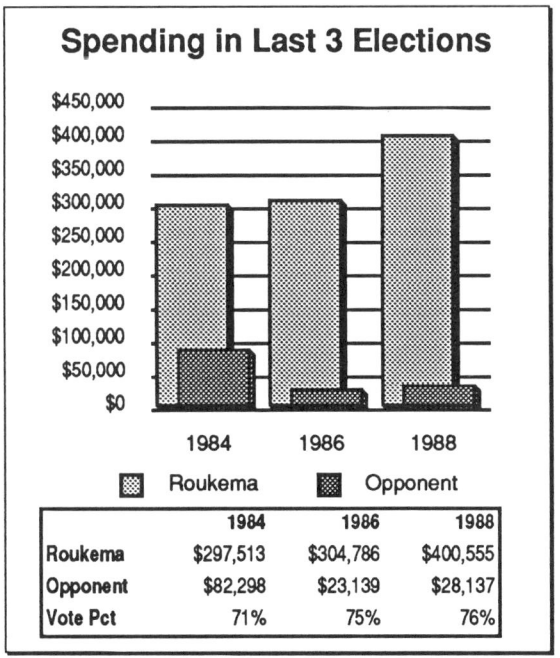

Spending in Last 3 Elections

	1984	1986	1988
Roukema	$297,513	$304,786	$400,555
Opponent	$82,298	$23,139	$28,137
Vote Pct	71%	75%	76%

J. Roy Rowland, D-Ga (8)

First elected: 1982
Total receipts: $261,545
Total from PACs: $127,637

1988 Committees & Subcommittees

Public Works and Transportation
Aviation Investigations and Oversight
Surface Transportation

Veterans' Affairs
Hospitals and Health Care
Housing and Memorial Affairs

Select Children, Youth and Families

PAC Contribution Profile

Business

Automotive	**$5,900**
National Auto Dealers Assn	$3,100
Auto Dealers & Drivers for Free Trade	$2,500
Others	$300
Aviation & Aerospace	**$8,650**
Eastern Airlines	$1,700
Boeing Company	$1,100
Long Island Aerospace PAC	$1,000
Others	$4,850
Commercial Banks	**$3,900**
Citizens & Southern National Bank	$1,950
Others	$1,950
Construction	**$5,500**
National Assn of Home Builders	$1,800
Associated General Contractors	$1,300
Others	$2,400
Defense Aerospace	**$2,600**
Lockheed Corp	$2,000
Others	$600
Electric Utilities	**$3,100**
Southern Company*	$1,500
Others	$1,600

Campaign Revenue Sources

Other (10.5%)
PACs (45.7%)
Individuals (43.6%)

Health Professionals	**$17,800**
American Medical Assn	$10,250
American Dental Assn	$1,500
American Podiatry Assn	$1,500
American Academy of Ophthalmology	$1,000
American College of Emergency Physicians	$1,000
Cmte for Quality Orthopedic Health Care	$1,000
Georgia Medical Assn	$1,000
Others	$550
Insurance	**$3,950**
National Assn of Life Underwriters	$1,000
Others	$2,950
Real Estate	**$6,900**
National Assn of Realtors	$6,300
Others	$600
Telecommunications	**$5,250**
Southern Bell	$3,000
Continental Telecom	$1,500
Others	$750
Tobacco	**$4,500**
RJR Nabisco	$2,500
Others	$2,000
Trucking & Freight	**$4,300**
United Parcel Service	$2,900
Others	$1,400

Other Major Business PACs

Associated Milk Producers	$1,000	Dairy
Holiday Inns	$1,000	Hotel/Motel
King & Spalding	$1,000	Lawyers

PAC Totals by Category

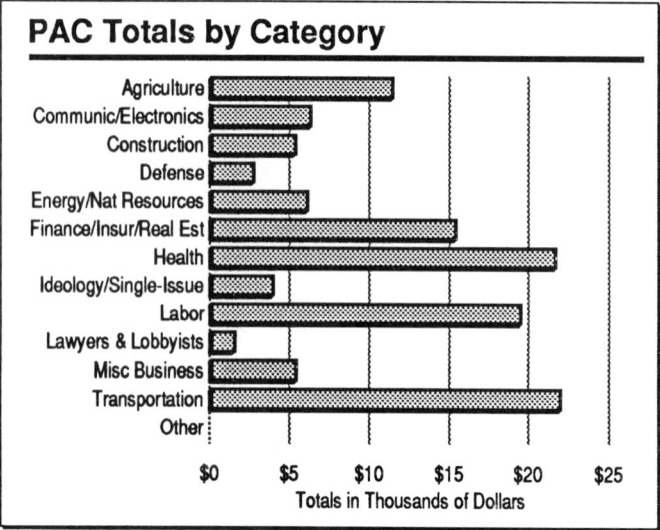

Agriculture
Communic/Electronics
Construction
Defense
Energy/Nat Resources
Finance/Insur/Real Est
Health
Ideology/Single-Issue
Labor
Lawyers & Lobbyists
Misc Business
Transportation
Other

$0 $5 $10 $15 $20 $25
Totals in Thousands of Dollars

Labor

Government & Postal Workers ***$7,700***
    National Assn of Retired Federal Employees $5,000
    National Assn of Letter Carriers $1,650
    Others $1,050

Other Unions ***$11,650***
    Air Line Pilots Assn $5,000
    United Transportation Union $2,600
    Marine Engineers District 2 Maritime Officers $1,000
    Others $3,050

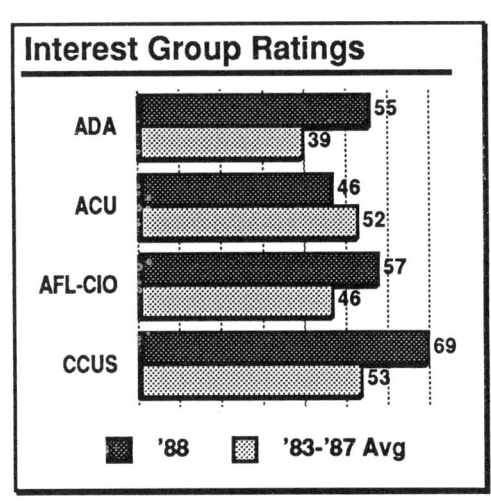

Interest Group Ratings

Group	'88	'83–'87 Avg
ADA	55	39
ACU	46	52
AFL-CIO	57	46
CCUS	69	53

Ideological/Single-Issue

Democratic Leadership PACs ***$3,000***
    Conservative Democratic PAC (Charles Stenholm) $2,000
    Valley Education Fund (Tony Coelho) $1,000

Independent expenditures supporting Rowland

American Medical Assn $2,000
National Cmte to Preserve Social Security $1,104

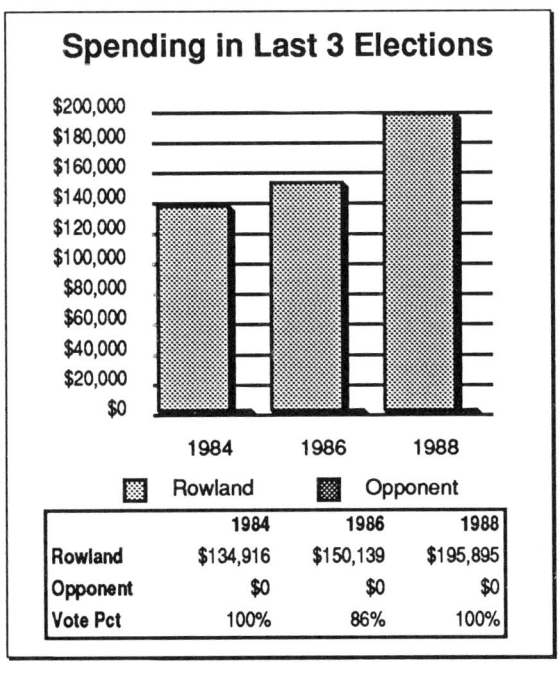

Spending in Last 3 Elections

	1984	1986	1988
Rowland	$134,916	$150,139	$195,895
Opponent	$0	$0	$0
Vote Pct	100%	86%	100%

John G. Rowland, R-Conn (5)

First elected: 1984
Total receipts: $440,084
Total from PACs: $147,635

1988 Committees & Subcommittees

Armed Services
Procurement and Military Nuclear Systems
Readiness

Veterans' Affairs
Hospitals and Health Care
Housing and Memorial Affairs

PAC Contribution Profile

Business

Auto Dealers	**$6,750**
National Auto Dealers Assn	$5,250
Auto Dealers & Drivers for Free Trade	$1,500
Chemicals & Plastics	**$2,750**
Dow Chemical/Eastern Employees	$1,000
Dow Corning Corp/Employees	$1,000
Others	$750
Commercial & Savings Banks	**$4,750**
Connecticut Bankers Assn	$1,250
Hartford National Corp	$1,000
Others	$2,500
Construction	**$4,550**
Associated General Contractors	$1,300
National Assn of Home Builders	$1,000
Others	$2,250
Defense	**$24,800**
United Technologies	$2,700
Lockheed Corp	$2,500
AT&T	$2,000
Textron Inc	$2,000
UNC Inc	$1,300
General Dynamics	$1,250
Northrop Corp	$1,250
ITT Corp	$1,000
McDonnell Douglas*	$1,000
Others	$9,800

Campaign Revenue Sources

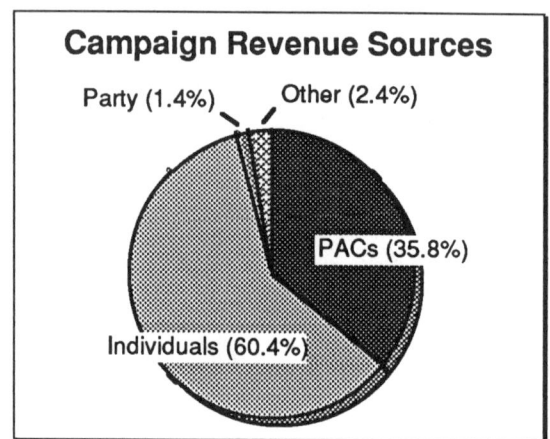

Party (1.4%)   Other (2.4%)
PACs (35.8%)
Individuals (60.4%)

Food & Beverage	**$5,125**
National Restaurant Assn	$1,000
Others	$4,125
Forest Products	**$5,400**
Westvaco Corp	$4,500
Others	$900
Health Professionals	**$6,900**
American Medical Assn	$2,250
American Academy of Ophthalmology	$2,000
American Dental Assn	$1,000
Others	$1,650
Insurance	**$26,249**
Independent Insurance Agents of America	$10,249
Insurance Assn of Connecticut	$5,000
National Assn of Life Underwriters	$4,500
National Assn Mutual Insurance Agents	$2,800
Others	$3,700
Oil & Gas	**$4,300**
Petroleum Marketers Assn	$2,000
Others	$2,300
Real Estate	**$6,250**
National Assn of Realtors	$5,500
Others	$750
Tobacco	**$5,100**
United States Tobacco Company	$4,250
Others	$850
Trucking & Freight	**$2,850**
United Parcel Service	$2,250
Others	$600

PAC Totals by Category

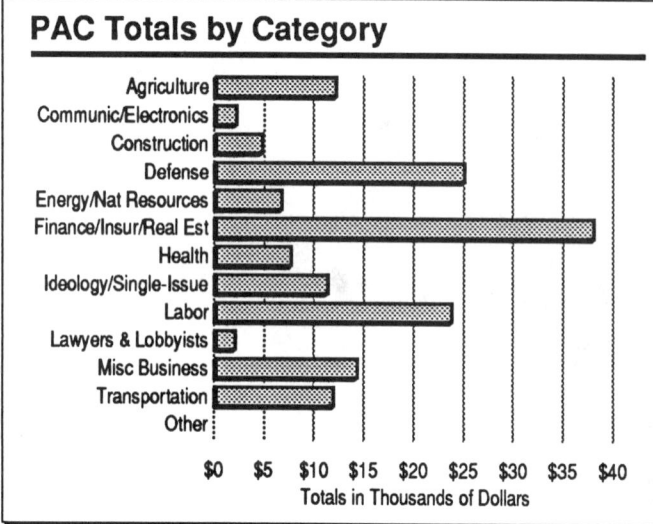

Agriculture
Communic/Electronics
Construction
Defense
Energy/Nat Resources
Finance/Insur/Real Est
Health
Ideology/Single-Issue
Labor
Lawyers & Lobbyists
Misc Business
Transportation
Other

$0 $5 $10 $15 $20 $25 $30 $35 $40
Totals in Thousands of Dollars

Other Major Business PACs

National Assn of Temporary Services ....$1,000   EmployAgency

Labor

Bldg Trades/Industrial/Misc Unions $5,800
Carpenters & Joiners Union $1,500
Connecticut Union of Telephone Workers $1,500
Ironworkers Union $1,000
Operating Engineers Union $1,000
Others $800

Teachers Unions $2,750
National Education Assn $2,750

Transportation Unions $15,000
Teamsters Union $10,000
Air Line Pilots Assn $2,000
Marine Engineers Union* $2,000
Seafarers International Union $1,000

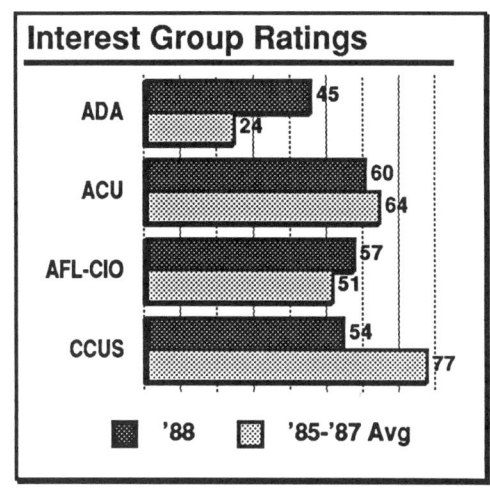

Ideological/Single-Issue

Pro-Israel $7,800
National PAC $5,000
Hudson Valley PAC $2,800

Other Major Ideological/Single-Issue PACs
GOP-5 Committee .... $1,100   Repub/Conser

Independent expenditures supporting Rowland
National Cmte to Preserve Social Security $4,240

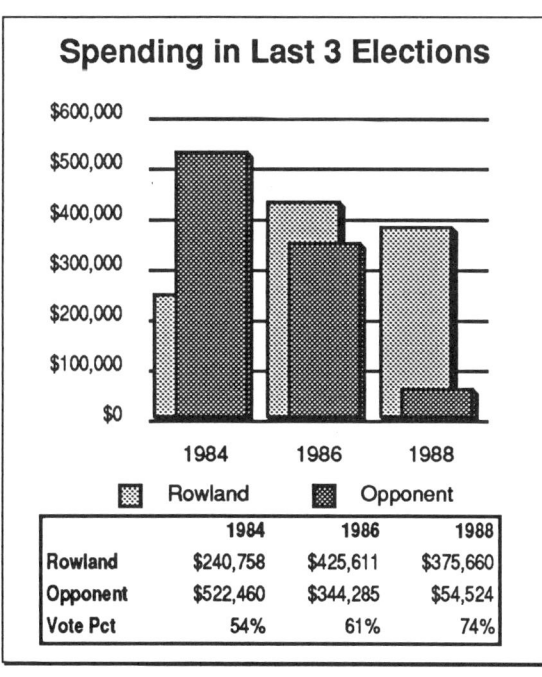

Spending in Last 3 Elections

	1984	1986	1988
Rowland	$240,758	$425,611	$375,660
Opponent	$522,460	$344,285	$54,524
Vote Pct	54%	61%	74%

---

* Contributions came from more than one PAC affiliated
with this sponsor.

Edward R. Roybal, D-Calif (25)

First elected: 1962
Total receipts: $86,724
Total from PACs: $46,800

1988 Committees & Subcommittees

Appropriations
Treasury, Postal Service and General Government (Chairman)
Labor, Health and Human Services, Education and Related Agencies

Select Aging (Chairman)
Retirement Income and Employment (Chairman)

PAC Contribution Profile
Business

Food & Beverage $1,500
    National Beer Wholesalers Assn $1,000
    McDonald's Corp $500

Fruit & Vegetable Growers $1,500
    Sunkist Growers $1,000
    California Almond Growers Exchange $500

Health Professionals $7,850
    American Medical Assn $3,500
    American Dental Assn $3,000
    American Society of Consultant Pharmacist $500
    Cmte for Quality Orthopedic Health Care $500
    Others $350

Import Auto Dealers $2,500
    Auto Dealers & Drivers for Free Trade $2,500

Real Estate $3,000
    National Assn of Realtors $3,000

Telecommunications $1,500
    AT&T $750
    Penn Central Corp $500
    Others $250

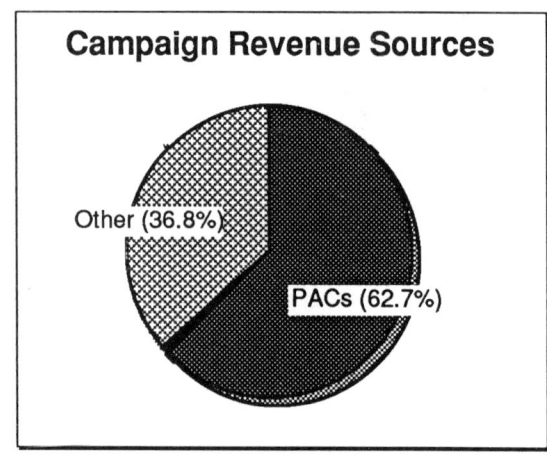

Campaign Revenue Sources

Other (36.8%)
PACs (62.7%)

Other Major Business PACs

Associated Milk Producers	$1,000	Dairy
National Assn of Social Workers	$1,000	Social Work
National Assn of Trade/Tech Schools	$1,000	Voc Tech
Xerox Corp	$1,000	Off Machines
Pacific Enterprises	$800	Natural Gas
Allied-Signal	$500	Air Defense
American Veterinary Medical Assn	$500	Veterinary
American Bankers Assn	$500	Comml Banks
Assn of Trial Lawyers of America	$500	Lawyers
BankAmerica	$500	Comml Banks
Hallmark Cards	$500	Publishing
MCA Inc	$500	Movies
TransAmerica Life Companies	$500	Life Insurance
United Parcel Service	$500	Delivery

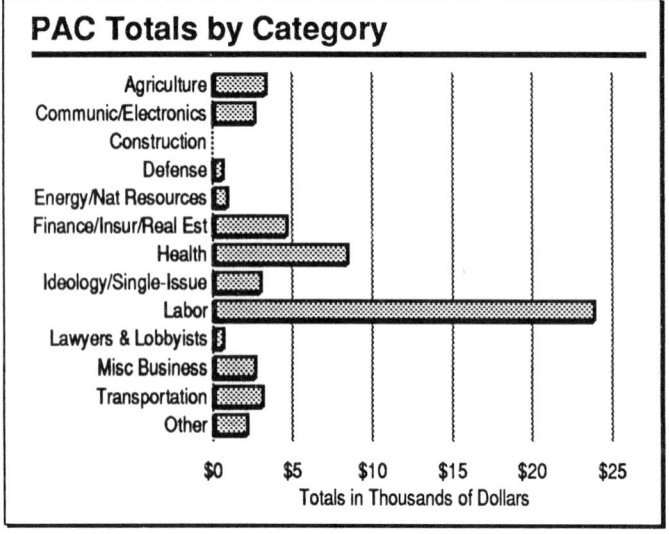

PAC Totals by Category

Categories: Agriculture, Communic/Electronics, Construction, Defense, Energy/Nat Resources, Finance/Insur/Real Est, Health, Ideology/Single-Issue, Labor, Lawyers & Lobbyists, Misc Business, Transportation, Other

Totals in Thousands of Dollars ($0, $5, $10, $15, $20, $25)

Labor

Bldg Trades/Industrial/Misc Unions $8,000
Laborers' Western Political League $2,000
Machinists/Aerospace Workers Union $1,500
Food & Commercial Workers Union $1,000
Operating Engineers Union $1,000
Seafarers International Union $1,000
United Auto Workers $1,000
Intl Brotherhood of Electrical Workers $500

Government & Postal Workers $11,200
National Assn of Letter Carriers $5,000
National Assn of Retired Federal Employees $5,000
American Postal Workers Union $1,000
Others $200

Teachers Unions $4,500
National Education Assn $4,500

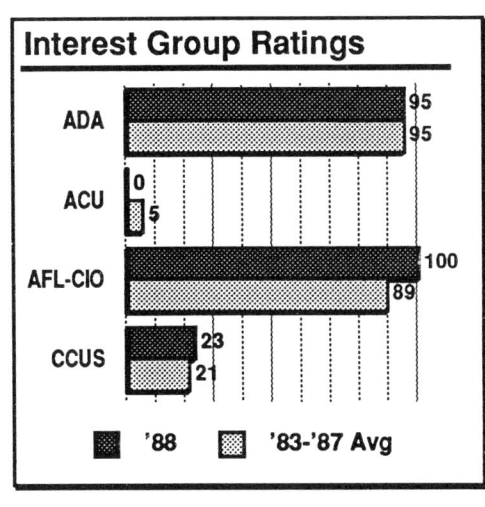

Interest Group Ratings

	'88	'83-'87 Avg
ADA	95	95
ACU	0	5
AFL-CIO	100	89
CCUS	23	21

Ideological/Single-Issue

Ideological/Single-Issue $2,870
Human Rights Campaign Fund .... $2,000   Gay/Lesbian
Women's Pro-Israel National PAC .... $500   Pro-Israel
Others $370

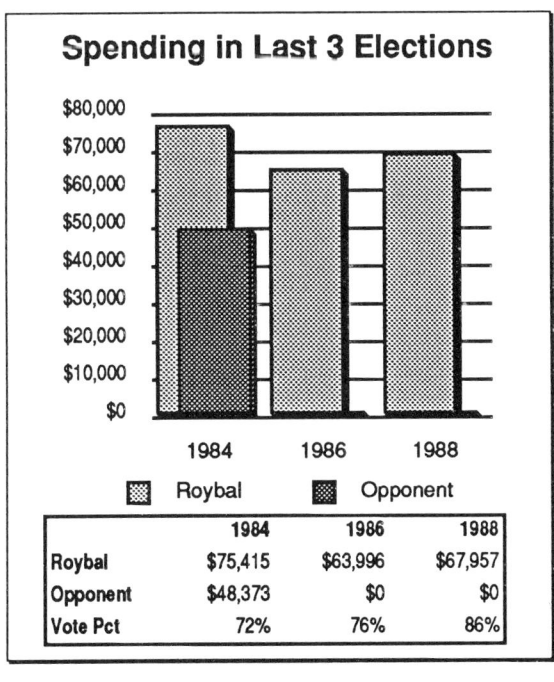

Spending in Last 3 Elections

	1984	1986	1988
Roybal	$75,415	$63,996	$67,957
Opponent	$48,373	$0	$0
Vote Pct	72%	76%	86%

Marty Russo, D-Ill (3)

First elected: 1974
Total receipts: $558,458
Total from PACs: $357,996

1988 Committees & Subcommittees

Budget
Income Security (Chairman)
Defense and International Affairs
Economic and Trade Policy

Ways and Means
Trade

PAC Contribution Profile

Business

Accountants	**$8,500**
American Institute of CPA's	$5,500
Others	$3,000
Automotive	**$6,500**
National Auto Dealers Assn	$3,000
Chrysler Corp	$1,500
Ford Motor Company	$1,500
Others	$500
Broadcasting/Entertainment	**$11,500**
Motion Picture Assn of America	$3,500
MCA Inc	$2,000
Warner Communications	$2,000
Others	$4,000
Casinos/Gambling	**$3,500**
Nevada Resort Assn	$2,000
Others	$1,500
Commodities/Securities Trading	**$31,000**
Chicago Board of Trade	$10,000
Chicago Mercantile Exchange	$10,000
Chicago Board of Options Exchange	$3,000
Investment Company Institute	$1,500
Others	$6,500
Consumer Credit & Loans	**$3,500**
American Express	$1,500
Household International	$1,500
Others	$500

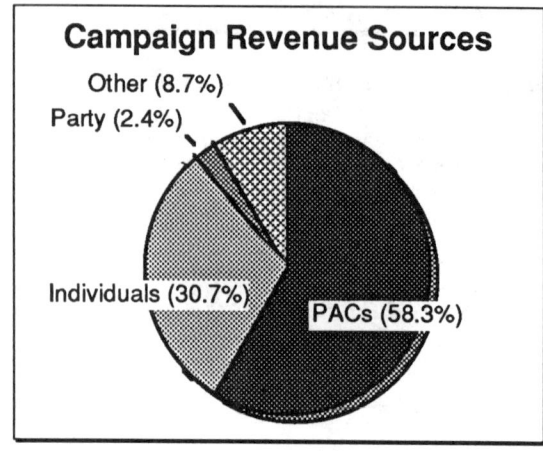

Campaign Revenue Sources

Other (8.7%)
Party (2.4%)
Individuals (30.7%)
PACs (58.3%)

Defense	**$4,500**
United Technologies	$1,500
Others	$3,000
Electric Utilities	**$3,500**
Commonwealth Edison	$1,500
Others	$2,000
Financial Institutions	**$13,750**
Talman Home Federal Savings & Loan	$2,750
Credit Union National Assn	$2,500
US League of Savings Assn	$2,500
Continental Illinois Corp	$1,500
Others	$4,500
Food & Beverage	**$12,500**
National Beer Wholesalers Assn	$3,000
Joseph E Seagram & Sons	$1,500
Wine & Spirits Wholesalers of America	$1,500
Others	$6,500
Health Professionals	**$11,550**
American Dental Assn	$4,000
Oral & Maxillofacial Surgeons	$1,500
American College of Emergency Physicians	$1,100
Others	$4,950
Insurance	**$41,200**
National Assn of Life Underwriters	$7,500
Torchmark Corp	$4,500
Massachusetts Mutual Life Insurance	$3,000
Aetna Life & Casualty	$2,500
CNA Financial Corp	$2,000
Blue Cross & Blue Shield Assn	$1,500
Cigna Corp	$1,500
Kemper Insurance	$1,500
New England Mutual Life	$1,500
Others	$15,700
Lawyers & Lobbyists	**$10,250**
Assn of Trial Lawyers of America	$5,000
Others	$5,250
Oil & Gas	**$5,300**
None over $1,000	
Real Estate	**$9,000**
National Assn of Realtors	$6,000
JMB Realty Corp	$2,000
Others	$1,000

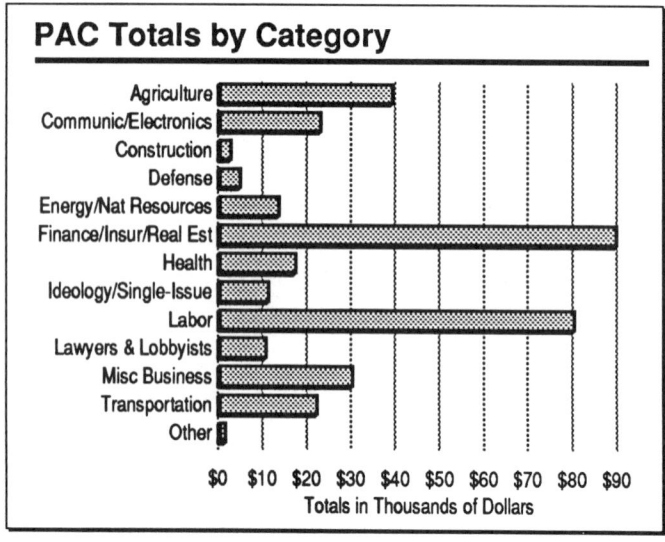

PAC Totals by Category

Agriculture
Communic/Electronics
Construction
Defense
Energy/Nat Resources
Finance/Insur/Real Est
Health
Ideology/Single-Issue
Labor
Lawyers & Lobbyists
Misc Business
Transportation
Other

$0 $10 $20 $30 $40 $50 $60 $70 $80 $90
Totals in Thousands of Dollars

Telecommunications *$9,000*
    AT&T $4,500
    Illinois Bell Telephone $3,000
    Others $1,500

Tobacco *$5,250*
    Philip Morris $4,500
    Others $750

Trucking & Freight *$5,800*
    United Parcel Service $2,800
    Consolidated Freightways $1,500
    American Trucking Assns $1,000
    Others $500

Venture Capital *$5,000*
    National Venture Capital Assn $5,000

Other Major Business PACs

American Assn of Equipment Lessors	$2,500	Rentals
Waste Management Inc	$2,000	Waste Mgmt
Marriott Corp	$1,500	Hotel/Motel
Mid-American Dairymen	$1,500	Dairy
United Airlines	$1,500	Airlines
American Hospital Assn	$1,250	Hospitals
American Horse Council	$1,000	Livestock

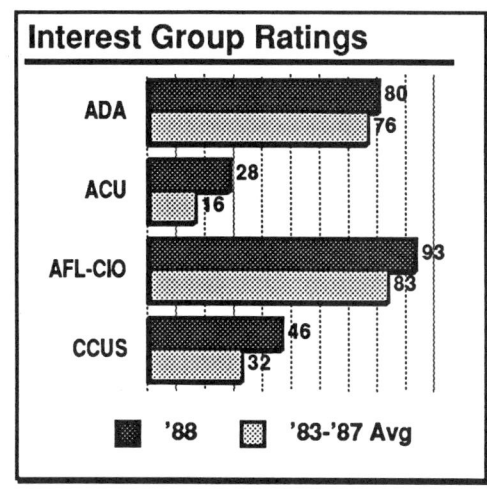

Interest Group Ratings

	'88	'83-'87 Avg
ADA	80	76
ACU	28	16
AFL-CIO	93	83
CCUS	46	32

Labor

Bldg Trades/Industrial/Misc Unions *$33,950*
    United Auto Workers $6,000
    Hotel/Restaurant Employees Union $5,500
    Carpenters & Joiners Union $3,500
    Intl Brotherhood of Electrical Workers $3,000
    AFL-CIO* $2,500
    Food & Commercial Workers Union $2,500
    Laborers' Political League $2,500
    Operating Engineers Union $2,000
    Others $6,450

Government & Postal Workers *$18,550*
    National Assn of Retired Federal Employees $7,000
    American Fedn of State/County/Munic Employees $5,000
    International Assn of Firefighters $1,500
    National Treasury Employees Union $1,500
    American Postal Workers Union $1,250
    Others $2,300

Teachers Unions *$11,000*
    National Education Assn $9,000
    American Federation of Teachers $2,000

Transportation Unions *$16,300*
    Teamsters Union $5,000
    Air Line Pilots Assn $3,500
    Marine Engineers Union* $3,000
    Seafarers International Union $2,000
    Others $2,800

Ideological/Single-Issue

Ideological/Single-Issue *$10,823*

National Cmte to Preserve Social Security	$5,000	Soc Secur
Valley Education Fund (Tony Coelho)	$3,000	Dem Leaders
Others	$2,823	

Independent expenditures supporting Russo

National Cmte to Preserve Social Security $4,272

---

* Contributions came from more than one PAC affiliated
  with this sponsor.

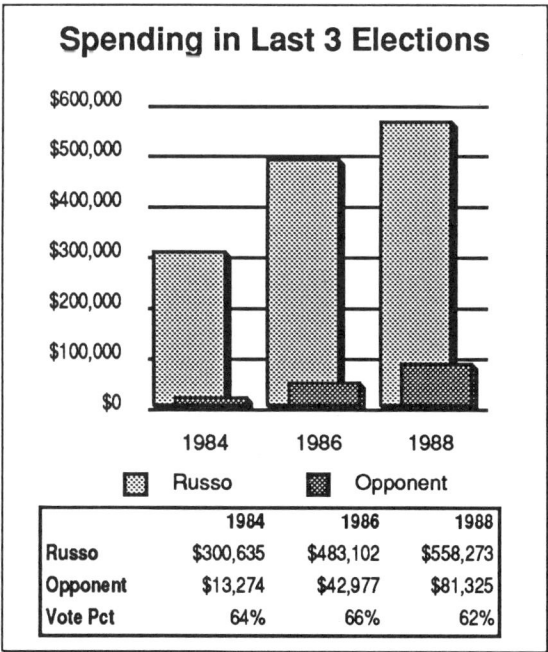

Spending in Last 3 Elections

	Russo	Opponent

	1984	1986	1988
Russo	$300,635	$483,102	$558,273
Opponent	$13,274	$42,977	$81,325
Vote Pct	64%	66%	62%

Martin Olav Sabo, D-Minn (5)

First elected: 1978
Total receipts: $363,965
Total from PACs: $237,550

1988 Committees & Subcommittees

Appropriations
Defense
HUD-Independent Agencies
Transportation and Related Agencies

Budget
Budget Process
Human Resources

PAC Contribution Profile

Business

Air Transport/Air Freight **$8,450**

Federal Express Corp	$3,000
Texas Air	$2,000
Aircraft Owners & Pilots Assn	$1,000
Northwest Airlines	$1,000
Others	$1,450

Construction **$3,600**

National Assn of Home Builders	$2,700
Others	$900

Dairy **$7,500**

Associated Milk Producers	$4,000
Land O'Lakes Inc	$2,000
Mid-American Dairymen	$1,000
Others	$500

Defense **$47,300**

AT&T	$7,500
Hughes Aircraft	$3,000
Northrop Corp	$3,000
McDonnell Douglas*	$2,750
General Dynamics	$2,000
Grumman	$2,000
Textron Inc	$2,000
FMC Corp	$1,700
Bath Iron Works	$1,500
General Electric	$1,500
LTV Aerospace & Defense Company	$1,500
United Technologies	$1,500
Honeywell Inc*	$1,100
Beech Aircraft	$1,000

(Continued in next column)

PAC Totals by Category

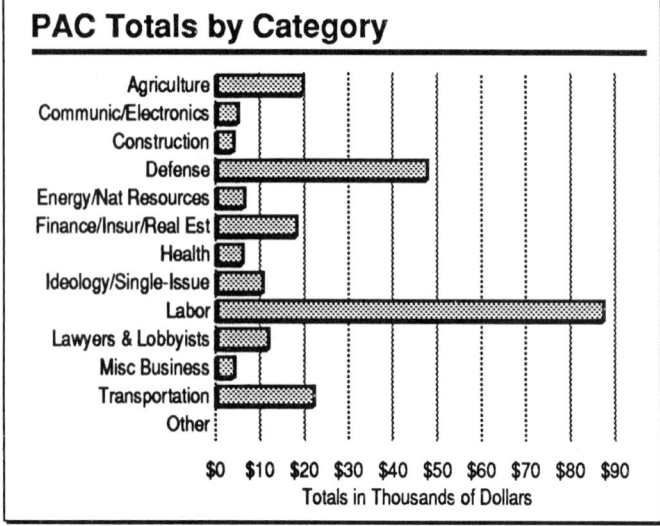

Totals in Thousands of Dollars

Campaign Revenue Sources

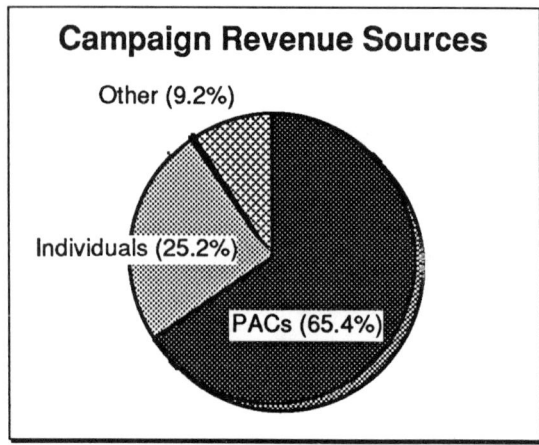

Other (9.2%)
Individuals (25.2%)
PACs (65.4%)

Defense (cont'd)

Boeing Company	$1,000
E-Systems/Corporate Division	$1,000
Emerson Electric	$1,000
General Motors	$1,000
Lockheed Corp	$1,000
Martin Marietta Corp	$1,000
Raytheon	$1,000
Rockwell International	$1,000
TRW Inc	$1,000
Unisys Corp	$1,000
Westinghouse Electric	$1,000
Others	$4,250

Electric Utilities & Equipment **$3,000**

ACRE (Action Committee for Rural Electrification)	$1,000
Northern States Power Company	$1,000
Others	$1,000

Financial Institutions **$7,100**

Norwest Corp	$2,150
Credit Union National Assn	$1,500
US League of Savings Assns	$1,150
American Bankers Assn	$1,000
Others	$1,300

Food & Beverage **$3,000**

Minnesota Beer Wholesalers Assn	$1,000
Others	$2,000

Health Professionals **$3,400**

American Optometric Assn	$1,000
Others	$2,400

Lawyers & Lobbyists **$11,395**

Assn of Trial Lawyers of America	$2,250
Faegre & Benson	$2,000
Holmes & Graven	$1,700
Akin, Gump, Hauer & Feld	$1,500
Dorsey, Windhorst, et al	$1,025
Hill & Knowlton	$1,000
Others	$1,920

Real Estate **$6,750**

National Assn of Realtors	$5,500
Mortgage Bankers Assn of America	$1,000
Others	$250

Sugar Growers *$7,550*

    American Crystal Sugar Corp $2,500
    Southern Minnesota Beet Sugar Co-op $2,500
    American Sugarbeet Growers Assn $1,000
    Others $1,550

Telecommunications *$3,000*

    North Western Bell Telephone $2,500
    Others $500

Trucking/Delivery *$6,390*

    United Parcel Service $2,850
    Minnesota Truck Operators $1,700
    American Trucking Assns $1,540
    Others $300

Other Major Business PACs

Philip Morris	$1,500	Tobacco
American Bus Assn	$1,000	Bus Svcs
Ashland Oil	$1,000	Refine/Mktg
Boat Owners Assn of the US	$1,000	Rec Boats
Coastal Corp	$1,000	Natural Gas
CSX Transportation Inc	$1,000	Railroads
National Auto Dealers Assn	$1,000	Auto Sales

Labor

Bldg Trades/Industrial/Misc Unions *$26,525*

    United Auto Workers $5,000
    Carpenters & Joiners Union $3,000
    Intl Brotherhood of Electrical Workers* $2,500
    AFL-CIO* $2,000
    Sheet Metal Workers Union $2,000
    Laborers' Political League $1,500
    Operating Engineers Union $1,500
    Machinists/Aerospace Workers Union $1,200
    Communications Workers of America $1,000
    Food & Commercial Workers Union $1,000
    Ladies Garment Workers Union $1,000
    United Steelworkers $1,000
    Others $3,825

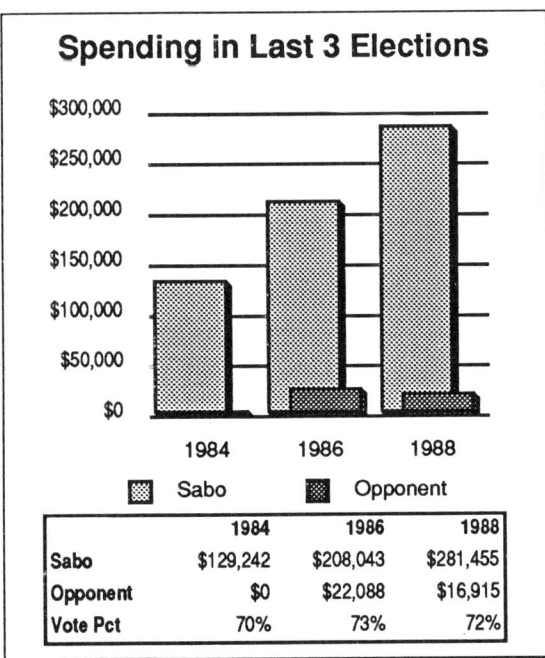

Spending in Last 3 Elections

	1984	1986	1988
Sabo	$129,242	$208,043	$281,455
Opponent	$0	$22,088	$16,915
Vote Pct	70%	73%	72%

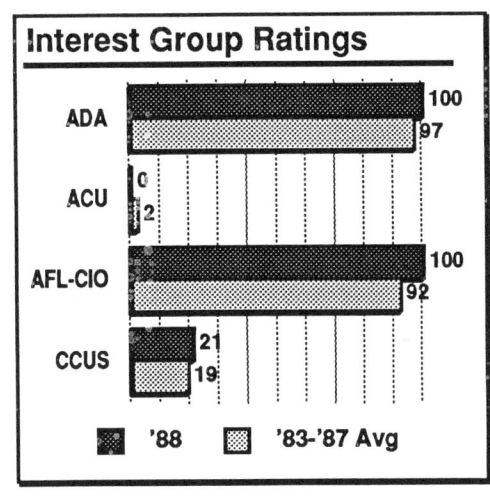

Interest Group Ratings

	'88	'83-'87 Avg
ADA	100	97
ACU	0	2
AFL-CIO	100	92
CCUS	21	19

Government & Postal Workers *$20,220*

    National Assn of Retired Federal Employees $5,000
    American Fedn of State/County/Munic Employees $4,500
    National Assn of Letter Carriers* $4,120
    American Postal Workers Union* $2,300
    American Federation of Government Employees $1,000
    Others $3,300

Teachers Unions *$8,500*

    American Federation of Teachers $5,000
    Minnesota Education Assn $1,750
    National Education Assn $1,750

Transportation Unions *$31,650*

    Teamsters Union* $11,100
    Air Line Pilots Assn $7,500
    United Transportation Union $3,500
    Marine Engineers District 2 Maritime Officers $2,500
    Amalgamated Transit Union $2,000
    Seafarers International Union $2,000
    Transportation Communication Union $1,700
    Others $1,350

Ideological/Single-Issue

Ideological/Single-Issue *$10,088*

Human Rights Campaign Fund	$3,000	Gay/Lesbian
National Cmte for an Effective Congress	$2,497	Dem/Liberal
National Cmte to Preserve Social Security	$2,000	Soc Secur
Valley Education Fund (Tony Coelho)	$1,000	Dem Leaders
Others	$1,591	

Independent expenditures supporting Sabo

National Cmte to Preserve Social Security $1,773

* Contributions came from more than one PAC affiliated
with this sponsor.

Patricia Saiki, R-Hawaii (1)

First elected: 1986
Total receipts: $708,391
Total from PACs: $261,634

1988 Committees & Subcommittees

Banking, Finance and Urban Affairs
Economic Stabilization
Housing and Community Development
International Development Institutions and Finance
International Finance, Trade and Monetary Policy

Merchant Marine and Fisheries
Coast Guard

Fisheries and Wildlife Conservation and the Environment
Oceanography

Select Aging
Housing and Consumer Interests
Human Services

PAC Contribution Profile

Business

Automotive **$9,400**
Auto Dealers & Drivers for Free Trade $6,500
National Auto Dealers Assn $1,550
Others $1,350

Business Associations **$7,620**
National Fedn of Independent Business $5,000
Business Industry PAC $2,353
Others $267

Commercial Banks **$43,500**
American Bankers Assn $10,000
Bancorp Hawaii $9,100
J P Morgan & Company $6,000
Bankers Trust $2,000
Barnett Banks of Florida $2,000
Citicorp $2,000
City Bank (Honolulu) $2,000
First Hawaiian Inc $2,000
Chase Manhattan $1,300
Others $7,100

Construction **$23,600**
National Assn of Home Builders $10,000
Associated General Contractors $3,250
Boise Cascade $2,500
Weyerhaeuser Company $1,300
Associated Builders & Contractors $1,250
Deere & Company $1,000
Kilohana Corp $1,000
Others $3,300

Campaign Revenue Sources

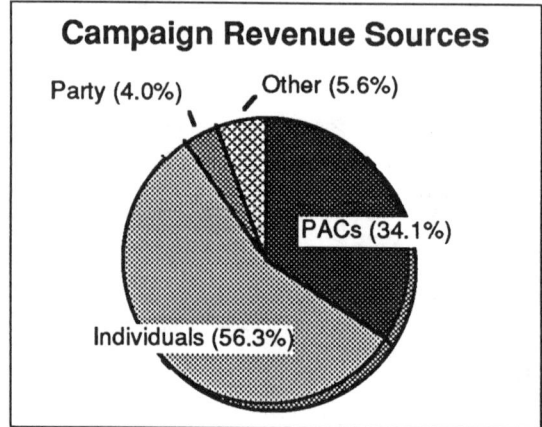

Party (4.0%)
Other (5.6%)
PACs (34.1%)
Individuals (56.3%)

Consumer Credit & Loans **$2,900**
None over $750

Dairy **$2,250**
Associated Milk Producers $1,500
Others $750

Food & Beverage **$5,900**
Nabisco Brands Inc $1,000
National Restaurant Assn $1,000
Others $3,900

Health Professionals **$18,900**
American Medical Assn $10,000
American Academy of Ophthalmology $5,000
American Dental Assn $4,000
Others .... -$100

Insurance **$6,800**
Casualty & Surety Agents Assn $1,000
National Assn of Life Underwriters $1,000
Others $4,800

Oil & Gas **$11,800**
Pacific Resources $4,300
Amoco Corp $1,550
Chevron Corp $1,400
Others $4,550

Real Estate **$15,200**
National Assn of Realtors $10,000
Mortgage Bankers Assn of America $3,900
Others $1,300

Savings Banks & Credit Unions **$10,200**
Credit Union National Assn $4,300
US League of Savings Assn $2,000
National Council of Savings Institutions $1,100
Honolulu Federal Savings & Loan $1,000
Others $1,800

PAC Totals by Category

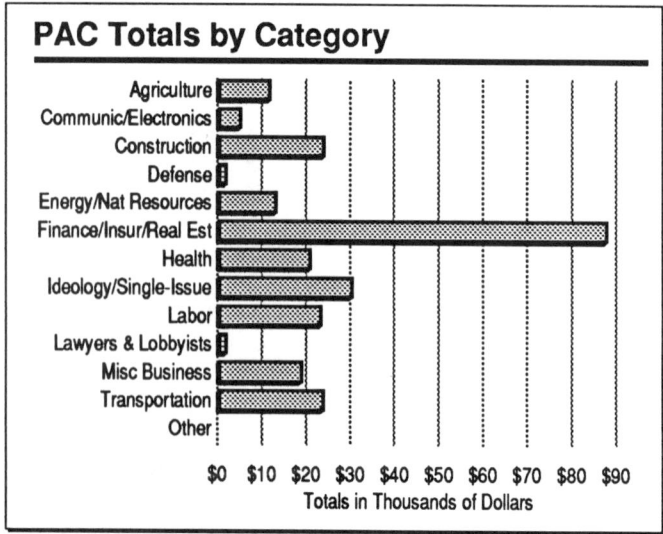

Agriculture
Communic/Electronics
Construction
Defense
Energy/Nat Resources
Finance/Insur/Real Est
Health
Ideology/Single-Issue
Labor
Lawyers & Lobbyists
Misc Business
Transportation
Other

$0 $10 $20 $30 $40 $50 $60 $70 $80 $90
Totals in Thousands of Dollars

Sea Transport **$11,300**

American Pilots Assn	$2,500
Matson Navigation	$2,500
Alexander & Baldwin Inc	$2,300
Tenneco Inc	$1,000
Others	$3,000

Securities Investment **$6,300**

Prudential-Bache Securities	$2,500
Goldman Sachs	$1,000
Municipal Securities Industry	$1,000
Others	$1,800

Sugar Growers **$3,800**

None over $850

Other Major Business PACs

Cooper Industries	$2,000	Electronics
Amfac Inc	$1,900	Wholesale
Dow Chemical*	$1,500	Chemicals
J C Penney Company	$1,250	Dept Store
Coopers & Lybrand	$1,100	Accountants
GTE Corp*	$1,100	Phone Util
Castle & Cooke	$1,000	Fruit/Veg
Equifax Inc	$1,000	CreditReport

Labor

Sea Transport Unions **$16,250**

Marine Engineers Union*	$12,000
Seafarers International Union	$3,500
Others	$750

Other Unions **$6,550**

National Assn of Retired Federal Employees	$3,000
Teamsters Union	$1,500
National Assn of Letter Carriers	$1,000
Others	$1,050

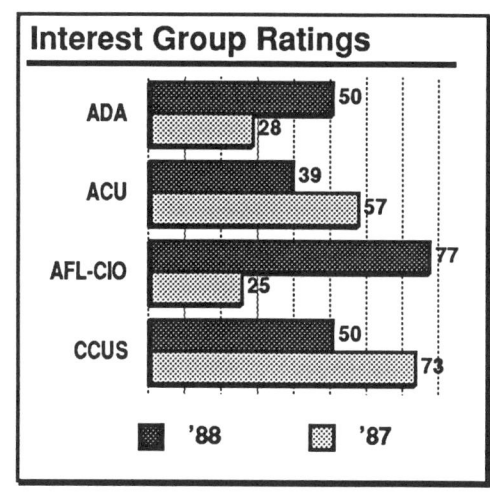

Interest Group Ratings

	'88	'87
ADA	50	28
ACU	39	57
AFL-CIO	77	25
CCUS	50	73

Ideological/Single-Issue

Republican Leadership PACs **$7,800**

Citizens for the Republic (Ronald Reagan)	$5,000
Campaign America (Bob Dole)	$2,800

Womens Issues/Pro-Choice **$15,000**

Women's Campaign Fund	$9,500
National Abortion Rights Action League	$5,000
Others	$500

Other Major Ideological/Single-Issue PACs

National Rifle Assn	$1,800	Pro-Guns
GOP Women's Political Action League	$1,000	Repub/Conser
National Cmte to Preserve Social Security	$1,000	Soc Secur

Independent expenditures supporting Saiki

National Cmte to Preserve Social Security	$1,477

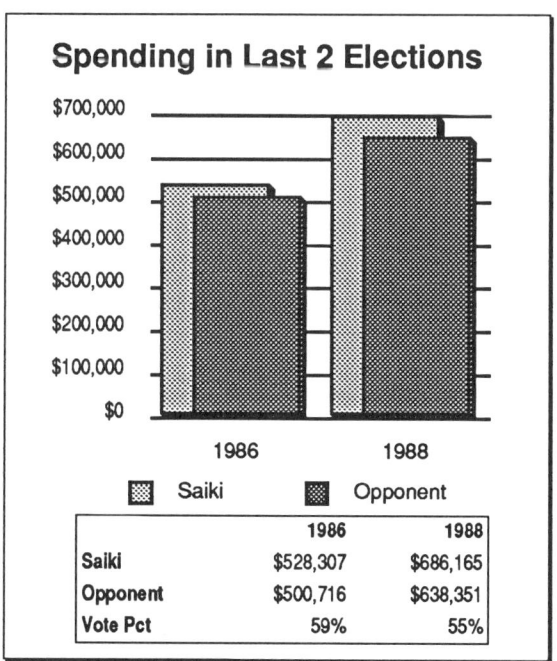

Spending in Last 2 Elections

Saiki   Opponent

	1986	1988
Saiki	$528,307	$686,165
Opponent	$500,716	$638,351
Vote Pct	59%	55%

---

* Contributions came from more than one PAC affiliated with this sponsor.

George E. Sangmeister, D-Ill (4)

First elected: 1988
Total receipts: $378,294
Total from PACs: $158,042

1988 Committees & Subcommittees

Judiciary
Courts, Civil Liberties and the Administration of Justice
Criminal Justice

Veterans' Affairs
Compensation, Pension and Insurance
Education, Training and Employment

PAC Contribution Profile

Business

Financial Institutions **$3,300**
American Bankers Assn $2,000
Credit Union National Assn $1,000
Others $300

Lawyers **$5,350**
Assn of Trial Lawyers of America $5,000
Others $350

Real Estate **$5,000**
National Assn of Realtors $5,000

Other Major Business PACs

American Nurses Assn	$1,000	Health Union
Mid-American Dairymen	$1,000	Dairy
National Assn of Life Underwriters	$1,000	Life Insurance
National Assn of Social Workers	$1,000	Social Work

Campaign Revenue Sources

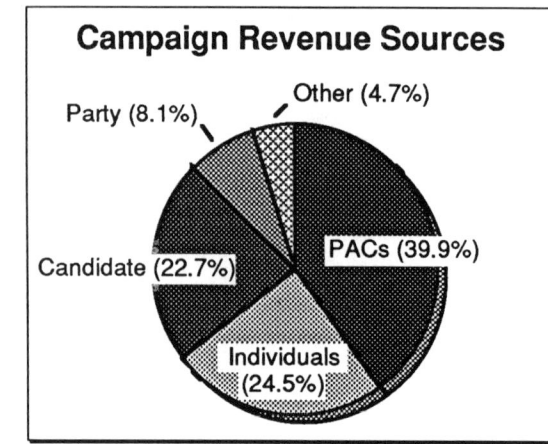

Other (4.7%)
Party (8.1%)
PACs (39.9%)
Candidate (22.7%)
Individuals (24.5%)

PAC Totals by Category

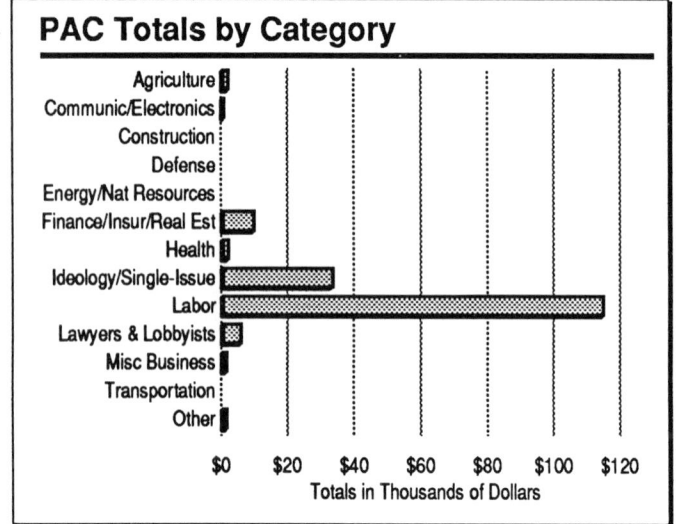

Totals in Thousands of Dollars

Labor

Bldg Trades/Industrial/Misc Unions $74,800

AFL-CIO $10,000
Intl Brotherhood of Electrical Workers $10,000
Machinists/Aerospace Workers Union $10,000
United Auto Workers $10,000
United Steelworkers $5,500
Communications Workers of America $5,000
Food & Commercial Workers Union $5,000
Carpenters & Joiners Union $4,000
Sheet Metal Workers Union $3,500
Service Employees International Union $3,000
United Mine Workers $2,500
Laborers' Political League $2,000
Graphic Communications Union $1,500
Plumbers/Pipefitters Union $1,000
Others $1,800

Government & Postal Workers $13,750

American Fedn of State/County/Munic Employees $10,000
National Assn of Retired Federal Employees $2,000
National Rural Letter Carriers Assn $1,000
Others $750

Teachers Unions $15,500

National Education Assn $10,000
American Federation of Teachers $5,500

Transportation Unions $10,200

Teamsters Union $5,000
Marine Engineers District 2 Maritime Officers $2,500
Amalgamated Transit Union $1,000
Others $1,700

Ideological/Single-Issue

Democratic/Liberal $8,499

National Cmte for an Effective Congress $7,499
Democratic Study Group Campaign Fund $1,000

Democratic Leadership PACs $11,000

Cmte for Democratic Opportunity (Bill Gray) $2,500
House Leadership Fund (Tom Foley) $2,000
Majority Congress Committee (Jim Wright) $2,000
Valley Education Fund (Tony Coelho) $2,000
Pax Americas (David Bonior) $1,500
Empire Leadership Fund (Mario Cuomo) $1,000

Pro-Peace $4,537

Council for a Livable World $2,283
Illinois SANE/Freeze $1,750
Others $504

Senior Citizens Issues $6,000

National Cmte to Preserve Social Security $5,000
National Council of Senior Citizens $1,000

Other Major Ideological/Single-Issue PACs

Handgun Control Inc .... $1,000   Anti-Guns
League of Conservation Voters .... $1,000   Environment

Independent expenditures supporting Sangmeister

National Cmte to Preserve Social Security $2,821

Spending in Last Election

	1988
Sangmeister	$359,142
Opponent	$266,768
Vote Pct	50%

Bill Sarpalius, D-Texas (13)

First elected: 1988
Total receipts: $374,645
Total from PACs: $231,450

1988 Committees & Subcommittees

Agriculture
Conservation, Credit and Rural Development
Cotton, Rice and Sugar
Domestic Marketing, Consumer Relations and Nutrition
Wheat, Soybeans and Feed Grains

Small Business
Procurement, Tourism and Rural Development

Select Children, Youth and Families

PAC Contribution Profile

Business

Auto Dealers	**$2,000**
National Auto Dealers Assn	$2,000
Commodities Trading	**$2,000**
Chicago Mercantile Exchange	$2,000
Construction	**$2,000**
Associated General Contractors	$2,000
Dairy	**$8,500**
Associated Milk Producers	$5,000
Mid-American Dairymen	$1,500
Dairymen Inc	$1,000
Dairymens Mountain Assn	$1,000
Electric Utilities	**$6,750**
Texas Utilities Electric Company	$5,000
ACRE (Action Committee for Rural Electrification)	$1,500
Others	$250
Farm Organizations	**$4,600**
Texas Farm Bureau	$3,750
Others	$850
Food & Beverage	**$2,000**
Winn-Dixie Stores	$1,000
Others	$1,000
Health Professionals	**$13,500**
American Medical Assn	$10,000
American Academy of Ophthalmology	$3,000
Others	$500

Insurance	**$2,800**
National Assn of Life Underwriters	$2,500
Others	$300
Lawyers	**$8,300**
Assn of Trial Lawyers of America	$7,000
Winstead, McGuire, Sechrest & Minick	$1,000
Others	$300
Oil & Gas	**$2,500**
Coastal Corp	$1,000
Others	$1,500
Real Estate	**$10,000**
National Assn of Realtors	$10,000
Sugar Growers	**$4,350**
American Sugarbeet Growers Assn	$1,500
Great Lakes Sugar Beet Growers	$1,000
Others	$1,850

Other Major Business PACs

Texas Cattle Feeders Assn	$2,000	Feedlots
Credit Union National Assn	$1,000	Credit Union
Motorola Inc	$1,000	Electronics
National Assn of Social Workers	$1,000	Social Work
National Assn of Temporary Services	$1,000	EmployAgency
Texas Air	$1,000	Airlines

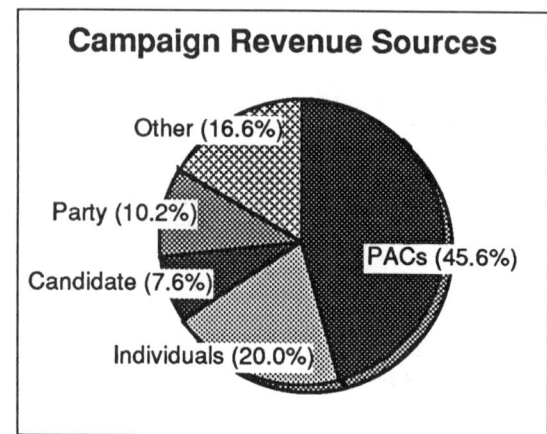

Campaign Revenue Sources

Other (16.6%)
Party (10.2%)
Candidate (7.6%)
Individuals (20.0%)
PACs (45.6%)

PAC Totals by Category

Agriculture
Communic/Electronics
Construction
Defense
Energy/Nat Resources
Finance/Insur/Real Est
Health
Ideology/Single-Issue
Labor
Lawyers & Lobbyists
Misc Business
Transportation
Other

$0 $10 $20 $30 $40 $50 $60 $70 $80 $90
Totals in Thousands of Dollars

Labor

Bldg Trades/Industrial/Misc Unions $38,000

Intl Brotherhood of Electrical Workers $5,000	
Machinists/Aerospace Workers Union $5,000	
United Auto Workers $5,000	
Carpenters & Joiners Union $3,500	
Sheet Metal Workers Union $3,500	
AFL-CIO* $2,000	
Communications Workers of America $2,000	
Food & Commercial Workers Union $2,000	
Ironworkers Union $2,000	
Operating Engineers Union $2,000	
Plumbers/Pipefitters Union $1,500	
Rubber Cork Linoleum Plastic Workers $1,500	
United Steelworkers $1,500	
Laborers' Political League $1,000	
Others $500	

Government & Postal Workers $20,750

American Fedn of State/County/Munic Employees $5,000	
National Assn of Letter Carriers $5,000	
National Assn of Retired Federal Employees $3,000	
American Postal Workers Union $2,500	
National Rural Letter Carriers Assn $2,500	
American Federation of Government Employees $1,000	
Others $1,750	

Teachers Unions $2,500

American Federation of Teachers $2,500

Transportation Unions $28,350

Seafarers International Union $10,000	
Teamsters Union* $10,000	
Air Line Pilots Assn $2,500	
United Transportation Union $2,500	
Amalgamated Transit Union $2,000	
Others $1,350	

Ideological/Single-Issue

Democratic Leadership PACs $29,750

Valley Education Fund (Tony Coelho) $7,000	
24th Cong Dist of California PAC (Henry Waxman) $5,000	
Cmte for a Democratic Consensus (Marvin Leath) $5,000	
Majority Congress Committee (Jim Wright) $5,000	
America's Leaders' Fund (Dan Rostenkowski) $2,000	
Conservative Democratic PAC (Charles Stenholm) $2,000	
Cmte for Democratic Opportunity (Bill Gray) $1,750	
Empire Leadership Fund (Mario Cuomo) $1,000	
House Leadership Fund (Tom Foley) $1,000	

Senior Citizens Issues $6,000

National Cmte to Preserve Social Security $5,000
National Council of Senior Citizens $1,000

Independent expenditures supporting Sarpalius

American Medical Assn $131,560

Spending in Last Election

	1988
Sarpalius	$384,738
Opponent	$476,220
Vote Pct	53%

---

* Contributions came from more than one PAC affiliated
with this sponsor.

Gus Savage, D-Ill (2)

1988 Committees & Subcommittees

Public Works and Transportation
Economic Development (Chairman)
Aviation
Water Resources

Small Business
Procurement, Innovation and Minority Enterprise Development
SBA and the General Economy

PAC Contribution Profile

Business

Commercial Banks **$1,750**
    First Chicago Corp $1,250
    Illinois Bankers Assn $500

Commodities Trading **$1,300**
    Chicago Board of Trade $1,000
    Others $300

Delivery Services **$3,550**
    United Parcel Service $3,550

Real Estate **$4,000**
    National Assn of Realtors $4,000

Sugar Growers **$1,450**
    Florida Sugar Cane League $600
    Others $850

Other Major Business PACs

Associated Milk Producers	$1,000	Dairy
National Assn of Home Builders	$1,000	Resid Constr
Metropolitan Life Insurance	$600	Life Insurance

First elected: 1980
Total receipts: $240,244
Total from PACs: $116,218

Campaign Revenue Sources

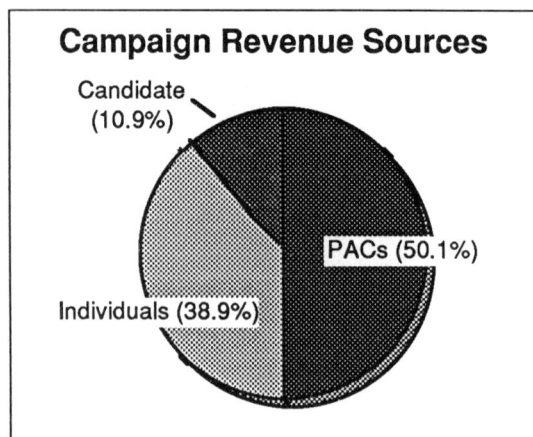

Candidate (10.9%)
Individuals (38.9%)
PACs (50.1%)

PAC Totals by Category

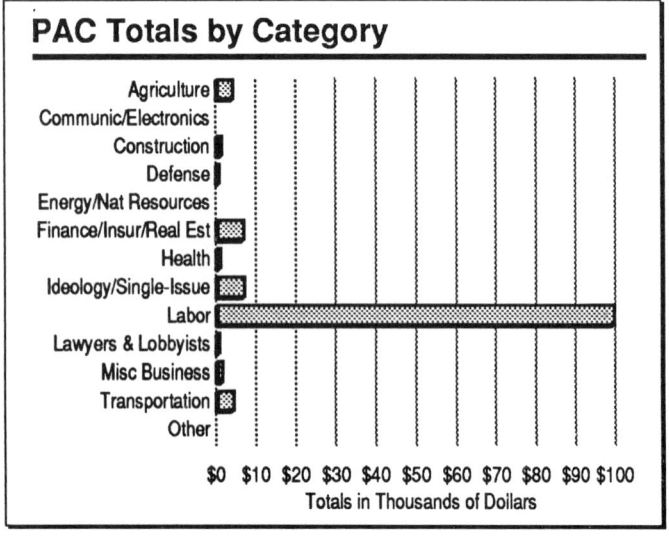

Agriculture
Communic/Electronics
Construction
Defense
Energy/Nat Resources
Finance/Insur/Real Est
Health
Ideology/Single-Issue
Labor
Lawyers & Lobbyists
Misc Business
Transportation
Other

$0 $10 $20 $30 $40 $50 $60 $70 $80 $90 $100
Totals in Thousands of Dollars

Labor

Bldg Trades/Industrial/Misc Unions $38,250

Machinists/Aerospace Workers Union $7,500	
Carpenters & Joiners Union $5,400	
United Auto Workers $5,000	
AFL-CIO $4,200	
Food & Commercial Workers Union $3,650	
Intl Brotherhood of Electrical Workers $2,500	
Laborers' Political League $2,100	
Operating Engineers Union $1,500	
Rubber Cork Linoleum Plastic Workers $1,500	
Ladies Garment Workers Union $1,300	
Plumbers/Pipefitters Union $1,250	
Painters & Allied Trades Union $1,000	
United Steelworkers $750	
Amalgamated Clothing & Textile Workers $550	
Others $50	

Government & Postal Workers $16,000

National Assn of Letter Carriers $5,600
American Fedn of State/County/Munic Employees $5,000
American Postal Workers Union $2,800
National Assn of Retired Federal Employees $2,000
Others $600

Teachers Unions $9,350

National Education Assn $8,000
American Federation of Teachers $1,350

Transportation Unions $35,550

Teamsters Union $10,000
Marine Engineers Union* $6,500
Air Line Pilots Assn $5,000
Seafarers International Union $5,000
Amalgamated Transit Union $4,750
United Transportation Union $2,600
Transportation Communication Union $1,100
Others $600

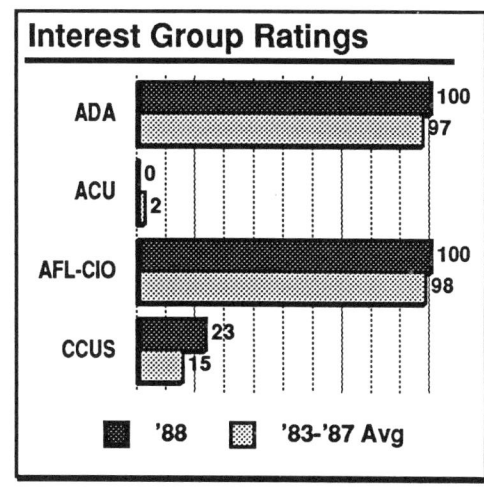

Interest Group Ratings

	'88	'83-'87 Avg
ADA	100	97
ACU	0	2
AFL-CIO	100	98
CCUS	23	15

Ideological/Single-Issue

Democratic Leadership PACs.........................$5,500

Majority Congress Committee (Jim Wright) $5,000
Valley Education Fund (Tony Coelho) $500

Other Major Ideological/Single-Issue PACs

National Cmte to Preserve Social Security ....$800   Soc Secur

Independent expenditures supporting Savage

National Cmte to Preserve Social Security $1,241

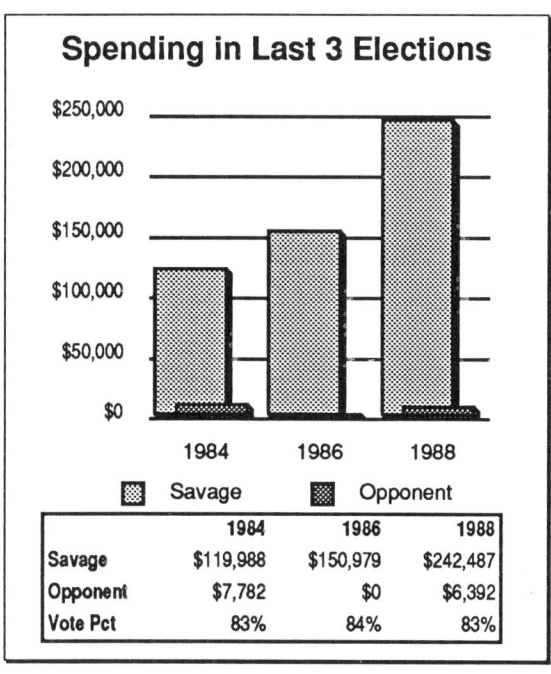

Spending in Last 3 Elections

	Savage	Opponent

	1984	1986	1988
Savage	$119,988	$150,979	$242,487
Opponent	$7,782	$0	$6,392
Vote Pct	83%	84%	83%

---

* Contributions came from more than one PAC affiliated
with this sponsor.

Thomas C. Sawyer, D-Ohio (14)

First elected: 1986
Total receipts: $447,420
Total from PACs: $312,904

1988 Committees & Subcommittees

Education and Labor
Elementary, Secondary and Vocational Education
Human Resources
Labor-Management Relations

Government Operations
Government Activities and Transportation
Human Resources and Intergovernmental Relations

Select Children, Youth and Families

PAC Contribution Profile

Business

Accountants	**$5,000**
American Institute of CPA's	$5,000
Automotive	**$3,200**
National Auto Dealers Assn	$2,000
Others	$1,200
Dairy	**$4,100**
Mid-American Dairymen	$1,800
Associated Milk Producers	$1,500
Others	$800
Defense	**$4,450**
Gencorp Inc	$2,850
Loral Corp	$1,600
Delivery Services	**$2,850**
Federal Express Corp	$1,500
United Parcel Service	$1,350
Electric Utilities & Equipment	**$5,450**
Ohio Edison	$2,300
Babcock & Wilcox	$2,000
Others	$1,150
Financial Institutions	**$7,875**
National City Corp	$1,875
Ohio Savings Assns League	$1,500
Credit Union National Assn	$1,300
Others	$3,200

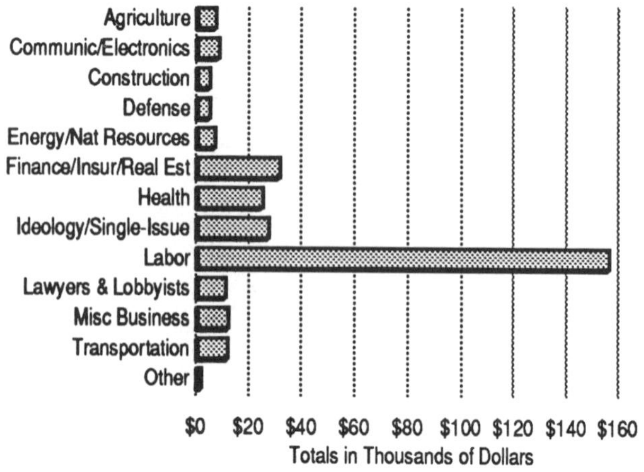

Campaign Revenue Sources

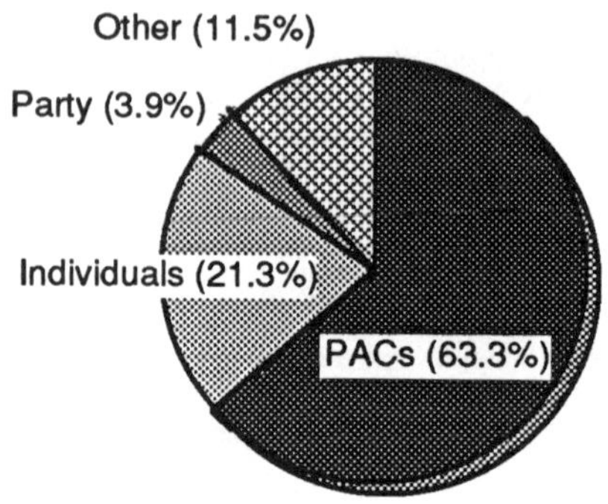

Other (11.5%)
Party (3.9%)
Individuals (21.3%)
PACs (63.3%)

Food & Beverage	**$4,350**
National Restaurant Assn	$2,500
Others	$1,850
Health Professionals	**$22,399**
American Medical Assn	$16,499
American Academy of Ophthalmology	$2,000
American Dental Assn	$1,200
Others	$2,700
Insurance	**$8,000**
National Assn of Life Underwriters	$3,500
Independent Insurance Agents of America	$1,500
Others	$3,000
Lawyers	**$10,600**
Assn of Trial Lawyers of America	$9,000
Others	$1,600
Real Estate	**$9,400**
National Assn of Realtors	$9,100
Others	$300
Residential Construction	**$4,500**
National Assn of Home Builders	$4,500
Retail Sales	**$6,900**
Revco DS Inc	$1,700
Limited Inc	$1,250
Federated Department Stores	$1,000
Others	$2,950
Telecommunications	**$6,850**
AT&T	$4,500
Ohio Bell Telephone	$1,800
Others	$550
Trucking Companies	**$3,940**
Roadway Services Inc	$2,500
Others	$1,440

PAC Totals by Category

Agriculture
Communic/Electronics
Construction
Defense
Energy/Nat Resources
Finance/Insur/Real Est
Health
Ideology/Single-Issue
Labor
Lawyers & Lobbyists
Misc Business
Transportation
Other

$0 $20 $40 $60 $80 $100 $120 $140 $160
Totals in Thousands of Dollars

Other Major Business PACs

American Hospital Assn	$1,150	Hospitals
National Assn of Social Workers	$1,000	Social Work

Labor

Bldg Trades/Industrial/Misc Unions **$60,900**

United Auto Workers $10,600
Machinists/Aerospace Workers Union $9,400
Carpenters & Joiners Union $5,950
Intl Brotherhood of Electrical Workers.................... $5,500
Rubber Cork Linoleum Plastic Workers $4,800
Operating Engineers Union $3,500
AFL-CIO* $3,050
Food & Commercial Workers Union.......................... $3,000
Sheet Metal Workers Union $3,000
United Steelworkers $2,750
Communications Workers of America........................ $2,000
Laborers' Political League $2,000
Service Employees International Union $1,050
International Chemical Workers Union...................... $1,000
Plumbers/Pipefitters Union $1,000
Others $2,300

Government & Postal Workers **$40,750**

National Assn of Retired Federal Employees $12,500
National Assn of Letter Carriers $10,550
American Fedn of State/County/Munic Employees $7,500
American Postal Workers Union $3,800
National Rural Letter Carriers Assn $3,000
National Treasury Employees Union $2,100
Others $1,300

Teachers Unions **$18,000**

National Education Assn $10,000
American Federation of Teachers $8,000

Transportation Unions **$36,100**

Teamsters Union $10,000
Air Line Pilots Assn $6,500
Marine Engineers Union* $6,100
Seafarers International Union $4,000
Amalgamated Transit Union $3,000
United Transportation Union $2,300
Transportation Communication Union...................... $1,900
International Longshoremen Assn $1,000
Others $1,300

Interest Group Ratings

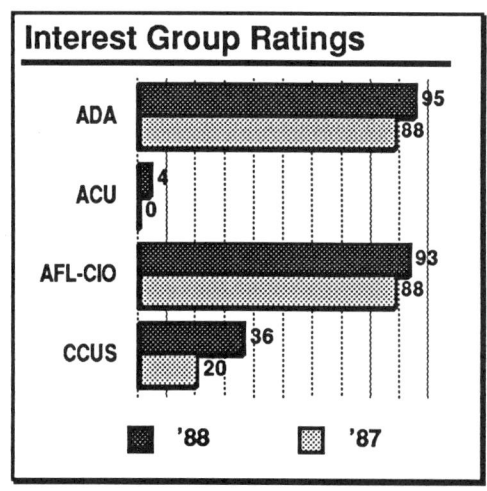

Ideological/Single-Issue

Democratic/Liberal **$3,499**

National Cmte for an Effective Congress $2,499
Teamwork America... $1,000

Democratic Leadership PACs **$3,580**

Valley Education Fund (Tony Coelho) $2,000
Participation 2000 (Gov. Richard Celeste) $1,500
Others $80

Pro-Israel **$9,500**

National PAC $5,000
Joint Action Cmte for Political Affairs $1,000
Others $3,500

Other Major Ideological/Single-Issue PACs

National Cmte to Preserve Social Security ...... $2,850   Soc Secur
National Abortion Rights Action League .... $2,500   Pro-Choice
Great Lakes Space Tech Assn .... $1,000   OtherIdeolog
National Council of Senior Citizens .... $1,000   Soc Secur

Independent expenditures supporting Sawyer

National Cmte to Preserve Social Security $1,556

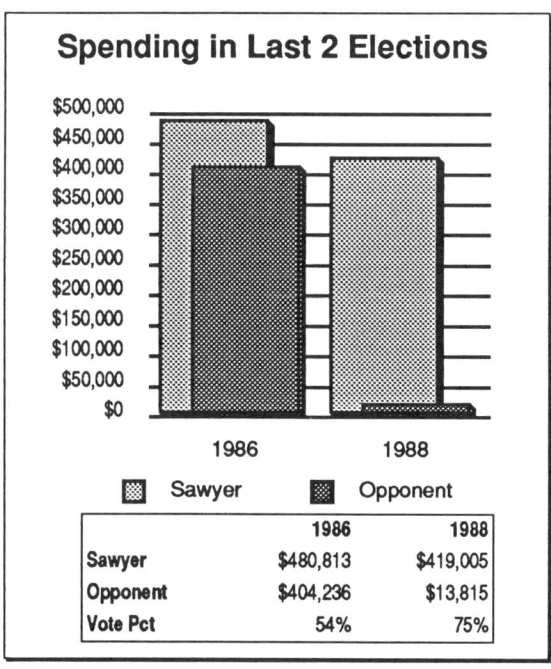

Spending in Last 2 Elections

	1986	1988
Sawyer	$480,813	$419,005
Opponent	$404,236	$13,815
Vote Pct	54%	75%

* Contributions came from more than one PAC affiliated
with this sponsor.

H. James Saxton, R-NJ (13)

First elected: 1984
Total receipts: $491,036
Total from PACs: $195,430

1988 Committees & Subcommittees

Banking, Finance and Urban Affairs
Domestic Monetary Policy
Economic Stabilization
Financial Institutions Supervision, Regulation and Insurance
Housing and Community Development

Merchant Marine and Fisheries
Fisheries and Wildlife Conservation and the Environment
Merchant Marine
Oceanography

Select Aging
Health and Long-Term Care

PAC Contribution Profile

Business

Automotive	**$5,850**
Auto Dealers & Drivers for Free Trade	$2,750
National Auto Dealers Assn	$2,550
Others	$550
Commercial Banks	**$7,850**
American Bankers Assn	$2,500
New Jersey Bankers Assn	$1,000
Others	$4,350
Computers & Electronics	**$2,900**
Computer Sciences Corp	$1,600
General Electric	$1,300
Construction	**$13,741**
National Assn of Home Builders	$7,791
Stone & Webster	$1,100
National Electrical Contractors Assn	$1,000
Others	$3,850
Consumer Credit & Loans	**$3,800**
American Express	$1,000
Others	$2,800
Dairy	**$2,000**
Associated Milk Producers	$1,500
Others	$500
Defense	**$3,400**
None over $800	

Campaign Revenue Sources

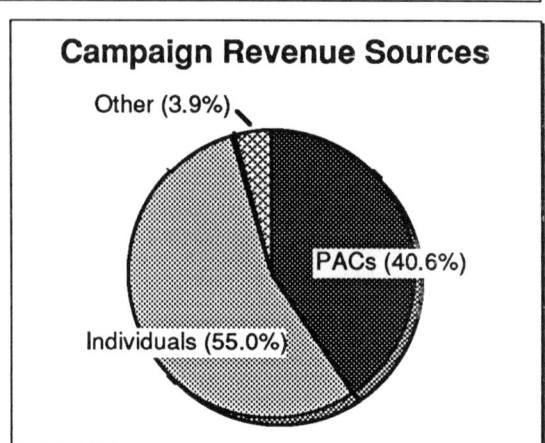

Other (3.9%)
PACs (40.6%)
Individuals (55.0%)

Electric Utilities	**$8,050**
General Public Utilities	$1,250
Public Service Electric & Gas	$1,000
Others	$5,800
Food & Beverage	**$4,200**
ARA Services Inc	$1,000
Others	$3,200
Fruit & Vegetable Growers	**$2,038**
Ocean Spray Cranberries Inc	$2,038
Health Professionals	**$7,300**
American Medical Assn	$3,250
American Dental Assn	$1,500
American Academy of Ophthalmology	$1,000
Others	$1,550
Insurance	**$34,923**
National Assn of Life Underwriters	$10,000
Independent Insurance Agents of America	$9,999
Casualty & Surety Agents Assn	$3,999
National Assn Mutual Insurance Agents	$3,300
American Council of Life Insurance	$1,850
National Assn of Independent Insurers	$1,300
Prudential Insurance	$1,300
Others	$3,175
Lawyers	**$3,050**
Assn of Trial Lawyers of America	$1,500
Delaware Valley Leadership Fund	$1,000
Others	$550
Oil & Gas	**$8,100**
Atlantic Richfield	$1,350
Others	$6,750
Pharmaceuticals	**$4,200**
Johnson & Johnson	$1,000
Others	$3,200

PAC Totals by Category

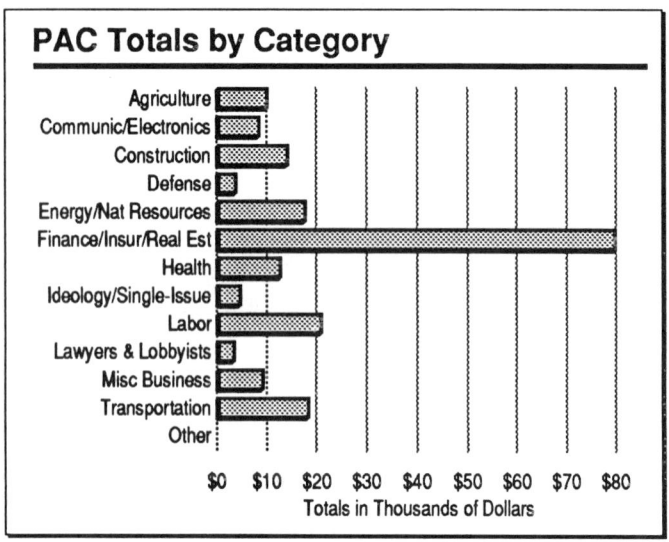

Agriculture
Communic/Electronics
Construction
Defense
Energy/Nat Resources
Finance/Insur/Real Est
Health
Ideology/Single-Issue
Labor
Lawyers & Lobbyists
Misc Business
Transportation
Other

$0 $10 $20 $30 $40 $50 $60 $70 $80
Totals in Thousands of Dollars

Real Estate **$11,700**
    National Assn of Realtors $8,000
    Mortgage Bankers Assn of America $1,100
    Others $2,600

Savings Banks & Credit Unions **$9,000**
    SAPEC/ NJ (New Jersey Savings Assn) $3,500
    Howard Savings Bank $1,000
    National Council of Savings Institutions $1,000
    US League of Savings Assn $1,000
    Others $2,500

Sea Transport **$10,050**
    American Pilots Assn $3,000
    Tenneco Inc $1,500
    Others $5,550

Securities/Commodities Investment **$13,400**
    PaineWebber $1,550
    Prudential-Bache Securities $1,500
    Chicago Board of Trade $1,000
    Drexel Burnham Lambert $1,000
    Ehrlich-Bober & Company $1,000
    Federated Investors Inc $1,000
    First Boston Corp $1,000
    Goldman Sachs $1,000
    Morgan Stanley & Company $1,000
    Philadelphia Stock Exchange $1,000
    Municipal Securities Industry $1,000
    Others $1,350

Telecommunications **$5,100**
    New Jersey Bell Telephone $2,000
    AT&T $1,750
    Others $1,350

Tobacco **$2,150**
    Philip Morris $1,300
    Others $850

Other Major Business PACs
J C Penney Company .... $1,100   Dept Store

Interest Group Ratings

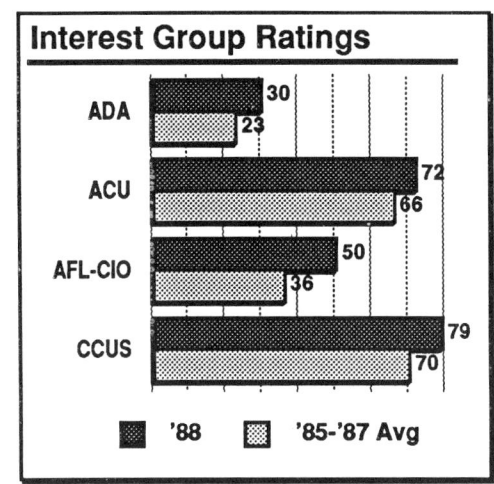

	'88	'85-'87 Avg
ADA	30	23
ACU	72	66
AFL-CIO	50	36
CCUS	79	70

Labor

Government & Postal Workers **$5,800**
    National Assn of Retired Federal Employees $5,000
    Others $800

Sea Transport Unions **$9,550**
    Marine Engineers District 2 Maritime Officers $7,500
    Masters, Mates & Pilots Union $1,050
    Seafarers International Union $1,000

Other Unions **$5,050**
    National Education Assn $2,000
    Air Line Pilots Assn $1,500
    Teamsters Union $1,000
    Others $550

Ideological/Single-Issue

Ideological/Single-Issue **$4,233**
National Cmte to Preserve Social Security ...... $1,500   Soc Secur
American Security Council .... $1,483   Pro-Defense
Others $1,250

Independent expenditures supporting Saxton
National Cmte to Preserve Social Security $4,865

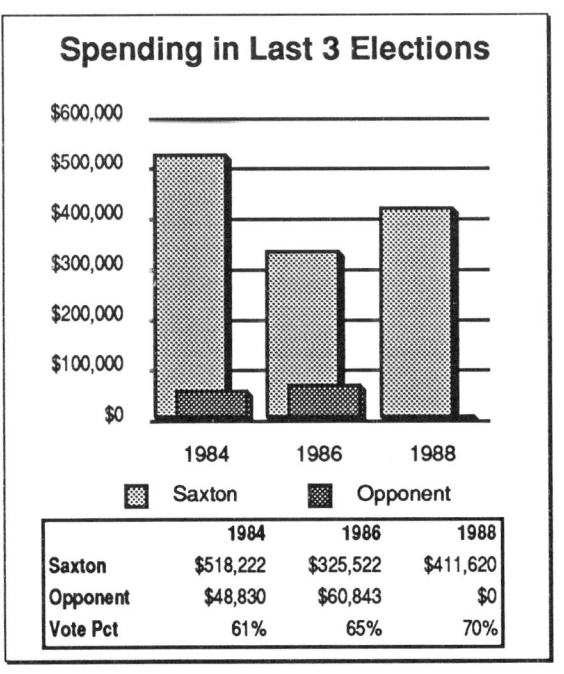

Spending in Last 3 Elections

	1984	1986	1988
Saxton	$518,222	$325,522	$411,620
Opponent	$48,830	$60,843	$0
Vote Pct	61%	65%	70%

Legend: Saxton, Opponent

Dan Schaefer, R-Colo (6)

First elected: 1983
Total receipts: $618,607
Total from PACs: $335,302

1988 Committees & Subcommittees

Energy and Commerce
Energy and Power
Oversight and Investigations
Transportation, Tourism and Hazardous Materials

PAC Contribution Profile

Business

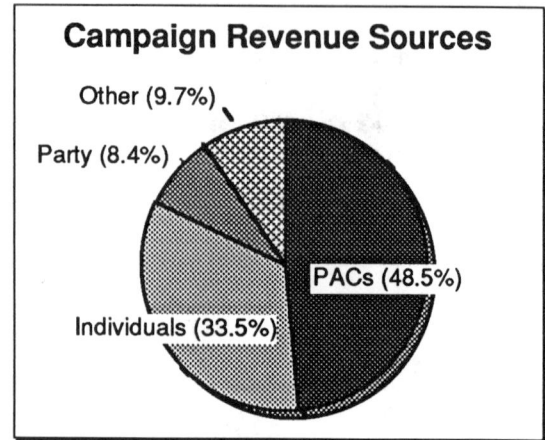

Campaign Revenue Sources

Other (9.7%)
Party (8.4%)
PACs (48.5%)
Individuals (33.5%)

Accountants	**$6,850**
American Institute of CPA's	$5,000
Others	$1,850
Automotive	**$18,650**
Auto Dealers & Drivers for Free Trade	$10,000
National Auto Dealers Assn	$5,850
Others	$2,800
Construction	**$25,550**
National Assn of Home Builders	$6,000
Sheet Metal/AirCon Contractors	$4,050
Associated General Contractors	$3,500
National Utility Contractors Assn	$3,000
Manville Corp	$2,000
Associated Builders & Contractors	$1,350
Others	$5,650
Defense	**$10,150**
Martin Marietta Corp	$2,200
Allied-Signal	$1,100
Litton Industries	$1,050
Textron Inc	$1,050
United Technologies	$1,050
Others	$3,700
Electric Utilities	**$9,900**
Southern Company*	$2,650
Public Service Company of Colorado	$2,350
Others	$4,900

Food & Beverage	**$14,670**
Coors Industries	$5,270
National Restaurant Assn	$4,000
Others	$5,400
Health Professionals	**$19,450**
American Medical Assn	$10,000
American Optometric Assn	$5,000
American Dental Assn	$2,500
Others	$1,950
Industrial Equipment & Materials	**$5,350**
C A Norgren Company	$5,350
Insurance	**$20,807**
National Assn of Life Underwriters	$5,000
Independent Insurance Agents of America	$2,200
American Council of Life Insurance	$1,557
Casualty & Surety Agents Assn	$1,550
National Assn of Independent Insurers	$1,400
Security Life of Denver	$1,350
American Family Corp	$1,200
Others	$6,550
Oil & Gas	**$38,169**
Phillips Petroleum	$4,998
Atlantic Richfield	$3,500
Dow Chemical*	$3,000
Amoco Corp	$2,700
Petroleum Marketers Assn	$2,500
Chevron Corp	$1,600
Coastal Corp	$1,200
Exxon Corp	$1,200
Union Oil	$1,071
CSX Transportation Inc	$1,050
Marathon Oil	$1,050
Texaco	$1,050
Others	$13,250
Real Estate	**$12,200**
National Assn of Realtors	$10,000
Others	$2,200
Telecommunications	**$22,397**
Mountain Bell	$6,500
AT&T	$6,200
BellSouth Services	$2,100
Motorola Inc	$1,697
Pacific Telesis Group	$1,100
Others	$4,800

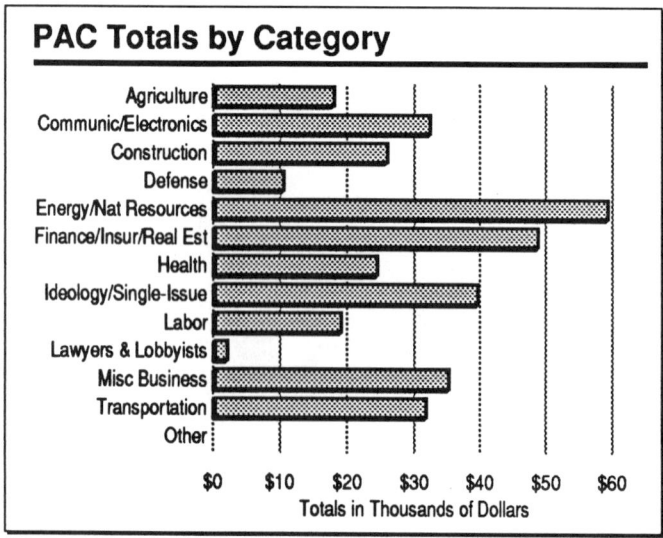

PAC Totals by Category

Agriculture
Communic/Electronics
Construction
Defense
Energy/Nat Resources
Finance/Insur/Real Est
Health
Ideology/Single-Issue
Labor
Lawyers & Lobbyists
Misc Business
Transportation
Other

$0 $10 $20 $30 $40 $50 $60

Totals in Thousands of Dollars

Television/Cable TV $8,100

National Cable Television Assn	$3,000
Tele-Communications Inc	$2,500
National Assn of Broadcasters	$1,350
Others	$1,250

Tobacco $7,950

Philip Morris	$3,550
RJR Nabisco	$2,000
Tobacco Institute	$1,050
Others	$1,350

Waste Management $5,200

Waste Management Inc	$2,000
Browning-Ferris Industries	$1,500
Ch2M Hill	$1,200
Others	$500

Other Major Business PACs

American Bankers Assn	$2,500	Comml Banks
United Parcel Service	$2,400	Delivery
National Fedn of Independent Business	$1,700	Sml Business
Westvaco Corp	$1,500	Paper Prod
Cyprus Minerals Company	$1,350	Metals/Mining
Whirlpool Corp	$1,300	Appliances
Norfolk Southern Corp	$1,200	Railroads
Business Industry PAC	$1,161	Bus Assns
American Sugarbeet Growers Assn	$1,050	Sugar
Santa Fe Southern Pacific	$1,050	Railroads
Securities Industry Assn	$1,050	StocksInvest
Southland Corp	$1,007	Dept Store

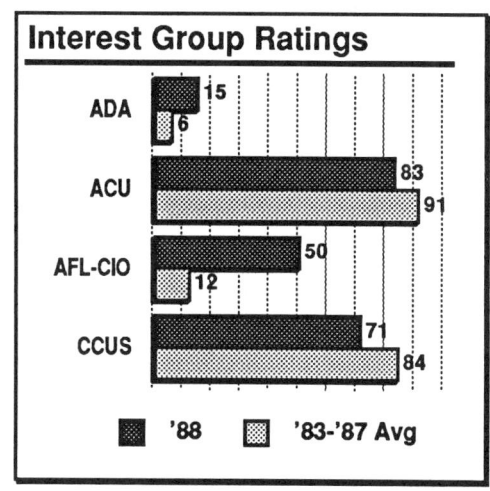

Interest Group Ratings

	'88	'83-'87 Avg
ADA	15	6
ACU	83	91
AFL-CIO	50	12
CCUS	71	84

Labor

Labor Unions $18,700

Marine Engineers Union	$8,500
National Assn of Retired Federal Employees	$5,000
Air Line Pilots Assn	$2,000
Masters Mates & Pilots Union*	$1,500
Seafarers International Union	$1,350
Others	$350

Ideological/Single-Issue

Pro-Gun Ownership $10,900

National Rifle Assn	$9,900
Others	$1,000

Republican Leadership PACs $13,646

Campaign America (Bob Dole)	$5,162
Citizens for the Republic (Ronald Reagan)	$4,999
Conservative Victory Fund (Steve Symms)	$1,485
Others	$2,000

Other Major Ideological/Single-Issue PACs

National PAC	$5,000	Pro-Israel
National Right to Life PAC	$4,477	Pro-Life
Public Service Research Council	$3,000	Anti-Union
Council for National Defense	$1,217	Pro-Defense

Spending in Last 3 Elections

Schaefer / Opponent

	1984	1986	1988
Schaefer	$163,104	$125,435	$636,204
Opponent	$0	$0	$489,303
Vote Pct	89%	65%	63%

* Contributions came from more than one PAC affiliated with this sponsor.

James H. Scheuer, D-NY (8)

First elected: 1964
Total receipts: $77,854
Total from PACs: $55,600

1988 Committees & Subcommittees

Energy and Commerce
Commerce, Consumer Protection and Competitiveness
Health and the Environment

Science, Space and Technology
Natural Resources, Agriculture Research and Environment (Chairman)
International Scientific Cooperation
Space Science and Applications

Select Narcotics Abuse and Control

Joint Economic
Education and Health (Chairman)
Economic Resources and Competitiveness
National Security Economics

PAC Contribution Profile

Business

Accountants	**$5,600**
American Institute of CPA's	$5,000
Others	$600
Computers & Electronics	**$1,100**
Computer Sciences Corp	$500
Others	$600
Health Professionals	**$5,350**
New York Medical Assn	$1,200
American College of Emergency Physicians	$1,000
American Nurses Assn	$1,000
American Podiatry Assn	$500
Warner-Lambert	$500
Others	$1,150
Lawyers & Lobbyists	**$5,900**
Assn of Trial Lawyers of America	$5,300
Others	$600
Pharmaceuticals	**$3,850**
Eli Lilly & Company	$1,000
Schering-Plough Corp	$1,000
Pfizer Inc	$500
Others	$1,350
Real Estate	**$2,100**
National Assn of Realtors	$2,100

Retail Sales	**$1,250**
International Council of Shopping Centers	$1,000
Others	$250
Securities Investment	**$1,300**
E F Hutton Group	$1,000
Others	$300
Telecommunications	**$1,600**
AT&T	$500
Pacific Telesis Group	$500
Others	$600

Other Major Business PACs

American Veterinary Medical Assn	$1,000	Veterinary
National Cable Television Assn	$1,000	CableTV
National Assn of Federal Credit Unions	$500	Credit Union
Waste Management Inc	$600	Waste Mgmt

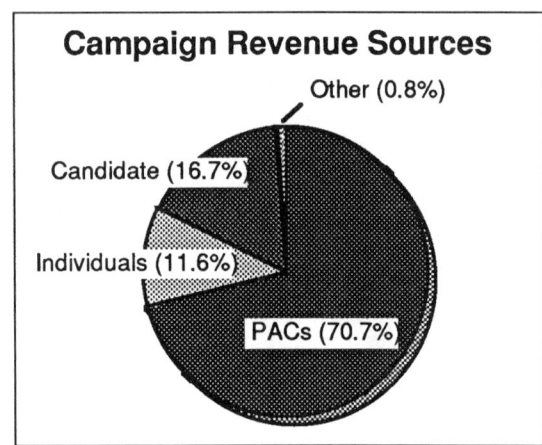

Campaign Revenue Sources

- Other (0.8%)
- Candidate (16.7%)
- Individuals (11.6%)
- PACs (70.7%)

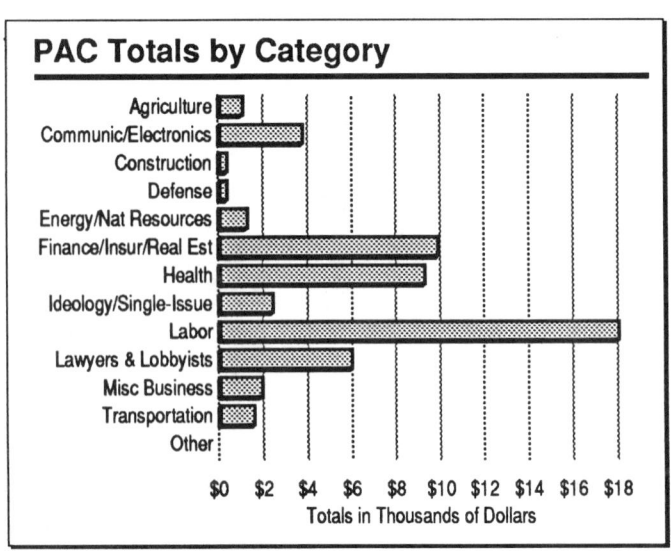

PAC Totals by Category

- Agriculture
- Communic/Electronics
- Construction
- Defense
- Energy/Nat Resources
- Finance/Insur/Real Est
- Health
- Ideology/Single-Issue
- Labor
- Lawyers & Lobbyists
- Misc Business
- Transportation
- Other

$0 $2 $4 $6 $8 $10 $12 $14 $16 $18

Totals in Thousands of Dollars

Labor

Bldg Trades/Industrial/Misc Unions $3,400
    Carpenters & Joiners Union $1,000
    Food & Commercial Workers Union $1,000
    Laborers' Political League $600
    Intl Brotherhood of Electrical Workers $500
    Others $300

Government & Postal Workers $4,600
    National Assn of Retired Federal Employees $3,000
    American Fedn of State/County/Munic Employees $1,000
    National Assn of Letter Carriers $600

Teachers Unions $4,800
    National Education Assn $4,500
    Others $300

Transportation Unions $5,150
    United Transportation Union $3,000
    Seafarers International Union $1,000
    Others $1,150

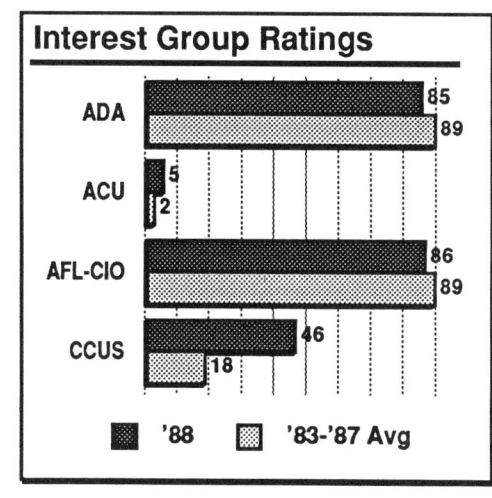

Interest Group Ratings

	'88	'83-'87 Avg
ADA	85	89
ACU	5	2
AFL-CIO	86	89
CCUS	46	18

Ideological/Single-Issue

Ideological/Single-Issue $2,350
Washington PAC .... $1,000 Pro-Israel
Human Rights Campaign Fund .... $500   Gay/Lesbian
National Cmte to Preserve Social Security .... $500   Soc Secur
Others $350

Independent expenditures supporting Scheuer

National Cmte to Preserve Social Security $1,790

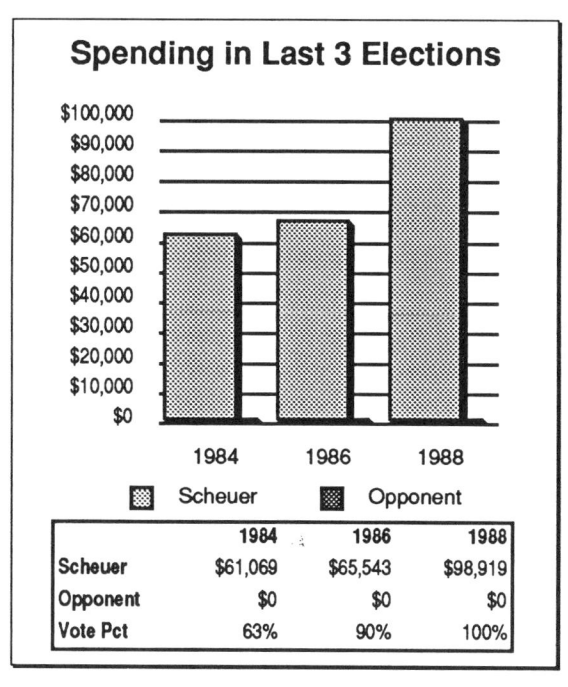

Spending in Last 3 Elections

	Scheuer	Opponent

	1984	1986	1988
Scheuer	$61,069	$65,543	$98,919
Opponent	$0	$0	$0
Vote Pct	63%	90%	100%

Steven H. Schiff, R-NM (1)

First elected: 1988
Total receipts: $563,429
Total from PACs: $158,911

Government Operations
Commerce, Consumer and Monetary Affairs
Government Information, Justice and Agriculture

Science, Space and Technology
Energy Research and Development
Space Science and Applications

Campaign Revenue Sources

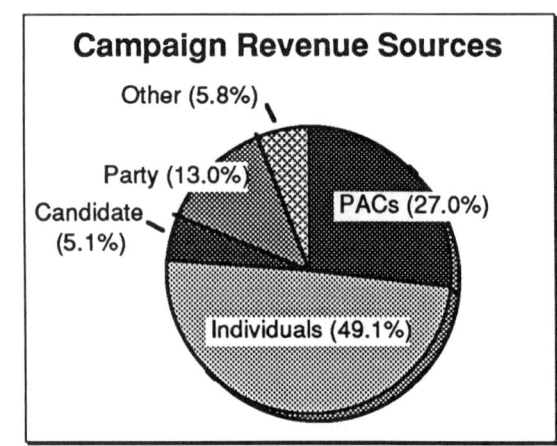

Other (5.8%)
Party (13.0%)
Candidate (5.1%)
PACs (27.0%)
Individuals (49.1%)

PAC Contribution Profile
Business

Automotive	**$8,250**
Auto Dealers & Drivers for Free Trade	$5,000
Eaton Corp	$2,000
National Auto Dealers Assn	$1,000
Others	$250
Business Associations	**$6,470**
National Fedn of Independent Business	$3,500
Business Industry PAC	$2,161
Others	$809
Chemicals & Plastics	**$2,650**
Dow Chemical	$2,000
Others	$650
Construction	**$18,500**
National Assn of Home Builders	$10,000
Associated General Contractors	$2,500
Sheet Metal/AirCon Contractors	$1,500
Wall & Ceiling/Gypsum Contractors	$1,000
Others	$3,500
Defense	**$10,500**
BDM International	$4,000
Harris Corp	$2,000
Lockheed Corp	$1,000
Tenneco Inc	$1,000
Others	$2,500
Electric Utilities	**$2,750**
None over $575	

Electronics & Computers	**$5,500**
Cooper Industries	$3,000
Honeywell Inc	$1,500
Others	$1,000
Financial Institutions	**$5,100**
American Bankers Assn	$1,000
Credit Union National Assn	$1,000
Others	$3,100
Food & Beverage	**$5,753**
Coors Industries	$2,753
National Restaurant Assn	$2,000
Others	$1,000
Health Professionals	**$9,500**
American Medical Assn	$5,000
American Academy of Ophthalmology	$3,000
American Optometric Assn	$1,000
Others	$500
Insurance	**$5,250**
National Assn of Life Underwriters	$2,500
Independent Insurance Agents of America	$2,000
Others	$750
Lawyers	**$5,300**
Assn of Trial Lawyers of America	$5,000
Others	$300
Oil & Gas	**$16,650**
Chevron Corp	$3,000
Phillips Petroleum	$3,000
Amoco Corp	$1,500
Hunt Oil Company	$1,000
Sun Company	$1,000
Others	$7,150
Real Estate	**$5,000**
National Assn of Realtors	$5,000
Telecommunications	**$3,350**
AT&T	$2,850
Others	$500

Other Major Business PACs

Southland Corp	$1,007	Dept Store
Stone Container Corp	$1,000	Paper Packg
Texas Cattle Feeders Assn	$1,000	Feedlots

PAC Totals by Category

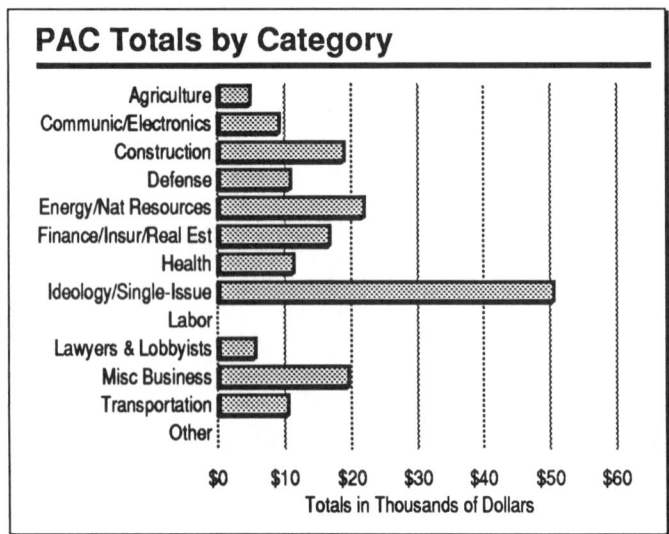

Agriculture
Communic/Electronics
Construction
Defense
Energy/Nat Resources
Finance/Insur/Real Est
Health
Ideology/Single-Issue
Labor
Lawyers & Lobbyists
Misc Business
Transportation
Other

$0 $10 $20 $30 $40 $50 $60
Totals in Thousands of Dollars

Ideological/Single-Issue

Anti-Union PACs **$6,500**

    Public Service Research Council $5,000
    Right to Work PAC $1,500

Pro-Israel **$15,500**

    National PAC $5,000
    Congressional Action Cmte of Texas $3,000
    Garden State PAC $1,500
    Delaware Valley PAC $1,000
    Hudson Valley PAC $1,000
    Roundtable PAC $1,000
    Washington PAC $1,000
    Others $2,000

Republican/Conservative **$4,550**

    Conservative Victory Cmte $3,000
    Republican Congressional Boosters Club $1,000
    Others $550

Republican Leadership PACs **$14,882**

    Citizens for the Republic (Ronald Reagan) $5,000
    Fund for America's Future (George Bush) $5,000
    Conservative Victory Fund (Steve Symms) $1,632
    Campaign America (Bob Dole) $1,000
    Republican Leader's Fund (Bob Michel) $1,000
    Others $1,250

Other Major Ideological/Single-Issue PACs

National Rifle Assn ....$4,950   Pro-Guns
Ruff PAC ....$3,000   Tax Policy

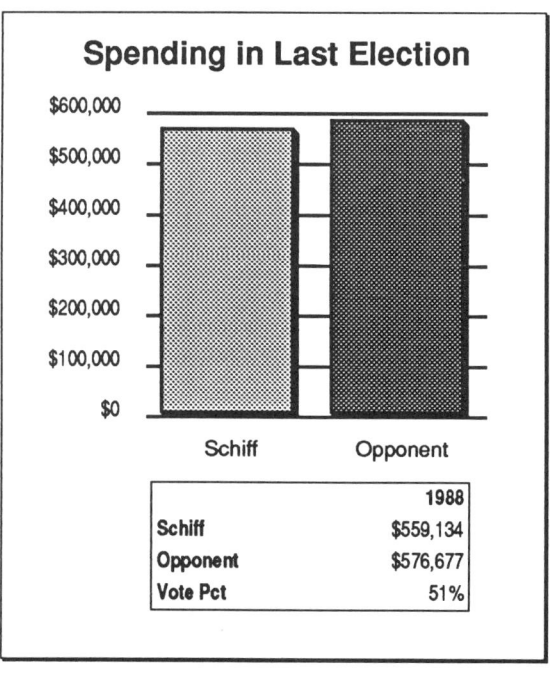

Spending in Last Election

	1988
Schiff	$559,134
Opponent	$576,677
Vote Pct	51%

Claudine Schneider, R-RI (2)

First elected: 1980
Total receipts: $419,633
Total from PACs: $193,656

1988 Committees & Subcommittees

Merchant Marine and Fisheries
Oversight and Investigations (Ranking Republican)
Fisheries and Wildlife Conservation and the Environment
Oceanography

Science, Space and Technology
Natural Resources, Agriculture Research and Environment (Ranking Republican)
Science, Research and Technology

Select Aging
Health and Long-Term Care

Campaign Revenue Sources

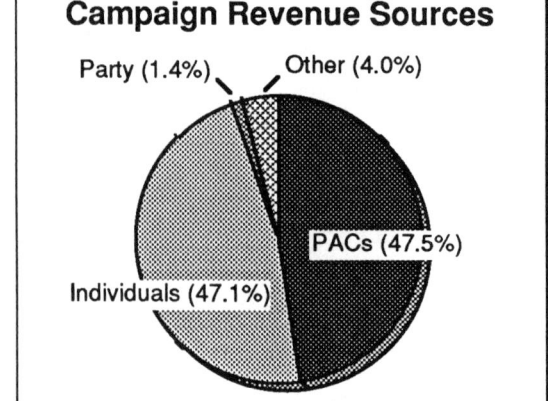

Party (1.4%)
Other (4.0%)
PACs (47.5%)
Individuals (47.1%)

PAC Contribution Profile

Business

Automotive	**$3,200**
Auto Dealers & Drivers for Free Trade	$1,500
Chrysler Corp	$1,100
Others	$600
Aviation & Aerospace	**$5,300**
Boeing Company	$1,600
Federal Express Corp	$1,300
TRW Inc	$1,100
Others	$1,300
Chemicals	**$2,000**
Monsanto Company	$1,000
Others	$1,000
Commercial & Savings Banks	**$4,400**
Marine Midland Banks	$1,000
Others	$3,400
Construction	**$15,300**
National Assn of Home Builders	$12,300
Associated General Contractors	$1,000
Others	$2,000
Cosmetics	**$2,000**
Avon Products	$1,050
Others	$950

Defense	**$12,900**
General Dynamics	$3,500
Textron Inc	$3,000
Allied-Signal	$2,000
Raytheon	$1,600
Others	$2,800
Electronics & Computers	**$3,050**
None over $600	
Food & Beverage	**$5,250**
Food Marketing Institute	$1,100
Coca-Cola Company	$1,050
Joseph E Seagram & Sons	$1,000
Others	$2,100
Health Professionals	**$9,550**
American Medical Assn	$2,300
American Academy of Ophthalmology	$2,000
American Dental Assn	$1,500
American Optometric Assn	$1,100
American Nurses Assn	$1,000
Others	$1,650
Insurance	**$11,500**
National Assn of Life Underwriters	$3,500
Equitable Financial Services	$1,300
Metropolitan Life Insurance	$1,100
New England Mutual Life	$1,100
Others	$4,500
Pharmaceuticals	**$10,500**
Schering-Plough Corp	$1,600
Johnson & Johnson	$1,500
Hoffman-La Roche	$1,400
Pfizer Inc	$1,000
Sandoz Pharmaceuticals	$1,000
Others	$4,000
Real Estate	**$5,750**
National Assn of Realtors	$5,750
Sea Transport	**$3,200**
American Pilots Assn	$2,000
Others	$1,200
Telecommunications	**$5,600**
AT&T	$3,000
New England Tel & Tel	$1,200
Others	$1,400

PAC Totals by Category

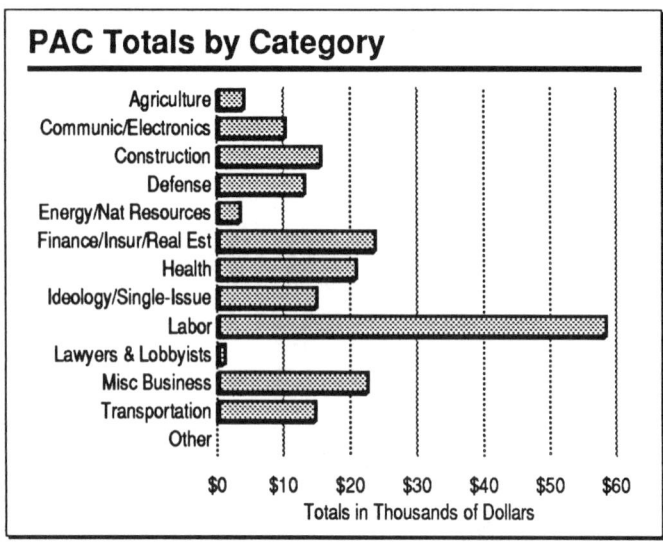

Agriculture
Communic/Electronics
Construction
Defense
Energy/Nat Resources
Finance/Insur/Real Est
Health
Ideology/Single-Issue
Labor
Lawyers & Lobbyists
Misc Business
Transportation
Other

$0 $10 $20 $30 $40 $50 $60
Totals in Thousands of Dollars

Textiles/Fibers	....	$3,850
Hoechst Celanese Corp	....	$1,800
Others	....	$2,050

Other Major Business PACs

Stanley Works	$1,500	Hardware
National Fisheries Institute	$1,248	Fishing
Merrill Lynch	$1,200	StocksInvest
Hallmark Cards	$1,050	Publishing
Associated Milk Producers	$1,000	Dairy
Corning Glass Works	$1,000	Glass Prod
Dun & Bradstreet	$1,000	Mkt Research
International Council of Shopping Centers	$1,000	Retail
Marriott Corp	$1,000	Hotel/Motel

Labor

Bldg Trades/Industrial/Misc Unions	....	$16,500
United Steelworkers	....	$4,000
Food & Commercial Workers Union	....	$2,800
Carpenters & Joiners Union	....	$2,600
Intl Brotherhood of Electrical Workers	....	$2,000
Operating Engineers Union	....	$2,000
Others	....	$3,100

Government & Postal Workers	....	$9,575
National Assn of Retired Federal Employees	....	$5,000
National Assn of Letter Carriers	....	$1,850
Others	....	$2,725

Sea Transport Unions	....	$11,800
Marine Engineers Union*	....	$6,500
International Longshoremen Assn	....	$1,800
Seafarers International Union	....	$1,500
Others	....	$2,000

Other Transportation Unions	....	$17,100
Teamsters Union	....	$7,500
Air Line Pilots Assn	....	$5,000
Amalgamated Transit Union	....	$2,500
Others	....	$2,100

Teachers Unions	....	$3,175
National Education Assn	....	$2,925
Others	....	$250

Ideological/Single-Issue

Pro-Israel	....	$6,050
National PAC	....	$5,000
Others	....	$1,050

Womens Issues/Pro-Choice	....	$4,300
Women's Campaign Fund	....	$2,500
Others	....	$1,800

Other Major Ideological/Single-Issue PACs

National Cmte to Preserve Social Security	$2,100	Soc Secur

Independent expenditures supporting Schneider

National Cmte to Preserve Social Security	....	$1,808

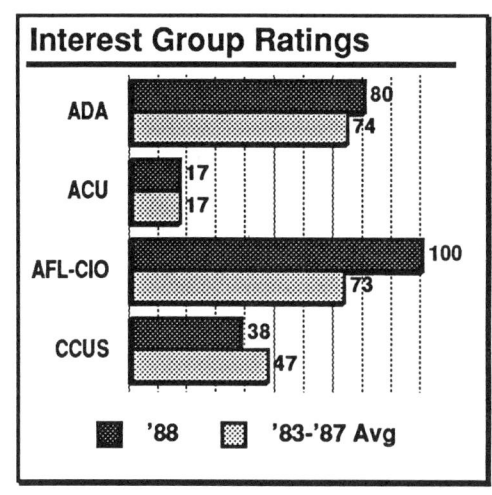

Interest Group Ratings

	'88	'83-'87 Avg
ADA	80	74
ACU	17	17
AFL-CIO	100	73
CCUS	38	47

■ '88   ▨ '83-'87 Avg

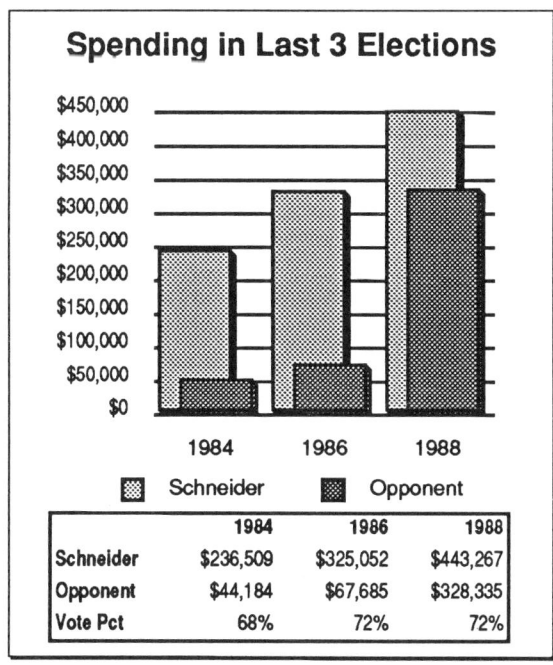

Spending in Last 3 Elections

	1984	1986	1988
Schneider	$236,509	$325,052	$443,267
Opponent	$44,184	$67,685	$328,335
Vote Pct	68%	72%	72%

▨ Schneider   ■ Opponent

---

* Contributions came from more than one PAC affiliated with this sponsor.

Patricia Schroeder, D-Colo (1)

First elected: 1972
Total receipts: $275,795
Total from PACs: $129,785

1988 Committees & Subcommittees

Armed Services
Military Installations and Facilities
Research and Development

Judiciary
Civil and Constitutional Rights
Courts, Civil Liberties and the Administration of Justice

Post Office and Civil Service
Civil Service (Chairwoman)

Select Children, Youth and Families

PAC Contribution Profile

Business

Broadcasting/Entertainment $9,600
    National Cable Television Assn $3,350
    Motion Picture Assn of America $1,500
    Warner Communications $1,500
    ASCAP $1,000
    MCA Inc $1,000
    Others $1,250

Construction $2,000
    Manville Corp $1,000
    National Assn of Home Builders $1,000

Defense..$3,050
    None over $600

Delivery Services $2,000
    United Parcel Service $2,000

Health Professionals $12,200
    American Dental Assn $5,000
    Assn for Advancement of Psychology $5,000
    Others $2,200

Import Auto Dealers $2,000
    Auto Dealers & Drivers for Free Trade $2,000

Insurance..$4,100
    Security Life of Denver $2,000
    National Assn of Life Underwriters $1,000
    Others $1,100

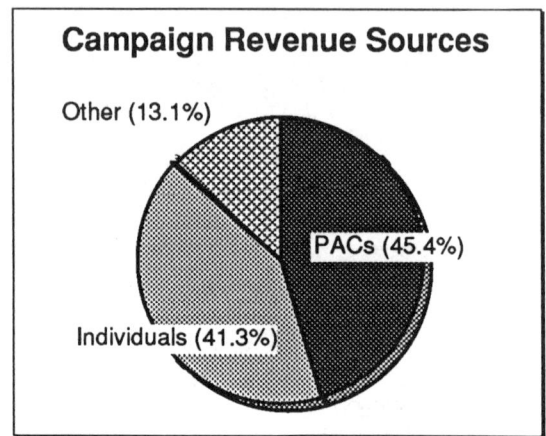

Campaign Revenue Sources

Other (13.1%)
PACs (45.4%)
Individuals (41.3%)

Lawyers & Lobbyists $6,850
    Assn of Trial Lawyers of America $5,500
    Others $1,350

Real Estate $2,700
    National Assn of Realtors $2,350
    Others $350

Other Major Business PACs

Kelly Service Inc	$1,000	EmployAgency
National Assn of Trade/Tech Schools	$1,000	Voc Tech
National Assn of Social Workers	$1,000	Social Work
West Publishing	$1,000	Books & Mags

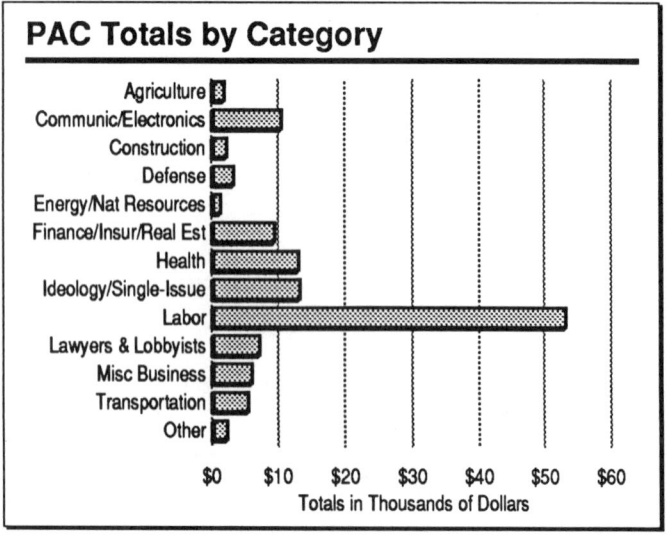

PAC Totals by Category

Agriculture
Communic/Electronics
Construction
Defense
Energy/Nat Resources
Finance/Insur/Real Est
Health
Ideology/Single-Issue
Labor
Lawyers & Lobbyists
Misc Business
Transportation
Other

$0 $10 $20 $30 $40 $50 $60
Totals in Thousands of Dollars

Labor

Bldg Trades/Industrial/Misc Unions $13,150

Food & Commercial Workers Union	$2,250
Carpenters & Joiners Union	$2,000
Machinists/Aerospace Workers Union	$1,500
Laborers' Political League	$1,350
Bakery, Confectioery & Tobacco Workers	$1,000
Operating Engineers Union	$1,000
United Steelworkers	$1,000
Others	$3,050

Government & Postal Workers $26,000

National Assn of Retired Federal Employees	$8,000
National Assn of Letter Carriers	$5,000
American Fedn of State/County/Munic Employees	$2,000
American Federation of Government Employees	$1,700
American Postal Workers Union	$1,700
National Assn of Postmasters	$1,700
National Treasury Employees Union	$1,700
National Assn of Postal Supervisors	$1,050
Others	$3,150

Teachers Unions $3,000

National Education Assn	$3,000

Transportation Unions $10,750

Teamsters Union	$5,000
Air Line Pilots Assn	$2,500
Assn of Flight Attendants	$1,000
Others	$2,250

Interest Group Ratings

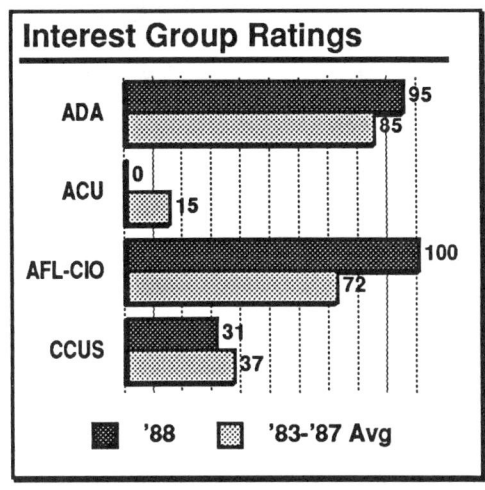

Ideological/Single-Issue

Gay/Lesbian Rights $5,000

Elections Cmte/Orange County	$4,000
Human Rights Campaign Fund	$1,000

Other Major Ideological/Single-Issue PACs

National Cmte to Preserve Social Security	$1,850	Soc Secur
Hollywood Women's Political Cmte	$1,000	Dem/Liberal
Valley Education Fund (Tony Coelho)	$1,000	Dem Leaders
Voters for Choice/Friends of Family Planning	$1,000	Pro-Choice

Independent expenditures supporting Schroeder

National Cmte to Preserve Social Security	$3,258

Independent expenditures opposing Schroeder

American Citizens for Political Action	$1,421

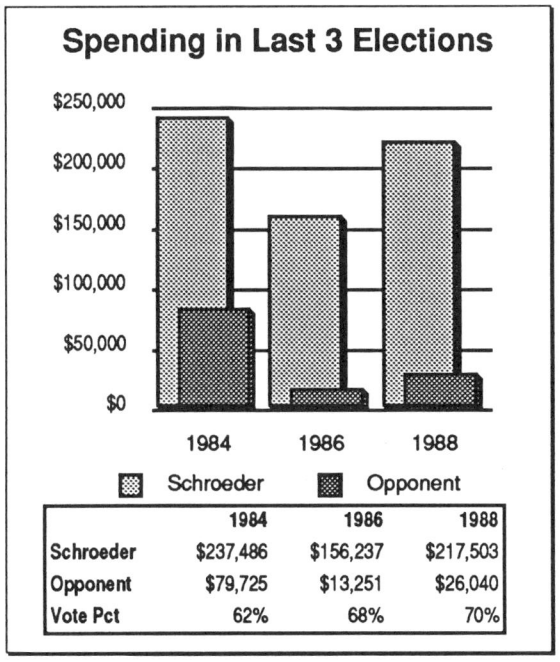

	1984	1986	1988
Schroeder	$237,486	$156,237	$217,503
Opponent	$79,725	$13,251	$26,040
Vote Pct	62%	68%	70%

Bill Schuette, R-Mich (10)

First elected: 1984
Total receipts: $782,377
Total from PACs: $292,987

1988 Committees & Subcommittees

Agriculture
Domestic Marketing, Consumer Relations and Nutrition
Forests, Family Farms and Energy
Wheat, Soybeans and Feed Grains

Select Aging
Housing and Consumer Interests
Retirement Income and Employment

PAC Contribution Profile

Business

Agricultural Chemicals	**$12,200**
Dow Chemical*	$6,200
Ecolab Inc	$1,000
FMC Corp	$1,000
Freeport-McMoran Inc	$1,000
Others	$3,000
Automotive	**$19,700**
Auto Dealers & Drivers for Free Trade	$10,000
National Auto Dealers Assn	$4,350
General Motors	$1,150
Ford Motor Company	$1,100
Federal-Mogul Corp	$1,000
Others	$2,100
Commodities/Securities Investment	**$6,850**
Commodity Exchange Inc	$1,800
Chicago Mercantile Exchange	$1,250
Chicago Board of Trade	$1,000
Smith Barney	$1,000
Others	$1,800
Construction	**$14,900**
National Assn of Home Builders	$5,500
Associated General Contractors	$2,500
Associated Builders & Contractors	$1,500
Sheet Metal/AirCon Contractors	$1,000
Others	$4,400

Campaign Revenue Sources

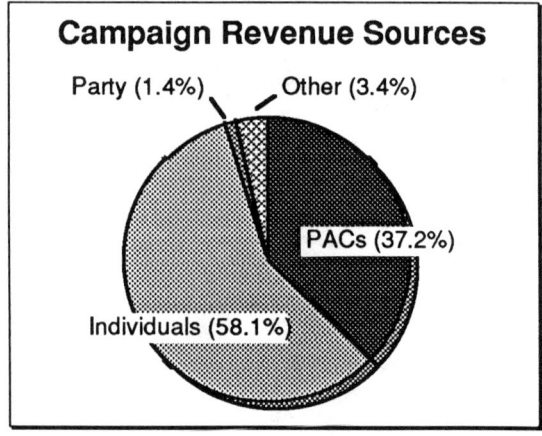

Party (1.4%) Other (3.4%)
PACs (37.2%)
Individuals (58.1%)

Dairy	**$19,150**
Associated Milk Producers	$7,500
Dairymen Inc	$4,250
Mid-American Dairymen	$3,600
Land O'Lakes Inc	$1,300
Michigan Milk Producers Assn	$1,300
Others	$1,200
Electric Utilities & Equipment	**$9,110**
Consumers Power Company	$4,260
Detroit Edison	$1,400
ACRE (Action Committee for Rural Electrification)	$1,300
Gilbert Associates	$1,000
Others	$1,150
Financial Institutions	**$14,250**
American Bankers Assn	$2,750
Comerica Inc	$2,500
Michigan League of Savings Institutions	$2,000
Independent Bankers Assn	$1,600
Michigan Credit Union League	$1,500
Security Bancorp	$1,000
Others	$2,900
Food & Beverage	**$20,700**
American Meat Institute	$2,150
Kellogg Company	$2,000
Food Marketing Institute	$1,900
ConAgra Inc	$1,550
Michigan Beer & Wine Wholesalers Assn	$1,550
Pillsbury Company	$1,300
A E Staley Manufacturing Company	$1,100
Coca-Cola Company	$1,050
General Mills	$1,000
National Restaurant Assn	$1,000
Others	$6,100
Forest Products	**$6,500**
Weyerhaeuser Company*	$2,600
Georgia-Pacific Corp	$1,150
Others	$2,750
Grain & Soybean Growing/Processing	**$7,900**
Archer-Daniels-Midland Corp	$2,500
Cargill Inc	$2,000
National Assn of Wheat Growers	$1,200
Central Soya Company	$1,000
Others	$1,200

PAC Totals by Category

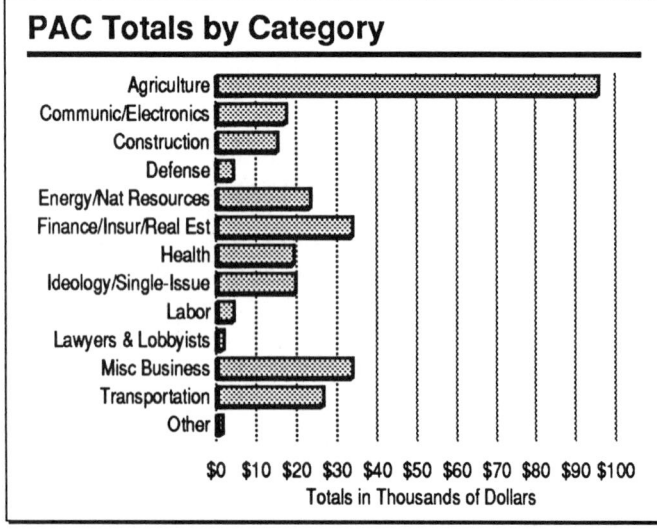

Category	
Agriculture	
Communic/Electronics	
Construction	
Defense	
Energy/Nat Resources	
Finance/Insur/Real Est	
Health	
Ideology/Single-Issue	
Labor	
Lawyers & Lobbyists	
Misc Business	
Transportation	
Other	

$0 $10 $20 $30 $40 $50 $60 $70 $80 $90 $100
Totals in Thousands of Dollars

Health Professionals $13,185

American Medical Assn	$8,635
American Academy of Ophthalmology	$2,000
American Dental Assn	$2,000
Others	$550

Insurance $9,000

National Assn of Life Underwriters	$4,500
Independent Insurance Agents of America	$2,150
Others	$2,350

Oil & Gas $12,400

Sun Company	$2,500
Michigan Consolidated Gas	$1,250
Amoco Corp	$1,050
Ashland Oil	$1,000
Phillips Petroleum	$1,000
Others	$5,600

Real Estate $7,550

National Assn of Realtors	$7,000
Others	$550

Sugar Growers $9,325

Great Lakes Sugar Beet Growers	$2,075
American Sugarbeet Growers Assn	$1,700
American Crystal Sugar Corp	$1,300
Southern Minnesota Beet Sugar Co-op	$1,250
Others	$3,000

Telecommunications $14,450

Michigan Bell Telephone	$7,500
AT&T	$1,500
US Telephone Assn	$1,100
Northern Telecom	$1,050
Others	$3,300

Textiles $5,600

Burlington Industries	$1,600
American Textile Manufacturers Institute	$1,500
Collins & Aikman Corp	$1,200
J P Stevens & Company	$1,000
Others	$300

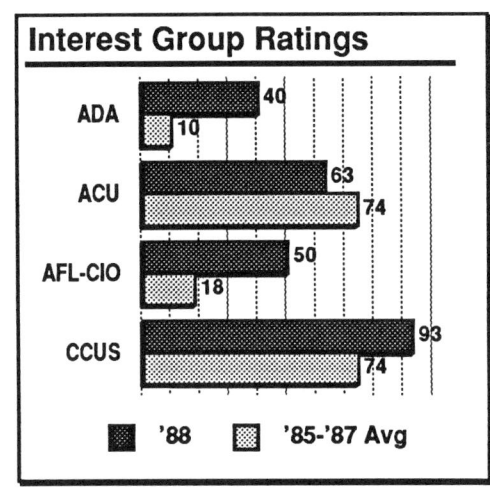

Interest Group Ratings

	'88	'85-'87 Avg
ADA	40	10
ACU	63	74
AFL-CIO	50	18
CCUS	93	74

Other Major Business PACs

National Pest Control Assn	$3,900	Pest Control
Dow Corning Corp/Employees	$2,500	PlasticRubb
Michigan Farm Bureau	$2,500	Farm Orgs
National Tooling & Machining Assn	$2,250	Indust Equip
Electronic Data Systems	$2,223	Data Process
Air Line Pilots Assn	$2,000	AirTrans Lab
Corning Glass Works	$2,000	Glass Prod
JSJ Corp	$2,000	Indust Equip
Philip Morris	$1,600	Tobacco
K Mart Corporation PAC	$1,500	Dept Store
American Feed Industry Assn	$1,300	Animal Health
American Airlines	$1,300	Airlines
Chicago & North Western Transport	$1,300	Railroads
Cleveland-Cliffs Iron Company	$1,250	Metals/Mining
Upjohn Company	$1,250	Pharmaceut
American Hospital Assn	$1,050	Hospitals
American Veterinary Medical Assn	$1,000	Veterinary
Harris Corp	$1,000	Defense
Merck & Company	$1,000	Animal Health
Precision Metalforming Assn	$1,000	MetalProduct
Schering-Plough Corp	$1,000	Pharmaceut

Major Labor PACs

Marine Engineers District 2 Maritime Officers	$1,000	Seamen Union

Ideological/Single-Issue

Pro-Israel $12,100

National PAC	$5,000
Hudson Valley PAC	$3,850
Garden State PAC	$1,000
Roundtable PAC	$1,000
Others	$1,250

Other Major Ideological/Single-Issue PACs

National Rifle Assn	$3,100	Pro-Guns
Campaign America (Bob Dole)	$1,648	Repub Leader
Pennsylvania Good Government Cmte	$1,000	Repub/Conser
Forum	$1,000	Unknown

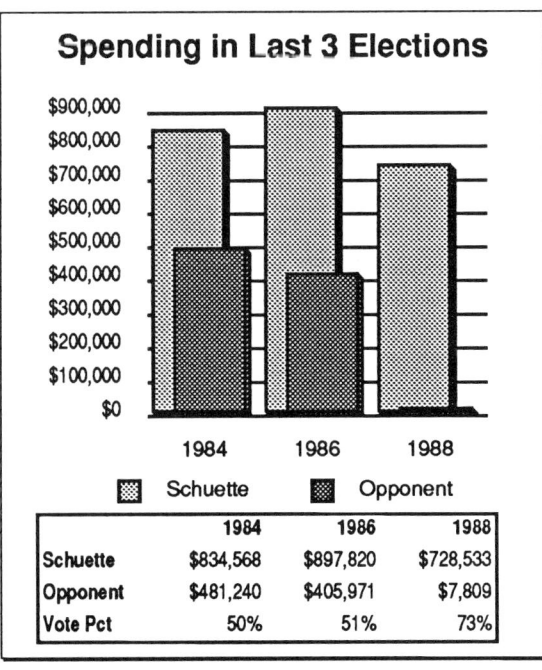

Spending in Last 3 Elections

	1984	1986	1988
Schuette	$834,568	$897,820	$728,533
Opponent	$481,240	$405,971	$7,809
Vote Pct	50%	51%	73%

* Contributions came from more than one PAC affiliated with this sponsor.

Richard T. Schulze, R-Pa (5)

First elected: 1974
Total receipts: $435,745
Total from PACs: $264,420

1988 Committees & Subcommittees

Ways and Means
Oversight (Ranking Republican)
Trade

PAC Contribution Profile

Business

Accountants	**$7,500**
American Institute of CPA's	$5,000
Others	$2,500
Automotive	**$8,500**
National Auto Dealers Assn	$3,500
Auto Dealers & Drivers for Free Trade	$1,500
Others	$3,500
Chemicals	**$9,100**
FMC Corp	$2,600
Others	$6,500
Construction	**$6,850**
National Assn of Home Builders	$3,000
Associated General Contractors	$1,500
Others	$2,350
Defense	**$6,350**
None over $1,000	
Electric Utilities	**$11,050**
Philadelphia Electric	$3,600
Florida Power & Light	$1,500
Others	$5,950
Financial Institutions	**$9,600**
American Bankers Assn	$3,000
Pennsylvania Savings League	$1,200
Others	$5,400

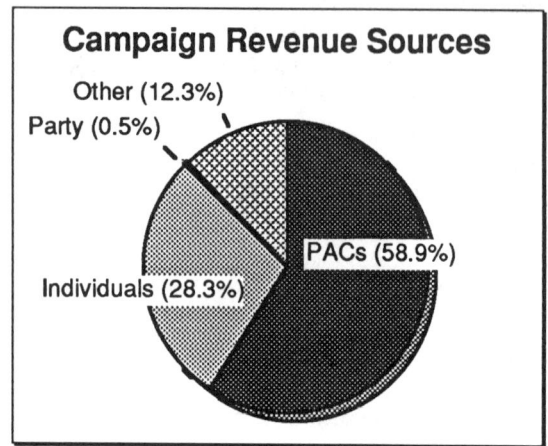

Campaign Revenue Sources

- Other (12.3%)
- Party (0.5%)
- PACs (58.9%)
- Individuals (28.3%)

Food & Beverage	**$14,700**
National Restaurant Assn	$2,000
National Beer Wholesalers Assn	$1,500
Whitman Corp	$1,300
Others	$9,900
Health Professionals	**$14,750**
American Medical Assn	$4,000
American Dental Assn	$3,000
National Assn of Pharmacists	$2,000
Pennsylvania Medical Assn	$1,750
Oral & Maxillofacial Surgeons	$1,500
Others	$2,500
Hospitals & Nursing Homes	**$5,000**
American Hospital Assn	$3,000
American Health Care Assn	$1,500
Others	$500
Insurance	**$46,221**
National Assn of Life Underwriters	$7,000
Torchmark Corp	$5,000
American Family Corp	$2,000
Massachusetts Mutual Life Insurance	$2,000
North Western Mutual Life	$2,000
Provident Mutual Life Insurance	$1,800
Metropolitan Life Insurance	$1,521
American Council of Life Insurance	$1,500
New England Mutual Life	$1,500
Travelers Corp	$1,500
Independent Insurance Agents of America	$1,200
Others	$19,200
Lawyers & Lobbyists	**$10,000**
Assn of Trial Lawyers of America	$5,000
Schnader Harrison Segal & Lewis	$2,500
Others	$2,500
Mining	**$5,300**
None over $1,000	
Oil & Gas	**$14,550**
Columbia Gas*	$2,000
Atlantic Richfield	$1,300
Others	$11,250
Pharmaceuticals	**$10,650**
Smithkline Beckman	$4,000
Others	$6,650

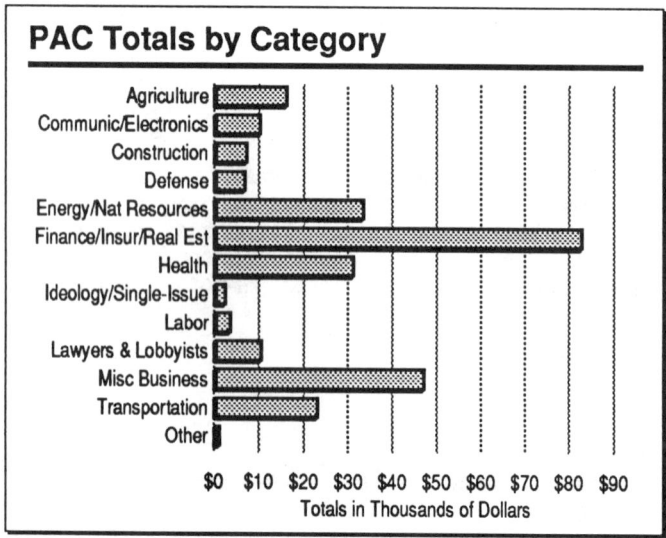

PAC Totals by Category

- Agriculture
- Communic/Electronics
- Construction
- Defense
- Energy/Nat Resources
- Finance/Insur/Real Est
- Health
- Ideology/Single-Issue
- Labor
- Lawyers & Lobbyists
- Misc Business
- Transportation
- Other

$0 $10 $20 $30 $40 $50 $60 $70 $80 $90
Totals in Thousands of Dollars

Real Estate *$7,500*
    National Assn of Realtors $6,000
    Others $1,500

Securities/Commodities Investment *$9,500*
    Chicago Board of Trade $2,000
    First Boston Corp $2,000
    Others $5,500

Steel Production *$7,200*
    Armco Inc $1,500
    LTV Steel $1,500
    Others $4,200

Telecommunications *$7,550*
    AT&T $2,500
    Bell Telephone of Pennsylvania $1,500
    Others $3,550

Textiles *$7,050*
    American Textile Manufacturers Institute $5,000
    Others $2,050

Other Major Business PACs

National Venture Capital Assn	$3,000	Venture Cap
Corning Glass Works	$2,000	Glass Prod
American Bus Assn	$1,500	Bus Svcs
United Parcel Service	$1,500	Delivery
Scott Paper Company	$1,300	Paper Prod

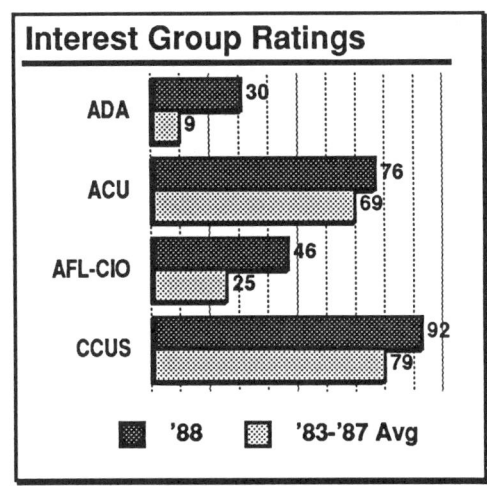

Interest Group Ratings

ADA: '88 = 30, '83-'87 Avg = 9
ACU: '88 = 76, '83-'87 Avg = 69
AFL-CIO: '88 = 46, '83-'87 Avg = 25
CCUS: '88 = 92, '83-'87 Avg = 79

■ '88   ▨ '83-'87 Avg

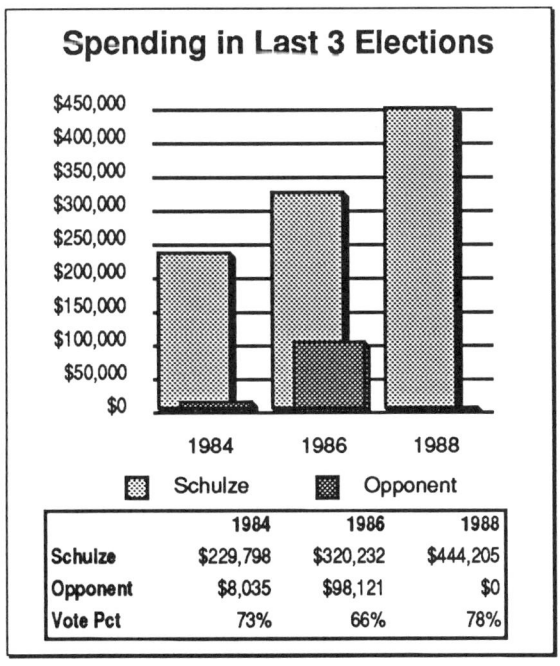

Spending in Last 3 Elections

▨ Schulze   ■ Opponent

	1984	1986	1988
Schulze	$229,798	$320,232	$444,205
Opponent	$8,035	$98,121	$0
Vote Pct	73%	66%	78%

* Contributions came from more than one PAC affiliated with this sponsor.

Charles E. Schumer, D-NY (10)

First elected: 1980
Total receipts: $437,574
Total from PACs: $137,325

1988 Committees & Subcommittees

Banking, Finance and Urban Affairs
Financial Institutions Supervision, Regulation and Insurance
Housing and Community Development
International Development Institutions and Finance

Budget
Economic and Trade Policy
Health
State and Local Government

Judiciary
Civil and Constitutional Rights
Immigration, Refugees and International Law

PAC Contribution Profile

Business

Accountants **$7,000**
    American Institute of CPA's $5,000
    Others $2,000

Automotive **$3,000**
    Auto Dealers & Drivers for Free Trade $2,500
    Others $500

Financial Institutions **$7,525**
    Anchor Savings Bank $1,000
    Bank of New York $1,000
    Columbia Savings & Loan (Beverly Hills) $1,000
    US League of Savings Assn $1,000
    Others $3,525

Health Professionals **$9,500**
    American Dental Assn $6,000
    New York Medical Assn $2,500
    Others $1,000

Insurance **$14,490**
    National Assn of Life Underwriters $2,500
    American Council of Life Insurance $1,740
    Connecticut Mutual Life Insurance $1,000
    Equitable Financial Services $1,000
    Home Group Inc $1,000
    Independent Insurance Agents of America $1,000
    Massachusetts Mutual Life Insurance $1,000
    Travelers Corp $1,000
    Others $4,250

Campaign Revenue Sources

Other (19.0%)
PACs (32.2%)
Individuals (48.8%)

Lawyers **$6,500**
    Assn of Trial Lawyers of America $5,500
    Others $1,000

Real Estate **$5,750**
    National Assn of Realtors $3,500
    Metropolitan Life Insurance $1,000
    Others $1,250

Securities/Commodities Investment **$53,500**
    Shearson Lehman Hutton $8,500
    First Boston Corp $8,000
    Bear, Stearns & Company $5,000
    Commodity Exchange Inc $5,000
    Goldman Sachs $5,000
    Investment Company Institute $5,000
    Oppenheimer Holdings Inc $3,000
    Prudential-Bache Securities $3,000
    Chicago Board of Trade $2,000
    Federated Investors Inc $2,000
    Chicago Mercantile Exchange $1,000
    Dean Witter Reynolds $1,000
    E F Hutton Group $1,000
    Morgan Stanley & Company $1,000
    New York Stock Exchange $1,000
    PaineWebber $1,000
    Others $1,000

Other Major Business PACs

American Express .... $1,000   Credit/Loans
International Council of Shopping Centers ...... $1,000   Retail
Joseph E Seagram & Sons .... $1,000   Wine&Liquor

PAC Totals by Category

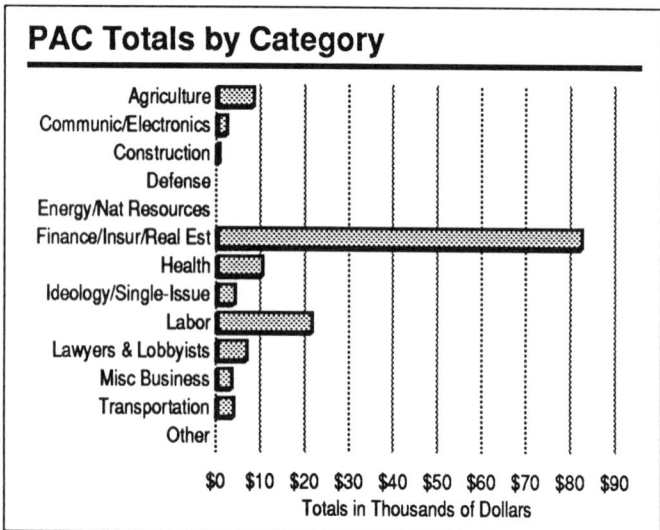

Category	
Agriculture	
Communic/Electronics	
Construction	
Defense	
Energy/Nat Resources	
Finance/Insur/Real Est	
Health	
Ideology/Single-Issue	
Labor	
Lawyers & Lobbyists	
Misc Business	
Transportation	
Other	

$0 $10 $20 $30 $40 $50 $60 $70 $80 $90
Totals in Thousands of Dollars

Labor

Bldg Trades/Industrial/Misc Unions **$4,450**
    Carpenters & Joiners Union $1,500
    Food & Commercial Workers Union $1,000
    Others $1,950

Government & Postal Workers **$8,000**
    National Assn of Retired Federal Employees $3,000
    American Fedn of State/County/Munic Employees $2,000
    American Postal Workers Union $1,500
    National Assn of Letter Carriers $1,000
    Others $500

Teachers Unions **$4,500**
    National Education Assn $4,500

Transportation Unions **$4,250**
    Seafarers International Union $1,000
    Teamsters Union $1,000
    Others $2,250

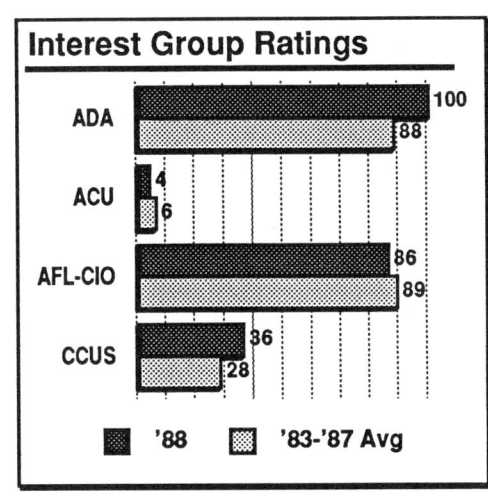

Interest Group Ratings

Group	'88	'83-'87 Avg
ADA	100	88
ACU	4	6
AFL-CIO	86	89
CCUS	36	28

Ideological/Single-Issue

Ideological/Single-Issue **$4,250**
National Cmte to Preserve Social Security ...... $1,000   Soc Secur
National Council of Senior Citizens .... $1,000   Soc Secur
Others $2,250

Independent expenditures supporting Schumer
National Cmte to Preserve Social Security $1,776

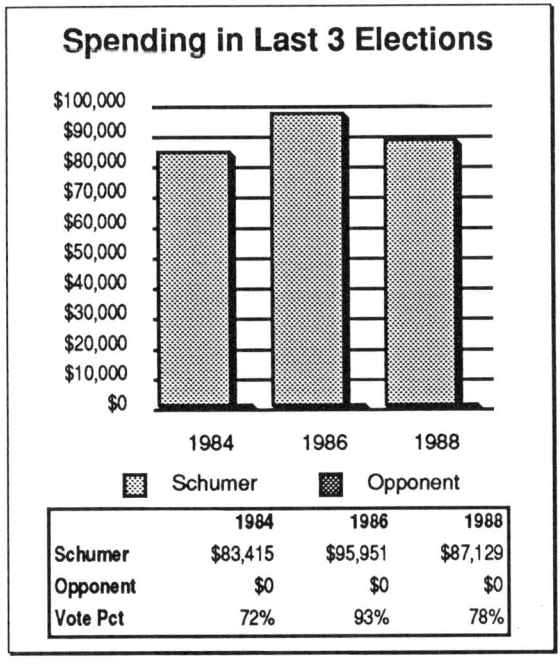

Spending in Last 3 Elections

	1984	1986	1988
Schumer	$83,415	$95,951	$87,129
Opponent	$0	$0	$0
Vote Pct	72%	93%	78%

F. James Sensenbrenner Jr., R-Wis (9)

First elected: 1978
Total receipts: $309,612
Total from PACs: $109,839

1988 Committees & Subcommittees

Judiciary
Civil and Constitutional Rights (Ranking Republican)
Monopolies and Commercial Law

Science, Space and Technology
International Scientific Cooperation (Ranking Republican)
Investigations and Oversight
Transportation, Aviation and Materials

Select Narcotics Abuse and Control

PAC Contribution Profile

Business

Accountants	**$6,300**
American Institute of CPA's	$5,000
Others	$1,300
Aerospace	**$6,250**
Boeing Company	$5,000
Others	$1,250
Automotive	**$3,750**
National Auto Dealers Assn	$2,000
Auto Dealers & Drivers for Free Trade	$1,500
Others	$250
Commercial & Savings Banks	**$3,300**
None over $500	
Construction	**$5,850**
Associated General Contractors	$2,500
National Assn of Home Builders	$1,500
National Electrical Contractors Assn	$1,000
Others	$850
Dairy	**$5,500**
Associated Milk Producers	$5,000
Others	$500

Campaign Revenue Sources

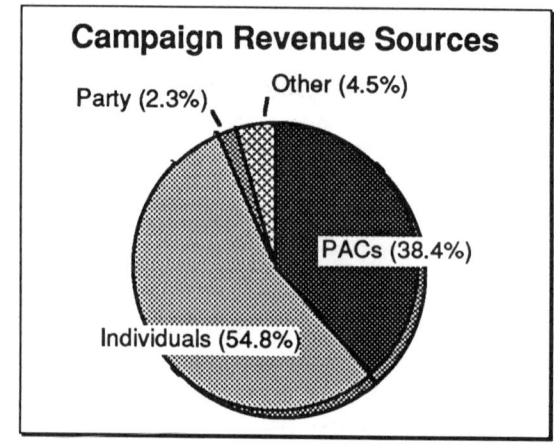

Party (2.3%)
Other (4.5%)
PACs (38.4%)
Individuals (54.8%)

Defense	**$3,500**
Rockwell International	$1,000
Tenneco Inc	$1,000
Others	$1,500
Electric Utilities	**$3,600**
Wisconsin Electric Power Company	$2,350
Others	$1,250
Food & Beverage	**$5,950**
National Beer Wholesalers Assn	$2,000
Food Marketing Institute	$1,500
Others	$2,450
Health Professionals	**$3,250**
American Medical Assn	$2,250
Others	$1,000
Industrial Equipment & Materials	**$3,650**
Square D Company	$1,500
Others	$2,150
Insurance	**$16,000**
National Assn of Life Underwriters	$4,000
North Western Mutual Life	$2,000
National Assn of Independent Insurers	$1,500
Others	$8,500
Lawyers & Lobbyists	**$11,000**
Assn of Trial Lawyers of America	$10,000
Others	$1,000
Oil & Gas	**$2,700**
None over $750	
Pharmaceuticals	**$2,800**
None over $350	
Real Estate	**$10,500**
National Assn of Realtors	$10,000
Others	$500
Telecommunications	**$4,750**
AT&T	$2,000
Wisconsin Bell Telephone	$1,000
Others	$1,750

PAC Totals by Category

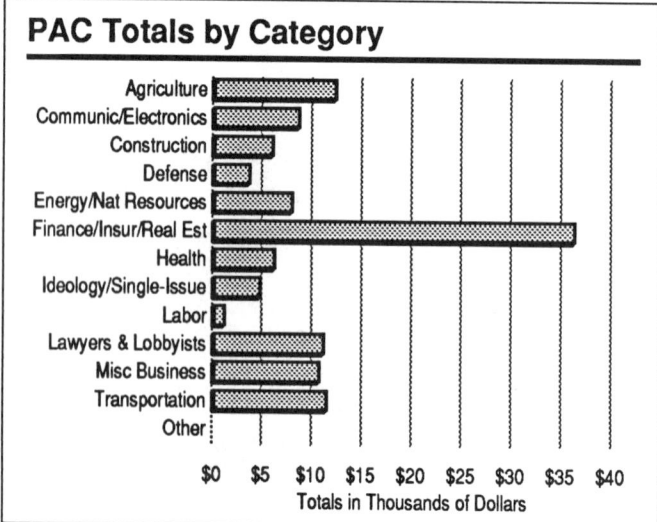

Agriculture
Communic/Electronics
Construction
Defense
Energy/Nat Resources
Finance/Insur/Real Est
Health
Ideology/Single-Issue
Labor
Lawyers & Lobbyists
Misc Business
Transportation
Other

$0 $5 $10 $15 $20 $25 $30 $35 $40
Totals in Thousands of Dollars

TV/Movies **$2,250**
     National Cable Television Assn $1,000
     Others $1,250

Other Major Business PACs

FMC Corp ....$1,000   Chemicals
Marriott Corp ....$1,000   Hotel/Motel
Philip Morris ....$1,000   Tobacco
Waste Management Inc ....$1,000   Waste Mgmt
West Publishing ....$1,000   Books & Mags

Major Labor PACs

National Assn of Retired Federal Employees ..$1,000   Fedl Workers

Ideological/Single-Issue

Ideological/Single-Issue **$4,587**
Council for National Defense ....$1,837   Pro-Defense
Handgun Control Inc ....$1,000   Anti-Guns
Others...$1,750

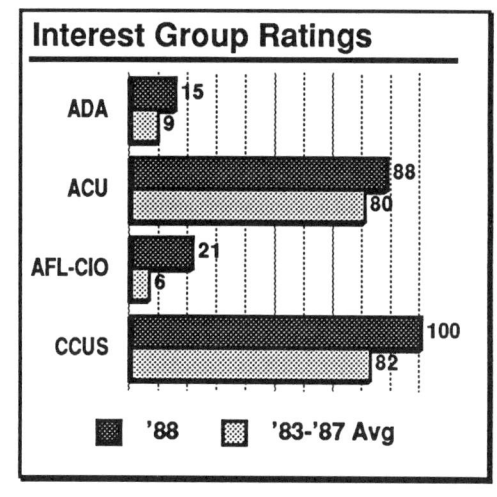

Interest Group Ratings

	'88	'83-'87 Avg
ADA	15	9
ACU	88	80
AFL-CIO	21	6
CCUS	100	82

■ '88   ▨ '83-'87 Avg

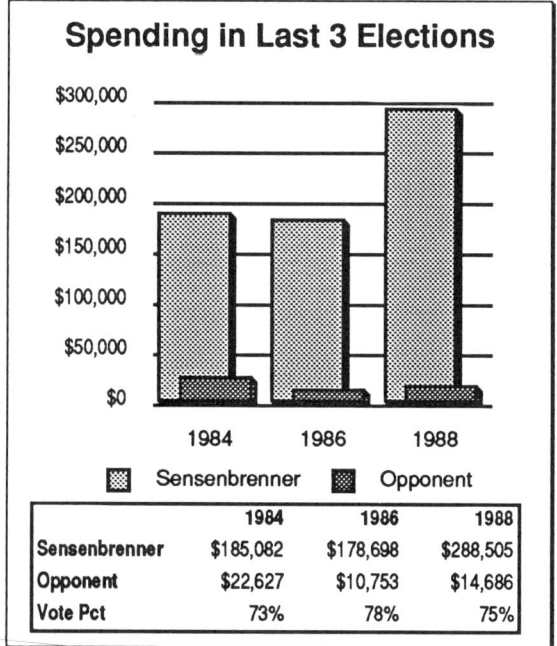

Spending in Last 3 Elections

▨ Sensenbrenner   ■ Opponent

	1984	1986	1988
Sensenbrenner	$185,082	$178,698	$288,505
Opponent	$22,627	$10,753	$14,686
Vote Pct	73%	78%	75%

Philip R. Sharp, D-Ind (2)

1988 Committees & Subcommittees

First elected: 1974
Total receipts: $465,414
Total from PACs: $310,981

Energy and Commerce
Energy and Power (Chairman)
Commerce, Consumer Protection and Competitiveness

Interior and Insular Affairs
Energy and the Environment
Water and Power Resources

PAC Contribution Profile

Business

Accountants	**$7,000**
American Institute of CPA's	$5,000
Coopers & Lybrand	$1,200
Others	$800
Commercial Banks	**$9,850**
American Bankers Assn	$4,000
Citicorp	$2,000
Banc One Corp*	$1,600
Indiana Bankers Assn	$1,125
Indiana National Corp	$1,000
Others	$125
Construction	**$8,300**
National Assn of Home Builders	$3,500
Manville Corp	$1,000
Others	$3,800
Electric Utilities	**$26,150**
ACRE (Action Committee for Rural Electrification)*	$3,400
American Electric Power*	$2,400
Southern California Edison	$2,300
Texas Utilities Electric Company*	$2,000
Consumers Power Company	$1,450
Southern Company*	$1,350
Pacific Gas & Electric	$1,300
Public Service Company of Indiana	$1,250
National Independent Energy Producers	$1,000
Others	$9,700

Campaign Revenue Sources

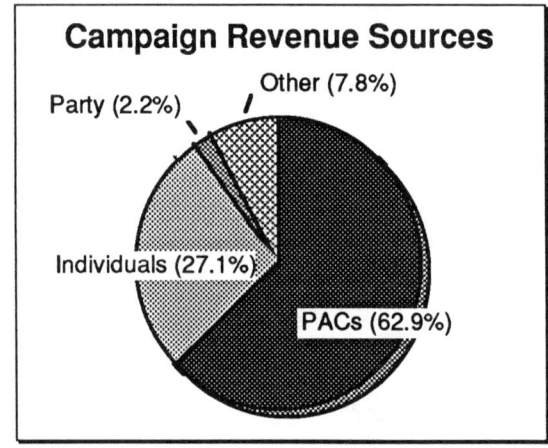

Party (2.2%)
Other (7.8%)
Individuals (27.1%)
PACs (62.9%)

Food & Beverage	**$5,000**
American Bakers Assn	$1,050
Others	$3,950
Lawyers & Lobbyists	**$13,200**
Akin, Gump, Hauer & Feld	$1,700
Van Ness, Feldman, Sucliffe & Curtis	$1,500
Dickstein, Shapiro & Morin	$1,300
Rivkin, Radler, Dunne & Baye Good Government Cmte	$1,300
Crowell & Moring	$1,150
Others	$6,250
Mining	**$6,950**
Alcoa	$1,300
National Coal Assn	$1,050
Freeport-McMoran Inc	$1,000
Independent Coal Operators Assn	$1,000
Others	$2,600
Oil & Gas	**$38,556**
Columbia Gas*	$2,800
Coastal Corp	$2,300
Interstate Natural Gas Assn	$2,206
Chevron Corp	$1,950
Atlantic Richfield	$1,500
Pacific Enterprises	$1,300
Transco Energy Company	$1,300
Enserch Corp	$1,250
Williams Companies*	$1,250
Petroleum Marketers Assn	$1,100
Ashland Oil	$1,000
Panhandle Eastern Corp	$1,000
Texas Eastern Gas Transmission	$1,000
Union Pacific Corp	$1,000
Others	$17,600
Real Estate	**$6,250**
National Assn of Realtors	$6,250
Telecommunications	**$16,575**
AT&T	$5,000
Continental Telecom	$2,500
Indiana Bell Telephone	$2,100
Corning Glass Works	$2,000
Pacific Telesis Group	$1,300
United Telecommunications	$1,000
Others	$2,675

PAC Totals by Category

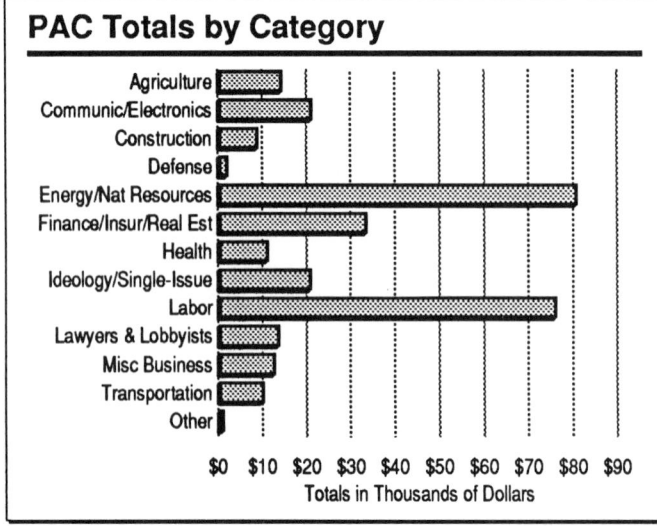

Agriculture
Communic/Electronics
Construction
Defense
Energy/Nat Resources
Finance/Insur/Real Est
Health
Ideology/Single-Issue
Labor
Lawyers & Lobbyists
Misc Business
Transportation
Other

$0 $10 $20 $30 $40 $50 $60 $70 $80 $90
Totals in Thousands of Dollars

Other Major Business PACs

Borg-Warner	$3,300	Indust Equip
Philip Morris	$2,700	Tobacco
Waste Management Inc	$2,600	Waste Mgmt
Indiana Farm Bureau	$2,500	Farm Orgs
Ford Motor Company	$2,250	Auto Mfrs
National Cable Television Assn	$2,000	CableTV
United Parcel Service	$1,950	Delivery
Westinghouse Electric	$1,550	NuclearEquip
American Dental Assn	$1,500	Dentists
National Society of Professional Engineers	$1,500	Energy
American College of Emergency Physicians	$1,300	Doctors
American Medical Assn	$1,250	Doctors
Eli Lilly & Company	$1,250	Pharmaceut
American Hospital Assn	$1,050	Hospitals
Associated Milk Producers	$1,000	Dairy
Combustion Engineering	$1,000	NuclearEquip
Investment Company Institute	$1,000	StocksInvest
Morgan Stanley & Company	$1,000	InvestmtBank
Travelers Corp	$1,000	Insurance

Labor

Bldg Trades/Industrial/Misc Unions $41,750

Sheet Metal Workers Union	$10,000
Operating Engineers Union*	$5,250
United Auto Workers	$5,000
AFL-CIO*	$3,800
Carpenters & Joiners Union	$3,100
Plumbers/Pipefitters Union	$2,500
Laborers' Political League	$2,300
Food & Commercial Workers Union	$2,000
Intl Brotherhood of Electrical Workers	$2,000
United Steelworkers	$2,000
United Mine Workers	$1,850
Ladies Garment Workers Union	$1,250
Others	$700

Government & Postal Workers $13,908

National Assn of Retired Federal Employees	$7,000
American Fedn of State/County/Munic Employees	$4,408
American Postal Workers Union	$1,000
Others	$1,500

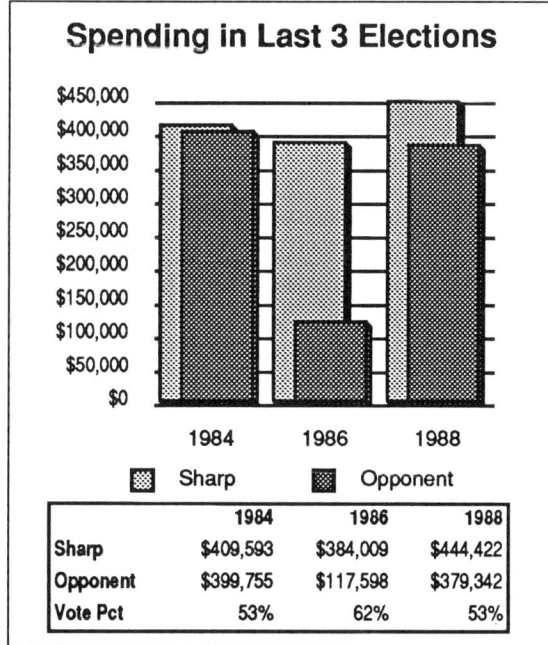

Spending in Last 3 Elections

	1984	1986	1988
Sharp	$409,593	$384,009	$444,422
Opponent	$399,755	$117,598	$379,342
Vote Pct	53%	62%	53%

Legend: Sharp, Opponent

Interest Group Ratings

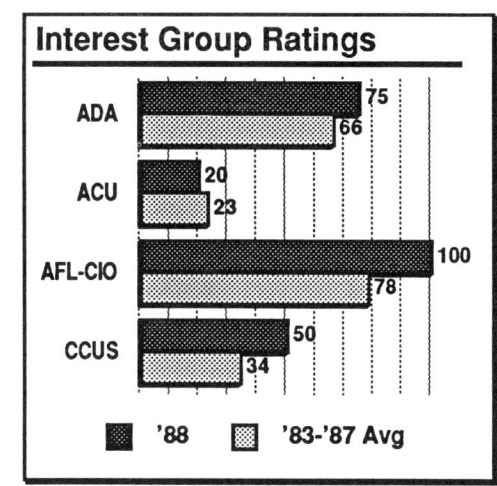

ADA 75 / 66
ACU 20 / 23
AFL-CIO 100 / 78
CCUS 50 / 34

■ '88   □ '83-'87 Avg

Teachers Unions $6,800

National Education Assn	$5,300
American Federation of Teachers	$1,500

Transportation Unions $13,000

Teamsters Union	$5,000
United Transportation Union	$3,250
Brotherhood of Railway Carmen	$1,000
Seafarers International Union	$1,000
Transport Workers Union	$1,000
Others	$1,750

Ideological/Single-Issue

Democratic Leadership PACs $13,500

24th Cong Dist of California PAC (Henry Waxman)	$5,000
Majority Congress Committee (Jim Wright)	$5,000
America's Leaders' Fund (Dan Rostenkowski)	$2,000
Valley Education Fund (Tony Coelho)	$1,000
Others	$500

Other Major Ideological/Single-Issue PACs

National Cmte to Preserve Social Security	$2,300	Soc Secur
KidsPAC	$1,000	HealthWelfare
National Council of Senior Citizens	$1,000	Soc Secur

Independent expenditures supporting Sharp

National Cmte to Preserve Social Security	$1,232

---

* Contributions came from more than one PAC affiliated
with this sponsor.

E. Clay Shaw Jr., R-Fla (15)

1988 Committees & Subcommittees

Ways and Means
Oversight
Public Assistance and Unemployment Compensation

First elected: 1980
Total receipts: $348,233
Total from PACs: $153,750

PAC Contribution Profile
Business

Accountants **$11,250**
- American Institute of CPA's $5,000
- Deloitte, Haskins & Sells $2,000
- Ernst & Whinney $2,000
- Coopers & Lybrand $1,250
- Others $1,000

Air Transport **$4,000**
- Texas Air $1,500
- Eastern Airlines $1,000
- Others $1,500

Automotive **$6,450**
- National Auto Dealers Assn $4,650
- Auto Dealers & Drivers for Free Trade $1,500
- Others $300

Chemicals & Explosives **$2,400**
- None over $650

Commercial Banks **$4,900**
- Barnett Banks of Florida $1,500
- Citizens & Southern National Bank $1,500
- Others $1,900

Construction **$16,850**
- Walter Industries $10,500
- National Utility Contractors Assn $2,500
- Associated General Contractors $1,650
- Sheet Metal/AirCon Contractors $1,300
- Others $900

Campaign Revenue Sources

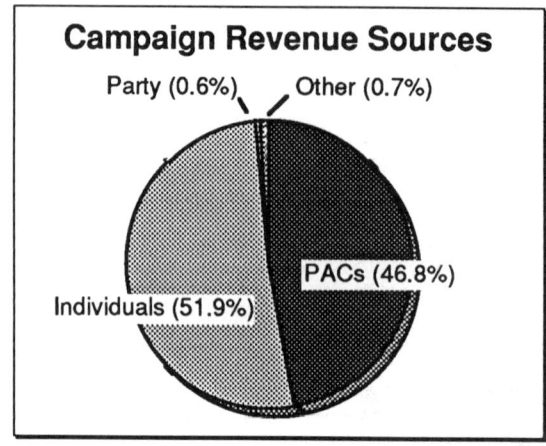

Party (0.6%)   Other (0.7%)
PACs (46.8%)
Individuals (51.9%)

Defense **$2,150**
- Harris Corp $1,000
- Others $1,150

Electric Utilities **$4,350**
- Florida Power & Light $1,500
- Others $2,850

Food & Beverage **$6,100**
- Winn-Dixie Stores $2,000
- Others $4,100

Health Professionals **$12,400**
- Florida Medical Assn $4,800
- American Dental Assn $3,000
- American Medical Assn $2,800
- American Academy of Ophthalmology $1,000
- Others $800

Hospitals **$3,050**
- None over $800

Hotels & Resorts **$2,150**
- Holiday Inns $1,000
- Others $1,150

Insurance **$15,650**
- National Assn of Life Underwriters $4,000
- American Council of Life Insurance $2,150
- Casualty & Surety Agents Assn $1,150
- National Assn of Independent Insurers $1,150
- Blue Cross & Blue Shield* $1,000
- Torchmark Corp $1,000
- Others $5,200

Oil & Gas **$5,300**
- None over $750

Pharmaceuticals **$2,500**
- None over $500

Real Estate **$11,900**
- National Assn of Realtors $8,750
- American Resort & Residential Developers Assn $1,500
- General Development Corp $1,000
- Others $650

PAC Totals by Category

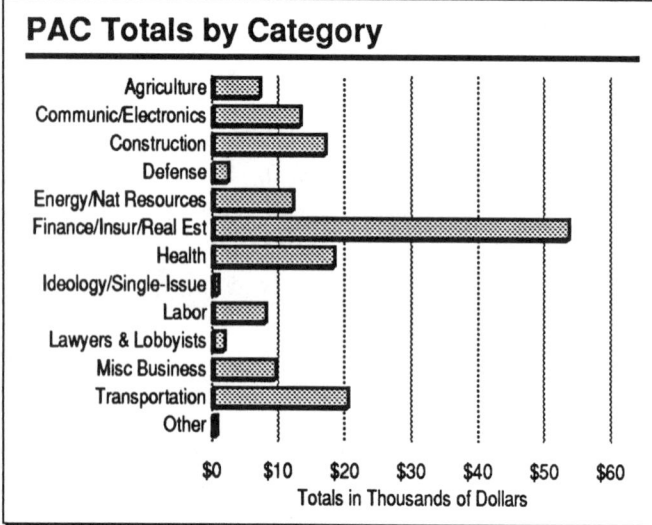

Categories (top to bottom): Agriculture, Communic/Electronics, Construction, Defense, Energy/Nat Resources, Finance/Insur/Real Est, Health, Ideology/Single-Issue, Labor, Lawyers & Lobbyists, Misc Business, Transportation, Other

Totals in Thousands of Dollars ($0, $10, $20, $30, $40, $50, $60)

Interest Group Ratings

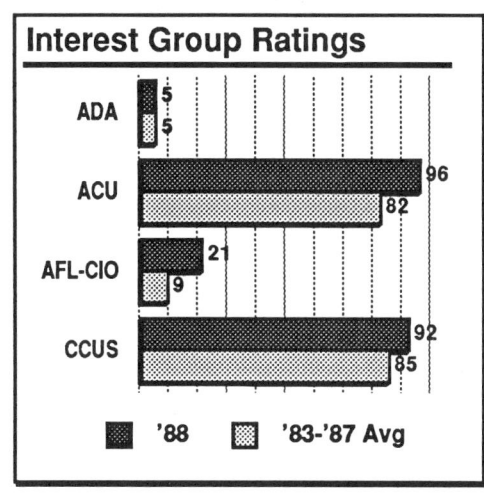

	'88	'83-'87 Avg
ADA	5	5
ACU	96	82
AFL-CIO	21	9
CCUS	92	85

Savings Banks **$5,200**

Florida League/Financial Institutions $2,000
Glendale Federal Savings & Loan $1,000
US League of Savings Assn $1,000
Others $1,200

Securities/Commodities Investment **$2,750**

Chicago Board of Trade $1,000
Others $1,750

Telecommunications **$11,250**

Southern Bell $4,000
AT&T $1,750
Motorola Inc $1,000
Others $4,500

Trucking/Delivery **$6,000**

United Parcel Service $1,750
Ryder System Inc $1,500
Consolidated Freightways $1,000
Others $1,750

Other Major Business PACs

American Express	$1,650	Credit/Loans
International Council of Shopping Centers	$1,000	Retail
National Assn of Temporary Services	$1,000	EmployAgency
National Venture Capital Assn	$1,000	Venture Cap
Waste Management Inc	$1,000	Waste Mgmt

Labor

Transportation Unions **$7,850**

Marine Engineers District 2 Maritime Officers $4,000
Air Line Pilots Assn $2,500
Seafarers International Union $1,000
Others $350

Spending in Last 3 Elections

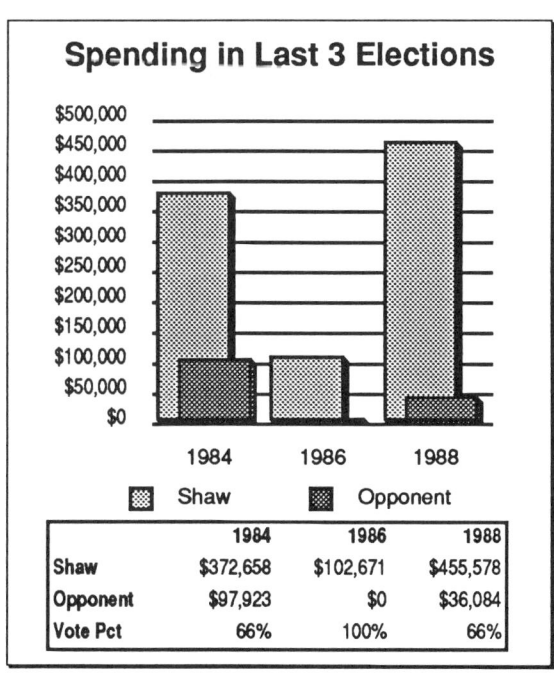

	Shaw	Opponent

	1984	1986	1988
Shaw	$372,658	$102,671	$455,578
Opponent	$97,923	$0	$36,084
Vote Pct	66%	100%	66%

* Contributions came from more than one PAC affiliated with this sponsor.

Christopher Shays, R-Conn (4)

1988 Committees & Subcommittees

First elected: 1987
Total receipts: $340,602
Total from PACs: $79,702

Government Operations	**Science, Space and Technology**
Commerce, Consumer and Monetary Affairs	Energy Research and Development
Employment and Housing	Science, Research and Technology
Human Resources and Intergovernmental Relations	
	Select Narcotics Abuse and Control

PAC Contribution Profile

NOTE: The PAC contributions listed on these pages include funds that Shays received both in 1988 and in the 1987 special election in which he was first elected to Congress. The total receipts listed in the box above, and the percentages in the pie chart at right, refer only to his 1988 general election race.

Business

Accountants	**$2,000**
American Institute of CPA's	$2,000
Automotive	**$1,500**
Eaton Corp	$1,000
Others	$500
Aviation & Aerospace	**$4,300**
United Technologies	$2,000
Aircraft Owners & Pilots Assn	$1,000
Others	$1,300
Commercial Banks	**$8,275**
Marine Midland Banks	$3,500
Hartford National Corp	$1,250
Others	$3,525
Construction	**$2,900**
Associated General Contractors	$1,000
Southdown Inc	$1,000
Others	$900
Consumer Credit & Loans	**$4,000**
Primerica Corp	$4,000
Food & Beverage	**$2,600**
National Restaurant Assn	$1,000
Pepsico Inc	$1,000
Others	$600

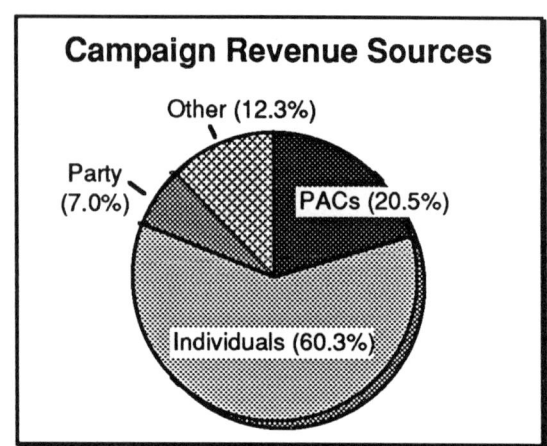

Campaign Revenue Sources

- Other (12.3%)
- Party (7.0%)
- PACs (20.5%)
- Individuals (60.3%)

Health Professionals	**$8,300**
American Academy of Ophthalmology	$5,000
American Medical Assn	$1,300
American Dental Assn	$1,000
Connecticut Medical Assn	$1,000
Insurance	**$3,000**
National Assn of Life Underwriters	$1,000
Others	$2,000
Lawyers & Lobbyists	**$1,700**
Cummings & Lockwood	$1,000
Others	$700
Pharmaceuticals	**$5,150**
Ciba-Geigy Corp	$2,300
Others	$2,850
Power Plant Equipment	**$1,500**
Combustion Engineering	$1,500
Real Estate	**$2,100**
National Assn of Realtors	$1,800
Others	$300
Savings Banks	**$6,029**
People's Bank (Bridgeport, Connecticut)	$2,643
National Council of Savings Institutions	$1,500
Others	$1,886
Telecommunications	**$4,800**
AT&T	$1,500
Southern New England Telecom	$1,050
Continental Telecom	$1,000
Others	$1,250
Tobacco	**$5,975**
United States Tobacco Company	$5,975
Other Major Business PACs	
Xerox Corp	$1,000 Off Machines

PAC Totals by Category

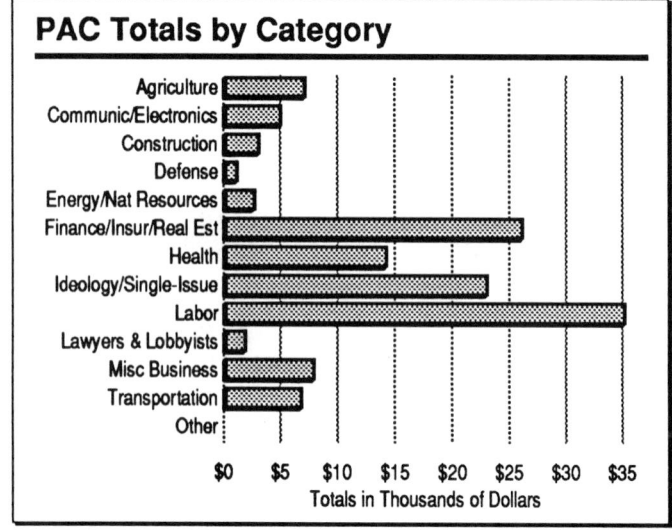

Agriculture
Communic/Electronics
Construction
Defense
Energy/Nat Resources
Finance/Insur/Real Est
Health
Ideology/Single-Issue
Labor
Lawyers & Lobbyists
Misc Business
Transportation
Other

$0 $5 $10 $15 $20 $25 $30 $35
Totals in Thousands of Dollars

Labor

Bldg Trades/Industrial/Misc Unions **$18,000**

    Carpenters & Joiners Union* $6,500
    Connecticut Union of Telephone Workers $5,500
    AFL-CIO Bldg/Construction Trades Dept $1,600
    Ironworkers Union $1,600
    Intl Brotherhood of Electrical Workers $1,000
    Plumbers/Pipefitters Union $1,000
    Others $800

Government & Postal Workers **$6,400**

    American Fedn of State/County/Munic Employees $2,500
    National Assn of Letter Carriers $2,000
    Others $1,900

Teachers Unions **$2,000**

    National Education Assn $2,000

Transportation Unions **$8,600**

    Marine Engineers Union* $5,000
    Teamsters Union $2,000
    Air Line Pilots Assn $1,000
    Others $600

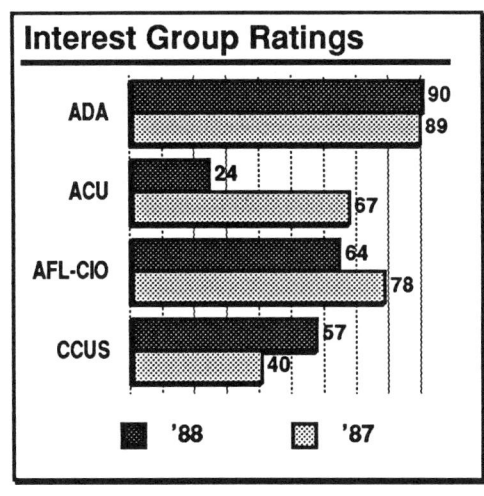

Interest Group Ratings

	'88	'87
ADA	90	89
ACU	24	67
AFL-CIO	64	78
CCUS	57	40

Ideological/Single-Issue

Gay/Lesbian Rights **$7,236**

    Human Rights Campaign Fund $7,236

Pro-Israel **$4,000**

    Hudson Valley PAC $2,000
    National PAC $2,000

Republican Leadership/Conservative PACs..............**$9,600**

    Republican Congressional Boosters Club $4,000
    Fund for America's Future (George Bush) $2,500
    Constitution Federal PAC (Lowell Weicker) $1,100
    Republican Majority Fund (Richard Lugar) $1,000
    Others $1,000

Other Major Ideological/Single-Issue PACs

Sierra Club ....$1,000   Environment

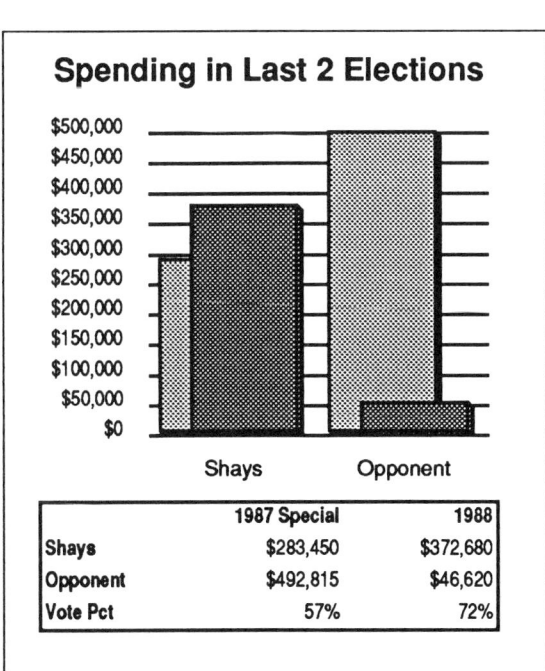

Spending in Last 2 Elections

	1987 Special	1988
Shays	$283,450	$372,680
Opponent	$492,815	$46,620
Vote Pct	57%	72%

---

* Contributions came from more than one PAC affiliated
with this sponsor.

Norman D. Shumway, R-Calif (14)

First elected: 1978
Total receipts: $390,233
Total from PACs: $151,635

1988 Committees & Subcommittees

Banking, Finance and Urban Affairs
Economic Stabilization (Ranking Republican)
Financial Institutions Supervision, Regulation and Insurance
International Finance, Trade and Monetary Policy

Merchant Marine and Fisheries
Oceanography (Ranking Republican)
Merchant Marine
Panama Canal/Outer Continental Shelf

Select Aging
Human Services
Retirement Income and Employment

PAC Contribution Profile

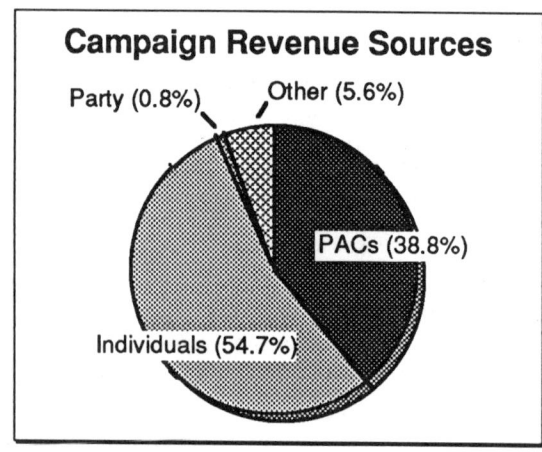

Campaign Revenue Sources

Party (0.8%)
Other (5.6%)
PACs (38.8%)
Individuals (54.7%)

Business

Automotive	**$2,750**
Auto Dealers & Drivers for Free Trade	$1,500
Others	$1,250
Commercial Banks	**$42,020**
American Bankers Assn	$10,000
Bank of Stockton	$5,350
J P Morgan & Company	$5,000
BankAmerica	$3,920
Bankers Trust	$3,000
Wells Fargo	$3,000
Barnett Banks of Florida	$2,000
Chase Manhattan	$1,750
Union Bank	$1,500
Assn of Bank Holding Companies	$1,250
Security Pacific Corp	$1,250
Others	$4,000
Construction	**$3,100**
Associated General Contractors	$1,500
National Assn of Home Builders	$1,000
Others	$600

Consumer Credit & Loans	**$2,800**
American Financial Services Assn	$1,250
Others	$1,550
Department Stores	**$2,600**
J C Penney Company	$1,000
Others	$1,600
Food & Beverage	**$3,050**
None over $500	
Fruit & Vegetable Growers	**$7,250**
California Almond Growers Exchange	$5,000
Tri/Valley Growers	$1,000
Others	$1,250
Health Professionals	**$8,500**
American Medical Assn	$6,750
American Dental Assn	$1,000
Others	$750
Insurance	**$9,500**
TransAmerica*	$4,000
Pacific Mutual Life	$1,000
Travelers Corp	$1,000
Others	$3,500
Oil & Gas	**$4,300**
None over $750	
Real Estate	**$6,750**
National Assn of Realtors	$6,000
Others	$750
Savings Banks	**$18,000**
California League of Savings Institutions	$2,000
Great Western Financial Corp	$2,000
Coast Federal Savings & Loan	$1,750
Glendale Federal Savings & Loan	$1,750
Mercury Savings & Loan	$1,250
American Savings & Loan Assn	$1,000
Home Federal Savings & Loan	$1,000
Home Savings of America	$1,000
US League of Savings Assn	$1,000
Others	$5,250

PAC Totals by Category

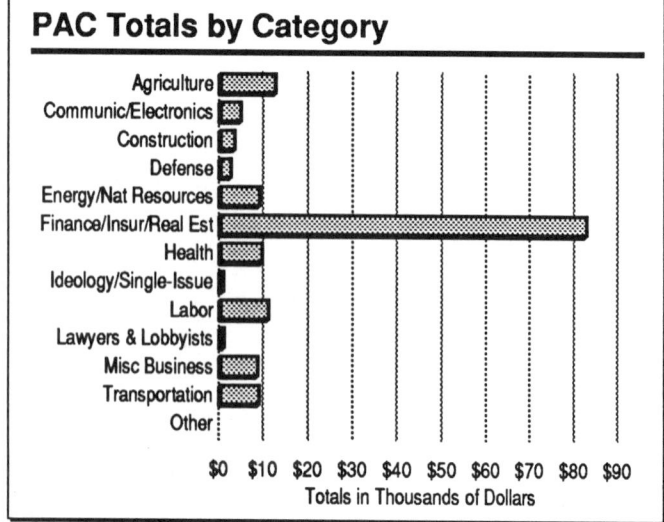

Agriculture
Communic/Electronics
Construction
Defense
Energy/Nat Resources
Finance/Insur/Real Est
Health
Ideology/Single-Issue
Labor
Lawyers & Lobbyists
Misc Business
Transportation
Other

$0 $10 $20 $30 $40 $50 $60 $70 $80 $90
Totals in Thousands of Dollars

Sea Transport *$3,000*
    Matson Navigation $1,500
    Others $1,500

Securities/Commodities Investment *$2,750*
    Chicago Mercantile Exchange $1,000
    Dean Witter Reynolds $1,000
    Others $750

Telecommunications *$4,250*
    Continental Telecom $1,500
    Pacific Telesis Group $1,250
    AT&T $1,000
    Others $500

Other Major Business PACs

Marriott Corp	$1,500	Hotel/Motel
Credit Union National Assn	$1,000	Credit Union
FMC Corp	$1,000	Chemicals

Labor

Sea Transport Unions *$10,700*
    Marine Engineers Union* $8,000
    Seafarers International Union $2,000
    Others $700

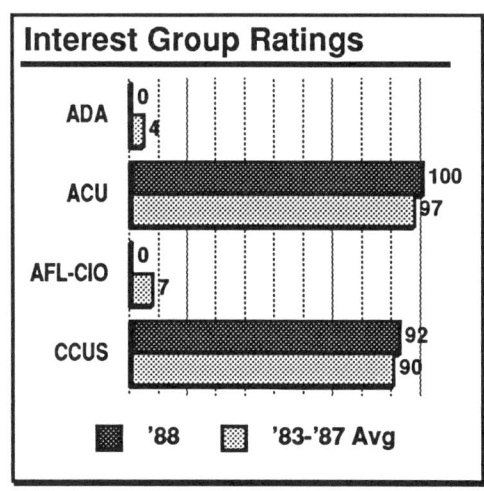

Interest Group Ratings

	'88	'83–'87 Avg
ADA	0	4
ACU	100	97
AFL-CIO	0	7
CCUS	92	90

■ '88   ▨ '83-'87 Avg

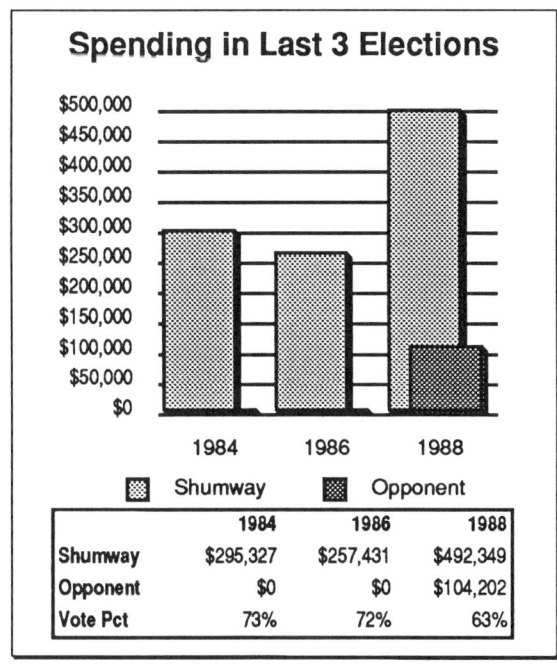

Spending in Last 3 Elections

▨ Shumway   ▦ Opponent

	1984	1986	1988
Shumway	$295,327	$257,431	$492,349
Opponent	$0	$0	$104,202
Vote Pct	73%	72%	63%

---

* Contributions came from more than one PAC affiliated with this sponsor.

Bud Shuster, R-Pa (9)

1988 Committees & Subcommittees

Public Works and Transportation
Surface Transportation (Ranking Republican)
Aviation
Investigations and Oversight

Select Intelligence
Legislation
Oversight and Evaluation

First elected: 1972
Total receipts: $402,210
Total from PACs: $152,815

PAC Contribution Profile

Business

Air Transport	**$8,800**
Federal Express Corp	$2,100
Eastern Airlines	$1,000
Others	$5,700
Automotive	**$2,950**
National Auto Dealers Assn	$1,300
Others	$1,650
Buses & Taxis	**$3,000**
American Bus Assn	$1,100
Others	$1,900
Chemicals	**$2,800**
Greyhound Corp	$1,300
Betz Laboratories	$1,000
Others	$500
Commercial & Savings Banks	**$2,500**
American Bankers Assn	$1,000
Others	$1,500
Construction	**$22,050**
Associated General Contractors	$6,000
National Utility Contractors Assn	$4,500
National Assn of Home Builders	$2,600
American Road & Transportation Builders Assn	$1,100
STV Engineers	$1,000
Others	$6,850

Defense	**$3,650**
Rockwell International	$1,550
Litton Industries	$1,500
Others	$600
Electric Utilities	**$2,250**
ACRE (Action Committee for Rural Electrification)	$1,250
General Public Utilities	$1,000
Health Professionals	**$6,100**
American Medical Assn	$5,250
Others	$850
Industrial Equipment & Materials	**$3,100**
Minnesota Mining & Manufacturing (3M)	$2,500
Others	$600
Lawyers	**$2,100**
Williams & Jensen	$1,300
Others	$800
Oil & Gas	**$3,100**
Sun Company	$1,000
Others	$2,100
Outdoor Advertising	**$3,482**
Penn Advertising	$2,700
Others	$782
Paper Mills	**$4,800**
Westvaco Corp	$4,500
Others	$300
Railroads	**$4,700**
Union Pacific Corp	$2,500
Others	$2,200
Real Estate	**$7,350**
National Assn of Realtors	$6,000
Lamar Corp	$1,000
Others	$350
Steel Production	**$2,750**
Standard Steel	$1,500
Others	$1,250
Telecommunications	**$4,750**
Bell Telephone of Pennsylvania	$1,350
AT&T	$1,050
Continental Telecom	$1,000
Others	$1,350

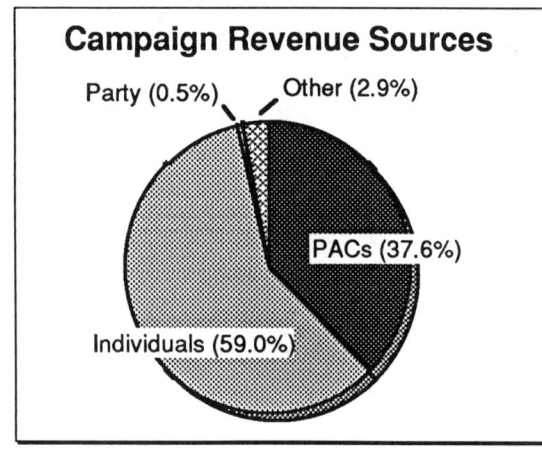

Campaign Revenue Sources

Party (0.5%)
Other (2.9%)
PACs (37.6%)
Individuals (59.0%)

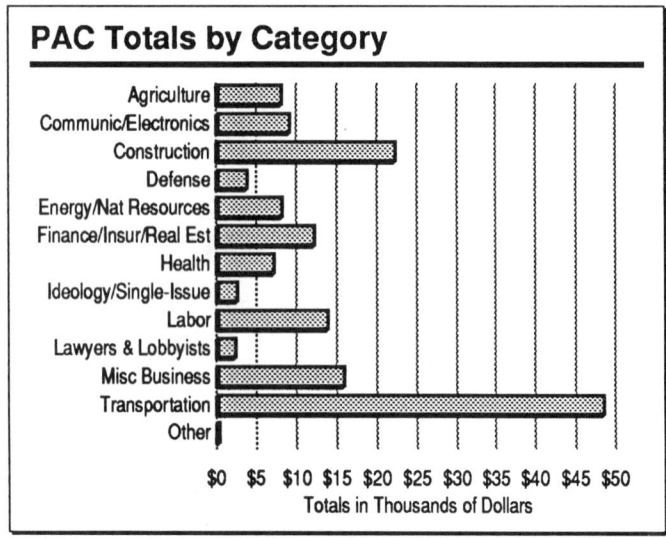

PAC Totals by Category

Agriculture
Communic/Electronics
Construction
Defense
Energy/Nat Resources
Finance/Insur/Real Est
Health
Ideology/Single-Issue
Labor
Lawyers & Lobbyists
Misc Business
Transportation
Other

$0 $5 $10 $15 $20 $25 $30 $35 $40 $45 $50
Totals in Thousands of Dollars

Interest Group Ratings

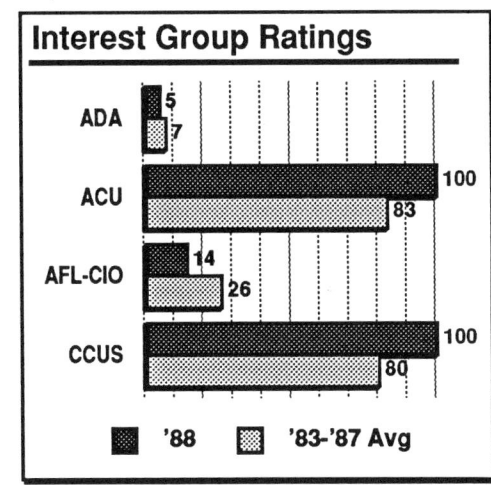

Group	'88	'83-'87 Avg
ADA	5	7
ACU	100	83
AFL-CIO	14	26
CCUS	100	80

■ '88   ▨ '83-'87 Avg

Trucking & Delivery Services **$26,450**

United Parcel Service	$7,400
Consolidated Freightways	$4,000
North American Van Lines	$4,000
American Trucking Assns	$3,000
Roadway Services Inc	$2,800
Yellow Freight System	$2,550
IU International Corp	$1,000
Others	$1,700

Waste Management **$2,100**

Waste Management Inc	$1,100
Chambers Development Company	$1,000

Other Major Business PACs

National Assn of Life Underwriters	$1,500	Life Insurance
Printing Industries of America	$1,250	Printing
Holiday Inns	$1,000	Hotel/Motel
National Beer Wholesalers Assn	$1,000	Liquor Whlsl
Warner Communications	$1,000	Broadcast

Labor

Transportation Unions **$12,050**

Teamsters Union	$6,500
Amalgamated Transit Union	$2,000
United Transportation Union	$1,600
Others	$1,950

Ideological/Single-Issue

Ideological/Single-Issue **$2,353**

National Rifle Assn	$1,503	Pro-Guns
Others	$850	

Spending in Last 3 Elections

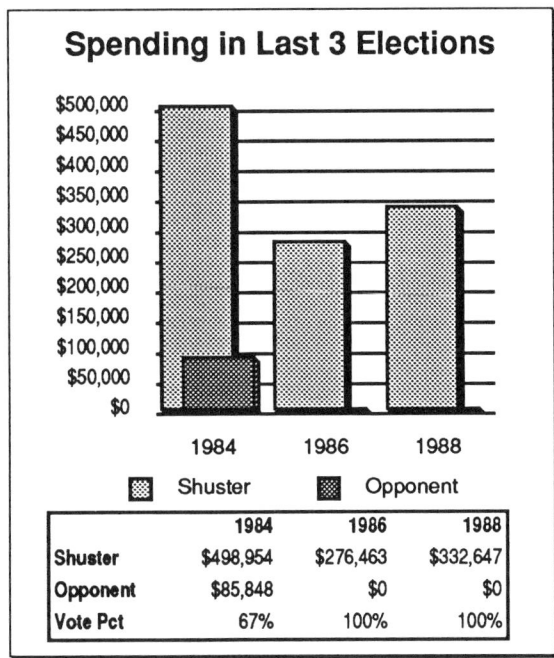

	1984	1986	1988
Shuster	$498,954	$276,463	$332,647
Opponent	$85,848	$0	$0
Vote Pct	67%	100%	100%

▨ Shuster   ■ Opponent

Gerry Sikorski, D-Minn (6)

1988 Committees & Subcommittees

First elected: 1982
Total receipts: $547,198
Total from PACs: $356,982

Energy and Commerce
Health and the Environment
Oversight and Investigations
Transportation, Tourism and Hazardous Materials

Post Office and Civil Service
Human Resources (Chairman)
Census and Population

Select Children, Youth and Families

PAC Contribution Profile

Business

Accountants	**$10,100**
American Institute of CPA's	$5,000
Touche Ross	$2,550
Others	$2,550
Broadcasting/Entertainment	**$5,100**
National Cable Television Assn	$2,000
National Assn of Broadcasters	$1,500
Others	$1,600
Dairy	**$10,050**
Associated Milk Producers	$6,000
Mid-American Dairymen	$2,300
Land O'Lakes Inc	$1,750
Financial Institutions	**$11,650**
Credit Union National Assn	$2,000
J P Morgan & Company	$2,000
Norwest Corp	$2,000
First Bank System/Minnesota	$1,550
Others	$4,100
Food & Beverage	**$6,800**
Wine & Spirits Wholesalers of America	$2,700
General Mills*	$1,500
Others	$2,600

Campaign Revenue Sources

Other (2.6%)
Individuals (30.2%)
PACs (66.7%)

Health Professionals	**$28,050**
American Medical Assn	$5,250
Corp for the Advancement of Psychiatry	$5,000
American Academy of Ophthalmology	$2,500
American Dental Assn	$2,500
American Physical Therapy Assn	$1,900
National Assn of Pharmacists	$1,800
American Podiatry Assn	$1,500
Oral & Maxillofacial Surgeons	$1,500
American Optometric Assn	$1,100
Others	$5,000
Hospitals & Nursing Homes	**$6,050**
American Health Care Assn	$3,000
National Assn of Private Psychiatric Hospitals	$1,500
Others	$1,550
Insurance	**$8,400**
Blue Cross & Blue Shield Assn	$1,500
American Council of Life Insurance	$1,200
Prudential Insurance	$1,150
Health Insurance Assn of America	$1,100
Others	$3,450
Lawyers & Lobbyists	**$26,036**
Assn of Trial Lawyers of America	$10,000
Opperman & Paquin	$7,065
Akin, Gump, Hauer & Feld	$2,000
Faegre & Benson	$1,450
Burson-Marsteller	$1,100
Others	$4,421
Real Estate	**$6,050**
National Assn of Realtors	$5,750
Others	$300
Securities/Commodities Investment	**$13,575**
Chicago Board of Trade	$2,000
Federated Investors Inc	$2,000
Investment Company Institute	$1,500
Securities Industry Assn	$1,400
Dain Bosworth	$1,200
Others	$5,475

PAC Totals by Category

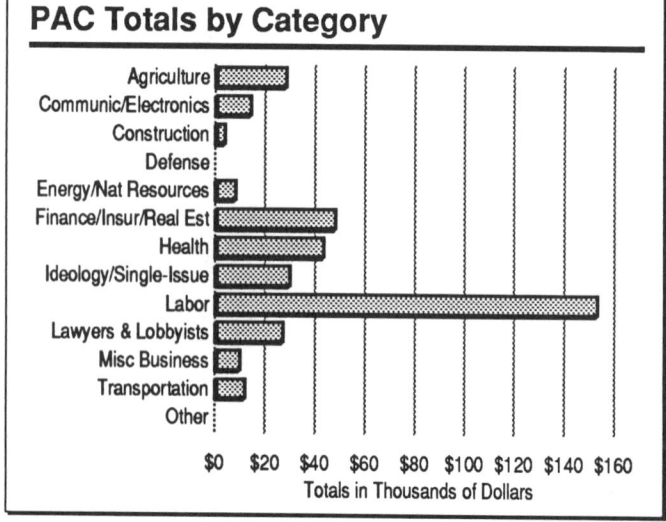

Totals in Thousands of Dollars

Sugar Growers **$6,750**

American Crystal Sugar Corp	$2,550
Southern Minnesota Beet Sugar Co-op	$2,500
American Sugarbeet Growers Assn	$1,100
Others	$600

Telecommunications **$6,900**

North Western Bell Telephone	$2,500
AT&T	$1,950
Pacific Telesis Group	$1,050
Others	$1,400

Other Major Business PACs

United Parcel Service	$2,800	Delivery
National Auto Dealers Assn	$2,300	Auto Sales
FMC Corp	$2,000	Chemicals
American Veterinary Medical Assn	$1,500	Veterinary
National Assn of Home Builders	$1,400	Resid Constr
Southern California Edison	$1,400	ElectricUtil
Medtronic Inc	$1,250	Med Supply
Philip Morris	$1,200	Tobacco
Sheet Metal/AirCon Contractors	$1,200	Plumbing/AC
Archer-Daniels-Midland Corp	$1,100	Grain Trader

Labor

Bldg Trades/Industrial/Misc Unions **$58,362**

Intl Brotherhood of Electrical Workers*	$7,500
Machinists/Aerospace Workers Union	$6,000
AFL-CIO*	$5,000
Carpenters & Joiners Union	$5,000
Food & Commercial Workers Union	$5,000
United Auto Workers	$4,100
Communications Workers of America	$3,500
Ironworkers Union	$3,000
Electronic Machine Furniture Workers	$2,500
Operating Engineers Union	$2,500
Sheet Metal Workers Union	$2,500
Laborers' Political League	$1,900
Ladies Garment Workers Union	$1,800
Boilermakers Union	$1,700
Hotel/Restaurant Employees Union	$1,587
Amalgamated Clothing & Textile Workers	$1,100
Others	$3,675

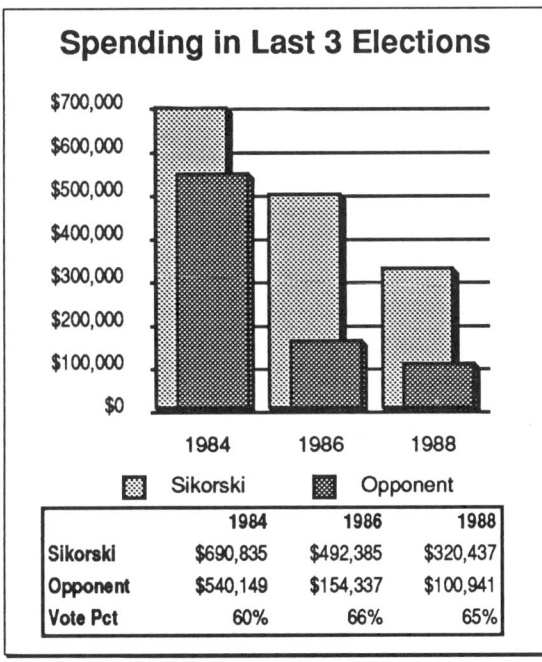

Spending in Last 3 Elections

Legend: ▨ Sikorski ▨ Opponent

	1984	1986	1988
Sikorski	$690,835	$492,385	$320,437
Opponent	$540,149	$154,337	$100,941
Vote Pct	60%	66%	65%

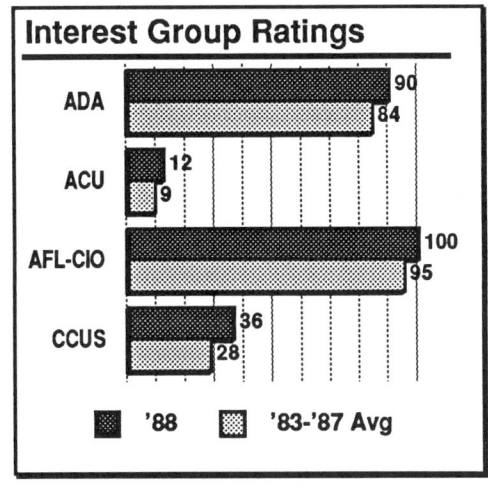

Interest Group Ratings

Legend: ▨ '88   ▨ '83-'87 Avg

	'88	'83-'87 Avg
ADA	90	84
ACU	12	9
AFL-CIO	100	95
CCUS	36	28

Government & Postal Workers **$39,650**

National Assn of Letter Carriers*	$10,300
American Fedn of State/County/Munic Employees	$10,000
National Assn of Retired Federal Employees	$8,000
American Postal Workers Union*	$4,300
National Federation of Federal Employees	$1,800
American Federation of Government Employees	$1,100
Others	$4,150

Teachers Unions **$9,700**

American Federation of Teachers	$5,000
National Education Assn	$3,000
Minnesota Education Assn	$1,700

Transportation Unions **$44,550**

Teamsters Union*	$10,000
United Transportation Union	$10,000
Air Line Pilots Assn	$5,000
Transportation Communication Union	$4,700
Marine Engineers District 2 Maritime Officers	$4,100
Maintenance of Way Employees	$3,200
Amalgamated Transit Union	$3,000
Brotherhood of Railroad Signalmen	$1,650
Seafarers International Union	$1,500
Brotherhood of Locomotive Engineers	$1,100
Others	$300

Ideological/Single-Issue

Democratic Leadership PACs **$12,500**

24th Cong Dist of California PAC (Henry Waxman)	$10,000
Valley Education Fund (Tony Coelho)	$2,000
Others	$500

Pro-Israel **$6,850**

| National PAC | $5,000 |
| Others | $1,850 |

Other Major Ideological/Single-Issue PACs

National Cmte to Preserve Social Security	$2,600	Soc Secur
National Cmte for an Effective Congress	$2,497	Dem/Liberal
Christians for Life	$2,000	Pro-Life

Independent expenditures supporting Sikorski

| American Medical Assn | $83,782 |
| National Cmte to Preserve Social Security | $1,118 |

* Contributions came from more than one PAC affiliated with this sponsor.

Norman Sisisky, D-Va (4)

First elected: 1982
Total receipts: $185,555
Total from PACs: $101,886

1988 Committees & Subcommittees

Armed Services
Investigations
Procurement and Military Nuclear Systems
Seapower and Strategic and Critical Materials

Small Business
Exports, Tourism and Special Problems (Chairman)
SBA and the General Economy

Select Aging
Health and Long-Term Care

PAC Contribution Profile

Business

Auto Dealers	**$6,150**
National Auto Dealers Assn	$3,650
Auto Dealers & Drivers for Free Trade	$2,500
Commercial Banks	**$3,500**
Virginia Bankers Assn	$2,500
Sovran Financial Corp	$1,000
Construction	**$2,000**
None over $700	
Defense	**$27,650**
Mantech International	$2,450
Tenneco Inc	$2,000
BDM International	$1,600
Advanced Technology Inc	$1,500
Textron Inc	$1,300
McDonnell Douglas*	$1,250
Atlantic Research Corp	$1,000
Boeing Company	$1,000
General Dynamics	$1,000
General Electric	$1,000
Grumman	$1,000
Lockheed Corp	$1,000
Northrop Corp	$1,000
Others	$10,550
Electric Utilities	**$4,850**
ACRE (Action Committee for Rural Electrification)	$2,500
Dominion Resources Inc	$1,700
Others	$650

Campaign Revenue Sources

Other (13.6%)
Individuals (17.4%)
PACs (69.0%)

Food & Beverage	**$11,800**
Pepsi-Cola Bottlers Assn	$5,000
Pepsico Inc	$2,000
Coca-Cola Company	$1,000
National Restaurant Assn	$1,000
Others	$2,800
Health Professionals	**$5,500**
American Medical Assn	$2,350
American Dental Assn	$1,500
National Assn of Pharmacists	$1,300
Others	$350
Insurance	**$2,850**
National Assn of Life Underwriters	$2,000
Others	$850
Lawyers	**$3,850**
Assn of Trial Lawyers of America	$2,000
Kleinfeld, Kaplan & Becker	$1,050
Others	$800
Real Estate	**$2,800**
National Assn of Realtors	$2,500
Others	$300
Telecommunications	**$2,200**
AT&T	$1,500
Others	$700
Tobacco	**$6,000**
Philip Morris	$1,500
RJR Nabisco	$1,500
Pinkerton Tobacco	$1,000
Others	$2,000

Other Major Business PACs

Stone Container Corp	$1,000	Paper Packg
Texas Air	$1,000	Airlines

PAC Totals by Category

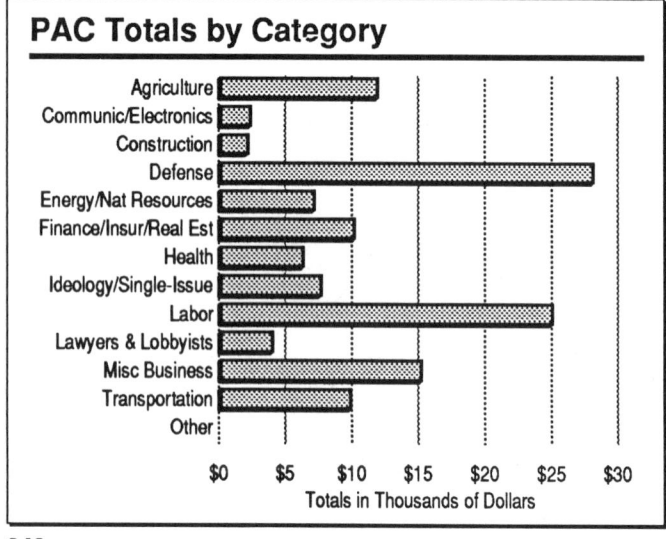

Category	
Agriculture	
Communic/Electronics	
Construction	
Defense	
Energy/Nat Resources	
Finance/Insur/Real Est	
Health	
Ideology/Single-Issue	
Labor	
Lawyers & Lobbyists	
Misc Business	
Transportation	
Other	

$0 $5 $10 $15 $20 $25 $30
Totals in Thousands of Dollars

Labor

Bldg Trades/Industrial/Misc Unions $4,050
Sheet Metal Workers Union $2,500
Others $1,550

Government & Postal Workers $9,450
American Fedn of State/County/Munic Employees $2,000
National Assn of Retired Federal Employees $2,000
National Assn of Letter Carriers $1,600
Others $3,850

Teachers Unions $3,350
National Education Assn $3,350

Transportation Unions $8,000
Marine Engineers Union* $3,350
United Transportation Union $1,800
Seafarers International Union $1,500
Others $1,350

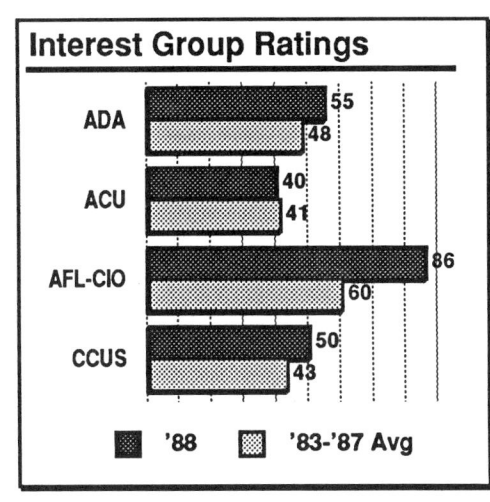

Interest Group Ratings

ADA — '88: 55, '83-'87 Avg: 48
ACU — '88: 40, '83-'87 Avg: 41
AFL-CIO — '88: 86, '83-'87 Avg: 60
CCUS — '88: 50, '83-'87 Avg: 43

■ '88   ▨ '83-'87 Avg

Ideological/Single-Issue

Democratic Leadership PACs $3,950
Valley Education Fund (Tony Coelho) $3,000
Others $950

Other Major Ideological/Single-Issue PACs
National Cmte to Preserve Social Security ......$1,100   Soc Secur
Washington PAC ....$1,000   Pro-Israel

Independent expenditures supporting Sisisky
National Cmte to Preserve Social Security $1,343

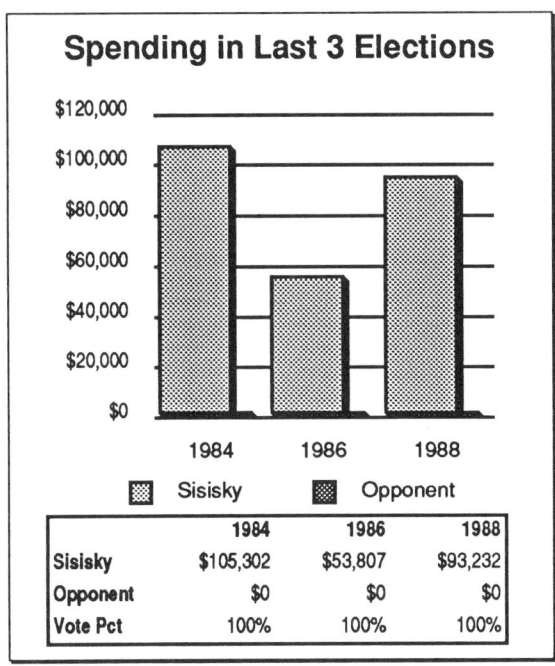

Spending in Last 3 Elections

	1984	1986	1988
Sisisky	$105,302	$53,807	$93,232
Opponent	$0	$0	$0
Vote Pct	100%	100%	100%

▨ Sisisky   ■ Opponent

---

* Contributions came from more than one PAC affiliated
with this sponsor.

David E. Skaggs, D-Colo (2)

1988 Committees & Subcommittees

First elected: 1986
Total receipts: $730,990
Total from PACs: $452,772

Public Works and Transportation	Science, Space and Technology
Aviation	Science, Research and Technology
Public Buildings and Grounds	Space Science and Applications
Water Resources	
	Select Children, Youth and Families

PAC Contribution Profile

Business

Auto Dealers **$14,000**
    Auto Dealers & Drivers for Free Trade $12,000
    National Auto Dealers Assn $2,000

Aviation & Aerospace **$19,825**
    Federal Express Corp $5,000
    Aircraft Owners & Pilots Assn $3,225
    Eastern Airlines $2,000
    Martin Marietta Corp $2,000
    Texas Air $2,000
    Boeing Company $1,050
    Others $4,550

Construction **$13,050**
    National Assn of Home Builders $11,000
    Others $2,050

Dairy **$4,500**
    Associated Milk Producers $3,000
    Others $1,500

Financial Institutions **$7,250**
    Credit Union National Assn $4,000
    Others $3,250

Health Professionals **$15,500**
    American Medical Assn $10,000
    American Academy of Ophthalmology $2,000
    American Nurses Assn $2,000
    Others $1,500

Insurance **$5,750**
    National Assn of Life Underwriters $4,000
    Independent Insurance Agents of America $1,500
    Others $250

Campaign Revenue Sources

Other (8.5%)
Party (7.5%)
Candidate (0.6%)
Individuals (31.0%)
PACs (52.3%)

Lawyers & Lobbyists **$11,180**
    Assn of Trial Lawyers of America $10,000
    Others $1,180

Real Estate **$8,000**
    National Assn of Realtors $8,000

Telecommunications **$8,550**
    AT&T $3,500
    Mountain Bell $2,500
    BellSouth* $1,050
    Others $1,500

Trucking/Delivery **$4,950**
    United Parcel Service $1,700
    American Trucking Assns $1,300
    Others $1,950

Other Major Business PACs

Huffy Corp ....$3,500   Bikes
National Assn of Social Workers ....$2,000   Social Work

PAC Totals by Category

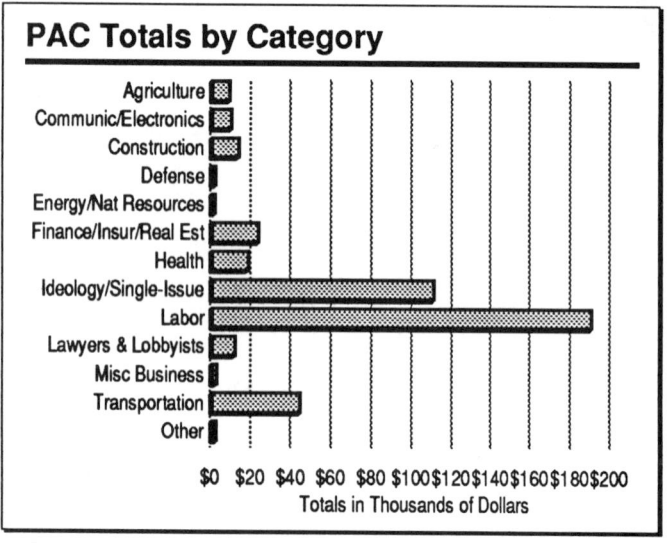

Category	
Agriculture	
Communic/Electronics	
Construction	
Defense	
Energy/Nat Resources	
Finance/Insur/Real Est	
Health	
Ideology/Single-Issue	
Labor	
Lawyers & Lobbyists	
Misc Business	
Transportation	
Other	

$0 $20 $40 $60 $80 $100 $120 $140 $160 $180 $200
Totals in Thousands of Dollars

Labor

Bldg Trades/Industrial/Misc Unions $93,950

AFL-CIO*	$10,000
Food & Commercial Workers Union	$10,000
Machinists/Aerospace Workers Union	$10,000
United Auto Workers	$10,000
United Steelworkers	$10,000
Carpenters & Joiners Union	$6,850
Intl Brotherhood of Electrical Workers	$6,500
Sheet Metal Workers Union	$6,000
Communications Workers of America	$5,500
Plumbers/Pipefitters Union	$5,000
Operating Engineers Union	$3,500
Laborers' Political League	$2,100
Oil, Chemical & Atomic Workers Union	$2,050
Bakery, Confectionery & Tobacco Workers	$2,000
Rubber Cork Linoleum Plastic Workers	$2,000
Others	$2,450

Government & Postal Workers $38,150

American Fedn of State/County/Munic Employees	$10,000
National Assn of Letter Carriers	$10,000
National Assn of Retired Federal Employees	$8,000
National Rural Letter Carriers Assn	$3,500
American Postal Workers Union	$3,300
International Assn of Firefighters	$1,500
Others	$1,850

Teachers Unions $20,000

American Federation of Teachers	$10,000
National Education Assn	$10,000

Transportation Unions $28,550

Teamsters Union	$10,000
Amalgamated Transit Union	$5,000
Marine Engineers Union	$5,000
United Transportation Union	$4,000
Transportation Communication Union	$2,000
Seafarers International Union	$1,500
Others	$1,050

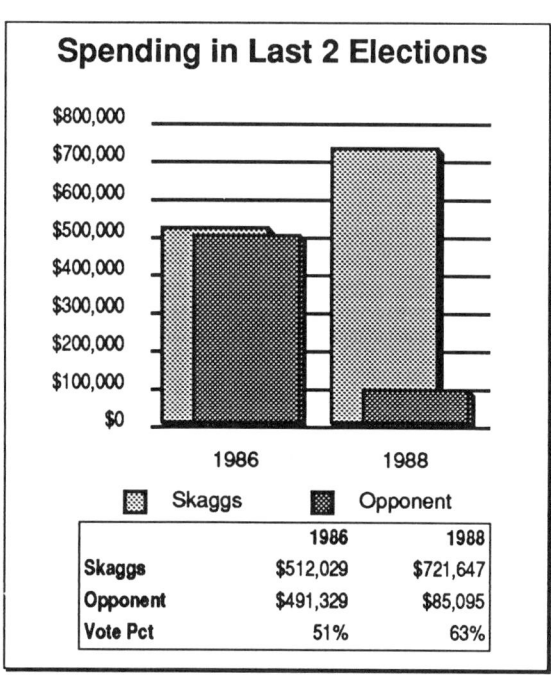

Spending in Last 2 Elections

	1986	1988
Skaggs	$512,029	$721,647
Opponent	$491,329	$85,095
Vote Pct	51%	63%

Interest Group Ratings

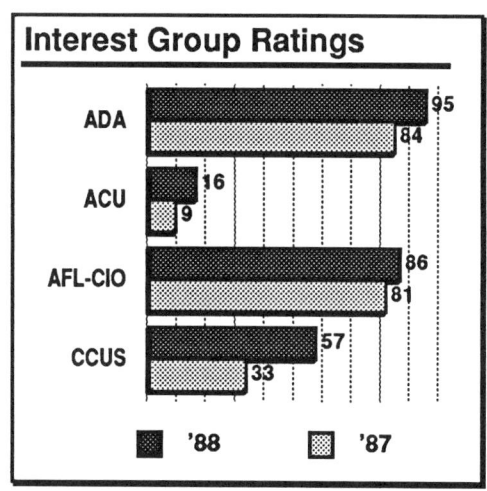

	'88	'87
ADA	95	84
ACU	16	9
AFL-CIO	86	81
CCUS	57	33

Ideological/Single-Issue

Democratic/Liberal $17,500

National Cmte for an Effective Congress	$7,500
Class PAC	$5,000
Hollywood Women's Political Cmte	$3,000
Others	$2,000

Democratic Leadership PACs $33,500

Valley Education Fund (Tony Coelho)	$10,000
24th Cong Dist of California PAC (Henry Waxman)	$5,000
Majority Congress Committee (Jim Wright)	$5,000
Cmte for Democratic Opportunity (Bill Gray)	$4,000
America's Leaders' Fund (Dan Rostenkowski)	$3,000
Cmte for the 100th Congress (Charles Rangel)	$3,000
Pax Americas (David Bonior)	$1,500
Others	$2,000

Environmental PACs $10,646

Sierra Club	$5,718
Environmental Action	$2,913
League of Conservation Voters	$2,015

Pro-Choice $13,000

National Abortion Rights Action League	$7,000
Voters for Choice/Friends of Family Planning	$6,000

Pro-Israel $19,000

National PAC	$5,000
Joint Action Cmte for Political Affairs	$2,000
Maryland Assn for Concerned Citizens	$1,500
Roundtable PAC	$1,500
Hudson Valley PAC	$1,250
Others	$7,750

Pro-Peace $5,791

Council for a Livable World	$2,584
SANE/Freeze Inc	$2,300
Others	$907

Other Major Ideological/Single-Issue PACs

Human Rights Campaign Fund	$3,000	Gay Rights
KidsPAC	$2,500	HealthWelfare
National Cmte to Preserve Social Security	$2,250	Soc Secur

Independent expenditures supporting Skaggs

Auto Dealers & Drivers for Free Trade	$80,000
National Cmte to Preserve Social Security	$2,077

* Contributions came from more than one PAC affiliated
  with this sponsor.

949

Joe Skeen, R-NM (2)

First elected: 1980
Total receipts: $143,944
Total from PACs: $87,050

1988 Committees & Subcommittees

Appropriations
Treasury, Postal Service and General Government (Ranking Republican)
Rural Development, Agriculture and Related Agencies

Campaign Revenue Sources

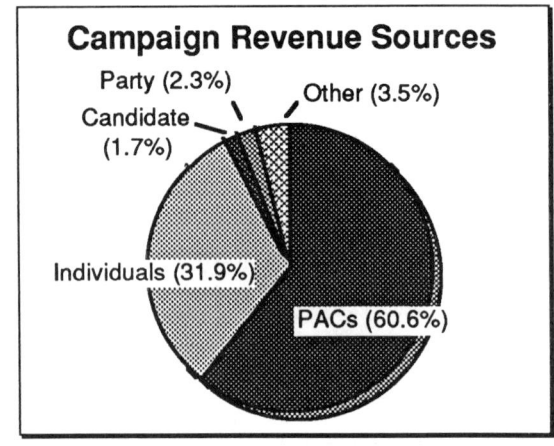

Party (2.3%)
Other (3.5%)
Candidate (1.7%)
Individuals (31.9%)
PACs (60.6%)

PAC Contribution Profile

Business

Agricultural Chemicals	**$2,800**
American Cyanimid*	$1,300
Others	$1,500
Agricultural Services	**$2,700**
American Assn of Crop Insurers	$1,450
Others	$1,250
Auto Dealers	**$2,600**
Auto Dealers & Drivers for Free Trade	$2,000
National Auto Dealers Assn	$600
Commodity Trading	**$2,000**
Chicago Board of Trade	$1,000
Chicago Mercantile Exchange	$1,000
Construction	**$6,600**
Associated General Contractors	$1,000
National Assn of Home Builders	$1,000
National Electrical Contractors Assn	$1,000
National Society of Professional Engineers	$1,000
Fluor Corp	$750
Others	$1,850
Cotton	**$1,861**
National Cotton Council	$1,611
Others	$250

Defense	**$4,450**
Lockheed Corp	$1,450
BDM International	$950
Dyncorp	$600
Others	$1,450
Electrical Utilities	**$4,600**
Southwestern Public Service Company	$2,100
Public Service Company of New Mexico	$1,300
Southern California Edison	$600
Others	$600
Food & Beverage	**$2,900**
National Beer Wholesalers Assn	$900
American Meat Institute	$750
Others	$1,250
General Aviation	**$1,200**
Aircraft Owners & Pilots Assn	$1,200
Health Professionals	**$7,500**
American Dental Assn	$2,500
American Medical Assn	$2,250
New Mexico Medical Assn	$2,000
Others	$750
Insurance	**$1,350**
National Assn of Life Underwriters	$1,000
Others	$350
Livestock	**$2,100**
National Cattlemen's Assn	$850
National Wool Growers Assn	$750
Others	$500
Mining	**$2,150**
Phelps Dodge Corp	$850
Others	$1,300
Oil & Gas	**$10,350**
Atlantic Richfield	$1,500
Chevron Corp	$1,050
El Paso Company	$1,000
Amoco Corp	$850
Shell Oil	$750
Pennzoil Company	$600
Others	$4,600

PAC Totals by Category

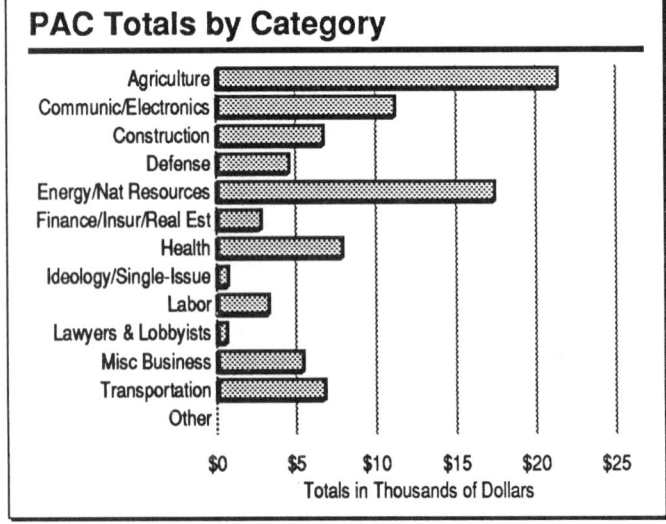

Agriculture
Communic/Electronics
Construction
Defense
Energy/Nat Resources
Finance/Insur/Real Est
Health
Ideology/Single-Issue
Labor
Lawyers & Lobbyists
Misc Business
Transportation
Other

$0 $5 $10 $15 $20 $25
Totals in Thousands of Dollars

Railroads *$1,850*
    Santa Fe Southern Pacific $1,100
    Union Pacific Corp $750

Real Estate *$1,100*
    Mortgage Bankers Assn of America $850
    Others $250

Sugar Growers *$2,850*
    American Crystal Sugar Corp...$750
    American Sugarbeet Growers Assn $600
    Others $1,500

Telecommunications *$9,450*
    AT&T $3,000
    GTE (Southwest) $2,700
    Mountain Bell $2,000
    Continental Telecom $1,000
    National Telephone Co-op Assn $750

Textiles *$2,000*
    American Textile Manufacturers Institute $750
    Burlington Industries $750
    Others $500

Other Major Business PACs

Westinghouse Electric	$1,350	Electronics
United Parcel Service	$1,000	Delivery
Greyhound Corp	$850	Home Chem

Labor

Labor Unions *$3,150*
    Marine Engineers Dist 2 Retirees $1,000
    National Assn of Retired Federal Employees $1,000
    Others $1,150

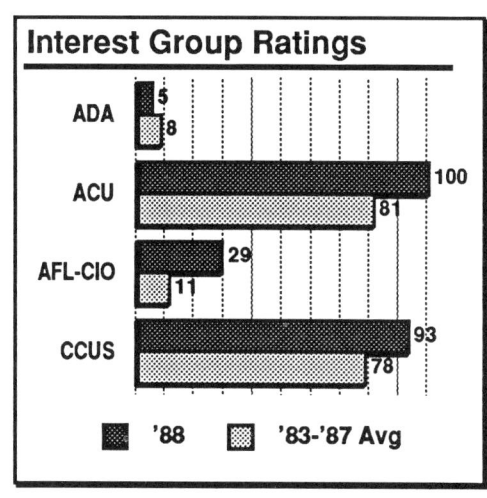

Interest Group Ratings

	'88	'83-'87 Avg
ADA	5	8
ACU	100	81
AFL-CIO	29	11
CCUS	93	78

■ '88   ▨ '83-'87 Avg

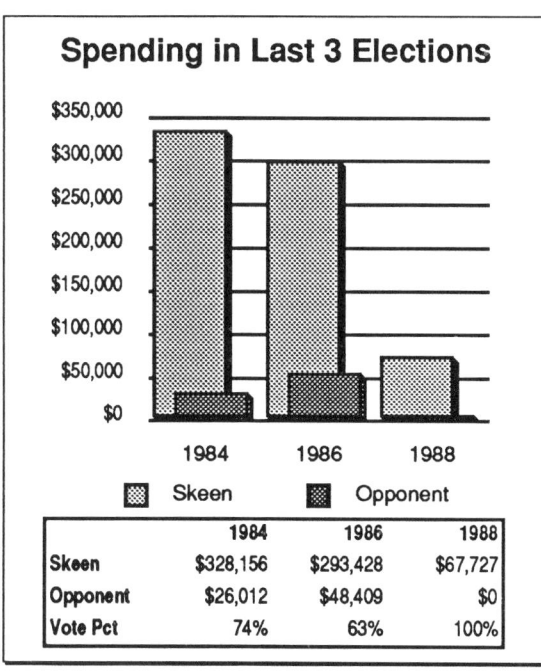

Spending in Last 3 Elections

■ Skeen   ▨ Opponent

	1984	1986	1988
Skeen	$328,156	$293,428	$67,727
Opponent	$26,012	$48,409	$0
Vote Pct	74%	63%	100%

---

* Contributions came from more than one PAC affiliated
with this sponsor.

Ike Skelton, D-Mo (4)

1988 Committees & Subcommittees

First elected: 1976
Total receipts: $314,323
Total from PACs: $195,725

Armed Services
Military Installations and Facilities
Military Personnel and Compensation
Procurement and Military Nuclear Systems

Small Business
Procurement, Innovation and Minority Enterprise Development (Chairman)
Exports, Tourism and Special Problems (Chairman)

Select Aging
Health and Long-Term Care

PAC Contribution Profile

Business

Auto Dealers **$5,500**
    National Auto Dealers Assn $5,500

Commercial & Savings Banks **$5,700**
    Commerce Bancshares $1,000
    US League of Savings Assn $1,000
    Others $3,700

Construction **$6,150**
    National Assn of Home Builders $1,500
    American Consulting Engineers Council $1,000
    Others $3,650

Dairy **$7,300**
    Associated Milk Producers $5,000
    Mid-American Dairymen $2,000
    Others $300

Defense **$44,200**
    McDonnell Douglas* $5,000
    Northrop Corp $2,500
    Continental Telecom $2,000
    Lockheed Corp $2,000
    Rockwell International $2,000
    United Technologies $2,000
    Boeing Company $1,500
    Chrysler Corp $1,500
    E-Systems/Corporate Division $1,500
    General Dynamics $1,500
    Grumman $1,500
    Hughes Aircraft $1,500
    LTV Aerospace & Defense Company $1,500
    (Continued in next column)

Campaign Revenue Sources

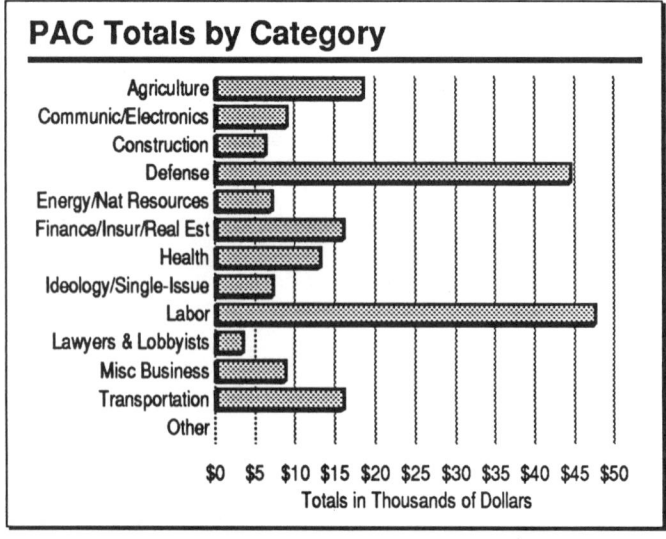

Individuals (37.6%)
PACs (62.0%)

Defense (cont'd)
    Textron Inc $1,500
    Olin Corp $1,100
    Allied-Signal $1,000
    AT&T $1,000
    Colt Industries $1,000
    Emerson Electric $1,000
    Emhart Corp $1,000
    General Electric $1,000
    Martin Marietta Corp $1,000
    Raytheon $1,000
    Others $7,600

Electric Utilities **$3,675**
    ACRE (Action Committee for Rural Electrification) $1,000
    Others $2,675

Food & Beverage **$3,450**
    National Beer Wholesalers Assn $1,000
    Pepsi-Cola Bottlers Assn $1,000
    Others $1,450

Health Professionals **$10,050**
    American Medical Assn $3,800
    American Dental Assn $2,000
    American Optometric Assn $1,500
    Missouri Medical Assn $1,250
    Others $1,500

Insurance **$5,250**
    General American Life Insurance $1,000
    Kansas City Life Insurance $1,000
    National Assn of Life Underwriters $1,000
    Shelter Mutual Insurance $1,000
    Others $1,250

Lawyers **$3,250**
    Assn of Trial Lawyers of America $3,250

Railroads **$3,000**
    Kansas City Southern $2,000
    Burlington Northern $500
    Union Pacific Corp $500

PAC Totals by Category

Agriculture
Communic/Electronics
Construction
Defense
Energy/Nat Resources
Finance/Insur/Real Est
Health
Ideology/Single-Issue
Labor
Lawyers & Lobbyists
Misc Business
Transportation
Other

$0 $5 $10 $15 $20 $25 $30 $35 $40 $45 $50
Totals in Thousands of Dollars

Interest Group Ratings

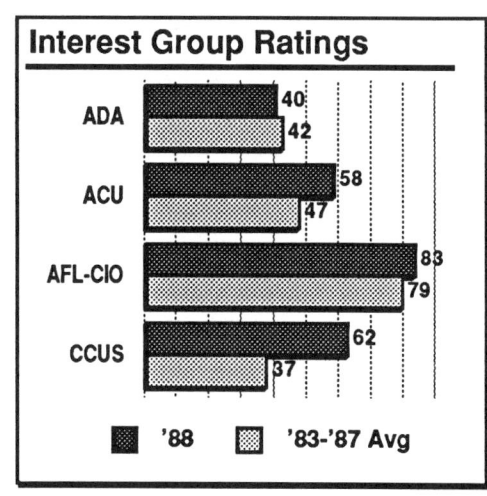

Group	'88	'83-'87 Avg
ADA	40	42
ACU	58	47
AFL-CIO	83	79
CCUS	62	37

■ '88   ▨ '83-'87 Avg

Real Estate **$4,000**

    National Assn of Realtors $4,000

Sugar Growers **$3,300**

    None over $750

Telecommunications **$8,800**

    Southwestern Bell $2,500
    US Telephone Assn $2,000
    United Telecommunications $1,800
    Others $2,500

Tobacco **$2,250**

    Tobacco Institute $1,000
    Others $1,250

Travel Agents **$2,000**

    American Society of Travel Agents $1,500
    Others $500

Other Major Business PACs

Deere & Company	$1,500	Farm Equip
National Tooling & Machining Assn	$1,250	Indust Equip
American Textile Manufacturers Institute	$1,000	Textiles
National Assn of Chain Drug Stores	$1,000	Drug Stores
National Assn of Sm Bus Invest Companies	$1,000	Sml Business
National Assn of Truck Stop Operators	$1,000	Truck Svcs
Petroleum Marketers Assn	$1,000	Gas Stations
Pfizer Inc	$1,000	Pharmaceut
Trans World Airlines	$1,000	Airlines
Waste Management Inc	$1,000	Waste Mgmt

Labor

Bldg Trades/Industrial/Misc Unions **$24,717**

    Carpenters & Joiners Union $3,500
    Machinists/Aerospace Workers* $3,500
    United Auto Workers $3,500
    AFL-CIO* $2,500
    Hotel/Restaurant Empl Union $2,117
    (continued in next column)

Labor (cont'd)

    Communications Workers of America $1,500
    Food & Commercial Workers Union $1,500
    Laborers' Political League $1,500
    Intl Brotherhood of Electrical Workers $1,000
    Ladies Garment Workers Union $1,000
    Operating Engineers Union $1,000
    Plumbers/Pipefitters Union $1,000
    Others $1,100

Government & Postal Workers **$7,550**

    National Assn of Retired Federal Employees $4,000
    American Postal Workers Union $2,000
    National Assn of Letter Carriers $1,000
    Others $550

Teachers Unions **$2,300**

    National Education Assn $2,300

Transportation Unions **$12,800**

    Teamsters Union $5,000
    Seafarers International Union $2,500
    United Transportation Union $2,000
    Marine Engineers Union* $1,500
    Transportation Communication Union $1,050
    Others $750

Ideological/Single-Issue

Pro-Israel **$2,250**

    Chai PAC $1,000
    St Louisians for Better Government $1,000
    Others $250

Other Major Ideological/Single-Issue PACs

National Rifle Assn	$1,500	Pro-Guns
National Cmte to Preserve Social Security	$1,000	Soc Secur
Valley Education Fund (Tony Coelho)	$1,000	Dem Leaders

Independent expenditures supporting Skelton

    Missouri Citizens for Life $2,110
    National Cmte to Preserve Social Security $1,761

Spending in Last 3 Elections

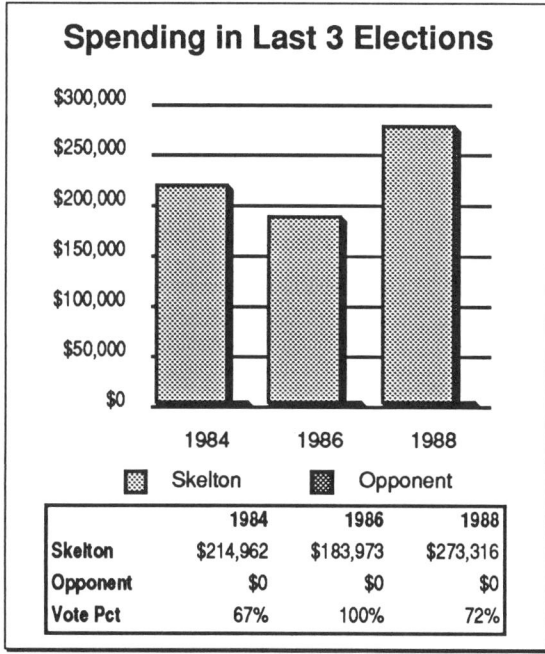

	1984	1986	1988
Skelton	$214,962	$183,973	$273,316
Opponent	$0	$0	$0
Vote Pct	67%	100%	72%

▨ Skelton   ▨ Opponent

---

* Contributions came from more than one PAC affiliated
  with this sponsor.

Jim Slattery, D-Kan (2)

1988 Committees & Subcommittees

Budget
Community and Natural Resources
Defense and International Affairs
Economic and Trade Policy

Energy and Commerce
Oversight and Investigations
Telecommunications and Finance
Transportation, Tourism and Hazardous Materials

First elected: 1982
Total receipts: $453,832
Total from PACs: $266,122

PAC Contribution Profile

Business

Accountants	*$7,250*
American Institute of CPA's	$5,000
Coopers & Lybrand	$1,250
Ernst & Whinney	$1,000
Automotive	*$5,000*
National Auto Dealers Assn	$2,250
Others	$2,750
Construction	*$4,200*
Heavy Constructors Assn	$1,250
National Electrical Contractors Assn	$1,000
Others	$1,950
Defense	*$4,250*
BDM International	$1,250
Rockwell International	$1,250
Others	$1,750
Electric Utilities	*$8,250*
Southern Company*	$1,000
Others	$7,250
Financial Institutions	*$9,950*
American Bankers Assn	$2,500
J P Morgan & Company	$2,000
US League of Savings Assn	$1,750
Kansas Bankers Assn	$1,250
Kansas League of Savings Institutions	$1,000
Others	$1,450

Food & Beverage	*$4,650*
National Restaurant Assn	$1,000
Wine & Spirits Wholesalers of America	$1,000
Others	$2,650
Health Professionals	*$15,000*
American Medical Assn	$4,250
American Dental Assn	$2,500
National Assn of Pharmacists	$2,000
American Academy of Ophthalmology	$1,000
American College of Emergency Physicians	$1,000
American Optometric Assn	$1,000
Cmte for Quality Orthopedic Health Care	$1,000
Kansas Chiropractic Assn	$1,000
Others	$1,250
Insurance	*$22,697*
National Assn of Life Underwriters	$6,500
Great-West Life Assurance	$5,007
Security Benefit Group	$1,640
Travelers Corp	$1,500
American Council of Life Insurance	$1,000
Others	$7,050
Lawyers & Lobbyists	*$7,550*
Assn of Trial Lawyers of America	$2,750
Verner, Liipfert, Bernhard & McPherson	$1,000
Others	$3,800
Oil & Gas	*$15,400*
Petroleum Marketers Assn	$1,750
KPL Gas Service	$1,500
Union Pacific Corp	$1,100
Burlington Northern	$1,050
Atlantic Richfield	$1,000
Williams Companies	$1,000
Others	$8,000
Pharmaceuticals	*$5,638*
Abbott Laboratories	$1,050
Others	$4,588
Railroads & Railroad Svcs	*$6,050*
Santa Fe Southern Pacific	$1,500
Chicago & North Western Transport	$1,250
Kansas City Southern	$1,050
Others	$2,250

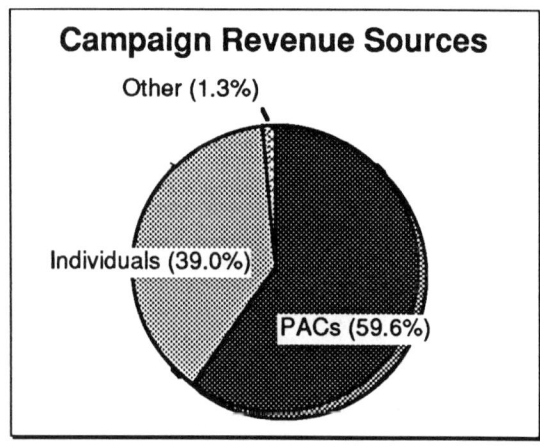

Campaign Revenue Sources

Other (1.3%)
Individuals (39.0%)
PACs (59.6%)

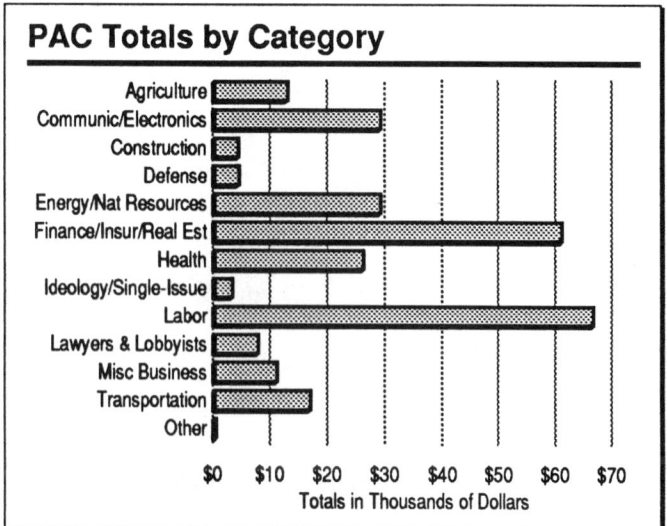

PAC Totals by Category

Agriculture
Communic/Electronics
Construction
Defense
Energy/Nat Resources
Finance/Insur/Real Est
Health
Ideology/Single-Issue
Labor
Lawyers & Lobbyists
Misc Business
Transportation
Other

$0 $10 $20 $30 $40 $50 $60 $70
Totals in Thousands of Dollars

Real Estate $9,000
    National Assn of Realtors $8,000
    Others $1,000

Securities/Commodities $15,500
    First Boston Corp $3,000
    Investment Company Institute.........................$2,000
    Chicago Board of Trade $1,250
    Securities Industry Assn $1,250
    Chicago Board of Options Exchange $1,000
    Chicago Mercantile Exchange $1,000
    Morgan Stanley & Company $1,000
    Others $5,000

Telecommunications $22,050
    BellSouth* $3,750
    AT&T $2,000
    Continental Telecom $2,000
    Southwestern Bell $2,000
    Pacific Telesis Group $1,750
    Bell Atlantic $1,500
    Corning Glass Works $1,000
    DSC Communications Corp $1,000
    NYNEX Corp $1,000
    United Telecommunications* $1,000
    Others $5,050

TV/Movies $4,000
    National Cable Television Assn $2,000
    National Assn of Broadcasters $1,500
    Others $500

Other Major Business PACs

FMC Corp	$3,000	Chemicals
Hallmark Cards	$2,800	Publishing
Waste Management Inc	$2,000	Waste Mgmt
American Hospital Assn	$1,700	Hospitals
Mid-American Dairymen	$1,500	Dairy
Boeing Company	$1,000	Aircraft
Farmland Industries	$1,000	Ag Svcs
Holiday Inns	$1,000	Hotel/Motel
Independent Coal Operators Assn	$1,000	Coal
National Society of Professional Engineers	$1,000	Engineers

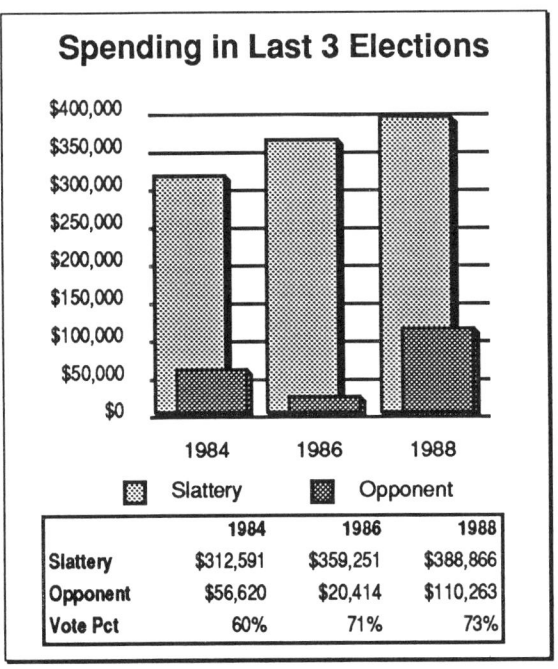

Spending in Last 3 Elections

	1984	1986	1988
Slattery	$312,591	$359,251	$388,866
Opponent	$56,620	$20,414	$110,263
Vote Pct	60%	71%	73%

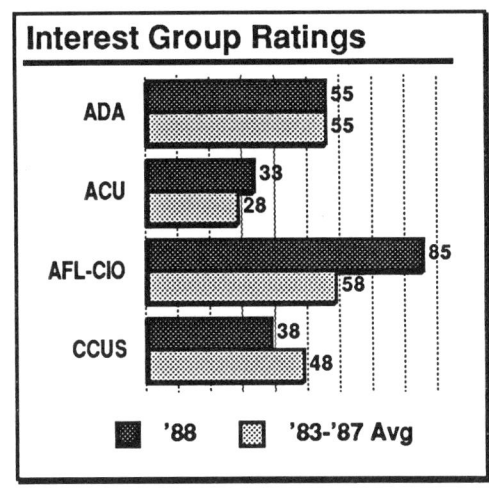

Interest Group Ratings

	'88	'83-'87 Avg
ADA	55	55
ACU	33	28
AFL-CIO	85	58
CCUS	38	48

Labor

Bldg Trades/Industrial/Misc Unions $26,950
    Rubber Cork Linoleum Plastic Workers $6,000
    United Auto Workers $3,500
    Communications Workers of America $2,750
    Machinists/Aerospace Workers Union $2,500
    Sheet Metal Workers Union $2,500
    Operating Engineers Union* $2,100
    Plumbers/Pipefitters Union* $2,000
    Intl Brotherhood of Electrical Workers* $1,900
    Laborers' Political League $1,700
    Food & Commercial Workers Union $1,250
    Others $750

Government & Postal Workers $16,100
    National Assn of Letter Carriers $7,100
    National Assn of Retired Federal Employees $5,000
    National Rural Letter Carriers Assn $1,250
    Others $2,750

Teachers Unions $4,000
    National Education Assn $3,500
    Others $500

Transportation Unions $14,850
    Teamsters Union $5,000
    United Transportation Union $3,100
    Brotherhood of Locomotive Engineers $1,600
    Transportation Communication Union $1,050
    Air Line Pilots Assn $1,000
    International Longshoremen Assn $1,000
    Others $2,100

Major Ideological/Single-Issue PACs
Valley Education Fund (Tony Coelho) ....$1,000   Dem Leaders

---

* Contributions came from more than one PAC affiliated with this sponsor.

D. French Slaughter Jr., R-Va (7)

First elected: 1984
Total receipts: $219,559
Total from PACs: $94,496

1988 Committees & Subcommittees

Judiciary
Courts, Civil Liberties and the Administration of Justice
Immigration, Refugees and International Law

Science, Space and Technology
Science, Research and Technology
Space Science and Applications

Small Business
Antitrust, Impact of Deregulation and Privatization
Exports, Tourism and Special Problems

PAC Contribution Profile

Business

Aerospace	**$1,950**
Martin Marietta Corp	$550
TRW Inc	$550
Others	$850
Automotive	**$6,400**
National Auto Dealers Assn	$3,550
Auto Dealers & Drivers for Free Trade	$2,000
Chrysler Corp	$550
Others	$300
Broadcasting/Entertainment	**$3,100**
National Assn of Broadcasters	$800
ASCAP	$750
Others	$1,550
Construction	**$6,200**
National Assn of Home Builders	$2,500
Associated Builders & Contractors	$550
Associated General Contractors	$550
Stone & Webster	$550
Wall & Ceiling/Gypsum Contractors	$550
Others	$1,500
Defense	**$5,000**
Tenneco Inc	$1,000
Rockwell International	$800
Hughes Aircraft	$550
Others	$2,650

Campaign Revenue Sources

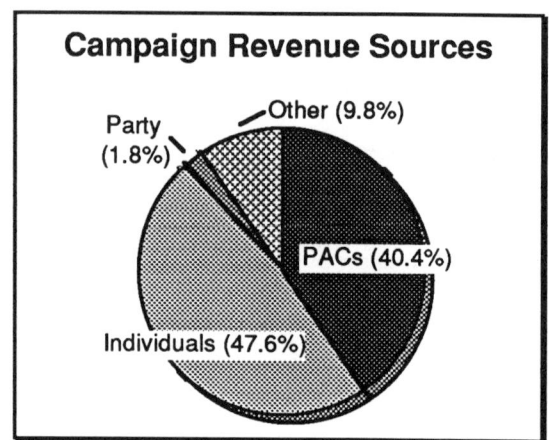

Other (9.8%)
Party (1.8%)
PACs (40.4%)
Individuals (47.6%)

Electric Utilities	**$3,950**
ACRE (Action Committee for Rural Electrification)	$2,350
Dominion Resources Inc	$1,100
Others	$500
Financial Institutions	**$5,200**
Virginia Bankers Assn	$2,750
Credit Union National Assn	$1,000
Rochester Community Savings Bank	$1,000
Others	$450
Food & Beverage	**$3,650**
National Beer Wholesalers Assn	$1,050
Food Marketing Institute	$800
ConAgra Inc	$750
Coca-Cola Company	$550
Others	$500
Health Professionals	**$3,800**
American Medical Assn	$2,800
Others	$1,000
Insurance	**$9,000**
National Assn of Life Underwriters	$2,000
National Assn Mutual Insurance Agents	$1,150
Travelers Corp	$1,000
Aetna Life & Casualty	$600
American Council of Life Insurance	$600
Casualty & Surety Agents Assn	$550
Others	$3,100
Power Plant Equipment	**$2,750**
Cooper Industries	$2,250
Others	$500
Real Estate	**$3,000**
National Assn of Realtors	$3,000

PAC Totals by Category

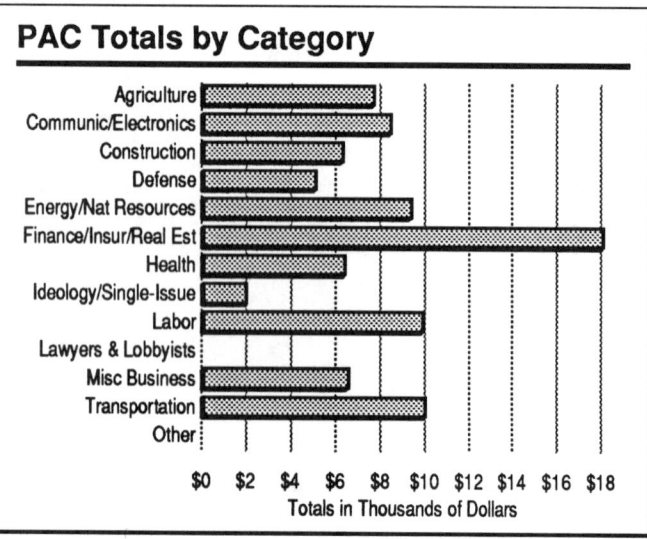

Agriculture
Communic/Electronics
Construction
Defense
Energy/Nat Resources
Finance/Insur/Real Est
Health
Ideology/Single-Issue
Labor
Lawyers & Lobbyists
Misc Business
Transportation
Other

$0 $2 $4 $6 $8 $10 $12 $14 $16 $18
Totals in Thousands of Dollars

Telecommunications **$4,450**

AT&T	$1,500
Chesapeake & Potomac Telephone	$600
Centel Corp	$550
Others	$1,800

Tobacco **$3,650**

Philip Morris	$1,500
Brown & Williamson Tobacco	$550
Tobacco Institute	$550
Others	$1,050

Other Major Business PACs

American Health Care Assn	$1,000	Nursing Home
West Publishing	$1,000	Books & Mags
Westvaco Corp	$1,000	Paper Prod
Dairymen Inc-Virginia	$550	Dairy
General Electric	$550	Electronics
Hoffman-La Roche	$550	Pharmaceut
J P Stevens & Company	$550	Textiles
Shell Oil	$550	Major Oil

Labor

Labor Unions **$9,800**

Intl Brotherhood of Electrical Workers	$3,500
National Assn of Retired Federal Employees	$3,000
Marine Engineers Union*	$1,600
Service Employees International Union	$1,000
Others	$700

Major Ideological/Single-Issue PACs

American Security Council	$846	Pro-Defense

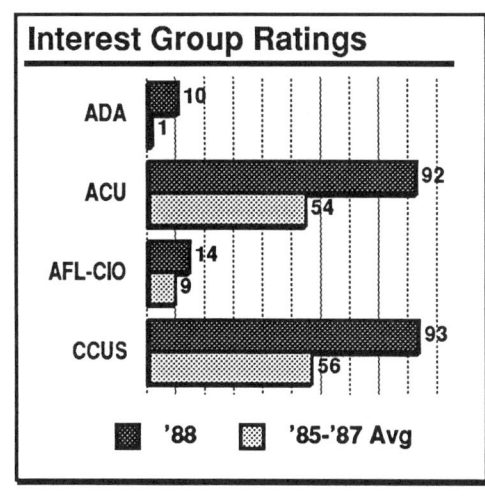

Interest Group Ratings

	'88	'85-'87 Avg
ADA	10	1
ACU	92	54
AFL-CIO	14	9
CCUS	93	56

◼ '88   ▨ '85-'87 Avg

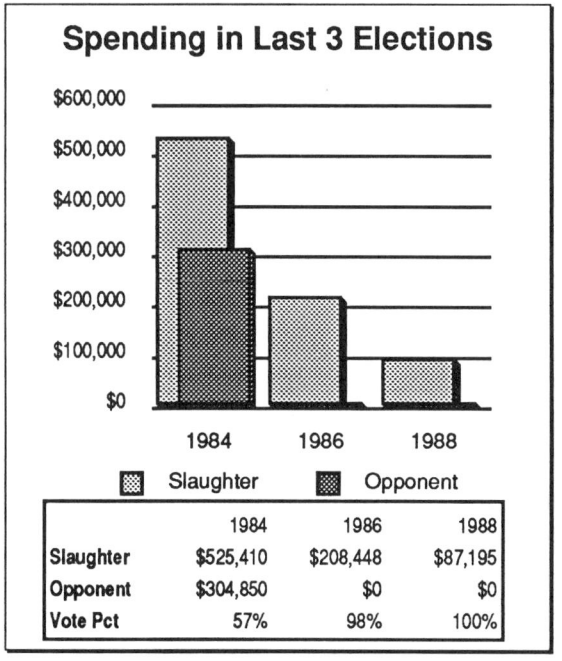

Spending in Last 3 Elections

▨ Slaughter   ◼ Opponent

	1984	1986	1988
Slaughter	$525,410	$208,448	$87,195
Opponent	$304,850	$0	$0
Vote Pct	57%	98%	100%

---

* Contributions came from more than one PAC affiliated with this sponsor.

Louise M. Slaughter, D-NY (30)

First elected: 1986
Total receipts: $778,946
Total from PACs: $387,871

1988 Committees & Subcommittees

Government Operations
Environment, Energy and Natural Resources
Government Information, Justice and Agriculture

Public Works and Transportation
Investigations and Oversight
Surface Transportation
Water Resources

Select Aging
Human Services

Campaign Revenue Sources

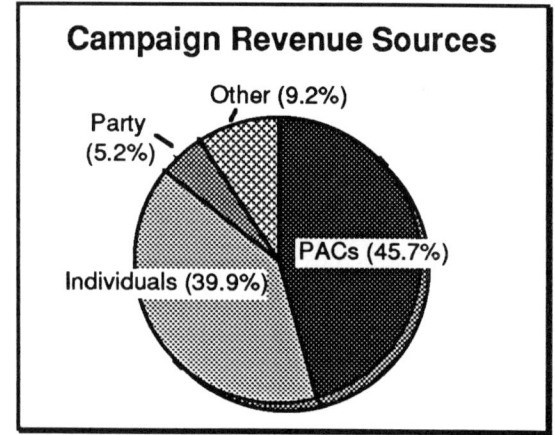

Other (9.2%)
Party (5.2%)
PACs (45.7%)
Individuals (39.9%)

PAC Contribution Profile

Business

Accountants	**$10,500**
American Institute of CPA's	$10,000
Others	$500
Commercial & Savings Banks	**$5,075**
Citicorp	$1,500
Sovran Financial Corp	$1,000
Others	$2,575
Construction	**$5,250**
National Assn of Home Builders	$3,750
National Electrical Contractors Assn	$1,000
Others	$500
Dairy	**$5,000**
Mid-American Dairymen	$2,250
Associated Milk Producers	$2,000
Others	$750
Health Professionals	**$20,999**
American Medical Assn	$9,499
American Nurses Assn	$2,750
New York Medical Assn	$2,500
American Academy of Ophthalmology	$2,000
American Dental Assn	$1,500
American Optometric Assn	$1,500
American Dietetic Assn	$1,000
Others	$250

Lawyers	**$10,500**
Assn of Trial Lawyers of America	$10,000
Others	$500
Real Estate	**$9,000**
National Assn of Realtors	$8,000
Others	$1,000
Securities/Commodities	**$3,325**
Chicago Board of Trade	$1,000
Chicago Mercantile Exchange	$1,000
PaineWebber	$1,000
Others	$325
Trucking/Delivery	**$5,281**
United Parcel Service	$2,600
Others	$2,681

Other Major Business PACs

National Assn of Life Underwriters	$1,500	Life Insurance
Philip Morris	$1,200	Tobacco
ACRE (Action Committee for Rural Electric)	$1,150	RuralElect
New York Telephone	$1,050	Phone Util
National Restaurant Assn	$1,000	Restaurants
National Assn of Social Workers	$1,000	Social Work
Tenneco Inc	$1,000	Ships
Xerox Corp	$1,000	Off Machines

PAC Totals by Category

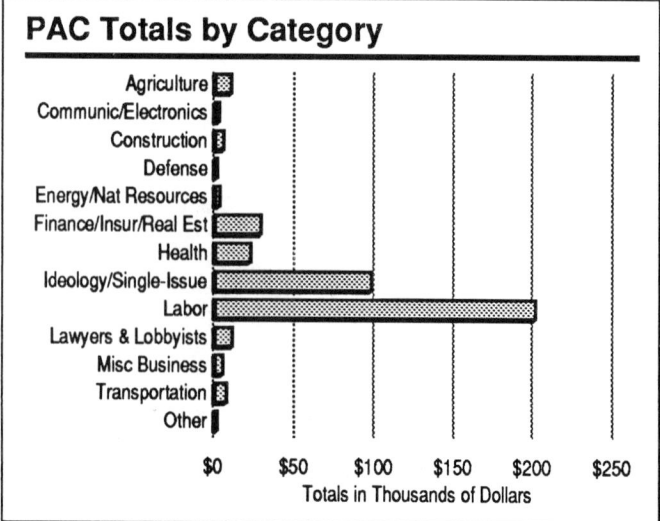

Agriculture
Communic/Electronics
Construction
Defense
Energy/Nat Resources
Finance/Insur/Real Est
Health
Ideology/Single-Issue
Labor
Lawyers & Lobbyists
Misc Business
Transportation
Other

$0 $50 $100 $150 $200 $250
Totals in Thousands of Dollars

Labor

Bldg Trades/Industrial/Misc Unions	**$109,100**
AFL-CIO*	$10,000
Food & Commercial Workers Union	$10,000
Machinists/Aerospace Workers Union	$10,000
Operating Engineers Local #832	$10,000
United Auto Workers	$10,000
Carpenters & Joiners Union	$6,750
Intl Brotherhood of Electrical Workers	$6,500
Bricklayers Union	$5,500
United Steelworkers	$5,000
Communications Workers of America	$4,750
Service Employees International Union	$4,000
Sheet Metal Workers Union	$4,000
Electrical Radio/Machine Workers	$2,450
Amalgamated Clothing & Textile Workers*	$2,200
Bakery, Confectionery & Tobacco Workers	$2,000

(continued in next column)

Labor (cont'd)

Plumbers/Pipefitters Union	$2,000
United Mine Workers	$1,800
Laborers' Political League	$1,750
Painters & Allied Trades Union	$1,700
Rubber Cork Linoleum Plastic Workers	$1,500
Electronic Machine Furniture Workers	$1,250
Ladies Garment Workers Union	$1,250
Ironworkers Union	$1,000
Others	$3,700

Government & Postal Workers $38,860

National Assn of Letter Carriers	$10,000
American Fedn of State/County/Munic Employees	$8,360
National Assn of Retired Federal Employees	$8,000
American Postal Workers Union	$7,500
International Assn of Firefighters	$1,500
National Assn of Postmasters	$1,250
Others	$2,250

Teachers Unions $20,000

American Federation of Teachers	$10,000
National Education Assn	$10,000

Transportation Unions $32,750

Air Line Pilots Assn	$10,000
Seafarers International Union	$6,000
Amalgamated Transit Union	$4,000
Marine Engineers District 2 Maritime Officers	$4,000
Transport Workers Union	$2,250
(Continued in next column)	

Transportation Unions (con't)

United Transportation Union	$2,000
Brotherhood of Railroad Signalmen	$1,000
Transportation Communication Union	$1,000
Others	$2,500

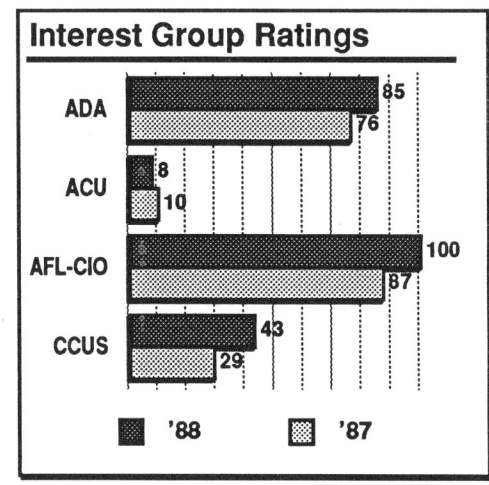

Interest Group Ratings

	'88	'87
ADA	85	76
ACU	8	10
AFL-CIO	100	87
CCUS	43	29

■ '88   ▨ '87

Ideological/Single-Issue

Democratic/Liberal $14,747

National Cmte for an Effective Congress	$9,997
Class PAC	$3,500
Others	$1,250

Democratic Leadership PACs $35,660

Cmte for Democratic Opportunity (Bill Gray)	$7,000
24th Cong Dist of California PAC (Henry Waxman)	$5,000
Majority Congress Committee (Jim Wright)	$5,000
America's Leaders' Fund (Dan Rostenkowski)	$4,910
Valley Education Fund (Tony Coelho)	$4,000
Cmte for the 100th Congress (Charles Rangel)	$3,500
House Leadership Fund (Tom Foley)	$3,000
Empire Leadership Fund (Mario Cuomo)	$2,500
Others	$750

Pro-Choice $13,250

National Abortion Rights Action League	$10,000
Voters for Choice/Friends of Family Planning	$2,500
Others	$750

Pro-Israel $13,500

National PAC	$5,000
Joint Action Cmte for Political Affairs	$2,000
Roundtable PAC	$2,000
Women's Pro-Israel National PAC	$2,000
Washington PAC	$1,000
Others	$1,500

Womens Issues $5,150

Women's Campaign Fund	$2,000
Emily's List	$1,000
National Womens Political Caucus	$1,000
Others	$1,150

Other Major Ideological/Single-Issue PACs

Sierra Club	$4,658	Environment
KidsPAC	$2,500	HealthWelfare
National Council of Senior Citizens	$2,000	Soc Secur
SANE/Freeze Inc	$2,000	Pro-Peace
Neighbor to Neighbor PAC	$1,553	ForeignPolcy
Council for a Livable World	$1,272	Pro-Peace

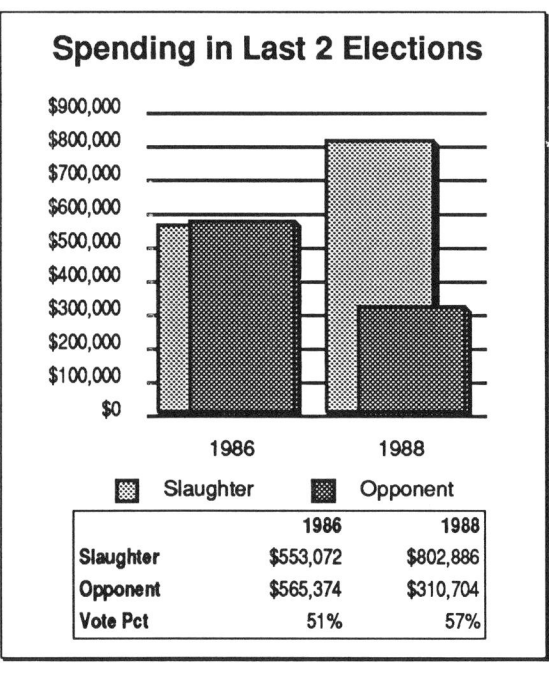

Spending in Last 2 Elections

	1986	1988
Slaughter	$553,072	$802,886
Opponent	$565,374	$310,704
Vote Pct	51%	57%

▨ Slaughter   ■ Opponent

* Contributions came from more than one PAC affiliated with this sponsor.

Bob Smith, R-Ore (2)

1988 Committees & Subcommittees

Agriculture
Forests, Family Farms and Energy
Livestock, Dairy and Poultry
Wheat, Soybeans and Feed Grains

Select Hunger

First elected: 1982
Total receipts: $381,363
Total from PACs: $153,366

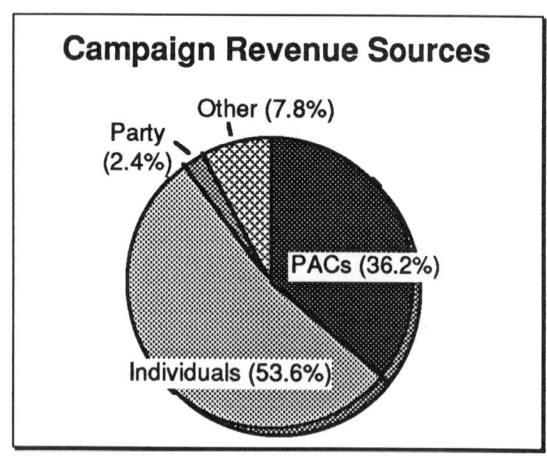

Campaign Revenue Sources

- Other (7.8%)
- Party (2.4%)
- PACs (36.2%)
- Individuals (53.6%)

PAC Contribution Profile

Business

Agricultural Chemicals	**$3,400**
None over $500	

Automotive	**$5,250**
National Auto Dealers Assn	$3,500
Auto Dealers & Drivers for Free Trade	$1,500
Others	$250

Aviation	**$5,000**
Aircraft Owners & Pilots Assn	$4,000
Boeing Company	$1,000

Commodities Trading	**$2,000**
Chicago Board of Trade	$1,000
Chicago Mercantile Exchange	$1,000

Construction	**$9,850**
National Assn of Home Builders	$4,000
Associated General Contractors	$3,500
Others	$2,350

Dairy	**$3,800**
Dairymen Inc	$1,800
Mid-American Dairymen	$1,000
Others	$1,000

Defense	**$3,500**
Harris Corp	$1,000
Litton Industries	$1,000
Others	$1,500

Department/Variety Stores	**$3,300**
Fred Meyer Inc	$2,500
Others	$800

Electric Utilities	**$3,650**
Pacific Power & Light	$1,000
Others	$2,650

Electronics & Computers	**$2,000**
Cooper Industries	$1,000
Others	$1,000

Financial Institutions	**$5,950**
American Bankers Assn	$2,500
US Bancorp	$1,500
Others	$1,950

Food & Beverage	**$5,150**
Food Marketing Institute	$1,500
McDonald's Corp	$1,000
Others	$2,650

Forest Products	**$13,150**
Boise Cascade	$4,000
Louisiana-Pacific Corp	$1,750
Weyerhaeuser Company*	$1,500
Stone Container Corp*	$1,400
Sun Studs Inc	$1,000
Others	$3,500

Health Professionals	**$11,500**
American Medical Assn	$10,000
American Dental Assn	$1,500

Insurance	**$5,000**
National Assn of Life Underwriters	$2,000
American Family Corp	$1,000
Standard Insurance Company	$1,000
Others	$1,000

Livestock & Poultry	**$6,150**
Texas Cattle Feeders Assn	$2,500
National Cattlemen's Assn	$1,600
National Broiler Council	$1,000
Others	$1,050

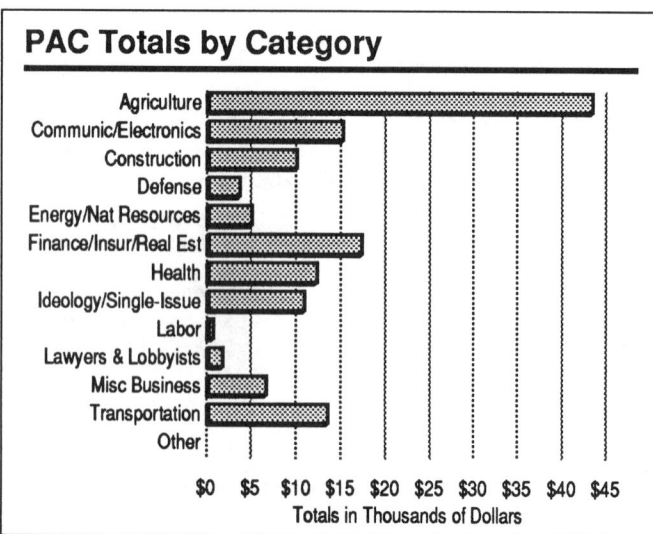

PAC Totals by Category

Categories (top to bottom): Agriculture, Communic/Electronics, Construction, Defense, Energy/Nat Resources, Finance/Insur/Real Est, Health, Ideology/Single-Issue, Labor, Lawyers & Lobbyists, Misc Business, Transportation, Other

Totals in Thousands of Dollars ($0, $5, $10, $15, $20, $25, $30, $35, $40, $45)

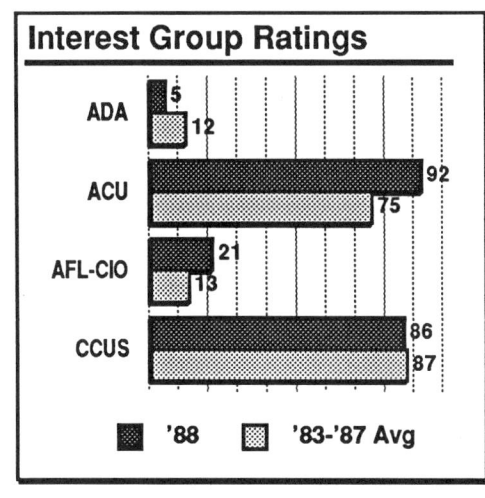

Interest Group Ratings

	'88	'83–'87 Avg
ADA	5	12
ACU	92	75
AFL-CIO	21	13
CCUS	86	87

Real Estate **$5,650**
  National Assn of Realtors $5,350
  Others $300

Sugar Growers **$3,800**
  American Sugarbeet Growers Assn $1,300
  Others $2,500

Telecommunications **$13,000**
  Pacific Northwest Bell $5,500
  United Telecommunications $4,500
  Continental Telecom $1,500
  Others $1,500

Tobacco **$2,250**
  Philip Morris $1,000
  Tobacco Institute $1,000
  Others $250

Other Major Business PACs

Stoel, Rives, Boley, Jones & Grey .... $1,300 Lawyers
National Fedn of Independent Business .... $1,000 Sml Business

Ideological/Single-Issue

Pro-Gun Ownership **$8,200**
  National Rifle Assn $6,450
  Safari Club International $1,750

Other Major Ideological/Single-Issue PACs

National Right to Life PAC .... $1,000 Pro-Life
Right to Life (Oregon) .... $1,000 Pro-Life

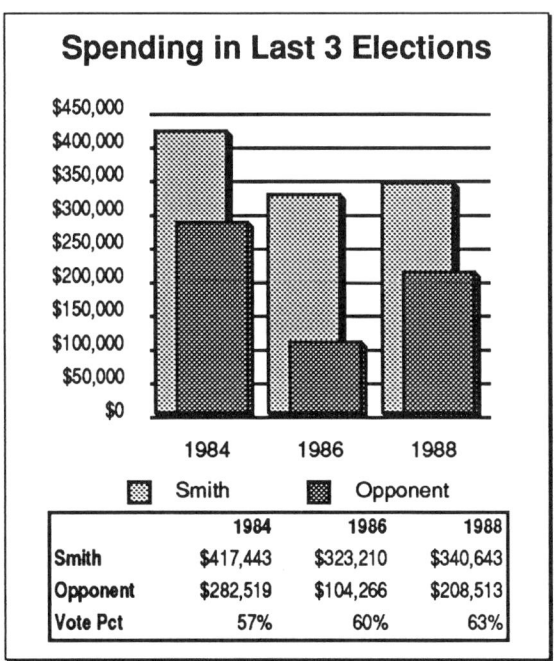

Spending in Last 3 Elections

	1984	1986	1988
Smith	$417,443	$323,210	$340,643
Opponent	$282,519	$104,266	$208,513
Vote Pct	57%	60%	63%

Smith   Opponent

* Contributions came from more than one PAC affiliated with this sponsor.

Christopher H. Smith, R-NJ (4)

First elected: 1980
Total receipts: $333,733
Total from PACs: $124,881

1988 Committees & Subcommittees

Foreign Affairs
Europe and the Middle East
Human Rights and International Organizations

Veterans' Affairs
Education, Training and Employment (Ranking Republican)
Hospitals and Health Care

Select Aging
Health and Long-Term Care

PAC Contribution Profile

Business

Auto Dealers	**$2,000**
National Auto Dealers Assn	$2,000
Construction	**$6,750**
National Assn of Home Builders	$6,000
Others	$750
Financial Institutions	**$3,324**
SAPEC/ NJ (New Jersey Savings Assn)	$1,300
American Bankers Assn	$750
Credit Union National Assn	$500
Others	$774
Food & Beverage	**$3,050**
Miller Brewing Company	$1,000
Brown-Forman Distillers	$750
Occidental Petroleum	$500
Papa Ginos	$500
Others	$300
Health Professionals	**$5,500**
American Medical Assn	$2,500
American Dental Assn	$2,000
American Society for Medical Technology	$1,000
Insurance	**$3,590**
National Assn of Life Underwriters	$2,500
Others	$1,090

Campaign Revenue Sources

Other (5.1%)
Party (6.3%)
PACs (36.6%)
Individuals (52.0%)

Pharmaceuticals	**$1,600**
Sandoz Pharmaceuticals	$550
Merck & Company	$500
Schering-Plough Corp	$500
Others	$50
Real Estate	**$6,250**
National Assn of Realtors	$6,000
Others	$250
Telecommunications	**$4,700**
New Jersey Bell Telephone	$3,500
AT&T	$1,200

Other Major Business PACs

Public Service Electric & Gas	$900	Gas & Electr
Mobil Oil	$750	Major Oil
Federated Investors Inc	$500	StocksInvest
Harsco Corp	$500	Indust Equip
NL Industries	$500	Chemicals
Owens-Illinois	$500	Paper Packg

PAC Totals by Category

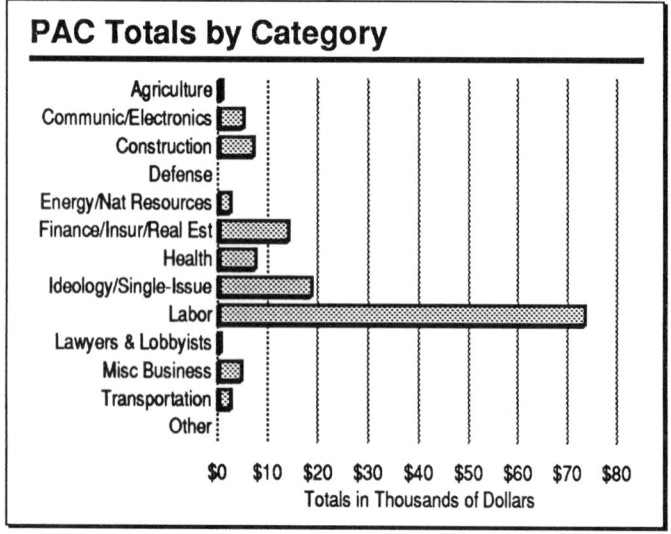

Agriculture
Communic/Electronics
Construction
Defense
Energy/Nat Resources
Finance/Insur/Real Est
Health
Ideology/Single-Issue
Labor
Lawyers & Lobbyists
Misc Business
Transportation
Other

$0 $10 $20 $30 $40 $50 $60 $70 $80

Totals in Thousands of Dollars

Labor

Bldg Trades/Industrial/Misc Unions $30,340
- Operating Engineers Union* $7,000
- United Auto Workers $6,500
- Carpenters & Joiners Union $4,000
- AFL-CIO* $3,000
- Plumbers/Pipefitters Union* $2,540
- Intl Brotherhood of Electrical Workers.............................$2,000
- Machinists/Aerospace Workers Union $2,000
- Laborers' Political League $1,500
- Ladies Garment Workers Union $1,000
- Boilermakers Union $500
- Others $300

Government & Postal Workers $9,216
- National Assn of Retired Federal Employees $6,500
- National Assn of Letter Carriers $1,966
- International Assn of Firefighters......................................$500
- Others $250

Teachers Unions $3,000
- National Education Assn $3,000

Transportation Unions $30,550
- Teamsters Union $10,000
- Air Line Pilots Assn $6,000
- Masters, Mates & Pilots Union $5,500
- Marine Engineers Union* $3,000
- International Longshoremen Assn $2,500
- Seafarers International Union $1,000
- Transportation Communication Union................................$800
- Amalgamated Transit Union $500
- Maritime Union of America $500
- United Transportation Union $500
- Others $250

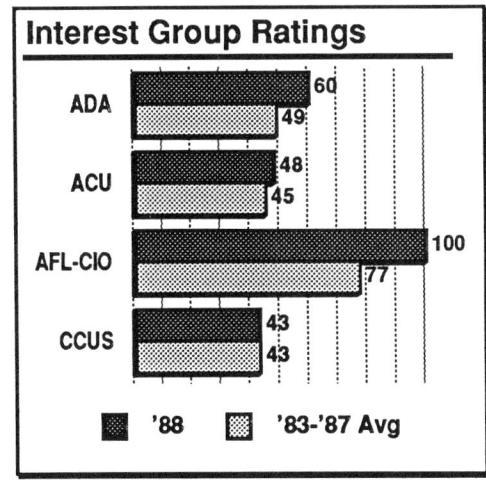

Ideological/Single-Issue

Pro-Israel $11,500
- National PAC $10,000
- Hudson Valley PAC $1,250
- Others $250

Pro-Life
- National Right to Life PAC..$2,254
- New Jersey Pro-Life PAC $750

Republican Leadership PACs $2,000
- Campaign for a New Majority (Jack Kemp).....................$2,000

Other Major Ideological/Single-Issue PACs

National Cmte to Preserve Social Security	$1,000	Soc Secur
Greek-American Progressive Political Fund	$500	Ethnic

Independent expenditures supporting Smith

National Cmte to Preserve Social Security $3,482

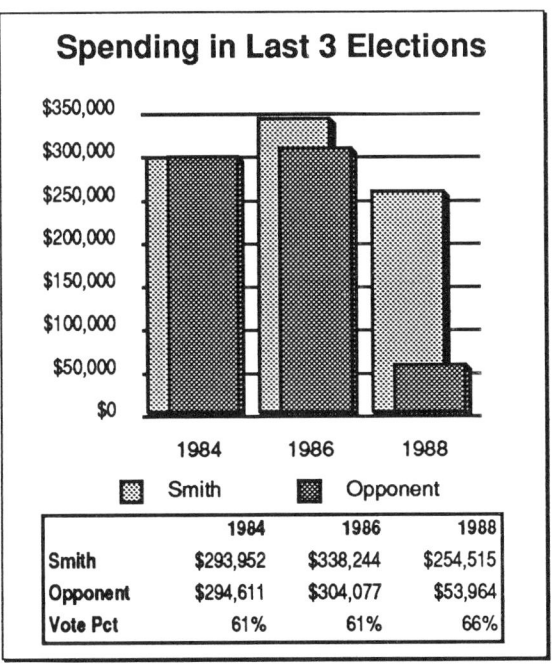

Spending in Last 3 Elections

	1984	1986	1988
Smith	$293,952	$338,244	$254,515
Opponent	$294,611	$304,077	$53,964
Vote Pct	61%	61%	66%

---

* Contributions came from more than one PAC affiliated with this sponsor.

Denny Smith, R-Ore (5)

First elected: 1980
Total receipts: $476,246
Total from PACs: $211,227

1988 Committees & Subcommittees

Budget
State and Local Government (Ranking Republican)
Budget Process
Defense, Foreign Policy and Space

Interior and Insular Affairs
General Oversight and Investigation (Ranking Republican)
Water and Power Resources

PAC Contribution Profile

Business

Air Transport	**$13,625**
Aircraft Owners & Pilots Assn	$7,400
General Aviation Manufacturers Assn	$1,175
Boeing Company	$1,000
Others	$4,050
Auto Dealers	**$11,300**
Auto Dealers & Drivers for Free Trade	$7,500
National Auto Dealers Assn	$3,800
Business Associations	**$3,258**
National Fedn of Independent Business	$3,193
Others	$65
Commercial & Savings Banks	**$4,400**
US Bancorp*	$2,300
Others	$2,100
Construction	**$18,148**
National Assn of Home Builders	$7,500
Ameron Inc	$3,000
Associated General Contractors	$2,000
National Electrical Contractors Assn	$1,000
Others	$4,648
Defense	**$14,950**
Northrop Corp	$2,100
Textron Inc	$2,100
Emerson Electric*	$1,800
Rockwell International	$1,600
United Technologies	$1,250
Colt Industries	$1,000

(Continued in next column)

Campaign Revenue Sources

Other (10.8%)
Party (8.9%)
PACs (38.8%)
Individuals (41.6%)

PAC Totals by Category

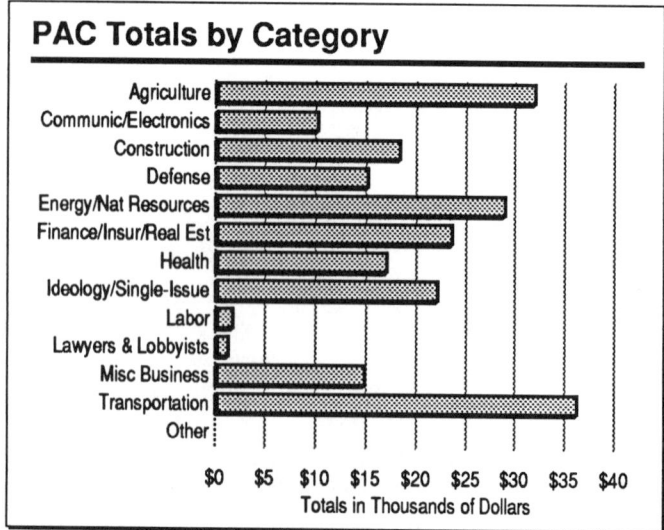

Agriculture
Communic/Electronics
Construction
Defense
Energy/Nat Resources
Finance/Insur/Real Est
Health
Ideology/Single-Issue
Labor
Lawyers & Lobbyists
Misc Business
Transportation
Other

$0 $5 $10 $15 $20 $25 $30 $35 $40
Totals in Thousands of Dollars

Defense (cont'd)	
General Dynamics	$1,000
Lockheed Corp	$1,000
Others	$3,100
Electric Utilities	**$12,850**
Idaho Power Company	$2,100
Texas Utilities Electric Company*	$1,400
Southern California Edison	$1,100
Pacific Power & Light	$1,000
Others	$7,250
Food & Beverage	**$3,700**
National Restaurant Assn	$1,000
Others	$2,700
Forest Products	**$15,350**
Louisiana-Pacific Corp	$2,250
National Forest Products Assn	$2,050
Boise Cascade	$2,000
Simpson Investment Company	$2,000
Weyerhaeuser Company*	$1,500
Georgia-Pacific Corp	$1,050
Sun Studs Inc	$1,000
Willamette Industries/Oregon	$1,000
Others	$2,500
Health Professionals	**$14,000**
American Medical Assn	$10,000
American Academy of Ophthalmology	$2,000
American Dental Assn	$1,500
Others	$500
Insurance	**$8,651**
National Assn of Life Underwriters	$4,000
Independent Insurance Agents of America	$1,151
Business Mens Assurance Company	$1,000
Standard Insurance Company	$1,000
Others	$1,500
Mining	**$2,050**
None over $500	
Oil & Gas	**$12,861**
Union Pacific Corp	$1,100
Dallas Energy PAC	$1,000
Mobil Oil	$1,000
Phillips Petroleum	$1,000
Rosewood Corp	$1,000
Others	$7,761

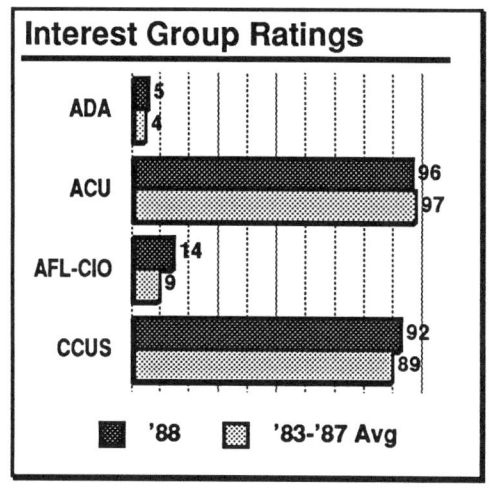

Interest Group Ratings

	'88	'83-'87 Avg
ADA	5	4
ACU	96	97
AFL-CIO	14	9
CCUS	92	89

◼ '88   ▨ '83-'87 Avg

Package Delivery **$9,900**
    United Parcel Service $8,800
    Federal Express Corp $1,100

Pharmaceuticals **$2,050**
    None over $550

Real Estate **$10,300**
    National Assn of Realtors $10,000
    Others $300

Sugar Growers **$4,600**
    American Crystal Sugar Corp $1,500
    Others $3,100

Telecommunications **$9,250**
    Pacific Northwest Bell $5,000
    Continental Telecom $1,500
    AT&T $1,000
    United Telecommunications $1,000
    Others $750

Textiles **$5,900**
    Burlington Industries $1,300
    J P Stevens & Company $1,300
    American Textile Manufacturers Institute $1,050
    Others $2,250

Tobacco **$4,500**
    Philip Morris $1,900
    Batus Inc* $1,800
    Others $800

Other Major Business PACs

Nevada Resort Assn .... $1,500   Casinos/Gamb
National Cattlemen's Assn .... $1,000   Livestock

Major Labor PACs

Marine Engineers Union .... $1,000   Seamen Union

Ideological/Single-Issue

Republican/Conservative **$7,900**
    Conservatives Acting Together $3,500
    Americans for Constitutional Action $2,500
    Conservative Victory Cmte $1,000
    Others $900

Other Major Ideological/Single-Issue PACs

National Rifle Assn .... $5,950   Pro-Guns
National Right to Life PAC .... $2,500   Pro-Life
Public Service Research Council .... $1,800   Anti-Union
National Security PAC .... $1,000   Pro-Defense

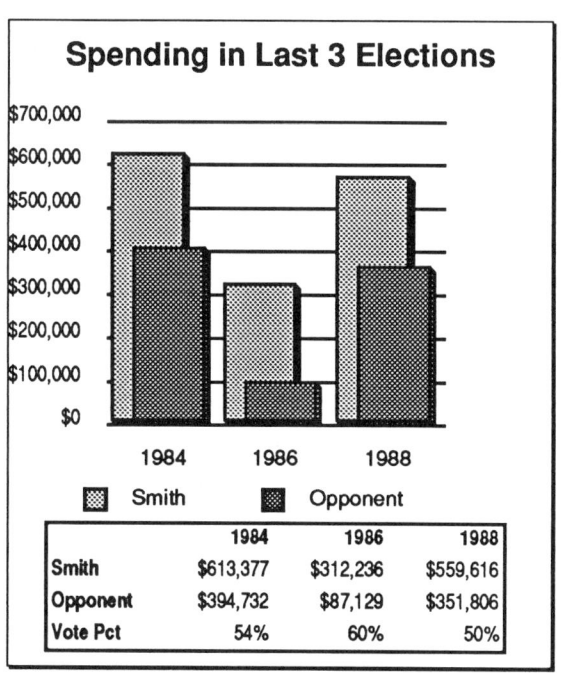

Spending in Last 3 Elections

	1984	1986	1988
Smith	$613,377	$312,236	$559,616
Opponent	$394,732	$87,129	$351,806
Vote Pct	54%	60%	50%

▨ Smith   ◼ Opponent

---

* Contributions came from more than one PAC affiliated with this sponsor.

Lamar Smith, R-Texas (21)

First elected: 1986
Total receipts: $567,201
Total from PACs: $95,732

1988 Committees & Subcommittees

Judiciary
Administrative Law and Governmental Relations
Crime

Science, Space and Technology
Energy Research and Development
Science, Research and Technology

PAC Contribution Profile

Business

Accountants **$6,350**

American Institute of CPA's $5,000
Others $1,350

Auto Dealers **$4,000**

National Auto Dealers Assn $2,500
Auto Dealers & Drivers for Free Trade $1,500

Construction **$6,250**

National Assn of Home Builders $1,500
Associated General Contractors $1,000
Ray Ellison Industries $1,000
Sheet Metal/AirCon Contractors $1,000
Others $1,750

Defense **$12,000**

Litton Industries $5,500
Harris Corp $1,000
Sequa Corp $1,000
Tenneco Inc $1,000
Others $3,500

Electric Utilities **$8,150**

Houston Industries $2,000
Texas Utilities Electric Company $2,000
Others $4,150

Financial Institutions **$4,577**

Centrust Savings Bank $2,000
Credit Union National Assn $1,000
Others $1,577

Campaign Revenue Sources

Party (0.5%)   Other (1.6%)
Candidate (6.5%)
PACs (23.7%)
Individuals (67.6%)

Food & Beverage **$3,050**

National Restaurant Assn $1,000
Others $2,050

Health Professionals **$6,117**

American Medical Assn $4,000
American Academy of Ophthalmology $1,500
Others $617

Insurance **$11,850**

National Assn of Life Underwriters $4,000
United Svcs Auto Assn Group $2,350
Others $5,500

Lawyers **$7,650**

Assn of Trial Lawyers of America $5,000
Sawtelle, Good, Davidson & Troilo $1,150
Others $1,500

Oil & Gas **$16,600**

Valero Energy Corp $2,800
Amoco Corp $1,000
El Paso Company $1,000
Mesa PAC II $1,000
Occidental Oil & Gas $1,000
Others $9,800

Real Estate **$8,250**

National Assn of Realtors $8,000
Others $250

Retail Sales **$2,750**

J C Penney Company $1,000
National Assn of Convenience Stores $1,000
Others $750

Telecommunications **$7,250**

GTE (Southwest) $2,500
AT&T $2,000
Southwestern Bell $2,000
Others $750

Textiles **$2,000**

None over $500

Other Major Business PACs

Texas Cattle Feeders Assn .... $1,000   Feedlots

PAC Totals by Category

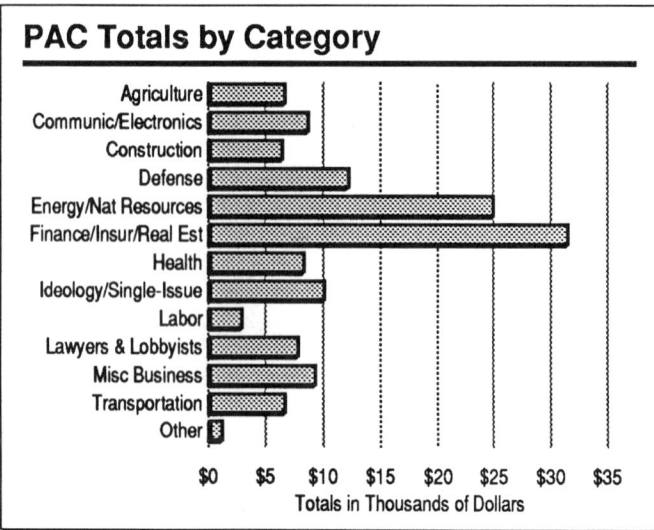

Totals in Thousands of Dollars

(Categories: Agriculture, Communic/Electronics, Construction, Defense, Energy/Nat Resources, Finance/Insur/Real Est, Health, Ideology/Single-Issue, Labor, Lawyers & Lobbyists, Misc Business, Transportation, Other; scale $0 $5 $10 $15 $20 $25 $30 $35)

Labor

Labor Unions **$2,750**
    Communications Workers of America $2,000
    Others $750

Ideological/Single-Issue

Pro-Israel **$6,000**
    National PAC $5,000
    Hudson Valley PAC $1,000

Other Major Ideological/Single-Issue PACs

Housing for America PAC ....$1,000   Unknown
Midland County Republican Womens Club .....$1,000   Repub/Conser

Independent expenditures supporting Smith

National Structured Settlements Assn $1,000

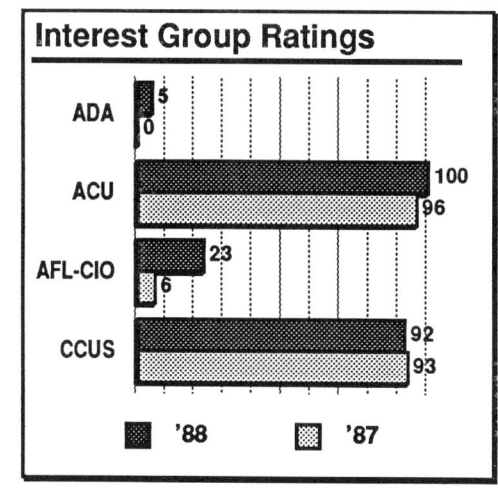

Interest Group Ratings

(Bar chart showing Interest Group Ratings)

	'88	'87
ADA	5	0
ACU	100	96
AFL-CIO	23	6
CCUS	92	93

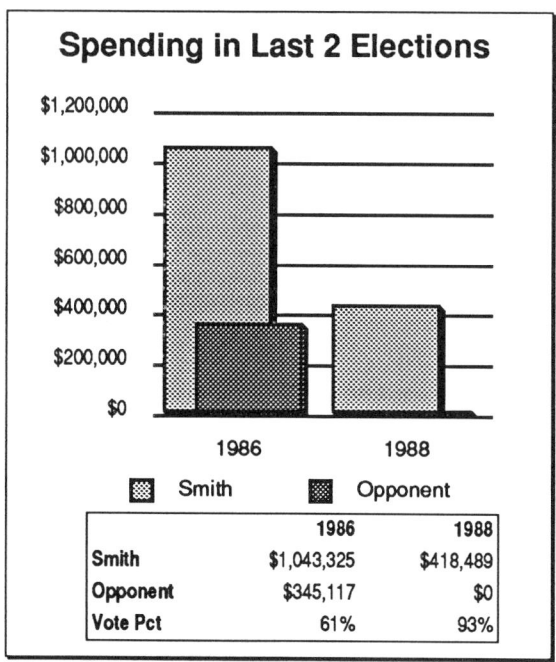

Spending in Last 2 Elections

	1986	1988
Smith	$1,043,325	$418,489
Opponent	$345,117	$0
Vote Pct	61%	93%

Smith ◻   Opponent ▨

Larkin Smith, R-Miss (5)

1989 Committees & Subcommittees

First elected: 1988
Total receipts: $588,552
Total from PACs: $135,150

Government Operations
Human Resources and Intergovernmental Relations (Ranking Republican)

Judiciary
Administrative Law and Governmental Relations
Criminal Justice

PAC Contribution Profile

Business

Campaign Revenue Sources

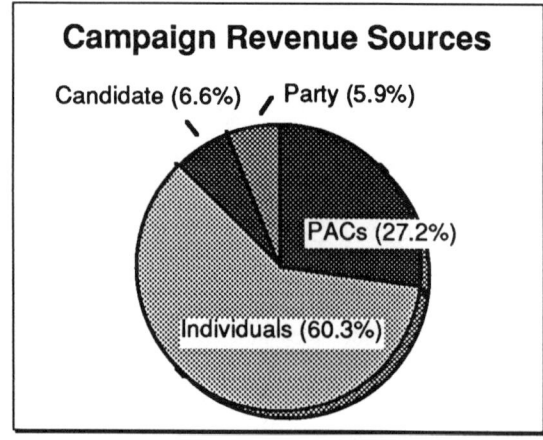

Candidate (6.6%) / Party (5.9%)
PACs (27.2%)
Individuals (60.3%)

Automotive	$5,750
Auto Dealers & Drivers for Free Trade	$2,500
National Auto Dealers Assn	$2,000
Eaton Corp	$1,000
Others	$250

Chemicals	$5,400
Dow Chemical*	$3,500
FMC Corp	$1,000
Others	$900

Commercial & Savings Banks	$9,800
First Magnolia Federal Savings & Loan	$4,600
Bank of Mississippi	$2,000
Forest Bancorp	$1,000
US League of Savings Assn	$1,000
Others	$1,200

Construction	$9,350
Associated General Contractors	$2,500
National Assn of Home Builders	$2,500
Texas Industries	$2,000
Others	$2,350

Dairy	$2,000
Associated Milk Producers	$1,000
Dairymen Inc-Mississippi	$1,000

Defense	$5,600
Mantech International	$1,600
Harris Corp	$1,000
Others	$3,000

Electric Utilities	$6,050
Southern Company*	$3,050
Middle South Utilities	$1,500
Mississippi ACRE	$1,000
Others	$500

Electronics & Computers	$3,500
Cooper Industries	$3,000
Others	$500

Food & Beverage	$9,800
Coors Industries	$1,250
Delchamps Inc	$1,000
Jitney-Jungle Inc	$1,000
Malone & Hyde Inc	$1,000
National Restaurant Assn	$1,000
Pepsi-Cola Bottlers Assn	$1,000
Others	$3,550

Health Professionals	$8,500
American Medical Assn	$5,000
American Academy of Ophthalmology	$2,500
American Chiropractic Assn	$1,000

Insurance	$7,300
National Assn of Life Underwriters	$5,000
Independent Insurance Agents of America	$1,000
Others	$1,300

Oil & Gas	$8,400
Phillips Petroleum	$2,000
Amoco Corp	$1,000
Chevron Corp	$1,000
Others	$4,400

Paper Production	$2,250
International Paper Company	$2,000
Others	$250

Real Estate	$5,000
National Assn of Realtors	$5,000

Telecommunications	$5,500
South Central Bell Telephone	$3,000
AT&T	$2,000
Others	$500

PAC Totals by Category

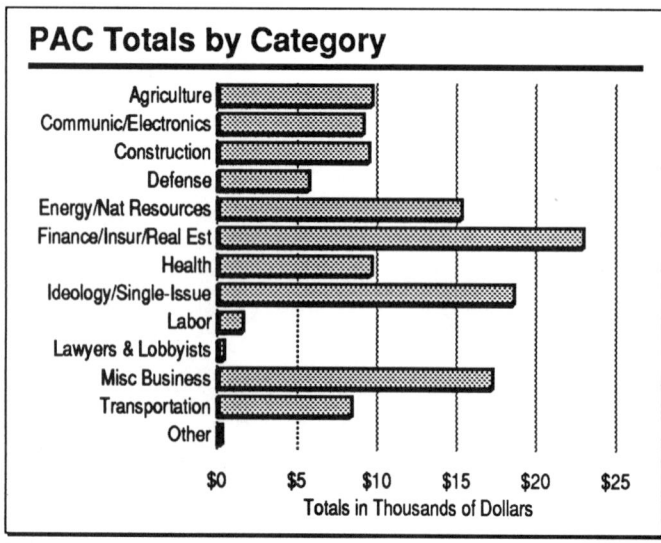

Agriculture
Communic/Electronics
Construction
Defense
Energy/Nat Resources
Finance/Insur/Real Est
Health
Ideology/Single-Issue
Labor
Lawyers & Lobbyists
Misc Business
Transportation
Other

$0 $5 $10 $15 $20 $25

Totals in Thousands of Dollars

Other Major Business PACs

American Hotel & Motel Assn	$1,000	Hotel/Motel
Business Industry PAC	$1,000	Bus Assns
Corning Glass Works	$1,000	Glass Prod
L. M. Berry & Company	$1,000	Mail Advert
National Assn of Temporary Services	$1,000	EmployAgency

Major Labor PACs

Marine Engineers Union	$1,500	Seamen Union

Ideological/Single-Issue

Pro-Israel	**$7,000**
National PAC	$5,000
Americans for Good Government Inc	$1,000
Women's Pro-Israel National PAC	$1,000
Republican Leadership PACs	**$2,350**
Republican Leader's Fund (Bob Michel)	$1,000
Others	$1,350

Other Major Ideological/Single-Issue PACs

National Rifle Assn	$2,500	Pro-Guns
Right to Work PAC	$2,500	Anti-Union
National Conservative PAC	$1,783	Repub/Conser
Public Service Research Council	$1,000	Anti-Union

Independent expenditures supporting Smith

American Medical Assn	$93,179

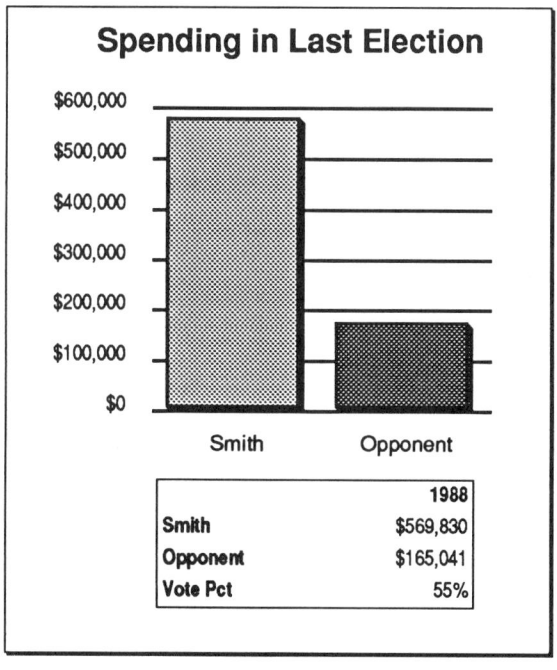

Spending in Last Election

	1988
Smith	$569,830
Opponent	$165,041
Vote Pct	55%

---

* Contributions came from more than one PAC affiliated with this sponsor.

Lawrence J. Smith, D-Fla (16)

First elected: 1982
Total receipts: $660,164
Total from PACs: $289,543

1988 Committees & Subcommittees

Foreign Affairs
Europe and the Middle East
International Operations

Judiciary
Crime
Monopolies and Commercial Law

Select Narcotics Abuse and Control

PAC Contribution Profile

Business

Campaign Revenue Sources

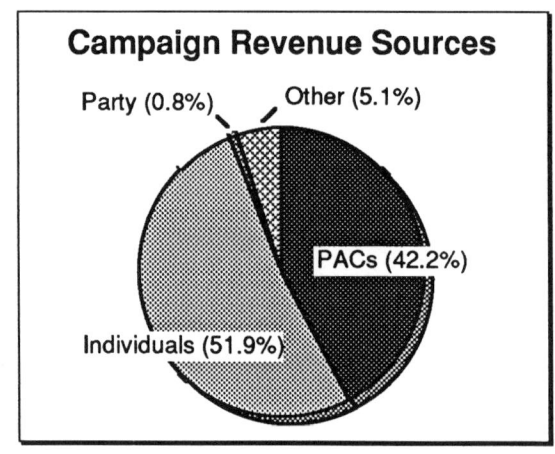

Party (0.8%) Other (5.1%)
PACs (42.2%)
Individuals (51.9%)

Accountants	**$6,400**
American Institute of CPA's	$5,000
Others	$1,400
Broadcasting/Entertainment	**$6,800**
Storer Administration Inc	$2,000
National Assn of Broadcasters	$1,200
ASCAP	$1,000
Others	$2,600
Commercial Banks	**$7,700**
Barnett Banks of Florida	$2,500
Citizens & Southern National Bank	$1,400
National Banks of Florida	$1,300
Others	$2,500
Construction	**$4,750**
National Assn of Home Builders	$2,500
Adler Group Inc	$1,000
Walter Industries	$1,000
Others	$250
Electric Utilities	**$2,400**
Florida Power & Light	$1,300
Others	$1,100
Food & Beverage	**$6,100**
National Beer Wholesalers Assn	$2,000
General Mills*	$1,500
Southern Wine & Spirits	$1,000
Winn-Dixie Stores	$1,000
Others	$600

Health Professionals	**$18,150**
Florida Medical Assn	$4,800
American Medical Assn	$3,800
American Dental Assn	$3,000
National Assn of Pharmacists	$1,500
American College of Emergency Physicians	$1,300
American Podiatry Assn	$1,000
Cmte for Quality Orthopedic Health Care	$1,000
Others	$1,750
Insurance	**$4,500**
National Assn of Life Underwriters	$1,500
Independent Insurance Agents of America	$1,300
Others	$1,700
Lawyers & Lobbyists	**$10,400**
Assn of Trial Lawyers of America	$5,300
Akin, Gump, Hauer & Feld	$1,200
Kirkpatrick & Lockhart	$1,000
Others	$2,900
Oil & Gas	**$2,800**
Chevron Corp	$1,100
Others	$1,700
Pharmaceuticals	**$2,750**
Schering-Plough Corp	$1,000
Others	$1,750
Real Estate	**$11,000**
National Assn of Realtors	$10,000
General Development Corp	$1,000
Savings Banks	**$10,100**
Centrust Savings Bank	$5,000
Florida League of Financial Institutions	$2,000
Guardian Savings & Loan	$1,200
Others	$1,900
Telecommunications	**$6,750**
Southern Bell	$3,000
AT&T	$2,100
Others	$1,650
Waste Management	**$2,100**
Waste Management Inc	$2,100

Other Major Business PACs

Ryder System Inc ... $1,500 TruckRental

PAC Totals by Category

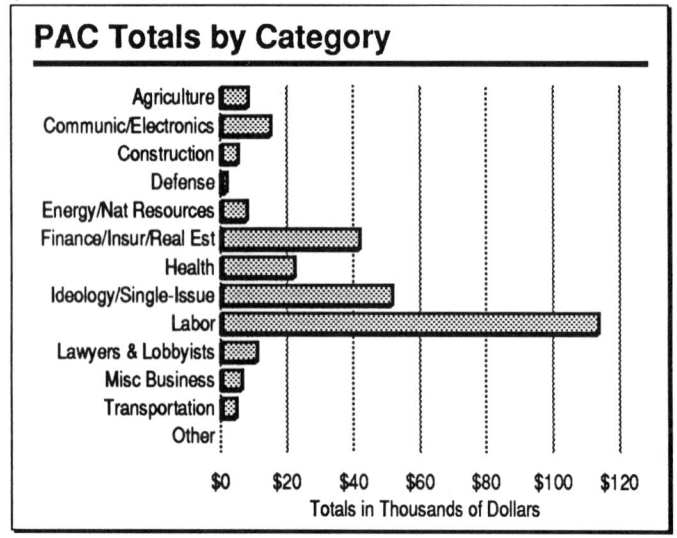

Agriculture
Communic/Electronics
Construction
Defense
Energy/Nat Resources
Finance/Insur/Real Est
Health
Ideology/Single-Issue
Labor
Lawyers & Lobbyists
Misc Business
Transportation
Other

$0 $20 $40 $60 $80 $100 $120
Totals in Thousands of Dollars

Labor

Bldg Trades/Industrial/Misc Unions $41,050
Intl Brotherhood of Electrical Workers* $6,100
Machinists/Aerospace Workers Union $5,000
Operating Engineers Union* $5,000
United Auto Workers $4,100
Carpenters & Joiners Union $3,300
Communications Workers of America $3,100
Plumbers/Pipefitters Union* $2,700
Food & Commercial Workers Union $2,300
Sheet Metal Workers Union $2,000
Laborers' Political League $1,600
Hotel/Restaurant Employees Union $1,250
AFL-CIO* $1,200
Boilermakers Union $1,200
Others $2,200

Government & Postal Workers $24,313
National Assn of Letter Carriers $9,900
National Assn of Retired Federal Employees $7,600
American Fedn of State/County/Munic Employees $2,563
American Postal Workers Union $1,500
International Assn of Firefighters $1,300
Others $1,450

Teachers Unions $9,150
American Federation of Teachers $4,950
National Education Assn $4,200

Transportation Unions $38,600
Marine Engineers Union* $10,000
Teamsters Union $10,000
Air Line Pilots Assn $5,000
Seafarers International Union $2,600
Amalgamated Transit Union $2,500
United Transportation Union $2,400
Transport Workers Union $2,200
Masters, Mates & Pilots Union $1,600
Others $2,300

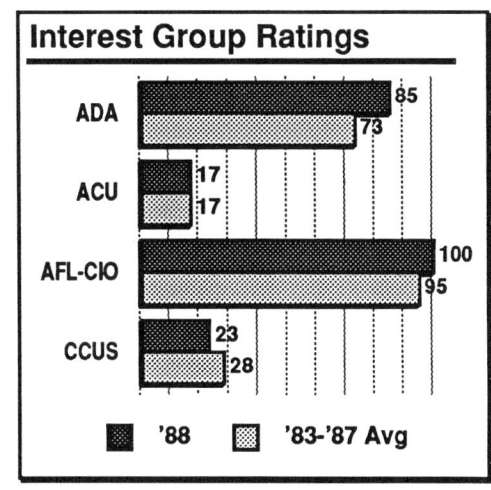

Interest Group Ratings

	'88	'83–'87 Avg
ADA	85	73
ACU	17	17
AFL-CIO	100	95
CCUS	23	28

Ideological/Single-Issue

Anti-Castro $9,500
Free Cuba PAC $9,500

Democratic Leadership PACs $3,500
Valley Education Fund (Tony Coelho) $3,000
Others $500

Pro-Israel $33,100
Florida Congressional Cmte $5,000
National Action Committee (NACPAC) $5,000
National PAC $5,000
East Midwood PAC $2,000
Washington PAC $2,000
Roundtable PAC $1,500
Citizens Organized PAC $1,000
Delaware Valley PAC $1,000
Hudson Valley PAC $1,000
Joint Action Cmte for Political Affairs $1,000
San Diego Community PAC $1,000
South Florida Caucus $1,000
St Louisians for Better Government $1,000
Others $5,600

Other Major Ideological/Single-Issue PACs
National Cmte for an Effective Congress .... $2,530   Dem/Liberal
National Cmte to Preserve Social Security ...... $1,500   Soc Secur

Independent expenditures supporting Smith
National Cmte to Preserve Social Security $4,205

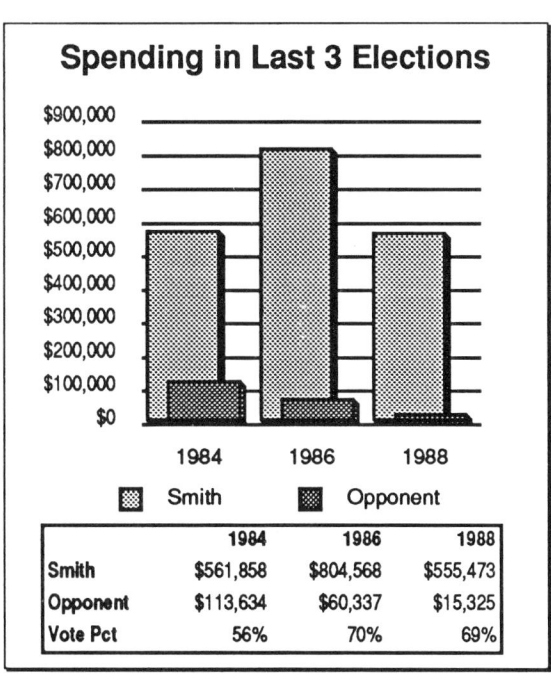

Spending in Last 3 Elections

	1984	1986	1988
Smith	$561,858	$804,568	$555,473
Opponent	$113,634	$60,337	$15,325
Vote Pct	56%	70%	69%

Legend: Smith / Opponent

* Contributions came from more than one PAC affiliated with this sponsor.

Neal Smith, D-Iowa (4)

First elected: 1958
Total receipts: $205,035
Total from PACs: $162,585

1988 Committees & Subcommittees

Appropriations
Commerce, Justice, State, the Judiciary and Related Agencies (Chairman)
Labor, Health and Human Services, Education and Related Agencies
Rural Development, Agriculture and Related Agencies

Small Business
SBA and the General Economy

PAC Contribution Profile

Business

Campaign Revenue Sources

Other (13.9%)
Party (3.5%)
Individuals (10.3%)
PACs (72.4%)

Automotive	**$6,500**
National Auto Dealers Assn	$3,750
Auto Dealers & Drivers for Free Trade	$2,500
Others	$250
Commercial & Savings Banks	**$7,500**
Hawkeye Bancorp	$3,000
American Bankers Assn	$2,250
Norwest Corp	$1,000
Others	$1,250
Construction	**$5,000**
National Utility Contractors Assn	$2,000
Sheet Metal/AirCon Contractors	$1,000
Others	$2,000
Dairy	**$2,750**
Associated Milk Producers	$1,500
Mid-American Dairymen	$1,250
Defense	**$3,000**
Rockwell International	$1,000
Others	$2,000
Electric Utilities	**$3,050**
Iowa Resources Inc	$1,000
Others	$2,050
Electronics & Computers	**$3,450**
Computer Sciences Corp	$1,000
General Electric	$1,000
Westinghouse Electric	$1,000
Others	$450

Farm Organizations	**$3,500**
Iowa Farm Bureau Federation	$2,500
Others	$1,000
Food & Beverage	**$2,750**
Food Marketing Institute	$1,000
National Beer Wholesalers Assn	$1,000
Others	$750
Health Professionals	**$20,000**
American Medical Assn	$10,000
American Dental Assn	$4,000
American Academy of Ophthalmology	$1,000
National Assn of Pharmacists	$1,000
Oral & Maxillofacial Surgeons	$1,000
Others	$3,000
Insurance	**$2,650**
Principal Mutual Life Insurance	$1,000
Others	$1,650
Lawyers & Lobbyists	**$9,513**
Assn of Trial Lawyers of America	$5,000
Akin, Gump, Hauer & Feld	$1,000
Kirkpatrick & Lockhart	$1,000
Preston, Thorgrimson, Ellis & Holman	$1,000
Others	$1,513
Oil & Gas	**$2,000**
Bass Brothers Enterprises	$1,000
Others	$1,000
Package Delivery	**$2,750**
United Parcel Service	$2,750
Real Estate	**$2,875**
National Assn of Realtors	$2,125
Others	$750
Sugar Growers	**$2,550**
None over $750	
Telecommunications	**$5,800**
North Western Bell Telephone	$1,500
AT&T	$1,000
Others	$3,300
TV/Cable TV	**$2,000**
National Cable Television Assn	$1,000
Others	$1,000

PAC Totals by Category

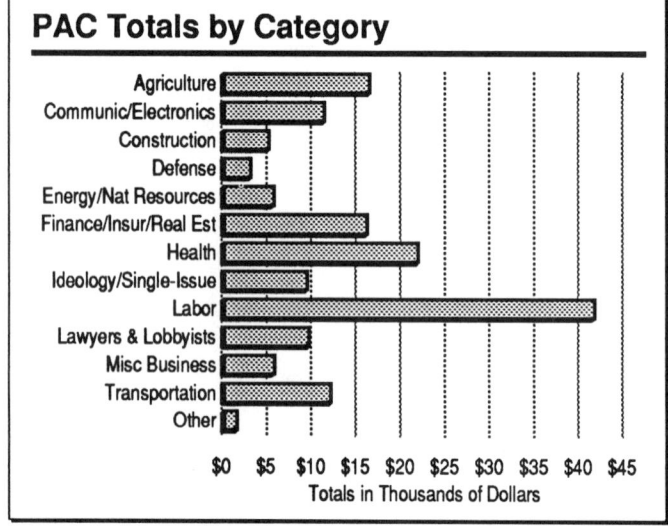

Agriculture
Communic/Electronics
Construction
Defense
Energy/Nat Resources
Finance/Insur/Real Est
Health
Ideology/Single-Issue
Labor
Lawyers & Lobbyists
Misc Business
Transportation
Other

$0 $5 $10 $15 $20 $25 $30 $35 $40 $45
Totals in Thousands of Dollars

Venture Capital *$3,000*

    National Venture Capital Assn $3,000

Other Major Business PACs

Health Industry Manufacturers Assn ....$1,250   Med Supply
American Soybean Assn ....$1,000   Grain
Deere & Company ....$1,000   Farm Equip
National Assn of Trade/Tech Schools ....$1,000   Voc Tech

Labor

Bldg Trades/Industrial/Misc Unions *$11,000*

    Carpenters & Joiners Union $2,500
    Food & Commercial Workers Union.................$1,500
    Laborers' Political League $1,500
    Operating Engineers Union $1,500
    Plumbers/Pipefitters Union $1,000
    Others $3,000

Government & Postal Workers *$10,500*

    National Assn of Retired Federal Employees $5,000
    National Assn of Letter Carriers $2,000
    American Fedn of State/County/Munic Employees $1,500
    American Postal Workers Union $1,000
    Others $1,000

Teachers Unions *$13,035*

    National Education Assn $10,000
    American Federation of Teachers $3,035

Transportation Unions *$7,050*

    Air Line Pilots Assn $2,500
    Seafarers International Union $2,000
    United Transportation Union $1,000
    Others $1,550

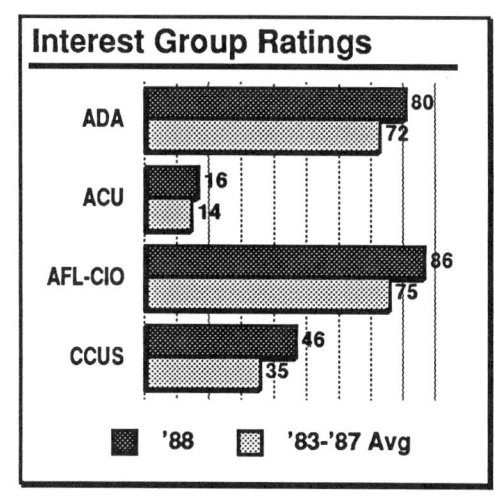

Ideological/Single-Issue

Ideological/Single-Issue *$8,800*

Free Cuba PAC ....$5,000   Anti-Castro
National Cmte to Preserve Social Security ......$2,000   Soc Secur
KidsPAC ....$1,000   HealthWelfare
Others $800

Independent expenditures supporting Smith

National Cmte to Preserve Social Security $3,232

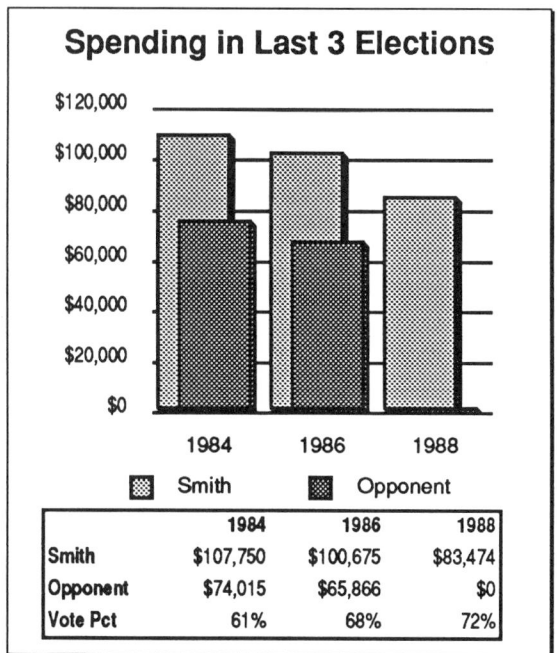

Peter Smith, R-Vt (At Large)

1989-90 Committees & Subcommittees

First elected: 1988
Total receipts: $457,737
Total from PACs: $158,811

Education and Labor
Elementary, Secondary and Vocational Education
Employment Opportunities
Select Education

Government Operations
Human Resources and Intergovernmental Relations
Legislation and National Security

Select Children, Youth and Families

PAC Contribution Profile

Business

Automotive **$11,100**
    National Auto Dealers Assn $6,350
    Auto Dealers & Drivers for Free Trade $2,500
    Eaton Corp $2,000
    Others $250

Business Associations **$2,334**
    Business Industry PAC $1,271
    National Fedn of Independent Business $1,000
    Others $63

Construction **$12,850**
    Associated General Contractors $5,000
    National Assn of Home Builders $5,000
    Associated Builders & Contractors $1,000
    Others $1,850

Dairy **$8,050**
    Associated Milk Producers $5,000
    Dairymen Inc $1,050
    Mid-American Dairymen $1,000
    Others $1,000

Defense **$4,000**
    Harris Corp $2,000
    Lockheed Corp $1,000
    Others $1,000

Electronics **$3,250**
    Cooper Industries $3,000
    Others $250

Campaign Revenue Sources

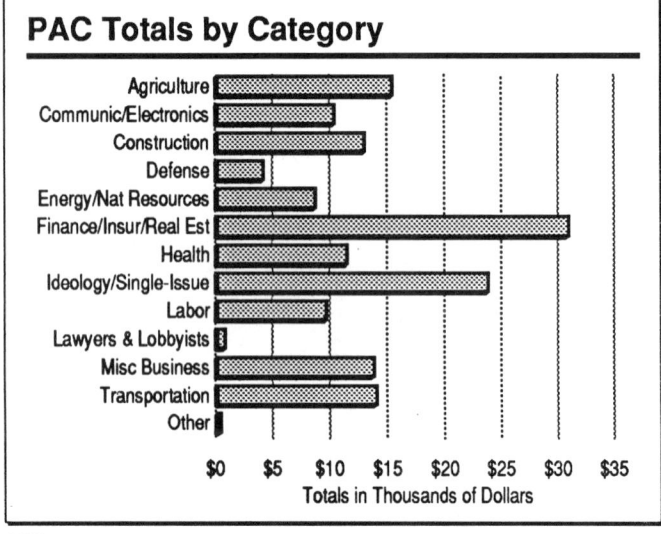

Other (15.9%)
PACs (24.4%)
Party (16.0%)
Individuals (43.7%)

Financial Institutions **$7,000**
    American Bankers Assn $3,000
    Credit Union National Assn $1,000
    US League of Savings Assn $1,000
    Others $2,000

Food & Beverage **$7,450**
    National Restaurant Assn $3,000
    American Meat Institute $1,000
    McDonald's Corp $1,000
    Others $2,450

Forest Products **$2,000**
    Boise Cascade $1,000
    International Paper Company $1,000

Health Professionals **$9,000**
    American Medical Assn $5,000
    American Dental Assn $2,500
    American Optometric Assn $1,000
    Others $500

Insurance **$12,300**
    National Assn of Life Underwriters $6,000
    Independent Insurance Agents of America $2,000
    American International Group inc $1,250
    Casualty & Surety Agents Assn $1,000
    Others $2,050

Oil & Gas **$7,300**
    Phillips Petroleum $2,500
    Sun Company $1,000
    Others $3,800

Real Estate **$10,500**
    National Assn of Realtors $10,000
    Others $500

Telecommunications **$6,950**
    New England Tel & Tel $2,500
    AT&T $2,200
    Continental Telecom $1,000
    Others $1,250

PAC Totals by Category

Category	Totals in Thousands of Dollars
Agriculture	
Communic/Electronics	
Construction	
Defense	
Energy/Nat Resources	
Finance/Insur/Real Est	
Health	
Ideology/Single-Issue	
Labor	
Lawyers & Lobbyists	
Misc Business	
Transportation	
Other	

$0 $5 $10 $15 $20 $25 $30 $35
Totals in Thousands of Dollars

Other Major Business PACs

FMC Corp	$1,000	Chemicals
National Assn of Temporary Services	$1,000	EmployAgency
Philip Morris	$1,000	Tobacco

Labor

Labor Unions *$9,500*

National Assn of Letter Carriers	$5,000
Air Line Pilots Assn	$2,500
National Assn of Retired Federal Employees	$2,000

Ideological/Single-Issue

Pro-Israel *$12,850*

National PAC	$5,000
Americans for Good Government Inc	$1,000
Bi-County PAC	$1,000
Delaware Valley PAC	$1,000
Hudson Valley PAC	$1,000
Others	$3,850

Republican Leadership/Conservative PACs *$9,800*

Fund for America's Future (George Bush)	$5,000
Campaign America (Bob Dole)	$2,000
Republican Congressional Boosters Club	$1,000
Republican Leader's Fund (Bob Michel)	$1,000
Others	$800

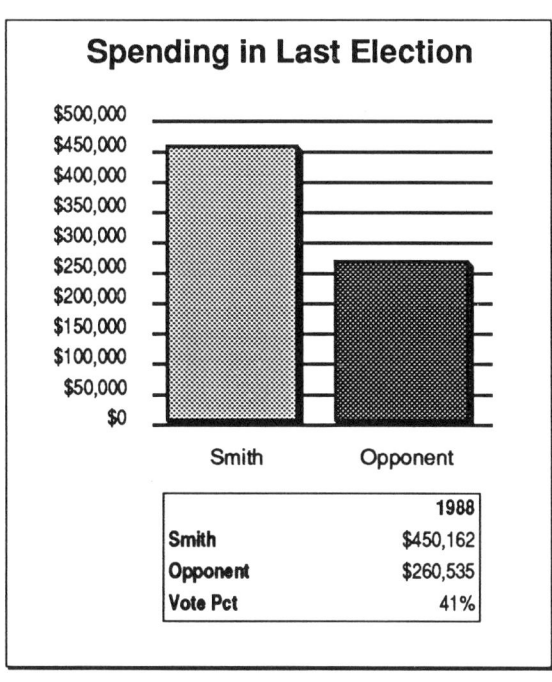

Spending in Last Election

	1988
Smith	$450,162
Opponent	$260,535
Vote Pct	41%

Robert C. Smith, R-NH (1)

First elected: 1984
Total receipts: $361,130
Total from PACs: $109,500

1988 Committees & Subcommittees

Science, Space and Technology
Natural Resources, Agriculture Research and Environment
Space Science and Applications

Veterans' Affairs
Compensation, Pension and Insurance
Housing and Memorial Affairs

PAC Contribution Profile

Business

Aerospace **$1,900**
　None over $500

Alternate Energy **$10,000**
　Henley Group Inc $10,000

Automotive **$14,900**
　National Auto Dealers Assn $8,300
　Auto Dealers & Drivers for Free Trade $6,000
　Others $600

Chemicals **$1,550**
　Dow Chemical/Eastern Employees $750
　Others $800

Commercial & Savings Banks **$4,750**
　New Hampshire Bankers Assn $3,000
　Bankeast Corp $1,000
　Others $750

Construction **$6,150**
　National Assn of Home Builders $2,500
　Associated General Contractors $1,300
　Others $2,350

Defense **$4,050**
　Lockheed Corp $1,000
　Bath Iron Works $600
　Others $2,450

Campaign Revenue Sources

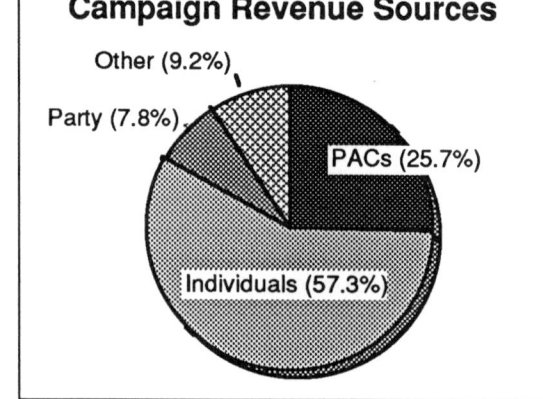

Other (9.2%)
Party (7.8%)
PACs (25.7%)
Individuals (57.3%)

Electric Utilities **$7,650**
　Middle South Utilities* $550
　Others $7,100

Food & Beverage **$2,650**
　Papa Ginos $1,500
　Others $1,150

Health Professionals **$11,000**
　American Medical Assn $10,000
　Cmte for Quality Orthopedic Health Care $1,000

Industrial Equipment & Materials **$1,100**
　Interlake Inc $600
　Others $500

Insurance **$8,200**
　National Assn of Life Underwriters $5,000
　National Assn Mutual Insurance Agents $1,000
　American International Group inc $800
　Independent Insurance Agents of America $600
　Others $800

Lawyers **$2,300**
　Assn of Trial Lawyers of America $2,000
　Others $300

Oil & Gas **$1,550**
　Mobil Oil $1,000
　Others $550

Real Estate **$8,850**
　National Assn of Realtors $8,550
　Others $300

Telecommunications **$3,000**
　AT&T $2,000
　New England Tel & Tel $1,000

Tobacco **$1,300**
　Philip Morris $1,000
　Others $300

PAC Totals by Category

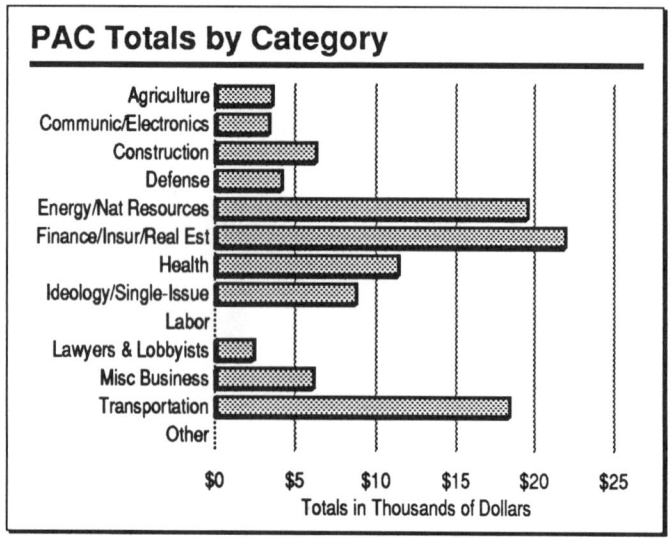

Agriculture
Communic/Electronics
Construction
Defense
Energy/Nat Resources
Finance/Insur/Real Est
Health
Ideology/Single-Issue
Labor
Lawyers & Lobbyists
Misc Business
Transportation
Other

$0　$5　$10　$15　$20　$25
Totals in Thousands of Dollars

Ideological/Single-Issue

Republican Leadership PACs $1,850

    Campaign America (Bob Dole)..$1,000
    Campaign for a New Majority (Jack Kemp).......................$600
    Others $250

Other Major Ideological/Single-Issue PACs

National Rifle Assn ....$4,300   Pro-Guns
National Right to Life PAC ....$1,000   Pro-Life

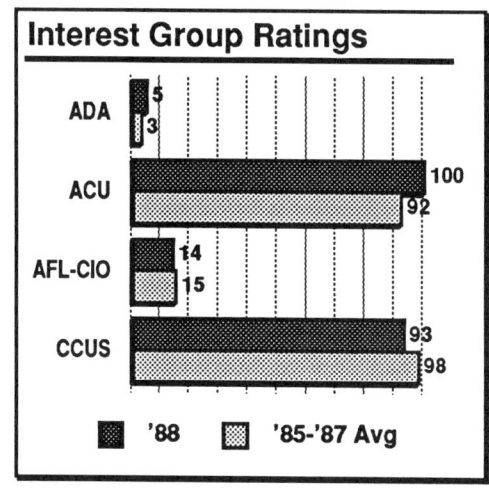

Interest Group Ratings

	'88	'85-'87 Avg
ADA	5	3
ACU	100	92
AFL-CIO	14	15
CCUS	93	98

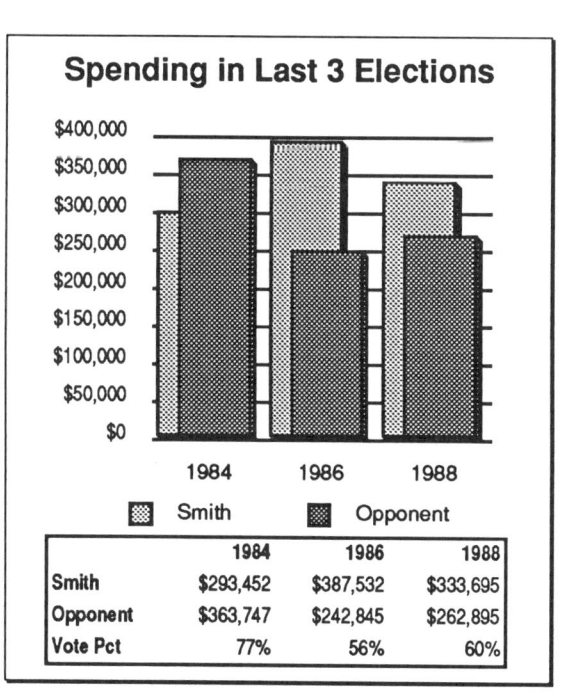

Spending in Last 3 Elections

Smith   Opponent

	1984	1986	1988
Smith	$293,452	$387,532	$333,695
Opponent	$363,747	$242,845	$262,895
Vote Pct	77%	56%	60%

---

* Contributions came from more than one PAC affiliated with this sponsor.

Virginia Smith, R-Neb (3)

First elected: 1974
Total receipts: $271,730
Total from PACs: $138,715

1988 Committees & Subcommittees

Appropriations
Rural Development, Agriculture and Related Agencies (Ranking Republican)
Energy and Water Development

Campaign Revenue Sources

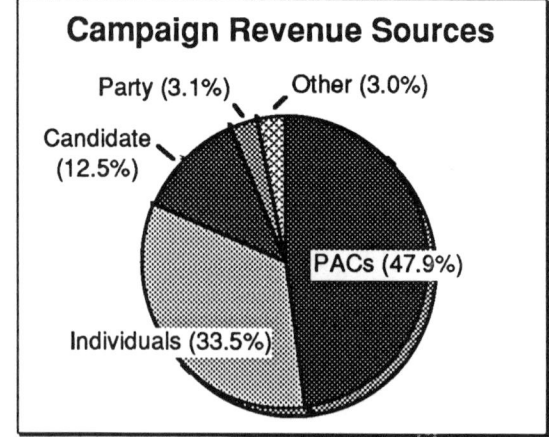

Party (3.1%)   Other (3.0%)
Candidate (12.5%)
PACs (47.9%)
Individuals (33.5%)

PAC Contribution Profile

Business

Agricultural Chemicals	**$2,600**
Fertilizer Institute	$1,250
Others	$1,350
Agricultural Services	**$3,100**
Farmland Industries	$1,000
Others	$2,100
Animal Feed & Health	**$3,150**
American Veterinary Medical Assn	$1,500
Animal Health Institute	$1,050
Others	$600
Auto Dealers	**$2,550**
Auto Dealers & Drivers for Free Trade	$1,500
National Auto Dealers Assn	$1,050
Commercial Banks	**$11,876**
Nebraska Bankers Assn	$5,500
American Bankers Assn	$4,500
Norwest Corp	$1,000
Others	$876
Construction	**$11,350**
National Assn of Home Builders	$3,200
Associated General Contractors	$2,400
National Utility Contractors Assn	$2,000
Nebraska Assoc General Contractors	$1,000
Others	$2,750

Dairy	**$6,050**
Associated Milk Producers	$4,500
Others	$1,550
Defense	**$2,200**
None over $700	
Electric Utilities	**$2,100**
ACRE (Action Committee for Rural Electrification)	$1,050
American Public Power Assn	$1,050
Food & Beverage	**$5,527**
ConAgra Inc	$1,527
American Meat Institute	$1,050
Food Marketing Institute	$1,050
Others	$1,900
Grain & Soybeans	**$2,350**
None over $700	
Health Professionals	**$9,050**
American Medical Assn	$5,350
Nebraska Medical Assn	$2,000
American Dental Assn	$1,350
Others	$350
Insurance	**$8,000**
National Assn of Life Underwriters	$5,000
Others	$3,000
Lawyers & Lobbyists	**$3,300**
Kutak, Rock & Campbell	$1,750
Others	$1,550
Livestock & Poultry	**$4,500**
National Cattlemen's Assn	$2,050
National Broiler Council	$1,050
Others	$1,400
Oil & Gas	**$7,750**
Chevron Corp	$1,050
Amoco Corp	$1,000
Others	$5,700
Pharmaceuticals	**$3,000**
Schering-Plough Corp	$1,500
Others	$1,500

PAC Totals by Category

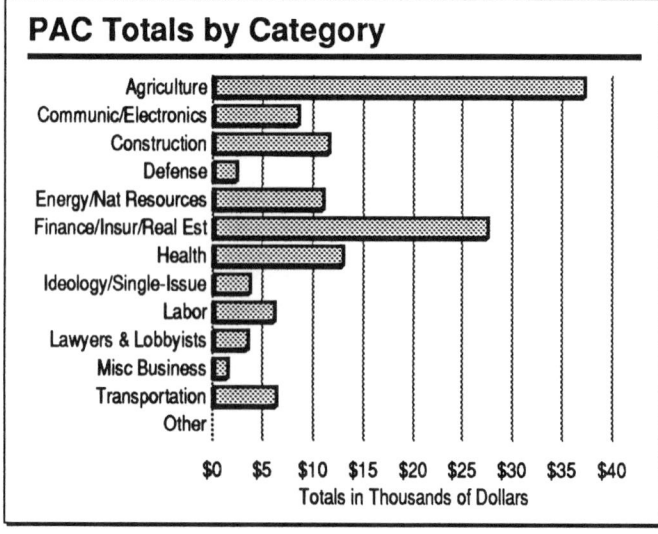

Agriculture
Communic/Electronics
Construction
Defense
Energy/Nat Resources
Finance/Insur/Real Est
Health
Ideology/Single-Issue
Labor
Lawyers & Lobbyists
Misc Business
Transportation
Other

$0 $5 $10 $15 $20 $25 $30 $35 $40
Totals in Thousands of Dollars

Railroads **$2,180**

    None over $950

Real Estate **$6,400**

    National Assn of Realtors $5,000
    Mortgage Bankers Assn of America $1,050
    Others $350

Sugar Growers **$4,300**

    American Sugarbeet Growers Assn $1,050
    US Beet Sugar Assn $1,050
    Others $2,200

Telecommunications **$6,600**

    AT&T $2,000
    North Western Bell Telephone $1,500
    National Telephone Co-op Assn $1,050
    Others $2,050

Other Major Business PACs

Valmont Industries	$1,400	Electronics
United Parcel Service	$1,050	Delivery
Ocean Spray Cranberries Inc	$1,000	Fruit/Veg

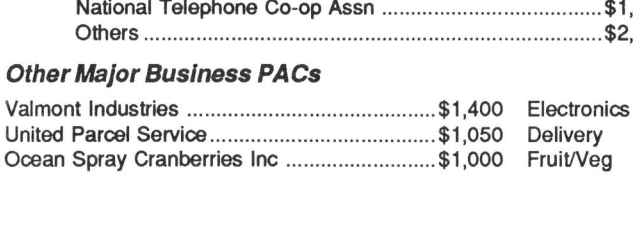

Interest Group Ratings

	'88	'83–'87 Avg
ADA	25	9
ACU	80	73
AFL-CIO	43	9
CCUS	93	79

Labor

Labor Unions **$5,950**

    National Assn of Retired Federal Employees $3,500
    United Transportation Union $1,050
    Others $1,400

Ideological/Single-Issue

Ideological/Single-Issue **$2,650**

    National Rifle Assn .... $2,050   Pro-Guns
    Others $600

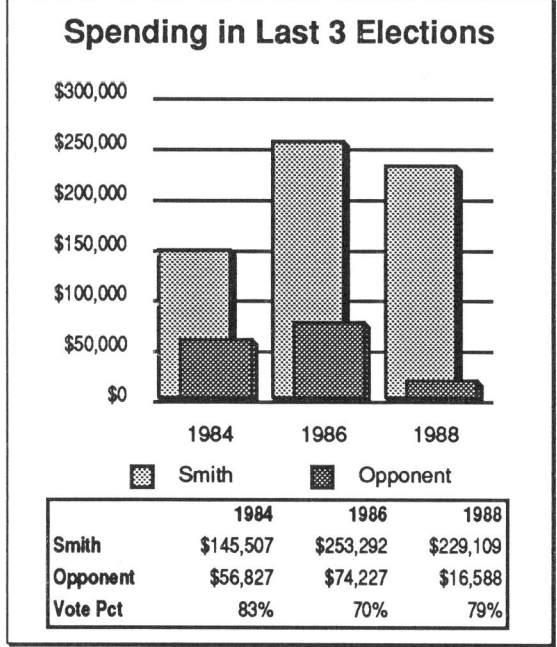

Spending in Last 3 Elections

	1984	1986	1988
Smith	$145,507	$253,292	$229,109
Opponent	$56,827	$74,227	$16,588
Vote Pct	83%	70%	79%

Olympia J. Snowe, R-Maine (2)

First elected: 1978
Total receipts: $229,929
Total from PACs: $72,300

1988 Committees & Subcommittees

Foreign Affairs
International Operations (Ranking Republican)
Arms Control, International Security and Science

Select Aging
Human Services (Ranking Republican)

Joint Economic
Economic Goals and Intergovernmental Policy
Education and Health
International Economic Policy

PAC Contribution Profile

Business

Commercial Banks	**$2,800**
Fleet Bank of Maine	$1,250
American Bankers Assn	$1,000
Others	$550
Construction	**$2,900**
Associated General Contractors	$1,300
National Assn of Home Builders	$600
Others	$1,000
Dairy	**$1,800**
Associated Milk Producers	$1,000
Others	$800
Defense	**$5,400**
Bath Iron Works	$4,000
Lockheed Corp	$800
Others	$600
Food & Beverage	**$2,900**
National Confectioners Assn	$1,000
Pepsi-Cola Bottlers Assn	$1,000
Food Marketing Institute	$600
Others	$300
Forest Products	**$9,150**
Great Northern Nekoosa Corp	$5,000
Boise Cascade	$1,500
Champion International Corp	$600
Georgia-Pacific Corp	$600
Scott Paper Company	$600
Others	$850

Campaign Revenue Sources

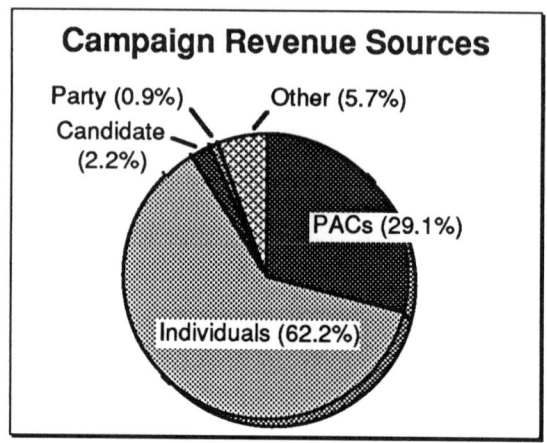

Party (0.9%)
Other (5.7%)
Candidate (2.2%)
PACs (29.1%)
Individuals (62.2%)

Health Professionals	**$4,500**
American Dental Assn	$1,500
American Medical Assn	$1,300
American Occupational Therapy Assn	$600
Others	$1,100
Insurance	**$4,950**
National Assn of Life Underwriters	$2,000
Independent Insurance Agents of America	$600
Casualty & Surety Agents Assn	$550
Others	$1,800
Real Estate	**$5,300**
National Assn of Realtors	$5,300
Telecommunications	**$2,000**
AT&T	$1,000
Others	$1,000
Textiles	**$1,850**
American Textile Manufacturers Institute	$800
Northern Textile Assn	$750
Others	$300

Other Major Business PACs

Corning Glass Works	$1,000	Glass Prod
Kelly Service Inc	$1,000	EmployAgency
Avon Products	$600	Cosmetics
Bay State Gas Company	$600	Natural Gas
Chrysler Corp	$600	Auto Mfrs

PAC Totals by Category

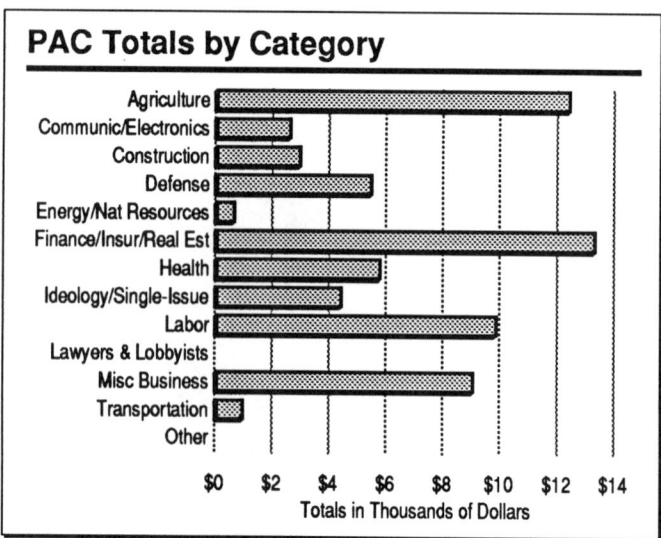

Agriculture
Communic/Electronics
Construction
Defense
Energy/Nat Resources
Finance/Insur/Real Est
Health
Ideology/Single-Issue
Labor
Lawyers & Lobbyists
Misc Business
Transportation
Other

$0 $2 $4 $6 $8 $10 $12 $14
Totals in Thousands of Dollars

Labor

Labor Unions **$9,800**

Marine Engineers Union $4,500
National Education Assn $2,500
Seafarers International Union $1,000
National Assn of Letter Carriers $600
United Transportation Union $600
Others $600

Ideological/Single-Issue

Ideological/Single-Issue **$4,350**

Bean-Jones Republican Congressional PAC ..$1,000   Repub Cands
Dynamis ....$1,000   GreekEthnic
Others..$2,350

Independent expenditures supporting Snowe

National Cmte to Preserve Social Security $1,659

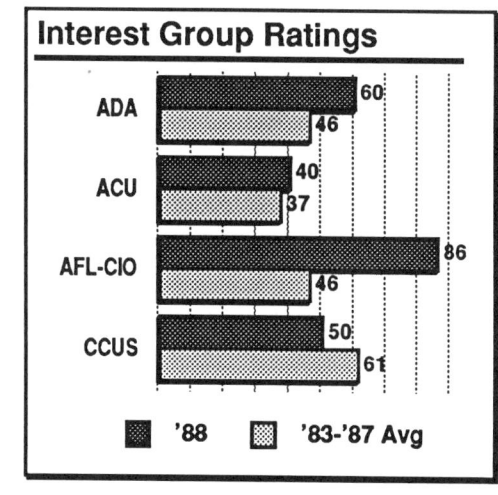

Interest Group Ratings

	ADA	ACU	AFL-CIO	CCUS
'88	60	40	86	50
'83-'87 Avg	46	37	46	61

■ '88   ▨ '83-'87 Avg

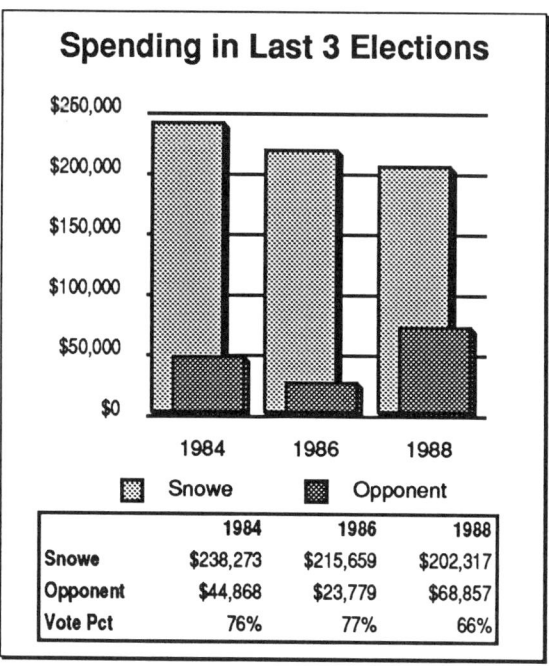

Spending in Last 3 Elections

▨ Snowe   ■ Opponent

	1984	1986	1988
Snowe	$238,273	$215,659	$202,317
Opponent	$44,868	$23,779	$68,857
Vote Pct	76%	77%	66%

Stephen J. Solarz, D-NY (13)

First elected: 1974
Total receipts: $899,313
Total from PACs: $59,605

1988 Committees & Subcommittees

Education and Labor
Elementary, Secondary and Vocational Education
Human Resources

Foreign Affairs
Asian and Pacific Affairs (Chairman)
Western Hemisphere Affairs

Post Office and Civil Services
Civil Service

Joint Economic
Fiscal and Monetary Policy
International Economic Policy
Investment, Jobs and Prices

PAC Contribution Profile

Business

Commercial Banks **$2,350**
  Citicorp $1,000
  J P Morgan & Company $1,000
  Others $350

Defense **$1,500**
  General Dynamics $500
  Grumman $500
  Lockheed Corp $500

Food & Beverage **$1,250**
  Joseph E Seagram & Sons $500
  Nabisco Brands Inc $500
  Others $250

Health Professionals **$3,750**
  American Medical Assn $2,250
  Philippine Physicians in America $1,000
  New York Medical Assn $500

Lawyers **$6,000**
  Assn of Trial Lawyers of America $5,000
  Powell, Goldstein, Frazer, & Murphy $500
  Others $500

Other Major Business PACs

SGS North America .... $1,000 BusinessSvcs
Ansell Inc .... $500 Health Prod
AT&T .... $500 LongDistance
United Parcel Service .... $500 Delivery

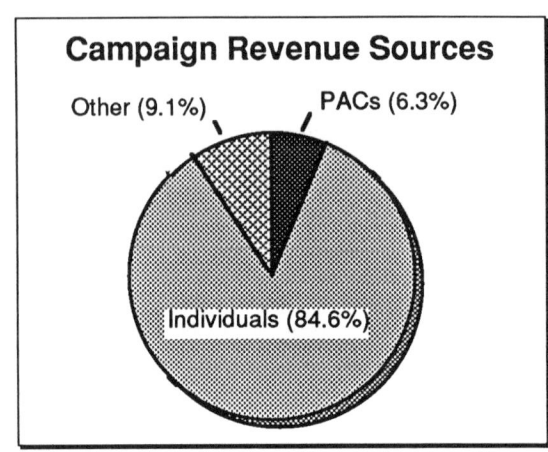

Campaign Revenue Sources

Other (9.1%)
PACs (6.3%)
Individuals (84.6%)

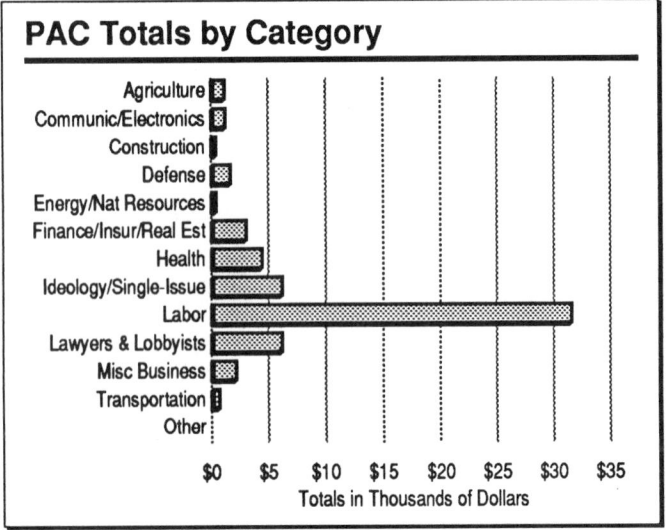

PAC Totals by Category

Agriculture
Communic/Electronics
Construction
Defense
Energy/Nat Resources
Finance/Insur/Real Est
Health
Ideology/Single-Issue
Labor
Lawyers & Lobbyists
Misc Business
Transportation
Other

$0 $5 $10 $15 $20 $25 $30 $35
Totals in Thousands of Dollars

Labor

Bldg Trades/Industrial/Misc Unions $6,250

    Carpenters & Joiners Union $1,500
    Laborers' Political League $1,500
    Food & Commercial Workers Union...............................$1,000
    Intl Brotherhood of Electrical Workers...........................$1,000
    Plumbers/Pipefitters Union $500
    Others $750

Government & Postal Workers $6,950

    National Assn of Retired Federal Employees $3,000
    American Fedn of State/County/Munic Employees $1,000
    American Postal Workers Union $1,000
    National Assn of Letter Carriers $1,000
    National League of Postmasters $500
    Others $450

Teachers Unions $5,000

    National Education Assn $4,500
    American Federation of Teachers $500

Transportation Unions $13,206

    Teamsters Union $7,500
    International Longshoremen Assn* $2,206
    Seafarers International Union $2,000
    Masters, Mates & Pilots Union $500
    United Transportation Union $500
    Others $500

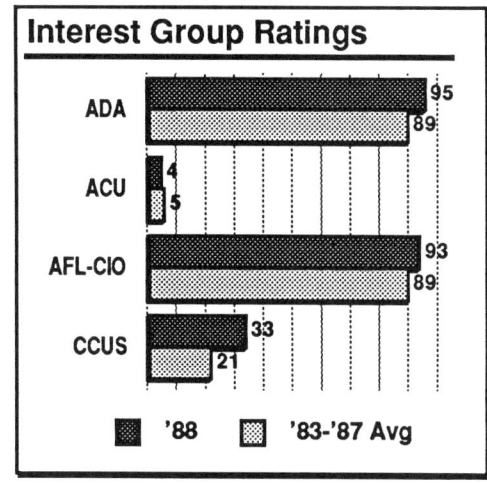

Interest Group Ratings

	'88	'83-'87 Avg
ADA	95	89
ACU	4	5
AFL-CIO	93	89
CCUS	33	21

Ideological/Single-Issue

Democratic/Liberal $2,898

    National Cmte for an Effective Congress $2,498
    Others $400

Other Major Ideological/Single-Issue PACs

Assembly of Turkish-American Assns	$1,000	Ethnic
National Abortion Rights Action League	$500	Pro-Choice
National Cmte to Preserve Social Security	$500	Soc Secur
Washington PAC	$500	Pro-Israel

Independent expenditures supporting Solarz

National Cmte to Preserve Social Security $1,126

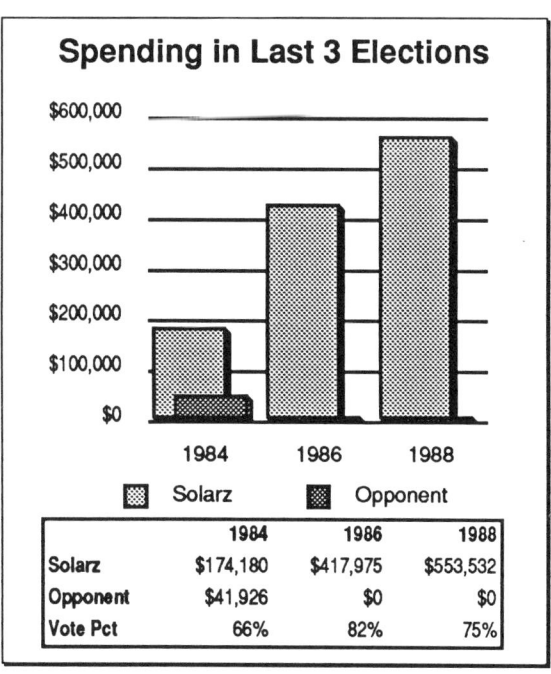

Spending in Last 3 Elections

	1984	1986	1988
Solarz	$174,180	$417,975	$553,532
Opponent	$41,926	$0	$0
Vote Pct	66%	82%	75%

Legend: ▨ Solarz ■ Opponent

* Contributions came from more than one PAC affiliated
with this sponsor.

Gerald B. H. Solomon, R-NY (24)

First elected: 1978
Total receipts: $195,033
Total from PACs: $74,650

1988 Committees & Subcommittees

Foreign Affairs
Human Rights and International Organizations (Ranking Republican)
International Economic Policy and Trade

Veterans' Affairs (Ranking Republican)

PAC Contribution Profile

Business

Campaign Revenue Sources

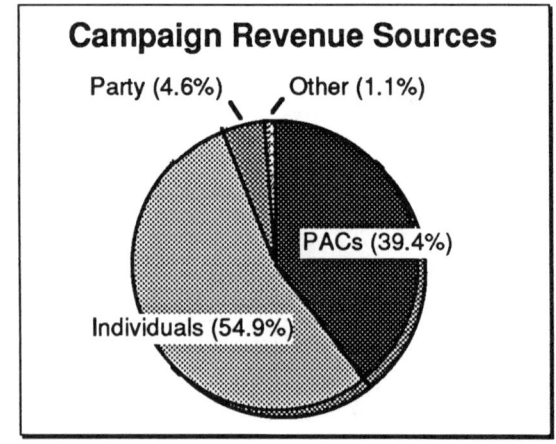

Party (4.6%) · Other (1.1%) · PACs (39.4%) · Individuals (54.9%)

Automotive	**$6,100**
National Auto Dealers Assn	$3,250
Auto Dealers & Drivers for Free Trade	$2,500
Others	$350
Commercial Banks	**$2,000**
Chase Lincoln First Bank	$1,500
Others	$500
Construction	**$5,050**
Gifford-Hill & Company	$2,500
Associated General Contractors	$1,000
Associated Builders & Contractors	$750
Others	$800
Dairy	**$1,500**
Associated Milk Producers	$1,000
Others	$500
Defense	**$3,750**
Northrop Corp	$1,000
General Dynamics	$750
Rockwell International	$750
Others	$1,250
Electric Utilities	**$1,650**
New York State Electric & Gas Corp	$1,000
Niagara Mohawk Power Corp	$650
Electronics	**$1,350**
General Electric	$1,350

Health Professionals	**$10,750**
New York Medical Assn	$4,000
American Medical Assn	$2,250
American Dental Assn	$2,000
American Academy of Ophthalmology	$1,000
American Chiropractic Assn	$1,000
Others	$500
Insurance	**$5,700**
National Assn of Life Underwriters	$1,500
Casualty & Surety Agents Assn	$1,250
Independent Insurance Agents of America	$750
Others	$2,200
Oil & Gas	**$1,500**
Mobil Oil	$1,000
Others	$500
Paper Production	**$3,000**
International Paper Company	$2,000
Others	$1,000
Pharmaceuticals	**$2,300**
Ciba-Geigy Corp	$1,000
Sterling Drug	$550
Others	$750
Real Estate	**$4,000**
National Assn of Realtors	$3,500
Others	$500
Telecommunications	**$4,930**
AT&T	$2,500
Continental Telecom	$1,250
New York Telephone	$1,180
Tobacco	**$2,250**
Philip Morris	$1,500
Others	$750

Other Major Business PACs

American Textile Manufacturers Institute	$750	Textiles
Corning Glass Works	$750	Glass Prod
FMC Corp	$750	Chemicals
United Parcel Service	$650	Delivery

PAC Totals by Category

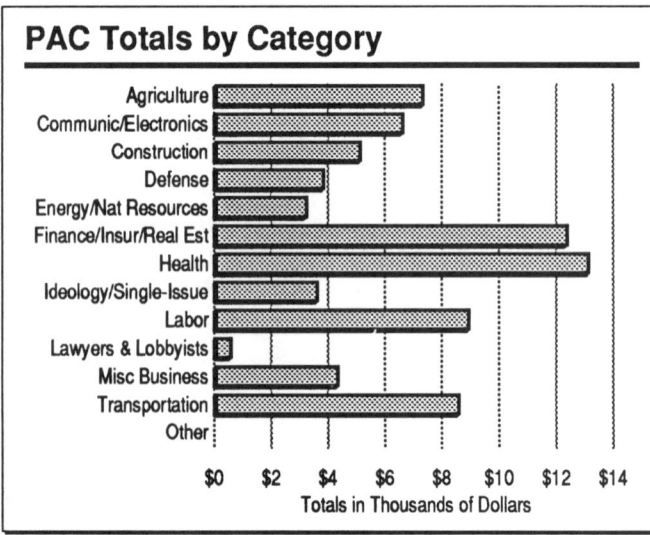

Agriculture
Communic/Electronics
Construction
Defense
Energy/Nat Resources
Finance/Insur/Real Est
Health
Ideology/Single-Issue
Labor
Lawyers & Lobbyists
Misc Business
Transportation
Other

$0 $2 $4 $6 $8 $10 $12 $14
Totals in Thousands of Dollars

Labor

Labor Unions **$8,860**
    Marine Engineers Union* $4,000
    National Assn of Retired Federal Employees $3,000
    Seafarers International Union $1,000
    Others $860

Ideological/Single-Issue

Ideological/Single-Issue **$3,537**
Veterans of Foreign Wars ....$750   Pro-Defense
Others...$2,787

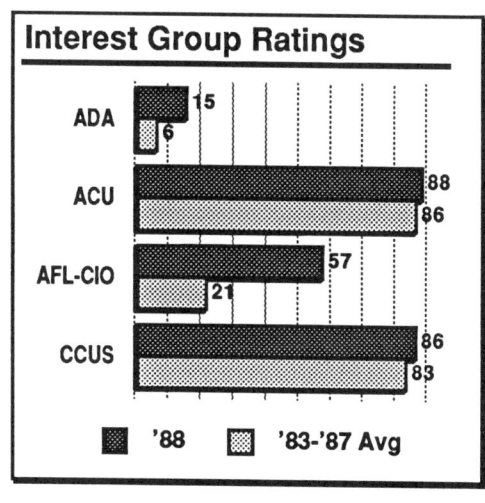

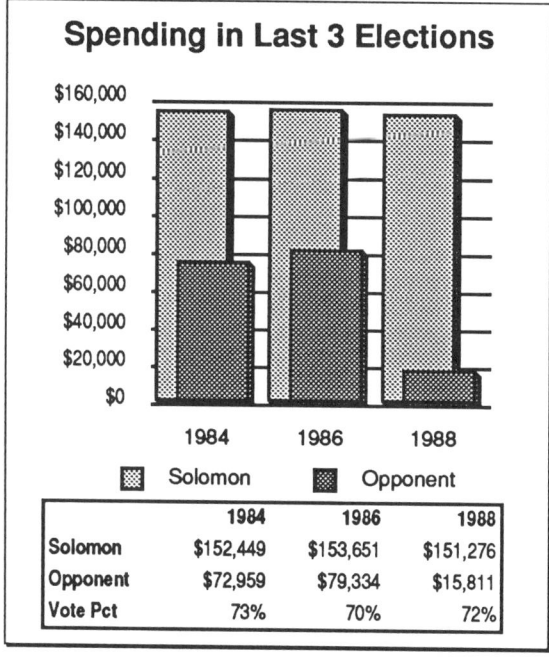

---

* Contributions came from more than one PAC affiliated with this sponsor.

Floyd D. Spence, R-SC (2)

First elected: 1970
Total receipts: $363,171
Total from PACs: $191,268

1988 Committees & Subcommittees

Armed Services
Seapower and Strategic and Critical Materials (Ranking Republican)
Military Installations and Facilities

Select Aging
Human Services
Retirement Income and Employment

PAC Contribution Profile

Business

Auto Dealers	**$12,250**
National Auto Dealers Assn	$6,250
Auto Dealers & Drivers for Free Trade	$6,000
Chemicals	**$4,000**
Eastman Kodak/Chemicals Division	$2,500
Others	$1,500
Construction	**$10,600**
Associated General Contractors	$4,000
National Assn of Home Builders	$4,000
Others	$2,600

Campaign Revenue Sources

Other (9.0%)
Party (12.4%)
PACs (43.7%)
Individuals (34.9%)

Defense	**$42,450**
General Dynamics	$3,000
Lockheed Corp	$3,000
Hughes Aircraft	$2,500
Northrop Corp	$2,500
Harris Corp	$2,000
Tenneco Inc	$2,000
McDonnell Douglas*	$1,800
Bath Iron Works	$1,750
United Technologies	$1,750
Allied-Signal	$1,250
General Electric	$1,250
Litton Industries	$1,250
LTV Aerospace & Defense Company	$1,250
Martin Marietta Corp	$1,250
FMC Corp	$1,200
AT&T	$1,000
Computer Sciences Corp	$1,000
Continental Telecom	$1,000
Gould Inc	$1,000
Others	$10,700
Electric Utilities & Equipment	**$15,750**
Gilbert Associates	$7,750
Duke Power Company	$3,000
ACRE (Action Committee for Rural Electrification)	$1,500
Carolina Power & Light	$1,500
Babcock & Wilcox	$1,000
Scana Corp	$1,000
Electronics & Computers	**$2,750**
Cooper Industries	$2,000
Others	$750
Financial Institutions	**$6,600**
South Carolina National Bank	$2,500
South Carolina Credit Union League	$1,050
Citizens & Southern National Bank	$1,000
Others	$2,050
Food & Beverage	**$7,050**
Flowers Industries	$2,000
National Beer Wholesalers Assn	$1,500
Winn-Dixie Stores	$1,000
Others	$2,550
Forest & Paper Products	**$4,300**
Westvaco Corp	$2,000
Stone Container Corp	$1,000
Others	$1,300

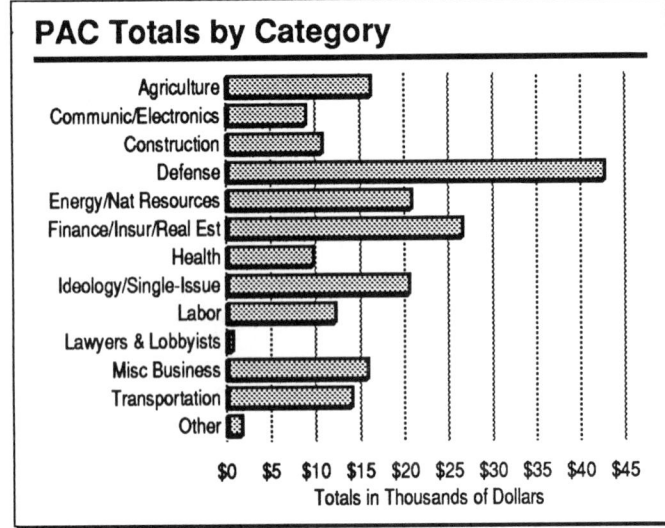

PAC Totals by Category

- Agriculture
- Communic/Electronics
- Construction
- Defense
- Energy/Nat Resources
- Finance/Insur/Real Est
- Health
- Ideology/Single-Issue
- Labor
- Lawyers & Lobbyists
- Misc Business
- Transportation
- Other

$0 $5 $10 $15 $20 $25 $30 $35 $40 $45
Totals in Thousands of Dollars

Interest Group Ratings

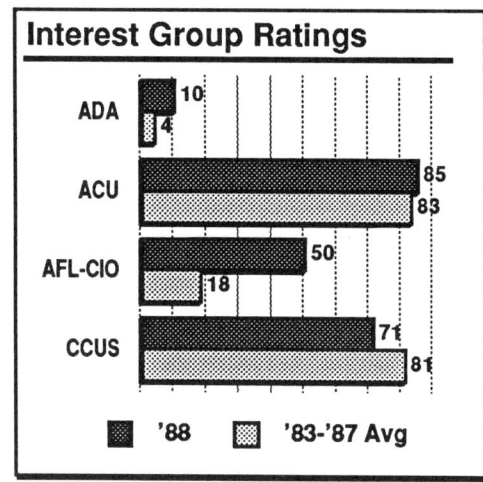

	'88	'83-'87 Avg
ADA	10	4
ACU	85	83
AFL-CIO	50	18
CCUS	71	81

Health Professionals *$7,250*
    American Medical Assn $5,000
    American Dental Assn $2,000
    Others $250

Home Appliances *$2,100*
    Whirlpool Corp $1,600
    Others $500

Insurance *$11,250*
    American International Group inc $2,500
    National Assn of Independent Insurers $2,250
    National Assn of Life Underwriters $1,500
    Liberty Mutual Insurance $1,000
    Others $4,000

Oil & Gas *$3,250*
    Phillips Petroleum $1,000
    Others $2,250

Real Estate *$8,250*
    National Assn of Realtors $8,000
    Others $250

Sugar Growers *$2,350*
    None over $750

Telecommunications *$5,500*
    Southern Bell $5,500

Textiles *$3,250*
    None over $800

Tobacco *$2,750*
    Philip Morris $1,000
    Others $1,750

Other Major Business PACs

Dairymen Inc	$1,000	Dairy
Square D Company	$1,000	Indust Equip
Waste Management Inc	$1,000	Waste Mgmt

Labor

Labor Unions *$12,000*
    Marine Engineers District 2 Maritime Officers $4,000
    National Assn of Retired Federal Employees $4,000
    Teamsters Union $2,500
    Seafarers International Union $1,500

Ideological/Single-Issue

Republican Leadership/Conservative PACs *$10,250*
    Fund for America's Future (George Bush) $5,000
    Republican Congressional Boosters Club $2,000
    15th District Committee (Edward Madigan) $1,000
    Campaign America (Bob Dole) $1,000
    Others $1,250

Other Major Ideological/Single-Issue PACs

National Rifle Assn	$5,950	Pro-Guns
Public Service Research Council	$1,500	Anti-Union
Council for National Defense	$1,362	Pro-Defense
Fund for Southern Progress	$1,000	Unknown

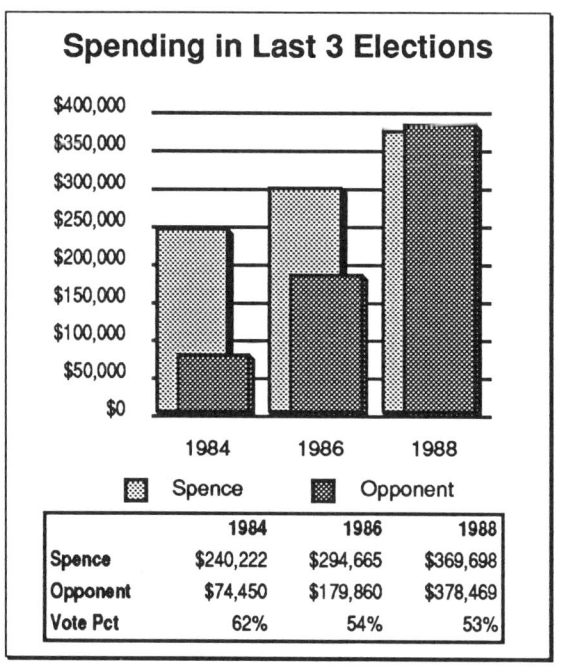

Spending in Last 3 Elections

	Spence	Opponent

	1984	1986	1988
Spence	$240,222	$294,665	$369,698
Opponent	$74,450	$179,860	$378,469
Vote Pct	62%	54%	53%

* Contributions came from more than one PAC affiliated
with this sponsor.

987

John M. Spratt Jr., D-SC (5)

First elected: 1982
Total receipts: $203,552
Total from PACs: $140,970

1988 Committees & Subcommittees

Armed Services
Investigations
Procurement and Military Nuclear Systems

Government Operations
Commerce, Consumer and Monetary Affairs
Government Information, Justice and Agriculture

PAC Contribution Profile

Business

Accountants	**$5,000**
American Institute of CPA's	$5,000
Auto Dealers	**$4,300**
National Auto Dealers Assn	$4,300
Commercial Banks	**$11,100**
American Bankers Assn	$2,000
Citizens & Southern National Bank	$2,000
South Carolina National Bank	$2,000
NCNB Corp*	$1,300
South Carolina Bankers Assn	$1,000
Others	$2,800
Construction	**$3,000**
National Assn of Home Builders	$1,000
Others	$2,000
Defense	**$29,050**
Torrington Company	$5,000
AT&T	$2,100
Lockheed Corp	$2,000
Northrop Corp	$1,800
McDonnell Douglas*	$1,450
Textron Inc	$1,300
Raytheon	$1,200
General Atomics	$1,000
General Dynamics	$1,000
Others	$12,200

Electric Utilities	**$6,550**
ACRE (Action Committee for Rural Electrification)	$3,100
Duke Power Company	$1,600
Carolina Power & Light	$1,050
Others	$800
Food & Beverage	**$2,000**
None over $600	
Forest & Paper Products	**$2,450**
Willamette Industries	$1,000
Others	$1,450
Health Professionals	**$7,000**
American Medical Assn	$5,000
American Dental Assn	$2,000
Insurance	**$5,600**
National Assn of Life Underwriters	$1,000
Others	$4,600
Real Estate	**$6,000**
National Assn of Realtors	$5,000
First Union Corp	$1,000
Savings Banks & Credit Unions	**$4,500**
Credit Union National Assn	$2,000
US League of Savings Assn	$2,000
Others	$500
Sugar Growers	**$1,950**
None over $750	
Telecommunications	**$4,900**
Southern Bell	$4,000
Others	$900
Textiles	**$9,800**
Hoechst Celanese Corp	$2,000
Springs Mills	$2,000
Clinton Mills Inc	$1,200
American Textile Manufacturers Institute	$1,000
Others	$3,600
Tobacco	**$1,950**
None over $600	

Other Major Business PACs

American Hospital Assn	$1,300	Hospitals
Aircraft Owners & Pilots Assn	$1,200	GenlAviation

Campaign Revenue Sources

Other (8.8%)
Individuals (22.9%)
PACs (68.0%)

PAC Totals by Category

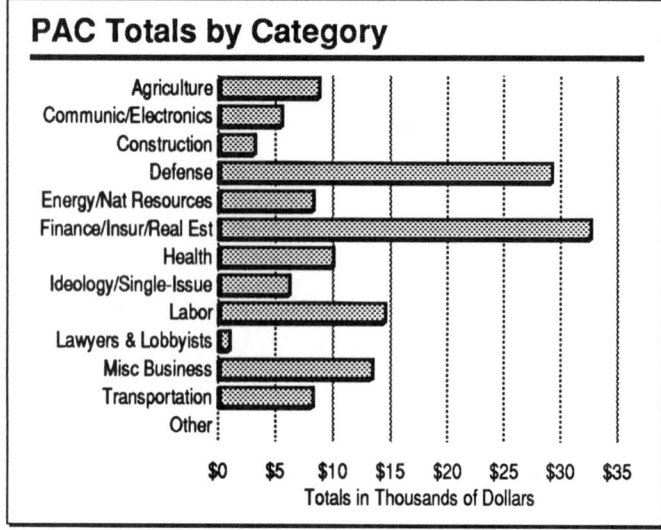

Agriculture
Communic/Electronics
Construction
Defense
Energy/Nat Resources
Finance/Insur/Real Est
Health
Ideology/Single-Issue
Labor
Lawyers & Lobbyists
Misc Business
Transportation
Other

$0 $5 $10 $15 $20 $25 $30 $35
Totals in Thousands of Dollars

Labor

Bldg Trades/Industrial/Misc Unions **$4,500**
    Food & Commercial Workers Union $1,600
    Others $2,900

Postal Worker Unions **$3,200**
    National Assn of Letter Carriers $1,600
    Others $1,600

Teachers Unions **$3,100**
    National Education Assn $3,100

Transportation Unions **$3,500**
    Marine Engineers Dist 2 Retirees $1,000
    Seafarers International Union $1,000
    Others $1,500

Ideological/Single-Issue

Democratic Leadership PACs **$3,000**
    Valley Education Fund (Tony Coelho) $2,000
    Citizens for a Competitive America (Ernest Hollings) $1,000

Pro-Israel **$2,650**
    Hudson Valley PAC $1,000
    South Carolinians for Representative Government $1,000
    Others $650

Independent expenditures supporting Spratt

National Cmte to Preserve Social Security $2,275

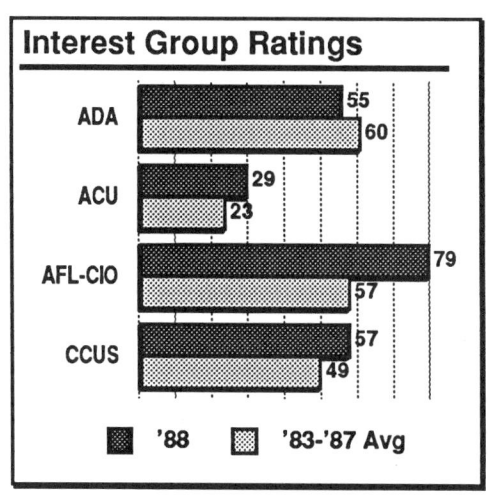

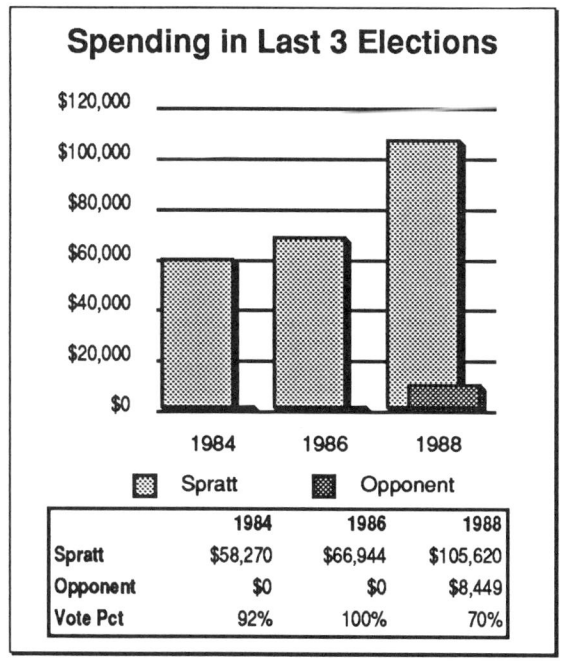

* Contributions came from more than one PAC affiliated
with this sponsor.

989

Harley O. Staggers Jr., D-WVa (2)

First elected: 1982
Total receipts: $146,928
Total from PACs: $131,953

1988 Committees & Subcommittees

Agriculture
Department Operations, Research and Foreign Agriculture
Domestic Marketing, Consumer Relations and Nutrition

Judiciary
Crime
Monopolies and Commercial Law

Veterans' Affairs
Hospitals and Health Care

Select Hunger

PAC Contribution Profile

Business

Accountants	**$5,600**
American Institute of CPA's	$5,000
Others	$600
Commodities Trading	**$1,850**
Chicago Board of Trade	$1,250
Others	$600
Defense	**$2,000**
None over $800	
Financial Institutions	**$2,500**
Credit Union National Assn	$1,000
Others	$1,500
Food & Beverage	**$4,450**
National Beer Wholesalers Assn	$2,000
Food Marketing Institute	$1,300
Others	$1,150
Health Professionals	**$5,700**
American Podiatry Assn	$2,500
American Academy of Ophthalmology	$1,000
Others	$2,200
Insurance	**$1,800**
National Assn of Life Underwriters	$1,500
Others	$300
Lawyers	**$5,550**
Assn of Trial Lawyers of America	$5,000
Others	$550

Livestock & Poultry	**$2,950**
None over $800	
Natural Gas	**$2,300**
Washington Gas Light Company	$1,100
Others	$1,200
Paper Production	**$2,000**
Westvaco Corp	$2,000
Real Estate	**$3,900**
National Assn of Realtors	$3,300
Others	$600
Sugar Growers	**$2,100**
None over $600	
Telecommunications	**$3,417**
AT&T	$1,167
Continental Telecom	$1,000
Others	$1,250
Tobacco	**$3,150**
Philip Morris	$2,000
Others	$1,150

Other Major Business PACs

National Assn for Home Care .... $1,000   HealthCare

Campaign Revenue Sources

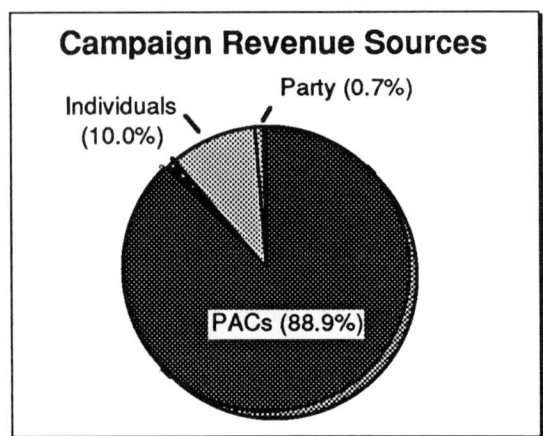

Individuals (10.0%)
Party (0.7%)
PACs (88.9%)

PAC Totals by Category

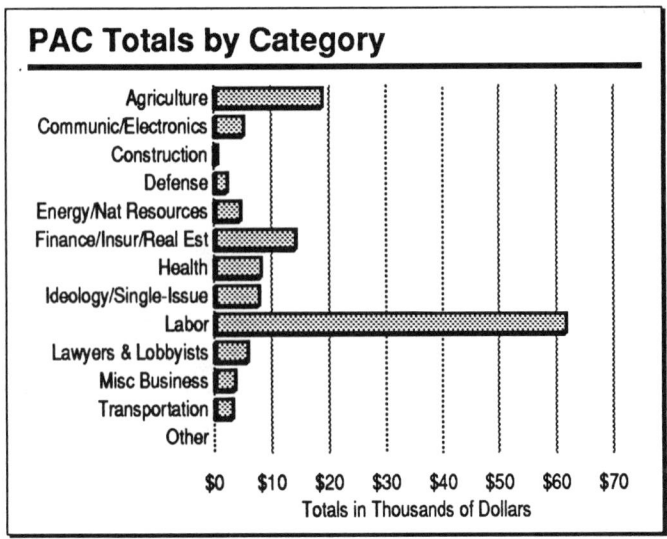

Agriculture
Communic/Electronics
Construction
Defense
Energy/Nat Resources
Finance/Insur/Real Est
Health
Ideology/Single-Issue
Labor
Lawyers & Lobbyists
Misc Business
Transportation
Other

$0 $10 $20 $30 $40 $50 $60 $70
Totals in Thousands of Dollars

Labor

Bldg Trades/Industrial/Misc Unions **$21,800**
- United Auto Workers $5,600
- Operating Engineers Union $4,500
- Intl Brotherhood of Electrical Workers.................$3,000
- Carpenters & Joiners Union $1,800
- Laborers' Political League $1,300
- Others $5,600

Government & Postal Workers **$11,900**
- National Assn of Retired Federal Employees $5,000
- American Fedn of State/County/Munic Employees $3,000
- National Assn of Letter Carriers $1,200
- Others $2,700

Teachers Unions **$2,600**
- National Education Assn $2,600

Transportation Unions **$25,050**
- Teamsters Union $10,000
- United Transportation Union $5,000
- Air Line Pilots Assn $2,000
- Marine Engineers Union* $2,000
- Seafarers International Union $2,000
- Masters, Mates & Pilots Union $1,500
- Others $2,550

Interest Group Ratings

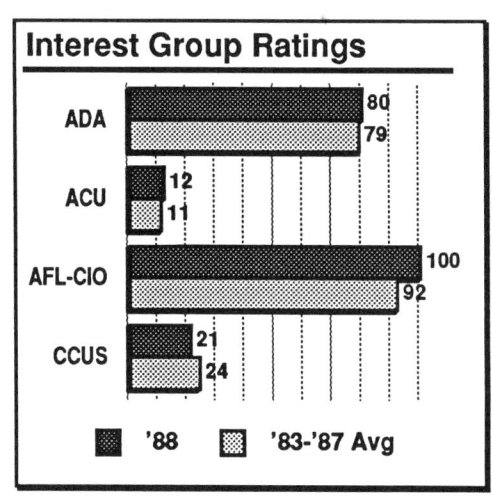

■ '88   ▨ '83-'87 Avg

Ideological/Single-Issue

Ideological/Single-Issue **$7,200**
National Rifle Assn ....$5,950   Pro-Guns
National Cmte to Preserve Social Security ......$1,000   Soc Secur
Others $250

Independent expenditures supporting Staggers
National Cmte to Preserve Social Security $1,674

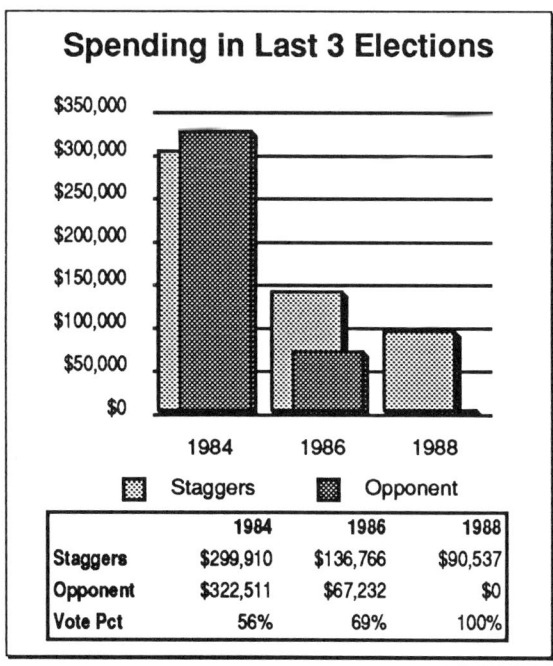

Spending in Last 3 Elections

	1984	1986	1988
Staggers	$299,910	$136,766	$90,537
Opponent	$322,511	$67,232	$0
Vote Pct	56%	69%	100%

---

* Contributions came from more than one PAC affiliated with this sponsor.

Richard Stallings, D-Idaho (2)

First elected: 1984
Total receipts: $498,997
Total from PACs: $265,739

1988 Committees & Subcommittees

Agriculture
Conservation, Credit and Rural Development
Cotton, Rice and Sugar
Forests, Family Farms and Energy

Science, Space and Technology
Energy Research and Development
International Scientific Cooperation

Select Aging
Retirement Income and Employment

PAC Contribution Profile

Business

Agricultural Chemicals	**$4,550**
FMC Corp	$2,500
Others	$2,050
Auto Dealers	**$6,550**
Auto Dealers & Drivers for Free Trade	$4,000
National Auto Dealers Assn	$2,550
Commercial Banks	**$10,200**
American Bankers Assn	$5,000
Citicorp	$2,500
Independent Bankers Assn	$2,000
Others	$700
Commodities/Securities	**$5,250**
Chicago Mercantile Exchange	$2,000
Chicago Board of Trade	$1,500
Chicago Board of Options Exchange	$1,000
Others	$750
Construction	**$4,700**
National Assn of Home Builders	$2,000
Others	$2,700
Dairy	**$9,600**
Associated Milk Producers	$5,500
Mid-American Dairymen	$2,250
Others	$1,850
Defense	**$2,300**
Rockwell International	$1,050
Others	$1,250

Campaign Revenue Sources

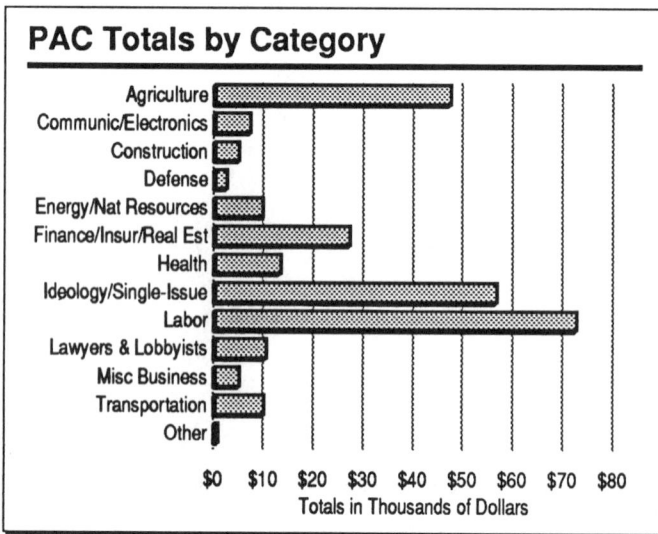

Other (8.3%)
Party (8.4%)
PACs (46.9%)
Individuals (36.4%)

Electric Utilities	**$7,450**
Idaho Power Company	$3,300
ACRE (Action Committee for Rural Electrification)	$1,550
Others	$2,600
Food & Beverage	**$7,950**
American Meat Institute	$2,050
American Bakers Assn	$1,050
Pillsbury Company	$1,000
Winn-Dixie Stores	$1,000
Others	$2,850
Forest Products	**$3,300**
Potlatch Corp	$1,500
Others	$1,800
Health Professionals	**$12,499**
American Medical Assn	$9,999
American Chiropractic Assn	$1,000
American Nurses Assn	$1,000
Others	$500
Insurance	**$4,550**
National Assn of Life Underwriters	$2,250
Others	$2,300
Lawyers & Lobbyists	**$10,116**
Assn of Trial Lawyers of America	$10,000
Others	$116
Real Estate	**$10,600**
National Assn of Realtors	$10,000
Others	$600
Sugar Growers	**$11,100**
American Crystal Sugar Corp	$3,000
American Sugarbeet Growers Assn	$2,800
Southern Minnesota Beet Sugar Co-op	$1,300
Amalgamated Sugar Company	$1,000
Others	$3,000

PAC Totals by Category

Agriculture
Communic/Electronics
Construction
Defense
Energy/Nat Resources
Finance/Insur/Real Est
Health
Ideology/Single-Issue
Labor
Lawyers & Lobbyists
Misc Business
Transportation
Other

$0 $10 $20 $30 $40 $50 $60 $70 $80
Totals in Thousands of Dollars

Telecommunications **$6,500**
       Mountain Bell $3,000
       AT&T $2,750
       Others $750

Other Major Business PACs

National Fedn of Independent Business ....$1,450   Sml Business
Cyprus Minerals Company ....$1,000   Metals/Mining
National Cotton Council ....$1,000   Cotton
Waste Management Inc ....$1,000   Waste Mgmt

Labor

Bldg Trades/Industrial/Misc Unions **$26,650**
       Food & Commercial Workers Union* $8,000
       Intl Brotherhood of Electrical Workers............................$5,000
       United Auto Workers $5,000
       AFL-CIO $4,500
       Laborers' Political League $1,800
       Oil, Chemical & Atomic Workers Union..........................$1,300
       Others $1,050

Government & Postal Workers **$23,975**
       National Assn of Letter Carriers $10,000
       National Assn of Retired Federal Employees $10,000
       American Postal Workers Union $2,100
       Others $1,875

Teachers Unions **$5,900**
       National Education Assn $5,900

Transportation Unions **$15,800**
       Teamsters Union $8,500
       United Transportation Union $2,600
       Air Line Pilots Assn $2,500
       Transportation Communication Union..............................$1,350
       Others $850

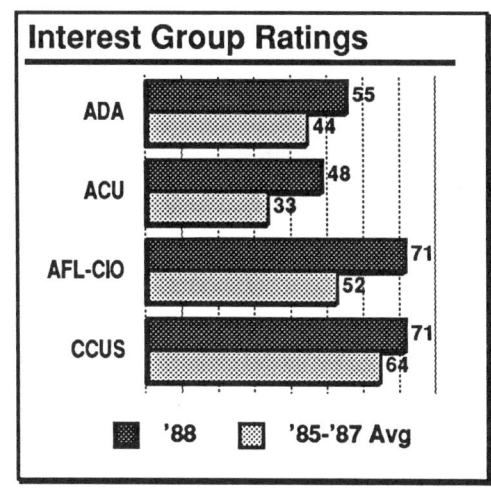

Interest Group Ratings

Bar chart showing ratings for ADA, ACU, AFL-CIO, CCUS with '88 and '85-'87 Avg values:
- ADA: '88 = 55, '85-'87 Avg = 44
- ACU: '88 = 48, '85-'87 Avg = 33
- AFL-CIO: '88 = 71, '85-'87 Avg = 52
- CCUS: '88 = 71, '85-'87 Avg = 64

Legend: ■ '88   ▨ '85-'87 Avg

Ideological/Single-Issue

Democratic/Liberal **$10,747**
       National Cmte for an Effective Congress $9,997
       Others $750

Democratic Leadership PACs.............................**$20,437**
       Valley Education Fund (Tony Coelho) $8,437
       Majority Congress Committee (Jim Wright) $5,000
       America's Leaders' Fund (Dan Rostenkowski) $3,000
       Cmte for Democratic Opportunity (Bill Gray) $2,000
       House Leadership Fund (Tom Foley) $1,000
       Pax Americas (David Bonior) $1,000

Pro-Gun Ownership **$7,450**
       National Rifle Assn $7,450

Pro-Israel **$9,550**
       National PAC $5,000
       Hudson Valley PAC $1,250
       Delaware Valley PAC $1,000
       Joint Action Cmte for Political Affairs $1,000
       Others $1,300

Other Major Ideological/Single-Issue PACs

Sierra Club ....$4,500   Environment
Council for a Livable World ....$1,169   Pro-Peace
National Cmte to Preserve Social Security ......$1,000   Soc Secur

Independent expenditures supporting Stallings

National Assn of Realtors $126,450
Auto Dealers & Drivers for Free Trade $45,000
National Cmte to Preserve Social Security $2,719

Independent expenditures opposing Stallings

Council for National Defense $6,044

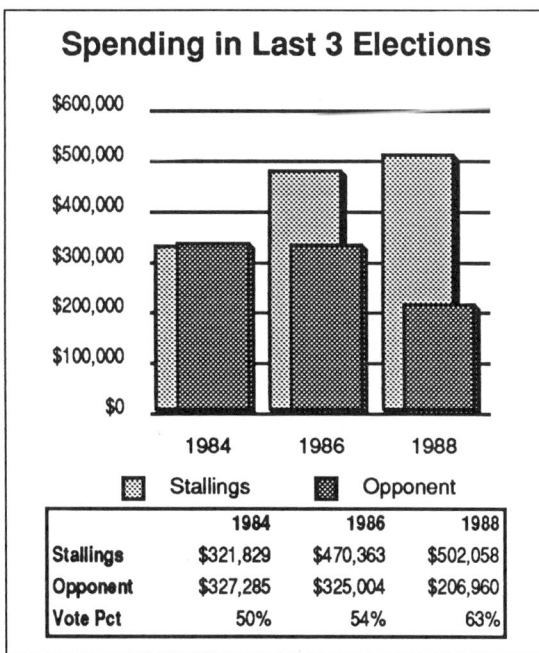

Spending in Last 3 Elections

Bar chart with y-axis $0 to $600,000, years 1984, 1986, 1988, legend: ▨ Stallings, ▨ Opponent

	1984	1986	1988
Stallings	$321,829	$470,363	$502,058
Opponent	$327,285	$325,004	$206,960
Vote Pct	50%	54%	63%

---

* Contributions came from more than one PAC affiliated
with this sponsor.

Arlan Stangeland, R-Minn (7)

First elected: 1977
Total receipts: $659,007
Total from PACs: $344,281

1988 Committees & Subcommittees

Agriculture
Cotton, Rice and Sugar (Ranking Republican)
Livestock, Dairy and Poultry
Wheat, Soybeans and Feed Grains

Public Works and Transportation
Water Resources (Ranking Republican)
Aviation
Public Buildings and Grounds

PAC Contribution Profile

Business

Agricultural Chemicals	$10,050
FMC Corp	$2,200
Dow Chemical*	$2,000
Ecolab Inc	$2,000
Others	$3,850

Automotive	$14,800
Auto Dealers & Drivers for Free Trade	$10,000
National Auto Dealers Assn	$3,650
General Motors	$1,150

Aviation & Aerospace	$16,600
Aircraft Owners & Pilots Assn	$3,800
Northwest Airlines	$2,150
Trans World Airlines	$1,750
Federal Express Corp	$1,500
Allied-Signal	$1,300
United Airlines	$1,150
Others	$4,950

Business Associations	$9,464
National Fedn of Independent Business	$7,237
Business Industry PAC	$2,121
Others	$106

Commercial & Savings Banks	$8,500
US League of Savings Assns	$2,650
American Bankers Assn	$2,500
Others	$3,350

Campaign Revenue Sources

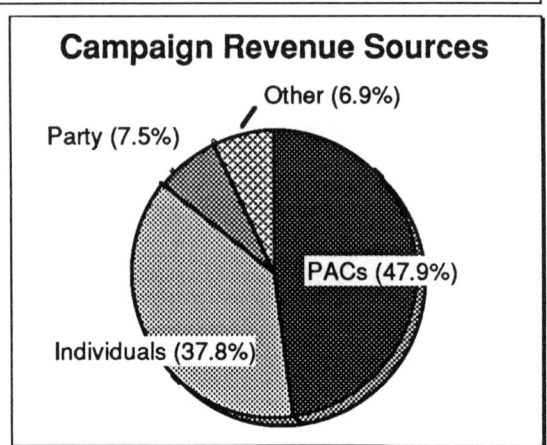

Other (6.9%)
Party (7.5%)
PACs (47.9%)
Individuals (37.8%)

Construction	$32,900
National Utility Contractors Assn	$7,500
National Assn of Home Builders	$5,500
Associated General Contractors	$4,300
Associated Builders & Contractors	$2,150
Ch2M Hill	$2,000
American Consulting Engineers Council	$1,500
Sheet Metal/AirCon Contractors	$1,500
Wall & Ceiling/Gypsum Contractors	$1,450
Deere & Company	$1,250
Others	$5,750

Dairy	$22,850
Associated Milk Producers	$9,000
Mid-American Dairymen	$7,600
Land O'Lakes Inc	$4,000
Dairymen Inc	$1,450
Others	$800

Electric Utilities	$7,065
Northern States Power Company	$1,800
Others	$5,265

Food & Beverage	$13,650
ConAgra Inc	$2,300
Food Marketing Institute	$1,700
General Mills	$1,500
A E Staley Manufacturing Company	$1,350
American Meat Institute	$1,150
Others	$5,650

Grain Processing & Trading	$8,250
Cargill Inc	$5,000
Archer-Daniels-Midland Corp	$2,000
Others	$1,250

Health Professionals	$12,535
American Medical Assn	$4,735
American Dental Assn	$4,500
American Academy of Ophthalmology	$2,000
Others	$1,300

Insurance	$9,500
National Assn of Life Underwriters	$5,000
Others	$4,500

PAC Totals by Category

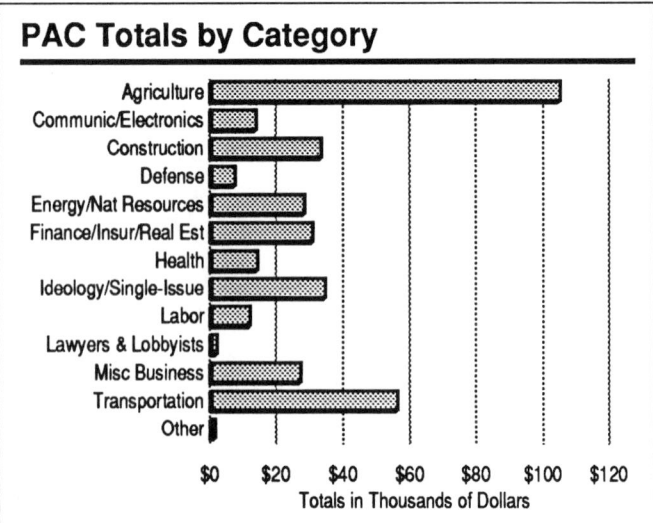

Agriculture
Communic/Electronics
Construction
Defense
Energy/Nat Resources
Finance/Insur/Real Est
Health
Ideology/Single-Issue
Labor
Lawyers & Lobbyists
Misc Business
Transportation
Other

$0 $20 $40 $60 $80 $100 $120
Totals in Thousands of Dollars

Oil & Gas	**$11,150**
Amoco Corp	$2,650
Mobil Oil	$1,500
Phillips Petroleum	$1,500
Texaco	$1,150
Others	$4,350

Real Estate	**$10,500**
National Assn of Realtors	$10,500

Sugar Growers	**$26,800**
American Crystal Sugar Corp	$9,200
American Sugarbeet Growers Assn	$5,150
Southern Minnesota Beet Sugar Co-op	$4,850
American Sugar Cane League	$2,000
Minn-Dak Farmers Co-op	$1,750
Others	$3,850

Telecommunications	**$8,700**
North Western Bell Telephone	$2,500
United Telecommunications	$2,000
Continental Telecom	$1,500
US West Inc	$1,000
Others	$1,700

Trucking/Delivery	**$13,970**
United Parcel Service	$4,720
American Trucking Assns	$2,350
Minnesota Truck Operators	$2,000
North American Van Lines	$1,500
Roadway Services Inc	$1,150
Others	$2,250

Interest Group Ratings

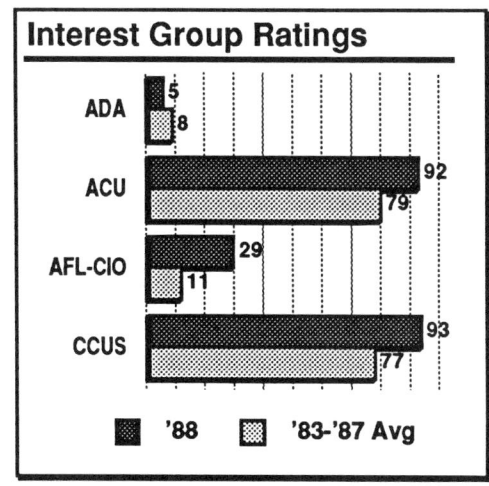

ADA — '88: 5, '83-'87 Avg: 8
ACU — '88: 92, '83-'87 Avg: 79
AFL-CIO — '88: 29, '83-'87 Avg: 11
CCUS — '88: 93, '83-'87 Avg: 77

■ '88   ▨ '83-'87 Avg

Other Major Business PACs

Minnesota Mining & Manufacturing (3M)	$6,000	Indust Equip
Waste Management Inc	$6,000	Waste Mgmt
National Cotton Council	$2,900	Cotton
American Cotton Shippers Assn	$2,400	Cotton
Chicago Board of Trade	$2,000	Commodities
Cooper Industries	$2,000	Electronics
Eaton Corp	$2,000	Water Util
Rockwell International	$1,950	Air Defense
American Coml Barge Line Company	$1,600	SeaTransport
Honeywell Inc	$1,600	Electronics
Lockheed Corp	$1,600	Air Defense
Philip Morris	$1,550	Tobacco
Holiday Inns	$1,500	Hotel/Motel
Potlatch Corp	$1,500	Forestry
Tobacco Institute	$1,200	Tobacco
Burlington Northern	$1,150	Railroads
Kansas City Southern	$1,150	Railroads
National Council of Farmer Co-ops	$1,150	Farm Orgs
American Waterways Operators	$1,100	SeaTransport
Bowling Proprietors Assn	$1,100	AmuseCtr
Society of American Florists	$1,100	Florists

Labor

Labor Unions	**$11,450**
Marine Engineers Union*	$5,500
Air Line Pilots Assn	$5,000
Others	$950

Ideological/Single-Issue

Ideological/Single-Issue	**$31,013**	
National Right to Life PAC	$9,054	Pro-Life
National Rifle Assn	$8,450	Pro-Guns
Public Service Research Council	$3,950	Anti-Union
Campaign America (Bob Dole)	$2,607	Repub Leader
Council for National Defense	$2,152	Pro-Defense
Others	$4,800	

Independent expenditures supporting Stangeland

Kansas City Southern	$5,000
Associated Milk Producers	$2,000
National Auto Dealers Assn	$1,500

* Contributions came from more than one PAC affiliated
  with this sponsor.

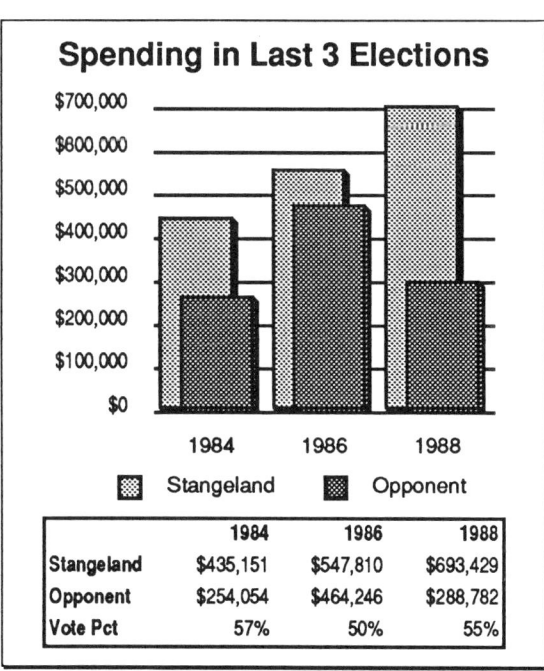

Spending in Last 3 Elections

▨ Stangeland   ▦ Opponent

	1984	1986	1988
Stangeland	$435,151	$547,810	$693,429
Opponent	$254,054	$464,246	$288,782
Vote Pct	57%	50%	55%

Pete Stark, D-Calif (9)

First elected: 1972
Total receipts: $504,558
Total from PACs: $325,428

1988 Committees & Subcommittees

District of Columbia
Fiscal Affairs and Health
Government Operations and Metropolitan Affairs

Ways and Means
Health (Chairman)
Select Revenue Measures

Select Narcotics Abuse and Control

Joint Economic
Fiscal and Monetary Policy (Vice Chairman)
Economic Growth, Trade and Taxes
Education and Health

PAC Contribution Profile

Business

Accountants	**$8,500**
American Institute of CPA's	$5,000
Coopers & Lybrand	$1,500
Others	$2,000
Automotive	**$9,000**
National Auto Dealers Assn	$5,000
Auto Dealers & Drivers for Free Trade	$2,500
Others	$1,500
Food & Beverage	**$8,750**
Food Marketing Institute	$3,000
ConAgra Inc	$1,500
Winn-Dixie Stores	$1,500
Others	$2,750
Health Professionals	**$49,100**
Assn for Advancement of Psychology	$10,000
American Dental Assn	$5,000
American Podiatry Assn	$3,500
Corp for the Advancement of Psychiatry	$3,500
National Assn of Pharmacists	$3,500
American Physical Therapy Assn	$2,500
American Assn of Nurse Anesthetist	$2,000
American Nurses Assn	$2,000
American Optometric Assn	$2,000
Oral & Maxillofacial Surgeons	$2,000
American Occupational Therapy Assn	$1,800
Co-op of American Physicians	$1,500
Pathology Practice Assn	$1,500
Others	$8,300

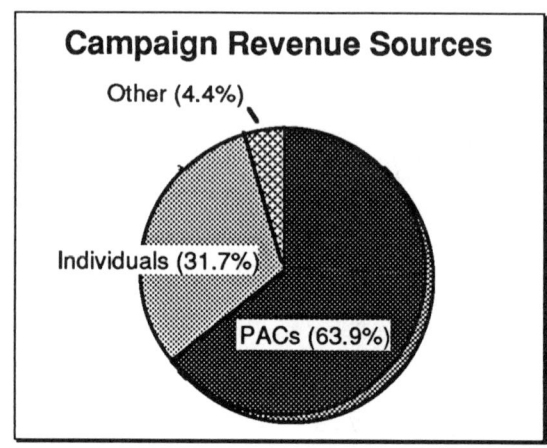

Campaign Revenue Sources

- Other (4.4%)
- Individuals (31.7%)
- PACs (63.9%)

Hospitals & Nursing Homes	**$15,500**
American Health Care Assn	$5,000
American Hospital Assn	$4,000
Manor Healthcare Corp	$2,000
National Assn of Private Psychiatric Hospitals	$2,000
Voluntary Hospitals of America	$2,000
Others	$500
Insurance	**$56,000**
Massachusetts Mutual Life Insurance	$6,000
TransAmerica Corp*	$5,500
Metropolitan Life Insurance	$5,000
Equitable Financial Services	$4,000
Prudential Insurance	$4,000
Lincoln National Corp	$2,500
Aetna Life & Casualty	$2,000
Blue Cross & Blue Shield Assn	$2,000
American Family Corp	$1,500
Cigna Corp	$1,500
Pacific Mutual Life	$1,500
Torchmark Corp	$1,500
Others	$19,000
Lawyers & Lobbyists	**$17,964**
Assn of Trial Lawyers of America	$5,500
Vinson, Elkins, Searls, Connally & Smith	$2,000
Arnold & Porter	$1,500
Baker & Hostetler	$1,500
Burson-Marsteller	$1,000
Kutak, Rock & Campbell	$1,000
Pillsbury, Madison & Sutro	$1,000
Western Enterprise PAC	$1,000
Others	$3,464
Medical Supply	**$5,941**
American Orthotic/Prosthetic Assn	$1,500
Medical Equipment Suppliers	$1,500
Health Industry Manufacturers Assn	$1,441
Others	$1,500

PAC Totals by Category

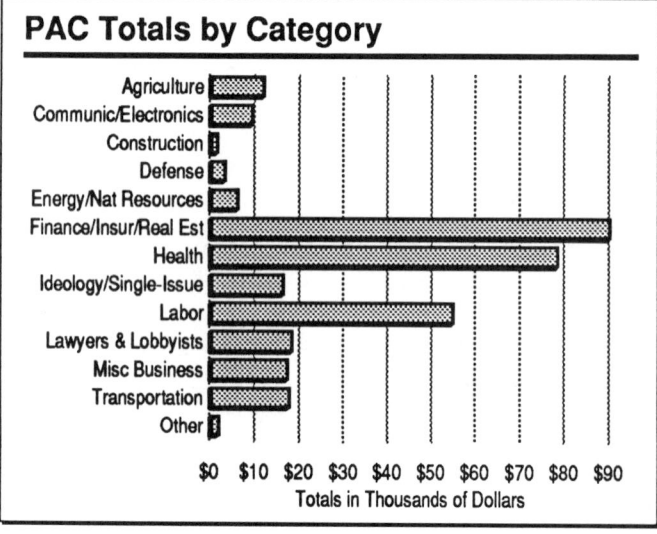

Agriculture
Communic/Electronics
Construction
Defense
Energy/Nat Resources
Finance/Insur/Real Est
Health
Ideology/Single-Issue
Labor
Lawyers & Lobbyists
Misc Business
Transportation
Other

$0 $10 $20 $30 $40 $50 $60 $70 $80 $90
Totals in Thousands of Dollars

Real Estate **$9,500**

    National Assn of Realtors $6,500
    Mortgage Bankers Assn of America $2,000
    Others $1,000

Retail Sales **$6,850**

    J C Penney Company $2,000
    National Assn of Chain Drug Stores $1,500
    Others $3,350

Savings & Commercial Banks **$6,250**

    Home Savings of America $4,000
    Others $2,250

Securities/Commodities Investment **$9,500**

    Securities Industry Assn $3,000
    Investment Company Institute $2,000
    Chicago Board of Trade $1,500
    Investors Diversified Services $1,500
    Others $1,500

Telecommunications **$5,250**

    Pacific Telesis Group $3,250
    AT&T $1,500
    Others $500

Other Major Business PACs

General Electric	$2,000	Electronics
Henley Group Inc	$1,500	Altern Energy
Family Health Program Inc	$2,000	HMOs
Footwear Distributors PAC	$1,100	Shoes
United Airlines	$1,500	Airlines
Texas Air	$2,000	Airlines

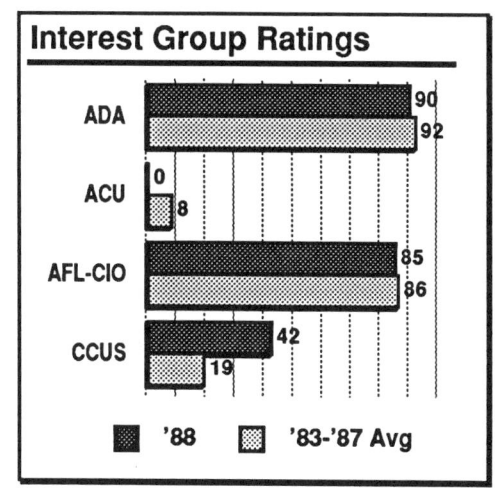

Interest Group Ratings

	'88	'83–'87 Avg
ADA	90	92
ACU	0	8
AFL-CIO	85	86
CCUS	42	19

Labor

Bldg Trades/Industrial/Misc Unions **$13,500**

    National Education Assn $4,500
    Carpenters & Joiners Union $4,000
    Machinists/Aerospace Workers Union $2,000
    Others $3,000

Government & Postal Workers **$19,700**

    National Assn of Letter Carriers* $5,200
    National Assn of Retired Federal Employees ... $5,000
    National Rural Letter Carriers Assn $3,000
    American Fedn of State/County/Munic Employees ... $2,500
    National Treasury Employees Union $2,000
    Others $2,000

Transportation Unions **$21,250**

    Teamsters Union $10,000
    Seafarers International Union $3,000
    Air Line Pilots Assn $2,500
    United Transportation Union $2,000
    Others $3,750

Ideological/Single-Issue

Ideological/Single-Issue **$13,370**

National Cmte to Preserve Social Security	$5,000	Soc Secur
National Right to Life PAC	$2,500	Pro-Life
Sierra Club	$1,300	Environment
Others	$4,570	

Independent expenditures supporting Stark

National Cmte to Preserve Social Security $2,066

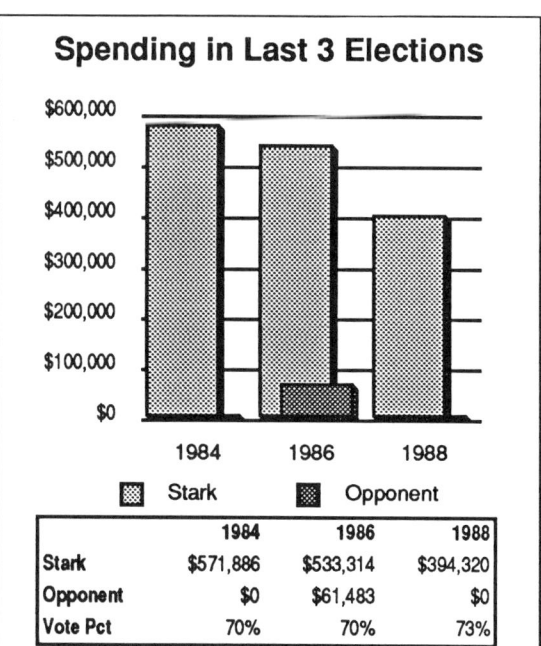

Spending in Last 3 Elections

	1984	1986	1988
Stark	$571,886	$533,314	$394,320
Opponent	$0	$61,483	$0
Vote Pct	70%	70%	73%

Stark   Opponent

---

* Contributions came from more than one PAC affiliated
with this sponsor.

Cliff Stearns, R-Fla (6)

1989-90 Committees & Subcommittees

Banking, Finance and Urban Affairs
Financial Institutions Supervision, Regulation and Insurance
Housing and Community Development
International Development, Finance, Trade and Monetary Policy

Veterans' Affairs
Oversight and Investigations

Select Aging
Retirement Income and Employment

PAC Contribution Profile

Business

Business Associations..**$1,000**	
National Fedn of Independent Business $1,000	
Citrus Growers..**$1,650**	
Florida Citrus Mutual $1,650	
Construction **$1,250**	
Associated Builders & Contractors $1,000	
Others $250	
Health Professionals **$6,000**	
American Medical Assn $5,000	
Florida Society of Anesthesiology $1,000	
Real Estate **$5,000**	
National Assn of Realtors $5,000	
Soft Drinks **$1,000**	
Pepsico Inc $1,000	
Telecommunications **$6,500**	
United Telecommunications $3,500	
Southern Bell $3,000	

Campaign Revenue Sources

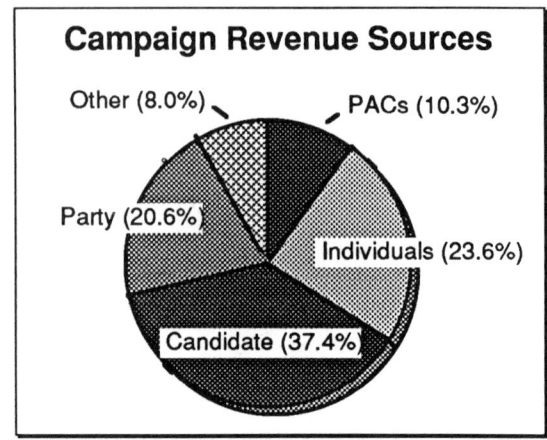

Other (8.0%)
PACs (10.3%)
Party (20.6%)
Individuals (23.6%)
Candidate (37.4%)

Other Major Business PACs

American Horse Council $500	Livestock
Browning-Ferris Industries $500	Waste Mgmt
Florida Power Corp $500	ElectricUtil
Jack Eckerd Corp $500	Drug Stores
Lockheed Corp $500	Air Defense
Mapco Inc $500	Refine/Mktg
Petroleum Marketers Assn $500	Gas Stations
Sun Banks $500	Comml Banks

PAC Totals by Category

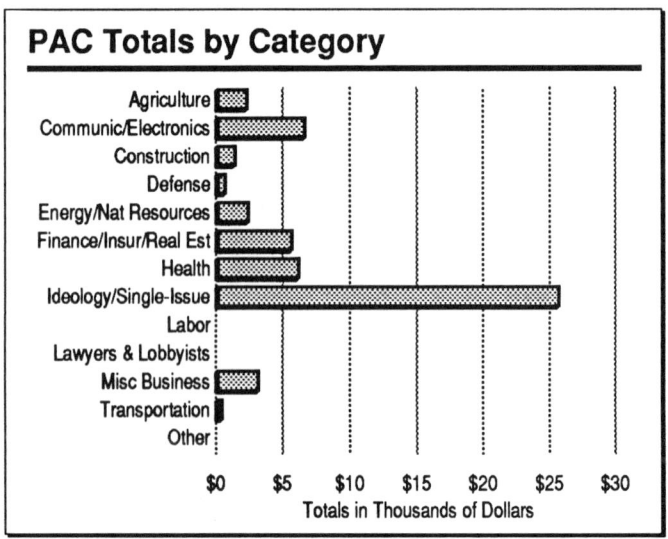

Agriculture
Communic/Electronics
Construction
Defense
Energy/Nat Resources
Finance/Insur/Real Est
Health
Ideology/Single-Issue
Labor
Lawyers & Lobbyists
Misc Business
Transportation
Other

$0 $5 $10 $15 $20 $25 $30
Totals in Thousands of Dollars

Ideological/Single-Issue

Anti-Union PACs ***$4,500***
      Public Service Research Council $3,500
      Right to Work PAC $1,000

Pro-Gun Ownership ***$4,970***
      National Rifle Assn $4,970

Republican/Conservative ***$1,450***
      Conservative Victory Committee $1,000
      Others $450

Republican Leadership PACs ***$12,850***
      Citizens for the Republic (Ronald Reagan) $5,000
      Fund for America's Future (George Bush) $5,000
      Campaign America (Bob Dole)....................................$1,000
      Policy Innovation PAC (Dick Armey) $1,000
      Conservative Victory Fund (Steve Symms) $750
      Others $100

Other Major Ideological/Single-Issue PACs

Ruff PAC ....$1,000   Tax Policy
National Right to Life PAC ....$509   Pro-Life

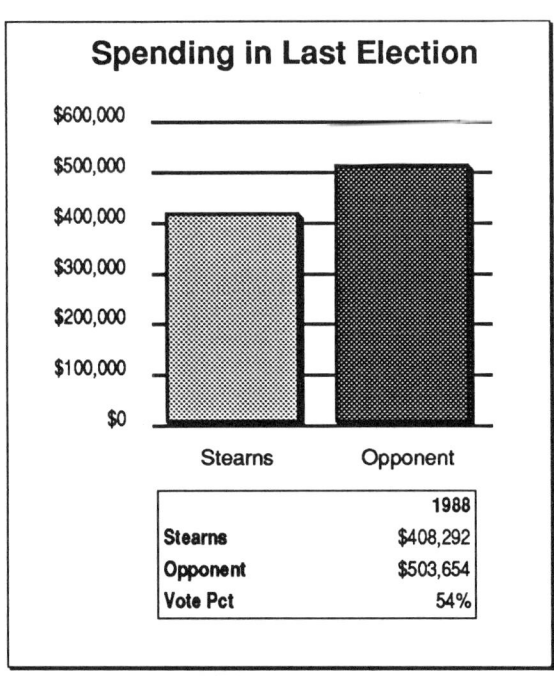

Spending in Last Election

	1988
Stearns	$408,292
Opponent	$503,654
Vote Pct	54%

Charles W. Stenholm, D-Texas (17)

First elected: 1978
Total receipts: $289,551
Total from PACs: $111,716

1988 Committees & Subcommittees

Agriculture
Livestock, Dairy and Poultry (Chairman)
Cotton, Rice and Sugar
Department Operations, Research and Foreign Agriculture
Tobacco and Peanuts

Veterans' Affairs
Hospitals and Health Care

PAC Contribution Profile

Business

Campaign Revenue Sources

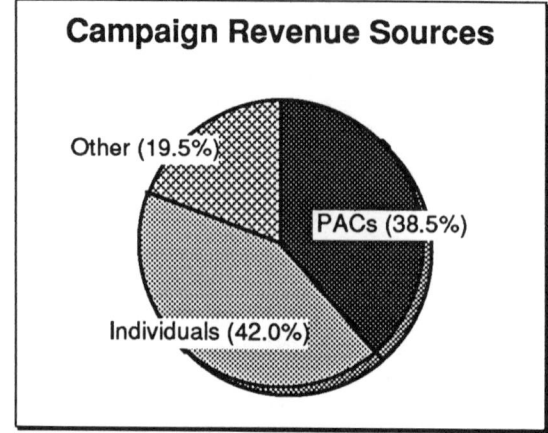

Other (19.5%)
PACs (38.5%)
Individuals (42.0%)

Agricultural Chemicals *$4,000*
- Dow Chemical $1,000
- Ecolab Inc $1,000
- Others $2,000

Agricultural Services *$2,750*
- American Veterinary Medical Assn $1,000
- Farmland Industries $1,000
- Others $750

Auto Dealers *$3,500*
- Auto Dealers & Drivers for Free Trade $2,500
- National Auto Dealers Assn $1,000

Commercial & Savings Banks *$2,700*
- American Bankers Assn $2,500
- Others $200

Commodities Trading *$3,500*
- Chicago Board of Trade $1,500
- Chicago Mercantile Exchange $1,000
- Commodity Exchange Inc $1,000

Construction *$5,250*
- National Utility Contractors Assn $2,000
- Associated Builders & Contractors $1,000
- Associated General Contractors $1,000
- Others $1,250

Cotton *$2,650*
- National Cotton Council $1,500
- Others $1,150

Dairy *$7,950*
- Associated Milk Producers $4,000
- Dairymen Inc $1,000
- Mid-American Dairymen $1,000
- Others $1,950

Electric Utilities *$5,550*
- Texas Utilities Electric Company* $3,200
- Houston Industries $1,000
- West Texas Utilities $1,000
- Others $350

Farm Organizations *$2,250*
- Texas Farm Bureau $1,500
- Others $750

Food & Beverage *$12,600*
- ConAgra Inc $1,000
- IBP Inc $1,000
- National Restaurant Assn $1,000
- Pepsico Inc $1,000
- Swift Independent Packing Company $1,000
- Texas Restaurant Assn $1,000
- Others $6,600

Health Professionals *$8,166*
- American Medical Assn $7,231
- Others $935

Insurance *$6,000*
- National Assn of Realtors $6,000

Livestock & Poultry *$7,900*
- Texas/Southwestern Cattle Raisers $2,000
- National Wool Growers Assn $1,000
- Texas Cattle Feeders Assn $1,000
- Others $3,900

Oil & Gas *$6,700*
- Valero Energy Corp $2,000
- Others $4,700

Pharmaceuticals *$3,000*
- Burroughs Wellcome $1,000
- Schering-Plough Corp $1,000
- Others $1,000

PAC Totals by Category

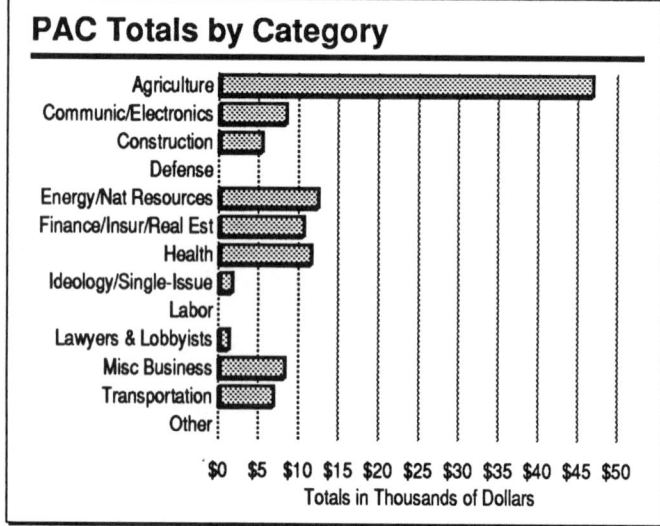

Agriculture
Communic/Electronics
Construction
Defense
Energy/Nat Resources
Finance/Insur/Real Est
Health
Ideology/Single-Issue
Labor
Lawyers & Lobbyists
Misc Business
Transportation
Other

$0 $5 $10 $15 $20 $25 $30 $35 $40 $45 $50
Totals in Thousands of Dollars

Sugar Growers *$2,550*

    American Crystal Sugar Corp $1,000
    Others $1,550

Telecommunications *$7,450*

    AT&T $4,000
    GTE (Southwest) $1,500
    Southwestern Bell $1,500
    Others $450

Tobacco *$2,250*

    Philip Morris $1,000
    RJR Nabisco $1,000
    Others $250

Other Major Business PACs

National Assn of Life Underwriters	$1,500	Life Insurance
Texas Air	$1,000	Airlines

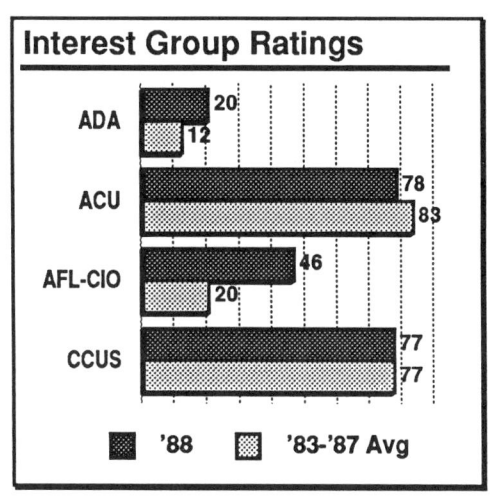

Interest Group Ratings

	'88	'83-'87 Avg
ADA	20	12
ACU	78	83
AFL-CIO	46	20
CCUS	77	77

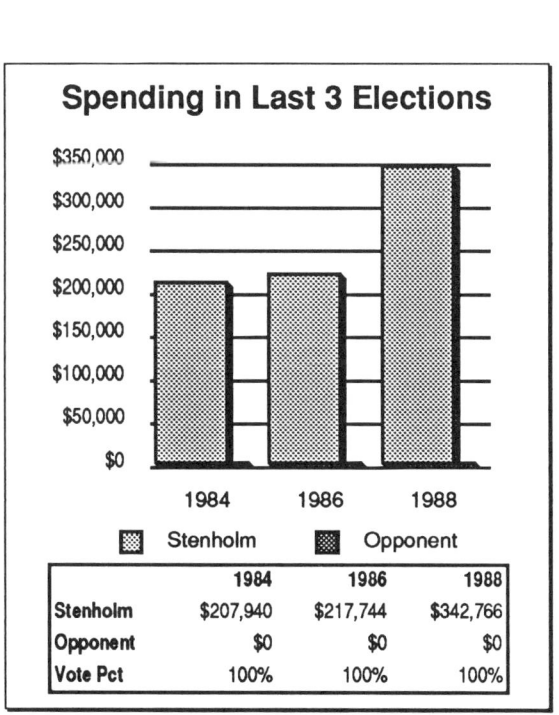

Spending in Last 3 Elections

	1984	1986	1988
Stenholm	$207,940	$217,744	$342,766
Opponent	$0	$0	$0
Vote Pct	100%	100%	100%

    □ Stenholm   ■ Opponent

* Contributions came from more than one PAC affiliated
with this sponsor.

Louis Stokes, D-Ohio (21)

First elected: 1968
Total receipts: $241,646
Total from PACs: $147,800

1988 Committees & Subcommittees

Appropriations
District of Columbia
HUD-Independent Agencies
Labor, Health and Human Services, Education and Related Agencies

Select Intelligence (Chairman)
Program and Budget Authorization (Chairman)
Legislation

PAC Contribution Profile

Business

Aviation & Aerospace	**$2,500**
TRW Inc	$1,500
Others	$1,000
Commercial & Savings Banks	**$2,000**
American Bankers Assn	$1,000
Others	$1,000
Construction	**$2,000**
National Assn of Home Builders	$1,000
National Utility Contractors Assn	$1,000
Defense	**$8,000**
Grumman	$2,000
Lockheed Corp	$2,000
Rockwell International	$1,500
Others	$2,500
Electric Utilities	**$2,500**
Potomac Electric Power Company	$1,000
Others	$1,500
Electronics & Computers	**$3,000**
Computer Sciences Corp	$1,000
General Electric	$1,000
Others	$1,000

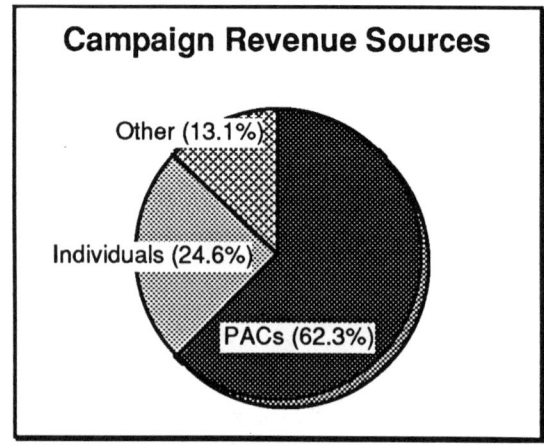

Campaign Revenue Sources

- Other (13.1%)
- Individuals (24.6%)
- PACs (62.3%)

Health Professionals	**$13,450**
American Podiatry Assn	$4,500
American Dental Assn	$2,500
American Optometric Assn	$1,500
Cmte for Quality Orthopedic Health Care	$1,500
Assn for Advancement of Psychology	$1,000
Others	$2,450
Lawyers	**$6,250**
Assn of Trial Lawyers of America	$3,500
Baker & Hostetler	$1,500
Others	$1,250
Real Estate	**$4,000**
National Assn of Realtors	$3,000
Mortgage Bankers Assn of America	$1,000
Sugar Growers	**$3,050**
American Crystal Sugar Corp	$1,000
Others	$2,050
Telecommunications	**$3,000**
AT&T	$2,500
Others	$500
Trucking/Delivery	**$3,000**
United Parcel Service	$2,000
American Trucking Assns	$1,000

Other Major Business PACs

Associated Milk Producers	$1,500	Dairy
Delaware North Companies	$1,500	Casinos/Gamb
Consolidated Rail Corp	$1,000	Railroads
Michigan Consolidated Gas	$1,000	Natural Gas
National Assn of Trade/Tech Schools	$1,000	Voc Tech
Ocean Spray Cranberries Inc	$1,000	Fruit/Veg

PAC Totals by Category

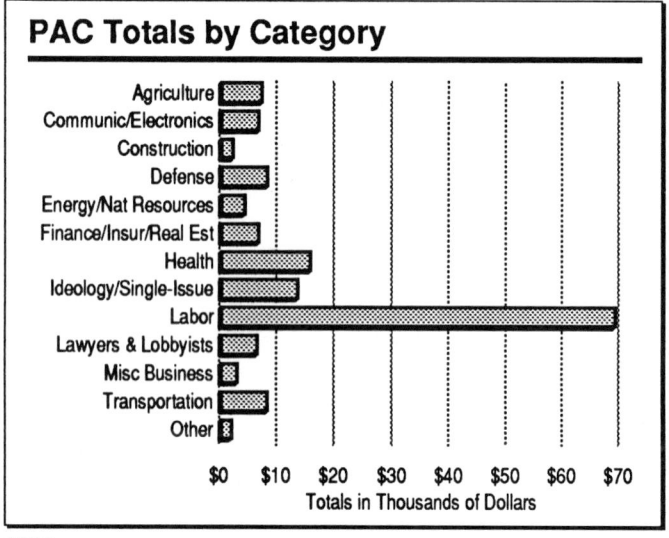

Categories: Agriculture, Communic/Electronics, Construction, Defense, Energy/Nat Resources, Finance/Insur/Real Est, Health, Ideology/Single-Issue, Labor, Lawyers & Lobbyists, Misc Business, Transportation, Other

Totals in Thousands of Dollars ($0 $10 $20 $30 $40 $50 $60 $70)

Labor

Bldg Trades/Industrial/Misc Unions **$27,200**

United Auto Workers $5,500
Communications Workers of America.............................$5,000
Machinists/Aerospace Workers Union $3,000
AFL-CIO* $2,000
Laborers' Political League $2,000
Carpenters & Joiners Union $1,500
Intl Brotherhood of Electrical Workers............................$1,500
Operating Engineers Union $1,500
United Steelworkers $1,500
Food & Commercial Workers Union.................................$1,000
Ladies Garment Workers Union $1,000
Others $1,700

Government & Postal Workers **$15,750**

American Fedn of State/County/Munic Employees $5,000
National Assn of Letter Carriers $4,000
American Postal Workers Union $2,000
National Assn of Retired Federal Employees $2,000
National Assn of Postal Supervisors $1,000
Others $1,750

Teachers Unions **$8,000**

National Education Assn $5,000
American Federation of Teachers $3,000

Transportation Unions **$18,005**

Teamsters Union $7,500
Amalgamated Transit Union....................................$2,000
Seafarers International Union $1,500
United Transportation Union $1,500
Air Line Pilots Assn $1,000
Brotherhood of Locomotive Engineers $1,000
International Longshoremen Assn $1,000
Marine Engineers District 2 Maritime Officers.................$1,000
Others $1,505

Interest Group Ratings

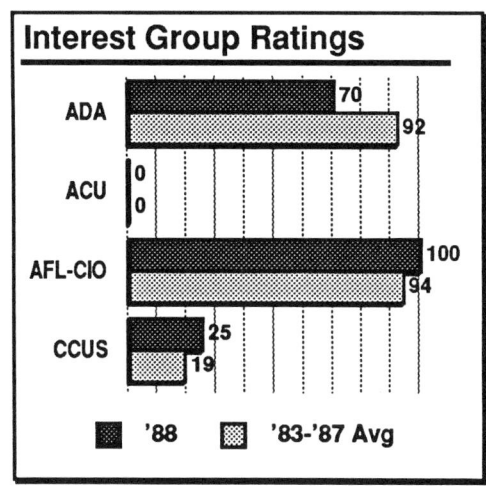

Ideological/Single-Issue

Pro-Israel **$5,500**

National PAC $5,000
Others $500

Other Major Ideological/Single-Issue PACs

Human Rights Campaign Fund ....$2,500   Gay Rights
National Cmte to Preserve Social Security ......$1,500   Soc Secur
Valley Education Fund (Tony Coelho) ....$1,500   Dem Leaders

Independent expenditures supporting Stokes

National Cmte to Preserve Social Security $1,070

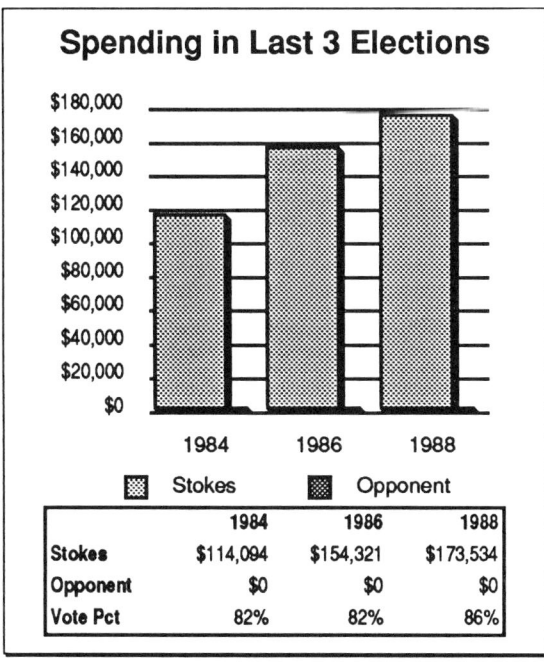

Spending in Last 3 Elections

	1984	1986	1988
Stokes	$114,094	$154,321	$173,534
Opponent	$0	$0	$0
Vote Pct	82%	82%	86%

---

* Contributions came from more than one PAC affiliated
with this sponsor.

Gerry E. Studds, D-Mass (10)

First elected: 1972
Total receipts: $243,095
Total from PACs: $83,545

1988 Committees & Subcommittees

Foreign Affairs
Arms Control, International Security and Science
Western Hemisphere Affairs

Merchant Marine and Fisheries
Fisheries and Wildlife Conservation and the Environment (Chairman)
Coast Guard and Navigation
Oceanography

PAC Contribution Profile

Business

Commercial Fishing **$5,445**
    National Fisheries Institute $4,820
    American Tunaboat Assn $625

Food & Beverage **$2,000**
    Pepsi-Cola Bottlers Assn $1,000
    Pacific Seafood Processors $500
    Others $500

Real Estate **$3,000**
    National Assn of Realtors $3,000

Sea Transport **$4,000**
    Boat Owners Assn of the US $1,500
    American Pilots Assn $1,000
    Boating PAC $1,000
    Matson Navigation $500

Telecommunications **$2,500**
    AT&T $2,000
    South Central Bell Telephone $500

Waste Management **$2,000**
    Waste Management Inc $2,000

Other Major Business PACs

Duchossois Industries	$1,000	RR Equip
National Assn of Home Builders	$1,000	Resid Constr
Ocean Spray Cranberries Inc	$1,000	Fruit/Veg
Garvey, Schubert & Barer	$500	Lawyers
US League of Savings Assn	$500	SavingsBanks

Campaign Revenue Sources

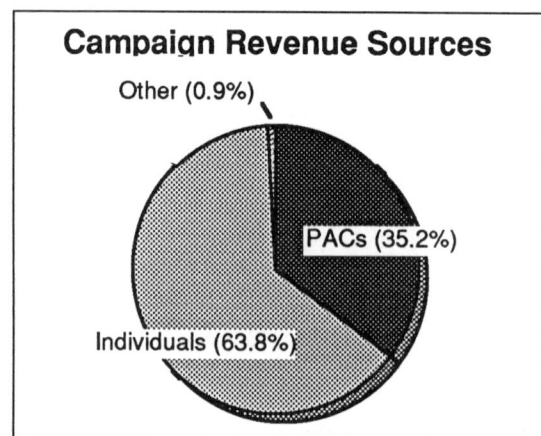

Other (0.9%)
PACs (35.2%)
Individuals (63.8%)

PAC Totals by Category

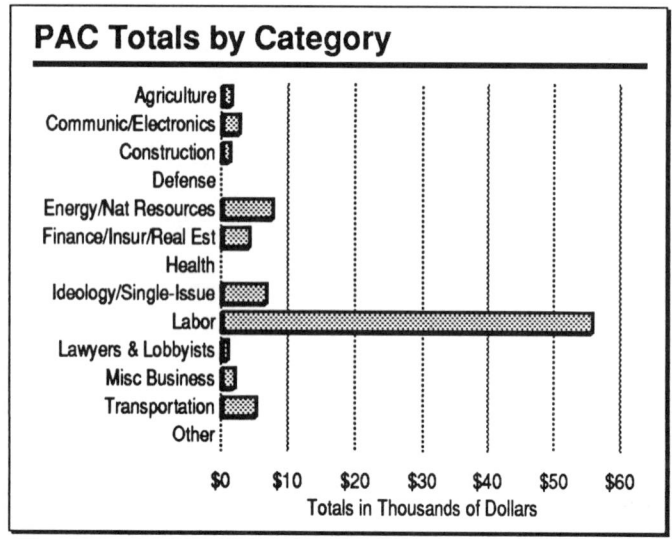

Agriculture
Communic/Electronics
Construction
Defense
Energy/Nat Resources
Finance/Insur/Real Est
Health
Ideology/Single-Issue
Labor
Lawyers & Lobbyists
Misc Business
Transportation
Other

$0 $10 $20 $30 $40 $50 $60
Totals in Thousands of Dollars

Labor

Bldg Trades/Industrial/Misc Unions **$15,950**
United Auto Workers $5,000
Machinists/Aerospace Workers Union $2,500
Carpenters & Joiners Union $1,500
Food & Commercial Workers Union $1,500
Laborers' Political League $1,500
Amalgamated Clothing & Textile Workers $1,000
Ladies Garment Workers Union $1,000
Sheet Metal Workers Union $1,000
AFL-CIO Bldg/Construction Trades Department $500
Others $450

Government & Postal Workers **$11,050**
National Assn of Retired Federal Employees $5,000
National Assn of Letter Carriers $3,000
American Postal Workers Union $2,000
American Fedn of State/County/Munic Employees $1,000
Others $50

Sea Transport Unions **$10,000**
Marine Engineers Union* $6,000
Seafarers International Union $3,000
Maritime Union of America $1,000

Other Transportation Unions **$11,000**
Teamsters Union $10,000
Transportation Communication Union $1,000

Teachers Unions **$7,500**
National Education Assn $7,500

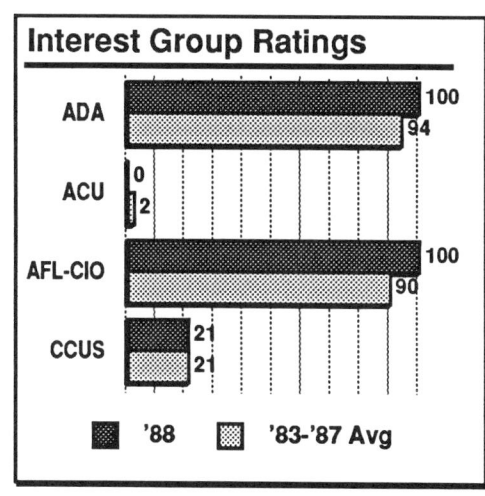

Interest Group Ratings

ADA — 100 ('88), 94 ('83-'87 Avg)
ACU — 0 ('88), 2 ('83-'87 Avg)
AFL-CIO — 100 ('88), 90 ('83-'87 Avg)
CCUS — 21 ('88), 21 ('83-'87 Avg)

■ '88   ▨ '83-'87 Avg

Ideological/Single-Issue

Ideological/Single-Issue **$6,500**

Human Rights Campaign Fund	$3,500	Gay Rights
Sierra Club	$1,500	Environment
Democratic Congressional Fund (Joe Moakley)	$500	Dem Leaders
National Abortion Rights Action League	$500	Pro-Choice
Valley Education Fund (Tony Coelho)	$500	Dem Leaders

Independent expenditures supporting Studds

National Cmte to Preserve Social Security $2,178

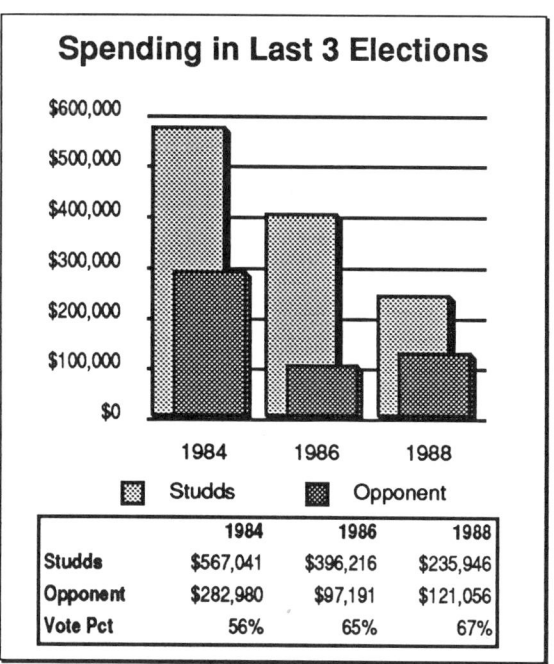

Spending in Last 3 Elections

	1984	1986	1988
Studds	$567,041	$396,216	$235,946
Opponent	$282,980	$97,191	$121,056
Vote Pct	56%	65%	67%

▨ Studds   ■ Opponent

---

* Contributions came from more than one PAC affiliated with this sponsor.

Bob Stump, R-Ariz (3)

First elected: 1976
Total receipts: $257,184
Total from PACs: $114,546

1988 Committees & Subcommittees

Armed Services
Investigations
Research and Development

Veterans' Affairs
Oversight and Investigations (Ranking Republican)
Hospitals and Health Care

PAC Contribution Profile

Business

Automotive	**$5,250**
National Auto Dealers Assn	$3,250
Auto Dealers & Drivers for Free Trade	$1,500
Others	$500
Commercial & Savings Banks	**$9,000**
Arizona Bankers Assn	$1,500
Chase Bank of Arizona	$1,500
Merabank Federal Savings Bank	$1,500
Valley National Bank of Arizona	$1,500
Others	$3,000
Construction	**$3,700**
Associated General Contractors	$1,000
National Assn of Home Builders	$1,000
Others	$1,700
Cotton	**$2,500**
Arizona Cotton Growers Assn	$1,500
National Cotton Council	$750
Others	$250

Campaign Revenue Sources

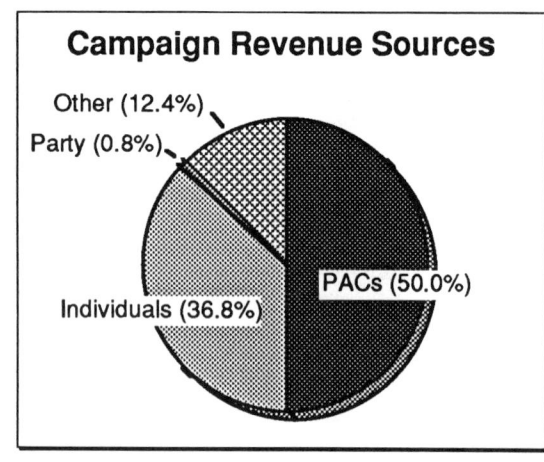

Other (12.4%)
Party (0.8%)
Individuals (36.8%)
PACs (50.0%)

Defense	**$36,350**
AT&T	$2,950
McDonnell Douglas*	$2,550
Northrop Corp	$2,500
FMC Corp	$2,000
Hughes Aircraft	$2,000
Rockwell International	$1,350
Emerson Electric*	$1,300
Lockheed Corp	$1,250
Textron Inc	$1,250
United Technologies	$1,250
Honeywell*	$1,050
Allied-Signal	$1,000
Boeing Company	$1,000
Continental Telecom	$1,000
General Dynamics	$1,000
Motorola Inc	$1,000
Westinghouse Electric	$1,000
Loral Corp	$900
Emhart Corp*	$750
Grumman	$750
Litton Industries	$750
LTV Aerospace & Defense Company	$750
Martin Marietta Corp	$750
Raytheon	$750
Others	$5,500
Electric Utilities	**$3,500**
Arizona Public Service Company	$1,000
Others	$2,500
Food & Beverage	**$2,000**
McLane Company	$1,000
Others	$1,000
Health Professionals	**$13,996**
American Medical Assn	$8,996
American Academy of Ophthalmology	$2,500
American Dental Assn	$2,000
Others	$500
Insurance	**$3,400**
Blue Cross/Shield of Arizona	$900
Others	$2,500
Mining	**$3,300**
Phelps Dodge Corp	$2,000
Others	$1,300

PAC Totals by Category

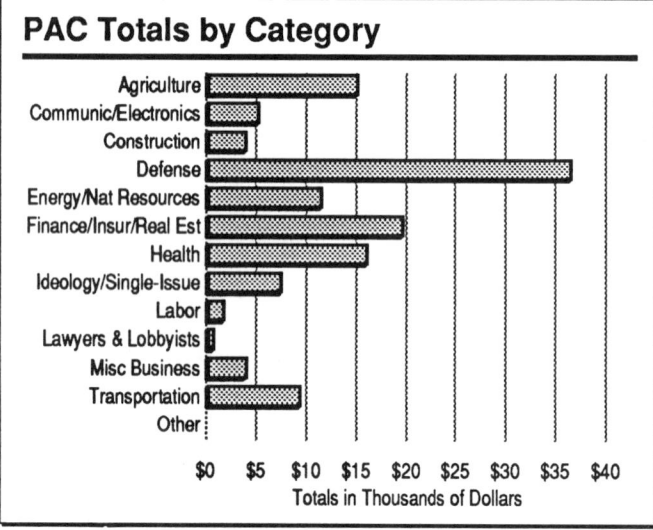

Agriculture
Communic/Electronics
Construction
Defense
Energy/Nat Resources
Finance/Insur/Real Est
Health
Ideology/Single-Issue
Labor
Lawyers & Lobbyists
Misc Business
Transportation
Other

$0 $5 $10 $15 $20 $25 $30 $35 $40
Totals in Thousands of Dollars

Oil & Gas $4,450
   Circle K Corp $1,500
   Southwest Gas Corp $1,500
   Others $1,450

Railroads $2,000
   Santa Fe Southern Pacific $1,250
   Others $750

Real Estate $7,000
   National Assn of Realtors $4,500
   Estes Company $1,500
   Others $1,000

Sugar Growers $2,600
   American Crystal Sugar Corp $750
   American Sugarbeet Growers Assn $750
   Florida Sugar Cane League $550
   Others $550

Telecommunications $5,000
   Mountain Bell $5,000

Tobacco $2,000
   Philip Morris $650
   Others $1,350

Other Major Business PACs

Greyhound Corp	$1,750	Home Chem
Salt River Valley Water Users	$1,750	Ag Svcs
Kaibab Industries	$1,500	Forestry
Stone Container Corp	$1,000	Paper Packg

Major Labor PACs

National Assn of Retired Federal Employees	$1,000	Fedl Workers

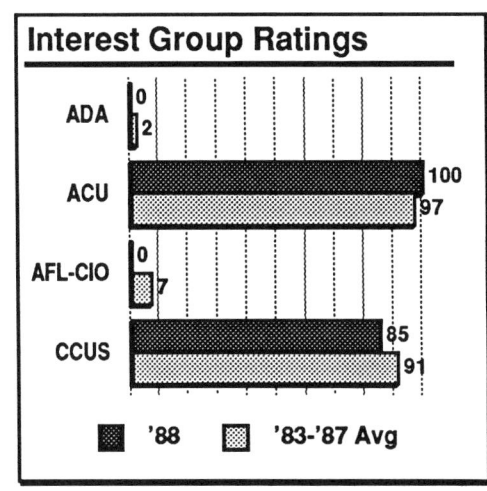

Interest Group Ratings

	'88	'83-'87 Avg
ADA	0	2
ACU	100	97
AFL-CIO	0	7
CCUS	85	91

■ '88 ▨ '83-'87 Avg

Ideological/Single-Issue

Ideological/Single-Issue $6,750

National Rifle Assn	$4,950	Pro-Guns
American Security Council	$1,300	Pro-Defense
Others	$500	

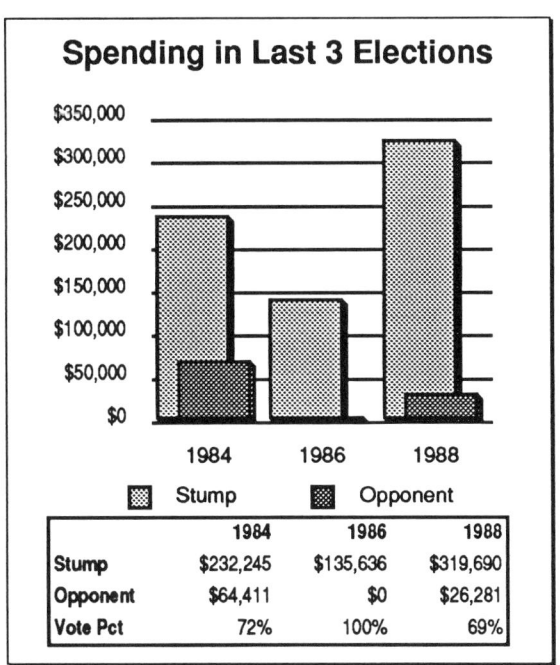

Spending in Last 3 Elections

▨ Stump ■ Opponent

	1984	1986	1988
Stump	$232,245	$135,636	$319,690
Opponent	$64,411	$0	$26,281
Vote Pct	72%	100%	69%

* Contributions came from more than one PAC affiliated with this sponsor.

Don Sundquist, R-Tenn (7)

First elected: 1982
Total receipts: $393,171
Total from PACs: $182,103

1988 Committees & Subcommittees

Budget
Budget Process
Defense and International Affairs
Economic and Trade Policy

Public Works and Transportation
Aviation
Public Buildings and Grounds
Water Resources

PAC Contribution Profile

Business

Automotive **$7,200**
National Auto Dealers Assn $4,600
Auto Dealers & Drivers for Free Trade $2,000
Others $600

Aviation & Aerospace **$5,100**
Boeing Company $1,000
Others $4,100

Chemicals & Plastics **$3,150**
None over $600

Construction **$16,350**
National Assn of Home Builders $5,000
National Utility Contractors Assn $2,000
Associated General Contractors $1,500
Manville Corp $1,000
Others $6,850

Defense **$3,900**
Litton Industries $1,000
Tenneco Inc $1,000
Others $1,900

Delivery Services **$11,000**
Federal Express Corp $10,000
United Parcel Service $1,000

Campaign Revenue Sources

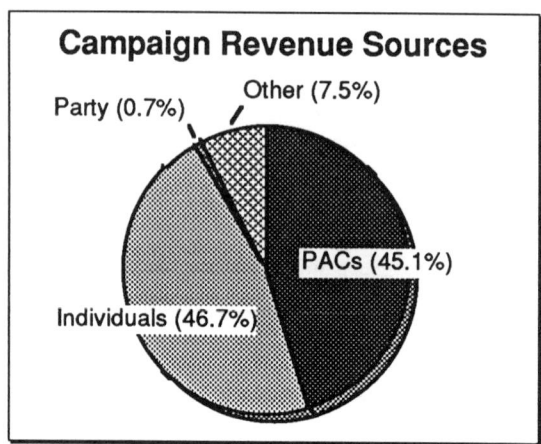

Other (7.5%)
Party (0.7%)
PACs (45.1%)
Individuals (46.7%)

Financial Institutions **$11,800**
US League of Savings Assn $2,800
American Bankers Assn $1,500
First Tennessee National Corp $1,500
First American Corp $1,000
National Bank of Commerce/Memphis $1,000
Sovran Bank $1,000
Tennessee League of Savings Institutions $1,000
Third National Corp $1,000
Others $1,000

Food & Beverage **$11,650**
Malone & Hyde Inc $5,000
Shoneys Inc $1,500
Kellogg Company $1,000
Others $4,150

Health Professionals **$5,650**
American Dental Assn $2,500
American Medical Assn $2,300
Others $850

Hotels & Motels **$2,800**
Holiday Corp $1,000
Holiday Inns $1,000
Others $800

Insurance **$13,365**
National Assn of Life Underwriters $5,000
American Family Corp $2,500
Casualty & Surety Agents Assn $1,390
National Assn Mutual Insurance Agents $1,250
Independent Insurance Agents of America $1,100
Others $2,125

Oil & Gas **$5,800**
Texas Gas Transmission Corp $1,000
Others $4,800

Paper Production **$4,050**
Westvaco Corp $2,500
International Paper Company $1,000
Others $550

PAC Totals by Category

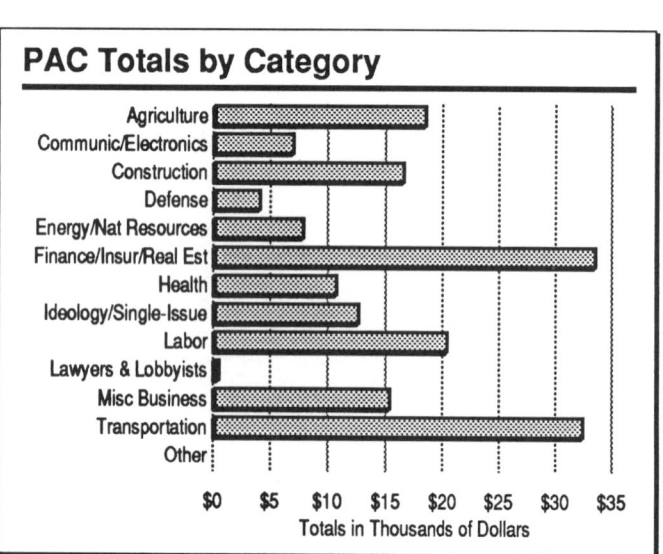

Agriculture
Communic/Electronics
Construction
Defense
Energy/Nat Resources
Finance/Insur/Real Est
Health
Ideology/Single-Issue
Labor
Lawyers & Lobbyists
Misc Business
Transportation
Other

$0 $5 $10 $15 $20 $25 $30 $35
Totals in Thousands of Dollars

Pharmaceuticals $4,500
Schering-Plough Corp $2,100
Pfizer Inc..$1,000
Others $1,400

Real Estate $7,400
National Assn of Realtors.............................$6,300
Mortgage Bankers Assn of America.................$1,100

Telecommunications $3,800
AT&T $1,500
South Central Bell Telephone $1,500
Others $800

Tobacco $4,250
Philip Morris $1,500
Tobacco Institute $1,100
Others $1,650

Trucking Companies $2,200
None over $800

Other Major Business PACs

Printing Industries of America $1,816	Printing
American Assn of Equipment Lessors $1,500	Rentals
Maytag Company $1,500	Appliances
American Coml Barge Line Company $1,000	SeaTransport
Computer Dealers & Lessors Assn $1,000	Computers

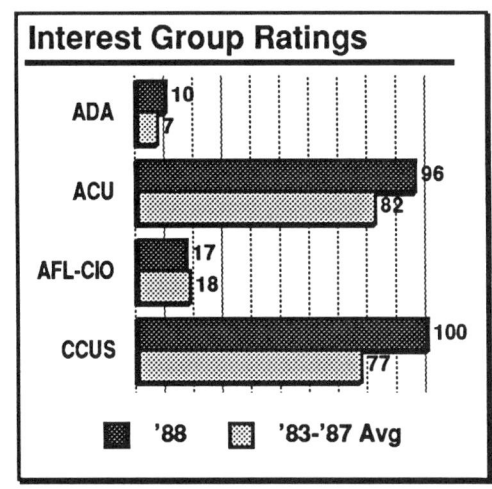

Interest Group Ratings

	'88	'83-'87 Avg
ADA	10	7
ACU	96	82
AFL-CIO	17	18
CCUS	100	77

Labor

Government & Postal Workers $6,900
National Assn of Retired Federal Employees $3,500
National Assn of Letter Carriers $1,500
National Assn of Postmasters $1,000
Others $900

Transportation Unions $13,300
Marine Engineers Union* $5,000
Air Line Pilots Assn...$3,500
Teamsters Union $3,000
Seafarers International Union.........................$1,000
Others $800

Ideological/Single-Issue

Pro-Israel $6,500
National PAC $5,000
Tennesseans for Better Government $1,500

Other Major Ideological/Single-Issue PACs

National Rifle Assn $2,300	Pro-Guns
Council for National Defense $2,010	Pro-Defense

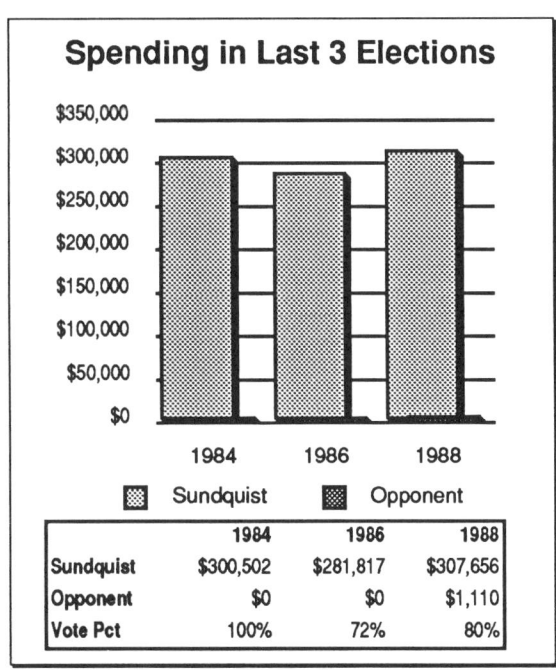

Spending in Last 3 Elections

Sundquist / Opponent

	1984	1986	1988
Sundquist	$300,502	$281,817	$307,656
Opponent	$0	$0	$1,110
Vote Pct	100%	72%	80%

---

* Contributions came from more than one PAC affiliated with this sponsor.

Al Swift, D-Wash (2)

1988 Committees & Subcommittees

Energy and Commerce
Energy and Power
Telecommunications and Finance

House Administration
Elections (Chairman)
Accounts
Libraries and Memorials

First elected: 1978
Total receipts: $376,189
Total from PACs: $286,312

Campaign Revenue Sources

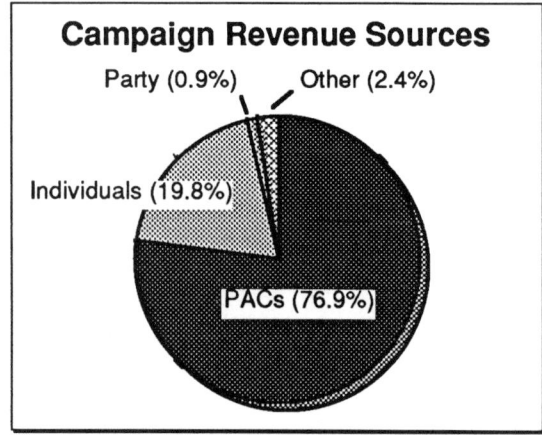

Party (0.9%)　Other (2.4%)
Individuals (19.8%)
PACs (76.9%)

PAC Contribution Profile

Business

Accountants	**$9,600**
American Institute of CPA's	$5,000
Touche Ross	$2,600
Coopers & Lybrand	$1,200
Others	$800
Automotive	**$6,400**
Auto Dealers & Drivers for Free Trade	$2,500
Ford Motor Company	$1,200
General Motors	$1,200
Others	$1,500
Commercial & Savings Banks	**$18,225**
American Bankers Assn	$2,300
Citicorp	$2,000
J P Morgan & Company	$2,000
US Bancorp	$2,000
Washington Mutual Savings Bank	$1,550
Barnett Banks of Florida	$1,000
Security Pacific Corp	$1,000
Washington Savings League	$1,000
Others	$5,375
Electric Utilities	**$10,850**
Southern California Edison	$2,100
Puget Sound Power & Light	$1,800
ACRE (Action Committee for Rural Electrification)	$1,500
Others	$5,450
Forest Products	**$5,075**
Georgia-Pacific Corp	$1,700
Others	$3,375

Health Professionals	**$8,500**
American Dental Assn	$2,000
Washington Medical Assn	$1,500
American Medical Assn	$1,300
American College of Emergency Physicians	$1,000
Cmte for Quality Orthopedic Health Care	$1,000
Others	$1,700
Lawyers & Lobbyists	**$15,450**
Assn of Trial Lawyers of America	$5,000
Verner, Liipfert, Bernhard & McPherson	$1,800
Garvey, Schubert & Barer	$1,650
Preston, Thorgrimson, Ellis & Holman	$1,000
Others	$6,000
Mining	**$5,100**
Independent Coal Operators Assn	$1,000
National Coal Assn	$1,000
Others	$3,100
Oil & Gas	**$12,825**
Burlington Northern	$1,725
Atlantic Richfield	$1,600
Michigan Consolidated Gas	$1,600
Columbia Gas*	$1,000
Others	$6,900
Securities/Commodities Investment	**$19,857**
Dean Witter Reynolds	$3,307
First Boston Corp	$3,000
Investment Company Institute	$2,600
E F Hutton Group	$1,900
Securities Industry Assn	$1,200
Goldman Sachs	$1,100
Chicago Board of Options Exchange	$1,000
Morgan Stanley & Company	$1,000
Others	$4,750

PAC Totals by Category

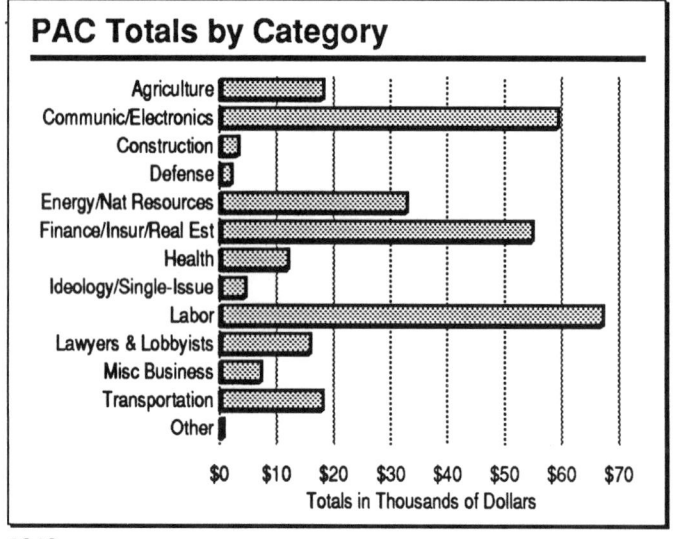

Totals in Thousands of Dollars

Agriculture
Communic/Electronics
Construction
Defense
Energy/Nat Resources
Finance/Insur/Real Est
Health
Ideology/Single-Issue
Labor
Lawyers & Lobbyists
Misc Business
Transportation
Other

$0　$10　$20　$30　$40　$50　$60　$70

Telecommunications $40,075

Pacific Telesis Group	$4,900
BellSouth Corp	$4,100
Pacific Northwest Bell	$3,975
AT&T	$3,500
Bell Atlantic	$2,900
Ameritech Corp	$2,400
United Telecommunications*	$2,100
Continental Telecom	$2,050
NYNEX Corp	$1,700
GTE Corp	$1,300
Comsat	$1,200
National Telephone Co-op Assn	$1,200
Competitive Telecom Assn	$1,100
Southwestern Bell	$1,100
Corning Glass Works	$1,000
DSC Communications Corp	$1,000
International Telecharge Inc	$1,000
Others	$3,550

Television/Entertainment $16,900

National Cable Television Assn	$5,000
National Assn of Broadcasters	$3,000
Assn of Independent TV Stations	$2,800
Tele-Communications Inc	$2,400
Turner Broadcasting System	$1,000
Others	$2,700

Other Major Business PACs

National Assn of Realtors	$3,425	Real Estate
Associated Milk Producers	$3,000	Dairy
Boeing Company	$2,600	Aircraft
National Assn of Home Builders	$1,800	Resid Constr
United Parcel Service	$1,500	Delivery
Waste Management Inc	$1,500	Waste Mgmt
Westinghouse Electric	$1,400	NuclearEquip
Mid-American Dairymen	$1,100	Dairy
National Assn of Life Underwriters	$1,000	Life Insurance
Paccar Inc	$1,000	Truck Mfrs
Pfizer Inc	$1,000	Pharmaceut
Philip Morris	$1,000	Tobacco

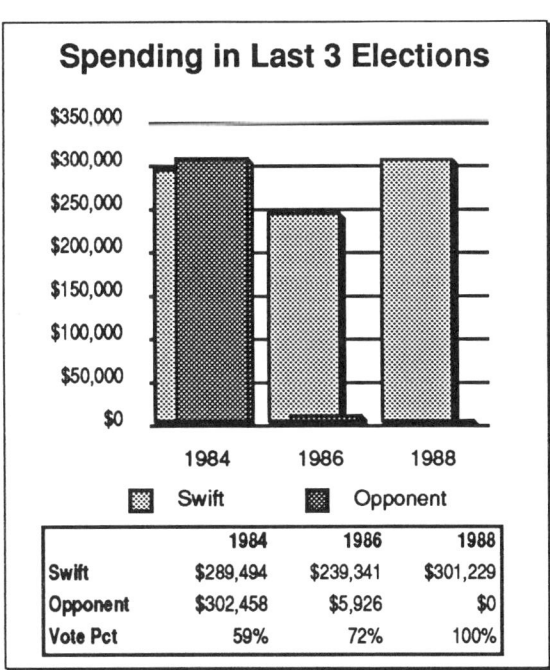

Spending in Last 3 Elections

	1984	1986	1988
Swift	$289,494	$239,341	$301,229
Opponent	$302,458	$5,926	$0
Vote Pct	59%	72%	100%

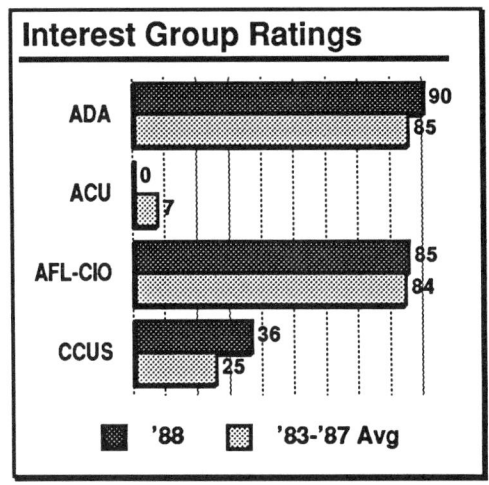

Interest Group Ratings

	'88	'83-'87 Avg
ADA	90	85
ACU	0	7
AFL-CIO	85	84
CCUS	36	25

Labor

Bldg Trades/Industrial/Misc Unions $29,550

Food & Commercial Workers Union	$5,300
National Education Assn	$4,000
Carpenters & Joiners Union	$2,600
Operating Engineers Union*	$2,600
Intl Brotherhood of Electrical Workers	$2,500
Communications Workers of America	$2,400
United Auto Workers	$2,100
Oil, Chemical & Atomic Workers Union	$1,800
Machinists/Aerospace Workers Union	$1,600
Laborers' Political League	$1,500
Hotel/Restaurant Employees Union	$1,100
Others	$2,050

Government & Postal Workers $14,000

National Assn of Retired Federal Employees	$5,000
American Fedn of State/County/Munic Employees	$2,000
National Assn of Letter Carriers	$2,000
National Rural Letter Carriers Assn	$1,500
National Treasury Employees Union	$1,400
Others	$2,100

Transportation Unions $22,925

Teamsters Union	$10,000
Marine Engineers Union	$2,500
United Transportation Union	$2,400
Seafarers International Union	$2,325
Maintenance of Way Employees	$1,200
Air Line Pilots Assn	$1,000
Others	$3,500

Major Ideological/Single-Issue PACs

Valley Education Fund (Tony Coelho)	$2,000	Dem Leaders
KidsPAC	$1,000	HealthWelfare

Independent expenditures supporting Swift

National Cmte to Preserve Social Security	$4,699

Independent expenditures opposing Swift

Life Amendment PAC	$1,725

---

* Contributions came from more than one PAC affiliated with this sponsor.

Mike Synar, D-Okla (2)

First elected: 1978
Total receipts: $310,865
Total from PACs: $0

1988 Committees & Subcommittees

Energy and Commerce
Energy and Power
Telecommunications and Finance

Government Operations
Environment, Energy and Natural Resources (Chairman)

Judiciary
Courts, Civil Liberties and the Administration of Justice
Criminal Justice

Select Aging
Health and Long-Term Care
Retirement Income and Employment

PAC Contribution Profile

Chemical Bank	$300	Comml Banks
Fluor Corp	$250	Comml Constr
Limited Inc	$250	ClothesStore
Southern Minnesota Beet Sugar Co-op	$100	Sugar
Sierra Club	$12	Environment

NOTE: Synar reported taking no PAC funds in his 1988 campaign. The PACs listed above did report making contributions to him during 1987-88, however, and those contributions are recorded in the official FEC records.

Independent expenditures supporting Synar

National Cmte to Preserve Social Security $2,635

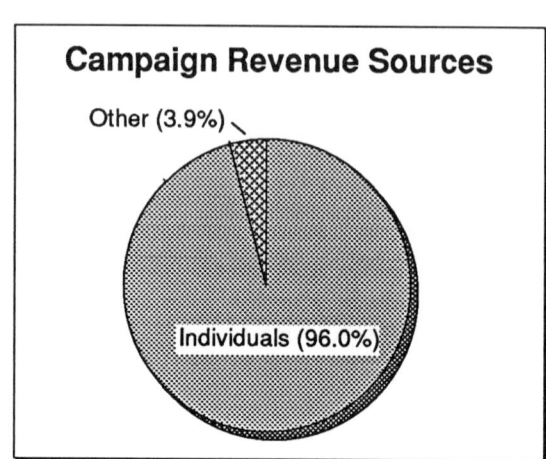

Campaign Revenue Sources

Other (3.9%)
Individuals (96.0%)

PAC Totals by Category

The candidate reported no PAC contributions in his 1988 campaign.

Agriculture	
Communic/Electronics	
Construction	
Defense	
Energy/Nat Resources	
Finance/Insur/Real Est	
Health	
Ideology/Single-Issue	
Labor	
Lawyers & Lobbyists	
Misc Business	
Transportation	
Other	

$0 $1 $2 $3 $4 $5 $6 $7 $8 $9 $10

Totals in Thousands of Dollars

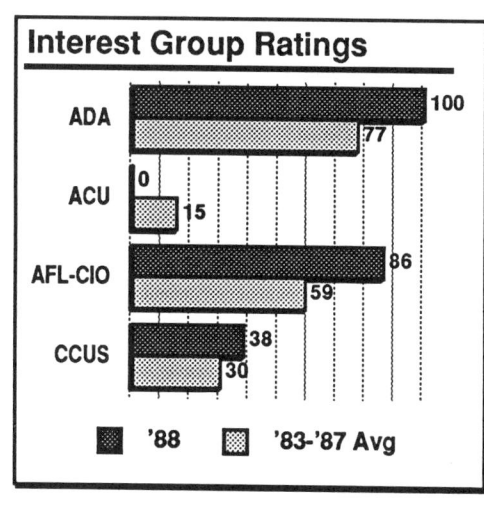

Interest Group Ratings

	ADA	ACU	AFL-CIO	CCUS
'88	100	0	86	38
'83-'87 Avg	77	15	59	30

■ '88   ▦ '83-'87 Avg

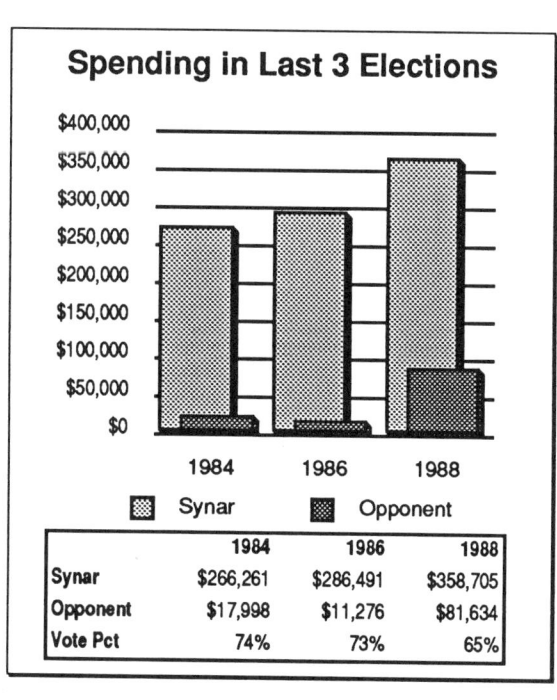

Spending in Last 3 Elections

▦ Synar   ■ Opponent

	1984	1986	1988
Synar	$266,261	$286,491	$358,705
Opponent	$17,998	$11,276	$81,634
Vote Pct	74%	73%	65%

Robin Tallon, D-SC (6)

1988 Committees & Subcommittees

Agriculture
Conservation, Credit and Rural Development
Cotton, Rice and Sugar
Tobacco and Peanuts

Merchant Marine and Fisheries
Merchant Marine
Oceanography

PAC Contribution Profile

Business

Auto Dealers	***$6,400***
National Auto Dealers Assn	$6,400
Commodities Trading	***$4,100***
Chicago Mercantile Exchange	$1,300
Chicago Board of Options Exchange	$1,000
Chicago Board of Trade	$1,000
Others	$800
Construction	***$6,350***
National Assn of Home Builders	$3,000
Associated General Contractors	$1,900
Others	$1,450
Dairy	***$5,500***
Associated Milk Producers	$2,500
Dairymen Inc	$1,700
Mid-American Dairymen	$1,300
Electric Utilities	***$5,500***
ACRE (Action Committee for Rural Electrification)	$2,100
Duke Power Company	$1,350
Carolina Power & Light	$1,250
Others	$800
Financial Institutions	***$13,050***
Citizens & Southern Corp*	$3,800
American Bankers Assn	$2,500
South Carolina National Bank	$2,000
Barnett Banks of Florida	$1,000
Others	$3,750

Food & Beverage	***$10,850***
Food Marketing Institute	$1,700
ConAgra Inc	$1,400
American Meat Institute	$1,200
Joseph E Seagram & Sons	$1,000
National Restaurant Assn	$1,000
Others	$4,550
Forest Products	***$6,450***
Westvaco Corp	$3,000
International Paper Company	$1,000
Willamette Industries	$1,000
Others	$1,450
Health Professionals	***$12,187***
American Medical Assn	$9,387
American Dental Assn	$1,500
American Academy of Ophthalmology	$1,000
Others	$300
Oil & Gas	***$5,421***
None over $900	
Real Estate	***$7,000***
National Assn of Realtors	$6,200
Others	$800
Sea Transport	***$7,150***
American Pilots Assn	$1,800
Boat Owners Assn of the US	$1,200
Others	$4,150
Sugar Growers	***$4,500***
American Crystal Sugar Corp	$1,600
American Sugarbeet Growers Assn	$1,200
Others	$1,700
Telecommunications	***$6,050***
Southern Bell	$3,600
AT&T	$1,700
Others	$750
Tobacco	***$11,650***
Philip Morris	$5,000
RJR Nabisco	$4,000
Tobacco Institute	$1,200
Others	$1,450

First elected: 1982
Total receipts: $381,464
Total from PACs: $203,958

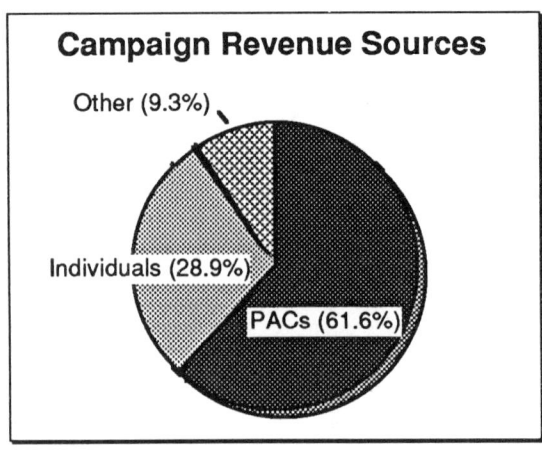

Campaign Revenue Sources

Other (9.3%)
Individuals (28.9%)
PACs (61.6%)

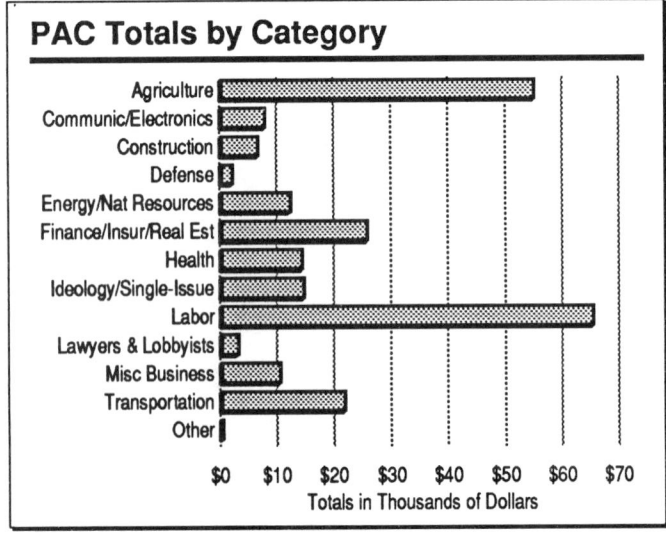

PAC Totals by Category

Agriculture
Communic/Electronics
Construction
Defense
Energy/Nat Resources
Finance/Insur/Real Est
Health
Ideology/Single-Issue
Labor
Lawyers & Lobbyists
Misc Business
Transportation
Other

$0 $10 $20 $30 $40 $50 $60 $70

Totals in Thousands of Dollars

Other Major Business PACs

Assn of Trial Lawyers of America ....$2,000   Lawyers
United Parcel Service.......................................$1,550   Delivery
National Cotton Council ....$1,500   Cotton
National Assn of Life Underwriters ....$1,500   Life Insurance
Springs Mills ....$1,500   Textiles
Transouth Financial Corp.................................$1,500   Credit/Loans
National Tour Brokers Assn ....$1,300   Travel Agent
Norfolk Southern Corp ....$1,300   Railroads
Aircraft Owners & Pilots Assn ....$1,200   GenlAviation
American Cotton Shippers Assn ....$1,200   Cotton
American Textile Manufacturers Institute ....$1,100   Textiles
FMC Corp ....$1,100   Ag Chemicals

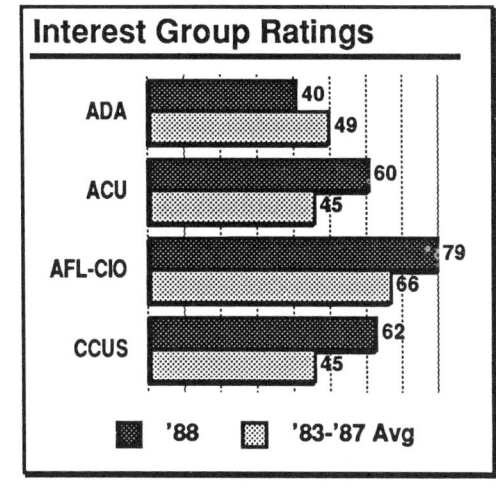

Interest Group Ratings

	'88	'83-'87 Avg
ADA	40	49
ACU	60	45
AFL-CIO	79*	66
CCUS	62	45

Labor

Bldg Trades/Industrial/Misc Unions	$20,300
United Steelworkers	$5,000
National Education Assn	$3,400
Food & Commercial Workers Union	$3,100
AFL-CIO	$1,500
Carpenters & Joiners Union	$1,400
Machinists/Aerospace Workers Union	$1,200
Bakery, Confectionery & Tobacco Workers	$1,000
Others	$3,700

Government & Postal Workers	$14,100
National Assn of Retired Federal Employees	$7,000
National Assn of Letter Carriers	$3,600
American Postal Workers Union	$1,500
Others	$2,000

Sea Transport Unions	$15,500
Marine Engineers Union*	$8,500
Masters, Mates & Pilots Union	$5,000
Seafarers International Union	$2,000

Other Transportation Unions	$15,150
Teamsters Union	$10,000
United Transportation Union	$1,500
Transportation Communication Union	$1,200
Air Line Pilots Assn	$1,000
Others	$1,450

Ideological/Single-Issue

Pro-Israel	$7,500
National PAC	$5,000
Hudson Valley PAC	$1,000
South Carolinians for Representative Government	$1,000
Others	$500

Other Major Ideological/Single-Issue PACs

National Rifle Assn ....$1,900   Pro-Guns
Citizens for a Competitive America (Hollings) .$1,000   Dem Leaders
House Leadership Fund (Tom Foley) ....$1,000   Dem Leaders
Majority Congress Committee (Jim Wright) .....$1,000   Dem Leaders

Independent expenditures supporting Tallon

National Cmte to Preserve Social Security $2,142

Spending in Last 3 Elections

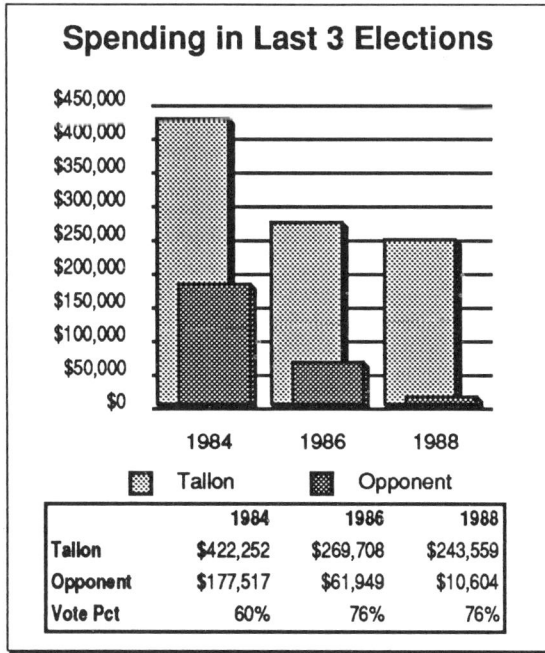

	1984	1986	1988
Tallon	$422,252	$269,708	$243,559
Opponent	$177,517	$61,949	$10,604
Vote Pct	60%	76%	76%

* Contributions came from more than one PAC affiliated
with this sponsor.

John Tanner, D-Tenn (8)

First elected: 1988
Total receipts: $931,539
Total from PACs: $283,861

1989-90 Committees & Subcommittees

Armed Services
Investigations
Readiness

Science, Space and Technology
Investigations and Oversight
Natural Resources, Agriculture Research and Environment
Space Science and Applications

PAC Contribution Profile

Business

Automotive **$7,000**
- National Auto Dealers Assn $5,000
- Auto Dealers & Drivers for Free Trade $1,000
- Others $1,000

Commercial Banks **$14,450**
- First American Corp $3,500
- Third National Corp $2,500
- American Bankers Assn $2,000
- First Tennessee National Corp $2,000
- Sovran Bank $1,500
- Citicorp $1,000
- Others $1,950

Construction **$11,050**
- National Assn of Home Builders $6,000
- Tennessee Road Builders Assn $2,000
- Associated General Contractors $1,000
- Others $2,050

Dairy **$11,750**
- Dairymen Inc-Tennessee $5,000
- Associated Milk Producers $4,500
- Mid-American Dairymen $2,000
- Others $250

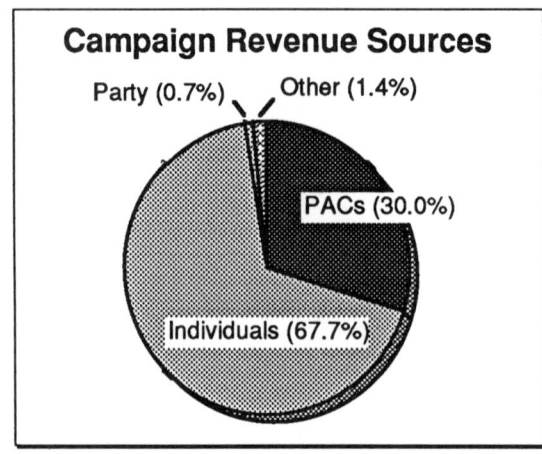

Campaign Revenue Sources

- Party (0.7%)
- Other (1.4%)
- PACs (30.0%)
- Individuals (67.7%)

Food & Beverage **$19,542**
- Malone & Hyde Inc $8,000
- Shoneys Inc $2,000
- Hardee's Food Systems $1,000
- Kroger Company $1,000
- McDonald's Corp $1,000
- National Beer Wholesalers Assn $1,000
- Pepsico Inc $1,000
- Winn-Dixie Stores $1,000
- Others $3,542

Health Professionals **$8,400**
- American Medical Assn $5,000
- American Dental Assn $1,000
- American Optometric Assn $1,000
- Others $1,400

Hospitals & Nursing Homes **$3,450**
- National Health Corp $2,500
- Others $950

Insurance **$12,523**
- National Assn of Life Underwriters $5,000
- Independent Insurance Agents of America $2,000
- Provident Life & Accident Insurance $1,500
- National Assn Mutual Insurance Agents $1,250
- Others $2,773

Lawyers & Lobbyists **$11,000**
- Assn of Trial Lawyers of America $8,000
- Williams & Jensen $1,250
- Vinson, Elkins, Searls, Connally & Smith $1,000
- Others $750

Oil & Gas **$8,350**
- Tenneco Inc $3,500
- Phillips Petroleum $1,000
- Others $3,850

Package Delivery **$10,000**
- Federal Express Corp $10,000

Real Estate **$11,750**
- National Assn of Realtors $10,000
- Mortgage Bankers Assn of America $1,000
- Others $750

PAC Totals by Category

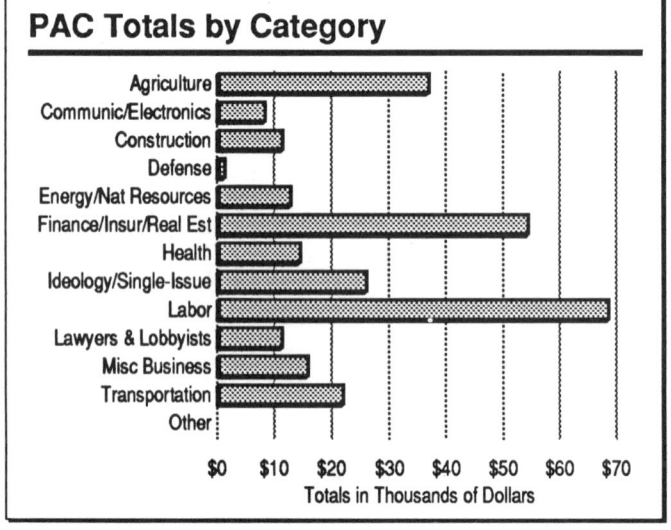

Totals in Thousands of Dollars

Agriculture
Communic/Electronics
Construction
Defense
Energy/Nat Resources
Finance/Insur/Real Est
Health
Ideology/Single-Issue
Labor
Lawyers & Lobbyists
Misc Business
Transportation
Other

$0 $10 $20 $30 $40 $50 $60 $70

Retail Sales $4,257
        Southland Corp $1,007
        Others $3,250

Savings Banks $11,500
        Tenn League of Savings Institutions $6,500
        Leader Federal Savings & Loan $2,500
        US League of Savings Assn $1,000
        Others $1,500

Telecommunications $6,750
        AT&T..$2,000
        South Central Bell Telephone $2,000
        Continental Telecom $1,000
        United Telecommunications $1,000
        Others $750

Other Major Business PACs

Westvaco Corp ....$2,000   Paper&Pulp
Schering-Plough Corp ....$1,750   Pharmaceut
American Trucking Assns ....$1,305   Trucking
ACRE (Action Committee for Rural Electric) ...$1,000   RuralElect
Alabama Power Company ....$1,000   Elec Util
Browning-Ferris Industries ....$1,000   Waste Mgmt
Dean Witter Reynolds ....$1,000   StocksInvest
Eastern Airlines ....$1,000   Airlines
Eastman Kodak/Chemicals Division ...$1,000   Chemicals
National Assn of Temporary Services ...$1,000   EmployAgency
National Fedn of Independent Business ...$1,000   Sml Business
Philip Morris ....$1,000   Tobacco
RJR Nabisco ....$1,000   Tobacco
Tyson Foods ....$1,000   Poultry/Egg

Spending in Last Election

	1988
Tanner	$863,425
Opponent	$106,028
Vote Pct	62%

Labor

Bldg Trades/Industrial/Misc Unions $28,000
        United Auto Workers $10,000
        Machinists/Aerospace Workers Union $5,000
        Communications Workers of America $4,000
        Carpenters & Joiners Union $2,000
        Laborers' Political League $1,500
        AFL-CIO..$1,000
        Intl Brotherhood of Electrical Workers $1,000
        Operating Engineers Union $1,000
        Rubber Cork Linoleum Plastic Workers $1,000
        Others $1,500

Government & Postal Workers $11,750
        National Assn of Letter Carriers $7,500
        National Assn of Retired Federal Employees $2,000
        American Postal Workers Union $1,000
        Others $1,250

Teachers Unions $10,000
        National Education Assn $10,000

Transportation Unions $18,500
        Teamsters Union $10,000
        Air Line Pilots Assn..$2,500
        Seafarers International Union $2,000
        Amalgamated Transit Union $1,500
        Marine Engineers District 2 Maritime Officers ...$1,000
        United Transportation Union $1,000
        Others $500

Ideological/Single-Issue

Democratic Leadership PACs $14,000
        Valley Education Fund (Tony Coelho) $6,000
        Majority Congress Committee (Jim Wright) $3,000
        Conservative Democratic PAC (Charles Stenholm) $2,000
        America's Leaders' Fund (Dan Rostenkowski) $1,000
        Cmte for Democratic Opportunity (Bill Gray) $1,000
        House Leadership Fund (Tom Foley) $1,000

Other Major Ideological/Single-Issue PACs

National Cmte to Preserve Social Security ......$5,000   Soc Secur
National Rifle Assn ....$4,950   Pro-Guns

Tom Tauke, R-Iowa (2)

First elected: 1978
Total receipts: $601,558
Total from PACs: $290,210

1988 Committees & Subcommittees

Education and Labor
Human Resources (Ranking Republican)
Postsecondary Education

Energy and Commerce
Health and the Environment
Telecommunications and Finance
Transportation, Tourism and Hazardous Materials

Select Aging
Retirement Income and Employment (Ranking Republican)

PAC Contribution Profile

Business

Accountants	**$8,000**
American Institute of CPA's	$5,000
Touche Ross	$2,000
Others	$1,000
Automotive	**$8,650**
National Auto Dealers Assn	$5,000
Auto Dealers & Drivers for Free Trade	$2,500
Others	$1,150
Commercial Banks	**$20,400**
American Bankers Assn	$7,500
J P Morgan & Company	$5,000
Hawkeye Bancorp	$3,000
Norwest Corp	$2,000
Barnett Banks of Florida	$1,000
Others	$1,900
Construction	**$11,050**
Sheet Metal/AirCon Contractors	$2,500
Assoc General Contractors/Iowa	$1,500
Associated General Contractors	$1,300
American Supply Assn	$1,000
Lennox Industries	$1,000
National Electrical Contractors Assn	$1,000
Others	$2,750
Dairy	**$9,000**
Associated Milk Producers	$6,000
Mid-American Dairymen	$1,500
Land O'Lakes Inc	$1,000
Others	$500

Campaign Revenue Sources

Party (0.7%)   Other (2.7%)
PACs (48.2%)
Individuals (48.3%)

Electric Utilities	**$9,450**
Midwest Energy Company	$2,500
Interstate Power Company	$1,100
Iowa Electric Light & Power	$1,000
Iowa Resources Inc	$1,000
Others	$3,850
Food & Beverage	**$15,050**
General Mills*	$2,000
National Restaurant Assn	$2,000
Hy-Vee Food Stores	$1,500
Nabisco Brands Inc	$1,500
Food Marketing Institute	$1,300
American Bakers Assn	$1,000
McDonald's Corp	$1,000
National Beer Wholesalers Assn	$1,000
Pepsi-Cola Bottlers Assn	$1,000
Others	$2,750
Health Professionals	**$27,711**
American Medical Assn	$8,761
American Dental Assn	$3,500
American Physical Therapy Assn	$3,000
American Optometric Assn	$2,800
American Academy of Ophthalmology	$2,000
American Podiatry Assn	$2,000
American College of Emergency Physicians	$1,500
National Assn of Pharmacists	$1,000
Others	$3,150
Hospitals & Nursing Homes	**$8,900**
American Health Care Assn	$5,500
Manor Healthcare Corp	$1,000
Others	$2,400
Insurance	**$22,350**
National Assn of Life Underwriters	$7,000
Casualty & Surety Agents Assn	$1,400
Health Insurance Assn of America	$1,400
Principal Mutual Life Insurance	$1,250
Blue Cross & Blue Shield Assn	$1,000
Others	$10,300

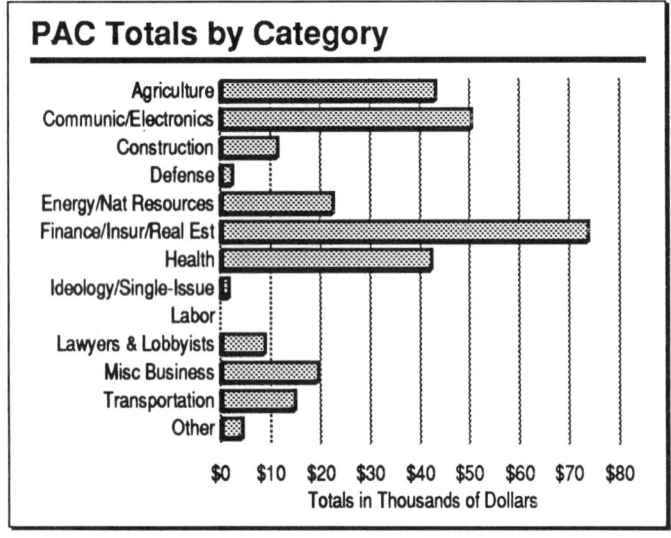

PAC Totals by Category

- Agriculture
- Communic/Electronics
- Construction
- Defense
- Energy/Nat Resources
- Finance/Insur/Real Est
- Health
- Ideology/Single-Issue
- Labor
- Lawyers & Lobbyists
- Misc Business
- Transportation
- Other

$0 $10 $20 $30 $40 $50 $60 $70 $80
Totals in Thousands of Dollars

Lawyers $8,450
    Assn of Trial Lawyers of America $5,000
    Others $3,450

Oil & Gas $8,950
    Dow Chemical* $1,000
    Petroleum Marketers Assn $1,000
    Sun Company $1,000
    Williams Companies $1,000
    Others $4,950

Real Estate $7,125
    National Assn of Realtors $5,625
    Century 21 Real Estate $1,000
    Others $500

Savings Banks & Credit Unions $5,600
    US League of Savings Assns* $4,900
    Others $700

Securities/Commodities Trading $11,350
    Chicago Board of Trade $1,000
    First Boston Corp $1,000
    Goldman Sachs $1,000
    Investment Company Institute $1,000
    Morgan Stanley & Company $1,000
    Travelers Corp $1,000
    Others $5,350

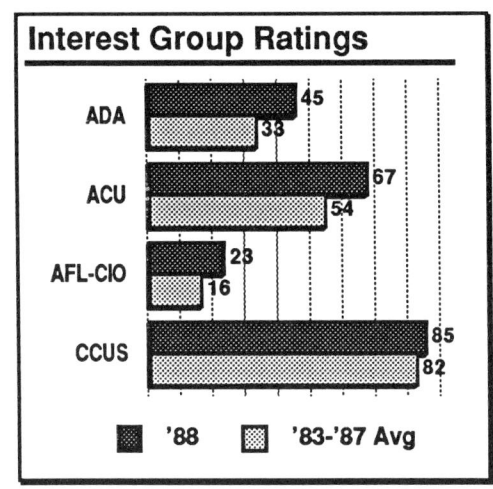

Interest Group Ratings

	'88	'83-'87 Avg
ADA	45	33
ACU	67	54
AFL-CIO	23	16
CCUS	85	82

Telecommunications $39,750
    North Western Bell Telephone $4,000
    BellSouth* $3,000
    Continental Telecom $3,000
    Pacific Telesis Group $3,000
    US Telephone Assn $3,000
    Ameritech Corp $2,000
    Bell Atlantic $2,000
    US West Inc $2,000
    United Telecommunications $2,000
    NYNEX Corp $1,800
    Southwestern Bell $1,800
    GTE Corp $1,750
    AT&T $1,500
    Michigan Bell Telephone $1,500
    DSC Communications Corp $1,000
    Palmer Communications $1,000
    Others $5,400

Television/Cable TV $7,000
    National Assn of Broadcasters $2,300
    National Cable Television Assn $2,000
    Assn of Independent TV Stations $1,100
    Others $1,600

Other Major Business PACs

Deere & Company	$4,000	Farm Equip
Iowa Farm Bureau Federation	$2,700	Farm Orgs
Maytag Company	$2,500	Appliances
Philip Morris	$2,500	Tobacco
Printing Industries of America	$2,300	Printing
American Veterinary Medical Assn	$1,500	Veterinary
Square D Company	$1,500	Indust Equip
Cargill Inc	$1,000	Grain Trader
Dun & Bradstreet	$1,000	Mkt Research
Farmland Industries	$1,000	Ag Svcs
Health Industry Manufacturers Assn	$1,000	Med Supply
National Coal Assn	$1,000	Coal
National Assn of Trade/Tech Schools	$1,000	Voc Tech
National Council of Farmer Co-ops	$1,000	Farm Orgs

Major Ideological/Single-Issue PACs

Constitution Club	$2,000	Unknown

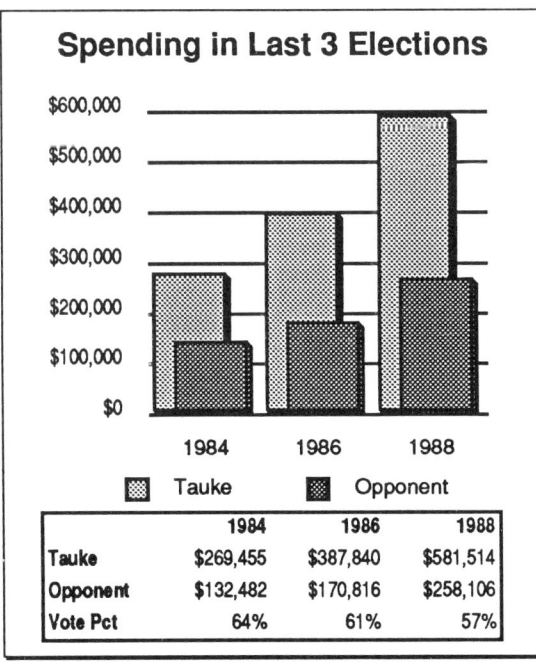

Spending in Last 3 Elections

	Tauke	Opponent

	1984	1986	1988
Tauke	$269,455	$387,840	$581,514
Opponent	$132,482	$170,816	$258,106
Vote Pct	64%	61%	57%

---

* Contributions came from more than one PAC affiliated
with this sponsor.

W. J. "Billy" Tauzin, D-La (3)

First elected: 1980
Total receipts: $347,890
Total from PACs: $263,228

1988 Committees & Subcommittees

Energy and Commerce
Energy and Power
Telecommunications and Finance
Transportation, Tourism and Hazardous Materials

Merchant Marine and Fisheries
Panama Canal/Outer Continental Shelf (Chairman)
Fisheries and Wildlife Conservation and the Environment

PAC Contribution Profile

Business

Accountants	**$7,400**
American Institute of CPA's	$5,000
Others	$2,400
Automotive	**$6,900**
National Auto Dealers Assn	$5,000
Others	$1,900
Broadcasting/Entertainment	**$5,770**
National Assn of Broadcasters	$2,370
National Cable Television Assn	$1,000
Others	$2,400
Chemicals	**$5,000**
Monsanto Company	$1,500
Others	$3,500
Commercial Banks	**$9,010**
American Bankers Assn	$2,500
J P Morgan & Company	$2,000
Others	$4,510
Defense	**$8,700**
Martin Marietta Corp	$5,000
Gencorp Inc	$2,000
Others	$1,700
Electric Utilities	**$24,598**
Middle South Utilities*	$10,750
Central Louisiana Electric	$3,000
ACRE (Action Committee for Rural Electrification)	$1,600
Public Service Company of NH/Yankee Division	$1,548
Others	$7,700

Campaign Revenue Sources

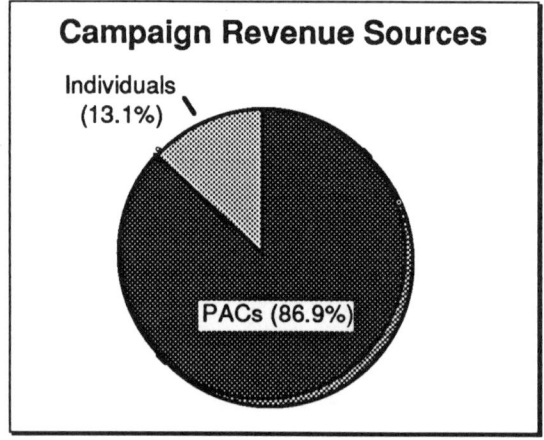

Individuals (13.1%)
PACs (86.9%)

Health Professionals	**$12,550**
National Assn of Pharmacists	$3,500
American Dental Assn	$2,500
American Academy of Ophthalmology	$1,500
Cmte for Quality Orthopedic Health Care	$1,500
Oral & Maxillofacial Surgeons	$1,500
Others	$2,050
Insurance	**$16,412**
National Assn of Life Underwriters	$5,000
Independent Insurance Agents of America	$2,500
Health Insurance Assn of America	$1,500
American Council of Life Insurance	$1,200
Aetna Life & Casualty	$1,175
Others	$5,037
Lawyers & Lobbyists	**$16,487**
Assn of Trial Lawyers of America	$10,000
Others	$6,487
Mining	**$8,600**
Freeport-McMoran Inc	$3,000
Peabody Coal	$2,000
Others	$3,600
Oil & Gas	**$46,500**
Pennzoil Company	$2,800
Columbia Hydrocarbon Corp	$2,700
Chevron Corp	$2,100
Atlantic Richfield	$2,000
Halliburton Company*	$2,000
Exxon Corp	$1,700
Michigan Consolidated Gas	$1,700
Petroleum Marketers Assn	$1,700
Shell Oil	$1,700
Amoco Corp	$1,500
Ashland Oil	$1,500
Occidental Petroleum*	$1,500
Internorth Inc	$1,200
BP America	$1,100
Others	$21,300
Real Estate	**$6,500**
National Assn of Realtors	$5,000
Others	$1,500
Sea Transport	**$8,337**
American Pilots Assn	$2,000
Others	$6,337

PAC Totals by Category

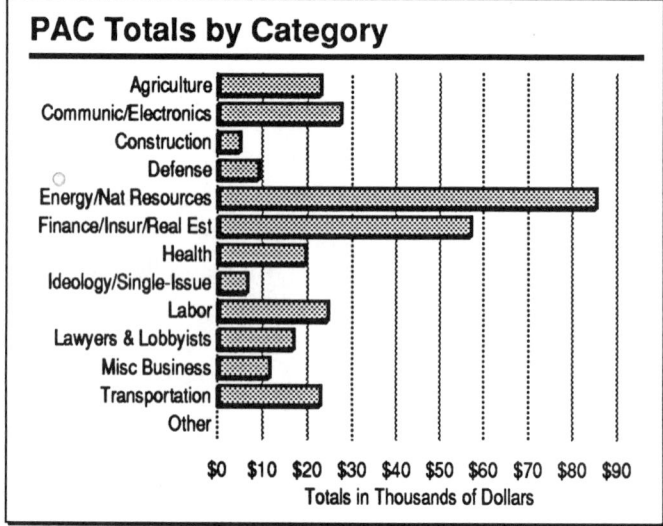

Agriculture
Communic/Electronics
Construction
Defense
Energy/Nat Resources
Finance/Insur/Real Est
Health
Ideology/Single-Issue
Labor
Lawyers & Lobbyists
Misc Business
Transportation
Other

$0 $10 $20 $30 $40 $50 $60 $70 $80 $90
Totals in Thousands of Dollars

Securities/Commodities Investment **$20,150**

Thomson McKinnon Securities	$4,000
Goldman Sachs	$3,000
Travelers Corp	$2,500
Chicago Board of Trade	$2,000
First Boston Corp	$2,000
Prudential-Bache Securities	$1,500
Securities Industry Assn	$1,200
Others	$3,950

Telecommunications **$21,350**

AT&T	$5,000
South Central Bell Telephone	$4,000
Continental Telecom	$2,000
US Telephone Assn	$1,500
Bell Atlantic	$1,400
Pacific Telesis Group	$1,400
Others	$6,050

Tobacco **$7,300**

Philip Morris	$3,500
RJR Nabisco	$1,500
Others	$2,300

Other Major Business PACs

International Paper Company	$2,000	Paper Prod
McDermott Inc	$2,000	PowerEquip
Westinghouse Electric	$1,870	NuclearEquip
Associated Milk Producers	$1,500	Dairy
General Mills*	$1,500	FoodProducts
National Medical Enterprises Inc	$1,500	Hospitals

Interest Group Ratings

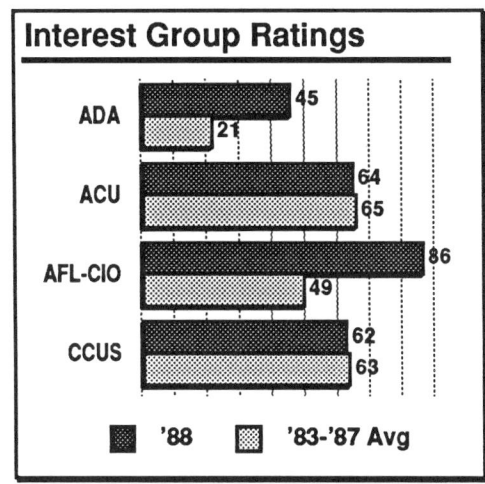

	'88	'83-'87 Avg
ADA	45	21
ACU	64	65
AFL-CIO	86	49
CCUS	62	63

■ '88   ▨ '83-'87 Avg

Labor

Sea Transport Unions **$14,700**

Marine Engineers Union*	$9,000
Masters, Mates & Pilots Union	$2,500
Seafarers International Union	$2,200
Others	$1,000

Other Unions **$9,369**

National Assn of Retired Federal Employees	$2,000
United Auto Workers	$2,000
National Assn of Letter Carriers	$1,625
National Education Assn	$1,200
Others	$2,544

Major Ideological/Single-Issue PACs

Louisiana for American Security	$2,500	Pro-Israel

Independent expenditures supporting Tauzin

National Cmte to Preserve Social Security	$1,696
Fleishman-Hillard	$1,500

Spending in Last 3 Elections

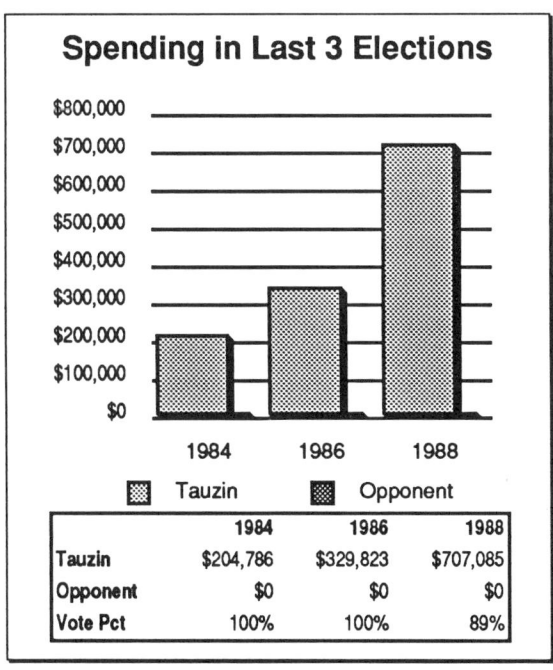

	1984	1986	1988
Tauzin	$204,786	$329,823	$707,085
Opponent	$0	$0	$0
Vote Pct	100%	100%	89%

---

* Contributions came from more than one PAC affiliated with this sponsor.

Bill Thomas, R-Calif (20)

First elected: 1978
Total receipts: $335,586
Total from PACs: $215,150

1988 Committees & Subcommittees

Budget
Budget Process
Economic and Trade Policy
Income Security

House Administration
Elections (Ranking Republican)
Office Systems(Ranking Republican)
Accounts

Ways and Means
Trade

PAC Contribution Profile

Business

Accountants	**$5,500**
American Institute of CPA's	$5,000
Others	$500
Automotive	**$3,750**
Auto Dealers & Drivers for Free Trade	$1,500
Others	$2,250
Construction	**$6,750**
Associated General Contractors	$2,500
Manville Corp	$1,000
National Assn of Home Builders	$1,000
National Electrical Contractors Assn	$1,000
Others	$1,250
Cotton	**$6,000**
National Cotton Council	$2,500
J G Boswell Company	$2,000
Calcot Ltd	$1,500
Defense	**$9,000**
Tenneco Inc	$2,000
Allied-Signal	$1,500
Others	$5,500
Electric Utilities	**$3,050**
Philadelphia Electric	$1,000
Southern California Edison	$1,000
Others	$1,050

Campaign Revenue Sources

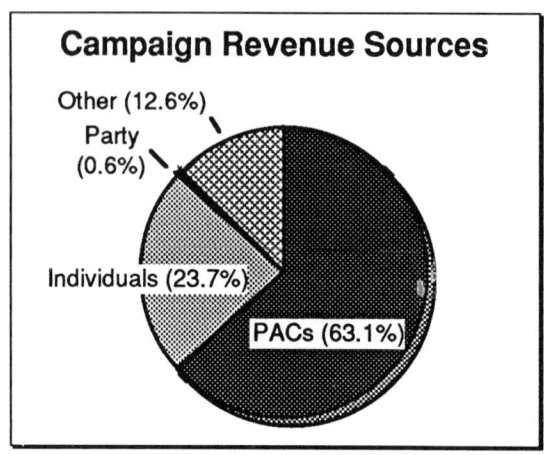

Other (12.6%)
Party (0.6%)
Individuals (23.7%)
PACs (63.1%)

Financial Institutions	**$9,250**
American Bankers Assn	$2,750
Credit Union National Assn	$2,000
BankAmerica	$1,000
California League of Savings Institutions	$1,000
Security Pacific Corp	$1,000
Others	$1,500
Food & Beverage	**$15,850**
Food Marketing Institute	$2,000
National Restaurant Assn	$2,000
National Beer Wholesalers Assn	$1,500
Wine & Spirits Wholesalers of America	$1,500
Wine Institute	$1,500
Kellogg Company	$1,000
Pepsico Inc	$1,000
Winn-Dixie Stores	$1,000
Others	$4,350
Fruit & Vegetable Growers	**$15,300**
California Almond Growers Exchange	$5,000
California Pistachio Assn	$3,000
Desert Grape Growers League/California	$2,000
Sun-Maid Growers of California	$1,000
Sunkist Growers	$1,000
Tri/Valley Growers	$1,000
Others	$2,300
Health Professionals	**$17,350**
American Medical Assn	$8,000
American Dental Assn	$4,000
Cmte for Quality Orthopedic Health Care	$1,500
American Academy of Ophthalmology	$1,000
American College of Emergency Physicians	$1,000
National Assn of Pharmacists	$1,000
Others	$850

PAC Totals by Category

Agriculture
Communic/Electronics
Construction
Defense
Energy/Nat Resources
Finance/Insur/Real Est
Health
Ideology/Single-Issue
Labor
Lawyers & Lobbyists
Misc Business
Transportation
Other

$0 $10 $20 $30 $40 $50 $60
Totals in Thousands of Dollars

Insurance **$19,150**
- TransAmerica Life Companies $3,150
- National Assn of Life Underwriters $2,000
- Torchmark Corp $2,000
- Health Insurance Assn of America $1,500
- Pacific Mutual Life $1,500
- Travelers Corp $1,500
- Chubb Corp $1,000
- Cigna Corp $1,000
- Independent Insurance Agents of America $1,000
- Others $4,500

Oil & Gas **$18,650**
- Shell Oil $2,200
- Chevron Corp $1,500
- Enserch Corp $1,500
- Internorth Inc $1,500
- Pacific Enterprises $1,300
- Independent Oil Producers Agency $1,200
- Atlantic Richfield $1,000
- Mobil Oil $1,000
- Sun Company $1,000
- Texaco $1,000
- Others $5,450

Pharmaceuticals **$4,500**
- Pfizer Inc $1,000
- Others $3,500

Real Estate **$18,250**
- National Assn of Realtors $10,000
- Century 21 Real Estate $5,000
- Mortgage Bankers Assn of America $1,000
- Others $2,250

Retail Sales **$4,100**
- Carter Hawley Hale Stores $1,000
- J C Penney Company $1,000
- International Council of Shopping Centers $1,000
- Others $1,100

Interest Group Ratings

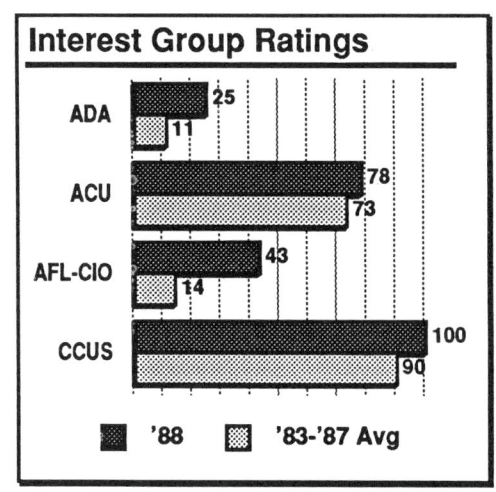

	'88	'83-'87 Avg
ADA	25	11
ACU	78	73
AFL-CIO	43	14
CCUS	100	90

Securities/Commodities Investment **$6,000**
- Chicago Board of Trade $1,000
- E F Hutton Group $1,000
- First Boston Corp $1,000
- Securities Industry Assn $1,000
- Others $2,000

Sugar Growers **$6,100**
- American Crystal Sugar Corp $2,800
- American Sugar Cane League $1,000
- Minn-Dak Farmers Co-op $1,000
- Others $1,300

Telecommunications **$9,500**
- AT&T $4,000
- Continental Telecom $2,250
- Pacific Telesis Group $2,000
- Others $1,250

Tobacco **$3,500**
- Philip Morris $2,500
- Tobacco Institute $1,000

Other Major Business PACs

American Hospital Assn	$1,500	Hospitals
FMC Corp	$1,500	Chemicals
General Electric	$1,500	Electronics
Alabama Farm Bureau Federation	$1,000	Farm Orgs
Computer Sciences Corp	$1,000	Data Process
H & R Block	$1,000	Tax Svcs
International Paper Company	$1,000	Paper Prod
Marriott Corp	$1,000	Hotel/Motel
Union Pacific Corp	$1,000	Railroads
United Parcel Service	$1,000	Delivery

Major Labor PACs

National Assn of Retired Federal Employees	$1,000	Fedl Workers

Spending in Last 3 Elections

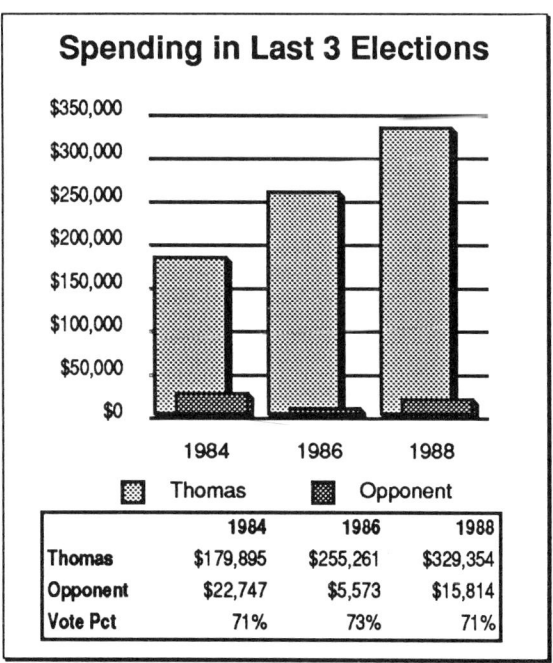

	Thomas	Opponent

	1984	1986	1988
Thomas	$179,895	$255,261	$329,354
Opponent	$22,747	$5,573	$15,814
Vote Pct	71%	73%	71%

Lindsay Thomas, D-Ga (1)

1988 Committees & Subcommittees

First elected: 1982
Total receipts: $339,987
Total from PACs: $149,969

Appropriations
Energy and Water Development
Military Construction

PAC Contribution Profile

Business

Automotive	**$8,300**
National Auto Dealers Assn	$4,100
Auto Dealers & Drivers for Free Trade	$2,500
Torrington Company	$1,000
Others	$700
Aviation & Aerospace	**$2,650**
Aircraft Owners & Pilots Assn	$1,600
Others	$1,050
Commercial Banks	**$14,270**
Citizens & Southern National Bank	$8,220
Barnett Banks of Florida	$1,500
First Atlanta Corp	$1,100
American Bankers Assn	$1,000
Georgia Bankers Assn	$1,000
Others	$1,450
Construction	**$4,350**
Associated General Contractors	$1,300
Manville Corp	$1,000
National Assn of Home Builders	$1,000
Others	$1,050
Dairy	**$5,500**
Dairymen Inc-Georgia	$2,400
Associated Milk Producers	$2,000
Others	$1,100
Defense	**$6,150**
Lockheed Corp	$3,750
Others	$2,400

Campaign Revenue Sources

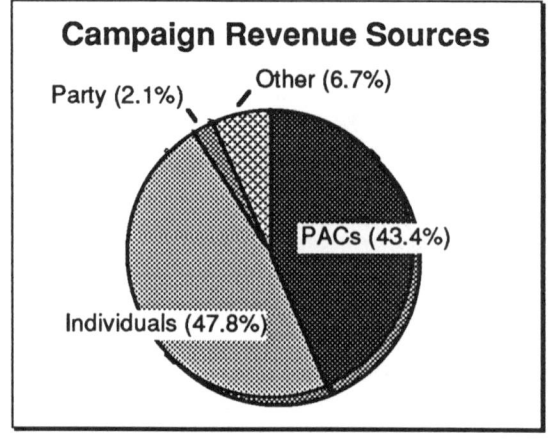

Party (2.1%)
Other (6.7%)
PACs (43.4%)
Individuals (47.8%)

Electric Utilities	**$5,300**
ACRE (Action Committee for Rural Electrification)	$3,000
Southern Company*	$2,000
Others	$300
Food & Beverage	**$7,000**
Coca-Cola Company	$2,000
American Meat Institute	$1,100
Others	$3,900
Forest Products	**$11,050**
Boise Cascade	$1,600
Stone Container Corp	$1,500
Westvaco Corp	$1,500
Union Camp Corp	$1,350
Mead Corp	$1,150
Others	$3,950
Health Professionals	**$7,800**
American Medical Assn	$6,000
American Dental Assn	$1,000
Others	$800
Insurance	**$3,300**
National Assn of Life Underwriters	$1,000
Others	$2,300
Oil & Gas	**$4,100**
Exxon Corp	$1,300
Atlanta Gas Light Company	$1,000
Others	$1,800
Real Estate	**$7,350**
National Assn of Realtors	$6,550
Others	$800
Sea Transport	**$3,100**
American Pilots Assn	$2,500
Others	$600
Sugar Growers	**$3,400**
Savannah Foods & Industries	$1,400
Others	$2,000
Telecommunications	**$7,600**
AT&T	$3,000
Southern Bell	$2,500
Continental Telecom	$1,500
Others	$600

PAC Totals by Category

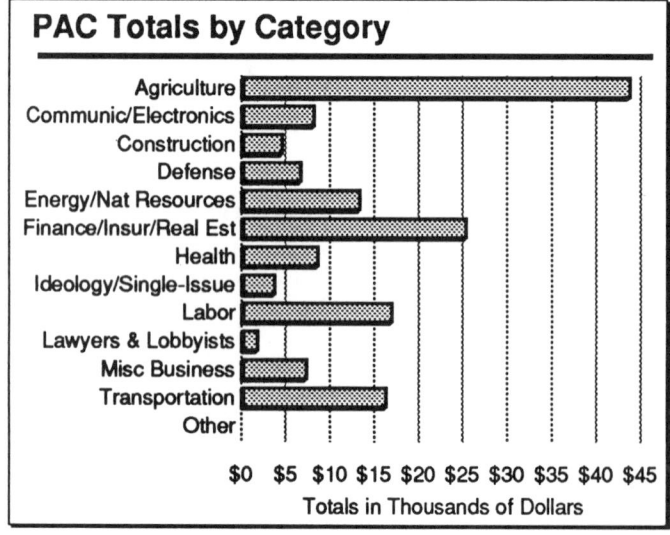

Agriculture
Communic/Electronics
Construction
Defense
Energy/Nat Resources
Finance/Insur/Real Est
Health
Ideology/Single-Issue
Labor
Lawyers & Lobbyists
Misc Business
Transportation
Other

$0 $5 $10 $15 $20 $25 $30 $35 $40 $45

Totals in Thousands of Dollars

Tobacco **$7,100**

> Philip Morris $3,200
> RJR Nabisco $2,000
> Others $1,900

Other Major Business PACs

Waste Management Inc $1,700	Waste Mgmt
Alabama Farm Bureau Federation $1,100	Farm Orgs
National Cotton Council $1,100	Cotton
Desert Grape Growers League/California $1,000	Fruit/Veg
King & Spalding $1,000	Lawyers

Interest Group Ratings

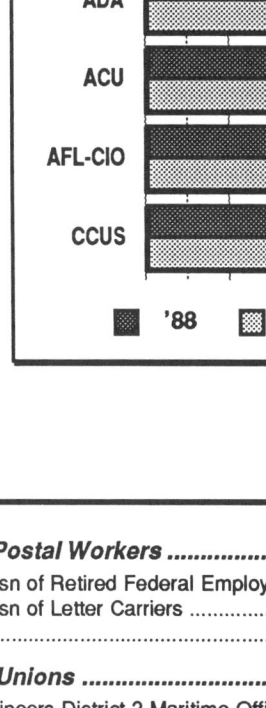

■ '88   ▨ '83-'87 Avg

Labor

Government & Postal Workers **$6,450**

> National Assn of Retired Federal Employees $4,000
> National Assn of Letter Carriers $1,600
> Others $850

Transportation Unions **$8,600**

> Marine Engineers District 2 Maritime Officers $3,500
> International Longshoremen Assn $2,100
> United Transportation Union $1,400
> Seafarers International Union $1,000
> Others $600

Ideological/Single-Issue

Democratic Leadership PACs **$2,000**

> Valley Education Fund (Tony Coelho) $2,000

Other Major Ideological/Single-Issue PACs

Safari Club International ....$1,000   Pro-Hunting

Spending in Last 3 Elections

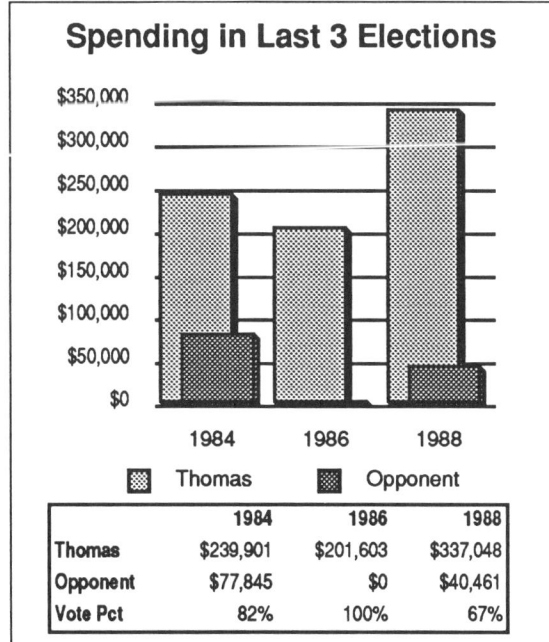

	1984	1986	1988
Thomas	$239,901	$201,603	$337,048
Opponent	$77,845	$0	$40,461
Vote Pct	82%	100%	67%

* Contributions came from more than one PAC affiliated with this sponsor.

Esteban E. Torres, D-Calif (34)

First elected: 1982
Total receipts: $226,964
Total from PACs: $106,780

1988 Committees & Subcommittees

Banking, Finance and Urban Affairs
Financial Institutions Supervision, Regulation and Insurance
Housing and Community Development
International Development Institutions and Finance

Small Business
Procurement, Innovation and Minority Enterprise Development
SBA and the General Economy

PAC Contribution Profile

Business

Commercial Banks	**$9,650**
American Bankers Assn	$3,000
Security Pacific Corp	$1,500
BankAmerica	$1,000
Barnett Banks of Florida	$1,000
Wells Fargo	$1,000
Assn of Bank Holding Companies	$600
Independent Bankers Assn	$550
Others	$1,000
Construction	**$3,350**
National Assn of Home Builders	$1,000
National Electrical Contractors Assn	$1,000
Others	$1,350
Health Professionals	**$2,750**
American Medical Assn	$2,500
Others	$250
Insurance	**$1,850**
TransAmerica Life Companies	$1,000
Others	$850
Lawyers	**$3,100**
Assn of Trial Lawyers of America	$2,300
Others	$800
Real Estate	**$9,200**
National Assn of Realtors	$8,300
Ticor Company	$600
Others	$300

Campaign Revenue Sources

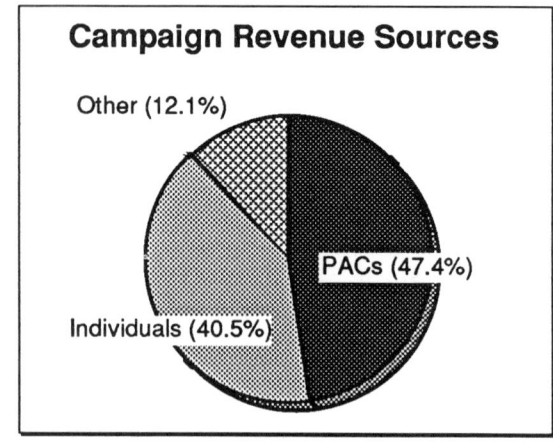

Other (12.1%)
PACs (47.4%)
Individuals (40.5%)

Retail Sales	**$2,111**
Southland Corp	$711
May Department Stores	$600
Others	$800
Savings Banks	**$14,000**
California League of Savings Institutions	$3,000
Glendale Federal Savings & Loan	$3,000
Great Western Financial Corp	$2,500
Coast Federal Savings & Loan	$1,750
Home Savings of America	$1,000
US League of Savings Assn	$1,000
Others	$1,750
Securities Investment	**$2,300**
Morgan Stanley & Company	$1,000
Others	$1,300

Other Major Business PACs

Associated Milk Producers	$1,000	Dairy
Northrop Corp	$800	Air Defense
Pacific Enterprises	$750	Natural Gas
Pacific Telesis Group	$550	Phone Util

PAC Totals by Category

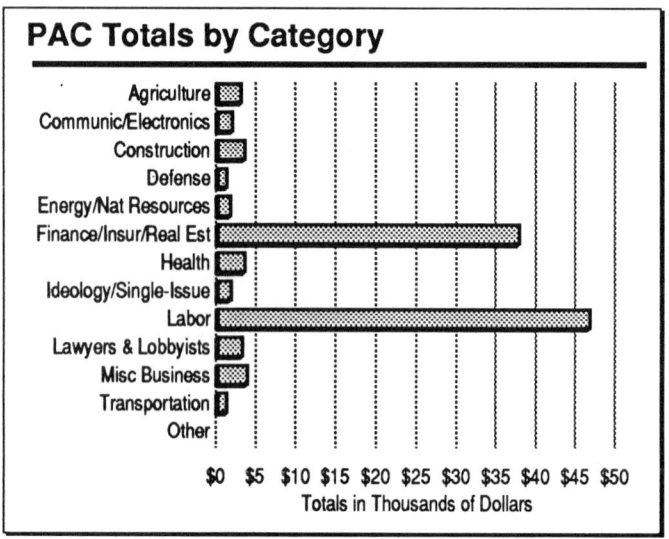

Agriculture
Communic/Electronics
Construction
Defense
Energy/Nat Resources
Finance/Insur/Real Est
Health
Ideology/Single-Issue
Labor
Lawyers & Lobbyists
Misc Business
Transportation
Other

$0 $5 $10 $15 $20 $25 $30 $35 $40 $45 $50
Totals in Thousands of Dollars

Labor

Bldg Trades/Industrial/Misc Unions $23,485

United Auto Workers $7,500
Laborers' Western Political League $4,000
Carpenters & Joiners Union* $2,750
Communications Workers of America $2,500
Machinists/Aerospace Workers Union $2,000
AFL-CIO $1,335
Food & Commercial Workers Union...................$1,300
Intl Brotherhood of Electrical Workers $1,000
Others $1,100

Government & Postal Workers $7,100

National Assn of Retired Federal Employees $5,000
American Fedn of State/County/Munic Employees $1,500
National Assn of Letter Carriers $600

Teachers Unions $5,200

National Education Assn $5,200

Transportation Unions $10,749

Teamsters Union $5,500
Seafarers International Union $2,000
Transportation Communication Union...............$1,449
Marine Engineers District 2 Maritime Officers $1,000
United Transportation Union $800

Major Ideological/Single-Issue PACs

Valley Education Fund (Tony Coelho) ....$1,000 Dem Leaders

Independent expenditures supporting Torres

National Cmte to Preserve Social Security $1,422

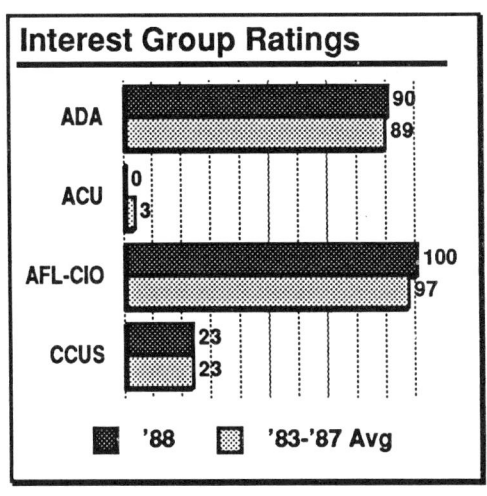

Interest Group Ratings

ADA — 90 / 89
ACU — 0 / 3
AFL-CIO — 100 / 97
CCUS — 23 / 23

■ '88   ▨ '83-'87 Avg

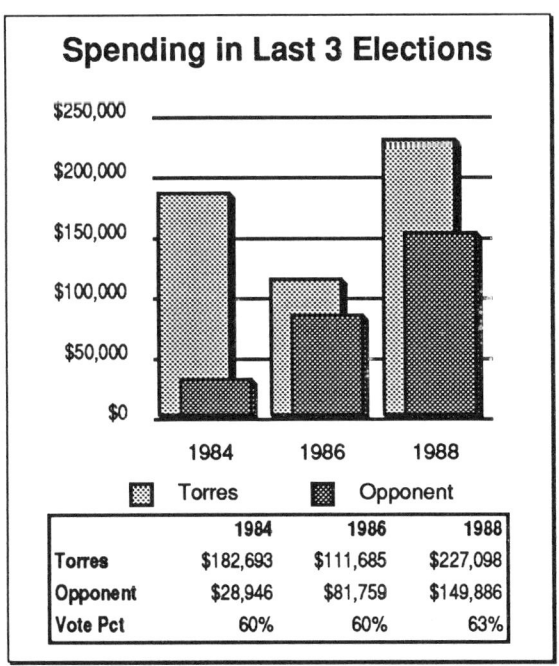

Spending in Last 3 Elections

	1984	1986	1988
Torres	$182,693	$111,685	$227,098
Opponent	$28,946	$81,759	$149,886
Vote Pct	60%	60%	63%

▨ Torres   ■ Opponent

* Contributions came from more than one PAC affiliated with this sponsor.

Robert G. Torricelli, D-NJ (9)

First elected: 1982
Total receipts: $653,659
Total from PACs: $173,057

1988 Committees & Subcommittees

Foreign Affairs
Asian and Pacific Affairs
Europe and the Middle East

Science, Space and Technology
International Scientific Cooperation
Space Science and Applications

PAC Contribution Profile

Business

Aviation & Aerospace **$3,250**
　　Boeing Company $1,000
　　Hercules Inc $1,000
　　Others $1,250

Dairy **$3,500**
　　Associated Milk Producers $2,500
　　Mid-American Dairymen $1,000

Defense **$5,730**
　　General Dynamics $1,000
　　Others $4,730

Electric Utilities **$5,888**
　　None over $900

Financial Institutions **$4,390**
　　SAPEC/ NJ (New Jersey Savings Assn) $2,500
　　American Bankers Assn $1,000
　　Others $890

Food & Beverage **$2,200**
　　Joseph E Seagram & Sons $1,000
　　Others $1,200

Health Professionals **$5,250**
　　American Medical Assn $3,750
　　International Chiropractors Assn $1,000
　　Others $500

Insurance **$4,500**
　　National Assn of Life Underwriters $3,000
　　Others $1,500

Campaign Revenue Sources

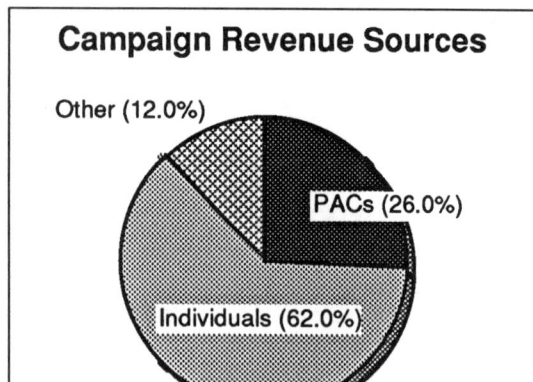

Other (12.0%)
PACs (26.0%)
Individuals (62.0%)

Lawyers & Lobbyists **$7,426**
　　Assn of Trial Lawyers of America $2,750
　　Akin, Gump, Hauer & Feld $1,000
　　Dow, Lohnes & Albertson $1,000
　　Others $2,676

Motion Pictures/Entertainment **$4,500**
　　MCA Inc $2,250
　　Gulf + Western Industries $1,250
　　Others $1,000

Package Delivery **$3,130**
　　United Parcel Service $3,130

Pharmaceuticals **$5,050**
　　Warner-Lambert $1,250
　　Hoffman-La Roche $1,000
　　Others $2,800

Real Estate **$3,250**
　　National Assn of Realtors $3,250

Telecommunications **$4,500**
　　New Jersey Bell Telephone $2,000
　　AT&T $1,750
　　Others $750

Other Major Business PACs

Kidder, Peabody	$2,000	Stocks Invest
Deere & Company*	$1,500	Farm Equip
National Assn of Home Builders	$1,500	Resid Constr
Corning Glass Works	$1,000	Glass Prod
GAF Corporation	$1,000	Chemicals

PAC Totals by Category

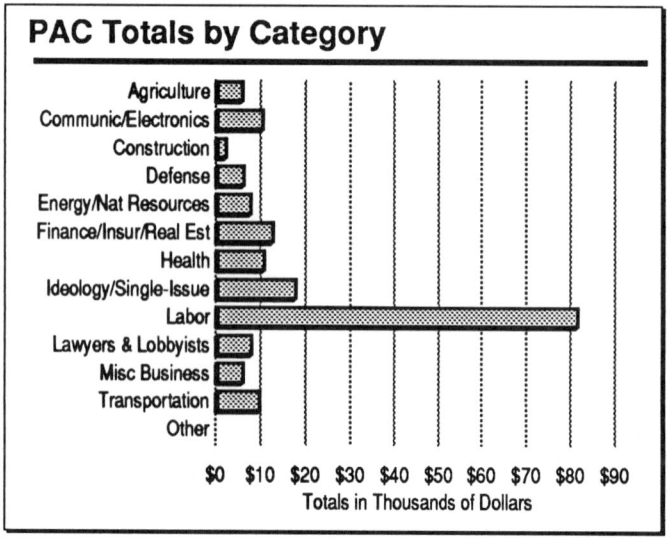

Agriculture
Communic/Electronics
Construction
Defense
Energy/Nat Resources
Finance/Insur/Real Est
Health
Ideology/Single-Issue
Labor
Lawyers & Lobbyists
Misc Business
Transportation
Other

$0 $10 $20 $30 $40 $50 $60 $70 $80 $90
Totals in Thousands of Dollars

Labor

Bldg Trades/Industrial/Misc Unions **$31,280**
    United Auto Workers $9,500
    Operating Engineers Union* $5,250
    Plumbers/Pipefitters Union* $2,980
    Carpenters & Joiners Union $2,500
    Intl Brotherhood of Electrical Workers............$1,500
    Laborers' Political League $1,500
    AFL-CIO* $1,000
    Food & Commercial Workers Union................$1,000
    Others $6,050

Government & Postal Workers **$12,550**
    National Assn of Retired Federal Employees $7,000
    American Fedn of State/County/Munic Employees $2,000
    National Assn of Letter Carriers $1,500
    Others $2,050

Teachers Unions **$5,130**
    National Education Assn $4,130
    American Federation of Teachers $1,000

Transportation Unions **$32,130**
    Teamsters Union $10,000
    Marine Engineers Union* $8,000
    Masters, Mates & Pilots Union $5,000
    Seafarers International Union $2,000
    Transport Workers Union $1,880
    Amalgamated Transit Union $1,500
    Air Line Pilots Assn $1,000
    United Transportation Union $1,000
    Others $1,750

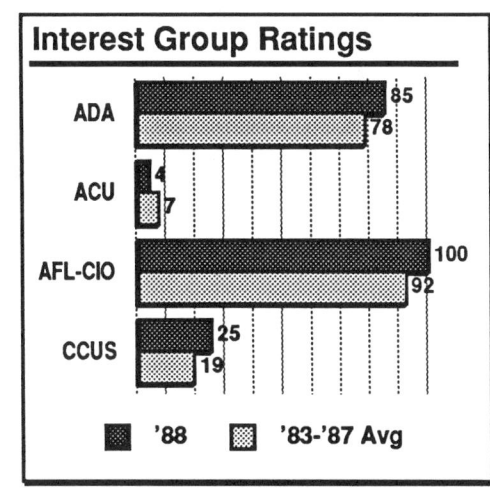

Interest Group Ratings

	'88	'83-'87 Avg
ADA	85	78
ACU	4	7
AFL-CIO	100	92
CCUS	25	19

Ideological/Single-Issue

Pro-Israel **$11,340**
    National PAC $5,000
    Delaware Valley PAC $1,000
    Five Towns PAC $1,000
    Hudson Valley PAC $1,000
    Mid Manhattan PAC $1,000
    Others $2,340

Other Major Ideological/Single-Issue PACs
National Cmte for an Effective Congress.........$2,498   Dem/Liberal
Valley Education Fund (Tony Coelho) ....$1,000   Dem Leaders

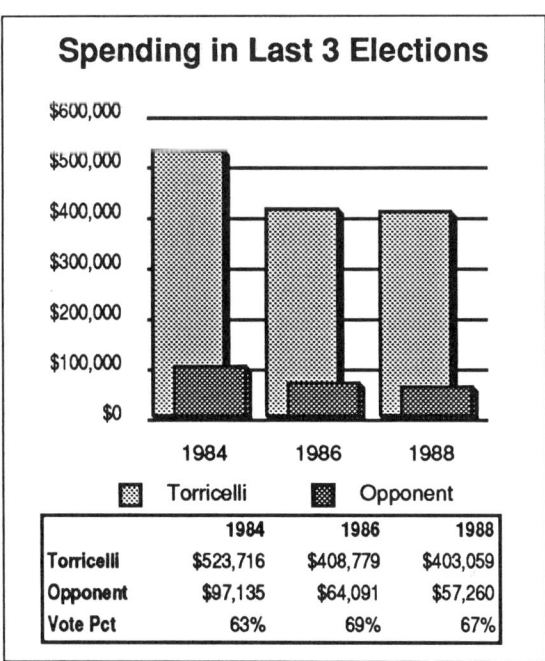

Spending in Last 3 Elections

	1984	1986	1988
Torricelli	$523,716	$408,779	$403,059
Opponent	$97,135	$64,091	$57,260
Vote Pct	63%	69%	67%

Torricelli   Opponent

---

* Contributions came from more than one PAC affiliated
  with this sponsor.

Ed Towns, D-NY (11)

1988 Committees & Subcommittees

First elected: 1982
Total receipts: $327,722
Total from PACs: $129,291

Government Operations
Environment, Energy and Natural Resources
Government Information, Justice and Agriculture

Public Works and Transportation
Aviation
Economic Development
Investigations and Oversight
Surface Transportation

Select Narcotics Abuse and Control

PAC Contribution Profile

Business

Accountants	*$5,000*
American Institute of CPA's	$5,000
Air Transport	*$2,000*
None over $900	
Commercial & Savings Banks	*$4,450*
Citicorp	$2,500
Others	$1,950
Dairy	*$2,100*
Associated Milk Producers	$1,500
Others	$600
Electric Utilities	*$1,505*
Consolidated Edison/New York	$1,205
Others	$300
Health Professionals	*$9,100*
American Medical Assn	$4,100
New York Medical Assn	$3,100
American Podiatry Assn	$1,000
Others	$900
Insurance	*$5,350*
National Assn of Life Underwriters	$1,000
Others	$4,350
Lawyers	*$2,950*
Assn of Trial Lawyers of America	$2,500
Others	$450

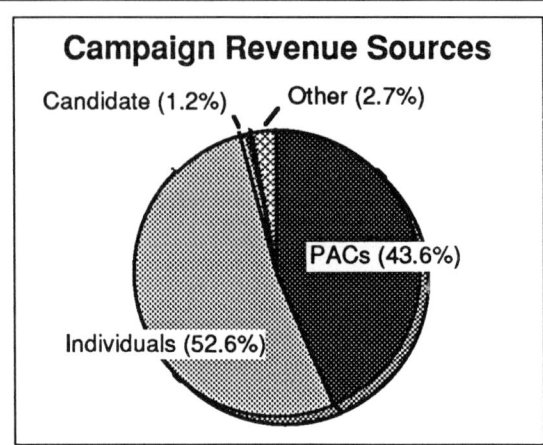

Campaign Revenue Sources

Candidate (1.2%)
Other (2.7%)
PACs (43.6%)
Individuals (52.6%)

Pharmaceuticals	*$3,550*
Johnson & Johnson	$1,200
Pfizer Inc	$1,000
Others	$1,350
Real Estate	*$2,300*
National Assn of Realtors	$2,050
Others	$250
Sugar Growers	*$2,850*
None over $850	
Telecommunications	*$3,180*
New York Telephone	$1,680
AT&T	$1,500
Tobacco	*$3,400*
Philip Morris	$1,000
RJR Nabisco	$1,000
Others	$1,400
Trucking/Delivery	*$6,200*
United Parcel Service	$4,250
Others	$1,950

PAC Totals by Category

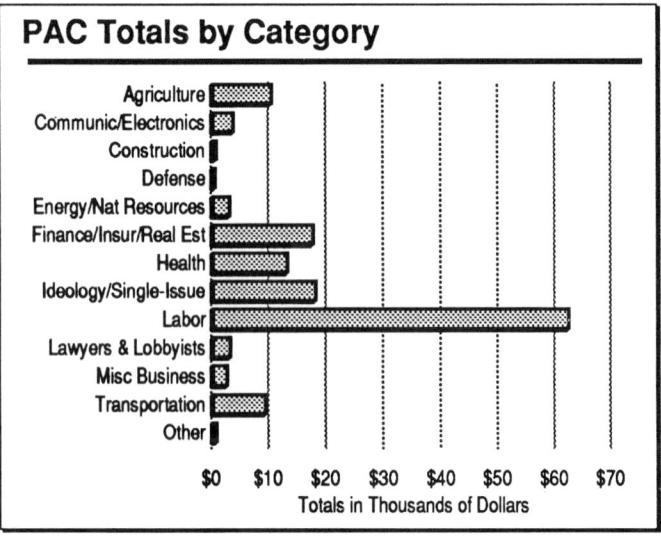

Agriculture
Communic/Electronics
Construction
Defense
Energy/Nat Resources
Finance/Insur/Real Est
Health
Ideology/Single-Issue
Labor
Lawyers & Lobbyists
Misc Business
Transportation
Other

$0 $10 $20 $30 $40 $50 $60 $70
Totals in Thousands of Dollars

Labor

Bldg Trades/Industrial/Misc Unions **$12,900**
- AFL-CIO* $1,950
- Food & Commercial Workers Union $1,900
- Machinists/Aerospace Workers Union $1,850
- Carpenters & Joiners Union $1,500
- Laborers' Political League $1,500
- Ladies Garment Workers Union $1,350
- Others $2,850

Government & Postal Workers **$13,900**
- American Fedn of State/County/Munic Employees $5,000
- National Assn of Letter Carriers $3,400
- National Assn of Retired Federal Employees $3,000
- American Postal Workers Union $1,200
- Others $1,300

Teachers Unions **$4,840**
- National Education Assn $4,500
- Others $340

Transportation Unions **$30,550**
- Teamsters Union $10,000
- Air Line Pilots Assn $6,000
- Marine Engineers District 2 Maritime Officers $4,000
- Amalgamated Transit Union $1,500
- Seafarers International Union $1,500
- United Transportation Union $1,400
- Transport Workers Union $1,300
- International Longshoremen Local #1814 .... $1,000
- Others $3,850

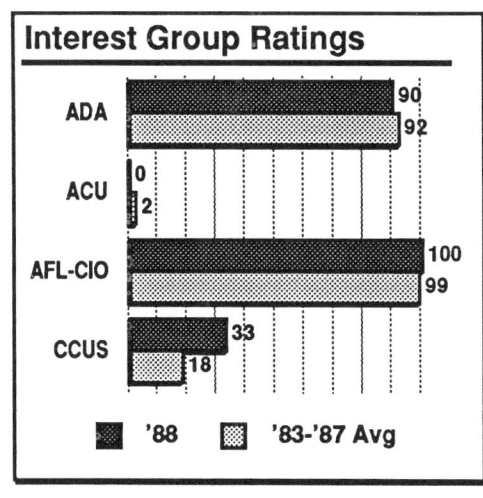

Interest Group Ratings

	'88	'83-'87 Avg
ADA	90	92
ACU	0	2
AFL-CIO	100	99
CCUS	33	18

Ideological/Single-Issue

Democratic Leadership PACs **$9,500**
- Majority Congress Committee (Jim Wright) $5,000
- Cmte for Democratic Opportunity (Bill Gray) $3,300
- Valley Education Fund (Tony Coelho) $1,000
- Others $200

Pro-Israel **$5,500**
- National PAC $5,000
- Others $500

Other Major Ideological/Single-Issue PACs

National Cmte to Preserve Social Security ...... $1,000   Soc Secur

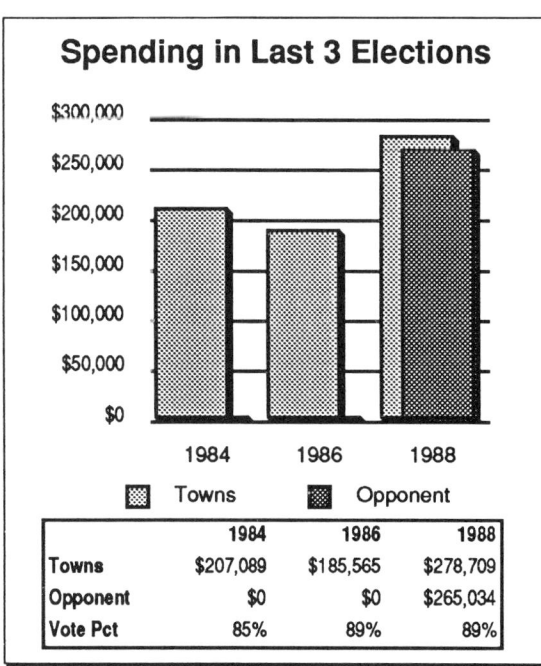

Spending in Last 3 Elections

	1984	1986	1988
Towns	$207,089	$185,565	$278,709
Opponent	$0	$0	$265,034
Vote Pct	85%	89%	89%

Legend: Towns, Opponent

---

* Contributions came from more than one PAC affiliated
with this sponsor.

James A. Traficant Jr., D-Ohio (17)

First elected: 1984
Total receipts: $100,063
Total from PACs: $49,500

1988 Committees & Subcommittees

Public Works and Transportation
Economic Development
Surface Transportation
Water Resources

Science, Space and Technology
Energy Research and Development
Investigations and Oversight
Space Science and Applications

Select Narcotics Abuse and Control

PAC Contribution Profile

Business

Trucking/Delivery **$1,520**
    United Parcel Service $1,000
    North American Van Lines $500
    Others $20

Other Major Business PACs

Associated Milk Producers	$1,000	Dairy
National Assn of Realtors	$1,000	Real Estate
National Utility Contractors Assn	$1,000	Comml Constr
Browning-Ferris Industries	$500	Waste Mgmt
Independent Insurance Agents of America	$500	Insurance
Valmont Industries	$500	Electronics

Campaign Revenue Sources

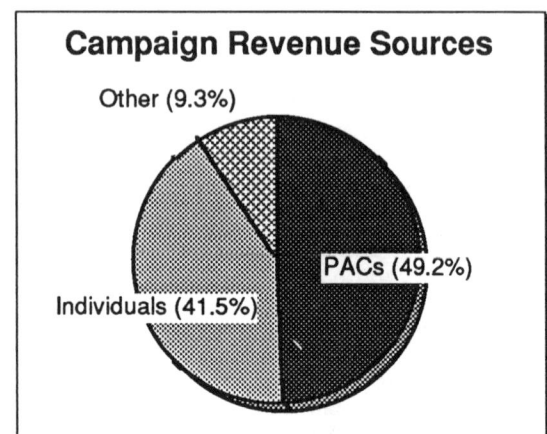

Other (9.3%)
PACs (49.2%)
Individuals (41.5%)

PAC Totals by Category

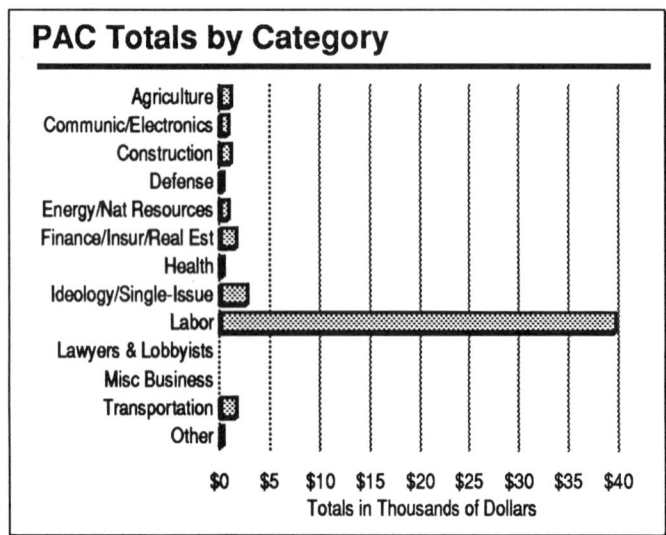

Agriculture
Communic/Electronics
Construction
Defense
Energy/Nat Resources
Finance/Insur/Real Est
Health
Ideology/Single-Issue
Labor
Lawyers & Lobbyists
Misc Business
Transportation
Other

$0 $5 $10 $15 $20 $25 $30 $35 $40
Totals in Thousands of Dollars

Labor

Bldg Trades/Industrial/Misc Unions $21,000
United Auto Workers $5,000
Machinists/Aerospace Workers Union $2,750
Electronic Machine Furniture Workers $2,500
Int'l Brotherhood of Electrical Workers $2,000
Carpenters & Joiners Union $1,500
Food & Commercial Workers Union $1,500
Laborers' Political League $1,500
AFL-CIO $1,000
Plumbers/Pipefitters Union $1,000
Rubber Cork Linoleum Plastic Workers $1,000
Ladies Garment Workers Union $750
Amalgamated Clothing & Textile Workers $500

Government & Postal Workers $3,500
American Fedn of State/County/Munic Employees $1,000
American Postal Workers Union $1,000
National Assn of Retired Federal Employees $1,000
American Federation of Govt Employees $500

Teachers Unions $2,500
National Education Assn $2,500

Transportation Unions $12,500
Teamsters Union $5,000
Air Line Pilots Assn $2,500
United Transportation Union $1,500
Seafarers International Union $1,000
Transport Workers Union $1,000
Assn of Flight Attendants $500
Others $1,000

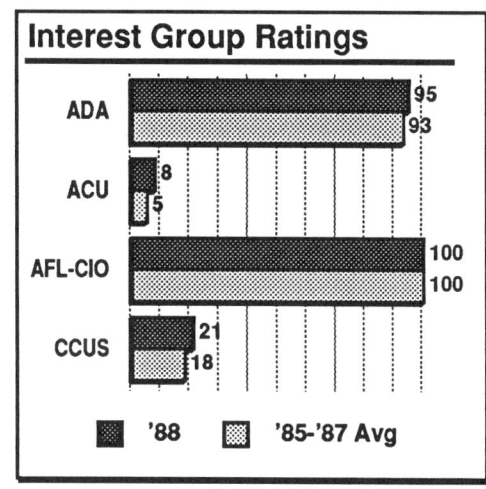

Ideological/Single-Issue

Ideological/Single-Issue $2,550
India Association .... $1,050   Ethnic
Valley Education Fund (Tony Coelho) .... $1,000   Dem Leaders
Others $500

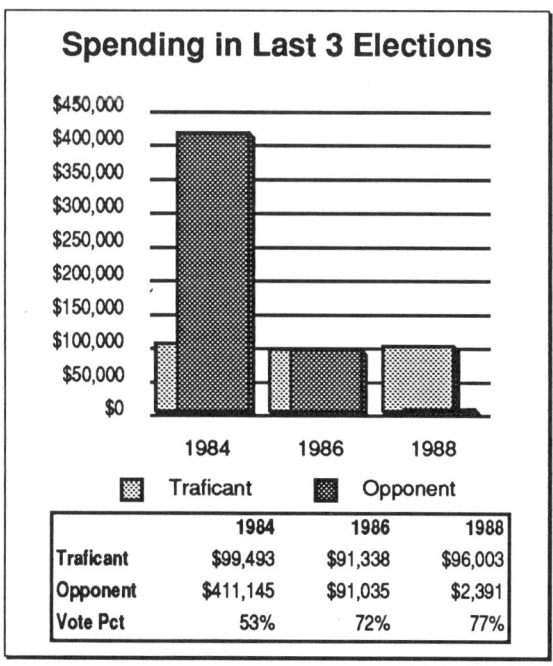

Bob Traxler, D-Mich (8)

1988 Committees & Subcommittees

Appropriations
HUD-Independent Agencies
Legislative Branch
Rural Development, Agriculture and Related Agencies

Select Hunger

First elected: 1974
Total receipts: $238,000
Total from PACs: $148,737

PAC Contribution Profile

Business

Automotive	**$4,400**
General Motors	$2,000
Ford Motor Company	$1,600
Others	$800
Aviation & Aerospace	**$4,900**
Boeing Company	$2,000
TRW Inc	$1,300
Others	$1,600
Construction	**$9,950**
National Utility Contractors Assn	$3,500
Jacobs Engineering Group	$1,100
Manufactured Housing Institute	$1,100
American Consulting Engineers Council	$1,000
Others	$3,250
Dairy	**$12,650**
Associated Milk Producers	$6,000
Mid-American Dairymen	$4,500
Others	$2,150
Defense Aerospace	**$5,600**
McDonnell Douglas	$1,600
Rockwell International	$1,100
Others	$2,900
Electric Utilities	**$3,830**
Consumers Power Company	$2,230
ACRE (Action Committee for Rural Electrification)	$1,100
Others	$500

Campaign Revenue Sources

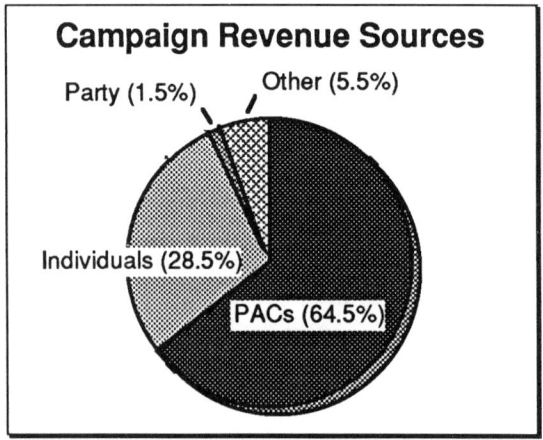

Party (1.5%)
Other (5.5%)
Individuals (28.5%)
PACs (64.5%)

Financial Institutions	**$2,675**
Michigan Credit Union League	$1,175
Atlantic Financial Federal	$1,000
Others	$500
Food & Beverage	**$6,500**
General Mills*	$1,500
Nutrasweet Company	$1,000
Others	$4,000
Fruit & Vegetable Growers	**$2,300**
Ocean Spray Cranberries Inc	$1,500
Others	$800
Health Professionals	**$4,000**
American Medical Assn	$2,000
American Dental Assn	$1,500
Others	$500
Insurance	**$2,500**
Massachusetts Mutual Life Insurance	$2,250
Others	$250
Lawyers & Lobbyists	**$2,700**
None over $800	
Real Estate	**$6,300**
National Assn of Realtors	$6,000
Others	$300
Sugar Growers	**$8,580**
American Sugarbeet Growers Assn	$2,300
Great Lakes Sugar Beet Growers	$1,770
American Crystal Sugar Corp	$1,500
Others	$3,010
Telecommunications	**$5,040**
AT&T	$2,000
Michigan Bell Telephone	$1,740
Others	$1,300
Veterinarians	**$2,000**
American Veterinary Medical Assn	$2,000

Other Major Business PACs

American Hospital Assn	$1,150	Hospitals
International Council of Shopping Centers	$1,000	Retail
National Tooling & Machining Assn	$1,000	Indust Equip
Philip Morris	$1,000	Tobacco

PAC Totals by Category

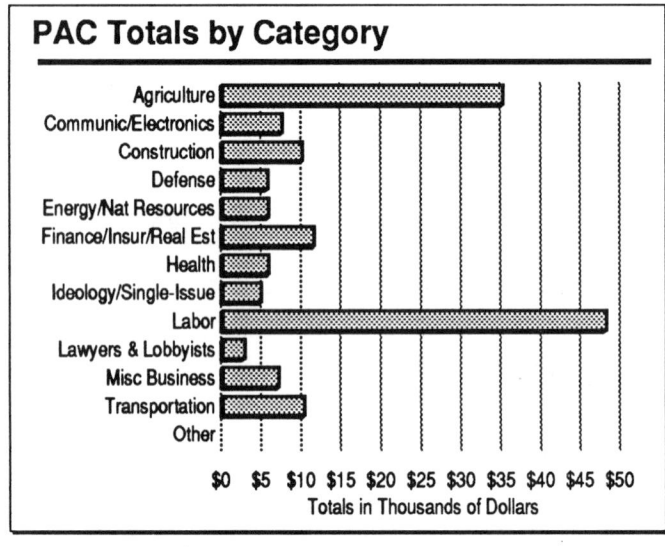

Agriculture
Communic/Electronics
Construction
Defense
Energy/Nat Resources
Finance/Insur/Real Est
Health
Ideology/Single-Issue
Labor
Lawyers & Lobbyists
Misc Business
Transportation
Other

$0 $5 $10 $15 $20 $25 $30 $35 $40 $45 $50
Totals in Thousands of Dollars

Labor

Bldg Trades/Industrial/Misc Unions $17,335

United Auto Workers $5,000
Machinists/Aerospace Workers Union $2,000
Carpenters & Joiners Union $1,600
Operating Engineers Union $1,500
Laborers' Political League $1,300
Intl Brotherhood of Electrical Workers $1,000
Plumbers/Pipefitters Union $1,000
Others $3,935

Government & Postal Workers $12,975

American Fedn of State/County/Munic Employees $5,000
National Assn of Retired Federal Employees $3,000
National Assn of Letter Carriers $2,650
American Postal Workers Union $1,100
Others $1,225

Teachers Unions $5,000

National Education Assn $5,000

Transportation Unions $12,700

Teamsters Union $10,000
United Transportation Union $1,100
Seafarers International Union $1,000
Others $600

Ideological/Single-Issue

Ideological/Single-Issue $4,750

National Cmte to Preserve Social Security ...... $2,500   Soc Secur
Valley Education Fund (Tony Coelho) .... $1,000   Dem Leaders
Others $1,250

Independent expenditures supporting Traxler

National Cmte to Preserve Social Security $1,687

Spending in Last 3 Elections

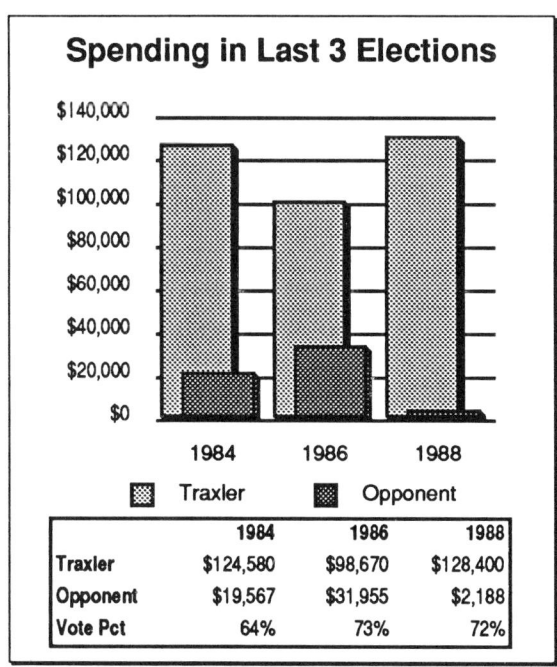

	1984	1986	1988
Traxler	$124,580	$98,670	$128,400
Opponent	$19,567	$31,955	$2,188
Vote Pct	64%	73%	72%

Interest Group Ratings

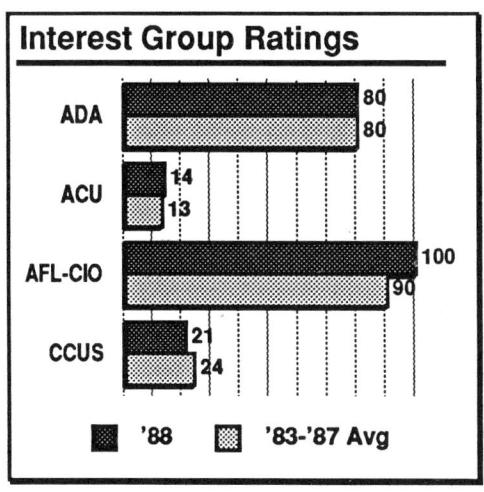

Morris K. Udall, D-Ariz (2)

First elected: 1961
Total receipts: $119,497
Total from PACs: $84,605

1988 Committees & Subcommittees

Interior and Insular Affairs (Chairman)
Energy and the Environment (Chairman)
Insular and International Affairs
Mining and Natural Resources
Water and Power Resources

Foreign Affairs
Arms Control, International Security and Science

Post Office and Civil Service
Investigations

PAC Contribution Profile

Business

Construction **$1,450**
    American Homebuilders PAC $1,000
    Others $450

Electric Utilities **$8,800**
    ACRE (Action Committee for Rural Electrification) $1,000
    Arizona Public Service Company $1,000
    Detroit Edison $750
    Southern Company* $750
    Dominion Resources Inc $500
    Middle South Utilities* $500
    Pacific Gas & Electric $500
    Others $3,800

Financial Institutions **$3,855**
    Merabank Federal Savings Bank $1,605
    First National Bank/Albuquerque $750
    American Bankers Assn $500
    Arizona Bank $500
    Others $500

Irrigation Services **$2,000**
    Salt River Valley Water Users $2,000

Lawyers **$5,500**
    Assn of Trial Lawyers of America $5,000
    Others $500

Mining **$2,500**
    Phelps Dodge Corp $1,250
    Cyprus Minerals Company $500
    National Coal Assn $500
    Others $250

Oil & Gas **$3,250**
    Southwest Gas Corp $2,250
    Union Pacific Corp $500
    W R Grace & Company $500

Package Delivery **$1,250**
    United Parcel Service $1,250

Power Plant Equipment **$1,250**
    General Electric $500
    Others $750

Other Major Business PACs

Mountain Bell	$1,000	Phone Util
Blue Cross/Shield of Arizona	$800	Health Insur
Stone Container Corp	$750	Paper Packg
Allied-Signal	$500	Air Defense
Associated Milk Producers	$500	Dairy
Conf of National Park Concessioners	$500	Lodging/Tour
Del Webb Corp	$500	Real Estate
Greyhound Corp	$500	Home Chem
Joseph E Seagram & Sons	$500	Wine&Liquor
Kaibab Industries	$500	Forestry
National Fed/Bus & Prof Women Clubs	$500	BusinessAssn
Sunkist Growers	$500	Fruit/Veg

Campaign Revenue Sources

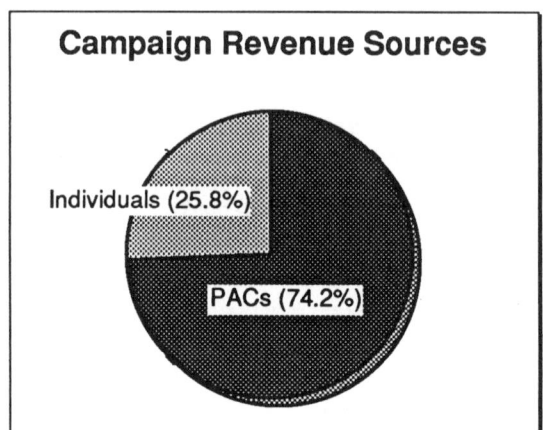

Individuals (25.8%)
PACs (74.2%)

PAC Totals by Category

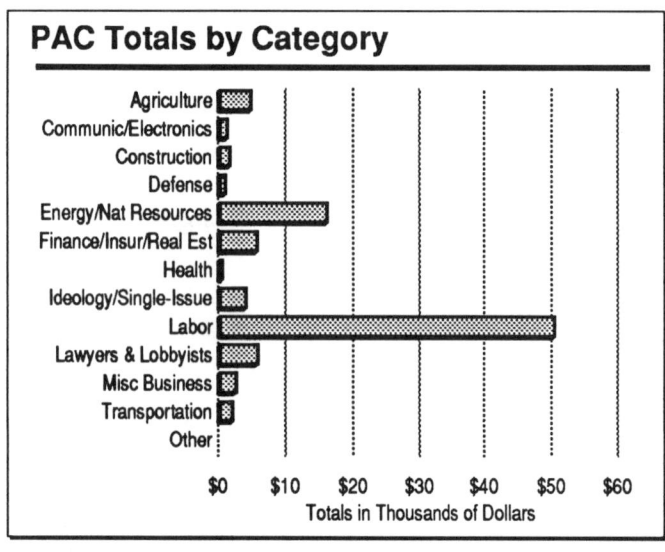

Agriculture
Communic/Electronics
Construction
Defense
Energy/Nat Resources
Finance/Insur/Real Est
Health
Ideology/Single-Issue
Labor
Lawyers & Lobbyists
Misc Business
Transportation
Other

$0 $10 $20 $30 $40 $50 $60
Totals in Thousands of Dollars

Labor

Bldg Trades/Industrial/Misc Unions **$23,000**
- Intl Brotherhood of Electrical Workers.............................$4,000
- Laborers' Western Political League $4,000
- Food & Commercial Workers Union.................................$3,000
- United Auto Workers $3,000
- AFL-CIO* $2,000
- Plumbers/Pipefitters Union $2,000
- Carpenters & Joiners Union $1,000
- Machinists/Aerospace Workers Union $1,000
- United Mine Workers $1,000
- Ironworkers Union $500
- National Education Assn $500
- Others $1,000

Government & Postal Workers **$11,850**
- American Fedn of State/County/Munic Employees $5,000
- National Assn of Letter Carriers $2,100
- National Assn of Retired Federal Employees $2,000
- American Federation of Government Employees $1,000
- American Postal Workers Union $1,000
- National League of Postmasters $500
- Others $250

Transportation Unions **$15,250**
- Teamsters Union $12,000
- Seafarers International Union $1,500
- Longshoremen/Warehousemen Union $500
- Transportation Communication Union...............................$500
- United Transportation Union $500
- Others $250

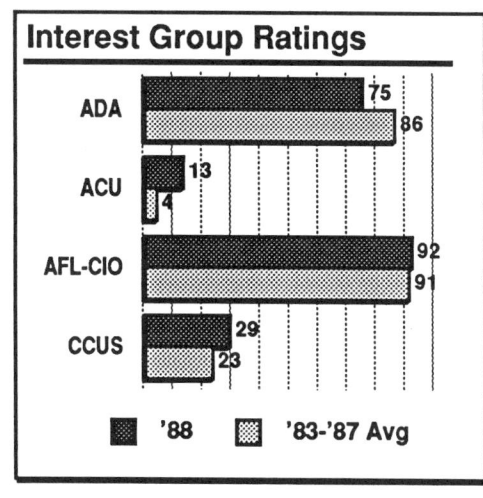

Interest Group Ratings

	'88	'83-'87 Avg
ADA	75	86
ACU	13	4
AFL-CIO	92	91
CCUS	29	23

Ideological/Single-Issue

Ideological/Single-Issue **$3,750**

National Cmte to Preserve Social Security $2,000	Soc Secur
Chicagoans for Better Congress $500	Pro-Israel
Human Rights Campaign Fund $500	Gay Rights
Others $750	

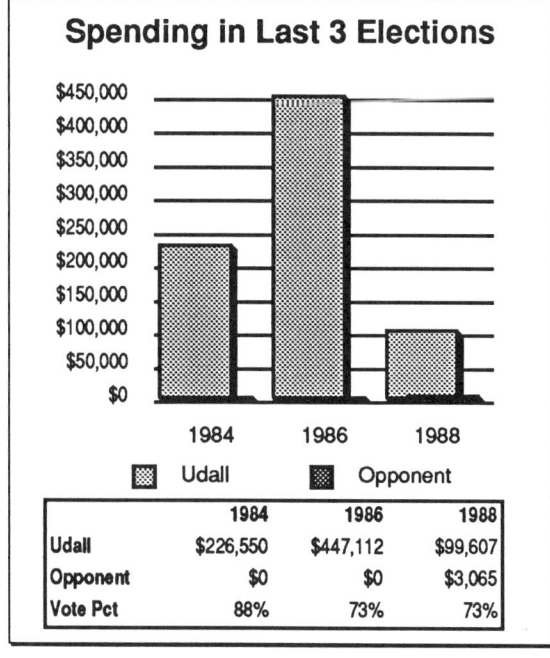

Spending in Last 3 Elections

	1984	1986	1988
Udall	$226,550	$447,112	$99,607
Opponent	$0	$0	$3,065
Vote Pct	88%	73%	73%

■ Udall   ■ Opponent

---

* Contributions came from more than one PAC affiliated with this sponsor.

Jolene Unsoeld, D-Wash (3)

First elected: 1988
Total receipts: $687,800
Total from PACs: $282,082

1989-90 Committees & Subcommittees

Education and Labor
Elementary, Secondary and Vocational Education
Health and Safety
Human Resources

Merchant Marine and Fisheries
Fisheries and Wildlife Conservation and the Environment
Merchant Marine

Select Aging
Housing and Consumer Interests

PAC Contribution Profile

Business

Commercial & Savings Banks	**$1,300**
None over $500	
Dairy	**$1,750**
Associated Milk Producers	$1,500
Others	$250
Lawyers	**$11,800**
Assn of Trial Lawyers of America	$10,000
Garvey, Schubert & Barer	$1,000
Others	$800
Social Workers	**$2,000**
National Assn of Social Workers	$2,000

Campaign Revenue Sources

Other (9.6%)
Party (4.5%)
Candidate (4.8%)
PACs (38.4%)
Individuals (42.6%)

Labor

Bldg Trades/Industrial/Misc Unions	**$80,050**
AFL-CIO	$10,000
Machinists/Aerospace Workers Union	$10,000
United Auto Workers	$10,000
Food & Commercial Workers Union	$9,100
American Nurses Assn	$7,000
Carpenters & Joiners Union	$6,500
Intl Brotherhood of Electrical Workers	$5,000
United Steelworkers	$5,000
Rubber Cork Linoleum Plastic Workers	$4,000
Laborers' Political League	$3,500
Bakery, Confectionery & Tobacco Workers	$2,000
Ironworkers Union	$2,000
Service Employees International Union	$2,000
Operating Engineers Union	$1,500
Plumbers/Pipefitters Union	$1,000
Sheet Metal Workers Union	$1,000
Others	$450
Government & Postal Workers	**$25,400**
American Fedn of State/County/Munic Employees	$10,000
National Assn of Letter Carriers	$10,000
American Postal Workers Union	$2,000
National Assn of Retired Federal Employees	$2,000
International Assn of Firefighters*	$1,100
Others	$300
Teachers Unions	**$18,000**
National Education Assn	$10,000
American Federation of Teachers	$8,000
Transportation Unions	**$25,750**
Teamsters Union	$10,000
Amalgamated Transit Union	$3,000
Air Line Pilots Assn	$2,500
Longshoremen/Warehousemen Union	$2,500
Seafarers International Union	$2,500
Marine Engineers Union	$2,000
United Transportation Union	$2,000
Others	$1,250

PAC Totals by Category

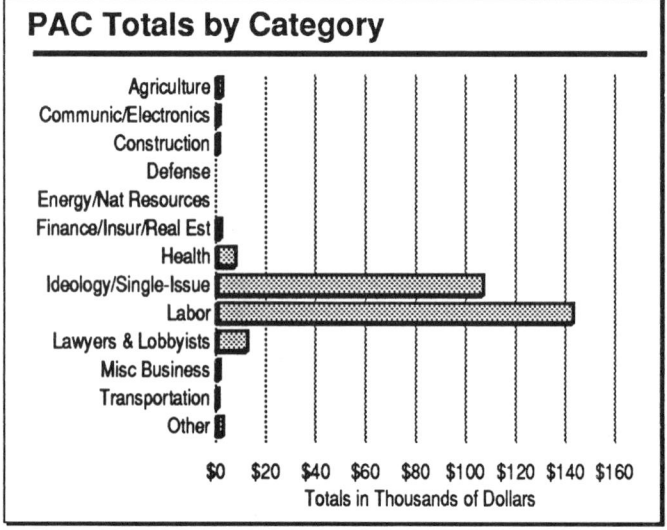

Agriculture
Communic/Electronics
Construction
Defense
Energy/Nat Resources
Finance/Insur/Real Est
Health
Ideology/Single-Issue
Labor
Lawyers & Lobbyists
Misc Business
Transportation
Other

$0 $20 $40 $60 $80 $100 $120 $140 $160
Totals in Thousands of Dollars

Ideological/Single-Issue

Central America Policy **$8,934**

Neighbor to Neighbor PAC $8,278
Others $656

Democratic/Liberal **$17,748**

National Cmte for an Effective Congress $9,998
Hollywood Women's Political Cmte $5,000
Americans for Democratic Action $1,500
Others $1,250

Democratic Leadership PACs **$17,616**

Majority Congress Committee (Jim Wright) $5,000
Valley Education Fund (Tony Coelho) $2,500
America's Leaders' Fund (Dan Rostenkowski) $2,000
Cmte for Democratic Opportunity (Bill Gray) $2,000
House Leadership Fund (Tom Foley) $2,000
Independent Action (Morris Udall) $2,000
Pax Americas (David Bonior) $1,000
Others $1,116

Environmental Policy **$6,019**

Sierra Club $3,500
League of Conservation Voters $1,519
Environmental Action $1,000

Gay/Lesbian Rights **$9,972**

Human Rights Campaign Fund $9,972

Pro-Choice **$11,858**

Voters for Choice/Friends of Family Planning $6,000
National Abortion Rights Action League $5,858

Pro-Peace **$3,275**

SANE/Freeze Inc $1,314
Council for a Livable World $1,311
Others $650

Social Security/Senior Citizens **$5,000**

National Cmte to Preserve Social Security $4,000
National Council of Senior Citizens $1,000

Womens Issues **$23,317**

Emily's List $9,335
Women's Campaign Fund $9,282
National Organization for Women $2,000
National Womens Political Caucus $1,250
National Womens Political Caucus $1,250
Others $200

Other Major Ideological/Single-Issue PACs

KidsPAC .... $1,500   HealthWelfare

Independent expenditures supporting Unsoeld

American Fedn of State/County/Munic Employees $5,000
Assn of Trial Lawyers of America $5,000
Majority Congress Committee (Jim Wright) $5,000
AFL-CIO $2,500
Machinists/Aerospace Workers Union $2,500
National Assn of Letter Carriers $2,500
American Postal Workers Union $1,000
American Nurses Assn $1,000
National Cmte to Preserve Social Security $1,000
Service Employees International Union $1,000

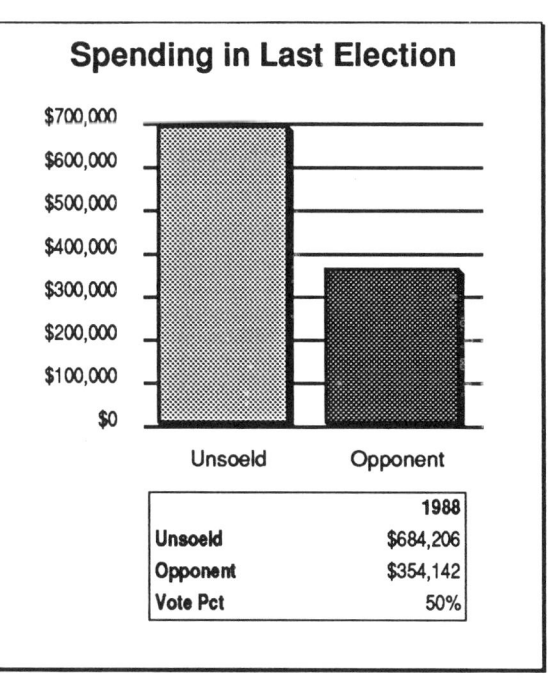

Spending in Last Election

	1988
Unsoeld	$684,206
Opponent	$354,142
Vote Pct	50%

---

* Contributions came from more than one PAC affiliated
with this sponsor.

Fred Upton, R-Mich (4)

1988 Committees & Subcommittees

First elected: 1986
Total receipts: $422,884
Total from PACs: $116,965

Public Works and Transportation
Surface Transportation
Water Resources

Small Business
Exports, Tourism and Special problems
Procurement, Innovation and Minority Enterprise Development

Select Hunger

PAC Contribution Profile

Business

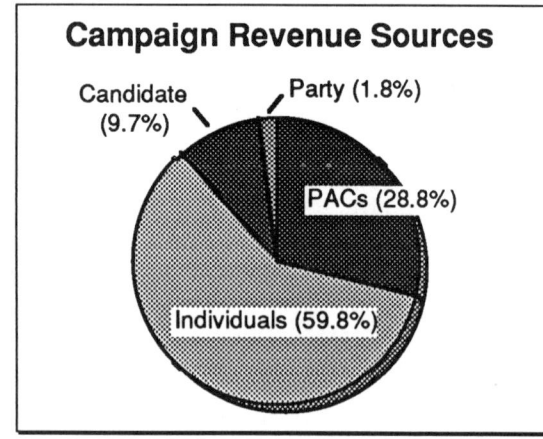

Campaign Revenue Sources

Candidate (9.7%)
Party (1.8%)
PACs (28.8%)
Individuals (59.8%)

Automotive	....	**$8,550**
National Auto Dealers Assn	....	$3,400
Auto Dealers & Drivers for Free Trade	....	$2,500
Chrysler Corp	....	$1,100
Others	....	$1,550

Aviation/Air Freight	....	**$3,600**
Federal Express Corp	....	$1,500
Aircraft Owners & Pilots Assn	....	$1,000
Others	....	$1,100

Construction	....	**$15,200**
Sheet Metal/AirCon Contractors	....	$5,000
National Assn of Home Builders	....	$2,500
Associated General Contractors	....	$2,350
Henley Group Inc	....	$1,000
National Electrical Contractors Assn	....	$1,000
Others	....	$3,350

Dairy	....	**$2,500**
Associated Milk Producers	....	$2,000
Others	....	$500

Defense	....	**$3,550**
United Technologies	....	$1,500
Allied-Signal	....	$1,000
Others	....	$1,050

Department/Convenience Stores **$3,157**

Southland Corp	....	$1,007
National Assn of Convenience Stores	....	$1,000
Others	....	$1,150

Electric Utilities **$4,800**

Consumers Power Company	....	$2,000
Detroit Edison	....	$1,550
American Electric Power*	....	$1,000
Others	....	$250

Electronics & Computers **$2,420**

Zenith Electronics Corp	....	$1,000
Others	....	$1,420

Financial Institutions **$4,850**

Michigan League of Savings Institutions	....	$2,000
Michigan Credit Union League	....	$1,000
Others	....	$1,850

Food & Beverage **$5,727**

Pepsico Inc	....	$1,250
National Restaurant Assn	....	$1,000
Others	....	$3,477

Health Professionals **$11,299**

American Medical Assn	....	$4,799
American Academy of Ophthalmology	....	$4,000
American Dental Assn	....	$2,500

Home Appliances **$2,500**

Whirlpool Corp	....	$1,500
Maytag Company	....	$1,000

Industrial Equipment & Materials **$3,250**

JSJ Corp	....	$3,000
Others	....	$250

Insurance **$5,200**
None over $750

Lawyers **$2,500**
Assn of Trial Lawyers of America $2,500

Oil & Gas **$3,700**
None over $850

PAC Totals by Category

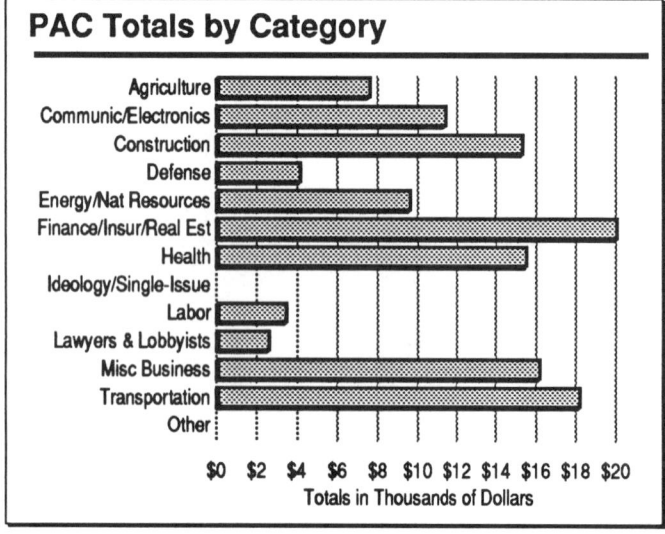

Agriculture	
Communic/Electronics	
Construction	
Defense	
Energy/Nat Resources	
Finance/Insur/Real Est	
Health	
Ideology/Single-Issue	
Labor	
Lawyers & Lobbyists	
Misc Business	
Transportation	
Other	

$0 $2 $4 $6 $8 $10 $12 $14 $16 $18 $20
Totals in Thousands of Dollars

Interest Group Ratings

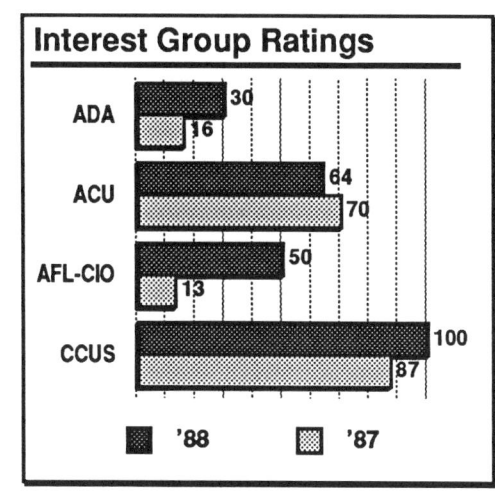

	'88	'87
ADA	30	16
ACU	64	70
AFL-CIO	50	13
CCUS	100	87

Pharmaceuticals **$3,100**
    Upjohn Company $1,250
    Abbott Laboratories $1,100
    Others $750

Real Estate **$7,000**
    National Assn of Realtors $6,500
    Others $500

Telecommunications **$7,800**
    Michigan Bell Telephone $6,000
    AT&T $1,250
    Others $550

Trucking/Delivery **$4,650**
    United Parcel Service $2,100
    Others $2,550

Other Major Business PACs

American Furniture Manufacturers Assn	$1,150	Furniture
Merrill Lynch	$1,100	StocksInvest
American Institute of CPA's	$1,000	Accountants
American Hospital Assn	$1,000	Hospitals
Michigan Farm Bureau	$1,000	Farm Orgs
National Grape Company-Operative Assn	$1,000	Fruit/Veg
Waste Management Inc	$1,000	Waste Mgmt

Labor

Labor Unions **$3,350**
    Air Line Pilots Assn $2,500
    Others $850

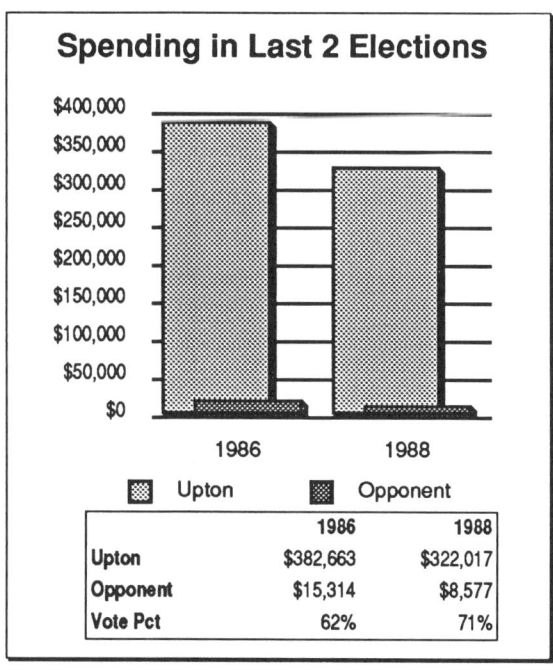

Spending in Last 2 Elections

	1986	1988
Upton	$382,663	$322,017
Opponent	$15,314	$8,577
Vote Pct	62%	71%

* Contributions came from more than one PAC affiliated with this sponsor.

Tim Valentine, D-NC (2)

First elected: 1982
Total receipts: $78,527
Total from PACs: $58,650

1988 Committees & Subcommittees

Public Works and Transportation
Aviation
Water Resources

Science, Space and Technology
Energy Research and Development
Natural Resources, Agriculture Research and Environment
Science, Research and Technology

PAC Contribution Profile

Business

Campaign Revenue Sources

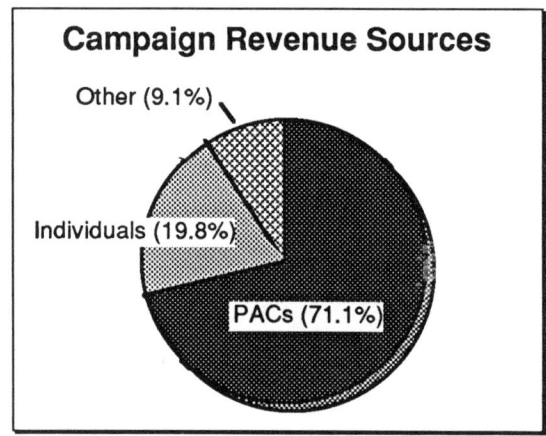

Other (9.1%)
Individuals (19.8%)
PACs (71.1%)

Auto Dealers	**$1,300**
National Auto Dealers Assn	$1,300
Aviation & Aerospace	**$2,400**
None over $300	
Chemicals	**$1,250**
NL Industries	$1,000
Others	$250
Commercial & Savings Banks	**$2,350**
US League of Savings Assn	$600
Branch Banking & Trust	$500
Central Carolina Bank & Trust	$500
Others	$750
Construction	**$1,400**
National Utility Contractors Assn	$500
Others	$900
Dairy	**$1,400**
Mid-American Dairymen	$800
Dairymen Inc-North Carolina	$600
Electric Utilities	**$5,700**
Carolina Power & Light	$800
Southern Company*	$750
Duke Power Company	$550
Dominion Resources Inc	$500
Middle South Utilities*	$500
Others	$2,600

Health Professionals	**$2,800**
American Medical Assn	$2,500
Others	$300
Insurance	**$2,500**
National Assn of Life Underwriters	$2,500
Lawyers	**$2,250**
Assn of Trial Lawyers of America	$2,000
Others	$250
Oil & Gas	**$1,350**
Texas Eastern Gas Transmission	$500
Others	$850
Pharmaceuticals	**$1,350**
Merck & Company	$500
Others	$850
Real Estate	**$3,300**
National Assn of Realtors	$3,000
Others	$300
Telecommunications	**$1,550**
Southern Bell	$750
Others	$800
Textiles	**$3,350**
Burlington Industries	$600
Collins & Aikman Corp	$600
American Yarn Spinners Assn	$500
Cone Mills Corp	$500
Others	$1,150
Tobacco	**$2,600**
RJR Nabisco	$2,000
Philip Morris	$600
Trucking/Delivery	**$2,400**
United Parcel Service	$1,000
National Assn of Truck Stop Operators	$500
Others	$900

Other Major Business PACs

General Atomics	$1,000	NuclearEquip
Archer-Daniels-Midland Corp	$600	Grain Trader
American Furniture Manufacturers Assn	$500	Furniture
American Veterinary Medical Assn	$500	Veterinary
American Hospital Assn	$500	Hospitals
Computer Sciences Corp	$500	Data Process
Kidder, Peabody	$500	StocksInvest

PAC Totals by Category

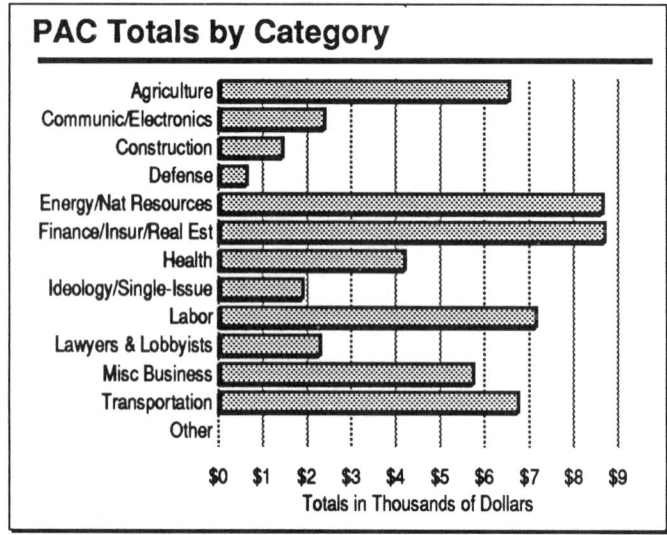

Agriculture
Communic/Electronics
Construction
Defense
Energy/Nat Resources
Finance/Insur/Real Est
Health
Ideology/Single-Issue
Labor
Lawyers & Lobbyists
Misc Business
Transportation
Other

$0 $1 $2 $3 $4 $5 $6 $7 $8 $9
Totals in Thousands of Dollars

Labor

Government & Postal Workers $1,900
    National Assn of Retired Federal Employees $1,000
    National Assn of Letter Carriers $600
    Others $300

Teachers Unions $1,700
    National Education Assn $1,700

Other Unions $3,500
    Seafarers International Union $1,500
    Amalgamated Transit Union $600
    United Transportation Union $500
    Others $900

Ideological/Single-Issue

Ideological/Single-Interest $1,850
National Cmte to Preserve Social Security .... $800   Soc Secur
Valley Education Fund (Tony Coelho) .... $500   Dem Leaders
Others $550

Independent expenditures supporting Valentine

National Cmte to Preserve Social Security $2,136

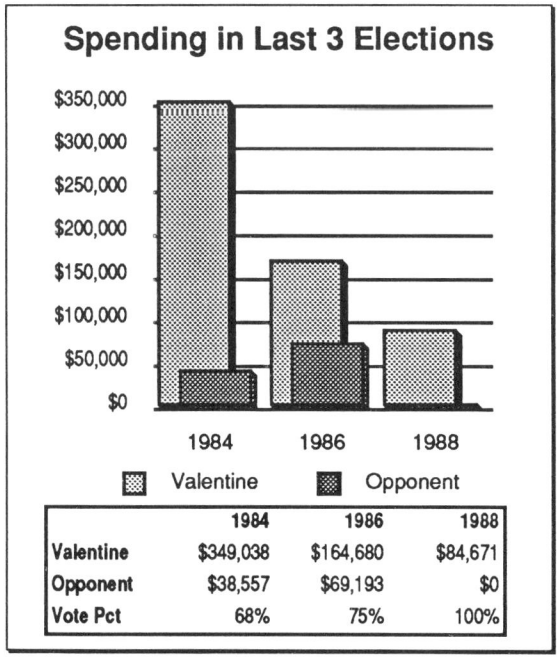

Spending in Last 3 Elections

	1984	1986	1988
Valentine	$349,038	$164,680	$84,671
Opponent	$38,557	$69,193	$0
Vote Pct	68%	75%	100%

Valentine   Opponent

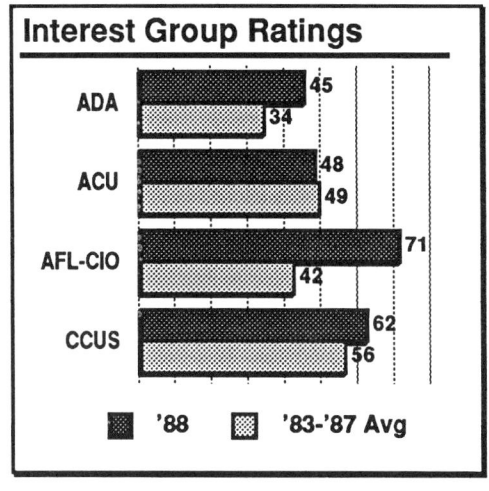

Interest Group Ratings

	'88	'83-'87 Avg
ADA	45	34
ACU	48	49
AFL-CIO	71	42
CCUS	62	56

* Contributions came from more than one PAC affiliated
with this sponsor.

Guy Vander Jagt, R-Mich (9)

1988 Committees & Subcommittees

Ways and Means
Select Revenue Measures (Ranking Republican)
Trade

Joint Taxation

First elected: 1966
Total receipts: $456,633
Total from PACs: $237,725

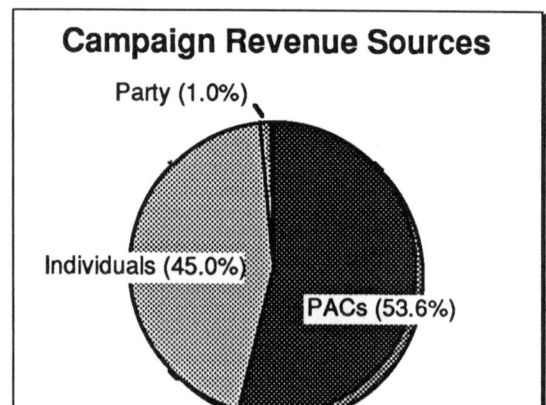

Campaign Revenue Sources

Party (1.0%)
Individuals (45.0%)
PACs (53.6%)

PAC Contribution Profile

Business

Accountants	$8,100
American Institute of CPA's	$4,900
Ernst & Whinney	$1,500
Price Waterhouse	$1,000
Others	$700

Air Transport	$4,150
United Airlines	$2,200
Others	$1,950

Automotive	$16,190
Auto Dealers & Drivers for Free Trade	$9,000
American Motors	$1,300
Budd Company	$1,000
Eaton Corp	$1,000
Federal-Mogul Corp	$1,000
Others	$2,890

Construction	$9,175
National Assn of Home Builders	$2,000
Sheet Metal/AirCon Contractors	$1,500
Manville Corp	$1,000
Others	$4,675

Defense	$7,200
None over $850	

Electric Utilities	$5,400
Consumers Power Company	$2,400
Others	$3,000

Financial Institutions	$6,360
US League of Savings Assn	$1,750
Michigan League of Savings Institutions	$1,500
Michigan Credit Union League	$1,080
Credit Union National Assn	$1,000
Others	$1,030

Food & Beverage	$16,050
Wine & Spirits Wholesalers of America	$5,800
National Beer Wholesalers Assn	$1,800
Food Marketing Institute	$1,050
Kellogg Company	$1,000
McDonald's Corp	$1,000
Pepsico Inc	$1,000
Others	$4,400

Health Professionals	$17,450
American Medical Assn	$6,250
American Dental Assn	$5,000
American Optometric Assn	$1,750
Cmte for Quality Orthopedic Health Care	$1,500
Others	$2,950

Hospitals & Nursing Homes	$5,030
American Hospital Assn	$3,830
Others	$1,200

Insurance	$18,220
National Assn of Life Underwriters	$3,000
Travelers Corp	$1,500
American Family Corp	$1,300
Massachusetts Mutual Life Insurance	$1,300
Independent Insurance Agents of America	$1,220
North Weatern Mutual Life	$1,150
Associated Life Insurance	$1,000
Others	$7,750

Lawyers & Lobbyists	$4,850
Jones, Day, Reavis & Pogue	$1,000
Kirkpatrick & Lockhart	$1,000
Others	$2,850

Oil & Gas	$10,530
Michigan Consolidated Gas	$1,130
Atlantic Richfield	$1,000
Mobil Oil	$1,000
Petroleum Marketers Assn	$1,000
Others	$6,400

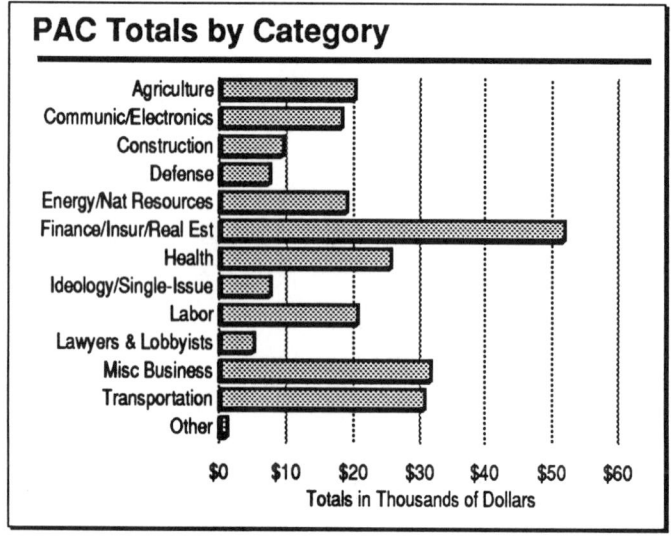

PAC Totals by Category

Agriculture
Communic/Electronics
Construction
Defense
Energy/Nat Resources
Finance/Insur/Real Est
Health
Ideology/Single-Issue
Labor
Lawyers & Lobbyists
Misc Business
Transportation
Other

$0 $10 $20 $30 $40 $50 $60

Totals in Thousands of Dollars

Real Estate **$8,510**
- National Assn of Realtors $4,410
- American Resort & Residential Developers Assn $2,150
- Others $1,950

Securities/Commodities Investment **$7,350**
- Morgan Stanley & Company $2,000
- Securities Industry Assn $1,600
- Chicago Board of Trade $1,000
- First Boston Corp $1,000
- Others $1,750

Telecommunications **$13,875**
- Michigan Bell Telephone $3,625
- AT&T $3,000
- Ameritech Corp $2,200
- Others $5,050

Tobacco **$7,600**
- Philip Morris $4,000
- RJR Nabisco $1,000
- United States Tobacco Company $1,000
- Others $1,600

Other Major Business PACs

National Venture Capital Assn	$2,000	Venture Cap
United Parcel Service	$1,300	Delivery
National Assn of Broadcasters	$1,200	TV/Radio
Great Lakes Sugar Beet Growers	$1,050	Sugar
Consolidated Freightways	$1,000	Trucking
Dow Chemical*	$1,000	Chemicals
General Electric	$1,000	Electronics
International Council of Shopping Centers	$1,000	Retail
Kelly Service Inc	$1,000	EmployAgency
Marriott Corp	$1,000	Hotel/Motel
National Assn of Temporary Services	$1,000	EmployAgency
Nevada Resort Assn	$1,000	Casinos/Gamb
Scott Paper Company	$1,000	Paper Prod
Union Pacific Corp	$1,000	Railroads

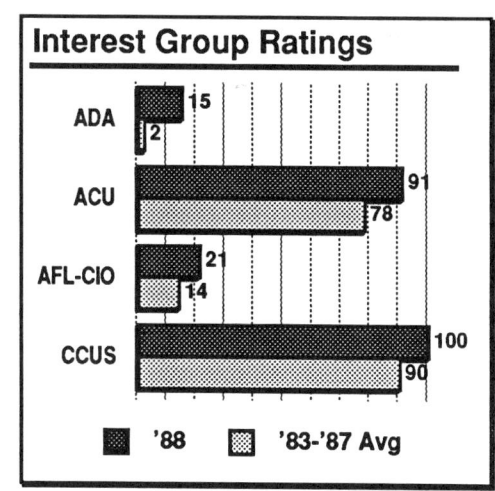

Labor

Government & Postal Workers **$6,300**
- National Assn of Letter Carriers $1,600
- National Assn of Postmasters $1,500
- National Rural Letter Carriers Assn $1,500
- National Assn of Retired Federal Employees $1,000
- Others $700

Transportation Unions **$13,400**
- Marine Engineers Union* $7,500
- Air Line Pilots Assn $3,500
- Seafarers International Union $2,000
- Others $400

Ideological/Single-Issue

Pro-Israel **$5,350**
- National PAC $5,000
- Others $350

Independent expenditures supporting Vander Jagt

National Cmte to Preserve Social Security $1,505

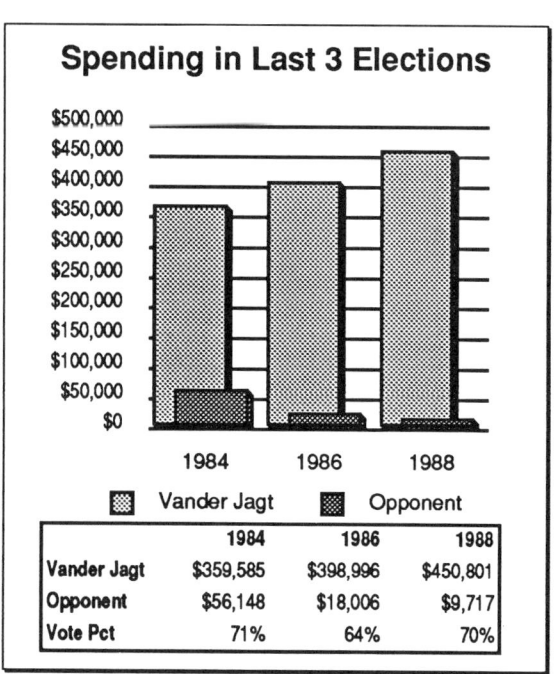

* Contributions came from more than one PAC affiliated with this sponsor.

Bruce F. Vento, D-Minn (4)

First elected: 1976
Total receipts: $268,237
Total from PACs: $188,459

1988 Committees & Subcommittees

Banking, Finance and Urban Affairs
Economic Stabilization
Financial Institutions Supervision, Regulation and Insurance
Housing and Community Development

Interior and Insular Affairs
National Parks and Public Lands (Chairman)
Insular and International Affairs

Select Aging
Health and Long-Term Care

PAC Contribution Profile

Business

Dairy **$7,650**
    Associated Milk Producers $4,000
    Land O'Lakes Inc $2,050
    Mid-American Dairymen $1,300
    Others $300

Electric Utilities **$2,262**
    None over $850

Financial Institutions **$18,975**
    US League of Savings Assns* $7,325
    Norwest Corp $3,000
    Credit Union National Assn $2,000
    Barnett Banks of Florida $1,500
    First Bank System/Minnesota $1,350
    Independent Bankers Assn $1,350
    Others $2,450

Health Professionals **$3,850**
    American Medical Assn $2,300
    American Dental Assn $1,000
    Others $550

Insurance **$4,150**
    National Assn of Life Underwriters $1,100
    Others $3,050

Lawyers & Lobbyists **$4,900**
    Assn of Trial Lawyers of America $2,500
    Others $2,400

Real Estate **$12,150**
    National Assn of Realtors $9,950
    Century 21 Real Estate $1,000
    Others $1,200

Securities Investment **$13,300**
    First Boston Corp $4,000
    Investment Company Institute $1,800
    Municipal Securities Industry $1,600
    Morgan Stanley & Company $1,500
    E F Hutton Group $1,050
    Federated Investors Inc $1,000
    Others $2,350

Sugar Growers **$6,000**
    Southern Minnesota Beet Sugar Co-op $2,500
    American Sugarbeet Growers Assn $1,600
    American Crystal Sugar Corp $1,300
    Others $600

Telecommunications **$2,025**
    North Weatern Bell Telephone $1,500
    Others $525

Other Major Business PACs

Aircraft Owners & Pilots Assn	$1,600	GenlAviation
National Assn of Home Builders	$1,000	Resid Constr
National Auto Dealers Assn	$1,000	Auto Sales

Campaign Revenue Sources

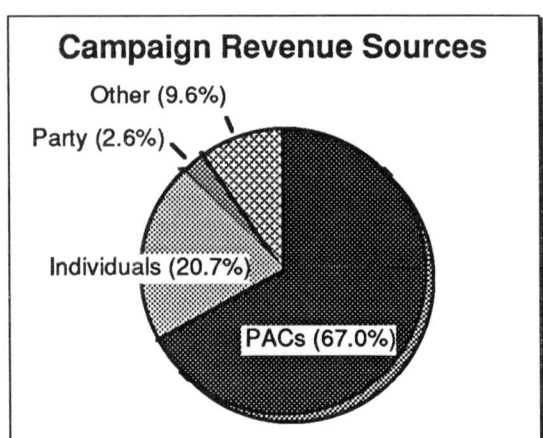

Other (9.6%)
Party (2.6%)
Individuals (20.7%)
PACs (67.0%)

PAC Totals by Category

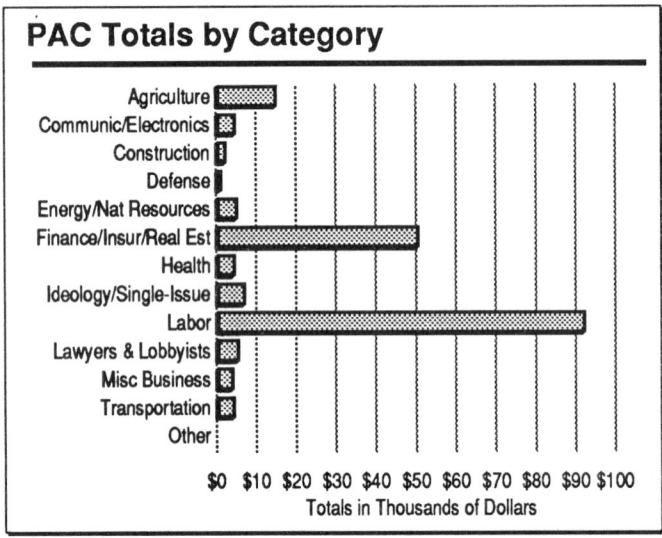

Agriculture
Communic/Electronics
Construction
Defense
Energy/Nat Resources
Finance/Insur/Real Est
Health
Ideology/Single-Issue
Labor
Lawyers & Lobbyists
Misc Business
Transportation
Other

$0 $10 $20 $30 $40 $50 $60 $70 $80 $90 $100
Totals in Thousands of Dollars

Labor

Bldg Trades/Industrial/Misc Unions $32,955

AFL-CIO*	$6,450
United Auto Workers	$4,600
Machinists/Aerospace Workers Union	$4,200
Operating Engineers Union	$3,200
Carpenters & Joiners Union	$2,500
Laborers' Political League	$1,900
Food & Commercial Workers Union	$1,000
Intl Brotherhood of Electrical Workers	$1,000
Ironworkers Union	$1,000
Painters & Allied Trades Union	$1,000
United Steelworkers	$1,000
Others	$5,105

Government & Postal Unions $26,550

National Assn of Retired Federal Employees	$8,000
American Postal Workers Union*	$5,000
National Assn of Letter Carriers*	$4,700
American Fedn of State/County/Munic Employees	$3,500
National Assn of Retired Federal Employees	$2,000
American Federation of Government Employees	$1,100
Others	$2,250

Teachers Unions $8,750

American Federation of Teachers	$5,000
National Education Assn	$2,500
Minnesota Education Assn	$1,250

Transportation Unions $24,200

Teamsters Union*	$10,300
Air Line Pilots Assn	$3,500
Marine Engineers District 2 Maritime Officers	$2,500
Amalgamated Transit Union	$1,850
United Transportation Union	$1,700
Seafarers International Union	$1,000
Others	$3,350

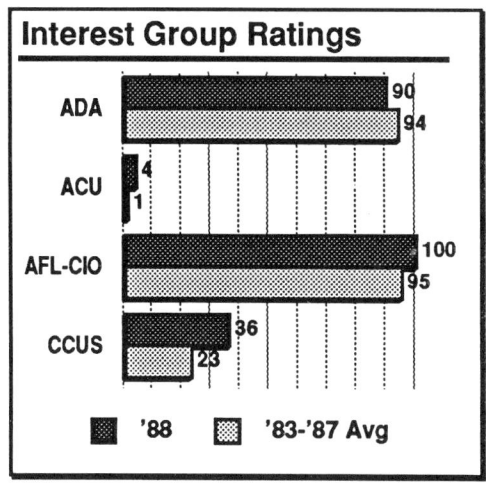

Interest Group Ratings

	'88	'83-'87 Avg
ADA	90	94
ACU	4	1
AFL-CIO	100	95
CCUS	36	23

■ '88   ▨ '83-'87 Avg

Ideological/Single-Issue

Ideological/Single-Issue $6,484

National Cmte for an Effective Congress	$2,496	Dem/Liberal
Sierra Club	$1,000	Environment
Valley Education Fund (Tony Coelho)	$1,000	Dem Leaders
Others	$1,988	

Independent expenditures supporting Vento

National Cmte to Preserve Social Security	$1,776

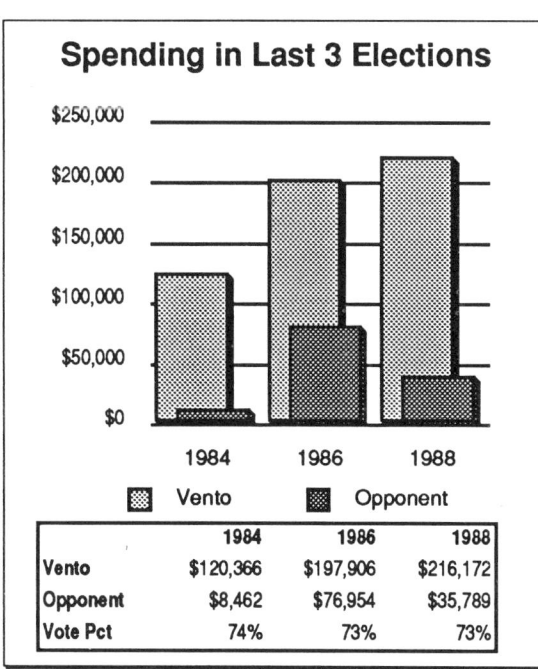

Spending in Last 3 Elections

	1984	1986	1988
Vento	$120,366	$197,906	$216,172
Opponent	$8,462	$76,954	$35,789
Vote Pct	74%	73%	73%

▨ Vento   ■ Opponent

---

* Contributions came from more than one PAC affiliated
with this sponsor.

Peter J. Visclosky, D-Ind (1)

First elected: 1984
Total receipts: $222,620
Total from PACs: $157,250

1988 Committees & Subcommittees

Education and Labor
Elementary, Secondary and Vocational Education
Human Resources

Interior and Insular Affairs
National Parks and Public Lands

Public Works and Transportation
Aviation
Water Resources

PAC Contribution Profile

Business

Aviation & Aerospace	**$2,950**
Aircraft Owners & Pilots Assn	$1,250
Others	$1,700
Commercial & Savings Banks	**$3,625**
Banc One Corp*	$1,200
American Bankers Assn	$1,000
Others	$1,425
Construction	**$3,550**
National Assn of Home Builders	$2,000
National Utility Contractors Assn	$1,000
Others	$550
Farm Organizations	**$4,375**
Indiana Farm Bureau	$4,375
Food & Beverage	**$3,000**
National Restaurant Assn	$2,000
Others	$1,000
Health Professionals	**$6,350**
American Medical Assn	$4,500
Others	$1,850
Insurance	**$2,000**
National Assn of Life Underwriters	$1,000
Others	$1,000
Lawyers & Lobbyists	**$6,250**
Assn of Trial Lawyers of America	$5,000
Others	$1,250

Oil & Gas	**$2,875**
None over $750	
Real Estate	**$7,250**
National Assn of Realtors	$7,000
Others	$250
Telecommunications	**$4,600**
Indiana Bell Telephone	$1,700
AT&T	$1,500
Continental Telecom	$1,000
Others	$400
Trucking/Delivery	**$4,300**
United Parcel Service	$2,600
Others	$1,700
Vocational Tech Schools	**$2,900**
National Assn of Trade/Tech Schools	$2,000
Others	$900

Other Major Business PACs

Waste Management Inc .... $1,250   Waste Mgmt

Campaign Revenue Sources

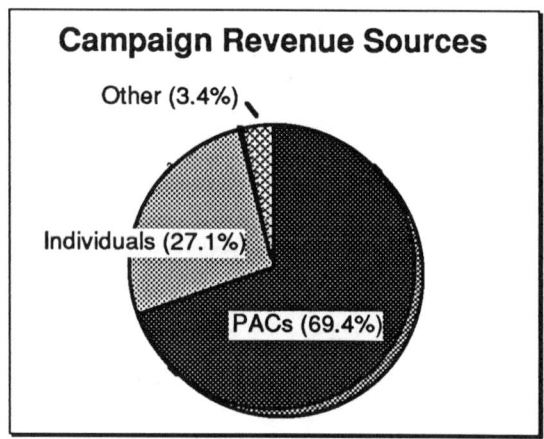

Other (3.4%)
Individuals (27.1%)
PACs (69.4%)

PAC Totals by Category

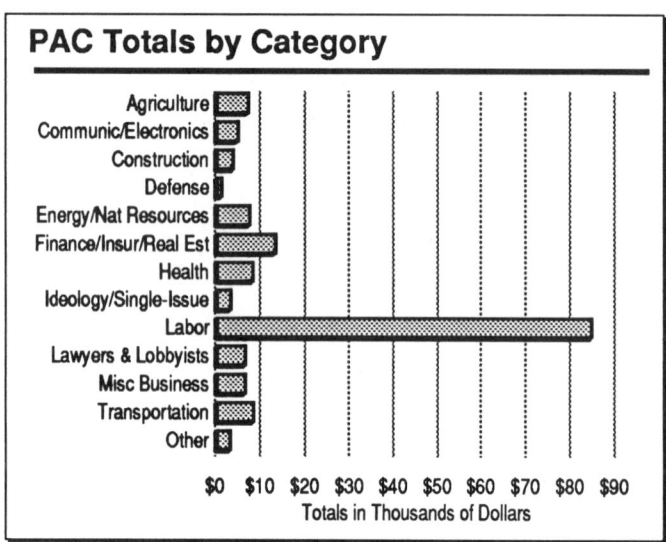

Agriculture
Communic/Electronics
Construction
Defense
Energy/Nat Resources
Finance/Insur/Real Est
Health
Ideology/Single-Issue
Labor
Lawyers & Lobbyists
Misc Business
Transportation
Other

$0 $10 $20 $30 $40 $50 $60 $70 $80 $90
Totals in Thousands of Dollars

Labor

Bldg Trades/Industrial/Misc Unions $44,800

United Auto Workers $10,000
Sheet Metal Workers Union $7,500
United Steelworkers $7,000
Machinists/Aerospace Workers Union $3,500
Carpenters & Joiners Union $2,750
Intl Brotherhood of Electrical Workers...........................$2,500
Operating Engineers Union $2,500
Laborers' Political League $2,000
Plumbers/Pipefitters Union $1,500
Food & Commercial Workers Union..............................$1,250
Others $4,300

Government & Postal Workers $9,750

American Fedn of State/County/Munic Employees $3,000
National Assn of Letter Carriers $3,000
National Assn of Retired Federal Employees $2,000
American Postal Workers Union $1,000
Others $750

Teachers Unions $8,750

National Education Assn $5,000
American Federation of Teachers $3,750

Transportation Unions $21,125

Teamsters Union $10,000
Air Line Pilots Assn $5,000
Amalgamated Transit Union $1,500
International Longshoremen Assn $1,500
United Transportation Union $1,000
Others $2,125

Major Ideological/Single-Issue PACs

Valley Education Fund (Tony Coelho) ....$1,000   Dem Leaders

Independent expenditures supporting Visclosky

National Cmte to Preserve Social Security $1,245

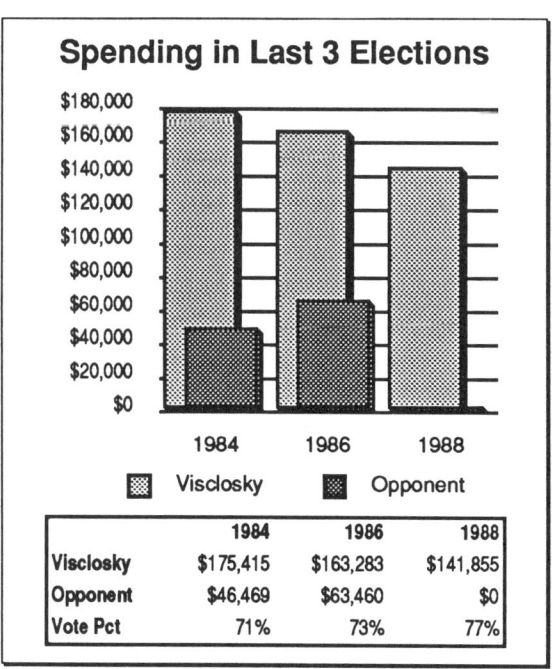

Spending in Last 3 Elections

Visclosky   Opponent

	1984	1986	1988
Visclosky	$175,415	$163,283	$141,855
Opponent	$46,469	$63,460	$0
Vote Pct	71%	73%	77%

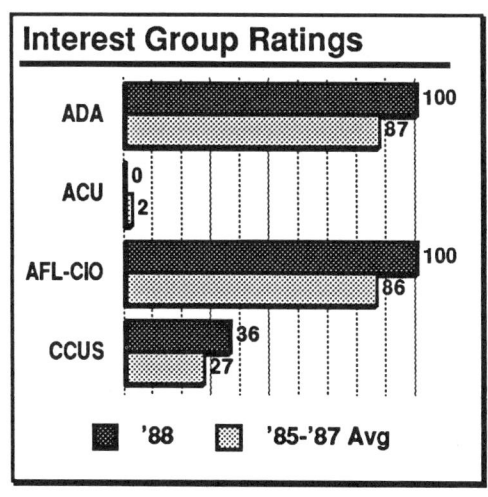

Interest Group Ratings

ADA — 100 ('88), 87 ('85-'87 Avg)
ACU — 0 ('88), 2 ('85-'87 Avg)
AFL-CIO — 100 ('88), 86 ('85-'87 Avg)
CCUS — 36 ('88), 27 ('85-'87 Avg)

■ '88   ▨ '85-'87 Avg

---

* Contributions came from more than one PAC affiliated with this sponsor.

Harold L. Volkmer, D-Mo (9)

First elected: 1976
Total receipts: $300,348
Total from PACs: $218,185

1988 Committees & Subcommittees

Agriculture
Forests, Family Farms and Energy (Chairman)
Livestock, Dairy and Poultry
Wheat, Soybeans and Feed Grains

Science, Space and Technology
Investigations and Oversight
Space Science and Applications

Select Aging
Housing and Consumer Interests
Retirement Income and Employment

PAC Contribution Profile

Business

Agricultural Chemicals **$3,150**
American Cyanimid* $1,050
Others $2,100

Automotive **$9,400**
National Auto Dealers Assn $8,300
General Motors $1,100

Aviation & Aerospace **$4,350**
None over $900

Dairy **$21,350**
Associated Milk Producers $10,000
Mid-American Dairymen $10,000
Dairymen Inc $1,350

Defense **$5,000**
Rockwell International $1,000
Others $4,000

Electric Utilities **$4,250**
Missouri ACRE $3,200
Others $1,050

Financial Institutions **$7,380**
American Bankers Assn $3,250
Credit Union National Assn $1,300
Others $2,830

Campaign Revenue Sources

Candidate (0.7%) Other (2.0%)
Individuals (25.2%)
PACs (71.7%)

Food & Beverage **$5,400**
American Meat Institute $1,300
Food Marketing Institute $1,300
Others $2,800

Forest Products **$2,600**
National Forest Products Assn $1,100
International Paper Company $1,000
Others $500

Health Professionals **$6,850**
American Medical Assn $5,300
Missouri Medical Assn $1,000
Others $550

Insurance **$6,550**
National Assn of Life Underwriters $2,000
Shelter Mutual Insurance $1,450
Business Mens Assurance Company $1,000
General American Life Insurance $1,000
Others $1,100

Lawyers **$2,300**
Assn of Trial Lawyers of America $2,000
Williams & Jensen $300

Real Estate **$7,000**
National Assn of Realtors $7,000

Sugar Growers **$3,100**
None over $850

Telecommunications **$7,950**
Continental Telecom $3,000
Southwestern Bell $2,000
AT&T $1,900
Others $1,050

Other Major Business PACs
Farmland Industries .... $1,000 Ag Svcs
Waste Management Inc .... $1,000 Waste Mgmt

PAC Totals by Category

Agriculture
Communic/Electronics
Construction
Defense
Energy/Nat Resources
Finance/Insur/Real Est
Health
Ideology/Single-Issue
Labor
Lawyers & Lobbyists
Misc Business
Transportation
Other

$0 $10 $20 $30 $40 $50 $60 $70 $80 $90
Totals in Thousands of Dollars

Labor

Bldg Trades/Industrial/Misc Unions $41,700

United Auto Workers $10,000
Machinists/Aerospace Workers* $6,600
Intl Brotherhood of Electrical Workers...........................$4,000
Carpenters & Joiners Union* $3,600
Communications Workers of America $3,000
AFL-CIO $2,500
Laborers' Political League $2,500
Operating Engineers Union $2,000
Sheet Metal Workers Union $1,800
Food & Commercial Workers Union................................$1,350
Ladies Garment Workers Union $1,050
United Steelworkers $1,000
Others $2,300

Government & Postal Workers $18,000

National Assn of Retired Federal Employees $8,000
National Assn of Letter Carriers* $4,300
National Rural Letter Carriers Assn $2,500
American Postal Workers Union $2,100
Others $1,100

Teachers Unions $10,000

National Education Assn $10,000

Transportation Unions $12,850

Teamsters Union $8,000
Seafarers International Union $2,000
United Transportation Union $2,000
Others $850

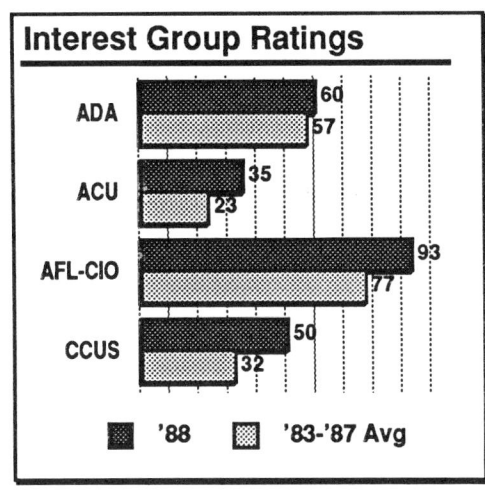

Interest Group Ratings

ADA 60 / 57
ACU 35 / 23
AFL-CIO 93 / 77
CCUS 50 / 32

■ '88   ▨ '83-'87 Avg

Ideological/Single-Issue

Democratic Leadership PACs.......................................$6,000

Majority Congress Committee (Jim Wright) $5,000
Valley Education Fund (Tony Coelho) $1,000

Pro-Gun Ownership...$10,900

National Rifle Assn $9,900
Safari Club International $1,000

Other Major Ideological/Single-Issue PACs

St Louisians for Better Government................$1,500   Pro-Israel

Independent expenditures supporting Volkmer

Letter Carriers Branch #343 ....$2,000
National Cmte to Preserve Social Security $1,766
Missouri Citizens for Life...$1,728

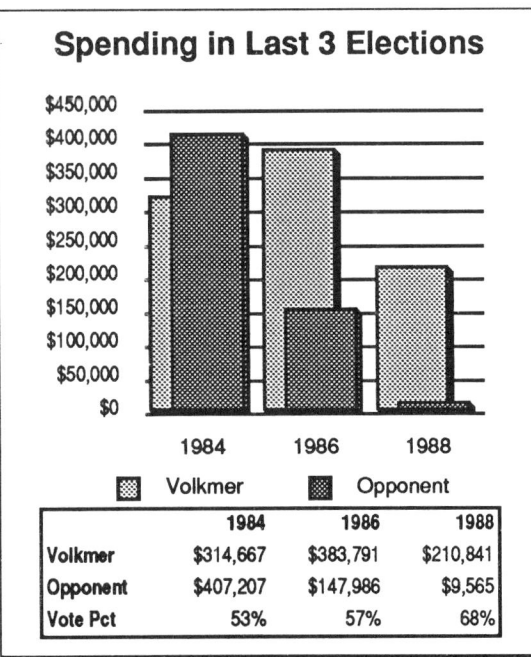

Spending in Last 3 Elections

	1984	1986	1988
Volkmer	$314,667	$383,791	$210,841
Opponent	$407,207	$147,986	$9,565
Vote Pct	53%	57%	68%

▨ Volkmer   ■ Opponent

---

* Contributions came from more than one PAC affiliated
with this sponsor.

Barbara Vucanovich, R-Nev (2)

1988 Committees & Subcommittees

Interior and Insular Affairs
Energy and the Environment
Mining and Natural Resources
National Parks and Public Lands

House Administration
Accounts
Elections

Select Children, Youth and Families

PAC Contribution Profile

Business

Automotive	**$11,400**
Auto Dealers & Drivers for Free Trade	$6,500
National Auto Dealers Assn	$4,150
Others	$750
Aviation & Aerospace	**$2,733**
Aircraft Owners & Pilots Assn	$1,983
Others	$750
Business Associations	**$5,977**
National Fedn of Independent Business	$3,659
Business Industry PAC	$2,296
Others	$22
Casinos/Gambling	**$22,841**
Circus Circus Enterprises	$5,391
Hilton Nevada Corp	$3,500
Harrah's	$2,500
California Hotel & Casino PAC	$2,000
Summa Corp	$2,000
Union Plaza	$2,000
Bally Manufacturing	$1,500
Sierra Development Company	$1,300
Bally's Grand Inc	$1,000
Caesars World	$1,000
Others	$650
Commercial Banks	**$3,650**
Nevada National Bancorp	$1,250
American Bankers Assn	$1,000
Others	$1,400

Campaign Revenue Sources

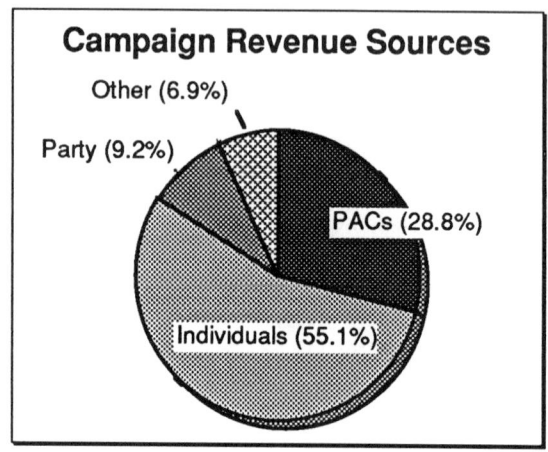

Other (6.9%)
Party (9.2%)
PACs (28.8%)
Individuals (55.1%)

Construction	**$15,650**
National Assn of Home Builders	$9,500
Associated General Contractors	$1,550
Associated Builders & Contractors	$1,250
National Electrical Contractors Assn	$1,000
Others	$2,350
Defense	**$6,250**
Gencorp Inc	$1,500
TRW Inc	$1,100
Rockwell International	$1,000
Others	$2,650
Electric Utilities	**$8,250**
Sierra Pacific Resources*	$2,800
ACRE (Action Committee for Rural Electrification)	$1,500
Idaho Power Company	$1,500
Others	$2,450
Food & Beverage	**$6,700**
National Restaurant Assn	$4,000
Others	$2,700
Health Professionals	**$6,750**
American Medical Assn	$2,500
American Dental Assn	$2,000
American Academy of Ophthalmology	$1,000
Cmte for Quality Orthopedic Health Care	$1,000
Others	$250
Hotels & Motels	**$2,300**
Holiday Corp	$1,000
Others	$1,300
Insurance	**$12,500**
National Assn of Life Underwriters	$4,500
National Assn Mutual Insurance Agents	$2,550
National Assn of Independent Insurers	$1,400
Independent Insurance Agents of America	$1,300
Others	$2,750

PAC Totals by Category

Agriculture
Communic/Electronics
Construction
Defense
Energy/Nat Resources
Finance/Insur/Real Est
Health
Ideology/Single-Issue
Labor
Lawyers & Lobbyists
Misc Business
Transportation
Other

$0 $5 $10 $15 $20 $25 $30 $35 $40 $45 $50
Totals in Thousands of Dollars

Interest Group Ratings

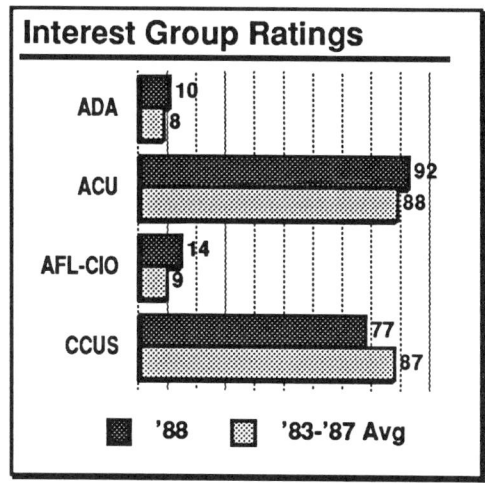

	'88	'83-'87 Avg
ADA	10	8
ACU	92	88
AFL-CIO	14	9
CCUS	77	87

Mining & Metal Processing **$13,950**

FMC Corp	$6,000
Cyprus Minerals Company	$1,500
Phelps Dodge Corp	$1,100
National Coal Assn	$1,050
Freeport-McMoran Inc	$1,000
Others	$3,300

Oil & Gas **$24,857**

Southwest Gas Corp	$3,000
Cooper Industries	$2,000
Exxon Corp	$2,000
Phillips Petroleum	$1,500
Sun Company	$1,500
Amoco Corp	$1,100
Southland Corp	$1,007
Chevron Corp	$1,000
Dow Chemical*	$1,000
Mesa PAC II	$1,000
Others	$9,750

Real Estate **$10,300**

National Assn of Realtors	$10,000
Others	$300

Retail Sales **$3,100**

J C Penney Company	$1,500
Others	$1,600

Telecommunications **$5,800**

Continental Telecom	$2,000
Pacific Telesis Group	$1,500
AT&T	$1,000
Others	$1,300

Other Major Business PACs

Boise Cascade	$1,000	Forestry

Major Labor PACs

Seafarers International Union	$1,000	Seamen Union

Ideological/Single-Issue

Pro-Gun Ownership **$9,900**

National Rifle Assn	$9,900

Other Major Ideological/Single-Issue PACs

Public Service Research Council	$1,250	Anti-Union
Americans for Constitutional Action	$1,000	Repub/Conser
Republican Congressional Boosters Club	$1,000	Repub/Conser

Spending in Last 3 Elections

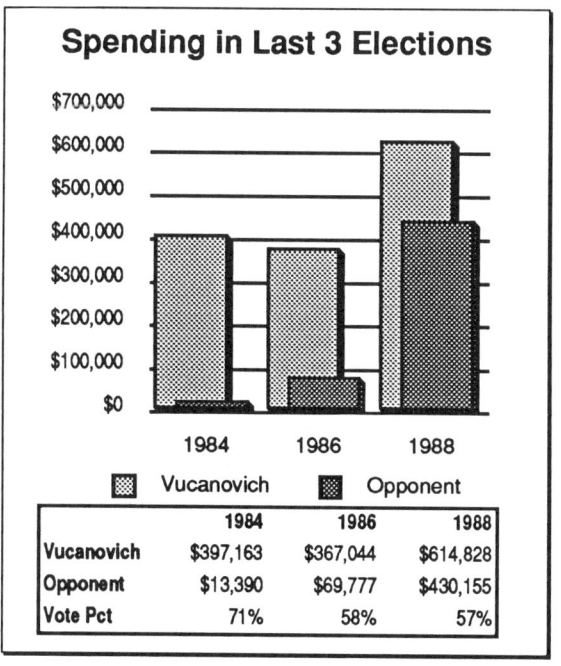

	Vucanovich	Opponent

	1984	1986	1988
Vucanovich	$397,163	$367,044	$614,828
Opponent	$13,390	$69,777	$430,155
Vote Pct	71%	58%	57%

---

* Contributions came from more than one PAC affiliated with this sponsor.

Doug Walgren, D-Pa (18)

1988 Committees & Subcommittees

First elected: 1976
Total receipts: $389,537
Total from PACs: $232,214

Energy and Commerce
Energy and Power
Health and the Environment
Oversight and Investigations

Science, Space and Technology
Science, Research and Technology (Chairman)
Energy Research and Development

PAC Contribution Profile

Business

Accountants	*$8,600*
American Institute of CPA's	$5,000
Coopers & Lybrand	$1,500
Arthur Young & Company	$1,250
Others	$850
Commercial & Savings Banks	*$8,850*
American Bankers Assn	$4,000
Citicorp	$2,000
Barnett Banks of Florida	$1,000
Others	$1,850
Construction	*$5,900*
National Concrete Masonry Assn	$2,500
National Assn of Home Builders	$1,250
Others	$2,150
Health Professionals	*$34,000*
American Podiatry Assn	$6,500
American Dental Assn	$4,000
American Optometric Assn	$2,500
American Nurses Assn	$2,000
American Physical Therapy Assn	$1,800
American College of Emergency Physicians	$1,600
American Academy of Ophthalmology	$1,500
American Society Cataract/Refract Surgery	$1,500
American Medical Assn	$1,500
Assn for Advancement of Psychology	$1,500
Oral & Maxillofacial Surgeons	$1,500
American Assn of Nurse Anesthetist	$1,250
American Chiropractic Assn	$1,250

(Continued in next column)

Campaign Revenue Sources

Other (4.8%)

Individuals (22.4%)

PACs (72.6%)

PAC Totals by Category

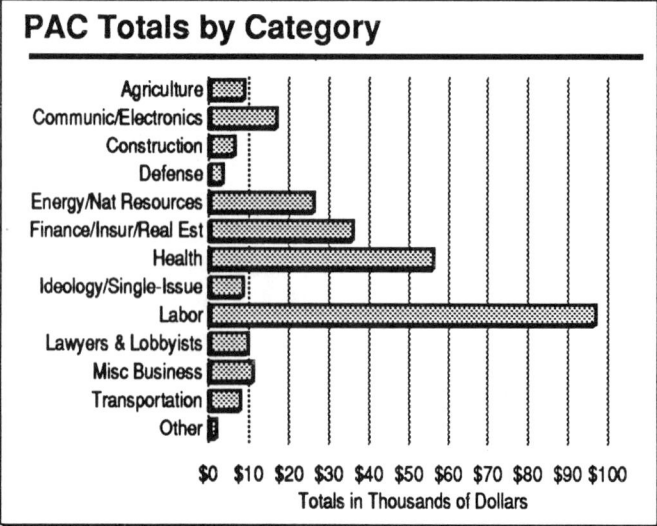

Agriculture
Communic/Electronics
Construction
Defense
Energy/Nat Resources
Finance/Insur/Real Est
Health
Ideology/Single-Issue
Labor
Lawyers & Lobbyists
Misc Business
Transportation
Other

$0 $10 $20 $30 $40 $50 $60 $70 $80 $90 $100
Totals in Thousands of Dollars

Health Professionals (cont'd)	
Corp for the Advancement of Psychiatry	$1,250
American Dietetic Assn	$1,000
Cmte for Quality Orthopedic Health Care	$1,000
Others	$2,350
Hospitals & Nursing Homes	*$7,550*
American Health Care Assn	$5,000
American Hospital Assn	$1,050
Manor Healthcare Corp	$1,000
Others	$500
Insurance	*$9,050*
Blue Cross & Blue Shield Assn	$2,250
American Council of Life Insurance	$1,300
National Assn of Life Underwriters	$1,250
National Assn Mutual Insurance Agents	$1,000
Travelers Corp	$1,000
Others	$2,250
Lawyers & Lobbyists	*$9,300*
Assn of Trial Lawyers of America	$5,000
Kirkpatrick & Lockhart	$1,300
Others	$3,000
Oil & Gas	*$14,031*
Columbia Gas*	$2,100
W R Grace & Company	$1,000
Others	$10,931
Pharmaceuticals	*$6,950*
Hoffman-La Roche	$1,050
Smithkline Beckman	$1,000
Others	$4,900
Securities/Commodities Investment	*$5,550*
Chicago Board of Trade	$1,000
Investment Company Institute	$1,000
Salomon Brothers	$1,000
Others	$2,550
Telecommunications	*$11,800*
AT&T	$3,000
Pacific Telesis Group	$1,750
Bell Telephone of Pennsylvania	$1,500
Continental Telecom	$1,000
United Telecommunications*	$1,000
Others	$3,550

Other Major Business PACs

National Assn of Realtors	$3,650	Real Estate
American Orthotic/Prosthetic Assn	$2,500	Med Supply
National Cable Television Assn	$2,000	CableTV
United Parcel Service	$1,750	Delivery
Waste Management Inc	$1,750	Waste Mgmt
American Veterinary Medical Assn	$1,500	Veterinary
National Society of Professional Engineers	$1,500	Energy
Valmont Industries	$1,250	Electronics
American Sugarbeet Growers Assn	$1,050	Sugar
Bethlehem Steel	$1,050	Steel
Health Industry Manufacturers Assn	$1,050	Med Supply
Allied-Signal	$1,000	Air Defense
Chrysler Corp	$1,000	Auto Mfrs
Cosmetic Toiletry & Fragrance Assn	$1,000	Cosmetics
Independent Coal Operators Assn	$1,000	Coal
Martin Marietta Corp	$1,000	Space Equip
McDermott Inc*	$1,000	PowerEquip
Medical Equipment Suppliers	$1,000	Med Supply
National Assn for Home Care	$1,000	Home Care
National Beer Wholesalers Assn	$1,000	Liquor Whlsl

Labor

Bldg Trades/Industrial/Misc Unions $28,300

United Auto Workers	$6,500
Carpenters & Joiners Union	$3,500
Ironworkers Union	$2,500
Operating Engineers Union	$2,000
Laborers' Political League	$1,550
Intl Brotherhood of Electrical Workers	$1,500
AFL-CIO*	$1,300
Ladies Garment Workers Union	$1,300
Machinists/Aerospace Workers Union	$1,300
Plumbers/Pipefitters Union	$1,250
Boilermakers Union	$1,050
Food & Commercial Workers Union	$1,000
Others	$3,550

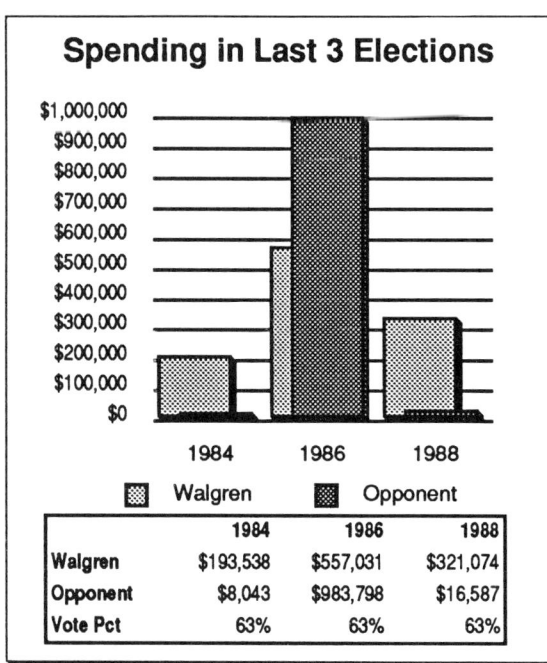

Spending in Last 3 Elections

Walgren · Opponent

	1984	1986	1988
Walgren	$193,538	$557,031	$321,074
Opponent	$8,043	$983,798	$16,587
Vote Pct	63%	63%	63%

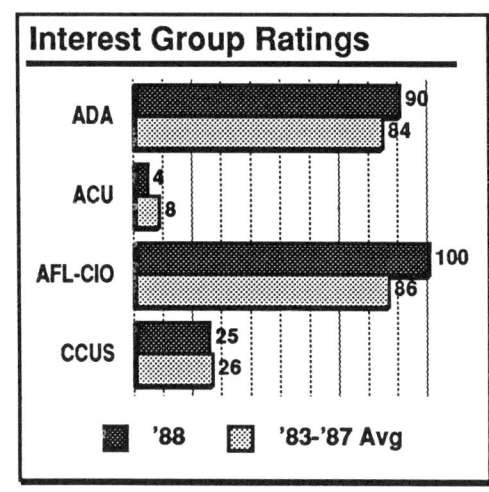

Interest Group Ratings

ADA 90 / 84
ACU 4 / 8
AFL-CIO 100 / 86
CCUS 25 / 26

■ '88   ▨ '83–'87 Avg

Government & Postal Workers $26,747

American Fedn of State/County/Munic Employees	$9,697
National Assn of Retired Federal Employees	$6,000
National Assn of Letter Carriers	$5,500
American Postal Workers Union*	$3,750
Others	$1,800

Teachers Unions $14,200

National Education Assn	$10,000
American Federation of Teachers	$4,200

Transportation Unions $27,100

Teamsters Union	$7,500
Marine Engineers Union*	$3,500
United Transportation Union	$3,500
Amalgamated Transit Union	$2,300
Air Line Pilots Assn	$2,000
Seafarers International Union	$1,500
Transportation Communication Union	$1,300
Brotherhood of Locomotive Engineers	$1,250
Brotherhood of Railroad Signalmen	$1,000
Transport Workers Union	$1,000
Others	$2,250

Ideological/Single-Issue

Ideological/Single-Issue $7,949

National Cmte to Preserve Social Security	$2,500	Soc Secur
National Cmte for an Effective Congress	$2,499	Dem/Liberal
KidsPAC	$1,000	HealthWelfare
Valley Education Fund (Tony Coelho)	$1,000	Dem Leaders
Others	$950	

---

* Contributions came from more than one PAC affiliated
with this sponsor.

Robert S. Walker, R-Pa (16)

First elected: 1976
Total receipts: $106,318
Total from PACs: $43,875

1988 Committees & Subcommittees

Government Operations
Legislation and National Security

Science, Space and Technology
Space Science and Applications (Ranking Republican)
Transportation, Aviation and Materials

PAC Contribution Profile

Business

Aerospace	**$3,700**
Boeing Company	$1,000
Martin Marietta Corp	$800
United Technologies	$800
Morton Thiokol	$500
Others	$600
Automotive	**$1,100**
Auto Dealers & Drivers for Free Trade	$500
Others	$600
Construction	**$3,100**
National Assn of Home Builders	$2,000
Ch2M Hill	$500
Others	$600
Defense	**$3,250**
McDonnell Douglas	$900
Harris Corp	$500
Hughes Aircraft	$500
Others	$1,350
Department Stores	**$1,350**
J C Penney Company	$500
Others	$850
Electronics & Computers	**$1,950**
National Computer Systems	$650
Computer Sciences Corp	$500
NCR Corp	$500
Others	$300

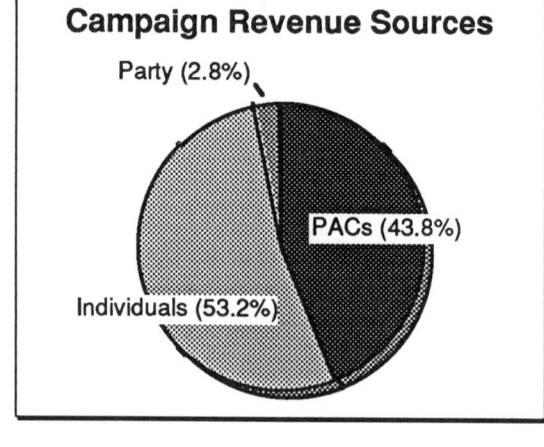

Campaign Revenue Sources

Party (2.8%)
PACs (43.8%)
Individuals (53.2%)

Financial Institutions	**$2,850**
Hamilton Bank	$550
American Bankers Assn	$500
Meridian Bancorp	$500
Pennsylvania Bankers Assn	$500
Pennsylvania Savings League	$500
Others	$300
Food & Beverage	**$2,700**
National Confectioners Assn	$800
Kellogg Company	$500
Nabisco Brands Inc	$500
Others	$900
Health Professionals	**$2,000**
American Medical Assn	$2,000
Industrial Equipment & Materials	**$1,900**
Fuller Company	$1,000
Emhart Corp	$600
Others	$300
Lawyers	**$1,600**
Assn of Trial Lawyers of America	$500
Garvey, Schubert & Barer	$500
Others	$600
Mining & Metal Processing	**$1,600**
Dravo Corp	$800
Alcoa	$500
Others	$300
Oil & Gas	**$1,100**
None over $350	
Pharmaceuticals	**$3,750**
Sterling Drug	$1,000
American Home Products Corp	$500
Smithkline Beckman	$500
Others	$1,750
Real Estate	**$1,300**
National Assn of Realtors	$1,300

PAC Totals by Category

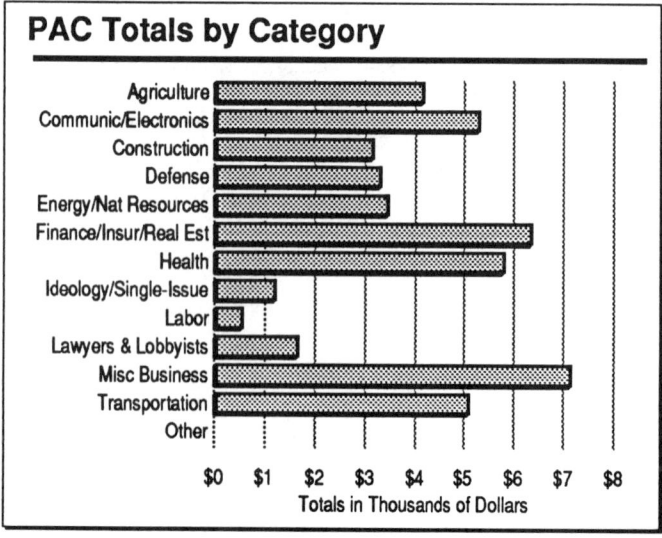

Totals in Thousands of Dollars

Telecommunications **$2,800**

Bell Telephone of Pennsylvania	$1,000
Comsat	$500
Continental Telecom	$500
United Telecommunications	$500
Others	$300

Other Major Business PACs

Milk Industry Foundation	$550	Dairy
American Institute of CPA's	$500	Accountants
Amway Corp	$500	Direct Sales
Bowling Proprietors Assn	$500	AmuseCtr
Equifax Inc	$500	CreditReport
FMC Corp	$500	Chemicals
Gilbert Associates	$500	NuclearEquip
National Assn of Life Underwriters	$500	Life Insurance
R R Donnelley & Sons	$500	Publishing

Major Labor PACs

Marine Engineers District 2 Maritime Officers	$500	Seamen Union

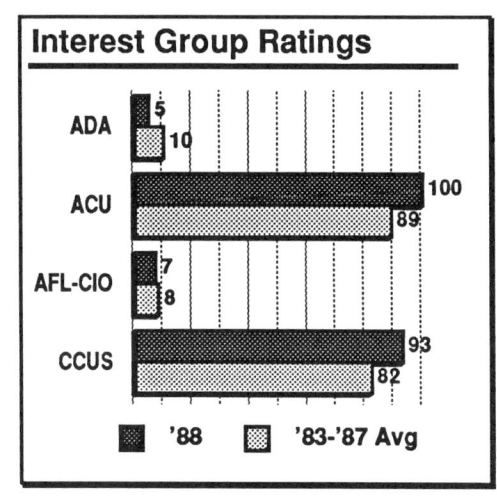

Interest Group Ratings

	'88	'83-'87 Avg
ADA	5	10
ACU	100	89
AFL-CIO	7	8
CCUS	93	82

■ '88   ▨ '83-'87 Avg

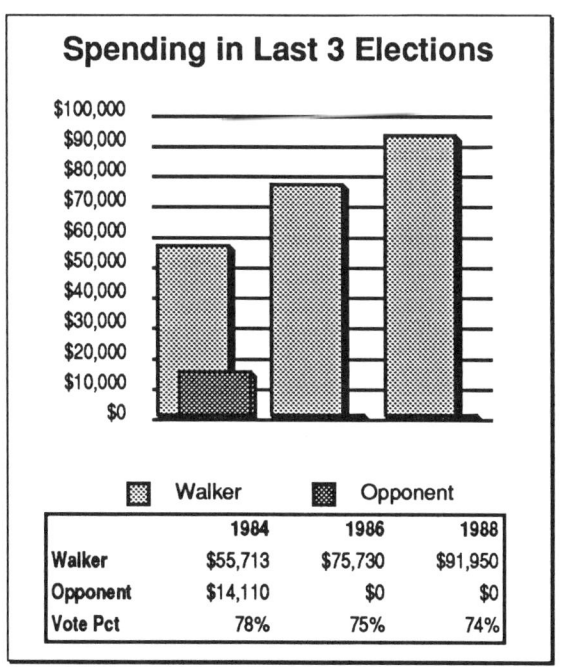

Spending in Last 3 Elections

▨ Walker   ■ Opponent

	1984	1986	1988
Walker	$55,713	$75,730	$91,950
Opponent	$14,110	$0	$0
Vote Pct	78%	75%	74%

James T. Walsh, R-NY (27)

First elected: 1988
Total receipts: $610,935
Total from PACs: $202,620

1989-90 Committees & Subcommittees

Agriculture
Department Operations, Research and Foreign Agriculture
Livestock, Dairy and Poultry

House Administration
Office Systems (Ranking Republican)
Elections
Libraries and Memorials

Select Children, Youth and Families

Joint Library

PAC Contribution Profile

Business

Automotive **$13,500**
National Auto Dealers Assn $6,000
Auto Dealers & Drivers for Free Trade $5,000
Eaton Corp $2,000
Others $500

Business Associations **$4,648**
Business Industry PAC $2,121
National Fedn of Independent Business $2,000
Others $527

Chemicals & Plastics **$3,000**
FMC Corp $1,000
Others $2,000

Commercial Banks **$19,925**
Marine Midland Banks $5,000
American Bankers Assn $3,000
Barnett Banks of Florida $2,500
Citicorp $2,500
Chase Manhattan* $2,000
Bankers Trust $1,000
J P Morgan & Company $1,000
Keycorp $1,000
Others $1,925

Construction **$9,000**
National Assn of Home Builders $5,000
Associated Builders & Contractors $1,250
Associated General Contractors $1,000
Others $1,750

Campaign Revenue Sources

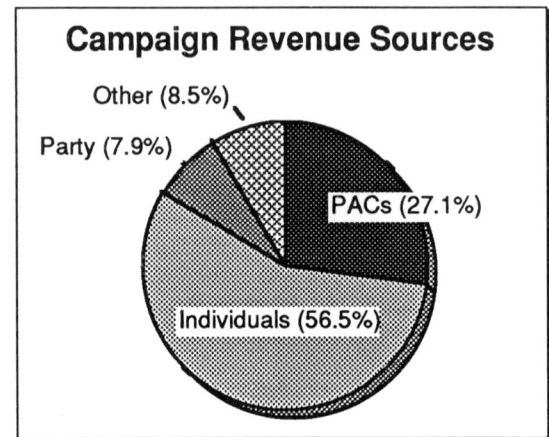

Other (8.5%)
Party (7.9%)
PACs (27.1%)
Individuals (56.5%)

Dairy **$3,000**
Associated Milk Producers $2,000
Others $1,000

Defense **$8,500**
United Technologies $3,500
Harris Corp $2,000
Others $3,000

Electric Utilities **$8,725**
Niagara Mohawk Power Corp $2,650
New York State Electric & Gas Corp $2,500
Others $3,575

Electronics **$2,300**
Cooper Industries $2,000
Others $300

Food & Beverage **$3,350**
National Restaurant Assn $1,000
Others $2,350

Health Professionals **$18,500**
American Medical Assn $10,000
American Academy of Ophthalmology $3,000
American Dental Assn $2,500
American Optometric Assn $2,500
Others $500

Industrial Equipment & Materials **$2,000**
Goulds Pumps Inc $1,000
Minnesota Mining & Manufacturing (3M) $1,000

Insurance **$15,500**
National Assn of Life Underwriters $5,000
American Family Corp $2,500
Casualty & Surety Agents Assn $1,000
Independent Insurance Agents of America $1,000
Nationwide Corp $1,000
Others $5,000

PAC Totals by Category

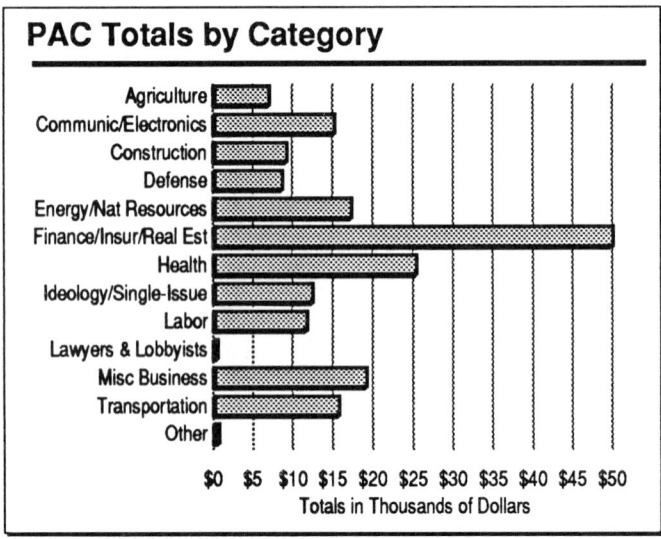

Agriculture
Communic/Electronics
Construction
Defense
Energy/Nat Resources
Finance/Insur/Real Est
Health
Ideology/Single-Issue
Labor
Lawyers & Lobbyists
Misc Business
Transportation
Other

$0 $5 $10 $15 $20 $25 $30 $35 $40 $45 $50
Totals in Thousands of Dollars

Nursing Homes	$2,250
American Health Care Assn	$2,250

Oil & Gas	$8,350
None over $800	

Pharmaceuticals	$4,450
Bristol-Myers	$1,000
Schering-Plough Corp	$1,000
Others	$2,450

Real Estate	$8,900
National Assn of Realtors	$8,400
Others	$500

Retail Sales	$2,007
Southland Corp	$1,007
Others	$1,000

Savings Banks & Credit Unions	$4,100
Credit Union National Assn	$2,000
Goldome Bank for Savings	$1,500
Others	$600

Telecommunications	$11,653
AT&T	$5,000
New York Telephone	$1,653
Continental Telecom	$1,000
Others	$4,000

Other Major Business PACs

Oneida Ltd	$1,500	Hous/Off Prd
Agway Inc	$1,250	Farm Equip
Corning Glass Works	$1,000	Glass Prod
Goldman Sachs	$1,000	InvestmtBank
Precision Metalforming Assn	$1,000	MetalProduct

Labor

Labor Unions	$11,500
American Fedn of State/County/Munic Employees	$5,000
Intl Brotherhood of Electrical Workers	$4,500
Air Line Pilots Assn	$1,000
Others	$1,000

Ideological/Single-Issue

Republican Leadership PACs	$4,977
Campaign America (Bob Dole)	$1,377
15th District Committee (Edward Madigan)	$1,000
Catch the Spirit PAC (Bob Kasten)	$1,000
Republican Leader's Fund (Bob Michel)	$1,000
Others	$600

Other Major Ideological/Single-Issue PACs

National PAC	$5,000	Pro-Israel
National Security PAC	$1,000	Pro-Defense
Public Svc Research Council	$1,000	Anti-Union

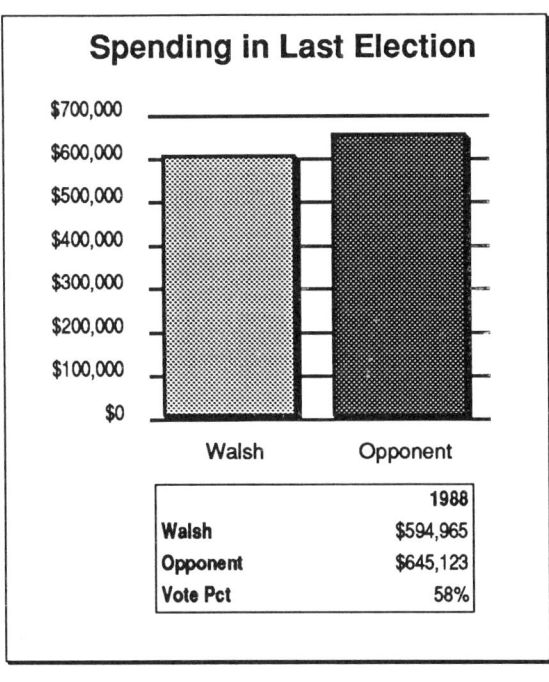

Spending in Last Election

	1988
Walsh	$594,965
Opponent	$645,123
Vote Pct	58%

* Contributions came from more than one PAC affiliated with this sponsor.

Wes Watkins, D-Okla (3)

1988 Committees & Subcommittees

Appropriations
District of Columbia
Energy and Water Development
Rural Development, Agriculture and Related Agencies

First elected: 1976
Total receipts: $241,418
Total from PACs: $73,900

PAC Contribution Profile
Business

Construction	**$4,900**
National Assn of Home Builders	$2,300
Associated General Contractors	$1,300
National Utility Contractors Assn	$1,000
Others	$300
Dairy	**$4,100**
Associated Milk Producers	$3,000
Mid-American Dairymen	$600
Dairymen Inc	$500
Defense	**$3,025**
Rockwell International	$1,025
LTV Aerospace & Defense Company	$800
Martin Marietta Corp	$600
Others	$600
Electric Utilities	**$2,700**
Oklahoma Gas & Electric	$1,000
ACRE (Action Committee for Rural Electrification)	$900
Others	$800
Financial Institutions	**$3,525**
Oklahoma League of Savings Institutions	$1,300
American Bankers Assn	$1,000
Others	$1,225
Food & Beverage	**$1,550**
ConAgra Inc	$750
Others	$800

Campaign Revenue Sources

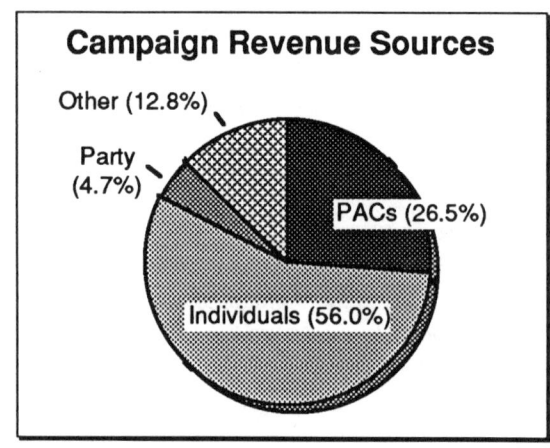

Other (12.8%)
Party (4.7%)
PACs (26.5%)
Individuals (56.0%)

Health Professionals	**$3,600**
Oklahoma Medical Assn	$1,300
American Dental Assn	$1,000
National Assn of Pharmacists	$1,000
Others	$300
Insurance	**$1,550**
National Assn of Life Underwriters	$1,000
Others	$550
Lawyers & Lobbyists	**$2,750**
Assn of Trial Lawyers of America	$1,000
Burson-Marsteller	$600
Others	$1,150
Oil & Gas	**$9,050**
Enserch Corp	$1,500
Phillips Petroleum	$1,000
Burlington Northern	$600
Mapco Inc	$600
Williams Companies	$600
Others	$4,750
Poultry & Livestock	**$2,650**
Texas Cattle Feeders Assn	$1,000
Others	$1,650
Real Estate	**$1,200**
Mortgage Bankers Assn of America	$600
National Assn of Realtors	$600
Sugar Growers	**$2,350**
American Crystal Sugar Corp	$600
American Sugarbeet Growers Assn	$600
Rio Grande Valley Sugar Growers	$550
Others	$600
Telecommunications	**$5,300**
AT&T	$2,000
Southwestern Bell	$1,500
GTE (Southwest)	$1,250
National Telephone Co-op Assn	$550
Trucking/Delivery	**$1,850**
United Parcel Service	$1,050
Others	$800

PAC Totals by Category

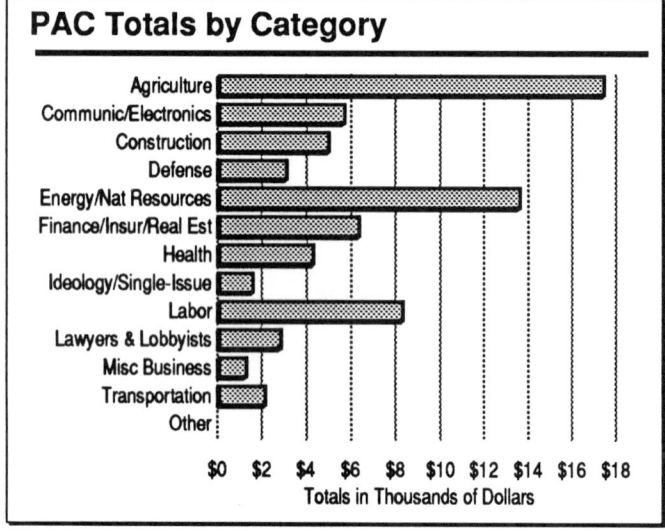

Agriculture
Communic/Electronics
Construction
Defense
Energy/Nat Resources
Finance/Insur/Real Est
Health
Ideology/Single-Issue
Labor
Lawyers & Lobbyists
Misc Business
Transportation
Other

$0 $2 $4 $6 $8 $10 $12 $14 $16 $18
Totals in Thousands of Dollars

Veterinarians *$2,000*
    American Veterinary Medical Assn $2,000

Other Major Business PACs

National Cotton Council $900	Cotton
American Textile Manufacturers Institute $600	Textiles
Chrysler Corp $600	Auto Mfrs
General Electric.. $600	NuclearEquip
Tobacco Institute $600	Tobacco
Southwest Peanut Membership Organization $550	Crops

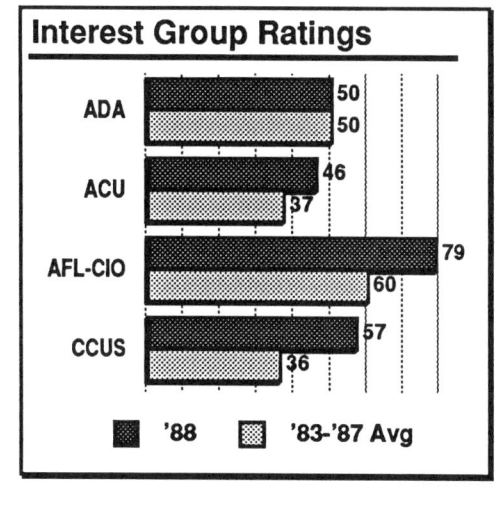

Labor

Government & Postal Workers *$5,200*
    National Assn of Retired Federal Employees $2,000
    National Assn of Letter Carriers $1,600
    National League of Postmasters $550
    Others $1,050

Other Unions *$3,000*
    Food & Commercial Workers Union $1,000
    Transportation Communication Union $600
    United Transportation Union $600
    Others $800

Ideological/Single-Issue

Democratic Leadership PACs *$1,500*
    Valley Education Fund (Tony Coelho) $1,500

Independent expenditures supporting Watkins

National Cmte to Preserve Social Security $2,553

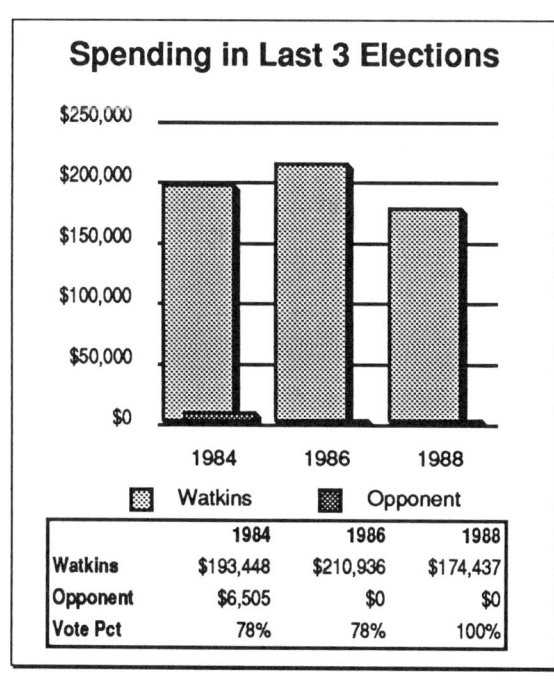

Henry A. Waxman, D-Calif (24)

First elected: 1974
Total receipts: $345,006
Total from PACs: $255,841

1988 Committees & Subcommittees

Energy and Commerce
Health and the Environment (Chairman)
Commerce, Consumer Protection and Competitiveness

Government Operations
Environment, Energy and Natural Resources
Human Resources and Intergovernmental Relations

Select Aging
Health and Long-Term Care

PAC Contribution Profile

Business

Automotive **$4,000**
- Auto Dealers & Drivers for Free Trade $3,500
- Others $500

Broadcasting/Entertainment **$10,800**
- MCA Inc $2,000
- National Assn of Broadcasters $2,000
- Warner Communications $2,000
- Columbia Pictures $1,000
- Motion Picture Assn of America $1,000
- National Cable Television Assn $1,000
- Recording Industry Assn $1,000
- Others $800

Commercial & Savings Banks **$6,800**
- Citicorp $2,000
- Security Pacific Corp $1,500
- American Bankers Assn $1,000
- California Bankers Assn $1,000
- Mercury Savings & Loan $1,000
- Others $300

Food & Beverage **$10,500**
- National Beer Wholesalers Assn $2,500
- Nutrasweet Company $2,000
- Coca-Cola Company $1,000
- Joseph E Seagram & Sons $1,000
- Quaker Oats $1,000
- Wine & Spirits Wholesalers of America $1,000
- Wine Institute $1,000
- Others $1,000

Campaign Revenue Sources

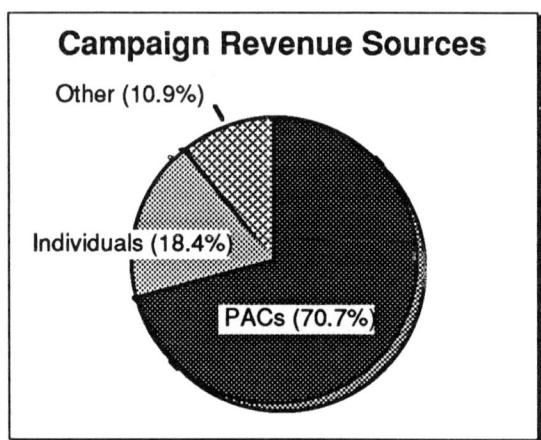

Other (10.9%)
Individuals (18.4%)
PACs (70.7%)

Health Professionals **$50,250**
- American Medical Assn $10,000
- American Dental Assn $5,000
- American Optometric Assn $5,000
- Oral & Maxillofacial Surgeons $5,000
- American Academy of Ophthalmology $4,500
- American Nurses Assn $3,000
- Outpatient Ophthalmic Surgery Society $2,500
- American Podiatry Assn $1,500
- American Assn for Marriage/Family Therapy $1,000
- American Assn of Nurse Anesthetist $1,000
- American Occupational Therapy Assn $1,000
- American Pharmaceutical Assn $1,000
- American Society Cataract/Refract Surgery $1,000
- Cmte for Quality Orthopedic Health Care $1,000
- Co-op of American Physicians $1,000
- Corp for the Advancement of Psychiatry $1,000
- Medivision Inc $1,000
- National Assn of Pharmacists $1,000
- Osteopathic PAC $1,000
- Others $2,750

Hospitals & Nursing Homes **$14,300**
- American Health Care Assn $5,500
- Federation of America Hospitals $3,000
- American Hospital Assn $2,500
- Manor Healthcare Corp $1,000
- National Assn of Private Psychiatric Hospitals $1,000
- Others $1,300

Insurance **$14,700**
- American Family Corp $5,000
- Blue Cross & Blue Shield Assn $4,000
- TransAmerica Life Companies $3,700
- Cigna Corp $1,000
- Others $1,000

Lawyers & Lobbyists **$16,300**
- Assn of Trial Lawyers of America $10,000
- Akin, Gump, Hauer & Feld $1,000
- Kirkpatrick & Lockhart $1,000
- Others $4,300

PAC Totals by Category

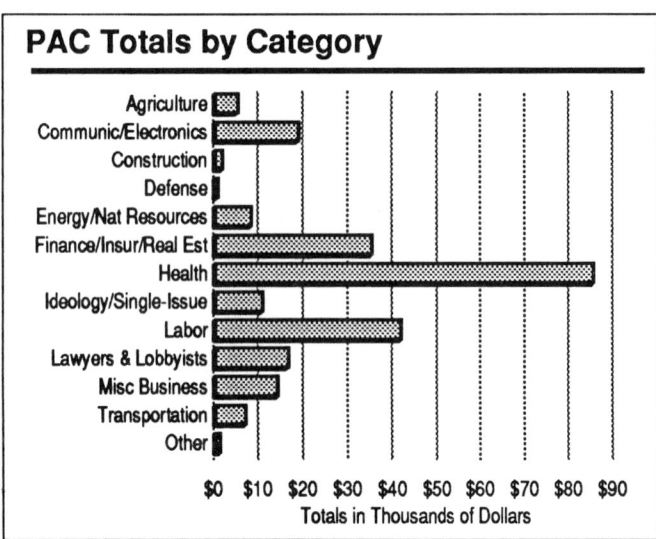

- Agriculture
- Communic/Electronics
- Construction
- Defense
- Energy/Nat Resources
- Finance/Insur/Real Est
- Health
- Ideology/Single-Issue
- Labor
- Lawyers & Lobbyists
- Misc Business
- Transportation
- Other

$0 $10 $20 $30 $40 $50 $60 $70 $80 $90
Totals in Thousands of Dollars

Medical Supplies *$5,065*

    Baxter Healthcare Corp $1,750
    Health Industry Manufacturers Assn $1,315
    American Orthotic/Prosthetic Assn $1,000
    Others $1,000

Oil & Gas *$7,000*

    Pacific Enterprises $2,500
    Coastal Corp $1,500
    Dow Chemical (Cincinnati Employees) $1,000
    Others $2,000

Pharmaceuticals *$8,600*

    Warner-Lambert $3,900
    Burroughs Wellcome $1,000
    McKesson Corp $1,000
    Others $2,700

Real Estate *$6,500*

    National Assn of Realtors $6,000
    Others $500

Securities Investment *$7,000*

    Investment Company Institute $2,000
    Morgan Stanley & Company $2,000
    Prudential-Bache Securities $1,000
    Others $2,000

Telecommunications *$7,500*

    AT&T $3,000
    Pacific Telesis Group $2,000
    Others $2,500

Other Major Business PACs

Group Health Assn of America	$2,000	HMOs
National Assn of Home Builders	$1,500	Resid Constr
American Ambulance Assn	$1,000	HlthCareSvcs
American Veterinary Medical Assn	$1,000	Veterinary
Contact Lens Manufacturers Assn	$1,000	Optical Svc
National Assn of Chain Drug Stores	$1,000	Drug Stores
National Assn of Social Workers	$1,000	Social Work

Interest Group Ratings

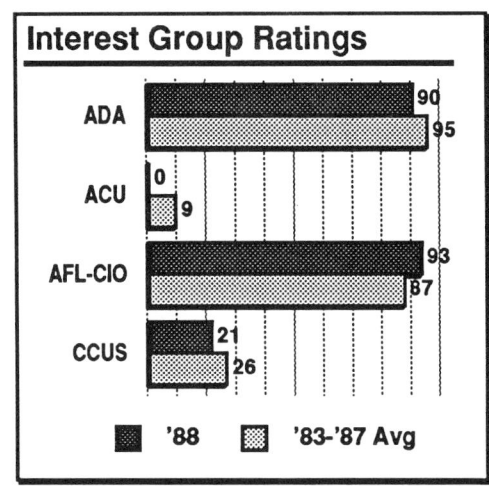

    ■ '88   ▨ '83-'87 Avg

Labor

Bldg Trades/Industrial/Misc Unions *$13,600*

    United Auto Workers $5,000
    Laborers' Western Political League $2,000
    Ironworkers Union $1,600
    Food & Commercial Workers Union $1,500
    Plumbers/Pipefitters Local #467 .... $1,500
    Others $2,000

Government & Postal Workers *$8,500*

    American Fedn of State/County/Munic Employees $5,000
    National Assn of Retired Federal Employees $5,000
    Others .... -$1,500

Teachers Unions *$6,500*

    National Education Assn $6,000
    Others $500

Transportation Unions *$12,850*

    Teamsters Union $7,500
    United Transportation Union $2,600
    Seafarers International Union $1,500
    Others $1,250

Ideological/Single-Issue

Ideological/Single-Issue *$10,070*

Human Rights Campaign Fund	$4,000	Gay Rights
KidsPAC	$2,000	HealthWelfare
National Council of Senior Citizens	$1,000	Soc Secur
Others	$3,070	

Independent expenditures supporting Waxman

National Cmte to Preserve Social Security $2,235

Spending in Last 3 Elections

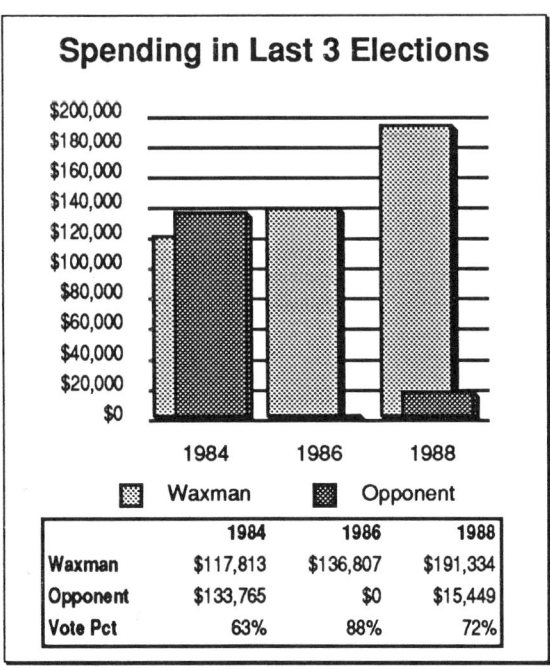

    ▨ Waxman   ■ Opponent

	1984	1986	1988
Waxman	$117,813	$136,807	$191,334
Opponent	$133,765	$0	$15,449
Vote Pct	63%	88%	72%

Vin Weber, R-Minn (2)

1988 Committees & Subcommittees

Appropriations
Labor, Health and Human Services, Education and Related Agencies
Rural Development, Agriculture and Related Agencies

First elected: 1980
Total receipts: $728,427
Total from PACs: $232,704

PAC Contribution Profile

Business

Agricultural Chemicals	**$7,300**
Dow Chemical/Midwest	$2,000
Ecolab Inc	$2,000
FMC Corp	$2,000
Others	$1,300
Agricultural Services	**$3,100**
Farmland Industries	$1,500
Others	$1,600
Air Transport	**$3,800**
Northwest Airlines	$2,850
Others	$950
Auto Dealers	**$4,350**
National Auto Dealers Assn	$2,850
Auto Dealers & Drivers for Free Trade	$1,500
Commodities/Securities Investment	**$3,300**
Chicago Mercantile Exchange	$1,000
Others	$2,300
Construction	**$11,950**
National Assn of Home Builders	$4,000
Associated General Contractors	$3,600
Sheet Metal/AirCon Contractors	$1,000
Others	$3,350
Dairy	**$21,400**
Mid-American Dairymen	$10,000
Associated Milk Producers	$8,000
Land O'Lakes Inc	$2,200
Others	$1,200

Campaign Revenue Sources

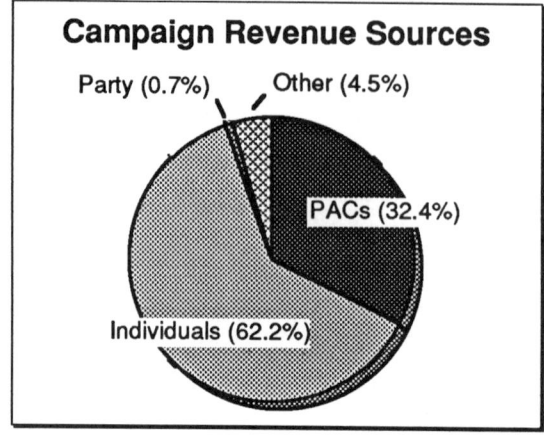

Party (0.7%)   Other (4.5%)
PACs (32.4%)
Individuals (62.2%)

Defense	**$6,800**
Harris Corp	$2,000
Lockheed Corp	$1,100
TRW Inc	$1,100
Northrop Corp	$1,000
Rockwell International	$1,000
Others	$600
Electric Utilities	**$3,300**
ACRE (Action Committee for Rural Electrification)	$1,500
Others	$1,800
Financial Institutions	**$5,950**
Credit Union National Assn	$1,750
Norwest Corp	$1,500
American Bankers Assn	$1,000
Others	$1,700
Food & Beverage	**$11,500**
National Restaurant Assn	$2,500
General Mills*	$2,000
Food Marketing Institute	$1,000
McDonald's Corp	$1,000
National Beer Wholesalers Assn	$1,000
Winn-Dixie Stores	$1,000
Others	$3,000
Grain/Soybean Processing	**$4,100**
Cargill Inc	$2,000
Others	$2,100
Health Professionals	**$11,706**
American Medical Assn	$6,156
American Dental Assn	$2,000
American Academy of Ophthalmology	$1,500
Others	$2,050
Insurance	**$9,000**
National Assn of Life Underwriters	$2,500
Casualty & Surety Agents Assn	$1,000
Health Insurance Assn of America	$1,000
St Paul Companies Inc	$1,000
Others	$3,500
Oil & Gas	**$6,350**
Ashland Oil	$1,500
Phillips Petroleum	$1,500
Others	$3,350

PAC Totals by Category

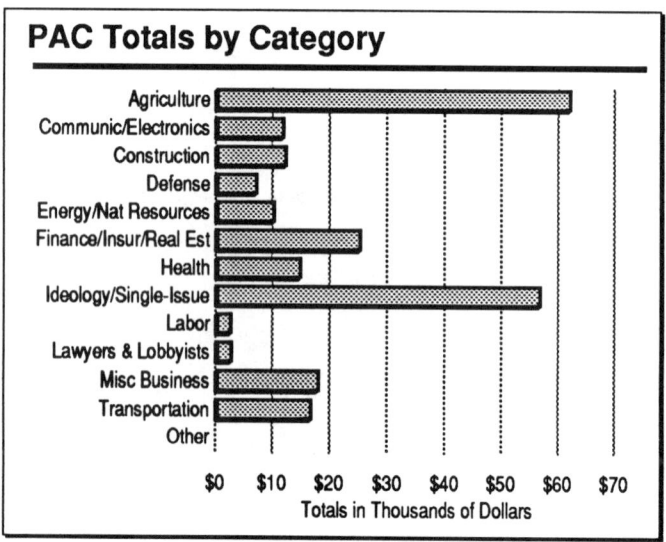

Agriculture
Communic/Electronics
Construction
Defense
Energy/Nat Resources
Finance/Insur/Real Est
Health
Ideology/Single-Issue
Labor
Lawyers & Lobbyists
Misc Business
Transportation
Other

$0 $10 $20 $30 $40 $50 $60 $70
Totals in Thousands of Dollars

Real Estate *$7,500*
    National Assn of Realtors $6,000
    American Land Title Assn $1,000
    Others $500

Sugar Growers *$8,600*
    Southern Minnesota Beet Sugar Co-op $3,900
    American Crystal Sugar Corp $2,500
    American Sugarbeet Growers Assn $1,000
    Others $1,200

Telecommunications *$8,250*
    North Weatern Bell Telephone $2,500
    United Telecommunications $2,000
    AT&T $1,400
    Continental Telecom $1,000
    Others $1,350

Tobacco *$2,450*
    Philip Morris $1,500
    Others $950

Trucking/Delivery *$4,876*
    Minnesota Truck Operators $2,000
    United Parcel Service $1,776
    Others $1,100

Other Major Business PACs

National Assn of Retired Federal Employees .. $2,000	Fedl Workers
Precision Metalforming Assn $2,000	MetalProduct
American Veterinary Medical Assn $1,500	Veterinary
National Tooling & Machining Assn $1,350	Indust Equip
Opperman & Paquin $1,200	Lawyers
Chicago & North Weatern Transport $1,000	Railroads
Deere & Company $1,000	Farm Equip
Honeywell Inc $1,000	Electronics
Medtronic Inc $1,000	Med Supply
Minnesota Mining & Manufacturing (3M) $1,000	Indust Equip
Potlatch Corp $1,000	Forestry
PPG Industries $1,000	Glass Prod

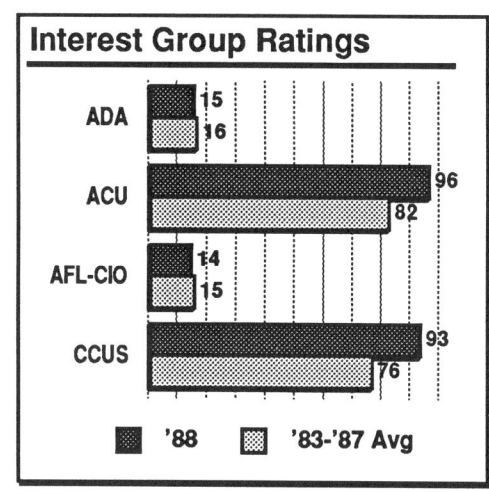

Interest Group Ratings

ADA: '88 15; '83-'87 Avg 16
ACU: '88 96; '83-'87 Avg 82
AFL-CIO: '88 14; '83-'87 Avg 15
CCUS: '88 93; '83-'87 Avg 76

■ '88   ▨ '83-'87 Avg

Ideological/Single-Issue

Pro-Israel *$38,200*
    Desert Caucus $5,000
    National PAC $5,000
    Garden State PAC $3,000
    Hudson Valley PAC $3,000
    Five Towns PAC $2,500
    Delaware Valley PAC $2,000
    Roundtable PAC $2,000
    Women's Pro-Israel National PAC $2,000
    Mid Manhattan PAC $1,500
    Washington PAC $1,500
    City PAC $1,000
    Committee for "18" $1,000
    East Midwood PAC $1,000
    Florida Congressional Cmte $1,000
    ICEPAC $1,000
    National Action Committee (NACPAC) $1,000
    San Diego Community PAC $1,000
    San Franciscans for Good Government $1,000
    Others $2,700

Other Major Ideological/Single-Issue PACs

National Right to Life PAC $6,998	Pro-Life
National Rifle Assn $4,000	Pro-Guns
Council for National Defense $2,152	Pro-Defense
Public Svc Research Council $1,500	Anti-Union

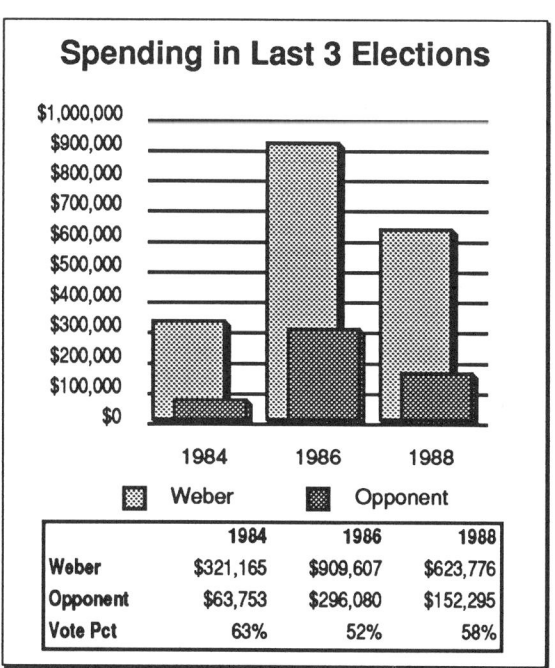

Spending in Last 3 Elections

▨ Weber   ■ Opponent

	1984	1986	1988
Weber	$321,165	$909,607	$623,776
Opponent	$63,753	$296,080	$152,295
Vote Pct	63%	52%	58%

* Contributions came from more than one PAC affiliated with this sponsor.

Ted Weiss, D-NY (17)

1988 Committees & Subcommittees

First elected: 1976
Total receipts: $171,815
Total from PACs: $64,890

Foreign Affairs
Arms Control, International Security and Science
Human Rights and International Organizations
Western Hemisphere Affairs

Government Operations
Human Resources and Intergovernmental Relations (Chairman)
Employment and Housing

Select Children, Youth and Families

PAC Contribution Profile

Business

Commercial & Savings Banks **$1,200**
    None over $350

Health Professionals **$6,100**
    New York Medical Assn $5,000
    Assn for Advancement of Psychology $500
    Others $600

Lawyers & Lobbyists **$4,400**
    Assn of Trial Lawyers of America $3,800
    Others $600

Music Production **$1,300**
    ASCAP $1,000
    Others $300

Package Delivery **$1,800**
    United Parcel Service $1,800

Telecommunications **$1,150**
    AT&T $600
    New York Telephone $550

Other Major Business PACs

Consolidated Edison/New York .... $650   Gas & Electr
Chrysler Corp .... $600   Auto Mfrs

Campaign Revenue Sources

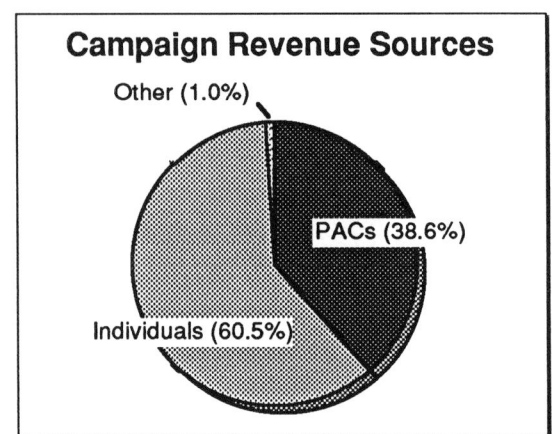

Other (1.0%)
PACs (38.6%)
Individuals (60.5%)

PAC Totals by Category

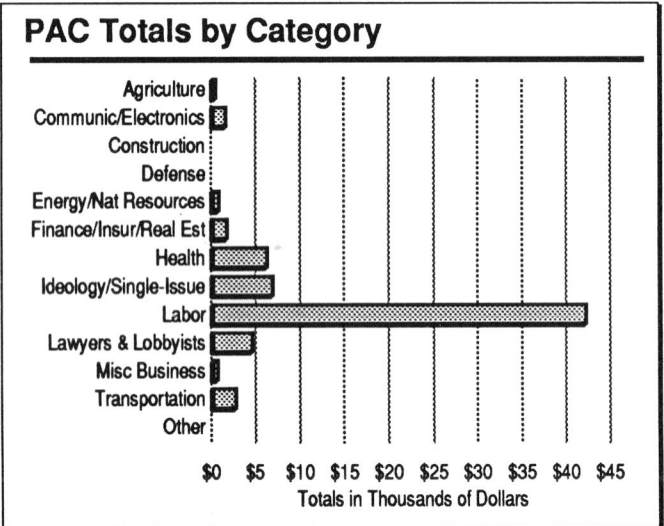

Agriculture
Communic/Electronics
Construction
Defense
Energy/Nat Resources
Finance/Insur/Real Est
Health
Ideology/Single-Issue
Labor
Lawyers & Lobbyists
Misc Business
Transportation
Other

$0 $5 $10 $15 $20 $25 $30 $35 $40 $45
Totals in Thousands of Dollars

Labor

Bldg Trades/Industrial/Misc Unions $11,500
    Carpenters & Joiners Union $3,100
    Food & Commercial Workers Union $2,300
    Laborers' Political League $1,500
    Communications Workers of America $1,300
    Ladies Garment Workers Union $600
    Machinists/Aerospace Workers Union $600
    AFL-CIO* $600
    United Auto Workers $600
    Others $900

Government & Postal Workers $11,600
    National Assn of Letter Carriers $4,100
    American Fedn of State/County/Munic Employees $3,000
    National Assn of Retired Federal Employees $3,000
    American Postal Workers Union $600
    Others $900

Teachers Unions $6,200
    National Education Assn $4,500
    American Federation of Teachers $1,700

Transportation Unions $12,750
    Teamsters Union $5,000
    Air Line Pilots Assn $2,500
    Marine Engineers Union $1,500
    Seafarers International Union $1,500
    United Transportation Union $1,100
    Brotherhood of Locomotive Engineers $600
    Transportation Communication Union $550

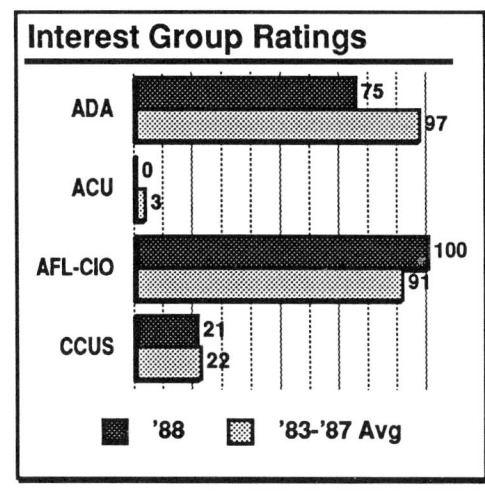

Interest Group Ratings

	'88	'83–'87 Avg
ADA	75	97
ACU	0	3
AFL-CIO	100	91
CCUS	21	22

Ideological/Single-Issue

Ideological/Single-Issue $6,700
Human Rights Campaign Fund .... $3,500 Gay Rights
National Cmte to Preserve Social Security ...... $1,300 Soc Secur
Handgun Control Inc .... $500 Anti-Guns
Valley Education Fund (Tony Coelho) .... $500 Dem Leaders
Others $900

Independent expenditures supporting Weiss
National Cmte to Preserve Social Security $1,628

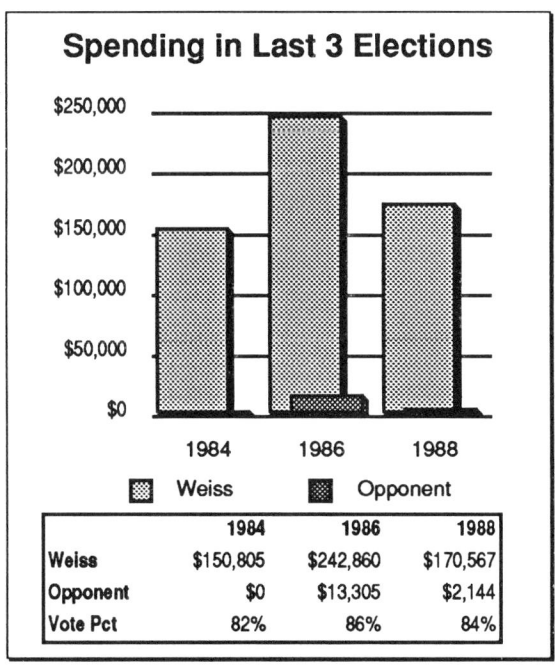

Spending in Last 3 Elections

	Weiss	Opponent

	1984	1986	1988
Weiss	$150,805	$242,860	$170,567
Opponent	$0	$13,305	$2,144
Vote Pct	82%	86%	84%

* Contributions came from more than one PAC affiliated with this sponsor.

Curt Weldon, R-Pa (7)

1988 Committees & Subcommittees

First elected: 1986
Total receipts: $659,218
Total from PACs: $251,617

Armed Services
Military Installations and Facilities
Military Personnel and Compensation
Seapower and Strategic and Critical Materials

Merchant Marine and Fisheries
Coast Guard and Navigation
Fisheries and Wildlife Conservation and the Environment
Panama Canal/Outer Continental Shelf

PAC Contribution Profile

Business

Automotive	**$5,250**
National Auto Dealers Assn	$3,250
Auto Dealers & Drivers for Free Trade	$1,500
Others	$500
Chemicals	**$7,250**
Betz Laboratories	$2,000
Pennwalt Corp	$1,500
Dow Chemical*	$1,000
Rohm and Haas Company	$1,000
Others	$1,750
Commercial & Savings Banks	**$5,400**
Mellon Bank	$1,250
American Bankers Assn	$1,000
Others	$3,150
Construction	**$7,500**
National Assn of Home Builders	$3,500
Associated General Contractors	$1,000
Mechanical Contractors Assn of America	$1,000
National Concrete Masonry Assn	$1,000
Sheet Metal/AirCon Contractors	$1,000

Campaign Revenue Sources

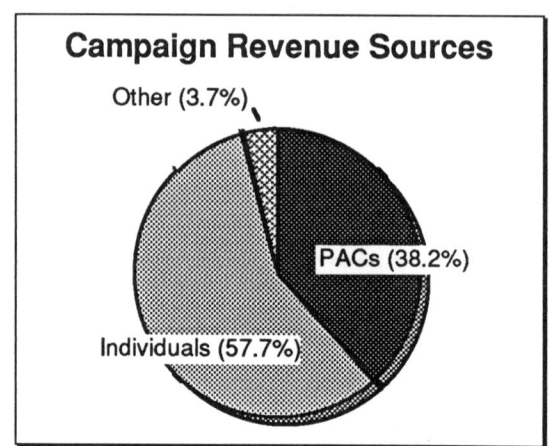

Other (3.7%)
PACs (38.2%)
Individuals (57.7%)

Defense	**$36,000**
Boeing Company	$5,000
Litton Industries	$3,500
FMC Corp	$3,000
AT&T	$2,250
Harris Corp	$2,000
Lockheed Corp	$2,000
Raytheon	$1,750
Eaton Corp	$1,000
Tenneco Inc	$1,000
United Technologies	$1,000
Others	$13,500
Electric Utilities	**$5,000**
Philadelphia Electric	$4,250
Others	$750
Food & Beverage	**$2,650**
None over $750	
Forest Products	**$3,500**
Scott Paper Company	$1,750
Willamette Industries	$1,750
General Aviation	**$2,750**
Aircraft Owners & Pilots Assn	$2,750
Health Professionals	**$8,275**
American Medical Assn	$3,775
American Academy of Ophthalmology	$2,000
American Dental Assn	$1,500
American Podiatry Assn	$1,000
Insurance	**$6,750**
National Assn of Life Underwriters	$3,000
Casualty & Surety Agents Assn	$1,000
Cigna Corp	$1,000
Others	$1,750

PAC Totals by Category

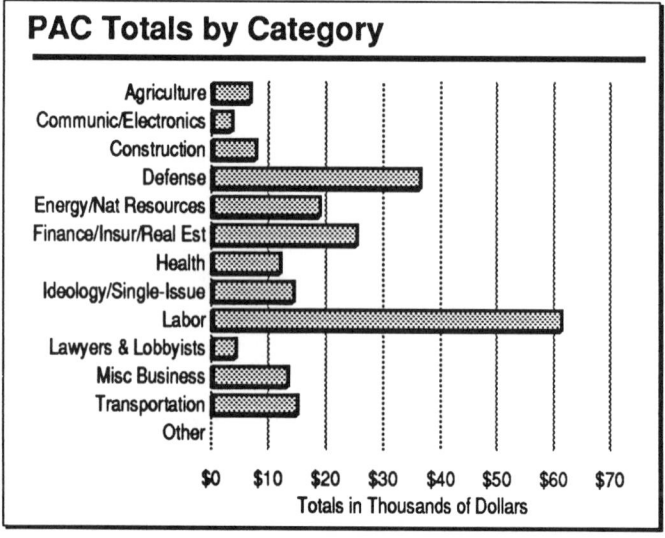

Agriculture
Communic/Electronics
Construction
Defense
Energy/Nat Resources
Finance/Insur/Real Est
Health
Ideology/Single-Issue
Labor
Lawyers & Lobbyists
Misc Business
Transportation
Other

$0 $10 $20 $30 $40 $50 $60 $70
Totals in Thousands of Dollars

Interest Group Ratings

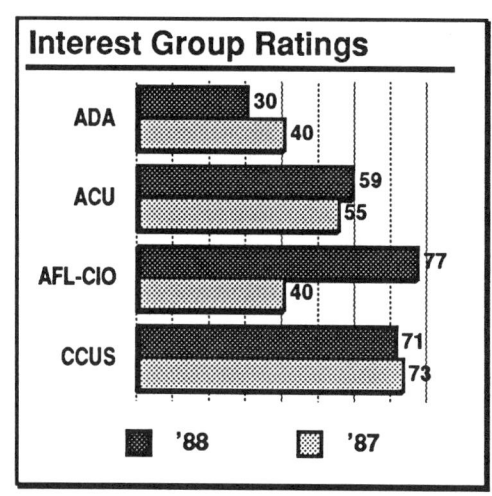

	'88	'87
ADA	30	40
ACU	59	55
AFL-CIO	77	40
CCUS	71	73

■ '88   ▦ '87

Lawyers & Lobbyists **$4,000**
    Schnader Harrison Segal & Lewis $1,500
    Wolf, Block, Schorr and Solis-Cohen $1,000
    Others $1,500

Oil & Gas **$11,050**
    Sun Company $2,500
    Atlantic Richfield $1,500
    Phillips Petroleum $1,500
    Others $5,550

Pharmaceuticals **$3,000**
    Smithkline Beckman $1,500
    Others $1,500

Railroads **$2,000**
    Union Pacific Corp $1,500
    Others $500

Real Estate **$10,500**
    National Assn of Realtors $10,000
    Others $500

Sea Transport **$3,250**
    CSX Transportation Inc* $1,000
    Maritrans Gp Inc $1,000
    Others $1,250

Securities Investment **$2,250**
    Smith Barney $2,000
    Others $250

Telecommunications **$2,250**
    Bell Telephone of Pennsylvania $1,250
    Others $1,000

Other Major Business PACs

United Parcel Service	$1,500	Delivery
Business Industry PAC	$1,121	Bus Assns
Cooper Industries	$1,000	Electronics
Gilbert Associates	$1,000	NuclearEquip

Labor

Bldg Trades/Industrial/Misc Unions **$20,750**
    Plumbers/Pipefitters Union* $4,500
    Intl Brotherhood of Electrical Workers $3,150
    Operating Engineers Union* $2,500
    Sheet Metal Workers Union $2,500
    Boilermakers Union $2,000
    Carpenters & Joiners Union $2,000
    Painters & Allied Trades Union $2,000
    Others $2,100

Government & Postal Workers **$11,300**
    National Assn of Retired Federal Employees $4,000
    American Fedn of State/County/Munic Employees $2,500
    National Assn of Letter Carriers $1,500
    International Assn of Firefighters $1,000
    Others $2,300

Sea Transport Unions **$11,500**
    Marine Engineers Union* $9,000
    Masters, Mates & Pilots Union $1,500
    Seafarers International Union $1,000

Other Transportation Unions **$17,500**
    Teamsters Union* $14,000
    Air Line Pilots Assn $2,500
    Transport Workers Union $1,000

Ideological/Single-Issue

Republican Leadership PACs **$2,000**
    15th District Committee (Edward Madigan) $1,000
    New Republican Victory Fund (Trent Lott) $1,000

Other Major Ideological/Single-Issue PACs

National PAC	$5,000	Pro-Israel
Council for National Defense	$4,277	Pro-Defense
Free Congress PAC	$1,000	Repub/Conser

Independent expenditures supporting Weldon

National Cmte to Preserve Social Security $3,862

---

* Contributions came from more than one PAC affiliated
  with this sponsor.

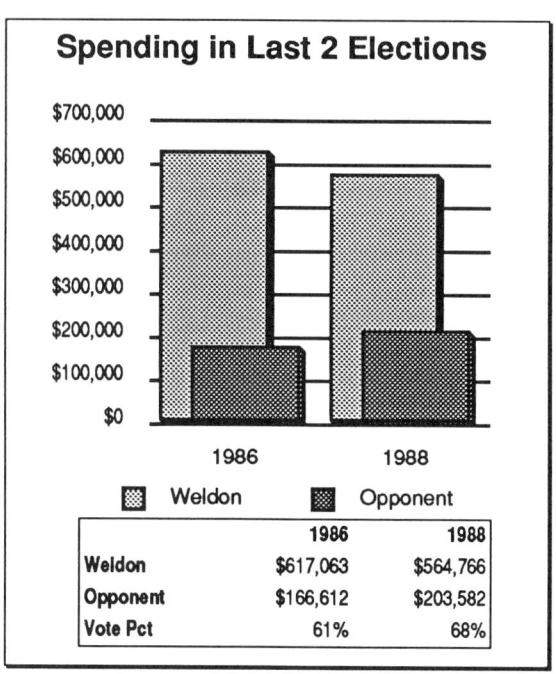

Spending in Last 2 Elections

	Weldon	Opponent

	1986	1988
Weldon	$617,063	$564,766
Opponent	$166,612	$203,582
Vote Pct	61%	68%

Alan Wheat, D-Mo (5)

First elected: 1982
Total receipts: $303,915
Total from PACs: $206,900

1988 Committees & Subcommittees

District of Columbia
Government Operations and Metropolitan Affairs (Chairman)
Judiciary and Education

Rules
Legislative Process

Select Children, Youth and Families

PAC Contribution Profile

Business

Automotive	**$3,800**
Auto Dealers & Drivers for Free Trade	$2,000
Others	$1,800
Construction	**$3,250**
Heavy Constructors Assn	$2,000
Others	$1,250
Dairy	**$2,100**
Mid-American Dairymen	$2,100
Electric Utilities	**$2,250**
None over $600	
Financial Institutions	**$8,050**
American Bankers Assn	$2,500
US League of Savings Assn	$1,100
Credit Union National Assn	$1,000
Others	$3,450
Food & Beverage	**$3,100**
National Beer Wholesalers Assn	$1,100
Joseph E Seagram & Sons	$800
Others	$1,200
Greeting Cards	**$4,660**
Hallmark Cards	$4,660
Health Professionals	**$4,700**
American Medical Assn	$2,800
Missouri Medical Assn	$1,000
Others	$900

Campaign Revenue Sources

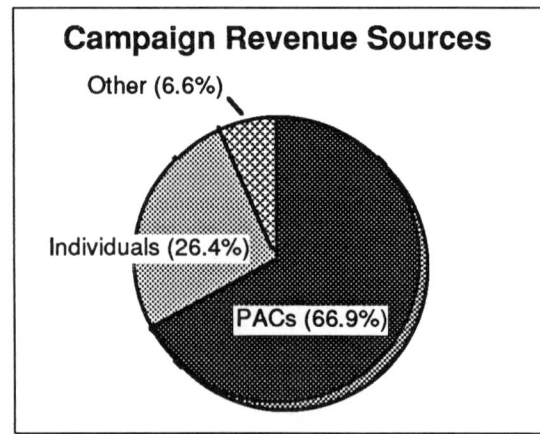

Other (6.6%)
Individuals (26.4%)
PACs (66.9%)

Hospitals & Nursing Homes	**$2,050**
American Hospital Assn	$1,000
Others	$1,050
Insurance	**$5,750**
National Assn of Life Underwriters	$1,000
Others	$4,750
Lawyers	**$8,100**
Assn of Trial Lawyers of America	$5,000
Others	$3,100
Oil & Gas	**$2,150**
Mobil Oil	$1,000
Others	$1,150
Pharmaceuticals	**$2,700**
Pfizer Inc	$1,000
Others	$1,700
Railroads	**$6,900**
Kansas City Southern	$3,800
Union Pacific Corp	$1,200
Others	$1,900
Real Estate	**$2,900**
National Assn of Realtors	$2,600
Others	$300
Securities Investment	**$4,050**
Investment Company Institute	$1,500
Morgan Stanley & Company	$1,000
Others	$1,550
Sugar Growers	**$2,900**
None over $900	
Teachers	**$9,780**
National Education Assn	$7,780
American Federation of Teachers	$2,000
Telecommunications	**$6,500**
AT&T	$2,500
Southwestern Bell	$2,500
Others	$1,500

PAC Totals by Category

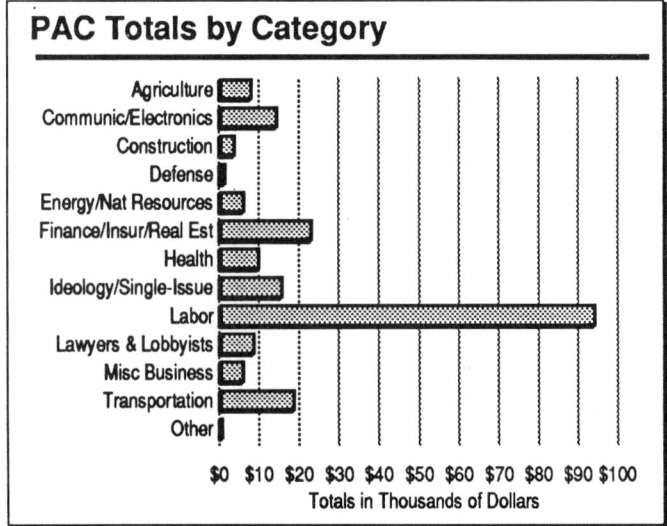

Agriculture
Communic/Electronics
Construction
Defense
Energy/Nat Resources
Finance/Insur/Real Est
Health
Ideology/Single-Issue
Labor
Lawyers & Lobbyists
Misc Business
Transportation
Other

$0 $10 $20 $30 $40 $50 $60 $70 $80 $90 $100
Totals in Thousands of Dollars

Trucking/Delivery..$6,300
    United Parcel Service $3,400
    Yellow Freight System $2,000
    Others $900

Other Major Business PACs

National Cable Television Assn ....$1,600   CableTV

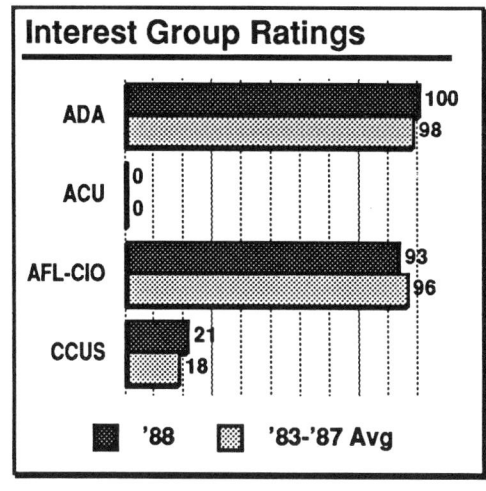
Labor

Bldg Trades/Industrial/Misc Unions $46,792
    United Auto Workers $10,000
    Machinists/Aerospace Workers* $6,500
    Intl Brotherhood of Electrical Workers* $6,100
    Operating Engineers Union $4,000
    Hotel/Restaurant Empl Union $3,932
    AFL-CIO* $2,800
    Carpenters & Joiners Union $2,200
    Painters & Allied Trades Union $2,000
    Plumbers/Pipefitters Local #533 ....$2,000
    Food & Commercial Workers Union....................$1,400
    Laborers' Political League $1,200
    Bakery, Confectionery & Tobacco Workers $1,000
    Others $3,660

Government & Postal Workers $18,330
    American Fedn of State/County/Munic Employees $5,000
    National Assn of Retired Federal Employees $5,000
    National Assn of Letter Carriers $4,430
    Others $3,900

Transportation Unions $18,660
    Teamsters Union $5,500
    Air Line Pilots Assn $4,500
    Seafarers International Union $2,100
    United Transportation Union $2,100
    Marine Engineers District 2 Maritime Officers.................$2,000
    Others $2,460

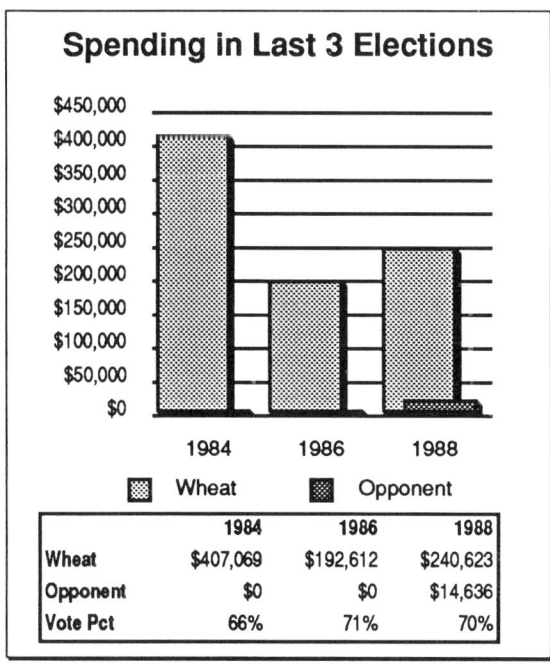

Spending in Last 3 Elections

	1984	1986	1988
Wheat	$407,069	$192,612	$240,623
Opponent	$0	$0	$14,636
Vote Pct	66%	71%	70%

▦ Wheat   ■ Opponent

Ideological/Single-Issue

Democratic Leadership PACs..$2,200
    Valley Education Fund (Tony Coelho) $1,000
    Others $1,200

Pro-Israel $8,500
    National PAC $5,000
    Chai PAC $1,500
    St Louisians for Better Government $1,000
    Others $1,000

Other Major Ideological/Single-Issue PACs

Health Care Concerns PAC ....$2,000   HealthWelfare

---

* Contributions came from more than one PAC affiliated
with this sponsor.

Bob Whittaker, R-Kan (5)

First elected: 1978
Total receipts: $222,261
Total from PACs: $155,056

1988 Committees & Subcommittees

Energy and Commerce
Transportation, Tourism and Hazardous Materials (Ranking Republican)
Health and the Environment

PAC Contribution Profile

Business

Accountants	**$5,300**
American Institute of CPA's	$5,000
Others	$300
Automotive	**$6,950**
National Auto Dealers Assn	$2,300
Auto Dealers & Drivers for Free Trade	$2,000
Others	$2,650
Commercial & Savings Banks	**$3,300**
Kansas Bankers Assn	$1,000
Others	$2,300
Construction	**$5,500**
Manville Corp	$1,000
National Assn of Home Builders	$1,000
Others	$3,500
Defense	**$2,000**
None over $500	
Electric Utilities	**$7,650**
Texas Utilities Electric Company*	$1,000
Others	$6,650
Food & Beverage	**$5,200**
IBP Inc	$1,000
National Beer Wholesalers Assn	$1,000
Pepsi-Cola Bottlers Assn	$1,000
Others	$2,200

Health Professionals	**$16,900**
American Dental Assn	$3,500
American Medical Assn	$3,100
American Optometric Assn	$3,000
American Podiatry Assn	$1,500
Cmte for Quality Orthopedic Health Care	$1,000
Kansas Chiropractic Assn	$1,000
Others	$3,800
Hospitals & Nursing Homes	**$3,250**
American Hospital Assn	$1,000
Others	$2,250
Insurance	**$12,650**
National Assn of Life Underwriters	$2,000
National Assn of Insurance Brokers	$1,300
American Council of Life Insurance	$1,100
American Family Corp	$1,000
Farmers Group Inc	$1,000
Travelers Corp	$1,000
Others	$5,250
Labor Unions	**$5,650**
United Transportation Union	$3,900
Others	$1,750
Oil & Gas	**$13,900**
Union Pacific Corp	$2,300
CSX Transportation Inc	$1,200
Atlantic Richfield	$1,000
Cooper Industries	$1,000
Others	$8,400
Pharmaceuticals	**$9,450**
Schering-Plough Corp	$1,000
Upjohn Company	$1,000
Others	$7,450
Railroads	**$5,500**
Santa Fe Southern Pacific	$1,000
Others	$4,500
Real Estate	**$6,600**
National Assn of Realtors	$6,300
Others	$300

Campaign Revenue Sources

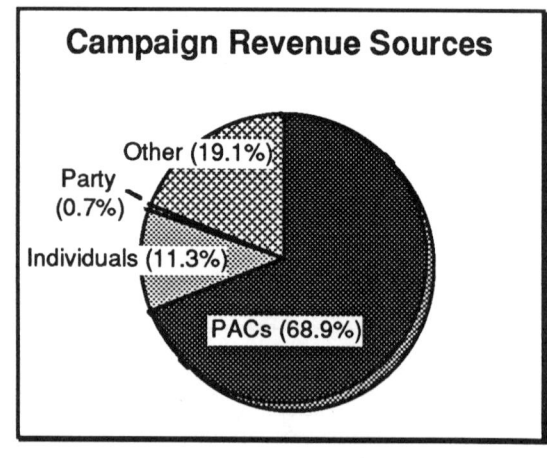

Other (19.1%)
Party (0.7%)
Individuals (11.3%)
PACs (68.9%)

PAC Totals by Category

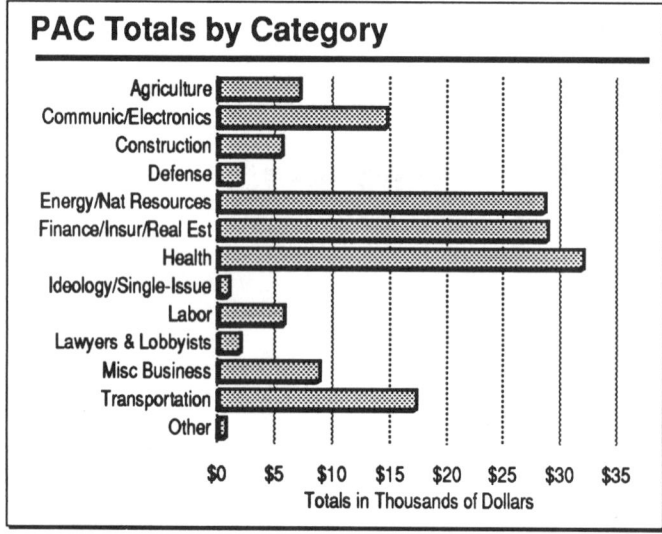

Agriculture
Communic/Electronics
Construction
Defense
Energy/Nat Resources
Finance/Insur/Real Est
Health
Ideology/Single-Issue
Labor
Lawyers & Lobbyists
Misc Business
Transportation
Other

$0 $5 $10 $15 $20 $25 $30 $35
Totals in Thousands of Dollars

Retail Sales **$2,150**
    International Council of Shopping Centers $1,000
    Others $1,150

Telecommunications **$10,650**
    AT&T $3,000
    Continental Telecom $2,000
    Southwestern Bell $1,300
    US Telephone Assn $1,000
    Others $3,350

TV/Cable TV **$3,100**
    National Cable Television Assn $2,500
    Others $600

Waste Management **$2,000**
    Waste Management Inc $1,200
    Others $800

Other Major Business PACs

Henley Group Inc	$1,600	Altern Energy
Contact Lens Manufacturers Assn	$1,200	Optical Svc
Mid-American Dairymen	$1,100	Dairy
American Veterinary Medical Assn	$1,000	Veterinary
Boeing Company	$1,000	Aircraft
Holiday Inns	$1,000	Hotel/Motel

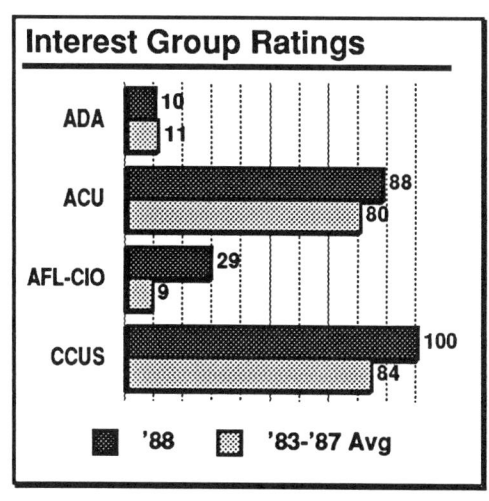

Interest Group Ratings

	'88	'83-'87 Avg
ADA	10	11
ACU	88	80
AFL-CIO	29	9
CCUS	100	84

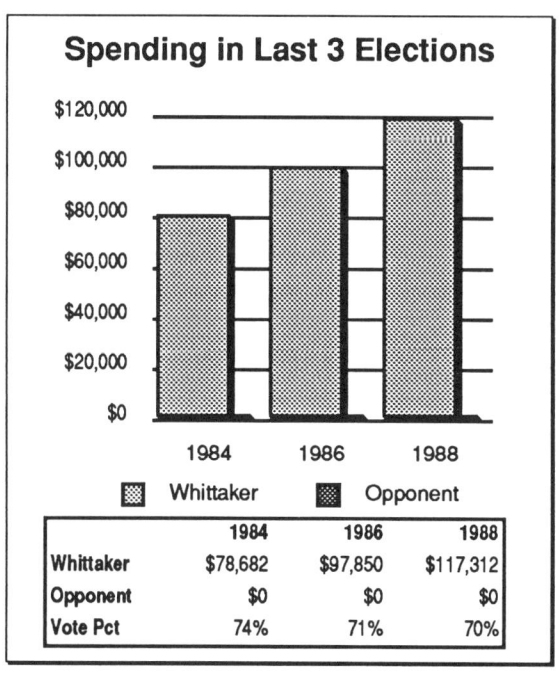

Spending in Last 3 Elections

	1984	1986	1988
Whittaker	$78,682	$97,850	$117,312
Opponent	$0	$0	$0
Vote Pct	74%	71%	70%

Whittaker ▪ Opponent

---

* Contributions came from more than one PAC affiliated with this sponsor.

Jamie L. Whitten, D-Miss (1)

First elected: 1941
Total receipts: $175,925
Total from PACs: $135,400

1988 Committees & Subcommittees

Appropriations (Chairman)
Rural Development, Agriculture and Related Agencies (Chairman)

Campaign Revenue Sources

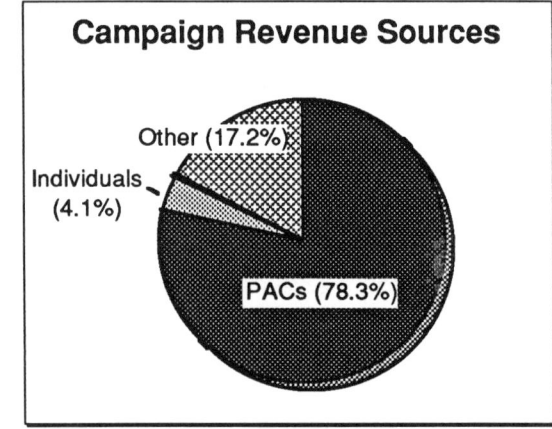

Other (17.2%)
Individuals (4.1%)
PACs (78.3%)

PAC Contribution Profile

Business

Automotive **$2,000**
    None over $500

Aviation/Air Cargo **$8,000**
    Federal Express Corp $6,000
    Boeing Company $1,000
    Others $1,000

Commercial Banks **$4,500**
    American Bankers Assn $2,500
    Bank of Mississippi $1,500
    Others $500

Commodities/Securities Investment **$2,000**
    Chicago Board of Trade $1,000
    Others $1,000

Construction **$8,000**
    National Utility Contractors Assn $4,500
    National Assn of Home Builders $1,500
    Others $2,000

Cotton **$2,750**
    National Cotton Council $1,500
    Others $1,250

Dairy **$6,500**
    Associated Milk Producers $4,000
    Dairymen Inc-Mississippi $1,000
    Mid-American Dairymen $1,000
    Others $500

Defense **$13,000**
    Lockheed Corp $2,000
    Colt Industries $1,500
    General Dynamics $1,000
    Grumman $1,000
    Hughes Aircraft $1,000
    McDonnell Douglas $1,000
    Rockwell International $1,000
    Others $4,500

Electric Utilities **$3,000**
    ACRE (Action Committee for Rural Electrification) $2,000
    Others $1,000

Food & Beverage **$7,500**
    National Beer Wholesalers Assn $4,000
    Pepsi-Cola Bottlers Assn $1,000
    Others $2,500

Forest Products **$2,500**
    Westvaco Corp $1,000
    Others $1,500

Fruit & Vegetable Growers **$3,100**
    Ocean Spray Cranberries Inc $1,000
    Others $2,100

Health Professionals **$7,000**
    American Dental Assn $4,000
    American Medical Assn $2,500
    Others $500

Lawyers & Lobbyists **$7,500**
    Assn of Trial Lawyers of America $5,000
    Hill & Knowlton $1,500
    Others $1,000

Oil & Gas **$3,250**
    Enserch Corp $1,000
    Others $2,250

Pharmaceuticals **$2,050**
    None over $500

Poultry & Livestock **$2,500**
    National Turkey Federation $1,000
    Others $1,500

PAC Totals by Category

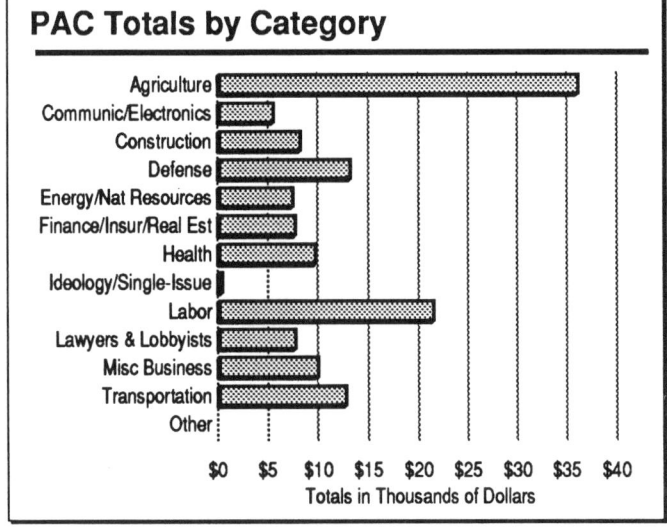

Agriculture
Communic/Electronics
Construction
Defense
Energy/Nat Resources
Finance/Insur/Real Est
Health
Ideology/Single-Issue
Labor
Lawyers & Lobbyists
Misc Business
Transportation
Other

$0 $5 $10 $15 $20 $25 $30 $35 $40

Totals in Thousands of Dollars

Sugar Growers **$4,000**

    American Crystal Sugar Corp $1,000
    American Sugar Cane League $1,000
    Others $2,000

Telecommunications **$3,000**

    AT&T $1,000
    Others $2,000

Tobacco **$3,000**

    Philip Morris $1,500
    RJR Nabisco $1,000
    Others $500

Other Major Business PACs

Alcoa $1,000	Metals/Mining
American Veterinary Medical Assn $1,000	Veterinary
Archer-Daniels-Midland Corp $1,000	Grain Trader
Farm Credit Council $1,000	Ag Svcs
FMC Corp $1,000	Ag Chemicals
International Council of Shopping Centers $1,000	Retail
National Assn of Broadcasters $1,000	TV/Radio
National Council of Farmer Co-ops $1,000	Farm Orgs

Interest Group Ratings

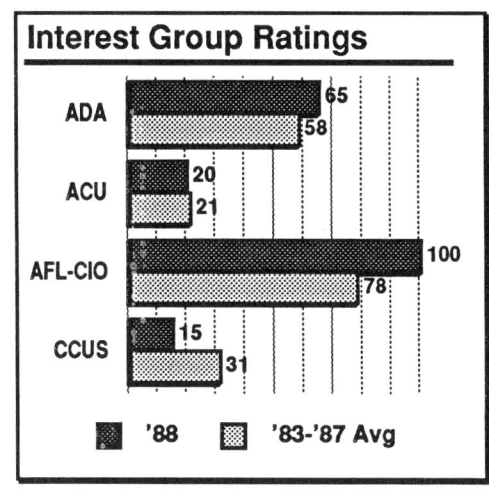

	'88	'83-'87 Avg
ADA	65	58
ACU	20	21
AFL-CIO	100	78
CCUS	15	31

Labor

Bldg Trades/Industrial/Misc Unions **$6,000**

    American Federation of Teachers $1,000
    Laborers' Political League $1,000
    Sheet Metal Workers Union $1,000
    Others $3,000

Government & Postal Workers **$4,000**

    American Fedn of State/County/Munic Employees $1,000
    American Postal Workers Union $1,000
    National Assn of Letter Carriers $1,000
    Others $1,000

Transportation Unions **$11,250**

    Air Line Pilots Assn $5,000
    Teamsters Union $2,500
    Seafarers International Union $1,500
    Amalgamated Transit Union $1,000
    Others $1,250

Independent expenditures supporting Whitten

National Cmte to Preserve Social Security $1,224

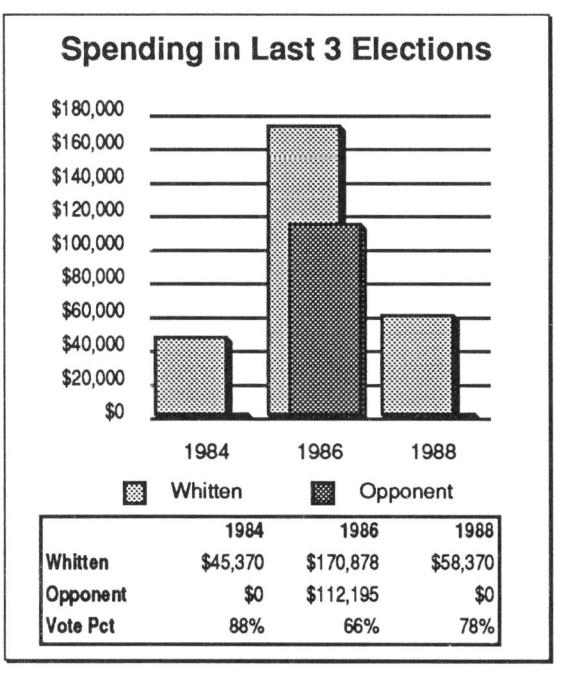

Spending in Last 3 Elections

	1984	1986	1988
Whitten	$45,370	$170,878	$58,370
Opponent	$0	$112,195	$0
Vote Pct	88%	66%	78%

Pat Williams, D-Mont (1)

1988 Committees & Subcommittees

First elected: 1978
Total receipts: $279,812
Total from PACs: $180,156

Budget
Human Resources (Chairman)
Community and Natural Resources
Economic and Trade Policy

Education and Labor
Postsecondary Education (Chairman)
Elementary, Secondary and Vocational Education
Employment Opportunities
Labor Standards
Select Education

PAC Contribution Profile

Business

Construction	**$2,600**
Manville Corp	$1,000
Others	$1,600
Dairy Producers	**$2,200**
Associated Milk Producers	$1,850
Others	$350
Financial Institutions	**$3,650**
Credit Union National Assn*	$1,100
Norwest Corp	$1,000
Others	$1,550
Food & Beverage	**$3,431**
National Restaurant Assn	$2,931
Others	$500
Health Professionals	**$3,550**
American Dental Assn	$1,500
Others	$2,050
Lawyers	**$5,750**
Assn of Trial Lawyers of America	$5,000
Others	$750
Railroads	**$2,700**
Burlington Northern	$1,350
Others	$1,350

Campaign Revenue Sources

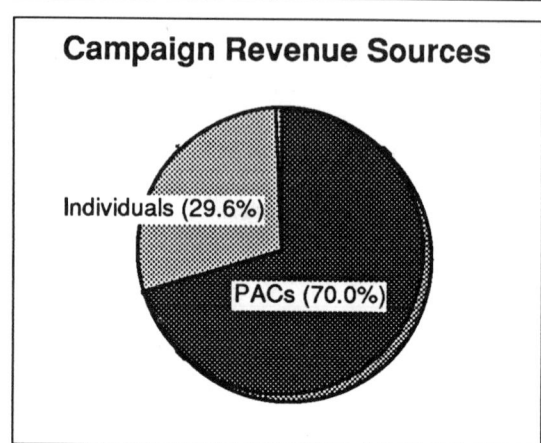

Individuals (29.6%)

PACs (70.0%)

Schools & Vocational Training	**$12,300**
National Assn of Trade/Technical Schools	$4,700
Assn of Independent Colleges/Schools	$4,100
National Assn of Cosmetology Schools	$1,350
Higher Education Mgmt/Resources Foundation	$1,200
Others	$950
Sugar Producers	**$2,000**
None over $850	
Textiles	**$3,100**
Burlington Industries	$1,000
Others	$2,100

Other Major Business PACs

AT&T	$1,500	Long Dist
National Assn Life Underwriters	$1,500	Life Insur
American Veterinary Medical Assn	$1,000	Veterinary
Cyprus Minerals Company	$1,000	Metal Mining
Precision Metalforming Assn	$1,000	Metal Prod

PAC Totals by Category

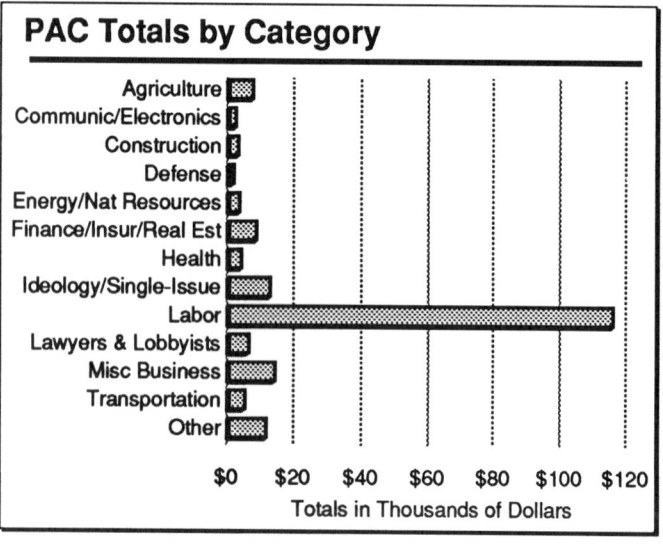

Agriculture
Communic/Electronics
Construction
Defense
Energy/Nat Resources
Finance/Insur/Real Est
Health
Ideology/Single-Issue
Labor
Lawyers & Lobbyists
Misc Business
Transportation
Other

$0 $20 $40 $60 $80 $100 $120

Totals in Thousands of Dollars

Labor

Bldg Trades, Industrial & Misc Unions $52,150

Intl Brotherhood of Electrical Workers	$8,500
Food & Commercial Workers Union	$5,500
Operating Engineers Union	$5,000
AFL-CIO*	$4,300
Carpenters & Joiners Union	$4,200
Laborers' Political League	$2,200
Ironworkers Union	$2,000
Plumbers/Pipefitters Union	$2,000
Boilermakers Union	$1,850
Machinists/Aerospace Workers Union	$1,850
Service Employees International Union	$1,850
United Auto Workers	$1,850
Ladies Garment Workers Union	$1,700
Painters & Allied Trades Union	$1,700
Amalgamated Clothing & Textile Workers	$1,350
Bricklayers Union	$1,350
United Steelworkers	$1,000
Others	$3,950

Civil Service & Postal Workers $28,250

National Assn of Letter Carriers	$10,000
National Assn of Retired Federal Employees	$6,050
American Fedn of State/County/Munic Employees	$4,850
American Postal Workers Union	$1,700
American Federation of Government Employees	$1,200
Others	$4,450

Teachers Unions $11,950

American Federation of Teachers	$6,750
National Education Assn	$5,200

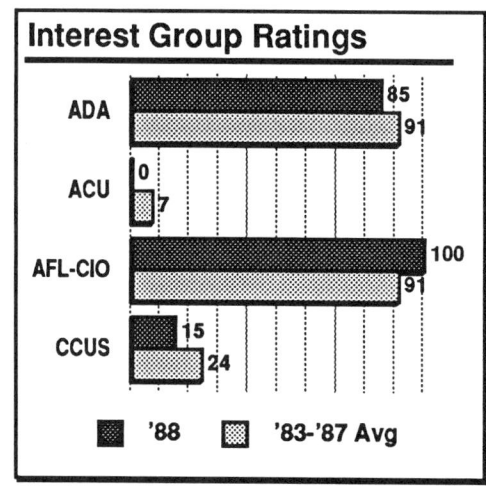

Interest Group Ratings

	'88	'83-'87 Avg
ADA	85	91
ACU	0	7
AFL-CIO	100	91
CCUS	15	24

Transportation Unions $23,100

Teamsters Union	$7,500
Air Line Pilots Assn	$5,000
Amalgamated Transit Union	$2,000
Seafarers International Union	$2,000
Transportation Communication Union	$1,700
United Transportation Union	$1,500
Marine Engineers Union	$1,000
Others	$2,400

Ideological/Single-Issue

Pro-Israel $5,750

National PAC	$5,000
Others	$750

Other Major Ideological/Single-Issue PACs

National Cmte to Preserve Social Security	$1,250	Soc Secur
KidsPAC	$1,000	Health/Welfare
Valley Education Fund (Tony Coelho)	$1,000	Dem Leaders

Independent expenditures supporting Williams

National Cmte to Preserve Social Security	$1,354

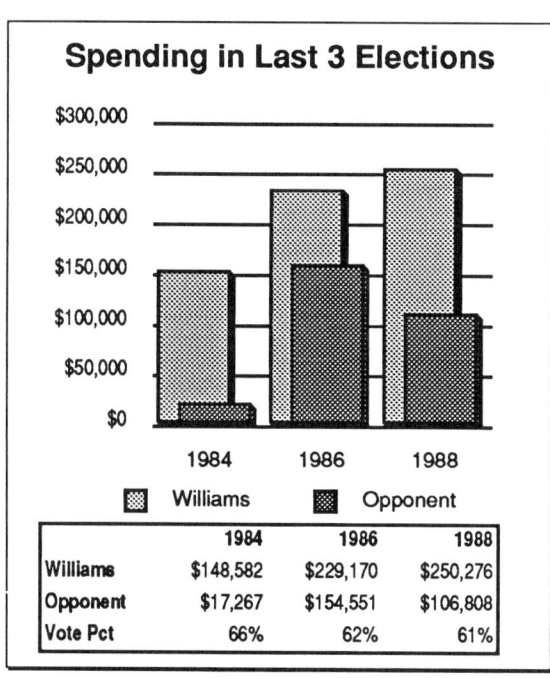

Spending in Last 3 Elections

	Williams	Opponent

	1984	1986	1988
Williams	$148,582	$229,170	$250,276
Opponent	$17,267	$154,551	$106,808
Vote Pct	66%	62%	61%

---

* Contributions came from more than one PAC affiliated with this sponsor.

Charles Wilson, D-Texas (2)

1988 Committees & Subcommittees

Appropriations
Defense
Foreign Operations

Select Intelligence
Oversight and Evaluation
Program and Budget Authorization

First elected: 1972
Total receipts: $338,839
Total from PACs: $253,350

PAC Contribution Profile

Business

Airlines	**$7,000**
Texas Air	$6,000
American Airlines	$1,000
Auto Dealers	**$3,000**
National Auto Dealers Assn	$3,000
Commercial Banks	**$2,750**
NCNB Texas	$2,000
Citizens St Bank/Woodville, Texas	$750
Construction	**$2,750**
Associated General Contractors	$1,000
Brown & Root	$1,000
Others	$750
Dairy	**$4,000**
Associated Milk Producers	$4,000
Defense	**$87,250**
Textron Inc	$10,000
Northrop Corp	$5,500
Grumman	$5,000
Singer Company	$4,500
McDonnell Douglas*	$4,000
FMC Corp	$3,500
LTV Aerospace & Defense Company	$3,500
AT&T	$3,000
E-Systems/Corporate Division	$3,000
Gencorp Inc	$3,000
General Dynamics	$3,000
Hughes Aircraft	$3,000

(Continued in next column)

Campaign Revenue Sources

Other (5.7%)
Individuals (24.9%)
PACs (69.4%)

PAC Totals by Category

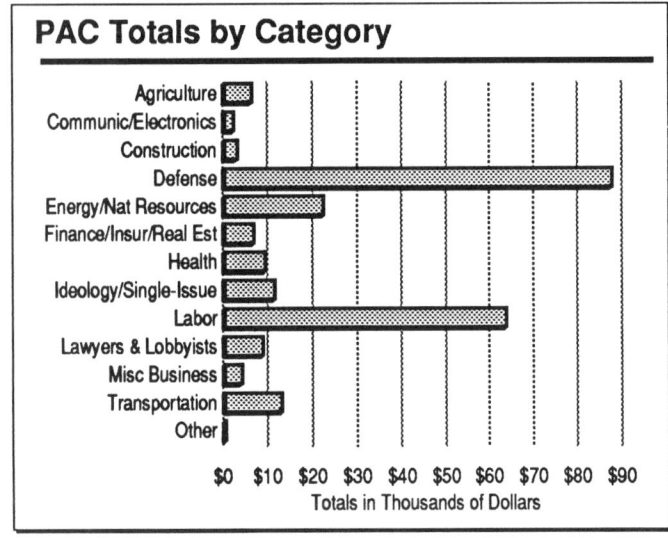

Agriculture
Communic/Electronics
Construction
Defense
Energy/Nat Resources
Finance/Insur/Real Est
Health
Ideology/Single-Issue
Labor
Lawyers & Lobbyists
Misc Business
Transportation
Other

$0 $10 $20 $30 $40 $50 $60 $70 $80 $90
Totals in Thousands of Dollars

Defense (cont'd)

Allied-Signal	$2,500
GTE Corp*	$2,500
Lockheed Corp	$2,500
Rockwell International	$2,500
Texas Instruments	$2,500
United Technologies	$2,500
General Electric	$2,000
Morton Thiokol	$2,000
TRW Inc	$2,000
Varo Inc	$2,000
Boeing Company	$1,500
Tenneco Inc	$1,500
Bath Iron Works	$1,000
Harsco Corp	$1,000
Long Island Aerospace PAC	$1,000
Martin Marietta Corp	$1,000
Westinghouse Electric	$1,000
Others	$5,250
Electric Utilities	**$5,750**
Houston Industries	$3,000
Texas Utilities Electric Company*	$2,000
Others	$750
Health Professionals	**$8,832**
American Medical Assn	$6,500
American Dental Assn	$2,000
Others	$332
Lawyers	**$8,500**
Vinson, Elkins, Searls, Connally & Smith	$4,000
Akin, Gump, Hauer & Feld	$3,000
Williams & Jensen	$1,000
Others	$500
Oil & Gas	**$16,250**
Coastal Corp	$6,000
Enserch Corp	$4,000
Atlantic Richfield	$1,000
Others	$5,250
Real Estate	**$3,500**
National Assn of Realtors	$3,000
Others	$500

Other Major Business PACs

Southwestern Bell	$2,000	TelephUtil
Temple-Eastex Inc	$2,000	Packaging
American Trucking Assns	$1,000	Trucking
National Beer Wholesalers Assn	$1,000	Liquor Whlsl
United Parcel Service	$1,000	Delivery

Labor

Bldg Trades/Industrial/Misc Unions **$30,850**

United Auto Workers $5,500
Carpenters & Joiners Union $5,000
Intl Brotherhood of Electrical Workers.................... $3,000
Machinists/Aerospace Workers Union $2,500
AFL-CIO* $2,000
Sheet Metal Workers Union $2,000
United Steelworkers $2,000
Communications Workers of America..................... $1,500
Amalgamated Clothing & Textile Workers $1,000
Boilermakers Union $1,000
Food & Commercial Workers Union........................ $1,000
Ladies Garment Workers Union $1,000
Operating Engineers Union $1,000
Plumbers/Pipefitters Union $1,000
Others $1,350

Government & Postal Workers **$5,000**

American Postal Workers Union $2,000
National Assn of Letter Carriers $2,000
American Federation of Government Employees $1,000

Teachers Unions **$4,000**

National Education Assn $4,000

Transportation Unions **$23,500**

Marine Engineers Union* $9,000
Seafarers International Union $7,000
Teamsters Union $5,000
United Transportation Union $1,500
Transportation Communication Union..................... $1,000

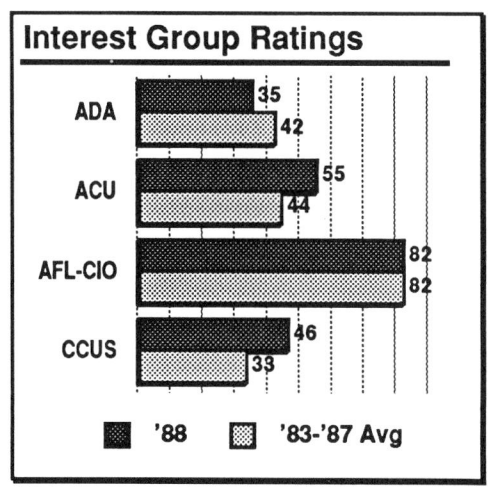

Interest Group Ratings

	'88	'83-'87 Avg
ADA	35	42
ACU	55	44
AFL-CIO	82	82
CCUS	46	33

Ideological/Single-Issue

Pro-Israel **$5,500**

National PAC $5,000
Others $500

Other Major Ideological/Single-Issue PACs

National Rifle Assn .... $4,950   Pro-Guns

Independent expenditures supporting Wilson

National Cmte to Preserve Social Security $1,435

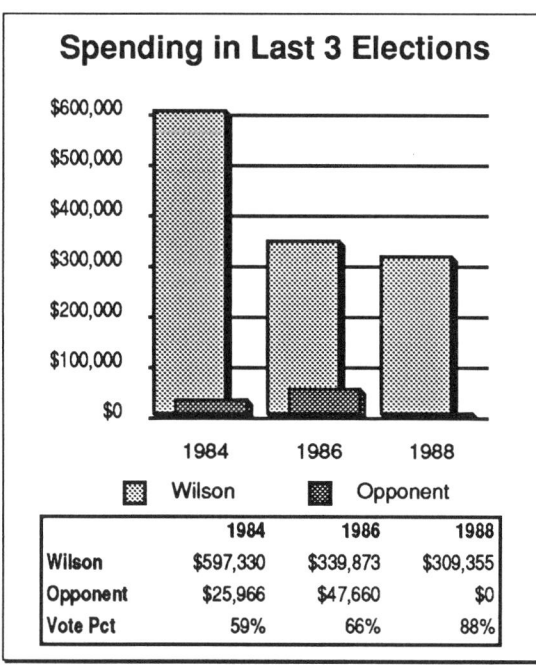

Spending in Last 3 Elections

	1984	1986	1988
Wilson	$597,330	$339,873	$309,355
Opponent	$25,966	$47,660	$0
Vote Pct	59%	66%	88%

■ Wilson   ■ Opponent

---

* Contributions came from more than one PAC affiliated
with this sponsor.

Bob Wise, D-WVa (3)

First elected: 1982
Total receipts: $173,893
Total from PACs: $122,952

1988 Committees & Subcommittees

Education and Labor
Elementary, Secondary and Vocational Education
Labor Standards

Government Operations
Government Activities and Transportation
Legislation and National Security

Public Works and Transportation
Surface Transportation
Water Resources

Select Aging
Retirement Income and Employment

PAC Contribution Profile

Business

Accountants	**$5,000**
American Institute of CPA's	$5,000
Automotive	**$2,150**
National Auto Dealers Assn	$1,000
Ford Motor Company	$850
Others	$300
Chemicals	**$4,700**
FMC Corp	$2,600
Union Carbide	$1,000
Others	$1,100
Construction	**$3,500**
National Utility Contractors Assn	$2,000
Ashland Oil	$1,000
Others	$500
Electric Utilities	**$1,600**
American Electric Power	$1,050
ACRE (Action Committee for Rural Electrification)	$550
Food & Beverage	**$3,000**
National Restaurant Assn	$2,500
Others	$500
Health Professionals	**$3,350**
American Dental Assn	$1,500
American Medical Assn	$1,300
Others	$550

Campaign Revenue Sources

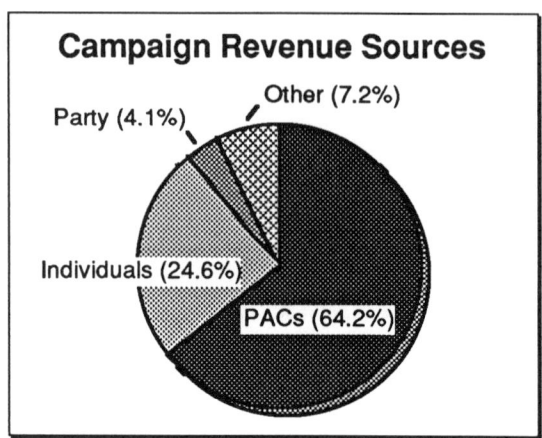

Other (7.2%)
Party (4.1%)
Individuals (24.6%)
PACs (64.2%)

Hotels & Motels	**$1,300**
American Hotel & Motel Assn	$800
Holiday Inns	$500
Insurance	**$1,350**
National Assn of Life Underwriters	$1,000
Others	$350
Lawyers	**$5,300**
Assn of Trial Lawyers of America	$5,300
Mining	**$2,300**
National Coal Assn	$1,050
Peabody Coal	$1,050
Others	$200
Oil & Gas	**$3,100**
Columbia Natural Resources	$1,000
Others	$2,100
Real Estate	**$3,300**
National Assn of Realtors	$3,300
Sugar Growers	**$1,700**
American Sugarbeet Growers Assn	$550
Others	$1,150
Telecommunications	**$2,967**
AT&T	$1,167
Continental Telecom	$1,000
Chesapeake & Potomac Telephone	$800
Trucking/Delivery	**$2,793**
United Parcel Service	$1,600
North American Van Lines	$550
Others	$643

Other Major Business PACs

CSX Transportation Inc	$850	Railroads
Tobacco Institute	$550	Tobacco

PAC Totals by Category

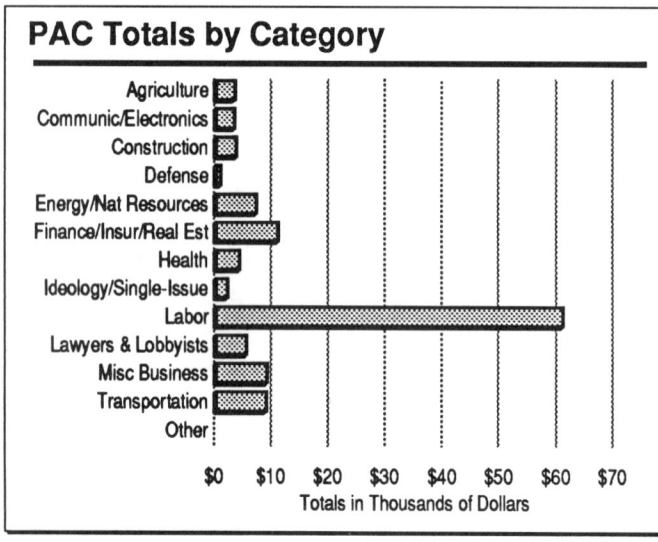

Agriculture
Communic/Electronics
Construction
Defense
Energy/Nat Resources
Finance/Insur/Real Est
Health
Ideology/Single-Issue
Labor
Lawyers & Lobbyists
Misc Business
Transportation
Other

$0 $10 $20 $30 $40 $50 $60 $70
Totals in Thousands of Dollars

Labor

Bldg Trades/Industrial/Misc Unions **$24,550**

United Auto Workers $5,550
Operating Engineers Union $3,500
United Mine Workers $2,600
American Federation of Musicians $1,500
Carpenters & Joiners Union $1,500
Laborers' Political League $1,500
Ladies Garment Workers Union $1,050
Food & Commercial Workers Union $1,000
Plumbers/Pipefitters Union $1,000
United Steelworkers $1,000
Amalgamated Clothing & Textile Workers $550
Machinists/Aerospace Workers Union $550
Others ....-$3,250

Government & Postal Workers **$11,150**

National Assn of Retired Federal Employees $5,000
National Assn of Letter Carriers $2,500
American Fedn of State/County/Munic Employees $1,000
Others $2,650

Teachers Unions **$4,300**

National Education Assn $4,300

Transportation Unions **$27,350**

Teamsters Union $10,000
Air Line Pilots Assn $5,000
Amalgamated Transit Union.............................$2,500
Marine Engineers Union* $2,500
Masters, Mates & Pilots Union $2,000
Seafarers International Union $2,000
United Transportation Union $2,000
Transportation Communication Union.................$800
Others $550

Interest Group Ratings

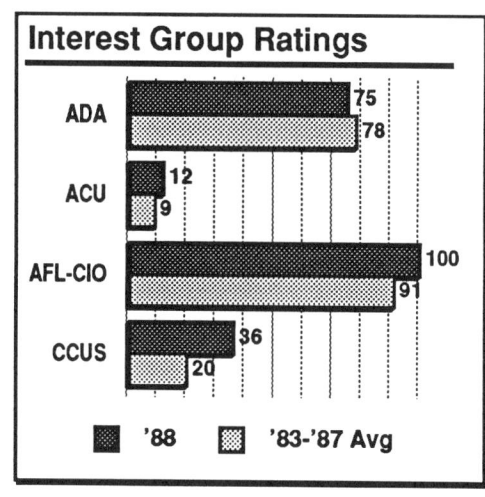

	'88	'83-'87 Avg
ADA	75	78
ACU	12	9
AFL-CIO	100	91
CCUS	36	20

Ideological/Single-Issue

Democratic Leadership PACs.......................................**$1,500**

Valley Education Fund (Tony Coelho) $1,000
Others $500

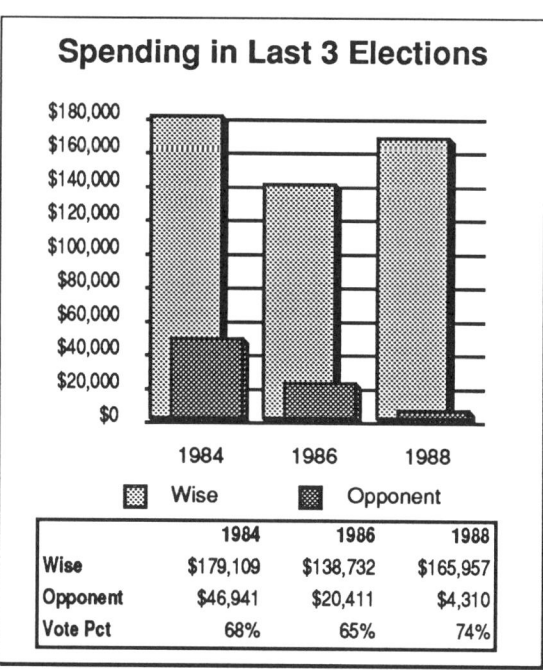

Spending in Last 3 Elections

	1984	1986	1988
Wise	$179,109	$138,732	$165,957
Opponent	$46,941	$20,411	$4,310
Vote Pct	68%	65%	74%

Wise ▨   Opponent ▨

* Contributions came from more than one PAC affiliated
with this sponsor.

Frank R. Wolf, R-Va (10)

1988 Committees & Subcommittees

Appropriations
Transportation and Related Agencies
Treasury, Postal Service and General Government

Select Children, Youth and Families

First elected: 1980
Total receipts: $803,080
Total from PACs: $235,615

Campaign Revenue Sources

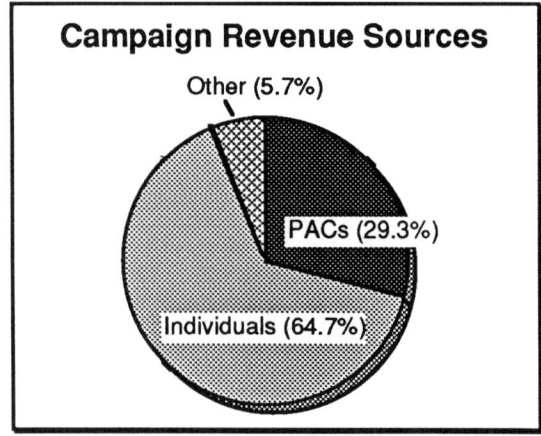

Other (5.7%)
PACs (29.3%)
Individuals (64.7%)

PAC Contribution Profile

Business

Accountants	**$2,000**
Touche Ross	$1,000
Others	$1,000
Automotive	**$10,150**
National Auto Dealers Assn	$6,100
Auto Dealers & Drivers for Free Trade	$1,500
Others	$2,550
Aviation & Aerospace	**$14,200**
Aircraft Owners & Pilots Assn	$2,000
Worldcorp Inc	$2,000
Orbital Sciences Corp	$1,750
Boeing Company	$1,500
Federal Express Corp	$1,500
McDonnell Douglas	$1,000
Others	$4,450
Business Associations	**$3,550**
Greater Washington Board of Trade	$3,550
Computers & Electronics	**$8,160**
Computer Sciences Corp	$2,110
Electronic Data Systems	$1,500
Planning Research Corp	$1,250
Unisys Corp	$1,000
Others	$2,300
Construction	**$17,100**
Associated General Contractors	$2,500
National Assn of Home Builders	$2,500
National Utility Contractors Assn	$2,500
National Electrical Contractors Assn	$1,000
Others	$8,600

Defense	**$36,207**
Tenneco Inc	$7,000
BDM International	$5,000
TRW Inc	$4,000
E-Systems*	$3,622
Lockheed Corp	$1,635
Dyncorp	$1,500
Hughes Aircraft	$1,500
Litton Industries	$1,500
Martin Marietta Corp	$1,150
Mantech International	$1,100
Rockwell International	$1,100
Textron Inc	$1,100
United Technologies	$1,100
Northrop Corp	$1,000
Others	$3,900
Electric Utilities	**$10,650**
Dominion Resources Inc	$2,350
Houston Industries	$1,000
Others	$7,300
Financial Institutions	**$11,050**
Virginia Bankers Assn	$5,000
MNC Financial Inc	$1,200
Crestar Financial Corp	$1,000
Sovran Financial Corp	$1,000
Others	$2,850
Food & Beverage	**$6,211**
Coors Industries	$1,186
Others	$5,025
Forest Products	**$2,600**
Westvaco Corp	$1,500
Others	$1,100
Health Professionals	**$13,000**
American Medical Assn	$10,000
American Dental Assn	$3,000
Industrial Equipment	**$3,700**
Emhart Corp	$1,400
National Tooling & Machining Assn	$1,000
Others	$1,300
Insurance	**$8,850**
National Assn of Life Underwriters	$3,500
Travelers Corp	$1,500
Others	$3,850

PAC Totals by Category

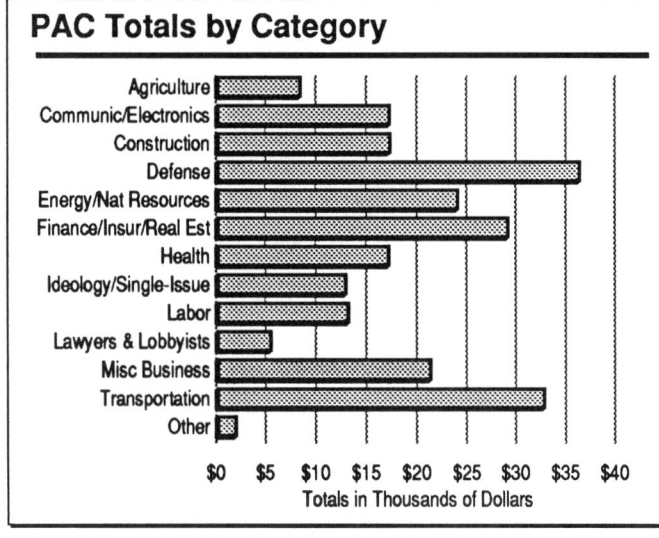

Agriculture
Communic/Electronics
Construction
Defense
Energy/Nat Resources
Finance/Insur/Real Est
Health
Ideology/Single-Issue
Labor
Lawyers & Lobbyists
Misc Business
Transportation
Other

$0 $5 $10 $15 $20 $25 $30 $35 $40
Totals in Thousands of Dollars

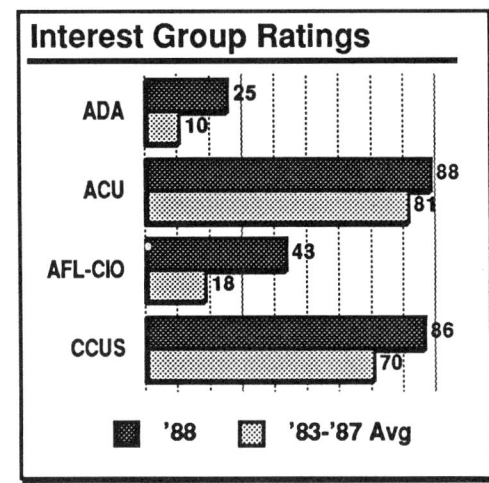
Lawyers **$5,300**

    O'Melveny & Myers $2,000
    Fullbright & Jaworski $1,000
    McGuire, Woods, Battle & Booth $1,000
    Others $1,300

Oil & Gas **$9,650**

    Mobil Oil $2,000
    Washington Gas Light Company $1,700
    Amoco Corp $1,000
    Others $4,950

Pharmaceuticals **$3,750**

    Abbott Laboratories $1,250
    Others $2,500

Real Estate **$7,100**

    National Assn of Realtors $6,250
    Others $850

Retail Sales **$2,561**

    None over $711

Telecommunications **$8,650**

    Continental Telecom $2,650
    AT&T $2,000
    Chesapeake & Potomac Telephone $1,700
    Others $2,300

Trucking/Delivery **$6,325**

    United Parcel Service $2,250
    American Trucking Assns $1,050
    Others $3,025

Other Major Business PACs

Philip Morris	$1,500	Tobacco
Waste Management Inc	$1,500	Waste Mgmt
Maytag Company	$1,000	Appliances
Xerox Corp	$1,000	Off Machines

Labor

Labor Unions **$13,000**

    National Assn of Retired Federal Employees $9,000
    American Postal Workers Union $1,000
    United Transportation Union $1,000
    Others $2,000

Ideological/Single-Issue

Pro-Israel **$6,500**

    National PAC $5,000
    Others $1,500

Other Major Ideological/Single-Issue PACs

National Assn for Uniformed Services	$1,500	Pro-Defense
Conservative Victory Fund (Steve Symms)	$1,123	Repub Leader
Public Service Research Council	$1,000	Anti-Union

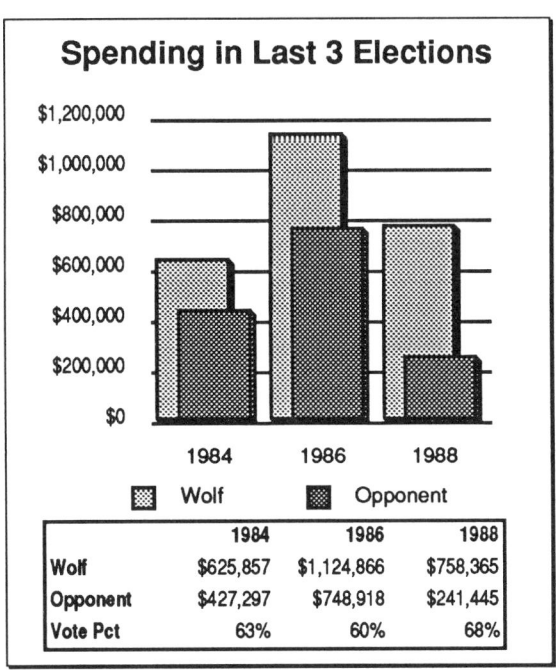

Spending in Last 3 Elections

	1984	1986	1988
Wolf	$625,857	$1,124,866	$758,365
Opponent	$427,297	$748,918	$241,445
Vote Pct	63%	60%	68%

* Contributions came from more than one PAC affiliated with this sponsor.

Howard Wolpe, D-Mich (3)

First elected: 1978
Total receipts: $576,393
Total from PACs: $262,274

1988 Committees & Subcommittees

Budget
Community and Natural Resources (Chairman)
Defense and International Affairs

Foreign Affairs
Africa (Chairman)
International Economic Policy and Trade

PAC Contribution Profile

Business

Automotive	**$2,050**
National Auto Dealers Assn	$1,000
Others	$1,050
Dairy	**$6,950**
Associated Milk Producers	$3,000
Mid-American Dairymen	$2,300
Others	$1,650
Electric Utilities	**$3,700**
Consumers Power Company	$2,300
Others	$1,400
Financial Institutions	**$2,400**
Michigan League of Savings Institutions	$1,000
Michigan Credit Union League	$1,000
Others	$400
Food & Beverage	**$2,175**
None over $925	
Health Professionals	**$2,550**
None over $750	
Lawyers & Lobbyists	**$5,850**
Assn of Trial Lawyers of America	$5,000
Others	$850
Oil & Gas	**$3,600**
Northville Industries Corp	$1,050
Tosco Corp	$1,000
Others	$1,550

Campaign Revenue Sources

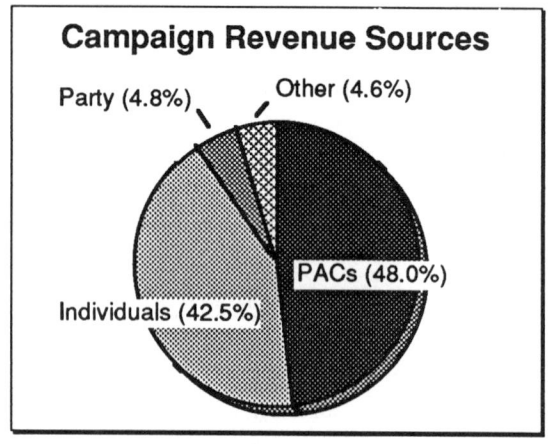

Party (4.8%)
Other (4.6%)
PACs (48.0%)
Individuals (42.5%)

Real Estate	**$6,100**
National Assn of Realtors	$5,600
Others	$500
Telecommunications	**$2,100**
Michigan Bell Telephone	$2,000
Others	$100

Other Major Business PACs

National Assn of Home Builders	$1,750	Resid Constr
Upjohn Company	$1,250	Pharmaceut
United Parcel Service	$1,200	Delivery
American Hospital Assn	$1,100	Hospitals
Ansell Inc	$1,000	Health Prod
Minn-Dak Farmers Co-op	$1,000	Sugar
Waste Management Inc	$1,000	Waste Mgmt

Labor

Bldg Trades/Industrial/Misc Unions	**$72,150**
Machinists/Aerospace Workers Union	$10,000
United Auto Workers	$10,000
AFL-CIO*	$7,500
Food & Commercial Workers Union	$6,000
Intl Brotherhood of Electrical Workers	$6,000
United Steelworkers	$5,000
Carpenters & Joiners Union	$4,850
Boilermakers Local #169	$4,800
Ironworkers Union	$2,500
Laborers' Political League	$2,500
Rubber Cork Linoleum Plastic Workers	$2,500
Bakery Confect & Tobacco Workers	$2,000
American Fed of of Grain Millers Local#3	$1,600
Ladies Garment Workers Union	$1,600
Plumbers/Pipefitters Union	$1,000
Service Employees International Union	$1,000
United Paperworkers	$1,000
Others	$2,300
Government & Postal Workers	**$32,400**
American Fedn of State/County/Munic Employees	$10,000
National Assn of Letter Carriers	$10,000
National Assn of Retired Federal Employees	$8,000
American Postal Workers Union	$3,600
Others	$800

PAC Totals by Category

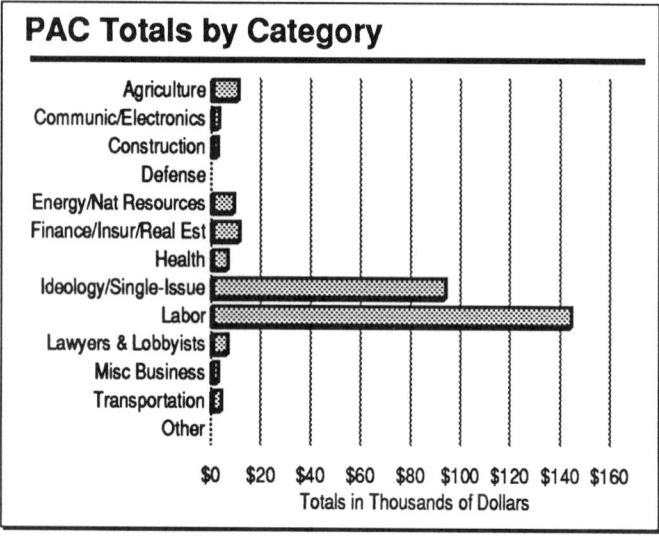

Agriculture
Communic/Electronics
Construction
Defense
Energy/Nat Resources
Finance/Insur/Real Est
Health
Ideology/Single-Issue
Labor
Lawyers & Lobbyists
Misc Business
Transportation
Other

$0 $20 $40 $60 $80 $100 $120 $140 $160
Totals in Thousands of Dollars

Teachers Unions *$9,550*
 National Education Assn $9,550

Transportation Unions *$29,300*
 Teamsters Union $10,000
 Marine Engineers Union* $8,000
 Seafarers International Union $6,000
 Amalgamated Transit Union $2,000
 Transportation Communication Union $1,200
 United Transportation Union $1,100
 Others $1,000

Ideological/Single-Issue

Democratic/Liberal *$16,450*
 Ingham County Democratic Party $9,250
 National Cmte for an Effective Congress $5,000
 Fifth Horseman PAC $1,000
 Hollywood Women's Political Cmte $1,000
 Others $200

Democratic Leadership PACs *$19,000*
 24th Cong Dist of California PAC (Henry Waxman) $5,000
 Majority Congress Committee (Jim Wright) $5,000
 America's Leaders' Fund (Dan Rostenkowski) $3,000
 Cmte for Democratic Opportunity (Bill Gray) $3,000
 Pax Americas (David Bonior) $2,000
 Valley Education Fund (Tony Coelho) $1,000

Environmental Issues *$3,249*
 Sierra Club $2,000
 League of Conservation Voters $1,000
 Others $249

Pro-Choice *$6,000*
 National Abortion Rights Action League $4,000
 Voters for Choice/Friends of Family Planning $2,000

Interest Group Ratings

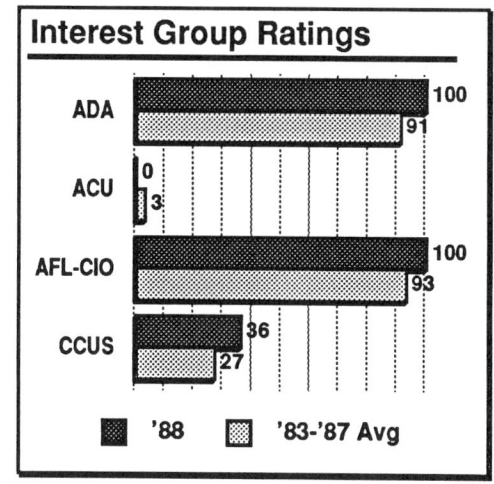

	'88	'83-'87 Avg
ADA	100	91
ACU	0	3
AFL-CIO	100	93
CCUS	36	27

Pro-Israel *$32,500*
 MOPAC $6,500
 National PAC $5,000
 Joint Action Cmte for Political Affairs $2,500
 Roundtable PAC $2,500
 Arizona Politically Interested Citizens $2,000
 Delaware Valley PAC $2,000
 Hudson Valley PAC $1,500
 City PAC $1,000
 Desert Caucus $1,000
 Garden State PAC $1,000
 Multi-Issue PAC $1,000
 San Franciscans for Good Government $1,000
 Washington PAC $1,000
 Others $4,500

Social Security/Senior Citizens *$7,300*
 National Cmte to Preserve Social Security $5,300
 National Council of Senior Citizens $2,000

Other Major Ideological/Single-Issue PACs

Americans Against Apartheid	$3,500	ForeignPolcy
Hellenic American Council	$1,300	Ethnic
Handgun Control Inc	$1,000	Anti-Guns
KidsPAC	$1,000	HealthWelfare

Independent expenditures supporting Wolpe

National Cmte to Preserve Social Security $1,589

Spending in Last 3 Elections

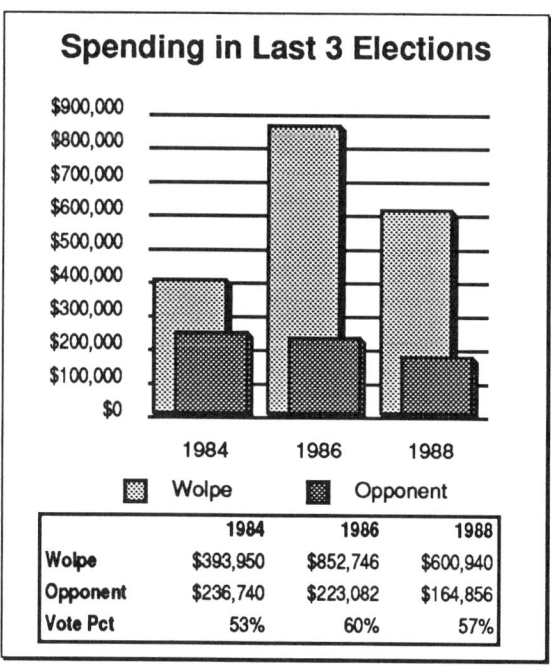

	1984	1986	1988
Wolpe	$393,950	$852,746	$600,940
Opponent	$236,740	$223,082	$164,856
Vote Pct	53%	60%	57%

Wolpe   Opponent

* Contributions came from more than one PAC affiliated
 with this sponsor.

Jim Wright, D-Texas (12)

1988 Committees & Subcommittees

First elected: 1954
Total receipts: $513,983
Total from PACs: $181,138

> **Speaker of the House**

PAC Contribution Profile

Business

Commercial Banks **$25,200**

MBank	$7,000
NCNB Texas	$5,200
Texas Commerce Bancshares	$5,000
J P Morgan & Company	$3,500
Barnett Banks of Florida	$2,500
Allied Bankshares	$2,000

Commodities/Securities Investment **$13,500**

Chicago Mercantile Exchange	$10,000
Morgan Stanley & Company	$2,500
Others	$1,000

Construction **$26,500**

National Assn of Home Builders	$10,000
Associated General Contractors	$5,000
Brown & Root	$5,000
National Utility Contractors Assn	$3,500
Others	$3,000

Dairy **$7,500**

Associated Milk Producers	$7,500

Defense **$15,000**

General Dynamics	$5,000
Tenneco Inc	$2,500
LTV Aerospace & Defense Company	$2,000
Singer Company	$2,000
Others	$3,500

Electric Utilities **$10,000**

Houston Industries	$5,000
Texas Utilities Electric Company*	$5,000

Campaign Revenue Sources

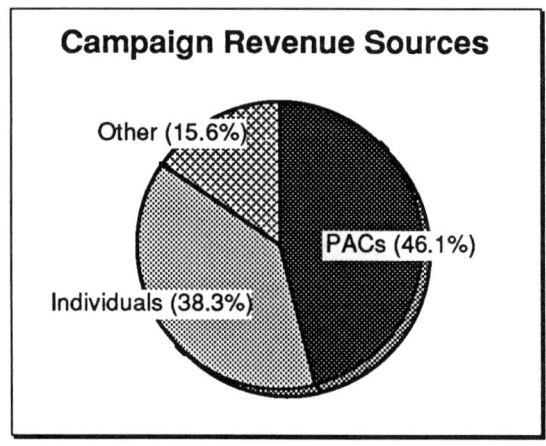

Other (15.6%)
PACs (46.1%)
Individuals (38.3%)

Food & Beverage **$10,000**

Coca-Cola Company	$5,000
Miller Brewing Company	$2,000
Others	$3,000

Health Professionals **$13,663**

American Academy of Ophthalmology	$5,000
American Dental Assn	$5,000
American Society Cataract/Refract Surgery	$2,500
Texas Medical Assn	$1,063
Others	$100

Insurance **$18,000**

National Assn of Life Underwriters	$8,000
Equitable Financial Services	$2,000
Massachusetts Mutual Life Insurance	$2,000
New England Mutual Life	$2,000
TransAmerica Life Companies	$2,000
Travelers Corp	$2,000

Lawyers **$39,250**

Fullbright & Jaworski	$7,250
Andrews, Kurth, Campbell & Jones	$5,000
Baker & Botts	$5,000
Bracewell & Patterson	$5,000
Butler & Binion	$5,000
Lidell, Sapp	$5,000
Vinson, Elkins, Searls, Connally & Smith	$5,000
McCamish, Martin, Brown & Loeffler	$2,000

Nursing Homes **$5,000**

American Health Care Assn	$5,000

Oil & Gas **$37,400**

Coastal Corp	$10,000
Arkla Inc	$5,000
Atlantic Richfield	$4,000
Conoco Inc	$2,500
Valero Energy Corp	$2,500
Mitchell Energy & Development	$2,000
Others	$11,400

Real Estate **$12,000**

Commonwealth Financial Group	$5,000
National Assn of Realtors	$5,000
Lamar Corp	$2,000

PAC Totals by Category

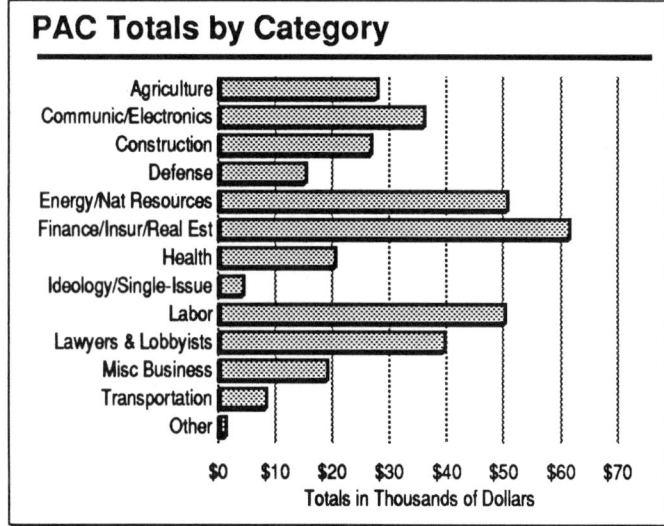

Agriculture
Communic/Electronics
Construction
Defense
Energy/Nat Resources
Finance/Insur/Real Est
Health
Ideology/Single-Issue
Labor
Lawyers & Lobbyists
Misc Business
Transportation
Other

$0 $10 $20 $30 $40 $50 $60 $70
Totals in Thousands of Dollars

Telecommunications **$30,000**

    AT&T $10,000
    GTE Corp* $10,000
    Southwestern Bell $10,000

Tobacco **$5,000**

    Philip Morris $5,000

Other Major Business PACs

Electrocom Automation Inc	$2,805	Comput Parts
E I Du Pont de Nemours & Company	$2,500	Chemicals
United Parcel Service	$2,125	Delivery
Archer-Daniels-Midland Corp	$2,000	Grain Trader
Browning-Ferris Industries	$2,000	Waste Mgmt

Interest Group Ratings

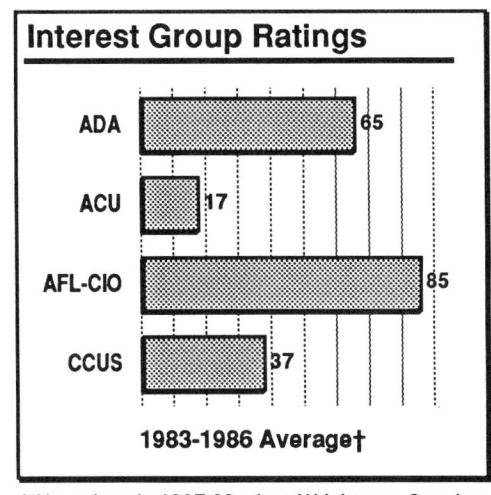

1983-1986 Average†

† No ratings in 1987-88 when Wright was Speaker

Labor

Bldg Trades/Industrial/Misc Unions **$25,025**

    Operating Engineers Union $10,000
    Sheet Metal Workers Union $10,000
    Electronic Machine Furniture Workers $2,000
    Others $3,025

Government & Postal Workers **$9,450**

    American Fedn of State/County/Munic Employees $5,000
    American Postal Workers Union $2,250
    National Star Route Mail Contractors $2,000
    Others $200

Teachers Unions **$5,000**

    National Education Assn $5,000

Transportation Unions **$10,490**

    Marine Engineers District 2 Maritime Officers $5,000
    United Transportation Union $2,000
    Others $3,490

Major Ideological/Single-Issue PACs

Alliance of Arts Advocates	$1,050	OtherIdeolog

Independent expenditures supporting Wright

National Cmte to Preserve Social Security $1,387

Independent expenditures opposing Wright

Fund for Conservative Majority $2,154

Spending in Last 3 Elections

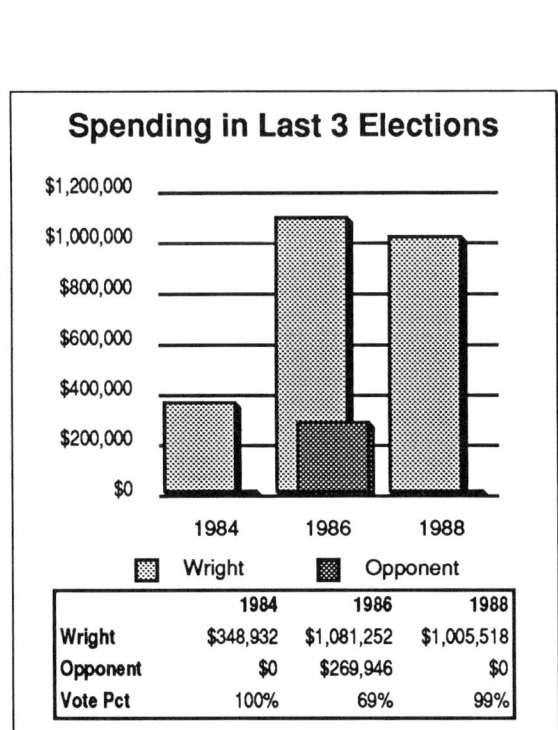

	1984	1986	1988
Wright	$348,932	$1,081,252	$1,005,518
Opponent	$0	$269,946	$0
Vote Pct	100%	69%	99%

---

* Contributions came from more than one PAC affiliated
with this sponsor.

Ron Wyden, D-Ore (3)

1988 Committees & Subcommittees

First elected: 1980
Total receipts: $596,224
Total from PACs: $316,772

Energy and Commerce
Energy and Power
Health and the Environment
Oversight and Investigations

Small Business
Regulation and Business Opportunities (Chairman)

Select Aging
Health and Long-Term Care

PAC Contribution Profile

Business

Automotive	**$9,050**
National Auto Dealers Assn	$4,850
Auto Dealers & Drivers for Free Trade	$3,500
Others	$700
Broadcasting/Entertainment	**$8,000**
National Cable Television Assn	$3,750
Others	$4,250
Construction	**$6,400**
National Assn of Home Builders	$5,700
Others	$700
Electric Utilities	**$6,425**
Idaho Power Company	$1,200
Pacific Power & Light	$1,200
Others	$4,025
Financial Institutions	**$6,000**
US Bancorp*	$2,100
American Bankers Assn	$1,000
Citicorp	$1,000
Others	$1,900
Food & Beverage	**$7,150**
Wine & Spirits Wholesalers of America	$1,400
Others	$5,750
Forest Products	**$9,600**
National Forest Products Assn	$2,650
Weyerhaeuser Company*	$1,100
Others	$5,850

Campaign Revenue Sources

Other (3.8%)
PACs (53.6%)
Individuals (42.6%)

PAC Totals by Category

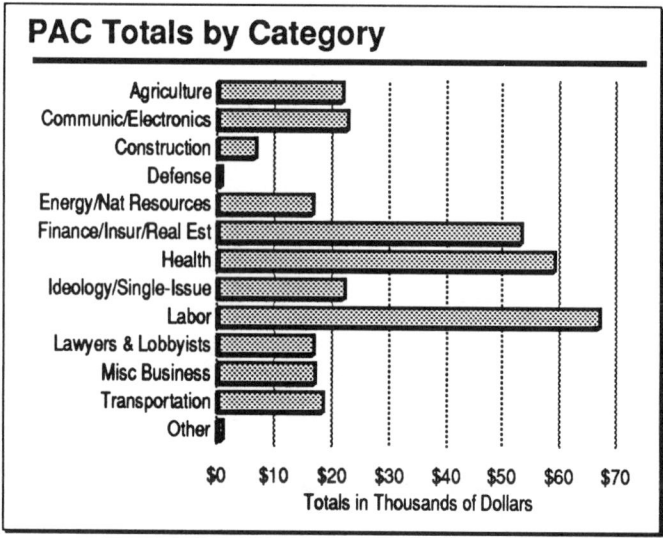

Agriculture
Communic/Electronics
Construction
Defense
Energy/Nat Resources
Finance/Insur/Real Est
Health
Ideology/Single-Issue
Labor
Lawyers & Lobbyists
Misc Business
Transportation
Other

$0 $10 $20 $30 $40 $50 $60 $70
Totals in Thousands of Dollars

Health Professionals	**$31,700**
American Dental Assn	$4,250
Corp for the Advancement of Psychiatry	$4,005
American Physical Therapy Assn	$2,100
American Podiatry Assn	$2,000
National Assn of Pharmacists	$1,750
American Chiropractic Assn	$1,645
American Pharmaceutical Assn	$1,550
American Optometric Assn	$1,550
American Academy of Ophthalmology	$1,500
American College of Emergency Physicians	$1,050
Others	$10,300
Hospitals & Nursing Homes	**$15,300**
American Health Care Assn	$4,000
American Hospital Assn	$3,850
Federation of America Hospitals	$2,850
National Assn of Private Psychiatric Hospitals	$1,550
Voluntary Hospitals of America	$1,350
Others	$1,700
Insurance	**$19,745**
Independent Insurance Agents of America	$3,295
Travelers Corp	$2,500
Aetna Life & Casualty	$1,200
American Council of Life Insurance	$1,200
Health Insurance Assn of America	$1,200
National Assn Mutual Insurance Agents	$1,050
Others	$9,300
Lawyers & Lobbyists	**$16,405**
Assn of Trial Lawyers of America	$5,000
Akin, Gump, Hauer & Feld	$2,600
Kirkland & Ellis	$1,234
Others	$7,571
Oil & Gas	**$6,198**
Interstate Natural Gas Assn	$1,198
Others	$5,000
Pharmaceuticals	**$5,500**
None over $1,000	

Real Estate **$9,800**

    National Assn of Realtors $5,900
    Arthur Andersen & Company $1,700
    Mortgage Bankers Assn of America...............................$1,200
    Others $1,000

Retail Sales **$4,300**

    Fred Meyer Inc $2,000
    National Assn of Chain Drug Stores $1,500
    Others $800

Securities/Commodities Investment **$16,350**

    Chicago Board of Trade $2,500
    Salomon Brothers $1,700
    Securities Industry Assn $1,200
    Investment Company Institute $1,050
    Others $9,900

Telecommunications **$13,350**

    Pacific Northwest Bell $3,000
    Pacific Telesis Group $1,750
    MCI Telecommunications $1,350
    US Telephone Assn $1,350
    Others $5,900

Other Major Business PACs

Medical Equipment Suppliers	$1,550	Med Supply
Coopers & Lybrand	$1,400	Accountants
Boeing Company	$1,350	Aircraft
National Assn for Home Care	$1,350	Home Care
American Crystal Sugar Corp	$1,050	Sugar
American Institute of CPA's	$1,050	Accountants
National Assn of Wholesale-Distributors	$1,050	Wholesale
Nike Inc	$1,050	Shoes
Pennwalt Corp	$1,050	Chemicals
Touche Ross	$1,050	Accountants
United Parcel Service	$1,050	Delivery

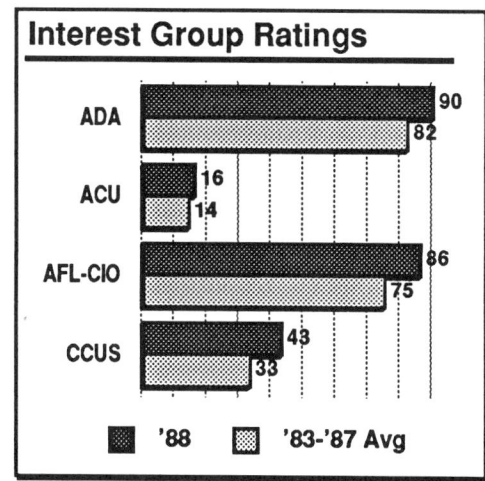

Interest Group Ratings

	'88	'83–'87 Avg
ADA	90	82
ACU	16	14
AFL-CIO	86	75
CCUS	43	33

Labor

Bldg Trades/Industrial/Misc Unions **$19,150**

    Machinists/Aerospace Workers Union $3,700
    Carpenters & Joiners Union $3,250
    Operating Engineers Union $2,400
    Intl Brotherhood of Electrical Workers............................$2,000
    Laborers' Political League $1,700
    AFL-CIO* $1,200
    Others $4,900

Government & Postal Workers **$18,550**

    National Assn of Letter Carriers $6,000
    National Assn of Retired Federal Employees $6,000
    American Fedn of State/County/Munic Employees $3,700
    Others $2,850

Teachers Unions **$8,750**

    American Federation of Teachers $4,400
    National Education Assn $2,850
    Oregon Education Assn $1,500

Transportation Unions **$20,300**

    Teamsters Union $8,000
    United Transportation Union $3,450
    Transportation Communication Union $1,450
    Marine Engineers Union* $1,350
    Others $6,050

Ideological/Single-Issue

Pro-Israel **$14,800**

    Citizens Organized PAC $5,000
    National PAC $5,000
    Others $4,800

Other Major Ideological/Single-Issue PACs

National Cmte to Preserve Social Security ......$3,000   Soc Secur

Independent expenditures supporting Wyden

National Cmte to Preserve Social Security $3,872

---

* Contributions came from more than one PAC affiliated
with this sponsor.

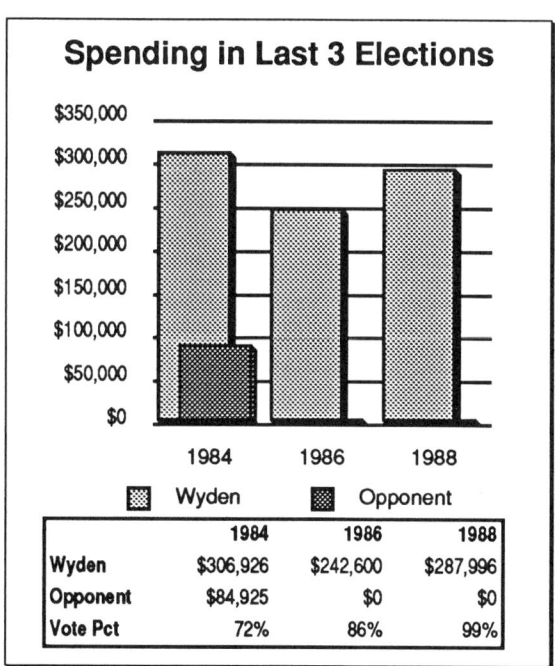

Spending in Last 3 Elections

    ☒ Wyden   ■ Opponent

	1984	1986	1988
Wyden	$306,926	$242,600	$287,996
Opponent	$84,925	$0	$0
Vote Pct	72%	86%	99%

Chalmers P. Wylie, R-Ohio (15)

First elected: 1966
Total receipts: $231,063
Total from PACs: $158,415

1988 Committees & Subcommittees

Banking, Finance and Urban Affairs (Ranking Republican)
Financial Institutions Supervision, Regulation and Insurance (Ranking Republican)
Consumer Affairs and Coinage
Housing and Community Development

Veterans' Affairs
Compensation, Pension and Insurance
Education, Training and Employment

Joint Economic
Economic Resources and Competitiveness
Fiscal and Monetary Policy
International Economic Policy

PAC Contribution Profile

Business

Automotive **$3,750**
    Auto Dealers & Drivers for Free Trade $2,000
    National Auto Dealers Assn $1,250
    Others $500

Commercial Banks **$19,650**
    American Bankers Assn $5,000
    Citicorp $2,500
    Barnett Banks of Florida $2,000
    Banc One Corp $1,500
    Independent Bankers Assn $1,500
    BankAmerica $1,000
    J P Morgan & Company $1,000
    Others $5,150

Construction **$16,719**
    National Assn of Home Builders $9,719
    Owens-Illinois $1,500
    Manville Corp $1,000
    National Concrete Masonry Assn $1,000
    Others $3,500

Consumer Credit & Loans **$2,850**
    Associated Credit Bureaus $1,000
    Others $1,850

Dairy **$2,250**
    Associated Milk Producers $2,000
    Others $250

Defense **$2,000**
    None over $500

Campaign Revenue Sources

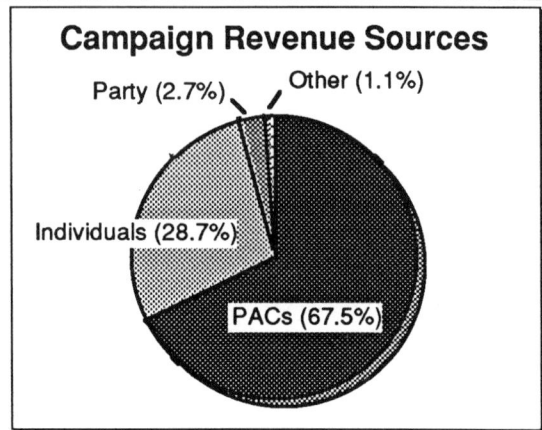

Party (2.7%)
Other (1.1%)
Individuals (28.7%)
PACs (67.5%)

Electric Utilities **$4,750**
    American Electric Power* $1,650
    ACRE (Action Committee for Rural Electrification) $1,250
    Others $1,850

Health Professionals **$5,250**
    American Medical Assn $2,500
    American Dental Assn $1,500
    American Academy of Ophthalmology $1,000
    Others $250

Insurance **$23,500**
    Independent Insurance Agents of America $5,250
    National Assn of Life Underwriters $5,000
    Nationwide Corp $3,500
    American Council of Life Insurance $2,500
    Travelers Corp $2,500
    National Assn Mutual Insurance Agents $2,250
    Others $2,500

Lawyers **$9,650**
    Assn of Trial Lawyers of America $5,250
    Baker & Hostetler $1,000
    Bricker & Eckler $1,000
    VSS&P FEDPAC $1,000
    Others $1,400

Oil & Gas **$2,272**
    Columbia Gas* $1,522
    Others $750

Real Estate **$15,000**
    National Assn of Realtors $10,000
    Mortgage Bankers Assn of America $2,000
    American Resort & Residential Developers Assn $1,000
    Commonwealth Financial Group $1,000
    Others $1,000

Retail Sales **$3,500**
    Limited Inc $1,500
    Federated Department Stores $1,000
    Others $1,000

PAC Totals by Category

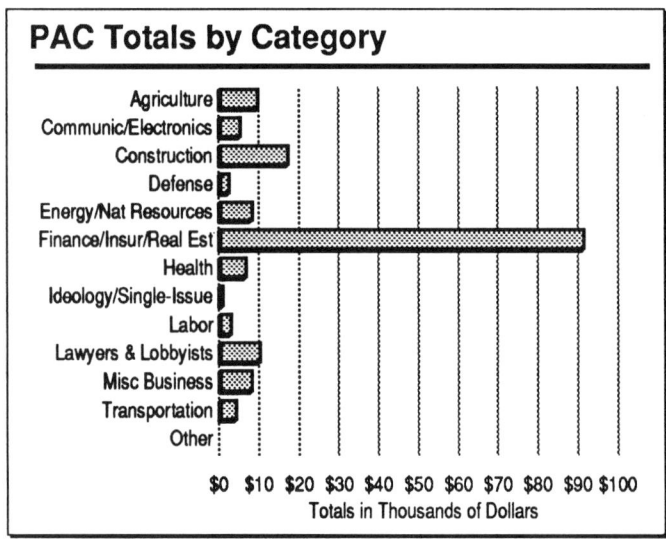

Agriculture
Communic/Electronics
Construction
Defense
Energy/Nat Resources
Finance/Insur/Real Est
Health
Ideology/Single-Issue
Labor
Lawyers & Lobbyists
Misc Business
Transportation
Other

$0 $10 $20 $30 $40 $50 $60 $70 $80 $90 $100
Totals in Thousands of Dollars

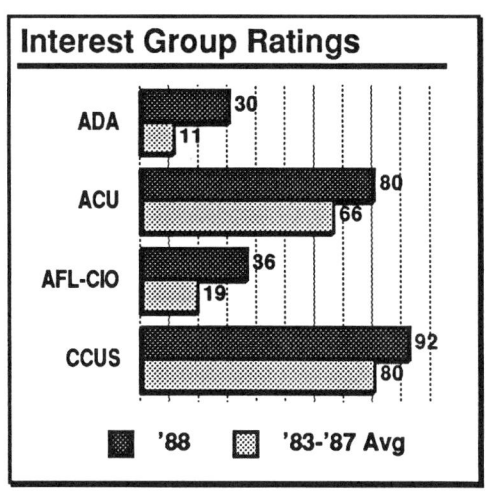
Savings Banks & Credit Unions **$10,150**
    Credit Union National Assn $4,000
    Ohio Savings Assns League $2,000
    National Council of Savings Institutions $1,000
    US League of Savings Assn $1,000
    Others $2,150

Securities/Commodities Investment **$22,550**
    Municipal Securities Institute $3,000
    Investment Company Institute $2,500
    Chicago Board of Trade $2,000
    Chicago Mercantile Exchange $2,000
    First Boston Corp $2,000
    E F Hutton Group $1,500
    Goldman Sachs $1,500
    Dain Bosworth $1,000
    Drexel Burnham Lambert $1,000
    Morgan Stanley & Company $1,000
    PaineWebber $1,000
    Prudential-Bache Securities $1,000
    Smith Barney $1,000
    Others $2,050

Telecommunications **$3,670**
    AT&T $2,500
    Ohio Bell Telephone $1,170

Other Major Business PACs

Ohio Farm Bureau Federation .... $1,750   Farm Orgs
Xerox Corp .... $1,000   Off Machines

Labor

Labor Unions **$2,500**
    Teamsters Union $2,000
    Others $500

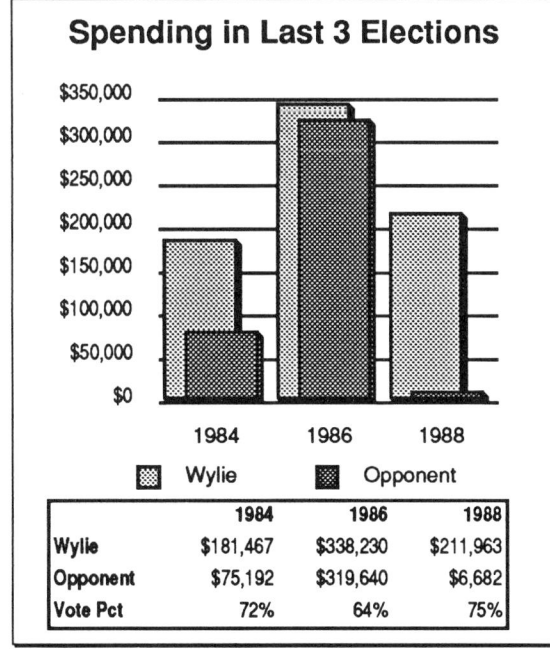

	1984	1986	1988
Wylie	$181,467	$338,230	$211,963
Opponent	$75,192	$319,640	$6,682
Vote Pct	72%	64%	75%

* Contributions came from more than one PAC affiliated with this sponsor.

Sidney R. Yates, D-Ill (9)

1988 Committees & Subcommittees

Appropriations
Interior and Related Agencies (Chairman)
Foreign Operations
Treasury, Postal Service and General Government

First elected: 1948
Total receipts: $126,705
Total from PACs: $25,250

PAC Contribution Profile

Business

Food & Beverage **$1,800**
    National Beer Wholesalers Assn $1,000
    Occidental Petroleum $500
    Others $300

Lawyers **$2,000**
    Assn of Trial Lawyers of America $2,000

Other Major Business PACs

American Dental Assn	$1,000	Dentists
Illinois Bell Telephone	$500	Phone Util
Martin Marietta Corp	$500	Air Defense
Mid-Continent Oil & Gas Assn	$500	Independ Oil
Tesoro Petroleum	$500	Independ Oil
United Technologies	$500	Air Defense

Campaign Revenue Sources

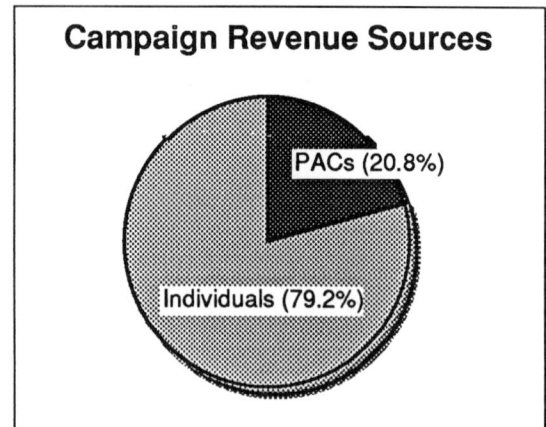

PACs (20.8%)
Individuals (79.2%)

PAC Totals by Category

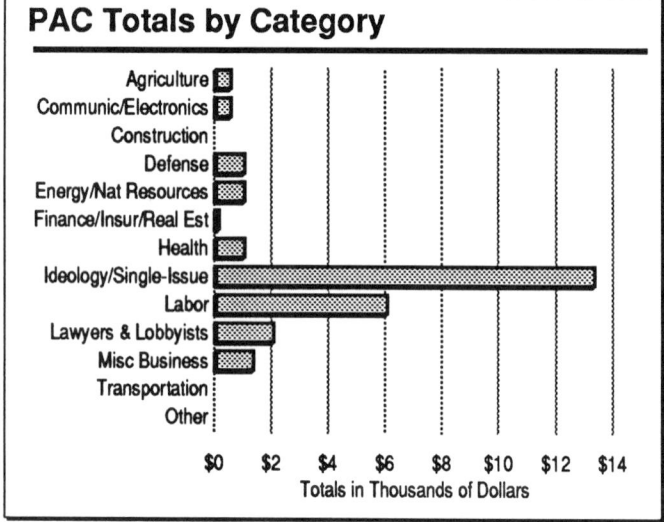

Totals in Thousands of Dollars

Labor

Labor Unions **$6,000**

    National Education Assn $4,000
    AFL-CIO $1,000
    American Fedn of State/County/Munic Employees $1,000

Ideological/Single-Issue

Pro-Israel **$7,750**

    National PAC $5,000
    San Franciscans for Good Government........................... $1,500
    Chicagoans for Better Congress $1,000
    Others $250

Other Major Ideological/Single-Issue PACs

KidsPAC $2,000	HealthWelfare
National Cmte to Preserve Social Security $1,000	Soc Secur
Sierra Club $999	Environment
Armenian Assembly of America $500	Ethnic
Handgun Control Inc $500	Anti-Guns

Independent expenditures supporting Yates

National Cmte to Preserve Social Security $2,925

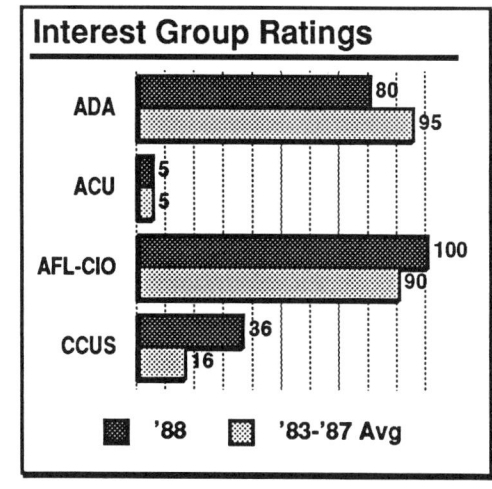

Interest Group Ratings

	'88	'83-'87 Avg
ADA	80	95
ACU	5	5
AFL-CIO	100	90
CCUS	36	16

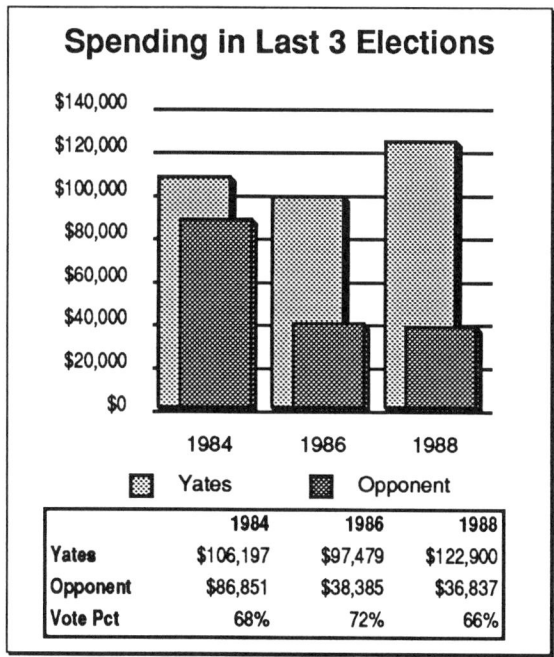

Spending in Last 3 Elections

	1984	1986	1988
Yates	$106,197	$97,479	$122,900
Opponent	$86,851	$38,385	$36,837
Vote Pct	68%	72%	66%

Gus Yatron, D-Pa (6)

1988 Committees & Subcommittees

Foreign Affairs
Human Rights and International Organizations (Chairman)
International Operations

Post Office and Civil Service
Human Resources
Investigations

First elected: 1968
Total receipts: $145,914
Total from PACs: $109,700

PAC Contribution Profile

Business

Defense	**$2,200**
General Dynamics	$750
Rockwell International	$700
Others	$750
Electric Utilities	**$1,100**
ACRE (Action Committee for Rural Electrification)	$750
Others	$350
Financial Institutions	**$1,250**
None over $500	
Food & Beverage	**$1,800**
McDonald's Corp	$1,000
Others	$800
Health Professionals	**$3,750**
American Medical Assn	$3,500
Others	$250
Lawyers & Lobbyists	**$5,750**
Assn of Trial Lawyers of America	$5,000
Others	$750
Package Delivery	**$1,300**
United Parcel Service	$1,300
Real Estate	**$6,000**
National Assn of Realtors	$6,000

Campaign Revenue Sources

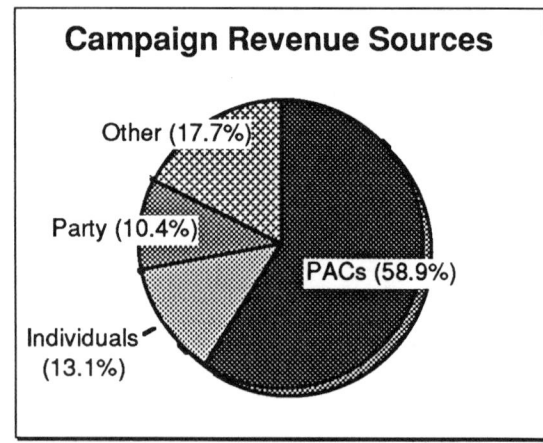

Other (17.7%)
Party (10.4%)
PACs (58.9%)
Individuals (13.1%)

Telecommunications	**$4,000**
AT&T	$2,000
Continental Telecom	$1,000
Bell Telephone of Pennsylvania	$750
Others	$250

Other Major Business PACs

Gilbert Associates	$1,000	NuclearEquip
Atlantic Apparel Contractors Assn	$800	Clothing

PAC Totals by Category

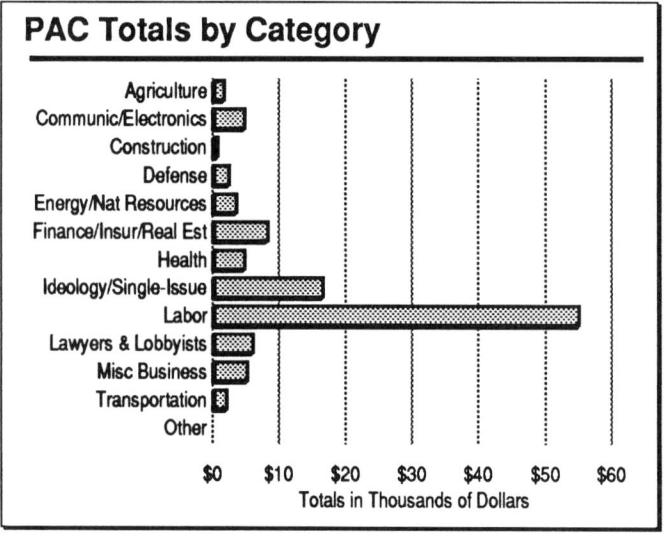

Agriculture
Communic/Electronics
Construction
Defense
Energy/Nat Resources
Finance/Insur/Real Est
Health
Ideology/Single-Issue
Labor
Lawyers & Lobbyists
Misc Business
Transportation
Other

$0 $10 $20 $30 $40 $50 $60
Totals in Thousands of Dollars

Labor

Bldg Trades/Industrial/Misc Unions $16,700
    Ironworkers Union $4,000
    United Auto Workers $2,500
    Laborers' Political League $2,000
    Carpenters & Joiners Union $1,750
    Plumbers/Pipefitters Union* $1,150
    Food & Commercial Workers Union $1,000
    Intl Brotherhood of Electrical Workers $1,000
    AFL-CIO* $700
    Ladies Garment Workers Union $650
    Others $1,950

Government & Postal Workers $13,750
    National Assn of Retired Federal Employees $7,000
    National Assn of Letter Carriers $2,000
    National Star Route Mail Contractors $1,500
    National League of Postmasters $1,000
    National Assn of Postal Supervisors $850
    American Postal Workers Union $750
    National Assn of Postmasters $650

Teachers Unions $2,750
    National Education Assn $2,750

Transportation Unions $21,500
    Marine Engineers Union $8,000
    Teamsters Union $7,500
    Air Line Pilots Assn $2,000
    United Transportation Union $1,500
    Seafarers International Union $1,000
    Transportation Communication Union $750
    Others $750

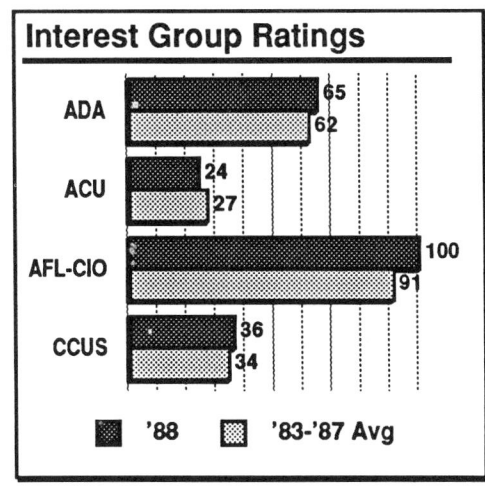

Interest Group Ratings

	'88	'83-'87 Avg
ADA	65	62
ACU	24	27
AFL-CIO	100	91
CCUS	36	34

Ideological/Single-Issue

Pro-Israel $7,500
    National PAC $5,000
    Washington PAC $1,500
    Others $1,000

Other Major Ideological/Single-Issue PACs

National Rifle Assn	$4,500	Pro-Guns
Dynamis	$1,000	Greek Ethnic
National Albanian American PAC	$1,000	Ethnic
National Cmte to Preserve Social Security	$1,000	Soc Secur
Valley Education Fund (Tony Coelho)	$1,000	Dem Leaders

Independent expenditures supporting Yatron

National Cmte to Preserve Social Security $3,665

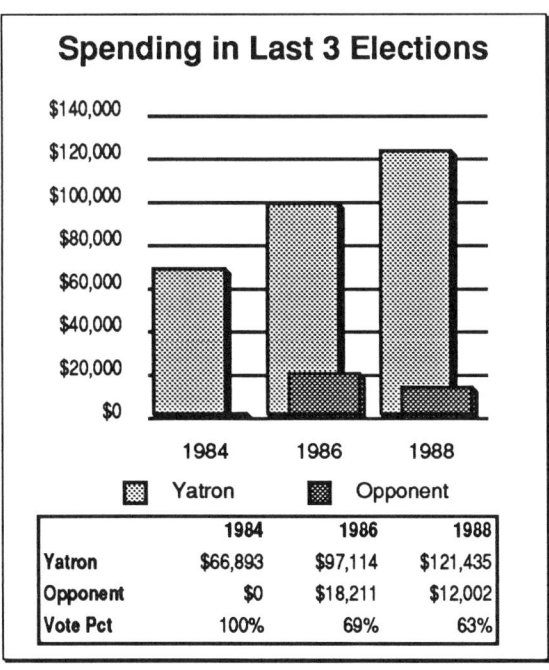

Spending in Last 3 Elections

	1984	1986	1988
Yatron	$66,893	$97,114	$121,435
Opponent	$0	$18,211	$12,002
Vote Pct	100%	69%	63%

---

* Contributions came from more than one PAC affiliated
with this sponsor.

C. W. Bill Young, R-Fla (8)

First elected: 1970
Total receipts: $212,972
Total from PACs: $109,600

1988 Committees & Subcommittees

Appropriations
Defense
Labor, Health and Human Services, Education and Related Agencies

PAC Contribution Profile

Campaign Revenue Sources

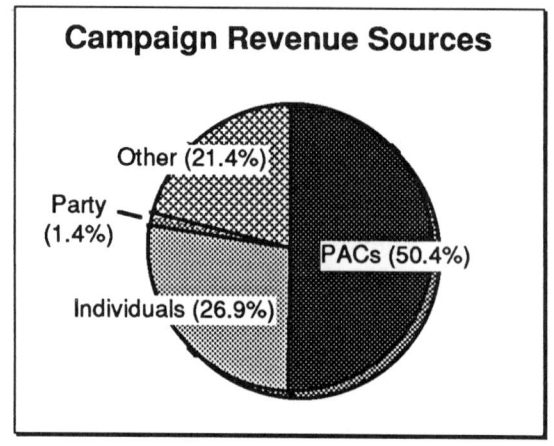

Other (21.4%)
Party (1.4%)
PACs (50.4%)
Individuals (26.9%)

Business

Auto Dealers **$6,000**
    National Auto Dealers Assn $4,500
    Auto Dealers & Drivers for Free Trade $1,500

Commercial & Savings Banks **$5,300**
    Barnett Banks of Florida $1,000
    Florida League of Financial Institutions $1,000
    National Banks of Florida $1,000
    Others $2,300

Construction **$4,000**
    Walter Industries $1,500
    Others $2,500

Defense **$45,274**
    McDonnell Douglas* $3,500
    TRW Inc $3,000
    General Electric $2,500
    Northrop Corp $2,200
    E-Systems* $2,024
    AT&T $2,000
    Boeing Company $2,000
    General Dynamics $2,000
    Grumman $2,000
    Hughes Aircraft $2,000
    Textron Inc $2,000
    Honeywell Florida $1,500
    Lockheed Corp $1,500
    LTV Aerospace & Defense Company $1,500
    Computer Sciences Corp $1,000
    (Continued in next column)

Defense (cont'd)
    FMC Corp $1,000
    Gencorp Inc $1,000
    Harris Corp $1,000
    Rockwell International $1,000
    Tenneco Inc $1,000
    United Technologies $1,000
    Figgie International $750
    Cubic Corp $550
    Others $7,250

Electric Utilities **$2,000**
    None over $500

Food & Beverage **$2,500**
    Food Marketing Institute $1,000
    National Beer Wholesalers Assn $1,000
    Others $500

Health Professionals **$16,000**
    American Medical Assn $5,000
    Florida Medical Assn $5,000
    American Dental Assn $3,000
    Oral & Maxillofacial Surgeons $1,500
    Others $1,500

Real Estate **$4,000**
    National Assn of Realtors $4,000

Retail Sales **$2,550**
    None over $500

Ship Building **$1,500**
    American Ship Building Company $1,500

Telecommunications **$3,000**
    Southern Bell $3,000

Other Major Business PACs

Intergraph Corp .... $1,000   Comput Parts
National Assn of Trade/Tech Schools .... $1,000   Voc Tech

PAC Totals by Category

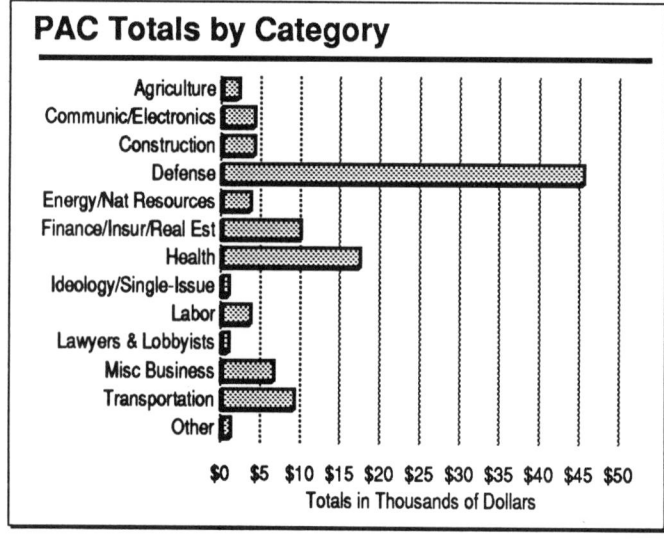

Agriculture
Communic/Electronics
Construction
Defense
Energy/Nat Resources
Finance/Insur/Real Est
Health
Ideology/Single-Issue
Labor
Lawyers & Lobbyists
Misc Business
Transportation
Other

$0 $5 $10 $15 $20 $25 $30 $35 $40 $45 $50
Totals in Thousands of Dollars

Labor

Labor Unions **$3,500**
    Air Line Pilots Assn $1,000
    National Assn of Retired Federal Employees $1,000
    Others $1,500

Independent expenditures supporting Young

National Cmte to Preserve Social Security $3,957

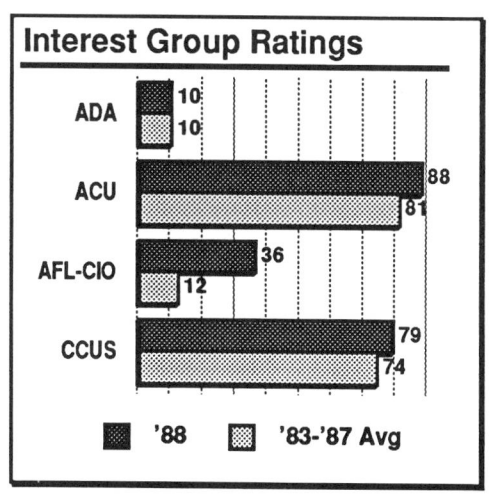

Interest Group Ratings

	'88	'83-'87 Avg
ADA	10	10
ACU	88	81
AFL-CIO	36	12
CCUS	79	74

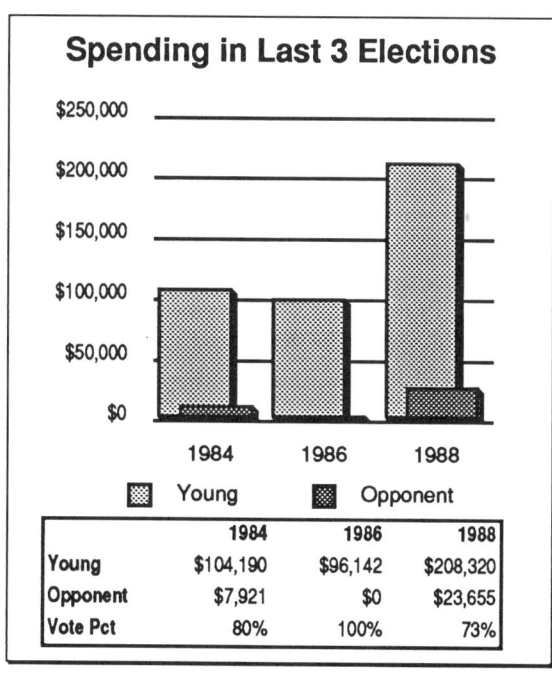

Spending in Last 3 Elections

	1984	1986	1988
Young	$104,190	$96,142	$208,320
Opponent	$7,921	$0	$23,655
Vote Pct	80%	100%	73%

* Contributions came from more than one PAC affiliated with this sponsor.

Don Young, R-Alaska (At Large)

First elected: 1973
Total receipts: $623,760
Total from PACs: $295,950

1988 Committees & Subcommittees

Interior and Insular Affairs (Ranking Republican)
Energy and the Environment
Water and Power Resources

Merchant Marine and Fisheries
Fisheries and Wildlife Conservation and the Environment (Ranking Republican)
Coast Guard and Navigation
Merchant Marine

Post Office and Civil Service
Postal Personnel and Modernization (Ranking Republican)
Postal Operations and Services

PAC Contribution Profile

Business

Air Transport	**$4,800**
Aircraft Owners & Pilots Assn	$3,000
Boeing Company	$1,000
Others	$800
Automotive	**$6,900**
Auto Dealers & Drivers for Free Trade	$3,500
National Auto Dealers Assn	$2,600
Others	$800
Construction	**$15,450**
Associated General Contractors	$2,800
Morrison-Knudsen	$2,500
National Assn of Home Builders	$2,500
National Utility Contractors Assn	$2,000
Associated Builders & Contractors	$1,000
Brown & Root	$1,000
Others	$3,650
Dairy	**$5,300**
Mid-American Dairymen	$3,000
Associated Milk Producers	$2,000
Others	$300
Defense Aerospace	**$5,000**
Martin Marietta Corp	$2,800
Others	$2,200
Electric Utilities	**$9,150**
ACRE (Action Committee for Rural Electrification)	$1,400
Philadelphia Electric	$1,250
Others	$6,500

Campaign Revenue Sources

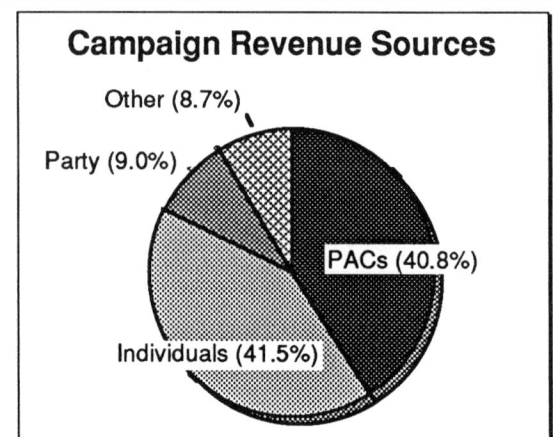

Other (8.7%)
Party (9.0%)
PACs (40.8%)
Individuals (41.5%)

Package Delivery	**$4,200**
United Parcel Service	$3,200
Federal Express Corp	$1,000
Forest Products	**$11,850**
Louisiana-Pacific Corp	$4,000
National Forest Products Assn	$2,500
Potlatch Corp	$1,300
Boise Cascade	$1,000
Others	$3,050
Health Professionals	**$10,750**
American Medical Assn	$5,550
American Optometric Assn	$1,800
American Chiropractic Assn	$1,300
American Physical Therapy Assn	$1,100
American Dental Assn	$1,000
Insurance	**$7,950**
National Assn of Life Underwriters	$5,250
Others	$2,700
Lawyers	**$5,000**
Garvey, Schubert & Barer	$1,500
Others	$3,500
Mining	**$8,250**
Inspiration Gold Inc	$2,000
Peabody Coal	$1,100
National Coal Assn	$1,000
Others	$4,150
Oil & Gas	**$57,325**
BP America	$9,800
Atlantic Richfield	$5,000
Amoco Corp	$3,750
Phillips Petroleum	$3,000
Chevron Corp	$2,800
Shell Oil	$2,550
Exxon Corp	$2,500
Cooper Industries	$2,000
Marathon Oil	$1,800

(Continued in next column)

PAC Totals by Category

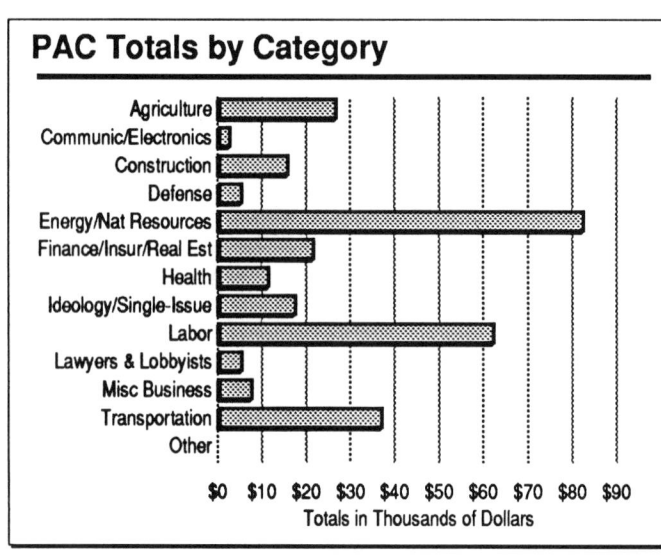

Agriculture
Communic/Electronics
Construction
Defense
Energy/Nat Resources
Finance/Insur/Real Est
Health
Ideology/Single-Issue
Labor
Lawyers & Lobbyists
Misc Business
Transportation
Other

$0 $10 $20 $30 $40 $50 $60 $70 $80 $90
Totals in Thousands of Dollars

Oil & Gas (cont'd)

Enserch Corp	$1,500
Sun Company	$1,500
Texaco	$1,500
Williams Companies	$1,500
Litton Industries	$1,300
Mapco Inc	$1,300
Texas Gas Transmission Corp	$1,100
Columbia Hydrocarbon Corp	$1,000
Interstate Natural Gas Assn	$1,000
International Assn of Drilling Contractors	$1,000
Mobil Oil	$1,000
Occidental Oil & Gas	$1,000
Tesoro Petroleum	$1,000
Union Oil	$1,000
Union Pacific Corp	$1,000
Others	$6,425

Real Estate $10,000

National Assn of Realtors	$10,000

Sea Transport $15,800

Matson Navigation	$3,000
Crowley Maritime	$2,575
American Pilots Assn	$2,100
Totem Ocean Trailer Express	$1,625
American President Lines	$1,400
Bath Iron Works	$1,400
Sea-Land Corp	$1,350
Others	$2,350

Sugar Growers $5,300

American Sugarbeet Growers Assn	$1,100
American Crystal Sugar Corp	$1,000
Southern Minnesota Beet Sugar Co-op	$1,000
Others	$2,200

Other Major Business PACs

McDermott Inc	$2,000	PowerEquip
Waste Management Inc	$2,000	WasteMgmt
Credit Union National Assn	$1,600	Credit Union
NL Industries	$1,000	Chemicals
Winn-Dixie Stores	$1,000	Food Stores

Spending in Last 3 Elections

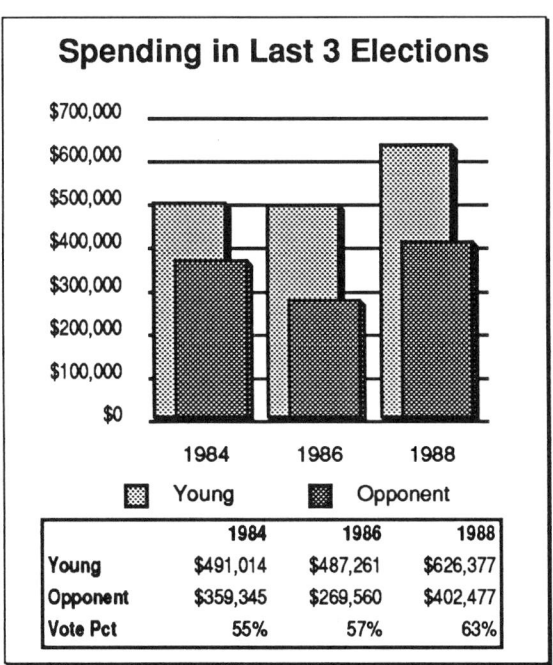

	1984	1986	1988
Young	$491,014	$487,261	$626,377
Opponent	$359,345	$269,560	$402,477
Vote Pct	55%	57%	63%

Interest Group Ratings

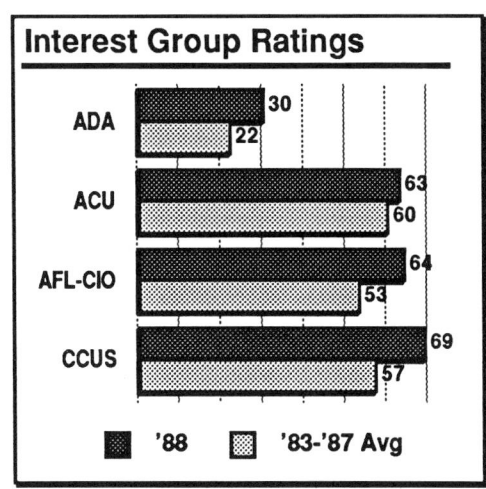

	'88	'83-'87 Avg
ADA	30	22
ACU	63	60
AFL-CIO	64	53
CCUS	69	57

Labor

Bldg Trades/Industrial/Misc Unions $4,500

Plumbers/Pipefitters Union	$2,000
Operating Engineers Union	$1,000
Others	$1,500

Government & Postal Workers $26,700

National Assn of Letter Carriers	$10,000
National Assn of Retired Federal Employees	$7,200
American Postal Workers Union	$5,000
National League of Postmasters	$1,600
National Assn of Postal Supervisors	$1,100
Others	$1,800

Sea Transport Unions $20,100

Seafarers International Union	$10,000
Marine Engineers Union*	$9,500
Others	$600

Other Transportation Unions $10,500

Teamsters Union	$8,500
Air Line Pilots Assn	$2,000

Ideological/Single-Issue

Pro-Gun Ownership $10,900

National Rifle Assn	$9,900
Safari Club International	$1,000

Other Major Ideological/Leadership PACs

Bristol Bay Native Corp	$2,000	Ethnic
National Right to Life PAC	$1,014	Pro-Life
Fund for a Repub Majority (Ted Stevens)	$1,000	Repub Leader
National Security PAC	$1,000	Pro-Defense

---

* Contributions came from more than one PAC affiliated
with this sponsor.

5.

PAC Profiles

pen Secrets

Introduction to the PAC Profiles

This final section of Open Secrets provides a directory of every political action committee that gave $20,000 or more in the 1987-88 election cycle. In all, these PACs contributed $147 million to federal candidates — 92.5 percent of the total given by all PACs in the 1988 elections.

The PACs are listed alphabetically by the name of the PAC sponsor, or the name of the PAC itself where there is no other sponsor.

What's included in the PAC profiles:

Short name of the PAC or PAC sponsor. This is the name used elsewhere in the book to identify the PAC. The term "sponsor" is used simply to identify the group whose members contribute to the PAC, and does not imply a formal relationship between the PAC and the organization. Many PACs *are* officially connected with their sponsoring organization; others operate independently, even though the PAC's contributors all work for the same company or belong to the same trade association, labor union, or other organization.

Official name of the PAC. The only abbreviation is the use of "PAC" for "Political Action Committee"

Total contributions in 1987-88 election cycle

AFL-CIO	$1,006,096	316 Candidates	Dems:	98.6%
AFL-CIO Committee on Political Education/Political Contributions Committee		Avg House: $2,674	House:	72.6%
Washington, DC AFL-CIO	Labor Unions	Avg Sen: $6,521	Incumb:	53.4%

Location of the PAC's headquarters

Category or thumbnail description. See Appendix A for a complete list of categories used to classify the PACs in this book.

Affiliated organization. When an organization is listed here, it means the PAC is one of several affiliated with this parent group. In the case of leadership PACs, the name of the PAC's sponsor is listed here.

Percentage of total dollars that went to Democratic or Republican candidates. Whichever party got more than 50 percent is listed.

Number of federal candidates receiving contributions from the PAC in 1987-88.

Alabama Farm Bureau Federation	$57,375	58 Candidates	Dems:	83.7%
ELECT - The PAC of Alabama Farm Bureau Federation		Avg House: $870	House:	56.1%
Montgomery, AL	Farm Orgs	Avg Sen: $1,329	Incumb:	96.1%

Average contribution to House candidates in 1987-88.

Average contribution to Senate candidates in 1987-88.

Percentage of dollars that went to incumbents.

Percentage of dollars that went to House, Senate, or Presidential candidates. The group that got the biggest share is listed.

Sponsor or Related Group/PAC Name	Affiliate	1987-88 Total	Where the money went...		
15th District Committee 15th District Committee Bloomington, IL — Rep Edward Madigan (R-Ill) / Repub Leaders		$21,050	26 Candidates Avg House: $825 Avg Sen: $625	Repubs: 100.0% House: 94.1% Incumb: 33.3%	
24th Congr Dist of California PAC 24th Congressional District of California PAC Beverly Hills, CA — Rep Henry Waxman (D-Calif) / Dem Leaders		$205,000	42 Candidates Avg House: $4,696 Avg Sen: $5,555	Dems: 100.0% House: 75.6% Incumb: 71.2%	
A E Staley Manufacturing Company Staley PAC of A E Staley Manufacturing Company Decatur, IL / Food Processing		$118,950	133 Candidates Avg House: $704 Avg Sen: $1,401	Dems: 66.5% House: 56.3% Incumb: 93.0%	
AAI Corp AAI Corporation PAC Hunt Valley, MD / Defense R&D†		$30,250	22 Candidates Avg House: $1,441 Avg Sen: $1,062	Repubs: 57.0% House: 81.0% Incumb: 87.6%	
Abbott Laboratories Abbott Laboratories Better Government Fund Abbott Park, IL / Pharmaceuticals†		$191,527	188 Candidates Avg House: $576 Avg Sen: $2,737	Repubs: 70.6% Senate: 52.8% Incumb: 75.0%	
Acacia Mutual Life Insurance Acacia Mutual PAC Washingon, DC / Life Insurance†		$32,850	46 Candidates Avg House: $595 Avg Sen: $1,058	Dems: 71.1% House: 59.8% Incumb: 97.7%	
ACRE (Action Committee for Rural Electrification) Action Committee for Rural Electrification (ACRE) Washington, DC — ACRE / Rural Electric		$447,178	372 Candidates Avg House: $893 Avg Sen: $3,834	Dems: 78.6% House: 66.6% Incumb: 78.3%	
Aetna Life & Casualty Aetna Life and Casualty Company PAC Hartford, CT / Insurance		$198,084	142 Candidates Avg House: $715 Avg Sen: $2,493	Repubs: 58.7% Senate: 61.6% Incumb: 77.8%	
AFL-CIO AFL-CIO Committee on Political Education/Political Contributions Committee Washington, DC — AFL-CIO / Labor Unions		$1,006,096	316 Candidates Avg House: $2,674 Avg Sen: $6,521	Dems: 98.6% House: 72.6% Incumb: 53.4%	
AFL-CIO Allied Industrial Workers Campaign Fund of the Allied Industrial Workers of America AFL-CIO Milwaukee, WI — AFL-CIO / Manuf Unions		$21,100	34 Candidates Avg House: $668 Avg Sen: $561	Dems: 100.0% House: 76.1% Incumb: 49.5%	
AFL-CIO Bldg/Construction Trades Dept Political Educational Fund of the Building and Construction Trades Department Washington, DC — AFL-CIO / Constr Unions		$150,826	185 Candidates Avg House: $780 Avg Sen: $1,239	Dems: 89.0% House: 88.5% Incumb: 91.7%	
AFL-CIO Industrial Union Dept Industrial Union Department AFL-CIO Voluntary Fund Washington, DC — AFL-CIO / Manuf Unions		$29,210	66 Candidates Avg House: $435 Avg Sen: $583	Dems: 97.3% House: 94.0% Incumb: 96.9%	
AG Processing Inc AG Processing Inc PAC, AGPAC Omaha, NE / Grain/Soybeans		$24,550	62 Candidates Avg House: $357 Avg Sen: $612	Repubs: 51.9% House: 77.2% Incumb: 87.8%	
Air Conditioning Contractors of America Air Conditioning Contractors of America PAC Washington, DC / Plumbing/AirCon		$27,250	65 Candidates Avg House: $310 Avg Sen: $783	Repubs: 95.4% House: 56.9% Incumb: 53.2%	
Air Line Pilots Assn Air Line Pilots Association PAC Washington, DC / Air Transport Union		$1,209,500	307 Candidates Avg House: $3,589 Avg Sen: $6,541	Dems: 78.7% House: 79.2% Incumb: 83.8%	
Air Products & Chemicals Inc Air Products Political Alliance Trexlertown, PA / Chemicals		$49,125	73 Candidates Avg House: $518 Avg Sen: $1,384	Repubs: 66.7% House: 63.4% Incumb: 89.4%	
Aircraft Owners & Pilots Assn Aircraft Owners and Pilots Association PAC Frederick, MD / Genl Aviation		$290,089	188 Candidates Avg House: $1,392 Avg Sen: $2,296	Dems: 53.7% House: 75.9% Incumb: 88.5%	
Akin, Gump, Hauer & Feld Akin, Gump, Strauss, Hauer & Feld Civic Action Committee Washington, DC / Lawyers		$197,490	182 Candidates Avg House: $888 Avg Sen: $1,762	Dems: 77.7% House: 63.4% Incumb: 98.3%	
Alabama Farm Bureau Federation ELECT - The PAC of Alabama Farm Bureau Federation Montgomery, AL / Farm Orgs		$57,375	58 Candidates Avg House: $870 Avg Sen: $1,329	Dems: 83.7% House: 56.1% Incumb: 96.1%	

† PAC Sponsor has other major interests in addition to this primary category

Sponsor or Related Group/PAC Name	Affiliate	1987-88 Total	Where the money went...
Alabama Peanut Producers Assn Peanut PAC of Alabama, PAC of Alabama Peanut Producers Association Dothan, AL	Misc Crops	$24,850	26 Candidates Dems: 77.5% Avg House: $717 House: 57.7% Avg Sen: $1,750 Incumb: 100.0%
Alabama Power Company Alabama Power Co Employees Federal PAC (APC Employees Federal PAC) Birmingham, AL	Southern Company Electric Utility	$81,110	133 Candidates Dems: 53.8% Avg House: $510 House: 62.9% Avg Sen: $882 Incumb: 84.2%
Alcoa Alcoa Employees Political Fund Pittsburgh, PA	Metal Mining/Processing†	$59,675	67 Candidates Dems: 51.9% Avg House: $630 House: 58.1% Avg Sen: $2,083 Incumb: 90.4%
Allied Bankshares First Interstate Texas Leadership Funds/Federal (Formerly Allied Bankshares Leadership) Houston, TX	Commercial Banks	$31,725	20 Candidates Dems: 58.3% Avg House: $1,072 Senate: 45.7% Avg Sen: $1,812 Incumb: 100.0%
Allied-Signal Allied-Signal PAC Morristown, NJ	Air Defense†	$296,125	316 Candidates Repubs: 51.7% Avg House: $606 House: 55.5% Avg Sen: $2,927 Incumb: 85.5%
Allstate Insurance Allstate Insurance Company PAC Northbrook, IL	Sears Insurance	$71,050	63 Candidates Repubs: 72.2% Avg House: $657 Senate: 63.9% Avg Sen: $1,891 Incumb: 68.3%
Alltel Corp Alltel Corporation PAC (APAC) Hudson, OH	Phone Utilities	$38,275	70 Candidates Dems: 56.8% Avg House: $490 House: 74.4% Avg Sen: $800 Incumb: 85.1%
Amalgamated Clothing & Textile Workers Amalgamated Clothing and Textile Workers Union - PAC (ACTWU-PAC) New York, NY	Clothing/Textile Workers Manuf Unions	$262,850	247 Candidates Dems: 93.3% Avg House: $605 House: 50.2% Avg Sen: $4,394 Incumb: 72.4%
Amalgamated Transit Union Amalgamated Transit Union-COPE Washington, DC	Transport Union	$543,687	247 Candidates Dems: 93.9% Avg House: $1,757 House: 65.9% Avg Sen: $4,367 Incumb: 61.9%
America's Leaders' Fund America's Leaders' Fund (Chicago Campaign Committee) Chicago, IL	Rep Dan Rostenkowski (D-Ill) Dem Leaders	$189,626	98 Candidates Dems: 100.0% Avg House: $1,864 House: 93.4% Avg Sen: $5,000 Incumb: 61.5%
America's PAC America's PAC Herndon, VA	Repub/Conservative†	$27,500	17 Candidates Repubs: 100.0% Avg House: $1,666 House: 54.5% Avg Sen: $1,562 Incumb: 25.5%
American Academy of Ophthalmology American Academy of Ophthalmology Inc Political Committee ("OPTHPAC") San Francisco, CA	Eye Doctors	$644,000	242 Candidates Repubs: 53.3% Avg House: $2,081 House: 65.3% Avg Sen: $5,587 Incumb: 66.1%
American Airlines American Airlines PAC Washington, DC	Airlines	$124,649	137 Candidates Dems: 60.0% Avg House: $773 House: 64.5% Avg Sen: $1,174 Incumb: 96.9%
American Assn for Marriage/Family Therapy American Association for Marriage & Family Therapy Washington, DC	Health Practitioners	$20,100	34 Candidates Dems: 66.4% Avg House: $592 House: 59.0% Avg Sen: $596 Incumb: 100.0%
American Assn of Crop Insurers American Association of Crop Insurers PAC (AACI PAC) Washington, DC	Ag Services†	$49,550	57 Candidates Dems: 68.0% Avg House: $722 House: 62.7% Avg Sen: $1,321 Incumb: 96.5%
American Assn of Equipment Lessors AAEL Lease-PAC (Formerly American Assoc of Equip Lessors CAP/Invest-Lease PAC) Arlington, VA	Rentals†	$87,900	41 Candidates Repubs: 52.2% Avg House: $1,440 Senate: 44.4% Avg Sen: $3,250 Incumb: 92.6%
American Assn of Nurse Anesthetists American Association of Nurse Anesthetists Separate Segregated Fund (CRNA-PAC) Park Ridge, IL	Health Unions	$33,650	58 Candidates Dems: 55.4% Avg House: $484 House: 56.2% Avg Sen: $883 Incumb: 97.0%
American Bakers Assn American Bakers Association (Bread PAC) Washington, DC	Food Processing	$65,849	61 Candidates Repubs: 86.0% Avg House: $500 Senate: 69.6% Avg Sen: $2,183 Incumb: 54.8%
American Bankers Assn American Bankers Association (BankPAC) Washington, DC	American Bankers Assn Commercial Banks	$1,151,050	412 Candidates Dems: 56.2% Avg House: $2,289 House: 71.8% Avg Sen: $6,360 Incumb: 88.9%

Sponsor or Related Group/PAC Name	Affiliate	1987-88 Total	Where the money went...			
American Bus Assn BusPAC-PAC of the American Bus Association Washington, DC	 Bus Services	$46,650	49 Candidates Avg House: $906 Avg Sen: $1,090	Dems: 72.8% House: 70.0% Incumb: 88.6%
American Chiropractic Assn American Chiropractic Association PAC Arlington, VA	 American Chiropractic Assn Chiropractors	$137,615	192 Candidates Avg House: $574 Avg Sen: $1,366	Dems: 74.9% House: 65.5% Incumb: 68.0%
American Citizens for Political Action American Citizens for Political Action Washington, DC	 Repub/Conservative	$67,400	64 Candidates Avg House: $1,182 Avg Sen: $822	Repubs: 100.0% House: 54.4% Incumb: 46.0%
American Collectors Assn American Collectors Association Inc (ACPAC) Minneapolis, MN	 Consumer Credit	$47,600	116 Candidates Avg House: $376 Avg Sen: $625	Repubs: 78.3% House: 79.0% Incumb: 87.3%
American College of Emergency Physicians National Emergency Medicine PAC of the American College of Emergency Physicians Irving, TX	 Doctors	$105,825	109 Candidates Avg House: $895 Avg Sen: $1,248	Dems: 61.4% House: 70.3% Incumb: 91.0%
American Commercial Barge Line Company American Commercial Barge Line Co/Jeffboat Inc - PAC (ACBL/JFFBT) Jeffersonville, IN	 CSX Corp Sea Transport	$39,075	62 Candidates Avg House: $613 Avg Sen: $875	Repubs: 57.1% House: 91.0% Incumb: 99.4%
American Consulting Engineers Council American Consulting Engineers PAC (ACE/PAC) Washington, DC	 Engineers†	$88,275	119 Candidates Avg House: $559 Avg Sen: $1,281	Repubs: 65.7% House: 56.4% Incumb: 79.6%
American Cotton Shippers Assn Cmte Organized for the Trading of Cotton - PAC of the American Cotton Shippers Assn Washington, DC	 Cotton	$43,200	51 Candidates Avg House: $689 Avg Sen: $1,000	Repubs: 60.3% House: 60.6% Incumb: 89.0%
American Council of Life Insurance American Council of Life Insurance, Life Insurance PAC Washington, DC	 Life Insurance	$283,271	273 Candidates Avg House: $797 Avg Sen: $2,109	Dems: 53.9% House: 62.8% Incumb: 90.5%
American Crystal Sugar Corp American Crystal Sugar PAC Moorhead, MN	 Sugar	$334,575	304 Candidates Avg House: $833 Avg Sen: $2,457	Dems: 58.4% House: 63.3% Incumb: 89.8%
American Cyanimid American Cyanamid Employee PAC Washington, DC	 American Cyanimid Pharmaceuticals†	$23,750	50 Candidates Avg House: $448 Avg Sen: $666	Repubs: 64.0% House: 83.2% Incumb: 95.8%
American Cyanimid American Cyanamid Company Good Government Fund Washington, DC	 American Cyanimid Pharmaceuticals†	$30,320	36 Candidates Avg House: $511 Avg Sen: $2,000	Dems: 67.2% Senate: 52.8% Incumb: 94.2%
American Dental Assn American Dental PAC Washington, DC	 American Dental Assn Dentists	$886,500	383 Candidates Avg House: $1,965 Avg Sen: $4,641	Repubs: 50.1% House: 73.4% Incumb: 84.0%
American Dietetic Assn American Dietetic Association PAC, The Washington, DC	 Health Practitioners	$28,000	40 Candidates Avg House: $438 Avg Sen: $1,019	Dems: 69.5% Senate: 65.5% Incumb: 87.1%
American Electric Power American Electric Power Committee for Responsible Government; The Columbus, OH	 American Electric Power Electric Utility†	$73,000	128 Candidates Avg House: $466 Avg Sen: $959	Dems: 58.6% House: 63.8% Incumb: 92.4%
American Electronics Assn American Electronics Association (ELECTRO PAC) Santa Clara, CA	 Electronics	$22,050	54 Candidates Avg House: $318 Avg Sen: $759	Repubs: 51.4% House: 62.1% Incumb: 89.3%
American Express American Express Company Committee for Responsible Governmennt Washington, DC	 American Express Consumer Credit†	$95,250	98 Candidates Avg House: $728 Avg Sen: $1,551	Dems: 65.7% House: 52.8% Incumb: 89.8%
American Family Corp American Family PAC (AF-PAC) Washington, DC	 Health Insurance	$334,900	145 Candidates Avg House: $1,443 Avg Sen: $3,833	Dems: 58.1% Senate: 54.9% Incumb: 75.9%
American Federation of Government Employees American Federation of Government Employees' PAC Washington, DC	 Federal Workers	$211,515	194 Candidates Avg House: $795 Avg Sen: $2,345	Dems: 92.5% House: 59.0% Incumb: 77.3%

† PAC Sponsor has other major interests in addition to this primary category

1105

Sponsor / Committee / City	Affiliate	1987-88 Total	Candidates / Avg House / Avg Sen	Party/Chamber/Incumb
American Federation of Musicians American Federation of Musicians - TEMPO Political Contributions Committee New York, NY	Entertainment Union	$43,255	87 Candidates Avg House: $308 Avg Sen: $1,087	Dems: 94.3% Senate: 50.2% Incumb: 91.2%
American Federation of Teachers American Federation of Teachers Committee on Political Education Washington, DC American Fedn of Teachers	Teachers Union	$865,063	247 Candidates Avg House: $3,026 Avg Sen: $6,290	Dems: 97.6% House: 72.8% Incumb: 56.8%
American Fedn of State/County/Munic Employees American Federation of State County & Municipal Employees - PEOPLE, Qualified Washington, DC	Local Govt Union	$1,658,386	365 Candidates Avg House: $4,287 Avg Sen: $6,650	Dems: 96.3% House: 82.0% Incumb: 57.2%
American Feed Industry Assn Feed Industry PAC (FIPAC/AFIA) Arlington, VA	Animal Health	$30,400	55 Candidates Avg House: $468 Avg Sen: $776	Repubs: 70.8% House: 61.7% Incumb: 81.7%
American Financial Services Assn American Financial Services Assn PAC (Formerly Nat'l Consumer Finance Assn PAC) Washington, DC	Consumer Credit	$82,321	86 Candidates Avg House: $800 Avg Sen: $1,595	Dems: 59.9% House: 67.1% Incumb: 100.0%
American Furniture Manufacturers Assn American Furniture Manufacturers Association PAC High Point, NC	Furniture Mfrs	$78,783	77 Candidates Avg House: $796 Avg Sen: $1,715	Repubs: 62.7% House: 58.6% Incumb: 81.8%
American Gas Assn Gas Employees PAC Arlington, VA	Natural Gas	$64,375	122 Candidates Avg House: $346 Avg Sen: $1,015	Dems: 60.0% Senate: 52.0% Incumb: 87.7%
American General Insurance Company American General PAC Houston, TX American General	Insurance†	$68,176	62 Candidates Avg House: $719 Avg Sen: $1,616	Dems: 52.5% Senate: 64.0% Incumb: 73.2%
American Health Care Assn American Health Care Association PAC (AHCA-PAC) Washington, DC	Nursing Homes	$253,528	175 Candidates Avg House: $1,014 Avg Sen: $3,214	Dems: 61.4% House: 54.8% Incumb: 91.3%
American Home Products Corp American Home Products Corporation-AHP Good Government Fund New York, NY	Pharmaceuticals†	$41,050	54 Candidates Avg House: $526 Avg Sen: $1,269	Repubs: 60.7% House: 50.1% Incumb: 92.7%
American Horse Council American Horse Council, Inc Committee on Legislation and Taxation (COLT) Washington, DC	Livestock†	$49,200	55 Candidates Avg House: $576 Avg Sen: $1,983	Dems: 53.2% House: 51.5% Incumb: 91.5%
American Hospital Assn PAC of the American Hospital Association Chicago, IL American Hospital Assn	Hospitals	$409,127	316 Candidates Avg House: $907 Avg Sen: $3,113	Dems: 67.9% House: 57.9% Incumb: 82.0%
American Hotel & Motel Assn American Hotel Motel PAC Washington, DC	Hotel/Motel	$120,400	192 Candidates Avg House: $502 Avg Sen: $1,274	Repubs: 52.1% House: 67.2% Incumb: 89.0%
American Institute of CPA's American Institute of Certified Public Accountants Effective Legis Cmte (AICPA) New York, NY	Accountants	$907,159	185 Candidates Avg House: $4,565 Avg Sen: $5,824	Dems: 56.8% House: 70.6% Incumb: 94.4%
American Insurance Assn American Insurance Association PAC Washington, DC	Insurance	$71,454	98 Candidates Avg House: $486 Avg Sen: $1,365	Repubs: 50.0% Senate: 50.7% Incumb: 77.0%
American International Group Inc American International Group Employee PAC New York, NY	Insurance	$113,400	69 Candidates Avg House: $930 Avg Sen: $2,244	Repubs: 51.3% Senate: 49.5% Incumb: 81.4%
American Land Title Assn Title Industry PAC Washington, DC	Title Insurance	$54,650	96 Candidates Avg House: $416 Avg Sen: $980	Dems: 56.2% House: 53.3% Incumb: 84.0%
American Meat Institute American Meat Institute PAC Arlington, VA	Meat Processing†	$140,650	129 Candidates Avg House: $820 Avg Sen: $1,780	Repubs: 54.3% House: 54.3% Incumb: 80.4%
American Medical Assn American Medical Association PAC Washington, DC American Medical Assn	Doctors	$2,315,646	479 Candidates Avg House: $4,823 Avg Sen: $4,923	Repubs: 52.7% House: 88.9% Incumb: 82.8%

Sponsor or Related Group/PAC Name	Affiliate	1987-88 Total	Where the money went...		
American National Can Company American National Can Company Employees' Good Government Committee Chicago, IL	Cans/Containers	$31,550	33 Candidates Avg House: $643 Avg Sen: $1,093	Repubs: 73.8% House: 46.9% Incumb: 90.5%	
American Nurses Assn American Nurses' Association PAC (ANA-PAC) (Formerly N-CAP) Washington, DC	Health Unions	$272,758	177 Candidates Avg House: $1,312 Avg Sen: $2,757	Dems: 89.5% House: 71.7% Incumb: 50.7%	
American Occupational Therapy Assn American Occupational Therapy PAC Rockville, MD	Health Practitioners†	$69,811	72 Candidates Avg House: $604 Avg Sen: $1,483	Dems: 85.7% Senate: 63.7% Incumb: 78.2%	
American Optometric Assn American Optometric Association PAC Alexandria, VA	American Optometric Assn Eye Doctors†	$335,186	240 Candidates Avg House: $1,125 Avg Sen: $2,751	Dems: 60.6% House: 67.2% Incumb: 79.3%	
American Orthotic/Prosthetic Assn American Orthotic & Prosthetic Association PAC (AOPAPAC) Alexandria, VA	Medical Supply	$21,225	12 Candidates Avg House: $1,580 Avg Sen: $2,333	Dems: 95.3% House: 67.0% Incumb: 76.4%	
American Petrofina American Petrofina PAC Dallas, TX	Oil & Gas Prod†	$20,700	33 Candidates Avg House: $480 Avg Sen: $872	Repubs: 68.1% Pres: 7.2% Incumb: 81.4%	
American Pharmaceutical Assn American Pharmaceutical Association PAC Washington, DC	Pharmacists	$41,050	58 Candidates Avg House: $534 Avg Sen: $1,253	Dems: 65.2% House: 57.2% Incumb: 96.3%	
American Physical Therapy Assn American Physical Therapy Congressional Action Committee Alexandria, VA	Health Practitioners	$102,258	98 Candidates Avg House: $794 Avg Sen: $1,733	Dems: 61.6% House: 55.9% Incumb: 85.5%	
American Pilots Assn American Pilots' Association PAC Washington, DC	Sea Transport	$69,550	48 Candidates Avg House: $1,434 Avg Sen: $1,666	Dems: 57.7% House: 92.8% Incumb: 100.0%	
American Podiatry Assn Podiatry PAC Bethesda, MD	MD Specialists	$249,800	144 Candidates Avg House: $1,243 Avg Sen: $3,323	Dems: 64.1% House: 54.8% Incumb: 93.2%	
American Postal Workers Union Political Fund Committee of the American Postal Workers Union, AFL-CIO Washington, DC	American Postal Workers Union Postal Workers	$898,075	364 Candidates Avg House: $2,129 Avg Sen: $4,479	Dems: 93.0% House: 74.2% Incumb: 68.8%	
American President Lines American President Lines Ltd PAC (APT/PAC) Oakland, CA	Sea Transport	$77,950	92 Candidates Avg House: $737 Avg Sen: $1,269	Dems: 61.5% House: 69.1% Incumb: 92.7%	
American Public Power Assn Public Ownership of Electric Resources PAC (POWERPAC) Washington, DC	Electric Utility	$32,583	72 Candidates Avg House: $410 Avg Sen: $611	Dems: 74.8% House: 71.8% Incumb: 97.9%	
American Rental Assn American Rental Association PAC (ARAPAC) Moline, IL	Rentals	$30,102	51 Candidates Avg House: $473 Avg Sen: $871	Repubs: 96.6% House: 56.6% Incumb: 63.4%	
American Resort & Residential Development Assn American Resort & Residential Development Ass'n PAC Washington, DC	Real Estate Devel†	$65,075	53 Candidates Avg House: $1,070 Avg Sen: $1,656	Dems: 59.7% House: 59.2% Incumb: 66.8%	
American Road & Transportation Bldrs Assn American Road & Transportation Builders Association (ARTBA) - 525 PAC Washington, DC	Heavy Construction	$47,450	59 Candidates Avg House: $632 Avg Sen: $1,357	Dems: 63.5% House: 60.0% Incumb: 96.3%	
American Security Council American Security Council PAC (Formerly National Security PAC) Washington, DC	Pro-Military	$65,446	105 Candidates Avg House: $547 Avg Sen: $1,218	Repubs: 72.7% House: 83.6% Incumb: 96.0%	
American Society of Assn Executives American Society of Association Executives A-PAC Washington, DC	Other	$25,350	36 Candidates Avg House: $547 Avg Sen: $981	Dems: 51.7% House: 47.5% Incumb: 93.7%	
American Society of Cataract/Refractive Surgery American Society of Cataract & Refractive Surgery PAC (EYEPAC) Fairfax, VA	Eye Doctors	$65,100	35 Candidates Avg House: $900 Avg Sen: $2,866	Dems: 83.7% Senate: 66.0% Incumb: 86.9%	

† PAC Sponsor has other major interests in addition to this primary category

Sponsor / PAC	Affiliate	Total	Candidates & Averages	Party / Chamber / Incumbency
American Society of Travel Agents American Society of Travel Agents PAC Alexandria, VA	Travel Agents	$72,450	134 Candidates Avg House: $457 Avg Sen: $943	Dems: 51.8% House: 70.0% Incumb: 96.4%
American Soybean Assn American Soybean Association PAC (SOYPAC) Washington, DC	Grain/Soybeans	$42,508	89 Candidates Avg House: $420 Avg Sen: $596	Dems: 52.1% House: 59.3% Incumb: 89.8%
American Space Frontier Cmte American Space Frontier Committee Arlington, VA — Rep Bob Dornan (R-Calif)	Repub Leaders	$20,100	16 Candidates Avg House: $450 Avg Sen: $2,214	Repubs: 100.0% Senate: 77.1% Incumb: 39.1%
American Speech-Language-Hearing Assn American Speech-Language-Hearing Association PAC Rockville, MD	Health Practitioners	$24,119	33 Candidates Avg House: $376 Avg Sen: $1,839	Dems: 67.9% Senate: 61.0% Incumb: 100.0%
American Subcontractors Assn American Subcontractors Association Inc PAC(ASA-PAC) Alexandria, VA	Subcontractors	$61,500	80 Candidates Avg House: $566 Avg Sen: $1,578	Repubs: 65.6% House: 58.9% Incumb: 78.5%
American Sugar Cane League American Sugar Cane League PAC Thibodaux, LA	Sugar	$148,500	249 Candidates Avg House: $456 Avg Sen: $1,325	Dems: 65.4% House: 64.3% Incumb: 88.2%
American Sugarbeet Growers Assn American Sugarbeet Growers Association PAC Washington, DC	Sugar	$220,700	250 Candidates Avg House: $760 Avg Sen: $1,524	Dems: 61.1% House: 72.4% Incumb: 89.2%
American Supply Assn American Supply Association PAC Chicago, IL	Pipe Products†	$77,808	88 Candidates Avg House: $625 Avg Sen: $1,574	Repubs: 79.7% House: 51.4% Incumb: 67.1%
American Systems Corp American Systems Corporation PAC (ASC-PAC) Chantilly, VA	Defense Electronics†	$36,610	59 Candidates Avg House: $500 Avg Sen: $918	Repubs: 50.4% House: 57.4% Incumb: 96.2%
American Textile Manufacturers Institute American Textile Manufacturers Institute, Inc Committee for Good Government Washington, DC	Textiles	$128,300	153 Candidates Avg House: $693 Avg Sen: $1,520	Dems: 57.1% House: 69.2% Incumb: 95.5%
American Trucking Assns Trucking PAC of the American Trucking Associations Inc Washington, DC — American Trucking Assns	Trucking	$279,872	291 Candidates Avg House: $702 Avg Sen: $2,415	Dems: 70.2% House: 62.0% Incumb: 90.8%
American Veterinary Medical Assn American Veterinary Medical Association PAC (AVMAPAC) Washington, DC	Veterinarians	$188,500	184 Candidates Avg House: $766 Avg Sen: $2,350	Dems: 52.8% House: 62.6% Incumb: 87.5%
American Waterways Operators American Waterways Operators-PAC Arlington, VA	Sea Transport	$57,102	99 Candidates Avg House: $485 Avg Sen: $1,090	Dems: 59.3% House: 71.4% Incumb: 95.4%
American Yarn Spinners Assn American Yarn Spinners Association PAC Gastonia, NC	Textiles	$21,500	40 Candidates Avg House: $409 Avg Sen: $1,100	Dems: 64.0% House: 62.8% Incumb: 97.7%
Americans for Democratic Action Americans for Democratic Action Inc PAC Washington, DC	Dem/Liberal	$42,000	49 Candidates Avg House: $817 Avg Sen: $1,062	Dems: 97.6% House: 79.8% Incumb: 26.2%
Americans for Good Government Inc Americans for Good Government Inc Jasper, AL	Pro-Israel	$79,200	54 Candidates Avg House: $971 Avg Sen: $2,000	Dems: 55.8% Senate: 65.6% Incumb: 61.5%
AmeriFirst Bank Amerifirst PAC of Amerifirst Bank, A Federal Savings Bank Miami, FL	Savings Banks	$23,600	21 Candidates Avg House: $550 Avg Sen: $1,500	Repubs: 72.4% Senate: 50.8% Incumb: 80.9%
Ameritech Corp American Information Technologies Corporation PAC (Ameritech PAC) Chicago, IL — Ameritech	Phone Utilities	$68,997	58 Candidates Avg House: $953 Avg Sen: $1,177	Repubs: 61.4% House: 42.8% Incumb: 87.5%
Ameritrust Company Ameritrust PAC (AMERIPAC) Cleveland, OH	Commercial Banks	$23,550	27 Candidates Avg House: $742 Avg Sen: $1,242	Dems: 58.6% House: 63.1% Incumb: 71.1%

Sponsor or Related Group/PAC Name	Affiliate	1987-88 Total	Where the money went...		
Amoco Corp Amoco PAC Chicago, IL	Oil & Gas Prod†	$318,764	247 Candidates Avg House: $786 Avg Sen: $4,562	Repubs: 77.3% House: 52.8% Incumb: 70.7%	
Amsouth Bancorp Amsouth PAC Birmingham, AL	Commercial Banks	$26,850	11 Candidates Avg House: $2,316 Avg Sen: $3,000	Dems: 77.7% House: 77.7% Incumb: 92.6%	
Andrews, Kurth, Campbell & Jones Andrews Kurth Lawyers for American Committee Houston, TX	Lawyers	$26,800	10 Candidates Avg House: $2,700 Avg Sen: $2,200	Dems: 64.6% Senate: 41.0% Incumb: 94.4%	
Anesthesia Service Medical Group Anesthesia Service Medical Group Inc Good Government Fund San Diego, CA	MD Specialists	$30,850	10 Candidates Avg House: $2,307 Avg Sen: $4,900	Repubs: 72.4% House: 52.4% Incumb: 83.8%	
Anheuser-Busch Anheuser-Busch Companies Inc PAC (AB-PAC) St. Louis, MO	Beer†	$58,200	70 Candidates Avg House: $639 Avg Sen: $1,250	Dems: 71.9% House: 52.7% Incumb: 91.8%	
Archer-Daniels-Midland Corp Archer Daniels Midland Company-ADM PAC Decatur, IL	Grain Traders†	$160,550	79 Candidates Avg House: $1,501 Avg Sen: $2,416	Dems: 56.6% Senate: 54.1% Incumb: 92.1%	
Arizona Politically Interested Citizens Arizona Politically Interested Citizens Phoenix, AZ	Pro-Israel	$46,750	24 Candidates Avg House: $656 Avg Sen: $2,593	Dems: 66.3% Senate: 88.7% Incumb: 88.2%	
Arkansas Best Corp Arkansas Best Corporation PAC Fort Smith, AR	Trucking†	$20,250	19 Candidates Avg House: $975 Avg Sen: $1,125	Dems: 79.0% House: 48.1% Incumb: 95.1%	
Arkla Inc Arkla, Inc PAC or ArklaPAC Shreveport, LA	Arkla Inc / Natural Gas	$29,070	33 Candidates Avg House: $582 Avg Sen: $1,120	Dems: 76.2% Senate: 61.6% Incumb: 85.2%	
Arkla Inc/Entex Entex (Arkla, Inc) Better Government Committee Houston, TX	Arkla Inc / Natural Gas	$22,300	22 Candidates Avg House: $941 Avg Sen: $1,142	Dems: 77.6% House: 50.7% Incumb: 87.7%	
Armco Inc Armco Employees' PAC (APAC) Washington, DC	Steel Mfrs	$30,050	34 Candidates Avg House: $580 Avg Sen: $1,317	Repubs: 59.4% Senate: 61.4% Incumb: 82.7%	
Armenian Assembly of America Armenian Assembly of America PAC Washington, DC	Ethnic/Minority	$22,100	35 Candidates Avg House: $496 Avg Sen: $1,022	Dems: 64.9% House: 58.4% Incumb: 79.6%	
Armenian-American PAC Armenian-American PAC New York, NY	Ethnic/Minority	$20,000	15 Candidates Avg House: $1,416 Avg Sen: $1,000	Dems: 70.0% House: 85.0% Incumb: 85.0%	
Arnold & Porter Arnold & Porter Partners PAC Washington, DC	Arnold & Porter / Lawyers†	$57,575	86 Candidates Avg House: $556 Avg Sen: $868	Dems: 73.1% House: 57.1% Incumb: 89.0%	
Arthur Andersen & Company Arthur Andersen & Company PAC Washington, DC	Accountants	$64,750	88 Candidates Avg House: $705 Avg Sen: $847	Repubs: 50.7% House: 75.1% Incumb: 96.9%	
Arthur Young & Company Federal Arthur Young & Company PAC New York, NY	Arthur Young / Accountants	$69,915	76 Candidates Avg House: $714 Avg Sen: $1,068	Repubs: 57.0% House: 50.1% Incumb: 89.4%	
ASCAP ASCAP Legislative Fund for the Arts New York, NY	Live Music Prod	$43,350	56 Candidates Avg House: $746 Avg Sen: $900	Dems: 82.1% House: 79.2% Incumb: 96.5%	
Ashland Oil Ashland Oil PAC for Employees (PACE) Russell, KY	Ashland Oil / Oil Refining/Marketing†	$134,525	145 Candidates Avg House: $655 Avg Sen: $2,184	Repubs: 50.6% House: 58.9% Incumb: 88.3%	
Assembly of Turkish-American Assns PAC-Assembly of Turkish American Associations Bethesda, MD	Ethnic/Minority	$20,200	36 Candidates Avg House: $405 Avg Sen: $906	Dems: 59.2% House: 54.2% Incumb: 93.1%	

† PAC Sponsor has other major interests in addition to this primary category

Sponsor or Related Group/PAC Name	Affiliate	1987-88 Total	Where the money went...
Assn for Advancement of Psychology Psychologists for Legislative Action Now (PLAN) Washington, DC	Psychol	$99,830	62 Candidates — Dems: 92.2% Avg House: $1,232 — House: 59.3% Avg Sen: $3,056 — Incumb: 92.0%
Assn of American Publishers Association of American Publishers PAC Washington, DC	Publishing	$23,500	40 Candidates — Dems: 57.9% Avg House: $392 — Senate: 64.8% Avg Sen: $802 — Incumb: 96.8%
Assn of Bank Holding Companies Association of Bank Holding Companies PAC (ABHC PAC) Washington, DC	Commercial Banks	$84,558	76 Candidates — Dems: 55.4% Avg House: $917 — House: 71.6% Avg Sen: $2,400 — Incumb: 98.5%
Assn of Flight Attendants Association of Flight Attendants PAC ("Flight PAC") Washington, DC	Air Transport Union	$67,527	81 Candidates — Dems: 94.7% Avg House: $578 — House: 54.8% Avg Sen: $1,794 — Incumb: 79.3%
Assn of Independent Colleges/Schools Association of Independent Colleges and Schools PAC Washington, DC	Education	$37,820	23 Candidates — Repubs: 55.2% Avg House: $1,256 — House: 59.8% Avg Sen: $3,040 — Incumb: 81.5%
Assn of Independent TV Stations Association of Independent Television Stations PAC (INTV PAC) Washington, DC	TV/Radio	$70,783	56 Candidates — Dems: 54.4% Avg House: $835 — House: 52.0% Avg Sen: $3,175 — Incumb: 85.2%
Assn of Private Pension Plans Association of Private Pension & Welfare Plans Washington, DC	Securities Investment	$26,683	36 Candidates — Dems: 60.3% Avg House: $513 — Senate: 51.9% Avg Sen: $1,259 — Incumb: 92.3%
Assn of Trial Lawyers of America Association of Trial Lawyers of America PAC Washington, DC — Assn of Trial Lawyers	Lawyers	$1,919,558	407 Candidates — Dems: 85.9% Avg House: $4,528 — House: 84.7% Avg Sen: $6,125 — Incumb: 70.2%
Associated Builders & Contractors Associated Builders and Contractors PAC (ABC/PAC) Washington, DC	Builders†	$180,876	181 Candidates — Repubs: 90.5% Avg House: $660 — House: 57.4% Avg Sen: $3,213 — Incumb: 66.3%
Associated Credit Bureaus Associated Credit Bureaus PAC Houston, TX	Consumer Credit	$29,425	60 Candidates — Dems: 56.9% Avg House: $432 — House: 74.9% Avg Sen: $819 — Incumb: 98.3%
Associated General Contractors Associated General Contractors PAC Washington, DC	Heavy Construction	$740,225	336 Candidates — Repubs: 72.2% Avg House: $1,621 — House: 65.7% Avg Sen: $7,051 — Incumb: 74.6%
Associated Milk Producers Cmte for Thorough Agricultural Political Education of Associated Milk Producers San Antonio, TX	Dairy	$836,350	322 Candidates — Dems: 68.1% Avg House: $2,457 — House: 84.3% Avg Sen: $3,648 — Incumb: 87.7%
AT&T American Telephone & Telegraph Company Inc PAC (AT&T PAC) Morristown, NJ	Long Distance†	$1,305,112	555 Candidates — Dems: 55.0% Avg House: $2,115 — House: 74.4% Avg Sen: $3,518 — Incumb: 88.6%
Atlantic Richfield Arco PAC, Atlantic Richfield Company Los Angeles, CA	Oil & Gas Prod†	$296,748	195 Candidates — Repubs: 56.9% Avg House: $1,121 — House: 61.2% Avg Sen: $3,837 — Incumb: 87.5%
Auto Dealers & Drivers for Free Trade Auto Dealers and Drivers for Free Trade PAC Jamaica, NY	Japanese Auto Dealers	$1,158,700	344 Candidates — Repubs: 73.8% Avg House: $3,318 — House: 78.8% Avg Sen: $3,544 — Incumb: 74.0%
Avon Products Avon Products, Inc. Fund for Responsible Government New York, NY — Avon Products	Cosmetics†	$56,636	64 Candidates — Dems: 57.2% Avg House: $583 — House: 47.4% Avg Sen: $1,517 — Incumb: 92.5%
Babcock & Wilcox Babcock & Wilcox Company Good Government Fund; The New Orleans, LA — McDermott Inc	Power Plant Equip†	$35,850	39 Candidates — Dems: 50.2% Avg House: $763 — House: 55.4% Avg Sen: $1,230 — Incumb: 70.7%
Baker & Botts Bluebonnet Fund (Baker & Botts), The Houston, TX	Lawyers	$49,591	32 Candidates — Dems: 59.4% Avg House: $1,199 — Senate: 35.9% Avg Sen: $1,369 — Incumb: 95.0%
Baker & Hostetler Baker & Hostetler PAC Cleveland, OH	Lawyers	$55,450	54 Candidates — Dems: 53.8% Avg House: $959 — House: 65.7% Avg Sen: $1,200 — Incumb: 91.0%

Sponsor or Related Group/PAC Name	Affiliate	1987-88 Total	Where the money went...		
Bakery, Confectionery & Tobacco Workers		$140,725	80 Candidates	Dems:	100.0%
Bakery, Confectionery and Tobacco Workers International Union PAC			Avg House: $1,639	House:	68.7%
Kensington, MD		Food Svc Unions	Avg Sen: $2,095	Incumb:	42.8%
Ball Corp		$29,225	41 Candidates	Repubs:	87.6%
Ball Corporation PAC (BAC PAC)			Avg House: $402	Senate:	63.8%
Muncie, IN		Packaging†	Avg Sen: $1,332	Incumb:	51.9%
Baltimore Gas & Electric		$54,650	67 Candidates	Repubs:	73.5%
Baltimore Gas and Electric Company PAC (BG&E PAC)			Avg House: $811	House:	81.7%
Baltimore, MD		Gas/Electric†	Avg Sen: $833	Incumb:	84.4%
Banc One Corp		$58,050	54 Candidates	Repubs:	55.7%
Banc One PAC			Avg House: $913	House:	64.5%
Columbus, OH	Banc One Corp	Commercial Banks	Avg Sen: $1,600	Incumb:	85.2%
Bancorp Hawaii		$23,650	7 Candidates	Dems:	61.5%
Bancorp Hawaii Special Political Education Committee			Avg House: $3,691	House:	93.7%
Honolulu, HI		Commercial Banks	Avg Sen: $1,500	Incumb:	53.3%
Bank of Boston		$25,500	43 Candidates	Dems:	64.9%
Bank of Boston Federal PAC			Avg House: $550	House:	69.0%
Boston, MA	Bank of Boston	Commercial Banks	Avg Sen: $718	Incumb:	93.1%
Bank of New York		$25,550	26 Candidates	Dems:	69.1%
Bank of New York Company PAC-BNY PAC			Avg House: $561	Senate:	62.6%
New York, NY		Commercial Banks	Avg Sen: $1,777	Incumb:	100.0%
BankAmerica		$96,748	108 Candidates	Repubs:	55.9%
BankAmerica Federal Election Fund			Avg House: $731	House:	61.2%
San Francisco, CA	BankAmerica	Commercial Banks	Avg Sen: $1,388	Incumb:	84.0%
Bankers Trust		$170,450	83 Candidates	Dems:	60.1%
Bankers Trust PAC			Avg House: $1,700	House:	61.9%
New York, NY		Commercial Banks	Avg Sen: $3,095	Incumb:	95.3%
Barnett Banks of Florida		$375,700	200 Candidates	Dems:	51.0%
Barnett People for Better Government Inc - Fed, a PAC of Barnett Banks of Florida			Avg House: $1,573	House:	66.6%
Tallahassee, FL		Commercial Banks	Avg Sen: $3,060	Incumb:	78.0%
Bath Iron Works		$69,850	66 Candidates	Dems:	62.8%
Bath Iron Works Corp Political Action Cmte (Formerly Congoleum Corp PAC)			Avg House: $1,029	House:	79.6%
Arlington, VA		Shipbuilding†	Avg Sen: $1,022	Incumb:	100.0%
Baxter Healthcare Corp		$62,600	68 Candidates	Repubs:	60.7%
Baxter Healthcare Corporation PAC			Avg House: $558	Senate:	46.6%
Deerfield, IL		Medical Supply	Avg Sen: $1,214	Incumb:	93.8%
BDM International		$137,100	97 Candidates	Repubs:	54.3%
BDM International, Inc. PAC (BDM-PAC)			Avg House: $1,159	Senate:	51.0%
McLean, VA	Ford Motor Co	Defense R&D	Avg Sen: $1,791	Incumb:	71.7%
Bear, Stearns & Company		$74,150	50 Candidates	Dems:	81.7%
Bear, Stearns and Company Political Campaign Committee			Avg House: $1,073	House:	40.5%
New York, NY		Investment Banking†	Avg Sen: $1,602	Incumb:	93.3%
Bechtel Corp		$90,650	115 Candidates	Repubs:	61.3%
Bechtel Group, Inc PAC			Avg House: $522	Senate:	54.4%
San Francisco, CA		Heavy Construction†	Avg Sen: $1,853	Incumb:	78.5%
Beech Aircraft		$44,290	54 Candidates	Dems:	65.0%
Beech Aircraft PAC (BEECHPAC)			Avg House: $643	House:	61.1%
Wichita, KS	Raytheon	Aircraft Mfrs†	Avg Sen: $1,175	Incumb:	94.9%
Bell Atlantic		$160,007	134 Candidates	Repubs:	51.0%
Bell Atlantic Corporation PAC			Avg House: $832	House:	49.4%
Philadelphia, PA	Bell Atlantic	Phone Utilities	Avg Sen: $1,887	Incumb:	80.1%
Bell Telephone of Pennsylvania		$31,523	25 Candidates	Repubs:	62.4%
Bell Telephone Company of Pennsylvania PAC (Pa Bell PAC)			Avg House: $1,114	House:	77.8%
Philadelphia, PA	Bell Atlantic	Phone Utilities	Avg Sen: $2,499	Incumb:	100.0%
BellSouth Corp		$92,540	100 Candidates	Repubs:	50.6%
BellSouth Federal PAC (BellSouth Fed PAC)			Avg House: $736	House:	55.7%
Atlanta, GA	BellSouth	Phone Utilities	Avg Sen: $1,209	Incumb:	90.5%

† PAC Sponsor has other major interests in addition to this primary category

Sponsor or Related Group/PAC Name	Affiliate	Industry	1987-88 Total	Where the money went...				
BellSouth Services BellSouth Services Federal PAC Birmingham, AL	BellSouth	Phone Utilities	$83,320	98 Candidates Avg House: $681 Avg Sen: $1,298	Repubs: 51.6% House: 55.6% Incumb: 92.8%
Beneficial Management Corp Beneficial Management Corporation and Affiliated Corporations PAC Peapack, NJ		Consumer Credit†	$82,300	68 Candidates Avg House: $883 Avg Sen: $2,271	Dems: 62.8% House: 55.8% Incumb: 91.9%
Bethlehem Steel Bethlehem Steel Good Government Committee Bethlehem, PA		Steel Mfrs	$85,363	85 Candidates Avg House: $733 Avg Sen: $2,100	Repubs: 50.4% House: 57.6% Incumb: 94.4%
Betz Laboratories Betz Laboratories, Inc PAC (Betz PAC) Trevose, PA		Chemicals	$21,000	13 Candidates Avg House: $1,450 Avg Sen: $2,750	Repubs: 83.3% House: 69.0% Incumb: 76.2%
Beverly Enterprises Beverly Health PAC Pasadena, CA		Nursing Homes	$59,370	79 Candidates Avg House: $602 Avg Sen: $1,097	Dems: 66.7% House: 55.8% Incumb: 87.8%
BHP-Utah International BHP-Utah International Inc PAC San Francisco, CA		Metal Mining/Processing	$32,350	58 Candidates Avg House: $344 Avg Sen: $933	Repubs: 80.9% Senate: 60.5% Incumb: 75.9%
Blount Inc Blount Inc Employees' PAC (BLTPAC) Montgomery, AL		Indust Construction	$25,450	22 Candidates Avg House: $527 Avg Sen: $1,592	Repubs: 84.2% Senate: 81.3% Incumb: 62.7%
Blue Cross & Blue Shield Assn CAREPAC, The Blue Cross and Blue Shield Association PAC Washington, DC	Blue Cross	Health Insurance	$132,667	151 Candidates Avg House: $618 Avg Sen: $1,709	Dems: 71.9% House: 53.6% Incumb: 90.5%
Blue Cross/Shield of Florida Florida Health PAC Jacksonville, FL	Blue Cross	Health Insurance	$21,850	18 Candidates Avg House: $737 Avg Sen: $2,400	Dems: 70.3% Senate: 54.9% Incumb: 25.6%
Boat Owners Assn of the US Boat Owners Association of the United States (BOAT/US) PAC Alexandria, VA		Pleasure Boats†	$32,400	42 Candidates Avg House: $678 Avg Sen: $1,111	Dems: 62.7% House: 69.1% Incumb: 94.4%
Boating PAC Boating PAC Washington, DC		Pleasure Boats†	$28,950	40 Candidates Avg House: $623 Avg Sen: $1,125	Dems: 50.9% House: 68.9% Incumb: 81.7%
Boatmens Bankshares BOBANCPAC, a PAC of Boatmen's Bancshares, Inc St Louis, MO		Commercial Banks	$27,800	20 Candidates Avg House: $1,020 Avg Sen: $1,933	Repubs: 69.7% Senate: 41.7% Incumb: 85.6%
Boeing Company Boeing Company PAC (BPAC) Seattle, WA		Aircraft Mfrs†	$325,485	175 Candidates Avg House: $1,669 Avg Sen: $2,860	Dems: 57.0% House: 75.4% Incumb: 93.4%
Boilermakers Local #169 Int'l B'hood of Boilermakers Blacksmiths Forgers & Helpers of America Local 169 Dearborn, MI	Boilermakers Union	Constr Unions	$26,935	12 Candidates Avg House: $2,283 Avg Sen: $2,100	Dems: 100.0% House: 84.8% Incumb: 66.4%
Boilermakers Union International Brotherhood of Boilermakers, in Sp Bldrs, Bkmths, Frgrs & Hlprs-Leg Ed Fund Kansas City, KS	Boilermakers Union	Manuf Unions†	$213,225	181 Candidates Avg House: $820 Avg Sen: $2,769	Dems: 92.8% House: 56.2% Incumb: 67.3%
Boise Cascade Boise Cascade Political Fund Boise, ID		Forest Prod†	$83,800	52 Candidates Avg House: $1,272 Avg Sen: $2,375	Repubs: 89.9% House: 54.7% Incumb: 63.0%
Borg-Warner Borg-Warner PAC Chicago, IL	Merrill Lynch	Indust Equip/Materials†	$69,600	58 Candidates Avg House: $645 Avg Sen: $2,517	Repubs: 72.5% Senate: 61.5% Incumb: 56.6%
Bowling Proprietors Assn Bowling Proprietors Assn of America PAC Arlington, TX		Amusement Centers	$52,050	93 Candidates Avg House: $462 Avg Sen: $1,107	Repubs: 85.4% House: 70.2% Incumb: 86.0%
BP America BPA-PAC (The BP American PAC) (Formerly Standard Oil Co PAC) Cleveland, OH		Oil & Gas Prod†	$98,575	94 Candidates Avg House: $693 Avg Sen: $2,781	Repubs: 66.1% House: 54.9% Incumb: 88.6%

Sponsor or Related Group/PAC Name	Affiliate	1987-88 Total	Where the money went...		
Bracewell & Patterson Bracewell & Patterson PAC Washington, DC	Lawyers	$33,550	22 Candidates Avg House: $914 Avg Sen: $4,000	Dems: 72.3% House: 46.3% Incumb: 98.5%	
Bricklayers Union International Union of Bricklayers and Allied Craftsmen PAC Washington, DC	Bricklayers Union Constr Unions	$197,300	105 Candidates Avg House: $1,024 Avg Sen: $3,844	Dems: 96.2% Senate: 56.5% Incumb: 56.1%	
Bristol-Myers Bristol-Myers Company PAC New York, NY	Pharmecuticals	$88,725	177 Candidates Avg House: $325 Avg Sen: $1,571	Repubs: 69.8% House: 55.7% Incumb: 80.9%	
Brotherhood of Locomotive Engineers Brotherhood of Locomotive Engineers Legislative League Cleveland, OH	Railroad Unions	$166,957	242 Candidates Avg House: $590 Avg Sen: $1,471	Dems: 95.4% House: 75.0% Incumb: 77.9%	
Brotherhood of Railway Carmen Railway Carmen Political League Kansas City, MO	Brthrhd of Railway Carmen Railroad Unions	$39,300	89 Candidates Avg House: $388 Avg Sen: $818	Dems: 88.4% House: 77.1% Incumb: 89.8%	
Brotherhood of Railroad Signalmen Brotherhood of Railroad Signalmen PAC Mt. Prospect, IL	Railroad Unions	$77,270	145 Candidates Avg House: $495 Avg Sen: $780	Dems: 91.9% House: 80.8% Incumb: 90.8%	
Brown & Root Brownbuilders PAC of Brown & Root, Inc Employees Houston, TX	Halliburton Heavy Construction†	$74,700	118 Candidates Avg House: $468 Avg Sen: $1,350	Repubs: 59.7% House: 61.4% Incumb: 91.9%	
Brown & Williamson Tobacco Brown & Williamson Tobacco Corporation Employee PAC (EMPAC) Louisville, KY	Batus Inc Tobacco	$103,650	176 Candidates Avg House: $445 Avg Sen: $1,260	Dems: 54.7% House: 63.6% Incumb: 91.0%	
Brown-Forman Distillers Brown-Forman Non-Partisan Committee for Responsible Government Louisville, KY	Wine/Liquor†	$90,333	85 Candidates Avg House: $656 Avg Sen: $1,486	Repubs: 65.0% Senate: 59.2% Incumb: 79.5%	
Browning-Ferris Industries Browning-Ferris Industries PAC (BFI PAC) Houston, TX	Waste Mgmt	$136,277	142 Candidates Avg House: $657 Avg Sen: $2,192	Dems: 63.0% House: 55.0% Incumb: 79.2%	
Brunswick Corp Brunswick Corporation Good Government Fund Skokie, IL	Indust Equip/Materials	$26,800	48 Candidates Avg House: $454 Avg Sen: $909	Repubs: 81.3% House: 62.7% Incumb: 69.8%	
Brush Wellman Brush Wellman Good Government Fund Cleveland, OH	Indust Equip/Materials	$32,000	5 Candidates Avg House: $4,666 Avg Sen: $9,000	Repubs: 100.0% Senate: 56.2% Incumb: 37.5%	
Budd Company Budd Company Citizenship Committee Troy, MI	Auto Parts†	$27,500	31 Candidates Avg House: $761 Avg Sen: $1,055	Repubs: 85.4% House: 58.2% Incumb: 80.0%	
Burlington Industries Burlington Industries Good Government Committee Greensboro, NC	Morgan Stanley Textiles†	$98,950	101 Candidates Avg House: $721 Avg Sen: $1,754	Dems: 60.8% House: 55.4% Incumb: 90.8%	
Burlington Northern Burlington Northern Employees Voluntary Good Government Fund Seattle, WA	Railroads†	$95,600	143 Candidates Avg House: $575 Avg Sen: $1,108	Dems: 58.6% House: 71.0% Incumb: 90.5%	
Burson-Marsteller Burson-Marsteller PAC Washington, DC	Lobbyist/PR	$56,312	77 Candidates Avg House: $520 Avg Sen: $1,060	Dems: 56.6% Senate: 56.5% Incumb: 87.6%	
Business Industry PAC Business Industry PAC Washington, DC	Business Assns	$136,487	89 Candidates Avg House: $1,366 Avg Sen: $2,190	Repubs: 94.2% House: 71.1% Incumb: 44.4%	
Business Mens Assurance Company Business Men's Assurance Company of America PAC-Federal (BMA-PAC Federal) Kansas City, MO	Insurance	$34,000	24 Candidates Avg House: $796 Avg Sen: $2,375	Repubs: 72.7% Senate: 41.9% Incumb: 98.5%	
Calcot Ltd Calcot Ltd Federal PAC Bakersfield, CA	Cotton	$24,820	26 Candidates Avg House: $803 Avg Sen: $1,350	Repubs: 77.3% House: 64.7% Incumb: 98.0%	

† PAC Sponsor has other major interests in addition to this primary category

Sponsor or Related Group / PAC Name / Location	Affiliate	1987-88 Total	Candidates / Avg House / Avg Sen	Party / Chamber / Incumb
California Almond Growers Exchange Blue Diamond Growers PAC (Formerly California Almond Growers Exchange PAC) Sacramento, CA	Fruit/Veg	$69,450	49 Candidates Avg House: $1,442 Avg Sen: $1,500	Repubs: 54.2% House: 91.4% Incumb: 97.1%
California Farm Bureau Federation California Farm Bureau Federation PAC (FARM PAC) Sacramento, CA	Farm Orgs	$22,550	9 Candidates Avg House: $1,821 Avg Sen: $4,900	Repubs: 96.2% House: 56.5% Incumb: 91.1%
California Hotel & Casino PAC California Hotel & Casino PAC (CAL-PAC) Las Vegas, NV	Casinos/Gambling†	$32,000	8 Candidates Avg House: $1,750 Avg Sen: $6,666	Repubs: 54.6% Senate: 62.5% Incumb: 64.1%
California League of Savings Institutions California League of Savings Institutions (FEDPAC) Los Angeles, CA — US League of Savings Assn	Savings Banks	$33,726	26 Candidates Avg House: $1,169 Avg Sen: $2,000	Dems: 50.3% House: 76.3% Incumb: 100.0%
California Pistachio Assn California Pistachio Association Nut PAC Fresno, CA	Fruit/Veg	$22,300	12 Candidates Avg House: $1,257 Avg Sen: $2,700	Repubs: 76.4% Senate: 60.5% Incumb: 100.0%
California Trial Lawyers Assn California Trial Lawyers Federal PAC (CTL FEDPAC) Sacramento, CA — Assn of Trial Lawyers	Lawyers	$42,500	22 Candidates Avg House: $1,547 Avg Sen: $10,000	Dems: 91.8% House: 76.5% Incumb: 60.0%
Camp, Barsh, Bates & Tate CAMPAC Washington, DC	Lawyers†	$70,680	84 Candidates Avg House: $628 Avg Sen: $1,422	Dems: 81.8% House: 58.7% Incumb: 97.8%
Campaign America Campaign America Washington, DC — Sen Bob Dole (R-Kans)	Repub Leaders	$313,861	98 Candidates Avg House: $1,700 Avg Sen: $5,790	Repubs: 100.0% Senate: 66.4% Incumb: 42.3%
Campaign for a New Majority Campaign for a New Majority (Federal) (Formerly Campaign for Prosperity) Falls Church, VA — Jack Kemp	Repub Leaders	$48,100	35 Candidates Avg House: $960 Avg Sen: $3,375	Repubs: 100.0% House: 57.9% Incumb: 40.5%
Campaign for America Campaign for America Morristown, NJ — Sen Frank Lautenberg (D-NJ)	Dem Leaders	$35,000	7 Candidates Avg House: $1,000 Avg Sen: $6,000	Dems: 100.0% Senate: 85.7% Incumb: 68.6%
Capital Holding Corp Capital Holding PAC - CAP-PAC Louisville, KY	Insurance	$39,475	50 Candidates Avg House: $542 Avg Sen: $1,138	Dems: 54.9% Senate: 51.9% Incumb: 96.7%
Capital PAC Capital PAC (CAPPAC) Washington, DC	Pro-Israel	$20,250	37 Candidates Avg House: $467 Avg Sen: $794	Dems: 67.9% House: 64.7% Incumb: 68.4%
Cargill Inc Cargill, Incorporated PAC Minneapolis, MN	Grain Traders†	$90,300	48 Candidates Avg House: $1,155 Avg Sen: $3,642	Repubs: 90.8% Senate: 56.4% Incumb: 62.9%
Carolina Power & Light Employees Federal PAC - Carolina Power & Light Company Raleigh, NC	Electric Utility	$54,100	96 Candidates Avg House: $537 Avg Sen: $657	Dems: 53.6% House: 74.5% Incumb: 88.0%
Carpenters & Joiners Union Carpenters' Legislative Improvement Committee Washington, DC — Carpenters Union	Constr Unions	$1,357,998	395 Candidates Avg House: $3,148 Avg Sen: $5,571	Dems: 94.1% House: 79.8% Incumb: 64.9%
Carter Hawley Hale Stores Carter Hawley Hale Stores Inc PAC Los Angeles, CA	Dept Stores	$46,900	54 Candidates Avg House: $645 Avg Sen: $1,850	Repubs: 60.7% House: 60.6% Incumb: 89.3%
Casualty & Surety Agents Assn National Association of Casualty & Surety Agents PAC (NACSAPAC) Bethesda, MD	Insurance	$235,614	211 Candidates Avg House: $819 Avg Sen: $2,347	Dems: 54.8% House: 59.1% Incumb: 80.8%
Catch the Spirit PAC Catch The Spirit PAC Inc Washington, DC — Sen. Bob Kasten (R-Wis)	Repub Leaders	$162,563	34 Candidates Avg House: $2,593 Avg Sen: $5,454	Repubs: 100.0% Senate: 87.2% Incumb: 41.8%
Caterpillar Tractor Caterpillar Tractor Company Committee for Effective Government Peoria, IL	Bldg Equip†	$59,855	67 Candidates Avg House: $686 Avg Sen: $1,753	Repubs: 87.3% House: 61.9% Incumb: 65.0%

Sponsor or Related Group/PAC Name	Affiliate	1987-88 Total	Where the money went...		
Centel Corp Centel Corporation Good Government Fund Washington, DC	Phone Utilities†	$41,975	78 Candidates Avg House: $426 Avg Sen: $835	Repubs: 51.6% House: 55.9% Incumb: 86.0%	
Central Bancshares of the South Central Bancshares of the South, Inc PAC ("Central BancPAC") Birmingham, AL	Commercial Banks	$28,700	8 Candidates Avg House: $3,990 Avg Sen: $1,875	Dems: 65.2% House: 69.5% Incumb: 100.0%	
Centrust Savings Bank Centrust Savings Bank Federal PAC Miami, FL	Savings Banks	$64,900	18 Candidates Avg House: $1,916 Avg Sen: $4,740	Dems: 95.4% Senate: 73.0% Incumb: 48.5%	
Century 21 Real Estate Century 21 PAC (CEN-PAC) Washington, DC	Metropolitan Life Real Estate	$74,250	47 Candidates Avg House: $1,135 Avg Sen: $2,875	Dems: 55.6% House: 53.5% Incumb: 86.5%	
CF Industries CF Industries Employees' Good Government Fund Long Grove, IL	Ag Chemicals†	$60,585	92 Candidates Avg House: $469 Avg Sen: $1,340	Dems: 66.4% House: 55.8% Incumb: 90.8%	
Ch2M Hill Ch2M Hill PAC Inc Corvallis, OR	Engineers†	$94,648	125 Candidates Avg House: $548 Avg Sen: $1,637	Repubs: 60.2% House: 58.5% Incumb: 91.4%	
Champion International Corp Champion International Corporation PAC Stamford, CT	Paper Prod†	$48,739	48 Candidates Avg House: $521 Avg Sen: $2,102	Dems: 57.9% Senate: 64.7% Incumb: 86.7%	
Chase Manhattan Chase Manhattan Corporation PAC - (ChasePAC) New York, NY	Chase Manhattan Commercial Banks	$127,320	114 Candidates Avg House: $925 Avg Sen: $1,651	Dems: 55.9% House: 61.1% Incumb: 81.2%	
Chemical Bank Chemical Bank Fund for Good Government New York, NY	Chemical Bank Commercial Banks	$148,890	134 Candidates Avg House: $918 Avg Sen: $1,665	Dems: 58.7% House: 55.5% Incumb: 91.5%	
Chesapeake & Potomac Telephone Chesapeake & Potomac Telephone Company Federal PAC, C&P of MD VA WV Washington, DC	Bell Atlantic Phone Utilities	$36,027	31 Candidates Avg House: $1,113 Avg Sen: $1,413	Dems: 63.7% House: 80.4% Incumb: 88.3%	
Chevron Corp Chevron Employees PAC San Francisco, CA	Oil & Gas Prod†	$277,815	243 Candidates Avg House: $781 Avg Sen: $3,528	Repubs: 61.9% House: 59.4% Incumb: 74.2%	
Chicago & North Western Transport North Western Officers Trust Account - Chicago & North Western Transportation Co Chicago, IL	Railroads	$56,804	68 Candidates Avg House: $659 Avg Sen: $1,321	Repubs: 60.3% House: 60.4% Incumb: 93.8%	
Chicago Board of Options Exchange Chicago Board of Options Exchange Inc PAC Chicago, IL	Commodity Trading	$96,200	55 Candidates Avg House: $1,212 Avg Sen: $3,180	Dems: 68.8% House: 50.4% Incumb: 97.9%	
Chicago Board of Trade Auction Markets PAC of the Chicago Board of Trade (AMPAC/CBT) Chicago, IL	Commodity Trading	$424,350	203 Candidates Avg House: $1,519 Avg Sen: $3,856	Dems: 67.1% House: 55.5% Incumb: 94.9%	
Chicago Mercantile Exchange Commodity Futures Political Fund of the Chicago Mercantile Exchange Chicago, IL	Commodity Trading	$449,400	206 Candidates Avg House: $1,362 Avg Sen: $4,510	Dems: 63.0% Pres: 54.0% Incumb: 87.2%	
Chicagoans for a Better Congress Chicagoans for a Better Congress Chicago, IL	Pro-Israel	$31,950	22 Candidates Avg House: $565 Avg Sen: $2,030	Dems: 69.5% Senate: 63.5% Incumb: 79.0%	
Chrysler Corp Chrysler Corporation Political Support Committee Highland Park, MI	Chrysler Corp Auto Mfrs†	$305,983	308 Candidates Avg House: $717 Avg Sen: $2,605	Dems: 70.1% House: 61.7% Incumb: 91.2%	
Chubb Corp Chubb Corporation PAC "ChubbPAC" Warren, NJ	Insurance	$33,000	34 Candidates Avg House: $952 Avg Sen: $1,000	Dems: 54.5% House: 60.6% Incumb: 90.9%	
Ciba-Geigy Corp Ciba-Geigy Employee Good Government Fund Ardsley, NY	Pharmaceuticals†	$77,830	99 Candidates Avg House: $586 Avg Sen: $1,446	Repubs: 66.7% House: 57.2% Incumb: 95.8%	

† PAC Sponsor has other major interests in addition to this primary category

Cigna Corp
Cigna Corporation PAC
Philadelphia, PA
Insurance
$178,487

195 Candidates
Avg House: $573
Avg Sen: $2,376
Repubs: 56.6%
House: 50.7%
Incumb: 84.2%

Circus Circus Enterprises
Circus Circus Enterprises Inc PAC (CC-PAC)
San Francisco, CA
Casinos/Gambling†
$49,798

31 Candidates
Avg House: $1,151
Avg Sen: $2,426
Dems: 61.2%
Senate: 48.7%
Incumb: 84.7%

Citicorp
Citicorp Voluntary Political Fund Federal
New York, NY
Commercial Banks†
$401,223

200 Candidates
Avg House: $1,693
Avg Sen: $3,160
Dems: 55.5%
House: 64.2%
Incumb: 89.0%

Citizens & Southern National Bank
Citizens and Southern Corporation Better Government Committee
Atlanta, GA   Citizens & Southern Corp   Commercial Banks
$177,101

112 Candidates
Avg House: $1,500
Avg Sen: $1,773
Dems: 65.7%
House: 61.9%
Incumb: 91.6%

Citizens Concerned for National Interest
Citizens Concerned for the National Interest
Chicago, IL
Pro-Israel
$35,600

9 Candidates
Avg House: $600
Avg Sen: $4,571
Dems: 61.8%
Senate: 89.8%
Incumb: 89.9%

Citizens for the Republic
Citizens for the Republic
Malibu, CA   Ronald Reagan   Repub Cands
$186,769

35 Candidates
Avg House: $4,990
Avg Sen: $6,090
Repubs: 100.0%
House: 64.1%
Incumb: 27.5%

Citizens Organized PAC
Citizens Organized PAC
Los Angeles, CA
Pro-Israel
$197,000

30 Candidates
Avg House: $5,100
Avg Sen: $7,421
Dems: 79.7%
Senate: 71.5%
Incumb: 74.6%

City PAC
City PAC
Deerfield, IL
Pro-Israel
$32,250

41 Candidates
Avg House: $685
Avg Sen: $1,100
Dems: 74.4%
House: 65.9%
Incumb: 60.5%

Class PAC
Class PAC
Washington, DC
Dem/Liberal
$50,000

14 Candidates
Avg House: $3,571
Avg Sen: $0
Dems: 100.0%
House: 100.0%
Incumb: 96.0%

Cleveland-Cliffs Iron Company
Cleveland-Cliffs Iron Company PAC (CliffsPAC)
Cleveland, OH
Metals Min & Proc
$26,550

32 Candidates
Avg House: $645
Avg Sen: $1,305
Repubs: 61.9%
House: 51.0%
Incumb: 87.0%

CNA Financial Corp
CNA Financial Corporation Citizens for Good Government
Chicago, IL
Insurance
$36,325

43 Candidates
Avg House: $743
Avg Sen: $1,019
Dems: 65.4%
House: 59.4%
Incumb: 92.0%

Co-op of American Physicians
Cooperative of American Physicians Federal Action Committee (CAP/FAC)
Los Angeles, CA
Doctors
$51,450

37 Candidates
Avg House: $1,085
Avg Sen: $2,942
Dems: 73.4%
House: 59.1%
Incumb: 73.3%

Coast Federal Savings & Loan
Coast FEDPAC - a PAC of Coast Savings and Loan
Granada Hills, CA
Savings Banks
$39,160

30 Candidates
Avg House: $1,007
Avg Sen: $2,000
Repubs: 58.7%
House: 54.0%
Incumb: 88.0%

Coastal Corp
Coastal Corp. Employee Action Fund
Houston, TX
Natural Gas†
$237,558

154 Candidates
Avg House: $1,107
Avg Sen: $2,771
Dems: 79.0%
House: 52.2%
Incumb: 82.7%

Coca-Cola Company
Coca-Cola Company Nonpartisan Committee for Good Government
Atlanta, GA   Coca-Cola   Soft Drinks†
$214,790

243 Candidates
Avg House: $663
Avg Sen: $1,257
Dems: 59.7%
House: 54.4%
Incumb: 86.5%

Collins & Aikman Corp
Collins & Aikman Corporation PAC
Charlotte, NC
Textiles
$40,900

46 Candidates
Avg House: $607
Avg Sen: $1,250
Dems: 55.1%
Senate: 55.0%
Incumb: 95.0%

Colt Industries
Colt Industries Inc Voluntary Political Committee
New York, NY
Air Defense†
$110,775

146 Candidates
Avg House: $614
Avg Sen: $1,460
Repubs: 50.9%
House: 66.6%
Incumb: 89.4%

Columbia Hydrocarbon Corp
Columbia Gas Employees Political Action Fund
Wilmington, DE   Columbia Gas   Natural Gas
$75,553

90 Candidates
Avg House: $740
Avg Sen: $1,099
Repubs: 61.9%
House: 64.7%
Incumb: 82.6%

Columbia Natural Resources
Columbia Employees Political Action Fund
Charleston, WV   Columbia Gas   Oil & Gas Prod
$33,860

46 Candidates
Avg House: $767
Avg Sen: $682
Dems: 60.9%
House: 65.7%
Incumb: 88.9%

Sponsor or Related Group/PAC Name	Affiliate	1987-88 Total	Where the money went...		
Columbia Pictures Columbia Pictures Entertainment Inc PAC New York, NY	Coca-Cola	$32,000 Movies	34 Candidates Avg House: $789 Avg Sen: $1,133	Dems: 87.5% Senate: 53.1% Incumb: 96.9%	
Columbia Savings & Loan (Beverly Hills) Columbia Savings and Loan Association Federal Political Contribution Fund Beverly Hills, CA		$35,300 Savings Banks	15 Candidates Avg House: $1,042 Avg Sen: $3,285	Dems: 63.7% Senate: 65.1% Incumb: 96.3%	
Combustion Engineering Combustion Engineering Inc PAC (COMPAC) Stamford, CT		$59,937 PowerEquip†	68 Candidates Avg House: $667 Avg Sen: $1,475	Dems: 51.0% House: 55.7% Incumb: 94.2%	
Comerica Inc Comerica Inc Committee for Responsible Political Action ("Comerica PAC") Detroit, MI		$26,955 Commercial Banks	19 Candidates Avg House: $1,327 Avg Sen: $1,843	Repubs: 63.1% House: 68.9% Incumb: 77.7%	
Communications Workers Union Local #13000 Local 13000 CWA AFL-CIO Philadelphia, PA	Communications Workers	$38,000 Communic Unions	8 Candidates Avg House: $5,428 Avg Sen: $0	Dems: 100.0% House: 100.0% Incumb: 59.2%	
Committee for "18" Committee for "18" Denver, CO		$23,500 Pro-Israel	16 Candidates Avg House: $1,000 Avg Sen: $1,576	Dems: 70.2% Senate: 87.2% Incumb: 42.6%	
Committee for a Democratic Consensus Committee for a Democratic Consensus; The Washington, DC	Sen Alan Cranston (D-California)	$261,800 Dem Leaders	37 Candidates Avg House: $5,833 Avg Sen: $7,316	Dems: 100.0% Senate: 86.6% Incumb: 40.9%	
Committee for Democratic Consensus Committee for Democratic Consensus Washington, DC	Rep Marvin Leath (D-Texas)	$67,423 Dem Leaders	19 Candidates Avg House: $3,464 Avg Sen: $4,000	Dems: 100.0% House: 82.2% Incumb: 18.5%	
Committee for Democratic Opportunity Committee for Democratic Opportunity Philadelphia, PA	Rep William Gray III (D-Pa)	$139,800 Dem Leaders	97 Candidates Avg House: $1,359 Avg Sen: $4,000	Dems: 100.0% House: 91.4% Incumb: 56.8%	
Committee for Quality Orthopedic Health Care Committee for Quality Orthopaedic Health Care Inc Washington, DC		$173,250 MD Specialists	182 Candidates Avg House: $840 Avg Sen: $1,541	Repubs: 52.9% House: 74.2% Incumb: 83.5%	
Committee for the 100th Congress Committee for the 100th Congress Washington, DC	Rep Charles Rangel (D-NY)	$51,000 Dem Leaders	24 Candidates Avg House: $2,173 Avg Sen: $0	Dems: 100.0% House: 98.0% Incumb: 94.1%	
Commodity Exchange Inc Commodity Exchange Inc PAC (COMPAC) New York, NY		$47,800 Commodity Trading	44 Candidates Avg House: $1,052 Avg Sen: $1,111	Dems: 69.1% House: 74.9% Incumb: 100.0%	
Commonwealth Financial Group Commonwealth Group PAC Houston, TX		$30,250 Mortgage Bank	14 Candidates Avg House: $1,805 Avg Sen: $3,000	Dems: 64.5% House: 53.7% Incumb: 100.0%	
Communications Workers of America CWA-COPE Political Contributions Committee Washington, DC	Communications Workers	$733,090 Communic Unions	257 Candidates Avg House: $2,438 Avg Sen: $5,111	Dems: 97.9% House: 72.2% Incumb: 52.5%	
Computer Dealers & Lessors Assn Computer Dealers and Lessors Association, Inc PAC Washington, DC		$29,473 Computers†	28 Candidates Avg House: $585 Avg Sen: $1,351	Dems: 70.8% Senate: 73.3% Incumb: 82.2%	
Computer Sciences Corp Computer Sciences Corporation PAC (CSC PAC) El Segundo, CA		$119,930 Computer Svcs†	125 Candidates Avg House: $798 Avg Sen: $1,409	Dems: 50.8% House: 61.2% Incumb: 91.7%	
Comsat ComsatPAC Washington, DC		$73,008 Satellite Communications†	82 Candidates Avg House: $632 Avg Sen: $1,421	Dems: 59.3% Senate: 52.5% Incumb: 83.6%	
ConAgra Inc ConAgra Good Government Association Omaha, NE	ConAgra	$176,577 Food Processing†	117 Candidates Avg House: $984 Avg Sen: $2,624	Repubs: 70.0% Senate: 52.0% Incumb: 84.3%	
Concerned Texans in Action Concerned Texans in Action Houston, TX	Lidell, Sapp	$25,450 Lawyers	14 Candidates Avg House: $1,635 Avg Sen: $1,750	Dems: 100.0% House: 45.0% Incumb: 96.1%	

† PAC Sponsor has other major interests in addition to this primary category

1117

Sponsor or Related Group/PAC Name	Affiliate	1987-88 Total	Where the money went...		
Cone Mills Corp Cone Mills Corporation PAC (Cone PAC) Greensboro, NC	Textiles	$31,150	25 Candidates Avg House: $1,067 Avg Sen: $1,571	Dems: 58.4% House: 58.3% Incumb: 99.4%	
Congressional Action Cmte of Texas Congressional Action Committee of Texas Houston, TX	Pro-Israel	$45,750	23 Candidates Avg House: $1,477 Avg Sen: $2,458	Dems: 66.7% Senate: 64.4% Incumb: 44.3%	
Congressional Agenda 80's Congressional Agenda 80's Washington, DC	Dem/Liberal	$22,810	40 Candidates Avg House: $557 Avg Sen: $442	Dems: 100.0% House: 78.3% Incumb: 61.9%	
Congressional Majority Committee Congressional Majority Committee Arlington, VA	Repub/Conservative	$20,350	37 Candidates Avg House: $348 Avg Sen: $1,464	Repubs: 97.7% Senate: 50.3% Incumb: 46.7%	
Connecticut Mutual Life Insurance Connecticut Mutual Life Insurance Co-PAC (CM-PAC;/CM PAC;/CML PAC) Hartford, CT	Life Insurance	$77,950	88 Candidates Avg House: $724 Avg Sen: $1,250	Dems: 51.5% House: 56.7% Incumb: 84.3%	
Connecticut Union of Telephone Workers PAC for Education - C U T W Hamden, CT	Communic Unions	$37,750	11 Candidates Avg House: $3,750 Avg Sen: $2,000	Dems: 76.2% House: 89.4% Incumb: 53.6%	
Conservative Democratic PAC Conservative Democratic PAC (Formerly Boll Weevil PAC) Washington, DC	Rep Charles Stenholm (D-Tex) — Dem Leaders	$28,000	16 Candidates Avg House: $1,750 Avg Sen: $0	Dems: 100.0% House: 100.0% Incumb: 42.9%	
Conservative Victory Committee Conservative Victory Committee Alexandria, VA	Repub/Conservative	$84,352	61 Candidates Avg House: $1,253 Avg Sen: $2,010	Repubs: 98.7% Senate: 52.4% Incumb: 40.4%	
Conservative Victory Fund Conservative Victory Fund Washington, DC	Sen Steve Symms (R-Idaho) — Repub Leaders	$73,179	81 Candidates Avg House: $879 Avg Sen: $1,008	Repubs: 100.0% House: 79.3% Incumb: 51.7%	
Conservatives Acting Together Conservatives Acting Together PAC Dallas, TX	Repub/Conservative	$20,500	8 Candidates Avg House: $2,125 Avg Sen: $2,333	Repubs: 100.0% House: 41.5% Incumb: 73.2%	
Consolidated Freightways Consolidated Freightways Inc PAC Menlo Park, CA	Trucking†	$114,800	100 Candidates Avg House: $1,005 Avg Sen: $1,405	Dems: 50.8% Pres: 50.3% Incumb: 88.2%	
Consolidated Rail Corp Consolidated Rail Corp Good Government Fund (Conrail Good Govt Fund) Philadelphia, PA	Railroads	$46,750	66 Candidates Avg House: $533 Avg Sen: $1,357	Dems: 50.7% House: 59.4% Incumb: 97.9%	
Consumer Bankers Assn Consumer Bankers Association PAC, The Arlington, VA	Banks	$32,950	56 Candidates Avg House: $558 Avg Sen: $857	Dems: 68.0% House: 81.4% Incumb: 98.5%	
Consumers Power Company Consumers Power Company Employees for Better Government - Federal Jackson, MI	Gas/Electric†	$86,039	89 Candidates Avg House: $897 Avg Sen: $1,238	Dems: 51.8% House: 74.1% Incumb: 92.4%	
Continental Illinois Corp Political Participation Fund of Continental Illinois Corp Chicago, IL	Commercial Banks	$90,775	84 Candidates Avg House: $894 Avg Sen: $1,736	Dems: 63.2% House: 63.1% Incumb: 93.6%	
Continental Telecom Continental Telecom Inc PAC (ContelPAC) Washington, DC	Phone Utilities†	$320,170	215 Candidates Avg House: $1,303 Avg Sen: $2,663	Repubs: 67.6% House: 74.9% Incumb: 77.9%	
Contran Corp Contran Corporation PAC (CONPAC) Dallas, TX	NL Industries — Chemicals†	$24,167	12 Candidates Avg House: $1,166 Avg Sen: $1,958	Repubs: 100.0% Senate: 64.8% Incumb: 75.2%	
Cooper Industries Cooper Industries PAC (CIPAC) Houston, TX	Electronics†	$292,250	141 Candidates Avg House: $1,283 Avg Sen: $5,258	Repubs: 95.9% Senate: 50.3% Incumb: 45.7%	
Coopers & Lybrand Coopers & Lybrand PAC Washington, DC	Coopers & Lybrand — Accountants	$133,862	122 Candidates Avg House: $980 Avg Sen: $1,303	Dems: 59.5% House: 62.3% Incumb: 90.7%	

Sponsor or Related Group/PAC Name	Affiliate	1987-88 Total	Where the money went...		
Coors Industries Political Action Coors Employees (PACE) Golden, CO	Beer	$84,456	46 Candidates Avg House: $1,536 Avg Sen: $3,066	Repubs: 98.8% House: 67.3% Incumb: 33.8%	
Corning Glass Works Corning Glass Works Employees PAC Corning, NY	Glass Products†	$100,200	86 Candidates Avg House: $1,124 Avg Sen: $1,375	Repubs: 58.6% House: 80.8% Incumb: 86.5%	
Corp for the Advancement of Psychiatry Corporation for the Advancement of Psychiatry PAC (CAPPAC) Washington, DC	Psychol	$99,280	100 Candidates Avg House: $947 Avg Sen: $1,115	Dems: 76.3% House: 69.7% Incumb: 73.5%	
Council for a Livable World Council for a Livable World Boston, MA	Council for Livable World Pro-Peace	$116,553	21 Candidates Avg House: $0 Avg Sen: $5,550	Dems: 94.0% Senate: 100.0% Incumb: 42.1%	
Council for National Defense Council for National Defense Inc, The Vienna, VA	Pro-Military	$234,332	341 Candidates Avg House: $626 Avg Sen: $984	Repubs: 99.1% House: 74.4% Incumb: 37.1%	
Credit Union National Assn Credit Union Legislative Action Council of Credit Union National Association Washington, DC	Credit Union National Assn Credit Unions	$431,875	254 Candidates Avg House: $1,352 Avg Sen: $3,504	Dems: 63.7% House: 66.7% Incumb: 85.5%	
Credithrift Financial Management Corp Credithrift of America PAC Evansville, IN	American General Consumer Credit	$36,075	34 Candidates Avg House: $1,009 Avg Sen: $785	Repubs: 80.9% House: 64.4% Incumb: 83.2%	
Crowell & Moring Crowell & Moring PAC Washington, DC	Lawyers	$37,804	74 Candidates Avg House: $407 Avg Sen: $701	Repubs: 50.0% House: 51.8% Incumb: 84.9%	
Crowley Maritime Crowley Maritime Federal PAC San Francisco, CA	Sea Transport	$30,575	47 Candidates Avg House: $639 Avg Sen: $686	Dems: 56.7% House: 75.3% Incumb: 86.1%	
Crum & Forster Insurance Crum & Forster Voluntary PAC Morristown, NJ	Insurance	$21,729	45 Candidates Avg House: $474 Avg Sen: $506	Repubs: 59.2% House: 72.0% Incumb: 88.3%	
CSX Transportation Inc CSX Transportation Inc PAC (Formerly Seaboard System Railroad PAC) Washington, DC	CSX Corp Railroads†	$115,458	151 Candidates Avg House: $627 Avg Sen: $1,570	Dems: 63.1% House: 69.0% Incumb: 91.7%	
Cubic Corp Cubic Employees' PAC (CUEPAC) San Diego, CA	Defense Electronics†	$27,400	25 Candidates Avg House: $745 Avg Sen: $2,250	Repubs: 82.3% House: 59.9% Incumb: 98.2%	
Cyprus Minerals Company Cyprus Minerals Company PAC/Cyprus PAC Englewood, CO	Metal Mining/Processing	$55,250	45 Candidates Avg House: $723 Avg Sen: $2,058	Repubs: 53.1% Senate: 63.3% Incumb: 96.4%	
Dairymen Inc Dairymen Inc-Special Political Agricultural Community Education (DI-SPACE) Louisville, KY	Dairymen Inc Dairy	$183,400	178 Candidates Avg House: $795 Avg Sen: $2,257	Dems: 70.7% House: 64.2% Incumb: 85.6%	
Dairymen Inc-Georgia Dairymen Inc-Georgia Committee for Political Action (DI-GCFPA) Culloden, GA	Dairymen Inc Dairy	$22,950	13 Candidates Avg House: $1,768 Avg Sen: $1,750	Dems: 78.0% House: 84.7% Incumb: 93.5%	
Dairymen Inc-Tennessee Dairymen Inc-Tennessee Committee for Political Action (DI-TCFPA) Cleveland, TN	Dairymen Inc Dairy	$34,683	12 Candidates Avg House: $3,020 Avg Sen: $3,250	Dems: 60.2% House: 78.4% Incumb: 69.7%	
Dallas Energy PAC Dallas Energy PAC (DALENPAC) Dallas, TX	Oil & Gas Prod	$108,000	18 Candidates Avg House: $2,428 Avg Sen: $8,272	Repubs: 95.3% Senate: 84.2% Incumb: 25.9%	
Dana Corp Dana Corporation PAC Toledo, OH	Auto Parts	$24,500	21 Candidates Avg House: $958 Avg Sen: $1,444	Repubs: 97.9% Senate: 53.0% Incumb: 28.6%	
Dayton Hudson Corp Dayton Hudson Corporation Committee for Effective Federal Government Minneapolis, MN	Dept Stores	$37,275	61 Candidates Avg House: $503 Avg Sen: $868	Repubs: 56.5% House: 56.7% Incumb: 88.6%	

† PAC Sponsor has other major interests in addition to this primary category

Dean Witter Reynolds
Dean Witter Reynolds PAC
New York, NY — Sears — Securities Investment — **$71,857**
94 Candidates — Dems: 57.5%
Avg House: $636 — House: 67.3%
Avg Sen: $1,305 — Incumb: 84.7%

Deere & Company
Deere & Company Civic Action Fund
Moline, IL — Deere & Co — Farm Equip — **$109,625**
90 Candidates — Repubs: 84.7%
Avg House: $916 — House: 56.9%
Avg Sen: $2,150 — Incumb: 66.9%

Delaware Valley PAC
Delaware Valley PAC
Southampton, PA — Pro-Israel — **$178,100**
87 Candidates — Dems: 70.4%
Avg House: $1,052 — Senate: 65.1%
Avg Sen: $4,142 — Incumb: 73.3%

Deloitte, Haskins & Sells
Deloitte, Haskins & Sells Good Government PAC (DH&S Good Gov't PAC)
Washington, DC — Deloitte, Haskins — Accountants — **$33,406**
42 Candidates — Repubs: 60.9%
Avg House: $727 — House: 63.2%
Avg Sen: $946 — Incumb: 79.8%

Delta Airlines
Delta Airlines Inc PAC
Atlanta, GA — Airlines — **$34,900**
70 Candidates — Dems: 53.6%
Avg House: $489 — House: 71.5%
Avg Sen: $497 — Incumb: 93.8%

Democratic Candidate Fund
Democratic Candidate Fund (Thomas P O'Neill, Jr Congress Fund)
Washington, DC — Former Rep Tip O'Neill (D-Mass) — Dem Cands — **$24,000**
33 Candidates — Dems: 100.0%
Avg House: $525 — Senate: 51.8%
Avg Sen: $1,131 — Incumb: 33.1%

Democratic Study Group Campaign Fund
Democratic Study Group Campaign Fund *
Washington, DC — Dem/Liberal — **$54,000**
23 Candidates — Dems: 100.0%
Avg House: $2,347 — House: 100.0%
Avg Sen: $0 — Incumb: 38.9%

Democrats for the 80's
Democrats for the 80's Inc
Washington, DC — Dem/Liberal — **$243,830**
57 Candidates — Dems: 100.0%
Avg House: $571 — Senate: 86.4%
Avg Sen: $7,022 — Incumb: 47.6%

Desert Caucus
Desert Caucus
Tucson, AZ — Pro-Israel — **$214,450**
67 Candidates — Dems: 64.6%
Avg House: $1,423 — Senate: 73.4%
Avg Sen: $5,833 — Incumb: 73.1%

Desert Grape Growers League/California
Desert Grape Growers League of California PAC
Palm Desert, CA — Fruit/Veg — **$31,500**
12 Candidates — Repubs: 60.3%
Avg House: $2,050 — House: 65.1%
Avg Sen: $5,500 — Incumb: 100.0%

Detroit Edison
Detroit Edison PAC-EDPAC-Federal
Detroit, MI — Electric Utility — **$49,948**
75 Candidates — Dems: 55.1%
Avg House: $613 — House: 72.5%
Avg Sen: $821 — Incumb: 94.5%

Dickstein, Shapiro & Morin
Dickstein, Shapiro & Morin PAC
Washington, DC — Lawyers — **$71,150**
121 Candidates — Dems: 65.2%
Avg House: $469 — House: 62.1%
Avg Sen: $1,000 — Incumb: 90.1%

Distilled Spirits Council
Distilled Spirits Council PAC
Washington, DC — Wine/Liquor — **$49,678**
75 Candidates — Dems: 68.8%
Avg House: $448 — Senate: 52.1%
Avg Sen: $1,178 — Incumb: 89.9%

Dominion Resources Inc
Committee for Responsible Govt-Dominion Resources Inc (Formerly Va Elec & Power)
Richmond, VA — Electric Utility — **$78,423**
122 Candidates — Dems: 60.1%
Avg House: $562 — House: 68.1%
Avg Sen: $926 — Incumb: 76.8%

Donaldson, Lufkin & Jenrette
Donaldson, Lufkin & Jenrette Better Government Fund
New York, NY — Equitable Life — Securities Investment — **$46,150**
26 Candidates — Dems: 51.5%
Avg House: $880 — Senate: 65.8%
Avg Sen: $2,334 — Incumb: 58.6%

Dow Chemical
Dow Chemical Company Employees' PAC
Freeport, TX — Dow Chemical — Chemicals† — **$62,000**
43 Candidates — Repubs: 96.0%
Avg House: $1,032 — House: 51.6%
Avg Sen: $2,500 — Incumb: 54.8%

Dow Chemical Consumer/Health Employees
Consumer & Health Employees PAC of the Dow Chemical Company-(KEYPAC)
Indianapolis, IN — Dow Chemical — Chemicals† — **$37,400**
54 Candidates — Repubs: 86.9%
Avg House: $461 — House: 51.9%
Avg Sen: $1,500 — Incumb: 65.2%

Dow Chemical/Eastern Emplyees
Dow Eastern Employees PAC of the Dow Chemical Company (DEEPAC)
Strongsville, OH — Dow Chemical — Chemicals† — **$23,700**
40 Candidates — Repubs: 88.8%
Avg House: $547 — House: 83.1%
Avg Sen: $1,000 — Incumb: 53.6%

Dow Chemical/HQ Unit
Dow Chemical Company-Headquarters Unit Employees PAC; The
Midland, MI — Dow Chemical — Chemicals† — **$52,350**
63 Candidates — Repubs: 88.5%
Avg House: $677 — House: 64.7%
Avg Sen: $1,423 — Incumb: 61.3%

Sponsor or Related Group/PAC Name	Affiliate	1987-88 Total	Where the money went...		
Dow Chemical/Midland Midland Committee for Employees of the Dow Chemical Company Midland, MI — Dow Chemical — Chemicals†		$28,400	36 Candidates Avg House: $604 Avg Sen: $1,136	Dems: 67.8% House: 48.9% Incumb: 94.7%	
Dow Chemical/Midwest Midwest Area PAC - Employees of the Dow Chemical Company (MAPAC) Midland, MI — Dow Chemical — Chemicals†		$44,600	36 Candidates Avg House: $1,112 Avg Sen: $2,250	Repubs: 100.0% House: 79.8% Incumb: 54.3%	
Dow Chemical/SE Region EmPAC (Employees' PAC, S. E. Region, The Dow Chemical Company) Plaquemine, LA — Dow Chemical — Chemicals†		$50,750	49 Candidates Avg House: $888 Avg Sen: $4,500	Repubs: 91.0% House: 82.3% Incumb: 55.2%	
Dow Chemical/Western Employees Western Employees PAC of the Dow Chemical Company (WESPAC) Pittsburg, CA — Dow Chemical — Chemicals†		$21,800	29 Candidates Avg House: $452 Avg Sen: $2,625	Repubs: 90.8% House: 51.8% Incumb: 77.1%	
Dow, Lohnes & Albertson Dow, Lohnes & Albertson PAC Washington, DC — Lawyers		$48,050	55 Candidates Avg House: $771 Avg Sen: $1,096	Dems: 73.2% House: 61.0% Incumb: 84.9%	
Dravo Corp Dravo Employees for Better Government Fund Pittsburgh, PA — Mining†		$35,150	40 Candidates Avg House: $705 Avg Sen: $1,400	Repubs: 59.4% House: 60.2% Incumb: 95.0%	
Dresser Industries Dresser Industries PAC (DIPAC) Dallas, TX — Oilfield Svc		$36,850	42 Candidates Avg House: $494 Avg Sen: $1,406	Repubs: 67.4% Senate: 61.0% Incumb: 75.8%	
Drexel Burnham Lambert Drexel Burnham Lambert PAC (DBL-PAC) New York, NY — Securities Investment		$122,833	109 Candidates Avg House: $741 Avg Sen: $1,976	Repubs: 56.1% Senate: 54.7% Incumb: 87.5%	
DSC Communications Corp DSC Communications Corporation PAC DSCPAC Washington, DC — Comm Equip		$33,850	31 Candidates Avg House: $741 Avg Sen: $1,541	Dems: 65.3% Senate: 54.6% Incumb: 61.6%	
Duchossois Industries Duchossois Industries Inc PAC Elmhurst, IL — Railroad Equip		$22,000	14 Candidates Avg House: $1,850 Avg Sen: $250	Repubs: 65.9% House: 84.1% Incumb: 88.6%	
Duke Power Company Employees Federal PAC - Duke Power Company Charlotte, NC — Electric Utility		$53,500	63 Candidates Avg House: $851 Avg Sen: $828	Repubs: 57.9% House: 89.2% Incumb: 93.4%	
Dun & Bradstreet PAC of the Dun & Bradstreet Corporation Washington, DC — Market Research†		$159,079	98 Candidates Avg House: $676 Avg Sen: $3,055	Repubs: 78.6% Senate: 74.9% Incumb: 77.3%	
Dyncorp Dyncorp Federal PAC (Formerly Dynalectron Corp Fed PAC) Reston, VA — Air Defense†		$31,600	43 Candidates Avg House: $567 Avg Sen: $1,468	Repubs: 50.1% House: 62.8% Incumb: 81.0%	
E F Hutton Group E F Hutton Group PAC; The New York, NY — American Express — Securities Investment		$151,421	148 Candidates Avg House: $633 Avg Sen: $2,657	Dems: 56.9% House: 49.8% Incumb: 98.7%	
E I Du Pont De Nemours & Company E I du Pont de Nemours & Company Good Government Fund Wilmington, DE — du Pont — Chemicals†		$72,000	121 Candidates Avg House: $517 Avg Sen: $943	Dems: 54.2% House: 71.2% Incumb: 95.1%	
E-Systems/Corporate Division E-Systems Corporate Division PAC Dallas, TX — E-Systems — Defense Electronics		$54,017	75 Candidates Avg House: $694 Avg Sen: $929	Repubs: 56.6% House: 81.0% Incumb: 82.0%	
Eagle Forum Eagle Forum PAC Alton, IL — Repub/Conservative		$49,590	85 Candidates Avg House: $486 Avg Sen: $921	Repubs: 98.3% House: 62.7% Incumb: 53.3%	
East Midwood PAC East Midwood PAC Brooklyn, NY — Pro-Israel		$24,000	24 Candidates Avg House: $666 Avg Sen: $1,333	Dems: 67.7% Senate: 66.6% Incumb: 81.3%	
Eastern Airlines Eastern Airlines PAC Miami, FL — Texas Air — Airlines		$101,050	62 Candidates Avg House: $1,328 Avg Sen: $2,366	Repubs: 57.0% House: 57.8% Incumb: 77.4%	

† PAC Sponsor has other major interests in addition to this primary category

Sponsor or Related Group/PAC Name	Affiliate	1987-88 Total	Where the money went...		
Eastman Kodak/Chemicals Division EASTPAC-PAC of Eastman Chemicals Division Eastman Kodak Company Kingsport, TN	Eastman Kodak Chemicals	$41,450	43 Candidates Avg House: $873 Avg Sen: $886	Repubs: 76.4% House: 63.2% Incumb: 63.7%	
Eaton Corp Eaton Corporation Public Policy Association Cleveland, OH	Auto Parts†	$183,050	84 Candidates Avg House: $1,623 Avg Sen: $4,078	Repubs: 97.1% House: 57.7% Incumb: 37.2%	
Ecolab Inc Ecolab Inc PAC St Paul, MN	Business Svcs†	$38,500	24 Candidates Avg House: $1,300 Avg Sen: $2,111	Repubs: 93.5% House: 50.6% Incumb: 75.3%	
Edison Electric Institute Power PAC of the Edison Electric Institute Washington, DC	Electric Utility	$85,300	182 Candidates Avg House: $437 Avg Sen: $620	Repubs: 54.5% House: 77.4% Incumb: 88.3%	
Effective Government Committee Effective Government Committee Washington, DC	Rep Richard Gephardt (D-Mo) Dem Leaders	$24,000	8 Candidates Avg House: $2,000 Avg Sen: $3,600	Dems: 100.0% Senate: 75.0% Incumb: 2.1%	
EG&G Inc EG&G, Inc. PAC Wellesley, MA	Defense R&D†	$21,100	30 Candidates Avg House: $509 Avg Sen: $1,268	Dems: 62.3% House: 50.7% Incumb: 75.1%	
El Paso Company El Paso Company PAC (PASPAC) El Paso, TX	Natural Gas†	$46,600	45 Candidates Avg House: $660 Avg Sen: $3,071	Dems: 60.9% House: 53.9% Incumb: 96.1%	
Elections Cmte/Orange County Elections Committee of the County of Orange Laguna Beach, CA	Gay/Lesbian Rights†	$25,562	11 Candidates Avg House: $2,501 Avg Sen: $1,850	Repubs: 65.5% House: 78.3% Incumb: 55.7%	
Electrocom Automation Inc Electrocom Automation Inc PAC Arlington, TX	Computers	$31,005	32 Candidates Avg House: $872 Avg Sen: $1,146	Repubs: 51.7% Senate: 51.7% Incumb: 89.5%	
Electronic Data Systems Electronic Data Systems Employees' PAC Dallas, TX	General Motors Computer Svcs†	$57,681	71 Candidates Avg House: $787 Avg Sen: $865	Repubs: 58.9% House: 68.3% Incumb: 92.5%	
Electronic Machine Furniture Workers IUE COPE Int'l Union/Electronic Electrical Tech Salaried Mach Workers AFL-CIO Washington, DC	Communic Unions†	$167,295	119 Candidates Avg House: $994 Avg Sen: $3,152	Dems: 97.3% House: 57.1% Incumb: 61.5%	
Eli Lilly & Company Eli Lilly and Company PAC Indianapolis, IN	Pharmaceuticals†	$133,140	107 Candidates Avg House: $629 Avg Sen: $3,064	Repubs: 74.3% Senate: 62.1% Incumb: 73.3%	
Emerson Electric Emerson PAC (EMPAC) St Louis, MO	Emerson Electric Defense Electronics†	$57,025	45 Candidates Avg House: $791 Avg Sen: $2,022	Repubs: 64.5% House: 44.4% Incumb: 90.4%	
Emhart Corp Emhart PAC Farmington, CT	Emhart Corp Indust Equip†	$46,855	46 Candidates Avg House: $719 Avg Sen: $1,764	Repubs: 60.0% House: 52.2% Incumb: 76.7%	
Emily's List Emily's List Washington, DC	Womens Issues	$67,984	15 Candidates Avg House: $4,844 Avg Sen: $2,505	Dems: 100.0% House: 92.6% Incumb: 9.6%	
Empire Leadership Fund Empire Leadership Fund New York, NY	Gov Mario Cuomo (D-NY) Dem Cands	$36,500	23 Candidates Avg House: $1,428 Avg Sen: $3,500	Dems: 100.0% House: 54.8% Incumb: 41.1%	
Employee Stock Ownership Assn Employee Stock Ownership Association Inc PAC Washington, DC	Other	$29,400	29 Candidates Avg House: $747 Avg Sen: $1,528	Dems: 84.7% House: 53.4% Incumb: 95.4%	
Enserch Corp Enserch Corporation Employees Political Support Association Dallas, TX	Natural Gas†	$112,263	121 Candidates Avg House: $682 Avg Sen: $1,609	Dems: 57.7% House: 54.1% Incumb: 93.3%	
Environmental Action Environmental Action's PAC (ENACT/PAC) Washington, DC	Environmental	$38,131	17 Candidates Avg House: $2,279 Avg Sen: $2,670	Dems: 98.5% House: 71.8% Incumb: 22.1%	

Sponsor or Related Group/PAC Name	Affiliate	1987-88 Total	Where the money went...		
Equifax Inc Equifax PAC EQUIPAC Atlanta, GA	Credit Svcs†	$42,675	56 Candidates Avg House: $653 Avg Sen: $913	Dems: House: Incumb:	62.5% 50.6% 89.5%
Equitable Financial Services Equitable Financial Services PAC (EQUI-PAC) New York, NY	Equitable Life Insurance†	$171,800	114 Candidates Avg House: $1,092 Avg Sen: $2,236	Dems: Senate: Incumb:	62.7% 54.7% 91.8%
Ernst & Whinney Ernst & Whinney PAC Washington, DC	Ernst & Whinney Accountants	$105,850	125 Candidates Avg House: $787 Avg Sen: $1,055	Dems: House: Incumb:	59.1% 72.1% 98.6%
Exxon Corp Exxon Corporation PAC (EXPAC) Houston, TX	Oil & Gas Prod†	$164,105	225 Candidates Avg House: $513 Avg Sen: $2,357	Repubs: House: Incumb:	73.3% 61.1% 73.5%
Fairchild Industries Fairchild PAC Chantilly, VA	Aerospace Equip†	$28,600	45 Candidates Avg House: $497 Avg Sen: $1,275	Dems: House: Incumb:	67.5% 64.3% 93.0%
Family Health Program Inc FHP, Inc - Health Services PAC (FHP-HESPAC) Fountain Valley, CA	HMOs	$28,350	37 Candidates Avg House: $505 Avg Sen: $1,885	Repubs: House: Incumb:	50.7% 53.4% 80.8%
Farm Credit Council Farm Credit Council PAC/Farm Credit PAC Washington, DC	Ag Services	$80,865	158 Candidates Avg House: $441 Avg Sen: $884	Dems: House: Incumb:	59.7% 72.7% 95.7%
Farmers Group Inc Farmers Group Inc PAC Los Angeles, CA	Insurance	$32,050	57 Candidates Avg House: $582 Avg Sen: $437	Repubs: House: Incumb:	59.7% 89.1% 96.9%
Farmland Industries Farmland Industries PAC (Farmland/PAC) Kansas City, MO	Ag Services†	$46,100	53 Candidates Avg House: $715 Avg Sen: $1,459	Repubs: House: Incumb:	64.1% 65.2% 89.6%
Federal Express Corp Federal Express Corporation PAC ("FEPAC") Memphis, TN	Air Freight	$573,537	188 Candidates Avg House: $2,471 Avg Sen: $3,827	Dems: Senate: Incumb:	66.1% 50.0% 80.6%
Federal Managers' Assn Federal Managers' Association PAC Washington, DC	Federal Workers	$20,600	49 Candidates Avg House: $431 Avg Sen: $370	Dems: House: Incumb:	78.6% 79.6% 89.1%
Federal National Mortgage Assn Federal National Mortgage Association PAC ("Fannie PAC") Washington, DC	Mortgage Bank	$39,150	43 Candidates Avg House: $722 Avg Sen: $1,477	Dems: House: Incumb:	59.0% 57.2% 99.2%
Federal-Mogul Corp Federal-Mogul Employees PAC Detroit, MI	Auto Parts†	$22,000	19 Candidates Avg House: $1,000 Avg Sen: $1,600	Repubs: House: Incumb:	84.0% 63.6% 81.8%
Federated Department Stores Federated Department Stores PAC Cincinnati, OH	Dept Stores	$57,000	37 Candidates Avg House: $1,192 Avg Sen: $2,363	Repubs: House: Incumb:	57.8% 54.4% 86.0%
Federated Investors Inc Financial Services Political Committee Pittsburgh, PA	Securities Investment	$41,300	32 Candidates Avg House: $1,021 Avg Sen: $1,562	Dems: Senate: Incumb:	54.5% 60.5% 91.5%
Federation of American Hospitals Federation of American Health Systems PAC Washington, DC	Hospitals	$135,517	110 Candidates Avg House: $738 Avg Sen: $2,334	Dems: Senate: Incumb:	60.0% 58.5% 85.3%
Fertilizer Institute FERT PAC Washington, DC	Ag Chemicals	$28,250	52 Candidates Avg House: $414 Avg Sen: $930	Dems: House: Incumb:	65.7% 57.2% 89.9%
Figgie International Figgie International Employees Better Government Committee Willoughby, OH	Security Svcs†	$57,150	84 Candidates Avg House: $529 Avg Sen: $1,106	Repubs: House: Incumb:	85.9% 57.4% 65.8%
First American Corp First American Corporation PAC Nashville, TN	Commercial Banks	$48,916	20 Candidates Avg House: $1,694 Avg Sen: $5,500	Dems: House: Incumb:	67.8% 52.0% 76.0%

† PAC Sponsor has other major interests in addition to this primary category

|---|---|---|---|---|---|
First Atlanta Corp First Atlanta Corporation Fund for Better Government Atlanta, GA	Commercial Banks	$23,450	25 Candidates Avg House: $1,103 Avg Sen: $722	Dems: 70.4% House: 65.9% Incumb: 88.3%	
First Bank System/Minnesota First Bank System Minnesota Good Government Committee Minneapolis, MN	First Bank System Commercial Banks	$29,250	46 Candidates Avg House: $514 Avg Sen: $886	Repubs: 53.9% House: 54.5% Incumb: 94.0%	
First Boston Corp First Boston-PAC (FB-PAC); The New York, NY	Investment Banking	$257,350	109 Candidates Avg House: $1,868 Avg Sen: $3,862	Dems: 67.2% House: 55.9% Incumb: 95.3%	
First Chicago Corp First Chicago Corp Government Affairs c/o The First National Bank of Chicago Chicago, IL	Commercial Banks	$119,483	106 Candidates Avg House: $1,036 Avg Sen: $1,401	Dems: 62.3% House: 65.9% Incumb: 94.0%	
First City Bancorp First City Bancorporation - PAC Houston, TX	Commercial Banks	$43,500	22 Candidates Avg House: $1,225 Avg Sen: $2,425	Dems: 58.0% Senate: 55.7% Incumb: 96.6%	
First Interstate Bank/California First Interstate Bank of California PAC Los Angeles, CA	First Interstate Commercial Banks	$37,350	35 Candidates Avg House: $859 Avg Sen: $1,419	Repubs: 61.7% House: 50.6% Incumb: 84.6%	
First Tennessee National Corp First Tennessee National Corp Federal PAC (First Tennessee Banks Federal PAC) Memphis, TN	Commercial Banks	$29,850	16 Candidates Avg House: $918 Avg Sen: $4,250	Dems: 61.3% Pres: 37.7% Incumb: 89.6%	
First Union Corp First Union Corporation Employees Good Government "F" Fund Charlotte, NC	Mortgage Bank	$62,300	55 Candidates Avg House: $975 Avg Sen: $1,840	Dems: 74.6% House: 70.5% Incumb: 80.7%	
Five Towns PAC Five Towns PAC Lawrence, NY	Pro-Israel	$21,750	17 Candidates Avg House: $900 Avg Sen: $1,437	Repubs: 50.5% Senate: 79.3% Incumb: 82.8%	
Fleetwood Enterprises Fleetwood Enterprises, Inc PAC Riverside, CA	Mobile Homes	$47,000	75 Candidates Avg House: $526 Avg Sen: $921	Repubs: 58.6% House: 62.8% Incumb: 81.3%	
Fleishman-Hillard Fleishman-Hillard PAC Washington, DC	Lobbyist/PR	$22,225	42 Candidates Avg House: $406 Avg Sen: $1,225	Repubs: 62.0% House: 58.5% Incumb: 89.2%	
Florida Citrus Mutual Florida Citrus Mutual PAC Inc Lakeland, FL	Fruit/Veg	$35,780	39 Candidates Avg House: $688 Avg Sen: $1,990	Dems: 66.2% House: 59.7% Incumb: 50.4%	
Florida Congressional Cmte Florida Congressional Committee Miami, FL	Pro-Israel	$133,250	49 Candidates Avg House: $1,645 Avg Sen: $3,750	Dems: 68.1% Senate: 70.3% Incumb: 71.5%	
Florida League/Financial Institutions Florida League of Financial Institutions PAC - FSPAC-Federal Orlando, FL	Savings Banks	$49,250	31 Candidates Avg House: $1,467 Avg Sen: $2,071	Dems: 68.5% House: 68.5% Incumb: 61.4%	
Florida Medical Assn Florida Medical PAC Jacksonville, FL	American Medical Assn Doctors	$85,100	22 Candidates Avg House: $3,652 Avg Sen: $5,233	Dems: 59.1% House: 81.6% Incumb: 59.2%	
Florida Power & Light Good Government Management Ass'n Florida Power & Light Company Employees PAC Juno Beach, FL	FPL Group Electric Utility	$63,545	95 Candidates Avg House: $524 Avg Sen: $987	Repubs: 56.3% House: 61.1% Incumb: 81.7%	
Florida Power Corp PAC of Florida Power Corporation Employees (Power PAC) St Petersburg, FL	Electric Utility	$25,950	52 Candidates Avg House: $435 Avg Sen: $736	Dems: 51.4% House: 68.8% Incumb: 66.3%	
Florida Sugar Cane League Florida Sugar Cane League PAC Clewiston, FL	Sugar	$112,950	209 Candidates Avg House: $426 Avg Sen: $1,246	Dems: 70.0% House: 68.0% Incumb: 89.7%	
Flowers Industries Flowers PAC Thomasville, GA	Food Processing	$73,000	19 Candidates Avg House: $2,833 Avg Sen: $4,250	Repubs: 100.0% Senate: 69.8% Incumb: 35.6%	

Sponsor or Related Group/PAC Name	Affiliate		1987-88 Total	Where the money went...		
Fluor Corp Fluor Corporation Public Affairs Committee (Fluor PAC) Irvine, CA	Fluor Corp	Heavy Construction†	$86,550	107 Candidates Avg House: $460 Avg Sen: $1,629	Repubs: 68.0% Senate: 47.1% Incumb: 92.2%	
FMC Corp FMC Corporation Good Government Program Chicago, IL		Chemicals	$382,345	263 Candidates Avg House: $1,076 Avg Sen: $3,993	Repubs: 73.8% House: 64.5% Incumb: 79.5%	
FMR Corp FMR Corp PAC Boston, MA		Securities Investment	$30,512	16 Candidates Avg House: $1,341 Avg Sen: $2,246	Dems: 59.8% Senate: 73.6% Incumb: 96.7%	
Food & Commercial Workers Local #1222 United Food & Commercial Workers, Local 1222 San Diego, CA	Food/Commercial Workers Union	Food Svc Unions	$27,600	12 Candidates Avg House: $2,760 Avg Sen: $0	Dems: 100.0% House: 100.0% Incumb: 74.6%	
Food & Commercial Workers Union Active Ballot Club, A Dept of United Food & Commercial Workers Int'l Union Washington, DC	Food/Commercial Workers Union	Retail Unions†	$1,147,610	363 Candidates Avg House: $2,846 Avg Sen: $5,849	Dems: 96.2% House: 79.9% Incumb: 60.1%	
Food Marketing Institute Food Marketing Institute PAC (Food PAC) Washington, DC		Food Stores	$358,574	302 Candidates Avg House: $956 Avg Sen: $2,710	Repubs: 56.7% House: 69.6% Incumb: 86.1%	
Footwear Distributors PAC Footwear Distributors PAC New York, NY		Shoe Mfrs†	$30,000	25 Candidates Avg House: $666 Avg Sen: $1,692	Repubs: 50.8% Senate: 73.3% Incumb: 96.7%	
Ford Motor Company Ford Motor Company Civic Action Fund Detroit, MI	Ford Motor Co	Auto Mfrs†	$203,458	241 Candidates Avg House: $688 Avg Sen: $1,984	Dems: 52.2% House: 71.7% Incumb: 92.6%	
Fort Howard Corp Fort Howard Corporation PAC Green Bay, WI		Paper Prod	$38,450	27 Candidates Avg House: $630 Avg Sen: $2,416	Repubs: 97.1% Senate: 75.4% Incumb: 35.0%	
Fox Inc FOXPAC (Fox Inc and Subsidiaries) (Formerly Twentieth Century Fox PAC) Beverly Hills, CA		Broadcast††	$25,933	38 Candidates Avg House: $639 Avg Sen: $718	Dems: 83.4% House: 51.8% Incumb: 92.3%	
Fred Meyer Inc Fred Meyer Federal PAC Portland, OR		Dept/Variety Stores†	$26,600	14 Candidates Avg House: $1,950 Avg Sen: $1,833	Dems: 75.6% House: 58.6% Incumb: 85.0%	
Free Cuba PAC Free Cuba PAC Inc Miami, FL		Foreign Policy (Anti-Castro)	$182,897	56 Candidates Avg House: $2,310 Avg Sen: $3,944	Dems: 69.1% Senate: 60.3% Incumb: 71.3%	
Freeport-McMoran Inc Freeport-McMoran Inc Citizenship Committee Washington, DC		Mining†	$123,400	149 Candidates Avg House: $650 Avg Sen: $1,311	Dems: 58.9% House: 57.5% Incumb: 93.6%	
Fulbright & Jaworski Freedom Fund; The Houston, TX		Lawyers	$65,750	37 Candidates Avg House: $1,453 Avg Sen: $1,735	Dems: 62.4% Senate: 44.9% Incumb: 89.0%	
Fund for a Democratic Majority Fund for a Democratic Majority Washington, DC	Sen Edward Kennedy (D-Mass)	Dem Leaders	$123,916	32 Candidates Avg House: $1,986 Avg Sen: $4,307	Dems: 100.0% Senate: 90.3% Incumb: 44.8%	
Fund for a Republican Majority Fund for a Republican Majority (Formerly-Republican Whip Leadership Fund) Washington, DC	Sen Ted Stevens (R-Alaska)	Repub Leaders	$60,881	21 Candidates Avg House: $1,000 Avg Sen: $3,099	Repubs: 100.0% Senate: 96.7% Incumb: 47.4%	
Fund for America's Future Fund for America's Future, Inc; The La Plata, MD	George Bush	Repub Cands	$271,660	71 Candidates Avg House: $3,277 Avg Sen: $5,166	Repubs: 100.0% House: 62.7% Incumb: 33.2%	
Garden State PAC Garden State PAC Union, NJ		Pro-Israel	$90,400	87 Candidates Avg House: $649 Avg Sen: $2,006	Dems: 63.6% Senate: 55.4% Incumb: 60.3%	
Garvey, Schubert & Barer Garvey, Schubert & Barer PAC Washington, DC		Lawyers	$41,050	55 Candidates Avg House: $680 Avg Sen: $950	Dems: 73.8% House: 64.7% Incumb: 76.9%	

† PAC Sponsor has other major interests in addition to this primary category

Sponsor or Related Group/PAC Name	Affiliate	1987-88 Total	Where the money went...
Gencorp Inc GenCorp Inc PAC (GENPAC) Fairlawn, OH	Air Defense†	**$74,215**	67 Candidates Dems: 59.9% Avg House: $953 House: 60.4% Avg Sen: $1,568 Incumb: 96.6%
Genentech Inc Genentech Inc PAC South San Francisco, CA	Pharmaceuticals	**$28,400**	25 Candidates Repubs: 58.8% Avg House: $520 Senate: 74.4% Avg Sen: $1,762 Incumb: 91.2%
General American Life Insurance General American Life Associates' Federal PAC St Louis, MO	Insurance	**$50,500**	28 Candidates Repubs: 50.5% Avg House: $1,272 Senate: 60.4% Avg Sen: $2,033 Incumb: 86.1%
General Atomics General Atomics PAC San Diego, CA	Nuclear Power Equip†	**$36,000**	28 Candidates Dems: 56.7% Avg House: $1,165 House: 64.7% Avg Sen: $1,587 Incumb: 94.4%
General Aviation Manufacturers Assn GAMAPAC (General Aviation Manufacturers Association PAC) Washington, DC	Aircraft Mfrs	**$34,905**	55 Candidates Repubs: 50.2% Avg House: $520 House: 64.1% Avg Sen: $684 Incumb: 98.7%
General Development Corp General Development Corporation Better Government PAC Miami, FL	Real Estate Devel†	**$43,400**	27 Candidates Dems: 67.7% Avg House: $1,122 Senate: 62.3% Avg Sen: $1,932 Incumb: 47.2%
General Dynamics General Dynamics Corporation Voluntary Political Contribution Plan St Louis, MO	Air Defense†	**$285,049**	202 Candidates Dems: 60.7% Avg House: $1,171 House: 68.6% Avg Sen: $2,483 Incumb: 95.8%
General Electric Non-Partisan Political Support Committee for General Electric Company Employees Fairfield, CT General Electric	Electronics†	**$317,745**	338 Candidates Dems: 61.7% Avg House: $742 House: 64.7% Avg Sen: $1,916 Incumb: 91.1%
General Mills General Mills Inc PAC (GM PAC) Minneapolis, MN General Mills	Food Processing†	**$95,300**	89 Candidates Repubs: 51.9% Avg House: $798 Senate: 50.9% Avg Sen: $1,616 Incumb: 80.1%
General Mills Restaurants General Mills Restaurants Inc Empl Good Government Fund (Red Lobster Emp Gd Govt Fd) Orlando, FL General Mills	Restaurants	**$64,500**	63 Candidates Dems: 62.0% Avg House: $711 Senate: 50.4% Avg Sen: $1,805 Incumb: 70.5%
General Motors Civic Involvement Program/General Motors Corp. Detroit, MI General Motors	Auto Mfrs†	**$198,688**	266 Candidates Repubs: 59.8% Avg House: $536 House: 61.3% Avg Sen: $1,972 Incumb: 82.5%
General Public Utilities General Public Utilities Political Participation Association Parsippany, NJ	Electric Utility	**$43,813**	73 Candidates Repubs: 53.4% Avg House: $564 House: 74.8% Avg Sen: $737 Incumb: 92.7%
Georgia Citizens for Good Government Georgia Citizens for Good Government Atlanta, GA	Pro-Israel	**$20,500**	14 Candidates Dems: 82.9% Avg House: $750 Senate: 92.6% Avg Sen: $1,583 Incumb: 68.3%
Georgia Power Company Georgia Power Company Federal PAC Inc Atlanta, GA Southern Company	Electric Utility	**$57,175**	112 Candidates Dems: 54.7% Avg House: $431 House: 65.6% Avg Sen: $800 Incumb: 82.2%
Georgia-Pacific Corp G-P Employees Fund of Georgia-Pacific Corporation Washington, DC Georgia-Pacific	Forest Prod†	**$99,141**	95 Candidates Repubs: 58.2% Avg House: $596 Senate: 55.3% Avg Sen: $2,029 Incumb: 68.2%
Gilbert Associates Gilbert Associates Inc PAC (Gilbert/Commonwealth PAC) Green Hill/Reading, PA	Nuclear Power Equip†	**$23,500**	21 Candidates Repubs: 73.4% Avg House: $1,197 House: 96.8% Avg Sen: $375 Incumb: 95.7%
Glendale Federal Savings & Loan Glendale Federal Savings Association Committee to Improve Our Nation Glendale, CA	Savings Banks	**$42,500**	45 Candidates Repubs: 64.9% Avg House: $730 House: 67.1% Avg Sen: $1,800 Incumb: 97.6%
Goldman Sachs GSMMI Holdings Inc PAC (Goldman Sachs PAC) Washington, DC	Investment Banking	**$230,300**	142 Candidates Dems: 65.3% Avg House: $1,278 House: 59.4% Avg Sen: $2,671 Incumb: 88.1%
Goldome Bank for Savings Goldome Bank for Savings PAC Buffalo, NY	Savings Banks	**$22,800**	21 Candidates Repubs: 65.1% Avg House: $1,268 House: 61.2% Avg Sen: $800 Incumb: 73.2%

Sponsor or Related Group/PAC Name	Affiliate	1987-88 Total	Where the money went...		
Gould Inc Gould Inc Responsible Government Association Rolling Meadows, IL	Computers†	$61,250	111 Candidates Avg House: $509 Avg Sen: $673	Dems: House: Incumb:	55.8% 69.0% 94.7%
Graphic Communications Union Graphic Communications International Union Political Contributions Committee Washington, DC	Communic Unions	$66,200	91 Candidates Avg House: $647 Avg Sen: $1,079	Dems: House: Incumb:	97.7% 71.5% 64.8%
Great American Federal Savings Great American First Savings Govt Action Cmte (Formerly Great American Federal) San Diego, CA	Savings Banks	$21,855	32 Candidates Avg House: $515 Avg Sen: $853	Repubs: Senate: Incumb:	59.6% 50.7% 85.4%
Great Lakes Sugar Beet Growers Great Lakes Sugar Beet Growers PAC (GLSBGPAC) Saginaw, MI	Sugar	$45,395	71 Candidates Avg House: $596 Avg Sen: $1,035	Dems: House: Incumb:	57.2% 84.0% 83.5%
Great Western Financial Corp Great Western Financial Corporation Good Government Committee Beverly Hills, CA	Savings Banks	$76,450	63 Candidates Avg House: $973 Avg Sen: $1,630	Dems: House: Incumb:	54.2% 50.9% 90.1%
Greater Washington Board of Trade Federal Commerce & Industry PAC of the Greater Washington Board of Trade Washington, DC	Chamb/Commerce	$43,300	27 Candidates Avg House: $1,490 Avg Sen: $1,416	Repubs: House: Incumb:	57.2% 68.8% 90.8%
Greyhound Corp Greyhound Good Government Project Phoenix, AZ	Hhold Chemicals†	$87,129	90 Candidates Avg House: $723 Avg Sen: $1,461	Repubs: House: Incumb:	62.5% 54.0% 89.4%
Grumman Grumman PAC Bethpage, NY	Air Defense†	$251,475	194 Candidates Avg House: $1,174 Avg Sen: $1,683	Dems: House: Incumb:	66.5% 65.9% 94.4%
GTE (Southwest) GTE Southwest Federal Political Action Club Austin, TX	GTE Phone Utilities†	$83,875	52 Candidates Avg House: $1,746 Avg Sen: $1,745	Dems: House: Incumb:	57.2% 85.4% 95.3%
GTE Corp GTE Corporation Good Government Club Washington, DC	GTE Phone Utilities†	$156,455	212 Candidates Avg House: $585 Avg Sen: $1,524	Repubs: House: Incumb:	53.4% 66.6% 85.1%
Guardian Life Insurance Guardian Life Insurance Company of America PAC (Guardian Life PAC) New York, NY	Insurance	$29,350	33 Candidates Avg House: $834 Avg Sen: $1,019	Dems: House: Incumb:	58.3% 54.0% 96.6%
Gulf + Western Industries Gulf + Western Industries Inc PAC New York, NY	Consumer Credit†	$80,550	47 Candidates Avg House: $810 Avg Sen: $4,333	Dems: Senate: Incumb:	65.2% 64.5% 96.9%
Gulfstream Aerospace Gulfstream Aerospace PAC Arlington, VA	Chrysler Corp Aircraft Mfrs	$23,750	39 Candidates Avg House: $522 Avg Sen: $833	Dems: House: Incumb:	69.5% 74.7% 96.8%
H & R Block H & R Block PAC (BlockPAC) Kansas City, MO	Tax Svcs	$22,200	27 Candidates Avg House: $606 Avg Sen: $1,150	Repubs: Senate: Incumb:	75.6% 51.8% 100.0%
Halliburton Company Halliburton PAC Duncan, OK	Halliburton Oilfield Svc†	$62,218	71 Candidates Avg House: $706 Avg Sen: $1,112	Repubs: House: Incumb:	80.4% 52.3% 75.9%
Hallmark Cards Hallmark PAC-Federal HALLPAC-Federal Kansas City, MO	Publish/Print	$92,183	55 Candidates Avg House: $1,081 Avg Sen: $2,389	Repubs: House: Incumb:	63.2% 42.3% 93.8%
Handgun Control Inc Handgun Control Inc PAC (HCI PAC) Washington, DC	Anti-Guns	$85,100	123 Candidates Avg House: $595 Avg Sen: $1,583	Dems: House: Incumb:	83.4% 77.7% 77.9%
Hardee's Food Systems Hardee's Food Systems Inc Good Government Fund Rocky Mount, NC	Restaurants	$41,825	54 Candidates Avg House: $734 Avg Sen: $1,095	Repubs: House: Incumb:	76.8% 84.3% 72.5%
Harris Corp Harris Corporation-Federal PAC Melbourne, FL	Defense Electronics†	$302,250	130 Candidates Avg House: $1,289 Avg Sen: $7,409	Repubs: Senate: Incumb:	91.7% 53.9% 61.5%

† PAC Sponsor has other major interests in addition to this primary category

Sponsor or Related Group/PAC Name	Affiliate	1987-88 Total	Where the money went...		
Harsco Corp Harsco Corporation PAC Camp Hill, PA	Indust Equipt†	$58,150	82 Candidates Avg House: $696 Avg Sen: $771	Repubs: 55.4% House: 81.4% Incumb: 92.3%	
Hartford Insurance Hartford Insurance Group - PAC Windsor, CT	ITT Corp	Insurance	$37,875	43 Candidates Avg House: $515 Avg Sen: $1,383	Dems: 51.6% Senate: 76.7% Incumb: 72.3%
Hawaiian Sugar Planters Assn Hawaiian Sugar Planters' Association-PAC (Hawaiian Sugar-PAC) Aiea, HI	Sugar	$69,150	155 Candidates Avg House: $353 Avg Sen: $978	Dems: 66.8% House: 67.5% Incumb: 91.1%	
Hazeltine Corp Hazeltine Corporation PAC Commack, NY	Emerson Electric	Defense Electronics	$25,625	38 Candidates Avg House: $692 Avg Sen: $350	Dems: 63.9% House: 97.3% Incumb: 100.0%
Health Industry Manufacturers Assn Health Industry Manufacturers Assn Washington, DC	Med Supply	$51,906	77 Candidates Avg House: $549 Avg Sen: $1,288	Dems: 58.9% House: 67.7% Incumb: 97.2%	
Health Insurance Assn of America Health Insurance PAC of the Health Insurance Association of America Washington, DC	Health Insurance	$175,879	195 Candidates Avg House: $622 Avg Sen: $1,782	Repubs: 58.7% House: 52.4% Incumb: 85.4%	
Heartland PAC Heartland PAC Formerly: Youngstown PAC Washington, DC	Pro-Israel	$61,250	45 Candidates Avg House: $718 Avg Sen: $2,095	Dems: 72.2% Senate: 71.8% Incumb: 66.1%	
Heat/Frost/Asbestos Workers Union International Association of Heat & Frost Insulators and Asbestos Workers PAC Washington, DC	Constr Unions	$39,395	34 Candidates Avg House: $963 Avg Sen: $1,825	Dems: 99.4% House: 56.3% Incumb: 48.9%	
Henley Group Inc Henley Group Inc Employees Cmte for Sensible Government (Henley COSIGN) Hampton, NH	Alternate Energy†	$131,400	72 Candidates Avg House: $1,216 Avg Sen: $2,319	Repubs: 55.8% House: 43.6% Incumb: 84.8%	
Hercules Inc Hercules Inc Voluntary Nonpartisan Political Contributions Cmte (Hercules PCC) Wilmington, DE	Chemicals†	$31,750	46 Candidates Avg House: $640 Avg Sen: $850	Repubs: 54.4% House: 70.6% Incumb: 81.6%	
Heublein Heublein Employees' Political Participation Committee Hartford, CT	RJR Nabisco	Wine/Liquor	$32,450	52 Candidates Avg House: $498 Avg Sen: $1,020	Dems: 68.1% House: 59.9% Incumb: 96.6%
Hewlett-Packard Hewlett-Packard Company PAC (HP PAC) Palo Alto, CA	Electronics†	$43,950	58 Candidates Avg House: $538 Avg Sen: $1,175	Repubs: 53.3% Senate: 53.4% Incumb: 73.3%	
Hill & Knowlton Hill & Knowlton Incorporated PAC (HillPAC) (Formerly Gray & Co PAC-GrayPAC) Washington, DC	Lobbyist/PR	$54,455	99 Candidates Avg House: $455 Avg Sen: $801	Dems: 69.6% House: 62.8% Incumb: 85.5%	
Hoechst Celanese Corp Hoechst Celanese Corporation PAC Somerville, NJ	Synthetic Fibers†	$67,300	81 Candidates Avg House: $655 Avg Sen: $1,444	Repubs: 58.4% House: 61.4% Incumb: 91.4%	
Hoffman-La Roche Hoffmann-La Roche Inc Good Government Committee Nutley, NJ	Pharmaceuticals†	$50,850	69 Candidates Avg House: $600 Avg Sen: $1,323	Repubs: 52.7% House: 66.2% Incumb: 93.4%	
Holiday Corp HI/PAC Holiday Corporation PAC Memphis, TN	Hotel/Motel	$24,000	25 Candidates Avg House: $640 Avg Sen: $1,041	Repubs: 60.4% House: 42.7% Incumb: 76.0%	
Holiday Inns INN/PAC Int'l Assn of Holiday Inns Inc PAC Memphis, TN	Holiday Inns	Hotel/Motel	$60,200	66 Candidates Avg House: $817 Avg Sen: $1,233	Repubs: 72.9% House: 69.3% Incumb: 80.1%
Holland & Knight Holland & Knight Committee for Effective Government Washington, DC	Lawyers†	$24,700	40 Candidates Avg House: $479 Avg Sen: $1,094	Dems: 70.6% House: 60.1% Incumb: 71.3%	
Hollywood Women's Political Cmte Hollywood Women's Political Committee Beverly Hills, CA	Dem/Liberal†	$117,590	31 Candidates Avg House: $3,421 Avg Sen: $4,382	Dems: 99.1% House: 55.3% Incumb: 38.7%	

Sponsor or Related Group/PAC Name	Affiliate	1987-88 Total	Where the money went...		
Home Federal Savings & Loan Home Federal Savings & Loan Assn of San Diego Cmte for Responsible Govt-Federal San Diego, CA	 Savings Banks	$25,750	40 Candidates Avg House: $585 Avg Sen: $1,050	Repubs: 58.2% House: 79.6% Incumb: 95.1%	
Home Group Inc Home Group Inc PAC New York, NY	 Insurance	$46,600	22 Candidates Avg House: $1,458 Avg Sen: $2,677	Dems: 60.8% Senate: 51.7% Incumb: 73.7%	
Home Savings of America Home Savings of America PAC San Francisco, CA	 Home Savings Savings Banks	$88,775	37 Candidates Avg House: $2,446 Avg Sen: $2,330	Dems: 84.0% House: 60.6% Incumb: 88.7%	
Honeywell Inc Honeywell Employees Citizenship Fund Minneapolis, MN	 Honeywell Electronics†	$59,900	45 Candidates Avg House: $779 Avg Sen: $2,331	Repubs: 79.6% Senate: 62.3% Incumb: 74.9%	
Hopkins & Sudder HS Political Fund Chicago, IL	 Lawyers	$37,771	50 Candidates Avg House: $618 Avg Sen: $1,137	Dems: 51.9% House: 54.0% Incumb: 89.3%	
Hotel/Restaurant Employees Union Hotel Employees & Restaurant Employees Int'l Union T I P - "To Insure Progress" Washington, DC	 Food Svc Unions	$208,320	224 Candidates Avg House: $710 Avg Sen: $2,079	Dems: 87.9% House: 64.5% Incumb: 78.5%	
HOUPAC HOUPAC Houston, TX	 Oil & Gas Prod	$47,298	68 Candidates Avg House: $357 Avg Sen: $1,293	Repubs: 97.3% Senate: 54.7% Incumb: 57.7%	
House Leadership Fund House Leadership Fund; The Washington, DC	 Rep Thomas Foley (D-Wash) Dem Leaders	$134,594	75 Candidates Avg House: $1,637 Avg Sen: $5,000	Dems: 100.0% House: 86.4% Incumb: 39.6%	
Household International Household International Inc & Subsidiary Companies PAC (HousePAC) Prospect Heights, IL	 Consumer Credit†	$142,600	130 Candidates Avg House: $783 Avg Sen: $1,918	Dems: 55.4% House: 52.7% Incumb: 85.1%	
Houston Industries Houston Industries PAC Houston, TX	 Electric Utility†	$81,212	34 Candidates Avg House: $2,274 Avg Sen: $2,466	Dems: 55.3% House: 75.6% Incumb: 97.5%	
Hudson Valley PAC Hudson Valley PAC Spring Valley, NY	 Pro-Israel	$289,615	173 Candidates Avg House: $932 Avg Sen: $4,496	Dems: 57.9% Senate: 55.9% Incumb: 80.9%	
Hughes Aircraft Hughes Aircraft Company Active Citizenship Fund Los Angeles, CA	 General Motors Defense Electronics†	$299,100	241 Candidates Avg House: $1,053 Avg Sen: $1,852	Dems: 54.2% House: 69.4% Incumb: 93.7%	
Human Rights Campaign Fund Human Rights Campaign Fund Washington, DC	 Gay/Lesbian Rights	$285,823	122 Candidates Avg House: $2,219 Avg Sen: $3,156	Dems: 77.6% House: 82.3% Incumb: 55.5%	
Humana Inc HUMPAC - A PAC Sponsored by Humana Inc Louisville, KY	 Hospitals†	$21,000	17 Candidates Avg House: $777 Avg Sen: $1,150	Repubs: 50.2% Pres: 39.3% Incumb: 88.1%	
IBP Inc IBP-PAC IBP Inc PAC Dakota City, NE	 Occidental Petroleum Meat Processing	$45,250	54 Candidates Avg House: $583 Avg Sen: $1,270	Repubs: 72.7% Senate: 56.1% Incumb: 72.9%	
ICI Americas Inc ICI Americas PAC Wilmington, DE	 Pharmaceuticals†	$31,050	50 Candidates Avg House: $487 Avg Sen: $1,000	Dems: 53.3% House: 58.1% Incumb: 93.6%	
Idaho Power Company IDA-PAC PAC Boise, ID	 Electric Utility	$22,450	16 Candidates Avg House: $1,495 Avg Sen: $1,200	Repubs: 65.2% House: 73.3% Incumb: 73.3%	
Illinois Bell Telephone Illinois Bell Citizenship Responsibility Committee Chicago, IL	 Ameritech Phone Utilities	$53,700	22 Candidates Avg House: $2,485 Avg Sen: $1,500	Repubs: 59.8% House: 97.2% Incumb: 92.6%	
Illinois Central Railroad Illinois Central Railroad Good Government Fund (Formerly ICG Good Gov't Fund) Chicago, IL	 Railroads	$24,750	47 Candidates Avg House: $387 Avg Sen: $933	Dems: 65.9% House: 54.7% Incumb: 88.1%	

† PAC Sponsor has other major interests in addition to this primary category

Sponsor or Related Group/PAC Name	Affiliate	1987-88 Total	Where the money went...		
Illinois Tool Works Illinois Tool Works Inc PAC Chicago, IL	Indust Equip	$28,299	33 Candidates Avg House: $703 Avg Sen: $986	Repubs: 91.1% Senate: 62.7% Incumb: 62.0%	
IMC Fertilizer Inc International Minerals & Chemicals Corp PAC (IMC PAC) Northbrook, IL — Intl Minerals & Chemicals	Ag Chem	$24,550	50 Candidates Avg House: $472 Avg Sen: $533	Repubs: 62.9% House: 67.4% Incumb: 95.3%	
Independent Action Independent Action Inc Arlington, VA — Rep Morris Udall (D-Ariz)	Dem Leaders	$213,115	55 Candidates Avg House: $2,575 Avg Sen: $6,890	Dems: 100.0% Senate: 51.7% Incumb: 19.6%	
Independent Bakers Assn BAKEPAC - The PAC of the Independent Bakers Association Washington, DC	Food Processing	$35,250	56 Candidates Avg House: $317 Avg Sen: $933	Repubs: 70.3% Senate: 55.6% Incumb: 78.3%	
Independent Bankers Assn Independent Bankers - PAC Washington, DC	Commercial Banks	$177,290	185 Candidates Avg House: $723 Avg Sen: $2,005	Dems: 65.1% House: 61.3% Incumb: 90.0%	
Independent Coal Operators Assn Independent Coal Operators Assoc PAC (ICOA PAC) Bristol, VA	Coal Mining	$32,500	34 Candidates Avg House: $953 Avg Sen: $1,000	Dems: 86.2% House: 93.8% Incumb: 84.6%	
Independent Insurance Agents of America Independent Insurance Agents of America Inc PAC (INSURPAC) Washington, DC	Insurance	$612,167	340 Candidates Avg House: $1,361 Avg Sen: $4,137	Dems: 60.8% House: 63.4% Incumb: 77.8%	
Indiana Bell Telephone Indiana Bell Telephone Company, Incorporated PAC (INBELLPAC) Indianapolis, IN — Ameritech	Phone Utilities	$21,975	14 Candidates Avg House: $1,627 Avg Sen: $1,225	Repubs: 62.7% House: 88.9% Incumb: 82.7%	
Indiana Farm Bureau Indiana Farm Bureau Inc (ELECT PAC Inc) Indianapolis, IN	Farm Orgs	$37,675	10 Candidates Avg House: $3,630 Avg Sen: $5,000	Dems: 50.9% House: 86.7% Incumb: 100.0%	
Ingham County Democratic Party Ingham County Democratic Party Federal PAC Lansing, MI	Dem/Liberal	$22,350	7 Candidates Avg House: $4,370 Avg Sen: $500	Dems: 100.0% House: 97.8% Incumb: 86.1%	
Institute/Scrap Recycling Industries ISRI PAC (Formerly Institute of Scrap Iron & Steel PAC) Washington, DC	Recycling	$26,300	51 Candidates Avg House: $424 Avg Sen: $890	Dems: 60.8% House: 66.2% Incumb: 86.3%	
Insurance Assn of Connecticut Insurance Association of Connecticut PAC Hartford, CT	Insurance	$34,003	7 Candidates Avg House: $4,800 Avg Sen: $5,000	Repubs: 50.0% House: 70.6% Incumb: 79.4%	
Intel Corp Intel PAC Santa Clara, CA	Computers	$26,000	40 Candidates Avg House: $425 Avg Sen: $1,115	Repubs: 64.4% Senate: 55.7% Incumb: 66.3%	
Interlake Inc Interlake PAC Oak Brook, IL	Indust Equip†	$24,179	31 Candidates Avg House: $787 Avg Sen: $754	Repubs: 75.6% House: 78.2% Incumb: 89.9%	
International Assn for Financial Planning International Association for Financial Planning PAC Inc (IAFP-PAC) Atlanta, GA	Finance Svcs	$23,500	49 Candidates Avg House: $343 Avg Sen: $702	Dems: 50.4% Senate: 50.8% Incumb: 92.1%	
International Assn of Drilling Contractors International Association of Drilling Contractors PAC Houston, TX	Oilfield Svc	$47,750	41 Candidates Avg House: $583 Avg Sen: $2,285	Repubs: 65.7% Senate: 67.0% Incumb: 64.8%	
International Assn of Firefighters Int'l Assn of Firefighters Interested in Registration and Education PAC Washington, DC — Intl Assn of Firefighters	Public Safety	$151,975	172 Candidates Avg House: $794 Avg Sen: $1,261	Dems: 95.9% House: 71.6% Incumb: 62.3%	
Intl Brotherhood of Electrical Workers International Brotherhood of Electrical Workers Committee on Political Education Washington, DC — IBEW	IBEW	$1,194,690	347 Candidates Avg House: $3,064 Avg Sen: $6,023	Dems: 96.1% House: 76.9% Incumb: 54.8%	
International Chemical Workers Union International Chemical Workers Union Labor's Investment In Voter Education Akron, OH	Manuf Unions	$25,400	103 Candidates Avg House: $221 Avg Sen: $321	Dems: 100.4% House: 64.6% Incumb: 50.4%	

Sponsor or Related Group/PAC Name	Affiliate	1987-88 Total	Where the money went...		
International Council of Shopping Centers International Council of Shopping Centers Inc PAC (ICSC PAC) New York, NY		$74,000 Retail Sales	74 Candidates Avg House: $1,000 Avg Sen: $1,000	Dems: House: Incumb:	64.9% 73.0% 97.3%
International Longshoremen Assn Int'l Longshoremen's Association AFL-CIO Cmte on Political Education ILA-COPE New York, NY	Intl Longshoremen Assn	$198,640 Sea Trans Union	99 Candidates Avg House: $1,841 Avg Sen: $2,502	Dems: House: Incumb:	76.4% 70.5% 86.1%
International Mass Retail Assn International Mass Retail Association PAC (Formerly IMRAPAC) Secaucus, NJ		$32,000 Retail Sales	34 Candidates Avg House: $805 Avg Sen: $1,100	Repubs: Senate: Incumb:	79.6% 51.5% 85.9%
International Paper Company Voluntary Contributors for Better Government: Employees of Int'l Paper Company Washington, DC		$139,200 Paper Prod	80 Candidates Avg House: $1,150 Avg Sen: $3,697	Repubs: House: Incumb:	80.6% 51.3% 63.9%
International Sanitary Supply International Sanitary Supply Association PAC (ISSA Clean PAC) Lincolnwood, IL		$31,450 Hhold/Office Prod†	48 Candidates Avg House: $577 Avg Sen: $950	Repubs: House: Incumb:	62.6% 69.8% 95.2%
International Telecharge Inc International Telecharge Inc PAC (ITI-PAC) Washington, DC		$20,700 Long Distance	27 Candidates Avg House: $629 Avg Sen: $1,000	Dems: House: Incumb:	75.8% 51.7% 68.6%
Internorth Inc Enron PAC (Formerly HNG/Internorth PAC) Houston, TX		$117,383 Natural Gas	141 Candidates Avg House: $515 Avg Sen: $1,915	Repubs: Pres: Incumb:	50.5% 49.1% 87.9%
Interstate Natural Gas Assn Interstate Natural Gas Association of America PAC Washington, DC		$54,140 Natural Gas	74 Candidates Avg House: $527 Avg Sen: $1,132	Dems: Senate: Incumb:	70.9% 52.2% 87.7%
Investment Company Institute Investment Mgmt PAC of the Investment Company Institute (IMPAC) Washington, DC		$206,572 Securities Investment	97 Candidates Avg House: $1,669 Avg Sen: $3,610	Dems: House: Incumb:	78.1% 59.8% 97.1%
Investors Diversified Svcs IDS PAC Minneapolis, MN	American Express	$26,004 Securities Investment†	41 Candidates Avg House: $473 Avg Sen: $1,023	Dems: House: Incumb:	51.0% 52.8% 86.5%
Irell & Manella I & M PAC Los Angeles, CA	Lawyers	$27,500 	9 Candidates Avg House: $2,125 Avg Sen: $4,000	Repubs: Senate: Incumb:	74.6% 43.6% 72.7%
Ironworkers Union Ironworkers Political Action League Washington, DC	Ironworkers Union	$428,050 Constr Unions	180 Candidates Avg House: $2,044 Avg Sen: $3,750	Dems: House: Incumb:	94.5% 70.2% 54.2%
Irvine Company Irvine Company Employees' PAC, The Newport Beach, CA		$47,465 Real Estate Devel	33 Candidates Avg House: $1,392 Avg Sen: $1,269	Repubs: House: Incumb:	53.0% 55.7% 86.6%
Irving Bank Irving Bank Corporation Committee for Responsible Government New York, NY		$38,050 Commercial Banks	43 Candidates Avg House: $685 Avg Sen: $1,346	Dems: House: Incumb:	76.9% 54.0% 98.7%
ITEL Corp ITEL Corporation PAC Chicago, IL		$22,650 Railroad Svcs	14 Candidates Avg House: $1,741 Avg Sen: $1,600	Dems: Senate: Incumb:	76.8% 49.4% 95.6%
ITT Corp Corporate Citizenship Committee (ITT) New York, NY	ITT Corp	$110,900 Insurance†	170 Candidates Avg House: $527 Avg Sen: $1,258	Repubs: House: Incumb:	61.9% 67.1% 82.0%
IU International Corp IU-PAC, The PAC of IU International Corporation Philedelphia, PA		$20,154 Trucking†	21 Candidates Avg House: $761 Avg Sen: $1,625	Repubs: House: Incumb:	67.7% 52.9% 100.0%
J C Penney Company J C Penney Company PAC (Penney PAC) Dallas, TX		$237,668 Dept Stores†	264 Candidates Avg House: $752 Avg Sen: $1,448	Dems: House: Incumb:	62.0% 65.9% 92.3%
J G Boswell Company J.G. Boswell Company Employees' PAC Los Angeles, CA		$41,050 Cotton	39 Candidates Avg House: $691 Avg Sen: $1,777	Repubs: House: Incumb:	73.3% 48.8% 84.7%

† PAC Sponsor has other major interests in addition to this primary category

Sponsor or Related Group/PAC Name	Affiliate	1987-88 Total	Where the money went...			
J P Morgan & Company Morgan Companies PAC (MorganPAC) New York, NY	Commercial Banks†	$445,900	128 Candidates Avg House: $3,095 Avg Sen: $4,514	Dems: House: Incumb:	51.6% 64.6% 90.6%
J P Stevens & Company Good Government Committee of J P Stevens & Company Inc Greenville, SC	Textiles	$59,825	55 Candidates Avg House: $815 Avg Sen: $1,975	Repubs: House: Incumb:	69.7% 58.6% 79.5%
Jack Eckerd Corp Eckerd Committee for Responsible Government (ECKPAC) Clearwater, FL	Drug Stores	$36,600	56 Candidates Avg House: $480 Avg Sen: $1,363	Dems: House: Incumb:	54.2% 59.0% 64.1%
Jefferson-Pilot Corp Jefferson-Pilot Corp Federal Good Govt Cmte Jefferson-Pilot FEDPAC Greensboro, NC	Insurance†	$41,250	24 Candidates Avg House: $1,486 Avg Sen: $2,416	Dems: House: Incumb:	75.2% 64.8% 74.5%
Jerrico Inc Jerrico PAC (J-PAC) Lexington, KY	Restaurants	$40,550	45 Candidates Avg House: $661 Avg Sen: $1,432	Repubs: House: Incumb:	93.4% 50.6% 69.2%
JMB Realty Corp JMB Realty Corporation PAC/JMB PAC Chicago, IL	Real Estate Devel	$23,000	11 Candidates Avg House: $1,300 Avg Sen: $2,625	Dems: Senate: Incumb:	93.5% 45.7% 91.3%
John Hancock Financial Service John Hancock Financial Services PAC Boston, MA	Insurance†	$41,950	47 Candidates Avg House: $757 Avg Sen: $1,180	Dems: House: Incumb:	66.7% 57.8% 91.5%
Johnson & Gibbs Fund for Quality In Government Dallas, TX	Lawyers	$32,500	18 Candidates Avg House: $1,156 Avg Sen: $3,250	Dems: Senate: Incumb:	59.2% 40.0% 98.5%
Johnson & Johnson Johnson & Johnson Employees' Good Government Fund New Brunswick, NJ	Health Care Prod†	$75,950	80 Candidates Avg House: $694 Avg Sen: $1,664	Repubs: House: Incumb:	50.6% 54.0% 94.9%
Joint Action Cmte for Political Affairs Joint Action Committee for Political Affairs Highland Park, IL	Pro-Israel	$236,450	149 Candidates Avg House: $1,052 Avg Sen: $4,115	Dems: House: Incumb:	83.1% 54.7% 68.5%
Jones, Day, Reavis & Pogue Jones, Day, Reavis & Pogue Good Government Fund Cleveland, OH	Lawyers†	$97,294	110 Candidates Avg House: $552 Avg Sen: $1,596	Repubs: Senate: Incumb:	55.1% 57.4% 71.2%
Joseph E Seagram & Sons Joseph E Seagram & Sons, Inc PAC New York, NY	Wine/Liquor†	$173,150	153 Candidates Avg House: $755 Avg Sen: $2,741	Dems: House: Incumb:	75.1% 54.1% 83.5%
JSJ Corp JSJ Corporation PAC Grand Haven, MI	Indust Equip	$27,500	23 Candidates Avg House: $970 Avg Sen: $1,833	Repubs: House: Incumb:	98.1% 60.0% 61.8%
K Mart Corporation PAC K Mart Corporation PAC Troy, MI	Dept Stores	$81,250	228 Candidates Avg House: $307 Avg Sen: $694	Repubs: House: Incumb:	81.4% 75.7% 81.0%
Kaman Corp Kaman Corporation Good Government Fund Bloomfield, CT	Defense Electronics†	$37,734	37 Candidates Avg House: $1,063 Avg Sen: $889	Dems: House: Incumb:	68.9% 84.5% 99.3%
Kansas City Southern Kansas City Southern Employees PAC Kansas City, MO	Railroads†	$113,070	122 Candidates Avg House: $693 Avg Sen: $1,529	Dems: House: Incumb:	61.7% 54.0% 90.4%
Kellogg Company Kellogg Better Government Committee Battle Creek, MI	Food Processing	$93,989	99 Candidates Avg House: $730 Avg Sen: $1,672	Dems: House: Incumb:	50.9% 59.1% 84.0%
Kelso & Company Kelso PAC Washington, DC	Investment Banking	$24,650	38 Candidates Avg House: $471 Avg Sen: $1,357	Dems: House: Incumb:	79.9% 57.4% 81.7%
Kemper Insurance Kemper Campaign Fund Long Grove, IL	Insurance	$41,775	66 Candidates Avg House: $559 Avg Sen: $1,000	Repubs: House: Incumb:	71.7% 73.7% 86.2%

Sponsor or Related Group/PAC Name	Affiliate	1987-88 Total	Where the money went...		
Kerr-McGee Kerr-McGee Corporation PAC Oklahoma City, OK		$35,750 Oil Refining/Marketing†	52 Candidates Avg House: $492 Avg Sen: $1,055	Repubs: 68.5% Senate: 53.1% Incumb: 74.8%	
Kidder, Peabody Nonpartisan Political Support Committee for Kidder, Peabody Employees New York, NY	General Electric	$52,700 Securities Investment	37 Candidates Avg House: $1,418 Avg Sen: $1,400	Dems: 63.9% Senate: 53.1% Incumb: 72.5%	
KidsPAC KidsPAC Cambridge, MA		$287,400 Health/Welfare	154 Candidates Avg House: $1,046 Avg Sen: $5,903	Dems: 90.6% Senate: 53.4% Incumb: 72.0%	
Kimberly-Clark Kimberly-Clark Good Government Committee Neenah, WI		$36,050 Paper Prod	54 Candidates Avg House: $401 Avg Sen: $1,300	Repubs: 81.5% Senate: 57.7% Incumb: 63.1%	
King & Spalding King & Spalding Nonpartisan Committee for Good Government Atlanta, GA		$37,399 Lawyers	42 Candidates Avg House: $704 Avg Sen: $1,138	Dems: 79.7% Senate: 54.8% Incumb: 89.2%	
Kirkland & Ellis Kirkland & Ellis PAC (Formerly WSS PAC) Chicago, IL		$56,384 Lawyers†	53 Candidates Avg House: $637 Avg Sen: $1,325	Dems: 84.7% Senate: 47.0% Incumb: 92.2%	
Kirkpatrick & Lockhart Kirkpatrick & Lockhart PAC Washington, DC		$69,071 Lawyers†	76 Candidates Avg House: $732 Avg Sen: $1,340	Dems: 61.6% House: 57.3% Incumb: 91.4%	
Kraft Inc Kraft, Inc PAC (Formerly Dart & Kraft Inc PAC) Glenview, IL	Philip Morris	$46,550 Food Processing	54 Candidates Avg House: $615 Avg Sen: $1,250	Repubs: 67.5% Senate: 56.4% Incumb: 77.4%	
Kroger Company Kroger Better Government Committee/ KROPAC Cincinnati, OH		$42,100 Food Stores	51 Candidates Avg House: $545 Avg Sen: $1,845	Repubs: 52.9% House: 51.8% Incumb: 63.2%	
Kutak, Rock & Campbell Kutak Rock & Campbell PAC Washington, DC		$93,000 Lawyers†	78 Candidates Avg House: $687 Avg Sen: $1,725	Dems: 67.0% Senate: 57.5% Incumb: 77.4%	
L. M. Berry & Company L. M. Berry and Company PAC Dayton, OH	BellSouth	$46,500 Direct Mail Advert†	61 Candidates Avg House: $369 Avg Sen: $1,666	Repubs: 98.4% Senate: 64.5% Incumb: 58.1%	
Laborers' Political League Laborers' Political League Washington, DC	Laborers Union	$685,925 Constr Unions	331 Candidates Avg House: $1,651 Avg Sen: $4,495	Dems: 93.3% House: 67.2% Incumb: 67.8%	
Laborers' Western Political League Laborers' Western Political League Sacramento, CA	Laborers Union	$190,850 Constr Unions	46 Candidates Avg House: $3,606 Avg Sen: $8,600	Dems: 97.9% House: 77.5% Incumb: 61.2%	
Ladies Garment Workers Union International Ladies Garment Workers Union Campaign Commmittee New York, NY		$393,929 Manuf Unions	325 Candidates Avg House: $872 Avg Sen: $3,055	Dems: 92.7% House: 61.6% Incumb: 75.3%	
Land O'Lakes Inc Land O'Lakes Inc PAC Minneapolis, MN		$95,000 Dairy	60 Candidates Avg House: $1,462 Avg Sen: $1,825	Dems: 55.7% House: 61.6% Incumb: 87.9%	
Leadership - USA Leadership - USA Washington, DC	Sen James McClure (R-Idaho)	$34,127 Repub Leaders	14 Candidates Avg House: $1,500 Avg Sen: $2,509	Repubs: 100.0% Senate: 95.6% Incumb: 20.5%	
League for Effective Government League for Effective Government Houston, TX	Lidell, Sapp	$21,500 Lawyers	5 Candidates Avg House: $0 Avg Sen: $3,833	Repubs: 100.0% Senate: 53.5% Incumb: 100.0%	
League of Conservation Voters League of Conservation Voters Washington, DC		$89,431 Environmental	41 Candidates Avg House: $1,778 Avg Sen: $3,048	Dems: 74.4% House: 55.7% Incumb: 36.0%	
Liberty Mutual Insurance Liberty Mutual Insurance Company PAC Boston, MA		$41,050 Insurance	37 Candidates Avg House: $729 Avg Sen: $1,666	Repubs: 80.5% Senate: 60.9% Incumb: 58.6%	

† PAC Sponsor has other major interests in addition to this primary category

Sponsor or Related Group/PAC Name	Affiliate	1987-88 Total	Where the money went...			
Lincoln National Corp Lincoln National Corporation PAC Fort Wayne, IN	Lincoln National Insurance	$57,350	50 Candidates Avg House: $799 Avg Sen: $1,643	Dems: 51.3% Senate: 51.6% Incumb: 91.9%
Litton Industries Litton Industries Inc Employees Political Assistance Committee (LEPAC) Beverly Hills, CA	Naval Ships†	$217,975	164 Candidates Avg House: $1,064 Avg Sen: $2,483	Repubs: 65.2% House: 64.4% Incumb: 90.3%
Lockheed Corp Lockheed Employees PAC Burbank, CA	Air Defense†	$441,834	281 Candidates Avg House: $1,369 Avg Sen: $2,436	Repubs: 52.3% House: 69.8% Incumb: 87.7%
Loews Corp/Lorillard Loews Corporation/Lorillard Public Affairs Committee (LOPAC) New York, NY	Insurance†	$22,250	52 Candidates Avg House: $343 Avg Sen: $833	Dems: 50.6% House: 66.3% Incumb: 100.0%
Long Island Aerospace PAC Long Island Aerospace Political Committee Federal Baldwin, NY	Aerospace Equip†	$45,738	29 Candidates Avg House: $1,036 Avg Sen: $2,916	Dems: 63.6% House: 45.3% Incumb: 96.7%
Longshoremen/Warehousemen Union International Longshoremen's & Warehousemen's Union - Political Action Fund San Francisco, CA	Sea Trans Union	$89,472	60 Candidates Avg House: $1,324 Avg Sen: $2,250	Dems: 100.0% House: 69.6% Incumb: 41.3%
Loral Corp Civic Action Fund - Loral Systems Group (Formerly Goodyear Aerospace Corp PAC) Akron, OH	Defense Electronics†	$46,450	60 Candidates Avg House: $631 Avg Sen: $1,350	Dems: 69.4% House: 66.6% Incumb: 99.4%
Louisiana for American Security Louisiana for American Security PAC Baton Rouge, LA	Pro-Israel	$33,750	16 Candidates Avg House: $2,613 Avg Sen: $1,000	Repubs: 58.5% House: 85.2% Incumb: 71.9%
Louisiana Land & Exploration Louisiana Land and Exploration Company PAC (LL&E-PAC); The New Orleans, LA	Oilfield Svc†	$30,750	40 Candidates Avg House: $586 Avg Sen: $1,066	Repubs: 55.2% Senate: 52.0% Incumb: 78.9%
Louisiana Power & Light Louisiana Employees Cmte on Pol Action of La. Power & Light Co (LECOPA-LP&L) New Orleans, LA	Middle South Utilities Electric Utility	$27,250	47 Candidates Avg House: $547 Avg Sen: $700	Dems: 50.6% House: 74.3% Incumb: 88.6%
Louisiana-Pacific Corp Louisiana-Pacific Corp Federal PAC Portland, OR	Forest Prod	$33,878	25 Candidates Avg House: $1,301 Avg Sen: $1,468	Repubs: 71.8% House: 65.3% Incumb: 74.9%
LTV Aerospace & Defense Company LTV Aerospace and Defense Company Active Citizenship Campaign Dallas, TX	LTV Corp Air Defense†	$173,284	147 Candidates Avg House: $1,013 Avg Sen: $1,635	Dems: 64.1% House: 66.1% Incumb: 97.7%
LTV Steel LTV Steel Active Citizenship Campaign Cleveland, OH	LTV Corp Steel Mfrs	$41,850	47 Candidates Avg House: $552 Avg Sen: $2,000	Dems: 51.7% Senate: 47.8% Incumb: 87.8%
Lykes Bros Steamship Company Lykes Bros Steamship Company Inc Active Citizenship Campaign New Orleans, LA	Sea Transport	$27,612	43 Candidates Avg House: $613 Avg Sen: $750	Dems: 68.1% House: 75.6% Incumb: 92.8%
Machinists/Aerospace Local #837 Aerospace District Lodge 837-IAMAW-PAC Hazelwood, MO	Machinists/Aerospace Workers Manuf Unions	$32,000	10 Candidates Avg House: $3,277 Avg Sen: $2,500	Dems: 100.0% House: 92.2% Incumb: 45.3%
Machinists/Aerospace Workers Union Machinists Non-Partisan Political League Washington, DC	Machinists/Aerospace Workers Manuf Unions	$1,492,780	351 Candidates Avg House: $3,906 Avg Sen: $7,008	Dems: 98.9% House: 80.3% Incumb: 57.9%
Maintenance of Way Employees Maintenance of Way Political League Detroit, MI	Railroad Unions	$138,127	165 Candidates Avg House: $572 Avg Sen: $2,120	Dems: 98.0% House: 56.7% Incumb: 75.8%
Majority Congress Committee Majority Congress Committee Washington, DC	Rep Jim Wright (D-Tex) Dem Leaders	$447,220	104 Candidates Avg House: $4,300 Avg Senate: $0	Dems: 100.0% House: 100.0% Incumb: 52.6%
Malone & Hyde Inc Malone & Hyde Committee for Responsible Government, The Memphis, TN	Malone & Hyde Food Wholesale†	$110,750	57 Candidates Avg House: $1,550 Avg Sen: $3,100	Repubs: 65.9% House: 63.0% Incumb: 60.7%

Sponsor or Related Group/PAC Name	Affiliate	1987-88 Total	Where the money went...		
Manatt, Phelps, Rothenberg & Tunney Golden State PAC (Formerly Manatt, Phelps, Rothenberg & Tunney PAC) Los Angeles, CA	Lawyers	$60,600	100 Candidates Avg House: $460 Avg Sen: $1,154	Dems: 61.1% House: 60.0% Incumb: 96.6%	
Manor Healthcare Corp Manor Healthcare Federal PAC (Formerly Four Seasons Fed PAC) Silver Spring, MD	Nursing Homes	$24,000	22 Candidates Avg House: $892 Avg Sen: $1,437	Dems: 68.8% House: 52.1% Incumb: 97.9%	
Mantech International Mantech International Corp PAC Alexandria, VA	Defense Svcs†	$60,220	41 Candidates Avg House: $1,360 Avg Sen: $1,656	Repubs: 52.0% House: 58.7% Incumb: 63.4%	
Manufactured Housing Institute Manufactured Housing Institute PAC (MHI PAC) Arlington, VA	Mobile Homes	$47,749	48 Candidates Avg House: $844 Avg Sen: $1,500	Repubs: 56.3% House: 65.4% Incumb: 96.9%	
Manufacturers Hanover Manufacturers Hanover Association for Responsible Government Fund New York, NY	Commercial Banks	$95,875	96 Candidates Avg House: $554 Avg Sen: $2,128	Dems: 57.5% Senate: 57.7% Incumb: 92.0%	
Manville Corp Manville Corporation PAC Washington, DC	Bldg Materials†	$159,760	112 Candidates Avg House: $1,040 Avg Sen: $2,481	Repubs: 56.0% House: 53.4% Incumb: 82.5%	
Mapco Inc Mapco Inc PAC Tulsa, OK	Oil Refining/Marketing†	$86,460	106 Candidates Avg House: $463 Avg Sen: $2,159	Repubs: 88.4% Senate: 54.9% Incumb: 64.6%	
Marathon Oil Marathon Oil Company Employees Political Action Commttee (MEPAC) Findlay, OH	USX Corp — Oil & Gas Prod	$29,400	36 Candidates Avg House: $560 Avg Sen: $1,712	Repubs: 65.3% House: 53.4% Incumb: 78.1%	
Marine Engineers District 2 Maritime Officers District 2 Marine Engineers Beneficial Assn-Associated Maritime Officers Brooklyn, NY	Marine Engineers Union — Sea Trans Union	$720,771	289 Candidates Avg House: $2,487 Avg Sen: $2,555	Dems: 65.2% House: 89.7% Incumb: 89.1%	
Marine Engineers District 2 Retirees District 2 Marine Engineers Beneficial Assn-Assoc Maritime Officers, Retirees Brooklyn, NY	Marine Engineers Union — Sea Trans Union	$106,500	50 Candidates Avg House: $2,032 Avg Sen: $3,250	Repubs: 69.5% House: 87.8% Incumb: 89.7%	
Marine Engineers Radio Officers Dist #3 Radio Officers Union - District No 3 (ROU PAC) Panama City Beach, FL	Marine Engineers Union — Sea Trans Union	$43,300	44 Candidates Avg House: $970 Avg Sen: $1,043	Dems: 89.1% House: 80.7% Incumb: 95.7%	
Marine Engineers Union Marine Engineers' Beneficial Assn Pol Action Fund (MEBA Political Action Fund) Washington, DC	Marine Engineers Union — Sea Trans Union	$560,200	187 Candidates Avg House: $2,797 Avg Sen: $3,629	Dems: 78.9% House: 71.9% Incumb: 79.8%	
Marine Midland Banks Marine Midland Banks Inc Buffalo, NY	Commercial Banks	$104,425	89 Candidates Avg House: $971 Avg Sen: $1,788	Repubs: 58.6% House: 62.3% Incumb: 82.4%	
Marion Laboratories Marion Laboratories Inc PAC (MLPAC) Kansas City, MO	Dow Chemical — Pharmaceuticals	$45,900	136 Candidates Avg House: $297 Avg Sen: $500	Dems: 56.6% House: 70.6% Incumb: 89.3%	
Maritime Union of America NMU Political & Legislative Organization on Watch Jersey City, NJ	Sea Trans Union	$37,300	60 Candidates Avg House: $579 Avg Sen: $863	Dems: 75.7% House: 74.5% Incumb: 96.5%	
Marriott Corp Marriott PAC Washington, DC	Hotel/Motel†	$110,750	123 Candidates Avg House: $696 Avg Sen: $1,950	Repubs: 63.8% House: 64.8% Incumb: 84.7%	
Martin Marietta Corp Martin Marietta Corporation PAC Bethesda, MD	Air Defense†	$253,404	268 Candidates Avg House: $775 Avg Sen: $1,837	Repubs: 50.5% House: 68.8% Incumb: 87.5%	
Maryland Assn for Concerned Citizens Maryland Association for Concerned Citizens PAC Pikesville, MD	Pro-Israel	$60,500	22 Candidates Avg House: $954 Avg Sen: $4,545	Dems: 71.9% Senate: 82.6% Incumb: 84.3%	
Maryland Medical Assn Maryland Medical PAC Baltimore, MD	American Medical Assn — Doctors	$20,000	8 Candidates Avg House: $2,571 Avg Sen: $2,000	Dems: 75.0% House: 90.0% Incumb: 100.0%	

† PAC Sponsor has other major interests in addition to this primary category

Sponsor / PAC	Affiliate	1987-88 Total	Candidates / Averages	Party / Chamber / Incumbent
Massachusetts Mutual Life Insurance Massachusetts Mutual Life Insurance Company PAC Springfield, MA	Life Insurance	$163,265	101 Candidates Avg House: $1,385 Avg Sen: $2,010	Dems: 73.6% House: 52.6% Incumb: 90.5%
Masters Mates & Pilots/Pensioners Fund Pensioners Action Fund Baltimore, MD Masters, Mates & Pilots	Sea Trans Union	$69,000	19 Candidates Avg House: $3,000 Avg Sen: $5,000	Dems: 73.9% House: 56.5% Incumb: 62.3%
Masters, Mates & Pilots Union Masters, Mates and Pilots Political Contribution Fund Linthicum Heights, MD Masters, Mates & Pilots	Sea Trans Union	$147,448	101 Candidates Avg House: $1,380 Avg Sen: $1,852	Dems: 73.5% House: 78.6% Incumb: 91.7%
Matson Navigation Matson Federal Election Committee San Francisco, CA	Sea Transport	$47,300	36 Candidates Avg House: $1,241 Avg Sen: $1,568	Repubs: 54.8% House: 73.5% Incumb: 93.6%
Maxus Energy Corp Maxus Energy Corporation Employees' PAC Dallas, TX	Oil & Gas Prod	$23,600	32 Candidates Avg House: $644 Avg Sen: $1,462	Repubs: 61.6% House: 73.7% Incumb: 83.5%
May Department Stores May Department Stores Company PAC (MayPAC) St Louis, MO	Dept Stores	$95,650	189 Candidates Avg House: $296 Avg Sen: $2,021	Repubs: 70.2% House: 51.4% Incumb: 82.2%
Maytag Company Maytag Good Government Committee Newton, IA	Appliance Mfrs	$83,500	73 Candidates Avg House: $925 Avg Sen: $1,763	Repubs: 94.6% House: 59.9% Incumb: 57.2%
MBank MBank PAC Houston, TX	Commercial Banks	$60,600	36 Candidates Avg House: $1,818 Avg Sen: $1,218	Dems: 53.6% House: 48.0% Incumb: 92.2%
MCA Inc MCA PAC Universal City, CA	Movies†	$139,211	103 Candidates Avg House: $965 Avg Sen: $2,205	Dems: 87.2% Senate: 50.6% Incumb: 84.9%
McDermott Inc Better Government Fund of McDermott Incorporated New Orleans, LA McDermott Inc	Power Plant Equip†	$22,350	25 Candidates Avg House: $785 Avg Sen: $1,125	Dems: 59.3% House: 59.7% Incumb: 86.6%
McDonald's Corp McDonald's Corporation PAC Oak Brook, IL	Restaurants	$230,100	218 Candidates Avg House: $630 Avg Sen: $4,196	Repubs: 67.5% House: 52.6% Incumb: 73.7%
McDonnell Douglas McDonnell Douglas Good Government Fund St Louis, MO McDonnell Douglas	Air Defense†	$256,650	191 Candidates Avg House: $1,128 Avg Sen: $2,039	Dems: 53.1% House: 65.1% Incumb: 93.8%
McDonnell Douglas Helicopter McDonnell Douglas Helicopter Company PAC San Francisco, CA McDonnell Douglas	Air Defense†	$64,150	89 Candidates Avg House: $618 Avg Sen: $1,152	Dems: 68.3% House: 69.4% Incumb: 97.9%
MCI Telecommunications MCI Telecommunications PAC (MCI PAC) Washington, DC	Long Distance	$56,433	77 Candidates Avg House: $463 Avg Sen: $1,405	Dems: 78.9% Senate: 54.8% Incumb: 92.8%
McKesson Corp McKesson Corp Employees Political Fund (Formerly Foremost-McKesson Inc Empl Pol Fund) San Francisco, CA	Pharmaceuticals†	$32,000	35 Candidates Avg House: $604 Avg Sen: $1,590	Repubs: 65.6% Senate: 54.6% Incumb: 78.1%
McLane Company McLane Company Inc. Federal PAC Temple, TX	Food Stores	$27,000	23 Candidates Avg House: $846 Avg Sen: $857	Repubs: 70.3% House: 40.7% Incumb: 79.6%
Mead Corp Mead Corporation Effective Citizenship Fund Dayton, OH	Paper Prod†	$68,340	71 Candidates Avg House: $670 Avg Sen: $1,597	Repubs: 63.8% Senate: 51.4% Incumb: 72.8%
Mechanical Contractors Assn of America Mechanical Contractors-PAC (MC-PAC) Bethesda, MD	Plumb/AirCon	$25,075	34 Candidates Avg House: $620 Avg Sen: $1,063	Repubs: 73.2% House: 61.8% Incumb: 70.1%
Mellon Bank Bipartisan PAC Mellon Bank Corporation (BIPAC/MBC) Pittsburgh, PA	Commercial Banks	$49,814	67 Candidates Avg House: $592 Avg Sen: $1,450	Repubs: 52.4% House: 63.1% Incumb: 97.5%

Sponsor or Related Group/PAC Name	Affiliate	1987-88 Total	Where the money went...			

Merck & Company
Merck & Company, Inc PAC (Merck PAC)
Rahway, NJ — Pharmaceuticals†
$63,850

89 Candidates	Repubs:	57.2%
Avg House: $557	House:	58.5%
Avg Sen: $1,204	Incumb:	71.8%

Mercury Savings & Loan
Mercury Savings PAC; The
Huntington Beach, CA — Savings Banks
$42,750

24 Candidates	Dems:	78.8%
Avg House: $1,596	House:	56.0%
Avg Sen: $2,287	Incumb:	83.6%

Meridian Bancorp
Meridian Bancorp Inc PAC
Reading, PA — Commercial Banks
$23,842

37 Candidates	Repubs:	82.1%
Avg House: $495	House:	54.0%
Avg Sen: $996	Incumb:	96.9%

Merrill Lynch
Merrill Lynch PAC
Washington, DC — Merrill Lynch — Securities Investment†
$138,007

146 Candidates	Repubs:	55.2%
Avg House: $519	Senate:	59.6%
Avg Sen: $2,056	Incumb:	82.4%

Mesa PAC II
Mesa PAC II
Amarillo, TX — Oil & Gas Prod
$70,150

41 Candidates	Repubs:	76.9%
Avg House: $1,126	Senate:	62.0%
Avg Sen: $2,416	Incumb:	67.9%

Metropolitan Life Insurance
Metropolitan Employees' Political Participation Fund A
New York, NY — Metropolitan Life — Life Insurance†
$245,595

158 Candidates	Dems:	69.0%
Avg House: $1,252	House:	53.0%
Avg Sen: $2,110	Incumb:	90.6%

Michigan Bell Telephone
Michigan Bell Telephone Company PAC (MICHBELLPAC)
Detroit, MI — Ameritech — Phone Utilities
$74,632

34 Candidates	Repubs:	53.4%
Avg House: $2,428	House:	91.1%
Avg Sen: $1,413	Incumb:	98.6%

Michigan Consolidated Gas
Michigan Consolidated Gas Company Federal PAC (MICHCON FED PAC)
Detroit, MI — Natural Gas
$46,660

55 Candidates	Dems:	74.7%
Avg House: $752	House:	74.2%
Avg Sen: $1,378	Incumb:	86.5%

Michigan Credit Union League
Michigan Credit Union League Legislative Action Fund
Detroit, MI — Credit Union National Assn — Credit Unions
$24,055

19 Candidates	Dems:	64.7%
Avg House: $1,141	House:	85.5%
Avg Sen: $3,500	Incumb:	100.0%

Mid Manhattan PAC
Mid Manhattan PAC (MID PAC)
New York, NY — Pro-Israel
$80,450

68 Candidates	Dems:	79.2%
Avg House: $488	Senate:	70.8%
Avg Sen: $2,850	Incumb:	64.6%

Mid-American Dairymen
Mid-American Dairymen Inc Agricultural & Dairy Educational Political Trust Adept
Springfield, MO — Dairy
$458,650

278 Candidates	Dems:	66.2%
Avg House: $1,378	House:	72.2%
Avg Sen: $3,344	Incumb:	80.8%

Milk Industry Foundation
Ice Cream & Milk PAC, PAC of the Int'l Ice Cream Assn & Milk Industry Foundation
Washington, DC — Dairy
$75,250

63 Candidates	Repubs:	65.9%
Avg House: $841	Senate:	51.3%
Avg Sen: $1,754	Incumb:	87.2%

Milk Marketing Inc
Milk Marketing Inc PAC
Strongsville, OH — Dairy
$26,150

43 Candidates	Dems:	59.5%
Avg House: $605	House:	88.0%
Avg Sen: $630	Incumb:	85.7%

Minn-Dak Farmers Co-op
Minn-Dak Farmers Cooperative PAC (MDFPAC)
Wahpeton, ND — Sugar
$42,450

71 Candidates	Dems:	53.7%
Avg House: $467	House:	55.0%
Avg Sen: $909	Incumb:	91.5%

Minnesota Education Assn
Independent Minnesota PAC for Education Minnesota Education Assn
St Paul, MN — National Education Assn — Teachers Union
$21,650

9 Candidates	Dems:	100.0%
Avg House: $2,081	House:	76.9%
Avg Sen: $5,000	Incumb:	30.3%

Minnesota Mining & Manufacturing (3M)
Minnesota Mining & Manufacturing Company PAC (3M PAC)
St. Paul, MN — Indust Equip†
$85,850

75 Candidates	Repubs:	78.3%
Avg House: $685	Senate:	53.7%
Avg Sen: $2,711	Incumb:	66.2%

MNC Fianancial Inc
MNC Financial PAC-Federal Fund (Formerly Maryland National Corp PAC)
Baltimore, MD — Commercial Banks
$28,075

28 Candidates	Repubs:	55.5%
Avg House: $1,119	House:	67.8%
Avg Sen: $605	Incumb:	92.0%

Mobil Oil
Mobil Oil Corporation PAC (Mobil PAC)
New York, NY — Oil & Gas Prod†
$242,550

251 Candidates	Repubs:	80.4%
Avg House: $674	House:	62.3%
Avg Sen: $3,388	Incumb:	76.6%

Monsanto Company
Monsanto Citizenship Fund
St. Louis, MO — Monsanto — Chemicals†
$98,650

109 Candidates	Repubs:	72.0%
Avg House: $575	House:	48.4%
Avg Sen: $1,815	Incumb:	83.4%

† PAC Sponsor has other major interests in addition to this primary category

Sponsor or Related Group/PAC Name	Affiliate	1987-88 Total	Candidates	Party	House/Senate	Incumb
Montgomery Ward Montgomery Ward & Company Incorporated PAC (WardPAC) Chicago, IL	Dept Stores	$37,250	46 Candidates Avg House: $701 Avg Sen: $1,033	Dems: 53.2% House: 58.4% Incumb: 80.4%		
MOPAC MOPAC Troy, MI	Pro-Israel	$96,000	40 Candidates Avg House: $1,815 Avg Sen: $2,928	Dems: 94.8% Senate: 64.0% Incumb: 55.2%		
Morgan Stanley & Company Morgan Stanley Better Government Fund New York, NY	Morgan Stanley / Investment Banking†	$206,000	123 Candidates Avg House: $1,284 Avg Sen: $3,000	Dems: 58.0% House: 59.2% Incumb: 96.8%		
Morrison Inc Morrison's PAC Mobile, AL	Restaurants†	$55,300	87 Candidates Avg House: $488 Avg Sen: $1,070	Repubs: 87.1% House: 57.4% Incumb: 73.9%		
Morrison-Knudsen Morrison-Knudsen PAC Boise, ID	Heavy Construction†	$39,600	31 Candidates Avg House: $975 Avg Sen: $2,314	Repubs: 88.3% House: 59.1% Incumb: 84.6%		
Mortgage Bankers Assn of America Mortgage Bankers Association of America PAC Washington, DC	Mortgage Bank	$309,858	312 Candidates Avg House: $746 Avg Sen: $2,347	Dems: 58.8% House: 63.6% Incumb: 91.7%		
Mortgage Insurance Companies of America Mortgage Insurance PAC Washington, DC	Mortgage Insurance	$40,050	48 Candidates Avg House: $607 Avg Sen: $1,819	Dems: 57.1% House: 59.1% Incumb: 100.0%		
Morton Building Inc Morton Building Inc PAC Morton, IL	Heavy Construction	$20,000	42 Candidates Avg House: $500 Avg Sen: $333	Repubs: 100.0% House: 90.0% Incumb: 97.5%		
Morton Thiokol Morton Thiokol PAC Chicago, IL	Air Defense†	$65,550	84 Candidates Avg House: $714 Avg Sen: $952	Repubs: 59.8% House: 66.5% Incumb: 91.9%		
Motion Picture Assn of America Motion Picture Association of America Inc PAC Washington, DC	Movies	$89,962	111 Candidates Avg House: $668 Avg Sen: $1,180	Dems: 76.2% House: 57.9% Incumb: 93.1%		
Motorola Inc Motorola Employees Good Government Committee Washington, DC	Electronics†	$131,578	128 Candidates Avg House: $661 Avg Sen: $2,128	Repubs: 61.4% House: 52.6% Incumb: 82.6%		
Mountain Bell Mountain Bell PAC Denver, CO	US West / Phone Utilities	$90,140	30 Candidates Avg House: $3,271 Avg Sen: $2,128	Repubs: 68.1% House: 83.5% Incumb: 91.2%		
MSU System Services MSU System Services Inc New Orleans, LA	Middle South Utilities / Gas/Electric†	$51,100	96 Candidates Avg House: $461 Avg Sen: $743	Repubs: 52.3% House: 65.1% Incumb: 83.1%		
Multi-Issue PAC Multi-Issue PAC (MI-PAC) Highland Park, IL	Pro-Israel	$107,000	58 Candidates Avg House: $689 Avg Sen: $3,880	Dems: 97.9% Senate: 76.1% Incumb: 49.1%		
Municipal Elections Cmte of Los Angeles MECLA: Municipal Elections Cmte of Los Angeles Los Angeles, CA	Gay/Lesbian Rights†	$21,500	9 Candidates Avg House: $2,142 Avg Sen: $3,250	Dems: 86.0% House: 69.8% Incumb: 4.7%		
Municipal Securities Industry PAC Municipal Securities Industry PAC Washington, DC	Securities Industry Assn / Securities	$47,000	103 Candidates Avg House: $838 Avg Sen: $1,339	Dems: 68.9% House: 62.6% Incumb: 98.0%		
Mutual Benefit Life Insurance Mutual Benefit Life Federal PAC Newark, NJ	Insurance	$37,350	25 Candidates Avg House: $921 Avg Sen: $3,308	Dems: 76.6% Senate: 53.1% Incumb: 96.3%		
Mutual Life Insurance of New York Mutual Life Insurance Company of New York MONY PAC New York, NY	Insurance	$47,957	38 Candidates Avg House: $1,206 Avg Sen: $1,357	Dems: 69.9% House: 60.4% Incumb: 88.5%		
Mutual of Omaha Mutual of Omaha Companies PAC (IMPAC) Omaha, NE	Mutual of Omaha / Insurance	$48,462	59 Candidates Avg House: $509 Avg Sen: $1,432	Repubs: 70.7% Senate: 50.3% Incumb: 63.9%		

Sponsor or Related Group/PAC Name	Affiliate	1987-88 Total	Where the money went...		
Mutual of Omaha/General Agents Assn General Agents Association PAC (COMPAC) Winston-Salem, NC	Mutual of Omaha Insurance	$58,100	88 Candidates Avg House: $519 Avg Sen: $990	Repubs: 89.2% House: 59.0% Incumb: 65.9%	
Nabisco Brands Inc Nabisco Brands, Inc Program for Active Citizenship (NABPAC) East Hanover, NJ	Food Processing	$103,350	127 Candidates Avg House: $641 Avg Sen: $1,929	Repubs: 60.5% House: 68.3% Incumb: 82.3%	
Nalco Chemical Company Nalco Chemical Company PAC Naperville, IL	Chemicals	$24,250	28 Candidates Avg House: $723 Avg Sen: $1,187	Repubs: 78.3% House: 56.7% Incumb: 74.2%	
National Abortion Rghts Action League National Abortion Rights Action League - PAC (NARAL-PAC) Washington, DC	Pro-Choice	$264,924	117 Candidates Avg House: $1,936 Avg Sen: $4,069	Dems: 86.3% House: 72.4% Incumb: 56.9%	
National Action Committee (Dave Evans) National Action Committee (Formerly Dave Evans for Congress Committee) Arlington, VA	Lobbyists	$21,200	33 Candidates Avg House: $632 Avg Sen: $700	Dems: 84.4% House: 83.5% Incumb: 93.9%	
National Action Committee (NACPAC) National Action Committee - NACPAC Coconut Grove, FL	Pro-Israel	$104,000	42 Candidates Avg House: $1,480 Avg Sen: $4,093	Dems: 78.8% Senate: 62.9% Incumb: 68.5%	
National Aggregates Assn National Aggregates Association PAC (SANDPAC) (Formerly National Sand & Gravel PAC) Silver Spring, MD	Stone/Concrete	$24,404	75 Candidates Avg House: $264 Avg Sen: $548	Repubs: 90.7% House: 64.0% Incumb: 63.0%	
National Albanian American PAC National Albanian American PAC Palm Beach Gardens, FL	Ethnic/Minority	$25,500	14 Candidates Avg House: $2,500 Avg Sen: $1,142	Repubs: 76.4% House: 68.6% Incumb: 92.2%	
National Alliance Postal/Federal Employees National Alliance for Political Action (NAPA) Washington, DC	Postal Workers	$30,830	39 Candidates Avg House: $803 Avg Sen: $375	Dems: 99.2% House: 88.6% Incumb: 87.0%	
National Apartment Assn Apartment Political Committee of the National Apartment Association Washington, DC	Bldg Mgmt	$27,034	38 Candidates Avg House: $443 Avg Sen: $1,122	Repubs: 65.2% Senate: 62.2% Incumb: 79.7%	
National Assn for Home Care National Association for Home Care Congressional Action Committee Washington, DC	Home Care	$24,200	29 Candidates Avg House: $676 Avg Sen: $1,135	Dems: 94.2% House: 53.1% Incumb: 87.2%	
National Assn for Uniformed Services National Association for Uniformed Services PAC Springfield, VA	Pro-Military	$27,300	60 Candidates Avg House: $500 Avg Sen: $0	Repubs: 57.9% House: 102.6% Incumb: 95.8%	
National Assn of Arab-Americans NAAA PAC Washington, DC	Foreign Policy†	$28,950	48 Candidates Avg House: $561 Avg Sen: $891	Dems: 69.8% House: 81.5% Incumb: 78.4%	
National Assn of Broadcasters National Association of Broadcasters Television and Radio PAC Washington, DC	TV/Radio	$193,204	202 Candidates Avg House: $764 Avg Sen: $1,709	Dems: 52.0% House: 63.7% Incumb: 88.8%	
National Assn of Chain Drug Stores National Association of Chain Drug Stores, Inc. PAC Alexandria, VA	Drug Stores	$64,208	100 Candidates Avg House: $521 Avg Sen: $1,070	Dems: 68.0% House: 63.3% Incumb: 92.2%	
National Assn of Convenience Stores National Association of Convenience Stores Alexandria, VA	Dept Stores	$79,550	81 Candidates Avg House: $650 Avg Sen: $1,770	Repubs: 72.5% Senate: 53.4% Incumb: 72.7%	
National Assn of Federal Credit Unions National Association of Federal Credit Unions PAC (NACFUPAC) Arlington, VA	Credit Unions	$44,608	69 Candidates Avg House: $602 Avg Sen: $911	Dems: 73.3% House: 77.0% Incumb: 95.5%	
National Assn of Home Builders BUILD PAC of the National Association of Home Builders Washington, DC	National Assn of Home Bldrs Resid Construction†	$1,452,958	458 Candidates Avg House: $2,843 Avg Sen: $5,915	Repubs: 52.3% House: 79.8% Incumb: 82.4%	
National Assn of Independent Insurers National Association of Independent Insurers PAC Des Plaines, IL	Insurance	$244,608	188 Candidates Avg House: $722 Avg Sen: $3,376	Repubs: 78.8% Senate: 56.6% Incumb: 78.9%	

† PAC Sponsor has other major interests in addition to this primary category

Sponsor or Related Group/PAC Name	Affiliate	1987-88 Total	Where the money went...		
National Assn of Insurance Brokers National Association of Insurance Brokers PAC (NAIBPAC) Washington, DC	Insurance	$36,250	50 Candidates Avg House: $525 Avg Sen: $1,051	Repubs: 53.7% Senate: 55.1% Incumb: 94.5%	
National Assn of Letter Carriers Committee on Letter Carriers Political Education (Letter Carriers Pol Action Fund) Washington, DC Letter Carriers Union	Postal Workers	$1,732,482	391 Candidates Avg House: $4,304 Avg Sen: $5,250	Dems: 89.8% House: 83.7% Incumb: 70.9%	
National Assn of Life Companies National Association of Life Cos PAC (NALC/PAC) Washington, DC	Life Insurance	$28,125	37 Candidates Avg House: $582 Avg Sen: $950	Repubs: 56.8% Senate: 47.3% Incumb: 88.3%	
National Assn of Life Underwriters National Association of Life Underwriters PAC Washington, DC	Life Insurance	$1,329,150	432 Candidates Avg House: $2,790 Avg Sen: $5,311	Dems: 54.6% House: 80.4% Incumb: 77.8%	
National Assn of Mutual Insurance Agents Professional Insurance Agents PAC Alexandria, VA	Insurance	$317,283	224 Candidates Avg House: $947 Avg Sen: $3,136	Repubs: 50.8% House: 52.6% Incumb: 81.2%	
National Assn of Pharmacists National Association of Pharmacists PAC Alexandria, VA	Pharmacists†	$151,194	117 Candidates Avg House: $1,013 Avg Sen: $2,001	Dems: 77.3% House: 56.3% Incumb: 91.6%	
National Assn of Postal Supervisors National Association of Postal Supervisors PAC Washington, DC	Postal Workers	$92,075	126 Candidates Avg House: $614 Avg Sen: $1,170	Dems: 85.8% House: 65.4% Incumb: 92.3%	
National Assn of Postmasters NAPUS PAC for Postmasters (Formerly Political Education for Postmasters) Alexandria, VA	Postal Workers	$169,035	244 Candidates Avg House: $591 Avg Sen: $1,072	Dems: 72.9% House: 67.6% Incumb: 87.3%	
National Assn of Private Psychiatric Hospitals National Association of Private Psychiatric Hospitals PAC Washington, DC	Hospitals	$59,412	46 Candidates Avg House: $854 Avg Sen: $2,118	Dems: 58.6% Senate: 53.4% Incumb: 94.4%	
National Assn of Realtors Realtors PAC Chicago, IL National Assn of Realtors	Real Estate	$3,045,769	542 Candidates Avg House: $5,851 Avg Sen: $4,565	Dems: 53.5% House: 89.7% Incumb: 84.7%	
National Assn of Retired Federal Employees National Association of Retired Federal Employees PAC (NARFE-PAC) Washington, DC	Federal Workers	$1,974,850	445 Candidates Avg House: $4,291 Avg Sen: $5,674	Dems: 81.6% House: 86.5% Incumb: 79.5%	
National Assn of Small Business Investment Companies National Association of Small Business Investment Companies PAC Washington, DC	Small Business†	$36,025	50 Candidates Avg House: $551 Avg Sen: $1,757	Dems: 57.2% House: 65.9% Incumb: 100.0%	
National Assn of Social Workers National Association of Social Workers Political Action for Candidate Election Silver Spring, MD	Social Workers	$122,490	114 Candidates Avg House: $971 Avg Sen: $1,459	Dems: 96.9% House: 69.0% Incumb: 52.0%	
National Assn of Temporary Services National Association of Temporary Services PAC Alexandria, VA	Employ Agency	$66,650	69 Candidates Avg House: $992 Avg Sen: $913	Repubs: 56.8% House: 67.0% Incumb: 65.1%	
National Assn of Trade/Technical Schools National Association of Trade and Technical Schools PAC Washington, DC	Vocational Tech	$88,650	39 Candidates Avg House: $2,020 Avg Sen: $3,250	Dems: 59.1% House: 70.7% Incumb: 94.4%	
National Assn of Truck Stop Operators National Association of Truck Stop Operators Alexandria, VA	Trucking	$48,090	73 Candidates Avg House: $540 Avg Sen: $1,049	Repubs: 68.1% House: 62.9% Incumb: 79.5%	
National Assn of Water Companies National Association of Water Companies PAC (NAWC - PAC) Washington, DC	Water Utilities	$35,050	56 Candidates Avg House: $396 Avg Sen: $928	Repubs: 67.7% Senate: 60.9% Incumb: 81.3%	
National Assn of Wheat Growers National Association of Wheat Growers PAC (WHEATPAC) Washington, DC	Grain/Soybeans	$32,975	51 Candidates Avg House: $607 Avg Sen: $775	Dems: 60.6% House: 71.8% Incumb: 98.5%	
National Assn/Wholesale-Distributors Wholesaler-Distributor PAC of the National Association of Wholesale-Distributors Washington, DC	Wholesalers	$133,622	160 Candidates Avg House: $473 Avg Sen: $1,916	Repubs: 74.9% Senate: 54.5% Incumb: 68.9%	

Sponsor or Related Group/PAC Name	Affiliate	1987-88 Total	Where the money went...		
National Auto Dealers Assn Dealers Election Action Cmte of the Nat'l Automobile Dealers Assn (NADA) McLean, VA	 Auto Sales	$1,202,420	386 Candidates Avg House: $2,965 Avg Sen: $4,168	Repubs: 60.7% House: 83.4% Incumb: 80.9%	
National Banks of Florida Florida National Good Government Committee Inc Jacksonville, FL	 Commercial Banks	$54,348	59 Candidates Avg House: $725 Avg Sen: $1,405	Dems: 67.5% House: 56.0% Incumb: 60.1%	
National Beer Wholsalers Assn National Beer Wholesalers' Association PAC (NBWA PAC) Falls Church, VA	 Liquor Wholesale	$440,301	282 Candidates Avg House: $1,144 Avg Sen: $3,815	Dems: 62.9% House: 61.9% Incumb: 94.8%	
National Bipartisan PAC National Bipartisan PAC Washington, DC	 Pro-Israel	$24,400	31 Candidates Avg House: $335 Avg Sen: $1,335	Dems: 100.0% Senate: 76.6% Incumb: 62.9%	
National Broiler Council National Broiler Council PAC Washington, DC	 Poultry/Egg	$52,150	83 Candidates Avg House: $531 Avg Sen: $1,005	Dems: 60.0% House: 67.2% Incumb: 92.9%	
National Cable Television Assn National Cable Television Association's PAC (Cable PAC) Washington, DC	 CableTV	$302,190	144 Candidates Avg House: $1,791 Avg Sen: $3,020	Dems: 56.1% House: 64.0% Incumb: 94.5%	
National Cattlemen's Assn National Cattlemen's Association PAC Englewood, CO	National Cattlemens Assn Livestock	$146,596	232 Candidates Avg House: $522 Avg Sen: $1,313	Repubs: 56.5% House: 71.3% Incumb: 86.3%	
National City Corp National City Corporation PAC (National City PAC or NC PAC) Cleveland, OH	 Commercial Banks	$40,765	44 Candidates Avg House: $797 Avg Sen: $1,383	Repubs: 56.0% House: 64.6% Incumb: 70.7%	
National Coal Assn COALPAC - The PAC of the National Coal Association Washington, DC	National Coal Assn Coal Mining	$101,750	147 Candidates Avg House: $559 Avg Sen: $1,342	Repubs: 54.2% House: 67.0% Incumb: 87.1%	
National Cmte for an Effective Congress National Committee for an Effective Congress Washington, DC	 Dem/Liberal	$684,616	125 Candidates Avg House: $5,201 Avg Sen: $6,524	Dems: 100.0% House: 75.2% Incumb: 45.5%	
National Cmte to Preserve Social Security National Committee to Preserve Social Security PAC Washington, DC	 Elderly/Soc Security	$744,650	342 Candidates Avg House: $1,808 Avg Sen: $4,794	Dems: 95.3% House: 72.9% Incumb: 62.0%	
National Community Action Foundation Community Action Program-PAC (SSF of National Community Action Foundation Inc) Washington, DC	 Health/Welfare	$61,500	38 Candidates Avg House: $973 Avg Sen: $2,039	Dems: 82.9% Senate: 76.2% Incumb: 61.4%	
National Concrete Masonry Assn National Concrete Masonry Association PAC Herndon, VA	 Stone/Concrete	$39,100	39 Candidates Avg House: $982 Avg Sen: $961	Dems: 52.4% House: 57.8% Incumb: 98.7%	
National Confectioners Assn National Confectioners Association of the United States Inc PAC McLean, VA	 Candy	$27,775	55 Candidates Avg House: $419 Avg Sen: $795	Repubs: 70.4% House: 64.9% Incumb: 89.6%	
National Congressional Club National Congressional Club Raleigh, NC	Sen Jesse Helms (R-NC) Repub Leaders	$26,899	16 Candidates Avg House: $2,172 Avg Sen: $927	Repubs: 100.0% House: 72.7% Incumb: 24.0%	
National Conservative PAC National Conservative PAC Alexandria, VA	 Repub/Conservative	$83,481	92 Candidates Avg House: $1,052 Avg Sen: $583	Repubs: 98.3% House: 83.2% Incumb: 17.6%	
National Cotton Council National Cotton Council Committee for the Advancement of Cotton Memphis, TN	 Cotton	$156,603	164 Candidates Avg House: $759 Avg Sen: $1,662	Dems: 62.4% House: 63.1% Incumb: 97.0%	
National Council of Farmer Co-ops National Council of Farmer Cooperatives PAC (Co-op/PAC) Washington, DC	 Farm Orgs	$102,850	176 Candidates Avg House: $470 Avg Sen: $1,307	Dems: 69.1% House: 69.5% Incumb: 93.8%	
National Council of Savings Institutions National Council of Savings Institutions (THRIFTPAC) Washington, DC	 Savings Banks	$130,857	160 Candidates Avg House: $674 Avg Sen: $1,440	Dems: 55.0% House: 67.0% Incumb: 88.9%	

† PAC Sponsor has other major interests in addition to this primary category

National Council of Senior Citizens
National Council of Senior Citizens PAC
Washington, DC
Elderly/Soc Security — $190,700

124 Candidates		Dems:	98.4%
Avg House:	$1,356	House:	63.3%
Avg Sen:	$2,058	Incumb:	35.5%

National Crushed Stone Assn
National Stone Association (STONEPAC)
Washington, DC
Stone/Concrete — $29,000

39 Candidates		Repubs:	75.8%
Avg House:	$574	House:	53.4%
Avg Sen:	$1,125	Incumb:	77.6%

National Education Assn
National Education Association PAC
Washington, DC — National Education Assn
Teachers Union — $2,104,689

393 Candidates		Dems:	94.3%
Avg House:	$5,279	House:	86.0%
Avg Sen:	$5,949	Incumb:	66.1%

National Electrical Contractors Assn
Electrical Construction PAC-Nat'l Electrical Contractors Assn Inc (ECPAC)
Bethesda, MD
Electr Contr — $217,500

96 Candidates		Repubs:	85.2%
Avg House:	$1,352	Senate:	57.7%
Avg Sen:	$4,482	Incumb:	63.2%

National Farmers Organization
National Farmers Organization (Grass Roots in Politics)
Washington, DC
Farm Orgs — $34,050

73 Candidates		Dems:	88.8%
Avg House:	$466	House:	79.4%
Avg Sen:	$503	Incumb:	90.0%

National Fedn/Business & Prof Women Clubs
National Federation of Business & Professional Women's Clubs, Inc. PAC; The
Washington, DC
Business Assns — $22,750

56 Candidates		Dems:	84.0%
Avg House:	$395	House:	78.2%
Avg Sen:	$450	Incumb:	47.3%

National Fedn of Federal Employees
National Federation of Federal Employees Public Affairs Council
Washington, DC
Federal Workers — $31,100

61 Candidates		Dems:	92.8%
Avg House:	$513	House:	75.9%
Avg Sen:	$500	Incumb:	85.5%

National Fedn of Independent Business
National Federation of Independent Business Free Enterprise PAC
San Mateo, CA
Small Business — $310,349

204 Candidates		Repubs:	88.4%
Avg House:	$1,113	House:	59.6%
Avg Sen:	$3,303	Incumb:	62.6%

National Fisheries Institute
National Fisheries Institute Fisheries PAC (FISHPAC)
Washington, DC
Fishing — $69,769

48 Candidates		Repubs:	55.2%
Avg House:	$1,067	Senate:	55.6%
Avg Sen:	$2,043	Incumb:	64.2%

National Forest Products Assn
Forest Industries PAC
Washington, DC
Forest Prod — $80,388

90 Candidates		Repubs:	55.3%
Avg House:	$743	House:	58.3%
Avg Sen:	$1,242	Incumb:	83.1%

National Health Corp
National Health Corporation PAC
Murfreesboro, TN
Nursing Homes — $30,350

15 Candidates		Dems:	78.3%
Avg House:	$1,666	House:	49.4%
Avg Sen:	$2,333	Incumb:	67.1%

National Intergroup
NII Political Action Fund
Pittsburgh, PA — National Intergroup
Pharm Sales† — $40,385

34 Candidates		Repubs:	59.0%
Avg House:	$464	Senate:	60.4%
Avg Sen:	$2,216	Incumb:	89.6%

National League of Postmasters
National League of Postmasters PAC
Alexandria, VA
Postal Workers — $182,270

271 Candidates		Dems:	67.4%
Avg House:	$532	House:	64.9%
Avg Sen:	$1,306	Incumb:	94.9%

National Machine Tool Builders Assn
Machine ToolPAC
McLean, VA
Indust Equip — $55,299

93 Candidates		Repubs:	68.7%
Avg House:	$388	House:	49.2%
Avg Sen:	$1,231	Incumb:	82.2%

National Medical Enterprises Inc
National Medical Enterprises Inc PAC
Los Angeles, CA
Hospitals† — $79,577

83 Candidates		Dems:	57.5%
Avg House:	$696	House:	57.7%
Avg Sen:	$1,789	Incumb:	93.4%

National Multi Housing Council
National Multi Housing Council PAC
Washington, DC
Resid Construction — $43,743

101 Candidates		Dems:	54.4%
Avg House:	$329	House:	57.3%
Avg Sen:	$769	Incumb:	97.0%

National Organization for Women
NOW/PAC (National Organization for Women PAC)
Washington, DC
Womens Issues — $34,448

34 Candidates		Dems:	89.6%
Avg House:	$921	House:	69.5%
Avg Sen:	$1,312	Incumb:	8.3%

National PAC
National PAC
Washington, DC
Pro-Israel — $1,134,500

215 Candidates		Dems:	63.5%
Avg House:	$5,011	House:	75.1%
Avg Sen:	$6,381	Incumb:	80.6%

National Parking Assn
National Parking Association PAC
Washington, DC
Bldg Mgmt — $20,000

12 Candidates		Dems:	75.0%
Avg House:	$1,333	Senate:	70.0%
Avg Sen:	$1,750	Incumb:	90.0%

Sponsor or Related Group/PAC Name	Affiliate	1987-88 Total	Where the money went...		
National Pest Control Assn National Pest Control Association PAC Dunn Loring, VA	Pest Control	$36,850	68 Candidates Avg House: $537 Avg Sen: $557	Repubs: 70.4% House: 78.8% Incumb: 88.2%	
National Pork Producers Council National Pork Producers Council (Pork PAC) Des Moines, IA	Livestock	$28,900	65 Candidates Avg House: $385 Avg Sen: $613	Dems: 61.2% House: 61.4% Incumb: 98.1%	
National Propane Gas Assn National Propane Gas Association PAC (PropanePAC) Oak Brook, IL	LPG/Propane	$45,925	102 Candidates Avg House: $372 Avg Sen: $789	Repubs: 78.8% House: 66.5% Incumb: 75.3%	
National Ready Mixed Concrete Assn National Ready Mixed Concrete Association Political Committee Silver Spring, MD	Stone/Concrete	$24,279	75 Candidates Avg House: $275 Avg Sen: $487	Repubs: 91.7% House: 65.9% Incumb: 62.8%	
National Realty Committee National Realty PAC (REALPAC) Washington, DC	Real Estate Devel	$71,613	50 Candidates Avg House: $970 Avg Sen: $1,794	Dems: 68.6% Senate: 42.6% Incumb: 93.9%	
National Restaurant Assn National Restaurant Association PAC Washington, DC — National Restaurant Assn	Restaurants	$361,300	170 Candidates Avg House: $1,561 Avg Sen: $4,982	Repubs: 70.3% House: 61.4% Incumb: 71.8%	
National Rifle Assn NRA Political Victory Fund Washington, DC	Pro-Guns	$772,756	237 Candidates Avg House: $3,127 Avg Sen: $4,038	Repubs: 63.2% House: 80.1% Incumb: 81.0%	
National Right to Life PAC National Right to Life PAC Washington, DC	Pro-Life	$254,132	135 Candidates Avg House: $1,946 Avg Sen: $2,716	Repubs: 79.6% House: 78.9% Incumb: 62.8%	
National Rural Letter Carriers Assn National Rural Letter Carriers' Association PAC Alexandria, VA	Postal Workers	$398,280	272 Candidates Avg House: $1,101 Avg Sen: $3,672	Dems: 81.2% House: 64.2% Incumb: 81.9%	
National Screw Machines Prod Assn National Screw Machines Products Association-PAC (NSMPA-PAC) Brecksville, OH	Indust Equip	$50,326	27 Candidates Avg House: $500 Avg Sen: $2,666	Repubs: 100.0% Senate: 90.0% Incumb: 37.8%	
National Security PAC National Security PAC Washington, DC	Pro-Military	$116,774	65 Candidates Avg House: $700 Avg Sen: $4,298	Repubs: 97.6% Senate: 73.6% Incumb: 54.2%	
National Semiconductor Corp National Semiconductor Corporation Employees PAC Santa Clara, CA	Computers	$29,800	13 Candidates Avg House: $2,883 Avg Sen: $1,785	Repubs: 78.1% House: 58.1% Incumb: 56.4%	
National Society of Professional Engineers National Society of Professional Engineers - PAC (NSPE-PAC) Alexandria, VA	Engineers†	$101,650	140 Candidates Avg House: $631 Avg Sen: $1,261	Repubs: 61.8% House: 73.9% Incumb: 76.4%	
National Society of Professional Surveyors American Congress on Surveying & Mapping/National Society of Prof Surveyors PAC Falls Church, VA	Surveyors	$22,200	52 Candidates Avg House: $386 Avg Sen: $622	Repubs: 54.9% House: 74.8% Incumb: 86.0%	
National Soft Drink Assn Soft Drink PAC Washington, DC	Soft Drinks	$26,150	36 Candidates Avg House: $528 Avg Sen: $1,076	Dems: 53.0% Senate: 53.5% Incumb: 83.7%	
National Telephone Co-op Assn National Telephone Cooperative Assn Telephone Education Cmte Organization Washington, DC	Phone Utilities	$44,384	94 Candidates Avg House: $451 Avg Sen: $535	Dems: 72.5% House: 77.2% Incumb: 97.0%	
National Tooling & Machining Assn Tooling & Machining PAC of the National Tooling and Machining Association Ft Washington, MD	Indust Equip	$60,400	61 Candidates Avg House: $826 Avg Sen: $1,352	Repubs: 76.4% House: 57.5% Incumb: 82.2%	
National Treasury Employees Union National Treasury Employees Union PAC (TEPAC) Washington, DC	Federal Workers	$172,970	131 Candidates Avg House: $882 Avg Sen: $2,944	Dems: 94.2% House: 52.0% Incumb: 66.2%	
National Turkey Federation National Turkey Federation Political Action Commitee/TURPAC Reston, VA	Poultry/Egg	$29,500	44 Candidates Avg House: $522 Avg Sen: $1,023	Repubs: 60.3% House: 54.9% Incumb: 93.9%	

† PAC Sponsor has other major interests in addition to this primary category

1143

Sponsor or Related Group/PAC Name	Affiliate	1987-88 Total	Where the money went...		
National Utility Contractors Assn National Utility Contractors Assn Legislative Information & Action Committee Arlington, VA	Heavy Construction	$337,500	143 Candidates Avg House: $1,937 Avg Sen: $3,887	Repubs: 56.8% House: 64.3% Incumb: 87.0%	
National Venture Capital Assn National Venture Capital Association PAC (NVCA PAC) Washington, DC	Venture Capital	$256,500	64 Candidates Avg House: $3,621 Avg Sen: $4,571	Dems: 57.9% Pres: 52.0% Incumb: 88.7%	
National Wholesale Grocers Assn National American Wholesale Grocers' Association PAC (NAWGAPAC) Falls Church, VA	Food Wholesale	$50,428	103 Candidates Avg House: $250 Avg Sen: $1,004	Repubs: 83.5% Senate: 55.7% Incumb: 68.4%	
National Womens Political Caucus National Women's Political Caucus Campaign Support Committee Washington, DC	Womens Issues	$28,100	21 Candidates Avg House: $1,360 Avg Sen: $1,125	Dems: 91.1% House: 92.0% Incumb: 9.8%	
National Wool Growers Assn National Wool Growers Assn-PAC (RAMS-Responsible Activity) Washington, DC	Livestock	$24,875	41 Candidates Avg House: $440 Avg Sen: $910	Dems: 61.8% Senate: 51.2% Incumb: 93.0%	
Nationwide Corp Nationwide Political Participation Committee Columbus, OH	Insurance	$27,975	21 Candidates Avg House: $942 Avg Sen: $9,075	Repubs: 78.1% House: 64.0% Incumb: 54.7%	
Navistar International Navistar Int'l Transportation Corp Good Gov't Cmte (Formerly International Harvester) Chicago, IL	Farm Equip	$43,110	43 Candidates Avg House: $834 Avg Sen: $1,236	Repubs: 68.4% Senate: 51.6% Incumb: 85.5%	
NCNB Corp NCNB Corporation PAC (NCNB PAC) Charlotte, NC	NCNB Corp Commercial Banks	$62,858	84 Candidates Avg House: $667 Avg Sen: $1,026	Dems: 70.7% House: 69.0% Incumb: 88.5%	
NCNB Texas NCNB Texas PAC (Formerly First Republic Bank (FRB)) Dallas, TX	NCNB Corp Commercial Banks	$58,377	29 Candidates Avg House: $1,770 Avg Sen: $2,464	Dems: 67.6% House: 54.6% Incumb: 99.0%	
NCR Corp NCR Corporation PAC Dayton, OH	Computers†	$41,625	58 Candidates Avg House: $565 Avg Sen: $1,400	Repubs: 66.8% House: 59.8% Incumb: 79.6%	
Neighbor to Neighbor PAC Neighbor to Neighbor PAC San Francisco, CA	Foreign Policy (Central America)†	$49,893	16 Candidates Avg House: $3,571 Avg Sen: $2,749	Dems: 100.0% House: 71.6% Incumb: 21.6%	
Nestle Enterprises Inc Nestle Enterprises Inc PAC Solon, OH	Food/Beverage†	$71,050	174 Candidates Avg House: $343 Avg Sen: $859	Repubs: 91.2% House: 73.4% Incumb: 74.3%	
Nevada Resort Assn Nevada Resort Association PAC Las Vegas, NV	Casinos/Gambling†	$64,150	66 Candidates Avg House: $574 Avg Sen: $2,117	Dems: 51.7% Senate: 56.1% Incumb: 87.5%	
New England Mutual Life New England Mutual Life Insurance Company PAC/New England Life PAC (NELPAC) Boston, MA	Life Insurance	$74,800	67 Candidates Avg House: $956 Avg Sen: $1,625	Dems: 64.4% House: 65.2% Incumb: 94.9%	
New England Power Service Company New England Electric PAC Establ by New England Power Service Co (NEEPAC) Westborough, MA	Electric Utility	$43,900	90 Candidates Avg House: $447 Avg Sen: $586	Repubs: 59.9% House: 65.3% Incumb: 93.6%	
New England Tel & Tel New England Telephone and Telegraph Company Federal PAC (NET-FED-PAC) Boston, MA	NYNEX Phone Utilities	$39,838	27 Candidates Avg House: $1,337 Avg Sen: $2,050	Dems: 68.1% House: 70.5% Incumb: 74.9%	
New Jersey Bell Telephone New Jersey Bell Telephone Company Federal PAC (NJB PAC) Newark, NJ	Bell Atlantic Phone Utilities	$44,260	19 Candidates Avg House: $2,062 Avg Sen: $4,600	Dems: 63.3% House: 79.2% Incumb: 92.7%	
New Orleans Public Service Inc New Orleans Public Service Inc Committee for Responsible Government New Orleans, LA	Middle South Utilities Gas/Electric†	$24,050	47 Candidates Avg House: $514 Avg Sen: $500	Dems: 54.5% House: 79.2% Incumb: 92.7%	
New Republican Victory Fund New Republican Victory Fund Alexandria, VA	Sen Trent Lott (R-Miss) Repub Leaders	$22,000	9 Candidates Avg House: $1,500 Avg Sen: $3,750	Repubs: 100.0% Senate: 68.1% Incumb: 29.5%	

Sponsor or Related Group/PAC Name	Affiliate	1987–88 Total	Where the money went...			

New York Life
New York Life PAC - Federal Fund (New York Life PAC - Federal)
New York, NY — Life Insurance
$92,647

83 Candidates		Dems:	74.2%
Avg House:	$942	House:	64.1%
Avg Sen:	$1,644	Incumb:	94.6%

New York Medical Assn
New York Medical PAC
Lake Success, NY — American Medical Assn — Doctors
$102,409

36 Candidates		Repubs:	50.8%
Avg House:	$2,676	House:	88.9%
Avg Sen:	$5,700	Incumb:	86.9%

New York State Electric & Gas Corp
New York State Electric & Gas Corporation PAC (NYSEGPAC)
Binghamton, NY — Gas/Electric†
$25,090

23 Candidates		Repubs:	83.0%
Avg House:	$1,179	House:	94.0%
Avg Sen:	$500	Incumb:	58.2%

New York Stock Exchange
New York Stock Exchange Inc PAC (NYSE PAC)
Washington, DC — Securities
$45,900

44 Candidates		Dems:	60.2%
Avg House:	$772	Senate:	51.2%
Avg Sen:	$1,566	Incumb:	94.6%

New York Telephone
New York Telephone Federal PAC
New York, NY — NYNEX — Phone Utilities
$45,834

46 Candidates		Repubs:	51.2%
Avg House:	$927	House:	85.0%
Avg Sen:	$2,131	Incumb:	91.4%

Nike Inc
Nike Inc PAC
Beaverton, OR — Shoe Mfrs†
$25,812

36 Candidates		Dems:	60.2%
Avg House:	$667	House:	69.9%
Avg Sen:	$864	Incumb:	89.2%

NL Industries
NL Industries Inc PAC
Houston, TX — NL Industries — Chemicals
$104,950

63 Candidates		Repubs:	86.1%
Avg House:	$500	Senate:	77.1%
Avg Sen:	$3,854	Incumb:	49.0%

Norfolk Southern Corp
Norfolk Southern Corporation Good Government Fund
Norfolk, VA — Norfolk Southern — Railroads†
$118,900

176 Candidates		Dems:	63.3%
Avg House:	$583	House:	72.2%
Avg Sen:	$1,223	Incumb:	91.4%

Norstar Bancorp
Norstar Bancorp Inc PAC
Albany, NY — Commercial Banks
$32,925

20 Candidates		Repubs:	53.2%
Avg House:	$1,143	House:	41.7%
Avg Sen:	$1,533	Incumb:	71.4%

North American Van Lines
North American Van Lines, Inc PAC (NAPAC)
Fort Wayne, IN — Norfolk Southern — Trucking
$77,850

111 Candidates		Dems:	59.3%
Avg House:	$662	House:	79.1%
Avg Sen:	$902	Incumb:	94.7%

Northern States Power Company
Northern States Power Employee Political Interest Committee
Minneapolis, MN — Gas/Electric†
$37,175

69 Candidates		Repubs:	60.3%
Avg House:	$456	House:	57.7%
Avg Sen:	$714	Incumb:	80.2%

Northern Telecom
Northern Telecom Inc PAC
Nashville, TN — Comm Equip
$23,550

51 Candidates		Dems:	51.6%
Avg House:	$426	House:	85.1%
Avg Sen:	$875	Incumb:	92.4%

Northern Trust Company
Northern Trust Company Good Government Committee
Chicago, IL — Commercial Banks
$23,500

39 Candidates		Repubs:	54.2%
Avg House:	$500	House:	59.6%
Avg Sen:	$863	Incumb:	91.5%

Northrop Corp
Northrop Employees PAC (NEPAC)
San Francisco, CA — Air Defense†
$383,517

247 Candidates		Repubs:	60.0%
Avg House:	$1,144	House:	60.3%
Avg Sen:	$3,514	Incumb:	86.5%

Northwest Airlines
Northwest Airlines PAC (Formerly Republic Airlines PAC)
St Paul, MN — Airlines
$50,211

58 Candidates		Dems:	51.9%
Avg House:	$705	House:	63.2%
Avg Sen:	$1,420	Incumb:	92.0%

Northwestern Bell Telephone
Northwestern Bell Telephone Company Federal PAC (NWB Fed PAC)
Omaha, NE — US West — Phone Utilities
$84,400

35 Candidates		Repubs:	56.8%
Avg House:	$1,984	House:	58.8%
Avg Sen:	$3,480	Incumb:	73.3%

Northwestern Mutual Life
Northwestern Mutual Life Insurance Company Federal PAC (NML FedPAC)
Milwaukee, WI — Life Insurance
$99,870

59 Candidates		Dems:	58.1%
Avg House:	$1,642	House:	65.8%
Avg Sen:	$1,787	Incumb:	95.0%

Norwest Corp
Norwest Corporation PAC (Norwest PAC)
Minneapolis, MN — Commercial Banks
$62,775

60 Candidates		Repubs:	52.1%
Avg House:	$931	House:	59.3%
Avg Sen:	$1,276	Incumb:	87.7%

Nutrasweet Company
Nutrasweet Company PAC
Deerfield, IL — Monsanto — Artif Sweeteners
$21,850

21 Candidates		Dems:	57.7%
Avg House:	$1,090	House:	74.8%
Avg Sen:	$916	Incumb:	100.0%

† PAC Sponsor has other major interests in addition to this primary category

Sponsor or Related Group/PAC Name	Affiliate	1987-88 Total	Where the money went...		
NYNEX Corp NYNEX Federal PAC New York, NY	NYNEX — Phone Utilities†	$101,154	119 Candidates Avg House: $590 Avg Sen: $1,173	Repubs: 71.7% House: 49.0% Incumb: 85.2%	
O'Melveny & Myers O'Melveny & Myers PAC Washington, DC	Lawyers†	$38,200	40 Candidates Avg House: $715 Avg Sen: $1,059	Repubs: 52.3% Senate: 58.2% Incumb: 77.7%	
Occidental Oil & Gas Occidental Oil & Gas Corp PAC (OOGPAC) (Cities Service Oil & Gas Corp PAC) Tulsa, OK	Occidental Petroleum — Oil & Gas Prod†	$68,657	112 Candidates Avg House: $501 Avg Sen: $1,281	Repubs: 84.3% House: 70.1% Incumb: 72.3%	
Occidental Petroleum Occidental Petroleum Corporation PAC Los Angeles, CA	Occidental Petroleum — Oil & Gas Prod†	$111,769	82 Candidates Avg House: $744 Avg Sen: $2,366	Dems: 78.1% Senate: 42.3% Incumb: 88.5%	
Ocean Spray Cranberries Inc Ocean Spray PAC Plymouth, MA	Fruit/Veg	$65,898	52 Candidates Avg House: $954 Avg Sen: $1,768	Dems: 63.5% Senate: 53.6% Incumb: 96.4%	
Ocean State PAC Ocean State PAC Providence, RI	Pro-Israel	$30,300	24 Candidates Avg House: $628 Avg Sen: $2,150	Dems: 80.9% Senate: 70.9% Incumb: 87.5%	
Office & Professional Employees Union Office and Professional Employees International Union-Voice of the Electorate Washington, DC	$60,350 Misc Unions		51 Candidates Avg House: $732 Avg Sen: $2,340	Dems: 100.0% House: 44.9% Incumb: 49.0%	
Ohio Bell Telephone Ohio Bell Telephone Company Federal PAC; The (OBT PAC) Cleveland, OH	Ameritech — Phone Utilities	$23,570	23 Candidates Avg House: $1,118 Avg Sen: $1,030	Dems: 49.5% Senate: 97.8% Incumb: 12.5%	
Ohio Farm Bureau Federation Ohio Farm Bureau Federation Inc-Agriculture Pol Educ Program (OFBF-APEP) Columbus, OH	Farm Orgs	$21,600	17 Candidates Avg House: $1,203 Avg Sen: $2,550	Repubs: 61.5% House: 83.6% Incumb: 86.8%	
Ohio Freeze Voter Freeze Voter Washington, DC	Pro-Peace	$43,440	16 Candidates Avg House: $1,509 Avg Sen: $4,265	Dems: 100.0% Senate: 68.7% Incumb: 27.7%	
Ohio Savings Assns League Savings Associations' League PAC Ohio Columbus, OH	US League of Savings Assn — Savings Banks	$21,250	17 Candidates Avg House: $1,250 Avg Sen: $0	Dems: 60.0% House: 100.0% Incumb: 90.6%	
Oil, Chemical & Atomic Workers Union Oil, Chemical & Atomic Workers Int'l Union Cmte on Pol Educ Fund (OCAW-COPE) Denver, CO	Oil Chemical & Atomic Wkrs — Energy Unions	$106,375	128 Candidates Avg House: $637 Avg Sen: $1,541	Dems: 97.6% House: 59.9% Incumb: 74.7%	
Olin Corp Olin Corporation Good Government Fund Washington, DC	Chemicals†	$38,086	60 Candidates Avg House: $466 Avg Sen: $1,027	Repubs: 69.2% House: 51.4% Incumb: 75.2%	
Operating Engineers Local #12 Operating Engineers Local 12 Voluntary Legislative Fund Los Angeles, CA	Operating Engineers Union — Constr Unions	$28,845	9 Candidates Avg House: $2,355 Avg Sen: $10,000	Dems: 100.0% House: 65.3% Incumb: 17.0%	
Operating Engineers Local #15 International Union of Operating Engineers Local 15 PAC New York, NY	Operating Engineers Union — Constr Unions	$23,500	9 Candidates Avg House: $2,357 Avg Sen: $3,500	Repubs: 61.7% House: 70.2% Incumb: 66.0%	
Operating Engineers Local #3 SELEC: Supporters of Engineers Local 3 Endorsed Candiates San Francisco, CA	Operating Engineers Union — Constr Unions	$27,560	14 Candidates Avg House: $1,927 Avg Sen: $2,500	Dems: 100.0% House: 90.9% Incumb: 38.7%	
Operating Engineers Local #68 International Union of Operating Engineers Local 68 PAC West Caldwell, NJ	Operating Engineers Union — Constr Unions	$41,055	11 Candidates Avg House: $4,083 Avg Sen: $2,150	Dems: 91.5% House: 89.5% Incumb: 54.9%	
Operating Engineers Local #825 Int'l Union of Operating Engineers Lo 825 Pol Action and Education Cmte Little Falls, NJ	Operating Engineers Union — Constr Unions	$83,670	22 Candidates Avg House: $4,161 Avg Sen: $1,533	Dems: 61.9% House: 94.5% Incumb: 85.0%	
Operating Engineers Union Engineers Pol Education Cmte (EPEC)/Int'l Union of Operating Engineers Washington, DC	Operating Engineers Union — Bldg Trades	$678,731	261 Candidates Avg House: $2,129 Avg Sen: $6,141	Dems: 93.4% House: 71.5% Incumb: 80.3%	

Sponsor or Related Group/PAC Name	Affiliate	1987-88 Total	Where the money went...		
Opperman & Paquin Opperman & Paquin Political Fund Minneapolis, MN	Lawyers	$35,045	15 Candidates Avg House: $1,722 Avg Sen: $2,873	Dems: 83.8% Senate: 65.6% Incumb: 60.8%	
Oral & Maxillofacial Surgeons Oral and Maxillofacial Surgery PAC (OMSPAC) Rosemont, IL	Dentists	$143,500	66 Candidates Avg House: $1,817 Avg Sen: $2,760	Repubs: 51.2% House: 51.9% Incumb: 78.7%	
Oregon Education Assn Oregon Education Association People for Improvement of Education Tigard, OR — National Education Assn	Teachers Union	$23,340	10 Candidates Avg House: $2,315 Avg Sen: $2,500	Dems: 100.0% House: 89.3% Incumb: 36.9%	
Owens-Corning Fiberglas Owens-Corning Fiberglas Corporation Employees' Better Government Fund Toledo, OH	Bldg Materials†	$80,338	59 Candidates Avg House: $844 Avg Sen: $2,231	Repubs: 77.5% Senate: 61.1% Incumb: 57.2%	
Owens-Illinois Owens-Illinois Inc Employees Good Citizenship Fund Toledo, OH	Paper Packaging†	$114,800	86 Candidates Avg House: $992 Avg Sen: $2,250	Repubs: 60.1% House: 52.7% Incumb: 85.0%	
Paccar Inc Paccar Employees Political Action Fund Bellevue, WA	Truck Mfrs†	$29,425	26 Candidates Avg House: $968 Avg Sen: $1,571	Dems: 51.8% House: 59.2% Incumb: 84.7%	
Pacific Enterprises Pacific Enterprises Political Assistance Committee Los Angeles, CA	Natural Gas†	$142,314	138 Candidates Avg House: $725 Avg Sen: $1,778	Dems: 55.2% House: 53.0% Incumb: 93.7%	
Pacific Gas & Electric Pacific Gas and Electric Company Employees' Federal Good Government Fund San Francisco, CA	Gas/Electric†	$89,363	97 Candidates Avg House: $738 Avg Sen: $1,582	Repubs: 58.4% House: 62.8% Incumb: 89.9%	
Pacific Mutual Life Pacific Mutual Life Insurance Company PAC (PMPAC) Newport Beach, CA	Life Insurance	$56,675	68 Candidates Avg House: $674 Avg Sen: $1,276	Dems: 53.8% House: 59.5% Incumb: 84.9%	
Pacific Northwest Bell Pacific Northwest Bell Employees' Public Interest Committee - Federal Seattle, WA — US West	Phone Utilities	$64,575	24 Candidates Avg House: $2,860 Avg Sen: $2,278	Dems: 54.6% House: 75.3% Incumb: 78.3%	
Pacific PAC Pacific PAC Los Angeles, CA	Pro-Israel	$111,000	16 Candidates Avg House: $5,000 Avg Sen: $7,285	Dems: 100.0% Senate: 91.8% Incumb: 62.2%	
Pacific Resources Pacific Resources PAC Honolulu, HI	Oil Refining/Marketing	$25,100	40 Candidates Avg House: $369 Avg Sen: $791	Repubs: 60.9% House: 38.2% Incumb: 88.0%	
Pacific Telesis Group Pacific Telesis Group Federal PAC (Pacific Telesis Federal PAC) San Francisco, CA	Phone Utilities†	$260,460	185 Candidates Avg House: $1,233 Avg Sen: $1,746	Dems: 60.0% House: 62.5% Incumb: 95.8%	
PaineWebber PaineWebber Fund for Better Government New York, NY — Paine Webber	Securities Investment	$81,550	57 Candidates Avg House: $698 Avg Sen: $2,295	Dems: 59.6% Senate: 61.9% Incumb: 85.3%	
Painters & Allied Trades Union Int'l Brotherhood of Painters & Allied Trades Political Action Together Pol Cmte Washington, DC — Painters & Allied Trades	Constr Unions	$94,055	89 Candidates Avg House: $868 Avg Sen: $1,986	Dems: 94.5% House: 68.3% Incumb: 51.5%	
Pan Am Pan Am PAC Washington, DC	Airlines	$22,850	57 Candidates Avg House: $350 Avg Sen: $711	Dems: 60.6% House: 72.0% Incumb: 97.2%	
Panhandle Eastern Corp Panhandle Eastern Corporation PAC Houston, TX	Natural Gas	$20,550	41 Candidates Avg House: $379 Avg Sen: $795	Dems: 65.7% House: 53.5% Incumb: 94.9%	
Papa Ginos Papa Ginos 128 PAC Dedham, MA	Restaurants	$26,500	22 Candidates Avg House: $850 Avg Sen: $1,500	Repubs: 100.0% Senate: 67.9% Incumb: 37.7%	
Parsons Corp Parsons Corporation PAC Pasadena, CA — Ralph M Parsons Co	Engineers/Architects†	$23,150	27 Candidates Avg House: $739 Avg Sen: $1,137	Dems: 59.2% House: 60.7% Incumb: 95.7%	

† PAC Sponsor has other major interests in addition to this primary category

Sponsor or Related Group/PAC Name	Affiliate	1987-88 Total	Where the money went...		
Pax Americas Pax Americas (Formerly Priorities PAC) Washington, DC	Rep David Bonior (D-Mich) Dem Leaders	$56,600	42 Candidates Avg House: $1,405 Avg Sen: $1,000	Dems: 97.3% House: 89.4% Incumb: 45.2%	
Peabody Coal Peabody PAC St Louis, MO	Coal Mining	$103,180	101 Candidates Avg House: $698 Avg Sen: $1,543	Dems: 51.4% Senate: 47.9% Incumb: 90.1%	
Peace PAC/Council for a Livable World Peace PAC Boston, MA	Council for Livable World Pro-Peace	$72,854	42 Candidates Avg House: $1,757 Avg Sen: $810	Dems: 97.3% House: 98.9% Incumb: 37.4%	
Pelican PAC Pelican PAC Washington, DC	Sen J Bennett Johnston (D-La) Dem Leaders	$201,647	36 Candidates Avg House: $750 Avg Sen: $6,246	Dems: 100.0% Senate: 96.0% Incumb: 44.5%	
Penn Central Corp Penn Central PAC-PENNPAC Cincinnati, OH	Comm Equip†	$33,600	48 Candidates Avg House: $604 Avg Sen: $1,750	Repubs: 51.1% House: 79.2% Incumb: 82.9%	
Penn Mutual Life Insurance Penn Mutual PAC Philadelphia, PA	Life Insurance	$21,000	32 Candidates Avg House: $480 Avg Sen: $1,105	Dems: 56.0% House: 52.6% Incumb: 96.9%	
Pennzoil Company Pennzoil PAC Houston, TX	Oil Refining/Marketing†	$45,000	61 Candidates Avg House: $517 Avg Sen: $965	Dems: 58.3% House: 46.0% Incumb: 92.0%	
Pepsi-Cola Bottlers Assn Pepsi-Cola Bottlers Association-PAC Irving, TX	Bevg Bottling	$51,150	47 Candidates Avg House: $1,085 Avg Sen: $964	Repubs: 56.6% House: 65.8% Incumb: 88.3%	
Pepsico Inc Pepsico Concerned Citizens Fund Purchase, NY	Food/Beverage†	$183,292	150 Candidates Avg House: $857 Avg Sen: $2,318	Repubs: 70.2% House: 54.7% Incumb: 78.2%	
Petroleum Marketers Assn Petroleum Marketers Association of America Small Businessmen's Committee Washington, DC	Gas Stations†	$182,700	190 Candidates Avg House: $741 Avg Sen: $1,974	Repubs: 68.7% House: 65.4% Incumb: 73.3%	
Pfizer Inc Pfizer PAC New York, NY	Pharmaceuticals†	$193,545	192 Candidates Avg House: $613 Avg Sen: $2,374	Repubs: 51.5% Senate: 52.7% Incumb: 88.4%	
Pharmaceutical Manufacturers Assn Pharmaceutical Manufacturers Association Better Government Committee Washington, DC	Pharmaceuticals	$37,538	60 Candidates Avg House: $476 Avg Sen: $972	Dems: 58.8% House: 52.0% Incumb: 95.7%	
Phelps Dodge Corp Phelps Dodge Employees Fund for Good Government Phoenix, AZ	Metal Mining/Processing	$31,925	43 Candidates Avg House: $632 Avg Sen: $1,105	Repubs: 58.7% House: 65.4% Incumb: 95.3%	
PHH Group PHH Group Inc PAC (GROUPAC) Hunt Valley, MD	Car/Truck Rent†	$22,075	42 Candidates Avg House: $399 Avg Sen: $807	Dems: 54.4% House: 52.4% Incumb: 95.5%	
Philadelphia Electric Philadelphia Electric Company Federal PAC (PECOPAC) Philadelphia, PA	Gas/Electric†	$70,400	87 Candidates Avg House: $685 Avg Sen: $1,234	Repubs: 57.6% House: 65.3% Incumb: 96.5%	
Philadelphia Stock Exchange Philadelphia Stock Exchange, Inc PAC Philadelphia, PA	Securities	$20,000	17 Candidates Avg House: $923 Avg Sen: $2,000	Dems: 70.0% House: 60.0% Incumb: 97.5%	
Philip Morris Philip Morris PAC (PHIL-PAC) New York, NY	Philip Morris Tobacco†	$558,530	316 Candidates Avg House: $1,617 Avg Sen: $2,496	Dems: 60.3% House: 75.9% Incumb: 87.6%	
Philips Industries Philips Industries Inc. PAC Dayton, OH	Construction Products†	$21,050	9 Candidates Avg House: $970 Avg Sen: $3,733	Dems: 55.1% Senate: 53.2% Incumb: 99.0%	
Phillips Petroleum Phillips Petroleum Company PAC Bartlesville, OK	Oil & Gas Prod†	$249,037	177 Candidates Avg House: $1,240 Avg Sen: $2,419	Repubs: 78.7% House: 75.7% Incumb: 65.3%	

Pillsbury Company
Pillsbury Company PAC
Minneapolis, MN — Pillsbury — Food Processing†
$66,697

39 Candidates	Repubs: 73.8%
Avg House: $921	Senate: 59.8%
Avg Sen: $3,989	Incumb: 67.0%

Pillsbury, Madison & Sutro
Pillsbury, Madison & Sutro PAC
San Francisco, CA — Lawyers
$42,750

23 Candidates	Repubs: 50.8%
Avg House: $1,225	Senate: 42.1%
Avg Sen: $2,000	Incumb: 67.4%

Pirelli Cable
Pirelli Cable Corporation PAC
Union, NJ — Indust Equip†
$39,500

35 Candidates	Dems: 67.1%
Avg House: $1,210	House: 58.2%
Avg Sen: $1,031	Incumb: 91.1%

Pittston Company
Pittston Company PAC
Greenwich, CT — Air Freight††
$40,500

47 Candidates	Dems: 64.2%
Avg House: $608	Senate: 54.9%
Avg Sen: $1,308	Incumb: 74.7%

Planning Research Corp
Planning Research Corporation PAC
McLean, VA — Emhart Corp — Computer Svcs†
$20,075

26 Candidates	Repubs: 75.3%
Avg House: $500	Senate: 60.2%
Avg Sen: $1,207	Incumb: 95.0%

Plasterers/Cement Masons Union
Plasterers' and Cements Masons' Action Committee
Washington, DC — Constr Unions
$21,550

40 Candidates	Dems: 98.6%
Avg House: $532	House: 76.6%
Avg Sen: $561	Incumb: 38.3%

Plumbers/Pipefitters Union
United Assn of Journeymen and Apprentices of the Plumb and Pipeftrs Indus
Washington, DC — Plumbers/Pipefitters Union — Constr Unions
$472,686

297 Candidates	Dems: 94.5%
Avg House: $1,283	House: 71.4%
Avg Sen: $4,096	Incumb: 57.7%

Pneumo Abex Corp
Pneumo Abex Corporation PAC (Pneumo Abex PAC)
Boston, MA — Aerospace Equip†
$37,771

55 Candidates	Dems: 51.0%
Avg House: $562	House: 64.0%
Avg Sen: $1,007	Incumb: 82.8%

Policy Innovation PAC
Policy Innovation PAC
Lewisville, TX — Rep Dick Armey (R-Tex) — Repub Leaders
$53,550

71 Candidates	Repubs: 100.0%
Avg House: $754	House: 100.0%
Avg Senate: $0	Incumb: 28.9%

Potato Chip/Snack Food Assn
SnackPAC-Potato Chip/Snack Food Ass'n PAC
Alexandria, VA — Food Processing
$22,850

32 Candidates	Repubs: 70.2%
Avg House: $469	Senate: 56.8%
Avg Sen: $1,181	Incumb: 69.4%

Potlatch Corp
Potlatch Employees' Political Fund
San Francisco, CA — Forest Prod
$37,849

18 Candidates	Repubs: 50.3%
Avg House: $2,149	House: 79.5%
Avg Sen: $1,937	Incumb: 97.4%

Potomac Electric Power Company
Pepco PAC
Washington, DC — Electric Utility
$21,825

32 Candidates	Dems: 77.5%
Avg House: $618	House: 79.4%
Avg Sen: $1,125	Incumb: 96.6%

Powell, Goldstein, Frazer & Murphy
Powell, Goldstein, Frazer & Murphy PAC
Atlanta, GA — Lawyers
$99,840

183 Candidates	Dems: 86.4%
Avg House: $458	House: 58.8%
Avg Sen: $765	Incumb: 85.7%

PPG Industries
PPG Employees Voluntary Political Campaign Fund
Pittsburgh, PA — Glass Products†
$53,000

46 Candidates	Repubs: 88.6%
Avg House: $939	House: 58.5%
Avg Sen: $1,692	Incumb: 53.8%

Precision Metalforming Assn
Precision Metalforming Association PAC (Formerly American Metal Stamping Assn PAC)
Richmond Hts., OH — Metal Products
$65,200

38 Candidates	Repubs: 92.3%
Avg House: $1,125	Senate: 58.5%
Avg Sen: $2,728	Incumb: 49.1%

Premark International
Premark International, Inc PAC
Deerfield, IL — Plastic/Rubber†
$26,750

22 Candidates	Repubs: 81.3%
Avg House: $1,375	Senate: 59.8%
Avg Sen: $1,066	Incumb: 66.4%

Preston, Thorgrimson, Ellis & Holman
Preston, Thorgrimson, Ellis & Holman PAC
Washington, DC — Lawyers†
$86,028

170 Candidates	Dems: 72.5%
Avg House: $459	House: 79.5%
Avg Sen: $839	Incumb: 88.5%

Price Waterhouse
Price Waterhouse Partners' PAC
Washington, DC — Accountants
$30,500

39 Candidates	Dems: 50.8%
Avg House: $703	House: 62.3%
Avg Sen: $958	Incumb: 93.4%

Primerica Corp
Primerica Corporation PAC (Formerly American Can Company PAC)
Greenwich, CT — Consumer Credit†
$34,940

27 Candidates	Repubs: 51.2%
Avg House: $877	Senate: 61.6%
Avg Sen: $1,436	Incumb: 73.3%

† PAC Sponsor has other major interests in addition to this primary category

Principal Mutual Life Insurance
Principal Mutual Life Insurance Company - Federal PAC (Formerly Bankers Life Co PAC)
Des Moines, IA — Insurance — **$49,100**
66 Candidates — Dems: 59.8%
Avg House: $606 — House: 53.2%
Avg Sen: $1,000 — Incumb: 83.2%

Printing Industries of America
Printing Industries of America PAC (Print PAC)
Arlington, VA — Printing — **$73,773**
62 Candidates — Repubs: 90.3%
Avg House: $735 — Senate: 61.7%
Avg Sen: $1,898 — Incumb: 50.5%

Provident Life & Accident Insurance
Provident Life and Accident Insurance Company PAC (PROPAC)
Chattanooga, TN — Insurance — **$33,025**
22 Candidates — Dems: 72.4%
Avg House: $1,188 — House: 54.0%
Avg Sen: $2,000 — Incumb: 88.5%

Provident Mutual Life Insurance
Provident Mutual Life Insurance Company PAC
Philadelphia, PA — Life Insurance — **$21,500**
26 Candidates — Repubs: 61.6%
Avg House: $555 — House: 46.5%
Avg Sen: $1,357 — Incumb: 90.9%

Prudential Insurance
Prudential Insurance Company of America Federal PAC ("Prudential PAC")
Newark, NJ — Prudential Insurance — Insurance† — **$183,329**
161 Candidates — Dems: 62.6%
Avg House: $866 — House: 54.4%
Avg Sen: $1,801 — Incumb: 89.6%

Prudential-Bache Securities
Prudential-Bache Securities Inc PAC
New York, NY — Prudential Insurance — Securities Investment — **$122,633**
95 Candidates — Dems: 60.5%
Avg House: $1,023 — House: 48.4%
Avg Sen: $1,669 — Incumb: 93.7%

Public Securities Assn
Public Securities Association
Washington, DC — Securities — **$68,664**
97 Candidates — Dems: 69.6%
Avg House: $517 — House: 55.8%
Avg Sen: $1,330 — Incumb: 91.9%

Public Service Company of NH/Yankee Division
Public Service Company of New Hampshire, NH Yankee Division PAC (NHY-PAC)
Seabrook, NH — Public Service Co of NH — Electric Utility — **$27,298**
44 Candidates — Repubs: 56.8%
Avg House: $612 — House: 80.8%
Avg Sen: $656 — Incumb: 96.3%

Public Service Electric & Gas
Public Service Electric and Gas Company PAC (PEGPAC)
Newark, NJ — Gas/Electric† — **$41,055**
58 Candidates — Dems: 54.2%
Avg House: $593 — House: 63.6%
Avg Sen: $1,066 — Incumb: 78.1%

Public Service Research Council
Public Service PAC
Vienna, VA — Anti-Union — **$299,787**
182 Candidates — Repubs: 97.7%
Avg House: $1,241 — House: 67.1%
Avg Sen: $4,936 — Incumb: 46.5%

Puget Sound Power & Light
Puget Power Good Government Committee - Federal
Bellevue, WA — Electric Utility — **$21,400**
18 Candidates — Repubs: 70.7%
Avg House: $1,093 — House: 76.6%
Avg Sen: $1,666 — Incumb: 57.7%

Quaker Oats
Public Interest Committee of the Quaker Oats Company; The
Chicago, IL — Food Processing† — **$34,000**
36 Candidates — Repubs: 58.8%
Avg House: $794 — Senate: 60.2%
Avg Sen: $1,078 — Incumb: 88.2%

R R Donnelley & Sons
R R Donnelley & Sons Company PAC
Chicago, IL — Publishing/Printing† — **$31,000**
36 Candidates — Repubs: 74.5%
Avg House: $653 — Senate: 66.2%
Avg Sen: $1,027 — Incumb: 65.2%

Raytheon
Raytheon Company PAC
Lexington, MA — Raytheon — Defense Electronics† — **$167,500**
172 Candidates — Repubs: 50.4%
Avg House: $893 — House: 69.9%
Avg Sen: $1,230 — Incumb: 89.7%

Real Estate Investment PAC
Real Estate Investment PAC
Washington, DC — Real Estate Devel — **$21,000**
29 Candidates — Dems: 58.8%
Avg House: $529 — Senate: 57.1%
Avg Sen: $1,000 — Incumb: 77.1%

Recognition Equipment Inc
Recognition Equipment Incorporated PAC
Dallas, TX — Electronics† — **$65,421**
47 Candidates — Repubs: 63.2%
Avg House: $1,054 — Senate: 55.5%
Avg Sen: $1,816 — Incumb: 73.1%

Recording Industry Assn
Recording Industry Assn of America Inc PAC (Formerly Recording Arts PAC)
Washington, DC — Music Prod — **$45,700**
60 Candidates — Dems: 83.6%
Avg House: $623 — House: 57.3%
Avg Sen: $1,083 — Incumb: 90.7%

Religion and Tolerance PAC
Religion and Tolerance PAC (RATPAC)
Washington, DC — Dem/Liberal — **$69,200**
28 Candidates — Dems: 100.0%
Avg House: $1,337 — Senate: 75.1%
Avg Sen: $3,058 — Incumb: 56.6%

Republican Congressional Boosters Club
Republican Congressional Boosters Club
Washington,, DC — Repub Leaders — **$84,500**
59 Candidates — Repubs: 94.6%
Avg House: $1,091 — House: 63.3%
Avg Sen: $3,100 — Incumb: 23.1%

Sponsor or Related Group/PAC Name	Affiliate	1987-88 Total	Where the money went...		
Republican Leader's Fund Republican Leader's Fund Washington, DC	Rep Bob Michel (R-Ill) Repub Leaders	$27,500	31 Candidates Avg House: $887 Avg Sen: $0	Repubs: 100.0% House: 100.0% Incumb: 0.0%	
Republican Majority Fund Republican Majority Fund Washington, DC	Sen Richard Lugar (R-Ind) Repub Leaders	$170,000	30 Candidates Avg House: $1,000 Avg Sen: $7,363	Repubs: 100.0% Senate: 95.2% Incumb: 54.1%	
Reynolds Metals Reynolds Metals Company Political Participation Program Fund (RAPPP) Richmond, VA	Metal Mining/Processing	$31,420	61 Candidates Avg House: $484 Avg Sen: $595	Repubs: 57.7% House: 67.8% Incumb: 78.4%	
Right to Work PAC Right to Work PAC Springfield, VA	Anti-Union	$148,091	107 Candidates Avg House: $1,037 Avg Sen: $3,218	Repubs: 98.8% House: 63.0% Incumb: 37.5%	
Rivkin, Radler, Dunne & Baye RRD & B Good Government Committee Washington, DC	Lawyers	$48,237	61 Candidates Avg House: $488 Avg Sen: $1,119	Dems: 86.5% Senate: 60.3% Incumb: 80.2%	
RJR Nabisco RJR PAC, RJR Nabisco Inc Winston-Salem, NC	RJR Nabisco Tobacco†	$260,675	212 Candidates Avg House: $940 Avg Sen: $3,390	Dems: 51.9% House: 67.5% Incumb: 76.9%	
Roadway Services Inc Roadway Services Inc (REXPAC) Akron, OH	Trucking	$52,275	79 Candidates Avg House: $591 Avg Sen: $898	Dems: 61.0% House: 69.1% Incumb: 82.7%	
Rockwell International Rockwell International Corporation Good Government Committee Pittsburgh, PA	Air Defense†	$379,768	286 Candidates Avg House: $1,019 Avg Sen: $3,382	Repubs: 60.1% House: 67.1% Incumb: 85.3%	
Rohm and Haas Company Rohm and Haas Employees Association for Better Government Philadelphia, PA	Chemicals†	$21,400	28 Candidates Avg House: $666 Avg Sen: $1,583	Repubs: 63.3% House: 77.8% Incumb: 90.7%	
Roundtable PAC Roundtable PAC New York, NY	Pro-Israel	$120,000	94 Candidates Avg House: $979 Avg Sen: $2,309	Dems: 69.6% House: 59.6% Incumb: 73.7%	
Rubber Cork Linoleum Plastic Workers COPE Cmte of the United Rubber Cork Linoleum and Plastic Workers of America AFL-CIO Akron, OH	Manuf Unions	$198,850	90 Candidates Avg House: $1,790 Avg Sen: $4,163	Dems: 98.0% House: 64.8% Incumb: 49.0%	
Ruff PAC Ruff PAC Washington, DC	Tax Policy	$125,079	68 Candidates Avg House: $1,456 Avg Sen: $2,989	Repubs: 100.0% House: 59.4% Incumb: 31.4%	
Ryder System Inc Ryder System, Inc Committee for Effective Government Miami, FL	Car/Truck Rent†	$44,350	47 Candidates Avg House: $731 Avg Sen: $1,636	Dems: 58.9% House: 59.4% Incumb: 80.4%	
S & A Restaurant Corp S & A Restaurant Corp Employees PAC Dallas, TX	Restaurants	$54,300	22 Candidates Avg House: $1,200 Avg Sen: $3,625	Repubs: 78.8% Senate: 80.1% Incumb: 70.5%	
Sacramento Area Good Govt Assn Sacramento Area Good Government Assoc (SAGGA) Sacramento, CA	Pro-Israel	$29,500	8 Candidates Avg House: $3,000 Avg Sen: $3,916	Dems: 79.7% Senate: 79.6% Incumb: 44.1%	
Safari Club International Safari Club International PAC Livonia, MI	Hunting/Pro-Guns†	$29,150	28 Candidates Avg House: $1,041 Avg Sen: $1,037	Repubs: 71.7% House: 85.8% Incumb: 94.0%	
Safeco Corp Safeco-PAC Seattle, WA	Insurance†	$24,225	24 Candidates Avg House: $473 Avg Sen: $1,760	Repubs: 93.2% Senate: 72.6% Incumb: 34.6%	
Safeway Stores Safeway Stores, Incorporated PAC (SAFEPAC) Oakland, CA	Food Stores	$29,100	31 Candidates Avg House: $543 Avg Sen: $1,800	Repubs: 79.0% Senate: 43.3% Incumb: 79.4%	
St Louisans for Better Government St Louisans for Better Government St Louis, MO	Pro-Israel	$127,000	44 Candidates Avg House: $1,233 Avg Sen: $6,428	Dems: 66.5% Senate: 70.8% Incumb: 79.5%	

† PAC Sponsor has other major interests in addition to this primary category

Sponsor or Related Group/PAC Name	Affiliate	1987-88 Total	Where the money went...		
St Paul Companies Inc St Paul Companies Inc Volunteer Committee for Good Federal Government St Paul, MN	Insurance	$26,850	33 Candidates Avg House: $356 Avg Sen: $1,727	Repubs: 83.3% Senate: 70.7% Incumb: 74.7%	
Salomon Brothers Salomon Brothers Inc PAC New York, NY	Securities Investment	$121,162	114 Candidates Avg House: $601 Avg Sen: $2,209	Dems: 54.6% Senate: 54.7% Incumb: 88.6%	
San Diego Community PAC San Diego Community PAC Inc (SANCPAC) San Diego, CA	Pro-Israel	$32,100	25 Candidates Avg House: $640 Avg Sen: $2,250	Dems: 63.2% Senate: 70.0% Incumb: 66.4%	
San Diego Gas & Electric San Diego Gas & Electric Co. Citizens for Good Government Committee San Diego, CA	Gas/Electric	$30,525	59 Candidates Avg House: $475 Avg Sen: $781	Repubs: 50.7% House: 79.5% Incumb: 91.8%	
San Franciscans for Good Government San Franciscans for Good Government San Francisco, CA	Pro-Israel	$104,000	31 Candidates Avg House: $1,730 Avg Sen: $4,527	Dems: 78.8% Senate: 78.3% Incumb: 80.3%	
Sandoz Pharmaceuticals Sandoz Pharmaceuticals Corp PAC East Hanover, NJ	Pharmaceuticals†	$53,825	110 Candidates Avg House: $457 Avg Sen: $560	Repubs: 73.6% House: 68.0% Incumb: 89.3%	
SANE/Freeze Inc SANE/Freeze PAC Washington, DC	Pro-Peace	$58,237	35 Candidates Avg House: $1,467 Avg Sen: $2,660	Dems: 99.5% House: 68.0% Incumb: 22.5%	
Santa Fe International Corp Santa Fe International Corporation PAC Alhambra, CA	Trucking	$26,700	30 Candidates Avg House: $757 Avg Sen: $1,118	Repubs: 95.3% House: 53.9% Incumb: 43.3%	
Santa Fe Southern Pacific Santa Fe Southern Pacific Corporation PAC Chicago, IL	Railroads†	$90,127	129 Candidates Avg House: $569 Avg Sen: $1,208	Repubs: 61.6% House: 65.1% Incumb: 92.5%	
SAPEC/ NJ (New Jersey Savings Assn) SAPEC, N J Cranford, NJ	US League of Savings Assn / Savings Banks	$33,250	18 Candidates Avg House: $1,910 Avg Sen: $1,533	Repubs: 52.3% House: 86.2% Incumb: 89.8%	
Savannah Foods & Industries Savannah Foods & Industries Inc Nonpartisan Cmte for Better Federal Govt Savannah, GA	Sugar†	$20,550	45 Candidates Avg House: $408 Avg Sen: $521	Dems: 50.4% House: 59.6% Incumb: 74.9%	
Schering-Plough Corp Schering-Plough Corporation Better Government Fund Madison, NJ	Pharmaceuticals†	$117,600	93 Candidates Avg House: $1,052 Avg Sen: $1,565	Repubs: 64.2% House: 60.9% Incumb: 80.4%	
Scott Paper Company Scott Paper Company PAC (SCOTTPAC) Washington, DC	Paper Prod†	$46,950	83 Candidates Avg House: $415 Avg Sen: $981	Repubs: 65.5% House: 54.0% Incumb: 83.9%	
Sea-Land Corp Sea-Land Good Government Fund Sea-Land Industries Inc Washington, DC	CSX Corp / Sea Transport†	$40,084	55 Candidates Avg House: $512 Avg Sen: $1,504	Repubs: 52.0% House: 54.9% Incumb: 86.9%	
Seafarers International Union Seafarers Political Activity Donation (SPAD) Camp Springs, MD	Seafarers Intl Union / Sea Trans Union	$1,083,415	397 Candidates Avg House: $2,410 Avg Sen: $5,283	Dems: 85.9% House: 78.3% Incumb: 73.9%	
Sears Sears PAC Chicago, IL	Sears / Retail Sales†	$68,400	151 Candidates Avg House: $374 Avg Sen: $868	Repubs: 60.2% House: 69.5% Incumb: 75.8%	
Securities Industry Assn Securities Industry PAC Washington, DC	Securities Industry Assn / Securities Investment	$100,366	47 Candidates Avg House: $965 Avg Sen: $1,113	Dems: 62.8% House: 73.9% Incumb: 95.2%	
Security Life of Denver Security Life of Denver Insurance Company PAC (Security Life PAC) Denver, CO	Life Insurance	$23,543	22 Candidates Avg House: $1,123 Avg Sen: $993	Dems: 65.2% House: 62.0% Incumb: 78.1%	
Security Pacific Corp Security Pacific Corporation Active Citizenship Today Committee (SPACT) Los Angeles, CA	Commercial Banks	$104,000	83 Candidates Avg House: $1,077 Avg Sen: $1,738	Dems: 63.7% House: 63.2% Incumb: 98.1%	

Sponsor or Related Group/PAC Name	Affiliate	1987-88 Total	Where the money went...		
Senate Majority Fund Senate Majority Fund Washington, DC — Sen Daniel Inouye (D-Hawaii)	Dem Leaders	$258,100	31 Candidates Avg House: $10,000 Avg Sen: $8,270	Dems: 100.0% Senate: 96.1% Incumb: 54.7%	
Senate Victory Fund Senate Victory Fund PAC (Formerly Cochran Committee) Jackson, MS — Sen Thad Cochran (R-Miss)	Repub Leaders	$24,961	22 Candidates Avg House: $0 Avg Sen: $1,134	Repubs: 100.0% Senate: 100.0% Incumb: 64.1%	
Service Corporation Inernational Service Corporation International PAC (SRV/PAC) Houston, TX	Funeral Svcs	$28,150	34 Candidates Avg House: $530 Avg Sen: $1,318	Dems: 85.6% Senate: 51.5% Incumb: 81.3%	
Service Employees International Union Service Employees Int'l Union COPE Political Campaign Comm Washington, DC	Misc Unions	$319,808	160 Candidates Avg House: $1,401 Avg Sen: $4,125	Dems: 95.8% House: 54.8% Incumb: 50.8%	
Services Group of America Services Group of America PAC Seattle, WA	Food Wholesale†	$24,750	12 Candidates Avg House: $1,763 Avg Sen: $2,958	Repubs: 75.2% House: 64.1% Incumb: 46.0%	
Shearson Lehman Hutton Action Fund of Shearson Lehman Hutton Inc New York, NY — American Express	Securities Investment	$169,725	137 Candidates Avg House: $807 Avg Sen: $2,323	Dems: 67.2% Senate: 53.4% Incumb: 77.5%	
Sheet Metal Workers Union Sheet Metal Workers International Association Political Action League (PAL) Washington, DC — Sheet Metal Workers	Constr Unions	$801,000	207 Candidates Avg House: $3,399 Avg Sen: $6,393	Dems: 98.7% House: 71.7% Incumb: 53.2%	
Sheet Metal/Air Conditioning Contractors Sheet Metal and Air Conditioning Contractors' PAC Vienna, VA	Plumb/AirCon	$205,535	121 Candidates Avg House: $1,406 Avg Sen: $2,820	Repubs: 71.9% House: 65.7% Incumb: 74.0%	
Shell Oil Shell Oil Company Employees' Political Awareness Committee Houston, TX	Oil & Gas Prod†	$155,075	179 Candidates Avg House: $608 Avg Sen: $1,860	Repubs: 69.6% House: 57.2% Incumb: 84.7%	
Shoneys Inc Shoney's PAC Nashville, TN	Restaurants	$27,850	20 Candidates Avg House: $1,603 Avg Sen: $1,000	Dems: 80.3% House: 74.9% Incumb: 49.7%	
Sierra Club Sierra Club Committee on Political Education San Francisco, CA	Environmental	$286,904	162 Candidates Avg House: $1,453 Avg Sen: $3,906	Dems: 88.5% House: 71.4% Incumb: 59.1%	
Simpson Investment Company Simpson Investment Company PAC (Simpson Pol Act Cmte/SIMPAC) Seattle, WA	Forest Prod	$48,424	32 Candidates Avg House: $996 Avg Sen: $3,062	Repubs: 78.0% Senate: 50.5% Incumb: 62.8%	
Singer Company Singer Company PAC (Shortened Form: Singer PAC) Stamford, CT	Defense Electronics†	$92,900	58 Candidates Avg House: $1,315 Avg Sen: $2,500	Dems: 65.3% House: 62.3% Incumb: 100.0%	
Smith Barney Smith Barney Better Government Committee New York, NY	Securities Investment	$55,450	34 Candidates Avg House: $889 Avg Sen: $1,940	Repubs: 55.1% Senate: 52.4% Incumb: 71.8%	
Smithkline Beckman Smithkline Beckman PAC (SKB-PAC) Philadelphia, PA	Pharmaceuticals†	$92,400	91 Candidates Avg House: $851 Avg Sen: $1,511	Repubs: 75.0% House: 62.7% Incumb: 92.2%	
Smokeless Tobacco Council Smokeless Tobacco Council Inc PAC (STCPAC) Washington, DC	Tobacco	$25,150	40 Candidates Avg House: $336 Avg Sen: $986	Repubs: 56.0% Senate: 70.5% Incumb: 98.0%	
Society Corp Society Corporation PAC Cleveland, OH	Commercial Banks	$25,450	16 Candidates Avg House: $845 Avg Sen: $10,000	Repubs: 65.0% House: 39.9% Incumb: 58.0%	
Society for Advancement of Ambulatory Care Society for the Advancement of Ambulatory Care PAC (SAAC/PAC) Washington, DC	Outpatient Svcs	$24,800	32 Candidates Avg House: $552 Avg Sen: $1,146	Dems: 81.7% Senate: 60.0% Incumb: 81.3%	
Society of American Florists Society of American Florists PAC (SAF-PAC) Alexandria, VA	Florists	$56,412	107 Candidates Avg House: $476 Avg Sen: $840	Repubs: 83.2% House: 77.7% Incumb: 91.0%	

† PAC Sponsor has other major interests in addition to this primary category

Society of Independent Gasoline Marketers
Society of Independent Gasoline Marketers of America
Washington, DC — Gas Stations — **$62,963**
86 Candidates — Dems: 55.3%
Avg House: $551 — House: 57.8%
Avg Sen: $1,292 — Incumb: 88.2%

Society of Real Estate Appraisers
Society of Real Estate Appraisers PAC (APPAC)
Chicago, IL — Real Est Svcs — **$20,800**
50 Candidates — Repubs: 52.4%
Avg House: $370 — House: 82.0%
Avg Sen: $937 — Incumb: 100.0%

South Carolina National Bank
South Carolina National Bank PAC
Columbia, SC — Commercial Banks — **$28,583**
27 Candidates — Dems: 59.6%
Avg House: $1,043 — House: 69.4%
Avg Sen: $1,093 — Incumb: 89.3%

South Carolinians for Representative Government
South Carolinians for Representative Government
Charleston, SC — Pro-Israel — **$21,000**
19 Candidates — Dems: 90.5%
Avg House: $818 — Senate: 57.1%
Avg Sen: $1,500 — Incumb: 42.9%

South Central Bell Telephone
South Central Bell Telephone Company Federal PAC (SCB FPAC)
Birmingham, AL — BellSouth — Phone Utilities — **$136,461**
59 Candidates — Dems: 67.5%
Avg House: $2,271 — House: 76.6%
Avg Sen: $2,743 — Incumb: 77.1%

Southern Bell
Southern Bell Telephone and Telegraph Company Federal PAC (SOUBELL PAC)
Atlanta, GA — BellSouth — Phone Utilities — **$219,835**
71 Candidates — Dems: 64.2%
Avg House: $3,292 — House: 80.9%
Avg Sen: $2,629 — Incumb: 83.3%

Southern California Edison
Federal Citizenship Responsibility Group/The Southern California Edison Company
Rosemead, CA — Electric Utility — **$161,270**
155 Candidates — Dems: 61.5%
Avg House: $890 — House: 70.7%
Avg Sen: $1,684 — Incumb: 91.8%

Southern Company
Southern Company Services PAC
Atlanta, GA — Southern Company — Electric Utility — **$99,930**
165 Candidates — Repubs: 55.8%
Avg House: $481 — House: 62.1%
Avg Sen: $1,052 — Incumb: 76.4%

Southern Minnesota Beet Sugar Co-op
Southern Minnesota Sugar Cooperative PAC
Renville, MN — Sugar — **$108,300**
130 Candidates — Repubs: 52.4%
Avg House: $807 — House: 66.4%
Avg Sen: $892 — Incumb: 88.5%

Southern Natural Resources
Sonat Inc PAC
Birmingham, AL — Natural Gas† — **$42,775**
50 Candidates — Dems: 78.8%
Avg House: $659 — House: 50.9%
Avg Sen: $1,187 — Incumb: 94.3%

Southern Wine & Spirits
Southern Wine & Spirits PAC
Miami, FL — Wine/Liquor — **$21,180**
11 Candidates — Dems: 97.6%
Avg House: $1,125 — Senate: 76.3%
Avg Sen: $2,696 — Incumb: 21.2%

Southland Corp
Southland Corporation Employee's PAC; The
Dallas, TX — Dept Stores† — **$59,049**
55 Candidates — Repubs: 79.9%
Avg House: $828 — House: 57.5%
Avg Sen: $1,792 — Incumb: 64.7%

Southwest Gas Corp
Southwest Gas Corporation PAC
Las Vegas, NV — Natural Gas — **$30,385**
18 Candidates — Repubs: 57.0%
Avg House: $1,414 — House: 60.5%
Avg Sen: $2,400 — Incumb: 85.1%

Southwest Marine
Southwest Marine Inc PAC
San Diego, CA — Ship Mfrs — **$35,350**
23 Candidates — Repubs: 72.7%
Avg House: $1,373 — House: 58.3%
Avg Sen: $1,892 — Incumb: 84.4%

Southwest Peanut Membrship Organization
Southwest Peanut PAC
Washington, DC — Misc Crops — **$28,900**
49 Candidates — Dems: 86.2%
Avg House: $444 — House: 58.5%
Avg Sen: $1,090 — Incumb: 93.1%

Southwestern Bell
Southwestern Bell Corporation Employee Federal PAC (SWB EMPAC or EMPAC)
St Louis, MO — Phone Utilities — **$154,300**
98 Candidates — Dems: 52.9%
Avg House: $1,533 — House: 73.5%
Avg Sen: $1,278 — Incumb: 94.9%

Springs Mills
Springs Mills Inc PAC (SpringsPAC)
Fort Mill, SC — Textiles — **$32,250**
41 Candidates — Repubs: 53.1%
Avg House: $719 — House: 73.6%
Avg Sen: $928 — Incumb: 86.2%

Square D Company
Square D Company PAC
Palatine, IL — Indust Equip — **$25,500**
26 Candidates — Repubs: 100.0%
Avg House: $894 — House: 66.7%
Avg Sen: $1,214 — Incumb: 66.7%

Squibb Corp
Squibb Good Govovernment Fund
Washington, DC — Pharmaceuticals — **$71,983**
89 Candidates — Repubs: 64.3%
Avg House: $502 — Senate: 55.2%
Avg Sen: $1,530 — Incumb: 86.7%

Sponsor or Related Group/PAC Name	Affiliate	1987-88 Total	Where the money went...		
Stephens Overseas Services Stephens Overseas Services PAC Little Rock, AR		$29,100	13 Candidates Avg House: $1,500	Repubs: 57.0% Senate: 68.7%	
		Financial Svcs	Avg Sen: $2,222	Incumb: 65.6%	
Sterling Drug Sterling Drug Inc PAC (STERLPAC) New York, NY	Eastman Kodak	$35,358	55 Candidates Avg House: $573	Repubs: 71.6% House: 73.0%	
		Pharmaceuticals	Avg Sen: $955	Incumb: 89.9%	
Stone & Webster Stone & Webster PAC New York, NY		$61,600	116 Candidates Avg House: $479	Dems: 53.7% House: 74.7%	
		Engineers	Avg Sen: $780	Incumb: 93.1%	
Stone Container Corp Stone Container Corporation PAC Chicago, IL	Stone Container Corp	$80,825	72 Candidates Avg House: $1,026	Repubs: 66.9% House: 62.2%	
		Paper Packaging†	Avg Sen: $1,327	Incumb: 80.8%	
Sun Banks Sun Banks Inc PAC (Sun BankPAC) Tallahassee, FL	Suntrust Banks	$74,350	64 Candidates Avg House: $636	Dems: 71.7% Senate: 62.2%	
		Commercial Banks	Avg Sen: $2,102	Incumb: 50.9%	
Sun Company Sun Company Inc PAC Radnor, PA		$152,000	135 Candidates Avg House: $827	Repubs: 82.2% House: 63.2%	
		Oil & Gas Prod†	Avg Sen: $2,947	Incumb: 69.1%	
Sun-Maid Growers of California Sun-Maid Growers of California PAC Kingsburg, CA		$35,000	23 Candidates Avg House: $1,333	Repubs: 57.1% House: 57.1%	
		Fruit/Veg	Avg Sen: $1,428	Incumb: 92.9%	
Sundstrand Corp Sundstrand Good Government Support Fund (SGGSF) Rockford, IL	Sundstrand Corp	$23,595	39 Candidates Avg House: $586	Repubs: 55.0% House: 74.6%	
		Aerospace Equip†	Avg Sen: $687	Incumb: 94.7%	
Sunkist Growers Sunkist Growers, Inc PAC Sherman Oaks, CA		$56,275	59 Candidates Avg House: $812	Repubs: 50.7% House: 75.1%	
		Fruit/Veg	Avg Sen: $1,500	Incumb: 98.2%	
Sunsweet Growers Sunsweet Growers Inc PAC Pleasanton, CA		$20,200	10 Candidates Avg House: $1,450	Repubs: 82.6% House: 43.1%	
		Fruit/Veg†	Avg Sen: $2,166	Incumb: 92.6%	
Teamsters Union Democratic Republican Independent Voter Education Committee (DRIVE) Washington, DC	Teamsters Union	$2,865,224	428 Candidates Avg House: $6,785	Dems: 88.9% House: 87.2%	
		Teamsters	Avg Sen: $6,263	Incumb: 69.4%	
Teamwork America Teamwork America Washington, DC		$22,250	23 Candidates Avg House: $1,000	Dems: 100.0% House: 58.4%	
		Dem/Liberal	Avg Sen: $925	Incumb: 44.9%	
Tele-Communications Inc Tele-Communications, Inc PAC (TCI PAC) Denver, CO		$41,025	17 Candidates Avg House: $2,105	Repubs: 50.0% Senate: 59.2%	
		CableTV	Avg Sen: $2,698	Incumb: 89.0%	
Tenneco Inc Tenneco Inc. Employees Good Govt Fund (Tenneco Employees Good Govt Fund) Houston, TX		$279,600	168 Candidates Avg House: $1,228	Repubs: 84.2% House: 63.3%	
		Shipbuilding†	Avg Sen: $4,281	Incumb: 68.7%	
Texaco Texaco Political Involvement Committee White Plains, NY		$152,815	197 Candidates Avg House: $573	Repubs: 74.6% House: 62.3%	
		Oil & Gas Prod†	Avg Sen: $1,858	Incumb: 88.6%	
Texas Air Texas Air Corporation PAC (TAC PAC) Houston, TX	Texas Air	$231,855	140 Candidates Avg House: $1,276	Dems: 64.4% House: 60.0%	
		Airlines	Avg Sen: $2,989	Incumb: 87.3%	
Texas Cattle Feeders Assn Beef-PAC (Beef PAC of Texas Cattle Feeders Association) Amarillo, TX	National Cattlemens Assn	$89,325	89 Candidates Avg House: $947	Repubs: 50.1% House: 72.2%	
		Feedlots	Avg Sen: $1,184	Incumb: 89.5%	
Texas Commerce Bancshares* Texas Commerce PAC Houston, TX	Chemical Bank	$33,000	25 Candidates Avg House: $1,046	Dems: 74.2% House: 50.8%	
		Commercial Banks	Avg Sen: $1,812	Incumb: 98.5%	
Texas Eastern Gas Transmission Texas Eastern PAC Houston, TX		$75,050	116 Candidates Avg House: $540	Dems: 53.4% House: 63.4%	
		Natural Gas†	Avg Sen: $981	Incumb: 89.0%	

† PAC Sponsor has other major interests in addition to this primary category

Sponsor or Related Group/PAC Name	Affiliate	1987-88 Total	Where the money went...		
Texas Farm Bureau Texas Farm Bureau Friends of Agriculture Fund (AGFUND), Inc Waco, TX	Farm Orgs	$32,587	17 Candidates Avg House: $1,916 Avg Sen: $0	Repubs: 51.0% House: 100.0% Incumb: 78.7%	
Texas Gas Transmission Corp Texas Gas Transmission Corporation PAC Owensboro, KY	Natural Gas	$29,158	45 Candidates Avg House: $535 Avg Sen: $995	Dems: 61.5% House: 62.4% Incumb: 92.1%	
Texas Industries TXI PAC Dallas, TX	Stone/Concrete	$20,050	11 Candidates Avg House: $1,756 Avg Sen: $2,000	Repubs: 75.0% House: 70.1% Incumb: 65.1%	
Texas Instruments Constructive Citizenship Program of Texas Instruments Dallas, TX	Computers†	$62,200	67 Candidates Avg House: $717 Avg Sen: $1,600	Repubs: 54.2% House: 58.8% Incumb: 95.6%	
Texas Utilities Company Texas Utilities Company PAC Dallas, TX	Texas Utilities / Electric Utility	$36,600	53 Candidates Avg House: $702 Avg Sen: $657	Repubs: 59.6% House: 74.9% Incumb: 86.6%	
Texas Utilities Electric Co/Tesco Division Tesco Div of Texas Utilities Electric Company PAC Fort Worth, TX	Texas Utilities / Electric Utility	$33,075	96 Candidates Avg House: $323 Avg Sen: $425	Repubs: 65.7% House: 74.3% Incumb: 80.0%	
Texas Utilities Electric Co/TP&L Division Texas Utilities Electric Company TP&L Division Employee PAC (Em-PAC) Dallas, TX	Texas Utilities / Electric Utility	$48,750	88 Candidates Avg House: $601 Avg Sen: $355	Repubs: 52.5% House: 87.6% Incumb: 84.8%	
Textron Inc Textron Inc PAC Providence, RI	Air Defense†	$411,431	246 Candidates Avg House: $1,204 Avg Sen: $4,081	Dems: 59.3% House: 60.3% Incumb: 86.9%	
Third National Corp Third National Corporation Good Government Fund Nashville, TN	Suntrust Banks / Commercial Banks	$27,340	13 Candidates Avg House: $1,736 Avg Sen: $3,240	Dems: 81.7% House: 69.9% Incumb: 68.9%	
Thomson McKinnon Securities Thomson McKinnon Securities Inc PAC (TMSI-PAC) New York, NY	Securities Investment	$24,000	8 Candidates Avg House: $3,333 Avg Sen: $2,250	Dems: 75.0% House: 41.7% Incumb: 75.0%	
Tobacco Institute Tobacco Institute PAC Washington, DC	Tobacco	$194,557	264 Candidates Avg House: $675 Avg Sen: $1,267	Dems: 53.4% House: 81.6% Incumb: 95.6%	
Torchmark Corp Torchmark Corporation Political Action Committe (TORCH-PAC) Birmingham, AL	Insurance	$188,798	59 Candidates Avg House: $2,450 Avg Sen: $4,326	Repubs: 57.3% Senate: 52.7% Incumb: 82.5%	
Torrington Company Torrington Company PAC Torrington, CT	Ingersoll-Rand / Auto Parts†	$26,950	28 Candidates Avg House: $1,041 Avg Sen: $825	Dems: 59.4% House: 65.7% Incumb: 97.4%	
Totem Ocean Trailer Express Totem Ocean Trailer Express Inc/Foss Maritime Company PAC (TOTE/Foss PAC) Seattle, WA	Sea Transport	$22,350	23 Candidates Avg House: $709 Avg Sen: $2,000	Repubs: 59.7% House: 50.8% Incumb: 74.5%	
Touche Ross Touche Ross Partners Federal PAC (TRPAC) Washington, DC	Accountants	$159,354	78 Candidates Avg House: $1,583 Avg Sen: $2,961	Dems: 51.7% House: 51.7% Incumb: 86.8%	
Trammell Crow Company Trammell Crow Partners Political Committee Dallas, TX	Real Estate Devel†	$30,125	20 Candidates Avg House: $1,152 Avg Sen: $1,531	Dems: 57.3% Senate: 40.7% Incumb: 94.2%	
Trans World Airlines Trans World Airlines PAC (TWA-PAC) Washington, DC	Airlines	$41,300	52 Candidates Avg House: $662 Avg Sen: $1,250	Dems: 59.9% House: 64.2% Incumb: 99.4%	
TransAmerica Insurance TransAmerica Insurance Company PAC Woodland Hills, CA	TransAmerica / Insurance	$32,000	10 Candidates Avg House: $3,000 Avg Sen: $3,500	Repubs: 90.6% House: 56.3% Incumb: 81.3%	
TransAmerica Life Companies TransAmerica Life Companies PAC ("TALCPAC") Los Angeles, CA	TransAmerica / Life Insurance	$62,300	69 Candidates Avg House: $903 Avg Sen: $902	Dems: 71.0% House: 66.7% Incumb: 96.8%	

Sponsor or Related Group/PAC Name	Affiliate	1987-88 Total	Where the money went...		
Transco Energy Company Transco Energy Company PAC (Formerly TRANSPAC) Houston, TX	Natural Gas	$52,490	89 Candidates Avg House: $464 Avg Sen: $923	Repubs: 51.6% House: 58.4% Incumb: 85.1%	
Transport Workers Union Transport Workers Union Political Contributions Committee New York, NY	Transport Workers Union Transport Union	$221,780	114 Candidates Avg House: $1,565 Avg Sen: $3,665	Dems: 92.5% House: 64.9% Incumb: 71.3%	
Transportation Communication Union Responsible Citizens Pol League - A Project of the Trans Comm Intl Union (TCU) Rockville, MD	Transport Union	$375,398	343 Candidates Avg House: $793 Avg Sen: $3,056	Dems: 94.3% House: 63.2% Incumb: 70.6%	
Travelers Corp Travelers Corporation PAC (T-PAC); The Hartford, CT	Travelers Corp Insurance†	$195,750	135 Candidates Avg House: $1,157 Avg Sen: $2,390	Repubs: 51.2% House: 60.9% Incumb: 89.7%	
Triangle Industries Triangle Industries Inc PAC New York, NY	Cans/Containers†	$92,000	19 Candidates Avg House: $4,800 Avg Sen: $5,083	Dems: 80.4% Senate: 66.3% Incumb: 94.6%	
Trust Company of Georgia Trust Company of Georgia Good Government Group Atlanta, GA	Suntrust Banks Commercial Banks	$23,250	24 Candidates Avg House: $955 Avg Sen: $1,000	Dems: 71.2% House: 69.9% Incumb: 85.2%	
TRW Inc TRW Good Government Fund Lyndhurst, OH	Defense Electronics†	$208,648	225 Candidates Avg House: $723 Avg Sen: $2,528	Repubs: 54.6% House: 68.3% Incumb: 86.5%	
Turner Broadcasting System Turner Broadcasting System PAC Inc Atlanta, GA	CableTV†	$23,950	25 Candidates Avg House: $465 Avg Sen: $1,833	Dems: 53.7% Senate: 68.8% Incumb: 92.5%	
TX PAC TX PAC (Formerly Texans for Sound Middle East Policy) Dallas, TX	Pro-Israel	$23,550	30 Candidates Avg House: $419 Avg Sen: $1,333	Dems: 73.5% Senate: 67.9% Incumb: 64.3%	
Tyson Foods Tyson Foods Inc PAC (TYPAC) Springdale, AR	Poultry/Egg†	$50,490	50 Candidates Avg House: $825 Avg Sen: $1,086	Dems: 87.0% House: 47.4% Incumb: 88.4%	
UNC Inc UNC Incorporated Public Responsibility Fund Annapolis, MD	Aerospace Equip	$25,700	27 Candidates Avg House: $805 Avg Sen: $1,222	Dems: 59.5% House: 53.3% Incumb: 96.1%	
Union Camp Corp Union Camp Corporation PAC Wayne, NJ	Paper Prod†	$75,882	65 Candidates Avg House: $581 Avg Sen: $2,168	Repubs: 68.4% Senate: 68.5% Incumb: 57.8%	
Union Carbide Union Carbide Corporation PAC New York, NY	Chemicals	$24,100	38 Candidates Avg House: $503 Avg Sen: $1,000	Repubs: 58.7% House: 58.5% Incumb: 79.9%	
Union Oil Union Oil (Unocal) Political Awareness Fund Los Angeles, CA	Oil & Gas Prod†	$118,951	153 Candidates Avg House: $460 Avg Sen: $2,250	Repubs: 73.1% House: 50.0% Incumb: 71.2%	
Union Pacific Corp Union Pacific Fund for Effective Government New York, NY	Railroads†	$358,450	237 Candidates Avg House: $829 Avg Sen: $3,930	Repubs: 60.1% Senate: 57.0% Incumb: 79.2%	
Unisys Corp Unisys Corporation Employees PAC Washington, DC	Unisys Computers†	$57,600	111 Candidates Avg House: $411 Avg Sen: $890	Repubs: 52.5% House: 61.4% Incumb: 87.4%	
United Airlines United Airlines PAC Chicago, IL	Airlines	$68,500	81 Candidates Avg House: $683 Avg Sen: $1,484	Repubs: 52.2% House: 63.9% Incumb: 87.6%	
United Auto Workers UAW - V - CAP (UAW Voluntary Community Action Program) Detroit, MI	United Auto Workers Auto Unions	$1,953,099	375 Candidates Avg House: $5,148 Avg Sen: $6,037	Dems: 98.8% House: 87.3% Incumb: 60.2%	
United Mine Workers United Mine Workers of America - Coal Miners PAC Washington, DC	Mining Union	$309,068	212 Candidates Avg House: $1,182 Avg Sen: $2,576	Dems: 97.2% House: 64.7% Incumb: 72.7%	

† PAC Sponsor has other major interests in addition to this primary category

Sponsor or Related Group/PAC Name	Affiliate	1987-88 Total	Where the money went...		
United Paperworkers United Paperworkers International Union Political Education Program Washington, DC	Manuf Unions	$64,850	53 Candidates Avg House: $892 Avg Sen: $1,823	Dems: 100.0% House: 52.3% Incumb: 51.6%	
United Parcel Service UPSPAC Greenwich, CT	Express Delivery	$771,768	424 Candidates Avg House: $1,642 Avg Sen: $2,660	Dems: 59.8% House: 74.5% Incumb: 96.6%	
United Services Auto Assn Group United Services Automobile Association Group PAC (USAA Group PAC) San Antonio, TX	Property Insurance	$37,700	19 Candidates Avg House: $1,063 Avg Sen: $3,583	Repubs: 51.3% Senate: 57.0% Incumb: 81.4%	
United States Lines United States Lines PAC (USL-PAC) New York, NY	Sea Transport	$28,600	31 Candidates Avg House: $623 Avg Sen: $1,395	Dems: 56.5% Senate: 58.5% Incumb: 80.1%	
United States Tobacco Company U S Tobacco Executives, Administrators and Managers PAC (USTEAM PAC) Greenwich, CT	Tobacco	$146,775	81 Candidates Avg House: $1,321 Avg Sen: $2,196	Repubs: 60.7% House: 48.5% Incumb: 72.0%	
United Steelworkers United Steelworkers of America Political Action Fund Pittsburgh, PA	Manuf Unions	$902,150	210 Candidates Avg House: $3,877 Avg Sen: $7,264	Dems: 99.6% House: 76.9% Incumb: 49.9%	
United Technologies United Technologies Corporation, PAC Hartford, CT	Air Defense†	$343,996	240 Candidates Avg House: $1,128 Avg Sen: $3,186	Repubs: 58.3% House: 66.3% Incumb: 84.7%	
United Telecommunications United Telecommunications, Inc PAC (UNIPAC) Westwood, KS	United Telecom Phone Utilities†	$213,984	166 Candidates Avg House: $939 Avg Sen: $2,754	Repubs: 83.4% House: 58.8% Incumb: 66.0%	
United Transportation Union Transportation Political Education League Cleveland, OH	Railroad Unions	$803,385	395 Candidates Avg House: $1,681 Avg Sen: $4,684	Dems: 91.2% House: 72.8% Incumb: 79.8%	
Universal Health Services Universal Health Services Employees' Good Government Fund King of Prussia, PA	Hospitals	$21,500	29 Candidates Avg House: $738 Avg Sen: $642	Dems: 54.7% House: 72.1% Incumb: 96.5%	
Unum Life Insurance Company Unum PAC (Formerly Union Mutual PAC) Portland, ME	Insurance	$23,950	23 Candidates Avg House: $705 Avg Sen: $1,300	Dems: 82.0% Senate: 70.5% Incumb: 74.9%	
Upjohn Company Upjohn Employees PAC Kalamazoo, MI	Pharmaceuticals	$69,550	122 Candidates Avg House: $487 Avg Sen: $885	Dems: 53.0% House: 68.0% Incumb: 96.0%	
US Bancorp U S Bancorp PAC Portland, OR	US Bancorp Commercial Banks	$26,607	25 Candidates Avg House: $1,126 Avg Sen: $970	Repubs: 57.9% House: 63.5% Incumb: 76.9%	
US Beet Sugar Assn United States Beet Sugar Association PAC Washington, DC	Sugar	$39,196	78 Candidates Avg House: $435 Avg Sen: $821	Dems: 66.0% House: 70.0% Incumb: 84.7%	
US Fidelity & Guaranty United States Fidelity & Guaranty Company PAC (USF&G PAC) Baltimore, MD	Insurance	$42,822	44 Candidates Avg House: $705 Avg Sen: $1,181	Repubs: 60.2% Senate: 60.7% Incumb: 72.9%	
US League of Savings Assn U S League-Savings Association Political Elections Committee Washington, DC	US League of Savings Assn Savings Banks	$537,550	256 Candidates Avg House: $1,579 Avg Sen: $4,136	Dems: 66.9% House: 59.9% Incumb: 92.4%	
US Telephone Assn United States Telephone Assn PAC Washington, DC	Phone Utilities	$122,354	117 Candidates Avg House: $826 Avg Sen: $1,343	Dems: 64.1% House: 54.7% Incumb: 85.7%	
US West Inc U S West Inc PAC(U S West PAC) Englewood, CO	US West Phone Utilities	$59,613	78 Candidates Avg House: $611 Avg Sen: $1,178	Repubs: 56.7% House: 58.5% Incumb: 76.0%	
USA Committee USA Committee Los Angeles, CA	Former Calif Gov Jerry Brown Dem Leaders	$25,000	5 Candidates Avg House: $5,000 Avg Sen: $5,000	Dems: 100.0% House: 80.0% Incumb: 40.0%	

Sponsor or Related Group/PAC Name	Affiliate	1987-88 Total	Where the money went...		
USAir Corp US-Air PAC (Allegheny PAC) Washington, DC	Airlines	$33,500	66 Candidates Avg House: $417 Avg Sen: $873	Repubs: House: Incumb:	54.9% 66.1% 93.1%
USX Corp USXPAC (Formerly USX Good Government Fund) Washington, DC	USX Corp Oil & Gas Prod†	$76,300	69 Candidates Avg House: $758 Avg Sen: $2,256	Dems: House: Incumb:	58.8% 52.7% 93.8%
Valero Energy Corp Valero Energy Corporation PAC (VALPAC) San Antonio, TX	Oil Refining/Marketing†	$60,792	34 Candidates Avg House: $1,376 Avg Sen: $2,375	Dems: House: Incumb:	72.0% 49.8% 95.5%
Valley Education Fund Valley Education Fund Washington, DC	Former Rep Tony Coelho (D-Calif) Dem Leaders	$553,576	249 Candidates Avg House: $2,183 Avg Sen: $2,818	Dems: House: Incumb:	100.0% 93.5% 59.5%
Valmont Industries Valmont PAC Valley, NE	Electronics†	$32,099	28 Candidates Avg House: $743 Avg Sen: $1,381	Repubs: Senate: Incumb:	58.4% 47.4% 95.8%
Van Ness, Feldman, Sutcliffe, & Curtis Van Ness, Feldman, Sutcliffe & Curtis PAC Washington, DC	Lawyers	$41,906	77 Candidates Avg House: $439 Avg Sen: $902	Dems: House: Incumb:	74.9% 60.8% 87.7%
Veda Inc Veda Incorporated Employees PAC Alexandria, VA	Defense Electronics	$22,400	37 Candidates Avg House: $570 Avg Sen: $1,000	Repubs: House: Incumb:	75.8% 86.6% 69.2%
Verner, Liipfert, Bernhard, McPherson & Hand Verner, Liipfert, Bernhard, McPherson & Hand PAC Washington, DC	Lawyers†	$82,954	81 Candidates Avg House: $583 Avg Sen: $1,531	Dems: Senate: Incumb:	83.9% 70.1% 87.4%
Veterans of Foreign Wars Veterans of Foreign Wars PAC Inc Washington, DC	Pro-Military	$52,500	178 Candidates Avg House: $287 Avg Sen: $409	Dems: House: Incumb:	51.0% 91.4% 99.0%
Vinson, Elkins, Searls, Connally & Smith National Good Government Fund; The Houston, TX	Lawyers†	$116,640	79 Candidates Avg House: $1,261 Avg Sen: $1,419	Dems: Senate: Incumb:	65.8% 42.6% 85.3%
Virginia Bankers Assn Virginia Bankpac Richmond, VA	American Bankers Assn Commercial Banks	$44,750	13 Candidates Avg House: $3,840 Avg Sen: $1,250	Dems: House: Incumb:	51.4% 94.4% 75.4%
Voluntary Hospitals of America Voluntary Hospitals of America Inc PAC Washington, DC	Hospitals	$64,563	53 Candidates Avg House: $803 Avg Sen: $1,903	Dems: Senate: Incumb:	60.3% 58.9% 97.7%
Voters for Choice/Friends of Family Planning Voters for Choice/Friends of Family Planning Washington, DC	Pro-Choice	$174,450	98 Candidates Avg House: $1,505 Avg Sen: $3,088	Dems: House: Incumb:	90.8% 69.9% 49.1%
W R Grace & Company GracePAC New York, NY	Chemicals†	$90,809	150 Candidates Avg House: $501 Avg Sen: $1,005	Dems: House: Incumb:	56.9% 65.7% 93.9%
Walgreen Company Walgreen PAC Deerfield, IL	Drug Stores	$30,848	43 Candidates Avg House: $605 Avg Sen: $906	Dems: House: Incumb:	50.6% 53.0% 77.3%
Wall & Ceiling/Gypsum Contractors Wall and Ceiling PAC Washington, DC	Subcontractors	$93,439	99 Candidates Avg House: $607 Avg Sen: $1,939	Repubs: Senate: Incumb:	95.0% 51.8% 62.6%
Walt Disney Company Walt Disney Company Employees' PAC Burbank, CA	Resorts†	$63,000	49 Candidates Avg House: $833 Avg Sen: $1,552	Repubs: Senate: Incumb:	53.9% 46.8% 79.4%
Walter Industries Walter Industries Inc PAC (WALTPAC) (Formerly Jim Walter Corp PAC) Tampa, FL	Jim Walter Corp Resid Construction†	$120,200	71 Candidates Avg House: $1,591 Avg Sen: $1,891	Dems: House: Incumb:	70.5% 62.2% 86.4%
Warner Communications Warner Communications Inc PAC New York, NY	Entertainment†	$77,516	71 Candidates Avg House: $744 Avg Sen: $1,550	Dems: Senate: Incumb:	78.4% 50.0% 87.7%

† PAC Sponsor has other major interests in addition to this primary category

Sponsor or Related Group/PAC Name	Affiliate	1987-88 Total	Where the money went...		
Warner-Lambert Warner-Lambert PAC ("WALPAC") Morris Plains, NJ	Health Care Prod†	$108,060	75 Candidates Avg House: $848 Avg Sen: $2,750	Dems: 56.7% Pres: 49.6% Incumb: 95.2%	
Washington PAC Washington PAC Washington, DC	Pro-Israel	$308,650	202 Candidates Avg House: $813 Avg Sen: $3,513	Dems: 77.1% Senate: 60.3% Incumb: 75.5%	
Waste Management Inc Waste Management Inc Employees' Better Government Fund ("WMI PAC") Oak Brook, IL	Waste Mgmt	$418,116	305 Candidates Avg House: $1,034 Avg Sen: $2,216	Dems: 62.8% House: 56.9% Incumb: 82.7%	
Watkins Associated Industries Watkins Associated Industries Inc Employees for Good Govt Cmte (Watkins-PAC) Atlanta, GA	Trucking	$20,650	26 Candidates Avg House: $806 Avg Sen: $717	Repubs: 66.3% Senate: 59.0% Incumb: 70.0%	
Watkins-Johnson Company Watkins-Johnson PAC Palo Alto, CA	Defense Electronics†	$36,625	8 Candidates Avg House: $4,025 Avg Sen: $5,750	Repubs: 97.2% House: 54.9% Incumb: 79.5%	
Wells Fargo Wells Fargo & Company Impact Fund San Francisco, CA	Commercial Banks	$52,600	47 Candidates Avg House: $1,023 Avg Sen: $1,431	Repubs: 57.5% House: 70.1% Incumb: 89.5%	
West Publishing West Publishing Company PAC (West Publishing PAC) Minneapolis, MN	Publishing	$35,000	40 Candidates Avg House: $833 Avg Sen: $937	Repubs: 52.8% House: 57.1% Incumb: 91.4%	
Western Growers Assn Western Growers Association PAC Federal Irvine, CA	Fruit/Veg	$25,494	27 Candidates Avg House: $600 Avg Sen: $2,166	Repubs: 79.4% Senate: 50.9% Incumb: 96.1%	
Westinghouse Electric Westinghouse Electric Corporation Employees Political Participation Program Pittsburgh, PA	Electronics†	$177,570	230 Candidates Avg House: $644 Avg Sen: $1,516	Dems: 63.4% House: 70.4% Incumb: 93.9%	
Westpoint Pepperell Westpoint Pepperell Employees PAC West Point, GA	Textiles	$35,725	51 Candidates Avg House: $551 Avg Sen: $1,344	Repubs: 50.8% House: 63.3% Incumb: 86.6%	
Westvaco Corp Westvaco Corporation Political Participation Program New York, NY	Paper Prod†	$208,500	82 Candidates Avg House: $2,016 Avg Sen: $4,071	Repubs: 65.2% House: 59.0% Incumb: 82.5%	
Wexler Reynolds Harrison & Schule Wexler Reynolds Harrison & Schule Inc PAC (WRHSPAC) Washington, DC	Lobbyist/PR	$70,653	123 Candidates Avg House: $421 Avg Sen: $949	Dems: 70.0% House: 51.3% Incumb: 82.1%	
Weyerhaeuser Company Weyerhaeuser Company PAC Federal Way, WA	Weyerhaeuser	Forest Prod†	$36,191	31 Candidates Avg House: $1,007 Avg Sen: $1,998	Repubs: 63.6% House: 72.4% Incumb: 64.6%
Weyerhaeuser Company/Shareholders PAC Weyerhaeuser Company Special Shareholders PAC St. Paul, MN	Weyerhaeuser	Forest Prod†	$63,349	61 Candidates Avg House: $585 Avg Sen: $2,312	Repubs: 86.8% Senate: 58.4% Incumb: 68.4%
Whirlpool Corp Whirlpool PAC Benton Harbor, MI	Appliance Mfrs	$51,250	52 Candidates Avg House: $752 Avg Sen: $1,464	Repubs: 99.4% House: 51.4% Incumb: 55.1%	
White Castle System White Castle System, Inc PAC Columbus, OH	Restaurants	$29,600	45 Candidates Avg House: $487 Avg Sen: $1,076	Repubs: 98.3% House: 52.7% Incumb: 64.5%	
Willamette Industries Willamette Industries PAC (WILPAC) Portland, OR	Willamette Industries	Forest Prod	$44,750	37 Candidates Avg House: $824 Avg Sen: $2,250	Repubs: 86.6% Senate: 50.3% Incumb: 47.5%
Williams & Jensen Williams & Jensen PC PAC (W & J PAC) Washington, DC	Lawyers†	$89,156	142 Candidates Avg House: $469 Avg Sen: $1,178	Dems: 67.7% House: 57.4% Incumb: 89.7%	
Williams Companies Williams Companies PAC ("Willco PAC"); The Tulsa, OK	Williams Companies	Natural Gas	$29,450	44 Candidates Avg House: $515 Avg Sen: $1,000	Repubs: 70.8% House: 52.5% Incumb: 94.1%

Sponsor or Related Group/PAC Name	Affiliate	1987-88 Total	Where the money went...			
Wine & Spirits Wholesalers of America Wine and Spirits Wholesalers of America PAC Washington, DC	Liquor Wholesale	$165,679	116 Candidates Avg House: $1,227 Avg Sen: $1,809	Dems: House: Incumb:	60.8% 56.3% 90.8%	
Wine Institute Wine Institute PAC San Francisco, CA	Wine/Liquor	$56,761	41 Candidates Avg House: $1,043 Avg Sen: $2,608	Dems: House: Incumb:	72.9% 58.8% 95.3%	
Winn-Dixie Stores Sunbelt Good Government Committee of Winn-Dixie Stores, Inc. Jacksonville, FL	Food Stores†	$117,000	89 Candidates Avg House: $1,086 Avg Sen: $2,100	Dems: House: Incumb:	55.6% 64.1% 71.8%	
Winstead, McGuire, Sechrest & Minick Winstead, McGuire, Sechrest & Minick PC PAC Dallas, TX	Lawyers	$31,500	12 Candidates Avg House: $1,666 Avg Sen: $4,166	Repubs: Senate: Incumb:	55.5% 39.7% 93.7%	
Wolf, Block, Schorr and Solis-Cohen Tercentenary Fund Philadelphia, PA	Lawyers	$53,600	31 Candidates Avg House: $1,066 Avg Sen: $1,941	Repubs: Senate: Incumb:	63.6% 61.5% 79.9%	
Women's Action/Nuclear Disarmament Women's Action for Nuclear Disarmament: A Citizen's Organization Inc (WAND-PAC) Arlington, MA	Pro-Peace	$20,400	53 Candidates Avg House: $386 Avg Sen: $377	Dems: House: Incumb:	95.3% 83.3% 30.6%	
Women's Campaign Fund Women's Campaign Fund Inc Washington, DC	Womens Issues	$121,012	37 Candidates Avg House: $3,242 Avg Sen: $3,500	Dems: House: Incumb:	67.8% 88.4% 23.6%	
Women's Political Committee Women's Political Committee Los Angeles, CA	Womens Issues	$29,000	5 Candidates Avg House: $6,000 Avg Sen: $5,000	Dems: House: Incumb:	100.0% 82.8% 0.0%	
Women's Pro-Israel National PAC Women's Pro-Israel National PAC ("WIN PAC") Washington, DC	Pro-Israel	$134,250	98 Candidates Avg House: $1,070 Avg Sen: $2,291	Dems: House: Incumb:	50.3% 59.0% 63.9%	
Xerox Corp Team Xerox PAC ("TXP") Stamford, CT	Office Machines†	$75,250	91 Candidates Avg House: $710 Avg Sen: $1,214	Repubs: House: Incumb:	60.4% 66.1% 82.7%	
Yellow Freight System Yellow Freight System Inc PAC Shawnee Mission, KS	Trucking	$183,680	196 Candidates Avg House: $651 Avg Sen: $1,966	Dems: House: Incumb:	64.3% 56.0% 83.9%	

† PAC Sponsor has other major interests in addition to this primary category

Appendix A: PAC Categories

This is a listing of the categories used in classifying all the PACs that contributed to federal candidates in the 1987-88 elections. Included are the full category name, the shorthand name used on the member profile pages, and the total contributions given during 1987-88 by PACs that fall within that category.

Classification of PACs is not always a straightforward matter, particularly among PACs operated by diversified corporations. The same PAC could be placed under several different categories, depending on the committee assignment of the member receiving the contribution. For that reason, the PAC totals listed here can be assumed to be conservative — particularly within the Defense sector, as many defense contractors earn the majority of their revenues from non-defense activities. In such cases, the contributions are classified as defense-related only when they are made to a member who sits on a defense-related committee or subcommittee. A similar format was used for all other diversified companies; the PAC's main classification represents its sponsor's primary profit center; but its secondary classification was applied if it related to a member's particular committee assignments.

Readers are encouraged to adapt this classification system to their own needs, and the author welcomes any suggestions for possible rearrangement of categories to more accurately reflect the business and political interests of the PAC community.

Agriculture

	Short name	87-88 PAC Total
Agricultural Services & Equipment		
Animal feed & health products	Animal Hlth	$50,250
Agricultural services & related industries	Ag Svcs	$229,892
Agricultural chemicals (fertilizers & pesticides)	Ag Chemicals	$421,340
Veterinarians	Veterinary	$189,400
Grain traders & terminals	Grain Trader	$268,414
Pest control, agricultural	Pest Control	$36,950
Farm machinery & equipment	Farm Equip	$162,835
Crop Production & Basic Processing		
Cotton	Cotton	$283,403
Vegetables, fruits and tree nuts	Fruit/Veg	$480,022
Wheat, corn, soybeans and cash grains	Grain	$120,983
Other commodities (including rice, peanuts, honey)	Misc Crops	$123,350
Farmers, crop unspecified	Farmers	$3,900
Sugar cane & sugar beets	Sugar	$1,186,301
Tobacco		
Tobacco & tobacco products	Tobacco	$1,351,087
Dairy Producers		
Milk & dairy producers	Dairy	$1,911,107
Poultry & Livestock		
Poultry & eggs	Poultry/Egg	$165,040
Livestock	Livestock	$274,486
Sheep and wool producers	Sheep/Wool	$25,275
Feedlots & related livestock services	Feedlots	$92,825
Food Production & Sales		
Food processors	Food Products	$1,020,378
Meat processing & products	Meat Process	$299,362
Food stores	Food Stores	$621,699
Food wholesalers	Food Whlsale	$195,528
Forest Products		
Forestry & forest products, generally	Forestry	$585,019
Paper & pulp mills and paper products	Paper Prod	$723,299
Miscellaneous Agriculture		
Farm organizations & cooperatives	Farm Orgs	$424,266
Florists & nursery services	Florists	$61,812
Commodity Trading		
Commodity brokers/dealers	Commodities	$1,044,050

Communications & Electronics

	Short name	87-88 PAC Total
Printing & Publishing		
Printing, publishing & allied industries	Publishing	$124,683
Book, newspaper & periodical publishing	Books & Mags	$86,250
Commercial printing & typesetting	Printing	$81,973
Broadcasting, Music & Motion Pictures		
Broadcasting & motion pictures	Broadcast	$87,949
Commercial TV & radio stations	TV/Radio	$263,987
Cable & satellite TV operators	CableTV	$432,411
Motion picture production & distribution	Movies	$322,073
Recorded music & music production	Music Produc	$63,400
Telecommunications		
Telephone utilities	Phone Util	$2,928,293
Long-distance telephone services	Long Dist	$1,209,329
Paging and cellular phones & services	CellularPhon	$7,900
Satellite communications	Sat Comm	$73,008
Other communications services	Commun Svc	$4,050
Telephone & communications equipment	Commun Equip	$179,926
Electronics & Computers		
Electronics manufacturing & services	Electronics	$816,797
Computer manufacture & services	Computers	$72,798
Computers, components & accessories	ComputerPart	$231,055
Computer software	Software	$3,500
Data processing & computer services	Data Process	$180,761

Construction

	Short name	87-88 PAC Total
Commercial & Industrial Contractors		
Builders associations	Builders	$180,876
Public works, industrial & commercial construction	Comml Constr	$1,565,346
Residential Contractors		
Residential construction	Resid Constr	$1,680,007
Mobile home construction	Mobile Home	$110,249
Subcontractors		
Special trade contractors	Sub Contract	$160,639
Electrical contractors	ElectricCont	$217,500
Plumbing, heating & air conditioning	Plumbing/AC	$274,727
Landscaping & excavation services	Landscape	$16,350
Construction Services		
Engineering, architecture, & construction mgmt svcs	Engineers	$503,078
Architectural services	Architects	$4,125
Surveying	Surveying	$23,200
Building Materials & equipment		
Building materials	Bldg Material	$275,708
Stone, clay, glass & concrete products	Stone/Concrete	$224,223
Lumber and wood products	Lumber	$107,423
Plumbing & pipe products	Pipe Prod	$84,658
Other construction-related products	Const Prod	$42,100
Construction equipment	Bldg Equip	$82,759

Defense

	Short name	87-88 PAC Total
Defense aerospace contractors	Air Defense	$4,144,658
Defense electronic contractors	Defense	$2,114,192
Defense research & development	Defense R&D	$207,700
Ground-based & other weapons systems	Weapons	$133,461
Defense-related services	Defense Svcs	$80,179
Defense shipbuilders	Ships	$501,325

Energy & Natural Resources

	Short name	87-88 PAC Total

Oil & Gas

Oil & gas, diversified	Oil & Gas	$112,350
Major (multinational) oil & gas producers	Major Oil	$2,355,142
Independent oil & gas producers	Independ Oil	$532,804
Natural gas transmission & distribution	Natural Gas	$1,550,206
Oilfield service, equipment & exploration	Oilfield Svc	$313,318
Petroleum refining & marketing	Refine/Mktg	$371,414
Gasoline service stations	Gas Stations	$271,523
Fuel oil dealers	Fuel Oil	$3,050
LPG/liquid propane dealers & producers	LPG	$45,925

Mining

Mining, diversified	Mining	$19,550
Coal mining	Coal	$300,810
Metal mining & processing	MetalMinProc	$340,295
Non-metallic mining	Other Mining	$134,550
Mining services & equipment	Mine Svcs	$7,000

Power Generation

Electric power utilities	Electric Util	$1,783,378
Gas & electric utilities	Gas & Electr	$734,560
Rural electric cooperatives	Rural Elect	$508,138
Power plant construction & equipment	Power Equip	$120,587

Nuclear Energy

Nuclear energy	Nuke Energy	$19,300
Nuclear plant construction, equipment & services	NuclearEquip	$138,120

Alternate Energy

Alternate energy production & services	Altern Enrgy	$128,150

Other Energy

Misc Energy production & distribution	Energy	$47,250

Waste Management & Pollution Control

Waste management	Waste Mgmt	$593,401
Pollution control services & equipment	Pollut Cntrl	$8,500

Other Natural Resources

Commercial fishing	Fishing	$79,519

Water Utilities

Water utilities	Water Util	$41,800

Finance, Insurance & Real Estate

	Short name	87-88 PAC Total

Banks & Lending Institutions

General banks & lending institutions	Banks	$43,200
Commercial banks & bank holding companies	Comml Banks	$6,456,883
Savings banks and savings & loans	Sav Banks	$1,970,335
Credit unions	Credit Union	$516,238
Credit agencies & finance companies	Credit/Loans	$637,993

Securities

Investment banking	InvestmtBank	$812,800
Securities & commodities investment	Securities	$204,841
Security brokers & investment companies	Stock Invest	$1,755,819

Insurance

Insurance companies, brokers & agents	Insurance	$4,272,864
Accident & health insurance	Health Insur	$717,904
Life insurance	Life Insur	$2,733,318
Property & casualty insurance	P
roprtyInsur	$98,462

Real Estate

Real estate developers & subdividers	Real Estate	$387,406
Real estate agents & managers	Real Estate	$3,166,688
Mortgage bankers and brokers	MortgageBank	$449,698
Title insurance & title abstract offices	Title Insur	$61,600
Building operators and managers	Bldg Mgmt	$48,434
Misc real estate	Real Estate	$1,500
Other real estate services	RE Svcs	$22,800

Financial Services

Accountants	Accountants	$1,524,526
Credit reporting services & collection agencies	CreditReport	$36,125
Tax return services	Tax Svcs	$23,450
Venture capital	Venture Cap	$256,500
Other financial services	Finance Svcs	$90,840

Health

	Short name	87-88 PAC Total

Health Professionals

Physicians	Doctors	$2,849,077
Psychiatrists & psychologists	Psychol	$204,330
Optometrists & ophthalmologists	Eye Docs	$1,065,036
Other physician specialists	Other MD	$518,495
Dentists	Dentists	$1,040,500
Chiropractors	Chiropractor	$172,490
Other non-physician health practitioners	Health Pract	$259,767
Nurses	Nurses	$306,408
Pharmacists	Pharmacists	$210,594

Health Services

Health care services	HlthCareSvcs	$7,133
Home care services	Home Care	$27,150
Outpatient health services	OutpatntCare	$24,800
Optical services (glasses & contact lenses)	Optical Svc	$11,650
Medical laboratories	Med Labs	$850
HMOs	HMOs	$39,900

Health Care Institutions

Hospitals	Hospitals	$826,749
Nursing homes	Nursing Home	$386,898
Other health care institutions	HlthCareInst	$700

Pharmaceuticals/Health Care Products

Health care products	Health Prod	$108,060
Medical supplies manufacturing	Med Supply	$194,065
Personal health care products	HlthCareProd	$96,700
Pharmaceutical manufacturing	Pharmaceut	$1,476,215
Pharmaceutical wholesale/retail sales	Pharm Sales	$39,085

Lawyers & Lobbyists

	Short name	87-88 PAC Total
Attorneys & law firms	Lawyers	$4,557,750
Lobbyists & public relations counseling	Lobbyist/PR	$238,995

Miscellaneous Business

	Short name	87-88 PAC Total

Business Associations

General business associations	BusinessAssn	$67,700
Chambers of commerce	Chamb/Cmrce	$55,482
Small business organizations	Sml Business	$369,230
Pro-business organizations	Pro-Business	$167,662

Business Services

Beauty & barber shops	Hair Shops	$2,000
Advertising agencies & billboards	Advertising	$52,120
Direct mail advertising services	Mail Advert	$52,350
Employment agencies	EmployAgency	$85,650
Marketing research services	Mkt Research	$159,079
Security services	Security Svc	$60,653
Equipment rental & leasing	Rentals	$118,002
Funeral services	Funeral Svcs	$30,750
Pest control, home & commercial	Pest Control	$5,900
Warehousing	Warehouse	$3,500
Other business services	BusinessSvcs	$81,335

Food & Beverage

Food & beverage products and services	Food & Bevg	$292,342
Artificial sweeteners and food additives	Artif Sweet	$21,850
Confectionery processors & manufacturers	Candy	$44,625
Fish processing	Fish Process	$10,971
Food catering & food services	Food Svcs	$8,500
Beer	Beer	$181,201
Wine & distilled spirits manufacturing	Wine&Liquor	$456,202
Liquor stores	Liquor Store	$2,850
Liquor wholesalers	Liquor Whlsl	$626,470
Restaurants & drinking establishments	Restaurants	$976,736
Beverages (non-alcoholic)	Soft Drinks	$243,190
Beverage bottling & distributing	BevgBottling	$64,450

Wholesale & Retail Sales

Wholesale trade, general	Wholesale	$169,747
Retail trade, general	Retail	$173,700
Apparel & accessory stores	ClothesStore	$14,577
Department, variety & convenience stores	Dept Store	$771,531
Furniture & appliance stores	Furn Stor	$1,250
Miscellaneous retail stores	Misc Stores	$18,450
Catalog & mail order houses	Mail Order	$26,225
Direct sales	Direct Sales	$33,600
Drug stores	Drug Stores	$171,276

Recreation & Tourism

Lodging & tourism	Lodging/Tour	$8,300
Hotels & motels	Hotel/Motel	$327,553
Travel agents	Travel Agent	$88,000
Resorts & amusement parks	Resorts	$72,900
Amusement/recreation centers & movie theaters	Amuse Ctr	$57,750
Bands, orchestras & other live music production	Live Music	$43,350
Professional sports, arenas & related equip & svcs	Pro Sports	$7,400
Casinos & other gambling establishments & equipment	Casinos/Gamb	$287,814

Chemicals & Related Manufacturing

Chemicals	Chemicals	$1,148,596
Explosives	Explosives	$10,500
Household cleansers & chemicals	Hhold Chem	$89,100
Plastics & rubber processing & products	PlasticRubb	$100,350
Paints, solvents and coatings	Paint Etc	$3,750
Adhesives & sealants	Adhesives	$1,600

Heavy Industry

Steel	Steel	$245,265
Industrial/commercial equipment & materials	Indust Equip	$733,590
Recycling of metal, paper, plastics, etc	Recycling	$28,000

Misc Manufacturing

Clothing & accessories	Clothing	$40,566
Shoes & leather products	Shoes	$60,162
Toiletries & cosmetics	Cosmetics	$70,871
Sporting goods sales & manufacturing	Sport Goods	$1,625
Household & office products	Hous/Off Prod	$36,950
Furniture & wood products	Furniture	$82,283
Office machines	Off Machines	$104,350
Household appliances	Appliances	$148,655
Fabricated metal products	MetalProduct	$72,501
Hardware & tools	Hardware	$18,900
Electroplating, polishing & related services	Metalwork	$3,375
Small arms & ammunition	Guns & Ammo	$200
Electrical lighting products	LightingProd	$500
Paper, glass & packaging materials	Packaging	$37,575
Paper packaging materials	Paper Packg	$81,200
Glass products	Glass Prod	$134,750
Metal cans & containers	Cans	$132,000
Textiles & fabrics	Textiles	$515,711
Synthetic fibers	Synth Fiber	$65,650
Precision instruments	Instruments	$375
Clocks & watches	Clocks	$4,450

Transportation

	Short name	87-88 PAC Total

Air Transport

Air transport, general	AirTransport	$13,600
Airlines	Airlines	$737,572
Aircraft manufacturers	Aircraft	$327,755
Aircraft parts & equipment	AerospacePts	$159,865
Air freight & express delivery	Air Freight	$605,537
Aviation services & airports	AviationSvcs	$16,650
General aviation (private pilots)	GenlAviation	$290,089
Space vehicles & components	Space Equip	$120,250

Automotive

Auto manufacturers	Auto Mfrs	$584,664
Truck/automotive parts & accessories	Auto Equipmt	$314,050
Auto dealers, new & used	Auto Sales	$1,202,420
Auto dealers, Japanese imports	JapanAutoSal	$1,158,700
Auto repair	Auto Repair	$300

Trucking, Buses & Delivery

Car/truck rental agencies	Car/Trk Rent	$85,575
Trucking	Truck Indust	$1,825
Trucking companies & services	Trucking Cos	$940,039
Truck & trailer manufacturers	Truck Mfrs	$33,925
Delivery (UPS)	Delivery	$771,768
Freight & delivery services	Delivery Svc	$14,350
Bus services	Bus Svcs	$81,500
Taxicabs	Taxis	$17,951

Railroads & Railroad Services

Railroads	Railroads	$925,456
Railroad equipment	RR Equip	$23,200
Railroad services	RR Svcs	$50,000

Sea Transport

Sea transport, general	Sea	$40,275
Ship building & repair	ShipBld/Repr	$74,246
Sea freight & passenger services	SeaTransport	$432,110
Pleasure boats	Rec Boats	$61,100

Recreational Vehicles

Motorcycles, snowmobiles & other motorized vehicles	Motorcycles	$26,100
Bicycles & other non-motorized vehicles	Bikes Etc	$35,025

Other

	Short name	87-88 PAC Total
Schools & colleges	Schools	$3,000
Technical, business and vocational schools	Voc Tech	$159,420
Welfare & Social Work	Social Work	$129,090
Other	Other	$64,650
Unknown	Unknown	$117,202

Labor

	Short name	87-88 PAC Total
Labor unions, general	Labor Unions	$1,006,096

Public Sector Unions

	Short name	87-88 PAC Total
Civil service & government unions	Govt Workers	$7,700
Federal employees unions	Fedl Workers	$2,423,085
State & local govt employee unions	LocalGovWrk	$1,665,136
Teachers unions	Teachers	$3,021,709
Police & firefighters unions	Pub Safety	$169,377
US Postal Service unions & associations	Postal Union	$3,558,977

Bldg Trades, Misc & Industrial Unions

	Short name	87-88 PAC Total
Agricultural labor unions	Ag Labor	$1,600
Auto workers	Auto Unions	$1,955,099
Construction unions	Constr Union	$5,706,655
Communications & hi-tech unions	Commun Union	$1,042,335
Electrical workers (IBEW)	IBEW	$1,237,170
Mining unions	Mine Workers	$309,068
Energy-related unions (non-mining)	Enrgy Union	$118,075
Food service & related unions	FoodSvcUnion	$379,916
Retail trade unions	Retail Union	$1,162,689
Commercial service unions	ComlSvcUnion	$5,800
Entertainment unions	Entrtain Lab	$43,255
Other commercial unions	Misc Unions	$319,808
Health worker unions	Health Union	$10,625
Manufacturing unions	Manuf Union	$3,665,469
Other unions	Other Labor	$66,742

Transportation Unions

	Short name	87-88 PAC Total
Air transport unions	AirTrans Lab	$1,287,977
Railroad unions	RR Unions	$1,226,339
Sea transport unions	Seamen Union	$3,111,791
Teamsters Union	Teamsters	$2,925,164
Other transportation unions	Transp Labor	$1,147,665

Ideological/Single-Issue

	Short name	87-88 PAC Total

Ideological PACs

	Short name	87-88 PAC Total
Conservative/Republican	Repub/Conser	$590,241
Liberal/Democrat	Dem/Liberal	$1,442,212
Third party committees	Third Party	$1,995

Human Rights

	Short name	87-88 PAC Total
Human rights, generally	Human Rights	$13,800
Abortion policy, pro-life	Pro-Life	$301,711
Abortion policy, pro-choice	Pro-Choice	$457,374
Elderly issues/social security	Elderly	$935,350
Gay & lesbian rights	Gay/Lesbian	$354,582
Minority/ethnic groups	Ethnic Group	$165,747
Women's issues	Womens Issues	$311,194

Other Issues

Animal rights	Animal Rights	$2,150
Consumer groups	Consumer	$22,501
Defense policy, pro-military	Pro-Military	$498,852
Defense policy, pro-peace	Pro-Peace	$354,815
Environmental policy	Environment	$459,951
Fiscal & tax policy	Tax Policy	$126,679
Gun ownership advocates	Pro-Guns	$802,906
Gun control advocates	Anti-Guns	$87,900
Health & welfare policy	HealthWelfare	$360,740
Labor, anti-union	Anti-Union	$447,878
Pro-Israel	Pro-Israel	$4,642,372
Other foreign policy	ForeignPolcy	$286,443
Other single-issue/ideological PACs	OtherIdeolog	$57,565

Leadership PACs

Democratic leadership PACs	Dem Leaders	$3,121,200
Republican leadership PACs	Repub Leader	$1,220,875
Other Democratic officials & candidates	Dem Cands	$80,693
Other Republican officials & candidates	Repub Cands	$498,454
Non-Congressional candidate committees	NonCong Cand	$117,279

Appendix B: State Delegation Index

The supplementary index below lists all members of each state's congressional delegation as of November 1988. A number of changes have taken place since that time, but this was the membership of the U.S. Congress immediately after the 1988 general elections.

Members are listed by state and district. The page number indicates the location of that member's two-page campaign finance profile. A notation of NL in the page listing indicates that the member did not run in 1988, so he or she has no listing on the profile pages. Readers wishing to find all other references to the members listed here should consult the regular index.

* Switched party affiliation to Republican after the election

New Jersey

Senate

	Bill Bradley (D)	NL
	Frank R. Lautenberg (D)	196

House of Representatives

1	James J. Florio (D)	472
2	William J. Hughes (D)	588
3	Frank Pallone Jr. (D)	812
4	Christopher H. Smith (R)	962
5	Marge Roukema (R)	892
6	Bernard J. Dwyer (D)	430
7	Matthew J. Rinaldo (R)	872
8	Robert A. Roe (D)	880
9	Robert G. Torricelli (D)	1028
10	Donald M. Payne (D)	826
11	Dean A. Gallo (R)	490
12	Jim Courter (R)	376
13	H. James Saxton (R)	914
14	Frank J. Guarini (D)	530

New Mexico

Senate

	Pete V. Domenici (R)	NL
	Jeff Bingaman (D)	164

House of Representatives

1	Steven H. Schiff (R)	920
2	Joe Skeen (R)	950
3	Bill Richardson (D)	868

New York

Senate

	Daniel Patrick Moynihan (D)	212
	Alfonse M. D'Amato (R)	NL

House of Representatives

1	George J. Hochbrueckner (D)	572
2	Thomas J. Downey (D)	422
3	Robert J. Mrazek (D)	770
4	Norman F. Lent (R)	662
5	Raymond J. McGrath (R)	728
6	Floyd H. Flake (D)	468
7	Gary L. Ackerman (D)	230
8	James H. Scheuer (D)	918
9	Thomas J. Manton (D)	694
10	Charles E. Schumer (D)	930
11	Ed Towns (D)	1030
12	Major R. Owens (D)	804
13	Stephen J. Solarz (D)	982
14	Guy V. Molinari (R)	754
15	Bill Green (R)	528
16	Charles B. Rangel (D)	858
17	Ted Weiss (D)	1066
18	Robert Garcia (D)	492
19	Eliot L. Engel (D)	446
20	Nita M. Lowey (D)	684
21	Hamilton Fish Jr. (R)	466
22	Benjamin A. Gilman (R)	506
23	Michael R. McNulty (D)	736
24	Gerald B. H. Solomon (R)	984
25	Sherwood Boehlert (R)	288
26	David O'B. Martin (R)	700
27	James T. Walsh (R)	1058
28	Matthew F. McHugh (D)	730
29	Frank Horton (R)	578
30	Louise M. Slaughter (D)	958
31	Bill Paxon (R)	824
32	John J. LaFalce (D)	642
33	Henry J. Nowak (D)	792
34	Amo Houghton (R)	580

North Carolina

Senate

	Jesse Helms (R)	NL
	Terry Sanford (D)	NL

House of Representatives

1	Walter B. Jones (D)	614
2	Tim Valentine (D)	1042
3	H. Martin Lancaster (D)	646
4	David E. Price (D)	850
5	Stephen L. Neal (D)	784
6	Howard Coble (R)	354
7	Charlie Rose (D)	886
8	W. G. "Bill" Hefner (D)	560
9	Alex McMillan (R)	732
10	Cass Ballenger (R)	258
11	James McClure Clarke (D)	344

North Dakota

Senate

	Quentin N. Burdick (D)	168
	Kent Conrad (D)	NL

House of Representatives

At Large	Byron L. Dorgan (D)	416

Ohio

Senate

	John Glenn (D)	NL
	Howard M. Metzenbaum (D)	208

House of Representatives

1	Thomas A. Luken (D)	686
2	Bill Gradison (R)	520
3	Tony P. Hall (D)	536
4	Michael G. Oxley (R)	808
5	Paul E. Gillmor (R)	504
6	Bob McEwen (R)	726
7	Mike DeWine (R)	404
8	Donald E. "Buz" Lukens (R)	688
9	Marcy Kaptur (D)	620
10	Clarence E. Miller (R)	744
11	Dennis E. Eckart (D)	438
12	John R. Kasich (R)	622
13	Don J. Pease (D)	830
14	Thomas C. Sawyer (D)	912

Index

NOTE: Profiles of individual PACs that gave $20,000 or more are listed alphabetically in Section 5 of this book, which begins on page 1101. They are listed here only if referred to elsewhere in the book. **Boldface page numbers** indicate main entries.

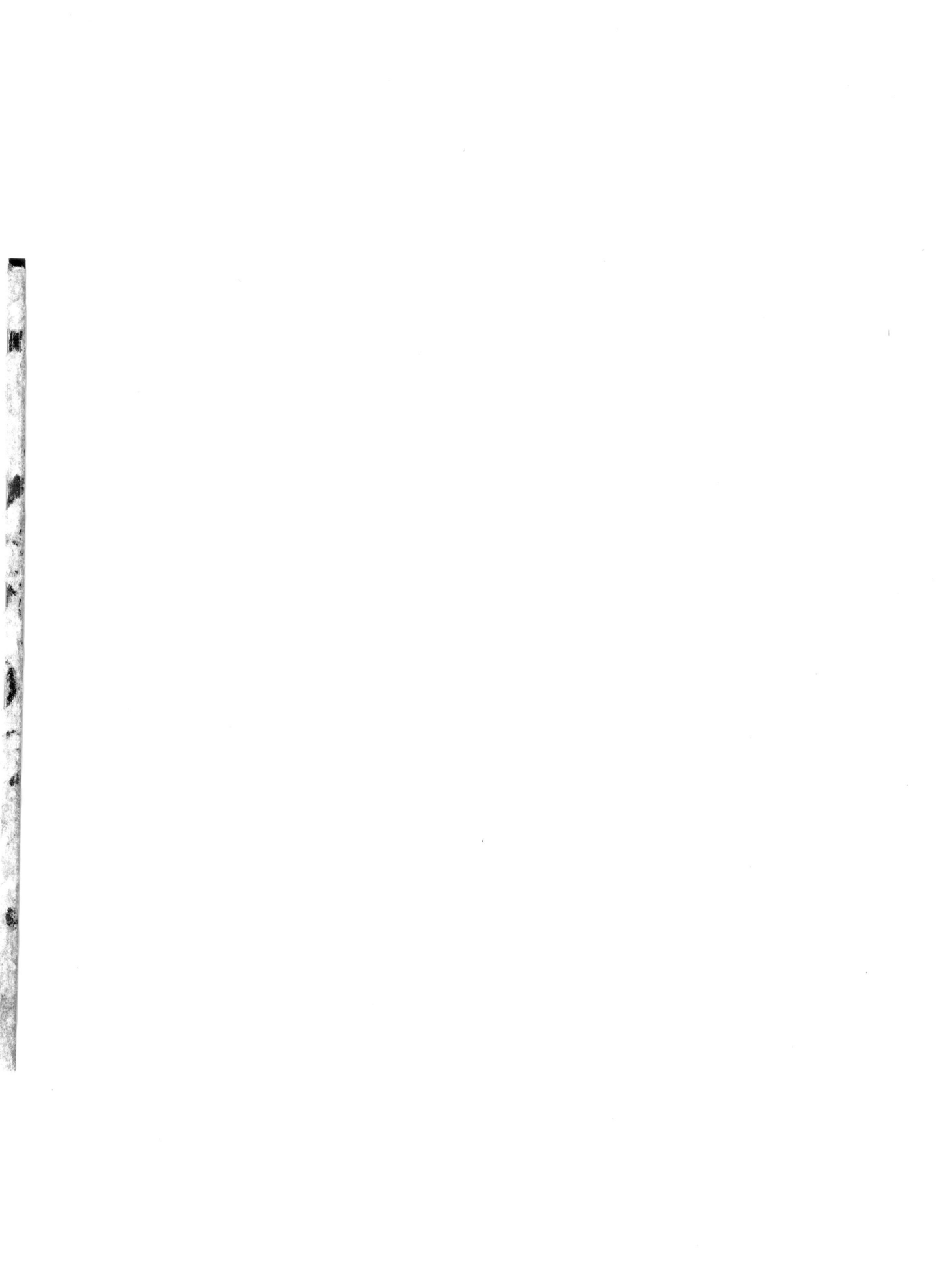